Bibliography of Canadian Bibliographies

Bibliographie des bibliographies canadiennes

Bibliographie des Bibliographies Canadiennes

Troisième édition

Mise à jour, révisée et augmentée

Éditeur et compilateur

Ernie Ingles

Chercheur principal et compilateur

Gordon R. Adshead

Adjoints à la recherche

Donna Brockmeyer-Klebaum
Sue Fisher
Suzanna Loeppky

UNIVERSITY OF TORONTO PRESS
Toronto Buffalo London

Bibliography of Canadian Bibliographies

Third Edition

Updated, Revised and Enlarged

Editor and Compiler

Ernie Ingles

Principal Researcher and Compiler

Gordon R. Adshead

Research Assistants

Donna Brockmeyer-Klebaum
Sue Fisher
Suzanna Loeppky

UNIVERSITY OF TORONTO PRESS
Toronto Buffalo London

University of Toronto Press Incorporated 1994
Toronto Buffalo London
Printed in Canada

ISBN 0-8020-2837-3

Printed on acid-free paper

Canadian Cataloguing in Publication Data

Ingles, Ernest, 1948–
Bibliography of Canadian bibliographies =
Bibliographies des bibliographies canadiennes

3rd ed.
Second ed. compiled by Douglas Lochhead.
Entries in English or French according to the
language of the title.
Added t.p. in French.
Includes bibliographical references and index.
ISBN 0-8020-2837-3

1. Bibliography – Bibliography – Canada.
2. Canada – Bibliography, I. Lochhead, Douglas,
1922–   . Bibliography of Canadian bibliographies.
II. Title. III. Title: Bibliographie des
bibliographies canadiennes.

Z1365.A1I54 1994   016.016971   C94-931389-OE

Données de catalogage avant publication (Canada)

Ingles, Ernest, 1948–
Bibliography of Canadian bibliographies =
Bibliographies des bibliographies canadiennes

3e éd.
Deuxième éd. sous la direction de Douglas Lochhead.
Notices en français ou en anglais selon la
langue de titre.
Page de titre additionelle en anglais.
Comprend des références bibliographiques et un index.
ISBN 0-8020-2837-3

1. Bibliographie de bibliographies – Canada.
2. Canada – Bibliographie, I. Lochhead, Douglas,
1922–   . Bibliography of Canadian bibliographies.
II. Titre. III. Title: Bibliographie des
bibliographies canadiennes.

Z1365.A1I54 1994   016.016971   C94-931389-OF

Contents

Introduction

The current *Bibliography of Canadian Bibliographies/Bibliographie des bibliographies canadiennes (BCB:3)* is a work in progress – a work with honourable antecedents, and a work in need of ongoing attention as scholars continue to require bibliographic awareness of the sources available for Canadian studies.

Previous Editions of the *Bibliography of Canadian Bibliographies/Bibliographie des bibliographies canadiennes (BCB),(BCB:1) and (BCB:2)*

Progress began in the academic years of 1929 and 1930 when bibliography classes at McGill University Library School, under the direction of Marion Higgins, listed some 550 relevant items (*BCB*). These were arranged under 31 broad subjects (themselves alphabetically arranged) and, within each category, entries were ordered alphabetically by compiler or corporate body. This work was recognized at the time as a small but valuable beginning, though it was by no means a complete listing of Canadian bibliography to that date. Although no inclusion criteria or specific exclusions were outlined, examination shows that library catalogues, indexes to library catalogues, bibliographies that appeared as part of books (consisting of as few as three pages), bibliographies in journals and annuals, sales catalogues, and biographical dictionaries containing lists of works, were all included.

While the entries found in the initial *BCB* seem to have been incorporated into Raymond Tanghe's first edition of the *Bibliography of Canadian Bibliographies/Bibliographie des bibliographies canadiennes* (1960) (*BCB:1*), the latter defined 'bibliography' as " . . . a list of books, brochures, newspapers, periodicals, maps or their reproductions, with information for their identification . . ." [1] Tanghe noted also the following exclusions: bibliographies or catalogues on cards; bibliographies included in a monograph or periodical article; catalogues and price lists of publishers, booksellers and second-hand book-dealers; analytical writings on bibliography or on source material; subject or name indexes; and directories, trade lists and biographical dictionaries.

Unlike the initial *BCB*, *BCB:1* included manuscript bibliographies compiled by students of library schools – these, in fact, comprised a substantial portion of the 1,375 entries.

BCB:1 listings are arranged under 29 broad bilingual subject headings, and by author within each category.

Indexes are provided for compilers, authors (referring to the subjects within the large category – 751 items – of 'author bibliographies'), and subject. The subject index is bilingual: entries are listed twice if English and French do not coincide in the alphabetical filing order, regardless of the language of the bibliography to which the index entry refers.

Douglas Lochhead's commendable second edition of the *Bibliography of Canadian Bibliographies/Bibliographie des bibliographies canadiennes* (1972) (*BCB:2*) incorporated the contents of Tanghe's first edition as well as those of three supplements that had embraced the years 1961–65. To this body of entries was added information on bibliographies up to June, 1970, yielding 2,325 entries.

Lochhead adopted the same definition of bibliography as was used in the first edition, and the exclusions and noted inclusions (i.e. a few bibliographies that are parts of other texts, and library school bibliographies) were repeated verbatim. The only additional exclusion noted was bibliographies in theses.

The arrangement of the second edition was the major change from the first. The revised and enlarged second edition was ordered alphabetically by author (main entry), with an integrated subject and author/editor index.

The Third Edition of the *Bibliography of Canadian Bibliographies/Bibliographie des bibliographies canadiennes (BCB:3)*

The production of Canadian bibliographies has increased substantially in the past twenty or so years. Indeed, the number that have appeared constitutes a significant body of literature in itself. It was tempting, therefore, to limit the *BCB:3* to a twenty-year supplement – but this was not to be the case.

Consultation with the bibliographical community, as well as with Canadian studies researchers, indicated that such a plan would have some considerable drawbacks from the user's point of view. Some examples: a user desiring complete chronological coverage (i.e. both current and historical bibliographies on a subject) would have to use both *BCB:2* and *BCB:3*; any changes in inclusion criteria, arrangement or indexing, would make the two editions difficult to use in tandem; anomalies which managed to survive the previous editions would not be addressed (i.e. pre-1972 bibliographies which had been overlooked would remain marginally accessible); and finally, as *BCB:2* is out-of-print it may not be readily available in libraries and to individuals who do not currently own a copy.

In addition, in a 1977 paper to the Bibliographical Society of Canada/ Société bibliographique du Canada, Douglas Lochhead and Peter Greig, made a series of recommendations toward the future production of the *BCB:3*.

They proposed major changes to the scope and form of entries, including: expansion of the scope to include bibliographies appearing as articles in serials; catalogues of significant library, private or booksellers' collections, inclusion of only published and near-published works; exclusion of indexes; the listing of locations; the physical examination of all works listed; the addition of annotations to each entry; and, adherence of bibliographic style to national and international standards. [2]

And finally, perhaps the most compelling reasoning for undertaking a substantially new *BCB:3* was that proffered by Theodore Besterman. He stated in his classic work *A World Bibliography of Bibliographies* . . .

> We look, above all, for completeness, . . . We desire completeness even more than accuracy . . . for in most cases a bibliography is intended to give us particulars of publications to which we wish to refer; thus we can always judge for ourselves (waiving gross errors) whether the bibliographer has correctly described these publications. On the other hand, anything that is omitted is lost until rediscovered. [3]

In the end, it seemed appropriate that Lochhead's work be utilized as a basis upon which to build a *BCB:3* which is substantially **enlarged** (including omissions from the first and second editions), **updated** (including all works that fit the inclusion criteria which have become available in the past twenty years), and **revised**, (excluding previous anomalous entries and making other adjustments to the inclusion/ exclusion criteria).

Inclusion/Exclusion Criteria

Defining 'bibliography'

For purposes of framing inclusion/exclusion parametres for the *BCB:3*, 'bibliography' was defined as 'a listing, arranged according to some system, of books or other documentary materials, that have a formal relationship one with another'. Encompassed within this definition would be lists which might be entitled as something else: 'catalogue', 'guide', 'index', 'directory', 'checklist', 'database', etc.

Defining 'Canadian' and 'Canadian Studies'

'Canadian' was defined as 'relating in subject to Canada', which was in turn interpreted to be listings, whether published in Canada or abroad, which had substantial Canadian content or interest. Such an interpretation of 'Canadian' was intended to encompass all bibliographies which systematically listed works dealing with Canada in general; with the geographic area of Canada (past and present); with an individual Canadian or a group of Canadians; with any thematic aspect of Canadian studies; or, with the Canadian aspect of, contribution to, or perspective upon, any subject in the universe of knowledge.

Such definition was considered to be consistent with that employed by the Commission on Canadian Studies in 1975 which framed the discipline as "... any field that, as one of its major purposes, promotes knowledge about Canada by dealing with some aspects of the country's culture, social conditions, physical setting, or place in the world". [4]

Unlike the *BCB:2*, those bibliographies which were published in Canada, or of Canadian authorship, but which are foreign in subject, i.e. which do not further our understanding of things, people or events Canadian, or Canada's place in the world, have not been included. In this, *BCB:3* was instructed by D.C. Appelt's review of *BCB:2*:

> It is a simple criterion, but one of questionable significance if one judges by such examples as *Pakistan: a selected, annotated bibliography; Public finance: information sources . . .; or, Theology in transition.* The first was published in Canada; the second, though having a United States imprint, may be supposed to have a Canadian compiler; the only evident reason for the third is that, along with New York, it has a Montreal imprint. My point is: who would think of looking for bibliographies on these subjects in a bibliography of Canadian bibliographies? [5]

These criterion were not without difficulties in application. There was need for evaluative judgment with regard to many titles, both in terms of the concept of direct Canadian connection, and of substantial Canadian content.

In terms of Canadian connection, some liberal interpretation was required, for example: in assessing the national or cultural dimensions within scientific or technological disciplines; or, when dealing with geopolitical jurisdictions which changed often over some 500 years; or, in appreciating native cultures which were continental in scope. Many additional examples would be possible.

While on the matter of Canadian content, substantial content was not always easily defined, even utilizing the guiding principles set forth by the National Library of Canada for *Canadiana*, the national bibliography; that is, the rule of one-third Canadian content. This was particularly the case if the universe of Canadian contribution within a thematic listing was itself small, but nonetheless identifiable and perhaps all encompassing. All in all, compilers erred on the side of inclusiveness.

'Published' as a Criterion for Inclusion

BCB:2 contained a large percentage of citations for manuscript bibliographies produced by students in library schools. Sensitive to the recommendations made by Lochhead and Greig, *BCB:3* has excluded these works.

In terms of coverage, the 7,375 entries, representing over 10,000 editions and supplements, span a time frame from 1789 to mid-1993. No finite cut-off date was chosen, compilers opting instead to include at least major works up to the delivery of the final manuscript.

'Publicly Available' as a Criterion for Inclusion

Again, in deference to Lochhead and Greig, every item listed has been examined, and a known location has been included in each entry. In addition, it has been determined that at the time of examination every item listed was accessible to the general public, either by way of in-person examination or through the interlibrary loan network.

Forms of Bibliographies and Categories of Inclusions/Exclusions

There are innumerable forms in which bibliographical enterprise can appear. These include, but are probably not limited to: bibliographic monographs; titles in a monographic series; parts of a multi-volume set; part of a monograph, separately paged/numbered or not; thesis, or appended to a thesis; bibliographic serials (in which all issues are individual or cumulative bibliographies); periodical articles; part of a periodical article; periodical issues; bibliographic databases; and, bibliography produced in ephemeral formats, or in the 'grey literature. In addition, there are listings of documentary materials which, while in effect fitting the definition of 'bibliography', are of questionable form or availability and are not always included in bibliographies of bibliographies. These analogous listings include: library catalogues; booksellers or auction catalogues; library accession or acquisition lists; literature guides; abstract and indexing publications; etc.

BCB:3 attempts to apply objective inclusion/exclusion criteria, as outlined below, to decision-making. Nonetheless, some subjective judgments were required. These judgments were made with regard to bibliographic form, however, and were not made on any critical or evaluative basis.

BCB:3 generally includes the following forms of bibliographies or categories of related material:

- bibliographic monographs;
- titles in monographic series;
- parts of multi-volume sets;
- bibliographic serial titles;
- bibliographies produced as thesis;
- regular bibliographic issues or recurring articles in serials;
- bibliographic articles appearing occasionally in serials (see 'Appendix B' for those titles searched);
- library or collection catalogues specifically supporting Canadian studies;
- bibliographic pamphlets or ephemera;
- bibliographic literature guides/bibliographic essays.

BCB:3 generally excludes the following forms of bibliographies or categories of related material:

- bibliographies appended to monographs;
- bibliographies appended to articles in serials;
- bibliographies appended to thesis;
- general library catalogues;
- library accession, new acquisition and backlog lists;
- archives and manuscript catalogues and finding aids;
- catalogues or price lists of commercial publishers, booksellers or antiquarian or second-hand booksellers (some judgment was applied in this category);
- periodical and other types of indexes;
- union lists of serials (if not substantially of Canadian content);
- lists of academic faculty publications;
- directories;
- electronic formats/databases.

All in all, there will be questions as to the judgment of including or excluding particular items. There will also be errors of omission. Since the *BCB* is a work in progress, the search for relevant bibliographies has not ended with the publication of this volume. Notices of additional items would be gratefully appreciated.

Structure of the Bibliography

Bibliographic Style

Entries are formatted in a manner consistent with the stylistic conventions established in the *Bibliographic Style Manual/Guide de rédaction bibliographique*, prepared by Danielle Thibault and published in 1989/1990 by the National Library of Canada/Bibliothèque nationale du Canada. The outline for the *Manual's* entry is taken from: ISO Standard 690, *Documentation, bibliographic references, content, form and structure* – 2nd ed. – [Geneva]: The Organization, c1987; the punctuation forms based on those in: *ISBD(G): General international standard bibliographic description* ... – Prepared by the Working Group on the General International Standard Bibliographic Description set up by the IFLA Committee on Cataloguing.- – London: IFLA International Office for UBC, 1977. The *Manual's* recording rules are derived from: *Anglo-American Cataloguing Rules.* – 2nd ed. – Ottawa: Canadian Library Association, 1988.

Notes

The *BCB:3* record includes notes of varying length and content, which supply relevant information with regard to the described publication. The following elements generally comprise the scope of the note, but may not be incorporated into every record:

- number of entries (provided if immediately evident, or easily approximated);
- period of coverage (if significant and readily available);
- brief descriptors of subjects covered (as determined from preliminary materials, i.e. preface, introduction, etc.);
- types of material (frequently expressed as inclusions and exclusions);
- extent of Canadian content, if such content is limited in terms of the overall scope of the work;
- names of compilers, editors, etc. which do not appear in the author field (these names will also be accessible by way of the Author Index);
- location of copy described (identified by the standard library symbol as assigned by the National Library and published in *Symbols of Canadian Libraries/Sigles des bibliothèques canadiennes. –* Ottawa: National Library of Canada/Bibliotheque nationale du Canada, 1993). For convenience symbols employed have been reproduced and identified in a listing following this introduction.

Previous Editions, Supplements, Reprints, Microforms

The note field also includes, when appropriate, a publishing history of the item. Supplements to the described work are listed from earliest to the most recent; previous editions are similarly listed, but from the latest to the earlier imprint. In both cases the description has been limited to only that information which is different from the main entry. In the case of a reprint, the original edition has been described and the reprint recorded in the note field.

Language and Bilingual Documents

Inclusion of documents into the *BCB:3* has not been restricted by language. However, for documents in other than the official languages, notes have been prepared in English. For English and French documents, the content of the entry, and the notes, appear in the language of publication. Canadian documents, or documents directed at a Canadian audience, are frequently published in two languages. These publications have been variously entered and described, depending upon their nature.

Published as one physical item

Documents compiled as one bilingual information source have been described only once, with the content of entry and notes in the language of the first title. Bilingual text is noted by the phrase: 'Text in English and French/texte en français et en anglais'. Bilingual documents in 'tête-bêche' or 'tumble' format have been entered and described twice, once in English and once in French. The version other than that described in the record is noted by the phrase: 'Text in English and French with French text on inverted pages. – Title of additional title-page: < >'

Published as two physical items

A document published in two separate English and French versions has also been treated as two distinct works. Other document title is noted by the phrase: 'Titre en français: < >, or English title: < >'

Sample Records

Following are sample entries for both monographic and serial publications. Key entry elements have been identified.

Monograph

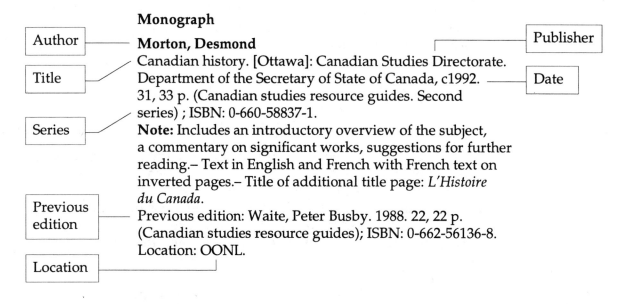

Author — **Morton, Desmond**

Title — Canadian history. [Ottawa]: Canadian Studies Directorate.
Department of the Secretary of State of Canada, c1992. — Date
31, 33 p. (Canadian studies resource guides. Second
Series — series) ; ISBN: 0-660-58837-1.
Note: Includes an introductory overview of the subject,
a commentary on significant works, suggestions for further
reading.– Text in English and French with French text on
inverted pages.– Title of additional title page: *L'Histoire
du Canada.*
Previous edition — Previous edition: Waite, Peter Busby. 1988. 22, 22 p.
(Canadian studies resource guides); ISBN: 0-662-56136-8.
Location — Location: OONL.

Publisher

Monograph

Leclerc, Charles
Bibliotheca americana: histoire, voyages, archéologie et
linguistique des deux Amériques et des îles Philippines.
Paris: Maisonneuve, 1878. vii, 424 p.
Note: 2,628 entrées.
Microforme: ICMH collection de microfiches ; no 09017; ISBN:
0-665-09017-X. 9 microfiches (401 images).
Suppléments:
... : *supplément no 1.* 1881. 102 p.
Microform — Microforme: ICMH collection de microfiches ; no 09018; ISBN:
0-665-09018-8. 2 microfiches (59 images).
Supplement — ... : *supplément no 2.* 1887. 127 p.
Microforme: ICMH collection de microfiches ; no 09019; ISBN:
0-665-09019-6. 2 microfiches (69 images).
Reprint — Réimpression: Paris: Maisonneuve et Larose, 1961. xx, 737 p. Le
vol. principal et les suppléments sont reliés ensemble.
Localisation: OONL.

Periodical

Article title

Lavoie, Pierre
"Bibliographie commentée [de Michel Tremblay]."
Dans: *Voix et images*; Vol. 7, no 2 (hiver 1982) p. 225-306.
ISSN: 0318-9201.
Note: Oeuvres: théâtrographie (oeuvres originales, adaptations), filmographie, bibliographie (romans, contes, nouvelles, divers); études sur Tremblay et son oeuvre.
Localisation: AEU.

Periodical title

Serial Publication

Hogan, Brian F.
"A current bibliography of Canadian church history/Bibliographie récente de l'histoire de l'église canadienne."

In: *Canadian Catholic Historical Association. Study Sessions*;
Vol. 42 (1975) p. 110-141; vol. 43 (1976) p. 91-119; vol. 44 (1977) p. 111-144; vol. 45 (1978) p. 101-141; vol. 46 (1979) p. 99-137; vol. 47 (1980) p. 69-108; vol. 48 (1981) p. 101-139; vol. 49 (1982) p. 135-167; vol. 50 (1983) p. 655-691; vol. 51 (1984) p. 145-199; vol. 53 (1986) p. 121-148; vol. 55 (1988) p. 149-193.; ISSN: 0318-6172.
Note: Books and articles: regional history (diocese, religious orders, synods), Communions, sources, bibliographies, parish histories, institutions, biography, missions, church and the arts, church and society, church and politics/labour/social thought.- Continues: Michael M. Sheehan (1965-1969), James Hanrahan (1970-1973).- Text in English and French/texte en français et en anglais.
Location: OONL.

Recurring bibliographic article

Arrangement

BCB:3 is seen to be primarily useful as a point-of-entry into research on a subject: that is, its use constituting a first step in a lengthy and multiple-stage investigative process. The premise of arrangement by subject-class underpinned the compilation of the BCB:3 from the outset, although as the body of entries took shape, the nature of the subject classifications was altered. The final list of broad subject classes is as noted in the 'Table of Contents'.

The subject class arrangement is itself modified in several significant ways. The listing includes sections for: 'Area Bibliographies' (sub-grouped by way of standard regional groupings); 'Types of Material Bibliographies' (i.e. 'Serials', 'Newspapers', 'Theses', 'Official Publi-cations', 'Maps', and 'Audio-Visual Materials'); 'Institutional' or 'Personal' Catalogues; and, 'Bibliographies of Individuals'.

The classes have been grouped and ordered somewhat arbitrarily, but nonetheless with an eye to their juxtaposition within broad subject areas. In making this determination it was felt, because of relationships and the overlap between classes, that the user would benefit from their being in proximity.

Publications enjoy only one entry point in the body of the listing (see also section on subject indexes), and they are arranged in ascending date order within subject classes. Thus, users are provided with a chronology of bibliographic activities within each subject discipline, and in consequence, they are provided with some sense of the evolving disciplinary/bibliographic inventory – the latter intended also to guide bibliographers in identifying lacunae within the Canadian bibliographical record. The choice of this ordering mechanism was felt to be reasonable, as well as useful, given that no subject class is unmanageable in terms of number of entries for those users needing to browse the entire thematic subject listing.

There is one caveat to this ordering by date of publication. The section devoted to listing bibliographies of individuals has been ordered alphabetically by the person's name used as subject.

Indexes

The above arrangement of entries will satisfy the requirements of many users, however, additional access points (over 50,000) are also provided by way of a number of indexes.

Author Index

The 'Author Index' has been generated from those fields of the entry in which personal or corporate authorship, or the responsibility for the intellectual content of the work, have been recorded. In addition, compilers, editors, etc., who do not appear in the main entry, but who are identified within a note, are also listed.

Title Index

The 'Title Index' has been created from the title fields of the main entry. It includes, also, titles which are to be found within the note field of the record. In a few instances when a title is not in itself explanatory, i.e. 'Bibliography', a note has been created and appended in square brackets to the title ([]).

Subject Indexes

Additional subject access is provided by way of an 'English Subject Headings Index' and a 'French Subject Headings Index'.

Appreciating the nature of usage which the *BCB:3* is most likely to serve, as well as the inter- or multi-disciplinary nature of a great many of the publications listed, considerable attention was given to enhanced subject access. This access is provided by way of a controlled bilingual vocabulary, taken from the *Canadian Thesaurus: a guide to the subject headings used in the Canadian Periodical Index and CPI Online/Thésaurus canadien: Un guide des vedettes-matière utilisées dans l'In dex de périodiques canadiens et CPI Online — Second edition/Deuxième édition* — Toronto: Info Globe, 1989. Use of this tool has also allowed the easy incorporation of 'See also' (suggesting related or more specific search terms), and 'See' (leading the user from unused to used terms) references.

Short Entry Listing — Appendix A

Although recognizing that the interests of the *BCB:3* are best served by a modified subject arrangement, further enhanced by subject heading access, the compilers did not wish to lose the important attributes of the straight alphabetical arrangement. [6]

The record of bibliographical achievement as presented in *BCB:2*, and the comparative purposes to which an alphabetical enumeration can be put, whether for individual researchers, for libraries or for booksellers, are believed to be served by incorporating a 'Short Entry Listing' into the present volume. The entry is limited to the bibliographical description and does not include information found in the note fields.

1. Raymond Tanghe, *Bibliography of Canadian Bibliographies/Bibliographie des bibliographies canadiennes.* Toronto: University of Toronto Press in association with the Bibliographical Society of Canada, 1960, p.v.

2. Douglas Lochhead; Peter Greig, "The Bibliography of Canadian Bibliographies: Some Proposals for its Future." *Papers of the Bibliographical Society of Canada/Cahiers de la societe bibliographique du Canada*, Vol. 16, 1977. pp. 8-12.

3. Theodore Besterman, *A World Bibliography of Bibliographies and of* ... Lausanne: Societas Bibliographica, 1965. col. 33/34.

4. T.H.B. Symons, *To Know Ourselves: The Report of the Commission on Canadian Studies.* Ottawa: Association of Universities and Colleges of Canada, 1975. p.5.

5. *Papers of the Bibliographical Society of America.* Vol. 68, no. 2, 1974. p. 196.

6. The alphabetical arrangement of *BCB:2* was viewed positively by some reviewers at the time of its publication. William F. E. Morley wrote that it made for "... more convenient use than the classified arrangement of the first edition consolidation of the indices ..." (*Choice.* Vol. 9, no. 7, September, 1972, p. 792.). However, Jean-Pierre Chalifoux in his review saw the change as an unfortunate compromise born of budget constraints. (*Bulletin de l'association canadienne des bibliothécaires de langue français.* Vol. 18, no. 4, December, 1972, p. 282.).

Acknowledgements

I am indebted to my predecessors — Marion Higgins, Raymond Tanghe and Douglas Lochhead, together with their students, associates and colleagues — for their contribution to the development of a Canadian bibliography of bibliographies. Without the foundation which they laid over the years, this current contribution may well not have been initiated, let alone completed.

Similarly, I extend sincerest thanks to those bibliographers, past and present, who produced the works which have been listed. If *BCB:3* serves no other purpose, it stands as a tribute to the industry and contribution of the Canadian bibliographic community. My hope is that the work done here will in turn be instructive to them or to their successors.

Without financial assistance this volume would not have been feasible. Support was provided by the Social Sciences and Humanities Research Council of Canada through the Canadian Studies Research Tools Program. In addition, the University of Alberta, by way of the Endowment Fund for the Advancement of Scholarship, contributed measurably to the resources available for the project. The University also supplied many of the infrastructure supports which contribute to the successful execution of any research initiative.

The National Library of Canada/Bibliothèque nationale du Canada, and the National Librarian/Directeur général, Marianne Scott, have been long-time supporters of the *BCB:3* initiative, and are very much a part of this volume. Incentive to prepare a revised edition of the work was first provided by the National Library's Committee on Bibliography and Information Services for the Social Sciences and Humanities (CBISSSH).

Essential research support, in the person of Susan Haigh, was assigned by way of CBISSSH, to prepare the initial feasibility study. Working facilities for project personnel were made available, and ongoing staff assistance was always at hand — ranging from access to collections, for which we thank the Circulation Department staff for their patience and good nature — to reference services, for which we are particularly indebted to Mary Bond, and the entire staff of the Reference Service division for their unflagging support.

Whether at the National Library/Bibliothèque nationale du Canada, or at the University of Alberta, or in a host of institutions throughout the country, there is a group of often unrecognized but extremely dedicated librarians and library workers who perform essential services on behalf of researchers. I refer to those individuals, whom I have always admired, and vigorously applauded, who comprise the interlibrary loan network. The project is indebted to Carol Smale at the National Library, and Alexis Gibb at the University of Alberta, and their respective staff persons, for their dedication to the research enterprise. I would also thank the staff of those libraries which supplied materials for review.

From time to time over the course of the project, I have drawn advice and counsel from a group of colleagues who acted informally as the 'Editorial Board' for the project. They are: Bertrum MacDonald (School of Library and Information Studies, Dalhousie University), Patricia Fleming (Faculty of Library and Information Science, University of Toronto), Richard Hopkins (School of Library, Archival and Information Studies, University of British Columbia), Mary Bond (National Library of Canada), and David Kotin (Metropolitan Toronto Library). Anne Piternick (retired, University of British Columbia), and again Douglas Lochhead (retired, Mount Allison University), must also be recognized as friends whose timely conversations were most helpful. Similarly, interventions by various individuals who have served on the Council of the Bibliographical Society of Canada/Société bibliographique du Canada have been instrumental in moving the project forward.

Indispensable have been numerous colleagues who contributed their own work to the project. In particular I would thank: Bertrum MacDonald, whose expertise in the field of the bibliography of Canadian science and technology is without peer; Paul Aubin (Institut québécois de recherche sur la culture), whose bibliographic scholarship is incomparable, as demonstrated by his multi-volume *Bibliographie de l'histoire du Québec et du Canada . . ./Bibliography of the history of Quebec and Canada . . .*; Joyce Banks (Rare Books Department, National Library of Canada) whose considerable expertise in the area of native studies and bibliography was invaluable; and, Maria Calderisi (Music Department, National Library of Canada) whose scholarship in the field of Canadian music bibliography is very much in harmony with the works she so aptly describes.

To Gord Ripley of Reference Press, and especially to Elizabeth Lumley, at the University of Toronto Press, I express sincerest thanks for their assistance and patience, particularly in waiting for a manuscript the delivery of which was always . . . imminent!

Key acknowledgments are to those members of the *BCB:3* team who worked with me, from time to time, over a period of four years. I thank research assistants Donna Brockmeyer-Klebaum, Sue Fisher, and Suzanna Loeppky for their energy and dedication to the project.

But in the end, my manifold and lasting obligation is to my Principal Researcher, Gordon Adshead. His skill and prodigious labours were immeasurable, whether identifying, locating, retrieving or describing thousands of the works which represent the content of the present volume, or coordinating the myriad of details, as the manuscript made its way through the various stages of production to publication.

And finally, our joint debt is to our families who have lived, not only with us, but with the *BCB:3* since its inception, and who have foregone many of the attentions which were their due.

E. Ingles, July 1994

Table des Matières

Introduction

La présente *Bibliographie des bibliographies canadiennes/Bibliography of Canadian Bibliographies (BCB:3)* est un ouvrage en cours de réalisation, un ouvrage aux antécédents honorables et qui requiert une mise à jour soutenue, étant donné que les chercheurs ont toujours besoin de se tenir au courant des sources bibliographiques qui sont disponibles pour les études canadiennes.

Éditions antérieures de la *Bibliographie des bibliographies canadiennes/Bibliography of Canadian Bibliographies* : *(BCB), (BCB:1) et (BCB:2)*.

Le travail a commencé avec les cours de bibliographie de 1929 et 1930, à la McGill University Library School, alors qu'on dressait, sous la direction de Marion Higgins, la liste de quelque 550 ouvrages pertinents (*BCB*), qu'on répartissait sous 31 rubriques générales (ces dernières rangées par ordre alphabétique); à l'intérieur de chaque catégorie, les notices étaient classées par ordre alphabétique d'après le nom du compilateur ou de la collectivité responsable. A l'époque, bien qu'il ne s'agissait certes pas d'une liste complète des bibliographies canadiennes existantes, cet ouvrage a été reconnu en tant que début modeste mais précieux. Bien qu'il n'y soit pas fait état de critères d'inclusion ni des bibliographies exclues, on se rend compte, à l'examen, que les catalogues des bibliothèques, les index de ces derniers, les bibliographies parues en tant que parties de livres (certaines ne comptant que trois pages à peine), les bibliographies incluses dans les revues et les publications annuelles, les catalogues de vente et les dictionnaires biographiques renfermant des listes d'ouvrages, avaient tous été retenus.

Si les notices de la première *BCB* semblent avoir été incorporées dans la première édition, par Raymond Tanghe, de la *Bibliographie des bibliographies canadiennes/Bibliography of Canadian Bibliographies* (1960, *BCB:1*), celui-ci définissait le mot «bibliographie» comme suit : «. . . a list of books, brochures, newspapers, periodicals, maps or their reproductions, with information for their identification . . .». [1] Tanghe notait aussi qu'étaient exclus : les bibliographies ou catalogues sur fiches; les bibliographies incluses dans une monographie ou un article de périodique; les catalogues et les tarifs des éditeurs, des libraires et des bouquinistes; les analyses portant sur la bibliographie ou les sources documentaires; les index de matières ou de noms propres; enfin, les répertoires, les listes de publications commerciales et les dictionnaires biographiques.

A la différence de la *BCB* du début, la *BCB:1* comprenait des bibliographies manuscrites compilées par des étudiants des écoles de bibliothéconomie; il s'agissait là, en fait, d'une partie considérable des quelques 1 375 notices.

Les notices de la *BCB:1* sont classées sous 29 vedettes-matières bilingues générales et, à l'intérieur de chaque catégorie, elles sont classées par auteurs. On trouve des index des compilateurs, des auteurs (avec renvois aux matières incluses dans la grande catégorie des «bibliographies d'auteurs») et des matières. L'index des matières est bilingue : si l'anglais et le français ne coïncident pas dans l'ordre alphabétique, les notices figurent deux fois, quelle que soit la langue de rédaction des bibliographies auxquelles elles renvoient.

L'estimable deuxième édition, par Douglas Lochhead, de la *Bibliographie des bibliographies canadiennes/Bibliography of Canadian Bibliographies* (1972, *BCB:2*) comprenait le contenu de la première édition (Tanghe) ainsi que trois suppléments correspondant aux années 1961-1965. A cet ensemble de notices, on ajoutait des données sur des bibliographies parues jusqu'à juin 1970, pour en arriver à un total de 2 325 notices.

M. Lochhead adopta la définition de la bibliographie qui avait servi à la première édition et répéta mot à mot les exclusions et les inclusions soulignées dans cette dernière (à savoir quelques bibliographies incorporées dans d'autres textes et les bibliographies d'écoles de bibliothéconomie). L'unique nouvelle exclusion mentionnée : les bibliographies de thèses.

C'est dans la disposition qu'intervenait le principal changement de la deuxième édition, par rapport à la première. Révisée et augmentée, cette deuxième édition était classée par ordre alphabétique des noms d'auteurs (notice principale), avec un index intégrant les matières et les noms d'auteurs et d'éditeurs.

Troisième édition de la *Bibliographie des bibliographies canadiennes/Bibliography of Canadian Bibliographies* (BCB:3)

La production de bibliographies canadiennes a considérablement augmenté au cours des quelques vingt dernières années. En effet, il s'agit en soi d'un ensemble de publications notable. On était donc tenté de limiter la *BCB:3* à un supplément portant sur une période de vingt années, mais cela ne s'est pas produit.

En consultant la collectivité des bibliographes ainsi que les chercheurs du domaine des études canadiennes, on s'est rendu compte que ce plan présentait quelques sérieux désavantages du point de vue de l'utilisateur.

Par exemple, un utilisateur désireux de consulter l'ensemble des bibliographies concernant une matière donnée, c'est-à-dire tant celles qui sont disponibles à l'heure actuelle que celles du passé, devrait se servir et de la *BCB:2* et de la *BCB:3*. Tout changement apporté aux critères d'inclusion, à la disposition ou au système d'index, rendrait difficile l'utilisation des deux éditions à la fois; aucune solution ne serait apportée aux anomalies qui avaient persisté dans les éditions antérieures (c'est-à-dire que les bibliographies d'avant 1972, qui avaient été laissées de côté, resteraient d'un accès limité); et enfin, vu que la *BCB:2* est épuisée, il se peut qu'elle ne soit pas facilement disponible dans les bibliothèques, ni aux particuliers qui n'en possèdent pas d'exemplaire.

En outre, Douglas Lochhead et Peter Greig, dans un exposé destiné à la Société bibliographique du Canada/Bibliographical Society of Canada, avaient formulé une série de recommandations en vue de la production de la *BCB:3*. Il s'agissait de changements majeurs qui seraient apportés à l'objet et à la forme des notices, entre autres : expansion de l'objet, qui serait applicable aux bibliographies qui figurent à titre d'articles dans des publications en série ainsi qu'aux catalogues des collections notables des bibliothèques, des particuliers ou des libraires; inclusion des seuls ouvrages publiés ou en cours de publication; exclusion des index; listage des lieux d'accès aux bibliographies; description matérielle de tous les ouvrages mentionnés; ajout de notes à chacune des notices; adhésion de la rédaction bibliographique aux normes nationales et internationales. [2]

Enfin, la raison la plus décisive, peut-être, pour entreprendre une édition essentiellement nouvelle, soit la *BCB:3*, correspond à une réflexion de Theodore Besterman. Dans son ouvrage classique, *A World Bibliography of Bibliographies...* , il affirme:

> We look, above all, for completeness, . . . We desire completeness even more than accuracy . . . for in most cases a bibliography is intended to give us particulars of publications to which we wish to refer; thus we can always judge for ourselves (waiving gross errors) whether the bibliographer has correctly described these publications. On the other hand, anything that is omitted is lost until rediscovered. [3]

On a fini par trouver à propos de se servir du travail de M. Lochhead comme d'une base sur laquelle élaborer une édition considérablement *élargie* (incluant les bibliographies omises des deux premières éditions), *mise à jour* (incluant tous les ouvrages, parus au cours des dernières vingt années, qui satisfont aux critères) et *révisée* (excluant les notices irrégulières des autres éditions et apportant d'autres ajustements aux critères d'inclusion et d'exclusion) : la *BCB:3*.

Critères d'inclusion et d'exclusion

Définition de «bibliographie»

Afin de déterminer des critères d'inclusion et d'exclusion pour la *BCB:3*, on a défini le terme «bibliographie» comme suit : «une liste, disposée d'après un système quelconque, de livres ou d'autres documents qui ont un rapport explicite entre eux». Cette définition pourrait comprendre des listes susceptibles d'autres appellations que «bibliographie» : «catalogue», «guide», «index», «répertoire», «liste de contrôle», «base de données», etc.

Définition de «canadien» et d'«études canadiennes»

On a défini «canadien» comme suit : «dont la matière se rapporte au Canada», définition interprétée comme applicable à des listes, publiées au Canada ou à l'étranger, qui présentent un contenu ou un intérêt canadien considérable. On voulait que cette interprétation soit applicable à toutes les bibliographies qui font systématiquement état des ouvrages traitant du Canada en général, au territoire canadien (passé et présent), à tout Canadien ou groupe de Canadiens, à tout thème des études canadiennes ou à l'aspect canadien de toute matière du monde de la connaissance, de même qu'à la contribution des Canadiens à cette matière et qu'à leur point de vue sur elle.

On a jugé que cette définition concordait avec celle dont la Commission sur les études canadiennes s'était servie en 1975 : «. . . any field that, as one of its major purposes, promotes knowledge about Canada by dealing with some aspects of the country's culture, social conditions, physical setting, or place in the world». [4]

A la différence de la *BCB:2*, on n'a pas inclus ici les bibliographies, publiées au Canada ou dont les auteurs sont des Canadiens, dont la matière est étrangère, c'est-à-dire qui ne font pas avancer notre compréhension du Canada, des choses, des gens ou des événements canadiens, ni de la place du Canada dans le monde. A cet égard, la *BCB:3* a profité du compte rendu de la *BCB:2* par D.C. Appelt :

> It is a simple criterion, but one of questionable significance if one judges by such examples as *Pakistan: a selected, annotated bibliography; Public finance: information sources* . . .; or, *Theology in transition.* The first was published in Canada; the second, though having a United States imprint, may be supposed to have a Canadian compiler; the only evident reason for the third is that, along with New York, it has a Montreal imprint. My point is: who would think of looking for bibliographies on these subjects in a bibliography of Canadian bibliographies? [5]

Ce n'était pas sans difficultés qu'on pourrait appliquer ces critères. Il faudrait faire preuve de jugement dans l'évaluation de plusieurs titres, tant en ce qui concerne la question du lien direct avec le Canada qu'en ce qui a trait à celle du contenu canadien notable.

Pour ce qui est du lien avec le Canada, il fallait quelque ampleur d'interprétation; par exemple, lorsqu'il s'agissait d'évaluer la dimension nationale ou culturelle dans le cadre des disciplines scientifiques ou technologiques; d'aborder la question des zones géopolitiques, qui ont souvent changé au cours de quelques 500 ans; ou d'évaluer la pertinence d'ouvrages traitant de cultures autochtones dont la sphère débordait nos frontières. On pourrait multiplier les exemples.

Puisque nous touchons à la question du contenu canadien, il faut dire que la notion de contenu notable n'a pas toujours été facile à définir, même en se servant des principes directeurs énoncés par la Bibliothèque nationale du Canada aux fins de *Canadiana*, la bibliographie nationale : principes qui se ramènent à la règle du tiers de contenu canadien. Cette difficulté était particulièrement sensible lorsque l'ensemble de la contribution canadienne, dans une liste thématique, était modeste tout en restant identifiable et peut-être compréhensif. A tout prendre, les compilateurs ont plutôt erré du côté de l'inclusion.

La publication comme critère d'inclusion

La *BCB:2* contenait un fort pourcentage de notices portant sur des bibliographies manuscrites produites par des étudiants des écoles de bibliothéconomie. Conscients des recommandations de MM. Lochhead et Greig, les compilateurs de la *BCB:3* ont exclu ces ouvrages.

Les 7 375 notices, soit plus de 10 000 éditions et suppléments, correspondent à une période qui va de 1789 au milieu de 1993. Les compilateurs n'ont fixé aucune date limite, préférant inclure au moins les ouvrages importants jusqu'au moment de la mise sous presse du manuscrit final.

La disponibilité au public comme critère d'inclusion

Ici encore, pour tenir compte des recommandations de MM. Lochhead et Greig, on a examiné chaque unité listée et inclus la mention d'un lieu d'accès connu dans chaque notice. En outre, on a déterminé qu'à l'époque de l'examen, le grand public avait accès à toutes les unités listées, que ce soit en personne ou grâce au réseau des prêts entre bibliothèques.

Les formes de bibliographies et les catégories d'inclusions et d'exclusions

Les travaux bibliographiques peuvent revêtir une infinité de formes. Ce sont, entre autres : les monographies bibliographiques; les titres d'une série monographique; les différents volumes d'un ensemble; une partie de monographie, paginée ou numérotée de façon distincte ou non; une thèse, ou l'annexe d'une thèse; les publications bibliographiques en série (dont tous les numéros sont des bibliographies distinctes ou constituent une bibliographie cumulative); des articles de périodiques; une partie d'un article de périodique; des numéros de périodiques; des bases de données bibliographiques; enfin, des bibliographies éphémères ou qui font partie de la «littérature grise». En outre, il existe des listes de documents auxquelles la définition de la bibliographie s'applique, mais dont la forme ou la disponibilité sont douteuses et qui ne figurent pas toujours dans les bibliographies de bibliographies. Ces listes d'ouvrages analogues comprennent : les catalogues de bibliothèques; les catalogues de libraires ou d'encanteurs; les listes d'acquisitions des bibliothèques; les guides littéraires; les publications d'abrégés et d'index; etc.

Les compilateurs de la *BCB:3* ont tenté d'appliquer des critères d'inclusion et d'exclusion objectifs; on en verra la description ci-dessous. Cependant, il fallait porter quelques jugements subjectifs. Toutefois, ces derniers portaient sur la forme bibliographique et il ne s'agissait pas de jugements de valeur.

En général, la *BCB:3* retient les formes de bibliographies ou les catégories de documents connexes qui suivent :

• les monographies bibliographiques;
• les titres d'une série monographique;
• les différents volumes d'un ensemble;
• les titres d'une publication bibliographique en série;
• les bibliographies présentées comme thèses;
• les numéros bibliographiques réguliers ou les articles bibliographiques réguliers des publications en série;
• les articles bibliographiques qui paraissent à l'occasion dans les publications en série (voir les titres recherchés à l'Annexe B);
• les catalogues de bibliothèques ou de collections qui sont expressément destinés à faciliter les études canadiennes;
• les brochures ou documents éphémères bibliographiques;
• les guides littéraires bibliographiques ou les essais bibliographiques.

D'une manière générale, la *BCB:3* exclut les formes de bibliographies ou les catégories d'ouvrages connexes qui suivent :

• les bibliographies annexées à des monographies;
• les bibliographies annexées à des articles parus dans des publications en série;

- les bibliographies annexées à des thèses;
- les catalogues de bibliothèques généraux;
- les listes des acquisitions et des arriérés des bibliothèques;
- les catalogues d'archives et de manuscrits ainsi que les instruments de recherche connexes;
- les catalogues ou les tarifs des éditeurs, des libraires spécialisés ou non dans le livre ancien et des bouquinistes (on a dû faire preuve de jugement dans ce genre de cas);
- les index sous forme de périodiques ou autres;
- les catalogues collectifs des publications en série (si le contenu canadien n'en est pas suffisant);
- les listes de publications des corps enseignants;
- les répertoires;
- les documents sous forme électronique et les bases de données.

À tout prendre, certaines inclusions ou exclusions seront discutées. Des erreurs par omission ont dû se produire. Vu que la *BCB* reste un ouvrage en cours de réalisation, la publication du présent volume n'a pas mis fin à la recherche de bibliographies pertinentes. Nous serons reconnaissants à tous ceux qui nous en signaleront l'existence.

Structure de la bibliographie

La rédaction bibliographique

Le présentation des notices est conforme aux normes de rédaction établies dans le *Guide de rédaction bibliographique/Bibliographic Style Manual* élaboré par Danielle Thibault et publié en 1989-1990 par la Bibliothèque nationale du Canada/National Library of Canada. Le plan du *Guide* provient de la norme ISO 690 : *Documentation, références bibliographiques, contenu, forme et structure*, deuxième édition, Genève (ISO, c1987); les normes de ponctuation sont basées sur celles de la *Description internationale normalisée* (ISBD), élaborée par le Groupe de travail nommé par le Comité de l'IFLA sur le catalogage, Londres, Bureau international de l'IFLA pour le CBU (1977). Les règles du *Guide* en matière d'inscription dérivent des *Règles de catalogage anglo-américaines*, deuxième édition, Ottawa, Canadian Library Association (1988).

Les notes

Les notices de la *BCB:3* comprennent des notes, de longueur et de contenu variables, qui fournissent des données pertinentes sur la publication décrite. Les éléments qui suivent, qu'on ne retrouve pas nécessairement dans toutes les notices, constituent en général la teneur d'une note :

- le nombre de notices (s'il est évident ou facile à citer approximativement);
- la période visée (si elle est notable et facile à déterminer);

- une brève mention descriptive des matières abordées (d'après les textes préliminaires, soit la préface, l'introduction, etc.);
- les genres de matériel (souvent exprimés sous forme d'inclusions ou d'exclusions);
- l'ampleur du contenu canadien, si ce contenu est limité par rapport à la portée d'ensemble de l'ouvrage en question;
- les noms des compilateurs, des éditeurs, etc., qui ne figurent pas dans la zone des auteurs (ces noms sont également accessibles grâce à l'Index des auteurs);
- le lieu d'accès à l'exemplaire décrit (identifié au moyen du sigle normalisé attribué par la Bibliothèque nationale et publié dans *Sigles des bibliothèques canadiennes/Symbols of Canadian Libraries*, Ottawa, Bibliothèque nationale du Canada, 1993). Pour plus de commodité, on a reproduit et identifié les sigles employés en les regroupant dans une liste qui suit la présente introduction.

Éditions, suppléments, réimpressions et microformes précédents

La zone des notes comprend aussi, s'il y a lieu, un historique de l'ouvrage en question. On en cite les suppléments par ordre chronologique; la liste des éditions précédentes est également fournie, mais dans l'ordre inverse. Dans les deux cas, la description se limite à l'information qui diffère de la notice principale. Dans le cas d'une réimpression, on décrit l'édition originale et la réimpression est mentionnée dans la zone des notes.

Langue de rédaction et documents bilingues

La langue n'a pas constitué un facteur restreignant l'inclusion de documents dans la *BCB:3*. Cependant, pour ce qui est des documents écrits dans des langues autres que les langues officielles, les notes ont été rédigées en anglais. Dans le cas de documents anglais et français, la notice et les notes sont rédigées dans la langue de publication de chaque document.

Les documents canadiens ou destinés à un public canadien sont fréquemment publiés dans deux langues. Ces publications ont fait l'objet de notices et de descriptions de type variable, d'après leur nature.

Publication bilingue en une seule unité matérielle

Les documents compilés en tant que source d'information bilingue unique ne sont décrits qu'une fois; la notice et les notes sont rédigées dans la langue du premier titre. Le caractère bilingue d'un texte est signalé par la phrase : «Texte en français et en anglais/text in English and French»

Les documents bilingues en présentation tête-bêche font l'objet de deux notices et de deux descriptions, à savoir en français et en anglais. La version autre que celle qui est décrite dans la notice est signalée par la phrase : «Texte en français et en anglais disposé tête-bêche. – Titre de la p. de t. additionnelle : <   >»

Publication en deux unités matérielles

Tout document publié en versions française et anglaise séparées est traité comme deux documents distincts. Le titre autre que celui dont il s'agit est signalé par la phrase : «English title: < >; ou, Titre en français: < >»

Exemples de notices

Voici des exemples de notices qui correspondent à des publications monographiques et en série. On en a signalé les éléments clés.

Monographie

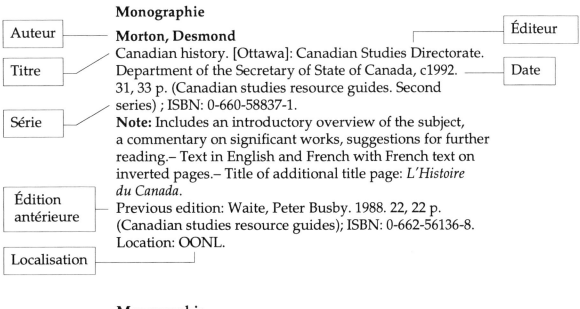

Morton, Desmond
Canadian history. [Ottawa]: Canadian Studies Directorate. Department of the Secretary of State of Canada, c1992. 31, 33 p. (Canadian studies resource guides. Second series) ; ISBN: 0-660-58837-1.
Note: Includes an introductory overview of the subject, a commentary on significant works, suggestions for further reading.– Text in English and French with French text on inverted pages.– Title of additional title page: *L'Histoire du Canada*.
Previous edition: Waite, Peter Busby. 1988. 22, 22 p. (Canadian studies resource guides); ISBN: 0-662-56136-8.
Location: OONL.

Labels: Auteur, Titre, Série, Édition antérieure, Localisation, Éditeur, Date

Monographie

Leclerc, Charles
Bibliotheca americana: histoire, voyages, archéologie et linguistique des deux Amériques et des îles Philippines.
Paris: Maisonneuve, 1878. vii, 424 p.
Note: 2,628 entrées.
Microforme: ICMH collection de microfiches ; no 09017; ISBN: 0-665-09017-X. 9 microfiches (401 images).
Suppléments:
... : *supplément no 1*. 1881. 102 p.
Microforme: ICMH collection de microfiches ; no 09018; ISBN: 0-665-09018-8. 2 microfiches (59 images).
... : *supplément no 2*. 1887. 127 p.
Microforme: ICMH collection de microfiches ; no 09019; ISBN: 0-665-09019-6. 2 microfiches (69 images).
Réimpression: Paris: Maisonneuve et Larose, 1961. xx, 737 p. Le vol. principal et les suppléments sont reliés ensemble.
Localisation: OONL.

Labels: Microforme, Supplément, Réimpression

Périodique

Titre : article

Lavoie, Pierre

Titre : périodique

"Bibliographie commentée [de Michel Tremblay]."
Dans: *Voix et images*; Vol. 7, no 2 (hiver 1982) p. 225-306.
ISSN: 0318-9201.
Note: Oeuvres: théâtrographie (oeuvres originales, adaptations),
filmographie, bibliographie (romans, contes, nouvelles, divers);
études sur Tremblay et son oeuvre.
Localisation: AEU.

Publication en série

Hogan, Brian F.

"A current bibliography of Canadian church history/Bibliographie
récente de l'histoire de l'église canadienne."

Article bibliograph-ique régulier

In: *Canadian Catholic Historical Association. Study Sessions*;
Vol. 42 (1975) p. 110-141; vol. 43 (1976) p. 91-119; vol. 44
(1977) p. 111-144; vol. 45 (1978) p. 101-141; vol. 46 (1979) p.
99-137; vol. 47 (1980) p. 69-108; vol. 48 (1981) p. 101-139;
vol. 49 (1982) p. 135-167; vol. 50 (1983) p. 655-691; vol. 51
(1984) p. 145-199; vol. 53 (1986) p. 121-148; vol. 55 (1988) p.
149-193.; ISSN: 0318-6172.
Note: Books and articles: regional history (diocese, religious
orders, synods), Communions, sources, bibliographies, parish
histories, institutions, biography, missions, church and the
arts, church and society, church and politics/labour/social
thought.- Continues: Michael M. Sheehan (1965-1969), James
Hanrahan (1970-1973).- Text in English and French/texte en
français et en anglais.
Location: OONL.

Disposition

Nous estimons que la principale utilité de la *BCB:3*, c'est qu'elle permet d'amorcer la recherche sur une matière; c'est le premier pas d'un processus de longue haleine et à multiples étapes. Depuis le début, le principe de l'arrangement par classes-matières sous-tendait la compilation de la *BCB:3*; toutefois, au fur et à mesure que l'ensemble des notices prenait forme, la nature de la classification a été modifiée. La Table des matières fournit la liste finale des classes-matières générales.

La disposition des classes-matières a elle-même subi diverses modifications notables. La liste comporte des sections pour les «bibliographies de secteurs» (avec sous-groupes correspondant à des regroupements régionaux standard); les «bibliographies de de genres matériel» (c'est-à-dire les «publications en série», les «journaux», les «thèses», les «publications officielles», les «cartes» et les «documents audio-visuels»); les catalogues «institutionnels» ou «personnels»; et les «bibliographies de particuliers».

On a regroupé et ordonné les classes de façon quelque peu arbitraire, mais en tâchant tout de même de les juxtaposer à l'intérieur de domaines généraux. On estimait que, compte tenu des rapports et des chevauchements entre les classes, l'utilisateur profiterait de cette proximité.

Les publications ne font l'objet que d'une seule notice dans le corps de l'ouvrage (voir aussi la section sur les index de matières) et sont rangées, à l'intérieur des classes-matières, en ordre chronologique. Ainsi, on fournit aux utilisateurs une chronologie des activités bibliographiques au sein de chaque discipline et de cette façon, ils peuvent se faire une idée de l'évolution de cette discipline et de son inventaire bibliographique; en outre, nous voulions ainsi faciliter aux bibliographes le repérage des lacunes dans le corpus bibliographique canadien. On estimait que ce mécanisme d'agencement était raisonnable et s'avérerait utile, étant donné que, pour l'utilisateur qui aurait besoin de parcourir toute la liste des sujets thématiques, aucune classe-matière ne serait trop encombrante, pour ce qui est du nombre des notices qu'elle renferme.

Il faut bien prendre note d'une particularité de cet agencement par ordre de publication. La section consacrée à la liste des bibliographies de particuliers a été rangée par ordre alphabétique, en se servant des noms de personnes comme matières.

Les index

La disposition susmentionnée des notices satisfera aux exigences de plusieurs utilisateurs; toutefois, quelques index fournissent d'autres points d'accès (plus de 50 000).

Index des auteurs

L'Index des auteurs a été élaboré à partir des zones de notices où les noms des auteurs-individus ou des collectivités-auteurs, ou encore la responsabilité du contenu intellectuel de l'ouvrage en question, ont été inscrits. En outre, cet index comprend les noms des compilateurs, des éditeurs, etc., qui ne figurent pas dans les notices principales mais sont identifiés dans les notes.

Index des titres

L'Index des titres a été élaboré à partir des zones de titres des notices principales. Il comprend aussi les titres qui se trouvent dans la zone des notes de chaque notice. Dans quelques cas, lorsque le sens du titre lui-même n'est pas évident (c'est-à-dire ne contient pas l'indication «bibliographie») on a créé une note qu'on a annexée, entre crochets, au titre lui-même ([ ]).

Les index des matières

On peut aussi avoir accès aux matières grâce à l'Index français des vedettes-matières et à l'Index anglais des vedettes-matières.

Pour tenir compte de l'utilisation la plus probable de la *BCB:3*, de même que de la nature inter- ou multidisciplinaire d'un grand nombre de publications parmi celles qui ont été recensées, on a particulièrement soigné l'accès aux matières, qui peut être effectué grâce à un vocabulaire bilingue contrôlé provenant du *Thésaurus canadien : Un guide des vedettes-matières utilisées dans l'Index de périodiques canadiens et CPI Online/Canadian Thesaurus: a Guide to the subject headings used in the Canadian Periodical Index and CPI Online*, deuxième édition, Toronto, Info Globe, 1989. L'utilisation de cet instrument a également permis d'incorporer facilement les renvois «Voir aussi» (pour indiquer les termes de recherche connexes ou plus précis) et «Voir» (pour permettre à l'utilisateur de passer de termes inusités aux termes en usage).

Liste des notices abrégées — Annexe A

Tout en reconnaissant qu'il valait mieux, aux fins de la *BCB:3*, modifier la disposition des matières et développer l'accès au moyen des Index des vedettes-matières, les compilateurs ne voulaient pas sacrifier les importantes caractéristiques de l'ordre alphabétique simple. [6] On estime qu'en incorporant une «liste des notices abrégées» dans le présent ouvrage, on respecte la réalisation bibliographique de la *BCB:2* et on permet les diverses utilisations de type comparatif dont une liste alphabétique est susceptible, que ce soit de la part des chercheurs, des bibliothèques ou des libraires. La notice abrégée se limite à la description bibliographique et ne comporte pas l'information qu'on trouve dans les zones des notes.

1. Raymond Tanghe, *Bibliographie des bibliographies canadiennes/Bibliography of Canadian Bibliographies*, Toronto, University of Toronto Press, de concert avec la Société bibliographique du Canada, 1960, p. v.

2. Douglas Lochhead et Peter Greig, «The Bibliography of Canadian Bibliographies: Some Proposals for its Future», *Cahiers de la Société bibliographique du Canada/Papers of the Bibliographical Society of Canada*, vol. 16, 1977, p. 8 à 12.

3. Theodore Besterman, *A World Bibliography of Bibliographies and of. . .*, Lausanne, Societas Bibliographica, 1965, coll. 33/34.

4. T.H.B. Symons, *To Know Ourselves: The Report of the Commission on Canadian Studies*, Ottawa, Association des universités et collèges du Canada, 1975, p. 5.

5. *Papers of the Bibliographical Society of America*, vol. 68, n° 2, 1974, p. 196.

6. Au moment de la publication de la *BCB:2*, certains critiques ont vu sa disposition alphabétique d'un oeil favorable. William F. E. Morley écrivait qu'elle permettait «. . . more convenient use than the classified arrangement of the first edition . . . » (*Papers of the Bibliographical Society of Canada/Cahiers de la Société bibliographique du Canada*, vol. 10, 1971, p. 87). Dans la même veine, le compte rendu de Choice notait que la disposition «. . . has been improved by using an alphabetical arrangement of entries regardless of subject and by a consolidation of the indices . . .» (*Choice*, vol. 9, n° 7, septembre, 1972, p. 792). Toutefois, Jean-Pierre Chalifoux, dans son compte rendu, estimait que ce changement n'était qu'un malheureux compromis résultant des contraintes budgétaires. (*Bulletin de l'Association canadienne des bibliothécaires de langue française*, vol. 18, n° 4, décembre, 1972, p. 282).

Remerciements

En premier lieu, je suis reconnaissant envers mes prédécesseurs, Marion Higgins, Raymond Tanghe et Douglas Lochhead, ainsi qu'envers leurs élèves, associés et collègues, de leur contribution au développement de la bibliographie canadienne des bibliographies. Sans les bases qu'ils ont jetées au cours des années, la présente contribution n'aurait peut-être jamais été amorcée et encore moins menée à terme.

J'exprime également mes plus sincères remerciements aux bibliographes du passé et d'aujourd'hui, qui ont produit les ouvrages que nous avons recensés. Quand elle n'aurait eu d'autre fin, la *BCB:3* constituerait au moins un hommage au zèle et à l'apport de la collectivité bibliographique du Canada. J'espère qu'à son tour, le présent travail sera utile aux bibliographes actuels ou à leurs successeurs.

Sans aide financière, le présent ouvrage n'aurait pu être réalisé. Le Conseil de recherches en sciences humaines, par l'intermédiaire du programme relatif aux outils de recherche des études canadiennes, nous a donné son appui. En outre, l'Université de l'Alberta a contribué de façon notable, au moyen de son Endowment Fund for the Advancement of Scholarship (fondation pour le progrès du savoir), aux ressources disponibles pour le projet. L'Université a également fourni plusieurs soutiens de l'infrastructure, qui aident à mener à bien toute entreprise de recherche.

La Bibliothèque nationale du Canada/National Library of Canada et son Directeur général/National Librarian, Marianne Scott, appuient depuis longtemps le projet de la *BCB:3* et leur part dans le présent ouvrage est très réelle. C'est le Comité de la bibliographie et des services d'information en sciences humaines de la BNC qui a d'abord proposé l'élaboration d'une édition révisée de l'ouvrage. C'est par l'intermédiaire du Comité que Susan Haigh a été chargée de fournir le soutien essentiel à la recherche, en vue de préparer l'étude de faisabilité. On a mis des installations de travail à la disposition des membres du projet, qui pouvaient toujours compter sur l'aide du personnel dans un champ d'activité qui allait de l'accès aux collections (nous remercions les gens du Service de la circulation pour leur patience et leur naturel accommodant) aux services de la référence, et nous sommes particulièrement redevables à Mary Bond et à tout le personnel de la Division du service de la référence pour leur inlassable soutien.

Que ce soit à la Bibliothèque nationale du Canada ou à l'Université de l'Alberta, ou encore dans une foule d'institutions partout au pays, il existe un groupe de bibliothécaires et de travailleurs de bibliothèques dont on ne reconnaît pas toujours la valeur mais qui sont extrêmement dévoués et rendent des services essentiels aux chercheurs. Je fais allusion à ces gens que j'ai toujours admirés et que j'applaudis chaleureusement : les membres du réseau de prêts entre bibliothèques.

Nous sommes redevables à Carol Smale de la Bibliothèque nationale, à Alexis Gibb de l'Université de l'Alberta, ainsi qu'aux membres de leurs personnels respectifs, pour leur dévouement dans le cadre des recherches exigées par le projet. Je remercie également les membres du personnel des bibliothèques qui ont soumis des documents à notre examen.

De temps à autre, pendant toute la durée du projet, j'ai profité des conseils d'un groupe de collègues qui ont officieusement agi en tant que «comité de rédaction». Ce sont : Bertrum MacDonald (School of Library and Information Studies, Dalhousie University), Patricia Fleming (Faculty of Library and Information Science, University of Toronto), Richard Hopkins (School of Library, Archival and Information Studies, University of British Columbia), Mary Bond (Bibliothèque nationale du Canada) et David Kotin (Metropolitan Toronto Library). Ce groupe d'amis, tant individuellement que collectivement, a servi le projet d'innombrables façons. Anne Piternick (retraitée, University of British Columbia) et, encore une fois, Douglas Lochhead (retraité, Mount Allison University), doivent aussi être salués comme des amis dont les entretiens opportuns ont été grandement utiles. De même, les interventions de plusieurs personnes qui ont fait partie du conseil de la Société bibliographique du Canada/Bibliographical Society of Canada ont contribué à faire avancer le projet.

Nous n'aurions pu nous passer des nombreux collègues qui ont contribué leur propre travaux au projet et nous ont ainsi épargné une infinité d'heures de recherche. En particulier, j'aimerais remercier Bertrum MacDonald, dont la compétence en bibliographie des sciences et de la technologie canadiennes est sans égale; Paul Aubin (Institut québécois de recherche sur la culture), dont l'érudition bibliographique est incomparable, comme le montre bien sa *Bibliographie de l'histoire du Québec et du Canada .../Bibliography of the History of Quebec and Canada ...*; Joyce Banks (Service des livres rares, Bibliothèque nationale du Canada), dont les grandes connaissances dans le domaine des études et de la bibliographie autochtones se sont avérées inestimables; et Maria Calderisi (Division de la musique, Bibliothèque nationale du Canada), dont la compétence en bibliographie de la musique canadienne est tout à fait en harmonie avec les ouvrages qu'elle décrit de façon si pertinente.

À Gordon Ripley de Reference Press, qui était responsable de la copie prête-à-photographier, et surtout à Elizabeth Lumley, de University of Toronto Press, j'offre mes remerciements les plus sincères pour leur aide et leur patience, en particulier lorsqu'ils attendaient un manuscrit dont la livraison était toujours... imminente!

Les membres de l'équipe de la BCB:3 qui ont travaillé avec moi, de façon intermittente, pendant une période de quatre ans, méritent des remerciements pour leur rôle clé. Je remercie les adjoints à la recherche, Donna Brockmeyer-Klebaum, Sue Fisher et Suzanna Loeppky, pour leur énergie et leur dévouement au projet.

Mais en fin de compte, c'est à mon chercheur principal, Gordon Adshead, que je suis redevable de façon multiple et durable. Son habileté et son activité prodigieuse étaient sans limites, qu'il se soit agi d'identifier, de repérer ou de décrire des milliers d'ouvrages parmi ceux qui forment le contenu du présent volume, ou de coordonner les myriades de détails du manuscrit, à mesure que ce dernier franchissait les diverses étapes, de la production à la publication.

Enfin, nous sommes tous deux redevables à nos familles qui ont partagé non seulement notre vie à chacun, mais celle de la *BCB:3* depuis le début, et qui se sont privées de plusieurs des attentions auxquelles elles avaient droit.

E. Ingles, juillet 1994

Symbols of Canadian Libraries
Sigles des bibliothèques

ABA	Whyte Museum of the Canadian Rockies (Archives), Banff
ACCP	Canadian Petroleum Association, Calgary
ACG	Glenbow-Alberta Institute, Calgary
ACIA	Western Regional Office, Parks Canada
ACPC	Petro-Canada, Calgary
ACU	University of Calgary
ACUIA	Arctic Institute of North America, University of Calgary
ADTMP	Tyrrell Museum of Palaeontology, Drumheller
AE	Edmonton Public Library
AEAU	Athabasca University
AEECW	Conservation and Protection, Western and Northern Region, Environment Canada, Edmonton
AEU	University of Alberta, Edmonton
AEUB	Boreal Institute for Northern Studies, University of Alberta, Edmonton
AEUL	Law Library, University of Alberta, Edmonton
BBIT	British Columbia Institute of Technology, Burnaby
BVA	Vancouver Public Library
BVAS	Simon Fraser University, Burnaby
BVAU	University of British Columbia, Vancouver
BVAWC	Workers Compensation Board of British Columbia
BVIF	Pacific Forestry Centre, Victoria
BVILFW	British Columbia Ministry of Environment, Victoria
BVIP	Legislative Library, Victoria
BVIPA	Provincial Archives of British Columbia, Victoria
DLC	United States Library of Congress
KHayF	Fort Hays Kansas State Library
KyU	University of Kentucky, Lexington
MBC	Brandon University
McBJ	Johns Hopkins University
MWIAP	Prairie Regional Office, Parks Canada
MWSJ	St. John's College, Winnipeg
MWUC	University of Winnipeg
NBAB	Biological Station, Fisheries and Oceans Canada: Station de biologie, Pêches et océans Canada, St. Andrews
NBEBR	Bibliothèque régionale du Haut Saint-Jean, Edmundston
NBFL	Legislative Library, Fredericton
NBFU	University of New Brunswick, Fredericton
NBFUL	Law Library, University of New Brunswick, Fredericton
NBS	Saint John Regional Library
NBSAM	Mount Allison University, Sackville

NBSM	New Brunswick Museum, Saint John
NBSU	University of New Brunswick, Saint John
NFSF	Northwest Atlantic Fisheries Centre, St. John's
NFSM	Memorial University of Newfoundland, St. John's
NFSNM	Marine Dynamics Branch, Canada Institute for Scientific and Technical Information, St. John's
NNM	American Museum of Natural History, New York
NSAS	St. Francis Xavier University, Antigonish
NSDE	Environment Canada, Dartmouth
NSHIAP	Atlantic Regional Library, Parks Canada, Halifax
NSHDE	Nova Scotia Dept. of the Environment, Halifax
NSHL	Legislative Library, Halifax
NSHMS	Nova Scotia Museum, Halifax
NSHPL	Nova Scotia Provincial Library, Halifax
NSHS	St. Mary's University, Halifax
NSHT	Technical University of Nova Scotia, Halifax
NSWA	Acadia University, Wolfville
OBUC	Canada Centre for Inland Waters, Burlington
OCKE	Petawawa National Forestry Institute, Chalk River
OGU	University of Guelph
OH	Hamilton Public Library
OHM	McMaster University, Hamilton
OKF	Fort Frontenac Library, Kingston
OKQ	Queen's University, Kingston
OKQL	Law Library, Queen's University, Kingston
OLU	University of Western Ontario, London
OLUL	Law Library, University of Western Ontario, London
OMIH	Huronia Historical Park, Midland
OOA	National Archives: Archives nationales, Ottawa
OOAG	Agriculture Canada, Ottawa
OOAGE	Entomology Research Library, Agriculture Canada, Ottawa
OOAMA	National Map Collection, National Archives: Collection nationale des cartes et plans, Archives nationales, Ottawa
OOB	Bank of Canada: Banque du Canada, Ottawa
OOCC	Carleton University, Ottawa
OOCI	Consumer and Corporate Affairs: Consommation et corporations Canada, Ottawa
OOCIHM	Canadian Institute for Historical Microreproductions: Institut canadien de microreproductions historiques, Ottawa
OOCM	Canadian Housing Information Centre: Centre canadien de documentation sur l'habitation, Ottawa
OOCO	Department of Communications: Ministère des communications, Ottawa
OOCS	Public Service Commission: Commission de la fonction publique, Ottawa
OOCT	Canadian Teachers' Federation, Ottawa
OOCW	Canadian Council on Social Development, Ottawa

OOEC	Economic Council of Canada: Conseil économique du Canada, Ottawa
OOEPC	Emergency Planning Canada: Planification d'urgence Canada, Ottawa
OOEPSE	Socio-economic Research Division, Environment Canada: Division de la recherche socio-économique, Environnement Canada, Ottawa
OOF	Department of Finance: Ministère des finances, Ottawa
OOFF	Environment Canada: Environnement Canada, Ottawa
OOFI	Fisheries and Oceans Canada: Pêches et océans Canada, Ottawa
OOFP	Forintek Canada Corporation, Ottawa
OOG	Geological Survey of Canada: Commission géologique du Canada, Ottawa
OOJ	Department of Justice Canada: Ministère de la justice Canada, Ottawa
OOMR	Energy, Mines and Resources Canada: Énergie, mines et ressources Canada, Ottawa
OONG	National Gallery of Canada: Galerie nationale du Canada, Ottawa
OONHHS	Health Services and Promotion Branch, Health and Welfare Canada: Direction générale des services et de la promotion de la santé, Santé et bien-être social Canada, Ottawa
OONHL	Laboratory Centre for Disease Control, Health and Welfare Canada: Laboratoire de lutte contre la maladie, Santé et bien-être social Canada, Ottawa
OONHM	Medical Services Branch, Health and Welfare Canada: Direction générale des services médicaux, Santé et bien-être social Canada, Ottawa
OONL	National Library of Canada: Bibliothèque nationale du Canada, Ottawa
OONM	National Museums of Canada: Musées nationaux du Canada, Ottawa
OONMM	National Museum of Civilization: Musée canadien des civilisations, Ottawa
OONMNS	National Museum of Natural Sciences: Musée national des sciences naturelles, Ottawa
OOP	Library of Parliament: Bibliothèque du Parlement, Ottawa
OOPAC	Chaudière Branch, Environment Canada: Succursale Chaudière, Environnement Canada, Ottawa
OOPW	Public Works Canada: Travaux publics Canada, Ottawa
OORD	Indian and Northern Affairs Canada: Affaires indiennes et du Nord Canada, Ottawa
OORT	Canadian Radio-Television and Telecommunications Commission: Conseil de la radiodiffusion et des télécommunications canadiennes, Ottawa
OOS	Statistics Canada: Statistiques Canada, Ottawa
OOSC	Supreme Court of Canada: Cour suprême du Canada, Ottawa
OOSG	Solicitor General Canada: Solliciteur général Canada, Ottawa
OOSS	Secretary of State: Secrétariat d'état, Ottawa

OOSSHRC	Social Sciences and Humanities Research Council of Canada: Conseil de recherches en sciences humaines du Canada, Ottawa
OOT	Transport Canada: Transports Canada, Ottawa
OOU	University of Ottawa: Université d'Ottawa
OOUM	Vanier Library, University of Ottawa: Bibliothèque Vanier, Université d'Ottawa
OPAL	Lakehead University, Thunder Bay
OPET	Trent University, Peterborough
OS	Sarnia Public Library
OSTCB	Brock University, St. Catharines
OSUU	University of Sudbury: Université de Sudbury
OTDRE	Ontario Ministry of Treasury and Economics, Toronto
OTDT	Ontario Ministry of Transportation and Communications, Toronto
OTEAO	Atmospheric Environment Service, Ontario region: Service de l'environnement atmosphérique, Région de l'Ontario, Toronto
OTER	Ontario Institute for Studies in Education, Toronto
OTL	Legislative Library of Ontario, Toronto
OTMCL	Metropolitan Toronto Reference Library
OTP	Toronto Public Libraries
OTRM	Royal Ontario Museum, Toronto
OTSTM	St. Michael's College, Toronto
OTU	University of Toronto
OTUTF	Thomas Fisher Rare Book Library, University of Toronto
OTY	York University, Toronto
OTYL	Law Library, York University, Toronto
OW	Windsor Public Library
OWA	University of Windsor
OWAL	Law Library, University of Windsor
OWTU	University of Waterloo
QLB	Bishop's University, Lennoxville
QMAC	Macdonald College Library, Ste Anne de Bellevue
QMAI	See ACUAI
QMBM	Bibliothèque de la ville de Montréal
QMBN	Bibliothèque nationale du Québec, Montréal
QMECB	Centrale de bibliothèques, Ministère de l'éducation du Québec, Montréal
QMHE	École des hautes études commerciales, Montréal
QMJB	Jardin botanique, Montréal
QMM	McLennan Library, McGill University, Montreal
QMME	Physical Sciences and Engineering Library, McGill University, Montreal
QMML	Law Library, McGill University, Montreal
QMMMCM	McCord Museum, McGill University, Montreal
QMMO	Osler Library, McGill University, Montreal

QMNF	National Film Board: Office national du film, Montreal
QMTD	Transportation Development Centre: Centre de développement des transports, Montreal
QQE	Services de bibliothèque, Environnement Canada, Ste-Foy
QQEN	Ministère de l'environnement du Québec, Ste-Foy
QQERM	Centre de documentation — Mines, Ministère de l'énergie et des ressources du Québec, Québec
QQERT	Centre de documentation — Terres et forêts, Ministère de l'énergie et des ressources du Québec, Québec
QQL	Bibliothèque de l'Assemblée nationale, Québec
QQLA	Bibliothèque générale, Université Laval, Québec
QQLAS	Bibliothèque scientifique, Université Laval, Québec
QQPCQ	Parks Services, Environment Canada: Service des parcs, Environnement. Canada, Québec
QQPSM	Fisheries and Oceans Canada: Pêches et océans Canada, Mont-Joli
QQS	Séminaire de Québec
QRCN	Collège de l'Abitibi-Témiscamingue, Rouyn-Noranda
QRUQR	Université du Québec en Abitibi-Témiscamingue, Rouyn-Noranda
QSHERSH	Société d'histoire des Cantons de l'Est, Sherbrooke
QSHERU	Université de Sherbrooke
QSTJ	Collège militaire royal de Saint-Jean
SRU	University of Regina
SSU	University of Saskatchewan, Saskatoon
WaU	University of Washington, Seattle

BIBLIOGRAPHIES

General/Canada

Généralités/Canada

— 1789 —

0001 **Rede, L.T.**
Bibliotheca Americana, or, A chronological catalogue of the most curious and interesting books, pamphlets, state papers, &c .... London: Printed for J. Debrett ..., J. Sewell ..., R. Baldwin and J. Bew ..., and E. Harlowe ..., 1789. 271 p.
Note: Represents "a chronological catalogue ... upon the subject of North and South America, from the earliest period to the present, in print and manuscript, for which research has been made in the British Museum, and the most celebrated public and private libraries, reviews, catalogues, &c., with an introductory discourse on the present state of literature in those countries."
Microform: CIHM Microfiche series ; no. 39988; ISBN: 0-665-39988-X. 3 microfiches (145 fr.).
Location: OONL.

— 1832 —

0002 **Rich, Obadiah**
A catalogue of books relating principally to America: arranged under the years in which they were printed. London: O. Rich, 1832. 129 p.
Note: 486 entries.– Period covered is 1500 to 1700.
Microform: CIHM Microfiche series ; no. 35377; ISBN: 0-665-35377-4. 2 microfiches (70 fr.).
Location: OOA.

— 1837 —

0003 **Ternaux-Compans, Henri**
Bibliothèque américaine ou Catalogue des ouvrages relatifs à l'Amérique qui ont paru depuis sa découverte jusqu'à l'an 1700. Paris: Arthus-Bertrand, 1837. viii, 191, 16 p.
Note: Microforme: ICMH collection de microfiches ; no 48807; ISBN: 0-665-48807-6. 3 microfiches (116 images).
Localisation: OONL.

— 1843 —

0004 **Catalogue of pamphlets relating to Canada.** Montreal: Lovell and Gibson, 1843. 3 p.
Note: Microform: CIHM Microfiche series ; no. 21926; ISBN: 0-665-21926-1. 1 microfiche (5 fr.).
Location: OOA.

— 1850 —

0005 **Catalogue of books relating to America, including a large number of rare works printed before 1700.** Amsterdam: [s.n.], 1850. 98, 103-104 p.
Note: Microform: CIHM Microfiche series ; no. 47182; ISBN: 0-665-47182-3. 3 microfiches (60 fr.).
Location: QQS.

— 1858 —

0006 **Bibaud, Maximilien**
Bibliothèque canadienne: ou, Annales bibliographiques. Montréal: Cérat et Bourguignon, [1858]. 52 p.
Note: Approx. 800 entrées.– Liste chronologique, 1658 à 1858.
Microforme: ICMH collection de microfiches ; no 32619; ISBN: 0-665-32619-X. 1 microfiche (31 images).
Localisation: OONL.

— 1866 —

0007 **British Museum. Department of Printed Books**
Catalogue of the American books in the library of the British Museum at Christmas MdcccLvi. London: C. Whittingham, 1866. xxxii, 628, 14, 62, 17 p.
Note: Part 2: "Catalogue of Canadian books in the Library of the British Museum, Christmas 1856, including those printed in the other British North American provinces." 14 p.
Reprint: Nendeln, Liechtenstein: Kraus Reprint, 1969. 4 pt. in 1.
Location: OONL.

0008 **Harrisse, Henry**
Bibliotheca americana vetustissima: a description of works relating to America published between the years 1492 and 1551. New York: G. Philes, 1866. iv, 519 p.
Note: 304 entries.
Microform: CIHM Microfiche series ; no. 05616; ISBN: 0-665-05616-8. 7 microfiches (310 fr.).
Supplement: ... : additions. Paris: Tross, 1872. xl, 199 p.
Microform: CIHM Microfiche series ; no. 05617; ISBN: 0-665-05616-8. 3 microfiches (132 fr.).
Location: OONL.

— 1867 —

0009 **Morgan, Henry J.**
Bibliotheca Canadensis, or, A manual of Canadian literature. Ottawa: Printed by G.E. Desbarats, 1867. xiv, 411 p.
Note: Approx. 3,000 entries.– Books, pamphlets, periodical and newspaper articles written in Canada, by Canadians or relating to Canada for the period 1763 to 1867.– Includes works in English and French.
Reprint: Detroit: Gale Research, 1968. 411 p.
Microform: CIHM Microfiche series ; no. 11068; ISBN: 0-665-11068-5. 5 microfiches (223 fr.).
Location: OONL.

— 1869 —

0010 **Booker, Alfred**
Catalogue de raretés bibliographiques canadiennes. Montréal: [s.n.], 1869. 16 p.
Note: "Comprenant 200 ouvrages (richement reliés) sur le Canada, près de 600 brochures canadiennes, cartes, plans, gravures, etc.: aussi de livres de droit, à être vendus, sans réserve."
Microforme: ICMH collection de microfiches ; no. 00852; ISBN: 0-665-00852-X. 1 microfiche (12 images).
Localisation: OONL.

— 1870 —

0011 **Stevens, Henry**
Bibliotheca historica, or A catalogue of 5000 volumes of books and manuscripts relating chiefly to the history and literature of North and South America: among which is included the larger portion of the extraordinary library

of the late Henry Stevens, senior, ... Boston: Houghton, 1870. xv, 234 p.
Note: Microform: CIHM Microfiche series ; no. 09238; ISBN: 0-665-09238-5. 3 microfiches (135 fr.).
Location: OONL.

— 1878 —

0012 **Filteau, J.O.**
Catalogue de livres canadiens et de quelques ouvrages français sur le Canada anciens et modernes. St.–Roche de Québec: Laberge & Gingras, 1878. 22 p.
Note: Microforme: ICMH collection de microfiches ; no 05459; ISBN: 0-665-05459-9. 1 microfiche (16 images).
Localisation: OONL.

0013 **Leclerc, Charles**
Bibliotheca americana: histoire, géographie, voyages, archéologie et linguistique des deux Amériques et des îles Philippines. Paris: Maisonneuve, 1878. vii, 424 p.
Note: 2,638 entrées.
Microforme: ICMH collection de microfiches ; no 09017; ISBN: 0-665-09017-X. 9 microfiches (401 images).
Suppléments:
... : supplément no 1. 1881. 102 p.
Microforme: ICMH collection de microfiches ; no 09018; ISBN: 0-665-09018-8. 2 microfiches (59 images).
... : supplément no 2. 1887. 127 p.
Microforme: ICMH collection de microfiches ; no 09019; ISBN: 0-665-09019-6. 2 microfiches (69 images).
Réimpression: Paris: Maisonneuve et Larose, 1961. xx, 737 p.– Le vol. principal et les suppléments sont reliés ensemble.
Localisation: OONL.

— 1884 —

0014 **Gagnon, Philéas**
Catalogue of rare old books: read attentively, English & French, Americana and miscellanies, but specially a Canadian collection. [Quebec: s.n., 1884]. 12 p.
Note: Microform: CIHM Microfiche series ; no. 47184; ISBN: 0-665-47184-X. 1 microfiche (10 fr.).
Location: OONL.

— 1885 —

0015 **Catalogue d'ouvrages historiques et littéraires sur le Canada.** Québec: Filteau, 1885. 8 p.
Note: Microforme: ICMH collection de microfiches ; no 11765; ISBN: 0-665-11765-5. 1 microfiche (10 images).
Localisation: QMBM.

0016 **Oct. Lemieux et Cie.**
Catalogue, vente à l'encan d'une bibliothèque de livres rares et précieux par Oct. Lemieux & Cie: 2,000 volumes: ouvrages sur l'Amérique, et en particulier sur le Canada: droit, littérature, science, poésie, etc. .... [S.l.: s.n.], 1885. 24 p.
Note: 467 entrées.
Microforme: ICMH collection de microfiches ; no 35561; ISBN: 0-665-35561-0. 1 microfiche (18 images).
Localisation: OTUTF.

— 1886 —

0017 **Gagnon, Philéas**
Catalogue d'ouvrages rares sur le Canada et les États-Unis. [S.l.: s.n.], 1886. 12 p.
Note: Microforme: ICMH collection de microfiches ; no 57739; ISBN: 0-665-57739-7. 1 microfiche (10 images).
Localisation: QQS.

0018 **Morgan, Henry J.**
"Review of literature, science and art."
In: _Dominion Annual Register and Review_; (1879) p. 263-305; (1880-1881) p. 279-326; (1882) p. 268-310; (1883) p. 206-242; (1884) p. 168-213; (1885) p. 329-356; (1886) p. 210-258.
Note: Bibliographical essays discussing events and publications in literature, which includes history, geography, biography, linguistics, politics and economics, as well as poetry, fiction and drama.– Two other sections deal broadly with the sciences and the arts.
Location: OONL.

— 1891 —

0019 **Baillairgé, Frédéric-Alexandre**
La littérature au Canada en 1890. Joliette, Québec: s.n., 1891. vii, 352 p.
Note: "Nous prenons le mot littérature dans son sens le plus large: travaux de l'esprit; nous prenons le mot Canada dans le sens de Canada-Français, sans cependant exclure systématiquement la littérature de langue anglaise."
Réimpression: Saint-Jacques, Québec: Éditions du Pot de fer, 1990. xxxiv, 354 p. (Collection Les Oubliés du 19e siècle québécois ; 9); ISBN: 2-921176-22-X.
Microforme: ICMH collection de microfiches ; no 00081; ISBN: 0-665-00081-2. 4 microfiches (190 images).
Localisation: OONL.

— 1892 —

0020 **Complete catalogue of blue books relating to Canada and the Arctic regions from the earliest times to 1892.** [S.l.: s.n., 1892]. 58 l.
Note: Includes a list of laws and command papers relating to Newfoundland.
Location: OTP.

— 1894 —

0021 **Bourinot, Sir John George**
Bibliography of the members of the Royal Society of Canada. [Ottawa: Printed by order of the Society], 1894. 79 p.
Note: Approx. 1,500 entries.– Listing of members, with publications from 1882 to 1894.
Microform : CIHM Microfiche series ; no. 00218; ISBN: 0-665-00218-1. 1 microfiche (44 fr.).
Location: OONL.

0022 **Bourinot, Sir John George**
"Bibliography of the members of the Royal Society of Canada."
In: _Proceedings and Transactions of the Royal Society of Canada_; Series 1, Vol. 12 (1894) p. 5-79.; ISSN: 0316-4616.
Note: Location: OONL.

— 1895 —

0023 **Emerson, Mabel E.**
"Reference lists: Canada."
In: _Monthly Bulletin of the Providence Public Library_; Vol. 1, no. 10 (October 1895) p. 176-180.
Note: Location: OONL.

— 1896 —

0024 **Haight, Willet Ricketson**
Canadian catalogue of books. Part one. Toronto: Haight, 1896. 130 p.
Note: 1,006 entries.– Compiled from publishers' catalogues.
Microform: CIHM Microfiche series ; no. 05134; ISBN: 0-

665-05134-4. 2 microfiches (75 fr.).
Supplements:
The annual Canadian catalogue of books, 1896: first supplement to the Canadian catalogue of books, 1791-1895. Toronto: Haight, 1898. 48 p.
Microform: CIHM Microfiche series ; no. 05125; ISBN: 0-665-05125-5. 1 microfiche (36 fr.).
Annual Canadian catalogue of books, 1897: second supplement to the Canadian catalogue of books, 1791-1895. Toronto: Haight, 1904. 57 p.
Reprint: *Canadian catalogue of books, 1791-1897: 1791-1895 and the two annual supplements for 1896 and 1897.* London: H. Pordes, 1958. 130, 48, 57 p.
Location: OONL.

— 1898 —

0025 **Imprimerie générale A. Côté et Cie**
Catalogue avec quelques notes des livres, brochures, journaux, etc. sortis de l'Imprimerie générale A. Côté et Cie depuis sa fondation, le 1er décembre, 1842. 2e éd. [Québec]: A. Côté, 1898. 32 p.
Note: Approx. 500 entrées.
Microforme: ICMH collection de microfiches ; no 07178; ISBN: 0-665-07178-7. 1 microfiche (16 images).
Édition antérieure: 1895. 23 p.
Microforme: ICMH collection de microfiches ; no 00161; ISBN: 0-665-00161-4. 1 microfiche (16 images).
Localisation: OONL.

0026 **Williamson & Company**
Catalogue of a valuable collection of Canadian books and rare pamphlets: includes some items of remarkable value and great scarcity, choice extra illustrated works, history, biography, travel, politics, geology, topography, agriculture, the Indian tribes, etc. : for sale at the affixed prices. Toronto: Printed for Williamson & Co. at the Robinson-Arbuthnot Press, 1898. 34 p.
Note: Microform: CIHM Microfiche series ; no. 26709; ISBN: 0-665-26709-6. 1 microfiche (23 fr.).
Location: OONL.

— 1899 —

0027 **Gareau, C.A.**
Liste de livres canadiens rares et précieux: au nombre desquels se trouvent plusieurs incunables. Montréal: 1899. 15 p.
Note: Microforme: ICMH collection de microfiches ; no 03291; ISBN: 0-665-03291-9. 1 microfiche (11 images).
Localisation: OONL.

— 1900 —

0028 **Carswell Company**
Catalogue of Canadian publications including historical and general books, statutes and other government imprints, pamphlets, magazines and miscellaneous books. Toronto: Carswell, 1900. 71 p.
Note: Microform: CIHM Microfiche series ; no. 26823; ISBN: 0-665-26823-8. 1 microfiche (42 fr.).
Location: OONL.

— 1901 —

0029 **Canadian Pacific Railway Company**
Catalogue of Canadian books provided for the tour of the Duke and Duchess of Cornwall and York. Montreal: [s.n.], 1901. 3 p.
Note: In Lochhead.– No location.

0030 **Courrier du livre.** Québec: Brosseau, 1897-1901. 5 vol.
Note: Revue mensuelle de bibliophilie et de bibliographie publié en anglais et en français, mai 1896-juin 1900. Organe officiel de la Société littéraire et historique de Québec.– Thèmes: histoire, archéologie, bibliographie, numismatique, philatélie et généalogie canadienne.
Microforme: ICMH collection de microfiches ; no P04139.
Localisation: OONL.

— 1902 —

0031 **Canadian Society of Authors**
Bibliography and general report. Toronto: 1902. 29 p.
Note: Location: OONL.

— 1906 —

0032 **Granger Frères**
Bibliographie canadienne: catalogue annoté d'ouvrages canadiens-français. [Montréal: s.n., 1906]. 295, [1] p.
Note: Approx. 2,500 entrées.– Histoire et mémoires, ouvrages religieux, littérature, géographie et voyages, droit et législation, sciences, éducation, agriculture, politique et polémique.
Édition antérieure: *France-Canada: bibliographie canadienne: catalogue d'ouvrages canadiens-français, accompagné de notes bibliographiques, et préparée pour l'Exposition universelle de Paris.* Montréal: Granger [1900]. 83 p.
Microforme [de l'édition antérieure]: ICMH collection de microfiches ; no 54221; ISBN: 0-665-54221-6. 1 microfiche (46 images).
Réédition: Saint-Jacques, Québec: Éditions du Pot de fer, 1992. ii, 295 p.; ISBN: 2-92117-693-9.– Ed. par Sylva Clapin.
Localisation: OONL.

— 1910 —

0033 **Moir, Elizabeth**
"List of books on Canadian bibliography in the reference department of the Toronto Public Library."
In: *Library World*; Vol. 13, no. 52 (October 1910) p. 111-113.; ISSN: 0024-2616.
Note: Location: OONL.

— 1915 —

0034 **United States. Library of Congress. Division of Bibliography**
List of references on Canadian independence. Washington: Library of Congress, 1915. 2 l.
Note: Location: OOP.

— 1916 —

0035 **Toronto. Public Library**
Books and pamphlets published in Canada, up to the year eighteen hundred and thirty-seven, copies of which are in the Public Reference Library, Toronto, Canada. Toronto: Public Library, 1916. 76 p.
Note: Approx. 550 entries.– Includes section of government documents and reports of Upper Canada, Lower Canada.– Compiled by Frances M. Staton.
Supplement: *... : supplement.* 1919. 8 p.
Location: OONL.

— 1917 —

0036 **Shortt, Adam; Doughty, Arthur George**
Canada and its provinces: a history of the Canadian people and their institutions by one hundred associates. Archives ed. Toronto: Glasgow, Brook, 1914-1917. 23 vol.
Note: Vol. 23 contains the bibliography, p. 233-283, arranged by the 11 sections and 22 volumes of the set.

Location: OONL.

— 1923 —

0037 **Toronto. Public Library. Reference Division**
Canadian books: an outline for the people. Toronto: Department of Education of Ontario, Public Libraries Branch, [1923]. 20 p.
Note: Approx. 600 entries.– List of books and articles issued during Canadian Book Week, 1923.– Excludes scholarly and technical works, fiction and poetry.
Location: OONL.

— 1924 —

0038 **Wallace, William Stewart**
"The bibliography of Canadiana."
In: *Canadian Historical Review*; Vol. 5, no. 1 (March 1924) p. 4-9.; ISSN: 0008-3755.
Note: Bibliographical essay in which "the chief sources of bibliographical information in regard to Canadiana are briefly indicated."
Location: OONL.

— 1925 —

0039 **British Empire Exhibition (1924-1925: London, England)**
Catalogue of Canadian books (English section): British Empire Exhibition, Wembley Park, 1925. 2nd and rev. ed. [London]: The Exhibition, 1925. 63 p.
Note: Approx. 450 entries.– Compiled by editorial committee of Toronto Public Library, the " ... list of books is fairly representative of what is current in Canadian literature ..."
Previous edition: 1924. 57 p.
Location: OONL.

0040 **Exposition de l'Empire britannique (1924-1925: Londres, Angleterre)**
Catalogue de livres canadiens (section française): Exposition de l'Empire britannique, Parc Wembley, Londres, 1925. Londres: l'Exposition, 1925. 38 p.
Note: Approx. 225 entrées.
Édition antérieure: 1924. 32 p.
Localisation: OONL.

— 1927 —

0041 **Books of French Canada: an exhibit prepared for the annual meeting of the American Library Association, Toronto, June 1927 under the distinguished patronage of the Hon. Athanase David, Secretary of the Province of Quebec.** Montreal: Louis Carrier, 1927. 47 p.
Note: Location: OONL.

— 1930 —

0042 **McGill University. Library School**
A bibliography of Canadian bibliographies compiled by the 1929 and 1930 classes in bibliography of the McGill University Library School under the direction of Marion V. Higgins. Montreal: [s.n.], 1930. iv, 45 p. (McGill University publications, series VII: Library ; no. 20)
Note: Approx. 480 entries.
Location: OONL.

— 1931 —

0043 **McCoy, James Comly**
Canadiana and French Americana in the library of J.C. McCoy: a hand-list of printed books. Montreal: Grasse, 1931. 87 p.
Note: Reprint: Montreal: Osiris, 1978. 87 p.: ill.
Location: OONL.

— 1932 —

0044 **Queen's University (Kingston, Ont.). Douglas Library**
Canadiana, 1698-1900: in the possession of the Douglas Library, Queen's University, Kingston, Ontario. Kingston, Ont.: 1932. ii, 86 p.
Note: Approx. 2,500 entries.– Covers all books and pamphlets published in Canada, or about Canada as well as those by Canadian writers, up to 1900, in the possession of Queen's University Library.– Chronological arrangement to 1850, alphabetically by author from 1850 to 1900.– Compiled by Janet S. Porteous.
Location: OONL.

— 1933 —

0045 **Bull, William Perkins**
M 'n N Canadiana: books by Canadians or about Canada: a national wedding present from Wm. Perkins Bull, K.C. to his son Michael Bull, B.A., Oxon., Barrister of the Inner Temple and his bride Noreen Hennessy, on the occasion of their visit (while on their honeymoon) to the parental home, Lorne Hall, Rosedale, Toronto, Canada, where Michael was born. [Toronto: W.P. Bull, 1933]. xxi, [171] p.: ill.
Note: 446 entries.– Printed for private circulation by Charters Publishing, Brampton, Ontario.
Location: OONL.

0046 **Sykes, William John**
Canada: a reading list. Ottawa: Carnegie Public Library, 1933. 23 p.
Note: Location: OONL.

— 1934 —

0047 **Toronto. Public Library**
A bibliography of Canadiana: being items in the Public Library of Toronto, Canada, relating to the early history and development of Canada. Toronto: The Public Library, 1934. 828 p.: facsims.
Note: 4,646 entries.– Full bibliographic description for books, pamphlets and broadsides selected from the Reference collection of the Library to form a chronological record of the history of Canada from discovery to 1867.– Excludes manuscripts, maps, prints, magazines, newspapers, transactions of societies.– Edited by Frances M. Staton and Marie Tremaine, with an introduction by G.H. Locke.
Supplements:
Boyle, Gertrude M. ... . *First supplement:* ... . Toronto: The Public Library; 1959. [10], 333 p.: ill. (1,640 entries).– Compiled with the assistance of Marjorie Colbeck.
Alston, Sandra. ... . *Second supplement:* ... . Toronto: Metropolitan Toronto Library Board; 1985-1989. 4 vol. : facsims.; ISBN: 0-88773-029-9. (3,271 entries).– Covers the years 1521 to 1867.– Indexes: name, title, subject, illustrations, maps, place of publication, printer, publisher.– Compiled with the assistance of Karen Evans.
Location: OONL.

— 1936 —

0048 **Association of Canadian Bookmen**
Books about Canada. Toronto: Association of Canadian Bookmen, [1936]. 25 p.
Note: General works, history and biography, social conditions, travel.
Location: OONL.

0049 **Sabin, Joseph; Eames, Wilberforce; Vail, R.W.G.**
Bibliotheca americana. A dictionary of books relating to America, from its discovery to the present time. Begun by Joseph Sabin, continued by Wilberforce Eames, and completed by R.W.G. Vail for the Bibliographical Society of America. New York: 1868-1936. 29 vol.
Note: Issued in 172 parts.– 106,413 entries, representing approx. 250,000 different publications, with library locations for about one million copies.– Original intention was to "include everything dealing with the political, governmental, military, economic, social and religious history of the Western Hemisphere from the discovery of the New World..." With vol. 21, inclusion was restricted to pre-1876 imprints, broadsides up to 1800.– Excludes newspapers, government publications, legal and medical works.
Index: Molnar, John Edgar. *Author-title index to Joseph Sabin's Dictionary of books relating to America.* Metuchen, N.J.: Scarecrow Press; 1974. 3 vol.
Reprint: Amsterdam: N. Israel, 1961-1962. 29 vol. (bound in 15 vol.).
Microform: CIHM Microfiche series ; nos. 25885-29513; ISBN: 0-665-25884-4 (set).
Location: OONL.

— 1938 —

0050 **Gregory, Winifred**
International congresses and conferences, 1840-1937: a union list of their publications available in libraries of the United States and Canada. New York: H.W. Wilson, 1938. 229 p.
Note: Reprint: Kraus Reprint Corp., 1967. 229 p.
Location: OONL.

— 1939 —

0051 **Canada, Newfoundland, Labrador and the Canadian Arctic: a selection of six hundred and fifty books, with 44 illustrations.** London: Maggs Bros., 1939. 118 p., [38] p. of pl.: ill., facsims.
Note: 658 entries.– Canadiana catalogue (no. 678) of London antiquarian dealer.
Location: OONL.

— 1941 —

0052 **Loosely, Elizabeth W.; Wickson, Ethelwyn**
"Canada: a reading guide and bibliography."
In: *Booklist*; Vol. 37, no. 10 (February 1, 1941) p. 247-257.
Note: Bibliography in eight sections follows a brief discussion of principal works: the people, Canadian art and literature, the country, history and politics, Canada and the United States, Canadian economy, Canada at war, reference books, general works.
Location: OONL.

0053 **United States. Library of Congress. Division of Bibliography**
Selected list of recent books and pamphlets on Canada. [Washington]: 1941. 145 p.
Note: 1,081 entries.– Covers 1930-1940.– Includes books, pamphlets, government publications.– Compiled by Ann Duncan Brown under the direction of Florence S. Hellman, chief bibliographer.
Location: OONL.

— 1945 —

0054 **Crombie, Jean Breakell; Webb, Margaret Alice**
Bibliography of Canadiana, 1944. Montreal: Sir George Williams College, 1945. 322 l.

Note: Supplement: 1946. 55 l.
Location: OONL.

0055 **Morrison, Hugh M.; Whitworth, Fred E.**
A guide to reading on Canada for high school teachers and students of social studies. Ottawa: Canadian Council of Education for Citizenship, [1945]. 116 p.
Note: Approx. 1,000 entries.– Emphasis on material published between 1930 and 1945 on geography, history, primary industries and manufacturing, transportation and communications, business and finance, external relations, labour relations, constitution and government.
Location: OONL.

— 1948 —

0056 **Barnstead, Winifred G.**
"University of Toronto Library School bibliographies 1928-1948."
In: *Ontario Library Review*; Vol. 32, no. 3 (August 1948) p. 230-240.; ISSN: 0030-2996.
Note: Location: OONL.

0057 **Child, Philip, et al.**
"Many called, but few chosen: a roll call of 350 outstanding Canadian books."
In: *Canadian Author and Bookman*; Vol. 24, no. 2 (June 1948) p. 34-42.; ISSN: 0008-2937.
Note: Location: AEU.

0058 **Reynolds, Grace**
"Bibliographies by Library School students."
In: *Ontario Library Review*; Vol. 32, no. 2 (May 1948) p. 142-145.; ISSN: 0030-2996.
Note: Bibliographies compiled during the years 1927 to 1942 by students at the McGill University Library School on a variety of subjects with Canadian focus.
Location: OONL.

— 1949 —

0059 **Canada. Library of Parliament**
Bibliography of Canadiana: a list of Canadian books and references for public libraries, universities, the film industry, and others. Ottawa: 1949. 28 l.
Note: "Prepared in co-operation with the Canadian Dept. of Trade and Commerce and the Motion Picture Association of America, Inc."
Location: OOP.

— 1950 —

0060 **Tod, Dorothea D.; Cordingley, Audrey**
A check list of Canadian imprints, 1900-1925: preliminary checking edition/Catalogue d'ouvrages imprimés au Canada: liste à vérifier. Ottawa: Canadian Bibliographic Centre, Public Archives of Canada, 1950. 370 l.
Note: Approx. 4,300 entries.– Excludes serial publications, government documents, pamphlets under fifty pages.– Text in English and French/texte en anglais et en français.
Location: OONL.

— 1952 —

0061 **Tremaine, Marie**
A bibliography of Canadian imprints, 1751-1800. Toronto: University of Toronto Press, 1952. xxvii, 705 p.: facsim.
Note: 1,204 entries.– Books, pamphlets, leaflets, broadsides, government documents, newspapers and magazines.– Detailed notes on history of document, type of paper, illustrations, typography and binding.– Locations for all copies examined, with notes on

condition.

Microform: Canada. Public Archives. Library. *Canadian imprints, 1751-1800, identified and arranged by Tremaine numbers; reproductions of items listed in M. Tremaine's A Bibliography of Canadian imprints, 1751-1800.* London: Public Record Office, 1962. 22 reels.

Location: OONL.

— 1954 —

0062 **Campbell, Catherine**
Canada's two heritages: the effect of the two predominant heritages on the French Canadians and English Canadians as revealed in their writings of the present century: a bibliography to the end of 1952. London [Ont.]: Lawson Memorial Library, University of Western Ontario, 1954. 53 p.

Note: Approx. 800 entries.– Books, pamphlets, periodical articles, theses produced in the twentieth century in the fields of religion, history, politics and government, social conditions, education, economics, some forms of literature.– Excludes individual works of poetry, drama and fiction.– Writings chosen to illustrate contemporary thought concerning recent development and past trends and events as expressed by French and British (English, Irish, Scottish) Canadians.

Location: OONL.

0063 **Dafoe, Elizabeth**
Canada: nation of the new world: a book list. [S.l.: s.n.], 1954. 14 l.

Note: Approx. 110 entries.– Emphasis on government and economics.– Compiled for publication in the *A.L.A. Booklist*, a selective list of works printed in Canada and written by Canadians.

Location: OONL.

— 1957 —

0064 **Hewitt, A.R.**
Guide to resources for Commonwealth studies in London, Oxford and Cambridge, with bibliographical and other information. London: Published for the Institute of Commonwealth Studies by Athlone Press, University of London, 1957. vii, 219 p.

Note: Includes references to Canada and the provinces.

Location: OONL.

0065 **Manitoba. Legislative Library**
Canadian imprints and books about Canada, 1949-1956. Winnipeg: The Library, [1957]. 71 l.

Note: Approx. 700 entries.– Designed to assist smaller libraries in Manitoba with selection of Canadian books.

Location: OONL.

— 1958 —

0066 **Canada. Department of Trade and Commerce**
Books sent to the Library, Canadian Pavilion, Brussels Universal and International Exhibition, 1958. Ottawa: [s.n.], 1958. [27] l.

Note: Location: OONL.

— 1960 —

0067 **A Canadian reading list.** Toronto: National Committee for Friendly Relations with Overseas Students, [1960]. 12 p.

Note: Approx. 280 entries.– Prepared as introductory list of books and periodicals about Canada for foreign students.– Emphasis on publications from 1950 to 1960.– Topics range from arts and literature to university histories.– Compiled with the cooperation of the University of Toronto Library.

Location: OONL.

— 1961 —

0068 **Canadian printed books, 1752-1961: an exhibition.** London: Times Bookshop, 1961. 27 p.

Note: 116 entries.– Includes Canadian imprints in categories: early printing, literature, history and geography, biography.

Location: OONL.

0069 **Watt, Frank A.**
"Early Canadiana."
In: *Book Collector*; Vol. 10, no. 1 (Spring 1961) p. 28-39.; ISSN: 0006-7237.

Note: Location: OONL.

— 1962 —

0070 **Drolet, Antonio**
Répertoire de la bibliographie canadienne (ouvrages imprimés). [Québec]: 1962. 36 f.

Note: 269 entrées.

Localisation: OONL.

— 1963 —

0071 **Book Publishers' Association of Canada**
Books & music [presented by the Book Publishers' Association of Canada & the Canadian Music Publishers' Association, Stratford Festival, Canada, 1963]. Toronto: [s.n.], 1963. 30 p.

Note: Location: OONL.

0072 **The Canadian book at the Frankfurt Book Fair, 1963.** Ottawa: Queen's Printer, 1963. 41 p.

Note: "An exhibition of books published during recent years sponsored by the Canada Council and organized by a joint committee of the Book Publishers' Association of Canada and l'Association des éditeurs canadiens, with the collaboration of the Queen's Printer for Canada."

Location: OTU.

0073 **Canadian Teachers' Federation**
Books about Canada/Livres concernant le Canada. Ottawa: 1963. [16] p.

Note: Location: OOCT.

— 1964 —

0074 **Amtmann, Bernard**
A catalogue of the catalogues issued by Bernard Amtmann since 1948. Montreal: 1964. 20 p.

Note: 259 entries.

Location: OONL.

0075 **Canadian booklist.** Toronto: Published by *Quill & Quire* in cooperation with the National Library, 1961-1964. 18 no.; ISSN: 0576-4696.

Note: Bimonthly.– Compiled by the National Library from deposit copies of Canadian imprint books.– Ceased publication with January-February 1964 issue.

Location: OONL.

0076 **"Catalogue of a valuable collection of Canadian books and rare pamphlets."**
In: *Papers of the Bibliographical Society of Canada*; Vol. 3 (1964) p. 61-99.; ISSN: 0067-6896.

Note: "Includes some items of remarkable value and great scarcity & choice extra illustrated works: history, biography, travel, politics, geology, topography, agriculture, the Indian tribes, etc."
Facsimile reproduction of catalogue issued in Toronto, 1898. 34 p.

Location: OONL.

— 1965 —

0077 **The Canadian book at the Frankfurt Book Fair in West Germany, 1965.** Ottawa: Queen's Printer, 1965. 54 p.
Note: "An exhibition of books published during recent years sponsored by the Canada Council and the Department of Cultural Affairs of the Province of Quebec, and organized by a joint committee of the Book Publishers' Association of Canada and l'Association des éditeurs canadiens, with the collaboration of the Queen's Printer for Canada."
Location: OH.

0078 **Canadian Library Association**
[Exhibition of Canadian books. Catalogue]. [Ottawa: 1965]. i, 37 p.
Note: Exhibition of books chosen by the National Library of Canada, the Ministry of Cultural Affairs of Quebec and the Canadian Library Association, held at Cobo Hall, Detroit, during the American Library Association Conference, July 1965.
Location: OTU.

0079 **De Varennes, Rosario**
"Panorama de la bibliographie canadienne."
Dans: *Bulletin de l'Association canadienne des bibliothécaires de langue française*; Vol. 11, no 1 (mars 1965) p. 13-17.; ISSN: 0004-5314.
Note: Localisation: OONL.

0080 **Horne, A.J.; Bradley, Kenneth**
The Commonwealth today: a select bibliography on the Commonwealth and its constituent countries. [London]: Library Association, 1965. 107 p. (Library Association Special subject list ; no. 45)
Note: 720 entries.– Books and government publications about Commonwealth countries including Canada.– Excludes serial publications, with the exception of some yearbooks.
Location: OONL.

0081 **University of Alberta. Library**
Bibliographies (national and trade) available in the Cameron Library. Edmonton: University of Alberta, 1965. iv, 65 l.
Note: Includes Canadian sections.
Location: OONL.

— 1966 —

0082 **Besterman, Theodore**
A world bibliography of bibliographies, and of bibliographical catalogues, calendars, abstracts, digests, indexes and the like. 4th ed. rev. and greatly enl. throughout. Lausanne: Societas Bibliographica, 1965-1966. 5 vol.
Note: Approx. 117,000 entries.– Covers to 1963 inclusive.– Includes Canadian listings under the term "Canada" (p. 1100-1119) for general works, history, cartography, law, official publications, topography and local history.– Other listings occur in the geographical subdivision "Canada" under specific subjects.
Previous editions:
1955-1956. 3 vol.
1947-1949. 3 vol.
1939-1940. 2 vol.
Supplement: Toomey, Alice F. *A world bibliography of bibliographies, 1964-1974: a list of works represented by Library of Congress printed catalog cards: a decennial supplement to Theodore Besterman, "A world bibliography of*

bibliographies". Totowa, N.J.: Rowman and Littlefield, 1977. 2 vol.; ISBN: 0-8747-1999-2.
Location: OONL.

— 1967 —

0083 **Campbell, Henry Cummings**
How to find out about Canada. Oxford: New York: Pergamon Press, 1967. xiv, 248 p.: ill., facsims.
Note: Bibliographical essays on Canadian education, social sciences, religion and humanities, economics and business, science and technology, medicine, art, literature, sports, geography, biography, history.
Location: OONL.

0084 **The Canadian catalogue of books published in Canada, about Canada, as well as those written by Canadians, with imprint 1921-1949 (consolidated English language reprint edition) with cumulated author index.**
[Toronto]: Toronto Public Libraries, 1967. 1 vol. (in various pagings).
Note: Consolidated reprint edition of the English sections of the *Canadian catalogue*, published annually 1921-22 to 1949.– Listing of books and pamphlets published in Canada, English and foreign books about Canada, and those by Canadians published abroad.– Includes a selection of federal and provincial government publications.
Succeeded by *Canadiana: Canada's national bibliography*, published by the National Library of Canada, Ottawa.
Previous edition: 1959. 2 vol.: vol. 1, 1921-1939; vol. 2, 1940-1949.
Location: OONL.

0085 **Canadiana library [Expo 67]/Bibliothèque de Canadiana [Expo 67].** Montreal: 1967. 4 vol.
Note: List 1: "Books."- List 2: "Periodicals."- List 3: "Books for children."- List 4: "Titles added to collection from April 1 to August 31, 1967."- Catalogues of the collection contained in the Canadian Pavillion at Expo 67, Montreal.– Text in English and French/texte en français et en anglais.
Location: OONL.

0086 **Cotnam, Jacques**
"Essai de guide bibliographique des études canadiennes-françaises."
Dans: *Enseignement secondaire*; Vol. 46, no. 5 (novembre-décembre 1967) p. 318-351.
Note: Approx. 450 entrées.
Localisation: OONL.

0087 **Jain, Sushil Kumar**
A classified guide to Canadian biographical sources. Windsor, Ont.: University of Windsor Library, 1967. 16 l.
Note: Location: NBFU.

0088 **St. James, Man. Public Library**
A bibliography of Canadiana. Centennial edition. [St. James, Man.]: 1967. 1 vol. (in various pagings).
Note: Previous edition: 1961. 1 vol. (in various pagings). Supplement: 1963. 1 vol. (in various pagings).
Location: OONL.

— 1968 —

0089 **Flint, John E.**
Books on the British Empire and Commonwealth. London: Published on behalf of the Royal Commonwealth Society by Oxford University Press, 1968. vi, 65 p.
Note: Sections on Canada: geographical and descriptive,

contemporary economic affairs, history/politics and government, literature and the arts.
Location: OONL.

0090 **Quill & Quire cumulative catalogue.** Toronto: Quill & Quire, 1940-1968. vol.
Note: Bi-annual.– "Compiled by the editorial staff of *Quill & Quire* from listings supplied by the major English-speaking publishing houses."
Location: OONL.

— 1969 —

0091 **Canada. Department of External Affairs. Information Division**
A list of Canadian books for young people: for the guidance of those responsible for the selection of books for school libraries. Ottawa: Information Division, Department of External Affairs, 1969. 29 p.
Note: Approx. 175 entries.
Location: OONL.

0092 **Festival international du livre (1er: 1969: Nice, France)**
Le Livre canadien: premier Festival international du livre, Nice, 1969/Canadian books [International Book Festival, Nice, 1969]. Ottawa: Conseil des arts du Canada, 1969. 120 p.
Note: Texte en français et en anglais/text in English and French.
Localisation: OONL.

— 1970 —

0093 **Chalifoux, Jean-Pierre**
Bio-bibliographies et bibliographies. Liste des travaux bibliographiques des étudiants en bibliothéconomie de l'Université de Montréal. Montréal: Ministère des affaires culturelles du Québec, 1970. 60 p.
Note: Couvre les années 1938-1960.– Comprend deux listes: bio-bibliographies par ordre alphabétique d'auteurs étudiés, bibliographies par ordre alphabétique de titres. Index des étudiants cités.
Localisation: OONL.

0094 **Proulx, Jeanne**
Bio-bibliographies canadiennes-françaises. Montréal: Université de Montréal, 1970. 59, [11] l.
Note: Comprend l'ensemble des travaux bio-bibliographiques présentés par les élèves de l'Ecole bibliothécaires de l'Université de Montréal, entre 1938 et 1962, compilée sous la direction de Anna Poray-Wybranowski.
Localisation: OONL.

0095 **"Répertoire bibliographique."**
Dans: *Culture*; (1940-1970) ; ISSN: 0317-2066.
Note: Liste régulière de vol. 1, 1940 à vol. 31, 1970 sur bibliographie et bibliothéconomie, religion, philosophie, éducation, science politique, économie, droit, histoire, littérature, sciences, beaux arts.
Localisation: AEU.

0096 **Snow, Kathleen M.; Hauck, Philomena**
Canadian materials for schools. Toronto: McClelland and Stewart, [c1970]. 200 p.; ISBN: 0-7710-8198-7.
Note: Sections include "Newspapers and periodicals," "Government publications," "Canadian literature," "Elementary materials," "Films."
Location: OONL.

— 1971 —

0097 **Agence littéraire des éditeurs canadiens-français**
Ouvrages canadiens-français et titres québécois traduits et publiés au Canada, traduits et publiés à l'étranger et-ou publiés à l'étranger. 2e éd. rev., corr., mise à jour. Montréal: Conseil supérieur du livre, 1971. 27 f.
Note: Édition antérieure: *Titres canadiens-français traduits au Canada et-ou traduits et publiés à l'étranger.* 1969. 1 vol.
Localisation: OONL.

0098 **MacKenzie, Margaret**
Canadiana: a select bibliography of bibliographies in the Elizabeth Dafoe Library. Winnipeg: University of Manitoba Libraries, 1971. 4, 3 l. (Reference series / University of Manitoba Libraries ; no. 2)
Note: Approx. 40 entries.
Location: OONL.

0099 **National Book League**
Commonwealth in North America: an annotated list. 2nd rev. ed. London: National Book League and the Commonwealth Institute, 1971. 213 p.; ISBN: 0-85353-073-4.
Note: Includes section on Canada: non-fiction, imaginative literature, children's books.
Previous edition: *An annotated reading list of Canadian English-language titles prepared for the Commonwealth in Books exhibition, Canada House, London, June 1969.* 1969. 21 p.– 96 entries.
Location: OONL.

— 1972 —

0100 **Amtmann, Bernard**
Contributions to a short-title catalogue of Canadiana. Montreal: [s.n.], 1971-1972. 22 parts.
Note: 45,000 entries.– Based largely on booksellers records, with sale prices listed.
Two bound versions of the 22 part catalogue were also issued: 1973. 4 vol.; 1973. 5 vol.
Location: OONL.

0101 **Biblioteca Centrală de Stat a Republicii Socialiste România**
Expositia de carte canadiana: catalog. Bucuresti: Tipografia Bibliotecii Centrale de Stat, 1972. 30 p.: ill., facsims.
Note: Approx. 120 English-language entries, 200 French-language entries, 43 phonograph records.
Location: OONL.

0102 **Choate, Ray**
North American studies: a bibliography of reference materials relevant to the study of the United States and Canada. Bundoora [Australia]: La Trobe University Library, 1972. Approx. 200 p. (Library publications / La Trobe University Library ; no. 3)
Note: Approx. 1,000 entries.– Covers to 1970.
Location: OONL.

0103 **Fulford, Robert; Godfrey, David; Rotstein, Abraham**
Read Canadian: a book about Canadian books. Toronto: James Lewis & Samuel, 1972. xi, 275 p.; ISBN: 0-88862-018-7.
Note: Current titles with emphasis on history, economics and politics, Canadian society, literature and the arts.
Location: OONL.

0104 **Lochhead, Douglas**
Bibliography of Canadian bibliographies/Bibliographie des bibliographies canadiennes. 2nd ed., rev. and enl. Toronto: Published in association with the Bibliographical Society of Canada by University of Toronto Press, 1972. xiv, 312 p.; ISBN: 0-8020-1865-3.

Note: 2,325 entries.– Covers up to June 1970.– Includes material with Canadian focus, by subject, compiler, geographical location.– Excludes bibliographies in monographs, theses, periodical articles; catalogues and price lists of publishers, booksellers; writings about bibliography; directories, trade lists, biographical dictionaries.– Index compiled by Peter E. Greig.– Text in English and French/texte en français et en anglais.
Previous edition: Tanghe, Raymond. 1960. vii, 206 p.– 1,665 entries.
Supplements (to 1960 edition):
... : supplement, 1960 & 1961. 1962. 24 p.
... : supplement, 1962 & 1963. 1964. 27 p.
... : supplement, 1964 & 1965. 1966. 32 p.
Location: OONL.

— 1973 —

0105 **Amtmann, Bernard**
Contributions to a dictionary of Canadian pseudonyms and anonymous works relating to Canada/Contributions à un dictionnaire des pseudonymes canadiens et des ouvrages anonymes relatifs au Canada. Montreal: B. Amtmann, 1973. 144 p.
Note: Compiled from Bernard Amtmann catalogues published between 1950 and 1972, and from Montreal Book Auction catalogues, 1967-1972.– Introduction in English and French/Introduction en français et en anglais.
Location: OONL.

0106 **Brown, Gerald R.**
Canada: the provincial look. [Ottawa]: Canadian School Library Association, Canadian Library Association, 1973. 103 p. (in various pagings), [32] p.: ill.
Note: Approx. 800 entries.– Lists multi-media items of both provincial and regional nature, fiction and non-fiction, feature and documentary films.– Suggested levels for use are indicated.
Location: OONL.

0107 **Canadian publications, books-periodicals, out of print, 1967-1972/Publications canadiennes, livres-périodiques, épuisées, 1967-1972.** Vancouver: Versatile Publishing, 1973. xxxiv, 651, 185 p.
Note: Approx. 30,000 entries.– Compilation of non-current materials held by antiquarian and other Canadian booksellers.– Includes books, pamphlets, serials, government publications, speeches.– Text in English and French/texte en français et en anglais.
Location: OONL.

0108 **Mailloux, Pierre**
Bibliographie annotée d'ouvrages de référence. Montréal: Ministère des affaires culturelles, 1973. ix, 131 p.: fac.-sim.
Note: 330 entrées.
Suppléments:
... : supplément, 1967-1974. Montréal: Ministère des affaires culturelles, 1975. 305 p.
Bibliographie annotée des ouvrages de référence en usage au Bureau de la bibliographie rétrospective. 1981. 103 p.
Localisation: OONL.

0109 **Thibault, Claude**
Bibliographia Canadiana. Don Mills, Ont.: Longman Canada, 1973. lxiv, 795 p.
Note: 25,660 entries.– Covers books to 1970, periodical articles to the end of 1969.– Contains printed works (books, articles) on Canadian history and historiography.– Text in English and French/texte en français et en anglais.
Location: OONL.

— 1974 —

0110 **Canadian books in print/Catalogue des livres canadiens en librairie.** Toronto: University of Toronto Press, 1967-1974. 8 vol.; ISSN: 0702-0201.
Note: Annual.– Compiled from Canadian publishers' lists, includes all titles with Canadian imprint, Canadian subsidiaries of international publishing companies.– Lists textbooks, some government publications.– Excludes pamphlets, periodicals, maps, newspapers, sheet music.– 1974, edited by Harald Bohne and Martha Pluscauskas; 1970-1973, edited by Harald Bohne; 1968-1969, edited by Gerald Simoneau; 1967, edited by Rita Butterfield and Julia Richer.
Location: OONL.

0111 **Rapoport, Joseph**
Une liste abrégée sélective de Canadiana rare comprenent cent livres, mémoires et brochures imprimés pendant le 17e, 18e, et 19e siècle ainsi que plusieurs anciennes cartes géographiques de l'Amérique du Nord et des Canadas et contenant plus particulierement quelques items d'intérêt juif dans la bibliothèque privée de Joseph Rapoport/A selective checklist of rare Canadiana consisting of one hundred books, memoirs and pamphlets printed during the 17th, 18th & 19th century as well as several early maps of North America & of the Canadas and containing more particularly some items of Jewish interest in the private library of Joseph Rapoport. Montréal: Osiris, 1974. 58 p.: facsims.
Note: Texte en français et en anglais/text in English and French.
Localisation: OONL.

0112 **Simard, Sylvain**
"Bibliographie des écrits français sur le Canada."
Dans: *Les Relations entre la France et le Canada au XIXe siècle.* Paris: Centre culturel canadien, 1974. P. 85-109. (Les Cahiers du Centre culturel canadien ; no 3); ISBN: 2-900434-03-3.
Note: Localisation: OONL.

— 1975 —

0113 **Alberta. Culture, Youth and Recreation. Libraries Division**
A slice of Canada: a list of Canadian books of interest to small Alberta public libraries. 2nd ed. Edmonton: Alberta Culture, Youth and Recreation, Libraries Division, 1975. 250 p.
Note: Approx. 1,000 entries.– Includes material published up to and including 1974 on Canadian history, politics, business and economics, literature, science and technology, biography, travel and description.
Previous edition: *A suggested buying guide to Canadian books for small Alberta libraries.* 1957. 36 p.
Supplements:
1963. 1 vol. (unpaged).
Buccini, Anne. ... : a checklist ... . 1973. 216 l.
Location: OONL.

0114 **Lande, Lawrence M.**
Canadian imprints: a checklist. Montreal: McGill University, 1975. 62 p.: facsims. (Lawrence Lande Foundation for Canadian Historical Research ; no. 13); ISBN: 0-88940-029-

6.
Note: 474 entries.
Location: OONL.

0115 **Lande, Lawrence M.**
Canadian miscellanies: a checklist. Montreal: McGill University, 1975. 68 p.: facsims. (Lawrence Lande Foundation for Canadian Historical Research; no. 12); ISBN: 0-88940-028-8.
Note: 366 entries.
Location: OONL.

0116 **McAndrew, William J.; Elliott, Peter J.**
Teaching Canada: a bibliography. Orono, Me.: New England-Atlantic Provinces-Quebec Center, University of Maine at Orono, [1975]. 102 p.
Note: Approx. 800 entries.– Books, serials, audio-visual materials in areas of Canadian literature, history, social studies for teachers and school libraries in United States.
Location: OONL.

0117 **National Library of Canada**
National Library of Canada presents Canadian books for the exhibition at the National Library in Warsaw/ Bibliothèque nationale du Canada présente livres canadiens pour l'exposition de la Bibliothèque nationale à Varsovie/Biblioteka Narodowaw Kanadzie przedstawia ksiezki [sic] Kanadyjskie na wystawie w Bibliotece Narodowej w Warszawie. Ottawa: National Library of Canada, [1975]. 19 l.
Note: Approx. 700 entries.– Lists books on Canadian history, biography, geography, native peoples, political science, economics, social sciences, poetry, fiction, drama, fine arts, folklore, library science.– Text in English, French and Polish/texte en anglais, français et en polonais.
Location: OONL.

0118 **Notices en langue française du** *Canadian catalogue of books*, 1921-1949 avec index établi par Henri-Bernard Boivin. Montréal: Ministère des affaires culturelles, 1975. ix, 263, 199 p., 17 f. de pl.: ill.
Note: Approx. 6,250 entrées.– En tête du titre: Bibliothèque nationale du Québec.
Localisation: OONL.

0119 **Wasserman, Paul; Herman, Esther**
Library bibliographies and indexes: a subject guide to resource material available from libraries, information centers, library schools, and library associations in the United States and Canada. Detroit: Gale Research, 1975. ix, 301 p.; ISBN: 0-8103-0390-6.
Note: Approx. 5,000 entries.– Includes bibliographies or indexes from 75 Canadian libraries and information centres on various subjects.
Location: OONL.

— 1976 —

0120 **Cowan, Ann S.; Corcoran, Frank**
"Museum publications."
In: *Communiqué: Canadian Studies*; Vol. 2, no. 4/5 (May 1976) p. 11-34, 72-92.; ISSN: 0318-1197.
Note: Newsletters and journals, books, papers, leaflets published by museums, arranged by museum and publication series or subject group, films, prints, videotapes, list of Canadian Museums Association publications.
Location: OONL.

0121 **Directory of Canadian reports: a guide to Canadian report literature/Répertoire des rapports canadiens: guide des publications techniques canadiennes.**
Vancouver: Versatile, c1976. xxviii, 683 p.
Note: For this publication, a report is a statement, account, or presentation of facts of an administrative or research nature.– Issuing agencies are associations, institutions, individuals, committees, government departments.– Subjects include science and technology, humanities, commerce, industry, law, religion.– Includes catalogues and bibliographies.
Location: OONL.

— 1977 —

0122 **Canada. Department of Industry, Trade and Commerce**
Books from Canada/Livres du Canada. Ottawa: Department of Industry, Trade and Commerce, 1977. 1 portfolio.
Note: On cover: XVII International Book Exhibition, Chicago, Illinois.
Location: OONL.

0123 **Canadian studies bibliographies/Bibliographies des études canadiennes.** [Ottawa]: External Affairs Canada, Bureau of Public Affairs, [1977]. 1 vol. (in various pagings).
Note: Contains four sections: "Introduction to Canadian studies: selected bibliography," compiled by Institute of Canadian Studies, Carleton University; "Introduction au Canada français: bibliographie sélective," par Pierre Savard, revue, corrigée et augmentée par Jacques Grimard; "Canadian studies: series bibliography," compiled by Joseph J. Jurkovic; "Survey of microform resources in Canadian studies disciplines," prepared for the Department of External Affairs by John A. Moldenhauer.
Location: OONL.

0124 **Robinson, Paul**
After survival: a teacher's guide to Canadian resources. Toronto: P. Martin Associates, c1977. 329 p.; ISBN: 0-88778-147-0.
Note: Lists books, periodicals, newspapers, textbooks, books for teachers, recordings, multi-media kits in 25 subject areas from Art to Vocational: resource materials organized thematically and evaluated for kindergarten through high school; in English and French languages; related to ethnic groups, Canadian regions, native peoples, women's studies.
Location: OONL.

— 1978 —

0125 **"Books on Canada."**
In: *American Review of Canadian Studies*; Vol. 3, no. 1 (Spring 1973) p. 210-218; vol. 4, no. 1 (Spring 1974) p. 99-112; vol. 5, no. 1 (Spring 1975) p. 114-188; vol. 5, no. 2 (Autumn 1975) p. 146-204; vol. 8, no. 1 (Spring 1978) p. 65-95.; ISSN: 0272-2011.
Note: Abstracts or brief reviews of new publications in all fields.– Includes reference works.– Title varies: *Book notes*, (Vol. 3, no. 1, Spring 1973).
Location: AEU.

0126 **Canada. National Capital Commission**
A bibliography of history and heritage of the National Capital Region/Une bibliographie de l'histoire et du patrimoine de la région de la Capitale nationale. Rev. ed. [Ottawa]: National Capital Commission, 1978. xv, 310 l.

Note: Manuscripts arranged by archival collection, biographies, church histories, government documents, local histories, maps, serials.– Text in English and French/texte en français et en anglais.
Previous edition: 1976. xv, 310 l.
Supplement: 1982. xv, 71 l.
Location: OONL.

0127 **Canadian resources listing.** [Edmonton]: Alberta Education, 1978. xix, 676 p.; ISSN: 0708-4439.
Note: Listing of print and non-print materials authored, edited, designed or produced by Canadians, about Canada or presenting a Canadian perspective and evaluated by teachers for their value in language arts or social studies curricula, with appropriate grade level indicated.
Previous edition: *Canadian resources.* 1975. 141 p.; ISSN: 0708-4420.
Location: OONL.

0128 **Phillips, Donna**
In search of Canadian materials. Rev. ed. Winnipeg: Department of Education, 1978. iii, 336 p.
Note: 2,100 entries.– Commissioned by Canadian Studies Project Committee as an aid to selection of Canadian materials for school libraries.– Topics covered include activity books, art, business, Canadian studies (biography, geography, history), language and literature, Manitoba subjects, native studies, science, sports, women's studies, reference materials.
Previous edition: 1976. vi, 205 p.– Approx. 1,000 entries.
Supplements:
1977. iii, 94 p.
1979. 46 p.
1983. iii, 63 p.
1984. viii, 121 p.
1986. viii, 65 p.
1988. vii, 62 p.
1990. vii, 35 p.
1991. vii, 45 p.
Location: OONL.

— 1979 —

0129 **Canadian Book Information Centre**
Read: a selected list of Canadian books. Toronto: The Centre, [1979]. 24 l.
Note: Location: OONL.

0130 **Olivier, Réjean**
Livres québécois, canadiens et américains antérieurs à 1878 de la bibliothèque Olivier. Joliette [Québec: s.n.], 1979. 37 f.; ISBN: 2-920249-04-5.
Note: Approx. 450 entrées.
Localisation: OONL.

— 1980 —

0131 **A lesson in history: Canadiana collected by Dr. Lawrence Lande/Une page d'histoire: livres et documents historiques de la collection Lawrence Lande.** Ottawa: National Library of Canada: Public Archives Canada, 1980. 35 p.: ill., facsim.; ISBN: 0-662-50696-0.
Note: 11 entries.– Catalogue of an exhibition held at National Library, Mar. 27 – June 3, 1980.– Text in English and French/texte en français et en anglais.
Location: OONL.

0132 **Robeson, Virginia R.; Sylvester, Christine**
Teaching Canadian studies: an evaluation of print materials, grades 1-13. Toronto: OISE Press, 1980. ix, 340 p. (Curriculum series / Ontario Institute for Studies in Education ; 40); ISBN: 0-7744-0184-2.
Note: Approx. 500 entries.– Inventory of texts, resource books, reference books in Canadian history, geography, government and politics, economics, consumer education, law, social studies and social issues.– Annotations describe contents, organization of material and presentation approach, physical features (layout, illustrations, etc.).– Includes index of recommended titles by subject and grade level.
Location: OONL.

0133 **Thouin, Richard**
Les bibliographies du cours de bibliothéconomie de l'Université Laval, 1947-1961 [microforme]: index. Montréal: Ministère des affaires culturelles, Bibliothèque nationale du Québec, 1980. 1 microfiche.
Note: Localisation: QQLA.

0134 **Wasserman, Paul; Herman, Esther**
Catalog of museum publications & media: a directory and index of publications and audiovisuals available from United States and Canadian institutions. 2nd ed. Detroit: Gale Research, 1980. xi, 1044 p.; ISBN: 0-8103-03880-4.
Note: Lists books, booklets, periodicals, monographs, catalogues, pamphlets and leaflets, films and filmstrips, maps/charts, video programs which have been prepared and distributed by museums, art galleries, etc. in United States and Canada, a total of 922 institutions.
Previous edition: *Museum media: a biennial directory and index of publications and audiovisuals available from United States and Canadian institutions.* 1973. vii, 455 p.
Location: OONL.

— 1981 —

0135 **Ryder, Dorothy E.**
Canadian reference sources: a selective guide. 2nd ed. [Ottawa]: Canadian Library Association, 1981. viii, 311 p.; ISBN: 0-88802-156-9.
Note: Approx. 2,300 entries.– Covers reference material up to and including December 1980.– Includes bibliographies, encyclopedias, federal and provincial government publications, manuscripts, newspapers, periodicals, theses, year books and almanacs relating to history, humanities, science, social sciences.
Previous edition: 1973. x, 185 p.
Supplement: *... : supplement.* 1975. xi, 121 p.; ISBN: 0-88802-106-2.
Location: OONL.

0136 **University of Birmingham. Library**
Études canadiennes-Canadian studies: books, atlases and other illustrative materials relating to social, political, economic and cultural affairs in Canada, selected from the holdings of the Library of the University of Birmingham: exhibition celebrating the designation of the university as a Regional Canadian Study Centre, May 1981, the Library, University of Birmingham, May 15th – May 22nd, 1981. Birmingham, England: Department of Geography, University of Birmingham, 1981. 35 p.: ill.
Note: 137 entries.– Compiled by Alan F. Williams and David R. Ingram.
Location: OONL.

— 1982 —

0137 **Books in Canada, past and present: an exhibition/ Livres canadiens d'hier et d'aujourd'hui: une exposition.** Ottawa: National Library of Canada, 1982. 34 p.: ill.; ISBN: 0-662-51972-8.
Note: Catalogue prepared for exhibition in McLennan Library of McGill University in honour of forty-eighth General Conference of International Federation of Library Associations and Institutions, 22-28 August, 1982.– Includes early works on Canada (books, maps, illustrations), early Canadian imprints (books and pamphlets), livres d'artistes.– Text in English and French in parallel columns/texte en anglais et en français sur des col. parallèles.
Location: OONL.

0138 **Georgian Bay Regional Library System**
Sélection de livres français. [Barrie, Ont.]: The System, 1982. 132 p.
Note: Approx. 5,000 entrées.– Comporte des références québécoises.
Localisation: OONL.

0139 **Toronto. Public Library**
Experience Canada. 2nd ed. [Toronto]: The Library, 1982. 36 p.
Note: 215 entries.– Includes books published between 1976 and 1982 in areas of literature, history, politics.– Compiled by Linda Ashley, et al.
Previous edition: Hutcheson, Stephanie, et al. 1975. 40 p.– 250 entries.
Location: OONL.

0140 **Universitet i Oslo. Amerikansk Institutt**
List of books concerning the study of Canada at the American Institute, University of Oslo. Oslo: The University, 1982. 41, 15 p.
Note: Approx. 1,000 entries.– Compiled by Berit Timm Marcussen, Randi Tobiassen and Edel Fearnley.– Text in English and French with French text on inverted pages.– Title of additional title-page: *Liste de livres concernant l'étude du Canada à l'Institut des langues romanes, Section française, Université d'Oslo.*
Location: OONL.

0141 **Universitet i Oslo. Romansk Institutt. Avdeling A (Fransk)**
Liste de livres concernant l'étude du Canada à l'Institut des langues romanes, Section française, Université d'Oslo. Oslo: L'Université, 1982. 15, 41 p.
Note: Approx. 500 entrées.– Comp. par Berit Timm Marcussen, Randi Tobiassen and Edel Fearnley.– Texte en français et en anglais disposé tête-bêche.– Titre de la p. de t. additionnelle: *List of books concerning the study of Canada at the American Institute, University of Oslo.*
Localisation: OONL.

— 1983 —

0142 **Cameron, William J.**
A short-title catalog of Canadiana in English: from Hakluyt to Hennepin, 1599-1698 in the Rare Book Room: la Réserve, the National Library of Canada: la Bibliothèque nationale du Canada. London: University of Western Ontario, 1983. v, 10 l. (WHSTC library catalog ; no. 14; ISSN: 0712-9297); ISBN: 0-7714-0452-2.
Note: Location: OONL.

0143 **Underwood, Lisa**
Secondary level bibliographies: Canada studies, Canadian literature, multiculturalism. [Vancouver]: Education Services Group, Vancouver School Board, 1983. 51 p. (Curriculum resources / Education Services Group, Vancouver School Board ; 58)
Note: Approx. 1,000 entries.– Recommended books for high schools in areas of Canadian studies in general, Canadian literature, ethnic studies.
Location: OONL.

— 1984 —

0144 **Atlantic book choice: recommended Canadian and regional titles for a junior-senior high school library collection.** Halifax, N.S.: Canadian Learning Materials Centre, 1984. vi, 235 p. (Model Library Project / Canadian Learning Materials Centre ; vol. 2)
Note: "A joint project of the Canadian Learning Materials Centre and the Nova Scotia School Library Association with assistance from Newfoundland Model Library Committee, Association of Canadian Publishers, Atlantic Publishers Association."
Location: OONL.

— 1985 —

0145 **Aarhus universitet. Institut for engelsk filologi**
Canadiana at the University of Aarhus: the Canadian collection of the library of the English Department, University of Aarhus, Denmark. Aarhus, Denmark: The English Department, 1985. 94 p.
Note: Approx. 1,200 entries.– Compiled by Connie Relsted.
Location: OONL.

0146 **"Books about Canada."**
In: *Canada Year Book*; (1965) p. 1101-1114; (1966) p. 1121-1136; (1967) p. 1185-1200; (1968) p. 1174-1190; (1969) p. 1204-1220; (1970-71) p. 1285-1300; (1972) p. 1289-1302; (1973) p. 913-919; (1974) p. 878-885; (1975) p. 896-904; (1976-77) p. 1104-1113; (1978-79) p. 936-947; (1980-81) p. 946-965; (1985) p. 823-842; ISSN: 0068-8142.
Note: Selective list of books compiled by the National Library of Canada, "emphasizes the latest editions of books published within the last ten years, and includes titles issued in either or both English and French."
Location: OONL.

0147 **Breen, William J.; Marshall, Julie G.**
Resources for North American studies: an annotated list of microform collections in Australian libraries relating to the United States and Canada. Bundoora, Vic.: Borchardt Library, La Trobe University, 1985. vi l., 86 p.; ISBN: 0-85816-595-3.
Note: 335 entries.– Chronological arrangement.
Location: OONL.

0148 **Brundin, Robert E.**
Price guide to books on Canada and the Canadian Arctic. 2nd ed. Edmonton: University of Alberta Printing Services, 1985. vii, 124 p.; ISBN: 0-88864-950-9.
Note: Approx. 1,700 entries.– Books and pamphlets.– Excludes ephemeral material (photo albums, postcards, letters, etc.).– Emphasis on history, geography, politics, social development, early accounts of travel.
Previous edition: Ann Arbor, Mich.: Published for the Faculty of Library Science, University of Alberta by University Microfilms International; 1979. ix, 204 p.
Location: OONL.

0149 **Canada. Bureau des traductions. Direction de la documentation**
Répertoire des bibliographies [Bureau des traductions]/ Directory of bibliographies [Translation Bureau. 4e éd. [Ottawa: Le Bureau], 1985. vii, 21 p.
Note: Liste de bibliographies compilées à la Division des services d'information et de référence de la Direction de la documentation.– Sujets couverte sont multiples.– Texte en français et en anglais/text in English and French.
Éditions antérieures:
Répertoire des bibliographies disponibles/List of available bibliographies. 1982. 24, 21, 21 f.
1981. 14, 14, 14 f.
Localisation: OONL.

0150 **Cariou, Mavis; Cox, Sandra J.; Bregman, Alvan**
Canadian selection: books and periodicals for libraries. 2nd ed. Toronto: Published for the Ontario Ministry of Citizenship and Culture and the Centre for Research in Librarianship, University of Toronto [by] University of Toronto Press, c1985. xvi, 501 p.; ISBN: 0-8020-4630-4.
Note: 5,427 entries.– Lists English-language books, originals and translations, published in Canada, about Canada, or written by Canadians at home or abroad, up to December 31, 1983.– Excludes nonprint materials, children's and young adults' books, music scores, maps, county atlases, unpublished theses, works in languages other than English, highly specialized publications.
Previous edition: Jarvi, Edith T.; McLean, Isabel; MacKenzie, Catharine. c1978. xii, 1060 p.; ISBN: 0-8020-4554-5.
Supplement: McLean, Isabel; Jarvi, Edith. ... : *1977-1979.* c1980. 398 p.; ISBN: 0-8020-4593-6.
Location: OONL.

0151 **"Ouvrages sur le Canada."**
Dans: *Annuaire du Canada*; (1965) p. 1165-1178; (1966) p. 1219-1235; (1967) p. 1270-1286; (1968) p. 1262-1278; (1969) p. 1294-1310; (1970-71) p. 1382-1398; (1972) p. 1393-1407; (1973) p. 991-997; (1974) p. 969-976; (1975) p. 984-992; (1976-77) p. 1224-1233; (1978-79) p. 1028-1039; (1980-81) p. 1053-1073; (1985) p. 865-884.; ISSN: 0316-8557.
Note: Répertoire des principaux ouvrages sur le Canada, établi par la Bibliothèque nationale du Canada, "couvre de nombreux aspects de la vie canadienne, signale les plus récentes éditions de livres parus durant la dernière décennie, et comprend des ouvrages publiés en anglais, en français ou dans les deux langues."
Localisation: OONL.

— 1986 —

0152 **Canada. Bibliothèque du Parlement**
Brochures canadiennes index [microform]. [Ottawa: Micro Can, 1986]. 11 microfiches.
Note: Approx. 20,000 entrées.– Index des brochures historiques canadiennes par auteur, titre et sujet dans une séquence alphabétique.
English title: *CPV index.*
Localisation: OONL.

0153 **Canada. Library of Parliament**
CPV index [microform]. [Ottawa: Micro Can, 1986]. 20 microfiches.
Note: Card file index to collection of approximately 20,000 Canadian pamphlets in English language held in Rare Books collection of National Library of Canada.
Titre en français: *Brochures canadiennes index.*

Location: OONL.

0154 **Clarkson, Thora K.**
Selections from the Canadiana collection of the Ontario Legislative Library. Toronto: Ontario Legislative Library, 1986. v, 72 p. ill., facsims.; ISBN: 0-7729-1032-4.
Note: Includes books, newspapers, government publications in six categories: explorers, travel narratives, native peoples, Lower Canada, Upper Canada, law and government.
Location: OONL.

0155 **Zysman, Ewa**
Stany Zjednoczone Ameryki i Kanada w pismiennictwie polskim 1945-1985: bibliografia drukow zwartych. Warszawa: Polski Instytut Spraw Miedzynarodowych, 1986. 272 p.
Note: Includes a section of books on Canada in Polish.
Location: OONL.

— 1987 —

0156 **Bellemare, Louis**
L'information électronique au Québec: guide pratique des services d'information en ligne. Québec: Gouvernement du Québec, Direction des technologies de l'information, 1987. 93 p.; ISBN: 2-550-17536-0.
Note: 130 entrées.– Index des banques de données par secteurs d'activités: politique et actualité, économie et finances, sciences humaines, relations de travail, éducation, santé et sécurité au travail, sciences et technologies industrielles, communication et culture.– Annexes: index: banques de données, producteurs d'information, serveurs, producteurs-diffuseurs.
Localisation: OONL.

0157 **Rogers, Helen F.**
Bases de données canadiennes lisibles par machine: un répertoire et un guide. Ottawa: Bibliothèque nationale du Canada, 1987. 140, 134 p.; ISBN: 0-660-53734-6.
Note: Approx. 400 entrées.– Décrit les bases de données produites au Canada, chaque fichier en français et en anglais, sur tous les sujets, par ordre alphabétique avec leur nom énuméré au complet, ensuite quatre index: sujets, producteurs, fournisseurs de services en direct, liste maîtresse des noms anciens et actuels des fichiers.– Description des bases contenu et la portée, le type, le sujet, territoire géographique étudié, période recensée, périodicité des mises à jour, le producteur, le service en directe et les modalités d'access.– Texte en français et en anglais disposé tête-bêche.– Titre de la p. de t. additionnelle: *Canadian machine-readable databases: a directory and guide.*
Localisation: OONL.

0158 **Rogers, Helen F.**
Canadian machine-readable databases: a directory and guide. Ottawa: National Library of Canada, 1987. 134, 140 p.; ISBN: 0-660-53734-6.
Note: Approx. 400 entries.– Lists databases produced in Canada on all subjects, described in both English and French, arranged by name of database, followed by indexes: subject, database producer, online and offline service vendors, names.– Information provided includes content and scope, type, subject, coverage, languages, time span, updating frequency, producer, online service, conditions of use.– Text in English and French with French text on inverted pages.– Title of additional title-page: *Bases de données canadiennes lisibles par machine: un*

répertoire et un guide.
Location: OONL.

0159 **Università di Pisa**
Catalogo dei libri e dei periodici di interesse Canadese presso l'Università degli studi di Pisa a cura di Algerina Neri, Giovanni Pizzorusso. Pisa, [Italy]: Servizio Editoriale Universitario di Pisa, 1987. 168 p.
Note: Approx. 900 entries.– Covers to Dec. 31, 1986.– Project of the Centro Interuniversitario di studi sul Canada (Università di Milano – Università di Pisa).– Includes history, biography, literature in French and English.
Location: OONL.

— 1988 —

0160 **Henning, J.; Hogan, K.; Lipton, S.**
"Databases for research in Canadian studies: humanities and related disciplines (preliminary list)."
In: *Canadian Issues*; Vol. 10, no. 4 (1988) p. 77-109.; ISSN: 0318-8442.
Note: Approx. 100 entries.
Location: OONL.

0161 **Kanada kankei hogo bunken mokuroku: 1977-1988.**
Tokyo: Nihon Kanada Gakkai, 1988. 150 p.
Note: Bibliography of Canadian studies in Japan, 1977-1988.– Text in Japanese.
Previous edition: 1979. 102 p.
Supplement: 1989. 15 p.
Location: OONL.

— 1989 —

0162 **Black, Joseph Laurence**
Soviet perception of Canada, 1917-1987: an annotated bibliographic guide. Kingston, Ont.: Ronald P. Frye, c1989. ix, 139, xiv, 242 p. (Centre for Canadian Soviet Studies, Bibliographic series ; no. 1); ISBN: 0-919741-94-0.
Note: Approx. 3,000 entries.– Includes books, articles, chapters of books, newspaper articles, Soviet dissertations on Canada (1945-1986), Canadian works translated into Russian.
Location: OONL.

0163 **Ettlinger, John R.T.; O'Neill, Patrick B.**
A checklist of Canadian copyright deposits in the British Museum, 1895-1923. Halifax, N.S.: Dalhousie University, School of Library Service, 1984-1989. 5 vol.; ISBN: 0-7703-0179-7 (v.1); 0-7703-0178-9 (v.2); 0-7703-9706-9 (v.3, pt. 1); 0-7703-9726-3 (v.3, pt.2); 0-7703-9730-1 (v.4, pt. 1); 0-7703-9736-0 (v.4, pt.2); 0-7703-9732-8 (v.5).
Note: Series of checklists of Canadian material deposited at British Museum under copyright law in the years from 1895 to 1923.
Vol. 1: *Maps.* 1984. xvii, 96 p.– Approx. 950 entries.
Vol. 2: *Insurance plans.* 1985. xiii, 157 p.– 1,675 entries.
Vol. 3, part 1: *City and area directories.* 1986. xi, 138 p.– 887 entries.
Vol. 3, part 2: *Telephone and miscellaneous directories.* 1988. vii, 86 p.– 288 entries.
Vol. 4, parts 1 and 2: *Sheet music.* 1989. vii, 893 p.– 11,338 entries.– Lists all sheet music copyrighted in Canada between 1895 and 1924.– Indexes: Composers and lyricists; Titles.
Vol. 5: *Photographs.* 1989. ix, 228 p.– 4,263 entries.
Location: OONL.

0164 **Grünsteudel, Günther**
Canadiana-Bibliographie: Veröffentlichungen deutschsprachiger Kanadisten, 1980-1987. Bochum [Germany]: N. Brockmeyer, 1989. 89 p. (Kanada-Studien ; Bd. 1); ISBN: 3-88339-703-2.
Note: 761 entries.
Location: OONL.

— 1990 —

0165 **Artibise, Alan F.J.**
Interdisciplinary approaches to Canadian society: a guide to the literature. Montreal: Published for the Association for Canadian Studies by McGill-Queen's University Press, 1990. 156 p.; ISBN: 0-7735-0788-4.
Note: Reviews recent literature in four fields of Canadian studies: labour studies, religious studies, immigration and ethnic studies, native studies (with separate treatment of Amerindian studies in Quebec).
Location: OONL.

0166 **Artibise, Alan F.J.**
"Pacific views of Canada: Canadian studies research in Asia-Oceania."
In: *International Journal of Canadian Studies*; No. 1-2 (Spring-Fall 1990) p. 259-278.; ISSN: 1180-3991.
Note: Analysis and documentation of Canadian studies research in Japan, Australia, New Zealand, China, India, Korea.
Location: OONL.

0167 **Canadian Institute for Historical Microreproductions**
Canada, the printed record [microform]: a bibliographic register with indexes to the microfilm series of the Canadian Institute for Historical Microreproductions/ Catalogue d'imprimés canadiens [microforme]: répertoire bibliographique avec index de la collection de microfiches de l'Institut canadien de microreproductions historique. Ottawa: The Institute, 1990. 2 vol. (loose-leaf: [40] p. + 285 microfiches); ISBN: 0-665-99966-6.
Note: Approx. 66,000 entries.– Collection of pre-1900 Canadiana in microform, entries providing access to the pre-1901 Canadian monographs reproduced in full on microfiche by the CIHM: documents published or printed in Canada, documents published or printed outside Canada and written by Canadians, documents published or printed outside Canada having Canadian subject matter.– Includes monographs, pamphlets, playbills, pictures, advertisements, municipal and county publications, annual publications (reports, almanacs, directories).– Excludes for the most part: manuscripts, journals, newspapers, engravings, provincial and territorial government publications.– Indexes: author, title, series, subjects (English), subjects (French).– Updated register and indexes will be published annually.– Titles microfilmed are distributed annually to subscribers.– Text in English and French/texte en français et en anglais.
Location: OOCIHM.

0168 **Codignola, Luca**
"The view from the other side of the Atlantic."
In: *International Journal of Canadian Studies*; No. 1-2 (Spring-Fall 1990) p. 217-258.; ISSN: 1180-3991.
Note: Review of scholarly research literature on Canada by Europeans.
Location: OONL.

0169 **Davis, John F.; Howard, Susan V.**
Catalogue of Canadian holdings in Birkbeck College libraries. London: Birkbeck College, Centre for Canadian Studies, 1990. 86 p.
Note: Approx. 800 entries.– Listing of books which are largely or exclusively about Canada or on Canadian topics.– Sections include "General reference books," "Geography," "History and politics," "Regional materials."
Location: OONL.

0170 **Hafstrom, Ole; Stenderup, Vibeke**
Litteratursogning: Canada almen bibliografi. Aarhus: Statsbiblioteket, 1990. 24 p. (Canadiana / Statsbiblioteket, Aarhus ; 3); ISBN: 87-7507187-8.
Note: Listing of Canadian reference works.
Location: OONL.

0171 **Ingles, Ernest**
Canada. Oxford: Clio Press, c1990. xxx, 393 p.: map. (World bibliographical series / Clio Press ; 62); ISBN: 1-85109-005-3.
Note: 1,316 annotated entries.– Monographs, periodicals, reference works (bibliographies, dictionaries, atlases, almanacs, yearbooks, indexing and abstracting publications) dealing with Canadian history, geography, politics and economics, education, culture, religion, social organization, science and technology.– Emphasis is on books published between 1960 and 1990.– Majority of titles are in the English language.– Due to an international readership, availability is a factor in the inclusion decision.
Location: OONL.

0172 **Waldon, Freda Farrell**
Bibliography of Canadiana published in Great Britain, 1519-1763/Bibliographie des ouvrages sur le Canada publiés en Grande-Bretagne entre 1519 et 1763. Toronto: Published by ECW Press in collaboration with the National Library of Canada, c1990. lxv, 535 p.: port., facsims.; ISBN: 1-55022-087-X.
Note: Approx. 750 entries.– Printed works published in Britain to 1763 which concern in some way any part of the present area of Canada: books, pamphlets, broadsides and broadsheets, ballads and maps.– British imprints of translations, reprints, and other works originally published elsewhere are included.– Excludes manuscripts, articles from journals, extracts, and other parts of larger works not published separately, periodicals.– Chronological arrangement.– Text in English and French in parallel columns/texte en anglais et en français sur des col. parallèles.– Based on unpublished typescript of detailed bibliographical notes to about 600 works, compiled between 1930 and 1950 by Freda Waldon: *Canadiana published in Great Britain, 1519-1763: a list of books, pamphlets, broadsides, etc.* [manuscript]. 688 l.– Revised and edited by William F.E. Morley.
Location: OONL.

— 1991 —

0173 **Canada. Canadian Studies Directorate**
Decisions: projects funded from 1984 to 1989. Ottawa: The Directorate, c1991. 152 p.: ill.; ISBN: 0-662-19287-7.
Note: Presents projects supported by Canadian Studies Directorate, 1984-1989: publications completed, in progress; film, video and audio completed, in progress.– Topics include Canadian society, the media in Canadian society, Canadian comparisons, Canada in the World.

Title en français: *Décisions: projets subventionnées entre 1984 et 1989.*
Location: OONL.

0174 **Canada. Direction des études canadiennes**
Décisions: projets subventionnées entre 1984 et 1989. Ottawa: La Direction, 1991. 152 p.; ISBN: 0-662-97228-7.
Note: Projets qui ont été appuyés par la Direction des études canadiennes de 1984 à 1989: études sociales, politiques, culturelles et économiques, alphabétisation, participation des citoyens, connaissance des médias.
English title: *Decisions: projects funded from 1984 to 1989.*
Localisation: OONL.

0175 **Dublin Public Libraries**
Dublin Public Libraries and the Canadian Embassy present an exhibition of Canadian books: Monday 15th-Wednesday 31st July 1991, Central Library, ILAC Centre. Dublin: The Central Library, 1991. 21 l.
Note: Approx. 40 entries.– Part of the Canadian Studies Travelling Books Displays, a collection of 300 books in English and French donated by Canadian publishers.– Categories include history, women's studies, literature, art and architecture, reference works.
Location: OONL.

0176 **Senécal, André Joseph**
Canada: a reader's guide: introduction bibliographique. Ottawa: International Council for Canadian Studies, c1991. xviii, 444 p.; ISBN: 0-9691862-4-X.
Note: 1,500 entries.– Selective annotated listing of reference materials and representative titles in English and French languages in major disciplines comprising Canadian studies: economics and political science, history, geography, sociology and ethnology, language and literature, fine arts and music.– Most titles published since 1980.– Includes annotated listing of newspapers, periodicals, scholarly journals, providing information on indexing and microform availability.– Excludes most primary material (historical documents, state papers, statutes), textbooks, government documents under sixty pages.– Text in English and French/texte en français et en anglais.
Location: OONL.

— 1992 —

0177 **Jones, Linda M.**
Canadian studies: foreign publications and theses/ Études canadiennes: publications et thèses étrangères. 4th ed. Ottawa: International Council for Canadian Studies for External Affairs Canada: Conseil international d'études canadiennes pour Affaires extérieures Canada, 1992. xvii, 525 p.; ISBN: 0-9691862-7-4.
Note: Approx. 1,500 entries.– Books and serials published outside Canada which have Canada as principal subject, theses from non-Canadian universities: 1980-1989.– Includes material in English, French and other languages.– Text in English and French/texte en français et en anglais.
Previous editions:
1989. xvi, 175 p.; ISBN: 0-96918-622-3.
Monographs and periodicals published abroad in the context of Canadian studies/Monographies et revues publiées à l'étranger dans le cadre des études canadiennes. Ottawa: External Affairs Canada, 1987. 177 p.
1985. iv, 134 p.
Location: OONL.

— 1993 —

0178 **Cotterrell, Ann**
"Listings: recent articles in Canadian studies."
In: *British Journal of Canadian Studies*; Vol. 2, no. 1 (June 1987) p. 191-193; vol. 2, no. 2 (December 1987) p. 379-382; vol. 3, no. 1 (1988) p. 197-202; vol. 3, no. 2 (1988) p. 391-397; vol. 4, no. 1 (1989) p. 215-216; vol. 4, no. 2 (1989) p. 418-426; vol. 5, no. 1 (1990) p. 260-266; vol. 6, no. 1 (1991) p. 270-273; vol. 6, no. 2 (1991) p. 517-523; vol. 7, no. 1 (1992) p. 210-212; vol. 8, no. 1 (1993) p. 151-160.; ISSN: 0269-9222.
Note: Each issue focuses on a group of journals, with annotated listings of contents pertaining to aspects of Canadian studies.
Location: AEU.

0179 **Gale directory of databases.** Detroit: Gale Research, 1993. 2 vol.; ISBN: 0-8103-5746-1 (set).
Note: Approx. 8,100 entries.– "Formed by the merger of Gale's *Computer-readable databases* and Cuadra-Gale's *Directory of online databases* and *Directory of portable databases*."- Volume 1, *Online databases*, (5,200 entries), lists active and defunct databases, arranged alphabetically by database name.– Includes Canadian databases.– Volume 2, *CD-ROM, diskette, magnetic tape, handheld, and batch access database products*, (2,900 entries).– Includes Canadian products.
Location: AEU.

— Ongoing/En cours —

0180 **Campbell, Henry Cummings**
The Espial data base directory: a guide to current Canadian information contained in national and international data bases and data banks. Toronto: Espial Productions, 1987-. vol.; ISSN: 0834-3888.
Note: Irregular.– Latest edition: 1992-93.– Some issues are updated with supplements.– Includes general databases, social sciences, physical and applied science, technology.– Indexes: title, subject, producer, vendor.
Titre en français: *Guide Espial des banques de données canadiennes*.
Location: OONL.

0181 **Canadian books in print. Author and title index.** Toronto: University of Toronto Press, 1975-. vol.; ISSN: 0068-8398.
Note: Annual (published in January).– From 1980, available in microfiche format (issued in April, June, and October).– Since 1989, available online through InfoGlobe, the *BIP-Canadian books in print* database, updated quarterly.– 1981-1993, edited by Marian Butler; 1979-1980, edited by Martha Pluscauskas and Marian Butler; 1975-1978, edited by Martha Pluscauskas.
Location: OONL.

0182 **Canadian books in print. Subject index.** Toronto: University of Toronto Press, 1975-. vol.; ISSN: 0315-1999.
Note: Annual.– Since 1989, available online from InfoGlobe, the *BIP-Canadian books in print* database, updated quarterly.– 1981-1993, edited by Marian Butler; 1979-1980, edited by Martha Pluscauskas and Marian Butler; 1974-1978, edited by Martha Pluscauskas.
Location: OONL.

0183 **Canadiana 1867-1900, monographs [microform]: Canada's national bibliography/Canadiana 1867-1900, monographies [microforme]: la bibliographie nationale**
du Canada. [Ottawa]: National Library of Canada, 1980-. microfiches; ISSN: 1183-6849.
Note: Biennial.– Cumulates previous issues, with inclusion of new material and changes to previous listings.– Includes books, pamphlets, leaflets, offprints, broadsides, atlases, printed music.– Excludes periodicals, newspapers, maps, most government publications, audiovisual material.– Indexing is provided by author, title, year of publication, publisher/printer, place of publication/printing, subject.– Retitled for the 1991 issue: *Canadiana pre-1901: monographs/Canadiana d'avant 1901: monographies*.– Available on microfiche only.
Location: OONL.

0184 **Canadiana: Canada's national bibliography: La bibliographie nationale du Canada.** Ottawa: National Library of Canada, 1951-. vol.; ISSN: 0008-5391.
Note: Issued eleven times a year (January-June, July/August, September-December) from January 1950 to December 1991, with annual cumulations to 1988.– Print format ceased as of December, 1991.– Lists publications of Canadian origin or interest.– Includes material published in other countries if the author is a Canadian citizen, a resident of Canada, or if publication is Canadian in subject.– Types of material include monographs, serials, pamphlets, theses, atlases, microforms, sheet music and scores, sound recordings, government publications.– Excludes foreign imprints with less than one-third Canadian content, films, filmstrips and videotapes, videodiscs and videocassettes, other visual non-book material, maps issued as separate publications, letters, sales catalogues, timetables, course calendars, printings appearing after listing of first available printing of any edition.– Records from 1973 are available online as *NLCATBN* database on CAN/OLE.
Cumulative index: *Canadiana, 1968-1976: index*. Ottawa: National Library of Canada, 1978. 10 vol.; ISBN: 0-660-01656-7.
Microform:
Canadiana (Microfiche).– Available since January 1978.– Arranged in two parts with six indexes: Register 1, "Canadian imprints"; Register 2, "Foreign imprints".– Each monthly issue of the indexes cumulates entries from previous months.
Cumulation: *Canadiana, 1973-1980*. Ottawa: National Library of Canada; 1981. 336 microfiches. Includes 72,000 monographs, 32,000 theses, 15,000 serial titles, 44,000 government publications, pamphlets and sound recordings.– From 1981, the microfiche edition is issued monthly and cumulated in 5 year periods, of which two are available: *Canadiana 1981-1985*, and *Canadiana 1986-1990*.
Location: OONL.

0185 **Forthcoming books/Livres à paraître.** Ottawa: National Library of Canada, 1987-. vol.; ISSN: 1187-6301.
Note: Monthly.– "Distributed by *Quill & Quire* and *Livre d'ici*."- Text in English and French/texte en français et en anglais.
Location: OONL.

0186 **Guide Espial des banques de données canadiennes.** Montréal: Services documentaires multimédia, 1989-. vol.; ISSN: 0849-1453.
Note: Irrégulier.– "Répertoire des sources d'information courantes d'intérêt canadien dans les banques de

données canadiennes et étrangères."
English title: *The Espial data base directory: ....*
Localisation: OONL.

0187 **Les Livres disponibles canadiens de langue française/ Canadian French books in print.** Outremont, Québec: Bibliodata, 1987-. vol.; ISSN: 0836-7078.

Note: Quatre fois par an en édition imprimée.– Dix fois par an en édition microfiche.– La présente édition rend caduque toutes les précedentes.

Édition antérieure: *La Liste des livres disponibles de langue française des auteurs et des éditeurs canadiens/Canadian authors & publishers, French books in print.* Ottawa: Biblio-Informatica, 1981-1987. 6 vol.; ISSN: 0708-4889.– Quatre fois par année.

Localisation: OONL.

0188 **"New books."**

In: *Journal of Canadian Studies*; (1980-) vol.; ISSN: 0021-9495.

Note: Regular listing from Vol. 15, no. 3 (Fall 1980) of Canadian works in all disciplines arranged in broad subject categories and alphabetically by author.

Location: AEU.

0189 **"Recent publications relating to Canada."**

In: *Canadian Historical Review*; (1920-) vol.; ISSN: 0008-3755.

Note: Appears as a regular listing in each issue from vol. 1, no. 1, 1920.– Includes published scholarly and popular sources: monographs, journal articles, theses in the following categories: "Aboriginal history," discovery and exploration," "New France and Acadia," "British North American before 1867," "History of Canada since 1867" (general, foreign relations and military affairs, political history, social and labour history, women's history, economic and business history, intellectual and cultural history), "Regional and local history" (by provinces and regions).

Location: AEU.

0190 **Thompson, Lawrence Sidney**

The new Sabin: books described by Joseph Sabin and his successors, now described again on the basis of examination of originals, and fully indexed by title, subject, joint authors, and institutions and agencies. Troy, N.Y.: Whitston Publishing, 1974-. vol.

Note: Projected to include most Sabin listings, with enhanced descriptive notes, additional materials in some areas, accompanied by yearly indexes which will be replaced every five years by a cumulative index volume.

Location: OONL.

Area Bibliographies

Bibliographies par régions

— 1886 —

0191 Catalogue or List of manuscript documents, arranged, bound and catalogued under the direction of the commissioner of public records: together with a list of books of entry consisting of minutes of His Majesty's Council ... from year 1710 to year 1867, ... Halifax, N.S.: Commissioner of Public Works and Mines, 1886. 42 p.
Note: Microform: CIHM Microfiche series ; no. 54014; ISBN: 0-665-54014-0. 1 microfiche (25 fr.).
Location: NBSM.

— 1891 —

0192 **Bourinot, Sir John George**
"[Cape Breton Island]: bibliographical, historical and critical notes."
In: *Proceedings and Transactions of the Royal Society of Canada*; Series 1, vol. 9, section 2 (1891) p. 291-343.; ISSN: 0316-4616.
Note: "Complete summary of all the historical and other works which relate, in whole or in part, to Cape Breton, or Ile Royale."
Location: AEU.

0193 **Packard, Alpheus Spring**
"Bibliography of books and articles relating to the geography and civil and natural history of Labrador."
In: *The Labrador coast: a journal of two summer cruises to that region ...* . New York: Hodges, 1891. P. 475-501.
Note: Location: OONL.

— 1895 —

0194 **MacFarlane, William Godsoe**
New Brunswick bibliography: the books and writers of the province. Saint John, N.B.: Sun Printing, 1895. 98 p.
Note: Approx. 400 entries.– Books and pamphlets by New Brunswick authors, and printed in or related to the province.– Includes biographies and critical sketches of the writers and brief descriptions of many works.– Preface: "... appeared in the columns of the *St. John Sun* at intervals between November, 1893, and February 1895."
Microform: CIHM Microfiche series ; no. 09418; ISBN: 0-665-09418-3. 2 microfiches (57 fr.).
Location: OONL.

— 1896 —

0195 **Ganong, William F.**
Materials for a history of the province of New Brunswick. [S.l.: s.n.], 1896. 21 p.
Note: Contains a section: "The bibliography of New Brunswick."
Microform: CIHM Microfiche series ; no. 12509; ISBN: 0-665-12509-7. 1 microfiche (14 fr.).
Location: OOA.

— 1906 —

0196 **MacMechan, Archibald**
"Halifax in books."
In: *Acadiensis*; Vol. 6, no. 2 (April 1906) p. 103-122; vol. 6, no. 3 (July 1906) p. 201-217.; ISSN: 0701-4368.
Note: Two-part bibliographical essay on the City of Halifax referencing a variety of literary works, travel literature, and books of collected letters.
Location: OONL.

— 1918 —

0197 **Long, Robert James**
Nova Scotia authors and their work: a bibliography of the province. East Orange, N.J.: The Author, 1918. 312 [4] p.
Note: Books, pamphlets, magazines, newspaper articles, lectures, biographical notes published in Nova Scotia or written about Nova Scotia.
Location: OONL.

— 1922 —

0198 **Morse, Hazel G.**
"Acadia authors: a bibliography."
In: *Acadia Bulletin*; Vol. 11, no. 11 (December 1922) p. 1-43.; ISSN: 0044-5843.
Note: Listing of works by alumni of Acadia University, Wolfville, Nova Scotia, with appendix of student work.
Location: OONL.

— 1927 —

0199 **Robb, Marion Dennis**
Sources of Nova Scotian history, 1840-1867. Halifax, N.S.: Dalhousie University, 1927. 296 l.
Note: Location: NBFU.

— 1933 —

0200 **Couillard-Després, Azarie**
"Aux sources de l'histoire de l'Acadie."
Dans: *Mémoires de la Société royale du Canada*; Série 3, vol. 27, section 1 (1933) p. 63-81.; ISSN: 0316-4616.
Note: Localisation: AEU.

— 1939 —

0201 **Allan, Charlotte E.**
Bibliography of books and monographs printed and published in Nova Scotia, 1895-1920. Toronto: 1939. [4], 36 l.
Note: Approx. 300 entries.– Books, pamphlets, government documents, publications of societies and institutions.– Excludes manuscripts, newspapers, periodicals, publications of less than ten pages.– Chronological arrangement.
Microform: Ottawa: National Library of Canada, [1975]. 1 microfiche. (Canadian theses on microfiche ; no. 22736).
Location: OONL.

— 1942 —

0202 **Tanner, Väinö**
A bibliography of Labrador (specially Newfoundland-Labrador). Helsingfors: [s.n.], 1942. 83 p.
Note: 1,294 entries.– Books, periodical articles, government publications, maps.
Location: OONL.

— 1953 —

0203 **Rogers, Amos Robert**
Books and pamphlets by New Brunswick writers, 1890-1950. [Fredericton, N.B.: 1953]. vi, 73 l.

Note: Approx. 850 entries.– Includes English-language publications only.– Excludes publications with corporate authorship, articles and reprints.– For the purposes of this bibliography the definition of a New Brunswick writer is someone who was born in New Brunswick or who resided in New Brunswick while actively writing and publishing.
Location: OONL.

— 1955 —

0204 **Segura, Pearl Mary**
The Acadians in fact and fiction: a classified bibliography of writing on the subject of Acadians in the Stephens Memorial Library, Southwestern Louisiana Institute, Layfayette, Louisiana. Baton Rouge, La.: Department of Commerce and Industry, 1955. 88 p.
Note: Approx. 600 entries.– Books and articles on biography, genealogy, cookery, costumes, education, history and customs, language and literature, religion in Canada and Louisiana.
Location: OONL.

— 1962 —

0205 **Tremblay, Marc-Adélard**
"L'État des recherches sur la culture acadienne."
Dans: *Recherches sociographiques*; Vol. 3, no 1-2 (janvier-août 1962) p. 145-167.; ISSN: 0034-1282.
Note: Inventaire bibliographique: travaux historiques, études se rattachant au thème général de la survivance.
Localisation: AEU.

— 1966 —

0206 **Story, G.M.**
"Bacon and the fisheries of Newfoundland: a bibliographical ghost."
In: *Newfoundland Quarterly*; Vol. 65, no. 2 (November 1966) p. 17-18.; ISSN: 0380-5824.
Note: Brief bibliographical essay dealing with various works linking Francis Bacon, Newfoundland and the fisheries.
Location: OONL.

— 1967 —

0207 **Elliott, Shirley B.; Webster, Ellen**
Nova Scotia in books, from the first printing in 1752 to the present time, commemorating the centennial of Confederation. Halifax, N.S.: Halifax Library Association in cooperation with the Nova Scotia Provincial Library, 1967. 40 p.: ill., facsims.
Note: 216 entries.– Annotated catalogue of exhibition of books and related materials illustrating the history and development of printing and publishing in Nova Scotia.
Location: OONL.

0208 **Morley, William F.E.**
The Atlantic provinces: Newfoundland, Nova Scotia, New Brunswick, Prince Edward Island. [Toronto]: University of Toronto Press, [c1967]. xx, 137 p.: maps, plans, facsims. (Canadian local histories to 1950: a bibliography ; vol. 1)
Note: Approx. 1,000 entries.
Location: OONL.

— 1971 —

0209 **Stewart, Alice R.**
The Atlantic provinces of Canada: union lists of materials in the larger libraries of Maine. 2nd ed. [Orono, Me.]: New England-Atlantic Provinces-Quebec Center, University of Maine at Orono, 1971. 70 p.

Note: Holdings on Atlantic Provinces of serials, newspapers, non-fiction books and pamphlets in libraries of Bates, Bowdoin, Colby, the University of Maine, Maine Historical Society, Bangor and Portland Public Libraries.
Previous edition: 1965. 85 p.
Location: OONL.

0210 **Stewart, Alice R.**
"Recent historical literature and the New England-Atlantic provinces region."
In: *Acadiensis*; Vol. 1, no. 1 (Autumn 1971) p. 90-93.; ISSN: 0044-5851.
Note: Location: OONL.

0211 **Taylor, Hugh A.**
New Brunswick history: a checklist of secondary sources. Fredericton: Provincial Archives of New Brunswick, Historical Resources Administration, 1971. xii, 254 p.
Note: Approx. 3,500 entries.– Books, periodical articles, government publications, unpublished theses in English and French.– Excludes manuscripts and records, fiction and literature, directories and almanacs.
Supplements:
Swanick, Eric L. ... , *first supplement*. 1974. vi, 96 p.
Swanick, Eric L. ... , *second supplement*. 1984. vi, 214 p.; ISBN: 0-88838-783-0.
Location: OONL.

— 1972 —

0212 **Macdonald, Allan F.**
Selected annotated bibliography of recent research on rural life on Prince Edward Island. Charlottetown, P.E.I.: Department of Sociology and Anthropology, University of Prince Edward Island, 1972. iv, 70 l. (P.E.I. community studies, report ; no. 1)
Note: 80 entries.– Lists references to research studies carried out between 1960 and 1971 relating to agriculture, fisheries, tourism, business, economics and finance, development and planning, education, health and welfare.
Location: OONL.

— 1973 —

0213 **Halifax City Regional Library**
Around our lovely province. 3rd ed. [Halifax]: Halifax City Regional Library, 1973. 32 p.
Note: Approx. 150 entries.
Previous editions:
1968. 27 p.
Halifax Memorial Library. 1964. 22 p.
Location: OONL.

— 1974 —

0214 **Atlantic provinces checklist: a guide to current information in books, pamphlets, magazine articles and documentary films relating to the four Atlantic Provinces: New Brunswick, Newfoundland, Nova Scotia, Prince Edward Island.** Halifax, N.S.: Atlantic Provinces Library Association, 1958-1966; 1974.
Note: Arranged by province with a general section for material on two or more provinces, sub-arranged by subject and then by author.– Excludes annual reports of provincial government departments.– Volumes 1-9, 1957-1965, edited by Shirley B. Elliott and Douglas G. Lochhead. Volume 16, 1972, edited by Constance Dickson.– Annual listing to 1965, revived for 1972.– Retrospective for 1966-1971 was planned but not publish-

ed.
Location: OONL.

0215 **Baker, Melvin**
St. John's bibliography, 1870-1914. [St. John's: Memorial University of Newfoundland], 1974. 6 l.
Note: Location: OWTU.

0216 **Canada. Department of External Affairs**
Documents on relations between Canada and Newfoundland/Documents relatifs aux relations entre le Canada et Terre-Neuve. Ottawa: Department of External Affairs, 1974. 2 vol. (bound in 3): ill. (some folded), folded col. maps, ports. (Documents on Canadian external relations); ISBN: 0-660-52445-7.
Note: Vol. 1: *1935-1949: Defence, civil aviation and economic affairs/1935-1949: Défence, aviation civile et affaires économiques.* lxxiv, 1446 p.– 1,328 entries.
Vol. 2: *1940-1949: Confederation/1940-1949: Confédération.* li, 2106 p.– 1,239 entries.
Edited by Paul Bridle.
Location: OONL.

0217 **Nova Scotia. Legislative Library**
"Novascotiana: in-print titles as of May 1974."
In: *Nova Scotia Historical Quarterly*; Vol. 4, no. 2 (June 1974) p. 179-205.; ISSN: 0300-3728.
Note: Supplement: "Novascotiana 1976". In: *Nova Scotia Historical Quarterly*; Vol. 7, no. 1 (March 1977) p. 161-174.
Location: AEU.

0218 **Polegato, Lino L.**
Bibliography of reports, papers and studies prepared for the Strait of Canso area compiled for Nova Scotia Department of the Environment. [S.l.: s.n.], 1974. ca. 1000 p. (in various pagings): ill., maps.
Note: Contains a group of lists of various documents pertaining to the Strait of Canso region, arranged generally by issuing body, federal and Nova Scotia provincial departments and agencies, Bedford Institute of Oceanography, reports by other private or university organizations, mainly dealing with environmental conditions.– Canso region is broadly defined as including George Bay, western Bras D'or Lake and Chedabucto Bay, and the lands between.– Loose-leaf.
Location: NSHDE.

— 1975 —

0219 **Macdonald, William S.**
Productivity in Nova Scotia: a review of the literature and annotated bibliography. Halifax, N.S.: Institute of Public Affairs, Dalhousie University, 1975. ix, 123 p.; ISBN: 0-88926-011-7.
Note: 273 entries.– Books, conference reports, policy statements concerning productivity (half dealing directly with Nova Scotia), and factors affecting productive efficiency.
Location: OONL.

0220 **"Selected Islandia bibliography, 1963-1973."**
In: *Abegweit Review*; Vol. 1, no. 1 (March 1974) p. 66-67; vol. 2, no. 1 (Spring 1975) p. 110; vol. 2, no. 2 (Fall 1975) p. 150-151.; ISSN: 0045-3129.
Note: Location: OONL.

0221 **Sterns, Maurice A.; Hiscock, Philip; Daley, Bruce**
Newfoundland and Labrador: social science research: a selected bibliography. St. John's, Nfld.: Department of Sociology, Memorial University of Newfoundland, 1975. iii, 70 p.

Note: 510 entries.– Books, studies, government documents, theses on social change (community development, resettlement), culture (folklore, linguistics), education, politics (section on post-Confederation political culture), work and economy (general, fishing, unionism).
Location: OLU.

0222 **Surette, Paul; Bérubé, Claude**
"Bibliographie de l'Acadie."
Dans: *Cahiers: Société historique acadienne*; Vol. 6, no 1 (mars 1975) p. 48-57.; ISSN: 0049-1098.
Note: Comprend les titres qui ont paru durant 1973 et 1974.– Classification chronologique et géographique.– Principaux thèmes traités: histoire, biographie, politique, économie, géographie, société, arts et éducation.
Voir aussi: Bernard Léger et Raymond Léger (juin 1976); Raymond Léger (juin 1977); Bernard Léger (mars 1978); Suzanne Boucher (mars 1979); Adélard Comeau (décembre 1980).
Localisation: AEU.

— 1976 —

0223 **Léger, Bernard; Léger, Raymond**
"Bibliographie de l'Acadie."
Dans: *Cahiers: Société historique acadienne*; Vol. 7, no 2 (juin 1976) p. 93-99.; ISSN: 0049-1098.
Note: Comprend les titres qui ont paru durant 1975.– Classification chronologique et géographique.– Principaux thèmes traités: histoire, biographie, politique, économie, géographie, société, arts et éducation.
Voir aussi: Paul Surette et Claude Bérubé (mars 1975); Raymond Léger (juin 1977); Bernard Léger (mars 1978); Suzanne Boucher (mars 1979); Adélard Comeau (décembre 1980).
Localisation: AEU.

0224 **Nova Scotia Museum**
Gleaning Nova Scotia's history: a bibliography for use in local history studies. Halifax, N.S.: Nova Scotia Museum, 1976. [12] l.
Note: Location: OONL.

0225 **Vaison, Robert**
Nova Scotia past and present: a bibliography and guide. 2nd rev. and enl. ed. Halifax, N.S.: Nova Scotia, Department of Education, 1976. 164 p.
Note: Approx. 2,100 entries.– Covers materials dated to 1975.– Includes books, essays, articles, government publications arranged by subject: history and development, politics and government, economy, education.– Excludes memoirs and personal correspondence, documents not publicly available, non English-language materials.
Previous edition: *Studying Nova Scotia: its history and present state, its politics and economy: a bibliography and guide.* Mount Saint Vincent University Press, 1974. 123 l.
Location: OONL.

— 1977 —

0226 **Baglole, Harry**
Exploring Island history: a guide to the historical resources of Prince Edward Island. Belfast, P.E.I.: Ragweed Press, 1977. xi, 310 p.; ISBN: 0-920304-00-1.
Note: Resource guide containing articles dealing with themes related to the history of Prince Edward Island, most of which include lists of publications.
Location: OONL.

0227 **Barter, Geraldine**
A critically annotated bibliography of works published and unpublished relating to the culture of French Newfoundlanders. [St. John's]: Memorial University of Newfoundland, 1977. xiii, 52 l., [2] l. of pl.
Note: 155 entries.– Published works, manuscripts, works in French and English.
Location: OONL.

0228 **Cyr, Hermel**
Relevé de sources et d'ouvrages se rapportant au Madawaska des XVIIIe et XIXe siècles. [S.l.: s.n.], 1977. 43 f.
Note: Localisation: NBEBR.

0229 **Fisher, Gerald**
"Atlantic Canada studies."
In: *Communiqué: Canadian Studies*; Vol. 3, no. 2 (January 1977) p. 2-68.; ISSN: 0318-1197.
Note: Lists bibliographies, biographical studies, literature, works on economy, folklore, labour studies, Maritime union, natural science studies, Acadians, historical studies and travel literature.
Location: OONL.

0230 **Léger, Raymond**
"Bibliographie de l'Acadie."
Dans: *Cahiers: Société historique acadienne*; Vol. 8, no 2 (juin 1977) p. 93-96.; ISSN: 0049-1098.
Note: Comprend les titres qui ont paru durant 1976.– Classification chronologique et géographique.– Principaux thèmes traités: histoire, biographie, politique, économie, géographie, société, arts et éducation.
Voir aussi: Paul Surette et Claude Bérubé (mars 1975); Bernard Léger et Raymond Léger (juin 1976); Bernard Léger (mars 1978); Suzanne Boucher (mars 1979; Adélard Comeau (décembre 1980).
Localisation: AEU.

0231 **Pacey, Margaret**
"Recent publications relating to the history of the Atlantic region."
In: *Acadiensis*; Vol. 7, no. 1 (Autumn 1977) p. 148-156.; ISSN: 0044-5851.
Note: Books, articles, theses: general listing for Atlantic provinces, separate sections for New Brunswick, Newfoundland, Nova Scotia, Prince Edward Island.
See also: Swanick, Eric L. (Spring 1975-Spring 1977; Spring 1978-Spring 1990); McGahan, Elizabeth W. (Autumn 1991-Spring 1993).
Location: AEU.

0232 **Université de Moncton. Centre d'études acadiennes**
Inventaire général des sources documentaires sur les Acadiens. Moncton: Éditions d'Acadie, 1975-1977. 3 vol.
Note: Tome I: *Les sources premières (manuscrits, archives publiques et privées)*. 526 p.– Tome II: *Bibliographie acadienne: liste des volumes, brochures et thèses concernant l'Acadie et les Acadiens des débuts à 1975*. xiv, 463 p.– Tome III: *Bibliographie acadienne: liste des articles de périodiques concernant l'Acadie et les Acadiens des débuts à 1976*. vii, 212 p.
Localisation: OONL.

— 1978 —

0233 **Goff, T.W.**
Resource material for social analysis of the Chignecto region: a preliminary bibliography. Sackville, N.B.: Chignecto Research Group of Mount Allison University, 1978. [6], 20 l. (Chignecto Research Group of Mount Allison University Internal note ; no. 7); ISBN: 0-88828-015-7.
Note: Studies relating to socio-economic impact of a tidal power project in the Chignecto region of New Brunswick, general works on the impact of large projects in other areas, works on economy of the Atlantic region.
Location: OONL.

0234 **Kealey, Gregory; McKay, Ian; Reilly, Nolan**
"Canada's "eastern question": a reader's guide to regional underdevelopment."
In: *Canadian Dimension*; Vol. 13, no. 2 (1978) p. 37-40.; ISSN: 0008-3402.
Note: Bibliographical essay on economic history of Atlantic provinces.
Location: OONL.

0235 **Léger, Bernard**
"Bibliographie de l'Acadie."
Dans: *Cahiers: Société historique acadienne*; Vol. 9, no 1 (mars 1978) p. 38-43.; ISSN: 0049-1098.
Note: Comprend les titres qui ont paru durant 1977.– Classification chronologique et géographique.– Principaux thèmes traités: histoire, biographie, politique, économie, géographie, société, arts et éducation.
Voir aussi: Paul Surette et Claude Bérubé (mars 1975); Bernard Léger et Raymond Léger (juin 1976); Raymond Léger (juin 1977); Suzanne Boucher ((mars 1979); Adélard Comeau (décembre 1980).
Localisation: AEU.

0236 **Magee, Eleanor E.**
Pre-twentieth century literature of and about the Maritime Provinces: a bibliography of titles held in the special collections of Mount Allison University Library. Preliminary ed. [Sackville, N.B.]: Ralph Pickard Bell Library, Mount Allison University, c1978. iv, 25 p. (Maritime Studies Bibliography ; 2); ISBN: 0-88828-021-1.
Note: 321 entries.– Includes letters, personal narratives, essays.
Location: OONL.

0237 **Tennyson, Brian**
Cape Breton: a bibliography. Halifax, N.S.: Department of Education, Nova Scotia, 1978. vi, 114 p.
Note: 1,352 entries.– Covers earliest records and imprints to the end of 1976.– Includes books, documents, periodical articles, theses.– Excludes newspaper articles, unpublished manuscripts and technical material.
Location: OONL.

— 1979 —

0238 **Boucher, Suzanne**
"Bibliographie de l'Acadie."
Dans: *Cahiers: Société historique acadienne*; Vol. 10, no 1 (mars 1979) p. 56-69.; ISSN: 0049-1098.
Note: Comprend les titres qui ont paru durant 1978.– Classification chronologique et géographique.– Principaux thèmes traités: histoire, biographie, politique, économie, géographie, société, arts et éducation.
Voir aussi: Paul Surette et Claude Bérubé (mars 1975); Bernard Léger et Raymond Léger (juin 1976); Raymond Léger (juin 1977); Bernard Léger (mars 1978); Adélard Comeau (décembre 1980).
Localisation: AEU.

0239 **Brault, Helen, et al.**
Sources of information: an annotated directory of vertical file materials of interest to libraries in Nova Scotia. Halifax, Nova Scotia: [University Libraries/School of Library Service, Dalhousie University], 1979. iii, 54 l. (Dalhousie University Libraries and Dalhousie University School of Library Service Occasional papers ; no. 25; ISSN: 0318-7403); ISBN: 0-7703-0161-4.
Note: Approx. 250 entries.– Brochures and pamphlets, free or inexpensive, on Nova Scotia subjects.
Location: OONL.

0240 **Melanson, Lloyd J.**
Thirty-four Atlantic provinces authors/Trente-quatre auteurs des provinces de l'Atlantique. Halifax, N.S.: Atlantic Provinces Library Association, 1979. 38 p.; ISBN: 0-920844-00-6.
Note: Biobibliographical notes on 34 authors from New Brunswick, Nova Scotia, Prince Edward Island, Newfoundland.– Text in English and French/texte en français et en anglais.
Location: OONL.

0241 **Milner, Philip**
Nova Scotia writes. Antigonish, N.S.: FORMAC Publishing, 1979. 100 p.: ill.; ISBN: 0-88780-036-X.
Note: 86 authors represented.
Location: OONL.

0242 **Swanick, Eric L.**
New Brunswick regional development during the '60s and the 70s: an introductory bibliography. rev. ed. Monticello, Ill.: Vance Bibliographies, 1979. 37 l. (Public administration series: Bibliography ; P-204; ISSN: 0193-970X)
Note: 434 entries.– Government publications, consultants' studies, research papers, theses, conference proceedings, periodical articles.
Previous edition: 1976. 34 p. (Council of Planning Librarians Exchange bibliography ; 1122).
Location: OONL.

— 1980 —

0243 **Arsenault, Georges**
Bibliographie acadienne: bibliographie sélective et commentée préparée à l'intention des enseignants de l'Ile-du-Prince-Édouard. Summerside, P.E.I.: Société Saint-Thomas d'Aquin, 1980. 26 f.
Note: 90 entrées.– Livres, articles: ouvrages se rapportant particulièrement à l'héritage culturel du peuple acadien de P.E.I.: histoire, institutions acadiennes, église et religion, généalogie, folklore, cuisine, littérature, chansons folkloriques.
Localisation: OOSS.

0244 **Comeau, Adélard**
"Bibliographie de l'Acadie."
Dans: *Cahiers: Société historique acadienne*; Vol. 11, no 4 (décembre 1980) p. 367-382.; ISSN: 0049-1098.
Note: Comprend les titres qui ont paru durant 1979.– Classification chronologique et géographique.– Principaux thèmes traités: histoire, biographie, politique, économie, géographie, société, arts et éducation.
Voir aussi: Paul Surette et Claude Bérubé (mars 1975); Bernard Léger et Raymond Léger (juin 1976); Raymond Léger (juin 1977); Bernard Léger (mars 1978); Suzanne Boucher (mars 1979).
Localisation: AEU.

0245 **Hiscock, Audrey M.; Braine, Linda**
Annotated bibliography of Newfoundland materials for school libraries, part 1–print. [St. John's, Nfld.]: Division of Instruction, Department of Education, 1980. 137 p.
Note: Approx. 425 entries.– Includes books, booklets, periodicals, government documents.– Criteria for inclusion: material written by Newfoundlanders, about Newfoundland, with some element relating to Newfoundland.– Suggested appropriate grade levels are included.
Location: OONL.

0246 **Kemshead, Alison**
Newfoundland: a bibliography of social, economic and political conditions. Monticello, Ill.: Vance Bibliographies, 1980. 33 p. (Public administration series: Bibliography ; P-449; ISSN: 0193-970X)
Note: Approx. 275 entries.– Emphasis on post-1945 period.– Sections on population, settlement, resettlement, community development, education, recreation, industries (agriculture, forestry, mining, transportation).
Location: OONL.

0247 **Kemshead, Alison**
Prince Edward Island: a bibliography of social, economic, and political conditions. Monticello, Ill.: Vance Bibliographies, 1980. 16 p. (Public administration series: Bibliography ; P-529; ISSN: 0193-970X)
Note: Approx. 200 entries.– Books, pamphlets, theses: history, settlement and population, politics and government, economic conditions, social organization, agriculture, fisheries, tourism and recreation, transportation, community development.
Location: OOP.

0248 **Spray, W.A.**
"Recent publications in local history: New Brunswick."
In: *Acadiensis*; Vol. 9, no. 2 (Spring 1980) p. 115-121.; ISSN: 0044-5851.
Note: Bibliographical essay on New Brunswick local history.
Location: OONL.

— 1981 —

0249 **Halifax City Regional Library. Reference Department**
Halifax, N.S., social, economic and municipal studies, 1970-1980. Halifax: The Library, 1981. 13 l.
Note: Approx. 150 entries.
Location: OONL.

0250 **Hartling, Philip L.**
"A bibliographical selection of local history sources at the Public Archives of Nova Scotia."
In: *Nova Scotia Historical Review*; Vol. 1, no. 2 (1981) p. 42-49.; ISSN: 0227-4752.
Note: Location: AEU.

0251 **Memorial University of Newfoundland. Maritime History Group**
Check list of research studies pertaining to the history of Newfoundland in the archives of the Maritime History Group. 5th ed. St. John's: Memorial University of Newfoundland, 1981. 38 p.
Note: Previous editions:
1978. 37 p.
1975. 30 l.
1974. 29 l.
1973. 22 l.
Location: OONL.

— 1982 —

0252 **Nova Scotia. Legislative Library**
Travel in the Maritime Provinces, 1750-1867. Halifax,
N.S.: Nova Scotia Legislative Library, 1982. 14 l.
Note: Approx. 125 entries.– Listing of travel accounts
within the Atlantic provinces, 1750-1867.– Compiled by
Shirley B. Elliott.
Location: OONL.

— 1983 —

0253 **Canadian Learning Materials Centre**
Atlantic book choice: recommended Canadian and
regional titles for an elementary school library collection.
[Halifax]: Canadian Learning Materials Centre, [1983]. 2
vol.
Note: Titles published 1970-1982 with emphasis on
Atlantic region.
Location: OONL.

0254 **Dindial, Frances A.**
"A selected bibliography of people and places."
In: *Abegweit Review*; Vol. 4, no. 1 (Spring 1983) p. 113-125.;
ISSN: 0382-4632.
Note: Approx. 150 entries.– Books, pamphlets,
periodicals, government documents, diaries, theses,
reports, in printed and non-printed format, from the
Robertson Library special collection on Prince Edward
Island.
Location: OONL.

0255 **Potvin, Claude**
Acadiana 1980-1982: une bibliographie annotée/
[Acadiana 1980-1982]: an annotated bibliography.
Moncton, N.-B.: Éditions CRP, 1983. 110 p.; ISBN: 0-
9690939-1-8.
Note: 225 entrées.– Énumère des ouvrages de langue
française: romans, essais, poésie, monographies, théâtre,
livres pour jeunes, périodiques publiés en Acadie et des
ouvrages qui traitent de sujets acadiens.– Annotée en
français et en anglais.
Localisation: OONL.

— 1984 —

0256 **Bibliothèque régionale du Haut-Saint-Jean**
Découvrons le Nouveau-Brunswick: bibliographie
sélective sur l'histoire du Nouveau-Brunswick/Discover
New Brunswick: selective bibliography on New
Brunswick history. Edmundston, N.-B.: La Bibliothèque,
[1984]. 32 f.
Note: 121 entrées.– Cinq thèmes: biographies, coutumes
et légendes, généalogie, histoire et géographie,
monographies d'histoire locale.– Annotations en français
et en anglais/annotations in English and French.
Localisation: OONL.

0257 **Elliott, Shirley B.**
"Novascotiana."
In: *Journal of Education*; Vol. 7, no. 3, series 5 (June
1958) p. 29-35; vol. 8, no. 2-3, series 5 (April-June 1959) p.
66-72; vol. 9, no. 2, series 5 (June 1960) p. 51-56; vol. 10,
no. 2-3, series 5 (April-June 1961) p. 79-86; vol. 11, no. 3,
series 5 (June 1962) p. 42-47; vol. 12, no. 2, series 5 (April-
June 1963) p. 36-42; vol. 13, no. 3, series 5 (June 1964) p.
18-21; vol. 14, no. 4, series 5 (June 1965) p. 32-35; vol. 15,
no. 4, series 5 (April 1966) p. 26-28; vol. 16, no. 3, series 5
(February-April 1967) p. 36-39; vol. 17, no. 3, series 5
(February 1968) p. 41-44; vol. 18, no. 2, series 5 (May-June
1969) p. 30-32; vol. 19, no. 3, series 5 (May 1970) p. 47-49;

vol. 20, no. 3, series 5 (Spring 1971) p. 29-32; vol. 21, no. 3,
series 5 (Spring 1972) p. 52-55; vol. 22, no. 4, series 5
(Spring 1973) p. 60-64; vol. 1, no. 4, series 6 (Summer
1974) p. 38-41, vol. 2, no. 3, series 6 (Spring 1975) p. 29-33;
vol. 3, no. 2, series 6 (Winter 1975-76) p. 28-31; vol. 4, no.
3, series 6 (Spring 1977) p. 28-34; vol. 5, no. 2, series 6
(Winter 1977-78) p. 30-33; vol. 6, no. 2, series 6 (Spring
1979) p. 33-37; vol. 6, no. 4, series 6 (1979-1980) p. 39-42;
vol. 7, no. 3, series 6 (1982) p. 38-45; no. 398 (September
1984) p. 34-37.; ISSN: 0022-0566.
Note: Listing of books, pamphlets and documents
concerning Nova Scotia or written by Nova Scotia
authors.– Topics include history and biography,
agriculture, fiction and poetry, description and travel,
music, philosophy and religion, sociology, industry.
Location: OONL.

0258 **Smith, Leonard H.**
Nova Scotia, genealogy and local history: a trial
bibliography. 2nd ed. Clearwater, Fla.: Owl Books, 1984.
98 p.; ISBN: 0-932022-28-6.
Note: Approx. 1,500 entries.– Listing by author or title.
Previous edition: 1983. 38 l.
Location: OONL.

— 1985 —

0259 **De Leon, Lisa**
Writers of Newfoundland and Labrador: twentieth
century. St. John's, Nfld.: Jesperson Press, 1985. 380 p.:
ill.; ISBN: 0-920502-58-X.
Note: Selected authors include essayists, novelists, poets,
lyricists, historians, journalists, folklorists, biographers.–
Contains biographies with synopses of authors' published books, followed by bibliographies listing works by
and about the author.
Location: OONL.

0260 **Doiron, Jean**
Bibliographie acadienne. Halifax: Fondation d'éducation
des provinces maritimes, [1985]. iv, 38 p.
Note: Approx. 250 entrées.
Localisation: OONL.

0261 **Socio-economic development in Labrador: a select
bibliography.** [St. John's]: Department of Rural,
Agricultural and Northern Development, Government of
Newfoundland and Labrador, 1985. iv, 35 p.
Note: Approx. 350 entries.– Lists references pertaining to
environment, fisheries, planning (social and economic
development), communications, health care, education,
resource issues, transportation.
Location: OONL.

— 1986 —

0262 **Elliott, Shirley B.**
Nova Scotia in books: a quarter century's gatherings,
1957-1982. Halifax, N.S.: Department of Education,
Education Resources Services, 1986. [4], 110, [12] p.;
ISBN: 0-88871-088-7.
Note: Approx. 1,200 entries.– Books, pamphlets and
documents concerning Nova Scotia or written by Nova
Scotia authors.– Topics include history and biography,
fiction and poetry, description and travel, music,
religion, agriculture and other industries.
Location: OONL.

0263 **O'Dea, Agnes C.; Alexander, Anne**
Bibliography of Newfoundland. Toronto: Published by
University of Toronto Press in association with Memorial

University of Newfoundland, c1986. 2 vol. (xx, 1450 p.): facsims.; ISBN: 0-8020-2402-5.
Note: 6,289 entries.– Covers the period from early voyages of discovery to 1975.– Includes books, pamphlets, government publications, atlases, theses, films, music scores, lectures, speeches.– Excludes works by Newfoundlanders not related to Newfoundland, except in the field of literature.
Previous edition: *A Newfoundland bibliography: preliminary list.* St. John's: Memorial University of Newfoundland, 1960. Photocopy in 5 vol.
Location: OONL.

— 1987 —

0264 **Charest-Knoetze, Claire; Lefrançois, Guy**
L'Acadie, l'Acadie: bibliographie des ouvrages en bibliothèque. Edmundston, N.-B.: Bibliothèque, Centre universitaire Saint-Louis-Maillet, Université de Moncton, 1987. [90] f.
Note: 739 entrées.– Inventaire des ouvrages surtout imprimés sur l'Acadie et traitent substantiellement de l'Acadie: économique, historique, littéraire, politique, religieuse.
Localisation: OONL.

0265 **Ralph Pickard Bell Library**
Catalogue, the Winthrop Pickard Bell Collection of Acadiana. 2nd ed. Sackville, N.B.: Mount Allison University, 1987. 6 vol.; ISBN: 0-88828-061-0.
Note: Approx. 7,000 entries.– Collection concentrates on area once known as Acadia, which includes provinces of Nova Scotia, Prince Edward Island, New Brunswick and part of State of Maine, prior to 1940.– Includes books, pamphlets, journals, broadsides, slides, maps and ephemera.– Edited by Margaret Foley and Gwendolyn Creelman.
Previous edition: *A catalogue of the Winthrop Pickard Bell Collection of Acadiana held in the Ralph Pickard Bell Library, Mount Allison University as of January 1, 1973.* 1973. x, 181 p. (Ralph Pickard Bell Library Publication ; no. 3).
Location: OONL.

0266 **Service de diffusion sélective de l'information de la Centrale des bibliothèques**
L'Acadie. Montréal: Le Service, 1987. 2 vol. (DSI/CB ; 103, 104; ISSN: 0825-5024); ISBN: 2-89059-320-7 (série).
Note: Vol. I: *L'Acadie et les Acadiens.* 37 p. 319 entrées.– Livres, articles de revues, documents audiovisuels relatifs à l'Acadie et aux Acadiens (incluant les Cajuns) sous divers aspects: histoire, géographie, politique, religion, musique, littérature.– Vol. II: *Livres et auteurs d'Acadie.* 32 p. 273 entrées.– Notices de documents publiés en Acadie ou par des Acadiens hors de l'Acadie: ouvrages pour les jeunes; ouvrages didactiques pour les enseignants; ouvrages pour adolescents et pour adultes; ouvrages pour lecteurs cultivés et pour spécialistes.
Localisation: OONL.

— 1988 —

0267 **Bibliography on Maritime regionalism and multi-government partnerships/Bibliographie sur le régionalisme dans les Maritimes et la collaboration entre les gouvernements.** Halifax, N.S.: Council of Maritime Premiers, 1988. 13 l.
Note: Approx. 150 entries.– Includes books, studies, journal articles dealing with the concept of the Maritime region, regional economic development and regional

disparity, and a listing of material devoted to cooperation among Maritime governments, both broad issues and specific programs and agencies of the Council of Maritime Premiers.– Text in English and French/texte en français et en anglais.
Location: OONL.

0268 **Harbec, Hélène**
Guide bibliographique de l'Acadie, 1976-1987. [Moncton, N.-B.]: Centre d'études acadiennes, Université de Moncton, 1988. xvii, 508 p.; ISBN: 0-919691-30-7.
Note: 4,515 entrées.– Articles, monographies, publications officielles, thèses sur les Acadiens des Maritimes, au Québec, en Louisiane, en France et en Nouvelle-Angleterre, classés par sujets: ouvrages généraux, histoire, démographie, économie, science politique, droit, religion, éducation, famille, arts et littérature, anthropologie et sociologie, géographie, ethnographie, biographie.– Liste des journaux acadiens.– Sans compter: documents non publiés sauf les thèses.– Collaboratrice et consultante: Paulette Lévesque.– Oeuvre réalisée sous la direction de Muriel Kent Roy.
Supplément: Robichaud, Norbert. *Guide bibliographique de l'Acadie: supplément et mise à jour, 1988-1989.* 1991. 91 p.
Localisation: OONL.

0269 **New Brunswick. Legislative Library**
Regional development/Développement régional. Fredericton: New Brunswick Legislative Library, 1988. 8 l. (Bibliography / New Brunswick Legislative Library)
Note: Includes publications in English and French.– Focus on Atlantic provinces.
Location: OONL.

— 1990 —

0270 **Key people: writers in Atlantic Canada.** Halifax, N.S.: Writers' Federation of Nova Scotia, 1990. 201 p.; ISBN: 0-920636-15-2.
Note: Bio-bibliography.– Lists the published writings of 218 authors who live or work in Atlantic Canada.
Location: OONL.

0271 **Swanick, Eric L.**
"Recent publications relating to the history of the Atlantic region."
In: *Acadiensis;* Vol. 4, no. 2 (Spring 1975) p. 133-147; vol. 5, no. 1 (Autumn 1975) p. 150-164; vol. 5, no. 2 (Spring 1976) p. 163-172; vol. 6, no. 1 (Autumn 1976) p. 152-167; vol. 6, no. 2 (Spring 1977) p. 145-155; vol. 7, no. 2 (Spring 1978) p. 165-179; vol. 8, no. 1 (Autumn 1978) p. 140-154; vol. 8, no. 2 (Spring 1979) p. 143-153; vol. 9, no. 1 (Autumn 1979) p. 134-150; vol. 9, no. 2 (Spring 1980) p. 122-136; vol. 10, no. 1 (Autumn 1980) p. 178-192; vol. 10, no. 2 (Spring 1981) p. 179-191; vol. 11, no. 1 (Autumn 1981) p. 180-189; vol. 11, no. 2 (Spring 1982) p. 146-174; vol. 12, no. 1 (Autumn 1982) p. 164-185; vol. 12, no. 2 (Spring 1983) p. 181-201; vol. 13, no. 1 (Autumn 1983) p. 184-209; vol. 13, no. 2 (Spring 1984) p. 150-165; vol. 14, no. 1 (Autumn 1984) p. 155-178; vol. 14, no. 2 (Spring 1985) p. 167-188; vol. 15, no. 1 (Autumn 1985) p. 187-205; vol. 15, no. 2 (Spring 1986) p. 191-210; vol. 16, no. 1 (Autumn 1986) p. 198-222; vol. 16, no. 2 (Spring 1987) p. 138-166; vol. 17, no. 1 (Autumn 1987) p. 189-218; vol. 17, no. 2 (Spring 1988) p. 218-239; vol. 18, no. 1 (Autumn 1988) p. 257-283; vol. 18, no. 2 (Spring 1989) p. 175-202; vol. 19, no. 1 (Autumn 1989) p. 209-231; vol. 19, no. 2 (Spring 1990) p. 239-264.; ISSN: 0044-5851.

Note: Listing of books, articles, theses dealing with the Atlantic provinces in general, with separate sections for New Brunswick, Newfoundland, Nova Scotia, Prince Edward Island.

See also: Pacey, Margaret (Autumn 1977); Continued by: McGahan, Elizabeth W. (Autumn 1991-Spring 1993).

Location: AEU.

— 1991 —

0272 **Baker, Melvin**

Bibliography of Newfoundland history books in print. 6th ed. [St. John's, Nfld.]: Newfoundland Historical Society, c1991. 36 l.

Note: Approx. 500 entries.– Lists works published in Newfoundland, published elsewhere, relating to the history of Newfoundland.– Provides a list of pamphlets published by the Newfoundland Historical Society, list of forthcoming titles.

Previous editions:

1990. 32 p.

1989. 26 p.

1988. 24 l.

Bibliography of Newfoundland history. 1987. 18 p.

Bibliography of Newfoundland history. 1986. 15 p.

Location: OONL.

0273 **Fleming, Patricia Lockhart**

Atlantic Canadian imprints, 1801-1820: a bibliography. Toronto: University of Toronto Press, c1991. xviii, 188 p.: ill.; ISBN: 0-8020-5872-8.

Note: 338 entries.– Books, pamphlets, government publications, broadsides, serials.– Excludes newspapers, separately published maps and illustrations, tickets and forms.– Imprints arranged chronologically by year of publication with each of the four Atlantic provinces: New Brunswick, Newfoundland, Nova Scotia, Prince Edward Island.– Indexes: name, title, genre and subject, language trades (bookbinders, printers, publishers), place of publication.– Includes notes: contents, paper, typography, descriptive/historical.

Location: OONL.

— 1993 —

0274 **McGahan, Elizabeth W.**

"Recent publications relating to the history of the Atlantic region."

In: *Acadiensis;* Vol. 21, no. 1 (Autumn 1991) p. 200-224; vol. 21, no. 2 (Spring 1992) p. 191-222; vol. 22, no. 2 (Spring 1993) p. 186-206.; ISSN: 0044-5851.

Note: Books, articles, theses relating to Atlantic provinces history.– General listing for the region, individual listings for New Brunswick, Newfoundland, Nova Scotia, Prince Edward Island.

See also: Pacey, Margaret (Autumn 1977); Swanick, Eric L. (Spring 1975-Spring 1977; Spring 1978-Spring 1990).

Location: OONL.

— Ongoing/En cours —

0275 **"Bibliography of recent publications [Newfoundland and Labrador]."**

In: *Newfoundland Studies;* (1985-) vol.; ISSN: 0823-1737.

Note: Appears regularly in Spring issue from Vol. 1, no. 1 (Spring 1985).– Lists selected publications and studies related to Newfoundland and Labrador.

Location: OONL.

— 1898 —

0276 **Rouillard, Eugène**
Les premiers almanachs canadiens. Lévis: P.–G. Roy, 1898. 80 p.
Note: Microforme: ICMH collection de microfiches ; no 12976; ISBN: 0-665-12976-9. 1 microfiche (44 images).
Localisation: OONL.

— 1900 —

0277 **"Reading list on Canada and Montreal."**
In: *Library Journal*; Vol. 25 (March 1900) p. 120-141.; ISSN: 0000-0027.
Note: Location: OONL.

— 1909 —

0278 **Dionne, Narcisse-Eutrope**
Inventaire chronologique .... Québec: Société royale du Canada, 1905-1909. 4 vol.
Note: T. 1: *Inventaire chronologique des livres, brochures, journaux et revues publiés en langue française dans la province de Québec, depuis l'établissement de l'imprimerie au Canada jusqu'à nos jours, 1764-1905.* viii, 175 p.– 3,892 entrées.– t. 2: *Québec et Nouvelle France, bibliographie: inventaire chronologique des ouvrages publiés à l'étranger en diverses langues ... 1534-1906.* viii, 155, vi p.– 2,000 entrées.– t. 3: *Inventaire chronologiques des livres, brochures, journaux et revues publiés en langue anglaise dans la province du Québec ... 1764-1906.* 228 p.– 2,602 entrées.– t. 4: *Inventaire chronologiques des cartes, plans, atlas, etc. relatifs à la Nouvelle-France et à la province de Québec, 1508-1908.* viii, 124, vi p.– 1,252 entrées.
Supplément: *Inventaire chronologique des livres, brochures, journaux et revues publiés en diverses langues dans et hors la province de Québec, 1904-1912.* 1912. 76 p.– 1,068 entrées.
Réimpression: New York: Burt Franklin, 1969. 5 t. en 2 vol. (Burt Franklin Bibliography and reference series ; 289).
Microforme: Montréal: Bibliothèque nationale du Québec, 1985. 10 microfiches.
Localisation: OONL.

— 1919 —

0279 **Chartier, Armand B.**
"Introduction bibliographique à la civilisation du Québec."
Dans: *Contemporary French Civilization*; Vol. 3, no. 2 (Winter 1919) p. 265-296.; ISSN: 0147-9156.
Note: Localisation: OONL.

— 1924 —

0280 **Burpee, Lawrence J.**
"Quebec in books."
In: *Proceedings and Transactions of the Royal Society of Canada*; Series 3, vol. 18, section 2 (1924) p. 75-85.; ISSN: 0316-4616.
Note: Location: AEU.

— 1932 —

0281 **Roy, Pierre-Georges**
Bibliographie lévisienne. Lévis: [s.n.], 1932. 24 p.

Note: Approx. 250 entrées.– Livres et brochures publiés à Lévis ou ailleurs sur les hommes et les choses de Lévis.
Localisation: OONL.

0282 **Roy, Pierre-Georges**
"Bibliographie lévisienne."
Dans: *Bulletin des recherches historiques*; Vol. 38, no 8 (août 1932) p. 449-470.
Note: Localisation: OONL.

— 1934 —

0283 **Quebec in books.** Montreal: Unity Press, [1934]. 56 p.: ill.
Note: Approx. 110 entries.– Compiled under the direction of Marion V. Higgins by the class of 1934, McGill University Library School, for the fifty-sixth annual convention of the American Library Association, Montreal, June 25-30, 1934.– Selective reading list to acquaint members of A.L.A. with Quebec through its literature, history, folklore, handicrafts and architecture.
Location: OONL.

— 1939 —

0284 **Dubuc, J.–H.**
Bibliographie des monographies paroissiales du diocèse de Sherbrooke. [Montréal: s.n., 1939]. 11 l.
Note: Approx. 40 entrées.
Localisation: OONL.

— 1942 —

0285 **French Institute in the United States**
Publications contemporaines de langue française aux États-Unis et au Canada; exposition. New York: French Institute, 1942. 45 p.
Note: Localisation: QQLA.

— 1953 —

0286 **Lemieux, Marthe**
Essai d'une bibliographie sur la ville de Chicoutimi. Montréal: 1953. viii, 96 f.
Note: 583 entrées.
Localisation: OONL.

— 1954 —

0287 **Rousseau, Jacques**
Essai bibliographique sur la région du lac Mistassini. Montréal: [s.n.], 1954. 155 f.
Note: Approx. 700 entrées.– Monographies et articles de revues.– Annotations.– Catégories: exploration sous le régime français; explorations géographiques et géologiques; botanique; zoologie; ethnologie; linguistique; météorologie; littérature; cartographie ancienne et moderne; manuscrits.
Localisation: OONL.

— 1955 —

0288 **Québec (Province). Ministère de l'Industrie et du Commerce. Service de géographie**
Bibliographie du Nouveau-Québec/Bibliography of New Quebec. Québec: Le Ministère, 1955. 321 p.: carte. (Publication / Québec Ministère de l'Industrie et du Commerce, Service de géographie ; no 1)
Note: Approx. 1,500 entrées.– Nouveau Québec inclut la

partie septentrionale des comtés d'Abitibi, de Roberval, de lac Saint-Jean et de Chicoutimi, les territoires de l'Abibiti, de Mistassini, d'Ashuanipi et le Nouveau-Québec proprement dit.– Livres, articles de revue, manuscrits et publications diverses, quelques articles de journaux publiés après 1940: études générales, exploration et histoire, climat, études de sol et du sous-sol, hydrographie, végetation et faune, population, établissements, commerce et industrie.
Localisation: OONL.

— 1956 —

0289   Garigue, Philippe
A bibliographical introduction to the study of French Canada. [Montreal]: Department of Sociology and Anthropology, McGill University, 1956. 133 p.
Note: 2,984 entries.– Books, periodical articles, theses, government publications.– Focus on Quebec, with section of 170 listings on French-speaking groups outside the Province of Quebec.– Intended for use in anglophone universities.
Reprint: Westport, Conn.: Greenwood Press, 1977. 133 p.; ISBN: 0-8371-9807-0.
Location: OONL.

— 1959 —

0290   Cone, Gertrude
A selective bibliography of publications on the Champlain Valley. [Plattsburgh, N.Y.: c1959]. viii, 144 p.
Note: Mainly U.S. material, with a selection of Canadian and Quebec references.– Lists books, pamphlets, magazine and newspaper articles: history, biography, travel books, tourist literature, almanacs/gazetteers, journals and diaries.– Excludes periodicals, films, manuscripts, maps.– Separate sections for bibliographies, atlases, fiction (adult and juvenile).
Location: OONL.

— 1961 —

0291   Bonenfant, Jean-Claude
"Livres et périodiques canadiens d'expression française publiés de 1946 à 1961/Canada's French language books and periodicals published from 1946 to 1961."
Dans: *Annuaire du Québec*; (1961) p. 265-289.
Note: Localisation: OONL.

— 1965 —

0292   Daveluy, Marie-Claire
La Société de Notre-Dame de Montréal, 1639-1663: son histoire, ses membres, son manifeste. Montréal: Fides, [c1965]. 326, 127 p.: fac-sims. (Collection Fleur de lys)
Note: Première partie: "Bibliographie de la Société de Notre-Dame (1639-1663) accompagné de notes historiques et critiques."- 86 entrées.– Deuxième partie: "Bio-bibliographie des associés de Montréal."- 46 entrées.
Localisation: OONL.

0293   John Bassett Memorial Library
Catalogue of the Eastern Townships historical collection in the John Bassett Memorial Library. Lennoxville, Quebec: Bishop's University Library, 1965. 38 p.
Note: Location: OONL.

0294   Lacoste, Norbert
"Bibliographie sommaire des études sur Montréal, 1958-1964."
Dans: *Recherches sociographiques*; Vol. 6, no 3 (septembre-décembre 1965) p. 277-281.; ISSN: 0034-1282.
Note: Localisation: AEU.

0295   Saint-Denis, soeur
Gaspésiana. Montréal: Paris: Fides, [c1965]. xix, 180 p.: ill., fac-sims., carte.
Note: 107 entrées.– La période couverte est de 1565 à 1963.– Premier partie: livres, brochures, articles de revues, documents gouvernementales, périodiques, films sur: histoire, histoire religieuse, géographie et anthropologie, histoire économique, politique et colonisation, littérature, linguistique, histoire naturelle.– Deuxième partie: ouvrages écrits par des auteurs gaspésiens sur des sujets qui ne toucher pas directement à la Gaspésie.
Localisation: OONL.

— 1966 —

0296   "Bibliographie [relative à la vie sociale, économique et politique au Québec]."
Dans: *Relations*; No 309 (octobre 1966) p. 288-292.; ISSN: 0034-3781.
Note: Approx. 175 entrées.– Livres, périodiques: ouvrages généraux, enseignement social et morale publique, sociologie, économie, travail, politique, Nouveau-Québec.
Localisation: OONL.

— 1967 —

0297   Garigue, Philippe; Savard, Raymonde
Bibliographie du Québec (1955-1965). Montréal: Presses de l'Université de Montréal, 1967. 227 p.
Note: 2,270 entrées.– Monographies, articles de revues, publications officielles.– Divisée par sujets: histoire, géographie, population, institutions sociales, politiques et économiques, idéologie, culture.
Localisation: OONL.

0298   Hare, John; Wallot, Jean-Pierre
Les imprimés dans le Bas-Canada, 1801-1840: bibliographie analytique. Montréal: Presses de l'Université de Montréal, 1967. xxiii, 381 p.
Note: Vol. 1: 1801-1810: 272 entrées.– Publication no 1 du Groupe de recherche sur les idéologies dans la société canadienne-française.
Localisation: OONL.

— 1968 —

0299   Cooke, Alan; Caron, Fabien
Bibliography of the Quebec-Labrador peninsula/ Bibliographie de la péninsule du Québec-Labrador. Boston: G.K. Hall, 1968. 2 vol. (viii, 430; [4], 383 p.).
Note: Approx. 9,000 entries.– Books, pamphlets, periodical articles, government publications relating to Quebec-Labrador peninsula and islands.– Commissioned and published in collaboration with le Centre d'Études Nordiques, Université Laval.– Provides *Arctic bibliography* numbers for some entries.– Text in English and French/texte en français et en anglais.
Location: OONL.

0300   Pigeon, Marc; Bernier, Gaston
"Le Québec contemporain: éléments bibliographiques."
Dans: *Canadian Journal of Political Science*; Vol. 1, no. 2 (1968) p. 107-118.; ISSN: 0008-4239.
Note: 229 entrées.– Ouvrages de référence, documents officiels du gouvernement du Québec, livres, revues et journaux paraissant au Québec, articles, thèses.
Localisation: AEU.

0301 **Vézina, Germain**
Québec métropolitain: répertoire bibliographique. [Québec]: Université Laval, Faculté de théologie, Centre de recherches en sociologie religieuse, 1968. 64 p.
Note: 395 entrées.– Rapports, études, mémoires, articles, ouvrages, thèses: géographie, histoire, population, écologie, économie, transports et communications, gouvernement et services municipaux, organisation sociale et religieuse.
Localisation: OONL.

— 1969 —

0302 **Bosa, Réal**
Les ouvrages de référence du Québec: bibliographie analytique. [Québec]: Ministère des affaires culturelles du Québec, 1969. xiii, 189 p.
Note: 609 entrées.– Couvre les titres paru depuis novembre 1967.– Ouvrages de consultation publiés au Québec ou par des Québécois ou sur le Québec, dans toutes les disciplines.
Suppléments:
Lauzier, Suzanne; Cormier, Normand. ... *Supplément 1967-1974.* Montréal: Bibliothèque nationale du Québec, 1975. xv, 305 p. ill.– 585 entrées.– Compilé avec la collaboration de Ghislaine Houle et Yvon-André Lacroix.
Boivin, Henri-Bernard. ... *Supplément 1974-1981.* Montréal: Bibliothèque nationale du Québec; 1984. xii, 344 p.– 560 entrées.
Localisation: OONL.

0303 **Olivier, Réjean**
Bibliographie sur la ville de Joliette. Joliette, Québec: Société historique de Joliette, 1969. 2 p.
Note: Localisation: OONL.

0304 **Olivier, Réjean; Olivier, Yolande**
Bibliographie chronologique des livres publiés à Joliette depuis sa fondation. Joliette, Québec: Société historique de Joliette, [1969]. 3 f.
Note: Localisation: OONL.

— 1970 —

0305 **Bélanger, Pierre-A.**
"Bibliographie générale sur les Iles-de-la-Madeleine."
Dans: *Recherches sociographiques*; Vol. 11, no 3 (septembre-décembre 1970) p. 393-407.; ISSN: 0034-1282.
Note: Approx. 250 entrées.– Livres, articles de revues, rapports, films, journaux: général, économique, bio-physique, socio-culturel.
Localisation: AEU.

0306 **Durocher, René; Linteau, Paul-André**
Histoire du Québec: bibliographie sélective (1867-1970). Trois-Rivières: Boréal Express, 1970. 189 p.
Note: 1,897 entrées.– Livres, articles de revues, thèses, publications gouvernementales, brochures.
Localisation: OONL.

0307 **O'Bready, Maurice**
Les Cantons de l'Est: début de bibliographie. [S.l.: s.n., 1970]. 12 f.
Note: Géographie et préhistoire, période indienne, période loyaliste, période britannique, période canadienne-française, monographies paroissiales, périodiques, fonds de manuscrits.
Localisation: QSHERSH.

— 1971 —

0308 **Beaulieu, André; Morley, William F.E.**
La Province de Québec. Toronto: University of Toronto Press, 1971. xxvii, 408 p. (Histoires locales et régionales canadiennes des origines à 1950 ; vol. II); ISBN: 0-8020-1733-9.
Note: Approx. 1,500 entrées.– Avec la collaboration de Benoit Bernier et Agathe Garon.
Localisation: OONL.

0309 **Brassard, Léo**
"Bibliographie commentée des travaux suscités par les Jeunes Explos dans la région du Saguenay."
Dans: *Saguenayensia*; Vol. 13, no 4 (juillet-août 1971) p. 101-105.; ISSN: 0581-295X.
Note: Localisation: AEU.

0310 **Couture, Murielle, et al.**
Catalogue [des volumes et des publications concernant le Nord-Ouest: Abitibi-Témiscamingue]. Rouyn, Québec: Information Abitibi-Témiscamingue, 1971. 2 vol.
Note: Publications gouvernementales, publications d'associations, publications individuelles: agriculture, éducation, forêts, géographie, histoire, mines, socio-économique, tourisme.
Localisation: OONL.

0311 **Linteau, Paul-André; Thivierge, Jean**
Montréal au 19e siècle: bibliographie. [Montréal]: Groupe de recherche sur la société montréalaise au 19e siècle, Université du Québec à Montréal, [1971]. viii, 79 f.
Note: 1,086 entrées.– Compilée avec la collaboration de Huguette Beauséjour, André Cyr, Robert Paradis et Jean-Claude Robert.
Localisation: OONL.

— 1972 —

0312 **Arts plastiques de Rimouski (Projet). Section recherche en histoire**
Bibliographie annotée d'articles de journaux du comté de Rimouski. Rimouski: [s.n.], 1972. x p., 412 f.
Note: Localisation: OONL.

0313 **Arts plastiques de Rimouski (Projet). Section recherche en histoire**
Répertoire bibliographique du comté de Rimouski. Rimouski: Secrétariat-Jeunesse, 1972. xii, 197 p.
Note: 760 entrées.– Livres, périodiques, publications, journaux, documentation sonore: agriculture et colonisation, éducation et maisons d'enseignement, forêt, géographie et sciences voisines, religion, vie économique, vie politique, vie sociale, villes/villages/paroisses.
Localisation: OONL.

0314 **Bibliographie analytique régionale: études sur l'Estrie: [étude preparée dans le cadre du projet ESTRAE et presentée à l'Office de planification et de développement du Québec].** [Sherbrooke, Québec]: Université de Sherbrooke, Centre de recherches en aménagement régional, 1972. ii, 220 p.
Note: Approx. 1,500 entrées.– La période couverte est de 1940 à 1971.– Des ouvrages consacrés à l'Estrie couvrant les secteurs suivants: l'agriculture et la forêt, la géologie, le transport, l'industrie, l'environnement, l'aménagement du territoire, l'enseignement, les sciences sociales, les loisirs, la culture, la géographie, l'histoire.– Preparée sous la direction de Pierre Lacasse.
Localisation: OONL.

0315 **Boult, Jean-Claude**
"Bibliographie de l'histoire de Hull: inventaire préliminaire."
Dans: *Asticou*; No 9 (septembre 1972) p. 31-42.; ISSN:

0066-992X.
Note: 177 entrées.– Journaux, sources manuscrites, sources imprimées, études.
Localisation: OONL

0316 **Communication-Québec. Centre de documentation**
Répertoire bibliographique de la documentation dans l'Outaouais. Hull: Communication-Québec, 1972. 9 t. en 1 vol.
Note: T. 1: *Ouvragres généraux*; t. 2: *Bien-être*; t. 3: *Santé*; t. 4: *Culture*; t. 5: *Agriculture, forêt*; t. 6: *Éducation*; t. 7: *Industrie, commerce*; t. 8: *Main-d'oeuvre*; t. 9: *Loisirs, sports, tourisme, récréation*.
Localisation: QQE.

0317 **Dion, Louise**
"L'Est du Québec: bibliographie 1966-1971."
Dans: *Cahiers de géographie de Québec*; Vol. 16, no 37 (avril 1972) p. 130-139.; ISSN: 0007-9766.
Note: Approx. 200 entrées.– Couvre la Gaspésie, les îles-de-la-Madeleine, la Côte-Nord, le Saguenay, Lac Saint-Jean, le Bas estuaire et la Golfe de Saint-Laurent: généralités et milieu humain; milieu bio-physique.
Localisation: AEU.

0318 **Fortin, Suzanne, et al.**
La Beauce et un peu plus: bibliographie commentée, des ouvrages écrits sur la Beauce et la périphérie. Saint-Georges: [s.n.], 1972. 1 vol. (en pagination multiple).
Note: Volumes, publications et articles de journaux écrits sur la Beauce, Québec: histoire, éducation, industries et commerce, tourisme, agriculture, bois, démographie, transports et communications, travail.
Localisation: QQERT.

0319 **Gowling, Linda**
Contemporary French Canada: a select bibliography. [Waterloo, Ont.]: Reference Department, Dana Porter Arts Library, University of Waterloo, 1972. 77 l.
Note: Approx. 750 entries.– Monographs and journal articles on French Canadian and particularly Quebec institutions, social problems, economy, education, agriculture, urbanization, cultural characteristics, human geography.
Location: OONL.

0320 **Pouliot, Richard**
Influences culturelles des États-Unis sur le Québec: état sommaire des travaux. Québec: Centre québécois de relations internationales: Institut canadien des affaires internationales, 1972. 21, 34 f. (Notes de recherche / Centre québécois de relations internationales ; no 4)
Note: Approx. 300 entrées.– Monographies, articles de périodiques, thèses sur les thèmes: relations États-Unis-Canada; histoire du Québec; relations Québec-États-Unis (images "étasuniennes" au Canada-français, mouvements migratoire, le syndicalisme, l'Église, coopération franco-québécoise); société et culture québécoise: influences américaines; les Canadiens-français aux États-Unis.
Localisation: OONL.

0321 **Southam, Peter**
Bibliographie des bibliographies sur l'économie, la société et la culture du Québec, 1940-1971. Québec: Institut supérieur des sciences humaines, Université Laval, 1972. vi [i.e. vii], 86 f. (Cahiers de l'ISSH, Collection Instruments de travail / Institut supérieur des sciences humaines, Université Laval ; no 6)
Note: 357 entrées.– Exclut les biobibliographies, les bibliographies très spécialisées et les index de périodiques.
Localisation: OONL.

— 1973 —

0322 **Cotnam, Jacques**
Contemporary Quebec: an analytical bibliography. [Toronto]: McClelland and Stewart, [c1973]. 112 p.; ISBN: 0-7710-2249-2.
Note: Approx. 1,500 entries.– Focus on 1950 to 1970.– Includes books, periodicals, government publications, special issues of journals devoted to a particular subject.– Designed to assist English-speaking high-school and college students in researching Quebec topics.
Location: OONL.

0323 **Gourd, Benoît-Beaudry**
Bibliographie de l'Abitibi-Témiscamingue. Édition préliminaire. Rouyn: Université du Québec, Direction d'études universitaires dans l'Ouest québécois (Nord-Ouest), 1973. x, 270 p.
Note: 2,787 entrées.– Livres, articles de périodiques, thèses, publications officielles, études et rapports concernant: histoire, agriculture et colonisation, économie et société, éducation, géographie, terres et forêts, mines et géologie.– Comprend aussi des publications en langue anglais.
Suppléments:
... : *supplément*. 1975. ix, 214 p.
Gourd, Benoît-Beaudry; Lavallée, Denis. ... : *deuxième supplément*. 1977. ix, 202 p.
Béland, André. ... : *troisième supplément*. Rouyn: Université du Québec, Centre d'études universitaires dans l'Ouest québécois, Service des bibliothèques, Centre de documentation régionale, 1979. x, 94 p.
Localisation: OONL.

0324 **Greer-Wootten, Bryn; Wolfe, Jeanne**
"Bibliographie sur Montréal et sa région/Bibliography on Montreal and region."
Dans: *Revue de géographie de Montréal*; Vol. 27, no 3 (1973) p. 305-317.; ISSN: 0035-1148.
Note: Approx. 350 entrées.– Livres, articles, rapports, thèses: histoire, caractéristiques physiques, climat, géographie urbaine, qualité de milieu, démographie, aspects sociaux, économie, transport, aménagement, aspects politiques et administratifs.
Localisation: OONL.

0325 **McGill University. Centre d'études canadiennes-françaises**
Le Québec: guide bibliographique en histoire. [Montréal]: Centre d'études canadiennes-françaises; Service de la référence, Bibliothèque McLennan, Université McGill, 1973. 14 p.
Note: Approx. 100 entrées.– Comprend des titres d'ouvrages de référence, principalement de bibliographies, concernant l'histoire du Québec publiés récemment.
Localisation: OONL.

— 1974 —

0326 **Barbeau, Victor; Fortier, André**
Dictionnaire bibliographique du Canada français. Montréal: Académie canadienne-française, 1974. 246 p.; ISBN: 0-969008-14.
Note: Approx. 13,000 entrées.– Les auteurs précisent le contenu du dictionnaire: les auteurs, de naissance ou

d'adoption, du Canada français (en plus de quelques auteurs franco-américains) ainsi que les auteurs de France qui ont écrit sur le Canada.– La description bibliographique exclut la collation.– Les auteurs répertoriés font l'objet, la plupart du temps, de notes biographiques allant de quelques mots à plusieurs paragraphes.
Localisation: OONL.

0327 **"Bibliographie relative au drapeau québécois."**
Dans: *Le drapeau québécois*, par Jacques Archambault et Eugénie Lévesque. Québec: Éditeur officiel du Québec, 1974. P. 62-75.
Note: Localisation: OONL.

0328 **Fournier, Marcel**
Guide des monographies de paroisses de la région Joliette-Lanaudière. Chertsey, Québec: [s.n.], 1974. 30 f.
Note: Localisation: OONL.

0329 **Lemay, Henri-Paul**
Bibliographie sur le Saint-Laurent. Saint-Foy: Institut national de la recherche scientifique, Université du Québec, 1974. iii, iv, 159 p.
Note: Approx. 1,500 entrées.– Littérature traitant du fleuve Saint-Laurent: sources documentaires, études générales sur l'ensemble du Saint-Laurent et son bassin, le bassin québécois du Saint-Laurent, études socio-économiques québécoises, études diverses sur l'eau.
Localisation: OOFF.

0330 **Tawell, Rachel; Beaumont-Moisan, Renée**
L'île d'Anticosti (bibliographie). Québec: Ministère des terres et forêts, Service de l'information, Bibliothèque, 1974. 43, 7, 14 p.
Note: 492 entrées.– Livres, articles de périodiques et journaux, publications gouvernementales: géologie, sciences naturelles, histoire, tourisme, pêcheries, descriptions et voyages, chasse, aménagement du territoire, Consolidated Bathurst.– Compilée sous la direction de Kathleen Mennie-de Varennes.
Localisation: QQL.

— 1975 —

0331 **Bibliothèque municipale de Mulhouse**
Livres du Québec. Mulhouse, France: Mairie de Mulhouse, [1975]. 24 p.
Note: Approx. 125 entrées.
Localisation: OONL.

0332 **Bibliothèque nationale du Québec**
Le livre québécois 1764-1975. Montréal: Bibliothèque nationale du Québec, 1975. 182 p.: ill.
Note: 591 entrées.
Localisation: OONL.

0333 **Dion, Henriette**
Histoire régionale: bibliographie. Drummondville, Québec: Bibliothèque, [Collège régional Bourgchemin], Campus de Drummondville, 1975. 27 f.
Note: Approx. 150 entrées.– Livres, brochures, cartes, publications gouvernementales, documents audio-visuels, articles de périodiques d'histoire régionale de Drummondville.
Localisation: OONL.

0334 **Frappier, Monique; Heap, Margaret; Robert, Jean-Claude**
"Montréal dans les récits de voyage: bibliographie."
Dans: *Rapport et travaux, 1973-1975: Groupe de recherche sur la société montréalaise au 19e siècle*. Montréal: Départe-

ment d'histoire, Université du Québec à Montréal, 1975. 50 p.; ISSN: 0225-6959.
Note: Localisation: OONL.

0335 **Pelletier-Olivier, Yolande; Olivier, Réjean**
Bibliographie joliettaine. L'Assomption [Québec]: Collège de l'Assomption, Bibliothèque, 1975. 62 f.: facsim.
Note: 350 entrées.– Livres, brochures, revues, journaux publiés à Joliette depuis sa fondation jusqu'à 1970.
Localisation: OONL.

0336 **Québec (Province). Ministère des richesses naturelles. Bibliothèque**
Bibliographie du bassin de la rivière Saint-François. Québec: Gouvernement du Québec, Ministère des richesses naturelles, Service de la bibliothèque et des archives, 1975. 114 p.
Note: 508 entrées.
Localisation: OONL.

0337 **Rheault, Marie**
Bibliographie sommaire sur la Côte-Nord et les régions circonvoisines. Sept-Iles: Bibliothèque municipale, [1975]. 36 f.
Note: Approx. 350 entrées.– Livres, études, rapports gouvernementales, articles de périodiques: archéologie & géologie, économie, géographie de la Côte-Nord, littérature, politique, sociologie.
Localisation: OONL.

0338 **Université de Sherbrooke. Groupe de recherche en histoire régionale**
Bibliographie d'histoire des Cantons de l'Est. [Sherbrooke]: Département d'histoire, Université de Sherbrooke, 1975. 120 p.
Note: 871 entrées.– Livres, articles, thèses, brochures, publications officielles, chapitres complets ou les tranches d'ouvrages généraux qui concernant directement les Cantons de l'Est.
Localisation: OOFF.

— 1976 —

0339 **Fournier, Marcel**
Guide bibliographique Joliette-Lanaudière: [livres et journaux, 1847-1976]. Joliette [Québec]: Société historique de Joliette, 1976. 96 f.: fac.–sim.
Note: 234 entrées.
Localisation: OONL.

0340 **Lamonde, Yvan**
Guide d'histoire du Québec. Sillery: Boréal Express, c1976. 94 p. (Collection Mékinac); ISBN: 0-88503-051-6.
Note: Sources primaires (manuscrits, iconographiques, imprimés), sources secondaires (études), renseignements généraux.
Localisation: OONL.

0341 **Manseau, Édith**
Semaine des études québécoises, 1976: culture: bibliographie indicative. Trois-Rivières: Université du Québec à Trois-Rivières, [1976]. 7 f.
Note: Localisation: OONL.

0342 **Répertoire de l'édition au Québec.** Montréal: Edi-Québec, 1972-1976. 3 vol.; ISSN: 0315-5943.
Note: Répertoire des ouvrages en langue française du Québec.– Comporte trois parties: auteurs, titres, sujets.– Publiés avec le concours de l'Association des éditeurs canadiens, de la Société des éditeurs de manuels scolaires du Québec, et la collaboration du Conseil supérieur du

livre et de la Bibliothèque nationale du Québec.
Localisation: OONL.

0343 **Vlach, Milada; Buono, Yolande**
Laurentiana parus avant 1821. Montréal: Bibliothèque nationale du Québec, 1976. xxvii, 416, 120 p.
Note: 768 entrées.– Textes imprimés d'auteurs québécois ou de voyageurs de passage qui ont influencé cette société au niveau artistique, économique, politique ou religieux: documents produits par le Québec ou dont le sujet principal est le Québec.
Localisation: OONL.

— 1977 —

0344 **Beaumont-Moisan, Renée; Hudon, Céline**
Bibliographie sur les Iles-de-la-Madeleine. Québec: Ministère des Terres et Forêts, Service de l'Information, Bibliothèque, 1977. [24] f.
Note: 214 entrées.
Localisation: QQEN.

0345 **Côté, André**
Sources de l'histoire du Saguenay-Lac-Saint-Jean: Tome III: guide bibliographique. [Québec]: Centre de documentation, Direction de l'Inventaire des biens culturels, 1977. 273 p.: cartes. (Direction générale du patrimoine Dossier ; no 30)
Note: 3,059 entrées.– Instruments de travail et des études, documents réalisés au cours des XIXe et XXe siècles.
Localisation: OONL.

0346 **Hardy, René; Trépanier, Guy; Belleau, Jacques**
La Mauricie et les Bois-Francs: inventaire bibliographique, 1760-1975. Montréal: Éditions du Boréal Express, [1977]. 389 p.: cartes. (Collection Mékinac ; 2); ISBN: 0-88503-062-1.
Note: 3,802 entrées.– Livres, brochures, articles, publications officielles, cartes, films.
Localisation: OONL.

0347 **Lacroix, Benoît; Chrestien, Jean-Pierre**
"Initiation bibliographique à la connaissance du Canada français."
Dans: *Annales de Normandie*; Vol. 27, no 2 (juin 1977) p. 219-228.; ISSN: 0003-4134.
Note: Premiers instruments de travail, principaux accès aux sources, grandes synthèses et production courante, sciences auxiliaires.
Localisation: AEU.

0348 **LeMoyne, Beryl; Millette, Robert**
A Quebec bibliography. Montreal: ABQ/QLA, 1977. 10 p.
Note: 70 entries.– Compiled as the ABQ/QLA contribution to Canadian Library Association annual convention held in Montreal, June, 1977.
Location: OONL.

0349 **Lepage, Francia G., et al.**
Guide bibliographique: recherches historiques sur la ville de Sainte-Foy, 1534-1975. Sainte-Foy: Bureau de l'information de la Ville de Sainte-Foy, 1977. v, 207 p.
Note: 1,141 entrées.– Comprend des volumes, rapports, articles de journaux, documents officiels sur l'histoire de Sainte-Foy.– Index des sujets.
Localisation: QQLA.

0350 **Québec (Province). Bibliothèque de la Législature**
Catalogue des livres exposés au Musée de l'Assemblée nationale du Québec à l'occasion du 175e anniversaire de la Bibliothèque de la Législature. Québec: Bibliothèque de la Législature, 1977. 66 p.: ill.
Note: Localisation: OONL.

— 1978 —

0351 **Aubé, Pierre-Yvan**
Bibliographie d'histoire régionale. Drummondville: P.-Y. Aubé, 1978. 118 f.
Note: 311 entrées.
Localisation: QQAM.

0352 **Bibliothèque nationale du Québec. Service de microphotographie**
Catalogue des microéditions [Service de microphotographie, Bibliothèque nationale du Québec]. Montréal: Ministère des affaires culturelles, Bibliothèque nationale du Québec, 1974-1978. 5 vol.; ISSN: 0384-9724.
Note: Objectifs du Service de microphotographie: conservation et diffusion des laurentiana: toute microéditions réalisée au Québec ou relatif au Québec.
Localisation: OONL.

0353 **Boivin, Henri-Bernard**
"Contribution à la bibliographie du Comté des Deux-Montagnes."
Dans: *Cahiers d'histoire de Deux-Montagnes*; Vol. 1, no 1 (janvier 1978) p. 24-41.; ISSN: 0226-7063.
Note: Approx. 60 entrées.– Monographies, périodiques, publications officielles.
Localisation: OONL.

0354 **Deslongchamps, Jocelyne**
Répertoire de la collection entrevues des pionniers de l'Abitibi-Témiscamingue. Rouyn: Université du Québec, Centre d'études universitaires dans l'Ouest québécois, Service des bibliothèques, 1978. 85, [9] f.: ill. (Publication du Centre des archives de l'Abitibi-Témiscamingue ; no 7)
Note: Localisation: OONL.

0355 **St-Amour, Jean-Pierre F.**
L'Outaouais québécois: guide de recherche et bibliographie sélective. Hull, Québec: Université du Québec, Centre d'études universitaires dans l'Ouest québécois, [1978]. x, 178 p.
Note: 1,315 entrées.– Monographies, études, historiques, articles de revues, rapports techniques, thèses, brochures.– Sans compter mémoires présentés à des commissions d'étude ou d'enquête, textes non publiés et des documents d'archives.– Chronologie, liste des municipalités avec notes historiques.
Localisation: OONL.

0356 **Théberge, Jean-Yves**
Bibliographie du Haut-Richelieu. Saint-Jean [Québec]: Service des moyens d'enseignement, Commission scolaire régionale Honoré-Mercier, 1978. 86 p.
Note: 457 entrées.– Livres, brochures, articles de périodiques, publications officielles.
Localisation: OONL.

0357 **Zinman, Rosalind**
"Selected bibliography on Quebec."
In: *Canadian Review of Sociology and Anthropology*; Vol. 15, no. 2 (1978) p. 246-251.; ISSN: 0008-4948.
Note: List of books, articles, government publications in English and French, mainly from the period 1965 to 1977: bibliographies, works on history, government and politics, economy, sociology, demography, the national question.
Location: AEU.

— 1979 —

0358 **Bibliothèque nationale du Québec. Centre bibliographique**
Bibliographie de bibliographies québécoises. Montréal: Bibliothèque nationale du Québec, 1979. 2 vol.; ISBN: 2-400-00074-3 (Édition complète).
Note: 3,036 entrées.– Couvre jusqu'en 1977 inclusivement.– Un inventaire exhaustif des bibliographies québécoises, des origines à nos jours.– Inclut monographies et périodiques bibliographies.– Chaque document répertorié répond à au moins un des critères: est l'oeuvre d'un auteur québécois, concerne le Québec ou un sujet québécois, a été publié au Quebec.– Aucune annotation.– Index: auteurs, titres, sujets.– Comp. par Le Centre bibliographique sous la direction d'Henri-Bernard Boivin.
Suppléments:
1980. 145 p.; ISBN: 2-550-00630-5.– 674 entrées.
1981. 175 p.; ISBN: 2-550-02157-6.– 902 entrées.
Localisation: OONL.

0359 **Léveillé, Lionel**
Bibliographie sommaire de la Côte-du-Sud. La Pocatière, [Québec]: Cégep de La Pocatière, Service de l'éducation aux adultes, 1979. 66 p.
Note: Approx. 450 entrées.– Livres, brochures, thèses, documents gouvernementales, articles de périodiques, extraits (chapitres ou parties) de monographies sur le région du Québec qui s'étend de Berthier-en-Bas à Rivière-du-Loup.
Localisation: OONL.

— 1980 —

0360 **Boivin, Aurélien; Bourgeois, Jean-Marc**
Littérature du Saguenay-Lac-Saint-Jean: répertoire des oeuvres et des auteurs. Alma [Québec]: Éditions du Royaume, c1980. 147 p.: ill., fac.–sims.; ISBN: 2-920164-00-7.
Note: Approx. 1,200 entrées.
Localisation: OONL.

0361 **Lamy, Jean-Christian**
Le Québec: guide documentaire élaboré par Jean-Christian Lamy avec le concours des bibliographes de la Centrale des bibliothèques du Québec. Paris: Centre national de documentation pédagogique, 1980. 108 p. (Collection guides documentaires / Centre national de documentation pédagogique ; no 7)
Note: 519 entrées.– Cartes, diapositives, films, films fixes, livres, microformes, périodiques, phonogrammes, transparents, vidéogrammes.
Localisation: OONL.

0362 **Lepage, Françoise; Boyer, Denis**
Inventaire des documents de la Bibliothèque sur Hull et la région. Hull [Québec]: Bibliothèque municipale, 1980. [4], 172 f.
Note: 635 entrées.– Documents contenus dans la Salle de Hull: monographies, journaux et périodiques, articles, microfilms, documents sonores: arts, littérature, histoire et géographie, religion, technologie, langage, sciences sociale/exactes.
Localisation: OONL.

0363 **Livres du Québec.** Montréal: Société de développement du livre et du périodique, 1980. 58 p.
Note: Approx. 750 entrées qui portent sur l'art et les traditions populaires, l'histoire, la géographie, la politique, la linguistique, la littérature, la littérature pour la jeunesse, le management, la pédagogie, la psychologie et sociologie.
Supplément: [Québec]: Gouvernement du Québec, Ministère des affaires intergouvernementales, 1981. 17 p.; ISBN: 2-550-01678-5.– Approx. 200 entrées.
Localisation: OONL.

0364 **Monière, Denis; Vachet, André**
Les idéologies au Québec: bibliographie. 3e éd. rev. et augm. Montréal: Bibliothèque nationale du Québec, 1980. 175 p.; ISBN: 2-550-00821-9.
Note: 1,411 entrées.– Livres, revues, thèses de maîtrise et de doctorat.– Thèmes: classe sociale, clergé, confédération, culture, économie, éducation, église, fédéralisme, indépendance, littérature, nationalisme, séparatisme-indépendantisme, socialisme, syndicalisme.
Éditions antérieures:
1977. 176 p.
Montréal: Gouvernement du Québec, Ministère des affaires culturelles, 1976. 155 p.
Localisation: OONL.

0365 **Petit album des auteurs des cantons de l'Est.** Saint-Elie d'Orford, Qué.: Association des auteurs des Canton de l'Est, 1980. 126 p.: ill.
Note: Sous la responsabilité de Jean Civil avec la collaboration de Jocelyne Valence, André Bernier et Jacques Côté.
Localisation: OONL.

0366 **Sénécal, André Joseph**
"Quebec studies: a guide to the bibliographies."
In: *American Review of Canadian Studies*; Vol. 10, No. 2 (Autumn 1980) p. 85-88.; ISSN: 0272-2011.
Note: Location: AEU.

0367 **Tousignant, André**
Données sur l'histoire régionale: bibliographie annotée avec index et autres sources de référence. [Châteauguay, Québec]: Société historique de la vallée de la Châteauguay/Chateauguay Valley Historical Society, 1980. viii, 151 p.
Note: Approx. 900 entrées.– Ouvrages généraux et spécialisés, périodiques, biographies, section sur Kateri Tékakwitha, littérature, documents pédagogiques.
Localisation: OONL.

— 1981 —

0368 **Bernier, Hélène; Caron, Diane**
La tradition populaire québécoise: une base bibliographique. [Québec]: Gouvernement du Québec, Ministère du loisir, de la chasse et de la pêche, 1981. v, 207 f.
Note: Approx. 800 entrées.– Livres, brochures, articles, films, thèses: ouvrages décrivant divers aspects de la vie traditionnelle québécoise: chansons, danse, architecture, conte, coutumes, légende, techniques de transformation.
Localisation: OONL.

0369 **Cardinal, Claudette**
The history of Quebec: a bibliography of works in English. [Montreal]: Centre for the Study of Anglophone Quebec, Concordia University, 1981. vi, 202 p.; ISBN: 0-88947-002-2.
Note: 3,437 entries.– Books, journal articles, theses, pamphlets issued to 1976 on the history of Quebec.– Compiled under the direction of Graeme Decarie and Ronald Rubin.

Location: OONL.

0370 **Grenier, Ginette**
Bibliographie annotée de l'histoire de Sherbrooke. Trois-Rivières: Cegep de Trois-Rivières, 1981. iv, 58 f.
Note: 124 entrées.
Localisation: QSHERU.

0371 **Hamelin, Jean; Beaulieu, André; Gallichan, Gilles**
Brochures québécoises, 1764-1972. [Québec]: Gouvernement du Québec, Ministère des communications, Direction générale des publications gouvernementales, c1981. vii, 598, [2] p.; ISBN: 2-551-03737-9.
Note: 10,232 entrées.– Tout imprimé dont le nombre de pages est inférieur à 49.– Exclut les périodiques, publications gouvernementales, tirés à part, circulaires, calendriers, manuels.
Localisation: OONL.

0372 **Lambert, Ronald D.**
The sociology of contemporary Quebec nationalism: an annotated bibliography and review. New York: Garland Publishing, 1981. lxvi, 148 p. (Canadian review of studies in nationalism ; v. 2) (Garland reference library of social sciences ; v. 78); ISBN: 0-8240-9480-8.
Note: 586 entries.– Covers from 1945 to December, 1979.– Includes books, journal articles, theses and dissertations, government publications in French and English languages.– Annotations in English.
Locations: OONL.

0373 **Olivier, Réjean**
Catalogue de laurentiana, de canadiana et de livres anciens de la bibliothèque de la famille Olivier répertoriant 12,000 volumes et 120 collections de périodiques pour la plupart du Québec. Joliette [Québec: s.n.], 1981. 3 vol.; ISBN: 2-920249-00-2.
Note: Localisation: OONL.

0374 **Poirier, Jean**
Eléments de bibliographie: est du Québec. [Québec]: Ministère de l'éducation, Direction régionale du Bas-Saint-Laurent-Gaspésie, 1981. 86 f.; ISBN: 2-550-04310-3.
Note: Articles de revues, livres, brochures, albums qui concerne l'histoire, la géographie et le développement de la région gaspésienne.
Localisation: OONL.

0375 **Université du Québec à Trois-Rivières. Bibliothèque**
Catalogue collectif régional: Mauricie et centre du Québec. Trois-Rivières: Université du Québec à Trois-Rivières, 1977-1981. 2 fasc.
Note: Fascicule 1: *Monographies.* 1977. 327 p. (Bibliothèque, publication ; no 14).– Approx. 1,700 entrées.– Livres, brochures, films, montage audio-visuel, documentation qui concerne la région Mauricie et qui existe dans la région.– Fascicule 2: *Journaux et revues.* 1981. xiii, 48 f. (Bibliothèque, publication ; no 22).– Approx. 375 entrées.– Compilé par Philippe Houyoux et Micheline Xeropaides.
Supplément: 1979. xiv p. 315 f. (Bibliothèque, publication ; no 20).– Approx. 1,700 entrées.
Localisation: OONL.

— 1982 —

0376 **Gauvin, Lise; Mailhot, Laurent**
Guide culturel du Québec. Montréal: Boréal Express, 1982. 533 p.: ill.; ISBN: 2-89052-044-7.
Note: Choix des livres et articles: langage et langues, littérature, art, théâtre, géographie, histoire, science politique, sociologie, économique, psychologie et philosophie.
Localisation: OONL.

0377 **Giguère, Rita; Larrivée, Jean; Castonguay, Lise**
Répertoire de données compilées par le GRIDEQ. Rimouski: Université du Québec à Rimouski, 1982. viii, 137 p.
Note: Travaux réalisés ou en train par le Groupe de recherche en développement de l'Est du Québec: communications, condition féminine, condition ouvrière, de travail et syndicalisme, démographie, économie, éducation, milieu rurale, organisation et représentation de l'espace, pratiques d'intervention sociales.
Localisation: QQLA.

0378 **Laurin, Clément**
"Bibliographie de la bataille de Saint-Eustache."
Dans: *Cahiers d'histoire de Deux-Montagnes*; Vol. 5, no 2 (octobre 1982) p. 10-14.; ISSN: 0226-7063.
Note: Approx. 40 entrées.– Sources, études spéciales sur les troubles de 1837-1838, en particulier à St-Eustache.
Localisation: OONL.

— 1983 —

0379 **Collège d'enseignement général et professionnel de Rivière-du-Loup. Centre d'étude régionale**
Liste des documents disponibles au Centre d'étude régionale. Rivière-du-Loup [Québec]: Le Centre, 1983. 23 p. (Publications du Centre d'étude régionale ; no 1); ISBN: 2-920571-00-1.
Note: Approx. 200 entrées.– Ouvrages historiques régionaux et locaux, ouvrages à caractère géographique et socio-économique, ouvrages généalogiques, journaux et périodiques.– Colligé par Alain Roberge.
Localisation: OONL.

0380 **Dionne, André**
Bibliographie de l'Ile Jésus. [Québec]: Institut québécois de recherche sur la culture, 1983. 319, [4] p.: cartes. (Documents de recherche / Institut québécois de recherche sur la culture ; no 2; ISSN: 0823-0447); ISBN: 2-89224-035-2.
Note: Approx. 1,000 entrées.– Deux sections: 1. Références bibliographiques: livres, articles de revue, thèses, mémoires et rapports d'enquête, études techniques, documents divers sur l'histoire, l'économie, l'organisation politique et sociale et la culture à l'Ile Jésus (Ville de Laval); 2. Inventaires d'archives: dépôts d'archives gouvernementales, municipales, scolaires, religieuses, professionelles et privées.
Localisation: OONL.

— 1984 —

0381 **Gauthier, Serge**
Bibliographie de Charlevoix. [Québec]: Institut québécois de recherche sur la culture, 1984. 316 p.: cartes. (Documents de recherche / Institut québécois de recherche sur la culture ; no 3: ISSN: 0823-0447); ISBN: 2-89224-037-9.
Note: 1,810 entrées.– Monographies, articles de périodiques, thèses, publications officielles, instruments de travail, monographies paroissiales, biographies de personnalités, fonds d'archives (avec sources régionales).– Thèmes: le territoire, vie économique, aspects sociaux, aspects politiques, culture, religion, généalogie.
Localisation: OONL.

0382 **McGill University. Department of Rare Books and Special Collections**
Catalogue of the Rodolphe Joubert Collection on French Canada in the Department of Rare Books and Special Collections. Montreal: McGill University Libraries, 1984. 321 p.
Note: Approx. 3,200 entries.
Location: OONL.

0383 **Vlach, Milada; Buono, Yolande**
Catalogue collectif des impressions québécoises, 1764-1820. Québec: Direction générale des publications gouvernementales, 1984. xxxiii, 251, 195 p.; ISBN: 2-551-08919-0.
Note: 1,115 entrées.– Catalogue des imprimés québécois antérieurs à 1821 conservés dans les plus riches bibliothèques du Québec.– Comprend livres, brochures, publications gouvernementales, publications en série annuelles, tout autant que les textes imprimés sur une seule feuille.– Ne sont pas compris les revues, les journaux, ni les formulaires à remplir.– Divers index: titres, noms, sujets, genres, lieux d'édition, imprimeurs, dates d'édition, provenances.
Localisation: OONL.

— 1985 —

0384 **Duval, Marc**
Bibliographie d'articles de périodiques sur la Côte-Nord. Sept-îles [Québec]: Éditions Infodoc, 1985. 149 f.
Note: 942 entrées.– La période couverte est de 1973 à 1985.– Principaux thèmes traités: culture, éducation, géographie, histoire, sciences naturelles, tourisme, sport, économie, écologie, les autochtones (Inuit, Montagnais).
Localisation: OONL.

0385 **Hare, John; Motard, Chantal; Vigneault, Robert**
"Bibliographie représentative de la prose d'idées au Québec, des origines à 1980."
Dans: L'essai et la prose d'idées au Québec. Montréal: Fides, 1985. P. 783-921. (Archives des lettres canadiennes ; Tome 6); ISBN: 2-7621-1279-6.
Note: Approx. 2,000 entrées.– Essai socio-politiques, essai critiques, études (art, droit, éducation, histoire, littérature, philosophie, politique, psychologie, sociologie, théologie et religion), autobiographies, mémoires, journaux intimes, récits de voyage.
Localisation: OONL.

0386 **John Bassett Memorial Library**
Lists of Eastern Townships material in the John Bassett Memorial Library. Lennoxville, Quebec: Bishop's University Library, 1985. 2 vol.; ISBN: 0-920917-01-1 (set).
Note: Approx. 7,000 entries.– Lists archival material: manuscripts, minute-books, correspondence, diaries, photographs, scrap-books, etc. from private individuals, companies and institutions: maps, oral history tapes, pamphlet files, vertical files, books, theses, microforms and government documents relating to the Eastern Townships.
Location: OONL.

0387 **Laurin, Serge; Lagrange, Richard**
Bibliographie des Laurentides. [Québec]: Institut québécois de recherche sur la culture, 1985. 370 p.: cartes. (Documents de recherche / Institut québécois de recherche sur la culture ; no 7; ISSN: 0823-0447); ISBN: 2-89224-052-4.
Note: 2,048 entrées.– Livres, brochures, thèses universitaires, articles de revues, un choix d'articles de journaux, études gouvernementales.– Définition de la région des Laurentides: Antoine-Labelle, Argenteuil, Deux-Montagnes, La Rivière-du-Nord, Les Laurentides, Les Pays-d'en-Haut, Thérèse-de-Blainville, Mirabel, Les Moulins.– Sujets: histoire du peuplement, aspects économiques, aspects sociaux, politiques, culture, religion, histoire locale, biographies, généalogie, instruments de travail, liste des revues et journaux régionaux, filmographie, fonds d'archives, index des thèses.– Cartes: 1. "Début du 17e siècle." 2. "Les seigneuries vers 1852." 3. "La région des Laurentides en 1985."
Localisation: OONL.

0388 **Lennoxville-Ascot Historical and Museum Society**
Lennoxville-Ascot Historical and Museum Society: preliminary catalogue of documents, manuscripts and papers. Lennoxville, Quebec: The Society, 1985. 44 l.
Note: Location: OONL.

0389 **O'Donnell, Brendan**
Printed sources for the study of English-speaking Quebec: an annotated bibliography of works published before 1980. Lennoxville, Quebec: Bishop's University, 1985. ii, 298 p. (Eastern Townships Research Centre series ; no. 2); ISBN: 0-920917-04-6.
Note: 2,698 entries.– Books, articles, theses relating to development of English-speaking Quebec: biographies, clubs, culture, education, finance/commerce/economics, Eastern Townships, geography, history, newspapers and journalists, politics, religion, sociology, English-French relations.
Location: OONL.

0390 **Olivier, Réjean**
Le Lanaudois: bibliographie de la région de Lanaudière ou Extraits du catalogue de la collection de la famille Olivier de Joliette. Joliette [Québec: s.n.], 1985. 134 f., [12] f. de pl.: ill., fac-sims. (Collection Oeuvres bibliophiliques de Lanaudière ; no 15); ISBN: 2-920249-90-8.
Note: 575 entrées.
Localisation: OONL.

0391 **Service de diffusion sélective de l'information de la Centrale des bibliothèques**
Guides de voyage au Québec. Montréal: Le Service, 1985. 63 p. (DSI/CB ; no 69; ISSN: 0825-5024); ISBN: 2-89059-269-3.
Note: 210 entrées.– Volumes, articles de périodiques, documents audiovisuels.– "On a donné à 'guide' un sens général, de manière à inclure plusieurs ouvrages descriptifs et reportages photographiques qui ne sont pas sans intérêt pour le voyageur éventuel."
Localisation: OONL.

— 1986 —

0392 **Beauregard, Yves**
Bibliographie du centre du Québec et des Bois-Francs. Québec: Institut québécois de recherche sur la culture, 1986. 495 p.: cartes. (Documents de recherche / Institut québécois de recherche sur la culture ; no 9; ISSN: 0823-0447); ISBN: 2-89224-061-1.
Note: 3,157 entrées.– Monographies, articles de périodiques, publications officielles, instruments de travail, liste des revues et journaux régionaux, filmographie, thèses, monographies paroissiales, biographies.– Sections sur le territoire, vie économique,

aspects sociaux, aspects politiques, culture, religion, généalogie.
Localisation: OONL.

0393 **Hébert, Yves**
Bibliographie de la Côte-du-Sud. [Québec]: Institut québécois de recherche sur la culture, 1986. 339 p.: cartes. (Documents de recherche / Institut québécois de recherche sur la culture ; no 8; ISSN: 0823-0447); ISBN: 2-89224-060-3.
Note: 1,979 entrées.– Définition de la Côte-du-Sud: la ligne du fleuve, de Beaumont à Cacouna, et la frontière américaine, de Sainte-Sabine à Estcourt.– Comprend livres, brochures, thèses, publications gouvernementales, articles de revues sur les catégories suivant: territoire, aspects économiques, aspects sociaux, politiques et militaires, culture, religion, histoire locale, L'Archipel de Montmagny, biographies, généalogie, instruments de travail, journaux, revues et périodiques divers, filmographie.– Exclut les sources d'archives, articles de journaux.– Cartes: 1. "Relief." 2. "Vers 1850." 3. "En 1985."
Localisation: OONL.

0394 **Laperrière, Guy**
Bibliographie d'histoire des Cantons de l'Est/History of the Eastern Townships: a bibliography. 2e rev. et augm. éd. [Sherbrooke, Québec]: Département d'histoire, Université de Sherbrooke, 1986. 210 p. (Collection Histoire des Cantons de l'Est ; no 1); ISBN: 2-89343-006-6.
Note: 1,553 entrées.– Couvre la période de 1765 à 1984.– Livres, brochures, thèses, articles de périodiques sur les douze comtés qui composent traditionnellement les Cantons de l'Est.– Les sujets: Amérindiens, colonisation, événements politiques, économie, société, éducation, religion, vie socio-culturelle.– Recherche: Michel Sharpe. - Texte en français et en anglais/text in English and French. Édition antérieure: 1975. 120 p.– 693 entrées.
Localisation: OONL.

0395 **Lapointe, Raoul**
Guide bibliographique sur la région du Saguenay-Lac-Saint-Jean. [Chicoutimi]: Université du Québec à Chicoutimi, Service de documentation en études et interventions régionales, 1986. 35 f.; ISBN: 2-920751-04-2.
Note: Approx. 150 entrées.– Guides bibliographiques, répertoires, ouvrages généraux, documents géographiques, géologiques et ethnographiques, périodiques, histoires des paroisses et des municipalités. Édition antérieure: 1985. 26 f.
Localisation: OONL.

0396 **Société des écrivains de la Mauricie**
Répertoire des publications des membres de la Société des écrivains de la Mauricie. Trois-Rivières, Québec: La Société: Distribution, Diffusion Collective Radisson, [1986]. 19 p.; ISBN: 2-9800582-0-3.
Note: Approx. 150 entrées.
Localisation: OONL.

— 1987 —

0397 **Bernier, Gérald; Boily, Robert**
Le Québec en transition: 1760-1867: bibliographie thématique. [Montréal: Association canadienne-française pour l'avancement des sciences, c1987]. 193 p. (Politique et économie / Association canadienne-française pour l'avancement des sciences ; no 5); ISBN: 2-89245-068-3.
Note: 1,417 entrées.– Couvre jusque l'été 1980.– Livres, brochures, thèses, articles de périodiques, rapports de sociétés savantes sur les transformations du système politique québécois, en cinq parties: développement économique, classes sociales, institutions politiques, partis politiques, mouvement patriote et les événements de 1837-38.
Localisation: OONL.

0398 **Desjardins, Marc**
Bibliographie de la Gaspésie. [Québec]: Institut québécois de recherche sur la culture, 1987. 436 p.: ill., cartes. (Documents de recherche / Institut québécois de recherche sur la culture ; no 16; ISSN: 0823-0447); ISBN: 2-89224-100-6.
Note: 4,395 entrées.– Titres publiés jusqu'en 1987.– Livres, études, articles, thèses, journaux, documents cinématographiques ayant pour objet direct ou indirect le territoire s'étendant de la zone de Grosses-Roches, au nord, à celle de Matapédia, au sud soit les comtés de Gaspé-Nord et de Gaspé-Sud et de Bonaventure.– Principaux thèmes: démographie, territoire, aménagement et développement régional, économie, société, culture, religion, monographies locales et paroissiales, biographies, généalogie, bibliographies, presse régionale, filmographie.
Localisation: OONL.

0399 **Desjardins, Marc**
Bibliographie des Iles-de-la-Madeleine. [Québec]: Institut québécois de recherche sur la culture, 1987. 281 p.: carte. (Documents de recherche / Institut québécois de recherche sur la culture ; no 13; ISSN: 0823-0447); ISBN: 2-89224-089-1.
Note: 1,413 entrées.– Titres publiés jusqu'en 1986.– Livres, brochures, thèses, documents et études locales et régionales, articles de revues, documents cinématographiques.– Exclut documents constitutifs, rapports annuels, albums de finissants ou de graduation, les offres de service, dépliants, bulletins internes, comptes rendus.– Thèmes: Chroniques descriptives et récits de voyages, peuplement, territoire, aménagement et développement régional, économie, société, politique, culture, religion, monographies locales et paroissiales, biographies, bibliographies, filmographie, fonds d'archives.
Localisation: OONL.

0400 **Tessier, Daniel**
Bibliographie de Lanaudière. [Québec]: Institut québécois de recherche sur la culture, 1987. 270 p.: cartes. (Documents de recherche / Institut québécois de recherche sur la culture ; no 14; ISSN: 0823-0447); ISBN: 2-89224-097-2.
Note: 1,659 entrées.– Couvre jusque la fin de l'année 1984.– Livres, brochures, articles de revues, thèses, films sur le territoire, aspects économiques, sociaux et politiques, culture, religion, histoire locales, biographies, généalogie, instruments de travail.
Localisation: OONL.

0401 **Le Tourisme à Montréal: bibliographie annotée.**
[Montréal]: Centre d'études du tourisme, 1987. 138 p.
Note: 324 entrées.– Rassemble toutes les études, rapports, enquêtes et autres sources de données, produit entre 1980 et 1987 sur les différents aspects du tourisme à Montréal: évaluation de la situation actuelle, emploi, promotion, transports, hébergement, restauration, accueil et information, situation économique, le tourisme

en périphérie de Montréal.
Localisation: OONL.

— 1988 —

0402 **Lamontagne, Richard; Ménard, Marleine**
Le royaume du Saguenay: exposition de livres anciens.
Chicoutimi, Québec: Bouquinerie Jacques-Cartier, 1988.
42 p.
Note: 98 entrées.
Localisation: OONL.

0403 **Les Livres du Québec: 40ième Foire du livre de Francfort, 5 au 10 octobre 1988, Groupe Québec (Canada), Hall 4.1:A:906.** [S.l.]: SOGIC, Société générale des industries culturelles, Québec, [1988]. 81 p.
Note: Approx. 1,200 entrées.
Localisation: OONL.

0404 **McGill University. McLennan Library. Reference Department**
Quebec studies: a guide to reference sources. [Montreal]: The Library, 1988. 21 p.; ISBN: 0-7717-0181-0.
Note: Approx. 100 entries.– Focus on sociological and political aspects of Quebec life and culture.
Location: OONL.

0405 **Sénécal, André Joseph**
A reader's guide to Quebec studies. Québec: Gouvernement du Québec, Ministère des affaires internationales, [1988]. xi, 145 p.; ISBN: 2-550-19125-0.
Note: 1,205 entries.– Books (multidisciplinary, French and English titles): art and architecture, cinema, Quebec economy, geography, ethnology, history, language, literature, music, government and politics, sociology.– Includes listing of periodicals and newspapers.– Period covered: 1960 to June 1988.– Excludes periodical articles, brochures, unpublished works, textbooks, primary materials.
Previous editions:
1985. 127 p.; ISBN: 2-550-12388-3.
Sénécal, André Joseph; Crane, Nancy. *Quebec studies: a selected annotated bibliography.* Burlington, Vt.: Information Center on Canada, 1982. vii, 215 p.
Location: OONL.

0406 **Université du Québec à Chicoutimi**
Travaux en études régionales, résumés des mémoires de maîtrise, 1980-1988. [Chicoutimi]: Université du Québec à Chicoutimi, 1988. iv, 77 p.
Note: 28 entrées.– Principaux thèmes traités: famille, institutions et structures socio-historique, mise en valeur des ressources, impact de l'urban et de l'urbanisation, mouvement associatif et auto développement, politique et facteurs du développement.
Localisation: OONL.

— 1989 —

0407 **Montigny-Pelletier, Françoise de**
Bibliographie de la Rive-Sud de Québec, (Lévis-Lotbinière). Québec: Institut québécois de recherche sur la culture, 1989. 263 p.: cartes. (Documents de recherche / Institut québécois de recherche sur la culture ; no 19; ISSN: 0823-0447); ISBN: 2-89224-122-7.
Note: 2,006 entrées.– Géographie: les trois municipalités régionales de Comté de Desjardins, Les Chutes-de-la-Chaudière, et Lotbinière (les anciens comtés de Lévis et de Lotbinière).– Comprend volumes, thèses, rapports de recherche, articles de revues.– Exclut articles de journaux, documents internes, offres de service, rapports

annuels d'organismes, archives.– Thèmes: le territoire, vie économique, aspects sociaux, aspects politiques et militaires, culture, religion, monographies paroissiales, biographies, généalogie, instruments de travail, presse régionale, documentation audiovisuelle.– Index: thèses, auteurs, onomastique.
Localisation: OONL.

— 1990 —

0408 **Lahaise, Robert**
Le Québec, 1830-1939: bibliographie thématique: histoire et littérature. LaSalle, Québec: Hurtubise HMH, 1990. 173 p.; ISBN: 2-89045-862-8.
Note: 57 thèmes: Abitibi, Acadie à éducation, musique, rougisme, théâtre, et Zouaves.– Pour chaque thème, une liste des sources, inventaires, périodiques, archives, études.
Localisation: OONL.

0409 **Perron, Monique**
Bibliographie du Haut-Saint-Laurent (sud-ouest de la Montérégie). Québec: Institut québécois de recherche sur la culture, 1990. 318 p.: cartes. (Documents de recherche / Institut québécois de recherche sur la culture ; no 24; ISSN: 0823-0447); ISBN: 2-89224-140-5.
Note: 3,051 entrées.– Monographies, articles de périodiques, thèses, travaux d'étudiants, rapports gouvernementaux, brochures.– Exclut fonds d'archives, articles de journaux, textes manuscrits, généalogie.– Principaux thèmes traités: histoire et géographie, découvertes et explorations, le territoire, aspects contemporains en démographie et en aménagement du territoire, vie économique, aspects sociaux, culture, religion, monographies locales, politique, biographies, presse régionale, filmographie.– Compilé avec la collaboration de Luc Boisvert, Roland Viau.
Localisation: OONL.

0410 **Saint-Hilaire, Gaston**
Bibliographie de la Côte-Nord. Québec: Institut québécois de recherche sur la culture, 1990. 340 p.: 3 cartes pliées. (Documents de recherche / Institut québécois de recherche sur la culture ; no 26; ISSN: 0823-0447); ISBN: 2-89224-150-2.
Note: 3,933 entrées.– Monographies, thèses et mémoires universitaires, articles de périodiques, rapports gouvernementaux ou d'organismes divers.– Exclut les fonds d'archives, articles de journaux, manuscrits.– Thèmes: histoire et géographie, l'environnement physique, Amérindiens et Inuit, aménagement du territoire, économie, société, vie politique et militaire, culture, religion, monographies locales, biographies, généalogie, bibliographies régionales, presse régionale, documentation audio-visuelle.
Localisation: OONL.

— 1991 —

0411 **Hardy, René; Trépanier, Guy**
Bibliographie de la Mauricie. Québec: Institut québécois de recherche sur la culture, 1991. 294 p. (Documents de recherche / Institut québécois de recherche sur la culture ; no 27; ISSN: 0823-0447); ISBN: 2-89224-159-6.
Note: 3,427 entrées.– Livres, articles de périodiques, publications officielles, thèses sur la Mauricie: histoire et géographie, milieu physique, démographie, aménagement du territoire, économie, transports et communications, politiques, aspects sociaux, religion,

éducation, vie culturelle, généalogie, monographies et notices historiques des localités, biographies, instruments de travail.– Exclut articles de journaux, rapports internes, rapports annuels, les lois et règlements.
Localisation: OONL.

— 1992 —

0412 **Burgess, Joanne, et al.**
Clés pour l'histoire de Montréal: bibliographie. Montréal: Boréal, 1992. 247 p.; ISBN: 2-89052-486-8.
Note: 3,988 entrées.– Ouvrages, brochures, articles scientifiques et thèses de doctorat consacrés à l'histoire de Montréal des origines jusqu'en 1991.– Six grands sections: "Instruments de travail," "L'histoire générale," "Période avant 1642," "Période de 1642 à 1760," "Période de 1760 à 1867," "Période de 1867 à nos jours."- Sous sections: population, économie, société, institutions publiques, espace, culture.
Localisation: OONL.

0413 **McTernan, D.J.**
French Quebec: imprints in French from Quebec, 1764-1990, in the British Library: a catalogue/Le Québec français: imprimés en français du Québec, 1764-1990, à la British Library: catalogue. London: British Library, 1992. 2 vol.; ISBN: 2-551-12801-3 (vol. 1).
Note: Listing of imprints in French from Quebec held by the Humanities and Social Sciences Division, Collection Development, British Library.– Excludes manuscripts, maps, music, prints, drawings.– Inclusion based on date of publication (1764-1990), place (Quebec Province) and language (French).– Volume 1 covers books, libraries, publishing, literature, language and linguistics, philosophy and psychology, visual and plastic arts, music, architecture, travel writings and tourist guides.– Volume 2 will deal with social and political institutions, history, social order, geophysical features.
Location: OONL.

0414 **O'Donnell, Brendan**
Sources for the study of English-speaking Quebec: an annotated bibliography of works published between 1980 and 1990/Sources pour l'étude du Québec d'expression anglaise: bibliographie annotée d'ouvrages produit de 1980 à 1990. Lennoxville, Quebec: Eastern Townships Research Centre of Bishop's University with the assistance of the Secretary of State of Canada, 1992. li, 264 p.; ISBN: 0-662-58983-1.
Note: 1,584 entries.– References dealing with aspects of English-speaking Quebec, arranged in subject categories: culture, economics, education, ethnic studies, health care studies, history, politics, regional studies, religion, sociology (including English-French relations), women's studies.– Prefatory material in English and French, annotations in English only.– Texte prélim. en anglais et en français, annotations en anglais seulement.
Location: QLB.

— 1993 —

0415 **Breton, Jean-René**
Bibliographie de Beauce-Etchemin. Québec: Institut québécois de recherche sur la culture, 1993. 195 p.: cartes. (Documents de recherche / Institut québécois de recherche sur la culture ; no 33; ISSN: 0823-0447); ISBN: 2-89224-18-0.
Note: 1,817 entrées.– Monographies, articles de périodiques, thèses, rapports gouvernementaux, brochures, titres relatifs aux régions de l'Etchemin et de la Beauce: le territoire, présence amérindienne, peuplement euro-québécois, économie, société, démographie, culture, monographies locales, biographies, instruments de travail, presse régionale.
Localisation: OONL.

0416 **Rouillard, Jacques**
Guide d'histoire du Québec: du régime français à nos jours: bibliographie commentée. Laval, Québec: Méridien, 1993. 354 p.; ISBN: 2-89415-052-0.
Note: Volumes et articles dans les principaux domaines de recherche en histoire du Québec.– Trois grandes parties: "Régime français," "Régime britannique (1760-1867)," "Québec contemporaine (1867-1991)."- Thèmes: évolution politique, aspects économiques, sociaux et culturels, comportements démographiques, femmes et familles, histoire locale, vie intellectuelle, histoire religieuse, études littéraires, arts visuel et médias de communication.– Comporte une section consacrée aux guides bibliographiques et aux ouvrages de référence.
Édition antérieure: Montréal: 1991. 367 p.; ISBN: 0-89415-052-0.
Localisation: OONL.

— Ongoing/En cours —

0417 **Bibliographie du Québec.** Montréal: Bibliothèque nationale du Québec, 1970-. vol.; ISSN: 0006-1441.
Note: Comprend les documents publiés au Québec acquis principalement par dépôt légal (livres, brochures, publications en série, microformes, musique imprimée et documents cartographiques).– Douze numéros mensuels et l'index annuel.
Microforme: Montréal: Bibliothèque nationale du Québec, 1984- .
Localisation: OONL.

0418 **Bibliothèque nationale du Québec. Bureau de la bibliographie rétrospective**
Bibliographie du Québec, 1821-1967. [Québec]: Éditeur officiel du Québec, 1980-. vol.; ISBN: 2-551-03716-6 (édition complète).
Note: Comprend: livres, brochures, thèses, tirages à part, les publications faisant partie d'une série, ouvrages illustré, les programmes de spectacles, d'expositions, de foires, etc., les oeuvres musicales, les atlas.– Prévision pour le nombre de titres de cette période (1821-1967): 150,000.– Exclut cartes, publications en série, publications officielles.
Chaque tome comprend deux volumes: un volume de 1,000 notices et un volume de six index.
Localisation: OONL.

0419 **Bibliothèque nationale du Québec. Service de microphotographie**
Microéditions de la Bibliothèque: catalogue. Montréal: Bibliothèque nationale du Québec, 1979-. vol.; ISSN: 0707-848X.
Note: Publications en série courantes et rétrospectives, des secteurs privés et publics; monographies anciennes, contemporaines et précieuses (livres rare, livres d'artistes); atlas, cartes et plans; fonds d'écrivains et d'artistes; documents de travail (rapports, catalogues, etc.); thèses; microéditions originales.
Localisation: OONL.

Ontario

— 1892 —

0420 **Kingsford, William**
The early bibliography of the province of Ontario, Dominion of Canada, with other information. A supplemental chapter of Canadian archaeology. Toronto: Rowsell & Hutchison; Montreal: Eben Picken, 1892. 140 p.
Note: Annotated listing of books and pamphlets from 1783 to 1840, arranged chronologically.
Microform: CIHM Microfiche series ; no. 06712; ISBN: 0-665-06712-7. 2 microfiches (76 fr.).
Reprint: New York: AMS Press, 1977. 140 p.; ISBN: 0-4040-3704-6.
Location: OONL.

— 1934 —

0421 **Dow, Robena M.**
"The County of Wellington: a bibliography."
In: *Ontario Historical Society Papers and Records*; Vol. 30, (1934) p. 96-105.; ISSN: 0380-6022.
Note: Books and pamphlets relating to history of Wellington: source material (crown land papers, letters, land transfers); atlases and maps; directories and gazetteers; monographs.
Location: AEU.

— 1948 —

0422 **Morley, E. Lillian**
A Perth County bibliography. [Milverton, Ont.: Milverton Sun, 1948]. [14] p.
Note: List of publications about Perth County or by authors who are or were resident in the county.
Location: OTP.

— 1949 —

0423 **Hunter, Elizabeth**
"History of Ottawa and district: a selected list."
In: *Ontario Library Review*; Vol. 33, no. 4 (November 1949) p. 342-344.; ISSN: 0030-2996.
Note: Approx. 25 entries.
Location: OONL.

— 1950 —

0424 **Dyde, Dorothy F.**
"History of Kingston and District: a selected list."
In: *Ontario Library Review*; Vol. 34, no. 3 (August 1950) p. 226-228.; ISSN: 0030-2996.
Note: Location: OONL.

0425 **Talman, J.J.**
"History of south western Ontario: a selected list."
In: *Ontario Library Review*; Vol. 34, no. 2 (May 1950) p. 119-122; vol. 34, no. 4 (November 1950) p. 291-296.; ISSN: 0030-2996.
Note: Location: OONL.

— 1952 —

0426 **Leigh, Dawson M.**
Huronia in print. Midland, Ont.: Huronia Historic Sites and Tourist Association, 1952. [9] l.
Note: Books and pamphlets on Huronia found in public libraries of Barrie, Collingwood, Meaford, Midland,
Orillia, Owen Sound, Penetang, Stayner.
Location: OONL.

— 1954 —

0427 **Brault, Lucien**
"Bibliographie d'Ottawa."
Dans: *Revue de l'Université d'Ottawa*; Vol. 24, no 3 (juillet-Septembre 1954) p. 345-375.; ISSN: 0041-9206.
Note: Approx. 500 entrées.– Manuscrits, imprimés, ouvrages anonymes.– Thèmes: histoire, affaires municipales, capitale du Canada, éducation, district fédéral, religion, canal Rideau, commerce/industries, revues et journaux, Women's Canadian Historical Society of Ottawa Transactions (liste des principaux notes sur Ottawa).
Localisation: OONL.

— 1955 —

0428 **Jarvi, Edith T.**
Bibliography of Windsor and Essex County. [Rev. ed.]. [Windsor, Ont.]: Windsor Public Libraries, 1955. 35 l.
Note: Books, pamphlets, official publications, newspaper and periodical articles related to Windsor and Essex County held by Windsor Public Library.
Previous edition: *Windsor and Essex County, Ontario: bibliography*. 1954. [1], 24 l.
Location: OONL.

— 1959 —

0429 **Phelps, Edward**
"Lambton County: some bibliographical notes."
In: *Western Ontario Historical Notes*; Vol. 15, no. 4 (December 1959) p. 64-67.; ISSN: 0382-0157.
Note: Lists biographies, directories, histories (including local church histories), official publications.
Location: AEU.

0430 **Rankin, Reita A.**
"Bibliography of materials in Fort William Public Library relating to Fort William, Port Arthur, and northwestern Ontario."
In: *Ontario Library Review*; Vol. 43, no. 2 (May 1959) p. 140-146.; ISSN: 0030-2996.
Note: Topics include history and description, geology and mining, books by local writers or set in Fort William/Port Arthur area.
Location: OONL.

— 1962 —

0431 **Bishop, Olga B.**
"Checklist of historical works on western Ontario in the libraries of the University of Western Ontario."
In: *Western Ontario Historical Notes*; Vol. 14, no. 1 (December 1957) p. 24-30; vol. 14, no. 2 (March 1958) p. 30-37; vol. 14, no. 3 (June 1958) p. 42-47; vol. 14, no. 4 (September 1958) p. 31-39; vol. 15, no. 2 (June 1959) p. 19-27; vol. 15, no. 3 (September 1959) p. 11-24; vol. 16, no. 1 (March 1960) p. 32-39, 85-93; vol. 17, no. 1 (March 1961) p. 53-66; vol. 18, no. 1 (March 1962) p. 37-51.; ISSN: 0382-0157.

Note: Listing of historical works on the fourteen counties of western Ontario: atlases, biographies, diaries and journals, directories, histories of the counties and places within the counties (including agricultural, military, medical, transportation as well as general social and political histories).– Excludes church and parish histories.
Location: AEU.

— 1963 —

0432 **Hart, Patricia W.**
"North York history: a bibliography."
In: *Ontario Library Review*; Vol. 47, no. 4 (November 1963) p. 174-176.; ISSN: 0030-2996.
Note: Location: OONL.

0433 **Weber, Eileen**
"Niagara Falls in history: a bibliography."
In: *Ontario Library Review*; Vol. 47, no. 3 (August 1963) p. 107-111.; ISSN: 0030-2996.
Note: Location: OONL.

— 1967 —

0434 **Sudbury Public Library**
The Sudbury basin: a guide to the local collection. [Sudbury]: Sudbury Public Library, 1967. 17, [4] p.
Note: Approx. 120 entries.– Books, articles, government publications, guidebooks, periodicals, directories relating to Sudbury region: geology, climate, mining, politics and planning, history.
Location: OONL.

— 1968 —

0435 **Bucksar, R.G.**
Bibliography of socio-economic development of northern Ontario (northwestern and northeastern regions), 1968. Ottawa: Canadian Research Centre for Anthropology; Toronto: Department of Treasury and Economics, Regional Development Branch, 1968. 112 l.
Note: Approx. 900 entries.– Books, journal articles, theses, government publications, geological reports related to agriculture, economy and finance, history (economic, political, local), manufacturing and industry, mining and minerals, planning and development, transportation, water resources.– Compiled under direction of James Lotz.
Supplements:
1969. 64 l.– Approx. 500 entries.
1972. 86, v l.– Approx. 600 entries.
Location: OONL.

0436 **Spencer, Loraine; Holland, Susan**
Northern Ontario: a bibliography. [Toronto]: University of Toronto Press, [c1968]. x, 120 p.
Note: Approx. 800 entries.– Books, periodical articles, government publications relating to area of Ontario north of line from Cochrane-Kapuskasing-Sioux Lookout.– Some French-language publications.– Excludes fiction, newspaper articles, unpublished materials with the exception of theses.
Location: OONL.

0437 **Stirrett, George M.**
An annotated bibliography: Point Pelee National Park and the Point Pelee region of Ontario. [Ottawa]: National Parks Service, Dept. of Indian Affairs and Northern Development, [1968]. 76 p.
Note: Approx. 2,000 entries.– Covers to June 1966.– All references to the area, published or unpublished, are given: magazine and newspaper articles, diaries, field

notebooks, administrative reports, maps, plans, sketches.– Special emphasis on biology, geology, geography, park administration.
Supplement: 1971. 141 p.
Location: OONL.

— 1970 —

0438 **Phelps, Edward**
Bibliography of Lambton County and the City of Sarnia, Ontario. London, Ont.: General Library, University of Western Ontario, 1970. viii, 146 p.: ill., map. (University of Western Ontario Library Bulletin ; no. 8)
Note: 661 entries.– Books, pamphlets, journal articles, official publications from 1835 to 1969.– Excludes articles from local newspapers and weekly journals.
Location: OONL.

0439 **Tudor, Dean**
Regional development and regional government in Ontario. Monticello, Ill.: Council of Planning Librarians, 1970. 53 l.: map. (Council of Planning Librarians Exchange bibliography ; 157)
Note: Approx. 350 entries.– Includes reference guides, books, periodical articles dealing with planning, policies, economic development and implementation in the ten economic regions of Ontario.
Location: OONL.

— 1971 —

0440 **Crooks, Grace**
Huronia: a list of books and pamphlets concerning Simcoe County and the Lake Simcoe region. Barrie, Ont.: Simcoe County Historical Association, 1971. 10 l.
Note: Location: OONL.

0441 **Olling, Randy**
A guide to research resources for the Niagara region. St. Catharines: Brock University, 1971. 299 p.
Note: List of books, periodicals, newspapers, official publications, pamphlets, maps, newspapers clipping files, archival records related to the Niagara region.
Location: OSTCB.

— 1972 —

0442 **Barrie Public Library**
Huronia: a selection of books and pamphlets on this historic region. [Barrie, Ont.]: Barrie Public Library, 1972. 9 l.
Note: Approx. 100 entries.
Location: OONL.

0443 **Jones, Richard C.**
An annotated bibliography of the Sudbury area. 2nd ed., rev. and enl. Sudbury, Ont.: Sudbury Public Library, 1972. 55 p.
Note: 666 entries.– Books, periodical articles, theses, government publications, commission briefs in French and English, arranged by subject.
Previous edition: *Bibliography of the Sudbury area.* Laurentian University Press, 1970. 1 vol.
Location: OONL.

0444 **MacPhail, Cathy**
A bibliography of works on the two Soos and their surroundings, giving locations of the libraries holding each title. [Sault Ste. Marie, Ont.]: Sault Area International Library Association, 1972. 94 l. (in various foliations).
Note: Lists books, documents, pamphlets: history, geography, religion and education, politics and government, community development, commerce and

industry, Indians, autobiographies and biographies, literature.
Location: OONL.

0445 **Stelter, Gilbert A.; Rowan, John**
Community development in northeastern Ontario: a selected bibliography. [Sudbury: Laurentian University Press, 1972]. 56 p.
Note: Approx. 1,100 entries.– Designed as a guide to students engaged in research in community development in Northeastern Ontario, and to further an interdisciplinary study of characteristics of single-industry company towns of the area.– Lists general material pertaining to Northeastern Ontario and specific references to individual communities.
Location: OONL.

— 1973 —

0446 **Cumming, Alice; Cumming, Ross**
Bibliography of Bruce. Port Elgin, Ont.: Alice & Ross Cumming in co-operation with Bruce County Library, 1973. 8 l.
Note: 85 entries.– Books, pamphlets, church histories, genealogy.
Location: OONL.

0447 **Heritage of York: an historical bibliography, 1793-1840.**
[York, Ont.: s.n.], 1973. 1 vol. (in various pagings).
Note: Part of the project "Heritage of York," financed through Local Initiatives Program 1973, sponsored by the Borough of York, coordinated by Ivar Heissler.
Part I, "Land use and development, 1793-1840," by Michael and Ruth Gotthardt; Part II, "Social and cultural development, 1793-1834," by Pamela Roy; Part III, "Administrative and political development, 1793-1838," by Zenon Strzelzcyk.
Location: OTTC.

0448 **Ripley, Gordon M.**
A bibliography of Elgin County and St. Thomas, Ontario. St. Thomas: [St. Thomas History Project], 1973. 55 l.
Note: 246 entries.– Books, pamphlets, periodical articles, unpublished material (scrapbooks, manuscripts, family histories, genealogies).– Based on Warren C. Miller collection, St. Thomas Public Library, and Elgin Country Library collection.
Location: OONL.

— 1974 —

0449 **Heissler, Ivar**
Township of York historical sources, volume 2: a descriptive bibliography. [Weston, Ont.: s.n.], 1974. i, 224 l.
Note: Finding aid and bibliography for research in local history of former Township of York as it existed until the early 1920s.– Continuation of *Heritage of York, an historical bibliography, 1793-1840*, published in 1973.
Location: OTSTM.

0450 **McCullough, Donna, et al.**
Annotated bibliography: Peterborough and Lakefield. [S.l.: s.n.], 1974. 203 l.: ill., facsims., maps.
Note: Listing of books, periodical and newspaper articles, maps, government publications relating to Peterborough.– Some annotations and locations.– Appendix lists archival holdings of Peterborough Centennial Museum.
Location: OPET.

— 1975 —

0451 **Dale, Ronald J.**
Bibliography of 19th century Ontario. [Ottawa: s.n.], 1975. 101 p.; ISBN: 0-88884-582-0.
Note: Location: OOPAC.

0452 **Fleming, Patricia Lockhart**
"A bibliography of Ontario directories to 1867."
In: *Ontario Library Review*; Vol. 59, no. 2 (June 1975) p. 98-107.; ISSN: 0030-2996.
Note: Survey with brief history and description of contents, followed by listing of directories for "The Canadas," "Canada West," "Cities and towns," "Counties."- At least one Ontario location is given for all entries.
Location: OONL.

0453 **Fortin, Benjamin; Gaboury, Jean-Pierre**
Bibliographie analytique de l'Ontario français. [Ottawa]: Éditions de l'Université d'Ottawa, 1975. xii, 236 p. (Cahiers du Centre de recherche en civilisation canadienne-française ; 9); ISBN: 0-776-4089-5.
Note: 1,233 entrées.– La période couverte est de 1900 à l'automne 1973.– Comprend livres, articles de revue, rapports de comité d'études ou de commission d'enquête, documents gouvernementaux, brochures, mémoires, thèses et travaux de recherche dans tous les aspects de la vie française en Ontario: culturels, économiques, sociaux, politiques.
Localisation: OONL.

— 1976 —

0454 **District of Parry Sound bibliography.** [Parry Sound, Ont.: s.n.], 1975-1976. 63 l.
Note: 386 entries.– Compiled by District of Parry Sound Local History Project, organized by Reed Osborne.– Coordinator: Brenda Hackett.– Based on local history collection, Parry Sound Public Library.– Includes books, government publications, unpublished material (oral histories, clipping files).
Location: OONL.

0455 **Emard, Michel**
Inventaire sommaire des sources manuscrites et imprimées concernant Prescott-Russell, Ontario. Rockland [Ont.]: M. Emard, 1976. 172 p.: cartes.
Note: Localisation: OONL.

— 1978 —

0456 **Aitken, Barbara B.**
Local histories of Ontario municipalities, 1951-1977: a bibliography, with representative trans-Canada locations of copies. Toronto: Ontario Library Association, 1978. ix, 120 p.; ISBN: 0-88969-012-X.
Note: Approx. 1,700 entries.– Published books, pamphlets, Ontario Hydro local histories, Tweedsmuir (Women's Institutes) histories on microfilm at Archives of Ontario.– Topics include agricultural, educational, military, medical, transportation histories, atlases, biographies, as well as local histories of municipal public utilities commissions.– Excludes planning studies, tourist brochures, federal and provincial government publications, serials.
Supplement: *Local histories of Ontario municipalities, 1977-1987.* 1989. x, 74 p.; ISBN: 0-88969-030-8.– Approx. 1,050 entries.
Location: OONL.

0457 **Hazelgrove, A.R.**
A tercentennial contribution to a checklist of Kingston imprints to 1867. Kingston, Ont.: Special Collections, Douglas Library, Queen's University, 1978. xix, 118 p.: ill., facsim. (Douglas Library Occasional papers ; no. 5)
Note: Approx. 450 entries.– Monographs, serials, newspapers and periodicals.– Some locations are provided.– Compiled by Queen's University librarians.
Location: OONL.

0458 **Morley, William F.E.**
Ontario and the Canadian North. Toronto: University of Toronto Press, c1978. xxxii, 322 p. (Canadian local histories to 1950: a bibliography ; vol. 3); ISBN: 0-8020-2281-2.
Note: Approx. 1,000 entries.– Excludes manuscripts, typescripts, scrapbooks, serials, journal articles, offprints, documentary histories, reminiscences, pictorial histories, genealogical works, most church histories, gazetteers, directories, guidebooks.
Location: OONL.

0459 **Northern Ontario: a selected bibliography relating to economic development in northern Ontario, 1969-1978.**
[Toronto]: Economic Development Branch, Ministry of Treasury, Economics and Intergovernmental Affairs, 1978. 51, [8] l.
Note: Approx. 260 entries.– Published and unpublished reports and sources of information relating to economic conditions and developments in northern Ontario: forestry and wood processing, mining, tourism, service industries, transportation, communications, environment, community and regional planning and development.– Includes lists of additional bibliographies, directories, etc.
Location: OOP.

— 1979 —

0460 **Une bibliographie de sources historiques du district de Nipissing.** North Bay, Ont.: Société historique du Nipissing, 1979. vi, 21 p. (Société historique du Nipissing Études historiques ; no 1)
Note: Approx. 200 entrées.– Catégories principaux: guides et sources bibliographiques, découvertes, explorations, colonisation et histoire, géographie et biologie, économie et politique, vie sociale, les journaux.
Localisation: OONL.

0461 **A bibliography of Oxford County.** [Woodstock, Ont.]: Oxford Historical Research Project, 1979. [8], 88 p.: maps.
Note: Approx. 480 entries.– Published and unpublished material, local histories, atlases, directories, archival sources related to the county.
Previous edition: Evans, Mary. *A bibliography of Oxford County and the City of Woodstock, Ontario.* 1974. 49 p.
Location: OONL.

0462 **"Book notes."**
In: *Ontario History*; (1948-1979) ; ISSN: 0030-2953.
Note: Regular feature from vol. 40 (1948) to vol. 71, no. 4 (December 1979).– Includes books, historical and genealogical society publications, journal articles, theses.– Topics include local history, geography, biography, bibliographies, general history, business history.– Between 1948 and 1968, no compiler is listed.– In 1969, 1971, the compiler is Rienzi Crusz; from 1972 to 1979, Hilary Bates.
Continued by: *Annual bibliography of Ontario History:*

Bibliographie annuelle d'histoire ontarienne. Sudbury, Ont.: Laurentian University, 1980-1986.
Location: OONL.

0463 **Milette, Jean-Luc**
Répertoire de brochures relatives à l'Ontario français. Ottawa: Centre de recherche en civilisation canadienne-française, Université d'Ottawa, 1979. 67 p. (Documents de travail du Centre de recherche en civilisation canadienne-française ; 9)
Note: 307 entrées.– Documents publiés entre 1885 et 1977 conservés dans le depôt d'archives du Centre de recherche en civilisation canadienne française.– Marthe Beauparlant et Francine Gauthier, chercheuses.
Localisation: OONL.

0464 **Rees, D.L.; Topps, K.H.; Brozowski, R.S.**
Bibliographic guide to North Bay and area. [North Bay, Ont.: Dept. of Geography, Nipissing University College], 1979. [22], 259 p.: ill., maps.; ISBN: 0-9690905-0-1.
Note: Approx. 2,500 entries.– Books, articles, reports, official publications, theses, maps.– Covers environmental, social, economic and educational subjects, local histories.– Research and compilation: Carrie A. Woroniuk, et al.
Location: OONL.

0465 **Simcoe Public Library**
A bibliography of local history collection (Town of Simcoe and Haldimand-Norfolk region) at Simcoe Public Library. Simcoe, Ont.: Simcoe Public Library, 1979. 12 l.
Note: Approx. 180 entries.– Books, booklets, pamphlets, newspapers, periodical articles, biographies, family histories, memoirs, church histories, maps related to Haldimand-Norfolk region and town of Simcoe.– List of local authors.– Compiled by Autar K. Ganju.
Location: OONL.

0466 **Vallières, Gaétan; Grimard, Jacques**
"L'Ontario français: guide bibliographique."
Dans: *Cahiers de géographie de Québec*; Vol. 23, no 58 (avril 1979) p. 165-178.; ISSN: 0007-9766.
Note: Localisation: OONL.

— 1980 —

0467 **Bishop, Olga B.; Irwin, Barbara I.; Miller, Clara G.**
Bibliography of Ontario history, 1867-1976: cultural, economic, political, social. 2nd ed. Toronto: University of Toronto Press, [1980]. 2 vol. (Ontario historical studies series; ISSN: 0380-9188); ISBN: 0-8020-2359-2 (set).
Note: Approx. 15,000 entries.– Monographs, pamphlets, periodical articles, theses, government publications (limited to those related to royal commissions, advisory and select committees, task forces, and conservation reports), local histories, directories of cities and counties published between 1867 and 1912.– Excludes manuscripts, maps, histories of individual churches and schools.
Previous edition: *Ontario since 1867: a bibliography.* Ontario Ministry of Colleges and Universities, 1973. 330 p.– Approx. 4,000 entries.
Location: OONL.

0468 **Emard, Michel**
"Bibliographie des Comtés-Unis de Prescott-Russell, Ontario."
Dans: *Ontario History*; Vol. 72, no. 1 (March 1980) p. 49-55.; ISSN: 0030-2953.
Note: Principales études et sources sur les deux comtés

francophones de l'Ontario.
Localisation: AEU.

0469   **Hart, Patricia W.**
Local history of the regional municipalities of Peel, York and Durham: an annotated listing of published materials located in the public libraries in the regional municipalities of Peel, York and Durham. Richmond Hill: Central Ontario Regional Library System, 1980. 2 vol.
Note: 1,599 entries.– Covers to December 31, 1978.– Includes books, periodical articles, pamphlets which describe people, places, and events relating to the history of the area within the present boundaries of the regional municipalities of Peel, York and Durham.– Excludes general works on history of Canada and Ontario, unless they contain specific reference to this area.
Location: OONL.

— 1981 —

0470   **Explorations et enracinements français en Ontario, 1610-1978.** [Toronto]: Ontario Ministère de l'Éducation, 1981.; ISBN: 0-7743-6187-5.
Note: Comprend quatre parties: "Les Pays d'en haut: de l'Outaouais aux Rocheuses," "Le Sud: développement et enracinements français," "L'Est et les concentrations francophones," "Le Nord et les maillons d'une chaîne de peuplement francophone."
Localisation: OONL.

— 1982 —

0471   **Cox, Mark; Proudfoot, Geraldine**
Pittsburgh Township, 1783-1948: an annotated bibliography of history sources. Kingston, Ont.: Pittsburgh Historical Society, [1982]. iii, 99 p.: maps.
Note: Lists unpublished sources: government records (land, military and naval, legal, census, Rideau Canal), municipal administration; private sources: church, business, family papers; unpublished studies, histories, theses; published sources: books, pamphlets, directories, maps, atlases, periodicals, newspapers; pictorial sources: paintings and drawings, photographs, postcards.
Location: OONL.

0472   **Defoe, Deborah**
Kingston: a selected bibliography. 2nd ed. Kingston, Ont.: Kingston Public Library Board, 1982. 76 p.
Note: Books, periodical articles, government publications, addresses, letters, theses, planning documents.
Revision and expansion of "Kingston and district: selected publications," compiled by the Reference Division, Douglas Library, Queen's University, published in *Historic Kingston*, No. 15 (Jan. 1967), P. 67-83; No. 21 (1973), P. 78-102.
Previous edition: 1973. iii, 40 l.
Supplement: 1977. 24 l.
Location: OONL.

0473   **Huizenga, Angie; Stuart, Rob; Scott, Judy**
Our Prince Edward County: a source reference. Bloomfield, Ont.: [s.n.], 1982. vi, 214 p.
Note: 1,195 entries.– Published and unpublished material, archival sources, books, government publications, periodicals, newspapers, maps and atlases.– Entries are annotated and locations are given.
Location: OONL.

— 1983 —

0474   **Milligan, Janet; Wilson, Catherine**
Historical bibliography of Amherst Island. Kingston, Ont.: Kingston Branch, Ontario Genealogical Society, 1983. 10 p.
Note: 77 entries.– Compiled to provide background material for the Amherst Island Oral History Project.– List of books, journal articles, government documents, manuscripts (business records, personal papers, scrapbooks), newspapers.
Location: OONL.

— 1984 —

0475   **Jarvis, Eric; Baker, Melvin**
"Clio in Hogtown: a brief bibliography."
In: *Ontario History*; Vol. 76, no. 3 (September 1984) p. 287-294.; ISSN: 0030-2953.
Note: Review of literature relating to the history of Toronto, including books, articles and theses.
Location: AEU.

0476   **Lehmann, Cathy; Iles, Janet**
A bibliography of the Ioleen A. Hawken Memorial Local History Collection of the Owen Sound Public Library: including materials on deposit from the Bruce and Grey Branch, Ontario Genealogical Society. Owen Sound, Ont.: The Library, 1984. 2, 108 l.; ISBN: 0-9691650-0-5.
Note: Approx. 1,200 entries.– Books, pamphlets, reprints, privately printed family histories, periodicals and newspapers, microfilms of historical documents, census records dealing with Grey and Bruce counties, books by and about Grey and Bruce people, Georgian Bay region, Owen Sound.
Location: OONL.

0477   **Liste des bibliographies pour l'étude de l'Ontario français: dictionnaire des écrits de l'Ontario français.** Sudbury [Ont.]: Université Laurentienne, 1984. ii, 48 p. (Document de travail / Université Laurentienne ; 1)
Note: 250 entrées.– Bibliographies des bibliographies, générales, histoires, linguistique, littérature, religion, sciences sociales.
Localisation: OONL.

0478   **North York Public Library. Canadiana Collection**
Ontario bicentennial and Toronto sesquicentennial: a selected bibliography of some holdings of the Canadiana Collection of the North York Public Library. [North York, Ont.]: North York Public Library, [1984]. 9 p.
Note: Location: OONL.

0479   **Toronto. Public Library**
Toronto past and present: a multi-media list. rev. ed. [Toronto]: Toronto Public Library, 1984. 31 p.
Note: Approx. 180 entries.– Includes books, recordings, films and video cassettes.– Compiled by Rosemary Dale, et al.
Previous edition: 1980. 28 p.
Location: OONL.

— 1985 —

0480   **Gervais, Gaétan; Thomson, Ashley; Hallsworth, Gwenda**
Bibliographie: histoire du nord-est de l'Ontario/ Bibliography: history of north-eastern Ontario. Sudbury: La Société historique du Nouvel-Ontario, 1985. 112 p. (Documents historiques / Société historique du Nouvel-Ontario ; no 82)
Note: 2,280 entrées.– Texte en français et en anglais/text

in English and French.
Localisation: OONL.

— 1986 —

0481 **Ontario Historical Society**
Annual bibliography of Ontario history/Bibliographie annuelle d'histoire ontarienne. Sudbury, Ont.: Laurentian University, 1980-1986. 6 vol.; ISSN: 0227-6623.
Note: 6,602 entries.– Listing of monographs, theses, government publications, journal articles.– Sections include "Research aids" (bibliographies, etc.), "Ontario before 1783," "Economic/social/political/military history," "History of culture and civilization," "Regional and local history."- Continuation of "Book notes", a regular listing in *Ontario History*.– Compilers/editors: 1980, David B. Kotin; 1981-1984, Gaétan Gervais and Ashley Thomson; 1985, Gaétan Gervais, Ashley Thomson and Gwenda Hallsworth.– Text in English and French/ texte en français et en anglais.
Location: OONL.

0482 **Université laurentienne de Sudbury. Bibliothèque**
Collection franco-ontarienne: catalogue. Version prélim. Sudbury [Ont.]: Université laurentienne de Sudbury, Institut franco-ontarien, 1986. xi, 106 p.
Note: 799 entrées.
Localisation: OONL.

— 1987 —

0483 **Barr, Elinor**
Northwestern Ontario books: a bibliography: alphabetical by title, 1980s. [Thunder Bay, Ont.: Ontario Library Service Nipigon], 1987. 31 p.; ISBN: 0-9692949-0-5.
Note: Approx. 230 entries.– Published works by local authors and/or about the northwestern Ontario region (north of Lake Superior west to Manitoba border).
Location: OONL.

0484 **University of Windsor. Data Bank Research Group**
An annotated bibliography of studies related to the Windsor economy, 1975-1985. Windsor, Ont.: Data Bank Research Group, 1987. ii, 43 l.
Note: 76 entries.– Studies on economic activity in Windsor or topics closely related to or affecting Windsor's economic, business or social sector.– Excludes newspaper articles, government data sources such as Statistics Canada series.
Location: OW.

— 1988 —

0485 **Bloomfield, Elizabeth; Stelter, Gilbert A.**
Guelph and Wellington County: a bibliography of settlement and development since 1800. [Guelph, Ont.]: Guelph Regional Project, University of Guelph, 1988. 329 p.: map.; ISBN: 0-88955-133-2.
Note: 3,762 entries.– Annotated list of books, pamphlets, theses, journal articles to 1940.
Location: OONL.

0486 **Fleming, Patricia Lockhart**
Upper Canadian imprints, 1801-1841: a bibliography. Toronto: University of Toronto Press in co-operation with the National Library of Canada and the Canadian Government Publishing Centre, Supply and Services Canada, [c1988]. xviii, 555 p.; ISBN: 0-8020-2585-4.
Note: 1,605 entries.– Includes books, pamphlets, government publications, broadsides, printed ephemera, with appendices listing newspapers and journals.– Excludes separately published maps and illustrations.–

Provides references to other bibliographies and all copies examined are given locations.– Detailed notes on contents, type of paper, illustrations, typography and binding, authorship, printing, publishing, distribution and sales.
Location: OONL.

— 1989 —

0487 **Gervais, Gaétan; Hallsworth, Gwenda; Thomson, Ashley**
The bibliography of Ontario history, 1976-1986/La bibliographie d'histoire ontarienne, 1976-1986. Toronto: Dundurn Press, 1989. xxxiv, 605 p.; ISBN: 1-55002-031-5.
Note: Approx. 12,500 entries.– Monographs, periodicals, government publications, organized into broad groups: general works, Ontario before 1783, economy, history (social, political, military), culture, local history.– Includes pre-Confederation references.
Incorporates: *Annual bibliography of Ontario history, 1981-1985.* Sudbury, Ont.: Laurentian University; 1981-1986.
Location: OONL.

0488 **Pelletier, Jean Yves**
Bibliographie sélective de l'Ontario français. 2e éd., rev., corr. et augm. [Ottawa]: Centre franco-ontarien de ressources pédagogiques, [c1989]. 65 p.; ISBN: 1-55043-221-4.
Note: 706 entrées.– Un guide références qui s'adresse à la clientèle scolaire: enseignants des niveaux primaire et secondaire des écoles françaises de l'Ontario.– Le choix des oeuvres est basé sur de nombreux critères: les oeuvres de langue française publiées depuis 1960; publiées en Ontario par des Franco-ontariens; les oeuvres traitant de l'Ontario français ou d'un sujet d'actualité franco-ontarienne.– Comprend livres (historiques, romans, pièces de théâtre), rapports d'études, documents pédagogiques.– Exclut les inédits, thèses, articles de revue.
Édition antérieure: Beaudry, Cléo, et al. *Bibliographie sur l'Ontario français.* 1981. 42 p.
Localisation: OONL.

— 1991 —

0489 **Campbell, Geraldine**
Notes on microfilmed Tweedsmuir books. Ridgetown, Ont.: Federated Women's Institutes of Ontario, 1991. [25] l.
Note: Approx. 200 entries.– Listing of Ontario local histories published by Women's Institutes which are available on microfilm, with locations.
Location: OONL.

0490 **Campbell, Geraldine**
Notes on published [Tweedsmuir] books. Ridgetown, Ont.: Federated Women's Institutes of Ontario, 1991. [12] l.
Note: Approx. 100 entries.– Listing of Tweedsmuir books, local histories published by Ontario Women's Institutes.
Location: OONL.

0491 **Fraser, Alex W.**
Title guide of local histories for the counties of Glengarry, Dundas, Prescott, Stormont: including the HH-GGS titles. Lancaster, Ont.: Highland Heritage/ Glengarry Genealogical Society, 1991. 83 p.: ill.; ISBN: 0-921307-40-3.
Note: Lists books and pamphlets dealing with local

history and family history for eastern Ontario counties of Dundas, Stormont, Glengarry, Prescott.– Provides information on sources: historical/genealogical societies, newspapers, museums, libraries.
Location: OONL.

0492 **Scarborough Public Library Board**
A history of the City of Scarborough: an annotated bibliography. Scarborough, Ont.: Scarborough Public Library Board, 1991. 174 p.
Note: 753 entries.– Monographs, periodical articles, maps, atlases, manuscripts and unpublished materials.– Topics include cultural, economic and social history, biography, politics and government, religion, education, architecture, transportation and communications.
Location: OONL.

— 1992 —

0493 **Sullivan, Elinor**
A bibliography of Simcoe County, Ontario, 1790-1990: published works and post-graduate theses relating to the British colonial and post-Confederation periods: with representative locations. Penetanguishene, Ont.: SBI, 1992. 269 p.; ISBN: 0-969664-90-7.
Note: 2,624 entries.– Monographs, journal articles, theses at doctoral level, published or completed by 1990, covering a wide range of topics from agriculture to weather and climate.– Includes an extensive listing of directories and gazetteers, local histories.
Location: OONL.

— 1936 —

0494 **Lawrence, Bertha**
A survey of the materials to be found in the Provincial Legislative Library, Alberta, for a study of Canadian history and more particularly that of western Canada. Edmonton: 1936. 419 l.
Note: M.A. thesis, University of Alberta, 1936.– Lists books, pamphlets, government documents.– Detailed descriptive annotations for selected entries.
Location: AEU.

— 1949 —

0495 **Winnipeg Public Library**
A selective bibliography of Canadiana of the prairie provinces: publications relating to western Canada by English, French, Icelandic, Mennonite, and Ukrainian authors. [Winnipeg]: Winnipeg Public Library, 1949. 33 p.
Note: Approx. 400 entries.– History, biography, fiction, poetry, newspapers and magazines.– Edited by A.F. Jamieson.
Location: OONL.

— 1953 —

0496 **Peel, Bruce Braden**
"Saskatchewan imprints before 1900."
In: *Saskatchewan History*; Vol. 6, no. 3 (Autumn 1953) p. 91-94.; ISSN: 0036-4908.
Note: Location: OONL.

— 1955 —

0497 **Peel, Bruce Braden**
"Alberta imprints before 1900."
In: *Alberta Historical Review*; Vol. 3, no. 3 (Summer 1955) p. 41-46.; ISSN: 0002-4783.
Note: Location: OONL.

— 1958 —

0498 **MacDonald, Christine**
"Jubilee local histories."
In: *Saskatchewan History*; Vol. 8, no. 3 (Autumn 1955) p. 113-116; vol. 9, no. 1 (Winter 1956) p. 32-33; vol. 9, no. 3 (Autumn 1956) p. 110-115; vol. 11, no. 3 (Autumn 1958) p. 115-117.; ISSN: 0036-4908.
Note: Location: OONL.

— 1967 —

0499 **Scott, Michael M.**
A bibliography of western Canadian studies relating to Manitoba. Winnipeg: [Western Canada Research Council], 1967. 79 p.
Note: Approx. 700 entries.– Selected theses, research reports, books, periodical articles relating to Manitoba written between 1860 and 1967.
Location: OONL.

— 1970 —

0500 **Morley, Marjorie**
A bibliography of Manitoba from holdings in the Legislative Library of Manitoba. Winnipeg: [s.n.], 1970. 267 p.: map.
Note: 2,245 (plus approx. 700) entries.– Covers from earliest imprints to July 1970.– Includes books, theses, newspapers, periodicals, government publications relating to the history of Manitoba.
Previous editions:
1953. [2], 45 l.
A bibliography of Manitoba, selected from holdings in the Legislative Library of Manitoba. 1948. 16 p.
Microform: *Peel bibliography on microfiche.* Ottawa: National Library of Canada, 1976-1979. No. 4362.
Location: OONL.

0501 **National Library of Canada**
Manitoba authors/Écrivains du Manitoba. Ottawa: The Library, 1970. 1 vol. (unpaged).
Note: 263 entries.– Exhibit catalogue provides a brief history of printing, publishing and literature in Manitoba.– Arranged in five sections: arrival of printing, travellers' impressions, immigrants and pioneer settlers, chronicles of the province, poetry and prose.– Text in English and French/texte en français et en anglais.
Location: OONL.

— 1971 —

0502 **Corley, Nora T., et al.**
A selected bibliography on the Peace and Athabasca rivers and the Peace-Athabasca Delta region. Montreal: Arctic Institute of North America, 1971. [30] l.
Note: 134 entries.– Books, government publications, journal articles dealing with Peace and Athabasca rivers: history, geography, geology, natural history (birds, botany, mammals), meteorology, hydrology, navigation.– Excludes material on the Athabasca tar sands.
Location: AEUB.

0503 **Historical and Scientific Society of Manitoba**
A checklist of centennial publications in Manitoba, 1967-1970. Winnipeg: [s.n.], 1971. 11 p.
Note: Approx. 125 entries.
Location: OONL.

0504 **Livermore, Ronald P.**
Bibliography of primary sources for classroom study of the history of Alberta [microform]. Calgary: University of Calgary, 1971. 1 reel of microfilm (x, 298 p.): ill., map, facsim. (Canadian theses on microfilm ; 10194)
Note: Approx. 3,000 entries.– Documents (maps, manuscripts, articles, diaries) and photographs related to study of Alberta environment, people, explorers, surveyors, travellers, fur trade, rebellions, railway, settlement, agriculture, politics and government, education, religion, literature.– Thesis: M.Ec., University of Calgary.
Location: OONL.

0505 **Saskatchewan Provincial Library. Bibliographic Services Division**
Saskatchewan homecoming '71: a bibliography. Regina: The Library, [1971]. 29 p.
Note: Location: OONL.

— 1972 —

0506 **Manitoba School Library Audio Visual Association**
Manitoba: a provincial look. [Winnipeg: Manitoba School
Library Audio Visual Association], 1972. 48 p.
Note: Location: OONL.

— 1973 —

0507 **Dorge, Lionel**
Introduction à l'étude des Franco-Manitobains: essai
historique et bibliographique. Saint-Boniface: La Société
Historique de Saint-Boniface, 1973. v, 298 p.
Note: 2,885 entrées.
Localisation: OONL.

0508 **Glenbow-Alberta Institute. Library**
Catalogue of the Glenbow historical library, the
Glenbow-Alberta Institute Library, Calgary, Alberta.
Boston: G.K. Hall, 1973. 4 vol.; ISBN: 0-8161-0994-X.
Note: Reproduction of card catalogue.– Collection focus
on western Canadiana, native art and antiquities, history,
reference support for Glenbow museum curatorial staff.
Location: OONL.

0509 **MacKenzie, Margaret**
A preliminary check-list of writings by native
Manitobans and residents of Manitoba, and of material
written about Manitoba and Manitobans. [Winnipeg:
Elizabeth Dafoe Library, University of Manitoba, 1973].
44 l.
Note: Alphabetic listing by author of literature, history,
biography, politics and government.
Location: MWSJ.

0510 **Peel, Bruce Braden**
A bibliography of the prairie provinces to 1953, with
biographical index. 2nd ed. Toronto: University of
Toronto Press, c1973. xxviii, 780 p.; ISBN: 0-8020-1972-2.
Note: 4,408 entries.– Books and pamphlets relating to the
Prairie provinces, arranged chronologically from 1692 to
1953.
Previous edition: Published in co-operation with the
Saskatchewan Golden Jubilee Committee and the
University of Saskatchewan by University of Toronto
Press, 1956. xix, 680 p.
Supplement: 1963. x, 130 p.
Microform: *Peel bibliography on microfiche/Bibliographie
Peel sur microfiche*. Ottawa: National Library of Canada,
1975-. microfiches.; ISSN: 0065-5996.– Reproduces items
listed in the bibliography.
Location: OONL.

0511 **Regehr, T.D.**
"Historiography of the Canadian plains after 1870."
In: *A region of the mind: interpreting the western Canadian
plains*, edited by Richard Allen. Regina: Canadian Plains
Studies Centre, University of Saskatchewan, c1973. P. 87-
101.; ISBN: 0-889770085.
Note: Review of historical writings about the post-1870
period of western Canada.
Location: OONL.

0512 **Saskatchewan Provincial Library. Bibliographic
Services Division**
Saskatchewan history: a bibliography. Regina: Provincial
Library, 1973. 23 p.
Note: Location: OONL.

— 1974 —

0513 **Sloane, D. Louise; Roseneder, Jan; Hernandez, Marilyn
J.**
Winnipeg: a centennial bibliography. Winnipeg:
Manitoba Library Association, 1974. xi, 140 p.
Note: 1,437 entries.– Books, periodical articles, theses,
manuscripts and government publications relating to
city of Winnipeg and region.– Includes sections on
history, politics, planning, business, transportation,
sports, the arts, science and medicine.– Excludes
personal material on Louis Riel and Rebellion of 1885.
Location: OONL.

0514 **St. James-Assiniboia Public Library**
Winnipeg in print: a bibliography: books about
Winnipeg or by Winnipeggers in the St. James-Assiniboia
Public Library. [Winnipeg: St. James-Assiniboia Public
Library], 1974. 59 p.
Note: Approx. 460 entries.– Includes fiction and non-fic-
tion materials.
Location: OONL.

— 1975 —

0515 **Davies, W.H.; Wilson, J.S.**
A picture primer on the Churchill River Basin.
Saskatoon: Churchill River Study, 1975. 56 p.: ill., map.
(Bulletin / Churchill River study, Missinipe probe ; 7)
Note: Contains reading lists on the Churchill River Basin:
geology, geography, history, people, vegetation, wildlife,
fishes.
Location: OONL.

0516 **Dew, Ian F.**
Bibliography of material relating to southern Alberta
published to 1970. [Lethbridge, Alta.]: University of
Lethbridge, Learning Resources Centre, 1975. viii, 407 p.
Note: Approx. 3,600 entries.– Monographs, articles,
government publications, theses relating to life and
history of southern Alberta arranged in nine broad
subject fields.– Locations are given for monographs and
newspapers in larger Alberta libraries.
Location: OONL.

0517 **Dibb, Sandra**
Northern Saskatchewan bibliography. Saskatoon:
Institute for Northern Studies, University of
Saskatchewan, 1975. xii, 80 p. (Maudsley memoir series /
Institute for Northern Studies, University of
Saskatchewan ; 2)
Note: Part I: "Bibliography on human development in
northern Saskatchewan."- Approx. 600 entries.– Books,
periodical articles, government publications.
Part II: "Annotated bibliography on eco-biology of
northern Saskatchewan."- Approx. 275 entries.
Location: OONL.

0518 **P.S. Ross & Partners**
The economy of northern Alberta: a bibliography.
[Edmonton]: Northern Development Group, Department
of Business Development and Tourism, Government of
Alberta, 1975. iii, 71 p.
Note: Approx. 300 entries.– Planning reports, theses,
government publications on geographic area defined by
census divisions 12 – 15 for the period 1965 to 1974.–
Topics include industry and resource development,
community planning and development, manufacturing,
recreation and tourism, transportation.
Location: OONL.

0519 **Saskatchewan. Department of Education**
Social studies year one: "Saskatchewan": bibliography,
Division two, resource materials. Regina: Department of

Education, Saskatchewan, 1975. vi, 40 p.
Note: Multi-media listing of student materials and teachers' reference material about Saskatchewan and the prairie provinces.
Location: OONL.

— 1977 —

0520 **Gill, Dhara S.**
A bibliography of socio-economic studies on rural Alberta, Canada. Monticello, Ill.: Council of Planning Librarians, 1977. 206 p. (Council of Planning Librarians Exchange bibliography ; 1260-1261-1262)
Note: Approx. 2,400 entries.– Books, government reports and studies, journal articles, theses.
Location: OONL.

0521 **Saskatchewan Library Association**
Saskatchewan publications. Regina: Saskatchewan Library Association, 1975-1977. 3 vol.
Note: University, government and association publications.– Excludes periodicals and audiovisual material.
Location: OONL.

— 1978 —

0522 **Artibise, Alan F.J.**
Western Canada since 1870: a select bibliography and guide. Vancouver: University of British Columbia Press, [c1978]. xii, 294 p.; ISBN: 0-7748-0090-9.
Note: 3,662 entries.– Books, pamphlets, periodical articles, unpublished B.A. essays, M.A. and Ph.D. theses.– Excludes most fictional material, government publications.– Author index, select subject index, and index of organizations, institutions and serials.
Location: OONL.

0523 **Ryder, Dorothy E.**
The Canadian West & the North: a bibliographical overview. [Toronto]; Edmonton: Published for the Bibliographical Society of Canada by the University of Alberta Library, 1978. 13 l.
Note: 51 entries.– Limited to general and current bibliographies on western and northern Canada.– Emphasis on the 1970s.– Excludes specific subject and regional bibliographies.
Location: OONL.

0524 **Université du Québec à Montréal. Service des recherches arctiques et sub-arctiques**
Communications, Manitoba/Communications, Manitoba. Montréal: Université du Québec à Montréal, [1978]. 33 l. (Catalogue des coupures de presse, Collection Gardner ; catalogue 50)
Note: Approx. 500 entrées.
Localisation: OONL.

0525 **Ward, W. Peter**
"Western Canada: recent historical writing."
In: *Queen's Quarterly*; Vol. 85, no. 2 (Summer 1978) p. 271-288.; ISSN: 0033-6041.
Note: Location: OONL.

— 1979 —

0526 **Artibise, Alan F.J.**
Gateway city: documents on the City of Winnipeg, 1873-1913. Winnipeg: Manitoba Record Society, 1979. xiv, 288 p.: ill., maps. (Manitoba Record Society Publications ; vol. 5)
Note: 12 entries.
Location: OONL.

0527 **Huston, Barbara, et al.**
A preliminary guide to archival sources relating to southern Alberta. [Lethbridge, Alta.: Department of History, University of Lethbridge], 1979. iii, 21, [77] l.
Note: 716 entries.– Compiled and edited by members of the University of Lethbridge Regional History Project: Barbara Huston, James Tagg, William M. Baker, Don C. Wick.
Location: OONL.

0528 **Saskatchewan. Department of Education**
Celebrate Saskatchewan: a bibliography of instructional resources. Regina, Sask.: The Department, 1979. iii, 60 p.
Note: Approx. 150 entries.– Listing of print and non-print materials with a Saskatchewan theme: environment, native people, agriculture, Riel rebellion, history, Saskatchewan in literature, arts, politics and government.
Location: OONL.

0529 **Smith, Dwight L.**
The American and Canadian west: a bibliography. Santa Barbara, Calif.: American Bibliographical Center-Clio Press, c1979. xi, 558 p. (Clio bibliography series ; no. 6); ISBN: 0-87436-272-5.
Note: 4,157 entries.– Abstracted periodical articles, 1964 to 1973.– Geographical coverage: trans-Mississippi west and the trans-Shield Canadian west (Ontario-Manitoba provincial boundary).
Location: OONL.

0530 **Teillet, D.J.**
A northern Manitoba bibliography. [Ottawa]: Regional Economic Expansion; [Winnipeg]: Manitoba Department of Mines, Natural Resources and Environment, 1979. iv, 82 p. (Technical report / Manitoba Department of Mines, Natural Resources and Environment ; 79-5)
Note: Approx. 2,250 entries.– Works written since 1950 on resource management in Manitoba region north of 53rd parallel.
Location: OONL.

0531 **University of Manitoba. Library**
A selected bibliography of materials held in the libraries of the University of Manitoba pertaining to the history and historical geography of the Canadian Northwest, with particular reference to the Hudson Bay Lowlands, 1610-1930. [Winnipeg: University of Manitoba, 1979]. 103 p.
Note: Approx. 1,300 entries.– Books, pamphlets, journal articles.– Topics include discovery and exploration, fur trade, native peoples, immigration and settlement, Red River and Northwest rebellions (1869-70 and 1885), general history.– Includes government publications, serials, atlases and maps, bibliographies.
Location: OTU.

— 1980 —

0532 **Arora, Ved**
The Saskatchewan bibliography. Regina: Saskatchewan Provincial Library, 1980. ix, 787 p.; ISBN: 0-919059-00-7.
Note: 6,377 entries on Saskatchewan subjects published between 1905 and October, 1979.– Books, theses, selected government publications.– Excludes serials, maps, music scores, records, films, political and trade brochures.
Supplement: *... . First supplement.* Published by Saskatchewan Library Association with the cooperation of Saskatchewan Provincial Library, 1993. 1 vol.; ISBN: 0-9690714-4-2.

Location: OONL.

— 1981 —

0533 **DeGrâce, Eloi**
Inventaire des documents sur les Franco-albertains. Edmonton: Archives provinciales de l'Alberta, 1981. 10 f.
Note: Approx. 70 entrées.– Documents sur individus et familles, associations, documents religieux, documents du gouvernement, journaux, notes sur les archives sonores, photographie.
Localisation: OONL.

0534 **Friesen, Gerald; Potyondi, Barry**
A guide to the study of Manitoba local history. Winnipeg: Published by the University of Manitoba Press for the Manitoba Historical Society, c1981. 182 p.: ill.; ISBN: 0-88755-121-1.
Note: Describes local history as a field for research and provides detail on location and use of sources of information.– Themes include agriculture, the environment, population studies, business, politics, local government, education, religion, law/medicine/social services.– Appendices deal with land records, directories, archival sources.– Selected bibliography.
Location: OONL.

0535 **"Recent publications in local history."**
In: *Saskatchewan History*; Vol. 17 (1964) p. 39; vol. 24, no. 2 (Spring 1971) p. 78-80; vol. 31, no. 1 (Winter 1978) p. 39-40; vol. 33, no. 2 (Spring 1980) p. 78-79; vol. 34, no. 2 (Spring 1981) p. 78-80.; ISSN: 0036-4908.
Note: Location: OONL.

— 1982 —

0536 **Strathern, Gloria M.**
Alberta, 1954-1979: a provincial bibliography. Edmonton: University of Alberta, 1982. xv, 745 p.; ISBN: 0-88864-949-X.
Note: 3,513 entries.– Books, pamphlets and theses relating to Alberta, by Albertans, or published by Alberta regional presses.– Excludes serials and government publications, scientific, technical and specialized professional materials.
Location: OONL.

0537 **Wagner, Henry R.; Camp, Charles L.**
The Plains & the Rockies: a critical bibliography of exploration, adventure, and travel in the American West, 1800-1865. San Francisco: John Howell-Books, 1982. xx, 745 p., [32] p. of pl.: ill.; ISBN: 0-910760-11-1.
Note: 690 entries.– Geographical coverage: Arctic circle to U.S.–Mexico border and the hundredth meridian to the Cascades and Sierra Nevada.– Includes many Canadian references.– All documents examined and described in detail.– Locations are provided.– Revised, enlarged and edited by Robert H. Becker.
Location: OONL.

— 1983 —

0538 **Krotki, Joanna E.**
Local histories of Alberta: an annotated bibliography. Edmonton: Department of Slavic and East European Studies, University of Alberta, 1983. xviii, 430 p.
Note: 1,144 entries.– Books, pamphlets and unpublished material dated to 1982.– Covers history of settlement in Alberta, with emphasis on ethnic composition of population, focus on central and eastern Europe.– Compiled with the assistance of Jean Wilman and Jane Lamont.

Location: OONL.

— 1986 —

0539 **Books by Manitoba authors: a bibliography.**
[Winnipeg]: Manitoba Writers' Guild, [1986]. 88 p.; ISBN: 0-9692525-0-1.
Note: 148 entries.– Titles currently in print in 1986 by 74 Manitoba authors.
Location: OONL.

0540 **Boultbee, Paul G.**
A central Alberta bibliography. [Red Deer]: Red Deer College Press, 1986. 58 p.; ISBN: 0-88995-031-8.
Note: 788 entries.– Privately and commercially published monographs about central Alberta, or by central Alberta writers.
Location: OONL.

0541 **Edmonton Public Library. Western Canadiana Collection**
Supplementary bibliography [Edmonton Public Library, Western Canadiana Collection]. [Edmonton]: The Library, [1986]. iv, 184 p.
Note: Monographs, serials, official publications relating to Alberta, with emphasis on northern Alberta and Edmonton region, held in the Western Canadiana Collection of Edmonton Public Library.– The title derives from the intention of this publication to provide a supplement to: Peel, Bruce Braden: *A bibliography of the prairie provinces to 1953, with biographical index*; Strathern, Gloria M.: *Alberta, 1954-1979: a provincial bibliography*; Forsyth, Joseph: *Government publications relating to Alberta*.
Location: OONL.

0542 **Friesen, Jean; Angel, Michael**
"Manitoba bibliography of bibliographies."
In: *Manitoba History*; No. 12 (Fall 1986) p. 18-24 (Insert, 8 p.).; ISSN: 0226-5036.
Note: 115 entries.– General bibliographies on Manitoba and the prairie provinces, bibliographies produced by Manitoba government departments and agencies, Manitoba indexes and directories, general bibliographies containing substantial sections on Manitoba.– Covers to January 1985.
Location: AEU.

— 1987 —

0543 **Anderson, Alan B.**
Guide to bibliographic sources in francophone communities in Saskatchewan/Guide des sources bibliographiques des communautés francophones de la Saskatchewan. Saskatoon: Research Unit for French-Canadian Studies, University of Saskatchewan, 1987. 10 p. (Research report / Research Unit for French-Canadian Studies, University of Saskatchewan ; no. 13)
Note: Text in English only.
Location: OONL.

0544 **Stephen, Marg; Mah, Judy**
Alberta bibliography, 1980-1987 for adults and young adults. [Edmonton]: Young Alberta Book Festival Society, [1987]. 48 p.; ISBN: 0-9693147-0-1.
Note: Approx. 600 entries.
Location: OONL.

— 1989 —

0545 **Alberta. Provincial Archives. Historical Resources Library**
Alberta's local histories in the Historical Resources Library. 8th ed. [Edmonton]: The Library, 1989. 204 p.;

ISSN: 1180-9442.

Note: Approx. 2,600 entries.– Contains local, church, school and other histories on Alberta communities

Previous editions:

1987. 191 p.

1986. 178 p.

1983. 97, [39] p.

1979. 64, 17 p.

Location: OONL.

0546 **Hackett, Christopher**
A bibliography of Manitoba local history: a guide to local and regional histories written about communities in Manitoba. 2nd ed. [Winnipeg]: Manitoba Historical Society, c1989. xvi, 156 p.; ISBN: 0-921950-00-4.

Note: 971 entries.– Traditional works covering towns, rural municipalities, churches, schools, as well as those dealing with ethnic and religious groups, province-wide associations; research papers, theses, municipal, provincial and federal government publications.

Previous edition: Historical and Scientific Society of Manitoba. History Committee. *Local history in Manitoba: a key to places, districts, schools and transport routes.* 1976. 166 p.

Location: OONL.

0547 **Index of research in northern Alberta sponsored by the Northern Alberta Development Council.** [Peace River, Alta.]: Northern Alberta Development Council, [1989]. 19 l.: map.

Note: 125 entries.– Covers 1975 to 1989.– List includes all studies or research activities sponsored directly or indirectly by the N.A.D.C. or the Northern Development Branch.

Location: OONL.

— 1990 —

0548 **Pannekoek, Frits**
"A selected western Canada historical resources bibliography to 1985."
In: *Prairie Forum*; Vol. 15, no. 2 (Fall 1990) p. 329-374.; ISSN: 0317-6282.

Note: Approx. 1,000 entries.– Includes mainly research reports, published and unpublished, from Parks Canada, heritage and historic sites agencies of Alberta, British Columbia, Manitoba and Saskatchewan.

Location: OONL.

— 1991 —

0549 **Enns, Richard A.**
A bibliography of northern Manitoba. Winnipeg: University of Manitoba Press, 1991. 128 p. (Manitoba studies in native history occasional papers); ISBN: 0-88755-625-6.

Note: Approx. 1,875 entries.– Books, periodical articles, theses, government pamphlets dealing with the northern regions of Manitoba, the fur trade, aboriginal peoples, exploration and travel accounts, church and mission histories, northern geography and resources, community histories, resource exploitation.

Location: OONL.

0550 **Rek, Joseph**
Edmonton: an annotated bibliography of holdings in the Canadiana collection, Edmonton Public Library. 3rd updated ed. [Edmonton: Edmonton Public Library], 1991. 81 p.

Note: 463 entries.– Arrangement is by subject and types

of material.– Categories include the arts, civic government, economy, military history, social conditions, sports, bibliographies, directories, periodicals and newspapers.

Previous edition: 1989. 70 p.– 384 entries.

Location: OONL.

— 1992 —

0551 **Gillespie, Kay M.**
"Manitoba bibliography."
In: *Manitoba History*; No. 6 (Fall 1983) p. 29-32; no. 8 (Fall 1984) p. 33-35; no. 10 (Fall 1985) p. 35-37; no. 12 (Fall 1986) p. 14-16; no. 14 (Fall 1987) p. 33-36; no. 16 (Fall 1988) p. 17-20; no. 18 (Fall 1989) p. 33-35; no. 20 (Fall 1990) p. 29-31; no. 22 (Fall 1991) p. 16-18; no. 24 (Fall 1992) p. 36-38.; ISSN: 0226-5036.

Note: Annual listing of books, articles, government publications about Manitoba.

Location: AEU.

0552 **Stephen, Marg**
Alberta bibliography: books by Alberta authors and Alberta publishers. Edmonton: Young Alberta Book Festival Society, 1992. 73 p.; ISBN: 0-9693147-3-6.

Note: Approx. 1,050 entries.

Previous editions:

1991. 54 p.; ISBN: 0-9693147-2-8.

1989. 78 p.; ISBN: 0-9693147-0-1.

Location: OONL.

— Ongoing/En cours —

0553 **Northern Alberta Development Council**
List of current publications [Northern Alberta Development Council]. Peace River, Alta.: The Council, 1982-. vol.; ISSN: 0833-7918.

Note: Location: OONL.

— 1923 —

0554 Rockwood, Eleanor Ruth
Books on the Pacific northwest for small libraries. New York: H.W. Wilson, 1923. 55 p.
Note: Approx. 250 entries.– History, Indians, voyages of exploration, fur trade, missionaries, description and travel, natural history.
Location: OONL.

— 1924 —

0555 Howay, F.W.
"The early literature of the Northwest coast."
In: *Proceedings and Transactions of the Royal Society of Canada*; Series 3, vol. 18, section 2 (1924) p. 1-31.; ISSN: 0316-4616.
Note: Location: AEU.

— 1928 —

0556 Reid, R.L.
"British Columbia: a bibliographical sketch."
In: *Papers of the Bibliographical Society of America*; Vol. 22, part 1 (1928) p. 20-44.; ISSN: 0006-128X.
Note: Location: AEU.

— 1935 —

0557 British Columbia Library Association. Bibliography Committee
Bibliography on the Columbia River Basin. [Vancouver: The Association], 1935. [2], 46, [3] p.
Note: Approx. 500 entries.– Books, periodical articles, government documents dealing with topics related to the Columbia River Basin, British Columbia: agriculture, mines and mineral resources, exploration, Doukhobors, Indians, cities and towns (Fernie, Fort Steele, Nelson, Revelstoke, Rossland, Slocan, Trail), politics and government.
Location: BVIPA.

0558 British Columbia Library Association. Bibliography Committee
The Oregon question. [Vancouver: The Association], 1935. [17] p.
Note: Approx. 150 entries.– Books, articles, documents.– Part 1, "The Oregon boundary question," compiled by Franklin K. Lewis.– Part 2, "The Oregon question."
Location: BVIPA.

0559 Fairley, Helen
Bibliography of Prince George District. [Vancouver: British Columbia Library Association], 1935. 5 p.
Note: Approx. 60 entries.– Books, government publications, periodical articles dealing with history, geology and mining, natural history of the Prince George District, British Columbia.
Location: BVIPA.

0560 Fairley, Helen
Bibliography on the Cariboo District. [Vancouver: British Columbia Library Association], 1935. [1], 8 p.
Note: Approx. 125 entries.– Books, magazine articles, government documents dealing with exploration, natural history, mining, road-building and public works in the Cariboo District, British Columbia.
Location: BVIPA.

0561 Goodfellow, John; Lanning, Mabel M.
Similkameen Tulameen Valleys. [Vancouver: British Columbia Library Association], 1935. [8] p.
Note: Approx. 100 entries.– Books, periodical articles, government documemts dealing with topics related to the Similkameen and Tulameen Valleys, British Columbia: history, mining, public works, Indians, cities and towns.
Location: BVIPA.

0562 Ormsby, Margaret
The Okanagan District. [Vancouver: British Columbia Library Association], 1935. [1], 21 p.
Note: Approx. 250 entries.– Books, pamphlets, periodical articles, manuscripts, official published reports dealing with topics related to the Okanagan District, British Columbia: biography, history, agriculture, mining, roads and trails, natural history.
Location: BVAU.

0563 Prevost, Gerald
Duncan-Cowichan District, V.I. [Vancouver: British Columbia Library Association], 1935. [21] p.
Note: Approx. 300 entries.– Pamphlets, manuscripts, articles from the *Cowichan Leader* dealing with biography, Indians, institutions, history of Cowichan District, Vancouver Island.
Location: BVIPA.

0564 Stewart, Jean; Swan, J.O.
Nanaimo District, V.I. [Vancouver: British Columbia Library Association], 1935. [1], 14 p.
Note: Approx. 250 entries.– Books, newspaper and periodical articles, government publications relating to the Nanaimo District, British Columbia.– Topics include history, education, biography, coal mining, railway history, fisheries, politics and government, sports.
Location: BVIPA.

— 1936 —

0565 Matheson, Frances
Cranbrook Herald, 1900-1908. [Vancouver: British Columbia Library Association], 1935-1936. [2], 22 p.
Note: Approx. 400 entries.– Articles from the *Cranbrook Herald* dealing with Cranbrook District, British Columbia, with focus on the city of Cranbrook, and the towns in the area: Fort Steele, Marysville, Kimberley, Moyie, Creston and Elko.– General topics covered include agriculture, lumbering, mining and railroads.
Location: BVIPA.

— 1941 —

0566 Hanley, Annie Harvey (Ross) Foster
British Columbia authors' index. White Rock, B.C.: [1941]. 84, 29, [10] l.
Note: Books by British Columbia writers, books about British Columbia.– Addenda to 1949.– Mimeograph

format
Location: OONL.

— 1943 —

0567 **"Checklist of Crown Colony imprints."**
In: *British Columbia Historical Quarterly*; Vol. 1, no. 4 (October 1937) p. 263-271; vol. 4, no. 2 (April 1940) p. 139-141; vol. 7, no. 3 (July 1943) p. 226-227.; ISSN: 0706-7666.
Note: 63 entries in total.– Listing of imprints in the Crown Colonies of Vancouver Island and British Columbia, 1858-1870.– Excludes regularly issued government documents, newspapers.
Location: OONL.

— 1950 —

0568 **Smith, Charles Wesley**
Pacific northwest Americana: a check list of books and pamphlets relating to the history of the Pacific northwest. Edition 3, revised and extended by Isabel Mayhew. Portland, Ore.: Binfords & Mort, 1950. 381 p.
Note: Approx. 7,500 entries.– Union list of holdings of 38 libraries in the region, not a comprehensive bibliography of imprints.– Covers to July 1, 1949.– Contains substantial listings of material relating to British Columbia.
Previous editions:
New York: Wilson, 1921. xi, 329 p.
Check-list of books and pamphlets relating to the history of the Pacific northwest to be found in representative libraries of that region. 1909. 191 p.
Supplement: *Pacific northwest Americana, 1949-1974.* Portland, Ore.: Binford[sic] & Mort; 1981. 365 p.; ISBN: 0-8323-0389-5.– Approx. 4,000 entries.– Section on British Columbia, containing about 600 entries, compiled by Linda Webster, Provincial Archives of British Columbia.
Location: OONL.

— 1956 —

0569 **British Columbia. Department of Education. Division of Curriculum**
A bibliography on British Columbia for elementary and secondary schools. Victoria, B.C.: The Department, 1956. 8 l.
Note: Location: OONL.

— 1957 —

0570 **Colman, Mary Elizabeth**
British Columbia books past and present. Victoria, B.C.: British Columbia Government Travel Bureau, 1957. 1 folder: ill., map.
Note: Location: OONL.

— 1958 —

0571 **Napier, Nina**
"British Columbia: a bibliography of centennial publications, 1957-1959."
In: *British Columbia Historical Quarterly*; Vol. 21 (1957-1958) p. 199-220.; ISSN: 0706-7666.
Note: Books, pamphlets, articles, centennial issues of newspapers.– Includes general and local histories, business history, church histories.
Location: OONL.

— 1961 —

0572 **Peel, Bruce Braden**
"The Columbia drainage basin in Canada: a bibliographical essay."
In: *Pacific Northwest Quarterly*; Vol. 52, no. 4 (October 1961) p. 152-154.; ISSN: 0030-8803.
Note: Location: OONL.

— 1962 —

0573 **Freer, Katherine M.**
Vancouver, a bibliography compiled from material in the Vancouver Public Library and the Special Collections of the University of British Columbia Library. [London, Eng.]: University of London, 1962. [ix], 234 l.
Note: Unpublished Dipl. Lib. thesis.
Location: OONL.

— 1967 —

0574 **Webber, Bert**
The Pacific Northwest in books. [Tigard, Or.]: Lanson's, [1967]. 45 p.: ill.
Note: Includes Canadian (British Columbia) references.
Location: OONL.

— 1968 —

0575 **Lowther, Barbara J.**
A bibliography of British Columbia: laying the foundations, 1849-1899. [Victoria, B.C.: University of Victoria, 1968]. xii, 328 p.
Note: 2,173 entries.– Books, government publications, serials, offprints of periodical articles which relate to the first 50 years of settlement in British Columbia.– One location is provided for each entry.– Compiled with the assistance of Muriel Laing.
Location: OONL.

— 1969 —

0576 **Parke-Bernet Galleries**
The celebrated collection of Americana formed by the late Thomas Winthrop Streeter. New York: [s.n.]. 1969. 7 vol.: ill., facsims. (part col.).
Note: Volume 6: *The Pacific West, Oregon, British Columbia, Alaska and the Klondike 1873-1925, Canada, Hawaii, Maps.*
Location: OONL.

— 1970 —

0577 **Strathern, Gloria M.**
Navigations, traffiques & discoveries, 1774-1848: a guide to publications relating to the area now British Columbia. Victoria, B.C.: Social Sciences Research Centre, University of Victoria, 1970. xv, 417 p.: maps; ISBN: 0-9690418-2-9.
Note: 631 entries.– Published monographic works, small group of offprints from periodicals, facsimile reprints.– Emphasis on publications relating to area within present provincial boundaries.– Excludes newspapers, unpublished manuscripts and archival material, unpublished theses and photo reproductions.– Compiled with the assistance of Margaret H. Edwards.
Location: OONL.

— 1971 —

0578 **British Columbia. Provincial Archives. Library**
Dictionary catalogue of the Library of the Provincial Archives of British Columbia, Victoria. Boston: G.K. Hall, 1971. 8 vol.; ISBN: 0-8161-0912-5.
Note: Reproduction of card catalogue.– Books, pamphlets, reports, periodical literature relating to British Columbia, the Pacific Northwest, western Canada, Northwest Territories and the Yukon in all fields, with the exception of the natural sciences.
Location: OONL.

0579 **Goard, Dean S.; Dickinson, Gary**
A bibliography of social and economic research pertaining to rural British Columbia. Ottawa: Regional

Economic Expansion Canada, 1971. iv, 44 p. (Canada Land Inventory Project ; no. 49015)
Note: 314 entries.– Books, federal/provincial/municipal government studies and reports, journal articles, theses.– Covers to the end of 1970.– Excludes studies on Greater Vancouver and Victoria, technical reports dealing with specific industries such as fishing, forestry, mining, studies of Indians except as they relate to general social and economic conditions.
Previous edition: *Rural British Columbia: a bibliography of social and economic research*. Vancouver: Department of Adult Education, Faculty of Education, University of British Columbia, 1967. 26 p.– 227 entries.
Location: OONL.

0580 **Okanagan Regional Library**
British Columbia books. 3rd ed. Kelowna, B.C.: Okanagan Regional Library, 1971. 47 l.
Note: Approx. 375 entries.– Books about British Columbia and books by British Columbia authors from collections of Okanagan Regional Library.
Previous editions:
1965. 23 p.
1958. 12 p.
Location: OONL.

— 1972 —

0581 **University of Washington. Libraries**
The dictionary catalog of the Pacific Northwest Collection of the University of Washington Libraries, Seattle. Boston: G.K. Hall, 1972. 6 vol.; ISBN: 0-8161-0985-0.
Note: Reproduction of card catalogue.– Pacific Northwest Collection includes books, pamphlets and other materials relating to British Columbia and the Yukon: discovery and exploration, native peoples, fur trade era, missionaries, immigration, settlement, mining, agriculture, shipping, lumber industry, education.
Location: OONL.

— 1974 —

0582 **Armstrong, C.**
"A selected bibliography of maritime voyages to the Q.C.I."
In: *Charlottes*; Vol. 3 (December 1974) p. 56.; ISSN: 0316-6724.
Note: Location: OONL.

0583 **Cuddy, Mary Lou; Scott, James J.**
British Columbia in books: an annotated bibliography. Vancouver: J.J. Douglas, 1974. 144 p.: ill., maps.; ISBN: 0-88894-066-1.
Note: Approx. 1,000 entries.– Selection of materials about British Columbia in print as of December 31, 1973.– Includes a list of British Columbia organizations and associations, government agencies and their publications, listing of newspapers and periodicals.
Location: OONL.

— 1975 —

0584 **Edwards, Margaret H.; Lort, John C.R.**
A bibliography of British Columbia: years of growth, 1900-1950. Victoria, B.C.: Social Sciences Research Centre, University of Victoria, 1975. x, 446 p.: maps (on lining papers).; ISBN: 0-9690418-3-7.
Note: 4,125 annotated entries.– Published monographic books and pamphlets in English to 1974.– Excludes manuscripts, serials, unpublished briefs and theses,

directories, juvenile literature, maps, technical publications, government publications.– Provides one location.– Compiled with the assistance of Wendy J. Carmichael.
Location: OONL.

0585 **Gilbert, S.R.**
"British Columbia studies: basic references: selected bibliography."
In: *Communiqué: Canadian Studies*; Vol. 1, no. 4 (May 1975) p. 2-7.; ISSN: 0318-1197.
Note: Approx. 60 entries.
Location: OONL.

— 1976 —

0586 **Buri, Thomas**
A preliminary annotated bibliography of the Stikine River country and its people. Telegraph Creek, B.C.: T. Buri, 1976. 36 l.
Note: 124 entries.
Location: OONL.

0587 **Welwood, Ronald J.**
Kootenaiana: a listing of books, government publications, monographs, journals, pamphlets, etc., relating to the Kootenay area of the Province of British Columbia and located in the libraries of Notre Dame University of Nelson, B.C. and-or Selkirk College, Castlegar, B.C., up to 31 March 1976. Nelson: Notre Dame University Library; Castlegar: Selkirk College Library, 1976. 167 p.: ill., maps.
Note: 1,724 entries.
Previous edition: Turnbull, Jean. *Periodicals, articles, pamphlets, government publications and books relating to the West Kootenay region of British Columbia in the Selkirk College Library, Castlegar, B.C.* Castlegar: Selkirk College, 1968. 36 l.
Supplement: Turnbull, Jean; Port, Susan. *... : supplement I.* 1969. 33 l.
Location: OONL.

— 1977 —

0588 **Bowman, James**
Big country: a bibliography of the history of the Kamloops Region & Southern Cariboo. [Burnaby, B.C.]: Simon Fraser University, Department of Sociology and Anthropology, 1977. 79 p.: ill., map.
Note: 526 entries.– Covers 1812 to 1950.– Books, pamphlets, journal articles, theses, unpublished essays.– Excludes ethnological and archaeological works, materials in natural and applied sciences.
Location: OONL.

— 1978 —

0589 **Kent, Duncan**
British Columbia: a bibliography of industry, labour, resources & regions for the social sciences. Vancouver, B.C.: University of British Columbia Press, 1978. xi, 199 p.: ill., map.
Note: Approx. 2,000 entries.– Covers up to December, 1977.– Includes monographs, theses, journal articles, government and corporate reports, bibliographies, audiotapes, archival materials from the disciplines of anthropology, history, economics, geography, sociology, political science, urban studies and community planning.– Excludes popular magazine and newspaper articles.– Sections on industry case studies, labour force studies, resource use and development, regions and

regional communities, urban development, urban and rural relationships.
Location: BVIP.

— 1980 —

0590 **Ralston, H. Keith**
"Select bibliography on the history of British Columbia."
In: *Historical essays on British Columbia*, edited by Jean Friesen and H.K. Ralston. Toronto: Gage, 1980. P. 281-293.; ISBN: 0-7715-5694-2.
Note: Location: OONL.

— 1981 —

0591 **Woodward, Frances M.**
"British Columbia books of interest."
In: *B.C. Historical News*; (June 1971-Summer 1981) ; ISSN: 0045-2963.
Note: Regular listing from vol. 4, no. 4 (June 1971) to vol. 14, no. 4 (Summer 1981) of current publications about British Columbia: biography, history, art and architecture, travel and guidebooks.– Title varies: "B.C. books of interest", "Selected bibliography of British Columbia", "Books of interest", and "Bibliography".
Location: OONL.

— 1982 —

0592 **Hale, Linda Louise**
"Bibliography of British Columbia."
In: *BC Studies*; No. 55 (Autumn 1982) p. 107-123.; ISSN: 0005-2949.
Note: Regular select listing of books, articles, government publications on all subjects related to British Columbia.– Continues: Frances M. Woodward (Winter 1968-69-Summer 1982); continued by: Eve Szabo (Winter 1982-83-Autumn 1987); Melva J. Dwyer (Winter 1987-88-).
Location: AEU.

0593 **Woodward, Frances M.**
"Bibliography of British Columbia."
In: *BC Studies*; No. 1 (Winter 1968-69) p. 57-61; no. 2 (Summer 1969) p. 64-73; no. 3 (Fall 1969) p. 69-85; no. 4 (Spring 1970) p. 68-80; no. 5 (Summer 1970) p. 65-73; no. 8 (Winter 1970-71) p. 60-77; no. 9 (Spring 1971) p. 66-75; no. 10 (Summer 1971) p. 75-85; no. 11 (Fall 1971) p. 77-84; no. 12 (Winter 1971-72) p. 89-103; no. 13 (Spring 1972) p. 137-147; no. 14 (Summer 1972) p. 102-111; no. 15 (Autumn 1972) p. 96-103; no. 16 (Winter 1972-73) p. 83-93; no. 17 (Spring 1973) p. 80-89; no. 18 (Summer 1973) p. 90-100; no. 20 (Winter 1973-74) p. 94-109; no. 21 (Spring 1974) p. 62-71; no. 22 (Summer 1974) p. 89-95; no. 23 (Fall 1974) p. 69-77; no. 24 (Winter 1974-75) p. 102-109; no. 25 (Spring 1975) p. 143-152; no. 26 (Summer 1975) p. 78-91; no. 27 (Autumn 1975) p. 74-81; no. 28 (Winter 1975-76) p. 80-92; no. 29 (Spring 1976) p. 52-67; no. 30 (Summer 1976) p. 92-108; no. 31 (Autumn 1976) p. 83-95; no. 33 (Spring 1977) p. 58-79; no. 34 (Summer 1977) p. 71-87; no. 35 (Autumn 1977) p. 80-94; no. 36 (Winter 1977-78) p. 61-80; no. 37 (Spring 1978) p. 72-85; no. 38 (Summer 1978) p. 74-81; no. 39 (Autumn 1978) p. 75-85; no. 40 (Winter 1978-79) p. 92-103; no. 41 (Spring 1979) p. 70-86; no. 42 (Summer 1979) p. 72-85; no. 43 (Autumn 1979) p. 104-114; no. 44 (Winter 1979-80) p. 83-99; no. 45 (Spring 1980) p. 142-160; no. 46 (Summer 1980) p. 105-114; no. 47 (Autumn 1980) p. 94-102; no. 49 (Spring 1981) p. 104-126; no. 50 (Summer 1981) p. 79-94; no. 51 (Autumn 1981) p. 95-106; no. 53 (Spring 1982) p. 84-111; no. 54 (Summer

1982) p. 124-138.; ISSN: 0005-2949.
Note: Regular selected listing of books, articles, government publications on all subjects related to British Columbia.– Continued by Linda Louise Hale (Autumn 1982); Eve Szabo (Winter 1982-83-Autumn 1987); Melva J. Dwyer (Winter 1987-88-).
Location: AEU.

— 1986 —

0594 **Hale, Linda Louise**
Vancouver centennial bibliography: a project of the Vancouver Historical Society. [Vancouver]: Vancouver Historical Society, 1986. 4 vol. (xi, 1791 p.): ill., maps.; ISBN: 0-9692378-0-4 (set).
Note: 15,086 entries.– Books, pamphlets, broadsides, theses, periodical articles, films, recordings, microforms and machine-readable data files relating to Vancouver.– Covers from 1886 to 1985, with some earlier imprints, most important being ships' logs and published accounts of voyages of discovery.– Includes geographical studies, sociological surveys, geological papers, church histories, architectural designs, company reports, exhibition catalogues, musical scores.– Entries include notes and locations.– Cartobibliography by Frances M. Woodward.
Location: OONL.

0595 **Irvine, Susan; Rafferty, J. Pauline**
British Columbia Heritage Trust Student Employment Program: selected bibliography, 1982-1985. [Victoria]: British Columbia Heritage Trust, 1986. 36 p.: ill. (Information series / British Columbia Heritage Trust ; 1); ISBN: 0-7726-0427-4.
Note: 165 entries.– Annotated list of heritage reports.
Location: OONL.

— 1987 —

0596 **Szabo, Eve**
"Bibliography of British Columbia."
In: *BC Studies*; No. 56 (Winter 1982-83) p. 104-115; no. 58 (Summer 1983) p. 80-97; no. 59 (Autumn 1983) p. 74-83; no. 60 (Winter 1983-84) p. 87-98; no. 61 (Spring 1984) p. 97-109; no. 62 (Summer 1984) p. 81-88; no. 63 (Autumn 1984) p. 86-98; no. 64 (Winter 1984-85) p. 94-103; no. 65 (Spring 1985) p. 81-89; no. 66 (Summer 1985) p. 71-80; no. 67 (Autumn 1985) p. 79-86; no. 68 (Winter 1985-86) p. 77-85; no. 71 (Autumn 1986) p. 60-88; no. 72 (Winter 1986-87) p. 60-71; no. 73 (Spring 1987) p. 82-92; no. 74 (Summer 1987) p. 55-64; no. 75 (Autumn 1987) p. 78-89.; ISSN: 0005-2949.
Note: Regular select listing of books, articles, government publications on all subjects related to British Columbia.– Continues: Frances M. Woodward (Winter 1968-69-Summer 1982); Linda Louise Hale (Autumn 1982); continued by: Melva J. Dwyer (Winter 1987-88-).
Location: AEU.

— 1988 —

0597 **Knowlan, Anne McIntyre**
The Fraser Valley: a bibliography. Abbotsford, B.C.: Fraser Valley College, [c1988]. vi, 132 p.: ill.
Note: Approx. 1,000 entries.– Includes all published materials (books, government publications, magazine articles) held at Fraser Valley College or Fraser Valley Regional Library, as of December 1986, on history, geography, social and economic conditions, ethnic groups and cultural life of the Fraser Valley.
Location: OONL.

0598 **Lutz, John S.; Young, George**
The researcher's guide to British Columbia nineteenth
century directories: a bibliography & index. [Victoria,
B.C.]: Public History Group, University of Victoria, 1988.
162 p.; ISBN: 0-92127800-4.
Note: Approx. 140 entries.– Covers 1860-1900.– Place and
subject index.
Location: OONL.

— 1990 —

0599 **British Columbia. Ministry of Municipal Affairs,
Recreation and Culture**
Starting line-up: a directory of British Columbia writers
for public libraries. Victoria: Province of British
Columbia, Ministry of Municipal Affairs, Recreation and
Culture, [1990]. [59] l.: ill.
Note: Written and prepared by B.C. Bookworld.–
Includes bibliographical references.
Location: OONL.

0600 **Zilm, Glennis**
"Early books and printing in British Columbia."
In: *AB Bookman's Weekly*; Vol. 85, no. 9 (February 26,
1990) p. 837-845.; ISSN: 0001-0340.
Note: Bibliographic essay discusses British Columbia
imprints during the period 1858-1868.
Location: OONL.

— 1991 —

0601 **British Columbia. Ministry of International Business
and Immigration**
Immigration to British Columbia: a selected annotated
bibliography. Victoria: Province of British Columbia,
Ministry of International Business and Immigration,
1991. iii, 40 p.; ISBN: 0-77261-327-3.
Note: Co-published by the British Columbia Ministry of
Education.
Location: OONL.

0602 **Hale, Linda Louise; Barman, Jean**
British Columbia local histories: a bibliography. Victoria,
B.C.: British Columbia Heritage Trust, 1991. 196 p.: map.;
ISBN: 0-7718-9078-8.
Note: Listing of local histories for 889 different British
Columbia communities, from the nineteenth century to
1990: books, pamphlets, theses, special editions of
newspapers.– Excludes histories of churches and
schools.– All histories are given locations.
Location: OONL.

— 1992 —

0603 **Twigg, Alan**
Twigg's directory of 1001 B.C. writers. Victoria, B.C.:
Crown Publications, 1992. 194 p.: ill., ports.; ISBN: 0-
9696417-0-2.
Note: Listing of about 5,000 English-language works by
1,325 British Columbia writers.
Location: OONL.

0604 **Young, George; Lutz, John S.**
Researcher's guide to British Columbia directories, 1901-
1940: a bibliography & index. Victoria, B.C.: Public
History Group, University of Victoria, 1992. xviii, 255 p.;
ISBN: 0-921278-08-X.
Note: 212 entries.– Includes city and regional directories,
as well as professional, telephone, business, industry,
institutional and ethnic directories and social registers.
Location: OONL.

— 1993 —

0605 **Dwyer, Melva J.**
"Bibliography of British Columbia."
In: *BC Studies*; No. 76 (Winter 1987-88) p. 99-108; no. 77
(Spring 1988) p. 80-97; no. 78 (Summer 1988) p. 96-104;
no. 79 (Autumn 1988) p. 97-111; no. 80 (Winter 1988-
89) p. 85-96; no. 81 (Spring 1989) p. 97-117; no. 82
(Summer 1989) p. 83-98; no. 83 (Autumn 1989) p. 109-125;
no. 84 (Winter 1989-90) p. 117-134; no. 85 (Spring 1990) p.
77-90; no. 86 (Summer 1990) p. 93-108; no. 87 (Autumn
1990) p. 99-114; no. 88 (Winter 1990-91) p. 117-130; no. 90
(Summer 1991) p. 91-125; no. 91-92 (Autumn/Winter
1991-92) p. 235-261; no. 93 (Spring 1992) p. 94-108; no. 94
(Summer 1992) p. 97-107; no. 95 (Autumn 1992) p. 93-107;
no. 96 (Winter 1992-93) p. 129-142; no. 97 (Spring 1993) p.
90-103; no. 98 (Summer 1993) p. 113-127.; ISSN: 0005-2949.
Note: Regular select listing of books, articles,
government publications on all subjects related to British
Columbia.– Continues: Frances M. Woodward (Winter
1968-69-Summer 1982); Linda Louise Hale (Autumn
1982); Eve Szabo (Winter 1982-83-Autumn 1987).
Location: AEU.

— Ongoing/En cours —

0606 **Association of Book Publishers of British Columbia**
Books from British Columbia. Vancouver: The Associa-
tion, 1976-.   vol.; ISSN: 0823-8707.
Note: Annual.
Location: OONL.

— 1945 —

0607 **Dutilly, Arthème**
Bibliography of bibliographies on the Arctic. Washington, D.C.: Catholic University of America, 1945. 47 p. (Catholic University of America Department of Biology publication ; no. 1 B)
Note: Approx. 600 entries.
Location: OONL.

— 1947 —

0608 **Mitchell, Elaine Allan**
"Bibliography of the Canadian north."
In: *The new North-west*, edited by C.A. Dawson. Toronto: University of Toronto Press, 1947. P. 315-334.
Note: Location: OONL.

— 1949 —

0609 **Baird, P.D.**
"Expeditions to the Arctic."
In: *Beaver*; Outfit 279 (March 1949) p. 44-46; outfit 280 (June 1949) p. 41-44; outfit 280 (September 1949) p. 44-48.; ISSN: 0005-7517.
Note: Listing of various expeditions to the Canadian Arctic from 1000 to 1918 A.D.– Provides information about leader of expedition and other important members of the party, names of vessels, object of expedition, results and important discoveries.– Includes publications describing each expedition.
Location: AEU.

— 1958 —

0610 **Berton, Pierre**
A Klondike bibliography. [Kleinburg, Ont.]: 1958. 23 l.
Note: 229 entries.– Books, magazine articles dealing with the years 1896 to 1899, and relating to the gold discoveries on the Klondike watershed.– Includes entries on Yukon and Alaska history.
Location: OONL.

— 1962 —

0611 **Hanessian, John**
A select bibliography of the polar regions. New York: American Universities Field Staff, c1962. 30 p.
Note: Approx. 400 entries.– Lists works on polar regions in general, polar international law, internationalization of polar regions.– Specific references to Arctic and Antarctic regions, as well as a section on Canada and the North American Arctic.
Location: OONL.

— 1965 —

0612 **Arctic Institute of North America**
A selected reading list of books about the Arctic. Montreal: Arctic Institute of North America, 1965. 6 l.
Note: Location: OTU.

0613 **Hamelin, Louis-Edmond; Bussières, Aline**
Repertoire des travaux sur le nord publiés par le Centre d'études nordiques et l'Institut de géographie de l'Université Laval, 1953-1964. Québec: Université Laval, 1965. 42 f.: carte. (Centre d'études nordiques Travaux divers ; no 8)
Note: 176 entrées.– Ouvrages, thèses, rapports, articles, notes et recherches en cours en français et en anglais: sciences physiques et biologiques, science humaines, bibliographie, toponymie et cartographie, rapports administratifs et mémoires, nécrologie.
Localisation: QLB.

— 1967 —

0614 **Northern Co-ordination and Research Centre (Canada)**
A bibliography on the Canadian arctic. Ottawa: 1967. 10 p.
Note: Location: NBFU.

0615 **Stefansson Collection**
Dictionary catalog of the Stefansson Collection on the Polar regions in the Dartmouth College Library. Boston: G.K. Hall, 1967. 8 vol.
Note: Reproduction of card catalogue.– Emphasis on historical works, polar exploration.– Includes a substantial number of Canadian references.– "Represents the Stefansson Collection as of 1982."
Location: OONL.

— 1968 —

0616 **Arctic Institute of North America. Library**
Catalogue of the Library of the Arctic Institute of North America, Montreal. Boston: G.K. Hall, 1968. 4 vol.
Note: Approx. 34,000 entries.– Covers 1599 to 1968.– Includes books, pamphlets, theses, reprints, periodicals, microfilms, audio recordings, phonograph records dealing with arctic and subarctic in broadest terms: cold weather conditions, snow and ice studies, applied and basic research in the physical, biological and social sciences, ecology, oil and gas pipelines, native land claims, northern engineering problems.– Most publications in English language: many in Russian, Scandinavian languages, French, German, Japanese.
Supplements:
... : first supplement. 1971. 902 p.– Approx. 4,700 entries.
... : second supplement. 1974. 2 vol.; ISBN: 0-8161-1030-1.– Approx. 4,500 entries.
Catalogue of the Library of the Arctic Institute of North America, Calgary: third supplement. 1980. 3 vol.; ISBN: 0-8161-1162-6.– Approx. 1,200 entries.
Location: OONL.

— 1969 —

0617 **Jones, Mary Jane**
Bibliographie sur le delta du Mackenzie. Ottawa: Imprimeur de la Reine et contrôleur de la papeterie, 1969. xiii, 108 p.: ill., carte. (Travaux de recherches sur le delta du Mackenzie ; 6)
Note: 478 entrées.– Livres, publications officielles, thèses, articles de périodiques, rapports d'expéditions.
English title: *Mackenzie Delta bibliography.*
Localisation: OONL.

0618 **Jones, Mary Jane**
Mackenzie Delta bibliography. Ottawa: Queen's Printer and Controller of Stationery, 1969. xiii, 119 p.: map. (Mackenzie Delta research project ; 6)
Note: 478 entries.– Books, periodical articles, official publications, theses, expedition and research reports.– *Arctic bibliography* numbers provided.
Titre en français: *Bibliographie sur le delta du Mackenzie.*
Location: OONL.

— 1970 —
0619 **Corley, Nora T.; Coulter, K.; Anand, T.**
A selected bibliography on S.W. Devon Island (Radstock Bay and Maxwell Bay areas). Montreal: Arctic Institute of North America, 1970. [50] l.: map.
Note: 50 entries.– Topics include ice conditions, meteorology, geography, navigation, biology, geology, oceanography.
Location: QMAI.

0620 **Mid-Canada bibliography.** [Toronto: Maclean-Hunter, 1970]. 141 l. (in various foliations).
Note: Books, articles, government studies and reports relating to northern Canada: general references (development, environment, resources, future prospects); human resources (living conditions in the north, anthropology, northern administration, socio-economic features); natural resources (atmosphere, land, water, flora and fauna, underground); industrialization; urbanization; transportation; trade and finance.
Location: OOP.

0621 **University of Manitoba. Center for Settlement Studies**
Bibliography: resource frontier communities. [Winnipeg]: Center for Settlement Studies, University of Manitoba, 1969-1970. 3 vol.
Note: 1,541 entries.– Government publications, corporate documents, newspaper and periodical articles, monographs, consultant's reports, conference proceedings.– Vol. 1 concentrates on Manitoba, Vol. 2 covers northern Canada in general with the focus on the Northwest Territories, Vol. 3 provides a complete list of holdings of Center for Settlement Studies to 1970.
Location: OONL.

— 1971 —
0622 **Connor, Sylvia**
"Books of our northern North."
In: *British Columbia Library Quarterly*; Vol. 34, no. 2-3 (October 1970-January 1971) p. 22-24.; ISSN: 0007-053X.
Note: Location: OONL.

0623 **Université Laval. Centre d'étude nordiques**
Une décennie de recherches au Centre d'études nordiques, 1961-1970: résumés des principaux travaux publiés et manuscrits. Québec: Université Laval, 1971. 113 f. (Centre d'études nordiques Collection bibliographie ; no 4)
Note: Principaux thèmes: sciences de l'atmosphère, sciences de la terre et des eaux, sciences biologiques, sciences humaines (anthropologie, ethnographie, géographie, histoire, archéologie).
Localisation: OONL.

— 1973 —
0624 **Corley, Nora T.**
A bibliography of expeditions to the Canadian Arctic 1576 to 1966: with special emphasis on the classics of Canadian exploration. Ottawa: Arctic Institute of North America, 1973. [100] l.
Note: "Lists 328 expeditions of which 82 have accounts, totalling 184 books that can be classified as classics."-Covers expeditions to the areas of Canada north of 60.– Excludes northern Quebec and Labrador.– Expeditions listed in chronological order, with alphabetical index.
Location: OONL.

— 1974 —
0625 **Bollinger, Irene**
Northern development: people, resources, ecology, and transportation in the Yukon and the Northwest Territories: a bibliography of government publications with selected annotations. Monticello, Ill.: Council of Planning Librarians, 1974. 13 p. (Council of Planning Librarians Exchange bibliography ; 643)
Note: Approx. 75 entries.
Location: OONL.

0626 **Caron, Fabien; Bouchard, Jacqueline**
Bibliographie des travaux du Centre d'études nordiques. Québec: Université Laval, 1974. 26 l.
Note: 180 entrées.– Travaux et documents, Nordicana (travaux divers), bibliographie, articles scientifiques, cartes/croquis/tableaux, manuscrits scientifiques/rapports/thèses, documents administratifs et informatifs, notes et documents de cours, matériel audio-visuel.
Localisation: QQE.

— 1975 —
0627 **Arctic bibliography.** Montreal: McGill-Queen's University Press, 1953-1975. 16 vol.: folded col. maps.; ISSN: 0066-6947.
Note: Multi-lingual, multi-national bibliography of material pertaining to the Arctic, with small majority relating to Canadian Arctic.– 16 volumes comprise titles and English abstracts of 108,723 books and papers, published in 40 languages, in the fields of science, technology and the arts, with Canadian and U.S. library locations.– Authors list with subjects-geographic index.– Imprint varies: 1953-1965, Washington: Department of Defense.– Vol. 1-14 (1953-1969), edited by Marie Tremaine; vol. 15-16 (1971-1975), edited by Maret Martna. Microform: Ann Arbor, Mich.: University Microfilms, 1975. 8 microfilm reels.; ISSN: 0570-7307.
Location: OONL.

— 1976 —
0628 **Henley, Thomas J.; Eyler, Phillip L.**
Hudson Bay Lowlands bibliography. Winnipeg: Natural Resource Institute, University of Manitoba, 1976. ix, 82 p., [1] l. of pl.: ill., maps.
Note: Select listing of annotated references on lowlands west of Hudson Bay stretching from Chesterfield Inlet in the north to Nottaway River at bottom of James Bay.– Includes studies on geography, geology, climate, soils, flora and fauna, economic development, transportation, energy, parks and tourism, history, native peoples.
Location: AEUB.

0629 **Lanari, Robert**
Northwest Territories community bibliography/Bibliographie par communauté Territoires du Nord-Ouest. Ottawa: Indian and Northern Affairs, 1976. 79 p.: map (folded).; ISBN: 0-662-00263-6.
Note: Books, periodical articles, government publications related to the history, demography, social, economic and cultural organization of the Northwest Territories.– Sixty-

nine communities are represented.– Includes English and
French-language publications.
Location: OONL.

0630 **McGill University. Centre for Northern Studies and
Research**
Bibliography of McGill northern research, 1887-1975.
Montreal: Centre for Northern Studies and Research,
McGill University, 1976. iv, 92 p.: folded col. map.
(Information series / Centre for Northern Studies and
Research, McGill University ; no. 1; ISSN: 0709-6364)
Note: 1,504 numbered entries, plus a list of about 250
McGill theses relating to the North.– Alphabetic author
listing of all publications about the North written by
persons associated with McGill: staff, graduate students,
members of university-sponsored expeditions, etc. in 131
subject categories ranging from Administration and
Government, Geotechnical engineering, to Sea ice and
Wildlife conservation.– Provides *Arctic bibliography*
numbers.– Index: *Bibliography of McGill northern research:
index to subjects and regions.* [Montreal]: Centre for
Northern Studies and Research, McGill University; 1977.
i, 16 p.
Supplement: 1977. 16 p.– Includes a list of McGill
graduate theses relating to the North for 1973-1976.
Location: OONL.

0631 **Symons, I.J.**
Northern development in Canada: the impact of change:
economic, social, transportation and environmental: a
bibliography. [Ottawa]: Lands Directorate, Environment
Canada, 1976. ii, 124 l.
Note: Approx. 500 entries.– Includes books, research
papers, periodical articles, governmental papers,
proceedings, consultants' reports, theses.– Arranged in
geographic units, territories and provinces, and further
subdivided into four thematic sections: growth pole/
region impact (impact of economic activity produced by
growth point such as a mine, hydro development, etc.);
environmental impact; transportation impact; social
impact.
Location: OONL.

— 1977 —

0632 **Castonguay, Rachelle; Lanari, Robert**
Socio-economic impact studies relating to pipeline
projects and certain northern development projects:
bibliography/Études d'impact socio-économique
relatives à des projets de pipeline et à certains projets de
developpement nordique: bibliographie. Ottawa:
Northern Research Division, Department of Indian
Affairs and Northern Development, 1977. 27 l.
Note: Approx. 200 entries.– Text in English and French in
parallel columns/texte en français et en anglais sur des
col. parallèles.
Location: OORD.

0633 **Friesen, Richard J.**
The Chilkoot: a literature review. Ottawa: National
Historic Sites Service, Department of Indian Affairs and
Northern Development, 1977. iv, 111 p.: ill. (Manuscript
report / National Historic Parks and Sites Branch ; 203)
Note: Location: OONL.

0634 **Friesen, Richard J.**
The Chilkoot Pass: a preliminary bibliography. [Ottawa]:
National Historic Parks and Sites Branch, Parks Canada,
1977. 36 p. (National Historic Parks and Sites Branch

Research bulletin ; no. 50)
Note: Approx. 350 entries.– Books, magazine articles,
pamphlets, government documents written from 1890s
to 1970s on aspects of history of Chilkoot Pass, White
Pass and environs, designed to form basis of
historiographical essay on Chilkoot Pass, a component of
proposed International Gold Rush Park.
Location: OONL.

— 1978 —

0635 **Clancy, Peter**
Northern Canada bibliography. Kingston, Ont.: Centre
for International Relations, Northern Studies
Programme, Queen's University, 1978. 99 p.
Note: Approx. 1,600 entries.– Books, journal articles,
government publications, area economic surveys, theses
and dissertations.– Deals mainly with policy areas of
political and economic development, education, housing,
environment and land use, communications and
transportation, justice and legal, sovereignty and
security.– General sections covering history and
biography, social studies.
Location: OONL.

0636 **Cooke, Alan; Holland, Clive**
"Bibliography [Northern exploration]."
In: *The exploration of northern Canada: 500 to 1920, a
chronology.* Toronto: Arctic History Press, c1978. P. 447-
505.; ISBN: 0-7710-2265-4.
Note: Location: OONL.

— 1979 —

0637 **Yukon land and resource inventory: bibliographic
index.** Whitehorse, Y.T.: Government of Yukon, 1979. 1
vol. (in various pagings).
Note: Approx. 3,500 entries.– Contains references to
published and unpublished research data on Yukon
meteorology, hydrology, geology, pedology,
demography, non-renewable resources, renewable
resources.– Map listings refer to: *Yukon land and resource
inventory atlas.*
Location: OONL.

— 1980 —

0638 **Canada. Archives publiques. Division des archives
fédérales**
Documents pour l'étude du Nord canadien. Ottawa:
Archives publiques Canada, 1980. 24, 21 p.; ISBN: 0-662-
50848-3.
Note: Texte en français et en anglais disposé tête-bêche.–
Titre de la p. de t. additionnelle: *Sources for the study of the
Canadian North.*– Comp. par Terry Cook.
Localisation: OONL.

0639 **Canada. Public Archives. Federal Archives Division**
Sources for the study of the Canadian North. Ottawa:
Public Archives Canada, 1980. 21, 24 p.; ISBN: 0-662-
50848-3.
Note: Text in English and French with French text on
inverted pages.– Title of additional title-page: *Documents
pour l'étude du Nord canadien.*– Compiled by Terry Cook.
Location: OONL.

— 1981 —

0640 **Millar, J.F.V.; Ervin, Alexander M.**
A status report and bibliography of cultural studies in
the Canadian Arctic to 1976. Saskatoon: Institute for
Northern Studies, University of Saskatchewan, 1981.
113 p.: graphs.

Note: 1,489 entries.– Covers from 1744 to 1976.– References primarily in English pertaining to the Canadian Arctic, dealing with human conditions, social behaviour and values.– Includes material from the disciplines of anthropology, education, economics, psychology, history, geography, public health sciences.
Location: AEU.

— 1983 —

0641   **De la Barre, Kenneth; Harvey, Denise; Legat, Allice**
A bibliography on labour, employment and training in the Canadian North: some important issues/ Bibliographie sur la main d'oeuvre, l'emploi et la formation dans le Nord canadien: aspects majeurs de la question. Montréal: Committee on Northern Population Research: Comité de recherche sur les populations nordiques, c1983. xv, 106 p. (ASTIS occasional publication / Arctic Science and Technology Information System ; no. 8; ISSN: 0225-5170); ISBN: 2-920393-02-2.
Note: 495 entries.– Books, documents, journal articles describing the economic impact of large energy and mineral extraction projects as they affect training and employment of northerners.
Location: OONL.

0642   **Slavin, Suzy M.**
Polar regions: a guide to reference sources. Montreal: McLennan Library, Reference Department, McGill University, 1983. 12 p.; ISBN: 0-7717-0105-5.
Note: Approx. 75 entries.– Focus on literature of social sciences as it relates to the Canadian north.
Location: OONL.

— 1984 —

0643   **Brown, M.P. Sharon**
Eastern Arctic Study: annotated bibliography. Kingston, Ont.: Centre for Resource Studies, Queen's University, [c1984]. iv, 69 p.; ISBN: 0-88757-043-7.
Note: Approx. 500 entries.– Documents collected during course of research related to Eastern Arctic Study, the purpose of which was to examine potential impact of Inuit land claim settlements and constitutional changes in NWT on both local government and regulation of mineral industries.
Location: OONL.

0644   **Goodwin, C. Ross; Howard, Lynne M.**
The Beaufort Sea, Mackenzie delta, Mackenzie valley, and northern Yukon: a bibliographical review. Ottawa: Arctic Science and Technology Information System, 1984. v, 310 p.: map.
Note: 1,547 entries.– Coverage of documents in ASTIS database from mid-1970s to August, 1984.– Topics include geology, geography, oceanography, land use, native peoples, history, ecology, communications and transportation, petroleum, natural gas and pipelines.– Includes journal articles, scientific papers, government documents, theses, symposium proceedings.– Prepared for the Office of the Northern Research and Science Advisor, DIAND, by the Arctic Science and Technology Information System, the Arctic Institute of North America, University of Calgary.
Location: OONL.

0645   **Howard, Lynne M.**
Issues of public interest regarding northern development [microform]: an annotated bibliography. Calgary: Pallister Resource Management Ltd., 1984. 8 microfiches (451 fr.).
Note: Listing of government documents, contributions to periodicals and conference proceedings, reports of research in progress, impact assessments, published and unpublished books, pamphlets and reports dating from about 1970 to 1984.– Geographical areas covered: western Arctic, Arctic islands, Northwest Passage, eastern Arctic, including Labrador and Greenland.– Topics include land and resources, employment, political economy and land claims, development, environmental impact assessment, northern populations, northern economics, health, culture, resource industries.– Includes a list of additional bibliographies.
Location: OONL.

0646   **Minion, Robin**
Land use in northern Canada and Alaska. Edmonton: Boreal Institute for Northern Studies, University of Alberta, 1984. 67 p. (Boreal Institute for Northern Studies Bibliographic series ; no. 2; ISSN: 0824-8192); ISBN: 0-919058-36-1.
Note: 161 entries.– Series contains monographs, theses, government documents, consultants' reports, conference proceedings, children's publications, microforms.– BINS series produced monthly from January 1984 to May 1986 (no. 29).– Online access: *Boreal Northern Titles (BNT)*, available through QL Systems Limited.
Location: OONL.

0647   **Minion, Robin**
Nineteenth century expeditions in the Arctic and Canada. Edmonton: Boreal Institute for Northern Studies, University of Alberta, 1984. 98 p. (Boreal Institute for Northern Studies Bibliographic series ; no. 4; ISSN: 0824-8192); ISBN: 0-919058-38-8.
Note: 255 entries.– Covers from 1977 to 1984, with the addition of more important older material.– Compiled from *BOREAL, The Northern Database*, includes monographs, theses, government documents.– BINS series produced monthly from January 1984 to May 1986 (no. 29).– Includes an index to expedition leaders and ships.– Online access: *Boreal Northern Titles (BNT)*, available through QL Systems Limited.
Location: OONL.

— 1985 —

0648   **Bergeron, Raymond**
Bibliographical listing of studies conducted or supported by the Northern Affairs Program, Department of Indian Affairs and Northern Development, 1973-1984/Liste bibliographique des études effectuées ou appuyées par le Programme des affaires du Nord, Ministère des affaires indiennes et du Nord canadien. Ottawa: Indian and Northern Affairs Canada, 1985. ii, 203 p.
Note: Listing of northern studies relating to socio-economic concerns, renewable resources and environmental concerns, cultural topics, Arctic Land Use Research Program, Environmental-social Program, Northern pipelines, Eastern Arctic Marine Environmental Studies Program, Lancaster Sound regional study.– Text in English and French/texte en français et en anglais.
Location: OONL.

0649   **Bergeron, Raymond; Guimont, Pierre**
Ten years of northern research in Canada, 1974-1984/Dix ans de recherche nordique au Canada, 1974-1984. Ottawa: Indian and Northern Affairs Canada, 1985. 1 vol.

(115+ pages); ISBN: 0-662-54065-4.

Note: 5,324 entries.– Research papers and studies relevant to the Canadian north supported by the federal government.– Focuses on research projects selected from lists of awards, grants and scholarships of the federal granting councils and federal research contracts.– Grouped under 75 headings which correspond to research themes within four major areas of research: physical environment, biological environment, ecological environment, man-made environment.

Location: OONL.

0650 **Minion, Robin**
Hydroelectric development in northern regions. Edmonton: Boreal Institute for Northern Studies, University of Alberta, 1985. 78 p. (Boreal Institute for Northern Studies Bibliographic series ; no. 21; ISSN: 0824-8192); ISBN: 0-919058-55-8.

Note: 189 entries.– Series contains monographs, theses, government documents, consultants' reports, children's books, conference proceedings, microforms on topics related to northern environment and people.– BINS series produced monthly from January 1984 to May 1986 (no. 29).– Online access: *Boreal Northern Titles (BNT)*, available through QL Systems Limited.

Location: OONL.

— 1986 —

0651 **Andrews, Martha**
List of publications, 1968-1985: Institute of Arctic and Alpine Research. Boulder, Colo.: Institute of Arctic and Alpine Research, University of Colorado, 1986. iv, 97 p. (Institute of Arctic and Alpine Research Occasional paper ; no. 42; ISSN: 0069-6145)

Note: 901 entries.– Listing of published research undertaken by members and associates of the Institute of Arctic and Alpine Research.– Covers arctic and alpine areas worldwide, concentrating on Alaska, Arctic Canada, Colorado Rocky Mountains and related palaeoenvironments.– Chronological arrangement with author index.

Location: OOFF.

0652 **Cameron, Nancy P.**
Yukon economic planning studies, 1965-1985: an annotated bibliography. Whitehorse: Yukon Archives, 1986. vii, 317 p.

Note: 450 entries.– Books, government and consultant reports, theses, articles, published and unpublished, dealing with Yukon economic planning in the areas of agriculture, fisheries, community and regional development, hunting and trapping, hydrocarbon development, electric power, mining, tourism and outdoor recreation, transportation.
Supplement: Krangle, Wynne; Long, Peter. ... , *1986-1992: an annotated bibliography*. Yukon Economic Development, 1992. 68 p.: map.; 1-55018-524-1.– 329 entries.

Location: OONL.

0653 **Minion, Robin**
Biographies – Canada. Edmonton: Boreal Institute for Northern Studies, University of Alberta, 1986. 122 p. (Boreal Institute for Northern Studies Bibliographic series ; no. 25; ISSN: 0824-8192)

Note: 344 entries.– Series contains monographs, theses, government documents, consultants' reports, children's books, conference proceedings, microforms on topics related to northern environment and people.– This volume is a listing of biographies of persons connected with the Arctic and the north in general.– Excludes native artists, which are covered in a volume in this series entitled *Inuit art and artists*.– BINS series produced monthly from January 1984 to May 1986 (no. 29).– Online access: *Boreal Northern Titles (BNT)*, available through QL Systems Limited.

Location: OONL.

0654 **Minion, Robin; Saffran, Marion A.**
20th century Canadian Arctic expeditions. Edmonton: Boreal Institute for Northern Studies, University of Alberta, 1986. 116 p. (Boreal Institute for Northern Studies Bibliographic series ; no. 29; ISSN: 0824-8192); ISBN: 0-919058-64-7.

Note: 304 entries.– Series contains monographs, theses, government documents, consultants' reports, children's books, conference proceedings, microforms on topics related to northern environment and people.– This volume includes citations from the Scott Polar Research Institute, Cambridge, England.– BINS series produced monthly from January 1984 to May 1986 (no. 29).– Online access: *Boreal Northern Titles (BNT)*, available through QL Systems Limited.

Location: OONL.

— 1987 —

0655 **Adams, W. Peter**
Field research on Axel Heiberg Island, N.W.T., Canada: bibliographies and data reports. Montreal: Centre for Northern Studies and Research, McGill University, 1987. i, 207 p.: ill., maps. (McGill Subarctic Research paper ; no. 41; ISSN: 0076-1982) (McGill Axel Heiberg research report, Miscellaneous paper ; no. 2) (Trent University Department of Geography Occasional paper ; no. 12)

Note: *Axel Heiberg Island bibliography*, compiled by C. Simon L. Ommanney, located on pages 5-55, contains a listing of approximately 650 documents published about the island since the period of modern exploration and study which commenced in the late 1950s.– Includes grey literature, popular items from books and newspapers, and a list of maps produced in connection with the research projects.

Location: OONL.

0656 **Yukon bibliography.** Edmonton: Boreal Institute for Northern Studies, University of Alberta, 1964-1987. 11 vol.

Note: Preliminary edition, compiled by James Lotz.– Ottawa: Northern Co-ordination and Research Centre, 1964. vii, 155 p. (Yukon Research Project series ; no. 1).– Approx. 2,000 entries.– Includes books, periodical articles, government and industrial reports, theses.– Excludes maps, newspaper articles, air-photos, films and other non-book materials.– Geographically, limited to present boundaries of the Territory.– Arranged in broad subject groupings: agriculture, economic development, history, etc.– Supplementary issues contain indexes: author, subject, place names.– Provides *Arctic bibliography* numbers.
Supplements:
Hemstock, C. Anne; Cooke, Geraldine A. ... . *Update 1963-1970.* 1973. ix, 420 p. (Occasional publication (Boreal Institute for Northern Studies) ; no. 8-1; ISSN: 0068-0303)
Hemstock, C. Anne. ... . *Update to 1973.* 1975. x, 384 p.

(Occasional publication (Boreal Institute for Northern Studies) ; no. 8-2; ISSN: 0068-0303). Covers 1971-1973.– 655 entries.

Ridge, Marian F.; Cooke, Geraldine A. ... . *Update to 1975.* 1977. xi, 408 p. (Occasional publication (Boreal Institute for Northern Studies) ; no. 8-3; ISSN: 0068-0303). Covers 1974-1975.– 685 entries.

Thomas, Heather L. ... . *Update to 1977.* 1978. x, 476 p.; ISBN: 0-919058-15-9. (Occasional publication (Boreal Institute for Northern Studies) ; no. 8-4; ISSN: 0068-0303). Covers 1976-1977.– 756 entries.

Singh, Irina G. ... . *Update to 1979.* 1980-1981. 2 vol.; ISBN: 0-919058-18-3 (Part 1); 0-919058-19-1 (Part 2). (Occasional publication (Boreal Institute for Northern Studies) ; no. 8-5; 8-6; ISSN: 0068-0303). Covers 1978-1979.– 895 entries (Part 1), 320 entries (Part 2).

Singh, Irina G. ... . *Update to 1980.* 1982. x, 231 p.; ISBN: 0-919058-21-2. (Occasional publication (Boreal Institute for Northern Studies) ; no. 8-7; ISSN: 0068-0303). Covers 1980.– 300 entries.

Singh, Irina G. ... . *Update to 1981.* 1983. x, 306 p.; ISBN: 0-919058-25-6. (Occasional publication (Boreal Institute for Northern Studies) ; no. 8-8; ISSN: 0068-0303). Covers 1981.– 405 entries.

Singh, Irina G.; McPherson, Lynn. ... . *Update to 1982.* 1984. x, 398 p.; ISBN: 0-919058-28-0. (Occasional publication (Boreal Institute for Northern Studies) ; no. 8-11; ISSN: 0068-0303). Covers 1982.– 462 entries.

Singh, Irina G.; Pope, Lois. ... . *Update to 1983.* 1986. x p., 431 col.; ISBN: 0-919058-31-0. (Occasional publication (Boreal Institute for Northern Studies) ; no. 8-12; ISSN: 0068-0303). Covers 1983.– 573 entries.

Saffran, Marion A., et al. ... . *Update to 1984.* 1987. x p., 337 col.; ISBN: 0-919058-63-9. (Occasional publication (Boreal Institute for Northern Studies) ; no. 8-13; ISSN: 0068-0303). Covers 1984.– 516 entries.

Indexes:

Cumulated author index to 1980. Compiled by Janet MacDonald. 1983. vi, 167 p.; ISBN: 0-919058-26-4. (Occasional publication (Boreal Institute for Northern Studies) ; no. 8-9; ISSN: 0068-0303).

Cumulated subject index to 1980. Compiled by Janet MacDonald. 1983. vi, 153 p.; ISBN: 0-919058-27-2. (Occasional publication (Boreal Institute for Northern Studies) ; no. 8-10; ISSN: 0068-0303).

Location: OONL.

— 1988 —

0657 **Dobrowolsky, Helen**
Fort Selkirk bibliography: a listing of sources for Fort Selkirk and the Yukon field force found in Yukon Archives & elsewhere. Whitehorse: Yukon Tourism, Heritage Branch, 1988. ii, 32 p.
Note: Books, articles, pamphlets, corporate records, films & videos, government records, manuscripts and photographs, maps, tape recordings, anthropological and archaeological reports.
Location: OONL.

— 1989 —

0658 **King, Harold Godfrey Rudolf**
The Arctic. Oxford: Clio Press, c1989. xvi, 272, [3] p.: map. (World bibliographical series / Clio Press ; 99); ISBN: 1-85109-072-X.
Note: 935 entries.– Mainly books, monographs,

government publications.– Excludes newspaper articles, ephemera.– Topics covered include geography, flora and fauna, prehistory and archaeology, history, biographies of arctic explorers, philately, languages, religion, arctic in international law, science policy and programs, environment, literature, native arts, sports and recreation.
Location: OONL.

0659 **Pretes, Michael**
Sustainable development and the entrepreneur: an annotated bibliography of small business development in circumpolar and developing regions. Whitehorse: Department of Economic Development, Mines and Small Business, Government of the Yukon, 1989. vii, 52 l.
Note: Approx. 350 entries.– References dealing with sustainable development in practice, in particular with the role of the entrepreneur and small-scale development initiatives with emphasis on northern Canada, arranged in seven subject groups: agriculture, business and entrepreneurship, fisheries, forestry, tourism and wildlife.
Location: OONL.

— 1990 —

0660 **Andrews, Martha**
"Computerized information retrieval and bibliographic control of the polar and-or cold regions literature: a review."
In: *Bulletin (Special Libraries Association, Geography and Map Division)*; No. 159 (March 1990) p. 21-42.; ISSN: 0036-1607.
Note: Describes online reference services, bibliographic utilities, CD-ROM, electronic networks for access and control of polar and cold-regions literature.– Includes a bibliography.– Many Canadian references.
Location: OOG.

— 1992 —

0661 **Amor, Norman L.**
Beyond the Arctic Circle: materials on Arctic explorations and travels since 1750 in the Special Collections and University Archives Division of the University of British Columbia Library. Vancouver: University of British Columbia Library, 1992. 36 p.: ill., maps. (Occasional publication / University of British Columbia Library, Special Collections and University Archives Division ; no. 1); ISBN: 0-88865-196-1.
Note: Location: OONL.

— 1993 —

0662 **Yukon Archives**
Alaska Highway, 1942-1991: a comprehensive bibliography of material available in the Yukon Archives & MacBride Museum. Whitehorse: Yukon Education, Libraries and Archives Branch, [1993]. iv, 83 p.: ill., map.; ISBN: 1-55018-558-6.
Note: Approx. 500 entries.– Books, pamphlets, recordings, films and videos, manuscripts, maps and plans.
Location: OONL.

— Ongoing/En cours —

0663 **Arctic Science and Technology Information System**
ASTIS bibliography [microform]. Calgary: Arctic Institute of North America, 1979-. microfiches (& 9 l. introductory notes); ISSN: 0226-1685.
Note: Annual.– Interdisciplinary bibliography on the North: books, serials, articles, theses, conference

proceedings, research reports: natural and social sciences, humanities, technology.– Emphasis on Canadian Arctic.– Each issue is cumulative, including all entries in ASTIS database from May 1978 to present year.– Provides abstracts, locations.– Annual list is updated by *ASTIS current awareness bulletin.*

ASTIS database available online through QL Systems, 1978 to present.

CD ROM: available as part of *Arctic and Antarctic regions.* Baltimore, Md.: National Information Services, 1989-   , updated semi-annually.

Not available in print format.

Location: OONL.

0664 **Northern Political Studies (Program)**
Northern politics review: an annual publication of Northern Political Studies Program. Calgary: University of Calgary, 1984-. vol.; ISSN: 0823-9576.

Note: Annual.– Government publications, native organization documents, research institute studies and reports, petroleum industry documents.– Surveys political, social and economic issues: constitutional development and aboriginal rights, fiscal issues, oil and gas, environmental protection and land use, communications, transport and utilities, defence and foreign relations, circumpolar affairs.– Appendix lists comprehensive reference works and other sources.

Location: OONL.

0665 **Northern titles: KWIC index.** Edmonton: Boreal Institute for Northern Studies, University of Alberta, 1973-.   vol.; ISSN: 0704-6839.

Note: Listing in KWIC index permutation format of English-language titles of articles in journals, newspapers and government documents received by the Library of the Boreal Institute for Northern Studies, since 1991 reconstituted as the Canadian Circumpolar Institute.– Emphasis on northern regions of North America and native peoples.

Available online: *BNT-Boreal Northern Titles,* through QL Systems, iNet 2000, updated monthly.

Location: OONL.

Arts and Humanities

Arts et sciences humaines

Arts and Design

Arts et conception

— 1938 —

0666 **Harding, Anne D.; Bolling, Patricia**
Bibliography of articles and papers on North American Indian art. Washington: United States Department of the Interior, Indian Arts and Crafts Board, 1938. 365 p.
Note: Approx. 1,500 entries.– Articles and papers on Indian arts and crafts: basketry, weaving, stone, wood work, ceremonial, masks, painting, pottery.– Substantial listings on Mackenzie delta and Northwest Coast.
Reprint: New York: Kraus Reprint, 1969. 365 p.
Location: OONL.

— 1958 —

0667 **Dwyer, Melva J.**
A selected list of books and periodicals on industrial design. Vancouver, B.C.: University of British Columbia Library, 1958. 12 l. (Reference publication / University of British Columbia Library ; no. 13)
Note: Location: OONL.

— 1964 —

0668 **Martijn, Charles A.**
"Canadian Eskimo carving in historical perspective: bibliography."
In: *Anthropos*; Vol. 59 (1964) p. 584-596.; ISSN: 0003-5572.
Note: Location: OONMM.

— 1966 —

0669 **Pantazzi, Sybille**
"Book illustration and design by Canadian artists 1890-1940, with a list of books illustrated by members of the Group of Seven."
In: *Bulletin (National Gallery of Canada)*; Vol. 4, no. 1 (1966) p. 6-24: ill., facsims.; ISSN: 0027-9323.
Note: Location: OONL.

— 1967 —

0670 **National Gallery of Canada. Library**
Canadiana in the library of the National Gallery of Canada/Canadiana dans la bibliothèque de la Galerie nationale du Canada. Ottawa: The Gallery, 1967. [294] p.
Note: Photocopy of catalogue cards in the shelf list of the Canadian collection, with added subject key, and author and artist indexes.– Text in English and French/texte en français et en anglais.
Previous edition: *Canadian collection, author catalogue.* 1965. 1 vol. (unpaged).
Supplements:
... : *supplement 1968/... : supplément 1968.* 1968. v l., 98 p.
... : *second supplement/... : deuxième supplément.* 1969. vi l., [64] p.
... : *third supplement/... : troisième supplément.* 1970. vi l., 88 p.
... : *fourth supplement/... : quatrième supplément.* 1971. vi l., 147 p.
... : *fifth supplement/... : cinquième supplément.* 1973. vi l., 265 p.
... : *sixth supplement and cumulative indexes/... : sixième supplément et tables récapitulatives.* 1974. vi l., 248 p.

Location: OONL.

0671 **"A selected bibliography of literature relative to Eskimo art."**
In: *Beaver*; Outfit 298, no. 2 (Autumn 1967) p. 95-98.; ISSN: 0005-7517.
Note: Location: AEU.

— 1968 —

0672 **Mayrand, Pierre**
Sources de l'art en Nouvelle-France. Québec: [s.n.], 1968. 36 p., [6] f.
Note: Localisation: QQLA.

— 1970 —

0673 **Wardwell, Allen; Lebov, Lois**
Annotated bibliography of Northwest Coast Indian art. New York: Library, Museum of Primitive Art, 1970. 25 p. (Primitive art bibliographies / Museum of Primitive Art Library ; no. 8)
Note: 452 entries.– References to art produced by Tlingit, Tsimshian, Haida, Bella Coola, Kwakiutl and Nootka tribes in the coastal regions of British Columbia and Washington State.
Location: OONL.

— 1971 —

0674 **Reid, Dennis**
A bibliography of the Group of Seven. Ottawa: National Gallery of Canada, 1971. 89 p.
Note: Approx. 1,600 entries.
Location: OONL.

— 1972 —

0675 **Lebel, Maurice**
Bibliographie des ouvrages publiés avec le concours du Conseil canadien de recherches sur les humanités et du Conseil des arts du Canada, 1947-1971. Ottawa: Conseil canadien de recherches sur les humanités, 1972. 45 p.
Note: 320 entrées.
Localisation: OONL.

0676 **Saskatchewan Provincial Library. Bibliographic Services Division**
Art and architecture. Regina: The Library, 1972. 93 p.
Note: Location: OONL.

— 1973 —

0677 **National Gallery of Canada. Library**
Catalogue of the Library of the National Gallery of Canada, Ottawa, Ontario/[Catalogue de la Bibliothèque de la Galerie nationale du Canada, Ottawa, Ontario]. Boston: G.K. Hall, 1973. 8 vol.; ISBN: 0-8161-1043-3.
Note: Monographs on artists, reports and bulletins of art museums and societies, catalogues of individual artists' shows and group exhibitions, catalogue of permanent collections of Canadian galleries and private holdings, offprints of periodical articles on art in Canada, art auction records, books and calendars illustrated by Canadian artists, materials on decorative arts, photography, architecture, works of fiction and poetry collected for their illustrations.

Supplement: 1981. 6 vol.; ISBN: 0-8161-0291-0.
Location. OONL.

— 1974 —

0678 **Drolet, Gaëtan**
Bibliographie sur la sculpture québécoise. [Montréal]:
École de bibliothéconomie, Université de Montréal, 1974.
28 f.
Note: 267 entrées.– Livres, articles de périodiques et
journaux, publications gouvernementales, catalogues
d'expositions, diapositives, films.
Localisation: OONL.

0679 **York University (Toronto, Ont.). Programme in Arts
Administration**
A selective bibliography of Canadian and international
readings in arts administration and cultural development. [Toronto]: Canadian Conference of the Arts, 1974.
24 l.
Note: Approx. 480 entries.– Selective list of works
concerned with problems related to administration of the
arts, education and the arts, the economics and financing
of cultural activity, government and the arts and the
formulation and implementation of cultural policy.–
Includes special studies, research reports, policy papers.–
Prepared by the Programme in Arts Administration at
York University at the request of the Canadian
Conference of the Arts.
Location: OONL.

— 1975 —

0680 **Bradley, Ian L.**
"A bibliography on the arts and crafts of northwest coast
Indians."
In: *BC Studies*; No. 25 (Spring 1975) p. 78-123.; ISSN: 0005-
2949.
Note: 719 entries.– Scholarly studies, catalogues of
exhibitions, books, articles, government publications
relating to native plastic and graphic art (painting,
carving, basketry, etc.), dance and music.
Location: AEU.

0681 **Johnston, Joan L.**
Canada in the Victorian image, 1837-1887: a selective
guide to reading. [Guelph, Ont.]: Library, University of
Guelph, c1975. 15 p. (Bibliography series / University of
Guelph Library ; no. 4)
Note: Approx. 180 entries.– Books and pamphlets on
general Victoriana, architecture and town planning,
furniture, china, glass and silver, art and books, textiles
and clothing.
Location: OONL.

0682 **Phillips, David**
"Fine arts and Canadian studies."
In: *Communiqué: Canadian Studies*; Vol. 2, no. 1/2
(October 1975) p. 2-44.; ISSN: 0318-1197.
Note: General and period surveys, directories, Inuit and
Indian arts, individual studies, selected articles in
Canadian art history (1963-1974), films, audio and video
tapes.– Also includes a list of Canadian art journals,
materials on arts funding, government and the arts, and
art and education.
Location: OONL.

— 1976 —

0683 **"Canadian materials on the arts."**
In: *Ontario Library Review*; Vol. 60, no. 4 (December
1976) p. 226-235.; ISSN: 0030-2996.

Note: Location: OONL.

0684 **Williamson, Mary F.**
Canadian art: a guide to reference sources. [Downsview,
Ont.]: Scott Library, York University, 1976. 22 l.
Note: Approx. 150 entries.– Art collections (catalogues),
biography, bibliography, periodicals, indexes/
directories, annuals and yearbooks, art auction records,
reproductions of Canadian paintings, unpublished
sources.
Location: OONL.

0685 **Williamson, Mary F.**
The study of art in Canada. Toronto: York University
Libraries, 1976. 23 l.
Note: 300 entries.– Books and articles on Canadian art,
including the literature of painting: history, criticism,
exhibitions, reviews.– Topics include architecture,
sculpture, folk art, academies/art societies, art in the
community, criticism of Canadian art by non-Canadians,
art of native people.– Excludes photography, handicrafts,
decorative and industrial arts.
Location: OONL.

— 1977 —

0686 **Blazuk, Julia, et al.**
The music, art and drama of Commonwealth countries: a
source book for secondary teachers. Edmonton: 1977.
73 p.: ill.
Note: Listing of books, magazines, films, kits, recordings,
maps, slide sets in the areas of art, drama and music
compiled to assist Alberta teachers in designing
programs about Commonwealth countries to coincide
with the Commonwealth Games (1978) and Festival '78.–
Canadian materials are listed within the "America Block"
section.
Location: OONL.

0687 **Bradley, Ian L.; Bradley, Patricia**
A bibliography of Canadian native arts: Indian and
Eskimo arts, crafts, dance and music. [Agincourt, Ont.:
GLC Publishers, c1977]. [6], 107, [2] p.; ISBN: 0-88874-051-
4.
Note: 1,516 entries.– Bibliographies, theses, books,
periodical articles from mid-nineteenth century to 1976.–
Emphasis on Indians of Northwest coastal region.
Location: OONL.

0688 **Johnston, Joan L.**
Bibliography: Symposium 1977: Prepared for
Symposium 1977, The end of an era, 1880 – Canada –
1914/Bibliographie: Symposium 1977, La fin d'une
époque, 1880 – Canada – 1914. [S.l.: s.n., 1977]. 22 p.
Note: Approx. 175 entries.– Books and pamphlets,
published or reprinted between 1965 and 1977 dealing
with architecture, decorative and fine arts, clothing and
furniture, home furnishings of Canada during the years
1837 to 1914.– Text in English and French/texte en
français et en anglais.
Location: OONL.

— 1978 —

0689 **Andoniadis, Katherine L.**
Canadian art publications: an annotated bibliography for
the secondary school. [Victoria, B.C.]: Canadian Society
for Education through Art, 1978. vi, 138 p. (Canadian
Society for Education through Art Booklet ; no. 4)
Note: 380 entries.– Books (1960-1978), exhibition
catalogues (dating from 1970), periodicals, sources for

audio-visual materials directly related to the study of Canadian visual arts, applied arts and architecture, in English or bilingual.
Location: OONL.

0690 **Huffman, James; Huffman, Sybil**
Occupations in the arts, recreation, and equipment operation/Carrières dans les arts, les loisirs et l'outillage technique. Toronto: Guidance Centre, Faculty of Education, University of Toronto, c1978. 34 p. (Career information: a bibliography of publications about careers in Canada ; book 7); ISBN: 0-7713-0060-3.
Note: Approx. 250 entries.– Books, booklets, pamphlets, information sheets on Canadian arts, recreation, and related occupations.– Text in English and French/texte en français et en anglais.
Location: OPET.

— 1979 —

0691 **Lindsay, Doreen; McCutcheon, Sarah**
Women's bookworks: a survey exhibition of contemporary artists' books by Canadian women including unique book-objects and printed editions/Livres d'artistes-femmes: une exposition de livres contemporains réalisés par des artistes canadiennes comprenant des "livres-objets" uniques ou des livres faisant partie d'éditions à petits tirages. Montreal: Powerhouse Gallery, c1979. [ca. 100] p.: ill.
Note: Location: OONL.

0692 **Moulton, Donalee**
Antiques and restoration. Monticello, Ill.: Vance Bibliographies, 1979. 4 p. (Architecture series: Bibliography ; A-121; ISSN: 0194-1356)
Note: Location: OON.

0693 **Research bibliography on the cultural industries.**
[Ottawa: Futures, 1979]. 86 p. (Arts research monograph ; no. 4)
Note: Approx. 1,300 entries.– Journal articles, documents on the artistic cultural industries: broadcasting, computer services, crafts, libraries, motion pictures, museums, performing arts, publishing, recording, visual arts.– Excludes physical, religious and scientific culture and related industries.
Location: OONL.

— 1980 —

0694 **National Gallery of Canada**
National Gallery of Canada exhibition catalogues on microfiche, 1919-1959. Prelim. ed. [Ottawa]: McLaren Micropublishing, 1980. [51] l.
Note: Finding aid to microfiche collection of exhibition catalogues issued by the National Gallery of Canada from 1919 to 1959.
Location: OONL.

0695 **Sanderson, Paul**
Artists' legal bibliography. Toronto: CARO (Canadian Artists' Representation Ontario), 1980. 9 l.
Note: Approx. 75 entries.– Books and periodical articles on art law: legal forms, contracts, marketing, royalties, pricing, copyright, artists' agents.
Location: OONL.

— 1981 —

0696 **Loslier, Sylvie**
Répertoire sur les métiers d'art. Montréal: Centre de documentation Jean-Marie-Gauvreau, 1981. 50 f.; ISBN: 2-92027-300-0.

Note: Localisation: OONL.

— 1982 —

0697 **Blodgett, Jean**
"Bibliographie de l'art inuit canadien contemporain."
Dans: *Art et l'artisanat*; Vol. 5, no 2 (1982) p. 1-35.; ISSN: 0706-0203.
Note: Approx. 450 entrées.– Livres, articles, catalogues d'exposition sur l'art inuit canadien contemporain (de 1948 à 1982).– Exclut les articles de journaux.
English title: "A bibliography of contemporary Canadian Inuit art."
Localisation: OONL.

0698 **Blodgett, Jean**
"A bibliography of contemporary Canadian Inuit art."
In: *About Arts and Crafts*; Vol. 5, no. 2 (1982) p. 1-35.; ISSN: 0706-0203.
Note: Approx. 450 entries.– Books, articles, exhibition catalogues on contemporary (1948 to 1982) Canadian Inuit art, with some listings of major publications on prehistoric and historic Inuit art.– Excludes newspaper articles.
Titre en français: "Bibliographie de l'art inuit canadien contemporain."
Location: OONL.

0699 **Falk, Gathie**
"What's it like to be a woman artist? Selected bibliography."
In: *Capilano Review*; No. 24 (1982) p. 59-61.; ISSN: 0315-3754.
Note: Location: AEU.

0700 **Hould, Claudette**
Répertoire des livres d'artistes au Québec, 1900-1980. Montréal: Bibliothèque nationale du Québec, 1982. 240 p.: ill. (certaines en coul.); ISBN: 2-550-02456-7.
Note: 284 entrées.– L'auteur définit le livre d'artiste comme l'association d'un texte et d'estampes obtenues par les habituels procédés de gravure sur bois, métal, pierre lithographique, écran sérigraphique.
Supplément: *Répertoire des livres d'artistes au Québec, 1981-1990*. 1993. 346 p.: ill. (certaines en coul.); ISBN: 2-551-13060-3.
Localisation: OONL.

0701 **Mattison, David**
"British Columbia photographers of the nineteenth century: an annotated, select bibliography."
In: *BC Studies*; No. 52 (Winter 1981-1982) p. 166-170.; ISSN: 0005-2949.
Note: Approx. 40 entries.– Covers to March 1981.– Includes books, articles, exhibition catalogues.
Location: AEU.

— 1983 —

0702 **Singer, Loren**
"Canadian art publications: history and recent developments."
In: *Art Libraries Journal*; Vol. 8, no. 1 (Spring 1983) p. 4-57.; ISSN: 0307-4722.
Note: 175 entries.– Details of recently published works in fields of architecture, sculpture, painting, drawing, graphic arts, folk decorative arts, photography, Indian and Inuit art.
Location: OONL.

0703 **Carr, Sheridan**
Catalogue of slides for sale to educational institutions. Ottawa: National Gallery of Canada, 1984. 75 p.; ISBN: 0-88884-513-8.
Note: Listing of Canadian and international singles and sets of slides of art works in the permanent collection of the National Gallery of Canada.
Titre en français: *Répertoire de diapos en vente aux établissements d'éducation.*
Location: OONL.

0704 **Carr, Sheridan**
Répertoire de diapos en vente aux établissements d'éducation. Ottawa: Galerie nationale du Canada, 1984. 76 p.; ISBN: 0-88884-514-6.
Note: Liste de diapositives, individuelles et séries (Canada/international), oeuvres d'art, partie de la collection permanente de la Galerie nationale du Canada.
English title: *Catalogue of slides for sale to educational institutions.*
Localisation: OONL.

0705 **Holmes, Janet**
"Papers completed in North American decorative arts, graduate course, University of Toronto, 1968-82."
In: *Material History Bulletin*; No. 20 (Fall 1984) p. 83-85.; ISSN: 0703-489X.
Note: 37 entries.
Location: OONL.

0706 **McCaughey, Claire**
A survey of arts audience studies: a Canadian perspective, 1967-1984. Ottawa: Research & Evaluation, Canada Council, 1984. v, 76, 20, 10 p.
Note: 215 entries.– Articles, surveys, conference proceedings, government research reports dealing with size, characteristics, behaviour and motivation of Canadian arts audiences.
Location: OONL.

0707 **Service de diffusion sélective de l'information de la Centrale des bibliothèques**
La peinture québécoise. Montréal: Le Service, 1984. 90 p. (DSI/CB ; no 41; ISSN: 0825-5024); ISBN: 2-89059-241-3.
Note: Rassemble 129 volumes et 105 documents audiovisuels sur la peinture québécoise, depuis les débuts du Régime français jusqu'à nos jours, concernant plus de 70 artistes québécois.
Localisation: OONL.

0708 **Hyttenrauch, David**
Where it's at: pertinent publications on the arts. [Windsor, Ont.]: Arts Council Windsor & Region, 1985. [12], 315 p.
Note: Approx. 800 entries.– Topics include arts administration, art marketing, arts economics, arts education, government grants, arts and the law, restoration and conservation (buildings, paintings), vocational guidance, volunteerism and the arts.– Includes lists of theses, Canada Council publications.
Location: OONL.

0709 **Retfalvi, Andrea**
"Les expositions de l'année au Canada/The year's exhibitions in Canada."
Dans: *RACAR (Revue d'art canadienne, Canadian Art Review)*; Vol. 5, no 1 (1978) p. 57-64; vol. 6, no 1 (1979) p.

54-61; vol. 7, no 1 (1980) p. 116-125; vol. 8, no 1 (1981) p. 71-81; vol. 9, no 1 (1982) p. 99-108; vol. 10, no 1 (1983) p. 91-98; vol. 11, no 1-2 (1984) p. 137-146; vol. 12, no 1 (1985) p. 65-72.; ISSN: 0315-9906.
Note: Liste des catalogues des expositions organisées par les musées canadiens.– La liste des expositions au Québec a été compilée par Lorraine Groulx, Université de Montréal.
Localisation: OONL.

0710 **Hayes, Janice E.**
Bibliography on Canadian feminist art. Montreal: Graduate School of Library and Information Studies, McGill University, 1986. 43 p. (McGill University Graduate School of Library and Information Studies Occasional papers ; 9)
Note: 89 entries.– Monographs, journal articles, exhibition catalogues, theses, newspaper articles, journal titles, from 1960 to December 1984, dealing with decorative (applied) arts and visual arts in Canada with significant feminist content.– References to individual artists are not included.– Includes English-language material only.
Location: OONL.

0711 **Minion, Robin**
Inuit art and artists. Edmonton: Boreal Institute for Northern Studies, University of Alberta, 1986. 80 p. (Boreal Institute for Northern Studies Bibliographic series ; no. 26; ISSN: 0824-8192); ISBN: 0-919058-48-5.
Note: 226 entries.– Series contains monographs, theses, government documents, consultants' reports, children's books, conference proceedings, microforms on topics related to northern environment and people.– BINS series produced monthly from January 1984 to May 1986 (no. 29).– Online access: *Boreal Northern Titles (BNT),* available through QL Systems Limited.
Location: OONL.

0712 **Saint-Pierre, Louise**
Bibliographie québécoise de l'artisanat et des métiers d'art (1689-1985). [Québec]: Centre de formation et de consultation en métiers d'art, c1986. xxi, 205 p.; ISBN: 2-920790-01-3.
Note: Approx. 4,000 entrées.– Livres, articles de revues et journaux, catalogues d'expositions, mémoires et thèses, documents audio-visuels, bibliographies.– Comprend une section sur les autochtones Amérindiens et Inuits.
Édition antérieure: *Bibliographie de l'artisanat québécois.* Ministère des affaires culturelles, 1981. 195 p.; ISBN: 2-550-01628-9.
Localisation: OONL.

0713 **Hudon, Jean-Paul**
Répertoire bibliographique d'articles de périodiques sur les arts en général: dépouillement de seize (16) revues disponibles à la bibliothèque de l'UQAC. [Chicoutimi]: Bibliothèque, Université du Québec à Chicoutimi, 1987. v, 87 p.; ISBN: 2-920751-05-0.
Note: Approx. 700 entrées.– Articles sur peinture, sculpture, gravure, musique, théâtre, photographie.
Localisation: OONL.

0714 **Béland, Mario**
Marius Barbeau et l'art au Québec: bibliographie

analytique et thématique. 2e éd. rev. et corr. [Sainte-Foy, Québec: CELAT], 1988. xi, 135 p.: ill.; ISBN: 2-920576-19-4.
Note: Comprend volumes (ouvrages personnels, ouvrages en collaboration), articles (périodiques, journaux).
Édition antérieure: 1985. xiii, 139 p.: ill.; ISBN: 2-920576-05-4.
Localisation: OONL.

0715 **Chamberlain, K.E.**
Design in Canada, 1940-1987: a bibliography. [Richmond, B.C.: K. Chamberlain, c1988]. [48] p.
Note: Approx. 900 entries.– Books, pamphlets, periodical articles on design in Canada from 1940 to 1987.
Location: OONL.

0716 **Duhaime, Carole P.; Trudeau, Sylvain**
La clientèle des musées d'art: une revue de littérature. Montréal: École des hautes études commerciales, 1988. 52 f. (Rapport de recherche / École des hautes études commerciales ; no 88-03; ISSN: 0709-986X)
Note: Revue de littérature sur la clientèle des musées et galeries d'art.– La majeure partie des recherches examinées étudient le profil socio-démographique des visiteurs de musée; quelques études examinent les attitudes, les intérêts, les motivations et le comportement des visiteurs et des non-visiteurs de musée.
Localisation: OONL.

0717 **Holcomb, Adele M.; Williamson, Mary F.**
Bibliography: women's studies in art in Canadian universities and schools of art, 1985. [Lennoxville, Que.]: Distributed by Universities Art Association of Canada/ Association d'art des universités du Canada, 1988. 11 p.
Note: Approx. 120 entries.
Location: OONL.

0718 **Milne, David**
Canadian cultural industries: a bibliography/Industries culturelles canadiennes: une bibliographie. [Ottawa]: Library, Department of External Affairs, 1988. 47 p.
Note: Approx. 400 entries.– Books and documents, articles on government policy, copyright, cultural industries (broadcasting, film, publishing, recording), cultural industries and free trade, funding of cultural industries, cultural statistics.– Includes English and French language publications.
Location: OONL.

— 1989 —
0719 **Canadian Conference of the Arts**
Municipalities and the arts: inventory of municipal cultural material in the resource centre of the Canadian Conference of the Arts/Les municipalités et les arts: répertoire de la documentation sur les municipalités et la culture disponible au centre de ressources de la Conférence canadienne des arts. Ottawa: Canadian Conference of the Arts, 1989. 27 p.
Note: Reports, studies, speeches, conference papers, government documents, periodical articles in English and French dealing with municipal arts policies and cultural issues, economic impact and funding.– Text in English and French/texte en français et en anglais.
Location: OOCO.

0720 **Macnaughton, Elizabeth**
"Researching ceramics."
In: *Museum Quarterly*; Vol. 17, no. 4 (November 1989) p. 34-38.; ISSN: 0822-5931.

Note: Bibliography of research sources on British and Canadian ceramics.– List includes indexes, dictionaries and encyclopedias, bibliographies, general histories and guides.
Location: OONL.

— 1990 —
0721 **Boilard, Gilberte**
Statut de l'artiste: bibliographie sélective et annotée. Québec: Bibliothèque de l'Assemblée nationale, Division de la référence parlementaire, 1990. 92 p. (Bibliographie / Bibliothèque de l'Assemblée nationale du Québec ; no 37; ISSN: 0836-9100)
Note: 297 entrées.– Documents, articles pour Québec, Canada, autres pays (études comparatives).
Localisation: OONL.

0722 **Lerner, Loren R.**
"Recent publications on Canadian art."
In: *Journal of Canadian Art History*; Vol. 10, no. 2 (1987) p. 169-178; vol. 13, no. 1 (1990) p. 98-111.; ISSN: 0315-4297.
Note: Location: AEU.

0723 **Tobin, Mary A.T.; Mongrain, Susan; Finn, Julia**
Departmental Library Canadian Indian art and artists: a bibliography/Bibliothèque ministérielle art et artistes indiens du Canada: une bibliographie. Ottawa: Indian and Northern Affairs Canada, 1990. 26 p.; ISBN: 0-662-57509-1.
Note: Approx. 200 entries.– Lists items on native art from Indian and Northern Affairs Library collection.
Location: OONL.

— 1991 —
0724 **École des hautes études commerciales de Montréal. Groupe de recherche et de formation en gestion des arts**
Bibliographie sélective et synthèses de documents: rapport préparé pour le Groupe d'études sur la formation professionnelle dans le secteur culturel au Canada. Montréal: Le Groupe, 1991. 156 f.
Note: Localisation: OONL.

0725 **Légaré, Benoît**
Le marketing en milieu muséal: une bibliographie analytique. Montréal: École des hautes études commerciales, Chaire de gestion des arts, 1991. 179 f. (Cahiers de recherche de la Chaire de gestion des arts ; GA91-01B; ISSN: 0847-5148)
Note: 408 entrées.– Articles, monographies, thèses et textes d'allocution en français et en anglais.– Annotations en français seulement.– Inclut un nombre d'ouvrages canadiens.
Localisation: OONL.

0726 **Lerner, Loren R.; Williamson, Mary F.**
Art and architecture in Canada: a bibliography and guide to the literature to 1981/Art et architecture au Canada: bibliographie et guide de la documentation jusqu'en 1981. Toronto: University of Toronto Press, 1991. 2 vol.: maps.; ISBN: 0-8020-5856-6 (set).
Note: 9,555 entries.– Descriptive references to published books, reports, pamphlets, exhibition catalogues, periodical articles, theses.– A broad definition of "Canadian" artist includes: those born in Canada, those from elsewhere who have committed time and talent to Canada, those from elsewhere, in Canada briefly, but still with Canadian associations.– Only publications relating to work in Canada are included.– Buildings in Canada

designed by foreign architects are treated as Canadian.– Excludes the category of livres d'artistes/artists' books.– Subject divisions include: painting/sculpture/graphic arts/photography; decorative arts/fine crafts/industrial arts; arts of Native peoples; artists (individuals); architecture.– Text in English and French/texte en français et en anglais.
Location: OONL.

— 1992 —

0727 **Canada. Indian and Northern Affairs Canada. Inuit Art Section**
Inuit art bibliography/Bibliographie de l'art inuit. 2nd ed. Ottawa: The Section, 1992. 733, 69 p.
Note: 2,368 entries.– Exhibition catalogues and brochures, books, periodical articles, essays, theses, museum bulletins and video recordings.– Publications are mainly in English or French, with annotations in English only.
Previous edition: 1987. 265 p.– 1,269 entries.
Location: OONL.

0728 **Canada Council. Research and Evaluation**
The Canada Council Arts Research bibliography/Le Conseil des arts du Canada Répertoire des travaux de recherche sur les arts. [Ottawa]: Canada Council, 1988-1992. 3 vol.; ISSN: 0837-4910.; ISBN: 0-660-57315-6 (vol. 1); 0-660-57335-0 (vol. 2); 0-660-57477-2 (vol. 3).
Note: Lists all studies held in the Arts Research Library of the Research and Evaluation Section, Canada Council.– Arranged in three sections: "Environment" (demographics, research, education, private finance, public finance, socio-economic); "Copyright" (economics, legal, technology); "Artistic sectors."– Text in English and French/texte en français et en anglais.
Location: OONL.

0729 **Colbert, François; Turgeon, Normand**
La commandite dans le domaine des arts et de la culture: bibliographie. Montréal: Chaire de gestion des arts, École des hautes études commerciales de Montréal, 1992. 152 p. (Cahiers de la Chaire de gestion des arts / École des hautes études commerciales de Montréal ; GA92-01; ISSN: 0847-5148)
Note: 540 entrées.– Articles, monographies, thèses, mémoires, actes de colloques et bibliographies publiés au Canada et l'étranger entre décembre 1969 et décembre 1991.
Localisation: OONL.

0730 **Musée d'art contemporain de Montréal**
Répertoire des catalogues du Musée d'art contemporain de Montréal, 1965-1990. Montréal: Le Musée, c1992. 87 p.: ill.; ISBN: 2-551-12880-3.
Note: 215 entrées.
Localisation: OONL.

— Ongoing/En cours —

0731 **National Library of Canada**
Made in Canada: artists in books, livres d'artistes. Ottawa: National Library of Canada, 1981-. vol.: ill. (some col.); ISSN: 0228-7749.
Note: Series of exhibition catalogues of books and albums illustrated by Canadian artists, drawn from the National Library's Rare Books Division collection of about 500 bookworks or livres d'artistes.
Location: OONL.

0732 **University of British Columbia. Library**
Exhibition catalogues [microform]. Vancouver: University of British Columbia Library, 1988-. microfiches; ISSN: 1181-3091.
Note: Annual.– Published catalogues from public and commercial galleries.– International in scope, with emphasis on Canadian publications.– Includes student exhibition catalogues.
Location: OONL.

Architecture

— 1926 —

0733 **Gordon Home Blackader Library**
A catalogue of books on art and architecture in McGill University Library and the Gordon Home Blackader Library of Architecture. 2nd and rev. ed. Montreal: McGill University Library, 1926. 192, [2] p.: front., port. (McGill University publications series ; no. 9)
Note: Previous edition: *Catalogue of books on architecture and the fine arts in the Gordon Home Blackader Library and in the Library of McGill University.* Montreal: Dominion Press, 1922. 65 p. (McGill University publications, series 7, Library ; no. 4).
Location: OONL.

— 1959 —

0734 **Brass, Allen E.**
An annotated bibliography on laboratory buildings. Ottawa: Division of Building Research, National Research Council Canada, 1959. 17 l.
Note: Location: OONL.

— 1965 —

0735 **Doelle, Leslie L.**
Acoustics in architectural design: an annotated bibliography on architectural acoustics. Ottawa: National Research Council Canada, Division of Building Research, 1965. 543 p. (National Research Council Canada, Division of Building Research Bibliography ; no. 29)
Note: Books, booklets, articles, research papers, standards, codes on architectural acoustics, published in English, French and German: general works, room acoustics, noise control.– Includes Canadian references.
Location: OONL.

— 1966 —

0736 **Hedley, Alan**
Privacy as a factor in residential buildings and site development: an annotated bibliography. Ottawa: National Research Council Canada, Division of Building Research, 1966. 63 l. (National Research Council Canada, Division of Building Research Bibliography ; no. 32)
Note: Includes Canadian material.
Location: OON.

— 1967 —

0737 **"A guide to articles & architects."**
In: *Canadian Architect*; Vol. 12, no. 12 (December 1967) p. 51-60.; ISSN: 0008-2872.
Note: Articles in 9 journals published between October 1966 and September 1967 listing critiques, information about architects and their projects, articles of general interest: educational buildings, Expo 67, houses and housing, medical buildings, offices and plants, religious buildings, restaurants and hotels, urban/civic/government buildings.
Location: OONL.

— 1972 —

0738 **Fortier, John**
"The Fortress of Louisbourg and its cartographic evidence."
In: *Bulletin: Association for Preservation Technology*; Vol. 4, no. 1-2 (1972) p. 3-40.; ISSN: 0044-9466.
Note: Plans, elevations, profiles and views: cartographic evidence concerning military, civil and domestic architecture in eighteenth-century Louisbourg.
Location: OONL.

0739 **Kalman, Harold**
"Recent literature on the history of Canadian architecture."
In: *Journal of the Society of Architectural Historians*; Vol. 31, no. 4 (December 1972) p. 315-323.; ISSN: 0037-9808.
Note: Books and selection of articles from about 1960 to 1972: general studies (surveys, studies of particular styles), regional and local studies.
Location: OONL.

— 1974 —

0740 **Bourgeois, Annette E.**
Bibliography on the Parliament Buildings. [Ottawa: Public Works Library, 1974]. 12 l.
Note: 46 entries.– Government documents, monographs, periodicals, plans and drawings.
Location: OONL.

0741 **Central Mortgage and Housing Corporation. Data and Information Group**
Bibliography of background material on building in northern communities. Ottawa: Data and Information Group, Central Mortgage and Housing Corporation, 1974. [33] l.
Note: Location: OOCM.

0742 **Gauthier-Larouche, Georges**
"Évolution de la maison rurale traditionnelle dans la région de Québec: bibliographie."
Dans: *Archives de Folklore*; Vol. 15 (1974) p. 279-287.; ISSN: 0085-5243.
Note: Localisation: AEU.

0743 **Heritage Canada Conference on Area Conservation**
Bibliography of Canadian materials relevant to heritage conservation. Ottawa: Heritage Canada, 1974. 16 l.
Note: Approx. 200 entries.– Books and articles pertaining to heritage conservation in Canada.– Emphasis on historical and architectural writings.
Location: OOPW.

— 1975 —

0744 **Some materials for the study of Nova Scotia architecture.** [S.l.: s.n., 1975]. 3 l.
Note: Location: OONL.

0745 **Thibault, Marie-Thérèse**
Bibliographie pour la conservation et la restauration de lieux et de bâtiments historiques. [Québec]: Ministère des affaires culturelles, Direction générale du patrimoine, Service de l'inventaire des biens culturels, Centre de documentation, 1975. iii, 43 p. (Direction générale du patrimoine Dossier ; no 1)
Note: Approx. 450 entrées.– Thèmes: architecture

militaire, architecture (conservation et restauration), architecture (Ontario/Québec), architecture rurale, charpenterie, cheminée/chauffage, iconographie, maçonnerie, moulins, ouvrages historiques et géographiques, quincaillerie, récits de voyage et guides touristiques.
Localisation: OONL.

0746 **Université de Montréal. Faculté de l'aménagement. Bibliothèque**
Architecture et arts anciens du Québec: répertoire d'articles de revues disponibles à la Bibliothèque de la Faculté de l'aménagement, Université de Montréal. [S.l.: s.n.], 1975. 2, 92 p.; ISBN: 0-88529-003-8.
Note: Approx. 300 entrées.– Sujets: architectes, architecture, art, conservation et restauration, histoire, meubles, moulins, ponts, rénovation, sculpture, sites historiques.
Comp. par Jacqueline Pelletier.
Localisation: OONL.

0747 **Volz, John R.**
"Brick bibliography."
In: *APT Bulletin*; Vol. 7, no. 4 (1975) p. 38-49.; ISSN: 0044-9466.
Note: Approx. 150 entries.– Books and articles on the history of brickmaking, brick and mortar science and technology and application to preservation of historic structures.– Includes some Canadian references.
Location: OONL.

— 1976 —

0748 **Central Mortgage and Housing Corporation. Library**
Canadian architecture: bibliography/Architecture canadienne: bibliographie. [Ottawa: Central Mortgage and Housing Corporation], 1976. 12 l.
Note: Approx. 120 entries.– Books, periodical articles on Canadian architects, architecture (legal aspects, history, designs and plans, study and teaching, awards and competitions).
Location: OONL.

0749 **Crawford, Patricia; Monk, Philip; Wood, Marianna**
Architecture in Ontario: a select bibliography on architectural conservation and the history of architecture: with special relevance to the Province of Ontario: for "New Life for Old Buildings," a symposium sponsored jointly by Frontenac Historic Foundation and Ontario Heritage Foundation, Kingston, Ontario, September 9-12, 1976. Toronto: Department of Fine Arts, University of Toronto, 1976. ix, 140 p.; ISBN: 0-88365-404-0.
Note: Approx. 1,000 entries.– Books, articles, studies and reports on the history of the preservation movement, concepts of conservation, principles of townscape and planning, area preservation, adaptive use, examples of conservation, political strategies and preservation campaigns, technical aspects, bibliographies, works on history of architecture, by region and province.
Location: OOFF.

0750 **Heritage Ottawa**
A bibliography for the conservation of structures in Ottawa. Ottawa: Heritage Ottawa, 1976. 24 l.
Note: Location: OONL.

0751 **Wade, Jill**
Manitoba architecture to 1940: a bibliography. Winnipeg: University of Manitoba Press, 1976. xvi, 109 p., [8] l. of pl.: ill.; ISBN: 0-88755-116-5.

Note: 747 entries.– Includes material on buildings erected in Manitoba before 1940: books, articles, papers, minute books, photo collections, theses, maps, building specifications and plans.
Location: OONL.

— 1977 —

0752 **Buggey, Susan**
"Researching Canadian buildings: some historical sources."
In: *Histoire sociale: Social History*; Vol. 10, no 20 (novembre 1977) p. 409-426.; ISSN: 0018-2257.
Note: Bibliographical essay.
Location: OONL.

— 1978 —

0753 **Carlson, Alvar W.**
"Bibliography on barns in the United States and Canada."
In: *Pioneer America*; Vol. 10, no. 1 (June 1978) p. 65-71.; ISSN: 0032-0005.
Note: 120 entries.
Location: OKQ.

0754 **Priess, Peter J.**
An annotated bibliography for the study of building hardware. Ottawa: National Historic Parks and Sites Branch, Parks Canada, 1978. 79 p. (History and archaeology / National Historic Parks and Sites Branch ; 21); ISBN: 0-660-01775-X.
Note: Approx. 200 entries.– Archaeological site reports, books, journal articles.– Arranged by hardware categories (bolts, latches, wall anchors, etc.).
Titre en français: *Bibliographie annotée pour l'étude de la quincaillerie du bâtiment*.
Location: OONL.

0755 **Priess, Peter J.**
Bibliographie annotée pour l'étude de la quincaillerie du bâtiment. Ottawa: Parcs Canada, 1978. 80 p. (Histoire et archéologie / Direction des lieux et des parcs historiques nationaux ; 21); ISBN: 0-660-90035-1.
Note: Approx. 200 entrées.– Documentation générales, ouvrages de référence classés par catégories: jambes, grilles, serrures, ancres, clous, etc.
English title: *An annotated bibliography for the study of building hardware*.
Localisation: OONL.

— 1979 —

0756 **Calkins, Charles F.**
The barn as an element in the cultural landscape of North America: a bibliography. Monticello, Ill.: Vance Bibliographies, 1979. 20 p. (Architecture series: Bibliography ; A-84; ISSN: 0194-1356)
Note: Approx. 150 entries.– Books, monographs, periodical articles, scholarly and popular, published in the United States and Canada dealing with the character and distribution of barns in North America.– Includes entries on specialty barns, such as tobacco barns or hop houses.
Location: OOFF.

— 1980 —

0757 **Bradshaw, Janice**
Heritage conservation: a selected bibliography, 1979. [Victoria]: British Columbia Heritage Trust, [1980]. 71 p. (Technical paper series / British Columbia Heritage Trust ; no. 1; ISSN: 0229-9976); ISBN: 0-7719-9281-5.
Note: Approx. 275 entries.– Books, periodicals, museum

publications, journal articles on archaeology, architecture, care of materials, documentation, funding/ finance, interpretation, museology, planning, urban development and adaptive reuse of old buildings.
Supplement: Adam, Robert. 1983. 28 p.
Location: OONL.

0758 **Swanick, Eric L.**
British Columbia architecture: an introductory bibliography. Monticello, Ill.: Vance Bibliographies, 1980. 10 l. (Architecture series: Bibliography ; A-212; ISSN: 0194-1356)
Note: Approx. 150 entries.– Books, periodical articles.
Location: OONL.

0759 **Swanick, Eric L.**
Canadian library architecture: an introductory bibliography. Monticello, Ill.: Vance Bibliographies, 1980. 10 p. (Architecture series: Bibliography ; A-189; ISSN: 0194-1356)
Note: Location: OHM.

0760 **Swanick, Eric L.**
The Canadian lighthouse: an introductory bibliography with supplementary materials on lighthouses. Monticello, Ill.: Vance Bibliographies, 1980. 8 p. (Architecture series: Bibliography ; A-394; ISSN: 0194-1356)
Note: Approx. 100 entries.
Location: OONL.

0761 **Swanick, Eric L.**
Conservation architecture in Canada: an introductory bibliography. Monticello, Ill.: Vance Bibliographies, 1980. 7 p. (Architecture series: Bibliography ; A-174; ISSN: 0194-1356)
Note: Approx. 90 entries.
Location: OONL.

0762 **Swanick, Eric L.**
Current writings on Nova Scotia architecture: an introductory bibliography. Monticello, Ill.: Vance Bibliographies, 1980. 6 p. (Architecture series: Bibliography ; A-318; ISSN: 0194-1356)
Note: Approx. 75 entries.
Location: OONL.

0763 **Swanick, Eric L.**
Housing and architecture in North American northern regions. Monticello, Ill.: Vance Bibliographies, 1980. 7 p. (Architecture series: Bibliography ; A-186; ISSN: 0194-1356)
Note: Approx. 70 entries.
Location: OONL.

0764 **Swanick, Eric L.**
New Brunswick architecture: an introductory bibliography. Monticello, Ill.: Vance Bibliographies, 1980. 5 p. (Architecture series: Bibliography ; A-187; ISSN: 0194-1356)
Note: Approx. 60 entries.
Location: OONL.

0765 **Swanick, Eric L.**
Religious architecture of Canada. Monticello, Ill.: Vance Bibliographies, 1980. 8 p. (Architecture series: Bibliography ; A-188; ISSN: 0194-1356)
Note: Location: OON.

0766 **Vance, Mary**
Historical society architectural publications: Canada. Monticello, Ill.: Vance Bibliographies, 1980. 37 p.

(Architecture series: Bibliography ; A-179; ISSN: 0194-1356)
Note: Approx. 300 entries.– Lists publications of societies of interest to architectural historians and architecture students.
Location: OONL.

— 1981 —

0767 **Cullen, Mary K.**
"Highlights of domestic building in pre-confederation Quebec and Ontario as seen through travel literature from 1763 to 1860."
In: *Association for Preservation Technology Bulletin*; Vol. 13, no. 1 (1981) p. 16-34.; ISSN: 0044-9466.
Note: Location: OONL.

0768 **O'Dea, Shane**
"A selective annotated bibliography for the study of Newfoundland vertical-log structures with some comments on terminology."
In: *Association for Preservation Technology Bulletin*; Vol. 13, no. 1 (1981) p. 35-37.; ISSN: 0044-9466.
Note: Location: OONL.

0769 **Ontario. Ministry of Municipal Affairs and Housing. Library**
Energy conservation in housing and building: a bibliography: a listing of books, pamphlets and periodical information available from the Library. [Toronto]: Ontario Ministry of Municipal Affairs and Housing, 1981. 36, 20 p.
Note: Approx. 550 entries.– Period covered: 1974-1981.
Location: OONL.

— 1982 —

0770 **White, Anthony G.**
The architecture of Vancouver, British Columbia: a selected bibliography. Monticello, Ill.: Vance Bibliographies, 1982. 7 l. (Architecture series: Bibliography ; A-772; ISSN: 0194-1356)
Note: 100 entries.– Books, periodical articles.
Location: OONL.

— 1983 —

0771 **Canadian Housing Information Centre**
A selected bibliography on architecture in Canada/Une bibliographie sélective sur l'architecture au Canada. Ottawa: The Centre, 1983. 18 p.
Note: Approx. 150 entries.
Location: OONL.

0772 **Leggat, Portia**
A union list of architectural records in Canadian public collections/Catalogue collectif de recherche documentaire sur l'architecture provenant de collections publiques canadiennes. Montreal: Canadian Centre for Architecture, 1983. xxiii, 213 p.
Note: Results of Canadian Architectural Records Survey: overview of holdings of architectural records (plans and drawings, photographs, postcards, specifications, correspondence, atlases), materials dealing with Canadian architects and development of architecture in Canada, in federal, provincial and municipal archives, libraries, museums, historical societies, church organizations, corporate archives.– Index to architects.– Index to institutions.– Text in English and French/texte en français et en anglais.
Location: OONL.

0773 "Newfoundland architecture: a bibliography."
In: *Bulletin (Society for the Study of Architecture in Canada)*;
Vol. 8, no. 2 (June 1983) p. 20.; ISSN: 0712-8517.
Note: Location: OONL.

— 1984 —

0774 **Brousseau, Francine; Chabot, Line**
Architecture in *Canadian Illustrated News* and *L'Opinion
publique*: inventory of references/L'architecture dans le
Canadian Illustrated News et *L'Opinion publique*: inventaire
des références. Ottawa: Parks Canada, 1984. 203 p.; ISBN:
0-662-53167-1.
Note: 1,260 entries.– Citations concerning architecture in
Canada (excepting references to bridges), text or
illustrations, or both from the two illustrated papers
listed in the title, and the *Portfolio and Dominion Guide* for
1873.– Excludes general views of towns or villages
(unless certain buildings are identified), advertisements
containing only names and addresses of establishments,
unidentified sketches, fictitious structures.– Text in
English and French/texte en français et en anglais.
Location: OONL.

0775 **Swanick, Eric L.**
Canadian writings on architecture for the disabled: an
introduction to recent writings. Monticello, Ill.: Vance
Bibliographies, 1984. 5 p. (Architecture series:
Bibliography ; A-1281; ISSN: 0194-1356); ISBN: 0-89028-
171-8.
Note: 63 entries.
Location: OONL.

— 1985 —

0776 **Johnson, Melvin W.**
The cobblestone architecture of the Great Lakes region:
an annotated bibliography. Monticello, Ill.: Vance
Bibliographies, 1985. 46 p. (Architecture series:
Bibliography ; A-1416; ISSN: 0194-1356); ISBN: 0-89028-
446-6.
Note: 155 entries.– Monographs, periodical articles,
theses, photographic records related to cobblestone style
found mainly in western New York state from the period
1830-1860.– Descriptive annotations.– Includes Canadian
(Ontario) references.
Location: OON.

0777 **Kerr, Alastair**
"The growth of architectural history in British Columbia."
In: *Bulletin (Society for the Study of Architecture in Canada)*;
Vol. 10, no. 1 (March 1985) p. 21-24.; ISSN: 0712-8517.
Note: Literature review of B.C. architectural history:
journal articles, educational books, biographies and
monographs on individual architects, monographs on
individual buildings, writings on classes of buildings,
guide books, government publications.
Location: OONL.

0778 **Vance, Mary**
Selected architectural books published in Canada, 1974-
1984. Monticello, Ill.: Vance Bibliographies, 1985. 62 p.
(Architecture series: Bibliography ; A-1478; ISSN: 0194-
1356); ISBN: 0-89028-608-6.
Note: Approx. 700 entries.
Location: QQLA.

— 1986 —

0779 **Allan, Norman**
"Some random notes on Manitoba architectural
bibliography."

In: *Bulletin (Society for the Study of Architecture in Canada)*;
Vol. 11, no. 2 (June 1986) p. 9-10.; ISSN: 0712-8517.
Note: Location: OONL.

0780 **Mortsch, Linda D., Dolohan, Ken**
Applied climate bibliography for architects, planners,
landscape architects and builders/Bibliographie de
climatologie appliquée pour les architectes, les
planificateurs, les paysagistes et les entrepreneurs et
bâtiment. Downsview, Ont.: Environment Canada,
Atmospheric Environment Service, 1986. vi, 46 p.
Note: Approx. 500 entries.– Covers 1910-1985.–
References on climate as it relates to or is incorporated
into architecture, planning, landscape architecture,
municipal management, building science.– Emphasis on
climate and land use and land-capability.– Includes
journal articles, seminar and workshop results,
conference proceedings, technical manuals, government
agency reports, theses, unpublished government
documents.– Text in English and French/texte en
français et en anglais.
Location: OONL.

— 1987 —

0781 **Casper, Dale E.**
Canadian domestic architecture: trends and projects.
Monticello, Ill.: Vance Bibliographies, 1987. 5 p.
(Architecture series: Bibliography ; A-1772; ISSN: 0194-
1356); ISBN: 1-55590-222-7.
Note: Approx. 50 entries.
Location: OOPAC.

0782 **Casper, Dale E.**
Preserving Canadian architecture in the 1980's.
Monticello, Ill.: Vance Bibliographies, 1987. 7 p.
(Architecture series: Bibliography ; A-1771; ISSN: 0194-
1356); ISBN: 0-55590-221-9.
Note: 75 entries.
Location: OOPAC.

0783 **Doumato, Lamia**
Contemporary architecture in Canada. Monticello, Ill.:
Vance Bibliographies, 1987. 9 p. (Architecture series:
Bibliography ; A-1893; ISSN: 0194-1356); ISBN: 1-55590-
463-7.
Note: Approx. 100 entries.– Bibliographies, books,
periodical articles, exhibition catalogues and reviews,
awards.
Location: QQLA.

0784 **Husted, Deborah**
The architecture of Toronto: a selected bibliography.
Monticello, Ill.: Vance Bibliographies, 1987. 100 p.
(Architecture series: Bibliography ; A-1911; ISSN: 0194-
1356); ISBN: 0-1-55590-501-3.
Note: Approx. 1,300 entries.– Books, pamphlets, journal
and magazine articles, from late nineteenth century to
1987.– Includes studies of individual buildings and types
of buildings, planning and development, history,
waterfront, description and illustration, bibliographies
and indexes.
Location: OHM.

0785 **Kortman, Gregory M.; Butler, H. Julene**
Cordwood masonry construction: an annotated
bibliography. Monticello, Ill.: Vance Bibliographies, 1987.
24 p. (Architecture series: Bibliography ; A-1797; ISSN:
0194-1356); ISBN: 0-55590-267-7.
Note: Approx. 100 entries.– Canadian and American

references to wood-block masonry or stackwall (cordwood) construction method.
Location: OON.

0786 **White, Anthony G.**
Architecture of Arctic regions: a selected bibliography. Monticello, Ill.: Vance Bibliographies, [1987]. 7 p. (Architecture series: Bibliography ; A-1840; ISSN: 0194-1356); ISBN: 1-555903-50-9.
Note: Location: AEUB.

0787 **White, Anthony G.**
The architecture of Calgary, Alberta, Canada: a selected bibliography. Monticello, Ill.: Vance Bibliographies, [1987]. 5 p. (Architecture series: Bibliography ; A-1842; ISSN: 0194-1356); ISBN: 1-555903-52-5.
Note: Location: OOFF.

— 1989 —

0788 **Doumato, Lamia**
Arthur Charles Erickson's Canadian Chancery: a bibliography. Monticello, Ill.: Vance Bibliographies, 1989. 17 p. (Architecture series: Bibliography ; A-2226; ISSN: 0194-1356); ISBN: 0-7920-0276-8.
Note: Approx. 200 entries.– Books and articles on Erickson and his architectural work in general, with a section of writings on the Canadian embassy building, Washington, D.C.
Location: OON.

— 1990 —

0789 **Lord, Jules**
Bibliographie analytique sur les grands domaines et jardins: Villa Bagatelle, Société d'histoire de Sillery. Sillery, Québec: J. Lord, 1990. 182 p.
Note: Localisation: OONL.

0790 **White, Anthony G.**
The architecture of Ontario Province, Canada, Toronto metropolitan area: a selected bibliography. Monticello, Ill.: Vance Bibliographies, [1990]. 31 p. (Architecture series: Bibliography ; A-2339; ISSN: 0194-1356); ISBN: 0-792005-69-4.
Note: Location: OON.

0791 **White, Anthony G.**
The architecture of Quebec Province, Canada: Quebec metropolitan area: a selected bibliography. Monticello, Ill.: Vance Bibliographies, 1990. 7 p. (Architecture series: Bibliography ; A-2340; ISSN: 0194-1356); ISBN: 0-792005-70-8.
Note: Location: OON.

0792 **White, Anthony G.**
Canadian architecture: Alberta: a selected bibliography. Monticello, Ill.: Vance Bibliographies, 1990. 8 p. (Architecture series: Bibliography ; A-2293; ISSN: 0194-1356); ISBN: 0-792004-43-4.
Note: Location: OON.

0793 **White, Anthony G.**
Canadian architecture: British Columbia: a selected bibliography. Monticello, Ill.: Vance Bibliographies, 1990. 16 p. (Architecture series: Bibliography ; A-2294; ISSN: 0194-1356); ISBN: 0-792004-44-2.
Note: Location: OON.

0794 **White, Anthony G.**
Canadian architecture: Manitoba: a selected bibliography. Monticello, Ill.: Vance Bibliographies, 1990. 7 p. (Architecture series: Bibliography ; A-2292; ISSN: 0194-1356); ISBN: 0-792004-42-6.

Note: Location: OON.

0795 **White, Anthony G.**
Canadian architecture: Ontario Province, Ottawa northward: a selected bibliography. Monticello, Ill.: Vance Bibliographies, 1990. 11 p. (Architecture series: Bibliography ; A-2319; ISSN: 0194-1356); ISBN: 0-792004-89-2.
Note: Location: OON.

0796 **White, Anthony G.**
Canadian architecture: Prince Edward Island Province: a selected bibliography. Monticello, Ill.: Vance Bibliographies, 1990. 5 p. (Architecture series: Bibliography ; A-2313; ISSN: 0194-1356); ISBN: 0-792004-63-9.
Note: Location: OON.

0797 **White, Anthony G.**
Canadian architecture: Saskatchewan Province: a selected bibliography. Monticello, Ill.: Vance Bibliographies, 1990. 5 p. (Architecture series: Bibliography ; A-2314; ISSN: 0194-1356); ISBN: 0-792004-64-7.
Note: Location: OON.

0798 **White, Anthony G.**
Canadian architecture: southwestern Quebec Province, Montreal area: a selected bibliography. Monticello, Ill.: Vance Bibliographies, 1990. 18 p. (Architecture series: Bibliography ; A-2318; ISSN: 0194-1356); ISBN: 0-792004-88-4.
Note: Location: OON.

0799 **White, Anthony G.**
Canadian architecture: the Maritime Provinces: a selected bibliography. Monticello, Ill.: Vance Bibliographies, 1990. 6 p. (Architecture series: Bibliography ; A-2291; ISSN: 0194-1356); ISBN: 0-792004-41-8.
Note: Location: OON.

0800 **White, Anthony G.**
Canadian architecture: Yukon and Northwest Territories: a selected bibliography. Monticello, Ill.: Vance Bibliographies, 1990. 5 p. (Architecture series: Bibliography ; A-2295; ISSN: 0194-1356); ISBN: 0-792004-45-0.
Note: Location: OON.

— 1991 —

0801 **Blackader-Lauterman Library of Architecture and Art**
The libraries of Edward and W.S. Maxwell in the collections of the Blackader-Lauterman Library of Architecture and Art, McGill University/Les bibliothèques de Edward et W.S. Maxwell dans les collections de la Bibliothèque Blackader-Lauterman d'architecture et d'art, Université McGill. Montréal: Blackader-Lauterman Library of Architecture and Art, McGill University, 1991. iii, 110 p.; ISBN: 0-7717-0245-0.
Note: Selection of titles from the Maxwell brothers' collections on architectural and urban history, design and decorative arts, including monographs on architects and artists, books on building types, pamphlets on building safety and construction, works on painting, drawing and geometry.– Compiled by Cindy Campbell, Kathryn Jackson, and Judith Maxwell.– Text in English and French/texte en français et en anglais.
Location: OONL.

— 1992 —

0802 **Lord, Jules**
Bibliographie sur les grands domaines de la
Communauté urbaine de Québec: villas, jardins et
cimetières-jardins. Québec: Institut québécois de
recherche sur la culture, 1992. 129 p.: carte.; ISBN: 2-
89224-175-8.
Note: Localisation: OONL.

0803 **Simmins, Geoffrey**
Bibliography of Canadian architecture/Bibliographie
d'architecture canadienne. Ottawa: Society for the Study
of Architecture in Canada, 1992. 28 p.; ISBN: 0-919525-18-
0.
Note: Books and documents, exhibition catalogues,
articles in scholarly and popular journals, theses, journal
titles.– Focus on material published since 1981.–
Categories include bibliographies and general reference,
journals, indigenous architecture, work of individuals
and firms, studies of single buildings and building types,
style, thematic studies, national and period styles,
regional studies, urban planning, conservation and
preservation.– Index to authors, editors, compilers.– Text
in English and French/texte en français et en anglais.
Location: OONL.

— Ongoing/En cours —

0804 **"AID: architect's information directory."**
In: *Canadian Architect*; (1971-)   vol.; ISSN: 0008-2872.
Note: Regular listing from Vol. 16, nos. 10-11 (October-
November 1971 of brochures, folders, bulletins: literature
of interest to architects and builders.
Title varies: from Vol. 33 (1988), "Literature SpecGuide."
Location: OONL.

0805 **Canada. Lieux et parcs historiques nationaux. Section
des publications de recherches**
Manuscrits et bulletins [Lieux et parcs historiques
nationaux, Environnement Canada]. Ottawa: Environnement Canada, Parcs, 1987-.   vol.; ISSN: 0840-2027.
Note: Comprend trois listes: 1. Travaux inédits: rapports
de recherche non révisés et non publiées, rédigés pour
répondre aux besoins immédiats en matière de recherche
ou d'aménagement de sites. Fin de la collection, 1982,
remplace par 2. Rapports sur microfiches.– 3. Bulletins de
recherches: courts textes portant sur les recherches en
cours à Environnement Canada, Parcs tant au bureau
central que dans les régions.– Title in English:
Manuscripts and bulletins.
Localisation: OONL.

0806 **Canada. National Historic Parks and Sites. Research
Publications Section**
Manuscripts and bulletins [National Historic Parks and
Sites, Environment Canada]. Ottawa: Environment
Canada, Parks, 1987-.   vol.; ISSN: 0840-2019.
Note: Contains three separate listings: 1. Manuscript
report series: reference collection of unedited, unpublish-
ed research reports in printed form.– Discontinued in
1982, replaced by 2. Microfiche report series.– 3. Research
bulletins: short papers describing current Environment
Canada, Parks headquarters and regional research
projects.
Titre en français: *Manuscrits et bulletins.*
Location: OONL.

Music

Musique

— 1889 —

0807 **Complete list of Canadian copyright musical compositions, entered from 1868 to January 19th, 1889, compiled from the official register at Ottawa.** [Toronto: s.n., 1889]. [32] p.
Note: Approx. 1,400 entries.– Information includes title, authors, date of entry, no. of entry, publisher.
Location: OONL.

— 1930 —

0808 **Smitherman, Mary**
"Canadian composers."
In: *Ontario Library Review*; Vol. 15, no. 1 (August 1930) p. 3-6.; ISSN: 0030-2996.
Note: Mainly biographical references in magazines, yearbooks, Toronto Public Library files to approximately 80 composers.
Location: OONL.

— 1940 —

0809 **MacMillan, Jean Ross**
"Music in Canada: a short bibliography."
In: *Ontario Library Review*; Vol. 24, no. 4 (November 1940) p. 386-396.; ISSN: 0030-2996.
Note: Writings (books and articles) on Canadian music and writings on music by Canadians.– Emphasis on folk music, music methods, musical activities.– Intended "to form the basis of a permanent bibliography of Canadian music."
Location: OONL.

— 1946 —

0810 **Canadian Federation of Music Teachers' Associations**
A list of Canadian music. Toronto: Oxford University Press, 1946. 23 p.
Note: Lists instrumental and vocal works by type of work and alphabetically by composer.– Separate listing of composers, publishers.
Location: OONL.

— 1949 —

0811 **May, Lucille**
"Music and composers of Canada."
In: *Ontario Library Review*; Vol. 33, no. 3 (August 1949) p. 264-270.; ISSN: 0030-2996.
Note: References from books and periodicals on Canadian music and musicians.
Location: OONL.

— 1952 —

0812 **Kallmann, Helmut**
Catalogue of Canadian composers. Rev. and enl. ed. [Toronto]: Canadian Broadcasting Corporation, [1952]. 254 p.
Note: Biobibliographical information about 356 composers, " ... a record of musical composition of serious aspiration in Canada, from the earliest known examples up until the present time."
Previous edition: Gagnier, J.J.; Beaudet, Jean-Marie. Montreal: C.B.C., 1947. 9, 19, 105 p.– Reproduced from a typewritten copy.
Reprint: St. Clair Shores, Mich.: Scholarly Press, 1972. 254 p.; ISBN: 0-403-01375-5.
Location: OONL.

— 1954 —

0813 **Williamson, Nancy J.**
"Canadian music and composers since 1949."
In: *Ontario Library Review*; Vol. 38, no. 2 (May 1954) p. 118-122.; ISSN: 0030-2996.
Note: Books and articles in English on Canadian music and musicians.
Location: OONL.

— 1956 —

0814 **Beckwith, John**
"Canadian recordings: a discography."
In: *Canadian Library Association Bulletin*; Vol. 12, no. 5 (April 1956) p. 182-183.; ISSN: 0316-6058.
Note: Listing of recordings by Canadian composers and performers.– Includes folk music.
Location: OONL.

— 1957 —

0815 **Canadian League of Composers**
Catalogue of orchestral music (including works for small orchestra and band, concertos, vocal-orchestral and choral-orchestral works) composed by members of the Canadian League of Composers. Toronto: Canadian League of Composers, 1957. 58 p.
Note: Location: OONL.

— 1958 —

0816 **Canadian record guide.** Toronto: ECC Publications, 1958. 2 no.; ISSN: 0821-2163.
Note: Listing of all records available in Canada at time of publication, not exclusively Canadian productions.– Two numbers were published: Vol. 1, no. 1 (August 1958), and Vol. 1, no. 2 (September 1958).
Location: OONL.

— 1959 —

0817 **Canadian Music Library Association**
Standards for music collections in medium-sized libraries. Ottawa: Canadian Library Association, 1959. ii, 42 l.
Note: Recommended list of printed music, records, books, periodicals.– Includes Canadian references.
Location: OONL.

— 1964 —

0818 **Composers, Authors and Publishers Association of Canada**
CAPAC presents 3000 all-time song hits, 1892-1963. Toronto: The Association, [1964]. 101 p.
Note: Approx. 3,000 entries.– Information on top songs of each year in Canada, many written by Canadians.– Chronological arrangement, title index.
Location: OONL.

— 1965 —

0819 **Cook, D.F.**
"A survey of hymnody in the Church of England in eastern Canada to 1909."
In: *Journal of the Canadian Church Historical Society*; Vol. 8, no. 3 (September 1965) p. 36-61.; ISSN: 0008-3208.
Note: Includes a chronological list of psalm and hymn collections for the Church of England, published in Canada from 1800 to 1909.
Location: OONL.

— 1967 —

0820 **Canadian Music Library Association**
Musical Canadiana: a subject index. Ottawa: Canadian Library Association, 1967. v, 62 p.
Note: "800 vocal and instrumental pieces of music published in or outside Canada up to 1921, composed by Canadians or non-Canadians and significantly associated with the social life, physical features and political events of Canada by virtue of title, lyrics, plot, cover illustrations or dedication to groups or eminent individuals."- Compiled by a committee of the Canadian Music Library Association.
Location: OONL.

0821 **Cross, Lowell M.**
A bibliography of electronic music. Toronto: University of Toronto Press, 1967. ix, 126 p.
Note: 1,562 entries.- Books and articles dealing with experimental electronic music forms, ranging from highly technical works to generalized or popular pieces.- Includes Canadian references.
Location: OONL.

— 1968 —

0822 **Kasemets, Udo**
Canavangard: music of the nineteen sixties and after series. Don Mills, Ont.: BMI Canada, c1968. 112 p.: ill., ports.
Note: Catalogue of Canadian contemporary composers: biographies, description of compositions, data about performances, publication.
Location: OONL.

— 1969 —

0823 **Dwyer, Melva J.**
A selected list of music reference materials. Rev. ed. Ottawa: Canadian Library Association, 1969. 15 l.
Note: Previous edition: Edmonton: Edmonton Public Library, 1967. 15 l.
Location: OONL.

— 1970 —

0824 **"Canada on records."**
In: *Musicanada*; No. 26 (January-February 1970) p. 2-15.; ISSN: 0580-3152.
Note: Listing of 75 albums containing 182 works by Canadian composers.
Supplement: *List of recordings of works by Canadian composers supplementary to Musicanada No. 26.* Toronto: Canadian Music Centre, 1974. 8 p.
Location: OONL.

0825 **Hall, Frederick A., et al.**
A basic bibliography of musical Canadiana. Toronto: [s.n.], 1970. 38 l.
Note: Approx. 750 entries.- Books, articles, theses: a listing of literature on Canadian music in all areas: historical, bibliographical, biographical, compositional, ethnomusicological, educational.
Location: OONL.

0826 **Legendre, Victor**
Musique canadienne. Bibliographie. [Cap-Rouge, Québec]: Bibliothèque, Séminaire Saint-Augustin, 1970. 28 f.
Note: Approx. 300 entrées.- Articles de périodiques et journaux, livres: compositeurs canadiens, histoire de la musique canadienne, institutions musicales au Canada, vie musicale au Canada.
Localisation: OONL.

— 1971 —

0827 **BMI Canada Limited**
"Yes, there is Canadian music." "Oui, notre musique existe!". Montreal: 1971. 221 p.
Note: "A comprehensive listing of Canadian music licenced by BMI Canada Limited, with the respective artists and record labels indicated."- Title page and introductory matter in English and French/page de titre et préface bilingues, anglais et français.
Supplements: Monthly.- January 1971 to April 1977, when publication ceased. ISSN: 0381-579X.
Location: OONL.

0828 **Canadian Music Centre**
Catalogue of Canadian keyboard music available on loan from the library of the Canadian Music Centre/ Catalogue de musique canadienne à clavier disponible à titre de prêt à la bibliothèque du Centre musical canadien. Toronto: The Centre, c1971. 91 p.
Note: Provides information on keyboard works by composers resident in Canada for at least five years: piano (solos, four hands, two pianos) and organ.- Text in English and French/texte en français et en anglais.
Supplement: *List of Canadian keyboard music.* 1976. 5 l.
Location: OONL.

0829 **Matejcek, Jan**
Catalogue of Canadian music suitable for community orchestras. Toronto: Canadian Music Centre, 1971. 40 [i.e. 46] l.
Note: Selective catalogue of Canadian orchestral music, mainly from the period 1930-1970: one-movement, more than one movement, string orchestra, solo instrument with orchestra, solo voice and/or choir with orchestra.- "Produced in collaboration with the Province of Ontario Council for the Arts."
Location: OONL.

— 1972 —

0830 **Brassard, François**
"French-Canadian folk music studies: a survey."
In: *Ethnomusicology*; Vol. 16, no. 3 (September 1972) p. 351-359.; ISSN: 0014-1836.
Note: Approx. 40 entries.- Bibliographical essay.- Part of a special Canadian issue of *Ethnomusicology*.
Location: OONL.

0831 **Cavanagh, Beverley**
"Annotated bibliography: Eskimo music."
In: *Ethnomusicology*; Vol. 16, no. 3 (September 1972) p. 479-487.; ISSN: 0014-1836.
Note: References to the music and musical traditions of Inuit of Greenland, Canadian Arctic, and Alaska.- Part of a special Canadian issue of *Ethnomusicology*.
Location: OONL.

0832 **Couturier, Gaston; Archambault, Roger**
Chansons et thèmes. Montréal: Office des communications sociales, 1972. 96 f.
Note: Localisation: OONL.

0833 **Fowke, Edith**
"Anglo-Canadian folksong: a survey."
In: *Ethnomusicology*; Vol. 16, no. 3 (September 1972) p. 335-350.; ISSN: 0014-1836.
Note: Approx. 125 entries.– Bibliographical essay with a listing of books and articles.– Part of a special Canadian issue of *Ethnomusicology*.
Location: OONL.

0834 **Guédon, Marie-Françoise**
"Canadian Indian ethnomusicology: selected bibliography and discography."
In: *Ethnomusicology*; Vol. 16, no. 3 (September 1972) p. 465-478.; ISSN: 0014-1836.
Note: Listing of published studies and recordings (tapes, discs, films) arranged in five cultural areas: Eastern woodlands-Great Lakes; Plains; Yukon-Mackenzie basins; Plateau; Northwest coast.– Part of a special Canadian issue of *Ethnomusicology*.
Location: OONL.

0835 **Keillor, Elaine**
A bibliography of items on music in Canada. [Toronto]: E. Keillor, c1972. 89 l.
Note: 1,214 entries compiled from music journals (*Canadian Journal of Music, Conservatory Quarterly Review, The Etude, Musical Canada*) and from music columns in *The Globe, The Week, Saturday Night*.
Location: OONL.

0836 **Robertson, Alex**
Canadian Gennett and Starr-Gennett 9000 numerical. Pointe Claire, Quebec: [s.n.], 1972. iv, 30 l.
Note: Catalogue of phonograph records issued by the Starr Company of Canada, 1919-1925.
Location: OONL.

— 1973 —

0837 **Hollett, Gary**
An annotated bibliography of songs, ballads and poetry either about Newfoundland or by Newfoundlanders. [St. John's: Centre for Newfoundland Studies, Memorial University of Newfoundland, 1973]. 20 l.
Note: Approx. 100 entries.– Books and pamphlets located in the Newfoundland Room of Henrietta E. Harvey Library, Memorial University of Newfoundland.– Unpublished manuscript.
Location: NFSM.

0838 **Lande, Lawrence M.**
A checklist of early music relating to Canada, collected, compiled and annotated by Lawrence M. Lande from his private library. Montreal: McGill University, 1973. 23 p.: facsims. (Lawrence Lande Foundation for Canadian Historical Research ; no. 8)
Note: 112 entries.
Location: OONL.

— 1974 —

0839 **Magee, Eleanor E.; Fancy, Margaret**
Catalogue of Canadian folk music in the Mary Mellish Archibald Library and other special collections. [Sackville, N.B.]: Ralph Pickard Bell Library, Mount Allison University, [1974]. iv l., 88 p. (Library publications / Ralph Pickard Bell Library, Mount Allison University ; no. 5)
Note: 264 entries.– Books, periodicals, phonograph records, music scores dealing with music of native Canadians, traditional Canadian music, and music written or adapted by Canadians to the extent that it has become part of folk culture of Canada.– Excludes most works about modern folk music.
Location: OONL.

0840 **Mercer, Paul**
"A supplementary bibliography on Newfoundland music."
In: *Canadian Folk Music Journal*; Vol. 2 (1974) p. 52-56.; ISSN: 0318-2568.
Note: Books, articles, pamphlets: a bibliography of Newfoundland music to supplement: Fowke, Edith. "A reference list on Canadian folk music," in *Canadian Folk Music Journal*, Vol. 1 (1973) p. 46-56.
Location: AEU.

0841 **Robertson, Alex**
The Apex 8000 numerical. [Pointe Claire, Quebec: A. Robertson], 1974. vii, 58 l.
Note: Numerical catalogue of 78 rpm. phonograph records issued on the Apex label of the Compo Company, Lachine, Quebec.
Location: OONL.

— 1975 —

0842 **Canadian Music Centre**
Some reference sources for information on Canadian composers/Ouvrages de références sur les compositeurs canadiens. Toronto: The Centre, 1975. 13 l.
Note: Approx. 75 entries.– Books and booklets, articles in encyclopedias, periodicals.– Text in English and French/ texte en français et en anglais.
Location: OONL.

0843 **Cooke, Esther**
Canadian women in music: a bibliography of Canadian women composers and artists in the Alfred Whitehead Memorial Library. [Sackville, N.B.: Alfred Whitehead Memorial Library, 1975]. i, 8 p.
Note: Lists musical works by Canadian women.– Two sections: composer's works by scores and recordings; artists on recordings.
Location: OONL.

0844 **Cormier, Normand, et al.**
La chanson au Québec, 1965-1975. Montréal: Bibliothèque nationale du Québec, 1975. ix, 219 p. (Bibliographies québécoises / Bibliothèque nationale du Québec, Centre bibliographique ; no 3)
Note: 2,049 entrées.– Composé presque exclusivement d'ouvrages et d'articles de périodiques.– Préparé par le Centre bibliographique de la Bibliothèque nationale du Québec: Normand Cormier, Ghislaine Houle, Suzanne Lauzier, Yvette Trépanier.
Localisation: OONL.

0845 **Demers, Pierre**
"Filmographie succincte de la musique traditionnelle au Québec."
Dans: *Cinéma Québec*; Vol. 4, no 9-10 ([1975]) p. 29.; ISSN: 0319-4647.
Note: Localisation: OONL.

0846 **MacMillan, Keith; Beckwith, John**
Contemporary Canadian composers. Toronto: Oxford University Press, 1975. xxiv, 248 p.: [4] l. of pl.; ISBN: 0-

19-540244-8.

Note: Biobibliographical information about 144 composers who have produced all or most of their work since 1920.– Excludes composers or arrangers of popular or commercial music.

Titre en français: *Compositeurs canadiens contemporains.*

Location: OONL.

0847 **Moogk, Edward B.**
En remontant les années: l'histoire et l'héritage de l'enregistrement sonore au Canada, des débuts à 1930. Ottawa: Bibliothèque nationale du Canada, 1975. xii, 447 p.: ill., fac-sim., portr., disque (dans une pochette).

Note: Histoire du disque au Canada (1878 à 1930), documentation bibliographique, notes biographiques, discographie: interprètes, compositeurs et paroliers (nés, naturalisés ou qui ont reçu leur éducation musicale au Canada); séries canadiennes.– Title in English: *Roll back the years: history of Canadian recorded sound and its legacy: genesis to 1930.*

Localisation: OONL.

0848 **Moogk, Edward B.**
Roll back the years: history of Canadian recorded sound and its legacy: genesis to 1930. Ottawa: National Library of Canada, 1975. xii, 443 p.: ill., facsims., ports., phonodisc (in pocket).

Note: History of Canadian recorded sound (1878 to 1930) with extensive discography: performers, composers, lyricists (Canadian born/adopted/trained): lists the title of each performance, accompaniment, record company, size and type of record and catalogue number, Canadian series.

Titre en français: *En remontant les années: l'histoire et l'héritage de l'enregistrement sonore au Canada, des débuts à 1930.*

Location: OONL.

0849 **Taft, Michael**
A regional discography of Newfoundland and Labrador, 1904-1972. [St. John's, Nfld.]: Memorial University of Newfoundland Folklore and Language Archive, 1975. xxx, 102 p. (Bibliographical and special series / Memorial University of Newfoundland Folklore and Language Archive ; no. 1)

Note: Approx. 1,500 entries.– Covers to mid-1972.

Location: OONL.

— 1976 —

0850 **Bradley, Ian L.**
"Indian music of the Pacific northwest: an annotated bibliography of research."

In: *BC Studies*; No. 31 (Autumn 1976) p. 12-22.; ISSN: 0005-2949.

Note: 40 entries.– Books, journal articles, theses relating to musical forms, musical instruments, songs of the native people of the Pacific northwest.

Location: AEU.

0851 **Bradley, Ian L.**
A selected bibliography of musical Canadiana. rev. ed. Victoria, B.C.: University of Victoria, [c1976]. 177 p.; ISBN: 0-88874-050-6.

Note: Approx. 2,100 entries.– Books, articles, theses on biography, composition, education, ethnomusicology, history, section of song books.

Previous edition: Vancouver, Versatile Pub. Co., 1974. vii, 106 p.

Location: OONL.

0852 **Canadian Music Centre**
Canadian vocal music: available on loan from the libraries of the Canadian Music Centre/Musique vocale canadienne: disponible aux musicothèques du Centre de musique canadienne. 3rd ed. Toronto: The Centre, 1976. 108 l.

Note: Published and unpublished works by composers resident in Canada for at least five years: solos, duets/trios, collections.– Listing intended principally for the serious or professional singer, encompasses music suitable for recital, broadcast, church use.– Provides information on voice range, accompaniment, publication.– Text in English and French/texte en français et en anglais.

Previous editions:
Canadian vocal music available for perusal from the library of the Canadian Music Centre/Musique vocale canadienne disponible pour examen de la musicothèque du Centre musical canadien. 1971. 81 l.

1967. 64 l.

Location: OONL.

0853 **Canadian Music Centre**
Catalogue of Canadian music for orchestra, including concertos and works with choir and/or solo voice(s) in the libraries of the Canadian Music Centre/Catalogue de musique canadienne pour orchestre, comprenant également les concertos ainsi que les oeuvres avec choeur ou soliste(s) disponible dans les bibliothèques du Centre de musique canadienne. Toronto: The Centre, 1976. ca. 500 p.

Note: Lists 1,000 works by 130 Canadian composers, with emphasis on compositions since 1945.– Provides information on movements (tempo, etc.), instrumentation, degree of difficulty, duration, date of composition, first performance, recordings.– Includes descriptive notes supplied by composers.– Has an index of compositions by forms (symphonies, suites, overtures, etc.).– Text in English and French/texte en français et en anglais.

Supplements:
1979. ca. 150 p.; ISBN: 0-9690836-3-7.

Canadian music for string orchestra: supplement 1983/ Musique canadienne pour orchestra à cordes: supplément 1983. 1983. 4 p.

Location: OONL.

0854 **Creelman, Gwendolyn; Cooke, Esther; King, Geraldine L.**
Canadian music scores and recordings: a classified catalogue of the holdings of Mount Allison University libraries. Sackville, N.B.: Ralph Pickard Bell Library, Mount Allison University, c1976. viii, 192 p. (Publications in music / Ralph Pickard Bell Library, Mount Allison University ; no. 3); ISBN: 0-88828-000-9.

Note: 2,662 entries.– Covers to April 1976.– Includes works by Canadian citizens, present or past residents of Canada, or persons having some Canadian background in training or teaching.– Excludes arrangements of traditional compositions, Canadian folk songs for voice or chorus.

Location: OONL.

0855 **Jarman, Lynne**
Canadian music: a selected checklist, 1950-73: a selective listing of Canadian music from the Fontes artis musicae, 1954-73 based on the catalogued entries of Canadiana from 1950/La musique canadienne: une liste sélective, 1950-73: répertoire sélective de musique canadienne extrait de Fontes artis musicae, 1954-73 d'après les notices catalographiques de Canadiana depuis 1950. Toronto: University of Toronto Press, [1976]. xiv, 170 p.; ISBN: 0-8020-5327-0.
Note: Approx. 400 entries.– Works chosen for inclusion are of serious intent and of a certain length and substance.– Excludes popular music, teaching pieces, minor church music, most educational material.– Text in English and French/texte en français et en anglais.
Location: OONL.

0856 **Laforte, Conrad**
"Poétiques de la chanson traditionnelle française: bibliographie."
Dans: *Archives de Folklore*; Vol. 17 (1976) p. 127-142.; ISSN: 0085-5243.
Note: Localisation: AEU.

0857 **Tremblay, Jean-Pierre**
"La chanson: essai bibliographique."
Dans: *Cahiers de Cap-Rouge*; Vol. 4, no 4 (1976) p. 45-79.; ISSN: 0227-2822.
Note: Localisation: OONL.

— 1977 —

0858 **Bradley, Ian L.**
"Revised bibliography of Indian musical culture in Canada."
In: *Indian Historian*; Vol. 10, no. 4 (Fall 1977) p. 28-32.; ISSN: 0019-4840.
Note: Approx. 150 entries.
Location: AEU.

0859 **Canadian Music Centre**
Canadian compositions for band/Oeuvres canadiennes pour fanfare et harmonie. Toronto: The Centre, 1977. 5 l.
Note: Location: OONL.

0860 **Canadian Music Research Council**
Survey of research in music and music education in Canada. [Victoria, B.C.: s.n.], 1977. 15 p.
Note: Lists work of about 50 music scholars, by title.– No bibliographical details.
Location: OONL.

0861 **Laplante, Louise**
Compositeurs canadiens contemporains. Montréal: Presses de l'Université du Québec, 1977. xxviii, 382 p.: [8] f. de pl., ill.; ISBN: 0-7770-0205-1.
Note: Renseignements biographiques, listes d'oeuvres et bibliographies de compositeurs de toutes les parties du Canada, informations relatives aux styles et aux recherches propres à chacun d'eux.– La période couverte est de 1920 à janvier 1977.
English title: *Contemporary Canadian composers*.
Localisation: OONL.

0862 **McMillan, Barclay**
"Tune-book imprints in Canada to 1867: a descriptive bibliography."
In: *Papers of the Bibliographical Society of Canada*; Vol. 16 (1977) p. 31-57; facsims., music.; ISSN: 0067-6896.
Note: List of Canadian impressions and editions of publications of tune-books (collections of music for use in conjunction with words-only psalm and hymn books).
Location: OONL.

— 1978 —

0863 **Canadian Folk Music Society**
A reference list on Canadian folk music. Rev. and updated ed. Calgary: Canadian Folk Music Society; Toronto: Canadian Music Centre, 1978. 16 p.
Note: Approx. 400 entries.– Books of traditional songs and records by traditional singers, with some representative articles on aspects on Canadian folk music (Indian and Inuit, French Canadian, Anglo-Canadian, other language groups), compositions based on folk songs.– Includes published and unpublished works.
Previous edition: Cass-Beggs, Barbara; Fowke, Edith. 1973. 12 p.
Location: OONL.

0864 **Canadian Music Centre**
Catalogue of Canadian choral music/Catalogue de musique chorale canadienne. Toronto: The Centre, 1978. [400] p.; ISBN: 0-9690836-2-9.
Note: 1,650 entries.– Mainly repertoire appropriate for adult choirs, in English and French, for the period from 1900.– Information includes voice, accompaniment, duration, date of composition, publication, movements and first lines, descriptive notes supplied by the composers.– Text in English and French/texte en français et en anglais.
Location: OONL.

0865 **Feihl, John; Murphy, Brian**
List of controversial and obscure CanCon material. Ottawa: B. Murphy, 1978. 13 l.
Note: "Cites Canadian content recorded by Canadian, partly Canadian, formerly Canadian and non-Canadian performers."
Location: OONL.

0866 **Gaulin, Jean-Guy; Gaulin, André**
"Petite discographie de la chanson québécoise."
Dans: *Québec français*; No 29 (mars 1978) p. 32-36.; ISSN: 0316-2052.
Note: Localisation: OONL.

0867 **Lyttle, Brendan J.**
A chartology of Canadian popular music: January 1965 to December 1976. [Toronto: RPM Music Publications, 1978]. 82 p.
Note: Surveys single recordings and albums defined as Canadian Content by CRTC regulations that appeared on Top 100 single and album charts of *RPM* and *Billboard*.
Supplement: *A chartology of Canadian popular music: part two, 1977 to 1980*. Calgary: Record Research Services; [1980]. [37] l.
Location: OONL.

0868 **Mercer, Paul**
A bio-bibliography of Newfoundland songs in printed sources. St. John's: Memorial University of Newfoundland, 1978. xiii, 382 l.
Note: 208 entries.– Descriptive bibliography of sources of printed song in Newfoundland from 1807, with biographical sketches.– Includes broadside ballads, sheet music, scholarly folk song collections, other miscellany.
Location: OONL.

0869 **Moody, Lois**
"Contemporary Canadian jazz recordings: a selected bibliography."

In: *Jazz Ottawa*; No. 19 (September 1978) p. 7-10.; ISSN: 0383-9206.
Note: Recordings produced in Canada covering both native-born and "adopted" Canadian artists.
Location: OONL.

0870 **Robertson, Alex**
Canadian Compo numericals. Pointe Claire, Quebec: A. Robertson, 1978. v, 82 l.
Note: Numerical catalogue of 78 rpm. disc sound recordings issued on labels of the Compo Company of Lachine, Quebec.
Location: OONL.

0871 **Shand, Patricia Martin**
Canadian music: a selective guidelist for teachers. Toronto: Canadian Music Centre, 1978. viii, 186 p.; ISBN: 0-9690836-0-2.
Note: Published Canadian music suitable for large and small choral and instrumental student ensembles: evaluations of 160 compositions for choirs, bands, orchestras, chamber ensembles.– Information includes duration, grade level, rating (easy to very difficult), effectiveness in performance.– Excludes solo works, pop music.
Titre en français: *Musique canadienne: oeuvres choisies à l'intention des professeurs.*
Location: OONL.

0872 **Vomberg, Elisabeth**
Music for the physically disabled child: a bibliography. Toronto: E. Vomberg, 1978. 34 p.
Note: Approx. 850 entries.– Books and articles relating to effect of music on physically disabled children.
Location: OONL.

— 1979 —

0873 **Barron, John P.**
A selected bibliography of the Kodaly concept of music education. Willowdale, Ont.: Avondale Press; published in collaboration with the Kodaly Institute of Canada, c1979. 81 p.; ISBN: 0-9690452-7-1.
Note: Approx. 500 entries.– Monographs, collected works, articles in periodicals, published lectures/reports on research activities/reprints, theses, song collections/ textbooks/instruction books, discography.– Many references to Canadian application of Kodaly system.
Location: OONL.

0874 **Chartier, Yves**
"Situation de la recherche sur la musique au Canada français."
Dans: *Bulletin du Centre de recherche en civilisation canadienne-française de l'Université d'Ottawa*; No 19 (décembre 1979) p. 1-14.; ISSN: 0045-608X.
Note: Approx. 120 entrées.– Bibliographies, dictionnaires biographiques, histoire, périodiques, folklore musical (anthologies, études), discographie.
Localisation: AEU.

0875 **Keillor, Elaine**
Bibliography of items on music in Canada in *The Musical Courier*, 1898-1903. Ottawa: E. Keillor, 1979. 27 l.
Note: 249 entries about Canadian music and musicians from U.S. journal *Musical Courier*.– Numerous references to Albani, Lavallée, music scene in Montreal, Ottawa, Toronto.
Location: OONL.

0876 **Lee, Dorothy Sara**
Native North American music and oral data: a catalogue of sound recordings, 1893-1976. Bloomington: Indiana University Press, c1979. xiv, 463 p.; ISBN: 0 25319 877-6
Note: Approx. 1,600 entries.– Listing and guide to North American Indian and Inuit music and oral data holdings at the Indiana University Archives of Traditional Music.– Includes field, commercial and broadcast recordings.– Information provided includes name of collector and performer, culture group, quality of recording and a listing of available documentation.
Location: OONL.

0877 **Mercer, Paul**
Newfoundland songs and ballads in print, 1842-1974: a title and first-line index. St. John's, Nfld.: Memorial University of Newfoundland, 1979. 343 p.: ports. (Memorial University of Newfoundland Folklore and language publications, Bibliographical and special series ; no. 6); ISBN: 0-88901-038-2.
Note: Approx. 1,500 entries derived from about 100 publications, including contents of five regional magazines.– Excludes broadsides, newspaper articles.
Location: OONL.

0878 **Proctor, George A.**
Sources in Canadian music: a bibliography of bibliographies/Les sources de la musique canadienne: une bibliographie des bibliographies. 2nd ed. [Sackville, N.B.]: Ralph Pickard Bell Library, Mount Allison University, 1979. 36 p. (Publications in music / Ralph Pickard Bell Library, Mount Allison University ; no. 4); ISBN: 0-88828-027-0.
Note: 157 entries.– Includes only those items which contain bibliographies, lists or catalogues relating to Canadian music in areas of biography, discography, criticism, pedagogy, literature, ethnomusicology.– Types of materials include books, periodicals, theses.
Previous edition: 1975. 38 p.
Also issued in the Canadian Association of University Schools of Music *Journal*; Vol. 4, nos 1-2 (Fall 1974) P. 44-73.
Location: OONL.

0879 **Washburn, Jon**
CBC Choral Concert's 1979 Canadian choral records list. Vancouver: Canadian Broadcasting Corporation, 1979. 3, 16, 2 p.
Note: 113 entries.– Includes CBC Canadian Collection, records from commercial companies and privately produced recordings from individual choral organizations.
Location: OONL.

— 1980 —

0880 **Canadian Music Centre**
Canadian chamber music/Musique de chambre canadienne. Toronto: The Centre, 1980. c. 900 p.; ISBN: 0-9690836-4-5.
Note: 1,738 entries.– Information includes instrumentation, movements, degree of difficulty, duration, publication details, date of composition, recordings, descriptive notes supplied by the composers.– Text in English and French/texte en français et en anglais.
Previous edition: *Catalogue of chamber music available on loan from the library of the Canadian Music Centre/Catalogue de musique de chambre disponible à la musicothèque de Centre*

musical canadien. c1967. 288 p.
Supplements:
List of Canadian chamber music/Musique de chambre canadienne. 1971. 18 l.
List of Canadian chamber music: supplementary to the CMC 1967 Catalogue of Canadian chamber music/Musique de chambre canadienne: liste supplémentaire au catalogue de 1967 de Musique de chambre canadienne. 1976. 59 l.
Location: OONL.

0881 **Canadian Music Centre**
Canadian music for guitar/Musique canadienne pour guitare. Toronto: The Centre, 1980. 18 p.
Note: Approx. 75 entries.– Published and unpublished works: guitar solos/duets, guitar with one other instrument, chamber ensembles with guitar, voice and guitar with or without other instruments.– Notes on duration, date of composition, publication, recordings.– Text in English and French/texte en français et en anglais.
Location: OONL.

0882 **Canadian Music Centre**
List of Canadian music inspired by the music, poetry, art and folklore of native peoples. Toronto: The Centre, 1980. 22 l.
Note: Work of 27 Canadian composers.– Provides information on duration, date of composition, publication, recordings, descriptive notes.
Location: OONL.

0883 **Canadian Recording Industry Association**
Cancon releases. Toronto: Canadian Recording Industry Association, 1975-1980. 6 vol.; ISSN: 0706-8255.
Note: Discography of Canadian music.
Location: OONL.

0884 **Chants pour la liturgie: onze années de bibliographie canadienne (1968-1978): suivie d'un index général descriptif.** Ste-Foy, Québec: Alpec, 1980. 59 p.; ISBN: 2-920198-00-9.
Note: 30 ouvrages contenant des chants pour la liturgie publiés en français au Canada, parus dans le commerce de 1968 à 1978 inclusivement, suivie d'un index général, multiple, alphabétique et descriptif, de tous les chants dans ces ouvrages, en total, plus de 800 titres, dont 750 d'origine ou de contribution canadienne.
Localisation: OONL.

0885 **Hurn, Nancy J.**
Listing of sheet music available from the CNE archives. Toronto: The Archives, [1980]. [14] l.
Note: 94 entries.
Location: OONL.

0886 **Legere, Bill**
[List of Canadian artists]. [S.l.: B. Legere], 1980. [180] l.
Note: Discography of Canadian country music.– Typescript with holograph additions.
Location: OONL.

0887 **Rosenberg, Neil V.**
"A preliminary bibliography of Canadian old time instrumental music books."
In: *Canadian Folk Music Journal*; Vol. 8 (1980) p. 20-22.; ISSN: 0318-2568.
Note: Location: OONL.

— 1981 —

0888 **Association of Canadian Orchestras**
Canadian "pops" music project: music for orchestra by Canadian composers/Projet du musique "pop" canadienne: musique pour orchestre de compositeurs canadiens. Toronto: The Association, 1981. [60] p.
Note: Approx. 120 entries.– Compositions arranged in two sections: music for pops concerts; music for children's, youth & family concerts.– Provides information on movements, duration, instrumentation or staging, degree of difficulty, availability, performances, recordings.– Includes descriptive notes.– Text in English and French/texte en français et en anglais.
Location: OONL.

0889 **Calderisi, Maria**
L'édition musicale au Canada, 1800-1867. Ottawa: Bibliothèque nationale du Canada, 1981. x, 124, 128, x p.: fac-sim., musique.; ISBN: 0-660-50454-5.
Note: Publications musicales canadiennes antérieures à la Confédération: livres de musique (méthodes, recueils de cantiques et de chansons), journaux et périodiques, et après 1840, musique en feuille.– Comprend: répertoire de livres contenant de la musique, par éditeur ou imprimeur; liste chronologique de livres contenant de la musique; liste chronologique de journaux et de périodiques contenant de la musique (1831-1867); répertoire des éditeurs et imprimeurs canadiens de musique en feuille (1840-1868).– Texte en français et en anglais disposé tête-bêche.– Titre de la p. de t. additionnelle: *Music publishing in the Canadas, 1800-1867.*
Localisation: OONL.

0890 **Calderisi, Maria**
Music publishing in the Canadas, 1800-1867. Ottawa: National Library of Canada, 1981. x, 128, 124, x p.: facsims., music.; ISBN: 0-660-50454-5.
Note: Survey of music publishing in Canada: book publishers, newspaper and periodical publishers, sheet music publishers, music printing, copyright.– Includes publisher/printer index to books known to contain musical notation; chronological list of books known to contain musical notation; chronological list of newspapers and periodicals known to contain printed music (1831-1867); directory of Canadian sheet music publishers and printers (1840-1868).– Text in English and French with French text on inverted pages.– Title of additional title-page: *L'édition musicale au Canada, 1800-1867.*
Location: OONL.

0891 **Canadian Music Centre**
Canadian music for clarinet/Musique canadienne pour clarinette. Toronto: The Centre, 1981. 45 p.
Note: Approx. 200 entries.– Clarinet solo, clarinet and keyboard, clarinet choirs, solo clarinet with chamber ensemble, solo clarinet with orchestra.– Provides information on degree of difficulty, duration, date of composition, publication, recordings.– Text in English and French/texte en français et en anglais.
Previous edition: *Canadian music featuring clarinet.* 1978. 5 l.
Location: OONL.

0892 **Canadian Music Centre**
Canadian music for saxophone/Musique canadienne pour saxophone. Toronto: The Centre, 1981. 20 p.
Note: Approx. 100 entries.– Saxophone solo, sax with piano, sax quartets, sax with orchestra, ensembles with saxophone(s).– Provides information on degree of difficulty, duration, composition date, publication, recordings.– Text in English and French/texte en français

et en anglais.
Location: OONL.

0893 **Canadian Music Centre**
Canadian music for viola/Musique canadienne pour
alto. Toronto: The Centre, 1981. 38 p.
Note: Approx. 80 entries.– Works for viola solo, viola
and piano, duos with viola, string trios, ensembles with
viola, solo viola with orchestra, ensembles with viola and
voice.– Includes information on degree of difficulty,
duration, publication, recordings.– Text in English and
French/texte en français et en anglais.
Location: OONL.

0894 **Dubois, Monique**
Répertoire de chansons folkloriques. [Québec]: Gouverne-
ment du Québec, Ministère de l'éducation, 1981. 65 p.
(Document d'information / Gouvernement du Québec,
Ministère de l'éducation ; 16-3505-03); ISBN: 2-550-04851-
2.
Note: 21 références, liste des maisons d'éditions
musicales.
Localisation: OONL.

0895 **Edwards, Barry**
"A critical discography of Canadian music/Une
discographie critique de musique canadienne."
In: *Musicanada*; No. 46 (June 1981) p. 22-24; no. 47
(December 1981) p. 21-23.; ISSN: 0700-4745.
Note: Location: OONL.

0896 **Gallat-Morin, Élizabeth; Bouchard, Antoine**
Témoins de la vie musicale en Nouvelle-France.
Montréal: Ministère des affaires culturelles, Archives
nationales du Québec, 1981. 74 p.; ISBN: 2-550-04322-0.
Note: 57 entrées.– Foreword and annotations in English.
Localisation: OONL.

0897 **Matteau-Beaumier, Murielle**
Répertoire de chansons québécoises. [Québec]: Gouverne-
ment du Québec, Direction générale du développement
pédagogique, 1981. 76 p.; ISBN: 2-550-04777-X.
Note: Approx. 500 entrées.
Localisation: OONL.

0898 **Pille, John M.**
Catalogue of band music by Canadian composers.
[Lennoxville, Quebec: J.M. Pille], c1981. 80 l.
Note: Works by 142 Canadian composers, published and
unpublished.
Previous edition: 1973. 28 l.
Location: OONL.

0899 **Toomey, Kathleen M.; Willis, Stephen C.**
Musicians in Canada: a bio-bibliographical finding list/
Musiciens au Canada: index bibliographique. Ottawa:
Canadian Association of Music Libraries, 1981. xiv,
185 p. (Publications / Canadian Association of Music
Libraries ; no. 1); ISBN: 0-9690583-1-4.
Note: Approx. 3,300 entries derived from 218 sources.–
Includes musicians who were, have been or are active in
Canada.– Separate list of specialized works, mainly
biographical monographs on Canadian musicians.– Text
in English and French/texte en français et en anglais.
Previous edition: Dwyer, Melva J.; Brochu, Lucien;
Kallmann, Helmut. *A bio-bibliographical finding list of Can-
adian musicians and those who have contributed to music in
Canada*. Ottawa: Canadian Music Library Association;
[1961]. v, 53 p.– Approx. 1,300 entries.
Location: OONL.

0900 **Vineer, Bill**
The Vineer Organ Library. Ottawa: B. Vineer, [1981]. vi,
63 p.
Note: Private collection of books, pamphlets, theses,
films, recordings, organ builders trade catalogues,
periodicals.– Includes Canadian references.
Location: OONL.

— 1982 —

0901 **Canadian Music Centre**
Canadian music for accordion/Musique canadienne
pour accordéon. Toronto: The Centre, 1982. 14 p.
Note: Approx. 60 entries.– Solo, chamber and orchestral
works.– Provides information on degree of difficulty,
publication, recordings.– Text in English and French/
texte en français et en anglais.
Location: OONL.

0902 **Canadian Music Centre**
Canadian music for bassoon/Musique canadienne pour
basson. Toronto: The Centre, 1982. 27 p.
Note: Approx. 100 entries.– Instrumentation: bassoon
solo, bassoon and keyboard, bassoon choirs, ensembles
with bassoon, solo bassoon with chamber ensemble, solo
bassoon with orchestra.– Information provided about
degree of difficulty, duration, publication, recordings.–
Text in English and French/texte en français et en anglais.
Location: OONL.

0903 **Canadian Music Centre**
List of Canadian operas (including operettas & stage
works): December 1982, available from Canadian Music
Centre/Liste des opéras canadiens (incluant opérettes et
musique de scène): décembre 1982, disponible au Centre
de musique canadienne. Toronto: The Centre, 1982. 20 p.
Note: Approx. 60 entries.– Provides information on
casting, instrumentation, date of composition, publication, sources, librettist.
Previous edition: 1978. 15 l.
Location: OONL.

0904 **Centre de musique canadienne au Québec**
Compositeurs au Québec. Montréal: Centre de musique
canadienne au Québec, 1974-1982. 14 vol.: ill., portr.
Note: Chaque volume comprend une catalogue des
oeuvres et une sélection bibliographique.
Vol. 1: Laplante, Louise. *Gilles Tremblay*. 1974. 15 p.
Vol. 2: Richer-Lortie, Lyse. *François Morel*. 1974. 15 p.
Vol. 3: Bail-Milot, Louise. *Jean Papineau-Couture*. 1974.
26 p.
Vol. 4: Hambraeus, Bengt. *Bruce Mather*. 1974. 15 p.
Vol. 5: Hétu, Jacques. *André Prévost*. 1975. 19 p.
Vol. 6: Billette, Gaby. *Serge Garant*. 1975. 19 p.
Vol. 7: Potvin, Gilles. *Micheline Coulombe Saint-Marcoux*.
1975. 15 p.
Vol. 8: Brisson, Irène. *Roger Matton*. 1975. 15 p.
Vol. 9: Bernier, Françoys. *Pierre Mercure*. 1976. 31 p.
Vol. 10: Bourassa-Trépanier, Juliette. *Jacques Hétu*. 1978.
15 p.
Vol. 11: Pépin, Clermont. *Claude Champagne*. 1979. 39 p.
Vol. 12: Saint-Marcoux, Micheline Coulombe. *Otto
Joachim*. 1980. 18 p.
Vol. 13: Samson, Marc. *Jean Vallerand*. 1981. 15 p.
Vol. 14: Potvin, Gilles. *Guillaume Couture*. 1982. 39 p.
Localisation: OONL.

0905 **Litchfield, Jack**
The Canadian jazz discography: 1916-1980. Toronto: University of Toronto Press, c1982. 945 p.; ISBN: 0-8020-2448-3.
Note: Comprehensive listing of jazz recordings by Canadian artists, from the earliest in 1916 to 1980.– Includes audio tapes, piano rolls, Canadian motion pictures containing jazz, recorded titles that contain substantial jazz passages.
Location: OONL.

0906 **Musique: liste de ressources pédagogiques, cycles intermédiaire et supérieur.** [Toronto]: Ministère de l'Éducation, [1982]. iii, 43 p.: ill.; ISBN: 0-7743-7785-2.
Note: Localisation: OONL.

0907 **Shand, Patricia Martin**
Musique canadienne: oeuvres choisies à l'intention des professeurs. Toronto: Centre de musique canadienne, 1982. viii, 133 p.; ISBN: 0-9690836-1-0.
Note: Approx. 110 entrées.
English title: *Canadian music: a selective guidelist for teachers.*
Localisation: OONL.

— 1983 —

0908 **Bergeron, Chantal, et al.**
Répertoire bibliographique de textes de présentation générale et d'analyse d'oeuvres musicales canadiennes (1900-1980)/Canadian musical works 1900-1980: a bibliography of general and analytical sources. Ottawa: Association canadienne des bibliothèques musicales, c1983. xiv, 96 p. (Publications / Association canadienne des bibliothèques musicales ; no 3); ISBN: 0-9690583-2-2.
Note: 1,995 références à quatre-vingt-deux sources secondaires traitant de quelque mille cinquante oeuvres de musique savante écrites entre 1900 et 1980 par 165 compositeurs canadiens: volumes de références, monographies, thèses, périodiques.– Établi par Chantal Bergeron, et al., sous la direction de Lucien Poirier.– Texte en français et en anglais/text in English and French.
Localisation: OONL.

0909 **Canadian Music Centre**
New works accepted into the library of the Canadian Music Centre from January 1, 1982 to December 31, 1982/ Nouvelles oeuvres acceptées à la musicothèque du Centre de musique canadienne du 1er janvier, 1982 à 31 décembre, 1982. Toronto: The Centre, [1983]. 27 p.; ISSN: 0822-8264.
Note: Approx. 250 entries.– Published and unpublished Canadian works for orchestra, band, chamber ensemble, choir, vocal, piano, organ.– Text in English and French/ texte en français et en anglais.
Location: OONL.

0910 **Fowke, Edith**
"A reference list on Canadian folk music."
In: *Canadian Folk Music Journal*; Vol. 1 (1973) p. 46-56; vol. 6 (1978) p. 41-56; vol. 11 (1983) p. 43-60.; ISSN: 0318-2568.
Note: Books of traditional songs and records by traditional singers, articles on aspects of Canadian folk music, some folk song records by non-traditional singers.– Published material arranged in language groupings: Indian, Inuit, French, English, Other language groups.– Includes listing of compositions based on folk songs.
Location: OONL.

0911 **Kallmann, Helmut**
"The German contribution to music in Canada: a bibliography."
In: *German-Canadian Yearbook*; Vol. 7 (1983) p. 228-238.; ISSN: 0316-8603.
Note: Four sections: German contribution to musical life in Canada; musical life among minorities of German descent; some musicians and music administrators of German-speaking ancestry; German scholars and commentators on music in Canada.
Location: OONL.

0912 **"Ouvrages et articles publiés par les membres [de l'Association pour l'avancement de la recherche en musique du Québec]."**
Dans: *Cahiers de l'ARMUQ*; No 2 (mai 1983) p. 13-23.; ISSN: 0821-1817.
Note: Localisation: OONL.

— 1984 —

0913 **Bowers, Neal**
Index to Canadian children's records. Bridgewater, N.S.: Lunenburg County District Teacher's Centre, c1984. 48 p.
Note: 700 songs, rhymes and stories on 47 record albums produced in Canada between 1975 and 1983.
Location: OONL.

0914 **Canadian Music Centre**
Almanac/Almanach. Toronto: The Centre, c1984. iii, 94 p.; ISSN: 0827-7575.
Note: Approx. 900 entries.– Contains a listing of musical works catalogued and added to the Canadian Music Centre Library from January 1 to December 31, 1983: orchestra, band, chamber music, choral, vocal, piano, organ.– Includes a list of premieres.– Text in English and French/texte en français et en anglais.
Continues under the title *Acquisitions*, 1985- vol.; ISSN: 0827-7567.
Location: OONL.

0915 **Canadian record catalogue/Catalogue de disques canadiens.** Toronto: Canadian Independent Record Production Association, 1982-1984. 2 vol. (loose-leaf); ISSN: 0714-8070.
Note: Annual with quarterly updates.– Catalogue of current Canadian recordings indexed by song title, album title, performer and composer.– Co-published by the Association du disque et de l'industrie du spectacle québécoise.– Text in English and French/texte en français et en anglais.
Location: OONL.

0916 **McIntosh, Robert Dale**
Catalogue of the sheet music collection. Vancouver: Provincial Archives of British Columbia, 1984. 1 vol. (in various pagings).
Note: Approx. 650 entries.– Listing of sheet music written or published in British Columbia.
Location: OONL.

0917 **Morley, Glen**
The Glen Morley collection of historical Canadian music of the nineteenth century: a catalogue of Canadian music published between 1832 and 1914. [Ottawa: Kingsmere Concert Enterprises, c1984]. 18 l.
Note: 365 entries.– Pieces for pianoforte, songs, choral works, dramatic readings, works for organ.
Location: OONL.

0918 **Shand, Patricia Martin**
A guide to unpublished Canadian string orchestra music suitable for student performers. Ann Arbor, Mich.; University Microfilms International, 1984. 7 microfiches (687 fr.).
Note: Thesis.– Restricted to unpublished compositions for string orchestra by Canadian composers (Canadian citizens or 5-year residents), including original compositions based on Canadian folk music.– Excludes string orchestra compositions with added wind/percussion/piano/harp/vocal or tape parts, solo concerti with string orchestra accompaniment, transcriptions/arrangements of previously composed music, compositions written after July 1980.
Location: OONL.

— 1985 —

0919 **Calderisi, Maria**
"Music publishers in the Maritimes: 1801-1900."
In: *APLA Bulletin*; Vol. 49, no. 2 (September 1985) p. 10-11.; ISSN: 0001-2203.
Note: Checklist of known 19th-century music publishers in New Brunswick, Nova Scotia and Prince Edward Island and their products, arranged alphabetically by city, and divided into two alphabets of books and sheet music publishers.
Location: OONL.

0920 **Legere, Bill**
Hillbilly heaven: discography. Mississauga, Ont.: B. Legere, 1985. 1 vol. (loose-leaf).
Note: List of country artists, many Canadian.– Includes biographical information, list of songs, composers, codes to indicate Canadian connection.
Location: OONL.

0921 **Massey, Michael**
Canadian repertoire manual for youth orchestras. Banff, Alta.: Canadian Association of Youth Orchestras, c1985. 1 vol. (loose-leaf).
Note: 64 entries.– Provides information on duration, orchestration.– Includes descriptive notes with indications about tempo, phrasing, musical challenges.
Location: OONL.

0922 **Maxwell, Karen A.**
A guide to solo Canadian trombone literature available through the Canadian Music Centre. Toronto: Canadian Music Centre, 1985. i, 14 p.
Note: 9 entries.– Evaluations of Canadian solo trombone repertoire suitable for novice and professional players, and guidance as to degree of difficulty, musical characteristics, technical aspects.
Location: OONL.

0923 **Zuk, Ireneus**
The piano concerto in Canada (1900-1980): a bibliographic survey. Baltimore, Md.: Peabody Conservatory of Music, Peabody Institute of the Johns Hopkins University, 1985. xxxi, 429 l.
Note: Thesis.– Lists 103 works by 59 composers active in Canada from the beginning of the century to 1980.– For each composition, information includes composition date, publisher(s), duration, tempo indications, instrumentation, first performance(s), recordings.– Includes biographical sketch and selected bibliography of primary and secondary sources.
Location: OONL.

— 1986 —

0924 **Alberta Band Association. Lending Library**
A.B.A. Lending Library band catalogue. [Calgary: The Library, 1986]. 34 p.
Note: Approx. 850 entries.– Concert, stage and marching band titles for woodwind, brass and percussion ensembles at beginner, easy, medium and difficult levels of performance.– Many titles composed or arranged for band by Canadian composers.
Location: OONL.

0925 **Grondines, Hélène**
Bibliographie analytique des monographies, des thèses et essais concernant la musicothérapie et conservés à la bibliothèque de l'Université Laval [microforme]. Ottawa: Bibliothèque nationale du Canada, 1986. 3 microfiches (227 images).; ISBN: 0-315-22621-8.
Note: 61 entrées.– Thèse.
Localisation: OONL.

0926 **Shand, Patricia Martin**
Guidelist of unpublished Canadian string orchestra music suitable for student performers. Toronto: Canadian Music Centre, 1986. viii, 138 p.; ISBN: 0-921519-00-1.
Note: 62 pieces, arranged alphabetically by composer according to degree of difficulty.– Provides information on instrumentation, duration, availability, with notes on technical challenges, musical characteristics, and pedagogical value.
Location: OONL.

— 1987 —

0927 **Audio key: the record, tape & compact disc guide.** 3rd ed. Winnipeg: Audio Key Publications, 1987. x, 379 p.; ISSN: 9820-1691.
Note: Listings for popular, country, jazz, religious, children's records and soundtracks.– Includes Canadian listings.
Previous editions:
Audio key: the record, tape & compact disc catalogue. 1986. C18, 279 p.
Audio key: the Canadian record & tape guide. 1985. 291 p.
Location: OONL.

0928 **Gibeault, André**
Canadian records: a discography & price guide of Canadian 45's and LP's from 1955 to 1975. St-Lambert, Québec: André Gibeault, 1987. 1 vol. (in various pagings).
Note: Approx. 4,000 entries.– Alphabetical listing by individual artists and groups, with a list of their production of popular music singles and albums.– Includes a section of "punk/psychedelic obscurities and rareties," and a section of French Canadian groups from Quebec.– Excludes country and western music.
Location: OORT.

0929 **Laforte, Conrad**
Le catalogue de la chanson folklorique française. Nouv. éd. augm. et entièrement refondue. Québec: Presses de l'Université Laval, 1977-1987. 6 vol.: cartes. (Archives de folklore ; 18-23)
Note: Approx. 70,000 versions des chansons folkloriques françaises d'Amérique (Québec, Acadie, Louisiane), et l'Europe (France, Belgique et Suisse).– Vol. I: *Chansons en laisse.* 1977. 676 p.; ISBN: 9-7746-6824-5.– Vol. II: *Chanson strophiques.* 1981. 864 p.; ISBN: 2-7637-6917-9.– Vol. III: *Chansons en forme de dialogue.* 1982. 164 p.; ISBN: 2-7637-

6883-0.– Vol. IV: *Chansons énumératives*. 1979. 342 p.; ISBN: 2-7637-6883-0.– Vol. V: *Chansons brèves (les enfantines)*. 1987. 1017 p.; ISBN: 2-7637-7125-4.– Vol. VI: *Chansons sur les timbres*. 1983. 649 p.; ISBN: 2-7637-7000-2. Édition antérieure: 1958. xxix, 397 p.
Localisation: OONL.

0930 **Shand, Patricia Martin**
Guidelist of unpublished Canadian band music suitable for student performers. Toronto: Canadian Music Centre, 1987. xi, 76 p.; ISBN: 0-921519-01-X.
Note: 63 entries.– Includes original unpublished compositions for band, written by Canadian composers before July 1983.– Arranged by composer according to level of difficulty.
Location: OONL.

— 1988 —

0931 **Beaudry, Claude**
"Catalogue des imprimés musicaux d'avant 1800 conservés à la bibliothèque de l'Université Laval."
Dans: *Musical Canada: words and music honouring Helmut Kallmann*, edited by John Beckwith and Frederick A. Hall. Toronto: University of Toronto Press, 1988. P. 29-49.; ISBN: 0-8020-5759-4.
Note: Approx. 150 entrées.– Ouvrages liturgiques (antiphonaires, graduels), ouvrages datant du régime français depuis 1667 (oeuvres musicales et traités sur la musique), publications postérieures à la conquête de 1760.
Localisation: OONL.

0932 **Beckwith, John**
"Tunebooks and hymnals in Canada, 1801-1939."
In: *American Music*; Vol. 6, no. 2 (1988) p. 193-234.; ISSN: 0734-4392.
Note: 61 entries.– Bibliographical essay and chronological checklist of published Canadian tunebooks and hymnals, from *Union harmony*, (Saint John: 1801) to *The Canadian youth hymnal*, (Toronto: 1939).
Location: OONL.

0933 **Calderisi, Maria**
"John Lovell (1810-93): Montreal music printer and publisher."
In: *Musical Canada: words and music honouring Helmut Kallmann*, edited by John Beckwith and Frederick A. Hall. Toronto: University of Toronto Press, 1988. P. 79-99; facsim., music.; ISBN: 0-8020-5759-4.
Note: Contains a section entitled: "Music imprints of John Lovell from 1840 to 1888, chronological listings representing the known and reported Lovell imprints in libraries and private collections: sheet music; books and pamphlets."
Location: OONL.

— 1989 —

0934 **Beatty, Carolyn**
Directory of associate composers. Toronto: Canadian Music Centre, 1989. 1 vol. (loose-leaf).; ISBN: 0-921519-08-7.
Note: Bio-bibliography.– Listing of compositions for 200 Canadian composers.
Titre en français: *Répertoire des compositeurs agrées*.
Location: OONL.

0935 **Beatty, Carolyn**
Répertoire des compositeurs agrées. Toronto: Centre de musique canadienne, 1989. 1 vol. (f. mobiles); ISBN: 0-

921519-09-5.
Note: Biobibliographie.– Descriptions sur la vie et l'oeuvre des 238 compositeurs canadiens.
English title: *Directory of associate composers*.
Localisation: OONL.

0936 **Stubley, Eleanor Victoria**
A guide to unpublished Canadian brass chamber music suitable for student performers. Toronto: Canadian Music Educators' Association, c1989. x, 106 p.; ISBN: 0-92151-902-8.
Note: 44 entries.– Canadian compositions for brass trios, quartets, and quintets.– Annotations describe level of difficulty, technical/musical/ensemble challenges, pedagogical value.
Location: OONL.

— 1990 —

0937 **Peters, Diane E.**
Music reference and research materials in W.L.U. Library. Waterloo, Ont.: Library, Wilfrid Laurier University, 1990. v, 148 p.; ISBN: 0-921821-09-3.
Note: Approx. 1,200 entries.– Listing of bibliographies of music and music literature, discographies, dictionaries and encyclopaedias, thematic catalogues, directories, indexes and manuals.– Includes Canadian references in all categories.
Location: OONL.

0938 **Stubley, Eleanor Victoria**
A guide to solo french horn music by Canadian composers. Toronto: Canadian Music Centre, 1990. ix, 75 p.: ill., music.; ISBN: 0-921519-06-0.
Note: Approx. 50 entries.– Original published and unpublished Canadian compositions to July 1986 for solo horn and solo horn with keyboard, tape, electronic, or percussion accompaniment.– Provides information on instrumentation, duration, level of difficulty, musical style, technical challenges, ensemble co-ordination.
Location: OONL.

0939 **Tremblay-Matte, Cécile**
La chanson écrite au féminin: de Madeleine de Verchères à Mitsou, 1730-1990. Laval, Québec: Éditions Trois, [1990]. 391 p.: ill. (Collection Trois Guinées); ISBN: 2-920887-16-5.
Note: Comprend 409 créatrices, 6,628 chansons.– Comprend des références bibliographiques, discographies.
Localisation: OONL.

— 1991 —

0940 **MacInnis, Peggy**
Guidelist of solo free bass accordion music suitable for student performers. Toronto: Canadian Music Centre, 1991. x, 92 p.; ISBN: 0-921519-05-2.
Note: 72 entries.– Original Canadian compositions written for solo free bass accordion at the easy and medium levels of difficulty.– Excludes stradella or standard bass accordion music, as well as arrangements from piano music and transcriptions.
Location: OONL.

0941 **Peters, Diane E.**
Music in Canada: a bibliography of resources in W.L.U. Library. Waterloo, Ont.: Library, Wilfrid Laurier University, 1991. 24 p.; ISBN: 0-921821-15-8.
Note: Approx. 200 entries.– Books on the Canadian music industry, church music, ethnomusicology, history

and biography of individual composers and musicians, music education.– Includes a listing of bibliographies, catalogues, indexes, dictionaries, encyclopaedias, directories, conference proceedings.
Location: OONL.

— 1992 —

0942 **Thérien, Robert; D'Amours, Isabelle**
Dictionnaire de la musique populaire au Québec, 1955-1992. Québec: Institut québécois de recherche sur la culture, 1992. xxv, 580 p.: portr.; ISBN: 2-89224-183-9.
Note: 351 interprètes, groupes, auteurs, compositeurs, producteurs de musique populaire: biographies, discographies, références bibliographiques.
Localisation: OONL.

— 1993 —

0943 **Manley, Frank**
Smash the state: a discography of Canadian punk, 1977-92. Westmount, Quebec: No Exit, 1993. vi, 138 p.: ill., ports.; ISBN: 0-9696631-0-2.
Note: Approx. 500 entries.– Listing of vinyl recordings featuring Canadian punk rock bands, as well as international compilations which include these bands.
Location: OONL.

— Ongoing/En cours —

0944 **Canadian Music Centre. Library**
Acquisitions: Canadian Music Centre Library/ Bibliothèque du Centre de musique canadienne. Toronto: The Centre, 1985-. vol.; ISSN: 0827-7567.
Note: Annual.– First issue, 1984.– Lists musical works added to collection of Canadian Music Centre Library.– Classified by voice or instrument, with index of works by composer.– Provides information on instrumentation, date of composition (or copyright date), duration, availability of parts.– In the 1990 issue, a new section entitled "Electroacoustic archive" was added, a listing of a resource collection of electroacoustic music on cassette tape.– Text in English and French/texte en français et en anglais.
Location: OONL.

0945 **Canadian Society for Musical Traditions**
Folk music catalogue: LP's, cassettes and books. Calgary: CSMT Mail Order Service, 1989-. vol.; ISSN: 1186-7523.
Note: Annual.– Annotated listing of Canadian folk music records and books.– Categories include traditional, which is arranged by region, contemporary, music for children, music of native communities and multicultural communities.– Title varies: 1989, *Catalogue of LP's, cassettes and books.*
Location: OONL.

— 1949 —

0946 **Ouellet, Thérèse**
Bibliographie du théâtre canadien-français avant 1900. Québec: [Université Laval], 1949. 53 f.
Note: 55 entrées.
Localisation: OONL.

— 1956 —

0947 **Bilodeau, Françoise**
Bibliographie du théâtre canadien-français de 1900-1955. [S.l.: s.n.], 1956. 93 f.
Note: Localisation: QQLA.

— 1962 —

0948 **Ball, John L.**
"Theatre in Canada."
In: *Canadian Literature*; No. 14 (Autumn 1962) p. 85-100.; ISSN: 0008-4360.
Note: 451 entries.– List of materials outlining theatre history in Canada from the earliest recorded performance in 1606 to the end of 1959.
Location: AEU.

— 1968 —

0949 **Pearson, Willis Barry**
A bibliographical study of Canadian radio and television drama produced on the Canadian Broadcasting Corporation's national network, 1944-1967. [Saskatoon]: 1968. xix, 123 l.
Note: Photocopy: Thesis, M.A., University of Saskatchewan.
Location: OOCC.

— 1970 —

0950 **Du Berger, Jean**
Bibliographie du théâtre québécois de 1935 à nos jours. Québec: Université Laval, Département d'études canadiennes, 1970. 18 f.
Note: Approx. 300 entrées.
Localisation: OONL.

0951 **Guilmette, Pierre**
Bibliographie de la danse théâtrale au Canada. Ottawa: Bibliothèque nationale du Canada, 1970. 150 p.: ill.
Note: 1,717 entrées.– La période couverte est jusqu'en 1967.– Comprend livres, articles de journaux, parties de livres, articles de revues canadiennes et étrangères, spécialisées et générales sur les sujets: philosophie et esthètique, relations de la danse avec les autres arts, problèmes financiers, compagnies et groupes canadiens, personnalités canadiennes, étude et enseignement, chorégraphie canadienne, histoire de la danse au Canada.
Localisation: OONL.

— 1972 —

0952 **Clark, Diane**
"La recherche en mass-media au Québec."
Dans: *Bulletin de l'Association canadienne des bibliothécaires de langue française*; Vol. 18, no 4 (décembre 1972) p. 233-243.; ISSN: 0004-5314.
Note: Localisation: OONL.

0953 **Deschamps, Marcel; Tremblay, Deny**
Dossier en théâtre québécois: volume 1: bibliographie. [Jonquière]: Cegep de Jonquière, c1972. xii, 230 p.
Note: 1,428 entrées.– Couvre jusqu'à 1970.– Inclut références aux textes concernant des thèmes généraux du théâtre québécois (histoire, financement, édition, etc.); les oeuvres et les aspects particuliers du théâtre québécois concernant une troupe, une pièce, ou un auteur.
Localisation: OONL.

— 1974 —

0954 **Canadian Radio-Television Commission**
Bibliography: some Canadian writings on the mass media/Bibliographie: études canadiennes sur les mass media. Ottawa: Canadian Radio-Television Commission, c1974. 99 p.
Note: Approx. 1,000 entries.– Listing of books, documents, articles, theses prepared by the Journalism Department, Université Laval: general reference works, studies on sociology, history, politics and economics of the media.– Focus on Canadian media, with some international coverage.– Text in English and French/ texte en français et en anglais.
Location: OONL.

0955 **Gregory, Paul**
A bibliography: television violence and its effect on the family. Montreal: [Abused Children – Violence in the Family Project, 1974]. 14 p.
Note: 132 entries.– Books, articles, surveys, reviews and summaries, research reports.– Includes Canadian references.
Supplement: Krams, Earl. *Addenda to A bibliography: television violence and its effect on the family.* Montreal: Tree Foundation of Canada, 1976. 11 l.
Location: OONL.

— 1975 —

0956 **Gillespie, Gilbert**
Public access cable television in the United States and Canada: with an annotated bibliography. New York: Praeger, 1975. vii, 157 p. (Praeger special studies in U.S. economic, social and political issues); ISBN: 0-275-09980-6.
Note: Approx. 150 entries.
Location: OONL.

0957 **Pagé, Pierre**
Répertoire des oeuvres de la littérature radiophonique québécoise, 1930-1970. Montréal: Fides, c1975. 826 p.; ISBN: 0-7755-0533-1.
Note: Approx. 2,000 entrées.– Comprend les oeuvres originales, écrites pour la radio, par opposition aux adaptations.– Exclut le théâtre classique français ou étranger, écrit pour la scène, qui a été abondamment utilisé par la radio québécoise.– Comp. avec la collaboration de Renée Legris et Louise Blouin.
Localisation: OONL.

— 1976 —

0958 **Ball, John L.; Plant, Richard**
A bibliography of Canadian theatre history, 1583-1975, [Toronto: Playwrights Co-op, c1976]. 160 p.: ill.; ISBN: 0-919834-02-7.
Note: Approx. 2,000 entries.– Excludes ballet, music, opera, radio and television drama, newspaper articles.– Illustrations include drawings, playbill facsims., photographs, sketches.
Supplement: ... : *supplement, 1975-1976.* 1979. 75 p.; ISBN: 0-88754-136-4.– Approx. 1,000 entries.
Location: OONL.

0959 **Canadian Human Rights Commission**
An annotated bibliography: analysis of television content. Ottawa: Canadian Human Rights Commission, 1976. 8, [55] l.
Note: Location: OONL.

0960 **Hare, John**
"Bibliographie du théâtre canadien-français (des origines à 1973)."
Dans: *Le théâtre canadien français: évolution, témoignages, bibliographie.* Montréal: Fides, c1976. P. 951-999. (Archives des lettres canadiennes ; Tome 5); ISBN: 0-7755-0583-8.
Note: Approx. 700 entrées.– Liste des pièces de théâtre imprimées ainsi qu'une liste des études sur le théâtre au Québec.
Localisation: OONL.

0961 **Lamonde, Yvan**
La radiodiffusion au Canada et au Québec: guide préliminaire de recherche. Montréal: Centre d'études canadiennes-françaises, McGill University, 1976. 8 f.
Note: Localisation: OONL.

0962 **Sedgwick, Dorothy**
A bibliography of English-language theatre and drama in Canada, 1800-1914. Edmonton: Nineteenth Century Theatre Research, 1976. 48 p.: ill. (Occasional publications / Nineteenth Century Theatre Research ; no. 1; ISSN: 0316-5329)
Note: 525 entries.– List of plays, selection of articles about Canadian dramatists, theatres and theatre history, stage-tours and visits, bibliographies and other reference works.
Location: OONL.

— 1977 —

0963 **Canadian Radio-Television and Telecommunications Commission**
A bibliography of basic books on Canadian broadcasting/Bibliographie de références sur la radiodiffusion canadienne. Ottawa: Canadian Radio-Television and Telecommunications Commission, Library, 1977. 9 p.
Note: Location: OORT.

0964 **Conolly, L.W.; Wearing, J.P.**
"Nineteenth-century theatre research: a bibliography."
In: *Nineteenth Century Theatre Research*; Vol. 1, no. 2 (Autumn 1973) p. 109-123; vol. 2, no. 2 (Autumn 1974) p. 93-109; vol. 3, no. 2 (Autumn 1975) p. 97-124; vol. 4, no. 2 (Autumn 1976) p. 89-108; vol. 5, no. 2 (Autumn 1977) p. 93-112.; ISSN: 0316-5329.
Note: Annual list of nineteenth-century theatre and drama studies.– Includes a small section on Canadian theatre.
Continued by: J.P. Wearing (Autumn 1978-Winter 1982).
Location: AEU.

0965 **Ontario. Royal Commission on Violence in the Communications Industry**
Violence and the media: a bibliography. Toronto: Royal Commission on Violence in the Communications Industry, [1977]. 171 p.
Note: 3,000 entries.– Books, articles, government documents, research reports and studies dealing with issues relating to violence and the media: television, radio, film, news media, magazines, comics, sports, music.– Includes general sections on law, policy and regulations, education and social science, crime and violence.
Location: OONL.

— 1978 —

0966 **Duchesnay, Lorraine**
Vingt-cinq ans de dramatiques à la télévision de Radio-Canada. [Ottawa: Relations publiques, Services français, Société Radio-Canada], 1978. xxi, 684 p.
Note: Téléthéâtres: 746 entrées.– Téléromans: 200 entrées.– Détails d'information: genre, année de composition et d'adaptation, numéro d'émission, date de diffusion, minutage, reprises, nombres d'épisodes, indicatif musical, musique de scène, auteur et adaptateur, équipe de production.
Localisation: OONL.

0967 **Rinfret, Gabriel-Édouard**
Le théâtre canadien d'expression française: répertoire analytique des origines à nos jours. [Montréal]: Leméac, 1975-[1978]. 4 vol.; ISBN: 0-7761-9408-9.
Note: Vol. 1-3: index des pièces de théâtre.– Vol. 4: index des pièces de théâtre télévisées.
Localisation: OONL.

— 1980 —

0968 **Sainte-Pierre, Annette**
"Bibliographie du théâtre français au Manitoba."
Dans: *Cefco: Centre d'études franco-canadiennes de l'Ouest*; No 5 (mai 1980) p. 17-18.; ISSN: 0226-0670.
Note: Liste chronologique: 1924-1977.
Localisation: OONL.

0969 **Tourangeau, Rémi**
Tables provisoires du théâtre de Drummondville: index établi d'après les articles et les comptes rendus de presse parus dans les périodiques drummondvillois. Trois-Rivières: Centre de documentation en lettres québécoises de l'Université du Québec à Trois-Rivières, 1980. 184 f. (Guides bibliographiques du théâtre québécois ; no 1); ISBN: 2-89125-001-X.
Note: Couvre la période 1903-1977.
Localisation: OONL.

— 1981 —

0970 **Buller, Edward**
Indigenous performing and ceremonial arts in Canada: a bibliography: an annotated bibliography of Canadian Indian rituals and ceremonies (up to 1976). [Toronto: Association for Native Development in the Performing and Visual Arts, c1981]. x, 151 p.
Note: Includes all major books, articles, reports written from time of first contact to 1973.– Focusses on dance, drama, music, song, ceremonial dramas, masks.
Location: OONL.

0971 **Legris, Renée**
Dictionnaire des auteurs du radio-feuilleton québécois. Montréal: Fides, 1981. 200 p.; ISBN: 2-7621-1090-4.

Note: Biographies et bibliographies des 30 auteurs du radio-feuilleton québécois.

Localisation: OONL.

0972 **Tourangeau, Rémi**
Bibliographie du théâtre en Mauricie. Trois-Rivières: Centre de documentation en lettres québécoises, Université du Québec à Trois-Rivières, 1981. 2 vol.: ill. (Guides bibliographiques du théâtre québécois ; no 2, 4); ISBN: 2-89060-007-6 (Vol. 1); 2-89060-011-4 (Vol. 2).
Note: 546 entrées (vol. 1); 3,951 entrées (vol. 2).– Inventaire descriptif et analytique des articles et des comptes rendus de presse parus dans *Le Constitutionnel* (1868-1883), *Le Bien Public* (1909-1921), et *Le Nouvelliste* (1920-1940).
Localisation: OONL.

— 1982 —

0973 **Canadian Radio-Television and Telecommunications Commission**
Bibliography of CRTC studies. [Ottawa]: Canadian Radio-Television and Telecommunications Commission, 1982. vi, 75, 77 p.; ISBN: 0-662-52054-8.
Note: 356 entries.– Special reports, studies, working papers on aspects of broadcasting industry and government policy: advertising, cable TV, pay TV, children, freedom of expression, Canadian content, violence in television, portrayal of women, educational broadcasting.– Text in English and French with French text on inverted pages.– Title of additional title-page: *Bibliographie des études du C.R.T.C.*
Location: OONL.

0974 **Conseil de la radiodiffusion et des télécommunications canadiennes**
Bibliographie des études du C.R.T.C. [Ottawa]: Conseil de la radiodiffusion et des télécommunications canadiennes, 1982. vi, 77, 75 p.; ISBN: 0-662-52054-8.
Note: 356 entrées.– Comprend rapports spéciaux, études, documents de travail sur les sujets aux domaines de la radiodiffusion et des télécommunications: contenu canadien, liberté d'expression, politiques/réglementation, enfants, femmes, radiodiffusion éducative, télévision payante, violence, Société Radio-Canada, Radio Québec.– Texte en français et en anglais disposé tête-bêche.– Titre de la p. de. t. additionnelle: *Bibliography of CRTC studies.*
Localisation: OONL.

0975 **Fournier-Renaud, Madeleine; Véronneau, Pierre**
Écrits sur le cinéma: bibliographie québécoise, 1911-1981. Montréal: Cinémathèque québécoise-Musée du cinéma, c1982. 180 p.: ill. (Dossiers de la Cinémathèque / Cinémathèque québécoise-Musée du cinéma ; no 9); ISBN: 2-89207-022-8.
Note: 1,685 entrées.– Inclut toutes les publications québécoises, imprimées ou polycopiées, portant sur le cinéma et toutes les publications étrangères portant sur le cinéma québécois.
Localisation: OONL.

0976 **Tourangeau, Rémi**
Le théâtre à Nicolet, 1803-1969: bibliographie régionale. Trois-Rivières, Québec: Éditions CÉDOLEQ, 1982. 394 p. (Guides bibliographiques du théâtre québécois ; no 5); ISBN: 2-89060-013-0.
Note: 843 entrées.– Comprend un inventaire descriptif et analytique: articles, comptes rendus, annonces.– Présenta-

tion chronologique.– Index.
Localisation: OONL.

0977 **Wearing, J.P.**
"Nineteenth-century theatre research: a bibliography."
In: *Nineteenth Century Theatre Research*; Vol. 6, no. 2 (Autumn 1978) p. 95-115; vol. 7, no. 2 (Autumn 1979) p. 99-118; vol. 8, no. 2 (Autumn 1980) p. 91-104; vol. 9, no. 2 (Winter 1981) p. 107-129; vol. 10, no. 2 (Winter 1982) p. 93-109.; ISSN: 0316-5329.
Note: Annual list of nineteenth-century theatre and drama studies.– Includes a small section on Canadian theatre.
Continues: L.W. Conolly (Autumn 1973-Autumn 1977).
Location: AEU.

— 1983 —

0978 **Fink, Howard**
Canadian national theatre on the air, 1925-1961: CBC-CRBC-CNR radio drama in English, a descriptive bibliography and union list. Toronto: University of Toronto Press, c1983. ix, 48 p. (+ 25 microfiches) (The Concordia Radio Drama Project); ISBN: 0-8020-0358-3.
Note: 7,900 broadcasts cited (4,000 original English-language Canadian plays).– Arranged in two sets: individual plays and serials (with sequence numbers of individual plays in a series).– Information provided includes author of script, original author (in the case of adaptations), title, holdings.– Broadcast information includes producer, place, duration, network and date of broadcast, descriptive information about the play contents (themes, characters, plot).– Forms of holdings: paper, microfilm, sound.
Location: OONL.

— 1984 —

0979 **Service de diffusion sélective de l'information de la Centrale des bibliothèques**
Le théâtre québécois, 1980-1983. Montréal: Le Service, 1984. 54 p. (DSI/CB ; no 5; ISSN: 0825-5024); ISBN: 0-289059-205-7.
Note: 175 entrées.– Livres, articles de périodiques.
Localisation: OONL.

— 1985 —

0980 **Deschênes, Marc; Haeberlé, Viviane; Tremblay, Nicole**
Radiodiffusion et État: bibliographie des documents en langue française établie à l'intention du Groupe de travail sur la politique de la radiodiffusion. Québec: Département d'information et de communication, Université Laval, 1985. iv, 129 p.
Note: 344 entrées.– Documents (articles de périodiques, livres, rapports de recherche) de langue française parus entre 1975 et 1985 et portant sur les aspects culturel, économique, juridique et politique de la radiodiffusion, ouvrages fondamentaux relatifs à la politique de la radiodiffusion canadienne.
Localisation: OORT.

0981 **Lavoie, Pierre**
Pour suivre le théâtre au Québec: les ressources documentaires. Québec: Institut québécois de recherche sur la culture, 1985. 521 p. (Documents de recherche / Institut québécois de recherche sur la culture ; no 4; ISSN: 0823-0447); ISBN: 2-89224-047-6.
Note: 1,684 entrées.– Sept parties: bibliographies spécialisées, bibliographies générales, documents audiovisuels, études théâtrales, fonds d'archives,

mémoires et thèses, publications gouvernementales.
Localisation: OONL.

— 1986 —

0982 **Bruck, Peter A., et al.**
Canadian broadcasting: a working bibliography. Ottawa:
Centre for Communication, Culture and Society,
Carleton University, 1986. iii, 284 p.
Note: Approx. 850 entries.– English-language research
(scholarly and other documents) on technological and
cultural aspects of the Canadian broadcasting system.–
Includes material on programming and distribution.–
Arranged in 26 subject categories with author index.
Location: OOSS.

0983 **Hainaux, René; Leclerc, Nicole**
Les Arts du spectacle: Canada: bibliographie des
ouvrages en français publiées au Canada entre 1960 et
1985, concernant le théâtre, la musique, la danse, le
mime, les marionnettes, les spectacles de variétés, le
cirque, la radio et la télévision, le cinéma. Liège,
Belgique: Recherches et formation théâtrales en Wallonie,
1986. 79 f.
Note: Approx. 400 entrées.
Localisation: OONL.

0984 **Olivier, Réjean**
Catalogue de la collection Etienne-F. Duval en théâtre
québécois et français conservée à la bibliothèque du
Collège de l'Assomption. Joliette, Québec: [s.n.], 1986.
164 p.: portr. (Collection Oeuvres bibliophiliques de
Lanaudière ; no 15); ISBN: 2-920249-97-5.
Note: 907 entrées.
Localisation: OONL.

— 1988 —

0985 **Bélanger, Pierre C.**
Recherche bibliographique: impacts culturels et
linguistiques de la consommation de produits culturels
étrangers (émissions de télévision et musique à la radio).
Québec: Direction de la coordination et des politiques,
Ministère des communications, 1988. v, 75 p.; ISBN: 2-
550-19006-8.
Note: 626 entrées.
Localisation: OONL.

— 1989 —

0986 **Québec (Province). Ministère des communications.
Bibliothèque administrative**
Répertoire des recherches faites par ou pour le Ministère
des communications. 2e version. [Québec]: Ministère des
communications, Direction générale de la coordination et
des politiques, c1989. xiii, 128 p.; ISBN: 2-550-19262-1.
Note: 685 entrées.– Regroupe documents parus entre
1969 et 1988: rapports de recherche, revues de presse,
allocutions, rapports annuels, répertoires de médias;
documents parus suite à des Conférences socio-
économiques auxquelles le ministère a participé.–
Thèmes traités: métiers et fonctions de la communication, éducation et communication, médias
communautaires, communication de masse,
informatique, télécommunication.– Analyse et
indexation: Sylvie Bergeron, et al.
Édition antérieure: 1986. 104 p.
Localisation: OONL.

0987 **Théâtre québécois: ses auteurs, ses pièces: répertoire du
Centre d'essai des auteurs dramatiques.** Outremont,
Québec: VLB, c1989. xi, 307 p.: ill. [24] p. de pl.; ISBN: 2-

89005-374-1.
Note: Approx. 700 résumés de pièces québécoises,
incluant la durée et la distribution des oeuvres destinées
aux publics adulte, adolescent et enfant; théâtrographies
de 133 auteurs ainsi que leurs notes biographiques.
Localisation: OONL.

— 1990 —

0988 **Blum, Eleanor; Wilhoit, Frances Goins**
Mass media bibliography: an annotated guide to books
and journals for research and reference. 3rd ed. Urbana:
University of Illinois Press, c1990. viii, 344 p.; ISBN: 0-252-
01706-4.
Note: 1,947 entries.– Covers to 1987.– Listing of books
dealing with some aspect of mass communication:
theory, structure, economics, function, research, content,
effects.– Includes some Canadian references.
Previous editions:
*Basic books in the mass media: an annotated, selected booklist
covering general communications, book publishing, broadcasting, editorial journalism, film, magazines, and advertising.*
1980. xi, 426 p.; ISBN: 0-252-00814-6.
*Basic books in the mass media: an annotated, selected booklist
covering general communications, book publishing, broadcasting, film, magazines, newspapers, advertising, indexes, and
scholarly and professional periodicals.* 1972. ix, 252 p.; ISBN:
0-252-00178-8.
Location: OONL.

0989 **Lavoie, Pierre; Lépine, Stéphane**
"Théâtrographie: [théâtre et homosexualité au Québec]."
Dans: *Jeu*; No 54 (1990) p. 127-133.; ISSN: 0382-0335.
Note: Liste chronologique, 1966-1989.
Localisation: OONL.

— 1992 —

0990 **Ball, John L.; Plant, Richard**
Bibliography of theatre history in Canada: the
beginnings through 1984/Bibliographie d'histoire du
théâtre au Canada: des débuts-fin 1984. Toronto: ECW
Press, 1992. xxii, 445 p.; ISBN: 1-55022-120-5.
Note: 10,870 entries.– Books and articles in scholarly
journals and popular magazines in English and French
concerning theatre or drama history.– Includes general
works (bibliographies and reference works), theses,
history by region and period, references to little theatre,
festivals, radio and television drama, stage design,
biography, theatre education, puppetry.– Includes some
text in French.
Location: OONL.

0991 **Pelletier, Sylvie**
Bibliographie commentée sur le théâtre. Québec: Service
de la recherche et de l'évaluation, Musée de la civilisation, 1992. 46 f. (Document / Service de la recherche et de
l'évaluation, Musée de la civilisation ; no 8); ISBN: 2-551-
12898-6.
Note: Localisation: OONL.

Literature

Littérature

— 1899 —

0992   James, Charles Canniff
A bibliography of Canadian poetry (English). Toronto: Printed for the [Victoria University] Library by William Briggs, 1899. 71 p. (Victoria University Library publication ; no. 1)
Note: Approx. 600 entries.– "Based on a collection of about four hundred volumes and pamphlets ... now in the Library of Victoria University."–Preface.
Microform: CIHM Microfiche series ; no. 07356. ISBN: 0-665-07356-9. 1 microfiche (40 fr.).
Location: OONL.

— 1900 —

0993   Roy, Pierre-Georges
Bibliographie de la poésie franco-canadienne. Lévis, Québec: [s.n.], 1900. 14 p.
Note: Microfiche: ICMH collection de microfiches ; no 14784; ISBN: 0-665-14784-8. 1 microfiche (12 images).
Localisation: OONL.

— 1902 —

0994   Burpee, Lawrence J.
"A Canadian bibliography of the year 1901."
In: *Proceedings and Transactions of the Royal Society of Canada*; Series 2, vol. 8, section 2 (1902) p. 233-344.; ISSN: 0316-4616.
Note: Books, pamphlets, papers in society transactions, magazine articles in the English language, in the fields of history, biography, fiction, poetry, archaeology, being mainly material included within the English Literature section of the Royal Society of Canada.– Includes Canadian work in English and American periodicals.– Excludes newspaper articles.
Location: AEU.

— 1904 —

0995   Horning, Lewis Emerson; Burpee, Lawrence J.
A bibliography of Canadian fiction (English). Toronto: Printed for the [Victoria University] Library by William Briggs, 1904. 82 p. (Victoria University Library publication ; no. 2)
Note: Approx. 800 entries.– Includes a section listing works of unknown authorship; section of foreign authors.
Location: OONL.

— 1914 —

0996   Geddes, James
"Bibliographical outline of French-Canadian literature."
In: *Papers of the Bibliographical Society of America*; Vol. 8, no. 1-2 (1914) p. 7-42.; ISSN: 0006-128X.
Note: Location: OONL.

— 1926 —

0997   Bertrand, Camille
Bulletin bibliographique. Montréal: Bertrand, 1920-1926. 1 vol.; ISSN: 0703-8461.
Note: "Revue trimestrielle des publications traitant de littérature, d'histoire, de sciences et d'arts."- Suspendu: septembre 1926.

Localisation: OONL.

— 1928 —

0998   "Presentable plays for use in Canada."
In: *Ontario Library Review*; Vol. 13, no. 1 (August 1928) p. 14-46.; ISSN: 0030-2996.
Note: Approx. 400 entries.– Descriptive list of Canadian, British and American plays "suited to Canadian high school students, teachers, and teachers-in-waiting."- Categories include Christmas plays, junior plays, plays for girls and women, costume romances.
Location: OONL.

— 1930 —

0999   Crombie, Jean Breakell
A list of Canadian historical novels. Montreal: McGill University Library School, 1930. iv, 10 p. (McGill University publications, series VII: Library ; no. 21)
Note: Location: OONL.

— 1933 —

1000   Bellerive, Georges
Nos auteurs dramatiques, anciens et contemporains: répertoire analytique. Québec: Garneau, 1933. 162 p.
Note: Liste des auteurs dramatiques canadiennes-françaises, biographies, oeuvres, critiques.
Localisation: OONL.

1001   Bellerive, Georges
"Nos auteurs dramatiques: leurs noms et leurs oeuvres."
Dans: *Canada français*; Vol. 20, no 8 (avril 1933) p. 748-757.
Note: Approx. 350 entrées.
Supplément: Robert, Georges-H.; Senay, P.–E. Dans: *Canada français*; Vol. 21, no 3 (novembre 1933) p. 237-243.– Approx. 150 entrées.
Localisation: OONL.

— 1935 —

1002   Bonar Law Bennett Library
A catalogue of the Rufus Hathaway collection of Canadian literature, University of New Brunswick. Fredericton: [s.n.], 1935. vi, 53 p.
Note: Approx. 1,250 entries.– Manuscripts, biographical and critical works, letters.
Location: OONL.

1003   A catalogue of plays by Canadian authors: (including a select list of other publishers' plays). London, Ont.: Peter L. Morris, 1935. 29 p.
Note: Location: OONL.

1004   Fraser, Ian Forbes
Bibliography of French-Canadian poetry. Part 1: From the beginnings of the literature through the École littéraire de Montréal. New York: Institute of French Studies, Columbia University, c1935. vi, 105 p.
Note: 1,005 entries.– General works on French-Canadian literature and poetry, individual bibliographies of French-Canadian poets.
Location: OONL.

— 1944 —

1005 Barbeau, Victor
La Société des écrivains canadiens, son règlements, son action, bio-bibliographie de ses membres. Montréal: Éditions de la Société des écrivains canadiens, 1944. 117 p.
Note: Localisation: OONL.

— 1945 —

1006 MacPike, E.F.
"American and Canadian diaries, journals and notebooks: a short list."
In: Bulletin of Bibliography; Vol. 18, no. 4 (May-August 1944) p. 91-92; vol. 18, no. 5 (September-December 1944) p. 107-115; vol. 18, no. 6 (January-April 1945) p. 133-135; vol. 18, no. 7 (May-August 1945) p. 156-158.
Note: 657 entries.
Location: OONL.

— 1946 —

1007 Thomas, Clara
Canadian novelists, 1920-1945. Toronto: Longmans, Green, 1946. 129 p.
Note: Bio-bibliographical sketches on 122 English-Canadian writers.
Location: OONL.

— 1948 —

1008 Chabot, Juliette
Bio-bibliographie d'écrivains canadiens-français: une liste des bio-bibliographies présentées par les élèves de l'École de Bibliothécaires, Université de Montréal, 1937-1947. Montréal: [s.n.], 1948. 1 f., 12 p.
Note: Approx. 300 entrées.
Localisation: OONL.

1009 Duhamel, Roger, et al.
"The literature of French Canada."
In: Canadian Author and Bookman; Vol. 24, no. 4 (December 1948) p. 42-45.; ISSN: 0008-2937.
Note: Location: AEU.

— 1950 —

1010 Matthews, William
Canadian diaries and autobiographies. Berkeley: University of California Press, 1950. 130 p.
Note: 1,276 entries.– Published and unpublished works in English and French languages.– Excludes French material prior to 1759, diaries and travel books of Americans travelling in Canada, diaries of fur traders who worked in what is now American territory, journals of world explorers like Cook, and Arctic explorers.– Writings of travellers are included when in diary form or when they have distinctly autobiographical content.
Location: OONL.

— 1952 —

1011 Magee, William Henry
A checklist of English-Canadian fiction, 1901-1950. [S.l.: s.n.], 1952. 65 p.
Note: Location: NBSAM.

— 1954 —

1012 Société des écrivains canadiens
Répertoire bio-bibliographique de la Société des écrivains canadiens, 1954. Montréal: Éditions de la Société des écrivains canadiens, c1954. xviii, 248 p.: planches.
Note: Comprend approx. 350 écrivains.– Oeuvres personnelles de l'auteur, oeuvres en collaboration, des ouvrages collectifs, préfaces, compilations, etc., pièces de théâtre, de radio, de télévision, jouées mais non publiées, journaux, revues et autres périodiques auxquels l'auteur a collaboré.
Localisation: OONL.

1013 "Toronto and York in literature."
In: York Pioneer and Historical Society Annual Report; Vol. 86 (1954) p. 11-14.; ISSN: 0315-5269.
Note: Location: OONL.

— 1955 —

1014 Drolet, Antonio
Bibliographie du roman canadien-français, 1900-1950. Québec: Presses universitaires de Laval, 1955. 125 p.
Note: 886 entrées.– Comporte seulement les romans, les contes et les nouvelles qui ont paru en librairie, de langue française écrits par des auteurs canadiens-français et publiés au Canada ou à l'étranger, ainsi que les ouvrages de même genre en langue française par des auteurs étrangers mais publiés d'abord au Canada.
Localisation: OONL.

1015 St. James Literary Society (Montreal, Quebec)
List of papers and debates presented before the St. James Literary Society, 1898-99 to 1954-55. Montreal: [s.n.], 1955. 87 p.
Note: Location: QMBM.

— 1957 —

1016 Canadian Association for Adult Education
A selective bibliography of Canadian plays. Toronto: Commission for Continuous Learning, Canadian Association for Adult Education, 1957. 15 l.
Note: Approx. 225 entries.– Includes English-Canadian titles only.
Location: OONL.

1017 University of British Columbia. Library
French Canadian literature: La littérature canadienne française: a preliminary list of the holdings of the University of British Columbia Library. Vancouver: The Library, 1957. 68 l.
Note: Location: OONL.

— 1959 —

1018 Matthews, William
American diaries: an annotated bibliography of American diaries written prior to the year 1861. Boston: Canner, 1959. 383 p.
Note: Covers 1629 to 1860.– For the Northeast and Pacific Northwest, includes "all Canadian diaries written in English."- Note in preface to Matthews' companion volume, Canadian diaries and autobiographies, that in diaries written by Americans " ... there are numerous items of Canadian interest written by Americans which are not repeated here ..."
Location: OONL.

1019 Société des écrivains canadiens
Bulletin bibliographique de la Société des écrivains canadiens. Montréal: Société des écrivains canadiens, 1937-1959. 23 vol.; ISSN: 0700-6756.
Note: Annuel.– Liste des livres et brochures avec description bibliographique.– Répertorie tous les ouvrages dont un exemple a été adressé à la Société ou dont la publication est revue "d'une manière ou d'une autre, à la connaissance du compilateur."- Index: auteurs/collaborateurs/traducteurs, etc.; titres.
Localisation: OONL.

— 1964 —

1020 **Bell, Inglis Freeman**
"Canadian literature, a checklist."
In: *Canadian Literature*; No. 3 (Winter 1960) p. 91-108; no. 7 (Winter 1961) p. 86-102; no. 11 (Winter 1962) p. 79-89, 96-103; no. 15 (Winter 1963) p. 87-108; no. 19 (Winter 1964) p. 71-82, 90-98.; ISSN: 0008-4360.
Note: Listing of English- and French-Canadian literature in current publication.– Continued (Winter 1965-Spring 1971) by Rita Butterfield.
Location: OONL.

1021 **Milne, William Samuel**
Canadian full-length plays in English: a preliminary annotated catalogue. Ottawa: Dominion Drama Festival, c1964. viii, 47 p.
Note: Approx. 200 entries.– Defines a Canadian play as "one written by a Canadian citizen or a person who was, or is, normally resident in Canada."- Excludes musicals, television and radio scripts.
Supplement: 1966. vii, 39 p.– Approx. 90 entries.
Location: OONL.

1022 **Rome, David**
Jews in Canadian literature: a bibliography. rev. ed. Montreal: Canadian Jewish Congress and Jewish Public Library, 1964. 2 vol.
Note: Works by and about 56 published Jewish-Canadian writers, contributors to literary journals, notes on Jewish contribution to Canadian literature in French language.
Previous edition: Montreal: Jewish Public Library, 1962. xii, 218 p.
Supplement: *Recent Canadian Jewish authors and la langue française*. Montreal: Jewish Public Library, 1970. lxii, 25 l.
Location: OONL.

1023 **Roy, G. Ross; Gnarowski, Michael**
Canadian poetry: a supplementary bibliography. Quebec: Culture, 1964. 13 p.
Note: Approx. 200 entries.– Covers to 1950.
Location: OONL.

1024 **Wyczynski, Paul**
"Histoire et critique littéraires au Canada français: bibliographie."
Dans: *Recherches sociographiques*; Vol. 5, no 1-2 (janvier-août 1964) p. 52-69.; ISSN: 0034-1282.
Note: Histoire littéraire, ouvrages et articles généraux d'histoire et de critique littéraires, études sur le roman, la poésie, le théâtre.
Localisation: AEU.

— 1965 —

1025 **Bouquiniste**
Le guide du lecteur canadien-français. [Montréal: Imprimerie judiciaire], 1965. 77 p.: ill.
Note: 65 entrées.
Localisation: OONL.

1026 **Hare, John**
Bibliographie du roman canadien-français, 1837-1962. Montréal: Fides, [1965]. 82 p.
Note: Trois parties: bibliographie du roman canadien-français précédée d'une liste d'études sur le roman (livres, thèses, articles de revues et de journaux); chronologie du roman canadien-français; liste des romans pour adolescents.
Réimpression du: *Roman canadien-français: évolution,*

témoignages, bibliographie. Montréal, Fides [c1964] p. 375-456.
Supplément:
"Supplément bibliographique, 1963-1969." Dans: *Roman canadien-français*. 3e éd. Montréal: Fides, c1977. P. 497-511.
Localisation: OONL.

1027 **Hare, John**
"Literary sociology and French-Canadian literature: a summary bibliography."
In: *Culture*; Vol. 26 (1965) p. 419-423.; ISSN: 0317-2066.
Note: Approx. 60 entries.– Includes studies on external influences on literary production, as well as studies on the "image of society" in literary works.
Location: AEU.

1028 **Jain, Sushil Kumar**
French Canadian literature in English translation: a short list compiled from the library catalogues of the Regina Campus Library. Regina: Regina Campus Library, University of Saskatchewan, 1965. 9 l.
Note: Location: OONL.

1029 **Jain, Sushil Kumar**
Poetry in Saskatchewan: a bibliography. Regina, Sask.: University of Saskatchewan, 1965. 10 l.
Note: 62 entries.
Location: OONL.

1030 **Rhodenizer, Vernon Blair**
Canadian literature in English. [Montreal: Printed by Quality Press, c1965]. 1055 p.
Note: Includes sections on Indians in literature, travel (discovery and exploration), sports, scientific literature, juvenile literature, biography and autobiography, creative non-fiction, drama, poetry, the essay, humour and satire, criticism.– For author/title index see: Thierman, Lois Mary. *Index to Vernon Blair Rhodenizer's Canadian literature in English*. Edmonton: [1968]. ix, 469 p.
Location: OONL.

— 1966 —

1031 **Bell, Inglis Freeman; Port, Susan**
Canadian literature, Littérature canadienne, 1959-1963: A checklist of creative and critical writings. Bibliographie de la critique et des oeuvres d'imagination. [Vancouver]: Publications Centre, University of British Columbia, 1966. 140 p.
Note: Approx. 2,400 entries.– Amended cumulation of annual lists from *Canadian Literature*.– Text in English and French/texte en français et en anglais.
Location: OONL.

1032 **Chalifoux, Jean-Pierre**
Liste préliminaire de sources bibliographiques relatives à la littérature canadienne-française. Montréal: Bibliothèque, Centre d'études canadienne-françaises, McGill University, 1966. 7 f.
Note: Dans Lochhead.– Pas localisation.

1033 **Hamel, Réginald**
Bibliographie des lettres canadiennes-françaises, 1965. Montréal: Les Presses de l'Université de Montréal, 1966. 111 p.
Note: Bibliographies et catalogues, généralités (anthologies, conte, nouvelle, roman, critique, enseignement, littérature comparée, poésie, théâtre, thèmes littéraire); auteurs et leurs critiques.
Localisation: OONL.

1034 **Jain, Sushil Kumar**
Saskatchewan in fiction: a bibliography of works of fiction about Saskatchewan & fiction written by Saskatchewanians. Regina: Regina Campus Library, University of Saskatchewan, 1966. viii, 15 l.
Note: 86 entries.
Location: OONL.

1035 **Klinck, Carl F.**
"Annual bibliography of Commonwealth literature, ... : Canada."
In: *Journal of Commonwealth Literature*; 1964 in no. 1 (September 1965) p. 27-43; 1965 in no. 2 (December 1966) p. 39-55.; ISSN: 0021-9894.
Note: Lists bibliographies, dramatic works, fiction, poetry, anthologies, criticism (of individual authors, general studies), journals.– Continued by: Mary M.S. Brown: 1966 (December 1967), 1967 (January 1969); Robert Weaver: 1968 (December 1969); William H. New: 1969, 1971-1977 (December 1970-December 1977); Mary Burnett: 1970 (December 1971); Marilyn G. Flitton: 1978 (December 1979); Doreen Ingram: 1979 (December 1980); Moshie Dahms: 1980-1990 (February 1982-1991).
Location: AEU.

1036 **Watters, Reginald Eyre; Bell, Inglis Freeman**
On Canadian literature, 1806-1960: a check list of articles, books, and theses on English-Canadian literature, its authors, and language. [Toronto]: University of Toronto Press, [c1966]. ix, 165 p.; ISBN: 0-8020-5166-9.
Note: Approx. 3,200 entries.– Sections include general bibliographies, Canadian culture and background, Canadian English, language and linguistics, drama and theatre, fiction, poetry, literary criticism and history, regionalism, songs and folklore, journalism and publishing, censorship and copyright.
Location: OONL.

— 1967 —

1037 **Chalifoux, Jean-Pierre**
"Liste de sources bibliographiques relatives à la littérature canadienne-française."
Dans: *Bulletin de l'Association canadienne des bibliothécaires de langue française*; Vol. 13, no 3 (septembre 1967) p. 137-141.; ISSN: 0004-5314.
Note: 93 entrées.
Localisation: OONL.

1038 **Coan, Otis W.; Lillard, Richard G.**
America in fiction: an annotated list of novels that interpret aspects of life in the United States, Canada, and Mexico. Palo Alto, Calif.: Pacific Books, 1967. viii, 232 p.
Note: Novels, volumes of short stories, collections of folklore, listed in groups reflecting phases and aspects of life frequently treated by writers of fiction in Canada and the United States: pioneering, farm and village life, industrial life, politics and institutions, religion, minority ethnic groups.
Location: OONL.

1039 **"Études sur le roman canadien-français: essai bibliographique."**
Dans: *Relations*; No 320 (octobre 1967) p. 278-279.; ISSN: 0034-3781.
Note: Localisation: OONL.

1040 **Gnarowski, Michael**
A reference and bibliographical guide to the study of English Canadian literature. Ottawa: [s.n.], 1967.

Note: Thesis: Ph.D., University of Ottawa, 1967.
Location: OONL.

1041 **Klinck, Carl F.**
"Canadian literature in English: a select reading list."
In: *Bulletin (Association for Commonwealth Literature and Language Studies)*; No. 4 (1967) 32 p.
Note: Location: OLU.

— 1968 —

1042 **Hayne, David M.; Tirol, Marcel**
Bibliographie critique du roman canadien-français, 1837-1900. [Toronto]: University of Toronto Press, c1968. viii, 144 p.; ISBN: 0-8020-1541-7.
Note: 1,150 entrées.– Sources bibliographiques, biographiques et critiques; les principales éditions en volume ou en feuilleton, les traductions en langue anglaise et les reproductions partielles parues dans des périodiques pour 43 romanciers canadiens; une liste sous le nom de chaque romancier, des principaux livres et articles consacrés aux ouvrages romanesques de cet écrivain.
Localisation: OONL.

1043 **Livres et auteurs canadiens: panorama de la production littéraire de l'année, 1961-1968.** Montréal: [Éditions Jumonville], 1962-1968. 8 vol.: ill., ports.; ISSN: 0076-0153.
Note: Annuel.– Revue critique de la production littéraire canadienne-française pour l'année en cours dans les domaines: lettres, arts et sciences humaines.– Bibliographie générale.– Direction générale: Adrien Thério.– Continué par: *Livres et auteurs québécois: revue critique de l'année littéraire, 1969-1982*. Québec: Presses de l'Université Laval, 1969-1983. 14 vol.; ISSN: 0316-2621.
Localisation: OONL.

1044 **McGill University. Centre d'études canadiennes-françaises. Bibliothèque**
Bibliographie préliminaire de poésie canadienne-française. [Montréal: s.n.], 1968. 26 f.
Note: Approx. 400 entrées.– Couvre 1883 jusqu'en 1967.
Localisation: OONL.

1045 **Rhodenizer, Vernon Blair**
At the sign of the Hand and Pen: Nova Scotian authors. Toronto: Canadiana House, 1968. 42 p.
Note: Bio-bibliographical listing of Nova Scotia authors.
Location: OONL.

1046 **Stratford, Philip**
"French-Canadian literature in translation."
In: *Meta*; Vol. 13, no 4 (décembre 1968) p. 180-187.; ISSN: 0026-0452.
Note: Includes a selected bibliography listing novels, short fiction, poetry, drama, essays, autobiography.
Location: OONL.

— 1969 —

1047 **Brown, Mary M.S.**
"Annual bibliography of Commonwealth literature, ... : Canada."
In: *Journal of Commonwealth Literature*; 1966 in no. 4 (December 1967) p. 46-62; 1967 in no. 6 (January 1969) p. 43-63.; ISSN: 0021-9894.
Note: Lists bibliographies, research aids, poetry, fiction, anthologies, translations, criticism (of individual authors, general studies, journals.– Continues: Carl F. Klinck: 1964-1965 (September 1965, December 1966.– Continued by: Robert Weaver: 1968 (December 1969); William H. New: 1969, 1971-1977 (December 1970, December 1972-

1978); Mary Burnett: 1970 (December 1971); Marilyn G. Flitton: 1978 (December 1979); Doreen Ingram: 1979 (December 1980); Moshie Dahms: 1980-1990 (February 1982-1991).
Location: AEU.

1048 **Edwards, Mary Jane**
"Fiction and Montreal, 1769-1885: a bibliography."
In: *Papers of the Bibliographical Society of Canada*; Vol. 8 (1969) p. 61-75.; ISSN: 0067-6896.
Note: Approx. 250 entries.– Review of works in which Montreal was used as a point of reference, a partial setting, or a complete setting.
Location: OONL.

1049 **Hamel, Réginald**
Cahiers bibliographiques des lettres québécoises. Montréal: Centre de documentation des lettres canadiennes-françaises, Université de Montréal, 1966-1969. 4 vol.
Note: Chaque cahier comprend anthologies, bibliographies, dictionnaires; généralités; auteurs et leurs critiques; auteurs québécois sur la littérature étrangère.– Le dernier cahier d'une année (sauf celui de 1967) renferme un index des sujets et auteurs.– Comp. avec la collaboration de Madeleine Corbeil et Nicole Vigeant.
Localisation: OONL.

1050 **Hamel, Réginald**
"Un choix bibliographique des lettres québécoises (1764-1967)."
Dans: *Revue d'histoire littéraire de la France*; Vol. 69, no 5 (septembre-octobre 1969) p. 808-821.
Note: Les instruments de travail, les principaux genre littéraires depuis 1764.
Localisation: OONL.

1051 **Malycky, Alexander**
"A preliminary check list of studies on Ukrainian-Canadian creative literature: Part I. General studies."
In: *Canadian Ethnic Studies*; Vol. 1, no. 1 (1969) p. 161-163.; ISSN: 0008-3496.
Note: Location: OONL.

1052 **Weaver, Robert**
"Annual bibliography of Commonwealth literature, 1968: Canada."
In: *Journal of Commonwealth Literature*; No. 8 (December 1969) p. 89-106.; ISSN: 0021-9894.
Note: Lists bibliographies, poetry, fiction, drama, anthologies, non-fiction, translations, criticism (of individual authors, general studies), journals.– Continues: Carl F. Klinck: 1964-1965 (September 1965, December 1966); Mary M.S. Brown: 1966-1967 (December 1967, January 1969).– Continued by: William H. New: 1969, 1971-1977 (December 1970, December 1972-1978); Mary Burnett: 1970 (December 1971); Marilyn G. Flitton: 1978 (December 1979); Doreen Ingram: 1979 (December 1980); Moshie Dahms: 1980-1990 (February 1982-1991).
Location: AEU.

— 1970 —

1053 **Catalogue de l'édition au Canada français.** Montréal: Conseil supérieur du livre, 1958-1970. 7 vol.
Note: Publié avec le concours du Ministère des affaires culturelles du Québec.– Le titre varie: 1958, 1962, *Catalogue collectif de l'édition canadienne.*– L'éditeur varie: 1958, Société des éditeurs canadiens du livre français; 1962, 1965, Association des éditeurs canadiens.–

Responsable de la compilation et l'édition: Julia Richer.
Localisation: OONL.

1054 **Harasymiw, Elaine Verchomin; Malycky, Alexander**
"Ukrainian-Canadian creative literature: a preliminary check list of imprints."
In: *Canadian Ethnic Studies*; Vol. 2, no. 1 (June 1970) p. 205-227.; ISSN: 0008-3496.
Note: Supplement: Prokopiw, Orysia L. and Malycky, Alexander: Vol. 5, no. 1/2 (1973) p. 365-378.– 320 entries in total.
Location: OONL.

1055 **Leland, Marine; Hare, John**
"French literature of Canada."
In: *The literatures of the world in English translation: a bibliography.* Vol. 3, *The romance literatures* (Part 2: French literature), edited by George B. Parks and Ruth Z. Temple. New York: Ungar, [1970]. P. 576-590.; ISBN: 0-8044-3239-2.
Note: Approx. 125 entries.– Background studies, bibliographies, literary studies, collections, literature of exploration, individual authors.
Location: OONL.

1056 **Malycky, Alexander; Harasymiw, Elaine Verchomin**
"A preliminary check list of studies on Ukrainian-Canadian creative literature: Part II. Specific studies."
In: *Canadian Ethnic Studies*; Vol. 2, no. 1 (June 1970) p. 229-244.; ISSN: 0008-3496.
Note: 142 entries.– Listing of material on individual authors, literary criticism of those works written in Canada, as well as biographical, autobiographical and bibliographical materials.
Supplement: Malycky, Alexander and Prokopiw, Orysia L.: Vol. 5, no. 1/2 (1973) p. 387-408.– 355 entries.
Location: OONL.

1057 **Parker, George L.**
"A brief annotated bibliography of available titles in Canadian fiction, poetry, and related background material."
In: *Twentieth Century Literature*; Vol. 16, no. 3 (July 1970) p. 217-224.; ISSN: 0041-462X.
Note: Approx. 75 entries.– Background materials, fiction, poetry in English.
Location: OONL.

1058 **Watt, Roy MacGregor (Mrs.)**
Catalogue of ranking plays. Ottawa: Ottawa Little Theatre, 1970. 9 p.
Note: 56 entries.– Covers 1937-1970.– Listing of plays from the Canadian one-act playwriting competition.
Location: OONL.

1059 **Windthorst, Rolf E.B.**
"German-Canadian creative literature: a preliminary check list of imprints."
In: *Canadian Ethnic Studies*; Vol. 2, no. 1 (June 1970) p. 55-62.; ISSN: 0008-3496.
Note: Supplement: Gilby, William R.: Vol. 5, no. 1/2 (1973) p. 85-90.– 93 entries in total.
Location: OONL.

— 1971 —

1060 **Bell, Inglis Freeman; Gallup, Jennifer**
A reference guide to English, American and Canadian literature: an annotated checklist of bibliographical and other reference materials. Vancouver: University of British Columbia Press, [c1971]. xii, 139 p.; ISBN: 0-7748-0002-X.

Note: 569 entries.– Bibliographies, indexes, and annual surveys, handbooks, biographical reference tools, indexes to collections, dictionaries, literary historico and critical surveys.
Location: OONL.

1061 **Burnett, Mary**
"Annual bibliography of Commonwealth literature, 1970: Canada."
In: *Journal of Commonwealth Literature*; Vol. 6, no. 2 (December 1971) p. 43-67.; ISSN: 0021-9894.
Note: Lists bibliographies, research aids, poetry, drama, fiction, criticism, journals.– Continues: Carl F. Klinck: 1964-1965 (September 1965, December 1966); Mary M.S. Brown: 1966-1967 (December 1967, January 1969); Robert Weaver: 1968 (December 1969); William H. New: 1969, 1971-1977 (December 1970, December 1972-1977).– Continued by: Marilyn G. Flitton: 1978 (December 1979); Doreen Ingram: 1979 (December 1980); Moshie Dahms: 1980-1990 (February 1982-1991).
Location: AEU.

1062 **Butterfield, Rita**
"Canadian literature: a checklist."
In: *Canadian Literature*; No. 23 (Winter 1965) p. 81-100; no. 27 (Winter 1966) p. 83-100; no. 32 (Spring 1967) p. 83-104; no. 36 (Spring 1968) p. 101-120; no. 40 (Spring 1969) p. 101-120; no. 44 (Spring 1970) p. 99-119; no. 48 (Spring 1971) p. 95-119.; ISSN: 0008-4360.
Note: Listing of English and French Canadian literature and criticism, bibliographies.– Continues: Bell, Inglis Freeman (Winter 1960-Winter 1964).
Location: AEU.

1063 **Lemire, Maurice; Landry, Kenneth**
Répertoire des spécialistes de littérature canadienne-française. [Québec]: Archives de littérature canadienne, Université Laval, 1971. vi, 93 p.
Note: Inclut recherches inédites, publications, enseignement, liste des thèses de littérature canadienne-française de 1923 à 1970.
Localisation: OONL.

1064 **Séminaire Saint-Augustin. Bibliothèque**
Références bibliographiques d'auteurs canadiens. Cap-Rouge [Québec]: Séminaire Saint-Augustin, Bibliothèque, 1971. 55 f.
Note: Approx. 900 entrées.
Localisation: OONL.

— 1972 —

1065 **Endres, Robin**
"Women authors in Canada."
In: *Canadian Newsletter of Research on Women*; Vol. 1, no. 2 (October 1972) p. 46-52.; ISSN: 0319-4477.
Note: Fiction, poetry, plays, travel literature, autobiographies.
Location: AEU.

1066 **Moyles, Robert Gordon; Siemens, Catherine**
English-Canadian literature: a student guide and annotated bibliography. Edmonton: Athabascan Publishing, 1972. 44 p.
Note: Includes primary and secondary materials: collections of poetry and short stories, paperback novel series, reprints and micro-reproductions of early travel and descriptive literature, reference guides to early periodicals and newspapers, bibliographies, literary histories, encyclopaedias, dictionaries, newspaper

indexes, indexes to theses.– Selected references to studies in history, linguistics, folklore, Canadian culture and French-Canadian literature.
Location: OONL.

1067 **New, William H.**
"A checklist of major individual short story collections."
In: *World Literature Written in English*; Vol. 11, no. 1 (April 1972) p. 11-13.; ISSN: 0093-1705.
Note: Excludes anthologies and individual writers whose work has appeared only in anthologies.
Location: AEU.

1068 **Nichol, bp**
Ganglia Press index. Toronto: Ganglia Press, 1972. [49] p.
Note: Lists the poetry series published by Ganglia Press between 1964 and 1972.– Author index.
Location: OONL.

1069 **Pontaut, Alain**
Dictionnaire critique du théâtre québécois. Montréal: Leméac, 1972. 161 p.
Note: Bio-bibliographies d'auteurs dramatiques québécois.
Localisation: OONL.

1070 **Thomas, Clara**
Our nature – our voices: a guidebook to English-Canadian literature. Toronto: New Press, 1972. ix, 175 p.: ill.; ISBN: 0-88770-618-5.
Note: Bio-bibliographical listings.– Vol. 1 of 2 vol. set.– For vol. 2, please refer to: Davey, Frank. *From there to here: a guide to English-Canadian literature since 1960.* Erin, Ont.: Press Porcepic; 1974. 288 p.; ISBN: 0-88878-036-2.
Location: OONL.

1071 **University of Manitoba. Library**
Literary works by Jewish writers in Canada in the Elizabeth Dafoe Library. Winnipeg: University of Manitoba Libraries, 1972. 21 l. (Reference series / University of Manitoba Libraries ; no. 4)
Note: Approx. 160 entries.– Compiled by Verona M. Dechene.
Location: OONL.

1072 **Watters, Reginald Eyre**
A checklist of Canadian literature and background materials, 1628-1960. 2nd ed., rev. and enl. Toronto: University of Toronto Press, 1972. xxiv, 1085 p.; ISBN: 0-8020-1866-1.
Note: Approx. 16,000 entries.– In two parts: a comprehensive list of the books which constitute Canadian literature written in English; a selective list of other books by Canadian authors which reveal the background of that literature.– Includes poetry, fiction, drama, biography, essays and speeches, literary criticism, scholarship, local history, religion, social history, travel and description.– Excludes military, economic, constitutional history, writings in law, commerce and the sciences.
Previous edition: ... , *1628-1950.* [Toronto]: University of Toronto Press, [1959]. xx, 789 p.– Approx. 12,000 entries.
Location: OONL.

— 1973 —

1073 **Bellingham, Susan**
A catalogue of the modern Canadian poetry collection in the Division of Archives and Special Collections. Hamilton, Ont.: University Library Press at McMaster University, 1973. [75] p.

Note: Location: OTU.

1074 **Cardinal, Clive H.**
"Preliminary check list of studies on German-Canadian creative literature."
In: *Canadian Ethnic Studies*; Vol. 1, no. 1 (1969) p. 38-39; vol. 2, no. 1 (June 1970) p. 63-69; vol. 5, no. 1/2 (1973) p. 91-93.; ISSN: 0008-3496.
Note: 17 general studies, 77 specific studies related to published works of drama, poetry or prose in German, Low German and Pennsylvania German by German-Canadian authors (formative years in Canada, or settled in Canada as adults).
Location: OONL.

1075 **Du Berger, Jean**
"Bibliographie du théâtre québécois de 1935 à nos jours."
Dans: *Nord*; Nos 4-5 (automne-hiver 1973) p. 207-228.; ISSN: 0315-3789.
Note: Localisation: OONL.

1076 **Miska, John P.**
"Hungarian-Canadian creative literature: a preliminary check list of imprints."
In: *Canadian Ethnic Studies*; Vol. 5, no. 1/2 (1973) p. 131-137.; ISSN: 0008-3496.
Note: Location: OONL.

1077 **Saskatchewan Provincial Library. Bibliographic Services Division**
Canadian fiction: a bibliography. Regina: Bibliographic Services Division, Provincial Library, 1973. 33 p.
Note: Approx. 500 entries.– Selected listing compiled from Saskatchewan Union Catalogue.
Location: OONL.

1078 **Sigvaldadottir-Geppert, Margrét**
"Icelandic-Canadian creative literature: a preliminary check list of imprints."
In: *Canadian Ethnic Studies*; Vol. 5, no. 1/2 (1973) p. 139-151.; ISSN: 0008-3496.
Note: 97 entries.
Location: OONL.

1079 **Tougas, Gérard**
A checklist of printed materials relating to French-Canadian literature, 1763-1968/Liste de référence d'imprimés relatifs à la littérature canadienne-française, 1763-1968. 2nd ed. Vancouver: University of British Columbia Press, 1973. xvi, 174 p.; ISBN: 0-7748-0007-0.
Note: Approx. 3,000 entries.– Novels, poetry, drama, short stories, chronicles, literary criticism, biographies, parliamentary oratory, travellers' chronicles, folklore in translation and in various editions.– Excludes pulpit oratory, philosophy and history, newspapers, periodicals, anonymous works pertaining to literature of French Canada.– Text in English and French/texte en français et en anglais.
Previous edition: 1958. 93 p.
Location: OONL.

1080 **Tremblay, Jean-Pierre**
Bibliographie québécoise: roman, théâtre, poésie, chanson. Inventaire des Écrits du Canada français. [Cap-Rouge, Québec]: Educo média, 1973. 252 p.
Note: Localisation: OONL.

— 1974 —

1081 **Bibliothèque nationale du Québec**
Contes et légendes du Québec: liste de volumes localisés à la Bibliothèque nationale du Québec et exposés à la Bibliothèque municipale de Longueuil, du 16 au 25 août 1974. Montréal: Bibliothèque nationale du Québec, Service d'orientation du lecteur, 1974. 9 f.
Note: Localisation: QQLA.

1082 **Biggins, Patricia**
An annotated bibliography of Canadian radio drama produced by CBC Vancouver between 1939 and 1945. Burnaby, B.C.: Simon Fraser University, 1974. 103 l.
Note: Bound with two other pieces: "Virginia Woolf as a social novelist...," and "Christopher Marlowe and the theatre of the absurd," three extended essays submitted in partial fulfillment of the requirements for the degree of Master of Arts, Department of English, Simon Fraser University.– Includes indexes: Authors/adapters/dramatizers, producers, series, performers.
Location: BVAS.

1083 **Connections: writers and the land.** Winnipeg: Manitoba School Library Audio-Visual Association, 1974. viii, 136 p.: ill.
Note: Contains bio-bibliographical information on 28 Manitoba authors who have published works of fiction, non-fiction and poetry since 1920.
Location: OONL.

1084 **Davey, Frank**
From there to here: a guide to English-Canadian literature since 1960. Erin, Ont.: Press Porcepic, 1974. 288 p.: ill.; ISBN: 0-88878-036-2.
Note: Vol. 2 of 2 vol. set. For vol. 1, refer to: Thomas, Clara. *Our nature – our voices: a guidebook to English-Canadian literature.* Toronto: New Press; 1972.– Includes brief biographies, works by and about English-Canadian writers (excluding dramatists) who have emerged since 1960.
Location: OONL.

1085 **McLeod, Gordon Duncan**
A descriptive bibliography of the Canadian prairie novel, 1871-1970. Winnipeg: University of Manitoba, 1974. xviii, 253 l.
Note: Approx. 170 entries.– Novels of the Canadian prairie (Alberta, Manitoba, Saskatchewan) written for adults and published in English from 1871 to 1970; novels written by someone living on the prairie at the time regardless of subject matter, or with a prairie setting written by someone who once lived on the prairie.– Excludes short stories, novels written for a juvenile audience.– Thesis: Ph.D., University of Manitoba, Department of English. (Canadian theses on microfiche ; 20399).
Location: OONL.

1086 **Rogers, Amos Robert**
American recognition of Canadian authors writing in English, 1890-1960. [Ann Arbor, Mich.: University Microfilms, 1974]. 2 vol.
Note: Listings include a checklist of American editions and reprints of works by 278 Canadian writers; checklist of editions of works by 278 Canadian writers published outside the United States; poems by Canadian authors published in American anthologies; American anthologies which contain works by Canadian authors; poems, short stories published in American magazines; book reviews in American periodicals, 1890-1960.– Thesis: Ph.D., University of Michigan, 1964.
Location: OONL.

— 1975 —

1087 Boivin, Aurélien
Le conte littéraire québécois au XIXe siècle: essai de bibliographie critique et analytique. Montréal: Fides, c1975. xxxviii, 385 p.; ISBN: 0-7755-0557-9.
Note: 1,138 entrées.
Localisation: OONL.

1088 Harrison, Dick
"Mountie fiction: a reader's guide."
In: *Royal Canadian Mounted Police Quarterly*; Vol. 40, no. 4 (October 1975) p. 39-46.; ISSN: 0317-8250.
Note: Books about Mounties, books in which Mounties appear, short stories in collections and magazines.
Location: AE.

1089 Houle, Ghislaine; Lafontaine, Jacques
Écrivains québécois de nouvelle culture. Montréal: Bibliothèque nationale du Québec [Centre bibliographique], 1975. 137 p. (Bibliographies québécoises / Bibliothèque nationale du Québec, Centre bibliographique ; no 2)
Note: 743 entrées, 10 écrivains.– Biographie, volumes publiés, articles de périodiques, critiques de l'oeuvre de Paul Chamberland, Leonard Cohen, Raoul Duguay, Lucien Francoeur, Louis Geoffroy, Georges Khal, Pierre Léger, Claude Péloquin, Patrick Straram, Denis Vanier.
Localisation: OONL.

1090 Houyoux, Philippe
Théâtre québécois: M. Dubé, J. Ferron, G. Gélinas, G. Lamarche, J. Languirand, A. Laurendeau, F. Leclerc, Y. Thériault: bibliographies de travail. Trois-Rivières, Québec: Université du Québec à Trois-Rivières, Bibliothèque, Centre bibliographique, 1975. 175 f. (Publication / Université du Québec à Trois-Rivières, Bibliothèque ; no 6)
Note: Approx. 2,000 entrées.
Localisation: OONL.

1091 Jukelevics, Nicette
A bibliography of Canadian concrete, visual and sound poetry, 1965-1972 with an introduction [microform]. [Ottawa: Canadian Theses Division, National Library of Canada, c1975]. 2 microfiches: ill. (Canadian theses on microfiche ; 25376; ISSN: 0227-3845)
Note: Includes anthologies, periodicals, critical and theoretical articles, individual authors' publications and reviews of their work.– Thesis: M.A., Department of English, Sir George Williams University, 1974.
Location: OONL.

1092 Marlatt, Daphne
"B.C. poets: a bibliography for 1970-75."
In: *Communiqué: Canadian Studies*; Vol. 1, no. 4 (May 1975) p. 8-21.; ISSN: 0318-1197.
Note: Works of poets living and writing in B.C. during the period covered by the bibliography, or those residing elsewhere whose writing has been "informed by B.C. experiences."- Includes a list of anthologies and literary magazines.
Location: OONL.

1093 New, William H.
Critical writings on Commonwealth literatures: a selective bibliography to 1970, with a list of theses and dissertations. University Park: Pennsylvania State University Press, [1975]. 333 p.; ISBN: 0-271-01166-1.
Note: 6,576 entries (1,560 Canadian).– Research aids, general works, works about individual authors, theses and dissertations.
Location: OONL.

1094 Newman, Maureen; Stratford, Philip
"Bibliographie des livres canadiens en traduction: 1580-1974."
Dans: *Meta*; Vol. 20, no 1 (mars 1975) p. 83-105.; ISSN: 0026 0452.
Note: 370 entrées.– Traductions du français en anglais (250 titres); traductions de l'anglais en français (120 titres).– Deux parties subdivisées en catégories: roman, poésie, théâtre, folklore, lettres, relations de voyages, essais, anthologies, bibliographies.
Localisation: OONL.

— 1976 —

1095 Bindoff, Stanley Thomas; Boulton, James T.
Research in progress in English and history in Britain, Ireland, Canada, Australia and New Zealand. London: St. James Press; New York: St. Martin's Press, 1976. 284 p.; ISBN: 0-900997-28-1.
Note: Lists the work of 3,800 scholars from universities, museums, archives, societies in the fields of English literature and history.– Canada is included with the "Commonwealth Literature" section on pp. 55-61, and in the "Historical Studies" section on pp. 76-83.
Location: OONL.

1096 Dechene, Verona M.
Liste de référence de la littérature canadienne-française dans les bibliothèques manitobaines/A checklist of French-Canadian literature in Manitoba libraries. Winnipeg: University of Manitoba Libraries, 1976. 317 p. (Bibliography series / University of Manitoba Libraries ; no. 2)
Note: Approx. 2,200 entrées.– Couvre jusqu'en 1973.– Inclut roman, poésie, conte et nouvelle, théâtre, critique littéraire et biographie.– Exclut histoire, essai (sauf dans le domaine de la critique littéraire), folklore, roman juvénile.– Texte en français et en anglais/text in English and French.
Localisation: OONL.

1097 Fee, Margery; Cawker, Ruth
Canadian fiction: an annotated bibliography. Toronto: Peter Martin Associates, c1976. xiii, 170 p.; ISBN: 0-88778-134-9.
Note: Approx. 1,200 entries.– English- and French-Canadian adult novels and short story anthologies, autobiography and fictionalized history by authors who had at least one work in print during 1973 or 1974.– No fiction with a copyright date later than 1974 is listed or annotated, but critical works issued in 1975 and 1976 are listed.– Secondary sources include bibliographies, historical and biographical sources, general critical works, periodicals and indexes.
Location: OONL.

1098 Ferres, John H.
"Criticism of Canadian fiction since 1945: a selected checklist."
In: *Modern Fiction Studies*; Vol. 22, no. 3 (Autumn 1976) p. 485-500.; ISSN: 0026-7724.
Note: Approx. 275 entries.– Research aids (bibliographies, indexes, dictionaries), general studies (books and articles of general criticism and history), individual authors (criticism, including theses and

dissertations, of 16 leading writers).
Location: OONL.

1099 **Hamel, Réginald; Hare, John; Wyczynski, Paul**
Dictionnaire pratique des auteurs québécois. Montréal: Fides, c1976. xxv, 723 p.; ISBN: 0-7755-0597-8.
Note: Comprend quelque six cents auteurs de langue française au Québec et dans les autres provinces de Canada depuis Jacques Cartier jusqu'à nos jours: les romanciers, les poètes, les dramaturges, et les essayistes de marque: leurs écrits, livres et brochures, essais, poèmes, contes dans des revues et journaux.
Localisation: OONL.

1100 **Harger-Grinling, Virginia A.**
Aide bibliographique pour l'étude du nouveau roman canadien-français. [Regina]: University of Regina, [1976]. iii, 57 f.
Note: Approx. 750 entrées.– Bibliographies, revues, thèses, livres, articles.
Localisation: OONL.

1101 **Mount Allison University. Canadian Studies Programme**
A preliminary checklist of nineteenth century Canadian poetry in English. Sackville, N.B.: Canadian Studies Programme, Mount Allison University, 1976. 185 l.
Note: Approx. 1,000 entries.– Based on entries in Watters' *A checklist of Canadian literature and background materials, 1628-1960* (1972), with additions from other sources.
Location: OONL.

1102 **Moyles, Robert Gordon**
English-Canadian literature to 1900: a guide to information sources. Detroit: Gale Research, c1976. xi, 346 p. (American literature, English literature, and world literatures in English Information guide series ; vol. 6); ISBN: 0-8103-1222-0.
Note: Approx. 3,000 entries.– Includes bibliographies, biographical reference works, literary histories and criticism, anthologies, works of major authors, travel literature, selected nineteenth-century journals.
Location: OONL.

1103 **Université du Québec à Trois-Rivières. Bibliothèque**
Liste de bio-bibliographies d'auteurs canadiens-français. Trois-Rivières: Université de Québec à Trois-Rivières, 1976. 17 f.
Note: Approx. 300 entrées.– Les bio-bibliographies présentées sont le resultat du travail des candidats au titre de bibliothécaires à l'École de Bibliothécaires de l'Université de Montréal entre 1937-1962.
Localisation: OONL.

1104 **Urbas, Jeannette**
From thirty acres to modern times: the story of French-Canadian literature. Toronto: McGraw-Hill Ryerson, 1976. xiv, 158 p.; ISBN: 0-07-082323-5.
Note: History of French-Canadian literature built around major authors, with brief biographies, listing of works and critical studies.
Location: OONL.

1105 **Woodcock, George**
Canadian poets, 1960-1973: a list. Ottawa: Golden Dog Press, 1976. x, 69 p.; ISBN: 0-919614-14-0.
Note: Approx. 1,200 entries.– Includes works by individual poets, anthologies.
Location: OONL.

— 1977 —

1106 **Archambault, Michèle**
"Les instruments de travail."
Dans: *Études françaises*; Vol. 13, no 3-4 (octobre 1977) p. 191-218.; ISSN: 0014-2085.
Note: 85 entrées.– Principaux ouvrages de référence: bibliographies, dictionnaires et quelques manuels d'histoire littéraire.– Numéro spécial: "Pétit manuel de littérature québécoise."
Localisation: OONL.

1107 **Frittaion, Franco, et al.**
"Bibliography of Canadian plays in English 1800-1945."
In: *Canadian Drama*; Vol. 3, no. 1 (Spring 1977) p. 42-74.; ISSN: 0317-9044.
Note: Approx. 750 entries.
Location: OONL.

1108 **Linden, Marjorie; Teeple, Diane**
"The evolving role of Canadian women writers."
In: *Ontario Library Review*; Vol. 61, no. 2 (June 1977) p. 114-131.; ISSN: 0030-2996.
Note: Approx. 300 entries.– General works, individual authors (selected criticism, book reviews, bibliographies).
Location: OONL.

1109 **McIntyre, Sheila**
"A bibliography of scholarship on literature on and by Canadian women."
In: *Canadian Newsletter of Research on Women*; Vol. 6, no. 1 (February 1977) p. 99-114.; ISSN: 0319-4477.
Note: Listing of published scholarship and unpublished theses (1972-1977) about literature written by Canadian women or about the image of women in Canadian literature.– Excludes book reviews, theses in progress and biographical sketches in popular magazines.
Location: AEU.

1110 **New Play Centre**
The catalogue: plays by British Columbia playwrights. Vancouver, B.C.: Athletica Press for New Play Centre, [c1977]. 40 p.; ISBN: 0-920294-00-6.
Note: Approx. 200 entries.– Plays by British Columbia resident playwrights published or professionally produced since 1950, unpublished scripts from amateur productions or New Play Centre workshops.– Annotations include summary of play, cast size, length and setting requirements.– Edited by Suzann Zimmering.
Location: OONL.

1111 **Pagé, Pierre; Legris, Renée**
Répertoire des dramatiques québécoises à la télévision, 1952-1977: vingt-cinq ans de télévision à Radio-Canada, téléthéâtres, feuilletons, dramatiques pour enfants. Montréal: Fides, c1977. 252 p. (Archives québécoises de la radio et de la télévision ; vol. 3); ISBN: 0-7755-0664-8.
Note: 477 entrées.– Inclut les oeuvres originales écrites directement en français pour la télévision québécoise.– Les informations se rapportent à trois catégories: identité de l'auteur et de l'oeuvre; renseignements sur la diffusion (dates, durée, etc.); renseignements sur l'interprétation (réalisateur, comédiens).– Exclut les sketches (textes très brefs: moins de quinze minutes); les adaptations et traductions.
Localisation: OONL.

1112 **Québec (Province). Musée d'art contemporain**
Solstice de la poésie québécoise: poèmes, affiches, vidéogrammes: une exposition itinérante. Montréal:

Musée d'art contemporain, 1977. [42] p.: ill.
Note: Localisation: OONL

1113 Robinson, Jill M.
Seas of earth: an annotated bibliography of Saskatchewan literature as it relates to the environment. Regina: Canadian Plains Research Center, University of Regina, 1977. x, 139 p.: ill., ports., 19 l. of pl. (Canadian Plains reports / Canadian Plains Research Center, University of Regina ; 2); ISBN: 0-88977-010-7.
Note: Approx. 100 entries.
Location: OONL.

1114 Simon Fraser University. Library. Humanities Division
A bibliographical guide to French-Canadian literature/ Guide bibliographique de la littérature canadienne-française. [Burnaby, B.C.]: Simon Fraser University Library, Humanities Division, 1977. 33 p.
Note: 104 entries.– Lists mainly reference materials: bibliographies, dictionaries, encyclopedias in French language or bilingual.– Introduction and annotations are entirely in English.
Location: OONL.

1115 Writers' Development Trust. Atlantic Work Group
Social realism: [a resource guide for the teaching of Canadian literature]. [Toronto]: Writers' Development Trust, [1977]. 68 p.
Note: Representative Canadian novels, plays, poetry and short stories: major writers and works in social realism tradition, social issues and literature which illustrate literary characteristics of the genre.
Location: OONL.

1116 Writers' Development Trust. Atlantic Work Group
Women in Canadian literature: [a resource guide for the teaching of Canadian literature]. [Toronto]: Writers' Development Trust, [1977]. 93 p.
Note: Selected and recommended readings on four themes: images of women in early Canadian literature, societal roles of women, emerging female, women writers as innovators in Canadian literature: autobiographies, novels, short stories, poetry, film.
Location: OONL.

1117 Writers' Development Trust. British Columbia Work Group
Coming of age in Canada: [a resource guide for the teaching of Canadian literature]. [Toronto]: Writers' Development Trust, [1977]. 52 p.
Note: Selection of Canadian novels, short stories, poems, plays, non-fiction dealing with themes such as parent-child relationships, peer group pressures, decisions of youth entering adult world, cultural conflicts, confrontation with death.
Location: OONL.

1118 Writers' Development Trust. British Columbia Work Group
The North, native peoples: [a resource guide for the teaching of Canadian literature]. [Toronto]: Writers' Development Trust, [1977]. 76 p.
Note: Selection of novels, short stories, poetry, legends, drama, films, resource books arranged in units which detail the native experience alone, the native-white interrelationship from early settlers to the present, and the North of Canadian literary imagination.
Location: OONL.

1119 Writers' Development Trust. Ontario Work Group
Action, adventure: [a resource guide for the teaching of Canadian literature]. [Toronto]: Writers' Development Trust, [1977]. 200 p.
Note: Selection of literary works illustrating the theme of survival in harsh winter climate as central to understanding of Canadian character.– Topics include winter brutality, historical adventures, animals, mystery and supernatural, native peoples, sports, science fiction, folk tales.
Location: OONL.

1120 Writers' Development Trust. Ontario Work Group
Family relationships: [a resource guide for the teaching of Canadian literature]. [Toronto]: Writers' Development Trust, [1977]. 65 p.
Note: Selection of novels, short stories, plays, poetry, films, reference works dealing with the theme of the family as dynasty, in women's experience, the French-Canadian family, Jewish-Canadian family, marital relations, parent-child relations, estrangement.
Location: OONL.

1121 Writers' Development Trust. Prairie Work Group
The immigrant experience: [a resource guide for the teaching of Canadian literature]. [Toronto]: Writers' Development Trust, 1977. 43 p.
Note: Selection of novels, drama, short stories, films, video recordings, non-fiction, books of songs dealing with the process of moving from another country to Canada, settling and adapting to the new land.
Location: OONL.

1122 Writers' Development Trust. Prairie Work Group
New land, new language: [a resource guide for the teaching of Canadian literature]. [Toronto]: Writers' Development Trust, [1977]. 52 p.
Note: List of works dealing with Canadian authors' response to landscape of the north: memoirs, novels, short stories, drama, film, poetry.
Location: OONL.

1123 Writers' Development Trust. Quebec Work Group
Images of biculturalism: [a resource guide for the teaching of Canadian literature]. [Toronto]: Writers' Development Trust, [1977]. 32 p.
Note: List of readings (prose and poetry) which illustrate how English and French linguistic groups in Quebec view one another.– Includes a bibliography of background material.
Location: OONL.

1124 Writers' Development Trust. Quebec Work Group
Quebec literature in translation: [a resource guide for the teaching of Canadian literature]. [Toronto]: Writers' Development Trust, [1977]. 63 p.
Note: Selection of novels, short stories, poetry, drama, non-fiction arranged chronologically to illustrate development of literature of French Quebec.
Location: OONL.

— 1978 —

1125 Anthony, Geraldine; Usmiani, Tina
"A bibliography of English Canadian drama written by women."
In: *World Literature Written in English*; Vol. 17, no. 1 (April 1978) p. 120-143.; ISSN: 0093-1705.
Note: Location: AEU.

1126 **Association des littératures canadiennes et québécoise. Comité de recherche francophone**
Situation de l'édition et de la recherche: littérature québécoise ou canadienne-française. Ottawa: Centre de recherche en civilisation canadienne-française, Université d'Ottawa, 1978. 182 p. (Documents de travail du Centre de recherche en civilisation canadienne-française ; 18)
Note: Recueillis et présentés par René Dionne.– Catégories: bibliographies générales, bibliographies de la littérature canadienne-française, oeuvres de la Nouvelle-France, le roman, la poésie, l'essai, la littérature acadienne, instruments de travail et recherches.
Localisation: OONL.

1127 **Bentley, D.M.R.**
A checklist of literary materials in *The Week* (Toronto, 1883-1896). Ottawa: Golden Dog Press, 1978. vi, 161 p.; ISBN: 0-919611-30-2.
Note: Approx. 3,200 entries.– Includes articles, poetry, fiction, book reviews.
Location: OONL.

1128 **Dowler, Linda**
"Two year's work in Canadian poetry studies: 1976-1977."
In: *Canadian Poetry*; No. 2 (Spring/Summer 1978) p. 111-126.; ISSN: 0704-5646.
Note: Listing of criticism on English-Canadian poetry, arranged in periods: Pre-Confederation, Confederation, Modern, Contemporary, General studies.– Continued under title: "The year's work in Canadian poetry studies"; compiled by Linda Dowler (Spring/Summer 1979), Linda Dowler and Mary Ann Jameson (Spring/Summer 1980), Mary Ann Jameson (Spring/Summer 1981-Spring/Summer 1987).
Location: AEU.

1129 **Gagnon, Claude-Marie; Provost, Sylvie**
Bibliographie sélective et indicative de la paralittérature. Québec: Institut supérieur des sciences humaines, Université Laval, c1978. 88 f. (Cahiers de l'ISSH, Collection Instruments de travail / Institut supérieur des sciences humaines, Université Laval ; no 24)
Note: 659 entrées.– Comprend titres anglais et français sur: roman d'espionnage, roman policier, roman populaire, roman noir, roman fantastique, science-fiction, roman western, bande dessinée.
Localisation: OONL.

1130 **Gnarowski, Michael**
A concise bibliography of English-Canadian literature. Rev. ed. Toronto: McClelland and Stewart, c1978. 145 p.; ISBN: 0-7710-3362-1.
Note: Approx. 3,000 entries.
Previous edition: c1973. 125 p.; ISBN: 0-7710-3360-5.
Location: OONL.

1131 **Licht, Merete**
Et udvalg af bibliografier og monografier om Commonwealth litteratur i Det kongelige Bibliotek. København: Det Kongelige Bibliotek, 1978. 51 p. (Det Kongelige Bibliotek Fagbibliografier ; 8)
Note: Contains a section on Canadian literature: periodicals, bibliographies and handbooks, critical works.
Location: OONL.

1132 **Lillard, Charles**
"Daylight in the swamp: a guide to the west coast renaissance."
In: *Malahat Review*; No. 45 (January 1978) p. 319-340.;

ISSN: 0025-1216.
Note: Review of British Columbia literature discusses sources, periods and books; provides lists of anthologies; dramatic works, fiction, poetry, literary magazines, publishing houses.
Location: AEU.

1133 **McCaffery, Steve; Nichol, bp**
Sound poetry: a catalogue for the eleventh International Sound Poetry Festival, Toronto, Canada, October 14 to 21, 1978. Toronto: Underwhich Editions, [1978]. 111 p.: ill.
Note: Statements and listing of works of authors represented at festival, including Canadians Earle Birney, Bill Bissett, bp Nichol, Raôul Duguay, and others.
Location: OONL.

1134 **New, William H.**
"Annual bibliography of Commonwealth literature, ... : Canada."
In: *Journal of Commonwealth Literature*; 1969 in no. 10 (December 1970) p. 51-79; 1971 in vol. 7, no. 2 (December 1972) p. 59-86; 1972 in vol. 8, no. 2 (December 1973) p. 59-97; 1973 in vol. 9, no. 2 (December 1974) p. 54-94; 1974 in vol. 10, no. 2 (December 1975) p. 72-107; 1975 in vol. 11, no. 2 (December 1976) p. 30-81; 1976 in vol. 12, no. 2 (December 1977) p. 24-84; 1977 in vol. 13, no. 2 (December 1978) p. 51-110.; ISSN: 0021-9894.
Note: Lists bibliographies, research aids, poetry, drama, fiction, anthologies, criticism (of individual authors, general studies), journals.– Continues: Carl F. Klinck: 1964-1965 (September 1965, December 1966); Mary M.S. Brown: 1966-1967 (December 1967, January 1969); Robert Weaver: 1968 (December 1969).– Continued by: Mary Burnett: 1970 (December 1971); Marilyn G. Flitton: 1978 (December 1979); Doreen Ingram: 1979 (December 1980); Moshie Dahms: 1980-1990 (February 1982-1991).
Location: AEU.

1135 **Norris, Ken**
"Montreal English poetry in the seventies."
In: *Contemporary Verse Two*; Vol. 3, no. 3 (January 1978) p. 8-13.
Note: Listing of publications of Montreal small presses and a list of little magazines appended: "A Montreal bibliography."
Location: AEU.

1136 **O'Neill, Patrick B.**
Canadian plays: a supplementary checklist. Halifax, N.S.: Dalhousie University, University Libraries, School of Library Service, 1978. 69 l. (Occasional papers / Dalhousie University Libraries and Dalhousie University School of Library Service ; no. 19; ISSN: 0318-7403); ISBN: 0-7703-0158-4.
Note: 820 entries.
Location: OONL.

1137 **O'Neill, Patrick B.**
"Unpublished Canadian plays, copyrighted 1921-1937."
In: *Canadian Drama*; Vol. 4, no. 1 (Spring 1978) p. 52-63.; ISSN: 0317-9044.
Note: List of Canadian plays compiled through a search of records at Canadian Copyright Office, written by Canadians or persons residing in Canada and copyrighted in Canada.
Location: AEU.

1138 **Runte, Hans R.**
"Réquisitoire acadien."
Dans: *Contemporary French Civilization*; Vol. 2, no. 2
(Winter 1978) p. 295-311.; ISSN: 0147-9156.
Note: Localisation: OONL.

1139 **Stevens, Peter**
Modern English-Canadian poetry: a guide to information
sources. Detroit, Mich.: Gale Research, c1978. xi, 216 p.
(American literature, English literature, and world
literatures in English Information guide series ; vol. 15);
ISBN: 0-8103-1244-1.
Note: Approx. 2,100 entries.– Lists bibliographies,
biographical reference material, periodical indexes,
indexes to theses, manuscript collections and special
collections, literary histories, general and critical studies,
major anthologies, periodicals, works by and about
individual twentieth-century Canadian authors.
Location: OONL.

1140 **Wawrzyszko, Aleksandra**
"A bibliographic guide to French-Canadian literature."
In: *Canadian Library Journal*; Vol. 35, no. 2 (April 1978) p.
115-133.; ISSN: 0008-4352.
Note: Location: AEU.

1141 **Zimmering, Suzann; Nesbitt, Bruce**
"Canadian literature, 1971: an annotated bibliography:
une bibliographie avec commentaire."
In: *Essays on Canadian Writing*; No. 9 (Winter 1977-
1978) p. 190-313.; ISSN: 0316-0300.
Note: Books, articles, theses, reviews of books and
theatrical productions published during 1971 directly
related to the study of Canadian literature.
Location: AEU.

— 1979 —

1142 **Alberta novelists.** [Edmonton]: Alberta Culture, Library
Services, 1979. 16 p.
Note: Approx. 300 entries.– Alberta novelist defined as
one who is living in Alberta, lived in Alberta and made
an impact on life of the province, or whose writing was
influenced by living in Alberta.– Excludes short stories,
articles, plays, humour, reminiscences, travelogues,
essays and most translations.
Location: OONL.

1143 **Amprimoz, Alexandre L.**
"Bibliographie de la poésie franco-canadienne de l'Ouest."
Dans: *Cefco: Centre d'études franco-canadiennes de l'Ouest*;
No 2 (mai 1979) p. 9-14.; ISSN: 0226-0670.
Note: 56 entrées.
Localisation: OONL.

1144 **Anctil, Pierre**
A Franco-American bibliography: New England.
Bedford, N.H.: National Materials Development Center,
1979. ix, 137 p.: ill., map.
Note: Approx. 800 entries.–Includes books and
pamphlets related to Québécois diaspora.– Focus on
New England states.– Franco-American writing as
regional branch of Quebec literature.– Text in English
and French/texte en français et en anglais.
Location: OONL.

1145 **Cantin, Pierre; Harrington, Normand; Hudon, Jean-
Paul**
Bibliographie de la critique de la littérature québécoise
dans les revues des XIXe et XXe siècles. Ottawa: Centre
de recherche en civilisation canadienne-française,
Université d'Ottawa, 1979. 5 vol. (Documents de travail
du Centre de recherche en civilisation canadienne-
française , 12-16)
Note: 18,439 entrées.– Comprend les études générales et
particulières: périodes, mouvements, écoles, sociétés,
théories de la littérature, jeunesse et littérature; les
genres: roman, poésie, théâtre, conte et nouvelle, l'essai,
littérature orale, folklore et chanson; études sur les
auteurs individuels.
Localisation: OONL.

1146 **Colombo, John Robert, et al.**
CDN SF & F: a bibliography of Canadian science fiction
and fantasy. Toronto: Hounslow Press, c1979. viii, 85 p.;
ISBN: 0-88882-036-4.
Note: Approx. 600 entries.– Includes titles in English and
French languages, by Canadians or set in Canada.
Location: OONL.

1147 **Dionne, René**
"Le roman du XIXe siècle (1837-1895)."
Dans: *Revue de l'Université d'Ottawa*; Vol. 49, nos 1-2
(janvier-avril 1979) p. 30-45.; ISSN: 0041-9206.
Note: Localisation: OONL.

1148 **Dowler, Linda**
"The year's work in Canadian poetry studies: 1978."
In: *Canadian Poetry*; No. 4 (Spring/Summer 1979) p. 131-
142.; ISSN: 0704-5646.
Note: Listing of criticism on English-Canadian poetry,
arranged in periods: Pre-Confederation, Confederation,
Modern, Contemporary, General studies.– Continuation
of "Two year's work in Canadian poetry studies: 1976-
1977," (Spring/Summer 1978), compiled by Linda
Dowler.
Location: AEU.

1149 **Flitton, Marilyn G.**
"Annual bibliography of Commonwealth literature, 1978:
Canada."
In: *Journal of Commonwealth Literature*; Vol. 14, no. 2
(December 1979) p. 42-62.; ISSN: 0021-98944.
Note: Lists bibliographies, research aids, poetry, drama,
fiction, anthologies, criticism, journals.– Continues: Carl
F. Klinck: 1964-1965 (September 1965, December 1966);
Mary M.S. Brown: 1966-1967 (December 1967, January
1969); Robert Weaver: 1968 (December 1969); William H.
New: 1969, 1971-1977 (December 1970, December 1972-
1978); Mary Burnett: 1970 (December 1971).– Continued
by: Doreen Ingram: 1979 (December 1980); Moshie
Dahms: 1980-1990 (February 1982-1991).
Location: AEU.

1150 **Gottlieb, Lois C.; Keitner, Wendy**
"Bird at the window: an annotated bibliography of
Canadian fiction written by women, 1970-1975."
In: *American Review of Canadian Studies*; Vol. 9, no. 2
(Autumn 1979) p. 3-56.; ISSN: 0272-2011.
Note: 74 entries.– Includes novels, novellas, collections of
short stories by individual authors.– Lists first Canadian
publication, British and American editions, paperback
reprints.– Annotations provide objective information
about the fiction, factual bibliographic details,
classifications of the literature by genre and fictional
technique while highlighting various socio-political
influences in women's lives.– Intended as preliminary
work to test approach and method for larger
comprehensive bibliography of Canadian fiction by

women from beginnings to the present.
Location: OONL.

1151 **Hayne, David M.**
"État actuel des études bibliographiques de la littérature canadienne-française (avant 1945)."
Dans: *Revue de l'Université d'Ottawa*; Vol. 49, nos 1-2 (janvier-avril 1979) p. 14-25.; ISSN: 0041-9206.
Note: 82 entrées.
Localisation: OONL.

1152 **Hayne, David M.**
"Preliminary bibliography of the literary relations between Quebec and the francophone world."
In: *Canadian Review of Comparative Literature*; Vol. 6, no. 2 (Spring 1979) p. 206-218.; ISSN: 0319-051X.
Note: Location: AEU.

1153 **Latham, Sheila**
Canadian poetry 1970-1979: a multi-media list. [Toronto]: Toronto Public Library, 1979. 16 p.
Note: 88 entries.– Books, periodicals, audio recordings, films, video recordings.
Location: OONL.

1154 **Lillard, Charles**
"Fifty works of British Columbia fiction, 1908-1969."
In: *Malahat Review*; No. 50 (April 1979) p. 23-26.; ISSN: 0025-1216.
Note: List of fictional works by B.C. writers, the majority of which have a B.C. setting.
Location: AEU.

1155 **Maillet, Marguerite**
"Littérature acadienne (1874-1960): les oeuvres (liste chronologique)."
Dans: *Revue de l'Université d'Ottawa*; Vol. 49, nos 1-2 (janvier-avril 1979) p. 92-98.; ISSN: 0041-9206.
Note: Localisation: OONL.

1156 **Nesbitt, Bruce**
"Canadian literature: an annotated bibliography/ Littérature canadienne: une bibliographie avec commentaire."
In: *Journal of Canadian Fiction*; Vol. 2, no. 2 (Spring 1973) p. 97-150; vol. 3, no. 4 (1975) p. 103-142; no. 17/18 (1976) p. 70-239; no. 23 (1979) p. 76-331.; ISSN: 0047-2255.
Note: Books, articles, theses, reviews of books and theatrical productions: anthologies and collections, poetry/prose/drama, juvenile works, bibliographies and surveys.– Text in English and French/texte en français et en anglais.
Location: AEU.

1157 **Roux, Françoise**
"La littérature intime au Québec: éléments de bibliographie."
Dans: *Revue de l'Université d'Ottawa*; Vol. 49, nos 1-2 (janvier-avril 1979) p. 84-88.; ISSN: 0041-9206.
Note: Mémoires et souvenirs, journaux intimes, correspondance, roman autobiographique.
Localisation: OONL.

1158 **Stuart, Ross; Vincent, Thomas Brewer**
A chronological index of locally written verse published in the newspapers and magazines of Upper and Lower Canada, Maritime Canada, and Newfoundland through 1815. Kingston, Ont.: Loyal Colonies Press, 1979. viii, 386 p.; ISBN: 0-920832-00-8.
Note: Approx. 1,300 entries.– Indexes include genre, subject, first-line, title, author.

Location: OONL.

1159 **Sutherland, Fraser**
Scotland here: a checklist of Canadian writers of Scottish ancestry. [Scotsburn, N.S.: F. Sutherland, 1979]. 13 l.
Note: Approx. 230 entries.– Includes only authors born in 1918 or earlier whose ancestry was principally Scottish.– Those who wrote in Gaelic are included.
Location: OONL.

1160 **Vigneault, Robert**
"Bibliographie sélective de l'essai au Québec de 1895 à 1945."
Dans: *Revue de l'Université d'Ottawa*; Vol. 49, nos 1-2 (janvier-avril 1979) p. 79-81.; ISSN: 0041-9206.
Note: Localisation: OONL.

— 1980 —

1161 **Amprimoz, Alexandre L.**
"French poets of western Canada: a selected checklist."
In: *Essays on Canadian Writing*; Nos. 18/19 (Summer/Fall 1980) p. 320-321.; ISSN: 0316-0300.
Note: Location: AEU.

1162 **"Bibliographies on contributors [to *Prism International*]."**
In: *Prism International*; Vol. 18, no. 1 (Spring/Summer 1979) p. 118-123; vol. 18, no. 2 (Winter 1979-1980) p. 140-143; vol. 19, no. 1 (Spring 1980) p. 109-112.; ISSN: 0032-8790.
Note: Listings of additional writing by people published in the magazine.
Location: AEU.

1163 **"Bio-bibliographie sommaire de la plupart des écrivains ayant participé à la Rencontre québécoise internationale des écrivains."**
Dans: *Liberté*; No 84 (décembre 1972) p. 147-153; no 87-88 (juillet 1973) p. 189-191; no 90 (novembre-décembre 1973) p. 295-304; no 97-98 (janvier-avril 1975) p. 293-301; no 106-107 (juillet-octobre 1976) p. 331-340; no 112-113 (juillet-octobre 1977) p. 313-326; no 130 (juillet-août 1980) p. 134-143.; ISSN: 0024-2020.
Note: Localisation: OONL.

1164 **Boivin, Aurélien; Landry, Kenneth**
"Guide bibliographique de la littérature québécoise."
Dans: *Stanford French Review*; Vol. 4, no. 1-2 (Spring-Fall 1980) p. 265-285.; ISSN: 0163-657X.
Note: Instruments de travail (bibliographies, catalogues), études à consulter, anthologies, revues québécoises et étrangères.
Localisation: AEU.

1165 **Bullock, Chris; Peck, David**
Guide to Marxist literary criticism. Bloomington: Indiana University Press, c1980. ix, 176 p.; ISBN: 0-253-13144-8.
Note: Approx. 1,500 entries.– Listing of works on English, Canadian and U.S. literatures related to the contribution of Marxism to literary criticism.
Location: OONL.

1166 **"Chronologie de la littérature français de l'Ouest canadien."**
Dans: *Cefco: Centre d'études franco-canadiennes de l'Ouest*; No 6 (octobre 1980) p. 5-12.; ISSN: 0226-0670.
Note: Troisième partie: oeuvres romanesques, 1907-1980.
Localisation: OONL.

1167 **Cooley, Dennis**
"A selected checklist of Prairie poetry in English."
In: *Essays on Canadian Writing*; Nos. 18/19 (Summer/Fall 1980) p. 304-319.; ISSN: 0316-0300.

Note: Approx. 275 entries.– Collections by individuals, anthologies: "titles of reasonably well-known writers produced mainly within the last ten years."
Location: AEU.

1168 **Dionne, René**
Répertoire des professeurs et chercheurs: littérature québécoise et canadienne française. 2e éd. Sherbrooke, Qué.: Éditions Naaman, 1980. 120 p.; ISBN: 2-89040-146-4.
Note: Comprend les livres et articles publiés sur les sujets québécois ou canadiens-français uniquement pour 195 professeurs et chercheurs.
Édition antérieure: 1978. 120 p.
Localisation: OONL.

1169 **Dowler, Linda; Jameson, Mary Ann**
"The year's work in Canadian poetry studies: 1979."
In: *Canadian Poetry*; No. 6 (Spring/Summer 1980) p. 89-103.; ISSN: 0704-5646.
Note: Listing of criticism on English-Canadian poetry, arranged in periods: Pre-Confederation, Confederation, Modern, Contemporary, General studies.
Location: AEU.

1170 **Gauthier, Louis-Guy**
Littérature québécoise (romans, contes, nouvelles): bibliographie pour le 1er cycle du secondaire. Montréal: Association des institutions d'enseignement secondaire, 1980. vi, 8 f.
Note: Localisation: OONL.

1171 **Ingram, Doreen**
"Annual bibliography of Commonwealth literature, 1979: Canada."
In: *Journal of Commonwealth Literature*; Vol. 15, no. 2 (December 1980) p. 59-86.; ISSN: 0021-9894.
Note: Lists bibliographies, research aids, poetry, drama, fiction, anthologies, criticism, journals.– Continues: Carl F. Klinck: 1964-1965 (September 1965, December 1966); Mary M. S. Brown: 1966-1967 (December 1967, January 1969); Robert Weaver: 1968 (December 1969); William H. New: 1969, 1971-1977 (December 1970, December 1972-1978); Mary Burnett: 1970 (December 1970); Marilyn G. Flitton: 1978 (December 1979).– Continued by: Moshie Dahms: 1980-1990 (February 1982-1991).
Location: AEU.

1172 **Maillet, Marguerite**
"Littérature d'acadie: bibliographie."
Dans: *Les Acadiens des Maritimes: études thèmatiques*. Moncton, N.B.: Centre d'études acadiennes, Université de Moncton, 1980. P. 557-594.
Note: English title: "Acadian literature: bibliography". In: *The Acadians of the Maritimes: thematic studies*. 1982. P. 513-549.
Localisation: OONL.

1173 **Miska, John P.**
Canadian prose written in English 1833-1980 [microform]: a bibliography of secondary material. Lethbridge, Alta.: Microform Biblios, 1980. 5 microfiches (Canadian literature bibliographic series ; no. 2); ISBN: 0-919279-00-7.
Note: 3,360 entries.– Books, monographs, serial publications, bibliographies, checklists, directories, research reports, review articles, theses, book reviews about Canadian prose and authors of fiction.
Location: OONL.

1174 **Riedel, Walter E.**
"Verzeichnis kanadischer Literatur in deutscher Übersetzung."
In: *Das literarische Kanadabild: eine Studie zur Rezeption kanadischer Literatur in deutscher Übersetzung*. Bonn: Bouvier, 1980. P. 116-140. (Studien zur Germanistik, Anglistik und Komparatistik ; Bd. 92; ISSN: 0340-594X); ISBN: 3-416-01544-4.
Note: Checklist of Canadian literary works translated into German.
Location: OONL.

1175 **Rubin, Don; Cranmer-Byng, Alison**
Canada's playwrights: a biographical guide. Toronto: Canadian Theatre Review Publications, c1980. 191 p.: ports.; ISBN: 0-920-644-49-X.
Note: Bio-bibliographical notes on 70 Canadian playwrights: stage writing, published and unpublished, works in progress, radio writing, film scripts.
Location: OONL.

1176 **Wagner, Anton**
The Brock bibliography of published Canadian plays in English, 1766-1978. Toronto: Playwrights Press, c1980. xi, 375 p.; ISBN: 0-88754-157-7.
Note: 2,469 entries.– "Canadian" means those plays written by Canadians, native, naturalized or landed immigrant.– Includes plays reproduced by any means and distributed through a public agency, publisher or organization.– Excludes scripts for film, television, radio, unless these works were adapted for the stage, and stage-plays in French or other heritage languages (unless these were subsequently translated into and published in English).
Previous edition: Cummings, Richard, et al. *The Brock bibliography of published Canadian stage plays in English, 1900-1972*. St. Catherines, Ont.: Brock University; 1972. vi l., 35, [12] p.– Approx. 900 entries.
Supplement: *The First supplement to the Brock bibliography of published Canadian plays*. 1973. v, 32, [11] p.
Location: OONL.

— 1981 —

1177 **Boivin, Henri-Bernard**
Littérature acadienne, 1960-1980: bibliographie. Montréal: Bibliothèque nationale du Quebec, 1981. 63 p.: ill.; ISBN: 2-550-01639-4.
Note: 86 entrées.– Le terme "littérature" a été employé au sens strict pour designer les oeuvres d'imagination: la poésie, le roman, le théâtre, la nouvelle, le récit, la légende, la chanson des provinces de l'Atlantique.– Les catégories d'imprimés retenues sont les monographies et les périodiques.– Liste des sources consultées.
Localisation: OONL.

1178 **British Columbia in fiction.** [Vancouver]: Education Services Group, Vancouver School Board, 1981. 14 p.
Note: 82 entries.– Developed by a committee of teacher-librarians, provides a comprehensive list of materials for use by teachers, teacher-librarians and students, kindergarten to grade 7.– Arranged in broad geographic sections.
Locations: OONL.

1179 **Camerlain, Lorraine**
"Chronologie fragmentaire des créations québécoises depuis 1975."
Dans: *Jeu*; No 21 (1981) p. 129-169.; ISSN: 0382-0335.

Note: Approx. 400 entrées.– Liste bibliographique des pièces dramatiques québécoises, 1975-1981.
Localisation: OONL.

1180 **Dionne, René**
Bibliographie de la littérature outaouaise et franco-ontarienne. 2e éd. rev. et augm. Ottawa: Centre de recherche en civilisation canadienne-française, Université d'Ottawa, 1981. viii, 204 p. (Documents de travail du Centre de recherche en civilisation canadienne-française ; 10)
Note: Approx. 1,800 entrées.– Auteurs francophones nés en Ontario ou dans l'Outaouais québécois (Pontiac, Gatineau, Papineau et Hull); les auteurs francophone d'origine canadienne ou québécoise qui habitent l'Ontario ou l'Outaouais québécois; les auteurs d'origine ou de langue étrangères qui ont publié, du temps qu'ils habitaient, ou depuis qu'ils habitent, ces régions, des oeuvres de création littéraire (roman, poésie, théâtre, nouvelles, essai, etc.) ou des études sur des sujets canadiens-français ou québécois.
Édition antérieure: 1978. 91 p.– Approx. 1,000 entrées.
Localisation: OONL.

1181 **Hayne, David M.**
Bibliographie analytique de la critique littéraire au Québec. [Kingston, Ont.]: Association des professeurs de français des universités et collèges canadiens, 1981. 15 p. (Fascicule pédagogique / Association des professeurs de français des universités et collèges canadiens ; no 4)
Note: Approx. 125 entrées.– Inclut bibliographies, anthologies, histoire de la critique littéraire, nouvelles approches au Québec depuis 1960, critique des genres.
Localisation: OONL.

1182 **Henry, Jon Paul**
A select bibliography and a biographical dictionary of B.C. poets, 1970-1980. [Vancouver]: 1981. 78 l.
Note: Location: BVAS.

1183 **Mantz, Douglas**
Landscape in Canadian poetry: an annotated bibliography sampling the use of landscape in Canadian poetry, based upon the poetical works of major poets published in single-author book form between 1860 and 1960. Vancouver: [s.n.], c1981. 242 l. (TCP bibliography ; series 1, no. 1)
Note: 1,053 entries.– Principal arrangement by landscape type: seacoast, hill, tree, flower, river, sky, building, city, foreign location.– Categories selected by computer-generated frequency tabulation.– Indexes: geopolitical locations, poem titles, authors, seasons, topographical features, motifs.
Location: OONL.

1184 **Nadel, Ira Bruce**
Jewish writers of North America: a guide to information sources. Detroit, Mich.: Gale Research, c1981. xix, 493 p. (American studies information guide series ; vol. 8); ISBN: 0-8103-1484-3.
Note: 3,291 entries.– General reference guides: bibliographies, biographical references, periodical indexes, research catalogues, special collections, literary history and criticism, anthologies.– Includes bio-bibliographies on Canadian-Jewish poets, short-story writers, novelists, dramatists, and a section on Yiddish literature.
Location: OONL.

1185 **Olivier, Réjean**
Répertoire des auteurs contemporains de la région de Lanaudière. Joliette, Qué.: Éditions Pleins Bords, c1981. 320 p.: ill.; ISBN: 2-89197-019-5.
Note: Comprend notes biobibliographiques sur 153 écrivains.
Localisation: OONL.

1186 **Répertoire des textes du Centre d'essai des auteurs dramatiques.** Montréal: Cead, [1981]. 151 p.: ill.
Note: Liste des titres d'environ 500 pièces, écrites par plus de 200 auteurs, publiées et inédites.– Conception et rédaction: Hélène Dumas, Denis Lagueux, Pierre MacDuff.
Localisation: OONL.

1187 **Shek, Ben-Zion**
"Beyond the basics in selecting Quebec literature."
In: *Ontario Library Review*; Vol. 65, no. 2 (June 1981) p. 103-118.; ISSN: 0030-2996.
Note: Review and listing of fiction, poetry, theatre, literary history, bibliography and criticism.
Location: OONL.

— 1982 —

1188 **Bessette, Émile; Hamel, Réginald; Mailhot, Laurent**
Répertoire pratique de littérature et de culture québécoises. Montréal: Fédération internationale des professeurs de français, 1982. 63 p.; ISBN: 2-901106-02-1.
Note: Comprend les titres essential dans les domaines de la littérature, la langue, des arts et des science sociales, le cinéma, les disques, la chanson, les périodiques.
Localisation: OONL.

1189 **Brunet-Lamarche, Anita**
"Auteurs et oeuvres: bio-bibliographie."
Dans: *Revue du Nouvel Ontario*; No 4 (1982) p. 21-43.; ISSN: 0708-1715.
Note: 43 entrées.– Littérature sudburoise: poèmes, théâtre, contes et légendes, didactique, romans, biographie, essai, mélanges, récit.
Localisation: OONL.

1190 **Coppens, Patrick**
Littérature québécoise contemporaine. Québec: Gouvernement du Québec, Ministère de l'éducation, Direction générale des moyens d'enseignement; La Pocatière, Québec: Société du stage en bibliothéconomie de La Pocatière, [1982]. 77 p. (Bibliothèmes / Société du stage en bibliothéconomie de La Pocatière ; no 1; ISSN: 0229-639X); ISBN: 2-89123-084-1.
Note: 460 entrées.– La période couverte est jusqu'au 31 décembre 1981.– Comprend les ouvrages généraux, anthologies, dictionnaires, périodiques; poésie, théâtre, roman, nouvelle, conte.– Indices de niveau et d'utilité.
Localisation: QRCN.

1191 **Killaly contributors: being an index to *Stuffed Crocodile*** and Killaly chapbook contributors and a list of their recent publications, together with Twenty found poems signed on a floor by Frank B. Arnold. London, Ont.: Killaly Press, 1982. [48] p. (Killaly chapbooks, 5th series ; no. 1); ISBN: 0-920438-24-5.
Note: Location: OONL.

1192 **Laugher, Charles T.**
Atlantic Province authors of the twentieth century: a bio-bibliographical checklist. Halifax, N.S.: Dalhousie University, 1982. vi, 620 p. (Occasional papers / Dalhousie University Libraries and Dalhousie University

School of Library Service ; no. 29; ISSN: 0318-7403); ISBN: 0-7703-0163-0.
Note: Includes all writers of both juvenile and adult poetry, fiction and drama who were either born in the Atlantic Provinces or lived in the region long enough to have published a body of work.
Location: OONL.

1193 **Lister, Rota Herzberg**
"Canadian plays in English about older women: a bibliography."
In: *Resources for Feminist Research*; Vol. 11, no. 2 (July 1982) p. 238-240.; ISSN: 0707-8412.
Note: Location: OONL.

1194 **Maillet, Marguerite**
"Acadian literature: bibliography."
In: *The Acadians of the Maritimes: thematic studies.* Moncton, N.B.: Centre d'études acadiennes, Université de Moncton, 1982. P. 513-549.
Note: Titre en français: "Littérature d'acadie: bibliographie". Dans: *Les Acadiens des Maritimes: études thèmatiques.* 1980. P. 557-594.
Location: OONL.

1195 **McGill University. McLennan Library. Reference Department**
Canadian literature: a guide to reference sources. [Montreal]: McLennan Library, Reference Department, McGill University, 1982. 28 p.
Note: Approx. 175 entries.– Bibliographies, reference works, periodical titles for both English- and French-Canadian literature.– Literature means creative works, including fiction, short stories, poetry, drama, essays.– Excluded are children's literature, film, folklore, mass media, performing arts, author bibliographies.
Location: OONL.

1196 **Pivato, Joseph**
"The arrival of Italian-Canadian writing."
In: *Canadian Ethnic Studies*; Vol. 14, no. 1 (1982) p. 127-137.; ISSN: 0008-3496.
Note: Reviews and lists fiction, poetry, drama, prose non-fiction.
Location: OONL.

1197 **Rousseau, Guildo**
Contes et récits littéraires de la Mauricie, 1850-1950: essai de bibliographie régionale. Trois-Rivières, Québec: Éditions CEDOLEQ, [1982]. 178 p. (Guides bibliographiques / Éditions CEDOLEQ ; 8); ISBN: 2-89060-012-2.
Note: Localisation: OONL.

1198 **Tellier, Sylvie**
Chronologie littéraire du Québec, 1760 à 1960. Québec: Institut québécois de recherche sur la culture, 1982. 347 p. (Instruments de travail / Institut québécois de recherche sur la culture ; no 6); ISBN: 2-89224-024-7.
Note: 6,200 entrées.– Romans, contes, nouvelles, légendes et feuilletons, drames, poésie, essais.
Localisation: OONL.

1199 **Wagner, Anton**
"A selected bibliography of Canadian theatre and drama bibliographies and guides."
In: *Canadian Theatre Review*; No. 34 (Spring 1982) p. 77-83.; ISSN: 0315-0836.
Note: Approx. 50 entries.– Lists of published and unpublished plays, Canadian theatre history

bibliographies and checklists.– Includes a section on Quebec theatre.
Location: OONL.

1200 **Young, Judy**
"Canadian literature in the non-official languages: a review of recent publications and work in progress."
In: *Canadian Ethnic Studies*; Vol. 14, no. 1 (1982) p. 138-149.; ISSN: 0008-3496.
Note: 57 entries.– Lists and describes Canadian literary works published since 1970 in non-official languages or in translation.– Reference is made to bibliographies, anthologies, individual works of prose and poetry.
Location: OONL.

— 1983 —

1201 **Connections two: writers and the land.** Winnipeg: Manitoba School Library Audio-Visual Association, 1983. 123 p.; ISBN: 0-920082-009.
Note: Contains biographical and bibliographical information on 57 writers who have published works of poetry, fiction, drama, music and cartoons since 1970; writers born in Manitoba, worked or lived in Manitoba.– Excludes writers of non-fiction.
Location: OONL.

1202 **Godard, Barbara**
Inventory of research in Canadian and Quebec literature/ Répertoire des recherches en littératures canadiennes et québécoises. Downsview, Ont.: York University, 1983. 126 p.
Note: 958 entries.– Sections include: "Research in progress," "Publications since 1980," "In press," "Papers," "Theses."
Location: ACU.

1203 **Gross, Konrad**
"Literary criticism in German on English-Canadian literature: commentary and bibliography."
In: *German-Canadian Yearbook*; Vol. 6 (1981) p. 305-310; vol. 7 (1983) p. 234-238.; ISSN: 0316-8603.
Note: Location: OONL.

1204 **Hoy, Helen**
Modern English-Canadian prose: a guide to information sources. Detroit: Gale Research, c1983. xxiii, 605 p. (American literature, English literature, and world literatures in English Information guide series ; vol. 38); ISBN: 0-8103-1245-X.
Note: 5,259 entries.– Covers to January 1, 1981.– Includes general reference sources, literary history, criticism and theory, and for each individual author, a listing of primary and secondary works, criticism, book reviews.
Location: OONL.

1205 **Lamonde, Yvan**
Je me souviens: la littérature personnelle au Québec, 1860-1980. Québec: Institut québécois de recherche sur la culture, 1983. 275 p. (Instruments de travail / Institut québécois de recherche sur la culture ; no 9; ISSN: 0714-0576); ISBN: 2-89224-028-X.
Note: 366 entrées.– Inventaire de quatre genres littéraires spécifiques: le journal personnel, les souvenirs, les mémoires, autobiographie.
Localisation: OONL.

1206 **Légaré, Yves**
Dictionnaire des écrivains québécois contemporains. Montréal: Québec/Amérique, c1983. 399 p.; ISBN: 2-89037-158-1.

Note: Ce dictionnaire regroupe: les membres de l'Union des écrivains québécois; les écrivains qui ont publié au moins deux oeuvres en littérature (roman, essai, poésie, théâtre, littérature de jeunesse) depuis 1970: nés au Québec, ou y vivre y avoir vécu suffisamment longtemps pour y être identifiés.– Exclut les écrivains acadiens, les écrivains anglophones.– La bibliographie comprend l'ensemble des oeuvres d'un écrivain, ses oeuvres traduites, ses traductions ainsi que les études portant sur son oeuvre.– Exclut les rééditions, articles de revues (exception faite des numéros spéciaux consacrés à un auteur).
Localisation: OONL.

1207 **Livres et auteurs québécois: revue critique de l'année littéraire, 1969-1982.** Québec: Presses de l'Université Laval, 1969-1983. 14 vol.: ill.; ISSN: 0316-2621.
Note: Annuel.– Revue critique de la production littéraire québécoise de langue française pour l'année en cours dans tous les domaines.– Bibliographie générale.
1969-1972: publ. à Montréal par Éditions Jumonville.
A paru sous le titre: *Livres et auteurs canadiens* de 1961 à 1968. Montréal: Éditions Jumonville, 1962-1968. 8 vol.; ISSN: 0076-0153.
Localisation: OONL.

1208 **O'Neill, Patrick B.**
"A checklist of Canadian dramatic materials to 1967."
In: *Canadian Drama*; Vol. 8, no. 2 (1982) p. 173-303; vol. 9, no. 2 (1983) p. 369-506.; ISSN: 0317-9044.
Note: Approx. 5,000 listings, by author, of dramatic works by authors resident in Canada, under Canadian copyright, or in the Canadian collections of libraries consulted in the compilation.
Location: OONL.

1209 **Reimer, Louise**
Canadian fiction classics: a booklist prepared in commemoration of the centennial year of the Toronto Public Library. [Toronto]: The Library, [1983]. 12 p.
Note: Approx. 50 entries.– Selection of Canadian novels of enduring value.
Location: OONL.

— 1984 —

1210 **Coppens, Patrick**
La poésie québécoise, 1980-1983. Montréal: Service de diffusion sélective de l'information de la Centrale des bibliothèques, 1984. 84 p. (DSI/CB ; no 55; ISSN: 0825-5024); ISBN: 2-89059-255-3.
Note: 253 entrées.– Volumes et articles publiés entre 1980 et 1983.
Suppléments:
... , *1984-1985*. SDM, 1988. (DSI ; no 138); ISBN: 2-89059-085-2.
... , *1986-1987*. SDM, 1988. (DSI ; no 137); ISBN: 2-89059-351-7.
... , *1988-1989*. SDM, 1990. (DSI ; no 158); ISBN: 2-89059-378-9.
Localisation: OONL.

1211 **Dionne, René**
"Classiques de la littérature québécoise: essai de bibliographie fondamentale."
Dans: *Le Québécois et sa littérature*. Sherbrooke, Québec: Éditions Naaman; Paris: Agence de Coopération Culturelle et Technique, 1984. P. 407-424. (Collection littératures ; no 7); ISBN: 2-89040-299-1.

Note: Localisation: OONL.

1212 **Flack, David; Hunt, Lynn J.; Murray, Danielle**
History through drama: sourcebook. [Ontario: s.n.], c1984. 125 p.; ISBN: 0-9691747-0-5.
Note: Annotated bibliography of scripts and source material pertaining to Canadian history for developing drama.– Subjects include native peoples, settlement and immigration, regional history, Confederation, wars and rebellions, labour, women's issues, transportation, contemporary issues.
Location: OONL.

1213 **Giguère, Richard; Elder, Jo-Anne**
"Bibliographie sélective."
Dans: *Voix et Images*; Vol. 10, no 1 (automne 1984) p. 59-65.; ISSN: 0318-9201.
Note: Poésie canadienne, roman canadien.
Localisation: OONL.

1214 **Kermond, Lesley; Money, Christine**
Commonwealth women novelists: catalogue of an exhibition of novels, critical works and biographies, held in the Exhibition Galleries of the Commonwealth Institute 5-22 January, 1983. London: Library & Resource Centre, Commonwealth Institute, c1984. iii, 26 p.; ISBN: 0-946140-05-7.
Note: 330 entries.– Selection of works by Commonwealth women writers from late nineteenth century to 1980s: novels, short stories, critical and biographical studies.
Location: OONL.

1215 **Literary publications supported by Multiculturalism Canada/Publications littéraires subventionnées par Multiculturalisme Canada.** Ottawa: Multiculturalism Canada, 1984. 53 p.; ISBN: 0-662-53666-5.
Note: Catalogue of works of fiction, poetry, drama, children's literature, folktales supported by the Multiculturalism Directorate between the years 1971 to 1984.– Alphabetical by title, with an index of authors, editors, illustrators, translators, subjects.– Text in English and French/texte en français et en anglais.
Location: OONL.

1216 **McGrath, Robin**
Canadian Inuit literature: the development of a tradition. Ottawa: National Museum of Man, 1984. x, 230 p.: ill., maps. (Canadian Ethnology Service paper ; no. 94; ISSN: 0316-1862)
Note: Approx. 900 entries.– Books, articles, stories and poems by Inuit authors are documented and examined.– The bibliography, on pages 165-211, represents a significant listing of material in this area.– Résumé en français.
Location: OONL.

1217 **Mount Saint Vincent University. Library**
Catalogue of the Canadian drama collection in the Library of Mount Saint Vincent University, Halifax, Nova Scotia, 1984. Halifax, N.S.: The University, 1984. 29, 22, 62 p.
Note: 781 entries.– Listing of Canadian plays, published and unpublished, in the Canadian Drama Collection of Mount Saint Vincent University Library.
Location: OONL.

1218 **Rudnicki, Diane**
A bibliography of Canadian literature. Halifax, N.S.: Canadian Learning Materials Centre, 1984. 21 p.
Note: Approx. 120 entries.– Anthologies, history and criticism, reference and resource materials, guides to the

literature (reviewing sources, booklists).– Designed to provide secondary school teachers with basic listing of materials on Canadian literature (mainly English).
Location: OONL.

— 1985 —

1219 **Coach House Press**
Tweny/20. Toronto: Coach House Press, c1985. 142 p.; ISBN: 0-88910-295-3.
Note: 286 entries.– Twentieth anniversary catalogue.– Annotations, excerpts from reviews.– Chronological arrangement.
Location: OONL.

1220 **Coppens, Patrick**
Le roman québécois, 1980-1983. Montréal: Service de diffusion sélective de l'information de la Centrale des bibliothèques, 1985. 71 p. (DSI/CB ; no 67; ISSN: 0825-5024); ISBN: 2-89059-267-7.
Note: 180 entrées.– Oeuvres de création littéraire régroupées dans trois sections: "Romans pour adolescents," "Romans pour adultes," "Romans pour lecteurs cultivés et pour spécialistes."- Une section rassemble les études historiques ou critiques, biographies, journaux intimes, correspondance, anthologies et bibliographies.
Suppléments:
... , *1984-1986*. 1988. 41 p. (DSI/CB ; no 100); ISBN: 2-89059-305-3.
... , *1987*. 1988. 25 p. (DSI/CB ; no 132); ISBN: 2-89059-345-2.
... , *1988*. 1989. 32 p. (DSI/CB ; no 148); ISBN: 2-89059-363-0.
... , *1989*. 1990. 32 p. (DSI (Diffusion sélective de l'information) ; no 173); ISBN: 0-89059-394-0.
... , *1990*. 1991. 32 p. (DSI ; no 176); ISBN: 2-89059-399-1.
... , *1991*. 1992. 46 p. (DSI ; no 190); ISBN: 2-89059-415-7.
Localisation: OONL.

1221 **Hudon, Jean-Paul**
Guide bibliographique des lettres françaises et québécoises à l'intention des étudiants de l'Université du Québec à Chicoutimi. [Chicoutimi]: Bibliothèque, Université du Québec à Chicoutimi, 1985. vii, 109 p.; ISBN: 2-920751-02-6.
Note: Approx. 500 entrées.
Localisation: OONL.

1222 **Noonan, Gerald**
Guide to the literary heritage of Waterloo and Wellington Counties from 1830 to the mid-20th century: an historical bibliography of authors and poets. Waterloo, Ontario: [Wilfrid Laurier University], 1985. 152 p.; ISBN: 0-9692184-0-0.
Note: Location: OONL.

1223 **Platnick, Phyllis**
Canadian poetry: index to criticisms, 1970-1979/Poésie canadienne: index de critiques, 1970-1979. [Ottawa]: Canadian Library Association, c1985. xxviii, 337 p.; ISBN: 0-88802-194-1.
Note: Listing of books, journal articles, theses, bibliographies on individual poets (general works, individual books, individual poems).
Location: OONL.

1224 **Université de Montréal. Bibliothèque des sciences humaines et sociales**
Guide de la documentation en lettres françaises et québécoises: à l'intention des usagers de la Bibliothèque des sciences humaines et sociales. 3e éd. rev., corr. et augm. [Montréal]: Université de Montréal, Bibliothèque des sciences humaines et sociales, 1985. vi, 166 p ; ISBN: 0-88529-040-2.
Note: 365 entrées.– Comprend les ouvrages de référence concernant la littérature et la langue: bibliographies générales et spécialisées, synthèses historiques et chronologies, dictionnaires, répertoires des thèses et périodiques.
Éditions antérieures:
1977. v, 120 p.
Archambault, Michèle. *Guide bibliographique des lettres françaises et québécoises*. 1973. viii, 141 f.
Localisation: OONL.

— 1986 —

1225 **Cheverie, Carol Anne**
A brief history and bibliography of the Fredericton Tuesday Night Writers, 1966-1983 [microform]. Ottawa: National Library of Canada, 1986. 2 microfiches (135 frames); ISBN: 0-315-25119-0.
Note: Part Two (p. 18-50), is a bibliography of published works read by members of the Tuesday Night Writers workshop group, founded in 1966 by Dorothy Livesay when writer-in-residence at the University of New Brunswick.– Listing includes works of poetry, prose, drama, novels, songs.– Place of publication varies, from small town newspapers to national publishing companies.– Thesis: M.A., Department of English, University of New Brunswick, 1984.
Location: OONL.

1226 **Elliott, Lorris**
The bibliography of literary writings by Blacks in Canada. Toronto: Williams-Wallace Publishers, 1986. 48 p.; ISBN: 0-88795-047-7.
Note: Lists all published works, Canadian and foreign, of prose and poetry by Blacks living in Canada or who have lived in Canada for a period of time.– Definition of "Black" includes native Blacks and immigrants.
Location: NBS.

1227 **Heath, Jeffrey M.**
Profiles in Canadian literature. Toronto: Dundurn Press, 1980-1986. 6 vol., ill., ports.; ISBN: 0-919670-46-6 (vol. 1); 0-919670-50-4 (vol. 2); 0-919670-58-X (vol. 3); 0-919670-59-8 (vol. 4); 1-55002-001-3 (vol. 5); 1-55002-002-1 (vol. 6).
Note: Bio-bibliographical information on 90 authors.– Selected bibliographies include works of the author (books, articles), writings about the author (book reviews, criticism, dissertations).
Location: OONL.

1228 **Houle, Guy**
"Bibliographie de la littérature récente en Ontario, en Acadie et dans l'Ouest canadien."
Dans: *Revue de l'Université d'Ottawa*; Vol. 56, no 3 (juillet-septembre 1986) p. 145-154.; ISSN: 0041-9206.
Note: Poésie franco-ontarienne, roman et théâtre franco-ontarien depuis 1970, poésie acadienne, roman et théâtre acadien depuis 1950, roman, poésie et théâtre dans l'Ouest canadien depuis 1950.
Localisation: AEU.

1229 **Melançon, Benoît**
"Filmo-bibliographie: cinéma et littérature au Québec."
Dans: *Revue d'histoire littéraire du Québec et du Canada*

français; No 11 (hiver-printemps 1986) p. 167-221.; ISSN: 0713-7958.

Note: 348 entrées.– Six sections: Bibliographie générale; cinéma québecois et littérature québécoise; cinéma étranger et littérature québécoise; cinéma québécois et littérature étrangère; films sur la littérature; écrivains-scénaristes et réalisateurs.– Index des noms.

Localisation: OONL.

1230 **Melançon, Carole**
Bibliographie descriptive et critique de la réception canadienne de *Bonheur d'occasion*, 1945-1983 [microforme]. Ottawa: Bibliothèque nationale du Canada, 1986. 5 microfiches.; ISBN: 0-315-2094-5.
Note: 391 entrées.– Textes de Gabrielle Roy; ouvrages et articles publiés au Canada sur *Bonheur d'occasion.*– Mémoire (M.A.), Française, Université de Sherbrooke.
Localisation: OONL.

1231 **Mukherjee, Arun P.**
"A select bibliography of South Asian poetry in Canada."
In: *World Literature Written in English*; Vol. 26, no. 1 (Spring 1986) p. 97-98.; ISSN: 0093-1705.
Note: Location: AEU.

1232 **New, William H.**
Canadian writers since 1960. First series. Detroit, Mich.: Gale Research, 1986. xiii, 445 p.: ill. (Dictionary of literary biography ; vol. 53); ISBN: 0-8103-1731-1.
Note: Bio-bibliographical essays and listing of works for 63 English- and French-Canadian writers.– Includes a select list of critical writings.
Location: OONL.

1233 **Olivier, Réjean**
Bibliographie sur Nöel et le temps des fêtes: établie à partir du catalogue de la collection de la famille Olivier de Joliette. Joliette, Québec: R. Olivier, 1986. 29 f. (Collection Oeuvres bibliophiliques de Lanaudière ; no 14); ISBN: 2-920249-98-3.
Note: 146 entrées.
Localisation: OONL.

1234 **Slavutych, Yar**
An annotated bibliography of Ukrainian literature in Canada: Canadian book publications, 1908-1985. 2nd enl. ed. Edmonton: Slavuta, 1986. 155, 23 p.; ISBN: 0-919452-44-2.
Note: Approx. 1,500 entries.
Previous edition: Edmonton, Slavuta, 1984. 161, 20 p.
Location: OONL.

— 1987 —

1235 **Clavet, Jocelyn**
La critique littéraire des oeuvres canadiennes-françaises dans le journal *Le Canada*, 1940-1946 [microforme]: bibliographie descriptive et analytique. Ottawa: Bibliothèque nationale du Canada, 1987. 2 microfiches (143 images): (ii, 135 p.); ISBN: 0-315-33745-1.
Note: 250 entrées.– Thèse, M.A., Faculté des lettres, Université Laval, 1986.
Localisation: OONL.

1236 **Dionne, René; Cantin, Pierre**
"Bibliographie de la critique."
Dans: *Revue d'histoire littéraire du Québec et du Canada français*; No 1 (1979) p. 130-257; no 2 (1980-1981) p. 180-304; no 3 (hiver-printemps 1982) p. 151-266; no 4 (été-automne 1982) p. 117-234; no 5 (hiver-printemps 1983); p. 147-285; no 6 (été-automne 1983) p. 100-246; no 8 (été-

automne 1984) p. 109-248; no 9 (hiver-printemps 1985) p. 161-166; no 10 (été-automne 1985) p. 131-280; no 13 (hiver-printemps 1987) p. 255-261; no 14 (été-automne 1987) p. 175-345.; ISSN: 0713-7958.
Note: Inventaire de la critique récente en littérature québécoise et canadienne-française.– (1) Livres: dictionnaires des auteurs et des oeuvres, répertoires, inventaires d'archives, bibliographies, index, manuels d'histoires littéraire.– (2) Revues: études sur la littérature québécoise en général; études aux genres (roman, poésie, théâtre, conte et nouvelle, essai, presse, littérature orale); études qui concerne un auteur en particulier; index des auteurs des articles répertories; liste des revues dépouillées.
Localisation: OONL.

1237 **Guilmette, Bernadette**
"Bibliographie du *Nigog*."
Dans: *Le Nigog*. Montréal: Fides, 1987. P. 343-367. (Archives des lettres canadiennes ; Tome 7); ISBN: 2-7621-1381-4.
Note: Correspondance, thèses et mémoires, livres et brochures, périodiques, ouvrages collectifs et publications annuelles et sériées, colloques sur la revue littéraire *Nigog*, publié de janvier à décembre 1918.
Localisation: OONL.

1238 **Hayne, David M.; Sirois, Antoine**
"Preliminary bibliography of comparative Canadian literature (English-Canadian and French-Canadian)."
In: *Canadian Review of Comparative Literature*; Vol. 3, no. 2 (Spring 1976) p. 124-136; vol. 4, no. 2 (Spring 1977) p. 205-209; vol. 5, no. 1 (Winter 1978) p. 114-119; vol. 6, no. 1 (Winter 1979) p. 75-81; vol. 7, no. 1 (Winter 1980) p. 93-98; vol. 8, no. 1 (Winter 1981) p. 93-98; vol. 9, no. 2 (June 1982) p. 235-240; vol. 10, no. 1 (March 1983) p. 80-85; vol. 11, no. 1 (March 1984) p. 84-90; vol. 12, no. 3 (September 1985) p. 462-468; vol. 13, no. 3 (September 1986) p. 450-457; vol. 14, no. 2 (June 1987) p. 251-256.; ISSN: 0319-051X.
Note: Listings include bibliographies, reference works, bilingual anthologies, comparative works (authors, literary genres, language and style), literary translation (bibliographies, anthologies, theory and history, criticism).– Additional compiler for September 1986: Jean Vigneault; for June 1987: Jean Vigneault and Maria Van Sundert.
Location: AEU.

1239 **Jameson, Mary Ann**
"The year's work in Canadian poetry studies."
In: *Canadian Poetry*; No. 8 (Spring/Summer 1981) p. 100-110; no. 10 (Spring/Summer 1982) p. 138-146; no. 12 (Spring/Summer 1983) p. 99-111; no. 14 (Spring/Summer 1984) p. 95-111; no. 16 (Spring/Summer 1985) p. 94-107; no. 18 (Spring/Summer 1986) p. 148-169; no. 20 (Spring/Summer 1987) p. 123-141.; ISSN: 0704-5646.
Note: Annual listing of criticism on English-Canadian poetry, arranged in periods: Pre-Confederation, Confederation, Modern, Contemporary, General studies.– Continues: Linda Dowler (Spring/Summer 1978-Spring/Summer 1980).
Location: AEU.

1240 **Lochhead, Douglas**
A checklist of nineteenth century Canadian poetry in English: the Maritimes. Preliminary ed. Sackville, N.B.: Centre for Canadian Studies, Mount Allison University,

1987. 75 l.

Note: Approx. 375 entries.– Compiled as part of a larger work which will be a census of every known title of nineteenth century English Canadian poetry.

Location: OONL.

1241 **New, William H.**
Canadian writers since 1960. Second series. Detroit, Mich.: Gale Research, 1987. xiii, 470 p.: ill., ports. (Dictionary of literary biography ; vol. 60); ISBN: 0-8103-1738-9.

Note: Bio-bibliographical essays and listing of works for 82 English- and French-Canadian writers.– Includes a select list of critical writings.

Location: OONL.

1242 **Noroît 1971-1986.** Saint-Lambert, Québec: Éditions du Noroît, 1987. 78 p.: ill.; ISBN: 2-89018-160-X.

Note: 140 titres de soixante auteurs: la liste complète des titres de tout poète publié au Noroît avec la description bibliographique.– Pour les ouvrages de bibliophilie ou de livres d'artistes s'ajouteront les précisions concernant le nombre d'exemplaires, le papier utilisé, la reliure, le format, etc.

Localisation: OONL.

1243 **"A selected bibliography of Franco-manitoban writing."**
In: *Prairie Fire*; Vol. 8, no. 3 (Autumn 1987) p. 123-124.; ISSN: 0821-1124.

Note: Location: AEU.

1244 **"Ten years of Manitoba fiction in English: a selected bibliography."**
In: *Prairie Fire*; Vol. 8, no. 3 (Autumn 1987) p. 124-125.; ISSN: 0821-1124.

Note: Location: AEU.

— 1988 —

1245 **Bisztray, George**
Canadian-Hungarian literature: a preliminary survey. [Ottawa]: Department of the Secretary of State of Canada, Multiculturalism, 1988. 48 l.; ISBN: 0-662-16033-9.

Note: Contains biographical and bibliographical information on 46 Hungarian-Canadian authors.

Location: OONL.

1246 **Czaykowski, Bogdan**
Polish writing in Canada: a preliminary survey. [Ottawa]: Department of the Secretary of State of Canada, Multiculturalism, 1988. 57 l.; ISBN: 0-662-16030-4.

Note: Contains primary and critical works, bio-bibliographical information on Polish-Canadian authors.

Location: OONL.

1247 **Dionne, René**
Canadian literature in French. [Ottawa]: Canadian Studies Directorate, Department of the Secretary of State of Canada, c1988. 31, 35 p. (Canadian studies resource guides); ISBN: 0-662-56209-7.

Note: Approx. 180 entries.– Includes an introductory overview of the subject, a commentary on significant works, and suggestions for further reading.– Text in English and French with French text on inverted pages.– Title of additional title-page: *La littérature canadienne de langue française.*

Location: OONL.

1248 **Dionne, René**
La littérature canadienne de langue française. [Ottawa]: Direction des études canadiennes, Secrétariat d'État du Canada, c1988. 35, 31 p. (Guides pédagogiques des études canadiennes); ISBN: 0-662-56209-7.

Note: Approx. 180 entrées.– Comporte un exposé préliminaire, des observations sur les principaux travaux et une liste de lectures recommandées.– Texte en français et en anglais disposé tête-bêche.– Titre de la p. de t. additionnelle: *Canadian literature in French.*

Localisation: OONL.

1249 **Dionne, René; Cantin, Pierre**
Bibliographie de la critique de la littérature québécoise et canadienne-française dans les revues canadiennes (1974-1978). [Ottawa]: Presses de l'Université d'Ottawa, 1988. 480 p. (Histoire littéraire du Québec et du Canada français); ISBN: 2-7603-0147-8.

Note: 9,677 entrées.– Comprend les textes qui traitent de la littérature québécoise et canadienne-française en général: histoire, théorie de la littérature, langue, culture, enseignement, édition, etc.; les textes qui se rapportent aux genres: roman, poésie, conte et nouvelle, essai, presse (journalisme), littérature orale; les textes concernant un auteur en particulier.

Localisation: OONL.

1250 **Elliott, Lorris**
Literary writing by Blacks in Canada: a preliminary survey. [Ottawa]: Department of the Secretary of State of Canada, Multiculturalism, 1988. 40 l.; ISBN: 0-662-16029-0.

Note: Contains bibliographies and checklists, historical and general works, bio-bibliographical profiles.

Location: OONL.

1251 **Fortin, Marcel; Lamonde, Yvan; Ricard, François**
Guide de la littérature québécoise. [Montréal]: Boréal, 1988. 155 p.; ISBN: 2-89052-248-2.

Note: Dictionnaires d'oeuvres et d'auteurs, bibliographies, histoires littéraires, études comparées, travaux sur les genres littéraires.

Localisation: OONL.

1252 **The Italian connection: 25 years of Canadian literature and Italian translation, 1963-1988.** Toronto: Thomas Fisher Rare Book Library, University of Toronto, 1988. 24 p.

Note: Approx. 250 entries.– Includes Canadian literary works in original editions, in Italian translation, and in manuscript form, as well as studies by Italian critics of Canadian literature, together with Italian translations of Canadian works of criticism.– An exhibition on the occasion of the international symposium on the reception of Canadian literature in Italy organized by the Istituto italiano di cultura, Toronto, April 21-22, 1988.

Location: OONL.

1253 **Khan, Nuzrat Yar**
Urdu literature in Canada: a preliminary survey. [Ottawa]: Department of the Secretary of State of Canada, Multiculturalism, 1988. 45 l.; ISBN: 0-662-16028-2.

Note: Contains bio-bibliographical information on 31 Urdu poets and writers of Canada.

Location: OONL.

1254 **League of Canadian Poets**
Who's who in the League of Canadian Poets. 3rd ed.
Toronto: The League, 1988. 227 p.: ill.; ISBN: 0-9690327-4-9.
Note: Contains a list of major book publications, selected
list of anthologies in which work has appeared, selection
of critical comments for 214 poets.– Edited by Stephen
Scobie.
Previous editions:
League of Canadian poets. 1980. 180 p.; ISBN: 0-9690327-0-6.
Catalogue of members [League of Canadian poets]. 1976. 135 p.
Location: OONL.

1255 **Machalski, Andrew**
Hispanic writers in Canada: a preliminary survey of the
activities of Spanish and Latin-American writers in
Canada. [Ottawa]: Department of the Secretary of State
of Canada, Multiculturalism, 1988. 51 l.; ISBN: 0-662-16031-2.
Note: Contains biographical and bibliographical informa-
tion on 70 writers.
Location: OONL.

1256 **Melanson, Holly**
Literary presses in Canada, 1975-1985: a checklist and
bibliography. Halifax, N.S.: Dalhousie University, School
of Library and Information Studies, 1988. iii, 187 p.
(Occasional papers / Dalhousie University School of
Library and Information Studies ; no. 43; ISSN: 0318-7403); ISBN: 0-7703-9717-4.
Note: 4,300 entries.– Bibliographical record of 240
English-Canadian literary presses which published at
least two original literary works between 1975 and 1985.–
Literary press is defined as one which was created solely
to encourage and provide a forum for new Canadian
poets, novelists, dramatists and other creative artists.–
Includes novels, short stories, poetry, humour, literary
criticism, memoirs (books, pamphlets, broadsides).
Location: OWA.

1257 **Miska, John P.**
Hungarian writing in Canada: a bibliography of primary
and secondary material. Ottawa: Microform Biblios,
1988. i, 45 l. (Canlit bibliographic series / Microform
Biblios ; no. 5); ISBN: 0-919279-04-X.
Note: Approx. 700 entries.– Reference works,
bibliographies, directories, monographs, research papers,
theses, review articles, books of poetry and short stories,
novels, plays by Hungarian-Canadian authors.
Location: OONL.

1258 **Nesbitt, Bruce**
Canadian literature in English. [Ottawa]: Canadian
Studies Directorate, Department of the Secretary of State
of Canada, c1988. 41, 43 p. (Canadian studies resource
guides); ISBN: 0-662-56134-1.
Note: Approx. 250 entries.– Includes an introductory
overview of the subject, a commentary on significant
works, and suggestions for further reading.– Text in
English and French with French text on inverted pages.–
Title of additional title-page: *La littérature canadienne de
lange anglaise*.
Location: OONL.

1259 **Nesbitt, Bruce**
La littérature canadienne de langue anglaise. [Ottawa]:
Direction des études canadiennes, Secrétariat d'État du
Canada, c1988. 43, 41 p. (Guides pédagogiques des
études canadiennes); ISBN: 0-662-56134-1.
Note: Approx. 250 entrées.– Comporte un exposé
préliminaire, des observations sur les prinicipaux
travaux et une liste de lectures recommandées.– Texte en
français et en anglais disposé tête-bêche.– Titre de la p.
de t. additionnelle: *Canadian literature in English*.
Localisation: OONL.

1260 **New, William H.**
Canadian writers, 1920-1959. First series. Detroit, Mich.:
Gale Research, 1988. xv, 417 p.: ill. (Dictionary of literary
biography ; vol. 68); ISBN: 0-8103-1746-X.
Note: Bio-bibliographical essays and listing of works for
63 English- and French-Canadian writers.– Includes a
select list of critical writings.
Location: OONL.

1261 **Pivato, Joseph**
Italian-Canadian writers: a preliminary survey. [Ottawa]:
Department of the Secretary of State of Canada,
Multiculturalism, 1988. 53 l.; ISBN: 0-662-16034-7.
Note: Lists general works on Italian Canadians, bio-
bibliographical information on individual writers.
Location: OONL.

1262 **Spehner, Norbert**
Écrits sur la science-fiction: bibliographie analytique des
études & essais sur la science-fiction publiés entre 1900 et
1987 (littérature-cinéma-illustration). Longueuil, Québec:
Le Préambule, c1988. 534 p.; ISBN: 2-89133-092-7.
Note: 4,289 entrées.– Comprend les études générales sur
la science-fiction et les études spécifiques sur les auteurs
(les écrivains anglo-saxons et français: précurseurs,
classiques et modernes; tous les écrivains québécois
ayant produit de la science-fiction et pour lesquels il y a
un matériel critique consistant).
Localisation: OONL.

1263 **Sugunasiri, Suwanda H.J.**
The search for meaning: the literature of Canadians of
South Asian origin. [Ottawa]: Department of the
Secretary of State of Canada, 1988. 215 p.; ISBN: 0-662-16032-0.
Note: Approx. 250 entries.– Poetry, short stories, novels,
drama in English, Punjabi and Gujarati languages,
written by Canadians of South Asian origin, published in
Canada, some with Canadian content.– Critical essays
and a bibliography.
Location: OONL.

1264 **Union des écrivains québécois**
Les écrivaines du Québec. Montréal: L'Union, 1988. 53 p.:
ill., portr.; ISBN: 2-920088-18-1.
Note: Bio-bibliographies des femmes écrivains
canadiennes-françaises.
Localisation: OONL.

1265 **Weiss, Allan Barry**
A comprehensive bibliography of English-Canadian
short stories, 1950-1983. [Toronto]: ECW Press, [c1988].
973 p.; ISBN: 0-920763-67-7.
Note: 19,597 entries.– Limited to adult short stories;
children's and young adult fiction not included.–
Represents the work of 4,966 different authors.
Location: OONL.

— 1989 —

1266 **Alexander, Harriet Semmes**
English language criticism on the foreign novel: 1965-
1975. Athens: Swallow Press; Ohio University Press,

c1989. 285 p.; ISBN: 0-8040-0907-4.
Note: Approx. 13,000 entries.– 1,500 authors listed.– Includes novels and novellas.– Selection of major Canadian authors.– First volume of projected 2 volume set (vol. 2 to cover 1976-1985).
Location: OONL.

1267 **"Atlantic soundings: a checklist of recent literary publications of Atlantic Canada."**
In: *Fiddlehead*; No. 135 (January 1983) p. 136-143; no. 138 (January 1984) p. 95-99; no. 141 (Autumn 1984) p. 94-100; no. 145 (Autumn 1985) p. 63-71; no. 148 (Summer 1986) p. 71-79; no. 151 (Spring 1987) p. 97-106; no. 155 (Spring 1988) p. 89-98; no. 159 (Spring 1989) p. 91-103.; ISSN: 0015-0630.
Note: Anthologies, bibliographes, drama, juvenile, poetry, prose and prose fiction, general, critical works.
Location: OONL.

1268 **Balan, Jars**
"A selected bibliography of critical sources on Ukrainian-Canadian literature."
In: *Canadian Review of Comparative Literature*; Vol. 16, no. 3/4 (September-December 1989) p. 759-762.; ISSN: 0319-051X.
Note: Location: AEU.

1269 **Canadian plays for community theatres: a selected annotated bibliography.** Rev. 2nd ed. [Edmonton]: Alberta Culture and Multiculturalism, [1989]. 27 p.
Note: 90 entries.
Previous edition: 1988. 17 p.
Location: OONL.

1270 **Etcheverry, Jorge**
"Selected bibliography of Chilean writing in Canada."
In: *Canadian Review of Comparative Literature*; Vol. 16, no. 3/4 (September-December 1989) p. 863-865.; ISSN: 0319-051X.
Note: Location: AEU.

1271 **Harner, James L.**
Literary research guide: a guide to reference sources for the study of literatures in English and related topics. New York: Modern Language Association of America, 1989. 737 p.; ISBN: 0-87352-182-X.
Note: 6,630 entries.– Canadian literature section (p. 491-511) lists guides to reference works, histories and surveys, guides to primary works, guides to scholarship and criticism.
Location: OONL.

1272 **Maillet, Marguerite**
"La littérature acadienne: bibliographie sélective."
Dans: *Canadian Review of Comparative Literature*; Vol. 16, nos 3/4 (September-December 1989) p. 664-668.; ISSN: 0319-051X.
Note: Localisation: AEU.

1273 **McGrath, Robin**
"A selected bibliography of Inuit literature."
In: *Canadian Review of Comparative Literature*; Vol. 16, no. 3/4 (September-December 1989) p. 704-706.; ISSN: 0319-051X.
Note: Location: AEU.

1274 **Melançon, Benoît**
La littérature québécoise et l'Amérique: guide bibliographique. Montréal: Centre de documentation des études québécoises, Université de Montréal, 1989. 39 p.
Note: Textes critiques (livres et revues), depuis les années soixante, sur la littérature québécoise et l'Amérique (du Nord, centrale, du Sud).– Exclut articles de journaux, entrevues, mémoires et thèses, travaux sur la littérature franco-américaine.
Localisation: OONL.

1275 **New, William H.**
Canadian writers, 1920-1959. Second series. Detroit, Mich.: Gale Research, 1989. xiii, 442 p.: ill. (Dictionary of literary biography ; vol. 88); ISBN: 0-8103-4566-8.
Note: Bio-bibliographical essays and listing of works for 76 English- and French-Canadian writers.– Includes a select list of critical writings.
Location: OONL.

1276 **Sirois, Antoine, et al.**
Bibliography of studies in comparative Canadian literature, 1930-1987/Bibliographie d'études de littérature canadienne comparée, 1930-1987. Sherbrooke, Québec: Département des lettres et communications, Université de Sherbrooke, 1989. 130 p. (Cahiers de littérature canadienne comparée / Département des lettres et communications, Université de Sherbrooke ; no 1); ISBN: 2-893-43-010-4.
Note: 1,079 entries.– Consolidates the work done for the "Preliminary Bibliography" which has appeared annually since 1976 in the *Canadian Review of Comparative Literature*.– Includes bibliographies and checklists, reference works, anthologies and collections, current periodicals, literary histories, comparative studies (general works, authors, themes and influences, literary genres, form), epistemology and methodology.– Added authors: Jean Vigneault, Maria van Sundert, David M. Hayne.
Location: OONL.

1277 **Sirois, Antoine; Van Sundert, Maria**
"Supplementary bibliography of comparative Canadian literature (English-Canadian and French-Canadian)."
In: *Canadian Review of Comparative Literature*; Vol. 16, no. 1-2 (March-June 1989) p. 170-176.; ISSN: 0319-051X.
Note: Location: OONL.

1278 **Stenderup, Vibeke**
Litteratursongning: Canada Skonlitteratur pa engelsk: bibliografier, handboger, antologier. Aarhus: Statsbiblioteket, 1989. 36 p. (Canadiana / Statsbiblioteket, Aarhus ; 1); ISBN: 87-7507-179-7.
Note: Approx. 100 entries.– Listing of English-Canadian literary reference works and anthologies.
Location: OONL.

1279 **Totosy de Zepetnek, Steven**
"Literary works by German-speaking Canadians and their critical appraisal: a selected and annotated bibliography with an introduction."
In: *Canadian Review of Comparative Literature*; Vol. 16, no. 3/4 (September-December 1989) p. 669-686.; ISSN: 0319-051X.
Note: Bibliographies, anthologies, literary texts, criticism.
Location: AEU.

— 1990 —

1280 **Allard, Jacques**
"Où en sont les études sur la littérature québécoise?"
Dans: *Revue internationale d'études canadiennes*; No 1-2 (printemps-automne 1990) p. 115-134.; ISSN: 1180-3991.
Note: Localisation: OONL.

1281 **Drew, Bernard A.**
Lawmen in scarlet: an annotated guide to Royal Canadian Mounted Police in print and performance. Metuchen, N.J.: Scarecrow Press, 1990. xx, 276 p.: ill.; ISBN: 0-8108-2330-6.
Note: Approx. 700 entries (500 fiction works, 200 films).– Works are included if they feature a Mountie character in at least a minor speaking role.– Juvenile, romance and adventure titles are listed as well as mysteries and "Northerns."- Two parts: Prose and poetry (book fiction, magazine fiction, pulp magazine fiction, comic books, comic strips, big little books); Drama (motion pictures, television, radio, musical and dramatic theatre, opera).– Indexes: performers, author/title.
Location: OONL.

1282 **Kandiuk, Mary**
French-Canadian authors: a bibliography of their works and of English-language criticism. Metuchen, N.J.: Scarecrow Press, c1990. xii, 222 p.; ISBN: 0-8108-2362-4.
Note: Covers to January 1, 1989.– Primary sources include monographs only: contributions to periodicals and anthologies are excluded, as are reprints.– English translations are indicated.– Secondary sources include books, parts of books, journal articles, book reviews (brief reviews, newspaper reviews, and those appearing in minor or obscure periodicals, are omitted), dissertations.– Both popular and scholarly secondary materials are included.– Excludes newspaper articles, encyclopedia articles, audio-visual materials.– Includes criticism in English on works yet to be translated.
Location: OONL.

1283 **MacDonald, Mary Lu**
"Chronological checklist: Canadian literary works about, or referring to, Indians: 1817-1850."
In: *Canadian Literature*; No. 124-125 (Spring-Summer 1990) p. 106-109.; ISSN: 0008-4360.
Note: Location: AEU.

1284 **Miska, John P.**
Ethnic and native Canadian literature: a bibliography. 2nd ed. Toronto: University of Toronto Press, 1990. xv, 445 p.; ISBN: 0-8020-5852-3.
Note: 5,497 entries.– Primary and secondary material from earliest times to 1990.– Represents 65 nationality groups in over 70 languages; poetry, fiction, drama in any language: authors born outside Canada and settled in Canada as adolescent or adult; authors having written the work while residing in Canada.– Native authors included regardless of linguistic considerations.– Excludes writers from France, United States, Britain, Australia, New Zealand.
Previous edition: *Ethnic and native Canadian literature, 1850-1979 [microform]: a bibliography*. Lethbridge, Alta.: Microform Biblios; c1980. 7 microfiches (363 fr.).
Location: OONL.

1285 **New, William H.**
Canadian writers, 1890-1920. Detroit, Mich.: Gale Research, 1990. xv, 472 p.: ill., facsims., ports. (Dictionary of literary biography ; vol. 92); ISBN: 0-8103-4572-2.
Note: Bio-bibliographical essays and listing of works for 96 English- and French-Canadian writers.– Includes a select list of critical writings.
Location: OONL.

1286 **New, William H.**
Canadian writers before 1890. Detroit, Mich.: Gale Research, 1990. xiv, 434 p.: ill., ports. (Dictionary of literary biography ; vol. 99); ISBN: 0-8103-4579-X.
Note: Bio-bibliographical essays and listing of works for 101 English- and French-Canadian writers.– Includes a select list of critical writings.
Location: OONL.

1287 **New, William H.**
"Studies of English Canadian literature."
In: *International Journal of Canadian Studies*; No. 1-2 (Spring-Fall 1990) p. 97-114.; ISSN: 1180-3991.
Note: Survey of recent (1980-1990) studies of Anglophone Canadian literature: reference texts, generic and theoretical studies, biographical works.
Location: OONL.

1288 **Québec plays in translation: a catalogue of Québec playwrights and plays in English translation.** Montreal: Centre des auteurs dramatiques, c1990. xii, 86 p.: ill.; ISBN: 2-920308-14-9.
Note: Lists published and unpublished plays written by members of Le Centre des auteurs dramatiques.– Arrangement is alphabetical by author, with play titles chronologically listed within the playwright entry.– Information provided includes a synopsis, preceded by name of translator and English-language publisher, original title and publisher, running time, cast requirements.
Location: OONL.

1289 **Saskatchewan books! A selected annotated bibliography of Saskatchewan literature.** Regina: Saskatchewan Writers Guild, c1990. 65 p.; ISBN: 0-9690387-7-1.
Note: Lists drama, fiction, poetry (adult and children's), picture books, anthologies, bibliographies, miscellaneous resources by Saskatchewan writers or with a Saskatchewan theme.
Location: OONL.

— 1991 —

1290 **Chassay, Jean-François**
Bibliographie descriptive du roman montréalais. Montréal: Groupe de recherche Montréal imaginaire, Centre d'études québécoises, Département d'études françaises, Faculté des arts et des sciences, Université de Montréal, 1991. 230 p.; ISBN: 2-9802632-0-6.
Note: Localisation: QMBM.

1291 **Coppens, Patrick**
Ouvrages de base en littérature québécoise. Montréal: SDM, 1991. 60 p. (Services documentaires Multimedia ; no 178; ISSN: 0838-3189); ISBN: 2-89054-400-9.
Note: 300 entrées.– Sélection critique d'ouvrages sur la littérature québécoise ou canadienne d'expression française hors Québec.
Localisation: OONL.

1292 **Dahms, Moshie**
"Annual bibliography of Commonwealth literature, ... : Canada."
In: *Journal of Commonwealth Literature*; 1980 in vol. 16, no. 2 (February 1982) p. 52-79; 1981 in vol. 17, no. 2 (1982) p. 52-84; 1982 in vol. 18, no. 2 (1983) p. 54-91; 1983 in vol. 19, no. 2 (1984) p. 44-78; 1984 in vol. 20, no. 2 (1985) p. 42-81; 1985 in vol. 21, no. 2 (1986) p. 43-79; 1986 in vol. 22, no. 2 (1987) p. 30-60; 1987 in vol. 23, no. 2 (1988) p. 36-74; 1988

in vol. 24, no. 2 (1989) p. 36-72; 1989 in vol. 25, no. 2 (1990) p. 49-84; 1990 in vol. 26, no. 2 (1991) p. 44-86.; ISSN: 0021-9894.

Note: Lists bibliographies, research aids, poetry, drama, fiction, anthologies, criticism, journals (cessations, new journals).– Continues: Carl F. Klinck: 1964-1965 (September 1965, December 1966); Mary M.S. Brown: 1966-1967 (December 1967, January 1969); Robert Weaver: 1968 (December 1969); William H. New: 1969, 1971-1977 (December 1970, December 1972-1978); Mary Burnett: 1970 (December 1971); Marilyn G. Flitton: 1978 (December 1979); Doreen Ingram: 1979 (December 1980).

Location: AEU.

1293 **Froeschle, Hartmut**
Americana Germanica: Bibliographie zur deutschen Sprache und deutschsprachigen Literatur in Nord- und Lateinamerika. Hildesheim: Olms, 1991. xxi, 233 p. (Auslandsdeutsche Literatur der Gegenwart ; Band 15; ISSN: 0175-842X); ISBN: 3-487-08321-3.

Note: 2,270 entries.– Kanada: 542 entries.

Location: OONL.

1294 **Miska, John P.**
Literature of Hungarian-Canadians. Toronto: Rákòczi Foundation, 1991. 143 p.; ISBN: 0-919279-07-4.

Note: 608 entries.– Contains four essays and a bibliography, which includes bibliographies, directories, books, research papers, anthologies, works by individual authors.

Location: OONL.

1295 **Rudi, Marilynn J.**
Atlantic Canadian literature in English: a guide to sources of information. Halifax, N.S.: Dalhousie University, School of Library and Information Studies, 1991. iii, 60 p. (Occasional papers / Dalhousie University School of Library and Information Studies ; no. 51; ISSN: 0318-7403); ISBN: 0-7703-9752-2.

Note: Approx. 500 entries.– Arranged by type of publication: anthologies; literary presses and publications (bibliographies of literary presses, reviews, literary periodicals, indexes to early literary periodicals, directories of early literary periodicals); libraries and archives (directories, catalogues); literary histories and criticism (monographs, special issues of journals, theses); biographical reference works; bibliographies (regional/ Atlantic, individual authors, current bibliographies in serials); dictionaries; general reference sources for Canadian literature.

Location: OONL.

— 1992 —

1296 **Boivin, Aurélien; Émond, Maurice; Lord, Michel**
Bibliographie analytique de la science-fiction et du fantastique québécois, 1960-1985. Québec: Nuit blanche, 1992. 577 p. (Cahiers du Centre de recherche en littérature québécoise: Bibliographie ; no 3); ISBN: 2-021053-07-1.

Note: Approx. 2,000 entrées.

Localisation: OONL.

1297 **Holt, Faye Reineberg**
Alberta plays and playwrights: Alberta Playwrights' Network catalogue. Calgary: Alberta Playwrights' Network, c1992. 80 p.; ISBN: 0-9695459-0-8.

Note: Alphabetical list of Alberta playwrights, with listing of plays.– Entries include brief biography, plot outline, genre, audience level, number of acts, cast requirements, production date, awards, publishing information.– Index by play title or genre.

Location: OONL.

1298 **Maillet, Marguerite**
Bibliographie des publications d'Acadie, 1609-1990: sources premières et sources secondes. Moncton, N.–B.: Chaire d'études acadiennes, 1992. 389 p. (Collection Balises ; 2); ISBN: 2-921166-05-4.

Note: 3,674 entrées.– Auteurs: sources premières, sources secondes (auteurs acadiens nés aux provinces Maritimes, auteurs canadiens-français, auteurs d'ouvrages traitant de l'Acadie et édités en Acadie).– Généralités: littérature, roman et nouvelle, poésie, théâtre, presse, folklore et ethnographie, langue et linguistique, arts et culture.– Liste de publications, index des auteurs d'articles, liste de périodiques.

Localisation: OONL.

1299 **Saint-Germain, Richard; Bettinotti, Julia; Bleton, Paul**
Littérature en poche: collection "Petit format," 1944-1958: répertoire bibliographique. Sherbrooke, Québec: Éditions Ex Libris, 1992. 336 p.: ill.; ISBN: 2-921061-05-8.

Note: 442 entrées.– Répertoire descriptif de la littérature de grande consommation au Québec entre 1940 et 1960, le roman policier et le roman d'amour.– Inclut une section, "Bibliographie critique."

Localisation: OONL.

— 1993 —

1300 **Crime Writers of Canada**
In cold blood: a directory of criminous books by members of the Crime Writers of Canada. Toronto: Crime Writers of Canada, 1993. 43 p.; ISBN: 0-9696825-0-6.

Note: Listing of fiction (novels and short story anthologies), true crime, criticism and reference.

Location: OONL.

— Ongoing/En cours —

1301 **Dictionnaire des oeuvres littéraires du Québec.**
Montréal: Fides, 1980-. vol.: ill., fac.–sim., ports.; ISBN: 2-7621-1190-0 (série).

Note: Vol. 1: Des origines à 1900; vol. 2: 1900 à 1939; vol. 3: 1940-1959; vol. 4: 1960-1969; vol. 5: 1970-1975.

Dans chaque tome: oeuvres classés par ordre alphabétique des titres, chronologie comparée des événements littéraires, introduction à la littérature de l'époque, bibliographie générale des instruments de recherche, bibliographie des oeuvres, index onomastique.– Sous la direction de Maurice Lemire.

Localisation: OONL.

1302 **Lecker, Robert; David, Jack**
The annotated bibliography of Canada's major authors. Downsview, Ont.: ECW Press, 1979-. vol.; ISBN: 0-9208-0208-7 (set).

Note: Multi-volume series of annotated bibliographies of works by and on Canada's major French and English authors from the nineteenth and twentieth centuries.– A ten-volume set is projected.– Listings cover books, manuscripts, contributions to periodicals and books, audio-visual materials, miscellaneous works.– Many of these bibliographies are available as separate publications.

Location: OONL.

1303 **"Letters in Canada."**
In: *University of Toronto Quarterly*; (1936-)   vol.; ISSN: 0042-0247.
Note: Regular feature from 1936 of the Fall issue provides a critical round-up of Canadian imprints in the humanities, offering review articles on fiction, poetry and drama in both English and French, as well as translations, the social sciences and religion.– Volumes for 1936-1980 have one issue with a section called "Letters in Canada."- From 1981, the Fall issue has the distinctive title "Letters in Canada."
Location: OONL.

1304 **Letters in Canada.** Toronto: University of Toronto Press, 1981-.   vol.; ISSN: 0315-4955.
Note: Annual feature of *University of Toronto Quarterly* since 1936.– From 1980 it has also been published as a paperback book, paginated as a separate entity.– Provides a critical round-up of Canadian imprints in humanities, offering review articles on fiction, poetry, drama in both official languages, and on translations, religion and individual reviews of scholarly books.
Location: OONL

1305 **Who's who in Canadian literature.** Teeswater, Ont.: Reference Press, 1983-.   vol.; ISSN: 0715-9366.
Note: Biennial.– Latest edition, 1992-93.– Bio-bibliographical listing includes approximately 1,100 living Canadian poets, playwrights, story writers, novelists, children's writers, critics, editors and translators.– Bibliographical information includes anthologies, publications, work in progress, sources of additional biographical and bibliographical information.– Compiled and edited by Gordon M. Ripley and Anne V. Mercer.
Location: OONL.

— 1941 —

1306 **Smith, Lillian H.; Wright, Annie M.**
"Canada: a reading guide for children and young people."
In: *Booklist*; Vol. 37, no. 16 (May 1, 1941) p. 417-428.
Note: Supplements:
"Canada: a reading guide ... , 1941-1946"; In: *Ontario Library Review*; Vol. 30, no. 4 (November 1946) p. 353-358.
Canada: a reading guide ... , 1946-1951 supplement. Ottawa: Canadian Library Association, [1952]. [12] l.
"Canada: a reading guide ... , 1951-1958 supplement"; In: *Ontario Library Review*; Vol. 43, no. 1 (March 1959) p. 40-46.
Location: OONL.

— 1946 —

1307 **Saint-Pierre, Jeanne-M.**
"Choix de livres d'enfants se rapportant au Canada et à certains aspects de la vie canadienne."
Dans: *Canadian Library Association Bulletin*; Vol. 3 (October 1946) p. 14-16.; ISSN: 0316-6058.
Note: Localisation: OONL.

— 1948 —

1308 **Boulizon, Guy; Boulizon, Jeanne**
Nos jeunes liront: 1000 titres de livres. Montréal: École des parents du Québec, 1948. 40 p.
Note: Inclut des commentaires sur les différentes formes de la littérature enfantine et de nombreux ouvrages canadiens de langue française.
Localisation: OONL.

— 1949 —

1309 **"Livres canadiens pour la jeunesse canadienne."**
Dans: *École canadienne*; Vol. 24, no 7 (mars 1949) p. 446-448.
Note: Localisation: OONL.

— 1956 —

1310 **Bélisle, Alvine**
"Les écrivains canadiens racontent à nos jeunes."
Dans: *Canadian Library Association Bulletin*; Vol. 1, no. 1 (August 1956) p. 32-34.; ISSN: 0316-6058.
Note: Liste annotée d'ouvrages de langue française publiés au Canada pour les jeunes.
Localisation: OONL.

— 1957 —

1311 **Boulizon, Guy**
Livres roses et séries noires: guide psychologique et bibliographique de la littérature de jeunesse. Montréal: Beauchemin, 1957. 188 p.
Note: Comprend une section: "Littérature canadienne pour la jeunesse," p. 30-34.
Localisation: OONL.

1312 **McDowell, Marjorie**
A history of Canadian children's literature to 1900, together with a checklist [microform]. Fredericton: University of New Brunswick, 1957. 1 reel (iii, 342 p.)
Note: Includes travels and memoirs, adventure stories, history and biography, animal stories.– Thesis, M.A., University of New Brunswick.
Location: NBFU.

— 1960 —

1313 **Commission des écoles catholiques de Montréal. Bureau des bibliothèques scolaires**
Jeunes, voulez-vous des livres? ... 4000 suggestions pour tous les âges, pour tout les goûts. 2e éd. Montréal: Bureau des bibliothèques scolaires, Services des études, Commission des écoles catholiques de Montréal, 1960. 318 p.
Note: Inclut de nombreux ouvrages canadiens-français.– Collections de maison d'édition canadiennes-françaises à l'intention des jeunes sont analyses.
Édition antérieure: ... : 2,000 suggestions pour tous les âges, pour tout les goûts. 1956. 157 p.
Localisation: OONL.

— 1963 —

1314 **Bélisle, Alvine**
"Notre héritage français: choix de livres sur le Canada français."
Dans: *Canadian Library*; Vol. 20, no. 1 (July 1963) p. 26-28.; ISSN: 0316-604X.
Note: Localisation: OONL.

1315 **Bélisle, Alvine**
Notre héritage française [sic]: choix de livres sur le Canada français. Ottawa: Association canadienne des bibliothèques, [1963]. [4] p.
Note: Dans Lochhead.– Pas localisation.

— 1967 —

1316 **Winnipeg Public Library**
Canada in books for children. Winnipeg: [s.n.], 1967. 21 p.
Note: Location: OONL.

— 1968 —

1317 **Alberta Teachers' Association. English Council**
Canadian books for schools: a centennial listing. Edmonton: English Council and School Library Council of the Alberta Teachers' Association, 1968. 63 p.
Note: Edited by Kathleen M. Snow.
Location: OONL.

— 1970 —

1318 **Potvin, Claude**
"Sources bibliographiques sur la littérature enfantine au Canada français."
Dans: *Bulletin de l'Association canadienne des bibliothécaires de langue française*; Vol. 16, no 2 (juin 1970) p. 55-61.; ISSN: 0004-5314.
Note: Localisation: OONL.

— 1971 —

1319 **Canadian Library Association. Young People's Section**
Canadian books: a selection of books for young people's libraries. Ottawa: Canadian Library Association, 1960-1971. 16 vol.; ISSN: 0068-838X.
Note: Annual.– Compiled by the Committee on Canadian Books of the Young People's Section.– Ceased publication with 16th issue, 1970-71.

Previous editions:
Canadian books, 1958. 1959. 11 p. (Occasional paper (Canadian Library Association) ; no. 21).
Canadian books, 1957. 1958. 10 p. (Occasional paper (Canadian Library Association) ; no. 16).
Canadian books, 1956. 1957. 7 p. (Occasional paper (Canadian Library Association) ; no. 13).
Location: OONL.

— 1972 —

1320 **In review: Canadian books for children: 305 titles recommended, 1967-1972.** Toronto: Provincial Library Service, Ontario Ministry of Colleges and Universities, 1972. 45 p.
Note: "This booklet accompanied the Autumn, 1972 issue of *In Review*."
Location: OONL.

1321 **Potvin, Claude**
La littérature de jeunesse au Canada français, bref historique, sources bibliographiques, répertoire des livres. Montréal: Association canadienne des bibliothécaires de langue française, 1972. 110 p.
Note: Approx. 1,175 entrées.– Oeuvres publiées au Canada et rédigées en langue française, par les auteurs nés au Canada ou naturalisés canadiens.
Localisation: OONL.

— 1973 —

1322 **Bélisle, Alvine, et al.**
Guide de lecture pour les jeunes, 5 à 13 ans. Montréal: Association canadienne des bibliothécaires de langue française, 1973. 164 p.
Note: Localisation: OONL.

1323 **Cheda, Sherrill**
"Bibliography of non-sexist children's books."
In: *Canadian Newsletter of Research on Women*; Vol. 2, no. 1 (February 1973) p. 43-47.; ISSN: 0319-4477.
Note: Location: AEU.

— 1975 —

1324 **Chapman, Geoffrey**
"Canadian reference and information books for children."
In: *Canadian Children's Literature*; Vol. 1, no. 1 (Spring 1975) p. 42-52; vol. 1, no. 2 (Summer 1975) p. 47-65.; ISSN: 0319-0080.
Note: Literature review of dictionaries, encyclopedias, ready-reference books; works on the arts, sports, recreation, personal development, general science and natural history.
Location: OONL.

1325 **Communication-jeunesse (Montréal, Québec)**
Auteurs canadiens pour la jeunesse. Montréal: Communication-jeunesse, 1972-1975. 3 vol.
Note: Vol. 1: *20 biographies et bibliographies*; vol. 2: *22 biographies et bibliographies*; vol. 3: *Illustrateurs canadiens pour la jeunesse.*
Localisation: OONL.

1326 **Frayne, June; Laidley, Jennifer; Hadeed, Henry**
Print for young Canadians: a bibliographical catalogue of Canadian fiction for children from 1825-1920. Toronto: [s.n.], 1975. x, 80 p.: ill.
Note: Approx. 1,500 entries.– Listing of early Canadian children's literature in English.– Includes books written by Canadians or persons travelling through Canada, with the topic setting in Canada.– Emphasis on works written with the child reader in mind, up to the age of

sixteen.
Location: OONL.

1327 **Toronto Board of Education. Language Study Centre**
Bibliography of non-sexist books. Toronto: The Centre, 1975. 10 p.
Note: Location: OONL.

— 1976 —

1328 **Amtmann, Bernard**
Early Canadian children's books, 1763-1840: a bibliographical investigation into the nature and extent of early Canadian children's books and books for young people/Livres de l'enfance & livres de la jeunesse au Canada, 1763-1840: étude bibliographique. Montréal: B. Amtmann, 1976. xv, 150 p.: facsim.
Note: Lists publications in English and French.– Comprend des publications en anglais et en français.
Location: OONL.

1329 **Aubrey, Irene E.**
Canadian children's books: a treasury of pictures: list/ Livres canadiens d'enfants : un trésor d'images: liste. Ottawa: National Library of Canada, 1976. 18 p.
Note: Includes English and French publications.
Location: OONL.

1330 **Bélisle, Alvine**
"Children's literature in French-speaking Canada."
In: *Canadian Children's Literature*; No. 4 (1976) p. 59-65.; ISSN: 0319-0080.
Note: Location: AEU.

1331 **Fontannaz-Howard, Lucienne**
"Les livres d'images québécois."
Dans: *Documentation et bibliothèques*; Vol. 22, no 2 (juin 1976) p. 87-90.; ISSN: 0315-2340.
Note: Localisation: AEU.

— 1977 —

1332 **Amtmann, Bernard**
A bibliography of Canadian children's books and books for young people, 1841-1867/Livres de l'enfance & livres de la jeunesse au Canada, 1841-1867. Montréal: B. Amtmann, 1977. viii, 124 p.
Note: Lists works in English and French.– Comprend des publications en anglais et en français.
Location: OONL.

1333 **Egoff, Sheila; Bélisle, Alvine**
Notable Canadian children's books/Un choix de livres canadiens pour la jeunesse. 2nd ed. Vancouver: Vancouver School Board, 1977. vii, 94 p.
Note: Previous edition: Ottawa: National Library of Canada, 1973. x, 91 p.
Supplements and cumulations compiled by Irene E. Aubrey and published from 1977 by the National Library of Canada.
Location: OONL.

— 1978 —

1334 **Badger, Carole, et al.**
Enfin, je lis! Bibliographie sélective pour enfants de 7 à 10 ans. Montréal: Asted, 1978. 72 p.: ill.
Note: Localisation: OONL.

1335 **Bourneuf, Denise, et al.**
"Une bibliographie de livres pour enfants."
Dans: *Québec français*; No 30 (mai 1978) p. 40-44.; ISSN: 0316-2052.
Note: Comprend des titres français et québécois: livres d'images, les romans, la poésie, revues spécialisées en

littérature enfantine.
Localisation: OONL.

1336 **Grande, Ellen; Hansen, John Nørskov; Madsen, Nina**
Nordamerikanske indianere i børnelitteraturen: en genrebeskrivelse. København: Danmarks Biblioteksskole, 1978. 146 p. (Danmarks biblioteksskoles A4-serie ; nr 5); ISBN: 87-7415-090-1.
Note: Listing of literature for children and young adults, in Danish or translated into Danish, about North American Indians.– Includes Canadian references.
Location: OONL.

1337 **Sorfleet, John R.; Rubio, Mary**
"Canadian children's literature 1975: a bibliography."
In: *Canadian Children's Literature*; No. 11 (1978) p. 29-58.; ISSN: 0319-0080.
Note: 296 entries.– Alphabetical listing by author of children's fiction, poetry, drama, and non-fiction studies of children's literature published in 1975.– Continued by: Mary Rubio (1979-1989), assisted in various issues by John R. Sorfleet, Ramona Montagnes, Lenie Ott, and Jennifer Haire.
Location: AEU.

— 1979 —

1338 **Kimmitt, Marianne**
The World of Children's Books showcase: a selection of the best Canadian, British and American children's books: in celebration of the International Year of the Child 1979. Edmonton: World of Children's Books Magazine: Alberta Culture, Library Services Branch, 1979. iii, 31 p.: ill.
Note: Location: OONL.

1339 **Saskatoon Public Library**
Something to chew on: Canadian fiction for young adults. Saskatoon: Saskatoon Public Library, 1979. 35 p.
Note: Approx. 320 entries.– Annotated guide to novels and short stories about Canada or by Canadian writers for young adult readers.
Location: OONL

1340 **Warren, Louise**
"Quelques livres québécois pour la jeunesse."
Dans: *Dérives*; No 17-18 (1979) p. 95-102.; ISSN: 0383-7521.
Note: Localisation: OONL.

— 1980 —

1341 **ASTED. Congrès (1979: Montréal, Québec)**
Les tendances actuelles de la littérature de jeunesse en langue française: bibliographies d'ouvrages pour la jeunesse. Montréal: Secrétariat de l'ASTED, 1980. 50 p.; ISBN: 2-89055-008-7.
Note: Comporte les sections:
Laforest, Marthe. "Littérature enfantine canadienne pour les enfants jusqu'à dix ans." P. 11-17.– 23 entrées.
Aubrey, Irene E. "Livres québécois pour jeunes de 10 à 13 ans." P. 33-37.– 27 entrées.
Localisation: OONL.

1342 **Ford, Theresa M.**
Teacher resource book: western Canadian literature for youth. Edmonton: Alberta Education, c1980. 576 p.; ISBN: 0-920794-07-6.
Note: Accompanies ten anthologies published as part of the Alberta Heritage Learning Resources Project.
Location: OONL.

1343 **Provost, Michelle**
"Littérature québécois pour la jeunesse: de solides acquis et un avenir prometteur."
Dans: *Canadian Children's Literature*; No. 18/19 (1980) p. 72-94.; ISSN: 0319-0080.
Note: Approx. 80 entrées.
Localisation: AEU.

1344 **Robinson, Paul**
Indian, Inuit, Métis: selected bibliography. Halifax, N.S.: Atlantic Institute of Education, 1980. 19 l.
Note: Approx. 250 entries.– Includes fiction, non-fiction, periodicals, multi-media kits.
Location: OONL.

1345 **Rubio, Mary; Sorfleet, John R.**
"Canadian children's literature ... : a bibliography."
In: *Canadian Children's Literature*; 1976 in no. 13 (1979) p. 29-50; 1977 in no. 17 (1980) p. 27-55.; ISSN: 0319-0080.
Note: 1976 (266 entries).– 1977 (336 entries).– Fiction, fable, legend, drama, poetry, non-fiction, with general guidelines for primary, junior and senior levels of reading interest and ability.– Continues: John R. Sorfleet and Mary Rubio, No. 11 (1978).
Location: AEU.

1346 **Taylor, Donna**
The Great Lakes region in children's books: a selected annotated bibliography. Brighton, Mich.: Green Oak Press, c1980. xix, 481 p.; ISBN: 0-931600-01-4.
Note: 1,428 entries.– Lists books, pamphlets, magazines appropriate for children in grade K-8, related to Great Lakes states and Ontario: discovery, history, social/political/economic development.– Compiled by Elvia Carlino, Lois Curtis, Diane M. Gunn, Ernestine Mokede, Marilyn Solt, Grace Stageberg Swenson, Pat Tomey.
Location: OONL.

— 1981 —

1347 **Watt, Christine**
Children's books in the French language and books about Quebec in English. Vancouver: Education Services Group, Vancouver School Board, 1981. 25 p. (Curriculum resources / Education Services Group, Vancouver School Board ; no. 40; ISSN: 0714-6124)
Note: Location: OONL.

— 1982 —

1348 **Aubrey, Irene E.**
Sports and games in Canadian children's books: list/ Livres canadiens sur les sports et les jeux pour la jeunesse: liste. Ottawa: National Library of Canada, 1982. 6 p.; ISBN: 0-662-51763-6.
Note: 21 entries.– Text in English and French/texte en français et en anglais.
Location: OONL.

1349 **British Columbia. Ministry of Human Resources**
A bibliography of children's literature in the library. Vancouver: British Columbia Ministry of Human Resources, 1982. 40 p.
Note: Includes some Canadian references.
Location: OONL.

1350 **Hinke, C.J.**
Oz in Canada: bibliography. Vancouver: William Hoffer, c1982. 85 p. ill.; ISBN: 0-919758-00-2.
Note: Checklist of Canadian issues of Oz books for children by Copp Clark, Toronto.
Location: OONL.

1351 **In review: Canadian books for young people.** Toronto: Libraries and Community Information Branch, 1967-1982. 16 vol.; ISSN: 0019-3259.
Note: Lists and reviews current titles by Canadian authors or on a Canadian subject: fiction, poetry, non-fiction.– Edited by Irma McDonough.– Publication information: Vol. 1-16, no. 2 (Winter 1967-April 1982).– Published quarterly: (Winter 1967-February 1979); Bimonthly: (April 1979-April 1982).– Subtitle varies slightly: Winter 1967-Autumn 1978, *Canadian books for children.*– Index for 1967-1981 issued as Vol. 15, no. 6.– Includes some text in French.
Location: OONL.

— 1983 —

1352 **Aubrey, Irene E.**
Animal world in Canadian books for children and young people: list/Le monde animal dans les livres de jeunesse canadiens: liste. Ottawa: National Library of Canada, 1983. 24 p.; ISBN: 0-662-52331-8.
Note: Approx. 75 entries.– Text in English and French/texte en français et en anglais.
Location: OONL.

1353 **Aubrey, Irene E.**
Mystery and adventure in Canadian books for children and young people: list/Romans policiers et histoires d'aventures canadiens pour la jeunesse: liste. Ottawa: National Library of Canada, 1983. 18 p.; ISBN: 0-662-52484-5.
Note: Approx. 45 entries.– List prepared to accompany a display at National Library.– Text in English and French/texte en français et en anglais.
Location: OONL.

1354 **Aubrey, Irene E.; Greig, Peter E.**
Canadian children's books for Christmas: a selection of titles/Un choix de livres de jeunesse canadiens pour Noël. Ottawa: Ottawa Book Collectors, 1983. 37 p.
Note: Approx. 90 entries.– Text in English and French/texte en français et en anglais.
Location: OONL.

1355 **Martin, Sylvia**
An annotated bibliography of recommended titles for public libraries in western Canada to support the reading needs of children in early French immersion programs. Edmonton: [s.n.], 1983. 50 l.
Note: Fiction and non-fiction for children in French immersion programs between ages 4 and 9 (kindergarten to grade 4).– Selection preference given to works published in western Canada.– Excludes magazines, audio-visual materials, comic books, bilingual titles.
Location: OONL.

1356 **Roy, Zo-Ann**
Bibliographie des contes, récits et légendes du Canada-français. Boucherville, Québec: Éditions Proteau, [1983]. 326 p.; ISBN: 2-920369-17-2.
Note: 3,197 entrées.
Localisation: OONL.

— 1984 —

1357 **Alberta. Alberta Culture. Film & Literary Arts**
Alberta authors and their books for children and young adults. Edmonton: Alberta Culture, 1984. i, 45 p.: ill.
Note: Bio-bibliography listing and reviewing the works of 23 Alberta authors.
Location: OONL.

1358 **Aubrey, Irene E.**
Sources of French Canadian children's and young people's books: list/Sources d'information sur les livres de jeunesse canadiens-français: liste. Ottawa: National Library of Canada, 1984. 18 p.; ISBN: 0-662-52892-1.
Note: Approx. 100 entries.– Text in English and French/texte en français et en anglais.
Location: OONL.

1359 **Beauchamp, Hélène**
Bibliographie annotée sur le théâtre québécois pour l'enfance et la jeunesse, 1970-1983: suivie d'une Liste sélective d'articles de presse portant sur les productions de théâtre québécois pour l'enfance et la jeunesse, 1950-1980. Montréal: Université du Québec, 1984. 39 f.
Note: Livres, articles, thèses, pièces, documents vidéo, recensions, comptes-rendus de spectacles.
Localisation: OONL.

1360 **Canadian plays for young audiences: pre-school through grade 13.** Toronto: Playwrights Union of Canada, [1984]. [26] p.
Note: Plays, musicals, anthologies, with synopsis giving number of acts (scenes), size of cast.
Location: OONL.

1361 **Minion, Robin**
Children's books. Part I, social sciences. Edmonton: Boreal Institute for Northern Studies, University of Alberta, 1984. 95 p. (Boreal Institute for Northern Studies Bibliographic series ; no. 7; ISSN: 0824-8192); ISBN: 0-919058-41-8.
Note: 279 entries.– Series contains monographs, theses, government documents, consultants' reports, children's books, conference proceedings, microforms on topics related to northern environment and people.– BINS series produced monthly from January 1984 to May 1986 (no. 29).– Online access: *Boreal Northern Titles (BNT),* available through QL Systems Limited.
Location: OONL.

1362 **Minion, Robin**
Children's books. Part II, excluding social sciences. Edmonton: Boreal Institute for Northern Studies, University of Alberta, 1984. 122 p. (Boreal Institute for Northern Studies Bibliographic series ; no. 8; ISSN: 0824-8192); ISBN: 0-919058-42-6.
Note: 346 entries.– Series contains monographs, theses, government documents, consultants' reports, children's books, conference proceedings, microforms on topics related to northern environment and people.– BINS series produced monthly from January 1984 to May 1986 (no. 29).– Online access: *Boreal Northern Titles (BNT),* available through QL Systems Limited.
Location: OONL.

1363 **Rubio, Mary**
"Canadian children's literature ... : a bibliography."
In: *Canadian Children's Literature*; 1978 in no. 21 (1981) p. 25-57; 1979 in no. 26 (1982) p. 34-63; 1980 in no. 30 (1983) p. 42-60; 1981 in no. 35/36 (1984) p. 69-92.; ISSN: 0319-0080.
Note: 1978 (391 entries); 1979 (394 entries); 1980 (377 entries); 1981 (454 entries).– Record of creative output in the field of Canadian children's literature: fiction, drama, poetry, picture books, reference, with general guidelines for reading level.
For 1980 and 1981, introduction in English and French/

présentation en français et en anglais.
Location: AEU.
— 1985 —
1364 Charbonneau, Hélène
Livres en langue française pour les jeunes. Montréal:
Bibliothèque municipale de Montréal, 1985. xiii, 382 p.;
ISBN: 2-920374-00-1.
Note: 4,240 entrées.– Livres d'images, contes et légendes,
romans, bandes dessinées, poésie, théâtre.– Index:
auteurs, titres, collections, sujets.– Comprend un nombre
d'ouvrages canadiens.
Localisation: OONL.

1365 Denton, Vivienne
"Materials for the historical study of Canadian children's
literature: a survey of resources."
In: *Canadian Children's Literature*; No. 38 (1985) p. 35-50.;
ISSN: 0319-0080.
Note: 86 entries.– Resource books, collection guides and
listings, retrospective bibliographies of Canadian
children's literature, critical and historical studies,
historical listings and enumerative studies.
Location: AEU.

1366 Internationale Jugendbibliothek (Munich, Germany)
Canadian children's books at the International Youth
Library, Munich. [Munich: The Library, 1985]. [200] p.
Note: Approx. 2,000 entries.– Includes English, French,
Ukrainian and native Indian language titles published in
Canada.– Includes some adult works suitable for
children and young people.– Excludes works written by
Canadian authors published in other countries.
Location: OONL.

1367 Ontario. Ministry for Citizenship and Culture
Canadian books for young adults. Toronto: Ontario
Ministry for Citizenship and Culture, 1985. 26 l.
Note: Approx. 150 entries.– Prepared by the Children's
Book Centre for Youthtalk '85: public libraries and young
people, a symposium celebrating International Youth
Year.
Location: OONL.
— 1986 —
1368 Andrews, Christina Ann
The immigrant experience in Canadian children's
literature 1976 to 1985: an annotated bibliography.
Edmonton: [s.n.], 1986. 65 l.
Note: Literature review and annotated listing of 34
English-language titles representing 27 ethnic cultures,
dealing with the immigrant experience.
Location: OONL.

1369 Bibliothèque publique d'Ottawa
Liens entre les générations: livres pour enfants qui
mettant l'accent sur l'établissements de liens entre les
générations. Toronto: Ministère des affaires civiques et
culturelles de l'Ontario, 1986. 6 f.
Note: 25 entrées.– Comporte des références canadiennes.
English title: *Linking the generations: children's books with
an intergenerational focus.*
Localisation: OONL.

1370 Children's Book Centre
Canadian multicultural books for children and young
adults. Toronto: Ontario Ministry of Citizenship and
Culture, 1986. 14 l.
Note: Approx. 80 entries.– Includes picture books,
fiction, folk tales and legends, poetry, plays, history and
biography.
Location: OONL.

1371 McQuarrie, Jane; Dubois, Diane
Canadian picture books/Livres d'images canadiens.
Toronto: Reference Press, 1986. xv, 217 p.; ISBN: 0-919981-
12-7.
Note: Approx. 700 entries.– Covers to July 1985.–
Includes illustrated books written for pre-school and
primary school aged children by Canadian authors/
illustrators.– Text in English and French/texte en
français et en anglais.
Location: OONL.

1372 Ontario. Libraries and Community Information Branch
Linking the generations: children's books with an inter-
generational focus. Toronto: Ontario Ministry of
Citizenship and Culture, 1986. 15 l.
Note: Approx. 75 entries.– Listing of picture books,
fiction for older children and non-fiction which feature
relationships between children and their grandparents or
other older persons.– Includes Canadian titles.
Titre en français: *Liens entre les générations: livres pour
enfants qui mettant l'accent sur l'établissements de liens entre
les générations.*
Location: OONL.

1373 Stanbridge, Joanne
"An annotated bibliography of Canadian poetry books
written in English for children."
In: *Canadian Children's Literature*; No. 42 (1986) p. 51-61.;
ISSN: 0319-0080.
Note: 108 books by 82 different Canadian poets and
editors, hardcover and trade editions, published since
1867.– Excludes books which mix poetry with songs,
short stories, anecdotes or puzzles, plays written in
verse, books which mix Canadian poets with non-
Canadians.
Location: AEU.

1374 Thibault, Suzanne
Livres québécois pour enfants: une sélection de
Communication-jeunesse. Montréal: Communication-
jeunesse, 1986. 35 p.: ill.
Note: Approx. 200 entrées.– Titres québécois pour les 2 à
15 ans.
Édition antérieure: Provost, Michelle. *Livres québécois
pour les enfants.* 1981. 35 p.
Localisation: OONL.
— 1987 —
1375 Aubrey, Irene E.
Pictures to share: illustration in Canadian children's
books/Images pour tous: illustration de livres canadiens
pour enfants. 2nd ed. Ottawa: National Library of
Canada, 1987. 59 p.; ISBN: 0-660-53763-X.
Note: Approx. 200 entries.– Covers from beginning of
history of Canadian children's literature in the
nineteenth century to 1985.– Main entry under name of
illustrator, with alphabetical author/title index.
Previous edition: 1979. iv, 32 p.; ISBN: 0-662-50379-1.
Location: OONL.

1376 Gagnon, André
"Translations of children's books in Canada."
In: *Canadian Children's Literature*; No. 45 (1987) p. 14-53.;
ISSN: 0319-0080.
Note: Three listings: bilingual books; books translated
from English to French; livres traduits du français à

l'anglais.
Location: AEU.

1377 **Provost, Michelle**
Mieux connaître les Amérindiens et les Inuit en lisant avec les enfants: bibliographie sélective commentée. Québec: Gouvernement du Québec, Ministère de l'éducation, c1987. iii, 75 p.: carte.; ISBN: 2-550-13525-3.
Note: 59 entrées.– Livres pour la jeunesse écrits en français au Québec ou dans d'autres pays, publiés depuis 1978 (jusqu'en 1985 inclusivement), et qui concernant les Amérindiens et les Inuit du Canada, du Québec, des Territoires du Nord-Ouest.
Localisation: OONL.

— 1988 —

1378 **Gagnon, André; Gagnon, Anne**
Canadian books for young people/Livres canadiens pour la jeunesse. 4th ed. Toronto: University of Toronto Press, c1988. 186 p.; ISBN: 0-8020-6662-3.
Note: Includes board books, picture books, fiction, folklore, social sciences, arts, sciences, reference, professional media, magazines.– Indexes: author, title, illustrators.– Age range: pre-school to age eighteen.– Text in English and French/texte en français et en anglais.
Previous editions:
McDonough, Irma. 1980. 205 p.; ISBN: 0-8020-4594-4.
1978. 148 p.; ISBN: 0-8020-4547-2.
Canadian books for children/Livres canadiens pour enfants. 1976. 112 p.; ISBN: 0-8020-4533-2.
Location: OONL.

1379 **Nilson, Lenore**
The best of *Children's choices.* Ottawa: Citizens' Committee on Children, 1988. vi, 114 p.; ISBN: 0-9690205-5-4.
Note: 600 entries.– Annotated selection of Canadian children's books chosen by children.
Location: OONL.

1380 **Read across Canada: creative activities for Canadian readers.** Toronto: Canadian Children's Book Centre, 1988. 33 p.: ill.
Note: Approx. 200 entries.– Activity book with annotated listings of Canadian children's books.
Location: OONL.

1381 **Rubio, Mary; Montagnes, Ramona; Ott, Lenie**
"Canadian children's literature: ... /Bibliographie de la littérature canadienne pour la jeunesse: ...."
In: *Canadian Children's Literature*; 1982 in no. 44 (1986) p. 33-52; 1983 in no. 47 (1987) p. 29-56; 1984 in no. 52 (1988) p. 35-55.; ISSN: 0319-0080.
Note: 1982 (396 entries); 1983 (425 entries); 1984 (362 entries).– Record of creative output in field of Canadian children's literature: picture books, poetry, fiction, drama, reference, non-fiction, with general guidelines for reading level.– Excludes foreign children's books co-produced by Canadian publishers.– Text in English and French/texte en français et en anglais.
Location: AEU.

1382 **Stott, Jon C.**
Canadian books for children: a guide to authors & illustrators. Toronto: Harcourt Brace Jovanovich Canada, 1988. viii, 246 p.: ill.; ISBN: 0-7747-3081-1.
Note: Includes a section entitled "Recommended Canadian books for elementary and junior high: a graded reading list," p. 221-231.

Location: OONL.

1383 **Weller, Joan**
"A survey of Canadian picture books in recent years."
In: *Canadian Children's Literature*; No. 52 (1988) p. 23-34.; ISSN: 0319-0080.
Note: Review of production of English- and French-language children's picture books for the years 1986 and 1987.– Résumé en français.
Location: AEU.

— 1989 —

1384 **Aubrey, Irene E.**
Notable Canadian children's books: 1980-1984 cumulative edition/Un choix de livres canadiens pour la jeunesse: édition cumulative 1980-1984. Ottawa: National Library of Canada, 1989. 148 p.; ISBN: 0-660-54803-8.
Note: Approx. 200 entries.– Cumulates annual supplements.– Includes publications in English and French in separate sections.– Bilingual annotations are provided for all entries.– Indexes provide access to the books by author, title, illustrator, subject and literary award.
Previous edition: ... : *1975-1979 cumulative edition.* 1985. 103 p.; ISBN: 0-660-53040-6.
Location: OONL.

1385 **Rubio, Mary; Haire, Jennifer**
"Annual bibliography [Canadian children's literature] ... /Bibliographie de la littérature canadienne pour la jeunesse: 1985."
In: *Canadian Children's Literature*; No. 56 (1989) p. 52-73.; ISSN: 0319-0080.
Note: 431 entries.– Record of creative output in field of Canadian children's literature: poetry, picture books, non-fiction, fiction, drama, reference, with general guidelines for reading level.– Excludes foreign children's books co-produced by Canadian publishers.– Text in English and French/texte en français et en anglais.
Location: AEU.

— 1990 —

1386 **Communication-jeunesse (Montréal, Québec)**
Littérature pour la jeunesse: publications québécoises 1989. Montréal: Communication-jeunesse, 1990. 58 p.; ISBN: 2-92045-304-1.
Note: 157 entrées.– Livres et magazines d'éditeurs québécois, auteurs et illustrateurs québécois publiés hors Québec, traductions, québécoises d'oeuvres canadiennes.– Catégories: bébé-livres, livres-jeux, albums de fiction, romans, théâtre, nouvelles, poésie, contes et légendes, documentaires, livres d'activités, périodiques.
Localisation: OONL.

1387 **Egoff, Sheila; Salman, Judith**
The New republic of childhood: a critical guide to Canadian children's literature in English. Toronto: Oxford University Press, 1990. xiv, 378 p.: ill.; ISBN: 0-19-540576-5.
Note: Bibliographic essays with lists of titles of books written by Canadians or by writers long resident in Canada, most of which are also Canadian in content.– Categories include: Indian and Inuit legends, folktales, fiction, (historical, realistic, animal stories), science fiction, fantasy, picture books, poetry and verse.
Previous editions:
1975. vii, 335 p. ISBN: 0-19-540231-6.
1967. xiii, 287 p.

Location: OONL.

1388 **Manitoba. Instructional Resources Branch**
Images: a bibliography of Canadian children's and young adult literature. Winnipeg: Manitoba Education and Training, Instructional Resources Branch, 1990. 24 p.
Note: Approx. 400 entries.
Location: OONL.

— 1991 —

1389 **Baker, Gloria**
Changing roles: a bibliography of materials reflecting the roles of males and females in society. Vancouver, B.C.: Vancouver School Board, Program Services, 1991. viii, 157 p.; ISBN: 1-55031-318-5.
Note: Gender-neutral titles suitable for children and young adults: fiction, non-fiction, audio-visual materials.– Includes a section of professional materials.
Location: OONL.

1390 **The CANSCAIP companion: a biographical record of Canadian children's authors, illustrators and performers.** Markham, Ont.: Pembroke Publishers, c1991. 296 p.: ports.; ISBN: 0-921217-58-7.
Note: 262 bio-bibliographical profiles.– Lists published works.
Location: OONL.

1391 **Citizen's Committee on Children**
Children's choices of Canadian books. Ottawa: The Committee, 1979-1991. 7 vol.; ISSN: 0844-2932.
Note: "The books were read by children of the National Capital area and their reports were collated by the Citizens' Committee on Children, Ottawa."- Ceased publication with vol. 7, no. 2 (May 1991).– Editor, 1979-1984: Margaret Caughey; 1985-1991: M. Jane Charlton.
Location: OONL.

1392 **Coulombe, Johanne; Gamache, Sylvie; Provost, Michelle**
Le plaisir de lire sans sexisme: répertoire des livres québécois pour la jeunesse. Québec: Gouvernement du Québec, Ministère de l'éducation, 1991. 46 p.: ill.; ISBN: 2-550-15544-0.
Note: Préparée par Coordination à la condition féminine.
Localisation: OONL.

1393 **Ross, Elspeth**
"Children's books on contemporary North American Indian, Native, Métis life: a selected bibliography of books and professional reading materials."
In: *Canadian Children's Literature*; No. 61 (1991) p. 29-43.; ISSN: 0319-0080.
Note: Location: AEU.

— 1992 —

1394 **Canadian Children's Book Centre**
Our choice: your annual guide to Canada's best children's books. Toronto: Canadian Children's Book Centre, 1985-1992. 8 vol.: ill.; ISSN: 1192-2125.
Note: Annual.– Title varies: 1985-1987: *Our choice: your choice: Canadian children's books, authors and illustrators*; 1988-1990: *Our choice: memorable Canadian books for young people*.
Continues: Children's Book Centre. *Our choice*. Children's Book Centre, 1977-1984. 8 vol.: ill.; ISSN: 1185-281X.– Annual.– Issue for 1980 called: *Our choice catalogue*.
Location: OONL.

1395 **Simpson, Cathy**
"A select bibliography of Newfoundland children's books, 1970-1990."
In: *Canadian Children's Literature*; No. 66 (1992) p. 59-66.; ISSN: 0319-0080
Note: Includes only literature published in Newfoundland and books written by Newfoundland and Labrador residents for the trade market up to young adult level.– Excludes textbooks, anthologies, non-fiction, books in translation or under licence from foreign publishers.
Location: OONL.

1396 **University of British Columbia. Library. Special Collections and University Archives Division**
Canadian children's books, 1799-1939, in the Special Collections and University Archives Division, the University of British Columbia: a bibliographical catalogue. Vancouver: University of British Columbia, 1992. [391] p.: ill. (Occasional publication / University of British Columbia Library, Special Collections ; no. 2); ISBN: 0-88865-197-X.
Note: Compiled by Sheila Egoff, with the assistance of Margaret Burke, Ronald Hagler and Joan Pert.
Location: OONL.

— Ongoing/En cours —

1397 **Aubrey, Irene E.**
Un Choix de livres canadiens pour la jeunesse: supplément. Ottawa: Bibliothèque nationale du Canada, 1977-. vol.: ill.; ISSN: 0715-2604.
Note: Annuel.– Texte en français seulement, 1975-1976/1977; texte en français et en anglais disposé tête-bêche, 1978- .– Titre de la p. de t. additionnelle: *Notable Canadian children's books: supplement*.
Localisation: OONL.

1398 **Aubrey, Irene E.**
Notable Canadian children's books: supplement. Ottawa: National Library of Canada, 1977-. vol.: ill.; ISSN: 0715-2604.
Note: Annual.– Text in English only, 1975-1976/1977; text in English and French with French text on inverted pages, 1978- .– Title of additional title-page: *Un Choix de livres canadiens pour la jeunesse: supplément*.
Location: OONL.

1399 **CM: Canadian materials for schools and libraries.** Ottawa: Canadian Library Association, 1980-. vol.; ISSN: 0821-1450.
Note: Quarterly.– Lists and reviews Canadian children's and young adults' literature.– Includes fiction and non-fiction.
Previous edition: *Canadian materials*. 1971-1979. 9 vol.; ISSN: 0317-4654.
Location: OONL.

Linguistics and Translation

Linguistique et traduction

— 1858 —

1400 **Ludewig, Hermann E.**
The literature of American aboriginal languages. London: Trübner, 1858. xxiv, 258 p. (Trübner's bibliotheca glottica ; 1)
Note: Listing of vocabularies and grammars or grammatical notices, arranged by language groups and sub-groups, with index.– Additions and corrections by Wm. W. Turner.
Microform: CIHM Microfiche series ; no. 36368; ISBN: 0-665-36368-0. 4 microfiches (152 fr.).
Location: OONL.

— 1870 —

1401 **Bibliotheca hispano-americana: a catalogue of Spanish books ... : followed by a collection of works on the aboriginal languages of America.** London: Trübner, 1870. 184 p.
Note: Canadian language groups represented include Athapascan, Chinook, Chipewyan, Cree, "Eskimo," Micmac, Mohawk and Salish.
Microform: CIHM Microfiche series ; no. 32188; ISBN: 0-665-32188-0. 3 microfiches (102 fr.).
Location: OONL.

— 1876 —

1402 **Platzmann, Julius**
Verzeichniss einer Auswahl Amerikanischer Grammatiken Wörterbücher, Katechismen, u.s.w. Leipzig: K.F. Köhler, 1876. 38 p.
Note: Microform: CIHM Microfiche series ; no. 37866; ISBN: 0-665-37866-1. 1 microfiche (27 fr.).
Location: OONL.

— 1887 —

1403 **Pilling, James Constantine**
Bibliography of the Eskimo language. Washington: Government Printing Office, 1887. v, 116 p.: facsims. (Bulletin / Smithsonian Institution, Bureau of Ethnology ; no. 1; ISSN: 1066-1697)
Note: Approx. 400 entries.– Books, pamphlets, journal articles, manuscripts.
Microform: CIHM Microfiche series ; no. 12051; ISBN: 0-665-12051-6. 2 microfiches (67 fr.).
Reprint: Toronto: Canadiana House, 1969. v, 116 p.
Location: OONL.

— 1888 —

1404 **Pilling, James Constantine**
Bibliography of the Iroquoian languages. Washington: Government Printing Office, 1888. vi, 208 p., [1] folded l. of pl.: facsims. (Bulletin / Smithsonian Institution, Bureau of Ethnology ; no. 6; ISSN: 1066-1697)
Note: 949 entries.– Books, pamphlets, magazine articles and manuscripts.
Microform: CIHM Microfiche series ; no. 12050; ISBN: 0-665-12050-8. 3 microfiches (121 fr.).
Location: OONL.

— 1889 —

1405 **Pilling, James Constantine**
Bibliography of the Muskhogean languages. Washington: Government Printing Office, 1889. v, 114 p. (Bulletin / Smithsonian Institution, Bureau of Ethnology ; no. 9; ISSN: 1066-1697)
Note: 521 entries.– Books, pamphlets, magazine articles, tracts, manuscripts.
Microform: CIHM Microfiche series ; no. 12049; ISBN: 0-665-12049-4. 2 microfiches (65 fr.).
Location: OONL.

— 1891 —

1406 **Pilling, James Constantine**
Bibliography of the Algonquian languages. Washington: Government Printing Office, 1891. x, 614 p.: facsims. (Bulletin / Smithsonian Institution, Bureau of Ethnology ; no. 13; ISSN: 1066-1697)
Note: 2,245 entries.– Books, articles, pamphlets, manuscripts.
Microform: CIHM Microfiche series ; no. 12052; ISBN: 0-665-12052-4. 9 microfiches (424 fr.).
Location: OONL.

— 1892 —

1407 **Pilling, James Constantine**
Bibliography of the Athapascan languages. Washington: Government Printing Office, 1892. xiii, 125 p.: facsims. (Bulletin / Smithsonian Institution, Bureau of Ethnology ; no. 14; ISSN: 1066-1697)
Note: 544 entries.– Books, pamphlets, articles, manuscripts.
Microform: CIHM Microfiche series ; no. 15900; ISBN: 0-665-15900-5. 2 microfiches (75 fr.).
Location: OONL.

— 1893 —

1408 **Pilling, James Constantine**
Bibliography of the Chinookan languages (including the Chinook jargon). Washington: Government Printing Office, 1893. xiii, 81 p.: facsims. (Bulletin / Smithsonian Institution, Bureau of Ethnology ; no. 15; ISSN: 1066-1697)
Note: 270 entries.– Books, pamphlets, articles, manuscripts.– Deals mainly with linguistic amalgam of Chinook jargon, made up from several Indian languages (Chinookian, Salishan, Wakashan, Shahaptian) and English and French.
Microform: CIHM Microfiche series ; no. 15901; ISBN: 0-665-15901-3. 2 microfiches (54 fr.).
Reprint: Seattle: Shorey Book Store, 1972. xiii, 81 p.
Location: OONL.

1409 **Pilling, James Constantine**
Bibliography of the Salishan languages. Washington: Government Printing Office, 1893. xi, 86 p.: facsims. (Bulletin / Smithsonian Institution, Bureau of Ethnology ; no. 16; ISSN: 1066-1697)
Note: 320 entries.– Books, pamphlets, articles and manuscripts.

Microform: CIHM Microfiche series ; no. 15902; ISBN: 0-665-15902-1. 2 microfiches (56 fr.).
Location. OONL.

— 1894 —

1410 **Pilling, James Constantine**
Bibliography of the Wakashan languages. Washington: Government Printing Office, 1894. x, 70 p. (Bulletin / Smithsonian Institution, Bureau of Ethnology ; no. 19; ISSN: 1066-1697)
Note: 251 entries.– Books, pamphlets, magazine articles and manuscripts.
Microform: CIHM Microfiche series ; no. 15903; ISBN: 0-665-15903-X. 1 microfiche (45 fr.).
Location: OONL.

— 1897 —

1411 **Pilling, James Constantine**
Bibliography of the Siouan languages. Washington: Government Printing Office, 1897. v, 87 p. (Bulletin / Smithsonian Institution, Bureau of Ethnology ; no. 5; ISSN: 1066-1697)
Note: Approx. 250 entries.– Books, journal articles, pamphlets, manuscripts.
Microform: CIHM Microfiche series ; no. 12048; ISBN: 0-665-12048-6. 2 microfiches (52 fr.).
Location: OONL.

— 1902 —

1412 **Geddes, James**
Canadian French, the language and literature of the past decade, 1890-1900, with a retrospect of the causes that have produced them. Erlangen [Germany]: Junge & Sohn, 1902. 66 p.
Note: 350 entries.– Sonderabdruck aus: *Kritischer Jahresbericht über die Fortschritte der Romanischen Philologie*, Bd. 5, Heft 2.
Location: OONL.

— 1906 —

1413 **Geddes, James; Rivard, Adjutor**
Bibliographie du parler français au Canada: catalogue analytique des ouvrages traitant de la langue française au Canada. Paris: H. Champion; Québec: E. Marcotte, 1906. 99 p. (Publications de la Société du Parler français au Canada)
Note: 584 entrées.– Continuée par: Dulong, Gaston. Québec: Presses de l'Université Laval; Paris: Librairie C. Klincksieck, 1966. xxxii, 166 p.
Localisation: OONL.

— 1941 —

1414 **Edward E. Ayer Collection**
A bibliographical check list of North and Middle American Indian linguistics in the Edward E. Ayer Collection. Chicago: The Newberry Library, 1941. 2 vol.
Note: Location: OONL.

— 1947 —

1415 **Wolff, Hans**
"Bibliography of bibliographies of North American Indian languages still spoken."
In: *International Journal of American Linguistics*; Vol. 13, no. 4 (October 1947) p. 268-273.; ISSN: 0020-7071.
Note: Location: OONMM.

— 1951 —

1416 **Carrière, Gaston**
"Contribution des Oblats de Marie Immaculée de langue française aux études de linguistique et d'ethnologie du Nord canadien."
Dans: *Culture*; Vol. 12, no 2 (juin 1951) p. 213-226.; ISSN: 0317-2066.
Note: 210 entrées.– Ouvrages imprimés: livres, brochures, tirés à part.
Localisation: AEU.

— 1956 —

1417 **Haugen, Einar Ingvald**
Bilingualism in the Americas: a bibliography and research guide. [Gainesville, Fla.]: American Dialect Society, 1956. 159 p. (Publication of the American Dialect Society ; no. 26)
Note: Bibliography, p. 125-156.– Includes Canadian references.
Location: OONL.

— 1960 —

1418 **Robitaille, Lucie**
"Bibliographie: tableau approximatif des principaux ouvrages traitant de la langue française au Canada."
Dans: *Cahiers de l'Académie canadienne-française*; Vol. 5 (1960) p. 139-156.; ISSN: 0065-0528.
Note: Localisation: OONL.

— 1962 —

1419 **Dulong, Gaston**
"Bibliographie raisonnée du parler français au Canada."
Dans: *Revue de l'Université Laval*; Vol. 15, no 5 (janvier 1961) p. 461-468; vol. 15, no 6 (février 1961) p. 548-555; vol. 15, no 8 (avril 1961) p. 752-757; vol. 16, no 1 (septembre 1961) p. 75-82; vol. 16, no 2 (octobre 1961) p. 172-180; vol. 16, no 4 (décembre 1961) p. 364-370; vol. 16, no 5 (janvier 1962) p. 462-469; vol. 16, no 7 (mars 1962) p. 671-672.; ISSN: 0384-0182.
Note: 538 entrées.
Localisation: OONL.

— 1963 —

1420 **Association canadienne des éducateurs de langue française. Commission permanente de la langue parlée**
Éléments de bibliographie sur la langue parlée. Québec: Association canadienne des éducateurs de langue française, 1963. 11 p. (Publication / Association canadienne des éducateurs de langue française, Commission permanente de la langue parlée ; no 2)
Note: Location: OONL.

— 1965 —

1421 **Vinay, Jean-Paul**
"Éléments de bibliographie de la traduction automatique."
Dans: *Journal des traducteurs*; Vol. 10, no 3 (juillet-septembre 1965) p. 101-109.
Note: Localisation: OONL.

— 1966 —

1422 **Geddes, James; Rivard, Adjutor; Dulong, Gaston**
Bibliographie linguistique du Canada français. Québec: Presses de l'Université Laval; Paris: Librairie C. Klincksieck, 1966. xxxii, 166 p. (Bibliothèque française et romane. Série E: Langue et littérature françaises au Canada ; 1)
Note: 1,054 entrées.– Période couverte est de 1691 à 1965.– Reproduit et continue *Bibliographie du parler français au Canada*. Paris, H. Champion; Québec, E. Marcotte, 1906: 99 p.
Localisation: OONL.

— 1967 —

1423 **Viereck, Wolfgang**
"German dialects spoken in the United States and Canada and problems of German-English language contact especially in North America: a bibliography."
In: *Orbis: bulletin international de documentation linguistique*; Vol. 16, no. 2 (1967) p. 549-568.; ISSN: 0030-4379.
Note: Supplement: Vol. 17, no. 2 (1968) p. 532-535.
Location: AEU.

— 1969 —

1424 **"Bibliographic sources on Ukrainian in the New World, listed chronologically."**
In: *Canadian Ethnic Studies*; Vol. 1, no. 2 (December 1969) p. 202-212.; ISSN: 0008-3496.
Note: Location: AEU.

1425 **Vinay, Jean-Paul; Avis, Walter S.; Rudnyckyj, Jaroslav Bohdan**
"Linguistica Canadiana."
In: *Journal of the Canadian Linguistic Association*; Vol. 1, no. 2 (October 1955) p. 19-22; vol. 2, no. 2 (October 1956) p. 78-83; vol. 3, no. 2 (October 1957) p. 93-98; vol. 4, no. 2 (Fall 1958) p. 105-109; vol. 6, no. 1 (Spring 1960) p. 85-89; vol. 7, no. 2 (Spring 1962) p. 113-118; vol. 9, no. 2 (Spring 1964) p. 117-124; vol. 15, no. 1 (Fall 1969) p. 51-81.; ISSN: 0319-5732.
Note: Listing includes a section of bibliographical sources, followed by general works (applied linguistics, computer linguistics, translation and lexicography, socio- and ethno-linguistics, Canadian toponymy), Canadian English, Canadian French, Slavic languages, Amerindian languages.
From the Fall 1961 issue (Vol. 7, no. 1), the title of the journal changed to: *Canadian Journal of Linguistics*. ISSN: 0008-4131.
Location: OONL.

— 1971 —

1426 **Irving, E.**
"The relation between bilingualism and measured intelligence: a bibliographical guide."
In: *Cahiers linguistiques d'Ottawa*; No 1 (1971) p. 75-89.; ISSN: 0315-3967.
Note: Approx. 150 entries.– Books and articles pertaining to the relationship between bilingualism and intelligence.– Includes Canadian references.
Location: AEU.

— 1972 —

1427 **Mackenzie, M.E.**
"La Région de la Baie James (Québec): bibliographie linguistique."
Dans: *Recherches amérindiennes au Québec*; Vol. 2, Spécial 1 (juin 1972) p. 43-49.; ISSN: 0318-4137.
Note: Localisation: OLU.

— 1973 —

1428 **Pilling, James Constantine**
Bibliographies of the languages of the North American Indians. New York: AMS Press, 1973. 3 vol.; ISBN: 0-404-07390-5 (set).
Note: 9 parts in 3 volumes: Vol. 1, part 1: "Eskimo," part 2: "Siouan," part 3: "Iroquoian," part 4: "Muskhogean."- Vol. 2, part 5: "Algonquian."- Vol. 3, part 6: "Athapascan," part 7: "Chinookan," part 8: "Salishan," part 9: "Wakashan."- Reprint of the 1887-1894 editions, which

were published separately and issued as Smithsonian Institution, Bureau of Ethnology, Bulletin no. 1, 5-6, 9, 13-16, 19.
Location: OONL.

— 1974 —

1429 **Lamarche, Rolande; Sabourin, Conrad**
Psycholinguistique et sociolinguistique au Québec. [Montréal: Éditions fipf (Fédération internationale des professeurs de français)], 1974. 426 p.
Note: Approx. 400 entrées.– Comprend les livres, les articles de revues spécialisées, les monographies inédites, les thèses produites dans les universités québécoises, les rapports de recherche, les communications présentées devant des sociétés savantes et les recherches en cours: des travaux de psycholinguistique et de sociolinguistique effectués au Québec depuis 1960.
Localisation: OONL.

1430 **Parr, Richard T.**
A bibliography of the Athapaskan languages. Ottawa: National Museums of Canada, 1974. xiii, 333 p.: map. (National Museum of Man Mercury series: Ethnology Division paper ; no. 14)
Note: Approx. 5,000 entries.– Published materials, theses, dissertations, archive holdings of Smithsonian Institution and National Museum of Man relating to linguistics, anthropology, archaeology, folklore, ethnomusicology of Athapaskan Indian languages.
Location: OONL.

— 1975 —

1431 **Afendras, Evangelos A.; Pianarosa, Albertina**
Le bilinguisme chez l'enfant et l'apprentissage d'une langue seconde: bibliographie analytique/Child bilingualism and second language learning: a descriptive bibliography. Québec: Presses de l'Université Laval, 1975. xxiii, 401 p. (Travaux du Centre international de recherche sur le bilinguisme ; F-4); ISBN: 0-7746-6751-6.
Note: 1,661 entrées.– Comporte des références canadiennes et québécoises.
Localisation: OONL.

1432 **Brunet, Raymond**
Guide bibliographique de la traduction: à l'intention des usagers de la Bibliothèque des sciences humaines et sociales. Montréal: Bibliothèque des sciences humaines et sociales, Université de Montréal, 1975. iv, 119 p.
Note: 557 entrées.
Localisation: OONL.

1433 **Metropolitan Toronto Library. Languages Centre**
A bibliographical check-list of Canadian Indian linguistics in the Languages Centre of Metropolitan Toronto Central Library. Toronto: Languages Centre, Metropolitan Toronto Library Board, 1975. 31 p.
Note: Approx. 200 entries.
Supplement: *A supplement to "A bibliographical check-list ....* 1976. 4 p.
Location: OONL.

— 1976 —

1434 **Bibliographie des chroniques de langage publiées dans la presse au Canada.** [Montréal]: Département de linguistique et philologie, Université de Montréal, [1975-1976]. 2 vol.
Note: Vol. 1: xxix, 466 p.– 10,908 entrées.– Couvre 1950 à 1970.– Vol. 2: xxxvii, 1007 p.– 19,239 entrées.– Couvre 1879 à 1949.– Préparé sous la direction d'André Clas,

avec la collaboration de Paul Daoust et Claude Durand.
Localisation: OONL.

1435 **Gagnon, Claude-Marie**
Bibliographie critique du joual, 1970-1975. Québec:
Institut supérieur des sciences humaines, Université
Laval, 1976. 117 f. (Cahiers de l'ISSH, Collection
Instruments de travail / Institut supérieur des sciences
humaines, Université Laval ; no 19)
Note: 404 entrées.– Livres, articles de revues, articles de
journaux sur la question du français parle au Québec.
Localisation: OONL.

1436 **Landar, Herbert**
"An Innuit bibliography."
In: *Papers on Eskimo and Aleut linguistics*, edited by Eric P.
Hamp. Chicago: Chicago Linguistic Society, c1976. P. 108-
139.
Note: 383 entries.– Listing of manuscripts and printed
items examined at the Crosby Library, Gonzaga Univers-
ity, Spokane: grammars, dictionaries, texts in Inuit
language.
Location: OONL.

— 1977 —

1437 **Bähr, Dieter**
A bibliography of writings on the English language in
Canada: from 1857 to 1976. Heidelberg: Winter, 1977. xi,
51 p.; ISBN: 3-533-02565-9.
Note: 438 entries.– Books and journal articles on history,
pronunciation and spelling, grammar, vocabulary,
lexicography, social and geographical variation, dialect
studies, names.
Location: OONL.

1438 **De Haas, Patricia**
A bibliography of French-Canadian reference sources:
literature and language/Bibliographie des ouvrages
canadiens-français de référence: littérature et langue.
Edmonton: University of Alberta Library, 1977. 8 f.
Note: Lists publications in English and French.–
Comprend des publications en anglais et en français.
Location: OONL.

1439 **Gémar, Jean-Claude; Horguelin, Paul A.**
Bibliographie sélective du traducteur: commerce et
économie. Montréal: Linguatech, c1977. 187 p. (pagination variée).
Note: Bibliographie sélective presentée par secteur
d'activité: comptabilité, banque, finances publiques,
gestion, etc.– Pour chaque secteur, trois catégories
d'ouvrages: dictionnaires unilingues, dictionnaires de
traduction, ouvrages de référence.
Localisation: OONL.

1440 **Stratford, Philip**
Bibliography of Canadian books in translation: French to
English and English to French/Bibliographie de livres
canadiens traduits de l'anglais au français et du français
à l'anglais. 2nd ed. Ottawa: Humanities Research
Council of Canada, 1977. xvii, 78 p.
Note: 640 entries.– Translations of fiction, poetry, drama,
folklore, letters, reports, travel journals, essays,
anthologies, children's books.– Text in English and
French/texte en français et en anglais.
Previous edition: Newman, Maureen; Stratford, Philip.
1975. vi, 57 p.
Location: OONL.

— 1978 —

1441 **Allix, Beverley**
Annotated bibliography of English for special purposes.
Toronto: Newcomer Services Branch, Citizenship
Division, Ontario Ministry of Culture and Recreation,
1978. 91 p.
Note: Approx. 800 entries.– Books, monographs, reports,
conference papers, periodical articles, essays in
collections, theses and dissertations, bibliographies,
dictionaries, textbooks dealing with the English language
as developed in special fields: economics, medicine,
physical sciences and mathematics, technology.
Location: OONL.

1442 **Avis, Walter S.; Kinloch, A.M.**
Writings on Canadian English, 1792-1975: an annotated
bibliography. Toronto: Fitzhenry & Whiteside, [1978].
153 p.; ISBN: 0-88902-121-X.
Note: 723 entries.– Books, periodical and newspaper
articles, government publications, theses relating to
characteristics of Canadian-English language.– Excludes
works on onomastics, technical glossaries, manuals of
style, works dealing with influence of Canadian English
on other languages.
Previous edition: *A bibliography of writings on Canadian
English (1857-1965).* W.J. Gage, [c1965]. 17 p.– 103 entries.
Location: OONL.

1443 **Kinloch, A.M.; House, Anthony B.**
"The English language in New Brunswick and Prince
Edward Island: research published, in progress, and
required."
In: *Journal of the Atlantic Provinces Linguistic Association*;
Vol. 1 (1978) p. 34-45.; ISSN: 0706-6910.
Note: Literature review of dialect research on New
Brunswick and P.E.I. English.
Location: OONL.

1444 **Mackey, William Francis**
Le bilinguisme canadien: bibliographie analytique et
guide du chercheur. Québec: Centre international de
recherche sur le bilinguisme, 1978. [viii], 603 p.
(Publication / Centre international de recherche sur le
bilinguisme ; B-75)
Note: Approx. 8,000 entrées.– Documents, travaux
scientifiques, articles de périodiques et journaux: études
historiques, démographie linguistique, solutions
politiques, problèmes juridiques, langues et éducation,
dimension sociale, aspect géographique, contexte
culturel, rapports ethniques.
Localisation: OONL.

— 1979 —

1445 **Delisle, Jean; Albert, Lorraine**
Guide bibliographique du traducteur, rédacteur et
terminologue/Bibliographic guide for translators,
writers and terminologists. Éd. rev., corr. et augm.
Ottawa: Éditions de l'Université d'Ottawa, 1979. 207 p.
(Cahiers de traductologie ; no 1); ISBN: 2-7603-4651-X.
Note: 1,486 entrées.– Text en français et en anglais/text
in English and French.
Édition antérieure: Albert, Lorraine; Delisle, Jean.
*Répertoire bibliographique de la traduction/Bibliographic
guide to translation.* 1976. xi, 165 p.
Localisation: OONL.

1446 **Kerek, Andrew**
Bibliography of Hungarian linguistic research in the United States and Canada. [New Brunswick, N.J.]: American Hungarian Foundation, c1979. 28 p. (Hungarian reference shelf ; 5)
Note: 249 entries.
Location: OONL.

1447 **Sabourin, Conrad; Lamarche, Rolande**
Le français québécois: bibliographie analytique. Montréal: Service des publications, Office de la langue française, 1979. xv, 329 p.; ISBN: 2-551-03397-7.
Note: 3,357 entrées.– Livres, articles de revues spécialisées, thèses, communications présentées à des colloques, textes inédits de chercheurs reconnus, recherches en cours sur l'évolution et l'utilisation du français au Québec et en Amérique du Nord: la phonétique, la phonologie, la syntaxe et la lexicologie.
Localisation: OONL.

1448 **Sabourin, Conrad; Petit, Normand**
Langues et sociétés: bibliographie analytique. Montréal: Service de publications, Direction des communications, Office de la langue française, 1979. xv, 583 p.; ISBN: 2-551-03303-9.
Note: 5,063 entrées.– Références à des documents traitant de sociolinguistique, d'aménagement linguistique, de démographie linquistique, de politique linguistique, de multilinguisme, de droit et de jurisprudence en matière linguistique: travaux de recherche qui examinent les rapports entre les phénomènes linguistiques et sociaux.
Localisation: OONL.

— 1980 —

1449 **Gordon, W. Terrence**
Semantics: a bibliography, 1965-1978. Metuchen, N.J.: Scarecrow Press, 1980. xiv, 307 p.; ISBN: 0-8108-1300-9.
Note: 2,707 entries.– Books and journal articles.– Principal topics covered include semantics of parts of speech, semantics of child language, comparative semantics, definitions and models of meaning, semantics and syntax.– Lexical index, author index.– Substantial Canadian content.
Supplements:
... , *1979-1985*. 1987. xii, 292 p.; ISBN: 0-8108-2055-2.– 3,327 entries.
... , *1986-1991*. 1992. ix, 280 p.; ISBN: 0-8108-2598-8.– 1,350 entries.
Location: OONL.

1450 **Swanick, Eric L.**
Bilingualism in the federal Canadian public service. Monticello, Ill.: Vance Bibliographies, 1980. 6 p. (Public administration series: Bibliography ; P-425; ISSN: 0193-970X)
Note: Approx. 60 entries.– Government publications, theses, periodical articles, royal commission studies.
Location: OONL.

— 1981 —

1451 **Gardner, Robert C.; Desrochers, Alain**
"Second-language acquisition and bilingualism: research in Canada (1970-1980)."
In: *Canadian Psychology*; Vol. 22, no. 2 (April 1981) p. 146-161.; ISSN: 0708-5591.
Note: Approx. 125 entries.– Reviews research on second language acquisition and bilingualism conducted in Canada in the 1970s.

Location: OONL.

1452 **Goorachurn, Lynn-Dell**
Native languages: resources pertaining to native languages of Manitoba. [Winnipeg]: Province of Manitoba, Department of Education, 1981. i, 52 p. (Curriculum support series / Manitoba Department of Education)
Note: Approx. 250 entries.– Books, articles, government publications: Native (general), Algonquian, Chipewyan, Cree, Dakota, Ojibwa.– Selective annotation.
Location: OONL.

1453 **Roberts, R.P.; Blais, J.**
"Bibliographie annotée de la didactique de la traduction et de l'interprétation/The didactics of translation and interpretation: an annotated bibliography."
Dans: *Revue de l'Université d'Ottawa*; Vol. 51, no 3 (juillet-septembre 1981) p. 560-589.; ISSN: 0041-9206.
Note: 88 entries.– Publications in English and French dealing with training of professional translators, teaching methods and theory, selection of students, theses, practicums, on-the-job training, further training.– Excludes translation course manuals.
Location: AEU.

— 1982 —

1454 **Craven, Rita**
Indigenous languages of Manitoba: a select bibliography. [Winnipeg]: Elizabeth Dafoe Library, University of Manitoba, 1982. 19 l.
Note: Approx. 250 entries.– Select list of monographs on native languages of Manitoba held in collections of University of Manitoba Libraries: Assiniboin, Chipewyan, Cree, Dakota, Inuit, Ojibwa.– Includes texts in these languages.
Location: OONL.

1455 **Edwards, Barry; Love, Mary**
A bibliography of Inuit (Eskimo) linguistics in collections of the Metropolitan Toronto Library. Toronto: Metropolitan Toronto Library Board, Languages Centre, [1982]. iii, 36 p.
Note: Approx. 200 entries.
Location: OONL.

1456 **Langlois, Pierre**
Génie civil, travaux publics, terrassement, équipments de chantier et construction routière: bibliographies. Québec: Service des publications, Office de la langue française, 1982. 127 p.; ISBN: 2-551-04760-9.
Note: 332 entrées.– Répertoires terminologiques (vocabulaires, lexiques, dictionnaires), documents qui contiennent des termes normalisés, catalogues, ouvrages spécialisés avec index des termes.– Comprend un nombre d'ouvrages canadiens.
Localisation: OONL.

1457 **Pentland, David H.; Wolfart, H. Christoph**
Bibliography of Algonquian linguistics. [Winnipeg]: University of Manitoba Press, 1982. xix, 333 p.; ISBN: 0-88755-128-9.
Note: Approx. 2,800 entries.– Covers from the publication of Pilling's *Bibliography of the Algonquian languages*, 1891, to the end of 1981.– Includes books, journal articles, government documents, theses.
Location: OONL.

1458 **Pottier, Bernard**
Bibliographie américaniste: linguistique amérindienne. Paris: Musée de l'homme, 1967-1982. 9 vol.; ISSN: 0067-690X.
Note: Inclut un nombre considérable d'ouvrages canadiens.
Localisation: OONL.

— 1983 —

1459 **Anthony, Linda**
Heritage languages: a bibliography. Regina: Multicultural Council of Saskatchewan, c1983. 16 p.
Note: Approx. 240 entries.– Includes books, reports, papers, journal articles, bibliographies.
Location: OONL.

— 1984 —

1460 **Huot, Diane; Coulombe, Raymonde**
La classe de conversation en L2: une bibliographie sélective et descriptive. Québec: Centre international de recherche sur le bilinguisme, 1984. 308, 20 p. (Publication / Centre international de recherche sur le bilinguisme ; B-142); ISBN: 2-89219-150-5.
Note: Approx. 800 entrées.– Couvre la période de 1960 à 1983.
Localisation: OONL.

1461 **Lapierre, André**
"Bibliographie linguistique de l'Ontario français."
Dans: *Cahiers linguistiques d'Ottawa*; No 12 (février 1984) p. 1-38.; ISSN: 0315-3967.
Note: Comprend les livres, articles, thèses: bilinguisme, contact des langues, assimilation, transferts linguistiques.
Localisation: AEU.

1462 **Lightbown, Patsy**
Bibliography of research on the acquisition of French L1 and L2. Quebec: International Center for Research on Bilingualism, 1984. ii, 27, xviii p. (International Center for Research on Bilingualism Publication ; B-132); ISBN: 2-89219-137-8.
Note: Approx. 500 entries.
Location: OONL.

1463 **Schneider, Edgar W.**
"A bibliography of writings on American and Canadian English (1965-1983)."
In: *A bibliography of writings on varieties of English, 1965-1983*, compiled by Wolfgang Viereck, Edgar W. Schneider and Manfred Görlach. Amsterdam: John Benjamins, 1984. P. 89-223.; ISBN: 90-272-4861-3.
Note: 1,798 entries.– Books and scholarly articles in the disciplines of dialectology and sociolinguistics form the core of the bibliography.– Also includes works on bilingualism, language contact and language interference.– Excludes reviews, reprints of articles, articles in non-scholarly publications, unpublished manuscripts, onomastic studies.
Location: AEU.

— 1985 —

1464 **Minion, Robin**
Inuit and Indian languages, including educational concerns and materials in these languages. Edmonton: Boreal Institute for Northern Studies, University of Alberta, 1985. 77 p. (Boreal Institute for Northern Studies Bibliographic series ; no. 16; ISSN: 0824-8192); ISBN: 0-919058-50-7.
Note: 214 entries.– Series contains monographs, theses, government documents, consultants' reports, children's books, conference proceedings, microforms on topics related to northern environment and people.– BINS series produced monthly from January 1981 to May 1986 (no. 29).– Online access: *Boreal Northern Titles (BNT)*, available through QL Systems Limited.
Location: OONL.

— 1986 —

1465 **Cliche, Mireille**
Informatique: bibliographie sélective. Québec: Gouvernement du Québec, Office de la langue français, Direction de la recherche et du secrétariat, 1986. 134 p.; ISBN: 2-550-16720-1.
Note: 286 entrées.– Documents terminologiques (vocabulaires, lexiques, dictionnaires), normes de vocabulaire, ouvrages spécialisés avec index de termes.– Principaux domaines: informatique, micro-informatique, informatique de spécialités, téléinformatique, logiciel et programmation, matériel informatique.
Localisation: OONL.

1466 **Gesner, Edward**
Bibliographie annotée de linguistique acadienne. Québec: Centre international de recherche sur le bilinguisme, 1986. 89 p. (Publication / Centre international de recherche sur le bilinguisme ; B-155); ISBN: 2-89219-166-1.
Note: 430 entrées.– Phonétique et phonologie, morphologie et syntaxe, lexicologie, sémiotique, sociolinguistique, bilinguisme/anglicisation.
Localisation: OONL.

— 1987 —

1467 **Bulletin bibliographique sur la didactique des langues.** Québec: Centre international de recherche sur le bilinguisme, 1987. xiv, 559 p. (Publication / Centre international de recherche sur le bilinguisme ; J-1); ISBN: 2-89219-183-1.
Note: Approx. 480 entrées.– Monographies, articles de périodiques, rapports de recherche, thèses sur la didactique des langues vivantes, plus spécialement du français langue seconde ou étrangère, pour la période 1970-1985.– Banque de données: BIBELO (Bibliographie informatisée sur le bilinguisme et l'enseignement des langues officielles).
Localisation: OONL.

1468 **Bulletin bibliographique sur la linguistique appliquée à l'informatique.** Québec: Centre international de recherche sur le bilinguisme, 1987. xiv, 116 p. (Publication / Centre international de recherche sur le bilinguisme ; K-3); ISBN: 2-89219-182-3.
Note: 150 entrées.
Localisation: OONL.

1469 **Canada. Commission de la Fonction publique. Direction générale du programme de la formation linguistique**
Français langue seconde: catalogue/French as a second language: catalogue. [Ottawa]: La Commission, c1987. 63 p.: ill.; ISBN: 0-662-54691-1.
Note: Comprend le matériel d'enseignement du français langue seconde élaboré à la Commission de la Fonction publique du Canada: matériel de niveau élémentaire (*Dialogue Canada 1*), matériel de niveau intermédiaire et avancé (*Dialogue Canada 2* et *L'Atelier*), matériel spécialisé (modules à niveaux multiples), tests.

Localisation: OONL.

1470 **Canada. Public Service Commission. Language Training Program Branch**
English as a second language: ESL catalogue/Anglais langue seconde: catalogue ASL. [Ottawa]: Public Service Commission of Canada, c1987. 32 p.: ill.; ISBN: 0-662-54931-7.
Note: Materials developed for teaching English as a second language by the English Program Development Division of the Linguistic Service Directorate, Public Service Commission of Canada: *Contact Canada* core program and other modules which make use of different approaches depending upon subject matter.– Text in English and French/texte en français et en anglais.
Location: OONL.

1471 **Collectif de l'École de traducteurs et d'interprètes**
Bibliographie du traducteur/Translator's bibliography. [Ottawa]: Presses de l'Université d'Ottawa, 1987. xiii, 332 p. (Cahiers de traductologie ; no 6); ISBN: 2-7603-0120-6.
Note: Approx. 3,000 entrées.– Principaux thèmes traités: traduction, interprétation, terminologie (théorie, pédagogie, histoire, bibliographies); Langue française (grammaires, ouvrages spécialisés); English language (dictionaries and encyclopedias, grammars, specialized works); Dictionnaires bilingues (langue générale); Lengua y traducciòn española; Domaines spécialisés.– Inclut un nombre d'ouvrages canadiens.– Texte en français et en anglais/text in English and French.
Localisation: OONL.

1472 **Delisle, Jean**
La traduction au Canada, 1534-1984/Translation in Canada, 1534-1984. [Ottawa]: Presses de l'Université d'Ottawa, 1987. 436 p.: ill., ports.; ISBN: 2-7603-0182-6.
Note: Troisième partie: "Bibliographie annotée: Annotated bibliography," p. 243-434.– 2,472 entrées.– Livres, documents et articles de périodiques et journaux sur l'histoire de la traduction au Canada, l'évolution de la profession au Canada et de la place qu'elle y occupe du triple point de vue linguistique, politique et culturel.– Texte en français et en anglais/text in English and French.
Localisation: OONL.

1473 **Dumais, Hélène**
La féminisation des titres et du discours au Québec: une bibliographie. Québec: Groupe de recherche et d'échange multidisciplinaire féministe, Université Laval, [1987]. 35 p. (Cahiers de recherche du GREMF / Groupe de recherche et d'échange multidisciplinaire féministe, Université Laval ; 12); ISBN: 2-89364-012-5.
Note: Approx. 225 entrées.– Articles des revues et périodiques spécialisés et d'intérêt général, articles de journaux, publications gouvernementales: aménagement linguistique (autorité gouvernementale, autres groupes), réactions des gens face à l'emploi de certaines formes.
Localisation: OONL.

1474 **Foley, Kathryn Shred; Harley, Birgit; D'Anglejan, Alison**
Research in core French: an annotated bibliography/Recherches sur le français de base: bibliographie analytique. [Winnipeg]: Canadian Association of Second Language Teachers, 1987. v, 167 p.; ISBN: 0-921238-00-2.
Note: Summary of empirical research on core French programs since 1970.– Majority of studies involve

research conducted in Canada.– Includes research reports from school boards, reports of government-funded research, unpublished theses, published books, journal articles.
Location: OONL.

1475 **Sabourin, Conrad; Lamarche, Rolande; Tarrab, Elca**
La francité canadienne: bibliographie. Montréal: Université de Montréal, Faculté des sciences de l'éducation, 1985-1987. 2 vol.; ISBN: 2-920826-00-X (vol. 1); 2-920298-51-8 (vol. 2).
Note: Vol. 1: *Aspects linguistiques: bibliographie*: 3,270 entrées.– Vol. 2: *Sociologie et politicologie de la langue*: 3,348 entrées.
Localisation: OONL.

— 1988 —

1476 **Bibliographie sélective: terminologie et disciplines connexes/Selective bibliography: terminology and related fields.** [Ottawa]: Direction de la terminologie, Secrétariat d'État du Canada, c1988. vi, 87 p.; ISBN: 0-660-54120-3.
Note: Approx. 1,000 entrées.– Répertoire sélectif d'articles et d'ouvrages: sémantique, morphologie, systématique, langue de spécialité, planification linguistique, théorie et principes.– Texte en français et en anglais/text in English and French.
Localisation: OONL.

1477 **Boulanger, Jean-Claude; Nakos, Dorothy**
Le syntagme terminologique: bibliographie sélective et analytique. Québec: Centre international de recherche sur le bilinguisme, 1988. 81 p. (Publication / Centre international de recherche sur le bilinguisme ; K-7); ISBN: 2-89219-193-9.
Note: 75 entrées.– Couvre la période de 1960 à 1988.– Articles de revues québécoises et canadiennes, actes de colloques nationaux et internationaux, monographies consacrées en tout ou en partie à le syntagme terminologique.
Localisation: OONL.

1478 **Lamarche, Rolande; Tarrab, Elca; Daoust, Denise**
Bibliographie de travaux québécois. [Québec]: Office de la langue française, c1988. 2 vol.; ISBN: 2-550-19244-3 (vol. 1); 2-550-19245-1 (vol. 2).
Note: Vol. 1: *Psycholinguistique et pédagogie de la langue*. 176 p.– 2,040 entrées.– Comprend les travaux qui sont reliés à l'acquisition, à l'enseignement des langues et de façon générale à la psycholinguistique.– Vol. 2: *Linguistique générale, linguistique computationelle, terminologie, traduction*. 316 p.– 3,772 entrées.
Localisation: OONL.

1479 **Lougheed, W.C.**
Writings on Canadian English, 1976-1987: a selective, annotated bibliography. Kingston, Ont.: Strathy Language Unit, Queen's University, [1988]. xiii, 66 p. (Occasional papers / Strathy Language Unit, Queen's University ; no. 2); ISBN: 0-88911-510-9.
Note: Approx. 300 entries.– Books, journal and newspaper articles, conference papers, theses on General Canadian English (Central/Prairie English) or English of the Canadian Regions.– Excludes technical glossaries, works dealing with influence of Canadian English on other languages, pedagogical and prescriptive works, items concerning Canada's official languages policy.
Location: OONL.

1480 **Mezei, Kathy**
Bibliography of criticism on English and French literary translations in Canada: 1950-1986, annotated/ Bibliographie de la critique des traductions littéraires anglaises et françaises au Canada de 1950 à 1986 avec commentaires. [Ottawa]: University of Ottawa Press, [1988]. 177 p. (Translation studies: Cahiers de traductologie ; 7); ISBN: 0-7766-0198-9.
Note: 581 entries.– Books, journal articles, interviews, introductions by translators, reviews, theses relating to Canadian literary translation.– Compiled with assistance of Patricia Matson and Maureen Hole.– Text in English and French/texte en français et en anglais.
Location: OONL.

1481 **Service de diffusion sélective de l'information de la Centrale des bibliothèques**
Le Français au Québec. Montréal: Le Service, 1988. 48 p. (DSI/CB ; no 115; ISSN: 0825-5024); ISBN: 2-89059-321-5.
Note: 387 entrées.– Monographies, articles de périodiques, documents audiovisuels.– Principal questions: situation de la langue française au Québec, son statut, son avenir; politique linguistique du Québec; place de l'anglais au Québec; français comme langue du travail; lexicographie.
Localisation: OONL.

1482 **Service de diffusion sélective de l'information de la Centrale des bibliothèques**
La Francophonie. Montréal: Le Service, 1988. 34 p. (DSI/CB ; no 114; ISSN: 0825-5024); ISBN: 2-89059-321-5.
Note: 322 entrées.– Monographies, articles de périodiques, documents audiovisuels.– Principales questions: la francophonie et les francophones au Canada et dans divers pays du monde; les sommets de la francophonie; l'aspect de la langue, de la culture, des relations ethniques, de l'économie, de la coopération, de l'histoire.
Localisation: OONL.

1483 **Shaheen, Wali Alam; Nasim, Anwar; Mirza, Izhar**
Across continents: a review of Urdu language & literature in Canada. Ottawa: National Federation of Pakistani Canadians, 1988. 112 p.: ill.
Note: Location: OONL.

— 1989 —

1484 **Boulanger, Jean-Claude; Gambier, Yves**
Bibliographie fondamentale et analytique de la terminologie: 1962-1984. Québec: Centre international de recherche sur le bilinguisme, 1989. 104 p.; ISBN: 2-89219-207-2.
Note: 123 entrées.– Actes de colloques, ouvrages collectifs, articles de revues, livres, thèses, rapports.
Localisation: OONL.

1485 **Bulletin bibliographique sur le bilinguisme et le contact des langues.** Québec: Centre international de recherche sur le bilinguisme, 1989. xvii, 534 p. (Publication / Centre international de recherche sur le bilinguisme ; J-2); ISBN: 2-89219-201-3.
Note: Approx. 450 entrées.– Monographies, articles de périodiques, thèses, rapports de recherche, actes de colloques sur le bilinguisme et le contact des langues pendant la période des années '80.– Banque de données: BIBELO (Bibliographie informatisée sur le bilinguisme et l'enseignement des langues officielles).
Localisation: OONL.

1486 **Inventaire des travaux de terminologie récents: publiés et à diffusion restreinte.** Québec: Gouvernement du Québec, Office de la langue française, 1989. 429 p.; ISBN: 2-550-19816-6.
Note. 1,156 entrées.– Documents terminologiques parus depuis 1986 et rédigés en français, ou en français et dans une ou plusieurs autres langues.– Deux index: organismes et des auteurs; vedettes-matière et des descripteurs libres.
Localisation: OONL.

1487 **Manitoba. Multiculture Educational Resource Centre**
Heritage language resources: an annotated bibliography. Winnipeg: Multiculture Educational Resource Centre, Manitoba Education, 1989. iv l., 89 p.; ISBN: 0-7711-0796-X.
Note: Approx. 700 entries.– Contains materials appropriate for teaching languages other than English, French, Native.– Includes books on history and culture of ethnic groups.
Location: OONL.

1488 **Walz, Joel**
Annotated bibliography for developing oral proficiency in second and foreign languages. Québec: International Center for Research on Bilingualism, 1989. 63 p. (International Center for Research on Bilingualism Publication ; B-171); ISBN: 2-89219-200-5.
Note: Approx. 200 entries.– Contains references to articles and books published since 1970 that provide teachers with specific techniques to use in class to develop oral proficiency of students.
Location: OONL.

— 1990 —

1489 **Boulanger, Jean-Claude**
Bibliographie de la néologie: nouveaux fragments (1980-1989). Québec: Gouvernement du Québec, Office de la langue française, 1990. v, 192 p.
Note: 600 entrées.
Édition antérieure: Turcotte, Roselyne. *Bibliographie de la néologie: 300 apports nouveax (1980-1987).* 1988. 98 p.; ISBN: 2-550-18579-X.
Localisation: OONL.

1490 **Varin, Marie-Eve, et al.**
Inventaire des travaux en cours et des projets de terminologie. [3e éd.]. [Québec]: Gouvernement du Québec, Office de la langue française, c1990. 202 p.; ISBN: 2-550-20568-5.
Note: 450 entrées.– Glossaires, dictionnaires, lexiques, vocabulaires, thésaurus et nomenclatures de tous les domaines d'activités.
Éditions antérieures:
Bédard, Constant. 1987. 115 p.
Guérin, Huguette; Plourde, Marcel. *Inventaire des travaux de terminologie.* 1983. 101 p.; ISBN: 2-551-05787-6.
Localisation: OONL.

— 1991 —

1491 **Alberta. Alberta Education. Language Services**
Blackfoot language and culture: a selective bibliography of supplementary learning resources (early childhood services-grade 12). Edmonton: Language Services, Alberta Education, 1991. v, 97 p.; ISBN: 0-7732-0501-2.
Note: 62 entries.– Contains three sections: "Language learning resources," "Cultural learning resources," and "Professional references."– Includes print and non-print

materials to support the Alberta Education Blackfoot as a Second Language Program.
Location: OONL.

1492 **Annotated bibliography of the official languages of Canada/Bibliographie analytique des langues officielles au Canada.** [Ottawa]: Office of the Commissioner of Official Languages, [1991]. 53 p.
Note: 88 entries.– Covers 1960-1989.– Deals with general issue of the official languages in Canada under 15 themes, including attitudes of Canadians towards official bilingualism, costs of official bilingualism, linguistic rights, history of official bilingualism, language of work, linguistic minorities.– Text in English and French/texte en français et en anglais.
Location: OONL.

— Ongoing/En cours —

1493 **Canadian translations/Traductions canadiennes.** Ottawa: National Library of Canada, 1987-. vol.; ISSN: 0835-2291.
Note: Annual.– First issue: 1984-85.– Lists monographs translated and published in Canada, in any language.– Includes pamphlets and brochures.– Excludes government publications.– Two parts: subjects (arranged by UDC); author-title index (with full bibliographic records).– Text in English and French/texte en français et en anglais.
Location: OONL.

1494 **Index translationum. Répertoire international des traductions. International bibliography of translations.** Paris: Unesco, 1948-. vol.; ISSN: 0073-6074.
Note: Includes a section on Canadian works in translation, compiled by the National Library of Canada.
Location: OONL.

Religion et philosophie

— 1910 —

1495 Hugolin, père
Bibliographie antonienne, ou, Nomenclature des ouvrages, livres, revues, brochures, feuilles, etc., sur la dévotion à S. Antoine de Padoue, publiés dans la province de Québec de 1777 à 1909. Québec: Impr. de l'Événement, 1910. 76 p.
Note: Supplément: *Bibliographie antonienne de la province de Québec: supplément, 1910-1931.* Montréal: 1932. 35 p.
Localisation: OONL.

— 1915 —

1496 Hugolin, père
Les Franciscains et la croisade antialcoolique dans la province de Québec (Canada): aperçu sommaire de leurs travaux préparé pour le Chapître général de l'Ordre des frères mineurs. Montréal: [s.n.], 1915. xxix p.
Note: Localisation: OONL.

— 1916 —

1497 Hugolin, père
Bibliographie franciscaine: inventaire des revues, livres, brochures des autres écrits publié par les franciscains du Canada de 1890 à 1915. Québec: Imprimerie franciscaine missionaire, 1916. 141 p.
Note: Suppléments:
.... . *Supplément jusqu'à l'année 1931.* 1932. 214 p.
.... . *Second supplément.* Montréal: [s.n.], 1936. 76 p.
Localisation: OONL.

— 1921 —

1498 Hugolin, père
Bibliographie du Tiers-Ordre séculier de Saint François au Canada (province de Québec). Montréal: Ménard, 1921. 149 p.
Note: Approx. 500 entrées.
... : *supplément pour les années 1921 à 1931.* Montréal: 1932. 46 p.
Guilbert, Honoré. ... : *supplément pour les années 1931 à 1940.* 1940. 47 p.
Localisation: OONL.

— 1922 —

1499 Bernad, Marcel
Bibliographie des missionnaires oblats de Marie Immaculée. Liège: H. Dessain, 1922. 127 p.
Note: Localisation: OONL.

— 1933 —

1500 Hugolin, père
"Bibliographie des travaux édités ou imprimés en Europe sur les Récollets du Canada."
Dans: *Mémoires de la Société royale du Canada;* Série 3, vol. 27, section 1 (1933) p. 87-109.; ISSN: 0316-4616.
Note: Localisation: AEU.

— 1936 —

1501 Hugolin, père
Notes bibliographiques pour servir à l'histoire des Récollets du Canada. Montréal: Impr. des Franciscains, 1932-1936. 6 vol.

Note: Vol. 1: *Les écrits imprimés laissés par les Récollets;* vol. 2: *Le père Nicolas Viel;* vol. 3: *Le serviteur de Dieu, Frère Didace Pelletier, 1657-1699;* vol. 4: *Bibliographie des bibliographies du P. Louis Hennepin, récollet;* vol. 5: *Bibliograpie des travaux édités ou imprimés en Europe sur les Récollets du Canada;* vol. 6: *L'oeuvre manuscrite ou imprimée des Récollets de la Mission du Canada (Province de Saint-Denis), 1615-1629.*
Localisation: OONL.

— 1941 —

1502 Elphège, père
Bibliographie franciscaine: nos périodiques, nos auteurs, 1931-1941. Montréal: [s.n.], 1941. 21 p.
Note: Localisation: OONL.

— 1942 —

1503 Gervais, Émile
Pour mieux connaître nos fondateurs: bibliographie pratique. Montréal: Bureau de propagande, 1942. 32 p. (Collection "Textes" / Bureau de propagande, Église catholique ; no 1)
Note: Approx. 200 entrées.– Ouvrages et articles concernant l'Église canadienne en général et quatre fondateurs: Laval, Marie de l'Incarnation, Marguerite Bourgeoys et Mère Catherine de Saint-Augustin.
Localisation: OONL.

— 1944 —

1504 Lusignan, Lucien
"Essai sur les écrits de deux martyrs canadiens."
Dans: *Bulletin des recherches historiques;* Vol. 50, no 6 (juin 1944) p. 174-192.
Note: Localisation: OONL.

— 1949 —

1505 Provost, Honorius
"Le Séminaire de Québec et les missions d'Acadie."
Dans: *Revue d'histoire de l'Amérique française;* Vol. 2, no 4 (mars 1949) p. 613-620.; ISSN: 0035-2357.
Note: Liste des documents conservés aux archives du Séminaire, documents conservés aux archives de l'Archevêché de Québec.
Localisation: AEU.

— 1951 —

1506 Carrière, Gaston
Apôtres de la plume: contribution des professeurs des facultés ecclésiastiques de l'Université d'Ottawa (1912 [i.e. 1932]-1951) à la bibliographie des Oblats de M.I. Rome: Maison générale O.M.I., 1951. 32 p.
Note: Approx. 450 entrées.
Localisation: OONL.

1507 Carrière, Gaston
"Bibliographie des Oblats de langue française au Canada."
Dans: *Études oblates;* Vol. 10, no 2 (avril-juin 1951) p. 140-152; vol. 10, no 4 (octobre-décembre 1951) p. 291-304.; ISSN: 0318-9384.
Note: Approx. 500 entrées.– Volumes, brochures et

manuscrits miméographiés écrits par les Oblats de langue française au Canada.
Localisation: OONL.

1508 **Valois, Robert**
"Étude bibliographique sur les rapports de l'Association de la propagation de la foi à Montréal."
Dans: *Revue d'histoire de l'Amérique française*; Vol. 4, no 4 (mars 1951) p. 560-567.; ISSN: 0035-2357.
Note: Localisation: OONL.

— 1955 —

1509 **Acadia University. Library**
A catalogue of the Maritime Baptist historical collection in the Library of Acadia University. Kentville, N.S.: Kentville Pub. Co., 1955. 41 p.
Note: Approx. 1,000 entries.– Covers 1800 to 1955.– Includes minutes and yearbooks, handbooks, hymnbooks, periodicals, association records, biographies, diaries, correspondence, manuscripts of individual Maritime Baptists, church records and histories, missions, theses.
Location: OONL.

— 1956 —

1510 **Côté, Jean**
"L'institution des donnés à Sainte-Marie-Des-Hurons: bibliographie."
Dans: *Revue d'histoire de l'Amérique française*; Vol. 10, no 3 (décembre 1956) p. 448-453.; ISSN: 0035-2357.
Note: Manuscrits, guides, sources contemporaines, ouvrages généraux, articles de périodiques.
Localisation: AEU.

1511 **Hamelin, Louis-Edmond; Hamelin, Colette L.**
Quelques matériaux de sociologie religieuse canadienne. Montréal: Éditions du Lévrier, 1956. 156 p. (Collection Sociologie et pastorale ; 1)
Note: 268 entrées.– Sociologie religieuse générale, sociologie religieuse et Canada français, le diocèse de Trois-Rivières, autres diocèses, liste sommaire des revues et publications.
Localisation: OONL.

— 1957 —

1512 **Lamirande, Emilien**
"Unpublished academic literature concerning the Oblate missions of the Pacific coast."
In: *Études oblates*; Vol. 16, no 4 (octobre-décembre 1957) p. 360-379.; ISSN: 0318-9384.
Note: Location: OONL.

— 1962 —

1513 **Carrière, Gaston**
"Bibliographie des professeurs oblats des facultés ecclésiastiques de l'Université d'Ottawa (1932-1961)."
Dans: *Revue de l'Université d'Ottawa*; Vol. 32 (1962) p. 81-104, 215-244.; ISSN: 0041-9206.
Note: Localisation: OONL.

1514 **Falardeau, Jean-Charles**
"Les recherches religieuses au Canada français."
Dans: *Recherches sociographiques*; Vol. 3, no 1-2 (janvier-août 1962) p. 209-228.; ISSN: 0034-1282.
Note: 127 entrées.
Localisation: AEU.

— 1963 —

1515 **Canadian Church Historical Society**
Bibliography of printed books relating to the history of the Anglican Church of Canada. [Toronto: s.n., 1963]. 11 l.

Note: Approx. 120 entries.– Contains listings for Ecclesiastical provinces of Canada, Ontario, Rupert's Land, British Columbia.
Location: OONL.

1516 **Canadian Masonic Research Association**
List of papers read before the Association, May 9, 1949-Dec. 31, 1962. [Halifax, N.S.: s.n., 1963]. [7] p.
Note: Location: OONL.

— 1965 —

1517 **Riley, Marvin P.**
The Hutterian Brethren: an annotated bibliography with special reference to South Dakota Hutterite colonies. Brookings: Sociology Department, Agricultural Experiment Station, South Dakota State University, 1965. 188 p.: map.
Note: 332 entries.– Includes many Canadian references.– Lists books, field studies, popular articles on culture, history, intergroup relations, music, religion, social organization, agriculture, legal aspects of communal life and farming.
Location: OONL.

— 1966 —

1518 **"Bibliographie [L'Église au Québec]."**
Dans: *Relations*; No 302 (février 1966) p. 63-68.; ISSN: 0034-3781.
Note: Localisation: OONL.

— 1967 —

1519 **Greenfield, Katharine**
"Reference sources for the history of the Church of England in Upper Canada, 1791-1867."
In: *Journal of the Canadian Church Historical Society*; Vol. 9, no. 3 (September 1967) p. 50-74.; ISSN: 0008-3208.
Note: 89 entries.– General church history, histories of the Church of England in Canada, travellers' accounts and pioneer journals, diocesan histories, biographical works, periodicals and periodical indexes, theses, government publications, manuscripts.
Location: OONL.

1520 **Nadeau, Charles**
Saint Joseph dans l'édition canadienne: bibliographie. Montréal: Oratoire Saint-Joseph du Mont-Royal, 1967. v, 81 p.
Note: 352 entrées.– Comprend les oeuvres qui ont été publiées, au Canada, sur Saint Joseph: volumes, brochures, manuels de piété.– Exclut articles de périodiques et journaux.
Localisation: OONL.

1521 **Principe, Walter H.**
Bibliographies and bulletins in theology. Toronto: [s.n.], 1967. 44 l.
Note: Location: OONL.

— 1969 —

1522 **Guitard, André**
Bibliographie choisie d'études récentes sur le prêtre. Montréal: Office national de clergé, 1969. 70 p.
Note: Localisation: OONL.

1523 **Sheehan, Michael M.**
"A current bibliography of Canadian church history/ Bibliographie récente de l'histoire de l'église canadienne."
In: *Canadian Catholic Historical Association. Study Sessions*; Vol. 32 (1965) p. 81-91; vol. 33 (1966) p. 51-67; vol. 34 (1967) p. 77-93; vol. 35 (1968) p. 117-135; vol. 36 (1969) p. 79-101.; ISSN: 0318-6172.

Note: Books and articles: regional history (diocese, religious orders, synods), Communions, sources, bibliographies, parish histories, institutions, biography, missions, church and the arts, church and society, church and politics/labour/social thought.– Continued by: James Hanrahan (1970-1974), Brian F. Hogan (1975-1988). Text in English and French/texte en français et en anglais.

Location: OONL.

1524 **Veilleux, Bertrand**
Bibliographie sur les relations entre l'Église et l'État au Canada français, 1791-1914. Montréal: La Bibliothèque, Centre d'Études canadiennes-françaises, 1969. 92 f.
Note: Approx. 1,350 entrées.
Localisation: OONL.

— 1970 —

1525 **Hostetler, John A.**
"A bibliography of English language materials on the Hutterian brethren."
In: *Mennonite Quarterly Review*; Vol. 44 (1970) p. 106-113.; ISSN: 0025-9373.
Note: Listing of books, pamphlets, theses, articles in periodicals and encyclopedias, government documents.– Many Canadian references.
Location: OLU.

— 1972 —

1526 **Scollard, Robert J.**
Basilian novitiates in Canada and the United States: an annotated bibliography. Toronto: Basilian Press, 1972. 40 p. (Basilian historical bulletin ; no. 8)
Note: Location: OONL.

— 1973 —

1527 **Fisher, John**
"Bibliography for the study of Eskimo religion."
In: *Anthropologica*; Vol. 15, no. 2 (1973) p. 231-271.; ISSN: 0003-5459.
Note: Approx. 500 entries.– Books, journal articles (bibliographies, indexes, abstracts).– Includes general works, introductory works (origin/pre-history/ neighbouring cultures), accounts of explorers, missionaries, studies in Eskimo culture.– Topics include Eskimo religion (ritual, mythology, shamanism, art, burial customs, games).
Location: OONL.

1528 **Goertz, Richard O.W.; Malycky, Alexander**
"German-Canadian church history: Part II: Individual congregations: a preliminary bibliography."
In: *Canadian Ethnic Studies*; Vol. 5, no. 1/2 (1973) p. 95-123.; ISSN: 0008-3496.
Note: 91 entries.– Books, chapters of books, articles, sections of articles dealing with history of individual congregations established by German-Canadians.– Focus on church life, excludes materials dealing with history of settlements.– Churches include Baptist, Lutheran, Moravian, Mennonite, Roman Catholic, Pentecostal, German Church of God.
Location: OONL.

1529 **Hanrahan, James**
"A current bibliography of Canadian church history/ Bibliographie récente de l'histoire de l'église canadienne."
In: *Canadian Catholic Historical Association. Study Sessions*; Vol. 37 (1970) p. 101-126; Vol. 38 (1971) p. 71-94; Vol. 39 (1972) p. 83-104; Vol. 40 (1973) p. 69-93.; ISSN: 0318-6172.

Note: Books and articles: regional history (diocese, religious orders, synods), Communions, sources, bibliographies, parish histories, institutions, biography, missions, church and the arts, church and society, church and politics/labour/social thought.– Continues: Michael M. Sheehan (1965-1969), continued by Brian F. Hogan (1975-1988).– Text in English and French/texte en français et en anglais.

Location: OONL.

1530 **Horvath, Maria**
A Doukhobor bibliography, based on material collected in the University of British Columbia Library. Vancouver: University of British Columbia Library, 1970-1973. 3 vol.
Note: Part 1: *Books and periodical articles*. 144 p. (Reference publication ; no. 38).– 663 entries.– In addition to works on Doukhobors in Canada, includes listings on the sect's religious beliefs, philosophy and historical origins in Russia and Europe.– Part 2: *Government publications*. 37 p. (Reference publication ; no. 33).– 245 entries.– Part 3: *The Doukhobor file: audio-visual and unpublished writings by and about the Doukhobors*. ii, 61 p. (Reference publication ; no. 43).– 120 entries.– Based on the Doukhobor File, a collection housed in the Special Collections Division of the University of British Columbia Library.– Includes unpublished manuscripts, theses, pamphlets, photographs, tapes, other audio-visual materials.
Location: OONL.

1531 **Lande, Lawrence M.**
The Moravian missions to the Eskimos of Labrador: a checklist of manuscripts and printed material from 1715 to 1967, supplemented by other works on the Eskimo of Canada. Montreal: McGill University, 1973. 32 p.: ill., facsims. (Lawrence Lande Foundation for Canadian Historical Research ; no. 7)
Note: 132 entries.
Location: OONL.

— 1974 —

1532 **Crysdale, Stewart; Montminy, Jean-Paul**
La religion au Canada: bibliographie annotée des travaux en sciences humaines des religions (1945-1970)/Religion in Canada: annotated inventory of scientific studies of religion (1945-1970). Downsview, Ont.: York University; Québec: Presses de l'Université Laval, 1974. viii, 189 p. (Histoire et sociologie de la culture ; no 8); ISBN: 0-7746-6687-0.
Note: Approx. 450 entrées.– Essais, articles de revues, thèses, ouvrages spécialisés, publiés ou simplement miméographiés: anthropologie, ethnographie, folklore, herméneutique religieuse, histoire sociale, phénoménologie, psychologie, religiologie, sociologie.
Localisation: OONL.

1533 **Lalonde, Émile; Manseau, Edith**
Guide bibliographique en sciences religieuses. 2e éd. rev. et augm. Trois-Rivières: Université du Québec à Trois-Rivières, [1974]. 31 f. (Publication / Université du Québec à Trois-Rivières, Bibliothèque ; no 1)
Note: 141 entrées.– Comprend bibliographies générales et spécialisées, ouvrages de consultation (religion et mythologies, théologie, Église, Bible, atlas bibliques), liste des périodiques.
Édition antérieure: *Guide bibliographique de l'étudiant en sciences religieuses*. 1970.

Localisation: OONL.

1534 **Lucas, Glenn**
"Canadian Protestant church history to 1973."
In: *Bulletin (United Church of Canada. Committee on Archives and History)*; No. 23 (1974) p. 5-50.; ISSN: 0824-5843.
Note: Listing of monographs on Canadian Protestant church history from first published works in 1776 to end of 1972.– Excludes works on Canadian overseas missions.– Theses are omitted for all denominations except Lutherans and Pentecostals.– Copies of most items listed accessible through the United Church Archives, Victoria University, Toronto.
Location: NSAS.

1535 **"Petite bibliographie québécoise sur les groupes nouveaux chrétiens."**
Dans: *Relations*; No 389 (janvier 1974) p. 13.; ISSN: 0034-3781.
Note: Localisation: OONL.

1536 **Voisine, Nive**
"La production des vingt dernières années en histoire de l'Église du Québec."
Dans: *Recherches sociographiques*; Vol. 15, no 1 (janvier-avril 1974) p. 97-112.; ISSN: 0034-1282.
Note: Localisation: OONL.

— 1975 —

1537 **De Valk, Alphonse**
History collection: Canadian Catholic Church: catalogue/ Collection d'histoire: l'église catholique canadienne: catalogue. Saskatoon: St. Thomas More College, University of Saskatchewan, 1971-1975. 4 vol.; ISSN: 0315-3371.
Note: Approx. 1,400 entries.– Books and pamphlets in English and French dealing with Canadian Roman Catholic Church history: general works, biographies, institutions and congregations, diocese and church histories.– Includes a listing of church periodicals and newspapers.
Location: OONL.

1538 **Garceau, Benoît**
"La philosophie analytique de la religion: contribution canadienne 1970-1975."
Dans: *Philosophiques*; Vol. 2, no 2 (octobre 1975) p. 301-339.; ISSN: 0316-2923.
Note: Localisation: OONL.

— 1976 —

1539 **Bédard, Carole**
Politique et religion au Québec depuis 1960: bibliographie. Québec: [s.n.], 1976. v, 69 f.
Note: Approx. 500 entrées.
Localisation: QQLA.

1540 **Denault, Bernard**
"Jeunes et religion au Québec: revue des recherches."
Dans: *Cahiers de pastorale scolaire*; No 6 (février 1976) p. 7-22.
Note: Localisation: OONL.

1541 **Lee, Helen F. McRae Parker**
The Helen F. McRae collection: a bibliography of Korean relations with Canadians and other western peoples, which includes a checklist of documents and reports, 1898-1975. Halifax, N.S.: School of Library Service, Dalhousie University, 1976. vii, 201 p. (Occasional papers / Dalhousie University School of Library Service ; no. 12); ISBN: 0-7703-0149-5.

Note: Lists documents, books, pictures, records and reports, taped interviews, periodicals, periodical articles, official correspondence and records pertaining to Korean-Canadian relations, Canadian missions and missionaries in Korea and Manchuria (Presbyterian and United Churches).– Edited by Doreen E. Fraser.
Location: OONL.

— 1977 —

1542 **Smucker, Donovan E.**
The sociology of Canadian Mennonites, Hutterites and Amish: a bibliography with annotations. Waterloo, Ont.: Wilfrid Laurier University Press, c1977. xvi, 232 p.: ill.; ISBN: 0-88920-052-1.
Note: 800 entries.– Books, pamphlets, articles, unpublished manuscripts in English language (a few in German) on societies of three sectarian religious groups.– Focus on Canada, with some titles from United States and Great Britain.
Supplement: ... , *volume II, 1977-1990*. 1991. xix, 194 p.; ISBN: 0-88920-999-5.– Approx. 700 entries.
Location: OONL.

1543 **Springer, Nelson P.; Klassen, A.J.**
Mennonite bibliography, 1631-1961. Scottdale, Pa.; Kitchener, Ont.: Herald Press, 1977. 2 vol.; ISBN: 0-8361-1208-3.
Note: Volume 2: *North America*. Includes books, dissertations, periodical articles.– Many references to Canadian Mennonite communities, mainly in Manitoba, Ontario and Saskatchewan.
Location: OONL.

— 1978 —

1544 **Bédard, Marc-André**
"Les Protestants en Nouvelle-France: bibliographie."
Dans: *Cahiers d'histoire*; No 31 (1978) p. 127-138.
Note: Localisation: OONL.

1545 **Boyce, Gerald E.**
The St. Andrew's chronicles: bibliography and notes. Belleville, Ont.: St. Andrew's Presbyterian Church, [1978]. 57 p.; ISBN: 0-921385-08-0.
Note: Manuscripts and printed sources dealing with the history of the Presbyterian Church in the Belleville region, Ontario.
Location: OONL.

1546 **Drake, Paul Burton**
Protestantism on the Prairies to 1977: an annotated bibliography of historical and biographical publications. Edmonton: [s.n.], 1978. vii, 114 l.
Note: 577 entries.– Published materials (including theses) from the European settlement in the Red River Colony to 1977: historical materials arranged by denominations, congregational histories, biographical materials arranged by denominations.– List of additional bibliographies.
Location: OONL.

1547 **Pincoe, Grace**
"Bibliography of historical material in Friends House Library, Toronto."
In: *Canadian Quaker History Newsletter*; No. 3 (June 1973) p. 1-4; no. 6 (December 1973) p. 2-4; no. 8 (June 1974) p. 4-6; no. 12 (June 1975) p. 1-8; no. 22 (June 1978) p. 19.; ISSN: 0319-3934.
Note: Location: OONL.

— 1980 —

1548 **Pederson, Beverley**
Living with dying: philosophical and psychological aspects of death and dying: a selected bibliography of printed and audio-visual material available at the Saskatoon Public Library. Saskatoon: Saskatoon Public Library, 1980. 62 p. (in various pagings).
Note: Lists books, magazine articles, pamphlets and clippings, audio-visual materials (fiction and non-fiction), relating to philosophy and psychology of death and dying: attitudes toward death, experience of dying, personal narratives, terminal care, ministry to dying and bereaved, bereavement and grief, concepts of immortality, ethical issues and practical considerations.
Location: OONL.

— 1981 —

1549 **Gagnon, Claude-Marie**
Les manuscrits et imprimés religieux au Québec, 1867-1960: bibliographie. Québec: Université Laval, Institut supérieur des sciences humaines, c1981. 195 p. (Collection études sur le Québec ; no 12)
Note: 1,268 entrées.– Bibliographie en sept parties: ouvrages de référence et bibliographies générales, guide et bibliographies spécialisées, principaux fonds d'archives religieuses, principales revues religieuses, biographies et autobiographies, histoires des communautés religieuses et des paroisses, manuels de dévotion et d'exercice de piété.
Localisation: OONL.

1550 **Klippenstein, Lawrence**
"Canadian Mennonite writings: a bibliographical survey, 1970-1980."
In: German-Canadian Yearbook; Vol. 6 (1981) p. 284-293.; ISSN: 0316-8603.
Note: Location: OONL.

1551 **Wiebe, Victor G.**
Alberta-Saskatchewan Mennonite and Hutterite bibliography, 1962-1981. Saskatoon: Mennonite Historical Society of Alberta and Saskatchewan, 1981. 10 p.
Note: 122 entries.– Lists books, pamphlets, university theses.– Concentrates on Mennonite and Hutterite materials published or written in Alberta or Saskatchewan, or published elsewhere if subject is Alberta/Saskatchewan.– Excludes periodical articles, non-Mennonite materials written by Mennonite authors.
Location: OONL.

— 1982 —

1552 **Schawb, Robert**
The Church in northern Canada: a bibliography. Yellowknife: Northwest Territories Archives, [c1982]. 33 p. (Sources for Northwest Territories history ; 2)
Note: 242 entries.– Books, pamphlets, government publications, periodicals articles.– Focus on Mackenzie River area of Northwest Territories, selection on history of the Church throughout NWT and Yukon.
Location: OONL.

— 1983 —

1553 **Brunkow, Robert deV.**
Religion and society in North America: an annotated bibliography. Santa Barbara, Calif.: ABC-Clio, 1983.; ISBN: 0-87436-042-0.
Note: 4,304 entries.– Scholarly studies, published primary sources, bibliographies and review essays on the history and sociology of religion in the United States and Canada since the seventeenth century.
Location: OONL.

1554 **Germain, Élisabeth**
Les ordres religieux au Québec: bilan de la recherche: [bibliographie]. Québec: Groupe de recherche en science de la religion, Université Laval, 1983. iv, 80 p.: ill. (Études et documents en sciences de la religion: dossier documentaire ; 1)
Note: 235 entrées.– Livres, thèses, articles des périodiques.– Sujets principaux: histoire (histoire sociale), sociologie, sciences humaines des religions, psychologie et éducation, administration, statistiques, bibliographie.
Localisation: OONL.

1555 **Giesbrecht, Herbert**
The Mennonite Brethren: a bibliographic guide. 2nd ed. Fresno, Calif.: Board of Christian Literature, General Conference of Mennonite Brethren Churches, 1983. iv, 99 p.
Note: Books and articles dealing with Mennonite history, traditions, religious beliefs, Church polity and practice, missions, education, biography, music and imaginative literature.– Includes many Canadian references.
Previous edition: The Mennonite Brethren: a bibliographic guide to information. 1971. 17 p.
Location: OWOBC.

1556 **Olivier, Réjean**
La boîte à prières: boîte de brochures conservées par la supérieure des Petites soeurs de la Sainte-Famille du Collège de L'Assomption et remises au bibliothécaire avant leur départ en 1980. L'Assomption, Québec: Collège de L'Assomption, Bibliothèque, 1983. 8 f.; ISBN: 2-920248-77-4.
Note: 61 entrées.
Localisation: OONL.

— 1984 —

1557 **Boivin, Henri-Bernard; Jean, Claire; Bosa, Réal**
Histoire des communautés religieuses au Québec: bibliographie. Montréal: Bibliothèque nationale du Québec, 1984. 157, [16] p.: ill.; ISBN: 2-551-06457-0.
Note: 651 entrées.– La période couverte va des débuts de la colonie jusqu'à nos jours.– Les titres inclus ne devaient pas avoir obligatoirement paru au Québec, mais une partie importante de leur contenu devait être consacrée à ce territoire pour être inclus.– Cependant les activités des missionaires québécois et des missions de communautés québécoises ont également été admises.
Localisation: OONL.

1558 **Prud'homme, François**
Les publications des Clercs de Saint-Viateur. Montréal: Clercs de Saint-Viateur, 1984. xxi, 344, 58 p.: ill., fac-sim. (Cahiers du Regroupement des archivistes religieux ; no 1); ISBN: 2-920597-00-X.
Note: 4,174 entrées.– Liste en quatre parties: la congrégation, les provinces et leurs établissements (oeuvres); publications particulières et biographies de Clercs de Saint-Viateur; manuels scolaires; périodiques.
Éditions antérieures:
Trudeau, Paul-Albert; Prud'homme, François; Caron, A. Bibliographie viatorienne. 1967. 222 f.
Trudeau, Paul-Albert. Bibliographie viatorienne: travail présenté à l'École des [sic] bibliothécaires, Université de

Montréal, le 11 septembre 1939. 1939. 22 f.
Supplément: 1984. 13 p.
Localisation: OONL.

— 1985 —

1559 **Choquette, Diane**
New religious movements in the United States and Canada: a critical assessment and annotated bibliography. Westport, Conn.: Greenwood Press, 1985. xi, 235 p. (Bibliographies and indexes in religious studies ; no. 5; ISSN: 0742-6836); ISBN: 0-313-28772-7.
Note: 738 entries.– List of books and articles about movements having roots in 1960s and later.– Includes reference works; interdisciplinary collected essays; historical, anthropological, sociological, legal, psychological, psychiatric, theological and religious studies; personal accounts.
Location: OONL.

1560 **Lacroix, Benoît; Grammond, Madeleine**
Religion populaire au Québec: typologie des sources: bibliographie sélective (1900-1980). Québec: Institut québécois de recherche sur la culture, 1985. 175 p. (Instruments de travail / Institut québécois de recherche sur la culture ; no 10); ISBN: 2-89224-048-4.
Note: 961 entrées.– Comprend livres et brochures, articles de périodiques et de volumes, colloques, congrès, sessions savantes, thèses, manuscrits, documents audiovisuels.
Localisation: OONL.

1561 **Minion, Robin**
Religions of the circumpolar north. Edmonton: Boreal Institute for Northern Studies, University of Alberta, 1985. 92 p. (Boreal Institute for Northern Studies Bibliographic series ; no. 15; ISSN: 0824-8192); ISBN: 0-919058-49-3.
Note: 260 entries.– Produced from Boreal Institute Library SPIRES database.– Includes monographs, theses, government documents, consultants' reports, conference proceedings, periodicals.– BINS series produced monthly from January 1984 to May 1986 (no. 29).– Online access: *Boreal Northern Titles (BNT)*, available through QL Systems Limited.
Location: OONL.

— 1986 —

1562 **Grammond, Madeleine; Lacroix, Benoît**
"Mort et religion traditionnelle au Québec: bibliographie."
Dans: *Bulletin d'histoire de la culture matérielle*; No 23 (printemps 1986) p. 56-64.; ISSN: 0703-489X.
Note: Localisation: OONL.

— 1987 —

1563 **Arndt, John**
Christianity in Canada: a bibliography of books and articles to 1985. Waterloo, Ont.: Library, Wilfrid Laurier University, 1987. 195 p.: ill.
Note: Approx. 1,900 entries.– Monographs, journal articles and academic dissertations dealing with the history of the Christian churches in Canada.– Excludes local or congregational histories.
Location: OONL.

1564 **Harrison, Alice W.**
Checklist of United Church of Canada publications, 1925-1986. Halifax, N.S.: Atlantic School of Theology Library, 1987. 2 vol.
Note: Approx. 1,200 entries.– Includes published,

catalogued material only.– Excludes government documents, manuscripts.
Location: OONL.

— 1988 —

1565 **Anderson, Alan B.**
German, Mennonite and Hutterite communities in Saskatchewan: an inventory of sources. Saskatoon: Saskatchewan German Council, 1988. 17, 11, 4 p.
Note: Approx. 400 entries.– Books, local histories, research reports, monographs and booklets, graduate theses, bibliographies, government documents, journal articles, chapters in books, audiovisual materials in English and German dealing with German, Mennonite and Hutterite communities of Saskatchewan.
Location: OONL.

1566 **Hogan, Brian F.**
"A current bibliography of Canadian church history/ Bibliographie récente de l'histoire de l'église canadienne."
In: *Canadian Catholic Historical Association. Study Sessions*; Vol. 42 (1975) p. 110-141; vol. 43 (1976) p. 91-119; vol. 44 (1977) p. 111-144; vol. 45 (1978) p. 101-141; vol. 46 (1979) p. 99-137; vol. 47 (1980) p. 69-108; vol. 48 (1981) p. 101-139; vol. 49 (1982) p. 135-167; vol. 50 (1983) p. 655-691; vol. 51 (1984) p. 145-199; vol. 53 (1986) p. 121-148; vol. 55 (1988) p. 149-193.; ISSN: 0318-6172.
Note: Books and articles: regional history (diocese, religious orders, synods), Communions, sources, bibliographies, parish histories, institutions, biography, missions, church and the arts, church and society, church and politics/labour/social thought.– Continues: Michael M. Sheehan (1965-1969), James Hanrahan (1970-1973).– Text in English and French/texte en français et en anglais.
Location: OONL.

1567 **Laflèche, Guy**
"Bibliographie analytique et critique des saints Martyrs canadiens."
Dans: *Les saints Martyrs canadiens*. Laval, Québec: Singulier, 1988. P. 83-227.; ISBN: 2-920580-01-9.
Note: 603 entrées.– Bibliographies, sources et les études scientifiques, historiographie critique, ouvrages spécialisés (biographies, oeuvres littéraires, chants et chansons, cinéma).
Localisation: OONL.

— 1989 —

1568 **Griffin-Allwood, Philip G.A.; Rawlyk, George A.; Zeman, Jarold K.**
Baptists in Canada, 1760-1990: a bibliography of selected printed resources in English. Hantsport, N.S.: Published by Lancelot Press for Acadia Divinity College and the Baptist Historical Committee of the United Baptist Convention of the Atlantic Provinces, 1989. xix, 266 p. (Baptist heritage in Atlantic Canada: documents and studies ; 10); ISBN: 0-88999-399-8.
Note: 1,383 entries.– Books, pamphlets, articles, theses, manuscripts dealing with Canadian Baptist heritage: historical development and current divisions, biographical sources and studies, topical studies (ecumenism, education, evangelism, social issues, etc.), historiography and reference works, list of periodicals, list of archives/ libraries/schools.– Excludes histories of local churches, Baptist associations and summer camps, teaching materials and organizational manuals for Sunday schools, promotional materials, published minutes.

Location: OONL.

1569 **Lacroix, Benoît; Grammond, Madeleine**
Canada: Tome 1: Le Québec. Turnhout (Belgique): Brepols; Montréal: Bellarmin, [1989]. 153 p. (La Piété populaire: répertoire bibliographique); ISBN: 2-89007-690-3.
Note: 756 entrées.– Livres, articles de revues, thèses et travaux universitaires concernant la piété populaire.– Comprend une introduction en anglais/introduction in English.
Localisation: OONL.

1570 **Mathien, Thomas**
Bibliography of philosophy in Canada: a research guide/ Bibliographie de la philosophie au Canada: une[sic] guide à recherche. Kingston, Ont.: R.P. Frye, c1989. 157 p. (Frye library of Canadian philosophy supplementary ; vol. 1); ISBN: 0-919741-74-6.
Note: 1,110 entries.– Contains a guide to research, a list of secondary sources (historical pieces, bio-bibliographies) and published works by early English Canadian philosophers (active before 1950).– Excludes obituaries and memorial studies about deceased philosophers.– Text in English and French/texte en français et en anglais.
Location: OONL.

1571 **Redekop, Calvin W.**
A bibliography of Mennonites in Waterloo County and Ontario. Waterloo, Ont.: Institute of Anabaptist and Mennonite Studies, Conrad Grebel College, University of Waterloo, c1989. 19 p.
Note: Approx. 280 entries.– Books, journal and newspaper articles, encyclopedia articles, theses, unpublished papers.
Location: OONL.

— 1990 —

1572 **McGowan, Mark G.**
"Coming out of the cloister: some reflections on developments in the study of religion in Canada, 1980-1990."
In: *International Journal of Canadian Studies*; No. 1-2 (Spring-Fall 1990) p. 175-202.; ISSN: 1180-3991.
Note: Location: OONL.

1573 **Steckelberg, Warren Dean**
Lutheran rites in North America [microform]: an annotated bibliography of the hymnals, altar books, and selected manuals produced by or for Lutherans in North America from the late eighteenth century to the present. Ottawa: National Library of Canada, 1990. 5 microfiches (Canadian theses ; no. 51212); ISBN: 0-315-51212-1.
Note: Includes a section "The Nova Scotia Synod."
Location: OONL.

— 1991 —

1574 **Codignola, Luca**
Guide des documents relatifs à l'Amérique du Nord française et anglaise dans les archives de la Sacrée Congrégation de la Propagande à Rome, 1622-1799. Ottawa: Archives nationales du Canada, c1991. xi, 252 p.; ISBN: 0-660-93101-X.
Note: Ce guide présente une bibliographie des ouvrages relatifs à l'histoire religieuse de la période concernée ainsi qu'un index de les noms propres mentionés dans les descriptions des documents.
English title: *Guide to documents relating to French and British North America in the archives of the Sacred Congrega-*

tion "de Propaganda Fide" in Rome, 1622-1799.
Localisation: OONL.

1575 **Codignola, Luca**
Guide to documents relating to French and British North America in the archives of the Sacred Congregation "de Propaganda Fide" in Rome, 1622-1799. Ottawa: National Archives of Canada, c1991. viii, 250 p ; ISBN: 0 660 13758 5.
Note: Includes a bibliography of publications related to the religious history of the period covered and an index to all proper names mentioned in the *Calendar*.
Titre en français: *Guide des documents relatifs à l'Amérique du Nord française et anglaise dans les archives de la Sacrée Congrégation de la Propagande à Rome, 1622-1799.*
Location: OONL.

— 1870 —

1576 **Dawson Brothers (Montreal, Quebec)**
Books published by Dawson Brothers. Montreal: Dawson Brothers, [1870]. 33, 3, [26] p.
Note: Microform: CIHM Microfiche series ; no. 02617; ISBN: 0-665-02617-X. 1 microfiche (38 fr.).
Location: OONL.

— 1894 —

1577 **Wright, John**
Early bibles of America: being a descriptive account of bibles published in the United States, Mexico and Canada. New York: T. Whittaker, 1894. xv, 483 p.
Note: Microform: CIHM Microfiche series ; no. 39029; ISBN: 0-665-39029-7. 7 microfiches (298 fr.).
Location: OWA.

— 1896 —

1578 **Wright, John**
Early prayer books of America: being a descriptive account of prayer books published in the United States, Mexico and Canada. St. Paul, Minn.: Press of Evans & Bissell, 1896. xv, 492 p.: ill., facsims., pl.
Note: Microform: CIHM Microfiche series ; no. 29712; ISBN: 0-665-29712-2. 7 microfiches (304 fr.).
Location: OTMCL.

— 1949 —

1579 **Wilson, Lucy Roberta**
Regional and county library service in Canada: a bibliography. Ottawa: Canadian Library Association, 1949. 13 l.
Note: Location: OHM.

— 1954 —

1580 **Wallace, William Stewart**
The Ryerson imprint: a check-list of the books and pamphlets published by The Ryerson Press since the foundation of the House in 1829. Toronto: Ryerson Press, [1954]. 141 p.
Note: Approx. 2,300 entries.
Location: OONL.

— 1955 —

1581 **Clarke, Irwin & Company Limited**
Twenty-five years of Canadian publishing: W.H. Clarke: a memorial exhibition, 1930-1955. Toronto: 1955. 28 p.
Note: Contains a brief biographical sketch of W.H. Clarke, together with lists of publications of Clarke, Irwin, 1931-1955, and Oxford University Press (Canadian Branch), 1937-1949.
From Lochhead.– No location.

— 1956 —

1582 **A catalogue of the William Colgate Printing Collection: books, pamphlets, drawings.** Montreal: McGill University Library, 1956. 25 p.
Note: Many Canadian references, including the work of Thoreau MacDonald and William Colgate.
Location: OONL.

— 1957 —

1583 **Lamb, William Kaye**
"Seventy-five years of Canadian bibliography."
In: *Proceedings and Transactions of the Royal Society of Canada*; Series 3, vol. 51, section 2 (1957) p. 1-11.; ISSN: 0316-4616.
Note: Historical review of bibliographical literature in Canada.
Location: AEU.

— 1961 —

1584 **Desrochers, Edmond**
"Bibliographie sommaire sur la profession de bibliothécaire."
Dans: *Bulletin de l'Association canadienne des bibliothécaires de langue française*; Vol. 7, no 1 (mars 1961) p. 18-25.; ISSN: 0004-5314.
Note: 182 entrées.
Localisation: OONL.

1585 **Times Bookshop (London, England)**
Canadian printed books, 1752-1961: an exhibition. London: Times Bookshop, 1961. 27 p.
Note: Catalogue of exhibition of Canadian imprints, held in the Antiquarian Department, Times Bookshop, July 11-22, 1961.
Location: OONL.

— 1962 —

1586 **Adamson, Edith**
Public library finance: a literature review. Ottawa: Canadian Library Association, 1962. ii, 9 l. (Occasional paper / Canadian Library Association ; no. 36)
Note: Bibliography, l. 5-9.– Thesis: M.L.S., McGill University.
Location: OONL.

1587 **Tanghe, Raymond**
"Sources primordiales en bibliographie."
Dans: *Cahiers de la Société bibliographique du Canada*; Vol. 1 (1962) p. 49-56.; ISSN: 0067-6896.
Note: Localisation: OONL.

— 1963 —

1588 **Chartrand, Georges-Aimé**
"Bibliographie des publications de l'A.C.B.L.F., 1943-1963."
Dans: *Bulletin de l'Association canadienne des bibliothécaires de langue française*; Vol. 9, no 2 (juin 1963) p. 104-108.; ISSN: 0004-5314.
Note: 26 entrées.
Localisation: OONL.

— 1968 —

1589 **Anderson, Beryl L.**
Basic cataloguing tools for use in Canadian libraries. Ottawa: Canadian Library Association, 1968. 28 l. (Occasional paper / Canadian Library Association ; no. 59)
Note: "A report to the CLA Technical Services Section."- Includes Canadian references.

Location: OONL.

— 1969 —

1590 **Gnarowski, Michael**
"Contact Press, 1952-1967: a check list of titles."
In: *Culture*; Vol. 30, no. 3 (September 1969) p. 227-232.;
ISSN: 0317-2066.
Note: Chronological listing according to year of publication of all titles "clearly identifiable" as Contact Press publications.
Location: AEU.

— 1970 —

1591 **Anschutz, Martha**
A preliminary list of writings on Canadian archives and records management. Montreal: University Archives, McGill University, 1970. 27 l.
Note: Approx. 430 entries.
Supplement: Tremblay, Emilien. 1972. 21 p.
Location: OONL.

— 1971 —

1592 **Bibliothèque nationale du Québec**
Édition Erta: [exposition, mars-avril 1971]. Montréal: Ministère des affaires culturelles, 1971. 34 p.: ill.
Note: 33 entrées.
Localisation: OONL.

— 1972 —

1593 **British Columbia School Librarians' Association**
Index to BCSLA publications. Vancouver: British Columbia School Librarians' Association, 1970-1972. 3 vol.; ISSN: 0227-3446.
Note: Publications list.– Ceased with 1971-72 issue.
Location: OONL.

1594 **Dalhousie University. Library**
A bibliography for examination of forms of training for scientific and technical work. Halifax: Dalhousie University Library, 1972. 69 l. (Occasional paper / Dalhousie University Library ; no. 1)
Note: Approx. 1,200 entries.– Articles dealing with education and training of information workers in the fields of library science, information science, documentation and computer science.– Includes a number of Canadian references.
Location: OONL.

1595 **Mercure, Gérard**
"Microdocumentation: bibliographie."
Dans: *Bulletin de l'Association canadienne des bibliothécaires de langue française*; Vol. 18, no 4 (décembre 1972) p. 263-266.; ISSN: 0004-5314.
Note: Inclut un nombre d'ouvages canadiens.
Localisation: OONL.

1596 **Rivet-Panaccio, Colette; Awad, Amal; Cardinal, Robert**
Les bibliothèques canadiennes à l'ère de l'automatisation: synthèse bibliographique 1970-1972. Montréal: École de bibliothéconomie, Université de Montréal, 1972. 54 p. (Documentation en diagonale ; no 1)
Note: 75 entrées.
Localisation: OLU.

1597 **Saskatchewan Provincial Library. Bibliographic Services Division**
Books on library science. 2nd ed. Regina: The Library, 1972. 193 p.
Note: Approx. 2,250 entries.– Contains a substantial number of Canadian references.
Previous edition: 1971. 105 p.

Supplement: *Books on library service: first supplement.* 1971. 27 p.
Location: OONL.

— 1973 —

1598 **Bard, Thérèse, et al.**
Informatique: [bibliographie de base]. 3e éd. rev. et mise à jour. Montréal: Centre de la bibliographie, Centrale des bibliothèques, 1973. 147 p. (Cahiers de bibliographie / Centrale des bibliothèques, Centre de la bibliographie ; no 1; ISSN: 0383-4344); ISBN: 0-88523-002-7.
Note: Localisation: OONL.

1599 **Bergersen, Moira; Frigon, Claire**
"Management literature for librarians: an annotated list."
In: *Canadian Library Journal*; Vol. 30, no. 3 (May-June 1973) p. 227-233.; ISSN: 0008-4352.
Note: Includes Canadian references.
Location: AEU.

1600 **Dupuis, Onil**
Le centre de ressources: une bibliographie/Resource centers: a bibliography. Montréal: Cogito, 1973. 16 f.
Note: Approx. 150 entrées.– Volumes, articles, rapports et brochures, thèses, films.– La période couverte est de 1968 à 1973.– Inclut un nombre d'ouvrages canadiens en français et en anglais.– Text en français et en anglais/text in English and French.
Localisation: OONL.

1601 **Lavoie, Cécile**
312 volumes de bibliothéconomie et sciences connexes: liste bibliographique. Montréal: Fides, 1973. 27 p.
Note: 312 entrées.– Inclut un nombre considérable d'ouvrages canadiens.
Suppléments:
38 volumes de bibliothéconomie et sciences connexes: supplément 1973: liste bibliographique. 1973. [3] f.
97 volumes de bibliothéconomie et sciences connexes: liste bibliographique. 1974. [7] f.
Localisation: OONL.

1602 **Mennie-de Varennes, Kathleen; Gourdes, Irénée**
Bibliographie sur la bibliotechnique. Québec: Ministère des terres et forêts, Bibliothèque, 1973. 26 f.
Note: 213 entrées.– Comprend un nombre considérable d'ouvrages canadiens.
Localisation: OONL.

— 1974 —

1603 **Canadian Nurses' Association**
Libraries: resources and facilities: selected references/ Bibliothèques: ressources et facilités: bibliographie choisie. [Ottawa]: Canadian Nurses' Association, 1974. 29 l.
Note: 403 entries.– Lists books, documents, periodical articles on medical and hospital/patients' libraries: planning, history, automation, user education, administration.– Includes a substantial number of Canadian titles.
Location: OONL.

1604 **Cheda, Sherrill**
"Women in the library profession."
In: *Emergency Librarian*; Vol. 1, no. 5-6 (June-August 1974) p. 28-32.; ISSN: 0315-8888.
Note: Includes Canadian references.
Location: AEU.

1605 **Lamonde, Yvan**
"La recherche sur l'histoire de l'imprimé et du livre québécois."
Dans: *Revue d'histoire de l'Amérique française*; Vol. 28, no 3 (décembre 1974) p. 405-414.; ISSN: 0035-2357.
Note: Localisation: OONL.

1606 **McGill University. Archives**
Near-print publications of the McGill University Archives. Montreal: McGill University, 1974. 10 p.
Note: 87 entries.
Location: OONL.

1607 **Metropolitan Toronto Library Board**
Checklist of books presented by the Quebec Government to the Provincial Library Service of Ontario/Répertoire des livres offerts par le gouvernement [sic] du Québec au Provincial Library Service de l'Ontario. Toronto: Metropolitan Toronto Library Board, 1974. 77 p.
Note: Liste de livres français publiés au Québec.
En tête du titre: Metropolitan Toronto Bilingual Project.
Location: OONL.

1608 **Tratt, Grace**
Check list of Canadian small presses: English language. Halifax, N.S.: University Libraries; School of Library Service, Dalhousie University, 1974. 153 l. (Occasional papers / Dalhousie University Libraries and Dalhousie University School of Library Service ; no. 6; ISSN: 0318-7403)
Note: Lists publications of small, non-commercial presses.– Information includes name of founder, founding date, first publication, present owners/address, list of publications.– List of selected sources.– Geographic index.
Location: OONL.

— 1975 —

1609 **Beauvais, Gisèle D.; Lallier-Millot, Louise; St-Pierre, Normand**
Bibliographie: cours en archivistique/Bibliography: archives course. [Ottawa]: Archives publiques du Canada, 1975. 123 f.
Note: 1,176 entrées.– Manuels et ouvrages généraux, organisation et administration, la profession d'archiviste, histoire des archives, description et instruments de recherche, informatique, numismatique, généalogie, archives municipales/provinciales, archives spécialisées.– Inclut un nombre considérable d'ouvrages canadiens.
Supplément: Héroux, Réjean W. ... : supplément/ ... : supplément. 1976. 35 p.
Localisation: OONL.

1610 **Nova Scotia Provincial Library. Reference Services Section**
Professional reading materials. Halifax: Reference Services Section, Nova Scotia Provincial Libraries, 1975. 309 p.
Note: Includes Canadian references.
Previous editions:
Professional literature collection. Halifax: Provincial Library, 1963. 66 l.
1958. 40 p.
Location: OONL.

1611 **Schwebke, Paul**
Canadian library resources: a bibliography. [Ottawa, Ont.: Paul Schwebke, c1975].

Note: 2,513 entries.– Books, serials, government publications, pamphlets, periodical articles in reprint.
Location: OONL.

1612 **Stuart-Stubbs, Basil**
Étude et interprétation des ouvrages portant sur le prêt entre bibliothèques. Vancouver: University of British Columbia, Bibliothèque, 1975. 230 f.
Note: Histoire, évolution des codes, apparition des réseaux, prêt entre bibliothèques aujourd'hui: techniques et technologie, études récentes et faites nouveaux (importance des prêts, contenu, coûts).– Concentrés sur les ouvrages nord-américains (États-Unis).– Inclut quelques références canadiennes.
English title: *A survey and interpretation of the literature of interlibrary loan.*
Localisation: OONL.

1613 **Stuart-Stubbs, Basil**
A survey and interpretation of the literature of interlibrary loan. Vancouver: University of British Columbia Library, 1975. 158 l.
Note: History, evolution of codes, emergence of networks, contemporary interlibrary loan: technique and technology, recent surveys and developments (volume, content, costs).– Emphasis on current North American literature, particularly that of the United States.– Includes some Canadian references.
Titre en français: *Étude et interprétation des ouvrages portant sur le prêt entre bibliothèques.*
Location: OONL.

1614 **Union list of manuscripts in Canadian repositories/ Catalogue collectif des manuscrits des archives canadiennes.** 2nd ed., rev. and enl. Ottawa: Public Archives Canada, 1975. 2 vol.
Note: Approx. 26,000 entries from 171 archival repositories.– Lists collections of papers under names of individuals, corporate bodies, government agencies which received, created or accumulated the papers.– Provides information regarding the type of papers, inclusive dates, linear extent, location, ownership of originals and available finding aids.– Includes a catalogue by repositories and a subject index.– Text in English and French/texte en français et en anglais.
Previous edition: Gordon, Robert S. 1968. x, 734 p.
Supplements:
... : supplement, 1976/ ... : supplément, 1976. 1976. xxi, 322 p.
... : supplement, 1977-78/ ... : supplément, 1977-78. 1979. xxviii, 236 p.
... : supplement, 1979-80/ ... : supplément, 1979-80. 1982. xxiv, 243 p.; ISBN: 0-660-51601-2.
Yurkiw, Peter. ... : supplement, 1981-82/ ... : supplément, 1981-82. 1985. xxv, 616 p.; ISBN: 0-660-53090-2.
Location: OONL.

— 1976 —

1615 **Amey, L.J.**
"The combination school and public library: a bibliography with special emphasis on the Canadian experience."
In: *Canadian Library Journal*; Vol. 33, no. 3 (June 1976) p. 263-267.; ISSN: 0008-4352.
Note: Books and journal articles, newspaper articles dealing with concept of shared school/public library.
Location: AEU.

1616 **Côté, Lise**
Bibliographie sur la Bibliothèque nationale du Québec. Montréal: Ministère des affaires culturelles, Bibliothèque nationale du Québec, 1976. 6, 1, 4 p.
Note: 147 entrées.
Localisation: OONL.

1617 **Drolet, Gaëtan**
Bibliographie de publications officielles relatives aux archives et à la gestion des documents. Montréal: Faculté des études supérieures, École de bibliothéconomie, 1976. ii, 15 f.
Note: Publications sur l'administration des archives et la gestion des documents, les guides de base et les manuels d'organisation: Québec, Canada, États-Unis.
Localisation: OONL.

— 1977 —

1618 **Brault, Jean-Rémi; Auger, Roland**
"La bibliographie au Québec."
Dans: *Livre, bibliothèque et culture québécoise: mélanges offerts à Edmond Desrochers, s.j.* Montréal: ASTED, 1977. P. 161-190.; ISBN: 0-88606-000-1.
Note: Localisation: OONL.

1619 **Burdenuk, Gene**
Annotated guide to selection sources for secondary school resource centres. Toronto: Ontario Library Association, 1977. 30 p.
Note: Approx. 125 entries.– Arranged in six sections: "General bibliographic aids," "Bibliographies of selection aids," "Basic selection aids," "Specialized selection aids," "Aids to the selection of periodicals," "Current reviewing periodicals."- Includes Canadian references in all sections.
Location: OONL.

1620 **Catalogue collectif des presses universitaires de langue française.** Montréal: Association internationale des presses universitaires de langue française, c1977. 135 p.; ISBN: 0-919012-25-6.
Note: Localisation: OONL.

1621 **Ducharme, Jacques; Plante, Denis**
Catalogue des ouvrages traitant d'archivistique et de sujets connexes. Montréal: Secrétariat général de l'Université de Montréal, 1977. v, 238 p. (Publication / Université de Montréal, Service des archives ; no 25)
Note: Approx. 3,400 entrées.– Livres, brochures, périodiques.– Comporte des références canadiennes.
Localisation: OONL.

1622 **Klement, Susan**
"Selected annotated bibliography of articles relevant to alternatives in librarianship."
In: *Canadian Library Journal*; Vol. 34, no. 2 (April 1977) p. 137-140.; ISSN: 0008-4352.
Note: Includes Canadian references.
Location: AEU.

1623 **Robinson, Christopher D.**
PRECIS: an annotated bibliography, 1969-1977. 2nd ed. Toronto: C.D. Robinson, 1977. vi, 26 l.
Note: Includes Canadian references.
Previous edition: *PRECIS: an annotated bibliography, 1969-1975.* 1976. iv, 11 l.
Location: OONL.

1624 **Rousseau, Denis**
"L'édition en bibliothéconomie au Québec."
Dans: *Livre, bibliothèque et culture québécoise: mélanges offerts à Edmond Desrochers, s.j.* Montréal: ASTED, 1977. P.

219-267.; ISBN: 0-88606-000-1.
Note: 294 entrées.
Localisation: OONL.

— 1978 —

1625 **Koltun, Lilly, et al.**
"The photograph: an annotated bibliography for archivists."
In: *Archivaria*; No. 5 (Winter 1977-1978) p. 124-140.; ISSN: 0318-6954.
Note: Guide for archivists required to handle photographic material.– Topics include general photographic history, technique and image arrangement, photographic interpretation, copyright, storage/preservation/conservation, cataloguing, exhibiting and publishing, periodical literature.– Contains a substantial listing of Canadian material.
Location: AEU.

1626 **Renaud-Frigon, Claire**
Library and information science dictionaries and glossaries: a selective list based on National Library of Canada holdings/Dictionnaires et glossaires d'informatique et de bibliothéconomie: liste sélective basée sur la collection de la Bibliothèque nationale du Canada. Ottawa: National Library of Canada, 1978. [13] p.
Note: Includes Canadian references.
Location: OONL.

1627 **"A retrospective bibliography [on archives]."**
In: *Archivaria*; Vol. 1, no. 1 (Winter 1975-76) p. 131-142; vol. 1, no. 2 (Summer 1976) p. 126-141; No. 3 (Winter 1976-77) p. 150-157; no. 4 (Summer 1977) p. 256-268; no. 5 (Winter 1977-78) p. 240-254; no. 6, (Summer 1978) p. 221-268.; ISSN: 0318-6954.
Note: Books, articles, papers on archives and auxiliary sciences in six sections: "General" (bibliography, manuals, etc.), "Administrative archives," "Historical archives" (manuscripts and non-manuscripts), "Specialized archives" (business, church, etc.), "Technical services," "Auxiliary sciences" (heraldry, genealogy, numismatics).– Coverage is international, with a substantial selection of Canadian material.
Location: OONL.

1628 **South Central Regional Library System (Ont.)**
"Prime resort" catalogue: a professional collection housed in the Hamilton Public Library. [Hamilton, Ont.]: South Central Regional Library System, 1978. 476 p.
Note: Approx. 1,200 entries.– Books about libraries and librarianship: acquisitions, cataloguing, classification, library administration, library automation, library planning, library schools and training, etc.– Includes a substantial number of Canadian references.
Supplement: 1980. 102 p.
Location: OONL.

1629 **Vient de paraître: bulletin du livre au Canada français.** Montréal: Beauchemin, 1965-1978. 14 vol.; ISSN: 0042-5656.
Note: Périodicité multiple.– Ne paraît plus après le vol. 14, no 4, 1978.
Localisation: OONL.

— 1979 —

1630 **Brunet-Sabourin, Manon**
Documents pour une histoire de l'édition au Québec avant 1900: bibliographie analytique. Montréal: M. Brunet-Sabourin, 1979. vii, 278 f.

Note: 651 entrées.– Mémoire, M.A., Université de Montréal.

Localisation: OOU.

1631 **Cheng, Ivy; Macgregor, Robert**
Professional collection. Kingston [Ont.]: Lake Ontario Regional Library System, 1979. 88 p.
Note: Approx. 500 entries.– Books and reports in the fields of librarianship and information science.– Includes a substantial number of Canadian references.
Location: OONL.

1632 **Core reference for Manitoba schools, K-12: a selection guide for school libraries.** Winnipeg: Manitoba Department of Education, School Library Services, 1979. 59 p. (School library guide / Manitoba Department of Education, School Library Services ; no. 3)
Note: Approx. 300 entries.– Primarily a reference collection for students, rather than a resource collection for teachers and librarians.– Substantial Canadian content.
Location: OONL.

1633 **Drolet, Gaëtan**
Les bibliothèques universitaires du Québec: essai de bibliographie. [Québec]: Conférence des recteurs et des principaux des universités du Québec, 1979. 197 p.; ISBN: 2-920079-00-X.
Note: 1,945 entrées.– La période couverte est de 1960 à 1975.– Inclut guides du lecteur, de l'usager ou d'utilisation de la bibliothèque, guides bibliographiques, listes de périodiques, de nouvelles acquisitions, bulletins de nouvelles, catalogues de documents audio-visuels, rapports annuels.– Exclut documents qui sont strictement de régie interne (procès-verbaux, rapports de sous-comités, enquêtes internes, etc.).
Localisation: OONL.

1634 **Kotin, David B.**
"Graphic Publishers and the bibliographer: an introduction and checklist."
In: *Papers of the Bibliographical Society of Canada*; Vol. 18 (1979) p. 47-54.; ISSN: 0067-6896.
Note: Brief history of Graphic Publishers, founder Henry C. Miller, with checklist of Graphic and associated imprints, 1926 to 1932.
Location: OONL.

1635 **Larouche, Irma**
National Library of Canada: a bibliography/Bibliothèque nationale du Canada: une bibliographie. Ottawa: Reference and Bibliography Section, National Library of Canada, 1979. xxiii, 179 p.; ISBN: 0-660-50210-0.
Note: 656 entries.– Covers 1882 to 1978.– Includes briefs, interviews, monographs, papers, official publications (debates, laws, reports, Royal commissions), periodical and newspaper articles.– Text in English and French/ texte en anglais et en français.
Location: OONL.

1636 **Prince Edward Island. Provincial Library**
Professional books for school librarians available from the Prince Edward Island Provincial Library. Charlottetown: Prince Edward Island Provincial Library, 1979. 63, [9] p.
Note: Approx. 300 entries.– Includes Canadian references.
Location: OONL.

— 1980 —

1637 **Broten, Delores; Birdsall, Peter**
Studies in the book trade. Victoria, B.C.: CANLIT, c1980. 30 p.; ISBN: 0-920566-10-3.
Note: Approx. 125 entries.– Companion bibliography to: *Paper phoenix: a history of book publishing in English Canada.* Victoria: CANLIT; 1980. 84 p.– Omits material on copyright, regional histories of Canadian libraries, sources in trade journals, house organs, business periodicals, opinion pieces and letters to the editor, briefs from book trade organizations.
Location: OONL.

1638 **Dupuis, Susan L.; Perron-Croteau, Lise**
List of archival literature in the Public Archives Library/ Répertoire d'ouvrages et articles traitant d'archivistique conservés à la Bibliothèque des Archives publiques. [Ottawa]: Public Archives Canada, 1980. 111 p.
Note: Approx. 3,600 entries.– Lists books and journal articles in the field of archives and related sciences: records management, media archives, cartographical archives, film and photographic archives, sound archives, institutional archives, technical services.– International coverage with a substantial listing of Canadian titles.– Text in English and French/texte en français et en anglais.
Previous edition: *Bibliography of archival literature in the Public Archives of Canada/Bibliographie d'ouvrages et d'articles traitant d'archivistique conservés à la Bibliothèque des Archives publiques du Canada.* 1978. 102 p.– Approx. 2,000 entries.
Location: OONL.

1639 **Fleming, Patricia Lockhart**
A history of publishing in Toronto, 1841-1978, with a descriptive bibliography of imprints. London, (Eng.): [s.n.], 1980.
Note: Thesis: Ph.D., University of London.
Location: OONL.

1640 **Hall, Agnez; Ruthven, Patricia; Swanick, Eric L.**
An inventory of New Brunswick indexing projects/ Inventaire des projets d'indexation en cours au Nouveau-Brunswick. Fredericton: Council of Head Librarians of New Brunswick, 1980. 51 p.; ISBN: 0-9690287-1-7.
Note: 73 entries.– Indexes to newspapers, periodicals, map collections, subject indexes from various sources, genealogical indexes (cemeteries, etc.), correspondence.– Text in English and French/texte en français et en anglais.
Location: OONL.

1641 **Oak, Lydia**
Health science libraries: selected references/ Bibliothèques dans le domaine de la santé: bibliographie sélective. Ottawa: National Library of Canada, 1980. 5 p. (Bibliographies / Library Documentation Centre; ISSN: 0226-4226)
Note: Approx. 50 entries.– General works, standards, hospital libraries, clinical libraries, automation.– Includes Canadian references.
Supplement: Ozaki, Hiroko. *Health sciences libraries: selected references, 1981-1984/Bibliothèques des sciences de la santé: bibliographie sélective, 1981-1984.* 1985. 24 p.– Supplement includes a substantial number of Canadian references.
Location: OONL.

1642 **Saskatchewan. Department of Education**
Materials of interest to school librarians: a bibliography for school librarians. Regina: Saskatchewan Education, 1980. 12 p.
Note: 27 entries.– Includes Canadian references.
Location: OONL.

1643 **Saskatchewan. Department of Education**
Selection aids for Saskatchewan schools: a bibliography for school libraries. Regina: Saskatchewan Education, 1980. ii, 45 p.
Note: 90 entries.– Listing of specialized bibliographies to aid teachers in the selection of materials for students of special age groups and students with reading problems.– Various subjects and formats are covered, with the emphasis on Canadian titles.
Location: OONL.

— 1981 —

1644 **Kotin, David B.; Rueter, Marilyn**
Reader, lover of books, lover of heaven: a catalogue based on an exhibition of the book arts in Ontario. Willowdale, Ont.: North York Public Library, 1978-1981. 2 vol.: ill.; ISBN: 0-920552-01-3 (Vol. 1); 0-920552-02-1 (Vol. 2).
Note: Main body of both volumes is a checklist of Ontario private presses, with sections for Ontario bookbinders and a selected bibliography.– Indexes include artists and illustrators, authors and compilers, printers, presses.
Location: OONL.

1645 **MacLean, Ian A.**
Inventaire des bases de données bibliographiques dans les établissements canadiens décernant des diplômes. Ottawa: Bibliothèque nationale du Canada, 1981. 1 vol. (en pagination multiple).; ISBN: 0-662-51478-5.
Note: Décrit les fichiers bibliographiques et d'autorité lisibles par machine qu'ont créés la Bibliothèque nationale du Canada, l'Institut canadien de l'information scientifique et technique (ICIST), la Bibliothèque nationale du Québec, et les établissements d'enseignement canadiens qui décernent les diplômes.– Les enregistrements des bases de données couvertes par l'inventaire sont de nature permanente.– Texte en français et en anglais disposé tête-bêche.– Titre de la p. de t. additionnelle: *An inventory of bibliographic data bases in Canadian degree-granting institutions.*
Localisation: OONL.

1646 **MacLean, Ian A.**
An inventory of bibliographic data bases in Canadian degree-granting institutions. Ottawa: National Library of Canada, 1981. 1 vol. (in various pagings).; ISBN: 0-662-51478-5.
Note: Describes the machine-readable bibliographic and authority data bases created by the National Library of Canada, the Canadian Institute for Scientific and Technical Information (CISTI), the Bibliothèque nationale du Québec, and all of Canada's degree-granting educational institutions.– Includes library-processing oriented data bases (cataloguing, acquisitions, circulation, location of materials).– Includes permanent records only.– Text in English and French with French text on inverted pages.– Title of additional title-page: *Inventaire des bases de données bibliographiques dans les établissements canadiens décernant des diplômes.*

Location: OONL.

1647 **Ozaki, Hiroko**
Selected references for Canadian hospital libraries, 1974-1980/Bibliographie sélective à l'intention des bibliothèques d'hôpitaux canadiens, 1974-1980. Ottawa: National Library of Canada, 1981. 6 p. (Bibliographies / Library Documentation Centre; ISSN: 0226-4226)
Note: Approx. 60 entries.– Books, parts of books, journal articles on hospital libraries in general, Canadian hospital libraries, automation, bibliographies of recommended books and journals for medical libraries, psychiatric libraries, health care facility libraries.
Location: OONL.

1648 **Robinson, Douglas**
Videotex: a selective bibliography for librarians/Le vidéotex: une bibliographie sélective pour les bibliothécaires. Ottawa: National Library of Canada, 1981. 12 p. (Bibliographies / Library Documentation Centre; ISSN: 0226-4226)
Note: Approx. 135 entries.– Consists of items published since 1978 dealing with videotex (viewdata) and teletext (Antiope, Ceefax/Oracle, Prestel, Telidon).– Excludes highly technical or specialized articles.
Basically the same list also appears in *Ontario Library Review*; Vol. 66, no. 1 (March 1982) P. 54-61.
Location: OONL.

1649 **Zilm, Glennis**
Early B.C. books: an overview of trade book publishing in the 1800s with checklists and selected bibliography related to British Columbiana. [Burnaby, B.C.]: Simon Fraser University, 1981. xi, 303 p.
Note: Approx. 800 entries.– History of trade books published in area now British Columbia from 1858 to 1899, and overview of regional history of book publishing industry.– Includes checklist of B.C. imprints, checklist of trade books published in B.C., bibliography (books, articles, theses, government reports) relating to Canadian publishers and publishing with emphasis on British Columbia.– M.A. thesis, Communications, Simon Fraser University.
Location: OONL.

— 1982 —

1650 **Lafontaine, Suzanne**
Canadian government library handbooks: a list of orientation materials held in the Library Documentation Centre/Guides à l'intention des usagers des bibliothèques gouvernementales canadiennes: liste des manuels et brochures conservés au Centre de documentation sur les bibliothèques. Ottawa: National Library of Canada, 1982. 8 p. (Bibliographies / Library Documentation Centre; ISSN: 0226-4226)
Note: Approx. 125 entries.– Includes English and French publications.
Previous editions:
Davidson, Nadean. 1981. 7 p.
1980. 7 p.

1651 **Lakhanpal, S.K.**
Performance appraisal in libraries: a select annotated bibliography. Saskatoon: Collection Development, University of Saskatchewan Library, 1982. 37 l.
Note: 221 entries.– Books and journal articles on personnel evaluation in libraries.– Includes Canadian references.

Location: OONL.

1652 **McLeod, Donald W.**
"A chronological checklist of W.C. Chewitt and Company imprints."
In: *Papers of the Bibliographical Society of Canada*; Vol. 21 (1982) p. 30-45.; ISSN: 0067-6896.
Note: Listing of monographs, serial publications, maps, sheet music, broadsides, company trade catalogues from 1861 to 1869 with imprint of Toronto printer W.C. Chewitt and Co.
Location: OONL.

1653 **Rider, Lillian M.**
"Summary of developments in Canadian subject and area bibliography since 1974."
In: *Canadian Issues*; Vol. 4 (1982) p. 3-27.; ISSN: 0318-8442.
Note: Reviews bibliographic developments since 1974 and lists bibliographic tools in essay format within geographic (Canada, the regions, provinces, territories) and subject categories: arts, social sciences, sciences.
Location: AEU.

1654 **Robertson, Carolynn**
Surveys of library collections in Canada, 1955-1981/ Inventaire des collections des bibliothèques canadiennes, 1955-1981. Ottawa: National Library of Canada, 1982. i, 11 p. (Bibliographies / Library Documentation Centre; ISSN: 0226-4226)
Note: 83 entries.– National surveys, provincial and area studies, surveys in progress.– Excludes surveys in which the end product was a directory, statistical reports issued by library associations and provincial agencies.
Location: OONL.

— 1983 —

1655 **Lafontaine, Suzanne**
Canadian college library handbooks: a list of orientation materials held in the Library Documentation Centre/ Guides à l'intention des usagers des bibliothèques de collèges canadiens: liste des manuels et brochures conservés au Centre de documentation sur les bibliothèques. Ottawa: National Library of Canada, 1983. 9 p. (Bibliographies / Library Documentation Centre; ISSN: 0226-4226)
Note: Location: OONL.

1656 **Lamonde, Yvan; Olivier, Daniel**
Les bibliothèques personnelles au Québec: inventaire analytique et préliminaire des sources. Montréal: Ministère des Affaires culturelles, Bibliothèque nationale du Québec, 1983. 131 p. ill.; ISBN: 2-551-05267-X.
Note: Catalogues de bibliothèques privées au Québec vendues à l'encan.
Localisation: OONL.

1657 **Lyndsay Dobson Books**
The Canadian private presses in print: a list of books & broadsides, posters and pamphlets, ephemera, etc. Grimsby, Ont.: Lyndsay Dobson Books, 1983. [50] p.
Note: Listing and bibliographical description of examples of work by 22 private and 5 institutional presses in Canada.
Supplement: .... *Supplement*. 1984. [16] p.
Location: OONL.

1658 **Tomlinson, Jackie**
Sources of information for a listing of school libraries in Canada/Sources de renseignements sur les bibliothèques scolaires au Canada. Ottawa: National Library of

Canada, 1983. 6 p. (Bibliographies / Library Documentation Centre; ISSN: 0226-4226)
Note: 26 entries.– Directories and membership lists, school library agencies in Canada.– Text in English and French/texte en français et en anglais.
Location: OONL.

1659 **Verreault, Lucie; Taussig, Jeanne**
Relations publiques et communication documentaire: revue de la littérature. Montréal: Asted, 1983. 51 p.; ISBN: 2-89055-055-9.
Note: Approx. 100 entrées.– Principaux thèmes: études du milieu, analyse de la bibliothèque, organisation des programmes et services, présentation de la bibliothèque, production de matériel d'information et de promotion, relations publiques-communication.– Comporte des références québécoises.
Localisation: OONL.

— 1984 —

1660 **Bringhurst, Robert**
Ocean paper stone: the catalogue of an exhibition of printed objects which chronicle more than a century of literary publishing in British Columbia. Vancouver, B.C.: William Hoffer, 1984. 111 p.: ill., facsims.; ISBN: 0-919758-07-X.
Note: 215 entries.– Chronicles literary publishing in British Columbia from 1856 to spring 1984.– Includes books, chapbooks, literary magazines and broadsides from about 50 publishers.
Location: OONL.

1661 **British Columbia Systems Corporation. Library Services**
Bibliography on mini-microcomputers. [Victoria]: Library Services, British Columbia Systems Corporation, 1984. 27 p.
Note: Approx. 175 entries.– Books, periodicals and newsletters.
Location: OONL.

1662 **Inkster, Tim**
An honest trade: an exhibition of Canadian small press books printed and bound at the Porcupine's Quill in Erin, Ontario, 1974-1983. Erin, Ont.: Porcupine's Quill, 1984. [40] p.: ill.; ISBN: 0-88984-047-4.
Note: 40 entries.
Location: OONL.

1663 **Microcomputers in libraries: a bibliography.** Regina: Bibliographic Services Division, Saskatchewan Provincial Library, 1984. 31 p.; ISBN: 0-919059-09-0.
Note: Approx. 300 entries.– Books, periodicals, articles in professional journals on microcomputers in libraries.– Includes Canadian references.
Location: OONL.

1664 **Proulx, Serge; Harvey, Sylvie**
"L'informatisation au Québec: sélection bibliographique."
Dans: *Sociologie et sociétés*; Vol. 16, no 1 (avril 1984) p. 145-148.; ISSN: 0038-030X.
Note: 60 entrées.– Documentation gouvernementale, rapports de recherche concernant les impacts de la technologie de l'information au Québec.
Localisation: AEU.

1665 **Robinson, Douglas**
Automated acquisitions: a selective bibliography for librarians/Acquisitions automatisées: bibliographie sélective pour bibliothécaires. Ottawa: National Library

of Canada, 1984. 10 p. (Bibliographies / Library Documentation Centre; ISSN: 0226-4226)
Note: Approx. 120 entries.– Covers 1980-1984.– Excludes highly technical or very specialized articles.– Includes Canadian references.– Text in English and French/texte en français et en anglais.
Location: OONL.

1666 **Robinson, Douglas**
Telecommunications and libraries: a selective bibliography for librarians/Télécommunications et bibliothèques: bibliographie sélective pour bibliothécaires. Ottawa: National Library of Canada, 1984. 9 p. (Bibliographies / Library Documentation Centre; ISSN: 0226-4226)
Note: Approx. 100 entries.– Covers 1982 to 1984.– Lists material dealing with regulation, costs, library applications of telecommunications technology.– Includes Canadian references.
Location: OONL.

1667 **Saskatchewan Provincial Library. Bibliographic Services Division**
Library trustees: a bibliography. [Regina]: Saskatchewan Provincial Library, [1984]. 7 p.; ISBN: 0-919059-07-4.
Note: Books, handbooks, articles, newsletters, audiovisual materials on the topic of library trustees.– Includes Canadian references.
Location: OONL.

— 1985 —

1668 **Bergeron, Chantal; Tessier, Mario**
Bibliographie préliminaire sur le vidéodisque et les banques d'images. [Laval, Québec: s.n., c1985]. ii, 24 f.
Note: Approx. 200 entrées.– Couvre la littérature francophone et anglophone, de 1980 à 1984 inclusivement, sur le développement de la technologie du vidéodisque et ses applications pour emmagasiner, conserver et diffuser l'information.
Localisation: OONL.

1669 **Gaudreau, Liette**
"Bibliographie de l'édition au Québec, 1940-1960."
Dans: *L'Édition littéraire au Québec de 1940 à 1960.* Sherbrooke, Québec: Département d'études françaises, Université de Sherbrooke, 1985. P. 179-208. (Cahiers d'études littéraires et culturelles ; no 9); ISBN: 2-89343-000-7.
Note: Approx. 500 entrées.
Localisation: OONL.

1670 **Miska, John P.**
Celebration 1910-1985: an annotated bibliography of Agriculture Canada, Libraries Division. Ottawa: The Division, 1985. vii, 35 p.; ISBN: 0-662-14437-6.
Note: 178 entries.– Publications and mimeographed material relating to Agriculture Canada, Libraries Division: reports, articles, research papers, manuals, user's guides, catalogues, union lists, newsletters and bulletins, bibliographies, history, writings about the library and library staff.– Text in English and French/texte en français et en anglais.
Location: OONL.

1671 **Robertson, Carolynn**
The reference interview: a selective bibliography/L'entrevue de référence: bibliographie sélective. Ottawa: National Library of Canada, 1985. i, 9 p. (Bibliographies / Library Documentation Centre; ISSN: 0226-4226)

Note: Approx. 75 entries.– Books, articles, theses: reviews of the literature, general works, nonverbal communication, query negotiation, training, reference interview in computer-based setting, evaluation.– Includes Canadian references.– Text in English and French/texte en français et en anglais.
Location: OONL.

1672 **Robinson, Douglas**
Cooperative reference: a selective bibliography for librarians/Travail de référence en commun: bibliographie sélective pour bibliothécaires. Ottawa: National Library of Canada, 1985. 5 p. (Bibliographies / Library Documentation Centre; ISSN: 0226-4226)
Note: Approx. 60 entries.– Includes Canadian references.– Text in English and French/texte en français et en anglais.
Location: OONL.

1673 **Saskatchewan Provincial Library. Bibliographic Services Division**
Planning library buildings: a selected bibliography. Regina: Bibliographic Services Division, Professional Services Branch, Saskatchewan Library, 1985. 38 p.; ISBN: 0-919059-11-2.
Note: 360 entries.– Books, audio-visual material, periodical articles, floor plans of libraries.– Topics include library planning (case studies, layout, etc.), site selection, handicapped access, heating/lighting/ventilation, floors/furniture/equipment, remodelling/additions/interior decoration, shelving, security/insurance, etc.– Includes a number of Canadian references.
Previous edition: 1984. 28 p.
Location: OONL.

1674 **Whiteman, Bruce; Stewart, Charlotte; Funnell, Catherine**
A bibliography of Macmillan of Canada imprints 1906-1980. Toronto: Dundurn Press, 1985. xv, 474 p.; ISBN: 0-919670-89-X.
Note: 2,691 entries.– Chronological descriptive record of publishing activity of Macmillan of Canada.– All editions of a title given individual entries, reprints identified in notes.– Index provides access by author, title, contributor, illustrator, series.– Excludes books which Macmillan distributed as agency representive of other publishers; in-house ephemera such as newsletters and sales catalogues.
Supplement: Spadoni, Carl. "A bibliography of Macmillan of Canada imprints, 1906-1980: first supplement with corrigenda." In: *Papers of the Bibliographical Society of Canada*; Vol. 28 (1989) P. 38-69.
Location: OONL.

— 1986 —

1675 **Blanchard, Jim**
"A bibliography on mechanics' institutes with particular reference to Ontario."
In: *Readings in Canadian library history*, edited by Peter F. McNally. Ottawa: Canadian Library Association, 1986. P. 3-18.; ISBN: 0-88802-196-8.
Note: 174 entries.
Location: OONL.

1676 **British Columbia Systems Corporation. Library Services**
Bibliography on microcomputers. Victoria: Library Services, British Columbia Systems Corporation, 1984-

1986. 3 vol.; ISSN: 0827-0376.
Note: Retitled: 1982-1984, *Bibliography on mini-microcomputers*; ISSN: 0825-6128.
Location: OONL.

1677 **Burton, Melody C.**
Freedom of access and freedom of expression: an annotated bibliography of recent Canadian periodical literature. Edmonton: 1986. iv, 69 l.
Note: Approx. 600 entries.– Includes listing of periodical literature published between 1981 and 1985 on censorship and pornography issues in a Canadian context.
Location: OONL.

1678 **Caruso, Barbara; Nichol, bp**
"A Seripress bibliography, 1971-1979."
In: *Open Letter*; Series 6, no. 4 (Spring 1986) p. 71-77.; ISSN: 0048-1939.
Note: Lists all titles printed at Seripress (whether issued or unissued), with details on edition sizes, formats.
Location: OONL.

1679 **McNally, Peter F.**
"Canadian library history in English, 1964-1984: a survey and evaluation."
In: *Readings in Canadian library history*, edited by Peter F. McNally. Ottawa: Canadian Library Association, 1986. P. 19-30.; ISBN: 0-88802-196-8.
Note: 69 entries.– Bibliographic essay.
Location: OONL.

1680 **McNally, Peter F.**
"Canadian library history in French, 1964-1984: a survey and evaluation."
In: *Readings in Canadian library history*, edited by Peter F. McNally. Ottawa: Canadian Library Association, 1986. P. 31-39.; ISBN: 0-88802-196-8.
Note: 34 entries.– Bibliographic essay.
Location: OONL.

1681 **Murray, Heather D.**
Public lending right in Canada: a literature survey. Edmonton: H.D. Murray, 1986. v, 71 l.
Note: Approx. 125 entries.– Bibliographic essay, with a list of references.
Location: OONL.

1682 **Ozaki, Hiroko**
Library services to prisoners in Canada: a bibliography/ Services de bibliothèques aux détenus au Canada: une bibliographie. Ottawa: National Library of Canada, 1986. 4 p. (Bibliographies / Library Development Centre; ISSN: 0847-2467)
Note: 46 entries.– Articles and government publications.
Location: OONL.

1683 **Ozaki, Hiroko**
Subject headings and subject access to children's literature: a bibliography covering materials issued 1975-1985/Vedettes-matière et accès par sujet à la littérature de jeunesse: une bibliographie qui traite des publications parues entre 1975 et 1985. Ottawa: National Library of Canada, 1986. 4 l. (Bibliographies / Library Documentation Centre; ISSN: 0226-4226)
Note: 42 entries.– Subject heading lists and articles dealing with development of subject access to children's literature.– Includes Canadian references.
Location: OONL.

1684 **Seldon-MacFarlane, Betty D.; Mills, Patricia A.**
Records management: the Canadian contribution: a bibliography. London: Department of Secretarial and Administrative Studies, University of Western Ontario, 1986. 157 p.; ISBN: 0-7714-0652-5.
Note: Approx. 750 entries.– Topics include classification, electronic records, file control, health records, legality of records, micrographics, privacy and access, retention/disposition, security, text management and vital records management.– Text in English and French/texte en français et en anglais.
Location: OONL.

1685 **Tayler, Anne Hamilton; Nelson, Megan Jane**
From hand to hand: a gathering of book arts in British Columbia. Vancouver: Alcuin Society, 1986. 150 p.: ill.
Note: 326 entries.– Covers from 1868 to the 1980s.– Exhibition catalogue of British Columbia fine printing and publishing, bookbinding, papermaking, paper decoration, calligraphy, book design, typography and type design.
Location: OONL.

1686 **Van der Bellen, Liana**
"A checklist of books and articles in the field of the history of the book and libraries."
In: *Papers of the Bibliographical Society of Canada*; Vol. 23 (1984) p. 84-99; vol. 25 (1986) p. 139-152.; ISSN: 0067-6896.
Note: Lists the Canadian entries (1970 to 1986) from the *Annual bibliography of the history of the printed book and libraries*. The Hague: Martinus Nijhoff, 1970- . vol.; ISSN: 0303-5964.– Topics include history of the book and printing, publishing and the book trade, fine printing, small and private presses, livres d'artistes, retrospective Canadian bibliographies, bibliographical studies.
Location: OONL.

— 1987 —

1687 **Back, John**
Electronic book-detection systems: an annotated bibliography from 1975-1986. Edmonton: [J. Back], 1987. 75 l.
Note: 138 entries.– English-language journal articles dealing with electronic book-detection systems: case studies, technical reports, surveys, cost-benefit analyses related to protection of library materials from theft.– Includes Canadian references.
Location: OONL.

1688 **Brault, Jean-Rémi**
Bibliographie des Éditions Fides, 1937-1987. Montréal: Fides, 1987. 299 p.; ISBN: 2-7621-1358-X.
Note: Approx. 1,800 entrées.
Localisation: OONL.

1689 **Campbell, Dani Leigh**
A preliminary examination of the development of the public library and its antecedents, as institutions of public education in Ontario, 1851-1950: an annotated bibliography of the evidence found in the legislation and government reports of the province. Edmonton: [D.L. Campbell], 1987. 42 l.
Note: Location: OONL.

1690 **Centre canadien d'information et de documentation en archivistique**
"Bibliographie en archivistique, 1980-1986/Archival science bibliography, 1980-1986."
Dans: *Archives*; Vol. 19, no 1-2 (juin-septembre 1987) p. 1-

304.; ISSN: 0044-9423.

Note: Approx. 6,000 entrées.– Refonte des bibliographies publiées dans la revue *Archives* depuis 1980.– Publications traitant des principes et des techniques archivistiques, publications de dépôts d'archives canadiens et étrangers.– Inclut toute la production québécoise et canadienne, y compris les travaux ou documents non publiés.

Localisation: OONL.

1691 **Clay, D.**
Bibliography: computer programs for creating a bibliography with accompanying KWIC index. Moncton, N.B.: Fisheries and Oceans Canada, 1987. iii, 37 p. (Canadian manuscript report of fisheries and aquatic sciences ; no. 1910; ISSN: 0706-6473)

Note: Location: OONL.

1692 **Ozaki, Hiroko**
Interlibrary loan: a selected bibliography, 1982-1987 / Le prêt entre bibliothèques: une bibliographie sélective, 1982-1987. Ottawa: National Library of Canada, 1987. 21 p. (Bibliographies / Library Documentation Centre; ISSN: 0226-4226)

Note: Approx. 200 entries.– Sections include document delivery (automation, policies, handbooks, etc.), international lending, reviews and bibliographies.– Focus on Canadian topics.– Text in English and French / texte en français et en anglais.

Previous edition: *Recent developments in interlibrary loans: a select bibliography / Les développements récents concernant le prêt entre bibliothèques: une bibliographie sélective qui traite des publications parues depuis 1978.* Ottawa: National Library of Canada, 1981. 10 p.– Approx. 150 entries.

Location: OONL.

1693 **Ozaki, Hiroko**
Telefacsimile transmission being used for document delivery: cost studies: an annotated bibliography / Recours à la télécopie pour la livraison des documents: les analyses des coûts: bibliographie sommaire. [Ottawa]: National Library of Canada, 1987. 5 p. (Bibliographies / Library Documentation Centre; ISSN: 0226-4226)

Note: Approx. 25 entries.– Includes Canadian references.– Text in English and French / texte en français et en anglais.

Location: OONL.

1694 **La pénétration et l'utilisation de l'informatique au Québec: guide bibliographique.** [Québec]: Direction des technologies de l'information, Ministère des communications du Québec, c1987. 19 f.; ISBN: 2-550-17578-6.

Note: Approx. 90 entrées.– Recherches (monographies, mémoires, rapport d'enquête, répertoire statistiques, essai, etc.) sur l'informatisation de l'administration publique, l'informatisation des entreprises, l'informatisation des ménages.

Localisation: OONL.

1695 **Roberge, Michel**
L'expertise québécoise en gestion des documents administratifs: bibliographie thématique et chronologique, 1962-1987. 1re éd. Saint-Augustin, Québec: Gestar, 1987. 1 vol. (en pagination multiple); ISBN: 2-9800920-0-2.

Note: 1,515 entrées.

Localisation: OONL.

1696 **Robertson, Carolynn**
A bibliography of standards relevant to indexing and abstracting and the presentation of information / Bibliographie des normes relatives à l'analyse documentaire, à l'indexation et à la présentation de renseignements. Ottawa: National Library of Canada, 1987. 19 p. (Bibliographies / Library Documentation Centre; ISSN: 0226-4226)

Note: Includes Canadian publications in English and French.– Text in English and French / texte en français et en anglais.

Previous edition: 1980. ii, 17 p.; ISBN: 0-662-50776-2.

Location: OONL.

1697 **Sotiron, Minko**
An annotated bibliography of works on daily newspapers in Canada, 1914-1983 / Une bibliographie annotée des ouvrages portant sur les quotidiens canadiens, 1914-1983. Montréal: M. Sotiron, 1987. viii, 288 p.; ISBN: 0-9693102-0-X.

Note: 3,750 entries.– Periodical articles, government documents, books, theses on Canadian newspaper publishing, individual newspapers, journalists.– Text in English and French / texte en français et en anglais.

Location: OONL.

1698 **Zureik, Elia; Hartling, Dianne**
The social context of the new information and communication technologies: a bibliography. New York: P. Lang, 1987. x, 310 p.; ISBN: 0-82040-413-6.

Note: Approx. 4,000 entries.– Books, reports, studies, journal articles.– Topics include privacy, crime, transborder data flow, education, leisure, work, medicine, artificial intelligence, urban planning.– Includes Canadian references.

Previous edition: Kingston, Ont.: Queen's University at Kingston, Informatics and Social Research Unit, 1983. iv, 208 p.

Location: OHM.

— 1988 —

1699 **Alam, Ann; Creelman, Jan; Parsons, Ruth**
Public library service to senior citizens: an annotated bibliography of sources, 1979-1987. London, Ont.: School of Library and Information Science, University of Western Ontario, 1988. 40 p.

Note: Approx. 150 entries.– Selected list of books, reports, articles.– Topics covered include home services, library's responsibility to the aging, interagency cooperation with the library, descriptions of library programs, literature reviews.– Includes Canadian references.

Location: OONL.

1700 **Elsted, Crispin**
Utile dulci: the first decade at Barbarian Press, 1977-1987: a history & bibliography. Mission, B.C.: Barbarian Press, c1988. 52 p.; ISBN: 0-920971-07-5.

Note: 40 entries.– Books and portfolios, pamphlets and ephemera, commissioned pieces published by or printed at Barbarian Press.

Location: OONL.

1701 **Hendricks, Klaus B.; Whitehurst, Anne**
La conservation des documents photographiques: liste d'ouvrages de référence de base. [Ottawa]: Archives nationales du Canada, c1988. vi, 32, 32, vi p.; ISBN: 0-662-55591-0.

Note: 256 entrées.– Titres portant sur la préservation des

photographies créées au moyen de procédés fondés sur la photosensiblité des halogénures d'argent, documents traitant des propriétés et de la préservation des microfilms et des films cinématographiques.– Inclut un nombre d'ouvrages canadiens.– Texte en français et en anglais disposé tête-bêche.– Titre de la p. de t. additionnelle: *Conservation of photographic materials: a basic reading list.*
Localisation: OONL.

1702 **Hendricks, Klaus B.; Whitehurst, Anne**
Conservation of photographic materials: a basic reading list. [Ottawa]: National Archives of Canada, c1988. vi, 32, 32, vi p.; ISBN: 0-662-55591-0.
Note: 256 entries.– Covers references on the preservation of still photographic images made by processes based on light-sensitivity of silver halides, references on properties and preservation of microfilms and motion picture films, a few articles on stability of non-silver photographic materials used for microfilms.– Includes Canadian references.– Text in English and French with French text on inverted pages.– Added title page title; *La conservation des documents photographiques: liste d'ouvrages de référence de base.*
Location: OONL.

1703 **Lim, Eileen**
Automating the school library: a selective bibliography for librarians/L'informatisation des bibliothèques scolaires: une bibliographie sélective pour les bibliothécaires. Ottawa: National Library of Canada, 1988. 7 l. (Bibliographies / Library Documentation Centre; ISSN: 0226-4226)
Note: Approx. 70 entries.– Books, articles, reports and studies published since 1980 concerning automation of library processes in school libraries and media centres.– Excludes material on computer applications in school curricula.– Includes Canadian references.– Text in English and French/texte en français et en anglais.
Location: OONL.

1704 **Service de diffusion sélective de l'information de la Centrale des bibliothèques**
Télématique et téléinformatique. Montréal: Le Service, 1988. 36 p. (DSI/CB ; no 120; ISSN: 0825-5024); ISBN: 2-89059-335-5.
Note: 368 entrées.– Monographies, articles de périodiques, documents audiovisuels.
Localisation: OONL.

1705 **Stang, Anne**
"School libraries, K to 9: an annotated bibliography on the role of the school library and teacher-librarian in the strategies of teaching and learning."
In: *School Libraries in Canada*; Vol. 8, no. 3 (Spring 1988) p. 44–47.; ISSN: 0227-3780.
Note: Books, periodical articles, government documents on school library programs, planning, information skills and search strategies.– Emphasis on Canadian topics.
Location: AEU.

1706 **Université de Montréal. Service des archives**
Bibliographie des publications du Service des archives. 6e éd., rev. et augm. Montréal: Université de Montréal, Service des archives, 1988. ii, 17 p. (Publication / Université de Montréal, Service des archives ; no 21); ISBN: 2-8911907-3-4.
Note: Éditions antérieures:

1987. 17 p.; ISBN: 2-8911905-8-0.
1984. 14 p.; ISBN: 2-8911904-2-4.
1980. 11 p.; ISBN: 2-8911901-4-9.
1978. 8 p.
1976. 6 f.
Localisation: OONL.

— 1989 —
1707 **Friends of the library: a bibliography.** Regina: Provincial Library, Saskatchewan Education, 1989. 5 p.
Note: Lists resources on Friends of the library groups.– Includes Canadian references.
Location: OONL.

1708 **Needs assessment of the library's community: a bibliography.** Regina: Provincial Library, Saskatchewan Education, 1989. 7 p.
Note: Selection of materials on needs assessment for libraries: methodology, reports of needs assessment projects.– Focus on Canadian materials.
Location: OONL.

1709 **Poirier, René; Cournoyer, Sylvie**
L'impact des nouvelles technologies de l'information sur l'emplois et le travail: bibliographie thématique sélective/ New information technologies impact on employment and work: thematic and selective bibliography. Laval, Québec: Direction de la recherche organisationnelle, Centre canadien de recherche sur l'informatisation du travail, Ministère des communications du Canada, 1989. 192 p.; ISBN: 0-662-57057-X.
Note: 1,895 entrées.– La période couverte est de 1981 au début de l'année 1987.– Inclut monographies, articles de périodiques, chapitres de monographies reliés à la problèmatique des nouvelles technologies et de leur incidence sur l'emplois et le travail.– Texte en français et en anglais/text in English and French.
Localisation: OONL.

1710 **Robertson, Carolynn**
Marketing the special library: a selective bibliography/ Le marketing et la bibliothèque spécialisée: bibliographie sélective. Ottawa: National Library of Canada, 1989. 13 p. (Bibliographies / Library Development Centre ; no. 2; ISSN: 0847-2467)
Note: Approx. 125 entries.– Books and chapters of books, periodical articles dealing with marketing non-profit organizations, special libraries and online information services.– Contains a section on preparing marketing plans and a list of additional bibliographies.– Includes Canadian references.
Location: OONL.

1711 **Rogers, Helen F.**
Integrated systems: a selective bibliography on choosing, planning, implementing, managing, evaluating, and preparing RFPs for integrated library systems/Une bibliographie sélective sur le choix, la planification, la mise en oeuvre, la gestion, l'évaluation et la préparation d'appels d'offre pour les systèmes intégrés de bibliothèques. Ottawa: National Library of Canada, 1989. 6 p. (Bibliographies / Library Documentation Centre; ISSN: 0226-4226)
Note: Approx. 75 entries.– Includes Canadian references.
Location: OONL.

1712 **Rogers, Helen F.**
Library services for seniors: a selective bibliography/ Services de bibliothèque aux personnes âgées: une

bibliographie sélective. [Ottawa]: National Library of Canada, 1989. 10 p.

Note: Includes Canadian references in English and French.

Location: OONL.

1713 **Spadoni, Carl**
"Medical archives: an annotated bibliography."
In: *Archivaria*; No. 28 (Summer 1989) p. 74-119.; ISSN: 0318-6954.

Note: 216 entries.– Checklist of publications in English and French on medical archives, which is defined broadly to include archival literature on medicine and allied health sciences related to health care, research, education.– Topics include preservation/appraisal/records management, specific archives (by country, including Canada), confidentiality and the law, archives in medical libraries, oral history, union lists/directories/surveys.

Location: AEU.

1714 **Young, Rod**
"Labour archives: an annotated bibliography."
In: *Archivaria*; No. 27 (Winter 1988-1989) p. 97-110.; ISSN: 0318-6954.

Note: Approx. 75 entries.– Journal articles in the field of labour and trade union archives.– Focus on English North American literature, including a substantial number of Canadian titles.– Excludes published lists of archival acquisitions, unpublished papers, institutional and collection guides, archival inventories/finding aids.

Location: AEU.

— 1990 —

1715 **Boilard, Gilberte**
Édition du livre au Québec, 1980-1990: bibliographie sélective et annotée. Québec: Bibliothèque de l'Assemblée nationale, Division de la référence parlementaire, 1990. 20 p. (Bibliographie / Bibliothèque de l'Assemblée nationale du Québec ; no 33; ISSN: 0836-9100)

Note: 66 entrées.– Mise à jour du "L'industrie de l'édition au Québec" (Biblio Éclair ; no 49).

Localisation: OONL.

1716 **Bourget, Manon; Chiasson, Robert; Morin, Marie-Josée**
L'indispensable en documentation: les outils de travail. La Pocatière, Québec: Documentor, 1990. viii, 201 p.; ISBN: 2-89123-110-4.

Note: Approx. 250 entrées.– Quatre parties: "Documentation imprimée" (monographies, publications en série, documents officiels, ouvrages de référence; traitement documentaire, diffusion); "Documentation non-imprimée" (répertoires d'addresses, répertoires bibliographiques, normes de description, systèmes de classification); "Documents administratifs et les documents historiques;" "Information professionnelle courante."- Inclut un nombre considérable d'ouvrages canadiens et québécoises.

Localisation: OONL.

1717 **Donaldson, George; Fortin, Marcel**
Prison libraries: a bibliography/Bibliothèques des pénitenciers: une bibliographie. Ottawa: Solicitor General Canada, Ministry Library and Reference Centre, 1990. 14 l.

Note: Approx. 100 entries.– Sections include "Canada," and "Correctional services of Canada."

Location: OONL.

1718 **Saskatchewan Provincial Library**
Library science video cassette resources in the Provincial Library. Regina: Provincial Library, Saskatchewan Education, 1990. ii, 39 p.; ISBN: 0-919059-52-X.

Note: Includes Canadian references

Previous edition: 1988. 22 l.; ISBN: 0-919059-42-2.

Location: SSU.

1719 **Scott, Wendy; Herbert, Lynn**
Empowering librarians: meeting challenges of the 1990s/Plein pouvoir aux bibliothécaires: relever les défis des années 1990. Ottawa: National Library of Canada, 1990. 18 p. (Bibliographies / Library Development Centre ; no. 3; ISSN: 0226-4226)

Note: Approx. 250 entries.– Books and articles in English and French.– Topics include empowerment and management, librarians as leaders, recognition of librarians (position, status, remuneration), career development, impact of technology and the value of information.– Includes Canadian references.

Location: OONL.

1720 **Stephenson, Mary Sue**
Planning library facilities: a selected, annotated bibliography. Metuchen, N.J.: Scarecrow Press, c1990. ix, 249 p.; ISBN: 0-8108-2285-7.

Note: 800 entries.– Covers the period from 1970 to mid-1988.– Criteria for inclusion include: materials concerned with planning, design, evaluation of library buildings and facilities; English-language materials with emphasis on United States and Canada.– Excludes short announcements of new or renovated facilities, non-print source materials other than microforms, case studies and evaluation of existing or planned facilities.

Location: OONL.

1721 **Vallières, Ginette; Herbert, Lynn**
Canadian library statistics: a selective list of sources/Statistiques sur les bibliothèques canadiennes: une liste sélective des sources. Ottawa: National Library of Canada, 1990. 10 p. (Bibliographies / Library Development Centre ; no. 4; ISSN: 0847-2467)

Note: 68 entries.– Listing of reports, surveys and articles which provide statistical information about public, academic, school and special libraries in Canada.

Previous edition: Anderson, Beryl L. *Sources of Canadian library statistics: a bibliography/Sources des statistiques sur les bibliothèques canadiennes: une bibliographie*. Library Documentation Centre, National Library of Canada, 1987.

Location: OONL.

— 1991 —

1722 **Association québécoise pour l'étude de l'imprimé. Comité de bibliographie**
Bibliographie des études québécoises sur l'imprimé, 1970-1987. Montréal: Bibliothèque nationale du Québec, 1991. 124 p.: ill.; ISBN: 2-921241-00-5.

Note: 448 entrées.– Rédigée par Manon Brunet, et al.

Supplément: ... , *1988-1989. Premier supplément.* c1993. 73 p.; ISBN: 2-551-13066-2.

Localisation: OONL.

1723 **Canadian Centre for Information and Documentation on Archives**
Archival science bibliography, 1986-1988/Bibliographie en archivistique, 1986-1988. Ottawa: The Centre, c1991. xii, 164 p.; ISBN: 0-662-58342-6.

Note: 2,066 entries.– Continues the retrospective bibliography published in the special issue of the journal *Archives*, June-September 1987.– Lists publications in English, French, and other languages dealing with all aspects of archives administration, records management and auxiliary techniques.– Many Canadian references.– Text in English and French/texte en français et en anglais.
Location: OONL.

1724 **Gregorovich, Andrew**
Canadian ethnic press bibliography: ethnic, multilingual and multicultural press of Canada selected bibliography. Toronto: Canadian Multilingual Press Foundation, 1991. 31 p.; ISBN: 0-88969-032-4.
Note: Approx. 200 entries.– Books, popular and scholarly articles on the Canadian ethnic press, not a listing of the newspapers themselves.– Arrangement by author.
Location: OONL.

1725 **Herbert, Lynn**
Standards for Canadian libraries/Normes pour les bibliothèques canadiennes. Ottawa: National Library of Canada, 1991. 18 p. (Bibliographies / Library Development Centre ; no. 6; ISSN: 0847-2467)
Note: General works on standards for public, academic, school and special libraries; standards by topic: library services and administration, librarians, reference works.
Previous edition: Robertson, Carolynn. *Standards for Canadian libraries: a bibliography*. 1983. 5 p.
Location: OONL.

1726 **Latham, Sheila; Slade, Alexander L.; Budnick, Carol**
Library services for off-campus and distance education: an annotated bibliography. Ottawa: Canadian Library Association, c1991. xxii, 249 p.; ISBN: 0-88802-257-3.
Note: 535 entries.– Publications, theses, research reports produced between January 1930 and 1990 dealing with library support for post-secondary students and faculty involved with distance education courses in Canada, Australia, Great Britain, United States, New Zealand, other countries.– Topics include: role of libraries in distance education, guidelines and standards, organization and planning, collection management, document delivery, interlibrary cooperation.– Includes sections covering library surveys, user studies, library case studies.– Indexes: author, institution, subject.
Location: OONL.

1727 **Maillet, Lise; Scott, Wendy**
Law library networking: a list of references .../Réseaux de bibliothèques de droit: une liste de références .... Ottawa: National Library of Canada, 1991. 8 p. (Bibliographies / Library Development Centre ; no. 7; ISSN: 0847-2467)
Note: Approx. 100 entries.– Focus on cooperation and networking in law libraries, and legal information systems, within a Canadian context.– Introduction in English and French/Introduction en français et en anglais.
Location: OONL.

1728 **Mattison, David**
Catalogues, guides and inventories to the archives of Alberta, British Columbia, Northwest Territories, and the Yukon Territory: a selected bibliography of publications, 1968-1990. Vancouver: Archives Associations of British Columbia, 1991. 23 p. (Archives Association of British Columbia Occasional paper series ; 91-01; ISSN: 1183-

8574); ISBN: 1-895584-00-0.
Note: Lists published finding aids of archival materials produced either by the federal government or public institutions in Alberta, British Columbia, Northwest Territories, Yukon Territory issued between 1968 and December 31, 1990.– Includes research bibliographies describing archival (primary sources) and secondary (published) materials.– Excludes exhibition catalogues, information leaflets.
Location: OONL.

1729 **Michon, Jacques**
"Catalogue des Éditions de l'Arbre, 1941-1948."
Dans: *Éditeurs transatlantiques: études sur les Éditions de l'Arbre*, Lucien Parizeau, Fernand Pilon, Serge Brousseau, Mangin, B.D. Simpson. Sherbrooke, Québec: Éditions Ex Libris, 1991. P. [185]-225.; ISBN: 2-89031-128-7.
Note: 200 entrées.
Localisation: OONL.

— 1992 —

1730 **Bibliothèque nationale du Canada**
Catalogue de publications [Bibliothèque nationale du Canada]. Ottawa: La Bibliothèque, 1992. 30, 30 p.; ISBN: 0-662-59049-X.
Note: Liste commentée des publications en série et monographies: bibliographies, répertoires et catalogues collectifs, catalogues d'expositions, brochures, études et rapports.– Texte en français et en anglais disposé tête-bêche.– Titre de la p. de t. additionnelle: *Publications catalogue [National Library of Canada]*.
Éditions antérieures:
1989. 23, 23 p.; ISBN: 0-662-56714-5.
1988. 25, 25 p.; ISBN: 0-662-55889-8.
1983. 21, 19 p.; ISBN: 0-662-52486-1.
1982. 21, 21 p.; ISBN: 0-662-51933-7.
1981. 17, 17 p.; ISBN: 0-662-51465-3.
National Library of Canada: publications: a list/Bibliothèque nationale du Canada: publications: une liste. 1980. 31 p.; ISBN: 0-662-50832-7.– Couvre la période 1950 à 1980.– Texte en français et en anglais/text in English and French.
Localisation: OONL.

1731 **Bibliothèque nationale du Québec**
Publications éditées par la Bibliothèque nationale du Québec. Montréal: La Bibliothèque, 1992. 31 p.: ill.; ISBN: 2-550-26645-5.
Note: Comprend titres récemment publiés, bibliographie nationale, bibliographies générales et spécialisées, catalogues d'exposition.
Éditions antérieures:
Catalogue des publications. 1988. 69 p.; ISBN: 2-550-19004-1.
1987. 77 p.; 2-550-17692-8.
Catalogue des publications de la Bibliothèque nationale du Québec. 1986. 101 p.; 2-550-16102-5.
1982. 85 p.
1980. 90 p.
Localisation: OONL.

1732 **Boilard, Gilberte; Fortin, Jean-Luc**
Les bibliothèques parlementaires: histoire, fonctions, services: bibliographie sélective et annotée. Québec: Assemblée nationale, Direction générale de la bibliothèque, Service de la référence, 1992. 78 p. (Bibliographie / Bibliothèque de l'Assemblée nationale du Québec ; no 44; ISSN: 0836-9100)
Note: 247 entrées.– Partie II: "Canada," p. 9-24; Partie VI:

"Québec," p. 42-54.
Localisation: OONL.

1733 **Lakhanpal, S.K.**
User education in North American academic libraries: a select annotated bibliography. Saskatoon: Collection Development Department, University of Saskatchewan Library, 1992. 5, 67, 17 l.; ISBN: 0-88880-271-4.
Note: 391 entries.– Publications in the English language dealing with academic library user education published in Canada and the United States from 1980 to 1989.– Topics include bibliographic instruction, computer-assisted instruction, course-integrated instruction, freshman orientation, faculty cooperation, term paper assistance.
Location: OONL.

1734 **National Library of Canada**
Publications catalogue [National Library of Canada]. Ottawa: The Library, 1992. 30, 30 p.; ISBN: 0-662-59049-X.
Note: Lists and describes publications in series and monographs, including bibliographies, directories and union lists, exhibition catalogues, manuals, pamphlets, reports and studies.– Text in English and French with French text on inverted pages.– Title of additional title-page: *Catalogue des publications [Bibliothèque nationale du Canada]*.
Previous editions:
1989. 23, 23 p.; ISBN: 0-662-56714-5.
1988. 25, 25 p.; ISBN: 0-662-55889-8.
1983. 19, 21 p.; ISBN: 0-662-52486-1.
1982. 21, 21 p.; ISBN: 0-662-51933-7.
1981. 17, 17 p.; ISBN: 0-662-51465-3.
National Library of Canada: publications: a list/Bibliothèque nationale du Canada: publications: une liste. 1980. 31 p.; ISBN: 0-662-50832-7.– Covers the period 1950 to 1980.– Text in English and French/texte en français et en anglais.
Location: OONL.

1735 **"Reference titles."**
In: *Canadian Library Journal*; Vol. 44, no. 1 (February 1987) p. 56-58; vol. 45, no. 1 (February 1988) p. 53-55; vol. 46, no. 1 (February 1989) p. 48-51; vol. 47, no. 1 (February 1990) p. 45-50; vol. 48, no. 1 (February 1991) p. 63-68; vol. 49, no. 1 (February 1992) ; ISSN: 0008-4352.
Note: Annual.– Lists current Canadian reference works.
Location: AEU.

— 1993 —

1736 **Bartlett, Mark C.; Black, Fiona A.; MacDonald, Bertrum H.**
The history of the book in Canada: a bibliography. Halifax, N.S.: Dalhousie University, School of Library and Information Studies, 1993. xi, [xii], 260 p.; ISBN: 0-9697349-0-5.
Note: 2,041 entries.– Covers published secondary material, mainly in English and French.– Subject categories include printed books and printing, illustration, type founders and designers, book trade and publishing, book collecting, libraries and librarianship, periodicals, newspapers and journalism.
Location: OONL.

— Ongoing/En cours —

1737 **Annual bibliography of the history of the printed book and libraries.** The Hague: Martinus Nijhoff, 1970-. vol.; ISSN: 0303-5964.
Note: Includes Canadian references.
Location: OONL.

1738 **Canadian library–information science research projects, a list/Projets de recherche canadiens en bibliothéconomie et sciences de l'information, une liste.** Ottawa: Library Documentation Centre, National Library of Canada, 1981-. vol.; ISSN: 0826-1903.
Note: Annual.– Includes on-going and terminated investigations.– Information includes project title, project leader, institution where research is being done or was completed, sponsoring body, starting and completion dates, estimated costs.– The "Completed research projects" section lists publications resulting from the research process.
Location: OONL.

1739 **Canadian Library Association**
Publications catalogue [Canadian Library Association]. Ottawa: Canadian Library Association, 1969-. vol.; ISSN: 0381-5862.
Note: Location: OONL.

1740 **Directories of Canadian libraries/Répertoires des bibliothèques canadiennes.** Ottawa: National Library of Canada, 1980-. vol.; ISSN: 0825-8899. (Bibliographies / Library Documentation Centre; ISSN: 0226-4226)
Note: Includes English and French publications.
Location: OONL.

1741 **University of Toronto. Faculty of Library and Information Science. Library**
Bibliography series [Library and information science]. Toronto: The Library, 1983-. vol.; ISSN: 0838-7311.
Note: Canadian content in the following titles varies from slight to substantial.– In the interest of bibliographic completeness, the entire series has been listed.
No. 1: Jones, Ellen. *Selected references on electronic publishing.* 8, 2 l.
No. 2: Jones, Ellen; Wheeler, Jean. *Videodiscs: a selected list of references, 1981-November 1983.* 7 l.
No. 3: Jones, Ellen. *Literature search on: library budget and finance for special libraries.* 2 l.
No. 4: Jones, Ellen. *Bibliography on the user-friendly interface for online systems.* 5 l.
No. 5: Jones, Ellen; Wheeler, Jean. *Speech input-output via computer systems.* 5 l.
No. 6: Celsie, Mary Jane. *Library signage.* 2 l.
No. 7: Wheeler, Jean. *Evaluation of information retrieval systems.* 9 l.
No. 8: Jones, Ellen; Wheeler, Jean. *Selected references on online public access catalogues, November 1985.* 12 l.
No. 9: Wheeler, Jean. *Teletext, videotext.* 6 l.
No. 10: Jones, Ellen; Wheeler, Jean. *Selected references on UTLAS.* 4 l.
No. 11: Jones, Ellen. *Selected references on faculty governance.* 4 l.
No. 12: Jones, Ellen. *Selected references on cataloguing machine-readable data.* 3 l.
No. 13: Jones, Ellen; Wheeler, Jean. *Forecasts and futures for libraries and librarians.* 12 l.
No. 14: Wheeler, Jean. *Reference services for children.* 3 l.
No. 15: Wheeler, Jean; Jones, Ellen. *Book thefts and security systems.* 5 l.
No. 16: Wheeler, Jean. *Library automation with emphasis on special libraries.* 8 l.
No. 17: *Continuing education for professionals in Canada.* 2 l.
No. 18: Wheeler, Jean. *Recruitment to librarianship.* 2 l.

No. 19: Wheeler, Jean. *The information environment and users.* 4 l.

No. 20: Jones, Ellen; Wheeler, Jean. *Staffing the reference desk.* 2 l.

No. 21: Wheeler, Jean. *Accreditation of library schools.* 2 l.

No. 22: *International cataloguing codes and translations of AACR2.*

No. 23: Wheeler, Jean. *Selected references on women in librarianship, 1974-1984.* 9 l.

No. 24: Jones, Ellen; Wheeler, Jean. *FLIS bibliography: requests for proposals.* 2 l.

No. 25: Jones, Ellen; Wheeler, Jean. *Marketing of libraries and information centres.* 9 l.

No. 26: Jones, Ellen; Wheeler, Jean. *Selected references on user fees for library and information services.* 8 l.

No. 27: Wheeler, Jean. *Selected references on library school students.* 4 l.

No. 28: Jones, Ellen; Wheeler, Jean. *Services to business especially in public libraries.* 4 l.

No. 29: Jones, Ellen; Wheeler, Jean. *Librarians and burnout.* 2 l.

No. 30: Jones, Ellen; Wheeler, Jean. *Library services for the aged.* 6 l.

No. 32: *Microcomputer software: a list of sources found in U of T libraries.* 5 l.

No. 33: Black, Karen. *Library orientation for young children.* 6 l.

No. 34: Jones, Ellen; Wheeler, Jean. *MINISIS.* 4 l.

No. 35: Gallant, Kim. *Training and education of children's librarians in North American public libraries.* 5 l.

No. 36: Wheeler, Jean. *Bilingualism as it affects librarianship in Canada.* 4 l.

No. 37: Wheeler, Jean. *Library automation with emphasis on special libraries.* 4 l.

No. 38: Jones, Ellen, et al. *End-user searching.* 6 l.

No. 39: Wheeler, Jean. *Library publications.* 4 l.

No. 40: Black, Karen. *Electronic mail.* 11 l.

No. 41: *Questionnaires.* 3 l.

No. 42: Jones, Ellen; Wheeler, Jean. *Use of classification in online catalogues and online databases.* 3, 3 l.

No. 43: Jones, Ellen; Wheeler, Jean. *Selected references on the DBASE III database system.* 1 l.

No. 44: Jones, Ellen. *Using a micro for downloading online search results: a bibliography.* [6] l.

No. 45: Jones, Ellen. *Bibliography: evaluation of reference services.* 2 l.

No. 46: Jones, Ellen. *Bibliography: space problems in academic libraries.* 3 l.

No. 47: Jones, Ellen; Wheeler, Jean. *Bibliography on CD ROMs.* 4 l.

No. 48: Jones, Ellen; Wheeler, Jean. *Bibliometrics and library science literature.* 5 l.

No. 49: Jones, Ellen. *Bibliography on no main entry cataloguing.* 2 l.

No. 50: Jones, Ellen; Wheeler, Jean. *Online search services in public libraries.* 5 l.

No. 51: Wheeler, Jean. *Bibliography on the roles and responsibilities of librarians.* 6 l.

No. 52: Jones, Ellen. *User survey methodologies.* 2 l.

No. 53: Wheeler, Jean; Sutmoller, Saskia. *Online authority files.* 3 l.

No. 54: Wheeler, Jean. *Selected references on fund raising in libraries.* 7 l.

No. 55: Cox, Joseph P. *Retrospective conversion: selected bibliography.* 3 l.

No. 56: Jones, Ellen; Wheeler, Jean. *Selected references on online public access catalogues (1987).* 12 l.

No. 57: Jones, Ellen; Wheeler, Jean. *Expert systems in cataloguing or classification.* 3 l.

No. 58: Wheeler, Jean; Lohnes, Marilyn. *Selected references on library signage.* 4 l.

No. 59: Jones, Elllen; Wheeler, Jean. *Instruction and training for online public access catalogue users.* 3 l.

No. 60: Jones, Ellen; Wheeler, Jean. *Selected references on social science literature.* 7 l.

No. 61: Wheeler, Jean. *Selected references on statistical software, 1985-1988.* 8 l.

No. 62: Jones, Ellen. *Health sciences library networks.* 8 l.

No. 63: Jones, Ellen. *Community information databases.* 4 l.

No. 64: Wheeler, Jean. *Selected references on undergraduate programs in library science.* 3 l.

No. 65: Wheeler, Jean. *Selected references on Hypertext, 1987-1988.* 9 l.

No. 66: Wheeler, Jean. *Selected references on hypermedia.* 4 l.

No. 67: Wheeler, Jean. *Selected references on academic dissertations with emphasis on library and information science.* 10 l.

No. 68: Wheeler, Jean. *Selected references on interlibrary loans.* 9 l.

No. 69: Wheeler, Jean; Cole, Nancy. *Selected references on online public access catalogues, 1987-1989.* 11 l.

No. 70: Wheeler, Jean. *Selected references on the moving of libraries.* 6 l.

No. 71: Jones, Ellen. *Selected references on CDI/ISIS.* 7 l.

No. 72: Jones, Ellen. *Selected references on teaching automation in library schools.* 2 l.

Location: OONL.

Sports and Recreation

Sports et récréation

— 1886 —

1742 **Canadian numismatic bibliography.** Montreal: 1886. 16 p.
Note: Microform: CIHM Microfiche series ; no. 02826; ISBN: 0-665-02826-1. 1 microfiche (13 fr.).
Location: OONL.

— 1945 —

1743 **Fisher, Joel E.**
Bibliography of Canadian mountain ascents. [S.l.: The Author], 1945. 103 p.
Note: Lists all articles, notes, illustrations, maps through December 31, 1944 in a selection of mountaineering journals.– Includes only references of "actual climbing value."- Excludes references of a purely geological or historical nature.
Location: ABA.

— 1949 —

1744 **Duncan, Robert J.; Quarles, Mervyn V.; Crosby, Louis S.**
"Bibliography of Prince Edward Island [postage stamps]."
In: *British North America Philatelic Society Year Book*; (1949) p. 11, 13-14.
Note: Books, catalogues, articles on stamps of P.E.I.
Location: OONL.

— 1951 —

1745 **Canadian philatelic literature.** Cobden, Ont.: A.L. McCready, 1951. 39 l. ill.
Note: Lists books and booklets, catalogues, society yearbooks, stamp journals relating to postage stamps, revenue stamps, collectors and collecting.– "Additions and corrections:" 1 leaf laid in.
Location: OONL.

— 1952 —

1746 **McCready, A.L.**
Paper on Canadian philatelic literature. [Ottawa]: Ottawa Philatelic Society, 1952. [5] p.
Note: Lecture to Ottawa Philatelic Society comments on and recommends periodical and monographic literature on Canadian stamps and stamp collecting.
Location: OONL.

— 1954 —

1747 **Bowman, Fred**
A bibliography of Canadian numismatics. [Ottawa: Canadian Numismatics Association, 1954]. 35, v l.
Note: Approx. 900 entries.– Books, pamphlets, journal articles, papers.
Location: OONL.

1748 **Schonfeld, Josef; Larsen, R.W.**
A selective bibliography of literature on revenue stamps. Vancouver, B.C.: [s.n.], 1954. 34 p.
Note: Location: BVA.

— 1959 —

1749 **Bowman, Fred; Willey, R.C.**
"Bibliography of Canadian numismatics."
In: *Canadian Numismatic Journal*; Vol. 4, no. 6 (June 1959) p. 188-102; vol. 4, no. 7 (July 1959) p. 222-232; vol. 4, no. 8 (August 1959) p. 256-265; vol. 4, no. 9 (September 1959) p. 323-333; vol. 4, no. 10 (October 1959) p. 365-372.; ISSN: 0008-4573.
Note: Articles and pamphlets dealing with Canadian coins and tokens, banking history, paper currencies.– Continued by: Allen, H. Don (January 1960), and Willey, R.C. (January 1961-October 1986).
Location: OTP.

— 1960 —

1750 **Allen, Don H.; Willey, R.C.**
"Addenda to 'A bibliography of Canadian numismatics'."
In: *Canadian Numismatic Journal*; Vol. 5, no. 1 (January 1960) p. 28-32.; ISSN: 0008-4573.
Note: Articles and pamphlets dealing with Canadian coins and tokens, banking history, paper currencies.– Continues: Bowman, Fred; Willey, R.C. (June 1959-October 1959); continued by Willey, R.C. (January 1961-October 1986).
Location: OONL.

— 1962 —

1751 **Brière, Roger**
"Esquisse bibliographique de géographie touristique."
Dans: *Revue canadienne de géographie*; Vol. 16, nos 1/2/3/4 (1962) p. 57-68.; ISSN: 0316-3032.
Note: 224 entrées.– Thèses, articles de revues de géographie, communications, mémoires, rapports d'enquêtes, livres consacrés au tourisme.
Localisation: OONL.

— 1967 —

1752 **Goeldner, C.R.; Allen, Gerald L.**
Bibliography of tourism and travel: research studies, reports and articles. Boulder, Colo.: Business Research Division, Graduate School of Business Administration, University of Colorado, [c1967]. vi, 71 l.
Note: Approx. 600 entries.– Research references related to travel industry of Canada and United States for use in business and academic fields.– Covers from January 1, 1960 to 1967.– Excludes general descriptive material.
Location: OONL.

1753 **Willey, R.C.**
"A select bibliography of Canadian numismatics."
In: *Transactions of the Canadian Numismatic Research Society*; Vol. 3, no. 2 (April 1967) p. 13-19.; ISSN: 0045-5202.
Note: Approx. 80 entries.– General works and surveys, literature dealing with decimal coins, grading of coins, colonial coinages, patterns, numismatic art and designers, trade and transportation tokens, communion tokens, medals, paper money, periodical literature.
Location: OONL.

— 1969 —

1754 **Bowman, Fred**
Canadian numismatic research index. [Lachine, Quebec]: 1969. 176 p.

Note: 2,076 entries.– Journal articles on historical topics related to Canadian coins, tokens, medals.
Location: OONL.

— 1970 —

1755 **Bibliography: tourism research studies/Bibliographie: études de recherches de tourisme.** [Ottawa]: Canadian Government Travel Bureau, 1970. 86 p.
Note: 207 entries.– Reports and surveys on accommodation and services, advertising and promotional effectiveness, developing market potential, economic analysis, recreational needs and facilities, research procedures and methodologies.– Text in English and French/texte en français et en anglais.
Location: OONL.

1756 **Canada Land Inventory**
An initial bibliography on outdoor recreational studies in Canada with selected United States references/Une première bibliographie des études sur les loisirs de plein air au Canada, accompagnée d'un choix d'ouvrages de référence publiés aux États-Unis. Rev. ed. [Ottawa]: Canada Land Inventory, Department of Regional Economic Expansion, 1970. vi, 165, [109] l.
Note: Approx. 1,600 entries.– Focus on Canadian work from 1945 to 1970.– Subjects include administration and management, community and urban planning, land use, leisure, park system planning, tourism, user and travel studies.– Compiled by Elaine Baxter.– Text in English and French/texte en anglais et en français.
Previous edition: Munro, Neil; Anderson, Duncan M. Department of Forestry and Rural Development, 1967. v, 121 p.– Approx. 1,200 entries.
Location: OONL.

1757 **Walker, Elizabeth**
"Mountaineering in Canada, 1960-1969: a bibliography of periodical literature."
In: *Canadian Alpine Journal*; Vol. 53 (1970) p. 51-54.; ISSN: 0068-8207.
Note: Location: AEU.

— 1971 —

1758 **Irvine, Russell; Sealey, Gary**
A bibliography of selected topics related to park and recreation planning and management. Toronto: Parks and Recreation Areas Branch, Division of Outdoor Recreation, Department of Lands and Forests, 1971. ii, 187 l.
Note: Topical arrangement.– Includes some Canadian references.
Location: OONL.

1759 **Marsh, John S.**
Recreation trails in Canada: a comment and bibliography on trail development and use, with special reference to the Rocky Mountain national parks and proposed Great Divide Trail. Monticello, Ill.: Council of Planning Librarians, 1971. 17 l. (Council of Planning Librarians Exchange bibliography ; 175)
Note: Approx. 120 entries.– Lists journal articles and reports on trail design and management, trail use studies, trails in Canada and United States, skiing and snowmobile trails, bicycle trails, water and cave trails.
Location: OONL.

— 1972 —

1760 **British North America Philatelic Society**
Library list, 1972 [British North America Philatelic

Society]. [Burlington, Ont.]: British North America Philatelic Society, 1972. 19 p.
Note: Approx. 1,000 entries.– Books, pamphlets, handbooks, articles on postage stamps and stamp collecting: historical, pre-stamp and stampless, cancellations and cacheted envelopes.– Includes Canadian references.
Location: OONL.

1761 **National Library of Canada**
The philatelic collection of the National Library of Canada/La collection sur la philatelie de la Bibliothèque nationale du Canada. Ottawa: National Library, 1972. 36 l.
Note: Approx. 500 entries.– Monographs, journals, auction records and price lists, catalogues and exhibitions.
Location: OONL.

— 1973 —

1762 **Saskatchewan Provincial Library. Bibliographic Services Division**
Hockey: a bibliography. Regina: Bibliographic Services Division, Provincial Library, 1973. 21 p.
Note: Approx. 120 entries.– Books on history of hockey, how to play the game, accounts of great teams, biographies of players.
Location: NSWA.

— 1974 —

1763 **Bolduc, Jocelyn**
Equipements touristiques et politiques de développement: Tiers-Monde francophone et Canada: bibliographie sélective/Tourist facilities and development policies: French speaking Third World and Canada: selective bibliography. Ottawa: Institut de coopération internationale, Université d'Ottawa, 1974. vi, 71 f. (Travaux et documents de l'I.C.I. ; série C, no 7: bibliographies)
Note: 573 entrées.– Inclut études de synthèse, monographies, articles de périodiques, publications gouvernementales, publications d'organismes internationaux, comptes rendus de conférences, thèses et mémoires, rapports de recherche, études de consultants.– Preface in English.
Localisation: OONL.

1764 **Goeldner, C.R.**
Bibliographic sources for travel and tourism research. Burnaby, B.C.: Department of Economics and Commerce, Simon Fraser University, 1974. 22 l.
Note: Approx. 100 entries.– Indexing services, bibliographies, periodicals and statistical sources.– Includes Canadian references.
Location: OONL.

1765 **Guay, Donald**
Bibliographie québécoise sur l'activité physique, 1850-1973: hygiène, santé, éducation physique, sport, plein air, tourisme, loisirs. [Québec]: Éditions du Pélican, c1974. xix, 316 p. (Groupe de recherche sur l'histoire de l'activité physique ; 1); ISBN: 0-88514-009-5.
Note: 2,640 entrées.– Comprend les ouvrages québécois seulement: livres, brochures, articles de revue.– Exclut les articles de journaux, les lois et règlements, des thèses, des communications non publiées.
Localisation: OONL.

1766 **Leclerc, Pierre A.**
Aperçu de bibliophilatélie. Québec: [s.n.], 1974. P. A-T, [5] p., [1] f. de pl.: fac-sim.
Note: 20 entrées.– Inclut un nombre d'ouvrages canadiens.– Texte en français et en anglais/text in English and French.
Localisation: OONL.

1767 **Martin, Fred W., et al.**
Therapeutic recreation in Canada: an annotated bibliography. [Waterloo, Ont.]: Therapeutic Recreation Information Centre, c1974. 68 p. (TRIC Information monograph series / Therapeutic Recreation Information Centre)
Note: 131 entries.– Contains citations and abstracts of information pertaining to recreation service for ill and disabled persons from the Therapeutic Recreation Information Centre database.
Location: OONL.

1768 **Sawula, Lorne W.**
A repository of primary and secondary sources for Canadian history of sport and physical education: prepared as a project for the History of Sport and Physical Activity Committee of C.A.H.P.E.R. [Halifax, N.S.]: Dalhousie University, School of Physical Education, 1974. 170 l.
Note: Describes holdings of libraries, universities and archives and lists selected individual titles of works related to history of sport in Canada.
Location: OONL.

— 1975 —

1769 **Canada. Environment Canada. Land Use Studies Branch. Outdoor Recreation-Open Space Division**
OR-OS [Outdoor Recreation-Open Space] reference system: component 1 (bibliographic file)/Système de référence PA-GE [Plein-air-grand espaces]: composante no 1 (dossier bibliographique). Ottawa: Environment Canada, Lands Directorate, 1975. 2 vol.
Note: Listing of Canadian and United States references dealing with carrying capacity of parks, economic impact of parks on their regions, park location, delineation, zoning and design, survey and interviewing techniques, visitors to parks (length of stay, transportation, etc.).
Location: OONL.

1770 **Dooling, Peter J.; Herrick, Ramona**
Lakeshore and surface waters for recreational use: a bibliography with abstracts. Vancouver: Park and Forest Recreation Resources, Faculty of Forestry, University of British Columbia, 1975. 14 l. (Recreation land use review Report ; no. 3)
Note: 23 entries.– Reports dealing with lakes and lakeshore management guidelines for recreation.– Includes keyword index.
Location: OONL.

1771 **Dooling, Peter J.; Herrick, Ramona**
Recreation area maintenance and rehabilitation: a bibliography with abstracts. Vancouver: Park and Forest Recreation Resources, Faculty of Forestry, University of British Columbia, 1975. 23 l. (Recreation land use review Report ; no. 1)
Note: 57 entries.– Research reports dealing with aspects of British Columbia recreation maintenance and rehabilitation, including studies on physical carrying capacity, site planning and design, soil and vegetation measure-ment and management techniques.– Keyword index.
Location: OONL.

1772 **Dooling, Peter J.; Herrick, Ramona**
Wild, scenic and recreational waterways: classification and management and water quality criteria for recreational use. a bibliography with abstracts. Vancouver: Park and Forest Recreation Resources, Faculty of Forestry, University of British Columbia, 1975. 20 l. (Recreation land use review Report ; no. 2)
Note: 36 entries.– Focusses on problems and progress in stream preservation programs and retention of recreational attributes and potentials of free-flowing streams.
Location: OONL.

1773 **Dooling, Peter J.; Sheppard, Stephen**
Recreation site development: a bibliography with abstracts. Vancouver: Park and Forest Recreation Resources, Faculty of Forestry, University of British Columbia, 1975. 16 l. (Recreation land use review Report ; no. 5)
Note: 32 entries.– Reports and articles dealing with facility design, site development, construction and facility, equipment and maintenance.– Includes keyword index.
Location: OONL.

1774 **Dooling, Peter J.; Sheppard, Stephen**
Silvicultural techniques favoring visual resource management in recreation use influence zones and intensive use recreation sites: visitor reactions to timber harvesting: a bibliography with abstracts. Vancouver: Park and Forest Recreation Resources, Faculty of Forestry, University of British Columbia, 1975. 20 l. (Recreation land use review Report ; no. 6)
Note: 34 entries.– Research reports and articles dealing with visual resource management concerns: forest aesthetics, forestry in the landscape, inventory techniques, landscape design guidelines for forest management, silviculture for recreation area management.– Keyword index.
Location: OONL.

1775 **Dooling, Peter J.; Sheppard, Stephen**
Site selection criteria and the principles of design for planning recreational places: campgrounds: a bibliography with abstracts. Vancouver: Park and Forest Recreation Resources, Faculty of Forestry, University of British Columbia, 1975. 16 l. (Recreation land use review Report ; no. 4)
Note: 29 entries.– Annotated listing of reports focussed mainly on appraisal of potential recreation sites from use of aerial photo and ground reconnaissance surveys.– Includes reports on site design and development and visitor preferences related to campgrounds.– Keyword index.
Location: OONL.

1776 **Forkes, David**
Skiing: an English language bibliography, 1891-1971. Vancouver: [s.n.], 1975. 53 l.; ISBN: 0-96909-020-X.
Note: Approx. 500 entries.– Chronological listing, 1891-1971.– Includes many Canadian references.
Location: OONL.

1777 **Herrick, Ramona; Dooling, Peter J.**
Wilderness recreation management: a bibliography with abstracts. Vancouver: Park and Forest Recreation

Resources, Faculty of Forestry, University of British Columbia, 1975. 29 l. (Recreation land use review Report ; no. 7)

Note: 63 entries.– Reports, articles, legislation dealing with wilderness establishment, management and preservation, limitation of use for recreation.– Includes keyword index.

Location: OONL.

1778 **Provencher, Léo; Thibault, Jean-Claude**
Critères physiques en aménagement récréatifs à la campagne: recherches bibliographiques. Sherbrooke: Université de Sherbrooke, Département de géographie, 1975. 56 f. (Bulletin de recherche / Université de Sherbrooke, Département de géographie ; no 23)

Note: Approx. 500 entrées.– Principaux thèmes: caractéristiques biophysiques du site (études méthodologiques, études analytiques); exigences techniques des activités récréatives; standards de qualité.– Résumé en français et en anglais.

Localisation: OONL.

1779 **Redpath, D.K.**
Recreation residential developments: a review and summary of relevant material. [Ottawa]: Lands Directorate, Environment Canada, 1975. 32 p. (Occasional paper / Environment Canada, Lands Directorate ; no. 4)

Note: Location: OONL.

1780 **Rightmire, Robert W.**
"A research bibliography for Canadian large cents." In: *Canadian Numismatic Journal*; Vol. 20, no. 6 (June 1975) p. 241-242.; ISSN: 0008-4573.

Note: Location: OONL.

— 1976 —

1781 **Canada. Parks Canada. National Historic Parks and Sites Branch. Policy Co-ordination Division**
Recreation policy bibliography. Ottawa: The Division, 1976. [44] l.

Note: Location: OOFF.

1782 **Canadian Numismatic Association**
Library catalogue [Canadian Numismatic Association]. Stayner, Ont.: Canadian Numismatic Association, 1976. 70 p.

Note: Approx. 1,000 entries.– Books on history of coins and works on coin collecting: catalogues, directories, dictionaries, bibliographies, technical aspects, periodicals and auction catalogues.– Sections on paper money, tokens, banks and banking.– International in scope, with substantial Canadian listings.

Location: OONL.

1783 **Houle, Ghislaine; Lauzier, Suzanne; Cormier, Normand**
Les sports au Québec, 1879-1975: catalogue d'exposition. Montréal: Bibliothèque nationale du Québec, 1976. xiii, 185 p.: ill. (Bibliographies québécoises / Bibliothèque nationale du Québec, Centre bibliographique ; no 4)

Note: 365 entrées.– Présente les volumes et les périodiques choisis par ordre alphabétique des sports.– Inclut une liste de cartes et une liste d'associations sportives.

Localisation: OONL.

1784 **Jeux olympiques, Montréal, Québec, 1976. Comité organisateur. Centre de documentation**
Bibliographie traitent des jeux olympiques et sujets connexes: annexe "A". [Montréal]: Comité organisateur des jeux olympiques de 1976, Direction générale de l'administration, Centre de documentation, 1976. iv, 74 f.

Note: Rédaction: Louise Papineau.– Catalogage et classification: Michelle Coderre.

Localisation: OONL.

— 1977 —

1785 **Biron, Jean-Pierre**
Bibliographie sur le loisir de plein air. Trois-Rivières: Université du Québec à Trois-Rivières, 1977. 35 f.

Note: Approx. 550 entrées.– Monographies, documents des gouvernements, bibliographies, brochures, périodiques et index de périodiques.– Sujets principaux: alpinisme, camping, environnement, parcs, colonies de vacances, randonnée pédestre, véhicules récréatifs.

Localisation: OONL.

1786 **Smith, Stephen L.J.; Blair, Marilyn**
Information resources for students, scholars and researchers in outdoor recreation, University of Waterloo. [S.l: s.n.], 1977. 37 l.

Note: Lists journals, indexes, databases, bibliographies, reference works related to outdoor recreation.– Substantial Canadian content.

Location: OONL.

— 1978 —

1787 **Swanick, Eric L.**
Canadian lotteries: an introductory bibliography. Monticello, Ill.: Vance Bibliographies, 1978. 3 p.

Note: Location: OHM.

1788 **Thom, Douglas J., et al.**
The hockey bibliography: ice hockey worldwide. [Toronto]: Ontario Institute for Studies in Education: Ministry of Culture and Recreation, Ontario, 1978. v, 153 p.: ill. (Bibliography series / Ontario Institute for Studies in Education ; no. 4); ISBN: 0-7744-0166-4.

Note: Approx. 2,500 entries.– Books, articles, theses, papers, reports, films: history and biography, statistical and research material, selected material on European hockey, a selection of material of special interest to young people.

Location: OONL.

— 1979 —

1789 **Barney, Robert Knight**
The history of sport and physical education: a source bibliography. [London, Ont.]: D.B. Weldon Library, University of Western Ontario, 1979. 57 p.; ISBN: 0-7714-0098-5.

Note: 1,117 entries.– Lists works in English which describe and analyze the play, sport, games, dance, exercise and leisure activities of peoples of all civilizations throughout history and prehistory.– Many Canadian references.

Location: OONL.

1790 **Bibliographie sur les rivières du patrimoine: références choisies du fichier de la Direction des accords au sujet de la récréation et de la conservation, Parcs Canada.**
Ottawa: Parcs Canada, 1979. iv, 302 p.

Note: Références canadiennes et américaines concernant les rivières du patrimoine.

English title: *Heritage rivers bibliography: selected references from ARC Branch, Parks Canada card index.*

Localisation: QQLA.

1791 **Catalogue éducation physique et sports.** Ste-Foy: Service des communications du Conseil des loisirs – région de Québec, 1979. 64 p. (Librairie loisirs et sports)
Note: Approx. 1,500 entrées.– Inclut un nombre d'ouvrages canadiens.
Localisation: OONL.

1792 **Catalogue loisirs, plein air et socio-culturel.** Ste-Foy: Service des communications du Conseil des loisirs – région de Québec, 1979. 81 p.
Note: Approx. 2,200 entrées.– Inclut un nombre d'ouvrages canadiens.
Localisation: OONL.

1793 **Cox, Carole Ann**
A comprehensive bibliography on children and play. Owen Sound, Ont.: Toy Yard, Owen Sound Public Library, 1979. 46 l.
Note: Approx. 300 entries.– Books, pamphlets, periodical articles, non-print materials: pre-school facilities, toy libraries, child development, play, toys (games, puppets, toy industry, toymaking).– Includes Canadian references.
Location: OONL.

1794 **Heritage rivers bibliography: selected references from ARC Branch, Parks Canada card index.** Ottawa: Planning Division, ARC Branch, Parks Canada, 1979. 255 p.
Note: Canadian and American references relating to heritage rivers: classification and selection techniques, management techniques, legislation and policies, miscellaneous research activity, guidebooks, bibliographies.
Titre en français: *Bibliographie sur les rivières du patrimoine: références choisies ....*
Location: OOPAC.

1795 **L'abandon des voies ferrées au Canada: l'utilisation de historiques: bibliographie commentée.** [Ottawa]: Parcs Canada, 1979. 97 p.
Note: 297 entrées.– Études générales de planification, conservation du patrimoine, conservation des ressources naturelles, loisirs et l'interprétation, diverses utilisations, participation du public, exploitation et gestion des nouvelles installations, bibliographies.
Localisation: OORD.

1796 **Morin, Cimon**
Canadian philately: bibliography and index, 1864-1973/ Philatélie canadienne: bibliographie et index, 1864-1973. Ottawa: National Library of Canada, 1979. xxi, 281 p.: ill., facsims.; ISBN: 0-660-50175-9.
Note: 3,481 entries.– Monographs, brochures, periodical articles, auction catalogues, exhibition catalogues dealing with the postage stamp, postal stationery, postal history and postal markings of Canada and British North America.– Excludes unpublished manuscripts, official publications of the postal administration.– Text in English and French/texte en français et en anglais.
Supplement: ... . *Supplement/ ... . Supplément.* 1983. vi, 246 p.; ISBN: 0-660-52095-8. (5,772 entries).– Covers works published between 1974 and 1980, inclusive.
Location: OONL.

1797 **Ziegler, Ronald M.**
Wilderness waterways: a guide to information sources. Detroit, Mich.: Gale Research, c1979. x, 317 p. (Sports, games, and pastimes information guide series ; no. 1); ISBN: 0-8103-1434-7.
Note: Approx. 500 entries.– List of books, films, periodicals, pamphlets on canoeing, rafting, kayaking: technique and instruction, camping skills, history, biography and trip accounts, pictorial works, waterways guidebooks, maps.– Includes a number of Canadian references.
Location: OONL.

— 1980 —

1798 **Association canadienne pour la santé, l'éducation physique et la récréation**
Répertoire des documents publiés en français sur les sciences de l'activité physique et les loisirs. Vanier, Ont.: Centre de documentation pour le sport, 1980. 441 p.
Note: Approx. 2,200 entrées.– Comprend un nombre d'ouvrages canadiens.
Localisation: OONL.

1799 **Catalogue of sports books, films & video tapes/ Catalogue du sports livres, films et bandes magnétoscopique.** Ottawa: Coaching Association of Canada, [1980]. 260 p.: ill.
Note: Lists material designed to provide technical information on instruction and coaching of sport activities.– All publications and AV items have been screened and approved by the Coaching Association of Canada and the respective national sport governing agency.– Includes Canadian references.
Location: OONL.

1800 **Studies related to British Columbia tourism: a bibliography with selected annotations.** [Victoria, B.C.]: Ministry of Tourism in cooperation with the Ministry of Industry and Small Business Development and the Canadian Government Office of Tourism, [1980]. vi, 96, [11] l.: map.
Note: Approx. 700 entries.– Government authored or sponsored studies, surveys, reports written between 1970 and 1980 dealing with tourism in British Columbia: the travel industry (accommodation, outdoor recreation, transportation, travel services), natural resource management, regional and urban planning.– Compiled under the Tourism Studies 1980 program by Marilyn Brown and Ryan Hansen.
Location: OONL.

— 1981 —

1801 **Acadia University. Centre of Leisure Studies**
Volunteers and leadership bibliography. Wolfville, N.S.: Acadia University, Centre of Leisure Studies, 1981. 62 p.
Note: Includes Canadian references.
Location: NSHPL.

1802 **British Columbia. Recreation and Sport Branch**
Community recreation bibliography. Victoria: Province of British Columbia, Recreation and Sport Branch, [1981]. iii, 38 p.; ISBN: 0-7719-8777-3.
Note: Approx. 600 entries.– Books, articles, federal and British Columbia government publications.– Topics include leadership training, facilities planning, financial management and administration, fund raising, volunteers, therapeutic recreation, leisure education, adults and seniors recreation.– Includes a substantial number of Canadian references.
Location: OONL.

1803 **British Columbia. Recreation Division. Technical Services Unit**
Recreation and sport: technical resource index. Victoria,

B.C.: Province of British Columbia, Ministry of Provincial Secretary and Government Services, Recreation and Fitness Branch, [1981]. 139 p.; ISBN: 0-7719-8506-1.
Note: Publications dealing with recreational facilities: planning, building codes, energy conservation, management, maintenance, finance, funding, legislation, philosophical approaches.– Includes Canadian references.
Location: OONL.

1804 **Canada. Parks Canada. Socio-Economic Division**
Tourism: background reading list of interest to Parks Canada. [Ottawa]: Socio-Economic Division, Parks Canada, 1981. 36 l.
Note: Approx. 450 entries.– Books, reports and studies on tourist trade: cost-benefit analysis, tourism marketing and planning, research methodology, travel and destination surveys, participation: trends and patterns/forecasting.
Location: OONL.

1805 **Hayashida, D.L.**
Parks Canada visitor services: a bibliography. Ottawa: Interpretation and Visitor Services Division, National Parks Branch, Parks Canada, 1981. [5], 49 l.
Note: Approx. 600 entries.– Covers 1962 to 1981.– Arranged in five sections: visitor use, visitor services and facilities, parks access and circulation, visitor accommodation, planning and research.
Location: OOFF.

1806 **Marsland, T.A.**
An English language bibliography of computer chess. Edmonton: Department of Computing Science, University of Alberta, 1981. 42 (i.e. 21), 10 (i.e. 5) l. (Technical report / Department of Computing Science, University of Alberta ; TR81-1)
Note: Includes Canadian references.
Location: OONL.

1807 **Willey, R.C.**
"A select bibliography of Canadian decimal coins."
In: *Canadian Numismatic Journal*; Vol. 22, no. 11 (December 1977) P. 493-494; Vol. 26, no. 4 (April 1981) p. 164-165.; ISSN: 0008-4573.
Note: Location: OTP.

— 1982 —

1808 **Canadian Olympic Association. Library**
Library bibliography [Canadian Olympic Association]/ Bibliographie de la bibliothèque [Association olympique canadienne]. Montreal: Canadian Olympic Association, 1982. ii, 45, 1 l.
Note: Approx. 700 entries.– Listing of documents relating to Olympic Games and amateur sports in the collection of Canadian Olympic Association reference library.– Includes a substantial number of Canadian references.– Compiled by Sylvia Doucette.
Location: OONL.

1809 **Coaching Association of Canada. Sport Information Resource Centre**
Body composition and exercise: an annotated bibliography/Composition corporelle et exercise: bibliographie annotée. Ottawa: The Centre, c1982. [5] p.
Note: Includes Canadian references.– Text in English and French/texte en français et en anglais.
Location: OONL.

1810 **Coaching Association of Canada. Sport Information Resource Centre**
Dance aerobics: an annotated bibliography/Danse aérobie: bibliographie annotée. Ottawa: The Centre, c1982. [4] p.
Note: Includes Canadian references.– Text in English and French/texte en français et en anglais.
Location: OONL.

1811 **Coaching Association of Canada. Sport Information Resource Centre**
Exercise and pregnancy: an annotated bibliography/ Exercice et grossesse: bibliographie annotée. Ottawa: The Centre, c1982. [7] p.
Note: Includes Canadian references.– Text in English and French/texte en français et en anglais.
Location: OONL.

1812 **Coaching Association of Canada. Sport Information Resource Centre**
Lower back care: an annotated bibliography/Soins pour les bas du dos: bibliographie annotée. Ottawa: The Centre, c1982. [4] p.
Note: Includes Canadian references.– Text in English and French/texte en français et en anglais.
Location: OONL.

1813 **Coaching Association of Canada. Sport Information Resource Centre**
Stress and coping: an annotated bibliography/Stress et stratégies d'adaptation: bibliographie annotée. Ottawa: The Centre, c1982. [4] p.
Note: Includes Canadian references.– Text in English and French/texte en français et en anglais.
Location: OONL.

1814 **Craig, Helen C.**
Bibliography of Canadian Boy Scout materials. [Fredericton, N.B.: H.C. Craig, 1982]. [6] 57 p.; ISBN: 0-9691055-0-9.
Note: 1,346 entries.– Covers 1909 to 1981.– Books, magazine articles, serials, annual reports, films, filmstrips, slides, phonograph records, tape recordings.
Location: OONL.

1815 **Draayer, Ingrid**
Sport bibliography/Bibliographie du sport. Ottawa: Sport Information Resource Centre, 1981-1982. 8 vol.; ISBN: 0-920678-02-5 (vol. 1); 0-920678-04-1 (vol. 2); 0-920678-06-8 (vol. 3); 0-920678-08-4 (vol. 4); 0-920678-10-6 (vol. 5); 0-920678-12-2 (vol. 6); 0-920678-14-9 (vol. 7); 0-920678-16-5 (vol. 8).
Note: Approx. 70,000 entries.– Books, periodical articles, theses, microforms, conference proceedings on all subjects related to sport and physical activity for the years 1974 to 1980 inclusive.– Drawn from the SPORT database, compiled and maintained by the Sport Information Resource Centre, much of this material is available in the SIRC resource collection.– Substantial Canadian content.
Vol. 1: *Aquatic sports, outdoor sports, wintersports.* viii, 282 p.
Vol. 2: *Team sports, bowling sports and golf.* viii, 260 p.
Vol. 3: *Combat sports, gymnastics and dance, martial arts, racquet sports, track and field, weightlifting.* vii, 386 p.
Vol. 4: *Aeronautical sports, bicycling and cycling, equestrian sports, motor sports, target sports.* viii, 148 p.
Vol. 5: *Coaching, training and officiating.* viii, 89 p.

Vol. 6: *Sporting events and international competitions.* viii, 112 p.

Vol. 7: *Humanities and social sciences.* viii, 463 p.

Vol. 8: *Science and medicine.* viii, 535 p.

Text in English and French/texte en français et en anglais. Supplement. Wheeler, Linda. ... . *Update 1983/* ... . *Mise à jour 1983.* 1983. 2 vol.; ISBN: 0-920678-18-1.– 28,000 entries.– Includes all material from 1979 on added to the SPORT database since the 8-volume bibliography.
Location: OONL.

1816 **Forest, Paul**
Sports et loisirs: bibliographie, périodiques, films, diaporamas, organismes. Montréal: Collège Marie-Victorin, 1982. 31, [1] p.; ISBN: 2-920279-08-4.
Note: Approx. 300 entrées.– Inclut un nombre considérable d'ouvrages canadiens.
Localisation: OONL.

1817 **MacFarlane, John**
The bibliography of Canadian heritage interpretation, 1982/Bibliographie de l'interprétation du patrimoine canadien, 1982. Ottawa: Interpretation and Visitor Services Division, National Parks Branch, Parks Canada, [1982]. [37] l.
Note: Text in English and French/texte en français et en anglais.
Location: OOFF.

1818 **Ontario. Ministry of Labour. Library**
"Sex discrimination in sports: a selected bibliography."
In: *Labour Topics*; Vol. 5, no. 11 (November 1982) p. 1-4.; ISSN: 0704-8874.
Note: Approx. 50 entries.
Location: AEU.

1819 **Reid, Bob; Mongeon, Jean**
Employee fitness: an annotated bibliography/Condition physique de l'employé: bibliographie annotée. Ottawa: Coaching Association of Canada, Sport Information Resource Centre, c1982. [6] p.
Note: 20 entries.– Articles, documents.– Includes Canadian references.– Text in English and French/texte en français et en anglais.
Location: OONL.

1820 **Reid, Bob; Mongeon, Jean**
Fitness motivation: an annotated bibliography/Motivation et conditionnement physique: bibliographie annotée. Ottawa: Sport Information Resource Centre, c1982. [5] p.
Note: 11 entries.– Documents and articles on motivating factors influencing adult participation in vigorous physical activity.– Includes Canadian references.
Location: OONL.

— 1983 —

1821 **Archives ordinolingues (Canada)**
Dossiers des données sur les loisirs et la récréation. Ottawa: Archives publiques Canada, 1983. vi, 63, 62, vi p.; ISBN: 0-662-52335-0.
Note: Enquêtes dans les parcs nationaux, enquêtes faites aux lieux historiques nationaux, enquêtes faites près des canaux, enquêtes sur les activités de plein air (général).– Texte en français et en anglais disposé tête-bêche.– Titre de la p. de t. additionnelle: *Recreation and leisure data files.*
Localisation: OONL.

1822 **Canadian Government Office of Tourism. Tourism Reference and Data Centre**
Book catalogue of tourism research studies/Catalogue de livres des études de recherches de tourisme. Ottawa: Canadian Government Office of Tourism, 1980-1983. 5 vol.; ISSN: 0712-3469.
Note: Includes Canadian publications in English and French.– Text in English and French/texte en français et en anglais.
Location: OONL.

1823 **Graham, R.; Huff, Donald W.**
Annotated bibliography of underwater and marine park related initiatives in northern latitudes. Hull, Quebec: Parks Canada, 1983. [120] l.
Note: Approx. 400 entries.– Papers, reports, published articles dealing with marine and coastal conservation in northern latitudes.– Topics include marine parks planning and management, site classification, inventory, selection criteria, interpretation and environmental education, legislation and principles of marine resource policy, biological and ecological basis for establishment of marine parks.– Emphasis on European and Canadian experience.
Location: OOPAC.

1824 **Machine Readable Archives (Canada)**
Recreation and leisure data files. [Ottawa]: Public Archives Canada, 1983. vi, 62, 63, vi p.; ISBN: 0-662-52335-0.
Note: Canal surveys, general outdoor surveys, national historic sites surveys, national park surveys.– Text in English and French with French text on inverted pages.– Title of additional title-page: *Dossier des données sur les loisirs et la récréation.*
Location: OONL.

1825 **Malcolm, Ross**
A selected bibliography on regional and community park topics with particular reference to British Columbia. [Victoria, B.C.]: Parks and Outdoor Recreation Division, Ministry of Lands, Parks and Housing, 1983. (unpaged).
Note: Listing of parks planning and administration studies and reports with focus on British Columbia: general works, planning studies, design, regional and community park reports, parks and recreation master plans.– List of additional bibliographies.– List of periodicals.
Location: BVAS.

1826 **Pope, Judy L.**
A bibliographic survey of socio-economic studies relating to Canadian national heritage properties. Ottawa: Socio-economic Division, Program Management, Parks Canada, 1983. ix, 137 l.
Note: Approx. 600 entries.– Studies (unpublished government reports, research notes, planning studies) dealing specifically with the interaction of people and parks, produced from 1960 to 1980.– Arranged alphabetically by the five Parks Canada regions: Atlantic, Ontario, Prairie, Quebec and Western, which are subdivided into National Parks; National Historic Parks and Sites; Agreements for Recreation and Conservation areas; General references.– Includes a list of bibliographic sources.– All documents are given locations.
Titre en français: *Bibliographie sur les études socio-économiques relatives aux propriétés historiques du Canada.*
Location: OOEPSE.

1827 **Pope, Judy L.**
Bibliographie sur les études socio-économiques relatives aux propriétés historiques du Canada. Ottawa: Division socio-économique, Direction de la gestion du programme, Parcs Canada, 1983. ix, 140 p.
Note: Approx. 600 entrées.– Comprend les ouvrages produits durant la période de 1960 à 1980.– Études sur l'attitude des visiteurs face aux parcs, et notamment sur leur utilisation des parcs et des lieux.
English title: *A bibliographic survey of socio-economic studies relating to Canadian national heritage properties.*
Localisation: OOFF.

— 1984 —

1828 **Health, psychological and social factors: an annotated bibliography/La santé, les facteurs psychologiques et sociologiques: bibliographie annotée.** Vanier, Ont.: Secretariat for Fitness in the Third Age, 1984. 24 p.; ISBN: 0-919963-23-4.
Note: Approx. 60 entries.– Summaries of articles and documents published to 1982, dealing with physical fitness of senior citizens.– Includes Canadian references.– Text in English and French/texte en français et en anglais.
Location: OONL.

1829 **Holmes, Alison**
Children's play spaces and equipment: bibliography, prepared by Alison Holmes for the Canadian Institute of Child Health's Task Force for the Development of Guidelines for Children's Play Spaces and Equipment. Ottawa: The Institute, 1984. 19 l.
Note: Approx. 260 entries.– Reports and studies on playground equipment coded in four categories: injury, equipment, standards, statistics.– Excludes references to child development and related play concepts.– International coverage, with substantial Canadian content.
Location: OONL.

1830 **Kelly, Shirley; Stark, Richard**
Sport and recreation for the disabled: an index of resource materials/Sport et loisir pour handicapés: un répertoire de la littérature. Ottawa: Sport Information Resource Centre, 1984. xxxi, 186 p.; ISBN: 0-920678-38-6.
Note: Approx. 3,500 entries.– Holdings of 23 organizations and resource centres which have specialized material on sport and recreation for the handicapped.– Topics include administration, programs, professional development, facilities and equipment, accessibility, competitive sports, disabilities, motor ability and therapeutic recreation.– Substantial Canadian content.– Text in English and French/texte en français et en anglais.
Previous edition: Draayer, Ingrid. 1979. xxii, 67 p.
Location: OONL.

1831 **Perry, Lee**
For the comtemplative man: a bibliography of works on angling and on game fish in the University of British Columbia Library. Vancouver: The Library, 1984. 130 p.
Note: Approx. 1,600 entries.– Lists the general collection and the special collection of rare works housed in the Sherrington Room, supported by the Harry Hawthorn Foundation and dedicated to Roderick Haig-Brown.– Includes Canadian titles.
Previous edition: Starkman, Susan B.; Read, Stanley E. *The contemplative man's recreation: a bibliography of books on angling and game fish in the Library of the University of British Columbia.* Vancouver: 1970. 138 p.

Supplement: Daniells, Laurenda. *More recreation for the contemplative man: a supplemental bibliography of books on angling and game fish in the Library of the University of British Columbia.* Vancouver: 1971. 33 p.
Location: OONL.

1832 **Physical activity: annotated bibliography/Activité physique: bibliographie annotée.** Ottawa: Secretariat for Fitness in the Third Age, 1984. 28 p.; ISBN: 0-919963-20-X.
Note: Approx. 80 entries.– Covers up to 1982.– Lists articles and documents dealing with physical fitness of senior citizens.– Includes Canadian references.– Text in English and French/texte en français et en anglais.
Location: OONL.

1833 **Programming: an annotated bibliography/Programmation: bibliographie annotée.** Vanier, Ont.: Secretariat for Fitness in the Third Age, 1984. 18 p.; ISBN: 0-919963-31-5.
Note: Approx. 70 entries.– Includes summaries of articles and documents published to 1982 dealing with fitness programs for seniors, covering a wide range of exercises.– Includes Canadian references.– Text in English and French/texte en français et en anglais.
Location: OONL.

1834 **Research and studies: an annotated bibliography/Recherche et communiqué: bibliographie annotée.** Vanier, Ont.: Secretariat for Fitness in the Third Age, 1984. 24 p.; ISBN: 0-919963-20-X.
Note: Approx. 65 entries.– Includes summaries of articles and documents published to 1982 dealing with physical fitness of senior citizens, covering a range of topics, from physiological changes to general exercise program, to defined issues such as bone changes caused by running.– Text in English and French/texte en français et en anglais.
Location: OONL.

— 1985 —

1835 **McCarl, Henry N.; McConnell, David**
Bibliography on economic analysis for parks and recreation. Monticello, Ill.: Vance Bibliographies, 1985. 28 p. (Public administration series: Bibliography ; P-1709; ISSN: 0193-970X); ISBN: 0-89028-459-8.
Note: Books and articles on economic aspects of parks and outdoor recreation, United States and Canada.
Location: OOFF.

1836 **Saskatchewan. Saskatchewan Tourism and Small Business**
Bibliography of tourism surveys and reports. Regina: Saskatchewan Tourism and Small Business, 1985. 25 p.
Note: Location: OONL.

— 1986 —

1837 **Canada. Parks Canada. Socio-Economic Division**
Park fees reference list. Ottawa: Parks Canada, 1986. 10 l.
Note: Location: OOFF.

1838 **Willey, R.C.**
"Bibliography of Canadian numismatics."
In: *Canadian Numismatic Journal*; Vol. 6, no. 1 (January 1961) p. 18-22; vol. 8, no. 3 (March 1963) p. 95-96; vol. 10, no. 3 (March 1965) p. 93-95; vol. 11, no. 3 (March 1966) p. 95-98; vol. 12, no. 2 (February 1967) p. 46-49; vol. 14, no. 2 (February 1969) p. 44-47; vol. 15, no. 2 (February 1970) p. 45-47; vol. 19, no. 6 (June 1974) p. 204-209; vol. 20, no. 5 (May 1975) p. 225-227; vol. 21, no. 2 (February 1976) p. 54-57; vol. 22, no. 2 (February 1977) p. 55-66; vol. 22, no. 3

(March 1977) p. 111-120; vol. 22, no. 4 (April 1977) p. 154-169; vol. 22, no. 5 (May 1977) p. 222-224; vol. 22, no. 6 (June 1977) p. 269-278; vol. 22, no. 7 (July/August 1977) p. 323-325; vol. 22, no. 8 (September 1977) p. 363-373; vol. 22, no. 9 (October 1977) p. 398-405; vol. 22, no. 10 (November 1977) p. 458-463; vol. 31, no. 6 (June 1986) p. 245-252; vol. 31, no. 7 (July/August 1986) p. 318-321; vol. 31, no. 8 (September 1986) p. 367-370; vol. 31, no. 9 (October 1986) p. 416-421.; ISSN: 0008-4573.
Note: Articles and pamphlets dealing with Canadian coins and tokens, banking history, paper currencies.– Continues: Bowman, Fred; Willey, R.C. (June 1959-October 1959); Allen, Don H.; Willey, R.C. (January 1960).
Location: OONL.

— 1987 —

1839 **"Books and pamphlets authored by Fellows [of Canadian Numismatic Research Society]."**
In: *Transactions of the Canadian Numismatic Research Society*; Vol. 16, no. 2 (Summer 1980) p. 46-47; vol. 17, no. 1 (Spring 1981) P. 34-35; vol. 18, no. 1 (Spring 1982) p. 15-17; vol. 19, no. 2 (Summer 1983) p. 35-36; vol. 20, no. 4 (Winter 1984) p. 104-106; vol. 21 (1985) p. 119-120; vol. 23 (1987) p. 27-29.; ISSN: 0045-5202.
Note: Location: OLU.

1840 **Jay-Rayon, Jean-Claude**
Bibliographie plein-air: résumés d'ouvrages francophones québécois, 1972-1986. [Québec]: Loisir, chasse et pêche, Québec, 1987. xxi, 167 p.; ISBN: 2-550-17214-0.
Note: 165 entrées.– Fondements, politiques, éducation, études et évaluations, plans de développement, symposiums et colloques, organismes, activités.
Localisation: OONL.

1841 **Service de diffusion sélective de l'information de la Centrale des bibliothèques**
Le Hockey sur glace et sur gazon. Montréal: Le Service, 1987. 25 p. (DSI/CB ; no 101; ISSN: 0825-5024); ISBN: 2-89059-306-1.
Note: 241 entrées.– Monographies, articles de périodiques et documents audiovisuels sur aspects variés du hockey: techniques, règlements, équipes, joueurs, gardiens, équipement, entraînement.
Localisation: OONL.

1842 **"Station touristique et temps partage: deux formes de villégiature."**
Dans: *Notes du Centre d'études du tourisme*; Vol. 7, no 8 (février 1987) p. 1-4.; ISSN: 0229-2718.
Note: 49 entrées.– Inclut un nombre d'ouvrages canadiens.
Localisation: OONL.

1843 **"Le tourisme à Montréal."**
Dans: *Notes du Centre d'études du tourisme*; Vol. 7, no 9 (mars 1987) p. 1-4.; ISSN: 0229-2718.
Note: Localisation: OONL.

1844 **"Tourisme, culture, régions."**
Dans: *Notes du Centre d'études du tourisme*; Vol. 7, no 11 (mai 1987) p. 1-4.; ISSN: 0229-2718.
Note: 43 entrées.
Localisation: OONL.

1845 **Université de Montréal. Département d'éducation physique**
Département d'éducation physique, Université de Montréal: rétrospective 1982 à 1987. Montréal: Le

Département, 1987. 181 p.
Note: Publications et communications de recherche, contributions professionnelles: publications scientifiques, rapports techniques, conférences.
Localisation: OONL.

— 1988 —

1846 **Bibliothèque de la ville de Montréal**
L'Alimentation traditionnelle au Canada: une bibliographie. Montréal: Ville de Montréal, Service de loisirs et du développement communautaire, 1988. 8 p.; ISBN: 2-89417-028-9.
Note: Approx. 150 entrées.
Localisation: OONL.

1847 **Dubé, Carl**
Annotated bibliography on culture, tourism and multiculturalism. [Ottawa: Department of Communications], 1988. 23, 25 p.
Note: 127 entries.– Books, studies, reports: tourism and culture, audience profile, tourist profile, economic impact, bibliographies.– Text in English and French with French text on inverted pages.– Title of additional title-page: *Bibliographie commentée sur la culture, le tourisme et le multiculturalisme.*
Location: OOCO.

1848 **Dubé, Carl**
Bibliographie commentée sur la culture, le tourisme et le multiculturalisme. [Ottawa: Ministère des communications], 1988. 25, 23 p.
Note: 132 entrées.– Livres, rapports d'études: tourisme et culture, profil d'auditoire, profil des touristes, impact économique, bibliographies, divers.– Texte en français et en anglais disposé tête-bêche.– Titre de la p. de t. additionnelle: *Annotated bibliography on culture, tourism and multiculturalism.*
Localisation: OOCO.

1849 **"L'économie du tourisme."**
Dans: *Notes du Centre d'études du tourisme*; Vol. 8, no 1 (février 1988) p. 1-4.; ISSN: 0229-2718.
Note: Localisation: OONL.

1850 **"Le libre-échange et le champ récréotouristique."**
Dans: *Notes du Centre d'études du tourisme*; Vol. 8, no 6 (juillet 1988) p. 1-4.; ISSN: 0229-2718.
Note: Approx. 50 entrées.
Localisation: OONL.

1851 **"Le Québec touristique."**
Dans: *Notes du Centre d'études du tourisme*; Vol. 8, no 3 (avril 1988) p. 1-2.; ISSN: 0229-2718.
Note: Localisation: OONL.

1852 **"La recherche en tourisme."**
Dans: *Notes du Centre d'études du tourisme*; Vol. 8, no 5 (juin 1988) p. 1-2.; ISSN: 0229-2718.
Note: Deux parties: articles sur la recherche en général; produits de la recherche (plans de développement ou de marketing, résultats d'enquêtes, outils de mesure, études de comportements).
Localisation: OONL.

1853 **Samson, Marcel**
"La résidence secondaire et la région métropolitaine de Montréal: essai d'interprétation."
Dans: *Notes du Centre d'études du tourisme*; Vol. 8, no 2 (mars 1988) p. 1-4.; ISSN: 0229-2718.
Note: 63 entrées.
Localisation: OONL.

— 1990 —

1854 **Commercialization of amateur sport: a specialized bibliography from the SPORT database/Commercialisation du sport amateur: une bibliographie spécialisée de la base de données SPORT.** Gloucester, Ont.: Sport Information Resource Centre, 1990. 12 l. (SportBiblio ; no. 4; ISSN: 1180-5269)
Note: Approx. 250 entries.– Includes Canadian references.
Location: OONL.

1855 **Ethics in sport: a specialized bibliography from the SPORT database/Éthique du sport: une bibliographie spécialisée de la base de données SPORT.** Gloucester, Ont.: Sport Information Resource Centre, 1990. 10 l. (SportBiblio ; no. 1; ISSN: 1180-5269)
Note: Approx. 200 entries.– Includes Canadian references.
Location: OONL.

1856 **Gender issues in sport: a specialized bibliography from the SPORT database/L'équité dans le sport: une bibliographie spécialisée de la base de données SPORT.** Gloucester, Ont.: Sport Information Resource Centre, 1990. 49 l. (SportBiblio ; no. 15; ISSN: 1180-5269)
Note: Approx. 500 entries.– Books, magazine and journal articles, theses.– International scope, many Canadian references.
Location: OONL.

1857 **Nutrition and physical activity: a specialized bibliography from the SPORT database/Nutrition et l'activité physique: une bibliographie spécialisée de la base de données SPORT.** Gloucester, Ont.: Sport Information Resource Centre, 1990. 12 l. (SportBiblio ; no. 9; ISSN: 1180-5269)
Note: Approx. 250 entries.– Includes Canadian references.
Location: OONL.

1858 **Physical activity and mental health: a specialized bibliography from the SPORT database/L'activité physique et la santé mentale: une bibliographie spécialisée de la base de données SPORT.** Gloucester, Ont.: Sport Information Resource Centre, 1990. 13 l. (SportBiblio ; no. 6; ISSN: 1180-5269)
Note: Approx. 235 entries.– Includes Canadian references.
Location: OONL.

1859 **Physical fitness in the third age: a specialized bibliography from the SPORT database/Condition physique du troisième âge: une bibliographie spécialisée de la base de données SPORT.** Gloucester, Ont.: Sport Information Resource Centre, 1990. 18 l. (SportBiblio ; no. 5; ISSN: 1180-5269)
Note: Approx. 275 entries.– Includes Canadian references.
Location: OONL.

1860 **Spectator violence: a specialized bibliography from the SPORT database/Violence des spectateurs: une bibliographie spécialisée de la base de données SPORT.** Gloucester, Ont.: Sport Information Resource Centre, 1990. 10 l. (SportBiblio ; no. 2; ISSN: 1180-5269)
Note: Approx. 200 entries.– Includes Canadian references.
Location: OONL.

1861 **Sport violence: a specialized bibliography from the SPORT database/Violence du sport: une bibliographie spécialisée de la base de données SPORT.** Gloucester, Ont.: Sport Information Resource Centre, 1990. 9 l. (SportBiblio ; no. 8; ISSN: 1180-5269)
Note: Approx. 200 entries.– Includes Canadian references.
Location: OONL.

1862 **Stark, Richard, et al.**
Sport and recreation for the disabled: a bibliography, 1984-1989/Sport et loisirs pour handicapés: une bibliographie, 1984-1989. Gloucester, Ont.: Sport Information Resource Centre/Centre de documentation pour le sport, 1990. ii, 209 p.; ISBN: 0-921817-08-8.
Note: Approx. 4,000 entries.– Journal articles, books, conference proceedings, theses, microfiches.– Topics include administration, competitive sports, disabilities, facilities, professional development, sports and recreation activities, sports medicine, therapeutic recreation.– Many Canadian references.– Edited by Richard Stark, Marion Rogers, Jean-Michel Johnson, Gilles Chiasson.– Text in English and French/texte en français et en anglais.
Location: OONL.

— 1991 —

1863 **Canadian Coast Guard. Search and Rescue Branch**
Directory of safe boating information. Ottawa: Canadian Coast Guard, c1991. 50, [15] p.; ISBN: 0-662-18627-3.
Note: 251 entries.– Listing of Canadian documents dealing with safe boating, with a list of sources and a subject index.
Titre en français: *Répertoire de documents sur la sécurité nautique.*
Location: OONL.

1864 **Garde côtière canadienne. Direction de la recherche et du sauvage**
Répertoire de documents sur la sécurité nautique. Ottawa: Garde côtière canadienne, c1991. 51, [15] p.; ISBN: 0-662-96718-6.
Note: 251 entrées.– Documents portant sur la sécurité nautique, une section des sources, index analytique.
English title: *Directory of safe boating information.*
Localisation: OONL.

1865 **Liability and negligence: a specialized bibliography from the SPORT database/Responsabilité légale et négligence: une bibliographie spécialisée de la base de données SPORT.** Gloucester, Ont.: Sport Information Resource Centre, 1991. 15 l. (SportBiblio ; no. 11; ISSN: 1180-5269)
Note: Approx. 450 entries.– Includes Canadian references.
Location: OONL.

1866 **McBrien, Marlene; Buschert, Karen**
An introductory guide to coastal paddling information sources. [Ottawa]: Visitor Activities Branch, National Parks, Canadian Parks Service, 1991. 25 p.
Note: Books, articles, directories, guidebooks, reports, technical/standards information related to canoeing or kayaking along large freshwater or ocean shorelines, published after 1980, with emphasis on Canadian material.
Location: OOFF.

1867 Sport legislation: Europe and North America: a specialized bibliography from the SPORT Database/ Législation sportive: Europe et Amérique du Nord: une bibliographie spécialisée de la base de données SPORT. Gloucester, Ont.: Sport Information Resource Centre, 1991. 16 l.
Note: Includes Canadian references.– Text in English and French/texte en français et en anglais.
Location: OONL.

1868 Stark, Richard, et al.
The Drug file: a comprehensive bibliography on drugs and doping in sport/Dossier dopage: une bibliographie complète sur les drogues et le dopage dans le sport. Gloucester, Ont.: Sport Information Resource Centre, 1991. vi, 179 p.; ISBN: 0-921817-10-X.
Note: 4,000 entries.– Books, book chapters, journal articles, conference proceedings, theses, microfiches, pamphlets and brochures published between 1985 and 1991 dealing with aspects of drugs and doping in sports.– Selected references from 1980 to 1985.– Substantial Canadian content.– Online access: *SPORT Database*, available through CAN/OLE, DIALOG, DATA-STAR, BRS/MAXWELL.– CD-ROM: *SPORT Database* available as *SPORT Discus*, through SilverPlatter.– Text in English and French/texte en français et en anglais.
Location: OONL.

1869 Strength training for youth: a specialized bibliography from the SPORT database/Musculation pour les jeunes: une bibliographie spécialisées de la base de données SPORT. Gloucester, Ont.: Sport Information Resource Centre, 1991. 23 l. (SportBiblio ; no. 12; ISSN: 1180-5269)
Note: Approx. 400 entries.– Includes Canadian references.
Location: OONL.

— 1992 —

1870 Robson, Mark; Eagles, Paul F.J.; Waters, Joanne
Ecotourism: an annotated bibliography. Waterloo, Ont.: Department of Recreation and Leisure Studies, University of Waterloo, 1992. 59 p. (Occasional paper / Department of Recreation and Leisure Studies, University of Waterloo ; no. 19)
Note: 150 entries.– English-language journal articles, conference papers, theses, books and book chapters dealing with aspects of ecotourism.– Includes Canadian references.
Location: OONL.

Social Sciences

Sciences sociales

— 1808 —

1871 **Boucher de la Richarderie, Gilles**
Bibliothèque universelle des voyages ou Notice complète et raisonnée de tous les voyages anciens et modernes dans les différentes parties du monde .... Paris: Treuttel et Würtz, 1808. 6 vol.
Note: Microforme:
Vol. 1: ICMH collection de microfiches ; no 33265; ISBN: 0-665-33265-3. 6 microfiches (277 images).
Vol. 2: ICMH collection de microfiches ; no 33266; ISBN: 0-665-33266-1. 6 microfiches (282 images).
Vol. 3: ICMH collection de microfiches ; no 33267; ISBN: 0-665-33267-X. 6 microfiches (268 images).
Vol. 4: ICMH collection de microfiches ; no 33268; ISBN: 0-665-33268-8. 6 microfiches (288 images).
Vol. 5: ICMH collection de microfiches ; no 33269; ISBN: 0-665-33269-6. 6 microfiches (280 images).
Vol. 6: ICMH collection de microfiches ; no 33270; ISBN: 0-665-33270-X. 6 microfiches (259 images).
Localisation: OOU.

— 1837 —

1872 **Faribault, Georges Barthélemi**
Catalogue d'ouvrages sur l'histoire de l'Amérique, et en particulier sur celle du Canada, de la Louisiane, de l'Acadie, et autres lieux, ci-devant connus sous le nom de Nouvelle-France; avec des notes bibliographiques, critiques et littéraires. En trois parties. Québec: Cowan, 1837. 207 p.
Note: 969 entrées.
Microforme: ICMH collection de microfiches ; no 35093; ISBN: 0-665-35093-7. 3 microfiches (114 images).
Réimpression: [New York]: Johnson Reprint, 1966. 207 p.
Localisation: OONL.

— 1845 —

1873 **Canada. Legislature. Legislative Assembly. Library**
Catalogue of books relating to the history of America: forming part of the Library of the Legislative Assembly of Canada. Quebec: [s.n.], 1845. 29 p.
Note: Microform: CIHM Microfiche series ; no. 47181; ISBN: 0-665-47181-5. 1 microfiche (18 fr.).
Supplements:
Library of the Legislative Assembly: books added to the collection on the history of America, since the printing of the catalogue in 1845. [Montreal: s.n.], 1846. 8 p.
Supplement to the catalogue of books in the Library of the Legislative Assembly of Canada: containing the books added in the year 1846. Montreal: Lovell & Gibson, 1847. 24 p.
Microform: CIHM Microfiche series ; no. 53714; ISBN: 0-665-53714-X. 1 microfiche (16 fr.).
Supplementary catalogue of books, added to the collection on the history of America, during the year 1847. Montreal: Lovell & Gibson, 1848. 8 p.
Microform: CIHM Microfiche series ; no. 35890; ISBN: 0-665-35890-3. 1 microfiche (9 fr.).
Location: OONL.

— 1847 —

1874 **O'Callaghan, Edmund Bailey**
Jesuit relations of discoveries and other occurrences in Canada and the northern and western states of the Union, 1632-1672. New York: Press of the Historical Society, 1847. 22 p.
Note: Microform: CIHM Microfiche series ; no. 34056; ISBN: 0-665-34056-7. 1 microfiche (16 fr.).
Location: OONL.

— 1850 —

1875 **O'Callaghan, Edmund Bailey**
Relations des Jésuites sur les découvertes et les autres événements arrivés en Canada, et au nord et à l'ouest des États-Unis, 1611-1672. Montréal: Bureau des mélanges religieux, 1850. vi, 70 p.
Note: Microforme: ICMH collection de microfiches ; no 36458; ISBN: 0-665-36458-X. 1 microfiche (46 images).
Localisation: OONL.

— 1860 —

1876 **Catalogue of a large and valuable collection of English and French books: belonging to a private gentleman, among which are to be found a considerable number of scarce and rare books relating to the early history of America.** Quebec: [s.n.], 1860. 16 p.
Note: Microform: CIHM Microfiche series ; no. 47198; ISBN: 0-665-47198-X. 1 microfiche (19 fr.).
Location: QQS.

— 1864 —

1877 **Carayon, Auguste**
Bibliographie historique de la Compagnie de Jésus ou Catalogue des ouvrages relatifs à l'histoire des Jésuites depuis leur origine jusqu'à nos jours. London: Barthes and Lowell, 1864. viii, 612 p.
Note: Microforme: ICMH collection de microfiches ; no 44366; ISBN: 0-665-44366-8. 7 microfiches (326 images).
Localisation: OOU.

— 1883 —

1878 **Griffin, Appleton Prentiss Clark**
The discovery of the Mississippi: a bibliographical account, with a fac-simile of the map of Louis Joliet, 1674. To which is appended a note on the Joliet map by B.F. De Costa, with a sketch of Joutel's maps. New York: A.S. Barnes, 1883. 200 p., [1] folded l. of pl.: maps (1 col.).
Note: "Reprinted from the *Magazine of American History*, March and April, 1883."
Microform: CIHM Microfiche series ; no. 29025; ISBN: 0-665-29025-X. 1 microfiche (19 fr.).
Location: OONL.

1879 **Griffin, Appleton Prentiss Clark**
Discovery of the Mississippi, bibliographical account of the travels of Nicolet, Alloüez, Marquette, Hennepin and La Salle in the Mississippi Valley. Boston: [s.n.], 1883. P. [190]-199, [273]-280, [1] folded l. of pl.: col. map.
Note: Excerpt from the *Magazine of American History*; Vol. 9 (1883).

Microform: CIHM Microfiche series ; no. 06358; ISBN: 0-665-06358-X. 1 microfiche (11 fr.).
Location: OONL.

1880 **Griffin, Appleton Prentiss Clark**
"Discovery of the Mississippi, bibliographical account of the travels of Nicolet, Allouez, Marquette, Hennepin and La Salle in the Mississippi Valley."
In: *Magazine of American History*; Vol. 9 (1883) p. 190-199, [273]-280.; ISSN: 0361-6185.
Note: Location: OONL.

— 1885 —

1881 **Bibaud, Maximilien**
Mémorial des honneurs étrangers conférés à des Canadiens ou domiciliés de la puissance du Canada. Montréal: Beauchemin & Valois, 1885. 100 p.
Note: "Bibliographie canadienne en dehors du Canada," p. 83-94.
Microforme: ICMH collection de microfiches ; no 00111; ISBN: 0-665-00111-8. 2 microfiches (56 images).
Localisation: OONL.

1882 **Stewart, George**
"Sources of early Canadian history."
In: *Proceedings and Transactions of the Royal Society of Canada*; Series 1, vol. 3, section 2 (1885) p. 39-44.; ISSN: 0316-4616.
Note: Location: AEU.

— 1889 —

1883 **Boosé, James Rufus**
Titles of publications relating to the British colonies, their government, etc., in connection with imperial policy. London: Imperial Federation League, 1889. 24 p.
Note: Microform: CIHM Microfiche series ; no. 62056; ISBN: 0-665-62056-X. 1 microfiche (18 fr.).
Location: OONL.

— 1891 —

1884 **Remington, Cyrus Kingsbury**
The ship-yard of the Griffon: a brigantine built by René Robert Cavelier, sieur de La Salle, in the year 1679, above the falls of Niagara. Buffalo, N.Y.: [Press of J.W. Clement], 1891. 78 p.
Note: "Illustrated by views and maps, ancient and modern, together with the most complete bibliography of Hennepin that has ever been made in any one list and containing some editions not mentioned by Sabin and other authorities."- Bibliography of Hennepin: p. [51]-74.– Bibliography of La Salle: p. [75]-78.
Microform: CIHM Microfiche series ; no. 12327; ISBN: 0-665-12327-2. 1 microfiche (45 fr.).
Location: OONL.

1885 **Würtele, Fred C.; Strachan, J.W.**
Index of the lectures, papers and historical documents published by the Literary and Historical Society of Quebec, and also the names of their authors, together with a list of unpublished papers read before the society, 1829 to 1891. Quebec: Morning Chronicle, 1891. xlix p.
Note: Reprint: Quebec: Printed for the Society by L'Événement, 1927. xlix p.
Microform: CIHM Microfiche series ; no. 26287; ISBN: 0-665-26287-6. 1 microfiche (35 fr.).
Location: OONL.

— 1897 —

1886 **Dionne, Narcisse-Eutrope**
Hennepin, ses voyages et ses oeuvres. Québec: R.

Renault, 1897. 40 p.
Note: Réimpression: Montréal: Éditions Canadiana, [1970]. 40 p.
Microforme: ICMH collection de microfiches ; no 59008; ISBN: 0-665-59008-3. 1 microfiche (26 images).
Localisation: OONL.

1887 **LeMoine, Sir James MacPherson**
"Materials for Canadian history: the annals of towns, parishes, &c., extracted from church registers, and other sources."
In: *Proceedings and Transactions of the Royal Society of Canada*; Series 2, vol. 3, section 2 (1897) p. 309-311.; ISSN: 0316-4616.
Note: Location: AEU.

1888 **Plympton, Charles William**
Select bibliography on travel in North America. Albany: University of the State of New York, 1897. P. [37]-60. (New York State Library Bulletin; Bibliography ; no. 3)
Note: Microform: CIHM Microfiche series ; no. 37869; ISBN: 0-665-37869-6. 1 microfiche (16 fr.).
Location: OONL.

1889 **Renault, Raoul**
Mémoires et documents historiques: notice bibliographique. Québec: Brousseau, 1897. 14 p.
Note: Microforme: ICMH collection de microfiches ; no 12399; ISBN: 0-665-12399-X. 1 microfiche (13 images).
Localisation: OONL.

— 1900 —

1890 **Campbell, William Wilfred**
Bibliography: War of 1812-14. [S.l.: s.n., 1900]. 38 l.
Note: Attributed to William Wilfred Campbell.
Location: OOA.

— 1901 —

1891 **Doughty, Arthur George; Middleton, J.E.**
Bibliography of the siege of Quebec in three parts by A. Doughty and J.E. Middleton with a list of plans by R. [*sic*] Lee Phillips of the Library of Congress, Washington. Quebec: Dussault & Proulx, 1901. 161 p.: facsim.
Note: 536 entries (198 books and pamphlets, 173 manuscripts, including a separate listing of 156 pieces of "Correspondance de Bougainville"), 91 plans, 74 engravings.
Extract from the sixth volume of *The siege of Quebec and the battle of the Plains*, by A.G. Doughty and G.W. Parmelee.– One hundred and fifty copies were printed separately.
Location: OOP.

1892 **Thwaites, Reuben Gold**
The Jesuit relations and allied documents: travels and explorations of the Jesuit missionaries in New France, 1610-1791. Cleveland: Burrows Bros., 1896-1901. 73 vol.: ill., facsims., maps (some folded).
Note: "List of authorities cited or consulted in the preparation of the series." In: Vol. 71, p. 219-365.– Listing of bibliographies; archival reports (manuscripts, printed works); contemporary documents and publications; American Indians: anthropology, ethnology, history, religion and mythology, music and poetry, arts and industries, relations with whites; general history; periodicals and transactions; topography and statistics; natural sciences; list of maps and atlases.
Supplement: Donnelly, Joseph P. *Thwaites' Jesuit Relations: errata and addenda*. Chicago: Loyola University

Press, 1967.– "Bibliography, 1906-66," p. [211]-269.
Location: OONL.

— 1902 —

1893 **Larned, Josephus Nelson**
The literature of American history: a bibliographical guide in which the scope, character, and comparative worth of books in selected lists are set forth in brief notes by critics of authority. Boston: Published for the American Library Association by Houghton Mifflin, 1902. 596 p.
Note: Part 5, "Canada," p. 395-440.
Reprint: Columbus, Ohio: Long's College Book Co., 1953. 588 p.
Location: OONL.

1894 **Severance, Frank Hayward**
"Contributions towards a bibliography of the Niagara Region: the Upper Canada rebellion of 1837-38."
In: *Publications of the Buffalo Historical Society*; Vol. 5 (1902) p. [427]-495.
Note: Location: OONL.

— 1907 —

1895 **Church, Elihu Dwight**
A catalogue of books relating to the discovery & early history of North and South America, forming a part of the library of E.D. Church, compiled and annotated by George Watson Cole. New York: Dodd, Mead; [Cambridge University Press], 1907. 5 vol.: facsims.
Note: 1,385 entries.– Chronological arrangement.
Reprint: New York: P. Smith, 1951. 5 vol.: facsims.
Location: OONL.

1896 **Griffin, Appleton Prentiss Clark**
Bibliography of American historical societies (the United States and the Dominion of Canada). 2nd ed., rev. and enl. Washington: American Historical Association, 1907. 1374 p. (The Association reference series)
Note: Publications of historical societies through 1905.– Issued as Vol. 2 of the 1905 *Annual report of the American Historical Association*.
Location: OONL.
Previous edition: Government Printing Office, 1896. 677-1236 p.
Reprint: Detroit: Gale Research, 1966. 1374 p.
Location: OONL.

— 1909 —

1897 **Dionne, Narcisse-Eutrope**
Travaux historiques publiés depuis trente ans. Québec: Laflamme, 1909. 27 p.
Note: Approx. 150 entrées.– Livres et brochures, articles de revues et journaux.
Localisation: OONL.

— 1910 —

1898 **Burpee, Lawrence J.**
"A chapter in the literature of the fur trade."
In: *Papers of the Bibliographical Society of America*; Vol. 5 (1910) p. 45-60.; ISSN: 0006-128X.
Note: Review of literature dealing with history of the fur trade in western Canada.– Contains a list entitled "A working bibliography of the western Canadian fur trade" (p. 58-60).
Location: AEU.

— 1919 —

1899 **Review of historical publications relating to Canada, 1896-1917-18.** Toronto: University of Toronto Press [etc.],

1897-1919. 22 vol.
Note: Contains full-length reviews of contemporary Canadian historical works.
Edited by G.M. Wrong and others.– Succeeded by *Canadian Historical Review*.
Index, Vol. 1-10, by H.H. Langton. Toronto: Morang, 1907. 202 p.
Index, Vol. 11-20, by Laura Mason. Toronto: University of Toronto, 1918. 218 p.
Location: OONL.

1900 **Staton, Frances M.**
"Some unusual sources of information in the Toronto Reference Library on the Canadian rebellions of 1837-8."
In: *Papers and Records: Ontario Historical Society*; Vol. 17 (1919) p. 58-73.; ISSN: 0380-6022.
Note: Location: OONL.

— 1920 —

1901 **Hamilton, L.**
"German publications relating to Canada, 1914-1920."
In: *Canadian Historical Review*; Vol. 1, no. 3 (September 1920) p. 281-282.; ISSN: 0008-3755.
Note: Location: OONL.

— 1922 —

1902 **Scott, H.–A.**
"Au berceau de notre histoire."
Dans: *Mémoires de la Société royale du Canada*; Série 3, vol. 16, section 1 (1922) p. 39-74.; ISSN: 0316-4616.
Note: Localisation: AEU.

— 1923 —

1903 **Literary and Historical Society of Quebec**
Index to the archival publications of the Literary and Historical Society of Quebec, 1824-1924. Quebec: L'Événement, 1923. 215 p.
Note: Location: OONL.

— 1924 —

1904 **Toronto. Public Library**
The rebellion of 1837-38: a bibliography of the sources of information in the Public Reference Library of the City of Toronto, Canada. [Toronto]: Public Library of Toronto, 1924. 81 p.
Note: Approx. 1,500 entries.– Books, pamphlets, newspaper and periodical articles, chapters from books, fiction, government documents.– Compiled by Frances M. Staton.
Location: OONL.

— 1929 —

1905 **Leymarie, A. Léo**
Exposition rétrospective des colonies françaises de l'Amérique du Nord: catalogue illustré. Paris: Société d'éditions géographiques, maritimes et coloniales, 1929. lxv, 312 p., 139 p. de pl.: ill.
Note: Localisation: OONL.

— 1931 —

1906 **Toronto. Public Library**
The Canadian North West: a bibliography of the sources of information in the Public Reference Library of the City of Toronto, Canada in regard to the Hudson's Bay Company, the fur trade and the early history of the Canadian North West. Toronto: Public Library, 1931. 52 p.
Note: Approx. 1,125 entries.– Books and pamphlets, chapters from books, periodicals, society publications.– Compiled by Frances M. Staton.
Location: OONL.

— 1932 —

1907 **Newton, Arthur Percival, et al.**
"Bibliographie d'histoire coloniale, 1900-1930 : Grande Bretagne et Dominions."
Dans: *Bibliographie d'histoire coloniale, 1900-1930.* Paris: Société de l'histoire des colonies françaises, 1932. P. [103]-149.
Note: Liste des publications bibliographiques, publications historiques et sociétés savantes: histoire générale, histoire constitutionnelle, économique, religieuse, militaire, régionale.
Localisation: OONL.

1908 **Wallace, William Stewart**
"The literature relating to the Selkirk controversy."
In: *Canadian Historical Review*; Vol. 13, no. 1 (March 1932) p. 45-50.; ISSN: 0008-3755.
Note: Checklist of publications (books and pamphlets published between 1805 and 1820) relating to the struggle between Lord Selkirk and the North West Company over the Red River settlement.
Location: OONL.

— 1934 —

1909 **"Books relating to the Hudson's Bay Company."**
In: *Beaver*; Outfit 265, no. 3 (December 1934) p. 55-60.; ISSN: 0005-7517.
Note: Location: AEU.

1910 **Kerr, W.B.**
"Historical literature on Canada's participation in the Great War."
In: *Canadian Historical Review*; Vol. 14, no. 4 (December 1933) p. 412-436; vol. 15, no. 2 (June 1934) p. 181-190.; ISSN: 0008-3755.
Note: Listing of official and unofficial publications published during and immediately after World War I, general accounts of the Canadian military effort, private memoirs (1918-1933), histories of units, studies of Canadian organization and operations.
Location: AEU.

1911 **Trotter, Reginald George**
Canadian history: a syllabus and guide to reading. New and enl. ed. Toronto: Macmillan, 1934. xiv, 193 p.
Note: Approx. 2,000 entries.– Bibliographies, guides, handbooks and chronological works, constitutional history, geographical and descriptive works and atlases, biographies and memoirs, historical periodicals and reviews, official publications.
Previous edition: 1926. xiii, 162 p.
Location: OONL.

— 1935 —

1912 **British Columbia Library Association. Bibliography Committee**
Hudson's Bay Company. [Vancouver: The Association], 1935. [58] p.
Note: Approx. 350 entries.– Books and periodical articles dealing with the history of the Hudson's Bay Company.– Categories include general works, biography, charter, correspondence, forts and company life.
Location: BVIPA.

1913 **Hudson's Bay Company**
List of books relating to Hudson's Bay Company. [London: Hudson's Bay Company], 1935. 13 p.
Note: Approx. 120 entries.– Books about the Hudson's Bay Company, biographies of Company men, memoirs, etc., including novels; general works of history about the fur trade, exploration and discovery of the north-west, history of the western provinces and territories.
Location: OONL.

1914 **New York Public Library**
Canada: an exhibition commemorating the four-hundredth anniversary of the discovery of the Saint Lawrence by Jacques Cartier, 1534-1535: a catalogue with notes. New York: New York Public Library, 1935. 59 p.
Note: Location: OHM.

— 1937 —

1915 **McCoy, James Comly**
Jesuit relations of Canada, 1632-1673: a bibliography. Paris: Rau, 1937. xv, 310, [36] p.: front. (port.), ill. (facsims).
Note: 132 entries.– Contains descriptions of the editions and variants of the 41 separate relations published from 1632 to 1673 by the French Province of the Society of Jesus, the series of annual letters from the Superiors of the Jesuit missionaries of New France.
Location: OONL.

— 1938 —

1916 **Roy, Antoine**
"Bibliographie des monographies et histoires de paroisses."
Dans: *Rapport de l'archiviste de la Province de Québec*; Vol. 18 (1937-1938) p. 254-364.
Note: Localisation: OONL.

— 1939 —

1917 **"Bibliographie des matériaux déposés aux Archives publiques du Canada concernant l'insurrection de 1837-1838."**
Dans: *Rapport sur les Archives publiques du Canada*; (1939) p. 63-138.; ISSN: 0701-7790.
Note: Approx. 600 entrées.– Manuscrits, imprimés (proclamations, publications d'État, pièces judiciaires, publications et documents de l'époque, journaux de l'époque, documents iconographiques).
English title: "Bibliography of materials at the Public Archives of Canada relating to the rebellion of 1837-1838."
Localisation: OONL.

1918 **"Bibliography of materials at the Public Archives of Canada relating to the rebellion of 1837-1838."**
In: *Report of the Public Archives of Canada*; (1939) p. 63-138.; ISSN: 0701-7790.
Note: Approx. 600 entries.– Manuscripts, printed materials (official documents, publications and documents of the period, newspapers of the period).
Titre en français: "Bibliographie des matériaux déposés aux Archives publiques du Canada concernant l'insurrection de 1837-1838."
Location: OONL.

— 1941 —

1919 **Roy, Antoine**
"Bibliographie de généalogies et histoires de familles."
Dans: *Rapport de l'archiviste de la Province de Québec*; Vol. 21 (1940-1941) p. 95-332.
Note: Première partie: ouvrages généraux, articles de revues et de journaux sur les familles canadiennes françaises.– Deuxième partie: classée par ordre alphabétique des noms de familles, les titres des ouvrages, dictionnaires, monographies, etc. qui renferment des notes généalogiques sur les familles.

Localisation: OONL.
— 1942 —
1920 **Selected list of war time pamphlets: No. 1-3.** Ottawa: Department of National War Services, 1941-1942. 3 vol.
Note: Pamphlets on various subjects arranged by subject (Air Force, Canada, Democracy, War aims, etc.), with title and series indexes.
Location: OONL.
— 1948 —
1921 **"La querelle de l'eau-de-vie sous le régime français: bibliographie."**
Dans: *Revue d'histoire de l'Amérique française*; Vol. 1, no 4 (mars 1948) p. 615-624; Vol. 2, no 1 (juin 1948) p. 138-140.; ISSN: 0035-2357.
Note: Manuscrits, imprimés (documents officiels, journaux, lettres, mémoires, relations, monographs et essais).
Localisation: OONL.
— 1949 —
1922 **Lavoie, Amédée**
Bibliographie relative à l'histoire de la Nouvelle-France, 1516-1700. Giffard, Québec: [s.n.], 1949. 81 f.
Note: 223 entrées.
Localisation: OONL.
— 1951 —
1923 **Lanctot, Gustave**
L'oeuvre de la France en Amérique du Nord: bibliographie sélective et critique. Montréal: Fides, 1951. 185 p.
Note: 465 entrées.– Sources imprimées, histoire, culture, littérature, beaux-arts, folklore, questions sociales et politiques, institutions, droits, études et problèmes, guides bibliographiques.
Localisation: OONL.
— 1952 —
1924 **"Visits to Upper Canada, 1799-1867: a selected checklist of travel accounts in the Douglas Library."**
In: *Douglas Library Notes*; Vol. 1, no. 3 (April 1952) p. [3-4].; ISSN: 0012-5717.
Note: Location: OONL.
— 1954 —
1925 **Martin, Gérard**
Bibliographie sommaire du Canada français, 1854-1954. Québec: Secrétariat de la Province de Québec, 1954. 104 p.
Note: 900 entrées.– Une liste de volumes sur l'histoire du Canada en général, et en particulier sur les Canadiens français dans leur vie économique, culturelle, sociale, artistique et littéraire.
Localisation: OONL.
— 1955 —
1926 **A brief bibliography for a study of general naval history and the naval history of Canada.** Ottawa: Department of National Defence, [1955]. 6 p.
Note: Location: OKF.
1927 **Oleson, T.J.**
"The Vikings in America: a critical bibliography."
In: *Canadian Historical Review*; Vol. 36, no. 2 (June 1955) p. 166-173.; ISSN: 0008-3755.
Note: Location: AEU.
— 1957 —
1928 **Beers, Henry Putney**
The French in North America: a bibliographical guide to French archives, reproductions, and research missions.

Baton Rouge: Louisiana State University Press, c1957. xi, 413 p.
Note: Contains a chapter on Canadian institutions and historians.– Bibliography: p. 279-350.
Location: OONL.
— 1958 —
1929 **"Bibliographie raisonnée de l'anthroponymie canadienne."**
Dans: *Mémoires de la Société généalogique canadienne-française*; No 9 (1958) p. 153-173.; ISSN: 0037-9387.
Note: 185 entrées.– Livres, brochures, articles sur prénoms, patronymes, sobriquets et surnoms familiaux, gentilés, blasons populaires.– Comprend répertoires, études, sources bibliographiques.
Localisation: OOC.
1930 **Greenly, Albert Harry**
A selective bibliography of important books, pamphlets and broadsides relating to Michigan history. Lunenburg, Vt.: Stinehour Press, 1958. 165 p.: facsims.
Note: Contains references to documents relating to early exploration (Champlain, Hennepin, Lahontan, La Salle, Alexander Henry), and publications dealing with the War of 1812.
Location: OONL.
— 1959 —
1931 **Cambridge history of the British Empire.** New York: Macmillan; Cambridge: The University Press, 1929-1959. 8 vol.
Note: Vol. 6: *Canada and Newfoundland*. Bibliography, p. [813]-885. In three parts: Part 1: "The Manuscript sources of Canadian history," by Arthur George Doughty. Part 2: "Printed works," co-ordinated by Reginald George Trotter. Part 3: "Bibliography of the history of Newfoundland".– General bibliography of Canadian history (bibliographies, documents, historical journals, newspapers, handbooks of chronology, historical atlases and maps, general works, regional or topical works, biographical works, special selected bibliographies).
Location: OONL.
1932 **Martin, Gérard**
"Bibliographie du siège de Québec (1759)."
Dans: *Bulletin des recherches historiques*; Vol. 65, no 1 (janvier-mars 1959) p. 9-15.
Note: 72 entrées.
Localisation: OONL.
1933 **Winks, Robin W.**
Recent trends and new literature in Canadian history. Washington: Service Center for Teachers of History, c1959. v, 56 p. (Publication / Service Center for Teachers of History ; no. 19)
Note: Location: OONL.
— 1960 —
1934 **American Society of Genealogists**
Genealogical research: methods and sources. Washington: The Society, 1960. viii, 456 p.
Note: Includes a section "Canada," p. 261-288.
Location: OOP.
1935 **Canada. Department of Mines and Technical Surveys. Geographical Branch**
Colonization and settlement in the Americas: a selected bibliography/Colonisation et peuplement dans les Amériques: bibliographie choisie. Ottawa: [Queen's Printer], 1960. 68 p. (Bibliographical series / Canada

Department of Mines and Technical Surveys, Geographical Branch ; no. 25)
Note: Approx. 1,600 entries.– Lists books, articles, maps on settlement in each of the countries of North and South America.– Compiled by S.C. Wiley.– Text in English and French/texte en français et en anglais
Previous edition: *Selected bibliography on colonization and land settlement in Canada.* 1950. 5 p. (Bibliographical series ; no. 1). 5 p.– Compiled by J. Matheson.
Location: OONL.

— 1961 —

1936 **Hoffman, Bernard G.**
Cabot to Cartier: sources for a historical ethnography of northeastern North America, 1497-1550. [Toronto]: University of Toronto Press, 1961. xii, 287 p.: ill., maps, facsim.
Note: Approx. 500 entries.– Bibliography, p. 229-263.
Location: OONL.

— 1962 —

1937 **Mennie-de Varennes, Kathleen**
Sources généalogiques tirées de "Canadiana"/Genealogical materials compiled from "Canadiana". Ottawa: Canadian Library Association, 1962. 21 p. (Occasional paper / Canadian Library Association ; no. 38)
Note: Approx. 175 entries.
Location: OONL.

— 1963 —

1938 **Daveluy, Marie-Claire**
"Bibliographie de la Société de Notre-Dame de Montréal (1639-1663) et de ses membres, accompagné de notes historiques et critiques."
Dans: *Revue d'histoire de l'Amérique française*; (1951-1963) ; ISSN: 0035-2357.
Note: Bibliographie régulière.– Voir vol. 5, no 1 (juin 1951) à vol. 17, no 1 (juin 1963).
Localisation: OONL.

1939 **Gabriel-de-l'Annonciation, soeur**
Bibliographie analytique sur la méthodologie de l'histoire du Canada, 1950-1962. Québec: [s.n.], 1963. viii, 47 p.
Note: Localisation: QQLA.

1940 **Mennie-de Varennes, Kathleen**
Bibliographie annotée d'ouvrages généalogiques à la Bibliothèque du Parlement/Annotated bibliography of genealogical works in the Library of Parliament. Ottawa: Publiée à titre gracieux par la Bibliothèque du Parlement, 1963. 2 f. prélim., ix, 180 f.
Note: 1,137 entrées.– La période couverte, jusqu'en 1961.– Index des lieux, sujets, noms de familles.– Indiquant d'autres bibliothèques canadiennes possédant les mêmes ouvrages.
Localisation: OONL.

1941 **Toronto. Public Library**
The North West Passage, 1534-1859: a catalogue of an exhibition of books and manuscripts in the Toronto Public Library. Toronto: Baxter Publishing in co-operation with the Toronto Public Library, 1963. 26 p.: ill., facsims., maps, ports.
Note: 90 entries.– Compiled by Edith G. Firth, with an introduction by Henry Cummings Campbell.
Location: OONL.

— 1964 —

1942 **Beers, Henry Putney**
The French and British in the old Northwest: a bibliographical guide to archive and manuscript sources. Detroit: Wayne State University Press, 1964. 297 p.
Note: Approx. 700 entries.– Books, articles, manuscripts, journals, inventories, guides, calendars, bibliographies.– "Bibliographical sources," p. 195-255.
Location: OONL.

1943 **Hare, John**
Les Canadiens français aux quatre coins du monde: une bibliographie commentée des récits, de voyage, 1670-1914. Québec: Société historique du Québec, 1964. 215 p. (Cahiers d'histoire / Société historique du Québec ; no 16)
Note: 306 entrées.– Cette bibliographie étudie tous les récits de voyage écrits par des Canadiens français et publiés en édition séparée.
Localisation: OOCC

1944 **Nish, James Cameron**
"Bibliographie sommaire sur la Confédération."
Dans: *Action nationale*; Vol. 54, no 2 (octobre 1964) p. 198-207.; ISSN: 0001-7469.
Note: Localisation: OONL.

— 1965 —

1945 **"Bibliographie sommaire des événements de 1837-1838."**
Dans: *Liberté*; Vol. 7, no 1-2 (janvier-avril 1965) p. 174-182.; ISSN: 0024-2020.
Note: Localisation: OONL.

1946 **Jain, Sushil Kumar**
Louis "David" Riel & the North-West Rebellion: a list of references. Regina: Regina Campus Library, University of Saskatchewan, 1965. 19 l.
Note: Location: AEU.

— 1966 —

1947 **Dornbusch, Charles Emil**
The Canadian army, 1855-1965: lineages – regimental histories. Cornwallville, N.Y.: Hope Farm Press, 1966. viii, 179 p.
Note: Publications by and about the regiments, including manuals and periodicals.
Previous editions:
The Canadian army, 1855-1958: regimental histories and a guide to the regiments. 1959. 216 p.: ill.
Preliminary list of Canadian regimental histories. 1955. 45, [7] l.
Location: OONL.

1948 **United Empire Loyalists' Association of Canada. Dominion Council**
Bibliography of the United Empire Loyalists at the Toronto Public Library. Toronto: [s.n.], 1966. 10 l.
Note: Approx. 130 entries.
Location: OONL.

— 1967 —

1949 **Allen, Patrick**
"Confédération canadienne: bibliographie sommaire."
Dans: *Revue d'histoire de l'Amérique française*; Vol. 21, no 3a (décembre 1967) p. 697-719.; ISSN: 0035-2357.
Note: 380 entrées.
Localisation: AEU.

1950 **Dawson, Irene J.**
"The Dawson route, 1857-1883: a selected bibliography with annotations."

In: *Ontario History*; Vol. 59, no. 1 (March 1967) p. 47-55.; ISSN: 0030-2953.

Note: List of contemporary books and pamphlets related to history of the Dawson road (Red River route) from its beginning in 1857 until its abandonment in 1883.– Chronological arrangement with subject index.

Location: OONL.

1951 **Donnelly, Joseph P.**
Thwaites' *Jesuit Relations*: errata and addenda. Chicago: Loyola University Press, 1967. v, 269 p.

Note: "Bibliography, 1906-66," p. [211]-269.– Listing of books and articles in English and French pertaining to the Jesuits and New France which have appeared from 1906 to 1966, an addendum to Thwaites' "List of authorities cited or consulted in the preparation of the series," in *Jesuit Relations and allied documents*, Vol. 71, p. 219-365.

Location: OONL.

1952 **Exposition de documents d'histoire du Canada (1840-1880) à l'occasion du deuxième centenaire du Collège de Montréal avec l'aide financière de la Commission du Centenaire.** Montréal: [s.n.], 1967. [24] p.

Note: Localisation: OONL.

1953 **Fohlen, Claude**
"Au Canada, un siècle après la Confédération."
Dans: *Revue historique*; Vol. 238 (juillet-septembre 1967) p.135-146.; ISSN: 0035-3264.

Note: Localisation: OONL.

1954 **Lande, Lawrence M.**
Confederation pamphlets: a checklist – liste abrégée. Montreal: McGill University, 1967. 67 p.: facsims. (1 folded in pocket). (Lawrence Lande Foundation for Canadian Historical Research ; no. 3)

Note: Approx. 150 entries.– Introduction in English and French/introduction en français et en anglais.

Location: OONL.

1955 **Roy, Antoine**
"Court exposé sur notre bibliographie générale des voyageurs au Canada."
Dans: *Bulletin des recherches historiques*; Vol. 69, no. 1 (janvier 1967) p. 21-24.

Note: Localisation: OONL.

— 1968 —

1956 **Société historique de Montréal**
Inventaire sommaire des documents historiques de la Société historique de Montréal. Montréal: [s.n.], 1968. 174 p.

Note: Localisation: OTU.

— 1969 —

1957 **Beaulieu, André; Hamelin, Jean**
"Idéologies au Canada français, 1850-1900: orientations bibliographiques."
Dans: *Recherches sociographiques*; Vol. 10, no 2-3 (mai-décembre 1969) p. 449-463.; ISSN: 0034-1282.

Note: Approx. 280 entrées.– Livres, articles de revues: définition/méthode; contexte socio-économique; contexte socio-culturel; idéologies, idées, courants de pensée; idéologues.

Localisation: AEU.

1958 **Beaulieu, André; Hamelin, Jean; Bernier, Benoît**
Guide d'histoire du Canada. Québec: Presses de l'Université Laval, 1969. xvi, 540 p. (Les Cahiers de l'Institut d'histoire ; 13)

Note: Localisation: OONL.

1959 **Hurst, James W.**
"The Fenians: a bibliography."
In: *Eire: Ireland*; Vol. 4, no. 4 (1969) p. 90-106.; ISSN: 0013-2683.

Note: Approx. 400 entries.– Books, reference and bibliographical works, manuscript sources and official documents from Canada, Great Britain, Ireland and the United States dealing with the biography, history and politics of the Fenian movement.

Location: AEU.

1960 **Lachance, André**
Textes et documents pour servir à l'étude de l'histoire économique et sociale de la Nouvelle-France. Sherbrooke: Département d'histoire, Université de Sherbrooke, [1969]. 112 f.

Note: Bibliographie, p. 4-28: "Les principales sources imprimées et les principales synthèses."

Location: OONL.

1961 **Nish, James Cameron; Nish, Elizabeth**
Bibliographie pour servir à l'étude de l'histoire du Canada français. Montréal: Centre d'étude du Québec, Université Sir George Williams, 1966-1969. 5 vol.

Note: Guides bibliographiques, revues, journaux du Québec, documents originaux, monographies, articles de revues, journaux canadiens.

Localisation: OONL.

1962 **Smith, R.D. Hilton**
"Northwestern approaches: the first century of books."
In: *British Columbia Library Quarterly*; Vol. 32, no. 3 (January 1969) p. 3-67.; ISSN: 0007-053X.

Note: 80 entries.– Bibliographical essays, based on a lecture series, on the exploration of the Pacific coast of North America, the books written by the explorers of British Columbia and its approaches during the eighteenth and early nineteenth centuries.– Includes a checklist and index.

Location: OONL.

1963 **Smith, R.D. Hilton**
Northwestern approaches: the first century of books. Victoria, B.C.: Adelphi Book Shop, 1969. 67 p.

Note: 80 entries.– Bibliographical essays, based on a lecture series, on the exploration of the Pacific coast of North America, the books written by the explorers of British Columbia and the approaches during the eighteenth and early nineteenth centuries.– Includes a checklist and index.

Location: OONL.

1964 **Société historique de l'Ouest du Québec**
"Introduction bibliographique à l'histoire de l'ouest du Québec."
Dans: *Asticou*; No 2 (janvier 1969) p. 15.; ISSN: 0066-922X.

Note: Localisation: OONL.

— 1970 —

1965 **Alexandrin, Barbara; Bothwell, Robert**
Bibliography of the material culture of New France. [Ottawa: National Museums of Canada, 1970]. vii, 32 p. (National Museum of Man publications in history ; no. 4)

Note: 897 entries.– Books, articles, studies on economic, social, local history (parish, county, city, district), practical arts, architecture, folk arts, agricultural technology, furniture-making.

Location: OONL.

1966 **Cheung, Gretchen**
A preliminary list of photocopies in the collection of Collège militaire royal, St-Jean, P.Q., 1750-1917/Liste préliminaire de photocopies dans la collection du Collège militaire royal de St-Jean, Province de Québec, 1750 1917. St-Jean, Québec: Collège militaire royal, 1970, 10 l.
Note: Text in English.– Foreword and introduction in English and French/avant-propos et introduction en français et en anglais.
Location: QSTJ.

1967 **Harvey, Fernand**
Bibliographie de six historiens québécois: Michel Bibaud, François-Xavier Garneau, Thomas Chapais, Lionel Groulx, Fernand Ouellet, Michel Brunet. [Québec]: Institut supérieur des sciences humaines, Université Laval, 1970. 43 f.
Note: Comprend une section: "Aspects généraux et particuliers sur l'historiographie québécoise."
Localisation: OONL.

1968 **Morrell, W.P.**
British overseas expansion and the history of the Commonwealth: a select bibliography. 2nd ed. London: Historical Association, 1970. 48 p. (Historical Association Helps for students of history ; no. 63)
Note: Includes a section on Canada.
Previous edition: 1961. 40 p.
Location: OTY.

1969 **Scott, Joyce**
"A checklist of lodge and fraternal society material in the Regional History Collection."
In: *Western Ontario Historical Notes*; Vol. 25, no. 2 (Spring 1970) p. 7-16.; ISSN: 0382-0157.
Note: 82 entries.
Location: OONL.

1970 **Thibault, Henri-Paul**
"L'orientation des recherches historiques à Louisbourg."
Dans: *Revue d'histoire de l'Amérique française*; Vol. 24, no 3 (décembre 1970) p. 408-412.; ISSN: 0035-2357.
Note: Localisation: OONL.

— 1971 —

1971 **Centre de recherche en histoire économique du Canada français**
Documents, livres et journaux sur microfilms, microfiches et microcartes en dépôt au C.H.E. Montréal: Centre de recherche en histoire économique du Canada français, 1971. ii, 122 f.
Note: Inclut un nombre d'ouvrages canadiens.
Localisation: OONL.

1972 **Gwyn, Julian**
Reference works for historians: a list of reference works of interest to historians in the libraries of the University of Ottawa. [Ottawa]: Central Library, University of Ottawa, 1971. iv, 131 l.
Note: 1,181 entries (238 directly relating to Canadian history).– Contains a listing of reference material held by University of Ottawa to the end of January 1971: encyclopedias, historical/topographical/biographical dictionaries, bibliographies of historical literature, inventories of manuscripts, indexes of maps and historical atlases.
Location: OONL.

1973 **Lamonde, Yvan**
"Bibliographie des bibliographies des historiens canadiens-français du Québec."
Dans: *Recherches sociographiques*; Vol. 12, no 2 (mai-août 1971) p. 237-248.; ISSN: 0034-1282.
Note: Localisation: AEU.

1974 **Lelièvre, Francine**
Bibliographie annotée de l'histoire humaine du Parc national Forillon. Gaspé, Québec: Direction des parcs nationaux et des lieux historiques, Ministère des Affaires indiennes et du Nord canadien, 1971. viii, 111 l.
Note: Ouvrages et documents (articles de revues et journaux, cartes, plans, photographies aériennes, gravures, photos et films) concernant tous les aspects de l'histoire humaine du Parc national Forillon et de ses environs: politique, économique, social, culturel, religieux.
Localisation: OOFF.

— 1972 —

1975 **Clark, Jane**
Reference aids in Canadian history in the University of Toronto Library (Humanities and Social Sciences Division). Toronto: Reference Department, University of Toronto Library, 1972. iii, 75 p. (Reference series / University of Toronto Library ; no. 14)
Note: 203 entries.– Bibliographies, encyclopedias, dictionaries, directories, indexes, handbooks, yearbooks.– Prepared as a guide to students in Canadian history courses at University of Toronto.
Location: OONL.

1976 **Fellows, Jo-Ann; Calder, Kathryn**
"A bibliography of loyalist source material in Canada."
In: *Proceedings of the American Antiquarian Society*; Vol. 82 (1972) p. 67-270.; ISSN: 0044-751X.
Note: Listing of primary materials, published and unpublished, in private and institutional repositories, in New Brunswick, Nova Scotia, Prince Edward Island, Quebec and Ontario.– General definition for inclusion: material written by Loyalists, or about Loyalists during their lifetimes, or records or government documents, from approximately 1783 to 1830.– Includes a list of newspapers for this period with details of their publication and general description of contents.– Index: names and places.
Location: OONL.

— 1973 —

1977 **Berton, Pierre**
"A Klondike gold rush bibliography."
In: *Journal of Canadian Fiction*; Vol. 2, no. 3 (Summer 1973) p. 201-204.; ISSN: 0047-2255.
Note: Review of historical and biographical works relating to the Klondike gold stampede experience.
Location: AEU.

1978 **Lahaise, Robert**
Civilisation et vie quotidienne en Nouvelle-France: en 1000 diapositives, commentaire et bibliographie. Montréal: Guérin, [1973]. ix, 207 p.
Note: Approx. 1,000 entrées bibliographiques.– Principaux thèmes traités: société civile (cadres aristocratiques, le peuple: origines et classes sociales, l'habitant); vie religieuse (histoire et institutions); vie économique; vie militaire; vie intellectuelle (enseignement, littérature, beaux-arts, musique, folklore).

Localisation: OONL.

— 1974 —

1979 **Bates, Hilary**
Index to the publications of the Ontario Historical Society, 1899-1972. Toronto: Ontario Historical Society, 1974. x, 175 p.
Note: Chronological list of articles in the *Papers and Records*, 1899-1946, and *Ontario History*, 1947-1972, (including *Profiles of a Province*, which replaced the December 1967 and March 1968 issues).
Location: OONL.

1980 **Linteau, Paul-André**
"Sur quelques bibliographies récentes."
Dans: *Revue d'histoire de l'Amérique française*; Vol. 28, no 1 (juin 1974) p. 105-112.; ISSN: 0035-2357.
Note: Localisation: OONL.

1981 **Maltais, Madeleine**
Événements d'hier: recension de brochures et de plaquettes anciennes. Chicoutimi: Université du Québec à Chicoutimi, 1974. 235 f.
Note: Approx. 800 entrées.
Localisation: OONL.

1982 **Ontario Genealogical Society. Ottawa Branch. Library**
Library holdings [Ontario Genealogical Society, Ottawa Branch]. Ottawa: The Society, [1974]. [23] p.
Note: 353 entries.– Six main groupings: books, branch bulletins, cemeteries, genealogies, maps and atlases, miscellaneous publications.
Location: OONL.

1983 **Savard, Pierre**
"Un Quart de siècle d'historiographie québécoise, 1947-1972."
Dans: *Recherches sociographiques*; Vol. 15, no 1 (janvier-avril 1974) p. 77-96.; ISSN: 0034-1282.
Note: Localisation: OONL.

— 1975 —

1984 **Bruce, Anthony Peter Charles**
An annotated bibliography of the British Army, 1660-1914. New York: Garland Publishing, 1975. 255 p. (Garland reference library of social science; vol. 14); ISBN: 0-8240-9988-5.
Note: 2,246 entries.– Contains a section of references to the British Army in Canada.
Location: OONL.

1985 **Lamonde, Yvan**
"Inventaire des études et des sources pour l'étude des associations 'litteraires' québécoises francophones au XIXe siècle (1840-1900)."
Dans: *Recherches sociographiques*; Vol. 16, no 2 (mai-août 1975) p. 261-275.; ISSN: 0034-1282.
Note: Localisation: AEU.

1986 **"L'Invasion du Canada, 1775-1776: esquisse bibliographique."**
Dans: *Cahiers d'histoire*; No 28 (1975) p. 225-228.; ISSN: 0008-008X.
Note: Localisation: OONL.

1987 **Lyle, Guy R.**
British emigration into the Saskatchewan valley: the Barr colony, 1903: its bibliographical foundation. [S.l.: s.n.], 1975. iv, 57 l.
Note: Contains listings of background works, literature of the Barr colony, official correspondence, government publications, maps/plans/sketches, contemporary newspaper accounts, diaries and letters, reminiscences, secondary sources (books, theses, periodical articles).
Location: SRU.

— 1976 —

1988 **Careless, Virginia**
Bibliography for the study of British Columbia's domestic material history. Ottawa: National Museum of Canada, 1976. ii, 73 p.: ill. (National Museum of Man Mercury series, History Division paper; no. 20; ISSN: 0316-1900)
Note: Approx. 700 entries.– Books and articles, arranged in 46 subject categories in the areas of architecture, history, interior design, furniture, social life and lifestyle.
Location: OONL.

1989 **Stauffer, Ann Tholer**
"The French-Americans and the French-Canadians: a select bibliography of materials in the Library of the Vermont Historical Society."
In: *Vermont History*; Vol. 44, no. 2 (Spring 1976) p. 110-114.; ISSN: 0042-4161.
Note: Approx. 75 entries.– Books, articles, unpublished dissertations, maps, periodicals, fiction.
Location: OONL.

1990 **Stevens, Thomas J.**
"[Canadian military history]."
In: *Communiqué: Canadian Studies*; Vol. 2, no. 3 (February 1976) p. 2-26.; ISSN: 0318-1197.
Note: Audio-visual materials, military journals, general works, histories in chronological groupings by various events (War of 1812, Rebellion of 1837, etc.), selected documents and official records, journal articles.
Location: OONL.

— 1977 —

1991 **Desjardins-MacGregor, Louise**
Bibliographie annotée des études portant sur le régime français. Hamilton, Ont.: Department of Geography, McMaster University, 1977. 44 p. (Discussion paper / Department of Geography, McMaster University; no. 10)
Note: 137 entrées, organisée en fonction des divisions suivantes: administration de la Nouvelle-France, l'Église en Nouvelle-France, vie économique, société (études de population, colonisation et peuplement, le régime seigneurial, l'occupation du sol; sources imprimées, bibliographies, inventaires, atlas, dictionnaires biographiques et travaux généalogiques.
Localisation: OONL.

1992 **Kenny, William M.**
Literature of the Lakes. [S.l.: s.n., 1977]. 3 vol.; ISBN: 0-9203-3903-4 (vol. 1).
Note: Vol. 1: *Naval and marine history: Canada – Great Lakes region*. 126 p.– 306 entries.– Review of literature, monographs and periodicals, dealing with aspects of Great Lakes history, with emphasis on marine materials, excluding topics such as fishing, pollution, lake levels, maps.– Types of literature include general histories, naval studies, navigational aids, shipwrecks and lore, economic and commercial materials, social and area studies, Great Lakes art, marine periodicals and reference tools.– Historical works include both Canadian and American materials.
Location: OONL.

1993 **Laflèche, Guy**
Le récit de voyage en Nouvelle-France: (FRA 6661): Cahier bibliographique. Montréal: Université de Montréal, Département d'études françaises, 1977. v, 70 f.
Note: 293 entrées.– Littérature coloniale de la Nouvelle-France; études sur les écrits de la Nouvelle-France; écrits sur les saints Martyrs canadiens; écrits de/sur la Nouvelle-France; écrits des Jésuites de/sur Nouvelle-France; bibliographie et chronologie de Paul Ragueneau.
Localisation: QMBN.

1994 **Robeson, Virginia R.; Flow, A.F.**
Documents in Canadian history: a teacher's guide. Toronto: Ontario Institute for Studies in Education, c1977. v, 33 p.: ill. (Curriculum series / Ontario Institute for Studies in Education ; 26); ISBN: 0-7744-0150-8.
Note: List of books and articles in both French and English dealing with topics, people, issues of importance in four broad categories: "New France: 1713-1760;" "Upper Canada in the 1830s;" "Lower Canada in the 1830s;" "Debates about Canada's future: 1868-1896."
Location: OONL.

1995 **Université des sciences humaines de Strasbourg. Faculté des sciences historiques**
Les Amériques, de la découverte à l'indépendance: exposition du 18 mars au 30 avril 1977: catalogue. Strasbourg, France: Bibliothèque nationale et universitaire, [1977]. xvii, 160 p.: ill.
Note: 195 entrées.– Documents et cartes.– Comprend une section: "Le Canada (La Nouvelle France)."
Localisation: OONL.

— 1978 —

1996 **Bricker, Mary Anne**
"Genealogical materials for public libraries."
In: *Ontario Library Review*; Vol. 62, no. 3 (September 1978) p. 206-209.; ISSN: 0030-2996.
Note: Location: OONL.

1997 **Gibson, Rose Mary**
Genealogical sources in the Douglas Library, Kingston, Ont. Ottawa: Ottawa Branch, Ontario Genealogical Society, 1978. 15, 2, 6, 4 p.
Note: Location: OONL.

1998 **Hitchman, James H.**
"Pacific Northwest maritime history: a bibliographical survey."
In: *Pacific Northwest themes: historical essays, in honor of Keith A. Murray*, edited by James W. Scott. Bellingham, Wash.: Center for Pacific Northwest Studies, Western Washington University, 1978. P. 17-33.
Note: Location: OWTU.

1999 **McGill University. McLennan Library. Reference Department**
Canadian history: a student's guide to reference sources. [Montreal]: The Library, 1978. 52 p.
Note: Approx. 275 entries.
Previous edition: *Canadiana: a student's guide to bibliographic resources.* 1974. 23 p.
Location: OONL.

2000 **North York Public Library. Canadiana Collection**
Genealogy and family history catalogue. [Downsview, Ont.]: North York Public Library, c1978. 96 p.; ISBN: 0-920552-00-5.
Note: 504 entries.– Covers to the end of 1977.– Includes printed genealogies, loyalist literature, archives' reports, heraldic books, genealogical guides.– Excludes historical studies, local and church histories, biographies.
Location: OONL.

— 1979 —

2001 **Anctil, Pierre**
"Bibliographie commentée sur les Franco-américains de la nouvelle-angleterre."
Dans: *Cahiers de géographie de Québec*; Vol. 23, no 58 (avril 1979) p. 179-181.; ISSN: 0007-9766.
Note: 23 entrées.
Localisation: OONL.

2002 **Fredriksen, John C.**
Resource guide for the War of 1812. [S.l.: s.n.], c1979. vii, 156 p.
Note: 1,674 entries.– Separate listing of 119 manuscript sources in United States and Canada.– Contains Canadian, American and British publications.– Includes general texts, with geographical subdivisions for specific locations of battles.– Listings include references to the war at sea, politics and the peace process, military and biographical works, Indians, prisoners of war.
Location: OONL.

2003 **Messier, Jean-Jacques**
Bibliographie relative à la Nouvelle-France. [Montréal]: Éditions Univers: L'Aurore, c1979. 198 p.; ISBN: 2-89053-004-3.
Note: Approx. 2,300 entrées.– Ouvrages imprimés (documents officiels, documents publiés par les bureaux d'archives et par les sociétés privées, journaux); ouvrages de référence (bibliographies, encyclopédies, dictionnaires); atlas historiques et collections de cartes; sources secondaires (synthèse d'histoire générale, d'histoire nationale); études spécialisées telles les ouvrages spécialisés, les monographies, thèses, articles de revues et de périodiques, index de revues.
Localisation: OONL.

2004 **Waterston, Elizabeth**
"Literature of exploration: Canadian travel books of the 1870's."
In: *Studies in Canadian Literature*; Vol. 4, no. 2 (Summer 1979) p. 44-61.; ISSN: 0380-6995.
Note: 75 entries.– Survey of Canadian travel literature, 1870-1879.
Location: AEU.

— 1980 —

2005 **Barkley, Murray**
"Some recent publications relating to Loyalists."
In: *Loyalist Gazette*; Vol. 17, no. 2 (Autumn 1979) p. 12; vol. 18, no. 1 (Spring 1980) p. 12; vol. 18, no. 2 (Autumn 1980) p. 12-13.; ISSN: 0047-5149.
Note: Location: OONL.

2006 **Bennett, Paul W.**
"Beyond the textbook: a selected bibliography for the '80s."
In: *Rediscovering Canadian history: a teacher's guide for the '80s.* Toronto: OISE Press, 1980. P. 154-180. (Curriculum series / Ontario Institute for Studies in Education ; 39); ISBN: 0-7744-0192-3.
Note: Location: OONL.

2007 **Chandler, Dorothy, et al.**
A checklist of French-Canadian genealogical works at the Minnesota Historical Society Reference Library. St. Louis Park, Minn.: Northwest Territory French and Canadian

Heritage Institute, 1980. v, 96 p.

Note: 1,479 entries.– Family histories, local histories, parish registers, censuses, geographies, atlases and other materials of interest to French-Canadian genealogists.

Location: OTMCL.

2008 **Gauthier, Louis-Guy**

La généalogie: une recherche bibliographique. Précédée de Outils généalogique à la salle Gagnon de la Bibliothèque de la ville de Montréal, par Daniel Olivier. Montréal: Commissions des bibliothécaires: Association des institutions d'enseignement secondaire, 1980. xix, 150 p.

Note: Approx. 1,100 entrées.– Principaux thèmes traités: démographie, origines de nos ancêtres, Canadiens-français aux États-Unis et dans l'Ouest, répertoires de baptêmes, mariages et sépultures, sources archivistiques, histoire des paroisses.

Localisation: OONL.

2009 **Heritage history biography.** Toronto: Canadian Book Information Centre, 1980. [44] p. ill.

Note: Annotated catalogue designed to promote Canadian publications.

Location: OONL.

2010 **Lande, Lawrence M.**

John Law, Banque royale & Compagnie des Indes: a bibliographical monograph. Montreal: [s.n.], 1980. 2 vol.: facsims.

Note: 63 entries.– Documents relating to Scottish banker John Law, the history of banking in early eighteenth century France and French America.

Location: OONL.

2011 **McIntyre, W. John; McIntyre, Janet Houghton**

"Canadian furniture: an annotated bibliography."
In: *Material History Bulletin*; No. 11 (Fall 1980) p. 36-56.; ISSN: 0703-489X.

Note: Location: OONL.

— 1981 —

2012 **Aubin, Paul; Linteau, Paul-André**

Bibliographie de l'histoire du Québec et du Canada, 1966-1975. Québec: Institut québécois de recherche sur la culture, 1981. 2 vol.; ISBN: 2-89224-003-4.

Note: Livres, articles de périodiques, manuscrits.– Subdivisions principales: histoire générales, préhistoire, ethnohistoire, explorations, occupation eurocanadienne (colonisation française, colonisation anglaise, Confédération), répertoires démographiques et généalogiques.

Production informatique par Microfor Inc.– *HISCABEQ*, service interactif, disponible de Prima Télématic.– Mise à jour trimestrielle.

Localisation: OONL.

2013 **Grainger, Bruce**

"Information sources for oral history in Canada."
In: *Ontario Library Review*; Vol. 65, no. 2 (June 1981) p. 124-128.; ISSN: 0030-2996.

Note: Associations, periodicals, manuals, union lists, selected books.

Location: OONL.

2014 **Répertoire des publications des sociétés d'histoire et de généalogie du Québec.** [Montréal]: Fédération des sociétés d'histoire du Québec, 1979-1981. ISSN: 0228-3379.

Note: Irrégulier.

Localisation: OONL.

2015 **Simon Fraser University. Library**

Canadian history. [Burnaby, B.C.]: Simon Fraser University Library, 1981. 25 p.

Note: Approx. 170 entries.

Location: OONL.

— 1982 —

2016 **Allen, Robert S.**

Loyalist literature: an annotated guide to the writings on the Loyalists of the American Revolution. Toronto: Dundurn Press, 1982. 63 p. (Dundurn Canadian historical document series: Publication ; no. 2); ISBN: 0-919670-61-X.

Note: Bibliographical essays include general references (bibliographies, individual biographies, Loyalist papers, reprints, pamphlets, theses), sections on the American Revolution, The Diaspora (Quebec, Upper Canada, Nova Scotia, New Brunswick), the Loyalist legacy.

Location: OONL.

2017 **Bazinet, Jeanne, et al.**

Catalogue des biographies. Montréal: Société Radio-Canada. Bibliothèque, 1982. 1 vol.

Note: 393 entrées.– Biographies individuelles, biographies collectives (plus de trois personnages), ouvrages biographiques de référence (dictionnaires biographiques, les Who's who, répertoires biographiques).– Comp. en collaboration avec: Martine Bousquet, Sylvie Jetté, Pierre Richer.

Localisation: OONL.

2018 **Canada. Library of Parliament. Information and Reference Branch**

Governors General of Canada, 1867-1981: a select bibliography/Les Gouverneurs généraux du Canada, 1867-1981: une bibliographie sélective. [Ottawa: Information and Reference Branch, Library of Parliament, 1982]. ii, 58 p.: ports.

Note: 580 entries.– Contains all works by and about each of twenty-two Governors General since 1867: books, chapters of books, periodical articles held by the Library of Parliament.– Includes a section devoted to the constitutional role of the Governor General, the functions and powers.– Text in English and French/texte en français et en anglais.

Location: OOP.

2019 **Conrad, Glenn R.; Brasseaux, Carl A.**

A selected bibliography of scholarly literature on colonial Louisiana and New France. Lafayette: Center for Louisiana Studies, University of Southwestern Louisiana, c1982. 138 p.; ISBN: 0-940984-06-7.

Note: Approx. 1,500 entries.– Lists manuscripts, books, articles, theses and dissertations, microforms.– Focus on colonial Louisiana, Acadia and Acadians.

Location: OONL.

2020 **Feltner, Charles E.; Feltner, Jeri Baron**

Great Lakes maritime history: bibliography and sources of information. Dearborn, Mich.: Seajay Publications, 1982. xii, 111 p. ill., port.

Note: Approx. 1,000 entries.– Reference works, Great Lakes history, ship history, shipwreck history, shipbuilding, maps and cartography.– Many Canadian references.

Location: OONL.

2021 **Graves, Donald E.; MacLeod, Anne E.**
Nova Scotia military history: a resource guide. Halifax
[N.S.]: Army Museum, Halifax Citadel, 1982. 106 p.
Note: 865 entries.– Listing of published and legislative
sources for study of Nova Scotian military history,
arranged by period and military units, with a section on
forts and fortifications, select list on New Brunswick and
Prince Edward Island.
Location: OOFF.

2022 **Holdsworth, Rosalynd; Smit-Nielsen, Hendrika**
Scottish genealogy: a bibliographical guide to selected
sources in the University of Calgary Library, the LDS
Genealogical Library (Calgary), and the Calgary Public
Library. [Calgary]: Alberta Family Histories Society,
[1982]. 51 p.; ISSN: 0228-9288.
Note: 668 entries.– Includes a section on emigration and
listings of Canadian genealogies and settlement histories.
Location: OONL.

2023 **Manitoba Genealogical Society. Library**
The library holdings of the Manitoba Genealogical
Society, 1982. [Winnipeg]: The Society, [1982]. 2, [41], 3 p.
Note: Approx. 320 entries.– Lists books, periodicals,
vertical files.
Location: OONL.

2024 **Palmer, Gregory**
A bibliography of Loyalist source material in the United
States, Canada, and Great Britain. Westport [Conn.]:
Meckler, c1982. ix, 1064 p.; ISBN: 0-930466-26-8.
Note: Canadian section: "A bibliography of Loyalist
source material in Canada", edited by Jo-Ann Fellows. (p.
3-186).– Includes a list of repositories, primary unpublish-
ed material, primary published material.
Location: OONL.

2025 **A reader's guide to Canadian history.** Toronto: Univer-
sity of Toronto Press, 1982. 2 vol.; ISBN: 0-8020-6442-6
(vol. 1).– 0-8020-6490-6 (vol. 2).
Note: Bibliographical essays.– Vol. 1: *Beginnings to
Confederation.* Edited by D.A. Muise. vii, 253 p.–
Contents: "Canada during the French régime," by
Cornelius J. Jaenen; "Quebec, 1760-1867," by Fernand
Ouellet; "The Atlantic provinces," by D.A. Muise; "Upper
Canada," by J.K Johnson; "The north, the western
interior, and the Pacific coast," by David Richeson;
"Britain and British North America before Confedera-
tion," by Phillip Buckner; "Confederation," by D.A. Muise.
Vol. 2: *Confederation to the present.* Edited by J.L.
Granatstein and Paul Stevens. xi, 329 p.– Contents: "Na-
tional politics," by J.L. Granatstein and Paul Stevens;
"Foreign and defence policy," by J.L. Granatstein;
"Economic and business history," by Michael Bliss;
"Urban history," by Gilbert Stelter; "Labour and working-
class history," by Irving Abella; "Social and intellectual
history," by Carl Berger; "British Columbia," by Patricia
E. Roy; "The Prairie provinces," by Hartwell Bowsfield;
"Ontario," by Peter Oliver; "French Canada," by Ramsay
Cook; "Atlantic Canada," by William B. Hamilton; "The
North," by Morris Zaslow.
Previous editions:
Granatstein, J.L.; Stevens, Paul. *Canada since 1867: a
bibliographical guide.* 1977. ix, 204 p.; ISBN: 0-88866-584-9.
1974. x, 179 p.; ISBN: 0-88866-554-7.
Location: OONL.

— 1983 —

2026 **Filby, P. William**
American & British genealogy & heraldry: a selected list
of books. 3rd ed. Boston: New England Historic
Genealogical Society, 1983. xix, 736 p.; ISBN: 0-8808200-4-
7.
Note: Includes Canadian works.
Previous editions:
Chicago: American Library Association, 1975. xxi, 467 p.;
ISBN: 0-8389020-3-0.
Chicago: American Library Association, 1970. xix, 184 p.;
ISBN: 0-8389007-9-8.
Supplement: ... . *1982-1985 supplement.* 1987. xvii, 230 p.;
ISBN: 0-8808200-4-7.
Location: OONL.

2027 **Lande, Lawrence M.**
The political economy of New France: as developed by
John Law, Compagnie des Indes & the French-Canadian
traders: a bibliography, compiled by Lawrence M. Lande
from manuscripts and printed material in his private
collection. [Montreal: s.n.], 1983. xii, 98 p.: ill., facsims.
Note: 321 entries.– Contains a bibliography of related
works; sections listing books and other printed material,
(manuscripts, arrêts, edicts, etc., maps, numismatics)
pertaining to the banking/monetary and trading system
developed by John Law and established in France in 1716
as the Banque Générale (Banque Royale), and the
Compagnie des Indes, to control trading companies of
Canada and Louisiana.
Location: OONL.

2028 **Manitoba. Provincial Archives**
"Selected bibliography of genealogical publications."
In: *Saskatchewan Genealogical Society Bulletin*; Vol. 14, no. 1
(February 1983) p. 27-35.; ISSN: 0048-9182.
Note: Reference works, monographs, articles, brochures,
theses.
Location: AEU.

2029 **Peterson, Jean; Murphy, Lynn; MacDonald, Heather**
The Loyalist guide: Nova Scotian loyalists and their
documents. [Halifax]: Public Archives of Nova Scotia,
[1983]. 272 p.; ISBN: 0-088871-044-5.
Note: Part 1: Secondary sources: published material in
the Nova Scotia Archives Library, arranged by subject:
general, Cape Breton, Black loyalists, politics and
government, trade/commerce/transportation, societies,
religion, education, literature, newspapers, architecture,
cities and towns, genealogy, military, bibliographies.–
Part 2: Primary or manuscript sources in the Nova Scotia
Archives Manuscript Department.
Location: OONL.

2030 **Smith, Dwight L.**
The history of Canada: an annotated bibliography. Santa
Barbara, Calif.: ABC-CLIO Information Services, c1983.
xi, 327 p. (Clio bibliography series ; no. 10); ISBN: 0-
87436-047-1.
Note: 3,362 entries.– Based on database *America: History
and life*, contains periodical articles which appeared from
1973 through 1978, ranging from prehistory of Canada to
the present: native peoples, exploration and exploitation,
New France, British North America, achievement of
nationhood, contemporary scene (since 1945), the regions.
Location: OONL.

2031 **Vincent, Elizabeth**
Bibliographie choisie et commentée applicable à l'étude des techniques de construction du génie militaire en Amérique du Nord britannique, au XIXe siècle. [Ottawa]: Parcs Canada, 1983. 22 p. (Bulletin de recherches / Parcs Canada ; no 190; ISSN: 0228-1236)
Note: Préparée concurremment avec une étude de la construction militaire du XIXe siècle au Canada, les ouvrages datent essentiellement du XIXe siècle: encyclopédies, ouvrages généraux sur l'architecture, ouvrages sur des aspects particuliers de la construction, écrits militaires (principalement du génie militaire).
English title: *A select annotated bibliography applicable to the study of the Royal Engineers' building technology in nineteenth century British North America.*
Localisation: OONL.

2032 **Vincent, Elizabeth**
A select annotated bibliography applicable to the study of the Royal Engineers building technology in nineteenth century British North America. [Ottawa]: Parks Canada, 1983. 20 p. (Research bulletin / Parks Canada ; no. 190; ISSN: 0228-1228)
Note: Prepared in conjunction with a study of nineteenth-century military construction in Canada, works included date mainly from nineteenth-century: encyclopedias, general works on architecture, works on aspects of building, military writings (mainly in area of military engineering).
Titre en français: *Bibliographie choisie et commentée applicable à l'étude des techniques de construction du génie militaire en Amérique du Nord britannique, au XIXe siècle.*
Location: OONL.

2033 **Yukon Archives**
Dalton Trail: a bibliography of sources available at Yukon Archives. Whitehorse: Yukon, Education, Yukon Archives, 1983. 21 l.; ISBN: 1-55018-037-1.
Note: Location: OONL.

— 1984 —

2034 **Aitken, Barbara B.; Broughton, Dawn; Crouch, Yvonne J.**
Some Ontario references and sources for the family historian. Rev. and enl. ed. Toronto: Ontario Genealogical Society, c1984. 56 p.; ISBN: 0-920036-14-7.
Note: Lists references relating to sources of personal information, land acquisitions, estate records, military, naval records and militia rolls, immigration records, regional and biographical information, public repositories, genealogical and historical societies, computers as genealogical aid.
Previous edition: Keffer, Marion C.; Kirk, Robert F.; Kirk, Audrey L. 1976. 38 p.; ISBN: 0-920036-02-3.
Location: OONL.

2035 **Cameron, William J.**
A bibliography in short-title catalog form of Canadiana in French, 1545-1631. [London: University of Western Ontario], 1984. iii, 38 l. (WHSTC Bibliography ; no. 12; ISSN: 0712-9289); ISBN: 0-7714-0519-7.
Note: Approx. 150 entries.
Location: OONL.

2036 **Cooke, Owen Arnold**
The Canadian military experience, 1867-1983/ Bibliographie de la vie militaire au Canada, 1867-1983. 2nd ed. Ottawa: Directorate of History, Department of National Defence, 1984. xix, 329 p. (Monograph series / Department of National Defence, Directorate of History ; no. 2); ISBN: 0-660-52649-2.
Note: Approx. 4,000 entries.– Listing of published primary sources and secondary works on Canadian military topics, excluding poetry and fiction, covering the period from Confederation to the present.– Text in English and French/texte en français et en anglais.
Previous edition: *The Canadian military experience, 1867-1967: a bibliography/Bibliographie de la vie militaire au Canada, 1867-1967.* [Ottawa]: 1979. ix, 244 p. (Department of National Defence Occasional paper ; no. 2); ISBN: 0-660-50435-9.
Location: OONL.

2037 **Crochetière, Jacques; Dupont, L.**
"Genèse des structures d'habitat dans les seigneuries du Québec: une bibliographie sélective."
Dans: *Cahiers de géographie de Québec*; Vol. 28, nos 73-74 (avril-septembre 1984) p. 317-327.; ISSN: 0007-9766.
Note: Localisation: OONL.

2038 **Gephart, Ronald M.**
Revolutionary America, 1763-1789: a bibliography. Washington: Library of Congress, 1984. 2 vol. (xl, 1672 p.), ill.; ISBN: 0-8444-0359-8 (vol. 1); 0-8444-0379-2 (vol. 2).
Note: 14,810 entries.– Includes sections on "Non-revolutionary colonies" (Quebec, Upper Canada, Maritime provinces), and "Loyalists in exile" (Canada and the Maritime provinces).
Location: OONL.

2039 **History projects supported by Multiculturalism Canada/Activités de caractère historique subventionnées par Multiculturalisme Canada.** Ottawa: Multiculturalism Canada, 1984. 109 p.; ISBN: 0-662-53665-7.
Note: Approx. 300 entries.– Listing of history projects which received financial assistance from the Multiculturalism Program in the years 1977 to 1983, published, completed, or in progress.– Includes an index of associations and publishers, and a subject index.– Text in English and French/texte en français et en anglais.
Location: OONL.

2040 **Lande, Lawrence M.**
The founder of our monetary system, John Law, Compagnie des Indes & the early economy of North America: a second bibliography. Montreal: Lawrence Lande Foundation for Canadian Historical Research, McGill University, 1984. xxxix, 187, [1] p.: ill. facsims.
Note: 408 entries.– Contains a bibliography of related works; sections listing books and other printed material (manuscripts, arrêts, edicts, etc., maps, numismatics) pertaining to the banking/monetary and trading system developed by John Law and established in France in 1716 as the Banque Générale (Banque Royale), and the Compagnie des Indes, to control trading companies of Canada and Louisiana.
Location: OONL.

2041 **Marble, Allan Everett**
A catalogue of published genealogies of Nova Scotia families. 2nd ed. Halifax: Genealogical Association of the Royal Nova Scotia Historical Society, 1984. 77 p. (Publication / Genealogical Association of the Royal Nova Scotia Historical Society ; no. 2)

Note: 606 entries.
Previous edition: 1979. 59 p.
Location: OONL.

2042 **Simon Fraser University. Library**
The first British Empire: discovery & colonization, 1485-1775. [Burnaby, D.C.]. The Library, 1984. 29 p. (Simon Fraser University Library reference bibliography ; HIST 8)
Note: Lists material on Britain's exploration and expansion to 1775: books, government publications, private papers, diaries.
Location: OONL.

2043 **Warwick, Jack**
"Récits de voyages en Nouvelle-France au XVIIe siècle: bibliographie d'introduction."
Dans: *Scritti sulla Nouvelle-France nel seicento*. Bari, Italie: Adriatica, c1984. P. 283-319. (Quaderni del seicento francese ; 6)
Note: Appendice bibliografica, comp. par Paolo Carile et Giovanni Dotoli.
Location: OONL.

— 1985 —

2044 **Aubin, Paul; Côté, Louis-Marie**
Bibliographie de l'histoire du Québec et du Canada, 1976-1980/Bibliography of the history of Quebec and Canada, 1976-1980. [Québec]: Institut québécois de recherche sur la culture, 1985. 2 vol.; ISBN: 2-89224-055-7.
Note: Livres, articles de périodiques, manuscrits.– Subdivisions principales: histoire générales, préhistoire, ethnohistoire, explorations, occupation eurocanadienne (colonisation française, colonisation anglaise, Confédération), répertoire démographiques et généalogiques.– Avec la collaboration de l'équipe de bibliographie de la *Revue d'histoire de l'Amérique française* et de Microfor C.E.J. Inc.– Texte en français et en anglais/ text in English and French.
HISCABEQ, service interactif, disponible de Prima Télématic.– Mise à jour trimestrielle.
Localisation: OONL.

2045 **Cooke, Alan**
"A bibliographical introduction to Sir John Franklin's expeditions and the Franklin search."
In: *The Franklin era in Canadian Arctic history, 1845-1859*, edited by Patricia D. Sutherland. Ottawa: National Museum of Man, National Museums of Canada, 1985. P. 12-20. (National Museum of Man Mercury series; ISSN: 0316-1854 : Archaeological survey of Canada paper ; no. 131; ISSN: 0317-2244)
Note: Guide to published and unpublished literature related to Franklin and the Franklin search.– Emphasis on Arctic Blue Books, Hudson's Bay Company archives, manuscripts collections of Scott Polar Research Institute, Cambridge, England, with list of standard and secondary sources.
Location: OONL.

2046 **Fredriksen, John C.**
Free trade and sailors' rights: a bibliography of the War of 1812. Westport, Conn.: Greenwood Press, c1985. xiii, 399 p. (Bibliographies and indexes in American history ; no. 2; ISSN: 0742-6828); ISBN: 0-313-24313-1.
Note: Approx. 6,000 entries.– Sections listing British and Canadian texts; geographical divisions for western Ontario, Lake Ontario, Lower Canada, Nova Scotia, New Brunswick.

Location: OONL.

2047 **Hodgson, Maurice**
"The literature of the Franklin search."
In: *The Franklin era in Canadian Arctic history, 1845-1859*, edited by Patricia D. Sutherland. Ottawa: National Museum of Man, National Museums of Canada, 1985. P. 1-11. (National Museum of Man Mercury series; ISSN: 0316-1854 : Archaeological survey of Canada paper ; no. 131; ISSN: 0317-2244)
Note: Location: OONL.

2048 **Lande, Lawrence M.**
John Law, the French régime and the beginnings of exploration, trade and paper money in North America: a third bibliography. Montreal: Lawrence Lande Foundation for Canadian Historical Research, 1985. xii, 155 p.: ill. facsims.
Note: 345 entries.– Contains a bibliography of related works; sections listing books and other printed material, (manuscripts, arrêts, edicts, etc., maps, numismatics) pertaining to the banking/monetary and trading system developed by John Law and established in France in 1716 as the Banque Générale (Banque Royale), and the Compagnie des Indes, to control trading companies of Canada and Louisiana.
Location: OONL.

2049 **Ontario Genealogical Society**
Ontario Genealogical Society library holdings: housed with Canadiana Collection, North York Public Library. Toronto: The Society, c1985. 148 p.; ISBN: 0-920036-07-4.
Note: Approx. 1,500 entries.– Bibliographies and catalogues, church histories, historical atlases, maps and gazetteers, genealogy: (family histories and pioneer families; sources), heraldry, Ontario history and local history.– Appendix: cemeteries: Ontario and Quebec.– Edited by Barbara B. Aitken.
Location: OONL.

2050 **Parent, Jean-Claude**
Bibliographie commentée sur le régime seigneurial [microforme]. [Ottawa]: Parcs Canada, 1985. 4 microfiches (Parcs Canada Rapports sur microfiches ; no 220)
Note: 1,468 entrées.– Ouvrages académiques, albums souvenirs, articles de périodiques, thèses, brochures parus jusqu'en août 1985 sur le nature et fonctionnement du régime seigneurial, aspects économique et social, aspect géographique, monographies des seigneuries, seigneurs, censitaires et édifices, monographies de paroisses.– Deux index: auteurs, seigneuries.
Localisation: OONL.

2051 **Smith, Dwight L.**
The War of 1812: an annotated bibliography. New York: Garland Pub., 1985. xxiv, 340 p. (Wars of the United States ; v. 3) (Garland reference library of social science ; v. 250); ISBN: 0-8240-8945-6.
Note: 1,393 entries.– Covers through 1981.– Includes books, essays, articles, diaries, memoirs, speeches, satire, pamphlets, poems, songs, novels, juvenile literature, theses.– Excludes broadsides, government documents.
Location: OONL.

2052 **Yukon Archives**
Genealogy sources available at the Yukon Archives. Whitehorse: Yukon Archives, 1985. 11 l.; ISBN: 1-55018-041-X.

Note: Listing of books, imprint material, directories, indexes, manuscripts, corporate records, government records, municipal records, collections of photographs for genealogical research in the Yukon.
Location: OONL.

— 1986 —

2053 **Le Choc du passé: les années trente et les sans-travail: bibliographie sélective annotée.** Québec: Institut québécois de recherche sur la culture, 1986. 185 p. (Documents de recherche / Institut québécois de recherche sur la culture ; no 11; ISSN: 0823-0447); ISBN: 2-89224-082-4.
Note: 276 entrées.– Comporte articles de périodiques, études gouvernementales, monographies, thèses, manuscrits, documents et recueils de documents.– Documents audio-visuels on été exclus.– Thèmes: contexte économique et social, organisations de sans-travail, L'État, les partis, les politiques sociales, mouvement ouvrier et les mouvements sociaux, la culture.
Édition antérieure: Centre populaire de documentation, 1985. 138 f.
Localisation: OONL.

2054 **Day, Alan Edwin**
Search for the Northwest Passage: an annotated bibliography. New York: Garland, 1986. xiv, 632 p. (Garland reference library of social science ; vol. 186); ISBN: 0-8240-9288-0.
Note: 5,160 entries.– Section one contains a listing of general works, encyclopedic works, maps and atlases, collections of voyages and anthologies.– Following this introductory list, entries are arranged chronologically by the expedition or voyage.– Forms of material include books, pamphlets, newspaper and periodical articles, most in English language only.– Both Atlantic and Pacific approaches are covered.
Location: OONL.

2055 **Hamelin, Jean, et al.**
Guide du chercheur en histoire canadienne. Québec: Presses de l'Université Laval, 1986. xxxii, 808 p.; ISBN: 2-7637-7096-7.
Note: Regroupe en cinq parties: instruments de travail (ouvrages de référence, bibliographies, grandes synthèses d'histoire); les sources (archives, sources imprimées, histoire du Canada par les textes, sources statistiques); les études (synthèses, monographies, bilans historiographiques, matériel scolaire); sciences auxiliaires; pratique du métier.
Édition antérieure: *Guide de l'étudiant en histoire du Canada*. 1965. iv, 274 f.
Localisation: OONL.

2056 **Martin, Shirley A.; Makahonuk, Glen**
Louis Riel and the rebellions in the Northwest: an annotated bibliography of material in Special Collections, University of Saskatchewan Library. Saskatoon: University of Saskatchewan Library, 1986. 145 p.
Note: 396 entries.– Printed primary and secondary material on the Red River Rebellion, the Northwest Rebellion and biographical material on Louis Riel.– Manuscript collections include the Morton Collection (correspondence, clippings, photographs, government documents, reminiscences and personal papers), and the Griffin-Greenland Collection (photocopies of

correspondence, government records, medical records, articles and papers pertaining to William Henry Jackson and Louis Riel).
Location: MWIAP.

2057 **Ontario Genealogical Society. London Branch. Library**
London Branch Library holdings: a genealogical research aid. London, Ont.: London Branch, Ontario Genealogical Society, c1986. 39 p.
Note: Books and manuscripts, microfilms/fiche, tapes, periodicals.
Location: OONL.

— 1987 —

2058 **Aubin, Paul; Côté, Louis-Marie**
Bibliographie de l'histoire du Québec et du Canada, 1946-1965/Bibliography of the history of Quebec and Canada, 1946-1965. Québec: Institut québécois de recherche sur la culture, 1987. 2 vol.; ISBN: 2-89224-098-0.
Note: Livres, articles de périodiques, manuscrits.– Subdivisions principales: histoire générale, préhistoire, ethnohistoire, explorations, occupation eurocanadienne (colonisation française, colonisation anglaise, Confédération), répertoires démographiques et généalogiques.– Texte en français et en anglais/text in English and French.
HISCABEC, service interactif, disponible de Prima Télématic.– Mise à jour trimestrielle.
Localisation: OONL.

2059 **Goodwin, Daniel Corey**
A checklist of secondary sources for planter studies. Prelim. ed. Wolfville, N.S.: Acadia University, Department of History, Planter Studies Committee, 1987. iv, 64 l.
Note: Location: OONL.

2060 **Heraldry Society of Canada. Library**
Bibliography of the heraldic library of the Heraldry Society of Canada, la Société héraldique du Canada, at the City of Ottawa Archives. [Ottawa]: Heraldry Society of Canada, 1987. 1 vol. (in various foliations); ISBN: 0-9693063-1-8.
Note: Approx. 400 entries.– Books, booklets, brochures, leaflets.
Location: OONL.

2061 **Lande, Lawrence M.**
John Law: the creditability of land and the development of paper money and trade in North America: a fifth bibliography. Montreal: Lawrence Lande Foundation for Canadian Historical Research, 1987. liii, 263 p.: ill.
Note: 393 entries.– Books, maps, manuscripts, numismatics, arrêts, edicts, letters patent relating to the period 1676 to 1726.
Location: OONL.

2062 **Mennie-de Varennes, Kathleen**
Bibliographie annotée d'ouvrages généalogiques au Canada/Annotated bibliography of genealogical works in Canada. Markham, Ont.: Published by Fitzhenry & Whiteside in association with the National Library of Canada and the Canadian Government Publishing Centre, Supply and Services Canada, c1986-1987. 6 vol.; ISBN: 0-88902-911-3 (vol. 1); 0-88902-959-8 (vol. 2); 0-88902-905-9 (vol. 3); 0-88902-910-5 (vol. 4); 0-88902-986-5 (vol. 5); 0-88902-995-4 (vol. 6).
Note: Approx. 100,000 entries.– Monographs, brochures, pamphlets, manuscripts, microfilms, excerpts from

genealogical and historical periodicals; records of births, marriages and deaths.– Descriptive annotations, sources, locations.– Text in English and French/texte en français et en anglais.
Location: OONL.

2063 **Ontario Genealogical Society. Kingston Branch**
Library holdings: housed with Kingston Public Library. Kingston, Ont.: The Branch, c1987. i, 44 p.; ISBN: 1-55034-002-6.
Note: Approx. 450 entries.– Contains bibliographies and catalogues, family histories, genealogy sources, Ontario history and local histories.– Edited by Barbara B. Aitken.
Previous edition: Blackwell, John D. *Library list, Kingston Branch, Ontario Genealogical Society.* 1982. iv, 16 p.
Location: OONL.

2064 **Palmegiano, E.M.**
The British Empire in the Victorian press, 1832-1867: a bibliography. New York: Garland, 1987. xviii, 234 p. (Themes in European expansion ; vol. 8) (Garland reference library of social science ; vol. 389); ISBN: 0-8240-9802-1.
Note: 2,859 entries.– Articles from 50 London-based magazines which comment on events and personalities in the colonies in mid-nineteenth century.– Numerous references to Canada.
Location: OONL.

2065 **Sherman, George**
The Canada connection in American history: a guide for teachers: content backgrounders, teaching strategies, student materials and a multi-media bibliography. Plattsburgh, N.Y.: Center for the Study of Canada, SUNY Plattsburgh, 1987. vi, 199 l.: ill., maps.
Note: Contains reading lists on various topics of Canadian history and culture and a bibliography of books, pamphlets and audio-visual materials.
Location: OONL.

— 1988 —

2066 **Alberta Genealogical Society. Lethbridge and District Branch**
Lethbridge genealogical resources. Lethbridge: Lethbridge and District Branch, Alberta Genealogical Society, 1988. 185 p.; ISBN: 0-919224-79-2.
Note: Approx. 1,500 entries.– Local histories, cemetery recordings, family histories, bibliographies.– Main focus is on Lethbridge and area, with secondary emphasis on western Canada.
Location: OONL.

2067 **Cameron, William J.**
A bibliography in short-title catalog form of Jesuit relations, printed accounts of events in Canada, 1632-73, sent by Jesuit missionaries to France. Rev. ed. [London: University of Western Ontario], 1988. vi, 60 p. (WHSTC Bibliography ; no. 12; ISSN: 0712-9289); ISBN: 0-7714-0519-7.
Note: Approx. 180 entries.– Intended to simplify and interpret bibliographical information in McCoy's *Jesuit relations of Canada, 1632-1673: a bibliography,* to "correct, elaborate, or confirm the interpretations of earlier bibliographical descriptions."
Previous ed.: 1982. ii, 26 l.; ISBN: 0-7714-0333-X.
Location: OONL.

2068 **Cameron, William J.**
Sixteenth century Canadiana in English: a bibliography in short-title catalog form. [London: University of Western Ontario], 1988. vi, 27 p. (WHSTC Bibliography ; no. 52; ISSN: 0712-9289); ISBN: 0-7714-1036-0.
Note: Approx. 60 entries.
Location: OONL.

2069 **Filby, P. William**
Passenger and immigration lists bibliography, 1538-1900: being a guide to published lists of arrivals in the United States and Canada. Detroit, Mich.: Gale Research, c1988. xi, 324 p.; ISBN: 0-8103-2740-6.
Note: Approx. 2,500 entries.– Books, articles, pamphlets, journals.– Subject index provides access to names of places of emigration/immigration, ports of departure/arrival, places of settlement, ship names and dates of particular voyages.
Previous edition: 1981. 195 p.; ISBN: 0-8103-1098-8.
Location: OONL.

2070 **Kinnell, Susan K.**
People in history: an index to U.S. and Canadian biographies in history journals and dissertations. Santa Barbara, Calif.: ABC-Clio, c1988. 2 vol.; ISBN: 0-87436-493-0.
Note: 7,677 entries.– Biographical articles and theses on about 6,000 men and women in U.S. and Canadian history from earliest times to the present.
Location: OONL.

2071 **Lande, Lawrence M.**
John Law, early trade rivalries among nations and the beginnings of banking in North America: a sixth bibliography. Montreal: Lawrence Lande Foundation for Canadian Historical Research, 1988. xxi, 197 p.: ill.
Note: Books and other printed materials, manuscripts, maps, numismatic documents relating to John Law's banking and monetary system as it influenced trade in North America; early voyageurs contracts and history of trade and banking; war and conquest in America.
Location: OONL.

2072 **MacKenzie, David**
"Three sides of the same coin: some recent literature on Canada-Newfoundland relations in the 1940s."
In: *Newfoundland Studies;* Vol. 4, no. 1 (Spring 1988) p. 99-104.; ISSN: 0823-1737.
Note: Location: OONL.

2073 **Pichora, Anne**
Genealogical reference sources at the National Library of Canada: a selective bibliography/Ouvrages de référence en généalogie à la Bibliothèque nationale du Canada: une bibliographie sélective. [Ottawa]: National Library of Canada, Reference and Information Services Division, 1988. 14 p.
Note: Approx. 100 entries.– Bibliographies and catalogues, cemetery and parish registers, census documents, directories, name sources, handbooks, periodical indexes.– Revised by Mary E. Bond and Franceen Gaudet.
Location: OONL.

2074 **Stamp, Robert M.**
Royalty and royal tours: a Canadian bibliography. Toronto: Heritage Books, 1988. iv, 43 p. (Canadian Biblio-File series publication ; 002); ISBN: 0-921342-02-0.
Note: Approx. 600 entries.– Biographies, biographical

articles on specific visits by all members of the British royal family with connection to Canada, from Prince William Henry in the 1780s to the present generation.
Location: OONL.

— 1989 —

2075 **Eisenbichler, W.**
Genealogy at the Sault Ste. Marie Public Library. [Sault Ste. Marie, Ont.]: Sault Ste. Marie Public Library, 1989. 28 p.
Note: Books for preliminary research, gazetteers, guides and finding aids, passenger lists, prepared genealogies, periodicals, bibliographies, surnames dictionaries and local histories.
Previous edition: *Genealogy*. 1983. 20 p.
Location: OONL.

2076 **Lamonde, Yvan**
L'histoire des idées au Québec, 1760-1960: bibliographie des études. Montréal: Bibliothèque nationale du Québec, 1989. 167 p.: ill., fac.-sim.; ISBN: 2-551-12140-X.
Note: 795 entrées.– Présentation est chronologique, par période historique, et dans l'ordre chronologique, thématique: Conquête et révolutions (1760-1815); dynamique coloniale, conditions de vie intellectuelle; L'essor du nationalisme et du libéralisme (1815-1840); Vie intellectuelle active (1840-1880); libéralisme, ultramontanisme; Les idées, la ville et l'usine (1880-1929); L'affaire Riel et le nationalisme, les médias de masse, le renouveau nationaliste; Crise intellectuelle (1929-1945); Pour une pensée libre (1945-1960).
Localisation: OONL.

2077 **Lande, Lawrence M.**
The development of the voyageur contract (1686-1821): a monograph. Montreal: Lawrence Lande Foundation for Canadian Historical Research, 1989. xx, 151 p., [4] p. of pl.: ill., maps, facsims.; ISBN: 0-96941-850-7.
Note: 111 entries.– Lists and describes items from the Lande Collection.– Manuscripts voyageur contracts (1686-1789), and printed North West Company voyageur engagements (1780s-1820).
Location: OONL.

2078 **Lande, Lawrence M.**
John Law, the evolution of his system: a seventh bibliography. Montreal: Lawrence Lande Foundation for Canadian Historical Research, 1989. xl, 183 p.: ill.; ISBN: 0-9694185-1-5.
Note: 308 entries.– Books, numismatic documents (bills of exchange, warrants of various kinds, banknotes), manuscripts, maps, arrêts, edicts, etc. relating to the Law system of economics and its influence on North America through the Compagnie des Indes.
Location: OONL.

2079 **Waterston, Elizabeth**
The travellers: Canada to 1900: an annotated bibliography of works published in English from 1577. Guelph, Ont.: University of Guelph, 1989. viii, 321 p., [12] l. of pl.: ill., map.; ISBN: 0-88955-170-7.
Note: Approx. 700 entries.– Chronological listing of travel literature focussing on the period prior to 1900.– Subject index covers regions, towns and villages visited, climatic conditions noted, people, institutions, social customs, language patterns, health care and modes of transportation.– Includes a bibliography of secondary sources: bibliographies, collections and histories,

reference books, articles, books and dissertations on Canadian travel and exploration literature to 1900.– Canadian Institute for Historical Microreproduction numbers are provided for most entries.– Compiled with the assistance of Ian Easterbrook, Bernard Katz, Kathleen Scott.
Location: OOFF.

— 1990 —

2080 **Aubin, Paul; Côté, Louis-Marie**
Bibliographie de l'histoire du Québec et du Canada, 1981-1985/Bibliography of the history of Quebec and Canada, 1981-1985. Québec: Institut québécois de recherche sur la culture, 1990. 2 vol.; ISBN: 2-89224-142-1.
Note: 28,951 entrées.– Livres, articles de périodiques, thèses parues entre 1981-1985.– Classement par périodes, de la préhistoire à l'époque contemporaine; par régions, de Terre-Neuve à Yukon; par thèmes (politique, sports, littérature, syndicalisme, etc.).– Texte en français et en anglais/text in English and French.
HISCABEQ, service interactif, disponible de Prima Télématic.– Mise à jour trimestrielle.
Localisation: OONL.

2081 **Craig, Béatrice**
"Bibliographie relative aux transmissions de patrimoine en Amérique du Nord."
Dans: *Histoire sociale: Social History*; Vol. 23, no. 46 (novembre 1990) p. 269-270.; ISSN: 0018-2557.
Note: Trois parties: "Pour le Canada français," "Pour le Haut-Canada," "Pour le nord-est des États-Unis."
Localisation: OONL.

2082 **Gutteridge, Paul**
Canadian genealogical resources: a guide to the materials held in Surrey Public Library. [Surrey, B.C.]: Surrey Public Library, 1990. 168 p.; ISBN: 0-9692197-1-0.
Note: Listing of books (directories and handbooks, indexes, immigration and passenger lists, historical atlases, parish and biographical records, local histories), periodicals, microform materials (census records, estate records, loyalist lists, military records, parish and vital records, marriage records, naturalization records).
Previous editions:
Canadian genealogical resources: a guide to the materials held in Surrey Centennial Library. 1984. 115 p.
1984. 98 p.
1983. 78 p.
Location: OONL.

2083 **Peters, Diane E.**
Roots: genealogical resources in W.L.U. Library. Waterloo, Ont.: The Library, Wilfrid Laurier University, 1990. 161 p.; ISBN: 0-921821-05-0.
Note: Approx. 1,200 entries.– Bibliographies, census records and indexes, gazeteers/directories, guides to handwriting, selected historical works (family histories, ethnic group histories, local histories), heraldry, periodicals, dictionaries and histories of personal names and research guides.
Location: OONL.

2084 **Répertoire des historiens et historiennes de l'Amérique française.** Outremont [Québec]: Institut d'histoire de l'Amérique française, 1990. [env. 250] p.
Note: Publications historiques des membres de l'IHAF: livres d'histoire, articles d'histoire publiés dans les revues savantes, mémoires de maîtrise et/ou thèses de

doctorat dans la discipline historique.
Éditions antérieures:
Répertoire des historiens du Québec et du Canada français.
[Montréal]: Section québécoise du Comité international
des historiens et géographes de langue française, 1986.
Savard, Pierre. Québec: Section québécoise du Comité
international des historiens et géographes francophones,
1980. ix, 268 p.
1977. [200] p.
1973. 1 vol. (non paginé).
Répertoire des historiens du Québec. 1971. [100] p.
Localisation: OONL.

2085 **Robert, Jean-Claude**
"La recherche en histoire du Canada."
Dans: *Revue internationale d'études canadiennes*; No 1-2
(printemps-automne 1990) p. 11-33.; ISSN: 1180-3991.
Note: Localisation: OONL.

— 1992 —

2086 **Aubin, Paul; Linteau, Paul-André**
"Bibliographie d'histoire de l'Amérique française
(publications récentes)."
Dans: *Revue d'histoire de l'Amérique française*; Vol. 21, no 1
(juin 1967) p. 160-174; vol. 21, no 2 (septembre 1967) p.
340-353; vol. 21, no 3 (décembre 1967) p. 507-525; vol. 21,
no 4 (mars 1968) p. 853-880; vol. 22, no 1 (juin 1968) p.
152-162; vol. 22, no 2 (septembre 1968) p. 323-347; vol. 22,
no 3 (décembre 1968) p. 493-515; vol. 22, no 4 (mars
1969) p. 662-682; vol. 23, no 2 (septembre 1969) p. 341-
350; vol. 23, no 3 (décembre 1969) p. 504-522; vol. 23, no 4
(mars 1970) p. 649-664; vol. 24, no 1 (juin 1970) p. 143-163;
vol. 24, no 2 (septembre 1970) p. 301-325; vol. 24, no 3
(décembre 1970) p. 447-467; vol. 24, no 4 (mars 1971) p.
615-635; vol. 25, no 1 (juin 1971) p. 127-146; vol. 25, no 2
(septembre 1971) p. 271-292; vol. 25, no 3 (décembre
1971) p. 431-452; vol. 25, no 4 (mars 1972) p. 584-606; vol.
26, no 1 (juin 1972) p. 125-144; vol. 26, no 2 (septembre
1972) p. 290-312; vol. 26, no 3 (décembre 1972) p. 445-467;
vol. 26, no 4 (mars 1973) p. 601-621; vol. 27, no 1 (juin
1973) p. 126-148; vol. 27, no 2 (septembre 1973) p. 303-
312; vol. 27, no 3 (décembre 1973) p. 447-466; vol. 27, no 4
(mars 1974) p. 607-627; vol. 28, no 1 (juin 1974) p. 133-151;
vol. 28 no 2 (septembre 1974) p. 289-308; vol. 28, no 3
(décembre 1974) p. 454-468; vol. 28, no 4 (mars 1975) p.
604-626; vol. 29, no 1 (juin 1975) p. 119-140; vol. 29, no 2
(septembre 1975) p. 289-306; vol. 29, no 3 (décembre
1975) p. 447-465; vol. 29, no 4 (mars 1976) p. 604-622; vol.
30, no 1 (juin 1976) p. 126-141; vol. 30, no 2 (septembre
1976) p. 290-311; vol. 30, no 3 (décembre 1976) p. 448-469;
vol. 31, no 1 (juin 1977) p. 119-148; vol. 31, no 2
(septembre 1977) p. 281-305; vol. 31, no 3 (décembre
1977) p. 443-469; vol. 31, no 4 (mars 1978) p. 597-621; vol.
32, no 1 (juin 1978) p. 117-139; vol. 32, no 2 (septembre
1978) p. 281-303; vol. 32, no 4 (mars 1979) p. 649-678; vol.
33, no 1 (juin 1979) p. 107-142; vol. 33, no 2 (septembre
1979) p. 283-315; vol. 33, no 4 (mars 1980) p. 608-639; vol.
34, no 1 (juin 1980) p. 123-156; vol. 34, no 2 (septembre
1980) p. 296-314; vol. 34, no 3 (décembre 1980) p. 469-494;
vol. 35, no 1 (juin 1981) p. 122-150; vol. 35, no 2
(septembre 1981) p. 293-306; vol. 35, no 3 (décembre
1981) p. 444-463; vol. 35, no 4 (mars 1982) p. 605-628; vol.
36, no 1 (juin 1982) p. 129-150; vol. 36, no 2 (septembre
1982) p. 284-301; vol. 36, no 3 (décembre 1982) p. 451-468;
vol. 36, no 4 (mars 1983) p. 612-633; vol. 37, no 1 (juin

1983) p. 123-141; vol. 37, no 3 (décembre 1983) p. 480-509;
vol. 37, no 4 (mars 1984) p. 640-671; vol. 38, no 1 (été
1984) p. 114-146; vol. 38, no 2 (automne 1984) p. 281-311;
vol. 38, no 3 (hiver 1985) p. 452-485; vol. 38, no 4
(printemps 1985) p. 613-640; vol. 39, no 1 (été 1985) p. 126-
146; vol. 39, no 2 (automne 1985) p. 302-311; vol. 39, no 3
(hiver 1986) p. 446-471; vol. 39, no 4 (printemps 1986) p.
614-641; vol. 40, no 1 (été 1986) p. 117-143; vol. 40, no 2
(automne 1986) p. 305-325; vol. 40, no 3 (hiver 1987) p.
457-487; vol. 40, no 4 (printemps 1987) p. 630-657; vol. 41,
no 1 (été 1987) p. 113-137; vol. 41, no 2 (automne 1987) p.
296-325; vol. 41, no 3 (hiver 1988) p. 460-490; vol. 41, no 4
(printemps 1988) p. 639-669; vol. 42, no 1 (été 1988) p. 131-
151; vol. 42, no 2 (automne 1988) p. 313-349; vol. 42, no 3
(hiver 1989) p. 489-507; vol. 42, no 4 (printemps 1989) p.
641-669; vol. 43, no 1 (été 1989) p. 130-162; vol. 43, no 2
(automne 1989) p. 283-306; vol. 43, no 3 (hiver 1990) p.
443-468; vol. 43, no 4 (printemps 1990) p. 601-630; vol. 44,
no 1 (été 1990) p. 123-147; vol. 44, no 2 (automne 1990) p.
289-326; vol. 44, no 3 (hiver 1991) p. 459-495; vol. 44, no 4
(printemps 1991) p. 621-653; vol. 45, no 1 (été 1991) p.
133-167; vol. 45, no 2 (automne 1991) p. 299-326; vol. 45,
no 3 (hiver 1992) p. 473-500; vol. 45, no 4 (printemps
1992) p. 637-674; vol. 46, no 2 (automne 1992) p. 377-391.;
ISSN: 0035-2357.
Note: Bibliographie régulière de toutes les nouvelles
publications touchant l'histoire de l'Amérique française
et les civilisations qui la composent.
Localisation: AEU.

2087 **Morton, Desmond**
Canadian history. [Ottawa]: Canadian Studies
Directorate, Department of the Secretary of State of
Canada, c1992. 31, 33 p. (Canadian studies resource
guides. Second series); ISBN: 0-660-58837-1.
Note: Includes an introductory overview of the subject, a
commentary on significant works, suggestions for
further reading.– Text in English and French with French
text on inverted pages.– Title of additional title-page:
L'histoire du Canada.
Previous edition: Waite, Peter Busby. 1988. 22, 22 p. (Can-
adian studies resource guides); ISBN: 0-662-56136-8.
Location: OONL.

2088 **Morton, Desmond**
L'histoire du Canada. [Ottawa]: Direction des études
canadiennes, Secrétariat d'État du Canada, c1992. 33,
31 p. (Guides pédagogiques des études canadiennes.
Deuxième collection); ISBN: 0-660-58837-1.
Note: Comporte un exposé préliminaire, des
observations sur les principaux travaux et une liste de
lectures recommandées.– Texte en français et en anglais
disposé tête-bêche.– Titre de la p. de t. additionnelle: *Canadian history.*
Édition antérieure: Waite, Peter Busby. 1988. 22, 22 p.
(Guides pédagogiques des études canadiennes); ISBN: 0-
662-56136-8.
Localisation: OONL.

— 1993 —

2089 **Norton, Judith A.**
New England planters in the Maritime provinces of
Canada 1759-1800: bibliography of primary sources.
Toronto: University of Toronto Press in association with
Planter Studies Centre, Acadia University, c1993. xvii,
403 p.: map.; ISBN: 0-8020-2840-3.

Note: 3,181 entries.– Government documents, personal papers, business records, society documents, newspapers.– Geographic arrangement by county: documents located in the county to which they referred when created.– Subject index.– Planter index (persons who emigrated from New England to Nova Scotia between 1759 and 1774).– Non-Planter index.– New England town and church record index.– Nova Scotia and New Brunswick place index.
Location: OONL.

— Ongoing/En cours —

2090 **Alberta Genealogical Society. Library**
Alberta Genealogical Society Library holdings. [Edmonton]: Alberta Genealogical Society, [1989]-. vol.; ISSN: 0848-8762.
Note: Books, pamphlets, periodical articles.– New materials are listed in the AGS publication *Relatively Speaking*, under the heading "What's new in the library?".
Location: OONL.

2091 **Bibliografía de historia de América.** Ottawa: General Reference and Bibliography Section, National Library of Canada, 1977-. vol.; ISSN: 0708-2185.
Note: Semi-annual contribution of the National Library published in *Revista de historia de América* for Instituto Panamericano de Geografía, Caracas, Venezuela containing a selective list of books published during the current year on the history of Canada.– Compiled by Irma Larouche.– Text in English and French/texte en français et en anglais.
Location: OONL.

2092 **Bibliographic guide to North American history.** Boston: G.K. Hall, 1977-. vol.; ISSN: 0147-6491.
Note: Annual.– Listing of publications about United States and Canadian history catalogued during the year by the research libraries of the New York Public Library and the Library of Congress.– Canadian coverage: British America: political and constitutional history, history of nationalities and races, the French period, the British period, provincial history, local history.
Location: OONL.

2093 **Writings on American history.** Millwood, N.Y.: KTO Press, 1902-. vol.; ISSN: 0364-2887.
Note: Annual.– Editions for 1906-1920 subtitled: "A bibliography of books and articles on United States and Canadian history, published during the year ... , with some memoranda on other portions of America."- No bibliographies issued for 1904-1905, 1941-1947.– Suspended, 1962-1972.– Annual publication resumed with the 1973-74 edition.
Two sets of volumes covering the period 1962-1972 have been published:
Writings on American history, 1962-73: a subject bibliography of articles. Washington: American Historical Association, 1976. 4 vol.; ISBN: 0-527-00373-5 (set).
Writings on American history, 1962-73: a subject bibliography of books and monographs. Washington: American Historical Association, 1985. 10 vol.; ISBN: 0-527-98268-7 (set).
Location: OONL.

— 1876 —

2094 **Barreau de la province de Québec. Bibliothèque**
Catalogue de la bibliothèque du Barreau de Québec:
livres français. Québec: A. Coté, 1876. 65 p.
Note: Approx. 900 entrées.
Microforme: ICMH collection de microfiches ; no 55875;
ISBN: 0-665-55875-9. 1 microfiche (37 images).
Localisation: QQS.

— 1883 —

2095 **Périard, A. (Firm)**
Catalogue of law books, Canadian, French, English and
American: imported and for sale by A. Périard. Montreal:
A. Périard, 1883. 36 p.
Note: Microform: CIHM Microfiche series ; no. 41062;
ISBN: 0-665-41062-X. 1 microfiche (24 fr.).
Location: QMBM.

— 1891 —

2096 **Nouveau catalogue de livres de droit et de
jurisprudence de la Librairie A. Périard: français,
anglais, américains et canadiens.** Montréal: A. Périard,
1891. 62 p.
Note: Microforme: ICMH collection de microfiches ; no
45903; ISBN: 0-665-45903-3. 1 microfiche (37 images).
Localisation: BVAU.

— 1900 —

2097 **Catalogue de livres de droit et de jurisprudence de la
province de Québec (ci-devant Bas-Canada).** Montréal:
Theoret, 1900. 48, viii p.
Note: Microforme: ICMH collection de microfiches ; no
14941; ISBN: 0-665-14941-7. 1 microfiche (27 images).
Localisation: OKQ.

2098 **Law Society of Upper Canada. Library**
A subject index to the books in the Library of the Law
Society of Upper Canada at Osgoode Hall, Toronto,
January 1st, 1900. Toronto: Printed for the Law Society,
1900. 396 p.
Note: Compiled by W. George Eakins.
Microform: CIHM Microfiche series ; no. 10757; ISBN: 0-
665-10757-9. 5 microfiches (213 fr.).
Previous editions:
*Catalogue of the books in the Library of the Law Society of
Upper Canada: with an index of subjects.* Printed for the
Society by C.B. Robinson, 1886. 600 p.– Compiled by G.
Mercer Adam.
Microform: CIHM Microfiche series ; no. 10657; ISBN: 0-
665-10657-2. 7 microfiches (316 fr.).
1880. 381 p.– Compiled by G. Mercer Adam.
Microform: CIHM Microfiche series ; no. 10656; ISBN: 0-
665-10656-4. 5 microfiches (202 fr.).
*Catalogue of the books in the Library of the Law Society of
Upper Canada.* Printed for the Society by Rowsell &
Hutchison, 1876. 183 p.
Microform: CIHM Microfiche series ; no. 10744; ISBN: 0-
665-10744-7. 2 microfiches (98 fr.).
Printed for the Society by Rowsell & Ellis, 1863. 174 p.

Microform: CIHM Microfiche series ; no. 43304; ISBN: 0-
665-43304-2. 2 microfiches (95 fr.).
Supplements:
*Supplement to G. Mercer Adam's Catalogue of the books in the
library of the Law Society of Upper Canada: with a list of
subjects.* Printed for the Society by Rowsell & Hutchison,
1883. 69 p.
Microform: CIHM Microfiche series ; no. 10745; ISBN: 0-
665-10745-5. 1 microfiche (42 fr.).
*Supplement to the catalogue of books in the library of the Law
Society of Upper Canada, with an index of subjects.* Printed
for the Society by C. Blackett Robinson, 1888. 86 p.
Microform: CIHM Microfiche series ; no. 25015; ISBN: 0-
665-25015-0. 1 microfiche (49 fr.).
Location: OONL.

— 1908 —

2099 **Eakins, W. George**
"The bibliography of Canadian statute law."
In: *Index to Legal Periodicals and Law Library Journal*; Vol. 1,
no. 1 (January 1908) p. 61-78.; ISSN: 0023-9283.
Note: Brief bibliographical history of Canadian statute
law, accompanied by a checklist of laws of Upper
Canada, 1792-1818.
Location: AEU.

— 1909 —

2100 **Davie, Cyril Francis**
Catalogue of the text-books, reports, digests, statutes,
encyclopedias and periodicals, etc., which are to be
found in the library of the Attorney-General's
Department and in the Law Department of the library of
the Legislative Assembly of the Province of British
Columbia. Victoria, B.C.: King's Printer, 1909. vi, 117 p.
Note: Location: OONL.

— 1927 —

2101 **Brown, Charles R.**
"Bibliography of Quebec or Lower Canada laws."
In: *Law Library Journal*; Vol. 19, no. 4 (January 1927) p. 90-
109.; ISSN: 0023-9283.
Note: Brief bibliographical survey of Quebec legislation,
accompanied by a checklist of laws of Quebec and Lower
Canada to 1840-41.
Location: AEU.

— 1928 —

2102 **Trotter, Reginald George**
"The bibliography of Canadian constitutional history."
In: *Papers of the Bibliographical Society of America*; Vol. 22,
part 1 (1928) p. 1-12.; ISSN: 0006-128X.
Note: Location: AEU.

— 1933 —

2103 **"Bibliography of recommended works dealing with the
R.C.M. Police."**
In: *Royal Canadian Mounted Police Quarterly*; Vol. 1, no. 2
(October 1933) p. 62.; ISSN: 0317-8250.
Note: Location: AE.

— 1937 —

2104 Maxwell, William Harold; Brown, Charles R.
A complete list of British and colonial law reports and legal periodicals arranged in alphabetical and in chronological order with bibliographical notes [and] with a check list of Canadian statutes. Toronto: Carswell, 1937. viii, 141, 59 p.
Note: Supplement: ... . 1946 supplement. 1946. 15 p.
Location: OKQL.

— 1948 —

2105 Scott, Francis Reginald
Bibliography on constitutional law. [Montreal: Faculty of Law, McGill University, 1948]. [vii], 27, 5 l.
Note: Approx. 900 entries.– Covers 1867 to 1945.– Includes journal articles on federal Constitution, the Crown, political parties, distribution of legislative powers, Dominion-provincial relations, civil liberties and minority rights, citizenship, national status, local government.
Location: OOP.

— 1959 —

2106 Pépin, Eugène
Bibliographie du droit aérien et questions connexes: 1957-1958/Bibliography of air law and related problems: 1957-1958. Montréal: [s.n.], 1959. 2 vol.
Note: Texte en français et en anglais/text in English and French.
Localisation: OONL.

— 1962 —

2107 Bell, Emma H.
Bibliography of serials, topical cases, named reports, law reports, digests and statutes held by the University of Saskatchewan Law Library. Saskatoon: College of Law, University of Saskatchewan, 1962. 29 l.
Note: Supplement: The law library: a list of its holdings. Saskatoon: 1965. 1 vol. (various pagings).
Location: OONL.

2108 Roy, Jean
Bibliographie sélective des sources générales de documentation juridique canadienne et québécoise. Montréal: Ecole de bibliothécaires, Université de Montréal, 1962. 75 f.
Note: 360 entrées.
Localisation: OONL.

— 1964 —

2109 "Annotated bibliography of works written on the Supreme Court of Canada."
In: Osgoode Hall Law Journal; Vol. 3, no. 1 (April 1964) p. 173-177.; ISSN: 0030-6185.
Note: 15 entries.
Location: AEUL.

2110 A legal bibliography of the British Commonwealth of Nations. 2nd ed. London: Sweet and Maxwell, 1955-1964. 7 vol.
Note: Vol. 3: Canadian and British-American colonial law from earliest times to December, 1956. Compiled by Charles R. Brown, P.A. Maxwell and L.F. Maxwell. London: 1957. x, 218 p.
Previous edition: Sweet & Maxwell's complete law book catalogue. 1925. 6 vol.
Location: OONL.

— 1968 —

2111 Brierley, John E.C.
Bibliographical guide to Canadian legal materials. Montreal: Faculty of Law, McGill University, 1968. ii, 260 p.
Note: Location: OOCC.

2112 Conseil canadien des ministres des ressources
Bibliographie juridique des eaux canadiennes: revue de la doctrine et de la jurisprudence/Legal bibliography on Canadian waters: review of publications and decisions of the courts. [Montréal]: Le Secrétariat, Conseil canadien des ministres des ressources, 1968. xiii, 359 p.
Note: Bibliographie fut préparée par l'Université de Montréal (Institut de recherche en droit public, Faculté de droit).– Inclut livres, articles de revues, jurisprudence sur les sujets: droit administratif (conservation, irrigation, pouvoir hydrauliques, pollution, ressources naturelles, eaux, pêcheries, sous sol marins); droit civil (droits riverains, propriété et servitudes, responsabilités, dommages, injonction); droit constitutionnel; droit international public; droit maritime.– Texte en français et en anglais/text in English and French.
Localisation: OOCC.

2113 Courtois, Hélène
Essai de bibliographie sélective d'ouvrages et d'articles publiés en français relatifs au droit maritime privé anglais, américain et canadien. Chicago: University of Chicago Law School, 1968. 15 p.
Note: Location: OONL.

2114 Ravel d'Esclapon, Rysia de
"Bibliographie des assurances."
Dans: Revue juridique Thémis; No 1 (1968) p. 77-86.; ISSN: 0556-7963.
Note: Comprenant: commentaires d'arrêts, assurance automobile et accident, assurance-incendie, assurance-vie, divers.
Localisation: OONL.

— 1969 —

2115 Arthurs, H.W.; Bucknall, Brian D.
Bibliographies on the legal profession and legal education in Canada. [Toronto: York University Law Library, 1969]. viii, 95 p.
Note: 1,282 entries.– Books, journal articles, theses, government publications on history, government and sociology of the legal profession, practice of law, remuneration for legal services, professional and unprofessional conduct, law schools, law students and teachers, legal research, professional (bar admission) training.
Location: OONL.

2116 Waterman, Nairn
"Annotated bibliography of books on Canadian law published in 1968."
In: Osgoode Hall Law Journal; Vol. 7, no. 1 (November 1969) p. 87-103.; ISSN: 0030-6185.
Note: Location: AEUL.

— 1970 —

2117 Canada. Department of Consumer and Corporate Affairs. Library
Combines Investigation Act: selected references/Loi relative aux enquêtes sur les coalitions: bibliographie. [Ottawa]: Department of Consumer and Corporate Affairs, Library, 1970. 7 l.

Note: Approx. 100 entries.
Location: OONL.

2118 **Canada. Department of the Secretary of State**
Human rights research in Canada: a bibliography. Ottawa: Queen's Printer, 1970. 64 p.
Note: Approx. 900 entries.– Books, theses, articles, pamphlets and unpublished material, government publications.
Location: OOSC.

— 1971 —

2119 **Huang, Paul Te-Hsien**
Bibliography on copyright. 2nd ed. Halifax: T.–H. Huang, c1971. vi, 118 l.
Note: Previous edition: *Bibliography on copyright, 1965-1969.* Kingston, Ont.: Queen's University, 1970. vi, 61 p.
Location: OONL.

2120 **Mackaay, Ejan**
"Jurimétre, informatique juridique, droit de l'informatique: un résumé de la littérature."
Dans: *Revue juridique Thémis;* No 1 (1971) p. 3-29.; ISSN: 0556-7963.
Note: Localisation: OONL.

2121 **Rico, José M.**
"Commissions d'enquête sur la justice pénale au Canada."
Dans: *Acta criminologica;* Vol. 4, (janvier 1971) p. 209-219.; ISSN: 0065-1168.
Note: Description sommaire, selon l'ordre chronologique, des principales études sur le système pénal canadien.
Localisation: OONL.

2122 **Spencer, Maureen J.**
Shoplifting: a bibliography. Toronto: Centre of Criminology, University of Toronto, 1971. ii, 35 l.
Note: Approx. 180 entries.– Books and articles on various aspects of shoplifting including sociological, psychological, medical and legal investigation as well as some commercial material, articles in business periodicals dealing with losses due to shoplifting.
Location: OONL.

2123 **Thibault, Emilia**
"L'Information et les problèmes de la liberté de la presse: bibliographie annotée."
Dans: *Bulletin: Bibliothèque de l'Assemblée nationale du Québec;* Vol. 2, no 2 (avril 1971) p. 41-56.; ISSN: 0701-6808.
Note: Approx. 50 entrées.
Localisation: OONL.

2124 **Wilkins, James L.; Rogers, Judith; Greer, Marbeth**
Legal aid in criminal matters: a bibliography. [Toronto]: Centre of Criminology, University of Toronto, 1971. ii, 63 l.
Note: Approx. 750 entries.– Covers 1958 to June 1970.– Bibliography is part of a study of the Ontario legal aid system conducted in Centre of Criminology.– Lists articles in legal journals, government documents and reports concerning legal aid plans.– Excludes references to legal debates and court cases.
Location: OONL.

— 1972 —

2125 **Glenbow-Alberta Institute**
Royal Canadian Mounted Police: a bibliography of resource material. Calgary: Glenbow-Alberta Institute, [1972]. 102 p. (Glenbow Archives publication series / Glenbow-Alberta Institute ; no. 5)

Note: Approx. 1,000 entries.– Manuscripts, published material, photographs, works of art relating to the history of the R.C.M.P. in the West and North.
Location: OONL.

2126 **Maddaugh, Peter D.**
A bibliography of Canadian legal history. Toronto: York University, 1972. xii, 77 p.
Note: 845 entries.
Location: OONL.

— 1973 —

2127 **Armstrong, Douglas; Dworaczek, Marian**
A selective bibliography on human and civil rights. [Toronto]: Ontario Ministry of Labour, Research Library, 1973. 20 l.
Note: Approx. 250 entries.– Books and articles on human rights, civil rights in Canada and the United States.– Includes a list of periodicals.
Location: OONL.

2128 **Arora, Ved**
Royal Canadian Mounted Police: a bibliography. Regina: Bibliographic Services Division, Provincial Library, 1973. iv, 42 p.
Note: 385 entries.– Books, pamphlets, manuscripts, filmstrips, journal articles.
Location: OOP.

2129 **"A bibliography of the Royal Canadian Mounted Police."**
In: *Saskatchewan Genealogical Society Bulletin;* Vol. 4, no. 3 (Summer 1973) p. 73-76.; ISSN: 0048-9182.
Note: Location: AEU.

2130 **Dworaczek, Marian**
Human rights: a bibliography of government documents held in the Library. [Toronto]: Research Library, Ontario Ministry of Labour, 1973. 34 p.
Note: Approx. 450 entries.– Lists documents from Canadian federal and provincial governments, Great Britain and the United States (federal and state).
Location: OONL.

2131 **Hondius, E.H.; Peletier, W.M.**
Amerikaanse en Canadese rechtslitteratur in Nederlandse bibliotheken: lijst van Amerikaanse en Canadese juridische tijdschriften, jurisprudentierverzamelingen, serie-en standaardwerken/American and Canadian law literature in Dutch libraries: location guide to holdings of American and Canadian law journals, law reports, serials, digests and standard works. Deventer [Netherlands]: Kluwer, 1973. 80 p.; ISBN: 90-268-0686-8.
Note: Approx. 300 entries.– Includes, in addition to juridical journals, magazines on criminology, forensic psychiatry, polemology, administrative law.– Excludes jurisprudence collections, serial issues, loose-leaf editions, annual reports and proceedings of societies.
Location: OONL.

2132 **Jeffries, Fern**
Private policing: a bibliography. Toronto: Centre of Criminology, University of Toronto, 1973. iii, 39 p.; ISBN: 0-919584-07-1.
Note: Approx. 225 entries.– Literature on private police in industry, institutions, the community.
Location: OONL.

2133 **Scott, Marianne**
A selective bibliography of Canadian legal sources. Montreal: McGill University, Law Library, 1973. 29 l. (Bibliographical guides / McGill University Law Library ; no. 5)
Note: Location: OWAL.

2134 **Soong, H.M.**
Bibliography of land use planning law. Windsor, Ont.: University of Windsor, Faculty of Law Library, 1973. 37 l.
Note: Location: OTU.

2135 **Wiktor, Christian**
Automobile insurance publications. Halifax: Dalhousie University, Faculty of Law, 1973. xiii, 220 p.
Note: 1,556 entries.– Covers 1960 to June 1973.– For the period prior to 1960, very selective and limited to books only.– Includes books, government publications, articles from law reviews, case notes and comments.– Excludes newspaper and popular magazine articles, books which deal only in part with automobile insurance.– Confined mainly to legal aspects of automobile insurance, primarily publications in English language from Canada and United States.
Location: OONL.

— 1974 —

2136 **Barnett, Gregory; Perell, Paul**
Selected bibliography on sale of goods (other than warranties) and selected aspects of general contract law, together with supplement. [Toronto]: Ontario Law Reform Commission, 1974. 29, ii, 24 l. (Ontario Law Reform Commission Research paper ; no. I.5)
Note: Approx. 600 entries.– Provisional bibliography created as part of the Ontario Law Reform Commission Sale of Goods Project: history, modern developments, formation: adhesion contracts, formalities, uncertainty of terms, capacity, parties, modification of waiver, battle of forms, mistake, performance, good faith, termination, rights and remedies, dispute settlement, government contracts.
Location: OWAL.

2137 **Canadian Criminology and Corrections Association**
Correctional literature published in Canada/Ouvrages de criminologie publiés au Canada. Ottawa: Canadian Criminology and Corrections Association, 1968-1974. 6 vol.; ISSN: 0070-0509.
Note: Annual listing.– Contains only Canadian documents by Canadian authors published since 1959.– Cumulative: each issue supersedes previous issue.– Includes books, pamphlets, periodicals (journals, bulletins, inmate publications, ex-inmate publications, annual reports, directories, statistical reports, proceedings).– Title varies: 1964-1968: *Correctional and criminological literature published in Canada/Littérature criminologique publiée au Canada.*– Text in English and French/texte en français et en anglais.
Location: OONL.

2138 **Canadian Historical Association. Archives Section**
Bibliography on copyright. [S.l.: s.n.], 1974. 15 p.
Note: Location: OONL.

2139 **Fabien, Claude**
"Ordinateur et droit: bibliographie sélective."
Dans: *Revue du barreau*; Vol. 34, no 5 (novembre 1974) p. 561-567.; ISSN: 0383-669X.
Note: Localisation: OONL.

— 1975 —

2140 **Canada. Commission of Inquiry Relating to Public Complaints, Internal Discipline and Grievance Procedure within the Royal Canadian Mounted Police**
A bibliography on public complaints against the police, internal police discipline and related topics. [Ottawa: 1975]. 196 p.
Note: 705 entries.– Listings categories include: public complaints, police discipline, police misconduct, police discretion, Royal Canadian Mounted Police, civil rights and police power, police-community relations, police personality/culture.
Location: OOSG.

2141 **Chunn, Dorothy E.**
Bibliography on sentencing in Canada. Ottawa: [s.n.], 1975. 13 p.
Note: Approx. 125 entries.– Books, research monographs, reports, articles, conference proceedings.
Location: OOCC.

2142 **Dykstra, Gail S.**
A bibliography of legal materials for non-law libraries. Toronto: York University Law Library, c1975. 55 p.
Note: Part 1: statements of the law (statutes, bills, regulations, general report series, research guides, digests, bibliographies, encyclopedias, indexes and citators).
Part 2: subject arrangement of legal materials (law for the layman, loose-leaf services, texts and treatises, reports and journals pertaining to each subject, e.g. business, family, labour, etc.).
Location: OONL.

2143 **Macfarlane, Dianne; Giuliani, Gary**
Crime prevention: a selected bibliography. [Toronto]: Centre of Criminology, University of Toronto, 1975. v, 78 p.; ISBN: 0-919584-19-5.
Note: Approx. 350 entries.– Literature from 1965 to 1975 dealing with aspects of crime prevention: environmental design and modification, medical and psychological intervention, community involvement, police involvement, law reform.
Location: OONL.

2144 **Normandeau, André**
"[Criminology: a bibliography]."
In: *Canadian Journal of Criminology and Corrections*; Vol. 17, no. 1 (January 1975) p. 110-131.; ISSN: 0315-5390.
Note: Approx. 400 entries.– Three listings: publications from the Centre of Criminology, University of Toronto, 1963-1974; publications from the Centre of Criminology, University of Ottawa, 1967-1974; publications du Département de criminologie, du Groupe de recherche sur l'inadaptation juvénile, et du Centre internationale de criminologie comparée, Université de Montréal, 1960-1974.
Location: OONL.

2145 **Québec (Province). Bibliothèque de la Législature**
Documents du Comité Gauvin. Québec: Bibliothèque de la Législature, Assemblée nationale, 1975. 119 p. (Bibliographie et documentation / Bibliothèque de la Législature du Québec ; 4)
Note: 454 entrées.– Comprend les documents commandés, produits ou utilisés par les membres du comité et les recherchistes qui les ont assistés au cours de leurs trois années d'étude et de recherche sur l'assurance

automobile.
Localisation: OONL.

2146 **Ross, R.R.; McConkey, Nancy**
Behaviour modification with the offender: an annotated bibliography. Ottawa: [s.n.], 1975. 81 p.
Note: Location: OONL.

— 1976 —

2147 **Brunet-Aubry, Lise**
"Littérature carcérale québécoise."
Dans: *Criminologie*; Vol. 9, nos 1-2 (1976) p. 191-195.; ISSN: 0316-0041.
Note: 30 entrées.
Localisation: AEU.

2148 **Commission de réforme du droit du Canada**
La crainte du châtiment: la dissuasion. Ottawa: Commission de réforme du droit du Canada, c1976. vii, 160 p.
Note: Comprend: "Une revue de la littérature sur l'effet dissuasif de la peine," et bibliographies: p. 113-127; p.159-168.
English title: *Fear of punishment: deterrence.*
Localisation: OONL.

2149 **Hann, Robert G.**
Deterrence and the death penalty: a critical review of the research of Isaac Ehrlich. Ottawa: Research Division, Solicitor General of Canada, 1976. 96 p.
Note: Approx. 80 entries.– Focus on 1975 study by American economist Isaac Ehrlich pertaining to deterrent effect of the death penalty.– Bibliography contains some Canadian references.
Location: OONL.

2150 **Haynes, Jane Banfield**
Law and society: a bibliography. Downsview, Ont.: York University, Faculty of Arts, Division of Social Science, 1976. 20 l.
Note: Approx. 300 entries.– "A special attempt has been made to include Canadian materials."– Topics include jurisprudence, law and ethics, human and civil rights, legal systems and courts, legal profession, discrimination and equality, international law, law and urban problems, law and energy problems.
Location: OTYL.

2151 **Herman, Michael John**
"Bibliography of material on the Supreme Court of Canada."
In: *Ottawa Law Review*; Vol. 8, no. 1 (Winter 1976) p. 102-103.; ISSN: 0048-2331.
Note: Listing of books, journal articles, newspaper articles published as of December 31, 1975.– Excludes case comments and articles on substantive law.
Location: OONL.

2152 **Law Reform Commission of Canada**
Fear of punishment: deterrence. Ottawa: Law Reform Commission of Canada, c1976. vii, 149 p.
Note: Contains: "Deterrence: a review of the literature," by E.A. Fattah, and bibliographies, p. 105-119, p. 141.
Titre en français: *La crainte du châtiment: la dissuasion.*
Location: OONL.

2153 **Liepner, Michael; Chunn, Dorothy E.**
The secondary school law programme: an annotated bibliography. Toronto: Centre of Criminology, University of Toronto, 1976. iii, 46 p.; ISBN: 0-919584-29-2.
Note: Approx. 160 entries.– Contains annotated references to general texts, pamphlets, journal and newspaper articles, films and video recordings.– Topics include individual rights and obligations, family law, torts, landlord and tenant, criminal law, juvenile delinquency, courts and sentencing, compensation to victims of crime, punishment and rehabilitation, law reform.
Location: OONL.

2154 **Macdougall, Donald V.**
"Popularized Canadian trials: a bibliography."
In: *Gazette (Law Society of Upper Canada)*; Vol. 10, no. 3 (September 1976) p. 248-255.; ISSN: 0023-9364.
Note: Books and pamphlets which comment on Canadian trials.– Excludes judges' notebooks, factums of law prepared for appeal purposes, collections of verbatim reports of cases.
Location: AEU.

2155 **McCallum, John D.**
Gun control: a bibliography since 1970: Canada, Great Britain, United States. [Waterloo, Ont.]: Library, Wilfrid Laurier University, 1976. iii, 19 p.
Note: Approx. 300 entries.– Books, reports, theses, periodical and newspaper articles, legislation, briefs.
Location: OONL.

2156 **Murdoch, Laurel**
Bibliographie sélective concernant le bénévolat dans les services correctionnels. Toronto: Ministère des services correctionnels de l'Ontario, 1976. 21 f.
Note: English title: *Volunteerism in corrections: a selected bibliography.*
Localisation: OONL.

2157 **Murdoch, Laurel**
Volunteerism in corrections: a selected bibliography. Toronto: Ontario Ministry of Correctional Services, 1976. i, 20 l.
Note: Titre en français: *Bibliographie sélective concernant le bénévolat dans les services correctionnels.*
Location: OONL.

2158 **Renaud-Frigon, Claire; Robertson, Carolynn**
Copyright: a selective bibliography/Le droit d'auteur: bibliographie sélective. Ottawa: Library Documentation Centre, National Library of Canada, 1976. 12, 10, 7, [1] l.
Note: Approx. 270 entries.– Includes, as appendix 2: "A selected bibliography on Canadian copyright, 1970-75," compiled by Dorcas O'Reilly and Barbara Quinlan. Scarborough, Ont.: 1975. 8 p.
Location: OONL.

2159 **Royal Canadian Mounted Police. Library**
Industrial security: a bibliography. Ottawa: The Library, 1976. ii, 142 p.
Note: Approx. 1,400 entries.– Reports and articles dealing with topics related to industrial security, including private police, alarm systems, fire prevention, trade secrets, security measures for data processing departments.– Include Canadian references.
Location: OONL.

2160 **Royal Canadian Mounted Police. Library**
Riots: [a bibliography]. [Ottawa]: R.C.M.P., 1976. 204 p.
Note: Approx. 2,400 entries.– Books, articles, government studies and reports relating to civil disobedience, demonstrations and arrests, mobs, prison riots, race riots, riots (general), student movement, urban riots: causes, prevention, control techniques.– Period covered is 1940

to 1975 with emphasis on the 1960s.– Mainly U.S. material with some Canadian references.
Location: OONL.

2161 **Stanbury, W.T.**
"Anti-combines law and policy in Canada, 1888-1975: a bibliography."
In: *Canadian Business Law Journal*; Vol. 1, no. 3 (August 1976) p. 352-374.; ISSN: 0319-3322.
Note: Approx. 350 entries.– Books, articles, conference papers and government reports dealing with Canadian anti-trust law.– Excluded are industry studies, reports of the Restrictive Trade Practices Commission and judgements of cases relating to the Combines Investigation Act.
Location: OONL.

2162 **Thomson, Jennifer**
The law of the sea: with special reference to Canada: a select bibliography. Ottawa: Norman Paterson School of International Affairs, Carleton University, 1976. ii, 74 p. (Norman Paterson School of International Affairs Bibliography series ; no. 4)
Note: Emphasis on the period 1968 to 1976.– Series edited by Jane Beaumont.
Location: OONL.

2163 **Trethewey, Paul**
"Bibliography of the Supreme Court of Canada."
In: *Osgoode Hall Law Journal*; Vol. 14, no. 2 (October 1976) p. 425-443.; ISSN: 0030-6185.
Note: Approx. 250 entries.– Topics include jurisdiction, opinion writing and legal reasoning, history, the Constitution and federalism, selection of justices and composition of the Court, judicial writings and official pronouncements, the political role of the Supreme Court.
Location: AEUL.

— 1977 —

2164 **Boult, Reynald**
A bibliography of Canadian law/Bibliographie du droit canadien. New ed. Ottawa: Canadian Law Information Council, 1977. xxii, 661 p.; ISBN: 0-920358-00-4.
Note: 10,941 entries.– Covers to January 1, 1975 for periodical articles.– Includes statutes and statutory instruments, law reports, dictionaries, history of Canadian law, constitutional law, administrative law, military law, criminal and penal law, taxation, labour law, transport, civil law, commercial or business law, civil procedure and evidence, legal education.– Text in English and French/texte en français et en anglais.
Previous edition: Montreal: Wilson and Lafleur; 1966. xii, 393 p.
Supplement: ... . *First supplement*. 1982. xviii, 271 p.; ISBN: 0-920358-01-2. (3,329 entries).– Covers to January 1, 1980 for periodical articles.
Location: OONL.

2165 **British Columbia. Legal Services Commission**
A Basic legal collection for barristers and solicitors in British Columbia. Vancouver, B.C.: Centre for Continuing Education, University of British Columbia, 1977. vii, 58 p.
Note: Contains research materials required by lawyers practising in British Columbia: dictionaries and general reference, forms and precedents, case reports, digests and citators, periodicals, government documents, periodicals, loose-leaf services.– Excludes textbooks.

Location: OONL.

2166 **Canadian Association for the Prevention of Crime**
Publications [Canadian Association for the Prevention of Crime]. Ottawa: Canadian Association for the Prevention of Crime, 1977. 13, 13 p.: ill.
Note: Approx. 40 entries.– Lists bibliographies, periodicals, policy statements, conference proceedings and working papers.– Text in English and French with French text on inverted pages.– Title of additional title-page: *Publications [Société canadienne pour la prévention du crime]*.
Location: OONL.

2167 **Canadian Nurses' Association. Library**
Compilation of provincial nurses' acts and related legislation/Compilation des lois régissant les infirmières et de la législation qui s'y rapporte. [Ottawa]: Canadian Nurses' Association, 1977. 18 l. (in various foliations).
Note: Location: OONL.

2168 **Chunn, Dorothy E.**
Firearms control: a select bibliography. Toronto: Centre of Criminology, University of Toronto, 1977. 34 p.; ISBN: 0-919584-36-5.
Note: Approx. 400 entries.– Covers the period 1960-1976.– English-language publications from Canada, U.S., Great Britain pertaining to social, legislative and constitutional issues relating to firearms control.
Location: OONL.

2169 **De Plaen, Jacqueline; Czetwertynska, Aniela**
"Aperçu bibliographique des travaux de l'Université de Montréal, 1960-1978."
Dans: *Criminologie*; Vol. 10, no 2 (1977) p. 93-107.; ISSN: 0316-0041.
Note: Localisation: OONL.

2170 **Dykstra, Gail S.**
A bibliography of Canadian legal materials/Une bibliographie de documentation juridique canadienne. Toronto: Butterworths, 1977. xii, 113 p.; ISBN: 0-409-82824-6.
Note: Approx. 2,000 entries.– Includes books (bibliographies, digests, encyclopedias, directories), legal handbooks, law reports and journals, pamphlets, loose-leaf services, audiovisual materials published or available between 1973 and 1976 appropriate for inclusion in non-law library collections.– Excludes office consolidations, works dealing with sociology of law.– Jurisdictions included: Canada (federal government), ten provinces, Northwest Territories, Yukon.– Text in English and French/texte en français et en anglais.
Location: OONL.

2171 **Kiessling, Jerry J.; Andrews, Donald Arthur; Farmer, Colin**
An introduction to the CaVIC reports. Ottawa: Canadian Volunteers in Corrections Training Project, 1977. 7 p.
Note: 27 entries.– Publications produced by the Ottawa Volunteer Program (in probation and parole services), and the Canadian Volunteers in Corrections Training Project.
Location: OONL.

2172 **Kydd, Donna L.; Smith, Laurie J.**
Legal information and education: an annotated bibliography. [Saskatoon: Native Law Centre, University of Saskatchewan], 1977. iv, 64 l.
Note: 178 entries.– Books, periodical articles, government

publications dealing with law-related education programs and literature for native people and reflecting experience of Northwest Territories in adjusting to customs and traditions and Anglo-European legal principles.
Location: OONL.

2173 **Love, John L.**
Bibliography of legal materials for the Ontario region of the Canadian Penitentiary Service: a purchasing selection aid. [S.l.: s.n.], 1977. 7 p.
Note: Location: OONL.

2174 **Mayer, Katia Luce**
Criminologie canadienne: bibliographie commentée: la criminalité et l'administration de la justice criminelle au Canada/Canadian criminology: annotated bibliographie: crime and the administration of criminal justice in Canada. [Ottawa]: Solliciteur général Canada, Division de la recherche, [1977]. xviii, 726 p.
Note: 1,463 entrées.– La période couverte est de 1960 à 1976.– Principaux thèmes traités: étiologie de la délinquance, groupes particuliers de crimes, criminels et délinquants, administration de la justice, théories de la peine/système de correction/resocialisation du criminel, criminologie.– Préparé sous la direction de Gertrude Rosenberg, Centre international de criminologie comparée, Montréal.– Texte en français et en anglais/text in English and French.
Localisation: OONL.

2175 **Société canadienne pour la prévention du crime**
Publications [Société canadienne pour la prévention du crime]. Ottawa: Société canadienne pour la prévention du crime, 1977. 13, 13 p.: ill.
Note: Approx. 40 entrées.– Inventaire des bibliographies, périodiques, énoncés de politique, documents de travail.– Texte en français et en anglais disposé tête-bêche.– Titre de la p. de t. additionnelle: *Publications [Canadian Association for the Prevention of Crime]*.
Localisation: OONL.

2176 **Weeks, Thomas E.**
A survey of the collection of Canadian statutes and subordinate legislation held in the Sir James Dunn Law Library. Halifax, N.S.: Dalhousie University, 1977. ii, 71 p.
Note: Excludes sessional papers of Parliament and provincial legislatures.
Location: OONL.

— 1978 —

2177 **Asted. Comité du droit d'auteur**
Bibliographie de langue française sur le droit d'auteur. Montréal: Association pour l'avancement des sciences et des techniques de la documentation, 1978. 13 f.
Note: 152 entrées.– Inclut monographies, articles (périodiques et journaux).– La période couverte est de 1904 à 1978.
Localisation: OONL.

2178 **Bernier, Robert; Gagnon, Rosette**
Guide bibliographique: économique de la criminalité et planification des ressources de la justice criminelle/Bibliographical guide: the economics of crime and planning of resources in the criminal justice system. Ottawa: Solliciteur général Canada, Division de la recherche, 1978. x, 488 p.; ISBN: 0-662-01554-1.
Note: 430 entrées.– Bibliographie commentée sur l'économique de la criminalité et de la rationalisation de la politique criminelle: publications du gouvernement, livres, articles, rapports.– Texte en français et en anglais/text in English and French.
Localisation: OONL.

2179 **Blazina, Vesna**
"Bibliographie sélective sur la rééducation."
Dans: *Criminologie*; Vol. 11, no 1 (1978) p. 80-86.; ISSN: 0316-0041.
Note: 43 entrées.– Livres, thèses, publications officielles, en français et en anglais, publiés entre 1974 et 1977, sur la resocialisation des jeunes délinquants.
Localisation: OONL.

2180 **Canadian Council on International Law**
Canadian bibliography on international law, 1967-1977/Bibliographie canadienne en droit international, 1967-1977. [Ottawa: Canadian Council on International Law, 1978]. iv, 53 p.
Note: Approx. 550 entries.– Includes sections on maritime law, air and space law, human rights, treaties, international disputes, war crimes and terrorism, nuclear testing, international organizations, private international law (family, property, contracts, commercial law).– Text in English and French/texte en anglais et en français.
Location: OONL.

2181 **Correctional Service Canada**
Legal documentation for institutional libraries in Canadian corrections services. [Ottawa: Correctional Service Canada], 1978. [4], 20 l.
Note: Approx. 200 entries.– Lists basic legal materials intended to enable inmates to conduct research into various aspects of civil and criminal law: statutes, regulations, reports; reference tools; texts on human rights, criminal law, courts, law reform commission reports.
Location: OONL.

2182 **Gémar, Jean-Claude**
Bibliographie sélective du traducteur: droit et justice. Montréal: Linguatech, c1978. [283] p. (en pagination multiple).
Note: Approx. 3,200 entrées.– Annuaires, bibliographies, répertoires, catalogues et guides documentaires, périodiques, dictionnaires, encyclopédies, études et bulletins terminologiques: histoire du droit, droit administratif, droit civil, droit commercial, droit constitutionnel, droit international, droit pénal et judiciaire, théorie du droit.
Localisation: OONL.

2183 **Lisun, Luba**
People and law: a bibliography of public legal education. Edmonton: Legal Resource Centre, University of Alberta Extension, 1978. 147 p.
Note: 531 entries.– Lists books and articles.– Education areas are primary and secondary schools (including in-service teacher training), post-secondary and undergraduate law courses outside the law schools, community adult education.– Materials related to paralegals deal with training techniques, training materials, and kinds of work done by paralegals (or lay advocates).– Excludes some specific legal topics such as landlord and tenant rights, civil rights, etc. and the law as it relates to specific groups, e.g. women or native people.
Supplement: Brown, Gail. *Supplement to People and law: a*

bibliography of public legal education. 1984. 65 p.
Location: OONL.

2184 **McNaught, Hugh; Faulds, Jon**
The non-medical use of drugs by minors: a bibliography of legislative materials of the governments of Alberta and British Columbia. Vancouver: Non Medical Use of Drugs Directorate, Health and Welfare Canada, 1978. vii, 62 p.
Note: Legislation and case reports, background materials from provincial and municipal agencies, materials on the law and drugs for use by young people.– Provincial statutes' entries contain notes on the Act, notes on specific sections, political history of the Act, as well as background materials.
Location: OLUL.

2185 **Ouimet, Laurent**
Bibliographie de droit civil: ouvrages généraux. Montréal: Université de Montréal, Service des bibliothèques, Bibliothèque de droit, 1978. 22 p.; ISBN: 0-88529-029-1.
Note: Localisation: OONL.

2186 **Reid, Jean-Paul**
Bibliography on legal aid in Canada/Bibliographie sur l'aide juridique au Canada. Montreal: National Legal Aid Research Centre, 1978. ii, 62 l.
Note: Approx. 500 entries.– Books, journal articles, government reports and studies on legal aid in each provincial jurisdiction.– Excludes statutes and regulations concerning legal aid, annual reports of provincial legal aid organizations, case law, theses.– Text in English and French/texte en français et en anglais.
Location: OONL.

2187 **Université de Montréal. Bibliothèque de droit**
Catalogue des oeuvres des professeurs de la Faculté de droit de l'Université de Montréal: exposition réalisée par la Bibliothèque de droit à l'occasion du centenaire de la Faculté de droit, 1878-1978. [Montréal]: Université de Montréal, Service de bibliothèques, Bibliothèque de droit, 1978. 23 f.; ISBN: 0-88529-028-3.
Note: Approx. 275 entrées.– Exclut les articles de revue.
Localisation: OONL.

— 1979 —

2188 **Barnes, John**
"Canadian sports torts: a bibliographical survey."
In: *Canadian Cases on the Law of Torts*; Vol. 8 (1979) p. 198-206.; ISSN: 0701-1733.
Note: Bibliographical essay commenting on Canadian studies and case law relating to sports misadventures causing personal injuries.
Location: OONL.

2189 **Beugin, Sue**
Law library guide for Alberta practitioners. Calgary: Canadian Bar Association, Alberta Branch, 1979. iv, 162 p.
Note: List of legal materials for a model Alberta legal library.– Coded for small, medium, large law firm requirements: essential tools and specialized works and services.– Loose-leaf format.
Location: OONL.

2190 **A bibliography of the Royal Canadian Mounted Police.**
Ottawa: Historical Section, R.C.M.P. Headquarters, 1979. 69 p., 7 l.
Note: 1,020 entries.– Covers 1872 to 1979.– Includes books, pamphlets, periodical and newspaper articles,

government publications, theses, catalogues, unpublished papers, bibliographies, fiction.– Photocopy of typescript.
Location: OONL.

2191 **Clark, Lorenne M.G.; Armstrong, Simon**
A rape bibliography: with special emphasis on rape research in Canada/Bibliographie sur le viol: et plus particulièrement sur la recherche au Canada dans ce domaine. Ottawa: Solicitor General Canada, Research Division, 1979. xii, 130 p.; ISBN: 0-662-50513-1.
Note: Approx. 500 entries.– Contains periodical articles on topics related to sexual assault: the victim, the offender, law, medical and medico-legal, police investigation, rape in non-common law jurisdictions, rape research in Canada.– Text in English and French/texte en français et en anglais.
Location: OONL.

2192 **Daoust, Lucie**
Organized crime: a bibliography. Ottawa: RCMP HQ Library, 1979. ii, 201 p.
Note: Approx. 2,500 entries.– General works, criminal organizations, organized crime involvement (gambling, narcotics, smuggling, white-collar crime, etc.), control and prevention.– Some Canadian references.
Location: OONL.

2193 **De Plaen, Jacqueline**
"Bibliographie générale sur la probation."
Dans: *Criminologie*; Vol. 12, no 2 (1979) p. 101-105.; ISSN: 0316-0041.
Note: Localisation: OONL.

2194 **Gorecki, Paul K.; Stanbury, W.T.**
"Competition law and public policy in Canada, 1888-1979: a bibliography."
In: *Canadian competition policy: essays in law and economics*, edited by J. Robert S. Prichard, W.T. Stanbury and Thomas A. Wilson. Toronto: Butterworths, 1979. P. 555-609.; ISBN: 0-409-85950-8.
Note: Approx. 750 entries.– Books, articles, official reports dealing with Canadian competition policy over ninety years: general works, objectives of competition policy, changes in legislation, conspiracy/price fixing, mergers and monopoly, resale price maintenance, price discrimination, misleading advertising, administration and enforcement, competition policy.
Location: OONL.

2195 **Klancher, Donald James; Hearfield, J.D.**
The Royal Canadian Mounted Police: a bibliography. [Ottawa]: RCMP, [1979]. 111 p.
Note: 876 entries.– Books, articles, comic books from earliest references to 1979.– Excludes historical texts which make passing reference to the force, newspaper articles, debate of House of Commons and Senate.
Supplement: 1984. 4 p.
Location: OONL.

2196 **Knafla, Louis A.**
"Crime, criminal law and justice in Canadian history: a select bibliography, origins to 1940."
In: *Law and society in Canada in historical perspective*, edited by D.J. Bercuson and Louis A. Knafla. Calgary: University of Calgary, c1979. P. 157-171.
Note: Approx. 200 entries.– Monographs, journal articles, papers of historical societies, unpublished theses and dissertations dealing with criminal law and administra-

tion of justice from an historical perspective.
Location: OONL.

2197 **Lakos, Amos**
Terrorism, 1970-1978, a bibliography. Waterloo, Ontario: University of Waterloo Library, 1979. vi, 73 p. (University of Waterloo Library bibliography ; no. 4; ISSN: 0829-948X); ISBN: 0 920831 00 X.
Note: Approx. 900 entries.– Includes a section "U.S. and Canada," listing books, periodical and report literature.
Location: OONL.

2198 **Matthews, Catherine J.**
Police stress: a selected bibliography concerning police stress and the psychological evaluation and counseling of police. Toronto: Centre of Criminology, University of Toronto, 1979. viii, 43 p.; ISBN: 0-919584-44-6.
Note: Approx. 250 entries.– Books, articles and reports dealing with sociology of police work, police stress, police alcoholism and suicide, police family and social life, selection and recruitment (psychological testing, evaluation, counseling).– Section of audio-visual materials.
Location: OONL.

2199 **Matthews, Catherine J.; Chunn, Dorothy E.**
Congestion and delay in the criminal courts: a selected bibliography. Toronto: Centre of Criminology, University of Toronto, 1979. viii, 66 p.; ISBN: 0-919584-45-4.
Note: Approx 550 entries.– Canadian, American and British literature published in the 1970s: pre-trial criminal procedure, plea bargaining, alternatives to prosecution, organization and administration of court workload and resources.
Location: OONL.

2200 **Menzies, Robert J.**
Psychiatry and the judicial process: a bibliography. Toronto: Centre of Criminology, University of Toronto, 1979. 75 p.; ISBN: 0-919584-42-X.
Note: Approx. 750 entries.– Monographs and articles on forensic psychiatry from 1950 to 1978, a comprehensive collection of the Canadian literature, as well as American, British and European work.
Location: OONL.

2201 **Policewomen: a bibliography.** Ottawa: R.C.M.P. Library, 1979. 42 l.
Note: Approx. 500 entries.– Books, journal articles on women in policing, 1945 to 1979.
Location: OONL.

2202 **Resnick, Gary**
An annotated bibliography of current research on rape and other sexual offences. Toronto: Ontario Provincial Secretariat for Justice, 1979. 94 p.
Note: Location: OOCW.

2203 **Royal Canadian Mounted Police. Library**
Police misconduct – Canada: a bibliography. Ottawa: The Library, 1979. iii, 121 p.
Note: Listing of newspaper articles (January 1977-October 1978) and references to House of Commons debates (January 1977-June 1978) dealing with RCMP and provincial and municipal police force misconduct.
Location: OOSC.

2204 **Shearing, Clifford D.; Lynch, F. Jennifer; Matthews, Catherine J.**
Policing in Canada: a bibliography/La police au Canada: une bibliographie. Ottawa: Solicitor General Canada,

Research Division, 1979. xiv, 362 p.; ISBN: 0-662-50540-9.
Note: 578 entries.– Contains published and accessible unpublished information on research projects, reports, books and articles relevant to policing in Canada up to and including 1975.– Principal topics include administration, community relations, education, selection and training, history, private policing, duties and powers, arrest, discretion, police and youth.– Includes abstracts.– Text in English and French/texte en français et en anglais.
Location: OONL.

2205 **Swanick, Eric L.**
Rent control in Canada: an introductory bibliography. Monticello, Ill.: Vance Bibliographies, 1979. 5 l. (Public administration series: Bibliography ; P-205; ISSN: 0193-970X)
Note: 66 entries.– Studies, periodical articles.
Location: OONL.

2206 **Verdun-Jones, S.N.**
"Made in Canada: texts and readers for Canadian criminology and criminal justice courses."
In: *Canadian Journal of Criminology*; Vol. 21, no. 1 (January 1979) p. 86-104.; ISSN: 0704-9722.
Note: 36 entries.– Bibliographic essay reviewing readers and texts in criminology.
Location: OONL.

— 1980 —

2207 **Alberta. Bureau of Statistics**
Criminal justice statistical development: bibliography. [Edmonton]: Alberta Bureau of Statistics, 1980. ix, 91 p.
Note: References to published and unpublished documents, produced from 1965 to 1979, related to the development of criminal justice statistics, indicators and information systems, with focus on Province of Alberta.
Location: OONL.

2208 **Audet, Pierre H.**
The Canadian consumer and the regulatory process: a bibliography/Le consommateur canadien et le pouvoir réglementaire: une bibliographie. Ottawa: Consumer and Corporate Affairs Canada, Library, 1980. 10 l.
Note: Approx. 110 entries.– Books, articles, government publications on government regulation and consumers.
Location: OONL.

2209 **A bibliographic introduction to paralegals in two jurisdictions: Canada and the United States: 1970-1978.** Vancouver: Pacific Legal Education Association, c1980. vii, 47 p.
Note: 377 entries.– Monographs and articles on paralegalism.
Location: OONL.

2210 **A bibliography of Canadian material on freedom of information, individual privacy, and related topics.** Ottawa: Canadian Committee for the Right to Public Information, 1980. 55 l.
Note: Composite of Canadian listings from bibliographies compiled by the Library of Parliament and Ontario Commission on Freedom of Information and Individual Privacy, with additions.– Avant-propos en français.
Location: NBFU.

2211 **Canadian Human Rights Commission**
Bibliography on human rights/Bibliographie sur les droits de la personne. [Ottawa]: The Commission, 1980. iv, 262 p.; ISBN: 0-662-50837-8.

Note: Listing of books, theses, papers, government reports, periodical articles dealing with aspects of discrimination, human rights, basic freedoms: age, sex, race, ethnic origin, language, indigenous peoples, handicapped, sexual orientation, education, social conditions.
Location: NFSG.

2212 **Chodyniecki, JoAnn**
A bibliography on corrections, 1970-1979. Ottawa: Correctional Service of Canada, Information and Research Analysis Division, 1980. 37 l.
Note: Approx. 700 entries.– Articles published in criminal justice journals from 1970 to 1979.– Topics include community corrections, female offenders, history of corrections, juvenile corrections, rehabilitation programs, prison management, prisoners' rights and other issues, future of corrections.
Location: OONL.

2213 **Chrétien, Muriette; Perret, Diana-Lynn**
Répertoire des documents pédagogiques produits par les professeurs de droit du Québec. Montréal: Association des professeurs de droit du Québec, 1980. 33 f.
Note: Édition antérieure: Tanguay, Guy; Charest, Marie-Claire. 1978. 34 p.
Localisation: OONL.

2214 **Findlay, Joanna**
White collar crime: a bibliography. Ottawa: RCMP HQ Library, 1980. i, 105 p.
Note: Approx. 1,000 entries.– Books and reports, journal and newspaper articles dealing with topics related to white collar crime in Canada and the United States: fraud in general, embezzlement, stock market manipulation and fraud, corporate crime, accounting/auditing, banking, tax evasion.
Location: OONL.

2215 **Goulet, Jean**
"The Quebec legal system."
In: *Law Library Journal*; Vol. 73 (1980) p. 354-381.; ISSN: 0023-9283.
Note: Includes appendix: "A bibliography of materials written in English on the Quebec civil law systems."
Location: AEU.

2216 **Kozak, Elaine**
Applications of computer technology to law (1969-1978): a selected bibliography. Ottawa: Canadian Law Information Council, 1980. iii, 106 p. (Working paper / Canadian Law Information Council ; no. 4); ISBN: 0-920538-00-5.
Note: Approx. 600 entries.– Includes references in English and French which discuss impact of computer technology on creation and practice of law, computer-assisted legal research/information retrieval, litigation support, law office management and equipment, court administration, land and property registration, law libraries, computer law, research methods, education and training.
Location: OLU.
Supplement: Cameron, Judith M. *Applications of computer technology to law (1979-1982): a selected bibliography.* 1983. iii, 69 p. (Working paper ; no. 12).; ISBN: 0-920538-34-9.– Approx. 600 entries.
Location: OONL.

2217 **Martin, Maedythe J.; McGraw, Donna**
Canadian constitutional reform: a checklist and index to the papers presented at Federal-Provincial conferences, 1976-1979. Toronto: Legislative Library, Research and Information Services, 1980. ii, 34 p.
Note: Chronological listing of government statements on constitutional reform presented at federal-provincial and first ministers' conferences from 1976 to 1979.– Indexes: issuing bodies, personal names, titles, subjects.
Location: OONL.

2218 **Miller, Alan V.**
Capital punishment as a deterrent: a bibliography. Monticello, Ill.: Vance Bibliographies, 1980. 10 p. (Public administration series: Bibliography ; P-452; ISSN: 0193-970X)
Note: 150 entries.– Includes Canadian references.
Supplement: ... . *Supplement to P-452.* 1980. 23 p. (Public administration series: Bibliography ; P-592).
Location: OONL.

2219 **Moyer, Sharon**
La déjudiciarisation dans le système judiciaire pour les jeunes et ses répercussions sur les enfants: recension de la documentation. [Ottawa]: Solliciteur général Canada, Division de la recherche, 1980. v, 296 p.; ISBN: 0-662-90708-6.
Note: Approx. 400 entrées.– Rapports et articles sur le système judiciaire pour les jeunes.– Thèmes: organismes traditionnels, la "nouvelle" judiciarisation, la mise en oeuvre de la nouvelle déjudiciarisation, effets de la déjudiciarisation, répercussions sur le système judiciaire pour les jeunes au Canada.
English title: *Diversion from the juvenile justice system and its impact on children: a review of the literature.*
Localisation: OONL.

2220 **Moyer, Sharon**
Diversion from the juvenile justice system and its impact on children: a review of the literature. [Ottawa]: Solicitor General Canada, Research Division, 1980. xix, 201 p.; ISBN: 0-662-10979-1.
Note: Summarizes and assesses the research on agencies that stream young people to and from the juvenile justice system: community, family, school, social agencies, police; section on the "new" diversion (implementation, effects, implications for the juvenile justice system).
Titre en français: *La déjudiciarisation dans le système judiciaire pour les jeunes et ses répercussions sur les enfants: recension de la documentation.*
Location: OONL.

2221 **National Library of Canada. Resources Survey Division**
Checklists of law reports and statutes in Canadian law libraries/Listes de contrôle des recueils de jurisprudence et des statuts dans des bibliothèques de droit du Canada. Ottawa: National Library of Canada, 1977-1980. 4 vol.
Note: Vol. 1: *Canadian law reports.* xv, 293 p.; ISBN: 0-662-00442-6.– 682 entries.– Lists and holdings for general, regional, nominate and composite reports; special subject reports and administrative board decisions, arranged by jurisdictions, Canada, provinces, territories.– Vol. 4: *Canadian statutes and regulations.* xii, 249 p.; ISBN: 0-662-50452-9.– 1,702 entries.– Law library holdings of colonial, federal, provincial, territorial statutes and regulations.– Excludes publications containing summaries of statutes and regulations such as legal encyclopedias and digests.–

Volumes 2 and 3 do not contain bibliographical listings but do contain Canadian law library holdings of law reports for the United Kingdom (and Irish Republic) and the United States.– Text in English and French/texte en français et en anglais.
Location: OONL.

2222 **Oak, Lydla**
Copyright: a selective bibliography/Le droit d'auteur: une bibliographie sélective. Ottawa: Library Documentation Centre, National Library of Canada, 1980. [8] p.
Note: Approx. 100 entries.– Books, journal articles in the following sections: bibliographies, photocopy/ reprography, computer technology and nonbook material, copyright in Canada, copyright in U.S.A., laws and conventions.– Text in English and French/texte en français et en anglais.
Location: OONL.

2223 **Research in criminology by staff of the Centre of Criminology during the 1970's.** [Toronto]: Centre of Criminology, University of Toronto, 1980. vi, 95 p.; ISBN: 0-919584-53-5.
Note: Approx. 600 entries.– Books, monographs, journal articles, reviews, chapters in books, reports provided for federal and provincial governments: crime and deviance, criminal law and policy, administration of criminal justice, police, courts, sentencing, juveniles, medico-legal.
Location: OONL.

2224 **Resources law bibliography.** [Calgary]: Canadian Institute of Resources Law, c1980. xvi, 537 p.; ISBN: 0-919269-01-X.
Note: Approx. 2,250 entries.– Books, research reports and papers, conference proceedings, government publications, legislative committee reports, royal commission studies and reports related to natural resource law and legislation: energy resources (gas, petroleum, nuclear), mines and mineral resources, water resources, pollution and environmental policy and law.
Location: OONL.

2225 **Skinner, Shirley**
Annotated bibliography of Consortium members' current research, and published and unpublished materials. [Regina: Prairie Justice Research Consortium, School of Human Justice, University of Regina], 1980. 26 l.
Note: Approx. 75 entries.– Covers 1977 to 1980.– Includes publications, unpublished papers and reports, theses and dissertations, past research and forthcoming publications of members of the Consortium.
Location: OONL.

— 1981 —

2226 **Banks, Margaret A.**
"An annotated bibliography of statutes and related publications: Upper Canada, the Province of Canada, and Ontario 1792-1980."
In: *Essays in the history of Canadian law*, edited by David H. Flaherty. Toronto: Published for the Osgoode Society by the University of Toronto Press, 1981. P. 358-404.; ISBN: 0-8020-3382-2.
Note: Contains three sections: Statutes; Statutory indexes, citators, annotation services; Proclamations, regulations, gazettes.
Location: OONL.

2227 **Canada. Library of Parliament. Information and Reference Branch**
Constitutional review: select bibliography/Revision constitutionnelle: bibliographie sélective. Ottawa: The Branch, 1981. 55 l.
Note: Lists primary sources (federal and provincial documents) in chronological order from 1965 to 1980, selected general works (books, periodical and newspaper articles, theses).– Text in English and French/texte en français et en anglais.
Location: OOSS.

2228 **Cournoyer, Luce**
Bibliographie sur l'aide juridique/Bibliography on legal aid. Ottawa: Centre national d'information et de recherche sur l'aide juridique, 1981. ix, 33 p.; ISBN: 0-919513-00-X.
Note: Approx. 825 entrées.– Livres, articles, rapports.– Thèmes: administration, droit pénal, droits de la personne et libertés publiques, famille, femmes, jeunesse, pauvreté, prisons, statistiques.
Localisation: OONL.

2229 **Criminal justice research: a selective review.** Ottawa: Solicitor General Canada, Communication Division, c1981. ii, 88 p.; ISBN: 0-662-11844-8.
Note: Selection of Canadian and international material relating to criminal justice issues: police, sentencing, corrections, juvenile justice, crime victims, crime prevention.
Titre en français: *Revue sélective des recherches en matière de justice pénale.*
Location: OONL.

2230 **Dostaler, Ann**
Bibliographie sur l'aide juridique pour les handicapés/ Bibliography on legal aid for the handicapped. Ottawa: Centre national d'information et de recherche sur l'aide juridique, 1981. vii, 41 p.; ISBN: 0-919513-01-8.
Note: Approx. 900 entrées.– Livres, articles, périodiques, communiqués, matériaux audio-visuels et autres items publié avant 1981.– Inclut documentation canadienne, documentation américaines, documentation par sujets: éducation, patrimoine, euthanasie, code génétique, handicaps auditifs, service juridiques, déficience mentale, handicaps visuels.
Localisation: OONL.

2231 **Dykstra, Gail S.**
"Lockers, the strap, liability and the law."
In: *Emergency Librarian*; Vol. 8, no. 3-4 (January-April 1981) p. 20-22.; ISSN: 0315-8888.
Note: Location: AEU.

2232 **Florkow, David W.; Heitz, Thomas R.; Lounder, Shirley A.**
Case law reporting: a selected bibliography and checklist of Canadian law reporting studies. Ottawa: Canadian Law Information Council, [1981]. vi, 86 p. (CLIC Occasional paper ; no. 3); ISBN: 0-920358-05-5.
Note: Approx. 700 entries.– Part 1 includes citations to books and articles discussing law reporting in Canada, Great Britain, U.S. and other countries.– Part 2 is an annotated bibliography of early discussions of law reporting in Canada up to 1920, arranged chronologically.– Part 3 is a checklist of Canadian law reporting studies.
Location: OONL.

2233 **Henshel, Richard L.**
The Canadian civil liberties bibliography (indexed). 5th rev. ed., enl. [London, Ont.: Henshel], 1981. iv, 151 l.
Note: 1,126 entries.– Canadian civil liberties books, articles and theses from about 1960.– Topics include searches and seizures, electronic eavesdropping, police practices, access to the law, due process safeguards, bail problems, confessions, fitness to stand trial, lawyer-client relationship, double jeopardy, ombudsmen, War Measures Act.– Excludes works on freedom of expression, equality of treatment (civil rights).
Previous editions:
Civil liberty in Canada: an indexed bibliography on contemporary issues. 1979. ii, 75 l.
Liberty in Canada: a research bibliography on contemporary problems. 1977. 34 l.
Location: OLU.

2234 **Juliani, T.J.; Talbot, C.K.**
Military justice: a selected annotated bibliography. Ottawa: CRIMCARE, c1981. xii, 71 l.; ISBN: 0-919395-00-7.
Note: 175 entries.– Books, articles in specialized journals under eight subject divisions: historical, legal, offences, juvenile delinquency, sentencing, prisons/prisoners, treatment, prevention/prediction.– Includes some Canadian references.
Location: OONL.

2235 **Lane, Marion**
"Children's rights: an annotated bibliography."
In: *Emergency Librarian*; Vol. 8, no. 3-4 (January-April 1981) p. 23-26.; ISSN: 0315-8888.
Note: Location: AEU.

2236 **Nason, C.M.**
A checklist of Canadian sources in criminal justice. Monticello, Ill.: Vance Bibliographies, 1981. 10 p. (Public administration series: Bibliography ; P-682; ISSN: 0193-970X)
Note: 29 entries.– Lists bibliographies, scholarly journals in criminology, sources for criminal statistics, periodical indexes, directories related to criminal justice.
Location: OONL.

2237 **Revue sélective des recherches en matière de justice pénale.** Ottawa: Solliciteur général Canada, Division des communications, c1981. ii, 95 p.; ISBN: 0-662-91464-3.
Note: Sélection des documents canadiens et internationales sur les questions qui touchent la justice pénale: police, sentences, services de correction, système de justice applicable aux jeunes, victimes d'actes criminels, prévention.
English title: *Criminal justice research: a selective review.*
Localisation: OONL.

2238 **Simard, Michel**
Répertoire des documents parlementaires québécois relatifs à la justice pénale, 1867-1900. Montréal: École de criminologie, Université de Montréal, 1981. 111 f. (Cahiers de l'École de criminologie / Université de Montréal ; no 6)
Note: Approx. 1,000 entrées.– Documents de la session, statuts, débats relatifs à la justice pénale.– Quatre sections: "La police," "Le judiciaire," "Le correctionnel," "Divers."
Localisation: OONL.

2239 **Walsh, Sandra A.**
The Constitution of Canada and its amendment: a selected bibliography. Monticello, Ill.: Vance Bibliographies, 1981. 7 p. (Public administration series: Bibliography ; P-662; ISSN: 0193-970X)
Note: Approx. 75 entries.– Books and reports, conferences, periodical articles.
Location: OLU.

— 1982 —

2240 **Baker, G. Blaine**
"A course in Canadian legal history."
In: *Now and Then: A Newsletter For Those Interested in History and Law*; Vol. 2, no. 2 (September 1982) p. 56-62.; ISSN: 0229-690X.
Note: Reading list for course in legal history, Faculty of Law, McGill University.
Location: AEU.

2241 **Canadian Rights and Liberties Federation**
Bibliography [Human rights and civil liberties]. Ottawa: The Federation, [1982]. 208 p.
Note: Approx. 3,500 listings relating to various aspects of human rights and civil liberties, mainly post-1970.– Includes government documents, publications of non-governmental organizations, loose-leaf files.
Location: OONL.

2242 **Chao, Yen-pin**
Police literature: selected publications for a basic police library. Rev. ed. [Toronto]: Ontario Police College, 1982. iii, 61 l.
Note: Approx. 575 entries.– Books, government publications.– Lists of statutes and law reports, periodicals.
Previous edition: 1979. 32 p.
Location: OONL.

2243 **Chappell, Duncan; Gordon, Robert Macaire; Moore, Rhonda D.**
Criminal investigation: a selective literature review and bibliography. Ottawa: Communication Division, Programs Branch, Solicitor General Canada, 1982. 68 p.; ISBN: 0-662-12031-0.
Note: Approx. 350 entries.– Books, reports, articles dealing with criminal investigation.– Topics include history, evidence, management and organization, the investigative process and its impact.– Includes Canadian references.
Titre en français: *L'enquête criminelle: revue de documents choisis et bibliographie.*
Location: OONL.

2244 **Chappell, Duncan; Gordon, Robert Macaire; Moore, Rhonda D.**
L'enquête criminelle: revue de documents choisis et bibliographie. Ottawa: Division de communications, Direction des programmes, Solliciteur général Canada, 1982. 78 p.; ISBN: 0-662-91634-4.
Note: Approx. 350 entrées.– Monographies et articles de périodiques.– Comprend deux sections: "L'enquête criminelle," et "Les études sur le processus d'enquête et ses répercussions."
English title: *Criminal investigation: a selective literature review and bibliography.*
Localisation: OONL.

2245 Couse, Keith; Matonovich, Rae T.
Probation: North American literature review (1971-1981).
Regina: Prairie Justice Research, University of Regina,
1982. iv, 249 p.; ISBN: 0-7731-0051-2.
Note: Approx. 300 entries.– Journal articles, books,
published and unpublished conference papers,
manuscripts and government documents. Topics
include effectiveness of probation, levels of supervision,
classification for risk and need, program trends and
policy implications.
Location: OONL.

2246 De Plaen, Jacqueline
"Psychiatrie légale et criminalité: bibliographie sélective."
Dans: Criminologie; Vol. 15, no 2 (1982) p. 131-134.; ISSN:
0316-0041.
Note: 51 entrées.– Inclut un nombre d'ouvrages
canadiens.
Localisation: OONL.

2247 Ottawa Public Library. Reference Department
Legal reference materials at the Ottawa Public Library/
Documentation juridique au Service de consultation de
la Bibliothèque publique d'Ottawa. Rev. and enl. ed.
Ottawa: Reference Department, Ottawa Public Library,
1982. 58 p.
Note: Approx. 160 entries.
Location: OONL.

2248 Robichaud, Michèle
Revision and patriation of the Constitution 1965-1982:
select bibliography/Révision et repatriement de la
Constitution 1965-1982: bibliographie sélective. Ottawa:
Library of Parliament, Information and Reference
Branch, 1982. 89, A4, B24 l. (Select bibliography / Library
of Parliament, Information and Reference Branch ; no.
206)
Note: Lists primary sources in chronological order from
1965 to 1982, general works (books, pamphlets, articles,
publications by special interest groups and political
parties) by author or title.
Location: OOSC.

2249 Spence, Alex
Police brutality in Canada: a bibliography of books,
reports, magazine, journal and newspaper articles.
Toronto: Infolib Resources, c1982. 47 l.
Note: Approx. 1,200 entries.– Covers the period 1964 to
1982.– Deals with the use or alleged use of excessive
physical force by police officers in Canada.– Arrangement is geographic, by province and territory.
Location: OOP.

— 1983 —

2250 Audet, Pierre H.
"Competition law and public policy in Canada, 1979-
1982: a bibliography/Droit de la concurrence et politique
officielle au Canada, 1979-1982: une bibliographie."
In: Canadian Competition Policy Record; Vol. 4, no. 4
(December 1983) p. 19-34.; ISSN: 0228-1961.
Note: Approx. 300 entries.– Books, articles and reports in
English and French dealing with Canadian competition
policy.– Focus on items of legal or policy nature rather
than industry studies or economic analyses.– Excludes
general regulation studies and law reports.
Supplement: Droit de la concurrence et politique officielle au
Canada, 1983-1985: une bibliographie/Competition law and
public policy in Canada, 1983-1985: a bibliography. [Ottawa]:

Consumer and Corporate Affairs Canada, 1986. 33 p.
Location: OONL.

2251 B.C. Law Library Foundation
A legal bibliography for lawyers of B.C. 2nd ed.
Vancouver: The Foundation, 1983. 1 vol. (loose-leaf).
Note: Previous edition: 1982. 1 vol. (loose-leaf).
Location: OONL.

2252 Bibliographie C.L.E.F. Ottawa: Centre de référence de la
documentation juridique de langue française en matière
de Common Law, [1983]. 57 p. (en pagination multiple).
Note: Approx. 500 entrées.– Monographies, articles de
revue sur le droit des biens, contrats, délits, successions,
droit de la famille, droit criminel et pénal, droit municipal, droit administratif.
Localisation: OONL.

2253 Canada. Department of Justice
Bibliography of public legal information materials/
Bibliographie des documents juridiques de vulgarisation.
[S.l.]: Department of Justice, 1983. 172 p.
Note: Contains public legal information materials
developed between 1977 and 1983 by student summer
projects sponsored by the Department of Justice and
local agencies such as legal aid clinics, law schools,
community organizations.– Categories include consumer
law, family law, labour law, wills and estates, housing,
handicapped, senior citizens, small claims, list of guides
and directories.– Text in English and French/texte en
français et en anglais.
Location: OONL.

2254 Canada. Secrétariat d'État. Direction des droits de la
personne
Publications relatives aux droits de la personne. [Hull,
Québec]: La Direction, 1983. 7, 7 p.
Note: Texte en français et en anglais disposé tête-bêche.–
Titre de la p. de t. additionnelle: Human rights publications.
Localisation: OONL.

2255 Clarke, Lynn
An annotated bibliography of selected crime prevention
resource materials. Victoria, B.C.: Juvenile Crime
Prevention Project, 1983. i, 34 p.
Note: Approx. 120 entries.– Books and documents on
aspects of crime prevention: specific groups (children,
elderly, youth), school violence/vandalism prevention,
environmental design, specific crimes, crime prevention
research.
Location: OONL.

2256 Clarke, Lynn
Crime prevention literature: a catalogue of selected
library holdings. Victoria, B.C.: Juvenile Crime
Prevention Project, 1983. ii, 113 p.
Note: Approx. 350 entries.– Books and documents on
aspects of crime prevention: general issues, theories and
strategies, community organization and participation,
police services for children/youth, school violence/
vandalism prevention programs, crime prevention
through environmental design, research.– All documents
given library locations.
Location: OONL.

2257 Dandurand, Liette
Bibliographie sur le droit d'auteur: répertoires de centres
gouvernementaux de documentation et de la
bibliothèque de droit de l'Université Laval. [Québec]:
Ministère des Affaires culturelles, Service gouvernement-

al de la propriété intellectuelle, 1983. 501 p.
Note: Approx. 1,000 entrées.
Localisation: OONL.

2258 **Dworaczek, Marian**
Human rights legislation in Canada: a bibliography.
Monticello, Ill.: Vance Bibliographies, 1983. 35 p. (Public
administration series: Bibliography ; P-1145; ISSN: 0193-
970X); ISBN: 0-88066-395-2.
Note: 383 entries.– In three sections: "General readings"
(history, research, bibliographies, general background);
"Special issues" (judicial system and human rights legisla-
tion, native people, women, handicapped, labour);
"Federal and provincial jurisdictions."
Location: QQLA.

2259 **Ferguson, Margaret; Sy, San San**
Legal materials for high school libraries in Alberta.
Edmonton: Legal Resource Centre of Alberta, c1983. vi,
50 p.; ISBN: 0-919792-02-2.
Note: Approx. 200 entries.– Emphasis on materials
relating to the law as it applies in Alberta and designed
for the non-lawyer: material discussing the common law,
Alberta legislation, federal legislation.
Location: OONL.

2260 **Knight, Philip A.**
Issues in law and aging: an annotated bibliography of
legal literature. Winnipeg: Centre on Aging, University
of Manitoba, 1983. 5, 3, 56 l.
Note: Approx. 750 entries.– Articles, monographs, cases,
annotations, encyclopaedic treatments of law,
bibliographies.– Topics include gerontology, social
issues, human rights law, constitutional guarantees, anti-
discrimination law.
Location: OONL.

2261 **Lawson, Ian B.**
An annotated bibliography of public interest advocacy
literature/Bibliographie annotée sur la défense de
l'intérêt public. Ottawa: Research and Statistics Section,
Policy Planning and Development Branch, Department
of Justice Canada, 1983. iii, 233 p.
Note: Approx. 200 entries.– Reports and studies about
the legal representation of interests considered to be
inadequately represented in decision-making processes
of law, government, the marketplace.– Fields include
consumer protection, environmental protection.– Text in
English and French/texte en français et en anglais.
Location: OONL.

2262 **Public Legal Education Society of Nova Scotia. Schools
Committee**
Before the first day: teaching law for the first time: Nova
Scotia resources. Halifax, N.S.: The Society, 1983. ii, 50 p.;
ISBN: 0-88648-020-5.
Note: Includes a listing of pamphlets, handbooks and
other teaching materials dealing with Canadian and
Nova Scotia law.
Location: OONL.

2263 **Simon Fraser University. Library**
Canadian law. Rev. ed. Burnaby, B.C.: Simon Fraser
University Library, 1983. 34 p. (Bibliography / Simon
Fraser University Library ; GOV DOC 1)
Note: Previous editions:
1975. 32 p.
1973. 20 p.
Location: OONL.

— 1984 —

2264 **Canada. Department of the Secretary of State. Human
Rights Directorate**
Human rights publications. [Hull, Quebec]: The
Directorate, 1984. 7, 7 p.
Note: Text in English and French with French text on
inverted pages.– Title of additional title-page:
Publications relatives aux droits de la personne.
Location: OONL.

2265 **Elliott, Shirley B.**
"An historical review of Nova Scotia legal literature: a
select bibliography."
In: *Dalhousie Law Journal*; Vol. 8, no. 3 (1984) p. 197-212.;
ISSN: 0317-1663.
Note: Compilation of principal sources and related
literature to provide background to Nova Scotia legal
system: primary sources, secondary sources, statute law,
law reports, digests, manuals, history of the courts, legal
profession, legal education, biography, bibliographies.
Location: OONL.

2266 **Flaherty, David H.**
Privacy and data protection: an international
bibliography. White Plains, N.Y.: Knowledge Industry
Publications, 1984. xxvi, 276 p.; ISBN: 0-86729-121-4.
Note: 1,862 entries (240 on Canada).– Covers May, 1978-
mid 1984.– Focus on Canada, France, Great Britain,
Sweden, West Germany, United States.
Previous edition: *Privacy and access to government data for
research: an international bibliography.* London: Mansell,
1979. ix, 197 p.; ISBN: 0-72010-920-5.
Location: OONL.

2267 **Gingras, André; Perret, Diana-Lynn; Perret, Louis**
Legal bibliography on the Québec civil law published in
English. Ottawa: Éditions de l'Université d'Ottawa, 1984.
P. [713]-760
Note: Approx. 800 entries.– Quebec legal literature in
English language or bilingual texts covering the period
from 1866 to the end of 1984: statutes and regulations,
case law reports, monographs, theses, articles dealing
with the general system of civil law, private international
law, persons and family, property, successions and gifts,
obligations and offences, proof and civil procedure,
matrimonial regimes, suretyship and registration.
Excerpted from *Revue générale du droit*, vol. 16 (1985). P.
[713]-760.
Supplement: "... : supplement 1985-1988." In: *Revue
générale du droit*, vol. 20 (1989) P. 565-571; ISSN: 0035-
3086.
Location: OOJ.

2268 **Jenner, Catherine**
Bibliography of legal materials for non-law libraries.
Toronto: Ontario Ministry of Citizenship and Culture,
c1984. iv, 158 p.; ISBN: 0-7743-8963-X.
Note: Approx. 900 entries.– Covers to August 1982.–
Primary materials, including statutes, case reports,
reference works (dictionaries, directories, form manuals,
research guides, selection tools); secondary materials on
various subjects related to law.
Location: OONL.

2269 **Krueger, Donald R.**
The Canadian Charter of Rights and Freedoms: a selected
bibliography. Toronto: Ontario Legislative Library, 1984.
22 l.

Note: Location: OTL.

2270 **Myhal, Patricia J.**
"A selected bibliography of the Foreign Investment Review Act."
In: *Foreign investment review law in Canada*, edited by James M. Spence and William P. Rosenfeld. Toronto: Butterworths, 1984. P. 343-351 ; ISBN: 0 1098 6300 9.
Note: 103 entries.– Covers from 1967 to 1983.– Includes published material dealing with FIRA, a selected list of material on foreign investment generally and a list of publications produced by the Foreign Investment Review Agency.
Location: OONL.

2271 **Wiktor, Christian**
Canadian bibliography of international law. Toronto: University of Toronto Press, 1984. xxiii, 767 p.; ISBN: 0-8020-5615-6.
Note: 9,040 entries.– Monographs, articles, parts of books for the period 1755 to March, 1983 on a wide range of topics: Canada-United States relations in matters of boundary disputes, fishery rights; law of the sea, airspace and outer space, polar regions, conduct of armed conflict, international economic relations, environmental cooperation, communication and transportation, human rights, treaties.– Canadian writings are defined in a broad sense: works by Canadians published in Canada or elsewhere, single works by several authors, one of whom at least is a Canadian.– Excludes conflict of laws (private international law).
Location: OONL.

— 1985 —

2272 **Fritz, Linda**
Subject guide to native law cases and annotated text of the Indian Act of Canada. Saskatoon: University of Saskatchewan Native Law Centre, 1985. 267 p.
Note: Location: OONL.

2273 **Gélinas, Michel**
Droit à l'information et protection des renseignements personnels: bibliographie. Sainte-Foy, Québec: Centre de documentation, École nationale d'administration publique, 1985. 56 p. (ENAP Collection bibliographie ; no 1)
Note: 562 entrées.– Publications sur le droit à l'information gouvernementale et la protection des renseignements personnels.
Localisation: OONL.

2274 **Griffiths, Curt Taylor; Chunn, Dorothy E.**
Circuit and rural court justice in the North: a resource publication. [Burnaby, B.C.]: Northern Conference, [c1985]. 1 vol. (in various pagings).; ISBN: 0-86491-046-0.
Note: Lists of resource readings accompany the seven modules: dynamics of northern justice, aboriginal involvement in justice delivery, community involvement in justice delivery, sentencing alternatives, northern youth and the law, victim assistance, research on northern justice issues.
Location: OONL.

2275 **Hart, Keith**
An annotated bibliography of Canadian police history, 1651-1984. Edmonton: University of Alberta, Faculty of Library Science, 1985. 59 l.
Note: Approx. 300 entries.– Monographs, periodical articles, pamphlets, theses, archival materials on municip-

al or provincial police organizations.– Only those materials relating to the origin, development and history of a police force are listed.– Excludes annual reports, newspaper articles, material on the Royal Canadian Mounted Police.
Location: OONL.

2276 **Normandeau, André; Cusson, Maurice**
"Guide de lecteur sur le vol à main armée: si le coeur vous en dit!"
Dans: *Criminologie*; Vol. 18, no 2 (1985) p. 147-154.; ISSN: 0316-0041.
Note: Approx. 100 entrées.– Littérature scientifique et populaire sur le vol à main armée.– Consacrée principalement aux travaux réalisées au Québec.
Localisation: AEU.

2277 **Ontario. Ministry of Labour. Library**
"Canadian Charter of Rights and Freedoms: a selected bibliography."
In: *Labour Topics*; Vol. 8, no. 4 (April 1985) p. 1-6.; ISSN: 0704-8874.
Note: Approx. 75 entries.
Location: OONL.

2278 **Roy, Bernadette Kelly; Miller, Dallas K.**
The rights of indigenous peoples in international law: an annotated bibliography. [Saskatoon]: University of Saskatchewan Native Law Centre, 1985. [x], 97 p.; ISBN: 0-88880-163-7.
Note: Aboriginal rights, constitutional law, land and resources rights, self-determination, treaties, League of Nations and United Nations conventions, declarations; non-governmental organizations.– Specific attention given to position in international law of native peoples of Canada.
Supplement: *Supplement 1986: ... .* 33 p.; ISBN: 0-88880-176-9.
Location: OONL.

2279 **Sanderson, Paul**
"Musicians' legal problems: a select and annotated bibliography of Canadian and comparative law related materials."
In: *Queen's Law Journal*; Vol. 11 (1985) p. 90-133.; ISSN: 0316-778X.
Note: Approx. 200 entries.
Location: OONL.

2280 **University of Ottawa. Human Rights Research and Education Centre**
Charter bibliography: an indexed bibliography on the Canadian Charter of Rights and Freedoms/Bibliographie sur la Charte: une bibliographie annotée sur la Charte canadienne des droits et libertés. Saskatoon: Canadian Human Rights Reporter, 1985. 62 p.
Note: List of books and articles, collected essays, chronicles, annotations and reports of Charter decisions.– Compiled by Iva Caccia.
Supplements:
Charter bibliography: update no. 1/Bibliographie sur la Charte: mise à jour no 1. 1985. 22 p.
List of publications on the Canadian Charter of Rights and Freedoms. Ottawa: University of Ottawa, Human Rights Research and Educational Centre, 1987. 8 l.
Location: OONL.

2281 **Whittingham, Michael David**
Crowding and corrections: a bibliography. Toronto: [s.n.], 1985. 27 l.
Note: Approx. 340 entries.– Sources: criminological, sociopsychological, legal, medical, bibliographic.
Location: OONL.

— 1986 —

2282 **Canada. Library of Parliament. Information and Reference Branch**
Capital punishment/La peine de mort. Ottawa: Library of Parliament, 1986. 59 l.
Note: Approx. 600 entries.– Books, articles, reports and studies on the issue of capital punishment in Canada, Australia, Great Britain, France, United States.– Includes a section of additional bibliographies.– Text in English and French/texte en français et en anglais.
Supplement: *Capital punishment, 1982-1987: a reading list/ La peine de mort, 1982-1987: liste de lecture.* 1987. 6 l.
Location: OOSG.

2283 **Kaill, Robert C.**
Crime in the country: a literature review of crime and criminal justice in rural areas. [Ottawa]: Solicitor General Canada, Programs Branch, [1986]. 139 p. (Programs Branch user report / Ministry Secretariat, Solicitor General Canada ; 1986-39)
Note: Approx. 400 entries.– Review of literature on rural crime and criminal justice: corrections, courts, crime prevention, jails in rural areas, nature and extent of rural crime, police, victimization, young offenders.
Location: OONL.

2284 **McGinnis, Janice Dickin**
"Bibliography of the legal history of western Canada."
In: *Law and justice in a new land: essays in western Canadian legal history*, edited by Louis A. Knafla. Toronto: Carswell, 1986. P. 333-354.; ISBN: 0-459-38100-8.
Note: Approx. 250 entries.– Texts by historians and lawyers, law review articles, papers and essays from historical reviews, graduate theses.– Emphasis on criminal law and justice (especially the role of the police), and law and government.
Location: OONL.

2285 **Walker, Karen**
A legal collection for non-legal libraries in British Columbia. 4th ed. Vancouver: Library Services Program, Legal Services Society of British Columbia, 1986. 100 p.: ill.; ISBN: 0-77260-535-1.
Note: Books, government publications, mainly Canadian, on all aspects of law, politics, parliamentary practice, environmental protection, native people, women's issues, animal rights, free trade.
Previous editions:
Wilson, Margaret. 1981. viii, c1981.
Kublin, Joyce. 1978. iii, 83 p.
Flaherty, Shelagh; Kublin, Joyce; Adams, Darryl. *A legal collection for high school and other non-legal libraries in British Columbia.* Legal Services Commission of B.C., 1977. 48 p.
Supplements: ... *(supplement).* No. 1, Nov. 1986- . vol.–
Irregular.– Audio-visual material is included in the supplements, not in the main volume.
Location: OONL.

— 1987 —

2286 **Baker, G. Blaine, et al.**
Sources in the Law Library of McGill University for a reconstruction of the legal culture of Quebec, 1760-1890. [Montreal]: Faculty of Law and Montreal Business History Project, McGill University, 1987. ix, 276 p.
Note: Approx. 2,000 entries.– Lists works on Quebec judicial structure, judicial procedure, social control (crime and public disorder, labour relations, ecclesiastical matters), public investment, imperial relations, general legal literature, agencies of the law, property law, consensual legal relations, equity.– Compiled in collaboration with: Kathleen E. Fisher, Vince Masciotta, Brian Young.
Location: OONL.

2287 **Boilard, Gilberte**
Organisation policière: bibliographie sélective et annotée. Québec: Bibliothèque de l'Assemblée nationale, Division de la référence parlementaire, 1987. 26 p. (Bibliographie / Bibliothèque de l'Assemblée nationale du Québec ; no 12; ISSN: 0836-9100)
Note: Approx. 125 entrées.
Localisation: OONL.

2288 **Canada. Solicitor General Canada. Programs Branch**
Bibliography of Canadian criminal justice history [microform]/Bibliographie sur l'histoire de la justice pénale au Canada [microforme]. Toronto: Micromedia, 1987. 5 microfiches.
Note: Includes publications in English and French.
Location: NBFUL.

2289 **Canadian Intergovernmental Conference Secretariat**
Federal-provincial conferences on the Constitution, September 1978 – March 1987: list of public documents. [Ottawa]: The Secretariat, [1987]. 55, 2, 60, 2 p.
Note: Approx. 600 entries.– Lists documents tabled by delegations at federal-provincial constitutional conferences.– Text in English and French with French text on inverted pages.– Title of additional title-page: *Conférences fédérales-provinciales sur la Constitution, septembre 1978 – mars 1987: liste des documents publics.*
Location: OONL.

2290 **Donelan, Rita P.; Landau, Tammy**
Research in criminology by staff of the Centre of Criminology, January 1980 – December 1986. Toronto: Centre of Criminology, University of Toronto, c1987. 79 p.; ISBN: 0-919584-64-0.
Note: Approx. 550 entries.– Books, monographs, journal articles, chapters in books, book reviews and reports provided for federal and provincial governments: crime and deviance, criminal law and policy, police, sentencing and corrections, juveniles, domestic violence, medico-legal.
Location: OONL.

2291 **Dworaczek, Marian**
The Canadian Bill of Rights and the Charter of Rights and Freedoms: a bibliography. Monticello, Ill.: Vance Bibliographies, 1987. 71 p. (Public administration series: Bibliography ; P-2207; ISSN: 0193-970X); ISBN: 1-55590-407-6.
Note: Approx. 900 entries.– Monographs, articles, conference proceedings, cases, digests, indexes, dissertations, bibliographies, handbooks, manuals, guides, audiovisual materials, periodicals.

Location: OOSC.

2292 Felsky, Martin
The CLIC bibliography of computers and the law, 1983-1986. Ottawa: Canadian Law Information Council, 1987. 106 p.; ISBN: 0-921481-12-8.
Note: Approx. 800 entries.– Emphasis on Canadian materials in all subject areas: computer assisted legal research, law library automation, law office automation, expert systems and artificial intelligence, court and government administration, computers in legal education, computer law.
Location: OONL.

2293 Houle, France
La famille et le droit: bibliographie annotée. Montréal: Université de Montréal, Centre de recherche en droit public, 1987. 134 p.
Note: Approx. 750 entrées.– Couvre 1976 à 1986.– Monographies, articles, thèses et publications officielles des gouvernements fédéral et québécois.
Localisation: OONL.

2294 Janisch, H.N.; Rawson, S.G.; Stanbury, W.T.
Canadian telecommunications regulation bibliography/ Bibliographie de la réglementation des télécommunications au Canada. Ottawa: Canadian Law Information Council, 1987. xxii, 111 p.; ISBN: 0-9214810-6-3.
Note: 727 entries.– Books, studies and submissions, articles and chapters in books, government publications, legislation, judicial decisions, CRTC decisions, industry annual reports, newspaper and magazine articles.– Text in English and French/texte en français et en anglais.
Location: OONL.

2295 Li, Kuo Lee
World wide space law bibliography. Montreal: Center for Research of Air and Space Law, McGill University, 1978-1987. 2 vol.; ISBN: 0-9692703-3-X.
Note: Articles in legal journals, scientific and technical journals, monographs, documents, proceedings, etc., from the earliest found to 1986, relating to space law, including astronautics, astropolitics, astro-socio-economics.– Includes Canadian references.
Location: OONL.

2296 Lodhi, Abdul Q.; McNeilly, Russell A.
Human rights: sources and statutes. Fredericton, N.B.: Human Rights Research and Development, 1987. vii, 128 p.; ISBN: 0-920114-95-4.
Note: Approx. 150 entries.– Current books, government publications, periodical articles on Canadian human rights issues, together with a selection of U.N. declarations and Canadian statutes.
Location: OONL.

2297 Rangel, Yolanda
Le parrainage et la réunification de la famille: bibliographie annotée. [Québec]: Conseil des communautés culturelles et de l'immigration du Québec, 1987. [2], i, 34 f.; ISBN: 2-550-19148-X.
Note: Comprend législation fédérale et provinciale (Québec); législation étrangères; études et recherches (analyses juridiques, analyses historiques, analyses socio-économiques, éléments de politiques gouvernementales, données statistiques).
Localisation: OONL.

2298 Reid, Marianne E.
Enumerative bibliography of the University of Saskatchewan's holdings of Law Reform Commission publications for Australia, Canada, Great Britain and Scotland. [Saskatoon]: Publications Committee, University of Saskatchewan, 1987. 228 p.; ISBN: 0-88880-183-1.
Note: Approx. 1,000 entries.– Covers to June 1, 1986.– Includes publications of law reform commissions of Canadian common-law provinces (excludes Quebec).
Location: OONL.

2299 Secrétariat des conférences intergouvernementales canadiennes
Conférences fédérales-provinciales sur la Constitution, septembre 1978 – mars 1987: liste des documents publics. [Ottawa]: Le Secrétariat, [1987]. 60, 2, 55, 2 p.
Note: Approx. 600 entrées.– Liste des documents qui ont été déposés par les délégations au cours des conférences constitutionnelles fédérales-provinciales.– Texte en français et en anglais disposé tête-bêche.– Titre de la p. de t. additionnelle: *Federal-provincial conferences on the Constitution, September 1978 – March 1987: list of public documents.*
Localisation: OONL.

2300 Service de diffusion sélective de l'information de la Centrale des bibliothèques
Le droit d'auteur. Montréal: Le Service, 1987. 18 p. (DSI/ CB ; no 89; ISSN: 0825-5024); ISBN: 2-89059-290-1.
Note: 193 entrées.– Monographies, articles de revues, articles du quotidien *La Presse.*
Localisation: OONL.

2301 Smandych, Russell Charles; Matthews, Catherine J.; Cox, Sandra J.
Canadian criminal justice history: an annotated bibliography. Toronto: University of Toronto Press, c1987. xviii, 332 p.; ISBN: 0-8020-5720-9.
Note: 1,104 entries.– Contains published and unpublished scholarly materials in English and French written between 1867 and 1984, secondary sources for advanced research on the history and development of public policing, the criminal court system, the correctional system.– Excludes reports of royal commissions, annual reports, other government publications not exclusively historical studies.– Annotations in English only.
Location: OONL.

2302 Stanek, Edward
The Canadian Charter of Rights and Freedoms: a bibliography. Monticello, Ill.: Vance Bibliographies, [1987]. 10 p. (Public administration series: Bibliography ; P-2159; ISSN: 0193-970X); ISBN: 1-555903-19-3.
Note: Location: OOP.

2303 Watters, John G.
Reviews of the Young Offenders Act: a bibliography. [Ottawa]: Solicitor General Canada, Ministry Secretariat, [1987]. 84 p. (Programs Branch user report / Ministry Secretariat, Solicitor General Canada ; no. 1987-17)
Note: Approx. 150 entries.– Includes reports, reviews, critiques concerning the Young Offenders Act written up to April 30, 1987 in three categories: research, legal studies, commentary.
Location: OONL.

2304 Webster, Peter M.
Fine print: a guide to law materials for Nova Scotians. 2nd ed. [Halifax, N.S.]: Public Legal Education Society of

Nova Scotia, c1987. v, 99 p.; ISBN: 0-88648-076-0.
Note: 561 entries.– Covers 1976 to 1987.– Emphasis on legal materials for non-lawyers: primary sources (statutes and case law report series), primary reference materials (dictionaries, directories, guides, bibliographies), books, booklets, pamphlets, government materials.
Previous edition: 1984. v, 94 p.; ISBN: 0-88648-045-0.
Location: OONL.

— 1988 —

2305 Alderson Gill & Associates
An annotated bibliography of maintenance and custody literature. [Ottawa]: Department of Justice Canada, Family Law Research, c1988. 99, 112 p.; ISBN: 0-662-55723-9.
Note: Approx. 80 entries.– Books, articles and papers that provide information and analysis relevant to development of maintenance and custody policies in Canada, arranged in three sections: custody awards, maintenance awards, award violation and enforcement.– Text in English and French with French text on inverted pages.– Title of additional title-page: *Bibliographie annotée sur la documentation relative à la garde d'enfants et aux pensions alimentaires.*
Location: OONL.

2306 Alderson Gill & Associates
Bibliographie annotée sur la documentation relative à la garde d'enfants et aux pensions alimentaires. [Ottawa]: Ministère de la justice Canada, Recherche en droit de la famille, c1988. 112, 99 p.; ISBN: 0-662-55723-9.
Note: Approx. 80 entrées.– Ouvrages, articles et de mémoires qui fournissent information et analyses susceptibles d'aider à la définition de régles de conduite en matière de pensions alimentaires et de garde d'enfants au Canada, classées sous trois rubriques: attribution de la garde d'enfants, pensions alimentaires, infractions aux ordonnances et mécanismes d'exécution.– Texte en français et en anglais disposé tête-bêche.– Titre de la p. de t. additionnelle: *An annotated bibliography of maintenance and custody literature.*
Localisation: OONL.

2307 Beanlands, D. Bruce; Deacon, James
Contre-terrorisme: bibliographie. [Ottawa]: Solliciteur général Canada, Secrétariat du Ministère, [1988]. [iii], 362 p. (Rapport pour spécialistes / Solliciteur général Canada, Secrétariat du Ministère ; no 1988-14)
Note: Approx. 2,800 entrées.– Limite aux documents publiés après 1975.– Exclut articles de journaux ou de revues, des énoncés de politiques ni des discours.– Deux sections: ouvrages relatifs aux méthodes et aux enjeux de la lutte antiterroriste; ouvrages traitant des différentes tactiques des terroristes et des moyens d'endiguer et de prévenir les actions terroristes.
English title: *Counter-terrorism: bibliography.*
Localisation: OOP.

2308 Beanlands, D. Bruce; Deacon, James
Counter-terrorism: bibliography. [Ottawa]: Solicitor General Canada, Ministry Secretariat, [1988]. ii, 361 p. (User report / Solicitor General Canada, Ministry Secretariat ; no. 1988-14)
Note: Approx. 3,800 entries.– Restricted to material published after 1975, with some notable exceptions.– Excludes newspaper and magazine articles, policy statements or speeches.– Deals with issues relating to national and international developments in counter-terrorism policy, and with operations of counter-terror establishments, ideologies of terrorist groups and sponsor states.– Specific topics include legal/intelligence/military approaches concerning counter-terrorism; tactical variations of terrorism, their control and prevention.– Sub-division by nation/region.
Titre en français: *Contre-terrorisme: bibliographie.*
Location: OOP.

2309 Boilard, Gilberte; Desjardins, Joëlle
Clause nonobstant: (article 33 de la Charte canadienne des droits et libertés): bibliographie sélective et annotée. Québec: Division de la référence parlementaire, Bibliothèque de l'Assemblée nationale, 1988. 16 p. (Bibliographie / Bibliothèque de l'Assemblée nationale du Québec ; no 16; ISSN: 0836-9100)
Note: 43 entrées.– Articles de revues, monographies, articles de presse; Lois comportant une clause dérogatoire; Causes invoquant l'article 33; Causes dans lesquelles l'article 33 est cité.
Localisation: OONL.

2310 Canada. Library of Parliament. Information and Technical Services Branch
The Constitution since patriation/La Constitution depuis le rapatriement. Ottawa: The Library, 1988. 86 p. (Select bibliography / Library of Parliament ; no. 206A)
Note: Comprehensive listing of books, book chapters and scholarly articles published since patriation.– Excludes newspaper articles and articles in popular magazines.– Arranged in three sections: primary sources (official publications), general works, specific rights protected by the Constitution (aboriginal rights, democratic rights, economic rights, equality rights, language rights, legal rights, mobility rights).– Compiled by Audrey Dubé.– Text in English and French/texte en français et en anglais.
Previous edition: 1983. 21 l.
Location: OOP.

2311 Chappell, Duncan; Moore, Rhonda D.
Le recours à des sanctions pénales contre la pollution de l'environnement: bibliographie choisie et commentée. Ottawa: Ministère de la justice Canada, 1988. xvii, 109, 93, xvii p. (Recherches sur la réglementation et l'observation); ISBN: 0-662-55688-7.
Note: Approx. 200 entrées.– Comporte une liste de références dans les domaines de la criminologie, la jurisprudence, de la sociologie, psychologie et de l'industrie qui traitent de la réglementation portant sur les sanctions pénales relatives à la pollution de l'environnement.– Texte en français et en anglais disposé tête-bêche.– Titre de p. de t. additionnelle: *The use of criminal penalties for pollution of the environment: a selective and annotated bibliography of the literature.*
Localisation: OONL.

2312 Chappell, Duncan; Moore, Rhonda D.
The use of criminal penalties for pollution of the environment: a selective and annotated bibliography of the literature. Ottawa: Department of Justice Canada, 1988. xvii, 93, 109, xvii p. (Studies in regulation and compliance); ISBN: 0-662-55688-7.
Note: Approx. 180 entries.– Includes literature from Canada, United States and a number of other jurisdictions published from 1970 to 1988 in the fields of

criminology, jurisprudence, sociology, psychology and industry on the issue of criminal penalties for pollution of the environment.– Text in English and French with French text on inverted pages.– Title of additional title-page: *Le recours à des sanctions pénales contre la pollution de l'environnement: bibliographie choisie et commentée.*
Location: OONL.

2313 **Clifford, John Charles**
Inspection: a case study and selected references. Ottawa: Law Reform Commission of Canada, c1988. xi, 108, 117, xi p. (Administrative law series / Law Reform Commission of Canada); ISBN: 0-662-56316-6.
Note: 840 entries.– Articles and books, official publications, legislation, cases dealing with activities and powers associated with inspection, and the use, organization and control of inspection by the Canadian federal government.– Focus on materials which reflect contemporary Canadian law.– Text in English and French with French text on inverted pages.– Title of additional title-page: *Les régimes d'inspection: étude de cas et bibliographie sélective.*
Location; OONL.

2314 **Clifford, John Charles**
Les régimes d'inspection: étude de cas et bibliographie sélective. Ottawa: Commission de réforme du droit du Canada, c1988. xi, 117, xi, 108 p. (Série droit administratif / Commission de réforme du droit du Canada); ISBN: 0-662-56316-6.
Note: 840 entrées.– Articles, monographies, documentation officielle, législation, jurisprudence sur l'inspection au Canada.– L'accent soit placé sur les ouvrages reflétant le droit positif canadien.– Texte en français et en anglais disposé tête-bêche.– Titre de la p. de t. additionnelle: *Inspection: a case study and selected references.*
Localisation: OONL.

2315 **Cousineau, Douglas F.**
Legal sanctions and deterrence. Ottawa: Department of Justice Canada, Research and Development Directorate, Policy, Programs and Research Branch, 1988. vii, 214 p. (Research reports of the Canadian Sentencing Commission; ISSN: 0836-1797); ISBN: 0-662-15879-2.
Note: Approx. 1,300 entries.– Includes Canadian references.– Bibliography, p. 121-214.
Titre en français: *Sanctions légales et dissuasion.*
Location: OONL.

2316 **Cousineau, Douglas F.**
Sanctions légales et dissuasion. Ottawa: Ministère de la justice Canada, Direction générale de la recherche et du développement, Direction de la politique, des programmes et de la recherche, 1988. viii, 235 p. (Rapports de recherche de la Commission canadienne sur la détermination de la peine; ISSN: 0836-1800); ISBN: 0-662-94682-0.
Note: Approx. 1,200 entrées.– Comporte des références canadiennes.– Bibliographie, p. 147-235.
English title: *Legal sanctions and deterrence.*
Localisation: OONL.

2317 **Kirsh, Harvey J.**
Kirsh: selected bibliography of construction law writings in Canada. Toronto: Carswell, 1988. vii, 43 p.; ISBN: 0-459-31371-1.
Note: Approx. 225 entries.
Location: OONL.

2318 **New Brunswick. Legislative Library**
Meech Lake Constitutional Accord/Entente constitutionnelle du Lac Meech. Fredericton: Legislative Library, 1988. 6 l.
Note: 47 entries.– Includes books, documents, periodical articles.
Location: OONL.

2319 **Swanick, Eric L.; Whalen, Doreen**
The Lake Meech Accord (Canadian constitution): a bibliography. Monticello, Ill.: Vance Bibliographies, 1988. 22 p. (Public administration series: Bibliography ; P-2421; ISSN: 0193-970X); ISBN: 1-55590-811-X.
Note: Approx. 300 entries.– Articles and documents in English and French.
Location: OONL.

2320 **Yuille, John C.; King, Mary Ann; McDougall, Don**
Child victims and witnesses: the social science and legal literatures. Ottawa: Department of Justice Canada, 1988. vii, 61, 67, vii p. (Studies on the sexual abuse of children in Canada); ISBN: 0-662-55765-4.
Note: Part II of a review of literature pertaining to children as witnesses in the criminal justice system.– Part I: *Child victims and witnesses: an annotated bibliography,* was not published, but is available from the Research Section, Department of Justice Canada.– Many Canadian references.– Text in English and French with French text on inverted pages.– Title of additional title-page: *Enfants victimes et témoins: publications en droit et en sciences sociales.*
Location: OONL.

2321 **Yuille, John C.; King, Mary Ann; McDougall, Don**
Enfants victimes et témoins: publications en droit et en sciences sociales. Ottawa: Ministère de la justice Canada, 1988. vii, 67, 61, vii p. (Études sur les agressions sexuelles contre les enfants au Canada); ISBN: 0-662-55765-4.
Note: Partie II d'une revue critique de la littérature publiée en sciences sociales et en droit en ce qui concerne les enfants appelés à témoigner dans le système de justice pénale.– Partie I: *Enfants victimes et témoins: une bibliographie annotée,* n'a pas été publiée, mais disponible à la section Recherche du ministère de la justice à Ottawa.– Texte en français et en anglais disposé tête-bêche.– Titre de la p. de t. additionnelle: *Child victims and witnesses: the social science and legal literatures.*
Localisation: OONL.

— 1989 —

2322 **Boilard, Gilberte**
Avortement: prises de position et aspects juridiques: bibliographie sélective et annotée. Québec: Bibliothèque de l'Assemblée nationale, Division de la référence parlementaire, 1989. 43 p. (Bibliographie / Bibliothèque de l'Assemblée nationale du Québec ; no 25; ISSN: 0836-9100)
Note: 146 entrées.
Localisation: OONL.

2323 **Boilard, Gilberte**
Charte de la lange française (Loi 101): bibliographie annotée. 2e éd. Québec: Bibliothèque de l'Assemblée nationale, Division de la référence parlementaire, [1989]. 115 p. (Bibliographie / Bibliothèque de l'Assemblée nationale du Québec ; no 23; ISSN: 0836-9100)
Note: 427 entrées.– Articles de revues/périodiques, publications gouvernementales, monographies,

jurisprudence.
Supplément: 1989. 20 p.
Édition antérieure: 1987. 62 p. (Bibliographie ; no 3).
Localisation: OONL.

2324 **Canada. Library of Parliament. Bibliographies and Compilations Section**
The right to privacy/Le droit à la vie privée. Ottawa: Library of Parliament, Information and Technical Services Branch, 1989. 62 p. (Bibliographies / Library of Parliament, Bibliographies and Compilations Section ; no. 21)
Note: 564 entries.
Previous editions: *The right to privacy: select bibliography/ Le droit à la vie privée: bibliographie sélective.* 1982. 72 l. 1978. 46 p.
Location: OOP.

2325 **Canadian Law Information Council**
CLIC's legal materials letter. Bulletin d'information juridique. Ottawa: Canadian Law Information Council, 1977-1989. 12 vol.; ISSN: 0704-0393.
Note: Reviews of Canadian legal publications.– First issue: Vol. 1, no. 1 (October 1977).– Ceased with vol. 12, no. 6 (September-October 1989).– Text in English and French/texte en français et en anglais.
Location: OONL.

2326 **Lane, Kenneth**
Native land bibliography/Bibliographie sur le droit des autochtones. Ottawa: Library, Supreme Court of Canada, 1989. 19 l.
Note: 159 entries.– Books, documents, reports, microforms in the field of Native law.– Includes a listing of additional bibliographies.
Supplement: ... . Part II/... . 2e partie. 1990. 3, 37 l.– 330 entries.
Location: OONL.

2327 **National program for the integration of the two official languages in the administration of justice: publications/ Programme national de l'administration de la justice dans les deux langues officiels: publications.** Ottawa: Communications and Public Affairs, Department of Justice Canada, c1989. 24 p.; ISBN: 0-662-56864-8.
Note: List contains principal works published by various organizations under the National program.– Text in English and French/texte en français et en anglais.
Location: OONL.

2328 **Sheehy, Elizabeth A.; Boyd, Susan B.**
Canadian feminist perspectives on law: an annotated bibliography of interdisciplinary writings. Toronto: Resources for Feminist Research, Ontario Institute for Studies in Education, 1989. 79 p.
Note: Approx. 550 entries.– Books, parts of books, journal articles, government documents, most written between 1970 and 1988.– Topics include aboriginal women, constitution and the Charter, criminal law (pornography, prostitution, sexual assault, wife assault), employment (affirmative action, pay equity, sexual harrassment), family law, legal history, lesbian issues, racism, reproduction.
Location: OOP.

— 1990 —

2329 **Beavis, Joan; Cumming, Greta**
Organized crime: a bibliography. Ottawa: Law Enforcement Reference Centre, 1990. 39 l.

Note: Approx. 500 entries.– Books, journal articles, papers, newspaper articles dealing with organized criminal activities: gambling, narcotics trade, pornography, prostitution, racketeering and extortion, theft, white collar crime, with sections on crime control and prevention, gangs, mafia.– Includes a substantial number of Canadian references.
Location: OONL.

2330 **Beavis, Joan; Cumming, Greta**
Policewomen: a bibliography, 1980-1990. Ottawa: Law Enforcement Reference Centre, 1990. 20 l.
Note: Location: OONL.

2331 **Canada. Department of Justice**
The prevention of crime and the treatment of offenders: a source book of Canadian experiences. Ottawa: Communication and Public Affairs, Department of Justice Canada, c1990. vi, 74, 81, vi p.; ISBN: 0-662-57687-X.
Note: Listing of selected documents, databases, resource centres dealing with crime prevention and criminal justice, problems of imprisonment, organized crime and terrorism, juvenile crime.– Text in English and French with French text on inverted pages.– Title of additional title-page: *Prévention du crime et traitement des délinquants: recueil de ressources sur les expériences canadiennes.*
Location: OONL.

2332 **Canada. Ministère de la justice**
Prévention du crime et traitement des délinquants: recueil de ressources sur les expériences canadiennes. Ottawa: Direction des communications et affaires publiques, Ministère de la justice du Canada, c1990. vi, 81, 74, vi p.; ISBN: 0-660-57687-X.
Note: Liste de textes, bases de données choisis, centres d'information concernant prévention et justice pénale, politiques pénales et problème d'emprisonnement, crime organisé et terrorisme, délinquance juvénile et protection de la jeunesse.– Texte en français et en anglais disposé tête-bêche.– Titre de la p. de t. additionnelle: *The prevention of crime and the treatment of offenders: a source book of Canadian experiences.*
Localisation: OONL.

2333 **Canada. Solicitor General Canada. Ministry Library and Reference Centre**
Natives & criminal justice catalogue/Catalogue sur les autochtones et la justice pénale. [Ottawa]: Solicitor General Canada, Ministry Library and Reference Centre, 1990. 106 p.
Note: Approx. 1,800 entries.– Text in English and French/ texte en français et en anglais.
Location: OONL.

2334 **Canada. Solicitor General Canada. Ministry Library and Reference Centre**
Police: a reading list/La police: liste de lectures choisies. [Ottawa]: Solicitor General Canada, Ministry Library and Reference Centre, 1990. P. 1953-2078
Note: Approx. 2,500 entries.– Printout from library catalogue, subject section "Police."- Substantial Canadian content.– Text in English and French/texte en français et en anglais.
Location: OONL.

2335 **Desjardins, Joëlle**
L'Accord du lac Meech: bibliographie sélective et annotée. 3e éd. [Québec]: Division de la référence parlementaire, Bibliothèque de l'Assemblée nationale,

1990. 68 p. (Bibliographie / Bibliothèque de l'Assemblée nationale du Québec ; no 21; ISSN: 0836-9100)
Note: Comprend des publications en français et en anglais.
Éditions antérieures:
1989. 23 p.
1989. 12 p.
Localisation: OONL.

2336 **Farson, Anthony Stuart; Matthews, Catherine J.**
Criminal intelligence and security intelligence: a selective bibliography. Toronto: Centre for Criminology, University of Toronto, 1990. vii, 77 p. (Bibliography / Centre of Criminology, University of Toronto ; no. 14); ISBN: 0-919584-66-7.
Note: Approx. 500 entries.– Books, articles, papers, government publications.– Focus on English language materials about matters in Canada during the 1970s and 1980s.– Topics include domestic intelligence activities, political policing, surveillance techniques, undercover operations, role of informants and agents provocateurs.
Location: OONL.

2337 **Fritz, Linda**
Native law bibliography. 2nd ed. Saskatoon: University of Saskatchewan, Native Law Centre, 1990. ix, 167 p.; ISBN: 0-88880-233-6.
Note: Approx. 3,300 entries.– Cutoff date for entries is December 1988.– Includes journal articles, newspaper articles, books, government publications.– Emphasis on Canada with comparative works from common law jurisdictions of Australia, New Zealand and the United States.– Excludes anthropological and sociological works, legal cases.
Previous edition: 1984. [10], 100 p.; ISBN: 0-88880-141-6.– Approx. 1,400 entries.
Location: OONL.

2338 **Halévy, Balfour; Tanguay, Guy**
Inventory of Canadian secondary legal literature, 1970-1986. Ottawa: Canadian Legal Information Centre, 1990. vii, 115 p.; ISBN: 0-921481-21-7.
Note: Contains monographs covering substantive law and history of law in addition to finding tools: case and statute citators, bibliographies, dictionaries, lexicons, encyclopedias.– Includes legal education and law society publications.– Excludes government documents, law reform commission reports (except treatises), public legal education and audio-visual materials, pamphlets of fewer than 25 pages, law reports and digests, theses, bar admission course materials.– Text in English and French/texte en français et en anglais.
Location: OONL.

2339 **Herperger, Dwight**
"The Meech Lake Accord: a comprehensive bibliography."
In: *Canada: the State of the Federation*; (1990) p. 271-289.; ISSN: 0827-0708.
Note: Approx. 300 entries.
Location: OONL.

2340 **Lepkey, Gabriel**
Législation et politique canadienne en matière de concurrence: la bibliographie d'un centenaire: 1889-1989 / Canadian competition law and policy: a centennial bibliography, 1889-1989. Ottawa: Bureau de la politique de concurrence, c1990. 252 p.; ISBN: 0-662-57571-7.

Note: Approx. 3,250 entrées.– Les ouvrages contenus dans cette bibliographie ont trait au domaine légal ou à la politique publique.– Exclut les études industrielles ou des analyses purement économiques.– Texte en français et en anglais/text in English and French.
Localisation: OONL.

2341 **Lover, John G.; Pirie, A.J.**
Alternative dispute resolution for the community: an annotated bibliography. Victoria, B.C.: UVic Institute for Dispute Resolution, 1990. ix, 64 p.; ISBN: 1-550-58009-4.
Note: Approx. 250 entries.– Canadian and American publications dealing with negotiation, mediation, arbitration, conciliation and adjudication.
Location: OONL.

2342 **White, Anthony G.**
The Canadian Charter of Rights and Freedoms: a selected bibliography. Monticello, Ill.: Vance Bibliographies, 1990. 8 p. (Public administration series: Bibliography ; P-2907; ISSN: 0193-970X); ISBN: 0-792005-87-2.
Note: Location: OOP.

— 1991 —

2343 **Alberta. Task Force on the Criminal Justice System and Its Impact on the Indian and Metis People of Alberta**
Justice on trial: report of the Task Force on the Criminal Justice System and its Impact on the Indian and Metis People of Alberta. Edmonton: The Task Force, 1991. 6 vol.: ill.
Note: Vol. 3: *Working papers and bibliography.* (various pagings).
Location: OONL.

2344 **Boilard, Gilberte**
L'accès aux documents des organismes publics, 1980-1991: bibliographie sélective et annotée. Québec: Bibliothèque de l'Assemblée nationale, Division de la référence parlementaire, 1991. 81 p. (Bibliographie / Bibliothèque de l'Assemblée nationale du Québec ; no 41; ISSN: 0836-9100)
Note: Comprend des publications en français et en anglais.
Localisation: OONL.

2345 **Breem, Wallace; Phillips, Sally**
Bibliography of Commonwealth law reports. London, England; New York: Mansell, 1991. xix, 332 p.; ISBN: 0-720-12023-3.
Note: Location: OOSC.

2346 **Buttazzoni, Maria**
La vie privée et l'informatique: bibliographie sélective. Québec: Bibliothèque de l'Assemblée nationale, Division de la référence parlementaire, 1991. 44 p. (Bibliographie / Bibliothèque de l'Assemblée nationale du Québec ; no 43; ISSN: 0836-9100)
Note: Comprend des publications en français et en anglais.
Localisation: OONL.

2347 **Chao, Yen-pin**
Policing in Ontario: a bibliography. Aylmer, Ont.: Ontario Police College, 1991. vi, 187 p.
Note: 500 entries.– Published and unpublished material pertaining to policing in Ontario from 1970 to 1990, with the exception of a few earlier imprints of historical interest.– Excludes popular press articles, case law reports, non-print media, annual reports of police forces.
Location: OONL.

2348 **Gladstone, Jane; Ericson, Richard V.; Shearing, Clifford D.**
Criminology: a reader's guide. Toronto: Centre of Criminology, University of Toronto, 1991. vi, 275 p.; ISBN: 0-919584-67-5.
Note: Collection of essays, literature reviews, and reading lists on aspects of criminology: crime, policing and punishment; law reform and policy; social hierarchies, crime and justice.– Focus on Canada.
Location: OONL.

2349 **Harding, Jim; Forgay, Beryl**
Breaking down the walls: a bibliography on the pursuit of aboriginal justice. [Regina]: Prairie Justice Research, University of Regina, 1991. 108 p. (Aboriginal Justice Series report ; no. 2); ISBN: 0-7731-0191-8.
Note: Listing of books, newspaper articles, government reports, articles in aboriginal periodicals, films and videos dealing with native justice topics, including research methodology, criminal justice system, judicial inquiries, socio-economic issues, self-government, self-determination.– Includes listings of additional bibliographies.
Location: OONL.

2350 **Harding, Jim; Spence, Bruce**
An annotated bibliography of aboriginal-controlled justice programs in Canada. [Regina]: Prairie Justice Research, University of Regina, 1991. 89 p. (Aboriginal Justice Series report ; no. 3); ISBN: 0-7731-0190-X.
Note: Materials which discuss justice policies or developments aimed at encouraging increased aboriginal initiatives in the justice area.– Includes documentation of programs which are preventive in design.– Categories: general, policing, courts (native courtworker programs), corrections, diversion.
Location: OONL.

2351 **Herperger, Dwight**
"Constitutional reform in the post-Meech era: a select bibliography."
In: *Canada: the State of the Federation*; (1991) p. 241-249.; ISSN: 0827-0708.
Note: Approx. 125 entries.
Location: OONL.

2352 **Hutchinson, Elaine; Pahulje, Dani**
Legal materials for Alberta public libraries. Edmonton: Legal Resource Centre, Faculty of Extension, University of Alberta, 1991. iv, 93 p.
Note: Approx. 400 entries.– Focus on legal materials written for non-lawyers in Alberta.
Location: AEU.

2353 **Lakos, Amos**
Terrorism, 1980-1990: a bibliography. Boulder: Westview Press, 1991. x, 443 p.; ISBN: 0-8133-8035-9.
Note: Books, journal articles, conference reports, government documents, doctoral dissertations in the English language.– Contains a section on Canada with references to FLQ and the October Crisis, 1970, Canadian Security Intelligence Service and other topics.
Location: OONL.

2354 **Morgan, K.**
"Hate literature and freedom of expression in Canada: an annotated bibliography."
In: *Canadian Law Libraries*; Vol. 16, no. 3 (August 1991) p. 91-96.; ISSN: 1180-176X.

Note: 48 entries.– Covers from 1964 to 1984.
Location: OONL.

2355 **Normand, Sylvio**
Bibliographie sur le Code civil du Québec. Montréal: Wilson & Lafleur, 1991. x, 69 p.; ISBN: 2-89127-189-0.
Note: Ouvrages et articles portant sur le Code en quatre parties: travaux préparatoires, éditions du Code, modifications apportées au Code, commentaire et doctrine (personnes, famille, biens, obligations, sûretés, preuve, prescription, publicité des droits, droits international privé).
Localisation: OONL.

— 1992 —

2356 **Caccia, Iva**
"Bibliography on the Canadian Charter of Rights and Freedoms/Bibliographie sur la Charte canadienne des droits et libertés."
In: *Canadian Human Rights Yearbook: Annuaire canadien des droits de la personne*; Vol. 2 (1984-1985) p. 379-435; vol. 3 (1986) p. 199-297; vol. 4 (1987) p. 253-298; vol. 5 (1988) p. 263-297; vol. 6 (1989-1990) p. 313-366; vol. 7 (1991-1992) p. 265-294.; ISSN: 0824-5266.
Note: Location: OONL.

2357 **Chan, Janet B.L.; Matthews, Catherine J.**
Privatization of correctional services: a select bibliography. Toronto: Centre of Criminology, University of Toronto, 1992. 28 p. (Information paper / Centre of Criminology, University of Toronto ; no. 9); ISBN: 0-919584-70-5.
Note: Includes Canadian references.– Co-published by the Public Sector Research Centre, University of New South Wales.
Location: OONL.

2358 **Dunn, Christopher J.C.**
Select bibliography: the Canadian Charter of Rights and Freedoms. St. John's, Nfld.: [s.n.], 1992. 16 l.
Note: Approx. 225 entries.– Books and articles in English from 1968 to 1992.
Location: OONL.

— 1993 —

2359 **Brochu, Serge**
Bibliographie portant sur les drogues et les questions criminelles. Montréal: S. Brochu, 1993. 106 p.
Note: Approx. 1,400 entrées.– Inclut un nombre d'ouvrages canadiens.
Localisation: OONL.

2360 **Côté, Pauline; Kabano, John**
Recueil bibliographique sur les droits de l'enfant. Rimouski, Québec: Éditions GREME, 1993. 117 p.: ill. (Monographie / Université du Québec à Rimouski, Département des sciences de l'éducation); ISBN: 2-89241-113-0.
Note: Approx. 500 entrées.– Articles de périodiques, textes de conférences, rapports de recherche et publications gouvernementales.– Inclut un nombre d'ouvrages canadiens.
Localisation: OONL.

2361 **Matthews, Catherine J.; Jansen, Vivian A.**
Accountability in the administration of criminal justice: a selective annotated bibliography. Toronto: Centre of Criminology, University of Toronto, 1993. xi, 87 p. (Bibliography / Centre of Criminology, University of Toronto ; no. 16); ISBN: 0-919584-72-1.

Note: Approx. 250 entries.– Covers 1965-1991.– Focus on scholarly secondary sources which offer analysis of the criminal justice system.– Topics include police accountability, police complaints and civilian review of police, as well as issues in accountability pertaining to government and the criminal justice system.
Location: OONL.

2362 **Normandeau, André**
"Selective bibliography of North American commissions on criminal justice/Bibliographie sélective des commissions d'enquête nord-américaines en matière de justice pénale."
In: *Canadian Journal of Criminology*; Vol. 35, no. 3 (July 1993) p. 345-354.; ISSN: 0704-9722.
Note: 78 entries.
Location: OONL.

— Ongoing/En cours —

2363 **Canadian Human Rights Commission**
Publications of the Canadian Human Rights Commission. [Ottawa]: Canadian Human Rights Commission, 1982-. vol.
Note: Text in English and French with French text on inverted pages.– Title of additional title-page: *Publications de la Commission canadienne des droits de la personne.*
Location: OONL.

2364 **Clancy, Pam**
Square one: an index to CLE publications, 1978-1984-. Vancouver: Continuing Legal Education Society of British Columbia, c1985-. vol.; ISSN: 0830-9639.
Note: Comprehensive index and listing of CLE's collection of course materials and other publications.– Annual, loose-leaf format: in two parts, publication profiles and cumulative index.
Location: OONL.

2365 **Commission canadienne des droits de la personne**
Publications de la Commission canadienne des droits de la personne. [Ottawa]: Commission canadienne des droits de la personne, 1982-. vol.
Note: Texte en français et en anglais disposé tête-bêche.– Titre de la p. de t. additionnelle: *Publications of the Canadian Human Rights Commission.*
Localisation: OONL.

2366 **Legal Services Society of British Columbia**
Publications catalogue [Legal Services Society of British Columbia]. Vancouver: Legal Services Society, 1983-. vol.; ISSN: 0825-5075.
Note: Irregular.
Location: OONL.

2367 **Morrison, Linda**
A legal bibliography for lawyers of B.C. Vancouver: B.C. Law Library Foundation, 1983-. vol. (loose-leaf).
Note: Lists texts, loose-leaf services, law reform commission reports, periodicals, law reports, continuing legal education materials in 60 subject areas.– Emphasis on Canadian materials, but includes U.S. and British when considered standard works.– Updated annually.
Location: OONL.

2368 **Nadkarni, Meena**
Canadian legal materials in microform. Downsview, Ont.: York University Law Library in co-operation with the Canadian Association of Law Libraries, 1981-. vol. (loose-leaf).

Note: Lists periodicals, law reports, statutes and gazettes, court records, monographs, theses.– In addition to pure law, includes titles from subject areas of criminology, labour relations, sociology, business and economics, social work, history and politics.
Location: OONL.

2369 **Wiktor, Christian; Foster, Leslie A.**
Marine affairs bibliography: a comprehensive index to marine law and policy literature. Halifax, N.S.: Dalhousie Law School, 1980-. vol.; ISSN: 0226-8361.
Note: Quarterly.– Prepared under auspices of Dalhousie Ocean Studies Programme.
Location: OONL.

— 1891 —

2370 **Bourinot, Sir John George**
"Bibliography of parliamentary government in Canada."
In: *Annual report of the American Historical Association*;
(1891) p. 390-407.; ISSN: 0065-8561.
Note: Location: OONL.

— 1893 —

2371 **Bourinot, Sir John George**
"Comparative politics: bibliographical and critical notes."
In: *Proceedings and Transactions of the Royal Society of
Canada*; Series 1, vol. 2, section 2 (1893) p. 95-108.; ISSN:
0316-4616.
Note: "Special works and essays which relate to the
evolution of parliamentary government in the provinces
of the Dominion of Canada."- Sections include French
rule, establishment of representative institutions,
Constitution of Canada since concession of responsible
government, Cabinet system, parliamentary compared
with congressional government.
Location: AEU.

— 1909 —

2372 **United States. Library of Congress. Division of
Bibliography**
Select list of references on the annexation of Canada to
the United States. Washington: Library of Congress,
Division of Bibliography, [1909]. 8 l.
Note: Typescript.
Previous editions:
1907. 8 l.
1904. 4 l.
Location: OOP.

— 1949 —

2373 **Canada. Library of Parliament**
A bibliography relating to constitutional and economic
developments since the royal commission and the
Newfoundland Act of 1933. [Ottawa: The Library, 1949].
10, [1] p.
Note: Location: OOP.

2374 **Glazebrook, George P. de T.**
"Bibliographical article: Canadian foreign policy in the
twentieth century."
In: *Journal of Modern History*; Vol. 21, no. 1 (March
1949) p. 44-55.; ISSN: 0022-2801.
Note: Selective review of books, periodicals, primary
materials dealing with twentieth-century Canadian
foreign policy: governmental organization; relations with
the United States, Far East, Latin America; military,
economic and social history; international organization.
Location: AEU.

— 1951 —

2375 **So we may know more about Canada, citizenship &
democracy.** Ottawa: Canadian Citizenship Council, 1951.
14 l.
Note: 60 entries.– Includes books, pamphlets, films on
Canadian history, government, human rights, cultural

relations, citizenship.
Location: OONL.

— 1957 —

2376 **Bergeron, Gérard**
Problèmes politiques du Québec: répertoire
bibliographique des commissions royales d'enquête
présentant un intérêt spécial pour la politique de la
province de Québec, 1940-1957. Montréal: [Institut de
recherches politiques, Fédération libérale provinciale],
1957. xiii, 218 p.
Note: 328 entrées.– Mémoires, études, documents
publics.– Thèmes: structures politiques, relations
fédérales-provinciales, éducation, vie culturelle, bien-être
social, relations du travail, administration municipale,
voirie et transports, agriculture et colonisation, richesses
naturelles, commerce et industrie.
Localisation: OONL.

— 1960 —

2377 **Hamelin, Jean; Letarte, Jacques; Hamelin, Marcel**
"Les élections provinciales dans le Québec: orientations
bibliographiques."
Dans: *Cahiers de géographie de Québec*; Vol. 4, no 7
(octobre 1959-mars 1960) p. 204-207.; ISSN: 0007-9766.
Note: 50 entrées.– Brochures, journaux, mémoires,
sources statistiques, études spéciales et générales, cartes
historiques.
Localisation: OONL.

— 1961 —

2378 **Bonenfant, Jean-Charles**
"Matériaux pour une sociologie politique du Canada
français. III: Inventaire des sources."
Dans: *Recherches sociographiques*; Vol. 2, no 3-4 (juillet-
décembre 1961) p. 483-566.; ISSN: 0034-1282.
Note: Collaborateurs: Lemieux, Vincent. "Documents
publics ou semi-publics." p. 485-493.– Bonenfant, Jean-
Charles. "Les journaux." p. 495-506.– Chaloult, Michel.
"La propagande des partis politiques provinciaux:
bibliographie sommaire des brochures importantes
conservées dans les principales bibliothèques." p. 507-
520.– Corrivault, Claude. "Inventaire des sources:
bibliographie générale, 1867-1961." p. 521-566.– Deux
sections: manuscrits; imprimés (bibliographies, historie
politique, institutions politiques, biographies, politique
municipale, divers).
Localisation: OONL.

— 1962 —

2379 **Canadian Institute of International Affairs. Toronto.
Men's Branch. Defence Study Group**
Problems of national defence: a study guide and
bibliography. Toronto: Canadian Institute of Internation-
al Affairs, 1962. [1], 12, 14 l.
Note: Prepared by Brian A. Crane, Sydney Peck, Tom
Wickett.– Mimeograph.
Location: OOP.

— 1964 —

2380 Canadian Association for Adult Education
Discussion materials on Canadian unity. Ottawa: [1964].
[8] l.
Note: Text in English and French/texte en français et en
anglais.
Location: OOP

2381 Carleton University. Library
Sources of information for research in Canadian political
science and public administration: a selected and annotat-
ed bibliography prepared for the Department of Political
Science and the School of Public Administration. Ottawa:
The Library, 1964. 25 l.
Note: Location: OONL.

2382 Sinclair, Donald Michael
Reading reference to social credit: a bibliography about
the social credit movement. [Vancouver: s.n., 1964]. 26,
16 l.
Note: Covers from 1931 to December 1962.– Newspaper
files, pamphlets, books, magazine articles available at
Vancouver Public and University of British Columbia
libraries.
Location: OONL.

2383 Smith, Gordon S.
A selected bibliography on international peace-keeping.
Ottawa: Defence Research Board, Department of
National Defence Canada, 1964. 24 p., 2 l. (Systems
Analysis Group Memorandum ; 64:M.2)
Note: Approx. 100 entries.– Selected listing of books and
articles on military, political, legal aspects of internation-
al peace-keeping.– Includes Canadian references.
Location: OOP.

— 1965 —

2384 Canada. Library of Parliament
Select bibliography on parliamentary procedure/
Bibliographie sélective sur la procédure parlementaire.
Ottawa: The Library, 1965. 29 l.
Note: Approx. 340 entries.– Books, periodical articles in
English and French .– Topics include closure and
limitation of debate, privilege, procedure.
Location: OONL.

2385 Carleton University. Library
Selected list of current materials on Canadian public
administration. Ottawa: Carleton University, Library,
1954-1965. 19 vol.; ISSN: 0528-1504.
Note: Ceased publication with No. 19 (1965).– No. 18,
January 1964, is a cumulative issue replacing nos. 1-17,
September 1954 to December 1962.
Location: OONL.

2386 Université de Sherbrooke. Bibliothèque générale
Sens national, 1965: bibliographie de 400 articles et livres
pour mieux comprendre les orientations nouvelles du
sens national au Canada français. [Québec]: Association
canadienne des éducateurs de langue française, 1965. 20 f.
Note: "Compilée pour la session d'études patriotiques, 19
et 20 mars 1965 (Université de Sherbrooke, Québec)."
Localisation: QQLA.

— 1966 —

2387 McGill University. French Canada Studies Programme
Bibliography: Canadian political parties, 1791-1867, 1867-
(including books, review articles, graduate theses and
pamphlets). [Montreal: s.n., 1966]. 70 l.
Note: Approx. 1,400 entries.

Location: QMM.

2388 National Library of Australia
Select reading list on Canadian-Australian relations.
Canberra: National Library of Australia, [1966]. 61 l.
Note: Approx. 800 entries.– Books, pamphlets,
periodicals, periodical articles, treaties, parliamentary
papers, newspaper articles, conference papers on
cultural, commercial and political relations, constitutional comparisons, Empire and Commonwealth relations.
Location: OONL.

2389 North, R.A.
Bibliography on Canadian government and politics.
[Vancouver: s.n.], 1966. 47 l.
Note: Location: BVAS.

2390 United States. Information Service. Ottawa
A list of selected publications and sources of information
on Canadian-American relations. Ottawa: 1966. 75 p.
Note: 600 entries.– Mimeograph.– Books, government
publications, pamphlets, bibliographies, guides,
reference serials, list of bilateral public institutions and
private organizations in Canadian-American relations.
Location: OONL.

— 1967 —

2391 Liboiron, Albert A.
Federalism and intergovernmental relations in Australia,
Canada, the United States and other countries. Kingston,
Ont.: Institute of Intergovernmental Relations, Queen's
University, 1967. vi, 231 l.
Note: Approx. 4,000 entries.– Covers 1867-1967.–
Includes books, pamphlets, periodical articles, theses.
Supplements:
*Federalism and intergovernmental relations in Canada,
Australia, the United States and other countries: a supplement-
ary bibliography.* 1976. iv, 346 p. Covers 1967 to spring
1975.– Approx. 4,700 entries.
Ort, Karen. *Federalism and intergovernmental relations in
Canada and other countries: a supplementary bibliography.*
1977. 31 p. Covers from spring 1975 to September 1977.–
Approx. 350 entries.
Reynolds, Robert. *Federalism and intergovernmental
relations in Canada and other countries: a supplementary
bibliography.* 1979. 50 p.– Approx. 400 entries.
Location: OONL.

2392 Motiuk, Laurence
Canadian Forces college reading guide for the study of
war, national defence and strategy. [Ottawa: Department
of National Defence, 1967]. vii, 345 p.
Note: Contains a section (p. 69-130) entitled "National
security and the formulation of defence policy", which
includes a subdivision listing Canadian references.
Location: OONL.

2393 Overseas Institute of Canada
Bibliography on Canadian aid to the developing
countries/Bibliographie sur l'aide canadienne aux pays
en voie d'expansion. Ottawa: Overseas Institute of
Canada, 1967. 7, 4 l.
Note: Approx. 160 entries.– Books, pamphlets, federal
government publications, periodical articles,
bibliographies.– Text in English and French/texte en
français et en anglais.
Previous edition: 1964. 8 p.
Location: OONL.

— 1968 —

2394 **Chalifoux, Jean-Pierre**
Bibliographie sur des questions actuelles. [Montréal]: Bibliothèque, Centre d'études canadiennes-françaises, McGill University, 1968. [34] f.
Note: Approx. 350 entrées.– Livres, articles de revues sur la Constitution du Canada et Confédération, la Cour suprème, les aspirations nationales du Québec, urbanisation, aménagement, culture, économie, travail.
Localisation: OONL.

2395 **États-Unis. Service d'information**
Choix de publications et de sources de renseignements en français sur les relations canado-américaines. Ottawa: Service d'information des États-Unis, 1968. 28, iii f.
Note: Localisation: OONL.

2396 **Guide to the records of Royal and special commissions and committees of inquiry appointed by the Province of Saskatchewan.** [Regina: Legislative Assembly Office, 1968]. 103 l.
Note: Covers 1906-1967.
Location: OONL.

— 1969 —

2397 **Ontario. Department of Revenue. Library**
Provincial-municipal relations in Canada. Toronto: Department of Revenue Library, 1969. 5 p. (Bibliography series / Ontario Department of Revenue Library ; no. 6)
Note: Location: OONL.

— 1970 —

2398 **Bernier, Gaston**
"Carte electorale: modes de scrutin: liste bibliographique annotée."
Dans: *Bulletin: Bibliothèque de l'Assemblée nationale du Québec*; Vol. 1, no 3 (octobre 1970) p. 20-31.; ISSN: 0701-6808.
Note: Approx. 50 entrées.
Localisation: OONL.

2399 **Knight, Kenneth W.**
The literature of state budgeting in Australia, Canada, and the United States of America: a survey and select bibliography. St. Lucia, Queensland: University of Queensland Press, 1970. 51 p.; ISBN: 0-7022-0600-8.
Note: Approx. 400 entries.– Books and pamphlets, articles, official publications, unpublished papers, bibliographies dealing with the budget process in the U.S., Canada and Australia.
Location: OONL.

2400 **Vaison, Robert**
"Public financial administration in Canada: a bibliographic essay."
In: *Canadian Chartered Accountant*; Vol. 96, no. 3 (March 1970) p. 164-168.; ISSN: 0008-316X.
Note: Location: OONL.

— 1971 —

2401 **Bernier, Gaston**
"Études réalisées pour la Commission Laurendeau-Dunton."
Dans: *Bulletin: Bibliothèque de l'Assemblée nationale du Québec*; Vol. 2, no 4 (octobre 1971) p. 43-53.; ISSN: 0701-6808.
Note: Localisation: OONL.

2402 **Boily, Robert**
Québec 1940-1969: bibliographie: le système politique québécois et son environnement. Montréal: Presses de

l'Université de Montréal, 1971. xxii, 208 p.; ISBN: 0-8405-0153-6.
Note: 2,153 entrées.– Monographies, articles de journaux, thèses sur les problèmes québécois dans chacune des disciplines connexes: géographie, démographie, économie, sociologie, anthropologie et le système politique québécois.
Localisation: OONL.

2403 **Pelletier, Jocelyn**
"Activités politiques des fonctionnaires: bibliographie annotée."
Dans: *Bulletin: Bibliothèque de l'Assemblée nationale du Québec*; Vol. 2, no 2 (avril 1971) p. 57-73.; ISSN: 0701-6808.
Note: Localisation: OONL.

— 1972 —

2404 **Grasham, W.E.; Julien, Germain**
Canadian public administration: bibliography/Administration publique canadienne: bibliographie. [Toronto]: Institute of Public Administration of Canada, [c1972]. 261 p.
Note: Approx. 4,400 entries.– Covers the period 1930 to May 1971.– Includes books, journal articles, theses, government publications.– Excludes annual reports of government agencies.– Subjects covered include principles of public administration, administrative institutions, municipal administration, town planning, municipal finance, public service and bureaucracy, government information, administrative law, programming, budgeting and financial administration, public finance, planning and development.– Text in English and French/texte en français et en anglais.
Supplements:
... . *Supplement 1, 1971-1972/ ... Supplément 1, 1971-1972.* 1974. 122 p.– 1,999 entries.
... . *Supplement 2, 1973-1975/ ... Supplément 2, 1973-1975* . 1977. 96 p.– 1,439 entries.
... . *Supplement 3, 1976-1978/ ... Supplément 3, 1976-1978.* 1980. 131 p.; ISBN: 0-919400-76-7.– 1,872 entries.
... . *Supplement 4, 1979-1982/ ... Supplément 4, 1979-1982.* 1985. Comp. by W.E. Grasham and Jean-Marc Alain. xv, 269 p.; ISBN: 0-919696-30-9.– 3,779 entries.
... . *Supplement 5, 1983-1985/ ... Supplément 5, 1983-1985.* 1990. Comp. by R.V. Segsworth and Jean-Marc Alain. xvii, 413 p.; ISBN: 0-920715-01-X.– 4,920 entries.
Location: OONL.

2405 **Motiuk, Laurence; Grant, Madeline**
A reading guide to Canada in world affairs, 1945-1971. Toronto: Canadian Institute of International Affairs, c1972. x. 313 p.
Note: Approx. 5,000 entries.– Books, periodical articles, theses, government publications on foreign policy, foreign relations, defence policy, economic policies and relations.
Location: OONL.

2406 **Painchaud, Paul**
Francophonie: bibliographie 1960-1969. Montréal: Presses de l'Université du Québec, 1972. xvii, 136 p.; ISBN: 0-7770-0034-2.
Note: 1,602 entrées.– Livres, brochures, articles de revues, articles de journaux sur le concept de la francophonie (civilisation, langue, organisations internationales), rapports entre pays francophones (coopération, éducation, échanges culturels, relations

économiques, rapports politiques: Afrique-Canada; Canada-Québec-France, etc.).
Supplément.: *Communautées francophones: bibliographie, chroniques 1970-1972*. 1973.
Localisation: OONL.

— 1973 —

2407 **Kronström, Denis**
"La fonction d'orateur ou de président: bibliographie annotée."
Dans: *Bulletin: Bibliothèque de l'Assemblée nationale du Québec*; Vol. 4, no 3 (juillet 1973) p. 31-61.; ISSN: 0701-6808.
Note: Approx. 150 entrées.
Localisation: OONL.

2408 **Page, Donald M.**
A bibliography of works on Canadian foreign relations, 1945-1970. Toronto: Canadian Institute of International Affairs, c1973. 441 p.
Note: 6,279 entries.– Books, pamphlets, articles, theses on foreign policy, defence, foreign investment and ownership, immigration and emigration, international trade and finance.
Location: OONL.

2409 **Thibault, Claude**
Canada's external relations, 1600-1969 [microform]: a bibliography /Les relations extérieures du Canada, 1600-1969 [microforme]: une bibliographie. Rochester, N.Y.: University of Rochester, 1973. 2 vol. (on 1 reel microfilm).
Note: 10,867 entries.– Books, periodical articles, theses and dissertations.– A section of research tools, primary and secondary, is followed by listings in four main historical categories: French colonial regime, British North America, Dominion of Canada, the last thirty years.– Thesis, Ph.D., University of Rochester, 1972.
Location: OONL.

2410 **Université d'Ottawa. Institut de Coopération Internationale**
Recrutement, formation et promotion des fonctionnaires, Tiers-Monde francophone et Canada: bibliographie sélective/The recruitment, training and promotion of civil servants, French-speaking Third World and Canada: selective bibliography. Ottawa: L'Institut, 1973. vii, 98 f. (Travaux et documents de l'I.C.I. ; série C, no 3: bibliographies)
Note: 562 entrées.– Monographies, articles de périodiques, publications gouvernementales, rapports, thèses, comptes rendus de conférences.– Thèmes: l'administration publique, la fonction publique, l'administration du personnel, la formation et le perfectionnement des cadres.
Localisation: OONL.

— 1974 —

2411 **Bernier, Gaston**
"Parlements, parlementaires et parlementarisme: bibliographie sélective."
Dans: *Bulletin: Bibliothèque de l'Assemblée nationale du Québec*; Vol. 5, nos 1-2 (janvier-avril 1974) p. 29-71.; ISSN: 0701-6808.
Note: 390 entrées.– Couvre la période 1965 à 1974.
Localisation: OONL.

2412 **Cartigny, Sylvie**
"Bibliographie sur la Francophonie."
Dans: *Études internationales*; Vol. 5, no 2 (juin 1974) p. 399-

425.; ISSN: 0014-2123.
Note: 511 entrées.
Localisation: OONL.

2413 **International Development Research Centre (Canada)**
Publications of the International Development Research Centre, 1970-73/Publications du Centre de recherches pour le développement international, 1970-73. Ottawa: International Development Research Centre, c1974. 24 p.
Note: Location: OONL.

2414 **"Selected bibliography of literature on Canadian-American relations."**
In: *International Organization*; Vol. 28, no. 4 (Autumn 1974) p. 1015-1023.; ISSN: 0020-8183.
Note: Location: AEU.

— 1975 —

2415 **Brière, Jean-Marie**
L'information gouvernementale au Québec et au Canada: bibliographie analytique (texte provisoire). [Montréal]: Université de Montréal, Faculté des études supérieures, École de bibliothéconomie, 1975. 41 f.
Note: Localisation: OONL.

2416 **Dansereau, Bernard**
"Inventaire préliminaire des documents relatifs au mouvement communiste du Canada."
Dans: *Histoire des travailleurs québécois: Bulletin RCHTQ*; Vol. 2, no 3 (octobre-novembre 1975) p. 26-34.; ISSN: 0315-7938.
Note: Localisation: OONL.

2417 **Julien, Germain; Trudel, Denys**
"Bilan de la recherche sur l'administration publique québécoise."
Dans: *Recherches sociographiques*; Vol. 16, no 3 (septembre-décembre 1975) p. 413-438.; ISSN: 0034-1282.
Note: 128 entrées.
Localisation: OONL.

2418 **Lambert, Ronald D.**
Nationalism and national ideologies in Canada and Quebec: a bibliography. rev. ed. [S.l.: s.n.], 1975. 144 l.
Note: 1,529 entries.– Focus on period between 1960 and 1975.– Includes books, journal articles, theses and dissertations dealing with concepts of patriotism, loyalty, national identity, independence, sovereignty, separatism, continentalism, political myths, anti-Americanism.
Previous edition: Waterloo, Ont.: University of Waterloo, Department of Sociology, 1974. 82 l.
Location: OONL.

— 1976 —

2419 **Allaire, Daniel**
"La législation déléguée: liste annotée de documents disponibles à la bibliothèque."
Dans: *Bulletin: Bibliothèque de l'Assemblée nationale du Québec*; Vol. 7, no 1 (avril 1976) p. 15-25.; ISSN: 0701-6808.
Note: 19 entrées.– Comprend des monographies de langue française et anglaise traitant de la législation déléguée dans le contexte des institutions parlementaire d'origine britannique.
Localisation: OONL.

2420 **Dansereau, Bernard**
"Documentation sur le Parti Communiste du Canada."
Dans: *Histoire des travailleurs québécois: Bulletin RCHTQ*; Vol. 3, no 3 (octobre-novembre 1976) p. 19-25.; ISSN: 0315-7938.
Note: Localisation: OONL.

2421 **Donneur, André**
Politique étrangère canadienne: bibliographie 1972-1975. [Montréal]: Université du Québec à Montréal, Département de science politique, 1976. iii, 50 f. (Notes de recherche / Département de science politique, Université du Québec à Montréal ; no 1)
Note: Approx. 700 entrées.– Monographies, articles de revues et de magazines, thèses.
Suppléments:
... : bibliographie, 1976-1977. 1978. vi, 26 f. (Notes de recherche ; no 14).
Donneur, André; Gravel, Pierre. ... : bibliographie, 1978-1981. 1982. 58 f. (Notes de recherche ; no 23).
Donneur, André; Gravel, Pierre. ... : bibliographie, 1982-1984. 1985. 51 f. (Notes de recherche ; no 29).
Donneur, André; Roussel, Stéphane. ... : bibliographie, 1985-1989. Groupe de recherche et d'analyse de la politique étrangère, de la défense et des organisations internationales, 1990. 62 f.; ISBN: 2-980218-30-8.
Localisation: OONL.

2422 **Dreijmanis, John**
Canadian politics, 1950-1975: a selected research bibliography. Monticello, Ill.: Council of Planning Librarians, 1976. 16 p. (Council of Planning Librarians Exchange bibliography ; 1105)
Note: Contains listing of 241 scholarly books.– Excludes government publications.
Location: OONL.

2423 **Halary, Charles; Mascotto, J.; Soucy, P.-Y.**
"Sur la question nationale au Canada et au Québec."
Dans: *Pluriel*; No 7 (1976) p. 87-96.; ISSN: 0336-1721.
Note: Localisation: OOU.

2424 **Kreslins, Janis A.**
Foreign affairs bibliography: a selected and annotated list of books on international relations, 1962-1972. New York: Published for the Council on Foreign Relations by R.R. Bowker Company, 1976. xxi, 921 p.; ISBN: 0-8352-0784-6.
Note: Approx. 11,000 entries.– Includes listings for Canada under various topics: foreign relations, military policy, government and politics, economic problems.
Previous editions:
Roberts, Henry L. ... , 1952-1962. 1964. xxi, 752 p.
... , 1942-1952. Published for the Council on Foreign Relations by Harper & Brothers, 1955. xxii, 727 p.
Woolbert, Robert Gale. ... , 1932-1942. 1945. xxi, 705 p.
Langer, William L.; Armstrong, Hamilton Fish. ... , 1919-1932. 1933. xvii, 551 p.
Location: OONL.

2425 **National Library of Canada**
Select bibliography of books by parliamentarians, as displayed at the National Library of Canada from Mar. 12, to Apr. 11, 1976/Bibliographie sélective de livres par des membres du parlement, en montre à la Bibliothèque nationale du Canada du 12 mars au 11 avril 1976. Ottawa: National Library of Canada, 1976. 4 l.
Note: Text in English and French/texte en français et en anglais.
Location: OONL.

2426 **Québec (Province). Bibliothèque de la Législature. Service de documentation politique**
Bibliographie politique du Québec pour l'année 1975. Québec: Assemblée nationale, Bibliothèque de la Législature, 1976. xiii, 709 p.

Note: 1,760 entrées.– Articles des périodiques, publications officielles du Québec et quelques catégories de monographies à diffusion restreinte (mémoires, etc.), agencés systématiques sous quatre thèmes fondamentaux: les contextes politique, social et démographique, économique, éducatif et culturel.
Édition antérieure: 1975. xi, 346 p.
Localisation: OONL.

— 1977 —

2427 **Black, John B.**
Propaganda, mass media and politics [microform]: a computerized research bibliography. Toronto: Micromedia, c1977. 8 microfiches.
Note: Approx. 5,700 entries.– Books, journal articles, reports, government documents, theses dealing with role of propaganda in foreign policy and interaction between media and politics in Canada.– Focus on English-language materials published between 1960 and 1977.
Location: OONL.

2428 **Brière, Jean-Marie**
L'information gouvernementale au Québec: bibliographie analytique. Québec: Edi-GRIC, c1977. 135 p. (Travaux et recherches GRIC ; 1; ISSN: 0703-1297)
Note: 409 entrées.
Localisation: OONL.

2429 **Heggie, Grace F.**
Canadian political parties, 1867-1968: a historical bibliography. [Toronto]: MacMillan of Canada, [c1977]. 603 p.; ISBN: 0-7705-1341-7.
Note: Approx 8,850 entries.– Books, articles in books of collected essays, publications of Canadian historical and political societies, theses to 1970, and periodical articles to 1969.– Sections on biography, political history, individual political parties, Dominion-provincial relations, Constitution, legislation and judiciary.
Location: OONL.

2430 **Page, Donald M.**
A bibliography of works on Canadian foreign relations, 1971-1975. Toronto: Canadian Institute of International Affairs, c1977. ix, 300 p.
Note: 2,390 entries.– Books, articles, theses, speeches on foreign policy, defence, foreign investment and ownership, immigration and emigration.
Location: OONL.

2431 **Potts, Randall C.**
Public policy and natural resources in British Columbia: a bibliography. Vancouver, B.C.: [s.n.], 1977. 1 vol. (unpaged).
Note: 512 entries.– Listing of books, reports, articles dealing with resource policy in British Columbia.– Topics include forestry, mining, electric power development, petroleum and natural gas, agriculture.
Location: BVIP.

2432 **Quantrell, James**
Canada: federal provincial conferences of first ministers, 1887-1976: guide to microfiche edition. Toronto: Micromedia, 1977. 36 l.
Note: Contains references to 52 conferences held since 1887 involving the Prime Minister and premiers, and includes the Confederation of Tomorrow Conference, Toronto, 1967, involving only provincial premiers.– Conferences are described briefly and documents are listed.

Location: OONL.

2433 **Scotton, Anne**
Bibliography of all sources relating to the Cooperative Commonwealth Federation and the New Democratic Party in Canada. [S.l.]: Woodsworth Archives Project : Boag Foundation, c1977. 698 p.
Note: Includes books, pamphlets, papers, phonograph records, correspondence, convention minutes, speeches, theses, broadsides.– Locations in various libraries and special collections are given for all documents.
Location: OONL.

— 1978 —

2434 **Canada. Library of Parliament. Information and Reference Branch**
Government secrecy and the public's right to know: select bibliography/Secrets d'État et le droit du public à l'information. Ottawa: Library of Parliament, 1978. 40 p.
Note: Approx. 400 entries.– Journal articles, legislation, commission reports: general and comparative studies, works on Canada, Great Britain, United States, other countries.
Previous edition: 1976. 18 p.
Location: OOSS.

2435 **Lakos, Amos**
Comparative provincial politics of Canada: a bibliography of select periodical articles, 1970-1977. Waterloo, Ont.: University of Waterloo Library, c1978. iii, 67 p. (University of Waterloo Library bibliography ; no. 2; ISSN: 0829-948X); ISBN: 0-920834-02-7.
Note: Approx. 650 entries.– Selected papers presented at annual meetings of Canadian Political Science Association, 1970-1977.– Some articles on federal politics are included if dealing with federal-provincial matters.– Excludes monographs, pamphlets, government publications.
Location: OONL.

2436 **Painchaud, Paul**
Relations extérieures du Canada et du Québec: bibliographie. Québec: Centre québécois de relations internationales, 1978. 53 p.
Note: Références de langue anglaise et de langue française sur la politique internationale du Canada et du Québec: publications officielles, revues universitaires, périodiques.
Localisation: OONL.

2437 **Québec (Province). Bibliothèque de la Législature. Service de référence**
Le référendum: bibliographie sélective et annotée. 2e éd. Québec: Bibliothèque de la Législature, 1978. x, 114 p. (Bibliographie et documentation / Bibliothèque de la Législature du Québec ; 6)
Note: 344 entrées.
Édition antérieure: 1977. x, 88 p.
Localisation: OONL.

2438 **Seward, Shirley B.; Janssen, Helen**
Canadian development assistance: a selected bibliography, 1950-77. Ottawa: International Development Research Centre: Norman Paterson School of International Affairs, Carleton University, 1978. 62 p. (Norman Paterson School of International Affairs Bibliography series ; no. 6); ISBN: 0-88936-187-8.
Note: Approx. 750 entries.– Articles, government and non-governmental reports in such areas as Canadian

development assistance, regional aid programs (Africa, Asia, Latin America, Caribbean).– Includes a listing of bibliographies and reference works.
Location: OONL.

2439 **Swanick, Eric L.**
Canadian federal regulatory agencies: an introductory bibliography. Monticello, Ill.: Vance Bibliographies, 1978. 7 p. (Public administration series: Bibliography ; P-104; ISSN: 0193-970X)
Note: Approx. 90 entries.
Location: OONL.

2440 **Swanick, Eric L.**
The Office of the federal Canadian Auditor General: an introductory bibliography. Monticello, Ill.: Vance Bibliographies, 1978. 4 p. (Public administration series: Bibliography ; P-84; ISSN: 0193-970X)
Note: Approx. 50 entries.
Location: OONL.

2441 **Walsh, Sandra A.**
Freedom of information in Canada: bibliography of material in the Ontario Ministry of Treasury, Economics and Intergovernmental Affairs Library. Monticello, Ill.: Vance Bibliographies, 1978. 5 p. (Public administration series: Bibliography ; P-26; ISSN: 0193-970X)
Note: Approx. 55 entries.
Location: OONL.

— 1979 —

2442 **Alain, Jean-Marc**
Perceptions du député: une bibliographie. [Sainte Foy, Québec]: Centre de documentation, École nationale d'administration publique, Université du Québec, 1979. 10 f.
Note: 132 entrées.– Études et travaux traitant de diverses perceptions du député.
Localisation: OONL.

2443 **Andrew, Caroline**
"Espace et politique: le cas de Montréal: synthèse bibliographique."
Dans: *Revue canadienne de science politique*; Vol. 12, no 2 (juin 1979) p. 369-383.; ISSN: 0008-4239.
Note: Localisation: OONL.

2444 **Easson, A.J.**
Canada and the European communities: selected materials. Kingston, Ont.: Centre for International Relations, Queen's University, 1979. iii l., 359 p. (Canada-Europe series ; no. 2/1979)
Note: Approx. 400 entries.– Documents and articles in English and French on the relationship between Canada and the European Communities.
Location: OONL.

2445 **Hamel, Pierre; Léonard, Jean-François; Senécal, Francine**
Bibliographie sur les mobilisations populaires à Montréal, 1960-1978. [Montréal]: Département de science politique, Université du Québec à Montréal, 1979. 98 p. (Notes de recherche / Département de science politique, Université du Québec à Montréal ; no 17)
Note: 752 entrées.– Recherches, études, analyses: problèmes de mobilisation et d'organisation (animateurs, l'idéologie de la participation; financement; lieux d'intervention; composition sociale et caractéristiques des organisations populaires); secteurs d'intervention des organisations populaires (consommation, défense

des droits sociaux, éducation, logement).
Localisation: OONL.

2446 **Murdoch, Laurel; Hillard, Jane**
Freedom of information and individual privacy: a selective bibliography. [Toronto]: Commission on Freedom of Information and Individual Privacy, 1979. xii, 230 p. (Commission on Freedom of Information and Individual Privacy Research publication ; 12)
Note: 2,132 entries.– Books, periodical articles, some non-print materials: computers and privacy, eavesdropping, freedom of information, government and the media, government information and secrecy, ministerial responsibility, privacy, open meetings, privileges and immunities, security classification.
Location: OONL.

2447 **Reynolds, Robert; Sidor, Nicholas**
Research in progress on Canadian federalism and intergovernmental relations: September, 1979. Kingston, Ont.: Institute of Intergovernmental Relations, Queen's University, c1979. 34 p.
Note: Location: OWA.

2448 **Swanick, Eric L.**
Canadian provincial regulatory agencies: an introductory bibliography. Monticello, Ill.: Vance Bibliographies, 1979. 5 p. (Public administration series: Bibliography ; P-227; ISSN: 0193-970X)
Note: Approx. 50 entries.
Location: OONL.

2449 **Swanick, Eric L.**
Decentralization of government services in Canada. Monticello, Ill.: Vance Bibliographies, 1979. 5 p. (Public administration series: Bibliography ; P-300; ISSN: 0193-970X)
Note: Approx. 60 entries.
Location: OONL.

2450 **Swanick, Eric L.**
Introductory bibliography on the Canadian Treasury Board. Monticello, Ill.: Vance Bibliographies, 1979. 3 p. (Public administration series: Bibliography ; P-303; ISSN: 0193-970X)
Note: 30 entries.
Location: OONL.

2451 **Swanick, Eric L.**
Ombudsman bibliography. Monticello, Ill.: Vance Bibliographies, 1979. 39 p. (Public administration series: Bibliography ; P-302; ISSN: 0193-970X)
Note: Approx. 575 entries.– Journal articles, government committee reports, papers, books published from 1960 to 1977.
Location: OONL.

2452 **Swanick, Eric L.**
Public funding of political parties in Canada: an introductory bibliography. Monticello, Ill.: Vance Bibliographies, 1979. 5 p. (Public administration series: Bibliography ; P-212; ISSN: 0193-970X)
Note: 48 entries.
Location: QQLA.

2453 **Université de Montréal. Bibliothèque des sciences humaines et sociales**
Guide de la documentation en science politique: à l'intention des étudiants, des chercheurs et des professeurs en science politique. [Montréal]: Université de Montréal, 1979. vii, 95 p.; ISBN: 0-88529-030-5.

Note: Comprend les monographies, périodiques, publications officielles, microtextes, ouvrages de référence, atlas, répertoires biographiques.
Localisation: OONL.

2454 **Walsh, Sandra A.**
Quebec and Confederation: bibliography of material in the library of the Ontario Ministry of Treasury, Economics and Intergovernmental Affairs. Monticello, Ill.: Vance Bibliographies, 1979. 12 p. (Public administration series: Bibliography ; P-305; ISSN: 0193-970X)
Note: Approx. 150 entries.
Previous edition: 1978. 8 p. (Council of Planning Librarians Exchange bibliography ; 1509).
Location: OONL.

— 1980 —

2455 **Adshead, Gordon R.; Desrosiers, Danielle**
Referendum. [Ottawa]: Ottawa Public Library, [1980]. 39 p.
Note: Approx. 125 entries.– Annotated list of books published between 1970 and 1979 which deal with Canadian federal-provincial relations, Quebec nationalism, sovereignty-association, constitutional questions, economic aspects of Quebec independence.– Text in English and French/texte en français et en anglais.
Location: OONL.

2456 **Bibliothèque municipale de Loretteville**
Gros plan sur le Québec: bibliographie analytique sur la question référendaire au Québec. [Loretteville, Québec]: Bibliothèque municipale de Loretteville, 1980. viii, 87 p.
Note: 172 entrées.
Localisation: OONL.

2457 **Canada. Library of Parliament. Information and Reference Branch**
The speakership: select bibliography/La fonction d'orateur ou de président: bibliographie sélective. Ottawa: The Branch, 1980. 31 l.
Note: 455 entries.– Books, journal articles, government publications dealing with the office of the Speaker and parliamentary government in Canada and the provinces, other countries.
Location: BVAS.

2458 **Swanick, Eric L.**
Canadian government purchasing policies: an introductory bibliography. Monticello, Ill.: Vance Bibliographies, 1980. 5 p. (Public administration series: Bibliography ; P-445; ISSN: 0193-970X)
Note: Approx. 60 entries.
Location: OONL.

— 1981 —

2459 **Barrett, Jane R.; McTavish, Mary**
Reference aids in international relations. [Toronto]: University of Toronto Library, 1981. iv, 155 l. (Reference series / University of Toronto Library ; no. 25)
Note: 654 entries.– Publications since 1945.– Canadian emphasis.
Location: OONL.

2460 **Boismenu, Gérard; Ducatenzeiler, Graciela**
Transferts de technologie Canada-Québec: bibliographie annotée. Montréal: Département de science politique, Université de Montréal, 1981. 96 p. (Notes de recherche / Département de science politique, Université de Montréal ; no 3)
Note: Localisation: QQLA.

2461 **Canada. Library of Parliament. Information and Reference Branch**
The Office of prime minister: select bibliography/La fonction de premier ministre: bibliographie sélective. Ottawa: The Branch, 1981. 15 l.
Note: 200 entries.– Books, parts of books, journal articles in English and French: comparative studies, works on Canada, Great Britain, other countries.
Location: BVAS.

2462 **Kohler, Gernot; Hakim, Antjie; Bisci, Rosina**
Arms and disarmament: a bibliography of Canadian research, 1965-1980. Ottawa: Operational Research and Analysis Establishment, Department of National Defence, 1981. xiii, 168 p. (ORAE extra-mural paper / Operational Research and Analysis Establishment, Department of National Defence ; no. 15)
Note: 1,986 entries.– Background material concerning the scope of research in arms control and disarmament completed during period 1965-1980 in Canada.– Themes include peace-keeping, Canada and the United Nations, peace research.
Location: OOP.

2463 **Krueger, Donald R.**
Quebec politics in historical and cultural perspective: a selected bibliography. Monticello, Ill.: Vance Bibliographies, 1981. 77 p. (Public administration series: Bibliography ; P-848; ISSN: 0193-970X)
Note: Location: QQLA.

2464 **Roseman, Daniel**
"European Community-Canada relations: a selected bibliography, 1976-1981."
In: *Revue d'intégration européenne: Journal of European Integration*; Vol. 4, no. 3 (Spring 1981) p. 327-334.; ISSN: 0703-6337.
Note: Listing of scholarly works on EC-Canada relations.– Excludes material dealing with Canada's bilateral relations and works on Canada's relations with Europe through multilateral organizations (GATT, OECD, etc.).
Location: OONL.

2465 **Smith, Gaddis**
"Selected readings on Canadian external policy, 1909-1959."
In: *The growth of Canadian policies in external affairs.* Westport, Conn.: Greenwood Press, 1981. P. 164-168.; ISBN: 0-313-22850-7.
Note: Location: OONL.

2466 **Soren, Richard**
Political-strategic aspects of Canadian Pacific policy: an annotated bibliography of periodical literature and government documents, 1965 to 1980. Toronto: University of Toronto-York University Joint Centre on Modern East Asia, [1981]. 78 p. (Working paper series / University of Toronto-York University Joint Centre on Modern East Asia ; no. 7; ISSN: 0834-1664); ISBN: 0-921309-36-8.
Note: 253 entries.– English-language materials about Canada's interaction with the Pacific region between 1965 and 1980.– Includes primary (official) documentation (speeches, declarations, communiqués), and secondary (unofficial) documents (commentaries, analyses, discussion papers).
Location: OONL.

— 1982 —

2467 **Barrett, Jane R.; Beaumont, Jane**
A bibliography of works on Canadian foreign relations, 1976-1980. Toronto: Canadian Institute of International Affairs, c1982. xii, 306 p.; ISBN: 0-919084-40-0.
Note: 3,631 entries.– Books, articles, theses, government publications, speeches, conference papers, press releases on foreign relations, defence, peacekeeping, foreign investment and ownership, international economic relations.– Continues bibliographies compiled by Donald M. Page covering 1945 to 1975.
Location: OONL.

2468 **Beaudry, Lucille; Fournier, François; Villeneuve, Daniel**
Le souverainisme politique au Québec, le Parti québécois et les courants indépendantistes 1960-1980, recueil bibliographique. Montréal: Département de science politique, Université du Québec à Montréal, 1982. 103 p. (Notes de recherche / Département de science politique, Université du Québec à Montréal ; no 22)
Note: Approx. 1,100 entrées.– Documents sur le nationalisme et l'indépendantisme (1960-1980); le Parti québécois (1968-1980); forces politiques nationalistes et indépendantistes; groupes socio-politiques: livres, travaux, articles, dossiers de presse.
Localisation: OONL.

2469 **Bouchard, R.–Jean**
"Les premiers ministres du Québec de Duplessis à Lévesque: orientation bibliographique."
Dans: *Bulletin: Bibliothèque de l'Assemblée nationale du Québec*; Vol. 12, no. 3 (Septembre 1982) p. 83-97.; ISSN: 0701-6808.
Note: Biographies, oeuvres et ouvrages critiques: Duplessis, Sauvé, Barrette, Lesage, Johnson, Bourassa, Lévesque.
Localisation: OONL.

2470 **Bouchard, R.–Jean; Thériault, J.–Yvon**
Sources de documentation politique à l'usage des parlementaires. 2e éd. Québec: Service de l'édition de l'Assemblée nationale du Québec, 1982. ii, 61 p.
Note: Édition antérieure: 1981. ii, 67 p.
Localisation: OONL.

2471 **Walsh, Sandra A.**
Technological sovereignty: a selected bibliography with emphasis on Canada. Monticello, Ill.: Vance Bibliographies, 1982. 7 p. (Public administration series: Bibliography ; P-951; ISSN: 0193-970X)
Note: Approx. 90 entries.– Books, government publications, periodical and newspaper articles on industrial and technology policies which encourage indigenous technological capability.
Location: OONL.

2472 **Weinrich, Peter**
Social protest from the left in Canada, 1870-1970. Toronto: University of Toronto Press, [c1982]. xxiii, 627 p.; ISBN: 0-8020-5567-2.
Note: 6,006 entries.– Comprehensive listing of publications of CCF, NDP, Communist, Socialist, Labour parties, trade unions, movements such as "ban the bomb," secularism, native rights, feminism, documentation on riots, rebellions and strikes.– Works in languages other than English and French are excluded.
Location: OONL.

— 1983 —

2473 **Ducasse, Russell**
Le mode de scrutin au Québec: synthèse, chronologie, vocabulaire et bibliographie, 1970-1982. Québec: Bibliothèque de l'Assemblée nationale, 1983. 85 p. (Bibliographie et documentation / Bibliothèque de l'Assemblée nationale du Québec ; 12); ISBN: 2-551-05364-1.
Note: Approx. 150 entrées.
Localisation: OONL.

2474 **Fay, Terence J.**
"Canadian studies on the American relationship, 1945-1980."
In: *American Review of Canadian Studies*; Vol. 13, no. 3 (Autumn 1983) p. 179-200.; ISSN: 0272-2011.
Note: 326 books and articles by Canadian-based scholars which contain a "substantial amount of American historical content".
Location: AEU.

2475 **Krueger, Donald R.**
Backbenchers: a selected bibliography. Toronto: Ontario Legislative Library, Research and Information Services, 1983. 4 l. (Bibliographies and lists / Ontario Legislative Library, Research and Information Services ; no. 83-02; ISSN: 0833-2142)
Note: Location: OONL.

2476 **Krueger, Donald R.**
Business in the House: a selected bibliography. Toronto: Ontario Legislative Library, Research and Information Services, 1983. 3 l. (Bibliographies and lists / Ontario Legislative Library, Research and Information Services ; no. 83-09; ISSN: 0833-2142)
Note: Location: OONL.

2477 **Krueger, Donald R.**
Closure: an annotated bibliography. Toronto: Ontario Legislative Library, Research and Information Services, 1983. 3 l. (Bibliographies and lists / Ontario Legislative Library, Research and Information Services ; no. 83-07; ISSN: 0833-2142)
Note: Location: OONL.

2478 **Krueger, Donald R.**
Office of the Speaker: a selected bibliography. Toronto: Ontario Legislative Library, Research and Information Services, 1983. 4 l. (Bibliographies and lists / Ontario Legislative Library, Research and Information Services ; no. 83-03; ISSN: 0833-2142)
Note: Location: OONL.

2479 **Laberge, Raymond**
"Partis politiques québécois, 1968-1982: bibliographie sélective."
Dans: *Bulletin: Bibliothèque de l'Assemblée nationale du Québec*; Vol. 13, no 1 (janvier 1983) p. 21-57.; ISSN: 0701-6808.
Note: 445 entrées.
Localisation: OONL.

2480 **Moulary-Ouerghi, Josiane; Villemaire, Carmen**
Référendum québécois: bibliographie. Montréal: Éditions Bergeron, 1983. 276 p.; ISBN: 2-89247-113-3.
Note: 3,875 entrées.– Monographies, brochures, numéros spéciaux de périodiques, articles de périodiques et journaux uniquement de langue française produite avant le 31 mai 1980.
Localisation: OONL.

2481 **Québec (Province). Bibliothèque de l'Assemblée nationale**
Liste des ouvrages conservés au Service de la reconstitution des débats. Québec: La Bibliothèque, 1983. iv, 40 p.
Note: Approx. 200 entrées.– Livres en cinq catégories: bibliographies générales, répertoires et index; dictionnaires, linguistiques et guides de rédaction; droit, science politique et législation; parlementarisme (procédure et débats); histoire, géographie et biographie.
Localisation: OONL.

2482 **Simon Fraser University. Library**
Separatism. Burnaby, B.C.: Simon Fraser University Library, 1983. 45 p. (Bibliography / Simon Fraser University Library ; POL 6)
Note: Location: OONL.

2483 **Spazzapan, P.; Ternowetsky, Gordon W.**
"Comparative Canadian and Australian research in the social sciences: a bibliography."
In: *Australian-Canadian Studies: an interdisciplinary social science review*; Vol. 1 (January 1983) p. 96-105.; ISSN: 0810-1906.
Note: Approx 100 entries.– Listing of books, articles, book reviews, theses and dissertations.– Emphasis on politics and public administration.
Location: AEU.

2484 **Vaillancourt, Jean-Guy**
"The political economy of Quebec: a selective annotated bibliography."
In: *Socialist Studies*; (1983) p. 129-140.; ISSN: 0712-1970.
Note: Covers the years 1979 to 1982.– Books in French language with brief descriptive notes in English dealing with political economy of Quebec.
Location: OONL.

— 1984 —

2485 **Boismenu, Gérard; Ducatenzeiler, Graciela**
Technologie et politique au Canada: bibliographie, 1963-1983. Montréal: Association canadienne-française pour l'avancement des sciences, [1984]. 194 p. (Cahiers de l'ACFAS / Association canadienne-française pour l'avancement des sciences ; no 25); ISBN: 2-89245-016-0.
Note: 484 entrées.– Livres et articles concernant technologie et politique: production de la technologie (ressources humaines, innovation, recherche et développement, propriété intellectuelle, potential technologique, types de firmes, études de cas), transferts de technologie, politique gouvernementale.
Localisation: OONL.

2486 **Turcotte, Paul-André**
"General selective bibliography on French-Canadian or Quebec nationalism/Bibliographie générale sélective sur le nationalisme canadien-français ou québécois."
In: *Social Compass*; Vol. 31, no. 4 (1984) p. 427-438.; ISSN: 0037-7686.
Note: Two sections: "Sociology and history of nationalism;" "Nationalism and religion."
Location: AEU.

— 1985 —

2487 **Bernier, Gaston**
"Bibliographie parlementaire."
Dans: *Bulletin: Bibliothèque de l'Assemblée nationale du Québec*; Vol. 12, no 3 (septembre 1982) p. 99-105; vol. 12, no 4 (décembre 1982) p. 37-56; vol. 13, no 2 (mai 1983) p. 83-101; vol. 13, no 3 (août 1983) p. 41-58; vol. 13, no 4

(octobre 1983) p. 49-57; vol. 14, no 1 (janvier 1984) p. 61-77; vol. 14, no 4 (octobre 1984) p. 73-91; vol. 15, no 1 (janvier 1985) p. 53-75.; ISSN: 0701-6808.
Note: Liste de livres, brochures et articles sur les institutions parlementaires.
Localisation: OONL.

2488 **Black, Joseph Laurence**
Canadian-Soviet relations, 1917-1985: a bibliography. Ottawa: Institute of Soviet and East European Studies, Carleton University, 1985. iv, 142 p. (Institute of Soviet and East European Studies bibliography ; no. 4)
Note: 806 entries.– Part 1: "The Soviet perspective." Covers from 1945 to 1984.– Soviet books, journals, collections, magazine pieces which contain specific materials on Canada.– Part 2: "The Canadian perspective." Covers from 1917 to 1984.– Canadian references on Soviet-Canadian relations, with emphasis on trade and politics, and the popular Canadian perception of the U.S.S.R.
Location: OONL.

2489 **Cabatoff, Kenneth; Iezzoni, Massimo**
Bibliographie sur l'administration publique québécoise/ Quebec public administration: bibliography. Montréal: Université Concordia, Département de science politique, [1985]. 146 p. (Notes de recherche / Programme de maîtrise en politiques et en administration publiques, Université Concordia); ISBN: 0-88947-010-3.
Note: Approx. 1,250 entrées.– Comporte huite sections: ouvrages généraux, gestion de personnel, gestion financière, imputabilité, les organismes autonomes, locale et régionale, santé et services sociaux, administration de l'éducation.
Localisation: OONL.

2490 **Faulkner, Mary S.; Krueger, Donald R.**
The Ontario Cabinet: a selected annotated bibliography. Toronto: Ontario Legislative Library, Research and Information Services, 1985. 5 l. (Bibliographies and lists. New series / Ontario Legislative Library, Research and Information Services ; no. 9; ISSN: 0833-2150)
Note: Location: OOP.

2491 **Holland, William L.**
"Source materials on the Institute of Pacific Relations." In: *Pacific Affairs*; Vol. 58, no. 1 (Spring 1985) p. 91-97.; ISSN: 0030-851X.
Note: Location: AEU.

2492 **Institute for Research on Public Policy. Regional Employment Opportunities Program**
Canadian regionalism and political culture: a bibliography. [Montreal]: The Institute, [1985]. vii, 52 p.
Note: Approx. 600 entries.– Compiled by Shelagh Keene.
Localisation: OONL.

2493 **Krueger, Donald R.**
Legislative process in Ontario: a selected annotated bibliography. Toronto: Ontario Legislative Library, Research and Information Services, 1985. 5 l. (Bibliographies and lists. New series / Ontario Legislative Library, Research and Information Services ; no. 8; ISSN: 0833-2150)
Note: Location: OOP.

2494 **Mehlhaff, Carol J.**
Canada and the United States. Colorado Springs, Colo.: United States Air Force Academy Library, 1985. 45 p. (Special Bibliography series / United States Air Force Academy Library ; no. 69)
Note: Approx. 600 entries.– Books, periodical articles, government publications dealing with economic relations, environment, international relations, strategic relations, history of relations, political issues.
Location: QSTJ.

2495 **Mount, Graeme S.; Mahant, Edelgard E.**
"Review of recent literature on Canadian-Latin American relations."
In: *Journal of Interamerican Studies and World Affairs*; Vol. 27, no. 2 (Summer 1985) p. 127-151.; ISSN: 0022-1937.
Note: Reviews Canadian writings on Canada's relations with Latin America published between 1976 and 1983.
Location: OONL.

2496 **Nadkarni, Meena**
Citizenship in Canada: a retrospective bibliography. Monticello, Ill.: Vance Bibliographies, 1985. 29 p. (Public administration series: Bibliography ; P-1662; ISSN: 0193-970X); ISBN: 0-89028-372-9.
Note: Approx. 375 entries.– Covers 1875-1985.– English and French language books, journal articles, theses, newspaper articles, reports, published addresses, audio-visual materials on Canadian citizenship.
Location: OONL.

2497 **Normand, Sylvio**
Bibliographie sur les institutions parlementaires québécoises. Québec: Bibliothèque de l'Assemblée nationale, 1985. xiii, 90 p. (Bibliographie et documentation / Bibliothèque de l'Assemblée nationale du Québec ; 18); ISBN: 2-551-06573-9.
Note: Approx. 1,100 entrées.– Publications portant sur les institutions et le droit parlementaires québécois, parues depuis 1791 jusqu'à nos jours: publications parlementaires, législation, règles de procédure de la Chambre, jurisprudence, ouvrages de référence et études.– Index onomastique.
Localisation: OONL.

2498 **Ontario. Ministry of Treasury and Economics. Library Services**
Public sector accountability: a selected bibliography with emphasis on Canada. Toronto: Ontario Ministry of Treasury and Economics, Library Services, 1985. 18 p. (T & E Bibliographies / Ontario Ministry of Treasury and Economics, Library Services ; no. 11)
Note: Approx. 180 entries.– Books and reports, periodical articles, bibliographies dealing with issues of civil service power and responsibility in Canadian federal government and provinces.
Location: OONL.

2499 **Référendum 80: répertoire de la presse.** [Québec]: Directeur général des élections du Québec, [1985]. 3 vol.; ISBN: 2-551-06519-4 (éd. complète).
Note: Regroupe plus de 17,000 coupures de presse extraites des 164 quotidiens et hebdomadaires du Québec et du Canada pour la période du 15 avril au 15 juin 1980: les options politiques (les Québécois pour le non/le regroupement national pour le oui); les organes représentatifs; les groupes de pression; l'opinion internationale; le scrutin.– Annexe: émissions de radio et de télévision concernant la période référendaire.
Localisation: OONL.

2500 **Vanderwal, Andrew**
Canadian development assistance, a selected bibliography, 1978-1984. Ottawa: Norman Paterson School of International Affairs, Carleton University, 1985. 39 p. (Norman Paterson School of International Affairs Bibliography series ; no. 7)
Note: Approx. 450 entries.– General works on Canadian development assistance, regional aid programs, bibliographies and reference works.
Location: OONL.

— 1986 —

2501 **Bruck, Peter A.; Langille, David; Vardy, Jill**
Media, peace and security: a working bibliography. Ottawa: Centre for Communication, Culture and Society, Carleton University, 1986. 34 p.
Note: Approx. 500 entries.– Articles and books dealing with media coverage of peace/war events and social movements, the formation of public opinion and attitudes.– Includes Canadian material.
Location: OONL.

2502 **Canada. Library of Parliament. Information and Reference Branch**
The Senate/Le Sénat. Ottawa: Library of Parliament, 1986. 51 p.
Note: 809 entries.– Arranged in six sections: "Historical and general works," "Senate reform," "'Triple E' proposal," "Australian and German models," "Legislation," "British House of Lords."
Location: OOP.

2503 **Defence and arms control/Défense et contrôle des armements.** Ottawa: CSP Publications, 1986. xvi, 266 p. (Science and society: a directory to information sources ; vol. 1); ISBN: 0-9691021-3-5.
Note: Lists publications (periodicals, yearbooks, databases, UN and Canadian parliamentary documents, books, bibliographies, guides, sourcebooks), teaching aids, organizations and institutions.– Emphasis on Canadian sources in area of defence and arms control (including strategic studies, foreign policy, international relations, peace and conflict studies, peace education, economics of military spending, etc.).– Text in English and French/texte en français et en anglais.
Location: OONL.

2504 **Deschênes, Gaston**
Livres blancs et livres verts au Québec (1964-1984). 3e éd. Québec: Bibliothèque de l'Assemblée nationale, 1986. 52 p.; ISBN: 2-551-106592-5.
Note: Documents énonçant une politique gouvernementale (livre blanc) ou exposant diverses options face à un problème donné (livre vert).
Éditions antérieures:
... (1965-1981). 1981. 58 p.
Gélinas, Michel. Livres blancs et verts du Gouvernement du Québec (1960-1979). Québec: ENAP, Centre de documentation, 1980. 17 f.
Localisation: OONL.

2505 **Flem-Ath, Rand**
Canadian security and intelligence: a bibliography, 1945-1985. Victoria, B.C.: University of Victoria, 1986. 47 l.
Note: Approx. 400 entries.– Listing of unclassified materials published in Canada from September 1945 to September 1985.– Emphasis on espionage, counter-espionage, terrorism, counter-terrorism within the borders of Canada.– Includes material relating to the War Measures Act and the FLQ.– Excludes material on freedom of information, right to privacy, external affairs, industrial espionage and terrorism, book reviews, fiction, theses, newspapers, non-print material.
Location: QSTJ.

2506 **Gregor, Jan**
Bibliographical guide to Canadian government and politics, 1968-1980. Monticello, Ill.: Vance Bibliographies, 1986. 9 vol. (Public administration series: Bibliography ; P-1918-P-1926; ISSN: 0193-970X)
Note: 5,033 monographs, dissertations, research papers and documents divided into 9 sections by broad topics and 31 parts by specific issues.
Section 1: *Reference literature and general political readings.* 37 p.; ISBN: 0-89028-838-0.
Section 2: *The Canadian constitution and national institutions.* 40 p.; ISBN: 0-89028-839-0.
Section 3: *Foreign political and economic relations.* 36 p.; ISBN: 0-89028-840-2.
Section 4: *Issues in Canadian politics, federal-provincial responsibilities.* 119 p.; ISBN: 0-89028-841-0.
Section 5: *Political parties and elections.* 25 p.; ISBN: 0-89028-842-9.
Section 6: *Political behavior and public policy.* 35 p.; ISBN: 0-89028-843-7.
Section 7: *Canadian ethnic mosaic.* 33 p.; ISBN: 0-89028-844-5.
Section 8: *Provincial government and politics.* 60 p.; ISBN: 0-89028-845-3.
Section 9: *Municipal government and urban problems.* 47 p.; ISBN: 0-89028-846-1.
Previous edition: [Windsor, Ont.: 1974]. vii, 87 l.
Location: OONL.

2507 **Smith, Charles D.; Grmela, Sonia**
Le statut de réfugié au Canada: une bibliographie annotée. Montréal: [s.n.], 1986. ii, 70 f.
Note: Approx. 200 entrées.– Articles, papiers et livres concernant les politiques de réfugié, la détermination du statut, les services sociaux, la loi internationale sur les réfugiés, les mouvements des réfugiés, les femmes réfugiées et les immigrées.
Localisation: OONL.

— 1987 —

2508 **Barrett, Jane R.; Beaumont, Jane; Broadhead, Lee-Anne**
A bibliography of works on Canadian foreign relations, 1981-1985. Toronto: Canadian Institute of International Affairs, c1987. 157 p.; ISBN: 0-919084-57-5.
Note: Covers material on the period 1945-1985 published between 1981-1985.– Includes Canadian and foreign monographs, articles, theses, research papers, government documents, press releases in French and English.
Location: OONL.

2509 **Boilard, Gilberte**
Francophonie: bibliographie sélective et annotée. Québec: Bibliothèque de l'Assemblée nationale, Division de la référence parlementaire, 1987. 78 p. (Bibliographie / Bibliothèque de l'Assemblée nationale du Québec ; no 8; ISSN: 0836-9100)
Note: 280 entrées.– Thèmes: Francophonie (définition, histoire, prospective); langue française (situation, législation, prospective); rencontres et coopération

internationales; organismes internationaux; Afrique; Canada; États-Unis et Antilles; Europe; Québec.
Localisation: OONL.

2510 **Hemsley, Gordon D.; Park, Norman W.**
Literature review of personnel selection techniques: draft. Ottawa: Public Service Commission of Canada, 1987. 110 p.
Note: Location: OOCS.

2511 **Jamet, Virginie**
Commissions et comités gouvernementaux et parlementaires du Québec, 1867-1986: liste bibliographique annotée. Québec: Bibliothèque de l'Assemblée nationale, 1987. iv, 186 p. (Bibliographie et documentation / Bibliothèque de l'Assemblée nationale du Québec ; 26)
Note: Chaque notice comprend six types de renseignements sur les rapports: titre et l'addresse bibliographique; titre de l'édition anglaise s'il y en a une; instrument juridique par lequel le comité a été officiellement créé; le mandat; nom de président et des membres; description du contenu des rapports.
Édition antérieure: *Commissions et comités d'enquêtes au Québec depuis 1987*. Québec: Bibliothèque de l'Assemblée nationale, 1972. vii, 95 p.
Localisation: QQL.

2512 **Knight, David B.; Davies, Maureen**
Self-determination: an interdisciplinary annotated bibliography. New York: Garland Publishing, 1987. 254 p. (Canadian review of studies in nationalism ; vol. 8) (Garland reference library of social sciences ; vol. 394); ISBN: 0-8240-8495-0.
Note: 535 entries.– Documents and articles in English, French and German dealing with the concept of self-determination.– Topics include identity, territory and power, historical perspectives, international instruments, regional perspectives and state case studies.– Includes a number of references to Canada, Quebec, and Canadian indigenous peoples.
Location: OONL.

— 1988 —

2513 **Boilard, Gilberte**
Discipline de parti: bibliographie sélective et annotée. Québec: Division de la référence parlementaire, Bibliothèque de l'Assemblée nationale, 1988. 23 p. (Bibliographie / Bibliothèque de l'Assemblée nationale du Québec ; no 15; ISSN: 0836-9100)
Note: 115 entrées.– Canada, États-Unis, France, Grande-Bretagne, études comparatives.
Localisation: OONL.

2514 **Canada. Library of Parliament. Information and Technical Services Branch**
The role of the backbencher/Le role du député. Ottawa: Library of Parliament, 1988. 36 l. (Select bibliography / Library of Parliament, Information and Technical Services Branch ; no. 45)
Note: Approx. 350 entries.– Books, articles and government publications in English and French on the role and function of the backbencher in Canada (federal and provincial), Great Britain, United States, France and other countries, with a selection of general and comparative studies.
Location: OONL.

2515 **Desjardins, Joëlle**
Le whip: bibliographie sélective et annotée. Québec: Bibliothèque de l'Assemblée nationale, Division de la référence parlementaire, 1988. 11 p. (Bibliographie / Bibliothèque de l'Assemblée nationale du Québec ; no 14; ISSN: 0836-9100)
Note: 60 entrées.
Localisation: OONL.

2516 **Dionne, Guy**
Relations entre le Québec et les États-Unis: bibliographie. Québec: Bibliothèque de l'Assemblée nationale, Division de la référence parlementaire, 1988. 5 p. (Bibliographie / Bibliothèque de l'Assemblée nationale du Québec ; no 19; ISSN: 0836-9100)
Note: 29 entrées.– Monographies, articles de périodiques parus depuis 1980 et portant sur les relations politiques, économiques et culturelles entre le Québec et les États-Unis.
Localisation: OONL.

2517 **Donnelly, Michael W.; Arthy, Iain; Oki, Diane**
Canada-Japan: a selected bibliography. [Toronto]: University of Toronto-York University Joint Centre for Asia-Pacific Studies and Nakasone Programme of the Japan Foundation, [1988]. ii, 36 l.; ISBN: 0-921309-82-1.
Note: Approx. 500 entries.– Current books and periodical articles in English on Canada-Japan political and trade relations and on Japanese Canadians.
Location: OONL.

2518 **Gallichan, Gilles**
"Essai bibliographique sur les débats parlementaires du Québec (1792-1963)."
Dans: *Cahiers de la Société bibliographique du Canada*; Vol. 27 (1988) p. 54-79.; ISSN: 0067-6896.
Note: Approx. 250 entrées.– Sources imprimées originales ou reconstituées contenant des débats, des discours ou des extraits des discours parlementaires du Bas-Canada, du Canada uni et de la province de Québec avant 1964, sources non officielles qui précisent ou résument les sujets de délibérations des séances de l'Assemblée.
Localisation: OONL.

2519 **Lévesque, Michel**
L'Union nationale: bibliographie. Québec: Assemblée nationale, Bibliothèque, 1988. 51 p. (Bibliographie et documentation / Bibliothèque de l'Assemblée nationale du Québec ; 31); ISBN: 2-551-12063-2.
Note: 325 entrées.– Regroupe des monographies, thèses, biographies, mémoires de membres du parti, documents émanant de l'organisation unioniste, articles de journaux.
Localisation: OONL.

2520 **Mahler, Gregory S.**
Contemporary Canadian politics: an annotated bibliography, 1970-1987. New York: Greenwood Press, 1988. xiv, 400 p. (Bibliographies and indexes in law and political science ; no. 10; ISSN: 0742-6909); ISBN: 0-313-25510-5.
Note: 3,738 entries.– Books, articles, documents on the Canadian legal and constitutional system, political parties and elections, foreign policy, regionalism and local politics, federal-provincial relations, legislative and administrative process, English-Canadian politics, Quebec politics.
Location: OONL.

2521 **Pederson, Ann P., et al.**
Coordinating healthy public policy: an analytic literature review and bibliography. [Ottawa]: Health and Welfare Canada, 1988. vi, 71 p. (Health Services and Promotion Branch Working paper ; HSPB 88-1); ISBN: 0-662-16702-3.
Note: Approx. 350 entries.
Titre en français: *Coordination de la politique publique favorisant la santé: analyse documentaire et bibliographie.*
Location: OONL.

2522 **Reid, Darrel R.**
Bibliography of Canadian and comparative federalism, 1980-1985. Kingston, Ont.: Institute of Intergovernmental Relations, Queen's University, c1988. vii, 492 p.; ISBN: 0-88911-451-X.
Note: 3,418 entries.– Books, journal articles, government publications on federal-provincial, interprovincial, provincial-municipal relations.
Location: OONL.

2523 **Service de diffusion sélective de l'information de la Centrale des bibliothèques**
Personnalités politiques du Québec et du Canada. 2e éd. Montréal: Le Service, 1988. 43 p. (DSI/CB ; no 40; ISSN: 0825-5024); ISBN: 2-89059-330-4.
Note: 244 entrées.– Monographies, documents audiovisuels sur 83 personnalités politiques: biographies collectives, biographies individuelles.
Édition antérieure: 1984. 59 p.; ISBN: 2-89059-240-5.– 140 entrées.
Localisation: OONL.

2524 **Thérien, Jean-Philippe**
Relations Canada-Tiers Monde: bibliographie analytique, 1970-1987. Montréal: Département de science politique, Université de Montréal, 1988. iv, 63 p. (Notes de recherche / Département de science politique, Université de Montréal ; no 22)
Note: 1,002 entrées.– Publications officielles, livres, articles, notes de recherche et thèses.– Thèmes: économie, politique, coopération; études à base régionale: l'Afrique, l'Asie, l'Amérique latine.
Localisation: OONL.

— 1989 —

2525 **Canada. Department of External Affairs. Library Services Division**
"For the record: bibliography of recent publications on Canadian foreign relations."
In: *International Perspectives*; (1980-1989) ; ISSN: 0381-4874.
Note: Regular feature from January/February 1980 to February/March 1989.
Location: AEU.

2526 **Dufresne, Nicole**
Référendums (1979-1989): bibliographie sélective et annotée. Québec: Bibliothèque de l'Assemblée nationale, Division de la référence parlementaire, 1989. 50 p. (Bibliographie / Bibliothèque de l'Assemblée nationale du Québec ; no 29; ISSN: 0836-9100)
Note: 167 entrées.– Bibliographies, ouvrages théoriques sur le référendum au Québec, le référendum ailleurs qu'au Québec (États-Unis, Suisse, etc.).
Supplément: *Référendums (1989-1992):* .... 1992. 22 p. (Bibliographie (Assemblée nationale, Direction générale de la bibliothèque, Service de la référence) ; no 45).
Localisation: OONL.

2527 **Dufresne, Nicole; Chamberland, Diane**
Politiques d'immigration et d'accueil des réfugiés: bibliographie sélective et annotée. Québec: Bibliothèque de l'Assemblée nationale, Division de la référence parlementaire, 1989. 39 p. (Bibliographie / Bibliothèque de l'Assemblée nationale du Québec ; no 27; ISSN: 0836-9100)
Note: 148 entrées.– Comprend des publications en français et en anglais.– "Canada," p. 8-16; "Québec," p. 31-37.
Localisation: OONL.

2528 **Gélinas, Michel; Chabot, Josée**
Liste cumulative des publications et rapports de recherche du personnel de l'ÉNAP. [Sainte-Foy, Québec]: École nationale d'administration publique, Université de Québec, 1989. 193 p.; ISBN: 2-920112-47-3.
Note: Comprend monographies, thèses, articles de périodiques et journaux, conférences publiées et rapports de recherche du personnel actuellement à l'ÉNAP ou y ayant déjà travaillé.
Éditions antérieures:
1986. 119 p.
1985. 106 p.
Liste cumulative des publications du personnel de l'ÉNAP.
1984. 96 p.
Localisation: OONL.

2529 **Jones, Peter**
Peacekeeping: an annotated bibliography. Kingston, Ont.: R.P. Frye, c1989. xl, 152 p.; ISBN: 0-919741-15-0.
Note: Contains a selection of books and journal articles covering the period from 1945 to 1988.– Emphasis on Canadian role in international peacekeeping activities.
Location: OONL.

2530 **Levine, Marc V.**
"The language question in Quebec: a selected, annotated bibliography."
In: *Québec Studies*; No. 8 (Spring 1989) p. 37-41.; ISSN: 0737-3759.
Note: Location: OONL.

2531 **Pederson, Ann P., et al.**
Coordination de la politique publique favorisant la santé: analyse documentaire et bibliographie. [Ottawa]: Direction générale des services et de la promotion de la santé, 1989. viii, 85 p. (Document de travail / Direction générale des services et de la promotion de la santé ; HSPB 88-1); ISBN: 0-662-95288-X.
Note: Approx. 350 entrées.
English title: *Coordinating healthy public policy: an analytic literature review and bibliography.*
Localisation: OONL.

— 1990 —

2532 **Blais, André**
"Les études sur la politique canadienne: une contribution modeste mais *distincte.*"
Dans: *Revue internationale d'études canadiennes*; No 1-2 (printemps-automne 1990) p. 55-76.; ISSN: 1180-3991.
Note: Approx. 100 entrées.– Bilan des publications récentes sur la politique canadienne.
Localisation: OONL.

2533 **Boilard, Gilberte**
Conflits d'intérêt, 1988-1990: bibliographie sélective. Québec: Bibliothèque de l'Assemblée nationale, Division de la référence parlementaire, 1990. 46 p. (Bibliographie /

Bibliothèque de l'Assemblée nationale du Québec ; no 35; ISSN: 0836-9100)
Note: 190 entrées.– Droit, règles, articles de revues et journaux: Canada, États-Unis, Europe.
Localisation: OONL.

2534 **Canada. Library of Parliament. Bibliographies and Compilations Section**
Federal-provincial relations in Canada, 1970-1990/Les relations fédérales-provinciales au Canada, 1970-1990. Ottawa: Library of Parliament, 1990. 67 p. (Bibliographies / Library of Parliament Information and Technical Services Branch ; no. 195)
Note: 634 entries.– Books, articles, government publications arranged in the following divisions: bibliographies, general works, constitutional aspect, diplomatic aspect, economic aspect, political aspect.
Location: OOS.

2535 **Canada and international peace and security: a bibliography covering materials from January 1985 through December 1989/Le Canada, la paix et la sécurité internationales: une bibliographie comprenant des documents de janvier 1985 à décembre 1989.** Ottawa: Canadian Institute for International Peace and Security, 1990. v, 434 p.; ISBN: 0-660-55772-X.
Note: 10,070 entries.– Government documents, theses, conference papers, organizational newsletters, periodical articles.– Subject focus on arms control, disarmament, defence, conflict resolution.– Text in English and French/texte en français et en anglais.
Location: OONL.

2536 **Desjardins, Joëlle**
Ombudsman: statut, rôle, pouvoirs, organisation: bibliographie. Québec: Bibliothèque de l'Assemblée nationale, Division de la référence parlementaire, 1990. 48 p. (Bibliographie / Bibliothèque de l'Assemblée nationale du Québec ; no 34; ISSN: 0836-9100)
Note: 265 entrées.– Études générales et comparatives: Canada, États-Unis, France, autres pays, ombudsmen locaux ou de type particulier.
Localisation: OONL.

2537 **Drouilly, Pierre**
Les élections au Québec: bibliographie. Québec: Bibliothèque de l'Assemblée nationale, 1990. 62 p. (Bibliographie et documentation / Bibliothèque de l'Assemblée nationale du Québec ; 35); ISBN: 2-551-12406-9.
Note: 590 entrées.– Livres et monographies, thèses de doctorat et mémoires de maîtrise, articles de revues académiques, revues périodiques et journaux quotidiens: le système électorale, le personnel politique, l'analyse de sondages électoraux et des résultats électoraux.
Localisation: OONL.

2538 **Goehlert, Robert**
The Parliament of Canada: a select bibliography. Monticello, Ill.: Vance Bibliographies, 1990. 23 p. (Public administration series: Bibliography ; P-2957; ISSN: 0193-970X); ISBN: 0-7920-0657-7.
Note: Approx. 275 entries.
Location: OOP.

2539 **Inventaire des rapports d'intervention présentés à l'ÉNAP: septembre 1972-avril 1990.** [Sainte-Foy, Québec]: École nationale d'administration publique, Direction de l'enseignement et de la recherche,

Université de Québec, 1990. 1 vol. (en pagination multiple); ISBN: 2-920-112-48-1.
Note: 1,000 entrées.
Localisation: OONL.

2540 **Molot, Maureen Appel**
"Where do we, should we, or can we sit? A review of Canadian foreign policy literature."
In: *International Journal of Canadian Studies*; No. 1-2 (Spring-Fall 1990) p. 77-96.; ISSN: 1180-3991.
Note: Review of Canadian foreign policy literature, works analyzing Canada-U.S. relations, Quebec international relations.
Location: OONL.

— 1991 —

2541 **Boilard, Gilberte; Buttazzoni, Maria**
Guide de documentation politique. 2e éd. Québec: Bibliothèque de l'Assemblée nationale, 1991. 93 p. (Bibliographie et documentation / Bibliothèque de l'Assemblée nationale du Québec ; 20); ISBN: 2-551-12629-0.
Note: Approx. 500 entrées.
Édition antérieure: *Guide des sources de documentation politique.* 1985. 49 p.
Localisation: OONL.

2542 **Comeau, Robert; Lévesque, Michel**
Le Parti québécois: bibliographie rétrospective. Québec: Bibliothèque de l'Assemblée nationale, 1991. 132 p. (Bibliographie et documentation / Bibliothèque de l'Assemblée nationale du Québec ; 38); ISBN: 2-551-12602-9.
Note: 1,509 entrées.– Monographies, articles, thèses, mémoires, biographies.– Comprend des titres publiés entre 1968, date de la création du PQ, et décembre 1990.– Trois sections: (1) titres se rapportant au Parti et tous les écrits publiés par les trois chefs du parti (Lévesque, Johnson, Parizeau) ou par des députés et ministres; (2) documents produits par le PQ durant 22 années d'existence; (3) documents gouvernementaux.
Localisation: OONL.

2543 **Desjardins, Joëlle**
L'informatique dans les parlements: bibliographie sélective et annotée. Québec: Bibliothèque de l'Assemblée nationale, Division de la référence parlementaire, 1991. 21 p. (Bibliographie / Bibliothèque de l'Assemblée nationale du Québec ; no 42; ISSN: 0836-9100)
Note: 71 entrées.
Localisation: OONL.

2544 **Dufresne, Nicole; Chamberland, Diane**
Le député québécois: bibliographie sélective et annotée. Québec: Bibliothèque de l'Assemblée nationale, Division de la référence parlementaire, 1991. 37 p. (Bibliographie / Bibliothèque de l'Assemblée nationale du Québec ; no 40; ISSN: 0836-9100)
Note: Localisation: OONL.

2545 **Lévesque, Michel; Comeau, Robert**
Le Parti libéral du Québec: bibliographie rétrospective (1867-1990). Québec: Bibliothèque de l'Assemblée nationale, 1991. xii, 198 p. (Bibliographie et documentation / Bibliothèque de l'Assemblée nationale du Québec ; no 39; ISBN: 2-551-12692-4.
Note: 2,224 entrées.– Articles, thèses, ouvrages portant directement ou en partie sur le Parti libérale du Québec,

sur les députés ou des ministres de cette formation de 1867 à nos jours; documents publiés par le parti; livres et articles publié par les chefs du parti; les discours, les conférences et des rapports de ministres.
Localisation: OONL.

— 1992 —

2546 "Bibliographie sur les relations extérieures du Canada/ Canadian foreign relations: a bibliography."
Dans: *Chronique des relations extérieures du Canada*; (juillet-septembre 1989) p. 32-36; (octobre-décembre 1989) p. 41-44; (janvier-mars 1990) p. 31-35; (avril-juin 1990) p. 33-38; (juillet-septembre 1990) p. 33-38; (octobre-décembre 1990) p. 29-35; (janvier-mars 1991) p. 22-28; (avril-juin 1991) p. 24-31; (juillet-septembre 1991) p. 28-39; (octobre-décembre 1991) p. 28-36; (janvier-mars 1992) p. 27-39; (avril-juin 1992) p. 28-42; (juillet-septembre 1992) p. 26-37; (octobre-décembre 1992) p. 26-36.; ISSN: 0847-1304.
Note: Localisation: OONL.

2547 **Bickerton, James; Gagnon, Alain-G.**
Canadian politics. Ottawa: Canadian Studies Directorate, Department of the Secretary of State of Canada, 1992. 26, 28 p. (Canadian studies resource guides. Second series); ISBN: 0-662-58836-3.
Note: Includes an introductory overview of the subject, a commentary on significant works, suggestions for further reading.– Text in English and French with French text on inverted pages.– Title of additional title-page: *La politique canadienne.*
Previous edition: Jackson, Robert J. *Canadian government and politics.* 1988. [7], 20, [1], 21, [8] p. (Canadian studies resource guides); ISBN: 0-662-56208-9.
Location: OONL.

2548 **Bickerton, James; Gagnon, Alain-G.**
La politique canadienne. Ottawa: Direction des études canadiennes, Secrétariat d'État du Canada, 1992. 28, 26 p. (Guides pédagogiques des études canadiennes. Deuxième collection); ISBN: 0-662-58863-3.
Note: Comporte un exposé préliminaire, des observations sur les principaux travaux et une liste de lectures recommandées.– Texte en français et en anglais disposé tête-bêche.– Titre de la p. de t. additionnelle: *Canadian politics.*
Édition antérieure: Jackson, Robert J. *Le gouvernement du Canada et la politique canadienne.* 1988. [8], 21, [1], 20, [7] p. (Guides pédagogiques des études canadiennes); ISBN: 0-662-56208-9.
Localisation: OONL.

2549 **Comeau, Robert; Lévesque, Michel**
Partis politiques et élections provinciales au Québec: bibliographie rétrospective (1867-1991). Québec: Bibliothèque de l'Assemblée nationale, 1992. x, 391 p.; ISBN: 2-551-12997-4.
Note: Localisation: OONL.

2550 **Council of Maritime Premiers (Canada)**
Bibliography on regional cooperation/Bibliographie sur la coopération régionale. Halifax, N.S.: Council of Maritime Premiers, 1992. 5 p.; ISBN: 0-920925-08-1.
Note: 58 entries.– Focus on Atlantic provinces region of Canada.– Includes documents in English and French.– Foreword in English and French/avant-propos en français et en anglais.
Location: OONL.

2551 **Gélinas, Michel**
Guide bibliographique en administration publique (Québec). Sainte-Foy, Québec: École nationale d'administration publique, 1992. 71 p.; ISBN: 2-920112-56-2.
Note: Approx. 400 entrées.– Monographies, périodiques, thèses, publications gouvernementales, bases de données bibliographiques au service de l'administration publique, index bibliographiques.– Liste de répertoires d'adresses.
Localisation: OONL.

2552 **New Brunswick. Legislative Library**
Bill 88: bibliography/Projet de loi 88: bibliographie. Fredericton: New Brunswick Legislative Library, 1992. 4 p. (Bibliography / New Brunswick Legislative Library)
Note: Includes publications in English and French.
Location: OONL.

2553 **Québec (Province). Bibliothèque de l'Assemblée nationale**
Bibliographie du Parlement du Québec. Québec: Les Publications du Québec, 1992. 119 p.; ISBN: 2-551-14961-4.
Note: "Réalisé par la Direction générale du bicentenaire des institutions parlementaires du Québec, Assemblée nationale."
Localisation: OONL.

2554 **Saskatchewan. Legislative Library**
Annotated bibliography for the Special Committee on Rules and Procedures. [Regina]: The Library, 1992. 6 p.
Note: "Bibliography on rules, procedures, standing orders, legislative reform and other parliamentary issues".
Location: OONL.

— Ongoing/En cours —

2555 **Canadian Institute for International Peace and Security**
Peace and security bookshelf. [Ottawa]: The Institute, 1990-. vol.; ISSN: 1189-3680.
Note: Annual.– Selective annotated bibliography of current Canadian reference works, books, magazines for adults and children related to issues of peace and security.– Topics include international development, human rights, environment.
Titre en français: *La bibliothèque paix et sécurité.*
Location: OONL.

2556 **Institut canadien pour la paix et la sécurité internationales**
La bibliothèque paix et sécurité. [Ottawa]: L'Institut, 1990-. vol.; ISSN: 1189-3699.
Note: Annuel.– Bibliographie sélective et annotée, inclut les titres d'ouvrages canadien plus récents: ouvrages de consultation, périodiques, livres pour adultes et enfants concernant des domaines de la paix et de la sécurité.
English title: *Peace and security bookshelf.*
Localisation: OONL.

Business and Economics

Affaires et économie

— 1910 —

2557 **Canada. Library of Parliament**
Reference list on the subject of reciprocity in trade between Canada and the United States of America. Ottawa: Government Printing Bureau, 1910. 68 p.
Note: Chronological listings (1827-1910) of Canadian official documents, United States congressional documents, miscellaneous books, pamphlets, etc., magazine articles relating to reciprocity and commercial relations between Canada and the United States.
Supplement: *Additional references to reciprocity in trade between Canada and the United States of America*. 1911. 16 p.
Location: OOP.

2558 **United States. Library of Congress. Division of Bibliography**
List of references on reciprocity. Washington: U.S. Government Printing Office, 1910. 137 p.
Note: Approx. 1,000 entries, 300 dealing specifically with Canada and Newfoundland.– Covers 1816 to 1910.– Includes books, periodical articles, government documents.– Compiled under the direction of H.H.B. Meyer, Chief Bibliographer.
Previous editions:
Select list of books, with references to periodicals, on reciprocity with Canada. Compiled under the direction of Appleton Prentiss Clark Griffin. 1907. 14 p.
Griffin, Appleton Prentiss Clark. 1902. 38, 38 p.
Supplement: *Additional references relating to reciprocity with Canada*, compiled under the direction of H.H.B. Meyer. 1911. 44 p.
Location: OOP.

— 1929 —

2559 **Holland, William L.**
"Economic factors in the Pacific area: a review bibliography."
In: *Pacific Affairs*; Vol. 2, no. 6 (June 1929) p. 329-346.; ISSN: 0030-851X.
Note: Literature review related to economic developments and problems in five areas: China, Japan, North America, Australasia, Malaysia under topics: natural resources and population, economic development, investments and capital movements, trade and communications.
Location: AEU.

— 1934 —

2560 **Innis, Harold Adams; Bladen, M.L.**
"Bibliography of Canadian economics."
In: *Contributions to Canadian Economics*; Vol. 1 (1928) p. 86-100; vol. 2 (1929) p. 98-144; vol. 3 (1931) p. 57-132; vol. 4 (1932) p. 56-120; vol. 5 (1932) p. 77-112; vol. 6 (1933) p. 70-138; vol. 7 (1934) p. 131-186.; ISSN: 0383-6258.
Note: Topics covered include economic history, fur-trade and wildlife, fishing, agriculture, mining, forestry, manufacturing, electric power, transportation and communications, immigration and settlement, trade and commerce, banking and insurance, public finance and economic geography.– Includes a listing of additional bibliographies and reference works relating to Canadian economics.
Location: OONL.

— 1937 —

2561 **McDonald, Douglas Moore**
A select bibliography on the location of industry. Montreal: McGill University, 1937. xi, 84 p. (Social research bulletin / McGill University ; no. 2)
Note: 708 entries.– Books, bulletins, reports, articles, government publications, reference materials, unpublished materials on economic geography, industrial location, Canadian industrial development, industrial and economic surveys, statistical and bibliographical sources.
Location: OONL.

— 1940 —

2562 **Gras, N.S.B.**
"Books and articles on the economic history of the United States and Canada."
In: *Economic History Review*; Vol. 9, no. 2 (May 1939) P. 239-250; Vol. 10, no. 2 (November 1940) p. 185-192.; ISSN: 0013-0117.
Note: Location: OONL.

— 1952 —

2563 **"A bibliography of current publications on Canadian economics."**
In: *Canadian Journal of Economics and Political Science*; (1935-1952) ; ISSN: 0315-4890.
Note: Appears in each issue of this quarterly publication from vol. 1, no. 1 (February 1935) to vol. 18, no. 4 (November 1952).– Listing of books and articles in 20 categories, including economic history, fur trade, fisheries, agriculture, labour, mining, forestry, transportation, commerce, international relations, manufacturing, bibliography.
Location: AEU.

— 1953 —

2564 **Casselman, Paul Hubert**
Coopération: bibliographie des ouvrages et des articles publiés en français au Canada jusqu'à la fin de 1947. Ottawa: Centre social, Université d'Ottawa, [1953]. vii, 191 p.
Note: 2,637 entrées.– Comprend les livres et les articles sur les sources et les problèmes techniques de la coopération: administration, organisation, éducation, histoire, législation; les secteurs: agriculture, caisses populaires, consommation, mutuelles, loisirs, promotion des intérêts professionels et services d'art; coopération en relation avec les différentes formes sociétaires et communautaires: l'état, la famille, la religion, le capitalisme, le communisme, la démocratie, etc.
Localisation: OONL.

— 1955 —

2565 Hidy, Ralph W.; Hidy, Muriel E.
"List of books and articles on the economic history of the United States and Canada."
In: *Economic History Review*; Vol. 8 (2nd series), no. 2 (1955) p. 265-277.; ISSN: 0013-0117.
Note: Location: OONL.

— 1957 —

2566 Daniells, Lorna M.
Studies in enterprise: a selected bibliography of American and Canadian company histories. Boston: Baker Library, Harvard University Graduate School of Business Administration, 1957. xiv, 169 p.
Note: Includes a small section of Canadian company histories, p. 117-122.
Location: OONL.

— 1958 —

2567 Land, Brian
"Information desk: [Directory of publications issued by Canada's financial and investment community]."
In: *Canadian Business*; Vol. 31, no. 9 (September 1958) p. 102, 104+.; ISSN: 0820-9510.
Note: Location: OONL.

2568 Land, Brian
"Information desk: [Directory of publications issued periodically by chambers of commerce and boards of trade in Canada]."
In: *Canadian Business*; Vol. 31, no. 11 (November 1958) p. 82, 84+.; ISSN: 0820-9510.
Note: Location: OONL.

2569 Land, Brian
"Information desk: [list of city and trade directories published in Canada]."
In: *Canadian Business*; Vol. 31, no. 4 (April 1958) p. 32, 37-44+.; ISSN: 0820-9510.
Note: Location: OONL.

— 1959 —

2570 Rawkins, Reginald A.
Guide to publications: a guide by subject and author to the publications of the Canadian Tax Foundation to December 31st, 1958. Toronto: Canadian Tax Foundation, 1959. 42 p.
Note: Previous edition: *A subject catalogue of the Foundation's published material*. 1957. 30 l.
Location: OONL.

— 1960 —

2571 Business methods literature: a monthly classified index. Ottawa: Keith Business Library, 1959-1960. 10 no.; ISSN: 0380-4909.
Note: "American, Canadian, British books, pamphlets, articles selected from the weekly book trade lists, government catalogs, societies, universities & association releases, including the know-how articles from the leading business magazines."- Regular listing from Vol. 1, no. 1-10 (June 1959-April 1960).
Location: OONL.

2572 École des hautes études commerciales de Montréal
Contribution des professeurs de l'École des hautes études commerciales de Montréal à la vie intellectuelle du Canada ... : catalogue des principaux écrits. [Montréal]: 1960. iii, 132 f.
Note: "Livres, conférences, ouvrages en collaboration, brochures, mémoires, articles de revues, communications scientifiques, participation à des émissions à la radio et à la télévision."
Localisation: QQLA.

2573 National Committee for Research on Co-operatives
Bibliography of Canadian writings on co-operation, 1900 to 1959. Ottawa: Co-operative Union of Canada, 1960. 48 p. (Research paper / National Committee for Research on Co-operatives ; no. 1)
Note: Approx. 550 entries.– Includes books and pamphlets.– Compiled by the Saskatchewan Department of Co-operation and Co-operative Development for the National Committee for Research on Co-operatives.
Location: OONL.

— 1962 —

2574 Raynauld, André
"Recherches économiques récentes sur la province de Québec."
Dans: *Recherches sociographiques*; Vol. 3, no 1-2 (janvier-août 1962) p. 55-64.; ISSN: 0034-1282.
Note: Localisation: AEU.

— 1963 —

2575 Québec (Province). Conseil d'orientation économique
Répercussions économico-sociales de l'automatisation: bibliographie analytique. Montréal: Le Conseil, 1963. 68 f.
Note: Localisation: QQLA.

— 1964 —

2576 Canada. Department of Labour. Economics and Research Branch
A selected bibliography on the social and economic implications of electronic data processing. [Ottawa: s.n.], 1964. 75 l.
Note: Approx. 500 entries.– Lists journal articles from 1955 to 1963 on subject of office automation: planning and administration; education, selection and training; social and economic implications; worker displacement and unemployment; effects and adjustments; personnel management and industrial relations; surveys and bibliographies.
Location: OONL.

2577 Nish, James Cameron
"Bibliographie des bibliographies relatives à l'histoire économique du Canada français."
Dans: *Actualité économique*; Vol. 40, no 2 (juillet-septembre 1964) p. 456-466.; ISSN: 0001-771X.
Note: Localisation: BVAU.

2578 Nish, James Cameron
"Bibliographie sur l'histoire économique du Canada français."
Dans: *Actualité économique*; Vol. 40, no 1 (avril-juin 1964) p. 200-209.; ISSN: 0001-771X.
Note: Localisation: BVAU.

— 1965 —

2579 Atlantic Provinces Economic Council
Bibliography of research projects [Atlantic Provinces Economic Council]. Fredericton, N.B.: Atlantic Provinces Research Board, 1965. iii, 102 l.
Note: Approx. 600 entries.– Includes research reports and studies on Atlantic provinces' industries, mainly from government agencies, federal and provincial.– Some theses included.
Supplement: ... : addendum. 1967. 64 l.
Location: OONL.

— 1966 —

2580 **Allen, David E.**
Business books translated from English: 1950-1965. Reading, Mass.: Addison-Wesley Pub. Co., 1966. xiv, 414 p.
Note: Includes Canadian references.
Location: OONL.

2581 **Mallen, Bruce E.; Litvak, I.A.**
A basic bibliography on marketing in Canada. [Chicago: American Marketing Association, c1966]. x, 119 p. (AMA bibliography series / American Marketing Association ; no. 13)
Note: Approx. 1,000 entries.– Books and articles, from Canadian and American publications, dealing with all major phases of marketing, written between 1960-1966.
Location: OONL.

— 1967 —

2582 **Ontario. Department of Economics and Development. Office of the Chief Economist. Economic Analysis Branch**
Economic reports: a selected bibliography of economic reports produced by Ontario government departments. Toronto: Ontario Department of Economics and Development, Office of the Chief Economist, Economic Analysis Branch, 1967. 28 l.
Note: Location: OONL.

— 1969 —

2583 **Canada. Department of Industry, Trade and Commerce. Library**
Canadian investment abroad: selected bibliography, 1956 to 1968. Ottawa: Department of Industry, Trade and Commerce, 1969. 4, 5 l.
Note: Approx. 125 entries.– Books, documents, articles, speeches and statements by Cabinet ministers.
Supplements:
Addendum to Canadian investment abroad: selected bibliography, 1956-1968. 1970. 1 p.
Addendum to Canadian investment abroad: selected bibliography, 1956-1968. 1972. 2 p.
Location: OONL.

2584 **Canada. Department of Regional Economic Expansion. Planning Division**
Regional development and economic growth: problems, analyses, and policies: select bibliography/Expansion régionale et croissance économique: problèmes, analyses et politiques: bibliographie choisie. Ottawa: 1969. 285 p.
Note: Approx. 4,500 entries.– Books, pamphlets, journal articles, official documents and reports, unpublished reports and studies, news releases, addresses.
Location: OONL.

2585 **Canadian Construction Association. Manufacturers and Suppliers Council. Market Data Committee**
Guide to construction industry market data. Ottawa: Canadian Construction Association, 1969. 105 p.
Note: Lists publications of Dominion Bureau of Statistics, Central Mortgage and Housing, provincial bureaus of statistics.– Includes a list of trade magazines, bank newsletters.
Location: OONL.

2586 **Moore, Larry F.**
Guidelines for manpower managers: a selected annotated bibliography. Vancouver: Faculty of Commerce and Business Administration, University of British Columbia,

[1969]. 82 p. (Monograph series / Faculty of Commerce and Business Administration, University of British Columbia ; no. 3)
Note: 320 entries.– Some Canadian references.
Location: OONL.

— 1970 —

2587 **Nish, James Cameron**
Inventaire des documents relatifs à l'histoire économique du Canada français. Montréal: École des hautes études commerciales, 1967-1970. 14 fasc.
Note: Localisation: QQL.

2588 **Pillai, N.G.; Ling, Joyce**
Regional development and economic growth: Canada: a select bibliography. Monticello, Ill.: Council of Planning Librarians, 1970. 23 l. (Council of Planning Librarians Exchange bibliography ; 143)
Note: Approx. 350 entries.– Books, pamphlets, government publications, journal articles published from 1950 to 1969 on Canadian regional economics.
Location: OONL.

— 1971 —

2589 **Canadian Bankers' Association**
A bibliography of Canadian banking/Une bibliographie sur la banque au Canada. [Toronto: s.n., 1971]. 36 p.
Note: Approx. 900 entries.– Contains publications issued prior to December 31, 1970.– Includes books, pamphlets, articles.– Excludes speeches, newspaper articles, publications making only broad reference to banking.– Topics covered include history, Canadian banking practice, central banking, laws of banking, royal commissions, legislative proceedings relating to banking.– Text in English and French/texte en français et en anglais.
Location: OONL.

2590 **Canadian Tax Foundation**
Index of Canadian Tax Foundation publications to .... Toronto: Canadian Tax Foundation, 1965-1971. 2 vol.; ISSN: 0576-6214.
Note: Supplements:
Goodman, Millie. *Cumulative index of Canadian Tax Foundation publications, 1972-1977.* 1980. ix, 318 p.
Cumulative index, Canadian Tax Foundation publications, 1978-1980. 1982. ix, 204 p.
Cumulative index, Canadian Tax Foundation publications, 1981-1982. c1984. 303 p.
Robinson, Marjorie. *Cumulative index, Canadian Tax Foundation publications, 1981-1985.* c1987. vi, 624 p.
Location: OONL.

2591 **Directory of Canadian trade directories.** Rev. ed. Toronto: Ontario Department of Trade and Development, Technical Information Centre, 1971. 1 vol. (unpaged).
Note: Previous edition: 1969. 1 vol. (unpaged).
Location: OONL.

2592 **Hymer, Stephen**
"La firme plurinationale: une bibliographie sélective."
Dans: *Études internationales*; Vol. 2, no 1 (mars 1971) p. 115-129.; ISSN: 0045-2123.
Note: Localisation: OONL.

2593 **Lovett, Robert Woodberry**
American economic and business history information sources: an annotated bibliography of recent works pertaining to economic, business, agricultural, and labor

history and the history of science and technology for the United States and Canada. Detroit: Gale Research, [1971]. 323 p. (Management information guide ; 23)
Note: Approx. 2,500 entries.
Location: OONL.

— 1972 —

2594 **Arora, Ved**
Guide to sources of information on Canadian business and industry. Regina: Provincial Library, Bibliographic Services Division, [1972]. 11 p.
Note: Location: OONL.

2595 **Canada. Department of Industry, Trade and Commerce. Foreign Investment Division**
The international enterprise: a selected bibliography to May 1972. Ottawa: The Division, 1972. 29, 22, 1 l.
Note: Approx. 900 entries.– Books and documents, articles, speeches and statements by Canadian government officials.
Location: OONL.

2596 **Fortin, Donald**
Le développement organisationnel et le changement planifié: bibliographie. Montréal: Fédération des CEGEP, 1972. 31 f.
Note: Localisation: OONL.

2597 **Girouard, Laurie**
La consommation en dette: bibliographie. Montréal: Conseil de développement social du Montréal métropolitain, 1972. 2 vol.
Note: 355 entrées.
Localisation: OONL.

2598 **LeMinh, Canh**
Design management: bibliographie sélective. Montréal: École des hautes études commerciales, Bibliothèque, 1972. 52 f. (Sources d'information sur les problèmes nouveaux en relation avec les affaires)
Note: Localisation: QQLA.

2599 **Symansky, Judith**
Canadian federal Royal Commissions of interest to business libraries, 1955-1970. Montreal: Graduate School of Library Science, McGill University, 1972. iii, 35 l. (McGill University Graduate School of Library Science Occasional papers ; 3)
Note: 15 entries.
Location: OONL.

2600 **Tega, Vasile**
Franchising, 1960-1971: bibliographie internationale, sélective et annotée/Franchising, 1960-1971: an international, selective and annotated bibliography. Montréal: École des hautes études commerciales, Bibliothèque, 1972. vii, 64 p.
Note: 209 entrées.– Livres, brochures, articles de périodiques sur le franchising: aspects financiers, publicité et promotion, commerce de détail, types spécifiques d'opérations.– Texte en français et en anglais/ text in English and French.
Localisation: OONL.

2601 **Tudor, Dean**
"Basic tax library."
In: *Ontario Library Review*; Vol. 56, no. 2 (June 1972) p. 95-99.; ISSN: 0030-2996.
Note: Location: OONL.

— 1973 —

2602 **Boudreau, Gérald; Tournoux, Étienne**
Guide de documentation sur les affaires et l'économique au Québec. Montréal: École des hautes études commerciales de Montréal, Bibliothèque, 1973. 28 f.
Note: Approx. 75 entrées.
Localisation: OONL.

2603 **Canada. Department of Industry, Trade and Commerce. Foreign Investment Division**
Direct investment in Canada by non-residents: a selected bibliography to October 1973. Ottawa: Department of Industry, Trade and Commerce, Foreign Investment Division, 1973. 1 vol. (in various pagings).
Note: Approx. 700 entries.– Books and documents, articles, speeches and statements by Canadian government officials.
Supplement: ... . Addendum no. 1. 1974. [5] l.
Location: OONL.

2604 **Fortin, Donald**
Le développement des administrateurs et le perfectionnement: bibliographie. Montréal: Fédération des CEGEP, 1973. 14 f.
Note: Localisation: OONL.

2605 **Fortin, Donald**
La direction par objectifs: bibliographie. Montréal: Fédération des CEGEP, 1973. 12 f.
Note: Localisation: OONL.

2606 **Fortin, Donald**
L'évaluation des administrateurs: bibliographie. Montréal: Fédération des CEGEP, 1973. 9 f.
Note: Localisation: OONL.

2607 **Gutteridge, Paul**
Canadian economic history. Burnaby, B.C.: Simon Fraser University Library, 1973. 42 p. (Bibliography / Simon Fraser University Library ; no. 40)
Note: Location: OONL.

2608 **Lyn, D.E.; McDonald, L.**
A selective bibliography on the clothing and textile industry in Canada. Toronto: Ontario Ministry of Labour, Research Library, 1973. 5 l.
Note: Location: OONL.

2609 **Monty, Vivienne**
A bibliography of Canadian tax reform. Toronto: York University Law Library, 1973. 66 l.
Note: Briefs, submissions, studies related to Royal Commission on Taxation, 1966 (Chairman, K. Carter), periodical articles and various studies and reports on the commission report and its effect on several industries, additional material on general aspects of tax reform.
Location: OONL.

— 1974 —

2610 **Co-operative College of Canada. Publications Committee**
A guide to publications on co-operatives. Saskatoon: Co-operative College of Canada, [1974]. 56 p.
Note: Approx. 750 entries.– Books, pamphlets, journal articles, theses, papers and reports on cooperatives from 1964 to 1973.– Focus on Canadian material written in English.
Location: OONL.

2611 **Publicité-Club de Montréal**
Bibliographie du monde des communicateurs. Montréal: Publicité-Club, 1974. 24 p. (Cahiers Publicité-Club de

Montréal ; 3)
Note: Localisation: QQLA.

2612 **Saskatchewan Provincial Library. Bibliographic Services Division**
Consumer affairs: bibliography. Regina: Saskatchewan Department of Consumer Affairs, Education and Information Branch, 1974. 66 l.
Note: Approx. 350 entries.– Topics include consumer law, money management, housing, personal finance, credit.– Includes a list of teaching resource materials (films, kits, pamphlets and books).
Location: OONL.

— 1975 —

2613 **Alberta. Alberta Consumer and Corporate Affairs. Research Section**
A bibliography on consumer credit use and regulation. Edmonton: Alberta Consumer and Corporate Affairs. Research Section, 1975. ii, 27 l.
Note: Location: OONL.

2614 **British Columbia. Department of Consumer Services**
Consumer bibliography. Victoria: Department of Consumer Services, 1975. [27] l.
Note: Location: OONL.

2615 **Canada Institute for Scientific and Technical Information**
The Metric system: a bibliography of instructional guides, manuals and conversion tables/Le système métrique: liste bibliographique de guides, de manuels et de tables de conversion. Ottawa: CISTI, 1975. 8 l.
Note: Location: OON.

2616 **Giesbrecht, Irene**
The consumer crunch, or: meeting the challenge of rising prices. [Saskatoon]: Saskatoon Public Library, 1975. 21 p.
Note: Approx. 200 entries.– Lists books and pamphlets on consumerism and related topics: advertising, consumer protection, credit, wills, personal finance, housing.
Location: OONL.

2617 **Matthews, Catherine J.; Armstrong, Douglas**
The food processing industry in Canada: a selected bibliography, with particular emphasis on Ontario food processing. [Toronto]: Ontario Ministry of Labour, Research Library, 1975. 23 l.
Note: Approx. 200 entries.
Location: OONL.

— 1976 —

2618 **Bruneau, André**
Répertoire des sources d'information économique: Canada et États-Unis. Québec: Service de l'éducation économique, Direction des communications, Ministère de l'industrie et du commerce, 1976. 83 p.; ISBN: 0-775-42560-5.
Note: Localisation: OOP.

2619 **Swanick, Eric L.**
Agribusiness: an introductory bibliography. Monticello, Ill.: Council of Planning Librarians, 1976. 11 p. (Council of Planning Librarians Exchange bibliography ; 1019)
Note: Approx. 150 entries.– Research bulletins, books, journal and magazine articles, theses from Canada and the United States.
Location: OOCI.

2620 **Toronto Nutrition Committee**
Food: economics and politics: an annotated bibliography. [Toronto]: The Committee, 1976. 13 p.
Note: Approx. 30 entries.– Includes books, journal and magazine articles, government publications.– Compiled for professional workers interested in the interaction of politics/economics/food/consumers.
Location: OONL.

2621 **Velikov, Velitchko**
Provincial and federal land use and land ownership policies and their potential impact on political, economic and social conditions in Canada. Monticello, Ill.: Council of Planning Librarians, 1976. 22 p. (Council of Planning Librarians Exchange bibliography ; 993)
Note: Approx. 250 entries.
Location: OONL.

— 1977 —

2622 **Barker, Gordon; Beaudry, Richard**
Maintenir, rompre ou ... faire l'unité canadienne? Une bibliographie sur les aspects économiques de la Confédération. Ottawa: Conseil économique du Canada, 1977. iii, 130 p. (Conseil économique du Canada Document ; no 99); ISBN: 0-662-01291-7.
Note: Approx. 800 entrées.– Trois parties: "Historique": éléments sociaux, économiques et politiques; "L'État actuel de l'union" (vision globale, le cas particulier du Québec, le cas des provinces de l'Ouest); "Vers un nouveau fédéralisme" (diverses options, une politique économique régionaliste).– Abstract in English.
Localisation: OONL.

2623 **Bruneau, André; Germain, Geneviève**
Répertoire des sources d'information économique: Québec. 2e éd., rev. et mise à jour. Québec: Service de promotion de l'économie, Direction générale des services aux entreprises, Ministère de l'industrie et du commerce, 1977. 150 p.; ISBN: 0-775-42737-3.
Note: Édition antérieure: [Québec: Éditeur officiel du Québec], 1975. 101 p.; ISBN: 0-775-42202-0.
Localisation: QQLA.

2624 **Bruneau, Pierre; Larrivée, Jean**
Bibliographie: les inégalités de développement régional, au Québec et au Canada. Rimouski: Groupe de recherche interdisciplinaire en développement de l'est du Québec, Université du Québec à Rimouski, c1977. xvi, 152 p. (Cahiers du GRIDEQ / Groupe de recherche interdisciplinaire en développement de l'est du Québec ; no 1)
Note: 979 entrées.– Quatre thèmes: définition des concepts et l'identification des niveaux de perception des inégalités régionales; problèmes méthodologiques; manifestations concrètes des disparités régionales; origines et les causes des inégalités de développement.
Localisation: OONL.

2625 **C.D. Howe Research Institute**
Bibliography and index of C.D. Howe Research Institute publications, 1958-1976. [Montreal, Quebec: C.D. Howe Research Institute], 1977. viii, 75 p.; ISBN: 0-88806-027-0.
Note: 165 entries.– Includes all publications of C.D. Howe Research Institute, its predecessor, the Private Planning Association of Canada, and committees sponsored by these organizations on a wide range of economic policy issues and problems, from free trade to Bank of Canada and monetary policy to wage-price

controls.
Location: OOP.
Supplement: *Bibliography and index of publications: January 1, 1977-December 31, 1980.* 1981. xiii, 42 p.; ISBN: 0-88806-058-0. (75 entries.).
Location: OONL.

2626 **Cooney, Jane; Gervino, Joan; Hendsey, Susanne**
"United States and Canadian business and banking information sources."
In: *Law Library Journal*; Vol. 70, no. 4 (November 1977) p. 561-569.; ISSN: 0023-9283.
Note: Listing of bibliographies, dictionaries, indexes, biographies, directories, bank directories, corporate information, statistics (industry, bank and financial) and periodicals.
Location: AEU.

2627 **Demers, Henri**
Les investissements étrangers au Canada et au Québec: essai de bibliographie. Québec: Ministère de l'industrie et du commerce, Direction générale de l'administration, Centre de documentation, 1977. 83 p.
Note: 920 entrées.– Comprend des références à des livres, des thèses, des rapports de commissions d'enquête, des revues et des publications gouvernementales.
Localisation: OONL.

2628 **Gaspari, Carol; Kernaghan, Helgi**
Fund raising: the Canadian view, 1960-1976: a selective bibliography. [S.l.: s.n.], c1977. 45 p.
Note: Approx. 350 entries.– Journal articles, books, government documents, annual reports, magazines, films relating to fund-raising methods, campaign funds, charities, corporate contributions, foundations, gifts, grants and general philanthropy in Canada.
Location: OONL.

2629 **Passaris, Constantine E.A.**
Canadian regional monetary policy: introduction and extensive bibliography. Monticello, Ill.: Council of Planning Librarians, 1977. 20 p. (Council of Planning Librarians Exchange bibliography ; 1402)
Note: Approx. 200 entries.– Books, pamphlets, journal and magazine articles, theses, newsletters and speeches on regional economics, and particularly, monetary policy.
Location: OONL.

2630 **Sevigny, David C.**
The ethical pharmaceutical industry and some of its economic effects: an annotated bibliography. Toronto: Addiction Research Foundation of Ontario, c1977. xiv, 521 p. (Bibliographic series / Addiction Research Foundation of Ontario ; no. 13; ISSN: 0065-1885)
Note: 249 annotated entries, 527 listed entries.– Books, journal articles, research studies, government publications, prescription data studies, case studies, articles in popular magazines published in the English language between 1938 and 1976.– Topics include drug safety and efficacy, structure of the pharmaceutical industry, interaction with regulatory agencies, public policy issues.– Studies concerning proprietary (patent) drugs and the illicit drug trade are excluded.– Includes some Canadian references.– Provides an index by countries and regions.
Location: OONL.

2631 **Walsh, Sandra A.**
Crown corporations in Canada: bibliography of material in the Library of the Ontario Ministry of Treasury, Economics and Intergovernmental Affairs. Monticello, Ill.: Council of Planning Librarians, 1977. 2 l. (Council of Planning Librarians Exchange bibliography ; 1321)
Note: Location: OHM.

— 1978 —

2632 **Alberta. Alberta Consumer and Corporate Affairs. Research Section**
Annotated bibliography of research papers [Alberta Consumer and Corporate Affairs, Research Section]. [Edmonton]: Alberta Consumer and Corporate Affairs, Management Secretariat, Research Section, 1978. 8, 6, 1 l.
Note: Location: OONL.

2633 **Bonville, Jean de**
Communications: liste d'ouvrages disponibles à la Bibliothèque de l'Université Laval, 1974-1978. Québec: Bibliothèque de l'Université Laval, 1978. 417 p.
Note: 2,262 entrées.– Cinq listes chronologiques, chacune complétée d'un index des sujets et des auteurs.– Sujets couverts: cinéma, communications, économie de mass media, politique, publicité, radio, télévision, histoire de la presse.
Localisation: OONL.

2634 **Craven, Paul; Forrest, Anne; Traves, Tom**
Canadian company histories: a checklist. [Downsview, Ont.: Social Science Division, York University], 1978. 5, [75] l.
Note: 599 entries.– Pamphlets, journal articles, public relations volumes, scholarly studies: histories and related materials of companies operating in Canada.– All documents are given locations.
Location: OONL.

2635 **Crusz, Rienzi**
Business, a guide to select reference sources. Waterloo, Ont.: University of Waterloo Library, 1978. 50 p. (University of Waterloo Library bibliography ; no. 1; ISSN: 0829-948X); ISBN: 0-920834-00-0.
Note: Approx. 300 entries.– Listing of Canadian and American business and accounting reference works, including guides, bibliographies, directories, biographical sources, financial sources, dissertations, business journals.
Location: OONL.

2636 **Dick, Trevor J.O.**
Economic history of Canada: a guide to information sources. Detroit: Gale Research, c1978. xiii, 174 p. (Economics information guide series ; vol. 9); ISBN: 0-8103-1292-1.
Note: Approx. 1,300 entries.– Interpretive sources, bibliographic sources, texts and general works: sectors and industries, economic organization, technology, productivity change and welfare, resources, industrial organization, labour organization, role of government.
Location: OONL.

2637 **Huffman, James; Huffman, Sybil**
Construction trades occupations & Transport equipment operating occupations/Travailleurs du bâtiment [&] Personnel d'exploitation des transports. Toronto: Guidance Centre, Faculty of Education, University of Toronto, c1978. 40 p. (Career information: a bibliography of publications about careers in Canada ; book 3); ISBN:

0-7713-0052-2.
Note: Approx. 300 entries.– Includes books, booklets, pamphlets, government publications, information sheets.
Location: OONL.

2638 **Swanick, Eric L.**
The Canadian Anti-inflation Board: an introductory bibliography. Monticello, Ill.. Vance Bibliographies, 1978. 6 p. (Public administration series: Bibliography ; P-105; ISSN: 0193-970X)
Note: Approx. 85 entries.
Location: OONL.

2639 **Swanick, Eric L.**
The Canadian Royal Commission on Corporate Concentration. Monticello, Ill.: Vance Bibliographies, 1978. 6 p. (Public administration series: Bibliography ; P-102; ISSN: 0193-970X)
Note: Approx. 60 entries.– Report, background papers, case studies, periodical articles.
Location: OONL.

2640 **Swanick, Eric L.**
Registered retirement savings plans (RRSP'S) in Canada: an introductory selective bibliography. Monticello, Ill.: Vance Bibliographies, 1978. 4 p. (Public administration series: Bibliography ; P-83; ISSN: 0193-970X)
Note: Approx. 55 entries.
Location: OONL.

2641 **Venkateswarlu, Tadiboyina**
A bibliographic survey of microeconomics reading materials in North American universities: a comparative study between Canada and the United States of America. Windson, Ont.: Department of Economics, University of Windsor, 1978. 48 p. (Discussion paper series / Department of Economics, University of Windsor ; no. 51)
Note: 651 entries.
Location: OONL.

— 1979 —

2642 **Alain, Jean-Marc**
Le budget à base zéro-BBZ: une bibliographie. Sainte-Foy, Québec: Centre de documentation, ENAP, 1979. ii f, 68 p.
Note: Localisation: OONL.

2643 **Alain, Jean-Marc**
La rationalisation des choix budgétaires: une bibliographie. [Sainte-Foy, Québec]: Centre de documentation, ENAP, 1979. iv, 120 p.
Note: 820 entrées.– Comprend les sources documentaires sur la technique du P.P.B.S. (Planning, Programming, Budgeting System).
Édition antérieure: *Rationalisation des choix budgétaires: planning, programming, budgeting systems: une bibliographie.* 1973. iii, 84 p.
Localisation: OONL.

2644 **Anderson, Dennis; Cullen, Carman**
Energy research from a consumer perspective: an annotated bibliography. Ottawa: Consumer Research and Evaluation Branch, Consumer and Corporate Affairs Canada, 1979. 191 p.; ISBN: 0-662-10514-1.
Note: Approx. 300 entries.– Includes empirical studies and descriptive reports pertaining to consumers' energy-related attitudes and behaviours.
Titre en français: *Perspective du consommateur sur la recherche en matière d'énergie: une bibliographie annotée.*
Location: OONL.

2645 **Anderson, Dennis; Cullen, Carman**
Perspective du consommateur sur la recherche en matière d'énergie: une bibliographie annotée. Ottawa: Direction de l'évaluation et de la recherche en consommation, Consommation et corporations Canada, 1979. 191 p.; ISBN: 0-662-90307-2.
Note: Approx. 300 entrées.– Études empiriques et rapports descriptifs sur les attitudes et comportements des consommateurs en matière d'énergie.
English title: *Energy research from a consumer perspective: an annotated bibliography.*
Localisation: OONL.

2646 **Directory of faculty publications, 1975-1979.** Toronto: Faculty of Management Studies, University of Toronto, [1979]. 42 p.
Note: Approx. 500 entries.– Textbooks, edited publications, articles, government reports, contributions to conference proceedings, book reviews, working papers, cases.
Location: OONL.

2647 **Kallio, Edwin; Dickerhoof, Edward**
Business data and market information sourcebook for the forest products industry. Madison, Wis.: Forest Products Research Society, 1979. viii, 215 p.
Note: Listing of statistical sources, directories, forest products reports and newsletters, price reports, periodicals, bibliographies, databases.– Includes some Canadian references.
Location: OHM.

2648 **Kerbrat, Hervé**
Bibliographie sélective pour l'exportation. Montréal: École des hautes études commerciales, 1979. 36 p. (Cahiers du Centre d'études en administration internationale ; no 79-01; ISSN: 0709-986X)
Note: 69 entrées.– Annuaires, index, périodiques.
Localisation: OONL.

2649 **Swanick, Eric L.**
Canadian tax credit systems: an introductory bibliography. Monticello, Ill.: Vance Bibliographies, 1979. 5 p. (Public administration series: Bibliography ; P-229; ISSN: 0193-970X)
Note: Approx. 60 entries.
Location: OONL.

2650 **Swanick, Eric L.**
Reform of the Canadian banking act: a selected bibliography. Monticello, Ill.: Vance Bibliographies, 1979. 5 p. (Public administration series: Bibliography ; P-228; ISSN: 0193-970X)
Note: Approx. 60 entries.
Location: OONL.

2651 **Swanick, Eric L.**
Wage-price control in Canada: an introductory bibliography. Monticello, Ill.: Vance Bibliographies, 1979. 17 p. (Public administration series: Bibliography ; P-213; ISSN: 0193-970X)
Note: Approx. 230 entries.– Journal articles, reports and studies, conference proceedings.
Location: OONL.

2652 **Université de Sherbrooke. Bibliothèque générale**
Coopératives et bibliothèque: guide d'utilisation des collections de la bibliothèque à l'intention des usagers oeuvrant dans le domaine des coopératives. [S.l.: s.n.], 1979. 29, 24 f.

Note: Approx. 400 entrées.– Livres, articles, thèses, publications gouvernementales dans le domaine des coopératives.

Localisation: OONL.

2653 **Van Leusden, Karen; St-Jean, Charles; Dubuc, Marcel**
Canadian customs and excise: an annotated bibliography/Douanes et accise du Canada: une bibliographie annotée. Ottawa: Revenue Canada, Customs and Excise, 1979. xii, 642 p.; ISBN: 0-662-50365-1.
Note: 2,054 entries.– Text in English and French/texte en français et en anglais.
Location: OONL.

2654 **Walsh, Sandra A.**
The study of the future: a bibliography of material in the Library of the Ontario Ministry of Treasury, Economics and Intergovernmental Affairs. Monticello, Ill.: Vance Bibliographies, 1979. 8 p. (Public administration series: Bibliography ; P-306; ISSN: 0193-970X)
Note: Location: OONL.

2655 **Zins, Michael, et al.**
Consumer decision making: an annotated bibliography. [Ottawa]: Consumer Research and Evaluation Branch, Consumer and Corporate Affairs Canada, 1979. 398 p.
Note: Contains six sections: consumer information processing, problem recognition, pre-purchase search, buying situations, consumer purchasing processes, and consumer choice and satisfaction.
Location: OONL.

— 1980 —

2656 **Beauregard, Christian**
An annotated bibliography of Canadian public finance (revenue side) 1946-1979: a first round. Montréal: Département de science économique et Centre de recherche en développement économique, Université de Montréal, [1980]. 222, [7] p. (Cahier / Département de science économique et Centre de recherche en développement économique, Université de Montréal ; 8004)
Note: Approx. 600 entries.– Includes journal articles on Canadian fiscal policies, system of taxation, Carter (royal commission) report and studies, corporate income tax, taxation of cooperative and financial intermediaries, death/estate/gift taxation, federal-provincial tax relations, provincial-municipal tax relations, housing policies, international aspects of Canadian taxation, personal income tax, property taxation, tax expenditure analysis.
Supplement: *An annotated bibliography of Canadian public finance (revenue side) 1946-1979: extension and update.* [1980]. 43 p.
Location: OONL.

2657 **Bibliography on metric conversion/Bibliographie de la conversion au système métrique.** Ottawa: Metric Commission Canada, 1980. 130 p.
Note: Lists Metric Commission publications, other government and privately produced books and documents, legislation, standards, supplementary metric practice guides, bulletins/newspapers/periodicals on metric conversion, films, television pieces (MCC ads and educational videos).– Text in English and French/texte en français et en anglais.
Previous editions:
1977. ii, 49 p.
1975. [32] l.

Location: OONL.

2658 **Canada. Library of Parliament. Information and Reference Branch**
Canada-U.S. automotive pact: select bibliography/ Accord Canada-États-Unis sur les produits de l'industrie automobile: bibliographie sélective. Ottawa: Library of Parliament, Information and Reference Branch, 1980. 12 l.
Note: Location: OOP.

2659 **Deschênes, Gaston**
Le mouvement coopératif québécois: guide bibliographique. [Montréal]: Éditions du jour, [c1980]. xxiii, 291 p.; ISBN: 2-89044-029-X.
Note: 1,551 entrées.– Ouvrages et articles généraux, manuels, thèses, bibliographies, archives et périodiques du mouvement coopératif québécois: histoire, assurances et mutualité, épargne et crédit, agriculture, consommation, pêche, habitation, forêt, electrification; principes et philosophie; gestion/administration.
Localisation: OONL.

2660 **Duvall, D.**
Real estate development and market analysis: a selected bibliography/Aménagement des biens immobiliers et analyse du marché immobilier: bibliographie choisie. [Ottawa: Public Relations and Information Services], Public Works Canada, [1980]. xiv, 143 p.; ISBN: 0-660-50582-7.
Note: Approx. 1,100 entries.– Articles and books published from 1975 to 1980 dealing with methodologies, market information, current real estate issues, urban development and land use planning.– Separate section on bibliographies numbers 118 citations.– Text in English and French/texte en français et en anglais.
Location: OONL.

2661 **Lafrenière, Gilles R.**
Industrial security – Canada: bibliography. Ottawa: R.C.M.P. HQ Library, 1980. ii, 43 p.
Note: Approx. 300 entries.– Journal articles from 1973 to 1980 on topics related to industrial security: bank protection, bombs, retail trade security measures, computer data security, crime prevention, fraud, private police, shoplifting, trade secrets, and terrorism.
Location: OONL.

2662 **Ontario. Royal Commission on Electric Power Planning**
Report of the Royal Commission on Electric Power Planning. Toronto: The Commission, 1980. 9 vol.; ISBN: 0-7743-4672-8 (set).
Note: Volume 9: *Bibliography to the Report.* xi, 90 p.; ISBN: 0-7743-4671-X.– Books, reports, articles, and speeches accumulated by the Commission on energy-related topics: economics, energy conservation and utilization, load forecasting and management, renewable energy resources, waste management, social issues.
Location: OONL.

2663 **Roberts, Debra**
Selected bibliography on East-West commercial relations. Ottawa: East-West Project, Institute of Soviet and East European Studies, Carleton University, c1980. 134 p.; ISBN: 0-7709-0095-X.
Note: 911 entries.– Covers material published between August 1973 and September 1979.– Listing of general reference works, general economic and political aspects in the area of East-West trade, functional and organizational aspects (technology transfer, industrial coopera-

tion, joint ventures, etc.).– Includes Canadian references.
Location: OONL.

2664 **Semkow, Brian**
Pension reform in Canada: a bibliography with selected annotations. Kingston, Ont.: Industrial Relations Centre, Queen's University, 1980. 21 p. (Mimeographed bibliography series / Industrial Relations Centre, Queen's University ; no. 15)
Note: Approx. 225 entries.– Articles, books, monographs, newspaper articles.
Location: OONL.

2665 **Swanick, Eric L.**
Canadian small business financing: an introductory bibliography. Monticello, Ill.: Vance Bibliographies, 1980. 8 p. (Public administration series: Bibliography ; P-444; ISSN: 0193-970X)
Note: Approx. 110 entries.
Location: OONL.

2666 **Swanick, Eric L.**
Canadian trade missions: an introductory bibliography. Monticello, Ill.: Vance Bibliographies, 1980. 4 p. (Public administration series: Bibliography ; P-446; ISSN: 0193-970X)
Note: Approx. 50 entries.
Location: OONL.

2667 **Swanick, Eric L.**
Retirement, mandatory retirement and pensions in Canada: an introductory bibliography. Monticello, Ill.: Vance Bibliographies, 1980. 6 p. (Public administration series: Bibliography ; P-536; ISSN: 0193-970X)
Note: Location: OWTU.

— 1981 —

2668 **Amesse, Fernand**
Bibliographie sélective sur les transferts internationaux de technologie. Montréal: École des hautes études commerciales, 1981. 43 f. (Cahiers du Centre d'études en administration internationale ; no 81-08; ISSN: 0709-986X)
Note: 228 entrées.– Articles, livres, travaux et rapports portant sur les transferts internationaux de technologie: diffusion de l'innovation, évaluation et prévision technologique, technologie appropriée, coopération industrielle, études de productivité comparée, modèles du commerce international.
Localisation: OONL.

2669 **Clarke, Thomas E.**
R & D management bibliography, 1981. 3rd ed. Vancouver, B.C.: Stargate Consultants, c1981. 314 p.; ISBN: 0-9690-711-0-8.
Note: Approx. 3,000 entries.– Articles, conference papers, reports and books concerned with management of technological innovation, research and development in industrial and government laboratories: motivation, measurement, evaluation, planning and scheduling, patents and licencing.
Previous editions:
R & D management bibliography, 1976. 1977. 151 p.
R & D management bibliography. 1975. 138 p.
Location: OONL.

2670 **Gallina, Paul**
Electronic funds transfer: a bibliography. Ottawa: Socioscope, 1981. 94 p.; ISBN: 0-919539-02-5.
Note: 699 entries.– Covers 1969-1980.– Topics include marketing, consumer issues, data security and fraud,

legal, regulatory and public policy issues.
Location: OONL.

2671 **Ontario Economic Council**
Annotated list of Ontario Economic Council research publications, 1974-1980. Toronto: The Council, 1981. [10], 57 p.; ISBN: 0-7743-6681-8.
Note: Listing of Ontario Economic Council documents, arranged by year and series title: "Discussion papers," "Occasional papers," "Research studies," "Issues and alternatives."- Updated annually in appendix to OEC annual report.
Location: OONL.

2672 **Van-The, Nhut**
L'aspect humain du processus budgétaire: une revue de la littérature. Montréal: École des hautes études commerciales, 1981. 24 f. (Rapport de recherche / École des hautes études commerciales ; no 81-31; ISSN: 0709-986X)
Note: Localisation: OONL.

2673 **Walsh, Sandra A.**
Interest rates, the recent Canadian experience: a selected bibliography. Monticello, Ill.: Vance Bibliographies, 1981. 6 p. (Public administration series: Bibliography ; P-799; ISSN: 0193-970X)
Note: Approx. 60 entries.– Technical reports, discussion papers, theses, periodical articles.
Location: OONL.

— 1982 —

2674 **Arrowsmith, David**
Productivity trends: bibliography with selected annotations. Kingston, Ont.: Industrial Relations Centre, Queen's University, 1982. 16 p. (Mimeographed bibliography series / Industrial Relations Centre, Queen's University ; no. 21)
Note: Approx. 135 entries.
Location: OONL.

2675 **Barnabé, Clermont**
Personnel management: a bibliography/Gestion du personnel: une bibliographie. [LaSalle, Québec]: Gesper, Service des éditions, 1982. 194 p.; ISBN: 2-9800030-0-X.
Note: 2,924 entries.– Books, articles, theses, papers, reports: manpower planning, personnel policies, job analysis, recruitment, selection, promotion, evaluation, training and development, labour relations, organizational development.– Text in English and French/texte en français et en anglais.
Supplement: ... . *Supplement/... . Supplément.* 1984. 69 p.; ISBN: 2-9800030-1-3.
Location: OONL.

2676 **Bélanger, Yves; Fournier, Pierre; Painchaud, Claude**
Guide bibliographique pour l'étude du capital québécois. [Montréal]: Département de science politique, Université du Québec à Montréal, 1982. 72 f. (Notes de recherche / Département de science politique, Université du Québec à Montréal ; no 24)
Note: Approx. 650 entrées.– Ouvrages bibliographiques, répertoires et guides, ouvrages généraux, contextes américain et canadien, économie politique québécoise, les coopératives, l'État et l'économie du Québec.
Localisation: OONL.

2677 **Bouchard, Marie**
Une revue de la littérature sur les relations avec les membres dans les coopératives (et les fédérations de

coopératives). Montréal: École des hautes études commerciales, Centre de gestion des coopératives, 1982. 52 f.

Note: Localisation: OONL.

2678 **Canadian Network on the Informal Economy**
A bibliography on material pertinent to the informal economy/Bibliographie des sources de documentation sur l'économie informelle. Ottawa: Vanier Institute of the Family, 1982. 54, 2 p.

Note: Approx. 300 entries.– Text in English and French/texte en français et en anglais.

Location: OONL.

2679 **Davis, P.F.; Stevenson, J.H.; Suttie, I.P.**
Office automation: its impact on people, processes and procedures: selected resources. London, (Ont.): Department of Secretarial and Administrative Studies, Social Science Centre, University of Western Ontario, 1982. ix, [60] p.; ISBN: 0-7714-0383-6.

Note: 144 entries.– Covers 1978 to 1982.– Books, research reports, dissertations, literature reviews.– Topics include office information technology, business education trends, planning for office automation, impact of automation on the organization.– Emphasis on bibliographic works.– Includes Canadian references.

Location: OONL.

2680 **Directory of industry data sources, the United States of America and Canada.** Cambridge, Mass.: Ballinger, c1982. 3 vol.; ISBN: 0-88410-883-X (set).

Note: 22,056 entries.– General reference sources; specific industry sources.– Focus on marketing, financial and statistical data on specific industries.

Location: OONL.

2681 **Godavari, Sigrun Norma**
Electronic funds transfer: an annotated bibliography. [Ottawa: Canadian Home Economics Association], 1982. 78 p.

Note: 299 entries.– Covers 1979-April 1982.– Topics include aspects of banking law, privacy issue relating to EFTS, fraud, social aspects in Canada, Europe, United States.– Includes newspaper citations.

Location: OONL.

2682 **Lamy, Nicole**
Bibliographie sur les maisons de commerce. Montréal: École des hautes études commerciales, 1982. 21 f. (Cahiers du Centre d'études en administration internationale ; no 82-10; ISSN: 0709-986X)

Note: 169 entrées.– Articles, livres publiés après 1975 sur les maisons de commerce, particulièrement au Canada, aux États-Unis et au Japon.– Index des noms de lieux.

Localisation: OONL.

2683 **Miletich, John J.**
Hazardous substances in Canada: a selected, annotated bibliography. Chicago, Ill.: Council of Planning Librarians, 1982. v, 21 p. (CPL bibliography / Council of Planning Librarians ; no. 91); ISBN: 0-86602-091-8.

Note: 112 periodical articles and government publications published in English.– Covers August 1975 to August 1982.– Categories include transportation, accident prevention, storage, treatment, disposal, health and safety, legislation.

Location: OONL.

2684 **Miletich, John J.**
Noise pollution in Canada: a selected bibliography, 1971-1981. Chicago, Ill.: Council of Planning Librarians, 1982. v, 14 p. (CPL bibliography / Council of Planning Librarians ; no. 77); ISBN: 0-86602-077-2.

Note: 78 entries.– Annotated listing of journal articles, government publications, technical reports, conference proceedings: general information, industry, transportation, architecture, legislation.

Location: OONL.

2685 **Rahkra, A.S.**
Sources of economic and cost statistics for Canadian construction: a compilation. Ottawa: National Research Council Canada, Division of Building Research, 1982. iv, 37 p. (Bibliography / National Research Council Canada, Division of Building Research ; no. 44; ISSN: 0085-3828)

Note: Location: OONL.

2686 **Sutton, Michael J.D.**
Human impacts of office automation: a review of published information. Ottawa: Department of Systems and Computer Engineering, Carleton University, 1982. 33, 15, [28] p.

Note: Location: OOCC.

2687 **Walsh, Sandra A.**
Canadian corporate and industry information. Monticello, Ill.: Vance Bibliographies, 1982. 13 p. (Public administration series: Bibliography ; P-950; ISSN: 0193-970X)

Note: Directories, Financial Post surveys, Statistics Canada publications.

Location: OONL.

2688 **Walsh, Sandra A.**
A selected bibliography on wage and price controls in Canada. Monticello, Ill.: Vance Bibliographies, 1982. 7 p. (Public administration series: Bibliography ; P-1100; ISSN: 0193-970X); ISBN: 0-88066-310-3.

Note: Approx. 65 entries.

Location: OONL.

2689 **Yelle, André**
Income tax references/Références à la loi de l'impôt sur le revenu. Toronto: Richard De Boo, c1982. 2 vol. (looseleaf); ISBN: 0-88820-121-4.

Note: Lists publications on income taxation since major income tax reform of 1972, selected on basis of relevance and accessibility.– Includes periodical articles, government publications and court cases.– Text in English and French/texte en français et en anglais.

Previous editions:

1981. xxvii, 647 p.; ISBN: 0-88820-094-3.

1980. xxiv, 493 p.; ISBN: 0-88820-082-X.

Location: OONL.

— 1983 —

2690 **Canada. Public Service Staff Relations Board. Library**
Executive compensation: a selective bibliography/Rémunération des cadres: une bibliographie sélective. Ottawa: Library, Public Service Staff Relations Board, 1983. 30 p.

Note: Approx. 175 entries.– Includes documents from Canada, United States, Great Britain, Australia, western Europe, with major emphasis on Canadian works.– Coverage includes English and French materials, emphasizing current publications and articles.– Text in English and French/texte en français et en anglais.

Location: OONL.

2691 **Canadian Housing Information Centre**
Bibliography on real estate in Canada/Bibliographie sur la propriété immobilière au Canada. Ottawa: The Centre, 1983. 13 p.
Note: Approx. 125 entries.
Location: OONL.

2692 **Goldberg, Michael A.**
Bibliography re mobility of capital among Pacific Rim countries. Vancouver: Institute of Asian Research, University of British Columbia, 1983. 64 p. (Working paper / Institute of Asian Research, University of British Columbia ; no. 5)
Note: Approx. 350 entries.– Covers 1960 to 1983.– Includes books, newspaper articles, periodical articles, government publications, unpublished material (reports, theses).
Location: OONL.

2693 **Ontario. Ministry of Treasury and Economics**
Declining industries: profiles and prospects: a selected bibliography, 1977-1983. Toronto: Ontario Ministry of Treasury and Economics, 1983. 13 p.
Note: Approx. 130 entries.– Books and reports, periodical articles on various industries, conditions and prospects.
Location: OONL.

2694 **Perron, Bruno; Bonin, Bernard**
Les mandats mondiaux de production: une revue de littérature. Montréal: École des hautes études commerciales, 1983. 42, [6] f. (Cahiers du Centre d'études en administration internationale ; no 83-04; ISSN: 0709-986X)
Note: Revue de la littérature sur les mandats mondiaux de production: la stratégie industrielle et les mandats mondiaux, la rôle de la firme transnationale, le rôle du gouvernement.
Localisation: OONL.

2695 **Vaillancourt, François; Lacroix, Robert**
Revenus et langue au Québec: une revue des écrits. [Montréal]: Service des communications du Conseil de langue française, 1983. 32, 2 p. (Conseil de la langue française Notes et documents ; 27); ISBN: 2-550-02852-X.
Note: Études faites depuis 1970 et portant sur l'effet net des attributs linguistiques sur le revenu des Québécois.
Localisation: OONL.

— 1984 —

2696 **Hynes, Susan; Krueger, Donald R.**
Accountability and control of crown corporations: a selected bibliography. Rev. and expanded ed. [Toronto]: Ontario Legislative Library, Research and Information Services, 1984. 29 l.
Note: Books, journal articles, government reports and studies.– Covers Canada (federal), Ontario, Quebec, British Columbia, Saskatchewan, international.
Previous editions:
1982. 13 l.
[1980]. 7 l.
Location: OONL.

2697 **Metropolitan Toronto Library. Reference Division. Business Department**
Researching older Canadian companies at the Metropolitan Toronto Library. Toronto: The Department, 1984. 18 p.: ill. (Bibliographies on business topics ; no. 8)
Note: Approx. 60 entries.– Books, articles, pamphlets, annual reports: history of individual companies, directories, business histories, defunct companies.
Location: OONL.

2698 **Nova Scotia. Department of Agriculture and Marketing. Marketing and Economics Branch. Co-operatives Section**
Co-operative bibliography. Truro, N.S.: Co-operatives Section, [1984]. 42 p.
Note: Location: NSHL.

2699 **Ontario. Ministry of Treasury and Economics. Library Services**
Canada-United States trade relations: issues and options. Monticello, Ill.: Vance Bibliographies, 1984. 9 p. (Public administration series: Bibliography ; P-1367; ISSN: 0193-970X); ISBN: 0-88066-827-X.
Note: Supplement: *Canada-United States trade relations: the free trade debate, a selected bibliography*. 1986. 14 p. (Public administration series: Bibliography ; P-1873; ISSN: 0193-970X); ISBN: 0-89028-763-5.
Location: OOB.

2700 **Ontario. Ministry of Treasury and Economics. Library Services**
Financial services industry: emerging issues and trends, 1973-1984. Toronto: Ontario Ministry of Treasury and Economics, Library Services, 1984. [22] p. (T & E bibliographies / Ontario Ministry of Treasury and Economics, Library Services ; no. 9)
Note: Approx. 280 entries.– Includes books, reports, periodical articles, bibliographies, business and financial newsletters.
Location: OONL.

2701 **Ontario. Ministry of Treasury and Economics. Library Services**
Pensions in the Canadian economy: a selected bibliography, 1973-1984. Toronto: Ontario Ministry of Treasury and Economics, Library Services, 1984. 19 p.
Note: Location: OONL.

2702 **Ontario. Ministry of Treasury and Economics. Library Services**
Trade statistics with emphasis on Canada: a selected annotated bibliography. Monticello, Ill.: Vance Bibliographies, 1984. 12 p. (Public administration series: Bibliography ; P-1393; ISSN: 0193-970X); ISBN: 0-88066-863-6.
Note: Approx. 60 entries.
Location: OOF.

2703 **Ritchie, J.R. Brent; Mokkelbost, Per B.; Furlong, Carla B.**
Banking research from a Canadian perspective: an annotated bibliography. [Montreal]: Institute of Canadian Bankers, 1984. viii, 519 p.
Note: Approx. 700 entries.– Books, articles in professional and academic journals and periodicals with priority given to Canadian setting.– Includes a dictionary of banking terms, author index.– Topics include finance, human resources management, marketing, planning and strategy, regulation.
Location: OOCC.

2704 **Woodhead, Eileen**
Bibliographie de catalogues commerciaux de l'est du Canada, 1800-1880. [Ottawa]: Parcs Canada, 1984. 26 p. (Bulletin de recherches / Parcs Canada ; no 217; ISSN: 0228-1236)

Note: Approx. 200 entrées.– Catalogues classés par sujet.– Chaque entrée donne le nom et l'adresse de l'entreprise, la date du catalogue, son contenu ou son titre, le nombre de pages et d'illustrations qu'il contient, l'endroit où il se trouve et son code d'emplacement.
English title: *Bibliography of trade catalogues, 1800-1880, in eastern Canada.*
Localisation: OONL.

2705 **Woodhead, Eileen**
Bibliography of trade catalogues, 1800-1880, in eastern Canada. [Ottawa]: Parks Canada, 1984. 25 p. (Research bulletin / Parks Canada ; no. 217; ISSN: 0228-1228)
Note: Approx. 200 entries.– Catalogues listed by subject, with identity of the firm, content or title, paging and illustrations, location of catalogue and retrieval coding.
Titre en français: *Bibliographie de catalogues commerciaux de l'est du Canada, 1800-1880.*
Location: OONL.

— 1985 —

2706 **Bibliographie sur le développement régional/ Bibliography on regional development.** Moncton, N.-B.: Institut canadien de recherche sur le développement régional, 1985. iii, 348, 22 p.; ISBN: 0-88659-005-1.
Note: 4,300 entrées.– Quatre parties principales: généralités et bibliographies; économique et spatio-économique; politique, publique et parapublique; social.– Index thématique et géographique.– Texte en français et en anglais/text in English and French.
Localisation: OONL.

2707 **Bibliography of kind of business publications.** [Regina, Sask.]: Saskatchewan Tourism and Small Business, 1985. iii, 119 p.
Note: Approx. 550 entries.– Books on how to start and run specific kinds of businesses.
Location: OONL.

2708 **Canadian Housing Information Centre**
Bibliography on the construction industry in Canada/ Bibliographie sur l'industrie de la construction au Canada. Ottawa: The Centre, 1985. 16 p.
Note: Approx. 150 entries.
Location: OONL.

2709 **Drache, Daniel; Clement, Wallace**
The new practical guide to Canadian political economy. Updated and expanded ed. Toronto: J. Lorimer, 1985. xxiv, 243 p.; ISBN: 0-88862-785-8.
Note: 3,000 entries.– 25 subject bibliographies compiled and introduced by specialists in each area.– Topics include economic development, Canada's international economic relations, class formations, regional economics, women, Native peoples, nationalism, industrial and commercial policy, urban politics, banking and finance.
Previous edition: *A practical guide to Canadian political economy.* 1978. vi, 183 p.; ISBN: 0-88862-184-1.– 1,500 entries.
Location: OONL.

2710 **Land, Brian**
Sources of information for Canadian business. 4th ed. Ottawa: Canadian Chamber of Commerce, 1985. iv, 108 p.
Note: Emphasis on describing business resources in general: reference books, government publications, statistical sources, non-profit organizations.– Sections on periodicals, newspapers, working papers and pamphlets; business, economic and financial services.– Intended primarily for those conducting their own business research.
Previous editions:
Montreal: 1978. ii, 76 p.
Sources of information for the Canadian businessman. Montreal: 1972. ii, 32 p.
Avenues of research: a businessman's guide to sources of business information. Montreal: 1962. 40 p.
Location: OONL.

2711 **Marchak, Patricia**
"Canadian political economy [literature review]."
In: *Canadian Review of Sociology and Anthropology*; Vol. 22, no. 5 (December 1985) p. 673-709.; ISSN: 0008-4948.
Note: Approx. 250 entries.
Location: OONL.

2712 **Metropolitan Toronto Library. Reference Division. Business Department**
Biographies on Canadian business people. Toronto: The Department, 1985. [3] l. (Bibliographies on business topics ; no. 9)
Note: 20 entries.– List of directories and who's whos in business and finance.
Location: OONL.

2713 **Ontario. Ministry of Treasury and Economics. Library Services**
Budget and expenditure process and reforms: a bibliography with emphasis on Canada. Monticello, Ill.: Vance Bibliographies, [1985]. 16 p. (Public administration series: Bibliography ; P-1646; ISSN: 0193-970X); ISBN: 0-89028-336-2.
Note: Approx. 200 entries.– Includes books and reports, periodical articles, list of additional bibliographies.
Location: OONL.

2714 **Ontario. Ministry of Treasury and Economics. Library Services**
Canadian and provincial industrial policies – strategy debates since 1970: a bibliography. Monticello, Ill.: Vance Bibliographies, 1985. 28 p. (Public administration series: Bibliography ; P-1807; ISSN: 0193-970X); ISBN: 0-89028-637-X.
Note: Approx. 375 entries.– Books and reports, periodical articles.
Location: OTDRE.

2715 **P.G. Whiting and Associates**
Economic impacts of heritage institutions on the Canadian economy: bibliography. Ottawa: Canadian Museums Association, 1985. 54 l.; ISBN: 0-91910-618-8.
Note: Reports, studies, books, articles pertaining to the economic impact of heritage institutions.– Includes references to additional bibliographies.
Location: OONL.

— 1986 —

2716 **Alberta. Consumer Education and Information Resource Centre**
Consumer education materials: an annotated list. Rev. ed. [Edmonton]: Alberta Consumer and Corporate Affairs, 1986. 161 p.
Note: Lists books, films, periodicals, kits, video recordings, posters dealing with consumer education, consumer behaviour, financial management, buying practices, consumer protection and advocacy (rights, responsibilities, redress), economics.
Previous editions:

1985. 135 p.
1982. 146 p.
1979. v, 90 p.
Location: OONL.

2717 **Barnes, Eleanor; Fisher, Mary**
Beer and wine sales: different points of view: a selected bibliography. Toronto: Ontario Legislative Library, Research and Information Services, [1986]. 14 l. (Bibliographies and lists. New series / Ontario Legislative Library, Research and Information Services ; no. 14; ISSN: 0833-2150)
Note: Location: OOP.

2718 **Boilard, Gilberte**
Privatisation: bibliographie sélective et annotée. Québec: Bibliothèque de l'Assemblée nationale, Division de la référence parlementaire, 1986. 50 p. (Bibliographie / Bibliothèque de l'Assemblée nationale du Québec ; no 1; ISSN: 0836-9100)
Note: Approx. 250 entrées.– Articles de revues sur privatisation dans: Canada, Québec, États-Unis, Grande-Bretagne, France, autres pays, études comparatives. Supplément: *Privatisation, 1986-1988: bibliographie sélective et annotée.* 1988. 52 p.– Approx. 250 entrées.
Localisation: OONL.

2719 **Duval, Marc**
Incubateurs d'entreprises: bibliographie française et anglaise, 1986. Boucherville [Québec]: M. Duval, 1986. [8] l.
Note: Approx. 120 entrées.
Localisation: OONL.

2720 **Giroux, Nicole**
Gestion du crédit aux P.M.E. dans les banques: revues de la littérature. Montréal: École des hautes études commerciales, 1986. 41 f. (Cahier / École des hautes études commerciales, Montréal ; 86-3); ISBN: 2-893600-70-0.
Note: Localisation: OONL.

2721 **Nelson, Ruben**
Canadian directory of futures services and resources. Ottawa: Square One Management, 1986. vii, 189 p.; ISBN: 0-9690393-4-4.
Note: List of 42 firms providing forecasting services: technological and social forecasts, policy development, network development, "futures oriented" research.– Includes a section, "Futures Resources," listing newsletters, magazines, journals.
Location: OONL.

2722 **Nguyên, Vy-Khanh**
Déréglementation: bibliographie sélective et annotée. Québec: Bibliothèque de l'Assemblée nationale, Division de la référence parlementaire, 1986. 121 p. (Bibliographie / Bibliothèque de l'Assemblée nationale du Québec ; no 2; ISSN: 0836-9100)
Note: 598 entrées.– Couvre la documentation en français et en anglais publiée depuis 1980.
Localisation: OONL.

2723 **Northern Regulatory Review**
Some references relevant to regulation of industrial activity in the Canadian north, 1983-1986. [Ottawa]: Indian and Northern Affairs Canada, 1986. 26, 10, 40, 35 p.
Note: Approx. 400 entries.– Government reports, scholarly publications, journal articles, consultants'

studies.– Focus on regulation of mining and petroleum industries in the North: environmental protection, economic regulation.– Locations provided for all documents.
Location: OONL.

2724 **Ontario. Ministry of Treasury and Economics. Library Services**
The new services economy: free trade, labour and technology issues. Monticello, Ill.: Vance Bibliographies, 1986. 54 p. (Public administration series: Bibliography ; P-2051; ISSN: 0193-970X); ISBN: 1-55590-091-7.
Note: Approx. 600 entries.– Books and reports, periodical articles dealing with the service sector.– Many Canadian references.
Location: OOP.

2725 **Ostrye, Anne T.**
Foreign investment in the American and Canadian West, 1870-1914: an annotated bibliography. Metuchen, N.J.: Scarecrow Press, 1986. vii, 192 p.; ISBN: 0-8108-1866-3.
Note: 574 entries.– Scholarly, popular and personal accounts: monographs, articles, theses, government documents.– Includes the business and personal archival collections of those companies and individuals investing in the underdeveloped North American West during the decades between 1870 and 1914.
Location: OONL.

2726 **Taghvai, Hassan; Lamy, Nicole**
Bibliographie sélective sur l'économie de l'énergie/ Selective bibliography on the economics of energy. Montréal: École des hautes études commerciales, 1986. 71 f. (Cahiers du Centre d'études en administration internationale no 86-05; ISSN: 0825-5822)
Note: 330 entrées.– La période couverte est de 1979 à 1985.– Comporte cinq rubriques: énergie, pétrole brut, autres formes d'énergie, statistiques de l'énergie, divers.
Localisation: OONL.

2727 **Toth, Pierre**
La prévision des faillites: revue de la littérature financière et méthodologie. Montréal: École des hautes études commerciales, c1986. 73 f., 8 p. (Cahier / École des hautes études commerciales, Montréal ; 86-1); ISBN: 2-893600-68-9.
Note: Localisation: OONL.

— 1987 —

2728 **Bridault, Alain; Ouellet, Dominique**
Revue critique de la littérature en français sur la coopération ouvrière de production dans les pays industrialisés, 1975-1983. Sherbrooke, Québec: Institut de recherche et d'enseignement pour les coopératives, Université de Sherbrooke, 1987. xv, 99 p. (Collection Essais / Institut de recherche et d'enseignement pour les coopératives, Université de Sherbrooke ; no 9; ISSN: 0832-6037)
Note: Localisation: OONL.

2729 **Bridault, Alain; Ouellet, Dominique; Henry, Ronald**
Inventaire analytique des recherches universitaires canadiennes sur les coopératives, 1970-1985/Analytical inventory of Canadian university research on cooperatives, 1970-1985. Montréal: Centre interuniversitaires de recherche, d'information et d'enseignement sur les coopératives, c1987. xi, 321 p.: ill.; ISBN: 2-920258-06-0.
Note: Texte en français et en anglais/text in English and French.

Localisation: OONL.

2730 **Caron, Hélène; Denault, Bernard**
Bibliographie internationale: rapports états-coopératives. Sherbrooke, Québec: Institut de recherche et d'enseignement pour les coopératives, Université de Sherbrooke, 1987. vi, 65 f. (Collection Essais / Institut de recherche et d'enseignement pour les coopératives, Université de Sherbrooke ; no 13; ISSN: 0832-6037)
Note: Approx. 700 entrées.– Volumes, articles de revue: travaux qui traitent de l'État dans ses rapports avec les coopératives aux plans économique, législatif, politique, sociologique, administratif.– Inclut un nombre d'ouvrages canadiens.
Localisation: OONL.

2731 **Crown, Elizabeth Marie**
Economics of textiles and clothing: a bibliography and selected readings. Edmonton: University of Alberta, 1987. 1 vol. (in various pagings): ill.
Note: Approx. 225 entries.– Journal articles and government publications dealing with the structure of the textile industry, resource use, consumerism, international trade, future of the Canadian textile and apparel industries.
Location: OONL.

2732 **Darlington, Susan**
Home business information. Montreal: Info-Recherche, 1987. 14 p.
Note: Approx. 100 entries.– Books, government publications, selected articles from 1980 to 1986 on running home-based businesses.
Location: OONL.

2733 **Desjardins, Joëlle**
Les nouveaux libéralismes économiques: bibliographie sélective et annotée. Québec: Bibliothèque de l'Assemblée nationale, Division de la référence parlementaire, 1987. 48 p. (Bibliographie / Bibliothèque de l'Assemblée nationale du Québec ; no 4; ISSN: 0836-9100)
Note: Approx. 250 entrées.– Études générales, Reaganisme, Thatcherisme, autres pays, études comparatives.
Localisation: OONL.

2734 **Desjardins, Joëlle**
Politique industrielle: bibliographie sélective et annotée. Québec: Bibliothèque de l'Assemblée nationale, Division de la référence parlementaire, 1987. 28 p. (Bibliographie / Bibliothèque de l'Assemblée nationale du Québec ; no 7; ISSN: 0836-9100)
Note: Approx. 125 entrées.– Études comparatives, Canada, autres pays.
Localisation: OONL.

2735 **Desjardins, Joëlle**
Réforme de la taxe foncière: bibliographie sélective. Québec: Bibliothèque de l'Assemblée nationale, Division de la référence parlementaire, 1987. 10 p. (Bibliographie / Bibliothèque de l'Assemblée nationale du Québec ; no 6; ISSN: 0836-9100)
Note: Approx. 100 entrées.
Localisation: OONL.

2736 **Desjardins, Joëlle**
Réforme fiscale: bibliographie sélective et annotée. Québec: Bibliothèque de l'Assemblée nationale, Division de la référence parlementaire, 1987. 39 p. (Bibliographie /

Bibliothèque de l'Assemblée nationale du Québec ; no 10; ISSN: 0836-9100)
Note: 215 entrées.
Localisation: OONL.

2737 **Ketilson, Lou Hammond; Korthuis, Bonnie; Boyd, Colin**
The management of co-operatives: a bibliography. Saskatoon: Centre for the Study of Co-operatives, University of Saskatchewan, [1987]. 137 p.
Note: 522 entries.– Books, journal articles, pamphlets, working papers, conference proceedings relating to nature of management decision-making within co-operative institutions.– Listings by title, management function, type of co-operative institution.
Location: OONL.

2738 **Prince, Tim**
Personal tax reform, 1970-1987: a selected bibliography of sources in the Legislative Library. Regina: Saskatchewan Legislative Library, 1987. 4 l.
Note: 28 entries.
Location: OONL.

2739 **Service de diffusion sélective de l'information de la Centrale des bibliothèques**
Le Libre-échange Canada-États-Unis: bibliographie. Montréal: Le Service, 1987. 17 p. (DSI/CB ; no 96; ISSN: 0825-5024); ISBN: 2-89059-302-9.
Note: 206 entrées.– Livres, articles de périodiques, articles du quotidien *La Presse* couvrant les années 1985 à 1987 (jusqu'au 5 octobre), documents audiovisuels (vidéos produits par Radio-Québec).
Localisation: OONL.

— 1988 —

2740 **Boilard, Gilberte; Dufresne, Nicole**
Heures d'affaires dans les établissements commerciaux le dimanche: bibliographie. Québec: Bibliothèque de l'Assemblée nationale, Division de la référence parlementaire, 1988. 8 p. (Bibliographie / Bibliothèque de l'Assemblée nationale du Québec ; no 17; ISSN: 0836-9100)
Note: Localisation: OONL.

2741 **The Browning directory of Canadian business information.** Toronto: Browning Associates, 1988. 1 vol. (in various pagings).; ISBN: 0-920411-03-7.
Note: Listing and directory of Canadian business directories, buyers' guides, statistical sources, market surveys, special periodical issues which contain information on Canadian business activities.– Arranged in subject categories: agriculture, business law, retail trade, travel and hospitality, etc.
Previous edition: 1985. v, 538 p.; ISBN: 0-920411-01-0.
Location: OONL.

2742 **Connatty, Brad**
A bibliography of sustainable economic development literature available from the University of Calgary's MacKimmie Library. Calgary: Arctic Institute of North America, 1988. 55 p.
Note: Location: ACU.

2743 **Dworaczek, Marian**
Employment and free trade: a bibliography. Monticello, Ill.: Vance Bibliographies, 1988. 14 p. (Public administration series: Bibliography ; P-2482; ISSN: 0193-970X); ISBN: 1-55590-912-4.
Note: Approx. 200 entries.

Location: QQLA.

2744 Geahigan, Priscilla C.
U.S. and Canadian businesses, 1955 to 1987: a bibliography. Metuchen, N.J.: Scarecrow Press, 1988. xi, 589 p.; ISBN: 0-8108-2186-9.
Note: Approx. 4,000 entries.– Books and studies about individual companies in the United States and Canada, including some non-profit corporations.– Arrangement is by industry group: agriculture, mining, construction, manufacturing, transportation, retail trade, finance, services.– Indexes to company names, personal names, authors.
Location: OONL.

2745 Matyas, Cathy
Entrepreneurship and new business enterprise: a resource list. [Kingston, Ont.: Infomat, 1988]. 90 l.
Note: Lists books in print and forthcoming, magazine and serial titles, magazine and newspaper articles, government publications, audio-visual materials, publications available from banks and accounting firms, courses available, professional and small business advisory services.
Location: OONL.

2746 Murray, J. Alex
An international business library bibliography. 4th ed. Waterloo, Ont.: Laurier Trade Development Centre, Wilfrid Laurier University, 1988. i, 78 p.; ISSN: 0834-3373
Note: 947 entries.– Periodicals, directories, statistics, bibliographies, business research and intelligence services, business functions (management, marketing, etc.).– Includes Canadian listings in each category.
Previous editions:
1986. i, 81 p.
1984. i, 78 p.
1983. i, 74 p.
Location: OONL.

2747 Nadeau, Johan
Entreprises internationales, transnationales et multinationales: bibliographie sélective et annotée. Québec: Bibliothèque de l'Assemblée nationale, Division de la référence parlementaire, 1988. 64 p. [2] f. (Bibliographie / Bibliothèque de l'Assemblée nationale du Québec ; no 26; ISSN: 0836-9100)
Note: 243 entrées.– Couvre les ouvrages parus depuis 1980.– Aspects politiques, économiques, sociaux et environnementaux; organismes internationaux, pays en développement, droit et législation.
Localisation: OONL.

2748 Pauchant, Thierry C.
Crisis management: an annotated bibliography. Québec: Faculté des sciences de l'administration, Université Laval, 1988. 53 p. (Document spécial / Faculté des sciences de l'administration, Université Laval ; 88-110)
Note: 190 entries.– Includes Canadian references.
Location: OONL.

2749 Weiner, Alan R.
The insurance industry: an information sourcebook. Phoenix: Oryx Press, 1988. ix, 278 p. (Oryx sourcebook series in business and management ; no. 16); ISBN: 0-89774-307-5.
Note: 1,265 entries.– English-language reference material, published in the United States and Canada on a continuing basis, regularly or irregularly: yearbooks, directories, handbooks, policy and rate manuals, statistical compilations, periodicals, audiovisual programs, computerized databases.– Topics include general insurance, lines of insurance, insurance law, education and careers in insurance field, insurance operations.
Location: OONL.

— 1989 —

2750 Boilard, Gilberte
Taxe sur les produits et services (Phase II du Livre blanc sur la réforme fiscale): bibliographie sélective et annotée. Québec: Division de la référence parlementaire, Bibliothèque de l'Assemblée nationale, 1989. 30 p. (Bibliographie / Bibliothèque de l'Assemblée nationale du Québec ; no 30; ISSN: 0836-9100)
Note: 93 entrées.
Localisation: OONL.

2751 De Stricker, Ulla; Dysart, Jane I.
Business online: a Canadian guide. Toronto: John Wiley in association with the Canadian Institute of Chartered Accountants, c1989. xv, 335 p.; ISBN: 0-471-79676-X.
Note: Contains a section listing and describing Canadian online information services of interest to business: news databases, company databases, marketing databases (decision-support, statistical, trademarks and patents), securities databases, legal databases, financial and tax databases.
Location: OONL.

2752 Doucet, Ronald
Bibliographie sur "la qualité totale". Québec: Direction des communications, Ministère de l'industrie, du commerce et de la technologie, 1989. viii, 150 p.; ISBN: 2-550-19860-3.
Note: Approx. 1,200 entrées.– Livres, revues, audiovisuels, logiciels en langue française et en langue anglaise sur la question de la qualité dans l'entreprise.– Comprend une section: "Références bibliographiques d'origine canadienne et/ou québécoise."
Localisation: OONL.

2753 Jarjour, Gabi
Bibliographie sélectionée des articles sur l'économie du pétrole et du gaz, 1986-1989/Selected bibliography of articles on oil and gas economics, 1986-1989. Québec: Groupe de recherche en économie de l'énergie et des ressources naturelles, Université Laval, 1989. viii, 96, 6 p. (Cahier / Groupe de recherche en économie de l'énergie et des ressources naturelles ; 89-05)
Note: Comprend des articles, des analyses et des données factuelles concernant l'économie appliquée de pétrole et du gaz.
Localisation: OOMR.

2754 Lafortune, Andrée; Marchis-Mouren, Marie-Françoise
Revue de littérature: le micro-ordinateur comme outil de vérification dans les cabinets d'experts-comptables. Montréal: École des hautes études commerciales, 1989. 37 f. (Rapport de recherche / École des hautes études commerciales ; no 89-08; ISSN: 0709-986X)
Note: Approx. 100 entrées.
Localisation: OONL.

2755 Lewis, Pamela
Radio Frequency Spectrum Management Program evaluation: economic nature of the spectrum: a review of the literature. Ottawa: Government of Canada, Department of Communications, Program Evaluation

Division, 1989. vi, 43 p.

Note: Books, articles, government studies and reports dealing with the economic aspects of radio frequency spectrum management and regulation.– Topics include spectrum characteristics, spectrum management system, evaluation of the management system, the pure market alternative, policy options available to government.– International coverage with focus on Canadian materials.– Sommaire pour la direction en français.

Location: OONL.

2756 **McKitrick, Ross**
The Canada-U.S. Free Trade Agreement: an annotated bibliography of selected literature. Kingston, [Ont]: Industrial Relations Centre, Queen's University, [1989]. 27 p. (Bibliography series / Industrial Relations Centre, Queen's University ; no. 7; ISSN: 0075-613X); ISBN: 0-88886-223-7.

Note: Approx. 100 entries.– Books, articles, government publications, studies from economic think tank organizations (C.D. Howe Institute, Brookings Institution), and policy papers from trade unions on background issues, the agreement itself, and reaction and discussion on a range of topics from agriculture to social issues and sovereignty.

Location: OONL.

2757 **Milne, David**
Canada-United States free trade: a bibliography/Libre-échange entre le Canada et les États-Unis: une bibliographie. 5th ed. [Ottawa]: External Affairs and International Trade Canada, 1989. 147 p.

Note: Approx. 1,150 entries.– Books, periodicals, government documents, speeches, statements, news releases on political, economic, legal, cultural, regional aspects of free trade.– Text in English and French/texte en français et en anglais.

Previous editions:
1988. 74 p.
Bubic, Suzanne; Milne, David. 1987. 46 p.
Bubic, Suzanne. 1986. 33 p.

Location: OONL.

2758 **New Brunswick. Legislative Library**
Small business and entrepreneurship/Les petites entreprises et l'entrepreneurship. Fredericton: New Brunswick Legislative Library, 1989. 13 l. (Bibliography / New Brunswick Legislative Library)

Note: 144 entries.– Includes publications in English and French.

Location: OONL.

2759 **Ontario. Ministry of Labour. Library and Information Services**
"Sunday shopping legislation: a selected bibliography."
In: *Labour Topics*; Vol. 12, no. 1 (January 1989) p. 1-2.; ISSN: 0704-8874.

Note: 27 entries.

Location: AEU.

2760 **Ottawa Public Library**
Business information/Information sur les affaires. [Rev. ed.]. [Ottawa]: The Library, 1989. 40 p.

Note: Approx. 150 entries.– Reference materials (directories, dictionaries, biography, statistical works) in Canadian business and finance.– Compiled by Paul Schwebke, revised by Diana Pepall.– Text in English and French/texte en français et en anglais.

Previous edition: 1987. 30 p.

Location: OONL.

2761 **Poirier, René; Cournoyer, Sylvie**
Bibliographie thématique sélective sur l'économie de l'information/Thematic and selective bibliography on the information economy. Laval, Québec: Centre canadien de recherche sur l'information du travail, Direction de la recherche organisationnelle, 1989. 32 p.; ISBN: 0-662-57058-8.

Note: 299 entrées.– Couvre généralement la période 1981-1987.– Trois catégories thématiques: industries de l'information; diffusion des technologies de l'information; impacts régionaux et internationaux.– Inclut un nombre d'ouvrages canadiens.

Localisation: OONL.

2762 **Université de Montréal. École des relations industrielles**
La libéralisation des échanges Canada-États-Unis et les relations industrielles au Québec, négocier l'avenir: bibliographie sommaire. Montréal: L'Université, 1989. 24 p.

Note: Approx. 200 entrées.– Colloques, publications gouvernementales, syndicales et patronales, livres et publications universitaires, articles de journaux et périodiques.

Localisation: OOEC.

— 1990 —

2763 **Albala, Leila**
Catalogue of Canadian catalogues: shop at home from hundreds of mail order sources. Chambly, Quebec: ALPEL, c1990. 128 p.: ill.; ISBN: 0-921993-03-X.

Note: Approx. 500 entries.

Location: OONL.

2764 **Le commerce de détail et de gros au Canada: sources d'information.** [Ottawa]: Division des services de distribution, Industrie, sciences et technologie Canada, 1990. 40 p.; ISBN: 0-662-95998-1.

Note: Liste des répertoires de détaillants, grossistes et distributeurs au Canada, recueil des sources de statistiques sur le commerce de détail et de gros au Canada.

English title: *Retailing and wholesaling in Canada: information sources.*

Localisation: OONL.

2765 **Eiselt, Horst A.; Laporte, Gilbert; Thisse, Jacques-François**
Competitive location models: a framework and bibliography. Montréal: Centre de recherche sur les transports, Université de Montréal, 1990. 34 l. (Publication / Centre de recherche sur les transports, Université de Montréal ; no. 706)

Note: Approx. 100 entries.– Some Canadian references.

Location: OONL.

2766 **Le franchisage au Canada: sources d'information.** [Ottawa]: Direction générale des industries des services et des biens de consommation, Industrie, sciences et technologie Canada, 1990. 19, 19 p.; ISBN: 0-662-57349-8.

Note: Comprend une section des publications: bulletins et revues commerciales, presse commerciale, répertoires, livres et brochures sur l'achat et mise sur pied d'une franchise au Canada.– Texte en français et en anglais disposé tête-bêche.– Titre de la p. de t. additionnelle: *Franchising in Canada: information sources.*

Localisation: OONL.

2767 **Franchising in Canada: information sources.** [Ottawa]: Service Industries and Consumer Goods Branch, Industry, Science and Technology Canada, 1990. 19, 19 p.; ISBN: 0-662-57349-8.
Note: Includes a publications section listing newsletters, trade magazines, business press, directories, books and pamphlets on buying and developing a franchise in Canada.– Text in English and French with French text on inverted pages.– Title of additional title-page: *Le franchisage au Canada: sources d'information.*
Location: OONL.

2768 **Mack, Yvonne**
Goods and services tax: a reading list. Regina: Saskatchewan Legislative Library, 1990. 6 l.
Note: 17 entries.– Pamphlets, government publications, magazine articles.– Annotations.
Location: OONL.

2769 **Nantel, Jacques; Robillard, Renée**
Le concept de l'implication dans l'étude des comportements des consommateurs: une revue de la littérature. Montréal: École des hautes études commerciales, 1990. 59 f.: ill. (Rapport de recherche / École des hautes études commerciales ; 90-01; ISSN: 0709-986X)
Note: Localisation: OONL.

2770 **Retailing and wholesaling in Canada: information sources.** [Ottawa]: Distribution Services Division, Industry, Science and Technology Canada, 1990. 40 p.; ISBN: 0-662-17708-8.
Note: Includes a section listing directories for twenty industry groups, sources for industry statistics.
Titre en français: *Le commerce de détail et de gros au Canada: sources d'information.*
Location: OONL.

2771 **To, Minh Chau; Kryzanowski, Lawrence; Lessard, Michel**
La performance des fonds mutuels: une revue de la littérature. Montréal: École des hautes études commerciales, 1990. 46 f. (Rapport de recherche / École des hautes études commerciales ; no 90-07; ISSN: 0709-986X)
Note: Approx. 60 entrées.– Comprend quelques références canadiennes.
Localisation: OONL.

2772 **To, Minh Chau; Kryzanowski, Lawrence; Roy, Vincent**
Les anomalies dans les marchés des capitaux: une revue de la littérature. Montréal: École des hautes études commerciales, 1990. 55 f. (Rapport de recherche / École des hautes études commerciales ; no 90-06; ISSN: 0709-986X)
Note: Approx. 65 entrées.– Comprend quelques références canadiennes.
Localisation: OONL.

— 1991 —

2773 **Archambault, Guy**
Le perfectionnement des managers: une revue de la littérature: les années 80. Montréal: École des hautes études commerciales, 1991. 32 f. (Cahier de recherche / École des hautes études commerciales ; no 92-04; ISSN: 0846-0647)
Note: Localisation: OONL.

2774 **Income security: publications and sources of information/La sécurité du revenu: publications et sources de renseignements.** Montreal: Canadian Pension Conference, 1991. iv, 80 p.
Note: Books, studies, surveys and periodicals, published in Canada since 1980 in both English and French, in the fields of pensions and benefits: private pensions, public pensions, employee benefits, retirement and income planning, compensation, social security, royal commissions and task forces, government discussion papers and policy statements, law and legislation.– Text in English and French/texte en français et en anglais.
Location: OONL.

2775 **Miller, E. Willard**
United States trade: United States, Canada, and Latin America: a bibliography. Monticello, Ill.: Vance Bibliographies, 1991. 33 p. (Public administration series: Bibliography ; P-3064; ISSN: 0193-970X); ISBN: 0-792007-84-0.
Note: Location: OOF.

2776 **Monty, Vivienne**
The Canadian small business handbook. 2nd ed. Don Mills, Ont.: CCH Canadian, 1991. x, 201 p.; ISBN: 0-88796-622-5.
Note: Part 2, entitled "Bibliography of source materials on small business," and part 3, "Sources of business information," list publications, many Canadian, dealing with accounting and finance, forecasting, franchises, management, marketing, importing and exporting, location of business, starting a small business, business reference sources, government publications useful to small business.
Previous edition: 1985. viii, 152 p.; ISBN: 0-88796-285-8.
Location: OONL.

2777 **Nantel, Jacques; Robillard, Renée**
Le concept de la familiarité dans l'étude des comportements des consommateurs: une revue de la littérature. Montréal: Direction de la recherche, École des hautes études commerciales, 1991. ii, 44 f. (Cahier de recherche / Direction de la recherche, École des hautes études commerciales ; no 91-16; ISSN: 0846-0647)
Note: Localisation: OONL.

2778 **Robertson, Yves**
"Intelligence d'entreprise" et veille technologique: bibliographie sélective. Québec: Conseil de la science et de la technologie, Centre de documentation, 1991. 42 p.; ISBN: 2-550-22856-1.
Note: 118 entrées.
Localisation: OONL.

2779 **Yuan, Jing-dong; Cummins, Vivian**
Asian Pacific trade and Canada: a bibliography. Ottawa: Asian Pacific Research and Resource Centre, Carleton University, [1991]. 85 p. (Bibliography series / Asian Pacific Research and Resource Centre, Carleton University ; 1)
Note: Location: OOCC.

— 1992 —

2780 **Brown, Barbara E.**
Canadian business and economics: a guide to sources of information. 3rd ed. Ottawa: Canadian Library Association, c1992. xv, 675 p.; ISBN: 0-88802-256-5.
Note: Approx. 7,000 entries.– Lists current English and French monographs and serials with Canadian emphasis:

reference tools (bibliographies, demographic data sources, directories, indexes, statistical sources), theses, reports and digests.– Main body of work arranged in broad subject categories, e.g. business theory and practice, investment, labour, law, small business, transportation.– Index: authors, issuing bodies, editors, titles, subjects.– Excludes periodical articles, most government reports, technical publications.– Includes computer-based business information services.– Text in English and French/texte en français et en anglais.
Previous editions:
1984. xxxiv, 469 p.; ISBN: 0-88802-161-5.– 6,500 entries.
1976. xviii, 636 p.; ISBN: 0-88802-110-0.– 2,100 entries.
Location: OONL.

2781 **Dehem, Roger**
Canadian economics. [Ottawa]: Canadian Studies Directorate, Department of the Secretary of State of Canada, c1992. 22, 24 p. (Canadian studies resource guides. Second series); ISBN: 0-662-58839-8.
Note: Includes an introductory overview of the subject, a commentary on significant works, and suggestions for further reading.– Text in English and French with French text on inverted pages.– Title of additional title-page: *L'économie du Canada.*
Previous edition: 1988. 19, 21 p. (Canadian studies resource guides); ISBN: 0-662-56135-X.
Location: OONL.

2782 **Dehem, Roger**
L'économie du Canada. [Ottawa]: Direction des études canadiennes, Secrétariat d'État du Canada, 1992. 24, 22 p. (Guides pédagogiques des études canadiennes. Deuxième collection); ISBN: 0-662-58839-8.
Note: Comporte un exposé préliminaire, des observations sur les principaux travaux et une liste de lectures recommandées.– Texte en français et en anglais disposé tête-bêche.– Titre de la p. de t. additionnelle: *Canadian economics.*
Édition antérieure: 1988. 21, 19 p. (Guides pédagogiques des études canadiennes); ISBN: 0-662-56135-X.
Localisation: OONL.

2783 **Drummond, Christina S.R.**
Guide to accounting pronouncements & sources: a Canadian accountant's index of authoritative accounting and auditing literature including Canadian, international and relevant US and UK pronouncements. 3rd ed. Toronto: Canadian Institute of Chartered Accountants, 1992. 188 p.; ISBN: 0-88800-284-X.
Note: Previous editions:
1990. v, 157 p.; ISBN: 0-88800-229-7.
Butterworths, c1985. xi, 133 p. (Butterworths accounting series); ISBN: 0-409-80513-0.
Location: OONL.

2784 **Paquin, Benoît; Turgeon, Normand**
La gestion de la qualité dans les entreprises de services: une bibliographie sélective/Quality management in the services industry: a selective bibliography. Montréal: Direction de la recherche, École des hautes études commerciales, 1992. 42 f. (Cahier de recherche: Working paper / Direction de la recherche, École des hautes études commerciales ; no 92-09; ISSN: 0846-0647)
Note: 476 entrées.– Livres, articles de périodiques traitent des services (qualité, marketing, gestion des opérations, gestion du personnel, économie, management).– Texte en français et en anglais/text in English and French.
Localisation: OONL.

— Ongoing/En cours —

2785 **Directory of information sources in Canada/Répertoire des sources d'information au Canada.** Toronto: Micromedia, 1991-. vol.; ISSN: 0843-9494.
Note: Approx. 1,800 entries.– Listing of directories, handbooks, buyer's guides, membership lists, product guides, market surveys in a number of formats: books, serials, special issues of magazines, periodical articles.– Includes recent material only: publications in English and French from about 1988.– Excludes bibliographies, catalogues, indexes, statistical material, online and CD-ROM databases.– Text in English and French/texte en français et en anglais.
Formerly: *Access Canada: Micromedia's directory of Canadian information sources.* Toronto: Micromedia, c1990.
Location: OONL.

2786 **"In the library."**
In: *Canadian Tax Journal;* (1953-) vol.; ISSN: 0008-5111.
Note: Regular listing from Vol. 1, no. 1 (January-February 1953) of books and documents added to the Library of the Canadian Tax Foundation on topics dealing with taxation, finance, economics: Canadian, United States, international.
Location: AEUL.

2787 **Québec (Province). Office des ressources humaines. Direction de développement du personnel d'encadrement**
Bibliographie générale en management. Québec: Gouvernement du Québec, Office des ressources humaines, Direction de développement du personnel d'encadrement, 1983-. vol.; ISSN: 1181-8603.
Note: Semestriel.
Localisation: OONL.

— 1946 —

2788 **Queen's University (Kingston, Ont.). Department of Industrial Relations**
A selected bibliography on industrial relations. Kingston, Ont.: Department of Industrial Relations, Queen's University, 1946. 77 p. (Bulletin / Queen's University Department of Industrial Relations ; no. 11)
Note: Approx. 600 entries.– Books, pamphlets, documents dealing with aspects of industrial relations: labour organizations, collective bargaining, industrial psychology, industrial hygiene and safety, social security, women in industry, workers' education, biography.– Some Canadian references.
Location: OOL.

— 1955 —

2789 **Gulick, Charles Adams; Ockert, Roy A.; Wallace, Raymond J.**
History and theories of working-class movements: a select bibliography. Berkeley, Calif.: Published jointly by the Bureau of Business and Economic Research and Institute of Industrial Relations, University of California, Berkeley, [1955]. xix, 364 p.
Note: 120 entries specifically on Canada.– Covers 1800 to April 1954.– Arcticles, notes, occasional documents in journals and magazines ranging from scholarly to popular to propagandistic.– Working class movement is broadly defined to include trade unions, political parties, co-operative societies, cultural organizations of various kinds.
Location: OONL.

— 1956 —

2790 **"Guaranteed wages and supplemental unemployment benefits: an annotated bibliography with some historical notes."**
In: *Labour Gazette*; Vol. 56, no. 10 (October 1956) p. 1244-1249.; ISSN: 0023-6926.
Note: 69 entries.– Includes a section: "Canadian views."
Location: OONL.

— 1958 —

2791 **Land, Brian**
"Labor publications distributed in Canada."
In: *Canadian Business*; Vol. 31, no. 6 (June 1958) p. 40, 42-45.; ISSN: 0820-9510.
Note: Location: OONL.

— 1963 —

2792 **Jarvi, Edith T.**
Labour in Canada: basic books for Canadian public libraries. Ottawa: Canadian Library Association, 1963. 13 p. (Occasional paper / Canadian Library Association ; no. 40)
Note: Location: OONL.

— 1965 —

2793 **Farrell, David M.**
The contracting out of work: an annotated bibliography. Kingston, Ont.: Industrial Relations Centre, Queen's University, 1965. v, 61 p. (Bibliography series / Industrial Relations Centre, Queen's University ; no. 1)
Note: Approx. 250 entries.– Books, articles, cases related to subcontracting or contracting out of work.– Canadian references, p. 1-22.
Location: OONL.

2794 **Isbester, A. Fraser; Coates, Daniel; Williams, C. Brian**
Industrial and labour relations in Canada: a selected bibliography. Kingston, Ont.: Industrial Relations Centre, Queen's University, 1965. [ix], 120 p. (Bibliography series / Industrial Relations Centre, Queen's University ; no. 2; ISSN: 0075-613X)
Note: 1,169 numbered entries, plus a list of about 200 Canadian labour newspapers and journals.– Includes books, periodical articles, theses on collective bargaining (government relations and policy, disputes, adjustment procedures, labour law and legislation), labour union history and administration, wages, hours and working conditions, labour supply and unemployment.
Location: OONL.

— 1966 —

2795 **Canada. Civil Service Commission. Pay Research Bureau**
A selected bibliography on wage and salary administration, employee benefits and services and collective bargaining. [Ottawa: s.n., 1966]. ii, 80 l.
Note: Approx. 800 entries.– Includes books and pamphlets for 1954-1966, periodical articles for 1961-1966.– Excludes case studies, works of purely statistical nature.
Previous edition: 1964. iii, 55 l.
Location: OONL.

2796 **Canada. Department of Manpower and Immigration. Research Branch**
Manpower studies: a selected bibliography for policy and research. Ottawa: Research Branch, Program Development Service, Department of Manpower and Immigration, 1966. 56 p.
Note: Approx. 750 entries.– Books, articles in professional journals, papers and proceedings, government publications, unpublished theses and dissertations dealing with topics related to manpower and manpower mobility, vocational training, occupational studies.– Emphasis on North American sources relevant to the Canadian experience for the years 1945 to 1965.– Compiled by Barbara Alexandrin for the Manpower Mobility Unit.
Location: OONL.

— 1967 —

2797 **Hartson, Thalia, et al.**
"Canada at work: a bibliography."
In: *One World*; Vol. 5, no. 3 (February 1967) 24 p.; ISSN: 0475-0209.
Note: Pupil references, teacher references, free and inexpensive materials, poetry, broadcasts and

recordings, stories and poems in readers, music, maps, filmstrips, films, government publications.
Location: OONL.

— 1968 —

2798 **Canada. Department of Manpower and Immigration. Occupational Research Section. Occupational Analysis Unit**
Bibliography of career information publications/ Bibliographie de la documentation sur les carrières. 2nd ed. Ottawa: Queen's Printer, 1968. 2 vol.
Note: Vol. 1: *Federal government departments and agencies.–* Vol. 2: *Provincial agencies and private publishers.–* Text in English and French/texte en français et en anglais.
Previous edition: 1966. 35 p.
Location: OONL.

2799 **Page, Garnet T.; Caldwell, George**
Inventory of research on adult human resource development in Canada, 1963-1968/Inventaire de la recherche sur le développement des ressources humaines adultes au Canada. [Ottawa]: Department of Regional Economic Expansion, [1968]. xxiii, 215 p.
Note: 375 entries.– Listing of project reports relating to human resource development: effectiveness of providing skills and knowledge, levels of skills and knowledge, effectiveness of programs, program development.– Text in English and French/texte en français et en anglais.
Location: OONL.

2800 **Williams, C. Brian**
Manpower management in Canada: a selected bibliography. Kingston, Ont.: Industrial Relations Centre, Queen's University, 1968. 121 p. (Bibliography series / Industrial Relations Centre, Queen's University ; no. 3; ISSN: 0075-613X)
Note: 1,125 entries.– Covers 1960 to 1966 inclusive.– Includes books, journal articles, government publications dealing with specific aspects of employment and unemployment: measurement, public policy, impact of automation and technological change, manpower supply, labour mobility, forecasting labour requirements.– Section of bibliographies.
Location: OONL.

— 1969 —

2801 **British Columbia. Workmen's Compensation Board**
Safety literature catalogue: the printed word works for safety. Vancouver: B.C. Workmen's Compensation Board, [1969]. 32 p.
Note: Location: OONL.

2802 **Desmarteau, Leo M.**
Manpower training and retraining: a preliminary bibliography. Ottawa: Department of Manpower and Immigration, 1969. 24 l.
Note: Approx. 350 entries.– Books, articles, documents and papers.
Location: OONL.

2803 **Surry, Jean**
An annotated bibliography for industrial accident research and related fields: a companion volume to *Industrial accident research: a human engineering appraisal.* Toronto: Occupational Health and Safety Division, Ontario Ministry of Labour, 1969. 159 p.
Note: Approx. 1,000 entries.– Articles and reports dealing with accident prevalence, development, consequences, countermeasures.– Includes some

Canadian references.
Location: OONL.

2804 **Tremblay, Louis-Marie**
Bibliographie des relations du travail au Canada, 1940-1967. Montréal: Presses de l'Université de Montréal, 1969. ix, 242 p.; ISBN: 0-8405-0131-5.
Note: 1,269 entrées.– Monographies, articles de revues, bibliographies, thèses, publications officielles sur automation et changement technologique, conciliation, emploi, négociation collective, syndicats.– Avec la collaboration de Francine Panet-Raymond.
Localisation: OONL.

— 1970 —

2805 **Rothman, William A.**
A bibliography of collective bargaining in hospitals and related facilities, 1959-1968. Ann Arbor: Institute of Labor and Industrial Relations, University of Michigan-Wayne State University, 1970. 106 p.
Note: Listing of references related to labour relations in the health care industry.– Includes some Canadian references.
Supplements:
... , 1969-1971. 1972. 127 p.; ISBN: 0-877363-20-X.
... , 1972-1974. 1976. xxiv, 139 p.; ISBN: 0-875460-60-7.
Location: OHM.

2806 **Wood, W.D.; Campbell, H.F.**
Cost-benefit analysis and the economics of investment in human resources: an annotated bibliography. Kingston, Ont.: Industrial Relations Centre, Queen's University, 1970. vii, 211 p. (Bibliography series / Industrial Relations Centre, Queen's University ; no. 5; ISSN: 0075-613X)
Note: 389 entries.– Articles, papers, reports dealing with the theoretical aspects of cost-benefit analysis and the practical applications of the technique to evaluation of investment in human capital.
Location: OONL.

— 1972 —

2807 **Canada. Unemployment Insurance Commission. Library**
A selective bibliography on unemployment insurance in Canada, Great Britain and the United States, 1960-1971/ Bibliographie sélective de l'assurance-chômage au Canada, en Grande-Bretagne et aux États-Unis, 1960-1971. Ottawa: Unemployment Insurance Canada, 1972. 23 l.
Note: 178 entries.– Text in English and French/texte en français et en anglais.
Location: OONL.

2808 **Espesset, Hélène; Hardy, Jean-Pierre; Ruddell, Thierry**
"Le monde de travail au Québec au XVIIIe et au XIXe siècles: historiographie et État de la question."
Dans: *Revue d'histoire de l'Amérique française*; Vol. 25, no 4 (mars 1972) p. 499-539.; ISSN: 0035-2357.
Note: Localisation: OONL.

2809 **Jewett, Linda J.**
"The shortened work week: a selective bibliography."
In: *Ontario Library Review*; Vol. 56, no. 4 (December 1972) p. 230-237.; ISSN: 0030-2996.
Note: Books, periodical and newspaper articles, pamphlets relating to a work week of less than five days.– Excludes material on flexible hours and shorter daily or weekly hours within a standard work week.–

Includes Canadian references.
Location: OONL.

2810 **Rioux, Bernard; Bernier, Lise**
Travail, syndicalisme: bibliographie. Montréal: Conseil de développement social du Montréal métropolitain, 1972. 2 vol.
Note: 529 entrées – Livres, thèses, publications officielles, documents des syndicats, articles de revues sur le syndicalisme québécois.
Localisation: OONL.

— 1973 —

2811 **Armstrong, Douglas; Dworaczek, Marian**
The compressed work week: a bibliography. [Toronto]: Ontario Ministry of Labour, Research Library, 1973. 28 p.
Note: Approx. 300 entries.– Books, articles, government reports.– Many Canadian references.
Location: OONL.

2812 **Armstrong, Douglas; Dworaczek, Marian**
Plant closures, terminations, and layoffs: a bibliography. Toronto: Ontario Ministry of Labour, Research Library, 1973. 29 l.
Note: Approx. 300 entries.– Books, government reports, periodical articles.
Location: OONL.

2813 **Armstrong, Douglas; Krestensen, Kristeen**
Agricultural labour in Canada and United States: a bibliography. Toronto: Ontario Ministry of Labour, Research Library, 1973. 40 l.
Note: Approx. 400 entries.
Location: OONL.

2814 **Dworaczek, Marian**
Manpower training and utilization in Canada, 1955-1970: a bibliography. Toronto: Ontario Ministry of Labour, Research Library, 1973. 21 l.
Note: Approx. 250 entries.– Books, theses, periodical articles, government reports and studies.
Location: OONL.

2815 **Hann, Russell G., et al.**
Primary sources in Canadian working class history, 1860-1930. Kitchener, Ont.: Dumont Press, 1973. 169, [16] p.
Note: 3,347 entries.– Manuscripts, newspapers, pamphlets, government documents.– Topics include political activity, child labour, women, prisons, alms houses, asylums, agrarian protest, agricultural labour, freemasonry, education, hours of work, immigration, mining, labour newspapers, Mechanics Institutes, temperance, police, public health.– Includes numerous references to individual labour organizations.
Location: OONL.

2816 **LeBlanc, André E.; Thwaites, James D.**
Le monde ouvrier au Québec: bibliographie rétrospective. Montréal: Presses de l'Université du Québec, 1973. xv, 283 p. (Collection Histoire des travailleurs québécois); ISBN: 0-7770-0061-X.
Note: 2,927 entrées.– La période couverte est de 1660 à nos jours.– Principaux thèmes traités: le mouvement ouvrier, syndicats et métiers, les conflits de travail, le travail (salaire, conditions de travail, technologie/adaptation/éducation, emploi et chômage, la femme et l'enfant au travail), le milieu social, réponses et réactions, la presse ouvrière.– En collaboration avec Hélène Espesset, et al.
Localisation: OONL.

— 1974 —

2817 **Armstrong, Douglas; Dworaczek, Marian**
Industrial arbitration in Canada, 1965-1973: a selective bibliography. [Toronto]: Ontario Ministry of Labour, Research Library, 1974. 8 p.
Note: Approx. 100 entries.– Includes books, government documents, labour organization publications, periodical articles, list of serial publications dealing with industrial arbitration.
Location: OONL.

2818 **Greenberg, A. Morley; Wright, David M.**
The variable work week: a selected bibliography, 1967-1974. [Toronto]: Human, Social and Environmental Factors Section, Research and Development Division, Ontario Ministry of Transportation and Communications, 1974. 25 p.
Note: Approx. 375 entries.– Topics include variable work hours, shorter work week, altered work week, extended work week, compressed work week, four-day week, three-day week, staggered hours, flexible hours.– Within these subject areas are subdivisions: implementation, evaluation, effects on transportation, social impact, bibliographies.
Location: NBFU.

2819 **Taillon, Michèle**
Inventaire de sources de données sur la main-d'oeuvre et l'emplois. Québec: Ministère de l'éducation, Direction générale de la planification, 1974. 150 p. (Documents éducation et emploi / Québec Ministère de l'éducation, Direction générale de la planification ; 4-15)
Note: Localisation: OONL.

— 1975 —

2820 **Doughty, Howard**
"Industrial relations and labour history."
In: *Communiqué: Canadian Studies*; Vol. 1, no. 3 (March 1975) p. 2-22.; ISSN: 0318-1197.
Note: Books and pamphlets, articles, films, audio tapes, government publications, British and American comparative material.
Location: OONL.

2821 **Knight, Rolf**
Work camps and company towns in Canada and the U.S.: an annotated bibliography. [Vancouver]: New Star Books, [c1975]. 80 p.; ISBN: 0-919888-60-7.
Note: Approx. 325 entries.– Social history of primary resource workers, principally loggers and miners.– Focus on British Columbia and U.S.; Quebec is excluded.– Includes published and unpublished works.
Location: OONL.

2822 **Laperrière, Guy**
"Plan du cours: histoire du syndicalisme au Québec: bibliographie."
Dans: *Histoire des travailleurs québécois: Bulletin RCHTQ*; Vol. 2, no 2 (juin-juillet 1975) p. 29-40.; ISSN: 0315-7938.
Note: Localisation: OONL.

2823 **Moore, Larry F.**
Advances in manpower management: a selected annotated bibliography. Vancouver: Institute of Industrial Relations, University of British Columbia, 1975. vi, 69 p.
Note: Approx. 500 entries.– Books, monographs, articles, published speeches related to manpower management, excluding the area of labour-management relations.– Topics covered include employment levels, labour

market, migration and mobility, compensation, manpower planning, training and development, termination, discrimination and underutilization in employment.– Includes numerous Canadian references.
Location: OONL.

2824 **Queen's University (Kingston, Ont.). Industrial Relations Centre. Research Reference Section**
Collective bargaining in the public service of Canada: a bibliography. [Kingston, Ont.]: Industrial Relations Centre, Queen's University at Kingston, 1975. 18 p.
Note: Approx. 190 entries.– Government publications, conference proceedings, journal articles, theses from 1947 to 1975.
Location: OONL.

2825 **Queen's University (Kingston, Ont.). Industrial Relations Centre. Research Reference Section**
Cost of living adjustments (COLA): a bibliography. Kingston, Ont.: Industrial Relations Centre, Queen's University at Kingston, 1975. 9 l.
Note: Approx. 100 entries.
Location: OONL.

2826 **Queen's University (Kingston, Ont.). Industrial Relations Centre. Research Reference Section**
Final offer selection (FOS): a bibliography. Kingston, Ont.: Industrial Relations Centre, Queen's University, 1975. 7 l.
Note: Approx. 75 entries.– Publications dealing with one aspect of the collective bargaining process.– Includes Canadian references.
Location: OONL.

2827 **Queen's University (Kingston, Ont.). Industrial Relations Centre. Research Reference Section**
Wage-price controls: a selected bibliography. [Kingston, Ont.]: Industrial Relations Centre, Queen's University at Kingston, 1975. [10] p.
Note: General references on prices, wages and incomes policies in various countries, including Canada; background documents on Canadian experience (World War II, 1970s).
Location: OONL.

— 1976 —

2828 **Canada. Department of Labour. Accident Prevention Division. Technical Library**
Bibliography: occupational safety and health: selected holdings of Technical Library, Accident Prevention Division, Canada Department of Labour/Bibliographie: sécurité et hygiène professionnelles: choix de volumes de la Bibliothèque technique, Division de la prévention des accidents, Ministère du travail du Canada. Ottawa: Labour Canada, Occupational Safety and Health, 1976. x, 144 p.; ISBN: 0-662-00154-0.
Note: Approx. 1,000 entries.– Lists published materials in the areas of accident prevention, chemicals, construction, ergonomics/human engineering, fire protection, industrial health and welfare, management and supervision of safety programs, occupational disease, radiation, worker's compensation.– Excludes periodicals, annual reports, statutes and regulations, standards, catalogues, handbooks, technical data sheets.– Substantial Canadian content.– Compiled by W. Keith McLaughlin.– Text in English and French/texte en français et en anglais.
Previous editions:
1974. 139 p.– Compiled by Celia Bookman.

1971. 102 p.
1970. 2, 96 p.
Supplement: *Occupational safety and health, 1976-1980: a bibliography/Sécurité et hygiène au travail, 1976-1980: bibliographie.* [Hull, Quebec]: Labour Canada, 1981. x, 75 p.; ISBN: 0-662-51333-9.
Location: OONL.

2829 **Dworaczek, Marian**
Job satisfaction: a selected bibliography. Toronto: Research Library, Ontario Ministry of Labour, 1976. 38 p.
Note: Approx. 400 entries.– Includes books, documents from government and private agencies, university research studies, periodical articles.
Location: OONL.

2830 **Dworaczek, Marian; Perry, Elizabeth**
Labour-management cooperation: a selected bibliography. Toronto: Ontario Ministry of Labour, Research Library, 1976. 18 p. (Bibliography series / Ontario Ministry of Labour, Research Library ; no. 5)
Note: Location: OOP.

2831 **Haist, Dianne**
Equal pay for work of equal value: a selected bibliography. Toronto: Ontario Ministry of Labour, Research Library, 1976. 15 p. (Bibliography series / Ontario Ministry of Labour, Research Library ; no. 3)
Note: Location: OONL.

2832 **Moll, Marita**
Industrial relations in Canada. Ottawa: Canadian Teachers' Federation, 1976. 59 p. (Bibliographies in education / Canadian Teachers' Federation ; no. 57); ISBN: 0-88989-010-2.
Note: 325 entries.– Period covered is 1971-1976 for books, 1973-1976 for periodicals.– Includes sections on collective bargaining, dispute resolution, labour and politics, labour law, strikes and strike-breaking, unionization and professionalism, with sub-section relating to teachers.
Location: OONL.

2833 **Turgeon, Bernard**
Les horaires variable: examen de la littérature. Québec: Ministère du travail et de la main-d'oeuvre, Direction générale de la recherche, 1976. ii, 165 p.; ISBN: 0-7754-25-42-7.
Note: Localisation: OONL.

2834 **Williams, Carol**
Workers' participation: a bibliography of current books and articles. Kingston, Ont.: Industrial Relations Centre, Queen's University, 1976. 18 p.
Note: Includes a section entitled "References from Canadian sources."
Location: OONL.

— 1977 —

2835 **Anderson, Roselyn**
Employee benefits: a selected bibliography. Toronto: Ontario Ministry of Labour, Research Library, 1977. 24 p. (Bibliography series / Ontario Ministry of Labour, Research Library ; no. 7)
Note: Location: OONL.

2836 **Dworaczek, Marian**
Labour topics: a selected bibliography. Toronto: Ontario Ministry of Labour, Research Library, 1977. 78 p. (Bibliography series / Ontario Ministry of Labour, Research Library ; no. 9)
Note: Approx. 900 entries.

Location: OONL.

2837 **Newton, Keith; Leckie, Norman**
What's QWL?: definition, notes, and bibliography. Ottawa: Economic Council of Canada, 1977. iv, 124 p.; ISBN: 0-662-01346-8.
Note: Books, reports, articles on social, economic, political and technological factors related to quality of working life."- Topics include accessibility of work, aspects of the job context, sociopsychological relationships, workplace malaise, strategies of work humanization, measurement and methodology.
Location: OONL.

2838 **Queen's University (Kingston, Ont.). Industrial Relations Centre. Research Reference Section**
Collective bargaining and white collar employees: a bibliography, 1970-1977. Kingston, Ont.: Industrial Relations Centre, Queen's University, 1977. 10 p.
Note: Approx. 125 entries.
Location: OONL.

2839 **Queen's University (Kingston, Ont.). Industrial Relations Centre. Research Reference Section**
Collective bargaining in education in Canada: a bibliography, 1970-1977. Kingston, Ont.: Industrial Relations Centre, Queen's University, 1977. 6 p.
Note: Approx. 75 entries.- Articles, studies, briefs to commissions of inquiry in two categories: school teachers and universities and colleges.
Location: OONL.

2840 **Queen's University (Kingston, Ont.). Industrial Relations Centre. Research Reference Section**
Health care sector unionization and collective bargaining: a bibliography, 1970-1977. Kingston, Ont.: Industrial Relations Centre, Queen's University, 1977. 9 p.
Note: Approx. 100 entries.
Location: OONL.

— 1978 —

2841 **Canada. Emplois et immigration Canada. Analyse et développement–Professions et carrières**
Instruments d'orientation professionnelle. [Ottawa]: Emploi et immigration Canada, Analyse et développement–Professions et carrières, [1978]. [16, 16] p.
Note: Texte en français et en anglais disposé tête-bêche.- Titre de la p. de. t. additionnelle: *Career guidance material*.
Localisation: OONL.

2842 **Canada. Employment and Immigration Commission. Occupational and Career Analysis and Development**
Career guidance material. [Ottawa]: Employment and Immigration Canada, Occupational and Career Analysis and Development, [1978]. [16, 16] p.
Note: Text in English and French with French text on inverted pages.- Title of additional title-page: *Instruments d'orientation professionnelle*.
Location: OONL.

2843 **Chaison, Gary N.; Cockburn, Leslie; Morris, John**
Labour education: a bibliography of selected reading materials available at libraries in New Brunswick/ L'enseignement syndical: une bibliographie de matières choisies disponibles dans les bibliothèques du Nouveau Brunswick. Fredericton: Department of Extension and Summer Session[s], University of New Brunswick, c1978. ix, 62 p.
Note: Approx. 600 entries.- Reports, documents, studies on labour-management relations, labour organizations, industrial relations and public policy, labour economics, labour conditions and problems, lists of serials and reference materials.- Text in English and French/texte en français et en anglais.
Location: OONL.

2844 **Dechêne, Paul**
Le mouvement de restructuration du travail: bibliographie sélective commentée sur les nouvelles formes d'organisation du travail. Québec: Direction générale de la recherche, Ministère du travail et de la main-d'oeuvre, 1978. x, 187 p. (Études et recherches / Québec Ministère du travail et de la main d'oeuvre, Direction générale de la recherche ; 3); ISBN: 0-775-43271-7.
Note: Localisation: OONL.

2845 **Miller, Alan V.**
Homosexuality and employment: a selected bibliography. Toronto: Ontario Ministry of Labour, Research Branch, 1978. 111 p. (Bibliography series / Ontario Ministry of Labour, Research Branch ; no. 11)
Note: Location: OONL.

2846 **Neamtan, Judith; Paterson, Craig**
Workers' health, safety and compensation: a preliminary bibliography of Canadian federal and provincial government commissions and inquiries. North Vancouver, B.C.: Capilano College Labour Studies Program, 1978. vii, 53 l. (Labour Studies Program Publication series / Capilano College Labour Studies Program ; no. 1)
Note: 118 entries.- Covers 1867 to 1976.- Chronological listing within federal and provincial jurisdictions.- At least one location is given for each document.- Excludes select and standing committees of legislative bodies, white papers, briefs presented to investigating bodies.
Location: OONL.

2847 **Ontario. Ministry of Labour. Library**
"Tripartism."
In: *Labour Topics*; Vol. 1, no. 4 (April 1978) p. 1-3.; ISSN: 0704-8874.
Note: Approx. 40 entries.
Location: AEU.

2848 **Ontario. Ministry of Labour. Library**
"Unionization of bank employees."
In: *Labour Topics*; Vol. 1, no. 3 (March 1978) p. 1-2.; ISSN: 0704-8874.
Note: 35 entries.
Location: AEU.

2849 **Peitchinis, Stephen G.**
Effects of technological changes on employment and educational and skill requirements: an annotated bibliography. Calgary: University of Calgary, 1978. 2, 63 l. (Studies on employment effects of technology)
Note: Approx. 200 entries.
Location: OONL.

2850 **Queen's University (Kingston, Ont.). Industrial Relations Centre. Research Reference Section**
Cafeteria, deferred and flexible compensation: a bibliography, 1970-1978. Kingston, Ont.: Industrial Relations Centre, Queen's University, 1978. 4 p. (Compensation bibliographies series / Industrial Relations Centre, Queen's University ; no. 7)
Note: Approx. 50 entries.- Includes Canadian references.
Location: OONL.

2851 **Queen's University (Kingston, Ont.). Industrial Relations Centre. Research Reference Section**
Compensation administration: a bibliography 1970-1978. Kingston, Ont.: Industrial Relations Centre, Queen's University, 1978. 13 p. (Compensation bibliographies series / Industrial Relations Centre, Queen's University ; no. 5)
Note: Approx. 200 entries.– Includes Canadian references.
Location: OONL.

2852 **Queen's University (Kingston, Ont.). Industrial Relations Centre. Research Reference Section**
Employee benefits: a bibliography, 1970-1978. Kingston, Ont.: Industrial Relations Centre, Queen's University, 1978. 12 p. (Compensation bibliographies series / Industrial Relations Centre, Queen's University ; no. 10)
Note: Approx. 200 entries.– Articles, government reports, consultants' studies dealing with fringe benefits.– Includes a number of Canadian references.
Location: OONL.

2853 **Queen's University (Kingston, Ont.). Industrial Relations Centre. Research Reference Section**
Employee stock options and employee stock ownership plans: a bibliography, 1970-1978. Kingston, Ont.: Industrial Relations Centre, Queen's University, 1978. 7 p. (Compensation bibliographies series / Industrial Relations Centre, Queen's University ; no. 8)
Note: Approx. 100 entries.– Includes Canadian references.
Location: OONL.

2854 **Queen's University (Kingston, Ont.). Industrial Relations Centre. Research Reference Section**
Pay for performance: a bibliography, 1970-1977. Kingston, Ont.: Industrial Relations Centre, Queen's University, 1978. 9 p.
Note: Approx. 100 entries.
Location: OONL.

2855 **Queen's University (Kingston, Ont.). Industrial Relations Centre. Research Reference Section**
Performance appraisal: a bibliography, 1970-1977. Kingston, Ont.: Industrial Relations Centre, Queen's University, 1978. 16 p. (Compensation bibliographies series / Industrial Relations Centre, Queen's University ; no. 2)
Note: Approx. 200 entries.– Includes Canadian references.
Location: OONL.

2856 **Roberts, Wayne, et al.**
The Hamilton working class, 1820-1977: a bibliography. Hamilton, Ont.: McMaster University, Labour Studies Programme, 1978. 62 p.
Note: Contains a group of six bibliographical essays related to the history of the labour movement and working people in Hamilton, Ontario and area.
Location: OONL.

2857 **Venkateswarlu, Tadiboyina**
Labor and manpower economics library bibliography. Rev. 4th ed. Windsor, Ont.: University of Windsor, 1978. iv l., 114 p.
Note: Approx. 1,900 entries.– Reference sources, unpublished dissertations, government documents, periodicals, monographs: labour economics, labour history, wage theory and determination, manpower economics, unemployment and fringe benefits, labour legislation, international labour organization.
Previous editions:
1976. iii, 100 p.
1974. iii, 95 l.
1973. i, 102 l.
Location: OONL.

— 1979 —

2858 **David, Hélène**
L'évaluation des tâches: bibliographie annotée des documents disponibles à l'IRAT. Montréal: Institut de recherche appliquée sur le travail, Centre de documentation, [1979]. 11 p. (Centre de documentation bibliographie / Institut de recherche appliquée sur le travail ; no. 1)
Note: Approx. 75 entrées.
Localisation: OONL.

2859 **Kumar, Pradeep**
Canadian industrial relations information: sources, technical notes and glossary. Kingston, Ont.: Industrial Relations Centre, Queen's University, 1979. viii, 166 p.; ISBN: 0-88886-101-X.
Note: Contains technical notes on concepts, sources and methods of major information series relating to the economy, manpower and labour markets, labour legislation and public policy, trade unionism, collective bargaining and labour relations, wages, productivity and labour costs; bibliography of sources of information, including list of major industrial relations periodicals.
Location: OONL.

2860 **Wolfe, Carol Anne**
Employment of the physically handicapped: a selected bibliography, 1970-1978. Toronto: Ontario Ministry of Labour, Research Branch, 1979. 42 p. (Bibliography series / Ontario Ministry of Labour, Research Branch ; no. 14)
Note: Approx. 400 entries.
Location: OONL.

— 1980 —

2861 **Bujold, Charles**
"Signification du travail et valeurs de travail: revue de la littérature canadienne de langue française."
Dans: *Orientation professionnelle*; Vol. 16, no 1 (juin 1980) p. 5-47.; ISSN: 0030-5413.
Note: Localisation: OONL.

2862 **Canadian Centre for Occupational Health and Safety**
A review of the literature on attitudes and roles and their effects on safety in the workplace. [S.l.]: Canadian Centre for Occupational Health and Safety, 1980. 54 p.; ISBN: 0-660-11374-0.
Note: 106 entries.– Literature review and bibliography of reports, articles and documents dealing with the psychological aspects of industrial accidents and safety.– Includes Canadian references.
Titre en français: *Revue des publications traitant des attitudes et des rôles et de leurs effets sur la sécurité du travail*.
Location: OONL.

2863 **Centre canadien d'hygiène et de sécurité au travail**
Revue des publications traitant des attitudes et des rôles et de leurs effets sur la sécurité du travail. Hamilton, Ont.: Centre canadien d'hygiène et de sécurité au travail, 1980. 69 p.; ISBN: 0-660-91076-4.
Note: 106 entrées.

English title: *A review of the literature on attitudes and roles and their effects on safety in the workplace.*
Localisation: OONL.

2864 **Diamond, Sara**
Women's labour history in British Columbia: a bibliography, 1930-1948. [Vancouver, B.C.]: Press Gang Publishers, [c1980]. 80 p.; ISBN: 0-00074-033-8.
Note: Approx. 450 entries.– Periodical articles, government publications, trade union documents.
Location: OONL.

2865 **Ford, John; McTavish, Isabella**
Job sharing and work sharing: a selected bibliography. [Toronto]: Ontario Ministry of Labour, Library, 1980. 12 p.
Note: Approx. 175 entries.
Location: OONL.

2866 **Gower, Wendy**
Employee assistance programs. Kingston, Ont.: Industrial Relations Centre, Queen's University, 1980. 21 p. (Mimeographed bibliography series / Industrial Relations Centre, Queen's University ; no. 16)
Note: Approx. 350 entries.– Books, studies, articles on employee assistance programs in general and specific programs: alcoholism, career development, child care, counselling, financial, job separation/outplacement, fitness, retirement, stress.
Location: OONL.

2867 **Ontario. Ministry of Labour. Library**
"Severance pay: a selected bibliography."
In: *Labour Topics*; Vol. 3, No. 10 (October 1980) p. 1-3.; ISSN: 0704-8874.
Note: Approx. 40 entries.
Location: AEU.

2868 **Roberts, Hazel J.**
Faculty collective bargaining in Canadian universities, 1974-1979/La négociation collective chez les professeurs des universités canadiennes, 1974-1979. Ottawa: Association of Universities and Colleges of Canada, Library, 1980. iii l., 44 p.; ISBN: 0-88876-066-3.
Note: Approx. 650 entries.– Books, periodical articles, university newsletters, bibliographies, collective agreements (for specific universities and faculty associations).– Text in English and French/texte en français et en anglais.
Previous edition: *Collective bargaining in higher education: a bibliography/La convention collective sur l'enseignement supérieur: une bibliographie.* 1974. 17 l.
Location: OONL.

2869 **Swanick, Eric L.**
Workmen's compensation in Canada. Monticello, Ill.: Vance Bibliographies, 1980. 4 p. (Public administration series: Bibliography ; P-584; ISSN: 0193-970X)
Note: Approx. 50 entries.
Location: OONL.

2870 **Vaisey, G. Douglas**
"Bibliography on Canadian labour history."
In: *Labour: Le Travail*; Vol. 6 (Autumn 1980) p. 183-214.; ISSN: 0700-3862.
Note: Location: AEU.

2871 **Vaisey, G. Douglas**
The labour companion: a bibliography of Canadian labour history based on materials printed from 1950 to 1975. Halifax: Committee on Canadian Labour History,

[c1980]. 126 p.
Note: Approx. 1,900 entries.– Compiled with the assistance of John Battye, Marie deYoung, Gregory Kealey.– Based on working files of Battye and Kealey, Committee on Canadian Labour History.– Excludes archival collections or manuscripts, non-historical trade union publications.
Location: OONL.

— 1981 —

2872 **Kaliski, S.F.**
Labour turnover in Canada: a survey of literature and data. Kingston, Ont.: Industrial Relations Centre, Queen's University, 1981. iv, 27 p. (Research and current issues series / Industrial Relations Centre, Queen's University ; no. 41; ISSN: 0317-2546); ISBN: 0-88886-112-5.
Note: Location: OONL.

2873 **Luce, Sally R.; Ostling, Kristen**
"Women and white collar unions: an annotated bibliography."
In: *Resources for Feminist Research*; Vol. 10, no. 2 (July 1981) p. 95-106.; ISSN: 0707-8412.
Note: Covers 1975 to 1981.– Categories include statistics/bibliographies/fact sheets, earnings differentials, women's labour force characteristics, women and white collar occupations, women and trade unions.
Location: AEU.

2874 **Maguire, Robert K.; Scott, Allen J.; Willson, K.M.**
The structure and dynamics of intra-urban labour markets: a diagnostic bibliography. Toronto: University of Toronto-York University Joint Program in Transportation, 1981. 58 p. (University of Toronto-York University Joint Program in Transportation Research report ; no. 76; ISSN: 0316-9456)
Note: 350 entries.– References dealing with local labour market problems at intra-urban scale: intra-urban wage rate patterns and processes, geography of intra-urban labour supply and demand, journey to work, job search processes, dual labour markets, planning and policy issues.
Location: OONL.

2875 **Tascona, J.**
Grievance handling: issues and approaches: bibliography with selected annotations. Kingston, Ont.: Industrial Relations Centre, Queen's University, 1981. 12 p. (Mimeographed bibliography series / Industrial Relations Centre, Queen's University ; no. 17)
Note: Approx. 90 entries.
Location: OONL.

2876 **Tascona, J.**
Job evaluation systems and pay discrimination: a bibliography with selected annotations. Kingston, Ont.: Industrial Relations Centre, Queen's University, 1981. 10 p. (Mimeographed bibliography series / Industrial Relations Centre, Queen's University ; no. 19)
Note: Approx. 50 entries.
Location: OONL.

2877 **Tascona, J.**
Union mergers: bibliography with selected annotations. Kingston, Ont.: Industrial Relations Centre, Queen's University, 1981. 7 p. (Mimeographed bibliography series / Industrial Relations Centre, Queen's University ; no. 18)
Note: Approx. 50 entries.

Location: OONL.

2878 **Yanz, Lynda**
"Women and unions: a bibliography."
In: *Resources for Feminist Research*; Vol. 10, no. 2 (July 1981) p. 85-88.; ISSN: 0707-8412.
Note: Location: AEU.

— 1982 —

2879 **Arrowsmith, David**
Part-time workers: a selected bibliography. Kingston, Ont.: Industrial Relations Centre, Queen's University, 1982. 5 p. (Mimeographed bibliography series / Industrial Relations Centre, Queen's University ; no. 20)
Note: Approx. 75 entries.
Location: OONL.

2880 **Clarkson, Thora K.**
Miners and prospectors of Canada: a bibliography. Toronto: Thora Clarkson, 1982. vi, 80 p.; ISBN: 0-9691318-0-1.
Note: 434 entries.– Gathers references from 1850s to 1982.– Emphasis on labour history related to mining, not the industry as such.– Excludes material on mining legislation, economics, taxation, minerals marketing.– Includes a list of additional bibliographies.
Location: OOP.

2881 **Gascon, Denis; Roy, Paul-Martel**
La productivité dans le secteur public: les écrits récents, 1975-1982, sur le sujet, particulièrement ceux qui portent sur le Québec. Montréal: Laboratoire de recherche sur l'emploi, la répartition et la sécurité du revenu, 1982. 12, 4 f.
Note: Localisation: OONL.

2882 **Ontario. Ministry of Labour. Library**
"Bibliographies prepared by the Ontario Ministry of Labour Library, 1970-1982."
In: *Labour Topics*; Vol. 5, no. 12 (December 1982) p. 1-8.; ISSN: 0704-8874.
Note: Approx. 100 entries.
Location: AEU.

2883 **Richmond, Anthony H.**
Comparative studies in the economic adaptation of immigrants in Canada: a literature review. Downsview, Ont.: York University, Institute for Behavioural Research, 1982. viii, 226 p.; ISBN: 0-919604-95-1.
Note: Reviews major studies of immigrant economic adaptation undertaken between 1969 and 1981.– Topics include labour force participation, employment status, incidence of unemployment, relation between intended and actual occupations, job mobility, occupational status achievement, income levels, housing, job satisfaction.
Location: OONL.

2884 **Roy, Paul-Martel**
Politiques d'emploi des gouvernements au Québec: inventaire, bibliographie, éléments d'évaluation. Montréal: Laboratoire de recherche sur l'emploi, la répartition et la sécurité du revenu, Université du Québec à Montréal, 1982. [4], 79 f. (Cahier / Laboratoire de recherche sur l'emploi, la répartition et la sécurité du revenu, Université du Québec à Montréal ; 8202)
Note: Localisation: OONL.

— 1983 —

2885 **Alain, Jean-Marc; Bélanger, Jacqueline**
Qualité de vie au travail et productivité: lexique et bibliographie. [Sainte-Foy, Québec]: ENAP, [1983]. 70 p.;

ISBN: 2-92011-12-0.
Note: 238 entrées.– Monographies, périodiques, bibliographies.
Localisation: OONL.

2886 **Dworaczek, Marian**
History of the Canadian labour unions: a selective bibliography. Monticello, Ill.: Vance Bibliographies, [1983]. 7 p. (Public administration series: Bibliography ; P-1300; ISSN: 0193-970X); ISBN: 0-88066-710-9.
Note: Approx. 85 entries.
Location: OONL.

2887 **Ontario. Ministry of Labour. Library**
"Grievance arbitration: a selected bibliography."
In: *Labour Topics*; Vol. 6, no. 9 (September 1983) p. 1-4.; ISSN: 0704-8874.
Note: Approx. 50 entries.
Location: AEU.

2888 **Ontario. Ministry of Labour. Library**
"Women in labour unions: a selected bibliography."
In: *Labour Topics*; Vol. 6, no. 10 (October 1983) p. 1-4.; ISSN: 0704-8874.
Note: Approx. 50 entries.
Location: AEU.

— 1984 —

2889 **Couture, Denise, et al.**
Matériaux pour une sociologie appliquée à la santé et sécurité du travail: bibliographie. Montréal: Centre d'information et d'aide à la recherche, Département de sociologie, Université de Montréal, 1984. xxii, 258 p. (Les Cahiers du CIDAR / Centre d'information et d'aide à la recherche, Département de sociologie, Université de Montréal ; no 5); ISBN: 2-920770-00-4.
Note: Approx. 2,500 entrées.– Comprend trois grandes parties principales: la nature des problèmes en santé et sécurité du travail; les formes de gestion sociale de la santé et sécurité du travail et leurs resultats; les approches disciplinaires de la santé et securité du travail.– Inclut un nombre considérable d'ouvrages canadiens.
Localisation: OONL.

2890 **Laperrière, René**
Bibliographie du droit du travail canadien et québécois, 1964-1983. Cowansville, Québec: Éditions Y. Blais, c1984. xv, 70 p.; ISBN: 2-89073-515-X.
Note: Approx. 800 entrées.– Livres, périodiques, publications gouvernementales, revues de relations industrielles, compte-rendus de congrès/colloques: ouvrages général, code du travail, droit d'association, l'accréditation, négociation collective, convention collective, l'arbitrage des griefs, activités de pression, secteur public, normes du travail.
Localisation: OONL.

2891 **Ontario. Ministry of Labour. Library**
"Paid maternity leave: a selected bibliography."
In: *Labour Topics*; Vol. 5, no. 2 (February 1982) p. 1-4; vol. 7, no. 9 (September 1984) p. 1-3.; ISSN: 0704-8874.
Note: Approx. 100 entries.
Location: AEU.

2892 **Ontario. Ministry of Labour. Library**
"Technological change and employment in Canada: a selected bibliography."
In: *Labour Topics*; Vol. 7, no. 4 (April 1984) p. 1-4.; ISSN: 0704-8874.

Note: Approx. 50 entries.
Location: AEU.

2893 **Ontario. Ministry of Labour. Library**
"Worksharing: jobsharing: a selected bibliography."
In: *Labour Topics*; Vol. 7, no. 11 (November 1984) p. 1-3.;
ISSN: 0704-8874.
Note: Approx. 35 entries.
Location: AEU.

2894 **Ontario. Ministry of Treasury and Economics. Library Services**
Job creation: alternative approaches: a selective bibliography. Toronto: Ontario Ministry of Treasury and Economics, Library Services, 1984. 14 p. (T & E Bibliographies / Ontario Ministry of Treasury and Economics, Library Services ; no. 8)
Note: Location: OONL.

2895 **Service de diffusion sélective de l'information de la Centrale des bibliothèques**
Le chômage. Montréal: Le Service, 1984. 37 p. (DSI/CB ; no 17; ISSN: 0825-5024); ISBN: 2-89059-217-0.
Note: 137 entrées.– Livres, articles de périodiques, documents audiovisuels se rapportant au chômage.– La majorité de ces documents sont québécois ou canadiens.– La période couverte est de 1975 à 1983.
Localisation: OONL.

— 1985 —

2896 **Canadian Labour Congress**
Alphabetical list of Canadian Labour Congress briefs. [Ottawa: The Congress], 1985. 40 p.
Note: Covers 1959 to 1985.– Arranged by subject (health, labour legislation, transportation, etc.), and chronologically within each subject.
Location: OONL.

2897 **Leduc, Marcel; Vaisey, G. Douglas**
"The Canadian labour bibliography/Bibliographie du mouvement ouvrier canadien."
In: *Labour: Le Travail*; Vol. 8/9 (Autumn/Spring 1981/1982) p. 334-348; vol. 10 (Autumn 1982) p. 193-227; vol. 12 (Autumn 1983) p. 223-248; vol. 16 (Fall 1985) p. 245-270.; ISSN: 0700-3862.
Note: Continued by: Michael Lonardo (Fall 1989); Michael Lonardo and Robert Sweeny (Fall 1990, Spring 1991).
Location: AEU.

2898 **May, Louise**
A guide to labour records and resources in British Columbia. Vancouver: Special Collections Division, University of British Columbia Library, 1985. 197 p.
Note: Part 1, p. 1-42, is a select bibliography of articles, theses, pamphlets, books and newspapers which describe and analyze historical and current labour issues in British Columbia.
Location: OONL.

2899 **Ontario. Ministry of Labour. Library**
"Collective bargaining and first contracts: a selected bibliography."
In: *Labour Topics*; Vol. 8, no. 6 (June 1985) p. 1-2.; ISSN: 0704-8874.
Note: 25 entries.
Location: AEU.

— 1986 —

2900 **Benson, John**
"Canadian labour history: essay in bibliography."

In: *Bulletin: Society for the Study of Labour History*; Vol. 51, no. 1 (1986) p. 18-24.; ISSN: 0049-1179.
Note: Location: OONL.

2901 **Canadian Labour Congress. Educational Services**
CLC Educational Services catalogue. [Ottawa]: The Congress, 1986. xi, 202 p. (loose-leaf).
Note: Productions and holdings of CLC Educational Services Department in English language since 1977: books, booklets, leaflets, pamphlets, legislative briefs, manuals, video recordings, films and slides.
Location: OONL.

2902 **Curtis, Joanna B.**
Joint workplace health and safety committees and worker participation: a selected bibliography. Hamilton, Ont.: Canadian Centre for Occupational Health and Safety, 1986. 51 p.; ISBN: 0-660-12076-3.
Note: Approx. 300 entries.– Covers from early 1970s to 1985.– Includes government reports, journal articles, books, parts of books.– Abstracts for most items.
Location: OONL.

2903 **Dworaczek, Marian**
Workers' compensation: a bibliography. Monticello, Ill.: Vance Bibliographies, 1986. 38 p. (Public administration series: Bibliography ; P-1974; ISSN: 0193-970X); ISBN: 0-89028-934-4.
Note: Approx. 400 entries.– Monographs, articles, legislation, cases, collected works, periodicals, bibliographies.– Includes Canadian section.
Location: BVAWC.

2904 **Frank, David, et al.**
The New Brunswick worker in the 20th century: a reader's guide: a selective annotated bibliography/Les travailleurs au Nouveau-Brunswick au 20ième siècle: un guide au lecteur: bibliographie choisie et annotée. Fredericton: Department of History, University of New Brunswick, 1986. 178 p.
Note: 245 entries.– Published material only.– Excludes archival materials, government publications, documentary films.– Text in English and French/texte en français et en anglais.
Location: OONL.

2905 **Kerur, Sharad**
Factfinding, a dispute resolution procedure for collective bargaining: a review of the existing literature and an analysis of its use by school boards and teachers in Ontario. Kingston, Ont.: Industrial Relations Centre, Queen's University, 1986. xii, 109 [i.e. 119] p. (Research essay series / School of Industrial Relations, Queen's University ; no. 5); ISBN: 0-88886-136-2.
Note: 45 entries.– Literature review and bibliography dealing with factfinding as a procedure in the collective bargaining process.– Includes Canadian, mainly Ontario references.
Location: OONL.

2906 **Leduc, Marcel**
"Bibliographie sélective du monde ouvrier."
Dans: *Histoire des travailleurs québécois: Bulletin RCHTQ*; Vol. 12, no 1 (hiver 1986) p. 13-45.; ISSN: 0315-7938.
Note: 388 entrées.– Livres, articles, bibliographies, thèses de maîtrise et de doctorat.
Localisation: OONL.

2907 **Ontario. Ministry of Labour. Library and Information Services**
"Electronic monitoring & surveillance in the workplace: a selected bibliography."
In: *Labour Topics*; Vol. 9, no. 5 (May 1986) p. 1-2.; ISSN: 0704-8874.
Note: 19 entries.
Location: AEU.

2908 **Ontario. Ministry of Labour. Library and Information Services**
"Part-time work: a selected bibliography."
In: *Labour Topics*; Vol. 9, no. 7 (July 1986) p. 1-4.; ISSN: 0704-8874.
Note: Approx. 50 entries.
Location: OONL.

2909 **Richling, Joanne**
Work and workers: an annotated bibliography for secondary schools. Halifax, N.S.: Committee on Labour Education in the Schools, Henson College of Public Affairs and Continuing Education, Dalhousie University, 1986. 128 p. (Work and workers: a resource for teachers; ISSN: 0829-8955); ISBN: 0-7703-0966-6.
Note: Approx. 500 entries.– Books, government reports and studies in English on labour and trade unions for school use in Nova Scotia, all by Canadians, about Canadian subjects, published in Canada.– Topics include work and working conditions, health/safety/technology, unemployment, women and work, trade unions, co-operative and credit unions, music/poetry/drama/art, economic and social conditions.
Location: OONL.

2910 **Wybouw, George; Kanaan, Richard**
Office automation and productivity: review of the literature. Laval, Quebec: Canadian Workplace Automation Research Centre, Organizational Research Directorate, 1986. ii, 165 p.; ISBN: 0-662-16252-8.
Note: Approx. 125 entries.– Abstracts of documents dealing with workplace automation and productivity, employee motivation, training, supervision.
Titre en français: *La bureautique et la productivité: revue de la littérature.*
Location: OONL.

— 1987 —

2911 **Boulet, Marie-France**
Équité salariale: bibliographie sélective et annotée. Québec: Bibliothèque de l'Assemblée nationale, Division de la référence parlementaire, 1987. 71 p. (Bibliographie / Bibliothèque de l'Assemblée nationale du Québec ; no 9; ISSN: 0836-9100)
Note: 282 entrées.– Couvre la période de 1983 à 1987.– Inclut bibliographies, monographies, articles de périodiques, thèses, publications gouvernementales.
Localisation: OONL.

2912 **Brody, Bernard; Létourneau, Yves; Poirier, André**
Revue de littérature sur les coûts indirects des accidents du travail. Montréal: École de relations industrielles, Université de Montréal, 1987. 43 p. (Document de recherche / École de relations industrielles, Université de Montréal ; 87-13; ISSN: 0829-0121)
Note: 32 entrées.– Essai bibliographique.– Comprend quelques références canadiennes.
Localisation: OONL.

2913 **Cousineau, Eric**
Comparable worth: a list of readings. Kingston, Ont.: Industrial Relations Centre, Queen's University, 1987. 109 p. (Mimeographed bibliography series / Industrial Relations Centre, Queen's University ; no. 23); ISBN: 0-88886-168-0.
Note: Approx. 750 entries.– Books, periodical and newspaper articles related to job evaluation, pay equity, affirmative action, discrimination in employment.
Location: OONL.

2914 **LeBrasseur, Rolland, et al.**
Worker co-operatives: an international bibliography/ Coopératives de travailleurs: une bibliographie internationale. Saskatoon: Centre for the Study of Co-operatives, University of Saskatchewan, [1987]. v, 68 p.
Note: Approx. 1,300 entries.– Summarizes literature on worker cooperatives in English and French for the period 1970-1987: books, journal articles, research monographs, conference proceedings.– Text in English and French/ texte en français et en anglais.
Location: OONL.

2915 **Mercier, Jacques**
Les effets du salaire minimum sur l'emploi: revue de la littérature empirique américaine, canadienne et québécoise et estimations additionnelles pour le Québec. Québec: Département des relations industrielles, Université Laval, [1987]. i f., 106, [39] p. (Collection Instruments du travail / Département des relations industrielles, Université Laval ; 87-04); ISBN: 2-920259-08-3.
Note: Localisation: OONL.

2916 **Ontario. Ministry of Labour. Library**
"Free trade and collective bargaining: a selected bibliography."
In: *Labour Topics*; Vol. 10, no. 7 (July 1987) p. 1-2.; ISSN: 0704-8874.
Note: 32 entries.
Location: AEU.

2917 **Ontario. Ministry of Labour. Library and Information Services**
"Educational leave: a selected bibliography."
In: *Labour Topics*; Vol. 10, no. 3 (March 1987) p. 1-4.; ISSN: 0704-8874.
Note: Approx. 50 entries.
Location: AEU.

— 1988 —

2918 **Dworaczek, Marian**
Industrial relations and the Canadian Charter of Rights: a bibliography. Monticello, Ill.: Vance Bibliographies, [1988]. 11 p.; ISBN: 1-555907-70-9.
Note: Location: SSU.

2919 **Gower, Wendy**
Grievance arbitration: a bibliography. Kingston, Ont.: Industrial Relations Centre, Queen's University, 1988. [4] p. (Mimeographed bibliography series / Industrial Relations Centre, Queen's University ; no. 24)
Note: Approx. 50 entries.
Location: OONL.

2920 **New Brunswick. Legislative Library**
Employment equity/Équité en matière d'emplois. Fredericton: New Brunswick Legislative Library, 1988. 10 l. (Bibliography / New Brunswick Legislative Library)
Note: Includes publications in English and French.

Location: OONL.

2921 Ontario. Ministry of Labour. Library and Information Services
"Affirmative action: employment equity: a selected bibliography."
In: *Labour Topics*; Vol. 11, no 9 (September 1988) p. 1-4.; ISSN: 0704-8874
Note: Approx. 50 entries.
Location: OONL.

2922 Ontario. Ministry of Labour. Library and Information Services
"Pay equity – a Canadian perspective: a selected bibliography."
In: *Labour Topics*; Vol. 11, no. 4 (April 1988) p. 1-4.; ISSN: 0704-8874.
Note: Approx. 50 entries.
Location: AEU.

2923 Wybouw, George; Kanaan, Richard
La bureautique et la productivité: revue de la littérature. Laval, Québec: Centre canadien de recherche sur l'information du travail, c1988. ii, 162 p.; ISBN: 0-662-94940-4.
Note: Approx. 125 entrées.– Résumés des documents sur le sujet de la productivité dans l'environnement du bureau: systèmes informatisés de bureau, mesure de productivité, motivation, performance, supervision, bénéfices potentiels.
English title: *Office automation and productivity: review of the literature.*
Localisation: OONL.

— 1989 —

2924 Dworaczek, Marian
Labour legislation in Canada: a bibliography. Monticello, Ill.: Vance Bibliographies, 1989. 150 p. (Public administration series: Bibliography ; P-2776; ISSN: 0193-970X); ISBN: 0-7920-0366-7.
Note: Approx. 2,175 entries.– General materials (bibliographies, indexes, theses, audio-visual material, periodicals, reference works); specific issues (affirmative action, contracting out, drugs and employment, pay equity, pensions, working conditions, etc.).
Location: OOP.

2925 Lonardo, Michael
"The Canadian labour bibliography/Bibliographie du mouvement ouvrier canadien."
In: *Labour: Le Travail*; Vol. 24 (Fall 1989) p. 95-218.; ISSN: 0700-3862.
Note: Continues: Marcel Leduc and G. Douglas Vaisey (Autumn/Spring 1981-1982-Fall 1985).– Continued by: Michael Lonardo and Robert Sweeny (Fall 1990-Fall 1992).
Location: AEU.

2926 Ontario. Ministry of Labour. Library and Information Services
"Employee pensions: a selected bibliography."
In: *Labour Topics*; Vol. 12, no. 4 (April 1989) p. 1-4.; ISSN: 0704-8874.
Note: Approx. 50 entries.
Location: AEU.

2927 Ontario. Ministry of Labour. Library and Information Services
"Mandatory retirement: a selected bibliography."
In: *Labour Topics*; Vol. 12, no. 2 (February 1989) p. 1-3.;

ISSN: 0704-8874.
Note: Approx. 40 entries.
Location: AEU.

2928 Worker's Compensation Board of British Columbia. Films and Posters Department
Publications and posters catalogue. Inform, educate, remind, protect. [Richmond, B.C.]: Films and Posters Department, Worker's Compensation Board of British Columbia, 1989. 24 l.
Note: Location: OONL.

— 1990 —

2929 Burgess, Joanne
"Exploring the limited identities of Canadian labour: recent trends in English-Canada and Quebec."
In: *International Journal of Canadian Studies*; No. 1-2 (Spring-Fall 1990) p. 149-174.; ISSN: 1180-3991.
Note: Review of writings in the field of Canadian labour and working-class history from the 1970s and 1980s.
Location: OONL.

2930 Direction générale de la condition féminine de l'Ontario
L'équité d'emploi: une bibliographie commentée. Toronto: Direction générale de la condition féminine de l'Ontario, 1990. 12, 16 f.
Note: 47 entrées.– Thèmes: travail et les responsabilités familiales, garde des enfants, recrutement et la sélection, formation, syndicats, groupes-cible.– Annexe B: "Publications de la Direction générale de la condition féminine de l'Ontario."- Texte en français et en anglais disposé tête-bêche.– Titre de la p. de t. additionnelle: *Employment equity: an annotated bibliography.*
Localisation: OONL.

2931 Ontario. Ministry of Labour. Library and Information Services
"Employee dismissal – a Canadian perspective: a selected bibliography."
In: *Labour Topics*; Vol. 13, no. 1 (January 1990) p. 1-4.; ISSN: 0704-8874.
Note: Approx. 45 entries.
Location: AEU.

2932 Ontario Women's Directorate
Employment equity: an annotated bibliography. Toronto: Ontario Women's Directorate, 1990. 16, 12 l.
Note: 83 entries.– Topics include work-family issues, child care, recruitment and selection, training, labour unions.– Includes a list of Ontario Women's Directorate publications.– Text in English and French with French text on inverted pages.– Title of additional title-page: *L'équité d'emploi: une bibliographie commentée.*
Location: OONL.

2933 Walker, Catherine
Pay equity: the Ontario experience. Toronto: Pay Equity Commission of Ontario, 1990. ii l., 14 p. (Selected bibliography / Pay Equity Commission of Ontario ; no. 5)
Note: Location: OONL.

2934 Work and family employment policy: a selected bibliography. Victoria, B.C.: Work Well, 1990. 49 p.
Note: Approx. 1,000 entries.– Focus on Canadian literature dealing with work and family issues, effects of work life on the mental health of families, workplace survey literature.
Location: OONL.

— 1991 —

2935 **Alberta. Alberta Career Development and Employment**
An annotated bibliography of books on job-search related subjects. Edmonton: Information Development and Marketing Branch, Alberta Career Development and Employment, 1991. 40 p.
Note: Approx. 100 entries.– Covers 1986 to 1991.– Includes a substantial number of Canadian references.
Location: OONL.

2936 **Courchene, Melanie**
Training, retraining, and labour market adjustment: an annotated bibliography of selected literature. Kingston, Ont.: Industrial Relations Centre, Queen's University, 1991. 62 p. (Bibliography series / Industrial Relations Centre, Queen's University ; no. 8; ISSN: 0075-613X); ISBN: 0-88886-285-7.
Note: Approx. 200 entries.– Books, journal articles, monographs, reports by private and public research agencies, policy and position papers from government, labour and interest groups, conference proceedings, mimeographed articles, in the English language.– Emphasis on work published since 1980, with focus on Canadian perspective.– Excludes magazine articles, newspaper references, microdata sets.
Location: OONL.

— 1992 —

2937 **Auger, Michèle; Andersen, Heather**
Labour force adjustment for the 1990's: selective bibliography/L'adaptation de la main-d'oeuvre pour les années 1990: bibliographie sélective. Ottawa: Employment and Immigration Library, 1992. [6], 52 p.
Note: Approx. 400 entries.– All materials listed were published after 1988.– Books, articles, reports dealing with labour force development, skills, training, competitiveness, global economy, workforce adjustment in Canada, the United States, Great Britain, Australia and Europe.– Text in English and French/texte en français et en anglais.
Location: OONL.

2938 **Lonardo, Michael; Sweeny, Robert**
"The Canadian labour bibliography/Bibliographie du mouvement ouvrier canadien."
In: *Labour: Le Travail*; Vol. 26 (Fall 1990) p. 261-300; vol. 27 (Spring 1991) p. 371-423; vol. 28 (Fall 1991) p. 407-435; vol. 30 (Fall 1992) p. 339-367.; ISSN: 0700-3862.
Note: Continues: Marcel Leduc and G. Douglas Vaisey (Autumn:Spring 1981-1982-Fall 1985); Michael Londardo (Fall 1989).
Location: AEU.

2939 **Ontario. Ministry of Labour. Library and Information Services**
"Employment equity and the disabled: a selected bibliography."
In: *Labour Topics*; Vol. 15, no. 8-9 (September 1992) p. 1-4.; ISSN: 0704-8874.
Note: Approx. 50 entries.
Location: AEU.

2940 **Saint-Pierre, Céline; Rousseau, Thierry**
Bibliographie thématique sur le travail et la technologie. Québec: Service de la recherche et de l'évaluation, Musée de la civilisation, 1992. 70 p. (Document / Service de la recherche et de l'évaluation, Musée de la civilisation ; no 6); ISBN: 2-55112-841-2.

Note: Localisation: OONL.

— Ongoing/En cours —

2941 **Queen's University (Kingston, Ont.). Industrial Relations Centre. Research Reference Section**
Index of industrial relations literature. Kingston (Ont.): Industrial Relations Centre, Queen's University, 1977-. vol.; ISSN: 0226-1537.
Note: Annual compilation of articles, books, reports on all aspects of labour relations.– Approx. 2,000 entries in recent issues.
Location: OONL.

2942 **"[Selected bibliographies on Canadian labour issues]."**
In: *Labour Topics*; (1978-) vol.; ISSN: 0704-8874.
Note: Brief bibliographies (1-6 pages in length) on topics generally related to labour from a legal, social, medical, gender, economic, or educational perspective.– Appears in each issue from vol. 1, no. 1, 1978.
Location: OONL.

— 1897 —

2943 **Société de géographie de Québec**
Bibliographie: la Société de géographie de Québec vient de publier un bulletin de ses travaux depuis 1893 jusqu'à 1897. [Québec: s.n., 1897]. 1 f. (verso blanc).
Note: Microforme: ICMH collection de microfiches ; no 57879; ISBN: 0-665-57879-2. 1 microfiche (4 images).
Localisation: OONL.

— 1903 —

2944 **Clark, Edith**
"Niagara Falls: a partial bibliography."
In: *Bulletin of Bibliography*; Vol. 3, no. 6 (July 1903) p. 85-91.; ISSN: 0276-1602.
Note: 151 entries.– Some Canadian content.
Location: OONL.

— 1915 —

2945 **Sutherland, Betty**
"The Canadian Rockies: a short bibliography."
In: *Public Libraries*; Vol. 2, no. 5 (May 1915) p. 220-221.
Note: Location: OONL.

— 1918 —

2946 **"Geographical publications: reviews and titles of books, papers, maps."**
In: *Geographical Review*; (1916-1918) ; ISSN: 0016-7428.
Note: Regular listing of geographical publications, which from vol. 1, no. 1 (January 1916) to vol. 6, no. 4 (October 1918), includes a selection of Canadian publications.
Location: AEU.

— 1919 —

2947 **"Bibliography of the Canadian mountain region."**
In: *Canadian Alpine Journal*; Vol. 9 (1918) p. 159-164; vol. 10 (1919) p. 101-102.; ISSN: 0068-8207.
Note: Location: AEU.

— 1921 —

2948 **Dow, Charles Mason**
Anthology and bibliography of Niagara Falls. Albany: Published by the State of New York, J.B. Lyon Co., printers, 1921. 2 vol., [49] l. of pl. (1 folded): ill. (some col.), maps, port.
Note: References arranged in subject groupings, chronologically within each group.– Topics include discovery, history, travellers accounts, natural history (flora/fauna/geology), music and literature, industrialization, transportation (railroad, canals, bridges), preservation of falls.– Many Canadian listings.– List of additional bibliographies.
Location: OONL.

— 1926 —

2949 **Canada. Department of the Interior**
Bibliography on Hudson Bay: list of books and references contained in the Natural Resources Reference Library, Department of the Interior, Ottawa, March 24th, 1926. [S.l.: s.n., 1926]. 7 l.
Note: Location: OOP.

— 1930 —

2950 **Dietrich, B.**
"Britisch-Nordamerika, besonders Kanada [Bibliographie von 1916-1930]."
In: *Geographisches Jahrbuch*; 45 bd. (1930) S. 261-300.; ISSN: 0072-095X.
Note: Location: OOFF.

— 1933 —

2951 **Thorington, J. Monroe**
"A bibliography of the Canadian Rockies."
In: *Canadian Alpine Journal*; Vol. 22 (1933) p. 230-231.; ISSN: 0068-8207.
Note: Location: AEU.

— 1941 —

2952 **Tuckermann, Walther**
"Länderkunde der aussereuropäischen erdteile: Kanada und Neufundland [bibliographie von 1931-1939]."
In: *Geographisches Jahrbuch*; 56 Bd. II (1941) p. 357-432.; ISSN: 0072-095X.
Note: Location: BVAU.

— 1949 —

2953 **Robinson, Betty Belle**
Bibliography of population and immigration, with special reference to Canada. [Hamilton, Ont.: McMaster University], 1949. 20 l.
Note: Approx. 360 entries.
Location: OHM.

— 1950 —

2954 **Aumont, Gérard**
"Bibliographie sur l'enseignement de la géographie."
Dans: *Revue canadienne de géographie*; Vol. 4, nos 1-2 (janvier-avril 1950) p. 22-30.; ISSN: 0316-3032.
Note: Localisation: OONL.

2955 **Clark, Andrew H.**
"Contributions to geographical knowledge of Canada since 1945."
In: *Geographical Review*; Vol. 40, no. 2 (April 1950) p. 285-308.; ISSN: 0016-7428.
Note: Selective review of literature of interest to geographers.– Emphasis on writings by Canadians about Canada, particularly work of professional geographers: regional studies, systematic studies.– Excludes official government publications.
Location: OONL.

— 1954 —

2956 **Canada. Department of Mines and Technical Surveys. Geographical Branch**
A list of periodical literature on topics related to Canadian geography for the period 1940-1950. Ottawa: 1954. vi, 131 p. (Bibliographical series / Canada Department of Mines and Technical Surveys, Geographical Branch ; no. 9)
Note: Location: BVAS.

2957 **Canada. Department of Mines and Technical Surveys. Geographical Branch**
A selected list of periodical literature on topics related to Canadian geography for the period 1930-1939. Ottawa: 1954. iv l., 97 p. (Bibliographical series / Canada Department of Mines and Technical Surveys, Geographical Branch ; no. 11)
Note: Approx. 1,200 entries.
Location: BVAS.

— 1960 —

2958 **Canada. Department of Mines and Technical Surveys. Geographical Branch**
Bibliography of periodical literature on Canadian geography, 1930 to 1955. Ottawa: [Queen's Printer], 1959-1960. 6 parts. (Bibliographical series / Canada Department of Mines and Technical Surveys, Geographical Branch ; no. 22)
Note: Contents: Part 1, "Canada-General"; 2, "Atlantic Provinces"; 3, "Quebec and Ontario"; 4, "Prairie Provinces"; 5, "British Columbia and western Canada general"; 6, "Northern Canada" (Yukon, Northwest Territories, Arctic islands, Arctic sea areas, Alaska highway).– Sections in each part include: biogeography, description and travel, economic geography, historical geography, human geography, mathematical geography, physical geography, place names, political geography.
Location: OONL.

2959 **Canada. Department of Mines and Technical Surveys. Geographical Branch**
Selected bibliography on periglacial phenomena in Canada: annotations and abstracts. Ottawa: [Queen's Printer], 1960. 22 p. (Bibliographical series / Canada Department of Mines and Technical Surveys, Geographical Branch) ; no. 24)
Note: 93 entries.– Compiled by Frank A. Cook.
Location: OONL.

2960 **Hamelin, Louis-Edmond**
"Bibliographie annotée concernant la pénétration de la géographie dans le Québec."
Dans: *Cahiers de géographie de Québec*; Vol. 4, no 8 (avril-septembre 1960) p. 345-358.; ISSN: 0007-9766.
Note: Approx. 140 entrées.– Consacrée aux manuels de géographie qui ont été en usage dans le Québec, depuis la publication du premier en 1804.
Localisation: AEU.

— 1961 —

2961 **Brouillette, Benoît**
"Chronique pédagogique: les sources principales de documentation."
Dans: *Revue canadienne de géographie*; Vol. 14, nos 1-4 (1961) p. 72-99.; ISSN: 0316-3032.
Note: Quatre pays: Canada, France, Grande-Bretagne, États-Unis: manuels, atlas, cartes, auxiliaires visuels, sources de renseignements.
Localisation: OONL.

2962 **Schmelz, Oskar**
Jewish demography and statistics: bibliography for 1920-1960. Jerusalem: [s.n.], 1961. 1 vol. (in various pagings).
Note: Includes Canadian references.
Location: OONL.

— 1962 —

2963 **Michie, George H.**
A select annotated bibliography of Canadian geography.
Montreal: Canadian Association of Geographers, 1962. 19 p. (Canadian Association of Geographers Education Committee Bulletin ; no. 5; ISSN: 0068-8304)
Note: Approx. 175 entries.– Books, articles, government documents arranged by provinces, regions, territories.
Location: OONL.

— 1963 —

2964 **Canada. Bureau fédéral de la statistique**
Publications de recensement du Canada de 1961: liste. Ottawa: Bureau fédéral de la statistique, [1962-1963]. 3 vol.
Note: Texte en français et en anglais disposé tête-bêche.– Titre de la p. de t. additionnelle: *Publications of the 1961 census of Canada: list.*
Location: OONL.

2965 **Canada. Dominion Bureau of Statistics**
Publications of the 1961 census of Canada: list. Ottawa: Dominion Bureau of Statistics, [1962-1963]. 3 vol.
Note: Text in English and French with French text on inverted pages.– Title of additional title-page: *Publications du recensement du Canada de 1961: liste.*
Location: OONL.

— 1964 —

2966 **Canada. Department of Mines and Technical Surveys. Geographical Branch**
Selected bibliography on Canadian toponymy/ Bibliographie choisie d'ouvrages sur la toponymie au Canada. Ottawa: [Queen's Printer], 1964. 27 p. (Bibliographical series / Canada Department of Mines and Technical Surveys, Geographical Branch ; no. 30)
Note: Approx. 500 entries.– Regional arrangement of references pertaining to history and origin of place names, gazetteers and other compilations of names, reports and publications of Geographic Board of Canada (Canadian Permanent Committee on Geographical Names).– Text in English and French/texte en français et en anglais.
Location: OONL.

2967 **Towle, Edward L.**
Bibliography on the economic history and geography of the Great Lakes-St. Lawrence drainage basin. Rochester, N.Y.: University of Rochester, 1964. 41 l.
Note: Approx. 800 entries.– Books, journal articles, government publications, theses from Canada and U.S. pertaining to social science aspects of Great Lakes problems: regional analysis, transportation, trade and commerce in Canada-U.S. relations, industry and manufacturing, conservation and resource planning, urban development and land use.
Supplement: 1964. 34 l.– Topics added: hydrology-meteorology, geological structure, erosion and sedimentation, fisheries.
Location: OONL.

— 1966 —

2968 **Canada. Department of Mines and Technical Surveys. Geographical Branch**
Selected bibliography of Canadian geography/ Bibliographie choisie d'ouvrages sur la géographie au Canada. Ottawa: Queen's Printer, 1950-1966. 16 vol. (Bibliographical series / Canada Department of Mines and Technical Surveys, Geographical Branch ; nos. 2, 4-8, 10, 14-15, 17, 19, 23, 26-29, 32-33)
Note: Annual bibliography, 1949-1965, of books,

pamphlets, periodical literature relating to Canadian geography.– Includes section of maps.
Some issues are cumulations: no. 5 includes no. 2; no. 7 includes nos. 4 and 6.
Text in English and French/texte en français et en anglais.
Location: OONL.

2969 Stone, Maitlia B.; Kokich, George J.V.
A bibliography of Canadian demography. Ottawa: Dominion Bureau of Statistics, Census Division, 1966. 147 p. (Technical paper / Dominion Bureau of Statistics, Census Division ; no. 5)
Note: Approx. 1,070 entries.– Covers from early 1900s through 1965.– Books, government publications, periodical articles, unpublished material and work in progress in field of demographic analysis and related disciplines.
Location: OONL.

— 1967 —

2970 Harris, R. Colebrook
"Historical geography in Canada."
In: Canadian Geographer; Vol. 11, no. 4 (1967) p. 235-250.; ISSN: 0008-3658.
Note: 152 entries.– Brief overview of geographical writing in Canada followed by a bibliography of published material and theses.
Location: AEU.

2971 LeBlond, Robert
"Le Saint-Laurent: orientation bibliographique."
Dans: Cahiers de géographie de Québec; Vol. 11, no 23 (septembre 1967) p. 419-464.; ISSN: 0007-9766.
Note: Approx. 675 entrées.– Sources documentaire concernant la Voie maritime, le fleuve et le golfe du Saint-Laurent: aspects physiques (hydrologie, biologie, géomorphologie), aspects humaines (histoire, économie, droit et politique), aspects régionaux.
Localisation: AEU.

— 1968 —

2972 Mitchell, James Kenneth
A selected bibliography of coastal erosion, protection and related human activity in North America and the British Isles. [Toronto: Department of Geography, University of Toronto], 1968. 66 p. (Natural hazard research working paper / Department of Geography, University of Toronto ; no. 4)
Note: Approx. 700 entries.– Books, articles appearing in specialized periodicals, arranged in three categories: physical background, nature and control, human dimensions of coastal erosion.
Location: OONL.

— 1969 —

2973 Fiszhaut, Gustawa M.; Carrier, Lois J.
Guide to reference materials in geography in the Library of the University of British Columbia. Vancouver: University of British Columbia Library, 1969. 92 p. (Reference publication / University of British Columbia Library ; no. 27)
Note: Approx. 475 entries.– Includes general geographical aids (bibliographies, dictionaries, encyclopedias, indexes/abstracts), sections on geomorphology, biogeography and climatology, economic geography, social geography, regions.
Location: OONL.

— 1970 —

2974 Saint-Yves, Maurice; Dion, Louise
"Bibliographie sur la didactique de la géographie."
Dans: Cahiers de géographie de Québec; Vol. 14, no 31 (avril 1970) p. 117-147.; ISSN: 0007-9766.
Note: 630 entrées. Ouvrages portant sur les programmes, les méthodes, les recherches dans l'enseignement de la géographie, des études sur le milieu, sur les examens, sur les moyens audio-visuels.– Les manuels servant aux différent niveaux de l'enseignement sont exclus.
Localisation: AEU.

— 1971 —

2975 Atlantic Resource Planners
Annotated bibliography of Kouchibouguac National Park [microform]. Fredericton, N.B.: [s.n.], 1971. 2 microfiches (86 fr.).
Note: Topical listing of books, pamphlets, reports and studies on the area in Kent County, New Brunswick designated as Kouchibouguac National Park: human history, administration (land use, planning and development), natural history.– Includes a list of additional bibliographies.
Location: OOFF.

2976 Bendwell, André
Bibliographie annotée du Parc national La Mauricie. [Ottawa: Direction des parcs nationaux et des lieux historiques, Ministère des affaires Indiennes et du Nord Canadien, 1971. ii, 127 f.
Note: Approx. 600 entrées.– Études, ouvrages et cartes qui se rapportent au territoire du parc national de la Mauricie: anthropologie, conservation des ressources, écologie, faune, flore, géographie, histoire, hydrologie, météorologie, pédologie, planification, utilisation du sol et zoologie.
Localisation: OOFF.

2977 Beyer, Herman G.
Technical papers and technical memoranda issued by the Census Division, 1965-1968: an annotated list of studies and reports. Ottawa: Dominion Bureau of Statistics, Census Division, 1971. 36 p. (Working paper, General series / Dominion Bureau of Statistics, Census Division ; no. 1)
Note: Approx. 50 entries.
Location: OONL.

2978 Dodds, Donald G.
Annotated bibliography of Cape Breton Highlands National Park. [Ottawa]: National and Historic Parks Branch, Department of Indian Affairs and Northern Development, 1971. 128 l.
Note: Approx. 600 entries.– Articles, studies, maps related to the area within the park and to Cape Breton Island in general: natural history, human history, administration (land use, conservation, planning and development).– List of bibliographies.
Microform: Ottawa: Public Archives of Canada, 1972. 3 microfiches.
Supplement: Additions for the annotated bibliography of Cape Breton Highlands National Park. [Halifax: Atlantic Resource Planners, [1974]. 1 vol. (in various pagings).
Location: OOFF.

2979 **Dodds, Donald G.; Swain, Richard J.**
Bibliography of Kejimkujik National Park. [Ottawa: National and Historic Parks Branch, Department of Indian Affairs and Northern Development], 1971. [98] l.
Note: 500 entries.– Listing of references dealing with Kejimkujik National Park and the surrounding area in Nova Scotia: administration, human history, natural history.– List of maps.
Location: OORD.

2980 **Lefebvre, Claude-Jean**
"Bibliographie annotée des textes parus dans *Arctic*, de 1948 à 1969, sur le Nouveau-Québec, le Labrador et Baffin."
Dans: *Revue de géographie de Montréal*; Vol. 25, no 1 (1971) p. 53-57.; ISSN: 0035-1148.
Note: Localisation: AEU.

2981 **Mahy, Gérard D.**
Annotated bibliography of Fundy National Park. Bathurst, N.B.: National and Historic Parks Branch, 1971. 91, [2] l.
Note: 211 entries.– Books, articles, reports about Fundy National Park and adjacent areas; administration, human history, natural history, bibliographies.
Supplement: Mullen, E.C. *Additions to the Annotated bibliography of Fundy National Park, sections IV & V.* [S.l.: s.n.]; 1974. 34 p.
Location: OOFF.

2982 **Morisset, Pierre**
Bibliographie annotée sur l'histoire naturelle du Parc national Forillon (Québec). Québec: Parcs nationaux et des lieux historiques, 1971. 111 p.
Note: Localisation: OOPAC.

2983 **Oleson, Robert V.; Wilmat, Lloyd H.**
A selective and annotated bibliography of Riding Mountain National Park. Winnipeg, Man.: [s.n.], 1971. 125, 168 l.
Note: Approx. 900 entries arranged in two parts, by author and by subject groupings: monographs, journal articles, government reports and studies, theses, covering all aspects of the area within the boundaries of the park and the surrounding region.– Topics include administration, history, archaeology, natural history, native peoples, biography, tourism, wildlife management and land use.
Location: OOFF.

2984 **Russell, Marian**
Annotated bibliographies: Terra Nova and Gros Morne National Parks. St. John's, Nfld.: [s.n.], 1971. iv, 244 l.
Note: Approx. 1,400 entries.– Technical and popular studies and articles relating to fauna, flora, environment, people and planning within general vicinity of the two national parks arranged in two major sections: author listing, subject listing.– Includes a listing of additional bibliographies.
Supplement: Atlantic Resource Planners. *Additions for the Annotated bibliography of Terra Nova and Gros Morne National Parks.* Halifax: [s.n.], 1974. 117 p.
Location: QMAC.

— 1972 —

2985 **Canada. Ministère des travaux publics**
Bibliographie annotée des caractéristiques physiques de la côte nord de l'estuaire maritime et du golfe Saint-Laurent. Ottawa: Ministère des travaux publics, 1972. 191 l.
Note: Approx. 1,000 entrées.
Localisation: OONL.

2986 **Kienzle, Bob**
The Wood Buffalo National Park area: a bibliography. [Ottawa]: National and Historic Parks Branch, Department of Indian Affairs and Northern Development, 1972. xi, 61 l.
Note: 561 entries.– Books, articles (journal and newspaper), technical reports on Wood Buffalo National Park and adjacent areas.– Topics include administration and management, human history, birds, flora, mammals, natural history, planning and development, reserves, surveys, travel and description, wildlife, tourism.
Location: OOFF.

2987 **Padbury, Peter; Wilkins, Diane**
The future: a bibliography of issues and forecasting techniques. Monticello, Ill.: Council of Planning Librarians, 1972. 102 p. (Council of Planning Librarians Exchange bibliography ; 279)
Note: Approx. 1,000 entries.– Prepared for course series entitled "Ontario 2000: alternative futures."- Arranged in broad categories related to issues, e.g. ecology, resources, population, technology, food, lifestyle, with a separate section on forecasting techniques.
Location: OONL.

2988 **Paterson, Laura A.**
Annotated bibliography on Kluane National Park, Yukon Territory. Edmonton: Canadian Wildlife Service, 1972. 41 l.
Note: Approx. 200 entries.– Articles and reports dealing with geology, geomorphology and glaciology, hydrology, vegetation, wildlife and fish of the Kluane Park area from 1920s to 1972.– Includes general articles relating to potential of Kluane area as a national park.
Location: OOFF.

2989 **Scace, Robert C.**
An initial bibliography of the Elk Island National Park area. Calgary, Alta.: [s.n.], 1972. xvi, 97 l.: ill.
Note: 389 entries.– Selective, annotated listing of references pertaining to Elk Island National Park and surrounding public lands.– Topics include administration, land use, planning and development, human history (anthropology, history, exploration, settlement), natural history, maps, illustrations, photographs.
Location: BVAS.

2990 **Scace, Robert C.**
An initial bibliography of Waterton Lakes National Park, with additional references to Waterton-Glacier: the international peace park. Calgary: [s.n.], 1972. xvii, 249 l.
Note: 1,145 entries.– Selective, annotated list of references pertaining to geology, geomorphology, biology, natural and human history, admininstration of Waterton Lakes National Park and Glacier National Park.– Also includes literature on the Canadian national park system as a whole.
Location: BVAS.

2991 **Ship Harbour proposed national park: a bibliography.**
Halifax, N.S.: Dalhousie University, School of Library Service and University Library, 1972. 173 l.
Note: Approx. 800 entries.– Books, articles, documents, theses, films, maps relating to proposed national park at Ship Harbour, Nova Scotia.– Topics include administra-

tion (conservation, land use, planning and development), human history (anthropology, general history, socio-economic history), natural history, bibliographies and indexes.
Location: OOFF.

2992 **Thurlow and Associates**
A preliminary annotated bibliography for Pukaskwa National Park. Ottawa: Thurlow and Associates, 1972. vi, 266, [7] l.: maps.
Note: Approx. 700 entries.
Location: OORD.

2993 **Tudor, Dean**
Sources of statistical data for Ontario. Ottawa: Canadian Library Association, 1972. iv, 33 p.; ISBN: 0-88802-089-9.
Note: 361 entries (450 individual items).– Intended for current use, not historical purposes.– Omits monographic publications issued prior to 1960.– Emphasis on local and regional, rather than federal sources.– Publications of Statistics Canada are excluded.
Location: OONL.

— 1973 —

2994 **Adams, W. Peter; Barr, William**
"Annotated bibliography of the McGill sub-arctic research papers (1954-1970)."
In: *Revue de géographie de Montréal*; Vol. 27, no 4 (1973) p. 391-412.; ISSN: 0035-1148.
Note: Approx. 180 entries.– Listing of published field research undertaken at McGill Sub-Arctic Research Laboratory, Schefferville, Quebec.– Topics include lake ice, glacial geology, frost-heave, snow surveys, hydrology, climatology.
Location: OONL.

2995 **Scace, Robert C.**
Banff, Jasper, Kootenay and Yoho: an initial bibliography of the contiguous Canadian Rocky Mountains national parks. Ottawa: National and Historic Parks Branch, Department of Indian Affairs and Northern Development, 1973. 3 vol.: maps.
Note: 4,122 entries.– Covers 1885 to 1972.– Includes periodical and newspaper articles, government studies and reports, theses relating to geology, geomorphology, geography, biology, natural and human history, and administration of the four mountain parks, public lands adjacent to the parks, the national park system as a whole, national park systems in other countries.– Section on newspaper sources includes selected entries from the *Calgary Herald* between 1932 and 1973.– Brief section listing aerial photographs of the contiguous parks area.– Excludes fictional material, reports associated with surveying and mapping of the park, maps, photographic collections.
Updates and expands: *An annotated bibliography of the Banff National Park area.* [Ottawa: s.n.], 1970. xxiii, 229 l.– 2,098 entries.
Location: OONL.

2996 **Scace, Robert C.**
Glacier and Mount Revelstoke National Parks: an initial bibliography. Ottawa: National and Historic Parks Branch, Department of Indian Affairs and Northern Development, 1973. 173 l.
Note: 839 entries.– Published and unpublished non-fictional literature on Glacier and Mount Revelstoke National Parks and adjacent areas in the Selkirk

Mountains of British Columbia.– Includes notes on files in the National Archives, Ottawa pertaining to the parks.
Location: ACIA.

— 1974 —

2997 **Adams, W. Peter; Barr, William; Nicholson, Frank H.**
Annotated bibliography of the McGill Sub-arctic Research papers and theses, 1954-1974. Montreal: McGill University, 1974. iv, 98 p. (McGill Subarctic Research paper ; no. 26; ISSN: 0076-1982)
Note: Approx. 300 entries.– Articles and theses in hydrology, climatology, pedology, permafrost, physiologic ecology, snow hydrology and snow.
Location: OONL.

2998 **Addison, William D.**
A preliminary annotated bibliography of Nahanni National Park and the South Nahanni Watershed, N.W.T. [S.l.]: Department of Indian Affairs and Northern Development, National Parks Branch, 1974. ii, 149 l.
Note: 323 entries.– Books, articles, government studies and reports.– Topics covered include botany, climate, geology, hydrology, history, anthropology, ethnology, legends, recreation, Nahanni National Park (proposals, boundaries, planning), topography, zoology.– Includes an index to archival materials, a map index, a news clipping index, an analysis of resource base gaps.
Location: OORD.

2999 **Barnes, David H.**
A preliminary annotated bibliography of L'Anse aux Meadows National Historic Park. Ottawa: Department of Indian Affairs and Northern Development, National Parks Branch, 1974. 65 l.
Note: 124 entries.– Reports, theses, official publications, maps.– Emphasis on resource base of the park area: geology, geography, botany, climate, hydrology, with additional references pertaining to history, archaeology, anthropology, recreation, zoology.– Map index; aerial photograph index.– News clippings list.
Location: OOFF.

3000 **Canada. Statistics Canada**
1971 census catalogue, population, housing, agriculture, employment/Publications du recensement de 1971, population, logement, agriculture, emploi. Final ed. Ottawa: Statistics Canada, 1974. 70 p.
Note: Text in English and French/texte en français et en anglais.
Previous edition: 1972. 37, 37 p.
Location: OONL.

3001 **Dorion, Henri**
"Orientation bibliographique sur la théorie des frontières interétatiques."
Dans: *Cahiers de géographie de Québec*; Vol. 18, no 43 (avril 1974) p. 248-265.; ISSN: 0007-9766.
Note: Approx. 375 entrées.– Ouvrages et articles sur les thèmes: géographie politique, droit international, frontières et histoire, frontières naturelles, solutions pacifiques aux problèmes des frontières, frontières stratégiques, frontières et ethnies, fonctions des frontières, enclaves, frontières maritimes, terminologie des frontières.
Localisation: AEU.

3002 **Herrick, Ramona**
Wilderness preservation in North America: a conspectus and annotated bibliography. Cornwall, Ont.: Parks

Canada (Ontario Region), 1974. 255 p.
Note: 605 entries.– Books, journal articles, government reports, conservationist organization reports, theses, conference papers dealing with wilderness preservation in Canada and the United States.– Includes a list of Canadian national park bibliographies and other bibliographical sources.
Location: OONL.

3003 **Lacasse, Jean-Paul**
"Les nouvelles perspectives de l'étude des frontières politiques: revue de quelques contributions récentes."
Dans: *Cahiers de géographie de Québec*; Vol. 18, no 43 (avril 1974) p. 187-200.; ISSN: 0007-9766.
Note: Localisation: OONL.

3004 **Lawrence, Pauline, et al.**
Annotated bibliographies: Atlantic region national parks. Halifax, N.S.: Geomarine Associates, 1974. 4 vol.
Note: 2,500 entries.– Vol. 1-3 contain references to seven national parks in the Atlantic region: Baffin Island, Cape Breton Highlands, Forillon, Fundy, Kouchibouguac, Prince Edward Island, Terra Nova.– Topics include geography and archaeology, geophysics, oceanography, meteorology, ecology, flora-algae, fauna, bibliographies, marine parks.– Vol. 4 contains a synthesis of the material under various headings in the bibliography.
Location: BVAS.

3005 **Scace, Robert C.**
An initial bibliography of Prince Albert National Park. Calgary: Scace & Assoc., 1974. 69 l.
Note: 448 entries.– Guide to published and unpublished non-fictional literature, part of a group of bibliographies and literature reviews prepared for various units in Canadian national park system.
Supplement: Reid, Crowther & Partners. *Prince Albert National Park bibliography update and literature review*. Reid, Crowther, 1984. ii, 97, [58] l.
Location: OORD.

3006 **Scace, Robert C.**
An initial bibliography of Wood Buffalo National Park. Calgary: Scace & Assoc., 1974. 1 vol. (in various pagings).
Note: 824 entries.– Published and unpublished non-fictional literature on Wood Buffalo National Park, Alberta and Northwest Territories, prepared in conjunction with *Wood Buffalo National Park, a literature review* (Ottawa: Parks Canada, 1974).– Topics covered include history, botany, anthropology, geology, geography, ecology, hydrology, meteorology, zoology.– Includes an appendix listing archival file materials relating to land use and administration in the park, and a listing of maps, charts, graphs and photomosaics.
Location: OOFF.

— 1975 —

3007 **Bibliography and literature review of the resource base of St. Lawrence Islands National Park.** Ottawa: Indian and Northern Affairs, Ontario Region, Parks Canada, [1975]. 1 vol. (in various pagings): ill., maps.
Note: Literature review and annotated bibliography of Saint Lawrence Islands National Park region: archaeology, historical geography, anthropology, climatology, geology, hydrology, biology, limnology.– Compiled by D.W. Graham and Associates and A.D. Revill Associates.
Location: OOFF.

3008 **Biehl, Nancy**
Gazetteers in the History Section and the Baldwin Room of the Metropolitan Toronto Central Library. [Toronto]: Metropolitan Toronto Central Library, 1975. 32 p.
Note: Approx. 450 entries.
Location: OONL.

3009 **Mays, Herbert J.**
"Canadian Population Studies Group: report of research in progress."
In: *Histoire sociale: Social History*; Vol. 7, no. 13 (May 1974) p. 165-173; vol. 8, no. 16 (November 1975) p. 350-357.; ISSN: 0018-2257.
Note: Research in progress and cumulative bibliography focussing on demographic, social, structural and family oriented studies.– The Canadian Population Studies Group was formed in the fall of 1973 to facilitate communications among scholars engaged in historical study of populations.
Location: AEU.

3010 **McIntyre, Lillian**
Geography of British Columbia: a selected bibliography, 1930-1965. [Vancouver]: U.B.C. Library, Social Sciences Division, 1975. 59 l.
Note: Selection of books, pamphlets, articles, theses emphasizing economic geography, with sections on history, place names, human geography.
Location: BVAU.

3011 **Revill (A.D.) Associates**
Annotated bibliography and literature review of Auyuittuq National Park. Belleville: A.D. Revill Associates, 1975. 3 vol.
Note: Vol. one reviews literature on Auyuittuq Park and Baffin Island in three broad categories: physical geography (climatology, geology and geomorphology); biology (botany, zoology, limnology); human activity (anthropology, archaeology, historical geography).– Includes an author's list, and an appendix listing birds, mammals, vegetation.– Vol. 2: *Auyuittuq bibliography*; Vol. 3: *Baffin Island bibliography*.– Index numbers in the review volume refer to the bibliographies.
Location: OOFF.

3012 **Thurlow and Associates**
Annotated bibliography: Georgian Bay Islands National Park. [Ottawa]: Thurlow and Associates, 1975. vi, 197 l.: map.
Note: Published and unpublished reports and documents concerning Georgian Bay Islands National Park and surrounding area: climate, flora and fauna, geology, geomorphology, topography, pedology, hydrology, limnology, human activities.
Location: OORD.

— 1976 —

3013 **Bracher, Michael D.; Krishnan, P.**
"Family and demography: a selected Canadian bibliography."
In: *Journal of Comparative Family Studies*; Vol. 7, no. 2 (Summer 1976) p. 367-372.; ISSN: 0047-2328.
Note: Location: AEU.

3014 **Drolet, Jacques**
"Bibliographie concernant les congrès annuels de la S.P.G.Q. depuis sa fondation."
Dans: *Didactique-géographie*; Nouv. série, no 4 (décembre 1976) p. 130-137.; ISSN: 0318-6555.

Note: Localisation: QMBN.

3015 **Found, William C.**
Environment, migration, and the management of rural resources. Monticello, Ill.: Council of Planning Librarians, 1976. 4 vol. (Council of Planning Librarians Exchange bibliography ; 1143, 1144, 1145, 1146)
Note: Part 1: *Rural sociology, farm related decision-making and the influence of environment on behaviour.* 60 p.– Approx. 600 entries.
Part 2: *Interregional migration.* 21 p.– Approx. 250 entries.
Part 3: *Farm economics, land use and spatial analysis.* 42 p.– Approx. 550 entries.
Part 4: *Local studies: Canada, Ontario, and the counties of Kent, Essex, Lanark and Renfrew.* 26 p.– Approx. 400 entries.
Location: OONL.

3016 **Hope, S.**
A selected bibliography for aerial photograph interpretation of natural and cultural features. Victoria, B.C.: British Columbia Forest Service, 1976. 25 p. (Land management report / British Columbia Forest Service ; no. 1)
Note: Bibliographies and proceedings, general reference material, articles on interpretation of natural features (geology, hydrology, vegetation), specific applications from natural features (engineering, recreation, wildlife), interpretation of cultural features.
Location: OONL.

3017 **Lenz, Karl**
"Bibliography of geographic literature on Canada and its regions in the German language."
In: *German-Canadian Yearbook*; Vol. 3 (1976) p. 291-302.; ISSN: 0316-8603.
Note: Approx. 150 entries.– Review of the geographic literature on Canada in German with a list of recent general and regional works.
Supplement: "Deutschsprachige geographische Arbeiten über Kanada seit 1975". In: *German-Canadian Yearbook*, Vol. 6 (1981) p. 294-300.
Location: AEU.

3018 **Stone, Leroy O.**
"Bibliographie choisie sur la migration interne au Canada."
Dans: *Cahiers québécois de démographie*; Vol. 5, no 3 (décembre 1976) p. 135-145.; ISSN: 0380-1721.
Note: Approx. 100 entrées.
Localisation: OONL.

— 1977 —

3019 **Loveridge, Donald Merwin**
A preliminary bibliography on the proposed Grasslands National Park. Winnipeg: Parks Canada, Department of Indian and Northern Affairs, 1977. 212 l.
Note: Approx. 1,350 entries.– Annotated list of published and unpublished literature pertaining to the area in and near Frenchman River Valley in southwestern Saskatchewan, to be used in conjunction with, *A review of the literature on the proposed Grasslands National Park.*– In addition to direct references, materials dealing with historically and physically related areas are included: description, classification and analysis of the grasslands of the Northern Great Plains, dynamics of grassland ecosystems, impact of different types of use and abuse of the grasslands environment.– Where necessary,

Canadian listings are supplemented from American sources.
Location: OOFF.

3020 **O'Grady, K., et al.**
A bibliography of papers and reports issued in the Census Field internal series. 1965-1977 / Bibliographie des notes et des rapports publiés dans les séries internes du Secteur du recensement. Ottawa: Demographic Sector, Characteristics Division, Census Field, Statistics Canada, 1977. 1 vol. (in various pagings).
Note: Text in English and French/texte en français et en anglais.
Location: OONL.

3021 **Raveneau, Jean; Dion, Louise; Bélanger, Marcel**
"Ouvrages récents (1973-1977) pertinents à la géographie culturelle."
Dans: *Cahiers de géographie de Québec*; Vol. 21, nos 53-54 (septembre-décembre 1977) p. 309-318.; ISSN: 0007-9766.
Note: Approx. 240 entrées.– Comprend uniquement des titres d'ouvrages, à l'exclusion des articles de revues.
Localisation: AEU.

3022 **Ricci, Paolo F.; Maclaren, Virginia**
Selected and annotated readings on planning theory and practice. Ottawa: Department of Geography and Regional Planning, University of Ottawa, 1977. 72 p. (Research note / Department of Geography and Regional Planning, University of Ottawa ; no. 16)
Note: Approx. 450 entries.– Covers 1970-1976.– Topics include economic planning, environmental planning, law and planning, natural resources, social planning, transportation, urban design, urban renewal.
Location: OONL.

— 1978 —

3023 **De la Barre, Kenneth**
Northern population bibliography-Canada / Bibliographie sur les populations nordiques canadiennes. Calgary: Arctic Institute of North America, 1978. x, 167 p.
Note: 638 entries.– Covers 1878 to 1978.– Includes government documents, consultants' reports, bibliographies, theses.– Prepared under auspices of Committee on Northern Population Research, with the support of Louise Normandeau and Seth Rankin.– Text in English and French/texte en français et en anglais.
Location: OONL.

3024 **Granberg, Charlotte**
Annotated bibliography of recent research undertaken in the Labrador-Ungava area, near Schefferville, Quebec. Montreal: Centre for Northern Studies and Research, McGill University for the McGill Subarctic Research Station, 1978. iii l., 63 p.: ill. (McGill Subarctic Research paper ; no. 28; ISSN: 0076-1982)
Note: Approx. 350 entries.– Articles and theses on climate, ecology, geology, glaciation, hydroelectric development, mining, native people, permafrost, caribou, radiation, snow cover, transportation, vegetation, mainly in the Schefferville region.
Location: OONL.

3025 **Lebel-Péron, Suzanne; Péron, Yves**
"Bibliographie chronologique sur la mortalité au Canada."
Dans: *Cahiers québécois de démographie*; Vol. 7, no 2 (août 1978) p. 55-92.; ISSN: 0380-1721.
Note: Approx. 400 entrées.– La période couverte est de 1934 à 1977.– Thèmes: mortalité générale, mortalité

infantile, mortalité selon la cause du décès, mortalité selon quelques facteurs de risque, mortalité des groupes ethniques, mortalité selon l'état matrimonial ou la catégorie socio-professionnelle, étude prospective.
Localisation: OONL.

— 1979 —

3026 **Swanick, Eric L.**
Land use studies in Canada during the 1970s: an introductory bibliography. Monticello, Ill.: Vance Bibliographies, 1979. 24 p. (Public administration series: Bibliography ; P-304; ISSN: 0193-970X)
Note: Approx. 350 entries.– Federal, provincial and municipal documents, theses, journal articles on agricultural and urban land issues.
Previous edition: *Land use in Canada during the seventies: an introductory bibliography*. Council of Planning Librarians, 1976. 15 p. (Council of Planning Librarians Exchange bibliography ; 1180).
Supplement: *Land use in Canada during the seventies: a supplement to CPL Exchange bibliography no. 1180*. Council of Planning Librarians, 1978. 6 p.
Location: OONL.

— 1980 —

3027 **Duchesne, Louis; Messier, Suzanne; Sabourin, Conrad**
La population du Québec: bibliographie démographique. [Québec]: Gouvernement du Québec, Conseil de la langue française, Direction des études et recherches, 1980. 206 p. (Documentation du Conseil de la langue française ; 2); ISBN: 2-551-03900-2.
Note: Approx. 2,000 entrées.– Trois parties: "La population du Québec;" "Les francophones hors Québec;" "Étude économiques et sociologiques des groupes linguistiques."- Favorisé certains domaines de recherche: démolinguistique, travaux démométriques.
Localisation: OONL.

3028 **Dunbar, M.J., et al.**
The biogeographic structure of the Gulf of St. Lawrence. Montreal: McGill University, Marine Sciences Centre, 1980. 142 p.: maps. (Manuscript report / Marine Sciences Centre, McGill University ; no. 32; ISSN: 0828-1831)
Note: Approx. 450 entries.– Study and literature review designed to identify, describe and map the distribution of marine communities and fauna and flora elements in the Gulf of St. Lawrence.
Location: OONL.

3029 **Huff, Donald W.**
"Marine parks bibliography."
In: *Park News*; Vol. 16, no. 4 (Winter 1980) p. 26-28.; ISSN: 0553-3066.
Note: Approx. 90 entries.– Includes a listing "References to marine parks in Canada."
Location: OONL.

3030 **Jakle, John A.**
Past landscapes: a bibliography for historic preservationists. Rev. ed. Monticello, Ill.: Vance Bibliographies, 1980. 68 p. (Architecture series: Bibliography ; A-314; ISSN: 0194-1356)
Note: Approx. 850 entries.– Literature relating to modeling past landscapes, understanding past landscape perceptions, analyzing landscape change, and inventory-ing relic features in present day scene.– Draws only from literature of historical geography focussed on United States and Canada.

Location: OHM.

— 1981 —

3031 **Bell, Marcus A.M., et al.**
Pacific Rim National Park: an annotated bibliography. [Ottawa]: Social Science Federation of Canada, [c1981]. xii, 234 p.; ISBN: 0-920052-20-7.
Note: 1,570 entries.– Published and unpublished material from earliest records to June 30, 1977.– Subjects include human and natural history, land use and resource management of the west coast of Vancouver Island.– Locations provided for unpublished documents.– Co-authors: Brown, Jennifer M.; Downard, Katherine M.; Hubbard, William F.
Location: OONL.

3032 **Desrosiers, Denise; Gregory, Joel W.; Piché, Victor**
La migration au Québec: synthèse et bilan bibliographique. 2e éd. [Québec]: Gouvernement du Québec, Ministère de l'immigration, 1981. 106 p. (Études et documents / Gouvernement du Québec, Ministère de l'immigration ; no 2)
Note: 559 entrées.
Édition antérieure: 1978. 106 p.
Localisation: OONL.

3033 **Land-related Information Systems Co-ordination Project**
A consolidated bibliography on land-related information systems. Edmonton, Alta.: Treasury, Bureau of Statistics, 1981. iv, 408 p.; ISBN: 0-9690713-1-0.
Note: Approx. 2,000 entries.– References covering the period 1970 to 1980 dealing with collections of informa-tion which are gathered/stored/retrieved/analyzed/disseminated on the basis of spatial (geographic) criteria, and the systems (manual or computerized) which support them.– Indexes provided: author, title, subject, systems/software.
Location: OONL.

— 1982 —

3034 **Baillie, Murray**
Statistics published by provincial governments in Canada. Halifax, N.S.: Patrick Power Library, c1982. 7 p. (Documents fact sheet / Patrick Power Library ; no. 3)
Note: Approx. 25 entries.
Location: OONL.

3035 **Beak Consultants Limited**
A literature review of Grasslands National Park, 1977-1981. Winnipeg: Parks Canada, 1982. iii, 28 p.
Note: Location: MWIAP.

3036 **Canada. Statistics Canada**
Products and services of the 1981 census of Canada. Ottawa: Statistics Canada, c1982. 147 p.: ill., maps.
Note: Titre en français: *Produits et services du recensement du Canada de 1981*.
Location: OONL.

3037 **Canada. Statistique Canada**
Produits et services du recensement du Canada de 1981. Ottawa: Statistique Canada, c1982. 153 p.: ill., cartes.
Note: English title: *Products and services of the 1981 census of Canada*.
Localisation: OONL.

3038 **De la Barre, Kenneth; Harvey, Denise**
Northern population bibliography-Canada II/ Bibliographie sur les populations nordiques canadiennes-II. Calgary: Arctic Science and Technology Information

System, 1982. xv, 97 p. (ASTIS occasional publication / Arctic Science and Technology Information System ; no. 5; ISSN: 0225-5170); ISBN: 2-930393-00-6.

Note: 493 entries.– Covers 1972 to 1981.– Contains documents resulting from the Mackenzie Valley and Alaska Highway pipeline inquiries, regional social impact studies such as Lancaster Sound Regional Study and Ontario Commission on Northern Environment.– Additional material deals with public health research, employment and labour statistics, research on relationship between population and renewable resources, survey reports on Indian quality of life trends in provinces and territories.– Prepared under the auspices of the Committee on Northern Population Research, with the support of C. Ross Goodwin and Judy Flax.– Text in English and French/texte en français et en anglais.

Location: OONL.

3039 **Fauchon, André**
Bibliographie sur la population du Manitoba. [Saint-Boniface]: Collège universitaire de Saint-Boniface, 1982. iii, 64 f. (Travaux et documents de géographie / Collège universitaire de Saint-Boniface ; no 2)
Note: Approx. 500 entrées.– Livres, brochures, articles.
Localisation: OONL.

3040 **Sealock, Richard B.; Sealock, Margaret M.; Powell, Margaret S.**
Bibliography of place-name literature: United States and Canada. 3rd ed. Chicago: American Library Association, 1982. xii, 435 p.; ISBN: 0-8389-0360-6.
Note: 4,830 entries (886 on Canada).– Books, gazetteers, journal articles, historical society reports, papers and transactions, newspaper articles, government publications on the origin and meaning of geographical names and local histories.
Previous editions:
1967. x, 352 p.
Sealock, Richard B. and Seely, Pauline A. 1948. 331 p.
Location: OONL.

3041 **Wright, Maureen**
Canadian statistics: a guide to sources of information. [Montreal]: McLennan Library, McGill University, Government Documents Department, 1982. 12 p.
Note: Approx. 75 entries.– Includes compendia, catalogues, general guides, censuses and related guides.
Location: OONL.

— 1983 —

3042 **Baillie, Murray**
The census in Canada. Halifax, N.S.: Patrick Power Library, 1983. ii, 7 p. (Government publications guide ; no. 1)
Note: Previous edition: 1981. 5 p. (Documents fact sheet ; no. 1).
Location: OONL.

3043 **Corley, Nora T.**
Travel in Canada: a guide to information sources. Detroit, Mich.: Gale Research Co., 1983. xxi, 294 p. (Geography and travel information guide series ; vol. 4); ISBN: 0-8103-1493-2.
Note: 804 entries.– Current guidebooks, government publications, atlases and maps for the cities, regions and provinces of Canada.
Location: OONL.

3044 **Dubois, J.M.M.**
Vingt-cinq ans de géographie à l'Université de Sherbrooke, 1957-1982. Sherbrooke, Québec: Département de géographie, Université de Sherbrooke, 1983. 3 vol. (Bulletin de recherche / Université de Sherbrooke, Département de géographie ; no 65, 67/68, 76; ISSN: 0710-0868)
Note: Vol. 1: *Mémoires de maîtrise et rapports de baccalauréat.*– 462 entrées.– Vol. 2: *Publications*: comprend 664 contributions produits depuis 1957: articles, rapports scientifiques, volumes, communications scientifiques.– Thèmes: l'étude des petites villes et des sociétés en milieu rural, la cartographie et télédetection, l'étude du Quaternaire.– Vol. 3: *Axes de recherche.*– L'évolution des activités de recherche au Département de géographie de l'Université de Sherbrooke: liste chronologique des projets de recherche.
Supplément: *Publications et recherches en géographie à l'Université de Sherbrooke, 1983-85.* 1985. 53 p. (Bulletin de recherche ; no 83).
Localisation: OONL.

— 1984 —

3045 **Byam, Barbara**
Bibliography of statistical sources: sources of information of interest to writers, publishers, librarians and book and periodical distributors in Canada. [Toronto]: Book & Periodical Development Council, 1984. [3] l., 45 p.
Note: Approx. 100 entries.– Lists publications from federal and provincial departments and agencies, as well as non-governmental associations.
Location: OONL.

3046 **Wai, Lokky; Shiel, Suzanne; Balakrishnan, T.R.**
Annotated bibliography of Canadian demography, 1966-1982. [London, Ont.]: Centre for Canadian Population Studies, University of Western Ontario, [c1984]. v, 314 p.; ISBN: 0-7714-0586-3.
Note: 1,532 entries.– Includes materials of scholarly or scientific nature: journal articles, books, research monographs, doctoral dissertations, federal government publications.– Excludes newspaper and magazine articles and preliminary material such as working papers and internal series.
Supplements:
... , *1983-84 update.* 1985. iii, 34 p.; ISBN: 0-7714-0623-1.– 133 entries.
... , *1984-85 update.* 1986. iii, 31 p.; ISBN: 0-7714-0719-X.– 189 entries.
... , *1986 update.* 1987. iii, 31 p.; ISBN: 0-7714-0815-3.– 155 entries.
... , *1987 update.* 1988. 38 p.; ISBN: 0-7714-0719-X.– 180 entries).
Location: OONL.

— 1985 —

3047 **Minion, Robin**
Canadian national parks. Edmonton: Boreal Institute for Northern Studies, University of Alberta, 1985. 73 p. (Boreal Institute for Northern Studies Bibliographic series ; no. 22; ISSN: 0824-8192); ISBN: 0-919058-56-5.
Note: 183 entries.– Series contains monographs, theses, government documents, consultants' reports, children's books, conference proceedings, microforms on topics related to northern environment and people.– BINS series produced monthly from January 1984 to May 1986

(no. 29).– Online access: *Boreal Northern Titles (BNT)*, available through QL Systems Limited.
Location: OONL.

3048 **Rumney, Thomas A.**
A selected bibliography on the economic geography of Canada: industry, transportation, urban, and tertiary systems. Monticello, Ill.: Vance Bibliographies, 1985. 25 p. (Public administration series: Bibliography ; P-1762; ISSN: 0193-970X); ISBN: 0-89028-562-4.
Note: 275 entries.– Presents geographical research on Canada's industries, transport systems, urban economic dimensions, and tertiary activities since 1945.
Location: OOP.

3049 **Rumney, Thomas A.**
A selected bibliography on the economic geography of Canada: agriculture, land use, resources, energy, development, recreation and tourism. Monticello, Ill.: Vance Bibliographies, 1985. 25 p. (Public administration series: Bibliography ; P-1761; ISSN: 0193-970X; ISBN: 0-89028-561-6.
Note: 288 entries.– Covers material published since 1945.
Location: QQLA.

3050 **York University (Toronto, Ont.). Institute for Social Research**
Canadian social science data archive. North York, Ont.: The Institute, 1985. 136 l.; ISBN: 0-919-76280-8.
Note: Approx. 120 entries.– Covers 1963 to 1984.– Lists studies and social surveys generated by academic, governmental, and private institutions and individuals.– Includes abstracts.
Previous editions:
Canadian social science data catalog. Downsview, Ont.: Institute for Behavioural Research, York University, 1976. 1 vol. (loose-leaf); ISBN: 0-919-60432-3.
1974. 110 p.; ISBN: 0-919-60412-9.
Location: OONL.

— 1986 —

3051 **Herscovitch, Pearl; Hauck, Philomena**
"Geography and history skills: an annotated bibliography of recent Canadian teaching resources."
In: *History and Social Science Teacher*; Vol. 22, no. 1 (Fall 1986) p. 30-34.; ISSN: 0316-4969.
Note: Location: OONL.

— 1987 —

3052 **Hillman, Thomas A.**
Catalogue of census returns on microfilm, 1661-1891/ Catalogue de recensements sur microfilm, 1661-1891. Ottawa: Public Archives Canada, 1987. xv, 289 p.; ISBN: 0-660-53711-7.
Note: Text in English and French/texte en français et en anglais.
Location: OONL.

3053 **Québec (Province). Commission de toponymie**
Bibliographie toponymique du Québec. Éd. rev. et augm. Québec: Commission de toponymie, 1987. 160 p. (Dossiers toponymiques / Commission de toponymie du Québec ; 17); ISBN: 2-550-17744-4.
Note: 1,208 entrées.– Livres, publications gouvernementales, articles de revues, en français et en anglais, publiés sur le toponymie du Québec: ouvrages de référence, théorie de la toponymie, toponymie spécialisée, périodes chronologiques, couches linguistiques, types de lieux nommés, thématiques de désignation.– Index des noms de lieux étudiés.
Édition antérieure: Pâquet, Christiane. *Bibliographie sur la toponymie du Québec.* 1984. 222 p.– 714 entrées.
Localisation: OONL.

3054 **Rumney, Thomas A.**
The physical geography of Canada–geomorphology: a selected bibliography. Monticello, Ill.: Vance Bibliographies, 1987. 98 p. (Public administration series: Bibliography ; P-2241; ISSN: 0193-970X); ISBN: 1-55590-481-5.
Note: Approx. 1,100 entries.– Articles, monographs and books mainly published since 1945 arranged under broad headings: general works, glacial-quaternary studies, coastal geomorphology, landforms, fluvial-mass wasting, karst-arid regions, periglacial-permafrost.
Location: OONL.

— 1988 —

3055 **Canada. Statistics Canada**
Products and services: reference. Ottawa: Statistics Canada, 1988. ix, 136 p.: ill., maps.; ISBN: 0-660-12252-9.
Note: Contains a complete list of Census 1986 products (publications, machine-readable tables and profiles, maps, computerized files) and services (custom data products, geography information services, geocartographic services, agricultural tabulations, health and activity limitation survey information).
Titre en français: *Produits et services: référence.*
Location: OONL.

3056 **Canada. Statistique Canada**
Produits et services: référence. Ottawa: Statistique Canada, 1988. x, 144 p.; ISBN: 0-660-91852-8.
Note: Comprend toutes les produits et services relatives au recensement de 1986: publications, tableaux et profils lisibles par machine, cartes, fichiers géographiques informatisés, services des produits personnalisés, services d'information de la géographie, services de la géocartographie, autres services connexes au recensement.
English title: *Products and services: reference.*
Localisation: OONL.

3057 **LaRose, André**
"Bibliographie courante sur l'histoire de la population canadienne et la démographie historique au Canada/A current bibliography on the history of Canadian population and historical demography in Canada."
Dans: *Histoire sociale: Social History*; Vol. 12, no 23 (mai 1979) p. 192-197; vol. 13, no 25 (mai 1980) p. 225-231; vol. 13, no 26 (novembre 1980) p. 487-491; vol. 14, no 28 (novembre 1981) p. 509-515; vol. 15, no 30 (novembre 1982) p. 489-494; vol. 16, no 32 (novembre 1983) p. 443-449; vol. 17, no 34 (novembre 1984) p. 375-381; vol. 18, no 36 (novembre 1985) p. 439-445; vol. 19, no 38 (novembre 1986) p. 461-465; vol. 21, no 41 (mai 1988) p. 129-135.; ISSN: 0018-2257.
Note: Bibliographie établi à partir des chroniques parues dans *Acadiensis, BC Studies, Canadian Historical Review, Études ethniques au Canada, Revue canadienne des slavistes,* et la *Revue d'histoire de l'Amérique française.*
De novembre 1988, comp. par Yves Landry.
Localisation: AEU.

3058 **Rumney, Thomas A.**
The historical geography of Canada: a selected bibliography. rev., 2nd ed. Monticello, Ill.: Vance

Bibliographies, 1988. 44 p. (Public administration series: Bibliography ; P-2480; ISSN: 0193-970X); ISBN: 1-55590-910-8.

Note: Approx. 900 entries.– Articles, monographs, books, theses on the study of Canadian historical geography, from 1920, with emphasis from 1945 to present.

Previous edition. 1985. 34 p.; ISBN: 0-89028-560-8.

Location: OONL.

— 1990 —

3059 **Brosseau, Marc**
Bibliographie annotée des manuels de géographie au Canada français, 1804-1985. Ottawa: Université d'Ottawa, Centre de recherche en civilisation canadienne-française, 1990. 61 p.

Note: Approx. 300 entrées.

Localisation: OONL.

3060 **Chalmers, Lex**
Expert systems in geography and environmental studies: an annotated review of recent work in the field. [Waterloo, Ont.]: Department of Geography, University of Waterloo, 1990. v, 92 p. (Occasional paper publication series / Department of Geography, University of Waterloo ; no. 10; ISSN: 0843-7383); ISBN: 0-921083-35-1.

Note: 153 entries.– Journal articles and conference proceedings in the areas of urban and land use planning, landscape architecture, remote sensing, ecology, climatology, cartography.– Includes general references to tools, techniques and critiques of expert systems.– Excludes works in computer vision/image processing, cognitive science, decision support and robotics.

Location: OONL.

3061 **Lapierre-Adamcyk, Evelyne**
"Bibliographie des travaux réalisés dans le cadre des enquêtes de fécondité au Québec, 1971 et 1976."
Dans: Cahiers québécois de démographie; Vol. 9, no 1 (avril 1990) p. 139-141.; ISSN: 0380-1721.

Note: Livres, rapports de recherche, articles de revue, mémoires de maîtrise.

Localisation: OONL.

3062 **Powell, Margaret S.; Powell, Stephen S.**
"Bibliography of placename literature, United States and Canada, 1980-1988."
In: Names; Vol. 38, nos. 1-2 (March-June 1990) p. 49-141.; ISSN: 0027-7738.

Note: 655 entries.

Location: OONMM.

3063 **Shiel, Suzanne**
Annotated bibliography of Canadian demography, 1983-1989. London, Ont.: Population Studies Centre, University of Western Ontario, c1990. 237 p.; ISBN: 0-7714-1184-7.

Note: 1,146 entries.– Consolidation of supplements from 1983-1984 plus 1988-1989.– Includes books, journal articles, research monographs, doctoral dissertations, federal government publications, working papers.– Since 1986, annotations have been included for less scholarly material.

Location: OONL.

— 1991 —

3064 **LeBlanc, Robert G.**
"A critical survey of recent geographical research on la Franco-Américanie."
In: Le Québec et les francophones de la Nouvelle-Angleterre. Sainte-Foy: Presses de l'Université Laval, 1991. P. 107-

125. (Collection Culture française d'Amérique); ISBN: 2-7637-7273-0.

Note: Location: OONL.

3065 **Martin, Carol**
Canadian nomads: travel writing in the 20th century. Ottawa: National Library of Canada, 1991. 20, 20 p.; ISBN: 0-662-58147-4.

Note: Approx. 125 entries.– Books and articles from 1900 to 1990, with focus on the last 20 years.– Includes only works by Canadians about travel outside Canada.– Catalogue of exhibition held at National Library of Canada.– Text in English and French with French text on inverted pages.– Title of additional title-page: Des Canadiens nomades: récits de voyage du XXe siècle.

Location: OONL.

3066 **Martin, Carol**
Des Canadiens nomades: récits de voyage du XXe siècle. Ottawa: Bibliothèque nationale du Canada, 1991. 20, 20 p.; ISBN: 0-662-58147-4.

Note: Approx. 125 entrées.– Livres et articles parus entre 1900 et 1990, concentre principalement sur les vingt dernières années de cette période.– Exposition à la Bibliothèque nationale du Canada.– Seuls les ouvrages sur les voyages à l'extérieur du Canada, par des Canadiens, font l'objet de cette exposition.– Texte en français et en anglais disposé tête-bêche.– Titre de la p. de t. additionnelle: Canadian nomads: travel writing in the 20th century.

Localisation: OONL.

3067 **Taye, Haile Kebret**
A compendium of recent research on migration. Ottawa: Canada Mortgage and Housing Corporation, 1991. 27 p.

Note: Approx. 60 entries.– Résumé en français.

Location: OONL.

— 1992 —

3068 **Landry, Yves**
"Bibliographie courante sur l'histoire de la population canadienne et la démographie historique au Canada/A current bibliography on the history of Canadian population and historical demography in Canada."
Dans: Histoire sociale: Social History; Vol. 21, no 42 (novembre 1988) p. 347-353; vol. 22, no 44 (novembre 1989) p. 349-355; vol. 23, no 46 (novembre 1990) p. 363-370; vol. 24, no 48 (novembre 1991) p. 361-370; vol. 25, no 50 (novembre 1992) p. 379-389.; ISSN: 0018-2257.

Note: Bibliographie établi à partir des chroniques parues dans Acadiensis, BC Studies, Canadian Historical Review, Études ethniques au Canada, Revue canadienne des slavistes, Revue d'histoire de l'Amérique française, Revue d'histoire urbaine.

Mai 1979-mai 1988, comp. par André LaRose.

Localisation: AEU.

3069 **Villeneuve, Paul Y.**
Canadian geography. [Ottawa]: Canadian Studies Directorate, Department of the Secretary of State of Canada, 1992. 26, 28 p. (Canadian studies resource guides. Second series); ISBN: 0-662-58838-X.

Note: Includes an introductory overview of the subject, a commentary on significant works, and suggestions for further reading.– Text in English and French with French text on inverted pages.– Title of additional title-page: La géographie du Canada.

Previous edition: 1988. 22, 24 p. (Canadian studies

resource guides); ISBN: 0-662-56213-5.

Location: OONL.

3070 **Villeneuve, Paul Y.**

La géographie du Canada. [Ottawa]: Direction des études canadiennes, Secrétariat d'État du Canada, 1992. 28, 26 p. (Guides pédagogiques des études canadiennes. Deuxième collection); ISBN: 0-662-58838-X.

Note: Comporte un exposé préliminaire, des observations sur les principaux travaux et une liste de lectures recommandées.– Texte en français et en anglais disposé tête-bêche.– Titre de la p. de t. additionnelle: *Canadian geography*.

Édition antérieure: 1988. 24, 22 p. (Guides pédagogiques des études canadiennes); ISBN: 0-662-56213-5.

Localisation: OONL.

— 1993 —

3071 **Canada. Statistics Canada**

1991 census catalogue. Ottawa: Statistics Canada, 1993. ii, 239 p.: maps.; ISBN: 0-660-14252-X.

Note: Titre en français: *Catalogue de recensement de 1991*.

Location: OONL.

3072 **Canada. Statistique Canada**

Catalogue de recensement de 1991. Ottawa: Statistique Canada, 1993. 242 p.: cartes.; ISBN: 0-660-93502-3.

Note: English title: *1991 census catalogue*.

Localisation: OONL.

3073 **Canadian Permanent Committee on Geographical Names**

Native Canadian geographical names: an annotated bibliography/La toponymie autochtone du Canada: une bibliographie annotée. Ottawa: The Committee, 1993. v, 158 p.; ISBN: 0-660-58890-0.

Note: Location: OONL.

3074 **Conzen, Michael P.; Rumney, Thomas A.; Wynn, Graeme**

A scholar's guide to geographical writing on the American and Canadian past. Chicago: University of Chicago Press, 1993. xiii, 741 p.: ill., maps.; ISBN: 0-226-11569-0.

Note: 10,043 entries.– Covers from the mid-nineteenth century to the end of 1990.– Listing of published and unpublished material, including theses.– Excluded are working papers and discussion papers, book reviews, review essays and editorials.

Location: OONL.

3075 **Grenier, A.; Dubois, J.M.M.**

Publications et recherches en géographie et télédétection à l'Université de Sherbrooke, 1957-1993. Sherbrooke, Québec: Université de Sherbrooke, Département de géographie et télédétection, 1993. iii, 250 p. (Bulletin de recherche / Université de Sherbrooke, Département de géographie et télédétection ; no 110-112; ISSN: 0710-0868)

Note: Approx. 2,400 entrées.– Rapports, mémoires, thèses, publications et projets de recherche.

Localisation: OONL.

Sociology
Sociologie

—1910—

3076 **Hugolin, père**
Bibliographie des ouvrages concernant la tempérance: livres, brochures, journaux, revues, feuilles, cartes, etc., imprimés à Québec et à Lévis depuis l'établissement de l'imprimerie [1764] jusqu'à 1910, par le R.P. Hugolin. Québec: L'Événement, 1910. 165 p.
Note: 274 entrées.
Localisation: OONL.

—1915—

3077 **Hugolin, père**
Inventaire des travaux, livres, brochures, feuillets et autres écrits concernant la tempérance publiés par les pères franciscains du Canada de 1906 à 1915. Montréal: 1915. 50 p.
Note: Localisation: OONL.

—1944—

3078 **Barteaux, Eleanor**
Selected bibliography on problems of demobilisation, adjustment and rehabilitation of men and women from the armed forces. Ottawa: Made available by the Canadian Library Council and Wartime Information Board, 1944. 24 l.
Note: Books, documents, periodical articles, pamphlets dealing with problems of adjustment of discharged armed forces: national problems, community problems, employment, placement counselling, educational and vocational guidance, rehabilitation practises, veterans' laws.– Covers Canada, Great Britain, United States, United Nations.
Location: NBFU.

—1957—

3079 **Smith, T. Lynn**
"Rural sociology in the United States and Canada: classified and annotated bibliography."
In: *Current Sociology*; Vol. 6, no. 1 (1957) p. 24-75.; ISSN: 0011-3921.
Note: 597 entries.
Location: OONL.

—1962—

3080 **Canada. Department of Agriculture. Economics Division. Rural Sociology Unit**
A chronological summary of papers, reports and publications in the field of rural sociology and socio-economics of the Economics Division, Canada Department of Agriculture, Ottawa, Ontario. Ottawa: 1960-1962. 3 vol.
Note: Mimeograph.
Location: OONL.

3081 **Dussault, Christiane**
"Bibliographie du service social canadien-français."
Dans: *Service social*; Vol. 10, no 3/vol. 11, no 1 (octobre 1961-avril 1962) p. 122-141.; ISSN: 0037-2633.
Note: Localisation: OONL.

—1964—

3082 **McDonald, Michael**
Bibliography on the family from the fields of theology and philosophy. Ottawa: Vanier Institute of the Family, 1964. vi, 95 l.
Note: 1,249 entries.– Books, parts of books and articles.– Topics include marriage, divorce, sexuality, nature of the family, parenthood, love in philosophy and literature, parent-child relationship, evolution of the family.
Location: OONL.

—1965—

3083 **Schlesinger, Benjamin**
"La pauvreté: publications récentes."
Dans: *Service social*; Vol. 14, no 1 (janvier-juin 1965) p. 98-106.; ISSN: 0037-2633.
Note: Localisation: OONL.

—1966—

3084 **"Bibliographie [La famille au Québec]."**
Dans: *Relations*; No 305 (mai 1966) p. 162-164.; ISSN: 0034-3781.
Note: Localisation: OONL.

3085 **Paltiel, Freda L.**
Poverty: an annotated bibliography and references. [Ottawa: Canadian Welfare Council], 1966. x, 136 p.
Note: Approx. 600 entries.– Covers 1959 to 1965.– Books, pamphlets, periodicals, unpublished working papers, speeches, inventory of research and action programs on poverty and related subjects: aging, education, family, housing, income, welfare and social security.– Comprend aussi des références en français.
Supplements:
Woodward, Agnes. ... *Supplement I*. [1967]. viii, 245 p.– 881 entries.
Woodward, Agnes. ... *Supplement II*. [1967]. viii, 123 p.– 381 entries.
Woodward, Agnes. ... *Supplement III*. [1968]. viii, 76 p.– 282 entries.
Brighton, Wayne; Colby, Deanna. ... *Supplement IV*. [1969]. 80 p.– 393 entries.
Location: OONL.

3086 **Schlesinger, Benjamin**
Poverty in Canada and the United States: overview and annotated bibliography. [Toronto]: University of Toronto Press, 1966. xiii, 211 p.
Note: 741 entries.– Covers 1960 to June 1966.– Includes mainly published material.– Subjects include urban, regional and rural family life, social services and social work, the war on poverty.– Listing of 26 additional bibliographies.
Location: OONL.

—1967—

3087 **Vanier Institute of the Family**
An inventory of family research and studies in Canada, 1963-1967/Un inventaire des recherches et études sur la famille, au Canada [1963-1967]. Ottawa: The Institute,

1967. xiv, 161 p.

Note: 203 entries.– Principal topics include family structure and function, roles, relationships, demography and genetics, occupation, work, unemployment, external and internal migration, social problems, health and illness, law (property and divorce, separation), children and youth, counselling and treatment, family planning, housing and community development, native peoples.– Includes a section of theses from Canadian schools of social work.– Text in English and French/texte en français et en anglais.

Location: OONL.

— 1969 —

3088 **Canadian Welfare Council. Research Branch**
The day care of children: an annotated bibliography. Ottawa: The Branch, 1969. 68 l.

Note: 287 entries.– Focus on material published between 1960 and 1969.– Books, pamphlets, studies, surveys, government publications on various aspects of day care: standards and licensing, health and nutrition, administration of centres, parent and community participation.

Location: OONL.

3089 **Golant, Stephen**
Human behavior before the disaster: a selected annotated bibliography. [Toronto: Department of Geography, University of Toronto], 1969. 14 p. (Natural hazard research working paper / Department of Geography, University of Toronto ; no. 9)

Note: Approx. 40 entries.– Papers relating to human adjustments to natural hazards.

Location: OONL.

3090 **Klement, Susan**
The elimination of architectural barriers to the disabled: a selected bibliography and report on the literature in the field. Toronto: Canadian Rehabilitation Council for the Disabled, 1969. ii l., 36 p.

Note: 89 entries.– Books, articles, films, conference proceedings.

Location: OONL.

3091 **Martin, Janis A.**
An annotated bibliography of the literature on drinking and driving. Edmonton: Division of Alcoholism, Department of Health, Government of Alberta, 1969. 80, [4] p.

Note: 941 entries.– Literature in the English language from fields of law, medicine, alcoholism research, political science, pharmacology and chemistry related to drinking and driving.– Includes Canadian references.

Location: OONL.

3092 **Montreal Council of Social Agencies. Research Department**
Bibliographie des travaux de recherches dans le domaine du bien-être (1961-1967). Québec: Direction générale de la planification et de la recherche du Ministère de la famille et du bien-être social, 1969. 249 f.

Note: Approx. 400 entrées.

Localisation: OONL.

— 1970 —

3093 **Bahr, Howard M.**
Disaffiliated man: essays and bibliography on skid row, vagrancy, and outsiders. Toronto: University of Toronto Press, [1970]. xiv, 428 p.

Note: "Annotated bibliography": p. [94]-394.

Location: OONL.

3094 **Churchill, A.V.**
An annotated bibliography of reports, 1951-1970: human factors wing [Defence Research Establishment, Toronto]. Ottawa: Defence Research Board, Department of National Defence, 1970. 183 p.

Note: Location: OON.

3095 **Fox, Richard George**
The extra Y chromosome and deviant behavior: a bibliography. [Toronto]: Centre of Criminology, University of Toronto, 1970. 21 l.

Note: Approx. 150 entries.– Two sections: medicine and science articles, criminology and law articles.

Location: OONL.

3096 **Guilbeault, Marielle T.**
Famille québécoise: bibliographie. [Québec]: Université Laval, Bibliothèque, 1970. 37 f.

Note: Localisation: QQLA.

3097 **Schlesinger, Benjamin**
The multi-problem family: a review and annotated bibliography. 3rd ed. [Toronto]: University of Toronto Press, [c1970]. xii, 191 p.; ISBN: 0-8020-1726-6.

Note: 322 entries.– Studies, journal articles on services, costs, social work methods, reports on various approaches to problem of marginal social groupings drawn mainly from Canada, Great Britain and the United States.

Previous editions:
1965. xiv, 183 p.
1963. xiv, 173 p.

Location: OONL.

3098 **Schonfield, David; Stewart, Robert**
A bibliography of Canadian research in gerontology, 1949-1970. [Calgary: University of Calgary], 1970. iii, 62 l.

Note: Approx. 675 entries.– Published works in one of the fields of gerontology by authors residing in Canada at the time of publication: biology, clinical medicine and geriatrics, economics, education, employment, health and nutrition, housing, institutions, psychiatry, psychology, retirement and aging, social services, sociology, anthropology and politics.

Location: OONL.

— 1971 —

3099 **Bédard, Robert**
Clinique sociologique et profession de sociologue: bibliographie. Québec: Institut supérieur des sciences humaines, Université Laval, [1971]. 52 f.

Note: Localisation: OONL.

3100 **Berry, John W.; Wilde, G.J.S.**
Social psychology of Canada: an annotated bibliography. Kingston [Ont.]: 1971. iv, 96 p.

Note: Approx. 600 entries.– Books, theses, conference papers, journal articles up to the end of 1970.– Seven subject groupings: "Canadian people," "Canadian dualism," "Native people," "Ethnic groups," "Social groups," "Social movements," "Special problems" (delinquency, aged, poverty, women, drug and alcohol use, religion, industry/labour).

Location: OONL.

3101 **Henning, D.N.**
Annotated bibliography on building for disabled persons. Rev. ed. Ottawa: Division of Building Research, National Research Council Canada, 1971. 6 l. (National

Research Council Canada, Division of Building Research Bibliography ; no. 26)
Note: 28 entries.
Previous edition: Watson, W.B. *Annotated bibliography on building for the handicapped*. 1964. 6 l.
Location: OONL.

3102 **Richeson, Meg**
Canadian rural sociology bibliography. Monticello, Ill.: Council of Planning Librarians, 1971. 58 p. (Council of Planning Librarians Exchange bibliography ; 238)
Note: Approx. 750 entries.– Includes monographs, articles, films, recordings on demography (migration, settlement, stratification), levels of rural living, rural history, rural and regional development, rural poverty, rural institutions and organizations, biography, agricultural history.
Location: OONL.

3103 **Ross, R.R.; McKay, H.B.; Doody, K.**
The psychopath: a partially annotated bibliography. [Waterloo, Ont.]: University of Waterloo, 1971. 162 p.
Note: Approx. 950 entries.– Journal articles on psychopathic behaviour: diagnosis, dynamics, case studies, drug reactions, learning/conditioning, tests, psychometrics, social aspects.– Includes Canadian references.
Location: OONL.

— 1972 —

3104 **Canadian Nurses' Association**
Social and economic welfare: selected references/Le bien-être social et économique: bibliographie sélective. Ottawa: Canadian Nurses' Association, 1972. 45 p.
Note: Text in English and French/texte en français et en anglais.
Location: OONL.

3105 **Environics Research Group**
État des connaissances: recherches sur les personnes âgées de 1964 à 1972. Ottawa: Division de planification des politiques, Société centrale d'hypothèques et de logement, 1972. 69, 81 p.
Note: La seconde partie d'une documentation sur les besoins des personnes âgées dans le domaine du logement; une revue de la documentation canadienne actuelle dans le domaine du vieillissement.– Texte en français et en anglais disposé tête-bêche.– Titre de la p. de t. additionnelle: *State of the art: research on the elderly, 1964-1972*.
Localisation: OONL.

3106 **Environics Research Group**
State of the art: research on the elderly, 1964-1972. Ottawa: Policy Planning Division, Central Mortgage & Housing Corporation, 1972. 81, 69 p.
Note: Second volume of a background study on elder persons' housing needs, a review of existing Canadian literature in the field of aging.– Text in English and French with French text on inverted pages.– Title of additional title-page: *État des connaissances: recherches sur les personnes âgées de 1964 à 1972*.
Location: OONL.

3107 **Institut canadien d'éducation des adultes. Équipe de recherche**
Bibliographie générale sur l'animation. Montréal: Institut canadien d'éducation des adultes, 1972. v, 71, 36 f.
Note: Localisation: OOCC.

3108 **Institut national canadien-français pour la déficience mentale**
Bibliographie [Institut national canadien-français pour la déficience mentale: Centre d'information sur l'enfance inadaptées]. Montréal: Institut national canadien-français pour la déficience mentale, 1972. ? vol
Note: Vol. 1: *La déficience mentale: ouvrages et articles en langue anglaise*.– Vol. 2: *La déficience mentale: articles en langue française*.
Localisation: OONL.

3109 **Lalonde, Francine**
Bibliographie choisie sur les minorités francophones au Canada/Selected bibliography on Francophone minorities in Canada. [Ottawa]: Direction de la recherche et de la planification, Programme d'expansion du bilinguisme, Secrétariat d'État, 1972. 2 vol.
Note: Articles sociologiques, des livres, thèses sur les minorités francophone au Canada depuis 1945.– Compilée sous la direction du John A. Petrolias de la Direction de la recherche et de la planification du Secrétariat d'État.
Localisation: OONL.

3110 **Lederer, K.M.**
The nature of poverty: an interpretative review of poverty studies, with special reference to Canada. [Edmonton]: Human Resources Research Council, 1972. ii, 115 p.
Note: Approx. 185 entries.
Location: OONL.

3111 **National Day Care Information Centre (Canada)**
Day care services bibliography/Services de garde de jour: bibliographie. Ottawa: 1972. [74] l.
Note: Text in English and French/texte en français et en anglais.
Location: OONL.

3112 **National Institute on Mental Retardation. National Reference Service**
Catalogue of the John Orr Foster Reference Library. Downsview: The Institute, 1972. 142 p.
Note: Approx. 4,100 entries.– Books, pamphlets, reprints related to mental retardation and related developmental difficulties.
Location: OONL.

3113 **Nova Scotia NewStart Incorporated**
Abstracts of reports [Nova Scotia NewStart Incorporated]. Yarmouth: Nova Scotia NewStart Incorporated, 1972. 40 l.
Note: Location: NSWA.

3114 **Vanier Institute of the Family**
Canadian resources on the family: catalogue/Ressources canadiennes sur la famille: catalogue. Ottawa: Vanier Institute of the Family, 1972. 1 vol. (in various pagings).
Note: Covers 1965-1972.– Books, articles, pamphlets, audio-visual materials (films, filmstrips, tapes, records) dealing with social policy, housing, family planning, sex education, day care, aging, pressures on the family (poverty, alcoholism, drug abuse, mental illness, divorce, one-parent families, death.– Text in English and French/texte en français et en anglais.
Location: OONL.

— 1973 —

3115 **Canada. Department of the Secretary of State. Bilingualism Development Programme. Social Action**

Branch
Selected bibliography on Anglophone-Francophone relations in Canada/Bibliographie choisie sur les relations anglophones-francophones au Canada. [Ottawa]: Department of the Secretary of State, 1973. 56 p.
Note: Approx. 150 entries.– Covers from 1945.– Includes sociological articles, books, theses.– Compiled by Marie-France Albert.– Text in English and French/texte en français et en anglais.
Location: OONL.

3116 **Family Planning Federation of Canada**
Resource catalogue: family planning, sex education, population/Catalogue de ressources: le planning des naissances, l'éducation sexuelle, la population. [Toronto]: Family Planning Federation of Canada, [1973]. 52 p.
Note: Approx. 350 entries.– Booklets, posters, pamphlets, films.– Text in English and French/texte en français et en anglais.
Location: OONL.

3117 **Jacka, Alan A.**
Adoption in brief: research and other literature in the United States, Canada and Great Britain, 1966-72: an annotated bibliography. Windsor [Eng.]: National Foundation for Educational Research in England and Wales, 1973. 71 p.; ISBN: 0-85633-015-9.
Note: 236 entries.– Books, articles, research reports, theses related to adoption in areas of policy and practice, legal and medical, research, general literature.
Location: OONL.

3118 **Leroux, Paul-André**
"Une revue critique de la littérature sur l'homosexualité avec une emphase sur la science et la mesure."
Dans: *Bulletin de l'Association pour l'analyse et la modification du comportement*; Vol. 3, no 2 (Juin 1973) p. 23-32.
Note: Localisation: OONL.

3119 **Sève, Nicole de**
Animation sociale: bibliographie. Montréal: Conseil de développement social du Montréal métropolitain, 1973. [100] p.
Note: 227 entrées.– Animation, participation, développement des ressources communautaires, pauvreté, culture/ valeurs, leadership, éducation.
Localisation: OONL.

— 1974 —

3120 **Anderson, John C.; Moore, Larry F.**
Volunteerism and volunteer administration: an annotated bibliography. [Vancouver, B.C.]: Voluntary Action Resource Centre, Volunteer Bureau of Greater Vancouver, [1974]. iv, 111 p.
Note: Approx. 700 entries.– Books, reports and articles dealing with volunteerism: use of volunteers in medical services, correctional services, social services, education; volunteer administration (recruiting, selection, placement, training, motivation, public relations); list of additional bibliographies on volunteerism.
Location: OORD.

3121 **Beeston, John; Cramm, Karen M.; Robertson, Sheila M.**
Organize for action: a reading guide for community participants. Halifax: Institute of Public Affairs, Dalhousie University, 1974. vii, 32 l. (Dalhousie University Programmes in public administration ; no. 94)
Note: Approx. 75 entries.– Books, articles, films related to practical business of forming an organization, maintaining the organization, the role of the organizer: objectives/ strategies/tactics, case studies in citizen participation.
Location: OONL.

3122 **Béland, Denis**
La Revue des revues de *Recherches sociographiques*: bibliographie. Québec: Université Laval, 1974. iii f., 384 p. (Cahiers de l'ISSH, Collection Instruments de travail / Institut supérieur des sciences humaines, Université Laval ; no 14)
Note: 1,654 entrées.– La période couverte est de 1960 à 1971.
Localisation: OONL.

3123 **Canadian Nurses' Association**
Accidents and accident prevention: selected bibliography/Accidents et prévention des accidents: bibliographie choisie. [Ottawa]: Canadian Nurses' Association, 1974. 15 l.
Note: 174 entries.– Books and documents, journal articles.
Location: OONL.

3124 **De Pasillé, François B.**
"Bibliographie sur foyer nourricier et placement familial." Dans: *Famille*; Vol. 10, nos 110-111 (février-mars 1974) p. 4-25.; ISSN: 0046-3191.
Note: Localisation: OONL.

3125 **Gregory, Paul**
Child abuse bibliography. Montreal: [Abused Children – Violence in the Family Project, 1974]. 42 l.
Note: Location: OONL.

3126 **Harvey, Fernand; Samuel, Rodrigue**
Matériel pour une sociologie des maladies mentales au Québec. Québec: Institut supérieur des sciences humaines, Université Laval, 1974. xiii, 143 p. (Cahiers de l'ISSH, Collection Instruments de travail / Institut supérieur des sciences humaines, Université Laval ; no 15)
Note: 920 entrées.– La période couverte est des origines à 1974.– Exclut articles de journaux.
Localisation: OONL.

3127 **Munroe, Allan R.**
Research in sexual deviation and sexual offences: a bibliography. [Edmonton: Department of Psychological Services, Alberta Hospital], 1974. 86 p.
Note: Approx. 1,200 entries.– Books, journal articles, papers, reports on sexual deviation, incest, exhibitionism, pedophilia, sexual psychopathy.– Includes Canadian references.
Location: OONL.

3128 **Nadeau, Lise**
Pauvreté, province de Québec: bibliographie. Montréal: Ministère de la main-d'oeuvre et de l'immigration, Région du Québec, Bibliothèque régionale, 1974. 50 f.
Note: Approx. 700 entrées.
Localisation: OONL.

3129 **Rubin, Ken**
Information guide on citizen action and corporate power. [Ottawa: s.n.], 1974. 36 l.
Note: Approx. 700 entries.– Books and articles, newsletters, government publications relating to social participation: corporate power issues, citizen action, corporate research (guides, reference materials, studies).
Location: OONL.

3130 **Sicotte, Evelyne**
"Bibliographie sur les foyers nourriciers."
Dans: *Famille*; Vol. 10, nos 110-111 (février-mars 1974) p. 26-36.; ISSN: 0046-3191.
Note: Localisation: OONL.

3131 **Social service aspects of rehabilitation: a selective bibliography: une bibliographie sélective.** Ottawa: Health and Welfare Canada, Departmental Library Services, 1974. 67 p.
Note: Approx. 900 entries.– Books, studies, articles on aspects of rehabilitation: sociology, psychology, rehabilitation centres and counselling, sheltered workshops and halfway houses, volunteers, environmental and transportation barriers, rehabilitation of physically and mentally disabled.– Text in English and French/texte en français et en anglais.
Location: OONL.

3132 **Swanick, Lynne Struthers**
The young crusaders: the Company of Young Canadians: a bibliography. Monticello, Ill.: Council of Planning Librarians, 1974. 16 p. (Council of Planning Librarians Exchange bibliography ; 566)
Note: Approx. 50 entries.– Periodical literature, government publications, monographs, 1965 to 1973.
Location: OONL.

3133 **Valence, Jocelyne; Belisle, Monique**
Enfance et adolescence inadaptées: catalogue des ouvrages de la bibliothèque du C.I.E.A.I. Montréal: Centre d'information sur l'enfance et l'adolescence inadaptées, 1974. vi f., [69] p.
Note: Approx. 500 entrées.
Localisation: OONL.

— 1975 —

3134 **Canadian Nurses' Association. Library**
Family planning: selected references/Planification familiale: bibliographie choisie. Ottawa: Canadian Nurses' Association, 1975. 35 l.
Note: Includes English and French publications.
Location: OONL.

3135 **Day care: a guide to reading/Garde de jour: guide du lecteur.** Ottawa: National Day Care Information Centre, 1975. 168 p.
Note: Approx. 1,500 entries.– Journal articles, reports and studies by government and private agencies about issues related to day care: administration, funding, parent involvement, research and evaluation, standards and licensing, facilities and equipment, staffing, health and nutrition, social services.– Appendix: Canadian authors.– Text in English and French/texte en français et en anglais.
Location: OONL.

3136 **Desrochers, Alain; Smythe, Padric C.; Gardner, Robert C.**
The social psychology of second language acquisition and bilinguality: an annotated bibliography. London: Department of Psychology, University of Western Ontario, 1975. [150] p. (Research bulletin / Department of Psychology, University of Western Ontario ; no. 340; ISSN: 0316-4675)
Note: Location: QQLA.

3137 **Kannins, Malva, et al.**
"The changing Canadian society."
In: *Ontario Library Review*; Vol. 59, no. 3 (September 1975) p. 171-181.; ISSN: 0030-2996.

Note: Bibliography of books, periodical articles, bibliographies, films assembled for a seminar sponsored by the Ontario Provincial Library Service, April 3-4, 1975.
Location: OONL.

3138 **Project Child Care**
Family day care: an annotated bibliography. Toronto: Project Child Care, 1975. 38 p. (Project Child Care paper ; no. 1)
Note: 77 entries.– Reports and studies on quality of family day care, support systems (training, supervision, material supports).– Compiled by Carolyn T. Younger, et al.
Location: OONL.

3139 **Southam, Peter; Barry, Francine**
Caractéristiques de la pauvreté au Québec, 1940-1973: bibliographie. Québec: Institut supérieur des sciences humaines, Université Laval, 1975. v f., 221 p., 2 f. (Cahiers de l'ISSH, Collection Instruments de travail / Institut supérieur des sciences humaines, Université Laval ; no. 16)
Note: 819 entrées.– Livres, articles de périodiques, thèses, publications officielles sur le milieu rural et urbain, culture de pauvreté, familles, jeunes et personnes âgées, personnes seules, itinérantes, délinquance, santé physique et mentale, revenu, crédit et consommation, chômage.
Localisation: OONL.

3140 **Stinson, Arthur**
Citizen action: an annotated bibliography of Canadian case studies. Ottawa: Community Planning Association of Canada, 1975. 71 p.
Note: Approx. 150 entries.– Reports, research, evaluation studies, journalistic articles dealing with action-research, community planning, rural development, social welfare systems, strategies for change, urban development, resettlement and expropriation, transportation.
Location: OONL.

— 1976 —

3141 **Bakan, David; Eisner, Margaret; Needham, Harry G.**
Child abuse: a bibliography. Toronto: Canadian Council on Children and Youth, 1976. xxi, 89 p.; ISBN: 0-9690438-6-4.
Note: Approx. 800 entries.– Books and articles on nature of child abuse, causative factors, main issues and concerns: history, symptoms and diagnosis, effects of abuse on the child, etiology, management, legal intervention.
Location: OONL.

3142 **Canada. Department of National Health and Welfare. Departmental Library Services**
Rehabilitation and the handicapped: a layman's guide to some of the literature: a bibliography/Réadaptation des handicapés: guide populaire et bibliographie sélective. Ottawa: Health and Welfare Canada, 1976. x, 184 p.
Note: Approx. 1,300 entries.– Books, pamphlets, periodical articles published in the period 1965-1975, dealing with rehabilitation and the handicapped.– Arranged in subject groupings (education, employment, etc.), with an author index and a list of sources.– Text in English and French/texte en français et en anglais.
Location: OONL.

3143 **Cossette, Claude; Tessier, Yves**
Du mot à l'image: guide de lectures pour une approche systématique de l'image fonctionnelle. Québec: Groupe de recherche sur l'image fonctionnelle, École des arts visuels, Université Laval, 1976. 50 f.
Note: Localisation: QQLA.

3144 **Douglas College. Division of Libraries**
Child care bibliography. New Westminster, B.C.: Douglas College, 1976. 99 l.
Note: Location: BVAS.

3145 **Dwyer, John**
The poor in Vancouver: a preliminary checklist of sources. Vancouver, B.C.: Dwyer, 1976. 76 l.
Note: 636 entries.– Annotated list of books, government reports, articles dealing with topics related to social history of the poor in Vancouver.
Location: BVAU.

3146 **Hôpital Rivière-des-Prairies. Bibliothèque du personnel**
Développement personnel et social de l'enfant et de l'adolescent. Montréal: Hôpital Rivière-des-Prairies, 1976. 21 f.
Note: 288 entrées.– Livres, articles, tirés-à-part, monographies.– Comprend des publications en français et en anglais.– Comporte des références canadiennes.
Localisation: OONL.

3147 **Hôpital Rivière-des-Prairies. Bibliothèque du personnel**
L'enfant en foyer. Montréal: Hôpital Rivière-des-Prairies, 1976. 37 f.
Note: Approx. 200 entrées.– Comprend des publications en français et en anglais.
Localisation: OONL.

3148 **Houyoux, Philippe**
La propension aux accidents: thésaurus et bibliographie. Trois-Rivières: Université du Québec à Trois-Rivières, 1976. 116 f. (Publication / Université du Québec à Trois-Rivières, Bibliothèque ; no 11); ISBN: 0-885740-00-9.
Note: Comprend des publications en français et en anglais.
Localisation: OONL.

3149 **Jaque, Mervyn H.**
Research on youth: an annotated bibliography of selected current reports. Edmonton: Alberta Recreation, Parks & Wildlife, Youth Development Division, 1976. 24 l.
Note: Approx. 150 entries.– Selected list of research reports and related material pertaining to youth, with focus on Alberta.– Topics include attitudes and values, behaviour, delinquency, disadvantaged youth, education, employment, health, alcohol and drug abuse.
Location: OONL.

3150 **Ontario. Ministry of Community and Social Services. Ministry Library**
A select bibliography on alternatives to institutional care for the elderly. Toronto: Ministry of Community and Social Services, Ministry Library, 1976. 36 l.
Note: 187 entries.– Topics include social service delivery systems, nutrition programs, housing (living arrangements), home care programs, day care services.
Supplement: 1979. [13] l.– 81 entries.
Location: OONL.

— 1977 —

3151 **Barker, Maurice**
"L'adolescent normal: une revue de la littérature récente pertinente à l'expérience de l'adolescent québécois."
Dans: *Union médicale du Canada*; Vol. 106, no 9 (septembre 1977) p. 1237-1242.; ISSN: 0041-6959.
Note: Localisation: OONL.

3152 **British Columbia. Ministry of Human Resources**
Child abuse: a bibliography. Victoria: Province of British Columbia, Ministry of Human Resources, 1977. 15 p.
Note: Location: OONL.

3153 **Canada. Health and Welfare Canada. Departmental Library Services**
Divorce: a bibliographical look at the world/Le divorce: bibliographie internationale. Ottawa: Health and Welfare Canada, 1977. vi, 183 p.
Note: Approx. 1,500 entries.– Includes Canadian references, p. 102-118.– Text in English and French/texte en français et en anglais.
Location: OONL.

3154 **DuPerron, William A.**
Annotated research bibliography on rape. [Edmonton]: Correctional Justice Program, Grant MacEwan Community College, [1977]. 100 p.
Note: Approx. 400 entries.
Location: OWA.

3155 **Dupras, André**
Sexualité et éducation sexuelle des personnes déficientes mentales: bibliographie annotée. Montréal: Conseil du Québec de l'enfance exceptionnelle, 1977. 138 p.
Note: 407 entrées.– Comprend des publications en français et en anglais.– Annotations en français seulement.
Localisation: OONL.

3156 **Krayewski, Frances**
Human rights in intergroup relations: a community approach. Toronto: Ontario Ministry of Labour, Research Branch, 1977. 13 p. (Bibliography series / Ontario Ministry of Labour, Research Branch ; no. 6)
Note: Location: OONL.

3157 **Labrie, Gisèle; Tremblay, Marc-André**
"Études psychologiques et socioculturelles de l'alcoolisme: inventaire des travaux disponibles au Québec depuis 1960."
Dans: *Toxicomanies*; Vol. 10, no 2 (avril-juin 1977) p. 85-135.; ISSN: 0041-0098.
Note: Localisation: OONL.

3158 **Ontario Association for the Mentally Retarded**
Sexuality and the mentally handicapped: resource literature. Toronto: Ontario Association for the Mentally Retarded, [1977]. [14] l.
Note: Approx. 100 entries.– Reports and articles dealing with sex education, marriage, family planning and genetics.– Includes Canadian references.
Location: OONL.

3159 **Public participation: a general bibliography and annotated review of the Canadian experience.** [S.l.: s.n., 1977]. iii, 129 p.
Note: 100 case studies, 95 bibliographic references.– Arranged by province and territory.– Information includes scale (neighbourhood, city, town or village, region or province), nature of issue, techniques employed, objectives, case evaluation, type of participa-

tion, summary/abstract.– Prepared for the Canadian Conference on Public Participation.– Sponsored by the Environment Conservation Authority of Alberta and the Banff School of the Environment.– Bibliography compiled by Thomas L. Burton and Annette Wildgoose. Location: NSHIAP.

3160 **Ross, R.R.**
Reading disability and crime – link and remediation: an annotated bibliography. [Ottawa: s.n.], 1977. 37 p.
Note: Approx. 100 entries.– Books, reports, articles on relationship between reading problems and delinquent or criminal behaviour: reference materials, community-based programs, institutional settings for juveniles, correctional institutions for adults.
Location: OONL.

3161 **Sault College. Library Resource Centre**
Mental retardation counsellor: bibliography. Sault Ste. Marie, Ont.: Sault College, Library Resource Centre, 1977. 20 p.
Note: Approx. 200 entries.– Includes Canadian references.
Location: OONL.

3162 **Vanier Institute of the Family**
Varieties of family lifestyles: a selected annotated bibliography: phase I: innovative lifestyles. Ottawa: Vanier Institute of the Family, [1977]. 98 p.
Note: 326 entries.– Books and articles about the family in transition.– Topics include modifications within the the male-female couple-based family (union without legal contract, intentional childlessness, open marriage, extramarital sexuality), alternatives to the male-female couple-based family (singles, same-sex unions, family clusters).– Some Canadian references.
Location: OONL.

3163 **Vinet, Bernard; Jolicoeur, Louis-Philippe**
Bibliographie sur les personnes âgées: répertoire des livres et des périodiques de la collection de la Bibliothèque de l'Université Laval. Éd. provisoire. Québec: Bibliothèque de l'Université Laval, 1977. 167 f. (Guides bibliographiques / Bibliothèque de l'Université Laval ; 13)
Note: 962 entrées.
Localisation: OONL.

— 1978 —

3164 **Alberta. Alberta Advanced Education and Manpower. Career Resources Branch**
Pre-retirement bibliography: source book. Edmonton: The Branch, 1978. 26 p.
Note: Approx. 250 entries.– Research literature on retirement and retirement planning: general references, effectiveness of programs, "how to" books, employment, income and pensions, attitudes towards retirement, living arrangements, retirement and women, health, financial planning.– Emphasis on current Canadian material.
Location: OONL.

3165 **Association des directeurs de crédit de Montréal**
Répertoire des instruments et activités d'éducation sur le crédit à la consommation. Montréal: L'Association, [1978]. 15 p.
Note: Liste des brochures, cours, journaux et revues, audio-visuel, monographies.
Localisation: OONL.

3166 **Baker, Harold R.; Bantjes, June E.**
Education for rural development: an annotated bibliography of selected references, with emphasis on the Prairie region of Canada. Saskatoon: Rural Development Education Program, Extension Division, University of Saskatchewan, 1978. ii, 38 p. (Publication / University of Saskatchewan, Extension Division, Rural Development Education Program ; 388)
Note: 152 entries.– Covers the period 1970 to 1978.– Books, reports, pamphlets on rural development.– Topics include history, sociology, social change, disparity, poverty, land use, demography, research, policy and planning.– Arranged in four main categories: general and national, regional and provincial, area and local, bibliographies.
Location: AEU.

3167 **Canada. Transport Canada. Surface**
Transportation for the disadvantaged: a bibliography/ Transport pour les handicapés: bibliographie. [Montréal]: Transport Canada, 1978. 34 p.; ISBN: 0-662-01775-7.
Note: Approx. 300 entries.– Covers the period from 1972 to 1977.– Selected listing of journal articles, papers and reports on transportation for the physically handicapped, elderly and blind: rural and small community transportation, mass transit, paratransit, vehicles for the handicapped, accessibility and adaptation of facilities, bibliographies.– Text in English and French/texte en français et en anglais.
Location: OONL.

3168 **Dew, Ian F.**
A selected annotated bibliography of rural Canada/ Bibliographie annotée du Canada rural. [Ottawa]: Central Mortgage and Housing Corporation, [1978]. ix, 434 p.; ISBN: 0-662-02046-4.
Note: 1,800 entries.– Lists works of research and information about rural areas and small communities in Canada south of the Yukon and Northwest Territories.– Focus is socio-economic development and planning, rather than history and description.– Includes monographs, journal articles, theses and dissertations, documents produced by all levels of government.– Excludes newspaper articles, atlases, community directories, promotional literature, detailed technical reports, documents published by Statistics Canada.– Compiled with the assistance of Virginia E. Hassinger and Winstan M. Jones.– Text in English and French/texte en français et en anglais.
Location: NSHT.

3169 **Foreign Service Community Association. Committee on Mobility and the Family**
Mobility, cultural adaptation and the family: a selected annotated bibliography/Mobilité, adaptation culturelle et la famille: bibliographie commentée d'ouvrages choisis. Ottawa: Committee on Mobility and the Family, Foreign Service Community Association, 1978. iii, 47 p.
Note: 174 entries.– Covers the period 1960-1977.– Citations are grouped into four sections: "Children;" "Wives/Mothers/Women;" "Family;" "Cultural contact and adaptation."
Location: OONL.

3170 **Guay, Michelle**
Planification des naissances et développement professionnel: bibliographie. Québec: Laboratoire de recherche, École de service social, Université Laval,

[1978]. v, 153 p.

Note: Approx. 1,000 entrées.– Thèmes: nature et organisation des services, l'intervention, les professionnels, éléments de formation (méthodes de régulation des naissances).

Supplément: 1979. ii, 20 f.

Localisation: OONL.

3171 **Hôpital Rivière-des-Prairies. Bibliothèque du personnel**
La famille monoparentale. Montréal: Hôpital Rivière-des-Prairies, 1978. 20 f.

Note: 244 entrées.– Livres, monographies, articles de périodiques, tirés-à-part.– Comprend des publications en français et en anglais.– Comporte des références canadiennes.

Localisation: OONL.

3172 **Lapointe, Serge, et al.**
L'animation sociale au Québec: bibliographie. Rimouski: Groupe de recherche interdisciplinaire en développement de l'est du Québec, Université du Québec à Rimouski, 1978. xiv, 91 p. (Cahiers du GRIDEQ / Groupe de recherche interdisciplinaire en développement de l'est du Québec ; no 4)

Note: 516 entrées.– Articles, rapports, thèses sur animation sociale et participation, l'animation en action.

Localisation: OONL.

3173 **Lecompte, Louis-Luc**
Enfance et adolescence inadaptées: catalogue des ouvrages de la collection des sciences du comportement. 3e éd. revue et augm. Montréal: Centre d'information sur la santé de l'enfant, Hôpital Sainte-Justine, 1978. vi, 300, [272] p.

Note: Approx. 4,300 entrées.

Éditions antérieures:

Valence, Jocelyne; Bélisle, Monique. *Enfance et adolescence inadaptées: catalogue des ouvrages de la bibliothèque du C.I.E.A.I.* 1974. iv f., P. 157-226.

Valence, Jocelyne. 1973. 200 p.

Localisation: OONL.

3174 **McHenry, Wendie A.**
A fostering bibliography: based on material collected in the Library, Ministry of Human Resources. [Victoria] B.C.: [Library], Ministry of Human Resources, 1978. 16 p.; ISBN: 0-7719-8095-7.

Note: Approx. 125 entries.– Studies from Canada and other countries.– Topics include institutional care, child placements, natural parents, recruitment and selection, runaways, separation and grief, standards, guides and manuals, subsidized adoption and finance.

Location: OONL.

3175 **Miller, Alan V.**
Homosexuality and human rights: a selected bibliography. Toronto: Ontario Ministry of Labour, Research Branch, 1978. 67 p. (Bibliography series / Ontario Ministry of Labour, Research Branch ; no. 12)

Note: Location: OONL.

3176 **Miller, Alan V.**
Homosexuality in specific fields: the arts, the military, the ministry, prisons, sports, teaching, and transsexuals: a selected bibliography. Toronto: Ontario Ministry of Labour, Research Branch, 1978. 58 p. (Bibliography series / Ontario Ministry of Labour, Research Branch ; no. 13)

Note: Location: OONL.

3177 **Murphy, Lynn**
"Child abuse: an annotated bibliography."
In: *Emergency Librarian*; Vol. 5, no. 4 (March-April 1978) p. 6-11.; ISSN: 0315-8888.

Note: Location: AEU.

3178 **Sawka, Edward; Lind, Terry**
Evaluation of impaired driver programs: a literature review. Edmonton: AADAC, Program Development Division, [1978]. 9, [2] p.

Note: 19 entries.

Location: OONL.

3179 **Sell, Kenneth D.; Sell, Betty H.**
Divorce in United States, Canada, and Great Britain: a guide to information sources. Detroit: Gale Research, c1978. xv, 298 p. (Social issues and social problems information guide series ; vol. 1); ISBN: 0-8103-1396-0.

Note: Books, periodical articles, dissertations, databases, films in various subject fields: social and behavioural sciences, law, medicine, religion, philosophy, literature.

Location: OONL.

3180 **ServCom Côte-Nord (Québec)**
Bibliographie sur les personnes handicapées: documentation recueillie auprés des établissements de santé et de services sociaux de la Côte-Nord et auprés de la FRASC. Hautrive: CRSSS Côte-Nord, 1978. 67 f.

Note: Localisation: QQLA.

3181 **Swanick, Lynne Struthers**
The role of government in providing child care facilities: a checklist of sources. Monticello, Ill.: Vance Bibliographies, 1978. 9 p. (Public administration series: Bibliography ; P-85; ISSN: 0193-970X)

Note: Approx. 100 entries.– Emphasis on current books, periodicals and government publications within North American context.– Includes references to government regulations and guidelines for day care centres.

Location: OONL.

— 1979 —

3182 **Adams, David W.**
The psychosocial care of the child and his family in childhood cancer: an annotated bibliography. [Hamilton, Ont.]: McMaster University Medical Centre, c1979. vi, 92, xiv p.; ISBN: 0-9690051-0-5.

Note: Articles, books, studies on terminally ill children and terminal care.– Topics include psychosocial care of children and families, multidisciplinary teamwork, family responses, clinic visits and hospitalization, children and death, family after death of child.– Includes Canadian references.

Location: OONL.

3183 **Burtch, Brian E.; Ericson, Richard V.**
The silent system: an inquiry into prisoners who suicide and annotated bibliography. Toronto: Centre of Criminology, University of Toronto, 1979. ix, 113 p. (Research report / Centre of Criminology, University of Toronto); ISBN: 0-919584-43-8.

Note: Approx. 150 entries.– Books, articles and government reports dealing with suicide in prison.– Includes a number of Canadian references.

Location: OONL.

3184 **Canada. Department of Indian and Northern Affairs. Northern Social Research Division**
Ongoing and recently completed research studies

concerned with the social implications of the development of communications systems in northern Canada. Ottawa: Northern Social Research Division, Department of Indian and Northern Affairs, 1979. [70] l.

Note: 107 entries.– Northern Canada includes the Yukon, Northwest Territories, Nouveau-Québec, Labrador, and northern/isolated parts of B.C., Prairies, Ontario.– Communications systems refers to telecommunications undertakings as defined by *The CRTC Act, 1974-75, section 2*.– Social implications research means scientific investigation in both social sciences and hard sciences having an impact on social, economic, cultural milieu through communications systems.– Topics include cable television, education, native peoples, radio broadcasting, satellite use, socio-cultural impact, socio-economic impact, telemedicine and health-care delivery, telephone, television-video.

Location: OONL.

3185 **Canada. Health and Welfare Canada**
Canadians ask about child day care: a bibliography/Les canadiens veulent se renseigner sur la garde de jour des enfants: une bibliographie. [Ottawa]: Health and Welfare Canada, [1979]. 16 p.

Note: Books and articles on day care: programs, staff, buildings and equipment, costs, Canadian studies and reports.

Location: OONL.

3186 **Harvey, Fernand; Houle, Gilles**
Les classes sociales au Canada et au Québec: bibliographie annotée. Québec: Institut supérieur des sciences humaines, Université Laval, c1979. 282 p. (Collection études sur le Québec ; no 11)

Note: 843 entrées.– Livres, articles de périodiques généraux et spécialisées, thèses.– Principaux thèmes traités: société canadienne et québécoise, question nationale et question sociale, l'Église et la société québécoise, le Régime français, le Régime anglais (1760-1850), les débuts de l'industrialisation (1850-1914), les classes sociales au XXe siècle (bourgeoisies, classe ouvrière, classe agricole et milieu rural, aspects thèmatiques des classes sociales).

Localisation: OONL.

3187 **Lucyk, J.R.**
Communications and the physically handicapped: a literature review with some policy implications. [Ottawa]: Broadcasting and Social Policy Branch, Department of Communications, 1979. ii, 48 p.

Note: Approx. 100 entries.– Reviews literature relating to communications and the handicapped: categories of disability, mass media, telecommunications, communication aids and devices, current research, society, politics and the handicapped.

Location: OONL.

3188 **Midgley, Ellen**
The pre-school visually impaired child: a guide for parents and practitioners: a selected, annotated bibliography. Toronto: Ontario Foundation for Visually Impaired Children, 1979. 28 p.

Note: 165 entries.– Covers 1973-1978.– Includes books and articles in English from Canada and the United States dealing with pre-school visually impaired children.– Topics include attitudes, development, causes of blindness, family involvement, orientation and mobility, testing and assessment, teaching aids and programs.

Location: OONL.

3189 **N.D. Lea & Associates**
Transportation for the mobility disadvantaged: a bibliography/Transport pour les handicapés: bibliographie. Montreal: Transport Canada, Surface, 1979. 61 p.

Note: Approx. 780 entries.– Journal articles, papers and reports on transportation for the physically handicapped, elderly and blind: policies/programs/coordination, planning and information, transportation systems, equipment and facilities, additional bibliographies.

Location: OONL.

3190 **Pethick, Jane**
Battered wives: a select bibliography. [Toronto]: Centre of Criminology, University of Toronto, 1979. 114 p.; ISBN: 0-919584-41-1.

Note: Approx. 350 entries.– Books, journal articles, theses, reports, pamphlets, conference proceedings, articles from Toronto newspapers.– Includes violence in the family from assault to murder, social and legal aspects of the problem, police intervention in family crises, solutions offered by various agencies and self-help groups.– Excludes material on child abuse, general studies of violence, aggression, victimology.– Emphasis on scholarly literature in the 1970s from U.S., Canada, U.K., Australia.

Location: OONL.

3191 **Semkow, Brian**
Retirement: a bibliography, 1970-1979. Kingston, Ont.: Industrial Relations Centre, Queen's University, 1979. 72 p.

Note: Approx. 1,200 entries.– Includes Canadian references.

Location: OONL.

3192 **Sewell, W.R. Derrick**
Where is public participation going? An annotated bibliography focussing on Canadian experience. [Edmonton]: Environment Council of Alberta, [1979]. 146, [9] p.

Note: Approx. 250 entries.– Books, articles, newsletters, conference proceedings.– Categories include general works, philosophy, law, theory, techniques, interest groups, case studies, evaluative frameworks, bibliographies.

Location: OONL.

3193 **Stinson, Arthur**
Canadians participate. [Ottawa]: Centre for Social Welfare Studies, Carleton University, 1979. 167 p.; ISBN: 0-7709-0054-2.

Note: Lists case studies dealing with groups, communities, or collectivities of some kind: journalistic accounts, personal reconstruction of events by participants, reports of activities by group involved, academic evaluations of particular projects.– Themes include action research, community schools and education, cooperatives, housing, community planning, rural development, social welfare systems, transportation.

Location: OONL.

3194 **Tremblay, Jean-Marie**
Sociologie de la famille et de la société québécoise: bibliographie annotée, environ 750 titres. Québec: Ministère de l'éducation, Service des programmes de la direction de l'enseignement collégial, 1979. 102 f.
Note: Approx. 750 entrées.
Localisation: QRUQR.

— 1980 —

3195 **Abraham, Diana; Gomer, Mary; Herberg, Dorothy C.**
Cross-cultural social work in Canada: an annotated bibliography. Toronto: Multicultural Worker's Network, 1980. ii, 43 p.
Note: 90 entries.– Published and unpublished material related to ethno-racial-religious social work in Canada: service delivery (training, counselling, adoption, service to refugees); community studies; disease and illness (effects of ethnicity on modes of intervention); concept development.– Cross indexed by ethnic group.
Location: OWA.

3196 **Bibliography of studies on older people in Alberta.**
[Edmonton]: Senior Citizens Bureau, Alberta Social Services and Community Health, 1980. 28 l.
Note: Approx. 80 entries.– Journal articles, research papers, theses, government publications on demography, drug use, education, economic conditions, housing, mental health, social services related to Alberta senior citizens.
Location: OONL.

3197 **British Columbia. Ministry of Human Resources**
Adolescent pregnancy: a bibliography. Victoria: Province of British Columbia, Ministry of Human Resources, 1980. 6 p.
Note: Location: OONL.

3198 **Cadieux, Andrée**
Le phénomène de la femme battue: une bibliographie canadienne/Wife battering: a Canadian bibliography. Ottawa: Conseil consultatif canadien de la situation de la femme, 1980. 1 vol. (en pagination variée).
Note: Localisation: OOSS.

3199 **Canadian Council on Social Development**
Project information exchange: an inventory of studies, briefs and social action projects/Échange-renseignements: relevé d'études, de mémoires et de réalisations en action sociale. Ottawa: Canadian Council on Social Development; United Way of Canada, 1970-1980. 9 vol.; ISSN: 0704-6693.
Note: Listing of reports, studies, action projects initiated or completed by social planning councils, municipal and provincial social planning and research departments, schools of social work, research institutes, individual university researchers on aging, day care, family and child welfare, housing, community development, personal social services, volunteer services, women, youth, recreation and leisure.
Location: OONL.

3200 **Farnell, Margaret B.**
Screening procedures for the detection or prediction of child abuse: an annotated bibliography. [Toronto]: Centre of Criminology, University of Toronto, 1980. v, 29 p.; ISBN: 0-919584-47-0.
Note: Approx. 100 entries.
Location: OONL.

3201 **Heath, Jean**
Lone parent families: a selected and annotated bibliography. Vancouver: British Columbia Ministry of Education, Division of Continuing Education, 1980. 39 p.
Note: Location: OONL.

3202 **Krawetz, Donna**
The social impacts of layoffs: an annotated bibliography. Toronto: Social Planning Council of Metropolitan Toronto, 1980. 43 p. (Working papers for full employment ; no. 3)
Note: 80 entries.– One in a series of occasional papers dealing with problems of employment and unemployment in Metropolitan Toronto: research, analysis, planning.
Location: OONL.

3203 **Manitoba. Department of Consumer and Corporate Affairs and Environment**
Children and money: a bibliography. Winnipeg: Manitoba, Department of Consumer and Corporate Affairs and Environment, 1980. 16 p.
Note: Location: OONL.

3204 **Miller, Ann-Marie**
Consumer skills for disadvantaged adults: an annotated bibliography. Toronto: Ministry of Consumer and Commercial Relations, Consumer Information Centre, 1980. iii, 99 p.; ISBN: 0-7743-5547-6.
Note: Lists resources suitable for teaching consumer education to adults disadvantaged by reason of age, income, language, handicap, race, geography or culture.– Includes books, kits, games, films and other audio-visual materials.– Descriptive annotations.– Topics include daily living skills, money management (budgeting, credit), advertising and sales techniques, housing, nutrition, transportation, consumer rights and responsibilities.
Location: OONL.

3205 **Morgan, Jane**
Parenting: an annotated bibliography. Toronto: Library, Reference and Information Services, Ontario Institute for Studies in Education, 1980. ix, 70 p. (Current bibliography / Ontario Institute for Studies in Education ; no. 13)
Note: 268 entries.– Selection of books published 1970 to 1980 on aspects of parenting, including child care, management/communication/discipline, play and early learning activities, play groups/day care, education, reading, adolescence, sexuality, children and death, special needs children.
Location: OONL.

3206 **National Library of Canada**
Marriage and the family: preliminary check list of National Library holdings/Mariage et famille: inventaire préliminaire des fonds de la Bibliothèque nationale. Ottawa: National Library of Canada, 1980. viii, 130 p.; ISBN: 0-662-51091-7.
Note: Approx. 2,100 entries.– Lists monographs and periodicals on the following topics: history of the family, relationship between family and society, kinship organization, nuclear family, parent-child relationship, alternative lifestyles, future of the family, family violence, juvenile delinquency, separation and divorce, death and disorganization of family, history of marriage, marriage customs.– Includes Canadian references.–

Compiled by Maryna Nowosielski.– Text in English and French/texte en français et en anglais.
Location: OONL.

3207 **Pethick, Jane; Matthews, Catherine J.**
Vandalism: a bibliography. Toronto. Centre of Criminology, University of Toronto, 1980. x, 79 p.; ISBN: 0-919584-46-2.
Note: 475 entries.– Period covered: 1960-1979.– Books, articles, theses, government publications.– Topics include causes and theories of vandalism, prevention and intervention, school vandalism, transportation vandalism, vandalism of commercial and public buildings, parks and recreational facilities.
Location: OONL.

3208 **Shilling, Barbara A.**
Exclusionary zoning: restrictive definitions of family: an annotated bibliography. Chicago: Council of Planning Librarians, 1980. x, 38 p. (CPL bibliography / Council of Planning Librarians ; no. 31)
Note: Approx. 200 entries.– Books, law review and journal articles, monographs, reports, government publications.– American and Canadian references related to land use regulation, zoning, group homes, halfway houses, definitions of family, non-traditional households.
Location: OONL.

3209 **Wells, Lilian M.**
Chronic physical illness and disability: psychosocial perspectives: an annotated bibliography. [Toronto]: University of Toronto, Faculty of Social Work, 1980. 100 p. (University of Toronto Faculty of Social Work bibliographic series ; 1; ISSN: 0317-8382)
Note: Approx. 350 entries.– Covers 1965 to 1976.– Books and articles with focus on social and psychological factors faced by individuals and families in coping with chronic physical illness and disability where onset is in adulthood.
Location: OONL.

— 1981 —

3210 **Bibliography on disabled children: a guide to materials for young people aged 3 to 17 years.** Ottawa: Canadian Library Association, c1981. 50 p.; ISBN: 0-88802-159-3.
Note: Approx. 300 entries.– Covers 1970 to 1980.– Books and audiovisual materials, fiction and non-fiction.– Topics include emotional disorders, learning disabilities, hearing impairment, mental retardation, physical disabilities, visual impairment.
Location: OONL.

3211 **British Columbia. Ministry of Human Resources**
Adoption, special needs: a bibliography. Victoria: Province of British Columbia, Ministry of Human Resources, 1981. 13 p.
Note: Location: OONL.

3212 **Butler, Brian E.**
"Canadian studies of visual information-processing: 1970-1980."
In: *Canadian Psychology*; Vol. 22, no. 2 (April 1981) p. 113-128.; ISSN: 0708-5591.
Note: Location: OONL.

3213 **Canadian Association of Children's Librarians**
Bibliography of disabled children. [Ottawa]: Canadian Library Association, 1981. 50 p.
Note: Location: NBS.

3214 **Canadian Housing Information Centre**
A selected bibliography on housing and services for the disabled/Choix d'ouvrages sur le logement et les services pour les handicapés. Ottawa: Canada Mortgage and Housing Corporation, 1981. 28 p.; ISBN: 0-662-51450-5.
Note: Approx. 175 entries.– Books, research reports, journal articles, municipal documents, conference proceedings.– Text in English and French/texte en français et en anglais.
Location: OONL.

3215 **Canadian Paraplegic Association**
A core collection of materials on the disabled, suitable for public libraries: to observe the International year of disabled persons. Toronto: The Association, 1981. 30, viii p.
Note: Approx. 300 entries.– Lists directories, films, periodicals and newsletters, books and studies about rehabilitation in general, rehabilitation medicine, sexuality, housing and barrier-free design, technical aids, independent living, transportation and travel, accessibility, education and employment, recreation and sports, personal accounts, books for younger readers.
Location: OONL.

3216 **Chouinard, Charles; Collister, Edward A.; Tardif, Jean-François**
Bibliographie sélective sur les personnes âgées. Québec: Ministère des affaires sociales, Service de l'informathèque, 1981. 63 f. (Série bibliographiques / Ministère des affaires sociales, Service de l'informathèque ; no 4; ISSN: 0713-0740)
Note: Comprend un nombre d'ouvrages canadiens.
Localisation: OONL.

3217 **Collister, Edward A.; Chouinard, Charles**
Bibliographie sélective sur l'usage et l'abus des psychotropes par la population adulte. Québec: Ministère des affaires sociales, Service de l'informathèque, 1981. 25 p. (Série bibliographiques / Ministère des affaires sociales, Service de l'informathèque ; vol. 1, no 2; ISSN: 0713-0740)
Note: Comprend des publications en anglais.
Localisation: OONL.

3218 **Collister, Edward A.; Janik, Sophie**
La personne handicapée: documentation québécoise. Drummondville: Gouvernement du Québec, Ministère des affaires sociales, Direction des communications, 1981. v, 210 p.
Note: 1,269 entrées.– Documents québécois publiés depuis 1975 sur tous les aspects de la vie des personnes handicapées à partir de prevention, le diagnostic médical et la réadaptation jusqu'à l'intégration globale de la personne handicapée et la reconnaissance de ses droits de citoyen à part entière.
Localisation: OONL.

3219 **Fondation de l'arbre Canada**
Répertoire de la recherche et des projets pilotes réalisés au Canada sur l'enfance maltraitée et négligée: un rapport de recherches. [Ottawa]: Gouvernement du Canada, c1981. 369 p.; ISBN: 0-662-91348-5.
Note: English title: *Inventory of Canadian research and demonstration projects on child abuse and neglect: a research report.*
Localisation: OONL.

3220 **Furse, Alison; Levine, Elyse**
Food, nutrition and the disabled: an annotated bibliography. Toronto: Nutrition Information Service, Ryerson Polytechnical Institute Library, 1981. vii, 82 p.; ISBN: 0-919351-00-X.
Note: Approx. 260 entries.– Covers from 1960 to 1980.– Includes books, pamphlets, periodical articles, audiovisual materials related to those who suffer from a nutritional imbalance caused by their disability.– Excludes material on prenatal preventative nutrition for disabled, material related to cardiovascular, gastrointestinal and renal diseases.
Location: OONL.

3221 **Kearney, Hélène**
La planification différentielle de la main-d'oeuvre en service social: un relevé bibliographique. Montréal: Centre de services sociaux juifs à la famille, 1981. 30 f.
Note: Approx. 50 entrées.
Localisation: OONL.

3222 **Massel, Jo Anne, et al.**
Learning & growing: international year of disabled persons, 1981. [London, Ont.]: London Public Libraries and Museums, 1981. 46 p.
Note: Approx. 300 entries.– Includes books, periodicals, government documents, large print books relating to disabled adults and children.– Topics include rehabilitation, employment, recreation, travel, architecture, libraries and disabled.
Location: OONL.

3223 **Mieux vivre sa sexualité: qui consulter? quoi lire?** Saint-Lambert, Qué[bec]: Éditions Héritage, 1981. 121 p.: ill.; ISBN: 0-7773-5508-6.
Note: Bibliographie sommaire d'ouvrages de sexologie brièvement décrits et classés par thèmes: amout, avortement et contraception, corps, difficultés sexuelles, éducation sexuelle, érotisme, homosexualité, sexualité et société, violence.– Inclut un nombre d'ouvrages canadiens.
Localisation: OONL.

3224 **Poulin, Martin; Tanguay, Marc**
Bibliographie dans le domaine de la gestion des services sociaux (période recensée 1970-1980). Québec: Laboratoire de recherche, École de service social, Université Laval, 1981. xi, 81 f. (Rapports et outils de recherche / École de service social, Université Laval ; no 1)
Note: 528 entrées.– Services sociaux du Québec, gestion des services sociaux, formation, gestion de personnel, direction, système d'information, planification, contrôle et efficacité, budget.
Localisation: OONL.

3225 **Ruel, Ginette; Collister, Edward A.**
Bibliographie sélective sur le harcèlement sexuel. Québec: Ministère des affaires sociales, Service de l'informathèque, 1981. 20 f. (Série bibliographiques / Québec, Ministère des affaires sociales, Service de l'informathèque ; no 5; ISSN: 0713-0740)
Note: Comprend publications en français et en anglais.
Localisation: QQLA.

3226 **Saskatchewan Provincial Library. Bibliographic Services Division**
Rehabilitation of the handicapped: a bibliography. Regina: Saskatchewan Provincial Library, [1981]. i, [65] p.

(in various pagings).
Note: Approx. 650 entries.– Lists books, reports from associations and societies, government publications.– Principal topics covered are rehabilitation of physically and mentally handicapped, employment of handicapped, recreational activities, vocational rehabilitation, sex and the handicapped, transportation, travel and mobility for handicapped.
Location: OONL.

3227 **Savard, Réjean**
L'enfant handicapé au Québec: bibliographie. Montréal: Bibliothèque nationale du Québec, 1981. 72 p.; ISBN: 2-550-01899-0.
Note: 477 entrées.– Livres, périodiques, films, videocassettes, documents techniques sur trois types généraux d'handicapés: l'handicapé physique, intellectuel, social et culturel.
Localisation: OONL.

3228 **Schlesinger, Benjamin**
Sexual abuse of children: a selected annotated bibliography: 1937-1980. [Toronto]: Faculty of Social Work, University of Toronto, 1981. 74 l.
Note: 180 entries.– Journal articles, books on various aspects of sexual abuse of children: incest, historical background, legal aspects, medical treatment, psychiatric studies, sexual offenders, etc.
Location: OONL.

3229 **A selected bibliography on housing and services for the disabled/Choix d'ouvrages sur le logement et les services pour les handicapés.** Ottawa: Canada Mortgage and Housing Corporation, 1981. 28 p.; ISBN: 0-662-51450-5.
Note: Approx. 180 entries.– Books, documents, research reports.– Text in English and French/texte en français et en anglais.
Location: OONL.

3230 **Tree Foundation of Canada**
Inventory of Canadian research and demonstration projects on child abuse and neglect: a research report. [Ottawa]: Minister of Supply and Services Canada, 1981. 358 p.; ISBN: 0-662-11734-4.
Note: Titre en français: *Répertoire de la recherche et des projets pilotes réalisés au Canada sur l'enfance maltraitée et négligée: un rapport de recherches.*
Location: OONL.

3231 **Vallerand, Carole**
La vieillesse au Québec: essai de bibliographie signalétique avec mention de localisation. [Québec]: Bibliothèque, Université Laval, 1981. 120 p.
Note: 731 entrées.– L'ensemble des références couvre la période allant de 1960 à 1977 inclusivement.– Comprend thèses de maîtrise, monographies, rapports de recherches, mémoires, exposés, articles de journaux, articles de revues scientifiques et populaires, rapports d'activités, bibliographies, documents audio-visuels.– Principaux thèmes traités: démographie, nutrition, économie, environnement social, habitation, gérontologie, loisirs, politiques sociales, psychologie, retraite, santé, sexualité, transport.
Localisation: OONL.

3232 **Woodill, Gary**
Children with special needs: a manual of Canadian resources. Orillia, Ont.: Ptarmigan Publishing, 1981.

98 p.: ill.; ISBN: 0-9690349-0-3.

Note: Listing of books, articles, films, videos.– Topics covered include legal issues, medical services, specific special needs (allergies, autism, giftedness, learning disabilities, mental retardation, spina bifida, etc.).

Location: OONL.

— 1982 —

3233 **Alberta. Alberta Social Services and Community Health**

Selected list of bibliographies. [S.l.: s.n., 1982]. [32] p.

Note: Lists books and articles available from Alberta Social Services and Community Health Library on various topics related to human sexuality: abortion, birth control, sex education, family planning, infertility and pregnancy, sexuality and adolescence/aging/children/disability/illness/mentally retarded, sexually transmitted diseases.

Location: OONL.

3234 **British Columbia Federation of Foster Care Associations**

Foster care training resource catalogue. [Vancouver]: The Federation, 1982. 1 vol. (in various pagings).

Note: Books, training manuals, periodical articles, audiovisual materials on communication, parenting, behaviour management, self awareness, procedures-policies-practises, interaction and relationships with community agencies, special needs children, foster parent-natural parent involvement, ethics and standards.

Location: OONL.

3235 **Canada. Consumer and Corporate Affairs Canada**

Consumer sourcebook for the disabled/Sources d'informations du consommateur handicapé. Ottawa: Consumer and Corporate Affairs Canada, 1982. vi, 118 p.; ISBN: 0-662-52226-5.

Note: Approx. 600 entries.– Articles, books, audio-tapes.– Intended to meet needs of disabled consumers for material on food, clothing, shelter, aids to mobility.– Emphasis on information designed to enhance normal functioning of persons with a disability.– Topics include barrier-free design, independent living, leisure and recreation, rights, transportation and travel.– Text in English and French/texte en français et en anglais.

Location: OONL.

3236 **Collister, Edward A.**

Bibliographie sélective sur le bénévolat. Québec: Ministère des affaires sociales, Service de l'informathèque, 1982. 27 p. (Série bibliographiques / Ministère des affaires sociales, Service de l'informathèque ; no 11; ISSN: 0713-0740)

Note: Documentation relative au bénévolat publiée depuis 1970.– Comporte des références québécoises et européennes.

Localisation: QQLA.

3237 **Disabilities resources library bibliography: a Canada community development project sponsored by Participation House, Brantford.** [Brantford, Ont.: The House, 1982]. iv, 138 l.

Note: Approx. 2,000 entries.– Books, periodical articles and reprints, booklets and pamphlets, bibliographies on mental retardation, multiple sclerosis, muscular dystrophy, cerebral palsy, spina bifida, speech and hearing impairments, paralysis (paraplegia, etc.), physical disabilities.

Location: OONL.

3238 **Grant, Linda; Sai-Chew, Patricia; Natarelli, Fausto**

Work-related day care: an annotated bibliography. Toronto: Social Planning Council of Metropolitan Toronto, 1982. 26 l.

Note: Approx. 100 entries.– Books and papers, articles in journals and newspapers.– Materials issued by day care advocates and information services; employers sponsoring work-related day care; municipal, provincial and federal government departments.

Location: OONL.

3239 **LaHaye, Monique; Lefrançois, Richard**

Répertoire de la recherche sociale au Québec, 1975-1981. Sherbrooke, Québec: Département de service social, Université de Sherbrooke, [1982]. 157 p. (Collection recherche sociale / Département de service social, Université de Sherbrooke ; no 2)

Note: 611 entrées.– Les catégories de recherches: connaissance du milieu/clientèle, distribution des services, politiques sociales, méthodes d'intervention.– Principaux thèmes traités: criminologie, délinquance, adolescence, aide sociale, avortement, coopérative, discrimination, enfant, femme, logement, habitation, personne âgée, politique sociale, service sociale, travail et violence.

Localisation: OONL.

3240 **Lawton-Speert, Sarah; Wachtel, Andy**

Child sexual abuse and incest: an annotated bibliography. 2nd ed. Vancouver: United Way of the Lower Mainland, Social Planning and Research Department, 1982. iv, 42 p. (Working paper: Child Sexual Abuse Project / United Way of the Lower Mainland, Social Planning and Research Department ; 1)

Note: Previous edition: 1981. 35 l.

Location: OONL.

3241 **Manitoba's research on aging: an annotated bibliography, 1950-1982.** [Winnipeg]: Manitoba Association on Gerontology, [1982]. v, 269 p.

Note: Contains research literature arranged in two separate sections, one with annotations for general population, one with scientific abstracts.– Topics include clothing, housing, medical and dental, nutrition, recreation and leisure, social policy, program evaluations.

Location: OONL.

3242 **Schlesinger, Benjamin**

Sexual abuse of children: a resource guide and annotated bibliography. Toronto: University of Toronto Press, 1982. xiii, 200 p.; ISBN: 0-8020-6481-7.

Note: 180 entries.– Articles dealing with such topics as father-daughter incest, counselling, historical background of sexual abuse, legal aspects, media and incest, sexual offenders and offenses, treatment programs.

Location: OONL.

3243 **Scott, Norlayne L.**

In the mainstream: a bibliography on the disabled in Manitoba. Winnipeg: Library, Department of Education, 1982. xi, 102 p.; ISBN: 0-86497-063-3.

Note: Approx. 500 entries.– Books, pamphlets, articles, government publications, audio-visual materials (films, filmstrips, cassettes).– Includes novels, plays, stories which portray positive image of disabled and are notable for literary merit and sensitive treatment of subject

matter.– Topics covered include types of disabilities (emotional disorders, hearing impairments, learning disabilities, mental retardation, physical disabilities, visual impairments), the environment (architectural accessibility, recreation and sport, transportation, integration of disabled into society.– Includes a list of periodicals and bibliographies.
Location: OONL.

3244 **St. Clair, Barbara Elaine; Wong, Sandra Ann**
Nutrition and aging: a selected bibliography. Toronto: Nutrition Information Service, Ryerson Polytechnical Institute, 1982. 128 p.; ISBN: 0-919351-05-0.
Note: Approx. 750 entries.– Books, journal articles, pamphlets, bibliographies relating to nutrition and aging.– Sections on biology of aging, nutritional implications of aging, nutrition education programs, meal planning and food preparation.
Location: OONL.

— 1983 —

3245 **British Columbia. Ministry of Human Resources**
Mental retardation: a basic reading list. Victoria: Province of British Columbia, Ministry of Human Resources, Library, 1983. 10 p.
Note: Location: OONL.

3246 **Canada. Transport Canada. Transportation Development Centre**
Canadian travel guides for disabled persons, a bibliography. Montreal: Transport Canada. Transportation Development Centre, 1983. [3] p.
Note: Location: QMTD.

3247 **Canadian Rehabilitation Council for the Disabled**
Compendium of information resources on physical disability. Toronto: Canadian Rehabilitation Council for the Disabled, 1983. 1 vol. (in various pagings).; ISBN: 0-86500-013-1.
Note: Includes a section listing publications at the CRCD Resource Centre on various topics related to physical disability: architecture, education, employment, health care, recreation, rehabilitation and transportation.– Emphasis on Canadian material.– Contains a list of CRCD publications and films.
Location: OONL.

3248 **Gunn, Jonathan P.; Verkeley, Jacqueline; Newman, Lynda**
Older Canadian homeowners: a literature review. [Ottawa]: Canada Mortgage and Housing Corporation, 1983. [8], 71, [14] p.
Note: Approx. 125 entries.
Location: OOCM.

3249 **Johnson, Jenny**
Bibliography of selected titles on disability and disabled persons: procedures and selected sources. [North York, Ont.]: North York Public Library, 1983. 12, 19, 6 l.
Note: Approx. 160 entries.– Lists books, government publications, conference proceedings on aspects of disability.– Topics include architecture, attitudes, sexuality, sports and recreation, technical aids and devices, transportation, employment, advocacy and human rights.
Location: OONL.

3250 **Moscovitch, Allan**
The welfare state in Canada: a selected bibliography, 1840 to 1978. Waterloo, Ont.: Wilfrid Laurier University Press, c1983. xxiv, 246 p.; ISBN: 0-88920-114-5.
Note: 3,299 entries.– Books, journal articles, government studies and reports.– Emphasis on social welfare policies in such areas as people out of work, people who cannot work (physically disabled, mentally disabled), "marginal" people, natives and ethnic minorities, women and children.
Location: OONL.

3251 **Pouliot-Marier, Colette; Langlois, Simon**
Genres de vie et conditions de vie des ménages: bibliographie. Québec: Laboratoire de recherches sociologiques, Université Laval, 1983. 171 p. (Collection Outils de recherche / Laboratoire de recherches sociologiques, Université Laval ; cahier no 4); ISBN: 2-920495-13-5.
Note: Approx. 1,500 entrées.– Principaux thèmes traités: genre de vie, cycle de vie et sexe, budget et revenu, consommation, travail, population.– Inclut un nombre d'ouvrages canadiens.– Comprend du texte en anglais.
Localisation: OONL.

3252 **Saskatchewan aging: an annotated bibliography on research in Saskatchewan, 1945 to the present.** Regina: Senior Citizens' Provincial Council, 1983. vi, 166 p.
Note: Approx. 600 entries.– Books, articles in professional journals, government reports and studies dealing with research conducted in Saskatchewan relating to aging.– Many documents are given locations.
Location: OONL.

3253 **Schlesinger, Benjamin**
Canadian family studies: a selected, annotated bibliography, 1970-1982. Chicago, Ill.: Council of Planning Librarians, [1983]. v, 45 p. (CPL bibliography / Council of Planning Librarians ; no. 123); ISBN: 0-86602-123-X.
Note: 215 entries.– Articles, pamphlets, books dealing with aspects of Canadian family.– Topics include adoption, ethnic families, one-parent families, family violence, elderly, family trends, gender roles, marriage.
Location: OONL.

3254 **Stanek, Oleg**
L'influence de la localisation des logements sur la qualité de vie des personnes âgées: une bibliographie selectionée. Sherbrooke, Québec: Université de Sherbrooke, Département de géographie, 1983. 36 f. (Bulletin de recherche / Université de Sherbrooke, Département de géographie ; no 66)
Note: Approx. 500 entrées.
Localisation: OONL.

3255 **Szpakowska, Janina-Klara**
Le Québec jeune, 1978-1983: mini-banque d'information bibliographique sur la condition sociale des québécois et québécoises de 13 à 25 ans. Montréal: École de bibliothéconomie, Université de Montréal, 1983. 368 p. (Publications de l'École de bibliothéconomie / Université de Montréal ; no 8); ISBN: 2-920-537-00-8.
Note: 592 entrées.– Style de vie, vie quotidienne des jeunes (logement, alimentation, etc.), société des jeunes, vie étudiante, droits des jeunes, marché du travail, les jeunes en détresse sociale, délinquance juvénile, psychologie, santé et amour et sexualité.
Localisation: OONL.

— 1984 —

3256 **Bojanowski, Belle C., et al.**
Research on aging in British Columbia: an annotated bibliography, 1950-1983. Burnaby: Gerontology Research Centre, Simon Fraser University, c1984. v, 139 p.; ISBN: 0-86491-036-3.
Note: Approx. 250 entries.– Published and unpublished works (conference presentations, theses, documents produced by government departments, service agencies, local councils).– Twelve major subject groupings.– Classified by academic areas, such as education and psychology, concerns such as housing/living arrangements, and by aspects of the aging experience, such as retirement and leisure.
Location: OONL.

3257 **Carrier, Denis**
Répertoire des recherches gérontologiques publiées ou en cours (1977-1982). Montréal: Association québécoise de gérontologie, 1984. ii, 33 f.
Note: 129 entrées.
Localisation: OONL.

3258 **Carrière, Richard; Thomson, Ashley**
Child abuse & neglect: a compendium of community resources/Enfance maltraitée et négligée: un répertoire des ressources communautaires. Sudbury, Ont.: Laurentian University, 1984. xiv, 39, 94, 12, xxiv p.
Note: 1,062 entries.– Books, public documents, non-print materials, journal articles dealing with child abuse and neglect.– Includes many Canadian titles in English and French.– Text in English and French/texte en français et en anglais.
Location: OONL.

3259 **Crawford, William**
Homosexuality in Canada: a bibliography. 2nd ed. Toronto: Canadian Gay Archives, c1984. viii, 378 columns [iv, 189] p. (Canadian Gay Archives publication ; no. 9); ISBN: 0-9690981-3-8.
Note: Approx. 3,000 entries.– Includes books and articles on a wide range of topics related to homosexuality/lesbianism/transsexuality in Canada.– Topics include art, education, Canadian gay periodicals, history, film, literature, medicine, psychiatry and psychology, law, criminal cases, civil rights and censorship, religion, theses, bibliographies and indexes.– Introduction en français.
Previous edition: Spence, Alex. Toronto: Pink Triangle Press, 1979. 85 p.; ISBN: 0-920430-02-3.
Location: OONL.

3260 **Kurtz, Norman R.; Googins, Bradley; Howard, William**
Occupational alcoholism: an annotated bibliography. Toronto: Addiction Research Foundation of Ontario, c1984. xi, 218 p. (Bibliographic series / Addiction Research Foundation of Ontario ; no. 17; ISSN: 0065-1885); ISBN: 0-88868-101-1.
Note: Location: OONL.

3261 **Leroux, Denise; Leduc, Diane**
The aged in Canadian society: select bibliography/Les vieillards dans la société canadienne: bibliographie sélective. Ottawa: Library of Parliament, Information and Reference Branch, 1984. 17 l.
Note: Approx. 150 entries.– Books, government publications, journal articles dealing with social aspects of aging.– Topics covered include statistics, demographics, alcohol and drug dependence, health care, housing, retirement age policies, post-retirement income, women and aging.
Location: OOF.

3262 **Meredith, Colin**
Compte rendu sommaire et bibliographie annotée sur les besoins des victimes d'actes criminels. [Ottawa]: Ministère du Solliciteur général du Canada, [1984]. 289 p. (Rapport pour spécialistes / Ministère du Solliciteur général Canada ; no 1984-18)
Note: Approx. 250 entrées.– Accordé une attention particulière aux publications canadiennes traitant des besoins des victimes d'inceste et d'aggression sexuelle, des femmes battues et des enfants maltraités, ainsi que des personnes âgées, des autochtones et des résidents des régions rurales victimes d'actes criminels.
English title: *Overview and annotated bibliography of the needs of crime victims.*
Localisation: OONL.

3263 **Meredith, Colin**
Overview and annotated bibliography of the needs of crime victims. [Ottawa]: Ministry of the Solicitor General of Canada, [1984]. 138 p. (Programs Branch user report / Ministry Secretariat, Solicitor General Canada ; no. 1984-18)
Note: Approx. 350 entries.– Emphasis on Canadian literature which addresses needs of victims of wife abuse, child abuse/incest, sexual assault, and on elderly, natives and rural residents as crime victims.
Titre en français: *Compte rendu sommaire et bibliographie annotée sur les besoins des victimes d'actes criminels.*
Location: OONL.

3264 **Ruel, Ginette**
Bibliographie sélective sur le viol. Québec: Service de la documentation, Ministère des affaires sociales, 1984. 53 f.
Note: Approx. 300 entrées.– Bibliographies, répertoires, monographies, documents audio-visuels, articles de revues et de journaux en français et les articles de revues en anglais.– Les documents couvrent davantage les années quatre-vingt puisque les années soixante-dix.
Localisation: OONL.

3265 **Valade, Roxanne; Lips, Thomas; Mes, Femmy**
"Bibliography on child abuse."
In: *Canada's Mental Health*; Vol. 32, no. 2 (June 1984) p. B1-B8.; ISSN: 0008-2791.
Note: Selective listing of books, articles and reports in English and French languages dealing with child abuse.
Location: OONL.

— 1985 —

3266 **Aging and the aged: list of selected publications from Health and Welfare Canada.** [Ottawa]: Office on Aging, Policy, Planning and Information Branch, Health and Welfare Canada, [1985]. 63, 63 p.
Note: Lists documents produced by branches of Department of Health and Welfare that deal with issues of interest to the aged or to those responsible for their well-being.– Text in English and French with French text on inverted pages.– Title of additional title-page: *Vieillissement et personnes âgées: choix de publications de Santé et Bien-être social Canada.*
Location: OONL.

3267 **Bourgeois, Donald J.**
Annotated bibliography, public opinion and social policy. [Ottawa]: Ministry Secretariat, Solicitor General of Canada, [1985]. 3, 56, 4 p. (Programs Branch user report / Ministry Secretariat, Solicitor General Canada ; no. 1985-05)
Note: Approx. 350 entries.– Lists articles and books published between 1969 and 1981 on public opinion research related to social policy field, including criminal justice policy.
Titre en français: *Bibliographie annotée: opinion publique et politique sociale.*
Location: OONL.

3268 **Bourgeois, Donald J.**
Bibliographie annotée: opinion publique et politique sociale. [Ottawa]: Secrétariat du Ministère, Solliciteur général Canada, [1985]. 110 f. (Rapport pour spécialistes / Ministère du Solliciteur général Canada ; no 1985-05)
Note: Approx. 300 entrées.– Liste des textes publiés entre 1969 et 1981 inclusivement.
English title: *Annotated bibliography, public opinion and social policy.*
Localisation: OONL.

3269 **Carrière, Richard; Thomson, Ashley**
Family violence: a bibliography of Ontario resources, 1980-1984/La violence familiale: une bibliographie des ressources ontariennes, 1980-1984. Sudbury, Ont.: Laurentian University, 1985. xiv, 95 p.
Note: 789 entries.– Books, reports, articles, theses dealing with aspects of family violence, with emphasis on child abuse and neglect, spousal abuse, abuse of the elderly; all work produced in Ontario.
Location: OONHHS.

3270 **Child abuse: materials available from Manitoba Education Library.** [Winnipeg]: Manitoba Education, Instructional Resources, 1985. 15 p.
Note: Approx. 125 entries.– Books (fiction and non-fiction), audiovisual materials.
Location: OONL.

3271 **Fédération des enseignantes et des enseignants de l'Ontario. Comité de la condition féminine**
La violence au sein de la famille: une bibliographie sélective. [Toronto]: La Fédération, [1985]. 24, 82 p.; ISBN: 0-88872-064-5.
Note: Approx. 180 entrées.– Livres, articles de périodiques, publications officielles sur les thèmes: femmes battues, mauvais traitement de femmes âgées.– Texte en français et en anglais disposé tête-bêche.– Titre de la p. de t. additionnelle: *Family violence: a selective bibliography.*
Localisation: OONL.

3272 **Fisher, Honey Ruth**
Studies of drinking in public places: an annotated bibliography. Toronto: Addiction Research Foundation of Ontario, c1985. x, 85 p. (Bibliographic series / Addiction Research Foundation of Ontario ; no. 18; ISSN: 0065-1885); ISBN: 0-88868-106-2.
Note: Location: OONL.

3273 **Garant, Louise**
La déinstitutionnalisation en santé mentale: un tour d'horizon de la littérature. Québec: Ministère des affaires sociales, Secrétariat à la coordination de la recherche, 1985. 74 p.

Note: Localisation: QQLA.

3274 **Gaudette, Micheline**
Humanisation: bibliographie annotée. Montréal: Conseil de la santé et des services sociaux de la région de Montréal métropolitain, c1985. [62] p.
Note: Approx. 150 entrées.– Volumes et rapports, articles.– Principaux thèmes: qualité des soins et services, protection des droits, humanisation: bureaucratie, besoins des bénéficiaires et de la population.
Localisation: OONL.

3275 **Lawrence, Jean; Haddad, April**
Wife abuse: a bibliography of materials available at the Justice Institute. Vancouver: Justice Institute of British Columbia, 1985. 8 l.
Note: Selected list of books, articles, audiovisual materials dealing with battered women, part of a kit entitled *Victim support worker package: wife assault,* produced by the B.C. Ministry of Attorney General, Victim Assistance Program.
Location: OONL.

3276 **MacKinnon, Fred R.**
Annotated bibliography of social welfare in Nova Scotia. Halifax: Maritime School of Social Work, 1985. 221 p.
Note: 399 entries.– Monographs, articles, theses/dissertations, government documents, unpublished documents, archival documents to December 1981 on social welfare in Nova Scotia.– Topics include history, child welfare, Blacks in Nova Scotia, community development, economic development, public welfare history, social action, social planning, legislation.
Location: OONL.

3277 **Mayer-Renaud, Micheline; Berthiaume, Monique**
Les enfants du silence: revue de la littérature sur la négligence à l'égard des enfants. Montréal: Centre de services sociaux du Montréal métropolitain, Direction des services professionnels, 1985. 161, 12, 25 p.
Note: 322 entrées.– Articles, livres et rapports.– Comprend des publications en français et en anglais sur les types de négligence, les manifestations et impact de la négligence, les modes d'intervention, la prévention.– Comporte des références canadiennes et québécoises.
Localisation: OONL.

3278 **Ontario Teachers' Federation. Status of Women Committee**
Family violence: a selective bibliography. [Toronto]: The Federation, [1985]. 82, 24 p.; ISBN: 0-88872-064-5.
Note: Approx. 180 entries.– Books, government publications, periodical articles, audiovisual resources on historical aspects of family violence, causes of wife battering, effects on children, abuse and the older woman.– Text in English and French with French text on inverted pages.– Title of additional title-page: *La violence au sein de la famille: une bibliographie sélective.*
Location: OONL.

3279 **Pence, Alan R.**
Bibliography of Canadian day care research/Bibliographie des études sur la garde des enfants au Canada. [Ottawa: Status of Women Canada], c1985. 51 p.; ISBN: 0-662-54141-3.
Note: Approx. 500 entries.– Articles and studies from 1961 to 1984.
Supplement: Pence, Alan R.; Greenwood-Church, Margo L. *The 1989 update of "A bibliography of Canadian day care*

research." [S.l.: s.n.], 1989. [30] p.
Location: OONL.

3280 **Ryan, Nancy E.**
Rural aging in Canada: an annotated bibliography. Guelph, Ont.: Gerontology Research Centre, University of Guelph, c1985. iii, 150 p.; ISBN: 0-88955-033-6.
Note: 131 entries.– Theses, conference papers, journal articles, research papers, government documents from 1950s to 1985.– "Rural" means communities with population of less than 10,000.
Location: OONL.

3281 **Schlesinger, Benjamin**
The one-parent family in the 1980s: perspectives and annotated bibliography, 1978-1984. 5th ed. Toronto: University of Toronto Press, c1985. 284 p.; ISBN: 0-8020-6565-1.
Note: 490 entries.– Covers the period from January 1, 1978 to June 1, 1984.– Includes books, booklets, reports, articles written in English, with focus on Canada and United States.– Includes a section on remarriage.
Previous editions:
The one-parent family: perspectives and annotated bibliography. 1978. x, 224 p.; ISBN: 0-8020-2335-5. (750 entries covering the period from 1930 to 1978, revises and cumulates the material contained in earlier editions).
1975. ix, 186 p.; ISBN: 0-8020-2171-9.
1970. xiii, 138 p.; ISBN: 0-8020-1582-4.
1969. 132 p.; ISBN: 0-8020-1582-4.
Location: OONL.

3282 **Service de diffusion sélective de l'information de la Centrale des bibliothèques**
L'Homosexualité. Montréal: Le Service, 1985. 50 p. (DSI/CB ; no 72; ISSN: 0825-5024); ISBN: 2-89059-272-3.
Note: 160 entrées.– Livres, articles de périodiques, documents audiovisuels.– La période couverte est de 1973 à 1984.
Localisation: OONL.

3283 **Vieillissement et personnes âgées: choix de publications de Santé et Bien-être social Canada.**
[Ottawa]: Santé et Bien-être social Canada, [1985]. 63, 63 p.
Note: Liste des publications récentes dont le sujet concerne les personnes âgées ou les responsables de leur bien-être.– Texte en français et en anglais disposé tête-bêche.– Titre de la p. de t. additionnelle: *Aging and the aged: list of selected publications from Health and Welfare Canada.*
Localisation: OOCM.

— 1986 —

3284 **Boneca, Shirley; Clinton, Marshall**
Child abuse materials available in northwestern Ontario: a finding aid. 2nd ed. Thunder Bay, Ont.: Lakehead University Library, 1986. ii, 30 p.; ISBN: 0-88663-005-3.
Note: Approx. 250 entries.– Books, films and related material on child physical and sexual abuse in Thunder Bay and region.
Previous edition: ... : *a finding guide.* 1983.
Location: OONL.

3285 **Brym, Robert J.**
"Anglo-Canadian sociology: bibliography."
In: *Current Sociology*; Vol. 34, no. 1 (Spring 1986) p. 112-152.; ISSN: 0011-3921.
Note: Location: OONL.

3286 **Canada. Library of Parliament. Bibliographies and Compilations Section**
The handicapped, 1975-1986/Les handicapés, 1975-1986. Ottawa: Library of Parliament, Information and Reference Branch, 1986. 33 l.
Note: Approx. 300 entries.– Monographs, selected periodical articles dealing with physically handicapped, mentally handicapped, handicapped children, employment, transportation, housing and access to public buildings, law and civil rights, recreation.
Location: BVIP.

3287 **Family violence: an annotated bibliography.** Halifax: Public Legal Education Society of Nova Scotia, c1986. 43 p.; ISBN: 0-88648-066-3.
Note: Approx. 100 entries.– Lists material on battered women, child abuse, elder abuse, incest/sexual assault, crisis intervention, police/criminal justice system, health professionals, treatment groups.
Location: OONL.

3288 **Hayes, Janet; Souka, Jody**
Violence in society: a selective bibliography/Violence au sein de la société: biobibliographie [sic] choisie. [Ottawa]: Ministry Secretariat, Solicitor General Canada, [1986]. 215 p. (Programs Branch user report / Ministry Secretariat, Solicitor General Canada ; no. 1986-24)
Note: Approx. 2,000 entries.– Published and unpublished literature from 1979 to 1986.– Topics include alcohol/drug abuse and violence, child abuse, drunk driving, abuse of elderly, family violence, homicide, violence and the media, sexual violence, suicide, terrorism, victims of violence.– Text in English and French/texte en français et en anglais.
Location: OONL.

3289 **London Public Libraries and Museums (Ont.)**
Divorce: a multi-disciplinary approach. [London, Ont.]: London Public Libraries and Museums, [1986]. 13 p.
Note: List of books published from 1980 to 1986 on divorce, remarriage, stepparenting.– Some Canadian references.
Location: OONL.

3290 **Normandeau, André; Vauclair, Martin**
"Sociologie du milieu carcéral, bibliographie sélective."
Dans: *Revue canadienne de criminologie*; Vol. 28, no 4 (octobre 1986) p. 415-433.; ISSN: 0704-9722.
Note: Localisation: OONL.

3291 **Nova Scotia. Senior Citizens' Secretariat**
Aging and the aged in Nova Scotia: a list of writings from 1979 to 1985. [Halifax]: The Secretariat, 1986. ii, 10 l.
Note: Lists 80 articles and studies by individuals and agencies, from government, universities, private agencies.
Location: OONL.

3292 **Pocius, Gerald L.**
"An introductory bibliography on cultural studies relating to death and dying in Canada."
In: *Material History Bulletin*; No. 23 (Spring 1986) p. 53-55.; ISSN: 0703-489X.
Note: Lists works dealing with cultural practices and physical artifacts relating to death and dying.– Excludes works dealing with native peoples, demographic studies of mortuary trends, sociological material relating to bereavement, supernatural narratives.
Location: OONL.

3293 **Schlesinger, Benjamin**
Sexual abuse of children in the 1980's: ten essays and an annotated bibliography. Toronto: University of Toronto Press, c1986. 210 p.
Note: Bibliography: p. [95]-189.
Location: OONL.

3294 **Schlesinger, Benjamin**
"Single parent families: a bookshelf: 1978-1985."
In: *Family Relations*; Vol. 35, no. 1 (January 1986) p. 199-204.; ISSN: 0197-6664.
Note: 80 entries.– Books and special issues of journals dealing with single parents in Canada and the United States.
Location: OONL.

3295 **Warren, Nancy**
Bibliography on voluntarism: publications relevant to voluntarism and to the management of voluntary organizations. Toronto: Ontario Association of Volunteer Bureaux/Centres, 1986. x, 127 p.; ISBN: 0-7729-0381-6.
Note: Monographs, periodicals and newsletters published after 1970.– Excludes audio-visual materials, extracts from publications, periodical articles, individual conference papers and speeches, financial statements/ annual reports, promotional pamphlets and brochures.– Main criterion for entry focussed on materials to enhance effective management of voluntary organizations.– Ontario locations given for all documents.– Joint project of Ontario Ministry of Citizenship and Culture and Ontario Association of Volunteer Bureaux and Centres.– Préface, remerciements, introduction en français et en anglais.
Location: OONL.

— 1987 —

3296 **Bogo, Marion**
The practice of field instruction in social work: theory and process, with an annotated bibliography. Toronto: University of Toronto Press, 1987. xii, 167 p.: ill.; ISBN: 0-8020-6689-5.
Note: 149 entries.– Focusses on issues related to field instruction training in social work.– Includes a number of Canadian references.
Location: OONL.

3297 **Féger, Robert; Gauthier, Marcelle**
Bibliographie sur la violence à l'égard des enfants. Montréal: Commission des écoles catholiques de Montréal, Bureau de ressources en développement pédagogiques et en consultation personnelle, 1987. 129 p.; ISBN: 2-92076-638-4.
Note: 441 entrées.– Ouvrages, articles, rapports de recherche, textes de conférence et thèses en français et en anglais concernant la violence à l'endroit des enfants et des adolescents.– Thèmes: violence familiale, aspects jurido-médico-légaux de la violence, violence institutionnelle et programmes d'intervention.– Inclut un nombre d'ouvrages canadiens.
Localisation: OONL.

3298 **Homelessness: a selected, annotated bibliography.**
Calgary: City of Calgary, Social Services Department, 1987. i, 31 l.
Note: Approx. 125 entries.– Arranged in four sections: general information on the housing problem, subpopulation groups (mentally ill, alcohol abusers, women, families, youth, elderly, native people) and homelessness in Calgary.
Location: OONL.

3299 **Kenyon, Robert; Sawka, Edward**
Primary prevention of substance abuse: an annotated bibliography of related literature (1981-1987). [Edmonton]: Alberta Alcohol and Drug Abuse Commission, c1987. viii, 137, [12] p.
Note: Approx. 380 entries.– Books, booklets, journal articles, conference proceedings, papers dealing with the primary prevention of substance abuse, arranged in the following categories and subcategories: alcohol, illicit drugs, pharmaceuticals, solvent/inhalants, tobacco (research, policy, theory, programs, international, historical, general).– Excludes material on intervention and treatment.– Many Canadian references.
Location: OONL.

3300 **Lévesque, Gaétan**
Les facteurs déterminants du niveau des avantages sociaux: une revue de la littérature. Montréal: Institut de recherche et d'information sur la rémunération, 1987. vii, 67 f.
Note: Localisation: OONL.

3301 **Mastrocola-Morris, Elaine**
The assault and abuse of middle-aged and older women by their spouses and children: an annotated bibliography. [Ottawa]: National Clearing House on Family Violence, 1987. 5 p.; ISBN: 0-662-16663-9.
Note: Titre en français: *Voies de fait et mauvais traitements imposés aux femmes d'âge moyen et avancé par les conjoints et les enfants: bibliographie annotée.*
Location: OONL.

3302 **Mastrocola-Morris, Elaine**
Voies de fait et mauvais traitements imposés aux femmes d'âge moyen et avancé par les conjoints et les enfants: bibliographie annotée. [Ottawa]: Centre national d'information sur la violence dans la famille, 1987. 6 p.; ISBN: 0-662-95363-4.
Note: English title: *The assault and abuse of middle-aged and older women by their spouses and children: an annotated bibliography.*
Localisation: OONL.

3303 **Ouellet, Francine; Lampron, Christiane**
Bilan des évaluations portant sur les services sociaux. Québec: Commission d'enquête sur les services de santé et les services sociaux, 1987. 91 p.; ISBN: 2-551-08489-X.
Note: Approx. 250 entrées.– Documents et rapports de recherche, outils de référence sur la période 1980-1986.
Localisation: OONL.

3304 **Rempel, Judith Dianne**
Annotated bibliography of papers, articles and other documents resulting from the Aging in Manitoba [Project]: 1971, 1976, 1983 cross-sectional and panel studies (Betty Havens, Manitoba Health, Principal investigator). [Winnipeg: Aging in Manitoba Project, Manitoba Health], 1987. 54 l.
Note: Approx. 120 entries.
Location: OONL.

— 1988 —

3305 **Beland, François**
"La recherche en gérontologie sociale au Québec: une originalité obscure ou une obscurité méritée?"
Dans: *Canadian Journal on Aging: La revue canadienne du vieillissement*; Vol. 7, no 4 (hiver 1988) p. 257-292.; ISSN:

0714-9808.
Note: Annexe, p. 275-292: "Répertoire bibliographique des publiées au Québec de 1975 à nos jours."- Articles, compte rendus et communications scientifiques non-publiés, livres, rapports de recherche
Localisation: OONL.

3306 **Canadian Housing Information Centre**
Housing and the elderly: a bibliography/Le logement et les personnes âgées: une bibliographie. Ottawa: The Centre, [1988]. 78 p.
Note: Approx. 700 entries.
Location: OON.

3307 **Collectif Hommes et gars**
Répertoire de la condition masculine. Montréal: Éditions Saint-Martin, 1988. 160 p.; ISBN: 2-89035-151-3.
Note: Bibliographie, filmographie et discographie sur la condition masculine.- Comporte des références canadiennes et québécoises.
Localisation: OONL.

3308 **Haubrich, Dennis J.; McLeod, Donald W.**
Psychosocial dimensions of HIV and AIDS: a selected annotated bibliography. Ottawa: Health and Welfare Canada, Federal Centre for AIDS, 1988. v, 163 p.; ISBN: 0-662-16641-8.
Note: 742 entries.- English-language material on psychosocial aspects of HIV and AIDS, focussing on the period 1981 to September 1987: journal and magazine articles, books, theses, conference papers, Canadian and United States government reports, bibliographies.- Excludes popular articles, audiovisual materials, biomedical literature.- Examines personal, social and ethical issues generated by AIDS, which affect caregivers, persons at risk for AIDS or infected with HIV.
Location: OONHL.

3309 **Janik, Sophie**
Bibliographie québécoise sur les personnes handicapées. [Québec]: Office des personnes handicapées, 1988. vii, 253 p.; ISBN: 2-551-08230-7.
Note: 4,610 documents publiés avant 1986 au Québec et ayant trait aux personnes handicapées: livres, articles, documents de travail, bibliographies, répertoires.- Thèmes principaux: accessibilité, adaptation/réadaptation, communications, culture, diagnostic et traitement, droits et législation, famille, loisir, maintien à domicile, services et ressources, sexualité, situation et problématique, transport, travail, vie associative.
Localisation: OONL.

3310 **Lukawiecki, Teresa**
Elder abuse bibliography/Bibliographie sur les abus à l'égard des personnes âgées. [Ottawa]: National Clearing House on Family Violence, 1988. 87 p.; ISBN: 0-662-58951-3.
Note: Approx. 250 entries.- Books, reports, articles, government publications dealing with aspects of elder abuse.- Substantial Canadian content.
Previous edition: 1988. 103 p.; ISBN: 0-662-56466-9.
Location: OONL.

3311 **Pauls, Jake L.**
Life safety for people with disabilities: literature review. Ottawa: Public Works Canada, Architectural and Engineering Services, 1988. 75, 79 p.
Note: 361 entries.- Topics covered include building facilities, personal devices, disabilities, hazards and emergencies (accessibility, ergonomics, rescue, standards, training, communication systems).- Many Canadian listings.- Text in English and French with French text on inverted pages.- Title of additional title-page: *La sécurité des personnes handicapés: étude bibliographique*.
Location: OONL.

3312 **Pauls, Jake L.**
La sécurité des personnes handicapés: étude bibliographique. Ottawa: Travaux publics Canada, Service d'architecture et de génie, 1988. 79, 75 p.
Note: 361 entrées.- Principaux thèmes traités: aménagements des bâtiments, handicaps, affectations et installations, organismes et rôles, risques-urgences, ergonomie, accessibilité.- Quelques références canadiennes.- Texte en français et en anglais disposé tête-bêche.- Titre de la p. de t. additionnelle: *Life safety for people with disabilities: literature review*.
Localisation: OONL.

3313 **Perrault, Isabelle**
Autour des jeunes: reconnaissance bibliographique. Québec: Institut québécois de recherche sur la culture, 1988. 422 p. (Documents de recherche / Institut québécois de recherche sur la culture ; no 17; ISSN: 0823-0447); ISBN: 2-89224-108-1.
Note: 4,158 entrées.- Couvrant les diverses avenues de la recherche sociale sur les jeunes: fondation de l'identité, aspirations, système d'enseignement, milieu scolaire, abandon scolaire, économie, loisirs, religion, politique, langue, droits, délinquance, violence, santé (anorexie, toxicomanie), sexualité, famille.
Localisation: OONL.

3314 **Schlesinger, Benjamin; Schlesinger, Rachel Aber**
Abuse of the elderly: issues and annotated bibliography. Toronto: University of Toronto Press, [1988]. xxi, 188 p.; ISBN: 0-8020-6694-1.
Note: 267 entries.- Books, booklets, journal articles, reports, newsletters, surveys, published in Canada and the U.S. between 1979 and 1987, arranged in 44 subject categories, including crime against the elderly, familial abuse, incidence of abuse, professionals and elder abuse, legal aspects, protection services, research studies.
Location: OONL.

3315 **Schlesinger, Benjamin; Schlesinger, Rachel Aber**
Canadian families: a resource guide. Toronto: OISE Press-Guidance Centre, c1988. vii, 81 p. (Guidance series / Ontario Institute for Studies in Education ; 3); ISBN: 0-7744-0337-3.
Note: 399 entries.- Covers to January 1989.- Books, journals, monographs, reports, surveys, films and videos (156 from National Film Board of Canada).
Location: OONL.

3316 **Sobsey, Richard, et al.**
Annotated bibliography: sexual abuse and exploitation of people with disabilities. Edmonton: Severe Disabilities Program, Department of Educational Sociology, University of Alberta, 1988. 72 p.
Note: Approx. 300 entries.- Research studies, position papers, program descriptions, clinical reports, media accounts pertaining to the sexual abuse of the handicapped, children and adults.- English-language material is abstracted in English, French-language material abstracted in French.

Location: OKQ.

3317 **Swift, Karen**
Knowledge about neglect: a critical review of the literature. Toronto: University of Toronto, Faculty of Social Work, 1988. 74, [9] p. (Working papers in social welfare in Canada ; 23; ISSN: 0710-0299)
Note: Location: OONL.

— 1989 —

3318 **Brand, Judith**
You can say "no": an annotated resource guide for child abuse education. [Victoria]: Province of British Columbia, Ministry of Education, c1989. 124 p.; ISBN: 0-7726-1066-5.
Note: Approx. 600 entries.– Printed and audiovisual materials with focus on prevention of child abuse published from 1980 to date.– Includes materials for children, adolescents, adults, special educators and parents.
Location: OONL.

3319 **Canada. Health and Welfare Canada. Family Violence Prevention Division. National Clearinghouse on Family Violence**
Child sexual abuse overview: a summary of 26 literature reviews and special projects. [Ottawa]: National Clearinghouse on Family Violence, Health and Welfare Canada, 1989. 30, [1], [1], 36 p.; ISBN: 0-662-56641-6.
Note: Abstracts of literature reviews on various aspects of child sexual abuse outlining the purpose, method and key findings.– Text in English and French with French text on inverted pages.– Title of additional title-page: *Aperçu général sur les agressions sexuelles contre les enfants: résumé de 26 analyses de documentation et de projets spéciaux.*
Location: OONL.

3320 **Canada. Santé et Bien-être social Canada. Division de la prévention de la violence familiale. Centre national d'information sur la violence dans la famille**
Aperçu général sur les agressions sexuelles contre les enfants: résumé de 26 analyses de documentation et de projets spéciaux. [Ottawa]: Centre national d'information sur la violence dans la famille, Santé et Bien-être social Canada, 1989. 36, [1], [1], 30 p.; ISBN: 0-662-56641-6.
Note: Comprend 26 résumés qui indiquent l'objet, les méthodes et les principales constatations de la documentation relative à divers aspects des agressions sexuelles contre les enfants.– Texte en français et en anglais disposé tête-bêche.– Titre de la p. de t. additionnelle: *Child sexual abuse overview: a summary of 26 literature reviews and special projects.*
Localisation: OONL.

3321 **Conine, Tali A.**
The parent who is disabled: a selected annotated bibliography on childbearing and childcaring with a physical or sensory disability. Vancouver: School of Rehabilitation Medicine, University of British Columbia, 1989. ii, 30 p.; ISBN: 0-88865-509-6.
Note: Approx. 100 entries.– Topics include planning for motherhood, childcare (assessment of ability), family life, childcare techniques and adaptations.– Includes Canadian references.
Location: OONL.

3322 **Cooper, Mary; Mori, Monica**
Annotated bibliography of B.C. publications on aging: 1984-1988. Vancouver: Gerontology Research Centre,

Simon Fraser at Harbour Centre, c1989. 201 p.; ISBN: 0-86491-096-7.
Note: 390 entries.– Published and unpublished papers and reports describing quantitative and qualitative research, policy research, program evaluations, innovative programs and services for the elderly.
Location: OONL.

3323 **Deller, June**
Family day care internationally: an annotated bibliography. [Toronto]: Child Care Branch, c1989. i, 49 p.; ISBN: 0-7729-5339-2.
Note: Approx. 400 entries.– Documentation from Canada and other countries in the following areas: legislation and policy, research, training and supports, resources, organizations and people.
Location: OONL.

3324 **Descent, David, et al.**
Classes sociales et mouvements sociaux au Québec et au Canada: essai synthèse et bibliographie. Montréal: Éditions Saint-Martin, c1989. 206 p. (Cahiers du CIDAR / Centre d'information et d'aide à la recherche, Département de sociologie, Université de Montréal ; no 9); ISBN: 2-89035-154-8.
Note: Approx. 1,500 entrées.– Textes d'auteurs canadiens et québécois publiés principalement au Canada.– Couvre de la fin des années 1960 jusqu'en 1986.
Localisation: OONL.

3325 **Desjardins, Joëlle**
Adoption internationale, 1980-1989: bibliographie sélective et annotée. Québec: Bibliothèque de l'Assemblée nationale, Division de la référence parlementaire, 1989. 12 p. (Bibliographie / Bibliothèque de l'Assemblée nationale du Québec ; no 28; ISSN: 0836-9100)
Note: 49 entrées.– Articles, publications gouvernementales: Québec, autre pays, études générales et conventions internationales.
Localisation: OONL.

3326 **Doyle, Veronica M.**
Homesharing matchup agencies for seniors: a literature review. Burnaby, B.C.: Gerontology Research Centre, Simon Fraser University, 1989. 46 p.; ISBN: 0-8649109-5-9.
Note: Location: OONL.

3327 **Frankel-Howard, Deborah**
Family violence: review of theoretical and clinical literature. [Ottawa]: Policy, Communications and Information Branch, Health and Welfare Canada, 1989. 115, 129 p.; ISBN: 0-662-16951-4.
Note: Analytical overview of recent literature (published since 1980) in area of family violence.– Covers scholarly research, theoretical approaches and practical applications to prevention, protection and treatment of family violence, writings from the fields of sociology and psychology, history, politics, social work, education, medicine and law, with emphasis on Canadian literature.– Text in English and French with French text on inverted pages.– Title of additional title-page: *La violence familiale: examen des écrits théoriques et cliniques.*
Location: OONL.

3328 **Frankel-Howard, Deborah**
La violence familiale: examen des écrits théoriques et cliniques. [Ottawa]: Direction générale de la politique, des communications et de l'information, [1989]. 129,

115 p.; ISBN: 0-662-95439-4.

Note: Aperçu analytique des écrits récents (publiés depuis 1980) portant sur la violence familiale, recherches d'érudition, des approches théoriques et des applications pratiques relatives à la prévention, à la protection et au traitement des cas de violence familiale.– Disciplines: sociologie, psychologie, histoire, éducation, science politique, travail social, médecine et droit.– Inclut un nombre considérable d'ouvrages canadiens.– Texte en français et en anglais disposé tête-bêche.– Titre de la p. de t. additionnelle: *Family violence: review of theoretical and clinical literature.*

Localisation: OONL.

3329 **Inventory of data files on aging in Ontario.** Toronto: Centre for Studies on Aging, University of Toronto, 1989. 1 vol. (in various pagings).

Note: Approx. 200 entries.– Topics covered include social conditions, health, housing, transportation, income maintenance, recreation of aged in Ontario.– Inventory available in printed format or machine-readable database prepared on *R-BASE FOR DOS.*

Location: OONL.

3330 **Lacroix, Lucien**
Bibliographie 1975-1989, Service de la recherche [Centre de services sociaux de Québec]. Québec: Centre de services sociaux de Québec, 1989. 45 p.

Note: Approx. 200 entrées.

Localisation: OONL.

3331 **Patriquin, Larry**
Income, income security and the Canadian welfare state, 1978-1987: a selected bibliography. [Ottawa]: Canadian Centre for Policy Alternatives, 1989. iii, 69; ISBN: 0-88627-976-3.

Note: Approx. 800 entries.– Books, research studies, journal and magazine articles, government documents, theses relating to the history of welfare state, poverty, minimum wage, guaranteed annual income, job creation, taxation, and specific income security programs such as unemployment insurance, old age pensions, family allowances.

Location: OONL.

3332 **Peters, Diane E.**
Social work: a bibliography of directories in W.L.U. Library. [Waterloo, Ont.]: The Library, Wilfrid Laurier University, 1989. 32 p.; ISBN: 0-921821-08-5.

Note: Approx. 300 entries.– Lists directories of interest to social workers.– Many Canadian references.

Location: OONL.

3333 **Powell, Mary; Faghfoury, Nahid; Nyenhuis, Pat**
Encourager la participation du public: bref exposé et bibliographie choisie annotée. Ottawa: Conseil canadien de développement social, [1989]. 81 p.; ISBN: 0-88810-401-4.

Note: 204 entrées.

English title: *Fostering public participation: a brief discussion and selected annotated bibliography.*

Localisation: OONL.

3334 **Powell, Mary; Faghfoury, Nahid; Nyenhuis, Pat**
Fostering public participation: a brief discussion and selected annotated bibliography. Ottawa: Canadian Council on Social Development, [1989]. iii, 73 p.; ISBN: 0-88810-383-2.

Note: Titre en français: *Encourager la participation du*

public: bref exposé et bibliographie choisie annotée.

Location: OONL.

3335 **Trahan-Langlois, Lysette**
Les facteurs associés à l'orientation des personnes âgées dans des établissements d'hébergement: une revue de la littérature. Québec: Gouvernement du Québec, Ministère de la santé et des services sociaux, Direction générale de la planification et de l'évaluation, 1989. xi, 100 p. (Collection Études et analyses / Gouvernement du Québec, Ministère de la santé et des services sociaux, Direction générale de la planification et de l'évaluation ; no 5); ISBN: 2-550-1961-8.

Note: Localisation: OONL.

— 1990 —

3336 **Canada. Multiculturalism and Citizenship Canada**
Resource guide, eliminating racial discrimination in Canada: the challenge and the opportunity. Ottawa: Multiculturalism and Citizenship Canada, 1990. 16, 16 p.; ISBN: 0-662-58008-7.

Note: 86 entries.– Includes a list of additional bibliographies.– Text in English and French with French text on inverted pages.– Title of additional title-page: *Documents de référence: l'élimination de la discrimination raciale au Canada: le défi et la possibilité de le relever.*

Location: OONL.

3337 **Canada. Multiculturalisme et citoyenneté Canada**
Documents de référence, l'élimination de la discrimination raciale au Canada: le défi et la possibilité de le relever. Ottawa: Multiculturalisme et citoyenneté Canada, 1990. 16, 16 p.; ISBN: 0-662-58008-7.

Note: 86 entrées.– Comprend une liste des bibliographies additionnelle.– Texte en français et en anglais disposé tête-bêche.– Titre de la p. de t. additionnelle: *Resource guide, eliminating racial discrimination in Canada: the challenge and the opportunity.*

Localisation: OONL.

3338 **Chamberland, Claire**
Portrait de la littérature québécoise en toxicomanie. [Québec]: Ministère de la santé et des services sociaux, Direction générale de la planification et de l'évaluation, 1990. 2 vol.; ISBN: 2-550-20685-1 (vol. 1); 2-550-20686-X (vol. 2).

Note: Dossier 1: *La prévention.* Dossier 2: *La réadaptation.*

Localisation: OONL.

3339 **Forcese, Dennis P.**
"Sociology in Canada: a view from the eighties." In: *International Journal of Canadian Studies*; No. 1-2 (Spring-Fall 1990) p. 35-53.; ISSN: 1180-3991.

Note: Review of writings in the field of Canadian sociology, anglophone and francophone, with emphasis on the period from the 1960s through the 1980s.

Location: OONL.

3340 **Garant, Louise; Bolduc, Mario**
L'aide par les proches: mythes et réalités: revue de littérature et réflexions sur les personnes âgées en perte d'autonomie, leurs aidants et aidantes naturels et le lien avec services formels. Québec: Gouvernement du Québec, Ministère de la santé et des service sociaux, Direction générale de la planification et de l'évaluation, 1990. xviii, 157 p. (Collection Études et analyses / Gouvernement du Québec, Ministère de la santé et des service sociaux, Direction générale de la planification et de l'évaluation ; 8); ISBN: 2-550-21000-X.

Note: 189 entrées.
Localisation: OONL.

3341 **Lebeau, Mario, et al.**
Besoins de logements des groupes spéciaux: une synthèse des recherches francophones. [Ottawa]: Société canadienne d'hypothèques et de logement, 1990. 48, [32] p.
Note: Liste des principales recherches sur le logement des groupes particuliers produites en français au Canada: besoins élémentaires de logement, besoins de logements spéciaux, logement social.
English title: *Special housing needs: a synthesis of French language research.*
Location: OONL.

3342 **Lebeau, Mario, et al.**
Special housing needs: a synthesis of French language research. [Ottawa]: Canada Mortgage and Housing Corporation, 1990. 48, [32] p.
Note: Lists the main research work on housing of particular groups, written in French and produced in Canada: basic housing needs, special housing needs, social housing.
Titre en français: *Besoins de logements des groupes spéciaux: une synthèse des recherches francophones.*
Location: OONL.

3343 **People Against Crime Together**
Select annotated bibliography on abuse: child, domestic, elder, sexual, spouse, substance. Regina: People Against Crime Together, 1990. vi, 71 p.; ISBN: 0-9694625-0-6.
Note: Approx. 350 entries.– Books, booklets and pamphlets dealing with various forms of abuse.– Includes Canadian references.
Location: OONL.

3344 **Peters, Diane E.**
Social work: a bibliography of bibliographies in W.L.U. Library. Waterloo, Ont.: Library, Wilfrid Laurier University, 1990. 210 p.; ISBN: 0-921-821-11-5.
Note: Approx. 1,500 entries.– Lists bibliographies, indexes, abstracts relating to social work, social problems and policy.– Includes many Canadian references.
Previous editions:
Wilfrid Laurier University. Library. *Social work: a bibliography of bibliographies.* 1987. 122 p.
Wilkins, Diane. *Bibliographies: a bibliography of bibliographies of interest to social work.* Waterloo, Ont.: Wilfrid Laurier University; 1983. i, 67 p.
Location: OONL.

3345 **Sexual assault: annotated bibliography of sexual assault literature.** [Toronto]: Ontario Women's Directorate, [1990]. [12] p.
Note: 53 entries.– Provides resource information and sources for a series of fact sheets on sexual assault produced by the Ontario Women's Directorate.
Location: OONL.

3346 **Thomas, J., et al.**
"Aging and the aged: an eclectic annotated resource list." In: *Canadian Home Economics Journal*; Vol. 40, no. 3 (Summer 1990) p. 154-158.; ISSN: 0008-3763.
Note: Books, films, educational programs, pamphlets, research reports, selected journal articles concerning aging and the aged.– Includes Canadian resources, with emphasis on British Columbia.
Location: AEU.

— 1991 —

3347 **Aboussafy, David**
Bibliography of seniors and the family research, 1980-1991. Vancouver: B.C. Council for the Family, 1991. 42 p.; ISBN: 1-895342-32-5.
Note: Approx. 300 entries.– Books, articles, conference proceedings.– Topics include care issues, divorce, elder abuse, grandparenting, remarriage, relationships (senior parent-adult child; senior siblings), social supports, widowhood.
Location: OONL.

3348 **Aquan-Yuen, R. Margaret**
Homelessness in Canada: a selective bibliography. Waterloo, Ont.: University of Waterloo Library, 1991. vii, 29 p.; ISBN: 0-920834-15-9.
Note: 202 entries.– Focus on English-language material published after 1980.– Includes monographs, journal articles, government reports, conference proceedings, theses.
Location: OONL.

3349 **Canadian Housing Information Centre**
Bibliography on temporary shelter for battered women/ Bibliographie sur l'hébergement temporaire pour les femmes victimes de violence. Ottawa: Canada Mortgage and Housing Corporation, 1991. 11 p.
Note: Location: OOCM.

3350 **Desjardins, Joëlle**
Le vieillissement de la population, 1980-1991. Québec: Bibliothèque de l'Assemblée nationale, Division de la référence parlementaire, 1991. 39 p. (Bibliographie / Bibliothèque de l'Assemblée nationale du Québec ; no 39; ISSN: 0836-9100)
Note: Localisation: OONL.

3351 **Desrosiers, Danielle**
Family violence: a selective bibliography/La violence familiale: une bibliographie sélective. [Ottawa]: Supreme Court of Canada, 1991. 18 l.
Note: Approx. 120 entries.– Monographs and articles in English and French related to child abuse and wife battering: social, legal, public policy aspects.– List of sources.
Location: OOSC.

3352 **Dionne, Guy**
L'État et les personnes âgées, 1980-1991: bibliographie sélective et annotée. 2e éd. [Québec]: Bibliothèque de l'Assemblée nationale, Division de la référence parlementaire, 1991. 21 p. (Bibliographie / Bibliothèque de l'Assemblée nationale du Québec ; no 32; ISSN: 0836-9100)
Note: Liste des ouvrages généraux, Québec (aspects généraux, logement, soins à domicile); Canada et autres provinces; ailleurs dans le monde.
Édition antérieure: 1989. 13 p.
Localisation: OONL.

3353 **Friendly, Martha; Willis, Tricia**
Child care policy in Canada, 1990: selected topics: an annotated bibliography. Toronto: Childcare Resource and Research Unit, Centre for Urban and Community Studies, University of Toronto, 1991. 108 p.
Note: Location: OONL.

3354 **Mangham, Colin R.**
Prevention in action: a bibliography of research, programs and resources in substance abuse prevention.

[Victoria, B.C.]: Alcohol and Drug Program, Ministry of Labour and Consumer Services, c1991. 140 p.; ISBN: 0-7718-8996-8.

Note: Listing of articles, books, reports dealing with factors in drug usage, policy issues, prevention models and strategies, health promotion, program evaluation.– List of bibliographies and guides.

Location: OONL.

3355 **Paquet, Mario**
L'intervention de groupe pour les personnes soutien de personne âgée en perte d'autonomie: bibliographie. Joliette, Québec: Département de santé communautaire de Lanaudière, 1991. 8 f.; ISBN: 2-920924-47-8.

Note: 69 entrées.

Localisation: OONL.

3356 **Sobsey, Richard, et al.**
Disability, sexuality, and abuse: an annotated bibliography. Baltimore; Toronto: P.H. Brookes Pub. Co., 1991. xii, 185 p.; ISBN: 1-55766-068-9.

Note: 1,123 entries.– Books, reports and articles from Canada, Great Britain and the United States dealing with sexual exploitation of persons with disabilities.– Topics include effects of abuse, intervention, education, evaluation, families, institutions, law, services, therapy.

Location: OONL.

3357 **Willms, Sharon E.; Bates, Joanna M.**
Primary care for urban core disadvantaged patients: an annotated bibliography. Vancouver: Centre for Human Settlements, University of British Columbia, 1991. 30 p. (Housing and community planning series); ISBN: 0-88865-377-8.

Note: 139 entries.– Selection from literature relating to medical care for urban poor, including homeless, refugees, categories of people presenting problems such as mental illness, AIDS, alcohol and substance abuse.– Includes Canadian references.

Location: OONL.

3358 **Willms, Sharon E.; Hayes, Michael V.; Hulchanski, John David**
Housing options for persons with AIDS: an annotated bibliography. Vancouver: Centre for Human Settlements, University of British Columbia, 1991. 16 p.; ISBN: 0-88865-375-1.

Note: 113 entries.– Covers 1979-1990.– References in English and French dealing with palliative or hospice care with a focus on self-care or supported home care.– Includes a number of Canadian references.

Location: OONL.

— 1992 —

3359 **Elder Abuse Resource Centre**
Elder Abuse Resource Centre bibliography, May 1992: Canadian material. Winnipeg: Age & Opportunity, 1992. [17] p.

Note: Location: OONL.

3360 **Ray, Susan L.**
Selected review of literature on adult female and male incest survivors. London, Ont.: HMS Press, 1992. [29] l.; ISBN: 0-9199578-5-4.

Note: Location: OONL.

3361 **Sutherland, Neil; Barman, Jean; Hale, Linda Louise**
Contemporary Canadian childhood and youth: a bibliography. Westport, Conn.: Greenwood Press, 1992. ix, 492 p.; ISBN: 0-31328-586-1.

Note: 7,328 entries.– Covers to the end of 1990.– Listing of books, monographs, reports of government commissions, scholarly and professional articles, theses, arranged in geographical divisions: British Columbia, Prairies, Central Canada, Atlantic Canada, Northern Canada.

Location: OONL.

3362 **Sutherland, Neil; Barman, Jean; Hale, Linda Louise**
History of Canadian childhood and youth: a bibliography. Westport, Conn.: Greenwood Press, 1992. ix, 486 p.; ISBN: 0-31328-585-3.

Note: 7,998 entries.– Covers to the end of 1990.– Listing of books, monographs, reports of government commissions, scholarly and professional articles, theses, arranged in geographical divisions: British Columbia, Prairies, Central Canada, Atlantic Canada, Northern Canada.

Location: OONL.

3363 **Wachtel, Andy**
Sexually intrusive children: a review of the literature. Vancouver: Greater Vancouver Mental Health Services, 1992. 58 p.

Note: Prepared for the Child Sexual Abuse Advisory Committee, (incorporating the Ad Hoc Group on Sexually Intrusive Children).

Location: OONL.

— 1993 —

3364 **Allen, Marie-France**
Intervention interculturelle dans les services sociaux et de santé. Québec: Centre de recherche sur les services communautaires, 1993. 115, 16 f.; ISBN: 2-92100-856-4.

Note: Publ. en collaboration avec: Groupe d'études et de recherches sur l'Asie contemporaine, Université Laval.

Localisation: OONL.

3365 **Community living and intellectual disability in Canada, 1980-1992: an annotated bibliography.** North York, Ont.: Roeher Institute, 1993. vii, 278 p.; ISBN: 1-895070-39-2.

Note: 1,239 entries.– Articles and reports written in Canada or pertaining to the Canadian experience.– Focusses on issues affecting people who are mentally handicapped.– Themes include de-institutionalization, education, employment, social services and programs, friendship and leisure, behaviour, human rights and law.

Location: OONL.

— Ongoing/En cours —

3366 **Canadian union catalogue of library materials for the handicapped [microform]/Catalogue collectif canadien des documents de bibliothèque pour les personnes handicapées [microforme].** Ottawa: National Library of Canada, 1985-. microfiches; ISSN: 0822-2576.

Note: Quarterly with cumulating index.– Includes publications in English and French.

Location: OONL.

Education

Éducation

— 1897 —

3367 **Hodgins, J. George**
Catalogue of the books relating to education and educational subjects, also to history, geography, science, biography and practical life in the library of the Education Department for Ontario arranged in topical and alphabetical order. Toronto: Warwick Brothers & Rutter, 1897. vi, 268 p.
Note: Includes a section entitled "Education in Ontario, and other Canadian provinces," and Canadian references are included in most other sections.
Location: OONL.

— 1916 —

3368 **Chamberland, Constant-Alfred**
Catalogue des ouvrages utiles à l'enseignement religieux. Québec: Université Laval, 1916. 63 p.
Note: Location: OONL.

— 1922 —

3369 **Fauteux, Aegidius**
Bibliographie de la question universitaire Laval-Montréal, 1852-1921. Montréal: Arbour & Dupont, 1922. 62 p.
Note: 165 entrées.– Extrait de *l'Annuaire de l'Université de Montréal* pour 1922-1923.
Localisation: OONL.

— 1932 —

3370 **Woodley, Elsie Caroline**
The history of education in the province of Quebec: a bibliographical guide. [S.l.: s.n.], 1932. 199 l.
Note: Thesis: M.A., McGill University.– Bibliography: l. 142-194.
Location: OTY.

— 1934 —

3371 **Plumptre, A.F.W.; Gilroy, A.E.**
"Review of economics text-books for use in Canadian high schools."
In: *Contributions to Canadian Economics*; Vol. 7 (1934) p. 123-130.
Note: Location: OONL.

— 1938 —

3372 **Smith, Albert H.**
A bibliography of Canadian education. Toronto: Department of Educational Research, University of Toronto, [c1938]. 302 p. (Department of Educational Research Bulletin / University of Toronto ; no. 10)
Note: 2,324 entries.– Books, theses and dissertations; journal articles by Canadians; biographical material about Canadian educators; reports and records of departments of education which have assumed historical significance: school laws and regulations, departmental monographs, surveys, reports for the period pre-1900.– Excludes textbooks, curriculum material, tests and scales.
Location: OONL.

— 1946 —

3373 **Sheffield, Edward F.; Sheffield, Nora Morrison**
Educational and vocational guidance materials: a Canadian bibliography. Ottawa: Canadian Council of Education for Citizenship, 1946. 49 p.
Note: Contains materials written in Canada or referring specifically to Canadian conditions: guidance in general, psychological tests and testing, education and training, occupations and industries, labour legislation, placement aids.– Includes a section listing bibliographies, directories, catalogues.– Excludes periodical articles which have not been reprinted in pamphlet or book form, publications describing industries (as distinct from occupations).
Location: OONL.

— 1950 —

3374 **Brown, Brian E.**
Teaching aids obtainable from departments of the government at Ottawa. Ottawa: Canadian Citizenship Council, 1950. 23 p.
Note: Location: OONL.

— 1952 —

3375 **Ratté, Alice; Gagnon, Gilberte**
Bibliographie analytique de la littérature pédagogique canadienne-française. [Québec]: Association canadienne des éducateurs de langue française, 1952. 108 p.
Note: Approx. 500 entrées.– Thèmes: histoire et institutions, philosophie et théorie générale de l'éducation, méthodologie générale et spéciale, administration et organisation, psychologie, hygiène mentale et physique, orientation et documentation professionnelle.– Exclut les manuels scolaires.
Localisation: OONL.

— 1953 —

3376 **Donaldson, Helen**
A descriptive bibliography of manuscripts, pamphlets and books on education in Upper Canada particularly for the years 1791 to 1841. [S.l.: s.n.], 1953. x, 166 l.
Note: Manuscripts used are those registered to date as Educational Papers taken from Secretaries' Papers for Upper Canada, 1791 to 1841.– Pamphlets cover period 1840 to 1931.
Microform: Ottawa: National Library of Canada, 1976. 2 microfiches. (Canadian theses on microfiche ; no. 25472).– Thesis: M.A., University of Toronto, 1953.
Location: OONL.

— 1956 —

3377 **Thomson, Murray; Ironside, Diana J.**
A bibliography of Canadian writings in adult education. Toronto: Canadian Association for Adult Education, 1956. [ii], 56 p.
Note: Approx. 500 entries.– Covers the period 1935-1956.– Includes books, pamphlets, periodical articles by Canadians or about some phase of adult education in Canada in the English language only.– Topics include history, agriculture and co-operatives, the arts, citizenship and human rights, community development, labour and industry, libraries, social welfare, schools and

departments of education, universities, biographies of adult educators.
Location: OONL.

— 1960 —

3378 **Harris, Robin S.; Tremblay, Arthur**
A bibliography of higher education in Canada/ Bibliographie de l'enseignement supérieur au Canada. [Toronto]: University of Toronto Press; [Québec]: Presses Universitaires Laval, [c1960]. xxv, 158 p. (Studies in higher education in Canada ; no. 1/Études dans l'enseignement supérieur au Canada ; no 1)
Note: Approx. 4,000 entries.– List of secondary sources: books, pamphlets, theses, dissertations, articles in journals and magazines on Canadian culture and education (background materials).– Topics include history and organization of the institutions, curriculum and teaching (humanities, social sciences, mathematics and sciences, professional education, graduate study and research, adult education); professor and student.– Text in English and French/texte en français et en anglais.
Supplements:
Harris, Robin S. ... : supplement 1965/... : supplément. 1965. xxxi, 170 p. (Studies in higher education in Canada ; no. 3/Études dans l'enseignement supérieur au Canada ; no 3).– Approx. 3,000 entries.
Harris, Robin S. ... : supplement 1971/... : supplément 1971. 1971. xxxii, 311 p. (Studies in the history of higher education in Canada ; no. 5/Études sur l'histoire d'enseignement supérieur au Canada ; no 5); ISBN: 0-8020-1777-0.– Approx. 3,500 entries.
Harris, Robin S., et al. ... : supplement 1981/... : supplément 1981. 1981. xxv, 193 p. (Studies in the history of higher education in Canada ; no. 8/Études sur l'histoire d'enseignement supérieur au Canada ; no 8); ISBN: 0-8020-2440-8.– Approx. 3,500 entries.
Location: OONL.

3379 **Mezirow, Jack D.; Berry, Dorothea M.**
The literature of liberal adult education, 1945-1957. New York: Scarecrow Press, 1960. x, 308 p.
Note: Includes Canadian material.
Location: OONL.

3380 **Wigmore, Shirley K.**
An annotated guide to publications related to educational research. Toronto: Ontario College of Education, Department of Educational Research, 1960. 26 l. (Educational research series / Department of Educational Research, Ontario College of Education ; no. 32)
Note: Previous edition: *An annotated guide to certain educational research materials available in selected Toronto libraries.* 1949. ii, 47 l. (Educational research series ; no. 19).
Location: OONL.

— 1961 —

3381 **Canadian Association for Adult Education. Research Library**
The literature of adult education: a selected list of holdings from the the Research Library in Adult Education of the Canadian Association for Adult Education. [Toronto: Canadian Association for Adult Education, 1961]. xiv, 75 l.
Note: Approx. 800 entries.– Books, pamphlets, reports, reprints on adult education: theory, methods, practice.
Location: OONL.

— 1962 —

3382 **"Mémoire de la Société Saint-Jean-Baptiste de Montréal sur l'éducation nationale: bibliographie sommaire."**
Dans: *Action nationale*; Vol. 51, no 9-10 (mai-juin 1962) p. 834-839.; ISSN: 0001-7469.
Note: Localisation: OONL.

— 1963 —

3383 **Deverell, Alfred Frederick**
Canadian bibliography of reading and literature instruction (English) 1760 to 1959. Montreal: Copp Clark, [c1963]. viii, 241 p.
Note: Approx. 3,000 entries.– Books, journal articles, conference papers, theses.– Excludes government publications.– Subject sections include methods, psychology of reading, remedial reading, testing, readers, book reviews, books for children and youth (story books, art, music, social studies, science), reading and literature: teaching procedures, reading and philosophy of education, bibliographies.
Supplement: Deverell, Alfred Frederick; Buckley, L.P. *Canadian bibliography of reading and literature instruction (English) first supplement, 1960 to 1965.* Vancouver: Copp Clark, 1968. x, 158 p.
Location: OONL.

3384 **Hoy, Eileen Monica**
Select bibliography of recent material on teaching machines and programmed learning. Toronto: Ontario Educational Research Council, 1963. 18 p.
Note: 296 entries.– Includes Canadian references.
Location: OONL.

3385 **Stott, Margaret M.; Verner, Coolie**
A trial bibliography of research pertaining to adult education. Vancouver, B.C.: Extension Department, University of British Columbia, 1963. ii, 29 l.
Note: 289 entries.– Theses, reports, studies, journal articles pertaining to Canadian adult education: area studies, history and biography, evaluation, methods, administration and finance, institutions.
Location: OONL.

— 1964 —

3386 **Barbin, René**
Bibliographie de pédagogie religieuse: introductions et commentaires. Montréal: Éditions Bellarmin, 1964. 275 p.
Note: Localisation: QQLA.

3387 **Canada. Bureau of Statistics. Education Division. Research Section**
A bibliographical guide to Canadian education/Guide bibliographique de l'enseignement au Canada. [2nd ed.]. Ottawa: Queen's Printer, 1964. 55 p.
Note: 404 entries.– Books, theses and articles on history, organization and administration, school finance, vocational and special education, professional and adult education, education of native people, list of royal commissions and related reports, bibliographies and directories.– Excludes textbooks, books on methods, philosophical and controversial treatises, educational psychology, tests and measurements, child development.– Text in English and French in parallel columns/ Texte en anglais et en français sur des col. parallèles.
Previous edition: 1958. 55 p.– 306 entries.
Location: OONL.

— 1965 —

3388 Carney, R.J.; Ferguson, W.O.
A selected and annotated bibliography on the sociology of Eskimo education. Edmonton: Boreal Institute, University of Alberta, c1965. v, 59 l. (Occasional publication / Boreal Institute, University of Alberta ; no. 2)
Note: Approx. 350 entries.– Books, periodical articles, government publications on Eskimo education in Alaska, Canada, Greenland.
Location: OONL.

3389 Lebel, Marc
"Enseignement de la philosophie au Petit Séminaire de Québec (1765-1880)."
Dans: *Revue d'histoire de l'Amérique française*; Vol. 18, no 3 (décembre 1964) p. 463-473; vol. 19, no 2 (septembre 1965) p. 323-328.; ISSN: 0035-2357.
Note: Localisation: AEU.

— 1966 —

3390 Harris, Robin S.
An annotated list of the legislative acts concerning higher education in Ontario. Toronto: Innis College, University of Toronto, 1966. vi, 79 p.
Note: Location: OONL.

3391 Harris, Robin S.
A list of reports to the Legislature of Ontario bearing on higher education in the province. [Toronto]: Innis College, University of Toronto, 1966. v, 17 p.
Note: List of reports printed as appendices to proceedings of Legislature of Ontario pertaining to development of universities and colleges.
Location: OONL.

3392 Kapoor, Sudersan
Research and publication in adult education. Toronto: Adult Education Department, Ontario Institute for Studies in Education, [1966]. 14 p.
Note: Approx. 100 entries.– Includes theses, OISE bulletins, works of J.R. Kidd (chairman, Adult Education Department, OISE), studies in progress.
Location: OONL.

— 1967 —

3393 Canadian Teachers' Federation
School buildings and equipment: a bibliography. Ottawa: Canadian Teachers' Federation, 1967. 88 l. (Information note / Canadian Teachers' Federation ; no. 77)
Note: Location: NBFU.

3394 Finley, E. Gault
Sources à consulter en vue d'une compilation bibliographique sur l'évolution de l'éducation au Canada français. [Montréal: Université McGill, 1967]. 60 f.
Note: 875 entrées.
Localisation: OONL.

3395 Rideout, E. Brock; Najat, Sandra
City school district reorganization: an annotated bibliography; centralization and decentralization in the government of metropolitan areas with special emphasis on the organization, administration and financing of large-city school systems. [Toronto]: Ontario Institute for Studies in Education, [c1967]. v, 93 p. (Educational research series / Ontario Institute for Studies in Education ; no. 1)
Note: 161 entries.– Books, government studies and reports.– Listing of bibliographies and periodicals in the fields of educational administration and municipal government.
Location: OONL.

— 1968 —

3396 Brooke, W. Michael
Canadian adult basic education. Toronto: Canadian Association for Adult Education, [1968]. 49 l. (Trends / Canadian Association for Adult Education)
Note: Approx. 150 entries.– Research studies, with critical annotations, intended for teachers and administrators in adult education programs.– Includes manuals, literature on reading, curriculum, instructional materials, psychology, teacher training, educational technology, libraries and adult education.
Location: OONL.

3397 Canadian Education Association. Research and Information Division
Education studies completed in Canadian universities. Toronto: Canadian Education Association, 1967-1968. 2 vol.; ISSN: 0424-5652.
Note: Lists staff studies and graduate theses in field of education completed at Canadian universities.
Continued by: *Directory of education studies in Canada/ Annuaire d'études en éducation au Canada.* 1969- . ISSN: 0070-5454.
Location: OONL.

3398 Selby, Suzanne R.
"[Indian and Eskimo education, anthropology and the North: bibliography]."
In: *Musk-Ox*; No. 4 (1968) p. i-103.; ISSN: 0077-2542.
Note: Lists books, pamphlets, articles published since 1960 in five sections: education, English as a second language, cultural anthropology, cultural change, economic and community development.
Location: OONL.

— 1969 —

3399 Canadian Association for Adult Education
Non-degree research in adult education in Canada, 1968: an inventory/La recherche en éducation des adultes au Canada, 1968: un inventaire. Toronto: Jointly published by Canadian Association for Adult Education; Ontario Institute for Studies in Education; Montréal: Institut canadien d'éducation des adultes, 1969. 103 p.
Note: 118 entries.– Summarizes completed and in-progress studies reported to the three collaborating organizations.– Areas of research include adult learning, intellectual, psychological, social, physical characteristics of adults, sociology of continuing education, program planning, evaluation and methods of instruction, historical and philosophical foundations of adult education, organizational administration and financing of adult programs.– Text in English and French/texte en français et en anglais.
Location: OONL.

3400 Canadian School Library Association
Basic book list for Canadian schools. Ottawa: Canadian Library Association, 1968-1969. 3 vol.
Note: Vol. 1: *Elementary division, grades 1-6.* (1,067 entries).– Includes picture books, fiction, history, sciences.
Vol. 2: *Junior division, grades 7-9.* (871 entries).– Includes general reference materials, aids for teacher-librarians, fiction, curriculum subjects.
Vol. 3: *Senior division, grades 10-13.* (947 entries).–

Includes general reference materials, aids for teacher-librarians, curriculum subjects, fiction.
Location: OONL.

3401 **Ferguson, D.S.**
Student housing report: submitted by D.S. Ferguson to the Ontario Department of University Affairs, 1969, with bibliography and appendices. Toronto: Ontario Department of University Affairs, 1969. 111 p.
Note: Bibliography, p. [31]-77.– Approx. 600 entries.– International coverage with substantial Canadian content.
Location: OONL.

3402 **Lamb, Eila; Nevison, Myrne**
Annotated bibliography for guidance and counseling. Vancouver: Extension Department, University of British Columbia, [1969]. 26 l.
Note: Location: OONL.

3403 **McConnell, Ruth Ethel; Wakefield, P.**
Teaching English as an additional language: annotated bibliography. Vancouver: Extension Department, University of British Columbia, 1969. 74 l.
Note: Location: BVAU.

3404 **Séminaire Saint-Augustin. Bibliothèque**
Bibliographie sur l'éducation au Québec. [Cap-Rouge, Québec]: Bibliothèque du Séminaire Saint-Augustin, 1969. 42 f. (Document / Bibliothèque du Séminaire Saint-Augustin ; no 146)
Note: Approx. 480 entrées.
Localisation: OONL.

3405 **Tymchuk, Alexander J.; Knights, Robert M.**
A two thousand item bibliography: the description, etiology, diagnosis, and treatment of children with learning disabilities or brain damage. [Ottawa: s.n., 1969]. 186 l.
Note: 2,000 entries.
Location: OONL.

— 1970 —

3406 **Canadian Teachers' Federation**
Disadvantaged children in Canada. Ottawa: Canadian Teachers' Federation, 1970. 15 p. (Bibliographies in education / Canadian Teachers' Federation ; no. 9)
Note: 191 entries.– Books, articles and excerpts from books, theses and unpublished material on culturally disadvantaged children in Canada: native education, social class, inner city, inequalities in Canadian education.
Location: OONL.

3407 **Canadian Teachers' Federation**
Histories of teachers' associations in Canada. Ottawa: Canadian Teachers' Federation, 1970. 6 p. (Bibliographies in education / Canadian Teachers' Federation ; no. 14)
Note: Location: OLU.

3408 **Canadian Teachers' Federation**
Subject catalogue of CTF publications in print. Ottawa: Canadian Teachers' Federation, 1970. 8 l.
Note: Location: OOCT.

3409 **Green, Vicki A.**
Annotated bibliography on Indian education. [Vancouver]: Indian Education Resources Centre, University of British Columbia, [1970]. 33 p.
Note: Approx. 180 entries.– Covers the period 1870 to 1969.– Emphasis on Canadian Indians.– Includes articles, books, research documents, films, newspapers, periodicals in four main categories: Indian education and religion, cultural differences, historical and anthropological material, curriculum material.
Location: OONL.

3410 **Gue, Leslie R.**
A selected, annotated bibliography concerning future needs in all levels and forms of native education in Alberta, Canada. [S.l.: s.n.], 1970. 25 l.
Note: Arranged under three headings: situation in native education; native student; curriculum in native education.– Emphasis on formal education of native pupils.
Location: AEUB.

3411 **Indian-Eskimo Association of Canada**
Bibliography: Indians and education. Toronto: [s.n.], 1970. 7 p.
Note: Location: OWTU.

3412 **Ontario Institute for Studies in Education. Library. Reference and Information Services**
Nongrading: an annotated bibliography. [Toronto]: Ontario Institute for Studies in Education, 1970. viii, 32 p. (Current bibliography / Ontario Institute for Studies in Education ; no. 1)
Note: 88 entries.– Books, reports, journal articles on research and evaluating student progress in nongraded system: elementary, junior, secondary schools.
Location: OONL.

3413 **Wilson, J.D.**
"Common school texts in use in Upper Canada prior to 1845."
In: *Papers of the Bibliographical Society of Canada;* Vol. 9 (1970) p. 36-53.; ISSN: 0067-6896.
Note: Listing of arithmetics, grammars, readers, spellers, geographies, histories, Latins, arranged by imprint date, with schools where used and dates in use.
Location: OONL.

— 1971 —

3414 **Campbell, Gordon**
The community college in Canada: an annotated bibliography. Calgary: Department of Educational Administration, University of Calgary, [c1971]. v, 82 p. (University of Calgary Department of Educational Administration Series on tertiary and continuing education)
Note: Approx. 500 entries.– Government studies and reports, citizen's briefs, national/provincial/local conferences, legislation, speeches.– Categories include historical development, philosophy and policy, finance, facilities and plant planning, faculty and staff, students and student services, institutional studies, continuing education, research aids and evaluation.
Location: OONL.

3415 **Canadian Teachers' Federation**
Systems analysis in education. Ottawa: Canadian Teachers' Federation, 1971. 29 p. (Bibliographies in education / Canadian Teachers' Federation ; no. 25)
Note: 374 entries.– Covers 1966 to the end of 1971.– Includes books and papers, articles and excerpts from books, theses.
Location: OONL.

3416 **Child, Alan H.**
"The history of Canadian education: a bibliographical note."
In: *Histoire sociale: Social History;* No. 8 (November

1971) p. 105-117.; ISSN: 0018-2257.
Note: Bibliographical essay commenting on books and articles dealing with history of Canadian education.
Location: OONL.

3417 **Degree and non-degree research in adult education in Canada, 1970: an inventory/La recherche académique et non-académique en éducation des adultes au Canada, 1970: un inventaire.** Toronto: Ontario Institute for Studies in Education; Canadian Association for Adult Education; Montréal: Institut canadien d'éducation des adultes; Université de Montréal, Faculté des sciences de l'éducation, 1971. 151 p.
Note: 153 entries.– Degree research is that which relates to Canada and is in partial fulfilment of a university degree, in Canada or elsewhere.– Text in English and French/texte en français et en anglais.
Location: OONL.

3418 **Dupont, Pierrette**
Répertoire bibliographique d'information scolaire et professionnelle. Sherbrooke: Faculté des sciences de l'éducation, Université de Sherbrooke, 1971. 109 f.
Note: Localisation: OONL.

3419 **Konrad, Abram G.; Collin, Wilbur; Ottley, Horace**
Community college research in western Canada: an annotated bibliography. Edmonton: Department of Educational Administration, Faculty of Education, University of Alberta, 1971. iv, 16 p.
Note: Approx. 40 entries.– Theses, occasional papers, monographs, conference reports.– Topics include system-environment relations functions (human, physical and economic resources; legal, philosophical and historical considerations), teaching-learning subsystems (programs and services development), supportive functions (planning, technical services), administrative functions.
Location: OONL.

3420 **Mathews, Robin**
Some of the materials concerning the struggle for the Canadian universities (other-wise known as "Americanization", "takeover", "de-Canadianization of the universities"). [Ottawa: s.n., 1971]. 18 l.
Note: Approx. 125 entries.– Selection of books, reports, articles in journals, newspapers and college press relating to issue of American takeover of Canadian universities.
Location: OONL.

3421 **McMurray, J.G.**
The exceptional student of secondary school age: a bibliography for psychology and education, 1960-1970. [London, Ont.]: J.G. McMurray, [1971]. viii, 138 l.
Note: Approx. 1,400 entries.– Journal articles written in English and published in Canada, Great Britain and United States.– Intended primarily for students and practitioners in fields of psychology and education, particularly in the areas of special education and guidance.
Location: OONL.

3422 **Ontario. Department of Public Records and Archives**
A guide to pamphlets in the Ontario Archives relating to educational history, 1803-1967. [Toronto]: Department of History & Philosophy, Ontario Institute for Studies in Education, [1971]. iv, 104 p. (Educational record series / Department of History & Philosophy, Ontario Institute for Studies in Education ; no. 1)

Note: 697 entries.– Selection criteria define the term education broadly to include pamphlets in areas of professional education (medicine, law, theology, engineering), as well as teacher training, curriculum, textbooks, libraries, methods, psychology/philosophy, administration.– Items on adult education such as Women's Institutes and Frontier College are also included.– Focus on Ontario, with some items from neighbouring provinces and states (e.g. Manitoba School Question).
Location: OONL.

3423 **Ontario Institute for Studies in Education. Library. Reference and Information Services**
Differentiated staffing: an annotated bibliography. Toronto: Ontario Institute for Studies in Education, 1971. viii, 18 p. (Current bibliography / Ontario Institute for Studies in Education ; no. 3)
Note: 73 entries.– Books, research reports, theses, pamphlets, journal articles, ERIC reports on recruitment, preparation, induction and continuing education of school personnel, including utilisation of paraprofessionals.
Location: OONL.

3424 **Reynolds, Roy**
A guide to published government documents relating to education in Ontario. [Toronto]: Department of History and Philosophy, Ontario Institute for Studies in Education, [1971]. i, 47 l. (Educational record series / Department of History and Philosophy, Ontario Institute for Studies in Education ; 2)
Note: Lists educational sources appearing in *Journals* of Legislative Assembly of Upper Canada (1792-1840), the Province of Canada (1841-1866), and the Province of Ontario (1867-1967); annual reports, booklets on legal and administrative aspects of education published by Department of Education.
Location: OONL.

3425 **Rosenbaum, H.**
A survey of literature on televised language instruction. Toronto: Ontario Educational Communications Authority, Research and Development Branch, 1971. 9 p. (Papers and reports concerning educational communications ; no. 11)
Note: Location: OTMCL.

3426 **Tracz, George S.**
Annotated bibliography on determination of teachers' salaries and effective utilization of teacher manpower. Toronto: Department of Educational Planning, Ontario Institute for Studies in Education, 1971. 15 p. (Educational Planning Occasional papers / Ontario Institute for Studies in Education ; no. 10:71)
Note: Includes Canadian references.
Location: OONL.

3427 **University of New Brunswick. Harriet Irving Library**
Faculty publications, University of New Brunswick and St. Thomas University, 1970. [Fredericton, N.B.]: Harriet Irving Library, School of Graduate Studies, 1971. iii, 67 p.
Note: Approx. 700 entries.
Location: OONL.

— 1972 —

3428 **Canadian Nurses' Association**
Continuing education: selected bibliography/L'éducation permanente: bibliographie choisie. [Ottawa]:

Canadian Nurses' Association, 1972. 25 l.
Note: 418 entries.– Includes books, government documents, pamphlets, journal articles on continuing education for nursing.
Location: OONL.

3429 **Canadian Teachers' Federation**
Community colleges. Ottawa: Canadian Teachers' Federation, 1972. 61 p. (Bibliographies in education / Canadian Teachers' Federation ; no. 26)
Note: 842 entries.– Covers 1961 to 1971.– Includes books, articles, theses.
Location: OONL.

3430 **Canadian Teachers' Federation**
Early childhood education. Ottawa: Canadian Teachers' Federation, 1972. 47 p. (Bibliographies in education / Canadian Teachers' Federation ; no. 28)
Note: 612 entries.– Covers 1967 to 1972.– Includes books and papers, articles, theses on preschool learning systems, head start programs, the development of language and reading skills.
Location: OONL.

3431 **Canadian Teachers' Federation**
Intercultural education: Indians and Eskimos of North America. Ottawa: Canadian Teachers' Federation, 1972. 35 p. (Bibliographies in education / Canadian Teachers' Federation ; no. 30)
Note: 489 entries.– Covers from 1968 to 1972.– Includes books, articles, theses.
Location: OONL.

3432 **Clément, H.L.**
Inventory of Newstart documents: répertoire de documents des sociétés de relance. Ottawa: Social and Human Analysis Branch, 1972. 1 vol. (in various pagings).
Note: Approx. 500 entries.– Contains a comprehensive listing of materials produced by and for the Canada Newstart Program.– Includes unpublished an unedited drafts.– Subject groupings: program design, recruitment/motivation, adult basic education, occupational training, life skills, placement and counselling, administration.– Text in English and French/texte en français et en anglais.
Supplement: 1973. 17 l.
Location: OONL.

3433 **College Administration Project**
The multi-campus: an annotated bibliography for Canadian colleges. [Edmonton: Department of Educational Administration], University of Alberta, 1972. ii, 22 p.
Note: Approx. 50 entries.– Lists material dealing with decentralized structure and functions at individual college level, at state or provincial level; selected studies with reference to establishing multi-campus operations; bibliographies on community/junior college literature.
Location: OONL.

3434 **College Bibliocentre**
Adult basic education. Don Mills, Ont.: College Bibliocentre, 1972. 2 vol. (Current awareness lists / College Bibliocentre)
Note: 339 entries.– Adult learning, communication, life skills, mathematics, science, teaching of adults, audio-visual materials.
Location: OONL.

3435 **Collin, Wilbur; Bryce, Robert**
Self-development readings for community college personnel: an annotated bibliography. Edmonton:

Department of Educational Administration, Faculty of Education, University of Alberta, 1972. v, 38 p.
Note: Approx. 100 entries.– Selected list of books, periodical articles, ERIC documents related to self-development of college administrators and instructional faculty.
Location: OONL.

3436 **Collin, Wilbur; Konrad, Abram G.; Stewart, Peter**
Understanding community colleges: a review of institutional research and related literature produced by community colleges in western Canada. Edmonton: Department of Educational Administration, University of Alberta, 1972. iv, 19 p.
Note: Location: OONL.

3437 **Dennison, John D.; Tunner, Alex**
The impact of community colleges: bibliography. Vancouver: B.C. Research, 1972. 142 p. (in various pagings).
Note: Approx. 1,700 entries.– Covers the period from 1965 to 1971.– Includes books, journal articles, compiled as part of a research program of community colleges in British Columbia.– Topics include admissions, curriculum, history and philosophy, faculty and teaching, students and student personnel, systems analysis, establishment/organization/administration/financing.
Location: OONL.

3438 **Edmonds, E.L.**
An annotated bibliography on team teaching. [Charlottetown]: University of Prince Edward Island, [1972]. [89] p.; ISBN: 0-919013-03-1.
Note: Approx. 800 entries.– Books, reports, theses, pamphlets, periodical articles.
Location: OONL.

3439 **Geddie, Nancy**
Bibliography on student services at Canadian universities/Bibliographie des services aux étudiants dans les universités canadiennes. Ottawa: Association of Universities and Colleges of Canada, 1972. 69 p.
Note: Approx. 800 entries.– Lists student handbooks and guides to student services, athletics, career planning, chaplain services, counselling and orientation, financial assistance, food services, housing, work/study/travel programs, general readings.– Text in English and French/texte en français et en anglais.
Location: OONL.

3440 **MacKenzie, Margaret**
The University of Manitoba almost one hundred years. Winnipeg: University of Manitoba Libraries, 1972. 26 l. (Reference series / University of Manitoba Libraries ; no. 5)
Note: Approx. 225 entries.– Includes official publications, proceedings of governing bodies, student publications, royal commissions, general history (monographs, periodical articles).
Location: OONL.

3441 **Ontario. Department of Education**
Canadian curriculum materials: educational media for Ontario schools/Matériel didactique canadien: sources de référence pédagogique pour les écoles ontariennes. Toronto: 1972. 159 p. (Circular / Ontario Department of Education ; no. 15)
Note: Text in English and French/texte en français en

anglais.
Location: OONL.

3442 **Sève, Nicole de**
Éducation: bibliographie, vol. 1, no 1. Montréal: Conseil de développement social du Montréal métropolitain, 1972. 84, 18 p.
Note: N'a pas été continué.
Localisation: OONL.

3443 **Shapson, Stanley M.**
Optimum class size? A review of the literature. Toronto: Research Department, Toronto Board of Education, 1972. 18 p. (Research Service / Research Department, Toronto Board of Education ; no. 114; ISSN: 0316-8786)
Note: Relationship between class size and method of instruction, teachers' and students' attitudes on class size, interpretations of the literature.
Location: OONL.

3444 **Soroka, Diane**
Education of native people in Canada: an annotated bibliography of the writings of native people about education. [S.l.: s.n.], 1972. 15 l.
Note: Location: AEUB.

3445 **Stevenson, H.A.; Hamilton, William B.**
Canadian education and the future: a select annotated bibliography, 1967-1971. London, Ont.: University of Western Ontario, c1972. 59 p.
Note: 260 entries.– Selection limited to works written by Canadians, those published in Canada, or books and articles about Canadian education regardless of authorship or place of publication.– Principal themes include trends and descriptive futures with educational applications (demographic and environmental studies; politics, government and finance; social structure, media and communications), Canadian educational futures (statistical analyses; pre-school, elementary and secondary education; post-secondary, technical, vocational; teacher education; educational technology; curriculum; minority groups; design and architecture).
Location: OWA.

— 1973 —

3446 **Bouthillette, Jean**
Répertoire de la collection Trefflé Boulanger. Sherbrooke: Université de Sherbrooke, Bibliothèque générale, 1973. 72 f. (en foliotation multiple).
Note: 64 entrées.– Articles, allocutions, causeries, émissions radiophoniques par Boulanger, livres données par Boulanger.– Inclut un nombre d'ouvrages canadiens ou québécoises.
Localisation: OONL.

3447 **Canadian Teachers' Federation**
Differentiated staffing. Ottawa: Canadian Teachers' Federation, 1973. 14 p. (Bibliographies in education / Canadian Teachers' Federation ; no. 36)
Note: 169 entries.– Covers 1971 to September 1973.– Includes books, articles and excerpts from books, theses dealing mainly with professional staff with some reference to paraprofessionals.
Previous edition: 1970. 12 p. (Bibliographies in education ; no. 15). (113 entries).– Covers 1965 to December 1970.
Location: OONL.

3448 **Canadian Teachers' Federation**
Independent study. Ottawa: Canadian Teachers' Federation, 1973. 20 p. (Bibliographies in education / Canadian Teachers' Federation ; no. 38)
Note: 264 entries.– Covers 1970 to November 1973.– Includes books, articles, theses.
Previous edition: 1970. 19 p. (Bibliographies in education ; no. 12). (248 entries).– Covers 1965 to October 1970.
Location: OONL.

3449 **Canadian Teachers' Federation**
Paraprofessional school personnel. Ottawa: Canadian Teachers' Federation, 1973. 24 p. (Bibliographies in education / Canadian Teachers' Federation ; no. 35)
Note: 299 entries.– Covers 1969 to June 1973.– Includes books and papers, articles, theses.
Previous edition: 1970. 33 p. (Bibliographies in education ; no. 16). (438 entries).– Covers 1965 to 1970.
Location: OONL.

3450 **Canadian Teachers' Federation**
The practicum in teacher education. Ottawa: Canadian Teachers' Federation, 1973. 65 p. (Bibliographies in education / Canadian Teachers' Federation ; no. 39)
Note: 462 entries.– Covers 1969 to December 1973.– Annotated listing includes books and papers, articles, theses.
Location: OONL.

3451 **Canadian Teachers' Federation**
Secondary education. Ottawa: Canadian Teachers' Federation, 1973. 21 p. (Bibliographies in education / Canadian Teachers' Federation ; no. 37)
Note: 284 entries.– Covers 1968 to October 1973.– Includes books and papers, articles, theses.
Location: OONL.

3452 **Canadian Teachers' Federation**
Teacher autonomy and teacher decision making. Ottawa: Canadian Teachers' Federation, 1973. 10 p. (Bibliographies in education / Canadian Teachers' Federation ; no. 34)
Note: 109 entries.– Covers 1969 to May 1973.– Includes books, articles, theses.
Location: OONL.

3453 **Cockburn, Ilze**
The open school: an annotated bibliography. Rev. ed. [Toronto]: Library, Reference & Information Services, Ontario Institute for Studies in Education, 1973. viii, 34 p. (Current bibliography / Ontario Institute for Studies in Education ; no. 4)
Note: 126 entries.– Books, pamphlets, research reports, theses, films, journal articles on the concept of open education and the design of open-plan schools.– Emphasis on material published between 1970 and 1973.
Previous edition: *Open plan: an annotated bibliography.* 1970. viii, 22 p. (Current bibliography ; no. 2).
Location: OONL.

3454 **College Administration Project**
A catalogue of C A P publications. Edmonton: Department of Educational Administration, University of Alberta, 1973. v, 12 p.
Note: 22 entries.
Location: OONL.

3455 **Contant, André**
Supervision et évaluation du personnel enseignant: bibliographie annotée. Montréal: Centre d'animation, de développement et de recherche en éducation, 1973. iii, 32 f.
Note: Approx. 90 entrées.
Localisation: OONL.

3456 **Dupuis, Onil**
L'administration scolaire et l'horaire modulaire flexible: une bibliographie/School administration and flexible modular scheduling: a bibliography. Montréal: Cogito, 1973. 17 f.
Note: Approx. 100 entrées.– Volumes, articles, rapports et brochures, films.– Texte en français et en anglais/text in English and French.
Localisation: OONL.

3457 **Dupuis, Onil**
L'école à aire ouverte: une bibliographie/Open schools: a bibliography. Montréal: Cogito, 1973. 15 f.
Note: Approx. 100 entrées.– Volumes, articles, rapports et brochures, films.– Texte en français et en anglais/text in English and French.
Localisation: OONL.

3458 **Dupuis, Onil**
L'enseignement micro-gradué ou programmé: une bibliographie/Programmed teaching and micro-teaching: a bibliography. Montréal: Cogito, 1973. 34 l.
Note: Approx. 300 entrées.– Volumes, articles, rapports et brochures, thèses, films.– Texte en français et en anglais/text in English and French.
Localisation: OONL.

3459 **Dupuis, Onil**
L'enseignement par équipe: une bibliographie/Team teaching: a bibliography. Montréal: Cogito, 1973. 19 l.
Note: Approx. 140 entrées.– Volumes, articles, rapports et brochures, thèses, films.– Texte en français et en anglais/text in English and French.
Localisation: OONL.

3460 **Dupuis, Onil**
Les objectifs pédagogiques: formulation, définition, classification, évaluation: une bibliographie/Behavioral objectives: stating, defining, classifying, evaluating: a bibliography. Montréal: Cogito, 1973. 30 f.
Note: Texte en français et en anglais/text in English and French.
Localisation: OONL.

3461 **Dupuis, Onil**
Techniques d'administration: P.P.B.S., processus de prise de décision, gestion par les objectifs, analyse de problèmes, appliquées au monde de l'éducation: une bibliographie/School management: P.P.B.S., decision taking, M.B.O., problem solving: a bibliography. Montréal: Cogito, 1973. 34 l.
Note: Approx. 300 entrées.– Volumes, articles, rapports et brochures, films.– Texte en français et en anglais/text in English and French.
Localisation: OONL.

3462 **Dupuis, Onil**
Le temps non-structuré: une bibliographie/Unstructured time: a bibliography. Montréal: Cogito, 1973. 16 f.
Note: Approx. 100 entrées.– Volumes, articles, rapports et brochures, thèses, films.– Texte en français et en anglais/text in English and French.

Localisation: OONL.

3463 **Dupuis, Onil**
Le travail individuel de l'étudiant: une bibliographie/Independent study: a bibliography. Montréal: Cogito, 1973. 23 l.
Note: Approx. 175 entrées.– Volumes, articles, rapports et brochures, thèses, films.– Texte en français et en anglais/text in English and French.
Localisation: OONL.

3464 **Dupuis, Onil**
L'utilisation pédagogique des petits et grands groupes: une bibliographie/ Small and large group instruction: a bibliography. Montréal: Cogito, 1973. 17 f.
Note: Approx. 100 entrées.– Volumes, articles, rapports et brochures, thèses, films.– Texte en français et en anglais/text in English and French.
Localisation: OONL.

3465 **Gajewsky, Stan**
Accreditation: review of the literature and selected annotated bibliography. Montreal: Faculty of Education, McGill University, c1973. 58 l. (Reports in education / Faculty of Education, McGill University ; no. 1)
Note: Review of research on school accreditation: standards and criteria, quality ratings and examiners, as a process of social control and professional sanction, advantages and criticisms.– Includes Canadian material.
Location: OONL.

3466 **Gajewsky, Stan**
Class size: review of the literature and selected annotated bibliography. Montreal: Faculty of Education, McGill University, c1973. 58 l. (Reports in education / Faculty of Education, McGill University ; no. 2)
Note: Presents research evidence for large classes and for small classes, opinions concerning best class size, interpretations of pupil-staff ratios and class sizes.– Includes Canadian references.
Location: OONL.

3467 **Gushue, W.J.; Singh, A.**
A bibliography of Newfoundland education. [St. John's]: Committee on Publications, Faculty of Education, Memorial University of Newfoundland, 1973. 22 l.
Note: Approx. 500 entries.– Books, journal and newspaper articles, theses, government reports and studies.
Location: OOU.

3468 **Leitch, Linda J.**
Learning disabilities: review of the literature and selected annotated bibliography. Montreal: Faculty of Education, McGill University, c1973. 59 l. (Reports in education / Faculty of Education, McGill University ; no. 3)
Note: Approx. 60 entries.– Review of literature on learning disabilities, here defined as children having average or above-average intelligence not performing at this level.– Sections include diagnosis, teacher qualifications and training, structuring the learning environment, curriculum, perceptual problems, integration versus segregation.– Includes Canadian references.
Location: OONL.

3469 **Ontario. Ministry of Education. Library**
Catalog of the teachers' professional collection/ Catalogue des ouvrages de perfectionnement professionnel pour les enseignants. Sudbury: The Library, 1973. v, 499 p.
Note: Approx. 6,000 entries.– Backup material for

teachers and school administrators, research material for teachers' workshops, in-service training, summer schools, extension courses, other professional development: books, bibliographies, pamphlets, etc.– Text in English and French/texte en français et en anglais.
Location: OONL.

3470 **Saskatchewan Provincial Library. Bibliographic Services Division**
Education: a bibliography. Regina: Bibliographic Services Division, Provincial Library, 1973. 107 p.
Note: Approx. 1,350 entries.
Location: OONL.

3471 **Tallboy, Felicity**
Open education: review of the literature and selected annotated bibliography. Montreal: Faculty of Education, McGill University, c1973. 109 l. (Reports in education / Faculty of Education, McGill University ; no. 4)
Note: Approx. 250 entries.– Review of literature pertaining to open space, team-teaching, and open education or open school.– Includes Canadian references.
Location: OONL.

3472 **Taylor, Ruth**
The non-graded school: an annotated bibliography. [Toronto]: Library, Reference & Information Services, Ontario Institute for Studies in Education, 1973. x, 40 p. (Current bibliography / Ontario Institute for Studies in Education ; no. 5)
Note: 132 entries.– Covers 1964 to 1972.– Includes books, research reports, films, journal articles, theses on non-grading in elementary, intermediate and secondary schools, as well as material related to instruments for placement and evaluation of pupil progress in the non-graded system.
Previous editions:
Nongrading: an annotated bibliography. 1970. viii, 32 p.
1969. 21 p.
Location: OONL.

3473 **Thom, Douglas J.; Hickcox, E.S.**
A selected bibliography of educational administration: a Canadian orientation. Toronto: Canadian Education Association, 1973. v, 32 l.
Note: Approx. 375 entries.– Includes books and journal articles.– Canadian educational subject matter with administrative perspective, based on Canadian data, dealing with uniquely Canadian issues, trends and conditions.– Themes include administrative theory, curriculum and instruction, economics of education, organizational development, planning, politics of education, research methods, school law, supervision.
Location: OONL.

3474 **Thwaites, James D.**
L'enseignant québécois: sources et études récentes. Québec: Institut supérieur des sciences humaines, Université Laval, 1973. x, 142 f. (Cahiers de l'ISSH, Collection Instruments de travail / Institut supérieur des sciences humaines, Université Laval ; no 8)
Note: 1,442 entrées.– Comprend les sections: syndicat et syndicalisme, conflits du travail, salaires, conditions du travail, statut et rôle.
Localisation: OONL.

— 1974 —

3475 **Allen, Harold Don**
Metric update: selected items from a column on metric conversion and metric education. And, Metric bibliography for the Canadian teacher. Truro, N.S.: Nova Scotia Teachers College, [1974]. 9, 4 l.
Note: Bibliography (4 l. at end) "revised April, 1974."
Location: OONL.

3476 **Amyot, Pierre; Pineau, Gaston**
Éducation permanente: répertoire bibliographique, 1957-1972. Montréal: Université de Montréal, Service d'éducation permanente, Division de la recherche, 1974. v, 245 p.
Note: 302 entrées.
Localisation: OONL.

3477 **Association canadienne d'éducation de langue française**
Liste des publications disponibles sur microfiche [Association canadienne d'éducation de langue française]. Québec: Association canadienne d'éducation de langue française, Service de diffusion de la documentation, 1974. 6 p.
Note: Localisation: OONL.

3478 **Blount, Gail**
Teacher evaluation: an annotated bibliography. Toronto: Library, Reference & Information Services, Ontario Institute for Studies in Education, 1974. x, 32 p. (Current bibliography / Ontario Institute for Studies in Education ; no. 8)
Note: 132 entries.– Covers 1970-1974.– Books, reports, journal articles, audiovisual materials on criteria and process of teacher evaluation, including student evaluation, classroom observation techniques, research on teaching effectiveness, merit rating.– Excludes material on evaluation at college and university level, teacher education programs.
Location: OONL.

3479 **Canadian Nurses' Association. Library**
Higher education with emphasis on nursing programs: selected references/Enseignement supérieur, principalement programmes d'enseignement infirmier: bibliographie choisie. Ottawa: Canadian Nurses' Association, 1974. 43 l.
Note: Includes publications in English and French.
Location: OONL.

3480 **Canadian Teachers' Federation**
Behaviour modification. Ottawa: Canadian Teachers' Federation, 1974. 34 p. (Bibliographies in education / Canadian Teachers' Federation ; no. 45)
Note: 433 entries.– Covers 1969 to June 1974.– Includes books, articles, theses related to modifying deviant social behaviour in classroom settings.
Location: OONL.

3481 **Canadian Teachers' Federation**
Curriculum development in Canada. Ottawa: Canadian Teachers' Federation, 1974. 16 p. (Bibliographies in education / Canadian Teachers' Federation ; no. 48)
Note: 203 entries.– Covers 1968 to 1974.– Includes books, articles and excerpts from books, theses.
Location: OONL.

3482 **Canadian Teachers' Federation**
Elementary education. Ottawa: Canadian Teachers' Federation, 1974. 39 p. (Bibliographies in education / Canadian Teachers' Federation ; no. 43)
Note: 507 entries.– Covers 1968 to April 1974.– Includes books and papers, articles, theses.
Location: OONL.

3483 **Canadian Teachers' Federation**
Microteaching. Ottawa: Canadian Teachers' Federation, 1974. 14 p. (Bibliographies in education / Canadian Teachers' Federation ; no. 40)
Note: 146 entries.– Covers 1969 to end of 1973.– Includes books, articles, theses,
Previous edition: 1969. 9 p. (Bibliographies in education ; no. 5). (86 entries).– Covers 1966 to end of 1969.
Location: OONL.

3484 **Canadian Teachers' Federation**
Moral and values education. Ottawa: Canadian Teachers' Federation, 1974. 30 p. (Bibliographies in education / Canadian Teachers' Federation ; no. 44)
Note: 414 entries.– Covers 1969 to May 1974.– Includes books, articles, theses.
Location: OONL.

3485 **Habiak, Marilyn J.; Baker, P.J.; James, I.R.**
Learning disabilities: a select bibliography of resources. Edmonton: Department of Education, Edmonton Regional Office, 1974. 97 p.
Note: Lists of resource materials for special educational settings identified and annotated.
Location: OONL.

3486 **Ontario Institute for Studies in Education. Library. Reference and Information Services**
Elementary teacher education-certification: an annotated bibliography, 1963-1973. Toronto: Ontario Institute for Studies in Education, 1974. x, 44 p. (Current bibliography / Ontario Institute for Studies in Education ; no. 9)
Note: 170 entries.– Selection of books, journal articles, reports, dissertations, audiotapes on trends in education and certification of elementary school teachers.
Location: OONL.

3487 **Rolfe, Brenda**
The credit system: an annotated bibliography. Toronto: Library, Reference & Information Services, Ontario Institute for Studies in Education, 1974. x, 21 p. (Current bibliography / Ontario Institute for Studies in Education ; no. 6)
Note: 86 entries.– Emphasizes Canadian material from 1967 to 1974.– Includes books, research reports, theses, pamphlets, journal articles on the credit system of grading and advancement of students in Canada, Ontario, general (questions and criticisms).
Location: OONL.

3488 **Roy, Jean-Luc; Contant, André**
L'agent de développement pédagogique: bibliographie sommaire sur ses principales tâches dans un collège. Montréal: Centre d'animation, de développement et de recherche en éducation, 1974. 21 f.
Note: Approx. 60 entrées.– Trois thèmes: innovation, recherche et expérimentation, perfectionnement des maîtres.
Localisation: OONL.

3489 **Saint-Pierre, Henri; Giroux, Richard**
Bibliographie annotée sur l'enseignement universitaire: volumes actuellement disponibles dans les différentes bibliothèques de l'Université Laval. Québec: Service de pédagogie universitaire, Université Laval, 1974. vii, 341 p. (Service de pédagogie universitaire bibliographie / Université Laval ; no 2)
Note: Approx. 1,000 entrées.– Thèmes: objectifs de l'université, l'université et le développement social, l'administration pédagogique, l'organisation du curriculum, liberté académique, formules pédagogique, caractéristiques des étudiants, l'orientation et consultation.
Localisation: OONL

3490 **Scott, Deborah**
The junior kindergarten: an annotated bibliography. Toronto: Library, Reference & Information Services, Ontario Institute for Studies in Education, 1974. x, 21 p. (Current bibliography / Ontario Institute for Studies in Education ; no. 7)
Note: 86 entries.– Books, reports, journal articles related to early childhood education.– Themes include theory, issues, trends, the junior kindergarten: program descriptions and curriculum guidelines, evaluation of benefits, government and school board studies of preschool education, specific preschool programs.
Location: OONL.

3491 **Small, James M.; Edey, J.H.**
Adult education: an annotated bibliography. Edmonton: Department of Educational Administration, Faculty of Education, University of Alberta, 1974. v, 24 p.
Note: 107 entries.– Articles and books about adult education.– Themes include role of university, psychology, methods, self-learning, older learners, disadvantaged, continuing education for women, administration, bibliographies.
Location: OONL.

3492 **Tracz, George S.**
Research into academic staff manpower and salary issues: a selective bibliography. Toronto: Department of Educational Planning, Ontario Institute for Studies in Education, 1974. ii, 35 p. (Educational Planning Occasional papers / Ontario Institute for Studies in Education ; no. 73/74-7)
Note: Approx. 350 entries.– Includes books, studies and articles in support of a system study on teacher cost models and university academic staff cost models.
Location: OONL.

— 1975 —

3493 **Blount, Gail**
Collective bargaining in Canadian education: an annotated bibliography. [Toronto]: Ontario Institute for Studies in Education, [c1975]. x, 38 p. (Bibliography series / Ontario Institute for Studies in Education ; no. 1); ISBN: 0-7744-0114-1.
Note: 176 entries.– Covers from early 1960s, with emphasis on 1970 to 1975.– Includes books, research reports, theses, pamphlets, journal articles on provincial teachers' associations, teacher militancy, collective bargaining in each province, with special subsection dealing with Reville report in Ontario, unionization of college and university faculty.
Location: OONL.

3494 **British Columbia School Trustees Association**
The community education collection. [Vancouver]: British Columbia School Trustees Association, [1975]. [66] l.
Note: Approx. 300 entries.– Collection of "quality material with as much Canadian content as possible" for use of BCSTA.– Arranged in subject categories: education, psychology, sociology, political science, social

welfare, economics, languages.

Location: OONL.

3495 Canadian Teachers' Federation

Continuing education for teachers. Ottawa: Canadian Teachers' Federation, 1975. 65 p. (Bibliographies in education / Canadian Teachers' Federation ; no. 53)

Note: 543 entries.– Covers 1970 to June 1975.– Includes books, articles, theses on competency-based programs, delivery systems, in-service programs, leadership development, planning and organizing in-service teacher education, released time/course credits, teacher centres, use of media in inservice programs.

Location: OONL.

3496 Canadian Teachers' Federation

A directory of curriculum guides used in Canadian schools. Ottawa: Canadian Teachers' Federation, [1975]. ii, 92 p.

Note: Includes book lists, administrative guides, elementary and secondary curriculum guides for all subjects, preschool and adult education programs, sources of curriculum guides.

Location: OONL.

3497 Canadian Teachers' Federation

School discipline. Ottawa: Canadian Teachers' Federation, 1975. 14 p. (Bibliographies in education / Canadian Teachers' Federation ; no. 49)

Note: 199 entries.– Covers 1972 to January 1975.– Includes books, articles, theses on classroom control, corporal punishment, self-regulation.

Previous edition: 1972. 23 p. (Bibliographies in education ; no. 27).

Location: OONL.

3498 Canadian Teachers' Federation

Teacher education programs for native people. Ottawa: Canadian Teachers' Federation, 1975. 18 p. (Bibliographies in education / Canadian Teachers' Federation ; no. 55)

Note: 74 entries.– Covers 1968 to 1975.– Includes books, papers, articles, excerpts from books, reports relating to teacher aide training programs.– Extensive annotation.

Location: OONL.

3499 Canadian Teachers' Federation

Teacher evaluation. Ottawa: Canadian Teachers' Federation, 1975. 26 p. (Bibliographies in education / Canadian Teachers' Federation ; no. 52)

Note: 370 entries.– Covers 1972 to May 1975.– Includes books, articles, theses on teaching performance evaluation.

Previous edition: 1972. (Bibliographies in education ; no. 29). 349 entries.– Covers 1967 to 1972.

Location: OONL.

3500 Caron, Louise; Leblanc, Nicole J.

Vie étudiante et services aux étudiants: bibliographie commentée sur les services aux étudiants au niveau collégial, le personnel de ces services, la clientèle étudiant concernée. Québec: Ministère de l'éducation, Direction générale de la planification, 1975. 144 f.

Note: Localisation: QQLA.

3501 Corman, Linda

Community education in Canada: an annotated bibliography. Toronto: Ontario Institute for Studies in Education, c1975. xi, 55 p. (Bibliography series / Ontario Institute for Studies in Education ; no. 2); ISBN: 0-7744-

0115-X.

Note: 219 entries.– Books, research reports, theses, pamphlets, journals, ERIC reports, films, filmstrips on theories and definitions of community schools (approaches, projects), community use of schools, community control of schools.

Location: OONL.

3502 Deosaran, Ramesh

Educational aspirations, what matters? A literature review. Toronto: Research Department, Toronto Board of Education, 1975. 94 p. (Research Service / Research Department, Toronto Board of Education ; no. 135; ISSN: 0316-8786)

Note: Approx. 175 entries.– Review of literature on postsecondary expectations and accessibility for Toronto students.– Topics include social class and sex, financial aid and educational aspirations, family and community characteristics.

Location: OONL.

3503 Desjarlais, Lionel; Carrier, Maurice

Étude de l'enseignement de l'anglais, langue seconde dans les écoles franco-ontariennes. [S.l.: s.n.], 1975. vi, 335 f.: ill.

Note: Suppléments en anglais:

Supplement 1. Further statistical analysis of the discrepancy evaluation questionnaire. 121 l.

Supplement 2. Selected and annotated bibliography on teaching and learning a second language with special emphasis on English as a second language. vi, 142 l.

Localisation: OONL.

3504 Locas, Claude

La réforme scolaire du Québec: bibliographie pour un bilan. [Québec]: Secrétariat, Direction générale de la planification, Ministère de l'éducation, 1975. 484 p.

Note: 2,187 entrées.– Principaux thèmes traités: histoire de l'éducation, histoire des idées, le système d'enseignement avant la réforme scolaire, une société en mutation, les prémisses de la reforme scolaire, le rapport Parent.

Localisation: OONL.

3505 Ottawa Public Library

Sexism in education. [Ottawa: Ottawa Public Library], 1975. [12] p.

Note: Approx. 60 entries.– Commissioned studies, government reports, investigations by parents, teachers, etc., in English language, on sex stereotyping in school systems.

Location: OONL.

3506 Québec (Province). Centrale des bibliothèques. Centre de bibliographie

Éducation sexuelle. Montréal: Centre de bibliographie de la Centrale des bibliothèques, 1975. 108 p. (Carnets de bibliographie / Centre de bibliographie de la Centrale des bibliothèques ; no 1); ISBN: 0-88523-015-9.

Note: Approx. 700 entrées.

Localisation: OONL.

3507 Roy, Jean-Luc; Contant, André

Bibliographie annotée sur l'analyse institutionnelle. Montréal: Centre d'animation, de développement et de recherche en éducation, [1975]. v, 155 p.

Note: Localisation: OONL.

3508 Sault College. Library Resource Centre

Early childhood education: bibliography. Sault Ste. Marie, Ont.: Sault College, Library Resource Centre,

1975. 23 p.
Note: Approx. 180 entries.– Includes Canadian references.
Location: OONL.

— 1976 —

3509 Boyce, Helena
Pre-service teacher education in Canada. Ottawa: Canadian Teachers' Federation, 1976. 29 p. (Bibliographies in education / Canadian Teachers' Federation ; no. 58); ISBN: 0-88989-011-0.
Note: 438 entries.– Covers from June 1969 to October 1976.– Includes books, articles, theses.
Previous edition: 1969: 26 p. (Bibliographies in education ; no. 1).– (368 entries).– Covers 1960 to 1969, with selected earlier material.
Location: OONL.

3510 Breton, Lise; Roy, Jean-Luc
Le collège québécois: introduction bibliographique. Montréal: Centre d'animation, de développement et de recherche en éducation, 1976. xvii, 98 p.
Note: 220 entrées.– Comprend les principaux textes susceptibles de donner une vue globale de l'historique des cégeps, de leur organisation administrative, des programmes d'études, du personnel, de la clientèle, de l'éducation des adultes, des services, des finances, des statistiques et des orientations de l'enseignement postsecondaire.
Localisation: OONL.

3511 Brooks, I.R.
Native education in Canada and the United States: a bibliography. [Calgary]: Office of Educational Development, Indian Students University Program Services, University of Calgary, c1976. xi, 298 p.
Note: 2,765 entries.– Surveys material published prior to January, 1975, with focus on period since 1900.– Restricted to works dealing with pedagogy, sociology or politics of native education.– Excludes curriculum materials, native studies programs, books by Native people, fiction featuring Native people.– Compiled with the assistance of A.M. Marshall.
Location: OONL.

3512 Canadian Teachers' Federation
Open area schools. Ottawa: Canadian Teachers' Federation, 1976. 27 p. (Bibliographies in education / Canadian Teachers' Federation ; no. 56); ISBN: 0-88989-008-0.
Note: 441 entries.– Covers 1971 to May 1976.– Includes books, articles, theses.
Previous edition: 1971. 10 p. (Bibliographies in education ; no. 17).– 100 entries.– Covers 1965 to end of 1970.
Location: OONL.

3513 Commission scolaire régionale de Chambly. Direction des services de recherche et de planification
Bilan des recherches, Direction des services de recherche et de planification, 1972-1976. [Saint-Lambert, Québec: Commission scolaire régionale de Chambly, Direction des services de recherche et de planification, 1976]. [73] f.: ill., carte.
Note: Approx. 70 entrées.
Localisation: OONL.

3514 Landsburg, June; Lee, Linda
Annotated bibliography of print materials on instructional development and related matters. Ottawa: Carleton University, 1976. [1] l., 83 p.
Note: Location: OWA.

3515 Lin, Suzane; Roberts, Hazel J.
Financing universities in Canada: a bibliography/Le financement des universités au Canada: bibliographie. Ottawa: Association of Universities and Colleges of Canada, 1976. 7 p.; ISBN: 0-88876-044-2.
Note: Location: OONL.

3516 Reynolds, Roy
A guide to periodicals and books relating to education in the Ontario Archives. [Toronto]: Department of History and Philosophy of Education, Ontario Institute for Studies in Education, c1976. iii l., 149 p. (Educational record series / Department of History and Philosophy of Education, Ontario Institute for Studies in Education ; 7)
Note: Approx. 1,500 entries.
Location: OONL.

3517 Swain, Merrill
"Bibliography: research on immersion education for the majority child."
In: *Canadian Modern Language Review*; Vol. 32, no. 5 (May 1976) p. 592-596.; ISSN: 0008-4506.
Note: Location: AEU.

3518 Vanier Institute of the Family
Perspectives on learning: a selected annotated bibliography/Perspectives sur l'apprentissage: bibliographie sélective annotée. Ottawa: Vanier Institute of the Family, [1976]. 121 l.
Note: Approx. 500 entries.– Books and articles on learning: contemporary issues, philosophical roots, humanistic learning, educational alternatives, learning in the family and community, learning as process, lifelong learning.– Includes brief listings of audio tapes, films, bibliographies, magazines.
Location: OONL.

3519 Yorio, Carlos Alfredo
A selected annotated bibliography for teacher training in Canada, 1976. [Toronto]: Ministry of Culture and Recreation, Citizenship Branch, 1976. 12 p.
Note: 69 entries.
Location: OONL.

— 1977 —

3520 Baccanale, Diane
Programme 04: cadre général de l'individualisation de l'enseignement professionnel: bibliographie sur l'élaboration, l'expérimentation et l'évaluation de programmes institutionnels. St-Lambert [Québec]: Commission scolaire régionale de Chambly, Direction des services de recherche et de planification, 1977. 64 f.
Note: Approx. 300 entrées.
Localisation: OONL.

3521 Canadian Teachers' Federation
Community schools. Ottawa: Canadian Teachers' Federation, 1977. 18 p. (Bibliographies in education / Canadian Teachers' Federation ; no. 60); ISBN: 0-88989-016-1.
Note: 253 entries.– Covers 1972 to 1977.– Includes books, articles, theses.
Previous edition: 1972. 32 p. (Bibliographies in education ; no. 31). 492 entries.– Covers 1967 to 1972.

Location: OONL.

3522 **Canadian Teachers' Federation**
Evaluation of student teachers. Ottawa: Canadian Teachers' Federation, 1977. 76 p. (Bibliographies in education / Canadian Teachers' Federation ; no. 59); ISBN: 0-88989-015-3.
Note: 278 entries.– Books, articles, theses from 1970 to 1977.
Location: OONL.

3523 **Casno, Pierre; Bernard, Jean-Paul; Lauzier, Suzanne**
Index des mémoires présentées à la Commission royale d'enquête sur l'enseignement dans la province de Québec, 1961-1963. Montréal: Université de Montréal, Service des bibliothèques, Bibliothèque E.P.C., 1977. 51 f.; ISBN: 0-88529-021-6.
Note: Approx. 300 entrées.
Localisation: OONL.

3524 **Dugan, Sylvia A.**
"Elementary French readers: a selective annotated bibliography."
In: *Canadian Modern Language Review*; Vol. 33, no. 3 (January 1977) p. 379-393.; ISSN: 0008-4506.
Note: Lists and describes readers suitable for students of French as a second language who have begun the study of French in Grade Six.
Location: AEU.

3525 **Lefebvre, Monique**
Techniques d'intervention auprès des enfants d'âge préscolaire: dossier bibliographique ouvert au Centre de documentation du C.A.D.R.E. Montréal: Centre d'animation, de développement et de recherche en éducation, 1977. 18 p.
Note: Localisation: OONL.

3526 **Moll, Marita**
Pupil transportation and school bus safety in Canada. Ottawa: Canadian Teachers' Federation, 1977. 27 p. (Bibliographies in education / Canadian Teachers' Federation ; no. 61); ISBN: 0-88989-035-8.
Note: 158 entries.– Books, articles, studies, papers, theses, federal and provincial legislation, driver's handbooks, vehicle inspection guides, films and filmstrips, posters, brochures, kits, etc. on school transportation.
Location: OONL.

3527 **National Council of Jewish Women of Canada**
Prejudice in educational material: a resource handbook. [Downsview, Ont.: National Council of Jewish Women of Canada], 1977. 18 p.
Note: Approx. 150 entries.– Books, pamphlets, papers, articles, speeches dealing with educational materials.– Topics include human rights, native peoples, labour, multiculturalism, prejudice, sexism.– Includes Canadian references.
Location: OONL.

3528 **Roy, Jean-Luc**
L'enseignement privé: liste annotée de quelques documents récents. Montréal: Centre d'animation, de développement et de recherche en éducation, 1977. 14 p.
Note: Approx. 40 entrées.
Localisation: OONL.

3529 **Savard, Jean-Guy**
Bibliographie analytique de tests de langues / Analytical bibliography of language tests. 2e éd. rev. et augm. Québec: Presses de l'Université Laval, 1977. xiv, 570 p.

(Travaux du Centre international de recherche sur le bilinguisme ; F-1); ISBN: 0-7746-6438-X.
Note: 495 entrées.
Édition antérieure: 1969. xviii, 372 p.
Localisation: OONL.

— 1978 —

3530 **Anderson, Ethel E.**
Annotated A.B.E. bibliography. Toronto: Movement for Canadian Literacy, 1978. ii, 106 p.: graph.; ISBN: 0-920588-01-8.
Note: Approx. 300 entries.– Listing of materials used in the 0 to 9 grade levels of adult basic education programs in Canada.– Categories include reading, language arts, reference materials, arithmetic/mathematics, evaluation materials, instructor's resource material.
Location: OONL.

3531 **Auster, Ethel**
Reference sources on Canadian education: an annotated bibliography. Toronto: Ontario Institute for Studies in Education, 1978. vii, 114 p. (Bibliography series / Ontario Institute for Studies in Education ; no. 3); ISBN: 0-7744-0163-X.
Note: 318 entries.– Covers material published from 1970 to March 1977.– Includes reference tools (almanacs, yearbooks, directories, abstracts, indexes, bibliographies) which deal with some aspect of education, are Canadian in content or origin, or deal especially with education in Ontario.– Excludes curriculum guides, reports of ministerial committees, commissions and task forces, acts, bills, laws, informally published materials.
Location: OONL.

3532 **Beslin, Ralph**
Education finance in Canada. Ottawa: Canadian Teachers' Federation, 1978. 13 p. (Bibliographies in education / Canadian Teachers' Federation ; no. 62); ISBN: 0-88989-040-4.
Note: 142 entries.– Covers from October 1974 to December 1977.– Includes books, articles, theses.
Previous editions:
1974. 17 p. (Bibliographies in education ; no. 47). (206 entries).– Covers from August 1970 to October 1974.
1970. 26 p. (Bibliographies in education ; no. 11). (354 entries).– Covers 1960 to 1970.
Location: OONL.

3533 **Beslin, Ralph**
Selection of teachers and student teachers. Ottawa: Canadian Teachers' Federation, 1978. 23 p. (Bibliographies in education / Canadian Teachers' Federation ; no. 64); ISBN: 0-88989-048-X.
Note: 99 entries.– Covers 1973 to July 1978.– Includes books, articles, theses on professional staff selection, hiring and promotion practices, evaluation of student teachers.
Location: OONL.

3534 **Beslin, Ralph**
Tenure. Ottawa: Canadian Teachers' Federation, 1978. 14 p. (Bibliographies in education / Canadian Teachers' Federation ; no. 66); ISBN: 0-88989-053-6.
Note: 55 entries.– Covers 1975 to 1978.– Includes books and articles on contract and tenure.– No entries on tenure in higher education are included.
Previous editions:
1975. 31 p. (Bibliographies in education ; no. 54). (182

entries).– Covers from April 1973 to October 1975. 1973. 20 p. (Bibliographies in education ; no. 33). (286 entries).– Covers 1963 to 1973.
Location: OONL.

3535 **Boisvert, Marcel**
Inventaire d'un stock d'anciens manuels de français. Montréal: Programme de perfectionnement des maîtres de français du secondaire, Faculté des sciences de l'éducation, Université de Montréal, 1978. 207 p. (Didactique du français au secondaire / Faculté des sciences de l'éducation, Université de Montréal ; série 1, no 2)
Note: Approx. 2,400 entrées.– La période couverte est de 1861 à 1978.
Localisation: OONL.

3536 **Cochrane, Donald B.**
Moral-values education in Canada: a bibliography and directory, 1970-1977. Toronto: Publication Division, Ontario Institute for Studies in Education, 1978. 13 p.
Note: Approx. 450 entries.
Location: OONL.

3537 **Dumas, Jean-Marc; Blais, Georgette**
Répertoire des écrits de l'INRS-Éducation. Sainte-Foy, Québec: INRS-Éducation, [1978]. 45 f.
Note: Approx. 300 entrées.– Écrits produits par les membres de l'INRS-Éducation depuis sa création en juillet 1972: rapports de recherche, communications de type varié, des articles de revue, des volumes, des instruments de mesure.
Localisation: OONL.

3538 **Enns, Carol**
The education of new Canadians: an annotated bibliography. Toronto: Library, Reference and Information Services, Ontario Institute for Studies in Education, 1978. ix, 50 p. (Current bibliography / Ontario Institute for Studies in Education ; no. 10)
Note: 162 entries.– Covers 1960 to 1978.– Books, research reports, theses, pamphlets, journal articles concerning cultural, social, and educational perspectives on immigrant needs; projects and programs: development and evaluation.
Location: OONL.

3539 **Houyoux, Philippe**
Bibliographie de l'histoire de l'éducation au Québec des origines à 1960. Trois-Rivières: Université du Québec à Trois-Rivières, 1978. viii, 227 p. (Publication / Université du Québec à Trois-Rivières, Bibliothèque ; no 18)
Note: 2,105 entrées.– Livres, articles de périodiques, thèses sur les sujets: philosophie de l'éducation, pédagogie, systèmes d'enseignement, formation des maîtres, niveaux d'enseignement, institutions, principales disciplines et programmes, figures dominantes et ses promoteurs.– Le Québec fait l'objet de l'étude: il y a une exception cependant, l'Université d'Ottawa.– Les francophones hors Québec en sont exclus.– Les secteurs anglophone, protestant et juif du Québec y trouvent place.
Localisation: OONL.

3540 **Huffman, James; Huffman, Sybil**
Occupations in social sciences, religion and teaching/ Travailleurs spécialisés des sciences sociales, membres du clergé et enseignants. Toronto: Guidance Centre, Faculty of Education, University of Toronto, c1978. 33 p.

(Career information: a bibliography of publications about careers in Canada ; book 4); ISBN: 0-7713-0054-9.
Note: Approx. 250 entries.– Includes books, pamphlets, booklets, information sheets.
Location: AEU.

3541 **Hulbert, Tina G.**
Educational resource materials for the hearing impaired: an annotated compilation for parents and teachers of deaf, deaf-blind and deaf multiply handicapped individuals. Victoria, B.C.: Ministry of Education, c1978. iii, 111 p.
Note: Location: BVAS.

3542 **Moll, Marita**
Teacher workload. Ottawa: Canadian Teachers' Federation, 1978. 68 p. (Bibliographies in education / Canadian Teachers' Federation ; no. 63); ISBN: 0-88989-046-3.
Note: 326 entries.– Covers 1971 to 1978.– Deals with teacher workload in elementary and secondary schools, post-secondary institutions.– Topics include assignment, distribution, supervisory and extra-curricular duties, class size and pupil-teacher ratio, hours of work, sources of stress and teacher morale.
Previous edition: 1971. 33 p. (Bibliographies in education ; no. 20). 467 entries.– Covers 1961 to 1971.
Location: OONL.

3543 **Perron, Yolande; Rousseau, Raymond; Thériault, Jacques**
Les organes officiels des syndicats des enseignants québécois. Québec: U.Q.A.R.–C.E.Q., 1978. ix, 901 p.
Note: 8,927 entrées.– Principaux thèmes: associations d'instituteurs, la corporation des instituteurs et institutrices catholiques du Québec, associations syndicales, la profession enseignante, les relations du travail, éducation et l'enseignement, l'organisation scolaire, politiques et législation scolaire, l'église, éléments biographiques et historiques.
Localisation: OONL.

3544 **Riverin-Simard, Danielle; Hamel, Lucie; Couture, Francine**
Bibliographie commentée sur l'apprenant-adulte. [Sainte-Foy, Québec]: INRS-Éducation: Téléuniversité, 1978. 14 f.
Note: Localisation: OONL.

3545 **Sault College. Library Resource Centre**
A broad look at education & related areas. Sault Ste. Marie, Ont.: Sault College, Library Resource Centre, 1978. a-f, 52 p.
Note: Approx. 500 entries.– Lists books and periodicals held at Sault College Resource Centre.
Location: OONL.

3546 **Thiele, Paul E.**
Educational materials for the handicapped: a preliminary union list. Victoria: British Columbia Ministry of Education, 1978. 2 vol.
Note: Location: OONL.

3547 **Troy, Kathleen**
Annotated bibliography of ESL testing. Toronto: Ministry of Culture and Recreation, Newcomer Services Branch, 1978. 49 p.
Note: Location: OONL.

— 1979 —

3548 **Bramwell, John R.; Vigna, Roxy**
Evaluation instruments locally developed in Ontario: an

annotated catalogue of material developed by school boards and other agencies. Toronto: Ministry of Education, c1979. xiv, 281 p.

Note: 270 entries.– Instruments for testing student achievement in both cognitive and affective areas (reading, science, mathematics, English, foreign languages, social sciences), attitude surveys and questionnaires, other evaluative instruments related to educational practice.

Location: OONL.

3549 Burkle, Eric F.
Resource materials for traffic safety programs in elementary schools: a bibliography. [Victoria, B.C.]: Division of Policy Development, Ministry of Education, Science and Technology, 1979. 19 p.; ISBN: 0-7719-8248-8.

Note: Includes pamphlets, films, posters.

Location: OONL.

3550 Corman, Linda
Declining enrolments: issues and responses: an annotated bibliography. Toronto: Ontario Institute for Studies in Education, 1979. x, 82 p. (Current bibliography / Ontario Institute for Studies in Education ; no. 11)

Note: 299 entries.– Books, research reports, theses, pamphlets, journal articles, ERIC and ONTERIS documents, audio-visual materials (films, filmstrips) relating to declining enrolments in elementary and secondary schools: demographic causes, school closure, use of surplus space, surplus staff, program contraction and reorganization, financial implications, management strategies.

Location: OONL.

3551 Fedigan, Larry
School-based elements related to achievement: a review of the literature. Edmonton: Minister's Advisory Committee on Student Achievement, 1979. 112 p.

Note: Approx. 175 entries.– Bibliographical review of research dealing with how educational outcomes are related to variables such as teaching behaviours, classroom climate, teacher expectations, student characteristics.– Section on research in Canadian schools.

Location: OONL.

3552 Mallea, John R.; Shea, Edward C.
Multiculturalism and education: a select bibliography. Toronto: Ontario Institute for Studies in Education; Ontario Ministry of Culture and Recreation, 1979. 290 p. (Informal series / Ontario Institute for Studies in Education ; 9); ISBN: 0-7744-5019-3.

Note: Approx. 2,200 entries.– Topics include culture and education, language and education, minorities and education, race and education, ethnicity and education, immigration and education, attitudes and education, multicultural education.– Sections listing audio-visual materials, additional bibliographies.

Location: OONL.

3553 Marchak, Nick
Assessing communication skills: a review of the literature: a study conducted under contract to Alberta Education, Edmonton, Alberta, Canada. Edmonton: Minister's Advisory Committee on Student Achievement, 1979. vii, 217 p.: ill.

Note: Reviews literature in five areas: reading literacy, writing literacy, functional literacy, oral communication, listening.– Bibliographies, p. 43-60; summaries of research, p. 61-217.

Location: OONL.

3554 Moll, Marita
Teaching French as a second language in Canada. Ottawa: Canadian Teachers' Federation, 1979. 95 p. (Bibliographies in education / Canadian Teachers' Federation ; no. 70); ISBN: 0-88989-067-6.

Note: 481 entries.– Emphasis on material published since 1967.– Includes books and articles in seven categories: aims and objectives of second-language instruction, bibliographies, bilingualism and effects, learning and retention, programs of instruction, research methodology, testing, measurement and evaluation.

Location: OONL.

3555 Québec (Province). Ministère de l'éducation. Service général des communications
Références pédagogiques. Québec: Service général des communications, Ministère de l'éducation, 1976-1979. 4 vol.; ISSN: 0225-7254.

Note: Vol. 1: Aylwin, Ulric; Lacroix, Claude. 1976. 352 p.
Vol. 2: Gatien, Louise; Aylwin, Ulric. 1977. 190 f.
Vol. 3: Aylwin, Ulric. 1978. 145 p.
Vol. 4: Aylwin, Ulric; Lacroix, Claude. 1979. 211 p.
Inclut un nombre considérable d'ouvrages canadiens et québécoises.
Édition antérieure: Cumulatif des références pédagogiques, 1974-1975. Montréal: Service de recherche et de développement, Cegep de Maisonneuve, 1975.

Localisation: OONL.

3556 Taylor, Sandra J.
Children: all different, all the same: a selected list of books available for loan through the Provincial Library System. Charlottetown: Prince Edward Island Provincial Library, 1979. 38 p.

Note: Approx. 150 entries.– Most works concerned with exceptional children or those with learning difficulties or disabilities, multi-handicapped children, standards of and resources for special education, sections on specific categories of exceptional children: gifted, hyperactive, mentally retarded, etc.– Includes Canadian references.

Location: OONL.

3557 Ward, Megan
Evaluating the arts in education: an annotated bibliography. Ottawa: Government of Canada, Department of Communications, 1979. ii, 73 p.

Note: 145 entries.– Includes books and articles on the arts in education: dance, drama and theatre, film and television, music, visual arts, art history.– Publications are categorized by type of information (descriptive, empirical, theoretical, statistical, bibliographical), and level of education (pre-school, elementary, secondary, post-secondary, adult).

Titre en français: Le rôle des arts dans l'enseignement: bibliographie commentée.

Location: OONL.

3558 Ward, Megan
Le rôle des arts dans l'enseignement: bibliographie commentée. Ottawa: Secrétariat d'État, 1979. ii, 73 p.

Note: 145 entrées.– Livres et articles sur les arts dans l'enseignement: danse, l'art dramatique, cinéma, télévision, musique, arts plastiques.– Les ouvrages ont en outre été rassemblés suivant le genre d'information qu'ils renferment, et le niveau d'enseignement auquel ils

s'adressent.– Title in English: *Evaluating the arts in education: an annotated bibliography*.
Localisation: OONL.

— 1980 —

3559 **Breton, Lise; Roy, Jean-Luc**
L'enseignement professionnel: bibliographie annotée. Montréal: Centre d'animation, de développement et de recherche en éducation, 1980. 262 p.; ISBN: 2-89169-002-8.
Note: Approx. 500 entrées.– Livres, articles de revues sur la planification et l'organisation de l'enseignement professionnel, programmes d'enseignement professionnel, méthodes d'analyse de programmes, pédagogie, enseignement coopératif et stage, personnel et clientèle de l'enseignement professionnel.
Localisation: OONL.

3560 **British Columbia. Ministry of Education, Science & Technology. Continuing Education Division**
Survey of leisure reading materials for A.B.E. students with emphasis on western Canada: a $500 collection. Victoria: The Division, [1980]. 46 p.
Note: Approx. 200 entries.– Lists material for adults with low reading skills, a beginning collection for libraries and Adult Basic Education instructors.– Categories include biography, Canadiana, life skills, novels, pictorial books, stories, Native materials, books with cassette tapes.– Compiled by Judy Ann Vetsch.
Location: OONL.

3561 **Cantin, Gabrielle; Chené-Williams, Adèle**
Aide-mémoire en andragogie. [Montréal]: Faculté des sciences de l'éducation, Université de Montréal, 1980. 79 p.
Note: Approx. 500 entrées.– Ouvrages généraux (éducation des adultes, recherche, méthodologie), recherche des références bibliographiques, périodiques, andragogie de Montréal (mémoires et thèses, cahiers, écrits des professeurs).
Localisation: OONL.

3562 **Casno, Pierre, et al.**
"Bibliographie sur l'éducation au Canada français."
Dans: *Revue des sciences de l'éducation*; Vol. 1, no 1 (printemps 1975) p. 77-87; vol. 1, no 2-3 (automne 1975) p. 191-202; vol. 2, no 1 (hiver 1976) p. 47-57; vol. 2, no 2 (printemps 1976) p. 137-145; vol. 2, no 3 (automne 1976) p. 267-276; vol. 3, no 1 (hiver 1977) p. 95-103; vol. 3, no 2 (printemps 1977) p. 239-247; vol. 3, no 3 (automne 1977) p. 381-390; vol. 4, no 1 (hiver 1978) p. 119-129; vol. 4, no 2 (printemps 1978) p. 325-333; vol. 4, no 3 (automne 1978) p. 425-435; vol. 5, no 1 (hiver 1979) p. 107-122; vol. 5, no 2 (printemps 1979) p. 281-293; vol. 5, no 3 (automne 1979) p. 441-451; vol. 6, no 1 (hiver 1980) p. 117-126; vol. 6, no 2 (printemps 1980) p. 351-359.; ISSN: 0318-479X.
Note: Localisation: AEU.

3563 **Cheng, Maisy; Wright, Edgar Norman; Larter, Sylvia**
Streaming in Toronto and other Ontario schools: a review of the literature. [Toronto]: Board of Education for the City of Toronto, 1980. 76 p. (Research Service / Research Department, Toronto Board of Education ; no. 157; ISSN: 0316-8786)
Note: Location: OONL.

3564 **Désy, Marguerite**
Education sexuelle: bibliographie. Montréal: Association des institutions d'enseignement secondaire, 1980. ii, 71 f.
Note: Localisation: OONL.

3565 **Ellis, Dormer**
An overview of literature pertaining to the presentation of students for and placement in post-secondary studies [microform]. [Toronto]: Ontario Ministry of Education, [1980]. 4 microfiches.
Note: 206 entries.– Books, research publications, journal articles, news-clippings, with focus on Ontario in the period 1960-1980.– Topics include Ontario grade 13 departmental exams, standardized aptitude and achievement tests, duplication of services among secondary schools/colleges/universities, admission tests, accessibility of post-secondary education to minorities.
Location: OONL.

3566 **Fedigan, Larry**
Classroom management and achievement: a review of the literature. Edmonton: Planning and Research Branch, Alberta Education, 1980. 60 p.
Note: Literature review related to classroom management and achievement in language arts and mathematics in lower elementary grades.– Many Canadian references.
Location: OONL.

3567 **Hardy, J. Stewart**
"A review of selected materials in the educational history of western Canada."
In: *Journal of Educational Thought*; Vol. 14, no. 2 (August 1980) p. 64-79.; ISSN: 0022-0701.
Note: Topics include education of native peoples, pre-provincial schooling, development of provincial schooling.
Location: OONL.

3568 **Lawton, Stephen B.; Currie, A. Blaine**
Handwriting: I. Instruction in handwriting in Ontario schools: II. Handwriting: an annotated bibliography. Toronto: Ontario Ministry of Education, 1980. x, 174 p.; ISBN: 0-7743-4756-2.
Note: 117 entries.– Historical, psychological, visuospatial literature on handwriting.– Some Canadian references.
Location: OONL.

3569 **Massey, D. Anthony; Potter, Joy**
A bibliography of articles and books on bilingualism in education. Ottawa: Canadian Parents for French, [1980]. [136] p.
Note: 279 entries.– Covers 1965 to 1979.– Focus on material dealing directly with topic of bilingualism in Canada for speakers of English who learn French in immersion or intensive courses.
Location: OONL.

3570 **Moll, Marita**
Declining enrolment. Ottawa: Canadian Teachers' Federation, 1980. 34 p. (Bibliographies in education / Canadian Teachers' Federation ; no. 72); ISBN: 0-88989-090-0.
Note: 221 entries.– Covers 1978 to 1980.– Includes books, articles, list of working papers, information bulletins, statistical appendices, occasional papers issued by Commission on Declining School Enrolments in Ontario (CODE).
Location: OONL.

3571 **Moll, Marita**
L'éducation spéciale au Canada. Ottawa: Fédération canadienne des enseignants, 1980. 34, 137 p. (Bibliographies en éducation / Fédération canadienne

des enseignants ; no 73); ISBN: 0-88989-093-5.

Note: 1,122 entrées.– La période couverte est de 1974 à 1980.– Inclut documents à caractère général portant sur les programmes, services, problèmes et questions en discussion; documents traitant de formes précises d'atypie.– Texte en français et en anglais disposé tête-bêche.– Titre de la p. de t. additionnelle: *Special education in Canada*.

Localisation: OOS.

3572 **Moll, Marita**
Part-time and substitute teaching. Ottawa: Canadian Teachers' Federation, 1980. 16 p. (Bibliographies in education / Canadian Teachers' Federation ; no. 71); ISBN: 0-88989-085-4.

Note: 95 entries.– Covers 1970 to 1980.– Contains books, articles, theses.

Location: OONL.

3573 **Moll, Marita**
Special education in Canada. Ottawa: Canadian Teachers' Federation, 1980. 137, 34 p. (Bibliographies in education / Canadian Teachers' Federation ; no. 73); ISBN: 0-88989-093-5.

Note: 1,122 entries.– Covers from 1974 to September 1980.– Includes general materials on programs, services, problems and issues, and specific materials on various forms of exceptionality.– Text in English and French with French text on inverted pages.– Title of additional title-page: *L'éducation spéciale au Canada*.

Location: OOS.

3574 **Riverin-Simard, Danielle**
"Apprentissage observationnel abstrait et éducation permanente: revue de littérature."
Dans: *Orientation professionnelle*; Vol. 16, no 4 (décembre 1980) p. 13-40.; ISSN: 0030-5413.

Note: Localisation: OONL.

3575 **Roberge-Brassard, Jocelyne**
L'École, son contexte social et le contexte de l'élève: relevé bibliographique commenté un vie d'une recherche. Ste-Foy, Québec: INRS-Éducation, 1980. 137 f.

Note: 300 entrées.– Volumes, articles de périodiques, thèses.– Comprend des références canadiennes.

Localisation: OONL.

3576 **Rochais, Gérard**
Bibliographie annotée de l'enseignement supérieur au Québec. Montréal: Commission d'étude sur les universités, 1979-1980. 2 vol.; ISBN: 2-550-00016-1 (édition complète).

Note: Vol. 1: *Les universités, 1968-1978*.– 1,326 entrées.– L'université québécoise (administration, planification, orientation et problèmes); fonctions de l'université (l'enseignement, recherche, fonction sociale); personnes (personnel administratif, professeurs, étudiants).
Vol. 2: *La formation des maîtres, 1962-1979*.– 367 entrées.– Formation des enseignants; perfectionnement des enseignants; l'enseignement professionnel: formation et perfectionnement; les enseignants; innovation pédagogique; Rapport Parent: mémoires et commentaires.

Localisation: Vol. 1: NSWA; Vol. 2: OONL.

3577 **Saskatchewan. Department of Continuing Education. Program Development Branch**
Annotated literacy bibliography. Regina: The Branch, 1980. 18 p.

Note: Student reading materials and workbooks in use in Saskatchewan literacy programs for adult new readers.

Location: OONL.

3578 **Stevenson, H.A.**
Public policy and futures bibliography: a select list of Canadian, American, and other book-length materials, 1970 to 1980, including highly selected works published between 1949 and 1969. Toronto: Ministry of Education, c1980. xvi, 413 p.: charts; ISBN: 0-7743-5231-0.

Note: 2,665 entries.– Monographs, anthologies, reports collections, conference proceedings, Canadian science fiction and utopian works.– Educational themes account for 901 citations, 1,467 represent other themes among general futures literature (global views of the future, peace, war, affluence, poverty, development and underdevelopment, the law, crime, violence, communications, health, learning, technology, environment, growth and its limits).– Focus on Canada and particularly Ontario.

Location: OONL.

3579 **A view of university financing: [bibliography]/Aperçu du financement des universités: [bibliographie].**
Ottawa: Association of Universities and Colleges of Canada, Library, 1980. 10 p.

Note: Approx. 150 entries.– Monographs, articles from Canadian university newspapers.

Location: OONL.

3580 **Woodward, Frances M.**
"The history of education in British Columbia: a selected bibliography."
In: *Schooling and society in twentieth century British Columbia*, edited by J.D. Wilson and David C. Jones. Calgary: Detselig Enterprises, c1980. P. 163-190.; ISBN: 0-920490-09-3.

Note: Approx. 325 entries.– Books, articles, theses dealing with the history and development of education in British Columbia.– Excludes local histories and school annuals.– Includes some short school histories and brief biographies of teachers.

Location: OONL.

— 1981 —

3581 **Bartram, Peter Edward Raven**
The Ontario colleges of applied arts and technology [microform]: a review and analysis of selected literature, 1965-1976. Ottawa: National Library of Canada, 1981. 4 microfiches (310 fr.). (Canadian theses on microfiche ; 47005; ISSN: 0227-3845)

Note: Bibliographical review.– Thesis: Ed.D., University of Toronto, 1980.

Location: OONL.

3582 **Bolduc, Anicette; Breton, Lise**
Apprentissage assuré: bibliographie annotée. Montréal: Centre d'animation, de développement et de recherches en éducation, 1981. 31 p.; ISBN: 2-89169-005-2.

Note: Approx. 80 entrées.

Localisation: OONL.

3583 **Breton, Lise; Roy, Jean-Luc**
L'évaluation de l'apprentissage: bibliographie annotée. Montréal: Centre d'animation, de développement et de recherche en éducation, 1981. 63 p.; ISBN: 2-89169-004-4.

Note: Approx. 175 entrées.– Livres, articles des périodiques sur l'évaluation de l'apprentissage dans le contexte d'un cours, sous la forme de tests, examens,

notation, évaluation formative, sommative, auto-évaluation et autres.
Localisation: OONL.

3584 **Bruneau, Sylvie; Larkin, Lise**
Pour une école nouvelle à Trois-Rivières: bibliographie annotée. [Trois-Rivières: s.n.], 1981. [3], iii, 100 f.
Note: Approx. 300 entrées.
Localisation: OONL.

3585 **Canadian Universities Foundation**
Select bibliography on higher education/Bibliographie sur l'enseignement supérieur. Ottawa: Canadian Universities Foundation, [1963-1981]. 18 vol.; ISSN: 0049-0091.
Note: Began with July-September 1963; ceased with January-March 1981.– Text in English and French/texte en français et en anglais.
Continues: *Items of interest/Articles à noter.* Ottawa: [1962-1963].
Absorbed by: *University Affairs/Affaires universitaires.* Ottawa: AUCC, 1959-. vol.; ISSN: 0041-9257.
Location: OONL.

3586 **Douglas College**
An annotated bibliography of adult basic education materials relevant to industrial and craft workers. Victoria: British Columbia, Ministry of Education, 1981. 25 p.
Note: Location: BVAWC.

3587 **Dow, Ian I.; O'Reilly, Robert R.**
L'enfance en difficulté: une revue de la documentation. Toronto: Ministère de l'Éducation: Ministère des Collèges et Universités, c1981. 210 p.; ISBN: 0-7743-6747-4.
Note: Documentation portant la définition et classification des difficultés d'apprentissage: l'intelligence, les processus d'apprentissage, le rendement scolaire, l'écart entre le rendement et les aptitudes, dysfonction neurologique, l'exclusion.
English title: *Exceptional pupils: a review of the literature.*
Localisation: OONL.

3588 **Dow, Ian I.; O'Reilly, Robert R.**
Exceptional pupils: a review of the literature. Toronto: Ministry of Education: Ministry of Colleges and Universities, c1981. 81 p.; ISBN: 0-7743-6746-6.
Note: Review of literature dealing with learning disabilities: definition, incidence, definitional components (intelligence, process, academic, discrepancy, neurological, exclusion).
Titre en français: *L'enfance en difficulté: une revue de la documentation.*
Location: OONL.

3589 **Dufour, Desmond**
Inventaire des travaux publiés par le Service de la démographie scolaire au 1 avril 1981. [Québec]: Gouvernement du Québec, Ministère de l'éducation, Direction des études économiques et démographiques, 1981. 105 p. (Document hors série / Gouvernement du Québec, Ministère de l'éducation, Direction des études économiques et démographiques ; no 20); ISBN: 2-550-04459-2.
Note: Approx. 250 entrées.– Publications en série: documents de démographie scolaire, documents de travail, documents statistiques, document "hors série"; articles et communications; documents "pré-série" (1968-

1971); documents commandités.
Localisation: OONL.

3590 **Dumas, Jean-Marc; Bergeron, Hélène; Hardy-Roch, Marcelle**
L'enseignement professionnel court au Québec: bibliographie analytique. Ste-Foy, Québec: INRS-Éducation, 1981. 60, 2 f.
Note: Approx. 100 entrées.
Localisation: OONL.

3591 **Eady, David**
Adult new readers: a bibliography of supplementary reading materials selected from the collection of the Windsor Public Library. [Windsor, Ont.]: Windsor Public Library, 1981. 25 l.
Note: Approx. 375 entries.– Compiled to supplement tutorial learning-to-read program for adults at Windsor Public Library, includes fiction and non-fiction materials and is marked for reading level.
Location: OONL.

3592 **Goulson, Cary F.**
A source book of royal commissions and other major governmental inquiries in Canadian education, 1787-1978. Toronto: University of Toronto Press, c1981. xxii, 406 p.; ISBN: 0-8020-2408-4.
Note: 367 entries.– Chronological arrangement by province: investigations into education in general, other matters of significance to education (municipal contracts, property assessment and taxation, social welfare and education, school bus operations, etc.).
Supplement: ... , *1979-1983.* Victoria: University of British Columbia, 1985. 140 p.
Location: OONL.

3593 **Knapper, Christopher K.**
"A decade review of college teaching research, 1970-1980."
In: *Canadian Psychology;* Vol. 22, no. 2 (April 1981) p. 129-145.; ISSN: 0708-5591.
Note: Review of research by Canadian psychologists on college and university teaching: effectiveness of instructional innovations, evaluation of effective teaching, characteristics of learners, teachers and courses.
Location: OONL.

3594 **Leboeuf, Jacques; Breton, Lise**
L'étudiant handicapé: vers une meilleure intégration au collège: bibliographie annotée. Montréal: CADRE, 1981. 40 p.; ISBN: 2-89169-022-2.
Note: Approx. 100 entrées.– Comprend un nombre d'ouvrages canadiens.
Localisation: OONL.

3595 **Lemelin, Clément**
La pratique de l'économie de l'éducation dans le Québec francophone de la dernière décennie, 1970-1980: une présentation bibliographique. Montréal: Département de science économique, Université de Québec à Montréal, 1981. 26, 15 f. (Cahier / Département de science économique, Université de Québec à Montréal ; no 8101)
Note: Approx. 200 entrées.– Cinq grands thèmes: l'effort relatif de la société québécoise, l'impact de la scolarité sur le marché du travail, la demande d'éducation, les tentatives de planification et les conditions de travail des professeurs.
Localisation: OONL.

3596 **Manitoba. Department of Education. Library**
Annotated bibliography on gifted children. Winnipeg: Manitoba Department of Education, Library, 1981. 7 p.
Note: Location: OONL.

3597 **Moll, Marita**
Teacher and administrator evaluation. Ottawa: Canadian Teachers' Federation, 1981. 107 p. (Bibliographies in education / Canadian Teachers' Federation ; no. 74); ISBN: 0-88989-121-4.
Note: 602 entries.– Lists material on teacher evaluation in general, self-evaluation, student evaluation of teachers, administrator evaluation in general.
Location: OONL.

3598 **Parker, Franklin; Parker, Betty June**
Women's education: a world view. Westport, Conn.: Greenwood Press, 1979-1981. 2 vol.; ISBN: 0-313-23205-9 (set).
Note: Vol. 1: *Annotated bibliography of doctoral dissertations.* xii, 470 p.– Approx. 2,000 entries.– Includes U.S. and Canadian dissertations in English that concern the education of girls and women at all ages and school levels in public and private institutions: studies of women in liberal or traditional academic education, as well as those in nursing education, home economics, physical education, other vocational or career education.
Vol. 2: *Annotated bibliography of books and reports.* xv, 689 p. (3,942 entries).
Location: OONL.

3599 **Select bibliography on higher education/Bibliographie sur l'enseignement supérieur.** Ottawa: Association of Universities and Colleges of Canada, [1965-1981]. 17 vol.; ISSN: 0049-0091.
Note: Quarterly list from the collections of the library of the Association of Universities and Colleges of Canada.– Text in English and French/texte en français et en anglais.
Location: OONL.

— 1982 —

3600 **An annotated list of selected library materials for early French immersion, kindergarten – grade 7.** Richmond, B.C.: Modern Languages Services Branch, Ministry of Education, 1982. vii, 312 p.; ISBN: 0-7719-9124-X.
Note: Approx. 900 entries.– List of fiction and non-fiction titles intended to assist teacher-librarians of schools with early French-immersion programs to select and catalogue basic materials in French.
Location: OONL.

3601 **An annotated list of selected library materials for late French immersion, grades 6 and 7.** 2nd ed. Richmond, B.C.: Modern Languages Services Branch, Ministry of Education, 1982. iv, 175 l.; ISBN: 0-7719-9010-3.
Note: Approx. 700 entries.– Lists fiction and non-fiction, intended to assist teacher-librarians of schools with late French-immersion programs to select and catalogue appropriate basic materials in French.
Previous edition: 1981. iv, 172 l.; ISBN: 0-7719-8786-2.
Location: OONL.

3602 **Birt, Heather; Gladman, Tina**
Maritime energy education bibliography/Bibliographie sur les programmes d'éducation sur l'énergie dans les Maritimes. Halifax, N.S.: Maritime Provinces Education Foundation, 1982. ix, 46 p.
Note: Designed to provide teachers in the Atlantic provinces with information on materials to augment lessons on energy topics: audio-visual, print materials dealing with solar energy, conservation, coal and peat, oil and gas, wood as fuel, electric power.– Includes a speakers list.– Text in English and French/texte en français et en anglais.
Location: OONL.

3603 **Breton, Lise; Dufresne, Jean-Pierre**
Enseigner aux adultes: bibliographie annotée. Montréal: Centre d'animation, de développement et de recherche en éducation, 1982. 143 p.; ISBN: 2-89169-025-2.
Note: Approx. 400 entrées.– Comporte des références québécoises.
Localisation: OONL.

3604 **Chapdelaine, Cécile**
Bibliographie: activités éducatives à l'environnement. Québec: Ministère de l'éducation, Direction générale de l'éducation des adultes, 1982. 94 p.
Note: Localisation: QQLA.

3605 **Charland, Jean-Pierre; Thivierge, Nicole**
Bibliographie de l'enseignement professionel au Québec, 1850-1980. Québec: Institut québécois de recherche sur la culture, 1982. 282 p. (Instruments de travail / Institut québécois de recherche sur la culture ; no 3); ISBN: 2-89224-006-9.
Note: 3,279 entrées.– Enseignement agricole, commercial, ménager, arts et metiers, formation féminine et familiale; enseignement spécialisé; réforme de l'enseignement, formation des apprentissage; l'après révolution (clientèle étudiante, personnel enseignant, pertinence de la formation).– Liste des bibliographies consultées.
Localisation: OONL.

3606 **Crewe, Donald Martin**
An annotated bibliography of published materials supplemental to the high school English program in Newfoundland [microform]. Ottawa: National Library of Canada, 1982. 3 microfiches (228 fr.). (Canadian theses on microfiche ; 53323; ISSN: 0227-3845)
Note: Thesis: M.Ed., Memorial University of Newfoundland, 1982.
Location: OONL.

3607 **Doutrelepont, Jean-François**
"Les ressources en éducation économique."
Dans: *Vie pédagogique*; No 21 (novembre 1982) p. 28-32.; ISSN: 0707-2511.
Note: Localisation: OONL.

3608 **Guillot, Andrée; Breton, Lise**
L'enseignement à distance: bibliographie annotée. Montréal: Centre d'animation, de développement et de recherche en éducation, 1982. 75 p.; ISBN: 2-89169-027-3.
Note: Approx. 200 entrées.– Documents, études, rapports sur l'enseignement à distance de niveau post-secondaire.
Localisation: OONL.

3609 **Harrison, David; Little, Barbara; Mallett, Graham**
Reading development: a resource book for adult education. Victoria: Province of British Columbia, Ministry of Education, 1982. 89 p.; ISBN: 0-771-99240-8.
Note: Location: OONL.

3610 **Huffman, Sybil; Huffman, James**
Career information: a bibliography of publications about careers in Canada. Toronto: Guidance Centre, Faculty of Education, University of Toronto, c1982. ix, 117 p.; ISBN: 0-7713-0104-9.
Note: Approx. 1,200 entries.

Location: OONL.

3611 Hull, Jeremy; Murphy, Michael; Regnier, Robert
Underdevelopment and education: selected annotated resources for Saskatchewan and Canadian educators. Saskatoon: Division of Extension and Community Relations, University of Saskatchewan, c1982. 280 p.; ISBN: 0-88880-117-3.
Note: Approx. 2,000 entries.– Books, kits, dossiers of materials, slide-tape shows, films, games.– Selected materials that analyze underdevelopment internationally, in Canada and in Saskatchewan.– Focusses on indigenous peoples, Métis, northern Saskatchewan, rural underdevelopment, women, uranium development in Saskatchewan, labour and underdevelopment.
Location: OONL.

3612 Index to Ontario education research: ONTERIS.
Toronto: Ontario Ministry of Education, c1982. 2 vol.; ISBN: 0-7743-7110-2 (set).
Note: 2,187 entries.– Ontario Education Resources Information System: provides online access by author, title, subject to comprehensive body of research material produced in Ontario.– Vol. 1 contains the list of documents, vol. 2 the subject index.– Introduction en français.
Location: OONL.

3613 Leduc, Marcel
"Complément bibliographique sur l'éducation des adultes."
Dans: *Histoire des travailleurs québécois: Bulletin RCHTQ*; Vol. 8, no 2 (été 1982) p. 45-53.; ISSN: 0315-7938.
Note: Localisation: OONL.

3614 Miller, Ann H.
School based programme options for gifted secondary students with a review of the literature and existing programmes. Vancouver: Educational Research Institute of British Columbia, 1982. 45 p. (Reports / Educational Research Institute of British Columbia ; no. 82:25)
Note: Location: OONL.

3615 Moll, Marita
Teacher stress. Ottawa: Canadian Teachers' Federation, 1982. 90 p. (Bibliographies in education / Canadian Teachers' Federation ; no. 75); ISBN: 0-88989-132-X.
Note: 387 entries.– Covers January 1977 to April 1982.– Includes books, articles, theses on teacher burnout, alienation, morale and job satisfaction.
Location: OONL.

3616 Québec (Province). Ministère de l'éducation. Direction des communications
Bibliographie sur l'éducation préscolaire. Québec: Direction générale du développement pédagogique, 1982. 42 p. (Guides pédagogiques du préscolaire); ISBN: 2-550-04984-5.
Note: Approx. 750 entrées.– Principaux thèmes traités: enfance en difficulté, expression musicale/plastique/rythmique, jeu, langage, pédagogie, principes de l'éducation préscolaire, psychologie, relations familiales.– Liste des revues recommandées pour le préscolaire.
Localisation: OONL.

3617 Shanks, Doreen
Guide to bibliographies in education. [Winnipeg]: University of Manitoba, c1982. v, 144 p. (Monographs in education / University of Manitoba ; no. 7; ISSN: 0709-6313)
Note: 947 entries.– Bibliography of bibliographies covering all areas of study and research in education, covering the time period 1964 to 1980.– Excludes ERIC materials, general listings of theses and dissertations from individual institutions.
Location: OONL.

— 1983 —

3618 Cummins, Jim
Heritage language education: a literature review. Toronto: Ontario Ministry of Education, c1983. v, 59 p.; ISBN: 0-7743-8375-5.
Note: Approx. 100 entries.– Reviews available research regarding effects of incorporating the heritage languages of minority students into the regular school curriculum as either a subject or a medium of instruction.– Many Canadian references.
Location: OONL.

3619 Moll, Marita
Principals and vice-principals. Ottawa: Canadian Teachers' Federation, 1983. 138 p. (Bibliographies in education / Canadian Teachers' Federation ; no. 76); ISBN: 0-88989-148-6.
Note: 759 entries.– Covers 1978 to 1983.– Includes books, articles, theses relating to work of school principals and vice-principals.– Topics include collective bargaining, professional associations, remuneration, legal issues, school and community relations, selection, appointment, evaluation and contractual status, stress, teacher supervision and evaluation, women and minorities.
Previous edition: 1978. 49 p. (Bibliographies in education ; no. 65); ISBN: 0-88989-051-X.
Location: OONL.

3620 Narang, H.L.
Multicultural education: an annotated bibliography. Regina, Sask.: Multicultural Council of Saskatchewan, c1983. 28 p.
Note: Approx. 150 entries.– Books, journal articles, ERIC documents, doctoral dissertations, audiovisual materials.– Includes Canadian references.
Location: OONL.

3621 Répertoire de matériel éducatif en nutrition. [Montréal]: Conseil scolaire de l'île de Montréal, [1983]. 1 vol. (f. mobiles).
Note: Comprend études et recherches, projets et programmes éducatifs, publications.– Thèmes: alimentation à l'école, adolescence, croissance humaine, conditionnement physique, distribution de lait, enseignement de la nutrition, milieux socio-économiquement faibles, obésité, santé publique.– Exclut documents audiovisuels.– Inclut un nombre d'ouvrages canadiens.
Localisation: OONL.

— 1984 —

3622 Gauthier, Louis-Guy
CRAPE [Commission des Responsables de l'aide personnelle aux élèves] et documentation en bibliothèque: [bibliographie]. Montréal: Association des institutions d'enseignement secondaire, 1984. [29] f.
Note: Approx. 150 entrées.– Inclut des index, liste de périodiques, bibliographie.– Comprend un nombre considérable d'ouvrages canadiens.
Localisation: OONL.

3623 **Gilliss, Geraldine; Moll, Marita**
Teacher effectiveness research. Ottawa: Canadian Teachers' Federation, 1984. 2 vol. (Bibliographies in education / Canadian Teachers' Federation ; nos. 77, 78); ISBN: 0-88989-160-5 (no. 77); 0-88989-161-3 (no. 78).
Note: Part I: "General works": 292 entries.– Covers 1978 to early 1984.– Includes reviews, critiques and reports of studies on wide selection of variables, observational instruments.
Part II: "Special topics": 723 entries.– Covers from 1978 to 1984.– Deals with specific aspects of the topic such as instructional time, classroom management, mastery learning, nonverbal behaviour, use of questions, reinforcement, planning and structure.
Location: OONL.

3624 **Karal, Pearl**
Parenting education for the young: a literature survey. Toronto: Ontario Ministry of Education, 1984. vi, 70 p.; ISBN: 0-7743-9195-2.
Note: Approx. 75 entries.– Books and articles on family life education.– Includes Canadian references.
Location: OONL.

3625 **Knopp, Edith**
Bibliography of development education material produced by Canadian NGOs/Bibliographie du matériel sur l'éducation au développement produit par les ONG canadiennes. Hull, Quebec: Canadian International Development Agency, Public Participation Program, 1984. iii, 70 p.
Note: Location: OWA.

3626 **Lapkin, Sharon, et al.**
"Annotated list of French tests."
In: *Canadian Modern Language Review*; Vol. 41, no. 1 (October 1984) p. 93-109.; ISSN: 0008-4506.
Note: Supplement: " ... : 1991 update." *Canadian Modern Language Review*; Vol. 48, no. 4 (June 1992) p. 780-807.
Location: AEU.

3627 **Nouveau-Brunswick. Ministère de l'éducation**
Répertoire des publications relatives à 'organisation de l'enseignement public et aux programmes d'enseignement en langue française dans la province du Nouveau-Brunswick. Fredericton: Gouvernement du Nouveau-Brunswick, Ministère de l'éducation, 1980-1984. 5 vol.; ISSN: 0825-690X.
Note: Localisation: OONL.

3628 **Press, Marian; Adams, Susan**
The Ontario Textbook Collection catalogue, 1846-1970 [microform]. Toronto: R.W.B. Jackson Library, Ontario Institute for Studies in Education, c1984. 12 microfiches.
Note: Approx. 3,600 entries.– Contains listing of textbooks authorized for use in Ontario schools from 1846 to 1970, as well as answer keys, manuals, guides and workbooks published to accompany the textbooks.
Location: OONL.

3629 **Recueil de documents pédagogiques préparées pour les classes d'immersion française, 1982-1984.** Ottawa: Association canadienne des professeurs d'immersion: Canadian Association for Immersion Teachers, [1982-1984]. 2 vol.
Note: Texte en français et en anglais/text in English and French.
Location: OONL.

3630 **Rosenberg, Gertrude**
Distance education in the Canadian North: annotated bibliography. Ottawa: Association of Canadian Universities for Northern Studies, c1984. iv, [1], 28 l. (Occasional publication / Association of Canadian Universities for Northern Studies ; no. 12); ISBN: 0-9690987-7-4.
Note: Approx. 110 entries.– For the bibliography, Canadian North means northern areas of provinces bordering on the Northwest Territories and Yukon as well as areas north of 60; distance education involves separation of teacher and learner, influence of an educational organization, use of technical media to unite learner and teacher, provision of two-way communication, teaching of people as individuals.
Location: OONL.

— 1985 —

3631 **Anisef, Paul**
L'accessibilité à l'enseignement postsecondaire au Canada: recension des ouvrages. Ottawa: Direction générale de l'aide à l'éducation, Secrétariat d'État du Canada, c1985. x, 267 p.; ISBN: 0-662-93490-5.
Note: English title: *Accessibility to postsecondary education in Canada: a review of the literature.*
Localisation: OONL.

3632 **Anisef, Paul**
Accessibility to postsecondary education in Canada: a review of the literature. Ottawa: Education Support Branch, Department of the Secretary of State of Canada, 1985. x, 243 p.: ill.; ISBN: 0-662-14410-4.
Note: Titre en français: *L'accessibilité à l'enseignement postsecondaire au Canada: recension des ouvrages.*
Location: OONL.

3633 **Boyd, J.A.; Mollica, Anthony**
"Core French: a selected annotated resource list."
In: *Canadian Modern Language Review*; Vol. 42, no. 2 (November 1985) p. 408-439.; ISSN: 0008-4506.
Note: List of material suitable for supplementing Core French programs from kindergarten to senior levels of high school.
Location: AEU.

3634 **Breton, Lise; Roy, Jean-Luc**
L'enseignement privé au Québec: bibliographie annotée. Montréal: Centre d'animation, de développement et de recherche en éducation, 1985. 100 p.; ISBN: 2-89169-032-X.
Note: 401 entrées.– La période couverte est de 1960 à 1985.
Localisation: OONL.

3635 **Carter, John C.**
"Community museums and schools: an annotated bibliography of resource and reference materials."
In: *History and Social Science Teacher*; Vol. 21, no. 2 (December 1985) p. 89-93.; ISSN: 0316-4969.
Note: Approx. 100 entries.– Books, articles and teaching materials dealing with museum interpretation, field trips and other learning activities associated with museum collections.– Includes Canadian references.
Location: AEU.

3636 **Cole, Elizabeth B.; Mischook, Muriel**
"Survey and annotated bibliography of curricula used by oral preschool programs."
In: *Volta Review*; Vol. 87, no. 3 (April 1985) p. 139-154.; ISSN: 0042-8639.

Note: Literature review on education of hearing-impaired children in United States and Canada.– Focus on materials used for organizing intervention in areas of cognition, audition, language and speech.
Location: OONL.

3637 **Creating success with native Indian students: a bibliographic source book on instructional strategies for teachers.** [Victoria]: British Columbia Ministry of Education, Indian Education Branch, c1985. 45 p.
Note: References on teaching styles, learning styles, communicative styles, thinking skills, teacher-child interactional styles, value systems: an attempt to link main currents of thought in Indian education with mainstream educational philosophy.
Location: OONL.

3638 **Dessureault, Guy**
Recherche documentaire sur les professeurs du collégial. [Québec]: Gouvernement du Québec, Ministère de l'éducation, Direction de la recherche, 1981-1985. 3 vol.; ISBN: 2-550-04718-4 (vol. 1); 2-550-06197-7 (vol. 2); 2-550-07711-3 (vol. 3).
Note: Vol. 1: *Formation et perfectionnement.*– 86 entrées.
Vol. 2: *Caractéristiques professionnelles et socio-culturelles.*– 146 entrées.
Vol. 3: *Le professeur de collège, tel que souhaité et perçu.*– 231 entrées.
La période couverte est de 1967, année de la création des premiers cegeps, à juin 1980.
Localisation: OONL.

3639 **LeBlanc, André E.**
"Collegial education in Quebec: a bibliography."
In: *McGill Journal of Education*; Vol. 20, no. 3 (Fall 1985) p. 273-280.; ISSN: 0024-9033.
Note: Location: AEU.

3640 **MacLean, Margaret**
"Reading in a second-foreign language: a bibliography 1974-1984."
In: *Canadian Modern Language Review*; Vol. 42, no. 1 (October 1985) p. 56-66.; ISSN: 0008-4506.
Note: Articles and books dealing with issues related to second language reading, with emphasis on English as a second language and French as a second language.– Includes Canadian references.
Location: AEU.

3641 **Manitoba. Department of Education**
Curriculum implementation in Manitoba: literature review. Winnipeg: Manitoba Education, Planning and Research, 1985. 12 p.
Note: Location: OONL.

3642 **Mock, Karen R.**
"Multicultural early childhood education bibliography and resource list."
In: *Multicultural preschool education: a resource manual for supervisors and volunteers.* Toronto: Ontario Ministry of Citizenship and Culture, 1985. P. 83-96.; ISBN: 0-7729-1093-6.
Note: Location: OONL.

3643 **Moll, Marita**
Job sharing for teachers. Ottawa: Canadian Teachers' Federation, 1985. 30 p. (Bibliographies in education / Canadian Teachers' Federation ; no. 79); ISBN: 0-88989-180-X.
Note: 131 entries.– Covers 1976 to November 1985.–

Includes books and articles.
Location: OONL.

3644 **Paquerot, Sylvie**
Éducation des adultes et développement régional: une étude exploratoire de la littérature nord-américaine (Québec exclu). Québec: Gouvernement du Québec, Ministère de l'éducation, Direction des politiques et des plans, 1985. 38, 15, 24 p.; ISBN: 2-550-08428-4.
Note: Localisation: OONL.

3645 **Ramrattan, Annette; Kach, Nick**
"Native education in Alberta: a bibliography."
In: *Canadian Journal of Native Education*; Vol. 12, no. 2 (1985) p. 55-68.; ISSN: 0710-1481.
Note: List of books, articles, reports, briefs, theses dealing with education of native people in Alberta.
Location: AEU.

3646 **Rowat, Louise**
A list of publications in the Ottawa ACLD Library. Ottawa: Ottawa Association for Children with Learning Disabilities, 1985. 73 p.
Note: Location: OOCC.

— 1986 —

3647 **An annotated list of selected library materials for early French immersion and programme-cadre: kindergarten/ Liste annotée de matériel bibliographique pour les programmes d'immersion et programme-cadre: maternelle.** [Victoria, B.C.]: Modern Languages Services Branch, Ministry of Education, 1986. vi, 53 p.
Note: Approx. 150 entries.– List designed to provide a thematic approach to high quality print resources for kindergarten teachers.– Includes Canadian materials.– Text in English and French/texte en français et en anglais.
Location: OONL.

3648 **Beauchesne, André; Mercier, Diane**
Promouvoir l'éducation interculturelle et l'éducation internationale: guide analytique des ressources éducatives de langue française. Montréal: Conseil scolaire de l'île de Montréal, c1986. 2 vol.
Note: Documents canadiens et européens de langue française qui sont disponibles au Québec, titre relativement récents, généralement diffusés après 1975, concernant l'éducation interculturelle.
Localisation: OONL.

3649 **Beharry, Hamblin**
Native education in Alberta: a selective bibliography. [Edmonton]: Policy and Planning Branch, Alberta Native Affairs, 1986. 25 l.
Note: Approx. 200 entries.– Journal and newspaper articles, government publications pertaining to research on contemporary issues in native education in Alberta.
Location: AEU.

3650 **Bouthillette, Jean; Tardif-Robitaille, Louise**
Revue de littérature et bibliographie indexée sur la recherche-action chez les professeurs de niveau collégial. Sherbrooke: Université de Sherbrooke, [1986]. 1 vol. (en pagination multiple).
Note: Localisation: QRCN.

3651 **Calgary Board of Education. Media Services Group. Educational Media Team**
Une bibliothèque fondamentale d'une école d'immersion française: 7e – 9e années. [Calgary]: The Board, c1986. vi, 145 p.
Note: Approx. 1,000 entrées.– Inclut un nombre

considérable d'ouvrages canadiens.– Introduction in English.

Localisation: OONL.

3652 **Cram, Jennifer; Cooke, Stefan**
A bibliography on northern and native education. Montreal: Hochelaga Research Institute, 1986. 159 p.
Note: Approx. 1,300 entries.
Location: AEUB.

3653 **Davie, Lynn; Suessmuth, Patrick; Thomas, Alan M.**
A review of the literature and field validation of the competencies of industrial and organizational trainers and educators. Toronto: Ontario Ministry of Education, 1986. iv, 40 p. (Review and evaluation bulletins / Ontario Ministry of Education ; vol. 6, no. 2; ISSN: 0226-7306); ISBN: 0-7729-1549-0.
Note: 78 entries.– Includes Canadian references.
Location: OONL.

3654 **Finley, Jean C.; Goodwin, C. Ross**
The training and employment of northern Canadians: an annotated bibliography. Calgary: Published under the auspices of the Environmental Studies Revolving Funds by the Arctic Institute of North America, c1986. xx, 206 p. (Environmental Studies Revolving Funds report ; no. 050); ISBN: 0-920-783-49-X.
Note: 861 entries.– Period covered is 1970 to June 1986.– Monographs, journal articles, conference proceedings, theses, pamphlets, government, corporate and institute reports on training of northern Canadians (mainly Northwest Territories and Yukon) for wage employment, and on employment opportunities in the North.– Areas covered include vocational schools, on-the-job training, apprenticeships, adult and distance education, northern teacher training programs.– Excluded are references to childhood learning, elementary school system, special education, school administration, school finance.– Introduction en français.
Location: OONL.

3655 **Gagné, Oscar**
L'oeuvre pédagogique des Frères de l'instruction chrétienne dans la province de Québec, 1886-1986. La Prairie [Québec]: Frères de l'instruction chrétienne, 1986. xiv, 229 p. (Cahiers du Regroupement des archivistes religieux ; no 2); ISBN: 2-9800558-0-8.
Note: 1,316 entrées.
Édition antérieure: ... , 1886-1953: essai de bibliographie. Montréal: École de bibliothécaires; 1955. xxii, 203 f.
Localisation: OONL.

3656 **Gilliss, Geraldine; Moll, Marita**
Administration de tests et évaluation du rendement des élèves au Canada. Ottawa: Fédération canadienne des enseignantes et des enseignants, 1986. 28, 172 p. (Bibliographies en éducation / Fédération canadienne des enseignantes et des enseignants ; no 80); ISBN: 0-88989-181-8.
Note: 937 entrées.– Comprend les ouvrages parus au Canada entre 1976 et 1984.– Inclut livres, brochures, articles de périodiques, mémoires et thèses.– Texte en français et en anglais disposé tête bêche.– Titre de la p. de t. additionelle: Testing and evaluation of student achievement in Canada.
Localisation: OONL.

3657 **Gilliss, Geraldine; Moll, Marita**
Testing and evaluation of student achievement in Canada. Ottawa: Canadian Teachers' Federation, 1986. 172, 28 p. (Bibliographies in education / Canadian Teachers' Federation ; no. 80); ISBN: 0-88989-181-8.
Note: 937 entries.– Includes Canadian materials published between 1976 and 1984.– Principal topics include diagnostic testing, achievement scores, longitudinal evaluation of achievement, standardized tests, test administration and scoring, test interpretation, test results for various subjects.– Text in English and French with French text on inverted pages.– Title of additional title page: Administration de tests et évaluation du rendement des élèves au Canada.
Location: OONL.

3658 **Lamarre, Patricia**
Professional development of core French teachers: selective review of general literature on inservice education and specific literature on inservice education of second language teachers. Winnipeg: Canadian Association of Second Language Teachers, 1986. iii, 168 p.; ISBN: 0-921238-04-5.
Note: 54 entries.– Annotated listing of books and articles on the professional development of teachers.– Includes Canadian references.
Location: OONL.

3659 **Moore, Barbara G.**
Equity in education: gender issues in the use of computers: a review and bibliography. Toronto: Ontario Ministry of Education, 1986. i, 68 p. (Review and evaluation bulletins: Education and technology series ; vol. 6, no. 1; ISSN: 0226-7306); ISBN: 0-7729-1543-1.
Note: Approx. 150 entries.– Literature on gender issues in education which relate specifically to computers, research undertaken in Canada, United States, Great Britain, Australia.
Location: OONL.

3660 **O'Bryan, Kenneth G.**
Requirements for the training and certification of teachers in early primary education: a review of the literature. Toronto: Ontario Ministry of Education, 1986. iv, 48 p.; ISBN: 0-7729-1255-4.
Note: Approx. 75 entries.– Covers 1975 to 1986.– Includes an annotated bibliography (p. 30-46) of literature from Canada, the United States, Great Britain, Europe and Australia.– Focus on selection criteria, competencies, models of teacher education, in-service training and certification.
Location: OONL.

3661 **Pegis, Jessica; Gentles, Ian; De Veber, L.L.**
Sex education: a review of the literature from Canada, the United States, Britain and Sweden. Toronto: Human Life Research Institute of Ottawa, 1986. 42 p.; ISBN: 2-92045-310-4.
Note: Location: OHM.

3662 **Ray, Douglas; Franco, Beatriz**
"Human rights in education: recently published Canadian sources and an index."
In: Canadian Journal of Education; Vol. 11, no. 3 (Summer 1986) p. 364-382.; ISSN: 0380-2361.
Note: Alphabetical author listing of studies emphasizing Canadian themes related to human rights in education: children's rights, language, racism, special education,

religion, ethnicity.
Location: AEU.

— 1987 —

3663 **Ambroise, Antoine; De Billy, Marie-Claude**
Les politiques éducatives récentes au Québec: chronologie et bibliographie sélective annotée, 1977-1983. Québec: Université Laval, Département de science politique, 1987. iv, 127 p. (Cahiers du LABRAPS: Série études et documents ; vol. 2; ISSN: 0824-0736); ISBN: 2-89326-008-X.
Note: Localisation: OONL.

3664 **Association des universités et collèges du Canada**
Bibliographie choisie et annotée sur l'enseignement postsecondaire au Canada. [Ottawa]: Comité du Colloque national, [1987]. 35, 31 p.
Note: Approx. 40 entrées.– La période couverte va de 1970 à 1987.– Documents se rapportant aux régions et provinces et les documents concernant le Canada.– Établie pour le Colloque national sur l'enseignement postsecondaire.– Texte en français et en anglais disposé tête-bêche.– Titre de la p. de t. additionnelle: *Selected and annotated bibliography on post-secondary education in Canada.*
Localisation: OONL.

3665 **Association of Universities and Colleges of Canada**
Selected and annotated bibliography on post-secondary education in Canada. [Ottawa]: National Forum Committee, [1987]. 31, 35 p.
Note: Approx. 40 entries.– Covers from 1970 to 1987.– Lists documents relating to regions and provinces and to Canada as a whole.– Prepared for National Forum on Post-secondary Education.– Text in English and French with French text on inverted pages.– Title of additional title-page: *Bibliographie choisie et annotée sur l'enseignement postsecondaire au Canada.*
Location: OONL.

3666 **Bellamy, Patricia**
Graduate schools and financial aid: a guide to reference sources in the Robarts Library. 3rd ed. [Toronto]: University of Toronto Library, 1987. 52 p.
Note: 161 entries.– Lists directories of graduate-level programs, guides to financial aid, guides to proposal writing and related material.– Includes Canadian references.
Previous edition: Stevenson, Mary-Jo. *... : a guide to reference sources in the John P. Robarts Library.* 1981. 23 p.
Location: OONL.

3667 **Bujea, Eleanor**
Business education practices and trends: a literature review. Regina: University of Regina, Saskatchewan Instructional Development & Research Unit, 1987. 52 l. (SIDRU Research report / Saskatchewan Instructional Development & Research Unit ; no. 4; ISSN: 0835-6580); ISBN: 0-77310-110-1.
Note: 64 entries.– Reviews studies relating to practices and trends of business education in Canada, Great Britain and the United States.
Location: OONL.

3668 **Christensen, Ernest Martin**
Annotated bibliography of the college union. Ithaca, N.Y.: Association of College Unions-International, 1967-1987. 5 vol. (College unions at work)
Note: Includes some Canadian references.
Location: OONL.

3669 **Hart, Earl Paul**
Science for Saskatchewan schools: a review of research literature, analysis, and recommendations. Regina: University of Regina, Saskatchewan Instructional Development & Research Unit, 1987. ii l., 205 p.: ill. (SIDRU Research report / Saskatchewan Instructional Development & Research Unit ; no. 7; ISSN: 0835-6580); ISBN: 0-77310-125-X.
Note: Approx. 500 entries.– Books, chapters in books, articles, government studies and reports dealing with science education.– Topics include science curricula in Saskatchewan, teacher education, instructional strategies, evaluation, integration of science and other school subjects.
Location: OONL.

3670 **Hedges, Donna M.; Wong, Betty; Macdonald, R. Bruce**
Employment of the learning disabled: an annotated bibliography of resource materials for education and training. Vancouver: Vancouver Association for Children and Adults with Learning Disabilities, 1987. xi, 159 p.; ISBN: 0-9693284-0-0.
Note: 511 entries.– Field studies, model projects, books, journal articles, theses, video recordings from 1980s.– Employers, adults with learning disabilities (pre-employment/employment, life/social skills, academic/education); instructors/training personnel (program planners, counsellors, educators).– Includes Canadian references.
Location: OONL.

3671 **Institut de recherches politiques. Secrétariat du Colloque national**
Bibliographie des documents déposés au Colloque national. [Ottawa]: Le Secrétariat, [1987]. 24, 24 p.
Note: Approx. 100 entrées.– Prises de position, déclarations, recommandations, rapports, discours, articles, documents, ouvrages, matériaux descriptifs d'organismes et d'activités d'intérêt pour ceux et celles procédant à l'examen du secteur de l'enseignement postsecondaire.– Texte en français et en anglais disposé tête-bêche.– Titre de la p. de t. additionnelle: *Bibliography of documents displayed at the National Forum.*
Localisation: OONL.

3672 **Institute for Research on Public Policy. National Forum Secretariat**
Bibliography of documents displayed at the National Forum. [Ottawa]: The Secretariat, [1987]. 24, 24 p.
Note: Approx. 100 entries.– Position papers, statements, recommendations, reports, speeches, articles, papers, books, descriptive material on organizations and activities of interest to those examining the post-secondary education sector.– Text in English and French with French text on inverted pages.– Title of additional title-page: *Bibliographie des documents déposés au Colloque national.*
Location: OONL.

3673 **Krawczyk, Andrew, et al.**
"Multicultural education bibliographies for elementary schools, secondary schools, and teachers."
In: *Multiculturalism;* Vol. 10, nos. 2-3 (1986-1987)
Note: Three bibliographies prepared for the Canadian Teachers' Federation: "Bibliography for elementary schools." p. 3-21; "Bibliography for secondary schools." p. 22-30; "Bibliography of teacher reference." p. 31-48.–

Topics covered include art forms, ethnic groups, language, religion, literature, education, ethnic and race relations, bibliographies.
Location: OONL.

3674 Melenchuk, Allan Samuel
Cultural literacy in education: a literature review. Regina: University of Regina, Saskatchewan Instructional Development & Research Unit, 1987. v l., 232 p.: ill. (SIDRU Research report / Saskatchewan Instructional Development & Research Unit ; no. 2; ISSN: 0835-6580); ISBN: 0-77310-108-X.
Note: 450 entries.– Review of books and articles dealing with ethnic/cultural literacy and the curriculum, multicultural education, the impact of culture on education, interaction of teachers and minority group students, interethnic contact and attitudes.– Includes Canadian references.
Location: OONL.

3675 Moll, Marita
Health and safety hazards in the school environment. Ottawa: Canadian Teachers' Federation, 1987. 247 p. (Bibliographies in education / Canadian Teachers' Federation ; no. 81); ISBN: 0-88989-196-6.
Note: 913 entries.– Lists materials on potential hazards to physical health and safety of teachers and students in school environment: acoustical, art materials, asbestos, communicable diseases, furniture, industrial arts shops, physical education, science labs, video display terminals.
Location: OONL.

3676 Ontario. Ministry of Citizenship. Citizenship Development Branch
Holdings on early childhood education: English as a second language and related topics. Toronto: The Ministry, 1987. 46 p.; ISBN: 0-7729-2921-1.
Note: Approx. 225 entries.– Includes professional literature, children's literature, audio-visual materials.– Designed for use by teachers and volunteers in pre-school ESL programs.– Includes Canadian references.
Location: OONL.

3677 Parkin, Michael; Morrison, Frances C.; Watkin, Gwyneth
French immersion research relevant to decisions in Ontario. Toronto: Ontario Ministry of Education, c1987. 181 p.
Note: Location: OONL.

— 1988 —

3678 Alberta. Language Services Branch
English as a second language: a selective bibliography of supplementary learning resources. Edmonton: Alberta Education, Language Services Branch, 1988. v, 34 p.; ISBN: 0-7732-0072-X.
Note: Annotated listing of mainly Canadian resources (with imprint 1980-) selected to support English as a second language instruction in Alberta schools.– Includes resources for teacher and student use, elementary through secondary levels.
Location: OONL.

3679 Andersen, Lorrie
"Resources on AIDS: the acquisition of instructional materials for schools."
In: School Libraries in Canada; Vol. 8, no. 2 (Winter 1988) p. 25-28.; ISSN: 0227-3780.
Note: Describes process of selecting AIDS resources and annotates selected Canadian and United States video and print materials.
Location: AEU.

3680 Blouin, Pierre, et al.
L'Institut canadien d'éducation des adultes et les communications, 1956-1987: bibliographie analytique. Sainte-Foy: Réseau québécois d'information sur la communication, c1988. 41 p.; ISBN: 2-921026-00-7.
Note: 87 entrées.
Localisation: OONL.

3681 Chartier, Jean-Pierre
Des difficultés d'apprentissage en milieu collégial: bibliographie. Shawinigan: Collège de Shawinigan, 1988. 142 p. (Collection: Repérer et aider des étudiants en difficulté d'apprentissage ; 2); ISBN: 2-9801095-1-7.
Note: Approx. 800 entrées.– Références sur les sections: "Concepts," "Manifestations et causes," "Instrumentation," "Interventions."- Inclut un nombre d'ouvrages canadiens.
Localisation: OONL.

3682 Confederation College. Native Programs Department
The native learner and distance education: annotated bibliography. Thunder Bay, Ont.: Confederation College, Native Programs Department, 1988. 43 l.
Note: Part of a project designed to encourage the participation of native peoples in planning and implementing distance education for native communities in northwestern Ontario.– Topics include community involvement/self-determination, learning styles/teaching strategies, distance education/use of technology, existing programs.
Location: AEUB.

3683 Deyell, Suzanne M.
Literacy: a selected bibliography. Calgary: Educational Media Team, Professional Resource Centre, Instructional Programs Department, Calgary Board of Education, 1988. 40 p. (Professional Resource Centre bibliography / Calgary Board of Education ; no. 35)
Note: Approx. 300 entries.– Books, periodical articles, ERIC microfiche documents dealing with literacy.– Topics include education and literacy, psychological aspects of the brain and literacy, language acquisition, reading, written language, adult literacy.– Includes Canadian references.
Location: OONL.

3684 Duguid, Stephen; Fowler, Terry A.
Of books and bars: an annotated bibliography on prison education. Burnaby, B.C.: Institute for the Humanities, Simon Fraser University, 1988. 138 p.; ISBN: 0-86491-064-9.
Note: Approx. 650 entries.– Studies, conference papers, journal articles on Canadian prison education, British prison education, literacy, vocational education, history of correctional education, moral development and education, recidivism and education, rehabilitation and education, women's programs, young offenders and juveniles.
Location: OONL.

3685 Ewing, Guy; Olson, David R.
The nature of literacy: a bibliography. Rev. ed. Toronto: McLuhan Program in Culture and Technology, University of Toronto, c1988. 74 p. (Working paper / McLuhan Program in Culture and Technology, University of

Toronto ; no. 14); ISBN: 0-77275-915-4.
Note: 223 entries.– Includes some Canadian references.
Previous edition: *The nature of literacy bibliography: thematic view: literacy and its technologies.*– 25 entries. 1986. 9 l.
Location: OONL.

3686 **Foley, Kathryn Shred; Harley, Birgit; D'Anglejan, Alison**
"Research in Core French: a bibliographic review."
In: *Canadian Modern Language Review*; Vol. 44, no. 4 (May 1988) p. 593-618.; ISSN: 0008-4506.
Note: Approx. 100 entries.– Research reports from school boards, reports of government-funded research, theses, books and journal articles.– The majority of the studies included involve research conducted in Canada.– Topics include program characteristics and outcomes, program supplements, student characteristics, factors affecting enrolment, teacher characteristics, opinion surveys of Core French programs, program implementation and administration, development and validation of tests and materials.
Location: OONL.

3687 **Landry, Francine**
Bibliographie des documents québécois sur la reconnaissance des acquis extrascolaires. Montréal: Fédération des cégeps, 1988. 45 p. (Fonds et réflexions / Fédération des cégeps ; 15); ISBN: 2-89100-048-X.
Note: Approx. 300 entrées.– Textes inédits, articles de périodiques et de journaux, rapports et documents divers diffusés au Québec depuis 1980.
Localisation: OONL.

3688 **Landry, Francine**
Revue de littérature sur le rôle des activités d'apprentissage dans l'enseignement à distance. Montréal: Télé-université, Direction de la recherche et des études avancées, 1988. 47 p. (Notes de recherche / Direction de la recherche et des études avancées, Université du Québec); ISBN: 2-76240-078-3.
Note: Approx. 40 entrées.– Inclut un nombre d'ouvrages canadiens en français et en anglais.
Localisation: OONL.

3689 **L'Institut canadien d'éducation des adultes et les communications, 1956-1987: bibliographie analytique.**
Sainte-Foy, Québec: Réseau québécois d'information sur la communication, c1988. 41 p.; ISBN: 2-921026-00-7.
Note: 87 entrées.– Regroupe des documents relatif aux communications produits par l'ICEA: mémoires, rapports de recherche, documents de travail, actes de colloque, numéros spéciaux de périodique: politique et réglementation de la communication, radiodiffusion et télédistribution, éducation et médias, médias parallèles, communication et informatisation, propriété et concentration des médias, médias écrits et électroniques.– Analyse et indexation: Pierre Blouin, et al.
Localisation: OONL.

3690 **Logiciels éducatifs québécois.** 3e éd. Montréal: Services documentaires multimedia, 1988. 146 p. (DSI/CB ; no 74; ISSN: 0825-5024); ISBN: 2-89059-346-0.
Note: 598 entrées.– Logiciels pédagogiques produits ou distribués par une centaine d'entreprises québécoises.– Comprend un index des titres, sujets, marques d'ordinateurs et systèmes d'exploitation, index des fournisseurs.

Éditions antérieures:
1987. 121 p.; ISBN: 2-89059-293-6.
1986. [253] p.; ISBN: 2-89059-274-X.
Localisation: OONL.

3691 **Olivier, Réjean**
Le Collège de l'Assomption et son rayonnement dans les écrits et les éditions de Réjean Olivier, bibliothécaire. Joliette, Québec: [s.n.], 1988. 30 f.: ill. (Collection Oeuvres bibliophiliques de Lanaudière ; no 17); ISBN: 2-920904-20-5.
Note: 64 entrées.– Publications en histoire, en patrimoine, en pédagogie, des biographies, des bibliographies ou des catalogues d'expositions.
Localisation: OONL.

3692 **Répertoire de documents relatifs aux mesures d'accueil et de francisation, au P.E.L.O. et l'éducation interculturelle: préscolaire, primaire, secondaire.** Québec: Gouvernement du Québec, Services aux communautés culturelles, 1988. 50, [2] p.; ISBN: 2-550-14451-1.
Note: Localisation: OONL.

3693 **Service de diffusion sélective de l'information de la Centrale des bibliothèques**
L'enseignement du français au Québec. Montréal: Le Service, 1988. 27 p. (DSI/CB ; no 116; ISSN: 0825-5024); ISBN: 2-89059-323-1.
Note: 202 entrées.– Monographies, articles de périodiques, documents audiovisuels.
Localisation: OONL.

3694 **Service de diffusion sélective de l'information de la Centrale des bibliothèques**
L'informatique et l'éducation: documents répertoriés dans ÉDUQ. Montréal: Le Service, 1988. 56 p. (DSI/CB ; no 108; ISSN: 0825-5024); ISBN: 2-89059-313-4.
Note: 267 entrées.– Documents québécois qui concernant l'informatique et son utilisation dans le contexte de la pédagogie et de l'administration scolaire.
Localisation: OONL.

3695 **Université Laval. Bibliothèque**
Catalogue des manuels scolaires québécois. 2e éd. Québec: Bibliothèque de l'Université Laval, [1988]. 2 vol.; ISBN: 2-920310-20-8.
Note: 4,694 entrées.– Comprend: "... tous les manuels scolaires québécois utilisés dans les institutions d'enseignement primaire et secondaire durant deux siècles, soit depuis les débuts de l'imprimerie au Québec, 1764, jusqu'à la creation du Ministère de l'éducation, en 1964."
Édition antérieure: 1983. [612] f. (f. multiple).– Approx. 2,300 entrées.
Localisation: OONL.

3696 **Vechter, Andrea**
Le maintien de l'acquis en langue seconde: bibliographie analytique. Ottawa: Commissariat aux langues officielles, 1988. ii, 91 p.
Note: 70 entrées.– Quelques références canadiennes.
English title: *Second-language retention: an annotated bibliography.*
Localisation: OONL.

3697 **Vechter, Andrea**
Second-language retention: an annotated bibliography. Ottawa: Office of the Commissioner of Official Languages, 1988. ii, 78 p.

Note: 70 entries.– Includes Canadian references.
Titre en français: *Le maintien de l'acquis en langue seconde: bibliographie analytique.*
Location: OONL.

— 1989 —

3698 **Alberta Education Response Centre**
Parent resources inventory. Edmonton: Alberta Education Response Centre, [1989]. 82 p. (in various pagings).; ISBN: 0-7732-0252-8.
Note: Approx. 500 entries.– Annotated list of articles related to child development and parenting.– Topics include child abuse, adoption, stress in children, developmental skills and training, moral and social development, parenting skills, safety/health issues, television/advertising and children.– Includes Canadian references.
Location: OONL.

3699 **Bibliographie pour les services de garde en milieu scolaire.** Québec: Gouvernement du Québec, Ministère de l'éducation, 1989. 36 p.; ISBN: 2-550-14751-0.
Note: Approx. 250 entrées.– Monographies et documents audiovisuels, dans la majorité des cas, de références québécoises.
Localisation: OONL.

3700 **Canadian School Trustees' Association**
Scholastic adaptation and cost effectiveness of programs for immigrant-refugee children in Canadian schools: [report and literature review]. [Ottawa]: Canadian School Trustees' Association, 1989. x l., 83, 33 p.; ISBN: 0-920632-229-7.
Note: Section 2 is a review of the literature and a bibliography on the education and integration of ethnic minorities: cognitive and cultural issues in bilingual education, types of programs.– Many Canadian references.
Location: OONL.

3701 **Duncan, Barry**
"Media literacy bibliography."
In: *History and Social Science Teacher*; Vol. 24, no. 4 (Summer 1989) p. 210-215.; ISSN: 0316-4969.
Note: Lists works on media education methodology, mass media, television, film, print media, advertising, gender and the media, popular culture, music videos.– List of periodicals in the field.– Emphasis on Canadian materials.
Location: AEU.

3702 **Finley, E. Gault**
Education in Canada: a bibliography/L'éducation au Canada: une bibliographie. Toronto: Published by Dundurn Press in cooperation with the National Library of Canada and the Canadian Government Pub. Centre, 1989. 2 vol.; ISBN: 1-55002-044-7 (vol. 1); 1-55002-047-1 (vol. 2).
Note: Approx. 14,000 entries.– Covers development of Canadian education from seventeenth century to early 1980s.– Includes a selection of secondary sources, published and unpublished: books, theses, reports, research studies, government documents.– Excludes periodical articles, briefs to commissions, courses of study, curriculum guides, directories, almanacs, educational statutes and regulations, newsletters, audio-visual materials, textbooks, tests and examinations, yearbooks, annual reports.– Education is broadly defined to include the formal system from pre-primary through post-

secondary levels, both academic and technical/vocational streams, as well as the informal system, adult education, etc.– Also available on diskettes and magnetic tape.– Text in English and French/texte en français et en anglais.– Bilingual works appear in both languages as separate entries.
Location: OONL.

3703 **Manitoba. Manitoba Education. Library**
AIDS 1989: a bibliography of resources available from Manitoba Education Library. [Winnipeg]: Instructional Resources, Manitoba Education, 1989. 18 p.; ISBN: 0-7711-0804-4.
Note: Includes books, audio-visual materials, periodical articles.– Intended as selective list of curriculum support materials for AIDS education in Manitoba.– Detailed annotations.– Includes Canadian references.
Location: OONL.

3704 **Steep, Barbara J.**
Drug education resources directory. Toronto: Addiction Research Foundation, c1989. 5 parts; ISBN: 0-88868-171-2 (set).
Note: Part 1. *Primary resources, kindergarten to grade 3.* vii, 47 p.; ISBN: 0-88868-170-2.
Part 2. *Junior resources, grades 4-6.* vii, 70 p.; ISBN: 0-88868-173-9.
Part 3. *Intermediate resources, grades 7-10.* vii, 110 p.; ISBN: 0-88868-174-7.
Part 4. *Senior resources, grades 11-13.* vii, 88 p.; ISBN: 0-88868-175-5.
Part 5. *Recommended films and videotapes.* vii, 146 p.; ISBN: 0-88868-176-3.
Includes pamphlets, curricula, teaching kits, reference materials for educators: print and audio-visual materials to be used for teaching children and adolescents about drugs (including alcohol and tobacco) and lifestyle choices.– Emphasis on Canadian materials.
Titre en français: *Répertoire des ressources éducatives sur les drogues: maternelle à fin du secondaire.*
Location: OONL.

3705 **Steep, Barbara J.**
Répertoire des ressources éducatives sur les drogues: maternelle à fin du secondaire. Toronto: Fondation de la recherche sur la toxicomanie, c1989. xii, 63 p.; ISBN: 0-88868-171-1.
Note: Approx. 60 entrées.– Inclut brochures, programmes d'études, films et vidéo, ressources destinées aux enseignants.
English title: *Drug education resources directory.*
Localisation: OONL.

3706 **Zuckernick, Arlene**
L'enseignement ouvert et la formation à distance au Canada. [Ottawa]: Secrétariat d'État du Canada, c1989. 51, 46 p. (Guides pédagogiques des études canadiennes); ISBN: 0-662-57210-6.
Note: Bref aperçu historique, principaux ouvrages canadiens.– Texte en français et en anglais disposé tête-bêche.– Titre de la p. de t. additionnelle: *Open learning and distance education in Canada.*
Localisation: OONL.

3707 **Zuckernick, Arlene**
Open learning and distance education in Canada. Ottawa: Canadian Studies Directorate, Department of the Secretary of State of Canada, c1989. 46, 51 p. (Canadian

studies resource guides); ISBN: 0-662-57210-6.
Note: Historical overview of the subject, list of key Canadian works.– Text in English and French with French text on inverted pages.– Title of additional title-page: *L'enseignement ouvert et la formation à distance au Canada.*
Location: OONL.

— 1990 —

3708 **Alberta Education. Planning and Policy Secretariat**
Educational quality indicators: annotated bibliography. 2nd ed. Edmonton: Planning and Policy Secretariat, Alberta Education, 1990. vi, 107 p.; ISBN: 0-7732-0299-4.
Note: Approx. 230 entries.– Studies relating to indicator systems (local, provincial, national, international), interpretative framework (accountability, educational finance, educational reform and improvement, school administrative effectiveness), outcomes (cognitive testing and achievement, issues, outcomes-results of education, standards).– Author-institution index.– Many Canadian references.
Supplement: ... . *Supplement to the second edition.*1990. vi, 56 p.; ISBN: 0-7732-0444-X.
Location: OONL.

3709 **"Bibliography of Canadian educational history/ Bibliographie d'histoire de l'éducation canadienne."**
In: *Historical Studies in Education*; Vol. 2, no. 1 (Spring 1990) p. 189-195.; ISSN: 0843-5057.
Note: Listing of books, journal articles, theses and essays in monographs.– Continues work begun in *CHEA Bulletin*, Vol. 4, no. 1 (March 1987) p. 45-50; Vol. 4, no. 3 (October 1987) p. 46-51.
Location: OLU.

3710 **Braun, Connie**
Bibliography of rural education in Canada. Brandon: WESTARC Group, [1990]. 61 p.
Note: Location: OONL.

3711 **Butler, Phyllis; Harris, Aphrodite**
English as a second language bibliography: the holdings of the King Edward Campus Library, Vancouver Community College. Vancouver: Vancouver Community College Press, c1990. v, 63 p.; ISBN: 0-921218-29-X.
Note: References arranged in broad subject areas: conversation and communication, listening comprehension, grammar, pronunciation, readers, literacy and language, writing, vocabulary, testing and study skills, audiovisual materials and computer software.– Some Canadian material.
Location: OONL.

3712 **Cumming, Alister**
"An annotated bibliography of Canadian ESL materials."
In: *TESL Canada Journal*; Special Issue 2 (June 1990) p. 1-64.; ISSN: 0826-435X.
Note: Listing of Canadian materials intended for classroom or independent study by English as a second language students, school-age ESL students, and materials for teacher reference to ESL curriculum and instruction, for professional development or applied research.
Location: OONL.

3713 **Dandurand, Pierre**
Les grandes orientations de la recherche en sociologie de l'éducation au Québec: un bilan bibliographique. Sainte-Foy, Québec: Université Laval, Laboratoire de recherche en administration et politique scolaires, 1990. vi, 154 p. (Cahiers du LABRAPS: Série études et documents ; 6; ISSN: 0824-0736); ISBN: 2-89326-015-2.
Note: Approx. 450 entrées.– Thèmes traités: éducation et emploi, organisation, socialisation et apprentissage, profession d'enseignant, accès différentiel des groupes sociaux à l'enseignement.
Localisation: OONL.

3714 **Dion, Judith**
Alphabétisation: répertoire 1975-1989. Ottawa: Réseau national d'action éducation femmes, [1990]. 55 p.; ISBN: 0-9693724-5-0.
Note: Approx. 350 entrées.– La majorité des documents répertoriés ont été publiés au Canada.– Trois sections: didactique, générale, vidéo.
Localisation: OONL.

3715 **Draper, James A.**
Writings relating to literacy: done at the Ontario Institute for Studies in Education. Toronto: OISE, 1990. xi, 31 p.
Note: Approx. 350 entries.– Publications by OISE faculty and research officers relating to literacy or basic education, student theses completed at OISE on literacy, list of graduates from OISE who have published materials on literacy.
Location: OONL.

3716 **Horsman, Jennifer**
Facilitating literacy: an introductory guide to readings on study circles and group process. Toronto: Toronto Board of Education, Continuing Education Department, Adult Basis Education Unit, [1990]. 21 p.; ISBN: 1-895282-06-3.
Note: Annotated resource list pertaining to concept of study circles for literacy facilitators.– Includes some Canadian references.
Location: OONL.

3717 **Manégre, Jean-François; Blouin, Louise**
Le rendement scolaire des élèves des communautés culturelles: bibliographie commentée. Montréal: Conseil des communautés culturelles et de l'immigration, 1990. 29 p.; ISBN: 2-550-20816-1.
Note: Approx. 100 entrées.– Description sommaire de chacune des onze études réalisées au Québec qui ont abordé la question du rendement scolaire selon la langue maternelle, et une bibliographie sur la question de l'intégration et de les enfants immigrants à l'école.
Localisation: OONL.

3718 **Ouellet, Micheline**
Synthèse historique de l'immersion française au Canada suivie d'une bibliographie sélective et analytique. Québec: Centre international de recherche sur l'aménagement linguistique, 1990. vii, 261 p. (Publication / Centre international de recherche sur l'aménagement linguistique ; B-175); ISBN: 2-89219-212-9.
Note: 409 entrées.– Ouvrages sur différents aspects de l'enseignement immersif: études linguistique, didactique, pédagogique, psychologique, social, politique et administratif traitent des multiples facettes de l'immersion.– Inclut une liste des rapports d'évaluation des provinces canadiennes.
Localisation: OONL.

3719 **Réginald Grigoire Inc.**
Les facteurs qui façonnent une bonne école: rapport d'une recherche bibliographique sélective et analytique. Québec: Ministère de l'éducation, Direction générale de

la recherche et du développement, 1990. 78 p.; ISBN: 2-550-15122-4.
Note: Localisation: OONL.

3720 **Valentini, Frances**
"Literacy titles."
In: *Canadian Library Journal*; Vol. 47, no. 3 (June 1990) p. 183-189.; ISSN: 0008-4352.
Note: Location: AEU.

3721 **Van Walleghem, Jean**
Multicultural educational resources: an annotated bibliography. [Winnipeg]: Multiculture Educational Resource Centre, 1990. vi, 18 p.; ISBN: 0-7711-0936-9.
Note: Approx. 150 entries.– Selective list of materials dealing specifically with multicultural education: professional development, resources guides, teaching strategies and activities, supplementary resources, periodicals.– Includes Canadian references.
Location: OONL.

— 1991 —

3722 **Duesterbeck, Florence; Veeman, Nayda**
Literacy materials produced in Saskatchewan: a bibliography. Saskatoon: Saskatchewan Literacy Network, 1991. 16 p.; ISBN: 0-919059-58-9.
Note: 32 entries.
Location: OONL.

3723 **Manitoba. Manitoba Education and Training**
Outdoor education resource catalogue. Winnipeg: Manitoba Education and Training, 1991. v, 95 p.; ISBN: 0-7711-1003-0.
Note: Approx. 700 entries.– Publications, books and audio visual resources produced by federal and provincial departments, and private organizations in Canada.
Location: OONL.

3724 **Memorial University of Newfoundland. Learning Resources Council**
Cooperative planning and teaching: annotated bibliography. St. John's, Nfld.: Learning Resources Council, Memorial University of Newfoundland, 1991. 5 p.
Note: 45 entries.– Reports and articles on cooperative planning and teaching involving teachers and teacher-librarians.– Includes Canadian references.
Location: OONL.

3725 **A Provincial bibliography of literacy learning materials, curricula and reference documents.**
Vancouver: Literacy BC, 1991. 25 p.; ISBN: 0-9695709-0-2.
Note: Listing of instructional material, research reports, books for adult learners, periodicals and newsletters, non-print media, work in progress.– Address list of agencies and publishers.– Prepared by Literacy BC with the assistance of the National Literacy Secretariat, the Department of Multiculturalism and Citizenship Canada.
Location: OONL.

— 1992 —

3726 **Burge, Elizabeth J.**
Computer mediated communication and education: a selected bibliography. Toronto: Distance Learning Office, Ontario Institute for Studies in Education, 1992. i, 87 p.
Note: Approx. 400 entries.– Books, articles and conference papers.– Topics include research and evaluation, distance mode institutions, teacher-related networks, participant/learner perspectives, tutor/moderator perspectives, messaging, tools and

techniques, group work and decision making, impact of CMC for specific communities.
Location: OONL.

3727 **Direction générale de la main-d'oeuvre féminine du Manitoba**
Matériel pédagogique sur la prévention de la violence utilisé dans les écoles: guide national. Winnipeg: Direction générale de la main-d'oeuvre féminine du Manitoba, 1992. 63, 59 p.
Note: Approx. 250 entrées.– Comprend documents pédagogiques et matériel complémentaire (publications, livres destinés aux enseignants).– Texte en français et en anglais disposé tête-bêche.– Titre de la p. de t. additionnelle: *Violence prevention materials in the schools: a national listing.*
Localisation: OONL.

3728 **Giles, Valerie M.E.**
Annotated bibliography of education history in British Columbia. Victoria: Royal British Columbia Museum, c1992. iii, 65 p. (Royal British Columbia Museum technical reports); ISBN: 0-7718-9188-1.
Note: Arrangement is by sections of books, theses, articles, subdivided chronologically, with an author index.
Location: OONL.

3729 **Manitoba. Instructional Resources Branch. Library**
Anti-racist education: kindergarten to senior 4: a bibliography of resources available from the Library, Instructional Resources Branch. Winnipeg: The Library, 1992. 7 p.
Note: Approx. 100 entries.– Books, reports and articles dealing with race relations and multicultural education.– Includes a number of Canadian references.
Location: OONL.

3730 **Manitoba Women's Directorate**
Violence prevention materials in the schools: a national listing. Winnipeg: Manitoba Women's Directorate, 1992. 59, 63 p.
Note: Approx. 250 entries.– Includes classroom materials and supplemental materials for teachers in English and French.– Emphasis on Canadian publications and audio-visual materials.– Text in English and French with French text on inverted pages.– Title of additional title-page: *Matériel pédagogique sur la prévention de la violence utilisé dans les écoles: guide national.*
Location: OONL.

— 1993 —

3731 **Weinrib, Alice**
"What's new in second-language teaching: a selected annotated bibliography."
In: *Canadian Modern Language Review*; Vol. 38, no. 1 (Autumn 1981) p. 111-114; vol. 39, no. 1 (October 1982) p. 90-103; vol. 40, no. 1 (October 1983) p. 94-104; vol. 41, no. 1 (October 1984) p. 79-92; vol. 42, no. 1 (October 1985) p. 93-102; vol. 43, no. 1 (October 1986) p. 117-122; vol. 44, no. 2 (January 1988) p. 361-365; vol. 45, no. 1 (October 1988) p. 155-160; vol. 46, no. 2 (January 1990) p. 365-371; vol. 47, no. 2 (January 1991) p. 351-357; vol. 48, no. 3 (April 1992) p. 602-609; vol. 49, no. 3 (April 1993) p. 589-594.; ISSN: 0008-4506.
Note: Includes professional books and reports as well as curriculum materials.
Title varies: "Recent Canadian publications in second

language teaching;" "Second language teaching in Canada: a review of recent publications;" "ESL/FSL: a review of recent publications;" "Canadian ESL and FSL publications in review;" "Recent publications for second language teachers;" "New Canadian ESL and FSL materials in second language pedagogy."
Location: AEU.

— Ongoing/En cours —

3732 **Association des institutions d'enseignement. Commission des bibliothécaires**
Répertoire de documents pédagogiques produits dans les établissements-membres de l'A.I.E.S. Montréal: Association des institutions d'enseignement secondaire, 1982-. vol. (f. mobiles).
Note: Localisation: OONL.

3733 **Directory of education studies in Canada/Annuaire d'études en éducation au Canada.** Toronto: Canadian Education Association, 1969-. vol.; ISSN: 0070-5454.
Note: Annual.– Lists education studies and theses completed by graduate students and staff in Canadian university faculties of education, provincial departments or ministries of education, school boards, teachers' associations, and other associations and institutions involved in education.– Arranged by subject, with author index.– Text in English and French/texte en français et en anglais.
Successor to: *Education studies completed in Canadian universities.* 1967-1968.; ISSN: 0424-5652.
Location: OONL.

3734 **Educational Research Institute of British Columbia**
Reports list [Educational Research Institute of British Columbia]. [Vancouver]: Educational Research Institute of British Columbia, 1976-. vol.; ISSN: 0706-9944.
Note: Annual.– New reports listed in *Edge*, the bi-monthly newsletter of ERIBC.– Includes reports based on studies funded by ERIBC, conducted by the Institute, or reports presented at conferences by ERIBC research associates.– Research topics include administration, computer-assisted instruction, enrichment, teaching methodology, industrial education, native Indian education, student attitudes and achievement.
Location: OONL.

3735 **ÉDUQ: bibliographie analytique sur l'éducation au Québec.** [Québec]: Gouvernement du Québec, Ministère de l'éducation, Direction de la recherche, [1981]-. vol.; ISSN: 0712-4635.
Note: La version imprimée est semestrielle: un numéro au printemps, l'autre à l'automne.– Ces documents se regroupent en neuf catégories: les documents de recherche proprement dits; les documents de développement pédagogique; les documents statistiques, les bibliographies; les répertoires ou inventaires méthodiques; les actes de colloques, de symposiums, etc.; les rapports de commissions, de comités, etc., les enonces de politiques (inclut les livres verts et blancs, les discours officiels); les avis présentés par les conseils consultatifs sur les questions d'éducation.– ÉDUQ englobe tous les documents, rédigés en français ou en anglais, produits au Québec ou qui, s'il proviennent de l'extérieur, concernant l'éducation au Québec.
Localisation: OONL.

3736 **Répertoire annoté des publications des commissions scolaires: documents pédagogiques et administratifs/ Annotated catalogue of school board publications: pedagogical and administrative documents.** Montréal: Conseil scolaire de l'île de Montréal, 1980-. vol.; ISSN: 0823-273X.
Note: Annuel.– Répertoire se divise en six parties: niveaux préscolaire et primaire, niveau secondaire, études administratives, documents en voie de réalisation, études du C.S.I.M., recherches financées par le C.S.I.M.– Texte en français et en anglais/text in English and French.
Localisation: OONL.

Women's Studies

Études sur la condition féminine

— 1965 —

3737 **Wigney, Trevor John**
Education of women and girls in a changing society: a selected bibliography with annotations. [Toronto]: Department of Educational Research, University of Toronto, 1965. v, 76 p. (Educational research series / Department of Educational Research, University of Toronto ; no. 36)
Note: 240 entries.– Lists books, journal articles, conference reports, theses, bibliographies, periodicals.– Topics covered include women's education in relation to role in society, women and work, recruitment and training of women in various occupations, vocational guidance and training, co-education, women college students and continuing education.
Location: OONL.

— 1972 —

3738 **Bayefsky, Evelyn**
"Women and work: a selection of books and articles."
In: *Ontario Library Review*; Vol. 56, no. 2 (June 1972) p. 79-90.; ISSN: 0030-2996.
Note: Books, pamphlets, and articles.– Section on women in librarianship.– Includes a list of additional bibliographies.
Location: OONL.

3739 **McEwen, Ruth**
"Bibliography on women in Canada: non-fiction."
In: *Canadian Newsletter of Research on Women*; Vol. 1, no. 2 (October 1972) p. 42-45.; ISSN: 0319-4477.
Note: Location: AEU.

3740 **Saskatchewan Provincial Library. Bibliographic Services Division**
Women: a selected bibliography. Regina: Bibliographic Services Division, Provincial Library, 1972. 52 p.
Note: Approx. 600 entries.– Books, pamphlets, articles on status of women (rights, liberation movement), history of women's rights, family planning, birth control, marriage, education, employment.– Includes a list of journals and periodicals about women.
Location: OONL.

— 1973 —

3741 **Eichler, Margrit**
An annotated selected bibliography of bibliographies on women. Ottawa: Association of Universities and Colleges of Canada, Committee on the Status of Women, c1973. 17 p.
Note: 41 entries.– Excludes bibliographies not readily available for purchase and those of less than 15 pages long.
Location: OONL.

3742 **Harrison, Cynthia Ellen**
Women's movement media: a source guide. New York: Bowker, c1973. x, 269 p.; ISBN: 0-8352-0711-0.
Note: A compendium of sources of information, U.S. and Canada.– Includes books and print media, children's books, films, mixed media, posters, records and audiotapes, video recordings, periodicals; directory of organizations and agencies.
Location: OONL.

— 1974 —

3743 **Armstrong, Douglas; Dworaczek, Marian**
Women: a bibliography of materials held in the Research Library. [Toronto]: Ontario Ministry of Labour, Research Library, 1974. 81 p.
Note: Approx. 1,000 entries.– Books, journal articles, government publications on women and work, women's rights in employment, feminism, social condition of women, women and trade unions.
Location: OONL.

3744 **Cheda, Sherrill**
"Women and management: a selective bibliography, 1970-73."
In: *Canadian Library Journal*; Vol. 31, no. 1 (January-February 1974) p. 18-20+.; ISSN: 0008-4352.
Note: Books, essays, articles, bibliographies.
Location: OONL.

3745 **Connelly, M. Patricia**
Women in the Canadian economy: an annotated selected bibliography. Toronto: Ontario Institute for Studies in Education, 1974. 24 l.
Note: Approx. 100 entries.– Books, monographs, pamphlets, articles in books and journals, government publications.– Listing of special journal issues on women.
Location: OTER.

3746 **Hamel, Réginald**
Bibliographie sommaire sur l'histoire de l'écriture féminine au Canada, 1769-1961. [Montréal]: Université de Montréal, 1974. 134 p.
Note: Approx. 1,000 entrées.– Livres, articles de périodiques en sept parties: la famille, la femme (écriture diverses), la fatalité (et les femmes), le roman (adultes), le roman (adolescents), la poésie, généralités (modernes et anciennes, et complémentaires).
Localisation: OONL.

3747 **Marvin, Maureen Woodrow**
"Annotated bibliography: women and drugs."
In: *Canada's Mental Health*; Vol. 22, no. 3 (September 1974) p. 13-19.; ISSN: 0008-2791.
Note: 75 entries.– Articles from popular and scholarly journals (medical, sociological, psychological) dealing with women and drugs.– Arranged in four sections: pregnancy, illegal drugs, prescription drugs, alcohol.– Some Canadian references.
Location: OONL.

3748 **"Some Canadian materials on women: a basic list."**
In: *Communiqué: Canadian Studies*; Vol. 1, no. 2 (December 1974) p. 5-13.; ISSN: 0318-1197.
Note: General works, biography and autobiography, literature, government publications, native women, periodicals, bibliographies.

Location: OONL.

3749 **Swanick, Lynne Struthers**
Women in Canadian politics and government: a bibliography. Monticello, Ill.: Council of Planning Librarians, 1974. 29 p. (Council of Planning Librarians Exchange bibliography ; 697)
Note: 245 entries.– Articles, books and documents concerning the role and rights of women in politics and government.
Location: OONL.

3750 **Swanick, Lynne Struthers**
"Women in New Brunswick: bibliography."
In: *Emergency Librarian*; Vol. 2, no. 2 (December 1974) p. 19-21.; ISSN: 0315-8888.
Note: Location: AEU.

3751 **Whaley, Sara S.; Eichler, Margrit**
"A bibliography of Canadian and United States resources on women."
In: *Women Studies Abstracts*; Vol. 2, no. 4 (Fall 1973) p. 1-104; vol. 3, no. 1 (Winter 1974) p. 1-106.; ISSN: 0049-7835.
Note: Lists material published from about 1963 to 1973 on the status of women in the U.S. and Canada: reference books, bibliographies, journal articles.– Subject areas covered are education, sex roles, employment, sexuality, family, society and government, religion, health issues, family planning and abortion, history/literature/art, media, women's movement.
Location: OONL.

— 1975 —

3752 **Atnikov, Pam, et al.**
Out from the shadows: a bibliography of the history of women in Manitoba. [Winnipeg]: Manitoba Human Rights Commission, 1975. 64 p.
Note: Approx. 500 entries.– Books, periodical articles, theses, government publications.– Arranged in five main subject areas: laws and legal position, politics, women in the work force, social and cultural (chronological arrangement, from 1806 to 1975), bibliographies.
Researchers: Reeva Finkel, Mary Hutchings, Mary Jensen, Chris Lane, Linda Lebedynski.
Location: OONL.

3753 **Deane, Marie, et al.**
"Women and film: a filmography."
In: *Ontario Library Review*; Vol. 59, no. 1 (March 1975) p. 44-51.; ISSN: 0030-2996.
Note: Includes some Canadian references.
Location: OONL.

3754 **Edmonton Public Library**
Of, by and about women: a bibliography for International Women's Year. [Edmonton: The Library, 1975]. [19] l.
Note: Approx. 230 entries.– Includes three categories: non-fiction on topics of women's rights, women's role in society, women's liberation movement; non-fiction by Canadian female authors; fiction by Canadian women authors, primarily contemporary.
Location: OONL.

3755 **Evans, Gwynneth**
Women in federal politics: a bio-bibliography/Les femmes au fédéral: une bio-bibliographie. Ottawa: National Library of Canada, 1975. 81 p.
Note: Presents a short biographical sketch of the 27 women members of the House of Commons and 14 women senators since 1921, sources of information, selected list of their publications. Includes a general bibliography on the subject of Canadian women in federal politics.– Text in English and French/texte en français et en anglais.
Location: OONL.

3756 **Houle, Ghislaine**
La femme et la société québécoise. Montréal: Bibliothèque nationale du Québec, Ministère des affaires culturelles, 1975. 228 p. (Bibliographies québécoises / Bibliothèque nationale du Québec, Centre bibliographique ; no 1)
Note: 1,380 entrées.– Livres, brochures, articles de periodiques, publications officielles.– Thèmes: droits politiques et condition juridique, femme et le travail, sexualité, la femme: sa promotion, littérature, biographies.
Localisation: OONL.

3757 **Latham, Sheila; Freedman, Gloria; Williamson, Michael**
Once upon a pedestal: multimedia list of material for reading, listening, and viewing prepared on the occasion of International Women's Year, 1975. [Toronto]: Young People's Service, Toronto Public Libraries, 1975. 13 p.
Note: Approx. 120 entries.– Books, pamphlets, periodicals, phonograph records, films on women's issues.
Location: OONL.

3758 **Pulyk, Marcia**
A bibliography of selected articles on women in the mass media. Ottawa: Canadian Radio-television and Telecommunications Commission, Library, 1975. iii, 43 l.
Note: Supplements:
Bibliography of selected articles on women in the mass media: an update. 1977. 63 l.
A bibliography of selected materials on women in the mass media: 1978 update. 1978. [28] p.
Location: OONL.

3759 **Smart, Anne; Parnell, Pat**
Rebirth of feminism: a selected list. Saskatoon: Saskatoon Public Library, 1975. 11 [i.e. 21] p.
Note: Location: OONL.

3760 **Strasser, Jean; Dirksen, Jean**
Festival of women in the arts: a multi-media list. Toronto: Metropolitan Toronto Library Board, 1975. 39 p.
Note: "Prepared to accompany the International Women's Year exhibit of the public libraries of Metropolitan Toronto."– Includes art prints, films, magazines, recordings, tapes, books.
Location: OONL.

3761 **University of Waterloo. Library. Reference Department**
Material pertaining to women in the reference collection, Dana Porter Arts Library, University of Waterloo. [Waterloo, Ont.]: Reference Department, Dana Porter Arts Library, University of Waterloo, 1975. 22 l.
Note: Approx. 150 entries.– Comprehensive coverage of Arts Reference Department's holdings in area of women's studies: encyclopedias, directories, biographical dictionaries, bibliographies, abstracts and indexes.– Includes some Canadian references.
Location: OONL.

— 1976 —

3762 **Canada. Health and Welfare Canada. Departmental Library Services**
Women and mental health: a selective bibliography

(1965-1975)/La femme et la santé mentale: une bibliographie choisie (1965-1975). Ottawa: Departmental Library Services, Health and Welfare Canada, 1976. ii, 48 p.
Note: Approx. 550 entries.– Books, articles, government reports and theses in English and French dealing with psychology of women and mental health.– Topics include sex roles, marital status, childbearing, aging, addiction, suicide and crime.– Includes some Canadian references.
Location: OONL.

3763 **Contandriopoulos, André-Pierre**
"L'activité professionnelle des femmes médecins au Québec: bibliographie/[Professional activity of female physicians in Québec: bibliography]."
Dans: *Bulletin: Corporation professionnelle des médecins du Québec*; Vol. 16, no 1 (janvier 1976) p. 42-43.
Note: Localisation: OONL.

3764 **Eichler, Margrit; Marecki, John; Newton, Jennifer L.**
Women: a bibliography of special periodical issues (1960-1975). [Toronto]: Canadian Newsletter of Research on Women, c1976. 76 p.
Note: Arranged in broad subject categories, e.g. arts and literature, health, political economy, sociology.
Location: OONL.

3765 **Haist, Dianne**
Women in management: a selected bibliography, 1970-1975. Toronto: Ontario Ministry of Labour, Research Library, 1976. 18 p. (Bibliography series / Ontario Ministry of Labour, Research Library ; no. 4)
Note: Approx. 180 entries.– Monographs, articles, bibliographies.
Location: OONL.

3766 **Québec (Province). Conseil du statut de la femme**
Les Québécoises: guide bibliographique suivi d'une filmographie. Québec: Éditeur officiel du Québec, 1976. 160 p. (Collection études et dossiers); ISBN: 0-7754-2451-X.
Note: 1,126 entrées.– Livres et brochures, articles de journaux et périodiques, biographies.– Thèmes: la femme et la société, conditions juridiques de la femme, participation de la femme à la vie politique, formation professionnelle et travail de la femme, la femme et son corps, la femme et religion, bibliographies, périodiques, filmographie.
Localisation: OONL.

3767 **Saskatchewan Provincial Library. Bibliographic Services Division**
Women and politics. Regina: Provincial Library, 1976. ii, 19 l.
Note: Approx. 125 entries.– Books and articles mainly from 1970 dealing with women's participation in the political process since the passage of women's suffrage legislation.
Location: OONL.

3768 **University of British Columbia. Women's Resources Centre**
Annotated bibliography for women's studies for high school students. Vancouver: Women's Resources Centre/ Daytime Program, Centre for Continuing Education, University of British Columbia, 1976. v, 126 p.
Note: Approx. 1,000 entries.– Books, films, video recordings, fiction and non-fiction on family, gender,

economy, history of women, politics, law, education, literature and arts.
Location: OONL.

— 1977 —

3769 **Bayefsky, Evelyn**
"Women and the status of part-time work: a review and annotated bibliography."
In: *Ontario Library Review*; Vol. 58, no. 2 (June 1974) p. 124-141; vol. 61, no. 2 (June 1977) p. 86-106.; ISSN: 0030-2996.
Note: 143 entries in total.
Location: OONL.

3770 **Eichler, Margrit; Newton, Jennifer L.; Primrose, Lynne**
"A bibliography of social science materials on Canadian women, published between 1950-1975."
In: *Women in Canada*. Rev. ed., edited by Marylee Stephenson. Don Mills, Ont.: General Publishing, 1977. P. 275-360.; ISBN: 0-7736-1026-X.
Note: 1,110 entries.– Books, journal articles, federal and provincial government publications (excepting parliamentary materials), theses.– Excludes publications in languages other than English or French, briefs of Royal Commission on the Status of Women, unpublished papers.– Topics include birth planning, day care, crime/ delinquency, education, family, labour market, law, social psychology, women's movement, women's organizations.
Previous edition: Toronto: New Press, 1973. P. 291-326.; ISBN: 0-8877-0727-0.
Location: OONL.

3771 **Maranda, Jeanne; Verthuy, Mair**
"Québec feminist writing/Les écrits féministes au Québec."
In: *Emergency Librarian*; Vol. 5, no. 1 (September-October 1977) p. 2-20.; ISSN: 0315-8888.
Note: Books, pamphlets, arranged chronologically and by genre, covering 1971 to 1977.– Text in English and French/texte en français et en anglais.
Location: OONL.

3772 **Ontario. Ministry of Education**
Girls and women in society: resource list. [Toronto]: Ministry of Education, [1977]. 21 p.: ill.
Note: Approx. 300 entries.– Lists non-sexist books, films, audio recordings, video recordings on roles and contributions of girls and women from contemporary and historical perspective.– Prepared by the Federation of Women Teachers in Ontario.
Location: OONL.

3773 **Strong-Boag, Veronica**
"Cousin Cinderella: a guide to historical literature pertaining to Canadian women."
In: *Women in Canada*. Rev. ed., edited by Marylee Stephenson. Don Mills, Ont.: General Publishing, 1977. P. 245-274.; ISBN: 0-7736-1026-X.
Note: Bibliographical essay reviews primary and secondary historical materials: autobiographies/ biographies, demography/marriage/family, sexuality, education, work, literature, sports, anti-feminism.
Previous edition: 1973. P. [291]-396.; ISBN: 0-8877-0727-0.
Location: OONL.

— 1978 —

3774 **Association féminine d'éducation et d'action sociale**
Pendant que les hommes travaillaient, les femmes elles... : entre 1820 et 1950. Montréal: Guérin, [1978]. 405 p.: ill.

Note: Notices bio-bibliographiques.
Localisation: OONL.

3775 **"Bibliographie des écrits féministes."**
Dans: *Canadian Women's Studies*; Vol. 1, no. 1 (Fall 1978) p.135-136.; ISSN: 0713-3235.
Note: Localisation: OONL.

3776 **"Bibliographies, Canadian and international."**
In: *Canadian Newsletter of Research on Women*; (1972-1978) ; ISSN: 0319-4477.
Note: Appears in each issue from vol. 1 (1972) to vol. 7 (1978).- Listing of bibliographies published in Canada, the United States and elsewhere on topics related to women's issues.- Includes monographs and serials.
Location: AEU.

3777 **Canadian Research Institute for the Advancement of Women**
Women and work: an inventory of research/La femme et le travail: un inventaire de recherches. Ottawa: The Institute, c1978. xvi, 85 p.
Note: 1,436 entries.- Covers from 1970 to 1977.- Inventory includes government reports, statistical surveys, theses, books, articles and research projects.- All material and topics limited to Canada and restricted to studies about women over fourteen years of age (research on child labour is excluded).- Principal categories include paid work, unpaid work, unemployment, education for work, images/myths/stereotypes.- Text in English and French/texte en français et en anglais.
Location: OONL.

3778 **Cross-Cultural Communication Centre**
Bibliography of Centre's resources on immigrant women in Canada and their countries of origin. Toronto: Cross-Cultural Communication Centre, [1978]. 17 p.
Note: Books, articles, papers, audio-visual resources related to immigrant women in Canada.- Topics include education, employment, family, health care, immigration, interaction, organizations, women's rights movement.- Separate section on condition of women in countries of origin.
Location: OWA.

3779 **DuPerron, William A.**
Annotated research bibliography on the female offender. Edmonton: Grant MacEwan Community College, Correctional Justice Program, 1978. 157 p.
Note: Approx. 400 entries.
Location: OONL.

3780 **Hale, Linda Louise**
Selected bibliography of manuscripts and pamphlets pertaining to women held by archives, libraries, museums and associations in British Columbia. [S.l.: s.n.], c1978. [185] l.
Note: Approx. 2,100 entries.- Personal papers; records of baptisms, marriages and burials; business, union, government and organization records; pamphlets.- Four types of organizations are listed: women's groups, girls' groups, women's clubs, organizations traditionally associated with women's activities such as children's aid and orphanages.
Location: OONL.

3781 **Newton, Jennifer L.; Zavitz, Carol**
Women: a bibliography of special periodical issues: volume II (updated through 1977). [Toronto]: Canadian Newsletter of Research on Women, c1978. vii, 280 p.;

ISSN: 0319-4477.
Note: Includes Canadian listings.- Arranged in broad subject categories, e.g. business, education, industrial and labour relations, psychology.- This publication is a special issue of the *Canadian Newsletter of Research on Women* (Special publication no. 4).
Location: OONL.

3782 **Rohrlick, Paula; Pellatt, Anna**
Canadian native women: an annotated bibliography. Montreal: Programme in the Anthropology of Development, McGill University, 1978. 146, 21 p.
Note: Approx. 600 entries.- Survey of published and unpublished material dating from 1846 to July 1977.- Includes monographs, periodical and newspaper articles, government publications, dissertations, legal case material, and films dealing with Indian, Inuit, Métis women, with specific tribes and regions, and topics such as involuntary sterilization of native women, native women and the law.
Location: OONL.

3783 **Samson, Marcelle Germain**
Des livres et des femmes: bibliographie. Québec: Conseil du statut de la femme, 1978. 254 p.
Note: 1,357 entrées.- Couvre particulièrement la période de 1940 à 1978, avec quelques références à des oeuvres classiques antérieures.- Thèmes principaux: féminisme, femmes et l'histoire, femmes, société et politique, femmes et le droit, femmes et le travail, femmes et l'éducation, affectivité et sexualité, famille, femmes et l'agression, roman et fiction.
Localisation: OONL.

3784 **Service, Dorothy Jane**
Women and the law: a bibliography of materials in the University of Toronto Law Library. 2nd ed. Toronto: [s.n.], 1978. i, 105 p.
Note: Approx. 750 entries.- Monographs, articles in Canadian legal journals, articles in non-Canadian legal journals, loose-leaf services, journals, reports. Previous edition: 1975. ii, 22 p.- Approx. 200 entries.- Material listed here is not duplicated in the 2nd edition.
Location: OONL.

3785 **Stevens, Alta Mae; McDowell, Linda**
"Filling in the picture: resources for teaching about women in Canada."
In: *History and Social Science Teacher*; Vol. 14, no. 1 (Fall 1978) p. 7-13.; ISSN: 0316-4969.
Note: Overview of resources concentrates on women in area of social history: non-fiction, memoirs, autobiographies and biographies, novels with historical backgrounds, as well as works dealing with women in local and regional history.
Location: AEU.

3786 **Swanick, Lynne Struthers**
Women as administrators: selected bibliography. Monticello, Ill.: Vance Bibliographies, 1978. 16 p. (Public administration series: Bibliography ; P-86; ISSN: 0193-970X)
Note: References to women in the business world, in supervisory, management and executive roles, in a North American context, mainly from 1972-1978.
Location: OHM.

— 1979 —

3787 **Anderson, Daphne; Connor, Mary**
Women and the Christian faith: a selected bibliography and resource catalogue. [Vancouver]: Division of Mission in Canada, United Church of Canada, [1979]. 51 p.
Note: Approx. 750 entries.– Books, periodical articles, essays in collections, unpublished materials.– Sections include history, theology, ministry, ordination, sexuality, abortion.
Location: OONL.

3788 **Feldman, Wendy A.**
"Women in Canadian politics since 1945: a bibliography."
In: *Resources for Feminist Research*; Vol. 8, no. 1 (March 1979) p. 38-42.; ISSN: 0707-8412.
Note: Books and articles arranged in sections dealing with general studies, specific levels of government, personalities, biographies, bibliographies.
Location: AEU.

3789 **Gulbinowicz, Eva**
Problems of immigrant women, past and present: a bibliography. [Toronto]: Ministry of Labour Library, 1979. 45 p.
Note: Approx. 500 entries.– Monographs, periodical articles, theses issued between 1900 and 1969.– Focus on Canadian material, with some British, American, European references.
Location: OONL.

3790 **Hauck, Philomena**
Sourcebook on Canadian women. Ottawa: Canadian Library Association, [c1979]. 111 p.: ill.; ISBN: 0-88802-126-7.
Note: Approx. 800 entries.– Current books, pamphlets, periodicals, audio-visual materials on women's rights, law, work and day care, health issues and biography.– Literature by and about women.– Illustrations: drawings, reproductions of book covers.– English-language sources only.
Location: OONL.

3791 **Sokoloff, Natalie J.**
"Bibliography on the sociology of women and work: 1970's."
In: *Resources for Feminist Research*; Vol. 8, no. 4 (1979) p. 48-74.; ISSN: 0707-8412.
Note: Major focus is on sociology of women and work in the United States, with substantial Canadian input by staff of *Resources for Feminist Research*: general works, feminist critique, mainstream sociology, radical sociology (Marxist feminism).
Location: OONL.

3792 **Swanick, Lynne Struthers**
Women and pensions: a checklist of publications. Monticello, Ill.: Vance Bibliographies, 1979. 9 p. (Public administration series: Bibliography ; P-273; ISSN: 0193-970X)
Note: Approx. 120 entries.– Covers 1973 to July 1979.– Periodical articles, government documents, books, conference papers on women and pensions primarily relating to North American situation.– Excludes general issue of women and work, women as volunteer workers and pensions.
Location: OONL.

3793 **Women's studies: video resource catalogue.** Toronto: Ontario Educational Communications Authority, 1979. 116 p.
Note: Listing of films, books, government publications, articles dealing with Canadian women writers, education, English literature, family and marriage, history of women, law, media, psychological and social problems, role models, sexuality, work.– Includes a list of film distributors.
Location: OONL.

— 1980 —

3794 **Dagg, A.I.**
76 terrific books about women: an annotated list. Waterloo, Ont.: Otter Press, 1980. 24 p.
Note: 76 entries.– Biographical and autobiographical works, including many Canadian references.
Location: OONL.

3795 **Dryden, Jean E.**
Some sources for women's history at the Provincial Archives of Alberta. [Edmonton]: Alberta Culture, Historical Resources Division, [1980]. viii, 189 p.: ill. (Provincial Archives of Alberta Occasional paper ; no. 2)
Note: Printed and manuscript material held in Provincial Archives of Alberta as of December 1979.– Includes personal and family papers, organizations and church records.– In general only those items or collections which provide information on thoughts, feelings, activities, accomplishments of women were listed.– Excludes odd items such as autograph books, dress patterns, bank books, invitations or certificates.
Location: OONL.

3796 **Light, Beth; Strong-Boag, Veronica**
True daughters of the North: Canadian women's history: an annotated bibliography. [Toronto]: OISE Press, [1980]. v, 210 p. (Bibliography series / Ontario Institute for Studies in Education ; no. 5); ISBN: 0-7744-0185-0.
Note: Approx. 1,200 entries.– Books, periodical articles, government publications, bibliographies, general histories, biographies, demographic studies.– Topics include education, political involvement, religion, sexuality, work.– Chronological arrangement.
Location: OONL.

3797 **Lips, Hilary M.**
"Social and psychological aspects of the normal pregnancy experience: a bibliography."
In: *Resources for Feminist Research*; Vol. 9, no. 2 (July 1980) p. 72-77.; ISSN: 0707-8412.
Note: Gathers research and theory in social sciences focussing on pregnancy as a normal life event.– Period covered is about 1950 to 1980.
Location: OONL.

3798 **Muldoon, Maureen**
Abortion: an annotated bibliography. New York; Toronto: E. Mellen Press, c1980. xv, [151] p. (Studies in women and religion ; vol. 3); ISBN: 0-88946-972-5.
Note: 3,397 entries.– Covers from 1968 to 1980.– Includes Canadian references.– Principal topics include ethical and theological aspects of abortion, medical and social aspects, legal aspects, abortion studies.– Includes a list of bibliographies on abortion and section listing collected articles and symposia proceedings.
Location: OONL.

3799 Weitz, Margaret Collins
"An introduction to 'Les Québécoises'."
In: *Contemporary French Civilization*; Vol. 5, no. 1 (Fall 1980) p. 105-129.; ISSN: 0147-9156.
Note: Bibliographical sources, general studies, anthologies, journals, essays by individuals and groups, contemporary Quebec women's publications.
Location: OONL.

— 1981 —

3800 Canada. Library of Parliament. Information and Reference Branch
Women in Canadian politics and government, 1974-1980: select bibliography/Les femmes en politique au Canada, 1974-1980: bibliographie sélective. Ottawa: The Library, 1981. 49 p.
Note: Approx. 400 entries.– Bibliographies, biographical works, general works, sections on women in federal, provincial and municipal politics, personalities, list of Canadian women's magazines and newsletters, directory of federal and provincial government bodies concerned about women in Canada.
Location: OOSS.

3801 Light, Beth
"Recent publications in Canadian women's history."
In: *Canadian Women's Studies*; Vol. 3, no. 1 (1981) p. 114-117.; ISSN: 0713-3235.
Note: 53 entries.
Location: AEU.

3802 Miller, Alan V.
Sexual harassment of women in the workplace: a bibliography with emphasis on Canadian publications. Monticello, Ill.: Vance Bibliographies, 1981. 22 p. (Public administration series: Bibliography ; P-801; ISSN: 0193-970X)
Note: Approx. 300 entries.– Canadian and United States periodical and newspaper articles, trade union and interest group documents.
Location: OONL.

3803 Sainte-Jarre, Chantal
"Bibliographies concernant la problématique femme-philosophie."
Dans: *Phi zéro*; Vol. 9, no 2 (février 1981) p. 149-157.; ISSN: 0318-4412.
Note: Localisation: OONL.

3804 St-Pierre, Nicole; Ruel, Ginette
Bibliographie sélective sur la condition des femmes. [Québec]: Gouvernement du Québec, Ministère des affaires sociales, 1981. 16 f.
Note: Approx. 110 entrées.– Monographies, articles portant sur féminisme, psychologie, femmes et santé, femmes et le travail, violence.
Localisation: OONL.

— 1982 —

3805 Bégin, Diane; Harel-Giasson, Francine; Marchis-Mouren, Marie-Françoise
Portraits de québécoises gestionnaires: une bibliographie annotée. Montréal: École des hautes études commerciales, 1982. iii, 64 f. (Rapport de recherche / École des hautes études commerciales ; no 82-07; ISSN: 0709-986X)
Note: 124 entrées.– Un inventaire des portraits de quatre-vingt six femmes gestionnaires québécoises à partir de la documentation parue dans des livres, revues et journaux.

Localisation: OONL.

3806 Cebotarev, E.A., et al.
"An annotated bibliography on women in agriculture and rural societies."
In: *Resources for Feminist Research*; Vol. 11, no. 1 (March 1982) p. 93-180.; ISSN: 0707-8412.
Note: Published and unpublished documents from academic and non-academic sources, grouped into four major sections: "Canada," "Other industrialized countries," "Developing countries," "General."- These are further subdivided by regions and countries.– The Canadian section focusses on women in agricultural production (participation in the family farm), with related subjects dealing with education, legal rights, off-farm work, socio-economic status.
Location: OONL.

3807 Jaffee, Georgina; Nett, Emily M.
"Annotated bibliography on women as elders."
In: *Resources for Feminist Research*; Vol. 11, no. 2 (July 1982) p. 253-288.; ISSN: 0707-8412.
Note: Location: AEU.

3808 Lemieux, Denise; Mercier, Lucie
La recherche sur les femmes au Québec: bilan et bibliographie. [Québec]: Institut québécois de recherche sur la culture, [1982]. 336 p. (Instruments de travail / Institut québécois de recherche sur la culture ; no 5); ISBN: 2-89-224-015-8.
Note: 2,140 entrées.– Couvre une période approximative de cent ans: de la fin du XIXe siècle jusqu'en décembre 1981.– Groupe surtout des ouvrages publiées et des articles de périodiques québécois portant sur la femme.– Les articles de revues proviennent en grande partie des années 1970 à 1981.– Thèmes: ouvrages généraux, histoire, femmes et ethnicité, cycles de l'existence (éducation, sexualité, mariage, reproduction, famille, troisième âge), pathologies et thérapies, participation sociale, vie culturelle, vie individuelle.
Localisation: OONL.

3809 L'Espérance, Jeanne
Vers des horizons nouveaux: la femme canadienne de 1870 à 1940. [Ottawa]: Archives publiques Canada, c1982. 69, 63 p.; ISBN: 0-662-52008-4.
Note: 135 entrées.– Documentaire sur l'histoire des femmes au Canada: catalogue d'une exposition.– Texte en français et en anglais disposé tête-bêche.– Titre de la p. de t. additionnelle: *The widening sphere: women in Canada, 1870-1940*.
Localisation: OONL.

3810 L'Espérance, Jeanne
The widening sphere: women in Canada, 1870-1940. [Ottawa]: Public Archives Canada, c1982. 63, 69 p.: ill.; ISBN: 0-662-52008-4.
Note: 135 entries.– Documentary presentation of history of women in Canada.– Catalogue of an exhibition.– Text in English and French with French text on inverted pages.– Title of additional title-page: *Vers des horizons nouveaux: la femme canadienne de 1870 à 1940*.
Location: OONL.

3811 McKay, Margaret
Women in the labour force with an emphasis on the clerical and service occupations: a selected bibliography. Ottawa: Social Sciences and Humanities Research Council of Canada, 1982. 59 p.; ISBN: 0-662-12070-1.

Note: Approx. 850 entries.– Books and monographs, journal articles and contributed papers, theses, statistical publications.– Prepared for seminar: "Women's work in the Toronto labour market: clerical and service workers," May 26, 1982, University of Toronto.
Location: OONL.

3812 **Storrie, Kathleen; Dykstra, Pearl**
"Bibliography on sexual harassment."
In: *Resources for Feminist Research*; Vol. 10, no. 4 (December 1981/January 1982) p. 25-32.; ISSN: 0707-8412.
Note: Lists newspaper articles from 1975 to 1981, legal cases, books and journal articles.
Location: OONL.

— 1983 —

3813 **Arnup, Katherine; Gottlieb, Amy**
"Annotated bibliography [Lesbianism]."
In: *Resources for Feminist Research*; Vol. 12, no. 1 (March 1983) p. 90-105.; ISSN: 0707-8412.
Note: Review of lesbian sources, historical and contemporary.– Excludes biography and literature.– Special lesbian issue of *Resources for Feminist Research*.
Location: AEU.

3814 **Bailey, Susan F.**
Women and the British Empire: an annotated guide to sources. New York: Garland, 1983. xiii, 185 p. (Garland reference library of social science ; vol. 159); ISBN: 0-8240-9162-0.
Note: Includes references to Canada.– Arranged in four main categories: wives of administrators, settlers, missionaries, native women.
Location: OHM.

3815 **Bégin, Diane**
Bibliographie sur la femme québécoise et le travail. Montréal: École des hautes études commerciales, [1983]. 77 f.
Note: 682 entrées.– Articles de journaux et de périodiques, chapitres ou parties de volumes, publications gouvernementales, thèses et mémoires.– Thèmes traités: histoire de la femme au Québec, femme et éducation, femme et travail, femme et conditions de travail, femme et égalité des chances, femme et syndicalisme, femme et politique.– La période couverte s'étend de 1975 à 1982.
Localisation: QMHE.

3816 **Dworaczek, Marian**
Women and the world of work: issues in the '80's: a selective bibliography, 1980-1982. Monticello, Ill.: Vance Bibliographies, 1983. 37 p. (Public administration series: Bibliography ; P-1243; ISSN: 0193-970X); ISBN: 0-88066-593-9.
Note: 318 entries.– Topics covered include sex discrimination in employment, sexual harassment at work, affirmative action, part-time employment, immigrant women, dual-career families, working mothers, women and unions, career development, impact of technology, maternity leave.– Additional bibliographies for most categories.– Many Canadian references.
Location: AEAU.

3817 **Fairbanks, Carol; Sundberg, Sara Brooks**
Farm women on the prairie frontier: a sourcebook for Canada and the United States. Metuchen, N.J.: Scarecrow Press, 1983. xiii, 237 p.: ill.; ISBN: 0-8108-1625-3.
Note: Part 1: *Essays*. Includes "Farm women on the

Canadian prairie frontier: the helpmate image."
Part 2: *Annotations*. Bibliographical section emphasizes the environment, homesteading, homemaking.– Includes books and journal articles, history and background, fiction and non-fiction, literary backgrounds.
Location: OONL.

3818 **Ferris, Kathryn**
"Child custody and the lesbian mother: an annotated bibliography."
In: *Resources for Feminist Research*; Vol. 12, no. 1 (March 1983) p. 106-109.; ISSN: 0707-8412.
Note: Articles and case law from Canadian and American sources.
Location: AEU.

3819 **Ford, John; Miller, Alan V.**
Women, microelectronics, and employment: a selected bibliography. [Toronto]: Ontario Ministry of Labour, Library, 1983. 16 p.
Note: Approx. 300 entries.
Location: OONL.

3820 **Khayatt, M. Didl; Brodribb, Somer**
"Bibliography of materials available in the Women's Educational Resource Centre."
In: *Resources for Feminist Research*; Vol. 12, no. 3 (November 1983) p. 32-45.; ISSN: 0707-8412.
Note: Unpublished papers, conference papers, government documents, books and articles.– Contains Canadian references only.
Location: OONL.

3821 **McPherson, Kathryn**
A 'round the clock job: a selected bibliography on women's work at home in Canada. Ottawa: Supply and Services Canada, 1983. 45 p.; ISBN: 0-662-12710-2.
Note: Approx. 450 entries.– Books, theses, articles, government publications, audio-visual materials.– Lists bibliographies, theoretical works by Canadian authors, material dealing with housework and maintenance of adults, paid domestic work, integrated domestic labour, childcare.
Location: OOSSHRC.

3822 **Ontario. Ministry of Labour. Library**
"Visible minority women and employment: a selected bibliography."
In: *Labour Topics*; Vol. 6, no. 8 (August 1983) p. 1-5.; ISSN: 0704-8874.
Note: Approx. 60 entries.
Location: AEU.

3823 **Veillette, Denise**
Bibliographie thématique sur la condition féminine. Québec: Laboratoire de recherches sociologiques, Université Laval, 1983. 255 p. (Collection Outils de recherche / Laboratoire de recherches sociologiques, Université Laval ; cahier 5); ISBN: 2-920495-15-1.
Note: 2,474 entrées.– Livres, articles, publications officielles.– Thèmes: éducation, femmes et corps, féminisme, femmes et hommes, femmes et pouvoir, religion, travail, violence, représentations des femmes dans les média.– Inclut un nombre considérable d'ouvrages canadiens.
Localisation: OONL.

3824 **Vothi, Nhu-y**
Bibliographie, forum sur la question économique. Québec: Gouvernement du Québec, Conseil du statut de

la femme, [1983]. 128 p.: ill.; ISBN: 2-550-10446-3.
Note: Approx. 400 entrées.– Bibliographie sélective et
annotée sur situation économique des femmes.– Thèmes:
production domestique, sécurité du revenu à la retraite,
conditions de travail, entrepreneurship au féminin.–
Comporte des références canadiennes et québécoises
Localisation: OONL.

3825 **Waiser, Joan**
Women's studies: a guide to reference sources.
[Montreal]: McGill University, McLennan Library,
Reference Department, 1983. 22 p.
Note: Approx. 150 entries.– Includes directories,
handbooks, biographical sources, bibliographies.–
Emphasis on Canadian material.
Location: OONL.

— 1984 —

3826 **Andersen, Marguerite**
"Bibliography [women and language]."
In: *Resources for Feminist Research*; Vol. 13, no. 3 (November 1984) p. 72-78.; ISSN: 0707-8412.
Note: Books, articles, theses on aspects of language,
culture, gender.
Location: AEU.

3827 **Andersen, Marguerite**
"Le Québec: féminisme contemporain et écrits de femmes
(1970-1983): une bibliographie pilote."
Dans: *Documentation sur la recherche féministe*; Vol. 12, no
4 (décembre/janvier 1983-1984) p. 18-28.; ISSN: 0707-8412.
Note: Approx. 500 entrées.
Localisation: AEU.

3828 **Canada. Public Service Commission. Staffing Programs
Branch. Operations, Staffing Support and Services
Division. Women's Programs Centre**
Resources for a new age: a selected annotated
bibliography on women and microtechnology/
Ressources pour une ère nouvelle: bibliographie annotée
d'ouvrages choisis concernant la femme et la
microtechnologie. [Ottawa]: The Centre, 1984. 38 p.
Note: Approx 225 entries.– Designed to assist women in
becoming aware of implications of microelectronics
technology.– Emphasis on current Canadian material.–
Topics include office of the future, employment impact
(women), health and safety, labour perspective, training
for the future.– List of additional bibliographies.– Text in
English and French/texte en français et en anglais.
Location: OONL.

3829 **Dworaczek, Marian**
Women at work: a bibliography of bibliographies.
Monticello, Ill.: Vance Bibliographies, 1984. 18 p. (Public
administration series: Bibliography ; P-1414; ISSN: 0193-970X); ISBN: 0-88066-894-6.
Note: Approx. 200 entries.– Many Canadian references.
Location: QQLA.

3830 **Mazur, Carol; Pepper, Sheila**
Women in Canada: a bibliography, 1965-1982. 3rd ed.
Toronto: OISE Press, c1984. xxi, 377 p.; ISBN: 0-7744-0288-1.
Note: 7,584 entries.– Books, parts of books, periodical
articles, theses, government publications.
Previous editions:
Women in Canada, 1965 to 1975: a bibliography. Hamilton,
Ont.: McMaster University Press, 1976. 187 p.; ISBN: 0-

919592-03-1.
Harrison, Cynthia Ellen. *Women in Canada, 1965-1972.*
Hamilton, Ont.: McMaster University Library Press,
1972. 54 p.; ISBN: 0-919592-01-5.
Location: OONL.

3831 **Murphy, Lynn**
Housework: an annotated bibliography. Halifax, N.S.:
International Education Centre, Saint Mary's University,
1984. [19] p.
Note: Approx. 100 entries.– Books and articles dealing
with economic aspects of housework.– Includes
Canadian references.
Location: OONL.

3832 **Murphy, Lynn**
Women and agriculture: an annotated bibliography.
Halifax, N.S.: International Education Centre, Saint
Mary's University, 1984. [12] p.
Note: Location: OONL.

— 1985 —

3833 **Dagenais, Huguette**
Approches et méthodes de la recherche féministe:
bibliographie multidisciplinaire. Québec: Groupe de
recherche et d'échange multidisciplinaire féministes,
Université Laval, 1985. 60 p. (Cahiers de recherche du
GREMF / Groupe de recherche et d'échange
multidisciplinaire féministes, Université Laval ; no 1);
ISBN: 2-89364-000-X.
Note: Approx. 500 entrées.
Localisation: OONL.

3834 **Eichler, Margrit**
"And the work never ends: feminist contributions."
In: *Canadian Review of Sociology and Anthropology*; Vol. 22,
no. 5 (December 1985) p. 619-644.; ISSN: 0008-4948.
Note: Approx. 185 entries.– Feminist writings in
Canadian social sciences.
Location: OONL.

3835 **Fahmy-Eid, Nadia; Dumont, Micheline**
"Bibliographie sur l'histoire de l'éducation des filles au
Québec."
Dans: *Documentation sur la recherche féministe*; Vol. 14, no
2 (juillet 1985) p. 45-70.; ISSN: 0707-8412.
Note: Comprends six grandes sections: "Les fonds
d'archives," "Les sources imprimées," "Les écrits et
témoignages d'époque sur l'éducation des filles," "Les
bibliographies et les instruments de recherches," "Les
études théoriques et méthodologiques," "Les synthèses
générales d'histoire de l'éducation."
Localisation: OONL.

3836 **Harrison, Cynthia Ellen**
Women in American history: a bibliography. Santa
Barbara, Calif.: American Bibliographical Center–Clio
Press, c1979-1985. 2 vol. (Clio bibliography series ; no. 5,
20); ISBN: 0-87436-260-1 (vol. 1); 0-87436-450-7 (vol. 2).
Note: 7,095 entries.– Covers 1963-1984.– Contains
abstracts and annotations of articles drawn from a list of
about 600 scholarly periodicals, newsletters, and
anthologies dealing with women's history and related
disciplines, United States and Canada.
Location: OONL.

3837 **Hawley, Donna Lea**
Women and aging: a comprehensive bibliography.
Burnaby, B.C.: Gerontology Research Centre, Simon
Fraser University, 1985. iii, 128 p. (Simon Fraser Univers-

ity Gerontology Research Centre Bibliography series 85-1); ISBN: 0-86491-048-7.
Note: Approx. 1,000 entries.– Articles, books, edited collections, theses, conference papers dealing with family issues (living arrangements, mothers, single women, widowhood/divorce), health issues (menopause, mental health/illness, reproduction), general issues.
Location: OONL.

3838 **Latham, Barbara; Carter, Connie; Reid, Jane**
Bibliography on women: a resource for other disciplines/ Bibliographie sur les femmes: ouvrage de référence pour d'autres disciplines. Toronto: Canadian Studies Bureau, Association of Canadian Community Colleges, 1985. xviii, 64 p.: ill.; ISSN: 0228-8451.
Note: Books, journal articles, audio-visual materials.– Bibliographical, statistical, reference sources on the arts, business, communications, education, history, native women, science, social sciences, social services, technology, women and work.– Text in English and French/texte en français et en anglais.
Special issue of *Communiqué*; Vol. 5, no. 1 (1985).
Location: OONL.

3839 **Poirier, Marie**
Les femmes immigrées au Québec: bibliographie annotée. [Montréal]: Direction de la recherche, Ministère des Communautés culturelles et de l'immigration, c1985. 51 p.; ISBN: 2-550-11976-2.
Note: Comprend livres et rapports, ouvrages inédits, numéros spéciaux de revues scientifiques, thèses et mémoires, articles de revues scientifiques et de journaux, liste de bibliographies.
Localisation: OONL.

3840 **Rooney, Frances**
"[Women and disability]: bibliography/[Les femmes handicapées]: bibliographie."
In: *Resources for Feminist Research*; Vol. 14, no. 1 (March 1985) p. 84-92.; ISSN: 0707-8412.
Note: Location: AEU.

3841 **Smith, Margaret; Waisberg, Barbara**
Pornography: a feminist survey. Toronto: Boudicca Books, 1985. 31 p. (Boudicca booklist ; 2); ISBN: 0-920223-01-X.
Note: 51 entries.– Books and articles pertaining to psychological and social aspects of pornography from a feminist perspective.– Themes: sexuality, social construction of perception, control of pornography.
Location: OONL.

— 1986 —

3842 **Ballou, Patricia K.**
Women: a bibliography of bibliographies. 2nd ed. Boston, Mass.: G.K. Hall, c1986. xv, 268 p.; ISBN: 0-81618-729-0.
Note: Includes a Canadian section.
Previous edition, 1980. xiii, 155 p.; ISBN: 0-81618-292-2.
Location: OOCC.

3843 **Doerkson, Lorna**
"Women and crime: a bibliography."
In: *Resources for Feminist Research*; Vol. 14, no. 4 (December/January 1985-1986) p. 60-61.; ISSN: 0707-8412.
Note: Location: AEU.

3844 **Hale, Linda Louise; Houlden, Melanie G.**
"The study of British Columbia women: a quarter-century review, 1960-1984."

In: *Resources for Feminist Research*; Vol. 15, no. 2 (July 1986) p. 58-68.; ISSN: 0707-8412.
Note: Overview of books, articles, pamphlets, serials, government publications, theses written about women in B.C. since 1960.
Location: AEU.

3845 **Hawley, Donna Lea**
"Prostitution in Canada: a bibliography."
In: *Resources for Feminist Research*; Vol. 14, no. 4 (December/January 1985-1986) p. 61-63.; ISSN: 0707-8412.
Note: Location: AEU.

3846 **Ontario. Ministry of Treasury and Economics. Library Services**
Working women in the economic future: a selected bibliography with emphasis on Canada. Monticello, Ill.: Vance Bibliographies, 1986. 39 p. (Public administration series: Bibliography ; P-1999; ISSN: 0193-970X); ISBN: 0-89028-999-9.
Note: Approx. 575 entries.– Lists books and reports, speeches and essays, periodical articles, editorials and bylined newspaper articles dealing with topics related to women in the labour force, including economic status, employment equity, affirmative action, sexual harassment, legal issues, entrepreneurship.
Location: OTY.

3847 **Women and the arts: bibliography/Les femmes et les arts: bibliographie.** [Ottawa: Canadian Conference of the Arts], c1986. iv, 67 l.
Note: Surveys the womens' and feminist presses.– Covers Canadian arts periodicals in five categories: general, visual arts, performing arts, media arts, writing and publishing.– Excludes critiques or reviews of artists' works.– Text in English and French/texte en français et en anglais.
Location: OONL.

3848 **Women in conflict with the law: a selected bibliography.** [Ottawa]: Ministry Secretariat, Solicitor General Canada, [1986]. 29 l. (Programs Branch user report / Ministry Secretariat, Solicitor General Canada ; no. 1986-36)
Note: Approx. 375 entries.– Lists books, journal articles, government publications, theses.– Topics include child and health care, education, natives, treatment, alcohol and drugs, young female offenders.
Location: OONL.

— 1987 —

3849 **Canada. Statistics Canada. Housing, Family and Social Statistics Division. Target Groups Project**
Guide to Statistics Canada data on women. Ottawa: Statistics Canada, 1987. 113 p.; ISSN: 0835-6300.
Note: Contains sources of data found separately in various Statistics Canada publications, generally wherever a male/female distinction or a theme devoted to women's issues was noted, e.g.: abortion, adoption, birth control, cancer, children, crime, divorce, education, employment, family, income distribution, marriage, single people, professional women.
Titre en français: *Guide des données de Statistique Canada sur les femmes*.
Location: OONL.

3850 **Canada. Statistique Canada. Division des statistiques sociales, du logement et des familles. Projet de groupes cibles**

Guide des données de Statistique Canada sur les femmes. Ottawa: Statistique Canada, 1987. 115 p.; ISSN: 0835-6319.

Note: Renferme des sources de données qu'on trouve séparément dans divers catalogues des publications de Statistique Canada, et il s'agit généralement des cas où l'on fait la distinction hommes/femmes ou des cas où l'on traite de questions concernant les femmes, e.g. adoption, avortement thérapeutiques, divorces, éducation, emploi, famille, fécondité, mariages, professions, santé, travailleurs.

English title: *Guide to Statistics Canada data on women.*

Localisation: OONL.

3851 **Godard, Barbara**
Bibliography of feminist criticism/Bibliographie de la critique féminist[e]. [Toronto]: ECW Press, [c1987]. 116 p.; ISBN: 0-920763-97-9.

Note: Approx. 1,800 entries.– Books, articles, sections of books, theses and dissertations.– Includes interviews, reviews on feminist literary theory, images of women in men's writing, feminist presses.– Text in English and French/texte en français et en anglais.

Extract from: *Gynocritics: feminist approaches to Canadian and Quebec women's writing.* Toronto: ECW Press; c1987. xxiv, 386 p.; ISBN: 0-920763-10-3.

Location: OONL.

3852 **Gotell, Lise**
"Employment equity for women in Canadian universities: a bibliography."
In: *Resources for Feminist Research*; Vol. 16, no. 4 (December 1987) p. 48-49.; ISSN: 0707-8412.

Note: Location: AEU.

3853 **Jackel, Susan**
Canadian prairie women's history: a bibliographic survey. Ottawa: Canadian Research Institute for the Advancement of Women, 1987. P. 1-22. (The CRIAW papers / Canadian Research Institute for the Advancement of Women ; no. 14); ISBN: 0-919653-14-6.

Note: Bibliographical paper presented at Canadian Historical Association annual meeting, Winnipeg, June 1986.

Location: OONL.

3854 **Leblanc, Thérèse**
Les femmes: guide des ressources documentaires à Montréal, with an introduction for English-speaking users and an English-French index. [Montréal]: Éditions F. Huot, 1987. 110 p.; ISBN: 2-9800-808-0-2.

Note: Information sur les centres de documentation et bibliothèques universitaires; liste sélective de divers types d'ouvrages de référence (thèses, documents audio-visuels, répertoires de groupes, de services, dictionnaires, bibliographies spécialisées).

Localisation: OONL.

3855 **Morgan, Kathryn Pauly**
"Bibliography of recent feminist philosophy and theory."
In: *Resources for Feminist Research*; Vol. 16, no. 3 (September 1987) p. 89-103.; ISSN: 0707-8412.

Note: Approx. 500 entries.– Includes Canadian references.

Location: AEU.

3856 **Pelletier, Lyse**
"Femmes, géographie et environnement: notes à propos de quelques titres."

Dans: *Cahiers de géographie de Québec*; Vol. 31, no 83 (septembre 1987) p. 301-307.; ISSN: 0007-9766.

Note: Comprend des ouvrages et des articles en langue française, parus à partir de 1980, et en langue anglaise, parus depuis 1985.

Localisation: OONL.

3857 **Scane, Joyce**
"Selected bibliography of community papers concerning immigrant women in Canada: 1975-1986."
In: *Resources for Feminist Research*; Vol. 16, no. 1 (March 1987) p. 47-53.; ISSN: 0707-8412.

Note: Listing of papers, articles, pamphlets relating to aspects of experience of immigrant women in Canada.– Excludes government reports, articles in scholarly journals.

Location: AEU.

3858 **Sheehy, Elizabeth A.**
Special defences for women: outline. Ottawa: National Association of Women and the Law, 1987. 5 p.; ISBN: 0-929049-22-5.

Note: 29 entries.– Articles about "battered woman syndrome," "premenstrual syndrome," "post-partum depression," "rape trauma syndrome."- Includes Canadian references.

Location: OONL.

3859 **Talbot, Christiane**
Index des organismes et répertoires féminins au Canada. Ottawa: Bureau de l'image de la femme dans la programmation, Société Radio-Canada, 1987. 65, 65 f.

Note: Approx. 50 entrées.– Comprend une liste sélective de répertoires, de publications et de banques de données sur les organismes féminins au Canada et sur les compétences féminines dans différents domaines.– Texte en français et en anglais disposé tête-bêche.– Titre de la p. de t. additionnelle: *Index to Canadian women's groups and directories.*

Localisation: OONL.

3860 **Talbot, Christiane**
Index to Canadian women's groups and directories. Ottawa: Office of the Portrayal of Women in Programming, Canadian Broadcasting Corporation, 1987. 65, 65 l.

Note: Approx. 50 entries.– Contains a selected list of directories, other publications and data banks of women's organizations and women in special fields.– Text in English and French with French text on inverted pages.– Title of additional title page: *Index des organismes et répertoires féminins au Canada.*

Location: OONL.

3861 **Wakil, F.A.**
Law and women: a select bibliography of cross-national relevance. [Saskatoon: University of Saskatchewan, 1987]. viii, 94 p.; ISBN: 0-88880-189-0.

Note: Approx. 800 entries.– Books, federal and provincial law reform commission studies and reports, law society studies, other government publications related to: contracts, family law, child custody, women and crime, violence against women, women in judiciary, women's rights (legal status, laws, etc.), women and the labour force.

Location: OONL.

— 1988 —

3862 **Brumpton, Cynthia**
A woman's place is in the House ... of Commons: an

annotated bibliography. [Toronto: C. Brumpton], 1988. 42 p.

Note: Approx. 350 entries.– Lists books, articles, audio visual materials, publications by women Members of Parliament, biographies.

Location: OONL.

3863 **Burke, Ronald J.; McKeen, Carol A.**
Women in management bibliography. London, Ont.: National Centre for Management Research and Development, University of Western Ontario, 1988. 185 p. (Working paper series / National Centre for Management Research and Development, University of Western Ontario ; no. NC 90-20)

Note: Location: OONL.

3864 **Carpentier, Louise E.; Lequin, Lucie**
"Bibliographie des écrits des femmes du Québec de 1945 à 1960."
Dans: *Resources for Feminist Research*; Vol. 17, no. 4 (December 1988) p. 49-61.; ISSN: 0707-8412.

Note: Localisation: AEU.

3865 **Ontario. Ministry of Labour. Library and Information Services**
"Sexual harassment: a Canadian perspective: a selected bibliography."
In: *Labour Topics*; Vol. 11, no. 7 (July 1988) p. 1-4.; ISSN: 0704-8874.

Note: Approx. 45 entries.

Location: AEU.

3866 **Parent, France; Cloutier, Renée**
"Recherches sur les femmes et l'éducation formelle au Canada et au Québec publiées dans la période 1975-1986."
Dans: *Recherches féministes*; Vol. 1, no 1 (1988) p. 129-148.; ISSN: 0838-4479.

Note: 223 entrées.– Huit catégories: statut, accès, formation et emploi, curriculum, culture, sexisme, performance scolaire, numéros spéciaux de périodiques.

Localisation: OONL.

— 1989 —

3867 **"Bibliography: Canadian refugee policy: a history."**
In: *Canadian Woman Studies*; Vol. 10, no. 1 (Spring 1989) p. 115-121.; ISSN: 0713-3235.

Note: Principal list is contained in section 2: "Women refugees: a literature review," which is preceded by a brief list of articles, government publications and legislation on the general topic of Canadian refugee policy.

Location: AEU.

3868 **Cloutier, Céline; Masson, Dominique**
Femmes et structures urbaines: bibliographie multidisciplinaire. Montréal: Faculté de l'aménagement, Université de Montréal, 1989. vi f., 101 p. (Notes de recherche / Faculté d'aménagement, Université de Montréal ; AME 04)

Note: Approx. 1,200 entrées.– Livres, articles, publications gouvernementales, rapports de recherche, thèses.– La période couverte: début des années 70 à 1988.– Sujets: habitation et logement, transport et mobilité, équipements collectifs et communautaires, sexualité, violence et sécurité, femmes et espaces urbains, planification et aménagement, architecture et design, interventions politiques, utopies.

Localisation: OONL.

3869 **Corbeil, Christine; Descarries, Francine**
Femmes, féminisme et maternité: une bibliographie sélective. [Montréal]: Université du Québec à Montréal, Centre de recherche féministe [et] Département de travail social, 1989. 79 p.; ISBN: 2-921080-03-6.

Note: Approx. 600 entrées.– Livres, articles, thèses, et rapports parus depuis 1975: principaux écrits théoriques issus du mouvement des femmes, maternité et maternage, maternité et travail, fécondité/grossesse/accouchment/naissance, nouvelles technologies de la reproduction.

Localisation: OONL.

3870 **Price, Lisa Sydney**
Patterns of violence in the lives of girls and women: a reading guide. Vancouver: Women's Research Centre, 1989. 97 p.; ISBN: 0-9692145-6-1.

Note: 51 entries.– Canadian and American books, essays, journal articles dealing with issues related to male violence.– Topics include wife assault, dating violence, child sexual abuse, sexual harassment in the workplace, rape, prostitution, pornography and patterns of violence.

Location: OONL.

3871 **Randall, Melanie**
"Feminist theory, political philosophy and the politics of reproduction: an annotated bibliography."
In: *Resources for Feminist Research*; Vol. 18, no. 3 (September 1989) p. 111-122.; ISSN: 0707-8412.

Note: Approx. 150 entries.– References on questions about feminism and political theory, motherhood and the social, scientific, political and economic aspects of the organization and control of reproduction.– Includes Canadian references.

Location: AEU.

3872 **Randall, Melanie**
The state bibliography: an annotated bibliography on women and the state in Canada. [Toronto: Ontario Institute for Studies in Education], 1989. 39 p. (Resources for feminist research Special publication)

Note: Approx. 400 entries.– Books, articles in journals and books, briefs in English from 1970s and 1980s relating to women and the state.

Location: OONL.

3873 **Vallée, Jacqueline**
Bibliographie sélective sur le "burn-out": compilée à l'occasion de la journée internationale des femmes de 1989. [Québec]: Ministère de la santé et des services sociaux, Direction générale de la planification et de l'évaluation, 1989. 23 f. (Collection méthodologie et instrumentation / Québec Ministère de la santé et des services sociaux, Direction générale de la planification et de l'évaluation ; no 1); ISBN: 2-550-19559-0.

Note: Approx. 200 entrées.– Deux parties: partie 1 porte sur le burn-out ou l'épuisement professionnel chez la femme; partie 2 recense les ouvrages qui étudient l'effet du burn-out sur les personnes en général.

Localisation: OONL.

— 1990 —

3874 **Andrew, Caroline**
"Laughing together: women's studies in Canada."
In: *International Journal of Canadian Studies*; No. 1-2 (Spring-Fall 1990) p. 134-148.; ISSN: 1180-3991.

Note: 61 entries.– Bibliographical article on the Canadian contribution to women's studies.

Location: OONL.

3875 **Bélisle Gouault, Denise**
Les femmes et le vieillissement au Canada: bibliographie annotée multidisciplinaire, 1975-1989. Ottawa: Chair conjointe en études des femmes, Carleton University: Université d'Ottawa, [1990]. xii, 133, 125, viii p.; ISBN: 0-9694670-0-1.
Note: Approx. 300 entrées.– Travaux scientifiques portant sur les femmes de 65 ans et plus, du moment qu'ils se penchaient sur la situation au Canada et qu'ils avaient été publiés entre 1975 et 1989: rapports de recherche, monographies, textes de conférences miméographiés, articles de revues scientifiques, publications gouvernementales.– Exclut témoignages personnels, histoires de vie individuelles, travaux de création littéraire.– Texte en français et en anglais disposé tête-bêche.– Titre de la p. de t. additionnelle: *Women and aging in Canada: multidisciplinary annotated bibliography, 1975-1989.*
Localisation: OONL.

3876 **Bélisle Gouault, Denise**
Women and aging in Canada: multidisciplinary annotated bibliography, 1975-1989. Ottawa: Joint Chair in Women's Studies, Carleton University: University of Ottawa, [1990]. viii, 125, 133, xii p.; ISBN: 0-9694670-0-1.
Note: Approx. 300 entries.– Lists research studies with Canadian content concerning women aged 65 and older, published between 1975 and 1989.– Includes research reports, monographs, mimeographed texts of conferences, journal articles, government publications, theses.– Excludes profiles or biographies of individual women, works of literary creation.– Text in English and French with French text on inverted pages.– Title of additional title-page: *Les femmes et le vieillissement au Canada: bibliographie annotée multidisciplinaire, 1975-1989.*
Location: OONL.

3877 **Canada. Solicitor General Canada. Ministry Secretariat**
Women and criminal justice collection/Collection sur les femmes et la justice pénale. [Ottawa]: Solicitor General Canada, Ministry Secretariat, [1990]. 3 l., 134, 139 p. (User report / Solicitor General Canada, Ministry Secretariat ; no. 1990-11); ISBN: 0-662-57665-9.
Note: 1,600 entries.– Books, reports, articles, audio and visual recordings relating to women and the criminal justice system.– Text in English and French/texte en français et en anglais.
Location: OONL.

3878 **Canadian Congress for Learning Opportunities for Women. Literacy Materials for Women Working Group**
Telling our stories our way: a guide to good Canadian materials for women learning to read. Toronto: Canadian Congress for Learning Opportunities for Women, c1990. 101 p.: ill.; ISBN: 0-921283-08-3.
Note: 49 books and pamphlets published in Canada of interest to women learning to read.
Location: OONL.

3879 **Courtemanche, Johanne**
La recherche sur les femmes cadres au Canada: une bibliographie annotée, 1980-1990. Montréal: Le Groupe Femmes, gestion et entreprises, 1990. v, 53 p.; ISBN: 2-9801355-1-8.
Note: 267 entrées.– Comprend les sections: présence des femmes cadres dans différents secteurs d'activités,

environnement organisationnel et femmes cadres, faire carrière au féminin, femmes cadres et conciliation famille-carrière, santé des femmes cadres, femmes entrepreneurs, statistiques sur les femmes cadres.
Supplément: Bégin, Diane. ... , 1990-1991. 25 p.
Localisation: OONL

3880 **Dorney, Lindsay**
Women's studies research handbook: a guide to relevant research at the University of Waterloo. 3rd ed., rev. and enl. Waterloo, Ont.: University of Waterloo Press, c1990. 88 p.; ISBN: 0-88898-100-7.
Note: Approx. 800 entries.– Covers from 1982 to 1990.– Listing of books, book chapters, articles, conference papers, book reviews, encyclopedia entries written by University of Waterloo faculty on women's issues or from feminist perspective.– Includes Canadian references.
Previous editions:
1988. 87 l.; ISBN: 0-88898-084-1.
1986. 57 l.; ISBN: 0-88898-069-8.
... : a guide to relevant research and publications at the University of Waterloo. 1985. 58 l.
Location: OONL.

3881 **Pettersen, Annie; Legault, Gaëtane**
Bibliographie: femmes et médias. [Toronto]: Évaluation-Médias, [1990]. ii, 40 p.; ISBN: 2-9802007-1-9.
Note: Approx. 300 entrées.– La période couverte est de 1965 à 1989.– Principaux thèmes traités: image des femmes, sexisme, pornographie, femmes et radiodiffusion, femmes et cinéma, femmes et journalisme.
Localisation: OONL.

3882 **Tremblay, Manon**
La participation des femmes aux structures politiques électorales: une bibliographie. Québec: Groupe de recherche et d'échange multidisciplinaire féministe, Université Laval, 1990. 142 p. (Cahiers de recherche du GREMF / Groupe de recherche et d'échange multidisciplinaire féministe, Université Laval ; 35); ISBN: 2-89364-037-0.
Note: 1,127 entrées.– Livres, articles, documents officiels.– Comprend un nombre d'ouvrages canadiens.
Localisation: OONL.

3883 **Vlach, Milada; Gallichan, Gilles; Tessier, Louise**
Le droit de vote des femmes au Québec: bibliographie sélective. Montréal: Bibliothèque nationale du Québec, 1990. 192 p.: ill.; ISBN: 2-551-12316-X.
Note: 626 entrées.– Deux parties: la partie chronologique, 1791-1940, composée de publications législatives et d'articles de journaux; la partie alphabétique: études, mémoirs, articles de revues et de journaux.
Localisation: OONL.

3884 **Watson, G. Llewellyn**
Feminism and women's issues: an annotated bibliography and research guide. New York: Garland Pub., 1990. 2 vol.; ISBN: 0-8240-5543-8.
Note: 7,364 entries.– Covers to 1986.– Topics include history, women and capitalism, work, education, sexism, sexuality, religion, health, legal system, sports, politics, sex-role specialization.– Compiled at the University of Prince Edward Island, the bibliography contains a substantial number of Canadian references.
Location: OONL.

3885 **Wylie, Alison, et al.**
"Philosophical feminism: a bibliographical guide to critiques of science."
In: *Resources for Feminist Research*; Vol. 19, no. 2 (June 1990) p. 2-36.; ISSN: 0707-8412.
Note: Approx. 125 entries.– Emphasis on literature which deals mainly with questions of methodology and epistemology.– Restricted to works in English language.– Includes core literature, discipline-specific critiques (social sciences, biological and applied sciences, women and technology), background literature (feminist background, non-feminist critiques of science, women in science).– Includes Canadian references.
Location: AEU.

— 1991 —

3886 **Bataille, Gretchen M.; Sands, Kathleen M.**
American Indian women: a guide to research. New York: Garland, 1991. xvii, 423 p.; ISBN: 0-8240-4799-0.
Note: 1,573 entries.– Primarily published works in the English language on Canadian and American Indian women.– Excludes conference records, dissertations, theses, pamphlets, popular fiction and works for children.– Includes a listing of additional bibliographies and other reference works.– Topics covered include ethnography, cultural history and social roles, politics and law, health, education and employment, visual and performing arts, literature and criticism, autobiography and biography, film and video.
Location: ACU.

3887 **Brandt, Gail Cuthbert**
"Postmodern patchwork: some recent trends in the writing of women's history in Canada."
In: *Canadian Historical Review*; Vol. 72, no. 4 (December 1991) p. 441-470.; ISSN: 0008-3755.
Note: Location: OONL.

3888 **Canada. Women's Bureau**
List of publications [Canada. Women's Bureau]. Ottawa: Labour Canada, Women's Bureau, 1991. [4] p.
Note: Location: OONL.

3889 **Connor, Cynthia**
Women with disabilities: documentation review and annotated bibliography. Ottawa: Disabled Persons Participation Program, Department of the Secretary of State, 1991. 154, 15 p.
Note: The bibliography includes a section "Canadian literature," p. 43-84.
Location: OONL.

3890 **DeCoste, Frederick Charles; Munro, K.M.; MacPherson, Lillian**
Feminist legal literature: a selective annotated bibliography. New York: Garland Publishing, 1991. x, 499 p. (Garland reference library of social science ; vol. 671); ISBN: 0-8240-7117-4.
Note: Multidisciplinary materials dealing with legal issues from a feminist perspective for the period January 1980 to November 1990.– Includes English-language journal articles and articles in French published in French-Canadian publications.– Topics covered include abortion and reproduction, constitutional law, criminal law, family law, feminist theory, judges and courts, First Nations and race, labour and employment.
Location: AEU.

3891 **Finson, Shelley Davis**
Women and religion: a bibliographic guide to Christian feminist liberation theology. Toronto: University of Toronto Press, c1991. xix, 207 p.; ISBN: 0-8020-5881-7.
Note: Approx. 2,700 entries.– Books, anthologies, journal articles, special issues of journals, dissertations, newsletters, reports, study kits published between 1975 and 1988, with the addition of a few significant resources published between 1969 and 1975.– Focus is on resources which relate to women and the Church from a Christian, feminist and liberation perspective.– Most publications are in English, including only the work of writers in Canada and the United States.– References are arranged in 11 sections: Bible, history, Judaism, language, Mariology, ministry, pastoral care, religion and the Church, spirituality, theology, worship, with an appendix listing additional bibliographies, journals, newsletters.
Location: OONL.

3892 **Lenskyj, Helen**
La femme, le sport et l'activité physique: recherche et bibliographie. 2e éd. Ottawa: Condition physique et sport amateur, c1991. 176 p.; ISBN: 0-660-92974-0.
Note: Revue féministe de la littérature sur la femme, le sport et l'activité physique, interdisciplinaire: sport, culture et société (socialisation, sport and genre, carrières dans le sport), psychologie, physiologie, exercice et la fonction de reproduction.– Inclut une liste des revues et périodiques féministe au Canada.
English title: *Women, sport and physical activity: research and bibliography.*
Édition antérieure: *Women, sport and physical activity: research and bibliography/La femme, le sport et l'activité physique: recherche et bibliographie.* 1988. 186 p.; 0-662-55922-3.
Location: OONL.

3893 **Lenskyj, Helen**
Women, sport and physical activity: research and bibliography. 2nd ed. Ottawa: Fitness and Amateur Sport, c1991. 165 p.; ISBN: 0-660-13608-2.
Note: Feminist review of literature on women in sport and physical activity across major disciplines.– Topics include sport, culture and society (socialization, sport and gender, careers in sport), psychology, physiology, exercise and the reproductive function.– Includes list of women's organizations, list of Canadian feminist periodicals and journals.
Titre en français: *La femme, le sport et l'activité physique: recherche et bibliographie.*
Previous edition: *Women, sport and physical activity: research and bibliography/La femme, le sport et l'activité physique: recherche et bibliographie.* 1988. 186 p.; ISBN: 0-662-55922-3.
Location: OONL.

3894 **Mori, Monica; McNern, Janet**
Women and aging: an annotated bibliography, 1968-1991. Vancouver, B.C.: Gerontology Research Centre, Simon Fraser University, 1991. xi, 223 p.; ISBN: 0-86491-112-2.
Note: 378 entries.– Covers 1985 to July 1991.– Includes such categories as attitudes toward elderly women, crime and victimization, demography, drug use, health care, housing, government policy, psycho-social aspects,

social relationships.
Location: OONL.

3895 **Mount Saint Vincent University. Library**
A guide to women's studies resources. [Halifax, N.S.]: The University, [1991]. 54 p.: ill.; ISBN: 1-895306-02-7.
Note: Women's studies reference works arranged by type of material and academic discipline. Includes some Canadian material.
Location: OONL.

3896 **Phillips, Gillian**
Reproduction: a guide to materials in the Women's Educational Resource Centre. Toronto: OISE Press, 1991. vi, 396 p. (WERC bibliography series / Women's Educational Resource Centre ; 1); ISBN: 0-7744-0373-X.
Note: 3,490 entries.– Published and unpublished literature dealing with topics related to human reproduction: abortion, sex education, reproductive rights, family planning, reproductive technologies, maternal mortality, birth control, surrogacy, teenage pregnancy, midwifery, genetic engineering, childbirth, infertility, fetal rights.
Location: OONL.

3897 **Yukon Territory. Women's Directorate. Library**
Yukon Women's Directorate Library containing a guide to using the library and library listings by category. [Whitehorse]: The Library, [1991]. 38 p.; ISBN: 1-55018-125-4.
Note: Approx. 1,200 entries.– Canadian books and documents dealing with women's issues.– Categories include employment, education, legal rights, political process, family, crime, reference materials, journals and videos.
Location: OONL.

— 1992 —

3898 **Desrosiers, Danielle; Lalonde, Nathalie**
Women and the criminal law: a selective bibliography of Canadian material/Les femmes et le droit criminel: une bibliographie sélective d'ouvrages canadiens. Ottawa: Library, Supreme Court of Canada, 1992. 20 l.
Note: Approx. 150 entries.– Canadian publications in English and French dealing with women as criminals and women as victims of crime.
Location: OONL.

3899 **Legros, Gisèle**
Histoire des femmes au Canada: bibliographie sélective/ Women's history in Canada: a selective bibliography. Ottawa: Secrétariat d'État du Canada, Bibliothèque ministérielle, 1992. 16 p.
Note: Approx. 150 entrées.– Livres, articles, publications officielles.– Comprend des publications en français et en anglais.
Localisation: OONL.

3900 **Répertoire de documents sur la femme.** 4e éd. [Ottawa]: Secrétariat d'État, 1992. 60, 58 p.; ISBN: 0-662-59260-3.
Note: Comprend un inventaire de titres de documents imprimés et audio-visuels par et pour les femmes produits de 1978 à 1991.– Texte en français et en anglais disposé tête-bêche.– Titre de la p. de t. additionnelle: *Women's resource catalogue.*
Éditions antérieures:
1984. 68, 81 p.; ISBN: 0-662-53308-9.
Catalogue de références de la femme. 1982. 64, 73 p.
Catalogue de références de la femme/Women's resource catalogue. 1978. 142 p.
Localisation: OONL.

3901 **Women's resource catalogue.** 4th ed. [Ottawa]: Secretary of State, Women's Program, c1992. 58, 60 p.; ISBN: 0-662-59260-3.
Note: Contains print and audio-visual materials by, for and about women produced from 1978 to 1991.– Text in English and French with French text on inverted pages.– Title of additional title-page: *Répertoire de documents sur la femme.*
Previous editions:
c1984. 81, 68 p.; ISBN: 0-662-53308-9.
c1982. 73, 64 p.
Women's resource catalogue/Catalogue de références de la femme. 1978. 142 p.
Location: OONL.

— 1993 —

3902 **Canadian Research Institute for the Advancement of Women**
Canadian women's studies: feminist research. Ottawa: Canadian Studies Directorate, 1993. 46, 50 p. (Canadian studies resource guides. Second series); ISBN: 0-662-60010-4.
Note: Approx. 200 entries.– Contains a section entitled "Key Canadian works," an interdisciplinary list which includes reference works such as bibliographies, indexes and resource guides.– Text in English and French with French text on inverted pages.– Title of additional title page: *Les études féministes au Canada.*
Location: OONL.

3903 **Institut canadien de recherche sur les femmes**
Les Études féministes au Canada. Ottawa: Direction des études canadiennes, 1993. 50, 46 p. (Guides pédagogiques des études canadiennes. Deuxième collection); ISBN: 0-662-60010-4.
Note: Approx. 200 entrées.– Comporte une section, "Principaux ouvrages canadiens."- Inclut des ouvrages de référence: bibliographies, index et répertoires.– Texte en français et en anglais disposé tête-bêche.– Titre de la p. de t. additionnelle: *Canadian women's studies: feminist research.*
Localisation: OONL.

Native Studies

Études autochtones

— 1873 —

3904 **Field, Thomas Warren**
An essay towards an Indian bibliography: being a catalogue of books relating to the history, antiquities, languages, customs, religion, wars, literature, and origin of the American Indians, in the library of Thomas W. Field. New York: Scribner, Armstrong, 1873. iv, 430 p.
Note: "With bibliographical and historical notes, and synopses of the contents of some of the works least known."
Reprints:
Columbus, Ohio: Long's College Book Co., 1951. iv, 430 p.
Detroit: Gale Research Co., 1967. iv, 430 p.
New Haven: W. Reese Co., 1991. 430 p.; ISBN: 0-93922-608-1.
Microform: CIHM Microfiche series ; no. 03100; ISBN: 0-665-03100-9. 5 microfiches (229 fr.).
Location: OONL.

— 1883 —

3905 **Littlefield, George Emery**
Catalogue of books and pamphlets relating to the American Indians. Boston: G.E. Littlefield, 1883. 24 p.
Note: Includes Canadian references.
Microform: CIHM Microfiche series ; no. 09181; ISBN: 0-665-09181-8. 1 microfiche (17 fr.).
Location: OONL.

— 1898 —

3906 **Scadding, Henry**
The Log shanty book-shelf for 1898, the pioneer's predecessor, the red man of North and South America: works on his origin, history, habits and language. Toronto: Copp, Clark, 1898. 5 p.
Note: Microform: CIHM Microfiche series ; no. 13237; ISBN: 0-665-13237-9. 1 microfiche (7 fr.).
Location: OONL.

— 1906 —

3907 **Catalogue des manuscrits et des imprimés en langues sauvages ainsi que des reliques indiennes, exposés à Québec à l'occasion du XVe Congrès international des américanistes, septembre 1906.** Québec: Dussault & Proulx, 1906. 50 p.
Note: Localisation: OONL.

— 1913 —

3908 **Hodge, Frederick Webb**
Handbook of Indians of Canada. Ottawa: Parmalee, 1913. x, 632 p.: maps.
Note: Bibliography, p. 550-593.
Reprint: Toronto: Coles, c1971. ix, 632 p. (Coles Canadiana collection).
Location: OONL.

— 1955 —

3909 **Fried, Jacob**
A survey of the aboriginal populations of Quebec and Labrador. Montreal: McGill University, 1955. iv, 121 p. (Eastern Canadian anthropological series ; no. 1)
Note: Approx. 650 entries in Part 1: "Bibliography and survey of the literature" (p. 1-64), by Jacob Fried and Joan Rothman.— Emphasis on field research: broad ethnographic studies and special interests (ethno-botany, religion, kinship, folklore, etc.).
Location: OONL.

— 1956 —

3910 **Bond, J. Jameson**
Selected bibliography on Eskimo ethnology with special emphasis on acculturation. Ottawa: Department of Northern Affairs and Natural Resources, Northern Administration and Lands Branch, 1956. 11 l.
Note: Location: OONM.

— 1958 —

3911 **Peel, Bruce Braden**
"How the Bible came to the Cree."
In: *Alberta Historical Review*; Vol. 6, no. 2 (Spring 1958) p. 15-19.; ISSN: 0002-4783.
Note: Bibliographical essay concerning translation and publication of religious texts in the Cree language.
Location: OONL.

— 1966 —

3912 **Honigmann, John J.**
Bibliography of northern North America and Greenland. [Chapel Hill]: University of North Carolina, Department of Anthropology, 1966. 19 l.
Note: Approx. 300 entries.— Books, journal articles, theses relating to Algonkian Indians, Athapaskan Indians, Inuit.
Location: OONL.

— 1967 —

3913 **McDiarmid, Garnet**
Culture contact, with special reference to the Indians of North America: an annotated bibliography. [Toronto]: Ontario Institute for Studies in Education, 1967. 214 l.
Note: Approx. 600 entries.— Books, journal articles pertaining to culture change and social structure, psychological processes and culture change, reformulative movements and cults, controlled acculturation.— Material collected by Larry J. Orton, research assistant.
Location: OORD.

— 1968 —

3914 **Indian-Eskimo Association of Canada**
An annotated bibliography of books for libraries serving children of Indian ancestry. Toronto: [s.n.], 1968. 13 p.
Note: Location: AEU.

— 1969 —

3915 **Ontario. Department of Education**
Multi-media resource list: Eskimos and Indians. [Toronto: s.n.], 1969. 50 p.
Note: Listing of books, films, filmstrips, records, picture sets, slide sets.
Location: OONL.

3916 **Ullom, Judith C.**
Folklore of the North American Indians: an annotated bibliography. Washington: Library of Congress, 1969. 126 p.
Note: 152 entries.– Studies, anthologies, children's anthologies, bibliographies.– Culture areas which contain Canadian references include the Central Woodland, Mackenzie and Plateau.
Location: OONL.

3917 **Weinman, Paul L.**
A bibliography of the Iroquoian literature, partially annotated. Albany: University of the State of New York, 1969. ix, 254 p. (Bulletin / New York State Museum and Science Service ; no. 411)
Note: Focus on Five Nations Iroquois.– Deals with archaeology, biography, history and culture contacts, language, material culture, physical anthropology, folklore, ethnology and history.– Includes a list of additional bibliographies.
Location: OONL.

— 1970 —

3918 **Alberta. Department of Education**
A bibliography of materials for and about native people. Edmonton: Alberta Department of Education, 1970. i, 53 p.
Note: Location: OONL.

3919 **Carrière, Gaston**
"Catalogue des manuscrits en langues indiennes conservés aux Archives historiques Oblates, Ottawa."
Dans: *Anthropologica*; Vol. 12, no. 2 (1970) p. 151-179.; ISSN: 0003-5459.
Note: Approx. 200 entrées.
Localisation: AEU.

3920 **Dalhousie University. Library**
The Eskimos: representative sources. Halifax: Dalhousie University Library, 1970. 17 l. (Dalhousie University Library bibliographies)
Note: Approx. 135 entries.– Bibliographies, history, social life and customs, economic conditions, language, legends and folklore, art and technology, periodicals.
Location: OONL.

3921 **Hippler, Arthur E.**
Eskimo acculturation: a selected annotated bibliography of Alaskan and other Eskimo acculturation studies. College, Alaska: Institute of Social, Economic and Governmental Research, University of Alaska, 1970. vi, 209 p.
Note: 199 entries.– 50 in section listing reports and studies on Canadian Inuit and Indians.– Sources selected on basis of contribution to understanding of process of cultural change.– Detailed descriptive notes.
Location: OONL.

3922 **Indian-Eskimo Association of Canada**
Bibliographies of materials relating to the Canadian Indian. [S.l.: s.n., 1970]. [39] p.
Note: Location: OMIH.

3923 **Johnson, Basil**
Bibliography of Indian history books. Toronto: Indian-Eskimo Association of Canada, 1970. 14 p.
Note: Location: OONL.

3924 **Tremblay, Marc-Adélard**
Bibliographie sur l'administration des Indiens du Canada et des États-Unis. [Québec: Université Laval], 1970. 76 f.
Note: Approx. 900 entrées.– Livres, articles, thèses, publications officielles.
Localisation: QQERM.

3925 **University of Saskatchewan. Indian and Northern Curriculum Resources Centre**
A syllabus on Indian history and culture. Saskatoon: The Centre, c1970. 46 l.
Note: Arranged in three sections: "Canadian Indians prior to the coming of the Europeans;" "European contact to the signing of the treaties;" "Contemporary Indians and Metis."- Provides listings of books, audio-visual materials in each section and subsection.
Location: OONL.

3926 **University of Saskatchewan. Indian and Northern Curriculum Resources Centre**
Teacher's guide to resource materials in cross-cultural education: Part one: Indians, Eskimos and early explorers. Saskatoon: University of Saskatchewn, 1970. 1 vol. (in various pagings).
Note: General reference material (history, arts and crafts, mythology), as well as resource material on early explorers of Canada and U.S.; Plains Indians; West Coast Indians; East Coast Indians; Inuit and northern Indians.– Includes annotated lists of filmstrips, films, pictures, recordings, tapes.
Location: OONL.

— 1971 —

3927 **Fenton, William Nelson**
American Indian and white relations to 1830: an essay & a bibliography. New York: Russell & Russell, [1971]. x, 138 p. (Needs and opportunities for study series)
Note: Bibliography, p. 31-122, by L.H. Butterfield, Wilcomb E. Washburn, and William N. Fenton.– Includes Canadian references.
Previous edition: Chapel Hill: Published for the Institute of Early American History and Culture, Williamsburg, Va., by the University of North Carolina Press, 1957. x, 138 p.
Location: OONL.

3928 **Gray, Viviane**
Bibliography of periodicals and articles on law related to Indians and Eskimos of Canada. [Ottawa]: Legal Services, Department of Indian Affairs and Northern Development, [1971]. [89] p.
Note: Approx. 800 entries.– Principal topics include government relations, history, treaties, citizenship, Indian lands and land tenure, reservations, Indian Act.
Location: OONL.

3929 **Meiklejohn, Christopher**
Annotated bibliography of the physical anthropology and human biology of Canadian Eskimos and Indians. [Toronto]: Department of Anthropology, University of Toronto, 1971. 169, xvi l.
Note: 643 entries.
Previous edition: *Bibliography of the physical anthropology and human biology of Canadian Eskimos and Indians.* 1970. 102 p.
Location: OONL.

3930 **Poppe, Roger**
Kutchin bibliography: an annotated bibliography of northern Yukon Kutchin Indians. Edmonton: Canadian Wildlife Service, 1971. 82 l.

Note: Approx. 750 entries.– Compiled as part of preliminary research activity for proposed project in and around village of Old Crow, Yukon.– Investigation of past and current attitudes and values of Kutchin (Loucheux) Indians on hunting, fishing and trapping and relationship to the land.– Study was preparatory to oil exploration and drilling.– Includes books, journal articles, theses, studies, government reports concerning ethnography, natural and physical sciences, culture change, folklore, environment, anthropology on Kutchin in general and Old Crow Vunta Kutchin in particular.
Location: AEUB.

— 1972 —

3931 **Arora, Ved**
Eskimos: a bibliography. Regina: Bibliographic Services Division, Provincial Library, 1972. 50 p.
Note: Approx. 250 entries.– Books, journal articles, government publications dealing with social, cultural and economic life of Canadian and Alaska Inuit.
Location: OOP.

3932 **Canadian Association in Support of the Native Peoples**
Publications list no. 18 [Canadian Association in Support of the Native Peoples]. Toronto: The Association, 1972. [16] p.
Note: 104 entries.– Booklets, leaflets on various topics: culture and conflict, economic conditions and development, education, legal status/laws/rights, urbanization, women.– Bibliographies.– Formerly the Indian-Eskimo Association of Canada.
Location: OONL.

3933 **Fehr, Helen**
Bibliography for professional development. Saskatoon: Indian and Northern Education Program, University of Saskatchewan, [1972]. 48, 15 l.
Note: Approx. 500 entries.– Booklist on Indians and Inuit to aid professional development in field of education.
Location: OONL.

3934 **Feit, Harvey A., et al.**
La Baie James des amérindiens, bibliographie/ Bibliography: native peoples, James Bay region. [Montréal]: s.n., 1972. 62 p.: carte.
Note: Approx. 900 entrées.– La période couverte est de 1882 à 1972.– Couvre toutes les bandes du bassin hydrographique de la baie James, ainsi que celles directment affectées par le projet hydroélectrique, en particulier la bande de Great Whale River, et enfin les groupes ayant des droits sur des territoires situés dans le bassin de la baie James.– Accent sur les écrits des ethnologues professionnels.– Ses trois parties, qui portent sur l'ethnologie et la linguistique des groupes autochtones ainsi que sur la préhistoire de la région, furent préparées respectivement par Harvey Feit et José Mailhot, M.E. MacKenzie, et Charles A. Martijn.– Texte en français et en anglais/text in English and French.
Localisation: OONL.

3935 **Kerri, James N.**
American Indians (U.S. and Canada): a bibliography of contemporary studies and urban research. Winnipeg: Department of the Secretary of State, Canadian Citizenship Branch, 1972. v l., 193 p.
Note: Approx. 1,200 entries.– Listing of studies and research (including theses and dissertations) on change, migration, urbanization, adjustment of people of North American Indian ancestry.
Location: OOP.

3936 **"Missionaries vs. native Americans in the Northwest: a bibliography for re-evaluation."**
In: *Indian Historian*; Vol. 5, no. 2 (Summer 1972) p. 46-48.; ISSN: 0019-4840.
Note: Includes some Canadian references.
Location: OONL.

3937 **Ryan, Joan**
Bibliography on Canadian Indians, 1960-1972. Calgary: Department of Anthropology, University of Calgary, 1972. 117 l.
Note: Approx. 1,000 entries.– Books and articles.– Topics include general anthropological and historical literature, archaeology, biographies and autobiographies, economics, education, Indian association publications.
Location: OONMNS.

3938 **University of Saskatchewan. Indian and Northern Education Program**
Annotated bibliography of articles pertaining to native North Americans. [Saskatoon, Sask.: Indian and Northern Education Program, University of Saskatchewan, 1972]. 44 l.
Note: Approx. 300 entries.– Covers 1959-1971.
Location: OONL.

— 1973 —

3939 **Carrière, Gaston**
"Imprimés en langues indiennes conservés aux Archives historiques Oblates, Ottawa."
Dans: *Anthropologica*; Vol. 15, no 1 (1973) p. 129-151.; ISSN: 0003-5459.
Note: Localisation: AEU.

3940 **Chance, David H.**
"Influences of the Hudson's Bay Company on the native cultures of the Colville District."
In: *Northwest Anthropological Research Notes*; Vol. 7, no. 1 (part 2) (1973) p. 138-166.; ISSN: 0029-3296.
Note: Bibliographical essay.
Location: OONMM.

3941 **Holzmueller, Diana Lynn**
Multi media resource list: Indian and Eskimo culture in the North. Anchorage: University of Alaska, Center for Northern Educational Research, 1973. iii, 59 p.
Note: Approx. 600 entries.– Books, pamphlets, periodicals, exhibits, lessons, audio-visual materials.– Substantial Canadian content.
Location: OONL.

3942 **Lanari, Robert**
"Bibliographie par village, de la population Inuit du Nouveau-Québec."
Dans: *Recherches amérindiennes au Québec*; Vol. 3, nos 3/4 (1973) p. 103-125.; ISSN: 0008-3496.
Note: Approx. 200 entrées.– Partie d'un projet bibliographique qui doit inclure tous les "villages" des Territoires du Nord-Ouest.
Localisation: AEU.

3943 **Marken, Jack W.**
The Indians and Eskimos of North America: a bibliography of books in print through 1972. Vermillion, S.D.: Dakota Press, 1973. ix, 200 p.; ISBN: 0-88249-016-8.
Note: 2,995 entries.– Books (general), bibliographies, handbooks, autobiographies, myths and legends.– Includes books by and about the American and

Canadian Indian and Inuit in print in 1972.
Location: OONL.

3944 **National Indian Brotherhood. Library**
Annotated list of holdings [National Indian Brotherhood Library]. Ottawa: National Indian Brotherhood, 1973. 76 l.
Note: Location: OONL.

3945 **Saskatchewan Provincial Library. Bibliographic Services Division**
Indians of the Americas: a bibliography. Regina: Bibliographic Services Division, Saskatchewan Provincial Library, 1973. 1 vol. (in various pagings).
Note: Approx. 1,700 entries.– List of published monographs on Indian culture and religion, myths and legends, language and literature, arts, crafts, hobbies, biography, status and legal rights, history, travel and fiction.
Location: OKQ.

3946 **Stearns, Louise**
Information Indian: [a list of books and other library materials about Cree Indians, Ojibway Indians, Sioux Indians]. Winnipeg: Manitoba Indian Brotherhood, 1973. 10 l.
Note: Approx. 60 entries.
Location: OONL.

3947 **Whiteside, Don**
Aboriginal people: a selected bibliography concerning Canada's first people. Ottawa: National Indian Brotherhood, c1973. i, 345 p.; ISBN: 0-919682-02-2.
Note: Approx. 4,000 entries.– Emphasizes unpublished materials: speeches, reports, proceedings of conferences, newspaper articles, works by native authors.
Location: OONL.

3948 **Whiteside, Don; Cook, Cyndi**
Contemporary Indian protests: reference aids–bibliographies. [Ottawa]: National Indian Brotherhood, 1973. 4 vol.
Note: Newspaper and periodical articles.– Vol. 1 contains listings for Kenora (Ont.) march, 1965-1966; Cornwall (Akwesasne) bridge blockade, 1968-1969; Indian Act, Canadian Bill of Rights and Lavell-Bedard cases, 1971-1973; Cold Lake boycott and sit-in; death of Fred Quilt, Williams Lake, B.C.; vol. 2 includes Wabasca, Alberta march, 1966; Blue Quills school sit-in, 1970; vol. 3, James Bay hydro-electric project, 1971-1973; vol. 4 has Six Nations controversy, 1890-1973.
Location: OONL.

3949 **Yukon Indian Resource Centre**
Indian education. Whitehorse: Yukon Indian Resource Centre, 1973. 10 l.: ill.
Note: Listing of resource materials about Indians and Inuit, including books, booklets, kits, handbooks, manuals.
Location: OONL.

— 1974 —

3950 **Abler, Thomas S.; Weaver, Sally M.**
A Canadian Indian bibliography, 1960-1970. Toronto: University of Toronto Press, 1974. xii, 732 p., [2] l. of pl.: maps.; ISBN: 0-8020-2092-5.
Note: 3,038 entries.– Covers Indian cultures within political boundaries of Canada.– In dealing with tribes such as the Iroquois and Blackfoot, whose traditional territories straddle Canada-U.S. border, the compilers focussed only on the Canadian community.– Includes

books and monographs, journals, theses, unpublished papers and reports, federal and provincial government publications, publications by Indians.– Contains a case law digest, prepared by Douglas E. Sanders with Paul C. Taylor, which includes all case law relating to Indian legal questions decided from July 1, 1867 to 1972.
Location: OONL.

3951 **Deer, A. Brian**
Bibliography of the Cree, Montagnais, and Naskapi Indians. Rupert House: Cree-Way Project, 1974. [4, 68] l.
Note: Approx. 950 entries.– Focus on ethnology, physical anthropology and linguistics of the Cree on east side of James Bay (Swampy Cree, Moose Cree, Mistassini-Cree, Montagnais, Montagnais-Naskapi).– Excludes prehistory, archaeology, historical materials on Cree contact with traders, explorers, missionaries and government agents.
Location: AEUB.

3952 **Deer, A. Brian**
Bibliography of the history of the James Bay people relating to the Cree people. Rupert House: Cree-Way Project, 1974. 28 l.
Note: Approx. 400 entries.– Books, periodical articles, government publications, theses.– Covers the geographic area bounded by east coast of James Bay to Great Whale River, to bottom of the Bay and southeastward by Lake Mistassini, the territories of eastern Cree of northern Quebec.
Location: AEUB.

3953 **Herisson, Michel R.P.**
An evaluative ethno-historical bibliography of the Malecite Indians. Ottawa: National Museums of Canada, 1974. vii, 260 p. (National Museum of Man Mercury series: Ethnology Division paper ; no. 16)
Note: Approx. 750 entries.– Books, journal articles, government documents, manuscripts to December 1970.
Location: OONL.

3954 **Hippler, Arthur E.; Wood, John R.**
The subarctic Athabascans: a selected annotated bibliography. [Fairbanks, Alaska]: Institute of Social, Economic and Government Research, University of Alaska, [1974]. 331 p. (in various pagings). (ISEGR report series / Institute of Social, Economic and Government Research, University of Alaska ; no. 39); ISBN: 0-88353-012-0.
Note: 518 entries.– Contains references of general or cultural anthropological nature.– Excludes technical material in fields of linguistics, archaeology, physical anthropology.– Includes Canadian references.
Location: OONL.

3955 **Javitch, Gregory**
A selective bibliography of ceremonies, dances, music & songs of the American Indian from books in the library of Gregory Javitch, with an annotated list of Indian dances. Montreal: Osiris, 1974. 71 p. ill.
Note: 97 entries.
Location: OONL.

3956 **Lande, Lawrence M.**
A checklist of printed and manuscript material relating to the Canadian Indian, also relating to the Pacific North West Coast. Montreal: McGill University, 1974. 78 p.: ill., facsims. (Lawrence Lande Foundation for Canadian Historical Research ; no. 9)

Note: 399 entries.– Includes reports, periodicals, dictionaries, grammars and texts in native languages of Canada.
Location: OONL.

3957 **Page, James E.**
"Native studies: an introductory bibliography."
In: *Communiqué: Canadian Studies*; Vol. 1, no. 1 (October 1974) p. 7-18.; ISSN: 0318-1197.
Note: General works about Indians and Inuit, works by native authors, section on native land claims, publications of National Indian Brotherhood, list of native people's newspapers and periodicals.
Location: OONL.

3958 **Raynauld, Françoy**
A bibliography of the Beothuk culture of Newfoundland. Ottawa: National Museum of Man, Ethnology Division, 1974. iv, 14 l.
Note: Approx. 150 entries.
Location: OONM.

3959 **Rogers, Helen F.**
Indian-Inuit authors: an annotated bibliography/ Auteurs indiens et inuit: bibliographie annotée. Ottawa: National Library of Canada, 1974. 108 p.
Note: Approx. 500 entries.– Covers to 1972.– Includes books, articles, addresses, conferences, reports, studies, theses.– Text in English and French in parallel columns/ texte en français et en anglais sur des cols. parallèles.
Location: OONL.

3960 **Union of Nova Scotia Indians**
Bibliography of the Micmac Indians of Nova Scotia and related materials thereto. [Sydney, N.S.]: Union of Nova Scotia Indians, [1974]. [94] l.
Note: Approx. 800 entries.– Books, government publications, periodical articles, theses, manuscripts from earliest records to 1973.
Location: OONL.

— 1975 —

3961 **Armstrong, Judy B.**
"Canadian Indians: a selective bibliography."
In: *Ontario Library Review*; Vol. 59, no. 1 (March 1975) p. 10-19.; ISSN: 0030-2996.
Note: Bibliographies, standard literature, newspapers, non-print materials, reference material, reprints and reassessments dealing with contemporary life, ethnography and biography, folklore and legends.
Location: OONL.

3962 **Boston, Janet Ellen Poth**
Indians of B.C. school package: book list and teacher's guide. [Vancouver]: Educational Research Institute of British Columbia, [1975]. 46 p. (ERIBC reports / Educational Research Institute of British Columbia ; no. 75:7)
Note: 127 entries.– Lists books dealing with Indian history and culture.– Emphasis on British Columbia.– Indicates appropriate grade levels.
Location: OONL.

3963 **Canada. Department of Indian and Northern Affairs. Program Reference Centre**
Economic development consultant reports: bibliography. [Ottawa: Research Reference Service, Indian and Northern Affairs, Government of Canada, 1975]. 192 p.
Note: Approx. 2,000 entries.
Location: OSUU.

3964 **Canada. Indian Claims Commission. Research Resource Centre**
Indian claims in Canada: an introductory essay and selected list of Library holdings/Revendications des Indiens au Canada: un exposé préliminaire et une sélection d'ouvrages disponibles en Bibliothèque. Ottawa: Research Resource Centre, Indian Claims Commission, [c1975]. viii, 278 p.
Note: Approx. 2,500 entries.– Books, serials, periodical articles, legal cases, manuscripts, indexes, tapes, maps.– Text in English and French/texte en français et en anglais.
Supplement: ... : *supplementary bibliography/... : bibliographie supplémentaire*. Ottawa: Published for the Canadian Indian Rights Commission by the National Library of Canada, 1979. iv, 116 p.– Approx. 1,000 entries.
Location: OONL.

3965 **Carter, James L.**
Canadian Eskimo in fact and fiction: a discursive bibliography. Toronto: Ontario Library Association, School Libraries Division, 1975. 21 p. (Ontario Library Association School Library Division Monograph ; no. 4)
Note: Approx. 80 entries.– Selection of literature in the English language, with emphasis on material published since 1965, relative to the study of Canadian Inuit people, designed as a basic collection for a high school library.
Location: OONL.

3966 **Clark, Donald Woodforde**
Koniag-Pacific Eskimo bibliography. Ottawa: National Museums of Canada, 1975. vii, 97 p. (National Museum of Man Mercury series; ISSN: 0316-1854 : Archaeological Survey of Canada paper ; no. 35; ISSN: 0317-2244)
Note: Approx. 500 entries.– Documents concerning prehistory, ethnohistory, cultural anthropology, language, human biology.– Résumé en français.
Location: OONL.

3967 **Haythorne, Owen; Layton, Carol; Laroque, Emma**
Natives of North America: a selected bibliography to improve resource availability in native studies programs. [Edmonton]: Alberta Education, 1975. iii, 156 p.
Note: 890 entries.– Current books (including fiction), films and other audio-visual material to assist in curriculum development.
Location: OONL.

3968 **Isto, Sarah A.**
Cultures in the North: Aleut, Athabascan Indian, Eskimo, Haida Indian, Tlingit Indian, Tsimpshian Indian: multimedia resource list. Fairbanks: Alaska Educational Program for Intercultural Communication, Center for Northern Educational Research, University of Alaska, 1975. v, 46 p.
Note: Approx. 250 entries.– Books, periodicals, films, filmstrips, slides, video recordings.
Location: OONL.

3969 **Lake Winnipeg, Churchill and Nelson Rivers Study Board (Canada)**
Social and economic studies. Winnipeg: The Board, [1975]. 8 vol. in 12: ill., maps (some folded).
Note: Appendix 8: *Social and economic studies*, part 3: "Literature review: socio-economic impact pertaining to native people." 84 p.– Reviews selected North American socio-economic literature pertaining to native people: impact of relocating native people, impact caused by hydro and other water development projects, impact

caused by construction of pipelines and transport systems in northern areas.
Location: OONL.

3970 **Murdock, George Peter; O'Leary, Timothy J.**
Ethnographic bibliography of North America. 4th ed. New Haven: Human Relations Area Files Press, 1975. 5 vol.: maps, (Behavior science bibliographies); ISBN: 0-87536-205-2 (vol. 1); 0-87536-207-9 (vol. 2); 0-87536-209-5 (vol. 3); 0-87536-211-7 (vol. 4); 0-87536-213-3 (vol. 5).
Note: Approx. 40,000 entries.– Restricted to published books and articles on native peoples of North America up to and including 1972.– Excludes manuscripts, maps, films and other audio-visual materials, newspaper articles, broadsides, articles in house organs, fictional materials.– Focus on ethnography (description of cultures and way of life), but includes material on linguistics, archaeology, history.
Vol. 1: *General North America.* xxxvi, 454 p. Canadian material included in sections: "Arctic coast," "Mackenzie-Yukon," "Northwest coast," "Eastern Canada," "Canadian Indians."
Vol. 2: *Arctic and subarctic.* xi, 255 p. Numerous Canadian references.
Vol. 3: *Far West and Pacific Coast.* xxxvi, 266 p. Canadian material in "Northwest Coast" section.– Covers British Columbia native cultures: Tlingit, Haida, Tsimshian, Kwakiutl, Comox, Cowichan, Nootka.
Vol. 4. *Eastern United States.* xxxvi, 253 p. Canadian references in "Northeast" section, which includes the lower Great Lakes.
Vol. 5: *Plains and Southwest.* xxxvi, 406 p. Canadian references in section: "Red River Métis."
Previous editions:
1960. 393 p.
1953. 239 p.
1941. xvi, 168 p.
Supplement: Martin, M.M. ... : *4th edition supplement, 1973-1987.* 1990. 3 vol.
Location: OONL.

3971 **Ontario. Ministry of Education**
People of native ancestry: resource list for the primary and junior divisions. Toronto: Ontario Ministry of Education, 1975. 28 p.
Note: Approx. 200 entries.– Books, films, videos, audiotapes and discs, filmstrips and slides recommended as learning materials.
Location: OONL.

3972 **Perkins, David; Tanis, Norman**
Native Americans of North America: a bibliography based on collections in the libraries of California State University, Northridge. Metuchen, N.J.: Scarecrow Press, 1975. x, 558 p. ill.; ISBN: 0-8108-0878-1.
Note: 3,419 entries.– Includes a selection of materials on Canadian native anthropology, antiquities, art, biography, history, literature, medicine.
Location: OONL.

3973 **Slobodin, Richard**
"Canadian subarctic Athapaskans in the literature to 1965."
In: *Canadian Review of Sociology and Anthropology*; Vol. 12, no. 3 (August 1975) p. 278-289.; ISSN: 0008-4948.
Note: Approx. 75 entries.– Bibliographic essay on ethnography of northern Athapaskan peoples.

Location: OONL.

3974 **Stearns, Louise**
Bibliography of Indians and Métis of Manitoba: preliminary draft. Winnipeg: [s.n.], 1975. [3] l.
Note: Location: OONL.

— 1976 —

3975 **Deer, A. Brian**
"Indians in Canada today: an annotated select bibliography."
In: *History and Social Science Teacher*; Vol. 12, no. 1 (Fall 1976) p. 46-49.; ISSN: 0316-4969.
Note: Lists autobiographies, bibliographies, works on law and native rights, history and culture, select list of native newspapers.
Location: AEU.

3976 **Deer, A. Brian**
Selected list of bibliographies on Indians of Canada. Ottawa: Library and Information Services, National Indian Brotherhood, 1976. [3] l.
Note: 30 entries.
Location: OONL.

3977 **Deer, A. Brian**
Unpublished material by Indian organizations in Canada: a list of holdings in the National Indian Brotherhood library. Ottawa: Library & Info Services, National Indian Brotherhood, 1976. 41 p.
Note: Approx. 400 entries.– Briefs, reports, papers relating to Indian concerns in areas of education, economic development, housing, health, criminal justice system, aboriginal rights and treaties, environment.
Location: OONL.

3978 **Feit, Harvey A.**
"Bibliographie [concernant la Baie James]."
Dans: *Recherches amérindiennes au Québec*; Vol. 6, no 1 (printemps 1976) p. 61-64.; ISSN: 0318-4137.
Note: Localisation: OONL.

3979 **Feit, Harvey A.**
James Bay debates: a bibliography. [Montreal]: Grand Council of Crees (of Quebec), 1976. 13 l.
Note: Approx. 100 entries.– Books, articles, documents, theses pertaining to the James Bay Development Project.– Themes include social impact, ecological impact, government positions, project description, political economy of the project.– Includes a list of additional bibliographies.
Location: QMME.

3980 **Helm, June**
The Indians of the subarctic: a critical bibliography. Bloomington: Indiana University Press, [c1976]. viii, 91 p. (Newberry Library Center for the History of the American Indian, Bibliographical series); ISBN: 0-253-33004-1.
Note: 272 entries.– Books, periodical articles, government publications.– Subarctic culture area defined as embracing the subarctic Algonkians of the Canadian Shield, Athapascans of the Shield and Mackenzie lowlands, Cordilleran Athapascans of northern British Columbia, Yukon and eastern Alaska.
Location: OONL.

3981 **Hodge, William H.**
A bibliography of contemporary North American Indians: selected and partially annotated with study guides. New York: Interland Publishing, 1976. xvi, 310 p.;

ISBN: 0-87989-102-5.
Note: 2,594 entries.– Includes a substantial group of Canadian listings, including government publications.– The term "contemporary" means from about 1875 to 1975.– Topics include anthropologists and Indians, social organization, reservations/rural areas as communities, stability and change in culture, city living, economics, education, religion, personality and culture (including folklore).
Location: OKQ.

3982 **Manitoba. Native Education Branch**
Teacher handbook: resource materials: Native peoples of Manitoba. [Winnipeg]: Manitoba Native Education Branch; School Library Services Branch, Department of Education, [1976]. 99 p.
Note: Approx. 1,500 entries.– Listings for the major Native groupings in Manitoba, sections on Manitoba archaeology, as well as the fur trade in western Canada.
Location: OONL.

3983 **Pageau, Pierrette**
Inuit du Nouveau-Québec: bibliographie. [Québec]: Centre de documentation, Service de l'inventaire des biens culturels, c1976. 175 f.: cartes. (Dossier / Centre de documentation, Service de l'inventaire des biens culturels ; 13)
Note: 1,800 entrées.– Articles de revues, livres, publications officielles, thèses.– Thèmes: histoire, langue, anthropologie physique, ethnologie traditionnelle, changements socio-économiques, art moderne et artisanat, administration et politiques gouvernementales, sources documentaires.– Cartes ethno-géographiques.
Localisation: OONL.

3984 **Rainey, Melvyn D.**
Native American materials for school libraries. Vancouver: British Columbia School Librarians' Association, 1976. 17 p. (BCSLA Occasional paper / British Columbia School Librarians' Association ; no. 9)
Note: Location: OONL.

3985 **Tanner, Helen Hornbeck**
The Ojibwas: a critical bibliography. Bloomington: Published for the Newberry Library [by] Indiana University Press, c1976. viii, 78 p. (Newberry Library Center for the History of the American Indian, Bibliographical series); ISBN: 0-253-34165-5.
Note: 275 entries.– Geographical area extends from the eastern end of Lake Ontario to Lake Winnipeg and Turtle Mountains of North Dakota.– Topics covered include accounts of travellers and explorers, missionaries and missions, regional studies, anthropology, language and tradition, treaties and claims.– Many Canadian listings.
Location: OONL.

— 1977 —

3986 **Canadian Association in Support of the Native Peoples**
Books by native authors. Toronto: Canadian Association in Support of the Native Peoples, [1977]. 2, 7 l.
Note: Approx. 100 entries.
Location: OONL.

3987 **Condon, Ann**
An informal annotated bibliography of materials related to native land claims: with editorial comment from the files and library of Inuit Tapirisat of Canada. [Ottawa]: Department of Indian and Northern Affairs, [1977]. 1 vol. (in various pagings).

Note: References to native claims and rights (Canada, United States, other countries), native proposals, briefs and statements, northern development, environmental issues, education, government relations, employment, anthropology, health, conferences, bibliographies.
Location: OSUU.

3988 **Gurstein, Michael**
Urbanization and Indian people: an analytical literature review. [Ottawa]: Indian and Northern Affairs Canada, 1977. 44, [7] p.
Note: 58 entries.– Reviews studies on Indian migration to urban areas: adjustment, assimilation, transients, types of urban natives, functional requirements for migrants, services required.
Location: OONL.

3989 **Hamilton, W.D.; Spray, W.A.**
Source materials relating to the New Brunswick Indian. Fredericton: Hamray Books, 1977. vii, 134 p.; ISBN: 0-920332-05-6.
Note: 71 entries.– Selection of documents relating history of Indian-white contact and relations from 1584 to 1865.
Location: OONL.

3990 **Indian and Eskimo Affairs Program (Canada). Education and Cultural Support Branch**
About Indians: a listing of books. 4th ed. [Ottawa]: Indian and Eskimo Affairs Program, Education and Cultural Support Branch, [c1977]. [382] p.: ill.; ISBN: 0-662-00714-8.
Note: 1,452 entries.– Compiled to assist librarians and teachers in collection and curriculum development.– Entries arranged by appropriate age groups.
Titre en français: *Les Indiens: une liste de livres à leur sujet.*
Previous editions:
About Indians: a listing of books/Les Indiens: une liste de livres à leur sujet. 1975. 321 p.
1973. 135 p.
1972. 27 p.
Location: OONL.

3991 **Programme des affaires indiennes et esquimaudes (Canada). Direction du soutien éducationel et culturel**
Les Indiens: une liste de livres à leur sujet. 4e éd. [Ottawa]: Programme des affaires indiennes et esquimaudes, Direction du soutien éducationel et culturel, [1977]. [399] p.: ill. en coul.; ISBN: 0-662-00715-8.
Note: 1,452 entrées.– Compilée à l'intention des enseignants, bibliothécaires s'intéressent aux livres écrits au sujet des Indiens.– Des étudiants indiens du Canada ont préparé des annotations.
English title: *About Indians: a listing of books.*
Éditions antérieures:
About Indians: a listing of books/Les Indiens: une liste de livres à leur sujet. 1975. 321 p.
1973. 135 p.
1972. 27 p.
Localisation: OONL.

3992 **Ray, Roger B.**
The Indians of Maine and the Atlantic Provinces: a bibliographical guide, being largely a selected inventory of material on the subject in the Society's library. Portland: Maine Historical Society, 1977. [85] p. (Maine history bibliographical guide series)
Note: Approx. 700 entries.
Previous edition: 1972. [44] p.

Location: OONL.

3993 **Wolf, Carolyn E.; Folk, Karen R.**
Indians of North and South America: a bibliography based on the collection at the Willard E. Yager Library-Museum, Hartwick College, Oneonta, N.Y. Metuchen, N.J.: Scarecrow Press, 1977. ix, 576 p.; ISBN: 0-8108-1026-3.
Note: 4,387 entries.– Covers to 1976.– Includes many references to Canadian subjects.
Supplement: Wolf, Carolyn E.; Chiang, Nancy S. 1988. viii, 654 p.; ISBN: 0-8108-2127-3.– 3,542 entries.
Location: OONL.

— 1978 —

3994 **Akwesasne Library and Cultural Center**
Bibliography of Indian books at the Akwesasne Library and Cultural Center. New York: [The Library and Cultural Center], 1978. 56 p.
Note: Approx. 800 entries.
Location: OONL.

3995 **Robinson, Paul**
Native writers and artists of Canada. Rev. ed. Halifax, N.S.: Atlantic Institute of Education, 1978. 29 p.: map.
Note: Lists and annotates work of about 60 native artists and authors.
Previous edition: 1976. 25 p.
Location: OONL.

3996 **Rouland, Norbert**
"L'ethnologie juridique des Inuit: approche bibliographique critique."
Dans: *Études Inuit Studies*; Vol. 2, no 1 (1978) p. 120-131.; ISSN: 0701-1008.
Note: Localisation: AEU.

3997 **Stebbings, Elizabeth**
Native Indians in British Columbia: a selected annotated bibliography. [Vancouver: B.C. Hydro], 1978. iv, 69 p.: map.
Note: 238 entries.– Deals with Indian land claims and other issues.– Includes books, government publications, journal articles.
Location: OONL.

3998 **Tooker, Elisabeth**
The Indians of the Northeast: a critical bibliography. Bloomington: Indiana University Press, c1978. xi, 77 p. (Newberry Library Center for the History of the American Indian, Bibliographical series); ISBN: 0-253-33003-3.
Note: 270 entries.– Geographical area ranges from Newfoundland to North Carolina, Atlantic Coast to the upper Great Lakes.– Concentrates on ethnological studies and early documentary sources.
Location: OONL.

— 1979 —

3999 **Algonquin Regional Library System**
The first Americans: an Indian, Eskimo resource list. 4th ed. [Parry Sound, Ont.]: Algonquin Regional Library System, 1979. 73 l.
Note: Approx. 500 entries.– Books, government publications. Subjects include antiquities, art, biography, government relations, language, social life and customs, wars, individual tribes and bands.
Previous editions:
The first Americans: Indian-Eskimo resource list, 1973. 1973. [15] l.

The first Americans: an Indian-Eskimo book list. 1971. 13 l.
Location: OONL.

4000 **An annotated list of books about Indians for grades 9 to 13.** Brantford: Woodland Indian Cultural Educational Centre, 1979. 67 l.
Note: 267 entries.
Location: NBFU.

4001 **Bramstedt, Wayne G.**
North American Indians in towns and cities: a bibliography. Monticello, Ill.: Vance Bibliographies, 1979. 74 p. (Public administration series: Bibliography ; P-234; ISSN: 0193-970X)
Note: Approx. 850 entries.– Books, chapters in books, periodical and newspaper articles, theses and dissertations in the social sciences related to Indian militancy in urban settings.– Substantial Canadian listings.
Location: OONL.

4002 **Buchanan, Jim**
Canadian Indian policy: a bibliography. Monticello, Ill.: Vance Bibliographies, 1979. 34 l. (Public administration series: Bibliography ; P-189; ISSN: 0193-970X)
Note: 370 entries.– Covers from the issuance of the 1969 "White paper" to 1979.– Includes government statements and policy documents, principally from the Dept. of Indian and Northern Affairs, and publications containing critical commentary on them.
Supplement: ...: a bibliography supplement, 1979-1986. 1986. 23 p. (Public administration series: Bibliography ; P-2054); ISBN: 1-55590-094-1.– 256 entries.
Location: OONL.

4003 **Gedalof, Robin**
An annotated bibliography of Canadian Inuit literature. [Ottawa]: Indian and Northern Affairs Canada, [1979]. 108 p.
Note: Approx. 300 entries.– Books, periodical articles by Canadian Inuit authors.– Annotations indicate language: English, French, syllabics.
Location: OONL.

4004 **Grumet, Robert Steven**
Native Americans of the Northwest Coast: a critical bibliography. Bloomington: Published for the Newberry Library [by] Indiana University Press, c1979. xvii, 108 p. (Newberry Library Center for the History of the American Indian, Bibliographical series); ISBN: 0-253-30385-0.
Note: 222 entries.– Geographical definition ranges from southeastern Alaskan Panhandle and British Columbia coast to the southern end of Puget Sound in northwestern Washington.– Narrative bibliographical essay of major publications of Northwest Coast archaeology, ethnohistory, ethnography.– Excludes historical tracts and specialized research papers, and all material dealing with myths, texts, languages, physical anthropology.
Location: OONL.

4005 **Hoover, Herbert T.**
The Sioux: a critical bibliography. Bloomington: Indiana University Press, 1979. xvi, 78 p. (Newberry Library Center for the History of the American Indian, Bibliographical series); ISBN: 0-253-34972-9.
Note: 213 entries.– Bibliographical essay and listing of books and articles dealing with Sioux (Assiniboine)

history, culture, biography, battles and wars, influence of non-Indian groups.– Includes Canadian references.
Location: OONL.

4006 **Kydd, Donna L.**
Towards a legal education and information program for native people: a review of the literature and annotated bibliography. [Saskatoon: Native Law Centre, University of Saskatchewan], 1979. vi, 73 p.
Note: 143 entries.– Concentrates on characteristics of native people as they relate to legal education and information programs; reviews material in fields of law, education and culture.– Annotated bibliography compiled by Laurie J. Smith.
Location: OONL.

4007 **Select bibliography on Canadian Indian treaties and related subjects/Bibliographie spéciale sur les traités indiens canadiens et des autres sujets alliés.** [Ottawa]: Treaties and Historical Research Centre (PRE Group), Indian and Northern Affairs, 1979. [38] p.
Note: Approx. 400 entries.– Books, periodical articles, government documents, archival collections, maps.– Text in English and French/texte en français et en anglais.
Location: OONL.

4008 **Snow, Dean R.**
Native American prehistory: a critical bibliography. Bloomington: Published for the Newberry Library [by] Indiana University Press, c1979. xiv, 75 p. (Newberry Library Center for the History of the American Indian, Bibliographical series); ISBN: 0-253-33498-5.
Note: 204 entries.– Books, articles in volumes of collected readings.– Includes some Canadian references, focussing on the B.C. coast, Arctic and Subarctic.
Location: OONL.

4009 **Taylor, Adrienne**
The native peoples of Canada: a checklist of uncatalogu-ed material in the Canadiana Collection. [Toronto]: Canadiana Collection, North York Public Library, 1979. 69 l.: ill., maps.
Note: 488 entries.– Books, pamphlets, government documents, ephemera, periodicals issued separately, microforms on Indians by regions, folklore, myths and legends, arts and crafts, Inuit art, folklore, and language.
Location: OONL.

4010 **Whiteside, Don**
Indians, Indians, Indians: a selected bibliography and resource guide. Ottawa: 1979. 3 vol.
Note: Approx. 7,000 entries.– Includes books, published articles, newspaper articles, unpublished reports and speeches.
Location: OORD.

— 1980 —

4011 **Brascoupé, Simon**
Bibliography related to Indian, Metis and non-status Indian socio-economic development. Ottawa: Regional Economic Expansion, 1980. 148 p.
Note: 606 entries.– Reports, studies, monographs and semi-published papers.– Includes over 200 references to other bibliographies, special library holdings and lists relating to native social and economic development.– Topics include urban adjustment and migration, employment and education, housing and social services.
Location: OONL.

4012 **Brassard, Denise; Lévesque, Lise; Reid, Doris**
Bibliographie sur les Amérindiens: une liste de documents répertoriés au Saguenay-Lac St-Jean. [Jonquière, Québec: s.n.], 1980. xxxviii, 633 p.
Note: 4,105 entrées.– Livres, brochures, publications officielles, thèses, articles de périodiques, bibliographies.
Localisation: OONL.

4013 **Canada. Department of Indian and Northern Affairs. Indian and Inuit Affairs Program. Research Branch**
A listing of research reports: Research Branch. Ottawa: Department of Indian and Northern Affairs, 1980. 55 p.
Note: 55 entries.– Listing of research reports prepared from 1975 to 1979 by or for the Research Branch of Indian and Inuit Affairs Program.– Topics covered include Indian self-government, justice, public attitudes, socio-economic issues, taxation.– Abstracts.
Location: OORD.

4014 **Dominique, Richard; Deschênes, Jean-Guy**
Bibliographie thématique sur les Montagnais-Naskapi. [Québec]: Direction générale du patrimoine, Ministère des affaires culturelles, 1980. 113 p.: cartes. (Direction générale du patrimoine Dossier ; no 48); ISBN: 2-550-01493-6.
Note: Approx. 1,200 entrées.– Livres, articles de revues, publications officielles, documents audio-visuels.– Thèmes: dimension diachronique, démographie, langue, ethnologie traditionnelle, droits aboriginaux, conditions de vie, éducation, changements socio-économiques.
Localisation: OONL.

4015 **Friesen, John W.; Lusty, Terry**
The Metis of Canada: an annotated bibliography. [Toronto]: OISE Press, [c1980]. viii, 99 p.; ISBN: 0-7744-0215-6.
Note: Approx. 700 entries.– Covers from about 1870 to 1980.– Lists books, government documents, pamphlets, reports, papers, theses, periodical articles, private correspondence on the history, sociology and experiences of Metis of western Canada, particularly Alberta.– Surveys writings by and about Metis.
Location: OONL.

4016 **Mail, Patricia D.; McDonald, David R.**
Tulapai to Tokay: a bibliography of alcohol use and abuse among native Americans of North America. New Haven: HRAF Press, 1980. xv, 356 p.
Note: 969 entries.– Covers 1900 to January 1, 1977.– Many Canadian references.
Location: OONL.

4017 **Mailhot, José**
Les Amérindiens et les Inuit du Québec, des stéréotypes à la réalité: orientation bibliographique à l'usage des enseignants du primaire. [Québec]: Service de recherche et expérimentation pédagogique, Direction générale du développement pédagogique, Ministère de l'Éducation, [1980]. 81 p. (Études et documents: Collection "S.R.E.P." / Service de recherche et expérimentation pédagogique); ISBN: 2-550-00969-X.
Note: Approx. 60 entrées.– Inclut livres, documents audiovisuels.
Localisation: OONL.

4018 **Martijn, Charles A.**
"Bibliographie préliminaire des Inuit de la Côte Nord du golfe Saint-Laurent, de la côte ouest de Terre-Neuve et du Labrador méridional: préhistoire et ethnohistoire/Pre-

liminary bibliography of the Inuit of the Gulf of St. Lawrence North Shore, the west coast of Newfoundland and southern Labrador: prehistory and ethnohistory."
Dans: *Études Inuit Studies*; Vol. 4, nos 1-2 (1980) p. 201-232.; ISSN: 0701-1008.
Note· Approx 300 ontróca.
Localisation: OONL.

4019 **McCardle, Bennett**
Canadian Indian treaties, history, politics and law: an annotated reading list. Ottawa: Treaty and Aboriginal Rights Research of the Indian Association of Alberta, 1980. 28 l.
Note: Approx. 250 entries.– Surveys generally available material on Canadian Indian treaties.– Concentrates on western or numbered treaties of 1871-1929, with major works on eastern and pre-Confederation treaties.– Excludes most background documents or position papers issued by regional Indian organizations on individual treaty rights issues.
Location: OLU.

4020 **Sandy Bay School. Library**
Native studies materials bibliography, Sandy Bay School Library. Sandy Bay, Man.: The School, 1980. 40 l.
Note: List of native studies materials in the Sandy Bay School Library.
Location: OONL.

4021 **Thornton, Russell; Grasmick, Mary K.**
Sociology of American Indians: a critical bibliography. Bloomington: Indiana University Press, c1980. xi, 113 p. (Newberry Library Center for the History of the American Indian, Bibliographical series); ISBN: 0-253-35294-0.
Note: 331 entries.– Articles and books produced in period 1880 to 1980 on sociology of Indians and Inuit in United States and Canada.
Location: OONL.

4022 **Whiteside, Don**
An annotated bibliography of articles in *The Globe* (Toronto), related to Indians (Indians, Inuit and Half-breeds) from January 1, 1848 through January 16, 1867, with special attention to the Hudson's Bay Company. (Plus selected items, August through September 1876). Ottawa: Aboriginal Institute of Canada, 1980. 205 p.
Note: Typewritten manuscript.
Location: AEUB.

— 1981 —

4023 **Brumble, H. David**
An annotated bibliography of American Indian and Eskimo autobiographies. Lincoln: University of Nebraska Press, c1981. 177 p.; ISBN: 0-8032-1175-9.
Note: 577 entries.– Includes Canadian references.
Location: OONL.

4024 **Decore, Anne Marie, et al.**
Native people in the curriculum. Edmonton: Alberta Education, 1981. ii, 143 p.
Note: Contains, as "Appendix B," an annotated bibliography, p. 35-134, which includes recommended learning resources, atlases, Kanata kits, Alberta Heritage Learning Resources (for young readers, senior students, adults), Western Canadian Literature for Youth series.
Location: OONL.

4025 **Lazarowich, Linda M.**
The costume of the North American Indian: an annotated bibliography of sources from journals. [Winnipeg]: University of Manitoba, College of Home Economics, 1981. 9 l.
Note: 38 entries.
Location: QMMMCM.

4026 **McCue, Harvey A.**
Subject bibliography: native studies [bibliography of bibliographies]. [Peterborough, Ont.: s.n., 1981]. 10 l.
Note: 56 entries.– Bibliographies, studies pertaining to native culture, ethnography.
Location: OONL.

4027 **Séminaire St-Joseph. Archives**
Les Indiens en Amérique du Nord: au Québec, aux États-Unis. Trois-Rivières, Québec: Les Archives, [1981]. 41 f.
Note: 260 entrées.– Livres, articles de périodiques et de journaux.
Localisation: OONL.

4028 **White, Louise, et al.**
"Indians and Metis of Manitoba: a bibliography."
In: *MSLAVA (Manitoba School Library Audio-visual Association Journal)*; Vol. 8, no. 3 (1981) p. 6-11.; ISSN: 0315-9124.
Note: Location: OONL.

— 1982 —

4029 **Bouchard, Serge; Vincent, Sylvie**
Pour parler des Amérindiens et des Inuit: guide à l'usage des professeurs du secondaire, histoire et géographie: bibliographie sélective commentée. [Québec]: Gouvernement du Québec, Coordination des activités en milieux amérindiens et inuit, Ministère de l'Éducation, 1982. 94 p.; ISBN: 2-550-05231-5.
Note: Approx. 60 entrées.
Localisation: OONL.

4030 **Gendron, Gaétan**
"Les métis et indiens sans statut du Québec: bibliographie sommaire."
Dans: *Recherches amérindiennes au Québec*; Vol. 12, no 2 (1982) p. 138-139.; ISSN: 0318-4137.
Note: Localisation: AEU.

4031 **Hirschfelder, Arlene B.**
Annotated bibliography of the literature on American Indians published in state historical society publications, New England and Middle Atlantic states. Millwood, N.Y.: Kraus International Publications, c1982. xv, 356 p.: ill.; ISBN: 0-527-40889-1.
Note: 1,182 entries.– Lists papers and articles dealing with Indian alliances, land concepts, religion, languages, place-names, trade, treaties, British-French rivalry for Indian allies, Indian-white conflict.– Includes some Canadian references.
Location: OONL.

4032 **Issenman, Betty**
Sources for the study of Inuit clothing. Montreal: B. Issenman, 1982. 60 l.
Note: Books and articles, listings of sources (research tools, periodicals, data centres), films, special collections dealing with Inuit clothing.
Location: ACU.

4033 **Johansson, S. Ryan**
"The demographic history of the native peoples of North America: a selective bibliography."
In: *Yearbook of Physical Anthropology*; Vol. 25 (1982) p. 133-

152.; ISSN: 0096-848X.

Note: Literature review dealing with native North American demography before contact, at-contact population estimates, nature and magnitude of contact shock, pre-modern patterns of demographic adjustment to conquest, recent trends among surviving native North Americans.– Includes some Canadian references.

Location: OONMM.

4034 **Madill, Dennis**
Select annotated bibliography on British Columbia Indian policy and land claims. Ottawa: Department of Indian and Northern Affairs Canada, 1982. i, 27 p.: ill., map.

Note: 89 entries.– Books, journal articles and government publications on specific tribes, treaties and land claims, legal and judicial aspects.

Titre en français: *Bibliographie choisie et annotée de la politique indienne et des revendications territoriales des Indiens de la Colombie-Britannique.*

Location: OONL.

4035 **Manitoba. Department of Education**
Native peoples: Department of Education resources pertaining to Indians, Inuit and Metis. [Rev. ed.]. [Winnipeg]: Province of Manitoba, Department of Education, 1982. vii, 287 p. (Curriculum support series / Manitoba Department of Education)

Note: Approx. 1,400 entries.– Books and documents, recordings, audio and video tapes, films, periodicals, bibliographies.– Topics covered include the arts, biography, education, history, literature, languages, religion/mythology.

Previous edition: 1980. 234 p.

Location: OONL.

4036 **Maud, Ralph**
A guide to B.C. Indian myth and legend: a short history of myth-collecting and a survey of published texts. Vancouver: Talonbooks, 1982. 218 p.; ISBN: 0-88922-189-8.

Note: Comprehensive survey of myth collecting and bibliography of ethnographic studies in British Columbia.– Discusses the work of Boas, Teit, Hill-Tout, Barbeau, Swanton, Jenness, Halpern, Sapir, Swanton, and others.

Location: OONL.

4037 **McCardle, Bennett**
Indian history and claims: a research handbook. [Ottawa]: Indian and Northern Affairs Canada, 1982. 2 vol.: ill., map.

Note: Approx. 500 entries.– Designed as a guide to research on Indian history, especially for projects which rely on written records, archival documents, ethnological studies.– Basic sources are listed, research techniques described.– Prepared for the Treaties and Historical Research Centre, Research Branch, Corporate Policy, Indian and Northern Affairs Canada.

Location: OONL.

4038 **McHoul, Alison**
Books to enjoy: a list for teachers on Indian reserves. Ottawa: Indian and Northern Affairs Canada, 1982. 23 p.: ill.

Note: Approx. 125 entries.– Booklist prepared to accompany display at convention of Alberta Indian Education Association.– Includes works by Indian authors or about Indian subjects, adult and juvenile.

Location: OONL.

4039 **Navet, Eric**
"Introduction à une bibliographie analytique des cultures amérindiennes sub-arctiques."
Dans: *Inter-Nord*; No. 16 (1982) p. 324-332.; ISSN: 0074-1035.

Note: 166 entrées.– Bibliographies, ouvrages de référence, études ethnographiques et sociologiques.

Localisation: OONL.

4040 **Surtees, Robert J.**
Canadian Indian policy: a critical bibliography. Bloomington: Indiana University Press, [c1982]. ix, 107 p. (Newberry Library Center for the History of the American Indian, Bibliographical series); ISBN: 0-253-31300-7.

Note: 293 entries.– Selection of books, articles, government publications covering the period 1608 to the present, with majority of imprints from 1950 to 1981.

Location: OONL.

4041 **Thornton, Russell; Sandefur, Gary D.; Grasmick, Harold G.**
The urbanization of American Indians: a critical bibliography. Bloomington: Published for the Newberry Library [by] Indiana University Press, c1982. viii, 87 p. (Newberry Library Center for the History of the American Indian, Bibliographical series); ISBN: 0-253-36205-9.

Note: 198 entries.– Includes Canadian references.

Location: OONL.

4042 **Van Hoorn, L.**
Index to Indian acts, 1876-1978 / Répertoire des lois relatives aux Indiens, 1876-1978. [Ottawa]: Indian and Northern Affairs Canada, 1982. 48 p.: ill.

Note: Contains a series of tables, chronologically arranged, tracing the development of the Indian Act from 1876, amendments and revisions.– Text in English and French / texte en français et en anglais.

Location: OONL.

— 1983 —

4043 **Barnett, Don C.; Dyer, Aldrich J.**
Research related to native peoples at the University of Saskatchewan, 1912-1983. [Regina: University of Saskatchewan], 1983. vi, 163 p.

Note: 62 entries.– Abstracts of studies focused on Canadian Indian, Inuit, Metis peoples: description of the study, research procedures, findings and conclusions.– Categories of contents: prehistoric excavations, role of forces/institutions/individuals, evaluation and assessment, attitudes and values, implications, processes.

Location: OONL.

4044 **Green, Howard; Sawyer, Don**
The NESA bibliography annotated for native studies. Vancouver: The Tillacum Library, 1983. 122 p.; ISBN: 0-88978-168-0.

Note: Approx. 500 entries.– Compiled by Native Education Services Associates to provide a tool for educators in preparation of programs and curriculum development.– Includes books, pamphlets, government documents, periodicals, newspapers, audio-visual materials.– Educational skill level assigned to each entry.

Location: OONL.

4045 **Green, Rayna**
Native American women: a contextual bibliography.
Bloomington: Indiana University Press, c1983. viii, 120 p.;
ISBN: 0-253-33976-6.
Note: 672 entries.– Lists items published from 1620 to
1983.– Substantial selection of Canadian books and
articles, films, conference papers.– Excludes material
contained in standard ethnographies or histories.–
Contains titles specifically about Native women as
members of groups or as individuals.
Location: OONL.

4046 **Haas, Marilyn L.**
Indians of North America: methods and sources for
library research. Hamden, Conn.: Library Professional
Publications, 1983. xii, 163 p.; ISBN: 0-208-01980-4.
Note: Three parts: library methodology and reference
works; annotated bibliography of topics related to native
studies; unannotated list of books on individual tribes.
Location: OONL.

4047 **Hirschfelder, Arlene B.; Byler, Mary Gloyne; Dorris,
Michael A.**
Guide to research on North American Indians. Chicago:
American Library Association, 1983. xi, 330 p.; ISBN: 0-
8389-0353-3.
Note: Approx. 1,100 entries.– Annotated list of English
language books, articles, government documents in 27
fields of study.– Geographical area covered: United
States, including Alaska, Canada (especially those tribes
whose traditional territory straddles the Canada-U.S.
border).– Excludes ethnographical studies.
Location: OONL.

4048 **Jamieson, Kathleen**
Native women in Canada: a selected bibliography.
[Ottawa]: Social Sciences and Humanities Research
Council of Canada, [1983]. 49 p.; ISBN: 0-662-12396-4.
Note: Approx. 550 entries.– Books, periodical articles,
theses, films, with emphasis on material since 1970.
Location: OONL.

4049 **Madill, Dennis**
Bibliographie annotée et choisie sur l'histoire et les
revendications des Métis. [Ottawa]: Centre de la
recherche historique et de l'étude des traités, Affaires
indiennes et du Nord Canada, 1983. iii, 54 p.: carte.
Note: 169 entrées.– Documents sur les rébellions de Riel,
les revendications foncières des Métis, des études
régionales, les organismes Métis, les questions
constitutionnelles.
English title: *Select annotated bibliography on Métis history
and land claims.*
Localisation: OONL.

4050 **Madill, Dennis**
Bibliographie choisie et annotée de la politique indienne
et des revendications territoriales des Indiens de la
Colombie-Britannique. Ottawa: Affaires indiennes et du
Nord Canada, 1983. 28 p.: carte.
Note: 89 entrées.– Monographies, articles de revues,
documents gouvernementales sur certaines tribus
particulières, la question territoriale, des traités, affaires
judiciaires.
English title: *Select annotated bibliography on British
Columbia Indian policy and land claims.*
Localisation: OONL.

4051 **Madill, Dennis**
Select annotated bibliography on Métis history and
claims. Ottawa: Treaties and Historical Research Centre,
Indian and Northern Affairs Canada, 1983. 45 p.: map.
Note: 169 entries.– Biographical studies, Riel rebellions,
Métis land claims, regional studies, Métis organizations,
constitutional issues.
Titre en français: *Bibliographie annotée choisie sur l'histoire
et les revendications des Métis.*
Location: OONL.

4052 **Narby, Jeremy; Davis, Shelton**
Resource development and indigenous peoples: a
comparative bibliography. Boston: Anthropology
Resource Center, 1983. 32 p.
Note: 326 entries.– Includes section on Canada.
Location: OONL.

4053 **Smith, Dwight L.**
Indians of the United States and Canada: a bibliography.
Santa Barbara: ABC-Clio, c1974-1983. 2 vol. (Clio
bibliography series ; no. 3, 9); ISBN: 0-87436-124-9 (vol.
1); 0-87436-149-4 (vol. 2).
Note: Vol. 1: 1,687 entries.– Contains history and social
science periodical literature published from 1954 to
1972.– Vol. 2: 3,213 entries.– Continues the coverage to
1983.
Location: OONL.

— 1984 —

4054 **Clements, William M.; Malpezzi, Frances M.**
Native American folklore, 1879-1979: an annotated
bibliography. Athens, Ohio: Swallow Press, c1984. xxiii,
247 p.; ISBN: 0-8040-0831-0.
Note: 5,450 entries.– Books and articles which treat oral
narratives, songs, chants, prayers, formulas, orations,
proverbs, riddles, word play, music, dance, games,
ceremonials of Native North Americans.– Arranged in
geographical regions, with index of subjects, index of
authors, editors and translators.– Includes Canadian
references in sections "Northwest Coast," "Sub-arctic,"
"Arctic," "Plains," and "Northeast."– Provides a list of
additional bibliographies and bibliographical articles.
Location: OONL.

4055 **Daugherty, Wayne**
Bibliographie choisie et annotée sur l'histoire des Indiens
des Maritimes. Ottawa: Ministère des affaires indiennes
et du nord, 1984. 25 p.
Note: English title: *Select annotated bibliography on
Maritime Indian history.*
Location: OONL.

4056 **Daugherty, Wayne**
Select annotated bibliography on Maritime Indian
history. Ottawa: Department of Indian and Northern
Affairs, 1984. 22 p.
Note: Titre en français: *Bibliographie choisie et annotée sur
l'histoire des Indiens des Maritimes.*
Location: OONL.

4057 **Echlin, Kim**
Bibliography of Canadian Indian mythology.
[Downsview? Ont.: s.n.], 1984. 48 col.
Note: Approx. 500 entries.– Intended to uncover lesser-
known sources of myth.– Researches museum reports,
geological surveys, anthropological papers.– Focus on
original-language materials.– Includes only early records
of myths and translations/adaptations for children are

omitted.

Location: OONL.

4058 Helm, June; Kurtz, Royce

Subarctic Athapaskan bibliography: 1984. Iowa City: Department of Anthropology, University of Iowa, [1984]. i, 515 p.

Note: Approx. 3,900 entries.– Coverage to June 1984.– Books, journal articles, theses, government publications dealing with archaeology, human biology, environment, ethnology, history and development, linguistics.

Location: AEUB.

Previous edition: *Subarctic Athapaskan bibliography, 1973.* 1973. i, 198, 23 l.– Approx. 1,500 entries.– Entries have been incorporated into the 1984 edition.

Supplement: *Addenda and corrigenda, 1974, to Subarctic Athapaskan bibliography, 1973.* [1974]. 23 l.

Location: OONL.

4059 Legros, Dominique

"Bibliographie des Amérindiens de la Côte Nord-Ouest (1973-1982)."

Dans: *Recherches amérindiennes au Québec*; Vol. 14, no 2 (1984) p. 57-70.; ISSN: 0318-4137.

Note: Approx. 500 entrées.– Ouvrages d'ordre général ou comparatif; ethnographies relatives à chacun des sous-groupes de la côte nord-ouest de l'Amérique.

Localisation: AEU.

4060 Logement dans les réserves: bibliographie annotée.

[Ottawa: Affaires indiennes et du Nord canadien], 1984. 24 f.

Note: Approx. 60 entrées.– Comporte une liste de références sur organization, planification, développement, construction, gestion du logement dans les réserves.

English title: *On-reserve housing: annotated bibliography.*

Localisation: OONL.

4061 Minion, Robin

Myths and legends. Edmonton: Boreal Institute for Northern Studies, University of Alberta, 1984. 79 p. (Boreal Institute for Northern Studies Bibliographic series ; no. 5; ISSN: 0824-8192); ISBN: 0-919058-39-6.

Note: 222 entries.– Series contains monographs, theses, government documents, consultants' reports, children's books, conference proceedings, microforms on topics related to northern environment and people.– BINS series produced monthly from January 1984 to May 1986 (no. 29).– Online access: *Boreal Northern Titles (BNT)*, available through QL Systems Limited.

Location: OONL.

4062 Minion, Robin

Native rights in Canada. Edmonton: Boreal Institute for Northern Studies, University of Alberta, 1984. 102 p. (Boreal Institute for Northern Studies Bibliographic series ; no. 1; ISSN: 0824-8192); ISBN: 0-919058-35-3.

Note: 280 entries.– Covers from 1977 to 1983.– Series includes monographs, theses, government documents, consultants' reports compiled from Boreal Institute's SPIRES database.– BINS series produced monthly from January 1984 to May 1986 (no. 29).– Online access: *Boreal Northern Titles (BNT)*, available through QL Systems Limited.

Location: OONL.

4063 Murdoch, John

A bibliography of Algonquian syllabic texts in Canadian repositories. [Rupert House, Quebec]: Project ASTIC, 1984. xiii, 147 p.: ill.; ISBN: 0-920245-08-0.

Note: 388 entries.– Bibles, gospels, hymn books, prayer books, readers, grammars.– All titles are listed in English or French with accompanying photographs of title pages which include syllabic characters.– All entries are given locations.

Location: OONL.

4064 Native Indian Pre-School Curriculum Research Project

Native Indian pre-school curriculum resources bibliography. Vancouver: Urban Native Indian Education Society, c1984. 107 p.: maps.; ISBN: 0-9691591-0-2.

Note: Approx. 500 entries.– Language arts, art, science, social studies pre-mathematics, music/movement and motor development.– Books and films of native Indian content suitable for pre-school curriculum.

Location: OONL.

4065 Ojibway-Cree Resource Centre

Ojibway Resource Centre catalogue. 2nd ed. [Timmins, Ont.]: The Centre, [1984]. 342, 262 p.

Note: Approx. 6,800 entries.– Monographs, serials, journal articles, government publications, briefs to commissions of inquiry on native history and archaeology, culture, legends and tales, literature and oratory, language, religion and philosophy, technology.

Previous edition: 1978. ii, 342 p.

Location: OONL.

4066 On-reserve housing: annotated bibliography. [Ottawa: Indian and Northern Affairs Canada], 1984. 24 l.

Note: Approx. 60 entries.– Lists references on organization, planning, development, construction, management of housing projects on Canadian Indian reserves.

Titre en français: *Logement dans les réserves: bibliographie annotée.*

Location: OONL.

4067 Seaton, Elizabeth; Valaskakis, Gail

New technologies and native people in northern Canada: an annotated bibliography of communications projects and research. Montreal: Concordia University, 1984. 72 l.

Note: Approx. 200 entries.– Covers 1970-1984.– Topics include native communication societies, radio, satellite communication, telephone, telidon, training, visual media.

Location: OORT.

4068 Vincent, Sylvie; Proulx, Jean-René

Bilan des recherches ethnohistoriques concernant les groupes autochtones du Québec. [Québec]: Ministère des affaires culturelles du Québec, 1984. 5 vol.: carte.

Note: Vol. 1: *État de la recherche.* v, 113 p. (annexes: pagination variée).– Notes sur objectifs, méthodes et organisation du bilan, évaluation quantitative de la recherche, les sources de l'ethnohistoire, organisation de la recherche, propositions pour la recherche future.

Vol. 2: *Bibliographie des ouvrages ethnohistoriques, 1960-1983.* xviii, 133, 6 p. Approx. 1,200 entrées.– Rassemble des titres d'articles, de rapports et de livres portant sur l'histoire des autochtones par des anthropologues et des historiens et publiés après 1960.

Vol. 3: *Bibliographie des sources publiées.* xiv, 153 p. Approx. 1,500 entrées.– Liste des ouvrages qui peuvent être considérés comme des sources pour l'histoire des autochtones du Québec: sources primaire et sources secondaire, entre le 15e siècle et 1950.

Vol. 4: *Tableaux des sources archivistiques* xix, 85 f, Liste des dépôts et des fonds d'archives qui contiennent des informations sur les groupes autochtones du Québec.

Vol. 5: *Bibliographie de guides et liste de dépôts d'archives.* v, 67 p. Répertoire des instruments de recherche et la liste des addresses des dépôts d'archives.

English title: *Review of ethnohistorical research on the native peoples of Quebec.*

Localisation: QMBN.

— 1985 —

4069 **Bandy, P.J.**
A selection of publications on the native Indians of British Columbia with particular reference to the struggle for native rights. Victoria: Ministry of Environment, 1985. 25 l.
Note: Location: OONL.

4070 **Banks, Joyce M.**
Books in native languages in the rare book collections of the National Library of Canada/Livres en langues autochtones dans les collections de livres rares de la Bibliothèque nationale du Canada. Rev. & enl. ed. Ottawa: National Library of Canada, 1985. [xvii], 190 p.: facsims.; ISBN: 0-660-53030-9.
Note: Approx. 500 entries.– Listing of pre-1950 imprints only: books in native languages, dictionaries and grammars.– Fifty-eight languages or dialects are represented.– Includes English and French publications.– Text in English and French/texte en français et en anglais. Previous edition: *Books in native languages in the collection of the Rare Books and Manuscripts Division of the National Library of Canada/Livres en langues autochtones dans la collection de la Division des livres rares et des manuscrits de la Bibliothèque nationale du Canada.* 1980. xiii, 93 p.; ISBN: 0-662-50733-9.
Location: OONL.

4071 **Canadian Housing Information Centre**
Bibliography on native housing. Ottawa: The Centre, 1985. 11 p.
Note: Approx. 100 entries.– Government studies and reports, theses, research by private and university agencies and institutes, native organizations.
Location: OONL.

4072 **Carrière, Richard, et al.**
Native child abuse and neglect: a bibliography of Canadian resources. Sudbury, Ont.: Laurentian University, 1985. 29, vii p.
Note: Approx. 300 entries.– Reports, studies, periodical and newspaper articles dealing with aspects of native child abuse and neglect. Topics include causative factors, manifestations, identification and reporting, treatment, foster care, prevention, child abuse and the law.– List of agencies.
Location: OONL.

4073 **Dominique, Richard; Deschênes, Jean-Guy**
Cultures et sociétés autochtones du Québec: bibliographie critique. Québec: Institut québécois de recherche sur la culture, 1985. 221 p.: cartes. (Instruments de travail / Institut québécois de recherche sur la culture ; no 11); ISBN: 2-89224-066-2.
Note: Approx. 1,200 entrées.– Comprend six grandes

parties: "Les Iroquoiens," "Les Algonquiens maritimes," "Les Algonquiens du subarctique," "Les Inuit," "Les Métis," "Les administration des Autochtones."
Localisation: OONL.

4074 **Dorais, Louis-Jacques**
"La recherche sur les Inuit du Nord québécois: bilan et perspectives."
Dans: *Études Inuit Studies*; Vol. 8, no 2 (1985) p. 99-115.; ISSN: 0701-1008.
Note: Localisation: AEU.

4075 **Evans, Karen**
Masinahikan: native language imprints in the archives and libraries of the Anglican Church of Canada. Toronto: Anglican Book Centre, 1985. xxiii, 357 p.; ISBN: 0-919891-33-0.
Note: 795 entries.– Represents holdings of 72 repositories and 44 native language categories.
Location: OONL.

4076 **Garratt, John G.**
The four Indian kings/Les quatre rois indiens. [Ottawa]: Public Archives Canada, 1985. xiv, 186 p.: ill., facsims.; ISBN: 0-660-53006-6.
Note: Short history of the Mohawk Indians who went to London in 1710 to plead for assistance of Queen Anne, together with a bibliographical record of works concerning them: the accounts, the ballad (in broadside and chapbook), the speech, the contemporary (eighteenth century) works, later works.– Text in English and French/texte en français et en anglais.
Location: OONL.

4077 **Native People's Resource Centre (London, Ont.)**
Catalogue: books, vertical files, videorecordings. London, Ont.: The Centre, [1982-1985]. [43] p.
Note: Approx. 500 entries.
Location: OONL.

4078 **People's Library**
Reference pamphlets listing, 1985-1986. [Winnipeg: The Library, 1985]. [128] p.
Note: Approx. 1,900 entries.– Emphasis on western Canadian and especially Manitoba native peoples.– Topics include culture, child welfare, criminal law/justice, education, government relations, history, Indian self-government, social conditions, urban issues, women.
Location: OONL.

4079 **Vincent, Sylvie; Proulx, Jean-René**
Review of ethnohistorical research on the native peoples of Quebec. [Québec]: Direction régionale du Nouveau-Québec et Service aux autochtones, Ministère des affaires culturelles du Québec, 1985. 5 vol.; ISBN: 2-550-12263-1 (complete set).
Note: Vol. 1: *Assessment of research.* v, 102 p. (appendices: various pagings).– Notes on objectives, methods, organization of review; sources of ethnohistory and evaluation of content, research proposals.
Vol. 2: *Bibliography of ethnohistorical works, 1960-1983.* xvii, 163 p. Approx. 1,200 entries.– Includes books, articles, theses, papers relating to native groups having lived or living within present boundaries of province of Quebec, presenting situation experienced between arrival of Europeans (fifteenth century) and mid-twentieth century: history, culture, relations with non-natives, economic activities, languages, social and political organization, narratives and music, biographies.

Vol. 3: *Bibliography of published works.* xiii, 172 p. Approx. 1,500 entries.– Primary and secondary sources about the life of native groups: books, booklets, maps, pictures, photographs, reports, memoirs, reports by explorers/ scientists/merchants/missionaries/Indian Affairs officials, public documents, linguistic documents.
Vol. 4: *Summary tables of archival sources.* xviii, 85 p.
Vol. 5: *Bibliography of guides and list of archives.* v, 74 p. Guides, inventories, catalogues of manuscript sources, cartographic sources, iconographic sources, archives related to ethnohistory of native peoples.
Titre en français: *Bilan des recherches ethnohistoriques concernant les groupes autochtones du Québec.*
Location: OONL.

4080 **Weist, Katherine M.; Sharrock, Susan R.**
An annotated bibliography of Northern Plains ethnohistory. Missoula, Mont.: Department of Anthropology, University of Montana, 1985. 299 p. (Contributions to anthropology / Department of Anthropology, University of Montana ; no 8)
Note: 718 entries.– Annotated list of primary and secondary sources: books, articles, reports.– Geographical coverage includes parts of Canada and the United States (bounded on the north by the Saskatchewan River and on the west by the Rocky Mountains.– Time period consists of observations which took place prior to 1880.– Excludes references to Red River Settlement, Métis and Riel Rebellion.– Emphasis on native tribes, not white settlement.
Location: ACG.

— 1986 —

4081 **British Columbia. Provincial Museum**
A selected list of publications on the Indians of British Columbia. [Victoria]: British Columbia Provincial Museum, 1986. 65 p.
Note: Books, articles, anthropological papers.
Previous editions:
A selection of publications on the Indians of British Columbia. 1982. 50 p.
1976. 30 p.
1970. 31 p.
1963. 32 p.
A selected list of publications pertaining to the Indians of British Columbia. 1961. 21 p.
1956. 21 p.
Location: OONL.

4082 **Cassidy, Frank; Dickson, Heather**
A selected and annotated bibliography on Indian self-government. [Victoria, B.C.]: School of Public Administration, University of Victoria, 1986. 34 l.
Note: 70 entries.– Prepared for the Gitksan-Wet'suwet'en Tribal Council as part of its Organizing for Self-Government Project.– Books, reports and studies, journal articles.– Topics covered include historical context of federal administration of Indian affairs, federal Indian policy, movement for self-government, aboriginal peoples and the constitutional process, aboriginal rights and the land question, colonialism and political conflict in British Columbia.
Location: OONL.

4083 **Dennis, Janet Lenoir**
An annotated bibliography of Canadian Plains Indian legends published in book form. Edmonton: [J.L. Dennis], 1986. 52 l.
Note: Approx. 200 entries.– Works in the English language from the oral tradition of Canadian Plains Indian tribes.– Includes bibliographies of native studies materials.
Location: OONL.

4084 **Deschênes, Jean-Guy**
Selective annoted [sic] bibliography for the study of the Amerindians and Inuit: a guide for secondary school history and geography teachers. [Québec]: Gouvernement du Québec, Ministère de l'Éducation, 1986. 110 p.; ISBN: 2-550-08669-4.
Note: Approx. 75 entries.– Selected reference material and cartographic references, with emphasis on administrative relations with native peoples, impact on Indian and Inuit societies of development projects in the North, resistance and diplomatic activity of native peoples, multiplicity of native cultures, principally within the province of Quebec.
Location: OONL.

4085 **Drolet, Gaëtan; Labrecque, Marie France**
Les femmes amérindiennes au Québec: guide annotée des sources d'information. [Québec]: Laboratoire de recherches anthropologiques, Département d'anthropologie, Université Laval, 1986. vii, 100 p. (Collection "Outils pédagogiques" / Laboratoire de recherches anthropologiques, Département d'anthropologie, Université Laval ; no 2)
Note: 253 entrées.– Livres, thèses, rapports, articles scientifiques et vulgarisés touchant les femmes amérindiennes au Québec depuis 1696.
Localisation: OONL.

4086 **Krech, Shepard**
Native Canadian anthropology and history: a selected bibliography. Winnipeg: Rupert's Land Research Centre, University of Winnipeg, 1986. 214 p.
Note: Approx. 2,150 entries.– Emphasis on current materials, post-1980.– Includes books, journal articles, research papers, grouped into three sections: reference, comparative and historical sources; tribal-specific materials; specific topics, including health and disease.– Excludes most government publications and unpublished material.
Location: OONL.

4087 **Peters, Evelyn J.**
Aboriginal self-government in Canada: a bibliography, 1986. Kingston, Ont.: Institute of Intergovernmental Relations, Queen's University, c1986. ix, 112 p. (Aboriginal peoples and constitutional reform); ISBN: 0-88911-423-4.
Note: Approx. 700 entries.– Current materials (1970s and 1980s): periodical articles, papers, reports, studies; documents related to first ministers' conferences on aboriginal constitutional matters.
Supplement: ... , *1987-90.* c1991. xii, 58 p.; ISBN: 0-88911-580-X.
Location: OONL.

4088 **Ryan, Helen**
Survey of documents available for research in the Treaties and Historical Research Centre/Catalogue des documents au Centre de recherches historiques et d'étude des traités. Rev. ed. Ottawa: Treaties and Historical Research Centre, 1986. v, 139 p.

Note: Approx. 1,300 entries.– Published and unpublished material, books and articles, working files, judicial cases and statutes, news clippings, government reports and studies.– List of bibliographies. Text in English and French/texte en français et en anglais.
Previous edition: 1983. v, 130 p.
Location: OONL.

— 1987 —

4089 **Micmac-Maliseet Institute**
The Micmac-Maliseet resource collection: a bibliographical listing. Fredericton: Micmac-Maliseet Institute, University of New Brunswick, 1987. 115 p.
Note: Approx. 1,500 entries.– Books, periodicals, articles, audio-visual materials concerning Micmac, Maliseet, Passamaquoddy, Penobscot, Beothuk peoples of Atlantic provinces and Maine.
Location: OONL.

4090 **Moskal, Susan**
Contemporary Canadian Indian statistics published by the federal government, 1960-1985: a selective bibliography and subject index to sources available in the University of Waterloo Library. Waterloo, Ont.: The Library, c1987. vii, 25 p. (University of Waterloo Library bibliography ; no. 16; ISSN: 0829-948X); ISBN: 0-920834-03-5.
Note: 95 entries.– Excludes all Statistics Canada publications, including the Census of Canada.
Location: OONL.

4091 **People's Library**
People's Library bibliography, 1987-88. Winnipeg: Manitoba Indian Cultural Education Centre, 1987. 204 p.
Note: Location: SSU.

4092 **Price, John A.**
"Recent publications in Canadian native studies."
In: *Native people, native lands: Canadian Indians, Inuit and Metis*, edited by Bruce Alden Cox. Ottawa: Carleton University Press, 1987. P. 266-298. (Carleton Library series ; no. 142); ISBN: 0-88629-062-7.
Note: Selection of about 300 titles published from 1966 to 1987.– Bibliographies, native authors, art, archaeology, religion, politics and law, cultural anthropology.
Location: OONL.

4093 **Stanek, Edward**
Native people: legal status, claims, and human rights: a bibliography. Monticello, Ill.: Vance Bibliographies, 1987. 18 p. (Public administration series: Bibliography ; P-2274; ISSN: 0193-970X); ISBN: 1-55590-534-X.
Note: Approx. 200 entries.
Location: OOSC.

4094 **Yukon Archives**
Yukon native history and culture: a bibliography of sources available at the Yukon Archives. Whitehorse: The Archives, 1987. ii, 65 p.
Note: Listing of sources for Yukon native history, culture and development: books and articles, theses, government records, films and videotapes, maps, manuscripts, corporate records, sound recordings, photographs.
Location: OONL.

— 1988 —

4095 **Alberta. Provincial Archives. Historical Resources Library**
Native peoples of Alberta: a bibliographic guide. [Edmonton]: Alberta Culture and Multiculturalism,

Historical Resources Division, 1988. 33 p.; ISBN: 0-919411-15-0.
Note: Approx. 200 entries.– Based on collection held by Historical Resources Library.– Includes books, periodicals, theses and dissertations, research papers, museum catalogues.
Location: OONL.

4096 **Barker, John**
"Bibliography of missionary activities and religious change in northwest coast societies."
In: *Northwest Anthropological Research Notes*; Vol. 22, no. 1 (Spring 1988) p. 13-57.; ISSN: 0029-3296.
Note: 505 entries.– Published books and papers, memoirs, unpublished manuscripts, grammars, theses and dissertations.
Location: AEU.

4097 **Davis, Lynne; Heidenreich, Barbara**
Aboriginal economic development: an annotated bibliography. Peterborough, Ont.: LHD, 1988. 107 p.
Note: Approx. 400 entries.– Includes both aboriginal and non-aboriginal sources, evaluative reports, business plans, community economic profiles, government strategy papers, feasibility and market studies.– Provides listings of additional bibliographies.
Location: OONL.

4098 **Johnson, Bryan R.**
The Blackfeet: an annotated bibliography. New York: Garland Publishing, 1988. xxiv, 231 p. (Garland reference library of social science ; vol. 441); ISBN: 0-8240-0941-X.
Note: 1,186 entries.– Comprehensive list in terms of format, language, date.– Includes scientific monographs, popular novels, magazine articles, films, phonograph records, government documents, religious tracts, manuscript collections.– Languages include English, Blackfeet, French, Spanish, German, Japanese.
Location: OONL.

4099 **Madill, Dennis**
"Riel, Red River, and beyond: new developments in Métis history."
In: *New directions in American Indian history*, edited by Colin G. Calloway. Norman: University of Oklahoma Press, 1988. P. 49-78. (D'Arcy McNickle Center bibliographies in American Indian history); ISBN: 0-80612-147-5.
Note: Bibliographical essay.
Location: OONL.

4100 **Martijn, Charles A.; Auger, Réginald**
La présence autochtone dans le détroit de Belle-Isle, est du Canada: bibliographie préliminaire/The native presence in the Strait of Belle-Isle, eastern Canada: preliminary bibliography. Québec: Direction du Nouveau-Québec et service aux autochtones, Ministère des affaires culturelles, 1988. 49 p.
Note: Localisation: QQLA.

4101 **Mongrain, Susan**
Aboriginal self-government: a selective annotated bibliography. Ottawa: Departmental Library, Indian and Northern Affairs Canada, 1988. 11 l.
Note: Location: OONL.

4102 **Mongrain, Susan**
Land claims: a selected annotated bibliography on specific and comprehensive claims. [Ottawa]: Departmental Library, Indian and Northern Affairs

Canada, 1988. 9 l.
Note: Approx. 55 entries.– Includes general works, departmental publications, legal issue references, bibliographies.
Location: OONL.

4103 **Stevens, Tina**
1988 Native peoples annotated bibliography: a listing of books, films, videos, newspapers, journals for and approved by native people. London, Ont.: Ontario Library Service-Thames, c1988. iv, 93 p.; ISBN: 0-9693736-0-0.
Note: Approx. 450 entries.– Designed as a demonstration model for native band library, specializing in native materials.
Location: OONL.

— 1989 —

4104 **Allen, Robert S.; Tobin, Mary A.T.**
Les études autochtones au Canada: guide de recherche. 3e éd. Ottawa: Centre de la recherche historique et de l'étude des traités, Direction générale des revendications globales, Affaires indiennes et du Nord canadien, 1989. iii, 197 p.
Note: Comprend une liste descriptive des divers cours et des programmes d'études, des associations autochtones et des centres de références.– Inclut une bibliographie sélective, p. 158-173.
English title: *Native studies in Canada: a research guide.*
Éditions antérieures:
1984. v, 203 p.
1982. iv, 199 p.
Localisation: OONL.

4105 **Allen, Robert S.; Tobin, Mary A.T.**
Native studies in Canada: a research guide. 3rd ed. Ottawa: Treaties and Historical Research Centre, Comprehensive Claims Branch, Indian and Northern Affairs Canada, 1989. iii, 195 p.
Note: Directory of native studies programs, courses, associations and resource centres.– Bibliography of selected works is included on p. 157-171.
Titre en français: *Les études autochtones au Canada: guide de recherche.*
Previous editions:
1984. ii, 185 p.
1982. iii, 185 p.
Location: OONL.

4106 **Allington-Baker, Amanda**
Our home and native land: books about Canada's native peoples. Toronto: Canadian Book Information Centre, 1989. 32 p.: ill.
Note: Approx. 300 entries.– Topics include self-determination, ethnology, children's legends and fiction, literature, social issues, women.
Location: OONL.

4107 **Bakker, Peter**
"Bibliography of Métis languages."
In: *Amsterdam Creole Studies*; Vol. 10, No. 56 (June 1989) p. 41-47.
Note: Covers to February 1989.– Includes papers and articles on Michif, Métis French, Métis Cree, Bungi.
Location: MdBJ.

4108 **Dempsey, Hugh A.; Moir, Lindsay**
Bibliography of the Blackfoot. Metuchen, N.J.: Scarecrow Press, 1989. viii, 245 p. (Native American bibliography series ; no. 13); ISBN: 0-8108-2211-3.
Note: 1,828 entries.– Covers to the end of 1986.– Includes books, monographs, reports, articles in periodicals, magazines, native press on three tribes of the Blackfoot nation: Blood, Blackfoot, Peigan.– Emphasis on works by Blackfoot writers.– Excludes fur trade and exploration books, articles in daily newspapers.
Location: OONL.

4109 **Horn, Charles; Griffiths, Curt Taylor**
Native North Americans: crime, conflict and criminal justice: a research bibliography. 4th ed. [Burnaby, B.C.]: Northern Justice Society, 1989. 275 p.; ISBN: 0-86491-074-6.
Note: Approx. 2,700 entries.– Books, periodical articles, government publications: research, policy and program materials relating to Native involvement with criminal justice system in Canada, United States and Greenland.
Previous editions:
McKechnie, Gail. Northern Conference, 1986. 156 p. (loose-leaf).; ISBN: 0-86491-058-4.
Griffiths, Curt Taylor; Weafer, Linda F. Criminology Research Centre, Simon Fraser University and the Northern Conference, 1984. v, 209 p.; ISBN: 0-86941-042-8.
Griffiths, Curt Taylor; Weafer, Linda F.; Williams, Gregory N. Criminology Research Centre, Simon Fraser University, 1982. vii, 172 p.; ISBN: 0-86941-030-4.
Supplement: Griffiths, Curt Taylor; Weafer, Linda F. ... . *Supplement to the 1st edition.* 1984. iii, 79 p.; ISBN: 0-86491-040-1.
Location: OONL.

4110 **Southern Ontario Library Service**
First Nations 1989 annotated bibliography: a listing of books, videos for and approved by First Nations. London, Ont.: Southern Ontario Library Service, 1989. iii, 27 p.; ISBN: 0-9693737-0-0.
Note: Approx. 150 entries.
Location: OONL.

4111 **Wai, Lokky**
The native peoples of Canada in contemporary society: a demographic and socioeconomic bibliography. [London, Ont.]: Population Studies Centre, University of Western Ontario, [c1989]. i, 82 p.; ISBN: 0-7714-1060-3.
Note: Approx. 425 entries.– Includes published and unpublished scholarly material in journal articles, books, monographs, working papers, reports, dissertations, government documents, including committee reports and position papers on four categories of natives.
Location: OONL.

— 1990 —

4112 **Canada. Solicitor General Canada. Ministry Secretariat**
Aboriginal peoples collection/Collection sur les autochtones. [Ottawa]: Solicitor General Canada, Ministry Secretariat, [1990]. 3 l., 106, 107 p. (User report / Solicitor General Canada, Ministry Secretariat ; no. 1990-10); ISBN: 0-662-57664-0.
Note: 1,600 entries.– Books, reports, articles, audio and video recordings held in the departmental library of the Solicitor General of Canada relating to aboriginal peoples in Canada.– Text in English and French/texte en français et en anglais.
Location: OONL.

4113 Rollins, Caron
"Canadian Indian treaties: a bibliography."
In: *Canadian Law Libraries*; Vol. 15, no. 2 (April 1990) p. 68-
72 ; ISSN: 1180-176X.
Note: Approx. 75 entries.
Location: OONL.

4114 Verrall, Catherine; McDowell, Patricia
Resource reading list 1990: annotated bibliography of
resources by and about native people. Toronto: Canadian
Alliance in Solidarity with the Native Peoples, c1990.
157 p.; ISBN: 0-921425-03-1.
Note: Lists books for children and elementary schools
(picture books, fiction, legends), teaching resources
(curriculum, film, video, kits, music), books for youth
and adults (arts, education, drama, fiction, native
languages), native periodicals, audio-visual sources.-
Priority is given to publications written, published,
produced by native people, and about native people and
issues within Canada.
Previous edition: 1987. v, 111 p.; ISBN: 0-921425-01-5.
Location: OONL.

— 1991 —

**4115 Canada. Solicitor General Canada. Ministry Library
and Reference Centre**
Library catalogue of aboriginal resources/Ouvrages
autochtones à la bibliothèque. Ottawa: Solicitor General
Canada, Ministry Secretariat, 1991. 2, 109, 108 p.; ISBN: 0-
662-58718-9.
Note: Approx. 1,600 entries.- Books, reports, articles,
video cassettes in English and French relating to aboriginal peoples and the criminal justice system, aboriginal
administration of justice, corrections.- Text in English
and French/texte en français et en anglais.
Location: OONL.

4116 Hoxie, Frederick E.
Native Americans: an annotated bibliography. Pasadena,
Calif.: Salem Press, c1991. xiii, 325 p.; ISBN: 0-89356-670-5.
Note: Approx. 1,200 entries.- Contains four main
sections: general studies and references (includes additional bibliographic listings); history; culture areas (Canadian entries in sections: Northeast, Plains, Northwest
and Plateau, Arctic and Subarctic); contemporary life.
Location: OONL.

4117 Shindruk, Cheryl; Carter, Tom
Selected sources on aboriginal issues. Winnipeg: Institute
of Urban Studies, University of Winnipeg, 1991. iv, 31 p.
(Bibliographica / Institute of Urban Studies, University
of Winnipeg ; 3); ISBN: 0-920213-55-3.
Note: 375 entries.- Topics include native housing,
community planning, economic development, education,
health and social welfare, culture and tradition.
Location: OONL.

4118 Snyder-Penner, Russel
"A select bibliography on indigenous peoples in Canada."
In: *Conrad Grebel Review*; Vol. 9, no. 2 (Spring 1991) p. 171-
178.; ISSN: 0829-044X.
Note: Published books dealing with issues and topics
relating to indigenous peoples in Canada: history and
culture, biography and autobiography, church and
missions, aboriginal rights, self-government, land claims,
education, environment and economic development,
religion.
Location: OONL.

— 1992 —

4119 Joseph, Gene
Sharing the knowledge: a First Nations resource guide.
Vancouver: Legal Services Society of British Columbia,
1992. ix, 101 p.: ill., ISBN: 0-919736 77 7.
Note: 288 entries.- Publications written from a First
Nations perspective which reflect current native and
government positions as well as judicial interpretations:
history and culture, foundations of aboriginal rights and
government relations, current issues, future directions.
Location: OONL.

— 1993 —

4120 Canadian Institute for Historical Microreproductions
Native studies collection: catalogue/La collection des
études autochtones: catalogue. Ottawa: CIHM, 1993. xii,
222 p.; ISBN: 0-665-91353-2.
Note: 1,515 entries.- Lists monograph titles included in
the CIHM Native Studies Microfiche Collection.- Topics
covered include Indian legends, traditions, religions,
laws, history and biography: documentation of native
North American culture from the time of European
contact to the late nineteenth century.- Includes
dictionaries and grammars, translations of religious
literature, works on archaeology and ethnology.
Location: OONL.

4121 Fortier, Marcel; Taylor, Marianne
First Nations public administration: an annotated
bibliography/Administrations publiques des Premières
nations: bibliographie annotée. Ottawa: Indian
Government Support Directorate, 1993. [11], 77 p.; ISBN:
0-662-59637-4.
Note: Approx. 250 entries.- "An annotated collection of
selected theses, publications, studies and other works
representative, but not exhaustive, of reference material
relevant to the Indian/Inuit Public Service sector."-
Topics include aboriginal society, law, self-government,
organizational development and planning, personnel
development.- Text in English and French/texte en
français et en anglais.
Location: OONL.

4122 Gilbert, Charlotte
Répertoire bibliographique: auteurs Amérindiens du
Québec/Bibliographic directory of Amerindian authors
in Quebec. Saint-Luc, Québec: Centre de recherche sur la
littérature et les arts autochtones du Québec, 1993. 46 p.;
ISBN: 2-9803426-0-2.
Note: Approx. 175 entrées.- Livres et articles publiés en
français par les Amérindiens du Québec.- Les auteurs
issus des deux groupes linguistiques amérindiens du
territoire, les Algonquiens et les Iroquoiens.- Texte en
français et en anglais/text in English and French.
Localisation: OONL.

4123 Graham, Katherine A.
Public policy and aboriginal peoples, 1965-1992. Volume
4, Bibliography. Ottawa: Royal Commission on Aborigin-
al Peoples, 1993. iv, 69 p.; ISBN: 0-660-58880-3.
Note: Approx. 1,000 entries.- Listing of primary sources,
such as reports and policy documents.- Includes English
and French publications.- Prepared for the Royal
Commission on Aboriginal Peoples by the Centre for
Policy and Program Assessment of the School of Public
Administration, Carleton University.
Location: OONL.

4124 **Morrison, Doreen**
Native peoples: a guide to reference sources. Montreal: Humanities and Social Sciences Library Reference Department, McGill University, 1993. 28 p.; ISBN: 0-7717-0161-6.
Note: Approx. 175 entries.– Emphasis on sources for ethnological research.– Includes materials in history and social anthropology.
Previous edition: Griffin, Meredith. *Native peoples of Canada: a guide to reference sources.* McLennan Library, Reference Department, 1986. 17 p.
Location: OONL.

— 1937 —

4125 Meynen, Emil
Bibliography on German settlements in colonial North America, especially on the Pennsylvania Germans and their descendants, 1688-1933. Leipzig: Harrassowitz, 1937. xxxvi, 636 p.
Note: Approx. 7,500 entries.– Listings for settlements in Canada generally, Nova Scotia, New Brunswick, Ontario (Mennonite settlements), as well as family histories and biographies.
Location: OONL.

— 1939 —

4126 Ory, François
Judéo-maçonnerie: petite bibliographie d'ouvrages surtout en français, à nos chers canadiens. Montréal: [s.n.], 1939. 17 p.
Note: Approx. 150 entrées.– "Ce n'est pas non plus une bibliographie sur la question juive: elle traite du juif seulement dans la ligne révolutionnaire et en tant qu'il est attaché à des mouvements subversifs. Indique les ouvrages les plus utiles ou qui intéressent spécialement les Canadiens."
Localisation: OONL.

— 1955 —

4127 Davies, Raymond Arthur
Printed Jewish Canadiana, 1685-1900: tentative checklist of books, pamphlets, pictures, magazine and newspaper articles and currency, written by or relating to the Jews of Canada. Montreal: Lillian Davies, 1955. 56 p.: ill., ports., facsims.
Note: Approx. 500 entries.
Location: OONL.

— 1956 —

4128 Canada. Department of Citizenship and Immigration. Canadian Citizenship Branch
Research on immigrant adjustment and ethnic groups: a bibliography of published material, 1920-1953/ Recherches sur l'adaptation des immigrants et les groupes ethniques: une bibliographie d'ouvrages publiées, 1920-1953. Ottawa: Research Division, Canadian Citizenship Branch, Department of Citizenship and Immigration, 1956. ii, 131 p.
Note: Approx. 500 entries.– Text in English and French/ texte en français et en anglais.
Supplement: ... : *an annual bibliography*. 1954-1956. 3 vol.– Issues for 1953-1954, 1954-1955, 1955-1956.
Location: OONL.

— 1957 —

4129 British Columbia Centennial Committee
Ethnic groups in British Columbia: a selected bibliography based on a check-list of material in the Provincial Library and Archives. Victoria: British Columbia Centennial Committee, 1957. 64 l.
Note: Approx. 500 entries.– Covers from 1858 to December 1956.– Includes books, articles, newspaper clippings, pamphlets, government documents, unpublished material (manuscripts and theses).– Many references on Chinese, Japanese, Doukhobors.
Location: OONL.

— 1958 —

4130 Canada. Department of Citizenship and Immigration. Library
Canadian immigration and emigration, 1946-1957: a bibliography. Ottawa: [s.n.], 1958. 38 p.
Note: 347 entries.– Concerned with general subject of immigration: policy, economic aspects, law, statistics.– Includes periodical articles, government publications.
Location: OONL.

4131 Turek, Victor
Polonica Canadiana: a bibliographical list of the Canadian Polish imprints, 1848-1957. Toronto: Polish Alliance Press, 1958. 138 p. (Polish Research Institute in Canada Studies ; 2)
Note: 779 entries.– Books and pamphlets issued in Canada in Polish language, by authors of Polish descent published in Canada and by Canadian authors published in Poland; works of authors of Polish origin on Canadian subjects and authors of Canadian origin on Polish subjects; translations of works of Polish authors published in Canada and of Canadian authors published in Poland.– Excludes periodicals, ephemeral material such as broadsides, book-trade catalogues, etc., maps and atlases, manuscripts, photographs, films, sound-recordings.
Supplements:
"Canadian Polish imprints, 1848-1957: additional entries." In: *The Polish past in Canada*. Toronto: Printed by Polish Alliance Press, 1960. P. 123-131.– 59 entries.
"Second supplement to *Polonica Canadiana* ..., *1848-1957*." In: *The Polish-language press in Canada: its history and a bibliographical list*. Toronto: Printed by Polish Alliance Press, 1962. P. 217-229.– 79 entries.
Zolobka, Vincent. ... , *1958-1970*. 1978. 414 p. (Canadian-Polish Research Institute Studies ; 13).– 4,225 entries.
Location: OONL.

— 1959 —

4132 Rome, David
A selected bibliography of Jewish Canadiana. Montreal: Canadian Jewish Congress and The Jewish Public Library, 1959. 1 vol. (unpaged).
Note: Approx. 2,000 entries.– Materials written or edited by Canadian Jews, books and pamphlets about Canadian Jews, books by Canadians on subjects of Jewish interest, such as Canadian Jewish history, education, sociology, art, religion, science, literature.
Location: OONL.

— 1960 —

4133 Canada. Department of Citizenship and Immigration. Economic and Social Research Branch
Citizenship, immigration and ethnic groups in Canada:

bibliography of research, published and unpublished sources, 1920-1958/Citoyenneté, immigration et groupes ethniques au Canada: une bibliographie des recherches, sources publiées et non publiées, 1920-1958. Ottawa: [Queen's Printer], 1960. [8], 190, xix p.
Note: Approx. 1,300 entries.– Monographs, periodical articles, government publications, theses on general demographic topics and specific ethnic groups and communities.– Excludes Indians and Inuit.– Text in English and French/texte en français et en anglais.
Supplements:
    ... , *1959-1961/...* , *1959-1961*. 1962: iv, iv, 55 p.– Approx. 320 entries.
    ... , *1962-1964/...* , *1962-1964*. 1964: iii, iv, 127 p.– Approx. 700 entries.
Location: OONL.

4134 **Chojnacki, Wladyslaw; Chojnacka, Jadwiga**
"Canadian items in Polish periodical literature: a bibliography for the period 1845-1958."
In: *The Polish past in Canada*, edited by Victor Turek. Toronto: Printed by Polish Alliance Press, 1960. P. 17-56. (Polish Research Institute in Canada Studies ; 3)
Note: 844 entries.– Articles and chapters of books dealing with Canada and Polish emigration and settlement in Canada, and missionary work of Polish clergy abroad.
Location: OONL.

— 1962 —

4135 **Rudnyckyj, Jaroslav Bohdan**
"Ukrainian Canadian bibliography."
In: *Papers of the Bibliographical Society of Canada*; Vol. 1 (1962) p. 44-48.; ISSN: 0067-6896.
Note: Location: OONL.

— 1965 —

4136 **Woycenko, Ol'ha**
Ukrainian contribution to Canada's cultural life. Winnipeg: [s.n.], 1965. iv, 116 l.
Note: Bibliography and review of contributions by Ukrainian Canadians to the arts, architecture, literature, science, linguistics, education.
Location: OONL.

— 1966 —

4137 **Lilley, Doreen A.**
East Indian immigration into Canada, 1880-1920: a bibliography. [Vancouver: University of British Columbia], 1966. 7 l.
Note: Location: BVAU.

— 1967 —

4138 **Dorotich, Daniel**
A bibliography of publications of Canadian Slavists. Vancouver: University of British Columbia, 1967. 51 [2] l.
Note: Approx. 750 entries.– Publications of members of Canadian Association of Slavists to the end of 1965.– Excludes newspaper articles, book reviews.– Includes a number of books and articles on Canadian subjects.
Location: OONL.

4139 **Jain, Sushil Kumar**
The Negro in Canada: a select list of primary and secondary sources for the study of [the] Negro community in Canada from the earliest times to the present days. Regina: Regina Campus Library, University of Saskatchewan, 1967. 30 l. (Unexplored fields of Canadiana ; vol. 3. Minorities in Canada series ; no. 1)
Note: 229 entries.– Books, theses, periodical articles, list

of periodicals, bibliographies.– Includes a list of libraries in the United States and Canada with strong Black studies collections.
Location: QMNF.

— 1968 —

4140 **Klymasz, Robert B.**
A bibliography of Ukrainian folklore in Canada, 1902-64. [Ottawa: Queen's Printer, 1968]. vi, 53 p. (National Museum of Canada Anthropology Papers ; no. 21)
Note: 463 entries.– Two general areas covered: Ukrainian folklore in Canada as reported in Canadian and foreign publications; materials published in Canada on traditional Ukrainian folklore.
Location: OONL.

— 1969 —

4141 **Anderson, Grace M.**
A selected bibliography on Portuguese immigration. Toronto: [s.n.], 1969. iv, 5 p.
Note: Listing of books, articles, theses and dissertations in English language on the subject of Portuguese immigration to Canada.– Includes a list of newspapers in Portuguese published in Canada, and a list of books in Portuguese.
Location: OONL.

4142 **Canada. Department of Manpower and Immigration**
Immigration, migration and ethnic groups in Canada: a bibliography of research, 1964-1968/Immigration, migration et groupes ethniques au Canada: une bibliographie de recherches, 1964-1968. Ottawa: [Queen's Printer], 1969. xiv, 56 p.
Note: Approx. 450 entries.– Text in English and French/texte en français et en anglais.
Location: OONL.

4143 **Pearlman, Rowena; Malycky, Alexander**
"Jewish-Canadian periodical publications: a preliminary check list."
In: *Canadian Ethnic Studies*; Vol. 1, no. 1 (1969) p. 44-49.; ISSN: 0008-3496.
Note: Supplement: Vol. 2, no. 1 (June 1970) p. 131-149.– 242 entries in total.
Location: OONL.

4144 **"Select bibliography on post-war immigrants in Canada."**
In: *International Migration Review*; Vol. 4, no. 1 (Fall 1969) p. 96-99.; ISSN: 0197-9183.
Note: Books, articles, Canadian government publications, miscellaneous reports.
Location: AEU.

— 1970 —

4145 **Blizzard, Flora Helena**
West Indians in Canada: a selective annotated bibliography. Guelph [Ont.]: The Library, University of Guelph, 1970. 41 p. (Bibliographic series / University of Guelph Library ; no. 1)
Note: Approx. 150 entries.– Emphasis on Blacks from West Indies in Toronto and Montreal.– Includes monographs, serials, government publications, newspaper articles.
Location: OONL.

4146 **Dalhousie University. Library**
Blacks in Canada: representative source materials. Halifax: Dalhousie University Library, 1970. 10 l.
Note: Approx. 80 entries.– Contains listings in the

following categories: bibliographies, indexes, biography, history, moral and social conditions, education, periodicals and newspapers.
Location: OONL.

4147 **Jain, Sushil Kumar**
East Indians in Canada: an essay with a bibliography. Windsor, Ont.: Canadian Bibliographic Centre, 1970. 25 l. (Unexplored fields of Canadiana ; vol. 3. Minorities in Canada series ; no. 2)
Note: Location: OONL.

4148 **Lifschutz, E.**
Bibliography of American and Canadian Jewish memoirs and autobiographies in Yiddish, Hebrew and English. New York: YIVO Institute for Jewish Research, 1970. 75 p.
Note: 364 entries.– Contains only published autobiographies and memoirs in book form.– Excludes fictionalized chronicles or accounts.
Location: QMM.

4149 **Luethy, Ivor C.E.**
"Swiss literature on Canada: a preliminary check list of imprints."
In: *Canadian Ethnic Studies*; Vol. 2, no. 1 (June 1970) p. 245-248.; ISSN: 0008-3496.
Note: 25 entries.– Topics include settlement, pioneers, experiences of immigrants, travel descriptions/ expeditions, fiction.
Supplement: "Canada in Swiss periodical literature." *Canadian Ethnic Studies*; Vol. 5, no. 1/2 (1973) p. 269-270.– 16 entries.
Location: OONL.

4150 **Piontkovsky, Roman**
"Russian-Canadian imprints: a preliminary check list."
In: *Canadian Ethnic Studies*; Vol. 2, no. 1 (June 1970) p. 177-185.; ISSN: 0008-3496.
Note: 79 entries.
Location: OONL.

4151 **Singh, Ganda**
The Sikhs in Canada and California. Patiala [India]: Punjabi University, Department of Punjab Historical Studies, 1970. 22 l.
Note: Approx. 200 entries.– Books, periodical and newspaper articles, government publications in English and Punjabi languages.
Location: OONL.

— 1971 —

4152 **Bell, Dorothy, et al.**
Canadian Black studies bibliography. [London, Ont.: s.n.], 1971. [108] l.
Note: Approx. 1,500 entries.– Books, periodical and newspaper articles on slavery, settlement, church history, black societies.– Compiled in collaboration with Pat Jasion, Karen Myers, Stephen Day.
Location: OONL.

4153 **Gregorovich, Andrew**
Multiculturalism and ethnic groups in Canada: a brief bibliography. Toronto: 1971. 24 l.
Note: 156 entries.– Books, journal articles, government publications treating Canadian ethnic groups generally.
Location: OONL.

4154 **Rome, David**
The early Jewish presence in Canada: a book lover's ramble through Jewish Canadiana. Montreal: Bronfman Collection of Jewish Canadiana, 1971. [163] l.

Note: Bibliographical essay describing early works of Jewish Canadian history and literature, works by Jewish Canadian authors, from the Bronfman Collection of Jewish Canadiana.
Location. OONL.

4155 **Schlesinger, Benjamin**
The Jewish family: a survey and annotated bibliography. [Toronto]: University of Toronto Press, [1971]. xii, 175 p.; ISBN: 0-8020-1749-5.
Note: 429 entries.– Books and articles on Jewish family life: home, marriage, intermarriage, sexuality, death and mourning, divorce, holocaust survivors, Jewish life in literature.
Location: OONL.

— 1972 —

4156 **Gregorovich, Andrew**
Canadian ethnic groups bibliography: a selected bibliography of ethno-cultural groups in Canada and the Province of Ontario. Toronto: Department of the Provincial Secretary and Citizenship of Ontario, 1972. xvi, 208 p.
Note: 2,120 entries.
Location: OONL.

4157 **Nemec, Thomas F.**
"The Irish emigration to Newfoundland: a critical review of the secondary sources."
In: *Newfoundland Quarterly*; Vol. 69, no. 1 (July 1972) p. 15-24.; ISSN: 0014-1836.
Note: Location: OONL.

— 1973 —

4158 **Buyniak, Victor O.**
"Ukrainian imprints of Saskatoon, Saskatchewan: a preliminary check list."
In: *Canadian Ethnic Studies*; Vol. 5, no. 1/2 (1973) p. 341-357.; ISSN: 0008-3496.
Note: 73 entries.– Books and brochures published in Ukrainian or in Ukrainian and any other language(s).
Location: OONL.

4159 **Dworaczek, Marian**
Minority groups in Metropolitan Toronto: a bibliography. [Toronto]: Ontario Ministry of Labour, Research Branch, Library, 1973. 57 p.
Note: Approx. 500 entries.– Books, theses, government publications, periodical articles.– Includes a list of ethnic periodicals.
Supplement: 1975. 48 p.
Location: OONL.

4160 **Froeschle, Hartmut**
"Deutschkanadische Bibliographie: eine auswahl."
In: *German-Canadian Yearbook*; Vol. 1 (1973) p. 327-344.; ISSN: 0316-8603.
Note: Location: AEU.

4161 **Jakle, John A.**
Ethnic and racial minorities in North America: a selected bibliography of the geographical literature. Monticello, Ill.: Council of Planning Librarians, 1973. 71 p. (Council of Planning Librarians Exchange bibliography ; 459, 460)
Note: Approx. 1,000 entries.– Books, articles, documents, theses, conference proceedings dealing with distribution of ethnic and racial communities in terms of land use, transportation, employment opportunities, political jurisdictions, community organization and community landscape.

Location: OONL.

4162 **Markotic, Vladimir**
"Croatian imprints of Canada: a preliminary check list."
In: *Canadian Ethnic Studies*; Vol. 5, no. 1/2 (1973) p. 19-25.;
ISSN: 0008-3496.
Note: 41 entries.– Books and brochures published in Croatian, or in Croatian and any other language(s).– Some relate to the Croatian-Canadian community.– Titles are translated into English.
Location: OONL.

4163 **Royick, Alexander**
"Ukrainian imprints of British Columbia: a preliminary check list."
In: *Canadian Ethnic Studies*; Vol. 5, no. 1/2 (1973) p. 293-301.; ISSN: 0008-3496.
Note: 29 entries.– Books and brochures published in Ukrainian in British Columbia.
Location: OONL.

4164 **Rudnyckyj, Jaroslav Bohdan**
Slavica Canadiana. Winnipeg: Ukrainian Free Academy of Sciences, 1952-1973. 21 vol.; ISSN: 0583-5364. (Slavistica, Proceedings of the Institute of Slavistics of the Ukrainian Free Academy of Sciences ; no. 15, 18, 21, 24, 27, 30, 33, 36, 39, 42, 45, 48, 51, 54, 57, 60, 63, 66, 69, 72, 75)
Note: Annual listing from 1952 to 1973.– Part 1: "A selected bibliography of Slavic books and pamphlets published in or related to Canada."- Sections include general works, religion, education, social sciences, economics, linguistics, technology, music, literature, history/biography.
Location: OONL.

4165 **Rudnyckyj, Jaroslav Bohdan, et al.**
Ukrainica Canadiana. Winnipeg: Ukrainian Free Academy of Sciences, 1954-1973. 20 vol.; ISSN: 0503-1095. (Bibliography / Ukrainian Free Academy of Sciences ; no. 1-20)
Note: Annual listing from 1953 to 1970.– Part 1: "A selected bibliography of Ukrainian books and pamphlets published in ... or related to Canada."- Categories include general works, religion, education, social sciences, linguistics, technology, music, literature, history/biography. Part 2: "Ukrainian Canadian newspapers and periodicals ... "- Compiled with the collaboration of D. Sokulski, Z. Horbay and O. Woycenko.
Location: OONL.

4166 **Suchowersky, Celestin N.**
"Ukrainian imprints of Edmonton, Alberta: a preliminary checklist."
In: *Canadian Ethnic Studies*; Vol. 5, no. 1/2 (1973) p. 303-341.; ISSN: 0008-3496.
Note: 199 entries.– Books and brochures published in Ukrainian or in Ukrainian and any other language(s).
Location: OONL.

— 1974 —

4167 **McLeod, Keith A.**
A select bibliography on ethnicity and multiculturalism for high schools. [Toronto: Faculty of Education, University of Toronto, 1974]. 24, 2 p.
Note: Approx. 450 entries.– Bibliographies, general sources, books dealing with concepts and problems; references on immigration, settlement, ethnic organizations, individual ethnic groups, native peoples.
Location: OONL.

4168 **"Select bibliography on ethnic groups and inter-ethnic relations in Alberta: 1972-1974."**
In: *Canadian Ethnic Studies*; Vol. 6, no. 1/2 (1974) p. 71-72.;
ISSN: 0008-3496.
Note: Location: OONL.

— 1975 —

4169 **Dyck, Ruth**
"Ethnic folklore in Canada: a preliminary survey."
In: *Canadian Ethnic Studies*; Vol. 7, no. 2 (1975) p. 90-101.;
ISSN: 0008-3496.
Note: 123 entries.– Lists publications which include references to oral traditions of ethnic communities in Canada since 1900.– Excludes Indian, Inuit, French and non-Gaelic British.– List of bibliographies.
Location: OONL.

4170 **Eterovich, Adam S.**
A guide and bibliography to research on Yugoslavs in the United States and Canada. San Francisco: [s.n.], 1975. xiii, 187 p.; ISBN: 0-88247-341-7.
Note: Listing of newspapers, magazines, journals, passenger lists, immigrant bibliography.– Books in English and Serbo-Croatian.
Location: OONL.

4171 **Iwaasa, David B.**
The Japanese Canadians: a bibliography. [S.l.: s.n.], c1975. ii, 27 l.
Note: 299 entries.– Books, pamphlets, articles; books in Japanese; Japanese-Canadian newspapers.
Location: OONL.

— 1976 —

4172 **Gakovich, Robert P.; Radovich, Milan M.**
Serbs in the United States and Canada: a comprehensive bibliography. [Minneapolis]: Immigration History Research Center, University of Minnesota, 1976. xii, 129 p.: ill.
Note: 793 entries.– Books, pamphlets, periodical articles.– Contains bibliographies, biographies, statistics, Serbian-Canadian literature, works on Yugoslavia by Canadian Serbs.
Location: OONL.

4173 **Jackson, Robin**
"A bibliography: development of the multicultural policy in Canada."
In: *Canadian Library Journal*; Vol. 33, no. 3 (June 1976) p. 237-243.; ISSN: 0008-4352.
Note: Books, federal and provincial government publications, from 1967 to 1976, that deal with development of multicultural policy.
Location: AEU.

4174 **Jerabek, Esther**
Czechs and Slovaks in North America: a bibliography. New York: Czechoslovak Society of Arts & Sciences in America, 1976. 448 p.
Note: 7,609 entries.– Books and pamphlets, serial publications, articles about Czechs and Slovaks in Canada, United States, Mexico, Central America.– Arrangement by broad subjects, with index.
Location: OONL.

4175 **Mallea, John R.; Philip, L.**
"Canadian cultural pluralism and education: a select bibliography."
In: *Canadian Ethnic Studies*; Vol. 8, no. 1 (1976) p. 81-88.;
ISSN: 0008-3496.

Note: Location: OONL.

4176 Sutyla, Charles M.
"Multicultural studies in Canada: a bibliography with introductory comments."
In: *Communique: Canadian Studies*; Vol. 3, no. 1 (October 1976) p. 4-65.; ISSN: 0318-1197.
Note: Books and articles arranged in sections: bibliographies, historical background (immigration history, government immigration policy/multicultural policy), ethnic group theory, inter-ethnic relations, periodical literature, ethnic groups, bibliographies of specific groups, multicultural literature and ethnic press, audio-visual materials.
Location: OONL.

4177 Swanick, Eric L.
Canadian immigration studies in the late 1960's and in the 1970's: an introductory bibliography. Monticello, Ill.: Council of Planning Librarians, 1976. 10 p. (Council of Planning Librarians Exchange bibliography ; 1179)
Note: Approx. 100 entries.– Books, journal articles, government publications, research reports.
Location: OONL.

— 1977 —

4178 Breyfogle, Donna; Dworaczek, Marian
Blacks in Ontario: a selected bibliography, 1965-1976. Toronto: Ontario Ministry of Labour, Research Library, 1977. 27 p. (Bibliography series / Ontario Ministry of Labour, Research Library ; no. 8)
Note: Approx. 250 entries.– Books, periodical articles, theses, government reports, bibliographies on history, immigration, education, employment, housing, race relations, human rights.– Focus is on Blacks in Toronto.
Location: OONL.

4179 Buchignani, Norman
"A review of the historical and sociological literature on East Indians in Canada."
In: *Canadian Ethnic Studies*; Vol. 9, no. 1 (1977) p. 86-108.; ISSN: 0008-3496.
Note: Approx. 200 entries.
Location: OONL.

4180 Liu, Gwen
"Ethnica Canadiana: a select bibliography."
In: *Ontario Library Review*; Vol. 61, no. 3 (September 1977) p. 203-216.; ISSN: 0030-2996.
Note: Listing of bibliographies, books, periodicals, special issues and articles, audio-tapes, films, videotapes, resource catalogues.– Includes works of fiction.
Location: OONL.

4181 Maxwell, Janet, et al.
Resource list for a multicultural society. [Toronto]: Ministry of Education; Ministry of Culture and Recreation, [1977]. viii, 626 p.
Note: Approx. 2,000 entries.– Books, periodicals, audio-visual materials on Canadian ethnic groups, excluding English and French.
Location: OONL.

4182 Schlichtmann, Hansgeorg
"Ethnic themes in geographic research on western Canada."
In: *Canadian Ethnic Studies*; Vol. 9, no. 2 (1977) p. 9-41.; ISSN: 0008-3496.
Note: Location: AEU.

4183 Shibata, Yuko
"The Japanese Canadians: a bibliography."
In: *The forgotten history of the Japanese-Canadians, volume one*. Vancouver: Published for the Japanese-Canadian History Group by New Sun Books, 1977. P. 23-85.
Note: Approx. 350 entries.– Covers 1907-1976.– Listing of books, reports, articles in English and Japanese dealing with aspects of Japanese-Canadian history, mainly based on University of British Columbia collections, primarily the Special Collection Division, and the Asian Study Library.– Annotations in English.
Location: OONL.

4184 Széplaki, Joseph
Hungarians in the United States and Canada: a bibliography: holdings of the Immigration History Research Center of the University of Minnesota. [Minneapolis]: Immigration History Research Center, University of Minnesota, 1977. viii, 113 p. [2] l. of pl. (Ethnic bibliography series / Immigration History Research Center, University of Minnesota ; no. 2)
Note: 916 entries.– History, religion, literature, textbooks, music, reference works, bibliographies, list of serials (newspapers, periodicals, annuals), manuscript collections.
Location: OONL.

— 1978 —

4185 Jonasson, Eric
"Ethnic groups in Manitoba: a select bibliography."
In: *Generations: the Journal of the Manitoba Genealogical Society*; Vol. 3, no. 2 (Summer 1978) p. 47-55.; ISSN: 0226-6105.
Note: Location: OONL.

4186 Nemec, Thomas F.
The Irish emigration to Newfoundland: a critical review of the secondary sources. St. John's: [Memorial University of Newfoundland], 1978. 29 l.
Note: Mimeograph of lecture delivered to the Newfoundland Historical Society, March 30, 1978.
Location: NFSM.

4187 Snyder, Ursula Kennedy
A selected and briefly annotated bibliography of sources relating to the Province of Nova Scotia and its major (and two minor) ethno-cultural groups. Halifax: St. Mary's University, [1978]. [30] l.
Note: Approx. 375 entries.– Books, articles, theses dealing with Acadians, Afro-Canadians, Germans, Irish, Loyalists, Micmacs, Scots.– Sections on Nova Scotia and Maritimes folklore, history, social conditions, education.
Location: NSHL.

4188 Swyripa, Frances A.
Ukrainian Canadians: a survey of their portrayal in English-language works. Edmonton: University of Alberta Press, 1978. xiii, 169 p. (Alberta Library in Ukrainian-Canadian Studies); ISBN: 0-88864-050-1.
Note: Chronological survey of government reports, theses, novels, magazines, and other sources which examine Ukrainian-Canadian development, with a bibliography (p. 147-166).
Location: OONL.

4189 Tapper, Lawrence F.
A guide to sources for the study of Canadian Jewry/ Guide des sources d'archives sur les juifs canadiens. [Ottawa]: National Ethnic Archives, Public Archives

Canada, 1978. 51 p.; ISBN: 0-662-50112-8.
Note: Includes a short bibliography, and a list of major collections in the Manuscript Division, Public Archives.– Text in English and French/texte en français et en anglais.
Location: OONL.

4190 **Wood, Dean D.**
Multicultural Canada: a teachers' guide to ethnic studies. Toronto: Ontario Institute for Studies in Education, 1978. vi, 138 p. (Curriculum series / Ontario Institute for Studies in Education ; 36); ISBN: 0-7744-0175-3.
Note: 766 entries.– Lists instructional materials, print and audio-visual, suitable for grades 5-12: bibliographies, ethnic studies, immigration, multiculturalism and bilingualism, individual ethnic groups.
Location: OONL.

— 1979 —

4191 **Benjamin, Steven M.**
The German-Canadians: a working bibliography. Morgantown, W. Va.: Department of Foreign Languages, West Virginia University, 1979. 41 p. (Occasional papers of the Society for German-American Studies ; no. 1)
Note: Approx. 480 entries.– Books, periodical articles, conference proceedings, theses in English and German.
Location: OWTU.

4192 **Desrochers, Alain; Clément, Richard**
The social psychology of inter-action contact and cross-cultural communication: an annotated bibliography. Quebec: International Center for Research on Bilingualism, 1979. 261 p. (International Center for Research on Bilingualism Publication ; B-83)
Note: 1,018 entries.– Articles dealing with inter-ethnic contact and cross-cultural communication.– Topics include bilingualism, intermarriage, contact in a work setting, simulated contact, foreign travel and foreign study, methodological issues and measurement.
Location: OONL.

4193 **Frideres, James S.**
"Recent publications relating to Canadian ethnic studies."
In: *Canadian Ethnic Studies*; Vol. 8, no. 2 (1976) p. 142-146; vol. 9, no. 2 (1977) p. 153-156; vol. 10, no. 2 (1978) p. 211-216; vol. 11, no. 2 (1979) p. 148-153.; ISSN: 0008-3496.
Note: Annual listing of research concerning Canadian ethnic studies with emphasis on articles in scholarly journals.– Excludes books, theses, popular publications.
Continued by: Jay Goldstein (1980-1982); Norma Milton (1983); Bob Hromadiuk (1984-1992).
Location: OONL.

4194 **Gregorovich, Andrew**
Ukraine and Ukrainian Canadians: books for high school, college and public libraries. Toronto: Ucrainica Research Institute, 1979. 58 p.
Note: 314 entries.– Sections include arts and culture, history and politics, Ukrainian-Canadian literature, reference and bibliography, maps, periodicals and journals, film and visual materials.
Location: OONL.

4195 **Lebel-Péron, Suzanne; Péron, Yves**
Bibliographie sur la démographie récente des groupes ethno-linguistiques au Canada. Calgary: Research Centre for Canadian Ethnic Studies, University of Calgary, 1979. iv, 52 p. (Canadian ethnic studies: Études ethniques au Canada / Research Centre for Canadian Ethnic Studies, University of Calgary ; no 1)

Note: Approx. 725 entrées.– La période couverte: postérieure à la seconde guerre mondiale.– Articles de périodiques et journaux, publications officielles, bibliographies, thèses: composition ethnique et linguistique de la population, transferts linguistiques et assimilation, études différentielles (mortalité, fécondité, etc.), études des groupes spécifiques.
Localisation: OOP.

— 1980 —

4196 **Gregorovich, Andrew**
"Ukrainian Canadiana: a selected bibliography of scholarly works 1970-1980."
In: *Canadian Ethnic Studies*; Vol. 12, no. 2 (1980) p. 102-124.; ISSN: 0008-3496.
Note: Approx. 250 entries.– Lists titles in English on Ukrainians in Canada.– Includes bibliographies, collective works, history and politics, sociology and anthropology, demography, linguistics and literary criticism, education, art and culture, economic and social life, religion.
Location: OONL.

4197 **Walker, James W. St. G.**
A history of Blacks in Canada: a study guide for teachers and students. Hull, Quebec: Minister of State, Multiculturalism, 1980. x, 181 p.; ISBN: 0-660-10735-X.
Note: Includes sections of bibliographical discussion for each subject category, (e.g. Black Loyalists, Black fugitives, Ontario's communal experiments, impact of the colour line), and a listing of resources for further reading.
Titre en français: *Précis d'histoire sur les Canadiens de race noire: sources et guide d'enseignement.*
Location: OONL.

4198 **Walker, James W. St. G.**
Précis d'histoire sur les Canadiens de race noire: sources et guide d'enseignement. Hull, Québec: Ministre d'État, Multiculturalisme, 1980. x, 197 p.; ISBN: 0-660-90535-3.
Note: Bibliographies annotées: publications portent sur les Noirs anglophones de l'Est du Canada, notamment ceux de la Nouvelle-Écosse et de l'Ontario.
English title: *A history of Blacks in Canada: a study guide for teachers and students.*
Localisation: OONL.

4199 **Wertsman, Vladimir**
The Romanians in America and Canada: a guide to information sources. Detroit: Gale Research, c1980. xvi, 164 p. (Ethnic studies information guide series ; vol. 5); ISBN: 0-8103-1417-7.
Note: Approx. 400 entries.– Includes books, pamphlets, periodical articles.– Descriptive and critical annotations.
Location: OONL.

— 1981 —

4200 **"Bibliography of the collection of A. Becker at the Adam Shortt Library of Canadiana, University of Saskatchewan, Saskatoon, Canada."**
In: *Saskatchewan Genealogical Society Bulletin*; Vol. 12, no. 3 (September 1981) p. 124-135.; ISSN: 0048-9182.
Note: Lists books and pamphlets dealing mainly with Germans and Mennonites from Russia.
Location: AEU.

4201 **Caruso, Naomi; Cukier, Golda; Finegold, Ronald**
A preliminary guide to the Jewish Canadiana Collection of the Jewish Public Library. Montreal: Jewish Public

Library, 1981. 24 p.

Note: Lists books, pamphlets, government publications, speeches, promotional and fund-raising literature.– Three topics selected for this preliminary guide are: "Canadian ties to the Holy Land before 1948," "Sephardic Jews in Canada;" "Educational rights of Jewish children in the Province of Quebec."

Location: OONL.

4202 **Kempeneers, Marianne; Massé, Raymond**
Les migrations antillaises: bibliographie sélective et annotée. [Montréal]: Centre de recherches caraïbes de l'Université de Montréal, c1981. 53 p.

Note: Regroupe les principales études traitant du phénomène de l'immigration antillaise au Québec (provenant d'Haïti, de Jamaïque, de Barbade et de Trinidad-Tobago).

Localisation: OONL.

4203 **Myroniuk, Halyna; Worobec, Christine**
Ukrainians in North America: a select bibliography. St. Paul, Minn.: Immigration History Research Center, University of Minnesota; Toronto: Multicultural History Society of Ontario, [c1981]. 236, [24] p.; ISBN: 0-919045-04-9.

Note: Approx. 2,000 entries.– Describes the Ukrainian Americana holdings at the Immigration History Research Center in St. Paul, Minn., and books and other printed material of Ukrainian life in U.S. and Canada at various libraries and depositories in Toronto.– Section II. "Ukrainians in Canada" contains approx. 600 entries.– Themes include history, biography, economic life, religious life, cultural and intellectual life.– Other broad categories deal with language, Ukrainian emigré literature in North America, and the arts.– Ukrainian titles are transliterated.– Publication information is given in English.

Location: OONL.

4204 **Rome, David; Nefsky, Judith; Obermeir, Paule**
Les Juifs du Québec: bibliographie rétrospective annotée. Québec: Institut québécois de recherche sur la culture, 1981. xvi, 317 p. (Instruments de travail / Institut québécois de recherche sur la culture ; no 1); ISBN: 2-89224-004-2.

Note: 1,696 entrées.– Livres, brochures, articles, thèses sur les thèmes: l'histoire, l'immigration, la religion, les institutions, la question des écoles, l'activité littéraire et artistique, les relations avec Israël et celles avec la société québécoise.

Localisation: OONL.

4205 **Sokolyszyn, Aleksander; Wertsman, Vladimir**
Ukrainians in Canada and the United States: a guide to information sources. Detroit, Mich.: Gale Research Company, [c1981]. xiv, 236 p. (Ethnic studies information guide series ; vol. 7); ISBN: 0-8103-1494-0.

Note: Approx. 1,000 entries.– Books, dissertations, periodical articles, pamphlets in English and Ukrainian languages.– Ukrainian titles are transliterated.– Includes descriptive annotations.

Location: OONL.

— 1982 —

4206 **Bombas, Leonidas C.**
Greeks in Canada (an annotated bibliography). [Montreal, Que.: Leonidas Bombas, 1982]. 139 p.

Note: Approx. 70 entries.– Published and unpublished

works, articles, reports, papers, theses.

Location: OONL.

4207 **Boshyk, Yury; Balan, Boris**
Political refugees and "displaced persons", 1945-1954: a selected bibliography and guide to research with special reference to Ukrainians. Edmonton: Canadian Institute of Ukrainian Studies, University of Alberta, 1982. xliv, 424 p. (Research report / Canadian Institute of Ukrainian Studies ; no. 2)

Note: Unpublished sources (bibliographies, guides to research, archival depositories and records, visual materials, sound recordings); primary sources (bibliographies, government publications, intergovernmental publications); publications by Ukrainian refugees; secondary sources (theses, articles, books).

Location: OONL.

4208 **Gee, Joyce**
Chinese Canadian bibliography. Toronto: Chinese Interpreter and Information Services, [1982]. 61 p.

Note: Approx. 600 entries.– Books, articles, theses on Chinese and other Asian Canadian groups.– Topics include history, immigration, culture, social conditions, directories, political activities.– Includes a section of books and articles in Chinese.

Location: OW.

4209 **Georges, Robert A.; Stern, Stephen**
American and Canadian immigrant and ethnic folklore: an annotated bibliography. New York: Garland Publishing, 1982. xix, 484 p. (Garland folklore bibliographies ; vol. 2); ISBN: 0-8240-9307-0.

Note: 1,900 entries.– Covers from 1888 through 1980.– Includes books and essays (from folklore periodicals) which document folklore of European and Asian immigrants and their American/Canadian-born descendants.

Location: OONL.

4210 **Goldstein, Jay**
"Recent publications relating to Canadian ethnic studies."
In: *Canadian Ethnic Studies*; Vol. 12, no. 3 (1980) p. 171-176; vol. 13, no. 3 (1981) p. 173-175; vol. 14, no. 3 (1982) p. 140-146.; ISSN: 0008-3496.

Note: Annual listing of research concerning Canadian ethnic studies with emphasis on articles in scholarly journals.– Excludes books, theses, popular publications.
Continues: James S. Frideres (1976-1979); Continued by: Norma Milton (1983); Bob Hromadiuk (1984-1992).

Location: OONL.

4211 **Janssen, Viveka K.**
"Bibliography on Swedish settlement in Alberta, 1890-1930."
In: *Swedish-American Historical Quarterly*; Vol. 33, no. 2 (April 1982) p. 124-129.; ISSN: 0730-028X.

Note: Monographs, periodical articles, biographies, memoirs, typescripts, letters relating to Swedish settlement in Alberta.– Excludes newspaper articles, personal interviews, oral histories.

Location: AEU.

4212 **Lee-Whiting, Brenda B.**
"A German-Canadian bibliography: studies on eastern Ontario."
In: *Canadiana Germanica*; No. 35 (August 1982) p. 28-33.; ISSN: 0703-1599.

Note: Articles by Lee-Whiting, newspaper articles by

various authors, parish histories published by churches founded by German immigrants, local histories of areas in eastern Ontario.
Location: OONL.

4213 **Liddell, Peter G.**
A bibliography of the Germans in British Columbia. Vancouver: Canadian Association of University Teachers of German, 1982. 89 p. (CAUTG publications / Canadian Association of University Teachers of German ; no. 5); ISBN: 0-91994404-3.
Note: 429 entries.– Covers early settlement period from mid-nineteenth century to 1981.– Includes books, periodical and newspaper articles, in English and German.
Location: OONL.

4214 **Young, Judy**
"Some thoughts about the present state of bibliography in the area of Canadian ethnic studies."
In: *Canadian Issues*; Vol. 4 (1982) p. 38-47.; ISSN: 0318-8442.
Note: Contains a listing of works on Canadian ethnic studies, general studies, by discipline, by specific ethnic group.– Provides a list of organizations and journals which publish information in the area of ethnic studies.
Location: OONL.

— 1983 —

4215 **Altfest, Karen C.**
"Ethnic studies in Canada."
In: *Ethnic and immigration groups: the United States, Canada, and England*. New York: Institute for Research in History: Haworth Press, c1983. P. 71-92.; ISBN: 0-917724-46-1.
Note: Bibliographical essay on Canadian ethnic studies.
Location: OONL.

4216 **Brye, David L.**
European immigration and ethnicity in the United States and Canada: a historical bibliography. Santa Barbara, Calif.: ABC-Clio Information Services, 1983. vii, 458 p.; ISBN: 0-87436-258-X.
Note: Contains 4,066 abstracts of articles selected from 585 periodicals.– Includes writings in political science, sociology, economics, psychology, health sciences, and literature, as well as general historical topics.– Limited to European immigration to United States and Canada from colonial period to 1982.– Topics include resources and general studies of immigration, response to immigration, immigrants and ethnic populations (by groups and by topics), special section on Canadian French-English relations.
Location: OONL.

4217 **Caldwell, Gary**
Les études ethniques au Québec: bilan et perspectives. Québec: Institut québécois de recherche sur la culture, 1983. 106 p.; ISBN: 2-89224-017-4.
Note: Localisation: OONL.

4218 **Malycky, Alexander**
"German-Albertans: a bibliography."
In: *German-Canadian Yearbook*; Vol. 6 (1981) p. 311-344; vol. 7 (1983) p. 239-325.; ISSN: 0316-8603.
Note: 2,468 entries.– Books, articles, special issues of periodicals dealing wholly or mainly with German-Albertans, from the 1890s to 1980.
Location: OONL.

4219 **Milton, Norma**
"Bibliography [recent publications relating to Canadian ethnic studies]."
In: *Canadian Ethnic Studies*; Vol. 15, no.3 (1983) p. 140-150.; ISSN: 0008-3496.
Note: Annual listing of research concerning Canadian ethnic studies with emphasis on articles in scholarly journals.– Excludes books, theses, popular publications. Continues: James S. Frideres (1976-1979); Jay Goldstein (1980-1982); Continued by: Bob Hromadiuk (1984-1992).
Location: OONL.

— 1984 —

4220 **Buchignani, Norman**
"Social science research on Asians in Canada."
In: *Asian Canadians: aspects of social change*, edited by K. Victor Ujimoto and Josephine Naidoo. [Guelph, Ont.: s.n., 1984]. P. 1-29.
Note: Approx. 80 entries.
Location: OONL.

4221 **Froeschle, Hartmut; Zimmerman, Lothar**
"The Germans in Ontario : a bibliography."
In: *German-Canadian Yearbook*; Vol. 8 (1984) p. 243-279.; ISSN: 0316-8603.
Note: 746 entries.
Location: AEU.

4222 **German-Canadian Historical Association**
"Activities in the field of German-Canadian studies and research/Aktivitäten im Bereich deutschkanadischer Studien und Forschung."
In: *Canadiana Germanica*; No. 41 (April 1984) p. 25-37.; ISSN: 0703-1599.
Note: Checklist, by author, of writings in the fields of history, biography, genealogy and immigrant studies.
Location: OONL.

4223 **Hessel, Peter**
"German immigration to the Ottawa Valley in the 19th century."
In: *German-Canadian Yearbook*; Vol. 8 (1984) p. 67-94.; ISSN: 0316-8603.
Note: Lists primary sources, secondary sources (books, booklets, journal articles, church anniversary booklets and other church publications, theses, local histories, family histories, newspaper articles, bibliographies).
Location: AEU.

4224 **Huggard, Turner**
An annotated list of resource material on the Irish in New Brunswick. Fredericton: [s.n.], 1984. iii, 53 l.
Note: 200 entries.– General history, Fenian movement, Irish genealogy, New Brunswick immigration, Orange Order, religion, Irish settlements in New Brunswick, ships and shipping.
Location: NBFU.

4225 **Indra, Doreen Marie**
Southeast Asian refugee settlement in Canada: a research bibliography. Ottawa: Canadian Asian Studies Association, 1984. 29 p.
Note: Approx. 250 entries.
Location: OONL.

4226 **Maltais, Claire**
Bibliographie sélective sur les communautés culturelles. Montréal: Ministère des Communautés culturelles et de l'Immigration, 1984. 65 p.; ISBN: 2-550-11284-9.
Note: Approx. 600 entrées.– Les documents sont

regroupés selon trois grands thèmes relatifs aux communautés culturelles: groupes spécifiques; aspects généraux et domaines d'activités.
Localisation: OONL.

4227 **Manitoba. Department of Education. Library**
Ethnic groups: bibliography materials in M.E.R.C. Winnipeg: Manitoba Department of Education, Multiculture Educational Resource Centre, 1984. 8 p.
Note: Location: OONL.

4228 **Morrison, James H.**
Common heritage: an annotated bibliography of ethnic groups in Nova Scotia. Halifax, N.S.: International Education Centre, Saint Mary's University, 1984. 130 p.: ill.
Note: Approx. 700 entries.– Includes books, periodicals, journal articles, theses, audio-visual materials.– Lists general sources, bibliographies, cross-cultural references, language, migration.– Extensive listings on Acadians, Blacks, Micmacs, Americans, Scots.
Location: OONL.

4229 **Ngatia, Therese**
The Blacks in Canada: a selective annotated bibliography. [Edmonton: T. Ngatia, 1984]. 45 l.
Note: Approx. 60 entries.– Monographs, pamphlets, periodical articles, theses.– Covers: 1971-1983.– Focus on scholarly materials.– Excludes popular works.
Location: OONL.

— 1985 —

4230 **Anderson, Wolseley W.**
Caribbean orientations: a bibliography of resource material on the Caribbean experience in Canada. Toronto: Organization for Caribbean Canadian Initiatives and Williams-Wallace Publishers, 1985. xi, 238 p.; ISBN: 0-88795-037-X.
Note: Approx 2,500 entries.– Includes published and unpublished materials.– General listings of materials on the region and individual countries and territories from which Caribbean Canadians come; materials about process of Caribbean integration into Canadian society: immigration, settlement, education, social and cultural adjustment, Canadian-Caribbean relations.– Includes a bibliography of bibliographies on the Caribbean and Canadian Blacks.
Location: OWA.

4231 **Canada. Department of the Secretary of State. Library**
Canadian ethnic groups bibliography/Bibliographie des groupes ethniques canadiens. 2nd ed. [Ottawa]: Secrétariat d'État du Canada, La Bibliothèque Department of the Secretary of State, The Library, [1985]. iv, 96 p.
Note: Approx. 700 entries.– Monographs, bibliographies, dictionaries, directories, periodicals received as of March 1985 concerning activities of sixty ethnic groups.– Text in English and French/texte en français et en anglais.
Previous edition: ... : an analytical list based on holdings in the Secretary of State Library. 1974. 1 vol. (various pagings).
Location: OONL.

4232 **Gough, C.J.**
Bibliography on topics related to immigrant settlement and ethnic minority concerns (in the Canadian context). Victoria, B.C.: Inter-cultural Association of Greater Victoria, [1982-1985]. 2 vol.
Note: Approx. 650 entries.– Journal articles on Canadian

ethnic issues, designed to meet needs of human service workers for specific information on ethno-cultural backgrounds of clients.
Location: OONL.

4233 **Metropolitan Toronto Library. Languages Department**
A selected bibliography of German Canadiana in the Languages Department of the Metropolitan Toronto Library/Deutschkanadische bücher aus der Sammlung der Sprachenabteilung der Metropolitan Toronto Library. Toronto: The Department, 1985. 17 p.
Note: Approx. 240 entries.– Includes works by German-Canadians published in Canada and Germany, translations of works by English and French Canadians published in Germany, works about Canada in the German language.
Location: OONL.

4234 **Ontario. Ministry of Citizenship and Culture**
Multicultural information: a selected bibliography of materials available in the Ministry, November, 1985. Toronto: Ontario Ministry of Citizenship and Culture, 1985. ii, 84 p.; ISBN: 0-7729-0904-0.
Note: Approx. 800 entries.– Subjects covered include business and employment, citizenship, cross-cultural communications, education, ethnic groups, francophone Canadians, immigrant women, media and ethnicity, multiculturalism, native people, refugees.
Location: OONL.

4235 **Pihach, John D.**
"Bibliography for Ukrainian researchers: resources at the Yorkton Public Library."
In: Saskatchewan Genealogical Society Bulletin; Vol. 16, no. 3 (July/September 1985) p. 127-129.; ISSN: 0048-9182.
Note: References to Ukrainians in Canada, genealogical sources, local histories.
Location: AEU.

4236 **Sawaie, Mohammed**
Arabic-speaking immigrants in the United States and Canada: a bibliographical guide with annotation. Lexington, Ky.: Mazdâ Publishers, c1985. xxiv, 158 p.; ISBN: 0-939214-27-X.
Note: Approx. 1,000 entries.– Includes published books and monographs, articles and book chapters, unpublished theses, newspapers and periodicals, annual reports, government documents.
Location: OONL.

4237 **Yip, Gladys**
Cross cultural childrearing: an annotated bibliography. Vancouver: Centre for the Study of Curriculum and Instruction, University of British Columbia, c1985. 81 p. (Early childhood series / Centre for the Study of Curriculum and Instruction, University of British Columbia); ISBN: 0-88865-372-7.
Note: Approx. 250 entries.– Books, studies, reports dealing with childrearing practices among different cultural groups.– Includes cross-cultural, cross-national and subcultural studies.
Location: OONL.

— 1986 —

4238 **Alberta. Alberta Culture. Library**
Multicultural resources in the Alberta Culture Library: an annotated bibliography. [Edmonton]: Alberta Culture, 1986. 173 p.
Note: Listing of books, pamphlets, documents on

individual ethnic groups, arts and crafts, cookbooks, dance and costume, music and songs, games, literature.– Section on multicultural education, multiculturalism and ethnic studies.– Additional bibliographies are listed in each major section.
Location: OONL.

4239 **Chandrasekhar, S.**
"A bibliography on immigration from India to Canada and the Asian Indian immigrant communities in Canada."
In: *From India to Canada: a brief history of immigration, problems of discrimination, admission and assimilation*, edited by S. Chandrasekhar. La Jolla, Calif.: Population Review Books, 1986. P. 175-205.; ISBN: 0-9609080-1-3.
Note: Approx. 450 entries.
Location: OONL.

— 1987 —

4240 **Alberta. Career Development and Employment. Immigration and Settlement Services.**
Resource Centre: bibliography of resource materials. [Edmonton]: Alberta Career Development and Employment, Immigration and Settlement Services, [1987]. 38 p.
Note: Collection of materials for people working with immigrants in Alberta.– Topics include ethnic issues, multiculturalism, refugees, cross-cultural counselling, Alberta (introductory guides), volunteer program management, orientation and adaptation.
Location: OONL.

4241 **Loades, Peter, et al.**
Canada's multicultural mosaic. [Toronto]: Toronto Public Library, 1987. 16 p.
Note: Approx. 100 titles.
Location: OONL.

4242 **Machalski, Andrew**
Multiculturalism in education resources: a user guide. [Ottawa]: Multiculturalism Sector, Department of the Secretary of State of Canada, 1987. 90 p.
Note: Approx. 300 entries.– Annotated list of resource materials in the area of ethnic studies, multiculturalism in education, race relations, cross-cultural communication, immigration.– Includes English- and French-language publications.– Provides a list of additional bibliographies and checklists.
Location: OONL.

4243 **McCreath, Peter L., et al.**
Multiculturalism in the Maritimes: a teacher's resource guide. Tantallon, N.S.: Four East Publications, 1987. 49 p.; ISBN: 0-920427-14-6.
Note: Includes a listing of educational materials to support programs in multiculturalism in the Atlantic provinces.
Location: OONL.

4244 **Metress, Seamus P.**
"The Irish in the Great Lakes: selected bibliography of sociohistorical sources."
In: *Ethnic Forum*; Vol. 7, no. 1 (1987) p. 97-109.; ISSN: 0278-9078.
Note: Includes a section on Canada.
Location: OTY.

4245 **Miska, John P.**
Canadian studies on Hungarians, 1886-1986: an annotated bibliography of primary and secondary sources.

Regina: Canadian Plains Research Center, University of Regina, 1987. xiii, 245 p. (Canadian Plains bibliographies / Canadian Plains Research Center, University of Regina ; 1; ISSN: 0821-8936); ISBN: 0-88977-034-4.
Note: 1,271 entries.– Books, newspaper and periodical articles, research papers, theses, church annals.
Supplement: *Canadian studies on Hungarians, a bibliography. Supplement.* Ottawa: Microform Biblios, 1992. x, 80 p.; ISBN: 0-91927-909-0.
Location: OONL.

4246 **Moreau, Bernice M.**
"Black Nova Scotian literature: a select bibliography."
In: *Journal of Education*; No. 400 (1987) p. 46-50.; ISSN: 0022-0566.
Note: Approx. 125 entries.– Books, studies, theses, articles on Nova Scotia Blacks.– Focus on socio-historical aspect of Black Nova Scotian life.– Themes include education, economic and political activities, religion, Black women.
Location: OHM.

4247 **Schlesinger, Benjamin**
Jewish family issues: a resource guide. New York: Garland, 1987. xvi, 144 p. (Garland library of sociology ; no. 10); ISBN: 0-8240-8460-8.
Note: 524 entries.– Covers 1960-1986.– Includes Canadian references.
Location: OONL.

— 1988 —

4248 **Burnet, Jean R.**
Multiculturalism in Canada. [Ottawa]: Canadian Studies Directorate, Department of the Secretary of State of Canada, c1988. 26, 29 p. (Canadian studies resource guides); ISBN: 0-662-56210-0.
Note: Approx. 150 entries.– Includes an introductory overview of the subject, a commentary on significant works, and suggestions for further reading.– Text in English and French with French text on inverted pages.– Title of additional title-page: *Le multiculturalisme au Canada*.
Location: OONL.

4249 **Burnet, Jean R.**
Le multiculturalisme au Canada. [Ottawa]: Direction des études canadiennes, Secrétariat d'État du Canada, c1988. 29, 26 p. (Guides pédagogiques des études canadiennes); ISBN: 0-662-56210-0.
Note: Approx. 150 entrées.– Comporte un exposé préliminaire, des observations sur les principaux travaux et une liste de lectures recommandées.– Texte en français et en anglais disposé tête-bêche.– Titre de la p. de t. additionnelle: *Multiculturalism in Canada*.
Localisation: OONL.

4250 **Communication Québec. Région de l'île de Montréal**
Répertoire des médias ethniques de la région de Montréal. 5e éd. Montréal: Communication-Québec, île-de-Montréal, 1988. 83 f.; ISBN: 2-550-19251-6.
Note: Approx. 100 entrées.
Éditions antérieures:
Communication Québec, Région de Montréal, 1985. 112 p.; ISBN: 2-550-11603-8.
Répertoire des médias des communautés culturelles du Québec. Gouvernement du Québec, Ministère des communautés culturelles et de l'immigration, Direction

des communications, 1982. 64 p.
Répertoire des médias des communautés ethniques du Québec.
Ministère de l'immigration, Direction des communications, 1979. 94 p.
Localisation: OONL.

4251 **De Vries, John**
Analytical overview of the literature on ethno-cultural community development and integration. [Ottawa]: Policy & Research, Multiculturalism & Citizenship Canada, 1988. [11], 16 l.
Note: Text in English and French with French text on inverted pages.– Title of additional title-page: *Coup d'oeil sur la littérature traitant du développement et de l'intégration des minorités ethnoculturelles.*
Location: OONL.

4252 **De Vries, John**
Coup d'oeil sur la littérature traitant du développement et de l'intégration des minorités ethnoculturelles. [Ottawa]: Politiques et recherches, Multiculturalisme et citoyenneté, 1988. 16, [11] f.
Note: Texte en français et en anglais disposé tête-bêche.– Titre de la p. de t. additionnelle: *Analytical overview of the literature on ethno-cultural community development and integration.*
Localisation: OONL.

4253 **De Vries, John**
L'intégration des communautés ethnoculturelles dans la société canadienne: bibliographie sélective. [Ottawa]: Multiculturalisme et Citoyenneté Canada, 1988. 117, 118 p.
Note: Approx. 800 entrées.– Texte en français et en anglais disposé tête-bêche.– Titre de la p. de t. additionnelle: *The integration of ethno-cultural communities into Canadian society: a selected bibliography.*
Localisation: OOSS.

4254 **De Vries, John**
The integration of ethno-cultural communities into Canadian society: a selected bibliography. [Ottawa]: Multiculturalism and Citizenship Canada, 1988. 118, 117 p.
Note: Approx. 800 entries.– Text in English and French with French text on inverted pages.– Title of additional title-page: *L'intégration des communautés ethnoculturelles dans la société canadienne: bibliographie sélective.*
Location: OOSS.

4255 **Denton, Vivienne**
"Ethnic and multicultural materials for children's reading: bibliographical sources."
In: *Canadian Children's Literature*; No. 49 (1988) p. 27-29.; ISSN: 0319-0080.
Note: Monographs, government publications, anthologies, journals, journal articles and bibliographies.
Location: AEU.

4256 **Govia, Francine; Lewis, Helen**
Blacks in Canada: in search of the promise: a bibliographical guide to the history of Blacks in Canada. Edmonton: Harambee Centre Canada, 1988. [viii], 102 p.; ISBN: 0-921550-00-6.
Note: Approx. 800 entries.
Location: OONL.

4257 **Gregorovich, Andrew**
"Ukrainians in Ontario: a selected bibliography."
In: *Polyphony*; Vol. 10 (1988) p. 271-285.; ISSN: 0704-7002.

Note: 175 entries.– Scholarly and popular material, mainly in English, relating to Ukrainians in Ontario.
Location: OONL.

4258 **Metress, Seamus P.; Baker, William M.**
"A bibliography of the history of the Irish in Canada."
In: *The Untold story: the Irish in Canada*, edited by Robert O'Driscoll and Lorna Reynolds. Toronto: Celtic Arts of Canada, 1988. P. 977-1001.; ISBN: 0-921745-00-1.
Note: Approx. 400 entries.– Emphasis on non-fictional, post-World War I, printed, secondary sources which focus on, or contain specific information about the Irish in Canada.
Location: OONL.

4259 **Nakonechny, Patricia; Kishchuk, Marie**
The monograph collections of the Ukrainian Museum of Canada: an integrated catalogue. Saskatoon: Ukrainian Museum of Canada, 1988. iv, 1174 p.; ISBN: 0-9693765-0-2.
Note: 14,600 entries.– Lists specialized materials relating to the history, settlement, cultural, economic, spiritual and community life of Canadians of Ukrainian origin.
Location: OONL.

4260 **Rome, David**
A bibliography of Jewish Canadiana [microform]. Montreal: National Archives, Canadian Jewish Congress, 1988. 118 microfiches (ca. 55 fr. each) in binder with 3 printed l.
Note: Approx. 15,000 entries.– Lists titles written, edited or compiled by Canadian Jews, books and pamphlets about Canadian Jews, books written by Canadians on subjects of Jewish interest.– Topics include Canadian Jewish history, arts, religion, education, sociology.– Entries in English, French, Yiddish, Hebrew.
Location: OONL.

4261 **Sturino, Franc**
Italian-Canadian studies: a select bibliography. [Toronto]: York University and Multicultural History Society of Ontario, [c1988]. 108 p. (Elia Chair publication series / York University and Multicultural History Society of Ontario ; no. 1); ISBN: 0-919045-37-5.
Note: Approx. 900 entries.– Covers selected material up to summer 1987.– Includes books, periodical articles, government publications.– Excludes fiction and poetry.
Location: OONL.

4262 **"Le tourisme ethno-culturel."**
Dans: *Notes du Centre d'études du tourisme*; Vol. 8, no 4 (mai 1988) p. 1-4.; ISSN: 0229-2718.
Note: 99 entrées.
Localisation: OONL.

— 1989 —

4263 **Akbari, Ather H.**
Economics of immigration and racial discrimination: a literature survey (1970-1989). [Ottawa]: Policy & Research, Department of Multiculturalism and Citizenship, 1989. 63, 32 p.
Note: Bibliographical essay reviewing articles and studies on economic aspects of immigration.– Text in English and French with French text on inverted pages.– Title of additional title-page: *Économique de l'immigration et de la discrimination raciale: une revue de la documentation (1970-1989).*
Location: OOSS.

4264 **Akbari, Ather H.**
Économique de l'immigration et de la discrimination raciale: une revue de la documentation (1970-1989). [Ottawa]: Politique et recherches, Ministère du Multiculturalisme et de la Citoyenneté, 1989. 32, 63 p.
Note: Essai bibliographique.– Revue des articles et des études sur l'aspect économique de l'immigration.– Texte en français et en anglais disposé tête-bêche.– Titre de la p. de t. additionnelle: *Economics of immigration and racial discrimination: a literature survey (1970-1989).*
Localisation: OOSS.

4265 **A bibliography of informational pamphlets and brochures to assist in immigrant settlement.** [Toronto]: Ontario Ministry of Citizenship, [1989]. 47 p.; ISBN: 0-7729-0946-6.
Note: Approx. 300 entries.– Listing of material describing programs and services offered by government and community agencies to assist in newcomers' integration and adaptation to Ontario.– Topics covered include education, consumer information, financial assistance, housing, rights, employment, women's issues.
Location: OONL.

4266 **Bombas, Leonidas C.**
Ho Hell-enismos tou Kanada: mia bibliographik-e parousias-e/Canada's Hellenism: a bibliographic guide. Athens: Leonidas C. Bombas, 1989. 76 p. (Greek-Canadian documentation series)
Note: 100 entries.– Publications in English, French or Greek dealing with aspects of Greek life in Canada: education, culture, ethnic identity, family, women, mass media, church, employment, socio-professional mobility and integration, general works.– Arranged in subject groups with author index.
Location: OONL.

4267 **Guttmann, David**
Jewish elderly in the English-speaking countries. New York: Greenwood Press, 1989. xvii, 140 p. (Bibliographies and indexes in gerontology ; no. 10); ISBN: 0-313-26240-3.
Note: 400 entries.– Topics include characteristics of Jewish elderly, special problems of Holocaust survivors, services, gerontological education.– Includes Canadian references.
Location: OONL.

4268 **Kim, Hyung-chan**
Asian American studies: an annotated bibliography and research guide. New York: Greenwood Press, 1989. x, 504 p. (Bibliographies and indexes in American history ; no. 11; ISSN: 0742-6828); ISBN: 0-313-26026-5.
Note: 3,396 entries.– Includes some Canadian references.
Location: OONL.

4269 **Laine, Edward W.**
Archival sources for the study of Finnish Canadians. Ottawa: National Archives of Canada, 1989. vii, 104, 104 v p. (Ethnocultural guide series / National Archives of Canada); ISBN: 0-662-56435-9.
Note: Includes a bibliography: books and pamphlets, list of newspapers, articles, theses and other unpublished works: archival and bibliographical reference works and research tools, historical literature.– Text in English and French with French text on inverted pages.– Title of additional title-page: *Sources d'archives sur les Finno-Canadiens.*
Location: OONL.

4270 **Laine, Edward W.**
Sources d'archives sur les Finno-Canadiens. Ottawa: Archives nationales du Canada, 1989. v, 104, 104, vii p. (Collection des guides ethnoculturels / Archives nationales du Canada); ISBN: 0-662-56435-9.
Note: Bibliographie, p. 75-93: Livres et brochures, articles, thèses et autres textes inédits: ouvrages de référence et instruments de recherche, littérature historique.– Liste de journaux et autres publications périodiques.– Texte en français et en anglais disposé tête-bêche.– Titre de la p. de t. additionnelle: *Archival sources for the study of Finnish Canadians.*
Localisation: OONL.

4271 **Mendis, Asoka**
Ethnocultural entrepreneurship: an overview and annotated bibliography. Ottawa: Multiculturalism and Citizenship Canada, 1989. 52 l.
Note: Books and journal articles, theses, government reports and studies arranged in four sections: theoretical works; empirical works; historical works; bibliographies, directories, newspapers, periodicals.
Location: OOSS.

4272 **Sanfilippo, Matteo**
"Pour l'histoire des communautés italiennes au Canada: essai bibliographique."
Dans: *Annali accademici Canadesi;* Vol. 5 (1989) p. 115-132.; ISSN: 0394-1736.
Note: Localisation: OONL.

4273 **Stymeist, David H.; Salazar, Lilia; Spafford, Graham**
A selected annotated bibliography on the Filipino immigrant community in Canada and the United States. Winnipeg: University of Manitoba, Department of Anthropology, 1989. xi, 131 p.: map. (University of Manitoba Anthropology papers ; no. 31)
Note: Survey of social science research on immigrant Filipino community in Canada and the U.S.– Detailed descriptive annotations.
Location: OONL.

— 1990 —

4274 **Froeschle, Hartmut; Zimmerman, Lothar**
German Canadiana: a bibliography/Deutschkanadische bibliographie. Toronto: Historical Society of Mecklenburg Upper Canada, 1990. xix, 420 p.; ISBN: 1-895503-12-4.
Note: Special issue of *German-Canadian Yearbook;* Vol. 11 (1990).
6,585 entries.– Covers through 1987.– Topics include German-Canadian history, German-Canadian group life, religious life, German language in Canada, German-Canadian press and periodicals, cultural contributions, economic contributions, German-Canadians as a literary theme.– Text in English and German.
Location: OONL.

4275 **Karim, Karim H.; Sansom, Gareth**
Bibliographie annotée sur les ethnies et les média au Canada. [Ottawa]: Politiques & Recherches, Secteur du multiculturalisme, Multiculturalisme et citoyenneté, 1990. 32, 30 f.
Note: Approx. 150 entrées.– Travaux de recherche, analyses de contenu, comptes rendu de conférences, rapports de groupes de travail, discours, textes de loi, codes de l'industrie.– Cet ouvrage est destiné aux chercheurs qui étudient la façon dont les Canadiens de

toutes les origines ethniques sont présentés et employés par les principaux médias du pays.– Texte en français et en anglais disposé tête-bêche.– Titre de la p. de t. additionnelle: *Ethnicity and the mass media in Canada: an annotated bibliography.*
Localisation: OOP.

4276 **Karim, Karim H.; Sansom, Gareth**
Ethnicity and the mass media in Canada: an annotated bibliography. [Ottawa]: Policy & Research, Multiculturalism Sector, Multiculturalism & Citizenship, 1990. 30, 32 l.
Note: Approx. 150 entries.– Studies, task force reports, conference proceedings, journal articles, theses dealing with portrayal and employment of Canadians of all ethnic backgrounds in mainstream Canadian media.– Text in English and French with French text on inverted pages.– Title of additional title-page: *Bibliographie annotée sur les ethnies et les média au Canada.*
Location: OOP.

4277 **Melançon, Benoît**
La littérature montréalaise des communautés culturelles: prolégomènes et bibliographie. Montréal: Groupe de recherche Montréal imaginaire, Université de Montréal, 1990. 31 f.
Note: Localisation: OONL.

4278 **Russell, Hilary**
A bibliography relating to African Canadian history. [Ottawa]: Historical Research Branch, National Historic Sites Directorate, 1990. 64 p.
Note: Approx. 480 entries.– Books, periodical articles, theses.– Arranged by regions of Canada.
Location: OONL.

4279 **Scantland, Anna Cecile**
Study of historical injustice to Japanese Canadians: text and bibliography. Rev. ed. Vancouver: Parallel Publishers, c1990. 392 p.; ISBN: 0-9690710-3-5.
Note: Covers 1890s to 1989.– Includes books, pamphlets, films, periodical and newspaper articles, government documents, legal case reports.
Previous edition: ... : *bibliography.* 1986. 195 l.
Location: OONL.

4280 **Wagle, Iqbal**
"Selected and annotated bibliography of South Asians in Ontario."
In: *Polyphony*; Vol. 12 (1990) p. 137-151.; ISSN: 0704-7002.
Note: 75 entries.
Location: OONL.

— 1991 —

4281 **Barr, Elinor**
Annotated bibliography of English-language books and articles relating to the Swedish experience in Canada. Växjö [Sweden]: Swedish Emigrant Institute; Thunder Bay, Ont.: Singing Shield Productions [distributor], 1991. 79 p.: port. (Proceedings from the Swedish Emigrant Institute ; 4; ISSN: 0283-4065); ISBN: 0-96917-173-0.
Note: Location: OONL.

4282 **Immigration to British Columbia: a selected annotated bibliography.** [Victoria]: Province of British Columbia, Ministry of International Business and Immigration, 1991. iii, 40 p.; ISBN: 0-7726-1327-3.
Note: Approx. 125 entries.– Books, articles, audio-visual materials which illustrate social, cultural, economic contributions of immigrants to British Columbia,

experiences of immigrants as individuals or groups, immigration history and policy in British Columbia.
Location: OONL.

4283 **Karim, Karim H.**
Images des Arabes et des Musulmans: recension de la recherche. Ottawa: Politiques et recherche, Secteur du multiculturalisme, Multiculturalisme et citoyenneté, 1991. 44 f. (Images des minorités: Recensions de la recherche)
Note: Approx. 400 entrées.– Livres, monographies, dépliants, articles, thèses et des ouvrages inédits, moyens audiovisuels: desciptions et critiques des études érudites menées sur les Arabes et Musulmans, analyses des médias de masse, de manuels scolaires et d'enquêtes menées auprès du public, ainsi que des publications sur la lutte aux stéréotypes.
English title: *Images of Arabs and Muslims: a research review.*
Localisation: OONL.

4284 **Karim, Karim H.**
Images of Arabs and Muslims: a research review. Ottawa: Policy & Research, Multiculturalism Branch, Multiculturalism & Citizenship, 1991. 44 l. (Images of minorities: Research reviews)
Note: Approx. 400 entries.– Books, monographs, booklets, articles, theses, unpublished papers, audio-visual materials: descriptive and critical writings on academic studies about Arabs and Muslims, analyses of the mass media, school textbooks and public surveys, publications on countering stereotypes.– Some Canadian references.
Titre en français: *Images des Arabes et des Musulmans: recension de la recherche.*
Location: OONL.

4285 **Lam, Van Be**
L'immigration et les communautés culturelles du Québec, 1968-1990: bibliographie sélective annotée. Québec: Documentor, 1991. 142 p.; ISBN: 2-89123-114-7.
Note: 726 entrées.– Monographies, publications gouvernementales, articles de périodiques, articles de journaux, documents audiovisuels concernant l'immigration au Canada et au Québec, les communautés culturelles du Québec.
Localisation: OONL.

4286 **Saskatchewan Organization for Heritage Languages. Resource Centre**
Saskatchewan Organization for Heritage Languages Resource Centre annotated bibliography. Regina: The Organization, 1991. vi, 160 p. (loose-leaf).
Note: 400 entries.– Books, pamphlets, periodicals, audio and video tapes on minorities and heritage languages.
Location: OONL.

4287 **Vadnay, Susan**
A selected bibliography of research on Canadian Jewry, 1900-1980. Ottawa: [S. Vadnay], 1991. iv, 81 p.
Note: Approx. 1,350 entries.– Reference works (bibliographies, year books, directories), general history, local history, social and communal history, economic history and the professions, religious and congregational history, education, cultural and literary history, biography.
Location: OONL.

— 1992 —

4288 Beguet, Véronique
Les réfugiés indochinois au Canada: une bibliographie/
Indochinese refugees in Canada: a bibliography. Québec:
Groupe d'études et de recherches sur l'Asie
contemporaine, Université Laval, c1992. x, 72 p.; ISBN: 0-
98024-072-9.
Note: 354 entrées.– Références sur les réfugiés
indochinois au Canada depuis 1980.
Localisation: OONL.

4289 Canada. Multiculturalism and Citizenship Canada
Recent publications supported by Multiculturalism and
Citizenship Canada/Publications récentes
subventionnées par Multiculturalisme et Citoyenneté
Canada. Ottawa: Multiculturalism and Citizenship
Canada, 1992. 21 p.: ill.
Note: Text in English and French/texte en français et en
anglais.
Location: OONL.

4290 Duryea, Michelle LeBaron
Conflict and culture: a literature review and
bibliography. Victoria, B.C.: UVic Institute for Dispute
Resolution, c1992. ix, 176 p.
Note: Approx. 500 entries.– Literature from psychology,
communications, law, sociology relating to culture
conflict and resolution.– Topics include acculturation,
communication and culture, conflict management, cross-
cultural orientation, ethnic attitudes, ethnic relations,
intercultural education, multiculturalism, race relations,
transcultural medical care.
Location: OONL.

4291 Hromadiuk, Bob
"Bibliography [recent publications relating to Canadian
ethnic studies]."
In: *Canadian Ethnic Studies*; Vol. 16, no. 3 (1984) p. 174-
179; vol. 17, no. 1 (1985) p. 145-162; vol. 17, no. 3 (1985) p.
168-190; vol. 18, no. 3 (1986) p. 169-203; vol. 19, no. 3
(1987) p. 187-219; vol. 20, no. 3 (1988) p. 195-266; vol. 21,
no. 3 (1989) p. 148-185; vol. 22, no. 3 (1990) p. 133-198;
vol. 23, no. 3 (1991) p. 193-244; vol. 24, no. 3 (1992) p. 191-
215.; ISSN: 0008-3496.
Note: Annual listing of research concerning Canadian
ethnic studies with emphasis on articles in scholarly
journals.– Excludes books, theses, popular publications.
Continues: James S. Frideres (1976-1979); Jay Goldstein
(1980-1982); Norma Milton (1983).
Location: OONL.

4292 Multicultural History Society of Ontario
A guide to the collections of the Multicultural History
Society of Ontario. Toronto: Multicultural History
Society of Ontario, 1992. xx, 695 p.; ISBN: 0-91904-558-8.
Note: Listing of documents held by the archives and
library of the MHSO relating to the history of cultural
minorities in Canada.
Location: OONL.

**4293 A Research bibliography on immigration to British
Columbia.** Victoria: Immigration Policy Branch,
Province of British Columbia, 1992. ii, 50 p.; ISBN: 0-7726-
1640-X.
Note: Approx. 600 entries.– Studies and papers related to
British Columbia immigration and immigrant issues:
history, demography, economic and policy issues, ethnic
and race relations, adaptation, immigrant services,

refugees, women's issues.– Excludes magazine, newspaper and newsletter articles, speeches, annual reports,
workshops.
Location: OONL.

4294 Strong, Lisa L.
Contemporary books reflecting Canada's cultural
diversity: a selective annotated bibliography for grades
K-12. Vancouver: British Columbia Teacher-Librarians'
Association, 1992. 120 p.: ill.; ISBN: 0-921140-20-7.
Note: Listing of fiction and information books on
Canadian racial, religious, cultural groups for students,
primary to grade 12.
Location: OONL.

4295 Teixeira, Carlos; Levigne, Gilles
The Portuguese in Canada: a bibliography/Les Portugais
au Canada: une bibliographie. Toronto: Institute for
Social Research, 1992. v, 79 p.; ISBN: 1-55014-163-5.
Note: 761 entries.– Books, journal and periodical articles,
theses, newspaper articles, reports, papers, manuscripts,
forthcoming works in English and French.– Portuguese-
language newspaper articles.
Location: OONL.

— 1993 —

4296 Canada. Canadian Heritage
Research results of projects funded by the Canadian
Ethnic Studies Program, 1973-1988: a bibliography/
Résultats des projets de recherche subventionnés par le
Programme des études ethniques canadiennes, 1973-
1988: une bibliographie. Ottawa: Canadian Heritage,
1993. x, 78 p.; ISBN: 0-662-60103-3.
Note: 667 entries.– Books, articles, conference papers,
research reports and review articles.– Text in English and
French/texte en français et en anglais.
Location: OONL.

4297 Harvey, Fernand
"An annotated bibliography on the Irish in Quebec."
In: *The Irish in Quebec: an introduction to the historiography*,
by Robert J. Grace. Québec: Institut québécois de
recherche sur la culture, 1993. P. 135-262. (Instruments de
travail / Institut québécois de recherche sur la culture ;
no 12; ISSN: 0714-0614)
Note: 1,089 entries.– Books, articles from specialized
journals and theses dealing with the history of the Irish
in Quebec.– Topics include immigration and settlement,
political life, culture, religion, biographies, genealogy.–
Includes a list of research aids.
Location: OONL.

4298 Woolford, Daniel
Resource guide of publications supported by
multiculturalism programs, 1973-1992/Guide des
publications subventionnées par les programmes du
multiculturalisme, 1973-1992. Ottawa: Multiculturalism
and Citizenship Canada, c1993. vii, 136 p.; ISBN: 0-662-
59679-X.
Note: Approx. 1,200 entries.– Listing of books and
periodicals funded by the multiculturalism programs of
Multiculturalism and Citizenship Canada.– Text in
English and French/texte en français et en anglais.
Location: OONL.

Urban Studies

Études urbaines

— 1907 —

4299 Wickett, Samuel Morley
"Bibliography of Canadian municipal government."
In: *Municipal government in Canada.* Toronto: [s.n.], 1907.
P. [121]-128.
Note: Approx. 150 entries.
Location: OONL.

— 1926 —

4300 McGill University. Blackader Library of Architecture
Books on town planning: a reference collection on view
in the Blackader Library of Architecture, McGill Univers-
ity Library, January to March 1926. Montreal: Mercury
Press, 1926. 20 p.
Note: Location: OTP.

— 1932 —

**4301 Special Libraries Association. Special Committee on
Municipal Documents**
Basic list of current municipal documents: a checklist of
official publications issued periodically since 1927 by the
larger cities of the United States and Canada. New York:
The Association, 1932. 71 p.
Note: Location: BVA.

— 1957 —

**4302 Canada. Department of Mines and Technical Surveys.
Geographical Branch**
Canadian urban geography. Rev. ed. Ottawa: E. Cloutier,
1957. 100 p. (Bibliographical series / Canada Department
of Mines and Technical Surveys, Geographical Branch ;
no. 13)
Note: Approx. 1,300 entries.– Journal articles, addresses,
planning association reports and studies, briefs to royal
commissions, master plans relating to geography and
planning of provinces, regions, cities and towns.
Previous edition: 1954. 80 p.
Location: OONL.

— 1959 —

4303 Saskatchewan Center for Community Studies
Developing Saskatchewan's community resources:
annotated bibliography for community leaders.
Saskatoon: University of Saskatchewan, Center for
Community Studies, 1959. 17 l.
Note: Location: OONL.

— 1961 —

4304 Oberlander, H. Peter; Lasserre, F.
Annotated bibliography: performance standards for
space and site planning for residential development.
Ottawa: National Research Council Canada, Division of
Building Research, 1961. iv, 33 l. (National Research
Council Canada, Division of Building Research
Bibliography ; no. 19)
Note: 113 entries.– References from Canada, Great
Britain, United States, 1931 to 1961 dealing with space
standards around and between buildings.
Location: OONL.

— 1963 —

4305 Bédard, Roger J.
"Finances municipales: une bibliographie."
Dans: *Cités et villes;* Vol. 6, no 5 (mai 1963) p. 43-47; vol. 6,
no 6 (juin 1963) p. 43.; ISSN: 0009-7500.
Note: Approx. 450 entrées.– Volumes, brochures, articles,
tirés-à-part.– Inclut statistiques officielles, commissions
royales d'enquête, finances municipales au Canada,
zones métropolitaines, évaluation de la propriété.
Localisation: OONL.

— 1965 —

4306 Canadian Federation of Mayors and Municipalities
Municipal reference library catalogue/Catalogue de la
bibliothèque de la Fédération [des maires et des
municipalités]. Montreal: Canadian Federation of
Mayors and Municipalities, 1956-1965. 1 vol. (loose-leaf).
Note: Arranged in six sections: "Government," "Municipal government," "Royal commissions" (submissions and
reports),"Conference proceedings and publications,"
"Reference tools" (bibliographies, directories, guides,
indexes), "Year books," "Periodicals."- Text in English and
French/texte en français et en anglais.
Previous edition: *Municipal reference library: a catalogue of
books and documents relating to municipal administration.*
1954. 115 l.
Location: OONL.

— 1966 —

**4307 Ontario. Department of Economics and Development.
Regional Development Branch**
Ontario, a bibliography for regional development:
classified list of limited references. 2nd ed. Toronto:
Regional Development Branch, Department of
Economics and Development, 1966. vi l., 126 p.
Note: Approx. 1,700 entries.– Contains mainly Ontario
provincial and municipal government studies and
reports, with a selection from other Canadian provinces
and the United States on topics relating to regional and
urban planning.– Topics include conservation, land use,
pollution, recreation, transportation, water resources.
Previous edition: *A bibliography for regional development:
classified list of limited references.* 1965. vi, 112 p.– 1,200
entries.
Location: OONL.

— 1968 —

4308 Central Mortgage and Housing Corporation. Library
Housing for the aged: bibliography. Ottawa: [s.n.], 1968.
17 l.
Note: 216 entries.– Books, pamphlets, periodical articles
dealing with architectural and social aspects of housing
for the aged, in Canada, Great Britain, the United States.
Location: OONL.

4309 Lessard, Marc-André
"Bibliographie des villes du Québec."
Dans: *Recherches sociographiques;* Vol. 9, no 1/2 (1968) p.
143-209.; ISSN: 0034-1282.

Note: 1,240 entrées.– Catégories: démographie, géographie, transport et circulation, économie, travail, urbanisme et rénovation urbaine, politique, finances municipales, organisation communautaire, groupes ethniques et immigrants, famille, logement, loisirs, écoles, religion.
Localisation: OONL.

— 1969 —

4310 **Central Mortgage and Housing Corporation. Library**
New towns bibliography. [S.l.: s.n.], 1969. 36 l.
Note: 576 entries.– Books, periodical articles, pamphlets on new town planning and development in Canada, Great Britain and United States.
Location: OONL.

4311 **Scott, Allen J.**
A bibliography on combinatorial programming methods and application in regional science and planning. [Toronto]: Centre for Urban and Community Studies, University of Toronto, 1969. 23 l. (University of Toronto Centre for Urban and Community Studies Bibliographic series ; no. 1)
Note: Approx. 235 entries.– Covers the period 1890 to the end of 1968.– Topics include general combinatorial analysis, computational procedures, network and graph-theoretic problems, grouping and partitioning problems.
Location: OONL.

— 1970 —

4312 **Blumenfeld, Hans**
The trend to the metropolis: bibliography. Monticello, Ill.: Council of Planning Librarians, 1970. 9 !. (Council of Planning Librarians Exchange bibliography ; 144)
Note: Approx. 100 entries.– Books, journal articles, government reports, theses.
Location: OONL.

4313 **Canadian Council on Urban and Regional Research**
Urban & regional references; [références] urbaines & régionales, 1945-1969. Ottawa: [The Council, 1970]. xi, 796 p.; ISBN: 0-919076-06-8.
Note: Approx. 7,000 entries.– Books, journal articles, theses, federal, provincial, municipal government documents related to urbanization and urban affairs in Canada: physical environment, population and social characteristics, urban regional settlement, economics, transportation and communication, government and administration, urban-regional development.– This is a cumulation of seven issues which appeared between 1945 and 1970.– Text in English and French/texte en français et en anglais.
Supplements:
... . Supplement, 1970/... . Supplément, 1970. [1971]. xi, 134 p.; ISBN: 0-919076-09-2.– Approx. 700 entries.
... . Supplement, 1971/... . Supplément, 1971. [1972]. xi, 121 p.; ISBN: 0-919076-11-4.– Approx. 800 entries.
... . Supplement, 1972/... . Supplément, 1972. [1973]. xi, 117 p.; ISBN: 0-919076-12-2.– Approx. 700 entries.
... . Supplement, 1973/... . Supplément, 1973. [1974]. xi, 141 p.; ISBN: 0-919076-13-0.– Approx. 700 entries.
... . Supplement, 1974/... . Supplément, 1974. [1975]. ix, 174 p.; ISBN: 0-919076-14-9.– Approx. 1,000 entries.
.... . Supplement, 1975-76/... . Supplément, 1975-76. [1976]. ix, 185 p.; ISBN: 0-919076-15-7.– Approx. 1,000 entries.
Location: OONL.

4314 **Chamberlain, Simon B.; Crowley, David F.**
Decision-making and change in urban residential space: selected and annotated references. [Toronto]: Centre for Urban and Community Studies, University of Toronto, 1970. iii, 67 p. (University of Toronto Centre for Urban and Community Studies Bibliographic series ; no. 2; ISSN: 0316-4691)
Note: 297 entries.– Arranged in two main sections: "The developer as producer of residential space (development, construction, urban growth);" "The household as consumer of residential space (intra-urban migration, urban residential structure, research strategies)."- Separate sections for Canadian studies, bibliographies.
Location: OONL.

4315 **Tudor, Dean**
Provincial-municipal relations in Canada. Monticello, Ill.: Council of Planning Librarians, 1970. 5 l. (Council of Planning Librarians Exchange bibliography ; 112)
Note: Approx. 60 entries.– Books, government publications, periodical articles from 1950 to 1968.
Location: OONL.

— 1971 —

4316 **Bernier, Gaston**
"Problèmes municipaux: liste bibliographique annotée."
Dans: Bulletin: Bibliothèque de l'Assemblée nationale du Québec; Vol. 2, no 1 (janvier 1971) p. 33-61.; ISSN: 0701-6808.
Note: Approx. 150 entrées.– Ouvrages de référence, études générales, droit municipale, finances municipales, administration et vie politique, transport, expropriation.
Localisation: OONL.

4317 **Black, A.; Powell, M.**
Municipal government and finance: an annotated bibliography/L'administration municipale et les finances: une bibliographie annotée. [Ottawa: Policy Planning Division, Central Mortgage and Housing Corporation, 1971]. 230 p.
Note: Approx. 1,000 entries.– Covers Canadian material written since 1960.– Includes books, periodical articles, theses, government documents on revenue sources, expenditures, intergovernmental tax relations, metropolitan government, regional government.– Text in English and French/texte en français et en anglais.
Location: OONL.

4318 **Brideau, Monique; Doré, Gérald**
Bibliographie du Québec métropolitain: rapport de recherche ézop-Québec. Québec (Ville): Conseil des oeuvres et du bien-être de Québec, 1971. 62 p.
Note: 689 entrées.– Livres, articles de périodiques, thèses, documents gouvernementales totalement ou partiellement consacré au Québec métropolitain ou à des villes du Québec métropolitain en les catégories suivant: administration/politique/finances municipales, économie, géographie/géologie, histoire, logement, organisation communautaire, tourisme, transport, urbanisme/rénovation urbaine, monographies générales.
Localisation: OONL.

4319 **Porteous, J. Douglas**
The single-enterprise community in North America. Monticello, Ill.: Council of Planning Librarians, 1971. 18 p. (Council of Planning Librarians Exchange bibliography ; 207)
Note: Approx. 450 entries.– Monographs, periodical and

newspaper articles, theses dealing with the subject of communities dependent upon one economic activity, mainly mining, forestry or fisheries.– Many Canadian references.
Location: OHM.

— 1972 —

4320 **Cardinal, Michel**
Urbanisme et logement: bibliographie. Montréal: Conseil de développement social du Montréal métropolitain, 1972. 169 p.: ill.
Note: 349 entrées.– Comprend thèses, manuels, recherches scientifiques, projets de recherche, travaux d'étudiants, compte-rendu de colloques ou de conférences, articles de revues, brochures.
Localisation: OONL.

4321 **Dhand, Harry; Miller, Thomas W.; Hynes, Ronald**
Selected and annotated bibliography on urbanization for Project Canada West. Saskatoon: Project Canada West: Saskatchewan Teacher's Federation, 1972. iii l., 47 p.
Note: Approx. 300 entries.
Location: OONL.

4322 **Edmonton Regional Planning Commission**
An annotated bibliography of works related to the Edmonton Regional Planning Commission. [Edmonton: Edmonton Regional Planning Commission], 1972. 276 l. (in various foliations).
Note: Includes listings on physical environment, population and social characteristics, urban-regional settlement, economics, transportation, communication and utilities, government and administration, planning and development.– Compiled for use of ERPC research staff.
Location: OONL.

4323 **Shelton, Valerie**
"Bibliography on Canadian urban policy."
In: *Plan Canada*; Vol. 12, no. 1 (July 1972) p. 123-128.; ISSN: 0032-0544.
Note: Location: OONL.

4324 **Stelter, Gilbert A.**
Canadian urban history: a selected bibliography. Sudbury: Laurentian University Press, 1972. ii, 61 p. (Laurentian University social science research publication ; no. 2)
Note: Approx. 1,000 entries.– Comparative and interdisciplinary approach, covers urban history by themes (architecture, suburban expansion, demography, planning) and by specific regions and cities.
Location: OONL.

4325 **United States. Department of Housing and Urban Development. Library and Information Division**
Condominium and cooperative housing, 1960-1971: a bibliography of economic, financial and legal factors. Washington: Superintendent of Documents, U.S. Government Printing Office, 1972. v, 32 p.
Note: 249 entries.– Books, periodical articles, surveys, reports, legal references to condominiums and cooperatives.– Contains a separate section on Canada.
Location: OOCM.

4326 **Wachtel, Andy**
Urbanism and urban social organization: recent Canadian studies. Monticello, Ill.: Council of Planning Librarians, 1972. 23 p. (Council of Planning Librarians Exchange bibliography ; 348)
Note: Approx. 100 entries.– Books, reports and articles on urban social organization in Canada, from 1965 to 1972.
Location: MBC.

— 1973 —

4327 **Brereton, Thomas F.**
Planning and government in the National Capital: a selected bibliography on Ottawa, Canberra, and Washington. Monticello, Ill.: Council of Planning Librarians, 1973. 25 p. (Council of Planning Librarians Exchange bibliography ; 461)
Note: Approx. 250 entries.– Includes a general comparative section on capital cities, in addition to listings for each city of books, theses, planning studies.– Excludes reports on individual projects by local planning agencies.
Location: OOS.

4328 **Pressman, Norman E.P.**
A comprehensive bibliography on new towns in Canada. Monticello, Ill.: Council of Planning Librarians, 1973. 22 p. (Council of Planning Librarians Exchange bibliography ; 483)
Note: 226 entries.– Books, planning studies, journal articles, government publications, mainly from the period 1950 to 1972, covering the development streams of both natural resources and urban-centred regions.
Location: OW.

4329 **Scollie, Frederick Brent**
"Regional planning in Ontario: an introduction to the literature."
In: *Ontario Library Review*; Vol. 57, no. 1 (March 1973) p. 5-14.; ISSN: 0030-2996.
Note: Location: OONL.

— 1974 —

4330 **Canada. Public Works Canada. Departmental Library**
Canadian urban profiles: Saskatoon. [Ottawa]: The Library, [1974]. 13 l. (Public Works Library bibliography ; no. 11)
Note: 68 entries.– Government documents (federal, provincial, regional/municipal), monographs, periodical articles, serials.
Location: OONL.

4331 **Canada. Public Works Canada. Departmental Library**
National capitals: Ottawa. [Ottawa]: The Library, [1974]. 3 parts. (Public Works Library bibliography ; no. 5)
Note: Listing of historical works, guidebooks, planning documents.
Location: OONL.

4332 **Dakin, John; Manson-Smith, Pamela**
Toronto urban planning: a selected bibliography, 1788-1970. Monticello, Ill.: Council of Planning Librarians, 1974. 31 p. (Council of Planning Librarians Exchange bibliography ; 670)
Note: Approx. 425 entries.– Includes books, planning studies by governments and private agencies and organizations, periodical articles.– Excludes routine annual reports of departments, boards, councils, etc., planning bylaws, routine real estate mortgage finance reports, newspaper articles.– Divisions include: "Historic period, 1788-1940;" "Pre-metropolitan period, 1941-1953;" "Modern period, 1954-1970" (government and law, housing and urban renewal, official plans and policies, parks and waterfront, planning, population, transporta-

tion, urbanization pattern).
Location: OONL.

4333 **Hulchanski, John David**
Citizen participation in planning: a comprehensive bibliography. [Toronto]: Department of Urban and Regional Planning, University of Toronto, 1974. 77 p. (Papers on planning and design / Department of Urban and Regional Planning, University of Toronto ; no. 2)
Note: Approx. 550 entries.– Covers from mid-1940s to late 1973.– Includes books, periodical articles, conference papers, government publications relating to community control, advocacy planning, decentralization, community organizing in the context of citizen participation in the planning process.
Location: OONL.

4334 **Lefebvre, Joan; Boulet, Francine**
L'aménagement du territoire: bibliographie. Québec: Ministère des terres et forêts, Service de l'information, Bibliothèque, 1974. 55 f.
Note: 514 entrées.
Localisation: OONL.

4335 **Lowenberg, Paul**
Windfalls for wipeouts: an annotated bibliography on betterment recapture and worsenment avoidance techniques in the United States, Australia, Canada, England and New Zealand. [Monticello, Ill.: Council of Planning Librarians], 1974. 220 p. (Council of Planning Librarians Exchange bibliography ; 618-620)
Note: Approx. 1,000 entries.– Books, articles, papers, official publications related to increases in land values by activity other than the landowner (windfalls) and means of mitigating losses in land values by similar activity (wipeouts).
Location: NBFUL.

4336 **Peters, Elizabeth**
The central business district of Canadian cities: an interdisciplinary approach. Monticello, Ill.: Council of Planning Librarians, 1974. 31 p. (Council of Planning Librarians Exchange bibliography ; 625)
Note: Approx. 300 entries.– Covers 1960 to 1973.– Books, theses, periodical articles, conference papers on urban sociology, retailing and marketing, economic geography and history, design and planning, human ecology, traffic and transportation patterns and problems.
Location: OONL.

4337 **Peters, Elizabeth**
The Toronto waterfront: planning and development. Monticello, Ill.: Council of Planning Librarians, 1974. 6 p. (Council of Planning Librarians Exchange bibliography ; 624)
Note: 53 entries.– Covers 1962-1973.– Listing of published and unpublished planning and development literature.– Topics include architecture, engineering studies, Ontario Place, redevelopment.
Location: OONL.

4338 **Rodgers, Evan**
An annotated bibliography on planning for pedestrians. Toronto: University of Toronto-York University Joint Program in Transportation, 1974. 23, 3 p. (University of Toronto-York University Joint Program in Transportation Research Report ; no. 15; ISSN: 0316-9456)
Note: Approx. 90 entries.
Location: OONL.

4339 **Saskatchewan. Urban Advisory Commission**
Bibliography of programs for urban municipalities. Regina: Urban Advisory Commission, 1974. 130 l. (in various foliations).
Note: Location: OONL.

4340 **Wellman, Barry, et al.**
Community, network, communication: an annotated bibliography. 2nd ed. Toronto: Centre for Urban and Community Studies, University of Toronto, 1974. 172 p. (Bibliographic series / Centre for Urban and Community Studies, University of Toronto ; no. 4)
Note: 277 entries.– Literature review providing an assessment of the current state of knowledge relating to intersection of concepts: community, network, communication.
Previous edition: Wellman, Barry; Whitaker, Marilyn. *Community-network-communication: an annotated bibliography.* 1971. 115 p. (Bibliographic series ; no. 3).
Location: OONL.

— 1975 —

4341 **Alberta. Alberta Task Force on Urbanization and the Future**
Index of urban and regional studies, Province of Alberta, 1950-1974. Edmonton: Alberta Municipal Affairs, 1973-1975. 7 vol.
Note: Approx. 3,000 entries.– Annotated bibliography of urban and regional research and planning studies relating to Alberta, undertaken in the province between 1950 and 1974.
Issue no. 1: *Regional planning commissions and non-metropolitan cities of Alberta.* 50 p.
Issue no. 2: *City of Calgary and City of Edmonton.* 28 p.
Issue no. 3: *Private consultants.* 53 p.
Issue no. 4: *Government of Alberta departments and agencies.* 68 p.
Issue no. 5: *Alberta universities.* 101 p.
Issue no. 6: *Government of Canada departments and agencies.* 64 p.
Issue no. 7: *Non-government, non-profit organizations.* 75 p.
Location: OONL.

4342 **Angers, Majëlla**
Liste de publications reliées aux 63 principales agglomérations du Québec. [Québec: Ministère des affaires municipales, 1975]. 63 p. (Collection du ministère des affaires municipales)
Note: Approx. 1,000 entrées.– La période couverte est de 1900 à 1974.– Liste des publications (livres, articles, études) concerne l'ensemble des municipalités comprises dans les 63 principales agglomérations du Québec.
Localisation: OTY.

4343 **Bélanger, Marcel; Trotier, Louis**
L'urbanisation de la région de Montréal: essai de bibliographie analytique. Québec: Département de géographie, Université Laval, 1975. 93 p.
Note: 688 entrées.– Sources bibliographiques, études politiques et administratives, études économiques, études écologiques.
Localisation: OTY.

4344 **Canada. Public Works Canada. Departmental Library**
Kitchener, Ontario: Canadian urban information for federal land management project. [Ottawa]: The Library, [1975]. 6 l. (Public Works Library bibliography ; no. 32)
Note: 33 entries.– Environmental studies, planning

documents, transportation studies.
Location: OONL.

4345 **Canada. Public Works Canada. Departmental Library**
London, Ontario: Canadian urban information for federal land managment project. [Ottawa]: Public Works Library, [1975]. 10 l. (Public Works Library bibliography ; no. 62)
Note: 64 entries.– Documents dealing with the economic development, environment, planning, transportation, sociology of London, Ontario.
Location: OONL.

4346 **Canada. Public Works Canada. Departmental Library**
Mississauga. [Ottawa]: Public Works Library, [1975]. [11] l. (Public Works Library bibliography ; no. 24)
Note: Includes a list of documents pertaining to Mississauga located in the Central Reference Department of the Mississauga Public Library.
Location: OONL.

4347 **Canadian Mobile Home Association**
Mobile home library index. Toronto: Canadian Mobile Home Association, [1975]. [70] p. (in various pagings).
Note: Books, government and privately sponsored reports and studies, periodicals, municipal bylaws and housing statistics in library of Canadian Mobile Home Association on subject of mobile home industry and development of mobile home communities in Canada.
Location: OONL.

4348 **Dill, John; Macri, Paula**
Current references relating to housing and land issues in Canada. Monticello, Ill.: Council of Planning Librarians, 1975. 33 p. (Council of Planning Librarians Exchange bibliography ; 842)
Note: Approx. 400 entries.– Books, reports, articles on housing policy and programs, land market and land speculation.
Location: OONL.

4349 **Foerstel, Hans**
Resources for teachers: local planning, development, environment. [S.l.: s.n.], 1975. 24, 8 p.: ill.
Note: 52 entries.
Location: OONL.

4350 **Lambert, Rosalind; Lavallée, Laval**
Bibliography on Canadian land market mechanisms and land information systems. Ottawa: Ministry of State for Urban Affairs, 1975. x, 50 p. (Urban paper / Canada Ministry of State for Urban Affairs ; A-76-1; ISSN: 0318-1286)
Note: Approx. 1,500 entries.– Articles, papers, reports, proceedings of conferences, and legislation pertaining to land banking, expropriation, land use, information systems, foreign ownership of land, speculation, zoning.
Location: OONL.

4351 **Nininger, J.R.; MacDonald, V.N.; McDiarmid, G.Y.**
Developments in the management of local government: a review and annotated bibliography. [Kingston, Ont.: School of Business, Queen's University at Kingston; Toronto: Ministry of Treasury, Economics and Intergovernmental Affairs], 1975. 79 p. (Local government management project: series D publications: periodic papers)
Note: Approx. 150 entries.– Lists references in the following areas: goal setting, performance measurement, management information systems, systems analysis,

financial resource management, organizational development and human resource management, labour relations, restructuring and reorganization, community data base, planning process.
Location: OONL.

4352 **Silzer, V.J.**
Housing rehabilitation and neighbourhood change: Britain, Canada and USA: an annotated bibliography. [Toronto]: Centre for Urban and Community Studies, University of Toronto, 1975. 72 p. (University of Toronto Centre for Urban and Community Studies Bibliographic series ; no. 5; ISSN: 0316-4691)
Note: 167 entries.– English language research literature.– Lists references in the following areas: government programs, financial institutions, rehabilitation industry, rehabilitation experience in particular cities, rehabilitation guides and handbooks, bibliographies.
Location: OONL.

4353 **Stelter, Gilbert A.**
"Current research in Canadian urban history."
In: *Urban History Review: Revue d'histoire urbaine*; No. 3 (1975) p. 27-36.; ISSN: 0703-0428.
Note: List of current literature on history of Canadian cities and towns, nineteenth and twentieth centuries.
Location: AEU.

4354 **Thouez, Jean-Pierre**
Bibliographie de géographie urbaine. Sherbrooke: Université de Sherbrooke, Département de géographie, 1975. 67 f. (Bulletin de recherche / Université de Sherbrooke, Département de géographie ; no 22; ISSN: 0710-0868)
Note: Localisation: OONL.

4355 **Turnbull, Allen A.; Barefoot, John C.; Strickland, Lloyd H.**
Privacy and community: a selected community. Ottawa: Carleton University, 1975. 27 l.
Note: Location: OOCM.

4356 **Weaver, John**
"Living in and building up the Canadian city: a review of studies on the urban past."
In: *Plan Canada*; Vol. 15, no. 2 (September 1975) p. 111-117.; ISSN: 0032-0544.
Note: Location: OONL.

— 1976 —

4357 **Canada. Public Works Canada. Departmental Library**
Parking in urban Canadian centres. [Ottawa]: The Library, 1976. 6 l. (Public Works Library bibliography ; no. 74)
Note: Approx. 50 entries.
Location: OONL.

4358 **Canada. Public Works Canada. Departmental Library**
Selected cities of the province of Quebec: Canadian urban information for federal land management project. [Ottawa]: The Library, [1976]. 21 l. (Public Works Library bibliography ; no. 70)
Note: Documents on environment, urban planning, economic development, transportation for 16 small cities in the province of Quebec.
Location: OONL.

4359 **Dalhousie University. Institute of Public Affairs. Library**
Municipal reference library catalogue. Halifax, N.S.: Institute of Public Affairs, Dalhousie University, 1957-

1976. 6 no.; ISSN: 0316-5027.
Note: Books and documents on municipal administration and local government, taxation and finance, sociology.– Listing of reference works, periodicals and serials.
Location: OONL.

4360 **Lauder, Kathleen; Lavallée, Laval**
A Canadian bibliography of urban and regional information system activity. Ottawa: Ministry of State for Urban Affairs, [1976]. ix, 39 p. (Urban paper / Canada Ministry of State for Urban Affairs ; A-76-2; ISSN: 0318-1286)
Note: Approx. 500 entries.– Conference proceedings, policy studies.– Land information system: geocoding, mapping, surveying, title/registration.
Location: OONL.

4361 **Ross, Aileen D.**
The people of Montreal: a bibliography of studies of their lives and behaviour. Montreal: Catholic Community Services, 1976. 30 l.
Note: Approx. 150 entries.– Selection of references published since 1950 about housing, employment, social characteristics of Montrealers.
Location: OONL.

4362 **Whitney, Joan**
Habitat bibliography: a selected bibliography of Canadian references on human settlements. Monticello, Ill.: Council of Planning Librarians, 1976. 98 p. (Council of Planning Librarians Exchange bibliography ; 1137-1138)
Note: Approx. 1,350 entries.– Articles and reports on quality of life in cities and towns, housing and shelter, human movement, ethnic groups, transportation, population, land, problems of certain areas regarding climate and terrain.
Location: OONL.

— 1977 —

4363 **Artibise, Alan F.J.**
"Canadian urban studies."
In: *Communiqué: Canadian Studies*; Vol. 3, no. 3 (April 1977) ; ISSN: 0318-1197.
Note: Special issue devoted to urban studies includes guides to sources such as government agencies, archives, libraries and information centres with their publications, lists of journals and newsletters, a select bibliography arranged by general topics, regions and cities (p. 51-124).
Location: OONL.

4364 **Baillie, Murray**
Municipal government in metropolitan Halifax: a bibliography. 2nd ed. Halifax, N.S.: Patrick Power Library, Saint Mary's University, 1977. vi, 51 p.
Note: Approx. 250 entries.– Lists books, pamphlets, government publications relating to municipal politics and administration, provincial-municipal relations, municipal finance, municipal reorganization, planning, regional environment and land use, municipal and regional transportation.
Previous edition: 1971. 18 p.
Supplement: 1978. ii, 18 p.
Location: OONL.

4365 **Bourne, L.S.; Biernacki, C.M.**
Urban housing markets, housing supply, and the spatial structure of residential change: a working bibliography. Toronto: Centre for Urban and Community Studies,

University of Toronto, 1977. ii, 56 p. (University of Toronto Centre for Urban and Community Studies Bibliographic series report ; no. 6; ISSN: 0316-4691)
Note: Approx. 700 entries.– Emphasis on macro housing policy, spatial patterning and change, environmental determinants of price variations within cities, the filtering process and neighbourhood turnover, Canadian housing issues and policies.– Most references are in English.
Location: OONL.

4366 **Levenson, Rosaline**
Company towns: a bibliography of American and foreign sources. Monticello, Ill.: Council of Planning Librarians, 1977. 25 p. (Council of Planning Librarians Exchange bibliography ; 1428)
Note: Contains a section listing Canadian references on the single-industry or company town.
Location: OONL.

— 1978 —

4367 **Auld, John W.**
Canadian housing references, 1975-1977. Monticello, Ill.: Vance Bibliographies, 1978. 182 p. (Public administration series: Bibliography ; P-11; ISSN: 0193-970X)
Note: Approx. 1,600 entries.– Reports, books and articles dealing with topics related to housing: land and land use, real estate, social housing, tenants and rent control, heritage, mobile homes, handicapped, taxation.
Location: OONL.

4368 **Choko, Marc H.**
Cent ans de crise du logement à Montréal: bibliographie chronologique. Montréal: Centre de recherches et d'innovation urbaines, Université de Montréal, 1978. 27 f.
Note: Approx. 200 entrées.
Localisation: OONL.

4369 **Cooper, Ian; Hulchanski, John David**
Canadian town planning, 1900-1930: a historical bibliography. Toronto: Centre for Urban and Community Studies, University of Toronto, 1978. 3 vol. (Bibliographic series / Centre for Urban and Community Studies, University of Toronto ; no. 7-9; ISSN: 0316-4691)
Note: Volume 1: *Planning.* 82 p.– 972 entries.
Volume 2: *Housing.* 21 l.– 179 entries.
Volume 3: *Public health.* 24 l.– 215 entries.
Articles from leading Canadian engineering, municipal affairs and public health journals as well as a selection of material on Canada published in American and British journals.
Location: OONL.

4370 **Hulchanski, John David**
Canadian town planning and housing, 1930-1940: a historical bibliography. Toronto: Centre for Urban and Community Studies, University of Toronto, 1978. 35 l. (Bibliographic series / Centre for Urban and Community Studies, University of Toronto ; no. 10; ISSN: 0316-4691)
Note: 297 entries.– Includes an outline history of town planning and housing, 1930-1940.
Location: OONL.

4371 **Human settlement issues in British Columbia 1968-1978: a selected bibliography.** [Vancouver]: Centre for Human Settlements, University of British Columbia, 1978. i, 36 l. (Occasional papers / Centre for Human Settlements, University of British Columbia; ISSN: 0706-2559)

Note: Approx. 550 entries.– Monographs, government documents, periodicals, journal articles, audio-visual presentations on aspects of city planning, community development, housing, land use, parks, pollution, port development, regional planning, suburbs, transportation, waste and sewage disposal, water supply, zoning.– Section of bibliographies and directories.
Location: OONL.

4372 **Stanek, Oleg**
Evolution des conceptions urbaines: bibliographie générale. Sherbrooke, Québec: Université de Sherbrooke, Département de géographie, 1978. 42 f. (Bulletin de recherche / Université de Sherbrooke, Département de géographie ; no 38)
Note: Localisation: OONL.

4373 **Swanick, Lynne Struthers**
Municipal administration in Canada: an introductory checklist of secondary sources. Monticello, Ill.: Vance Bibliographies, 1978. 12 p. (Public administration series: Bibliography ; P-95; ISSN: 0193-970X)
Note: Approx. 150 entries.– Lists bibliographies and indexing services, monographs, periodicals.
Location: OONL.

— 1979 —

4374 **Greater Vancouver Regional District. Planning Department**
Lower Mainland Regional Planning Board publications. Vancouver: Greater Vancouver Regional District, 1979. 31 p.
Note: Approx. 175 entries.– Regional publications on various subjects, including agriculture, industrial development, population, shorelines, etc. and contract planning service reports for towns and school districts in the Lower Mainland area of British Columbia.
Location: OONL.

4375 **Hulchanski, John David**
Canadian town planning and housing, 1940-1950: a historical bibliography. [Toronto]: Centre for Urban and Community Studies, University of Toronto, 1979. 51 p. (Bibliographic series / Centre for Urban and Community Studies, University of Toronto ; no. 12; ISSN: 0316-4691)
Note: 478 entries.– Citations from contemporary engineering, municipal affairs, architectural, public affairs journals relating to government programs and legislation, wartime housing measures, post-war planning, planning conferences, the Community Planning Association of Canada, public transit, transportation, municipal general plans.– Chronological arrangement to give historical perspective.
Location: OONL.

4376 **Lang, Reg; Lounds, John**
Information resources for municipal energy planning and management. Downsview, Ont.: York University, Faculty of Environmental Studies, 1979. 125 p. (Working paper / York University Faculty of Environmental Studies ; no. 1)
Note: Selected references in such areas as energy resources and conservation; energy, urban form and land use planning; energy, site planning, design and building; energy and municipal management.
Location: OONL.

4377 **Swanick, Eric L.**
Mobile homes in Canada: a revised bibliography. Monticello, Ill.: Vance Bibliographies, 1979. 9 p. (Public administration series: Bibliography ; P-301; ISSN: 0193-970X)
Note: Approx. 120 entries.
Previous edition: 1976. 5 p.
Location: OONL.

4378 **Tyrrell, Janice; Pawliuk, Nikki**
Research directory '79, Halton region: a compilation of studies dealing with community services and concerns in the region of Halton. [Burlington, Ont.]: Halton Regional Social Planning Council, 1979. iii, 71 p.
Note: Approx 270 entries.– Covers from 1969 to mid-1979.– Includes reports of committees in government and social service organizations, surveys, evaluations, experimental studies, action projects, theses or research papers completed for Honours B.A., M.A., or PhD. degree in geography, social work, sociology.
Location: OONL.

— 1980 —

4379 **Alsène, Éric; Hamel, Pierre; Patenaude, Jules**
Les politiques urbaines et régionales au Québec: éléments de bibliographie, 1940-1977. Montréal: Faculté de l'aménagement, Université de Montréal, [1980]. 80 p. (Cahier de recherche / Faculté de l'aménagement, Université de Montréal ; URB 01)
Note: Approx. 2,000 entrées.– Livres, articles de périodiques, publications officielles.– Exclut rapports annuels, projets de loi, répertoires statistiques.
Localisation: OONL.

4380 **Armstrong, F.H.; Artibise, Alan F.J.; Baker, Melvin**
Bibliography of Canadian urban history. [Monticello, Ill.]: Vance Bibliographies, [1980]. 6 vol. (Public administration series: Bibliography ; P-538-P-543; ISSN: 0193-970X)
Note: Part 1: *General works.* 17 p.
Part 2: *The Atlantic provinces.* 33 p.
Part 3: *Quebec.* 38 p.
Part 4: *Ontario.* 68 p.
Part 5: *Western Canada.* 72 p.
Part 6: *The Canadian north.* 8 p.
Location: Parts 1 and 2: OONL.– Parts 3-6: OW.

4381 **Canada Mortgage and Housing Corporation. Development Evaluation and Advisory Services Division**
CMHC demonstration projects: a selected annotated bibliography. [Ottawa]: CMHC, Demonstration Analysis Division, [1980]. 66, 68 p., ii l.; ISBN: 0-660-90545-0.
Note: Reference list of consultant reports and government studies on various demonstration projects, basically planning studies on a range of project components, from municipal infrastructure requirements to environmental impact studies: e.g. Le Vieux Port de Québec; Lebreton Flats Demonstration Project, Ottawa; Meadow Court, Calgary.– Text in English and French with French text on inverted pages.– Title of additional title-page: *Projets de démonstration SCHL: un choix de notices bibliographiques annotées.*
Location: OONL.

4382 **Corke, S.E.**
A selected, annotated bibliography of Canadian housing research, 1970-79. [Toronto]: Centre for Urban and Community Studies, University of Toronto, 1980. 264 p.

(Bibliographic series / Centre for Urban and Community Studies, University of Toronto ; no. 13; ISSN: 0316-4691); ISBN: 0-7727-1249-2.

Note: 520 entries.– Focus on social aspects of housing market, housing policy, housing environment and satisfaction, location and mobility, alternative tenures, special needs, general section of bibliographies, textbooks, anthologies.– Excludes literature on housing design, construction standards, costs and zoning.– Contains only Canadian work.

Location: OWA.

4383 **Hawkins, Ann**
Bibliography: energy-efficient community planning. Toronto: Ontario Ministry of Energy, 1980. 28 p.

Note: Approx. 450 entries.– Books, reports, articles on topics such as energy conservation policy formulation, site planning, house design, solar heating, district heating, public transit, car pools and integrated community energy systems.– Includes a substantial number of Canadian references.

Location: OONL.

4384 **Maguire, Robert K.**
Socio-economic factors pertaining to single-industry resource towns in Canada: a bibliography with selected annotations. Chicago, Ill.: Council of Planning Librarians, 1980. vi, 37 p. (CPL bibliography / Council of Planning Librarians ; no. 36); ISBN: 0-86602-036-5.

Note: Approx. 350 entries.– Topics covered include quality of life, family life, provision of social services, socio-economic implications, labour turnover, population mobility problems, health issues, planning considerations.– List of additional bibliographies.

Location: OONL.

4385 **Merrens, Roy**
Urban waterfront redevelopment in North America: an annotated bibliography. Toronto: University of Toronto-York University Joint Program in Transportation, 1980. xxvii, 104 p. (University of Toronto-York University Joint Program in Transportation Research report ; no. 66; ISSN: 0316-9456)

Note: 322 entries.– Reports and studies, journal and newspaper articles, theses and dissertations dealing with Canadian and American urban waterfront redevelopment, mainly from the 1960s and 1970s.– Focus on Toronto, Halifax (and Dartmouth), Vancouver.

Location: OONL.

4386 **Ontario. Ministry of Treasury and Economics. Library Services**
User fees for municipal services: a selected bibliography. Monticello, Ill.: Vance Bibliographies, 1980. 4 p.

Note: Location: OHM.

4387 **Société canadienne d'hypothèques et de logement. Division des services de consultation et d'évaluation du développement**
Projets de démonstration SCHL: un choix de notices bibliographiques annotées. [Ottawa]: SCHL, Division de l'analyse de nouveaux concepts, [1980]. ii f., 68, 66 p.; ISBN: 0-660-90545-0.

Note: Inventaire des rapports d'experts-conseil et des études gouvernementales traitant des projets de démonstration, essentiellement des études de planification, par exemple: Le Vieux Port de Québec; Quartier du Port, Toronto; Meadow Court, Calgary.– Texte en

français et en anglais disposé tête-bêche.– Titre de la p. de t. additionnelle: *CMHC demonstration projects: a selected annotated bibliography.*

Localisation: OONL.

4388 **Stanek, Oleg**
Aménagement de petites villes et de communautés rurales: bibliographie générale. Sherbrooke, Québec: Université de Sherbrooke, Département de géographie, 1980. 43 f. (Bulletin de recherche / Université de Sherbrooke, Département de géographie ; no 50; ISSN: 0710-0868)

Note: Approx. 500 entrées.

Localisation: OONL.

4389 **Urban and regional research in Canada: an annotated list/Recherches urbaines et régionales au Canada: répertoire annoté.** [Toronto]: Intergovernmental Committee on Urban and Regional Research, [1976-1980]. 3 vol.; ISSN: 0708-3823.

Note: Vol. 1, 1975-1976; Vol. 2, 1977-1978; Vol. 3, 1979-1980.– "Inventory of Canadian urban and regional research undertaken, in progress or published."– Topics include regional development, intra-urban structure and development, quality of the urban environment and leisure, planning systems and techniques.– Text in English and French/texte en français et en anglais.

Location: OONL.

— 1981 —

4390 **Artibise, Alan F.J.; Stelter, Gilbert A.**
Canada's urban past: a bibliography to 1980 and guide to Canadian urban studies. Vancouver: University of British Columbia Press, [c1981]. xxxix, 396 p.; ISBN: 0-7748-0134-4.

Note: 7,054 entries.– Contains a listing of general background works, sections on individual cities and towns arranged by region and province.– Subjects include building and architecture, housing, urban economics and demography, municipal politics and government, urban renewal.

Location: OONL.

4391 **Greater Vancouver Regional District. Planning Department**
Publications [Greater Vancouver Regional District, Planning Department]. Vancouver: Greater Vancouver Regional District, Planning Department, 1981. 26 l.

Note: Approx. 175 entries.– Bylaws, technical memoranda, maps, films and slides.– Annotated.

Location: OONL.

4392 **Simon Fraser University. Library**
Municipal politics and government. Burnaby, B.C.: Simon Fraser University Library, 1981. 24 p. (Bibliography / Simon Fraser University Library ; GOV DOC 6)

Note: Location: OONL.

— 1982 —

4393 **Cullingworth, J.B.**
A bibliography on rent control. [Toronto]: Centre for Urban and Community Studies, 1982. 11 p. (University of Toronto Centre for Urban and Community Studies Bibliographic series ; no. 14; ISSN: 0316-4691); ISBN: 0-7727-1250-6.

Note: Approx. 175 entries.– Government reports and studies, articles, books.

Location: OONL.

4394 **Hulchanski, John David**
Making better use of existing housing stock: a literature review. Toronto: Ministry of Municipal Affairs and Housing, Housing Renovation and Energy Conservation Unit, 1982. 155, 7 p.
Note: 244 entries.– Examines available reports and studies under various headings related to housing supply and demand in Ontario.– Themes include demographic factors, housing affordability, marketability of higher density units, conversion, infill and redevelopment, renovation and rehabilitation, community attitudes, demolition and abandonment, fiscal impact on municipalities, economic impact on existing neighbourhoods, social impact of conservation activities.
Location: OONL.

4395 **Laberge, Jacques**
Impacts de la télématique sur l'aménagement et l'habitat: essai et bibliographie. Montréal: I.N.R.S.–Urbanisation, 1982. 73 p. (Études et documents / Institut national de la recherche scientifique ; 32); ISBN: 2-89228-032-X.
Note: 186 entrées.– Thèmes: aménagement et urbanisme, transport et communications, impact social, impact économique, politiques des télécommunications, innovations technologiques.– Comprend un nombre d'ouvrages canadiens.
Localisation: OONL.

4396 **Ontario. Community Renewal Resource Centre**
Ontario renews bibliography: a listing of books, pamphlets and periodical information available from the Community Renewal Resource Centre. [Toronto]: Ontario Ministry of Municipal Affairs and Housing, 1982. 57, 21 p.
Note: Books, pamphlets, periodical articles arranged by subject: architecture and building, city planning, housing, neighbourhood rehabilitation, shopping centres, St. Lawrence redevelopment, urban renewal.– Emphasis on Ontario and especially Toronto.
Previous edition: 1981. 17 p.
Location: OONL.

4397 **Simard, Carole; Choko, Marc H.; Collin, Jean-Pierre**
Le développement urbain de Montréal, 1940-1960: bibliographie. Montréal: Institut national de la recherche scientifique, Université du Québec, 1982. 113 p. (Études et documents / Institut national de la recherche scientifique ; 35); ISBN: 2-89228-035-4.
Note: Approx. 1,300 entrées.– Livres et monographies, articles, thèses et travaux d'étudiants, rapports, brochures, documents officiels, législation, ordonnances: ouvrages généraux, logement, transport et infrastructures, activité économique, questions municipales.
Localisation: OONL.

— 1983 —

4398 **Canadian Housing Information Centre**
Bibliography on zoning in Canada/Bibliographie sur le zonage au Canada. Ottawa: The Centre, 1983. 5 p.
Note: 30 entries.
Location: OONL.

4399 **Québec (Province). Direction générale de l'urbanisme et de l'aménagement du territoire**
Répertoire des informations du Gouvernement du Québec en matière d'aménagement du territoire.
[Québec: Gouvernement du Québec, Direction générale de l'urbanisme et de l'aménagement du territoire], 1983. 352 p.: carte.; ISBN: 2-551-05584-9.
Note: Approx. 1,000 entrées.– Quatre types de documents: documents à référence spatiale (cartes, plans et photographies aériennes), documents et données statistiques, documents informatifs (brochures, guides et manuels, diaporamas, films), documents de recherche (rapports d'études).
Localisation: OONL.

4400 **White, Richard H.**
Human settlement issues in western Canada: a selected bibliography, 1975-1983. [Vancouver]: Centre for Human Settlements, University of British Columbia, 1983. iii, 48 l. (Occasional papers / Centre for Human Settlements, University of British Columbia ; 29; ISSN: 0706-2559)
Note: Approx. 500 entries.– Selection of federal, provincial, municipal government publications, theses, journal articles on urban, rural and regional planning issues in western provinces, Yukon, Northwest Territories.– Topics covered include agricultural land, central business district, development control, heritage preservation, housing, parks and recreation, transportation, urban design.
Location: OONL.

— 1984 —

4401 **Canadian Housing Information Centre**
Bibliography on public housing in Canada/Bibliographie sur les habitations à loyer modéré au Canada. Ottawa: The Centre, 1984. 15 p.
Note: Approx. 135 entries.– Reports and studies, theses in English and French languages dealing with public housing in Canada, from 1949 to 1983.– Text in English and French/texte en français et en anglais.
Location: OONL.

4402 **Klodawsky, Fran; Spector, Aron N.; Hendrix, Catrina**
Housing and single parents: an overview of the literature. [Toronto]: Centre for Urban and Community Studies, University of Toronto, 1984. 48 p. (University of Toronto Centre for Urban and Community Studies Bibliographic series ; no. 15; ISSN: 0316-4691); ISBN: 0-7727-1251-4.
Note: Approx. 80 entries.– Reports and studies on housing and single parents dealing with income constraints, concentration of single parents in public housing, accessibility and availability, housing and the community.
Location: OONL.

4403 **Reps, John W.**
Views and viewmakers of urban America: lithographs of towns and cities in the United States and Canada, notes on the artists and publishers, and a union catalog of their work, 1825-1925. Columbia: University of Missouri Press, 1984. xvi, 570 p.: ill. (some col.).; ISBN: 0-8262-0416-3.
Note: 4,480 entries.– Examination and catalogue of all separately published lithographic city views of United States and Canada.– Includes ground-level and moderately elevated panoramas as well as bird's-eye perspectives.– Information includes place, date, title, size, artist, lithographer, printer, publisher, legend/identification system/vignettes/advertisements, locations, catalogues/checklists.
Location: OONL.

— 1985 —

4404 Canadian Housing Information Centre
Bibliography on housing in Canadian municipalities/ Bibliographie sur l'habitation dans les municipalités canadiennes. Ottawa: The Centre, 1985. 44 p.
Note: Approx. 400 entries.
Location: OONL.

4405 Minion, Robin
Communities and towns of the Northwest Territories. Edmonton: Boreal Institute for Northern Studies, University of Alberta, 1985. 100 p. (Boreal Institute for Northern Studies Bibliographic series ; no. 23; ISSN: 0824-8192); ISBN: 0-919058-57-4.
Note: 183 entries.– Series contains monographs, theses, government documents, consultants' reports, children's books, conference proceedings, microforms on topics related to northern environment and people.– BINS series produced monthly from January 1984 to May 1986 (no. 29).– Online access: *Boreal Northern Titles (BNT)*, available through QL Systems Limited.
Location: OONL.

— 1986 —

4406 Adams, Eric; Ing, Pearl; Pringle, John
A review of the literature relevant to rent regulation. Toronto: Ontario Commission of Inquiry into Residential Tenancies, 1986. 311, 2 p. (Research study / Ontario Commission of Inquiry into Residential Tenancies ; no. 2); ISBN: 0-77291-456-7.
Note: Location: OOCM.

4407 Bowles, Roy T.; Brand, Rosemary; Johnston, Cynthia
Studies of community patterns and planning in the counties of Peterborough, Victoria and Haliburton: a bibliographical guide to unpublished reports. Peterborough, Ont.: Frost Centre for Canadian Heritage and Development Studies, Trent University, 1986. 106 p. (Frost Centre for Canadian Heritage and Development Studies Research bibliography ; no. 1)
Note: Approx. 600 entries.– Limited to unpublished reports which have a clear relevance to the human community: issues of social life, social planning, and government activities which pertain to these.– Excludes published books and articles, and those items which focus primarily on physical geography or biological patterns.
Location: OONL.

4408 Canadian Housing Information Centre
Bibliography of External Research Program reports/ Bibliographies des rapports du Programme de recherche à l'extérieur. Ottawa: The Centre, 1986. 20 p.
Note: Approx. 200 entries.
Location: OONL.

4409 Canadian Housing Information Centre
Bibliography on housing for single-parent families/ Bibliographie sur le logement et les familles monparentales. Ottawa: Canadian Housing Information Centre, Canada Mortgage and Housing Corporation, 1986. 6 p.
Note: Location: OGU.

4410 Canadian Housing Information Centre
Housing in New Brunswick: a bibliography. Ottawa: The Centre, [1986]. 5 p.
Note: 46 entries.– Government studies and reports, federal, provincial and municipal; consultants' planning studies.
Location: OONL.

4411 Hulchanski, John David
Co-operative housing in Canada: a comprehensive bibliography. Vancouver: University of British Columbia, School of Community and Regional Planning, 1986. iv, 14 p. (U.B.C. planning papers: bibliographies / University of British Columbia, School of Community and Regional Planning ; 4)
Note: Approx. 200 entries.– Covers 1950 to 1986.– Includes books, government reports, research studies, theses, periodical articles.
Location: OONL.

4412 MacGibbon, Diana
Towns, wheels or wings? for resource development: an annotated bibliography. [Victoria, B.C.]: Institute for Research on Public Policy, 1986. ix, 72 p.
Note: Approx. 250 entries.– References which deal with the subject of building new resource industry towns as opposed to providing commuting facilities from existing urban centres.– Geographic focus on western Canada and the North.– Topics include planning and developing new resource towns, conditions in resource towns, decline and abandonment of resource towns, commuting options, human resources and labour supply, including section on native workers, public policy environment.– List of related bibliographies.
Location: OORD.

4413 Robson, Robert
Canadian single industry communities: a literature review and annotated bibliography. Sackville, N.B.: Rural and Small Town Research Studies Program, Department of Geography, Mount Allison University, 1986. i, 148 p.: ill.; ISBN: 0-88828-055-6.
Note: Survey of literature and listing of studies and papers relating to single-industry towns.– Themes include economic considerations, planning, physical design, quality of life, issues and policies of future development, policy procedures.– List of bibliographic sources.– Townsite maps.
Location: OONL.

4414 Stevenson, Michael
Toronto and its metropolitan government: a bibliography. Monticello, Ill.: Vance Bibliographies, 1986. 18 p. (Public administration series: Bibliography ; P-1927; ISSN: 0193-970X)
Note: Approx. 175 entries.– Published material dealing with history and structure of Toronto's metropolitan government.– Topics include architecture, biography, city planning, transportation systems, urban renewal, economic geography, housing, politics and government, population, social conditions.
Location: AEAU.

— 1987 —

4415 Bloomfield, Elizabeth
"Bibliography: recent publications relating to Canada's urban past/Bibliographie: contributions récentes à l'histoire urbaine du Canada."
In: *Urban History Review: Revue d'histoire urbaine*; Vol. 10, no. 2 (October 1981) p. 41-55; vol. 11, no. 2 (October 1982) p. 59-84; vol. 12, no. 2 (October 1983) p. 107-135; vol. 13, no. 2 (October 1984) p. 121-159; vol. 14, no. 2 (October 1985) p. 135-191; vol. 15, no. 2 (October 1986) p.

175-200; vol. 16, no. 2 (October 1987) p. 196-221.; ISSN: 0703-0428.
Note: Annual list of books, articles, theses, reports and discussion papers relating to Canadian urban history.– Text in English and French/texte en français et en anglais.
Location: AEU.

4416 **Canadian Housing Information Centre**
Bibliography on public housing in Canada/Bibliographie sur les habitations à loyer modéré au Canada. Ottawa: Canada Mortgage and Housing Corporation, 1987. 40 p.
Note: Approx. 325 entries.
Location: OOFF.

4417 **Hulchanski, John David**
Cooperative housing in Canada. Chicago: Council of Planning Librarians, 1987. 14 p. (CPL bibliography / Council of Planning Librarians ; no. 191)
Note: Approx. 175 entries.– English-language books, articles, government documents pertaining to Canadian housing cooperatives.
Location: OONL.

4418 **Nguyên, Vy-Khanh**
Politique de l'habitation: bibliographie sélective et annotée. Québec: Bibliothèque de l'Assemblée nationale, Division de la référence parlementaire, 1987. 54 p. (Bibliographie / Bibliothèque de l'Assemblée nationale du Québec ; no 5; ISSN: 0836-9100)
Note: Approx. 250 entrées.– Documentation sur les politiques de l'habitat, sur les programmes de différents gouvernements tels que le logement pour personnes âgées, et sur les organismes administratifs ou à caractère coopératif ou social; documents traitant les formules d'occupation de l'espace résidential tels que le condominium et la conversion d'immeubles existants selon la formule de la copropriété.
Localisation: OONL.

4419 **Petrelli, Robert; Dubeau, Pierre**
Guide bibliographique en gestion municipale. Sainte-Foy, Québec: École nationale d'administration publique, 1987. 278 p.; ISBN: 2-9800104-6-4.
Note: 1,795 entrées.– Couvre la période 1976-1986.– Articles de périodiques, mémoires de maîtrise, monographies, thèses de doctorat, chapitres de monographies.– La bibliographie se concentre sur le Québec, Canada, France, États-Unis et Grande-Bretagne.– Thèmes: structures politico-administrative, droit municipale, gestion, fiscalité, urbanisme, environnement, transport, développement économique.
Localisation: OONL.

— 1988 —

4420 **Boilard, Gilberte**
Municipalités régionales de comté: bibliographie. Québec: Bibliothèque de l'Assemblée nationale, Division de la référence parlementaire, 1988. 12 p. (Bibliographie / Bibliothèque de l'Assemblée nationale du Québec ; no 18; ISSN: 0836-9100)
Note: 96 entrées.
Localisation: OONL.

4421 **McCann, Bernard**
Bibliographie annotée des sources d'information statistique sur l'habitation et les ménages. Québec: Société d'habitation du Québec, Direction de l'analyse et de la recherche, 1988. 73 p.
Note: 123 entrées.– Documents à contenu statistique provenant des secteurs publics fédéraux et québécois ainsi que d'organismes du secteur privé.
Localisation: QQLA.

4422 **Pressman, Norman E.P.**
The reduction of winter-induced discomfort in Canadian urban residential areas: an annotated bibliography and evaluation. Ottawa: Canada Mortgage and Housing Corporation, 1988. 103 p.
Note: 262 entries.– Covers 1947-1986.– Includes literature from the fields of architecture, landscape architecture, urban planning, applied climatology, social science, engineering dealing with reduction of human discomfort caused by Canadian winter climate.– Arranged in four categories: human needs, building design, urban and landscape design, applied climatology.
Location: OOCM.

4423 **Rumney, Thomas A.**
The urban geography of Canada: a selected bibliography. 2nd ed. Monticello, Ill.: Vance Bibliographies, 1988. 74 p. (Public administration series: Bibliography ; P-2534; ISSN: 0193-970X); ISBN: 1-55590-994-9.
Note: Approx. 900 entries.– Emphasis on the period from 1945.– Articles, monographs, books, theses on the study of Canadian urban geography.– Topics include land use and zoning, housing, social problems, history, commerce and industry, interurban systems, urban political geography, transportation and other services, employment, environment.
Previous edition: 1986. 65 p. (Public administration series: Bibliography ; P-2032; ISSN: 0193-970X); ISBN: 1-55590-052-6.
Location: OONL.

4424 **Stamp, Robert M.**
Street cars, subways and rapid transit: a Canadian bibliography. Toronto: Heritage Books, 1988. iv, 63 p. (Canadian Biblio-File series publication ; 001); ISBN: 0-921342-00-4.
Note: Approx. 900 entries.– Selection of books and articles on street cars and other urban transportation systems.– Concentrates on substantial historical works.– Largest sections devoted to Ontario and Toronto, but includes all provinces and main cities and towns as well.– General section on Canada: historical works, business and financial, technical and operational.
Location: OW.

4425 **Toronto. Planning and Development Department. Research and Information Section**
A bibliography of major planning publications (May 1942 - December 1988). Toronto: City of Toronto, Planning and Development Department, 1988. 89 p.
Note: Approx. 1,000 entries.– Contains reports on central area planning (core area studies, railway lands, central waterfront); community and neighbourhood planning; research and overall planning (health, housing, education, industry, official plan, parks and open space, social planning, transportation); legislation, development control, and zoning.– Compiled in co-operation with Metro Toronto Library Municipal Reference Department.
Location: OONL.

— 1989 —

4426 **Canadian Housing Information Centre**
Bibliography on non-profit housing/Logement sans but lucratif: une bibliographie. Ottawa: The Centre, 1989.

19 p.
Note: Approx. 200 entries.– Text in English and French/texte en français et en anglais.
Location: OONL.

4427 **Crossley, Diane**
A bibliography on local government in British Columbia. Victoria: Province of British Columbia, Ministry of Municipal Affairs, Recreation and Culture, 1989. vi, 68 p.; ISBN: 0-7718-8762-0.
Note: Approx. 600 entries.– Covers 1945 to December 1988, with emphasis on the period from the 1960s.– Focus on academic books and articles with policy orientation rather than such things as technical engineering studies.– Includes government documents, chiefly provincial, some theses.– Emphasis on published materials.– Excludes archival materials, unpublished consultants' reports, mimeographed conference speeches, etc.
Location: OONL.

4428 **Gallina, Paul**
"Research in urban history 1987-1988."
In: *Urban History Review: Revue d'histoire urbaine*; Vol. 18, no. 2 (October 1989) p. 166-175.; ISSN: 0703-0428.
Note: 385 entries.– Comprehensive compilation of urban history research, with emphasis on Canadian material, arranged under five broad headings: general works (bibliographies, historiography and methodology), growth and economic development, population, urban environment, municipal government.
Location: AEU.

4429 **Markham, Susan F.**
Research bibliography: the development of parks and playgrounds in selected Canadian Prairie cities, 1880-1930. Wolfville, N.S.: School of Recreation and Physical Education, Acadia University, 1989. 49 l.
Note: Approx. 900 entries.– Books, journal articles, theses dealing with urban history, development and reform, city planning, parks and recreation in Calgary, Edmonton, Regina, Saskatoon and Winnipeg, 1880-1930.
Location: OONL.

4430 **Merrens, Roy**
Bibliographie sommaire sur le port et le secteur riverain de Toronto. [Toronto: Commission royale sur l'avenir du secteur riverain de Toronto, 1989. [13] p. (Documents de travail du Centre canadien de documentation sur le secteur riverain ; no 1; ISSN: 0847-3218)
Note: 174 entrées.– Rapports, études, articles (revues et journaux) sur le port et le secteur riverain de Toronto.
English title: *A selected bibliography on Toronto's port and waterfront.*
Localisation: OONL.

4431 **Merrens, Roy**
A selected bibliography on Toronto's port and waterfront. [Toronto: Royal Commission on the Future of the Toronto Waterfront], 1989. [13] l. (Working papers of the Canadian Waterfront Resource Centre ; no. 1; ISSN: 0847-320X)
Note: 174 entries.– Reports, studies, journal and newspaper articles, theses pertaining to Toronto's port and waterfront.
Titre en français: *Bibliographie sommaire sur le port et le secteur riverain de Toronto.*
Location: OONL.

4432 **Robson, Robert**
Selected sources on northern housing and related community infrastructure: an annotated bibliography. [Winnipeg]: Institute of Urban Studies, University of Winnipeg, 1989. ii, 84 p. (Bibliographica / Institute of Urban Studies, University of Winnipeg ; 1); ISBN: 0-920213-66-9.
Note: Approx. 400 entries.– Journal articles, theses, government reports and studies, books, conference papers on northern housing and northern development, particularly in the prairie North, the Yukon and Northwest Territories.– Topics range from northern industrialization to provision of utility services.
Location: MWUC.

4433 **Selby, Joan Louise**
A bibliography on co-operative housing in Canada/Une bibliographie de l'habitation coopérative au Canada. Ottawa: Co-operative Housing Foundation of Canada, 1989. xii, 121 p. (Research paper / Co-operative Housing Foundation of Canada ; 4); ISBN: 0-9690660-4-X.
Note: Approx. 700 entries.– Books, manuals, booklets, unpublished theses and dissertations, articles, newsletters, periodicals, audio-visual materials on co-operative housing.– Excludes newspaper articles.– Emphasis on non-profit co-operatives.– Text in English and French/texte en français et en anglais.
Location: OONL.

— 1990 —

4434 **Dufresne, Nicole**
Gestion des déchets domestiques: bibliographie sélective et annotée. Québec: Bibliothèque de l'Assemblée nationale, Division de la référence parlementaire, 1990. 39 p. (Bibliographie / Bibliothèque de l'Assemblée nationale du Québec ; no 36; ISSN: 0836-9100)
Note: 120 entrées.– Études générales, Québec, Canada, Alberta, Colombie-Britannique, Nouveau-Brunswick, Ontario, autre pays.
Localisation: OONL.

4435 **Economic Council of Canada. Regional Development Research Team**
Bibliography on local and regional development. Ottawa: Economic Council of Canada, 1990. iii, 86 p.
Note: Approx. 800 entries.– Primarily Canadian books, journal articles, conference papers, government studies and reports, publications of university research institutes dealing with issues and problems related to urban and regional economic development: agricultural and rural, community and local, entrepreneurship, small business, environment, capital and investment, research and development, women and regional development, northern economic development.– Provides a list of additional bibliographies.
Previous edition: Aird, Rebecca. *Regional economic development in Canada: a selected annotated bibliography.* 1987. 56, 13 p.
Location: OOEC.

— 1991 —

4436 **An annotated bibliography of CED resources.** Vancouver: Westcoast Development Group, 1991. 75 p.; ISBN: 0-921424-06-X.
Note: Approx. 300 entries.– Reports, papers, studies, monographs pertaining to community economic development: analysis of economic development issues,

case studies and project documentation, special interest groups, development finance, practitioner resources, bibliographies and directories.

Location: OONL.

4437 **Canadian Urban Institute**

Managing regional urban growth I: an annotated bibliography. Toronto: Canadian Urban Institute, 1991. xiv, 78, 3 p. (Urban focus series / Canadian Urban Institute ; 90-1; ISSN: 1183-2304); ISBN: 1-895446-00-7.

Note: 320 entries.– Books, journal articles, government reports on urban growth management, mainly from 1980 to 1990, with emphasis on issues of special concern to the Greater Toronto Area.

Location: OONL.

4438 **Canadian Urban Institute**

Managing regional urban growth II: review of government documents. Toronto: Canadian Urban Institute, 1991. iii, 54, 3 p. (Urban focus series / Canadian Urban Institute ; 90-2; ISSN: 1183-2304); ISBN: 1-895446-02-3.

Note: Second component of a literature review dealing with policies, issues, and options for managing regional urban growth in major metropolitan areas.– Covers documents produced by authorities responsible for planning urban regions.– Canadian cities represented here are Montreal and Vancouver.

Location: OONL.

4439 **Poulin, André**

Bibliographie sur les coopératives d'habitation à capitalisation. [Ottawa]: Société canadienne d'hypothèques et de logement, 1991. 13 p.

Note: Approx. 150 entrées.– Documents, articles sur les formules de financement pour les coopératives d'habitation.

Localisation: OONL.

— 1992 —

4440 **Beavis, Mary Ann; Patterson, Jeffrey**

A select, annotated bibliography on sustainable cities. Winnipeg: Institute of Urban Studies, University of Winnipeg, 1992. v, 93 p. (Bibliographica / Institute of Urban Studies, University of Winnipeg ; 4); ISBN: 0-920213-77-4.

Note: Includes Canadian references.

Location: OONL.

4441 **Weiler, John; Bowering, Ann**

Reaching agreement on urban development: an annotated bibliography/La recherche de consensus dans le développement urbain: bibliographie annotée. Ottawa: Canadian Centre for Livable Places, 1992. 36 p.; ISBN: 0-88814-046-0.

Note: Approx. 100 entries.– Publications dealing with alternative methods of handling conflicts related to urban growth and development.– Some Canadian references.– Text in English and French/texte en français et en anglais.

Location: OONL.

— 1993 —

4442 **Beesley, Ken B.**

The rural-urban fringe: a bibliography. Peterborough, Ont.: Department of Geography, Trent University, 1993. ix, 89 p. (Occasional paper / Trent University, Department of Geography ; 15); ISBN: 0-921062-12-5.

Note: Approx. 1,500 entries.– Listing of books, articles and reports dealing with problems related to the town-country interface.– Topics include land use, agricultural land, suburban development.– Substantial Canadian content.

Location: OONL.

— Ongoing/En cours —

4443 **Canada Mortgage and Housing Corporation**

Compendium of research [CMHC]/Compendium de recherche [SCHL]. Ottawa: Canada Mortgage and Housing Corporation, 1984-. vol.; ISSN: 0838-892X.

Note: Irregular.– First issue covers 1980-1983; latest issue, 1990-1991.

Listing of research reports, reports produced under the External Research Program, dissertations produced under the CMHC Scholarship Program, dealing with the social, economic and technical aspects of housing and related fields.– Text in English and French/texte en français et en anglais.

Location: OONL.

Transportation

Transports

— 1922 —

4444 Johnsen, Julia E.
"St. Lawrence River ship canal."
In: *Reference Shelf*; Vol. 1, no. 3 (December 1922) p. 1-74.
Note: "Briefs, bibliographies, debates, reprints of selected articles and study outlines on timely topics."
Location: OONL.

— 1938 —

4445 Canada. Bureau of Statistics. Library
Bibliographical list of references to Canadian railways, 1829-1938. Ottawa: [s.n.], 1938. 99 p.
Note: 1,779 entries.– Books, government reports and studies, engineering reports, journal articles.– Topics include abandonment of lines, engineering, finance, government ownership, immigration, Hudson Bay Railway, government committees of inquiry, surveying, terminals.
Location: OOA.

— 1940 —

4446 Chew, Anne C.; Churchill, Arthur C.
References on the Great Lakes-Saint Lawrence waterway project. 2nd ed. Washington, D.C.: G.P.O., 1940. 189 p. (Bibliographical contributions / United States Department of Agriculture Library ; no. 30)
Note: 1,072 entries.– Books and pamphlets, articles, bibliographies, government documents (U.S. and Canada, state and provincial).– Special topics include Georgian Bay Canal, lake levels problem, Sault Ste. Marie Canal, Welland Canal.
Previous edition: Edwards, Everett Eugene. 1936. 185 p. (United States Department of Agriculture, Library, Bibliographical contributions ; no. 30).
Location: OOG.

— 1953 —

4447 Dechief, Helene A.
Trial bibliography: books and pamphlets relating to Canadian railways in libraries of Montreal. [Montreal: H.A. Dechief], 1953. viii, 118 l.
Note: 844 entries.– Bibliographies, historical works, biography, government publications dealing with railway law, the emerging Canadian National Railways system, the emerging Canadian Pacific Railways system, also miscellaneous railways (independent, unbuilt, or abandoned lines).– Includes entries on royal tours, and travel books with reference to railways.
Location: OONL.

— 1956 —

4448 Canadian Good Roads Association
Road reference library: a catalogue of publications on roads and road transport. Ottawa: The Association, 1956. iv, 149 p.
Note: Supplement: *Road reference library catalogue: supplement 1, August, 1961.* Ottawa: [1961]. viii, 51 p.
Location: OONL.

— 1957 —

4449 White, Bonney G.
Literature survey of papers dealing with the use of heat for keeping roads, sidewalks and parking areas free from snow and ice. Ottawa: Division of Building Research, National Research Council Canada, 1957. 10 l. (Bibliography / National Research Council Canada, Division of Building Research ; no. 8; ISSN: 0085-3828)
Note: Includes Canadian references.
Location: OONL.

— 1958 —

4450 St Lawrence Seaway Development Corporation. Office of Information
Seaway bibliography. Washington, D.C.: St Lawrence Seaway Development Corporation, 1958. 1 vol. (in various pagings).
Note: "Publications and articles relating to Great Lakes and St Lawrence River navigation and St Lawrence Seaway and power development."
Location: OONL.

— 1968 —

4451 Peckover, F.L.; Wong, W.W.
Annotated bibliography on track ballast to Dec. 1967. Montreal: Library Headquarters, Canadian National Railways, 1968. 43 l. (Special series / Canadian National Railways Library ; no. 43; ISSN: 0226-4889)
Note: Approx. 200 entries.– Includes Canadian references.
Supplements:
Supplement to Dec. 1969 of Annotated bibliography on track ballast to Dec. 1967. 1971. 15 p.
Supplement to Dec. 1972 of Annotated bibliography on track ballast. 1973. 32 p.
Location: OONL.

— 1970 —

4452 De Leeuw, J.H.; Reid, L.D.
"A bibliography of STOL technology."
In: *An assessment of STOL technology.* Ottawa: Canadian Transport Commission, 1970. P. 101-V-71. (UTIAS Report / University of Toronto Institute for Aerospace Studies ; no. 162; ISSN: 0082-5255)
Note: Emphasis on areas of Canadian interest.– Detailed annotations.– Includes five main sections: "Vehicle design and performance;" "Operational aspects;" "Navigation;" "Guidance and air traffic control;" "Non-passenger public acceptance;" "STOLports."
Supplement: *STOL technology bibliography update.* 1971. 21 p. (UTIAS Report (University of Toronto Institute for Aerospace Studies) ; no. 176; ISSN: 0082-5255).
Location: OONL.

4453 Tangri, Om P.
Transportation in Canada and the United States: a bibliography of selected references, 1945-1969. Winnipeg: Center for Transportation Studies, University of Manitoba, 1970. 2 vol. (Research report / University of

Manitoba Center for Transportation Studies ; no. 5-6)
Note: Approx. 3,242 entries.– Books, articles, bulletins and reports, theses, publications of boards, councils, commissions, etc. on all aspects of transportation.
Previous edition: ... , *1945-1967.* 1968. viii, 218 p. (Research progress report ; no. 2).
Location: OONL.

— 1972 —

4454 **Arctic Institute of North America**
A Bibliography on winter road construction and related subjects. Montreal: Arctic Institute of North America, 1972. 1 vol. (in various pagings).
Note: Location: ACU.

4455 **McLaren, William S.; Myers, Barry B.**
Guided ground transportation: a review and bibliography of advanced systems. Ottawa: Transport Canada, Development, 1972. 515 p.
Note: 289 entries.– Technical studies and reports on guided ground transportation systems.– Indexes: author, title, performing organization, NTIS numbers.– Some Canadian references.
Location: OONL.

— 1973 —

4456 **Bertrand, Denis**
Optimisation dans manutention des conteneurs: une bibliographie sélective/Optimising container handling: a selective bibliography. Montréal: Département de génie civil, Section transport, École polytechnique de Montréal, 1973. 25 f.
Note: 240 entrées.– Références en français et en anglais, recherche portant sur l'optimisation du fonctionnement d'un terminus de conteneurs.– Thèmes: manutention des conteneurs, conteneurs et informatique, location, entretien, standards, installations portuaires.– Texte en français et en anglais/text in English and French.
Localisation: OONL.

4457 **Mackay, Neilson A.M.; Martin, Brian D.**
Bibliography on railway signalling, 1960-1972. Kingston, Ont.: Canadian Institute of Guided Ground Transport, 1973. 50 l. (CIGGT report / Canadian Institute of Guided Ground Transport ; 73-9; ISSN: 0383-2449)
Note: Approx. 300 entries.– Topics include signalling hardware, automatic train control, signalling at level crossings, track-train communication, use of computers.
Location: OONL.

4458 **Meyer, Ron H.**
A selected bibliography on railways in British Columbia. Vancouver: Pacific Coast Branch, Canadian Railroad Historical Association, 1973. 2 vol. (B.C. rail guide / Canadian Railroad Historical Association, Pacific Coast Branch ; nos. 6 and 7)
Note: Approx. 350 entries.– Selective coverage from 1870 to 1973.– Includes books, periodical articles, government publications.
Location: OONL.

— 1975 —

4459 **Frisken, Frances; Emby, Gwynneth**
Social aspects of urban transportation: a bibliographic review. [Toronto]: University of Toronto/York University Joint Program in Transportation, 1975. 252 p. (University of Toronto-York University Joint Program in Transportation Research report ; no. 30; ISSN: 0316-9456)
Note: Approx. 300 entries.– Reviews literature which

considers social concerns related to urban transportation: identification of social factors, impact studies, transportation disadvantaged, characteristics and purposes of urban travel, alternative transportation, transit industry, social issues and social trends in urban transportation planning and policy-making.
Location: OONL.

4460 **Grains Group (Canada)**
Grain handling and transportation: a bibliography of selected references on transportation and rural sociology. [Ottawa]: Grains Group, 1975. iv, 102 l.
Note: Approx. 900 entries.– Books, federal and provincial publications, Canadian and American university research reports and studies, theses, royal commission reports, Canada Grains Council publications, railway company publications, periodical articles, reports from nongovernmental organizations and research institutions.
Location: OONL.

4461 **Melançon-Bolduc, Ginette**
"Bibliographie choisie sur la Voie maritime du Saint-Laurent entre 1967 et 1973."
Dans: *Revue de géographie de Montréal;* Vol. 29, no 1 (1975) p. 61-68.; ISSN: 0035-1148.
Note: Publications (livres, articles, brochures) en français et en anglais.
Localisation: OONL.

— 1976 —

4462 **Canadian Transport Commission. Research Branch**
Publications available from the Canadian Transport Commission. [Ottawa]: Canadian Transport Commission, 1976. 79 p.
Note: 184 entries.– Publications prepared by Research Branch staff and consultants' reports on transportation topics.– Text in English and French/texte en français et en anglais.
Location: OONL.

4463 **Hopkinson, Marvin W.**
The Beatrice Hitchins Memorial Collection of Aviation History: catalogue. London, Ont.: D.B. Weldon Library, University of Western Ontario, 1976. xix, 73 p.: ill., port. (Library bulletin / D.B. Weldon Library, University of Western Ontario ; no. 9)
Note: Lists manuscripts, books, periodicals, pamphlets, clippings.– Includes writings by Fred H. Hitchins, research sources, correspondence, illustrations, card files.
Location: OONL.

4464 **Patterson, Susan S.**
Canadian Great Lakes shipping: an annotated bibliography. Toronto: University of Toronto-York University Joint Program in Transportation, 1976. 72 l. (University of Toronto-York University Joint Program in Transportation Research report ; no. 37; ISSN: 0316-9456)
Note: Approx. 400 entries.– References from 1950 to 1976, with emphasis on the years following the opening of the St. Lawrence Seaway in 1959.– Arranged in three sections: "Economic history," "Labour," "Regulation."– Includes separate listings of theses and journal articles.– Locations are given for all documents in the main sections.
Location: OONL.

4465 **Ramlalsingh, Roderick D.**
Marine transportation in Canada and the U.S. Great Lakes region: a bibliography of selected references, 1950-

1975. Toronto: University of Toronto-York University Joint Program in Transportation, 1976. 32 l. (University of Toronto-York University Joint Program in Transportation Working paper ; no. 1; ISSN: 0380-9889)
Note: Approx. 300 entries.– References dealing with Saint Lawrence Seaway, ports in Canada and United States, containerization, government publications, Canada and the United States.
Location: OONL.

4466 **Tennant, Robert D.**
The quill-and-rail catalogue: a bibliographical guide to Canadian railroads. Halifax, N.S.: Tennant Publishing House, c1976. 92 p.; ISBN: 0-919928-00-5.
Note: Approx. 450 entries.– Books, government publications, serials, theses.
Location: OONL.

— 1977 —

4467 **Reid, Jean-Paul**
Bibliographie de bibliographies sur les transports et domaines connexes/Bibliography of bibliographies on transportation and related fields. Montréal: Université de Montréal, Centre de recherche sur les transports, 1977. 65 l. (Université de Montréal Centre de recherche sur les transports Publication ; no 84)
Note: 710 entrées.– Publiés entre 1972 et 1976 inclusivement.– Thèmes: conteneurisation, pipelines, transport de marchandises, transports urbains, transports maritimes.– Inclut un nombre d'ouvrages canadiens.– Texte en français et en anglais/text in English and French.
Localisation: OONL.

4468 **Whitaker, Marilyn; Wellman, Barry**
A catalogue of participatory transportation planning cases: Canada and the United States. [Toronto]: Joint Program in Transportation, 1977. i, 83 p. (University of Toronto-York University Joint Program in Transportation Working paper ; no. 9; ISSN: 0380-9889)
Note: 31 entries.
Location: OONL.

— 1978 —

4469 **Cunningham, Peter G.**
Canada's changing ports scene: an annotated classified bibliography. Toronto: University of Toronto-York University Joint Program in Transportation, 1978. 92 p. (University of Toronto-York University Joint Program in Transportation Research report ; no. 54; ISSN: 0316-9456)
Note: 367 entries.– Listing of references mainly from the 1970s dealing with aspects of Canadian ports development.– Topics include planning proposals, housing, industry, jurisdictional issues and public policy, port and shipping design and technology, recreation and access, trade and economics, waterfront redevelopment, additional bibliographies.
Location: OONL.

4470 **Rochon, James; O'Hara, Susan; Swain, Larry**
Exposure to the risk of an accident: a review of the literature, and the methodology for the Canadian study. Ottawa: Transport Canada, Road Safety, 1978. 1 vol. (in various pagings).
Note: Location: OON.

4471 **Systems Approach Ltd.**
Transportation for the disadvantaged: a bibliography/ Transport pour les handicapés: bibliographie. Montreal: Transport Canada, Surface, 1978. 34 p.; ISBN: 0-662-

01775-7.
Note: Listing of journal articles, papers and reports published between 1972 and 1977 on transportation for the physically handicapped, elderly and blind.– Text in English and French/texte en français et en anglais.
Location: OONL.

— 1979 —

4472 **Demers, Henri**
Le St-Laurent: bibliographie économique. [Québec]: Centre de documentation, Ministère de l'industrie et du commerce, 1979. 93 p.
Note: Livres, articles de périodiques, publications officielles concernant la vallée du Saint-Laurent et la voie maritime du Saint-Laurent.
Localisation: OONL.

4473 **Nawwar, A.M.**
Development of a research program for improving Arctic marine transportation technology: Volume III: Bibliography. Kanata, Ont.: Arctec Canada Limited, 1979. i, 41 p.
Note: 402 entries.– Listing of studies related to Arctic marine transportation technology, 1964 to 1977.– Topics include ship transmitting performance, environment characteristics, hull structural integrity, propulsion systems.
Location: OON.

4474 **Suen, Ling; Smith, B.A.; McCoomb, L.A.**
Urban Transportation Research Branch directory: publications, computer programs, data tapes, audio-visual material/Direction de la recherche sur les transports urbains, répertoire: publications, ensemble de programmes, données en mémoire, matériel audio-visuel. [Ottawa]: Transport Canada, Surface, 1979. 49 p.
Note: Approx. 400 entries.– Research work carried out by the Urban Transportation Research Branch, 1974-1979.– Text in English and French/texte en français et en anglais.
Location: OONL.

4475 **Swanick, Eric L.**
Transportation problems in Atlantic Canada: an introductory bibliography. Monticello, Ill.: Vance Bibliographies, 1979. 6 p. (Public administration series: Bibliography ; P-166; ISSN: 0193-970X)
Note: Approx. 60 entries.– Limited to studies written from about 1965 to 1977 which consider more than two of the Atlantic provinces.
Location: OONL.

4476 **University of Toronto. Centre for Urban and Community Studies**
Annotated bibliography on demand responsive scheduling systems. Montreal: Transport Canada, 1979. ii, 173 p. (Taxi dispatch report series ; vol. 6)
Note: Includes Canadian references.
Location: OONL.

— 1980 —

4477 **Canadian National Railways. Headquarters Library**
A selected bibliography on Canadian railways/Sélection de publications sur les chemins de fer canadiens. 8th ed. Montreal: [CN Library, Headquarters and St. Lawrence Region], 1980. 20 l. (Special series / CN Library, Headquarters and St. Lawrence Region ; no. 25)
Note: Approx. 200 entries.
Previous editions:
1972. 14 p.

1968. 5 p.
1966. 5 p.
1965. 5 p.
Location: NFSM.

4478 **Dechief, Helene A.**
A bibliography of published material and theses on Canadian railways/Liste des publications et thèses sur les chemins de fer canadiens. Montréal: CN Bibliothèque/Library, 1980. 72 p.; ISBN: 0-86503-000-6.
Note: 437 entries.– Lists published material and theses relating to history (general, Canadian National, Canadian Pacific, geographical divisions), railway executives, surveyors and builders, railway workers, politicians, journalists and the railways, railway facilities and rolling stock, immigration and settlement, transportation economics.– Includes a list of magazines and society newsletters.– Excludes unpublished pamphlets, periodical articles, monographs from railway and historical associations, federal and provincial government reports about railways.– Text in English and French/texte en français et en anglais.
Location: OONL.

4479 **Dunbar, M.J.**
Marine transportation and high Arctic development: a bibliography: scientific and technical research relevant to the development of marine transportation in the Canadian north. Ottawa: Canadian Arctic Resources Committee, 1980. v, 162 p.; ISBN: 0-919996-15-9.
Note: 1,397 entries.– Deals mainly with research publications and other documents which appeared in the period 1970 to 1980.– Purpose is to report on state of scientific and technological research in development of safe and rational marine transportation in Canadian Arctic and Subarctic.– Principal subjects covered are physical and biological oceanography, sea ice, marine biology, chemistry and geology, microbiology, engineering, navigation, coastal studies, human studies (native land claims, employment, education).
Location: OONL.

4480 **Québec (Province). Centrale des bibliothèques**
Sécurité routière: inventaire préliminaire de la documentation disponible. Montréal: La Centrale, 1980. 85 f.; ISBN: 2-89059-013-5.
Note: Localisation: OONL.

— 1981 —
4481 **Goodfellow, Gay; Hieatt, D.J.**
A literature review of research on the actions of drivers in emergencies. Downsview, Ont.: Policy Planning and Research Division, Ontario Ministry of Transportation and Communications, 1981. 60 p.
Note: Location: OTDT.

4482 **Jensen, Susan E.**
Crow-Rate, the great debate: a historical bibliography. Edmonton: Library, Alberta Agriculture, 1981. 31 p.
Note: Approx. 250 entries.– Books and pamphlets, periodical and newspaper articles, legislation, royal commissions and submissions to commissions on the special rail freight rate applied to grains and flour from points in western Canada to Thunder Bay, Churchill and British Columbia ports.
Location: OONL.

4483 **Miletich, John J.**
Light rail transit in Canada: a selected bibliography, 1970-1980. Chicago, Ill.: CPL Bibliographies, 1981. v, 10 p. (CPL bibliography / Council of Planning Librarians ; no. 62); ISBN: 0-86602-062-4.
Note: 57 entries.– Annotated list of technical reports, professional journal articles, books published in English concerning light rail transit/subways in Toronto, Montreal, Edmonton, Calgary and Vancouver.– In four categories: general, engineering, architectural, economic.
Location: OONL.

4484 **Munro, Douglas, et al.**
The relationship between age-sex and accident involvement-severity: a literature survey. Toronto: University of Toronto-York University Joint Program in Transportation, 1981. v, 44 p. (University of Toronto-York University Joint Program in Transportation Working paper ; no. 10; ISSN: 0380-9889)
Note: Bibliographical review of Canadian, U.S., and international studies related to driver involvement and severity studies, pedestrian involvement and severity studies, the relationship between age and sex.
Location: OONL.

4485 **Raymond, Jean-Claude**
Bibliographie sur le camionnage. Québec: Ministère des transports, 1981. 135 p.; ISBN: 2-550-02172-X.
Note: Approx. 1,200 entrées.– Principaux thèmes: structure de l'industrie du camionnage; marché de l'industrie du camionnage; tarification/taux de transport; législation, réglementation; coûts de transport, productivité; sécurité routière; equipements; généralités.
Localisation: QMBM.

4486 **Simpson-Lewis, Wendy; McKechnie, Ruth**
Land and the automobile: a selected bibliography/Les terres et l'automobile: bibliographie sélective. [Ottawa]: Lands Directorate, Environment Canada, 1981. iv, 95 p. (Working paper / Lands Directorate, Environment Canada ; no. 12; ISSN: 0712-4473); ISBN: 0-662-51259-6.
Note: Approx. 800 entries.– References mainly from 1950-1980 period.– Overview of land and automobile interface, subdivided into six categories: urban form and growth, environmental quality and impact on land, impact on rural and northern areas, planning, transportation and land use, energy and economics.
Location: OONL.

— 1982 —
4487 **Canada. Transport Canada. Transportation Development Centre**
Ships navigating in ice: a selected bibliography. [Montreal]: Transport Canada, [1982]. x, 129 p.
Note: Contains research reports, papers published in technical journals, articles selected from open literature and unpublished material from 1970 through 1980.– Topics covered include economic aspects, ice (accretion, breaking, collision damage, navigation), model testing/simulation, navigational aids and data gathering, propulsion systems, ship trials and performance, ship/ice interaction, related bibliographies.– Compiled by Daphne Sanderson and Gordon Smith.– Résumé en français.
Supplement: ... . *Volume 2, 1980-1984.* 1985. ix, 195 p.; ISBN: 0-660-11918-8.– Compiled by Judith C. Joba.
Location: OONL.

4488 **Canada. Transport Canada. Transportation Development Centre**
TDC publications, 1971-1982/Publications du CDT, 1971-1982. Montreal: The Centre, 1982. 70 p.
Note: Includes in-house reports, contractors' final reports, summary reports and working papers.– Excludes draft reports, confidential publications, papers presented at conferences and seminars.– Text in English and French/texte en français et en anglais.
Previous edition: ... , 1971-1979/... , 1971-1979. 1980. 37 p.
Supplements: Updated semi-annually from 1982. ISSN: 0837-8088.
Location: OONL.

4489 **Miletich, John J.**
Charter airline services in Canada: a selective bibliography. Monticello, Ill.: Vance Bibliographies, 1982. 5 p. (Public administration series: Bibliography ; P-980; ISSN: 0193-970X)
Note: 31 entries.– Covers from 1962 to 1981.– Lists periodical articles on both passenger and freight services.
Location: OONL.

4490 **Smith, Illoana M.**
Transportation in British Columbia: a bibliography. Vancouver: Centre for Transportation Studies, University of British Columbia, c1982. iv, 113 p.; ISBN: 0-919804-28-4.
Note: Approx. 2,000 entries.– Covers up to January, 1980.– Books, theses, corporate reports, government documents.– Broad subject coverage: air, rail, marine, road, urban, pipeline, transport history, transportation policy.– Geographic divisions for regions of British Columbia.
Location: OONL.

4491 **Vomberg, Mac**
Bibliography of legal materials on transportation of hazardous substances. Edmonton: Environmental Law Centre, 1982. 7 l.; ISBN: 0-921503-06-7.
Note: 110 entries.– Cases, articles, legislation.
Location: OONL.

— 1983 —

4492 **Gill, R.J.; Cammaert, A.B.**
Ice control for Arctic ports and harbours. Montreal: Transportation Development Centre, Transport Canada, 1983. 2 vol.
Note: Volume 2: *Annotated bibliography*.– Listing of studies dealing with types of ice problems that may occur in harbours operated in ice conditions, ice control techniques, harbour design.
Location: OON.

4493 **Mayhew, Daniel R.**
Motorcycle and moped safety: an annotated bibliography of the library holdings of the Traffic Injury Research Foundation of Canada. Ottawa: Traffic Injury Research Foundation of Canada, 1983. v, 195 p. (TIRF reports / Traffic Injury Research Foundation of Canada)
Note: 263 entries.– Books, technical reports, conference papers, journal articles.– Topics include rider characteristics, vehicle characteristics, accidents, injury, motorcycle safety, visibility, protective gear, driver education, licensing.
Location: OONL.

4494 **Rawson, Mary**
Transit: the nature and role of localized benefits: a selected annotated bibliography. Vancouver: Centre for Transportation Studies, University of British Columbia, 1983. 35 p.; ISBN: 0-919804-36-5.
Note: Approx. 200 entries.– Reports and articles dealing with economic and financial aspects of urban transit.– Includes Canadian references.
Location: OONL.

— 1984 —

4495 **Minion, Robin**
Arctic transportation. Edmonton: Boreal Institute for Northern Studies, University of Alberta, 1984. 138 p. (Boreal Institute for Northern Studies Bibliographic series ; no. 11; ISSN: 0824-8192); ISBN: 0-919058-45-0.
Note: 362 entries.– Series contains monographs, theses, government documents, consultants' reports, children's books, conference proceedings, microforms on topics related to northern environment and people.– BINS series produced monthly from January 1984 to May 1986 (no. 29).– Online access: *Boreal Northern Titles (BNT)*, available through QL Systems Limited.
Location: OONL.

4496 **Waters, William G.**
A bibliography of articles related to transportation in major economics journals, 1960-1981. Vancouver: Centre for Transportation Studies, University of British Columbia, 1984. [57] p. (Monographs / Centre for Transportation Studies, University of British Columbia)
Note: Includes Canadian references.
Previous edition: Waters, William G.; Keast, Thomas G.; Skene, Gordon D. *Articles related to transportation in major economics journals, 1960-1971*. 1972. 31 p.
Location: OHM.

— 1985 —

4497 **Joba, Judith C.**
Guide to marine transportation information sources in Canada. 2nd ed. Montreal: Transport Canada, Development, 1985. vii, 308 p.; ISBN: 0-660-11970-6.
Note: Includes a short bibliography followed by a directory of organizations in five sections: government, professional associations, academic-research establishments, commercial enterprises, selective list of international organizations.– Information provided on each organization includes a publications list.
Titre en français: *Répertoire des sources d'information sur le transport maritime au Canada*.
Previous edition: McKay, Margaret. Toronto: University of Toronto/York University Joint Program in Transportation, 1980. 221 p.
Location: OONL.

4498 **Joba, Judith C.**
Répertoire des sources d'information sur le transport maritime au Canada. 2e éd. Montréal: Centre de développement des transports, Tranports Canada, 1985. vii, 323 p.; ISBN: 0-660-91624-X.
Note: Comprend une courte bibliographie suivie d'un répertoire des organisations rassemblées en cinq catégories: organismes gouvernementaux, associations, établissements d'enseignement et de recherche, entreprises, entreprises et organisations étrangères.– Traduction de 2e éd. en anglais.
English title: *Guide to marine transportation information sources in Canada*.
Location: OONL.

— 1986 —

4499 Weatherby Bibliographics
Wheel-rail interaction: a selective bibliography/Interaction roue-rail: une bibliographie sélective. Montreal: Transportation Development Centre, Transport Canada, 1986. iv, 131 p.
Note: 400 entries.– International annotated listing of material published from 1970-1985 dealing with wheel-rail interaction.– Emphasis is on freight (heavy-haul) and not passenger rail transportation.– Text in English and French/texte en français et en anglais.
Location: OONL.

— 1987 —

4500 Espesset, Hélène
L'histoire des canaux du Québec: bilan et perspectives. [Ottawa]: Environnement Canada, Parcs, 1987. 36 p.: carte. (Bulletin de recherches / Environnement Canada Parcs ; no. 255; ISSN: 0228-1236)
Note: English title: *History of Quebec canals: a review of the literature.*
Localisation: OONL.

4501 Espesset, Hélène
History of Quebec canals: a review of the literature. [Ottawa]: Environment Canada, 1987. 17 p.: map. (Research bulletin / Environment Canada Parks ; no. 255; ISSN: 0228-1228)
Note: Titre en français: *L'histoire des canaux du Québec: bilan et perspectives.*
Location: OONL.

4502 Icebreakers and icebreaking (Jan 70 – May 87): citations from the NTIS bibliographic database. Springfield, Va.: National Technical Information Service, 1987.
Note: Contains citations concerning aspects of icebreaker vessels and icebreaking on navigable waterways and ocean bodies.– Topics include design aspects and performance evaluations of specific vessels and vessel types, ice navigation and forecasting, effects on shipping activity, design aspects of shipboard machinery and systems.
Location: NFSNM.

— 1988 —

4503 Fischer, Lewis R.; Salmon, M. Stephen
Canadian maritime bibliography for 1987. Ottawa: Canadian Nautical Research Society, 1988. 86 p.
Note: 986 entries.– Listing of books, articles, government documents dealing with archaeology, cartography, engineering, law, merchant shipping, naval studies, shipbuilding.
Location: OONL.

— 1989 —

4504 Maughan, R.G.
Rail transport of coal: a selective bibliography/Transport du charbon par chemin de fer: bibliographie sélective. Montreal: Transportation Development Centre, 1989. vii, 79 p.
Note: 105 entries.– Covers from 1978 to 1989.– Documents dealing with railway components or operating systems having to do with the transport of coal and the interfacing terminals.– Text in English and French/texte en français et en anglais.
Location: OONL.

4505 Robinson, Christopher D.; Smiley, Alison
Suspended drivers in Ontario: license disqualification: a review of the literature. Toronto: Safety Coordination & Development Office, Ontario Ministry of Transportation, 1989. 27 l.; ISBN: 0-77295-871-8.
Note: Location: OONL.

— 1990 —

4506 Billy, George J.
Shipping. Monticello, Ill.: Vance Bibliographies, 1990. 41 p. (Public administration series: Bibliography ; P-2880; ISSN: 0193-970X); ISBN: 0-7920-0540-6.
Note: 222 entries.– Includes basic references, statistical sources, directories, periodicals, bibliographies.– Additional Canadian references supplied by George Ludgate.
Location: OOP.

4507 Cortelyou, Catherine
Urban transportation. Monticello, Ill.: Vance Bibliographies, 1990. 52 p. (Public administration series: Bibliography ; P-2886; ISSN: 0193-970X); ISBN: 0-7920-0546-5.
Note: 242 entries.– Basic references (technology, government policy and finance, management, planning, modelling and methodology); directories, statistical sources, periodicals, databases, indexing and abstracting services, dictionaries and glossaries, bibliographies.– Many Canadian references.
Location: OOP.

4508 Hancock, Kenneth; Houghton, Conrad; Rogers, Dorothy
Advanced train control systems: a selective bibliography/Systèmes d'automatisation de la marche des trains: bibliographie sélective. Rev. 2nd ed. Montreal: Transportation Development Centre, 1990. viii, 75 p.: ill.
Note: International listing of selected works dealing with advanced train control systems, published between 1978 and September 1990.– Some Canadian references.– Text in English and French/texte en français et en anglais.
Previous edition: Houghton, Conrad; Rogers, Dorothy. 1989. vii, 37 p.: ill.
Location: OONL.

4509 Janiak, Jane M.
Air transportation. Monticello, Ill.: Vance Bibliographies, 1990. 78 p. (Public administration series: Bibliography ; P-2879; ISSN: 0193-970X); ISBN: 0-7920-0539-2.
Note: 692 entries.– Substantial Canadian content.
Location: OOP.

4510 Koeneman, Joyce; Martinello, Gilda
Railroads. Monticello, Ill.: Vance Bibliographies, 1990. 26 p. (Public administration series: Bibliography ; P-2881; ISSN: 0193-970X); ISBN: 0-7920-0541-4.
Note: 208 entries.– Includes numerous Canadian references.
Location: OOP.

4511 Krummes, Daniel C.
Highways. Monticello, Ill.: Vance Bibliographies, 1990. 67 p. (Public administration series: Bibliography ; P-2885; ISSN: 0193-970X); ISBN: 0-7920-0545-7.
Note: 513 entries.– Basic references (highway administration, economics, engineering, research, traffic safety); statistical sources; periodicals; bibliographies.– Additional Canadian references supplied by Diane L. Smith.
Location: OOP.

4512 **McHenry, Renée E.**
Intercity bus lines. Monticello, Ill.: Vance Bibliographies, 1990. 21 p. (Public administration series: Bibliography ; P-2887; ISSN: 0193-970X); ISBN: 0-7920-0547-3.
Note: 163 entries.– Listing includes bibliographies, directories, periodicals, statistical publications, government reports and studies.– Additional Canadian references supplied by Noreen Simpson, Ontario Ministry of Transportation Library.
Location: OTY.

4513 **Pearlstein, Toby; Dresley, Susan**
General transportation. Monticello, Ill.: Vance Bibliographies, 1990. 69 p. (Public administration series: Bibliography ; P-2878; ISSN: 0193-970X); ISBN: 0-7920-0538-4.
Note: 543 entries.– Includes basic references, statistical sources, directories, bibliographies, periodicals, conference proceedings, indexing and abstracting services, legislation and regulations.– Additional Canadian references supplied by Ann Poole and Alain Rochefort.
Location: OOP.

4514 **Rothbart, Linda S.**
Trucking. Monticello, Ill.: Vance Bibliographies, 1990. 63 p. (Public administration series: Bibliography ; P-2882; ISSN: 0193-970X); ISBN: 0-7920-0542-2.
Note: 486 entries.– General references, statistical sources, databases, directories and guidebooks, periodicals, bibliographies.– Additional Canadian references supplied by Christopher Hedges.
Location: OOP.

4515 **Roy, Mary L.**
Inland water transportation. Monticello, Ill.: Vance Bibliographies, 1990. 32 p. (Public administration series: Bibliography ; P-2883; ISSN: 0193-970X); ISBN: 0-7920-0543-0.
Note: 220 entries.– General studies, federal reports, contracted research reports, statistical sources, directories, periodicals, bibliographies.– Includes Canadian references.
Location: OOP.

4516 **Sletmo, Gunnar K.; Holste, Susanne**
The shipping and trade of Asia Pacific: trends and implications for Canada. Montréal: École des hautes études commerciales, Centre d'études en administration internationale, 1990. 2 vol.: ill., map. (Cahiers de recherche du Centre d'études en administration internationale ; no 90-16; ISSN: 0825-5822)
Note: Vol. 2: *An annotated bibliography.*– Books, articles, documents and government publications dealing with the potential for Canada of international ocean shipping and trade in Asia Pacific.– Résumé en français.
Location: OONL.

4517 **Tilson, Marie**
Pipelines. Monticello, Ill.: Vance Bibliographies, 1990. 28 p. (Public administration series: Bibliography ; P-2884; ISSN: 0193-970X); ISBN: 0-7920-0544-9.
Note: 164 entries.– Many Canadian references.
Location: OOP.

— 1991 —

4518 **British Columbia. Ministry of Transportation and Highways. Snow Avalanche Programs**
Literature review of snow avalanche research. Victoria: Ministry of Transportation and Highways British Columbia, Snow Avalanche Programs, Maintenance Branch, 1991. 328 p.
Note: Location: OON.

— 1992 —

4519 **Barnett, Le Roy**
Shipping literature of the Great Lakes: a catalog of company publications, 1852-1990. East Lansing: Michigan State University Press, 1992. ix, 165 p.: ill., maps.; ISBN: 0-87013-317-9.
Note: Approx. 3,500 entries.– Listing of publications of Great Lakes shipping companies, mainly folders and brochures.– Canadian companies, such as Canada Steamship Lines and Northern Navigation Company Limited, are well represented.
Location: OONL.

4520 **Turner, Larry**
Rideau Canal bibliography, 1972-1992. Smiths Falls, Ont.: Friends of the Rideau, 1992. 37 p.; ISBN: 0-9696052-0-X.
Note: Listing of books, historical reports, government studies, Canadian Parks Service Historical reports on the Rideau Canal, 1972-1992.
Location: OONL.

Anthropology/Archaeology/Prehistory/Palaeontology

Anthropologie/Archéologie/Préhistoire/Paléontologie

— 1878 —

4521 White, Charles A.; Nicholson, H. Alleyne
Bibliography of North American invertebrate paleontology. Washington: G.P.O., 1878. 132 p. (Miscellaneous publications / United States Geological Survey ; no. 10)
Note: Includes a section: "Publications made in British North America, West Indies, and Europe."
Microform: CIHM Microfiche series ; no. 27388; ISBN: 0-665-27388-6. 2 microfiches (74 fr.).
Location: OOG.

— 1880 —

4522 Chamberlain, A.F.
Contributions towards a bibliography of the archaeology of the Dominion of Canada and Newfoundland. Toronto: [s.n.], 1880. 6 p.
Note: Microform: CIHM Microfiche series ; no. 04119; ISBN: 0-665-04119-5. 1 microfiche (7 fr.).
Location: QMBN.

— 1891 —

4523 Chamberlain, A.F.
"Contributions towards a bibliography of the archaeology of the Dominion of Canada and Newfoundland."
In: *Annual Archaeological Report, Ontario*; Vol. 2 (1887-1888) p. 54-59; vol. 3 (1888-1889) p. 102-118; vol. 4 (1890-1891) p. 78-82.
Note: 276 entries.
Location: OONL.

— 1893 —

4524 Boyle, Cornelius Breckinridge
A catalogue and bibliography of North American mesozoic invertebrata. Washington: G.P.O., 1893. 315 p.
Note: Microform: CIHM Microfiche series ; no. 16872; ISBN: 0-665-16872-1. 4 microfiches (167 fr.).
Location: OOG.

— 1894 —

4525 Keyes, Charles Rollin
A bibliography of North American paleontology, 1888-1892. Washington: U.S.G.P.O., 1894. 251 p.
Note: Includes Canadian references.
Microform: CIHM Microfiche series ; no. 15204; ISBN: 0-665-15204-3. 3 microfiches (138 fr.).
Location: OONL.

— 1900 —

4526 Hunter, Andrew F.
"Bibliography of the archaeology of Ontario."
In: *Annual Archaeological Report, Ontario*; Vol. 10 (1896-1897) p. 98-116; vol. 12 (1897-1898) p. 67-87; vol. 15 (1900) p. 50-62.
Note: Location: OONL.

4527 Nickles, John M.; Bassler, Ray S.
A synopsis of American fossil Bryozoa: including bibliography and synonymy. Washington: G.P.O., 1900. 663 p. (United States Geological Survey Bulletin ; no. 173)

Note: Approx. 1,000 entries.– Includes Canadian references.
Microform: CIHM Microfiche series ; no. 14763; ISBN: 0-665-14763-5. 8 microfiches (349 fr.).
Location: OOG.

— 1902 —

4528 Hay, Oliver Perry
Bibliography and catalogue of the fossil vertebrata of North America. Washington: United States Government Printing Office, 1902. 868, iii p. (United States Geological Survey Bulletin ; 179)
Note: Approx. 4,600 entries.– List of books, memoirs and papers describing fossil vertebrates of North America north of Mexico to the end of 1900.
Supplement: *Second bibliography and catalogue of the fossil vertebrata of North America.* Carnegie Institution of Washington, 1929-1930. 2 vol. (Publication / Carnegie Institution of Washington ; no. 390, vol. 1-2; ISSN: 0099-4936).
Reprint: New York: Arno Press, 1974. 868 p. (Natural sciences in America); ISBN: 0-405-05741-5.
Location: ADTMP.

— 1948 —

4529 Lacourcière, Luc
"Comptines canadiennes."
Dans: *Archives de Folklore*; Vol. 3 (1948) p. 109-157.; ISSN: 0085-5243.
Note: Localisation: AEU.

— 1950 —

4530 Jury, Elsie McLeod
"A guide to archaeological research in Ontario."
In: *Ontario Library Review*; Vol. 34, no. 2 (May 1950) p. 123-133.; ISSN: 0030-2996.
Note: Listing of reports of field work in Ontario, the description of relics recovered from the terrain and the examination of sites and ossuaries.– Excludes works of Indian history, customs and related subjects.
Location: OONL.

4531 Popham, Robert E.
"A bibliography and historical review of physical anthropology in Canada: 1848-1949."
In: *Yearbook of Physical Anthropology*; Vol. 6 (1950) p. 161-184.; ISSN: 0096-848X.
Note: Approx. 250 entries.
Location: AEU.

4532 Popham, Robert E.
"A bibliography and historical review of physical anthropology in Canada: 1848-1949."
In: *Revue canadienne de biologie*; Vol. 9, no 2 (mai 1950) p. 175-198.; ISSN: 0035-0915.
Note: Approx. 250 entries.
Location: AEU.

— 1951 —

4533 Marie-Ursule, soeur
"Civilisation traditionnelle des Lavalois: bibliographie."

Dans: *Archives de Folklore*; Vol. 5-6 (1951) p. 391-395.; ISSN: 0085-5243.
Note: Localisation: AEU.

— 1960 —

4534 **Ives, Edward D.; Kirtley, Bacil**
"Bibliography of New England-Maritimes folklore, 1950-1957."
In: *Northeast Folklore*; Vol. 1 (Summer 1958) p. 18-31; vol. 2 (Summer 1959) p. 18-24; vol. 3 (1960) p. 20-23.; ISSN: 0078-1681.
Note: General folklore, material culture, folk art, customs, belief and superstition, folksay (riddles, proverbs, speech, place-names, etc.), folk narrative, folk music section (includes songs, poetry, drama, games, dance).– Includes a section listing collections and studies prior to 1950.
Location: OONM.

— 1961 —

4535 **Haywood, Charles**
A bibliography of North American folklore and folksong. 2nd rev. ed. New York: Dover Publications, [1961]. 2 vol.: maps (on lining papers).
Note: Approx. 40,000 entries, mainly American.– Vol. 1 includes a "Canada" section (general studies, folktales, customs/beliefs/superstitions, riddles, speech, place-names, folksong), and Vol. 2 lists references to Canadian Indian and Inuit folklore and music.
Previous edition: New York: Greenberg, [1951]. xxx, 1292 p.
Location: OONL.

— 1962 —

4536 **Clapp, Jane**
Museum publications. New York: Scarecrow Press, 1962. 2 vol.
Note: Listing of publications of 276 museums in United States and Canada.– Excludes serials, administrative reports, newsletters and bulletins, accession lists.– Part 1: "Anthropology, archaeology and art."- 4,416 entries.– Part 2: "Biological and earth sciences."- 9,231 entries.
Location: OONL.

4537 **Neuman, Robert W.**
"An archaeological bibliography: the central and northern Great Plains prior to 1930."
In: *Plains Anthropologist*; No. 15 (February 1962) p. 43-57.; ISSN: 0032-0447.
Note: 302 entries.– Annotated references to archaeological phenomena and investigations in the northern sector of the Great Plains (including portions of Manitoba, Alberta, Saskatchewan), 1840-1930.
Location: OONMM.

— 1963 —

4538 **Anthropological bibliography of the eastern seaboard.**
New Haven: Eastern States Archeological Federation, 1947-1963. 2 vol.
Note: Vol. 1, edited by Irving Rouse and John M. Goggin. 1947. 174 p. (Research publication (Eastern States Archeological Federation) ; no. 1).– Includes a section on eastern Canada in each section: "Archeology," "Ethnology," and "History."
Vol. 2, edited by Alfred K. Guthe and Patricia B. Kelly. 1963. 82 p. (Research publication (Eastern States Archeological Federation) ; no. 2).– Includes references to the Atlantic provinces.

Location: OONL.

— 1964 —

4539 **Kidd, Kenneth E.; Rogers, Edward S.; Kenyon, Walter Andrew**
Brief bibliography of Ontario anthropology. Toronto: Royal Ontario Museum, University of Toronto, 1964. 20 p. (Art and Archaeology Occasional paper / Royal Ontario Museum ; 7)
Note: Approx. 175 entries.– Books and journal articles on principal Indian groups in Ontario and surrounding regions (Cree, Ojibwa, Iroquois), general anthropology and archaeology, ethnology, linguistics and folklore.
Location: OOCC.

— 1966 —

4540 **Hlady, Walter M.; Simpson, Allan A.**
"Bibliography of Manitoba archaeology."
In: *Manitoba Archaeological Newsletter*; Vol. 1, no. 3 (Fall 1964) p. 3-20; vol. 2, no. 3 (Fall 1965) p. 7-12; vol. 3, no. 3 (Fall 1966) p. 3-6.; ISSN: 0025-2190.
Note: Published articles, monographs, books, manuscripts dealing with various aspects of Manitoba archaeology.– Excludes newspaper articles.
Location: AEU.

4541 **Kenyon, Walter Andrew**
"A bibliography of Ontario archaeology."
In: *Ontario Archaeology*; No. 9 (June 1966) p. 35-62.; ISSN: 0078-4672.
Note: Approx. 375 entries.
Location: OONL.

— 1967 —

4542 **McIlwraith, Thomas Forsyth**
"Bibliography of Canadian anthropology."
In: *Bulletin (National Museum of Canada)*; No. 142 (1956) p. 166-180; no. 147 (1957) p. 124-140; no. 162 (1960) p. 165-203; no. 167 (1960) p. 114-131; no. 173 (1961) p. 230-248; no. 190 (1963) p. 240-264; no. 194 (1964) p. 1-28; no. 204 (1967) p. 191-217.; ISSN: 0068-7944.
Note: Location: OONL.

4543 **Popham, Robert E.; Yawney, Carole D.**
Culture and alcohol use: a bibliography of anthropological studies. Toronto: Addiction Research Foundation of Ontario, 1967. v, 52 l. (Bibliographic series / Addiction Research Foundation of Ontario ; no. 1; ISSN: 0065-1885)
Note: 448 entries.– Studies on drinking behaviour (customary and pathological) in particular cultural contexts (literate/non-literate, past/present), or with theoretical implications of cross-cultural similarities and differences in such behaviour.– Includes Canadian references.
Location: OONL.

4544 **Rudnyckyj, Jaroslav Bohdan**
"Bibliographia onomastica: Canada."
In: *Onoma*; Vol. 3 (1952) p. 139; vol. 4 (1953) p. 154; vol. 5 (1954) p. 168; vol. 6 (1955/1956) p. 202; vol. 7 (1956/1957) p. 25; vol. 8 (1958/1959) p. 31-32; vol. 9 (1960/1961) p. 44-45; vol. 10 (1962/1963) p. 30-31; vol. 11 (1964/1965) p. 30; vol. 12 (1966-1967) p. 28.; ISSN: 0078-463X.
Note: Continued by Rudnyckyj and Jean Poirier (1968-1969).
Location: OONL.

4545 **Wagner, Frances J.E.**
Published references to Champlain Sea faunas 1837-1966 and list of fossils. Ottawa: Queen's Printer, 1967. v, 82 p.

(Geological Survey of Canada Paper ; 67-16)
Note: List of all published references to the Pleistocene Champlain Sea (Ottawa-St. Lawrence Lowland) faunas, arranged in chronological order.
Location: OONL.

— 1968 —

4546 **Guyot, Mireille**
Bibliographie américaniste: archéologie et préhistoire, anthropologie et ethnohistoire. Paris: Musée de l'homme, 1967-1968. 248 f.
Note: Approx. 2,750 entrées.
Localisation: OONL.

— 1969 —

4547 **Rudnyckyj, Jaroslav Bohdan; Poirier, Jean**
"Bibliographia onomastica: Canada."
In: *Onoma*; Vol. 13 (1968) P. 26-27; vol. 14 (1969) p. 513-515.; ISSN: 0078-463X.
Note: Continues: Rudnyckyj, Jaroslav Bohdan (1952-1966/1967).
Location: OONL.

— 1970 —

4548 **Carter, John Lyman; Carter, Ruth C.**
Bibliography and index of North American Carboniferous brachiopods (1898-1968). Boulder, Colo.: Geological Society of America, 1970. x, 382 p. (Geological Society of America Memoir ; 128)
Note: Approx. 350 entries.
Location: OONL.

4549 **Fladmark, K.R.**
"Bibliography of the archaeology of British Columbia."
In: *BC Studies*; No. 6-7 (Fall-Winter 1970) p. 126-151.; ISSN: 0005-2949.
Note: Approx. 375 entries.– Books, parts of books, journal and newspaper articles, theses from 1876 to 1969.
Location: AEU.

4550 **Jolicoeur, Catherine**
"Le vaisseau fantôme: légende étiologique: bibliographie."
Dans: *Archives de Folklore*; Vol. 11 (1970) p. 307-325.; ISSN: 0085-5243.
Note: Localisation: AEU.

4551 **Martijn, Charles A.; Cinq-Mars, Jacques**
"Aperçu sur la recherche préhistorique au Québec."
Dans: *Revue de géographie de Montréal*; Vol. 24, no 2 (1970) p. 175-188.; ISSN: 0035-1148.
Note: Esquisse de l'évolution et de l'orientation des études préhistoriques faites au Québec depuis 1850.
Localisation: OONL.

4552 **Rascoe, Jesse E.**
1200 treasure books: a bibliography. Fort Davis, Tex.: Frontier Book Co., 1970. 62 p.
Note: 1,200 entries.– Includes Canadian titles.
Location: OONL.

— 1971 —

4553 **Bernier, Hélène**
"La fille aux mains coupées (conte-type 706): bibliographie."
Dans: *Archives de Folklore*; Vol. 12 (1971) p. 175-183.; ISSN: 0085-5243.
Note: Localisation: AEU.

4554 **Maillet, Antonine**
"Rabelais et les traditions populaires en Acadie."
Dans: *Archives de Folklore*; Vol. 13 (1971) p. 189-196.; ISSN: 0085-5243.

Note: Localisation: AEU.

— 1972 —

4555 **Feit, Harvey A.; Mailhot, José**
"La région de la Baie James (Québec): bibliographie ethnologique."
Dans: *Recherches amérindiennes au Québec*; Vol. 2, Spécial 1 (juin 1972) p. 4-42.; ISSN: 0318-4137.
Note: Localisation: AEU.

4556 **University of British Columbia. Department of Anthropology and Sociology**
Bibliography of the archaeology of British Columbia. Vancouver: The Department, 1972. 31 l.
Note: Location: BVAU.

— 1973 —

4557 **Duff, Wilson; Kew, Michael**
"A select bibliography of anthropology of British Columbia."
In: *BC Studies*; No. 19 (Autumn 1973) p. 73-121.; ISSN: 0005-2949.
Note: Approx. 525 entries.– Books, studies, articles, theses.– Includes ethnographic sources (subdivided by tribal groupings), studies of ethnographic topics (material culture, economic life, social life, religious life, art, languages, prehistory), social change and current Indian affairs.
Location: OONL.

4558 **Olivier, Daniel**
Bibliographie sur la guignolée, Nöel, le jour de l'An, la quête de l'Enfant Jésus, l'Epiphanie et le temps des fêtes en général. [Ste-Elisabeth, Québec: D. Olivier, 1973]. [12] f.
Note: Approx. 100 entrées.
Localisation: OONL.

4559 **Pohorecky, Zenon S.**
"Archaeology and prehistory: the Saskatchewan case."
In: *A region of the mind: interpreting the western Canadian plains*, edited by Richard Allen. Regina: Canadian Plains Studies Center, University of Saskatchewan, c1973. P. 47-72.; ISBN: 0-88977-008-5.
Note: Literature review of archaeological and anthropological writings related to Saskatchewan.
Location: OONL.

— 1974 —

4560 **Moussette, Marcel, et al.**
"Bibliographie préliminaire pour la recherche en archéologie historique au Québec."
Dans: *Recherches amérindiennes au Québec*; Vol. 4, no 4/5 (octobre-décembre 1974) p. 48-60.; ISSN: 0318-4137.
Note: Approx. 400 entrées.– Trois parties: "Archéologie historique en général et analyse des artefacts;" "Archéologie historique au Québec;" "Archéologie du régime français."
Comp. par Marcel Moussette, Pierre Nadon, Gérard Gusset, Jean-Pierre Cloutier.
Localisation: AEU.

— 1975 —

4561 **McGee, Harold Franklin, Jr.; Davis, Stephen A.; Taft, Michael**
Three Atlantic bibliographies. [Halifax, N.S.]: Department of Anthropology, Saint Mary's University, 1975. 205 p. (Occasional papers in anthropology / Department of Anthropology, Saint Mary's University ; no. 1)

Note: Part 1: *Ethnographic bibliography of northeastern North America*, comp. by Harold Franklin McGee, Jr.– 722 entries.– Books, journal articles, government publications relating to archaeology and ethnology of Nova Scotia, New Brunswick, Prince Edward Island, the Gaspé, and Maine on Abenaki, Malecite, Micmac, Penobscot, and Beothuk.
Part 2: *Preliminary archaeology bibliography of Atlantic Canada and Maine*, comp. by Stephen A. Davis.– 380 entries.– Books, journal articles, theses.
Part 3: *A bibliography for folklore studies in Nova Scotia*, comp. by Michael Taft.– 762 entries.– Books, journal articles dealing with folk traditions of Nova Scotia: folktales, folksongs, beliefs, customs, material culture, local histories.
Location: OONL.

4562 **O'Leary, Timothy J.**
A preliminary bibliography of the archaeology of western Canada. [Calgary: s.n., 1975]. 23 l.
Note: Approx. 250 entries.– Books, journal articles, newspaper articles, museum publications.– Prepared for the Glenbow Institute.
Location: BVAS.

4563 **Storck, Peter L.**
A preliminary bibliography of early man in eastern North America, 1839-1973. Toronto: Royal Ontario Museum, 1975. 110 p. (Archaeology monograph / Royal Ontario Museum ; 4); ISBN: 0-88854-158-9.
Note: 1,242 entries.– Journal articles, reviews, monographs, books.– Term "early man" used in broad sense, including various manifestations of early and late Palaeo-Indian cultures, and antecedent cultures.– Eastern North America is defined as Canadian provinces east of Manitoba and the United States east of Mississippi River.
Location: OONL.

4564 **Stothers, David M.; Dullabaun, Marlene A.**
A bibliography of Arctic and sub-arctic prehistory and protohistory. Toledo, Ohio: Toldedo Area Aboriginal Research Club, 1975. iii, 58 p. (Toledo Area Aboriginal Research Bulletin Supplementary monograph ; no. 2)
Note: Approx. 600 entries (200 Canadian).– English language references: archaeology and anthropology of arctic and sub-arctic regions, Canada, Siberia, Scandinavia, Alaska, Greenland and Iceland.
Location: ACU.

— 1976 —

4565 **Canadian Museums Association**
Bibliography: an extensive listing of published material on the subjects of museology, museography and museum and art gallery administration/Bibliographie: un inventaire considérable de publications portant sur la muséologie, la muséographie et l'administration de musées et de galeries d'art. Ottawa: The Association, 1976. [235] p. (in various pagings: loose-leaf).
Note: Approx. 3,500 entries.– Books and articles on collection management, conservation, ethics, cultural policy, information storage and retrieval, history, education, personnel, restoration, technology.– Includes some publications in French.
Supplements:
... : Supplement I/ ... : Supplément I. 1976. 1 vol. (various pagings).
... : Supplement II/ ... : Supplément II. 1976. 1 vol. (various

pagings).
... : Supplement III/ ... : Supplément III. [1977]. 1 vol. (various pagings).
... : Supplement IV/ ... : Supplément IV. 1978. 1 vol. (various pagings).
... : Supplement V/ ... : Supplément V. 1980. 1 vol. (various pagings).
... : Supplements VI-VII/ ... : Suppléments VI-VII. 1981. 1 vol. (various pagings).
... : Supplement VIII/ ... : Supplément VIII. 1981. 1 vol. (various pagings).
... : Supplement IX/ ... : Supplément IX. 1982. 1 vol. (various pagings).
Canadian Museums Association bibliography: Supplement X/ Association des musées canadiens bibliographie: Supplément X. 1983. 1 vol. (various pagings).
Canadian Museums Association bibliography: Supplement XI/ Association des musées canadiens bibliographie: Supplément XI. 1984. 1 vol. (various pagings).
Canadian Museums Association bibliography: Supplement XII, 1984-1985/Association des musées canadiens bibliographie: Supplément XII, 1984-1985. 1987. 1 vol. (various pagings).
Location: OONL.

4566 **Jackson, L.J.**
"A bibliography of Huron-Petun archaeology."
In: *Ontario Archaeology*; no. 28 (1976) p. 33-69.; ISSN: 0078-4672.
Note: Approx. 500 entries.– Studies related to Huron-Petun branch of Iroquoian development in the Great Lakes region throughout the Late Woodland period.– Topics include prehistoric archaeology, historical archaeology, native habitat, native technology, trade goods and cultural studies.
Location: OONL.

— 1977 —

4567 **Fowke, Edith; Carpenter, Carole Henderson**
"A bibliography of Canadian folklore in English."
In: *Communiqué: Canadian Studies*; Vol. 3, no. 4 (August 1977) p. 3-72.; ISSN: 0318-1197.
Note: Covers to the end of 1975, with the addition of a few significant items from 1976.– Canadian folklore means folklore found in Canada: excludes works on non-Canadian folklore written by Canadians or published in Canada.– Sections include reference materials (bibliographies and checklists); general works (folktales, folk music and dance, folksay, superstitions/popular beliefs, folklife and customs, folk art, biographies).– Includes listings of audio-visual materials, theses and dissertations.
Location: OONL.

4568 **Joyes, Dennis C.**
"A bibliography of Saskatchewan archaeology, 1900-1975."
In: *Saskatchewan Archaeology Newsletter*; Vol. 52, no. 4-5 (1977) p. 41-115.; ISSN: 0581-832X.
Note: "Preliminary, basic bibliography of historic and prehistoric archaeology for the Province of Saskatchewan."– Includes unpublished theses, manuscripts held by Archaeological Survey of Canada.– Excludes newspaper articles.
Location: OONL.

4569 **"Material cultural research at Parks Canada."**
In: *Material History Bulletin*; No. 2 (1977) p. 70-78.; ISSN: 0703-489X.
Note: 158 entries.– Lists titles in the *Manuscript report series*, unedited manuscripts of research projects conducted by Parks Canada, Research Division, in the fields of Canadian archaeology and history.
Location: OONL.

4570 **Moeller, Roger W.; Reid, John**
Archaeological bibliography for eastern North America. New Haven: Eastern States Archeological Federation, 1977. xiii, 198 p.
Note: Approx. 8,000 entries.– Geographic coverage of references is eastern provinces of Canada and states east of the Mississippi.– Time period covered is 1959 to December 1976.– Excludes newspaper articles, unpublished papers.– Canadian references include National Museum manuscript reports.– Emphasis on prehistoric archaeology, rather than ethnological, ethnographic or historical material.
Location: NBFU.

4571 **Pettipas, Leo F.**
"A bibliography of Manitoba archaeology."
In: *Papers in Manitoba Archaeology*. Winnipeg: Department of Tourism, Recreation & Cultural Affairs, Historic Resources Branch, 1977. P. 55-74. (Miscellaneous papers / Historic Resources Branch, Manitoba Department of Tourism, Recreation & Cultural Affairs ; no. 4; ISSN: 0706-0483)
Note: Approx. 150 entries.– Covers 1970-1977.
Location: OONL.

— 1978 —
4572 **Dekin, Albert A.**
Arctic archaeology: a bibliography and history. New York: Garland Publishing, 1978. 279 p. (Garland reference library of science and technology ; v. 1); ISBN: 0-8240-1084-1.
Note: Approx. 1,300 entries.– Books, papers, articles, dissertations by and about explorers and ethnographers, chronologists and prehistorians, archaeologists and anthropologists dealing with recent developments/ current trends and problems related to Arctic archaeology.
Location: OONL.

4573 **Dominique, Richard; Trudel, François**
"Bibliographie sur les relations entre anthropologie et histoire, et sur l'ethnohistoire."
Dans: *Recherches amérindiennes au Québec*; Vol. 7, nos 3-4 (1978) p. 120-122.; ISSN: 0318-4137.
Note: Localisation: OONL.

4574 **Hunston, Jeffrey R.**
A bibliography of Yukon archaeology, anthropology, and Quaternary research. Burnaby, B.C.: Department of Archaeology, Simon Fraser University, 1978. 102 l.
Note: Approx. 1,000 entries.– Loose-leaf, typewritten listing of books, reports, studies, theses, conference papers dealing with geology, archaeology and anthropology of the Yukon Territory.
Location: ACUAI.

4575 **Leith, Harry**
Bibliography of books and articles on the relationship between science and pseudoscience. Toronto: York University, Department of Natural Sciences, Atkinson College, 1978. 61 p.
Note: Approx. 2,000 entries.– Includes some Canadian references.
Previous edition: [S.l.: s.n.], 1976. 49 p.
Location: OONL.

— 1979 —
4576 **Ontario Archaeological Society. Library**
Library and archives [Ontario Archaeological Society], September 1979. Toronto: Ontario Archaeological Society, 1979. 26 p.
Note: Approx. 500 entries.– Books, journals, occasional papers, newsletters, reports and manuscripts on aspects of prehistory, mainly Ontario.
Location: OONL.

— 1980 —
4577 **Karklins, Karlis; Sprague, Roderick**
A bibliography of glass trade beads in North America. Moscow, Idaho: South Fork Press, 1980. 51 p.
Note: 455 entries.– Reports and articles dealing with glass trade beads in Canada, the United States and Mexico.– Excludes reports concerned entirely with nonglass beads, Indian-made glass beads and prehistoric beads.
Supplement: ... . First supplement. Ottawa: Promontory Press, 1987. 72 p.; ISBN: 0-9692761-0-9.– 588 entries.
Location: OONL.

4578 **Krech, Shepard**
"Northern Athapaskan ethnology: an annotated bibliography of published materials, 1970-79."
In: *Arctic Anthropology*; Vol. 17, no. 2 (1980) p. 68-105.; ISSN: 0066-6939.
Note: 325 entries.– English-language publications, theses and dissertations relating to northern Athapaskan ethnology.– Linguistic, archaeological and biological material is omitted.
Location: AEU.

— 1981 —
4579 **Adams, Gary**
"Fur trade archaeology in western Canada: a critical evaluation and bibliography."
In: *Saskatchewan Archaeology*; Vol. 2, no. 1&2 (June/December 1981) p. 39-53.; ISSN: 0227-5872.
Note: Approx. 150 entries.
Location: AEU.

4580 **Fowke, Edith; Carpenter, Carole Henderson**
A bibliography of Canadian folklore in English. Toronto: University of Toronto Press, 1981. xx, 272 p.; ISBN: 0-8020-2394-0.
Note: 3,877 entries.– Covers to December 1979.– Emphasis on published material with the exception of theses and dissertations.– Includes books, periodical articles, films, records.– Subjects covered include folktales, folk music and dance, folk speech and naming, superstitions and popular beliefs, folklife and customs, folk art and material culture, biographies.
Previous edition: Downsview, Ont.: York University, 1976. v, 146 p.
Location: OONL.

4581 **Heath, Dwight B.; Cooper, A.M.**
Alcohol use and world cultures: a comprehensive bibliography of anthropological sources. Toronto: Addiction Research Foundation of Ontario, c1981. xv, 248 p. (Bibliographic series / Addiction Research

Foundation of Ontario ; no. 15; ISSN: 0065-1885); ISBN: 0-88868-045-7.
Note: 1,398 entries.– Some Canadian references.
Location: OONL.

4582 **Lafrenière, Normand**
Bilan des études spécifiques au site de Coteau-du-Lac. Québec: Parcs Canada, 1981. [150] f.
Note: Comprend une liste des études sur le site de Coteau-du-Lac, Québec, et un inventaire des nouvelles acquisitions iconographiques relatives à Coteau-du-Lac et aux premiers canaux militaires du Saint-Laurent.
Localisation: QQPCQ.

4583 **Milisauskas, Sarunas; Pickin, Frances; Clark, Charles**
A selected bibliography of North American archaeological sites. New Haven, Conn.: Human Relations Area Files, 1981. 2 vol. (HRAFlex Books bibliography series ; N4-001)
Note: Listing of North American archaeological site reports, including Canadian provinces and territories.
Location: NBFU.

4584 **Quinn, David B.**
Sources for the ethnography of northeastern North America to 1611. Ottawa: National Museums of Canada, 1981. iv, 93 p. (National Museum of Man Mercury series: Canadian Ethnology Service paper ; no. 76; ISSN: 0316-1862)
Note: Approx. 100 entries.– Printed and manuscript sources from earliest discoveries to establishment of European settlement (1497 to 1611).– Southern geographical limit is New York State.
Location: OONL.

4585 **Razzolini, E.M.; McIntyre, F.**
Bibliography of sources used in compiling and analyzing costume research and design information accumulated at the fortress of Louisbourg National Historic Park. [S.l.: s.n.], 1981. [27] l.
Note: Approx. 200 entries.– Bibliographical sources, background materials (manuscripts and published), dealing with civilian and military clothing and accessories of the Louisbourg period (first half of eighteenth century).
Location: OONM.

4586 **Smith, Margo L.; Damien, Yvonne M.**
Anthropological bibliographies: a selected guide. South Salem, N.Y.: Redgrave, c1981. 307 p.; ISBN: 0-913178-63-2.
Note: 3,200 entries.– Includes bibliographies, filmographies, discographies.– International in scope with a small Canadian section.– Emphasis on recent materials.
Location: OONL.

4587 **Université de Montréal. Bibliothèque des sciences humaines et sociales**
Guide de la documentation en anthropologie: à l'intention des usagers de la Bibliothèque des sciences humaines et sociales. 2e éd., rev. et corr. [Montréal]: La Bibliothèque, 1981. xii, 105 p.: ill.; ISBN: 0-88529-036-4.
Note: 385 entrées.– Compilé par Ghyslaine Brodeur.
Édition antérieure: 1978. vi f., 52 p.
Localisation: OONL.

— 1982 —

4588 **Blanchette, Jean-François; Bouchard, René; Pocius, Gerald L.**
"Une bibliographie de la culture matérielle traditionnelle au Canada 1965-1982/A bibliography of material culture in Canada 1965-1982."
Dans: *Canadian Folklore: Folklore canadien*; Vol. 4, no 1/2 (1982) p. 107-146.; ISSN: 0225-2899.
Note: Approx. 1,400 entrées.– Bibliographies, ouvrages généraux, études spécialisées (art populaire, artisans et technologie, meubles, textiles et costumes, alimentation, architecture).– Exclut manuscrits, compte-rendus de lecture, articles de revues populaires, domaines de l'artisanat classique, architecture classique, livres de recettes, oeuvres strictement d'intérêt local.
Localisation: OOCC.

4589 **Dugas, Jean-Yves**
"Bibliographie commentée des études concernant le problème des gentilés au Québec et au Canada."
Dans: *Onoma*; Vol. 26 (1982) p. 227-267.; ISSN: 0078-463X.
Note: Références sur les noms de personnes au Québec et au Canada.
Localisation: OONL.

4590 **Halpert, Herbert**
A Folklore sampler from the Maritimes: with a bibliographical essay on the folktale in English. St. John's: Published for the Centre for Canadian Studies, Mount Allison University by Memorial University of Newfoundland Folklore and Language Publications, 1982. xix, 273 p. (Bibliographical and special series / Centre for Canadian Studies, Mount Allison University ; no. 8); ISBN: 0-88901-086-2.
Note: Approx. 400 entries.– Bibliographical essay discusses folk-narrative publications of Atlantic Canada, with a survey of books from the rest of Canada.– Bibliography, p. 235-273.
Location: OONL.

4591 **Hardy, Kenneth J.**
Calgary archaeology, 1959-1980: a select annotated bibliography. Edmonton: Kenneth J. Hardy, 1982. vi, 57 p.
Note: 92 entries.– Heritage impact assessment reports, historical resources assessment reports, maps.
Location: OONL.

— 1983 —

4592 **Rodrigue, Denis**
"Le cycle de Pâques au Québec et dans l'Ouest de la France."
Dans: *Archives de Folklore*; Vol. 24 (1983) p. 313-329.; ISSN: 0085-5243.
Note: Localisation: AEU.

— 1984 —

4593 **Beaudoin-Ross, Jacqueline; Blackstock, Pamela**
"Costume in Canada: an annotated bibliography."
In: *Material History Bulletin*; No. 19 (Spring 1984) p. 59-92.; ISSN: 0703-489X.
Note: Lists and reviews material published to March 1984 from both French and English Canada on civilian clothing, everyday and fashionable, worn in the past in Canada, primarily of European influence.– Excludes literature on textile history, museological practices (storage and conservation), Indian/Inuit/Métis costume, theatrical costume, contemporary fashion and the garment industry.
Supplement: "Costume in Canada: the sequel." In: *Material History Review*; No. 34 (Fall 1991) p. 42-67.
Location: OONL.

4594 **Dawson, K.C.A.**
"A history of archaeology in northern Ontario to 1983 with bibliographic contributions."
In: *Ontario Archaeology*; No. 42 (1984) p. 27-92.; ISSN: 0078-4672.
Note: Approx. 900 entries.
Location: OONL.

4595 **Guse, Lorna; Koolage, William**
Medical anthropology, social science, and nursing: a bibliography. 2nd ed., rev. Winnipeg: Department of Anthropology, University of Manitoba, 1984. xvii, 106 p. (University of Manitoba Anthropology papers ; no. 28)
Note: Approx. 1,200 entries.– Lists books and articles on ethnicity and health care.– Topics include medical anthropology and sociology, transcultural nursing, poverty and social class.– Focus on Manitoba, native peoples.– Includes a listing of additional bibliographies.
Previous edition: 1979. xvii, 99 p. (University of Manitoba Anthropology papers ; no. 22).
Location: OONL.

4596 **Labelle, Ronald; Beaulieu, Jean; Breton, Marcel**
Inventaire des sources en folklore acadien. Moncton, N.-B.: Centre d'études acadiennes, Université de Moncton, 1984. viii, 194 p.: carte.; ISBN: 0-919241-20-4.
Note: 1,330 entrées.– Principaux thèmes traités: histoire orale et langue populaire, contes, chansons, croyances populaires, divertissements, sciences populaires, moeurs, folklore matériel.– Comprend: catalogue des contes, catalogue des chansons, catalogue des chansons locales.
Localisation: OONL.

— 1985 —

4597 **Minion, Robin**
Archaeology in northern Canada. Edmonton: Boreal Institute for Northern Studies, University of Alberta, 1985. 63 p. (Boreal Institute for Northern Studies Bibliographic series ; no. 20; ISSN: 0824-8192); ISBN: 0-919058-54-X.
Note: 165 entries.– Covers 1977 to 1985, with addition of limited amount of older material.– Includes monographs, theses, government documents, consultants' reports, conference proceedings.– BINS series produced monthly from January 1984 to May 1986.– Online access: *Boreal Northern Titles (BNT)*, available through QL Systems Limited.
Location: OONL.

— 1986 —

4598 **Lavoie, Marc C.**
A preliminary bibliography for historic artifact research in the Maritimes/Une bibliographie préliminaire sur les artefacts historiques pour les Maritimes. Fredericton, N.B.: Archaeology Branch, Department of Tourism, Recreation and Heritage, New Brunswick, 1986. ii, 66 p. (Manuscripts in archaeology / Archaeology Branch, New Brunswick Department of Tourism, Recreation and Heritage); ISBN: 0-88838-354-1.
Note: Approx. 600 entries.– Books and articles, mainly on subject of ceramics and glass, site reports and research summaries on various excavations, articles and books on history of Acadia and New France.– Text in English and French/texte en français et en anglais.
Location: OONL.

4599 **Turnbull, Christopher J.; Davis, Stephen A.**
An archaeological bibliography of the Maritime Provinces: works to 1984. Halifax, N.S.: Council of Maritime Premiers, Maritime Committee for Archaeological Cooperation, 1986. 118 p. (Reports in archaeology / Council of Maritime Premiers, Maritime Committee for Archaeological Cooperation ; 6); ISBN: 0-88838-360-6.
Note: Approx. 800 entries.– Includes reports which are of interest to archaeology, use archaeological data, or directly relate to an archaeological project in New Brunswick, Nova Scotia, Prince Edward Island.– Some ethnohistorical material and historic reports are included.
Location: OONL.

4600 **Vagné-Lebas, Mireille**
Irrationnel contemporain et survivance de la tradition au Québec. [Talence]: Maison des sciences de l'homme d'Aquitaine, 1986. 2 vol. (Publications de la M.S.H.A. / Maison des sciences de l'homme d'Aquitaine ; no 100); ISBN: 2-85892-104-0.
Note: Approx. 100 entrées.– "Bibliographie du conte québécois de l'irrationnel," vol. 1, p. 104-119.
Localisation: OONL.

— 1988 —

4601 **Danis, Jane**
"Bibliography of vertebrate palaeontology in Dinosaur Provincial Park."
In: *Alberta*; Vol. 1, no. 1 (1988) p. 225-234.
Note: Approx. 100 entries.
Location: AEU.

4602 **Jones, Tim E.H.**
Annotated bibliography of Saskatchewan archaeology and prehistory. Saskatoon: Saskatchewan Archaeological Society, 1988. ii, 196 p.; ISBN: 0-9691420-0-7.
Note: Approx. 1,100 entries.– Books, journal articles, government publications, theses, archaeological surveys pertaining to prehistoric and historic archaeology of lands within judicial boundaries of Saskatchewan.– Contributions by Dennis C. Joyes, David L. Kelly, Henry T. Epp.
Location: OONL.

4603 **Smith, Mary Margaret; Pyszczyk, Heinz W.**
A selected bibliography of historical artifacts: c. 1760-1920. Edmonton: Alberta Culture and Multiculturalism, Historical Resources Division, 1988. x, 325 p.: ill.
Note: Approx. 4,000 entries.– Published and unpublished works to 1986 dealing with historical artifacts (material goods) commonly found in western Canada between about 1760 and 1920.
Location: OONL.

— 1989 —

4604 **McMurdo, John**
Archaeological field research in British Columbia: an annotated bibliography. [Victoria]: Province of British Columbia, Archaeology and Outdoor Recreation Branch, Resource Information Services Program, [c1989]. viii, 343 p.: ill., map.; ISBN: 0-7718-8563-6.
Note: Approx. 1,700 entries.– Reports written in satisfaction of governmental requirements: manuscripts, publications, papers, theses categorized by project type: excavations, areal surveys, limited surveys.– Designed to provide an overview of the status of archaeological research.– Annotations by Ian R. Wilson.

Location: OONL.

4605 Pocius, Gerald L.
"Bibliography [Folklore]/Bibliographie [Folklore]."
In: *Bulletin of the Folklore Studies Association of Canada*; Vol. 8, nos 1/2 (May 1984) p. 28-32; vol. 8, nos 3/4 (November 1984) p. 28-30; vol. 9, nos 1/2 (May 1985) p. 31-32; vol. 9, nos 3/4 (November 1985) p. 30-34; vol. 10, nos 1/2 (May 1986) p. 34-5; vol. 10, nos 3/4 (November 1986) p. 42-44; vol. 11, nos 1/2 (May 1987) p. 25-26; vol. 11, nos 3/4 (November 1987) p. 50; vol. 12, nos 3/4 (November 1988) p. 15-16; vol. 13, nos 3/4 (November 1989) p. 42-43.; ISSN: 0705-1158.
Note: Location: OONM.

4606 Tyrrell Museum of Palaeontology
List of publications, by research, collections and library staff [Tyrrell Museum of Palaeontology]. Drumheller: Tyrrell Museum of Palaeontology, 1989. 16 l.
Note: Location: ACU.

— 1990 —

4607 Cardinal, Linda; Lapointe, Jean; Thériault, J.-Yvon
"Bibliographie sommaire sur les francophones hors Québec 1980-1989."
Dans: *Le déclin d'une culture: recherche, analyse et bibliographie: francophonie hors Québec, 1980-1989*, par Bernard Roger. Ottawa: Fédération des jeunes Canadiens français, c1990. P. 139-192.; ISBN: 0-921768-05-5.
Note: Approx. 500 entrées.
Localisation: OONL.

— 1991 —

4608 Hunston, Jeffrey R.
Prehistory of Canada: recommended general introductory reading. Whitehorse: Yukon Tourism, Heritage Branch, 1991. ii, 28 l.; ISBN: 1-550-18167-X.
Note: Approx. 250 entries.– Articles, leaflets, books dealing with archaeological research results in a popular and non-technical format.– Includes a list of additional bibliographies.
Location: OONL.

4609 Kerber, Jordan E.
Coastal and maritime archaeology: a bibliography. Metuchen, N.J.: Scarecrow Press, 1991. viii, 400 p.; ISBN: 0-8108-2465-5.
Note: 2,823 entries.– Papers, articles, books, theses dealing with prehistory, history and ethnography of indigenous peoples worldwide that have hunted, gathered, fished along shore or offshore.– Regional focus is northeastern North America, including Atlantic Canada, with many references to the Pacific Northwest as well.
Location: OONL.

— 1992 —

4610 Dupont, L.
Répertoire des publications du Musée de la civilisation. Québec: Service de la recherche et de l'évaluation, Musée de la civilisation, 1992. 49 p. (Document / Service de la recherche et de l'évaluation, Musée de la civilisation ; no 10); ISBN: 2-551-12941-9.
Note: 132 entrées.
Localisation: OONL.

4611 Pichette, Jean- Pierre
Le répertoire ethnologique de l'Ontario français: guide bibliographique et inventaire archivistique du folklore franco-ontarien. Ottawa: Presses de l'Université

d'Ottawa, 1992. x, 230 p.: ill. (Histoire littéraire du Québec et du Canada français ; no 3); ISBN: 2-7603-0340-3.
Note: 895 entrées.– Ouvrages généraux, littérature orale, vie sociale, culture matérielle.– Index: onomastique, toponymique, thématique.
Localisation: OONL.

4612 Steinfirst, Susan
Folklore and folklife: a guide to English-language reference sources. New York: Garland, 1992. 2 vol. (Garland folklore bibliographies ; vol. 16); ISBN: 0-8153-0068-9 (set).
Note: 2,577 entries.– Covers to 1987.– Topics include history of folklore, folk literature, ethnomusicology, folk belief systems, folk ritual, material culture.– Includes a number of Canadian references.
Location: OONL.

4613 Tokaryk, Tim T.; Storer, John E.; Nambudiri, E.M.V.
Selected bibliography of the Cretaceous-Tertiary boundary event, through 1989. Regina: Saskatchewan Museum of Natural History, c1992. 140 p. (Natural history contributions ; no. 11; ISSN: 0707-3887)
Note: 645 entries.– Literature search through 1989.– Articles dealing entirely or in part with the K-T boundary event which marks mass extinction of many species, including dinosaurs, and dramatic climatic changes.– Topics include extraterrestrial impact, flora, dinosaurs, iridium, impact site, magnetic polarity/reversals or stratigraphy, marine regression or transgression, shocked quartz, temperature, volcanism, wildfires.
Location: OONL.

Sciences and Applied Sciences

Sciences et Sciences appliquées

General Sciences

Sciences générales

— 1950 —

4614 **Ontario Research Foundation**
Scientific publications and papers by members of the staff of the Ontario Research Foundation covering the years 1929-1949. Toronto: [s.n., 1950]. 16 p.
Note: Location: OONL.

— 1953 —

4615 **National Research Council Canada. Division of Information Services**
Publications of the National Research Council of Canada, 1918-1952. 3rd ed. Ottawa: [s.n.], 1953. 263 p.
Note: Listing of N.R.C. numbers 1-2900.
Supplements:
... . *Supplement, 1953-1958.* [1959]. 180 p.
... . *Supplement, 1958-1963.* 1964. v, 438 p.
... . *Supplement, 1970-1976/Publications du Conseil national de recherches du Canada, 1970-1976.* Ottawa: Canada Institute for Scientific and Technical Information, 1976. 756 p.; ISSN: 0077-5584.
... . *Supplement, 1977-1981/... , 1977-1981: publications numérotées.* Ottawa: CISTI, 1982. 783 p.; ISSN: 0077-5584.
Location: OON.

— 1955 —

4616 **Besoushko, Wolodmyr; Rudnyckyj, Jaroslav Bohdan**
Publications of Ukrainian Free Academy of Sciences, 1945-1955. Winnipeg: Ukrainian Free Academy of Sciences, 1955. 22 p. (Ukrainian Free Academy of Sciences. Series: UVAN chronicle ; no. 13)
Note: Location: OONL.

4617 **Drolet, Antonio**
"Ouvrages scientifiques de la bibliothèque du Collège des Jésuites de Québec."
Dans: *Naturaliste canadien*; Vol. 82, nos 4-5 (avril-mai 1955) p. 102-107.; ISSN: 0028-0798.
Note: 54 entrées.
Localisation: OONL.

— 1967 —

4618 **Nova Scotia Research Foundation**
Research record, 1947-1967. Halifax, N.S.: Nova Scotia Research Foundation, 1967. 69 p.
Note: 350 entries.– List of publications produced by the Nova Scotia Research Foundation.
Previous edition: ..., *1947-1960.* 63 p.– 258 entries.
Location: OONL.

— 1970 —

4619 **National Science Library (Canada)**
Scientific policy, research and development in Canada: a bibliography/La politique des sciences, la recherche et le développement au Canada: bibliographie. Rev. ed. Ottawa: National Research Council of Canada, 1970. 112 p.
Note: 491 entries.– Covers the period 1935 to June 1970.– Includes reports, periodical articles, government documents, official speeches which discuss science policy and the role of scientific research in Canada.

Previous edition: 1968. 72 l.– 312 entries.
Supplements:
1972. 33 p.
1975. 91 p.
... : *supplement covering period June 1975-June 1977: a bibliography/... : supplément (juin 1975-juin 1977): bibliographie.* 1977. 98 p.
1979. 100 p.
Babbitt, John D. ... : *supplement covering period June 1979-1981/... : supplément (juin 1979-juin 1981).* 1981. 104 p.
Location: OONL.

— 1971 —

4620 **Gagné, Martine P.**
Catalogue de la bibliothèque [Québec Ministère des richesse naturelles]. Québec: Éditeur officiel du Québec, 1971. 338 p.
Note: Approx. 7,000 entrées.– Inventaire sélectif des documents catalogués depuis 1965 jusqu'au mois de février 1971.
Localisation: OONL.

— 1972 —

4621 **Sawchuk, John P.**
A natural resources bibliography for Manitoba. Winnipeg: Manitoba Department of Mines, Resources and Environmental Management, 1972. 1 vol. (in various pagings): map.
Note: Contains listings of published reports dealing with development, use and management of Manitoba natural resources.– Arrangement is by NTS map sheet area, and withing these, by topics: agriculture, fisheries, forestry, geology, hydrology, recreation, socio-economic, wildlife.
Location: OOFF.

— 1973 —

4622 **Saltiel, Marie-Louise**
Référence et bibliographie en sciences pures et appliquées. [Montréal]: Librairie de l'Université de Montréal, 1973. 87 f.
Note: Approx. 700 entrées.
Localisation: OONL.

4623 **Saskatchewan Research Council**
Saskatchewan Research Council reports, 1957-1972. [Saskatoon: The Council], 1973. 30, [7] l.
Note: Listing of approximately 500 reports in the fields of chemistry, engineering, geology, information sciences, physics.– Includes a list of confidential reports.
Location: OONL.

— 1974 —

4624 **Muhammad, A.F.; Jorgensen, E.**
Natural history in the National Capital Region: a bibliography. Ottawa: Forest Management Institute, Canadian Forestry Service, Department of the Environment, 1974. 97 p. (Forest Management Institute Information report ; FMR-X-65)
Note: 799 entries.– Monographs, articles, theses dealing with botany, zoology, environmental biology,

climatology, geology, nature study and appreciation in the Ottawa area.
Location: OONL.

— 1975 —

4625 **Rousseau, Camille; Alexandre, Claude; Labrecque, Olivette**
Répertoire des volumes et des revues accessibles aux jeunes scientifiques. [Montréal]: Conseil de la jeunesse scientifique, 1975. xi, 553 p.
Note: 1,831 entrées.
Localisation: OONL.

— 1980 —

4626 **Jarrell, Richard A.; Roos, Arnold E.**
"Select bibliography of the history of Canadian science, medicine and technology."
In: *Science, technology and Canadian history/Les sciences, la technologie et l'histoire canadienne,* edited by Richard A. Jarrell and Norman R. Ball. Waterloo, Ont.: Wilfrid Laurier University Press, 1980. P. 217-231.; ISBN: 0-88920-086-6.
Note: Approx. 250 entries.– Research tools, general works, sciences, specific technologies, scientific and technical education, scientific and technical institutions, biographical studies, social aspects.– Bibliography compiled to accompany papers of the First Conference on the Study of the History of Canadian Science and Technology, Kingston, Ontario, 1978.
Location: OONL.

— 1983 —

4627 **Jarrell, Richard A.; Roos, Arnold E.**
A bibliography for courses in the history of Canadian science, medicine, and technology. 2nd rev. ed. Thornhill, Ont.: HSTC Publications, 1983. vi, 62 p. (Research tools for the history of Canadian science and technology ; no. 1; ISSN: 0715-9668); ISBN: 0-9690475-2-5.
Note: Approx. 650 entries.– Monographs and articles on history of science and technology in Canada: works on specific branches or disciplines, biographical works, institutional history, educational history, science and technology policy.
Previous edition: 1979. 56, [1] p.
Location: OONL.

— 1984 —

4628 **Canada Institute for Scientific and Technical Information**
Directory of Canadian scientific and technical databases/ Répertoire des bases de données scientifiques et techniques au Canada. Ottawa: National Research Council Canada, 1984. 91, [15] p.
Note: 119 entries.– Information provided includes data type, status, time span covered, growth rate, update frequency, languages, subject coverage, accessibility (hours available, charges, etc.).– Indexes: producers/ maintainers, subject.– Text in English and French/texte en français et en anglais.
Location: OONL.

— 1985 —

4629 **Enros, Philip Charles**
Biobibliography of publishing scientists in Ontario between 1914 and 1939. Thornhill, Ont.: HSTC Publications, c1985. xxxvi, 526 p. (Research tools for the history of Canadian science and technology ; no. 2; ISSN: 0715-9668); ISBN: 0-9690475-3-3.

Note: 1,213 entries.– Includes scientists, including medical and engineering researchers, who studied or worked in Ontario for any length of time between 1914 and 1939, and who published during those years.– Excludes employees of federal government.– Compiled with assistance of Jim Peterson.
Location: OONL.

4630 **Pal, Gabriel**
How to find information on Canadian natural resources: a guide to the literature. Ottawa: Canadian Library Association, 1985. 182 p.; ISBN: 0-88802-178-X.
Note: Approx. 1,400 entries.– Books, articles, scientific studies and reports, maps, theses, films on fish, marine and wildlife resources, water resources, land resources, energy and mineral resources.
Location: OONL.

— 1986 —

4631 **Inuvik Scientific Resource Centre**
Bibliography of research publications, Inuvik Scientific Resource Centre: revised edition, 1964-1985/ Bibliographie des travaux de recherche, Centre de ressources scientifiques d'Inuvik: édition révisée, 1964-1985. Ottawa: Indian and Northern Affairs Canada, 1986. vi, 125 p.
Note: 973 entries.– Journal articles, papers, theses, conference proceedings related to scientific projects assisted or supported by the Inuvik Scientific Resource Centre.– Compiled by David Sherstone.– Text in English and French/texte en français et en anglais.
Previous edition: *Bibliography of research publications ... : 1964-1985.* 1985. 87 p. Compiled by Rachelle Castonguay and David Sherstone.
Location: OONL.

— 1987 —

4632 **Richardson, R. Alan; MacDonald, Bertrum H.**
Science and technology in Canadian history: a bibliography of primary sources to 1914. Thornhill, Ont.: HSTC Publications, c1987. 105 microfiches + 1 pamphlet in loose-leaf binder (17 p.). (Research tools for the history of Canadian science and technology ; no. 3; ISSN: 0715-9668); ISBN: 0-9690475-4-1.
Note: Approx. 58,000 entries.– Includes articles and monographs (including pamphlets) in science, engineering, architecture, technology published by Canadians or about Canada from the sixteenth century to 1914.– Excludes secondary publications (biographies, historical discussions of institutions, branches of science and technology, medicine).– Definition of Canada and Canadian for the purposes of this bibliography are: published/printed in Canada; published/printed outside Canada and written by Canadians; Canadian subject matter published outside Canada.
Location: OONL.
Previous edition: MacDonald, Bertrum H.; Richardson, R. Alan. *Preliminary bibliographical inventory of sources in the history of science, technology and medicine in Canada to the twentieth century.* London, Ont.: Department of History of Medicine and Science, Faculty of Medicine, University of Western Ontario, 1981. xiv, 275, 335 l.
Location: OLU.

— 1989 —

4633 **Hobson, G.D.; Voyce, J.**
Polar Continental Shelf Project: titles and abstracts of

scientific papers supported by PCSP/Étude du plateau continental polaire: titres et résumés scientifiques publiés grâce au soutien de l'ÉPCP. Ottawa: Energy, Mines and Resources Canada, 1971 1989. 8 vol.; ISSN: 0823-3543

Note: Biennial (irregular).– Listing of scientific research papers related to the Canadian Arctic, arranged by discipline, with an author index.

Location: OONL.

— 1991 —

4634 **Laverdière, Richard**
Bibliographie commentée, l'arbre en tête. Québec: Gouvernement du Québec, Ministère des forêts, 1991. 68 p.

Note: Approx. 200 entrées.– Bibliographie commentée pour l'enseignement des sciences de la nature au primaire.

Localisation: OONL.

— Ongoing/En cours —

4635 **Annotated bibliography of publications based on research supported by the Northern Scientific Training Program/Bibliographie annotée des publications fondées sur des recherches par le Programme de formation scientifique dans le Nord.** Ottawa: Northern Affairs Program, Office of the Northern Research and Science Advisor, 1985-. vol.; ISSN: 0837-3019.

Note: Annual listing of scientific papers, seminar or conference presentations, theses, based on projects supported by the Northern Scientific Training Program.– Topics include anthropology and archaeology, biology, geography, zoology, resource management, environmental sciences, earth sciences, sociology.– Arrangement is by university.– Text in English and French/texte en français et en anglais.

Location: OONL.

4636 **"Recent publications récentes."**
In: *Scientia canadensis*; (1984-) vol.; ISSN: 0829-2507.

Note: Regular listing from vol. 8, no. 1 (June 1984).– Listing of monographs and articles in scholarly and popular journals: history of Canadian science and technology, arranged under various topics: agriculture, astronomy, biography, medicine, urban technology, etc.– Additional bibliographies may be found under the heading "Reference."

Location: AEU.

Agricultural Sciences

Agronomie

— 1930 —

4637 **National Research Council Canada**
Review of the literature on apple by-products. Ottawa:
National Research Council Canada, 1930. 33 l.
Note: Includes Canadian references.
Location: OON.

— 1934 —

4638 **Bercaw, Louise O.; Hannay, A.M.; Colvin, Esther M.**
Bibliography on land settlement with particular
reference to small holdings and subsistence homesteads.
Washington: United States Government Printing Office,
1934. iv, 492 p. (United States Department of Agriculture
Miscellaneous publications ; no. 172)
Note: Includes a section on Canada, p. 228-243.
Location: OLU.

— 1942 —

4639 **Fowke, V.C.**
"An introduction to Canadian agricultural history."
In: *Canadian Journal of Economics and Political Science*; Vol.
8, no. 1 (February 1942) p. 56-68.; ISSN: 0315-4890.
Note: Bibliographical paper discusses and lists
monographs and articles concerning Canadian agricultur-
al history.
Location: AEU.

— 1953 —

4640 **Canada. Department of Agriculture. Economics
Division**
A list of published material by members of the
Economics Division, 1930-1953. Ottawa: The Division,
1953. 44 p.
Note: Supplements:
*List of published material, 1930-1956, by members of the
Economics Division.* 1957. 64 p. Compiled by Helen I.
Marquis.
*List of published material, 1957-1962, by members of the
Economics Division.* 1964. 40 p. Compiled by Helen I.
Marquis.
*List of published material, 1963-1967, by members of the
Economics Branch.* 1968. 23, 17 p.
*Publications: a list of material published from 1968-1972, by
members of the Economics Branch.* 1973. 20 p.
Location: NBFU.

— 1956 —

4641 **Dionne, J.L.; Robertson, George W.; Holmes, R.M.**
Agricultural meteorology: a brief literature review &
bibliography. [Ottawa]: Experimental Farms Service,
Canada Department of Agriculture, 1956. 59 p.
Note: 578 entries.– Review of research dealing with
agrometeorology, lists papers according to subject.–
Topics include plants and climate in general, weather
and crop yields, temperature, evaporation, effect of cold,
soil moisture, weather and diseases.
Location: OONL.

— 1957 —

4642 **Monette, René**
"Documentation sur la profession agronomique."
Dans: *Agriculture*; Vol. 14, no 5 (septembre-octobre
1957) p. 162-164.; ISSN: 0002-1687.
Note: Approx. 75 entrées.– Articles et publications
officielles concernant la profession agronomique au
Québec.
Localisation: OONL.

— 1958 —

4643 **Moss, Harold Charles**
A partial bibliography of Saskatchewan soil science, 1921-
1957. Saskatoon: Department of Soil Science, University
of Saskatchewan, 1958. 25 p.
Note: Approx. 250 entries.– Papers, reports, theses from
the Department of Soil Science and the Saskatchewan
Soil Survey.
Supplement: 1964. 7 l.– Covers 1958-1963.
Location: OOFF.

— 1960 —

4644 **Lawson, B.M.**
A review of literature on the problem of blackening in
cooked potatoes. Victoria, B.C.: Department of
Agriculture, [1960]. 6 l.
Note: Location: OONL.

— 1963 —

4645 **Siemens, Leonard Bernard**
Cropping systems: an evaluative review of the literature.
Winnipeg: Faculty of Agriculture and Home Economics,
University of Manitoba, 1963. vii, 89 p. (Technical
bulletin / Faculty of Agriculture and Home Economics,
University of Manitoba ; no. 1)
Note: 89 entries.
Location: OONL.

— 1965 —

4646 **Oliver, Kent D.**
Catalogue of the Buller Memorial Library/Catalogue de
la Bibliothèque commémorative Buller. Ottawa: Research
Branch, Canada Department of Agriculture, 1965. 84 p.:
ill.
Note: Text in English and French/texte en français et en
anglais.
Location: OONL.

— 1966 —

4647 **Anderson, William**
Bibliography of world literature on the strawberry, 1920-
1962. [S.l.: s.n.], 1966. 2 vol.
Note: Location: OONL.

4648 **Canada. Department of Forestry**
The ARDA catalogue [Agricultural Rehabilitation and
Development Administration]. Ottawa: Department of
Forestry, 1965-1966. 3 vol.
Note: Listing of ARDA projects and publications.
Supplement: *The ARDA catalogue [Department of Forestry
and Rural Development].* 1967-1968. 2 vol.

Location: OONL.

4649 Ontario Agricultural College. School of Agricultural Engineering
List of publications (School of Agricultural Engineering, University of Guelph). Guelph, Ont.: School of Agricultural Engineering, University of Guelph, 1966. 9 l.
Note: Listing of technical publications, miscellaneous publications, professional papers produced by the School of Agricultural Engineering at the University of Guelph.
Location: OONL.

— 1971 —

4650 Atkinson, H.J.
A bibliography of Canadian soil science. [Ottawa]: Research Branch, Canada Department of Agriculture, 1971. 303 p. (Canada Department of Agriculture Research Branch Publication ; 1452)
Note: 3,444 entries.– Lists studies carried out on the soils of Canada by Canadian and other scientists and on the soils of other countries by Canadians, published in journals, books, bulletins, theses, 1893 through 1969.
Location: OONL.

— 1972 —

4651 Canada. Department of Agriculture. Engineering Research Service
Bibliography of Canadian development equipment for field plot mechanization and related laboratory work. Ottawa: Engineering Research Service, Canada Department of Agriculture, 1972. 12 p.
Note: Location: OOAG.

4652 Frank, Thomas F.; Tarte, Frank C.
Marketing to farmers: an annotated bibliography. Guelph, Ont.: School of Agricultural Economics and Extension Education, Ontario Agricultural College, University of Guelph, 1972. [43] l.
Note: Location: OONL.

4653 Johansson, T.S.K.; Johansson, M.P.
Apicultural literature published in Canada and the United States. [New York: s.n.], c1972. 103 p.
Note: Approx. 1,300 entries.– Covers 1792 to 1971.– Lists publications by private individuals, beekeeping organizations, business enterprises, government departments and agencies.– Focus on writings directory concerned with honeybee biology and behaviour, technology of beekeeping and products of the hive.– Excludes technical or specialized topics such as pollination.
Location: OONL.

4654 McQuitty, J.B.; Barber, E.M.
An annotated bibliography of farm animal wastes. [Ottawa]: Water Pollution Control Directorate, Environmental Protection Service, 1972. vii, 522, [360] p. (Technical appraisal report / Water Pollution Control Directorate, Environmental Protection Service ; EPS 3-WP-72-1)
Note: 2,352 entries.– Covers the period from 1960 to 1971.– Journal articles, conference proceedings, books and monographs, government, research centre and university publications, unpublished scientific and technical papers, semi-technical publications (farming papers and magazines) pertaining to the subject of farm animal wastes as an environmental problem.
Location: OONL.

4655 Miska, John P.
Animal science [bibliography]. Lethbridge, Alta.: Agriculture Canada Research Station, [1972]. v, 25 l. (Bibliographic series / Canada Department of Agriculture Research Station, Lethbridge, Alberta ; no. 1)
Note: 192 entries.– Scientific and technical papers, bulletins and other departmental publications relating to animal science issued by the Research Station, Lethbridge, between 1906 and 1972.
Location: OONL.

4656 University of Manitoba. Department of Agricultural Economics and Farm Management
Publications of Department of Agricultural Economics and Farm Management, University of Manitoba. Winnipeg: Department of Agricultural Economics and Farm Management, University of Manitoba, 1972. 8 p.
Note: Approx. 85 entries.– Annual reports, bulletins, journal reprints, mimeographed reports, occasional papers/series, research bulletins, research reports, technical bulletins.
Location: OONL.

— 1973 —

4657 Anderson, E. William; Harris, Robert W.
References on grazing resources and associated elements of the Pacific Northwest range ecosystems (Oregon, Washington, British Columbia). [S.l.: Pacific Northwest Section, Society for Range Management, 1973. 103 p.
Note: Four sections: publications on grazing resources of Pacific Northwest; geology, soils, climate; plant identification publications; selected special publications applicable to the Pacific Northwest.
Location: WaU.

4658 Imperial Tobacco Products Limited. Library
Books and periodicals on tobacco: corporate library holdings. Montreal: Imperial Tobacco Products, 1973. ii, 33 l.
Note: Approx. 200 entries.– Books and articles dealing with the history and literature of tobacco, the tobacco industry and smoking, as well as bibliographical and statistical sources.– Includes Canadian references.
Previous edition: 1971. 22 l.
Location: OONL.

4659 Miska, John P.
Crop entomology [bibliography]. Lethbridge, Alta.: Research Station, Canada Department of Agriculture, 1973. v, 34 l. (Bibliographic series / Canada Department of Agriculture Research Station, Lethbridge, Alberta ; no. 4)
Note: 272 entries.– Scientific and technical papers, bulletins and other departmental publications relating to crop entomology issued by the Research Station, Lethbridge, between 1906 and 1972.
Location: OONL.

4660 Miska, John P.
Plant pathology and plant science [bibliography]. Lethbridge, Alta.: Research Station, Canada Department of Agriculture, 1973. vi, 50, ix l. (Bibliographic series / Canada Department of Agriculture Research Station, Lethbridge, Alberta ; no. 2)
Note: 523 entries.– Scientific and technical papers, bulletins and other departmental publications relating to plant pathology and plant science issued by the Research Station, Lethbridge, between 1906 and 1972.

Location: OONL.

4661 **Miska, John P.**
Soil science [bibliography]. Lethbridge, Alta.: Research Station, Canada Department of Agriculture, 1973. v, 35 l. (Bibliographic series / Canada Department of Agriculture Research Station, Lethbridge, Alberta ; no. 3)
Note: 282 entries.– Scientific and technical papers, bulletins and other departmental publications relating to soil science issued by the Research Station, Lethbridge, between 1906-1972.
Location: OONL.

4662 **Miska, John P.**
Veterinary medical entomology [bibliography]. Lethbridge, Alta.: Research Station, Canada Department of Agriculture, 1973. iv, 19 l. (Bibliographic series / Canada Department of Agriculture Research Station, Lethbridge, Alberta ; no. 5)
Note: 134 entries.– Scientific and technical papers, bulletins and other departmental publications relating to veterinary medical entomology issued by the Research Station, Lethbridge, between 1906 and 1972.
Location: OONL.

4663 **Saskatchewan Provincial Library. Bibliographic Services Division**
Gardening: a bibliography. Regina: The Library, 1973. 29 p.
Note: Selective list of books dealing with floriculture, soils, landscape design, nurseries, house plants and indoor gardening, greenhouses, fruit culture.
Location: OONL.

— 1974 —

4664 **Canada. Agriculture Canada. Economics Branch**
A bibliography of Canadian agricultural economics papers/Bibliographie des études canadiennes en économie agricole. Ottawa: Communications Unit, Economics Branch, Agriculture Canada, 1974. 65 p.
Note: Approx. 500 entries.– Federal and provincial government publications, publications of university departments of agricultural economics, journal articles.– Text in English and French/texte en français et en anglais.
Location: OONL.

4665 **Framst, G.E.**
Ontario and national marketing boards: a selected bibliography, 1955-1973. Toronto: Economics Branch, Ontario Ministry of Agriculture and Food, 1974. 4 p.
Note: Location: OONL.

— 1975 —

4666 **Klumph, S.G.; Haberer, A.**
Range: a selected bibliography of research and information. Edmonton: Alberta Department of Energy and Natural Resources, Lands Division, 1975. vii, 201 p.
Note: Approx. 1,800 entries.– Range research projects carried out in Alberta; selected topics relate to livestock production on range or pasture.– Section listing references of similar work conducted outside of Alberta.– Topics include climate, history, economics, hydrology and irrigation, livestock, predators, range, soils and geology, vegetation and wildlife.
Location: OONL.

4667 **Lancaster, John E.; Alexander, Dennis J.**
Newcastle disease virus and spread: a review of some of the literature. Ottawa: Canada Department of Agriculture, 1975. 79 p.: ill., maps (2 folded). (Monograph / Canada Department of Agriculture ; no. 11)
Note: Approx. 450 entries.– Review and bibliographic listing of studies dealing with the Newcastle poultry virus.– International coverage, with some Canadian references.
Location: OONL.

— 1976 —

4668 **Canada. Department of Agriculture. Library**
Chapais collection/Collection Chapais. [Ottawa]: Canada Department of Agriculture, 1976. xxi, 77 p.; ISBN: 0-662-00373-X.
Note: Approx. 800 entries.– Checklist of the collection of agricultural publications and documents developed by Jean-Charles Chapais (father and son): works by nineteenth-century French-Canadian agriculturalists, some works in English, a number of French works dealing with the agricultural sciences.– The collection is now part of the Library of the Department of Agriculture in Ottawa.– Text in English and French/texte en français et en anglais.
Location: OONL.

4669 **Hill, Stuart B., et al.**
Reading references on ecological agriculture: eight annotated bibliographies. [Regina]: University of Regina, 1976. [56] p. (in various pagings).
Note: Approx. 500 entries.– Topics include ecological farming and gardening, composting, soil biology, soil fertility, soils and fertilizers.– Includes Canadian references.
Location: OONL.

— 1977 —

4670 **Durand, Pierre**
"L'étude de l'agriculture québécoise: commentaires et bibliographie."
Dans: *Anthropologie et sociétés*; Vol. 1, no 2 (1977) p. 5-21.; ISSN: 0702-8997.
Note: Revue de la littérature consacrée à la question de l'agriculture québécoise: références théoriques, études.
Localisation: OONL.

4671 **Fuller, Anthony M.; Mage, Julius A.**
A directory of part-time farming studies. Vol. 1: North America and W. Europe. Guelph, Ont.: Department of Geography, University of Guelph, 1977. v, 81 p.
Note: 259 entries.– Covers 1965 to 1977.– Includes 42 annotated entries of works in progress.– Major disciplines (agricultural economics, socio-economic, economics, geography, extension education) applied to study of part-time farming and rural development.
Location: OONL.

4672 **Hill, Stuart B.**
Ecological soil management: an annotated bibliography. [Regina]: University of Regina, 1977. 32 p.
Note: Approx. 250 entries.– Includes Canadian publications dealing with natural fertilizers, mulches, influence of soil conditions on crop quality and animal and human health.
Location: OONL.

4673 **Miska, John P.**
Irrigation. Slough, Eng.: Commonwealth Agricultural Bureaux, 1976-1977. 4 vol.
Note: Vol. 1: *General works*.– 166 entries.
Vol. 2: *Specified methods*.– 195 entries.

Vol. 3: *Soil relations.*– 297 entries.

Vol. 4: *Crop response.*– 617 entries.

Covers 1965-1974.– Some Canadian references.

Location: OONL.

4674 Spector, David

A bibliographic study of field agriculture in the Canadian prairie west 1870-1940. [Ottawa]: National Historic Parks and Sites Branch, Parks Canada, 1977. 35 p. (National Historic Parks and Sites Branch Research bulletin ; no. 46)

Note: Literature review and bibliography: books, articles, theses, archival sources.

Location: OONL.

— 1978 —

4675 Kossatz, V. Christine; Millan, Carol A.

Bibliography of the Northern Research Group. Beaverlodge, Alta.: Agriculture Canada, Research Station, 1978. 48, vii p.: map.

Note: 617 entries.– Scientific papers and miscellaneous publications of the Northern Research Group of the Department of Agriculture, arranged by topics (bees, fertilizers, grasses, northern agriculture, etc.), and alphabetically by author.

Location: OONL.

4676 Miska, John P.

Nitrogen fixation 1970-1975: bibliography. Lethbridge, Alta.: Agriculture Canada Research Station, 1978. 18 l.

Note: 212 entries.

Location: OONL.

4677 Miska, John P.; Ronning, Cheryl

Bibliography of agriculture in northern Canada and the arctic tundra in Alaska, 1950-1970. Lethbridge: Agriculture Canada Research Station, 1978. 11 p.

Note: Location: OONL.

4678 Pal, Gabriel

Annotated bibliography of publications concerning Canada's food growing capacity. [Guelph, Ont.]: University of Guelph, Library, 1978. ii, 8 p. (Bibliography series / University of Guelph Library ; no. 6)

Note: Covers 1970 to 1976.– Includes monographs, magazine articles, maps, atlases relating to assessment of potential agricultural lands in Canada, their extent, location, possible use, problems involved in exploitation.– Also included are publications dealing with potential freshwater and marine resources.– Excludes publications dealing with methods of improving productivity on present agricultural lands.

Location: OONL.

4679 Saskatchewan Provincial Library. Bibliographic Services Division

Organic agriculture: a bibliography. Regina: Saskatchewan Provincial Library, 1978. i, 59 p.

Note: Approx. 500 entries.– Books, documents, periodicals dealing with aspects of organic farming and gardening, including agriculture and chemicals, ecological pest control, food preservation, soil composting, greenhouses, homesteading.

Location: OONL.

4680 Skelton, A.; Le Normand, J.; Ghanimé, Linda

Méthodes de conservation d'énergie dans les serres canadiennes: aperçu général et bibliographie. Ste. Anne de Bellevue, Québec: Institut de recherches Brace, Collège Macdonald de l'Université McGill, 1978. 5 p.

Note: English title: *Methods of energy conservation for Canadian greenhouses: outline and bibliography.*

Localisation: OONL.

4681 Skelton, A.; Le Normand, J.; Ghanimé, Linda

Methods of energy conservation for Canadian greenhouses, outline and bibliography. Ste. Anne de Bellevue, Quebec: Brace Research Institute, Macdonald College of McGill University, 1978. 4 p.

Note: Titre en français: *Méthodes de conservation d'énergie dans les serres canadiennes: aperçu général et bibliographie.*

Location: OONL.

4682 Spector, David

An annotated bibliography for the study of animal husbandry in the Canadian Prairie West, 1880-1925. Ottawa: National Historic Parks and Sites Branch, Indian and Northern Affairs Canada, 1978. 50 p. (National Historic Parks and Sites Branch Research bulletin ; no. 77)

Note: Part A: "Sources available in western Canada and the United States," lists materials related to animal husbandry as a part of mixed farming.– References to ranching are excluded.– Types of material include archival sources, books, articles and pamphlets, articles from contemporary journals, private papers.

Location: QQLA.

4683 Vallentine, John F.

U.S.–Canadian range management, 1935-1977: a selected bibliography on ranges, pastures, wildlife, livestock, and ranching. Phoenix, Ariz.: Oryx Press, 1978. xvii, 337 p.; ISBN: 0-912700-11-4.

Note: Approx. 20,000 entries.– Emphasis on literature dealing with core topics in range management in Canada and United States.– Excludes field day reports, unpublished items, bibliographies lacking substantial content.

Supplement: *U.S.–Canadian range management, 1978-1980: a selected bibliography ....* 1981. xiv, 166 p.; ISBN: 0-912700-96-3.

Location: OONL.

— 1979 —

4684 Bollman, Ray D.

Selected annotated bibliography of research on part-time farming in Canada. Monticello, Ill.: Vance Bibliographies, 1979. 64 p. (Public administration series: Bibliography ; P-262; ISSN: 0193-970X)

Note: 39 entries.

Location: NSHT.

4685 Harding, Howard

Cochliobolus sativus (Ito & Kurib.) Drechsl. ex Dastur (imperfect stage: bipolaris sorokiniana (Sacc. in Sorok.) Shoem.): a bibliography. Saskatoon: Research Station, Research Branch, Agriculture Canada, 1979. ca. 300 p.

Note: 1,988 entries.– Listing of papers dealing with the pathogen C. sativus, a major cause of cereal crop root rot.

Location: OOAG.

4686 Plant Research Institute (Canada). Agrometeorology Section

Selected Canadian agrometeorological publications. Ottawa: Agriculture Canada, [1966-1979]. 93 no.; ISSN: 0715-1772.

Note: Issue for January 1979 includes a cumulation for nos. 1-84 (May 1966-December 1978.

Location: OONL.

— 1980 —

4687 MacPherson, Arlean
Rapeseed and mustard: a selected bibliography. Rev. ed. Winnipeg: Rapeseed Association of Canada, 1980. 150, [28] p. (Publication / Rapeseed Association of Canada ; no. 52)
Note: Previous edition: Saskatoon: Agriculture Canada Research Station, 1978. 1 vol. (unpaged).
Location: OOAG.

4688 McRae, James Duncan
Les effets de l'établissement d'ex-citadins en milieu rural: une rétrospective de la littérature canadienne. [Ottawa]: Direction générale des terres, Environment Canada, 1980. v, 30 p. (Document de travail / Direction générale des terres, Environnement Canada ; no 3)
Note: 144 entrées.– Récentes recherches effectuées sur le repeuplement des zones rurales au pays ainsi que son influence sur les activités rurales et agricoles: effets sur les terres et la productivité agricole, sur les zones de loisirs, les incidences écologiques et les modifications de la structure économique et de la société rurale.
English title: *The influence of exurbanite settlement on rural areas: a review of the Canadian literature.*
Localisation: OONL.

4689 McRae, James Duncan
The influence of exurbanite settlement on rural areas: a review of the Canadian literature. [Ottawa]: Lands Directorate, Environment Canada, 1980. v, 30 p. (Working paper / Lands Directorate, Environment Canada ; no. 3; ISSN: 0712-4473); ISBN: 0-662-11085-4.
Note: Approx. 140 entries.– Lists studies related to effects of migration of urban residents to rural areas: on agricultural land and productivity, amenity lands and ecology, rural economy and society.
Titre en français: *Les effets de l'établissement d'ex-citadins en milieu rural: une rétrospective de la littérature canadienne.*
Location: OONL.

4690 Potter, Kathy
Bibliography of agricultural research in central British Columbia, 1938-1979. Victoria, B.C.: Ministry of Agriculture, 1980. 96 p.
Note: Location: OONL.

— 1981 —

4691 Abouguendia, Z.; Haraldson, J.; Valby, J.
Management and improvement of Saskatchewan rangeland: a selected bibliography. [Saskatoon]: Saskatchewan Research Council, 1981. ii, 80 p. (Saskatchewan Research Council Technical report ; no. 112)
Note: 534 entries.– References dealing mainly with range ecology, management and improvement of Saskatchewan rangeland, with emphasis on applied aspects of range science.
Location: OONL.

4692 Beattie, Kathleen G.; Bond, Wayne K.; Manning, Edward W.
The agricultural use of marginal lands: a review and bibliography. [Ottawa]: Lands Directorate, Environment Canada, 1981. v, 90 p.: ill., maps. (Working paper / Lands Directorate, Environment Canada ; no. 13; ISSN: 0712-4473); ISBN: 0-662-11454-8.
Note: Approx. 150 entries.– Reviews literature and provides annotated bibliography relating to physical,

economic and social factors which create retreating margins and advancing frontiers, conditions of the frontier and margins, socio-economic consequences and role of government.
Titre en français: *L'utilisation agricole des terres marginales: une rétrospective et une bibliographie.*
Location: OONL.

4693 Beattie, Kathleen G.; Bond, Wayne K.; Manning, Edward W.
L'utilisation agricole des terres marginales: une rétrospective et une bibliographie. [Ottawa]: Direction générale des terres, 1981. v, 98 p.: ill., cartes. (Document de travail / Direction générale des terres, Environnement Canada ; no 13); ISBN: 0-662-91113-8.
Note: Approx. 150 entrées.– Liste des études canadiennes sur les limites des marges agricoles, les terres marginales elles-mêmes et les conditions physiques, sociales et économiques qui expliquent le marginalité de ces terres.
English title: *The agricultural use of marginal lands: a review and bibliography.*
Localisation: OONL.

4694 Martel, Yvon
Liste des publications scientifiques, des articles récents de vulgarisation et des projets actuels de recherches/List of scientific publications, recent extension articles and actual research projects. Lennoxville, Québec: Direction générale de la recherche, Agriculture Canada, 1981. 19 p. (Bulletin technique / Station de recherches Lennoxville ; no 1; ISSN: 0319-9681)
Note: Approx. 200 entrées.– Production animale (bovins, moutons, porcs); production végétales et sols.– Texte en français et en anglais/text in English and French.
Localisation: OONL.

— 1982 —

4695 Ontario. Ministry of Agriculture and Food. Library
Bibliography on northern Ontario agriculture. Toronto: The Library, 1982. 4 l. (Ontario Ministry of Agriculture and Food Library Special bibliography ; no. 1)
Note: 35 entries.
Location: OONL.

4696 Shute, J.C.M.
Ghana-Guelph bibliography. [Guelph, Ont.: s.n.], 1982. 20 l.
Note: Approx. 200 entries.– Lists work produced from the Ghana-Guelph Project, an international effort by the University of Ghana and the University of Guelph to address Ghana's agricultural and food problems: theses, publications and presented papers on animal science, crop science, nutrition, agricultural economics, veterinary medicine.
Location: OONL.

4697 Stace-Smith, Richard; Matsumoto, T.
Virus diseases of small fruits: a bibliography, 1979-1981. Vancouver: Agriculture Canada, 1982. 20 p.
Note: 115 entries.– Includes Canadian references.
Previous edition: ... , 1973-1978. 1979. 39 p.
Location: OONL.

— 1983 —

4698 Duval, Raymond, et al.
Impacts de la loi 90, L.R.Q. chap. P-41.1, dans la région de Québec: bibliographie concernant la protection du territoire agricole. Québec: Centre de recherche en aménagement et en développement, Université Laval,

1983. 40 f. (Cahier spécial / Centre de recherche en aménagement et en développement, Université Laval ; no 9)

Note: Approx. 400 entrées.– Articles de périodiques, livres, thèses, publications officielles.– Littérature québécoise et canadienne.– Thèmes: zonage agricole, protection des terres rurales, agriculture québécoise, rente foncière et prix du sol, construction residentielle, frange urbaine et agriculture péri-urbaine, agriculture marginale.

Localisation: OONL.

4699 **Krogman, Ken K.**
Annotated bibliography on soil erosion by wind applicable to southern Alberta. [Edmonton]: Soils Branch, Alberta Agriculture, 1983. 38 p.

Note: 136 entries.– Articles, conference proceedings, government agricultural research studies and reports published between 1920 and 1982 on wind erosion, with focus on southern Alberta.– Topics include processes, prevention, control, cost (aesthetic, agricultural, social).

Location: OONL.

4700 **Mage, Julius A.; Clemenson, Heather; Lee, Grant**
Foreign ownership of farmland in Canada and the United States: legislative controls, literature review and bibliography. Guelph, Ont.: University School of Rural Planning and Development, University of Guelph, 1983. v, 59 l. (Publication (University School of Rural Planning and Development, University of Guelph) ; no. TSR-L10)

Note: Location: OONL.

4701 **Morrison, B.A.; Thuns, A.**
Energy reports (contributions) published by ESRI from 1973 to May 1983/Rapports concernant l'énergie (communication) publié par IRTS de 1973 à mai 1983. Ottawa: Engineering and Statistical Research Institute, Research Branch, Agriculture Canada, 1983. 32 p. (Engineering and Statistical Research Institute Contribution ; no. I-501)

Note: Location: OOAG.

— 1984 —

4702 **Canadian directory of agriculture and food markets information and services.** Ottawa: Agriculture Canada, Market Information Service, 1984. [144] p.

Note: Listing of publications and services provided by governments and industries in Canada, arranged in commodity groups: livestock, poultry, horticulture, dairy, grains and special crops.– Each publication is described, briefly identifying originator, format, frequency, sources, contents.

Location: OONL.

— 1985 —

4703 **Bircham, Paul D.; Bruneau, Hélène C.**
La dégradation des terres agricoles de la prairie canadienne: guide des publications et bibliographie annotée. [Ottawa]: Direction générale des terres, Environnement Canada, 1985. viii, 154 p. (Document de travail / Direction générale des terres, Environnement Canada ; no 37); ISBN: 0-662-93032-0.

Note: 71 entrées.– Livres, rapports et articles concernant la dégradation des terres agricoles de la prairie canadienne: pertes de matériaux, dégradation chimique, dégradation physique, solutions, role de gouvernements.

English title: *Degradation of Canada's prairie agricultural lands: a guide to literature and annotated bibliography.*

Localisation: OONL.

4704 **Bircham, Paul D.; Bruneau, Hélène C.**
Degradation of Canada's prairie agricultural lands: a guide to literature and annotated bibliography. [Ottawa]: Lands Directorate, Environmental Conservation Service, Environment Canada, 1985. viii, 137 p. (Working paper / Lands Directorate, Environment Canada ; no. 37; ISSN: 0712-4473); ISBN: 0-662-13797-3.

Note: 71 entries.– Books, reports, articles related to Canadian prairie agricultural land: loss of soil materials (erosion by water and wind, loss of organic materials and fertility), chemical deterioration, physical deterioration, solutions (erosion prevention, organic soil management, prevention of salinity), roles of governments.

Titre en français: *Le dégradation des terres agricoles de la prairie canadienne: guide des publications et bibliographie annotée.*

Location: OONL.

4705 **Canada. Agriculture Canada. Advisory Committee on Soil Survey**
Bibliography of soil survey and related works in Atlantic Canada/Bibliographie sur l'étude pédologique et oeuvres connexes au Canada atlantique. [Fredericton]: Atlantic Provinces Agricultural Services Coordinating Committee, 1985. v, 35 p.

Note: Approx. 300 entries.– Selected references to literature on soil surveys (by province), soil characterization, technical operations manuals and related information for Atlantic Canada.– Includes published and unpublished material.

Location: OONL.

4706 **Wikeem, Brian M.; Newman, Reg F.; Johnsen, Laila W.**
A bibliography on range, forages and livestock management in British Columbia. Victoria: Research Branch, Ministry of Forests, 1985. ix, 121 p. (Land management report / British Columbia Ministry of Forests ; no. 32; ISSN: 0702-9861); ISBN: 0-7718-8483-4.

Note: 3,868 entries.– Includes literature pertaining to animal husbandry, animal health, agronomy, agricultural engineering, economics and agri-business, ecology of natural ecosystems, and wildlife ecology where range use by domestic livestock and native fauna overlap.

Location: OONL.

— 1986 —

4707 **Sibbald, Ian Ramsay**
The T.M.E. system of feed evaluation: methodology, feed composition data and bibliography. Ottawa: Research Branch, Agriculture Canada, 1986. 114 p. (Technical bulletin / Agriculture Canada, Research Branch ; 1986-4E); ISBN: 0-662-14628-X.

Note: 561 entries.– Research papers and reports on the true metabolizable energy (TME) system of feed evaluation.– Many Canadian references.

Location: OONL.

4708 **Vineland Research Station. Library**
A bibliographic survey of publications of the Vineland Research Station, 1911-1986. Vineland Station, Ont.: Agriculture Canada, Research Branch, [1986]. iv, 79 p.

Note: 976 entries.– Research studies produced by employees of the Vineland Station published in scientific journals, government reports and bulletins.– Topics include acarology, insect pests and pest control, plant diseases, pesticides and chemical compounds.

Location: OONL.

4709 **Wolfe, J.S., et al.**
Farm family financial crisis: annotated bibliography. Guelph, Ont.: University School of Rural Planning and Development, University of Guelph, 1986. ii, 43 p. (University School of Rural Planning and Development technical series ; 129); ISBN: 0-88955-136-7.
Note: Approx. 250 entries.– Lists periodical and newspaper articles on farm management, farm family, economic factors, social supports, unemployment, family violence, role of the church in rural life, women's issues.– Compiled in collaboration with: Ruth Coursey, Michele Kempster, Farjam Masrour.
Location: OONL.

— 1987 —

4710 **Desjardins, Joëlle**
Subventions agricoles, 1980-1987: bibliographie sélective et annotée. Québec: Bibliothèque de l'Assemblée nationale, Division de la référence parlementaire, 1987. 23 p. (Bibliographie / Bibliothèque de l'Assemblée nationale du Québec ; no 13; ISSN: 0836-9100)
Note: 119 entrées.
Localisation: OONL.

4711 **Torn, M.S.; Degrange, J.E.; Shinn, J.H.**
The effects of acidic deposition on Alberta agriculture. Calgary: Acid Deposition Research Program, 1987. xvi, 160 p.; ISBN: 0-921625-10-3.
Note: Approx. 350 entries.– Reviews current literature on the effects of acidic precipitation on agricultural production, with focus on crops, pollutants and processes particularly relevant to Alberta.– Sources for pollutants covered are the petroleum industry and fossil fuel combustion for commercial industry, transportation, urban centres, and power generation.
Location: OONL.

4712 **Vesely, J.A.**
Highlights of research in sheep production in western Canada during the last thirty years. [Ottawa]: Research Branch, Agriculture Canada, 1987. i, 59 p. (Technical bulletin / Research Branch, Agriculture Canada ; 1987-4E; Lethbridge Research Station Contribution ; no. 11); ISBN: 0-662-15323-5.
Note: References dealing with topics of research in sheep breeding and management in western Canada: evaluation of breeds, selection experiments, crossbreeding, assessment of lifetime production, year-round breeding controlled by light.– Summarizes results of research at Manyberries Substation (1956-1970) and Lethbridge Research Station (1970-1986).
Location: OONL.

4713 **Von Baeyer, Edwinna**
L'histoire du jardinage au Canada: bibliographie sélective. Rév. et augm. éd. Ottawa: Direction des lieux et des parcs historiques nationaux, Environnement Canada–Parcs, 1987. 62 p.; ISBN: 0-662-94166-7.
Note: Approx. 1,000 entrées.– La bibliographie est restreinte aux ouvrages qui traitent de l'histoire des jardins crées de toutes pièces au Canada (par opposition aux jardins naturels) publiés avant 1950 et aux écrits contemporains qui portent sur les jardins aménagés avant 1950.
English title: *A selected bibliography for garden history in Canada.*

Édition antérieure: *L'histoire du jardinage au Canada: bibliographie provisoire.* Parcs Canada, Direction des lieux et des parcs historiques nationaux, 1983. 26, 24 p.
Localisation: OONL.

4714 **Von Baeyer, Edwinna**
A selected bibliography for garden history in Canada. Rev. and augm. ed. Ottawa: National Historic Parks and Sites Branch, Environment Canada, c1987. 62 p.; ISBN: 0-662-15269-7.
Note: Approx. 1,000 entries.– Limited to material on the history of designed (versus natural) gardens in Canada published before 1950, as well as contemporary literature on gardens existing before 1950.
Titre en français: *L'histoire du jardinage au Canada: bibliographie sélective.*
Previous edition: *A preliminary bibliography for garden history in Canada.* Parks Canada, National Historic Parks and Sites Branch, 1983. 24, 26 p.
Location: OONL.

— 1988 —

4715 **Morrison, B.A.; Thuns, A.; Feldman, M.**
List of engineering research contract reports under the DREAM, AERD and ERDAF programs of the Research Branch, 1973-1988/Liste des rapports de contrats de recherches techniques réalisés au titre des programmes DREMA, RDGR et RDEAA de la Direction générale de la recherche de 1973-1988. Ottawa: Engineering and Statistical Research Centre, Research Branch, Agriculture Canada, 1988. iv, 179 p.
Note: Text in English and French/texte en français et en anglais.
Location: OON.

— 1989 —

4716 **Bebee, Charles N.**
The protection of ornamental plants, 1979-April 1989: citations from AGRICOLA concerning diseases and other environmental considerations. Beltsville, Md.: United States Department of Agriculture, National Agriculture Library, 1989. 211 p. (Bibliographies and literature of agriculture ; no. 87)
Note: 1,808 entries.– Includes Canadian references.
Location: OOAG.

4717 **Cregier, Sharon E.**
Farm animal ethology: a guide to sources. North York, Ont.: Captus University Publications, 1989. xv, 213 p.; ISBN: 0-921801-40-8.
Note: Bibliography of works dealing with behaviour of five farm animals: horses, cows, sheep, pigs, and fowl.– Some Canadian references.
Location: OONL.

4718 **Kellogg, Catherine**
Speaking of food: an annotated bibliography of resources related to food issues. Toronto: FoodShare Metro Toronto, 1989. [132] p.; ISBN: 0-921030-06-1.
Note: 210 entries.– Books, periodicals, audiovisual materials, journal articles, pamphlets, newsletters related to agricultural policy, food supply, environmental impact, farming, food quality, food trade, hunger and poverty in First World/Third World, local policy/citizen action.
Location: OONL.

4719 **Shurtleff, William; Aoyagi, Akiko**
Bibliography of soya in Canada: 663 references from 1855 to 1989. Lafayette, Calif.: Soyfoods Center, 1989. 112 l.
Note: Location: OONL.

— 1990 —

4720 **Agricultural Energy Centre**
Agricultural Energy Centre bibliography (including videotapes and displays). Guelph, Ont.: The Centre, 1990. 20 l.
Note: Approx. 250 entries.– Studies related to farm energy, alternative fuels, biomass, solar energy, heat pumps, tobacco energy, livestock and poultry production, greenhouse energy.
Location: OONL.

4721 **Nichol, Paul**
A bibliography of agricultural and rural restructuring. Guelph, Ont.: School of Rural Planning and Development, University of Guelph, 1990. 27 p. (Technical study / School of Rural Planning and Development, University of Guelph ; 134); ISBN: 0-88955-203-7.
Note: 44 entries.– While focus is rural Canada, also contains commentaries and analyses from comparative settings, particularly the United States and Europe.– Includes books, briefs, articles, addresses.
Location: OONL.

— 1991 —

4722 **Faminow, Merle Douglas**
Bibliography of red meat research in Canada, 1980 to 1991. Winnipeg: Department of Agricultural Economics and Farm Management, University of Manitoba, 1991. iii, 43 p. (Occasional series / Department of Agricultural Economics and Farm Management, University of Manitoba ; no. 18)
Note: Location: OONL.

— 1992 —

4723 **Gagnon, Solange; Brassard, Hélène**
Répertoire des banques de données agricoles du Québec. Sainte-Foy, Québec: Groupe de gestion et d'économie agricoles, Comité collecte et accès à l'information technico-socio-économique, 1992. 152 f.
Note: Éditions antérieures:
1990. 117 p.; ISBN: 2-551-12460-3.
1989. 88 p.; ISBN: 2-551-12084-5.
Localisation: OONL.

— 1993 —

4724 **Ripley, Diane Lorraine; Rounds, Richard C.**
Rural communication: information and innovation in farming: a literature review. Brandon, Man.: Rural Development Institute, Brandon University, 1993. vii, 65 p.: ill.; ISBN: 1-89539-713-8.
Note: Location: OONL.

— Ongoing/En cours —

4725 **Prairie Agricultural Machinery Institute (Canada)**
Publications [Prairie Agricultural Machinery Institute]. [Humboldt, Sask.]: Prairie Agricultural Machinery Institute, 1979-. vol.; ISSN: 0319-9398.
Note: Location: OONL.

Earth Sciences and Mining

Sciences de la terre et mines

— 1867 —

4726 **Marsh, Othniel Charles**
Catalogue of official reports on geological surveys of the United States and British provinces. [S.l.: s.n.], 1867. 14 p.
Note: Microform: CIHM Microfiche series ; no. 40158; ISBN: 0-665-40158-2. 1 microfiche (10 fr.).
Location: DLC.

— 1879 —

4727 **Prime, Frederick**
A catalogue of official reports upon geological surveys of the United States and territories, and of British North America. Philadelphia: Sherman, 1879. 71 p.
Note: "From Vol. VII, *Transactions of the American Institute of Mining Engineers.*"
Microform: CIHM Microfiche series ; no. 24779; ISBN: 0-665-24779-6. 1 microfiche (49 fr.).
Supplements:
.... *Supplement I.* [Easton, Pa.: 1880]. 13 p.
.... *Supplement II.* [Easton, Pa.: 1881]. 12 p.
Location: OONL.

— 1896 —

4728 **Darton, Nelson Horatio**
Catalogue and index of contributions to North American geology, 1732-1891. Washington: U.S. Government Printing Office, 1896. 1045 p. (United States Geological Survey Bulletin ; no. 127)
Note: Geologic literature published in North America and about North American geology (excepting Greenland and Central America).– Includes many Canadian references.
Microform: CIHM Microfiche series ; no. 05413; ISBN: 0-665-05413-0. 12 microfiches (554 fr.).
Location: SRU.

— 1899 —

4729 **Ami, Henri Marc**
"Progress of geological work in Canada during 1898."
In: *Ottawa Naturalist*; Vol. 13, no. 2 (May 1899) p. 52-55.; ISSN: 0316-4411.
Note: Location: OONL.

4730 **Ami, Henri Marc**
Progress of geological work in Canada during 1898. Ottawa: [s.n.], 1899. 4 p.
Note: Reprint from *The Ottawa Naturalist*, Vol. 13, no. 2 (May 1899) P. 52-55.
Microform: CIHM Microfiche series ; no. 26426; ISBN: 0-665-26426-7. 1 microfiche (7 fr.).
Location: OONL.

— 1900 —

4731 **Ami, Henri Marc**
"Progress of geological work in Canada during 1899."
In: *Canadian Record of Science*; Vol. 8, no. 4 (July 1900) p. 232-246.; ISSN: 0383-0373.
Note: Location: OONL.

4732 **Ami, Henri Marc**
Progress of geological work in Canada during 1899. [Ottawa: s.n.], 1900. 15 p.
Note: Reprint from *The Canadian Record of Science*, Vol. 8, no. 4 (July 1900) P. 232-246.
Microform: CIHM Microfiche series ; no. 60944; ISBN: 0-665-60944-2. 1 microfiche (11 fr.).
Location: OONL.

— 1903 —

4733 **Bell, B.T.A.**
"Transactions of the Canadian Mining Institute: Indices to names of authors and subjects of the papers presented to the Canadian Mining Institute, the Federated Canadian Mining Institute, and the antecedent provincial mining societies, 1891 to 1903."
In: *Journal of the Canadian Mining Institute*; Vol. 6 (1903) p. 489-520.; ISSN: 0368-1688.
Note: Location: OONL.

— 1904 —

4734 **Bell, B.T.A.**
Transactions: indices to names of authors and subjects of the papers presented to the Canadian Mining Institute, and the antecedent provincial mining societies, 1891 to 1903. Ottawa: Orme's Hall, 1904. 31 p.
Note: Location: QMM.

— 1908 —

4735 **Gwillim, J.C.**
"A partial bibliography of publications referring to the geology and mineral industry of Alberta, British Columbia, and the Yukon."
In: *Canadian Mining Journal*; Vol. 29 (1908) p. 210-211, 242-243.; ISSN: 0008-4492.
Note: Location: OON.

— 1909 —

4736 **Ami, Henri Marc**
"Bibliography of Canadian geology and palaeontology."
In: *Proceedings and Transactions of the Royal Society of Canada*; Series 2, vol. 7, section 4 (1901) p. 123-133; series 2, vol. 8, section 4 (1902) p. 169-182; series 2, vol. 9, section 4 (1903) p. 173-188; series 2, vol. 10, section 4 (1904) p. 207-219; series 2, vol. 11, section 4 (1905) p. 127-142; series 2, vol. 12, section 4 (1906) p. 301-326; series 3, vol. 1, section 4 (1907) p. 143-156; series 3, vol. 3, section 4 (1909) p. 191-204.; ISSN: 0316-4616.
Note: Location: AEU.

— 1912 —

4737 **Reinecke, L.**
"Bibliography of Canadian geology for the years 1908 to 1911 (inclusive)."
In: *Proceedings and Transactions of the Royal Society of Canada*; Series 3, vol. 6, section 4 (1912) p. 139-226.; ISSN: 0316-4616.
Note: Location: AEU.

4738 **Malcolm, Wyatt**
"Bibliography of Canadian geology."
In: *Proceedings and Transactions of the Royal Society of Canada*; Series 3, vol. 8, section 4 (1914) p. 287-315, 317-350; series 3, vol. 9, section 4 (1915) p. 279-305; series 3, vol. 10, section 4 (1916) p. 131-168.; ISSN: 0316-4616.
Note: Location: AEU.

— 1937 —

4739 **Vancouver Public Library. Science and Industry Division**
Gold and gold mining in British Columbia. [Vancouver: British Columbia Library Association], 1936-1937. [2], 18 p.
Note: Approx. 150 entries.– Books, periodical and newspaper articles, government documents dealing with gold mining in British Columbia.– Arranged by mining divisions.
Location: BVIPA.

— 1941 —

4740 **Dresser, John A.; Denis, Théophile**
La géologie de Québec/Geology of Quebec. Québec: Paradis, Imprimeur du Roi, 1941. 3 vol.: ill., cartes.
Note: Vol. 1: *Bibliographie et index.*
Supplément: Québec (Province). Département des mines. *La géologie de Québec: bibliographie et index. Supplément, 1937-1949.* 1951. 91 p.
Localisation: NSWA.

— 1948 —

4741 **"Bibliography of Canadian seismology."**
In: *Canadian Geophysical Bulletin*; Vol. 2, no. 2 (April-June 1948) p. 1-12.; ISSN: 0068-8819.
Note: 144 entries.
Location: OON.

4742 **"Bibliography of radioactivity of rocks in Canada."**
In: *Canadian Geophysical Bulletin*; Vol. 2, no. 2 (April-June 1948) p. 13-27.; ISSN: 0068-8819.
Note: 172 entries.
Location: OON.

— 1949 —

4743 **"Bibliography of physical oceanography for Canada."**
In: *Canadian Geophysical Bulletin*; Vol. 3, no. 2 (April-June 1949) p. 11-25.; ISSN: 0068-8819.
Note: 237 entries.
Location: OON.

— 1950 —

4744 **"Bibliography of Canadian geophysics, 1951."**
In: *Canadian Geophysical Bulletin*; Vol. 4, no. 4 (Part 1) (October-December 1950) p. 1-49.; ISSN: 0068-8819.
Note: Location: OON.

4745 **"Canadian bibliography of geodesy."**
In: *Canadian Geophysical Bulletin*; Vol. 4, no. 4 (Part 2) (October-December 1950) p. 1-10.; ISSN: 0068-8819.
Note: 169 entries.
Location: OON.

— 1951 —

4746 **Kerr, Lillian B.**
Bibliography of geology, palaeontology, industrial minerals, and fuels in the post-Cambrian regions of Manitoba to 1950. Winnipeg: Province of Manitoba, Department of Mines and Natural Resources, Mines Branch, 1951. 38 p. (Mines Branch publication / Province of Manitoba, Department of Mines and Natural

Resources ; 51-2)
Note: Approx. 275 entries.
Previous edition: *Bibliography of geology, coal, oil, natural gas and industrial minerals in the post-Cambrian region of southern Manitoba to 1945.* 1949. 25 p.
Location: OONL.

4747 **Milligan, G.C.**
Bibliography of the geology of the Precambrian area of Manitoba to 1950. Winnipeg: Province of Manitoba, Department of Mines and Natural Resources, Mines Branch, 1951. 67 p. (Mines Branch publication / Province of Manitoba, Department of Mines and Natural Resources ; 51-1)
Note: Approx. 450 entries.– Technical studies, theses, journal articles: economic geology, historical geology, mineralogy, petrology, structural geology.
Location: OONL.

— 1954 —

4748 **Lang, A.H.**
A list of publications on prospecting in Canada and related subjects. Ottawa: Department of Mines and Technical Surveys, 1954. ii, 60 p. (Geological Survey of Canada Paper ; 54-1)
Note: Lists general Canadian publications on prospecting, geology, mineralogy, mining regulations; indexes and catalogues to Canadian geological literature; regional sections listing publications on prospecting and geology for particular provinces; sections covering books, articles and reports dealing with particular metals and minerals.– Annotations.
Location: OONL.

— 1956 —

4749 **Canada. Department of Mines and Technical Surveys. Geographical Branch**
Pedogeography of Canada. Rev. ed. Ottawa: [s.n.], 1956. 24 p. (Bibliographical series / Canada Department of Mines and Technical Surveys, Geographical Branch ; no. 12)
Note: Approx. 350 entries.– Lists studies relating to the relationship between the distribution and use of soils and the mapping and evaluation of natural resources.
Previous edition: *Bibliography of pedogeography of Canada.* 1953. 22 p. (Bibliographical series ; no. 12).
Location: OONL.

4750 **Griffith, J.W.**
A bibliography of the occurrence of uranium in Canada and related subjects. Ottawa: [Queen's Printer], 1956. iii l., 34 p. (Geological Survey of Canada Paper ; 56-5)
Note: Approx. 475 entries.– Geological Survey reports, papers from technical journals, provincial government reports, general publications, reports on specific deposits in provinces and territories, specific subjects (age determination, assaying, exploration, mineralogy and geochemistry, health precautions).– Excludes newspaper articles, general geological maps and reports.
Location: OONL.

— 1957 —

4751 **Jaster, Marion C.**
Selected annotated bibliography of high-grade silica of the United States and Canada through December 1954. Washington: United States Government Printing Office, 1957. P. 609-673. (United States Geological Survey Bulletin ; 1019-H)

Note: 282 entries.– References concerned with high-silica raw materials in the U.S. and Canada.– Topics include geology, geographic distribution, physical and chemical properties, mining, processing, utilization.
Extract from U.S. Geological Survey *Bulletin*.
Location: OLU.

4752 **Québec (Province). Ministère des mines**
Liste annotée des publications du Ministère des mines de la province de Québec, 1883-1957. Québec: Imprimeur de la Reine, 1957. 95 p.
Note: Localisation: OONL.

— 1958 —

4753 **Avery, Ruth Butler; Conant, Mary Lou; Weissenborn, Helen F.**
Selected annotated bibliography of asbestos resources in the United States and Canada. Washington: United States Government Printing Office, 1958. P. 817-865. (United States Geological Survey Bulletin ; 1019-L)
Note: 198 entries.– Lists publications on asbestos resources in U.S. and Canada that appeared before January 1956.– Topics include geology, mineralogy, origin of asbestos resources.
Extract from U.S. Geological Survey *Bulletin*.
Location: OLU.

4754 **Canada. Department of Mines and Technical Surveys. Geographical Branch**
Selected bibliography on Canadian permafrost: annotations and abstracts. Ottawa: [Queen's Printer], 1958. 23 p. (Bibliographical series / Canada Department of Mines and Technical Surveys, Geographical Branch ; no. 20)
Note: 102 entries.– Compiled by Frank A. Cook.
Location: OOCC.

4755 **McCrossan, R.G., et al.**
Annotated bibliography of geology of the sedimentary basin of Alberta and of adjacent parts of British Columbia and Northwest Territories, 1845-1955. Calgary: Alberta Society of Petroleum Geologists, 1958. xv, 499 p.: map (folded).
Note: Approx. 1,500 entries.– Though designed primarily to serve needs of the oil industry, includes all geologic subjects, such as vertebrate palaeontology, groundwater and pleistocene geology.– Separate list of masters and doctoral theses from major North American universities.
Location: OONL.

4756 **Pratt, Ethel M.; Cornwall, Henry R.**
Bibliography of nickel. Washington, D.C.: United States Government Printing Office, 1958. P. 755-815. (United States Geological Survey Bulletin ; 1019-K)
Note: "Contains references, to June 1956, on the geology, ore deposits, history, economics, and metallurgy of nickel."- Many Canadian references.
Extract from U.S. Geological Survey *Bulletin*.
Location: OLU.

— 1959 —

4757 **Badone, L.; Spence, N.S.**
Physical metallurgy and uses of gold: bibliography for the ten-year period 1950-1959/Métallurgie physique et usages de l'or: bibliographie pour la décade 1950-1959. Ottawa: Mines Branch, 1959. iii, 86 p. (Information circular / Mines Branch ; 116)
Note: Location: OONL.

4758 **Barry, G.S.**
Bibliography of geology of the Precambrian area of Manitoba, 1950-1957. Winnipeg: Province of Manitoba, Department of Mines and Natural Resources, Mines Branch, 1959. 39 p. (Mines Branch Publication / Province of Manitoba, Department of Mines and Natural Resources ; 57-3)
Note: Approx. 125 entries.
Location: OONL.

4759 **Luttrell, Gwendolyn W.**
Annotated bibliography on the geology of selenium. Washington, D.C.: United States Government Printing Office, 1959. P. 867-972. (United States Geological Survey Bulletin ; 1019-M)
Note: Approx. 400 entries.– Papers on geologic occurrence, mineralogy, geochemistry, metallurgy, analytical procedures, biologic effects, production and uses of selenium.– Some Canadian references.
Extract from U.S. Geological Survey *Bulletin*.
Location: OLU.

4760 **Mills, B.A.**
Bibliography of geology, palaeontology, industrial minerals, and fuels in the post-Cambrian regions of Manitoba, 1950 to 1957. Winnipeg: Province of Manitoba, Department of Mines and Natural Resources, Mines Branch, 1959. 32 p. (Mines Branch Publication / Province of Manitoba, Department of Mines and Natural Resources ; 57-4)
Note: Approx. 200 entries.
Location: OONL.

— 1963 —

4761 **Québec (Province). Service des gîtes minéraux**
Bibliographie annotée sur les minéralisations métalliques dans les Appalaches du Québec: pour accompagner les cartes nos B-790, B-791, B-792. Québec: Le Service, 1963. vi, 106 p.
Note: Localisation: QQLA.

— 1964 —

4762 **Davis, Harry Osmond**
Canadian coal geology: an annotated, toponymic bibliography of Geological Survey of Canada publications, 1845-1962. London, Ont.: University of Western Ontario, 1964. xiv, 277 p.
Note: 1,305 entries.– References arranged by province or territory, and subdivided by coal areas.
Location: OLU.

— 1965 —

4763 **Carrigy, M.A.**
Athabasca oil sands bibliography (1789-1964). Edmonton: Research Council of Alberta, 1965. ix, 91 p. (Research Council of Alberta Preliminary report ; 65-3)
Note: Approx. 450 entries.– Popular and technical publications relating to the Athabasca oil sands area.– Topics include history, geology, properties of oil sands, drilling, mining, recovery methods, refining, economics, utilization, government regulations, news reports.
Previous edition: *Bibliography of the Athabasca oil sands, Alberta*. 1962. ix, 66 p.
Location: OONL.

4764 **Hughes, G.T., et al.**
Bibliography of soil dynamics and soil structure interaction during dynamic or similar loadings. Ottawa: Defence Research Board, Department of National

Defence, 1965. iii, 106 p. (Report / Defence Research Board of Canada ; no. 170)
Note: Location: OON.

4765 **Terasmae, J.**
"A review of palynological studies in eastern Maritime Canada."
In: *Maritime Sediments*; Vol. 1, no. 2 (April 1965) p. 19-22.; ISSN: 0025-3456.
Note: Location: OONL.

— 1966 —

4766 **Bannatyne, Barry B.**
Bibliography of geology, palaeontology, industrial minerals, and fuels in the post-Cambrian regions of Manitoba, 1958 to 1965. Winnipeg: Province of Manitoba, Department of Mines and Natural Resources, Mines Branch, 1966. vii, 37 p. (Mines Branch publication / Province of Manitoba, Department of Mines and Natural Resources ; 66-1)
Note: Approx. 250 entries.
Location: OONL.

— 1967 —

4767 **Quebec (Province). Department of Natural Resources. Mineral Deposits Service**
Annotated bibliography on metallic mineralization in the regions of Noranda, Matagami, Val-d'Or, Chibougamau. Quebec: Geological Services, 1967. xii, 284 p. (Special paper / Quebec Geological Services ; 2)
Note: Approx. 1,400 entries.
Location: OONL.

— 1968 —

4768 **Norris, A.W.; Sanford, B.V.; Bell, R.T.**
Bibliography on Hudson Bay Lowlands. Ottawa: Geological Survey of Canada, 1968. P. 47-118: chart, map. (Geological Survey of Canada Paper ; 67-60)
Note: Compiled in preparation for Operation Winisk, the bibliography deals primarily with geology (bedrock and surficial deposits) of the Hudson Bay Lowlands and peripheral Precambrian terrain.– Includes some references dealing with outliers and larger outcrop belts of Paleozoic age surrounding the Lowlands.
Extract from Geological Survey of Canada *Paper.*
Location: NBFU.

4769 **Québec (Province). Ministère des richesses naturelles**
Liste des documents de levés geophysiques aériens/List of airborne geophysical documents. Québec: Ministère des richesses naturelles, 1968. 49 p.
Note: Texte en français et en anglais/text in English and French.
Localisation: OONL.

4770 **Radziminska-Lasalle, Jolanta; Lasalle, Pierre**
Une bibliographie sur les minéraux lourds/A bibliography of heavy minerals. Québec: Ministère des richesses naturelles du Québec, 1968. 56 p.
Note: Approx. 500 entrées.– Articles parus sur les minéraux lourds, 1913-1967: la séparation, identification et minéralogie, provenance.– Texte en français et en anglais/text in English and French.
Localisation: OONL.

— 1969 —

4771 **Butler, J.; Bartlett, G.**
Bibliography of the geology of Newfoundland and Labrador, 1814 through 1968. St. John's, Nfld.: Department of Mines, Agriculture and Resources, Mineral Resources Division, 1969. 273 p. (Bulletin / Newfoundland Mineral Resources Division ; 38)
Note: Lists reports and studies by government and private organizations and agencies.
Previous editions:
Baird, D.M.; Gillespie, C.R.; McKillip, J.H. *Bibliography of the geology of Newfoundland, 1936-1954; bibliography of the geology of Labrador, 1814-1954.* St. John's, Nfld.: Newfoundland Geological Survey, 1954. 47 p.
Betts, Rachel. *Bibliography of the geology of Newfoundland, 1818-1936.* St. John's, Nfld.: Department of Natural Resources, 1936. 35 p.
Location: OONL.

4772 **"Current bibliography [Sedimentary geology]."**
In: *Maritime Sediments*; (1965-1969) ; ISSN: 0025-3456.
Note: Appears in each issue from vol. 1, no. 2 (April 1965) to vol. 5, no. 2 (August 1969).
"Recently published works pertaining to sedimentary geology in the Maritime regions and environs."- Includes Canadian references.
Location: OONL.

4773 **Job, A.L.**
Transport of solids in pipelines, with special reference to mineral ores, concentrates, and unconsolidated deposits (a literature survey). Ottawa: Department of Energy, Mines and Resources, Mines Branch, 1969. vii, 96 p. (Mines Branch Information circular ; IC 230)
Note: 383 entries.– Literature on application of transport by pipeline: crude oil, natural gas, coal, mineral ores, industrial minerals, wood pulp.– Résumé en français.
Location: OONL.

— 1970 —

4774 **Bannatyne, Barry B.; Zoltai, Stephen C.; Tamplin, Morgan J.**
Annotated bibliography of the Quaternary in Manitoba and the adjacent Lake Agassiz region (including archaeology of Manitoba). Winnipeg: Province of Manitoba, Department of Mines and Natural Resources, Geological Division, 1970. vi, 142 p. (Geological Paper / Province of Manitoba, Department of Mines and Natural Resources, Geological Division ; 2/70)
Note: Part I: "Environmental studies (other than archaeology)." Approx. 500 entries.– Lists published reports and theses concerning groundwater, Pleistocene history, botany/bogs/flora, soils, industrial minerals, fossils, paleoecology of Lake Agassiz region.
Part II: "An annotated bibliography of Manitoba archaeology." Approx. 200 entries.– Includes published works and theses to the end of 1968.
Location: OONL.

— 1971 —

4775 **Hruska, Jan; Burk, C.F.**
Computer-based storage and retrieval of geoscience information: bibliography 1946-69. [Ottawa]: Department of Energy, Mines and Resources, [1971]. v, 52 p.
Note: 336 entries.– Papers dealing with aspects of geoscience information management, use of computers for storage and retrieval of geoscience information, including data, bibliographies, abstracts, indexes, text and graphical representations.
Supplement: Burk, C.F. ... : *bibliography, 1970-1972.* 1973. iii, 38 p.
Location: OONL.

— 1972 —

4776 **Dubois, J.M.M.; Dubois, Lise**
Bibliographie sur les caractéristiques physiques des
Cantons de l'Est, Province de Québec, Canada/
Bibliography on the physical characteristics of the
Eastern Townships of Quebec, Canada. Sherbrooke,
Québec: Laboratoire de géographie physique, Départe-
ment de géographie, Université de Sherbrooke, 1972. 74
f. (Bulletin de recherche / Université de Sherbrooke,
Département de géographie ; no 3; ISSN: 0710-0868)
Note: Approx. 1,800 entrées.– Comprend rapports,
thèses, cartes, articles sur les sujets: topographie,
géologie, mines et gîtes minéraux, géomorphologie,
hydrologie, pédologie.– Section des bibliographies.
Suppléments:
    ... : supplément no 1/... : supplement no. 1. 1972. 64 f.
(Bulletin de recherche ; no 12).
    ... : supplément no 2/... : supplement no. 2. 1975. 102 f.
(Bulletin de recherche ; no 24).
    ... : supplément no 3/... : supplement no. 3. 1976. 66 f.
(Bulletin de recherche ; no 29).
    ... : supplément no 4/... : supplement no. 4. 1979. 107 f.
(Bulletin de recherche ; nos 43-44).
    ... : supplément no 5/... : supplement no. 5. 1981. 93 f.
(Bulletin de recherche ; nos 59-60).
    ... : supplément no 6/... : supplement no. 6. 1983. 37 f.
(Bulletin de recherche ; no 69).
    ... : supplément no 7/... : supplement no. 7. 1988. iv, 168 f.
(Bulletin de recherche ; nos 99-100).
Localisation: OONL.

4777 **Greenwood, Brian; Davidson-Arnott, Robin G.D.**
"Quaternary history and sedimentation: a summary and
select bibliography."
In: *Maritime Sediments*; Vol. 8, no. 3 (December 1972) p.
88-100.; ISSN: 0025-3456.
Note: Location: OONL.

4778 **Mullens, Marjorie C.; Roberts, Albert E.**
Selected annotated bibliography on asphalt-bearing
rocks of the United States and Canada, to 1970.
Washington: U.S. Government Printing Office, 1972. iv,
218 p.: ill. (United States Geological Survey Bulletin ;
1352)
Note: Approx. 600 entries.
Location: OOUM.

4779 **Polis, Michel P.; Yansouni, P.A.**
Bibliographie annotée de la littérature concernant les
processus de broyage. Montréal: École Polytechnique,
Division d'automatique, 1972. 24 f.
Note: 122 entrées.– Liste des publications concernant la
représentation mathématique et la commande
automatique des processus de comminution.
Localisation: OONL.

— 1973 —

4780 **Kupsch, Walter Oscar**
Annotated bibliography of Saskatchewan geology (1823-
1970 incl.). Rev. ed. Regina: Department of Mineral
Resources, Saskatchewan Geological Survey, 1973. xxiii,
421 p.: ill., maps. (Geological Survey report ; no. 9,
revised edition, 1973)
Note: Approx. 3,000 entries.– Books, journal articles,
theses, publications of federal and provincial geological
agencies dealing with economic geology, geochemistry,
geomorphology and physiography, geophysics, glacial

geology, historical geology and stratigraphy,
hydrogeology, mineralogy, paleontology, petrology and
petrography, physical geology, research in geology, soils,
structural geology, topography.
Location: OOU.
Previous editions:
Kupsch, Walter Oscar; Wright, Michael D. *Annotated
bibliography of Saskatchewan geology (1823-1965 incl.).* 1967.
296 p.
*Annotated bibliography of Saskatchewan geology (1823-1958
incl.).* 1959. 198 p.
*Annotated bibliography of Saskatchewan geology 1823-1951
(incl.).* 1952. 106 p.
Supplements:
... , 1959 and 1960. 1961. 55 p.
*Annotated bibliography of Saskatchewan geology (1970-1976
inclusive).* 1979. xxx, 140 p.
Location: OLU.

— 1974 —

4781 **Armstrong, C.**
"Geological and mining index to the Q.C.I."
In: *Charlottes*; Vol. 3 (December 1974) p. 56-57.; ISSN:
0316-6724.
Note: Location: OONL.

4782 **Dionne, Jean-Claude**
Bibliographie annotée sur les aspects géologiques du
glaciel / Annotated bibliography on the geological aspects
of drift ice. Ste-Foy: Centre de recherches forestières des
Laurentides, Ministère de l'environnement, Service
canadien des forêts, 1974. 122 p. (Rapport d'information /
Centre de recherches forestières des Laurentides ; LAU-
X-9; ISSN: 0835-1589)
Note: 470 entrées.– Travaux entièrement ou partielle-
ment consacrés aux aspects géologiques des glaces
flottantes, suivie d'une orientation bibliographique.
Localisation: OONL.

4783 **Katz, Brian J.**
Arctic petroleum transportation bibliography. Winnipeg:
Natural Resource Institute, University of Manitoba, 1974.
v, 123 p.
Note: Approx. 1,000 entries.– Government reports and
hearings, unpublished materials, conference reports,
monographs, journal articles to August 1974.– Material
ranges from socio-political-economic to biological
sciences and engineering, relating to land use, native
land claims, pipeline construction in permafrost areas,
fishery and wildlife disruption, marine oil transportation
and pollution.
Location: OONL.

4784 **Richardson, W. George**
A survey of Canadian mining history. [Montreal]:
Canadian Institute of Mining and Metallurgy, 1974. iii,
115 p. (Special volume / Canadian Institute of Mining
and Metallurgy ; 14)
Note: Approx. 300 entries.– Bibliography, p. 50-115.
Location: OONL.

4785 **Smith, Annette L.**
The effects of effluents from the Canadian petrochemical
industry on aquatic organisms: a literature review.
Winnipeg: Research and Development Directorate,
Freshwater Institute, 1974. vi, 68 [i.e. 72] p. (Fisheries and
Marine Service Technical report ; no. 472; ISSN: 0701-
7626)

Note: Literature review and bibliographical listing describes petrochemical industry in Canada, summary of petrochemical processes, waste sources, treatments, characteristics.– Résumé en français.
Location: OONL.

— 1975 —

4786 **Baragar, W.R.A.**
National report for Canada on volcanology. Ottawa: Energy, Mines and Resources Canada, 1975. 12 p. (Geological Survey of Canada Paper ; 75-37; ISSN: 0068-7650)
Note: Approx. 200 entries.– Overview of volcanological research in Canada with bibliography.
Location: OONL.

4787 **Dionne, Jean-Claude**
"Bibliographie des dictionnaires, lexiques et vocabulaires du domaine des sciences de la terre."
Dans: *Revue de géographie de Montréal*; Vol. 29, no 4 (1975) p. 367-373.; ISSN: 0035-1148.
Note: Approx. 200 entrées.
Localisation: OONL.

4788 **Dufour, Jules**
"Géomorphologie du Saguenay et du Lac Saint-Jean: bibliographie."
Dans: *Protée*; Vol. 4, no 1 (printemps 1975) p. 163-170.; ISSN: 0300-3523.
Note: Localisation: OONL.

4789 **Gregory, Diane J.**
Bibliography of the geology of Nova Scotia. [Halifax]: Nova Scotia Department of Mines, 1975. vii, 237 p.: maps.
Note: 1,559 entries.– Listing of Nova Scotia Department of Mines publications, Geological Survey of Canada publications, Special papers of the Geological Association of Canada, theses, journal articles, reports (published and unpublished), maps.
Location: OONL.

4790 **Pal, Gabriel**
A bibliography of publications concerning proved and potential energy resources in Canada, 1970-1974. [Guelph, Ont.]: University of Guelph, Library, c1975. 22 p. (Bibliography series / University of Guelph Library ; no. 5)
Note: 204 entries.– Monographs, journal articles, government reports and studies on technology, future rate of supply and demand, energy policy relating to coal, petroleum, natural gas, tar sands, hydro, nuclear, geothermal energy, solar and wind energy potential.
Location: OONL.

4791 **Swanick, Eric L.**
The energy situation: crisis and outlook, an introductory non-technical bibliography. Monticello, Ill.: Council of Planning Librarians, 1975. 34 p. (Council of Planning Librarians Exchange bibliography ; 742)
Note: Approx. 500 entries.– Covers 1969 to 1975.– Journal articles, newspaper articles, conference papers.– Focus on non-technical aspects of energy crisis and future possibilities.
Supplement: *Canadian energy crisis: first supplementary bibliography*. 1976. 12 p. (Council of Planning Librarians Exchange bibliography ; 1188).
Location: OONL.

— 1976 —

4792 **Beaupré, Michel; Carpentier, Robert**
Les karsts et les cavernes du Québec: bibliographie inventaire de la littérature spéléologique québécoise, 1822-1975. Montréal: Société québécoise de spéléologie, 1976. 77 f. (Collection "Documents" / Société québécoise de spéléologie)
Note: Approx. 320 entrées.
Localisation: OONL.

4793 **Christie, R.L.**
Publications on the geology of the Arctic islands (District of Franklin) by the Geological Survey of Canada. Rev. ed. Ottawa: Energy, Mines and Resources Canada, 1976. iii, 37 p.: maps. (Geological Survey of Canada Paper ; 76-28; ISSN: 0068-7650)
Note: Listing of publications by officers of the Geological Survey that describe and illustrate the geology of the Canadian Arctic islands and surrounding continental shelves (the District of Franklin): bulletins, memoirs, papers, open file (unedited manuscript reports).
Previous editions:
Information Canada, 1973. iii, 39 p.: maps. (Geological Survey of Canada Paper ; 73-11).
Department of Energy, Mines and Resources, 1971. iii, 21 p.: maps. (Geological Survey of Canada Paper ; 71-10).
Location: OONL.

4794 **Envirocon Ltd.**
Environmental protection in strip mining. Calgary: Envirocon, 1976. 2 vol.
Note: Vol. 2: *Bibliography*. iv, 168 l.– Approx. 130 entries.– Includes journal articles, government documents, conference proceedings from Canada, U.S., Japan, United Kingdom, Yugoslavia.– Detailed annotations.
Location: OOFF.

4795 **Garneau, Denyse**
Selected bibliography on the geology of Canadian deposits and occurrences of uranium and thorium. Ottawa: Geological Survey of Canada, 1976. 41 p. (Geological Survey of Canada Paper ; 75-45; ISSN: 0068-7650)
Note: Approx. 1,000 entries.– Listing of geological and mineralogical references relating to deposits and occurences of uranium and thorium.
Location: OONL.

4796 **Gourd, Benoît-Beaudry**
"Aperçu critique des principaux ouvrages pouvant servir à l'histoire du développement minier de l'Abitibi-Témiscamingue (1910-1950)."
Dans: *Revue d'histoire de l'Amérique française*; Vol. 30, no 1 (juin 1976) p. 99-107.; ISSN: 0035-2357.
Note: Localisation: OONL.

— 1977 —

4797 **Clague, J.J., et al.**
Bibliography of marine geoscience information, Pacific regions of Canada, 1900-1976. [Ottawa]: Energy, Mines and Resources Canada, 1977. 43 p. (Geological Survey of Canada Paper ; 77-22; ISSN: 0068-7650); ISBN: 0-660-00840-8.
Note: Approx. 900 entries.– Published papers, maps, manuscript reports dealing with marine geology, geochemistry, geophysics: mainly studies of Quaternary sediments and the crust beneath the seafloor.– Excludes company reports, abstracts of papers presented orally at

scientific meetings, documents not publicly available.– Inventory area is bounded by the Dixon Entrance on the north, Juan de Fuca Strait on the south, inlets of mainland B.C. and the Fraser Delta on the east.
Location: OONL.

4798 **Fogwill, W.D.; Hawkins, V.**
Bibliography of the geology of Newfoundland and Labrador, 1969 to 1974. St. John's, Nfld.: Mineral Development Division, Department of Mines and Energy, Government of Newfoundland and Labrador, 1977. 258 p.
Note: Approx. 2,600 entries.– Comprehensive listing of geoscience literature concerning the province of Newfoundland and Labrador.
Location: OOCC.

4799 **Hubbard, William F.; Bell, Marcus A.M.**
Reclamation of lands disturbed by mining in mountainous and northern areas: a synoptic bibliography and review relevant to British Columbia and adjacent areas. Victoria: [British Columbia Ministry of Mines and Petroleum Resources, Inspection Branch], 1977. iii, 251 p.
Note: 171 entries.– Covers up to February 28, 1977.– Focus on surface coal mining in British Columbia and reclamation of coal mine wastes in alpine regions.– Topics covered include planning, operation preparation, site preparation, revegetation, site amelioration, site maintenance.– Prepared under contract for British Columbia Ministry of Mines and Petroleum Resources by Biocon Research Limited.
Location: OONL.

4800 **Peterson, Everett B.; Peterson, N. Merle**
Revegetation information applicable to mining sites in northern Canada. Ottawa: Supply and Services Canada, 1977. 405 p.: ill. (Environmental studies ; no. 3); ISBN: 0-662-01036-1.
Note: Approx. 200 entries.– Summarizes published information on revegetation techniques for application to disturbed surfaces created by mining in Yukon and Northwest Territories.– Topics include specific objectives for assisted revegetation, factors limiting revegetation, choice of revegetation species, revegetation methods, timing of revegetation steps, assisted revegetation costs, interactions between animals and assisted revegetation, time scale required for revegetation.
Location: OONL.

4801 **Pilon, C.A.**
Bibliography and index of coal in Saskatchewan and adjoining provinces and states. Saskatoon: Saskatchewan Research Council, 1977. 85 p. (Saskatchewan Research Council Geology Division report ; no. 18)
Note: 1,150 entries.– Reports and articles pertaining to occurrence of deposits, chemical and physical properties, calculation of reserves, geophysical exploration, mining conditions and economics, byproducts, transporting of lignite.
Location: AEU.

4802 **Powell, Wyley L.; Falby, Walter F.**
The Ontario energy catalogue: a directory of who's doing what in energy in Ontario and a bibliography of materials on energy available in Ontario. Toronto: Ontario Library Association, 1977. 170, [24] p.; ISBN: 0-88969-011-1.

Note: Approx. 400 entries.– Books, studies, government reports, conference papers, reference materials (encyclopedias and handbooks, bibliographies, directories), journals, audio-visual materials, databases, 1973 through 1977.– Topics covered include general social issues, technology, fossil fuels, nuclear energy, renewable sources, conversion processes, conservation and energy management.– Bibliography: p. 119-170.
Location: OONL.

— 1978 —

4803 **Alderman, John K.**
Uranium in coal and carbonaceous rocks in the United States and Canada: an annotated bibliography. Morgantown, W.Va.: West Virginia University, 1978. 21 p.
Note: 63 entries.– Papers and articles dealing with the association of uranium with coal or carbonaceous rocks.– Topics range from reconnaissance surveys to geochemistry of uranium emplacement in coal.– Chronological arrangement, from 1923 to 1977.
Location: OON.

4804 **Argue, Robert**
Renewable energy resources: a guide to the literature. Ottawa: Renewable Energy Resource Branch, Department of Energy, Mines and Resources, c1978. 29 p.; ISBN: 0-662-00980-0.
Note: Approx. 120 entries.– Includes books, reports, papers on solar heating, wind power, biomass energy, hydroelectric power, tidal power, geothermal energy, photovoltaics.
Location: OONL.

4805 **Bradford, Martin R.**
An annotated bibliographic and geographic review of Pleistocene and Quaternary dinoflagellates[sic] cysts and acritarchs. Calgary: Shell Canada Resources, 1978. 191 p. (American Association of Stratigraphic Palynologists Contribution series ; no. 6)
Note: Approx. 220 entries.– Indexed and arranged in four main divisions: marine dinoflagellate cysts, calcareous dinoflagellate cysts, marine acritarchs, freshwater dinoflagellate cysts and acritarchs, with author/species description and species/geographic locations.
Location: AEU.

4806 **Energy information index, 1978/Répertoire de renseignements sur l'énergie, 1978.** [Ottawa]: Energy, Mines and Resources Canada, c1978. 111 p. (Energy index series ; 78-1); ISBN: 0-662-01308-5.
Note: 363 entries.– Contains selected titles and subject index of general publications, reports, pamphlets, speeches, statements and news releases on energy, including nuclear energy, available from EMR and Crown companies and boards reporting to the Minister of Energy, Mines and Resources, 1974-1977.– Text in English and French/texte en français et en anglais.
Location: OONL.

4807 **Mann, Donald; Coakley, John Phillip**
An annotated bibliography of the geology and geomorphology of the Rondeau Peninsula and environs. [Waterloo, Ont.]: University of Waterloo, Department of Geography; Burlington, Ont.: Canada Centre for Inland Waters, Hydraulics Research Division, 1978. iii, 90 l.: map.

Note: Compilation of literature, illustrations, maps, databases on geology, geomorphology, physical geography of the Rondeau peninsula, Rondeau Bay, shoreline west to Port Crewe and east to Port Glasgow.
Location: OOFF.

4808 **Robertson, Paul B.**
Bibliography of Canadian meteorite impact sites. Ottawa: Earth Physics Branch, Department of Energy, Mines and Resources, 1978. [28] p.
Note: Approx. 375 entries.
Location: OONL.

4809 **Spratt, Albert A.**
"Efficient energy use: alternative energy sources: a bibliography."
In: *Ontario Library Review*; Vol. 62, no. 1 (March 1978) p. 28-33.; ISSN: 0030-2996.
Note: Location: OONL.

4810 **Stephenson, Robert, et al.**
Sudbury mining area: a selected bibliography. [Sudbury, Ont.]: Department of History, Laurentian University, [1978]. 29 p.
Note: 425 entries.– Compiled as part of a Young Canada Works Project, named "Inventory and Guide to Mining Sites in the Sudbury Region."- Primary sources (government documents, reports of professional associations, books), magazine articles, newspaper articles, theses, pamphlets pertaining to the mining industry and the history of Sudbury and region.
Location: OONL.

4811 **Yundt, S.E.; Booth, G.D.**
Bibliography: rehabilitation of pits, quarries, and other surface-mined lands. Toronto: Ontario Ministry of Natural Resources, 1978. vii, 27 p. (Ontario Geological Survey Miscellaneous paper ; 76; ISSN: 0704-2752)
Note: Location: OOFF.

— 1979 —

4812 **Parker, James McPherson**
Athabasca Oil Sands historical research project. Edmonton: Alberta Oil Sands Environmental Research Program, 1979. 3 vol.: ill., maps.
Note: Vol. 2: *Bibliography of published sources.* vii, 66 p. Approx. 2,000 entries.– Survey of published books, articles, and significant newspaper accounts: bibliographies, native peoples, fur trade, missionaries, travellers' accounts, transportation, settlement, oil sands scenarios, natural environment, trapping and fishing, Peace-Athabasca Delta Project, Mid-Canada development corridor.
Vol. 3: *Bibliography of government publications and primary sources.* xii, 165 p. Approx. 1,500 entries.– Arranged in two sections: "Government publications" (Canada Sessional papers, Alberta documents); "Primary documents" (Alberta Provincial Archives, University of Alberta, Glenbow-Alberta Institute Archives, Public Archives of Canada, theses).
Location: OONL.

— 1980 —

4813 **Andrews, Martha; Andrews, John T.**
Baffin Island Quaternary environments: an annotated bibliography. Boulder, Colo.: Institute of Arctic and Alpine Research, University of Colorado, 1980. xi, 123 p.: maps.
Note: 464 entries.– List of papers and theses on Quatern-

ary environment of Baffin Island.– Expeditions, field and reconnaissance reports dealing with bedrock geology, weathering and soils, geomorphology, climate and sea ice, climate change, glacial geology, marine geology, lichenometry, radiocarbon dating and holocene events.
Location: OOFF.

4814 **Armstrong, Jim**
The Canadian energy bibliography. Toronto: Ontario Library Association, 1980. xiv, 146 p.; ISBN: 0-88969-017-0.
Note: Approx. 600 entries.– Books, journals, journal articles, government reports, conference proceedings, reference works, databases, films, videotapes dealing with energy conservation and management, nuclear energy, conventional sources of energy, renewable sources of energy, planning and policy, social and political issues.– Compiled with the assistance of Glenn Garwood and Joyce Dinsmore.
Location: OONL.

4815 **Audet, Clément; Lacas, Robert**
Inventaire des travaux québécois de recherche et développement en énergie dans les universités, les sociétés d'état, les industries manufacturières. Sainte-Foy, Québec: Centre de recherche industrielle du Québec, 1980. 357 p.
Note: Localisation: OON.

4816 **Cameron, Neville S.C.**
The role of organic compounds in salinization of Plains coal mining sites: a literature review. Edmonton: Reclamation Research Technical Advisory Committee, Alberta Land Conservation & Reclamation Council, 1980. viii, 46 p.: ill. (Report / Reclamation Research Technical Advisory Committee, Alberta Land Conservation & Reclamation Council ; no. 80-3)
Note: Location: OONL.

4817 **Oil and gas technical reports, 1920-1980/Rapports techniques concernant la prospection petrolière et gazière, 1920-1980.** Ottawa: Indian and Northern Affairs Canada, 1980. 100 p.; ISBN: 0-662-51196-4.
Note: Approx. 1,500 entries.– Geological and geophysical reports for areas of the Yukon and Northwest Territories: Liard, Eagle Plain, Peel Plateau, Mackenzie Delta, Great Bear Plain, Great Slave Plain, Beaufort Sea, Arctic Lowlands, Arctic Islands, Baffin Bay/Davis Strait.
Previous edition: ..., *1921-1978.* 1978. 69 p.; ISBN: 0-662-10346-7.
Location: OONL.

4818 **Sanford, Cheryl**
A bibliography of the Athabasca oil sands Fort McMurray, Alberta area: socio-economic and environmental studies, 1980 cumulated update. Edmonton: Alberta Department of the Environment, 1980. 341 p.
Note: Reports, studies, papers, journal articles, maps relating to historical background, archaeology, geology, economy, social conditions, native peoples, community and regional planning, environmental topics (ecology, hydrology, soils, wildlife, pollution, climatology, mining) for the Athabasca oil sands region of Alberta.
Previous editions:
Moysa, Susan; Rost, Betty. ... , *1979 cumulated update.* 1979. 221 p.
Rost, Betty. ... , *1976 cumulated update.* 1977. vi, 121 p.
Moysa, Susan; Rost, Betty. ... , *1975 cumulated update.*

1976. vi, 93 p.
Supplements:
Sanford, Cheryl. ... , *1981 supplement*. 1981. 157 p.
Bramm, Susan. ... , *1982 supplement*. 1982. 236 p.
Location: OON.

4819 **Sangster, D.F.**
Bibliography of stratabound sulphide deposits of the
Caledonian-Appalachian orogen. Ottawa: Geological
Survey of Canada, 1980. 53 p. (Geological Survey of
Canada Paper ; 79-27; ISSN: 0068-7650); ISBN: 0-660-
10528-4.
Note: Approx. 1,100 entries.– Canadian contribution to
the International Geological Correlation Program,
established to promote geological research projects of
international scope.
Location: OONL.

— 1981 —

4820 **Kupsch, Walter Oscar**
"Nineteenth century geological writings and writers on
the Canadian Arctic."
In: *Musk-ox*; No. 28 (1981) p. 65-78.; ISSN: 0077-2542.
Note: Two listings: author list, with papers in
chronological order; subject list of these writers, with
biographical sketch and published biographical works.–
Topics covered include economic geology, historical
geology, mineralogy, palaeontology, petrology,
physiographic geology.
Supplement: "Further nineteenth century geological
writings on the Canadian Arctic". No. 30 (Summer 1982)
P. 72-73.
Location: AEU.

4821 **Leidemer, Nelle L.**
Geology of Halifax County: a selective bibliography. 2nd
ed. Halifax, N.S.: University Libraries; School of Library
Service, Dalhousie University, 1981. 60 p. (Occasional
papers / Dalhousie University Libraries and Dalhousie
University School of Library Service ; no. 5; ISSN: 0318-
7403); ISBN: 0-7703-0142-8.
Note: 495 entries.– List of monographs, theses, articles,
government publications, maps published between 1829
and 1981.
Location: OONL.

4822 **Olson, J.C.**
"Bibliography of oil sands, heavy oils, and natural
asphalts."
In: *The future of heavy crude oils and tar sands*, edited by
R.F. Meyer and C.T. Steele. New York: McGraw-Hill,
c1981. P. 855-897.; ISBN: 0-7-0606650-9.
Note: Retrospective survey of the literature on oil sands,
heavy oils, and natural asphalts for the years 1900 to
1979.– Papers cover geology, occurrence, resources,
reserves, composition, geochemistry, exploration and
development, recovery.– Excludes refining and utilization.– Section on Canada, p. 863-879.
Location: OONL.

— 1982 —

4823 **Alexander, Anne**
Newfoundland offshore oil and gas exploration and
development: a bibliography. St. Johns, Nfld.: Memorial
University of Newfoundland, Centre for Newfoundland
Studies, 1982. 9 p.
Note: Supplements:
1984. 10 p.

1986. 18 l.
Location: OONL.

4824 **Briggs, W.E., et al.**
Dielectric properties of Albert County oil shale.
Fredericton: New Brunswick Department of Natural
Resources, Minerals and Energy Division, 1982. 37 p.
(Open file report / New Brunswick Department of
Natural Resources, Minerals and Energy Division ; 82-18;
ISSN: 0712-4562)
Note: Appendix II: "Oil shale bibliography."
Location: OONL.

4825 **Cherry, M.E., et al.**
Gold: selected references. Toronto: Ontario Geological
Survey, 1982. v, 69 p. (Ontario Geological Survey Open
file report ; 5382)
Note: Approx. 250 entries.– Studies of geology and
genesis of gold deposits.
Location: OONL.

4826 **Cowell, Daryl William**
Earth sciences of the Hudson Bay Lowland: literature
review and annotated bibliography. Burlington, Ont.:
Lands Directorate, Environment Canada, 1982. xii, 309 p.
(Working paper / Lands Directorate, Environment
Canada ; no. 18; ISSN: 0712-4473); ISBN: 0-662-11539-2.
Note: 244 entries.– Papers related to aspects of bedrock
and economic geology of the Hudson Bay Lowland.–
Topics include glaciation, surficial geology, glacio-
isostacy, physiography, permafrost, soils,
geomorphology.
Location: OOFF.

4827 **Hawkes, Herbert Edwin**
Exploration geochemistry bibliography to January 1981.
Rexdale, Ont.: Association of Exploration Geochemists,
c1982. xi, 388 p. (Association of Exploration Geochemists
Special volume ; no. 11); ISBN: 0-9691014-1-4.
Note: Approx. 6,000 entries.– Principal theme focusses
on application of systematic measurement of chemical
properties of naturally occurring material to exploration
for deposits of solid minerals.
Previous edition: ... : *bibliography, period January 1965 to
December 1971*. 1972. v, 118 p. (Association of Exploration
Geochemists Special volume ; no. 1).
Supplements:
... : *bibliography, period January 1972 to December 1975*.
1976. v, 195 p.
Location: OONL.
*Exploration geochemistry bibliography: January 1981 to
October 1984*. Rexdale, Ont.: Association of Exploration
Geochemists, c1985. iv, 174 p.; ISBN: 0-9691014-2-2.
Location (1985 supplement): SSU.

4828 **Kent, Thomas D.**
Mackenzie Mountains region bibliography. Ottawa:
Environment Canada, Lands Directorate, 1982. 1 vol. (in
various pagings): maps.
Note: Approx. 250 entries.– Papers dealing with environ-
mental impact, geomorphology, geology, surficial
geology, wildlife, vegetation.– Listing compiled for the
Mackenzie Mountains Region Baseline Study.
Location: OOFF.

4829 **Moore, R.S.**
Beneficiation techniques applicable to Nova Scotian
coals: a literature review. Halifax: Atlantic Research
Laboratory, National Research Council Canada, 1982. 29,

30 p. (Atlantic Research Laboratory Technical report ; 39)

Note: 297 entries.– Books, major reports, articles, published searches, product literature, proceedings, personal communications in both hard copy and microfiche dealing with test facilities, process monitoring and control, timing considerations, cost and process modelling: physical techniques and chemical cleaning techniques.

Location: OON.

4830 **Powter, Christopher Barrett**
A bibliography of baseline studies in Alberta: soils, geology, hydrogeology, groundwater. Edmonton: Alberta Department of the Environment, Research Management Division, [1982]. xvii, 97 p. (Reclamation Research Technical Advisory Committee report ; no. 82-2)

Note: Approx. 600 entries.– Scientific references related to Alberta geology, soils, hydrogeology, groundwater and groundwater supply.– Within these broad categories, the material is arranged by geographic locations.

Location: OONL.

— 1983 —

4831 **Boirat, Jean-Michel**
"Le district à amas sulfurés polymétalliques de Bathurst-Newcastle (New-Brunswick, Canada) dans son environnement géotectonique: étude bibliographique."
Dans: *Chronique de la recherche minière*; No 473 (décembre 1983) p. 3-24.; ISSN: 0182-564X.

Note: Localisation: OOG.

4832 **Burr, S.V.**
The ten-year history and index of the Ontario Mineral Exploration Assistance Program (MEAP) 1971-1981. Toronto: Ontario Ministry of Natural Resources, 1983. v, 196 p.: ill., maps. (Ontario Geological Survey Miscellaneous paper ; 108; ISSN: 0704-2752); ISBN: 0-7743-8016-0.

Note: Index and listing of technical reports filed with the Ontario Mineral Exploration Assistance Program.

Location: OONL.

4833 **A general bibliography of the Lancaster Sound-Baffin Bay region: comprised of citations and abstracts of research documents in the public domain at the Arctic Institute of North America.** Calgary: Consolidex Magnorth Oakwood Joint Venture, 1983. xxviii, 207 p.

Note: Approx. 520 entries.– Prepared through the Arctic Science and Technology Information System, Arctic Institute of North America, at the request of the Consolidex Magnorth Oakwood Joint Venture in consultation with Pallister Resource Management Ltd.– Subjects include geology, geography, cartography, oceanography, ice, zoology, ecology, petroleum and gas pipelines, native peoples.

Location: OONL.

4834 **Holway, Debra; Fournier, Sandy**
A bibliography of Whitehorse Copper Belt material in the Yukon Archives. [Whitehorse]: Yukon Archives, c1983. [62] p.; ISBN: 1-55018-035-5.

Note: Listing of books, pamphlets, periodical articles, maps, government records, manuscripts and photographs relating to the history, geology, mineral developments and production, mining techniques, miners, geologists connected with the Whitehorse Copper Belt in the Yukon River valley.

Location: OONL.

4835 **Offshore Safety Task Force**
Offshore Safety Task Force report to the EPOA:APOA Safety Committee: selected references. Calgary: Eastcoast Petroleum Operators' Association, 1983. 74 p.

Note: Location: OONL.

4836 **Québec (Province). Ministère de l'énergie et des ressources. Direction générale de l'exploration géologique et minérale**
Catalogue du fichier géologique. Québec: Ministère de l'énergie et des ressources, Service des publications géologiques, 1983. v, 143 p.

Note: Approx. 1,000 entrées.

Localisation: OONL.

4837 **University of Calgary. Gallagher Library of Geology**
Selective bibliography of materials relating to the geology of Calgary, Alberta and vicinity. Rev. ed. Calgary: Gallagher Library of Geology, University of Calgary, 1983. 8 p.

Note: Approx. 80 entries.– Publications from the Alberta Society of Petroleum Geologists, Canadian Society of Petroleum Geologists, theses, articles from geological journals, Alberta Research Council publications.– Prepared by Yvonne Hinks with assistance of Moyra Mackinnon.

Previous edition: 1977. 5 p. Prepared by Elaine Bouey.

Location: OONL.

— 1984 —

4838 **Canada Oil and Gas Administration**
Released geophysical and geological reports, Canada lands/Divulgation des rapports géophysiques et géologiques, des terres du Canada. Ottawa: Canada Oil and Gas Administration, 1984. 131 p.: ill., maps.

Note: Contains listings of geophysical and geological reports which have been released in accordance with provisions of *Canada Oil and Gas Act*.– Text in English and French/texte en français et en anglais.

Location: OONL.

4839 **Dartmouth Regional Library**
Oil: gas bibliography. Dartmouth, N.S.: Dartmouth Regional Library, 1984. 20 l.

Note: Approx. 150 entries.– Publications dealing with the petroleum and natural gas industries, with the focus on the Atlantic region and offshore development.

Location: OONL.

4840 **Mortsch, Linda D.; Kalnins, Ingrid I.**
Bibliography pertinent to offshore energy exploration and development/Bibliographie concernant l'exploitation et la mise en valeur des ressources énergétiques en mer. Downsview, Ont.: Environment Canada, Atmospheric Environment Service, 1984. iv, 102 p.

Note: Approx. 850 entries.– Covers the period 1965 to 1983.– Organized into 17 major subject areas.– Topics include climatology, offshore industrial activities, atmospheric pressure, cyclones and anticyclones, winds, fog, clouds, humidity, precipitation, ice, waves, oil spills.– Text in English and French/texte en français et en anglais.

Location: OONL.

— 1985 —

4841 **Adams, John**
Canadian crustal stress data: a compilation to 1985. Ottawa: Division of Seismology and Geomagnetism,

Earth Physics Branch, Energy, Mines and Resources Canada, 1985. 16, [63] l.: ill., maps. (Earth Physics Branch Open file ; no. 85-31)

Note: 822 entries.

Location: OON.

4842 **Collins, Jim; Webb, Janis**
Update of *A peat research directory for Canada*. Ottawa: National Research Council Canada, Peat Energy Program, 1985. vi, 381 p.

Note: Contains project data sheets describing peat research, list of theses on peat in Canada, list of federally-funded peat research projects at Canadian universities, bibliography of about 650 references on the peat resource: mining, environmental aspects, dewatering, product development and standards, peatland transport, technical and economic studies.

Previous edition: *A peat research directory for Canada*. 1982. i, 200 p.

Location: OONL.

4843 **Goodwin, C. Ross; Finley, Jean C.; Howard, Lynne M.**
Ice scour bibliography. [Ottawa]: Environmental Studies Revolving Funds, 1985. xi, 99 p. (Environmental Studies Revolving Funds report ; no. 010); ISBN: 0-920783-09-0.

Note: 379 entries.– Documents in ASTIS (Arctic Science and Technology Information System) database on "disturbance of bottom sediments of water-body by floating ice," ice scour in oceans and lakes. Documents from Scandinavia and Soviet Union are included.– Introduction in English and French/Introduction en français et en anglais.

Location: OONL.

4844 **Maerz, Norbert H.; Smalley, Ian J.**
The nature and properties of very sensitive clays: a descriptive bibliography. Waterloo, Ont.: University of Waterloo Library, 1985. x, 135 p.: ill. (University of Waterloo Library bibliography ; no. 12; ISSN: 0829-948X); ISBN: 0-920834-36-1.

Note: Approx. 120 entries.– Selective listing of sensitive clay literature which appeared between about 1930 and 1985.– Sensitivity in soils or sediments is defined in terms of the ratio of the undisturbed strength to the disturbed or remoulded strength.

Location: OONL.

4845 **Minion, Robin**
Offshore development in northern Canada and Alaska. Edmonton: Boreal Institute for Northern Studies, University of Alberta, 1985. 83 p. (Boreal Institute for Northern Studies Bibliographic series ; no. 14; ISSN: 0824-8192); ISBN: 0-919058-48-5.

Note: 201 entries.– Monographs, theses, government documents, atlases, consultants' reports, annual reports, conference proceedings.– BINS series produced monthly from January 1984 to May 1986 (no. 29).– Online access: *Boreal Northern Titles (BNT)*, available through QL Systems Limited.

Location: OONL.

4846 **Moore, Kathryn E.; Curtis, Fred A.**
"Environmental management for pits and quarries: an annotated bibliography."
In: *CIM Bulletin*; Vol. 78, no. 879 (July 1985) p. 78-82.; ISSN: 0317-0926.

Note: List of selected articles on surface mining for mineral aggregates with emphasis on Ontario

experience.

Location: OONL.

4847 **Sanmugasunderam, V.; Brassinga, R.D.; Fulford, G.D.**
Biodegradation of silicate and aluminosilicate minerals: a literature review. Ottawa: Mineral Sciences Laboratories, 1985. ii, 33 l.: ill.

Note: Location: OONL.

— 1986 —

4848 **Canada. Department of Indian Affairs and Northern Development. Northern Regulatory Review**
Some references relevant to regulation of industrial activity in the Canadian north, 1983 to 1986. [Ottawa]: The Review, 1986. 26, 10, 40, 35 l.

Note: Approx. 225 entries.– Lists books, federal and provincial government reports, journal and newspaper articles, university research studies on subject of regulation of mining and petroleum industries.

Location: OONL.

4849 **Cavanagh, Joan**
Federal energy R&D task 6: oil, gas & electricity: bibliography 1975-1986/R-D énergétique du gouvernement fédéral activité 6: pétrole, gaz et électricité: bibliographie 1975-1986. [Ottawa]: Office of Energy Research and Development, Energy, Mines and Resources Canada, 1986. xiii, 148 p.; ISBN: 0-662-54699-7.

Note: Approx. 1,400 entries.– Lists reports produced from the eight programs funded by the federal Panel on Energy R&D which comprise PERD Task 6: Oil, Gas, Electricity.– Topics include geoscientific research, marine engineering, offshore geotechnics, enhanced oil recovery, materials for offshore structures, transportation of oil and gas, and environmental impact.– Text in English and French/texte en français et en anglais.

Location: OOFF.

4850 **Fricker, Aubrey; Samson, A.L.**
Bibliography of publications by staff of the Atlantic Geoscience Centre to December 1984. Dartmouth, N.S.: Fisheries and Oceans, 1986. v, 326 p. (Canadian data report of hydrography and ocean sciences ; no. 48; ISSN: 0711-6721)

Note: 1,604 entries.

Location: OOP.

4851 **Grenier, M.G.; Butler, K.C.**
Index of underground-environment dust reports: CANMET-Mining Research Laboratories, 1960-1985/ Liste de rapports sur la poussière en milieu souterrain: CANMET-Laboratoires de recherche minière, 1960-1985. Ottawa: Canada Centre for Mineral and Energy Technology, Energy, Mines and Resources Canada, 1986. vii, 13 p. (CANMET Special publication / Canada Centre for Mineral and Energy Technology ; SP 86-4); ISBN: 0-660-12240-5.

Note: 123 entries.– Reports prepared by staff of Mining Research Laboratory.– Topics include instrument design and calibration, results of underground dust surveys, dust measurement techniques.– Text in English and French/texte en français et en anglais.

Location: OONL.

4852 **Jakubick, A.T.; Church, W.**
Oklo natural reactors: geological and geochemical conditions: a review. Ottawa: Atomic Energy Control Board, 1986. ii, 53 p.

Note: Lists published and unpublished material on

natural reactors (precambrian nuclear fission reactions) evaluated with regard to long-term aspects of nuclear waste disposal.– Sections include geology and tectonics, petrology and mineralogy, nuclear geologic parameters, migration/retention.– Résumé en français.
Location: OONL.

4853 **Krause, F.F.; Collins, H.N.; French, R.**
Bibliography of geological and engineering studies of the Cardium Formation and its hydrocarbon reservoirs. Calgary: Petroleum Recovery Institute, 1986. 1 vol. (loose-leaf).
Note: Location: ACU.

4854 **Sangster, D.F.**
Classification, distribution, and grade-tonnage summaries of Canadian lead-zinc deposits. Ottawa: Geological Survey of Canada, 1986. 68 p.: ill. (Geological Survey of Canada, Economic geology report ; 37; ISSN: 0317-445X); ISBN: 0-660-12152-2.
Note: Appendix C: "Selected bibliography for Canadian lead-zinc deposits, arranged alphabetically by deposit-name." p. 39-68.– 748 entries.
Titre en français: *Classification, répartition et résumés des teneurs et des tonnages des gisements plombo-zincifères du Canada.*
Location: OONL.

4855 **Sangster, D.F.**
Classification, répartition et résumés des teneurs et des tonnages des gisements plombo-zincifères du Canada. Ottawa: Commission géologique du Canada, 1986. iv, 68 p.: ill. (certaines en coul.). (Commission géologique du Canada, Rapport de géologie économique ; 37; ISSN: 0317-445X); ISBN: 0-660-91774-2.
Note: Annexe C: "Bibliographie choisie des gisements plombo-zincifères du Canada, par ordre alphabétique des noms de gisement." p. 39-68.– Approx. 750 entrées.
English title: *Classification, distribution, and grade-tonnage summaries of Canadian lead-zinc deposits.*
Localisation: OONL.

— 1987 —

4856 **Beaudette, L.A.; McCready, R.G.L.**
Biotechnology bibliographies/Bibliographies de la biotechnologie. Ottawa: Canada Centre for Mineral and Energy Technology, c1987. v, 109 p. (CANMET Special publication / Canada Centre for Mineral and Energy Technology ; SP 86-2); ISBN: 0-660-53890-3.
Note: Approx. 1,600 entries in four topic areas: acid mine drainage (coal and metals) and bioadsorption of metals; solution mining; metabolism and physiology of Thiobacillus and other micro-organisms; bacterial leaching of metals.– Many Canadian references.
Location: OONL.

4857 **Gillespie-Wood, Janet**
Gold in Nova Scotia: a bibliography of the geology, and exploration and mining histories from 1832-1986. Halifax: Nova Scotia Department of Mines and Energy, 1987. xvi, 483 p.: map. (Nova Scotia Department of Mines and Energy report ; 87-02; ISSN: 0821-8188)
Note: Contains approx. 1,300 references documenting over 325 gold occurrences.– An occurrence refers to visible gold mineralization, not merely gold assay values.– Documents include Geological Survey of Canada publications, open files and maps; Nova Scotia Department of Mines and Energy publications, publish-

ed maps, open file reports, open file maps and assessment reports, company annual reports and prospectuses; newspaper articles, books, scientific journal literature, theses,
Location: OONL.

4858 **Gormely Process Engineering**
Heap leaching literature review. Ottawa: Indian and Northern Affairs Canada, 1987. 38, [7] p. (Environmental studies / Indian and Northern Affairs Canada ; no. 51); ISBN: 0-662-15946-2.
Note: 46 entries.– Review of the literature on cyanide heap leaching for gold recovery, with emphasis on references dealing with application of the technology in cold climates.– Focusses on engineering problems and solutions for waste treatment, containment, and disposal.– Résumé en français.
Location: OONL.

4859 **Hedley, D.G.F.**
Catalogue of rockburst literature. [Ottawa]: Mining Research Laboratories, Energy, Mines and Resources Canada, 1987. ii, 32 p. (Mining Research Laboratories Divisional report ; MRL 87-50-LS)
Note: Approx. 200 entries.– Lists reports and studies in English only in respect to hard rock mines (i.e., coal and potash mines not covered).– Topics include rockburst mechanics, seismic monitoring and source location, rockburst seismology, rockburst alleviation, controlling rockburst damage, rockburst prediction, case histories.– Résumé en français.
Location: OONL.

4860 **Kelly, Ross Ian; Barnett, R.S.; Delorme, R.J.**
An annotated bibliography of the Quaternary geology and history for the Don Valley Brickworks. Toronto: Mines and Minerals Division, Ministry of Northern Development and Mines, 1987. iv, 38 p. (Ontario Geological Survey Miscellaneous paper ; 135; ISSN: 0704-2752); ISBN: 0-7729-2505-4.
Note: Approx. 175 entries.– Assembles all relevant reports and studies concerning the Don Valley Brickworks.– Excavations at this site and various sedimentary units exposed over a period of 100 years (particularly the interglacial unit known as the Don Formation), provide a unique picture of Pleistocene history of the Great Lakes region.
Location: OONL.

4861 **Lakos, Amos; Cooper, Andrew F.**
Strategic minerals: a bibliography. Waterloo, Ont.: University of Waterloo Library, 1987. ix, 132 p. (University of Waterloo Library bibliography ; no. 14; ISSN: 0829-948X); ISBN: 0-920834-44-2.
Note: Approx. 1,100 entries.– Deals with the political, economic, international trade aspects of resource minerals, as well as North-South issues, supply issues, mineral cartels, seabed minerals and stockpiles.
Location: OONL.

4862 **McFarlane, Deborah**
Federal energy R&D, task 4: renewable energy bibliography, 1976-1986/R-D énergétique du gouvernement fédéral activité 4: énergies renouvelables bibliographie, 1976-1986. [Ottawa]: Office of Energy Research and Development, Energy, Mines and Resources Canada, [1987]. xii, 210 p.; ISBN: 0-662-54669-7.
Note: Approx. 2,400 entries.– Lists publications and

contract work titles which describe the focus and evolution of the federal interdepartmental Panel on Energy R&D renewables efforts since its inception.– Managing departments include Energy, Mines and Resources, Environment Canada and Canadian Forestry Service of Agriculture Canada.– Text in English and French/texte en français et en anglais.
Location: OONL.

4863 **Stefanski, M.J.**
Dewatering and self dewatering of concentrates. [Ottawa]: Mineral Sciences Laboratories, Canada Centre for Mineral and Energy Technology, 1987. iv, 72 l. (Mineral Sciences Laboratories Division report ; MSL 87-79 [IR])
Note: Part C: "Literature review."– 83 entries.– Covers 1960-1985.– Review of technical literature relating to dewatering/water migration processes of fine bulk materials, in particular Canadian iron ore concentrates.– Note liminaire et résumé en français.
Location: OONL.

— 1988 —

4864 **Caine, T.W., et al.**
Index to DIAND geology publications, Northwest Territories. Ottawa: Indian and Northern Affairs Canada, 1988. 95 p.; ISBN: 0-662-16638-8.
Note: Approx. 550 entries.– Lists geological publications written by staff of Geology divisions of Department of Indian Affairs and Northern Development from 1969 to December 1988.– Compiled with the collaboration of D.L. Dreger, P.T. Marion, S.M. Morton.– Introduction en français.
Location: OONL.

4865 **Caine, T.W., et al.**
Index to DIAND geology publications, Yukon. Ottawa: Indian and Northern Affairs Canada, 1988. 48 p.; ISBN: 0-662-16637-X.
Note: Approx. 350 entries.– Lists the geological publications written by staff of Geology divisions of Department of Indian Affairs and Northern Development from 1969 to December 1988.– Compiled with collaboration of D.L. Dreger, P.T. Marion, S.M. Morton.– Introduction en français.
Location: OONL.

4866 **Cameron, Nancy P.; Raines, Mary R.**
Hydrocarbon development: a Yukon perspective: an annotated bibliography of sources available in the Yukon Archives. Whitehorse: The Archives, 1986-1988. 2 vol.; ISBN: 1-55018-024-X (vol. 1); 1-55018-062-2 (vol. 2).
Note: Location: OONL.

4867 **Canadian Petroleum Association**
Bibliography: Canadian Petroleum Association publications. Calgary: Canadian Petroleum Association, 1988. xi, 37 p.
Note: Approx. 150 entries.– Reports, studies, manuals, booklets, brochures dealing with the petroleum industry.– Topics covered include health and safety, offshore and frontier, research and the environment, acid deposition research program.
Previous edition: 1985. vii, 21 l.
Location: ACCP.

4868 **Elson, J.A.**
"The Champlain Sea: evolution of concepts, and bibliography."

In: *The Late quaternary development of the Champlain Sea basin*, edited by N.R. Gadd. St. John's, Nfld.: Geological Association of Canada, 1988. P. 1-13.; ISBN: 0-919216-35-8.
Note: 312 entries.– Survey of the literature on the Champlain Sea through 1985.– The Champlain Sea is defined as the late Wisconsinan-Holocene marine waters in the St. Lawrence, Ottawa, and Champlain valleys west of the City of Quebec.
Location: OONL.

4869 **Harding, Jim; Forgay, Beryl; Gianoli, Mary**
Bibliography on Saskatchewan uranium inquiries and the northern and global impact of the uranium industry. Regina: Prairie Justice Research, School of Human Justice, University of Regina, 1988. 76 p. (In the public interest Research report ; no. 1); ISBN: 0-7731-0052-0.
Note: Approx. 1,400 entries.– Periodical and newspaper articles, government reports and studies on public inquiries related to uranium industry in Saskatchewan.– Includes references on other resource development and aboriginal concerns, references to methodology and impact assessment, ecological and energy analysis, social justice.
Location: OONL.

4870 **Knight, G.**
Noise and vibration control in mines: index of research reports, 1972-1986/Bruits et vibration dans les mines: répertoire des rapports des recherche, 1972-1986. [Ottawa]: Mining Research Laboratories, Canada Centre for Mineral and Energy Technology, [1988]. ix, 12, xii, 11 p. (Mining Research Laboratories Divisional report ; MRL 88-5-LS)
Note: Selected list of reports prepared by staff of Mining Research Laboratories dealing with noise and vibration in mining, arranged chronologically in seven categories: instrumentation, hearing protection tests, mine noise surveys, mill and surface plant noise surveys, noise abatement techniques, vibration studies, miscellaneous.– Text in English and French/texte en français et en anglais.
Location: OONL.

4871 **Martin, Gwen L.**
Neotechtonics in the Maritime Provinces. Ottawa: Atomic Energy Control Board, 1988. vii, 115 p.
Note: 288 entries.– Literature compilation and review of topics relating to earth movement and seismic risk assessment in the Atlantic provinces region, deformation of the geodetic reference level, including its mechanisms and geologic origin.
Location: OONL.

4872 **Scott, J.D., et al.**
A review of the international literature on mine spoil subsidence. Edmonton: Alberta Land Conservation and Reclamation Council, 1988. xxiv, 36 p. (Report / Alberta Reclamation Research Technical Advisory Committee ; RRTAC 88-12)
Note: Literature review of settlement behaviour of mine backfill: research methods, mechanisms of settlement, remedial measures for settlement, reclamation.– Some Canadian references.
Location: OONL.

— 1989 —

4873 **Chackowsky, Leonard Eugene**
Bibliography of Manitoba geology, 1795 to 1988. Winnipeg: Mines Branch, Minerals Division, Manitoba

Energy and Mines, 1989. iv, 221 p. (+ 5 microfiche in pocket).

Note: 5,598 entries. Lists references of Manitoba Energy and Mines, Geological Survey of Canada publications, papers in journal literature, theses, books, conference abstracts.– Includes NTS index (and NTS listing on microfiche) for geographic access.– Updated on a continuous basis.

Previous editions:

Bibliography of Manitoba geology 2. 1988. vii, 151 p. (Open File report ; OF 88-1).

Leskiw, P.D. *Bibliography of Manitoba geology 1.* 1986. iv, 198 p. (Open File report ; OF 86-1).

Location: OONL.

4874 **Chartrand, Francis; Couture, Jean-François; Pilote, Pierre**

Les gîtes de l'Abitibi du Nord-Ouest québécois: un inventaire des recherches récentes. Québec: Gouvernement du Québec, Service géologique du Nord-Ouest, 1989. 8 f.

Note: 58 entrées.

Localisation: OONL.

4875 **Coakley, John Phillip; Brodeur, Denis; Dionne, Jean-Claude**

Revue de la littérature et bibliographie des processus géologiques et des sédiments du Saint-Laurent. Burlington, Ont.: Institut national de recherche sur les eaux, 1989. 58 f.: carte.

Note: Localisation: OOFF.

4876 **Fyffe, L.R.; Blair, D.M.**

Bibliography of New Brunswick geology, (1839 to 1988). Fredericton: Minerals and Energy Division, Department of Natural Resources and Energy, New Brunswick, 1989. i, 225 p. (Geoscience report / Minerals and Energy Division, Department of Natural Resources and Energy, New Brunswick ; 89-3; ISSN: 0838-2565)

Note: Approx. 2,800 entries.– Federal and provincial government reports, papers from geoscientific and technical journals, theses, field guides, consultants' reports, newspaper articles.

Previous editions:

Abbott, D. *Bibliography of New Brunswick geology.* Research and Productivity Council, Mineral & Material Sciences Department, 1969. 105 p. (New Brunswick Research and Productivity Council Record ; 8).

1965. iv, 79 p. (New Brunswick Research and Productivity Council Record ; 2, Part C).

Location: OONL.

4877 **Ommanney, C. Simon L.**

Current research in the earth sciences: NHRI report for May 1988-April 1989. Saskatoon: National Hydrology Research Institute, 1989. 35 l.

Note: Location: OOFF.

— 1990 —

4878 **Munkittrick, Kelly Roland L.H.; Power, Elizabeth A.**

Literature review for biological monitoring of heavy metals in aquatic environments. Victoria: British Columbia Acid Mine Drainage Task Force, 1990. xi, 127 l.: ill.

Note: Location: OONL.

4879 **Riddell, Janet**

Information motherlode: geological source material for BC. Victoria: Province of British Columbia, Ministry of Energy, Mines and Petroleum Resources, Geological Survey Branch, 1990. 38 p. (Information circular / Province of British Columbia, Geological Survey Branch ; 1990-15; ISSN: 0825-5431); ISBN: 0-771-88965-8.

Note: Location: OONL.

— 1992 —

4880 **Canada. NOGAP Secretariat**

NOGAP bibliography: Northern Oil and Gas Action Program. Ottawa: NOGAP Secretariat, Constitutional Development and Strategic Planning Branch, Indian and Northern Affairs Canada, 1986-1992. 4 vol.; ISSN: 0837-4988.

Note: Contains references and summaries of publications and unpublished reports produced under the Northern Oil and Gas Action Program, an eight-year research and planning program related to federal and territorial hydrocarbon development north of 60.

Location: OONL.

— Ongoing/En cours —

4881 **Canadian Geoscience Council**

Current research in the geological sciences in Canada/ Travaux en cours dans le domaine des sciences géologiques au Canada. Ottawa: Energy, Mines and Resources Canada, 1951-. vol.; ISSN: 0526-4553.

Note: Annual.– Research reports, mainly from federal and provincial government departments and agencies and universities, are grouped under main headings covering the majority of disciplines within geological and allied sciences.– Began with 1950/51 issue.– Title varies slightly.– Text in English only, 1950-1978; text in English and French, 1978/79- .– Issued 1951-1952/53 by Geological Survey of Canada; 1965/66-1973/74 by the National Advisory Committee on Research in the Geological Sciences: volumes for 1953/54-1964/65 included as a section in annual report of the NACRGS (ISSN: 0373-6520); 1974/75- by the Canadian Geoscience Council.

Location: OONL.

4882 **Dominion Observatory (Canada)**

Bibliography of seismology. Ottawa: F.A. Acland, 1929-. vol.; ISSN: 0523-2988. (Publications of the Dominion Observatory Ottawa)

Note: Began as a quarterly publication in 1929.– From 1941, semiannual.

Published: Edinburgh, Scotland: International Seismological Centre, 1966- .

Location: OONL: 1929-1964.– OON: 1965- .

4883 **United States. Geological Survey**

Bibliography of North American geology. Washington: United States Government Printing Office, 1907-. vol.; ISSN: 0740-6347.

Note: Annual with cumulations.– Listing of papers relating to geology, palaeontology, petrology, mineralogy of North America: Canada (and Newfoundland), Arctic regions, United States, Mexico and Central America.– Volumes for 1927-1928, 1937-1939 not issued separately.

Cumulations:

Nickles, John M. *Geologic literature on North America, 1785-1918.* 1923. 2 vol. (United States Geological Survey Bulletin ; 746-747).

Nickles, John M. *... , 1919-1928.* 1931. iii, 1005 p. (United States Geological Survey Bulletin ; 823).

Thom, Emma M. ... , *1929-1939* 1944. 2 vol. (United States
Geological Survey Bulletin ; 937).
King, Ruth Rees, et al. ... , *1940-1949*. 1957. 2 vol. (United
States Geological Survey Bulletin ; 1049).
King, Ruth Rees, et al. ... , *1950-1959*. 1965. 4 vol. (United
States Geological Survey Bulletin ; 1195).
Location: OONL.

Fisheries

Pêches

— 1888 —

4884 Canada. Library of Parliament
List of British and American official documents relating to the history of the fisheries controversy. Ottawa: [s.n.], 1888. 21 l.
Note: Location: OOP.

— 1954 —

4885 International Commission for the Northwest Atlantic Fisheries
Guide to I.C.N.A.F. documents, proceedings, reports, and programs published or otherwise circulated up to 30 Sept. 1954. Dartmouth, N.S.: International Commission for the Northwest Atlantic Fisheries, [1954]. 17 l.
Note: 27 entries.– Listing of I.C.N.A.F. documents, arranged chronologically, 1951-1954.
Location: OONL.

— 1957 —

4886 McPhail, Marjorie E.
A selected bibliography of salt cod. Halifax, N.S.: Fisheries Research Board of Canada, 1957. iv, 30 p. (New series circular / Fisheries Research Board of Canada ; no. 5)
Note: Approx. 250 entries.– Studies and papers, journal articles dealing with the mechanism of salting, spoilage and preservation, processing, and the salt cod industry.
Location: OONL.

— 1967 —

4887 Roy, Jean-Marie; Beaulieu, Gérard; Talbot, Claire
Index des *Contributions du Département des Pêcheries*. Québec: Direction des pêcheries, Ministère de l'industrie et du commerce, 1967. 54 p.
Note: 92 entrées.– Comprend une liste chronologique (1912 à 1963) des *Contributions*.
Localisation: OONL.

— 1969 —

4888 British Columbia. Fish and Wildlife Branch
List of fisheries publications, 1947-1969. Victoria: [s.n., 1969]. 14, [3] l.
Note: Location: OONL.

— 1971 —

4889 Day, Dwane; Forrester, C.R.
A preliminary bibliography on the trawl fishery and groundfish of the Pacific coast of North America. [Ottawa: Information Canada, 1971]. 91 p. (Fisheries Research Board of Canada Technical report ; no. 246; ISSN: 0068-7553)
Note: 1,043 entries.– Excludes references found in popular outdoor and trade magazines, papers on fisheries science methodology, papers pertaining solely to Pacific halibut (Hippoglossus stenolepsis).
Location: OONL.

— 1972 —

4890 Nowak, W.S.W.
The lobster (Homaridae) and the lobster fisheries: an interdisciplinary bibliography. St. John's: Memorial University of Newfoundland, 1972. 313 p. (Marine Sciences Research Laboratory Technical reports ; no. 6)
Note: Approx. 3,200 entries.– Subjects covered include anatomy, aquaculture, biochemistry, conservation, ecology, economics of the lobster industry, fishery activity, gear technology, history of lobstering, law of fisheries, marine biology, marketing, physiology, statistics.
Location: OONL.

— 1976 —

4891 Dingle, J.R.
Technology of mackerel fishery: bibliography and survey of literature. Ottawa: Department of the Environment, Fisheries and Marine Service, 1976. viii, 63 p.: ill. (Fisheries and Marine Service Miscellaneous special publication ; 30)
Note: 184 entries.– Technical and scientific literature up to 1974 dealing with use of mackerel as human food: characteristics of mackerel muscle, handling of fresh mackerel, freezing, canning, salting and smoking, by-products.
Titre en français: *Procédés de traitement et de conservation de maquereau: étude et bibliographie annotée.*
Location: OONL.

4892 Mitchell, William Bruce; Mitchell, Joan
Law of the sea and international fisheries management. Monticello, Ill.: Council of Planning Librarians, 1976. 48 p. (Council of Planning Librarians Exchange bibliography ; 1162)
Note: Location: OONL.

— 1978 —

4893 Dingle, J.R.
Procédés de traitement et de conservation du maquereau: étude et bibliographie annotée. Ottawa: Services des pêches et de la mer, 1978. viii, 69 p. (Service des pêches et de la mer Publication diverse spéciale ; 30F)
Note: 184 entrées.– Documentation technique et scientifique parue avant 1974 et ayant trait au maquereau dans l'alimentation humaine: caractéristiques de la chair du maquereau, manutention du maquereau frais, congélation, mise en conserve, salage et fumage, sous-produits.
English title: *Technology of mackerel fishery: bibliography and survey of literature.*
Localisation: OONL.

4894 Pettigrew, Teresa, et al.
A review of water reconditioning re-use technology for fish culture, with a selected bibliography. St. Andrews, N.B.: Fisheries and Oceans Canada, 1978. iv, 19 p. (Fisheries and Marine Service Technical report ; no. 801; ISSN: 0701-7626)
Note: Approx. 200 entries.– Reviews published material on various aspects of construction and operation of water recycle systems with particular reference to those designed for rearing salmonid fishes.

Résumé en français.
Location: OONL.

— 1980 —

4895 **Cleugh, T.R.; Russell, L.R.**
Fisheries and fish related publications in Yukon Territory. Vancouver: Department of Fisheries and Oceans, 1980. [55] p. (Canadian technical report of fisheries and aquatic sciences ; no. 938; ISSN: 0706-6457)
Note: 444 entries.– Includes periodical articles, books, theses, government and industrial technical reports.– Excludes newspapers, maps and photo materials.
Location: OONL.

4896 **McLean, M.P.; McNicol, R.E.; Scherer, E.**
Bibliography of toxicity test methods for the aquatic environment. Winnipeg: Department of Fisheries and Oceans, 1980. vi, 29 p. (Canadian special publication of fisheries and aquatic sciences ; 50; ISSN: 0706-6481)
Note: 762 entries.– Technical papers dealing with methods for detecting lethal and sublethal toxic effects on aquatic organisms and communities, test compilations and reviews.– Résumé en français.
Location: OONL.

4897 **Nowak, W.S.W.**
Inventory of post-graduate, honours and senior undergraduate reports on the fishery and fishing industry in the data banks owned by the compiler. [St. John's, Nfld.]: Department of Geography, Memorial University of Newfoundland, [1980]. 48 l.
Note: Approx. 500 entries.
Location: OONL.

— 1981 —

4898 **Papst, M.H.; Ayles, G.B.; Lark, J.G.I.**
Current bibliography of publications on waste heat utilization in aquaculture. Winnipeg: Government of Canada, Fisheries and Oceans, 1981. iv, 13 p. (Canadian manuscript report of fisheries and aquatic sciences ; no. 1598; ISSN: 0706-6473)
Note: Approx. 180 entries.– Periodical articles, papers, technical reports and books containing information on utilization of waste heat in aquaculture to spring 1980.– Résumé en français.
Location: OONL.

— 1982 —

4899 **Ennis, G.L., et al.**
An annotated bibliography and information summary on the fisheries resources of the Yukon River basin in Canada. Vancouver: Water Use Unit, Habitat Management Division, Department of Fisheries and Oceans, 1982. v, 278 p. (Canadian manuscript report of fisheries and aquatic sciences ; no. 1657; ISSN: 0706-6473)
Note: 223 entries.– Periodical articles, theses, government and industrial technical reports, mapping projects, government records (open files, field notes, unpublished or incomplete studies) on Yukon River mainstem, and the White River, Stewart River, Pelly River, Teslin River, Aishinik River basin.
Location: OONL.

— 1983 —

4900 **Canadian Sealers' Association**
Bibliography of articles on seals and sealing published in the *Times* of London, 1960-1982. [S.l.]: Canadian Sealers' Association, [1983]. 52 p.
Note: Location: NFSM.

— 1985 —

4901 **Bernstein, J.W.**
Literature review of ultraviolet radiation systems and assessment of their use in aquaculture. Saskatoon: Saskatchewan Research Council, 1985. i, 39 l. (Saskatchewan Research Council Technical report ; no. 183)
Note: 32 entries.– Chapters include historical works, characteristics of UV equipment, mechanism of kill, maintenance, factors affecting efficiency, fail-safe devices, bacterial testing, hatcheries and UV systems.– Deals also with the limitations and advantages of UV water treatment.
Location: OONL.

4902 **Coady, L.W.; Maidment, J.M.**
Publications of the Fisheries Research Branch, Northwest Atlantic Fisheries Centre, St. John's Newfoundland: 1931 to 1984. St. John's, Nfld.: Fisheries Research Branch, Department of Fisheries and Oceans, 1985. v, 159 p. (Canadian manuscript report of fisheries and aquatic sciences ; no. 1790; ISSN: 0706-6473)
Note: Approx. 2,500 entries.– Includes primary, interpretive scientific and technical references to the end of 1984.– Popular and miscellaneous articles of long-term value are also included.– Résumé en français.
Location: OONL.

4903 **Minion, Robin**
Fish and fisheries of northern Canada and Alaska. Edmonton: Boreal Institute for Northern Studies, University of Alberta, 1985. 81 p. (Boreal Institute for Northern Studies Bibliographic series ; no. 18; ISSN: 0824-8192)
Note: 194 entries.– Covers from 1977 to 1985.– Compiled from Boreal Institute's SPIRES database, *BOREAL* includes monographs, government documents, theses, consultants' reports, microforms, periodicals.– BINS series produced monthly from January 1984 to May 1985 (no. 29).– Online access: *Boreal Northern Titles (BNT)*, available through QL Systems Limited.
Location: OONL.

4904 **Sawchyn, W.W.**
A review of crayfish literature relevant to the development of a crayfish industry in Saskatchewan. Saskatoon: Saskatchewan Research Council, 1985. iv, 64 l., [71] p.: ill. (Saskatchewan Research Council Technical report ; no. 174)
Note: Literature review of crayfish biology (characteristics, habitat, reproduction, etc.), crayfish harvesting (baits, trapping methods), marketing economics and regulation of crayfish industry, crayfish culturing.– Emphasis on Orconectes virilis, known to occur in Saskatchewan.
Location: OONL.

— 1986 —

4905 **McCullough, Alan Bruce**
Bibliographie annotée de travaux choisis sur l'historique des pêcheries commerciales des Grands Lacs canadiens. [Ottawa]: Parcs Canada, 1986. 20 p. (Bulletin de recherches / Parcs Canada ; no. 238; ISSN: 0228-1236)
Note: Approx. 130 entrées.– Préparée en relation avec "Les pêcheries commerciales de Grands Lacs canadiens."- Elle est un complement à cette étude et comprend travaux publiés, thèses, rapports manuscrits et

d'importantes sources puisées dans les archives.
English title: *A select, annotated bibliography on the history of the commercial fisheries of the Canadian Great Lakes*.
Localisation: OONL.

4906 **McCullough, Alan Bruce**
A select, annotated bibliography on the history of the commercial fisheries of the Canadian Great Lakes. [Ottawa]: Parks Canada, 1986. 20 p. (Research bulletin / Parks Canada ; no. 238; ISSN: 0228-1228)
Note: Approx. 130 entries.– Prepared in conjunction with the survey history "The commercial fisheries of the Canadian Great Lakes," this bibliography is designed as a supplement to this report.– Includes published works, theses, manuscript reports and major archival sources.
Titre en français: *Bibliographie annotée de travaux choisis sur l'historique des pêcheries commerciales des Grands Lacs canadiens*.
Location: OONL.

4907 **Smith, Shirleen**
Bibliography of bowhead whales, whaling, and Alaskan Inupiat and Yupik whaling communities. Edmonton: Boreal Institute for Northern Studies, University of Alberta, 1986. v, 55 p. (Miscellaneous publications / Boreal Institute for Northern Studies, University of Alberta); ISBN: 0-919058-32-9.
Note: Approx. 500 entries.– Central theme: subsistence hunting of bowhead whales by Inupiat and Yupik peoples.– References to bowhead biology, management policies, history.
Location: OONL.

— 1987 —

4908 **Halliday, R.G., et al.**
A history of Canadian fisheries research in the Georges Bank area of the northwestern Atlantic. Dartmouth, N.S.: Fisheries and Oceans Canada, 1987. iv, 37 p.: map. (Canadian technical report of fisheries and aquatic sciences ; no. 1550; ISSN: 0706-6457)
Note: Approx. 200 entries.– Provides a list of research reports which published the result of work by Canadians relevant to the fishery resources of the Georges Bank area to 1980.
Location: OONL.

4909 **Lamson, Cynthia; Reade, J.G.**
Atlantic fisheries and social sciences: a guide to sources. Halifax, N.S.: Fisheries and Oceans Canada, 1987. vi, 10 p.: map. (Canadian technical report of fisheries and aquatic sciences ; no. 1549; ISSN: 0706-6457)
Note: Approx. 200 entries.– Multidisciplinary listing of fisheries' human science materials with focus on Atlantic Canada: journal articles, government reports and studies, theses.– Résumé en français.
Location: OONL.

4910 **Macmillan, Stuart**
An annotated bibliography of the Arctic charr (Salvelinus alpinus) with emphasis on aquaculture, commercial fisheries, and migration and movements. Winnipeg: Natural Resources Institute, University of Manitoba, 1987. 20 p.
Note: Location: NFSF.

— 1988 —

4911 **New Brunswick. Legislative Library**
Aquaculture/Aquiculture. Fredericton: New Brunswick Legislative Library, 1988. 3 l. (Bibliography / New Brunswick Legislative Library)
Note: Includes publications in English and French.
Location: OONL.

4912 **Nicholson, H.F.; Moore, J.E.**
Bibliography on the limnology and fisheries of Canadian freshwaters. Burlington, Ont.: Fisheries and Marine Service, 1974-1988. 10 vol. (Canadian technical reports of fisheries and aquatic sciences; ISSN: 0706-6457)
Note: Series of technical reports listing scientific studies on physical features, biology and fisheries of Canadian lakes, creeks, rivers, ponds, reservoirs.– Covers from early nineteenth century to 1987.– The final volume, published in three parts, is cumulative, containing all references from nos. 1-9 inclusive, as well as additions through 1987.– Résumé en français.
Location: OONL.

— 1989 —

4913 **Sawada, Joel D.; Warner, Bing**
Abstracts of fisheries management reports, technical circulars, and project reports of the Recreational Fisheries Branch, British Columbia Ministry of Environment, 1985-88. Vancouver: Province of British Columbia, Ministry of Environment, 1989. i, 55 p. (Fisheries technical circular / British Columbia Ministry of Environment ; no. 86); ISBN: 0-7726-0979-9.
Note: 123 entries.
Location: OONL.

— 1990 —

4914 **Lane, Daniel E.**
Management science in the control and management of fisheries: an annotated bibliography. Ottawa: Faculty of Administration, University of Ottawa, 1990. i, 32 p. (Working papers series / Faculty of Administration, University of Ottawa ; 90-6; ISSN: 0701-3086)
Note: 133 entries.– Surveys and lists literature relating to applied management science models and methods in fisheries systems.
Location: OONL.

4915 **Magnan, Pierre; East, Pierre; Lapointe, Michèle**
Modes de contrôle des poissons indésirables: revue et analyse critique de la littérature. Québec: Ministère du loisir, de la chasse et de la pêche, 1990. xi, 198 p. (Rapport technique / Québec Ministère du loisir, de la chasse et de la pêche); ISBN: 2-550-20959-1.
Note: Localisation: OONL.

— 1992 —

4916 **Bourque, Christa; Lévesque, Paulette**
List of DFO-sponsored publications, Science Branch, Gulf Region, 1982-1991/Liste des publications subventionnées par le MPO, Direction des sciences, Région du golfe, 1982-1991. Revised edition. Moncton, N.B.: Department of Fisheries and Oceans, 1992. i, 38 p. (Canadian manuscript report of fisheries and aquatic sciences ; no. 2173; ISSN: 0706-6473)
Note: Approx. 400 entries.– Publications dealing with fisheries topics related to the Atlantic region.– Includes articles in scientific journals, books, symposium proceedings, published scientific and technical reports, book reviews in scientific journals.– Excludes working papers, unpublished contract reports, published abstracts.– Text in English and French/texte en français et en anglais.
Location: OONL.

Forestry

Sylviculture

— 1938 —

4917 **Candy, R.H.**
Review of reports of growth and regeneration surveys in Canada, conducted by the Dominion Forest Service and the Commission of Conservation, 1918-36. Ottawa: Department of Mines and Resources, Lands, Parks and Forests Branch, 1938. 50 p.
Note: 58 entries.– Review of reports includes notes on object of the survey, location of survey, area covered, methods of survey adopted, results and conclusions, comments and criticism of reviewer.
Location: OONL.

— 1940 —

4918 **Munns, Edward Norfolk**
A selected bibliography of North American forestry. Washington: U.S. Government Printing Office, 1940. 2 vol. (United States Department of Agriculture Miscellaneous publications ; no. 364)
Note: 21,413 entries.– "Includes references to the more important literature on forestry published in Canada, Mexico, and the United States prior to 1930".– Topics include forest botany, entomology, mensuration, forest production, logging, forest economics, wood technology, forest policy and legislation, forest aesthetics.
Location: OONL.

— 1949 —

4919 **Robertson, William Murdoch**
Selected bibliography of Canadian forest literature, 1917-1946. Ottawa: Department of Mines and Resources, Mines, Forests and Scientific Services Branch, 1949. 332 l. (in 3 parts). (Miscellaneous silvicultural research note / Canada Department of Mines and Resources, Mines, Forests and Scientific Services Branch ; no. 6)
Note: 3,744 entries.– Reports, studies, articles from technical journals and trade magazines related to general and applied silviculture, mensuration, woods operations, mills operations, fire protection, wood technology, administration.
Location: OONL.

— 1950 —

4920 **Flick, Frances Josephine; Brown, Elizabeth P.**
Economics of forestry: a bibliography for the United States and Canada, 1940-1947. Washington, D.C.: United States Department of Agriculture Library, 1950. vi, 126 p. (Library list / United States Department of Agriculture Library ; no. 52)
Note: Published works and post-graduate theses that emphasize the economic aspects of forestry, including forest management, wood-using industries, marketing and consumption of forest products and services.
Supplements:
... , 1948-1952. 1955. iv, 136 p.
Rumsey, Fay. ... , 1955-1959. Syracuse, N.Y.: State University College of Forestry at Syracuse University, 1964. 136 p.

Rumsey, Fay. ..., 1960-1962. U.S. Department of Agriculture, Forest Service, 1965. iv, 45 p. (Miscellaneous publication / U.S. Department of Agriculture, Forest Service ; 1003).
Location: OOFF.

— 1968 —

4921 **Adams, R.D.; El-Osta, M.L.; Wellwood, Robert William**
Index of selected articles from Canadian journals pertaining to the forest products industries, 1965-1967. Vancouver: Faculty of Forestry, University of British Columbia, 1968. iv, 22 l.
Note: Location: BVAU.

4922 **Lee, Yam (Jim)**
A review of research literature on forest fertilization. Victoria, B.C.: Department of Forestry and Rural Development, 1968. 40 p.
Note: Approx. 65 entries.– References dealing with nutrient requirements, nitrogen cycle, foliar analysis, growth and survival of planting stock, rate of fertilizer application, time and methods of application, insects and disease, economic aspects.
Location: OONL.

4923 **Pulp and Paper Research Institute of Canada**
List of Woodlands Research Department publications. Pointe Claire, Quebec: Pulp and Paper Research Institute of Canada, 1968. 14 p. (Woodlands Research index ; no. 36; ISSN: 0384-8663)
Note: Location: OOCC.

4924 **Walters, John**
An annotated bibliography of reports, theses, and publications pertaining to the campus and research forests of the University of British Columbia. Vancouver: Faculty of Forestry, University of British Columbia, 1968. viii, 71 p.
Note: 332 entries.– Covers the period 1935 to 1967.– Subjects covered include forest economics, ecology, entomology, fires, genetics, management, pathology, mensuration, soils, wood technology, silviculture.
Location: OONL.

— 1969 —

4925 **Forest Fire Research Institute (Canada). Information Centre**
Document list [Forest Fire Research Institute]. Ottawa: Forest Fire Research Institute, Department of Fisheries and Forestry, 1969. 1 vol. (loose-leaf).
Note: Listing of reports, theses, abstracts, publications related to forest fire research.
Location: OONL.

4926 **Fréchette, Jean-Guy**
Bibliographie de météorologie forestière. Québec: Éditeur officiel du Québec, 1969. 59 p.
Note: Localisation: QQLA.

— 1970 —

4927 **Richer, Suzanne**
Publications scientifiques – scientific publications,

Laboratoire de recherches forestières, région de Québec. Ste-Foy, Québec: Service canadien des forêts, Ministère des pêches et des forêts, 1970. [75] f. (Laboratoire de recherches forestières Rapports d'information ; Q-F-X-2)
Note: 748 entrées.– Publications émises par le personnel scientifique attaché au secteur de la recherche forestière du gouvernement canadien de la région de Québec, 1952-1970.
Localisation: OONL.

— 1971 —

4928 **Johnson, H.J., et al.**
Some implications of large-scale clearcutting in Alberta: a literature review. Edmonton: Canadian Forestry Service, Department of the Environment, 1971. 114 l. (Northern Forest Research Centre Information report ; NOR-X-6; ISSN: 0704-7673)
Note: Literature dealing with environmental factors affected by clearcutting, silvicultural implications of large block clearcutting, hydrological effects of clearcutting, fire hazard, effect of clearcutting on infection and development of disease in regeneration and insect problems associated with large block clearcutting.
Location: AEU.

4929 **Keays, J.L.**
Complete-tree utilization: an analysis of the literature. Vancouver, B.C.: Forest Products Laboratory, Canadian Forestry Service, Department of Fisheries and Forestry, 1971. 5 vol.: ill. (Canadian Forestry Service Information report ; VP-X-69,70,71,77,79)
Note: Part 1: *Unmerchantable top of bole.*– 315 entries.– Deals with the biomass and pulping characteristics of unmerchantable tops of boles.
Part 2: *Foliage.*– 158 entries.– Review of technical literature relating to foliage biomass, utilization of tree foliage for fiber and pulp in pharmaceutical preparations.
Part 3: *Branches.*– 119 entries.– Uses of tree branches, for pulp, power and fuel.
Part 4: *Crown and slash.*– 193 entries.– Focuses on tree foliage plus branches plus tops: construction materials, pulp and paper, power and fuel, agriculture, bulk chemicals, pharmaceuticals, oil, fodder.
Part 5: *Stump, roots and stump-root system.*– 81 entries.– Review of technical literature relating to tree stump-root systems and their potential uses in pulp and paper manufacture.
Supplement: Wellwood, Robert William. ... *(1970-1978).* [Hull, Quebec]: Canadian Forestry Service, 1979-1980. 3 vol. (ENFOR Project P (ENFOR Secretariat, Canadian Forestry Service) ; P-15).
Location: OONL.

— 1972 —

4930 **Bonnor, G.M.**
Forest sampling and inventories: a bibliography. Ottawa: Forest Management Institute, Canadian Forestry Service, Environment Canada, 1972. 27 p. (Forest Management Institute Internal report ; FMR-24)
Note: 252 entries.– English-language publications dating from 1945 to 1972 dealing with forest sampling and inventories, aerial photography, statistical analysis.– Excludes articles on point sampling, air photo measurements, mensuration studies, theses.
Location: OONL.

4931 **Dobbs, R.C.**
Regeneration of white and Engelmann spruce: a literature review with special reference to the British Columbia interior. Ottawa: Information Canada, 1972. 77 p.
Note: Location: OONL.

4932 **Johnson, Marion E.**
Forest products pollution control annotated bibliography (excluding pulp and paper). Vancouver: Department of the Environment, Canadian Forestry Service, Western Forest Products Laboratory, 1972. 20 p. (Information report / Western Forest Products Laboratory ; VP-X-100; ISSN: 0045-429X)
Note: Approx. 125 entries.– Selective listing of pollution control literature from 1965 to 1972 in area of forest products industry.– Excludes pulp and paper.
Location: OONL.

4933 **Masson, Gaétan**
Revue de la littérature sur le camionnage des produits forestiers en forêt. [S.l.: s.n.], 1972. 46 f.
Note: Localisation: QQLA.

— 1973 —

4934 **Adamovich, L.; Willington, R.P.; Lacate, D.**
Bibliography on forest roads and the environment. [S.l.: s.n.], 1973. 25 l.
Note: 272 entries.– Subjects covered include construction, cut and fill revegetation, erosion and sedimentation, environmental issues, fisheries, landslides, legal aspects, soils, water, wildlife.
Location: OONL.

4935 **Evert, F.**
Annotated bibliography on initial tree spacing. Ottawa: Canadian Forestry Service, Department of the Environment, 1973. 149 p. (Forest Management Institute Information report ; FMR-X-50)
Note: 388 entries.– References covering the period between 1920 and 1971.– Studies that involve initial spacing in plantations or in stands thinned to a uniform spacing before the start of intertree competition.– Résumé en français.
Supplement: *An update (1970-71-1982) of the Annotated bibliography on initial tree spacing.* Chalk River, Ont.: Petawawa National Forestry Institute, Canadian Forestry Service, 1984. iv, 157 p. (Information report (Petawawa National Forestry Institute) ; PI-X-44); ISBN: 0-662-13621-7.
Location: OONL.

4936 **Kimmins, J.P.; Fraker, P.N.**
Bibliography of herbicides in forest ecosystems. Victoria, B.C.: Canadian Forestry Service, 1973. 261 p.
Note: 1,614 entries.– Reports, studies, articles dealing with use of herbicides, their chemistry, methods, legislation.– Addresses themes of ecological effects of herbicides; effects of herbicides on soils; hydrology and aquatic ecosystems; herbicides and plants; effects of herbicides on birds, fish, mammals, humans; degradation of herbicides; herbicides and cells.
Location: OONL.

4937 **Richer, Suzanne**
Aménagement polyvalent de la forêt: une bibliographie rétrospective, 1960-1973. Sainte-Foy, Québec: Bibliothèque, Centre de recherches forestières des Laurentides, Service canadien des forêts, 1973. 30 p.

(Document / Centre de recherches forestières des Laurentides, Bibliothèque ; no 2)
Note: 401 entrées.
Localisation: OONL.

4938 **Richer, Suzanne**
Le sirop d'érable: une bibliographie rétrospective, 1949-1971. Sainte-Foy, Québec: Bibliothèque, Centre de recherches forestières des Laurentides, Service canadien des forêts, 1973. 5 p. (Document / Centre de recherches forestières des Laurentides, Bibliothèque ; no 1)
Note: 50 entrées.
Localisation: OONL.

4939 **Stanton, Charles R.**
Index to federal scientific and technical contributions to forestry literature 1901-1971. Ottawa: Canadian Forestry Service, Department of the Environment, 1973. 7 vol.
Note: Listing of books, journal articles, published work of congresses, conferences, symposiums, etc. on technical aspects of forestry published or prepared for publication during the period of an author's employment by the Government of Canada.– Introduction en français.
Location: OONL.

4940 **Sutherland, Jack R.**
List of references on forest nursery-disease research in British Columbia. Victoria, B.C.: Pacific Forest Research Centre, Canadian Forestry Service, 1973. 11 p. (Pacific Forest Research Centre Internal report ; BC-45)
Note: 74 entries.– References directly related to seedling disease research: non-pathogenic problems, pathogenic problems, including corky root disease, control, damping-off, nematodes, root rots, shoot and foliage problems.
Location: OONL.

4941 **Swan, Eric P.**
Resin acids and fatty acids of Canadian pulpwoods: a review of the literature. Vancouver: Department of the Environment, Canadian Forestry Service, Western Forest Products Laboratory, 1973. 21 p. (Information report / Western Forest Products Laboratory ; VP-X-115; ISSN: 0045-429X)
Note: Approx. 40 entries.
Location: OONL.

— 1974 —

4942 **Bell, Marcus A.M.; Beckett, Jennifer M.; Hubbard, William F.**
Impact of harvesting on forest environments and resources: a review of the literature and evaluation of research needs. Victoria: Pacific Forest Research Centre, Canadian Forestry Service, 1974. v, 141 p.
Note: Approx. 800 entries.– Summarizes available literature relevant to British Columbia concerning influence of harvesting and post-harvest practices on forest environment and resources.
Supplement: ... : a bibliography with abstracts. Ottawa: Canadian Forestry Service, Department of the Environment, 1976. 15 p.; ISBN: 0-662-00183-4.– 89 entries.
Location: OONL.

4943 **Campbell, A.E.; Pratt, R.H.M.**
Bibliography of North American shelterbelt research. Edmonton: Canadian Forestry Service, Department of the Environment, 1974. 52 p. (Northern Forest Research Centre Information report ; NOR-X-92; ISSN: 0704-7673)
Note: Approx. 600 entries.– Listing of technical literature to 1969 on establishing and maintaining shelterbelts: cultural practices, entomology, pathology, soils, climatic conditions, tree species selection.
Location: OONL.

4944 **Cooper, P.A.**
Improving durability of round timbers of some Canadian softwoods: an annotated bibliography. Vancouver: Western Forest Products Laboratory, 1974. 20 p. (Information report / Western Forest Products Laboratory ; VP-X-128; ISSN: 0045-429X)
Note: 61 entries.
Location: OONL.

4945 **Richer, Suzanne; Robidoux, Meridel D.**
Liste des publications scientifiques du personnel de recherche du CRFL. 2e éd. Ste-Foy, Québec: Centre de recherches forestières des Laurentides, 1974. 144 p.
Note: 1,037 entrées.– Liste complète des travaux scientifiques publiés par le personnel de recherche du CFRL depuis 1952 jusqu'en décembre 1973.– Summary in English.
Édition antérieure: *Publications scientifiques, Laboratoire de recherches forestières, région de Québec, 1952-1970.* Service canadien des forêts, Ministère des pêches et des forêts, 1970. [75] f.
Supplément: *Publications scientifiques: addendum, Centre de recherches forestières des Laurentides.* Environnement Canada, Service des forêts, 1972. 16 f.
Localisation: OONL.

— 1975 —

4946 **Murtha, Peter A.; Greco, Michael E.**
Appraisal of forest aesthetic values: an annotated bibliography. Ottawa: Canadian Forestry Service, 1975. v, 56 p. (Forest Management Institute Information report ; FMR-X-79)
Note: 87 entries.– Papers presenting four viewpoints or methods on appraisal of aesthetic values of forests: economic, visual analysis, preference analysis, aesthetic analysis.– Some Canadian references.– Résumé en français.
Location: OONL.

4947 **Ramsey, G.S.; Bruce, N.G.**
Bibliography of departmental forest fire research literature. 3rd ed. Ottawa: Forest Fire Research Institute, Canadian Forestry Service, Department of the Environment, 1975. [138] p. (in various pagings). (Information report / Forest Fire Research Institute ; FF-X-2; ISSN: 0068-757X)
Note: Lists all of the literature of forest fire research written by members of the Institute and the Regional establishments or their predecessors from 1909 to 1974.– Publications are listed by series: "Research notes," "Technical notes," etc.– Includes articles written by staff members for journals or papers delivered at conferences and meetings.
Previous editions:
1970. 1 vol. (in various pagings).
1966. 1 vol. (in various pagings).
Location: OONL.

4948 **Sault College. Library Resource Centre**
Bibliography: forestry. Sault Ste. Marie, Ont.: Sault College, Library Resource Centre, 1975. 26 p.
Note: Approx. 250 entries.– Includes Canadian references.

Location: OONL.

4949 **Wilford, David J.**
A review of literature to 1975 of forest hydrology pertinent to the management of mountainous watersheds. Victoria, B.C.: Ministry of Forests, 1975. [3], 50 l.: ill.
Note: Bibliography: l. 43-50.
Location: NFSM.

— 1976 —

4950 **Bell, Marcus A.M.; Beckett, Jennifer M.; Hubbard, William F.**
Establishment of forests after logging in north central British Columbia: an annotated bibliography. Victoria, B.C.: Pacific Forest Research Centre, 1976. 178 p. (Pacific Forest Research Centre Information report ; BC-X-109; ISSN: 0705-3274)
Note: Articles, reports, technical studies dealing with reforestation in the British Columbia Cariboo district.– Prepared by Biocon Research Limited under contract to the Pacific Forest Research Centre.
Location: OOFF.

4951 **Brazeau, Marcel; Veilleux, Jean-Marc**
Bibliographie annotée sur les effets de la fertilisation sur la production de cônes et de semences. [Sainte-Foy]: Service de la recherche, Direction générale des forêts, Ministère des terres et forêts du Québec, 1976. viii, 26 p. (Mémoire / Direction générale des forêts, Québec ; no 25)
Note: Approx. 60 entrées.– Comporte une bibliographie annotée accompagnée d'une orientation bibliographique.
Localisation: OONL.

4952 **Smith, R.M.**
Bibliography of forest pathology research publications, western and northern region. Edmonton: Northern Forest Research Centre, Canadian Forestry Service, 1976. 37 l.
Note: Approx. 420 entries.– Listing of all forest pathology research publications originating from the Canadian Forestry Service and its predecessors up to 1975 within the three prairie provinces.
Location: OONL.

4953 **Stanek, W.**
Annotated bibliography of peatland forestry/Foresterie des régions de tourbières: bibliographie annotée. Ottawa: Environment Canada, Library, 1976. 205 p. (Environment Canada Libraries Bibliography series ; 76/1)
Note: 598 entries.– Papers from Canada, U.S., Europe, U.S.S.R. on peatlands and their utilization for forestry purposes.– Topics include improvement of peatlands, ditching, drainage, fertilization, chemical properties of peat, peatland classification, regeneration of peatlands, tree species on peatlands, water-table in peat.
Location: OONL.

— 1977 —

4954 **Bickerstaff, A.; Hostikka, S.A.**
Growth of forests in Canada. [Ottawa]: Canadian Forestry Service, Fisheries and Environment Canada, 1977. v, 197 p. (Forest Management Institute Information report ; FMR-X-98)
Note: Part 1: "An annotated bibliography."– 634 entries.– Covers to the end of 1975.– Lists Canadian literature related to increment or yields at known ages of naturally established unmanaged forests.
Location: OONL.

4955 **Fahl, Ronald J.**
North American forest and conservation history: a bibliography. Santa Barbara, Calif.: Published under contract with the Forest History Society [by] A.B.C.–Clio Press, c1977. 408 p.; ISBN: 0-87436-235-0.
Note: Approx. 6.650 entries.– Includes books, articles, theses to mid-1975.– Excludes technical literature of forestry and related sciences, contemporary reports of forest industries, descriptive or polemical writings of conservation movement.
Location: OONL.

4956 **Kelsall, John P.; Telfer, Edmund S.; Wright, Thomas D.**
The effects of fire on the ecology of the boreal forest, with particular reference to the Canadian north: a review and selected bibliography. Ottawa: Canadian Wildlife Service, 1977. 58 p. (Canadian Wildlife Service Occasional paper ; no. 32); ISBN: 0-662-00638-0.
Note: Approx. 200 entries.– Résumé en français.
Location: OONL.

4957 **Lillard, Charles**
"Logging fact and fiction: a bibliography."
In: *Sound Heritage*; Vol. 6, no. 3 (1977) p. 73-77.; ISSN: 0316-2826.
Note: Location: OONL.

4958 **Sidhu, S.S.; Case, A.B.**
A bibliography on the environmental impact of forest resource roads: a list. St. John's: Newfoundland Forest Research Centre, 1977. 28 l.
Note: Approx. 325 entries.– Covers 1951-1976.
Location: OONL.

4959 **Simard, Albert J.**
Air tankers: a bibliography. Ottawa: Forest Fire Research Institute, 1977. 79 p. (Forest Fire Research Institute Information report ; FF-X-62)
Note: 703 entries.– Comprehensive listing of reports, articles, documents, brochures dealing with the use of air tankers in forest fire control.
Location: OONL.

4960 **Thurlow and Associates**
Étude des textes relatifs aux caractéristiques des eaux usées et aux techniques d'épuration dans l'industrie du traitement du bois. Hull, Québec: Service de la protection de l'environnement, Environnement Canada, 1977. ix, 60 p.: ill. (Étude économique et technique, Rapport / Service de la protection de l'environnement, Environnement Canada ; EPS 3-WP-77-2); ISBN: 0-662-90231-9.
Note: Approx. 150 entrées.– Quatre sections: stockage des billes, placage et contre-plaqué, panneaux de particles, préservation du bois.
English title: *Literature review of wastewater characteristics and abatement technology in the wood and timber processing industry.*
Localisation: OONL.

4961 **Thurlow and Associates**
Literature review of wastewater characteristics and abatement technology in the wood and timber processing industry. Ottawa: Environmental Protection Service, Fisheries and Environment Canada, 1977. 70 p. (Economic and technical review report / Environmental Protection Service, Fisheries and Environment Canada ; EPS 3-WP-77-2); ISBN: 0-662-00514-7.
Note: Approx. 150 entries.– Four sections: technical studies and papers dealing with log storage, veneer and

plywood, particleboard, wood preserving.– Topics include wastewater sources (industrial use of water and generation of wastewater), wastewater characteristics (contaminants discharged and potential environmental problems), abatement technology (current trends in industry).

Titre en français: *Étude des textes relatifs aux caractéristiques des eaux usées et aux techniques d'épuration dans l'industrie du traitement du bois.*

Location: OONL.

4962 **Zalasky, H.**
Bibliography of frost damage in tree nurseries. Edmonton: Northern Forest Research Centre, Canadian Forestry Service, Fisheries and Environment Canada, 1977. 8 l.
Note: 90 entries.– Canadian and U.S. references grouped under three headings: type of frost and frost nucleating agents, recognition and damage, protection.
Location: OONL.

— 1978 —

4963 **Feihl, O.**
Protection of veneer logs in storage in eastern Canada: a survey of the literature. Ottawa: Eastern Forest Products Laboratory, 1978. iii, 20 p.
Note: Location: OONL.

4964 **Fournier, François; Goulet, Marcel**
Propriétés physico-mécaniques de l'écorce: une étude bibliographique. Québec: Département d'exploitation et utilisation des bois, Université Laval, 1978. 44 f. (Notes de recherche / Département d'exploitation et utilisation des bois, Université Laval ; no 7)
Note: 38 entrées.
Localisation: OONL.

4965 **Smith, R.M.**
Bibliography of forest entomology research, 1927-77: Canadian Forestry Service, Prairies Region. Edmonton: Northern Forest Research Centre, Canadian Forestry Service, Environment Canada, 1978. ii, 34 p. (Northern Forest Research Centre Information report ; NOR-X-212; ISSN: 0704-7673)
Note: Approx. 1,000 entries.– Lists all forest entomology publications to 1977 with reference to the three prairie provinces.
Location: OONL.

— 1979 —

4966 **Alexander, Martin E.**
Bibliography and a résumé of current studies on fire history. Sault Ste. Marie, Ont.: Great Lakes Forest Research Centre, 1979. 43 p.: map. (Great Lakes Forest Research Centre report ; O-X-304; ISSN: 0704-7797)
Note: 332 entries.– Studies dating from 1900 on forest and rangeland fire history for Canada, United States, Scandinavia.– Includes general studies, historical references, charcoal analysis, tree-ring analysis, fire scar analysis.
Location: OONL.

4967 **McRae, Douglas J.**
Prescribed burning in jack pine logging slash: a review. Sault Ste. Marie, Ont.: Great Lakes Forest Research Centre, 1979. 57 p.: ill. (Great Lakes Forest Research Centre report ; O-X-289; ISSN: 0704-7797)
Note: 105 entries.– Literature review of prescribed fire in jack pine as forest management tool.– Topics include fuel hazard reduction, silvicultural and environmental effects, prescribed burn planning, economics, fire behaviour in jack pine logging slash.– Résumé en français.
Location: OONL.

4968 **Van Wagner, C.E.**
Annotated bibliography of forest fire research at the Petawawa Forest Experiment Station, 1961-1979. Rev. ed. Chalk River, Ont.: Petawawa Forest Experiment Station, 1979. 21 p. (Petawawa Forest Experiment Station Information report ; PS-X-52)
Note: 76 entries.– Journal articles, departmental publications, information reports, internal reports.– Topics include fire danger rating, fuel moisture relations, fire behaviour, fire control planning, fire ecology, fire damage to trees, Christmas tree flammability, prescribed fire.
Titre en français: *Bibliographie annotée de la recherche sur les feux de forêt effectuée à la Station d'expérimentation forestière de Petawawa de 1961 à 1979.*
Previous edition: 1974. 15 l.
Location: OON.

4969 **Wertman, Paul**
Small-scale technology for local forest development: an annotated bibliography. Vancouver: Forintek Canada Corp., Western Forest Products Laboratory, 1979. 189 p. (Review report / Western Forest Products Laboratory ; RR 1); ISBN: 0-86488-012-X.
Note: 484 entries.– Published references dealing with forestry technology: sawmills (economics, equipment), transport, debarkers and chippers, seasoning, wood preservation.– Résumé en français.
Location: OONL.

— 1980 —

4970 **Dendwick, F.M., et al.**
Forest research bibliography, 1968-1975; with 1976-1979 supplement compiled by F.M. Dendwick and R.M. Waldron. Edmonton: Northern Forest Research Centre, Canadian Forestry Service, 1980. x, 64, 19 p.
Note: Approx. 1,100 entries.– Lists forest research literature produced in prairie and northern regions of Canada.– Topics include climate, economics, fire, forest growth and yield, forest regeneration, insects and diseases, pollution and reclamation, watersheds.– Principal bibliography compiled with the assistance of G.R. Stevenson, C.L. Rentz and J.R. Gorman.
Location: OONL.

4971 **Perron, Normand**
"Bibliographie: La Compagnie de Pulpe de Chicoutimi."
Dans: *Saguenayensia*; Vol. 22, nos 3-4 (mai-août 1980) p. 184-186.; ISSN: 0581-295X.
Note: Localisation: AEU.

4972 **Strang, R.M.**
Ecology and management of the grassland and forested rangelands of interior British Columbia: an annotated bibliography. Rev. ed. Victoria: Province of British Columbia, Ministry of Forests, Information Services Branch, c1980. v, 129 p.
Note: 214 entries.– Reports and articles on British Columbia rangelands, including botanical studies, climate, grazing, ecological studies, herbage production and utilization, range administration, soils, weed control and wildlife.

Previous edition: Forest Service Information Division, B.C. Ministry of Forests, 1977. iii, 114 p.
Location: OONL.

— 1981 —

4973 Richardson, James
Black spruce research by the Canadian Forestry Service in Newfoundland. St. John's: Newfoundland Forest Research Centre, 1981. 36 l. (Newfoundland Forest Research Centre Information report ; N-X-206; ISSN: 0704-7657); ISBN: 0-662-11872-3.
Note: 137 entries.– Reports and publications on black spruce: ecology and growth, natural and artificial regeneration, stand treatment, tree improvement, damaging factors.– Résumé en français.
Location: OONL.

— 1982 —

4974 Feller, M.C.
The ecological effects of slashburning with particular reference to British Columbia: a literature review. Victoria: Information Services Branch, B.C. Ministry of Forests, 1982. vii, 60 p. (Land management report / British Columbia Ministry of Forests ; no. 13; ISSN: 0702-9861); ISBN: 0-7719-8890-7.
Note: Approx. 360 entries.– Technical studies, theses, conference reports, journal articles relating to ecological effects on soil, plant regeneration, wildlife, aquatic ecosystems, and atmosphere.
Location: OONL.

4975 Harvey, Daniel A.
A literature review of deer damage and controls in the Pacific Northwest with special reference to British Columbia [microform]. Ottawa: National Library of Canada, 1982. 3 microfiches (217 fr.): ill.; ISBN: 0-315-05548-0.
Note: Approx. 300 entries.– Review of current literature dealing with ecology, physiology and behaviour of white-tail and mule deer, and damage caused to British Columbia forests, orchards and vineyards.
Location: OONL.

4976 Hendrickson, O.; Robinson, J.B.; Chatarpaul, L.
The microbiology of forest soils: a literature review. Chalk River, Ont.: Petawawa National Forestry Institute, Canadian Forestry Service, 1982. ii, 75 p.; ISBN: 0-662-12257-7.
Note: Approx. 500 entries.– Review of literature dealing with two groups of forest soil microorganisms: bacteria and fungi, with focus on their participation in decay of major forest litter substrates, including leaves, branches and roots.– Résumé en français.
Location: OONL.

4977 Van Wagner, C.E.
Bibliographie annotée de la recherche sur les feux de forêt effectuée à la Station d'expérimentation forestière de Petawawa de 1961 à 1979. Chalk River, Ont.: Institut forestier national de Petawawa, 1982. i, 23 f. (Rapport d'information / Institut forestier national de Petawawa ; PS-X-52(F); ISSN: 0228-0736); ISBN: 0-662-91724-3.
Note: 76 entrées.– Articles de périodiques, publications du ministère, rapports d'information, publications diverses: tous les ouvrages publiés sur les feux de forêt par les chercheurs qui ont occupé un poste permanent à la Station de 1961 à 1979.
English title: *Annotated bibliography of forest fire research at*

the Petawawa Forest Experiment Station, 1961-1979.
Localisation: OONL.

— 1983 —

4978 Moore, Gary C.
A report on the feasibility of harvesting timber within buffer zones: a literature review. Fredericton, N.B.: Department of Natural Resources, 1983. iv, 138 l.; ISBN: 0-88838-538-2.
Note: Approx. 350 entries.– Review of literature relating to logging in riparian or buffer zones existing around bodies of water (streams and rivers, ponds, lakes, marshes), effects on water quality, prevention of sedimentation, usage by wildlife, aesthetics, effects on aquatic life.
Location: OONL.

4979 Peterson, Everett B.; Peterson, N. Merle; Kabzems, R.D.
Impact of climatic variation on biomass accumulation in the boreal forest zone: selected references. Edmonton: Canadian Forestry Service, Northern Forest Research Centre, 1983. x, 355 p. (Northern Forest Research Centre Information report ; NOR-X-254; ISSN: 0704-7673); ISBN: 0-662-12895-8.
Note: 329 entries.– Covers to the end of 1981.– Literature from North America, U.S.S.R., and Scandinavian countries, with emphasis on Canada, providing background information on climatic and nonclimatic factors that influence boreal biomass accumulation rates, influence of boreal biomass burning on atmospheric carbon dioxide levels, boreal climate-biomass relationships.– Résumé en français.
Location: OONL.

— 1984 —

4980 Gimbarzevsky, Philip
Remote sensing in forest damage detection and appraisal: selected annotated bibliography. Victoria: Pacific Forest Research Centre, 1984. 55 p. (Pacific Forest Research Centre Information report ; BC-X-253; ISSN: 0705-3274); ISBN: 0-662-13444-3.
Note: 187 entries.– Technical literature dealing with application of remote sensing technology for detection and appraisal of forest damage, primarily covering the years 1969 to 1983, classified by damage types (stress, insects, moisture, etc.), sensors, and geographic areas.– Résumé en français.
Location: OONL.

— 1985 —

4981 Baker, J.L.; Baskerville, G.L.
Growth and yield of New Brunswick forest species: an annotated bibliography. [Fredericton, N.B.]: Faculty of Forestry, University of New Brunswick, 1985. iii, 371 p.
Note: 412 entries.– Lists technical papers related to experimental trials for growth and yield of 16 species of trees native to New Brunswick.– Prepared under contract to New Brunswick Department of Natural Resources.
Location: OONL.

4982 El-Kassaby, Yousry Aly; White, Eleanor E.
Isozymes and forest trees: an annotated bibliography. Victoria: Pacific Forest Research Centre, Canadian Forestry Service, 1985. 79 p. (Pacific Forest Research Centre Information report ; BC-X-267; ISSN: 0705-3274); ISBN: 0-662-14070-2.
Note: 249 entries.– Covers the period 1970-1985.– Contains current references on the state of knowledge in

forest isozyme research.– Topics include genetic heterozygosity, population genetic structure, outcrossing rates, population dynamics, sampling strategies.– Résumé en français.

Location: OONL.

4983 **Hristienko, Hank**
The impact of logging on woodland caribou (Rangifer tarandus caribou): a literature review. Winnipeg: Manitoba Natural Resources, 1985. i, 46 l. (Technical report / Manitoba Natural Resources ; 40-46)
Note: Location: OONL.

4984 **Kimmins, J.P., et al.**
Biogeochemistry of temperate forest ecosystems: literature on inventories and dynamics of biomass and nutrients/Biochimie des écosystèmes des forêts tempérées: publications sur les inventaires et la dynamique de la biomasse et des éléments nutritifs. Chalk River, Ont.: Petawawa National Forestry Institute, Canadian Forestry Service, 1985. xxi, 227 p. (Information report / Petawawa National Forestry Institute ; PI-X-47 E/F; ISSN: 0706-1854); ISBN: 0-662-53946-X.
Note: Approx. 500 entries.– Review and bibliographic listing of studies dealing with nutrient inputs to ecosystems, nutrient dynamics within ecosystems, internal cycling of nutrients within trees, and outputs of nutrients from forest ecosystems.– Text in English and French/texte en français et en anglais.

Location: OONL.

4985 **Kimmins, J.P., et al.**
Whole-tree harvest – nutrient relationships: a bibliography/Exploitation des arbres entiers – rapport des éléments nutritifs: étude bibliographique. Chalk River, Ont.: Petawawa National Forestry Institute, Canadian Forestry Service, 1985. xi, 377 p. (Information report / Petawawa National Forestry Institute ; PI-X-60E-F; ISSN: 0714-3354); ISBN: 0-662-54154-5.
Note: Approx. 3,750 entries.– Research papers to July 1985 arranged in four subject categories: nutrient cycling, biomass, nutrient content of biomass, computer simulation models.– Authors listed alphabetically under each category.– Some Canadian references.– Text in English and French/texte en français et en anglais.

Location: OONL.

4986 **Nordstrom, Lance O.; Newman, Reg F.; Wikeem, Brian M.**
An annotated bibliography on forest-range ecosystems in the Pacific Northwest. Victoria: Information Services Branch, Ministry of Forests, c1985. iv, 96 p. (Land management report / British Columbia Ministry of Forests ; no. 38; ISSN: 0702-9861); ISBN: 0-7718-8510-5.
Note: 302 entries.– Listing of publications through August 1985 dealing with autecology and synecology of plants and animals in forest-range ecosystems, primarily in relation to resource management.– Economic and philosophical perspectives on forest-range issues also covered.

Location: OONL.

4987 **Owens, John N.; Blake, M.D.**
Forest tree seed production: a review of the literature and recommendations for future research. Chalk River, Ont.: Petawawa National Forestry Institute, 1985. vi, 161 p.: ill. (Information report / Petawawa National Forestry Institute ; PI-X-53; ISSN: 0706-1854); ISBN: 0-662-

14185-7.
Note: Approx. 900 entries.– Topics covered include reproductive cycles, floral initiation, environmental factors, pollen and pollination, gametophyte development and fertilization, embryo and seed development.
Titre en français: *Production de semences forestières: revue bibliographiques et suggestions de recherche.*
Location: OONL.

— 1986 —

4988 **Owens, John N.; Blake, M.D.**
Production de semences forestières: revue bibliographiques et suggestions de recherche. Chalk River, Ont.: Institut forestier national de Petawawa, 1986. iv, 216 p. (Rapport d'information / Institut forestier national de Petawawa ; PI-X-53F; ISSN: 0228-0736); ISBN: 0-662-93939-5.
Note: Approx. 900 entrées.– Principaux thèmes: cycles reproducteurs, initiation florale, facteurs du milieu, pollen et pollinisation, développement du gamétophyte et fécondation, développement de l'embryon et des graines.
English title: *Forest tree seed production: a review of the literature and recommendations for future research.*
Localisation: OONL.

— 1987 —

4989 **Ballak, A.J.F.**
Bibliography of reports produced under the assessment program of the Canada-Ontario Forest Management Subsidiary Agreement, 1978-1986. Sault Ste. Marie, Ont.: Great Lakes Forestry Centre, 1987. 29 p. (Great Lakes Forestry Centre Information report ; O-X-386; ISSN: 0832-7122); ISBN: 0-662-15550-5.
Note: Approx. 100 entries.– Catalogue of scientific, technical and popular reports produced by authors funded by Forest Management Subsidiary Agreement.– Topics include vegetative propagation of superior spruce planting stock, production of accelerated tranplants, greenhouse culture of container stock.– Résumé en français.
Location: OONL.

4990 **Grimble, D.G.**
"CANUSA publications useful to northeastern forest-land managers."
In: *Northern Journal of Applied Forestry*; Vol. 4, no. 2 (1987) p. 105-109.; ISSN: 0742-6348.
Note: List of references produced under the Canada-United States Spruce Budworms R&D Program (CANUSA), 1977-1987, arranged in four groups: budworm population monitoring and evaluation; budworm suppression; salvage and utilization of budworm damaged trees; forest management.
Location: OOFP.

4991 **Nietmann, K.**
Catalogue of Canadian forest inventory publications and manuals/Catalogue des manuels et publications de l'inventaire des forêts du Canada. Chalk River, Ont.: Canadian Forestry Service, c1987. 24 p. (Canadian Forestry Service Information report ; PI-X-76E/F; ISSN: 0714-3354); ISBN: 0-662-55501-5.
Note: Listing of forest inventory-related publications and manuals produced or used by the provinces and territories and by the Canadian Forestry Service.– Special attention given to unpublished manuals and technical

instructions.– Text in English and French/texte en français et en anglais.
Location: OONL.

4992 Plexman, C.A.
Bibliography of Great Lakes Forestry Centre publications, 1983-1987. [Sault Ste. Marie, Ont.]: Great Lakes Forestry Centre, Canadian Forestry Service, 1987. [6], 95, [15] p. (Great Lakes Forestry Centre Information report ; O-X-388; ISSN: 0832-7122); ISBN: 0-662-15775-3.
Note: Approx. 750 entries.– Lists scientific, technical and popular literature published by staff members of Great Lakes Forestry Centre.– Includes journal papers, "Information reports," "Joint reports," "Miscellaneous reports," "Survey bulletins," contributions to symposium proceedings, leaflets, pamphlets, newsletter articles.
Previous editions:
... , 1978-1982. 1982. 81, [13] p.; ISBN: 0-662-12299-2. (Information report ; O-X-345).
Bibliography of Great Lakes Forest Research Centre publications, 1965-1977. 1978. 108 p. (Report (Great Lakes Forest Research Centre) ; 279; ISSN: 0704-7797).
Supplements:
1990 bibliography: Forestry Canada, Ontario Region, Great Lakes Forestry Centre. 1991. 12 p. (Information report ; O-X-416); ISBN: 0-662-19200-1.
1991 bibliography: ... . 1992. 14 p. (Information report ; O-X-424); ISBN: 0-662-19907-3.
Location: OONL.

4993 Radvanyi, Andrew
Snowshoe hares and forest plantations: a literature review and problem analysis. Edmonton: Northern Forestry Centre, 1987. vi, 17 p. (Northern Forestry Centre Information report ; NOR-X-290; ISSN: 0704-7673); ISBN: 0-662-15628-5.
Note: Approx. 150 entries.– Review of literature on snowshoe hare damage to forest plantations in the prairie provinces.– Topics include damage control (silvicultural treatments, population control), habitat manipulation, physical barriers.– Résumé en français.
Location: OONL.

4994 Sauder, E.A.; Krag, R.K.; Wellburn, G.V.
Logging and mass wasting in the Pacific Northwest with application to the Queen Charlotte Islands, B.C.: a literature review. Victoria: Ministry of Forestry and Lands, 1987. vi, 26 p.: ill. (Forest Engineering Research Institute of Canada Special report ; no. SR-45) (Land management report / British Columbia Ministry of Forestry and Lands ; no. 53; ISSN: 0702-9861); ISBN: 0-7718-8606-3.
Note: Approx. 90 entries.– Review of research dealing with influence of yarding systems on erosional processes in the Pacific Northwest and the Queen Charlotte Islands.– Topics include erosion and mass wasting, soil mechanics, soil stability, timber harvesting and slope stability, cable yarding systems.
Location: OONL.

— 1988 —

4995 Addison, Paul Andrew; Rennie, P.J.
The Canadian Forestry Service air pollution program and bibliography. Ottawa: Canadian Forestry Service, 1988. iii, 133 p. (Canadian Forestry Service Information report ; DPC-X-26E; ISSN: 0705-324X); ISBN: 0-662-16584-5.
Note: 253 entries.– Publications produced between 1972

and 1988 related to air pollution impact on forest ecology: acid rain, heavy metals, climatology, soil chemistry, tree diseases and pests.
Titre en français: *Programme relatif à la pollution atmosphérique du Service canadien des forêts et bibliographie pertinente.*
Location: OONL.

4996 Hébert, Jacques; Bélanger, Johanne
Statistiques, études de marché et répertoires concernant l'industrie et l'exploitation forestières au Québec: une bibliographie. Québec: Ministère de l'énergie et des ressources, 1988. 30 f. (Études et bibliographies / Centre de documentation, Terres et forêts ; no 2; ISSN: 0838-2255)
Note: Approx. 300 entrées.
Localisation: OONL.

4997 Hébert, Jacques; Collister, Edward A.
Historique de la gestion des terres et des forêts au Québec: une bibliographie. 2e éd., rev. et augm. Québec: Ministère de l'énergie et des ressources, Direction des communications, Centre de documentation – Terres et forêts, 1988. iv, 149 p. (Collection: Études et bibliographies / Québec, Ministère de l'énergie et des ressources, Direction des communications, Centre de documentation: Terres et forêts); ISBN: 2-550-17778-9.
Note: Approx. 1,000 entrées.– Articles, monographies, publications gouvernementales, mémoires reliés à la gestion des terres et forêts au Québec.
Édition antérieure: 1984. 93 p.; ISBN: 2-550-18009-7.
Localisation: OONL.

4998 Macdonald, John Stevenson; Miller, G.; Stewart, R.A.
The effects of logging, other forest industries and forest management practices on fish: an initial bibliography. West Vancouver, B.C.: Fisheries and Oceans Canada, 1988. iv, 212 p. (Canadian technical report of fisheries and aquatic sciences ; no. 1622; ISSN: 0706-6457)
Note: 1,509 entries.– Published papers dealing directly with the interactions of fish and forestry up to and including 1986.– Topics covered selectively include water quality, stream channel morphology, streamflow, water supply, forest soils, forest fires, climate, toxicology and pollution.– Includes a list of additional bibliographical sources.– Résumé en français.
Location: OONL.

4999 Poulin, V.A.; Scrivener, James Charles
An annotated bibliography of the Carnation Creek Fish-forestry Project, 1970 to 1988. Nanaimo, B.C.: Pacific Biological Station, Biological Sciences Branch, Department of Fisheries and Oceans, 1988. iv, 35 p. (Canadian technical report of fisheries and aquatic sciences ; no. 1640; ISSN: 0706-6457)
Note: 147 entries.– Lists articles and research papers produced by participants in the Carnation Creek Fish-forestry Project: assessment of effects of forest practices including logging, prescribed burning, reforestation and herbicide use on salmonid production.
Location: OONL.

5000 Racey, G.D.
Moisture retaining materials for tree seedling packaging: a literature review. Maple, Ontario: Ontario Tree Improvement and Forest Biomass Institute, 1988. 16 p. (Forest Research report / Ontario Tree Improvement and Forest Biomass Institute ; 120; ISSN: 0301-3924); ISBN: 0-

7729-3606-4.

Note: Approx. 100 entries.– Review of literature and bibliography dealing with seedling packaging materials.– Includes Canadian references.

Location: OONL.

5001 **Rennie, P.J.**

Annotated bibliography of openly available published reports, 1950 to 1987. [Ottawa: Canadian Forestry Service], 1988. iii, 80 p.

Note: Listing of research reports and papers by staff of Canadian Forestry Service.

Location: OOFF.

5002 **Samoil, J.K.; Turtle, G.B.**

Northern Forestry Centre publications, 1980-86. Edmonton: Northern Forestry Centre, Canadian Forestry Service, 1988. vi, 36 p. (Northern Forestry Centre Information report ; NOR-X-297; ISSN: 0704-7673); ISBN: 0-662-16058-4.

Note: Approx. 500 entries.– "Information reports," "Forestry reports," "Forest management notes," "Program reviews," "Pest leaflets."- Lists journal and symposium articles, miscellaneous publications by staff members of the Northern Forestry Centre.– Subjects include fire, growth and yield, insects and diseases, regeneration, toxic substances, watersheds and hydrology, individual tree species, climate, economics.

Supplement: Leroy, D.A. *Northern Forestry Centre publications, 1987-1990.* 1991. vi, 30 p. (Information report ; NOR-X-321); ISBN: 0-662-19089-0.

Location: OONL.

5003 **Standish, J.T.; Commandeur, P.R.; Smith, R.B.**

Impacts of forest harvesting on physical properties of soils with reference to increased biomass recovery: a review. Victoria: Pacific Forestry Centre, 1988. 24 p. (Pacific Forestry Centre Information report ; BC-X-301; ISSN: 0830-0453); ISBN: 0-662-16364-8.

Note: Approx. 175 entries.– Summarizes literature dealing with physical soil impact of forest harvesting and effects on tree growth, with emphasis on material published since 1970.– Résumé en français.

Location: OONL.

— 1989 —

5004 **Bancroft, Bryce**

Response of aspen suckering to pre-harvest stem treatments: a literature review. Victoria: Forestry Canada, 1989. vii, 55 p.: ill. (FRDA report / Canada-British Columbia Forest Resource Development Agreement ; 087; ISSN: 0835-0752); ISBN: 0-7726-1013-4.

Note: Approx. 75 entries.– Emphasis on British Columbia forest management.

Location: OONL.

5005 **Bell, W.; Hanmore, C.J.; Willcock, A.J.**

Growth and yield of northwestern Ontario boreal (coniferous) forest species: an annotated bibliography. Thunder Bay: Northwestern Ontario Forest Technology Development Unit, 1989. iii l., 211 p. (Technical report / Northwestern Ontario Forest Technology Development Unit ; no. 31)

Note: 404 entries.– Subject areas include growth and development, spacing, thinning, fertilization, wood quality, as well as general information relating mainly to five key species: jack pine, lodgepole pine, red pine, black spruce, white spruce.

Location: OONL.

— 1990 —

5006 **Addison, Paul Andrew; Rennie, P.J.**

Programme relatif à la pollution atmosphérique du Service canadien des forêts et bibliographie pertinente. Ottawa: Service canadien des forêts, 1990. iii, 116 p. (Rapport d'information / Service canadien des forêts ; DPC-X-26F; ISSN: 0705-324X); ISBN: 0-662-96463-2.

Note: 253 entrées.– Présente un aperçu du Programme relatif à la pollution atmosphérique du Service canadien des forêts en plus expliquer la structure et la disposition de la bibliographie annotée des publications qui en découlent.– La bibliographie comprend des résumés de publications parues de 1972 à 1988.– Domaine d'études: études d'impact et bio-indicateurs, polluants (pluies acides, métaux lourds, dioxydes de soufre), changements climatiques, écologie forestière, chimie des sols.

English title: *The Canadian Forestry Service air pollution program and bibliography.*

Localisation: OONL.

5007 **Forest Engineering Research Institute of Canada**

FERIC publications, 1975-1989. Pointe-Claire, Quebec: FERIC, 1990. [40] p.

Note: 259 entries.– Technical reports, technical notes, special reports, handbooks on topics relating to forest harvesting and processing, transportation, silvicultural operations, small woodlot technology.

Location: OOFF.

5008 **Lindeburgh, S.B.**

Effects of prescribed fire on site productivity: a literature review. Victoria: B.C. Ministry of Forests, 1990. iv, 15 p. (Land management report / British Columbia Ministry of Forests ; no. 66; ISSN 0702-9861); ISBN: 0-7718-8908-9.

Note: 50 entries.

Location: OONL.

5009 **Lousier, J. Daniel**

Impacts of forest harvesting and regeneration on forest sites. Victoria: British Columbia Ministry of Forests, 1990. x, 92 p. (Land management report / British Columbia Ministry of Forests ; no. 67; ISSN: 0702-9861); ISBN: 0-7718-8927-5.

Note: Approx. 400 entries.– Selective annotated bibliography of studies reporting on impact of logging on soil properties and site productivity, costs and productivity of forest harvesting equipment used in interior British Columbia operations, and economics of soil degradation.

Location: OONL.

5010 **Morisette, Thomas**

Revue de littérature sur les divers concepts de vergers à graines. Québec: Service de la régénération forestière, Ministère de l'énergie et des ressources, 1990. v, 32 f.; ISBN: 2-550-20488.

Note: Localisation: OONL.

5011 **Nietfeld, Marie T.; Telfer, Edmund S.**

The effects of forest management practices on nongame birds: an annotated bibliography. Edmonton: Canadian Wildlife Service, c1990. v, 300 p. (Technical report series / Western & Northern Region, Canadian Wildlife Service ; no. 112; ISSN: 0831-6481); ISBN: 0-662-18315-0.

Note: 718 entries.– Contains references (scientific journal articles, technical papers, theses, government reports and studies) to the direct and indirect effects of forestry practices on nongame birds and their habitat.– Topics include logging, cut type, rotation period, thinning, site preparation, herbicide and pesticide use, reforestation, regeneration, burns, interaction between birds and habitat.

Location: OONL.

5012 **Preston, Caroline M.; Rusk, Ann C.M.**
A bibliography of NMR applications for forestry research. Victoria: Pacific Forestry Centre, Forestry Canada, 1990. vii, 42 p. (Pacific Forestry Centre Information report; BC-X-322; ISSN: 0830-0453); ISBN: 0-662-17942-0.

Note: 471 entries.– Lists references to the end of 1989 dealing with the application of nuclear magnetic resonance spectroscopy to forestry research, arranged in subject categories relevant to forestry problems: chemical applications, biological applications, bacteria, fungi, algae and higher plants, water in plants, invertebrates, wood, soils, pesticides.– Emphasis on in vivo biology, and on materials with complex or heterogeneous structures.– Résumé en français.

Location: OONL.

— 1991 —

5013 **Cadrin, Carmen; Campbell, Elizabeth; Nicholson, Alison**
A bibliography on old-growth forests in British Columbia: with annotations and abstracts. Victoria: Province of British Columbia, Ministry of Forests, 1991. v, 261 p. (Land management report / British Columbia Ministry of Forests; no. 72; ISSN: 0702-9861); ISBN: 0-7718-9000-1.

Note: 879 entries.– Books, review articles, bibliographies, theses, research papers to the end of 1990.– Topics include forest types, stand structure, harvesting and silviculture systems, biological diversity, wildlife and wildlife habitat, landscape ecology, values and conservation strategies, ecosystem function.

Location: OONL.

5014 **Leroy, D.A.**
Publications du Centre de foresterie du Nord, 1987-1990. Edmonton: Le Centre, 1991. vi, 30 p. (Rapport d'information / Centre de foresterie du Nord; NOR-X-321F); ISBN: 0-662-97178-7.

Note: Approx. 300 entrées.– Publications scientifiques et techniques, ouvrages de vulgarisation qui ont été rédigés par le personnel du Centre foresterie du Nord ou publié par le Centre entre 1987 et 1990.

English title: *Northern Forestry Centre publications, 1987-1990.*

Localisation: OONL.

— 1992 —

5015 **Hart, Denise; Comeau, P.G.**
Manual brushing for forest vegetation management in British Columbia: a review of current knowledge and information needs. Victoria: BC Ministry of Forests, 1992. vi, 36 p.: ill., maps. (Land management report / British Columbia Ministry of Forests; no. 77; ISSN: 0702-9861); ISBN: 0-7718-9172-5.

Note: 56 entries.– Literature review and listing of papers, studies and theses dealing with brush control in B.C. forests.– Topics include effectiveness of manual brushing, damage to crop trees, costs, constraints on use of manual brushing.

Location: OONL.

5016 **Hills, Steven C.; Morris, Dave M.**
The function of seed banks in northern forest ecosystems: a literature review. Sault Ste. Marie: Ontario Ministry of Natural Resources, 1992. iii, 25 p.: ill. (Forest research information paper; no. 107; ISSN: 0319-9118); ISBN: 0-7729-9722-5.

Note: Approx. 100 entries.– Research related to seed bank dynamics, physiology of seeds in a seed bank, boreal and deciduous forest seed banks.

Location: OONL.

5017 **Moody, B.H.; Amirault, P.A.**
Impacts of major pests on forest growth and yield in the prairie provinces and the Northwest Territories: a literature review. Edmonton: Northern Forestry Centre, Forestry Canada, 1992. vi, 35 p. (Northern Forestry Centre Information report; NOR-X-324; ISSN: 0704-7673); ISBN: 0-662-19535-3.

Note: Summarizes quantitative studies of tree mortality, growth reduction, growth reduction related to insect and disease damage in Alberta, Saskatchewan, Manitoba, and the Northwest Territories (Northwest region).

Location: OONL.

5018 **Rondeau, Guy; Desgranges, Jean-Luc**
Effets des perturbations naturelles et sylvicoles sur l'avifaune forestière: une synthèse bibliographique. Sainte-Foy, Québec: Service canadien de la faune, 1992. iv, 30 p. (Série de rapports techniques du Service canadien de la faune; no 148; ISSN: 0831-6481); ISBN: 0-662-97394-1.

Note: Approx. 100 entrées.– Littérature traitant des oiseaux forestiers pour évaluer les conséquences écologiques des différents types de perturbations forestières et les comparer entre elles.

Localisation: OONL.

5019 **Sarker, Rakhal; McKenney, Daniel William**
Measuring unpriced values: an economic perspective and annotated bibliography for Ontario. Sault Ste. Marie, Ont.: Forestry Canada, Great Lakes Forestry Centre, 1992. 29 p. (Great Lakes Forestry Centre Information report; O-X-422; ISSN: 0832-7122); ISBN: 0-662-19923-5.

Note: Approx. 125 entries.– References dealing with economics of public forestry, methods of valuing unpriced goods and services, Ontario case studies.

Location: OONL.

5020 **Savage, Graham David; Runyon, K.L.**
Economics of private woodlot management: a literature review/Les aspects économiques de l'aménagement des boisés privés: une étude documentaire. Fredericton: Forestry Canada, Maritimes Region, 1992. 111 p. (Information report / Forestry Canada, Maritimes Region; M-X-182E-F; ISSN: 1192-0033); ISBN: 0-662-059100-3.

Note: 477 entries.– Covers 1981-1991.– Text in English and French/texte en français et en anglais.

Location: OONL.

— 1993 —

5021 **Alemdag, I.S.; Richardson, James**
Annotated bibliography of ENFOR biomass reports 1979-1990/Bibliographie annotée des rapports ENFOR sur la biomasse 1979-1990. Ottawa: Forestry Canada, 1993. viii, 288 p. (Information report / ENFOR Secretariat, Forestry Canada; ST-X-6); ISBN: 0-660-58853-6.

Note: Text in English and French/texte en français et en anglais.

Location: OONL.

5022 **Harvey, Eileen M. Forestell; Mohammed, Gina H.; Noland, T.L.**

A bibliography on competition, tree seedling characteristics and related topics. Sault Ste. Marie: Ontario Ministry of Natural Resources, 1993. iv, 117 p. (Forest research information paper ; no. 108; ISSN: 0319-9118); ISBN: 0-7778-0969-9.

Note: 708 entries.– Focus is on interspecific competition with tree seedlings and nursery practices as they affect seedling morphology, physiology and field performance.– Substantial Canadian content.

Location: OONL.

— Ongoing/En cours —

5023 **Nova Scotia. Department of Lands and Forests**

Forest research report. Truro: Nova Scotia Department of Lands and Forests, 1987-.   vol.; ISSN: 0845-1788.

Note: Began with October 1987 issue.– Issued 15 times yearly.

Previous edition: *Inventory of forest research in Nova Scotia, 1985-1986.* Truro: [s.n.], 1986. 44, 3 p.

5024 **Pacific Forestry Centre**

Reports and publications [Pacific Forestry Centre]. Victoria: Pacific Forestry Centre, 1985-.   vol.; ISSN: 0846-6610.

Note: Annual listing of articles in scientific journals and reports by members of The Centre.– Topics include biology, ecology, economics, entomology, fire, hydrology, inventory/growth/yield.

Location: OONL.

— 1949 —

5025 "Bibliography of Canadian hydrology."
In: *Canadian Geophysical Bulletin*; Vol. 3, no. 2 (April-June 1949) p. 1-10.; ISSN: 0068-8819.
Note: 158 entries.
Location: OON.

— 1950 —

5026 "Bibliography of atmospheric ionization."
In: *Canadian Geophysical Bulletin*; Vol. 4, no. 2 (April-June 1950) p. 1-10.; ISSN: 0068-8819.
Note: 139 entries.– Four sections: atmospheric electricity, aurora, ionospheric ionization, meteor ionization.– Publications refer to or make use of observational material originating in Canada or prepared in Canadian laboratories.
Location: OON.

— 1951 —

5027 Pearce, D.C.
A bibliography on snow and ice. Ottawa: Division of Building Research, National Research Council, 1951. 69 l. (Bibliography / National Research Council Canada, Division of Building Research ; no. 1)
Note: References to articles on snow and ice and related topics in Canadian journals from their beginnings to December 1950: *Canadian Engineer*; *Engineering Journal*; Royal Society of Canada *Transactions*, (section 3); *Roads and Bridges*; *Water and Sewage*.
Location: BVAS.

— 1952 —

5028 American Geophysical Union
Annotated bibliography on hydrology, 1941-1950 (United States and Canada). [Washington: U.S. Government Printing Office, 1952]. 408 p. (Notes on hydrologic activities, Bulletin / U.S. Federal Inter-Agency River Basin Committee, Subcommittee on Hydrology ; no. 5)
Note: Supplements:
Annotated bibliography on hydrology (1951-54) and sedimentation (1950-54) United States and Canada. 1956. 207 p.
Riggs, H.C. *Annotated bibliography on hydrology and sedimentation, United States and Canada, 1955-58.* 1962. iv, 236 p.
Bradberry, Carroll E., and Associates. *Annotated bibliography on hydrology and sedimentation, 1959-1962 (United States and Canada).* 1964. xii, 323 p.
Location: OONL.

— 1957 —

5029 Canada. Department of Mines and Technical Surveys. Geographical Branch
Selected bibliography on sea ice distribution in the coastal waters of Canada. Ottawa: [Queen's Printer], 1957. 50 p.: maps (2 folded). (Bibliographical series / Canada Department of Mines and Technical Surveys, Geographical Branch ; no. 18)

Note: Approx. 560 entries.– Lists source material on sea ice conditions contained in the catalogue of the Canadian Ice Distribution Survey.– Includes the waters of the Canadian arctic archipelago, the Hudson-James Bay area, coastal waters of the Province of Newfoundland and Gulf of St. Lawrence.– Prepared by W.A. Black.
Location: OONL.

— 1959 —

5030 Williams, Gaynor P.
Frazil ice: a review of its properties with a selected bibliography. Ottawa: National Research Council Canada, Division of Building Research, 1959. 5 p. (National Research Council Canada, Division of Building Research Technical paper ; no. 81)
Note: Reprinted from *The Engineering Journal*; Vol. 42, no. 11 (November 1959) P. 55-60.
Location: OONL.

— 1960 —

5031 O'Riordan, Jonathan
A bibliography of Canadian writings in water resource management. [S.l.: s.n., 1960]. 1 vol. (in various pagings).
Note: Approx. 1,000 entries.– Lists books, government reports, journal articles dealing with aspects of water resource development and management within Canada.– Topics include water supply and conservation, water use, flood control, economics, legal aspects, water pollution, ground water.
Location: OOFF.

— 1961 —

5032 Annotated bibliography of selected documents pertaining to water allocation and utilization in the Saskatchewan River Basin. [S.l.: s.n.], 1961. 82 p.
Note: Listing of books, articles and government documents dealing with land, water, population, resources, economics of Saskatchewan River Basin.
Location: OONL.

5033 Thomas, Morley K.
A bibliography of Canadian climate, 1763-1957. Ottawa: Division of Building Research, National Research Council of Canada, 1961. 114 p.
Note: Approx. 1,400 entries.– Books, articles, papers.– Chronological arrangement for historical approach.– Published separately was: Stark, R.G. *A geographical index to A bibliography of Canadian climate, 1763-1957.* Toronto: Meteorological Branch, Department of Transport, 1961. 7 vol.
Location: OONL.

— 1964 —

5034 Hattersley-Smith, G.
Bibliography of "Operation Hazen," 1957-63. Ottawa: National Defence Department, Defence Research Board, Directorate of Physical Research Geophysics, 1964. 5 p.
Note: Articles and papers resulting from research undertaken at Hazen camp, northern Ellesmere Island: glaciology, oceanography, meteorology, marine biology,

botany.
Location: OOFF.

5035 **Myres, Miles Timothy**
An introduction to the literature of the effects of biocides on wildlife and fish: a select bibliography. Calgary: Department of Biology, University of Alberta at Calgary, 1964. 28, iii l.
Note: Location: OOFF.

— 1965 —

5036 **Arnell, Susan**
A bibliography on ice in navigable waters in Canada, 1945-1964. Ottawa: National Research Council of Canada, 1965. 64 p.
Note: 696 entries.– General works, bibliographies, atlases, works on pure physics and mechanics, applied physics and engineering, oceanography, description of natural ice covers, observed conditions, reconnaissance and forecasting techniques, ice navigation, icebergs, ice shelf and ice islands.
Location: QQLA.

5037 **Williams, John R.**
Ground water in permafrost regions: an annotated bibliography. Washington: United States Government Printing Office, 1965. iii, 294 p.: map. (Geological Survey Water-supply paper ; 1792)
Note: 862 entries.– Literature on the occurrence of ground water in permafrost regions.– Covers North American, Scandinavian and Russian material through 1960.– Includes a brief history of permafrost investigations and current trends in Canada, United States and Soviet Union.
Location: OWA.

— 1967 —

5038 **Michel, Bernard; Triquet, Claude**
Bibliographie de la mécanique des glaces de rivières et de lacs/Bibliography of river and lake ice mechanics. [Québec]: Université Laval, Faculté des sciences, Département de génie civil, Section mécanique des glaces, 1967. [250] l.
Note: Approx. 1,250 entrées.– Liste d'articles et de volumes traitant de la glace d'eau douce: propriétés physiques et mécaniques de la glace, problèmes de glace dans les structures hydrauliques, formation de la glace et débâcle sur les rivières et les lacs.– Texte en français et en anglais/text in English and French.
Localisation: OOPW.

— 1968 —

5039 **Bolsenga, S.J.**
River ice jams: a literature review. [Detroit]: Great Lakes Research Center, U.S. Lake Survey, 1968. iii, 568 p.: ill.
Note: Approx. 400 entries.– Published studies of river ice jams: ice-jam mechanism and methods for prevention and removal.– Includes Canadian references.
Location: AEU.

5040 **Canadian Council of Resource Ministers**
Pollution: bibliography/Pollution: bibliographie. [Montreal: s.n., 1968]. 74, 52 p.
Note: Approx. 1,100 entries.– Prepared for the conference "Pollution and Our Environment."- Topics include pollution control, measurement, legislation, surveys and toxicology.– Text in English and French/texte en français et en anglais.
Location: OONL.

5041 **Denike, C.C.E.**
A bibliography of climatology for British Columbia. Vancouver: [s.n.], 1968. vi, 70 l.
Note: 651 entries.– Listing of theses, graduating essays, term reports, studies from government and private agencies and institutions containing climatological data or dealing with theoretical or applied aspects of climatology in British Columbia.– Prepared for the Canada Land Inventory, A.R.D.A.
Location: SRU.

5042 **Dionne, Jean-Claude**
"Bibliographie du périglaciaire du Québec/A bibliography of periglacial studies in Quebec."
Dans: *Revue de géographie de Montréal*; Vol. 22, no 2 (1968) p. 175-180.; ISSN: 0035-1148.
Note: 144 entrées.
Localisation: AEU.

5043 **Hattersley-Smith, G.**
Bibliography of "Operation Hazen-Tanquary," 1964-1967. Ottawa: Defence Research Telecommunications Establishment (Canada), 1968. 10 p.
Note: Articles and papers resulting from research undertaken at Hazen and Tanquary camps, Ellesmere Island.– Themes: glaciology, oceanography, marine biology, botany.
Location: OTU.

5044 **Relph, E.C.; Goodwillie, S.B.**
Annotated bibliography on snow and ice problems. Toronto: Department of Geography, University of Toronto, 1968. 14 p. (Natural hazard research working paper / Department of Geography, University of Toronto ; no. 2)
Note: Approx. 100 entries.– Bibliographies and general studies, meteorological and climatic studies, studies of impact of snowfalls, perception of snow hazard, snow removal/ice control.
Location: OONL.

5045 **Selected bibliography of hydrology for the years ... annotated: Canada/Bibliographie choisie d'hydrologie des années ... annotée: Canada.** Ottawa: National Research Council, Associate Committee on Geodesy and Geophysics, Subcommittee on Hydrology: Department of Energy, Mines and Resources, Inland Waters Branch, 1959-1968. 4 vol.
Note: Years covered by the series: 1958-1967.– Includes bulletins and pamphlets from public and private agencies pertaining to hydrology in Canada.– Principal topics include hydrometeorology, rivers, lakes, glaciers, groundwater and springs, balance of the hydrologic cycle, application of sciences to hydrology.
Location: OONL.

— 1969 —

5046 **Dionne, Jean-Claude**
"Bibliographie annotée du glaciel: aspects morpho-sédimentologiques/An annotated bibliography of "glaciel" studies: morpho-sedimentological aspects."
Dans: *Revue de géographie de Montréal*; Vol. 23, no 3 (1969) p. 339-349.; ISSN: 0035-1148.
Note: Localisation: OONL.

5047 **El-Sabh, Mohammed I.; Forrester, W.D.; Johannessen, O.M.**
Bibliography and some aspects of physical oceanography in the Gulf of St. Lawrence. Montreal: Marine Sciences

Centre, McGill University, 1969. 65 p.: ill., charts, maps. (Manuscript report / Marine Sciences Centre, McGill University ; no. 14; ISSN: 0828-1831)
Note: Approx. 400 entries.– Chronological listing from 1837 to 1968 on oceanography of the Gulf of St. Lawrence.– Topics include air-sea interface, circulation, tides and sea level, water masses, ice, wave conditions.
Location: OONL.

5048 **Montreal Engineering Company**
Maritime provinces water resources study, stage 1: appendix 1: bibliography. [Ottawa]: Atlantic Development Board, 1969. [95] p. (in various pagings).
Note: 898 entries.– Reports and studies pertaining to water quality, demand, management, treatment in the Atlantic region.– Related material deals with climate, industrial wastes, pollution, fisheries, agriculture, recreation and transportation.
Location: OONL.

5049 **Parker, J.E.; Anderson, S.R.**
Guide to Canadian climatic data. Toronto: Meteorological Branch, Department of Transport, 1969. 1 vol. (in various pagings).
Note: Covers to June 1969.
Location: OOFF.

— 1970 —

5050 **Bibliography of hydrology. Canada, 1968-1970/ Bibliographie d'hydrologie. Canada, 1968-1970.**
[Ottawa]: Department of the Environment and National Research Council, [1970]. v, 336 p.
Note: 1,580 entries.– Lists reports and studies related to general hydrology and hydrometeorology, surface water, subsurface water, water quality/pollution, biohydrology, forest hydrology.– Includes a list of additional bibliographies.– Text in English and French/texte en français et en anglais.
Supplement: ... *1971-1973*/... *1971-1973*. 1973. v, 410 p.
Location: OONL.

5051 **Brunel, Pierre**
"Bibliographie choisie sur l'océanographie de l'estuaire du Saint-Laurent."
Dans: *Revue de géographie de Montréal*; Vol. 24, no 3 (1970) p. 277-282.; ISSN: 0035-1148.
Note: Localisation: AEU.

5052 **Hartman, Charles W.; Carlson, Robert F.**
A bibliography of Arctic water resources. College, Alaska: Institute of Water Resources, University of Alaska, [1970]. 344, [194] p. (Report / University of Alaska, Institute of Water Resources ; no. IWR-11)
Note: Location: OOCC.

5053 **Hedlin, Menzies & Associates**
Annotated bibliography of socio-economic references for water quality management studies in the Saint John River Basin. Toronto: [s.n.], 1970. 164 l.
Note: 741 entries.– Reports, studies, conference papers.– Sections include: background on the region (agriculture, forestry and fisheries, manufacturing, urban growth, recreation, regional development); role of water (municipal and industrial supply and demand, waste disposal, groundwater development, power generation, economic development, recreation); water quality management (costs and benefits, mathematical models).
Location: NBFU.

5054 **Laverdière, Camille; Bernard, Claude**
"Bibliographie annotée sur les broutures glaciaires/An annotated bibliography on glacial chattermarks."
Dans: *Revue de géographie de Montréal*; Vol. 24, no 1 (1970) p. 79-89.; ISSN: 0035-1148.
Note: Localisation: OONL.

5055 **Québec (Province). Ministère des richesses naturelles. Direction générale des eaux. Service de l'aménagement hydraulique**
Bibliographie sur le bassin de la Yamaska. Québec: Ministère des richesses naturelles, 1970. 51 p.: carte. (Mission technique pour l'aménagement des eaux du bassin de la Yamaska, Rapport ; no 1)
Note: Approx. 400 entrées.– Rapports, études, publications gouvernementales relatives à l'aménagement intégré du bassin de la Yamaska: développement économique, hydrologie, géologie, érosion et sedimentation, inondations et protection contre les inondations, navigation, aménagement des ressources agricoles, loisirs, gestion forestière, études d'aménagement.
Localisation: OONL.

5056 **Villeneuve, G.–Oscar**
Bibliographie climatologique du Québec. 2e éd. Québec: Ministère des richesses naturelles, Service de la météorologie, 1970. 17 p.
Note: Approx. 200 entrées.
Édition antérieure: 1969. 14 p.
Localisation: OONL.

— 1971 —

5057 **Brander, Leo G.; Graham, Bruce M.**
A bibliography of periodical articles concerning the management and economics of water resources. Wolfville, N.S.: Department of Economics, Acadia University, 1971. 22 l.
Note: Location: OONL.

5058 **"The environmental crisis: a select annotated list of books, films and magazine articles."**
In: *Ontario Library Review*; Vol. 55, no. 1 (March 1971) p. 21-26.; ISSN: 0030-2996.
Note: Sections include ecology, chemical pollution, air pollution, water pollution, bibliographies.
Location: OONL.

5059 **Longley, Richmond Wilberforce; Powell, John M.**
Bibliography of climatology for the Prairie provinces, 1957-1969. Edmonton: University of Alberta Press, 1971. 64 p. (University of Alberta studies in geography bibliographies ; 1); ISBN: 0-88864-002-1.
Note: 665 entries.– Journal articles, government studies, symposium papers published between 1957 and 1970.– Principal topics include climate in general, agricultural meteorology, atmospheric pollution, climatic change, evaporation, frost, hail, precipitation (general), soil erosion, temperature, thunderstorms and weather cycles.
Location: OONL.

5060 **Ward, E. Neville; Watson, Donna J.; White, S. Richard**
A selected bibliography of Canadian water management (1965-April 1970). Edmonton: Department of Geography, University of Alberta, 1971. 80 l.
Note: Approx. 1,500 entries.– Federal and provincial government studies and reports, periodical articles, theses.– Topics include agriculture and forestry, industrial and urban, recreation and conservation, flood control, hydrology and hydrogeology, international water and

water transfers.
Location: OONL.

— 1972 —

5061 **Bibliographie annotée des caractéristiques physiques de la côte nord de l'estuaire maritime et du golfe Saint-Laurent.** [Ottawa: Ministère des travaux publics], 1972. 191 l.
Note: Approx. 800 entrées.– Documents traitant des sujets: topographie et bathymétrie, physiographie, géologie, histoire du Quaternaire, géomorphologie, hydrologie et hydrographie, pédologie (sols), végétation, climatologie, océanographie et glaces flottantes.
Localisation: OONL.

5062 **Canada. National Advisory Committee on Water Resources Research**
Bibliography of water resources research/Bibliographie de la recherche sur les ressources hydrauliques. [Ottawa: s.n.], 1972. 80 l.
Note: Approx. 400 entries.– Contains three sections: published papers, unpublished papers and theses.– Text in English and French/texte en français et en anglais.
Location: OOFF.

5063 **Douglas College. Institute of Environmental Studies**
The environmental crisis: a bibliography of publications available in Douglas College Library. [New Westminster, B.C.]: Douglas College Institute of Environmental Studies, 1972. 31 l.
Note: Approx. 300 entries.– Lists books, studies, articles, reports, conference proceedings related to air pollution, environmental policy, population, noise, regional planning, water pollution, wildlife conservation.– Emphasis on British Columbia.
Location: OONL.

5064 **Emery, Alan R.**
A review of the literature of oil pollution with particular reference to the Canadian Great Lakes. [Toronto]: Ontario Ministry of Natural Resources, 1972. ii, 63 p. (Research information paper / Ontario Ministry of Natural Resources ; no. 40)
Note: Approx. 375 entries.– Lists government reports, journal articles, conference proceedings.– Topics include fate of oil in and on water, breakdown of oil, biological effects of oil pollution, oil spill clean-up and control and oil transportation.
Location: OOFF.

5065 **Hacia, Henry**
A selected annotated bibliography of the climate of the Great Lakes. Silver Spring, Md.: U.S. Environmental Data Service, 1972. iv, 70 p. (National Oceanic and Atmospheric Administration Technical memorandum ; EDS BS-7)
Note: 201 entries.– Covers January 1960 through April 1971.– Many Canadian references.
Location: OOCC.

5066 **Roberts-Pichette, Patricia**
Annotated bibliography of permafrost-vegetation-wildlife-landform relationships. Ottawa: Canadian Forestry Service, Department of the Environment, 1972. 350 p. (Forest Management Institute Information report ; FMR-X-43)
Note: 487 entries.– Covers 1945 to 1971.– Concerned primarily with land sensitivity in the North.– Includes studies and reviews in areas of taxonomy, ecology,

geology, geography, meteorology, permafrost related to revegetation of disturbed lands.
Location: OONL.

5067 **Thunder Bay Environmental Project**
The Thunder Bay environmental information index. Thunder Bay, Ont.: Thunder Bay Environmental Project, 1972. 99 p.
Note: References from Canadian and American sources: bibliographies, economics, geography, air/soil/water pollution, ecology, population, resource planning.– Filmography, p. 35-40.– Bibliography, p. 41-98.
Location: OONL.

5068 **United States. Water Resources Scientific Information Center**
Lake Huron: a bibliography. Washington: U.S. Department of the Interior, Office of Water Resources Research, [1972]. iv, 95 p.
Note: 58 entries.– Photocopy.– Topics include eutrophication, water quality, water pollution, limnological investigations, mercury in fish, shoreland management and erosion damage control.
Location: OONL.

5069 **United States. Water Resources Scientific Information Center**
Lake Ontario: a bibliography. Washington: Water Resources Scientific Information Center, U.S. Department of the Interior, 1972. iv, 200 p. (Bibliography series / United States Water Resources Information Center ; WRSIC 72-212)
Note: 130 entries.– Topics include eutrophication, water levels problem, wave action, sediments, erosion control, water pollution.
Location: OONL.

5070 **United States. Water Resources Scientific Information Center**
Lake Superior: a bibliography. Springfield, Va.: National Technical Information Service, United States Department of Commerce, [1972]. iv, 127 p.
Note: Approx. 80 entries.– Photocopy.– Topics include water pollution, eutrophication, water quality, lake sediments.
Location: OONL.

5071 **Université Laval. Centre de recherches sur l'eau**
Bibliographie du Fleuve Saint-Laurent de Trois-Rivières à l'île-aux-coudres. Québec: Université Laval, 1972. [22] f.
Note: Approx. 200 entrées.
Localisation: OONL.

5072 **Williams, Gaynor P.**
Summary of current research on snow and ice in Canada. Ottawa: National Research Council of Canada, Associate Committee on Geotechnical Research, 1972. 30 p. (Associate Committee on Geotechnical Research Technical memorandum ; no. 106)
Note: Approx. 200 entries.– Snow and ice properties and processes, atmospheric snow and ice, snow cover on ground, lake and river ice, sea ice, glaciers, soil ice, engineering structures (snow and ice problems).
Location: OONL.

— 1973 —

5073 **Brown, Roger J.E.; Péwé, Troy L.**
Distribution of permafrost in North America and its relationship to the environment: a review, 1963-1973. Ottawa: National Research Council Canada, Division of

Building Research, [1973]. [30] p. (National Research Council Canada, Division of Building Research Technical paper ; no. 411)
Note: 274 entries.– Literature review of progress (1963-1973) in knowledge of distribution of permafrost and relation of environmental factors in North America.
Excerpt from: *Permafrost: the North American contribution to the Second International Conference.* Washington, D.C.: 1973. P. 71-100.
Location: OONL.

5074 **Canada. Atmospheric Environment Service**
A selected list of articles and papers on the climatology of the Upper Great Lakes published from 1960 to 1972. Downsview, Ont.: Atmospheric Environment Service, Hydrometeorology and Marine Applications Division, 1973. 17 l.
Note: Approx. 200 entries.– Chronological listing.
Location: OTY.

5075 **Dingman, S. Lawrence**
The water balance in arctic and subarctic regions: annotated bibliography and preliminary assessment. Hanover, N.H.: Corps of Engineers, U.S. Army, Cold Regions Research and Engineering Laboratory, 1973. 134 p. (Cold Regions Research and Engineering Laboratory, Special report ; 187)
Note: Review of research literature dealing with elements of water balance in arctic regions, including Canada.– Topics include precipitation, evapotranspiration, runoff, streamflow, groundwater contributions to runoff, changes in glacial storage.
Location: NFSM.

5076 **Giffen, A.V.**
The occurrence and prevention of frazil ice blockage at water supply intakes: a literature review and field survey. [Toronto]: Ontario Ministry of the Environment, 1973. iii, 32 p. (Research Branch publication / Ontario Ministry of the Environment ; no. W 42)
Note: Location: OONL.

5077 **Indians of Quebec Association. James Bay Task Force**
Bibliography pertaining to environmental aspects of the James Bay Hydroelectric Development. Montreal: Indians of Quebec Association; Northern Quebec Inuit Association, 1973. 62 l.
Note: Location: OOCC.

5078 **LeClair, B.P.**
Selected references on phosphorus removal. Ottawa: Environment Canada, Environmental Protection Service, 1973. iii, 41 p. (Economic and technical review report / Water Pollution Control Directorate ; EPS 3-WP-73-2)
Note: Approx. 400 entries.– Literature survey arranged in order of categories related to chemicals used for precipitation of, or process used for, removal of phosphorus.– Some Canadian references.
Location: OONL.

5079 **Rybczywski, Witold**
"Bibliographie écologique."
Dans: *Architecture concept*; Vol. 28, no 314 (mai 1973) p. 17,19.; ISSN: 0003-8687.
Note: Localisation: OONL.

5080 **Thomas, Morley K.**
A bibliography of Canadian climate, 1958-1971/ Bibliographie du climat canadien, 1958-1971. Ottawa: Information Canada, 1973. 170 p.

Note: Approx. 1,400 entries.– Books, articles, reports dealing substantially with some aspect of Canadian climate.– Excludes publications dealing primarily with fundamental research, meteorological instruments, and methods used in forecasting.– Text in English and French/texte en français et en anglais.
Location: OONL.

5081 **United States. Environmental Protection Agency**
Annotated bibliography of Lake Ontario limnological and related studies. Washington, D.C.: Office of Research and Monitoring, U.S. Environmental Protection Agency, 1973. 3 vol.: maps. (Ecological research series)
Note: Vol. 1: *Chemistry*, by Daniel Proto and Robert A. Sweeney.– 187 entries.
Vol. 2: *Biology*, by Elaine P. Downing, James E. Hassan, Robert A. Sweeney.– 596 entries.
Vol. 3: *Physical*, by John Baldwin and Robert A. Sweeney.– 439 entries.
References dealing with physical properties and phenomena of Lake Ontario and tributaries: techniques and instrumentation, parameters, organisms and habitats.
Location: OKQ.

5082 **United States. Water Resources Scientific Information Center**
Lake Erie: a bibliography. Washington: U.S. Department of the Interior, Office of Water Resources Research, [1973]. iv, 240 p.
Note: 220 entries.– Photocopy.– Topics include water pollution, flood control, eutrophication, fish population studies, mercury pollution and fish, shoreland erosion.
Location: OONL.

5083 **Wilkie, Brian**
Energy in Canada: a selective bibliographic review. Waterloo, Ont.: Faculty of Environmental Studies, University of Waterloo, [1973]. 14 p. (Occasional papers / Faculty of Environmental Studies, University of Waterloo ; no. 8; ISSN: 0317-8625)
Note: Location: OON.

— 1974 —

5084 **Atton, F.M.; Johnson, Ronald P.; Smith, N.W.**
Bibliography of limnology and aquatic fauna and flora of Saskatchewan. Regina: Saskatchewan Department of Tourism and Renewable Resources, 1974. vi, 34 p. (Fisheries report / Saskatchewan Department of Tourism and Renewable Resources ; no. 10)
Note: Approx. 500 entries.– Covers from 1836 to the end of 1972.– Includes scientific papers, miscellaneous publications, technical reports, theses dealing with limnobiology of Saskatchewan lakes and streams.
Location: OONL.

5085 **Bibliography of land resource information for 17 estuaries in British Columbia.** Vancouver: Lands Directorate, Pacific Region, Environment Canada, 1974. 1 vol. (in various pagings): maps.
Note: Selected listing of published and unpublished surveys, reports and maps dealing with soils, geology, land capability of or near the 17 British Columbia estuaries.– For the Fraser River estuary only, there is a selection of references on recreation and wildlife, vegetation and ecology.
Location: OOFF.

5086 **Canada. Agriculture Canada. Research Station (Saskatoon). Library**
Pesticide application and spraying: a selected bibliography. Saskatoon: Agriculture Canada, 1974. 195 p. (Technical bulletin / Saskatoon Research Station, Agriculture Canada ; no. 2)
Note: Approx. 2,000 entries.– Topics covered include aerial application, drift, environmental factors, equipment, ground application, nozzles, safety, spreading, retention and persistence of sprays.– Includes a list of additional bibliographies.– Some Canadian references.
Location: OONL.

5087 **Clarke, R. McV.**
The effects of effluents from metal mines on aquatic ecosystems in Canada. Winnipeg: Freshwater Institute, Research and Development Directorate, Fisheries and Marine Service, Environment Canada, 1974. v, 150 p. (Fisheries and Marine Service Technical report ; no. 488; ISSN: 0701-7626)
Note: Location: OONL.

5088 **Hoos, Lindsay M.; Packman, Glen A.**
The Fraser River estuary: status of environmental knowledge to 1974: report of the Estuary Working Group, Department of the Environment, Regional Board Pacific Region. [Ottawa]: Environment Canada, 1974. xx, 518 p.: ill., maps. (Special estuary series / Estuary Working Group, Department of the Environment, Regional Board Pacific Region ; no. 1)
Note: Approx. 1,800 entries.– Journal articles, theses, government reports and studies dealing with environment of Fraser River estuary.– Topics include geology and soils, climatology, hydrology and water quality, oceanography, biology, land use, waste disposal.– Includes a list of maps.
Location: OONL.

5089 **Hunka, Diane Lynne**
The effects of effluents from the Canadian plastics industry on aquatic organisms: a literature review. Winnipeg: Freshwater Institute, Research and Development Directorate, Fisheries and Marine Service, Environment Canada, 1974. v, 64 p. (Fisheries and Marine Service Technical report ; no. 473; ISSN: 0701-7626)
Note: Location: OONL.

5090 **Québec (Province). Commission d'étude des problèmes juridiques de l'eau**
Bibliographie annotée de la Commission d'étude des problèmes juridiques de l'eau: documents remis à la bibliothèque. Québec: Ministère des richesses naturelles, Service de la bibliothèque et des archives, 1974. xi, 96 p.
Note: 342 entrées.– Regroupe uniquement les ouvrages ayant servi à la Commission pour son travail d'étude entrepris en juillet 1968 et terminé en juin 1971.– Classification géographique: pays, provinces, états, etc.– Le Canada et les provinces rassemblement 30% de la documentation.
Localisation: OONL.

5091 **Robinson, Susan E.; Scott, W.B.**
A selected bibliography on mercury in the environment, with subject listing. Toronto: Royal Ontario Museum, 1974. 54 p. (Royal Ontario Museum Life sciences miscellaneous publications; ISSN: 0082-5093); ISBN: 0-88854-166-X.

Note: 460 entries.– Papers from the mid 1960s to May 1973, with a few earlier papers from the 1930s through the 1950s for historical background.– Themes include analytical methods, properties of mercury compounds, biological and geochemical transformations, measurements of mercury levels.
Location: OONL.

5092 **Schick-Swanson Library and Information Consultants Ltd**
Pollution in Alberta: a bibliography. Edmonton: Schick-Swanson Library and Information Consultants, 1974. 31 p.
Note: Approx. 250 entries.– Lists reports and studies from municipal, provincial and federal agencies, university and private research institutions on air, water, noise pollution; solid waste management in Alberta.
Location: OONL.

5093 **Société de développement de la Baie James (Québec)**
Développement hydroélectrique de la Baie James: développement de l'environnement. Montréal: Société d'énergie de la Baie James, 1974. 235 p.: ill. (certaines en coul.), cartes (certaines en coul.), graphiques.
Note: "Ce document résume les connaissances de l'environnement humain, physique et biologique du territoire de la Baie James et des bassins des rivières adjacentes."- Bibliographie thématique, p. 210-235.
Localisation: QQLA.

5094 **Thompson, Barbara**
The effects of effluent from the Canadian textile industry on aquatic organisms: a literature review. Winnipeg: Environment Canada, Fisheries and Marine Service, Freshwater Institute, 1974. vi, 99 p. (Fisheries and Marine Service Technical report ; no. 489; ISSN: 0701-7626)
Note: Approx. 175 entries.– Review of technical studies related to toxicology of Canadian textile industry wastes.– Résumé en français.
Location: OONL.

5095 **Vermeer, Rebecca Arrieta; Vermeer, Kees**
The biological effects of oil pollution on aquatic organisms: a summarized bibliography. Ottawa: Pesticide Section, Canadian Wildlife Service, 1974. [4], 68 p. (Manuscript reports / Pesticide Section, Canadian Wildlife Service ; no. 31)
Note: Approx. 150 entries.– Covers to 1973.– Includes journal articles dealing with effects of oil pollution on fish, molluscs, crustaceans and other species.– Also covers the effects of dispersants.– Includes Canadian references.
Location: OONL.

5096 **Western Research & Development Limited**
Arctic air pollution bibliography. Calgary: Western Research & Development, 1974. [65] l.
Note: 135 entries.– Literature survey pertaining to air pollution in the Arctic in North America, Scandinavia, Russia, with particular emphasis on sources and effects of sulphur dioxide, fluorides, heavy metals, and the problem of ice fog.– Thirty papers are reviewed in detail.
Location: OOFF.

5097 **Williams, Gaynor P.**
Annotated bibliography on snow drifting and its control. Ottawa: Division of Building Research, National Research Council, [1974]. [43] p. (in various pagings). (National Research Council Canada, Division of Building

Research Bibliography ; no. 42)
Note: Approx. 120 entries.– Covers the period June 1964 to June 1973.– Selection of international references in five sections: drifting snow in the air; drifting snow on the ground; models and wind tunnels; railways, roads and buildings; snow fences, forests, hedges.
Previous edition: Gold, Lorne W. 1968. 30, 61 l. (National Research Council Canada, Division of Building Research Bibliography ; no. 38).– Covers to June 1964.
Location: OON.

— 1975 —

5098   Bell, Leonard M.; Kallman, Ronald J.
The Cowichan-Chemainus River estuaries: status of environmental knowledge to 1975: report of the Estuary Working Group, Department of the Environment, Regional Board Pacific Region. [Ottawa]: Environment Canada, [1975]. 328 p. (Special estuary series / Estuary Working Group, Department of the Environment, Regional Board, Pacific Region ; no. 4)
Note: Approx. 800 entries.– Journal articles, theses, government reports and studies dealing with environment of Cowichan-Chemainus River estuaries: geology and soils, climatology, hydrology and water quality, oceanography, biology, land use, waste disposal.– Includes a list of maps.
Location: OOFF.

5099   Grayson, Donald K.
A bibliography of the literature on North American climates of the past 13,000 years. New York: Garland Publishing, c1975. 206 p. (Garland reference library of natural science ; vol. 2); ISBN: 0-8240-9992-3.
Note: 1,398 entries.– Restricted to those studies which deal with periods of time for which modern observational data are not available.– Includes primarily archaeological, botanical, geological, meteorological, and zoological sources.
Location: OONL.

5100   Hoos, Lindsay M.
The Skeena River estuary: status of environmental knowledge to 1975: report of the Estuary Working Group, Department of the Environment, Regional Board Pacific Region. [Ottawa]: Environment Canada, 1975. xxvi, 418 p.: maps. (Special estuary series / Estuary Working Group, Department of the Environment, Regional Board, Pacific Region ; no. 3)
Note: Approx. 1,200 entries.– Journal articles, theses, government reports and studies dealing with environment of Skeena River estuary.– Topics include geology and soils, climatology, hydrology and water quality, oceanography, biology, land use, waste disposal.– Includes a list of maps.
Location: OONL.

5101   Hoos, Lindsay M.; Vold, Cecily L.
The Squamish River estuary: status of environmental knowledge to 1974: report of the Estuary Working Group, Department of the Environment, Regional Board, Pacific Region. [Ottawa]: Environment Canada, 1975. 361 p.: ill., maps. (Special estuary series / Estuary Working Group, Department of the Environment, Regional Board, Pacific Region ; no. 2)
Note: Approx. 1,000 entries.– Journal articles, theses, government reports and studies dealing with environment of Squamish River estuary: geology and soils,

climatology, hydrology and water quality, oceanography, biology, land use, waste disposal.– Includes a list of maps.
Location: OONL.

5102   Ontario Educational Communications Authority
Man builds – man destroys: a Canadian bibliographic supplement. Toronto: Ontario Educational Communications Authority, c1975. 48 p.: ill.
Note: List of Canadian references to accompany a television series on environmental problems.– Includes books, articles, films.
Location: OH.

5103   Schroeder, W.H.
Air pollution aspects of odorous substances: a literature survey. Ottawa: Air Pollution Control Directorate, Environment Canada, 1975. v, 53 p. (Economic and technical review report / Environmental Protection Service ; EPS 3-AP-75-1)
Note: 93 entries.– References dealing with nature of odorous substances, sensory characteristics, odor sources, human reactions and reponses to environmental odors, economic aspects, legislative aspects, measurement methods, odor abatement.
Location: OONL.

5104   Sparrow, Christopher J.; Foster, Leslie T.
An annotated bibliography of Canadian air pollution literature. Ottawa: Air Pollution Control Directorate, Air Pollution Protection Service, Environment Canada, 1975. xiv, 270 p. (Economic and technical review report / Air Pollution Control Directorate, Air Pollution Protection Service, Environment Canada ; EPS 3-AP-75-2)
Note: 1,012 entries.– Covers material published to end of 1973.– Includes books, academic journal articles, conference proceedings on air pollution.– Themes: sources, measurement and analysis, effects, adjustment and control, social aspects, research (government and university).
Supplement: 1978. viii, 69 p. (Economic and technical review report ; EPS 3-AP-77-1).– 329 entries.
Location: OONL.

5105   Sutton, R.M.D.; Quadling, C.
Inventory of pollution-relevant research in Canada/État des recherches sur la pollution au Canada. Ottawa: Environmental Secretariat, Division of Biological Sciences, National Research Council of Canada, 1975. 4 vol.
Note: Vol. 4, *Projects*, contains a listing of pollution research projects and publications.
Location: OONL.

— 1976 —

5106   Bell, Leonard M.; Kallman, Ronald J.
The Kitimat River estuary: status of environmental knowledge to 1976: report of the Estuary Working Group, Department of the Environment, Regional Board Pacific Region. [Ottawa]: Environment Canada, [1976]. 296 p. (Special estuary series / Estuary Working Group, Department of the Environment, Regional Board, Pacific Region ; no. 6)
Note: Approx. 700 entries.– Journal articles, theses, government reports and studies dealing with environment of Kitimat River estuary.– Topics include geology and soils, climatology, hydrology and water quality, oceanography, biology, land use, waste disposal.–

Includes a list of maps.
Location: OOFF.

5107 **Bell, Leonard M.; Kallman, Ronald J.**
The Nanaimo River estuary: status of environmental knowledge to 1976: report of the Estuary Working Group, Department of the Environment, Regional Board Pacific Region. [Ottawa]: Environment Canada, [1976]. xxix, 298 p., [1] l. of pl.: ill., maps. (Special estuary series / Estuary Working Group, Department of the Environment, Regional Board, Pacific Region ; no. 5)
Note: Approx. 700 entries.– Journal articles, theses, government reports and studies dealing with environment of Nanaimo River estuary.– Topics include geology and soils, climatology, hydrology and water quality, oceanography, biology, land use, waste disposal.– Includes a list of maps.
Location: OOFF.

5108 **Bernard, F.R.**
A selected bibliography on the biological effects of ocean dumping. Nanaimo, B.C.: Pacific Biological Station, Research and Development Directorate, Department of the Environment, 1976. iii, 22 p. (Fisheries and Marine Service Technical report ; no. 628; ISSN: 0701-7626)
Note: 195 entries.– Listing of journal articles, technical reports dealing with aspects of refuse disposal at sea.– Topics include dispersal and transportation by water, accumulation in food chains, ecology, mercury, cadmium, radioisotopes, metals, shellfish, sludge disposal, solid wastes, waste management.– Résumé en français.
Location: OONL.

5109 **Bloomfield, Janice; Harrison, Peter**
The shorezone: an annotated bibliography. [Ottawa]: Environment Canada, Lands Directorate, 1976. 53 p. (Occasional paper / Environment Canada, Lands Directorate ; no. 12)
Note: Approx. 100 entries.– Review of literature in shorezone and coastal management.– Topics include coastal management, shoreland use, land ownership and acquisition, land use planning and management, environmental law, decision-making/game theory/conflict resolution.
Location: OONL.

5110 **Canplan Oceanology Limited**
A literature survey of chemical oceanographic studies carried out in the Arctic. Halifax, N.S.: Canplan Oceanology, 1976. 233 p.
Note: 214 entries.– Includes waters above 60 North: all seas north of Canada, Alaska and seas surrounding Iceland and Greenland.– Provides name of water body surveyed, dates of survey, chemical measured, summary of discussions or conclusions.
Location: AEUB.

5111 **Chilton, C.E.**
Bibliography compiled for *A preliminary study on the environmental effects of various seabed exploitation schemes.* [Ottawa]: Resource Management and Conservation Branch, Department of Energy, Mines and Resources, 1976. 28 l.
Note: Approx. 200 entries.– Material dealing with marine ecology environmental baseline conditions and deep ocean mining, selected to emphasize the Central Pacific.
Location: OONL.

5112 **El-Sabh, Mohammed I.**
Bibliographie sur l'océanographie de l'estuaire du St-Laurent/Oceanographic bibliography for the St. Lawrence estuary. Rimouski, Québec: Section d'océanographie, Université du Québec à Rimouski, 1976. v f., 97 p.: cartes.
Note: Comprend 362 références en océanographie chimique, géochimique, géologique et physique ainsi qu'en météorologie.– La période couverte est de 1832 à 1974.– Texte en français et en anglais/text in English and French.
Localisation: OONL.

5113 **Frederking, R.**
Summary of current research on snow and ice in Canada, 1976. Ottawa: National Research Council Canada, Associate Committee on Geotechnical Research, 1976. 52 p. (Associate Committee on Geotechnical Research Technical memorandum ; no. 118)
Note: Approx. 135 entries.– Primary emphasis on snow and ice research as it relates to geotechnology, which includes aspects of hydrology and glacier studies, ice engineering, snow engineering, ice and environment, physics of ice, formation/movement/breakup of ice, remote sensing.
Location: OONL.

5114 **Institut de la médecine du travail et des ambiances**
Les projets de recherche subventionnés par l'IMTA et les publications scientifiques qui en découlent, 1966-1976. Montréal: Institut de la médecine du travail et des ambiances, 1976. xiii, 172 p.
Note: Aperçu des projets de recherche et 105 publications (à décembre 1976): littérature scientifique sur les effets physiologiques de l'amiante.
English title: *The research projects supported by IOEH and the scientific publications originating from them, 1966-1976.*
Localisation: OONL.

5115 **Institute of Occupational and Environmental Health**
The research projects supported by IOEH and the scientific publications originating from them, 1966-1976. Montreal: Institute of Occupational and Environmental Health, 1976. xiii, 172 p.
Note: Survey of research projects and 105 publications (to December 1976): scientific literature on biological effects of asbestos.
Titre en français: *Les projets de recherche subventionnés par l'IMTA et les publications scientifiques qui en découlent, 1966-1976.*
Location: OONL.

5116 **Johnson, Larry; Van Cleve, Keith**
Revegetation in arctic and subarctic North America: a literature review. Hanover, N.H.: U.S. Army Cold Regions Research and Engineering Laboratory, 1976. iv, 32 p. (CRREL report / U.S. Army Cold Regions Research and Engineering Laboratory ; 76-15)
Note: Approx. 135 entries.– Lists technical papers and journal articles on revegetation research connected with natural resource development, technologies designed to enable site restoration.
Location: OOFF.

5117 **Llamas, José**
"Rappel bibliographique [Centre de recherches sur l'eau]."
Dans: *Cahiers de Centreau*; Vol. 1, no 2 (1976) p. 1-66.;

ISSN: 0702-7214.

Note: 328 entrées.– Liste des documents, rapports et publications des chercheurs du Centre de recherches sur l'eau, 1968 jusqu'à 1975 inclusivement.

Localisation: OONL.

5118 **Miller, Gordon; Fehr, Laurene D.**
A contribution to the bibliography of the Mackenzie River Valley and northern Yukon: a list of Environment Canada reports and studies. Edmonton: Canadian Wildlife Service, 1976. 149 l.

Note: Listing of reports, studies, papers, articles relating to the Mackenzie River Valley and northern Yukon.– Includes a list of additional bibliographical sources.

Previous edition: *A preliminary bibliography of Environment Canada reports pertaining to the Mackenzie River Valley and the Mackenzie Valley gas pipeline route.* 1975. 1 vol. (in various pagings).

Location: OOFF.

5119 **Percy, Kevin E.**
Literature review of the controlled environment research completed on the sensitivity of coniferous tree species to air pollutants. Fredericton: Environment New Brunswick, 1976. [28] p. (in various pagings). (New Brunswick Department of the Environment Technical report series ; no. T-7601)

Note: Review in three sections: dose-response research, physiological research, histological research.– Literature presented according to the following criteria: air pollutants studied, species fumigated, fumigation apparatus used, prefumigation treatments, pollution concentration and duration of exposure, chamber environment during exposure, results and conclusions.

Location: OONL.

5120 **Strathy, Peter; Overboom, Fernande**
Natural resource management: a guide to reference and statistical materials for managers and economists. [Toronto]: Management Studies Library, Faculty of Management Studies, University of Toronto, 1976. vi, 107 p. (NR Publications / Faculty of Management Studies, University of Toronto ; no. 2)

Note: 354 entries.– General works, handbooks, bibliographies, abstracting services, directories, statistical publications.

Location: OONL.

— 1977 —

5121 **Bell, Leonard M.; Thompson, James M.**
The Campbell River estuary: status of environmental knowledge to 1977: report of the Estuary Working Group, Department of the Environment, Regional Board Pacific Region. [Ottawa]: Fisheries and Environment Canada, [1977]. xxxvi, 346 p., [2] l. of pl.: ill. (Special estuary series / Estuary Working Group, Department of the Environment, Regional Board, Pacific Region ; no. 7)

Note: Approx. 700 entries.– Journal articles, theses, government reports and studies dealing with environment of Campbell River estuary.– Topics include geology and soils, climatology, hydrology and water quality, oceanography, biology, land use, waste disposal.– Includes a list of maps.

Location: OOFF.

5122 **Canada. Inland Waters Directorate. Glaciology Division**
Bibliography: glaciology of the St. Elias Range, Yukon Territory and Alaska. Vancouver, B.C.: Inland Waters Directorate, Pacific Region, 1977. 54 p.

Note: 572 entries.– Based on information collected for the Canadian Glacier Inventory.– Includes references to snow, ice, glaciers and glacier-fed rivers, ice-dammed lakes, glacier flow, accumulation and ablation.– This bibliography forms part of the *Report on the influence of glaciers on the hydrology of streams affecting the proposed Alcan pipeline route.* Ottawa: 1977. [58] l. (in various foliations).

Location: OOFF.

5123 **Ficke, Eleanore R.; Ficke, John F.**
Ice on rivers and lakes: a bibliographical essay. Reston, Va.: Quality of Water Branch, U.S. Geological Survey, 1977. v, 173 p. (U.S. Geological Survey Water resources investigations ; 75-95)

Note: 752 entries.– Review of recent literature from Canada, United States, Soviet Union describing research and data collection.– Investigations of ice on rivers and lakes, such as processes of freezing and breakup, ice jams, effects of ice on navigation, water supply, flooding caused by ice jams and water quality.– Includes a section on the Great Lakes.

Location: OON.

5124 **Fingas, M.F.; Ross, C.W.**
An oil spill bibliography: March, 1975 to December, 1976. Ottawa: Fisheries and Environment Canada, 1977. 112 p. (Economic and technical review report / Fisheries and Environment Canada ; EPS-3-EC-77-10); ISBN: 0-66200663-1.

Note: Approx. 500 entries.– Lists journal articles, government reports and studies (Canada and U.S.).– Topics include Arctic oil spills and their cleanup, biodegradation of oil, dispersants, effects of oil on biota, land and underground spills, oil spill containment, prevention.

Location: OONL.

5125 **King, Geraldine L.**
Introductory bibliography of ground-water studies in New Brunswick, 1865-1977. Fredericton: Environment New Brunswick, 1977. iii, 25 l.

Note: Location: OONL.

5126 **Machniak, Kazimierz**
The impact of saline waters upon freshwater biota: a literature review and bibliography. Edmonton: Alberta Oil Sands Environmental Research Program, 1977. 258 p.: map. (Alberta Oil Sands Environmental Research Program report ; no. 8)

Note: Approx. 850 entries.– Prepared for the Aquatic Fauna Technical Research Committee of AOSERP to provide the committee with a review of current literature of the effects of saline water on freshwater aquatic plants and animals (invertebrates, fish, amphibians and reptiles, birds, mammals).

Location: OONL.

5127 **Renick, J.H.**
A bibliography of research on Alberta hailstorms and their modification. Three Hills: Alberta Agriculture, 1977. 19 l. (Alberta Weather Modification Board report ; no. 5)

Note: Approx. 300 entries.– Reports, papers, publications, theses dealing with or inspired by the Alberta hailstorm.– Includes studies by: Stormy Weather Group, McGill University; Alberta Weather Modification

Board; Alberta Research Council; Atmospheric Environment Service, Environment Canada.– Also included are theses from the University of Alberta and McGill University.
Location: OONL.

5128 **Rousselle, Jean**
Bibliographie sur les inondations: 1850-1976. Québec: Ministère des richesses naturelles, Direction générale des eaux, 1977. 2 vol.
Note: Localisation: QQE.

— 1978 —

5129 **Buchanan, Robert A.; Renaud, Wayne E.**
L'écologie marine du Détroit de Lancaster et des eaux adjacentes: bibliographie commentée. Ottawa: Affaires indiennes et du Nord [Canada], c1978. xxv, 378 p.: ill. (Étude environnementale / Affaires indiennes et du Nord Canada ; no 7); ISBN: 0-662-90550-4.
Note: Approx. 200 entrées.– Études interdisciplinaires, océanographie physique, production primaire, phytoplancton, zooplancton, benthos, necton, ornithologie, mammalogie marine, pollution, géologie marine.
English title: *The marine ecology of Lancaster Sound and adjacent waters: an annotated bibliography.*
Localisation: OONL.

5130 **Buchanan, Robert A.; Renaud, Wayne E.**
The marine ecology of Lancaster Sound and adjacent waters: an annotated bibliography. Ottawa: Indian and Northern Affairs Canada, c1978. xxiv, 262 p.; ISBN: 0-662-10188-X.
Note: Approx. 200 entries.– Research papers, studies, reports, theses issued from 1900 to 1977 related to assessment of impact of offshore exploratory drilling in Canadian eastern and central high arctic.
Titre en français: *L'écologie marine du Détroit de Lancaster et des eaux adjacentes: bibliographie commentée.*
Location: OONL.

5131 **Chawla, Rani J.K.**
Tsunamis: a selected bibliography. Ottawa: Marine Sciences Directorate, Department of Fisheries and the Environment, 1978. 4 p. (+ 2 microfiches in pocket): ill. (Manuscript report series / Marine Sciences Directorate ; no. 51)
Note: Approx. 1,900 entries.– Technical reports, articles, conference proceedings dealing with tsunami in disciplines of seismology, oceanography, aeronomy, geology, and tsunami generation from seismic and non-seismic sources.– Themes: volcanic explosions, nuclear explosions and landslides, tsunami propagation in the oceans, coastal problems, tsunami forecasting and warning systems, instrumentation and laboratory experiments dealing with tsunamis.– Some Canadian references.– Introduction in English and French/ introduction en français et en anglais.
Location: OONL.

5132 **Doe, Kenneth G.; Harris, Gary W.; Wells, Peter G.**
A selected bibliography on oil spill dispersants. Ottawa: Environmental Protection Service, Fisheries and Environment Canada, 1978. 98 p. (Environmental Impact Control Directorate Economic and technical review report ; EPS-3-EC-78-2); ISBN: 0-662-01573-8.
Note: 364 entries.– References to September 1977 dealing with chemistry, biological effects, use and effectiveness of oil spill dispersants (emulsifiers, solvent-emulsifiers, detergents).
Location: OONL.

5133 **Environment source book: a guide to environmental information in Canada: a joint project of the Department of the Environment, Ottawa and provincial and territorial environment and renewable resource departments.** [Ottawa: Department of the Environment], c1978. 115 p.; ISBN: 0-662-01622-X.
Note: Includes a section listing current literature and audio-visual aids: general works, federal and provincial publications.
Titre en français: *Références écologiques: répertoire des sources d'information écologiques ....*
Location: OONL.

5134 **Haworth, S.E.; Cowell, Daryl William; Sims, R.A.**
Bibliography of published and unpublished literature on the Hudson Bay Lowland. Ottawa: Canadian Forestry Service, Department of the Environment, 1978. 270 p.: maps. (Great Lakes Forest Research Centre report ; O-X-273; ISSN: 0704-7797)
Note: Approx. 1,900 references in the sociological and scientific fields pertaining to the Hudson Bay Lowland.– Listing of cultural and economic studies, earth sciences, limnology and oceanography, atmospheric sciences, life sciences, geographical surveys, bibliographies, conferences and symposia.
Location: OONL.

5135 **Références écologiques: répertoire des sources d'information écologiques: une réalisation conjointe du ministère fédéral de l'Environnement et des ministères et services provinciaux et territoriaux de l'environnement et des ressources renouvelables.** [Ottawa: Ministère de l'environnement], c1978. 124 p.; ISBN: 0-662-01622-8.
Note: Comprend une bibliographie sélective des ouvrages sur l'environnement: publications générales, publications des gouvernements fédérales et provinciaux, matériel audiovisuel.
English title: *Environment source book: a guide to environmental information in Canada ....*
Localisation: OONL.

5136 **Sefton, Joan; Miller, Gordon**
The Arctic islands pipeline route: a bibliography of unpublished Fisheries and Environment Canada reports. Ottawa: Department of Indian and Northern Affairs, 1978. x, 154 p. (ESCOM Report ; no. AI-12)
Note: 410 entries.– Compilation of unpublished reports prepared by employees of various agencies of Department of Fisheries and the Environment dealing with areas of the Northwest Territories and northern Manitoba likely to be affected by the construction of a pipeline to southern Canada.– Areas considered include the Queen Elizabeth Islands, Prince of Wales Island, Somerset Island, Coats Island, District of Keewatin and northeastern Manitoba.– Résumé en français.
Titre en français: *L'itinéraire du pipeline des îles de l'Arctique: une bibliographie des rapports inédits du Ministère des Pêches et de l'Environnement.*
Location: AEECW.

5137 **Sefton, Joan; Miller, Gordon**
L'itinéraire du pipeline des îles de l'Arctique: une bibliographie des rapports inédits du Ministère des

Pêches et de l'Environnement. Ottawa: Programme écologique et social, Pipe-lines du Nord, 1978. ix, 153 p. (Rapport ESCOM ; no AI-12)

Note: 410 entrées.– Rapports inédits sur l'évaluation de l'incidence environnementale du pipeline des îles de l'Arctique.– Les régions traitées comprennent les îles Reine-Élizabeth, l'île Prince de Galles, l'île Somerset, l'île Coats, le district de Keewatin et le nord-est du Manitoba. English title: *The Arctic islands pipeline route: a bibliography of unpublished Fisheries and Environment Canada reports.*

Localisation: OONL.

5138 **Shea, Mary; Mathers, John S.**
An annotated bibliography on the effects of roads on aquatic systems. Toronto: Ontario Ministry of Natural Resources; Ministry of Transportation and Communications, 1978. 55 p.

Note: 117 entries.– Papers dealing with physical, chemical and biological effects of roads on aquatic systems, with some references relating to impact on the terrestrial environment.– Other areas of study included are effects of sedimentation from mining, dredging, channelization and logging.

Location: OOFF.

5139 **Sikstrom, Calvin; Martin, John A.**
Review and annotated bibliography of stream diversion and stream restoration techniques and associated effects on aquatic biota. Edmonton: Alberta Oil Sands Environmental Research Program, 1978. xiv, 114 p.: ill.

Note: Approx. 250 entries.– Scientific references pertaining to effects of stream diversion on aquatic life, natural recovery of stream ecosystems from the effects of diversion, habitat restoration or enhancement techniques, potential applications of biomonitoring techniques for studying the effects of diversions, with special focus on the AOSERP study area.

Location: OONL.

5140 **Stansby, Maurice Earl; Diamant, Isabell**
Subject classified literature references on effects of oil pollution in Arctic and subarctic waters. Seattle, Wa.: Northwest and Alaska Fisheries Center, 1978. 201 p.

Note: Location: QMME.

5141 **Wigmore, Judy**
Literature review of previous oil pollution experience. Vancouver: Environment Canada, Environmental Protection Service, 1978. vii, 20 p. (Regional program report / Environmental Protection Service ; 78-24)

Note: Prepared for the West Coast Oil Ports Inquiry.– Abstracts in English and French/résumés en français et en anglais.

Location: OOFF.

— 1979 —

5142 **Andrews, Martha; Andrews, John T.**
"Bibliography of Baffin Island environments over the last 1000 years."
In: *Thule Eskimo culture: an anthropological perspective,* edited by Allan P. McCartney. Ottawa: National Museums of Canada, 1979. P. 555-569. (Archaeological Survey of Canada Paper ; no. 88)

Note: Selection of published papers on climate, glaciology, lichenometry and radiocarbon dating, glacial geology, changes of sea level, biotic studies on climatic change and review articles on holocene climatic change.– Text in English and French/texte en français et en anglais.

Location: OONL.

5143 **Audy, Réginald**
Inventaire de documents de base pour les études d'aménagement et d'environnement. Sherbrooke, Québec: Département de géographie, Université de Sherbrooke, 1979. 69 f. (Bulletin de recherche / Université de Sherbrooke, Département de géographie ; no 47; ISSN: 0710-0868)

Note: 60 entrées.

Localisation: OONL.

5144 **Bezanson, Donald S.; Moyse, Catherine M.; Byers, S.C.**
Research and related work on ocean dumping: an annotated bibliography. Ottawa: Department of Fisheries and Oceans, 1979. [2], 94 p. (Ocean dumping report / Canada Department of Fisheries and Oceans ; 2; ISSN: 0704:2701); ISBN: 0-662-10617-2.

Note: Approx. 300 entries.– Canadian research material to the end of 1978 dealing with dumping of substances in marine waters.

Titre en français: *Recherches et travaux connexes sur l'immersion de déchets en mer: bibliographie annotée.*

Location: OOFF.

5145 **Boyd, Gary L.**
Review of the literature concerning erosion and accretion of the Canadian shoreline of the Great Lakes. Burlington, Ont.: Canada Centre for Inland Waters, 1979. iii, 24 p. (Canada Centre for Inland Waters Technical note series ; no. 80-1)

Note: Approx. 175 entries.– Literature review of erosion and deposition of Great Lakes shoreline, from mid-eighteenth century to the 1970s.– Includes studies from the Canada-Ontario Erosion Monitoring Programme.

Location: OON.

5146 **Catalogue of environmental education materials/ Répertoire didactique sur l'environnement.** Ottawa: Department of the Environment, 1979. 12 vol.; ISBN: 0-662-50605-5.

Note: Listing of environmental publications suitable for classroom use, grouped under topics such as conservation, energy, land, pollutants, wildlife, noise.– The 12 volume set is made up of 10 provincial volumes, one for the Yukon and Northwest Territories, and a national (Canada) volume listing materials available from federal departments and agencies, crown corporations, national associations.– Text in English and French/texte en français et en anglais.

Location: OONL.

5147 **Chorley & Bisset Ltd**
Energy conservation in schools: review of Canadian and U.S. studies, surveys, programs and publications. Ottawa: Energy, Mines and Resources Canada, Conservation and Renewable Energy Branch, 1979. 86, [146] p. (Buildings series Publication ; no. 2a)

Note: Listing of energy conservation guidelines and manuals, technical papers and articles, reports on research and studies, standards for design and operation of facilities (including building codes and statistical publications).

Location: OONL.

5148 **Denison, P.J.; McMahon, T.A.; Kramer, J.R.**
Literature review on pollution deposition processes. Edmonton: Alberta Oil Sands Environmental Research Program, 1979. xx, 264 p.: ill., map. (Alberta Oil Sands

Environmental Research Program report ; no. 50)
Note: Approx. 350 entries.– Scientific references related to deposition of gases and particulates by dry deposition and precipitation scavenging.– Survey of experimental work done in the removal of pollutants from the atmosphere, with application to the AOSERP study area of northeast Alberta.
Location: OONL.

5149 **Fowle, Charles David; Baehre, Ralph K.**
A bibliography on acid rain. Don Mills, Ont.: Federation of Ontario Naturalists, 1979. 27 p.
Note: "Prepared for the Action Seminar on Acid Precipitation, Toronto, Ontario, November 1,2,3 1979."
Location: OOFF.

5150 **International Reference Group on Great Lakes Pollution from Land Use Activities**
Annotated bibliography of PLUARG reports. Windsor, Ont.: International Joint Commission, Great Lakes Regional Office, 1979. xii, 121 p.
Note: Describes all PLUARG Technical reports, as well as major unpublished reports, background documentation, data compilations prepared as part of the Reference Group's study, 1973-1978.
Location: OONL.

5151 **Marshall, K.E.**
Online retrieval of information: a comparison of different systems used to produce a bibliography on Ephemeroptera and pollution, 1969-78. Winnipeg: Fisheries and Marine Service, Department of Fisheries and the Environment, 1979. vi, 18 p. (Fisheries and Marine Service Technical report ; no. 878; ISSN: 0701-7626)
Note: Appendix 1: "A bibliography on Ephemeroptera and pollution, 1969-78."
Location: OONL.

5152 **Morris, Sahlaa, et al.**
The Courtenay River estuary: status of environmental knowledge to 1978: report of the Estuary Working Group, Department of the Environment, Regional Board Pacific Region. [Ottawa]: Fisheries and Environment Canada, 1979. xxxii, 355 p.: ill. (Special estuary series / Estuary Working Group, Department of the Environment, Regional Board, Pacific Region ; no. 8)
Note: Approx. 800 entries.– Journal articles, theses, government reports and studies dealing with environment of Courtenay River estuary.– Topics include geology and soils, climatology, hydrology and water quality, oceanography, biology, land use, waste disposal.– Includes a list of maps.
Location: AEU.

5153 **"Orientation bibliographique: [Océanographie de l'estuaire du Saint-Laurent]."**
Dans: Naturaliste canadien; Vol. 106, no 1 (janvier-février 1979) p. 273-276.; ISSN: 0028-0798.
Note: Localisation: OONL.

5154 **Saskatoon Public Library**
The conserver society: an annotated resource guide to selected books, films, periodicals & organizations. Saskatoon: Saskatoon Public Library, 1979. 80 p.
Note: Location: OONL.

5155 **Scott, Kevin M.**
Arctic stream processes: an annotated bibliography. Washington, D.C.: United States Government Printing

Office, 1979. iii, 78 p. (Geological Survey Water-supply paper ; 2065)
Note: Approx. 250 entries.– Papers dealing with the physical processes of streams in the Arctic published to 1978.– Numerous Canadian references.
Location: OON.

5156 **Social dimensions of environmental planning: an annotated bibliography.** Ottawa: Environment Canada, 1979. 206 p. (Office of the Science Advisor Report / Environment Canada ; no. 17)
Note: 813 entries.– Covers 1973 to 1978.– Contains a listing of published and unpublished English-language literature reflecting contemporary thinking, concepts, observations and methodologies related to social aspects of environmental planning.– Themes include state of the environment, natural resource planning, social impact assessment, resource communities, northern development, man-environment interactions, public participation, bibliographies.– A project of the Banff School of the Environment and Environment Canada.– Prepared by L.J. D'Amore & Associates Ltd.
Location: OONL.

5157 **Thomas, Morley K.; Phillips, David W.**
A bibliography of Canadian climate, 1972-1976/ Bibliographie du climat canadien, 1972-1976. [Hull, Quebec]: Environment Canada, Atmospheric Environment Service, 1979. 135 p.; ISBN: 0-660-50220-8.
Note: 902 entries.– Books, articles, reports dealing substantially with some aspect of Canadian climate, and/or with the direct effect or application of climate on Canadian society, the economy or the environment.– Excludes papers dealing with theoretical and fundamental research, with meteorological instruments, or with methods used in forecasting.– Text in English and French/texte en français et en anglais.
Location: OONL.

— 1980 —

5158 **Alberta. Alberta Environment. Communications Branch**
Government environmental resource materials guide. 4th ed. Edmonton: Alberta Environment, 1980. iv, 213 p.
Note: Annotated list of print and audio-visual materials on environmental topics produced by government departments and agencies for use by Alberta educators.
Previous editions:
Alberta. Department of the Environment. ... : for teachers in Alberta. 1979. 208 p.
1977. 116 p.
Location: OONL.

5159 **A bibliography: the long-range transport of air pollutants and acidic precipitation.** Downsview, Ont.: LRTAP Program Office, Atmospheric Environment Service, Environment Canada, 1980. 95 p.
Note: Approx. 1,350 entries.– Technical studies, journal articles, government reports.– Jointly sponsored by the Ontario Ministry of the Environment and the federal Atmospheric Environment Service.
Location: OONL.

5160 **Bradford, J.D.; Moline, M.**
Bibliography on northern sea ice and related subjects/ Bibliographie sur la glace de mer dans le Nord et autres sujets connexes. 2nd ed. Ottawa: Department of Fisheries and Oceans; Department of Transport, 1980. x, 194 p.

(Canadian special publication of fisheries and aquatic sciences ; 45; ISSN: 0706-6481)

Note: 2,340 entries.– Studies and reports dealing with problem that sea ice presents to vessels.– Topics include mechanics and strength, operations and ship design, sea ice observations, ice drift, sea ice environment, reconnaissance and forecasting.– Text in English and French/texte en français et en anglais.

Previous edition: Bradford, J.D.; Smirle, S.M. Marine Operations, Ministry of Transport: Marine Sciences Branch, Department of Energy, Mines and Resources, 1970. xiii, 188 p.

Location: OONL.

5161 **Cohen, Sanford F.**
Pollution from land use activities in the Great Lakes basin: a selected bibliography. Monticello, Ill.: Vance Bibliographies, 1980. 10 p. (Public administration series: Bibliography ; P-577; ISSN: 0193-970X)

Note: Approx. 80 entries.– Lists books, papers, articles, studies with impact of land use activities on water quality in Great Lakes basin.

Location: OONL.

5162 **The environmental reading list.** Toronto: Pollution Probe Foundation, [1980]. [5] l.; ISBN: 0-919764-10-X.

Note: Approx. 80 entries.– Books from the 1970s on ecology, pollution, energy issues, law, waste management.

Location: OONL.

5163 **Hawley, Norma J.**
A bibliography of AECL publications on environmental research/Une bibliographie des publications de l'EACL sur les recherches écologiques. Pinawa, Man.: Whiteshell Nuclear Research Establishment, 1980. 47 p. (AECL-6319-Rev. 1; ISSN: 0067-0367)

Note: 365 entries.– AECL reports, journal articles, conference papers on effects of radiation on plants, animals, insects, and in atmospheric, aquatic and terrestrial environments.– Résumé en français.

Previous edition: 1978. 40 p.

Location: OONL.

5164 **Lalonde, Girouard, Letendre & Associes**
Bibliographie annotée: documents comprenant des données de base pour la région du Québec. [Montréal]: Environnement Canada, Direction générale régionale, Région du Québec, 1980. 340 f.

Note: 340 entrées.– Rapports préparés par les organismes para-gouvernementaux et les firmes privées (consultants): évaluations environnementales.

Localisation: OOFF.

5165 **Marshall, I.B.**
The ecology and reclamation of lands disturbed by mining: a selected bibliography of Canadian references/ L'écologie et la récupération des terres perturbées par l'activité minière: bibliographie sélective de la litérature[sic] canadienne. Enl. 2nd ed. [Ottawa]: Lands Directorate, Environment Canada, 1980. 64 p. (Working paper / Lands Directorate, Environment Canada ; no. 1; ISSN: 0712-4473); ISBN: 0-662-50724-X.

Note: 592 entries.– Includes basic and applied research findings, reports on economic, legal and political considerations to the problem of land reclamation.– Bibliographies containing U.S. references are included.

Previous edition: 1979. 94 p. (Occasional paper ; no. 17);

ISBN: 0-662-10439-0.

Location: OONL.

5166 **Morris, Sahlaa, et al.**
The Somass River estuary: status of environmental knowledge to 1980: report of the Estuary Working Group, Joint Fisheries and Oceans-Environment Co-ordinating Committee on Environmental Affairs, Pacific and Yukon Region. [Ottawa]: Fisheries and Oceans Canada, 1980. 374 p. (Special estuary series / Estuary Working Group, Joint Fisheries and Oceans-Environment Co-ordinating Committee on Environmental Affairs, Pacific and Yukon Region ; no. 9)

Note: Journal articles, theses, government reports and studies dealing with environment of Somass River estuary.– Topics include geology and soils, climatology, hydrology and water quality, oceanography, biology, land use, waste disposal.– Includes a list of maps.

Location: OOFF.

5167 **Samson, A.L., et al.**
A selected bibliography on the fate and effects of oil pollution relevant to the Canadian marine environment/ Bibliographie sélective des travaux de recherche portant sur le devenir et les effets de la pollution par les hydrocarbures et pouvant s'appliquer au milieu marin canadien. 2nd ed. [Hull, Quebec]: Research and Development Division, Environmental Protection Service, Environment Canada, 1980. vii, 191 p. (Economic and technical review report / Research and Development Division, Environmental Protection Service, Environment Canada ; EPS-3-EC-80-5); ISBN: 0-662-51167-0.

Note: 1,794 entries.– Covers to October 1980.– Includes references selected from primary and technical scientific literature, Canadian and otherwise, on basis of relevance to Canadian marine temperate and northern/arctic waters.– Text in English and French/texte en français et en anglais.

Previous edition: 1977. vii, 174 p.– 598 entries.

Location: OONL.

5168 **Sandhu, H.S., et al.**
Environmental sulphur research in Alberta: a review. Edmonton: Research Secretariat, Alberta Department of the Environment, 1980. viii, 90 p.: maps (some col.).

Note: 254 entries.– Review and analysis of published environmental sulphur research from Alberta available up to August 1979.– Topics include sulphur emissions and technology, sulphur in the air, effects in the water, effects on soil and vegetation, effects on health.

Location: OONL.

5169 **Vinto Engineering Limited**
Energy conservation in office buildings: review of Canadian and U.S. studies, surveys, programs and publications. Ottawa: Energy, Mines and Resources Canada, Conservation and Renewable Energy Branch, 1980. 178, 18, 14 p. (Buildings series)

Note: 178 entries.– Energy conservation guidelines and manuals, technical papers and articles, reports on research and studies, standards for design and operation of facilities (including building codes and statistical publications).

Location: OOCC.

— 1981 —

5170 **Bezanson, Donald S.; Moyse, Catherine M.; Byers, S.C.**
Recherches et travaux connexes sur l'immersion de

déchets en mer: bibliographie annotée. Ottawa: Gouvernement du Canada, Ministère des pêches et des océans, 1981. 106 p. (Immersion de déchets en mer rapport ; no 2F; ISSN: 0226-3475); ISBN: 0-662-91334-5.

Note: Approx. 300 entrées.– Recherches et travaux connexes effectués au Canada jusqu'à la fin de 1978, sur l'immersion de substances en mer.

English title: *Research and related work on ocean dumping: an annotated bibliography.*

Localisation: OONL.

5171 **Canada water year book, 1979-1980: references/ Annuaire de l'eau du Canada, 1979-1980: références.** Ottawa: Environment Canada, 1981. v, 69 p.; ISSN: 0708-4285.; ISBN: 0-662-51566-8.

Note: Approx. 1,000 entries.– The *Canada Water Year Book* for 1979-1980 deals with research and a separate references volume was produced to accompany this edition.– Topics include physical processes in the aquatic environment, chemical and biological processes, water quality, wastewater treatment and disposal, water quantity management, water resources planning.– Avant-propos en français.

Location: OONL.

5172 **Leaney, Adelle J.; Morris, Sahlaa**
The Bella Coola River estuary: status of environmental knowledge to 1981: report of the Estuary Working Group, Fisheries and Oceans-Environment Joint Co-ordinating Committee on Environmental Affairs, Pacific and Yukon Region. [Ottawa]: Environment Canada, 1981. xxxiv, 266 p.: maps.

Note: Journal articles, theses, government reports and studies dealing with environment of Bella Coola River estuary.– Topics include geology and soils, climatology, hydrology and water quality, oceanography, biology, land use, waste disposal.– Includes a list of maps.

Location: BVAS.

5173 **Linzon, Samuel Nathan**
An annotated bibliography, terrestrial effects of acidic precipitation. Toronto: Phytotoxicology Section, 1981. 181 p.; ISBN: 0-77437-087-4.

Note: Location: OONL.

5174 **Mackenzie River Basin Committee**
Sensitive areas: literature review: WATDOC references. [Edmonton: Environment Canada], 1981. 1 vol. (in various pagings): ill., maps. (Mackenzie River Basin Study report. Supplement ; 1; ISSN: 0227-0285); ISBN: 0-919425-02-X.

Note: Covers to December 1979.– Literature review on 37 areas within the Mackenzie Basin expected to suffer in biologic productivity and cultural or social value if changes occur in hydrologic regime (river flows, water levels, water quality, sedimentation).

Location: OONL.

5175 **Sater, John E.**
Ice pressure ridges: a bibliography. Arlington, Va.: Arctic Institute of North America, 1981. [146] l.

Note: 439 entries.– Listing of studies related to ice pressure ridges as they concern arctic marine transportation.

Location: OON.

5176 **Stevens, R.D.S.**
The sampling and analysis of airborne sulphates and nitrates: a review of published work and synthesis of available information. Ottawa: Environment Canada, Environmental Protection Service, 1981. ix, 46 p. (Air Pollution Control Directorate Surveillance report ; EPS 5-AP-82-14); ISBN: 0-662-12166-X.

Note: 77 entries.

Location: OONL.

— 1982 —

5177 **Arctic Science and Technology Information System**
APOA bibliography. Calgary: Arctic Institute of North America, 1982. v, 113 p. (ASTIS occasional publication / Arctic Science and Technology Information System ; no. 1; ISSN: 0225-5170)

Note: 218 entries.– Contains all Arctic Petroleum Operators' Association research reports in the ASTIS database as of October 1982.– The purpose of APOA is to promote joint research in the Arctic towards obtaining engineering and environmental data related to petroleum development.

Previous edition: 1980. ii, 74 p.

Location: OONL.

5178 **Écologie de l'archipel arctique canadien: bibliographie sélective.** Ottawa: Affaires indiennes et du Nord, 1974-1982. 11 vol.; ISSN: 0715-8815.

Note: Couverture géographique: toutes les îles, depuis les îles Ellesmere, Prince-Patrick et Banks dans le nord-ouest, jusqu'aux îles Baffin, Mansel et Coates dans le sud-est.– Quelques régions du continent ont également été incluses: les presqu'îles Adélaïde, de Boothia, Simpson et de Melville.– Sujets traités: biologie, taxonomie, répartition, habitats terrestres, marins et d'eau douce.– Articles sur l'écologie humaine, l'anthropologie, l'archéologie et la sociologie n'ont pas été retenu.– Annotations par N. Merle Peterson.

English title: *Ecology of the Canadian Arctic archipelago: selected references.*

Localisation: OONL.

5179 **Ecology of the Canadian Arctic Archipelago: selected references.** [Ottawa]: Indian Affairs and Northern Development, 1974-1982. 11 vol.; ISSN: 0715-8807.

Note: Geographic coverage includes all islands from Ellesmere, Prince Patrick and Banks islands in the northwest to Baffin, Mansel and Coats islands in the southeast, with mainland areas such as Adelaide Peninsula, Boothia Peninsula, Simpson Peninsula and Melville Peninsula.– Marine coverage includes all water bodies surrounding these islands and peninsulas, from Amundsen Gulf in the west to Kane Basin and Davis Strait in the east and from Hudson Strait in the south to the edges of the Arctic Ocean and the Lincoln Sea in the north.– Subject matter coverage focuses on the following ecological subjects: terrestrial, freshwater and marine habitats, taxonomy, distribution, physiology, literature from physical sciences if subject of importance to ecosystem factor (e.g. articles on climate in relation to plant growth).– Excludes articles on human ecology, anthropology, archaeology, sociology.– Detailed annotations by N. Merle Peterson, Western Ecological Services, Sidney, B.C.

Titre en français: *Écologie de l'archipel arctique canadien: bibliographie sélective.*

Location: OONL.

5180 **Fallis, B.W.; Klenner, W.E.; Kroeker, D.W.**
Bibliography of trace metals (As, Cd, Hg, Pb, Zn) in marine ecosystems with emphasis on arctic regions, 1970-1980. Winnipeg: Government of Canada, Fisheries and Oceans, 1982. iv, 33 p. (Canadian technical report of fisheries and aquatic sciences ; no. 1087; ISSN: 0706-6457)
Note: Approx. 750 entries.– List of technical reports and studies of effects of heavy metals on marine biota, especially with respect to bioaccumulation of trace metals.– Résumé en français.
Location: OONL.

5181 **Goodwin, C. Ross**
EAMES bibliography. Calgary: Arctic Institute of North America, 1982. vii, 38 p. (ASTIS occasional publication / Arctic Science and Technology Information System ; no. 6; ISSN: 0225-5170)
Note: 130 entries.– Contains all reports and documents produced by the Eastern Arctic Marine Environmental Studies program, a comprehensive scientific investigation of a marine arctic ecosystem, in response to proposed oil and gas exploration.– The study area included all marine areas adjacent to north, east, and south coasts of Baffin Island.
Location: OONL.

5182 **Goodwin, C. Ross**
Norlands bibliography. Calgary: Arctic Institute of North America, 1982. iv, 10 p. (ASTIS occasional publication / Arctic Science and Technology Information System ; no. 7; ISSN: 0225-5170)
Note: 28 entries.– Contains reports on Lancaster Sound area produced by or for Norlands Petroleums between 1974 and 1981.– Includes geological, oceanographic and biological studies; 1978 environmental impact study with supporting documents on drilling systems and oil spills.
Location: OONL.

5183 **Merriman, J.C., et al.**
Water resources of the Hudson Bay lowland: a literature review and annotated bibliography. Sault Ste. Marie, Ont.: Canadian Forestry Service, Department of the Environment, 1982. 43 p.: map. (Great Lakes Forest Research Centre Information report ; 0-X-338; ISSN: 0704-7797); ISBN: 0-662-12028-0.
Note: Approx. 100 entries.
Location: OOCC.

5184 **Nordin, Richard Nels; McKean, Colin J.P.**
A review of lake aeration as a technique for water quality improvement. Victoria: Province of British Columbia, Ministry of Environment, Assessment and Planning Division, 1982. iv l., 30 p. (CAPD Bulletin / Province of British Columbia, Ministry of Environment, Assessment and Planning Division ; 22; ISSN: 0228-5304); ISBN: 0-7719-8888-5.
Note: Approx. 225 entries.– Reports and journal articles documenting experiences with aeration projects.– Includes Canadian references.
Location: OONL.

5185 **Ommanney, C. Simon L.**
Bibliography of Canadian glaciology/Bibliographie de la glaciologie. Ottawa: National Hydrology Research Institute, Inland Waters Directorate, 1978-1982. 3 vol. (Inland Waters Directorate Report series ; no. 58,59,73) (Glacier inventory note ; no. 9,10,11; ISSN: 0713-2875)
Note: Bibliography 1: *Bibliography of Canadian glaciology,*

1975/Bibliographie de la glaciologie, 1975. 1978. vii, 117 p.; ISBN: 0-662-10088-3.– 659 entries.– Lists all snow and ice studies in Canada published or printed in 1975: general glaciology, glaciological instruments and methods, physics of ice, land ice, glaciers, ice shelves, icebergs, glacial geology, frozen ground.
Bibliography 2: *Ellesmere Island glaciers and ice shelves/ Glaciers et plates-formes de glace de l'île Ellesmere.* 1982. v, 53 p.; ISBN: 0-662-12238-0.– Approx. 500 entries.
Bibliography 3: *Ice islands of the Arctic Ocean/îles de glace de l'océan Arctique.* 1982. v, 40 p.; ISBN: 0-662-52159-5.– Approx. 400 entries.
Location: OONL.

5186 **Sims, H.P.; Powter, Christopher Barrett**
Land surface reclamation: an international bibliography. Edmonton: Alberta Land Conservation and Reclamation Council, 1982. 2 vol. (Alberta Land Conservation and Reclamation Council report ; no. RRTAC 82-1; ISSN: 0713-1232)
Note: Approx. 1,900 entries.– Papers, research reports, studies dealing with land reclamation.– Topics include mine spoils, surface mining, topsoil replacement, acidity, contouring, drainage, erosion control, environmental law, revegetation, materials handling, introduced species.– Includes a listing of additional bibliographies and literature reviews.– Many Canadian references.
Previous edition: 1979. vi, 201 l.
Location: OONL.

5187 **Sprague, J.B.; Vandermeulen, J.H.; Wells, Peter G.**
Oil and dispersants in Canadian seas: research appraisal and recommendations. Ottawa: Environment Canada, Environmental Protection Service, 1982. xiii, 185 p.: ill. (Environmental Impact Control Directorate Economic and technical review report ; EPS 3-EC-82-2); ISBN: 0-662-11995-9.
Note: Approx. 600 entries.– Evaluates knowledge of the fate and effects of oil spilled at sea and implications of using dispersants, with special reference to Canadian marine environments.
Titre en français: *Le pétrole et les dispersants dans les mers baignant le littoral canadien: évaluation des recherches et recommandations.*
Location: OONL.

5188 **Sprague, J.B.; Vandermeulen, J.H.; Wells, Peter G.**
Le pétrole et les dispersants dans les mers baignant le littoral canadien: évaluation des recherches et recommandations. Ottawa: Environnement Canada, Service de la protection de l'environnement, 1982. xv, 199 p.: ill. (Direction générale du contrôle des incidences environnementales Analyse économique et technique, Rapport ; SPE 3-EC-82-2F); ISBN: 0-662-91605-0.
Note: Approx. 600 entrées.– Évalue connaissances actuelle sur le devenir du pétrole et ses effets en cas de déversement en mer, et les conséquences de dispersants dans le milieu marin au Canada.
English title: *Oil and dispersants in Canadian seas: research appraisal and recommendations.*
Localisation: OONL.

5189 **Washburn & Gillis Associates Ltd.**
Survey of literature on the assessment of the pollution potential of the peat resource: final report submitted to Environment Canada. Ottawa: National Research Council under the auspices of the Peat Forum, 1982. xv,

130 p.
Note: 157 entries.
Location: OOAG.

— 1983 —

5190 Bastedo, Jamie
Annotated bibliography for the Waterton Lakes
Biosphere Reserve, with discussion of management and
research priorities. [Ottawa]: Canada-MAB, 1983. 2 vol.:
ill., maps.
Note: Approx. 800 entries.– Part of the Canadian
contribution to Unesco's Man and the Biosphere
Programme (MAB), Waterton Lakes National Park is
designated a biosphere reserve, a representative example
of a major world landscape and a location for
management-oriented ecological research and environmental monitoring.– The bibliography which is a part of
the Waterton MAB program includes periodical articles,
books, chapters, reports, theses, papers, files, maps,
photos, newspaper articles relating to natural history
(biology, palaeoecology, geology, climatology,
hydrology, flora and fauna, soils), human history, land
use, planning and development, institutional arrangements, management issues, environmental education,
scientific research and environmental monitoring.
Location: OOFF.

5191 Chung, Yong-Seung; Dann, T.F.
A literature review of ozone in the atmosphere and on
interpretation of exceptionally high values of surface
ozone recorded at Regina, Saskatchewan. Downsview,
Ont.: Atmospheric Research Directorate, 1983. 32 l.
Note: Location: OOFF.

5192 Duinker, Peter N.; Beanlands, Gordon E.
Écologie et évaluation environnementale: bibliographie
annotée. Halifax, N.–E.: Institute for Resource and
Environmental Studies, Dalhousie University, et Bureau
fédéral d'examen des évaluations environnementales,
1983. 44, 40 p.
Note: Approx. 200 entrées.– Comprend les ouvrages
disponibles concernant divers sujets relatifs à l'utilisation
de la science écologique pour l'évaluation
environnementale: principes écologiques, philosophie et
théorie de l'EIE, la mer, modèle, contrôle, statistiques,
techniques et moyens pour l'EIE, terres.– Texte en
français et en anglais disposé tête-bêche.– Titre de la p.
de t. additionnelle: Ecology and environmental impact
assessment: an annotated bibliography.
Localisation: OONL.

5193 Duinker, Peter N.; Beanlands, Gordon E.
Ecology and environmental impact assessment: an
annotated bibliography. Halifax, N.S.: Institute for
Resource and Environmental Studies, Dalhousie University, in cooperation with Federal Environmental Review
Office, 1983. 40, 44 p.
Note: Approx. 200 entries.– Describes literature on
various topics related to application of ecological science
in environmental assessment: aquatic topics, arctic
topics, ecological principles, ecosystem theory, EIA
philosophy and theory, marine topics, monitoring,
techniques and tools in EIA.– Text in English and French
with French text on inverted pages.– Title of additional
title-page: Écologie et évaluation environnementale:
bibliographie annotée.
Location: OONL.

5194 Finley, Jean C.
Bibliography of the Lancaster Sound resource
management plan: supporting documentation. Calgary:
Arctic Institute of North America, University of Calgary,
1983. iv, 13 p. (ASTIS occasional publication / Arctic
Science and Technology Information System; no. 11;
ISSN: 0225-5170)
Note: Contains 23 reports, including the Resource
management plan, 15 support documents, and 5
background reports, all of which are intended to provide
information about the proposal to drill a test well, within
the context of projected activities and social and environmental effects which would follow an oil discovery in
Lancaster Sound.
Location: OONL.

5195 Habgood, Helen
Lake Wabamun literature review. [Edmonton]: Lake
Wabamun Watershed Advisory Committee, 1983. x,
136 p., 6 folded l.: ill., maps.
Note: Approx. 125 entries.– Summarizes available
published and unpublished scientific literature dealing
with Lake Wabamun, one of Alberta's largest and most
important recreational lakes.– Most references date from
1965 to 1982.– Subjects include physical features, climate,
hydrogeology, human use, power generation, physical
and chemical characteristics, lake biota, aquatic
macrophytes, control of aquatic macrophytes.
Location: OONL.

5196 Howard, Lynne M.; Goodwin, C. Ross
Beaufort E.I.S. bibliography. Calgary: Arctic Institute of
North America, 1983. iv, 66 p. (ASTIS occasional
publication / Arctic Science and Technology Information
System; no. 9; ISSN: 0225-5170)
Note: 198 entries.– Publications concerning the Beaufort
Sea Environmental Assessment Review received on or
before February 28, 1983: reference works, support
documents, government position statements, technical
reports.– Topics include oceanography, ice, zoology,
petroleum/natural gas/pipelines, land use and
management.
Location: OONL.

5197 Kwamena, Felix A.; Brassard, Charles; Wright, Don
Les incidences à terres de l'exploitation en mer des
hydrocarbures: bibliographie annotée. Ottawa: Service
de la protection de l'environnement, Environnement
Canada, 1983. iv, 123 p. (Rapport d'analyse économique
et technique; SPE 3-ES-83-4F); ISBN: 0-662-92198-4.
Note: Approx. 200 entrées.– Comporte des chapitres sur
les types d'installations et les besoins, les incidences
socio-économiques, les incidences sur l'environnement et
les expériences britannique, norvégienne et nord-
américaine.– Chaque notice présente les problèmes et les
recommandations qui ressortent de l'ouvrage examiné.
English title: Onshore impacts of offshore hydrocarbon
development: annotated bibliography.
Localisation: OONL.

5198 Kwamena, Felix A.; Brassard, Charles; Wright, Don
Onshore impacts of offshore hydrocarbon development:
annotated bibliography. Ottawa: Environmental
Protection Service, Environment Canada, 1983. iii, 108 p.
(Economic and technical review report / Environmental
Protection Service; EPS 3-ES-83-4); ISBN: 0-662-12686-6.
Note: Approx. 200 entries.– Articles, reports, studies:

facility types and requirements, socioeconomic impact, environmental impact, coastal zone management in North America, Norway, Great Britain.
Titre en français: *Les incidences à terres de l'exploitation en mer des hydrocarbures: bibliographie annotée.*
Location: OONL.

5199 **Lynch-Stewart, Pauline**
Changements d'utilisation des terres dans les milieux humides au sud du Canada: aperçu et bibliographie. Ottawa: Direction générale des terres, Environnement Canada, 1983. vii, 126 p. (Document de travail / Direction générale des terres, Environnement Canada ; no 26); ISBN: 0-662-92187-9.
Note: Approx. 75 entrées.– Critique des papiers concernant changements d'utilisation des terres dans les milieux humides, terres agricoles, développement industriel, étalement urbaine.
English title: *Land use change on wetlands in southern Canada: review and bibliography.*
Localisation: OOFF.

5200 **Lynch-Stewart, Pauline**
Land use change on wetlands in southern Canada: review and bibliography. [Ottawa]: Lands Directorate, Environment Canada, 1983. 115 p. (Working paper / Lands Directorate, Environment Canada ; no. 26; ISSN: 0712-4473); ISBN: 0-662-12675-0.
Note: Approx. 75 entries.– Review of papers dealing with issues of land use change on wetlands, land use pressures, agricultural reclamation, urban and industrial development, energy-related development, recreational use.
Titre en français: *Changements d'utilisation des terres dans les milieux humides au sud du Canada: aperçu et bibliographie.*
Location: OOFF.

5201 **Mackenzie, B.J.**
Bibliography of trace metals in marine and estuarine ecosystems, 1977-1981. Winnipeg: Government of Canada, Department of Fisheries and Oceans, 1983. iv, 20 p. (Canadian technical report of fisheries and aquatic sciences ; no. 1146; ISSN: 0706-6457)
Note: Approx. 320 entries.– List of technical reports and studies on heavy metals in marine and estuarine environments.– Résumé en français.
Location: OONL.

5202 **Miletich, John J.**
Acid rain in Canada: a selected bibliography. Chicago, Ill.: Council of Planning Librarians, 1983. v, 21 p. (CPL bibliography / Council of Planning Librarians ; no. 124); ISBN: 0-86602-124-8.
Note: 81 entries.– Annotated listing of journal articles on Canadian provinces, industry and environment, Canada-U.S. relations and general information concerning acidity in rain, snow, sleet, hail and mist and the resulting ecological problems: destruction of forests and marine life, human health effects.
Location: OONL.

5203 **Noseworthy, Ann**
A literature review of the marine environment, Terra Nova National Park and adjacent bays. [St. John's, Nfld.: Whale Research Group, Memorial University of Newfoundland], 1983. 245 l.: ill.
Note: Monographs, periodical articles, official publications, manuscripts related to marine environment

of the Park.– Subjects include history, folklore, sociology, oceanography, environment, fish, birds, mammals.
Location: OOFF.

5204 **Oil spill related research in the public domain at the Arctic Institute of North America: citations and abstracts: prepared through the Arctic Science and Technology Information System, Arctic Institute of North America, Calgary, Alberta at the request of The Consolidex Magnorth Oakwood Joint Venture in consultation with Pallister Resource Management Ltd.**
Calgary: Consolidex Magnorth Oakwood Joint Venture, 1983. xiii, 115 p.
Note: Approx. 350 entries.– Documents provide overview of research, include studies of biological effects and toxicity of oil in marine environments, behaviour of spilled oil, oil spill contingency planning, methods and technology.
Location: OONL.

5205 **Petro-Canada**
Offshore Queen Charlotte Islands initial environmental evaluation. Calgary: Petro-Canada, [1983]. 3 vol. (loose-leaf): ill., maps.
Note: Approx. 2,400 entries.– Topics include exploratory drilling, geology, climate, oceanography, biology, effects of oil, contingency planning.
Location: ACPC.

5206 **Phillips, David W.**
A bibliography of Canadian climate, 1977-1981/ Bibliographie du climat canadien, 1977-1981. Ottawa: Environment Canada, Atmospheric Environment Service, 1983. 169 p.; ISBN: 0-660-52326-4.
Note: 1,056 entries.– Books, articles, reports.– References are listed if they deal substantially with the climate of Canada or with the direct effect of an application of climate on Canadian society, its economy or environment.– Topics include climate change, regional climatology, carbon dioxide, glaciology, oceanography, permafrost, precipitation chemistry.– Excludes papers dealing principally with theoretical and fundamental research, meteorological instruments, weather forecasting techniques.– Text in English and French/texte en français et en anglais.
Location: OONL.

5207 **Wren, Christopher**
Literature review of the occurrence of toxicity of metals in wild mammals. Hull, Quebec: National Wildlife Research Centre, Canadian Wildlife Service, 1983. iv, 180, 29, [75] l.
Note: 372 entries.
Location: OOFF.

— 1984 —

5208 **Adams, W. Peter**
Ice, including snow research at Trent University ... with a bibliography for 1971-84. Peterborough, Ont.: Trent University, 1984. 13 p.
Note: Bibliography of papers and theses involving research in snow and ice at Trent University between 1971 and 1984.
Location: AEUB.

5209 **Anderson, Dennis; McDougall, Gordon H.G.**
Consumer energy research: an annotated bibliography/ Recherche sur la consommation d'énergie: une bibliographie annotée. Ottawa: Policy Research, Analysis

and Liaison Directorate, Policy Coordination Bureau, Consumer and Corporate Affairs Canada, c1984. 329 p.; ISBN: 0-662-62743-7.

Note: Approx. 250 entries.– Lists recent research studies on a wide range of issues dealing with consumers and energy falling generally into two basic categories: research focussing on understanding consumer attitudes and behaviour relating to energy; impact of energy conservation initiatives: actions taken by consumers in response to conservation programs.– Text in English and French/texte en français et en anglais.

Previous editions:
1983. 366 p.; ISBN: 0-662-52320-2.
1982. 510 p.
1981. 2 vol.; ISBN: 0-662-51574-9.
1980. 1 vol. (in various pagings).
Location: OONL.

5210 **Ashmore, Peter; Mescaniuk, Sheri**
The Fraser River estuary study: an annotated bibliography. Vancouver: Environment Canada, Pacific Yukon Region, 1984. v, 20 l.

Note: Provides references related to the Fraser River estuary: habitat, water quality, land use and transportation, recreation, cultural history, general works, audio-visual materials.
Location: OOFF.

5211 **Dzubin, Alex X.**
A selected bibliography of effects of dams, artificial impounds and reservoirs on the aquatic bird resource. Saskatoon: Ecological Assessment Section, Canadian Wildlife Service, Prairie Migratory Bird Research Centre, 1984. 226 l.

Note: Listing of books, papers, reviews, bibliographies on river basins, limnology, streams and lakes, water quality, man-made reservoirs, migratory birds, impoundments and waterfowl use, hydro projects, transmission lines and dams.
Location: OOFF.

5212 **Krueger, Donald R.**
Acid rain (part 1): a selected bibliography. Toronto: Ontario Legislative Library, Research and Information Services, 1984. 12 l.
Note: Location: OOP.

5213 **Krueger, Donald R.**
Acid rain (part 2): a selected bibliography. Toronto: Ontario Legislative Library, Research and Information Services, 1984. 12 l.
Note: Location: OOP.

5214 **Land, Bernard**
The toxicity of drilling fluid components to aquatic biological systems: a literature review. Winnipeg: Freshwater Institute, Research and Development Directorate, Fisheries and Marine Service, Environment Canada, 1984. iv l., 33 p. (Fisheries and Marine Service Technical report ; no. 487; ISSN: 0701-7626)
Note: Literature review (to January 31, 1974) on toxicity to aquatic biological systems of drilling fluid components used in northern Canada.
Location: OONL.

5215 **Lenentine, Beth L.**
New Brunswick-Maine border water resources, water use and related data: an annotated bibliography. Dartmouth, N.S.: Environment Canada, Inland Waters Directorate, Atlantic Region, 1984. iv, 101 l.: map.
Note: Approx. 100 entries.– Annotated list of reports and papers dealing with international boundary water issues involving New Brunswick and Maine.– Topics include water quality, water quantity, water use and related data (municipal, energy, agricultural, fisheries, wildlife and recreational uses).– At head of title: *A report prepared under the Environment 2000 Program.*– Résumé en français.
Location: OONL.

5216 **Minion, Robin**
Ice in the Beaufort Sea. Edmonton: Boreal Institute for Northern Studies, University of Alberta, 1984. 78 p. (Boreal Institute for Northern Studies Bibliographic series ; no. 6; ISSN: 0824-8192); ISBN: 0-919058-40-X.
Note: 204 entries.– Series contains monographs, theses, government documents, consultants' reports, children's books, conference proceedings, microforms on topics related to northern environment and people.– BINS series produced monthly from January 1984 to May 1986 (no. 29).– Online access: *Boreal Northern Titles (BNT)*, available through QL Systems Limited.
Location: OONL.

5217 **Mortsch, Linda D.; Kalnins, Ingrid I.**
A bibliography on storm surges and seiches/ Bibliographie sur les marées de tempête et les seiches. Downsview, Ont.: Environment Canada, Atmospheric Environment Service, 1984. iii, 42 p.
Note: Approx. 450 entries.– Covers 1960 to 1983.– Topics include storm surges (dynamics, statistics, core studies, models and engineering, impact and effect), and seiches (overview studies of lakes, seas, oceans).– Has substantial Canadian content.– Text in English and French/texte en français et en anglais.
Location: OONL.

5218 **Ommanney, C. Simon L.**
Bibliographic information on the Freshfield, Lyell and Mons glaciers, Alberta. Ottawa: National Hydrology Research Institute, 1984. 9 p.
Note: Location: ABA.

5219 **Shrybman, Steven**
Environmental mediation: bibliographies. Toronto: Canadian Environmental Law Association, 1984. 19, 22 l.
Note: Two sections: "Case studies" (facility siting and management, resource allocation standard setting and regulation); "Literature" (Canadian and American references).
Location: OOFF.

5220 **Smithers, Anne B.; Ghanimé, Linda; Harington, C.R.**
Climatic change in Canada, 4: annotated bibliography of quaternary climatic change in Canada. Ottawa: National Museums of Canada, National Museum of Natural Sciences, [1984]. 368 p.: ill., map. (Syllogeus / National Museum of Natural Sciences ; no. 51; ISSN: 0704-576X)
Note: 912 entries.– Published papers dealing with climatic change and variability in Canada during the last 2 million years.– Avant-propos en français.
Location: OONL.

— 1985 —

5221 **Canada. Environmental Conservation Service**
Long range transportation of airborne pollutants: bibliography, 1980-1984. [Ottawa]: Environment Canada, Environmental Conservation Service, 1985. iii, 27 p.; ISBN: 0-662-13962-3.

Note: Approx. 250 entries.– Published and unpublished reports, technical papers, workshop proceedings, working papers from the Canadian Wildlife Service, Inland Waters Directorate, Lands Directorate on acid rain and other airborne pollutants, mainly on research related to effect on lakes.
Titre en français: *Transport à grande distance des polluants atmosphériques: bibliographie 1980-1984*.
Location: OONL.

5222 **Canada. Service de la conservation de l'environnement**
Transport à grande distance des polluants atmosphériques: bibliographie 1980-1984. [Ottawa]: Environnement Canada, Service de la conservation de l'environnement, 1985. iii, 27 p.; ISBN: 0-662-93165-3.
Note: Approx. 250 entrées.– Inclut rapports, documents techniques, comptes-rendus des ateliers et autres documents de travail publiés et non-publiés.
English title: *Long range transportation of airborne pollutants: bibliography, 1980-1984*.
Localisation: OONL.

5223 **Delisle, Claude E.; Roy-Arcand, Line; Bouchard, Michel A.**
Effets des précipitations acides sur les divers écosystèmes: synthèse bibliographique. Québec: CINEP École polytechnique: Fondation canadienne Donner: Environnement Canada, Service de la protection de l'environnement, 1985. x, 307 p.
Note: Approx. 500 entrées.
Localisation: OOFF.

5224 **Jandali, Tarek; Hrebenyk, B.**
Urban air quality research needs in Alberta: a literature review and synthesis of available information. Edmonton: Alberta Environment, Research Management Division, 1985. xi, 188 p. (RMD report / Alberta Environment, Research Management Division ; 85-33)
Note: Approx. 400 entries.– Literature dealing with atmospheric processes in urban air quality, urban air quality monitoring, urban air quality modelling, effects/ consequences of air pollution.
Location: OONL.

5225 **MacFarlane, David S.; Fraser, James H.**
Water resources bibliography. Halifax: Province of Nova Scotia, Department of the Environment, 1985. ii, 111 p.
Note: Approx. 450 entries.– Lists studies, reports, research papers, theses, conference proceedings related to water resources of Nova Scotia.– Themes: hydro-geotechnical, tidal power, waste disposal, water quality, water resources, water supply.
Location: OONL.

5226 **Minion, Robin**
Aurora. Edmonton: Boreal Institute for Northern Studies, University of Alberta, 1985. 73 p. (Boreal Institute for Northern Studies Bibliographic series ; no. 24; ISSN: 0824-8192); ISBN: 0-919058-58-2.
Note: 222 entries.– Series contains monographs, theses, government documents, consultants' reports, children's books, conference proceedings, microforms on topics related to northern environment and people.– BINS series produced monthly from January 1984 to May 1986 (no. 29).– Online access: *Boreal Northern Titles (BNT)*, available through QL Systems Limited.
Location: OONL.

5227 **Minion, Robin**
Glacial deposition including moraines, drumlins and eskers. Edmonton: Boreal Institute for Northern Studies, University of Alberta, 1985. 90 p. (Boreal Institute for Northern Studies Bibliographic series ; no. 19; ISSN: 0824-8192); ISBN: 0-919058-53-1.
Note: 277 entries.– Series contains monographs, theses, government documents, consultants' reports, children's books, conference proceedings, microforms on topics related to northern environment and people.– BINS series produced monthly from January 1984 to May 1986 (no. 29).– Online access: *Boreal Northern Titles (BNT)*, available through QL Systems Limited.
Location: OONL.

5228 **Morin, Gérald; Potvin, Lise; Zubrzycki, Pierre**
Bibliographie analytique et description des banques de données dans le cadre des recherches sur le programme d'assainissement des eaux du Québec. [Sainte-Foy, Québec]: ÉNAP, 1985. iii, 282 p.
Note: 155 entrées.– Prinicpaux thèmes traités: assainissement agricole/industriel/urbain; milieu aquatic, aspects économiques/politiques/techniques, administration publique, législation, pesticides, aménagement du territoire, colloques/séminaires.
Localisation: OONL.

— 1986 —

5229 **Binda, Gilles G.; Day, T.J.; Syvitski, J.P.M.**
Terrestrial sediment transport into the marine environment of Canada: annotated bibliography and data. [Ottawa]: Environment Canada, Inland Waters Directorate, Water Resources Branch, [1986]. 1 vol. (in various pagings): ill., (1 map folded).
Note: 85 entries.
Location: OOFF.

5230 **British Columbia. Ecological Reserves Program**
List of reports and publications for ecological reserves in British Columbia. Victoria, B.C.: The Program, 1986. 1 vol. (loose-leaf): map.; ISBN: 0-7726-0515-7.
Note: 923 entries.– Contains reports and publications from 123 ecological reserves, documenting the research activity: graduate thesis projects, long-term monitoring or ecological studies.
Location: OONL.

5231 **Environmental resource book, 1986: environmental groups in Ontario and topical lists of their printed and audio-visual resources organized by issue category.**
Toronto: Ontario Environment Network, c1986. 42 p.: ill.
Note: Issue categories include energy conservation and alternatives, acid rain, herbicides and pesticides, municipal waste, nuclear issues, toxic wastes, water quality, policy and law.
Previous edition: *Environmental sourcebook*. 1982. 30 p.
Location: OONL.

5232 **Fitchko, J.**
Literature review of the effects of persistent toxic substances on Great Lakes biota. Windsor, Ont.: International Joint Commission, Great Lakes Regional Office, 1986. vii, 256 p.: map.
Note: Approx. 1,000 entries.
Location: OONL.

5233 **Free, Brian Michael**
Bibliography of recycling. Edmonton: Environment Council of Alberta, 1986. 56 p.

Note: Approx. 275 entries.– Contains a listing of reference materials used by Environment Council of Alberta in researching and writing reports on various aspects of recycling.– Three main topics covered are recycling, energy-from-waste and solid waste management.
Location: OONL.

5234 **Howard, Lynne M.**
Icebergs: a bibliography relevant to eastern Canadian waters. Ottawa: Environmental Studies Revolving Funds, 1986. xii, 277 p. (Environmental Studies Revolving Funds report ; no. 030); ISBN: 0-920783-29-5.
Note: 1,135 entries.– Geographic area covered ranges from Baffin Bay south to the Grand Banks and into the Atlantic.– Includes works on sea ice which also contain information on pack ice, ice floes, etc., works on ice scouring, iceberg towing, remote sensing of icebergs, iceberg surveying and measuring techniques.– Excludes works on properties of glacier ice in general.– Introduction in English and French/Introduction en français et en anglais.
Location: OONL.

5235 **Jones, Richard Edward**
The petrology and stratigraphy of arctic sea ice and relationships to formational processes [microform]: a critical review of the literature. Ottawa: National Library of Canada, 1986. 2 microfiches (118 fr.) (Canadian theses ; TH-26631); ISBN: 0-315-26631-7.
Note: Thesis (M.Sc.), Queen's University, 1984.
Location: OONL.

5236 **Meldrum, Janis**
Lake Superior bibliography: a compilation of references on the aquatic ecosystem. Houghton, MI.: Isle Royale National Park, 1986. ii, 95 l.
Note: Approx. 800 entries.– Journal articles, technical studies and reports from government agencies of Canada and the United States relating to Lake Superior ecology.– Most publications date from 1970, with a selection of earlier material.
Location: OPAL.

5237 **Neumeyer, Ronald N.**
The environmental effects of Canadian water diversion: a literature survey, 1985. Regina: Environment Canada, Inland Waters Directorate, 1986. iv, 87 p.: ill.
Note: 58 entries.– Published literature dealing with the ecological effects of existing Canadian water diversions.– Emphasis on biological, rather than hydraulic, hydrologic or physiographic effects.– Excludes social and economic implications.
Location: OOFF.

5238 **Taylor, Billie Louise**
An annotated bibliography of documentation relevant to acid precipitation in Atlantic Canada. Bedford, N.S.: Atmospheric Environment Service, 1986. iii, 77 p.
Note: Approx. 700 entries.– Published and unpublished reports and papers produced by researchers investigating various aspects of acid rain in Atlantic provinces, arranged in five categories: aquatic, atmospheric, controls, health, terrestrial.– Provides abstracts.
Location: OON.

5239 **Young, Stuart C.**
Bibliography on the fate and effects of Arctic marine oil pollution. Ottawa: Environmental Studies Revolving Funds, c1986. xii, 212 p. (Environmental Studies Revolving Funds report ; no. 026); ISBN: 0-920783-25-2.
Note: 748 entries.– Covers to December 1985.– Monographs, scientific journal articles, conference proceedings, theses, government publications dealing with physical, chemical and biological fate (dispersion, deposition, weathering, biodegradation) and biological effects (toxicity, sublethal effects, etc.) of petroleum and its hydrocarbon constituents.– Excludes work on detection and tracking of oil spills and oil spill dispersants.– Geographic coverage includes the Arctic regions plus Cook Inlet and the Gulf of Alaska.– Available online through the ASTIS database, (Arctic Science and Technology Information System), QL Systems Ltd.– Introduction en français.
Location: OONL.

— 1987 —

5240 **Binda, Gilles G.**
Ontario sediment-related literature: annotated bibliography. Ottawa: Environment Canada, Water Resources Branch, Inland Waters-Lands Directorate, Sediment Survey Section, 1987. iii, 250 p.
Note: 392 entries.– Compilation of references on subjects related to the quality, erosion, transportation and deposition of sediments in Ontario streams, rivers and lakes (excluding the Great Lakes).
Location: OOFF.

5241 **Boulet, Marie-France**
Politique de l'environnement: bibliographie sélective et annotée. Québec: Division de la référence parlementaire, Bibliothèque de l'Assemblée nationale, 1987. 41 p. (Bibliographie / Bibliothèque de l'Assemblée nationale du Québec ; no 11; ISSN: 0836-9100)
Note: 187 entrées.– Études générales, Québec, Canada, États-Unis, France, autres pays, études multinationales.
Localisation: OONL.

5242 **Campbell, K.W.**
Pollutant exposure and response relationships: a literature review: geological and hydrogeological aspects. Calgary: Acid Deposition Research Program, 1987. 151 p.: ill., maps.; ISBN: 0-921625-09-X.
Note: Approx. 285 entries.– Inventory and literature review of geological and hydrogeological aspects with specific reference to acidic deposition effects in Alberta.
Location: OONL.

5243 **Desiree Bradley Library and Technical Services**
An annotated bibliography of literature related to acid deposition in western Canada. Vancouver: Environment Canada, Atmospheric Environment Service, Scientific Services Division, 1987. 101 p.
Note: Approx. 200 entries.– Reports and papers on acidic deposition in the western provinces, Yukon and Northwest Territories, excluding the Arctic islands.– Topics include natural and anthropogenic emissions, aquatic processes and effects, terrestrial processes and effects, effects on vegetation, health effects, controls and legislation.
Location: OOFF.

5244 **Hooper, Tracey D.; Vermeer, Kees; Szabo, Ildy**
Oil pollution of birds: an annotated bibliography. Delta, B.C.: Canadian Wildlife Service, 1987. 180 p. (Technical report series / Canadian Wildlife Service ; no. 34; ISSN: 0831-6481); ISBN: 0-662-15904-7.

Note: 606 entries.– Covers from 1922 to early 1986.
Previous edition: Vermeer, Rebecca Arrieta; Vermeer, Kees. *Oil pollution of birds: an abstracted bibliography.* Canadian Wildlife Service, 1974. 68 p. (Canadian Wildlife Service Manuscript reports ; no. 29).
Location: OONL.

5245 **Knight, Kenneth Drew; Nelson, James Gordon; Priddle, George Burton**
Great Lakes shoreline resource management: a selected annotated bibliography. Waterloo, Ont.: Heritage Resources Centre, University of Waterloo, 1987. 43 p. (Occasional paper / Heritage Resources Centre, University of Waterloo ; 7; ISSN: 0829-0989); ISBN: 0-921245-12-2.
Note: Approx. 150 entries.– Covers 1974 to 1987.– Articles, manuals, technical reports, guidebooks and pamphlets.– Focus on technical and behavioural adjustments to fluctuating water levels and associated processes.
Location: OONL.

5246 **Krouse, Howard Roy**
Environmental sulphur isotope studies in Alberta: a review. Calgary: Acid Deposition Research Program, 1987. 89 p.; ISBN: 0-921625-05-7.
Note: Approx. 200 entries.
Location: OONL.

5247 **Legge, Allan H.; Crowther, Roy A.**
Acidic deposition and the environment: a literature overview. Calgary: Acid Deposition Research Program, 1987. ix, 235 p.: ill., map.; ISBN: 0-921625-13-8.
Note: Literature review of effects of acid rain on forests, agriculture, soils, soil microorganisms, geology and hydrogeology, surface water acidification.– Section of 73 references specifically dealing with acidic deposition in the Alberta context.
Location: OONL.

5248 **McLeay, D. and Associates Limited**
Aquatic toxicity of pulp and paper mill effluent: a review. Ottawa: Environment Canada, 1987. xlii, 191 p.; ISBN: 0-662-15335-9.
Note: Review and evaluation of publicly available documents dealing with toxic constituents in mill effluents, receiving waters and sediments.– Topics include laboratory monitoring for toxicity, toxic effects of mill effluents within receiving waters, bioaccumulation and elimination of organic constituents in mill effluents, bioassay tests for predicting impact of effluents in the aquatic environment.
Titre en français: *Enquête bibliographique sur la toxicité des effluents de l'industrie des pâtes et papiers pour les biocénoses aquatiques.*
Location: OONL.

5249 **McLeay, D. and Associates Limited**
Enquête bibliographique sur la toxicité des effluents de l'industrie des pâtes et papiers pour les biocénoses aquatiques. Ottawa: Environnement Canada, 1987. xliii, 183, [12] p.; ISBN: 0-662-94212-4.
Note: Une étude et une évaluation objectives des ouvrages et des rapports sur les sujets suivants: composition toxique des effluents, des eaux réceptrices et des sédiments; détermination en laboratoire de la toxicité de l'effluent de pâtes et papiers; prévision de la toxicité de l'effluent de pâtes et papiers pour la biocénose aquatique au moyen d'essai biologiques.

English title: *Aquatic toxicity of pulp and paper mill effluent: a review.*
Localisation: OONL.

5250 **New Brunswick. Water Resource Planning Branch**
Water resources in New Brunswick: a preliminary bibliography. Fredericton: Department of Municipal Affairs and Environment, Water Resource Planning Branch, 1987. 113 p.
Note: Approx. 1,500 entries.
Location: OONL.

5251 **Rafferty-Alameda Project environmental impact statement: bibliography.** [Regina]: Souris Basin Development Authority, [1987]. 53 l.
Note: Approx. 350 entries.– Studies related to Rafferty-Alameda (Souris River) dam project area in Saskatchewan.– Topics include anthropology and archaeology, ecology, geology, hydrology, biology, meteorology and climate, soils, limnology, pollution measurements.
Location: OONL.

5252 **Rosenthal, Harald; Wilson, J. Scott**
An updated bibliography (1845-1986) on ozone, its biological effects and technical applications. Ottawa: Department of Fisheries and Oceans, 1987. vii, 249 p. (Canadian technical report of fisheries and aquatic sciences ; no. 1542; ISSN: 0706-6457)
Note: Technical studies and papers on biological effects and chemical reactions of ozone, selected references related to general chemistry of ozone, effects of ozone on materials, toxicity to humans.
Previous edition: *Selected bibliography on ozone, its biological effects and technical applications.* Nanaimo, B.C.: Pacific Biological Station, Fisheries and Marine Service, 1974. 150 p. (Fisheries Research Board of Canada Technical report ; no. 456).
Location: OONL.

5253 **Rumney, Thomas A.**
The physical geography of Canada: climate, ice, water studies: a selected bibliography. Monticello, Ill.: Vance Bibliographies, 1987. 50 p. (Public administration series: Bibliography ; P-2275; ISSN: 0193-970X); ISBN: 1-55590-535-8.
Note: Approx. 575 entries.– Research literature published mainly since 1945, dealing with applied climatology, climatic change, ice and snow-related studies, climatological modelling and theoretical studies, physical and synoptic climatology, regional climatology, water-related topics.
Location: OONL.

5254 **Telang, S.A.**
Surface water acidification literature review. Calgary: Acid Deposition Research Program, 1987. x, 123 p.; ISBN: 0-921625-03-0.
Note: Approx. 375 entries.– Review of scientific literature dealing with effects of acidic atmospheric deposition on surface water chemistry.– Many Canadian references.
Location: OONL.

5255 **University of Western Ontario. Cross-cultural Learner Centre**
Annotated bibliography of environment-development issues. [London, Ont.]: London Cross Cultural Learner Centre, 1987. [54] p.
Note: Approx. 200 entries.– Books, periodicals, video

recordings, slides, kits.

Location: OONL.

5256 **Water resources in New Brunswick: a preliminary bibliography.** [Fredericton, N.B.]: Water Resource Planning Branch, Environmental Management, Land & Water Use Division, Department of Municipal Affairs and Environment, 1987. 113 p.

Note: Approx. 1,500 entries.– Lists material with which the Water Resource Planning Branch has been involved as author, sponsor, supervisor, participant, reviewer or recipient.– Principal topics include dams, floods and flood management, groundwater, ice and snow, hydrography, Saint John River, water and sewer services, water contamination, water quality, water supply, watercourse alteration, wells.

Location: OONL.

— 1988 —

5257 **Andrews, Thomas A.**
"Selected bibliography of native resource management systems and native knowledge of the environment."
In: *Traditional knowledge and renewable resource management in northern regions*, edited by Milton M.R. Freeman and Ludwig N. Carbyn. Edmonton: Boreal Institute for Northern Studies, University of Alberta, 1988. P. 105-124. (Boreal Institute for Northern Studies Occasional paper ; no. 23); ISBN: 0-919058-68-X.

Note: 246 entries.– Articles and papers dealing with traditional knowledge, use and management of Arctic sea ice environments and resources, boreal forest ecosystems, and reports on successful attempts at co-management.

Location: OONL.

5258 **Keleher, J.J.**
Manitoba: aquatic LRTAP data and bibliography. Winnipeg: Water Standards and Studies Section, 1988. ii, 272 p.

Note: 255 entries.– Covers 1933 to 1983.– Includes source publications and unpublished documents pertaining to long-range transport of atmospheric pollutants (acid rain) and its effect on water bodies of Manitoba.– Excludes Lake Winnipeg.

Location: OONL.

5259 **Kirby, Ronald E.; Lewis, Stephen J.; Sexson, Terry N.**
Fire in North American wetland ecosystems and fire-wildlife relations: an annotated bibliography. Washington, D.C.: Fish and Wildlife Service, U.S. Department of the Interior, 1988. vi, 146 p.: ill. (Biological report / Fish and Wildlife Service, U.S. Department of the Interior ; 88:1)

Note: Location: AEECW.

5260 **Phillips, David W.; Gullett, D.W.; Webb, M.S.**
Guide des sources des données climatiques du Service de l'environnement atmosphérique. 3e éd. Downsview, Ont.: Environnement Canada, Service de l'environnement atmosphérique, 1988. 1 vol. (en pagination multiple): ill., carte.; ISBN: 0-660-92270-3.

Note: Périodiques de données climatologiques actuelles nationales et régionales, périodiques de données climatologiques historiques, publications de données statistiques et spéciales, résumés et tableaux, archives climatologiques nationales.

English title: *Handbook on climate data sources of the Atmospheric Environment Service.*

Éditions antérieures:

Centre climatologique, 1982. 1 vol. (en pagination multiple); ISBN: 0-660-90996-0.

1979. 1 vol. (en pagination multiple); ISBN: 0-660-90180-3.

Localisation: OONL.

5261 **Phillips, David W.; Gullett, D.W.; Webb, M.S.**
Handbook on climate data sources of the Atmospheric Environment Service. 3rd ed. Downsview, Ont.: Environment Canada, Atmospheric Environment Service, 1988. 276 p. (in various pagings): ill., map.; ISBN: 0-660-12735-0.

Note: Lists current climatological data periodicals (national and regional), historical climatological data periodicals, statistical and special data publications, abstracts and tabulations, standard observing forms and charts, climatological digital archives.

Titre en français: *Guide des sources des données climatiques du Service de l'environnement atmosphérique.*

Previous editions:

Canadian Climate Centre, 1982. 1 vol. (various pagings); ISBN: 0-660-11258-2.

1979. 1 vol. (various pagings); ISBN: 0-660-10155-6.

Location: OONL.

5262 **Pross, Catherine; Dwyer-Rigby, Mary**
Sustaining earth: a bibliography of the holdings of the Ecology Action Resource Centre, Halifax, Canada. Halifax: School of Library and Information Studies, Dalhousie University, 1988. iv, 302 p. (Occasional papers / Dalhousie University School of Library and Information Studies ; no. 44; ISSN: 0318-7403); ISBN: 0-7703-9718-2.

Note: Approx. 6,000 entries.– Covers to July 1987.– List of books, studies, articles organized into six broad groupings: changes in the biosphere, energy, human habitat and society, institutional responses to environmental issues, pollution, resources and resource industries.

Location: OONL.

5263 **Répertoire de matériel éducatif dans le domaine de l'environnement.** Québec: Gouvernement du Québec, Ministère de l'environnement, [1988]. 128 p.; ISBN: 2-550-18724-5.

Note: Approx. 300 entrées.– Matériel écrit, audio-visuel et informatisé dans le domaine de l'environnement.– Partie 1: matériel didactique; partie 2: matériel utile.– Index thématique des productions.

Localisation: OONL.

5264 **Service de diffusion sélective de l'information de la Centrale des bibliothèques**
La pollution de l'air et les précipitations acides. 2e éd. Montréal: Le Service, 1988. 30 p. (DSI/CB ; no 56; ISSN: 0825-5024); ISBN: 2-89059-329-0.

Note: 277 entrées.– Monographies, articles de périodiques et journaux, documents audiovisuels.

Édition antérieure: 1984. 30 p.; ISBN: 2-89059-256-1.

Localisation: OONL.

5265 **Sullivan, Thomas Priestlay**
Non-target impacts of the herbicide Glyphosate: a compendium of references & abstracts. Victoria: Canadian Forestry Service, 1988. iii, 46 p. (FRDA report / Canada-British Columbia Forest Resource Development Agreement ; 013; ISSN: 0835-0752); ISBN: 0-7726-0827-X.

Note: 114 entries.– Articles and reports dealing with the effect of herbicide Glyphosate on mammals, birds, fish, aquatic invertebrates and algae, terrestrial invertebrates,

microflora.– Includes Canadian references.
Location: OONL.

— 1989 —

5266 Appleby, J.A.; Scarratt, D.J.
Physical effects of suspended solids on marine and estuarine fish and shellfish, with special reference to ocean dumping: a literature review. Halifax: Fisheries and Oceans Canada, 1989. v, 33 p. (Canadian technical report of fisheries and aquatic sciences ; no. 1681; ISSN: 0706-6457)
Note: Approx. 150 entries.– Literature concerning lethal and sublethal effects of suspended solids on marine and estuarine fish and shellfish, with reference to ocean and coastal zone dredging and dumping.– Résumé en français.
Location: OONL.

5267 Dave, Nand K.; Lim, T.P.
Wetlands and their role in treating acid mine drainage: a literature review. [Ottawa]: Canada Centre for Mineral and Energy Technology, Mining Research Laboratories, 1989. i, 37 p. (Mining Research Laboratory Divisional report ; MRL-107-LS)
Note: Approx. 225 entries.– Lists material pertaining to use of wetlands (swamps, marshes, bogs, wet meadows, fens, etc.) in controlling acid generation and metal release from mining wastes.– Some Canadian references.
Location: OONL.

5268 Dionne, Jean-Claude
"Bibliographie du périglaciaire du Québec, 1969-1989, incluant le glaciel pour la période 1960-1989."
Dans: *Géographie physique et quaternaire*; Vol. 43, no 2 (1989) p. 233-243.; ISSN: 0705-7199.
Note: Approx. 400 entrées.
Localisation: OONL.

5269 Dufresne, Nicole
Chartes, déclarations, recommandations et ententes concernant l'environnement: bibliographie sélective. Québec: Bibliothèque de l'Assemblée nationale, Division de la référence parlementaire, 1989. 17 p. (Bibliographie / Bibliothèque de l'Assemblée nationale du Québec ; no 31; ISSN: 0836-9100)
Note: Comprend des publications en français et en anglais.
Localisation: OONL.

5270 Higgins, Kenneth F., et al.
Annotated bibliography of fire literature relative to northern grasslands in south-central Canada and north-central United States. Brookings, S.D.: U.S. Fish and Wildlife Service, 1989. 20 p.
Note: 206 entries.
Location: DLC.

5271 Ommanney, C. Simon L.
Recent Canadian glacier references, 1986-1988. Saskatoon: Environment Canada, National Hydrology Research Institute, 1989. 22 l. (National Hydrology Research Institute Contribution ; no. 89001; ISSN: 0838-1992)
Note: Location: OOFF.

5272 Ommanney, C. Simon L.
Snow and ice research in Canada, 1988. Saskatoon: National Hydrology Research Institute, [1989]. 13 l. (National Hydrology Research Institute Contribution ; no. 89038; ISSN: 0838-1992)

Note: Location: OON.

— 1990 —

5273 Atomic Energy of Canada Limited. Technical Information Services Branch
Radioactive waste management in Canada: AECL research publications and other literature, 1953-1990/ Gestion des déchets nucléaires au Canada: publications d'EACL recherche et autres documents, 1953-1990. Chalk River, Ont.: Chalk River Laboratories, 1990. 217 p.; ISSN: 0067-0367.
Note: Approx. 2,500 entries.– AECL reports, journal articles, conference proceedings.– Includes publications from outside organizations of concern to the Canadian Nuclear Fuel Waste Management Program in addition to AECL Research reports and papers.– Text in English and French/texte en français et en anglais.
Previous edition: Wallace, Dianne E. Pinawa, Man.: Whiteshell Nuclear Research Establishment, 1983. 79 p.– Approx. 500 entries.– Covers from 1953 to 1982.
Location: OONL.

5274 Canadian Council of Ministers of the Environment. Research Advisory Committee
National inventory of environmental research and development projects/Inventaire national des projets de recherche et développement sur l'environnement. Ottawa: The Council, 1990. xii, 488 p. (Report / Canadian Council of Ministers of the Environment ; CCME-R-TRE-022); ISBN: 0-662-57656-X.
Note: Approx. 1,700 entries.– Summary listing of all significant environmental research and development projects and publications funded by Environment Canada, provincial governments, universities and private corporations and associations.
Location: OONL.

5275 Canadian Housing Information Centre
Bibliography on indoor air pollution/Bibliographie sur la pollution de l'air des habitations. Ottawa: Canada Mortgage and Housing Corporation, 1990. 29 p.
Note: Approx. 200 entries.
Location: OOCM.

5276 Charette, Jean-Yves
Bibliographie signalétique sur les précipitations acides. Québec: Environnement Canada, Conservation et protection, Région du Québec, 1990. v, 316 p.
Note: Approx. 2,000 entrées.– Articles, études techniques de gouvernement, institutions privée, universités.– Principaux thèmes traités: environnement atmosphérique, organismes aquatiques, hydrogéochimie, végétation terrestre, faune terrestre, lacs.
Éditions antérieures:
1987. v, 230 p.
Brunelle, Lucie. *Bibliographie signalétique: précipitations acides*. Environnement Canada, Direction générale des eaux intérieures, Région du Québec, 1984. v, 166 p.
1983. v, 128 p.
1982. v, 100 p.
Bibliographie sur les pluies acides. 1980. [72] p.
Localisation: OONL.

5277 Coakley, John Phillip; Long, B.F.N.
Étude de l'aide de traceurs du déplacement de sédiments à grain fin dans les systèmes aquatiques: étude documentaire. Burlington, Ont.: Direction générale des eaux intérieures, Institut national de recherche sur les

eaux, Centre canadien des eaux intérieures, 1990. v, 29 p. (Série scientifique, Étude / Direction générale des eaux intérieures, Institut national de recherche sur les eaux, Centre canadien des eaux intérieures ; no 174); ISBN: 0-662-96274-5.

Note: 100 entrées.

English title: *Tracing the movement of fine-grained sediment in aquatic systems: a literature review.*

Localisation: OONL.

5278 **Coakley, John Phillip; Long, B.F.N.**
Tracing the movement of fine-grained sediment in aquatic systems: a literature review. Burlington, Ont.: Inland Waters Directorate, 1990. v, 21 p. (Scientific series / Inland Waters Directorate, National Water Research Institute, Canada Centre for Inland Waters ; no. 174); ISBN: 0-662-18040-2.

Note: 100 entries.

Titre en français: *Étude de l'aide de traceurs du déplacement de sédiments à grain fin dans les systèmes aquatiques: étude documentaire.*

Location: OONL.

5279 **Dewailly, Éric**
Revue de la contamination dans la chaîne aquatique arctique: présentation de la banque de données. Sainte-Foy, Québec: Service Santé et environnement, Centre hospitalier de l'Université Laval, 1990. 21, [43] p.: ill., cartes.; ISBN: 2-921304-13-9.

Note: Approx. 300 entrées.– Documents publiés et non-publiés.– La territoire à l'étude comprend tout l'Arctique canadien situé au nord du 52e parallèle.

Localisation: OONL.

5280 **English, M.; Wong, R.K.W.; Kochtubajda, B.**
Literature review on the greenhouse effect and global warming. [Edmonton]: Alberta Department of Energy, 1990. 52 p.: ill.

Note: 501 entries.– Lists articles published in scientific journals, official studies and reports for the period 1980 to 1990.– Topics covered include climate modelling, monitoring of the atmosphere and climate, potential impact of climate change, strategies for responding to climate change, technological solutions to problems created by climate change.– Many Canadian references.

5281 **Hardy BBT Limited**
Reclamation of disturbed alpine lands: a literature review. Edmonton: Land Conservation and Reclamation Council, Reclamation Research Technical Advisory Committee, 1990. xviii, 198 [13] p. (Alberta Land Conservation and Reclamation Council report ; no. RRTAC 90-7; ISSN: 0713-1232)

Note: Review of North American sources on measures needed to reclaim alpine disturbances, in Alberta primarily associated with development and use of recreational facilities.– Much of this review deals with research on identification and selection of plant materials suitable for alpine revegetation, mulches and fertilization, addition of topsoil, transplantion.

Location: OONL.

5282 **Monenco Consultants Limited**
Literature review on the disposal of drilling waste solids. Edmonton: Alberta Land Conservation and Reclamation Council, Reclamation Research Technical Advisory Committee, 1990. xii, 83 p.

Note: Reviews Canadian and selected international literature to determine the environmental acceptability of burying drilling waste solids produced during petroleum exploration and production.

Location: OONL.

5283 **Ommanney, C. Simon L.**
Floating ice in Canada references (1988-1990) and recent work. Saskatoon: National Hydrology Research Institute, 1990. 120 p. (National Hydrology Research Institute Contribution ; no. 90052; ISSN: 0838-1992)

Note: Approx. 850 entries.– References to work done in Canada, on Canadian marine and freshwater floating ice, by Canadian glaciologists.– Includes unpublished reports and newspaper articles.

Location: OON.

5284 **Ommanney, C. Simon L.**
Permafrost in Canada: references (1988-1990) and recent work. Saskatoon: National Hydrology Research Institute, 1990. 47 p. (National Hydrology Research Institute Contribution ; no. 90053; ISSN: 0838-1992)

Note: Summarizes references to work done in Canada by Canadian glaciologists, on Canadian permafrost and ground ice, published between 1988 and 1990.– Includes unpublished reports and newspaper articles.

Location: OON.

5285 **Ommanney, C. Simon L.**
Snow in Canada references (1988-1990) and recent work. Saskatoon: Environment Canada, Conservation and Protection, Inland Waters Directorate, 1990. 53 p.

Note: Location: OOFF.

— 1991 —

5286 **Canada. Environment Canada**
Canada Water Act publications, 1970-1990 / Publications relatives à la Loi sur les ressources en eau du Canada, 1970-1990. [Ottawa]: Environment Canada, [1991]. xii, 197 p.: 1 col. map.

Note: 820 entries.– Documents dealing with planning and development of Canadian freshwater resources under the Canada Water Act, arranged in three main sections: water management, water management policy, river basins.– Online availability: AQUAREF database produced by WATDOC available on CAN/OLE through CISTI (Canada Institute for Scientific and Technical Information), provides access to bibliographic references to the general, scientific and technical literature on Canadian water resources and other environmental topics.– Updated bimonthly.– Text in English and French/texte en français et en anglais.

Location: OONL.

5287 **Christensen, John O.**
Acid rain and public policy: a selective bibliography of recent references. Monticello, Ill.: Vance Bibliographies, 1991. 15 p. (Public administration series: Bibliography ; P-3072; ISSN: 0193-970X); ISBN: 0-7920-0792-1.

Note: 250 entries.– Covers 1985-1991.– Includes references mainly in English dealing with acid rain policy issues in the United States and Canada.

Location: OONL.

5288 **Dufresne, Nicole**
Développement durable: bibliographie sélective et annotée. Québec: Bibliothèque de l'Assemblée nationale, Division de la référence parlementaire, 1991. 23 p. (Bibliographie / Bibliothèque de l'Assemblée nationale du Québec ; no 8; ISSN: 0836-9100)

Note: Localisation: OONL.

5289   **Joy, Albert H.**
Acid rain: a bibliography of Canadian federal and provincial government documents. Westport: Meckler, c1991. xxi, 237 p.; ISBN: 0-88736-527-2.
Note: 1,102 entries.– Comprehensive compilation of citations of Canadian government literature on acid precipitation, technical materials published by federal and provincial agencies, intergovernmental and government/industry organizations issued for the most part between 1975 and 1989.– Sections include general works, environmental effects, air and atmospheric processes, socio-economic aspects, political aspects, mitigative and corrective measures.
Location: OONL.
Previous edition: *Acid precipitation: a bibliography of Canadian federal and provincial documents and Canadian conference proceedings on acid precipitation: preliminary version*. Burlington: University of Vermont, 1988. 126 p.
Location: OKQ.

5290   **Koshida, G.; Mortsch, Linda D.**
Climate change and water level impacts on wetlands: a bibliography/Répercussions du changement climatique et du niveau des eaux sur les milieux humides: bibliographie. Downsview, Ont.: Canadian Climate Program, 1991. iv, 50 p.
Note: Approx. 540 entries.– Covers the period 1935 to 1991.– Journal articles, conference and symposium proceedings, technical manual, government agency reports arranged in four main subject groupings: wetlands, climate and water levels; wetland functions and values; wetlands of Canada and North America; climate change, water resources and the Great Lakes.– Text in English and French/texte en français et en anglais.
Location: OONL.

5291   **Mortsch, Linda D.**
Eastern Canadian boreal and sub-Arctic wetlands: a resource document. Ottawa: Environment Canada, Atmospheric Environment Service, 1991. xii, 169 p.: ill., maps (some folded).
Note: Includes bibliographical references.
Location: NFSM.

5292   **Pembina Institute for Appropriate Development**
The Canadian environmental education catalogue: a guide to selected resources and materials. Drayton Valley, Alta.: Pembina Institute for Appropriate Development, 1991. 1 vol. (in various pagings).; ISBN: 0-921719-07-8.
Note: Approx. 1,200 entries.– Annotated bibliographic listing of books, booklets, periodicals, kits, audio-visual materials dealing with environmental issues.– Focus is on Canadian materials in the English language.
Location: OONL.

5293   **Thomson, Bruce**
Annotated bibliography of large organic debris (LOD) with regards to stream channels and fish habitat. Victoria: BC Environment, 1991. iii, 93 p. (MOE Technical report ; 32; ISSN: 0840-9730); ISBN: 0-771-89028-1.
Note: Location: OONL.

— 1992 —

5294   **Barlow, D.P.**
Tsunami: annotated bibliography. Victoria: Province of British Columbia, Floodplain Management Branch, 1992.
28 p.; ISBN: 0-7726-1644-2.
Note: Approx. 200 entries.– Research documents on the nature of tsunamis, storm surges, tsunami studies on the west coast of Canada, flood insurance studies, floodplain management, coastal zone management.
Location: OONL.

5295   **Dufour, Jules**
Bibliographie thématique sur l'environnement. Québec: Service de la recherche et de l'évaluation, Musée de la civilisation, 1992. 50, [7] p. (Document / Service de la recherche et de l'évaluation, Musée de la civilisation ; no 7); ISBN: 2-551-12842-0.
Note: Localisation: OONL.

5296   **Holmberg, Robert George**
Pulp mills and the environment: an annotated bibliography for northern Alberta. Athabasca: Athabasca University; Edmonton: Canadian Circumpolar Institute, University of Alberta : Environmental Research and Study Centre, University of Alberta, 1992. 32 p.; ISBN: 0-919737-06-4.
Note: Approx. 350 entries.– Books, technical reports, periodical articles related to development and operation of pulp and paper mills in northern Alberta.– Topics include air pollution, economics, fish toxicology, forestry, human health, legal aspects, waste management, water pollution.
Location: OONL.

5297   **Larouche, Ursula; Boudreau, Francis**
Réserve écologique de Tantaré: bibliographie annotée des travaux et d'acquisition de connaissances. Québec: Ministère de l'environnement, Direction de la conservation et du patrimoine écologique, 1992. [4], i, 54 p.; ISBN: 2-550-26570-X.
Note: 53 entrées.– Rapports et publications scientifiques ayant trait à la réserve écologique Tantaré et à certains travaux régionaux englobant la réserve écologique, située à environ 40 km au nord-ouest de la ville de Québec.
Localisation: OONL.

5298   **Ommanney, C. Simon L.**
Canadian lake, river and sea ice references (1991-1992) and recent work. Saskatoon: National Hydrology Research Institute, 1992. 120 p. (National Hydrology Research Institute Contribution ; no. 92037; ISSN: 0838-1992)
Note: Previous edition: *Canadian lake, river and sea ice references (1990-1991) and recent work*. 1991. (National Hydrology Research Institute Contribution ; no. 91034).
Location: OON.

— 1993 —

5299   **Lonergan, David**
Le livre de mer: bibliographie commentée des livres de mer édités en français au Québec et au Canada et disponibles sur le marché. Bic, Québec: Isaac-Dion, 1993. 67 p.: ill.; ISBN: 2-9802497-2-6.
Note: 417 entrées.– Thèmes: histoire, voyages, arts et littérature, littérature de jeunesse, océanographie, droit, pêche et aquaculture, navigation, sports et loisirs.
Localisation: OONL.

— Ongoing/En cours —

5300   **Canadian environmental directory.** Toronto: Canadian Almanac & Directory Pub. Co., 1991-. vol.; ISSN: 1187-1202.

Note: Includes a bibliography listing and annotating books, brochures, directories and buyer's guides, handbooks, online databases and CD-ROMS, newsletters and newspapers, conference proceedings, statistical materials, yearbooks dealing with environmental issues.
Location: OONL.

5301 **Environmental resource directory.** [Toronto]: Public Focus, [1989]-. vol. (loose-leaf).
Note: Books, periodicals, pamphlets, booklets, factsheets, games, kits, audio-visual materials pertaining to environment and ecology, hazardous substances, acid rain, energy, conservation, water, wildlife, waste management, air pollution, wetlands.– Designed to facilitate location of materials for environmental education.– Updates published twice yearly, in March and September.
Location: OONL.

Biological Sciences

Sciences biologiques

— 1877 —

5302 Gill, Theodore Nicholas; Coues, Elliott; Allen, Joel Asaph
Material for a bibliography of North American mammals. Washington: U.S.G.P.O., 1877. P. [951]-1081.
Note: "Extracted from the eleventh volume of the final reports of the [United States Geological and Geographical] Survey, being Appendix B of the *Monographs of North American Rodentia*, by Elliott Coues and Joel Asaph Allen.
Microform: CIHM Microfiche series ; no. 06621; ISBN: 0-665-06621-X. 2 microfiches (74 fr.).
Location: OONL.

— 1878 —

5303 Strecker, Herman
Butterflies and moths of North America: ... with a full bibliography .... Reading, Pa.: B.F. Owen, 1878. [4], ii, 283 p.
Note: Microform: CIHM Microfiche series ; no. 28006; ISBN: 0-665-28006-8. 4 microfiches (158 fr.).
Location: OLU.

5304 Watson, Sereno
Bibliographical index to North American botany, or, Citations of authorities for all the recorded indigenous and naturalized species of the flora of North America: with a chronological arrangement of the synonymy. Washington: Smithsonian Institution, 1878. vi, 476 p. (Smithsonian miscellaneous collections ; vol. 15)
Note: Microform: CIHM Microfiche series ; no. 14775; ISBN: 0-665-14775-9. 6 microfiches (259 fr.).
Location: OONL.

— 1887 —

5305 Penhallow, D.P.
"A review of Canadian botany from the first settlement of New France to the nineteenth century."
In: *Proceedings and Transactions of the Royal Society of Canada*; Vol. 5, section 4 (1887) p. 45-61.; ISSN: 0316-4616.
Note: Location: OONL.

— 1889 —

5306 Edwards, Henry
Bibliographical catalogue of the described transformations of North American Lepidoptera. Washington: U.S.G.P.O., 1889. 147 p.
Note: Approx. 3,000 entries.– Listing of papers and articles dealing with life history of butterflies.– Includes many Canadian references.
Microform: CIHM Microfiche series ; no. 06611; ISBN: 0-665-06611-2. 2 microfiches (66 fr.).
Location: OONL.

— 1890 —

5307 "Canadian ornithological bibliography."
In: *Transactions of the Canadian Institute*; Vol. 1 (1889-1890) p. 60-64.; ISSN: 0384-823X.
Note: "Ornithological papers published in the *Canadian Journal* up to 1889 inclusive."

Location: OONL.

— 1893 —

5308 Smith, John Bernhard
A catalogue, bibliographical and synonymical of the species of moths of the Lepidopterous superfamily Noctuidae: found in boreal America. Washington: G.P.O., 1893. 424 p. (Bulletin / United States National Museum ; no. 44)
Note: Microform: CIHM Microfiche series ; no. 14772; ISBN: 0-665-14772-4. 5 microfiches (224 fr.).
Location: OOG.

— 1896 —

5309 Williston, Samuel W.
Bibliography of North American dipterology, 1878-1895. [S.l.: s.n.], 1896. P. 129-144.
Note: Excerpt from *Kansas University Quarterly*, Vol. 4, no. 3 (January 1896).
Microform: CIHM Microfiche series ; no. 28150; ISBN: 0-665-28150-1. 1 microfiche (12 fr.).
Location: OOAGE.

5310 Williston, Samuel W.
"Bibliography of North American dipterology, 1878-1895."
In: *Kansas University Quarterly*; Vol. 4, no. 3 (January 1896) p. [129]-144.; ISSN: 0885-4068.
Note: Location: OON.

— 1897 —

5311 Penhallow, D.P.
"A review of Canadian botany from 1800 to 1895."
In: *Proceedings and Transactions of the Royal Society of Canada*; Series 2, vol. 3, section 4 (1897) p. 3-56.; ISSN: 0316-4616.
Note: 470 entries.
Reprint: Montreal: McGill University, Department of Botany, 1898. 56 p. (Papers from the Department of Botany (McGill University) ; no. 7).
Location: OONL.

— 1907 —

5312 Whiteaves, J.F.
"Bibliography of Canadian zoology, exclusive of entomology."
In: *Proceedings and transactions of the Royal Society of Canada*; Series 2, vol. 7, section 4 (1901) p. 87-91; series 2, vol. 8, section 4 (1902) p. 151-155; series 2, vol. 9, section 4 (1903) p. 163-167; series 2, vol. 10, section 4 (1904) p. 161-166; series 2, vol. 11, section 4 (1905) p. 65-69; series 2, vol. 12, section 4 (1906) p. 27-32; series 3, vol. 1, section 4 (1907) p. 211-218.; ISSN: 0316-4616.
Note: Location: AEU.

— 1913 —

5313 Lambe, Lawrence M.
"Bibliography of Canadian zoology."
In: *Proceedings and Transactions of the Royal Society of Canada*; Series 3, vol. 2, section 4 (1908) p. 77-87; series 3, vol. 3, section 4 (1909) p. 169-176; series 3, vol. 4, section 4

(1910) p. 101-108; series 3, vol. 5, section 4 (1911) p. 155-163; series 3, vol. 6, section 4 (1912) p. 101-144; series 3, vol. 7, section 4 (1913) p. 187-199.; ISSN: 0316-4616.
Note: Location: AEU.

— 1916 —

5314 **Bethune, C.J.S.**
"Bibliography of Canadian entomology."
In: *Proceedings and Transactions of the Royal Society of Canada*; Series 2, vol. 7, section 4 (1901) p. 135-139; series 2, vol. 8, section 4 (1902) p. 161-167; series 2, vol. 9, section 4 (1903) p. 155-161; series 2, vol. 10, section 4 (1904) p. 147-152; series 2, vol. 11, section 4 (1905) p. 57-63; series 2, vol. 12, section 4 (1906) p. 55-65; series 3, vol. 1, section 4 (1907) p. 131-141; series 3, vol. 2, section 4 (1908) p. 89-103; series 3, vol. 3, section 4 (1909) p. 135-146; series 3, vol. 4, section 4 (1910) p. 109-120; series 3, vol. 5, section 4 (1911) p. 165-176; series 3, vol. 6, section 4 (1912) p. 115-127; series 3, vol. 7, section 4 (1913) p. 161-173; series 3, vol. 8, section 4 (1914) P. 53-68; series 3, vol. 9, section 4 (1915) p. 263-278; series 3, vol. 10, section 4 (1916) p. 169-187.; ISSN: 0316-4616.
Note: Listings for 1912 and 1913 compiled by Gordon C. Hewitt.
Location: AEU.

5315 **MacKay, A.H.**
"Bibliography of Canadian botany."
In: *Proceedings and Transactions of the Royal Society of Canada*; Series 2, vol. 7, section 4 (1901) p. 141-142; series 2, vol. 8, section 4 (1902) p. 157-60; series 2, vol. 9, section 4 (1903) p. 169-172; series 2, vol. 10, section 4 (1904) p. 153-160; series 2, vol. 11, section 4 (1905) p. 143-152; series 2, vol. 12, section 4 (1906) p. 33-48; series 3, vol. 4, section 4 (1910) p. 121-153 (contains listings for the years 1906-1909); series 3, vol. 5, section 4 (1911) p. 177-189; series 3, vol. 6, section 4 (1912) p. 129-137; series 3, vol. 7, section 4 (1913) p. 175-185; series 3, vol. 8, section 4 (1914) p. 25-35; series 3, vol. 9, section 4 (1915) p. 251-261; series 3, vol. 10, section 4 (1916) p. 189-199.; ISSN: 0316-4616.
Note: Location: AEU.

5316 **Walker, E.M.**
"Bibliography of Canadian zoology."
In: *Proceedings and Transactions of the Royal Society of Canada*; Series 3, vol. 8, section 4 (1914) p. 271-285; series 3, vol. 9, section 4 (1915) p. 307-318; series 3, vol. 10, section 4 (1916) p. 201-215.; ISSN: 0316-4616.
Note: Location: AEU.

— 1921 —

5317 **Huntsman, A.G.; Fraser, C.M.**
"List of publications based on results obtained at the biological stations of Canada, 1901-1921."
In: *Contributions to Canadian Biology: being studies from the biological stations of Canada*; No. 12 (1921) p. 167-183.
Note: Approx. 250 entries.
Location: OONL.

— 1930 —

5318 **Fox, W. Sherwood**
"The literature of Salmo salar in Lake Ontario and tributary streams."
In: *Proceedings and Transactions of the Royal Society of Canada*; Series 3, vol. 24, section 2 (1930) p. 45-55.; ISSN: 0316-4616.
Note: Location: AEU.

— 1932 —

5319 **Rigby, M.S.**
List of publications in connection with the work of the Biological Board of Canada 1922-1930. Ottawa: Biological Board of Canada, 1932. 22 p. (Biological Board of Canada Bulletin ; no. 28)
Note: Approx. 300 entries.
Location: OONL.

— 1934 —

5320 **Rousseau, Jacques**
Essai de bibliographie botanique canadienne. Montréal: Université de Montréal, Institut botanique, 1934. 101 p. (en pagination multiple).
Note: 599 entrées.– "Extrait, sans changement de pagination, du *Naturaliste canadien*, volumes 60 (1933) et 61 (1934)."- Index alphabétique des espèces, variétés et formes.
Localisation: OONL.

— 1938 —

5321 **Racine, Laurette**
Bibliographie sur le saumon de la province de Québec. [Montréal: s.n., 1938]. 21 f.
Note: Localisation: OONL.

— 1939 —

5322 **Rousseau, Jacques; Gauvreau, Marcelle; Morin, Claire**
Bibliographie des travaux botaniques contenus dans les *Mémoires et Comptes rendus de la Société royale du Canada*, de 1882 à 1936 inclusivement. Montréal: Institut botanique de l'Université de Montréal, 1939. 117 p. (Contributions de l'Institut botanique de l'Université de Montréal ; no 33)
Note: 306 entrées.– Liste des travaux, index analytique des sujets, index alphabétique des genres, espèces, variétés et formes.
Localisation: OONL.

— 1944 —

5323 **Rouleau, Ernest**
Bibliographie des travaux concernant la flore canadienne, parus dans *Rhodora*, de 1899 à 1943 inclusivement, précédée d'un index alphabétique de tous les noms botaniques nouveaux proposés dans cette revue. Montréal: Université de Montréal, Institute botanique, 1944. 367 p. (Contributions de l'Institut botanique de l'Université de Montréal ; no 54)
Note: 1,033 entrées.– Articles qui traitent directement ou indirectement de la flore du Canada, de Terre-Neuve, de Saint-Pierre et Miquelon, du Groenland, du Labrador et de l'Alaska.– Index des genres, espèces, variétés et formes.
Localisation: OONL.

— 1946 —

5324 **Schuette, H.A.; Schuette, Sybil C.; Ihde, A.J.**
"Maple sugar: a bibliography of early records."
In: *Transactions of the Wisconsin Academy of Sciences, Arts, and Letters*; Vol. 29 (1935) p. 209-236; vol. 38 (1946) p. 89-184.; ISSN: 0084-0505.
Note: 219 entries.– Includes many Canadian references, from discovery and exploration documents, travel literature, diaries, journals, ethnographic and botanical studies.
Location: OONMNS.

— 1947 —

5325 **Adams, J.; Norwell, M.H.; Senn, Harold A.**
"Bibliography of Canadian plant geography."
In: *Transactions of the Royal Canadian Institute*; Vol. 16, no. 2 (July 1928) p. 293-355; vol. 17, no. 1 (July 1929) p. 103-145; vol. 17, no. 2 (1930) p. 227-265, 267-295; vol. 18, no. 2 (1932) p. 343-373; vol. 21, no. 1 (1936) p. 95-134; vol. 21, no. 2 (October 1937) p. 95-119; vol. 26, no. 1 (1946) p. 9-151; vol. 26, no. 2 (1947) p. 153-344.; ISSN: 0080-4312.
Note: 5,402 entries in 9 parts.– Period covered is 1635 to 1945.– Geographic area covered is all of North America north of the United States: Canada, Newfoundland, Greenland, Alaska, St. Pierre and Miquelon.– Includes all papers making specific reference to the occurrence of a plant within this geographic area.
Part 9, covering the period 1941-1945, appeared as: Senn, Harold A. *Bibliography of Canadian plant geography.* Ottawa: Department of Agriculture, 1951. 183 p. (Department of Agriculture, Division of Botany and Plant Pathology Publication ; 863).
Location: OONL.

— 1949 —

5326 **Dutilly, Arthème**
Bibliography of reindeer, caribou and musk-ox. Washington, D.C.: Department of the Army, Environmental Protection Section, 1949. x, 462 p.
Note: 2,422 entries.– Books, periodical articles, government publications (Canadian, American, Russian) dealing with biology, description, distribution, ecology, economic aspects, diseases, domestication and ranching.
Location: OOU.

— 1951 —

5327 **Speirs, J. Murray, et al.**
Bibliography of Canadian biological publications. [Toronto]: Quebec Biological Bureau and the University of Toronto, [1949-1951]. 4 vol.
Note: Lists the biological literature written by Canadians, or dealing with Canadian wildlife, assembled by searching biological journals in local libraries.– Excludes medical and commercial papers, anonymous articles.– In the 1949 issue, the sections on arthropods, breeding habits, environment, food habits, and book reviews were discontinued, and a new section on microbiology was added.– Prepared with the support of the Research Council of Ontario, Advisory Committee on Fisheries and Wildlife.– Compilers include J.M. Johnston, Ruth Kingsmill and George W. North.– Text in English and French/texte en anglais et en français.
Location: OONL.

— 1955 —

5328 **MacFarlane, Ivan C.**
A preliminary annotated bibliography on muskeg. Ottawa: National Research Council Canada, Division of Building Research, 1955. 32 l. (National Research Council Canada, Division of Building Research Bibliography ; no. 11)
Note: Approx. 100 entries.
Location: OONL.

— 1957 —

5329 **Sansfaçon, Jacques; Legendre, Vianney**
Bibliographie des titres des documents sériés ayant [été] publié sur les poissons, la pêche et les pêcheries du Canada/Bibliography of the titles of serial documents

having [been] published on the fishes, fishing and fisheries of Canada. Montréal: Office de Biologie, Ministère de la Chasse et des Pêcheries, Province de Québec, Université de Montréal, 1957. xx, 107 f.
Note: 641 entrées.
Localisation: OONL.

5330 **Van Oosten, John**
Great Lakes fauna, flora and their environment: a bibliography. Ann Arbor, Mich.: Great Lakes Commission, 1957. x, 86 p.
Note: Approx. 3,000 entries.– Studies and papers dealing with fish, vertebrates other than fishes, invertebrates, plants, limnology, geology (mainly glacial), of the Great Lakes.– Excludes popular articles in newspapers and magazines.– Many Canadian references.
Location: OTRM.

— 1960 —

5331 **Crispens, Charles G.**
Quails and partridges of North America: a bibliography. Seattle: University of Washington Press, 1960. xii, 125 p. (University of Washington Publications in biology ; vol. 20)
Note: Includes Canadian references.
Location: OONL.

5332 **Judd, William W.**
A bibliography of the natural history of Hamilton to the year 1950. Hamilton, Ont.: Hamilton Naturalists' Club, 1960. 27 p.
Note: Reproduced from typewritten copy.– "Supplement" to Vol. 13, no. 5 (January 1960) of the *Wood Duck.*
Location: OHM.

5333 **McPhail, John Donald**
Annotated bibliography on Arctic North American freshwater fishes. Vancouver: Institute of Fisheries, University of British Columbia, 1960. 24 p. (Museum Contribution / Institute of Fisheries, University of British Columbia ; no. 6)
Note: Approx. 200 entries.– Geographic area covered includes Alaska, Yukon Territory, Northwest Territories, Quebec north of 60, and Labrador.
Location: OWA.

— 1962 —

5334 **Bergeron, Julien**
Bibliographie du saumon de l'Atlantique (Salmo salar L.). Québec: Ministère de la chasse et des pêcheries, 1962. 64 p. (Contributions / Ministère de la chasse et des pêcheries, Québec ; no 88)
Note: Approx. 1,800 entrées.
Localisation: QQL.

5335 **Clapp, Jane**
Museum publications. New York: Scarecrow Press, 1962. 2 vol.
Note: Listing of publications of 276 museums in United States and Canada.– Excludes serials, administrative reports, newsletters and bulletins, accession lists.– Part 1: "Anthropology, archaeology and art."- 4,416 entries.– Part 2: "Biological and earth sciences."- 9,231 entries.
Location: OONL.

5336 **Clarke, Arthur H.**
Annotated list and bibliography of the abyssal marine molluscs of the world. Ottawa: Department of Northern Affairs and National Resources, 1962. vi, 114 p.: col.

maps (on lining papers). (National Museum of Canada Bulletin ; no. 181)

Note: Approx. 225 entries.– Some Canadian references.

Location: OONL.

5337 **Smith, Anne Marie**

Guide to reference works in the aquatic sciences: a selected list of material to be found in the library of the University of British Columbia. Vancouver: University of British Columbia Library, 1962. 17 l.

Note: Approx. 135 entries.– Reference tools and standard texts in fisheries and oceanography.– International coverage with representative Canadian listings.

Location: OONL.

— 1963 —

5338 **Walters, John**

An annotated bibliography of western hemlock, Tsuga heterophylla (Raf.) Sarg. Vancouver: Faculty of Forestry, University of British Columbia, 1963. 86 p.: ill.

Note: Location: AEU.

— 1965 —

5339 **Bergeron, Julien**

Bibliographie du homard (Homarus americanus, Milne-Edwards et Homarus gammarus L.). Québec: Ministère de l'industrie et du commerce, 1965. 81 p. (Cahiers d'information / Station de biologie marine, Grande-Rivière ; no 34)

Note: Approx. 850 entrées.– Publications biologiques.– Comporte des références canadiennes et québécoises.

Localisation: OONL.

5340 **British Columbia. Provincial Museum. Department of Recreation and Conservation**

Selected literature concerning birds in British Columbia. Victoria, B.C.: British Columbia Provincial Museum, 1965. 9 p.

Note: Location: OONL.

— 1966 —

5341 **Arctic Institute of North America**

A polar bear bibliography. Washington, D.C.: Arctic Institute of North America, 1966. 25 p.

Note: Location: AEUB.

5342 **McGill University. Blacker-Wood Library of Zoology and Ornithology**

A dictionary catalogue of the Blacker-Wood Library of Zoology and Ornithology. Boston: G.K. Hall, 1966. 9 vol.

Note: Approx. 60,000 entries.

Location: OONL.

— 1967 —

5343 **Bernard, F.R.**

Prodrome for a distributional check-list and bibliography of the recent marine mollusca of the west coast of Canada. Nanaimo, B.C.: Fisheries Research Board of Canada, 1967. xxiv, 261 p.: ill. (Fisheries Research Board of Canada Technical report ; no. 2; ISSN: 0068-7553)

Note: Location: OONL.

5344 **Butler, T.H.**

A bibliography of the Dungeness crab, Cancer magister Dana. Nanaimo, B.C.: Fisheries Research Board of Canada, 1967. 12 p. (Fisheries Research Board of Canada Technical report ; no. 1; ISSN: 0068-7553)

Note: 131 entries.– Books, papers, articles dealing with Dungeness crab which occurs on Pacific coast from Alaska to Mexico.– Many references to British Columbia research.

Location: OONL.

5345 **Cayford, J.H.; Chrosciewicz, Z.; Sims, H.P.**

A review of silviculture research in jack pine. Ottawa: Queen's Printer, 1967. v, 255 p.: ill.

Note: Listing of published and unpublished reports from 1931, with project summaries of jack pine silvicultural research conducted by the Department of Forestry and Rural Development and its predecessors.– Topics include general habitat, sites and productivity, regeneration characteristics, natural variation, natural regeneration, artificial regeneration.

Location: OONL.

5346 **Eales, J. Geoffrey**

A bibliography of the eels of the genus Anguilla. St. Andrews, N.B.: Biological Station, Fisheries Research Board of Canada, 1967. 171 p. (Fisheries Research Board of Canada Technical report ; no. 28; ISSN: 0068-7553)

Note: Approx. 2,000 entries.– International author listing of scientific literature on the genus Anguilla.

Location: NSHS.

5347 **Jarvis, J.M., et al.**

Review of silvicultural research: white spruce and trembling aspen cover types, Mixedwood Forest Section, Boreal Forest Region, Alberta-Saskatchewan-Manitoba. Ottawa: Queen's Printer, 1967. iii, 189 p.: ill., map.

Note: Summary of research results and conclusions.– Topics include productivity, regeneration characteristics, growth, silvicultural systems, artificial regeneration, tending of stands and trees.

Location: OONL.

— 1968 —

5348 **Dalke, Paul D.**

Bibliography of the elk in North America. Moscow: Idaho Cooperative Wildlife Research Unit, University of Idaho, 1968. 87 p.

Note: Covers the literature through 1965.– Canadian and American references to elk distribution, diseases and parasites, habitat, hunting, behaviour, management.– Arrangement in two separate listings by subject and author.

Location: OOFF.

5349 **Gauthier, Monique**

Bibliographie sur le phototrophisme des animaux marins. Grande-Rivière, Québec: Ministère de l'Industrie et du Commerce, Station de biologie marine, 1968. 73 p. (Cahiers d'information / Station de biologie marine, Grande-Rivière ; no 44)

Note: Approx. 850 entrées.– Articles parus jusqu'en décembre 1965.

Localisation: OONL.

5350 **Shoup, J.M.; Nairn, L.D.; Pratt, R.H.M.**

Trembling aspen bibliography. Winnipeg, Man.: Forest Research Laboratory, 1968. 81 l.

Note: Approx. 800 entries.– Literature relating to the ecology, silviculture, growth, entomology, pathology and utilization of the trembling aspen (Populus tremuloides M.) up to and including 1966 publications.– Many Canadian listings.

Location: AEU.

5351 **Shoup, J.M.; Waldron, R.M.**

Red pine bibliography. Winnipeg: Canada Department of Forestry and Rural Development, 1968. 61 l.: ill. (Liaison and services note / Forest Research Laboratory,

Winnipeg ; MS-L-1)
Note: Approx. 700 entries.– Literature dealing with ecology, silviculture, growth, entomology, pathology of red pine (Pinus resinosa Ait.).
Location: AEU.

— 1969 —

5352 **Armstrong, Robert H.; Morton, William Markham**
Revised annotated bibliography on the Dolly Varden char. Juneau: Alaska Department of Fish and Game, 1969. 108 p. (Research report / Alaska Department of Fish and Game ; no. 7; ISSN: 0732-8486)
Note: 507 entries.– Published and unpublished literature on Dolly Varden, Salvelinus malma (Walbaum) through 1968.– Many Canadian references.
Previous edition: *Annotated bibliography on the Dolly Varden char.* 1965. 26 p. (Research report ; no. 4).
Location: OORD.

5353 **Dill, L.M.**
Annotated bibliography of the salmonid embryo and alevin. Vancouver, B.C.: Department of Fisheries, 1969. 190 p.
Note: 327 entries.– Journal articles, books, theses, manuscript reports, symposia transactions.– Many Canadian references.
Location: OOFI.

5354 **Shoup, J.M.; Nairn, L.D.**
Black spruce bibliography. Winnipeg: Canada Department of Fisheries and Forestry, 1969. 72 p. (Liaison and Services Note / Forest Research Laboratory, Winnipeg ; MS-L-6)
Note: Approx. 500 entries.– Literature relating to ecology, silviculture, growth, entomology, pathology, and utilization of the black spruce (Picea mariana).– Arranged in two sections: synopsis of subject matter, with authors and dates of publication; complete bibliographic listing.
Location: OOAG.

— 1970 —

5355 **Margolis, L.**
A bibliography of parasites and diseases of fishes of Canada: 1879-1969. Nanaimo, B.C.: Fisheries Research Board of Canada, 1970. 38 p. (Fisheries Research Board of Canada Technical report ; no. 185; ISSN: 0068-7553)
Note: 483 entries.– Publications concerned in whole or in part with research on parasites or diseases of fishes from Canadian waters.– Topics include fungi, bacteria, protozoa, monogenea, digenea, cestoda, nematoda, hirudinea, copepoda.
Location: OONL.

5356 **Marshall, K.E.; Keleher, J.J.**
A bibliography of the lake trout, Cristivomer namaycush (Walbaum) 1929-1969. Winnipeg: Freshwater Institute, Fisheries Research Board of Canada, 1970. 60 p. (Fisheries Research Board of Canada Technical report ; no. 176; ISSN: 0068-7553)
Note: Author listing with geographic and subject indexes.– Topics covered include acid precipitation, aquaculture and hatcheries, ecology and life history, embryology and reproduction, food and feeding, physiology, pollution, toxicology, survival.– Résumé en français.
Supplements:
    ... , *1970 through 1977.* 1978. 11 p. (Fisheries and Marine

Service Technical report ; no. 799; ISSN: 0701-7626).
Marshall, K.E.; Layton, M. ... , *1977 through 1984.* 1985. iv, 15 p. (Canadian technical report of fisheries and aquatic sciences ; no. 1346; ISSN: 0706-6457).
Marshall, K.E.; Layton, M.; Stobbe, C. ... , *1984 through 1990.* 1990. iv, 25 p. (Canadian technical report of fisheries and aquatic sciences ; no. 1749; ISSN: 0706-6457).
Location: OONL.

5357 **Milliron, H.E.**
A monograph of the western hemisphere bumblebees (Hymenoptera: Apidae, Bombinae). Ottawa: Entomological Society of Canada, 1970. lii p. (Memoirs of the Entomological Society of Canada ; no. 65)
Note: Articles and papers dealing with aspects of study of bumblebees complete through 1961, with other significant works to 1970.– Includes Canadian references.
Location: OONL.

5358 **Robins, G. Lewis**
A bibliography of the pike perch of the genus Stizostedion (including the genus known as Lucioperca). Winnipeg: Freshwater Institute, Fisheries Research Board of Canada, 1970. 67 p. (Fisheries Research Board of Canada Technical report ; no. 161; ISSN: 0068-7553)
Note: 581 entries.
Location: OONL.

— 1971 —

5359 **Erskine, Anthony J.**
A preliminary catalogue of bird census studies in Canada/Repertoire préliminaire des études de d'enombrement des oiseaux du Canada. Ottawa: Canadian Wildlife Service, 1971. 78 p. (Progress notes / Canadian Wildlife Service ; no. 20; ISSN: 0069-0023) (Cahiers de biologie / Service canadien de la faune ; no 20; ISSN: 0703-0967)
Note: Lists studies of bird census areas.– Includes a bibliography dealing with bird populations.– Text in English and French/texte en français et en anglais.
Supplements:
A preliminary catalogue of bird census plot studies in Canada, part 2/Répertoire préliminaire des études de d'enombrement des oiseaux du Canada par parcelles-échantillons, deuxième partie. 1972. 42 p. (Progress notes ; no. 30)(Cahiers de biologie ; no 30).
..., *part 3.* 1976. 26 p. (Progress notes ; no. 59).
..., *3e partie.* 1976. 26 p. (Cahiers de biologie ; no 59).
..., *part 4.* 1980. 26 p. (Progress notes ; no. 112).
..., *4e partie.* 1980. 26 p. (Cahiers de biologie ; no 112).
..., *part 5.* 1984. 34 p. (Progress notes ; no. 144).
..., *5e partie.* 1984. 35 p. (Cahiers de biologie ; no 144).
Location: OONL.

5360 **Marshall, K.E.; Woods, C.S.**
A bibliography of Coregonid fishes. Winnipeg: Fisheries Research Board of Canada, 1971. 63 p. (Fisheries Research Board of Canada Technical report ; no. 151; ISSN: 0068-7553)
Note: Approx. 2,650 entries.– World literature on Coregonid fishes from earliest published records to 1970.– Many Canadian references.
Location: OONL.

5361 **Renewable Resources Consulting Services**
A bibliography of wildlife studies for the Saskatchewan-Nelson River Basin. [S.l.]: Canadian Wildlife Service, Department of Environment, 1971. vii, 129 l.

Note: 903 entries.– Books, theses, published papers, unpublished reports from 1945 to 1971.– Includes research and reference material pertaining to wildlife habitat and populations, studies of land use, water transfers and manipulations affecting economically important wildlife species.– Saskatchewan-Nelson River basin defined as "that portion of the three prairie provinces south of 54 North latitude."
Location: OOFF.

5362 **Scrivener, James Charles; Butler, T.H.**
A bibliography of shrimps of the family Pandalidae, emphasizing economically important species of the genus Pandalus. Nanaimo, B.C.: Fisheries Research Board of Canada, 1971. 42 p. (Fisheries Research Board of Canada Technical report ; no. 241; ISSN: 0068-7553)
Note: 458 entries.– Covers from 1814 to 1969.– Arrangement by species, with geographical and subject indexes.– Many Canadian references.
Location: OONL.

5363 **Srivastava, V.M.**
Fish of the Gulf of St. Lawrence: an unabridged bibliography. Dartmouth, N.S.: Fisheries Research Board of Canada, Marine Ecology Laboratory, Bedford Institute, 1971. 141 p. (Fisheries Research Board of Canada Technical report ; no. 261; ISSN: 0068-7553)
Note: Approx. 800 entries.– Covers to March 1971.– Published and unpublished references on fish of the Gulf of St. Lawrence including St. Lawrence estuary to Quebec City, Saguenay fjord, Strait of Belle Isle, and Cabot Strait west of a line from Hermitage Bay to northern tip of Cape Breton.– Indexes by scientific names, common names, species.
Location: OONL.

— 1972 —

5364 **Barry, Thomas W.; Kear, Janet**
A bibliography of the swans. [Edmonton: Canadian Wildlife Service, 1972]. 181 l.
Note: Joint project of Canadian Wildlife Service and Wildfowl Trust (Slimbridge, England).– Covers world literature on swans through 1971.– Includes brief annotations.– Some Canadian references.
Location: OOFF.

5365 **British Columbia. Fish and Wildlife Branch**
List of wildlife publications, 1935-1972. Victoria, B.C.: 1972. 28 l.
Note: Location: OOCC.

5366 **Davies, R.W.**
Annotated bibliography to the freshwater leeches (Hirudinoidea) of Canada. Nanaimo, B.C.: Pacific Biological Station, Fisheries Research Board of Canada, 1972. 15 p. (Fisheries Research Board of Canada Technical report ; no. 306; ISSN: 0068-7553)
Note: Approx. 80 entries.
Location: OONL.

5367 **Fulton, John**
Keys and references to the marine copepoda of British Columbia. Nanaimo, B.C.: Fisheries Research Board of Canada, Pacific Biological Station, 1972. 63 p. (Fisheries Research Board of Canada Technical report ; no. 313; ISSN: 0068-7553)
Note: Approx. 100 entries.
Location: OONL.

5368 **Gruchy, I.M.; McAllister, Don E.**
A bibliography of the smelt family, Osmeridae. Ottawa: Fisheries Research Board of Canada, 1972. 104 p. (Fisheries Research Board of Canada Technical report ; no. 368; ISSN: 0068-7553)
Note: Approx. 1,800 entries.– Books and papers from the year 1553 to October 1972.
Location: QQPSM.

5369 **Paterson, Laura A.**
Caribou bibliography. Edmonton: Canadian Wildlife Service, 1972. [76] l.
Note: Approx. 450 entries.– Books, reports, articles on caribou and elk in western Canada, Alaska, western United States.– Excludes material on imported reindeer and references to caribou east of the Great Lakes.
Location: AEUB.

5370 **Pogue, Laura A.**
Bibliography on alpine vegetation in the Canadian Rockies. Edmonton: Canadian Wildlife Service, 1972. iii, 14 l.
Note: Approx. 80 entries.– Covers all aspects of alpine vegetation, plant succession, growth, plant communities, effects of animals, from about 1900 to 1972.
Location: AEUB.

5371 **Tietz, Harrison Morton**
An index to the described life histories, early stages and hosts of the macrolepidoptera of the continental United States and Canada. Sarasota, Fla.: Published by A.C. Allyn for the Allyn Museum of Entomology; Los Angeles: distributed by Entomological Reprint Specialists, 1972. 2 vol.; ISBN: 0-913492-01-9.
Note: Covers from 1899 to 1950.– Lists books and journal articles on butterflies and moths.
Location: OONL.

— 1973 —

5372 **Crossman, E.J.; Lewis, G.E.**
An annotated bibliography of the chain pickerel, Esox niger (Osteichthyes: Salmoniformes). Toronto: Royal Ontario Museum, c1973. 81 p. (Royal Ontario Museum Life sciences miscellaneous publications; ISSN: 0082-5093); ISBN: 0-88854-146-5.
Note: 630 entries.– Literature on distribution and range, anatomy, behaviour, food and food habits, parasites/pathology/diseases, predation, popular accounts, taxonomy/nomenclature/systematics, management.
Location: OONL.

5373 **Gibbons, Dave R.; Salo, Ernest O.**
An annotated bibliography of the effects of logging on fish of the western United States and Canada. Portland, Or.: Pacific Northwest Forest and Range Experiment Station, U.S. Department of Agriculture, 1973. 145 p. (USDA Forest Service General technical report ; PNW-10)
Note: 317 entries.– List of scientific and nonscientific literature published on effects of logging on fish and aquatic habitat.– Subject areas include erosion and sedimentation, water quality, related influences upon salmonids, multiple logging effects, alteration of streamflow, stream protection, stream improvement.
Location: OBUC.

5374 **Joyal, Robert**
"Volumes sur la faune du Québec."
Dans: *Québec chasse et pêche*; Vol. 2, no 6 (mars 1973) p. 30-31.

Note: Localisation: OONL.

5375 **Marcotte, Alexandre**
Bibliographie des travaux des laboratoires de biologie marine du gouvernement du Québec, 1938-1971. Québec: Direction générale des pêches maritimes, 1973. 131 p. (Cahiers d'information / Direction générale des pêches maritime, Direction de la recherche ; no 60)
Note: Approx. 600 entrées.– Articles traitant d'océanographie physique ou biologique, de pêche expérimentale et d'autres sujets se rapportant principalement aux pêches maritimes.
Localisation: OONL.

5376 **Marles, E.W.**
Bibliography of oceanographic information for the inside waters of the southern British Columbia coast. Victoria, B.C.: Marine Sciences Directorate, Pacific Region, Environment Canada, 1973. 2 vol. maps. (Pacific marine science report ; 73-1, 73-2)
Note: Vol. 1: *Physical oceanography*. 82 p. Focus on physical, chemical, water quality reports and studies. Vol. 2: *Biological oceanography*. vii, 46 p. Approx. 600 entries.– Emphasis on environmental biology.
Location: OOFF.

5377 **Phelps, V.H.**
Sitka spruce: a literature review with special reference to British Columbia. Victoria, B.C.: Pacific Forest Research Centre, Canadian Forestry Service, 1973. 39 p. (Canadian Forestry Service Information report ; BC-X-83)
Note: 100 entries.– Nomenclature, range and occurrence, morphology, natural variation, silvicultural characteristics, regeneration, management practices, damage (diseases and pests).
Location: OONL.

— 1974 —

5378 **AliNiazee, M.T.; Brown, R.D.**
"A bibliography of North American cherry fruit flies (Diptera: Tephritidae)."
In: *Bulletin of the Entomological Society of America*; Vol. 20, no. 2 (June 1974) p. 93-101.; ISSN: 0013-8754.
Note: 440 entries.
Location: OONMNS.

5379 **Atlantic salmon references.** Halifax: Maritimes Regional Library, Fisheries Service, 1971-1974. 2 vol.
Note: Volume 2 (1974) is a cumulated issue, including all references in volume 1, listing a total of about 3,000 entries.– Arranged by topic: age and growth, behaviour, physiology and genetics, spawning, migration, tagging studies, etc., with author index.
Location: OONL.

5380 **Evans, David**
A selected bibliography of North American literature on the European pine shoot moth. Victoria, B.C.: Canadian Forestry Service, 1974. 162 p.
Note: 990 entries.– Citations covering the period 1914-1972 inclusive, relating to North American publications that specifically mention Rhyacionia buoliana (Schiffermueller).
Location: OONL.

5381 **Field, William D.; Dos Passos, Cyril F.; Masters, John H.**
A bibliography of the catalogs, lists, faunal and other papers on the butterflies of North America north of Mexico arranged by state and province (Lepidoptera: Rhopalocera). Washington: Smithsonian Institution Press, 1974. 104 p. (Smithsonian contributions to zoology ; no. 157)
Note: Approx. 3,000 entries.
Location: BVAS.

5382 **MacBryde, Bruce**
"Bibliographical history of the botanical handbooks of the British Columbia Provincial Museum."
In: *Syesis*; Vol. 7 (1974) p. 255-258.; ISSN: 0082-0601.
Note: Location: OONL.

5383 **McInnes, B.E.; Nash, F.W.; Godfrey, H.**
A preliminary annotated bibliography on Georgia Strait fishes. Nanaimo, B.C.: Pacific Biological Station, 1974. 216 p. (Fisheries Research Board of Canada Manuscript report series ; no. 1332)
Note: 1,410 entries.– In addition to material on Georgia Strait fishes, the bibliography includes documents on oceanographic studies, shellfish and crustacea, fishing methods, catch statistics, stream surveys.– Consists primarily of publications of the Fisheries Research Board of Canada, some university theses, trade journal articles, statistical bulletins.
Location: NSHF.

5384 **Miska, John P.; Nelson, G.A.**
Bibliography of decay of potato seed pieces, 1930-1973. Lethbridge, Alta.: Research Station, Agriculture Canada, 1974. v, 49, xix p.
Note: 531 entries.– Scientific and technical papers published since 1930 relating to plant pathology and mycology.
Location: OONL.

5385 **Moore, Ian; Legner, E.F.**
"Bibliography (1758 to 1972) to the Staphylinidae of America north of Mexico (Coleoptera)."
In: *Hilgardia*; Vol. 42, no. 16 (December 1974) p. 511-547.; ISSN: 0073-2230.
Note: Publications concerning the taxonomy, developmental stages and biology of the Nearctic Staphylinidae.– Many Canadian references.
Location: QMJB.

5386 **Nicholls, H.B.; Sabowitz, N.C.**
Reports by staff of the Bedford Institute of Oceanography, 1962-1973: list of titles and index. [Dartmouth, N.S.]: Bedford Institute of Oceanography, 1974. 126 p. (Bedford Institute of Oceanography Report series ; BI-R-74-4)
Note: Listing by series: "Report series," "Data series," "Computer note series," "FRBC Technical reports," "FRBC Bulletins," "Geological Survey of Canada Papers," "Marine science papers."- Résumé en français.
Location: OONL.

5387 **Nova Scotia Research Foundation**
Selected bibliography on algae. Dartmouth, N.S.: Nova Scotia Research Foundation, 1952-1974. 14 vol.; ISSN: 0080-8571.
Note: Listing of references on both freshwater and marine algae, biology and utilization.– Themes: biophysical and biochemical studies, algae culture, genetics, fossil algae, physiology, nutrition and growth studies, taxonomy, reproduction, ecology and distribution, radiation studies, utilization (economic studies, food products, seaweed extracts, etc.).
Location: OONL.

— 1975 —

5388 British Columbia. Provincial Museum. Department of Recreation and Conservation
Recommended references to the flora of British Columbia. Victoria, B.C.: Provincial Museum, 1975. 13 p.
Note: Approx. 200 entries.
Previous edition: 1967. 12 p.
Location: OONL.

5389 De March, B., et al.
A compilation of literature pertaining to the culture of aquatic invertebrates, algae and macrophytes. Winnipeg: Freshwater Institute, Fisheries and Marine Service, Environment Canada, 1975. 2 vol. (Fisheries and Marine Service Technical report ; no. 576; ISSN: 0701-7626)
Note: Location: OONL.

5390 Eisenhauer, J.H.
A partial bibliography on Branta bernicla. Lethbridge: University of Lethbridge, 1975. 40 p.
Note: Approx. 500 entries.– Listing of papers on the Pacific Brant goose, Atlantic Brant, and Dark-bellied Brent.– Many Canadian references.
Location: OOFF.

5391 Feuerwerker, Elie; Ali, M.A.
"La vision chez les poissons: historique et bibliographie analytique."
Dans: *Revue canadienne de biologie*; Vol. 34, no 4 (décembre 1975) p. 221-285.; ISSN: 0035-0915.
Note: Approx. 1,100 entrées.
Localisation: OONL.

5392 Hillman, M.
Fish protein concentrate (FPC): a bibliography, 1970-1974/Les concentrés de protéines du poisson: bibliographie, 1970-1974. Ottawa: Environment Canada, Library, 1975. 7 l. (Environment Canada Libraries Bibliography series ; 75-1)
Note: Approx. 80 entries.– General literature on fish protein concentrate and its use in the human diet.– Excludes references to processing and manufacture, chemistry and nutritional studies.
Location: OONL.

5393 Johnson, Stephen R.; Adams, William J.; Morrell, Michael R.
The birds of the Beaufort Sea: an annotated bibliography. Edmonton: Canadian Wildlife Service, Department of the Environment, 1975. 169 p.
Note: Approx. 750 entries.– Journal articles, government reports and studies from Canada and the United States related to birds found in the Arctic Northwest Territories and Alaska dealing with distribution, migration, population studies, breeding biology, behaviour, environmental influence of oil and gas exploration in the Beaufort Sea.
Location: OONL.

5394 Kowand, Maureen
A bibliography of the river otter (Lutra canadensis). Edmonton: Canadian Wildlife Service, 1975. 27 l.
Note: Approx. 200 entries.– Covers from 1934 to June 1975.
Location: OONL.

5395 Machniak, Kazimierz
The effects of hydroelectric development on the biology of northern fishes (reproduction and population dynamics). Winnipeg: Freshwater Institute, Fisheries and Marine Service, Environment Canada, 1975. 4 vol. (Fisheries and Marine Service Technical report ; no. 527-530; ISSN: 0701-7626)
Note: Vol. 1: *Lake whitefish, Coregonus clupeaformis (Mitchill): a literature review and bibliography.* iv l., 67 p.– Approx. 250 entries.
Vol. 2: *Northern pike, Esox lucius (Linnaeus): a literature review and bibliography.* iv l., 82 p.– Approx. 500 entries.
Vol. 3: *Yellow walleye, Stizostedion vitreum vitreum (Mitchill): a literature review and bibliography.* iv l., 68 p.– Approx. 400 entries.
Vol. 4: *Lake trout, Salvelinus namaycush (Walbaum): a literature review and bibliography.* iv l., 54 p.– Approx. 125 entries.
Résumés en français.
Location: OONL.

5396 Mansfield, Arthur Walter; Smith, Thomas G.; Sergeant, David E.
Marine mammal research in the Canadian Arctic. Ste. Anne de Bellevue, Quebec: Arctic Biological Station, Fisheries and Marine Service, Department of the Environment, 1975. 23 l. (Fisheries and Marine Service Technical report ; no. 507; ISSN: 0701-7626)
Note: 35 entries.– Research carried out on marine mammals in the Arctic by staff of the Arctic Biological Station.– Résumé en français.
Location: OONL.

5397 Marshall, K.E.
An index to the publications of the staff of the Freshwater Institute, Winnipeg; the Biological Station and Technological Unit, London; and the Central Biological Station, Winnipeg: 1944-1973. Winnipeg: Environment Canada, Fisheries and Marine Service, 1975. 94 p. (Fisheries and Marine Service Technical report ; no. 505; ISSN: 0701-7626)
Note: Lists scientific and technical publications of the staff of the western region, including both reports and reprints of papers published in periodicals and books.
Supplements:
Marshall, K.E.; Kays, M. *An index to the publications of the staff of the Freshwater Institute, Winnipeg, 1974-75.* 1976. 55 p. (Technical report ; no. 620).
... , *1976-77.* 1978. 41 p. (Technical report ; no. 764).
Marshall, K.E.; Layton, M. *An index to the publications of the staff of the western region, Department of Fisheries and Oceans, 1978-79.* 1981. iv, 56 p. (Technical report ; no. 992).
... *1980-81.* 1984. iv, 82 p. (Canadian technical report of Fisheries and Aquatic Sciences ; no. 1273).
Location: OONL.

5398 Nicholls, H.B.; Scott, Wendy
Publications by staff of the Bedford Institute of Oceanography, 1962-1974: list of titles and index. [Dartmouth, N.S.]: Bedford Institute of Oceanography, 1975. 113 p. (Bedford Institute of Oceanography Report series ; BI-R-75-7)
Note: 454 entries.– Listing of BIO "Contributions," defined as a scientific publication by a BIO staff member designated by Institute directors as contributing to advancement of the marine sciences, arranged by Contribution number.– Résumé en français.
Location: OONL.

5399 **Russell, L.R.**
An annotated bibliography on the ecology of anadromous cutthroat trout and Dolly Varden char. Victoria: Province of British Columbia, Ministry of Environment, 1975. v, 86, 115 p. (Fisheries technical circular / British Columbia Ministry of Environment ; no. 17)
Note: 456 entries.– Articles on behaviour, feeding habits and diet, fish culture and hatchery propagation, habitat requirements, growth and survival, general life history, management studies, migration and distribution.
Location: OONL.

5400 **Russell, L.R.**
An annotated bibliography on steelhead trout and general salmonid ecology. Victoria, B.C.: Ministry of Environment, 1975. xi, 178, 66 p.
Note: 844 entries.– Articles dealing with steelhead trout behaviour, dietary physiology, feeding habits, habitat requirements, life history, management studies, migration and distribution, fish culture.
Location: OONL.

5401 **Safranyik, L.; Shrimpton, D.M.; Whitney, H.S.**
Mountain pine beetle bibliography. Victoria, B.C.: Canadian Forestry Service, Department of the Environment, 1975. 69 p.
Note: 424 entries.– References dealing with control, damage, infestation history, life history, morphology, parasites, predators, symptoms and tree susceptibility of the mountain pine beetle (Dendroctonus ponderosae H.).– Résumé en français.
Location: OONL.

5402 **Tynen, Michael J.**
A checklist and bibliography of the North American Enchytraeidae (Annelida: Oligochaeta). Ottawa: Natural Museum of Natural Sciences, National Museums of Canada, 1975. 14 p. (Syllogeus / Canadian Museum of Natural Sciences ; no. 9: ISSN: 0704-576X)
Note: Approx. 100 entries.
Location: OONL.

— 1976 —

5403 **Gauthier, Benoît**
"Bibliographie du phytobenthos laurentin, Québec (1850-1975)."
Dans: *Revue de géographie de Montréal*; Vol. 30, no 4 (1976) p. 359-366.; ISSN: 0035-1148.
Note: Localisation: AEU.

5404 **Griffiths, K.J.**
The parasites and predators of the gypsy moth: a review of the world literature with special application to Canada. Sault Ste. Marie, Ont.: Great Lake Forest Research Centre, 1976. 92 p. (Great Lakes Forest Research Centre report ; O-X-243; ISSN: 0704-7797)
Note: Approx. 200 entries.– Literature review makes reference to the nearly 400 species of parasites and vertebrate and invertebrate predators of the gypsy moth (Porthetria dispar L.).– Additional topics covered: native distribution, life history and effectiveness, attempts to colonize exotic species in North America.– Résumé en français.
Location: OONL.

5405 **Herman, Carlton M., et al.**
Bibliography of the avian blood-inhabiting protozoa. St. John's: International Reference Centre for Avian Haematozoa, Department of Biology, Memorial University of Newfoundland, 1976. v, 123 p.
Note: Approx. 3,700 entries.– Papers, articles, theses on avian haematozoa representing the genera: Plasmodium, Haemoproteus, Leucocytozoon, Akiba, Toxoplasma, Atoxoplasma, Lankesterella and Trypanosoma.
Supplement: Bennett, Gordon F., et al. ... . *Supplement 1.* 1981. 33 p.
Location: OONL.

5406 **Johnson, B.C.**
Labrador wildlife bibliography. St. John's, Nfld.: Canadian Wildlife Service, 1976. 7 l.
Note: Location: OOFF.

5407 **Jones, Barry C.; Geen, Glen H.**
Bibliography of spiny dogfish (Squalus acanthius L.) and related species. Nanaimo, B.C.: Fisheries and Marine Service, Environment Canada, 1976. 84 p. (Fisheries and Marine Service Technical report ; no. 655; ISSN: 0701-7626)
Note: 1,009 entries.– Covers 1900 to 1976.– Listing of references to 20 different aspects of spiny dogfish biology, research, management and utilization.– Résumé en français.
Location: OONL.

5408 **Judd, William W.**
Sources of information on the Byron Bog. [London, Ont.: s.n.], 1976. 10 l.
Note: Approx. 120 entries.– Contains articles and reports from scientific journals, letters to editor and editorials concerning preservation of acid bog lying south of London, Ontario, surrounded by Carolinian vegetation zone.
Location: OONL.

5409 **Milne, Henry; Dau, Christian P.**
Une bibliographie sur l'eider/A bibliography of eiders. Québec: Ministère du tourisme, de la chasse et de la pêche, 1976. 225, 23 p. (Bulletin / Service de la Faune du Québec ; no 20)
Note: Approx. 2,000 entrées.– Couvrent toutes les années jusqu'à 1974.– Publications qui traitent des différentes espèces de canards eiders: anatomie, comportement, reproduction, distribution et abondance, exploitation/ aménagement/conservation, habitat, maladies, physiologie, dynamiques des population.
Localisation: OONL.

5410 **Ronald, K., et al.**
An annotated bibliography on the Pinnipedia. Charlottenlund, Denmark: International Council for the Exploration of the Sea, 1976. 785 p.
Note: 9,500 entries.– References to seals, sea lions, walruses dating from earliest times to 1975.
Supplement: ... : *supplement 1.* Copenhagen: 1983. 346 l.
Location: OONL.

5411 **Westrheim, S.J.; Leaman, B.M.**
A selected bibliography of northeastern Pacific rockfishes (Sebastes and Sebastolobus) other than Sebastes alutus. Nanaimo, B.C.: Pacific Biological Station, Fisheries and Marine Service, Environment Canada, 1976. iii l., 20 p. (Fisheries and Marine Service Technical report ; no. 659; ISSN: 0701-7626)
Note: 171 entries.– Includes literature available to April 1976.– Emphasis on biology and distribution of commercially important rockfishes other than Pacific

ocean perch.– Excludes taxonomic references.
Location: OONL.

— 1977 —

5412 **Alderdice, D.F.; Bams, R.A.; Velsen, F.P.J.**
Factors affecting deposition, development, and survival of salmonid eggs and alevins: a bibliography, 1965-1975. Nanaimo, B.C.: Pacific Biological Station, Fisheries and Marine Service, Department of Fisheries and the Environment, 1977. 276 p. (Fisheries and Marine Service Technical report ; no. 743; ISSN: 0701-7626)
Note: 1,695 entries.– Literature relating to physical, chemical and biological factors that influence egg deposition, and development and survival of eggs and alevins of Pacific salmon.– Résumé en français.
Location: OONL.

5413 **Donaldson, Edward M.**
Bibliography of fish reproduction, 1963-1974. West Vancouver, B.C.: Research and Resource Services Directorate, Fisheries and Marine Service, Department of Fisheries and the Environment, 1977. 3 vol. (Fisheries and Marine Service Technical report ; no. 732; ISSN: 0701-7626)
Note: Approx. 6,600 entries.– Includes titles on all aspects of fish reproduction in all species.– Topics covered include ovarian and testicular development, ovulation and spermiation, reproductive behaviour, spawning, fertilization, fecundity, development of the egg, hatching and early larval development.
Location: OONL.

5414 **Hiltz, Linda L.**
The ocean clam (Arctica islandica): a literature review. Halifax, N.S.: Technology Branch, Fisheries and Marine Service, 1977. 161, 16 p.: ill. (Fisheries and Marine Service Technical report ; no. 720; ISSN: 0701-7626)
Note: 206 entries.– Studies conducted in Canada on definition of extent of clam resource in Canadian waters, biology and anatomy, commercial exploitation, processing techniques developed, flavour problems.– Résumé en français.
Location: OONL.

5415 **Miller, Gordon**
The American bison (Bison bison): an initial bibliography. Edmonton: Canadian Wildlife Service, 1977. vii, 89 p.
Note: 652 entries.– Published and unpublished materials dealing with management, biology, ecology and life history of American bison, with a short list of references on European bison.
Location: OONL.

5416 **Pfeifer, Wilma E.**
An annotated bibliography of the fishes of the Beaufort Sea and adjacent regions. [Fairbanks: University of Alaska], 1977. 76 p. (Biological papers of the University of Alaska ; no. 17)
Note: Approx. 500 entries.– References dealing with fishes of Beaufort Sea area, including streams of the arctic coast of North America, some Russian material containing information on distribution, utilization, biology, etc., of Beaufort Sea species in Russian waters.
Location: ACUAI.

5417 **Weir, R.D.**
Annotated bibliography of bird kills at man-made obstacles: a review of the state of the art and solutions.

Ottawa: Canadian Wildlife Service, Ontario Region, [1977]. ii, 85 p.
Note: 471 entries.– References from ornithological journals dealing with the problem of obstacles (lighthouses, chimneys, communication towers, telephone and power lines, etc.) and destruction of migrating birds.
Location: OONL.

— 1978 —

5418 **Amaratunga, T.; Balch, N.; O'Dor, R.K.**
Proceedings of the Workshop on the squid Illex illecebrosus: Dalhousie University, Halifax, Nova Scotia, May 1978: and a bibliography on the genus Illex. [Halifax, N.S.: Dalhousie University], 1978. 1 vol. (in various pagings).
Note: Location: OONL.

5419 **Austin, W.C.; Deutsch, M.M.**
Marine biota of the NE Pacific: a bibliography emphasizing systematics and distribution. Cowichan Station, B.C.: Khoyatan Marine Laboratory, 1978. 9, 14, 453, 3, 207 columns (ca. 400 p.).
Note: 7,749 entries.– Contains eight major categories: microbiology, protozoology, botany, zoology, ecology, methodology, directories, serials.
Location: OONL.

5420 **Crossman, E.J.**
An annotated bibliography of the muskellunge, Esox masquinongy (Osteichthyes: Salmoniformes). Toronto: Royal Ontario Museum, 1978. 131 p. (Life sciences miscellaneous publications; ISSN: 0082-5093); ISBN: 0-88854-208-9.
Note: Approx. 1,200 entries.– Literature concerning distribution and range, angling, popular accounts, habitat and environmental factors, parasites/diseases/pathology, taxonomy/nomenclature/systematics.
Location: OONL.

5421 **Dunn, Elizabeth; Stanlake, E.A.**
The family Mustelidae: a bibliography. Victoria: Wildlife Research and Technical Services Section, Ministry of Recreation and Conservation, Province of British Columbia, 1978. 73 p. (Fish and Wildlife bulletin ; B-4)
Note: Location: OONL.

5422 **Miller, Gordon**
Canadian Wildlife Service studies in Canada's national parks: a bibliography. Edmonton: Canadian Wildlife Service, 1978. v, 179 p.
Note: 1,216 entries.– Comprehensive listing of all reports and studies concerning Canadian national parks prepared or sponsored by the Canadian Wildlife Service: unpublished reports, published reports and papers, theses.
Location: OONL.

5423 **Rosenberg, D.M.**
Practical sampling of freshwater macrozoobenthos: a bibliography of useful texts, reviews and recent papers. Winnipeg: Western Region, Fisheries and Marine Service, Department of Fisheries and the Environment, 1978. 15 p. (Fisheries and Marine Service Technical report ; no. 790; ISSN: 0701-7626)
Note: Approx. 500 entries.– Covers mainly 1967 to 1976.– Includes references to reviews of sampling, sampling equipment and techniques and their comparisons, requisite numbers and size of samples, sorting

macrobenthos for identification.– Résumé en français.
Location: OONL.

5424 **Toussaint, Adéline**
Flore et faune canadiennes: inventaire de volumes et de documents audio-visuels au Canada français. [S.l.: s.n.], c1978. v, 66 p.
Note: Approx. 350 entrées.
Localisation: OONL.

— 1979 —

5425 **Bramall, L.; Clay, P.P.F.; Gridgeman, N.T.**
Personnel and publications in biological research at NRCC, 1929-1953. Ottawa: National Research Council of Canada, 1979. 183 p. (in various pagings).
Note: Location: OON.

5426 **British Columbia. Ministry of Forests**
Lodgepole pine: a bibliography. Victoria: British Columbia Ministry of Forests, [1979]. [25] p.
Note: Location: OONL.

5427 **Dagg, A.I.; Campbell, Craig A.**
An annotated bibliography on the status and ecology of the wolverine in Canada. [S.l.: s.n., 1979]. 1 vol. (in various pagings): map.
Note: 290 entries.– References dealing with distribution, populations, ecology, behaviour, breeding and management of the wolverine (Gulo gulo).
Location: OOFF.

5428 **Gilbert, F.F.; Brown, S.A.; Stoll, M.E.**
Semi-aquatic mammals: annotated bibliography. Edmonton: Alberta Oil Sands Environmental Research Program, [1979]. xii, 167 p. (Alberta Oil Sands Environmental Research Program report ; no. 59)
Note: 776 entries.– References relating to life history, mortality factors, physiology, environmental quality and management for four semi-aquatic mammal species: muskrat, beaver, mink and otter.– Literature not relevant to the AOSERP study area (northeastern Alberta) was excluded.
Location: OONL.

5429 **Harper, Alexander Maitland**
A bibliography of Alberta entomology, 1883 to 1977. Edmonton: Alberta Agriculture, 1979. 101 p.
Note: Location: AEAU.

5430 **Hodgins, James**
A guide to the literature on the herbaceous vascular flora of Ontario, 1978. Toronto: Botany Press, [1979]. 73 p.: ill.; ISBN: 0-920395-02-3.
Note: Approx. 850 entries.– Books, papers, maps, botanical surveys, journals, field guides.– Covers floras, ecology, history, horticulture, phytogeography, vegetation zones.
Location: OONL.

5431 **Hutchinson, Raymond**
"Liste des publications traitant de la faune Odonatologique du Québec de 1871 à 1979."
Dans: *Cordulia*; Vol. 5, no 2 (juin 1979) p. 21-33.; ISSN: 0700-4966.
Note: 253 entrées.– Publications, articles, notes brèves par des entomologistes amateurs et professionnels sur les Odonates de la province de Québec.
Localisation: OONL.

5432 **Jennings, Daniel T., et al.**
Spruce budworms bibliography, with author and key word indices. Orono, Me.: Canada-United States Spruce Budworms Program, School of Forest Resources, Univers-

ity of Maine at Orono, 1979. iii, 687 p. (Miscellaneous report / Life science and agriculture experimental station, University of Maine at Orono ; no. 213; ISSN: 0094-436X)
Note: 1,533 entries.– References to literature from published journals and unpublished reports from Canada and the United States on coniferophagous budworms.– Emphasis on spruce budworm, Choristoneura fumiferana (Clemens) and western spruce budworm, C. occidentalis Freeman.
Supplements:
... . *Supplement 1.* 1981. 139 p. (Miscellaneous report ; no. 255).
... . *Supplement 2.* 1982. 75 p. (Miscellaneous report ; no. 268).
... . *Supplement 3.* 1983. 59 p. (Miscellaneous report (Maine Agricultural Experiment Station) ; no. 292; ISSN: 0460-6426).
Location: NBFU.

5433 **Kennedy, Alan; Carbyn, Ludwig N.**
Selected annotated references concerning timber wolf (Canis lupus) predation. Edmonton: Canadian Wildlife Service, Western and Northern Region, 1979. 54 p.
Note: 133 entries.– Journal articles, government reports, conference proceedings, university theses on technical aspects of food habits research, papers on wolf diets, published in North America.
Location: OOFF

5434 **Larochelle, André**
"Liste des publications traitant de la faune des Coléoptères carabidae du Québec de 1859 à 1979."
Dans: *Cordulia*; Vol. 5, no 3 (septembre 1979) p. 41-63.; ISSN: 0070-4966.
Note: 468 entrées.– Publications traite de la taxonomie, la répartition géographique, l'écologie et la biologie des Coléoptères carabidae du Québec.
Localisation: OONL.

5435 **Lubinsky, G.A.; Loch, J.S.**
Ichthyoparasites of Manitoba: literature review and bibliography. Winnipeg: Western Region, Fisheries and Marine Service, Department of Fisheries and the Environment, 1979. vi, 29 p. (Fisheries and Marine Service Manuscript report ; no. 1513; ISSN: 0701-7618)
Note: 118 entries.– Covers to 1978.– Published papers, manuscript reports of federal and provincial governments, theses submitted to University of Manitoba on fish parasites of Manitoba.– Résumé en français.
Location: OONL.

5436 **Lynch, K.D.**
Partial bibliography of marine biomass resources of the Atlantic provinces. Halifax: Atlantic Research Laboratory, National Research Council of Canada, 1979. 60, [61] p. (Atlantic Research Laboratory Technical report ; no. 23)
Note: 339 entries.– Listing of articles, reports issued by government agencies and private institutions in the Atlantic region relating to the marine biology of the region.– Avant-propos en français.
Location: OON.

5437 **Maclellan, Delphine C.**
Theses and publications of the Marine Sciences Centre, 1964-1979. Montreal: Marine Sciences Centre, McGill

University, 1979. 61 l. (Manuscript report / Marine Sciences Centre, McGill University ; no. 31; ISSN: 0828-1831)

Note: Approx. 750 entries.– Refereed publications and reports pertaining to theses done at Marine Sciences Centre, Marine Sciences Centre manuscript reports, federal and provincial government bulletins, workshops and miscellaneous reports.

Previous edition: ..., *1964-1974*. 1974. 40 p.

Location: OONL.

5438 **Nicholson, H.F.**
List of the published and presented papers by the staff of the Great Lakes Biolimnology Laboratory, 1968-1978. [Ottawa]: Fisheries and Environment Canada, Fisheries and Marine Service, 1979. v, 30 l. (Fisheries and Marine Service Technical report ; no. 874; ISSN: 0701-7626)

Note: 245 entries.– Areas of research covered include descriptive biology, ecosystems metabolism, environmental toxicology, sedimentology.– Résumé en français.

Location: OONL.

5439 **Nijholt, W.W.**
The striped ambrosia beetle, Trypodendron lineatum (Oliver): an annotated bibliography. Victoria: Canadian Forestry Service, 1979. 35 p. (Pacific Forest Research Centre Report ; BC-X-121)

Note: 208 entries.– Covers to December 1, 1978.– Survey of international literature, including Canada, dealing with aspects of the ambrosia beetle.– Topics include control, attraction, beetle attack, geographical distribution, flight behaviour, hibernation, physiology, damage appraisal.– Résumé en français.

Location: OONL.

5440 **Sims, R.A.; Riley, J.L.; Jeglum, J.K.**
Vegetation, flora and vegetational ecology of the Hudson Bay Lowland: a literature review and annotated bibliography. Sault Ste. Marie, Ont.: Great Lakes Forest Research Centre, 1979. 177 p. (Hudson Bay Lowland environment baseline studies report ; 0-X-297: ISSN: 0704-7797)

Note: 265 entries.– Résumé en français.

Location: OONL.

5441 **Trudel, François**
Une bibliographie annotée sur le caribou (Rangifer tarandus) du Québec-Labrador. Québec: Ministère des affaires culturelles, Direction générale du patrimoine, 1979. 146 p.: ill. (Dossier / Direction générale du patrimoine, Québec ; 42)

Note: Approx. 1,200 entrées.– Archives; documentation parlementaire et juridique; rapports de recherche gouvernementale; littérature archéologique, historique, ethnologique et géographique; revues de chasse et pêche et journaux; documents audio-visuels sur le caribou du Québec-Labrador.

Localisation: OONL.

— 1980 —

5442 **Barton, B.A.; Toth, L.T.**
Physiological stress in fish: a literature review with emphasis on blood cortisol dynamics. Calgary: Alberta Energy and Natural Resources, 1980. 18 l. (Fisheries research report / Alberta Energy and Natural Resources ; no. 21)

Note: Approx. 100 entries.– Scientific references concerning stress in fish in relation to fish culture practices,

particularly capture, handling and transport.

Location: OONL.

5443 **Burk, William R.**
A bibliography of North American Gasteromycetes: I. Phallales. Vaduz [Liechtenstein]: A.R. Gantner, 1980. xv, 216 p. (Bibliotheca mycologica ; band 73); ISBN: 3-7682-1262-9.

Note: Approx. 750 entries.– Books and articles written by Canadian and American authors on mycology (fungi, mushrooms) of North America north of Mexico and including Hawaii.– Excludes publications dealing with general botany and plant pathology.

Location: OONL.

5444 **Crowther, Roy A.; Griffing, T.C.**
A literature review and bibliography of factors affecting the productivity of benthic invertebrates in running waters and the use of trophic classification in aquatic energy studies. Edmonton: Alberta Oil Sands Environmental Research Program, 1980. xvi, 216 p.: ill. (some folded, some col.), maps (some folded).

Note: Approx. 850 entries.– Review of scientific literature relating physical and chemical factors to the production of stream invertebrates and stream productivity, with focus on the Alberta Oil Sands Environmental Research Program study area of northeast Alberta.

Location: OONL.

5445 **Culver, Stephen John**
"Bibliography of North American Recent benthic foraminifera."

In: *Journal of Foraminiferal Research*; Vol. 10, no. 4 (October 1980) p. 286-302.; ISSN: 0096-1191.

Note: 691 entries.– Papers published between 1839 and 1979 on Recent benthic foraminifera from the margins of North America, including the Canadian Arctic.

Location: OOG.

5446 **Daye, Peter Graeme**
Effects of ambient pH on fish: an annotated bibliography. St. Andrews, N.B.: Government of Canada, Fisheries and Oceans, 1980. iii, 28 p. (Canadian technical report of fisheries and aquatic sciences ; no. 950; ISSN: 0706-6457)

Note: 316 entries.– Lists technical studies on effects of acid rain, acid mine drainage on fish.– Topics include biochemistry/physiology, embryo/reproduction, lethal levels, reclamation.

Location: OONL.

5447 **Griffiths, K.J.**
A bibliography of gypsy moth literature. Sault Ste. Marie, Ont.: Great Lakes Forest Research Centre, 1980. 2 vol.

Note: 4,140 entries.– Contains numerous Canadian references.

Location: OONL.

5448 **Harper, Alexander Maitland**
A bibliography of papers presented at the annual meetings of the Entomological Society of Alberta, 1953-1978. [Edmonton: s.n.], 1980. 56 p.

Note: 490 entries.

Location: OONL.

5449 **Hawthorn, R.S.; McCormick, W.A.**
A literature review of aquatic macrophytes with particular reference to those present in Windermere Lake, British Columbia. Vancouver: Province of British Columbia, Ministry of Environment, 1980. ii, 57 l.

Note: Location: OONL.

5450 **Hills, L.V.; Sangster, E.V.**
"A review of paleobotanical studies dealing with the last 20,000 years: Alaska, Canada and Greenland."
In: *Climatic change in Canada*, edited by C.R. Harington. Ottawa: National Museum of Natural Sciences, National Museums of Canada, c1980. P. 73-224: ill., maps; ISSN: 0704-576X.
Note: 366 entries.
Location: OONL.

5451 **Kossatz, V. Christine; Leavitt, Ferrin D.**
The biology, and the chemical and cultural control of Canada thistle (Cirsium arvense): a bibliography for the Canadian prairies. Edmonton: Weed Control and Field Services Branch, Alberta Department of Agriculture, 1980. ii, 97 p.
Note: 608 entries.– Canadian conference reports, articles and bulletins relating to Canada thistle biology and control in crops grown in Alberta, including wheat, barley, rapeseed, forage crops, vegetable crops.– Additional references deal with effects of zero and minimum tillage, irrigation and continuous cropping on Canada thistle.– References to distribution and biological control are not included.
Location: OONL.

5452 **Laird, Marshall**
Bibliography of the natural history of Newfoundland and Labrador. London: Academic Press, 1980. lxxi, 376 p.: ill., maps.; ISBN: 0-12-434050-4.
Note: Approx. 4,500 entries.– Books, chapters of books, technical reports from government and private agencies, journal articles on Newfoundland and Labrador plants and animals, environment, agriculture, fisheries, sealing.
Location: OONL.

5453 **Messieh, Shoukry N.**
A bibliography of herring (Clupea harengus L.) in the northwest Atlantic. St. Andrews, N.B.: Fisheries and Environment Canada, 1980. iii, 25 p. (Fisheries and Marine Service Technical report; no. 919; ISSN: 0701-7626)
Note: 385 entries.– Covers the period 1963 through 1978.– Subject list under seven major topics: age, stock identification, population dynamics, maturation, larvae, feeding/ecology, biochemistry/toxicology/disease.
Location: OONL.

5454 **Roberts, D.W.A.; Miska, John P.**
Cold hardiness and winter survival of plants, 1965-1975. Slough, England: Commonwealth Agricultural Bureaux, 1980. ix, 407 p. (Commonwealth Bureau of Soils Special publication; no. 8); ISBN: 0-85198-477-0.
Note: 2,886 entries.– References relating to publications on chilling injury, cold hardiness, winter survival of plants.
Location: OONL.

5455 **Swain, D.P.; Derksen, A.J.; Loch, J.S.**
A literature review of life histories of some species of fish: rainbow smelt Osmerus mordax, gizzard shad Dorosoma cepedianum, paddlefish Polydon spathula, shovelnose sturgeon Scaphirhynchus platorynchus, pallid sturgeon Scaphirhynchus albus, and shortnose gar Lepisosteus platostomus, that may be introduced into the Hudson Bay watershed from the Missouri River watershed as a result of the Garrison Diversion. [Winnipeg]:

Manitoba Department of Natural Resources, 1980. x, 168 p.: map. (MS report / Fisheries Branch, Manitoba Department of Natural Resources; 80-37)
Note: Approx. 200 entries.– Life histories in this report provide information on habitat and seasonal distribution, spawning sites, seasons and behaviour, sexual maturity, sex ratios, fecundity, early development, growth, food habits, parasites.
Location: OONL.

5456 **Swann, C.G.; Donaldson, Edward M.**
Bibliography of salmonid reproduction 1963-1979 for the family Salmonidae; subfamilies Salmoninae, Coregoninae and Thymallinae. West Vancouver, B.C.: Resources Services Branch, Department of Fisheries and Oceans, 1980. iv, 221 p. (Canadian technical report of fisheries and aquatic sciences; no. 970; ISSN: 0706-6457)
Note: 1,399 entries.– Books, papers, reports concerning reproduction in the family Salmonidae.– Topics covered include ovarian and testicular development, ovulation and spermiation, reproductive behaviour, fecundity, spawning and fertilization.– Résumé en français.

5457 **Triplehorn, Julia H.; Johnson, Lee E.**
Muskox bibliography. Fairbanks: Institute of Arctic Biology, University of Alaska, 1980. 216 p. (Institute of Arctic Biology Occasional publications on northern life; no. 3)
Note: Approx. 4,000 entries.– Books, government studies and reports, periodical and newspaper articles, ranging from technical to popular coverage.– Substantial representation of Canadian materials.– Topics include domestication, environmental impact studies, hunting, paleontology, social behaviour, stocking and transplanting, wildlife management, distribution, population dynamics, population numbers, habitat.
Location: OONL.

— 1981 —

5458 **Canada. Ocean Science and Surveys**
Pilot catalog of OSS marine data holdings. Ottawa: Department of Fisheries and Oceans, 1981. [58] l.: ill., maps.
Note: Location: OON.

5459 **Coad, Brian W.**
A bibliography of the sticklebacks (Gasterosteidae: Osteichthyes). Ottawa: National Museum of Natural Sciences, National Museums of Canada, 1981. 142 p. (Syllogeus / National Museum of Natural Sciences; no. 35; ISSN: 0704-576X)
Note: Approx. 2,000 entries.– Covers to the end of 1979.– Many Canadian references.
Location: OONL.

5460 **Craven, Scott R.**
The Canada goose (Branta Canadensis): an annotated bibliography. Washington, D.C.: U.S. Department of the Interior, Fish and Wildlife Service, 1981. 66 p. (Special scientific report: wildlife; no. 231)
Note: 646 entries.– Literature dealing with Canada goose biology, research, management, taxonomy, through 1977.– Excludes general ornithological texts, bird lists.
Location: OON.

5461 **Danks, H.V.**
Bibliography of the Arctic arthropods of the nearctic region. Ottawa: Entomological Society of Canada, 1981. 125 p.; ISBN: 0-9690829-1-6.

Note: 1,382 entries.– Deals with terrestrial arthropods of arctic North America and Greenland, including only animals that breathe air at some stage of life cycle.– Excludes freshwater crustaceans.
Location: OONL.

5462 **Jean, Michel**
Bibliographie-caribou (révision 1980). Québec: Ministère du loisir, de la chasse et de la pêche, 1981. iii, 139 p.
Note: Comprend des publications en français et en anglais.
Édition antérieure: *Bibliographie-caribou (à jour au 1er mai 1978)*. 1978. 43 p.
Localisation: OONL.

5463 **Judd, William W.**
A bibliography of the natural history of Middlesex County, Ontario to the year 1980: with an historical introduction. London, Ont.: Phelps Publishing, 1981. 157 p.; ISBN: 0-920298-32-X.
Note: Approx. 1,750 entries.– Lists journal articles concerning mainly birds, insects and flowering plants found in Middlesex County, Ontario.– Others on mammals, amphibians and reptiles, algae and fungi, lichens, etc.
Location: OONL.

5464 **Marshall, K.E.**
A bibliography of the arctic charr, Salvelinus alpinus (L.) complex to 1980. Winnipeg: Western Region, Department of Fisheries and Oceans, 1981. iv, 68 p. (Canadian technical report of fisheries and aquatic sciences ; no. 1004; ISSN: 0706-6457)
Note: 1,628 entries.– Covers from the seventeenth century to 1980.– Includes references to other closely related taxa, including the Dolly Varden.
Previous edition: ... to 1976. Freshwater Institute, Research and Development Directorate, 1977. iv, 49 p. (Technical report (Canada, Fisheries and Marine Service, Research and Development Directorate) ; no. 621; ISSN: 0701-7626/Technical report (Freshwater Institute ; no. 96).
Supplements:
Marshall, K.E.; Layton, M. ... : 1981 through 1984. 1985. iv, 16 p. (Canadian technical report of fisheries and aquatic sciences ; no. 1345; ISSN: 0706-6457).
Heuring, L.G.; Babaluk, J.A.; Marshall, K.E. ... : 1985-1990. 1991. iv, 46 p. (Canadian technical report of fisheries and aquatic sciences ; no. 1775; ISSN: 0706-6457).
Location: OONL.

5465 **Ogaard, Louis A.**
Wetland vegetation of the Prairie Pothole Region: research methods and annotated bibliography. Fargo, N.D.: Agricultural Experimental Station, North Dakota State University, 1981. iv, 50 p. (North Dakota Research report ; no. 85)
Note: Literature review and annotated bibliography of primary production, nutrient cycling, plant distribution of freshwater vegetation.– Canadian references deal with southern Manitoba, Saskatchewan, Alberta.
Location: KHayF.

5466 **Schooley, Hugh O.; Oldford, L.**
An annotated bibliography of the balsam woolly aphid (Adelges piceae (Ratzeburg)). St. John's: Newfoundland Forest Research Centre, 1981. 97 p. (Newfoundland Forest Research Centre Information report ; N-X-196; ISSN: 0704-7657)

Note: 607 entries.
Location: NSDE.

5467 **Spry, D.J.; Wood, C.M.; Hodson, P.V.**
The effects of environmental acid on freshwater fish with particular reference to the soft water lakes in Ontario and the modifying effects of heavy metals: a literature review. Burlington, Ont.: Department of Fisheries and Oceans, Great Lakes Biolimnology Laboratory, 1981. xi, 144 p. (Canadian technical report of fisheries and aquatic sciences ; no. 999; ISSN: 0706-6457)
Note: Approx. 250 entries.– Review of literature dealing with the physiology of acid stress and the toxic effects of selected metals in fish.– Résumé en français.
Location: OONL.

5468 **Wells, Peter G.; Moyse, Catherine M.**
A selected bibliography on the biology of Salmo gairdneri Richardson (rainbow, steelhead, Kamloops trout), with particular reference to studies with aquatic toxicants. Dartmouth, N.S.: Contaminants and Assessments Branch, Environmental Protection Service, Atlantic Region, 1981. vi, 90 p. (Economic and technical review report / Environmental Protection Service ; EPS-3-AR-81-1)
Note: 2,321 entries.– Primary and technical scientific literature to June 1979 dealing with rainbow trout and aquatic toxicants.– Includes Canadian references.– Résumé en français.
Location: NSDE.

— 1982 —

5469 **Banci, Vivian A.**
A bibliography on the wolverine Gulo gulo. Victoria: Published by the Ministries of Environment and Forests, 1982. i, 53 p. (Integrated Wildlife Intensive Forestry Research ; 9)
Note: Approx. 600 entries.
Location: OONL.

5470 **Bisson, Réal; Poulin, Pierre**
Les oiseaux de la Gaspésie: liste annotée et bibliographie. Percé, Québec: Club des ornithologues de la Gaspésie, 1982. 57 f.: carte.
Note: Approx. 80 entrées.
Localisation: OONL.

5471 **Borden, John H.**
Secondary attraction in the Scolytidae: an annotated bibliography. 3rd ed. Burnaby, B.C.: Pest Management Program, Department of Biological Sciences, Simon Fraser University, 1982. v l., 185 p. (Pest management papers / Centre for Pest Management, Simon Fraser University ; no. 26; ISSN: 0703-7643); ISBN: 0-86491-027-4.
Note: Research literature on secondary attraction, insect-produced, attractive compounds (pheromones) acting alone or in combination with host volatiles emanating from trees or logs, which results in the aggregation of a natural population and mass attack on the host.
Previous editions:
Pestology Centre, Simon Fraser University, 1975. 97 p.
Borden, John H.; Stokkink, Eveline. Victoria: Department of Fisheries and Forestry, 1971. 77 p. (Canadian Forestry Service Information report ; BC-X-57).
Location: OONL.

5472 **Butcher, G.A.; Davidson, R.B.**
A bibliography to Arctic grayling (Thymallus arcticus). [Victoria, B.C.]: Ministry of Environment, Aquatic

Studies Branch, 1982. 30 l.
Note: Approx. 450 entries.
Location: BVILFW.

5473 **Campbell, R. Wayne, et al.**
A bibliography of Pacific northwest herpetology.
Victoria: British Columbia Provincial Museum, 1982. v,
152 p.: ill., maps. (British Columbia Provincial Museum
Heritage record ; no. 14; ISSN: 0701-9556); ISBN: 0-7718-
8288-2.
Note: 1,156 entries.– Includes articles from herpetological
journals, zoological and natural history society
publications, museum publications, government
publications, books, field guides.– Indexes: species,
geographic, authors.
Location: OONL.

5474 **Crawford, Hewlette S.; Jennings, Daniel T.**
Relationships of birds and spruce budworms: literature
review and annotated bibliography. Washington, D.C.:
Forest Service, U.S. Department of Agriculture, 1982.
38 p. (Bibliographies and literature of agriculture ; no. 23)
Note: Approx. 150 entries.– Canadian and American
references dealing with predation and bird populations,
numerical and functional responses to spruce budworm
populations, habitat and bird population changes,
digestion rates, life histories of predaceous birds,
predator-prey models.– Publication of the Canada
United States Spruce Budworms Program (CANUSA).
Location: BBIT.

5475 **Enright, Catherine Theresa; Newkirk, G.F.**
Literature search on the growth of oysters as influenced
by artificial diets and natural diets. Halifax: Biology
Department, Dalhousie University, 1982. vii, 194 p.: ill.
Note: Some Canadian references.
Location: OON.

5476 **Gardner, Grant Allan; Szabo, Ildy**
British Columbia pelagic marine Copepoda: an identifica-
tion manual and annotated bibliography. Ottawa:
Department of Fisheries and Oceans, 1982. vi, 536 p.
(Canadian special publication of fisheries and aquatic
sciences ; 62; ISSN: 0706-6481); ISBN: 0-660-11250-7.
Note: List of studies pertaining to identification of
juvenile and adult copepods.– Emphasis on ecological
and distributional aspects rather than on taxonomy.–
Includes a systematic index to the orders Calanoida,
Cyclopoida, Monstrilloida, Harpacticoida, with separate
entries for naupliar and copepodite stages.
Location: OONL.

5477 **Goodyear, Carole D., et al.**
Atlas of the spawning and nursery areas of Great Lakes
fishes. Washington, D.C.: U.S. Fish and Wildlife Service,
Office of Biological Services, 1982. 14 vol.
Note: Vol. 14: *Literature cited*, contains the bibliography.–
Approx. 2,250 entries.– Compilation of current spawning
and nursery information concerning the fishes of the
Great Lakes.– Includes Canadian and American
references dealing with biology, breeding habits, distribu-
tion, life histories, effects of pollution, rehabilitation of
major species of the Great Lakes area.
Location: QMM.

5478 **LGL Limited Environmental Research Associates**
The biological resources of the southeastern Beaufort Sea,
Amundsen Gulf, northern Mackenzie delta and adjacent
coastal areas [microform]: a selected annotated

bibliography. Edmonton: LGL Limited, 1982. 12
microfiches (705 frames): negative, maps. (Arctic
Petroleum Operators' Association Project ; no. 173)
Note: Sections include mammals, birds, fish, zoobenthos,
zooplankton, ice biota, primary productivity,
geomorphology, physical oceanography, atlases, impact
studies.– Emphasis on aquatic biology.
Location: OONL.

5479 **Smith, Lynn M.; Addison, Edward M.**
A bibliography of parasites and diseases of Ontario
wildlife. Toronto: Ontario Ministry of Natural Resources,
1982. 267 p. (Wildlife research report / Ontario Ministry
of Natural Resources ; no. 99)
Note: 768 entries.– Journal articles, published papers
describing natural or experimental studies.– Includes
only parasites and disease agents originating in Ontario
(trematodes, cestodes, nematodes, acanthocephalans;
fleas, lice, mites, ticks, bugs, beetles; viruses, bacteria,
fungi, rickettsiae; environmental contaminants).–
Wildlife hosts include mammals, birds, amphibians,
reptiles from Ontario.– Excludes theses, conference
proceedings, symposia papers.
Location: OOCC.

5480 **Withler, Ruth Elinor; Healey, M.C.; Riddell, B.E.**
Annotated bibliography of genetic variation in the family
salmonidae. Nanaimo, B.C.: Department of Fisheries and
Oceans, Fisheries Research Branch, Pacific Biological
Station, 1982. v, 161 p. (Canadian technical report of
fisheries and aquatic sciences ; no. 1098; ISSN: 0706-6457)
Note: Approx. 300 entries.– References published
between 1920 and 1981 dealing with genetic variation in
the family Salmonidae.– Topics covered include the
heritability and genetic variation of morphological,
physiological, and behavioural characteristics of
salmonids, effects of stock manipulation and domestication on genetics.– Résumé en français.
Location: OONL.

— 1983 —

5481 **Dewar, D., et al.**
A bibliography of the arctic species of the Gadidae, 1982.
Winnipeg: Government of Canada, Department of
Fisheries and Oceans, 1983. iv, 29 p. (Canadian technical
report of fisheries and aquatic sciences ; no. 1141; ISSN:
0706-6457)
Note: Approx. 500 entries.– Technical articles and papers
on the toothed cod, polar cod, Arctic cod, saffron cod,
ogac (Greenland cod), navaga, species which form an
important part of the diet of marine and anadromous
fishes (Arctic char), marine mammals, birds in the
Arctic.– Résumé en français.
Location: OONL.

5482 **Dobson, W.R.; Drinnan, R.L.**
Harp seals and hooded seals (Phoca groenlandica and
Cystophora cristata): a guide to the scientific literature:
prepared for Greenpeace Foundation of Canada.
[Vancouver: Greenpeace Foundation of Canada], 1983. 2
vol.
Note: Vol. 1: *Annotated bibliography*. 165 entries.– Books,
papers, articles on seal population status, impact of seals
on fisheries, humane killing versus cruelty, mother-
young relationships, economic aspects of the sealing
industry.
Location: OONL.

5483 **Douglas, George W.; Ceska, Adolf; Ruyle, Gloria G.**
A floristic bibliography for British Columbia. Victoria: Information Services Branch, British Columbia Ministry of Forests, 1983. iv, 143 p. (Land management report / British Columbia Ministry of Forests ; no. 15; ISSN: 0702-9861); ISBN: 0-7719-9190-8.
Note: Approx. 1,500 entries.– Lists books, journal articles, papers on botany of British Columbia.– Types of papers include general texts, taxonomic papers on vascular plants, floristic vascular plant papers, bryophytes, lichens, general vegetation papers.
Location: OONL.

5484 **Frank, Peter G.**
A checklist and bibliography of the Sipuncula from Canadian and adjacent waters. Ottawa: National Museum of Natural Sciences, 1983. 47 p.: ill., maps. (Syllogeus / National Museum of Natural Sciences ; no. 46; ISSN: 0704-576X)
Note: Approx. 80 entries.– Listing of references relating to seventeen species of the Phylum Sipuncula, unsegmented marine worms found in Canadian waters from intertidal to great depths.
Location: OONL.

5485 **Henderson, V.; Sawatsky, W.**
Bibliography of vegetation studies in Manitoba. [Winnipeg]: Terrestrial Standards and Studies Section, Environmental Management Services Branch, Department of Environment and Workplace Safety and Health, [1983]. 33 l., map. (Terrestrial Standards and Studies report ; 83-6)
Note: 304 entries.
Location: OONL.

5486 **Kathman, R.D., et al.**
Benthic studies in Alice Arm and Hastings Arm, B.C. in relation to mine tailings dispersal. Sidney, B.C.: Institute of Ocean Sciences, Fisheries and Oceans Canada, 1983. vii, 30, [28] p.: ill., maps. (Canadian technical report of hydrography and ocean sciences ; no. 22; ISSN: 0711-6764)
Note: Approx. 150 entries.– Includes a review of the studies and a bibliographic listing of taxonomic references and references cited.– Bibliography, p. 20-30.
Location: OONL.

5487 **Sims, R.A.; Murtha, Peter A.**
Reindeer at Mackenzie: a selected annotated bibliography. Ottawa: Indian and Northern Affairs Canada, 1983. iv, 63 p.: ill., map. (Northern Affairs Program Environmental studies ; no. 31); ISBN: 0-662-12666-1.
Note: 119 entries.– Articles, technical studies, reports dealing with the Mackenzie Delta reindeer herd, a commercial reindeer operation that began as a government-sponsored experiment in the 1930s.
Titre en français: *Les rennes dans la région du Mackenzie: références choisies.*
Location: OONL.

5488 **Sims, R.A.; Murtha, Peter A.**
Les rennes dans la région du Mackenzie: références choisies. Ottawa: Affaires indiennes et du Nord Canada, 1983. iv, 75 p.: ill., carte. (Programme des affaires du Nord Étude environnementale ; no 31); ISBN: 0-662-92180-1.
Note: 119 entrées.– Articles, études, rapports: ouvrages traitant de l'exploitation commerciale du troupeau de rennes du delta du Mackenzie qui, à ses débuts dans les années 1930, était une entreprise expérimentale financée par le gouvernement.
English title: *Reindeer at Mackenzie: a selected annotated bibliography.*
Localisation: OONL.

5489 **Smits, C.M.M.**
An annotated bibliography and information summary on the furbearer resource and trapping industry of the Yukon River Basin. Whitehorse: Wildlife Management Branch, Yukon Department of Renewable Resources, 1983. ii, 168 l. (Yukon River Basin Study Project report: Wildlife ; no. 1, appendix 2)
Note: 154 entries.– Books, government and industrial technical reports, periodical articles, theses dealing with furbearers, the trapping industry and small mammals, pertaining to the Canadian portion of the Yukon River watershed (exclusive of the Porcupine River).
Location: AEUB.

5490 **Têtu-Bernier, P.; Allen, E.; Hiratsuka, Y.**
Bibliography of western gall rust. Edmonton: Canadian Forestry Service, Northern Forest Research Centre, c1983. iv, 10 p. (Northern Forest Research Centre Information report ; NOR-X-250; ISSN: 0704-7673); ISBN: 0-662-12712-9.
Note: Approx. 200 entries.
Location: OONL.

— 1984 —

5491 **Arthur, James Richard; Arai, H.P.**
Annotated checklist and bibliography of parasites of herring (Clupea harengus L.). Ottawa: Department of Fisheries and Oceans, 1984. iv, 26 p. (Canadian special publication of fisheries and aquatic sciences ; 70; ISSN: 0706-6481); ISBN: 0-660-11659-6.
Note: Approx. 250 entries.– Literature recording original observations on parasites of herring, from 1697 to 1984.– Some Canadian contributions.– Résumé en français.
Location: OONL.

5492 **Beck, Alfred Ernest**
Bibliography of mercury in Manitoba fish. Winnipeg: Government of Manitoba, Water Standards and Studies Section, 1984. ii, 9 l.
Note: Location: OONL.

5493 **Burns, Gordon R.**
A preliminary annotated bibliography of literature on small mammals relevant to Elk Island National Park. Edmonton: Canadian Wildlife Service, 1984. 69 p.
Note: Approx. 350 entries.– Prepared in conjunction with inventory of small (non-ungulate) mammals of Elk Island Park.– Includes journal articles, conference papers, government reports, theses.– Literature describing closely related species and publications for species formerly resident in the park are included.
Location: OOFF.

5494 **Campbell, R. Wayne; Forsman, E.D.; Van Der Raay, B.M.**
An annotated bibliography of literature on the spotted owl. Victoria: Province of British Columbia, Ministry of Forests, 1984. 115 p.: ill., map. (Land management report / British Columbia Ministry of Forests ; no. 24; ISSN: 0702-9861); ISBN: 0-7718-8454-0.
Note: 586 entries.– References from scientific journals

current through 1983 pertaining to the spotted owl.–
Topics include behaviour, distribution, foods,
management and conservation, human interaction, status
and population trends.

Location: OONL

5495 **Evans, David O.; Campbell, Bonnie A.**
An annotated listing of original field data books and
diaries of Ontario Fisheries Research Laboratory workers
(1921-1948). [Toronto]: Ontario Ministry of Natural
Resources, 1984. iii, 37 p. (Ontario fisheries technical
report series ; no. 11; ISSN: 0227-986X); ISBN: 0-7743-
8982-6.
Note: 167 entries.– Field trip diaries, accounts and
original data records of limnological, benthic,
entomological, fisheries and general aquatic surveys of
Ontario lakes and streams, primarily Lake Nipigon, Lake
Nipissing, and small lakes and streams in Algonquin
Park and southern Ontario.
Location: OONL.

5496 **Franzin, William Gilbert**
Bibliographies of beluga (Delphinapterus leucas),
narwhal (Monodon monocerus) and walrus (Odobenus
rosmarus) to June, 1982. Winnipeg: Government of
Canada, Fisheries and Oceans, 1984. iv, 20 p. (Canadian
manuscript report of fisheries and aquatic sciences ; no.
1740; ISSN: 0706-6473)
Note: Approx. 500 entries.
Location: OONL.

5497 **Harrison, P.J., et al.**
A bibliography of the biological oceanography of the
Strait of Georgia and adjacent inlets, with emphasis on
ecological aspects. Nanaimo, B.C.: Fisheries Research
Branch, Department of Fisheries and Oceans, 1984. vi,
140 p.: map. (Canadian technical report of fisheries and
aquatic sciences ; no. 1293; ISSN: 0706-6457)
Note: 830 entries.– Contains published and unpublished
reports (data reports, theses, etc.) on ecological aspects of
fauna and flora of pelagic and benthic environments:
phytoplankton, benthic microalgae, macrophytes or
seaweeds bacteria, zooplankton, benthic invertebrates.–
Limited reference made to taxonomic studies.– Includes
studies conducted in mesocosms located in Saanich Inlet
by CEPEX (controlled ecosystem/population
experiment).
Location: OONL.

5498 **Klaprat, D.A.; Hara, T.J.**
A bibliography on chemoreception in fishes, 1807-1983.
Winnipeg, Man.: Western Region, Department of
Fisheries and Oceans, 1984. iv, 47 p. (+ 1 errata sheet).
(Canadian technical report of fisheries and aquatic
sciences ; no. 1268; ISSN: 0706-6457)
Note: Approx. 900 entries.– Includes books and review
papers, symposium proceedings, journal articles and
technical reports.
Location: OONL.

5499 **Lambert, Elisabeth; Lavoie, André; Dubois, Jean-Marie**
Télédétection des algues marines des côtes du Québec: 1
– Bibliographie mondiale annotée. Québec: Gouverne-
ment du Québec, Ministère de l'agriculture, des
pêcheries et de l'alimentation, 1984. 44 p. (Cahier de
l'information / Direction des pêches maritimes ; no 112);
ISBN: 2-550-11666-6.
Note: 57 entrées.– Deux grands thèmes: télédétection des

algues marines; pénétration de la lumière dans l'eau.
Localisation: OONL.

5500 **Mason, E.; Maine, F.W.**
Tissue culture and micropropagation for forest biomass
production: literature review. Ottawa: National Research
Council of Canada, Division of Energy, 1984. vi, 81 p.: ill.
Note: 274 entries.– Review of books and papers dealing
with tissue culture methods, micropropagation of forest
trees, gymnosperms, angiosperms, haploids in tree
breeding, applications of protoplasts in plant breeding,
nitrogen fixation by genetic manipulation, germplasm
storage by cryopreservation.– Contains a general
bibliography and a selected annotated bibliography.
Location: OONL.

5501 **Minion, Robin**
Caribou and reindeer in Canada and Alaska. Edmonton:
Boreal Institute for Northern Studies, University of
Alberta, 1984. 65 p. (Boreal Institute for Northern Studies
Bibliographic series ; no. 3; ISSN: 0824-8192); ISBN: 0-
919058-37-X.
Note: 160 entries.– Covers from 1977 to 1984.– Compiled
from *BOREAL, The Northern Database*, includes
monographs, theses, government documents, conference
proceedings, consultants' reports.– BINS series produced
monthly from January 1984 to May 1986 (no. 29).– Online
access: *Boreal Northern Titles (BNT)*, available through QL
Systems Limited.
Location: OONL.

5502 **Minion, Robin**
Flora in the Yukon and NWT. Edmonton: Boreal Institute
for Northern Studies, University of Alberta, 1984. 95 p.
(Boreal Institute for Northern Studies Bibliographic
series ; no. 10; ISSN: 0824-8192); ISBN: 0-919058-44-2.
Note: 243 entries.– Covers 1977 to 1984.– Compiled from
BOREAL, The Northern Database, includes monographs,
theses, government publications, conference
proceedings, consultants' reports.– BINS series produced
monthly from January 1984 to May 1986 (no. 29).– Online
access: *Boreal Northern Titles (BNT)*, available through QL
Systems Limited.
Location: OONL.

5503 **Minion, Robin**
Seals. Edmonton: Boreal Institute for Northern Studies,
University of Alberta, 1984. 94 p. (Boreal Institute for
Northern Studies Bibliographic series ; no. 9; ISSN: 0824-
8192); ISBN: 0-919058-43-4.
Note: 258 entries.– Series contains monographs, theses,
government documents, consultants' reports, children's
books, conference proceedings, microforms on topics
related to northern environment and people.– BINS
series produced monthly from January 1984 to May 1986
(no. 29).– Online access: *Boreal Northern Titles (BNT)*,
available through QL Systems Limited.
Location: OONL.

5504 **Minion, Robin**
Swimmers and sea birds. Edmonton: Boreal Institute for
Northern Studies, University of Alberta, 1984. 79 p.
(Boreal Institute for Northern Studies Bibliographic
series ; no. 12; ISSN: 0824-8192); ISBN: 0-919058-46-9.
Note: 201 entries.– Series contains monographs, theses,
government documents, consultants' reports, children's
books, conference proceedings, microforms on topics
related to northern environment and people.– BINS

series produced monthly from January 1984 to May 1986 (no. 29).– Online access: *Boreal Northern Titles (BNT)*, available through QL Systems Limited.

Location: OONL.

5505 Olver, C.H.; Martin, N.V.

A selective bibliography of the lake trout, Salvelinus namaycush (Walbaum), 1784-1982. [Toronto]: Ontario Ministry of Natural Resources, 1984. iii, 109 p. (Ontario fisheries technical report series ; no. 12; ISSN: 0227-986X); ISBN: 0-7743-9061-1.

Note: Approx. 1,900 entries.– Journal articles, books, unpublished manuscripts, with emphasis on including reports by Ontario Ministry of Natural Resources and its predecessor, the Department of Lands and Forests.– Topics include taxonomy, distribution, morphology, physiology and biochemistry, life history and habits, population, exploitation, management.

Location: OONL.

5506 Sameoto, D.

Review of current information on Arctic cod (Boreogadus saida Lepechin) and bibliography. [Dartmouth, N.S.]: Ocean Science and Surveys Atlantic, Fisheries and Oceans Canada, 1984. 71 p.: ill., maps.

Note: Approx. 250 entries.– Journal articles, theses, government studies dealing with Arctic cod: taxonomy, distribution, life cycle, diet, predators, association with ice.

Location: OORD.

5507 Stockerl, Edward C.; Kent, Robert L.

The distribution, identification, biology and management of Eurasian water milfoil: an Alberta perspective. [Edmonton]: Pesticide Chemicals Branch, Pollution Control Division, Alberta Environment, 1984. vii l., 89 p.

Note: Approx. 120 entries.– Literature concerning this nuisance submergent aquatic plant is reviewed.– Topics include history, distribution, biology, identification, control measures.

Location: OONL.

— 1985 —

5508 Arthur, George W.

A buffalo roundup: a selected bibliography. Regina: Canadian Plains Research Center, c1985. xiv, 153 p. (Canadian plains bibliographies / Canadian Plains Research Center ; 2; ISSN: 0823-8936); ISBN: 0-88977-036-0.

Note: 2,521 entries.– Books, pamphlets, articles pertaining to the history, biology and ecology of the bison, with a sampling of anthropological, palaeontological, and taxonomic material.– Excludes most children's non-fiction literature, as well as children's and adult fiction.

Location: OONL.

5509 Brodo, Irwin M.

Guide to the literature for the identification of North American lichens. Ottawa: National Museums of Canada, National Museum of Natural Sciences, 1985. 39 p. (Syllogeus / National Museum of Natural Sciences ; no. 56; ISSN: 0704-576X)

Note: 360 entries.– Books, published articles, doctoral theses dealing with lichens by group and region, lichen parasites, Arctic species, boreal and hemiarctic lichens and maritime lichens.

5510 Ibach, Stephanie

Annotated bibliography of Rocky Mountain bighorn sheep specific to the management of bighorn sheep in Kootenay National Park. Edmonton: Produced by Canadian Wildlife Service for Parks Canada, Western Region, 1985. i, 242 [40] p.

Note: Approx. 1,200 entries.– Books, journal articles, reports, papers, theses.– Subjects covered include behaviour, diseases and parasites, management, mortality factors, nutrition, physiology, population dynamics, habitat, research techniques.

Location: OOFF.

5511 Ibach, Stephanie

Annotated bibliography on elk-livestock-range interactions in western Canada and northwestern U.S.A. specific to the management of elk and livestock within the Waterton Biosphere Reserve. Edmonton: Canadian Wildlife Service, 1985. i, 115, [43] p.

Note: Approx. 500 entries.

Location: OOFF.

5512 Lane, E. David

A bibliography on the white sturgeon, (Acipenser transmontanus) Richardson, 1836. Nanaimo, B.C.: Department of Fisheries and Oceans, 1985. iv, 33 p. (Canadian manuscript report of fisheries and aquatic sciences ; no. 1828; ISSN: 0706-6473)

Note: 224 entries.– Published and unpublished reports issued prior to January 1985 on the white sturgeon.– Some Canadian references.– Résumé en français.

Location: OONL.

5513 Lévesque, Frédéric; Magnan, Pierre

Bibliographie annotée sur le saumon atlantique (Salmo salar) au stade post-fraie. Québec: Pêches et océans Canada, 1985. v, 42 p. (Rapport manuscrit canadien des sciences halieutiques et aquatiques ; no 1823; ISSN: 0706-6589)

Note: 100 entrées.– Regroupe travaux au stade post-fraie du saumon atlantique, aussi appelé saumon noir, charognard, bécard et lingard: caractéristiques générales, dévalaison, maladies, mortalité, rapport des sexes et différences sexuelles, multiparisme, migrations.– Abstract in English.

Localisation: OONL.

5514 McDougall, Keith A.; McGillis, Joe R.; Holroyd, Geoffrey L.

Annotated wildlife references for Banff and Jasper National Parks. Edmonton: Canadian Wildlife Service, 1985. ii, 94 p.

Note: 315 entries.

Location: AEECW.

5515 McNicholl, Martin K.

Manitoba bird studies, 1744-1983: a bibliography. [Winnipeg]: Manitoba Natural Resources, 1985. 290 p.

Note: Approx. 3,200 entries.

Previous edition: *Manitoba bird studies: a bibliography of Manitoba ornithology.* Manitoba Department of Mines, Resources and Environmental Management, 1975. 146 p.

Location: OONL.

5516 Miska, John P.; Niilo, Alan

Animal diseases research, 1939-1985: a bibliography of research papers by ADRI scientists at Lethbridge. Ottawa: Agriculture Canada, 1985. 31 p.

Note: 307 entries.– Scientific publications by members of

the Animal Diseases Research Institute, Lethbridge, Alberta between 1939 and June 1985.
Location: OONL.

5517 **Shepard, C.; Miller, G.; Groot, C.**
Migration and movements of Pacific salmon, Atlantic salmon, and steelhead trout: a bibliography, 1900-1982. Nanaimo, B.C.: Department of Fisheries and Oceans, Fisheries Research Branch, 1985. iv, 450 p. (Canadian technical report of fisheries and aquatic sciences ; no. 1413; ISSN:0706-6457)
Note: 1,796 entries.– List of citations relating to physiological, behavioural, and ecological aspects of migration and movements of Pacific salmon, Atlantic salmon and steelhead trout in journal articles, technical papers, theses.– Résumé en français.
Location: OONL.

5518 **Vincent, Charles; Burgess, Larry**
Bibliographie sur les altises phytophages des crucifères au Canada/A bibliography relevant to crucifer-feeding flea beetle pests in Canada. Saint-Jean-sur-Richelieu, Québec: Agriculture Canada, 1985. 31 p. (Bulletin technique / Agriculture Canada ; no 22; ISSN: 0825-4559); ISBN: 0-662-53962-1.
Note: Approx. 300 entrées.– Présente une liste des références en rapport avec la recherche sur les espèces Phyllotreta cruciferae et Phyllotreta striolata au Canada.– Texte en français et en anglais/text in English and French.
Localisation: OONL.

5519 **West, Allen Sherman**
A review of insects affecting production of willows. St. John's: Newfoundland Forestry Centre, 1985. iv, 82 p. (Information report / Canadian Forestry Service, Newfoundland Forestry Centre ; N-X-232; ISSN: 0704-7657); ISBN: 0-662-14376-0.
Note: 66 entries.– List of references with abstracts to world literature (including Canadian) dealing with insect pests that may attack willows (Salix spp.).
Location: OONL.

5520 **Yurkowski, M.**
A bibliography on the biochemistry, nutrition, and related areas of aquatic mammals and Arctic people to 1983. Winnipeg: Fisheries and Oceans Canada, 1985. iv, 236 p. (Canadian technical report of fisheries and aquatic sciences ; no. 1361; ISSN: 0706-6547)
Note: 3,100 entries.– Includes a taxonomic index and a subject index.– Résumé en français.
Location: OONL.

— 1986 —

5521 **Brinkhurst, Ralph O.**
The Ocean Ecology Division, Institute of Ocean Sciences: the first decade, 1976-86. Sidney, B.C.: Fisheries and Oceans Canada, 1986. v, 24 p. (Canadian technical report of hydrography and ocean sciences ; no. 72; ISSN: 0711-6764)
Note: Includes a list of research literature by staff of the Ocean Ecology Division of the Institute of Ocean Sciences.– Focus on descriptive and process oriented plankton and benthos research.– Résumé en français.
Location: OONL.

5522 **Catling, P.M., et al.**
Bibliography of vascular plant floristics for New Brunswick, Newfoundland (insular), and Nova Scotia. Ottawa: Research Branch, Agriculture Canada, 1986.

28 p. (Technical bulletin / Research Branch, Agriculture Canada ; 1986-3E); ISBN: 0-662-14627-1.
Note: Approx. 525 entries.– Includes references to floristics and phytogeography for New Brunswick, Newfoundland, Nova Scotia (including Labrador, St. Pierre and Miquelon).– Résumé en français.
Location: OONL.

5523 **Clay, D.; Kenchington, T.J.**
World bibliography of the redfishes and rockfishes (Sebastinae, Scorpaenidae). Moncton, N.B.: Fisheries and Oceans Canada, 1986. iii, 303 p. (Canadian technical report of fisheries and aquatic sciences ; no. 1429; ISSN: 0706-6457)
Note: 3,374 entries.– Listing of published material which refers to any member of the subfamily Sebastinae (North Atlantic redfishes, Pacific rockfishes) from the eighteenth century to the end of 1984.– Excludes popular, industrial and unpublished works, purely administrative reports, routine data tabulations.– Many Canadian references.– Résumé en français.
Location: OONL.

5524 **De Groot, Pieter**
Cone and twig beetles (Coleoptera: Scolytidae) of the genus Conophthorus: an annotated bibliography. Sault Ste. Marie, Ont.: Forest Pest Management Institute, Canadian Forestry Service, 1986. iii, 36 p. (Forest Pest Management Institute Information report ; FPM-X-76; ISSN: 0704-772X); ISBN: 0-662-14986-6.
Note: 91 entries.– References address aspects of biology, behaviour, control, damage, ecology, taxonomy of Conophthorus beetle.
Location: OONL.

5525 **De Groot, Pieter**
Diptera associated with cones and seeds of North American conifers: an annotated bibliography. Sault Ste. Marie, Ont.: Forest Pest Management Institute, Canadian Forestry Service, c1986. iii, 38 p. (Forest Pest Management Institute Information report ; FPM-X-69; ISSN: 0704-772X); ISBN: 0-662-14533-X.
Note: 108 entries.– References address some aspect of biology, ecology, taxonomy, or control of North American species.– Includes publications dated December 1983, or earlier.
Location: OONL.

5526 **Haeussler, S.; Coates, D.**
Autecological characteristics of selected species that compete with conifers in British Columbia: a literature review. Victoria: Information Services Branch, Ministry of Forests, c1986. vi, 180 p. (Land management report / British Columbia Ministry of Forests ; no. 33; ISSN: 0702-9861); ISBN: 0-7718-8482-6.
Note: Approx. 400 entries.– Review of ecological, silvicultural and botanical literature pertaining to the management of 31 species of plants that interfere or compete with growth of coniferous tree species: description, distribution, habitat, growth and development, reproduction, predation and pests, effects on crop trees, response to disturbance or management.
Location: OONL.

5527 **McAllister, Don E.; Steigerwald, Michèle Bélanger**
Bibliography of the marine fishes of Arctic Canada, 1771-1985. Ste. Anne de Bellevue, Quebec: Fisheries and Oceans Canada, 1986. v, 108 p.: map. (Canadian

manuscript report of fisheries and aquatic sciences ; no. 1909; ISSN: 0706-6473)

Note: 1,111 entries.– Covers the geographic region from the Alaska-Yukon Territory boundary north to the North Pole, south to and along the Canada-Greenland boundary, west to Cape Chidley and west along the Arctic coasts of Quebec, Ontario, Manitoba, Northwest Territories and Yukon Territory to Alaska, including the waters of James Bay and Hudson Bay.– Includes scientific references dealing with taxonomy, distribution, ecology, biology, physiology, fisheries, growth, age and production.– Some bird and mammal studies are included if related to fish predation.– Résumé en français. Previous editions:

Robins, Kathleen; McAllister, Don E. *Bibliography of the marine fishes of Arctic Canada.* [S.l.]: Northern Social Research Information Service, 1979. 60 p.

McAllister, Don E. *Bibliography of the marine fishes of Arctic Canada.* Vancouver: Institute of Fisheries, University of British Columbia, 1966. 16 p.

Location: OOFI.

— 1987 —

5528 **Crossman, E.J.; Casselman, J.M.**
An annotated bibliography of the pike, Esox lucius (Osteichthyes: Salmoniformes). Toronto: Royal Ontario Museum, 1987. xix, 386 p. (Royal Ontario Museum Life Sciences miscellaneous publications; ISSN: 0082-5093); ISBN: 0-88854-331-X.

Note: Approx. 3,250 entries.– Professional and popular literature from international sources.– Substantial Canadian content.– Subject index in 37 categories (age and growth studies, behaviour, food and feeding habits, physiology and biochemistry, population dynamics, etc.).

Location: OONL.

5529 **Doucet, René; Boily, Jocelyn**
Bibliographie annotée sur le marcottage de l'épinette noire. [Québec]: Gouvernement du Québec, Ministère de l'énergie et des ressources, Direction de la recherche et du développement, 1987. x, 32 p. (Mémoire / Service de la recherche appliquée, Direction de la recherche et du développement, Ministère de l'énergie et des ressources, Gouvernement du Québec ; no 90); ISBN: 2-550-17281-7.

Note: 44 entrées.

Localisation: OONL.

5530 **Ealey, David M.**
A bibliography of Alberta mammalogy. [Edmonton]: Alberta Culture, Historical Resources Division, 1987. vii, 400 p.: map. (Natural history occasional paper / Provincial Museum of Alberta ; no. 8; ISSN: 0838-5971)

Note: 3,791 entries.– Lists unpublished and published reports, articles, books relating to mammalogy of Alberta, up to and including 1985: nomenclature and taxonomy, status and distribution, extinct and extirpated species, morphology and physiology, ecology and life history, behaviour, diseases and parasites, management and conservation, pesticides and pollution.

Location: OONL.

5531 **Grewal, H.**
Bibliography of lodgepole pine literature. Edmonton: Northern Forestry Centre, Canadian Forestry Service, 1987. vi, 327 p. (Northern Forestry Centre Information report ; NOR-X-291; ISSN: 0704-7673); ISBN: 0-662-15647-1.

Note: 1,418 entries.– Papers and reports on species description and characteristics, ecology, reproductive behaviour, growth and yield, damage and effects, silviculture, forest management.

Location: OONL.

5532 **Larochelle, André**
"A bibliography of papers on Cicindelidae published in *The Canadian Entomologist*, (1869-1979)."
In: *Cicindela*; Vol. 19, no. 2 (June 1987) p. 21-33.; ISSN: 0590-6334.

Note: 88 entries.

Location: KyU.

5533 **Lavallée, Robert**
Bibliographical review of Pachypappa tremulae (L): a root aphid of conifer seedlings in containers. Sainte-Foy, Quebec: Laurentian Forestry Centre, 1987. v, 16 p.: ill. (some col.). (Information report / Laurentian Forestry Centre ; LAU-X-73E; ISSN: 0835-1570); ISBN: 0-662-15184-4.

Note: Titre en français: *Revue bibliographique sur Pachypappa tremulae (L): un puceron des racines des plants de conifères en récipients.*

Location: OONL.

5534 **Lavallée, Robert**
Revue bibliographique sur Pachypappa tremulae (L): un puceron des racines des plants de conifères en récipients. Sainte-Foy, Québec: Centre de recherches forestières des Laurentides, Service canadien des forêts, 1987. v, 16 p.: ill. (quelques coul.). (Rapport d'information / Centre de recherches forestières des Laurentides ; LAU-X-73F; ISSN: 0835-1589); ISBN: 0-662-94098-9.

Note: English title: *Bibliographical review of Pachypappa tremulae (L): a root aphid of conifer seedlings in containers.*

Localisation: OONL.

5535 **Levy, Adrian R.; Lechowicz, Martin J.**
An annotated bibliography of research at Mont St. Hilaire, Quebec/Bibliographie annotée des recherches effectuées au Mont St-Hilaire (Québec). Ottawa: UNESCO Canada/MAB Committee, 1987. 75, v p.: ill., map. (UNESCO Canada/MAB Report ; no. 18)

Note: Approx. 200 entries.– Scientific literature (journal articles, graduate theses) related to the mountain of St. Hilaire.– Topics covered include botany, geology, mineralogy, pedology, hydrology, palynology, climatology, terrestrial animal ecology and behaviour.– Includes a section on human history of the area.– Complete through 1985.

Location: OONL.

5536 **McLaren Atlantic Limited**
Revised biological literature review of Davis Strait [microform]. Calgary: Arctic Petroleum Operators' Association, 1987. 3 microfiches (164 fr.). (Report / Arctic Petroleum Operators' Association ; APOA 138-8)

Note: Previous edition: *Biological literature review of Davis Strait.* Distributed by Palliser Resource Management, [1977]. 3 microfiches (120 fr.).

Location: OONL.

5537 **Noble, Willa J., et al.**
A second checklist and bibliography of the lichens and allied fungi of British Columbia. Ottawa: National Museum of Natural Sciences, c1987. 95 p.: ill., maps. (Syllogeus / National Museum of Natural Sciences ; no. 61; ISSN: 0704-576X)

Note: Approx. 300 entries.
Location: OONL.

5538 **Westheim, G.J.; Miller, G.**
A partial bibliography of Pacific cod (Gadus macrophalus) in the north Pacific Ocean, through December 1985. Nanaimo, B.C.: Fisheries and Oceans Canada, 1987. iii, 55 p. (Canadian technical report of fisheries and aquatic sciences ; no. 1518; ISSN: 0706-6457)
Note: 391 entries.– Lists published reports, including M.Sc. and Ph.D. theses, on Pacific cod.– Subjects include taxonomy, life history ecology, exploitation, processing, fisheries management.– Excludes unpublished reports, reports containing trivial references to Pacific cod, reports in foreign language lacking English abstract or summary.– Résumé en français.
Location: OONL.

— 1988 —

5539 **Campbell, R. Wayne, et al.**
A bibliography of British Columbia ornithology. Victoria: British Columbia Provincial Museum, 1979-1988. 2 vol. (British Columbia Provincial Museum Heritage record ; no. 7; ISSN: 0701-9556)
Note: 2,100 entries.– Includes references from ornithological journals, museum publications, theses, government reports, publications of natural history societies, reports of collectors, field biologists, naturalists and consultants.– Excludes books, bibliographies, book reviews, magazine and newspaper articles, avicultural society newsletters, sportsmen publications, game-farming bulletins.
Location: OONL.

5540 **Ebbers, Mark A.; Colby, Peter J.; Lewis, Cheryl A.**
Walleye-sauger bibliography. St. Paul: Minnesota Department of Natural Resources, 1988. 201 p. (Minnesota Department of Natural Resources Investigational report ; no. 396) (Ontario Ministry of Natural Resources, Fisheries Branch Contribution ; no. 88-02)
Note: 3,116 entries.– Technical and scientific publications on geographical distribution, age and growth, community dynamics, ecology, food studies, habitat degradation, impoundments, life history, morphology, mortality, movement and migrations, population and spawning studies, stocking, taxonomy.– Excludes material from popular magazines.
Location: OONL.

5541 **Favreau, Marc; Brassard, Guy R.**
Catalogue bibliographique des bryophytes du Québec et du Labrador. St. Jean, Terre-Neuve: Memorial University of Newfoundland, 1988. 114 p. (Memorial University of Newfoundland Occasional papers in biology ; no. 12; ISSN: 0702-0007)
Note: 350 entrées.– Compilation des mentions publiées de bryophytes pour le Québec et le Labrador.– Pour chaque taxon, les références bibliographiques sont énumérées par région.– Introduction en français et en anglais/Introduction in English and French.
Localisation: OON.

5542 **Hodgson, C.A.; Bourne, N.; Mottershead, D.**
A selected bibliography of scallop literature. Nanaimo, B.C.: Department of Fisheries and Oceans, 1988. iv, 133 p. (Canadian manuscript report of fisheries and aquatic sciences ; no. 1965; ISSN: 0706-6473)
Note: 589 entries.– Covers to March 1987.– Focus on

scallop culture literature.
Supplement: Townsend, L.D., et al. ... . *Supplement 1.* 1989 iii, 87 p (Canadian manuscript report of fisheries and aquatic sciences ; no. 2031).– 305 entries.– Covers to April 1989.
Location: OONL.

5543 **Langor, David William; Raske, A.G.**
Annotated bibliography of the eastern larch beetle, Dendroctonus simplex Leconte (Coleoptera: Scolytidae). St. John's: Newfoundland Forestry Centre, 1988. iii, 38 p. (Newfoundland Forestry Centre Information report ; N-X-266; ISSN: 0704-7657); ISBN: 0-662-16689-2.
Note: 192 entries.– Includes references from original description in 1868 to 1987.– Topics include life history, damage estimates, host species, control, morphology, surveys, taxonomy.
Location: OONL.

5544 **Laubitz, Diana R., et al.**
Bibliographia invertebratorum aquaticorum canadensium. Ottawa: National Museum of Natural Sciences, National Museums of Canada, 1983-1988. 8 vol.; ISBN: 0-662-11272-5 (set).
Note: Lists research studies, reports, articles on aquatic invertebrates in Canada, freshwater and marine.– Includes materials from several different fields: ecology, fisheries, physiology, biochemistry, genetics.
Location: OONL.

5545 **Linton, D.A.; Safranyik, L.**
The spruce beetle, Dendroctonus rufipennis (Kirby): an annotated bibliography, 1885-1987. Victoria: Pacific Forestry Centre, 1988. 39 p.: ill. (Pacific Forestry Centre Information report ; BC-X-298; ISSN: 0830-0453); ISBN: 0-662-16210-2.
Note: 311 entries.– Published literature dealing with the taxonomy, biology, ecology and management of the spruce beetle.– Résumé en français.
Location: OONL.

5546 **Medin, Dean E.; Torquemada, Kathryn E.**
Beaver in western North America: an annotated bibliography, 1966 to 1986. Ogden, Utah: Intermountain Research Station, 1988. 18 p. (Intermountain Research Station General technical report ; INT-242)
Note: 206 entries.– Technical reports and papers, popular articles, with emphasis on western United States and Canada.
Location: NSHIAP.

5547 **Puls, Robert**
Mineral levels in animal health: bibliographies. Clearbrook, B.C.: Sherpa International, c1988. 334 p.; ISBN: 0-9694329-1-8.
Note: Contains listing of general reference texts, bibliographies, by element, reviewed for the compilation of the diagnostic data.
Location: OONL.

— 1989 —

5548 **Benfey, Tillman J.**
A bibliography of triploid fish, 1943 to 1988. West Vancouver, B.C.: Department of Fisheries and Oceans, Biological Sciences Branch, 1989. iv, 33 p. (Canadian technical report of fisheries and aquatic sciences ; no. 1682; ISSN: 0706-6457)
Note: 311 entries.– Taxonomical listing of publications dealing with auto- and allo-triploids (genetically sterile)

of fish that are normally dioecious diploids.– Induction of triploidy is one method to delay or prevent sexual maturation of fish used for aquaculture.– Résumé en français.

Location: OONL.

5549 **Gollop, Bernie**
"A selected, annotated bibliography for Saskatchewan butterfly watchers."
In: *Blue Jay*; Vol. 47, no. 2 (June 1989) p. 83-88.; ISSN: 0006-5099.
Note: Location: OONL.

5550 **Larochelle, André**
"A bibliography of papers published on Cicindelidae in the *Annual Reports and Proceedings of the Entomological Society of Ontario*, 1871-1987."
In: *Cicindela*; Vol. 21, no. 3-4 (September-December 1989) p. 41-47.; ISSN: 0590-6334.
Note: 33 entries.
Location: NNM.

5551 **McLean, E.J.; McLean, C.C.; Donaldson, Edward M.**
A partially annotated guide to selected fish bibliographies (1738-1988). West Vancouver: Fisheries and Oceans Canada, 1989. iv, 43 p.: ill. (Canadian technical report of fisheries and aquatic sciences ; no. 1717; ISSN: 0706-6457)
Note: 228 entries.– Listing of bibliographies dealing with fish.– Includes specialized bibliographies, focussing on individual species and families, bibliographies relating to reproduction, early life history and larval rearing, and bibliographies relating to specific geographic areas.– Résumé en français.
Location: OONL.

5552 **Robitaille, J.A.; Mailhot, Yves**
Répertoire bibliographique des poissons d'eau douce et diadromes du Saint-Laurent, 1900-1987. Québec: Ministère du loisir, de la chasse et de la pêche, Direction de la gestion des espèces et des habitats, 1989. viii, 81 p.; ISBN: 2-550-20543-X.
Note: Approx. 400 entrées.– Articles, rapports, études, documentation par famille et par espèce sur les populations de poissons dans le Saint-Laurent et les mécanismes contrôlant leur abondance.
Localisation: OONL.

— 1990 —

5553 **Haeussler, S.; Coates, D.; Mather, J.**
Autecology of common plants in British Columbia: a literature review. [Victoria]: Forestry Canada; British Columbia Ministry of Forests, c1990. vi, 272 p. (Forest Resource Development Agreement report ; no. 158; ISSN: 0835-0752); ISBN: 0-7726-1270-6.
Note: Approx. 900 entries.– Summarizes autecological (interaction between plant species and the environment) characteristics of 35 vegetation species and response to silvicultural treatments in use on forest lands in British Columbia.– Topics include distribution, habitat, growth and development, reproduction, pests, effects on crop trees, response to disturbance or management, wildlife and range.
Location: OONL.

5554 **Lapointe, Michèle**
Modalités d'ensemencement pour l'omble de Fontaine: revue et analyse critique de la littérature, rapport. Québec: Direction de la gestion des espèces et des

habitats, 1990. vi, 51 p.; ISBN: 2-550-21139-1.
Note: Localisation: OONL.

5555 **Smith, Thomas G.; Hammill, Michael O.**
A bibliography of the white whale, Delphinapterus leucas. Ste. Anne de Bellevue, Quebec: Fisheries and Oceans Canada, 1990. ii, 45 p. (Canadian manuscript report of fisheries and aquatic sciences ; no. 2060; ISSN: 0706-6473)
Note: Location: OONL.

5556 **Williams, D. Dudley; Smith, Ian M.**
Spring habitats and their faunas: an introductory bibliography. Ottawa: Biological Survey of Canada (Terrestrial Arthropods), 1990. ii, 156 p. (Biological Survey of Canada Document series ; no. 4); ISBN: 0-9692727-5-8.
Note: 1,762 entries.– Published references on the geographical, physical, and chemical aspects of springs, detailed treatment of biological subjects related to fauna (distribution, ecology, evolution, food, growth, life history, migrations, parasitism, reproduction, systematics, zoogeography).
Location: OONL.

— 1991 —

5557 **Bruner, John Clay**
Bibliography of the family Catostomidae (Cypriniformes). Edmonton: Natural History Section, Provincial Museum of Alberta, 1991. viii, 213 p. (Natural history occasional paper / Provincial Museum of Alberta ; no. 14; ISSN: 0838-5971); ISBN: 0-7732-0539-X.
Note: 2,000 entries.– Articles, unpublished and published reports, theses and dissertations, maps, books relating to living and fossil forms of the family Catostomidae, commonly called suckers.– Indexes: theses, dissertations, common names, scientific names.
Location: OONL.

5558 **Choudhury, A.; Dick, T.A.**
Parasites of lake sturgeon, Acipenser fulvescens (Chondrostei: Acipenseridae), with special reference to the coelenterate parasite, Polypodium hydriforme, in Acipenseriform fishes: an annotated bibliography. Winnipeg: Central and Arctic Region, Department of Fisheries and Oceans, 1991. iv, 15 p. (Canadian technical report of fisheries and aquatic sciences ; no. 1772; ISSN: 0706-6457)
Note: 99 entries.– Scientific studies dating from 1871 to 1990 on Lake Sturgeon parasites.– Résumé en français.
Location: OONL.

5559 **Ealey, David M.; McNicholl, Martin K.**
A bibliography of Alberta ornithology. 2nd ed. Edmonton: Natural History Section, Provincial Museum of Alberta, 1991. vi, 751 p.: map. (Natural history occasional paper / Provincial Museum of Alberta ; no. 16; ISSN: 0838-5971); ISBN: 0-7732-0599-3.
Note: 7,444 entries.– Lists books, reports, articles, society bulletins related to 352 bird species recorded in Alberta up to and including 1989.– Themes: nomenclature and taxonomy, distribution and migration, extinct birds, morphology and physiology, ecology and life history, disease and parasitology, management and conservation. Previous edition: McNicholl, Martin K., et al. Alberta Culture, Historical Resources Division, 1981. iii, 377 p. (Natural history occasional paper ; no. 3).
Location: OONL.

5560 **Freemark, Kathryn; Dewar, Heather; Saltman, Jane**
A literature review of bird use of farmland habitats in the Great Lakes-St. Lawrence region/Une étude bibliographique de l'utilisation, par les oiseaux, des habitats agricoles dans la région des Grands Lacs et du Saint-Laurent. Ottawa: Canadian Wildlife Service, 1991. [200] p. (in various pagings): map. (Technical report series / Canadian Wildlife Service ; no. 114; ISSN: 8031-6481); ISBN: 0-662-18398-3.
Note: Reviews studies conducted in Canada and the United States since 1950.– Includes scientific publications, graduate theses, government reports dealing with bird use of farmland habitats.– Text in English and French/texte en français et en anglais.
Location: OONL.

5561 **Solar, I.I.; Donaldson, Edward M.; Douville, D.**
A bibliography of gynogenesis and androgenesis in fish (1913-1989). West Vancouver, B.C.: Biological Sciences Branch, Department of Fisheries and Oceans, 1991. iv, 41 p. (Canadian technical report of fisheries and aquatic sciences ; no. 1788; ISSN: 0706-6457)
Note: 347 entries.– Includes references dealing with induced and naturally occurring gynogenetic fish (unisexual reproduction), and with induced androgenesis in fish.
Location: OONL.

— 1897 —

5562 **Bibliothèque du Conseil d'hygiène de la province de Québec: catalogue/Library of the Board of Health of province of Quebec: catalogue.** Montréal: [s.n.], 1897. 40 p.
Note: Microforme: ICMH collection de microfiches ; no 53629; ISBN: 0-665-53629-1. 1 microfiche (26 images).
Localisation: QQS.

— 1928 —

5563 **Ahern, George**
Catalogue of books: being the complete library of late Geo. Ahern, Quebec, the well-known collector of rare and valuable Canadiana and Americana medical books. Montreal: [s.n.], 1928. 124 p.
Note: Location: OTU.

— 1955 —

5564 **Gowdey, C.D.; Pearce, J.W.**
A selected bibliography of the open literature on aviation medicine, 1945-1955. Ottawa: Defence Research Board, Department of National Defence, 1955. x, 59 p.
Note: 724 entries.– Topics given special emphasis: air sickness, altitude effects, anoxia and hypoxia, decompression aeroembolism, hyperventilation, oxygen toxicity, stress and fatigue.– Excludes references to technical and project reports.
Location: OONL.

— 1957 —

5565 **Canada. Department of National Health and Welfare. Epidemiology Division**
Selected Canadian public health references of epidemiological significance. [Ottawa: The Division], 1957. ii, 75 p.
Note: Approx. 800 entries.– Contains journal articles on communicable diseases, arctic medicine, accidents, air pollution, chronic diseases, public health services.
Location: OONL.

— 1962 —

5566 **Kerr, W.K.**
Bibliography of Canadian reports in aviation medicine, 1939-1945. [Ottawa]: Defence Research Board, Department of National Defence, 1962. 187 p.
Note: 1,085 entries.– Abstracts of reports submitted to the Associate Committee on Aviation Medical Research, National Research Council, Canada.
Location: OONL.

5567 **Popham, Robert E.; Schmidt, Wolfgang**
A decade of alcoholism research: a review of the research activities of the Alcoholism and Drug Addiction Research Foundation of Ontario, 1951-1961. Toronto: Alcoholism and Drug Addiction Research Foundation, 1962. vii, 64 p. (Brookside monograph ; no. 3; ISSN: 0068-2853)
Note: Includes bibliographical references.
Location: OONL.

— 1963 —

5568 **Meagher, Heather**
The medicare crisis in Saskatchewan (January 1, 1960 – July 31, 1962): a bibliography. Regina: Legislative Library, 1963. 201 p.
Note: Approx. 7,500 entries.– Mainly newspaper articles, some pamphlets, letters, press releases, periodical articles.– Chronological arrangement.
Location: OONL.

— 1964 —

5569 **Miller, Genevieve**
Bibliography of the history of medicine of the United States and Canada, 1939-1960. Baltimore: Johns Hopkins Press, [c1964]. xvi, 428 p.
Note: Approx. 120,000 entries.– Sections include biography, dentistry, diseases, hospitals, local history and societies, medical education, military medicine, nursing, pharmacy, professional history, public health and social medicine.
Location: OONL.

— 1965 —

5570 **Canada. Department of National Health and Welfare. Emergency Health Services Division**
Bibliography relating to disaster nursing. Ottawa: Department of National Health and Welfare, 1965. 30 p.
Note: Approx. 150 entries.– Papers, books, reports produced between 1960 and 1965 dealing with topics related to disaster nursing, planning and organization, disaster experience and preparedness plans, public health nursing.
Location: OONL.

5571 **Scott, D.M.**
An annotated bibliography (revised) of research on eye movements published during the period 1932-1962. Ottawa: Department of National Defence, Defence Research Medical Laboratories, 1965. 135 p. (DRML Publication / Defence Research Medical Laboratories ; no. 591)
Note: Listing of articles dealing with techniques or methods for measuring eye movements, experimental data.– Some Canadian references.
Location: OONL.

— 1967 —

5572 **Roland, Charles G.**
"Annotated bibliography of Canadian military medical history: preliminary checklist."
In: *Medical Services Journal Canada*; Vol. 23, no. 1 (January 1967) p. 42-59.; ISSN: 0368-9204.
Note: 127 entries.– Books, medical historical papers in scientific medical journals, medical history bulletins, general history transactions and periodicals.– Focus on the period prior to 1940.– Chronological arrangement.
Location: OONL.

— 1968 —

5573 **Fortuine, Robert**
The health of the Eskimos: a bibliography, 1857-1967.
Hanover, N.H.: Dartmouth College Libraries, [1968]. 87 p.
Note: 1,150 entries.– Lists articles, monographs, books
relating to health of Inuit.– Excludes consideration of
Arctic Indians.– Only writings by physicians, nurses,
medical scientists and anthropologists are included.
Location: OONL.

— 1969 —

5574 **Vinet, Alain**
Epistémologie et sociologie de la médecine:
bibliographie. Québec: Institut supérieur des sciences
humaines, Université Laval, 1969. 51 f. (Cahiers de
l'ISSH, Collection Instruments de travail / Institut
supérieur des sciences humaines, Université Laval ; no 2)
Note: Approx. 400 entrées.– Comporte des références
canadiennes en français et en anglais.
Localisation: OONL.

— 1970 —

5575 **Billings, Fred L.**
Biotin: an annotated bibliography. Montreal: Hoffman-
Laroche Limited, 1970. 241 l.
Note: Approx. 2,400 entries.– Listing of journal articles
and theses.– Includes Canadian references.
Location: OONL.

— 1971 —

5576 **Mitchell, William Bruce**
Fluoridation bibliography: background, behavioral and
Canadian aspects. Waterloo, Ont.: Department of
Geography, Division of Environmental Studies, University of Waterloo, 1971. 25 l.
Note: Period covered: 1945-1970.– "Canadian aspects", p.
18-25, contains sources ranging from research articles to
editorials which document the diffusion of fluoridation
in Canada.– Emphasis on development of viewpoints of
dental, medical and public health officials.
Location: OONL.

— 1972 —

5577 **Barrow, Mark V.; Niswander, Jerry D.; Fortuine, Robert**
Health and disease of American Indians north of Mexico:
a bibliography, 1800-1969. Gainesville: University of
Florida Press, 1972. xiii, 147 p.; ISBN: 0-8130-0331-8.
Note: 1,483 entries.– Lists publications (mainly medical
and anthropological journals) about health and disease
in North American Indians, including Canadian and
Arctic Indians.– Excludes Inuit, Indian beliefs regarding
disease, the Indian medicine man, and various folk
remedies and medicines, anthropological studies not
related to health, statistical studies about blood types.–
Topics covered include studies on healthy individuals,
health programs for Indians, infectious agents and
diseases, neoplasms, mental health and psychiatric
disorders, pregnancy and childbirth, congenital
malformations, child health and diseases of infancy.
Location: OONL.

5578 **Canadian Nurses' Association**
History of nursing in Canada: selected references/
Histoire de la profession infirmière au Canada:
bibliographie sélective. Ottawa: Canadian Nurses'
Association, 1972. 9 l.
Note: Text in English and French/texte en français et en
anglais.

Location: OOCN.

5579 **Environics Research Group**
The seventh age: a bibliography of Canadian sources in
gerontology and geriatrics, 1964-1972/Le septième âge:
une bibliographie des sources canadiennes de
gérontologie et de gériatrie, 1964-1972. [Ottawa: Policy
Planning Division, Central Mortgage and Housing
Corporation], 1972. xvii, 290 p.
Note: 1,217 entries.– Journal articles, government
publications, conference proceedings, briefs to
governments on living arrangements, working and
retirement, attitudes and behaviour, pharmacology,
psychiatry, health and nutrition.– Text in English and
French/texte en français et en anglais.
Location: OONL.

5580 **Liste des ouvrages subventionnés: soutien apporté à la
diffusion du manuel scientifique, technique et médical
francophone dans les universités du Québec (Entente
franco-québécoise sur l'éducation).** [S.l.: s.n.], 1972.
116 p.
Note: Localisation: OONL.

5581 **Lynas, Lothian**
Medicinal and food plants of the North American
Indians: a bibliography. New York: Library of the New
York Botanical Garden, 1972. 21 p.
Note: Approx. 400 entries.
Location: OONL.

5582 **Mercer, G.W.**
Non-alcoholic drugs and personality: a selected annotat-
ed bibliography. Toronto: Addiction Research
Foundation, 1972. 77 p. (Bibliographic series / Addiction
Research Foundation of Ontario ; no. 4; ISSN: 0065-1885)
Note: 182 entries.– Studies dealing with use of and
reactions to cannabis, psychedelic (LSD, mescaline),
amphetamine, tranquillizing and narcotic drugs.–
Includes Canadian references.
Location: OONL.

5583 **Nadeau, Pierre**
Santé: bibliographie. Montréal: Conseil de développement social du Montréal métropolitain, 1972. [95] p.
Note: 355 entrées.– Rapports, études, publications
gouvernementales, recherches sur les hôpitaux, les
cliniques, les produits pharmaceutiques, l'usage des
drogues, les problèmes de la santé.
Localisation: OONL.

5584 **Palko, Michael E.**
Annotated guide to health instruction materials in
Canada. 3rd ed. Ottawa: Canadian Health Education
Specialists Society, 1972. iv, 89 p.
Note: Booklets, pamphlets, leaflets, posters, folders, etc.
on physical, mental and social aspects of health.– Criteria
for selection: application to Canadian practices, scientific
accuracy, grade suitability, reading level, availability and
cost.
Previous editions:
1967. 105 p.
1964. iii, 87 p.
Location: OOU.

— 1973 —

5585 **Adams, David W.**
Therapeutic abortion: an annotated bibliography.
[Hamilton, Ont.]: McMaster University Medical Centre,
1973. 69, xi, [13] p.

Note: Catalogue of abstracts of current papers reflecting trend of thought and practice in area of therapeutic abortion.– Some Canadian material.
Location: OONL.

5586 **Canadian Nurses' Association. Library**
Nursing and northern health services: selected bibliography/Soins infirmiers et services de santé, région du nord canadien: bibliographie choisie. Ottawa: Canadian Nurses' Association, 1973. 5 l.
Note: Text in English and French/texte en français et en anglais.
Location: OONL.

5587 **Weise, C.E.**
Solvent abuse: an annotated bibliography with additional related citations. Toronto: Addiction Research Foundation, [c1973]. x, 231 p. (Bibliographic series / Addiction Research Foundation of Ontario ; no. 5; ISSN: 0065-1885)
Note: 510 entries.– References (including theses and book chapters) dealing with aspects involved in abuse of solvents, including gasoline and anaesthetics; related material on accidental overexposure and its treatment; experimental studies on toxicity.– Includes Canadian references.
Location: OONL.

5588 **Weise, C.E.; Busse, S.; Hall, R.J.**
Teratogenic and chromosomal damaging effects of illicit drugs: an annotated bibliography with selected related citations involving the use of licit drugs. Toronto: Addiction Research Foundation of Ontario, 1973. x, 175 p. (Bibliographic series / Addiction Research Foundation of Ontario ; no. 6; ISSN: 0065-1885)
Note: Includes Canadian references.
Location: OOCC.

— 1974 —

5589 **Bard, Thérèse**
Techniques infirmières. Montréal: Centrale des bibliothèques, Centre de la bibliographie, 1974. 202 p. (Cahiers de bibliographie / Centrale des bibliothèques, Centre de la bibliographie ; no 3; ISSN: 0383-4344); ISBN: 0-88523-005-1.
Note: Approx. 1,500 entrées.– Documents textuels et audiovisuels.– Comporte des références canadiennes.
Édition antérieure: Rimouski: Éditions du CEGEP, 1971. 194 p. (Guides bibliographiques (Collège d'enseignement général et professionnel de Rimouski, Bibliothèque) ; no 6).
Localisation: OONL.

5590 **Barnes, T.H.; Price, S.F.**
Drug use and driving: a bibliography of the scientific literature on the effects of drugs other than ethanol on driving or simulated driving of automobiles, piloting or simulated piloting of aircraft, and driving-related mental and motor performance. Toronto: Addiction Research Foundation of Ontario, 1974. xvii, 106 p. (Bibliographic series / Addiction Research Foundation of Ontario ; no. 7; ISSN: 0065-1885)
Note: Includes Canadian references.
Location: OOCC.

5591 **Boisvert, Bernard D.**
Rabies: a select bibliography. [S.l.: s.n.], 1974. ii, 64 p.
Note: 900 entries.– References from journals, magazines, reports dealing with rabies: public health aspects, distribution, taxonomy, biology, ecology, morphology, economic importance in agriculture, methods and materials for control of rabies.– Some Canadian references.
Location: OONL.

5592 **Chamberlain, Jane; Sendrovich, Pamela; Turl, L.H.**
A bibliography of papers and reports published by the Defence Research Establishment Toronto (formerly the Defence Research Medical Laboratories) 1950-1971. Downsview, Ont.: Defence and Civil Institute of Environmental Medicine, 1974. vii, 350 p. (DCIEM report / Defence and Civil Institute of Environmental Medicine ; no. 74-R-1000)
Note: 939 entries.– Subjects include: personnel selection and training, applied experimental psychology, human factors engineering, physiology, toxicology, food, protection from the environment, effects of noise.– Excludes publications arising from related DRB-supported research in universities.
Location: OONL.

5593 **Douglas College**
A bibliography of basic materials in the health sciences with emphasis on nursing. New Westminster, B.C.: Douglas College, 1974. 109 p.
Note: Approx. 1,500 entries.– Includes Canadian references.
Location: OONL.

5594 **Kalant, Oriana Josseau; Kalant, Harold**
Amphetamines and related drugs: clinical toxicity and dependence: a comprehensive bibliography of the international literature. Toronto: Addiction Research Foundation, c1974. xlviii, 210 p. (Bibliographic series / Addiction Research Foundation of Ontario ; no. 8; ISSN: 0065-1885)
Note: 802 entries.– Includes Canadian references.
Location: OONL.

5595 **Russell, Phyllis J.**
Guide to Canadian health science information services and sources. Ottawa: Canadian Library Association, c1974. ii, 34 p.; ISBN: 0-88802-103-8.
Note: Reference sources, Canadian health science serials, selection sources.
Location: OONL.

— 1975 —

5596 **Canadian Nurses' Association**
Abortion: selected references/L'avortement: bibliographie choisie. [Ottawa]: Canadian Nurses' Association, 1975. 23 l.
Note: 346 entries.– Lists books, government documents, periodical articles on medical and legal aspects of abortion issue.– Includes English and French publications.
Previous edition: *Selected references on abortion/ Bibliographie choisie: l'avortement.* 1972. 12 l.
Location: OONL.

5597 **Canadian Nurses' Association**
Public relations: selected bibliography/Relations publiques: bibliographie choisie. [Ottawa]: Canadian Nurses' Association, 1975. 16 l.
Note: 227 entries.– Books and documents, periodical articles.
Location: OONL.

5598 **Canadian Nurses' Association. Library**
Geriatrics: selected references/La gériatrie: bibliographie choisie. Ottawa: Canadian Nurses' Association, 1975. 48 p.
Note: Includes English and French publications.
Location: OONL.

5599 **Canadian Nurses' Association. Library**
School health: selected references/L'infirmière en santé scolaire: bibliographie choisie. Ottawa: Canadian Nurses' Association, 1975. 15 l.
Note: Includes publications in English and French.
Location: OONL.

5600 **Dussault, Gilles**
Le monde de la santé, 1940-1975: bibliographie. Québec: Institut supérieur des sciences humaines, Université Laval, c1975. vii f., 170 p. (Cahiers de l'ISSH, Collection Instruments de travail / Institut supérieur des sciences humaines, Université Laval ; no 17)
Note: 1,562 entrées.– Comprend des études et des analyses en trois grandes catégories: les professions de la santé, état de santé de la population (statistiques épidémiologiques), l'État et la santé.
Localisation: OONL.

5601 **Warner, Morton M.**
An annotated bibliography of health care teamwork and health centre development. [Vancouver]: Department of Health Care and Epidemiology, University of British Columbia, [1975]. vii, 274 p.
Note: Approx. 900 entries.– Includes some Canadian references.
Location: OONL.

5602 **Weise, C.E.**
Behaviour modification for the treatment of alcoholism: an annotated bibliography. Toronto: Addiction Research Foundation of Ontario, c1975. xv, 275 p. (Bibliographic series / Addiction Research Foundation of Ontario ; no. 10; ISSN: 0065-1885); ISBN: 0-88868-013-9.
Note: 347 entries.– Listing of English and other language articles and clinical reports dealing with classical and operant behaviour modification therapies for the treatment of alcoholism and illicit drug addiction.– Includes some Canadian references.
Location: OONL.

5603 **Weise, C.E.; Price, S.F.**
The benzodiazepines-patterns of use: an annotated bibliography. Toronto: Addiction Research Foundation of Ontario, c1975. xiii, 197 p. (Bibliographic series / Addiction Research Foundation of Ontario ; no. 9; ISSN: 0065-1885); ISBN: 0-88868-012-0.
Note: 203 entries.– Listing of chiefly Canadian and American papers dealing with the use of a class of compounds which includes "Librium" and "Valium."
Location: OONL.

— 1976 —

5604 **Canadian Nurses' Association**
Development of basic nursing education programs in Canada: selected references/Expansion des programmes d'enseignement infirmier de base au Canada: références choisies. Ottawa: Canadian Nurses' Association, 1976. 10 l.
Note: 107 entries.– Books and documents dealing with nursing education.– Includes publications in English and French.

Location: OONL.

5605 **Canadian Nurses' Association**
Health and health education: selected references/Santé et éducation sanitaire: bibliographie choisie. [Ottawa]: Canadian Nurses' Association, 1976. 29 l.
Note: 311 entries.– Text in English and French/texte en français et en anglais.
Location: OONL.

5606 **Canadian Nurses' Association**
Health and well being of nurses with emphasis on health hazards in the nurses' work environment/Santé et bien-être des infirmières plus particulièrement sur risques en milieu infirmier. [Ottawa]: Canadian Nurses' Association, 1976. 22 l.
Note: 253 entries. Books and documents, periodical articles.
Location: OONL.

5607 **Dubé, Viateur, et al.**
Bibliographie sur la préhistoire de la psychiatrie canadienne au dix-neuvième siècle. [Trois-Rivières, Québec]: Université du Québec à Trois-Rivières, Département de philosophie, 1976. xii, 117, 5 f.
Note: Quatre sections: documents inédits (manuscrits pour la plupart: archives des hôpitaux psychiatriques, archives judiciaires); documents concernant directement les institutions asiliaires: réglements, rapports annuels, rapports des commissaires du gouvernement; documents des commissions d'enquête et les textes législatifs; articles et volumes.
Localisation: OONL.

5608 **Frankel, B. Gail; Brook, Robert C.; Whitehead, Paul C.**
Therapeutic communities for the management of addictions: a critically annotated bibliography. Toronto: Addiction Research Foundation, c1976. xvii, 204 p. (Bibliographic series / Addiction Research Foundation of Ontario ; no. 12; ISSN: 0065-1885); ISBN: 0-88868-021-X.
Note: 322 entries.– Papers, information brochures, research papers.– Themes covered include types of residents, characteristics of residents, programs, research design and evaluation.
Location: OONL.

5609 **Green, Deirdre E.; Macdonald, Maggie**
Women and psychoactive drug use: an interim annotated bibliography. Toronto: Addiction Research Foundation of Ontario, c1976. x, 177 p. (Bibliographic series / Addiction Research Foundation of Ontario ; no. 11; ISSN: 0065-1885); ISBN: 0-88868-018-X.
Note: Location: OOCC.

— 1977 —

5610 **Canada. Health Consultants Directorate**
Review of the literature on home care. Ottawa: Health Consultants Directorate, 1977. viii, 93 p.
Note: Location: OONL.

5611 **Canadian Nurses' Association**
Nursing manpower: selected references/Main d'oeuvre infirmière: références choisies. [Ottawa]: Canadian Nurses' Association, 1977. 28 l.
Note: 204 entries.– Books, documents, periodical articles on nursing supply and demand.
Previous edition: *Selected references with annotations for study of nurse manpower requirements/Références choisies avec annotations pour l'étude des besoins de main-d'oeuvre infirmière. 1973. 15 l.*

Location: OONL.

5612 **Huffman, James; Huffman, Sybil**
Occupations in medicine and health. Toronto: Guidance Centre, Faculty of Education, University of Toronto, c1977. 29 p. (Career information: a bibliography of publications about careers in Canada ; book 1); ISBN: 0-7713-0048-4.
Note: Approx. 280 entries.– Books, chapters of books, pamphlets, information sheets pertaining to medical occupations: physicians, dentists, veterinarians, nurses, medical technicians, pharmacists, physiotherapists.– Text in English and French/texte en français et en anglais.
Location: OONL.

— 1978 —

5613 **Canadian Hospital Association. Library**
The health administrator's library: comprehensive bibliography of the materials available in the Canadian Hospital Association Library. Ottawa: Canadian Hospital Association, c1978. 144 p.; ISBN: 0-919100-15-5.
Note: 1,166 entries.– Classified list of books, theses, reports on hospitals and hospital administration, with listings for audio-visual materials and journals.
Location: OONL.

5614 **Canadian Nurses' Association**
Community health services with emphasis on the nurses' role, including mental health aspect: selected references/ Services communautaires de santé avec insistence [sic] particulière sur le rôle de l'infirmière, à l'inclusion de l'aspect de la santé mentale: bibliographie sélective. Ottawa: Canadian Nurses' Association, 1978. 43 p.
Note: Includes English and French publications.
Location: OONL.

5615 **Canadian Nurses' Association**
Occupational health nursing: selected references/ L'infirmière d'entreprise: soins en médecine du travail: bibliographie choisie. Ottawa: Canadian Nurses' Association, 1978. 27 p.
Note: 365 entries.– Books, documents and periodical articles dealing with industrial nursing.– Includes English and French publications.– Many Canadian references.
Previous edition: 1973. 22 l.
Location: OONL.

5616 **Canadian Nurses' Association**
Rehabilitation and the nurse: selected references/ L'infirmière et la réadaptation: bibliographie choisie. [Ottawa]: Canadian Nurses' Association, 1978. 24 p.
Note: 319 entries.– Books, documents, periodical articles, theses dealing with nursing role in rehabilitation of persons with physical injuries or mental disabilities.
Location: OONL.

5617 **Canadian Nurses' Association**
Selected references on Canadian Nurses' Association/ Bibliographie sélective on[sic] Association des infirmières et infirmiers du Canada. Ottawa: Canadian Nurses' Association, 1978. 4 p.
Note: Includes publications in English and French.
Location: OONL.

5618 **Thompson, Judy**
Alcohol and drug research in Saskatchewan, 1970-1978: subject index and abstracts. [Regina]: Saskatchewan Alcoholism Commission, Research Division, 1978. [38] p.
Note: Approx. 100 entries.

Location: OONL.

5619 **Torjman, Sherri Resin**
Mental health in the workplace: annotated bibliography. Toronto: Canadian Mental Health Association, 1978. iv, 78, 78, iii l.
Note: Approx. 175 entries.– Books and articles on theoretical and practical aspects of mental health in the workplace.– Includes Canadian references.– Text in English and French with French text on inverted pages.– Title of additional title-page: *La santé mentale et le lieu de travail: bibliographie annotée.*
Location: OONL.

5620 **Torjman, Sherri Resin**
La santé mentale et le lieu de travail: bibliographie annotée. Toronto: Association canadienne pour la santé mentale, 1978. iii, 78, 78, iv f.
Note: Approx. 150 entrées.– Livres et articles qui traitent des aspects théoriques et pratiques de la santé mentale sur les lieux du travail.– Comprend quelques références canadiennes.– Texte en français et en anglais disposé tête-bêche.– Titre de la p. de t. additionnelle: *Mental health in the workplace: annotated bibliography.*
Localisation: OONL.

— 1979 —

5621 **Canadian Nurses' Association**
Midwifery: selected references/Obstétrique: bibliographie sélective. Ottawa: Canadian Nurses' Association, 1979. 21 p.
Note: Approx. 275 entries.– Books and documents, periodical articles.– Includes English and French publications.– Many Canadian references.
Location: OONL.

5622 **Cunningham, Rosella**
Child abuse and family-centred care. Toronto: Faculty of Nursing, University of Toronto, c1979. 20 p. (Literature review monograph / Faculty of Nursing, University of Toronto ; 1)
Note: Approx. 60 entries.– Includes books and articles which relate to nursing practice and child abuse, and is broadened to include social and physical environment and precipitating factors in child abuse incidents.
Location: OONL.

5623 **Frank, K. Portland**
The anti-psychiatry bibliography and resource guide. 2nd ed., rev. & expanded. Vancouver: Press Gang, 1979. 159 p.; ISBN: 0-88974-008-9.
Note: Approx. 1,000 entries.– Books and articles on "political movement to free mental patients from psychiatric oppression."- Themes include: psychiatry and the law, mind control technology, psychiatry and women, alternatives to institutional psychiatry.
Previous edition: 1974. viii, 64 p.
Location: OONL.

5624 **Hamm, Carol A.**
Annotations from the literature on prevention and early intervention in mental health. Saskatoon: Saskatchewan Health, 1979. viii, 66 p.
Note: Summaries of publications from 1970-1979 dealing with prevention of mental illness and role of early intervention, including positive and negative viewpoints, role and training of service providers, service recipients.
Location: OONL.

5625 **Parkin, Margaret L.**
Index of Canadian nursing studies/Répertoire des études canadiennes sur les soins infirmiers. [Ottawa]: Canadian Nurses Association, 1979. 225, 97 p.; ISBN: 0-919108-00-8.
Note: Approx. 2,000 entries.– Includes studies done by Canadian nurses, or concerned with nursing in Canada, ranging from specific investigations to major research projects, including masters and doctoral theses, and reports by institutions, associations, and government departments.– Text in English and French/texte en anglais et en français.
Previous edition: 1974. ii, 109, 75 p.
Supplments:
Helen K. Mussallem Library. *Index of Canadian nursing research/Répertoire des travaux de recherche infirmière au Canada.* 1982. xvi, 64 p.; ISBN: 0-919108-73-3.
.... . *Supplement/... . Annexe.* 1983- .– Annual. ISSN: 0828-8186.
Location: OONL.

5626 **Storch, Janet L.; Meilicke, Carl A.**
Health and social services administration: an annotated bibliography. [Ottawa]: Foundation of the Canadian College of Health Service Executives, 1979. 112 p.; ISBN: 0-9690139-0-6.
Note: Books, articles and reports specific to Canada, anthologies, proceedings of conferences and symposia, bibliographies, case studies, periodicals, mainly from the 1970s.
Location: OONL.

5627 **Woods, Lance B.**
A bibliography of Canadian sources in gerontology, 1972-1978. Ann Arbor: Institute of Gerontology, University of Michigan, 1979. 26 l.
Note: Approx. 400 entries.– Books, articles and reports written by Canadians on topics related to aging: geriatrics, drugs and alcohol, institutional care, psychology, sexuality, social attitudes.
Location: OONL.

— 1980 —

5628 **Garant, Louise**
Revue des études sur la prévalence de la déficience mentale grave. Québec: Service des synthèses de recherche, Ministère des affaires sociales, 1980. 34 f.
Note: Inclut un nombre d'ouvrages canadiens.
Localisation: QQLA.

5629 **Jones, Phyllis E.**
Nurses in Canadian primary health care settings: a review of recent literature. [Toronto]: Faculty of Nursing, University of Toronto, c1980. iv, 26 p. (Literature review monograph / Faculty of Nursing, University of Toronto ; 2); ISBN: 0-7727-3601-4.
Note: Approx. 90 entries.– Covers 1966 to 1980.– Includes journal articles, books, reports which derive from research, demonstration or experience in Canada, focus on nurses' roles and functions, are based in primary health care settings and are written in the English language.
Location: OONL.

5630 **Purdham, James T.**
A review of the literature on health hazards of video display terminals. Hamilton: Canadian Centre for Occupational Health and Safety, 1980. 18 p.

Note: Location: OONL.

5631 **Rodgers, C.D.; Scott, Robert Nelson**
The congenital upper-extremity amputee: a review of the literature with emphasis on early fittings of powered prostheses. Fredericton: Bio-Engineering Institute, University of New Brunswick, 1980. 24 l.
Note: Literature review and bibliography (l. 18-24) on trends in initial fitting of the child amputee, age of fitting, role of parents, equipment and training.– Includes Canadian references.
Location: OONL.

5632 **Stewardson, Dawn; Thomas, Diane; Hughes, Linda**
Mirrors of the mind: a comprehensive bibliography of publications by staff of the Clarke Institute of Psychiatry. [Toronto: Clarke Institute of Psychiatry, 1980]. 164 l.
Note: Lists all books, articles, reviews published by individuals between 1966 and 1980, while on staff of the Institute.– Excluded are published abstracts of papers presented at conferences and items in press at publication of the bibliography.
Location: BVA.
Previous editions:
Stewardson, Dawn; Olley, Vanessa; Thomas, Diane. c1978. 120 l.
Stewardson, Dawn; Taylor, Elizabeth. *A decade of psychiatric issues, 1966-1976: a comprehensive bibliography of publications by the staff of the Clarke Institute of Psychiatry.* c1976. 65 l.
Location: OONL.

— 1981 —

5633 **Allard, François; Collister, Edward A.**
Bibliographie sélective sur la contribution des usagers aux frais médicaux et le ticket modérateur. Québec: Ministère des affaires sociales, Service de l'informathèque, 1981. 14 f. (Série bibliographiques / Ministère des affaires sociales, Service de l'informathèque ; no 3; ISSN: 0713-0740)
Note: Localisation: OONL.

5634 **Canadian Institute of Child Health**
Prenatal information in Canada: resources available on a national basis, 1981: major findings and recommendations. Ottawa: The Institute, 1981. xiv, 80 p.
Note: Listing of health education and public information materials intended to inform and educate the public and health professionals about pregnancy and birth.– Topics include family planning, immunization, nutrition, breastfeeding, effect of drugs and alcohol on pregnancy, birth process, preparation for parenthood.
Location: OONL.

5635 **Fraser, Doreen E.; Lloyd, Hazel A.**
The information needs of physiotherapists with a guide to physiotherapy collections for community general hospitals. Halifax: Dalhousie University Libraries, 1981. 72 p. (Occasional papers / Dalhousie University Libraries and Dalhousie University School of Library Service ; no. 13; ISSN: 0318-7403)
Note: Approx. 500 entries.– American, British and Canadian reference materials, journals, monographs, government publications.
Previous edition: *The information needs of physiotherapists in the Atlantic Provinces with suggested physiotherapy working collections for small hospitals.* 1977. 39 l.
Location: OONL.

5636 **Girard, Sonya**
Standards for medical and dental equipment and materials: bibliography/Normes traitant des produits et du matériel à usage médical et dentaire: bibliographie. [Ottawa]: Standards Council of Canada, 1981. 16 l.; ISBN: 0-920360-18-1.
Note: Lists standards in medical-dental field published by Canadian Standards Association, Canadian General Standards Board, American National Standards Institute, American Society for Testing and Materials, and International Organization for Standardization.
Location: OONL.

5637 **Hamm, Jean-Jacques**
Psychanalyse et littérature: essai de bibliographie. [Kingston, Ont.]: Association des professeurs de français des universités et collèges canadiens, 1981. 21 p. (Fascicule pédagogique / Association des professeurs de français des universités et collèges canadiens ; no 3)
Note: 159 entrées.
Localisation: OONL.

5638 **Kelso, Dianne R.; Attneave, Carolyn L.**
Bibliography of North American Indian mental health. Westport, Conn.: Greenwood Press, 1981. xxviii, 411 p.: map.; ISBN: 0-313-22930-9.
Note: 1,363 entries.– Books, government reports, scholarly articles.– Includes studies written in English of any age dealing with mental health issues related to North American Indians, Inuit and Metis.– Related subject areas include education, medicine, urbanization, foster care, religion, corrections, traditional healing.
Location: OONL.

5639 **McCardle, Bennett**
Bibliography of the history of Canadian Indian and Inuit health. Edmonton: Treaty and Aboriginal Rights Research (T.A.R.R.) of the Indian Association of Alberta, 1981. 89 p.
Note: Approx. 1,300 entries.– Selection of earlier material but focusses on period after 1968.– Comprehensive collection of historical and political references relating both to medical subjects and to mechanics of health service administration, in addition to technical material written by and for the medical profession.– Omits literature on major health issues (alcoholism and drug abuse) and influences (environmental health, poverty).
Location: OONL.

5640 **McKenzie, Donald; Collister, Edward A.**
Bibliographie sélective sur la répartition géographique des professionnels de la santé. Québec: Ministère des affaires sociales, Service de l'informathèque, 1981. 41 f. (Série bibliographiques / Ministère des affaires sociales, Service de l'informathèque ; no 6; ISSN: 0713-0740)
Note: Localisation: OONL.

5641 **Pérusse, Lyne**
Revue de littérature sur les écrans cathodiques. [Québec]: Département de santé communautaire, Hôpital du Saint-Sacrement, 1981. 81 f.; ISBN: 2-550-02265-3.
Note: Approx. 50 entrées.– Études concernant: problèmes généraux liés au travail sur écran cathodique et correctifs, l'opérateur d'écran cathodique.
Localisation: OONL.

5642 **Selected books & journals for Manitoba health care facilities.** Winnipeg: Manitoba Health Libraries Association, 1981. vi, 48 l.
Note: 245 entries.– Basic list of materials (books and journals) for small hospitals and personal care homes in Manitoba.
Location: OONL.

5643 **Vallée, Jacqueline; Allard, François**
Bibliographie sélective sur les actes médicaux inutiles. [Québec]: Ministère des affaires sociales, Service de l'informathèque, 1981. 18 f. (Série bibliographiques / Ministère des affaires sociales, Service de l'informathèque ; no 7)
Note: Localisation: OONL.

5644 **Visual display terminals: a selected bibliography/Les écrans cathodiques: une bibliographie sélective.** Hamilton, Ont.: Canadian Centre for Occupational Health and Safety, 1981. 29 p.; ISBN: 0-660-52253-5.
Note: Approx. 325 entries.– Books, reports, studies, periodical articles, newspaper articles published between 1956 and 1981, with emphasis on occupational health aspects.
Location: OONL.

— 1982 —

5645 **Crowhurst, Christine Marie; Kumer, Bonnie Lee**
Infant feeding: an annotated bibliography. Toronto: Nutrition Information Service, Ryerson Polytechnical Institute, 1982. 154 p.; ISBN: 0-919351-06-9.
Note: Approx. 700 entries.– Books, pamphlets, periodical articles, audio-visual material, mainly published since 1977, relating to infant feeding.– Inclusion is based on two criteria: definition of infancy as the first year of life and nutrition of the normal healthy infant.– Includes Canadian references.
Location: NFSM.

5646 **Dworaczek, Marian**
Health and safety of visual display terminals: a bibliography. Toronto: Ontario Ministry of Labour Library, 1982. 32 l. (Bibliographical guides to the sciences ; no. 5)
Note: 498 entries.– Some Canadian references.
Location: OONL.

5647 **Groupe de travail sur la surveillance de la santé et de la sécurité dans les laboratoires**
La santé et la sécurité dans les laboratoires: une étude de la documentation. Ottawa: Santé et bien-être social Canada, 1982. v, 46 p.
Note: 153 entrées.– Papiers sur les aspects médicaux et sanitaires, substances cancérogènes, radiation, produits chimiques, microbiologie, aspects de la sécurité dans les laboratoires.
English title: *Health and safety of laboratory workers in Canada: a review of the literature.*
Localisation: OONL.

5648 **McLaughlin, W. Keith**
Health and safety aspects of visual display terminals: a comprehensive bibliography. Edmonton: Occupational Health and Safety Library, Alberta Workers' Health, Safety and Compensation, [1982]. 28 l. (Occupational health and safety bibliographic series ; no. 7)
Note: Approx. 425 entries.
Location: OONL.

5649 **Working Group on Health Surveillance and Laboratory Safety (Canada)**
Health and safety of laboratory workers in Canada: a review of the literature. Ottawa: Health and Welfare

Canada, 1982. iii, 43 p.

Note: 153 entries.– Papers dealing with health and medical aspects, carcinogens, chemicals, radiation, microbiology, general aspects of laboratory safety.
Titre en français: *La santé et la sécurité dans les laboratoires: une étude de la documentation.*
Location: OONL.

— 1983 —

5650 **Association du Québec pour les déficients mentaux**
Répertoire audio-scripto-visuel en déficience mentale: bibliographie, documentation, ressources. Montréal: Association du Québec pour les déficients mentaux, 1983. 1 vol. (en pagination multiple).
Note: Localisation: QRCN.

5651 **Garant, Louise**
Habitudes de vie et santé: revue de la recherche. Québec: Gouvernement du Québec, Ministère des affaires sociales, 1983. 108 p. (Évaluation des programmes / Gouvernement du Québec, Ministère des affaires sociales ; 11)
Note: Localisation: OONL.

5652 **Kalant, Oriana Josseau, et al.**
Cannabis: health risks: a comprehensive annotated bibliography (1844-1982). Toronto: Addiction Research Foundation, 1983. xxxiv, 1100 p. (Bibliographic series / Addiction Research Foundation of Ontario ; no. 16; ISSN: 0065-1885); ISBN: 0-88868-081-3.
Note: 1,719 entries.– Focus on disturbances of behaviour, psychiatric complications, and development of tolerance.– Includes Canadian references.
Location: OONL.

5653 **Miller, Alan V.**
Gays and acquired immune deficiency syndrome (AIDS): a bibliography. Toronto: Canadian Gay Archives, 1983. ii, 67 l. (Canadian Gay Archives publication ; no. 7); ISBN: 0-9690981-0-7.
Note: Approx. 300 entries.– Covers to November 1982.
Location: OONL.

5654 **Morse, Janice M.; Tylko, Suzanne; English, Jennifer**
Canadian cultures and health bibliography. Edmonton: University of Alberta, Faculty of Nursing, 1983. 16 l.
Note: Listing of reports, studies, articles, theses dealing with health issues of Canadian native peoples and cultural minorities.
Location: AEUB.

5655 **Ottawa Public Library**
Medical information/Renseignements médicaux. [Ottawa]: The Library, 1983. 15 p.
Note: Approx. 50 entries.– Medical dictionaries and encyclopedias published between 1970 and 1982.
Location: OONL.

5656 **Royal College of Physicians and Surgeons of Canada**
Library and archival holdings in the Roddick Room, 1983/Contenu de la bibliothèque et archives dans la salle Roddick, 1983. [Ottawa]: The College, [1983]. 206 p.
Note: Books, pamphlets and reprints, journals in the Royal College Library collection on all branches of medicine, biography, hospitals, bibliographies.
Location: OONL.

— 1984 —

5657 **Association québécoise de gérontologie**
Répertoire des recherches gérontologiques publiées ou en cours (1977-1982). [Montréal]: L'Association, 1984. ii, 33 l.
Note: 129 entrées.– Livres, articles, rapports sur alimentation, demographie, hébergement, santé et problèmes de santé, services et soins, évaluation, éducation de la population âgée, programmes.
Localisation: OONL.

5658 **Evans, Judith E.M.**
Back injury prevention: a literature survey and compendium of programs and resources. [Edmonton]: Alberta Worker's Health, Safety and Compensation, Occupational Health and Safety Division, 1984. iii, 101 p.
Note: Reviews literature on back injury prevention strategies; describes work-related back injury prevention programs sponsored by organizations in Alberta, with listing of resource literature (books, pamphlets, booklets).– Many Canadian references.
Location: OONL.

5659 **Hôpital Rivière-des-Prairies. Bibliothèque du personnel**
Prévention en santé mentale: bibliographie annotée. Montréal: Service audio-visuel, Hôpital Rivière-des-Prairies, 1984. 42 p.
Note: 147 entrées.– Comporte des références canadiennes en français et en anglais.
Localisation: OONL.

5660 **Lemoine, Réjean**
"Les brochures publiées au XIXe siècle afin de lutter contre le choléra: essai bibliographique."
Dans: *Cahiers du livre ancien du Canada français*; Vol. 1, no 2 (été 1984) p. 35-41; ISSN: 0822-4315.
Note: 27 entrées.– Liste des brochures publiées au Québec, ou concernant le Québec, sur le choléra asiatique (1832-1893).
Localisation: OONL.

5661 **McDowell, Marilyn E., et al.**
Northern food habits, nutrition and health: an annotated bibliography. Halifax: Mount Saint Vincent University, 1984. 80 p.
Note: Approx. 250 entries.– Articles from scholarly and professional journals, and conference papers dealing with nutrition and health in northern Canada.– Topics include indigenous foods and diet, medical assessment, nutrition assessment, nutrition and health education.
Location: OONL.

5662 **Picot, Jocelyne; Roberts, Judy**
A Canadian telehealth sourcebook/Recueil de références sur la télésanté au Canada. Ottawa: Canadian Hospital Association, c1984. 98 l.
Note: List and description of health telecommunications projects with Canadian focus.– Includes bibliographic references.– Text in English and French/texte en français et en anglais.
Location: OOCO.

5663 **Richardson, Judith A.**
Mental health and aging: an annotated bibliography. Winnipeg: Centre on Aging, University of Manitoba, c1984. viii, 292 p.; ISBN: 0-920421-00-8.
Note: Approx. 900 entries.– Non-physiological, non-biological literature on mental health and illness, focussing on the elderly.
Location: OONL.

5664 **Roland, Charles G.**
Secondary sources in the history of Canadian medicine: a bibliography. Waterloo, Ont.: Hannah Institute for the History of Medicine, 1984. xxiii, 190 p.; ISBN: 0-88920-182-X.
Note: Approx. 26,000 entries.– Books, book chapters, journal and magazine articles, pamphlets, brochures and theses.– Extensive biographical listings, including obituaries.– Excludes most works on history of dentistry, pharmacy, nursing.
Location: OONL.

5665 **Service de diffusion sélective de l'information de la Centrale des bibliothèques**
L'Avortement. Montréal: Le Service, 1984. 41 p. (DSI/CB ; no 54; ISSN: 0825-5024); ISBN: 2-89059-254-5.
Note: 144 entrées.– La période couverte est de 1970 à 1984.– Volumes, articles de périodiques, documents audiovisuels.
Localisation: OONL.

5666 **The silent epidemic: childhood injuries: Canadian statistics (1978-82) and a selected bibliography of recent literature.** 2nd ed. Ottawa: Canadian Institute of Child Health, 1984. ii, 54 p.
Note: Approx. 600 entries.– Topics include general and background articles and papers on epidemiology, methodology, injuries and child development, prevention of childhood injuries, literature on specific types of childhood accidents and injuries, including motor vehicle, poisoning, burns, suffocation, drowning, sports and playground injuries, falls, animal bites, etc.
Previous edition: ... : *Canadian statistics (1977-81) and a selected bibliography of recent literature.* 1983. ii, 43 p.
Location: OONL.

— 1985 —

5667 **Anglin, Lise**
Cocaine: a selection of annotated papers from 1880 to 1984. Toronto: Addiction Research Foundation of Ontario, c1985. xxvi, 223 p. (Bibliographic series / Addiction Research Foundation of Ontario ; no. 19; ISSN: 0065-1885); ISBN: 0-88868-114-3.
Note: 277 entries.– Papers in English, French and German dealing with health effects of recreational use of cocaine.– Some Canadian references.
Location: OONL.

5668 **Frank, Jackie; Schonfield, David**
The running Canadian bibliography: a consolidation, 1978-1984/Bibliographie courante d'ouvrages canadiens: une consolidation, 1978-1984. Winnipeg: Canadian Association on Gerontology, [1985]. 1 vol. (in various pagings).
Note: Text in English and French/texte en français et en anglais.
Location: QQLA.

5669 **McLeod, Donald W.; Miller, Alan V.**
Medical, social & political aspects of the acquired immune deficiency syndrome (AIDS) crisis: a bibliography. Toronto: Canadian Gay Archives, c1985. iii, 314 p. (Canadian Gay Archives publication ; no. 10); ISBN: 0-9690981-2-X.
Note: Approx. 4,500 entries.– Covers April 1983 to September 1984.– Books, newspaper and periodical articles, pamphlets, unpublished works (conference papers), flyers, press releases.– Arranged in three

sections: "Medical Press," "Mainstream Press," "Gay Press."
Location: OONL.

5670 **Tari, Andor J.; Clewes, Janet L.; Semple, Shirley J.**
Annotated bibliography of autism, 1943-1983. Guelph: Ontario Society for Autistic Children, 1985. 454 p.; ISBN: 0-88955-035-2.
Note: 1,259 entries.– Comprehensive annotated listing of all published scientific articles on autism from 1943-1983, books with specific focus on autism, scientific and popular.
Location: OONL.

— 1986 —

5671 **Hunter, Isabel; Wotherspoon, Shelagh**
A bibliography of health care in Newfoundland. St. John's, Nfld.: Faculty of Medicine, Memorial University of Newfoundland, c1986. [158] p. (Occasional papers in the history of medicine ; no. 6); ISBN: 0-88901-113-3.
Note: 841 entries.– Books, articles, papers related to sickness and health, patients and caregivers, medical institutions in Newfoundland and Labrador for the years 1878 to 1984.– Excludes archival material, government documents, submissions, briefs to and reports of royal commissions, annual reports, statutes, directories, labour agreements, bylaws, obituaries.
Location: OONL.

5672 **Meiklejohn, Christopher; Rokala, D.A.**
The native peoples of Canada: an annotated bibliography of population biology, health, and illness. Ottawa: Canadian Museum of Civilization, National Museums of Canada, 1986. vi, 564 p. (Canadian Museum of Civilization Mercury series: Archaeological Survey of Canada paper ; no. 134; ISSN: 0317-2244)
Note: Approx. 2,100 entries.– Books, professional journal articles, reports, studies pertaining to the study of population biology, health and illness of native North Americans.– Topics include diseases, demography, dentition, ethnobotany, fitness, genetics, health care, mental health, mortality, nutrition, tuberculosis.
Location: OONL.

5673 **Wieler, Anne H.**
Gerontological resources: a reference. Ottawa: Medical Services Branch, Indian & Inuit Health Services, 1986. 36 p.
Note: Location: OONHM.

— 1987 —

5674 **Gelmon, Sherril B.; Fried, Bruce**
Multi-institutional arrangements and the Canadian health system. Ottawa: Canadian Hospital Association, 1987. v, 107 p.; ISBN: 0-919100-50-3.
Note: Approx. 200 entries.– Lists articles and documents with relevance to Canadian health services scene: multi-institutional development, governance of multi-institutional arrangements, strategy and structure, collaborative relationships, human resources, research issues, the Canadian experience.
Location: OONL.

5675 **University of Windsor. Data Bank Research Group**
An annotated bibliography of studies related to health in Windsor and Essex County, 1977-1987. Windsor, Ont.: Data Bank Research Group, c1987. ii, 79 l.
Note: 67 entries.– Municipal and federal studies, theses, journal articles, Health Council Task Force reports

pertaining to status of current health services, epidemiology of selected diseases/illnesses, aspects of mental and environmental health.– Excludes newspaper articles.
Location: OW.

— 1988 —

5676 **Annotated bibliography on reproductive health hazards in the workplace in Canada.** [Ottawa]: Women's Bureau, Labour Canada, c1988. 74 p.; ISBN: 0-662-16236-6.
Note: 120 entries.– Lists books, articles, reports, speeches, pamphlets, background papers (published and unpublished), primary research (published or in progress), legal decisions and cases instituted, legislation and regulations relating to safeguarding reproductive health.– Emphasis on Canadian material, 1980 to February 1987, and relevant legal cases, 1970 to 1987.– Includes social, legal, medical, economic, scientific and political research.
Titre en français: *Les risques pour la reproduction inhérants au milieu de travail au Canada: bibliographie annotée.*
Location: OONL.

5677 **Canadian Task Force on Mental Health Issues Affecting Immigrants and Refugees**
Review of the literature on migrant mental health. [Ottawa]: Multiculturalism and Citizenship Canada, c1988. ii, 51 p.; ISBN: 0-662-16393-1.
Note: Approx. 250 entries.– Reviews studies on mental health of immigrants and refugees, from emotional well-being, to psychological distress, to psychiatric disorders, as well as publications on mental health services (preventive programs, traditional healing practices, community treatment centres, hospital facilities).
Titre en français: *Revue des documents de référence portant sur la santé mentale des migrants.*
Location: OONL.

5678 **Groupe chargé d'étudier les problèmes de santé mentale des immigrants et des réfugiés**
Revue des documents de référence portant sur la santé mentale des migrants. Ottawa: Multiculturalisme et citoyenneté Canada, c1988. iii, 55 p.; ISBN: 0-662-95221-9.
Note: Approx. 250 entrées.– Documents de référence sur l'état de santé mentale des immigrants et des réfugiés, et sur les services de santé mentale.
English title: *Review of the literature on migrant mental health.*
Localisation: OONL.

5679 **Hayhurst, K.; Gutman, G.M.; Cooper, Mary**
Non-medical aspects of Alzheimer's disease and related disorders: a comprehensive bibliography, 1960-1988. Burnaby, B.C.: Gerontology Research Centre, Simon Fraser University, 1988. [12], 309 p.; ISBN: 0-86491-072-X.
Note: Approx. 1,600 entries.– Books, articles, theses and dissertations published in English.– Emphasis on non-medical aspects of dementia: research concerned with development and evaluation of programs, facilities and services designed to enhance functional status and quality of life of Alzheimer's victims and caregivers.– Topics include symptoms, assessment, diagnosis, stages of deterioration, case studies, epidemiology, etiology, health care system, treatment and management, environmental design, caregiver support, education, legal/ethical/research issues.

Location: OONL.
5680 **Marks, S.**
Radon epidemiology: a guide to the literature. Washington, D.C.: U.S. Department of Energy, Office of Health and Environmental Research, 1988. iii, 136 p.
Note: Includes Canadian references.
Location: OOCM.

5681 **Ontario. Ministry of Community and Social Services. Children's Services Branch**
Ontario Child Health Study: abstracts of research reports and literature reviews. Toronto: The Ministry, c1988. v, 21 p.
Note: Location: NBFU.

5682 **Paradis, André; Naubert, Hélène**
Recension bibliographique: les maladies infectieuses dans les périodiques médicaux québécois du XIXe siècle. [Trois-Rivières, Québec]: Centre de recherche en études québécoises, Université du Québec à Trois-Rivières, [1988]. 237 p.
Note: 2,816 entrées.– La période couverte est de 1826 à 1900.– Périodiques médicaux, rapports de comités, monographies médicales, séances de sociétés, éditoriaux, lettres, d'enseignements cliniques.– La dimension clinique et scientifique des maladies infectieuses, la dimension sociale et institutionnelle de la maladie: législation, encadrement hospitalier, mobilisation administrative et stratégies d'intervention sociale.
Localisation: OONL.

5683 **Les risques pour la reproduction inhérants au milieu de travail au Canada: bibliographie annotée.** Ottawa: Bureau de la main-d'oeuvre féminine, Travail Canada, c1988. 84 p.; ISBN: 0-662-94929-3.
Note: 120 entrées.– Couvre: depuis 1980.– Inclut livres, articles et autres documents, y compris rapports, allocutions, brochures et documents d'information (publiés ou inédits), travaux de recherche fondamentale publiés ou en cours, jurisprudence et litiges intentés, lois et règlements visant la protection d'une saine reproduction.
English title: *Annotated bibliography on reproductive health hazards in the workplace in Canada.*
Localisation: OOF.

5684 **Service de diffusion sélective de l'information de la Centrale des bibliothèques**
Les MTS: les maladies transmises sexuellement, sauf le SIDA. Montréal: Le Service, 1988. 20 p. (DSI/CB ; no 113; ISSN: 0825-5024); ISBN: 2-89059-319-3.
Note: 158 entrées.– Monographies, articles de périodiques, articles du journal *La Presse*, documents audiovisuels sur les maladies: herpès génital, syphilis, chlamydia.
Localisation: OONL.

— 1989 —

5685 **British Columbia Library Association**
Self health: a resource guide for healthy living. Vancouver: British Columbia Library Association, 1989. 69 p.
Note: Location: OONL.

5686 **Desjardins, Joëlle**
Privatisation des services de santé, 1985-1988: bibliographie sélective et annotée. Québec: Bibliothèque de l'Assemblée nationale, Division de la référence parlementaire, 1989. 13 p. (Bibliographie / Bibliothèque

de l'Assemblée nationale du Québec ; no 20; ISSN: 0836-9100)
Note: Localisation: OONL.

5687 **Dutil, Élisabeth; Filiatrault, Johanne; Arsenault, A. Bertrand**
Répertoire d'évaluations des fonctions sensori-motrices chez l'hémiplégique. [Montréal]: Centre de recherche, Institut de réadaptation de Montréal, [c1989]. 16 f.
Note: Approx. 75 entrées.
Localisation: OONL.

5688 **Fagnan, Vivianne M.**
Edentulousness: a bibliography of published reports, surveys and analyses of rates and trends of complete and partial edentulousness and of personnel requirements to satisfy the needs of the edentate in North American, Western European and other populations. Sherwood Park, Alta.: Alberta Denturist Society, 1989. vi, 30 p.
Note: 112 entries.– Covers 1960-1989.– Articles, monographs, reports and surveys on tooth loss and manpower requirements to serve future denture needs.– Includes a number of Canadian references.
Location: OONL.

5689 **Health help: children's health information: a guide to national resources.** Ottawa: Canadian Association of Paediatric Hospitals, 1989. vi, 93 p.
Note: Approx. 450 entries.– Books, pamphlets, booklets, factsheets, posters, videotapes related to health of children from conception to sixteen years.– Subjects include AIDS, asthma, cancer and leukemia, child abuse, eating disorders, ileitis and colitis, nutrition, safety, sudden infant death syndrome.
Location: OONL.

5690 **Lamothe, Emélie S.**
Literature review of the studies on uptake, retention and distribution of radionuclides by the foetus. Ottawa: Atomic Energy Control Board, 1989. 23 p.
Note: 62 entries.– Summarizes available literature from about 1970 to 1987 dealing with studies on uptake, retention and distribution of radionuclides by an embryo or foetus following maternal intakes.– Résumé en français.
Location: OONL.

5691 **Messely, Maryse**
Les Nouvelles technologies de la reproduction: bibliographie sélective par sujets. Québec: Centre de documentation, Conseil du statut de la femme, 1989. 79 p.; ISBN: 2-550-19791-7.
Note: Approx. 300 entrées.– Articles de périodiques publiés depuis 1984 au Québec, au Canada et à travers le monde.– Principaux thèmes traités: insémination artificielle, nouvelles technologies de reproduction, bioéthique, diagnostic prénatal, droits du foetus, fécondation in vitro.– Comprend des publications en français et en anglais.
Édition antérieure: 1987. 68 p.; ISBN: 2-550-17754-1.
Localisation: OONL.

5692 **New Brunswick. Legislative Library**
Health care costs/Le coût des soins médicaux. Fredericton: New Brunswick Legislative Library, 1989. 8 l. (Bibliography / New Brunswick Legislative Library)
Note: Includes publications in English and French.
Location: OONL.

5693 **Scott, Robert Nelson; Childress, D.S.**
A bibliography on myoelectric control of prostheses. Fredericton: Institute of Biomedical Engineering, University of New Brunswick, 1989. iii, 26 p. (UNB monographs on myoelectric prostheses ; no. 3); ISBN: 0-920114-51-2.
Note: Approx. 400 entries.– Contains material up to and including 1985.– Includes Canadian references.
Location: OONL.

— 1990 —

5694 **Flemming, Tom; Kent, Diana**
Sourcebook of Canadian health statistics. Toronto: Canadian Health Libraries Association, 1990. vi, 100 p.; ISBN: 0-9692171-2-9.
Note: 129 entries.– Publications providing statistical information about health and health care in Canada.– Categories include vital and hospital morbidity statistics, chronic conditions and life style concerns, health care expenditures, health personnel, journal literature.
Location: OONL.

5695 **Hospital governance: an annotated bibliography from Canadian sources in the English language, 1980-1989.** Don Mills, Ont.: Ontario Hospital Association, c1990. 56 p.; ISBN: 0-88621-142-5.
Note: Approx. 150 entries.– Books, journal articles, government reports on the subject of the function of the hospital trustee in Canadian institutions: relationships with medical staff, with the community, with the government; trustee education and board development, board maintenance, duties of the trustee.
Location: OONL.

5696 **Ketilson, Lou Hammond; Quennell, Michael**
Community-based models of health care: a bibliography. Saskatoon: Centre for the Study of Co-operatives, University of Saskatchewan, 1990. 49 p.
Note: Location: OONL.

5697 **Lamping, Donna L.**
Review of the literature on HIV infection and mental health. [Ottawa]: Health and Welfare Canada, 1990. iv, 66, 51, v, 2 p.; ISBN: 0-662-57720-5.
Note: Approx. 300 entries.– References cited include theoretical and conceptual works, clinical findings, case reports, empirical studies, methodological contributions.– Topics covered include mental health issues relevant to persons with HIV infection (sources of psychosocial stress, psychosocial stages and consequences of HIV infection); mental health issues relevant to other persons affected by HIV infection (caregivers, etc.), mental health services for persons infected with HIV, models of care.– Text in English and French with French text on inverted pages.– Title of additional title-page: *Revue de la documentation sur l'infection à VIH et la santé mentale.*
Location: OONL.

5698 **Lamping, Donna L.**
Revue de la documentation sur l'infection à VIH et la santé mentale. [Ottawa]: Santé et Bien-être social Canada, 1990. 2, v, 51, 66, iv p.; ISBN: 0-662-57720-5.
Note: Approx. 300 entrées.– Les références citées comprennent des ouvrages théoriques et conceptuels, des données cliniques, des rapports de cas, des études empiriques et des documents méthodologiques.– Trois sections: "Problèmes de santé mentale spécifiques aux personnes affectées par l'infection à VIH;" "Interventions

en santé mentale auprès des personnes affectées par l'infection à VIH;" "Modèles de soins."- Texte en français et en anglais disposé tête-bêche.- Titre de la p. de t. additionnelle: *Review of the literature on HIV infection and mental health.*

Localisation: OONL.

5699 **New reproductive technologies: a bibliography.** Winnipeg: Manitoba Advisory Council on the Status of Women, 1990. 26 p.

Note: Approx. 300 entries.- Books, periodical and newspapers articles, unpublished papers, government documents on medical/health, sociological/psychological, ethical and legal aspects of reproductive technologies.- In addition to Manitoba Advisory Council bibliography, appended lists include:
1. Overall, Christine. *Reproductive technologies and their social significance.*
2. Eichler, Margrit. *Bibliographic list: reproductive technologies.*
3. Women's Health Clinic. *A brief bibliography concerning the new reproductive technologies and their social significance.*
4. *CRIAW National Clearinghouse on New Reproductive Technologies: list of materials received to August 24, 1987.*
5. *Reproductive technologies: materials from FINRRAGE.*

Location: OONL.

5700 **Sproat, Bonnie; Feather, Joan**
Northern Saskatchewan health research bibliography. 2nd ed. Saskatoon: Northern Medical Services, Department of Family Medicine, University of Saskatchewan, c1990. x, 152 p.; ISBN: 0-88880-240-4.

Note: Collection of reports of scientific research, policy analysis and critical inquiry, published or unpublished.- Focus on communities, situations or health-related issues specific to northern Saskatchewan.- Health means clinical, medical or community health, epidemiology and health service studies, as well as social factors affecting health: economy, housing, employment, culture or education.

Previous edition: Feather, Joan. 1987. 76 p.

Location: OONL.

— 1991 —

5701 **Fitzpatrick, Diane E.**
The history of birth control in Canada: a working bibliography. Monticello, Ill.: Vance Bibliographies, 1991. 9 p. (Public administration series: Bibliography ; P-3039; ISSN: 0193-970X); ISBN: 0-7920-0759-X.

Note: 126 entries.- Books, theses, journal articles dealing with social, economic, religious, legal, medical aspects of Canadian birth control history.

Location: SSU.

5702 **Germain, Élisabeth**
Maladies chroniques et familles aidantes au Québec: une revue de la littérature. Matane, Québec: Centre local de services communautaires de Matane, 1991. vii, 106 p.

Note: Localisation: OONL.

5703 **Granger, Denise; Lefebvre, Christine**
Revue de littérature sur les modèles et les stratégies de prestation de service communautaires offerts aux personnes âgées en perte d'autonomie fonctionnelle et mentale et à leurs aidants naturels. Montréal: Université de Montréal, Faculté des sciences infirmières, 1991. vii, 200 p.

Note: Rapport de recherche présenté au Programme na-

tional de recherche et de développement en matière de santé, Santé et bien-être social Canada.

Localisation: OONL.

5704 **Jet lag and travel: a specialized bibliography from the SPORT database/Voyages et problèmes liés au décalage horaire: une bibliographie spécialisée de la base de données SPORT.** Gloucester, Ont.: Sport Information Resource Centre, 1991. 18 l.

Note: Text in English and French/texte en français et en anglais.

Location: OONL.

5705 **Mori, Monica**
Palliative care of the elderly: an overview and annotated bibliography. Vancouver: Gerontology Research Centre, Simon Fraser University, 1991. v, 191 p.; ISBN: 0-86491-106-8.

Note: 438 entries.- Literature review and annotated listing of journal articles and books dealing with past, present and future of palliative care in Canada and the United States.

5706 **Rokala, D.A.; Bruce, Sharon G.; Meiklejohn, Christopher**
Diabetes mellitus in native populations of North America: an annotated bibliography. Winnipeg: Northern Health Research Unit, University of Manitoba, c1991. 221 p. (Monograph series / Northern Health Research Unit, University of Manitoba ; no. 4); ISBN: 1-895034-05-1.

Note: 369 entries.- Papers and books dealing with native North American diabetes: epidemiology, prevalence, incidence, diagnosis, genetic studies, prevention and control, health care services, cultural concepts.- Indexes: author, subject, geographic and tribal.- Many Canadian references.

Location: OONL.

— 1992 —

5707 **AIDS resource directory.** Ottawa: National AIDS Clearinghouse, Canadian Public Health Association, 1992. iv, 22, 22, iv p.

Note: Books, pamphlets, reports, videos from a variety of private and government organizations dealing with AIDS.- Topics include aboriginal and northern peoples, street youth, women, epidemiology, biomedical research, treatment and caregivers, workplace issues.- Text in English and French with French text on inverted pages.- Title of additional title-page: *Répertoire de ressources sur le sida.*

Location: OONL.

5708 **Bernard, Claire**
Legal aspects of research and clinical practice with children: selected Canadian legal bibliography/ Questions de droit touchant la recherche et la pratique clinique auprès des enfants: bibliographie juridique canadienne sélective. Ottawa: National Council on Bioethics in Human Research, 1992. 15 p.; ISBN: 0-9696111-3-7.

Note: Text in English and French/texte en français et en anglais.

Location: OONL.

5709 **Harrigan, MaryLou**
Quality of care: issues and challenges in the 90s: a literature review. Ottawa: Canadian Medical Association, 1992. xv, 218 p.; ISBN: 0-92016-950-3.

Note: Location: OONL.

5710 **McClure, Lynn, et al.**
First nations urban health bibliography: a review of the literature and exploration of strategies. Winnipeg: Northern Health Research Unit, University of Manitoba, c1992. 89 p. (Monograph series / Northern Health Research Unit, University of Manitoba ; no. 5); ISBN: 1-895034-04-3.
Note: Location: OONL.

5711 **Mitchell, Alan Kenneth**
The yews and taxol: a bibliography (1970-1991). Victoria: Pacific Forestry Centre, Forestry Canada, 1992. v, 31 p. (Pacific Forestry Centre Information report ; BC-X-338; ISSN: 0830-0453); ISBN: 0-662-19896-4.
Note: Approx. 300 entries.– References dealing with cultivation, ecology, genetics, morphology, pathology, plant physiology, toxicology, taxol.– Author index.– Index of references pertinent to the Pacific Northwest.
Location: OONL.

5712 **Répertoire de ressources sur le sida.** Ottawa: Centre national de documentation sur le sida, Association canadienne de santé publique, 1992. iv, 22, 22, iv p.
Note: Livres, brochures, rapports, vidéos, affiches sur le sida.– Principaux thèmes: autochtones et populations du nord, jeunes de la rue, femmes, milieu de travail, épidémiologie, recherche biomédicale, traitement.– Texte en français et en anglais disposé tête-bêche.– Titre de la p. de t. additionnelle: *AIDS resource directory*.
Localisation: OONL.

5713 **Stinson, Shirley M.; Johnson, Joy L.; Zilm, Glennis**
History of nursing beginning bibliography: a proemial list with special reference to Canadian sources. Edmonton: Faculty of Nursing, University of Alberta, 1992. vii, 97 p.; ISBN: 0-88864-772-7.
Note: 1,001 entries.– Covers to 1991.– Emphasis on Canadian nursing history and politics.– Includes selected international sources.
Location: AEU.

5714 **Wakil, S. Parvez**
Reproduction, reproductive technologies, questions of law and ethics and the emergence of new family systems and policies in contemporary society: an annotated bibliography. Detroit, Mich.: Toronto: Farez-Savera, 1992. xiii, 66 p.; ISBN: 0-921230-03-6.
Note: Approx. 450 entries.– Monographs, periodical and newspaper articles.– Includes Canadian references.
Location: OONL.

— Ongoing/En cours —

5715 **British Columbia Medical Library Service**
Recent and recommended texts: a selective list for hospital libraries. Vancouver: British Columbia Medical Library Service, 1964-.   vol.; ISSN: 0228-0647.
Note: Annual.
Location: OONL.

Engineering and Technology

Ingénierie et technologie

— 1952 —

5716 Brodie, R.J.; O'Flanagan, J.; Anderson, M.K.
A bibliography of Canadian papers of interest in building research to June 30, 1951. Ottawa: Division of Building Research, National Research Council Canada, 1952. 43 l. (National Research Council Canada, Division of Building Research Bibliography ; no. 4)
Note: Papers selected from lists of publications issued by the Mines Branch, Department of Mines and Technical Surveys; Dominion Fuel Board; Forest Products Laboratories Division of Department of Resources and Development; National Research Council of Canada; Schools of engineering of Canadian universities.– All documents have a direct bearing on the subject of building research.
Location: OONL.

— 1956 —

5717 Brown, A.F.C.
Experimental stress analysis in the U.S.A. and Canada: a review of recent improvements in methods of stress analysis and of applications in various fields, with a classified bibliography. London: H.M.S.O., 1956. vi, 22 p. (Overseas technical reports / Department of Scientific and Technical Research ; no. 1)
Note: 107 entries.
Location: OOAG.

5718 Maclachlan, Wills
List of articles, books, and reports on electrical shock and correlated subjects. Maple, Ont.: W. Maclachlan, 1956. 98 l.
Note: Location: OTU.

— 1957 —

5719 Central Mortgage and Housing Corporation. Library
A selected list of references on cost-cutting in house construction. Ottawa: Central Mortgage and Housing Corporation, 1957. 15 p. (Central Mortgage and Housing Corporation Library Reference list ; no. 5)
Note: 173 entries.– Books, periodical articles, pamphlets pertaining to techniques of cutting costs of home building.
Location: OONL.

5720 Wachman, Constantin
An annotated bibliography on residential chimneys serving solid or liquid-fuel fired heating appliances. Ottawa: Division of Building Research, National Research Council Canada, 1957. 6 l.
Note: Location: OON.

— 1960 —

5721 Makepeace, Charles E.
The non-atomic uses of uranium: a bibliography of metallurgical abstracts. Ottawa: [s.n.], 1960. xxxvii, 165 p.: ill.
Note: Location: OONL.

— 1962 —

5722 Brearly, Anne; Warren, I.H.
Uranium nitrides: an annotated bibliography. Vancouver: Canadian Uranium Research Foundation, [1962]. 18 l.
Note: Includes Canadian references.
Location: OONL.

5723 McGill University. Mechanical Engineering Research Laboratories
Publications of the Mechanical Engineering Research Laboratories: McGill University. Montreal: McGill University, Mechanical Engineering Research Laboratories, 1962. 8 l.
Note: Location: OON.

— 1964 —

5724 Leach, Karen E.
A survey of literature on the lateral resistance of nails. Ottawa: Department of Forestry, 1964. 12 p. (Department of Forestry Publication ; no. 1085)
Note: 28 entries.– Sommaire en français.
Location: OONL.

— 1966 —

5725 Fang, Jin Bao; MacKay, G. David M.; Bramhall, George
Wood: fire behaviour and fire retardant: a review of the literature. Ottawa: Canadian Wood Council, 1966. 1 vol. (in various pagings).
Note: 395 entries.– References pertaining to ignition of wood and factors affecting ignition, thermal decomposition, analytical methods for pyrolysis studies, experimental work done on wood pyrolysis, fire retardant treatments for wood (pressure impregnation, paints and coatings), experimental treatments with various chemicals.– Includes Canadian material.
Location: OONL.

— 1967 —

5726 Hickey, Michael Daniel
A bibliography on the lateral strength of nails. Halifax: Nova Scotia Technical College, Department of Civil Engineering, 1967. iv, 37 l. (Essays on timber & timber structures / Nova Scotia Technical College, Department of Civil Engineering ; no. 23)
Note: 51 entries.– Handbooks, manuals, reports of laboratory findings.– Includes Canadian references.
Location: OONL.

— 1968 —

5727 Desai, R.L.
"Photodegradation of cellulosic materials: a review of the literature."
In: Pulp and Paper Magazine of Canada; Vol. 69, no. 16 (August 16, 1968) p. 53-61.; ISSN: 0380-2515.
Note: Location: OONL.

5728 Drennan, D.M.; Quinton, R.G.; Malhotra, S.K.
A literature survey on the application of computers to structural analysis. Halifax: Nova Scotia Technical College, 1968. 52 p.

Note: Includes some Canadian references.
Location: OONL.

5729 **Wilson, C.R.**
A review of literature on the lateral shear strength of nail-timber connections. Halifax: Nova Scotia Technical College, Department of Civil Engineering, 1968. 45 l. (Essays on timber & timber structures / Nova Scotia Technical College, Department of Civil Engineering ; no. 25)
Note: 177 entries.
Location: OONL.

— 1969 —

5730 **Davies, G.K.**
An annotated bibliography of unclassified reports issued by Defence Research Northern Laboratory, 1947-1965. Ottawa: Defence Scientific Information Service, 1969. 68 p. (Defence Scientific Information Service Report ; no. B-13)
Note: Approx. 250 entries.– Topics covered include arctic construction, atmospheric physics including auroral research, snow and ice, entomology, operational research (clothing, stoves, tents, navigation).
Location: OORD.

5731 **Heide, Cynthia**
Bibliography on technological forecasting and long range planning. Ottawa: Defence Research Board, 1969. ix, 22 p.
Note: Location: OOT.

— 1970 —

5732 **Greenshields, H.; Seddon, W.A.**
Pulse radiolysis: a comprehensive bibliography, 1960-March 1969 / Radiolyses pulsées: bibliographie complète, 1960-mars 1969. Chalk River, Ont.: Atomic Energy of Canada, 1970. ii, 62 p.; ISSN: 0067-0367.
Note: Supplements:
... , April 1969-December 1970. 1972. 42 p.
... , January 1971-December 1974. 1982. ii, 109 p.
Location: OONL.

5733 **MacFarlane, Ivan C.**
Annotated bibliography on engineering aspects of muskeg and peat (to 30 June 1969). Ottawa: National Research Council Canada, Division of Building Research, 1970. 1 vol. (in various pagings). (Bibliography / National Research Council Canada, Division of Building Research ; no. 39)
Note: Listing of books, research and technical reports, proceedings, general reports and popular articles.– Deals primarily with the origin and development, extent and distribution, geology/morphology, economic implications, classification, descriptions of specific muskeg areas, exploration and sampling, physical and mechanical properties of peat.– Additional topics include special engineering problems, road construction/ vehicles, utilization of peat, muskeg and permafrost.
Location: OON.

5734 **Searle, W.M.**
An annotated bibliography of unclassified reports issued by Defence Research Telecommunications Establishment, 1947-1969. Ottawa: Defence Scientific Information Service, 1970. viii, 206 p. (Defence Scientific Information Service Report ; no. B14)
Note: Approx. 800 entries.– Research reports produced by the Defence Research Telecommunications Establishment from 1947 to 1969, when it was renamed as

Communications Research Centre.– Topics include radar, communications, earth satellites, electricity and magnetism, radio astronomy, antennas, ionosphere and propagation.
Location: OONL.

— 1971 —

5735 **Canadian Pulp and Paper Association. Sulphite Committee**
Bibliography of multistage sulphite pulping of various wood species. Montreal: Technical section, Canadian Pulp and Paper Association, 1971. 52 p.
Note: Location: OONL.

5736 **Tibbetts, Donald Cleveland**
A bibliography on cold weather construction. Rev. ed. Ottawa: Division of Building Research, National Research Council Canada, 1971. 39 p. (National Research Council Canada, Division of Building Research Bibliography ; no. 10)
Note: Topics include buildings, highways and railways, foundations, scheduling and costs, concrete construction, brick and concrete masonry, equipment.
Previous editions:
1969. 38 l. Revised by Y. Fortier.
1965. 1 vol. (in various pagings). Revised by G.G. Boileau.
1962. 21 l. Revised by G.M. Price.
1956. 14 l. Revised by S.E. Caughey.
1955. 12 l.
Location: OONL.

— 1972 —

5737 **Dalgliesh, W.A.; Marshall, R.D.**
Research review: North and South America wind effects on tall buildings. Ottawa: Division of Building Research, National Research Council Canada, [1972]. [16] p.: ill. (National Research Council Canada, Division of Building Research Technical paper ; no. 401)
Note: 47 entries.
Location: OONL.

5738 **Hamoda, M.F.D.; Shannon, E.E.; Schmidtke, N.W.**
Advanced wastewater treatment: a selective, coded bibliography. Burlington, Ont.: Wastewater Technology Centre, Environmental Protection Service, 1972. 132 p. (Technical appraisal report / Water Pollution Control Directorate ; EPS 3-WP-73-1)
Note: 1,459 entries.– Papers, reports, articles in English for the period 1965 to July, 1972 dealing with advanced wastewater treatment processes, including adsorption, biological-chemical processes, electrodialysis, evaporation or distillation, filtration or microscreening, ionization, oxidation, sedimentation or clarification.
Location: OONL.

5739 **Heinke, Gary W.**
Bibliography of Arctic environmental engineering. Ottawa: Department of Indian Affairs and Northern Development, Northern Science Research Group, 1972. iii, 159 p.
Note: 500 entries.– Annotated listing of literature dealing with supply, distribution and treatment of water for municipal services in northern regions, with collection and treatment of waste water in the North and other problems related to environmental sanitation, municipal drainage and refuse disposal in northern regions.
Location: OONL.

— 1973 —

5740 **Bright, Norman F.H.**
Bibliography of high-temperature condensed states research published in Canada. Ottawa: Department of Energy, Mines and Resources, Mines Branch, 1960-1973. 13 vol.; ISSN: 0527-8023.
Note: Published quarterly from March 1960 to December 1972 on behalf of the Commission on High Temperatures and Refractory Materials of the International Union of Pure and Applied Chemistry; provides details of work published in Canadian scientific and technical journals.
Location: OONL.

5741 **Essai de bibliographie sur la filtration et quelques sujets connexes/Tentative bibliography on filtration and some related subjects.** Montréal: École polytechnique, Département du génie civil, Section du génie de l'environnement, 1973. 123 f.
Note: La période couverte est de 1930 à 1973.– Compilation d'articles dans diverses revues techniques publiées au Canada, aux États-Unis, et en France et traitant de la filtration et de quelques sujets connexes: coagulation, sédimentation, écoulement.– Foreword in English.
Localisation: OONL.

5742 **Johnston, H. Kirk; Lim, H.S.**
Bibliography on the application of reverse osmosis to industrial and municipal wastewaters. Ottawa: Information Canada, [1973]. iv, 117 p. (Research report / Research Program for the Abatement of Municipal Pollution under provisions of the Canada-Ontario Agreement on Great Lakes Water Quality ; no. 18)
Note: Approx. 600 entries.– Covers the period 1968-1973 (inclusive).– Résumé en français.
Location: OONL.

5743 **Larose, André; Vanderwall, Jake**
Bibliography of papers relevant to the scattering of thermal neutrons, 1963-1972. Hamilton, Ont.: McMaster University, c1973. 335 p.
Note: Includes Canadian papers.
Location: OONL.

5744 **Linell, Kenneth A.; Johnston, G.H.**
Engineering design and construction in permafrost regions: a review. Ottawa: Division of Building Research, National Research Council Canada, 1973. [23] p. (National Research Council Canada, Division of Building Research Technical paper ; no. 412)
Note: 190 entries.– Covers the period 1963-1973.
Location: OONL.

5745 **"La mécanisation de la construction: bibliographie."**
Dans: *Industrialisation forum*; Vol. 4, no 2 (1973) p. 27-34.; ISSN: 0380-3945.
Note: Localisation: OONL.

5746 **Metropolitan Toronto Library. Science and Technology Library**
Bibliography of standards. [Toronto]: Metropolitan Toronto Library Board, [1973]. 15 p.
Note: Approx. 120 entries.– Lists books relating to standards and standardizing activities.– Includes Canadian references.
Location: OONL.

5747 **Strasser, J.A.**
Roll compaction of metal powders: bibliography for period 1900 to 1973. Ottawa: Department of Energy, Mines and Resources, Mines Branch, 1973. iii, 91 p.

(Mines Branch Information circular ; IC 300)
Note: 487 entries.– Chronological listing of technical studies dealing with powder metallurgy, specifically the roll compaction of metal powders.– Avant-propos en français.
Location: OONL.

— 1974 —

5748 **Coleman, Brian**
A bibliography of the social effects of nuclear power, 1945-1973. Vancouver: Policy and Long-term Planning, British Columbia Hydro and Power Authority, 1974. [6] l., 188 p.
Note: Approx. 2,000 entries.– Sections include environment, health physics, location of nuclear power plants, radioactive wastes, reactor safety, social relations, thermal effects, transportation of radioactive materials.– Many Canadian references.
Location: OOU.

5749 **Mardon, Jasper**
Bibliography of references for Seminar on Basic Principles of Technical Papermaking: held at Lakehead University, Thunder Bay, Ontario, June 12, 13 and 14, 1974. Montreal: Technical Section, Canadian Pulp and Paper Association, [1974]. 64 p.
Note: Location: OONL.

5750 **National Science Library. Aeronautical and Mechanical Engineering Branch**
Wind power: a bibliography. [Ottawa]: National Research Council Canada, 1974. 25 l.
Note: Conference papers, books, journal articles, reports on wind energy systems.
Location: OONL.

5751 **Waters, William H.**
Bibliography: scientific papers resulting from Canadian space and upper atmosphere research, 1969-1973. Ottawa: National Research Council Canada, 1974. 87 p. (Space Research Facilities Branch Report ; 081)
Note: Previous edition: *Bibliography: scientific papers resulting from the Canadian upper atmosphere research program, 1965-1969.* 1970. (Space Research Facilities Branch Report ; 037).
Location: OTEAO.

— 1975 —

5752 **Filson, D.H.; Eyre, D.**
A bibliography of papers relevant to sanitary engineering practices in northern Saskatchewan townsites. [Saskatoon: Saskatchewan Research Council], 1975. 12 l.
Note: 29 entries.
Location: OONL.

5753 **Sault College. Library Resource Centre**
Aviation technology and pilot training program: bibliography. Sault Ste. Marie, Ont.: Sault College, Library Resource Centre, 1975. 17 p.
Note: Approx. 100 entries.– Includes Canadian references.
Location: OONL.

5754 **Stasko, Aivars B.**
Underwater biotelemetry: an annotated bibliography. St. Andrews, N.B.: Biological Station, Fisheries and Marine Service, 1975. 31 p. (Fisheries and Marine Service Technical report ; no. 534; ISSN: 0701-7626)
Note: Approx. 125 entries.– Covers from first publication in 1956 to January 1975- Includes refereed publications

and unpublished reports on underwater biotelemetry, the instrumentation and biological application of the technique of remote signalling.– Many Canadian references.– Résumé en français.
Location: OONL.

— 1976 —

5755 **Aeronautical and Mechanical Engineering Library (Canada)**
Remote handling: a bibliography. Ottawa: The Library, 1976. 27 l.
Note: Includes Canadian references.
Location: OON.

5756 **Brière, Jean-Marie**
Publications officielles canadiennes sur l'énergie atomique, la radioactivité et la sécurité: bibliographie signalétique. Montréal: Faculté des études supérieures, École de bibliothéconomie, Université de Montréal, 1976. 17 f.
Note: Approx. 125 entrées.– Les publications et documents officiels retenus dans cette bibliographie sont tous de provenance fédérale.– Thèmes principaux: l'énergie atomique et l'environnement, utilisations de l'énergie atomique, les dangers de la radioactivité, gestion des déchets radioactifs, les réacteurs nucléaires canadiens.
Localisation: OONL.

5757 **Bunn, Frank E.**
Remote sensing reflectance spectroscopy: a working bibliography. Rexdale, Ont.: Ph.D. Associates, 1976. ii, 350 l.
Note: Approx. 1,431 entries.– Journal articles, reports, books relating to reflection spectroscopy and its applications to remote sensing.– Topics covered include fundamental reflection spectroscopy, measurements of optical properties of materials, measurements on real world surfaces, interpretation of remote sensing imagery from the earth's surface, definitions, units and geometry.
Location: OONL.

5758 **Cooper, P.A.**
Waterborne preservative-treated railway ties: an annotated bibliography. Vancouver: Environment Canada, Forestry Directorate, Western Forest Products Laboratory, 1976. 12 p. (Information report / Western Forest Products Laboratory ; VP-X-143; ISSN: 0045-429X)
Note: 27 entries.
Location: OONL.

5759 **Hawaleshka, O.; Stasynec, G.**
Alternative energy: a bibliography of practical literature. Winnipeg: Agassiz Centre for Water Studies, University of Manitoba, 1976. vii, 54 l.: ill. (Agassiz Centre for Water Studies Research report ; no. 11)
Note: Listing of material dealing with practical aspects of nonconventional energy sources: biomass, geothermal, solar, wind.– Emphasis on Manitoba applications.– Includes a list of additional bibliographies.
Location: AEU.

5760 **Nadeau, Alphée**
Bibliographie de base en astronomie, astronautique, astrophysique: documents textuels avec index correspondants. [La Pocatière: A. Nadeau, 1976]. ii, 101 p.: ill.
Note: Localisation: OONL.

5761 **National Research Council Canada. Space Research Facilities Branch**
A bibliography of Canadian space science, 1971-1975. Ottawa: Space Research Facilities Branch, National Research Council Canada, 1976. 79, 42 p.
Note: Lists published papers in broad category of Canadian space and atmospheric science.
Previous editions:
Bibliography: scientific papers resulting from Canadian space and upper atmosphere research, 1969-1973. 1974. 87 p.
... , 1967-1971. 1971. 75 p.
Location: OON.

— 1977 —

5762 **Canadian Standards Association**
List of publications [Canadian Standards Association]. Rexdale, Ont.: Canadian Standards Association, 1951-1977. 26 vol.; ISSN: 0527-9771.
Note: Annual.– Ceased with issue for 1976.– Includes some text in French.
Location: OONL.

5763 **Couture, A.**
Impurity limits for cast copper alloys: a literature survey of tin bronze. Ottawa: Canada Centre for Mineral and Energy Technology, 1977. iii, 67 p. (CANMET Report / Canada Centre for Mineral and Energy Technology ; 76-37); ISBN: 0-660-00987-0.
Note: 55 entries.
Location: OONL.

5764 **Dumont, Rob**
Energy conservation in old and new buildings: bibliography. Saskatoon: College of Engineering, University of Saskatchewan, 1977. 84 p.
Note: Approx. 200 entries.– Five sections: "Heating," "Ventilation and air conditioning," "Electrical," "Insulation," "Solar."- Annotations.– Some Canadian references.
Location: OON.

5765 **McGrath, J.T.**
Literature review on fracture toughness of the heat-affected-zone. Ottawa: Canada Centre for Mineral and Energy Technology, 1977. vii, 48 p.: charts. (CANMET Report / Canada Centre for Mineral and Energy Technology ; 77-59); ISBN: 0-660-01582-X.
Note: 42 entries.– Reviews technical literature on methods available for evaluating fracture toughness of welding heat-affected zone in metals.– Résumé en français.
Location: OONL.

5766 **Skelly, H.M.**
A survey of powder forging literature, 1960-1974. Ottawa: Canada Centre for Mineral and Energy Technology, c1977. ii, 166 p. (CANMET Report / Canada Centre for Mineral and Energy Technology ; 76-38); ISBN: 0-660-00975-7.
Note: 347 entries.– Listing of articles on various powder forging techniques and procedures, utilizing ferrous and non-ferrous powders.– Includes references dealing with hot-compaction of powder into billets for subsequent forging, extruding or rolling.– Avant-propos en français.
Location: OONL.

— 1978 —

5767 **Burrage, David, et al.**
Catalogue of programs [McGill University, Computing Centre]. Montreal: McGill University, Computing Centre,

1978. 88 p.
Note: Location: OONL.

5768 **Holmes, Janet; Jones, Olive**
"Glass in Canada: an annotated bibliography."
In: *Material History Bulletin*; No. 6 (Fall 1978) p. 115-148.;
ISSN: 0703-489X.
Note: Lists material published since 1960 dealing with glass manufactured in Canada, glass used and found in Canada, focussing on tablewares, bottles, jars, stained glass, studio glass and beads.– Excludes newspaper articles, antique columns in magazines and newspapers, Canadian archaeological site reports, book reviews, articles in non-Canadian antiques magazines.
Location: OONL.

5769 **Québec (Province). Direction des énergies nouvelles**
Sommaire de la littérature disponible en français dans le domaine des énergies nouvelles. Québec: Gouvernement du Québec, Direction générale de l'énergie, 1978. 31 p.
Note: Localisation: OONL.

5770 **Swanick, Eric L.**
The Bay of Fundy tidal power project. Monticello, Ill.: Vance Bibliographies, 1978. 5 p. (Public administration series: Bibliography ; P-117; ISSN: 0193-970X)
Note: 61 entries.– Includes journal articles, government publications.
Location: OONL.

— 1979 —

5771 **Alberta Remote Sensing Centre**
Specialists involved in remote sensing in Alberta and a bibliography of remote sensing in Alberta. Edmonton: Alberta Environment, 1979. 27, [1] p.
Note: Approx. 100 entries.
Location: OONL.

5772 **Cluff, A.W.; Cluff, P.J.**
Energy conservation in hospitals: review of the Canadian and U.S. studies, programs and publications. Ottawa: Energy, Mines and Resources Canada, 1979. 198 p. (Buildings series Publication ; no. 2d)
Note: Contains an annotated bibliography of existing literature related to conservation and use of energy in health facilities: guidelines and manuals, technical papers and articles, reports on research and studies, standards for design and operation of facilities (including building codes and statistical publications).
Location: OON.

5773 **Hawley, Norma J.**
Fuel cycles: a bibliography of AECL publications. Pinawa, Man.: Atomic Energy of Canada Limited, Whiteshell Nuclear Research Establishment, 1979. 27 p.
Note: 239 entries.– Lists AECL publications from the open literature on fuels and fuel cycles used in CANDU reactors.– Chronological arrangement with subject index. Previous edition: 1983. 32 p.
Location: OONL.

5774 **MacDonald, E. Grant; Macdonald, William S.**
Fundy tidal power: a bibliography and guide to an assessment of its social impact. Halifax [N.S.]: Institute of Public Affairs, Dalhousie University, 1979. vi, 82 p.: map.; ISBN: 0-88926-019-2.
Note: Approx. 750 entries.– Contains annotated references to published and unpublished studies and reports prepared by private sector, universities and research institutions, departments and agencies of municipal, provincial, and federal governments pertaining to assessment of social, economic and community impact of tidal power.
Location: OONL.

5775 **Walli, Gary; Schwaighofer, Joseph**
A bibliography on silos: lateral pressure, field and model-measurements, theories. Toronto: Department of Civil Engineering, University of Toronto, 1979. 63 p. (Publication / Department of Civil Engineering, University of Toronto ; no. 79-05; ISSN: 0316-7968)
Note: Approx. 600 entries.– Includes Canadian references.
Location: OONL.

— 1980 —

5776 **Engineering Interface Limited**
Energy conservation in retail stores: review of Canadian and U.S. studies, surveys, programs and publications. Ottawa: Renewable Energy Branch, Energy, Mines and Resources Canada, 1980. 1 vol. (in various pagings). (Buildings series Publication ; no. 2b)
Note: Approx. 100 entries.– Annotated bibliography and critique of literature related to conservation and use of energy in the retail sector, including energy conservation guidelines and manuals, technical papers and articles, reports on relevant research and studies, standards for design and operation of facilities (including building codes and statistical publications).
Location: OOCC.

5777 **Graham, R.**
Biomass pyrolysis-gasification bibliography / Bibliographie pyrolyse et gazeification de la biomasse. Ottawa: Eastern Forest Products Laboratory, Forintek Canada Corporation, 1980. v, 17 p. (Review report / Eastern Forest Products Laboratory, Forintek Canada Corporation ; RR502FF; ISSN: 0709-4523)
Note: 274 entries.– Topics include pyrolysis/gasification chemistry, fundamental research papers, process development, engineering studies, economic analysis, catalysis, fluidization, gas purification, energy farming, industrial applications, biomass potential.
Location: OONL.

5778 **Jones, L.**
Energy conservation in schools [bibliography]. Ottawa: Division of Building Research, National Research Council Canada, 1980. 5 p. (Bibliography / National Research Council Canada, Division of Building Research ; no. 43)
Note: Approx. 65 entries.– Articles and reports on energy use and conservation in school buildings.
Location: OONL.

5779 **Ladanyi, Branko**
Literature review: field tests of foundations in permafrost. Montréal: École polytechnique de Montréal, 1980. 58 p.: ill.
Note: 103 entries.– Survey of published literature on full-scale field tests on foundations in permafrost, including footings, piles and pile groups.
Location: OON.

5780 **Townsend, Vera S.; Maydell, Ursula M.**
Computer network performance bibliography. Edmonton: Department of Computing Science, University of Alberta, 1980. 367 p. (Technical report / Department of Computing Science, University of

Alberta ; TR80-2) (Alberta Research Council Contribution ; no. 1036)
Note: Includes some Canadian studies.
Location: OONL.

— 1981 —

5781 **Armstrong, Bryan C.; Cameron, James J.; Smith, Daniel W.**
Annotated bibliography on northern environmental engineering. Hull, Quebec: Environment Canada, Environmental Protection Service, 1977-1981. 3 vol. (Economic and technical review reports / Environmental Protection Service; ISSN: 0713-9985); ISBN: 0-662-00558-9 (1974/75); 0-662-10321-1 (1976/77); 0-662-11638-0 (1978/79).
Note: 521 entries in 3 volumes.– Topics covered include air pollution, water supply, wastewater treatment, solid waste disposal, industrial camps and wastes, freeze protection of pipelines.
Location: OONL.

5782 **Haughton, E.R.; Huston, R.D.; Billingsley, W.A.**
Ethanol-alcohol from wastes: a literature review. Victoria: Province of British Columbia, Ministry of Environment, Waste Management Branch, 1981. iii, 57 p. (Report / Province of British Columbia, Ministry of Environment, Waste Management Branch ; no. 81-1)
Note: Literature review of background and current technology of ethanol production, Canadian demand for alternate fuels, options of substitution for liquid fuels.
Location: OONL.

5783 **Sanford, Cheryl**
Canadian energy-environment education bibliography. [Edmonton]: SEEDS Foundation, [1981]. viii, 54 p.
Note: Approx. 850 entries.– Annotated listing of Canadian materials (periodicals, books, films, filmstrips, slides).– Topics covered include sources of energy, how energy is produced, environmental implications of energy-production processes, energy conservation, pollution, recycling.
Previous edition: *Environmental education publications: a selective annotated listing of texts, activity guides and periodicals considered useful to teachers of environmental topics.* Alberta Environment, [1980]. 75 p.
Location: OONL.

— 1982 —

5784 **DeDuy, Anh**
Inventaire de la R&D sur l'hydrolyse enzymatique et la fermentation des matériaux lignocellulosiques en combustibles liquides et gazeux au Canada. Québec: Direction des programmes d'énergies nouvelles, Ministère de l'énergie et des ressources, Gouvernement du Québec, 1982. viii, 58 p.
Note: Localisation: OONL.

5785 **Hawley, Norma J.**
A bibliography of AECL publications on reactor safety/ Une bibliographie des publications de l'EACL sur la sûreté des réacteurs. Pinawa, Man.: Whiteshell Nuclear Research Establishment, 1982. 34 p. (AECL-6426-Rev. 1; ISSN: 0067-0367)
Note: 297 entries.– AECL reports, conference papers, journal articles on research in the field of nuclear reactor safety.– Topics include shutdown, emergency cooling and containment systems, analysis of experimental data and mathematical modelling.– Text in English and

French/texte en français et en anglais.
Previous edition: 1979. 26 p.
Location: OONL.

5786 **Stefanski, M.J.**
Characteristics and utilization of char: a literature survey. Halifax, N.S.: Atlantic Research Laboratory, National Research Council Canada, 1982. 33 p. (Atlantic Research Laboratory Technical report ; 40)
Note: 38 entries.– References from technical journals on characteristics and utilization of char as a boiler fuel, pyrolysis.
Location: OON.

5787 **Watson, M.; Sego, David Charles Cletus; Thomson, S.**
A literature review of settlement behaviour of sanitary landfills and their application to Alberta. Edmonton: Research Management Division, Alberta Environment, 1982. v, 82 p. (RMD report / Research Management Division, Alberta Environment ; RMD 81-20)
Note: Literature review of properties used to identify refuse and combined behaviour of municipal solid wastes as they relate to sanitary landfills.
Location: OONL.

— 1983 —

5788 **Berman, Gerald**
Graph theory bibliography with two level key-word index. [Waterloo, Ont.]: University of Waterloo Press, [1983]. 2 vol.; ISBN: 0-88898-046-9.
Note: 15,228 entries.– Books, papers published in refereed journals; conference proceedings to the middle of 1981.– Includes Canadian references.
Location: OONL.

5789 **Canadian Housing Information Centre**
Residential energy conservation: a selected bibliography of Canadian sources. Ottawa: Canada Mortgage and Housing Corporation, 1983. 19 l.
Note: Approx. 175 entries.– Prepared for a seminar sponsored by the Canada-United States Bilateral Program on Housing and Urban Affairs on residential energy conservation, July 26-29, 1983, Washington, D.C.
Location: OON.

5790 **Canadian steel industry factbook.** 2nd ed. Toronto: Canadian Steel Industry Research Association, 1983. 47 p.: ill.
Note: Includes a section: "Technology: recent publications (since 1977)."
Previous edition: 1980. 26 p.
Location: OONL.

5791 **Manitoba. Energy Information Centre**
Energy answers bibliography: a subject guide to the literature available at the Manitoba Energy Information Centre. Winnipeg: The Centre, 1983. [106] p. (in various pagings).
Note: Approx. 600 entries.– Lists reports, technical studies, bibliographies on types of energy generation: biomass, hydro, nuclear, solar, wind.– Additional themes include energy applications, such as commercial and industrial, agriculture, residential, energy education, heating, home construction, retrofit.
Location: OONL.

5792 **Source list of publications on housing.** Ottawa: Indian and Northern Affairs Canada, Technical Services and Contracts, 1983. 18 p. (Band technical publications)
Note: Approx. 50 entries.– Community planning, site planning and development, financial planning, house

construction (plumbing, heating, electrical wiring), home maintenance.

Titre en français: *Liste de référence des publications sur la construction domiciliaire.*

Location: OONL.

5793 **Weidmark, P.E.**
"Bibliography of Canadian contributions in the field of rock mechanics."
In: *CIM Bulletin*; (1963-1983) ; ISSN: 0317-0926.
Note: Published annually in the August issue from vol. 57 (1963) to vol. 76 (1983).– Includes published papers, university theses.
Location: AEU.

— 1984 —

5794 **Acadia University. Institute**
Bibliography on Fundy tidal power. Wolfville, N.S.: Acadia University Institute, 1984. 19 p.
Note: Location: NSWA.

5795 **Ciolkosz, A.; Baranowska, T.**
Selected annotated bibliography on application of satellite images to thematic mapping. Waterloo, Ont.: Department of Geography, University of Waterloo, 1984. x, 176 p. (Occasional paper publication series / Department of Geography, University of Waterloo ; no. 2; ISSN: 0843-7386)
Note: 380 entries.– Covers 1972-1983.– Includes papers, reports and studies related to the application of satellite imagery to thematic cartography.– Topics include geological mapping, mapping of soils, wetlands, oceans, flooding, water quality, ice and snow fields, vegetation, industrial areas.– International coverage, with a number of Canadian references.
Location: OONL.

5796 **Goodwin, C. Ross, et al.**
Cold ocean engineering bibliography. Calgary: Published jointly by the Arctic Science and Technology Information System and the Ocean Engineering Information Centre, Memorial University of Newfoundland, 1984. vi, 169 p. (ASTIS occasional publication / Arctic Science and Technology Information System ; no. 12; ISSN: 0225-5170) (C-CORE publication ; no. 84-12)
Note: 848 entries.– Contains research documents from the ASTIS database on the design, construction, and testing of structures, vessels, equipment for use on, or under the ocean: ships, offshore oil well drilling, underwater pipelines, navigation systems, ice management and control systems.
Location: OONL.

5797 **Hawley, Norma J.**
Radiation effects on living systems: a bibliography of AECL publications/Effets des rayonnements sur les organismes vivants: une bibliographie des publications de l'ÉACL. Pinawa, Man.: Whiteshell Nuclear Research Establishment, Atomic Energy of Canada Limited, 1984. 45 p.
Note: 447 entries.– Papers and reports by Atomic Energy of Canada Limited scientists concerning radiation effects on living systems: radiobiology, radiation biochemistry, radiation chemistry.– Résumé en français.
Location: OONL.

5798 **Liste de référence des publications sur la construction domiciliaire.** Ottawa: Affaires indiennes et du Nord Canada, Service techniques et marchés, 1984. 16 p.

(Publications techniques des bandes)
Note: Approx. 50 entrées.– Diverses publications sur la construction domiciliaire et les installations communautaires.
English title: *Source list of publications on housing.*
Localisation: OONL.

5799 **Miletich, John J.**
Canadian high technology since 1980: a selected bibliography. Chicago, Ill.: Council of Planning Librarians, c1984. v, 26 p. (CPL bibliography / Council of Planning Librarians ; no. 135); ISBN: 0-86602-135-3.
Note: 71 entries.– Annotated list of books, articles, government publications published between April 1980 and March 1984.– Categories: general information, business and investment, federal and provincial governments, sociological and psychological aspects.– Indexes: name, subject, company, author, periodical.
Location: OONL.

5800 **Sereda, Peter J.**
Durability of building materials: a bibliography using a keyword guide. Ottawa: National Research Council Canada, Division of Building Research, 1984. [32] p. (DBR Paper / National Research Council Canada, Division of Building Research ; no. 1212; ISSN: 0167-3890)
Note: Approx. 450 entries.
Reprint from *Durability of Building Materials*, 2 (1984) p. 97-128.
Location: OONL.

5801 **Villeneuve, Laurent; Riopel, Diane**
Critères d'identification des tâches à robotiser: revue de littérature. Montréal: Département de génie industriel, École polytechnique de Montréal, 1984. ii, 34 f. (Rapport technique / Département de génie industriel, École polytechnique de Montréal ; EPM:RT-84-2)
Note: Localisation: OONL.

— 1985 —

5802 **An annotated bibliography of literature in the field of energy-efficient construction.** [Toronto]: Canadian Home Builders' Association, 1985. 45 p.
Note: Studies on air quality, condensation, construction techniques, design, energy use/performance, foundations, materials, passive solar, retrofit, ventilation.
Location: OONL.

5803 **Canadian Housing Information Centre**
Bibliography on building in cold climates/Bibliographie sur la construction dans les pays froids. Ottawa: Canada Mortgage and Housing Corporation, 1985. 7 p.
Note: Location: AEUB.

5804 **Draper, Anne**
Bibliographie sur le formaldéhyde et la mousse isolante d'urée-formaldéhyde (MIUF)/Bibliography on formaldehyde and urea formaldehyde foam insulation (UFFI). [Ottawa]: Centre sur la MIUF, 1985. iv, 82 p.
Note: Approx. 400 entrées.– Documents de référence sur la MIUF et le formaldéhyde: qualité de l'air (intérieur), mesures correctives, risques pour la santé, allergies, cancer, instruments et méthodes de tests, lois et règlements, propriétés physiques-chimiques, toxicologie, effets génétiques.– Texte en français et en anglais/text in English and French.
Localisation: OONL.

5805 **Un guide index de la recherche et du développement en robotique au Canada.** Ottawa: Conseil national de recherches Canada, Division de génie électrique, 1985. vii, 256 p.

Note: Un guide et une bibliographie de la recherche en robotique au Canada: universités, collèges, organismes privés et publics: livres, articles de revues, rapports techniques, thèses, articles cités dans des comptes rendus de congrès.

English title: *An index and guide to robotics research and development in Canada.*

Localisation: OONL.

5806 **An index and guide to robotics research and development in Canada.** [Ottawa]: National Research Council Canada, Division of Electrical Engineering, 1985. vii, 238 p.

Note: Location guide and bibliography of Canadian robotics research and development: universities, industrial organizations and government agencies.– Lists of documents include books, articles, theses, conference papers, technical reports.

Titre en français: *Un guide index de la recherche et du développement en robotique au Canada.*

Location: OONL.

5807 **Kerr, Dale D.**
Annotated bibliography on the rain screen principle. Ottawa: National Research Council Canada, Division of Building Research, [1985]. 35 p. (Bibliography / National Research Council Canada, Division of Building Research ; no. 45)

Note: Approx. 300 entries.– References dealing with the study of open rain screens and pressure equalization.– Topics include building aerodynamics, joints, rain and water penetration, rainfall, rain screen principle, walls.

Location: OONL.

5808 **Minion, Robin**
Building construction in cold climates. Edmonton: Boreal Institute for Northern Studies, University of Alberta, 1985. 80 p. (Boreal Institute for Northern Studies Bibliographic series ; no. 17; ISSN: 0824-8192); ISBN: 0-919058-51-5.

Note: 207 entries.– Covers from 1977 to 1985.– Compiled from Boreal Institute's SPIRES database, *BOREAL*, includes books, periodicals, government documents, theses, consultants' reports, conference proceedings, microforms.– BINS series produced monthly from January 1984 to May 1986 (no. 29).– Online access: *Boreal Northern Titles (BNT)*, available through QL Systems Limited.

Location: OONL.

5809 **National Research Council Canada. Division of Building Research**
List of publications on snow and ice. [Ottawa]: National Research Council Canada, Division of Building Research, [1985]. [106] p.

Note: Approx. 300 entries.– Contains a listing of research and technical papers in the following series: "Technical memoranda," "Technical translations," "Canadian building digests," "Building research notes."– Includes a list of additional bibliographies.

Location: OON.

5810 **Plant, Sheila**
Bay of Fundy environmental and tidal power bibliography. 2nd ed. Dartmouth, N.S.: Fisheries and Oceans Canada, 1985. vi, 159, [270] p. (Canadian technical report of fisheries and aquatic sciences ; no. 1339; ISSN: 0706-6457)

Note: 1,486 entries.– Covers to September 1984.– Listing of scientific references which describe present knowledge of environmental characteristics of Bay of Fundy region.– Emphasis on marine aspects, but includes material from disciplines of physics, geology, chemistry, biology.– Also includes references to environmental impact of and engineering and economic aspects of tidal power development.

Previous edition: Moyse, Catherine M. 1978. 125 p. (Fisheries and Marine Service technical report ; 822).

Location: OONL.

5811 **Smith, Julian A.**
"Halley's comet: a bibliography of Canadian newspaper sources, 1835-36 and 1910."

In: *Journal of the Royal Astronomical Society of Canada*; Vol. 79, no. 2 (April 1985) p. 54-99.; ISSN: 0035-872X.

Note: Listing of newspaper reports covers Upper Canada, Lower Canada and Maritimes during the 1835-1836 appearance of Halley's comet, and in 1910, all provinces are represented, with articles arranged chronologically for each newspaper.

Location: OONL.

— 1986 —

5812 **Chappell, M.S.**
Recherche et développement en matière d'énergie éolienne au Conseil national de recherches du Canada, 1975-1985. Ottawa: Conseil national de recherches Canada, Division de l'énergie, Programme d'énergie éolienne, 1986. xi, 181 p.: ill.

Note: 231 entrées.– Rapports du Conseil national de recherches du Canada, rapports du Centre d'essais éoliens de l'Atlantique, rapports du Service de l'environnement atmosphérique, rapports d'entrepreneurs, références générales, références de l'Agence internationale de l'énergie.

English title: *Wind energy research and development at the National Research Council of Canada, 1975-1985.*

Localisation: OONL.

5813 **Chappell, M.S.**
Wind energy research and development at the National Research Council of Canada, 1975-1985. Ottawa: National Research Council Canada, Wind Energy Program, 1986. xi, 164 p.: ill.

Note: 231 entries.– Listing of National Research Council reports, Atlantic Wind Test Site reports, Atmospheric Environment Service reports, contractor reports, general references, International Energy Agency references.

Titre en français: *Recherche et développement en matière d'énergie éolienne au Conseil national de recherches du Canada, 1975-1985.*

Location: OONL.

5814 **Index of BETT's reports.** Ottawa: Energy, Mines and Resources Canada, 1986. 1 vol. (in various foliations).

Note: Listings of reports produced under the Buildings Energy Technology Transfer Program by Concordia University, Marbek Resource Consultants, Ontario Research Foundation, Saskatchewan Research

Foundation, University of Manitoba, University of Waterloo.
Location: OOMR.

5815 **Light, John D., Wylie, William N.T.**
Guide pour la recherche sur l'histoire de la forge. Ottawa: Parcs Canada, 1986. 30 p.: ill. (Bulletin de recherches / Parcs Canada ; no 243; ISSN: 0228-1236)
Note: Recherche archéologique, catalogue, manuels de forgeage et revues spécialisées, encyclopédies et dictionnaires de mécanique, recherche dans les archives.
English title: *A guide to research in the history of blacksmithing.*
Localisation: OONL.

5816 **Light, John D.; Wylie, William N.T.**
A guide to research in the history of blacksmithing. Ottawa: Parks Canada, 1986. 27 p.: ill. (Research bulletin / Parks Canada ; no. 243; ISSN: 0228-1228)
Note: Archaeological research, tools and hardware publications, blacksmithing manuals and journals, encyclopedias and mechanical dictionaries, archival research.
Titre en français: *Guide pour la recherche sur l'histoire de la forge.*
Location: OONL.

5817 **National Research Council Canada. Division of Electrical Engineering.**
Record of work of Electron Physics Section, 1949-1986 [i.e. 1985]. [Ottawa]: National Research Council Canada, Division of Electrical Engineering, c1986. vii, 72 p.
Note: 741 entries.– Publications by staff of NRC Electron Physics Section: journal articles, books and book chapters, presented papers, divisional reports.– Résumé en français.
Location: OONL.

5818 **Poon, C.**
Literature review on the design of composite mechanically fastened joints/Revue de la documentation sur la conception des joints à liaison mécanique en composites. Ottawa: National Research Council Canada, 1986. vi, 63 p.: ill. (Aeronautical note / National Aeronautical Establishment ; NAE-AN-37)
Note: Text in English only.– Résumé en français.
Location: OONL.

5819 **Yarranton, G.A.; Gray, B.J.; Yarranton, M.**
Methodologies for evaluation of AECB regulatory program. Ottawa: Atomic Energy Control Board, 1986. vi, 296 p.
Note: 280 entries.– Bibliography and literature review.– Publications describing methods applicable to the evaluation of regulatory programs.
Location: OONL.

— 1987 —

5820 **Amesse, Fernand, et al.**
L'univers des nouvelles technologies: une bibliographie sélective révisée et augmentée. Montréal: École des hautes études commerciales, 1987. 94 f.: ill. (Cahiers du Centre d'études en administration internationale ; no 87-09; ISSN: 0825-5822)
Note: 512 entrées.– Liste des publications sur nouvelles technologies: télécommunications, informatique, composants électroniques, aérospatiale, bureautique, robotique, laser, électronique, biotechnologie.
Édition antérieure: 1984. vi, 59 f.
English title: *The world of high technology: a revised and expanded selective bibliography.*
Localisation: OONL.

5821 **Amesse, Fernand, et al.**
The world of high technology: a revised and expanded selective bibliography. Montreal: École des hautes études commerciales, 1987. 94 l.: ill. (Cahiers du Centre d'études en administration internationale ; no 87-09; ISSN: 0825-5822)
Note: 512 entries.– List of publications about high technology: telecommunications, data processing, electronic components, aerospace, office automation, robotics, lasers, electronics, biotechnology.
Previous edition: 1984. v, 61 l.
Titre en français: *L'univers des nouvelles technologies: une bibliographie sélective révisée et augmentée.*
Location: OONL.

5822 **Gardner, L., et al.**
Alternative transportation fuels: review of research activity in Canada: report of the Task Force on Alternative Fuels, Associate Committee on Propulsion, National Research Council Canada/Combustibles de transport de remplacement: examen des travaux de recherche au Canada: rapport du Groupe de travail sur les combustibles de remplacement, Comité associé sur la propulsion, Conseil national de recherches du Canada. [Ottawa]: Division of Mechanical Engineering, National Research Council Canada, 1987. vii, 74, 64 p. (National Research Council Canada, Division of Mechanical Engineering report ; 1987-06)
Note: Review of research and development activities in alternative fuels for transportation in Canada, projects and publications.– Résumé en français.
Location: OONL.

5823 **Gold, Lorne W.**
"Fifty years of progress in ice engineering."
In: *Journal of Glaciology*; (Special Issue 1987) p. 78-85.; ISSN: 0022-1430.
Note: Review of literature reporting scientific and engineering investigations on ice.– Topics include ice formation in rivers, lakes, oceans; ice forces on structures; bearing capacity of ice covers; atmospheric ice.– Emphasis on difficulties faced by engineers due to unique physical and mechanical properties of ice.
Location: OON.

5824 **Handfield, Roger; Nollet, Jean**
Bibliographie annotée en robotique/Annotated bibliography on robotics. Montréal: École des hautes études commerciales, 1987. 5 vol. (Rapport de recherche / École des hautes études commerciales ; nos 87-12-87-16; ISSN: 0709-986X)
Note: Vol. 1. *Information générale.*– vol. 2. *Implantation.*– vol. 3. *Utilisation.*– vol. 4. *Aspects humains et enseignements.*– vol. 5. *Développements technologiques et perspectives.*
Localisation: OONL.

5825 **Monroe, Robin Lee; McLeish, Walter**
Small aircraft crashworthiness. Montreal: Transportation Development Centre, 1987. 2 vol.
Note: Vol. 2 comprises a bibliographic database on small aircraft crashworthiness, incorporating 1,331 references originating from Canada and nine other countries.– Topics covered include fuselage design, cockpit design, seats, harnesses, post-crash fire, medical aspects,

regulations, new materials.– Sommaire en français.
Location: OONL.

5826 **Pulp and Paper Research Institute of Canada**
Index to staff publications in the technical literature, 1968-1986. Pointe-Claire, Quebec: The Institute, 1987. 102 p.
Note: Previous editions:
... , *1968-1981*. 1982. 64 p.
Index to staff publications in the technical reports, 1968-1976.
1977. iii, 37 p.
Location: BVIF.

5827 **Scrimgeour, J.H.C.; Vernadat, F.**
Advances in CAD-CAM and robotics: NRC contributions: commentary and bibliography. Ottawa: National Research Council Canada, Division of Electrical Engineering, 1987. ix, 27 p.
Note: Approx. 150 entries.– Complete list of papers published by NRC researchers in the area of CAD/CAM and robotics.– Résumé en français.
Location: OONL.

5828 **Service de diffusion sélective de l'information de la Centrale des bibliothèques**
Logiciels québécois d'applications professionnelles générales. 2e éd. Montréal: Le Service, 1987. 146 p. (DSI/CB ; no 76; ISSN: 0825-5024); ISBN: 2-89059-297-9.
Note: 591 entrées.– Logiciels produits ou distribués par 154 entreprises québécoises.– Index: noms, titres, sujets, marques, fournisseurs.
Édition antérieure: 1986. [151] p.; ISBN: 2-89059-275-8.
Localisation: OONL.

— 1988 —

5829 **B.C. Hydro. Library Services**
Bibliography on biological effects of electric and magnetic fields, 1980-1987: literature held in B.C. Hydro Library. Vancouver: Library Services, B.C. Hydro, 1988. 53 p.; ISBN: 0-7726-0779-6.
Note: 472 entries.
Previous editions:
... , *1980-1986*. 1986. 44 p.; ISBN: 0-7726-0584-X.
... , *1980-1984*. 1984. 16 p.; ISBN: 0-7726-0110-0.
Location: OONL.

5830 **Brewer, Heather M.**
Anaerobic technology: a review of research, development and demonstration activity in the agrifood and pulp and paper industries/Technologie anaérobie: compte rendu des activités de recherche, de développement et de démonstration dans l'industrie agroalimentaire et celle des pâtes et papiers. Ottawa: Environment Canada, 1988. xiv, 105 p.; ISBN: 0-662-55802-2.
Note: 319 entries.– Papers and published reports from 1975 to 1988 dealing with anaerobic technologies: fundamentals of anaerobic digestion, agricultural applications, applications in food processing and pulp and paper industries.– Text in English and French/texte en français et en anglais.
Location: OONL.

5831 **Canada Centre for Mineral and Energy Technology**
Bibliography of CANMET publications on coprocessing. Ottawa: Canada Centre for Mineral and Energy Technology, Energy Research Laboratories, 1988. iii, 44 p.
Note: 102 entries.– Reports and publications generated at CANMET on processing of mixtures of coal and oil with the objective of liquefying the coal and upgrading the oil simultaneously.

Location: OONL.

5832 **Millar, Esther**
Bibliography of technical reports in the fields of computer science and computer engineering issued at the University of Waterloo from 1967-1987. Waterloo, Ont.: University of Waterloo Library, c1988. x, 215 p. + 1 microfiche. (University of Waterloo Library bibliography ; no. 17; ISSN: 0829-948X); ISBN: 0-920834-07-8.
Note: Approx. 1,300 entries.– Listing of technical reports produced by the Computer Communications Networks Group, the Departments of Computer Science, Electrical Engineering and Systems Design Engineering and the Institute for Computer Research.
Location: OONL.

5833 **Neufeld, Steve; Scott, Jude; D'Souza, Colleen**
Automating Ontario museums: computers in museums, a selected bibliography. Toronto: Ontario Museum Association, c1988. 15 p. (Technical Leaflet / Ontario Museum Association ; no. 4); ISBN: 0-920402-10-0.
Note: 553 entries.
Location: OONL.

5834 **Pauls, D.R.; Moran, S.R.; Macyk, T.**
Review of literature related to clay liners for sump disposal of drilling waste. Edmonton: Reclamation Research Technical Advisory Committee, 1988. xxiv, 61 p.: ill. (Report / Alberta Reclamation Research Technical Advisory Committee ; RRTAC 88-10)
Note: 111 entries.– Review of current literature (1985-1987) related to assessment of effectiveness of geological containment of drilling waste in sumps.
Location: OONL.

5835 **Sanger, Ann; Tillotson, J.**
Institute for Marine Dynamics reports, 1932-1985. St. John's, Nfld.: Institute for Marine Dynamics, 1988. ii, 142 p.
Note: Listing of reports done by the National Research Council's Institute for Marine Dynamics and its predecessors.
Supplement: 1990. ... : *publications 1986-1989*. 1990. 42 p.
Location: NFSNM.

5836 **Stefanski, M.J.**
Circuitry instrumentation and process control: literature review. [Ottawa]: Canada Centre for Mineral and Energy Technology, 1988. 92 p. (Mineral Sciences Laboratories Division report ; MSL 88-112 LS)
Note: 46 entries.– Abstracts of recent articles, mainly from the 1980s dealing with automatic process control in mineral processing.– Introduction en français.
Location: OONL.

5837 **Wastewater Technology Centre: publications and presentations, 1972-1988.** Burlington, Ont.: Environment Canada, Conservation and Protection, Technology Development and Technical Services Branch, [1988]. 48 p.
Note: Location: OOFF.

— 1989 —

5838 **Deschamps, Isabelle**
Current trends in technology-innovation literature: a new departure for the POM area. Montreal: École des hautes études commerciales, 1989. 66 l. (Rapport de recherche / École des hautes études commerciales ; no 89-01; ISSN: 0709-986X)
Note: Approx. 400 entries.– Studies dealing with

managerial/technical problems associated with new technology adoption, technology forecasting and business planning, in-house development of new technologies, transfer of technologies, management of innovation, general works on technology and organizations.
Location: OONL.

5839 **Les sources d'information sur l'automatisation industrielle.** [Québec]: Direction des communications, Ministère de l'industrie, du commerce et de la technologie, Gouvernement du Québec, 1989. 94 p.; ISBN: 2-550-19538-8.
Note: Approx. 300 entrées.
Localisation: OONL.

— 1990 —

5840 **Beatty, Carol Anne**
Managing technological change in manufacturing: an annotated bibliography of selected works. London, Ont.: National Centre for Management Research and Development, University of Western Ontario, 1990. 37 p. (Working paper series / National Centre for Management Research and Development, University of Western Ontario ; no. NC 90-18)
Note: Approx. 100 entries.
Location: OONL.

5841 **National Research Council Canada. Division of Mechanical Engineering**
Publications of the Division of Mechanical Engineering and the National Aeronautical Establishment. Ottawa: National Research Council Canada, 1965-1990. 8 no.; ISSN: 0077-5568.
Note: Series no. 2, supplements no. 1-8 (January 1965)-(June 1990).– Listing of reports, laboratory technical reports, miscellaneous papers, newsletters published since 1959 by the Canadian National Aeronautical Establishment and the NRC Division of Mechanical Engineering.
Location: OONL.

5842 **Patrickson, C.P.**
Bibliography on blast protection. [Ottawa]: Public Works Canada, 1990. 1 vol. (in various pagings).
Note: 989 entries.– Covers to December 1986.– Reports, reference material, published and unpublished, on methods of protecting people from the primary and secondary blast effects of nuclear weapons.– Includes a recommended list of references for shelter design.– Prepared for Emergency Preparedness Canada, H.Q. Accommodation.
Location: OOEPC.

5843 **Taylor, Peter**
A literature review of methods for handling solid residues arising from fuel recycle plant. Pinawa, Man.: Whiteshell Nuclear Research Establishment, 1990. 19 p.
Note: 35 entries.– Reviews technical literature on management of solid residues, principally Zircaloy fuel hulls, arising from fuel dissolution in nuclear fuel recycle plants.– Emphasis on information relevant to future recycling of CANDU fuel.– Résumé en français.
Location: OONL.

5844 **Taylor, Peter**
A review of phase separation in borosilicate glasses, with reference to nuclear fuel waste immobilization/Examen de la séparation des phases dans les verres aux

borosilicate quant à l'immobilisation des déchets de combustible nucléaire. Pinawa, Man.: Whiteshell Nuclear Research Establishment, 1990. 48 p.
Note: Approx. 150 entries.– Literature survey and account of experimental work performed within the Canadian Nuclear Fuel Waste Management Program.– Emphasis on measurement and depiction of miscibility limits in multicomponent systems and effects of individual components on occurrence of phase separation.– Résumé en français.
Location: OONL.

— 1991 —

5845 **Baras, Étienne**
A bibliography of underwater telemetry, 1956-1990. Ottawa: Department of Fisheries and Oceans, Communications Directorate, 1991. iv, 55 p. (Canadian technical report of fisheries and aquatic sciences ; no. 1819; ISSN: 0706-6457)
Note: 1,114 entries.– Publications dealing with techniques and applications of telemetry to aquatic vertebrates (fishes, amphibia, reptiles, and mammals) and invertebrates.– Includes conference and symposia papers and theses.– Species and thematic index.– Résumé en français.
Location: OONL.

5846 **Gaudert, P.C.**
Publications on composite materials (January 1983-June 1991). Ottawa: Institute for Aerospace Research, [1991]. i, 12 p. (Structures and Materials Laboratory Report ; LTR-ST-1833)
Note: Location: OON.

5847 **Nadeau, Élise; Paquet, Dominik; Robertson, Yves**
Les biotechnologies: bibliographie sélective. Québec: Conseil de la science et de la technologie, Centre de documentation, 1991. 73 p.; ISBN: 2-550-21871-X.
Note: 250 entrées.– Publications officielles québécoises et canadiennes, articles de périodiques, monographies.– Comporte des sections: "Les biotechnologies au Québec: 1980-1991," "Les biotechnologies au Canada, 1985-1991," "Les biotechnologies: évolution récente, politiques et programmes gouvernementaux: une revue internationale de 1985 à 1991."
Localisation: OONL.

5848 **Smith, Clinton William**
Analytical inductively coupled plasma mass spectrometry: advantages, limitations, research directions and applications: a literature review. Ottawa: Mineral Sciences Laboratories, 1991. 14 l.
Note: 53 entries.– Bibliographical review of literature on ICPMS.
Location: OONL.

— 1992 —

5849 **Canadian Water and Wastewater Association**
On-site wastewater treatment bibliography [computer file]. Ottawa: Canadian Water and Wastewater Association, c1992. 1 computer disk (5 1/4 in. + program user's manual: 15 p.); ISBN: 0-92912-808-7.
Note: Location: OONL.

5850 **Dhillon, Balbir Singh**
Reliability and quality control: bibliography on general and specialized areas. Gloucester, Ont.: Beta Publishers, 1992. ix, 313 p.; ISBN: 1-89560-300-5.
Note: Approx. 5,000 entries.– Books, documents,

conference proceedings, articles dealing with quality circles, reliability growth and testing, failure data, safety factors, software reliability, human reliability.– Includes Canadian references.
Location: OONL.

5851 **Dhillon, Balbir Singh**
Reliability engineering applications: bibliography on important application areas. Gloucester, Ont.: Beta Publishers, 1992. viii, 241 p.; ISBN: 1-895603-01-3.
Note: Approx. 3,600 entries.– Articles, conference papers dealing with electronics, computer hardware, testability, medical equipment, structural/civil engineering systems, robots, aerospace and telecommunication systems.– Includes Canadian references.
Location: OONL.

— 1993 —

5852 **Canadian Standards Association**
Construction plus: a guide to CSA construction standards (plus 4000). 3rd ed. [Rexdale, Ont.]: Canadian Standards Association, c1993. vi, 368 p.; ISBN: 0-921347-31-6.
Note: Summaries of standards: scope, purpose, products or services covered, requirements, test methodology of the standard, with full bibliographic citation of standards published by CSA as of March 31, 1990.
Previous editions:
1990. v, 342 p.; ISBN: 0-921347-05-7.
1988. v, 394 p.; ISBN: 0-921347-01-4.
Location: OONL.

5853 **Simpson, D.L.**
Review of Canadian aeronautical fatigue work, 1991-1993. Ottawa: National Research Council Canada, Institute for Aerospace Research, 1993. 94 p. (Structures and materials report / National Research Council Canada, Institute for Aerospace Research ; LTR-ST.1932)
Note: Review of aspects of aeronautical structural technology associated with fatigue.– Topics include loads monitoring, full scale tests, fracture mechanics, composite materials, engine fatigue.
Previous editions:
... , *1987-1989*. National Aeronautical Establishment, 1989. 34 p. (Structures and materials report ; LTR-ST.1706).
Campbell, Glen S. ... , *1981-1983*. 1983. 53 p. (Structures and materials report ; LTR-ST.1453).
... , *1979-1981*. 1981. 43 p. (Structures and materials report ; LTR-ST.1246/ICAF DOC) (International Committee on Aeronautical Fatigue ; no. 1199).
Location: OON.

— Ongoing/En cours —

5854 **Atomic Energy of Canada Limited**
List of publications [AECL]/Liste des publications [EACL]. Chalk River, Ont.: Atomic Energy of Canada Limited, 1987-. vol.; ISSN: 0571-8104.
Note: Annual from 1986-87.– Lists all scientific and technical publications issued by AECL, arranged in subject groupings: general, life sciences, chemistry, engineering, earth sciences, electronics, metals, mathematics, physics, reactor technology, waste management.– Text in English and French/texte en français et en anglais.
Previously issued in 5-year cumulations:
...: *April 1952 to August 1959*. 1959. 78 p.
...: *September 1959 to March 1966*. 1966. 125 p.
...: *April 1966 to March 1971*. 1971. 119 p.
...: *April 1971 to March 1976*. 1976. 137 p.
...: *April 1976 to March 1981/...*, *1976-1981*. 1981. 138 p.
...: *April 1981 to March 1986/...*, *1981-1986*. 1987. 123 p.
Location: OONL.

Types of Material Bibliographies

Bibliographies des genres de matériel

Publications en série

— 1883 —

5855 Liste des revues littéraires françaises publiées en Canada depuis la cession 1763 jusqu'à 1883. [S.l.: s.n.], 1883. 1 f.
Note: Microforme: ICMH collection de microfiches ; no 59533; ISBN: 0-665-59533-6. 1 microfiche (4 images).
Localisation: OTY.

— 1890 —

5856 Myers, R. Holtby & Co.
R. Holtby Myers & Co.'s Complete catalogue of Canadian publications: containing carefully prepared lists of all the newspapers and periodicals published in the Dominion of Canada, giving circulation, age and other valuable information. Toronto: R. Holtby Myers, 1890. 29 p.
Note: Copy examined: photocopy.
Location: OONL.

— 1895 —

5857 Elliott, A.R. (Firm)
Elliott's hand-book of medical, hygienic, pharmaceutical and dental journals of the United States and Canada. New York: A.R. Elliott, 1895. vi, 144 p.
Note: Microform: CIHM Microfiche series ; no. 32204; ISBN: 0-665-32204-6. 2 microfiches (90 fr.).
Location: OONL.

— 1904 —

5858 Jack, David Russell
"Acadian magazines."
In: Proceedings and Transactions of the Royal Society of Canada; Series 2, vol. 9, section 2 (1903-1904) p. 173-203.; ISSN: 0316-4616.
Note: Bibliographic essay.
Location: OONL.

— 1913 —

5859 Canadian Advertising Limited
French newspapers and periodicals of Canada and the United States. Montreal: [s.n., 1913]. 92, [1] p.: (incl. advertisements).
Note: Location: OONL.

— 1924 —

5860 Lomer, Gerhard Richard; Mackay, Margaret S.
A catalogue of scientific periodicals in Canadian libraries. Montreal: McGill University, 1924. xx, 255 p.
Note: International coverage with substantial Canadian listings.– Locations in 61 institutions.
Location: OONL.

— 1931 —

5861 Severance, Henry Ormal
A guide to the current periodicals and serials of the United States and Canada. 5th ed. Ann Arbor, Mich.: G. Wahr, 1931. 432 p.
Note: Previous editions:
1920. 3 l., [9]-564 p.
1914. 462 p.
1908. 435 p.

1907. 330 p.
Location: OONL.

5862 Wallace, William Stewart
"The periodical literature of Upper Canada."
In: Canadian Historical Review; Vol. 12, no. 1 (March 1931) p. 4-22.; ISSN: 0008-3755.
Note: 116 entries.– Chronological check-list of Upper Canadian periodicals, 1793 to 1840.
Location: AEU.

— 1932 —

5863 Tod, Dorothea D.; Cordingley, Audrey
"A bibliography of Canadian literary periodicals, 1789-1900."
In: Proceedings and Transactions of the Royal Society of Canada; Series 3, vol. 26, section 2 (1932) p. 87-96.; ISSN: 0316-4616.
Note: Part 1: "English-Canadian;" part 2: "French-Canadian."
Location: AEU.

— 1934 —

5864 MacDermot, Hugh Ernest
A bibliography of Canadian medical periodicals, with annotations. Montreal: Printed for McGill University by Renouf, 1934. 21 p.
Note: Location: QMMO.

— 1951 —

5865 Boone, Maurice P.
Union list of scientific and technical periodicals in libraries of the Maritime provinces and Newfoundland. Halifax: Imperial Press, 1951. 63 p.
Note: International coverage with substantial Canadian listings.– Locations in 27 institutions.– Prepared under the sponsorship of the Maritime Library Association and the Nova Scotia Research Foundation.
Previous edition: Hess, Ernest. A catalogue of scientific periodicals in libraries of the Maritime provinces. Published by the Nova Scotian Institute of Science with the assistance of the National Research Council of Canada, 1936. 82 p.
Location: OONL.

— 1953 —

5866 Blackburn, Robert H.
A joint catalogue of the serials in the libraries of the city of Toronto. 5th ed. [Toronto]: University of Toronto Press, 1953. 602 p.
Note: Approx. 11,000 entries.– Form and scope designed to conform to Union List of Serials.– Includes Canadian titles.– Excludes administrative and legislative serials issued by government agencies, universities and corporations; almanacs; annuals; newspapers; law reports and digests; publications of agricultural experimental stations, local trade unions, boards of trade, chambers of commerce; alumni, undergraduate and intercollegiate fraternity publications.
Previous editions:

Locke, G.H.; Wallace, William Stewart. *A joint catalogue of the periodicals and serials in the libraries of the city of Toronto.* 1934. 263 p.

A joint catalogue of the periodicals, publications and transactions of societies and other books published at intervals to be found in the various libraries of the city of Toronto. 1913. 112 p.

A joint catalogue of the periodicals, publications and transactions of societies and other books published at intervals to be found in the various libraries of the city of Toronto. Bryant Press, 1898. 96 p.

Microform: CIHM Microfiche series ; no. 24916; ISBN: 0-665-24916-0. 2 microfiches (56 fr.).

Location: OONL.

— 1955 —

5867   **Goggio, Emilio; Corrigan, Beatrice; Parker, J.H.**
A bibliography of Canadian cultural periodicals (English and French from colonial times to 1950) in Canadian libraries. Toronto: Department of Italian, Spanish and Portuguese, University of Toronto, 1955. 45 p.
Note: Approx. 400 entries.– Includes literary and historical periodicals, as well as those devoted to the fine arts.– Excludes mimeographed material, newspapers, publications of societies, annuals, anthologies of reprinted material, student publications, religious, political, humourous, juvenile publications.
Location: OONL.

— 1957 —

5868   **Kallmann, Helmut**
"A check-list of Canadian periodicals in the field of music."
In: *Canadian Music Journal*; Vol. 1, no. 2 (Winter 1957) p. 30-36.; ISSN: 0576-5773.
Note: Includes musical and partly-musical periodicals, printed house organs, sheet music published in periodical form.
Location: OONL.

— 1960 —

5869   **American Foundation for the Blind**
Periodicals of special interest to blind persons in the United States and Canada. New York: [s.n.], 1960. 48 p.
Note: Listing of braille and inkprint periodicals published in Canada and the United States.
Location: OONL.

5870   **United States. Air University. Library**
Union list of military periodicals. Maxwell Air Force Base, Ala.: Air University Library, 1960. viii, 121 p.
Note: Excludes classified materials, training bulletins, camp newsletters, annual reports, periodicals of less than semi-annual frequency.– Includes holdings of six Canadian libraries.– Includes Canadian titles.
Location: OONL.

— 1961 —

5871   **Harper, J. Russell**
Historical directory of New Brunswick newspapers and periodicals. Fredericton: University of New Brunswick, c1961. xxii, 121 p.: facsim.
Note: 461 entries.– Includes "every known New Brunswick newspaper and all periodicals of literary, historical, religious, educational or scientific nature."-Selection of school and college papers, trade journals, house organs, lodge/society/club journals.– Excludes year-books, almanacs, government periodicals.

Location: OONL.

— 1962 —

5872   **Duke, Dorothy Mary**
Agricultural periodicals published in Canada, 1836-1960. [Ottawa]: Information Division, Canada Department of Agriculture, 1962. iv, 101 p.
Note: 200 entries.
Location: OONL.

— 1963 —

5873   **Rudnyckyj, Jaroslav Bohdan**
"A bibliography of Ukrainian-Canadian press surveys."
In: *Papers of the Bibliographical Society of Canada*; Vol. 2 (1963) p. 74-78.; ISSN: 0067-6896.
Note: Lists in English and Ukrainian of directories and general surveys that provide historical information about Ukrainian serials published in Canada.
Location: OONL.

— 1964 —

5874   **Carrier, Lois J.**
Checklist of Canadian periodicals in the field of education. Ottawa: Canadian Library Association, 1964. iii, 17 p. (Occasional paper / Canadian Library Association ; no. 44)
Note: Approx. 90 entries.
Location: OONL.

— 1965 —

5875   **Canadian Cultural Information Centre**
Canadian cultural publications/Publications culturelles canadiennes. Ottawa: Canadian Cultural Information Centre, 1951-1965. 13 vol.; ISSN: 0576-5110.
Note: Listing of serial publications: literature, theatre, music.– Newsletters, bulletins and catalogues from cultural organizations (art galleries, crafts groups, arts councils).
Publisher varies: 1951-1961, issued by the Canada Foundation and Canadian Citizenship Council.– Editions 1-9 list English-language publications only.– First bilingual edition, March 1962.
Location: OONL.

5876   **Special Libraries Association. Montreal Chapter**
Union list of serials in Montreal and vicinity. Montreal: [s.n.], 1965. 1 vol. (unpaged).
Note: Holdings of 46 special libraries, as well as the Atwater Library, Bibliothèque de la Ville de Montréal, Sir George Williams University Library, McGill University McLennan Library (and fifteen departmental libraries), Université de Montréal (and three departmental libraries), Bibliothèque St. Sulpice.– A general list of serial titles with substantial Canadian listings.– Excludes daily newspapers, popular magazines, house organs, annual reports and government documents.– Preliminary matter in English and French/matière préliminaire en français et en anglais.
Previous edition: *Union list of periodicals in Montreal libraries.* Montreal Special Libraries Association, 1953. [7], 144 p.
Location: OONL.

— 1966 —

5877   **National Science Library (Canada)**
List of medical and related journals held in the National Science Library, National Research Council, January 1966. Ottawa: National Research Council of Canada, 1966. 92 p.

Note: Approx. 1,000 entries.– International list with a
substantial number of Canadian titles.
Location: OONL.

— 1967 —

5878 **Meister, Marilyn**
"The little magazines of British Columbia: a narrative
bibliography."
In: *British Columbia Library Quarterly*; Vol. 31, no. 2
(October 1967) p. 3-19.; ISSN: 0007-053X.
Note: Includes an appendix listing the holdings of the
British Columbia Provincial Library and University of
British Columbia Library.
Location: OONL.

5879 **Sansfaçon, Jacques**
Liste sélective de périodiques à l'intention des
bibliothèques de collèges du Canada français. Montréal:
Fédération des collèges classiques, 1967. 126 p.
Note: Localisation: OONL.

— 1969 —

5880 **Bohm, W.D.**
"Finnish-Canadian periodical publications: a preliminary
check list."
In: *Canadian Ethnic Studies*; Vol. 1, no. 1 (1969) p. 5-6.;
ISSN: 0008-3496.
Note: Supplement: Korvela, Aino. "First supplement."
Vol. 5, no. 1/2 (1973) p. 59-62.– 26 entries in total.
Location: OONL.

5881 **Breugelmans, René**
"Netherlandic-Canadian periodical publications: a
preliminary check list."
In: *Canadian Ethnic Studies*; Vol. 1, no. 1 (1969) p. 56-58.;
ISSN: 0008-3496.
Note: Supplement: "First supplement." Vol. 5, no. 1/2
(1973) p. 231-233.– 25 entries in total.
Location: OONL.

5882 **Kirschbaum, J.M.**
"Slovak-Canadian periodical publications: a preliminary
check list."
In: *Canadian Ethnic Studies*; Vol. 1, no. 1 (1969) p. 65-68.;
ISSN: 0008-3496.
Note: 33 entries.
Location: OONL.

5883 **Malycky, Alexander**
"Ukrainian-Canadian periodical publications: a prelimin-
ary check list."
In: *Canadian Ethnic Studies*; Vol. 1, no. 1 (1969) p. 77-142.;
ISSN: 0008-3496.
Note: Supplements:
"First supplement." Vol. 2, no. 1 (June 1970) p. 195-203.
"Second supplement." Vol. 5, no. 1/2 (1973) p. 275-292.–
701 entries in total.
Location: OONL.

5884 **Malycky, Alexander; Cardinal, Clive H.**
"German-Canadian periodical publications: a prelimin-
ary check list."
In: *Canadian Ethnic Studies*; Vol. 1, no. 1 (1969) p. 13-30.;
ISSN: 0008-3496.
Note: Supplements:
"First supplement." Vol. 2, no. 1 (June 1970) p. 47-54.
Malycky, Alexander; Goertz, Richard O.W. "Second
supplement." Vol. 5, no. 1/2 (1973) p. 67-84.– 318 entries
in total.
Location: OONL.

5885 **Olivier, Réjean**
Bibliographie des journaux et périodiques de la ville de
Joliette. Joliette, Québec: Société historique de Joliette,
[1969]. 2 f.
Note: Localisation: OONL.

5886 **Sauer, Serge A.**
"Russian-Canadian periodical publications: a preliminary
check list."
In: *Canadian Ethnic Studies*; Vol. 1, no. 1 (1969) p. 61-64.;
ISSN: 0008-3496.
Note: Supplement: "First supplement." Vol. 5, no. 1/2
(1973) p. 253-257.– 45 entries in total.
Location: OONL.

5887 **Skvor, George J.**
"Czech-Canadian periodical publications: a preliminary
check list."
In: *Canadian Ethnic Studies*; Vol. 1, no. 1 (1969) p. 3.; ISSN:
0008-3496.
Note: Zekulin, Nicholas G.A. "First supplement." Vol. 5,
no. 1/2 (1973) P. 31-34.– 16 entries in total.
Location: OONL.

— 1970 —

5888 **Bianchini, Luciano; Malycky, Alexander**
"Italian-Canadian periodical publications: a preliminary
check list."
In: *Canadian Ethnic Studies*; Vol. 2, no. 1 (June 1970) p. 121-
126.; ISSN: 0008-3496.
Note: Supplement: "First supplement." Vol. 5, no. 1/2
(1973) p. 197-204.– 97 entries in total.
Location: OONL.

5889 **Borys, Ann Mari**
"Swedish-Canadian periodical publications: a prelimin-
ary check list."
In: *Canadian Ethnic Studies*; Vol. 2, no. 1 (June 1970) p. 191-
192.; ISSN: 0008-3496.
Note: Supplement: Brook, Michael; Malycky, Alexander.
" ... . Supplement." Vol. 5, no. 1/2 (1973) p. 263-267.– 30
entries in total.
Location: OONL.

5890 **Duska, Leslie; Malycky, Alexander**
"Hungarian-Canadian periodical publications: a prelimin-
ary check list."
In: *Canadian Ethnic Studies*; Vol. 2, no. 1 (June 1970) p. 75-
81.; ISSN: 0008-3496.
Note: 50 entries.
Location: OONL.

5891 **Gaida, Pranas; Baltgailis, Peter**
"Lithuanian-Canadian periodical publications: a prelimin-
ary check list."
In: *Canadian Ethnic Studies*; Vol. 2, no. 1 (June 1970) p. 151-
155.; ISSN: 0008-3496.
Note: 37 entries.
Location: OONL.

5892 **Jensen, Karlo**
"Danish-Canadian periodical publications: a preliminary
check list."
In: *Canadian Ethnic Studies*; Vol. 2, no. 1 (June 1970) p. 27-
29.; ISSN: 0008-3496.
Note: Supplement: With, Peter K. "First supplement."
Vol. 5, no. 1/2 (1973) p. 35-39.– 28 entries in total.
Location: OONL.

5893 **Juricic, Zelimir B.; Malycky, Alexander**
"Croatian-Canadian periodical publications: a preliminary check list."
In: *Canadian Ethnic Studies*; Vol. 2, no. 1 (June 1970) p. 21-25.; ISSN: 0008-3496.
Note: Supplement: Markotic, Vladimir. "First supplement." Vol. 5, no. 1/2 (1973) p. 13-17.– 42 entries in total.
Location: OONL.

5894 **Kakabelaki, Helen**
"Greek-Canadian periodical publications: a preliminary check list."
In: *Canadian Ethnic Studies*; Vol. 2, no. 1 (June 1970) p. 71-74.; ISSN: 0008-3496.
Note: 20 entries.
Location: OONL.

5895 **Laurin, Christiane**
Périodiques canadiens sur microfilms: liste des microfilms disponibles au Québec dans les bibliothèques universitaires et à la Bibliothèque nationale. Montréal: Ministère des affaires culturelles du Québec, 1970. 89 p.
Note: Localisation: OONL.

5896 **Laychuck, Julian L.**
"Chinese-Canadian periodical publications: a preliminary check list."
In: *Canadian Ethnic Studies*; Vol. 2, no. 1 (June 1970) p. 15-20.; ISSN: 0008-3496.
Note: Supplement: " ... . Supplement." Vol. 5, no. 1/2 (1973) p. 7-11.– 38 entries in total.
Location: OONL.

5897 **Lindal, Walter J.**
"Icelandic-Canadian periodical publications: a preliminary check list."
In: *Canadian Ethnic Studies*; Vol. 2, no. 1 (June 1970) p. 85-90.; ISSN: 0008-3496.
Note: 54 entries.
Location: OONL.

5898 **Malycky, Alexander**
"Norwegian-Canadian periodical publications: a preliminary check list."
In: *Canadian Ethnic Studies*; Vol. 2, no. 1 (June 1970) p. 159-161.; ISSN: 0008-3496.
Note: Supplement: With, Peter K. "First supplement." Vol. 5, no. 1/2 (1973) p. 235-238. (24 entries in total).
Location: OONL.

5899 **Ogle, Robert W.; Malycky, Alexander**
"Periodical publications of Canada's Indians and Métis: a preliminary check list."
In: *Canadian Ethnic Studies*; Vol. 2, no. 1 (June 1970) p. 109-115.; ISSN: 0008-3496.
Note: Supplement: "First supplement." Vol. 5, no. 1/2 (1973) p. 183-192.– 127 entries in total.
Location: OONL.

5900 **Olvet, Jaan**
"Estonian-Canadian periodical publications: a preliminary check list."
In: *Canadian Ethnic Studies*; Vol. 2, no. 1 (June 1970) p. 35-40.; ISSN: 0008-3496.
Note: 44 entries.
Location: OONL.

5901 **Raduloff, Marianne**
"Bulgarian-Canadian periodical publications: a preliminary check list."
In: *Canadian Ethnic Studies*; Vol. 2, no. 1 (June 1970) p. 1-3.; ISSN: 0008-3496.
Note: 11 entries.
Location: OONL.

5902 **Scollard, Robert J.**
Basilian serial publications, 1935-1969. Toronto: Basilian Press, 1970. 28 p.: facsims. (Basilian historical bulletin ; no. 1)
Note: Describes 11 serial publications produced by the Basilian Fathers in Toronto.– Excludes publications of local Basilian houses.
Location: OONL.

— 1971 —

5903 **Association des universités partiellement ou entièrement de langue française**
Catalogue de l'exposition des publications périodiques et grandes collections des universités de langue française. Montréal: AUPELF, 1971. 95 p.
Note: "Canada," p. 34-44.
Localisation: OONL.

— 1972 —

5904 **Ogle, Robert W.; Malycky, Alexander**
"Periodical publications of Canada's Indians and Métis: a preliminary check list."
In: *Northian*; Vol. 8, no. 4 (March 1972) p. 39-43.; ISSN: 0029-3253.
Note: 61 entries.
Location: OONL.

5905 **Price, John A.**
"US and Canadian Indian periodicals."
In: *Canadian Review of Sociology and Anthropology*; Vol. 9, no. 2 (May 1972) p. 150-162.; ISSN: 0008-4948.
Note: 112 entries.– Bibliographic essay and listing of newsletters, newspapers and magazines produced by Indian groups and organizations in Canada and the United States.
Location: OONL.

5906 **Roy, J.–B.**
"La presse agricole au Québec."
Dans: *Agriculture*; Vol. 29, no 3 (septembre 1972) p. 20-22.; ISSN: 0002-1687.
Note: Deux sections: "Journaux et revues de 1877 à 1936," "Les journaux depuis 1936."
Localisation: OONL.

5907 **Woodsworth, Anne**
The 'alternative' press in Canada: a checklist of underground, revolutionary, radical and other alternative serials from 1960. Toronto: University of Toronto Press, c1972. xi, 74 p.; ISBN: 0-8020-1940-4.
Note: 413 entries.– Covers 1960-1971.– Listing of serials which present alternative points of view: "those expressing views which disagree with present governmental policies and social mores."– Includes papers issued by religious fringe groups, splinter groups of political parties.– Excludes neighbourhood/community papers, union-based serials, professional reviews, literary magazines, ethnic serials, serials indexed in conventional periodical indexes; includes those covered by the *Alternative Press Index*.
Location: OONL.

— 1973 —

5908 **Akmentins, Osvalds**
"Latvian-Canadian periodical publications: a preliminary

check list."
In: *Canadian Ethnic Studies*; Vol. 5, no. 1/2 (1973) p. 213-220.; ISSN: 0008-3496.
Note: 41 entries.
Location: OONL.

5909 **Arnason, David**
"Canadian literary periodicals of the nineteenth century."
In: *Journal of Canadian Fiction*; Vol. 2, no. 3 (Summer 1973) p. 125-128.; ISSN: 0047-2255.
Note: Review of English-language literary periodicals of the nineteenth century.
Location: AEU.

5910 **Basran, Gurcharn S.**
"East-Indian-Canadian periodical publications: a preliminary check list."
In: *Canadian Ethnic Studies*; Vol. 5, no. 1/2 (1973) p. 43-45.; ISSN: 0008-3496.
Note: 10 entries.
Location: OONL.

5911 **Directory of Canadian scientific and technical periodicals: a guide to currently published titles/ Répertoire des périodiques scientifiques et techniques canadiens: un guide de la littérature technique actuelle.**
5th ed. Ottawa: National Science Library, National Research Council of Canada, 1973. vii, 49 p.
Note: 526 periodicals in science and technology published in Canada.– Includes journals and technical and research report series issued by Canadian government departments, research institutions, universities, associations and industry, in addition to commercial publications.– Excludes house organs, trade journals, popular information publications, handbooks, surveys, etc., which do not cover research projects or technology.
Previous editions:
1969. 112 p.
1966. 49 p.
... : a classified guide to currently published titles. 1962. ii, 34 l.
1961. 31 l.
Location: OONL.

5912 **Fathi, Ashgar; Smeaton, B. Hunter**
"Arabic-Canadian periodical publications: a preliminary check list."
In: *Canadian Ethnic Studies*; Vol. 5, no. 1/2 (1973) p. 1-4.; ISSN: 0008-3496.
Note: 13 entries.
Location: OONL.

5913 **Heinrich, Albert C.**
"Periodical publications of Canada's Eskimos: a preliminary check list."
In: *Canadian Ethnic Studies*; Vol. 5, no. 1/2 (1973) p. 51-56.; ISSN: 0008-3496.
Note: 31 entries.
Location: OONL.

5914 **Izzo, Herbert J.**
"Romanian-Canadian periodical publications: a preliminary check list."
In: *Canadian Ethnic Studies*; Vol. 5, no. 1/2 (1973) p. 245-249.; ISSN: 0008-3496.
Note: 21 entries.
Location: OONL.

5915 **Stuntz, Stephen Conrad**
List of the agricultural periodicals of the United States and Canada published during the century July 1810 to July 1910. Wilmington, Del.: SR Scholarly Resources, 1973. vii, 190 p.; ISBN: 0-84201-500-0.
Note: Location: OKQ.

— 1974 —

5916 **Bouchard, Daniel**
Inventaire des périodiques de la bibliothèque du Ministère des terres et forêts. Québec: Ministère des terres et forêts, 1974. 118 f.
Note: Approx. 800 entrées.– Inclut des références canadiennes et québécoises.
Localisation: OONL.

5917 **Henry, Ginette**
Répertoire des périodiques québécois. Montréal: Ministère des affaires culturelles, 1974. xiv, 248 p.
Note: 1,221 entrées.– Publications du secteur commercial et aux périodiques qui originent des associations ou des organismes sociaux.– Exclut annuaires d'université, prospectus des maisons d'enseignement, périodiques publiés par le gouvernement québécois.– Couvre l'ensemble des périodiques parus au Québec des origines à nos jours.
Localisation: OONL.

5918 **National Library of Canada. Collections Development Branch**
Holdings of Canadian serials in the National Library/ Inventaire des publications canadiennes en série dans la Bibliothèque nationale. Ottawa: National Library of Canada, 1974. v, 278 p.
Note: 5,991 entries.– Includes regular serials, annuals, irregular serials, serials issued by government departments and agencies, annual reports of companies, etc.– Excludes university calendars, telephone and city directories.
Location: OONL.

5919 **Ontario Library Association. School Libraries Division**
Canadian periodicals for schools. Toronto: Ontario Library Association. School Libraries Division, 1974. [34] l.
Note: Location: OONL.

5920 **Parnell, Pat**
Serials list: Library, Prairie Migratory Bird Research Centre. Saskatoon: Canadian Wildlife Service, 1974. 23 l.
Note: Titles of journals, periodicals, bulletins, newsletters, annual reports held by the Library of the Prairie Migratory Bird Research Centre, June 1974.– Includes a substantial number of Canadian titles.
Location: OONL.

— 1975 —

5921 **Gauvin, Lise**
"Les revues littéraires québécoises de l'université à la contre-culture."
Dans: *Études françaises*; Vol. 11, no 2 (mai 1975) p. 161-189.; ISSN: 0014-2085.
Note: Localisation: OONL.

5922 **National Library of Canada. Union Catalogue of Serials Division**
Union list of serials in education and sociology held by Canadian libraries/Inventaire des publications en série dans les domaines de l'éducation et de la sociologie disponibles dans les bibliothèques canadiennes. Ottawa:

National Library of Canada, Union Catalogue of Serials Division, 1975. xxxv, 221 p.

Note: Approx. 1,000 entries.– While mainly a foreign listing, this is an important source for location of Canadian titles.– Text in English and French/texte en français et en anglais.

Location: OONL.

— 1976 —

5923 **Canadian Teachers' Federation**

Industrial relations periodicals: a selected and annotated directory of general and teacher-oriented periodicals. Ottawa: Canadian Teachers' Federation, 1976. iii, 20 p.; ISBN: 0-88989-005-6.

Note: Comprehensive listing of Canadian periodicals dealing with industrial and labour relations with emphasis on teacher collective bargaining (newsletters of teachers' associations).

Location: OONL.

5924 **Houyoux, Philippe**

Mauricie et centre du Québec: liste des journaux et périodiques régionaux. Trois-Rivières: Université du Québec à Trois-Rivières, Bibliothèque, 1976. 41 f.

Note: Approx. 250 entrées.

Localisation: OONL.

5925 **Periodicals for natural resource management: a listing with some locations for economists, managers, and students working in areas dealing with the economic management of Canadian natural resources.** [Toronto]: Natural Resources Information Center, Faculty of Management Studies, University of Toronto, [1976]. vii, 62, [5] l. (NR Publications / Natural Resources Information Center, Faculty of Management Studies, University of Toronto ; no. 1)

Note: 348 entries.– Academic or research periodicals in the English language with emphasis on Canadian publications.– General agricultural and recreational titles are excluded.

Location: OONL.

5926 **Québec (Province). Centrale des bibliothèques. Centre de bibliographie**

Périodiques pour les bibliothèques. Montréal: Centrale des bibliothèques, 1976. 273 p. (Sélections documentaires / Centrale des bibliothèques, Centre de bibliographie); ISBN: 0-88523-019-1.

Note: Approx. 1,000 entrées.– Comporte des titres canadiens et québécois.

Localisation: OONL.

5927 **Université du Québec à Trois-Rivières. Bibliothèque**

Guide de périodiques en langue française: psychologie et éducation. Trois-Rivières: Université du Québec à Trois-Rivières, Bibliothèque, 1976. 24 f. (Publication / Université du Québec à Trois-Rivières, Bibliothèque ; no 9)

Note: 72 entrées.– Comporte des références québécoises et canadiennes.

Localisation: OONL.

— 1977 —

5928 **Canada. Department of Agriculture. Library**

Union list of serials in Canada Department of Agriculture libraries/Répertoire collectif des publications en série des bibliothèques du Ministère de l'agriculture du Canada. 2nd ed. Ottawa: Canada Department of Agriculture, 1977. 745 p.; ISBN: 0-662-

01292-5.

Note: 30,000 entries.– Includes holdings of all 24 branch libraries of the Canadian Department of Agriculture.– International listing with a substantial number of Canadian titles.– Text in English and French/texte en français et en anglais.

Previous edition: 1973. 946 p.

Location: OONL.

5929 **Tega, Vasile**

Management and economics journals: a guide to information sources. Detroit: Gale Research, c1977. xxiv, 370 p.; ISBN: 0-8103-0833-9.

Note: 161 entries.– Includes Canadian titles.– Lists special issues and annual publications.

Location: OONL.

5930 **Vincent, Thomas Brewer**

An historical directory of Nova Scotia newspapers and journals before Confederation. Kingston, Ont.: Royal Military College of Canada, Department of English and Philosophy, 1977. vii, 67 p.

Note: 198 entries.

Location: OONL.

— 1978 —

5931 **Canada. Labour Canada. Library**

Canadian labour papers currently received in the Labour Canada Library/Journaux syndicaux canadiens que reçoit actuellement la Bibliothèque de Travail Canada. [Ottawa]: Labour Canada, Library, 1978. 9 p.

Note: Approx. 135 entries.

Location: OONL.

5932 **Cukier, Golda**

Canadian Jewish periodicals: a revised listing. Montreal: Collection of Jewish Canadiana, Jewish Public Library, 1978. 38 p.

Note: Approx. 260 entries.– Includes independently published serials, institutional organs published at time of compilation, as well as those which had ceased publication.– Excludes synagogue bulletins.

Previous edition: 1969. 2, 30 l.

Location: OONL.

5933 **National Library of Canada. Union Catalogue of Serials Division**

Union list of serials in fine arts in Canadian libraries/ Inventaire des publications en série dans la domaine des beaux-arts dans les bibliothèques canadiennes. Ottawa: National Library of Canada, 1978. vii, 236 p.; ISBN: 0-660-50131-7.

Note: Approx. 1,600 entries.– Holdings of about 200 libraries are represented.– While mainly a foreign listing, this is a principal source for location of Canadian titles.– Text in English and French/texte en français et en anglais.

Location: OONL.

— 1979 —

5934 **McKenzie, Karen; Williamson, Mary F.**

The art and pictorial press in Canada: two centuries of art magazines. Toronto: Art Gallery of Ontario, 1979. 71 p.: ill.; ISBN: 0-919876-47-1.

Note: Chronological check-lists of art and pictorial periodicals, architecture journals, photography journals, periodical publications of museums and art galleries accompany essays describing their history and contribution to the Canadian art scene.

Location: OONL.

5935 **Oxbridge directory of ethnic periodicals: the most comprehensive guide to U.S. & Canadian ethnic periodicals available.** New York. Oxbridge Communications, c1979. 247 p.; ISBN: 0-91746-006-5.
Note: Location: NSHD.

5936 **Roland, Charles G.; Potter, Paul**
An annotated bibliography of Canadian medical periodicals, 1826-1975. [Toronto]: Hannah Institute for the History of Medicine, c1979. xvii, 77 p.: ill., facsim.; ISBN: 0-7720-1243-1.
Note: 212 entries.– Locations given for all titles.– Includes historical chart.
Location: OONL.

5937 **Ryder, Dorothy E.**
Checklist of Canadian directories, 1790-1950/Répertoire des annuaires canadiens, 1790-1950. Ottawa: National Library of Canada, 1979. xvii, 288 p.; ISBN: 0-660-50409-X.
Note: Chronological listing of directories within geographical areas.– Text in English and French/texte en français et en anglais.
Location: OONL.

— 1980 —

5938 **Harris, Chauncey Dennison**
International list of geographical serials. 3rd ed., rev., expanded, and updated. Chicago: University of Chicago, Department of Geography, 1980. vi, 457 p. (University of Chicago Department of Geography Research paper ; no. 193; ISSN: 0069-3340); ISBN: 0-89065-100-0.
Note: 3,445 entries.– Includes a Canadian section.
Previous editions:
Harris, Chauncey Dennison; Fellmann, Jerome D. 1971. xxvi, 267 p. (University of Chicago Department of Geography Research paper ; no. 138).
1960. 194 p.
Location: OONL.

5939 **Mercer, Tom**
"Quelques périodiques autochtones."
Dans: *Recherches amérindiennes au Québec*; Vol. 9, no 4 (1980) p. 355-359.; ISSN: 0318-4137.
Note: Localisation: OONL.

— 1981 —

5940 **Bibliothèque nationale du Québec**
Catalogue de la Bibliothèque nationale du Québec: revues québécoises. Montréal: La Bibliothèque, 1981. 3 vol.; ISBN: 2-551-04239-9. (Édition complète).
Note: Comprend deux volumes de notices et un volume d'index (auteurs, vedettes-matières).
Localisation: OONL.

5941 **Bogusis, Ruth; Blazek, Liba**
Checklist of Canadian ethnic serials/Liste des publications en série ethniques du Canada. Ottawa: Newspaper Division, Public Services Branch, National Library of Canada, 1981. viii, 381 p.; ISBN: 0-660-50732-3.
Note: Approx. 3,000 entries of newspapers, periodicals, church bulletins, directories, almanacs, yearbooks and conference proceedings of about 60 cultural groups.– Excludes embassy periodicals, commercial publications, political publications, Indian and Inuit publications.– Canadian and foreign library locations are given for most publications.
Location: OONL.

5942 **Canada. Labour Canada. Library**
Canadian labour papers on microfilm in the Labour Canada Library/Journaux syndicaux canadiens sur microfilm dans la bibliothèque de Travail Canada. [Ottawa]: Labour Canada, Library, 1981. 48 p.
Note: Previous editions:
1978. 44 p.
Canadian labour papers available on microfilm from the Department of Labour Library. Department of Labour, 1958. 11 p.
1955. 13 p.
Location: OONL.

5943 **Gauthier, Benoît**
Liste des périodiques en sciences naturelles au Québec. 2e éd. augm. Ste-Foy: Société linnéene du Québec, 1981. ix, 53 p.; ISBN: 2-920125-01-X.
Note: 106 entrées.– Contient l'ensemble des périodiques publiés au Québec incluant quelques-uns en provenance du gouvernement fédéral.
Édition antérieure: 1978. 22 f.– 64 entrées.
Localisation: OONL.

5944 **A Guide to agricultural periodicals published in western Canada.** Edmonton: Alberta Agriculture, Library, 1981. iv, 16 l.
Note: Location: OONL.

5945 **Miller, Alan V.**
Lesbian periodical holdings in the Canadian Gay Archives as of June, 1981. Toronto: Canadian Gay Archives, 1981. 15 l.
Note: Approx. 110 entries.– Includes newsletters of lesbian and gay rights organizations, publications by agencies of women's liberation movement, as well as the main listing of lesbian periodicals.
Location: OONL.

5946 **Union list of music periodicals in Canadian libraries/ Inventaire des publications en série sur la musique dans les bibliothèques canadiennes.** 2nd ed. Ottawa: Canadian Association of Music Libraries, 1981. 293 col. (Publications / Canadian Association of Music Libraries ; no. 2); ISBN: 0-9690583-0-6.
Note: 1,783 entries with holdings of 45 participating libraries.– International coverage with listing of Canadian titles.– Text in English and French/texte en français et en anglais.
Previous edition: 1964. v, 32 p.
Supplement: 1967. v, 27 p.
Location: OONL.

— 1982 —

5947 **Bibliothèque nationale du Québec. Service des entrées**
Liste des revues et journaux courants québécois reçus à la Bibliothèque nationale du Québec. Montréal: Bibliothèque nationale du Québec, 1976-1982. 10 no.; ISSN: 0707-7823.
Note: Cessé avec no 10 (juillet 1982).
Localisation: OONL.

5948 **Cooke, Ronald J.**
Canadian publications listings: a listing of daily newspapers, trade journals, and consumer magazines. Beaconsfield, Quebec: R.J. Cooke, [1982]. 24 p.
Note: 360 entries.– English-language business publications, consumer magazines and daily newspapers.
Location: OONL.

— 1983 —

5949 Beaudry, Jacques
Philosophie et périodiques québécois: répertoire
préliminaire, 1902-1982. Trois-Rivières [Québec]:
Éditions Fragments, 1983. 131 f. (Collection Les cahiers
gris ; 2)
Note: 136 entrées.– Périodiques de langue française
publiés au Québec de philosophie ou consacrant une
partie de leurs contenu à la philosophie.
Localisation: OONL.

5950 Naslund, Colin H.
Curriculum related Canadian consumer magazines for
Alberta high school libraries: an annotated bibliography.
Edmonton: [s.n.], 1983. 25, [62] l.
Note: Location: OONL.

— 1984 —

5951 Danky, James P.; Hady, Maureen E.
Native American periodicals and newspapers, 1828-1982:
bibliography, publishing record, and holdings. Westport,
Conn.: Greenwood Press, 1984. xxxii, 532 p.: ill., 49 p. of
pl.; ISBN: 0-313-23773-5.
Note: Guide to the holdings and locations of 1,164
periodical and newspaper titles by and about native
North Americans.– Includes literary, political, and
historical journals, as well as general newspapers and
feature magazines.– Substantial Canadian listings.–
Arranged by title; indexes include subject, geographic,
editors, publishers, chronological.
Location: OONL.

— 1985 —

5952 "Bibliographie [revues littéraires québécoises]."
Dans: *Voix et Images*; Vol. 10, no 2 (hiver 1985) p. 173-176.;
ISSN: 0318-9201.
Note: Articles sur les périodiques au Québec en général,
sur *La Barre du Jour/La Nouvelle Barre du Jour*.
Localisation: AEU.

**5953 Canada. Indian and Northern Affairs Canada.
Departmental Library**
List of Canadian native periodicals held by the INAC
Library/Liste des périodiques canadiens sur les
autochtones conservés à la bibliothèque des AINC.
Ottawa: Indian and Northern Affairs Canada, 1983-1985.
2 vol.; ISSN: 0828-4342.
Note: Includes English and French publications.
Location: OONL.

5954 Dubois, Bernard
Choix bibliographique sur la bande dessinée: ouvrages
généraux, québécois, thèses. Sillery, Québec: B. Dubois,
1985. 32 f.
Note: Approx. 300 entrées.– Monographies et mémoires
d'universités en langue française sur la bande dessinée.
Localisation: OONL.

5955 Swyripa, Frances A.
Guide to Ukrainian Canadian newspapers, periodicals
and calendar-almanacs on microfilm, 1903-1970.
Edmonton: Canadian Institute of Ukrainian Studies,
1985. xv, 236 p. (Research report / Canadian Institute of
Ukrainian Studies ; no. 8)
Note: 210 entries.– Under transliterated title, each
publication is identified by last Cyrillic spelling of title
(with translation), inclusive dates of publication, volume
and issue numbers, place of publication, periodicity,
format, type, language, predecessors/successors, affilia-

tion, location of microfilm positive, description of
microfilm contents.
Location: OONL.

**5956 "Tableaux: périodiques littéraires et culturels du
Québec depuis 1954."**
Dans: *Voix et Images*; Vol. 10, no 2 (hiver 1985) p. 11-16.;
ISSN: 0318-9201.
Note: Localisation: AEU.

5957 Uhlan, Miriam
Guide to special issues and indexes of periodicals. 3rd
ed. Washington, D.C.: Special Libraries Association,
c1985. vi, 160 p.; ISBN: 0-87111-263-9.
Note: 1,362 U.S. and Canadian business, trade, technical
periodicals which publish special issues: directories,
buyer's guides, convention issues, statistical outlooks or
reviews.– Classified list of periodicals.– Subject index to
special issues.– List of Canadian periodicals.
Previous editions:
Devers, Charlotte M.; Katz, Doris B.; Regan, Mary
Margaret. xix, 289 p.; ISBN: 0-87111-224-3.
Katz, Doris B.; Madison, Charlotte; Regan, Mary
Margaret. ... : project of the Advertising Group of the New
York Chapter of Special Libraries Association. 1962. vi, 125 p.
Location: OONL.

— 1986 —

5958 Bell, John
Canuck comics: a guide to comic books published in
Canada. Montreal: Published and distributed to the
comic book trade by Matrix Books; Downsview, Ont.:
Distributed to the book trade by Eden Press, c1986.
154 p.: ill.; ISBN: 0-921101-00-7.
Note: Approx. 200 English Canadian and approx. 100
Quebec listings.– Covers from 1941 to 1985.– Includes
contributions from Luc Pomerleau and Robert
MacMillan.
Location: OONL.

5959 Canadian Institute for Historical Microreproductions
Preliminary checklist of pre-1901 Canadian serials
[microform]. Ottawa: Canadian Institute for Historical
Microreproductions, 1986. xiii, 267 p.: (10 microfiches;
515 fr.).; ISBN: 0-665-00000-6.
Note: Designed to aid in planning and management of
serials microfilming project, to determine number of
titles involved, location, and availability in microform.–
Includes periodicals, almanacs, reports, proceedings,
transactions, etc.– Excludes newspapers, government
documents.– Compiled by Linda M. Jones.
Location: OONL.

**5960 Multilingual newspapers & periodicals in Ontario
public libraries.** [Toronto]: Ontario Ministry of
Citizenship and Culture, [1986]. 124 p.; ISBN: 0-7729-
0162-7.
Note: Approx. 1,000 entries.– Mainly a foreign listing,
with a substantial representation of Canadian titles.
Location: OONL.

— 1987 —

5961 Bonavia, George
Ethnic publications in Canada: newspapers, periodicals,
magazines, bulletins, newsletters. Ottawa: Department of
the Secretary of State of Canada, 1987. xii, 158 p.
Note: Titre en français: *Répertoire des publications
ethniques du Canada: journaux, périodiques, magazines,
bulletins, lettres d'informations*.

Location: OONL.

5962 **Canadian serials directory/Répertoire des publications sériées canadiennes.** 3rd ed. Toronto: Reference Press, 1987. 396 p.; ISBN: 0-919981-10-0.

Note: Bibliographic listing of about 3,000 periodicals and serials currently published in Canada (to March 1987): magazines, newsletters, daily newspapers, annuals, yearbooks, journals, society proceedings and transactions.– Excludes weekly newspapers, monographic series, annual reports, company reports and financial statements, university and school calendars, city and telephone directories, most government publications.– Arrangement is alphabetical by title, with cross references provided for former titles and variations in style or name.– Indexes: subject, publisher.– French-language titles are described in French, all others in English.– Edited by Gordon M. Ripley.– Text in English and French/texte en français et en anglais.

Previous editions:

... , *1976/... , 1976.* University of Toronto Press, 1977. xii, 534 p.; ISBN: 0-8020-4507-3. Edited by Martha Pluscauskas.

1972. x, 961 p.

Location: OONL.

5963 **Klos, Sheila M.; Smith, Christine M.**

Historical bibliography of art museum serials from the United States and Canada. Tucson, Ariz.: Art Libraries Society of North America, 1987. 58 p. (Occasional papers of the Art Libraries Society of North America ; no. 5; ISSN: 0730-7160); ISBN: 0-942740-04-1.

Note: Listing of periodicals published by public museums and galleries primarily devoted to art which maintain permanent collections.– Subjects include antiques, classical archaeology, crafts, decorative arts, folk art, graphic arts, historical architecture, painting, photography, sculpture, textiles.– Excludes monographic series.

Location: OONL.

5964 **Répertoire de périodiques québécois en santé et services sociaux.** [Québec]: Service de l'évaluation, prévention et services communautaires, Ministère de la santé et des services sociaux, 1987. 2 f., 7, [270] p.: ill.; ISBN: 2-550-17408-9.

Note: Approx. 175 entrées.

Localisation: OONL.

— 1988 —

5965 **Bonavia, George**

Répertoire des publications ethniques du Canada: journaux, périodiques, magazines, bulletins, lettres d'informations. Ottawa: Multiculturalisme et citoyenneté Canada, 1988. xii, 165 p.

Note: English title: *Ethnic publications in Canada: newspapers, periodicals, magazines, bulletins, newsletters.*

Localisation: OONL.

5966 **Canada Institute for Scientific and Technical Information**

Union list of scientific serials in Canadian libraries/ Catalog collectif des publications scientifiques dans les bibliothèques canadiennes. 12th ed. Ottawa: National Research Council of Canada, 1988. 3 vol.; ISSN: 0082-7657.

Note: Approx. 88,000 entries.– Covers to April 1988.– Master file continuously updated at CISTI.– While mainly a foreign listing, this is a principal source for location of Canadian titles.– Includes titles in all fields of science, technology and medicine: journals, periodicals, transactions and proceedings of societies, annuals, and monographic series.– Excludes elementary or "popular" titles, newspapers, almanacs, directories, encyclopedias, handbooks, ephemeral publications, government statistical publications.– Text in English and French/texte en français et en anglais.

Database available on CISTI's CAN/OLE, and on DOBIS.

Previous editions:

1985. 3 vol.

1983. 3 vol.

1981. 2 vol.

1979. 2 vol.

1977. 2 vol.

1975. 2 vol.

National Science Library. 1973. 2 vol.

1971. 2 vol.

1967. 2 vol.

1957. xiii, 805 p.

Supplement: National Science Library. ... , *supplement, 1957-1959.* 1960. xiii, 290 p.

Microform: ... *[microform]/... [microforme].* 1957-. microfiches; ISSN: 0082-7657.

Location: OONL.

— 1989 —

5967 **Bond, Mary E.**

Canadian directories, 1790-1987: a bibliography and place-name index/Annuaires canadiens, 1790-1987: une bibliographie et un index des noms de lieux. Ottawa: National Library of Canada, 1989. 3 vol.; ISBN: 0-660-54786-4 (set).

Note: Approx. 1,200 entries.– Lists the Canadian directory holdings of National Library of Canada and library of National Archives of Canada for cities, towns, townships, counties, districts, regions and provinces.– Includes directories in hard copy and microform formats.– Excludes directories for specific professions and ethnic groups, telephone directories published by telephone companies.– Text in English and French/texte en français et en anglais.

Location: OONL.

5968 **Fort Frontenac Library**

Fort Frontenac Library periodical holdings/Bibliothèque Fort Frontenac: périodiques. [Kingston, Ont.]: The Library, 1989. 120 p.

Note: Approx. 1,900 entries.– Focus of collection is on serial publications dealing with international affairs, defence industries and military technology.– Includes a substantial number of Canadian titles.

Previous edition: 1983. 77 p.

Location: OONL.

5969 **Periodical title comparison list: alphabetical listing of serial titles indexed in** *Canadian Business Index, Canadian Education Index, Canadian Magazine Index, Canadian Periodical Index, Point de repère (édition abrégée).* Toronto: Micromedia, 1989. 13 p.

Note: Location: OON.

5970 **Québec (Province). Ministère des communications. Bibliothèque administrative**

Catalogue collectif des périodiques des bibliothèques

gouvernementales du Québec, 1989. 4e éd. [Québec]: La Bibliothèque, [1989]. xviii, 932 p.; ISBN: 2-551-12182-5.
Note: 11,300 entrées.– Périodiques couvrant tous les sujets des sciences pures et humaines reliés aux activités des ministères et organismes du Gouvernement du Québec.– Inclut un nombre considérable des titres canadiens et québécois.
Éditions antérieures:
1982. xv, 479 p.; ISBN: 0-551-05070-7.
1976. 399 p.
1975. 340 p.
Localisation: OONL.

— 1990 —

5971 **Beaulieu, André, et al.**
La presse québécoise: des origines à nos jours. Québec: Presses de l'Université Laval, 1973-1990. 10 vol.
Note: Liste des journaux et les revues publiés au Québec.– Exclut les périodiques des associations et institutions.
... . *Tome premier, 1764-1859.* 1973. xi, 268 p.; ISBN: 0-7746-6658-7.
... . *Tome deuxième, 1860-1879.* 1975. xv, 350 p.; ISBN: 0-7746-6771-0.
... . *Tome troisième, 1880-1895.* 1977. xv, 421 p.; ISBN: 0-7746-6834-2.
... . *Tome quatrième, 1896-1910.* 1979. xv, 417 p.; ISBN: 2-7637-6886-5.
... . *Tome cinquième, 1911-1919.* 1982. xv, 348 p.; ISBN: 2-7637-6969-1.
... . *Tome sixième, 1920-1934.* 1984. xv, 379 p.; ISBN: 2-7637-7036-3.
... . *Tome septième, 1935-1944.* 1985. xvii, 374 p.; ISBN: 2-7637-7066-5.
... . *Tome huitième, 1945-1954.* 1987. xviii, 368 p.; ISBN: 2-7637-7126-2.
... . *Tome neuvième, 1955-1963.* 1989. xx, 427 p.; ISBN: 2-7637-7157-2.
... . *Tome dixième, 1964-1975.* 1990. xx, 509 p.; ISBN: 2-7637-7211-0.
Index cumulatif: *La presse québécoise, index cumulatif, tome I à VII, 1764-1944.* Québec: Presses de l'Université Laval, 1987. xxiii, 504 p.; ISBN: 2-7637-7086-X.
Localisation: OONL.

5972 **Butling, Pauline**
"'Hall of fame blocks women': re-righting literary history: women and B.C. literary magazines."
In: *Open Letter*; Series 7, no. 8 (Summer 1990) p. 60-76.; ISSN: 0048-1939.
Note: Includes a chronological bibliography of British Columbia literary magazines, p. 73-76.– 33 entries.
Location: AEU.

5973 **Condon, Richard G.**
"Arctic bibliography: a guide to current Arctic and Subarctic periodicals."
In: *Arctic Anthropology*; Vol. 27, no. 2 (1990) p. 113-122.; ISSN: 0066-6939.
Note: List of current periodicals dealing with contemporary political, economic, social, environmental and educational issues in the North American Arctic and Subarctic: magazines, newspapers, newsletters/bulletins, journals.
Location: AEU.

5974 **Hafstrom, Ole; Stenderup, Vibeke**
Litteratursogning: Canada tidsskrifter: en annoteret liste. Aarhus: Statsbiblioteket, 1990. 22 p. (Canadiana / Statsbiblioteket, Aarhus ; 2); ISBN: 87-7507-183-5.
Note: Approx. 60 entries.– Listing of Canadian scholarly and professional journals.
Location: OONL.

5975 **Weller, Joan**
"Canadian English-language juvenile periodicals: an historical overview, 1847-1990."
In: *Canadian Children's Literature*; No. 59 (1990) p. 38-69.; ISSN: 0319-0080.
Note: Lists 66 children's magazines and 34 secondary sources (directories, indexes, guides, bibliographies).– Résumé en français.
Location: AEU.

— 1991 —

5976 **Miller, Alan V.**
Our own voices: a directory of lesbian and gay periodicals, 1890-1990. Toronto: Canadian Gay Archives, c1991. iv, 704 p. (Canadian Gay Archives publication ; no. 12); ISBN: 0-9690981-6-2.
Note: Approx. 7,200 entries.– International in scope.– Includes many Canadian references.
Location: OONL.

5977 **Mitchell, Mary E.**
Periodicals in Canadian law libraries: a union list. 6th ed. Vancouver: UBC Law Library, 1991. 332 p.
Note: International coverage with substantial Canadian listings.– Préface en français.
Previous editions:
1989. 321 p.
1987. [v], 308 p.
1984. 253 p.
Canadian Association of Law Libraries. Toronto: York University Law Library, 1973. vi, 190 l.
1968. 64 p.
Supplement: Sir James Dunn Law Library. ... : *supplement to the second edition.* Halifax, N.S.: Dalhousie Law School Library, 1977. iv, 18 l.
Location: OKQL.

5978 **Montreal Health Libraries Association**
Union list of serials in Montreal health libraries/ Catalogue collectif des périodiques dans les bibliothèques de santé de Montréal. 3rd ed. Montreal: INS Informatique, 1991. 285 p.; ISBN: 0-9801591-3-1.
Note: 3,997 entries.– Holdings of 68 institutions.– Excludes society newsletters, annual reports, titles not of medical or allied health subject matter.– Includes a substantial number of Canadian titles.– Text in English and French/texte en français et en anglais.
Previous editions:
Toronto: McAinsh & Co., 1988. 206 p.; ISBN: 0-92087-36-5.
McGill Medical and Health Libraries Association. Union List Committee. McGill University, 1980. 285 p.; ISBN: 0-7717-0025-3.
Location: OONL.

— 1992 —

5979 **Canada. Atmospheric Environment Service. Information Resource Centre**
Serials list (Atmospheric Environment Service)/Liste de périodiques (Service de l'environnement atmosphérique). Downsview: The Centre, 1992. 142 p.

Note: 1,100 entries.– Substantial Canadian listings.
Location: OONL.

5980 Canadian Centre for Information and Documentation on Archives
Directory of newsletters relating to archival administration and records management, published in Canada/ Annuaire de bulletins de nouvelles, concernant l'administration des archives et la gestion des documents, publiés au Canada. Ottawa: Canadian Centre for Information and Documentation on Archives, 1992. 8 l.
Note: 29 entries.– Includes English and French publications.
Location: OONL.

5981 Union list of serials in Ontario government libraries/ Liste collective des publications en série des bibliothèques du gouvernement de l'Ontario. 4th ed. Toronto: Ontario Government Libraries Council, 1992. [22], 339 p.; ISBN: 0-7729-9962-7.
Note: Approx. 8,500 entries.– 55 participating libraries.– Listing includes serials currently received as well as retrospective holdings.– International coverage with substantial Canadian listings.– Text in English and French/texte en français et en anglais.
Previous editions:
Willowdale: McAinsh, 1987. 274 p.; ISBN: 0-9208-2730-6.
1979. [200] p.
Union list of serials in Ontario government libraries as of February 28, 1975. 1976. iv, 190 p.
Location: OONL.

— 1993 —

5982 Canadian Institute for Historical Microreproductions
Catalogue of periodicals in CIHM's microfiche collection (as of June 1993)/Catalogue des périodiques dans la collection de microfiches de l'ICMH (à partir de juin 1993). Ottawa: The Institute, 1993. 77 p.; ISSN: 1194-9236.
Note: Approx. 1,200 entries.– Text in English and French/ texte en français et en anglais.
Location: OONL.

5983 Canadian Institute for Historical Microreproductions
Pre-1900 Canadian directories: catalogue/La Collection de répertoires d'avant 1900: catalogue. Ottawa: CIHM, 1993. xi, 75 p.; ISBN: 0-665-91354-0.
Note: Approx. 700 entries.– Lists all directories in the Pre-1900 Canadian Directories Microfiche Collection.– Includes directories and gazetteers from cities and towns, counties, townships and provinces, as well as medical registers, college handbooks, and other specialized directories.
Location: OONL.

5984 Lévesque, Albert
Répertoire des journaux et périodiques courants de langue française ou bilingues publiés au Canada à l'exception du Québec. Montréal: Association des responsables des bibliothèques et centre de documentation universitaires et de recherche d'expression française au Canada, 1993. xix, 73 p.; ISBN: 2-9802702-0-2.
Note: 551 entrées.
Localisation: OONL.

— Ongoing/En cours —

5985 Canada. Indian and Northern Affairs Canada. Departmental Library
List of Canadian native and northern periodicals held by the INAC Library/Liste des périodiques canadiens sur les autochtones et sur le Nord conservés à la bibliothèque du AINC. Ottawa: Indian and Northern Affairs Canada, 1989- vol.; ISSN: 0843-6401.
Note: Text in English and French/texte en français et en anglais.
Location: OONL.

5986 Catholic press directory. New York: Catholic Press Association, 1923-. vol.; ISSN: 0008-8307.
Note: Annual listing of Roman Catholic Church national newspapers, diocesan publications, magazines, newsletters, directories for United States and Canada.– Imprint varies: 1923-1976, Chicago: J.H. Meier.
Location: OONL.

5987 CONSER Microfiche [microform]. Ottawa: National Library of Canada, 1979-. microfiches; ISSN: 0707-3747.
Note: CONSER Microfiche is a COM (computer output microform) publication containing serials cataloguing information, a machine-readable database for Canadian and United States serial titles.– The base file, 1975-1978, is updated annually by supplements containing register entries added or changed during the period covered, with five cumulated indexes: author-title-series; ISSN; Canadiana serial number; LC card number; CONSER control number.
Location: OONL.

5988 Helen K. Mussallem Library
List of Canadian nursing related periodicals. Ottawa: Canadian Nurses Association, 1987-. vol.; ISSN: 0844-0999.
Note: Annual.
Location: OONL.

5989 The IMS directory of publications. Fort Washington, Pa.: IMS Press, 1986-. vol.; ISSN: 0892-7715.
Note: Annual.– Includes listings of Canadian periodicals and newspapers.
Continues:
IMS Ayer directory of publications. 1983-1985. 3 vol.; ISSN: 0738-372X. Annual.
Ayer directory of publications. Philadelphia: 1972-1982. 11 vol.; ISSN: 0145-1642. Annual.
Ayer directory, newspapers, magazines, and trade publications. Philadelphia: Ayer Press, 1970-1971. 2 vol.; ISSN: 0067-2696. Annual.
N.W. Ayer & Son's directory, newspapers and periodicals. Philadelphia: Ayer, 1880-1969.; ISSN: 0067-2696.– Annual.
Location: OONL.

5990 Journaux, bulletins et revues de l'Amérique française hors Québec: répertoire. Québec: Secrétariat permanent des peuples francophones, 1983-. vol.; ISSN: 0846-2488.
Note: Édition antérieure: *Répertoire des journaux, bulletins et revues de l'Amérique française hors Québec.* 1983-1989. 6 vol.; ISSN: 0840-3821.
Localisation: OONL.

5991 National Library of Canada
Romulus (Computer file)/Romulus (Fichier d'ordinateur). Ottawa: National Library of Canada, 1992-. compact disks; ISSN: 1188-8741.
Note: CD-ROM system for locating serials and ordering documents.– Combines about 200,000 records from: *Union list of serials in the Social Sciences and Humanities; Union list of scientific serials in Canadian libraries; Union list of Canadian newspapers; CISTI serials list.*– Updated annually.– Accompanied by a disk containing installa-

tion software and user guide.– In English and French/en français et en anglais.– Co-published by: Canada Institute for Scientific and Technical Information.
Location: OONL.

5992 **Oxbridge directory of newsletters.** New York: Oxbridge Communications, 1979-.   vol.; ISSN: 0163-7010.
Note: "The most comprehensive guide to U.S. and Canadian newsletters available."– Continues: *The Standard directory of newsletters*, 1971-1978.
Location: OONL.

5993 **Union list of serials in the social sciences and humanities held by Canadian libraries [microform]/ Liste collective des publications en série dans le domaine des sciences sociales et humaines dans les bibliothèques canadiennes [microforme].** [Ottawa: National Library of Canada], 1981-.   microfiches; ISSN: 0227-3187.
Note: COM version of selected serials contained in the Union Catalogue of Serials on DOBIS.– Unedited serial records in DOBIS are excluded.– Includes periodicals, newspapers, annuals (reports, yearbooks, directories), journals, memoirs, proceedings, transactions of societies, and monographic series, government documents published serially.– In addition to social sciences and humanities, general interest scientific or technical serials and interdisciplinary titles may be included.– All forms of material (microforms, reprints, hardcopy) are listed.– Excludes newspapers, city directories, house organs, school magazines.– While mainly a foreign listing, this is a principal source for location of Canadian titles.– Updated semi-annually (June and December): new titles, revised holdings or withdrawals.– Indexes: Index A (names/title/series); Index B (ISSN: International Standard Serial Number).– Indexes cumulate with each new supplement, include access points for all new or changed bibliographic records in the register.– Online availability: *CANUC:S*, through CAN/OLE, updated semi-annually.– Microfiche edition.– No print format.– Text in English and French/texte en français et en anglais.
Location: OONL.

Newspapers

Journaux

— 1858 —

5994 **Meikle, William**

The Canadian newspaper directory, or, Advertisers' guide: containing a complete list of all the newspapers in Canada, the circulation of each, and all the information in reference thereto. Toronto: Blackburn's City Steam Press, 1858. 60 p.

Note: "Alphabetical list of newspapers, with their designation, and a short criticism regarding the political position, and religious persuasion, circulation, &c., of each."

Microform: CIHM Microfiche series ; no. 43442.; ISBN: 0-665-43442-1. 1 microfiche (35 fr.).

Location: OONL.

— 1876 —

5995 **T.F. Wood & Co's Canadian newspaper directory, containing accurate lists of all the newspapers and periodicals published in the Dominion of Canada and province of Newfoundland.** Montreal: T.F. Wood, 1876. 79 p.

Note: Cover title: *Canadian newspaper directory, 1876.*

Microform: CIHM Microfiche series ; no. 26102; ISBN: 0-665-26102-0. 1 microfiche (47 fr.).

Location: OONL.

— 1881 —

5996 **Têtu, Horace**

Journaux et revues de Montréal: par ordre chronologique. Québec: [s.n.], 1881. 16 p.

Note: Microforme: ICMH collection de microfiches ; no 28012; ISBN: 0-665-28012-2. 1 microfiche (13 images).

Localisation: OONL.

— 1883 —

5997 **Têtu, Horace**

Journaux et revues de Québec: par ordre chronologique. Québec: [s.n.], 1883. 26 p.

Note: Microforme: ICMH collection de microfiches ; no 33918; ISBN: 0-665-33918-6. 1 microfiche (17 images).

Édition antérieure:

1881. 16 p.

Microforme: ICMH collection de microfiches ; no 56295; ISBN: 0-665-56295-0. 1 microfiche (12 images).

Localisation: OONL.

— 1886 —

5998 **Butcher, William W.**

W.W. Butcher's Canadian newspaper directory. London: Printed by the *Speaker* Printing Co., 1886. 46 p.

Note: Arranged by provinces or territories, cities: title, frequency, political affiliation, date established, circulation.– Includes commercial and church papers and magazines.– On cover: Issued by W.W. Butcher, proprietor "Canada Newspaper Advertising Agency," (established 1880) Toronto, Ontario, Canada.

Microform: CIHM Microfiche series ; no. 02005; ISBN: 0-665-02005-8. 1 microfiche (27 fr.).

Location: OONL.

— 1889 —

5999 **Têtu, Horace**

Historique des journaux de Québec. Nouv. éd., rev. augm. et annotée. Québec: [s.n.], 1889. 107 p.

Note: Essai bibliographique.

Microforme: ICMH collection de microfiches ; no 33987; ISBN: 0-665-33987-9. 2 microfiches (61 images).

Édition antérieure: 1875. 51 p.

Microforme: ICMH collection de microfiches ; no 24046; ISBN: 0-665-24046-5. 1 microfiche (29 images).

Localisation: OONL.

— 1898 —

6000 **Têtu, Horace**

Journaux de Lévis. 3e éd., rev. et augm. Québec: [s.n.], 1898. 29 p.

Note: Essai bibliographique.

Microforme: ICMH collection de microfiches ; no 37465; ISBN: 0-665-37465-8. 1 microfiche (19 images).

Éditions antérieures:

1894. 21 p.

Microforme: ICMH collection de microfiches ; no 33988; ISBN: 0-665-33988. 1 microfiche (15 images).

1890. 12 p.

Microforme: ICMH collection de microfiches ; no 24680; ISBN: 0-665-24680-3. 1 microfiche (11 images).

Localisation: OONL.

— 1908 —

6001 **Rowell's American newspaper directory.** New York: Rowell; Printers' Ink Publishing Co., 1869-1908. 40 vol.

Note: "Containing a description of all the newspapers and periodicals published in the United States and territories, Dominion of Canada and Newfoundland, and of the towns and cities in which they are published, together with a statement or estimate of the average number of copies printed by each publication catalogued."- Frequency varies: Annual, 1869-1877; Quarterly, January 1878-October 1879; Annual, 1880-1896; Quarterly, June 1897-December 1901; Semi-annual, April-October 1902; Annual, 1902-1908.

Title varies: 1869-1885, *Geo. P. Rowell & Co's American newspaper directory*; 1886-1904, *American newspaper directory*; 1905-1908, *Rowell's American newspaper directory*.– Absorbed by: *N.W. Ayer & Son's American newspaper annual and directory*.

Location: OONL.

— 1932 —

6002 **Desbarats Advertising Agency**

The Desbarats newspaper directory. Montreal: Desbarats Advertising Agency, 1904-[1932].

Note: Title varies: *Desbarats 'all Canada' newspaper directory, Canadian newspaper directory, Desbarats directory of Canada's publications*.

Location: OONL.

— 1933 —

6003 **Vallée, Henri**
Les journaux trifluviens de 1817 à 1933. Trois-Rivières: Éditions du Bien Public, 1933. 89 p.
Note: Localisation: OONL.

— 1937 —

6004 **Gregory, Winifred**
American newspapers, 1821-1936: a union list of files available in the United States and Canada. New York: H.W. Wilson, 1937. xvi, 791 p.
Note: "Canada" section, p. 758-786.
Location: OONL.

— 1939 —

6005 **Talman, J.J.**
"The Newspaper press of Canada West, 1850-60."
In: *Proceedings and Transactions of the Royal Society of Canada*; Series 3, vol. 33, section 2 (1939) p. 149-174.; ISSN: 0316-4616.
Note: Location: AEU.

— 1941 —

6006 **Lunn, Jean**
"Bibliography of the history of the Canadian press."
In: *Canadian Historical Review*; Vol. 22, no. 4 (December 1941) p. 416-433.; ISSN: 0008-3755.
Note: Lists bibliographies and directories, general items (relating to more than one province), listings for individual provinces.
Location: AEU.

— 1942 —

6007 **McKim's directory of Canadian publications.** Montreal: A. McKim, 1892-1942. ISSN: 0383-9451.
Note: Frequency varies.– Listing of newspapers and periodicals published in Canada and Newfoundland.– "A complete list of the newspapers and periodicals published in the Dominion of Canada and Newfoundland, with full particulars."- Title varies: 1st-16th ed., 1892-1923: *The Canadian newspaper directory.*
Location: OONL.

— 1944 —

6008 **Lunn, Jean**
"Canadian newspapers before 1921: a preliminary list."
In: *Canadian Historical Review*; Vol. 25, no. 4 (December 1944) p. 417-420.; ISSN: 0008-3755.
Note: Location: OONL.

— 1945 —

6009 **Harvey, D.C.**
"Newspapers of Nova Scotia, 1840-1867."
In: *Canadian Historical Review*; Vol. Vol. 26, no. 3 (September 1945) p. 279-301.; ISSN: 0008-3755.
Note: Bibliographical essay and listing of Nova Scotia newspapers.
Reprint: In: *Papers of the Bibliographical Society of Canada*; No. 26 (1987) p. 135-156.
Location: OONL.

— 1947 —

6010 **Murray, Elsie McLeod**
A check-list of early newspaper files located in local newspaper offices in western Ontario. London: University of Western Ontario, 1947. 23 l. (Western Ontario history nuggets ; 12)
Note: Location: OS.

— 1958 —

6011 **Saskatchewan. Legislative Library. Archives Division**
Catalogue of newspapers on microfilm in the Legislative Library (Archives Division) and Provincial Archives of Saskatchewan. [Regina: Queen's Printer, 1958]. 15 p.
Note: Primarily Saskatchewan newspapers.
Location: OONL.

— 1961 —

6012 **Firth, Edith G.**
Early Toronto newspapers, 1793-1867: a catalogue of newspapers published in the Town of York and the City of Toronto from the beginning to Confederation. Toronto: Published by the Baxter Pub. Co. in co-operation with the Toronto Public Library, 1961. 31 p.: facsims.
Note: 82 entries.
Location: OONL.

— 1962 —

6013 **Turek, Victor**
The Polish-language press in Canada: its history and a bibliographical list. Toronto: Polish Alliance Press, 1962. 248 p. (Polish Research Institute in Canada Studies ; 4)
Note: 118 entries.
Location: OONL.

— 1965 —

6014 **O'Bready, Maurice**
Les journaux publiés dans les Cantons de l'Est depuis 150 ans. Sherbrooke: [s.n.], 1965. 9 f.
Note: Composé en majeure partie de la liste de ces journaux.
Dans Lochhead.– Pas localisation.

— 1969 —

6015 **Queen's University (Kingston, Ont.). Douglas Library**
Catalogue of Canadian newspapers in the Douglas Library, Queen's University. Kingston, [Ont.]: The Library, 1969. xxi l., 195 p. (Douglas Library Occasional papers ; no. 1)
Note: Approx. 400 entries.– Includes listings of "periodical publications whose main purpose is to convey general news ... printed or published within the present-day boundaries of Canada."- Excludes magazines.– Information includes holdings, period of publication, names of founder, printer, editor, publisher, proprietor, political position or affiliation, sources of information.– Compiled by Lorraine C. Ellison, Peter E. Greig, William F.E. Morley.
Location: OONL.

— 1971 —

6016 **Savoie, Donat**
"Liste des publications indiennes, métis et esquimaudes."
Dans: *Recherches amérindiennes au Québec*; Vol. 1, no 3 (juin 1971) p. 21-24.; ISSN: 0318-4137.
Note: Liste des revues et journaux édités par des associations d'amérindiens.
Localisation: OONL.

— 1973 —

6017 **Arndt, Karl J.R.; Olson, May E.**
The German language press of the Americas, 1732-1968: history and bibliography/Die deutschsprachige Presse der Amerikas, 1732-1968: Geschichte und Bibliographie. Pullach-München: Verlag Dokumentation, 1973. 2 vol.; ISBN: 3-7940-3421-X.
Note: Vol. 2 includes a section on Canada, p. 223-262.
Location: OONL.

6018 **Boutet, Edgar**
"Les journaux de Hull: des origines à 1955."
Dans. *Asticou)* Nos 10 11 (mars 1973) p 45-70.; ISSN: 0066-992X.
Note: Localisation: OONL.

6019 **McLaren, Duncan**
Ontario ethno-cultural newspapers, 1835-1972: an annotated checklist. Toronto: University of Toronto Press, 1973. xviii, 234 p.; ISBN: 0-8020-2066-6.
Note: 500 entries.– Prepared in connection with the Ethnic Newspaper Microfilming Project undertaken by Ontario Council of University Libraries for preservation of primary research materials relating to ethnic studies.– Information includes place of publication, frequency, founding date, date of last issue (if defunct), related publications/supplements, publishers/editors, location of original issues, location of positive microfilm.– Chronological and geographic indexes.
Location: OONL.

— 1974 —
6020 **Glazier, Kenneth M.**
A list of newspapers in the university libraries of the prairie universities of Canada. Rev. and enl. ed. Calgary: [University of Calgary Library], 1974. iii, 104 l.
Note: Information on holdings through December, 1973.– Canadian section, p. 3-54.– Arrangement by country, province, city: alphabetic by title within each city.
Previous edition: 1972. ii, ii, 76 l.
Location: OONL.

6021 **Revai, Elisabeth**
Les périodiques de la collection Canadiana de Louis Melzack: journaux de langue française. Montréal: Service des collections des bibliothèques, Université de Montréal, 1974. iv, 59 f.
Note: Localisation: QQLA.

6022 **Smith, Ruell**
Canadian newspapers in the University of British Columbia Library. Rev. ed. Vancouver: University of British Columbia Library, 1974. [8], 91 p. (Reference publication / University of British Columbia Library ; no. 52)
Note: 646 entries.– General newspapers, labour newspapers, native newspapers, alternative press.
Previous edition: *Reference guide to Canadian newspapers: a check list of major holdings in the library of the University of British Columbia.* 1968. 19 l. (Reference publication ; no. 23).
Location: OONL.

— 1975 —
6023 **Fedynski, Alexander**
Bibliohrafichnyi pokazhchyk ukraïnskoï presy poza mezhmy Ukraïny/Bibliographical index of the Ukrainian press outside Ukraine. [Cleveland]: Ukrainian Museum-Archives in Cleveland, 1966-1975. 9 vol.; ISSN: 0067-737X.
Note: Includes a "Canada" section.
Location: OONL.

6024 **Smith, Ruell**
"The alternative press in British Columbia."
In: *British Columbia Library Quarterly*; Vol. 38, no. 3 (Winter 1975) p. 6-16.; ISSN: 0007-053X.
Note: Listing of post-1960 publications presenting an alternative lifestyle from the establishment press.– Includes underground newspapers.– Excludes ethnic publications.
Location: OONL.

— 1977 —
6025 **Canadian Library Association. Microfilm Committee**
Canadian newspapers on microfilm catalogue/ Catalogue de journaux canadiens sur microfilm. Ottawa: Canadian Library Association, 1959-1977. 1 vol. (loose-leaf).
Note: Part 1: *Cumulative catalogue of microfilms of the Canadian Library Association.*
Part 2: *Canadian newspapers microfilmed by the Canadian Library Association and other producers.*– Information provided includes dates of publication, changes of title and history, dates microfilmed, frequency, number of reels (or feet in small runs), price, proprietors/ publishers/editors, editorial policy and content, holders of files microfilmed, issues missing, institutions holding positive microfilm copies.– Compiled under the supervision of Sheila Egoff.
Location: OONL.

6026 **Demers, Pierre**
"Portrait des journaux au Saguenay-Lac-Saint-Jean."
Dans: *Focus*; Vol. 1, no 6 (novembre 1977) p. 30-36.; ISSN: 0705-5579.
Note: Localisation: OONL.

6027 **Kesteman, Jean-Pierre**
"Les premier journaux du District de Saint-François (1823-1845)."
Dans: *Revue d'histoire de l'Amérique française*; Vol. 31, no 2 (septembre 1977) p. 239-253.; ISSN: 0035-2357.
Note: Localisation: OONL.

— 1979 —
6028 **Tratt, Gertrude E.N.**
A survey and listing of Nova Scotia newspapers, 1752-1957: with particular reference to the period before 1867. Halifax: School of Library Service, Dalhousie University, 1979. 193 p. (Occasional papers / Dalhousie University Libraries and Dalhousie University School of Library Service ; no. 21; ISSN: 0318-7403); ISBN: 0-7703-0160-6.
Note: Contains a chronological table, a survey of development and a brief description of Nova Scotia newspapers arranged by the town in which they were published.
Thesis: M.A., Mount Allison University, 1957.
Location: OONL.

— 1980 —
6029 **McNaught, Hugh**
Newspapers of the modern Northwest Territories: a bibliographic study of their publishing history (1945-1978) and publishing record. Edmonton: Faculty of Library Science, University of Alberta, 1980. 106 l.: map.
Note: Listing and description of community-oriented publications in the Northwest Territories.– Includes newspapers, school publications, government publications, adult education publications, religious publications, special interest publications.
Location: OONL.

6030 **Québec (Province). Centre de services en communications. Service de médias**
Liste des journaux (quotidiens et hebdomadaires) et stations de télévision et de radio du Québec. Québec: Ministère des communications, 1980. 83 p.
Note: Localisation: QRCN.

— 1981 —

6031 **Loveridge, Donald Merwin**
A historical directory of Manitoba newspapers, 1859-1978. Winnipeg: University of Manitoba Press, c1981. 233 p.; ISBN: 0-887551-22-X.
Note: 906 entries.– Three listings: "English and French newspapers of rural Manitoba," "English and French newspapers of Metropolitan Winnipeg," "Ethnic newspapers of Manitoba."– Information includes title, language, frequency, dates, publishing history, political affiliations, editors/publishers, title variations, absorptions and mergers, supplements and related publications, holdings (principal location: Legislative Library of Manitoba).
Location: OONL.

— 1982 —

6032 **"The ethnic press in Ontario."**
In: *Polyphony*; Vol. 4, no. 1 (1982) p. 1-143.; ISSN: 0704-7002.
Note: Special issue devoted to Ontario ethnic newspapers.– Bibliographic essays on the publications of individual cultural groups provide brief histories and listings of titles.
Location: OONL.

— 1984 —

6033 **Landry, Charlotte**
Franco-Albertan newspapers 1898-1982: a guide. Edmonton: [C. Landry], 1984. 65 l.
Note: Listing of Franco-Albertan newspapers, urban and rural.– Identifies existing files of newspaper titles, with location and physical condition.
Location: OONL.

6034 **MacDonald, Christine**
Historical directory of Saskatchewan newspapers, 1878-1983. Regina: Saskatchewan Archives Board, 1984. vi, 87 p.: ill., facsims. (Saskatchewan Archives Reference series ; 4); ISBN: 0-9691445-3-9.
Note: Records facts about birth, life, and death of newspapers, names of publishers, owners, editors.– Lists microfilm availability.
Previous edition: *Historical directory of Saskatchewan newspapers, 1878-1950.* Saskatoon: Office of the Saskatchewan Archives, University of Saskatchewan, 1951. iii, 114 p.
Location: OONL.

6035 **United States. Library of Congress. Catalog Management and Publication Division**
Newspapers in microform: foreign countries, 1948-1983. Washington: Library of Congress, 1984. xxv, 504 p.
Note: Includes a "Canada" section, p. 32-101.
Location: OONL.

— 1985 —

6036 **Ellison, Suzanne**
Bibliography of Newfoundland newspapers. St. John's, Nfld.: Memorial University of Newfoundland Library, 1985. 32 p.; ISBN: 0-88901-107-9.
Note: 166 entries.– Newspapers published in Newfoundland containing a broad range of news on all subjects.– Excludes magazines, professional publications, church newspapers, school newspapers, company newsletters, political campaign literature, trade union publications, government publications.– Arrangement by city or town, subarranged by title.– Indexes: title, editor/

publisher, chronology.
Location: OONL.

— 1986 —

6037 **Manitoba Library Association**
Manitoba newspaper checklist with library holdings, 1859-1986. [Winnipeg]: Manitoba Library Association, 1986. 106 p.; ISBN: 0-9692814-0-4.
Note: Approx. 1,000 entries.– Listing of all Manitoba newspapers, arranged by place of publication.– Two listings: one for non-Winnipeg newspapers, one for Winnipeg newspapers.– Includes holdings for libraries which provide public access to newspaper collections.– Indexes: subject, language, chronology, title.
Location: OONL.

— 1987 —

6038 **Blue Pond Collaborative**
A union list of Nova Scotia newspapers: who has what for when and where. Halifax: [s.n.], 1987. xii, 432 p.
Note: Approx. 1,000 entries.– Covers 1752-1989.– Provides holdings information for Nova Scotia repositories, with brief historical notes for most titles.
Location: OONL.

6039 **Boylan, Heather**
Checklist and historical directory of Prince Edward Island newspapers, 1787-1986. Charlottetown: Public Archives of Prince Edward Island, 1987. 211 p.
Note: Approx. 175 entries.– Information includes dates of publication, frequency, names of proprietors/editors/publishers, brief prospectus outlining subject matter and editorial bias, locations in P.E.I. (gaps of one month or more are noted).– Indexes: geographical, chronological.
Location: OONL.

6040 **British Columbia Library Association**
British Columbia newspapers: register of microform masters. Vancouver: British Columbia Library Association, 1987. 7 p.
Note: Location: OONL.

6041 **Burrows, Sandra; Gaudet, Franceen**
Checklist of indexes to Canadian newspapers. Ottawa: National Library of Canada, 1987. 148, 154 p.; ISBN: 0-660-53735-4.
Note: Lists the results of a survey conducted to determine extent of indexing of newspapers and clipping files in Canadian libraries and newspaper offices.– Newspaper defined as publication which is printed and distributed daily, semi-weekly, weekly, or at some regular interval, and consisting of news, editorials, features, advertising.– Text in English and French with French text on inverted pages.– Title of additional title-page: *Liste de contrôle des index de journaux canadiens.*
Location: OONL.

6042 **Burrows, Sandra; Gaudet, Franceen**
Liste de contrôle des index de journaux canadiens. Ottawa: Bibliothèque nationale du Canada, 1987. 154, 148 p.; ISBN: 0-660-53735-4.
Note: Résultat d'enquête à déterminer l'étendue des travaux d'indexation des journaux canadiens au pays.– Définition: Un journal est une publication imprimée et distribuée quotidiennement, semi-hebdomadairement, hebdomadairement ou à des intervalles réguliers et courts.– Il contient des nouvelles, des éditoriaux, des articles de fonds, de la publicité et autres articles d'intérêt courant.– Texte en français et en anglais disposé

tête-bêche.– Titre de la p. de t. additionnelle: *Checklist of indexes to Canadian newspapers.*
Localisation: OONL

6043 **Gilchrist, J. Brian**
Inventory of Ontario newspapers, 1793-1986. Toronto: Micromedia, c1987. vi, 202, 72 p.; ISBN: 0-88892-596-4.
Note: Listing of Ontario newspapers arranged alphabetically by place of publication.– Information within entries includes dates of inclusive publication, frequency, publication history (interruptions in publication, variations in title), locations and holdings, geographic location (if newspaper associated with more than one community).
Location: OONL.

6044 **Komorous, Hana**
Union catalogue of British Columbia newspapers. Vancouver: British Columbia Library Association, 1987. 3 vol.
Note: 3,000 bibliographic entries and 7,000 holdings records from 266 locations.– Listing of all known newspapers published in British Columbia, including general-interest daily newspapers, non-daily general-interest newspapers, ethnic newspapers, alternative press newspapers, student press, financial and industrial newspapers, labour newspapers, religious newspapers, armed forces newspapers.– Arrangement: title list, place of publication list arranged by city or town, type of newspaper list, list of ethnic and native Indian newspapers, list of newspapers in languages other than English, list of indexed newspapers.– Indexes: geographic area index; names index (editors, publishers).
Location: OONL.

6045 **Wearmouth, Amanda**
Checklist of Yukon newspapers, 1898-1985. Whitehorse: Yukon Archives, 1987. iv, 47 p.
Note: Location: OONL.

— 1988 —

6046 **Ellison, Suzanne**
Historical directory of Newfoundland and Labrador newspapers, 1807-1987. St. John's: Memorial University of Newfoundland Library, 1988. 175 p.; ISBN: 0-88901-158-3.
Note: 240 entries.– Details the major newspaper holdings of libraries and archives in Newfoundland.– Information includes title, place of publication, dates of publication, title variations, frequency, name of publisher/proprietor/editor/printer, description of content and editorial policy, locations and holdings.
Location: OONL.

6047 **Lacroix, Jean-Michel**
Anatomie de la presse ethnique au Canada. [Bordeaux]: Presses universitaires de Bordeaux, 1988. 493 p.: ill.; ISBN: 2-85892-113-X.
Note: 368 entrées.– Liste des journaux ethniques courants: titre, adresse, rédacteur, éditeur, périodicité, date de création, politique éditoriale.– Index: nationalités, titres.
Localisation: OONL.

6048 **National Library of Canada. Newspaper Section**
Union list of Canadian newspapers held by Canadian libraries/Liste collective des journaux canadiens disponibles dans les bibliothèques canadiennes. Ottawa: Newspaper Section, Serials Division, Public Services Branch, National Library of Canada, 1977-1988. 11 vol.: ill., facsim.; ISSN: 0840-5832.
Note: Annual.– Lists holdings of 125 Canadian libraries.– Includes all Canadian newspapers reported by Canadian libraries published at any time, in any language, printed and distributed daily, semi-weekly, weekly or at some other regular and short interval.– Ethnic, political, student, labour, underground, religious and community publications are included.– Excludes papers solely devoted to a specific subject (financial, military, industrial papers).– Arranged by province, city, alphabetical under city.– Title index.– Microfiche edition since 1988.
Location: OONL.

6049 **Strathern, Gloria M.**
Alberta newspapers, 1880-1982: an historical directory. Edmonton: University of Alberta Press, 1988. xxxi, 568 p.: ill., [8] p. of pl.; ISBN: 0-88864-137-0.
Note: 1,090 entries.– Newspapers arranged chronologically by first date of issue under name of geographic area or place they served.– Information provided includes title, publication dates, frequency, special interest or ethnic affiliation, language, notes on history/publishing relationships/features, holdings locations.– Indexes: biographical, chronological, ethnic, title, subject.
Location: OONL.

— 1989 —

6050 **Craig, Helen C.**
New Brunswick newspaper directory, 1783-1988/Répertoire des journaux du Nouveau-Brunswick, 1783-1988. Fredericton: Council of Head Librarians of New Brunswick, 1989. xxiv, 254 p.; ISBN: 0-9690287-3-3.
Note: 670 entries.– In addition to daily and weekly regional and community newspapers, includes alternate, alumni, ethnic, labour, military, political, religious, and student newspapers.– Text in English and French/texte en français et en anglais.
Location: OONL.

— 1990 —

6051 **Murphy, Lynn; Hicks, Brenda**
Nova Scotia newspapers: a directory and union list, 1752-1988. Halifax: School of Library and Information Studies, Dalhousie University, 1990. 2 vol.; ISBN: 0-7703-9742-5 (vol. 1); 0-7703-9744-1 (vol. 2).
Note: 1,096 entries.– Prepared under the direction of the Ad Hoc Committee for the Preservation and Access of Nova Scotian Newspapers.
Location: OONL.

— 1992 —

6052 **Mavrinac, Mary Ann**
Guide to Canadian newspapers on microfilm in the D.B. Weldon Library. London: University Library System, University of Western Ontario, 1992. x, 150 p.; ISBN: 0-7714-1371-8.
Note: 602 entries.– Listing of Canadian newspapers on microfilm, with an emphasis on historical newspapers in southwestern Ontario cities, towns and villages.– Includes detailed notes which provide information on variations, changes, mergers, suspensions and continuations.
Location: OONL.

— Ongoing/En cours —

6053 **National Library of Canada**

Union list of Canadian newspapers [microform]/Liste collective des journaux canadiens [microforme]. Ottawa: National Library of Canada, 1988-. microfiches; ISSN: 0840-5832.

Note: Holdings for about 700 Canadian libraries.– Produced from DOBIS records, with title index and geographical index (provinces, cities and towns).– Available only in microform.– Continues: *Union list of Canadian newspapers held by Canadian libraries/Liste collective des journaux canadiens disponibles dans les bibliothèques canadiennes.*– Text in English and French/ texte en français et en anglais.

Location: OONL.

Theses

Thèses

Thèses

— 1932 —

6054 **Innis, Harold Adams**
"Bibliography of research work in economics in Canadian universities."
In: *Contributions to Canadian Economics*; Vol. 1 (1928) p. 69-85; vol. 2 (1929) p. 69-97; vol. 3 (1931) p. 53-56; vol. 4 (1932) p. 50-55.
Note: Location: OONL.

— 1933 —

6055 **Bladen, M.L.**
"Graduate theses in Canadian political science and economics."
In: *Contributions to Canadian Economics*; Vol. 6 (1933) p. 62-69.
Note: Location: OONL.

— 1940 —

6056 **Palfrey, Thomas R.; Coleman, Henry E.**
Guide to bibliographies of theses, United States and Canada. 2nd ed. Chicago: American Library Association, 1940. 54 p.
Note: Approx. 450 entries.
Previous edition: 1936. 48 p.
Location: OONL.

— 1947 —

6057 **Lebel, Maurice**
Thèses présentées à la Faculté des lettres de l'Université Laval, 1940-1947. Québec: Presses de l'Université Laval, 1947. 15 p.
Note: Localisation: QQLA.

— 1949 —

6058 **Bromberg, Erik**
"A Bibliography of theses and dissertations concerning the Pacific Northwest and Alaska."
In: *Pacific Northwest Quarterly*; Vol. 40, no. 3 (July 1949) p. 203-252.; ISSN: 0030-8803.
Note: 919 entries.– M.A. and Ph.D. theses written in the Pacific Northwest in the field of the social sciences which pertain to Washington, Oregon, British Columbia, Alaska.
Supplements:
Pacific Northwest Quarterly, Vol. 42, no. 2 (April 1951) p. 147-166.
Oregon Historical Quarterly, Vol. 59, no. 1 (March 1958) p. 27-84; vol. 65, no. 4 (December 1964) p. 363-391; vol. 72, no. 3 (September 1971) p. 225-279.
Location: OONL.

— 1951 —

6059 **Canadian graduate theses in the humanities and social sciences, 1921-1946/Thèses des gradués canadiens dans les humanités et les sciences sociales, 1921-1946.** [Ottawa: King's Printer, 1951]. 194 p.
Note: 3,043 entries.– Compiled and published under the auspices of the Humanities Research Council of Canada and the Social Science Research Council of Canada.
Location: OONL.

— 1952 —

6060 **Canadian Education Association**
Graduate theses in education, 1913-1952: partial list. Toronto: Canadian Education Association, 1952. 33, [1] p.
Note: Approx. 450 entries.
Location: OONL.

6061 **Ontario College of Education. Department of Educational Research**
Theses in education: Ontario College of Education, University of Toronto since 1898: including theses in pedagogy from Queen's University, 1911-1925. Toronto: Department of Educational Research, Ontario College of Education, University of Toronto, [1952]. i, 32 l. (Educational research series / Department of Educational Research, Ontario College of Education, University of Toronto ; no. 20)
Note: Location: OONL.

— 1954 —

6062 **"Canadian theses in psychology."**
In: *Canadian Journal of Psychology*; Vol. 3, no. 1 (March 1949) p. 44-46; vol. 4, no. 1 (March 1950) p. 33-37; vol. 5, no. 1 (March 1951) p. 43-48; vol. 6, no. 1 (March 1952) p. 49-53; vol. 7, no. 1 (March 1953) p. 44-48; vol. 8, no. 1 (March 1954) p. 46-48.; ISSN: 0008-4255.
Note: Location: AEU.

— 1955 —

6063 **Canada. Department of Citizenship and Immigration. Canadian Citizenship Branch**
Research on immigrant adjustment and ethnic groups: a bibliography of unpublished theses, 1920-1953/ Recherches sur l'adaptation des immigrants et les groupes ethniques: une bibliographie de thèses non publiées, 1920-1953. Ottawa: Research Division, Canadian Citizenship Branch, Department of Citizenship and Immigration, 1955. [3], 31 p.
Note: Approx. 150 entries.– Text in English and French/ texte en français et en anglais.
Location: OONL.

— 1956 —

6064 **List of graduate theses in forestry and allied subjects accepted by Canadian universities, 1917-1956.** [S.l.]: Pulp and Paper Research Institute of Canada, [1956]. [10] l.
Note: 74 entries.– Chronological arrangement.– Subject index.
Location: OONL.

— 1957 —

6065 **"Canadian theses in psychology, ..."**
In: *Canadian Psychologist*; Vol. 4, no. 1 (January 1955) p. 4-7; vol. 5, no. 1 (January 1956) p. 5-9; vol. 6, no. 1 (January 1957) p. 4-7.; ISSN: 0008-4832.
Note: Location: AEU.

— 1958 —

6066 **Chronic, John; Chronic, Halka**
Bibliography of theses written for advanced degrees in

geology and related sciences at universities and colleges in the United States and Canada through 1957. Boulder, Colo.: Pruett Press, 1958. 1 vol. (unpaged).
Note: 11,091 entries.– Postgraduate theses in geology and related fields: geophysics, geochemistry, geological engineering, petroleum engineering.– Arranged by author, with subject index and index of geologic names.
Supplements:
Bibliography of theses in geology, 1958-1963. Washington: American Geological Institute, 1964. 1 vol. (unpaged).
Bibliography of theses in geology, 1964. Washington: American Geological Institute, 1964. 1 vol. (unpaged).
Ward, Dederick C.; O'Callaghan, T.C. *Bibliography of theses in geology, 1965-66.* Washington: American Geological Institute, [1969]. v, 255 p.
Ward, Dederick C. *Bibliography of theses in geology, 1967-1970.* Boulder, Colo.: Geological Society of America, c1973. vii, 160, 274 p.; ISBN: 0-8137-2132-1.
Location: OONL.

6067 **Ontario. Department of Planning and Development. Community Planning Branch**
Geographic theses: a bibliography. Toronto: The Branch, 1958. 25 p.
Note: Listing of theses written at University of Toronto, McMaster University, University of Western Ontario, selected universities in the United States on geographic topics related to Ontario.
Location: OONL.

6068 **Tarbox, George E.**
Bibliography of graduate theses on geophysics in the U.S. and Canadian institutions. Golden, Colo.: Colorado School of Mines, 1958. vi, 55 p.
Note: Location: OOCC.

— 1959 —

6069 **Dassonville, Michel**
"Répertoire des thèses présentées à la faculté des lettres de l'Université Laval, 1946-1956."
Dans: *Culture*; Vol. 20, no 2 (juin 1959) p. 195-222.; ISSN: 0317-2066.
Note: 174 entrées.– Index analytique.
Localisation: OONL.

— 1960 —

6070 **Brehaut, Willard**
"A quarter century of educational research in Canada."
In: *Ontario Journal of Educational Research*; Vol. 2, no. 2 (April 1960) p. 109-222.; ISSN: 0474-2117.
Note: 574 entries.– Analysis of dissertations in English language in education accepted by Canadian universities, 1930 to 1955, with list by author.– A subject guide was subsequently published in "A classified index of Canadian theses (English) in education, 1930-1955." In: *Ontario Journal of Educational Research*; Vol. 3, no. 1 (October 1960) p. 35-37.
Location: AEU.

6071 **Gagné, Armand**
Répertoire des thèses des facultés ecclésiastiques de l'Université Laval, 1935-1960. Québec: [s.n.], 1960. iii, 19 f. (Études et recherches bibliographiques / Université Laval ; no 2)
Note: 129 entrées dans trois disciplines: théologie, droit canonique, philosophie.
Localisation: OONL.

6072 **Karrow, P.F.**
Bibliography of theses on Ontario geology (Cambrian to Quaternary inclusive). Toronto: Ontario Department of Mines, 1960. 11 l.
Note: 154 theses on post-Precambrian geology of Ontario completed before July 1959.
Location: OONL.

— 1961 —

6073 **Canadian Education Association**
Registry of Canadian theses in education. Toronto: Canadian Education Association, 1959-1961. 15 nos.
Note: Series 1: to 1955.– The first five numbers issued as inserts in the Association's newsletter, November 1959-April 1960.– Remaining numbers issued separately.
Supplement: ..., *1955-1962.* 1963. iii, 24 p.
Location: OOU.

6074 **Ginn, R.M.**
Bibliography of theses on the Precambrian geology of Ontario. [Toronto]: Ontario Department of Mines, 1961. ii, 49 l. (Miscellaneous paper / Ontario Department of Mines ; MP-2)
Note: 502 entries.– Theses on Ontario Precambrian geology completed before September 1960.
Location: OONL.

— 1962 —

6075 **Mailhiot, Bernard**
"Les recherches en psychologie sociale au Canada français (1946-1962)."
Dans: *Recherches sociographiques*; Vol. 3, no 1-2 (janvier-août 1962) p. 189-204.; ISSN: 0034-1282.
Note: Localisation: OONL.

6076 **Smith, Anne Marie; Wellwood, Robert William; Valg, Leonid**
Canadian theses in forestry and related subject fields, 1913-1962. [S.l: s.n.], 1962. [26] p.
Note: 388 entries.– Arranged by name of university, chronological.
Reprint from: *Forestry Chronicle*, Vol. 38, no. 3 (September 1962) p. 375-400.
Location: OONL.

— 1963 —

6077 **"An index of theses relating to the history of the Anglican Church of Canada."**
In: *Journal of the Canadian Church Historical Society*; Vol. 5, no. 2 (June 1963) p. [2-5].; ISSN: 0008-3208.
Note: 32 master's and 16 doctoral theses, 1915 to 1961.
Location: OONL.

6078 **LaNoue, George R.**
A bibliography of doctoral dissertations undertaken in American and Canadian universities (1940-1962) on religion and politics. New York: National Council of the Churches of Christ in the United States of America, c1963. 49 p.
Note: 649 dissertations (Ph.D. and Ed.D.) from disciplines of anthropology, education, history, law, philosophy, political science, sociology and religion dealing with relations and interactions of religion and politics.
Location: OONL.

6079 **National Research Council Canada. Associate Committee on Heat Transfer**
Abstracts of completed graduate theses in heat transfer in Canadian universities, to December 1961. Ottawa: Na-

tional Research Council Canada, 1963. 70 p.
Note: Location: OONL.

— 1964 —

6080 **Avison, Margaret**
The research compendium: review and abstracts of graduate research, 1942-1962, published in celebration of the fiftieth anniversary of the School of Social Work, University of Toronto. [Toronto]: University of Toronto Press, [c1964]. viii, 276 p.
Note: 412 entries.– Annotated listing of doctoral and masters' theses in social work at the University of Toronto School of Social Work.
Location: OONL.

— 1965 —

6081 **Black, Dorothy Miller**
Guide to lists of master's theses. Chicago: American Library Association, 1965. 144 p.
Note: Includes lists of master's theses written in colleges and universities of the United States and Canada through the year 1964: general lists, lists in special fields, lists by specific institutions.
Location: OONL.

6082 **"Graduate theses in Canadian history and related subjects."**
In: *Canadian Historical Review*; (1927-1965) ; ISSN: 0008-3755.
Note: Regular annual listing appears in the September issue from 1927 to 1965.– Includes "...titles not only in Canadian history but also in such related subjects as Canada's external relations, Canadian economics, law, and geography..."
Location: OONL.

6083 **Koester, C.B.**
A bibliography of selected theses on [i.e. in] the library of the University of Alberta (Edmonton) relating to western Canada, 1915-1965. Edmonton: [s.n.], 1965. 21 l.
Note: Approx. 200 entries.– Theses dealing with the social, economic, political, and cultural development of western Canada.– Excludes theses on scientific and technical subjects, even if generally located within the geographical scope of the bibliography.– Compiled for the Western Canada Research Project.
Location: OONL.

6084 **Kuehl, Warren F.**
Dissertations in history: an index to dissertations completed in history departments of United States and Canadian universities, 1873-1960. [Lexington]: University of Kentucky Press, 1965. 249 p.
Note: 7,635 entries.– Includes only those doctoral dissertations written under formally organized departments of history and for which the degree of doctor of philosophy has been conferred.– Excludes dissertations written in related fields such as religion, political science, economics, art, archaeology.
Supplements:
... , *1961-June 1970*. 1972. x, 237 p.; ISBN: 0-8131-1264-8.
Dissertations in history, 1970-June 1980: an index to dissertations completed in history departments of United States & Canadian universities. Santa Barbara, Calif.: ABC-Clio, c1985. xvii, 466 p.; ISBN: 0-87436-356-X.
Location: OONL.

— 1966 —

6085 **"Liste des thèses présentées à l'Institut d'histoire (Université de Montréal) 1947-1965."**
Dans: *Revue d'histoire de l'Amérique française*; Vol. 20, no 3 (décembre 1966) p. 515-521.; ISSN: 0035-2357.
Note: 108 entrées.
Localisation: OONL.

— 1967 —

6086 **Cruger, Doris M.**
A list of doctoral dissertations on Australia, covering 1933-34 through 1964-65; Canada, covering 1933-34 through 1964-65; New Zealand, covering 1933-34 through 1964-65. Ann Arbor, Mich.: Xerox, 1967. 20 p.
Note: Approx. 450 entries.– References taken from *American Doctoral Dissertations*.– Subject areas examined: economics, history, political science, sociology.– Includes dissertations accepted by American and Canadian universities.
Location: OONL.

6087 **Knill, William Douglas, et al.**
A classification of theses in education completed at the University of Alberta, 1929-1966. 3rd rev. ed. Edmonton: [s.n.], 1967. iv, 67 p.
Note: Previous editions:
... , *1929-1965*. 1965. 61 p.
Knill, William Douglas; Kowalski, A. ... , *1929-1964*. 1964. 61 p.
Location: AEU.

6088 **Roy, Jean**
"Liste des thèses et mémoires de maîtrise, D.E.S. et doctorat des facultés de droit du Québec."
Dans: *Revue du Barreau*; No 27 (1967) p. 680-687.; ISSN: 0383-669X.
Note: Localisation: OONL.

6089 **"Theses in geography completed for Department of Geography, University of Western Ontario."**
In: *Ontario Geography*; No. 1 (January 1967) p. 62-68.; ISSN: 0078-4850.
Note: Bachelor's theses, 1959 to December 1966; master's theses, 1947 to December 1966.
Location: OONL.

— 1968 —

6090 **McGill University. Faculty of Graduate Studies and Research**
List of McGill doctoral theses, 1907-1967. Montreal: McGill University, 1968.
Note: Location: BVAS.

6091 **Mills, Judy; Dombra, Irene**
University of Toronto doctoral theses, 1897-1967: a bibliography. [Toronto]: Published for the University of Toronto Library by University of Toronto Press, [c1968]. xi, 186 p.; ISBN: 0-8020-3224-9.
Note: 2,648 entries.
Supplement: ... , *1968-1975: a bibliography*. 1977. 166 p.; ISBN: 0-8020-3342-3.– 2,323 entries.
Location: OONL.

6092 **Parker, Franklin**
"Canadian education: a bibliography of doctoral dissertations."
In: *McGill Journal of Education*; Vol. 2, no. 2 (Fall 1967) p. 175-182; vol. 3, no. 1 (Spring 1968) p. 63-70.; ISSN: 0024-9033.
Note: Alphabetical author listing of 171 dissertations.

Location: AEU.

6093 University of British Columbia. Faculty of Forestry
U.B.C. theses in forestry and related subject fields (1920-1967). Vancouver: The Faculty, 1968. 8 l.
Note: Location: BVAS.

6094 University of Windsor. Department of Psychology
Graduate research in psychology, 1961-1968. Windsor, Ont.: Department of Psychology, University of Windsor, 1968. v l., 67 p.
Note: Location: OONL.

— 1969 —

6095 Breugelmans, René
"University research on Netherlandic-Canadians: a preliminary check list of dissertations and theses."
In: *Canadian Ethnic Studies*; Vol. 1, no. 1 (1969) p. 54-55.; ISSN: 0008-3496.
Note: Supplement: "First supplement." Vol. 5, no. 1/2 (1973) p. 229-230.– 14 entries in total.
Location: OONL.

6096 Cardinal, Clive H.; Malycky, Alexander
"University research on German-Canadians: a preliminary check list of dissertations and theses."
In: *Canadian Ethnic Studies*; Vol. 1, no. 1 (1969) p. 7-12.; ISSN: 0008-3496.
Note: Supplements:
"First supplement." Vol. 2, no. 1 (June 1970) p. 45-46.
"Second supplement." Vol. 5, no. 1/2 (1973) p. 63-65.
"Third supplement." *Canadiana Germanica*, No. 35 (August 1982) p. 34-37.– 115 entries in total.
Location: OONL.

6097 Con, Ronald J.
"University research on Chinese-Canadians."
In: *Canadian Ethnic Studies*; Vol. 1, no. 1 (1969) p. 1-2.; ISSN: 0008-3496.
Note: Supplements:
"First supplement." Vol. 2, no. 1 (June 1970) p. 13.
Laychuck, Julian L. "Second supplement." Vol. 5, no. 1/2 (1973) p. 5-6.– 30 entries in total.
Location: OONL.

6098 Malycky, Alexander
"University research on Jewish-Canadians."
In: *Canadian Ethnic Studies*; Vol. 1, no. 1 (1969) p. 40-43.; ISSN: 0008-3496.
Note: Supplements:
Goertz, Richard O.W. " ... . Supplement." Vol. 2, no. 1 (June 1970) p. 129.
" ... . Supplement." Vol. 5, no. 1/2 (1973) p. 207-212.– 89 entries in total.
Location: OONL.

6099 Malycky, Alexander
"University research on Ukrainian-Canadians: a preliminary checklist of dissertations and theses."
In: *Canadian Ethnic Studies*; Vol. 1, no. 1 (1969) p. 72-76.; ISSN: 0008-3496.
Note: Supplements:
"First supplement." Vol. 2, no. 1 (June 1970) p. 193-194.
"Second supplement." Vol. 5, no. 1/2 (1973) p. 271-273.
Location: OONL.

6100 Rosval, Sergei J.
"University research on Russian Canadians."
In: *Canadian Ethnic Studies*; Vol. 1, no. 1 (1969) p. 59-60.; ISSN: 0008-3496.
Note: Supplements:

"First supplement." Vol. 2, no. 1 (June 1970) p. 171-172.
Royick, Alexander. "Second supplement." Vol. 5, no. 1/2 (1973) p. 251-252.– 31 entries in total.
Location: OONL.

6101 Tirman, Jean-Louis
"Répertoire des thèses de maîtrise en géographie présentées à l'Institut de géographie de l'Université Laval, d'octobre 1959 à novembre 1968."
Dans: *Cahiers de géographie de Québec*; Vol. 13, no 30 (décembre 1969) p. 374-379.; ISSN: 0007-9766.
Note: Localisation: OONL.

— 1970 —

6102 Bianchini, Luciano
"University research on Italian-Canadians: a preliminary check list."
In: *Canadian Ethnic Studies*; Vol. 2, no. 1 (June 1970) p. 117-119.; ISSN: 0008-3496.
Note: Supplement: Malycky, Alexander. " ... . Supplement." Vol. 5, no. 1/2 (1973) p. 195-196.– 30 entries in total.
Location: OONL.

6103 Browning, Clyde E.
A bibliography of dissertations in geography, 1901-1969. Chapel Hill, N.C.: University of North Carolina at Chapel Hill, Department of Geography, 1970. 96 p. (Studies in geography / University of North Carolina at Chapel Hill, Department of Geography ; no. 1)
Note: 1,582 entries.– Includes theses with a Canadian focus in all subject categories.
Supplement: *A bibliography of dissertations in geography, 1969 to 1982: American and Canadian universities.* 1983. vii, 145 p. (Studies in geography ; no. 18).– 2,270 entries.
Location: OONL.

6104 Heinrich, Albert C.
"University research on Canada's Eskimos."
In: *Canadian Ethnic Studies*; Vol. 2, no. 1 (June 1970) p. 31-33.; ISSN: 0008-3496.
Note: Supplement: " ... . Supplement." Vol. 5, no. 1/2 (1973) p. 47-49.– 54 entries in total.
Location: OONL.

6105 Kiyooka, Harry M.
"University research on Japanese-Canadians: a preliminary check list of theses."
In: *Canadian Ethnic Studies*; Vol. 2, no. 1 (June 1970) p. 127-128.; ISSN: 0008-3496.
Note: Supplement: "First supplement." Vol. 5, no. 1/2 (1973) p. 205-206.– 21 entries in total.
Location: OONL.

6106 Malycky, Alexander
"University research on Canada's Indians and Métis."
In: *Canadian Ethnic Studies*; Vol. 2, no. 1 (June 1970) p. 95-107.; ISSN: 0008-3496.
Note: Supplement: "... . Supplement." Vol. 5, no. 1-2 (1973) p. 153-182.– 429 entries in total.
Location: OONL.

6107 Szucs, Lina
"University research on Polish-Canadians: a preliminary check list of theses."
In: *Canadian Ethnic Studies*; Vol. 2, no. 1 (June 1970) p. 163-164.; ISSN: 0008-3496.
Note: Supplement: "First supplement." Vol. 5, no. 1/2 (1973) p. 239.– 22 entries in total.
Location: OONL.

6108 **Wood, W.D.; Kelly, L.A.; Kumar, Pradeep**
Canadian graduate theses, 1919-1967: an annotated bibliography (covering economics, business and industrial relations). Kingston, Ont.: Industrial Relations Centre, Queen's University, 1970. xiv, 483 p. (Bibliography series / Industrial Relations Centre, Queen's University ; no. 4; ISSN: 0075-613X)
Note: 2,494 entries.– Inclusion is based on theses accepted by Canadian universities or completed at a U.S. university on a Canadian subject.– Both French- and English-language theses are included.– Industrial relations is given a broad meaning, to include all aspects of the employer-employee relationship: vocational choice, human rights and discrimination in the workplace, women's employment, employment law, unemployment and inflation, effects of automation, labour economics, personnel administration, collective bargaining, labour legislation, labour unions, industrial psychology and sociology.
Supplements:
Perry, Elizabeth. *Bibliography of masters and doctoral theses on Canadian industrial relations from 1967 to 1978.* Toronto: Centre for Industrial Relations, University of Toronto, 1981. iii, 93 p.
Perry, Elizabeth. *Bibliography of doctoral and masters theses on industrial relations, 1978-1985.* Toronto: Jean & Dorothy Newman Industrial Relations Library, 1991. 37, 15, 65, 24 p.
Location: OONL.

— 1971 —

6109 **Parker, Franklin**
American dissertations on foreign education: a bibliography with abstracts: volume 1: Canada. Troy, N.Y.: Whitston Publishing, 1971. 175 p.; ISBN: 0-87875-013-4.
Note: 171 entries.
Location: OONL.

6110 **Steeves, Allan D.**
A complete bibliography in sociology and a partial bibliography in anthropology of M.A. theses and Ph.D. dissertations completed at Canadian universities up to 1970. Ottawa: [s.n.], 1971. 83, 12 l.
Note: Approx. 800 entries.
Location: OONL.

6111 **Theses in Canadian political studies: completed and in progress/Thèses canadiennes en science politique: complétées et en cours de rédaction.** [Kingston, Ont.]: Canadian Political Science Association, [1971]. 71 p.
Note: Approx. 1,500 entries.– Covers all years up to and including 1970.– General categories cover political philosophy, analysis, sociology and methodology.– Specific topics include Canadian political parties and electoral studies, federalism and intergovernmental relations, local and municipal politics, French Canada, international organization and law, foreign policy, comparative politics (western, communist, Third World systems).– Text in English and French/texte en français et en anglais.
Supplements:
… . *Annual supplement.* Ottawa: Canadian Political Science Association, 1972-1973. 2 vol.; ISSN: 0316-5280.
… . *Supplement/… . Supplément.* Ottawa: Canadian Political Science Association, 1974-   . vol.; ISSN: 0228-3204.

Annual.– Prepared in association with the Société québécoise de science politique.– Text in English and French/texte en français et en anglais.
Location: OONL.

6112 **Woodward, Frances M.**
Theses on British Columbia history and related subjects in the Library of the University of British Columbia. Rev. and enl. ed. Vancouver: University of British Columbia Library, 1971. 57 p. (Reference publication / University of British Columbia Library ; no. 35)
Note: 411 entries.
Previous edition: 1969. 31 p. (Reference publication ; no. 29).
Microform: 1988. 6 microfiches.
Location: BVAU.

— 1972 —

6113 **Brodeur, Léo A.; Naaman, Antoine**
Répertoire des thèses littéraires canadiennes (janvier 1969-septembre 1971): 1786 sujets/Index of Canadian literary theses (January 1969-September 1971): 1786 subjects. [Sherbrooke, Québec]: Centre d'étude des littératures d'expression française, Université de Sherbrooke, [c1972]. 141 p. (Cahiers francophones / Centre d'étude des littératures d'expression française, Université de Sherbrooke ; 2)
Note: Sujets généraux (civilisation, folklore, mouvement des idées), genres littéraires (journalisme, poésie, roman, théâtre), études comparées (traduction, auteurs), auteurs.– Texte en français et en anglais/text in English and French.
Localisation: OONL.

6114 **Carleton University. Carleton Archives**
Theses and research essays accepted by Carleton University between 1950 and November 1969, and held in MacOdrum Library. Ottawa: Carleton Archives, Library, Carleton University, 1972. 62 l.
Note: Approx. 700 entries.– Compiled by D.M. Honeywell.
Location: OONL.

6115 **Clermont, Simonne**
Liste des thèses et des mémoires de l'Université de Moncton. Moncton, N.-B.: Bibliothèque Champlain, Université de Moncton, 1972. 24 f.
Note: Localisation: NBFL.

6116 **Fraser, J. Keith; Hynes, Mary C.**
List of theses and dissertations on Canadian geography/Liste des thèses et dissertations sur la géographie du Canada. Ottawa: Lands Directorate, Department of the Environment, 1972. vi, 114 p. (Geographical paper / Lands Directorate, Department of the Environment ; no. 51)
Note: 2,418 entries.– Baccalaureate, master's and doctoral theses produced at Canadian geography departments which concern the geography of Canada.– Also contains theses granted at foreign universities.– Excludes fields of economics, history, geology.– Text in English and French/texte en français et en anglais.
Previous editions:
Meyer, W.C. *Cumulative list of theses on Canadian geography/Liste des thèses sur la géographie du Canada.* 1966. 57 p. (Bibliographical series / Geographical Branch, Department of Energy, Mines and Resources ; no. 34).
Canada. Department of Mines and Technical Surveys.

Geographical Branch. 1964. 40 p. (Bibliographical series ; no. 31).

Canada. Department of Mines and Technical Surveys. Geographical Branch. *University dissertations, theses and essays on Canadian geography. Cumulative edition, 1953.* 1954. 19 p. (Bibliographical series ; no. 3).
Supplements:
... : supplement/... : supplément. Canadian Committee for Geography, 1973-1976. 4 vol.; ISSN: 0319-5392.– Annual.
Location: OONL.

6117 **Heinrich, Albert C.**
"University research on Canada's Eskimos: a preliminary check list of theses."
In: *Northian*; Vol. 8, no. 4 (March 1972) p. 29-30.; ISSN: 0029-3253.
Note: Location: OONL.

6118 **Klinck, Carl F.**
"Post-graduate theses in Canadian literature: English and French comparative."
In: *Journal of Canadian Fiction*; Vol. 1, no. 2 (Summer 1972) p. 68-73.; ISSN: 0047-2255.
Note: Continued by: Stephen Barnwell (Spring 1973-1976).
Location: AEU.

6119 **Malycky, Alexander**
"University research on Canada's Indians and Métis: a preliminary check list."
In: *Northian*; Vol. 8, no. 4 (March 1972) p. 31-37.; ISSN: 0029-3253.
Note: 129 entries.
Location: OONL.

6120 **Raveneau, Jean**
"Liste des thèses de maîtrise (1960-1971) et mémoires de licence (1964-1971) présentés au Département de géographie de l'Université Laval et concernant l'Est du Québec."
Dans: *Cahiers de géographie de Québec*; Vol. 16, no 37 (avril 1972) p. 122-129.; ISSN: 0007-9766.
Note: Localisation: OONL.

6121 **Université d'Ottawa. Bibliothèque générale. Informathèque**
Répertoire des thèses présentées à l'Université d'Ottawa dans le domaine des sciences sociales et des humanités: projet O3 – CE/Catalogue of social sciences and humanities theses presented at the University of Ottawa: O3 – CE project. [Ottawa]: Informathèque, Bibliothèque générale, 1972. v, 219 p.
Note: Approx. 1,600 entrées.– Texte en français et en anglais/text in English and French.
Localisation: OONL.

— 1973 —

6122 **Basran, Gurcharn S.**
"University research on East-Indian-Canadians: a preliminary check list of theses."
In: *Canadian Ethnic Studies*; Vol. 5, no. 1/2 (1973) p. 41-42.; ISSN: 0008-3496.
Note: 10 entries.
Location: OONL.

6123 **Canadian theses 1947-1960/Thèses canadiennes 1947-1960.** Ottawa: National Library of Canada, 1973. 2 vol.
Note: Theses accepted by Canadian universities.– Arranged in broad subject groupings, subdivided by university and by author.

Location: OONL.

6124 **Jobling, J. Keith**
"University research on Greek-Canadians: a preliminary check list of theses."
In: *Canadian Ethnic Studies*; Vol. 5, no. 1/2 (1973) p. 125-126.; ISSN: 0008-3496.
Note: 9 entries.
Location: OONL.

6125 **Laychuck, Julian L.**
"University research on Scottish-Canadians: a preliminary check list of theses."
In: *Canadian Ethnic Studies*; Vol. 5, no. 1/2 (1973) p. 259-261.; ISSN: 0008-3496.
Note: 21 entries.
Locations: OONL.

6126 **Malycky, Alexander**
"University research on Negro-Canadians: a preliminary check list of theses."
In: *Canadian Ethnic Studies*; Vol. 5, no. 1/2 (1973) p. 225-227.; ISSN: 0008-3496.
Note: 21 entries.
Location: OONL.

6127 **Miska, John P.**
"University research on Hungarian-Canadians: a preliminary check list of theses."
In: *Canadian Ethnic Studies*; Vol. 5, no. 1/2 (1973) p. 127-128.; ISSN: 0008-3496.
Note: 9 entries.
Location: OONL.

6128 **Moloney, Nancy M.**
"University research on Irish-Canadians: a preliminary check list of theses."
In: *Canadian Ethnic Studies*; Vol. 5, no. 1/2 (1973) p. 193-194.; ISSN: 0008-3496.
Note: 17 entries.
Location: OONL.

6129 **Stuart, Merrill M.**
A bibliography of master's theses in geography: American and Canadian universities. Tualatin, Or.: Geographic and Area Study Publications, c1973. x, 275 p.; ISBN: 0-88393-001-3.
Note: 5,054 entries.
Location: OONL.

6130 **Thwaites, James D.**
Thèses en sciences de l'éducation (universités du Québec et universités francophones ailleurs au Canada). Québec: Institut supérieur des sciences humaines, Université Laval, 1973. ii, 159 p. (Cahiers de l'ISSH, Collection Instruments de travail / Institut supérieur des sciences humaines, Université Laval ; no 9)
Note: 1,307 entrées.
Localisation: OONL.

6131 **Université Laval. École des gradués**
Répertoire des thèses, 1941-1973. 4e éd. [Québec]: Préparé par le Centre de documentation, Bibliothèque, pour l'École des gradués, Université Laval, 1973. 27, 186, 210 f.
Note: Éditions antérieures:
... , 1941-1970. 1971. 28, 136, 153 f.
Listes des thèses, 1940 à 1965. 1965. v, 82 p.
Gagne, Armand. *Catalogue des thèses de l'École des gradués de l'Université Laval, 1940-1960.* 1960. 76 p.
Localisation: QQLA.

— 1974 —

6132 **Dockstader, Frederick J.**
The American Indian in graduate studies: a bibliography of theses and dissertations. New York: Museum of the American Indian, Heye Foundation, 1973-1974. 2 vol. (Contributions from the Museum of the American Indian, Heye Foundation ; vol. 25)
Note: Vol. 1 covers the period from 1890 to 1955; vol. 2 covers from 1955 to 1970 inclusive.– Includes Canadian theses.
Location: OONL.

6133 **Hodson, Dean R.**
A bibliography of dissertations and theses in geography on Anglo-America, 1960-1972. Monticello, Ill.: Council of Planning Librarians, 1974. 202 p. (Council of Planning Librarians Exchange bibliography ; 583, 584)
Note: Approx. 3,000 entries.– Canadian section, p. 160-202, lists theses and dissertations in English and French on a wide range of geographical topics relating to all regions of Canada.
Location: NBSAM.

6134 **Narang, H.L.**
Canadian masters' theses in reading education: an annotated bibliography. Regina: Faculty of Education, University of Saskatchewan, 1974. 77 l.
Note: 131 entries.– Abstracts of master's theses in reading instruction, reading research, reading achievement, teaching methods, completed at 14 Canadian universities between 1922 and 1972.
Location: AEU.

6135 **Thwaites, James D.**
"Thèses récentes sur le travailleur, le syndicalisme et le patronat."
Dans: *Histoire des travailleurs québécois: Bulletin RCHTQ;* Vol. 1, no 2 (février 1974) p. 18-20.; ISSN: 0315-7938.
Note: Localisation: OONL.

— 1975 —

6136 **"Département de sociologie, Université de Montréal: maîtrise et doctorat, 1955-1975."**
Dans: *Sociologie et sociétés;* Vol. 7, no 2 (novembre 1975) p. 143-152.; ISSN: 0038-030X.
Note: Localisation: OONL.

6137 **Gnarowski, Michael**
Theses and dissertations in Canadian literature (English): a preliminary check list. Ottawa: Golden Dog Press, 1975. 41 p.; ISBN: 0-919614-12-4.
Note: Approx. 300 entries.
Location: OONL.

6138 **Narang, H.L.**
"Canadian research in Indian education."
In: *Northian;* Vol. 11, no. 1 (Spring 1975) p. 11-12.; ISSN: 0029-3253.
Note: Master's theses and doctoral dissertations completed through 1971.
Location: AEU.

6139 **Pane, Remigio U.**
"Doctoral dissertations on the Italian American experience completed in the United States and Canadian universities, 1908-1974."
In: *International Migration Review;* Vol. 9, no. 4 (Winter 1975) p. 545-556.; ISSN: 0197-9183.
Note: 156 entries.– Includes Canadian references.
Location: OONL.

6140 **University of Saskatchewan**
University of Saskatchewan postgraduate theses, 1912-1973. Saskatoon: University of Saskatchewan, 1975. 168 p.
Note: Approx. 3,000 entries.
Previous edition: *University of Saskatchewan postgraduate theses, 1912-1966.* 1967. iii, 93 p.
Location: OONL.

6141 **Wong, Chuck**
A checklist of university theses on northeastern Ontario/ Répertoire des thèses sur le nord-est de l'Ontario. Sudbury, Ont.: Laurentian University Library, 1975. 45 l.
Note: 149 entries.– Text in English and French/texte en français et en anglais.
Location: OONL.

— 1976 —

6142 **Barnwell, Stephen**
"Post-graduate theses in Canadian literature: English and English-French comparative."
In: *Journal of Canadian Fiction;* Vol. 2, no. 2 (Spring 1973) p. 78-82; vol. 3, no. 2 (1974) p. 87-92;, no. 16 (1976) p. 144-157.; ISSN: 0047-2255.
Note: Continues: Karl F. Klinck (Summer 1972).
Location: AEU.

6143 **Québec (Province). Ministère de l'éducation. Direction générale de la planification**
Thèses et mémoires relatifs à l'éducation, 1969-1974. Québec: Ministère de l'éducation, Direction générale de la planification, 1976. 258 p.
Note: Localisation: OONL.

6144 **Spitzer, Frank; Silvester, Elizabeth**
McGill University thesis directory. Montreal: Faculty of Graduate Studies and Research, McGill University, 1976. 2 vol.; ISBN: 0-7735-0278-5.
Note: Approx. 10,600 entries.– Covers the years 1881 to 1973.– Chronological arrangement with indexes: authors, departments, supervisors.
Location: OONL.

— 1977 —

6145 **Pronovost, Gilles**
Répertoire des thèses de maîtrise et de doctorat sur le loisir au Québec (des origines à 1976). Trois-Rivières: Groupe de recherche en loisir, Université du Québec à Trois-Rivières, 1977. 85 f.; ISBN: 0-919718-01-9.
Note: Localisation: QQLA.

6146 **University Microfilms International. Dissertations Publishing**
North American Indians: a dissertation index. Ann Arbor, Mich.: University Microfilms International, 1977. vii, 169 p.; ISBN: 0-8357-0134-4.
Note: Approx. 1,600 entries.– Listing of doctoral dissertations written between 1904 and 1976 concerning all Indian groups within the North American continent.– Substantial Canadian content.
Supplement: ... : *supplement 1.* 1979.– 557 entries.– 455 doctoral dissertations written in 1977 and 1978, 102 master's theses written between 1962 and 1978).
Location: OONL.

— 1978 —

6147 **Brunn, Stanley D.**
Key word identifiers of theses and dissertations from departments of geography in Canada and the United States on land use, water use, resource conflict, resource policy, and facility location. Monticello, Ill.: Council of

Planning Librarians, 1978. 71 p. (Council of Planning Librarians Exchange bibliography ; 1512)
Note: 782 entries.
Location: OWA.

6148 **Naaman, Antoine**
Répertoire des thèses littéraires canadiennes de 1921 à 1976. Sherbrooke: Éditions Naaman, [1978]. 453 p.
Note: 5,613 entrées.– Thèses soutenues ou en préparation dans les universités canadiennes et étrangères de 1921 au mois de mars 1976.
Édition antérieure: *Guide bibliographique des thèses littéraire canadiennes de 1921 à 1969.* Cosmos, 1970. 338 p.
Localisation: OONL.

6149 **Swyripa, Frances A.**
"Theses and dissertations on Ukrainian Canadians: an annotated bibliography."
In: *Journal of Ukrainian Graduate Studies;* Vol. 3, no. 1 (Spring 1978) p. 91-110.; ISSN: 0701-1792.
Note: Includes Ph.D. dissertations, master's theses, and degree-required essays at the bachelor level written on Ukrainian-Canadian topics at Canadian, American and European universities.– Arranged in two sections: humanities and social sciences; language, literature, linguistics.– Theses are annotated, giving author's purpose, summary of findings, relevance to Ukrainian-Canadian studies.
Location: AEU.

— 1979 —

6150 **Bibliothèque nationale du Québec**
Liste des thèses de l'Institut agricole d'Oka déposées à la Bibliothèque nationale du Québec. Montréal: La Bibliothèque, 1979. 25 f.
Note: Localisation: QQLAS.

6151 **Gribenski, Jean**
Thèses de doctorat en langue française relatives à la musique: bibliographie commentée/French language dissertations in music: an annotated bibliography. New York: Pendragon Press, 1979.; ISBN: 0-018728-09-6.
Note: 438 entrées.– La période couverte est de 1883 à 1976.– Catégories: histoire de la musique, ethnomusicologie, instruments, notation, théorie, pédagogie, musique et autres arts, musique et autres disciplines.– Comporte des références canadiennes et québécoises.
Localisation: OONL.

6152 **Markowitz, Arnold L.**
"Historic preservation: a survey of American and Canadian doctoral dissertations, 1961-1976."
In: *Journal of Architectural Education;* Vol. 32, no. 3 (February 1979) p. 10-11.; ISSN: 0047-2239.
Note: Presents a chronological overview of twelve dissertations concerned with the preservation of historic buildings, construction, sites; gives bibliographic data and description of content.
Location: OOCM.

6153 **"Mémoires et thèses de linguistique et de traduction soutenus à l'Université de Montréal de 1943 à 1971."**
Dans: *Vingt-cinq ans de linguistique au Canada: hommage à Jean-Paul Vinay.* Montréal: Centre éducatif et culturel, c1979. P. 125-135.; ISBN: 2-7617-0019-8.
Note: Localisation: OOCC.

6154 **Sandvoss, Joachim**
Canadian graduate theses in music and music education, 1897-1978. [S.l.: s.n., 1979]. [1], 38, [4] l.
Note: 496 entries.– Lists theses and dissertations accepted by Canadian universities in music and music education.– Also includes Canadian theses in experimental psychology, accoustics, literature of interest to music researchers, dissertations of Canadian interest completed at American universities.– Unpublished, typewritten copy.
Location: OONL.

— 1980 —

6155 **Libick, Helen**
A bibliography of Canadian theses and dissertations in urban, regional and environmental planning, 1974-1979 / Une bibliographie canadienne des thèses et dissertations en planification urbaine, régionale et environnementale, 1974-1979. [Montreal]: Canadian Association of Planning Students, 1980. xv, 286 p.
Note: Approx. 3,000 entries.– Survey of entire student output from Canadian universities, in addition to sampling from American and European universities, when subject is Canadian.– Includes thesis alternatives or research projects, theses in progress in planning and related disciplines.– Topics include city dynamics, settlement types and patterns, municipal policies/ politics and government, regional and rural development, housing, recreation, transportation, energy, man-environment interactions, planning.– Text in English and French/texte en français et en anglais.
Location: OONL.

6156 **Mutimer, Brian T.P.**
Canadian graduating essays, theses and dissertations relating to the history and philosophy of sport, physical education and recreation. Rev. ed. Ottawa: Canadian Association for Health, Physical Education and Recreation, 1980. 35 p.
Note: Compiled for the History of Sport and Physical Activity Committee, and the Philosophy of Sport and Physical Activity Committee of the Canadian Association for Health, Physical Education and Recreation.
Previous edition: Antigonish, N.S.: Saint Francis Xavier University, 1975. 14 l.
Location: QQLA.

6157 **Tupling, Donald**
Canada: a dissertation bibliography/Canada: une bibliographie de dissertations. [Ann Arbor, Mich.]: University Microfilms International, [1980]. vi, 131 p.
Note: 5,460 entries.– Covers the period 1884 to 1979.– Text in English and French/texte en français et en anglais.
Supplement: ... : 1983 supplement/... : 1983 supplément. 1983. x, 6, 31 p.– 760 entries.
Location: OONL.

— 1981 —

6158 **Draper, James A.**
Adult education theses, Canada. Toronto: Department of Adult Education, Ontario Institute for Studies in Education, 1981. iv, 165 p.
Note: 557 entries.– Master's and doctoral theses completed in adult education at seven Canadian universities, up to and including 1980.– Excludes M.Ed. and M.Sc. degrees which are not strictly theses, but rather "major projects," group projects, research relating to adult

education in Canada which is undertaken within other disciplines such as history, architecture, psychology, medical science, business administration.

Location: OONL.

6159 **Université de Montréal. Bibliothèque EPC.**
Liste des mémoires et des thèses en science de l'éducation, en psychologie et en communication disponibles à la Bibliothèque E.P.C.: licence, maîtrise, doctorat. Montréal: Service des bibliothèques, Université de Montréal, 1981. 2 vol.; ISBN: 0-88259-035-6.
Note: Localisation: OONL.

6160 **Veitch, Isobel G.**
Completed theses and undergraduate senior reports [Department of Geography, University of Western Ontario]. London: Department of Geography, University of Western Ontario, 1981. iv, 59 p. (Geographical papers / Department of Geography, University of Western Ontario ; no. 48; ISSN: 0706-487X); ISBN: 0-7714-0303-8.
Note: 656 entries.– Covers to December 31, 1981.– Lists undergraduate senior reports, master's theses, doctoral dissertations in chronological order.– Indexes: author, subject, geographic.
Location: OONL.

— 1982 —

6161 **Theses related to planning.** [Vancouver: University of British Columbia, Fine Arts Library], 1982. 124 p.
Note: Approx. 1,300 entries.
Location: OONL.

6162 **Wong, Chuck**
Master's theses and research essays accepted by Laurentian University between 1962 and June 1981, and held in the Main Library. Sudbury, Ont.: Laurentian University Library, 1982. 52 p. (Laurentian University Library special collections ; 2)
Note: 458 entries.– Text in English and French/texte en français et en anglais.
Location: OONL.

— 1983 —

6163 **Barnett, Don C.; Dyer, Aldrich J.**
"Research on native peoples at the University of Saskatchewan."
In: *Canadian Journal of Native Education*; Vol. 10, no. 4 (Summer 1983) p. 12-22.; ISSN: 0710-1481.
Note: Location: AEU.

6164 **Canadian theses/Thèses canadiennes.** Ottawa: Ministry of Supply and Services, 1962-1983. 15 vol.; ISSN: 0068-9874.
Note: Irregular annual.– Issues for 1960/61-1971/72, published annually; 1972/73-1974/75, issued in one volume (1980); 1976/77-1979/80, in one volume (1983).– Listing of all theses accepted by participating Canadian universities.– Arranged in broad subject divisions based on Dewey Decimal Classification.– Text in English and French/texte en français et en anglais.
Location: OONL.

6165 **Carleton University. Department of Geography**
Master and bachelor theses in geography, 1965-1983. Ottawa: Carleton University, 1983. 57 p.
Note: Location: OOCC.

6166 **Cohen, Yolande; Boucher, Andrée**
Les thèses universitaires québécoises sur les femmes, 1921-1981. 2e éd. rev., corr. et augm. Québec: Institut québécois de recherche sur la culture, 1983. 121 p. (Instru-

ments de travail / Institut québécois de recherche sur la culture ; no 7; ISSN: 0714-5608); ISBN: 2-89224-016-6.
Note: 731 entrées.– Thèmes: modèles littéraires, famille, "cas sociaux" et formes d'assistance, travail rémunéré, sexualité, différences sexuelles et stéréotypes sexistes, groupes d'âges et groupes ethniques, femmes dans l'histoire.
Édition antérieure: "La recherche universitaire sur les femmes au Québec (1921-1980): répertoire des thèses de maîtrise et de doctorat déposées dans les universités du Québec." Dans: *Documentation sur la recherche féministe*; Vol. 10, no 4 (décembre 1981-janvier 1982) p. 7-24; ISSN: 0707-8412.
Localisation: OONL.

6167 **Collette-Carrière, Renée**
Les études de la femme à l'Université de Montréal: répertoire des mémoires et des thèses complétés de 1962 à 1983 (juin). [S.l.: s.n.], 1983. 58 p.
Note: Approx. 500 entrées.
Localisation: OONL.

6168 **Concordia University**
Concordia University thesis directory. Montreal: Concordia University, 1979-1983. 2 vol.; ISBN: 0-88947-0006 (vol. 1); 0-88947-008-1 (vol. 2).
Note: Approx. 1,700 entries.– Covers the period 1967 to 1983.– Listings are chronological, author, supervisor, department.
Location: OONL.

6169 **Eiber, Thomas G.; King, Marjorie**
Forestry bibliography: theses, 1971-1983. Thunder Bay, Ont.: Lakehead University, 1983. 122 p.
Note: Approx. 400 entries.– Compiled from the *Forestry Theses Database*, a subset of Lakehead University's *Northern and Regional Studies Database*.– Principal subjects include ecology, growth and yield, genetics, entomology, management, silviculture, wood science, harvesting, mensuration, pathology, spruce (white and black).
Location: OONL.

6170 **National Library of Canada**
Theses of the Université de Montréal microfilmed since 1972/Thèses de l'Université de Montréal microfilmées depuis 1972. Ottawa: National Library of Canada, 1982-1983. 5 vol.; ISSN: 0713-5092.
Note: Location: OONL.

6171 **Noël, François**
Bibliographie des thèses et des mémoires sur les communautés culturelles et l'immigration au Québec. Montréal: Communautés culturelles et immigration Québec, 1983. ii, 43 p.; ISBN: 2-550-02925-9.
Note: 286 entrées.
Localisation: OONL.

6172 **Quance, Elizabeth J.; Cronk, Michael Sam**
"Museum studies dissertations at the University of Toronto: a selected bibliography."
In: *Material Studies Bulletin*; No. 18 (Fall 1983) p. 50-54.; ISSN: 0703-489X.
Note: Annotated selection of 29 dissertations, 1972-1983, in the field of material history relevant to museology.
Location: OONL.

6173 **Roseneder, Jan**
University of Calgary theses: a bibliography, 1959-1978. Calgary: University of Calgary Libraries, 1983. 2 vol. (Bibliography series / University of Calgary Libraries ;

no. 2); ISBN: 0-88953-048-3.

Note: 2,810 entries.– Includes master's, doctoral, master's projects completed at University of Calgary.– Citations list author, title, degree and year awarded, supervisor, National Library of Canada microfilm order number, LC subject headings, geographic location headings.– Indexes include author, title, supervisor, subject and geographic location.– Database updated annually.– Printouts on demand.

Location: OONL.

6174 **Université du Québec à Montréal. Département de science politique**
Sommaire des mémoires de maîtrise du Département de science politique. Montréal: Université du Québec à Montréal, 1983. 105 l. (Notes de recherche / Département de science politique, Université du Québec à Montréal ; no 25)

Note: Approx. 70 entrées.– Principaux thèmes: "La politique au Canada et au Québec;" "Relations internationales et systèmes politiques étrangers;" "Administration publique, théorie et la décision et analyse des politiques publiques;" "Théorie et analyse politiques."

Localisation: OONL.

— 1984 —

6175 **Gabel, Gernot U.**
Canadian literature: an index to theses accepted by Canadian universities, 1925-1980. Köln: Edition Gemini, 1984. 157 p.; ISBN: 3-922331-15-7.

Note: 1,531 entries.– Presented in two main sections: literary history and criticism (general studies, poetry, fiction, drama and theatre, periodicals); individual authors.

Location: OONL.

6176 **Gadacz, René R.**
Thesis and dissertation titles and abstracts on the anthropology of Canadian Indians, Inuit and Metis from Canadian universities, report 1, 1970-1982. Ottawa: National Museums of Canada, 1984. x, 128 p. (National Museum of Man Mercury series: Canadian Ethnology Service paper ; no. 95; ISSN: 0316-1862)

Note: Approx. 400 entries.– Guide to graduate research work undertaken in Departments of Anthropology in areas of ethnography, physical anthropology, archaeology and linguistics relating to Canadian native peoples.

Location: OONL.

6177 **Université Laval. Bureau de l'extension**
Répertoire des thèses de maîtrise et de doctorat (1962-1984) Faculté des sciences de l'agriculture et de l'alimentation, Université Laval. Québec: Le Bureau, 1984. 1 vol. (en pagination multiple); ISSN: 0843-2937.

Note: Inclut également quelques sujets d'essais de maîtrise de type A (sans thèse) réalisés aux départements d'économie rurale et de phytologie.– Les thèses et essais sont classés par département d'origine: nutrition humaine, économie rurale, génie rurale, phytologie, sols, sciences et technologie des aliments et zootechnie.

Localisation: OONL.

6178 **University of New Brunswick. Department of Sociology**
Abstracts of master of arts theses, 1960 to 1984. Fredericton: The Department, 1984. iii, 136 p.; ISBN: 0-

920114-66-0.

Note: Approx. 50 entries.– Abstracts of master's theses in sociology.

Location: OONL.

— 1985 —

6179 **Lefebvre, Marie-Thérèse**
"Répertoire des travaux universitaires sur la musique du Québec (1924-1984)."
Dans: *Canadian University Music Review: Revue de musique des universités canadiennes*; No. 6 (1985) p. 45-67.; ISSN: 0710-0353.

Note: Inventaire des travaux universitaires traitant de la musique québécoise: mémoires de maîtrise et thèses de doctorat déposés dans les universités canadiennes et étrangères.

Localisation: OONL.

6180 **Minion, Robin**
Partial list of theses related to native peoples. Edmonton: Boreal Institute for Northern Studies, University of Alberta, 1985. 133 p. (Boreal Institute for Northern Studies Bibliographic series ; no. 13; ISSN: 0824-8192); ISBN: 0-919058-47-7.

Note: 314 entries.– List produced from Boreal Institute Library's SPIRES database.– Includes master's and doctoral theses.– BINS series produced monthly from January 1984 to May 1986 (no. 29).– Online access: *Boreal Northern Titles*, available through QL Systems Limited.

Location: OONL.

— 1986 —

6181 **Dossick, Jesse J.**
Doctoral research on Canada and Canadians, 1884-1983/ Thèses et doctorat concernant le Canada et les canadiens, 1884-1983. Ottawa: National Library of Canada, 1986. xv, 559 p.; ISBN: 0-660-53227-1.

Note: 12,032 entries.– Inventory of doctoral research on Canadian subjects, completed at Canadian, American, British, European and Australian universities.– Text in English and French/texte en français et en anglais.

Location: OONL.

6182 **Dyer, Aldrich J.**
"An ore body of note: theses and dissertations on Indians, Metis and Inuit at the University of Alberta."
In: *Canadian Journal of Native Education*; Vol. 13, no. 2 (1986) p. 40-51.; ISSN: 0710-1481.

Note: 192 entries.

Location: AEU.

6183 **Gilbert, Anne**
Mémoires et thèses en géographie humaine dans les universités canadiennes de langue française: 1975-1985. Montréal: Université de Montréal, Département de Géographie, 1986. 60 p. (Notes et documents / Département de Géographie, Université de Montréal ; no 86-01)

Note: Localisation: QQLA.

6184 **Kerst, Catherine Hiebert**
Ethnic folklife dissertations from the United States and Canada, 1960-1980: a selected, annotated bibliography. Washington: American Folklife Center, Library of Congress, 1986. vi, 69 p. (Publications of the American Folklife Center ; no. 12)

Note: Approx. 250 entries.– Multidisciplinary selection of Ph.D. dissertations on subject of indigenous and ethnic folklife in U.S. and Canada.– Folklife is the traditional expressive culture: familial, ethnic, occupational, religious, regional in forms of custom, belief, technical skill, language, literature, art, architecture, music, play, dance, ritual, handicraft.

Location: OONL.

6185 **Minion, Robin**
Doctoral dissertations: northern Canada. Edmonton: Boreal Institute for Northern Studies, University of Alberta, 1986. 84 p. (Boreal Institute for Northern Studies Bibliographic series ; no. 27; ISSN: 0824-8192); ISBN: 0-919058-61-2.
Note: 193 entries.– Contains theses on topics related to northern environment and people.– BINS series produced monthly from January 1984 to May 1986 (no. 29).– Online access: *Boreal Northern Titles (BNT)*, available through QL Systems Limited.
Location: OONL.

6186 **Minion, Robin**
Master's theses – northern Canada. Edmonton: Boreal Institute for Northern Studies, University of Alberta, 1986. 108 p. (Boreal Institute for Northern Studies Bibliographic series ; no. 28; ISSN: 0824-8192); ISBN: 0-919058-62-0.
Note: 233 entries.– Contains theses on topics related to northern environment and people.– BINS series produced monthly from January 1984 to May 1986 (no. 29).– Online access: *Boreal Northern Titles (BNT)*, available through QL Systems Limited.
Location: OONL.

6187 **Perret, Diana-Lynn**
Répertoire des thèses de doctorat et de maîtrise soutenues dans les facultés de droit des universités du Québec et de l'Université d'Ottawa. 3e éd. [Ottawa]: Éditions de l'Université d'Ottawa, 1986. P. [947]-1030.
Note: Approx. 850 entrées.– Couverte jusqu'en la fin de l'année 1985.– Tiré à part de la *Revue générale de droit*, 17, (1986).
Éditions antérieures:
... , section de droit civil. 1983. 60 f.
Chrétien, Muriette. *... , section du droit civil*. Montréal: Association des professeurs de droit du Québec, Comité des bibliothécaires de droit, 1980. 11 f.
Localisation: OONL.

6188 **Robitaille, Denis; Waiser, Joan**
Theses in Canada: a bibliographic guide/Thèses au Canada: guide bibliographique. 2nd ed. Ottawa: National Library of Canada, 1986. xi, 72 p.; ISBN: 0-660-53228-X.
Note: 331 entries.– Includes general bibliographies, theses lists by university, specialized bibliographies (area studies, arts and music, history, native studies, social sciences, women's studies, etc.).– Excludes theses written by Canadians in universities abroad or theses on Canadian topics written in foreign universities by Canadians or others.– Text in English and French/texte en français et en anglais.
Previous edition: Bruchet, Susan; Evans, Gwynneth. *Theses in Canada: a guide to sources of information about theses completed or in preparation/Thèses au Canada: guide sur les sources documentaires relatives aux thèses complétées ou en cours de rédaction*. 1978. 25 p.; ISBN: 0-662-01620-3.
Location: OONL.

— 1987 —

6189 **Drapeau, Arnold J.**
Répertoire des travaux de recherche en génie de l'environnement a l'École polytechnique de Montréal, 1964-1986. Montréal: Département de génie civil, École polytechnique de Montréal, 1987. 41 p. (Rapport technique / Département de génie civil, École polytechnique de Montréal ; no EPM: RT-87/16); ISBN: 2-553-00193-2.
Note: Approx. 150 entrées.– Comprend: sommaires des mémoires de maîtrise (M.Sc.A., M. Ing.), sommaires des thèses de doctorat (Ph.D.).
Édition antérieure: *Répertoire des recherches effectuées en génie de l'environnement à l'École polytechnique de Montréal, 1964-1981*. 1981. 24 p.; ISBN: 2-553-00146-0.
Localisation: OONL.

6190 **Gall, Q.; Birkett, T.**
"Post-graduate theses in Canadian universities on geologic research related to mineral deposits, 1983-1986."
In: *CIM Bulletin*; Vol. 80, no. 905 (September 1987) p. 88-100.; ISSN: 0317-0926.
Note: Location: OONL.

6191 **Morrison, B.A.; Thuns, A.**
A catalogue of Canadian graduate theses in agricultural engineering and related fields 1942-1986/Répertoire des thèses maîtrise et de doctorat en génie rural ou autres domaînes connexes publiés au Canada de 1942 à 1986. Ottawa: Engineering and Statistical Research Centre, Research Branch, Agriculture Canada, 1987. 147 p. (Engineering and Statistical Research Centre Contribution ; no. I-946)
Note: 739 entries.– Theses are arranged in two sections: by university, subsorted by degree, year and author; by subject, subsorted by year and author, with abstracts for most entries.– Text in English and French/texte en français et en anglais.
Previous edition: *Index of graduate theses in agricultural engineering and related fields*. 1982. 110 p.
Location: OON.

6192 **Scott, Ian**
Environmental theses from Atlantic Canada universities: a natural resource information base. Halifax: Atlantic Provinces Council on the Sciences, 1987. i, 80 p.
Note: 888 entries.– Listing of theses to 1987 at honour's bachelor, master's and doctoral levels on topics related to the environment.– Indexes: author, keyword, universities.
Location: NBSU.

— 1988 —

6193 **L'Heureux, Lucie**
Thèses et cours sur le Québec dans les institutions d'enseignement supérieur en France. Paris: Centre de coopération universitaire franco-québécoise, 1988. 159 p.
Note: Localisation: QMM.

6194 **La Recherche universitaire en communication au Québec, 1960-1986: bibliographie analytique des thèses et mémoires.** Sainte-Foy, Québec: Réseau québécois d'information sur la communication, c1988. xxiii, 222 p.; ISBN: 2-921026-01-5.
Note: 983 entrées.– Comprend une liste des thèses et mémoires sur la méthodologie et théorie de la communication, langages et messages de la communication, métiers et fonctions de la communication, communication individuelle/de groupe, éducation et communica-

tion, communication de masse, télécommunication.
Localisation: OONL.

6195 **Steele, Apollonia**
Theses on English-Canadian literature: a bibliography of research produced in Canada and elsewhere from 1903 forward. Calgary: [University of Calgary Press], 1988. xxvi, 505 p.; ISBN: 0-919813-47-X.
Note: Approx. 6,100 entries.– Compiled with assistance from Joanne K. Henning.– Excludes theses on the teaching of literature, the subject of folklore and which discuss theatre rather than drama.
Location: OONL.

6196 **University of Alberta. Library. Special Collections Department**
University of Alberta theses. Edmonton: University of Alberta Library, Special Collections Department, 1971-1988. 17 vol.; ISSN: 0315-5870.
Note: Semi-annual.– Arranged by Department (subject), with author/department index.– First issue, Spring 1971.– Ceased publication with Spring 1988 issue.
Location: OONL.

— 1989 —

6197 **Dyer, Aldrich J.**
Indian, Metis and Inuit of Canada in theses and dissertations, 1892-1987. Saskatoon: University of Saskatchewan, c1989. 206, xxix, xl p.; ISBN: 0-88880-225-0.
Note: 3,162 entries.– Theses from Canadian, American and European universities, each containing one or more chapters directly concerning Indian, Metis or Inuit peoples of Canada.– Disciplines include anthropology, archaeology, art, education, literature, law, theology, economics.
Location: OONL.

6198 **Reid, Elspeth; McIlwaine, John**
Sub-doctoral theses on Canada: accepted by universities in the United Kingdom & Ireland, 1899-1986: together with a supplement to J.J. Dossick *Doctoral research on Canada and Canadians, 1884-1983*. [London, Eng.]: British Association for Canadian Studies, 1989. iii, 10 p.; ISBN: 0-9509063-1-X.
Note: 220 entries.
Location: OONL.

6199 **Singer, Loren**
"Canadian art history theses and dissertations/Mémoires et thèses en l'histoire de l'art au Canada."
In: *Journal of Canadian art history*; Vol. 5, no. 2 (1981) p. 122-128; vol. 6, no. 2 (1982) p. 220-224; vol. 10, no. 1 (1987) p. 48-60; vol. 12, no. 2 (1989) p. 199-201.; ISSN: 0315-4297.
Note: Location: AEU.

6200 **Université du Québec. Service du dossier étudiant. Section diplôme**
Répertoire des mémoires et des thèses de l'Université du Québec, 1969-88. 4e éd. Sainte-Foy: Université du Québec, 1989. 534 p.; ISBN: 2-7628-1866-4.
Note: Approx. 3,300 entrées.– Regroupe les informations relatives aux mémoires et thèses acceptés dans les différents établissements de l'Université du Québec depuis sa fondation en 1969 jusqu'au mois de décembre 1988.– Une liste pour les six établissements de l'Université du Québec: Chicoutimi (Abitibi-Témiscamingue, Hull), Montréal, Rimouski, Trois-Rivières, Institut Armand-Frappier, Institut national de

la recherche scientifique.
Éditions antérieures:
... , *1969-86.* 1987. 402 p.; ISBN: 2-7628-1079-5.
... , *1969-84.* 1985. 227 p.; ISBN: 2-7628-0165-6.
... , *1969-80.* 1981. 406 p.
Localisation: OONL.

— 1990 —

6201 **Drapeau, Arnold J.**
Répertoire des mémoires de maîtrise et thèses de doctorat de l'École polytechnique, 1983-1987. Montréal: École polytechnique, 1990. iv, 224 p.; ISBN: 2-553-00203-3.
Note: 610 entrées.
Supplément: *Répertoire des recherches en cours par les étudiants de maîtrise et de doctorat à l'École polytechnique.* Association des étudiants au cycles supérieurs de polytechnique, 1991-. vol.– Annuel.
Localisation: OONL.

6202 **Filotas, Paul K.G.**
A subject bibliography of theses bibliographies held in Carleton University Library. Ottawa: Carleton University, Library, 1990. 1 vol. (unpaged).
Note: Location: OOCC.

— 1991 —

6203 **Répertoire bibliographique: thèses de doctorat et mémoires de maîtrise en rapport avec la condition des femmes reçus à l'Université Laval, 1987-1991.** [Sainte-Foy]: Chaire d'étude sur la condition des femmes, Université Laval, [1991]. 16 p.; ISBN: 2-9801950-2-2.
Note: 98 entrées.
Localisation: OONL.

— 1992 —

6204 **Beauregard, Micheline; Tessier, Yves**
Répertoire bibliographique: thèses de doctorat et mémoires de maîtrise en rapport avec la condition des femmes reçus dans six universités du Québec, 1987-1991. Sainte-Foy, Québec: Chaire d'étude sur la condition des femmes, Université Laval, 1992. 113 p.; ISBN: 2-9801950-5-7.
Note: 445 entrées.
Localisation: OONL.

6205 **Bernhard, Paulette; Saint-Aubin, Diane**
"Recherches en éducation faites au Canada français."
Dans: *Revue des sciences de l'éducation*; Vol. 1, no 1 (printemps 1975) p. 89-92; vol. 1, no 2-3 (automne 1975) p. 203-212; vol. 2, no 3 (automne 1976) p. 277-282; vol. 3, no 1 (hiver 1977) p. 105-109; vol. 3, no 2 (printemps 1977) p. 249-252; vol. 3, no 3 (automne 1977) p. 391-396; vol. 4, no 1 (hiver 1978) p. 131-137; vol. 4, no 2 (printemps 1978) p. 335-339; vol. 4, no 3 (automne 1978) p. 437-442; vol. 5, no 1 (hiver 1979) p. 123-128; vol. 5, no 2 (printemps 1979) p. 295-298; vol. 5, no 3 (automne 1979) p. 453-457; vol. 6, no 1 (hiver 1980) p. 127-136; vol. 6, no 2 (printemps 1980) p. 361-368; vol. 6, no 3 (automne 1980) p. 563-571; vol. 7, no 1 (hiver 1981) p. 153-167; vol. 7, no 2 (printemps 1981) p. 335-343; vol. 7, no 3 (automne 1981) p. 523-530; vol. 8, no 1 (1982) p. 145-154; vol. 8, no 2 (1982) p. 329-341; vol. 8, no 3 (1982) p. 555-565; vol. 9, no 1 (1983) p. 141-148; vol. 9, no 2 (1983) p. 321-330; vol. 9, no 3 (1983) p. 481-490; vol. 10, no 1 (1984) p. 119-126; vol. 10, no 2 (1984) p. 331-340; vol. 10, no 3 (1984) p. 559-567; vol. 11, no 1 (1985) p. 131-139; vol. 11, no 2 (1985) p. 353-357; vol. 11, no 3 (1985) p. 507-511; vol. 12, no 1 (1986) p. 109-113; vol. 12, no 2 (1986) p. 277-281; vol. 12, no 3 (1986) p.

415-420; vol. 13, no 1 (1987) p. 125-129; vol. 13, no 2 (1987) p. 275-278; vol. 13, no 3 (1987) p. 463-467; vol. 14, no 1 (1988) p. 97-100; vol. 14, no 2 (1988) p. 267-271; vol. 14, no 3 (1988) p. 409-413; vol. 15, no 1 (1989) p. 139-144; vol. 15, no 2 (1989) p. 285-289; vol. 15, no 3 (1989) p. 449-454; vol. 16, no 2 (1990) p. 287-290; vol. 16, no 3 (1990) p. 471-475; vol. 17, no 1 (1991) p. 153-157; vol. 17, no 2 (1991) p. 305-313; vol. 17, no 3 (1991) p. 499-505; vol. 18, no 1 (1992) p. 129-144; vol. 18, no 2 (1992) p. 293-332; vol. 18, no 3 (1992) p. 475-489.; ISSN: 0318-479X.

Note: Comprend des essais, des mémoires de maîtrise et des thèses de doctorat en sciences de l'éducation: histoire, administration et organisation scolaire, méthodologie et technologie, philosophie, psychopédagogie, mésure et évaluation, personnel enseignant, programmes.

Localisation: AEU.

— Ongoing/En cours —

6206 **Canadian Historical Association**
Register of post-graduate dissertations in progress in history and related subjects/Répertoire des thèses en cours portant sur des sujets d'histoire et autres sujets connexes. [Ottawa]: Canadian Historical Association, [1966]-. vol.; ISSN: 0068-8088.

Note: Annual.– Compiled by the Public Archives of Canada, 1966-1980; compiled and published by the Canadian Historical Association, 1981- .– Lists completed theses, abandoned theses, doctoral theses in progress.– Includes theses being prepared for departments of history at Canadian universities; theses treating any aspect of Canadian history but undertaken outside history departments; theses being prepared at foreign universities dealing with topics in Canadian history.– Entries are arranged under broad geographical and chronological headings.– Text in English and French/texte en français et en anglais.

Location: OONL.

6207 **Canadian theses [microform]/Thèses canadiennes [microforme].** Ottawa: National Library of Canada, 1984-. microfiches; ISSN: 0068-9874.

Note: Semi-annual with 5 cumulating indexes; quinquennial cumulation.

Includes publications in English and French.

Previous editions:

Canadian theses on microfiche: catalogue/Thèses canadiennes sur microfiche: catalogue. 1974-1983. 32 no.; ISSN: 0316-0149.

Canadian theses on microfilm: catalogue – price list: numbers 1-2450/Thèses canadiennes sur microfilm: catalogue – prix: numéros 1-2450. 1969. 251 p.– Includes theses originally issued before 1968.

Location: OONL.

6208 **Masters theses in the pure and applied sciences accepted by colleges and universities of the United States and Canada.** New York: Plenum Press, c1974-. vol.; ISSN: 0736-7910.

Note: First published, vol. 1 (1957).– Effective with vol. 18 (1974) the coverage was extended to include Canadian universities.

Location: OONL.

— 1900 —

6209 **Canada. Geological Survey**
General index to the [Geological Survey of Canada] Reports of progress, 1863 to 1884. Ottawa: Queen's Printer, 1900. 475 p.
Note: Contains three parts: "Reports geographically analyzed and arranged under provinces, counties, districts," "Special examinations (ores, rocks, minerals or fossils subjected to assay, analysis, microscopic examination, etc.)," "General index."- Compiled by Donaldson Bogart Dowler.
Location: OONL.

— 1908 —

6210 **Canada. Geological Survey**
General index to reports, 1885-1906 [Geological Survey of Canada]. Ottawa: Government Printing Bureau, 1908. x, 1014 p.
Note: Approx. 180,000 references.– Index to "New Series" of Reports of the Survey, 1885-1906.– Compiled by Frank Nicolas.
Location: OONL.

— 1909 —

6211 **Canada. Geological Survey**
Catalogue of publications of the Geological Survey of Canada. Ottawa: King's Printer, 1909. 181 p.
Note: Previous edition: 1906. 129 p.
Supplement: *Supplementary list of publications of the Geological Survey, Canada.* 1912. 6 p.
Location: OONL.

— 1913 —

6212 **Adam, Margaret Isabella; Ewing, John; Munro, James**
Guide to the principal parliamentary papers relating to the Dominions, 1812-1911. Edinburgh: Oliver and Boyd, 1913. viii, 190 p.
Note: Chronological listing of sessional and command papers presented to the British House of Lords or House of Commons dealing with Canada, Newfoundland, Australia, New Zealand, South Africa, Dominions in general, emigration and colonization.
Location: OONL.

6213 **Canada. Commission of Conservation**
Catalogue of publications [Commission of Conservation]. [Ottawa]: Commission of Conservation, 1913. 35 p.
Note: Location: OONL.

— 1914 —

6214 **Burpee, Lawrence J.**
"Check-list of Canadian public documents."
In: *Papers of the Bibliographical Society of America;* Vol. 8, no. 1-2 (1914) p. 51-56.; ISSN: 0006-128X.
Note: Location: AEU.

— 1917 —

6215 **Ontario. Office of King's Printer**
Catalogue of publications issued by the government of Ontario (Revised to October 1st, 1917). Toronto: A.T. Wilgress, King's Printer, 1917. 16 p.
Note: Location: OONL.

— 1920 —

6216 **Canada. Geological Survey**
Annotated catalogue of and guide to the publications of the Geological Survey Canada, 1845-1917. Ottawa: King's Printer, 1920. 544 p.: maps.
Note: Includes publications of the Geological Survey from its inception to August 1, 1917: reports of progress, annual reports, summary reports, memoirs, museum bulletins, separate reports and special publications.– Compiled by W.F. Ferrier and Dorothy J. Ferrier.
Location: OONL.

— 1924 —

6217 **Canada. Department of Marine and Fisheries**
Catalogue of official Canadian government publications of use to mariners. Ottawa: King's Printer, 1924. 38 p.
Note: Location: OONL.

— 1929 —

6218 **Canada. Department of the Interior. Natural Resources Intelligence Branch**
Catalogue of publications [Natural Resources Intelligence Branch]. Ottawa: King's Printer, 1929. 21 p.
Note: Previous edition: 1924. 28 p.
Location: OONL.

— 1930 —

6219 **Canada. Mines Branch**
Catalogue of Mines Branch publications. Ottawa: Printer to the King, 1930. 29 p.
Note: Previous editions:
1927. 47 p.
Catalogue of Mines Branch publications with alphabetical guide. 1925. 43 p.
1924. 39 p.
1919. 29 p.
1918. 27 p.
1917. 28 p.
Catalogue of publications of the Mines Branch (1907-1911): containing tables of contents of the various technical reports, monographs, bulletins, etc., together with a list of magnetometric survey maps, working plans, etc.; including also a digest of technical memoirs and the annual summary reports of the superintendent of mines, issued by the Department of the Interior, 1902-1906. 1912. 134 p., [1] l.
Location: OONL.

— 1932 —

6220 **Gregory, Winifred**
List of the serial publications of foreign governments, 1815-1931. New York: H.W. Wilson, 1932. 720 p.
Note: Includes Canadian government serial publications.
Reprint: Kraus Reprint, 1973. [9], 720 p.; ISBN: 0-527-57400-7.
Location: OONL.

— 1935 —

6221 **Higgins, Marion Villiers**
Canadian government publications: a manual for librarians. Chicago: American Library Association, 1935. 582 p.: ill.
Note: Covers 1867 to 1931.– Includes history and organization of departments and agencies, listings of serials, special publications, catalogues and indexes.
Location: OONL.

— 1936 —

6222 **Murray, Florence**
"Canadian government catalogues and checklists."
In: *Library Quarterly*; Vol. 6, no. 3 (July 1936) p. 237-262.; ISSN: 0024-2519.
Note: Describes catalogues, lists and indexes available for Canadian government publications, legislative and departmental.– Includes a section on provincial documents.
Location: OOP.

— 1939 —

6223 **Cole, Arthur Harrison**
Finding-list of royal commission reports in the British Dominions. Cambridge, Mass.: Harvard University Press, 1939. 134 p.
Note: Includes listings for Canada, the provinces, Newfoundland, p. 87-106.
Location: OONL.

— 1940 —

6224 **Lewis, Grace S.**
"Reports of Dominion and provincial royal commissions, together with a selection of reports of British royal commissions having a bearing on Canada."
In: *Canada Year Book*; (1940) p. 1108-1116.
Note: Location: OONL.

— 1943 —

6225 **Parent, Raymond**
Étude bibliographique des publications du Bureau international du travail au Ministère du travail, Québec. Québec: Le Ministère, 1943. 67, [3] p., [2] f. de pl.: ill.
Note: Localisation: QQLA.

— 1945 —

6226 **Canada. Wartime Information Board**
List of Dominion government publications. Ottawa: The Board, 1944-1945. 6 nos.
Note: Location: OONL.

6227 **Holmes, Marjorie C.**
Royal commissions and commissions of inquiry under the "Public Inquiries Act" in British Columbia, 1872-1942: a checklist. [Victoria: King's Printer, 1945]. 68 p.
Note: 133 entries.
Location: OONL.

— 1946 —

6228 **Whitworth, Fred E.**
Teaching aids obtainable from departments of the government at Ottawa. Ottawa: Canadian Council of Education for Citizenship, 1946. 17 p.
Note: Books, pamphlets, bulletins, maps, posters, slides, films produced by departments and agencies of the federal government.
Location: OONL.

— 1948 —

6229 **Canada. Geological Survey**
Publications (1909-1947 inclusive) of the Geological Survey and National Museum. Ottawa: Department of Mines and Resources, Mines and Geology Branch, 1948. 103 p.
Note: Location: OONL.

— 1950 —

6230 **Holmes, Marjorie C.**
Publications of the government of British Columbia, 1871-1947. [Victoria: King's Printer, 1950]. 254 p.
Note: Approx. 4,000 entries.
Previous edition: Weston, Sydney Moss. *Publications of the government of British Columbia, 1871-1937*. 1939. 167 p.
Location: OONL.

— 1952 —

6231 **Canada. Geological Survey**
Publications of the Geological Survey of Canada (1917-1952). Ottawa: Department of Mines and Technical Surveys, 1952. v, 82 p.
Note: In two parts: list of reports issued since 1917; list by provinces and territories, of published geological maps.– Compiled by Lorne B. Leafloor.
Location: OONL.

6232 **Canada. National Museum**
Publications of the National Museum of Canada, 1913-1951. Ottawa: Department of Resources and Development, National Parks Branch, 1952. vi, 127 p.
Note: Supplement: *List of publications, 1913-1965 [National Museums of Canada*. [1965]. 1 vol. (unpaged).
Location: OOFF.

6233 **MacDonald, Christine**
Publications of the governments of the North-West Territories, 1876-1905, and of the Province of Saskatchewan, 1905-1952. Regina: Legislative Library, 1952. 109 [1] p.
Note: Commissions, boards, etc. and crown corporations.– Excludes maps, posters, office consolidations of acts and acts printed separately.– Preliminary mimeographed checklist dated 1948. 84 l.
Location: OONL.

6234 **Morley, Marjorie**
Royal commissions and commissions of inquiry under "The Evidence Act" in Manitoba: a checklist. [Winnipeg: Legislative Library, 1952]. 11, 10 l.
Note: Location: OONL.

— 1954 —

6235 **Canada. Department of National Health and Welfare**
Featuring fitness: a catalogue of the publications of the Physical Fitness Division, Dept. of National Health and Welfare, Ottawa. Ottawa: The Department, 1954. 19 p.
Note: Location: OONL.

— 1955 —

6236 **Alberta. Queen's Printer**
Catalogue of Alberta government publications. Edmonton: 1955. 2 vol.
Note: Vol. 1, no. 1-2, 1954-1955.– Cover title: *Catalogue: acts, regulations and publications of the Government of the Province of Alberta*.
Location: OONL.

6237 **British Columbia. Provincial Museum**
Publications of the Provincial Museum. Victoria, B.C.: British Columbia Provincial Museum, 1955. P. 87-99.
Note: Covers from the 1890s to 1954.– List of publications issued by the Museum or prepared by members of staff for publication elsewhere.

Excerpt: *Report* of the Provincial Museum of Natural History and Anthropology, 1954.
Location: OONL.

— 1956 —

6238   **Bishop, Yvonne, et al.**
Index to Manuscript reports of the biological stations, no. 1-600, and Manuscript reports of the technological stations, no. 1-57, together with the titles of the papers in these two series. [S.l.]: Fisheries Research Board of Canada, 1956. 142 p.
Note: 657 entries.– Contains a bibliographical listing of scientific papers in the Fisheries Research Board Manuscript reports series.
Location: OONL.

— 1957 —

6239   **Bishop, Olga B.**
Publications of the governments of Nova Scotia, Prince Edward Island, New Brunswick, 1758-1952. Ottawa: National Library of Canada, 1957. vi, 237 p.
Note: Includes only those pamphlets or books which have been printed with the imprint of, at the expense of, or by the authority of any one of the three governments of the Atlantic provinces.– Manuscripts are included only when they preceded a document which was later printed.– Excludes papers, broadsides, handbills, proclamations, maps, as well as reports, despatches, and other documents which appeared in appendix to the *Journals* of Council and Assembly and which did not have a separate existence.– Excludes also individual laws and statutes.
Location: OONL.

6240   **Bishop, Yvonne, et al.**
Index and list of titles, publications of the Fisheries Research Board of Canada, 1901-1954. Ottawa: Fisheries Research Board of Canada, 1957. xxi, 209 p. (Fisheries Research Board of Canada Bulletin ; no. 110)
Note: Covers the following seven series of publications: *Contributions to Canadian biology; Journal* of the Fisheries Research Board of Canada;bulletins of the Fisheries Research Board of Canada; *Canadian Atlantic Fauna; Canadian Pacific Fauna;* studies from stations; research bulletins and service bulletins of Newfoundland Government Laboratory.– Excludes annual reports, progress reports of Atlantic and Pacific stations.
Location: OONL.

6241   **Forget, Guy**
Bibliography of Canadian official publications on alcoholic beverages, 1921-1956. Ottawa: [s.n.], 1957. 1 vol. (unpaged).
Note: Location: OTU.

— 1959 —

6242   **Canada. Department of Public Printing and Stationery**
Documents relating to the St. Lawrence Seaway Development Project, obtainable from the Queen's Printer, Ottawa. Ottawa: Department of Public Printing and Stationery, 1959. 2 l. (Price list / Department of Public Printing and Stationery ; no. 3)
Note: Location: OONL.

— 1960 —

6243   **Quebec (Province). Department of Mines**
Annotated list of publications of the Department of Mines of the province of Quebec, 1883-1960. Quebec: [s.n.], 1960. 116 p.

Note: Location: QQLA.

— 1961 —

6244   **Canada. Geological Survey**
Index of publications of the Geological Survey of Canada (1845-1958). Ottawa: Department of Mines and Technical Surveys Canada, 1961. x, 378 p.: folded col. map (in pocket).
Note: Compiled by A.G. Johnston.– Listings for all publications of the Geological Survey of Canada from its inception to 1958.– Includes reports of progress, annual reports, summary reports, guide books, museum bulletins, memoirs, Geological Survey bulletins, Economic geology series, Preliminary series papers, water supply papers, indexes and catalogues, maps, finding lists.
Supplements:
Index to publications, 1959-1974/Index des publications, 1959-1974. [Ottawa: Information Canada, 1975]. 138 p. Compiled by P.J. Griffin.
Index to publications, 1975-1979/Index des publications, 1975-1979. [Ottawa: Supply and Services Canada, c1980]. 247 p. Compiled by P.J. Griffin.
Index to publications, 1980-1984/Index des publications, 1980-1984. [Ottawa: Supply and Services Canada, 1985]. 321 p.
Index to publications, 1985-1987/Index des publications, 1985-1987. [Ottawa: Supply and Services Canada, 1989]. 159 p.
For all supplements: Text in English and French/texte en français et en anglais.
Location: OONL.

— 1962 —

6245   **Canada. Geological Survey**
Index to reports of Geological Survey of Canada from 1927-50. Ottawa: Department of Mines and Technical Surveys Canada, 1962. viii, 723 p.
Note: Index to annual reports, economic geology series, geological bulletins, museum bulletins (1927-1950), geological papers (1935-1950), summary reports (1927-1933).– Compiled by W.E. Cockfield, E. Hall, and J.F. Wright.
Location: OONL.

— 1963 —

6246   **Bishop, Olga B.**
Publications of the government of the Province of Canada, 1841-1867. Ottawa: Queen's Printer, 1963. x, 351 p.
Note: Journals and proceedings, statutes, annual reports, reports compiled and published resulting from requests from Legislative Assembly to Governor General for certain information.– Includes reports of committees and commissions.
Location: OONL.

6247   **Canada. Department of Public Printing and Stationery. Documents Library**
Canadian government publications relating to labour/ Publications du gouvernement canadien sur les sujets relatifs au travail. 3rd ed.; 2e éd. bilingue. Ottawa: Queen's Printer, 1963. 337 p. (Canadian government publications sectional catalogue ; no. 10)
Note: Acts and regulations, publications of the Department of Labour, External Affairs documents (international labour agreements, etc.), Parliamentary documents, royal commissions, Unemployment Insurance Commission publications, international labour

publications.– English section, Section française, index.
Previous editions:
1959. 125 p.
Labour publications: a price list of the publications of the Department of Labour and publications relating to labour issued by Parliament and other agencies of the government of Canada. 1955. viii, 26 p.
Location: OONL.

6248 **Canada. Department of Public Printing and Stationery. Documents Library**
Canadian government publications sectional catalogue: Department of Forestry/Publications du Gouvernement canadien: Ministère des forêts. Ottawa: Queen's Printer, 1963. 137 p. (Canadian government publications sectional catalogue ; no. 13)
Note: Includes separate English and French sections.– Comprend des publications en français et en anglais.
Location: OOFF.

6249 **Canada. Department of Public Printing and Stationery. Documents Library**
Northern Affairs and National Resources publications/ Publications: Nord canadien et ressources nationales. 2nd ed. Ottawa: Queen's Printer, 1963. 182 p. (Queen's Printer Sectional catalogue ; no. 11)
Note: Listing of the publications of the Department of Northern Affairs and National Resources: administrative documents, Northern Administration Branch, National Parks Branch, Water Resources Branch, Council of the Northwest Territories, Council of the Yukon Territory.– Prepared by Marie-Louise Myrand.– Text in English and French/texte en français et en anglais.
Previous edition: 1956. 182 p.
Location: OONL.

— 1964 —

6250 **British Columbia Research Council**
Publications of the British Columbia Research Council. Vancouver: British Columbia Research Council, 1964. 26 l.
Note: Location: OONL.

6251 **MacTaggart, Hazel I.**
Publications of the Government of Ontario, 1901-1955: a checklist. Toronto: Printed and distributed by the University of Toronto Press for the Queen's Printer, 1964. xiv, 303 p.
Note: Approx. 4,000 entries.– Lists the publications of departments, boards and other publishing agencies of the government of the Province of Ontario.– Excludes maps, posters, internal administration documents, bills, separate printings of acts, extracts from government publications, reprints of articles by government officials appearing in non-government publications, publications of provincially-supported educational institutions.– All publications are given locations.
Location: OONL.

— 1965 —

6252 **Canada. Department of Public Printing and Stationery**
List of Canadian government periodicals/Liste des périodiques du gouvernement canadien. Ottawa: Queen's Printer, 1965. 15 p.
Note: Location: OONL.

6253 **Canada. Geological Survey**
Index to reports of Geological Survey of Canada from 1951-59. Ottawa: Department of Mines and Technical Surveys Canada, 1965. xii, 379 p.
Note: Seventh in a series of indexes issued by the Geological Survey of Canada.– Compiled by J.F. Wright.
Location: OONL.

6254 **Ontario. Department of Mines**
General index to the Reports of the Ontario Department of Mines. Toronto: Queen's Printer, 1921-1965. 7 vol.
Note: Vol. 1: ... , *volumes 1 to 25 (1891-1916)*. 1921. vi, 871 p.
Vol. 2: ... , *volumes 26 to 35 (1917-1927)*. 1928. vi, 668 p.
Vol. 3: ... , *volumes 36 to 49 (1927-1940)*. 1949. vii, 505 p.
Vol. 4: ... , *volumes 50 to 59 (1941-1950)*. 1954. vi, 333 p.
Vol. 5: ... , *volumes 60 to 64 (1951-1955)*. 1960. vi, 204 p.
Vol. 6: ... , *volumes 65-69 (1956-1960)*. 1962. vi, 153 p.
Vol. 7: ... , *volumes 70-73 (1961-1963)*. 1965. v, 166 p.
Annual reports covered by the indexes include: *Statistical review of the mineral industry, Mining accidents in Ontario, Mining operations in Ontario.*
Location: OONL.

6255 **Québec (Province). Comité permanent d'aménagement des ressources**
Inventaire bibliographique préliminaire des publications du gouvernement du Québec relatives à l'aménagement du territoire. Québec: Administration ARDA-Québec, 1965. v f., 290 p.
Note: Localisation: QQLA.

6256 **Québec (Province). Office d'information et de publicité**
Les publications gouvernementales du Québec. Québec: Office d'information et de publicité du Québec, 1965. [98] p.
Note: Localisation: OONL.

— 1966 —

6257 **British Columbia. Department of Mines and Petroleum Resources**
Index to publications of the British Columbia Department of Mines and Petroleum Resources. Victoria: Department of Mines and Petroleum Resources, 1966. vi, 142 p.
Note: Previous editions:
British Columbia. Department of Mines. *Index to publications of the British Columbia Department of Mines: annual reports of the Minister of Mines, 1937 to 1953 and bulletins nos. 1 to 35.* 1955. vi, 228 p.: map.
Nation, Harold T. *Index to annual reports of the Minister of Mines, 1937-1943: and bulletins 1-17, published by the Department of Mines, British Columbia.* C.F. Banfield, 1944. 123 p.
Nation, Harold T. *Index to annual reports of the Minister of Mines of the Province of British Columbia for the years 1874 to 1936, inclusive.* Printer to the King, 1938. 510 p.
Location: OONL.

6258 **Canada. Dominion Bureau of Statistics. Canada Year Book, Handbook and Library Division**
Historical catalogue of Dominion Bureau of Statistics publications, 1918-1960/Catalogue rétrospectif des publications du Bureau fédéral de la statistique, 1918-1960. Ottawa: Dominion Bureau of Statistics, DBS Library, 1966. xiv, 298 p.
Note: Lists all publications designed to provide statistical information for the public with the exception of special statements, press releases and preliminary or advance statements. Also excludes publications restricted to DBS internal or limited use, such as operating manuals.– Text in English and French/texte en français et en anglais.

Location: OONL.

6259 **Myrand, Marie-Louise**
Canada treaty series, 1928-1964/Recueil des traités du Canada, 1928-1964. Ottawa: Queen's Printer, 1966. 388 p. (Canadian government publications sectional catalogue ; no. 15)
Note: Supplement: *General index: Canada treaty series, 1965-1974/Index général: recueil des traités du Canada, 1965-1974.* Ottawa: 1977. 26, 26 p.; ISBN: 0-660-00602-2.
Location: OONL.

6260 **Ontario. Department of Mines**
List of publications, 1891-1965 [Ontario Department of Mines]. Toronto: Queen's Printer, 1966. viii, 112 p.: ill., maps. (Ontario Department of Mines Bulletin ; no. 25)
Note: Location: OONL.

— 1967 —

6261 **Canada. Department of Public Printing and Stationery. Documents Library**
Canadian government publications catalogue: Mines Branch and Mineral Resources Division, Energy, Mines and Resources/Publications du gouvernement canadien: Énergie, mines et ressources, Direction des mines et Division des ressources minérales. 3rd ed. Ottawa: Queen's Printer, 1967. 401 p. (Sectional catalogue series / Department of Public Printing and Stationery, Documents Library ; no. 12)
Note: Listing of Mines Branch publications: old series (to 1957), new series (from 1958)- Text in English and French/texte en français et en anglais.
Previous editions:
Canadian government publications: ..., Mines and Technical Surveys/... : Mines et relevés techniques, ... 1962. 301 p. (Sectional catalogue ; no. 12).
Canadian government publications: Mines Branch and Mines and Technical Surveys/... : Mines et relevés techniques, Division des Mines. 1957. 243 p. (Sectional catalogue ; no. 12).
Location: OONL.

6262 **Henderson, George Fletcher**
Federal royal commissions in Canada, 1867-1966: a checklist. Toronto: University of Toronto Press, c1967. xvi, 212 p.
Note: 396 entries.
Supplements:
Krywolt, Susan; Piush, Evelyn. *Federal royal commissions in Canada, 1966-1977: an update.* Edmonton: University of Alberta, Faculty of Library Science, 1977. [3], 20 p.
Bombak, Anna. *Canadian federal royal commissions, 1978-1988: an update.* Edmonton: Government Publications Unit, University of Alberta Library, 1989. 12 p.
Microform: *Guide to microform edition of the Reports of the royal commissions of Canada, 1867-1966.* [Toronto]: Micromedia, 1977. 12 l.
Location: OONL.

6263 **Lessard, Marc-André**
"Les publications du B.A.E.Q."
Dans: *Recherches sociographiques*; Vol. 8, no 3 (septembre-décembre 1967) p. 377-403.; ISSN: 0034-1282.
Note: 42 entrées.
Localisation: OONL.

— 1968 —

6264 **Beaulieu, André; Bonenfant, Jean-Charles; Hamelin, Jean**
Répertoire des publications gouvernementales du Québec de 1867 à 1964. Québec: Impr. de la Reine, 1968. 554 p.
Note: Rapports annuels ou spéciaux, périodiques ou revues, législation, publications des services, offices, bureaux, publications seriées, articles et documents spéciaux, extraits des rapports annuels.
Supplément: Beaulieu, André; Bonenfant, Jean-Charles; Bernier, Gaston. ... , *1965-1968.* [Éditeur officiel], 1970. 388 p.
Localisation: OONL.

6265 **Canada. Department of Forestry and Rural Development. Information and Technical Services Division**
List of available publications [Canada Department of Forestry and Rural Development]. Ottawa: Queen's Printer, 1968. 93 p.
Note: Preliminary matter in English and French/matière préliminaire en français et en anglais.– Publications en français, p. 82-93.
Location: OONL.

6266 **Canada. Department of Public Printing and Stationery**
Report of the Department of Public Printing and Stationery. Ottawa: Queen's Printer, 1887-1968. 62 vol.
Note: Reports for 1890-1934 contain a list of government publications issued during the year.
Location: OONL.

6267 **Carter, Neil M.**
Index and list of titles, Fisheries Research Board of Canada and associated publications, 1900-1964. Ottawa: Fisheries Research Board of Canada, 1968. xviii, 649 p. (Fisheries Research Board of Canada Bulletin ; no. 164)
Note: Subect-author index, and list of contents of 65 years of publications issued by predecessors of Fisheries Research Board of Canada (Board of Management for Canadian Government Marine Biological Stations, 1899-1911; succeeded by Biological Board of Canada, 1912-1937), and by present Board from 1938 to end of 1964.– Also listed are non-Board publications containing work by Board staff (2,301 entries, articles, reports, etc.).
Location: OONL.

6268 **Lamonde, Francine Neilson**
Répertoire bibliographique des documents du Bureau d'aménagement de l'est du Québec. Québec: Conseil d'orientation économique, Bureau d'étude en aménagement régional, 1968. ii, 118 p. (Planification du développement régional: série 1: Inventaire et méthodologie ; cahier 1-5)
Note: Localisation: QQLA.

6269 **Ontario. Department of Agriculture and Food**
Publications of the Ontario Department of Agriculture and Food. Toronto: Department of Agriculture and Food, 1968. 16 p.
Note: Location: OONL.

6270 **Québec (Province). Bureau de l'Imprimeur de la Reine**
Publications en vente au Bureau de l'Imprimeur de la Reine/Publications on sale at the Office of the Queen's Printer. Québec: Imprimeur de la Reine, 1966-1968. 3 vol.
Note: Localisation: OONL.

6271 **Quebec (Province). Department of Natural Resources**
Catalogue of publications since 1883 [Quebec Department of Natural Resources]. Quebec: Quebec Department of Natural Resources, 1968. [128] p. (loose-leaf).: ill., map (folded).

Note: Titre en français: *Catalogue des publications depuis 1883*.

Location: QQLA.

6272 **Québec (Province). Ministère des richesses naturelles**
Catalogue des publications depuis 1883 [Québec, Ministère des richesses naturelles]. Québec: [s.n.], 1968. 1 vol. (f. mobiles): ill., carte pliée.
Note: Comprend quatre parties: Mines, Nouveau-Québec, Eaux, Cartes.– En ce qui concerne les Mines, les rapports sont réunis par ordre chronologique jusqu'à 1937 et ensuite, par ordre numérique.– Index: auteurs, régions, substances, divers.
English title: *Catalogue of publications since 1883*.
Localisation: QMBN.

— 1970 —

6273 **British Columbia. Department of Agriculture. Publications Office**
List of publications [British Columbia Department of Agriculture]. Victoria: Department of Agriculture, [1954]-1970. [16] vol.
Note: Irregular.
Location: OONL.

6274 **Myrand, Marie-Louise**
National museums of Canada: publications/Musées nationaux du Canada: publications. Ottawa: Queen's Printer, 1970. 137 p. (Canadian government publications sectional catalogue ; no. 16)
Note: Location: OONL.

— 1971 —

6275 **Bhatia, Mohan**
Canadian federal government publications: a bibliography of bibliographies. Saskatoon: University of Saskatchewan, 1971. 33 l.
Note: 210 entries.– Bibliographic articles, bibliographies, catalogues, checklists, indexes in monographic and serial form: general bibliographies, bibliographies of parliamentary publications, bibliographies of departmental publications.
Location: OONL.

6276 **Bhatia, Mohan**
Canadian provincial government publications: a bibliography of bibliographies. Rev. and enl. ed. Saskatoon: University of Saskatchewan, Library, 1971. 19 l.
Note: 165 entries.
Previous edition: *Bibliographies, catalogues, checklists and indexes of Canadian provincial government publications*. 1970. 16 l.
Location: OONL.

— 1972 —

6277 **Ambeault, Georgia, et al.**
Union list of government documents. [S.l.: Sault Area International Library Association], 1972. 1 vol. (in various pagings).
Note: Lists documents of Canada, Ontario, United States departments and agencies, with locations and holdings of six participating Canadian and American libraries in the Sault area.
Location: OONL.

6278 **Forsyth, Joseph**
Government publications relating to Alberta: a bibliography of publications of the government of Alberta from 1905 to 1968, and of publications of the government of Canada relating to the province of Alberta from 1867 to 1968. High Wycombe [S. Buckingham]: University Microfilms, [1972]. 8 vol.
Note: Thesis submitted for Fellowship of Library Association, 1971.– Facsimile reproduction.
Location: OONL.

6279 **Janisch, Alice H.**
Publication of administrative board decisions in Canada. London, Ont.: Canadian Association of Law Libraries, 1972. xi, 66 l.
Note: Report and listing of publications of federal and provincial administrative agencies.
Location: OONL.

6280 **LeMoyne, Beryl**
An annotated list of Quebec government documents for a business library. [Montreal]: Graduate School of Library Science, McGill University, 1972. ii, 13 l. (McGill University Graduate School of Library Science Occasional papers ; 2)
Note: Books, periodicals, pamphlets arranged in categories.– Includes publications lists, laws, statistics, finance, directories, annual reports and royal commission reports.
Location: OONL.

6281 **Québec (Province). Bibliothèque de la Législature**
Commissions et comités d'enquêtes au Québec depuis 1867. Québec: Bibliothèque de la Législature, Assemblée nationale, 1972. vii, 95 p. (Bibliographie et documentation / Bibliothèque de la Législature du Québec ; 1)
Note: Approx. 150 entrées.
Localisation: OONL.

— 1973 —

6282 **Betts, Margaret; Krestensen, Kristeen**
A selected list of publications issued by the Ontario Ministry of Labour, 1955-1973. Toronto: Ontario Ministry of Labour, Research Library, 1973. 24 l.
Note: Approx. 350 entries.
Location: OONL.

6283 **Bruce, N.G.**
Forest fire control literature: an author bibliography of CFS publications. Ottawa: Forest Fire Research Institute, 1973. 1 vol. (loose-leaf). (Forest Fire Research Institute Miscellaneous report ; FF-Y-1)
Note: Publications issued from 1909 to 1972 dealing with aspects of Canadian forest fire research.– Updated by numbered supplements.
Location: OONL.

6284 **Carter, Neil M.**
Index and list of titles, Fisheries Research Board of Canada and associated publications, 1965-72. Ottawa: Fisheries Research Board of Canada, 1973. vi, 588 p. (Fisheries Research Board of Canada Miscellaneous special publication ; 18)
Note: Lists bulletins, circulars, technical reports, miscellaneous special publications, annual reports, reviews, studies, interpretative articles.
Supplement: *Publications December 1, 1972-December 31, 1975, Halifax Laboratory*. Halifax, N.S.: Fisheries and Marine Service, Environment Canada, 1976. 14 l. (Fisheries and Marine Service Technical report ; no. 614).
Location: OONL.

6285 **Guilbeault, Claude**
Guide des publications officielles de la Province de Nouveau-Brunswick, 1952-1970/Guide to official publications of the Province of New Brunswick, 1952-1970. Moncton: [s.n.], 1973. 382 l.
Note: 1,285 entrées.– Publications de l'Assemblée législative et comités, ministères et divisions, autres commissions et organismes.
Localisation: OONL.

6286 **Québec (Province). Éditeur officiel du Québec**
Publications: Bureau de l'Éditeur officiel du Québec/ Publications: Office of the Quebec Official Publisher. Québec: Éditeur officiel du Québec, 1969-1973. 5 vol.; ISSN: 0316-1579.
Note: Localisation: OONL.

— 1974 —

6287 **Canada. Department of Energy, Mines and Resources. Gravity Division**
Index of publications, 1948-1973 [Canada Department of Energy, Mines and Resources, Gravity Division]. Ottawa: Information Canada, 1974. 22 p.: ill., maps (folded).
Note: Lists all publications issued by the Gravity Division of the Dominion Observatory during the period 1948 to April 1970, and the Earth Physics Branch, April 1970 to December 1973.
Location: OONL.

6288 **Canadian Broadcasting Corporation**
C B C publications catalogue. Toronto: Canadian Broadcasting Corporation, 1969-1974. 4 vol.: ill.
Note: Location: OONL.

6289 **Fitzpatrick, Connie**
A selected list of current government publications dealing with pollution. Vancouver: University of British Columbia Library, 1974. ii, 77 p. (Reference publication / University of British Columbia Library ; no. 51)
Note: Approx. 700 listings of federal, provincial, municipal, international government publications dated 1970 and later.– Includes bibliographies, indexes, reports on air, water, oil, noise pollution, pesticides, radiation, recycling, waste management.
Previous edition: 1972. 58 p.
Supplement: 1974. ii, 30 p.
Location: OONL.

6290 **Hardisty, Pamela**
Publications of the Canadian Parliament: a detailed guide to the dual-media edition of Canadian parliamentary proceedings and sessional papers, 1841-1970. Washington, D.C.: United States Historical Documents Institute, 1974. viii, 57 p.; ISBN: 0-88222-033-0.
Note: Location: OONL.

6291 **Lebel, Clément**
Documents de la Commission d'enquête sur la situation de la langue française et les droits linguistiques au Québec (Commission Gendron): bibliographie. Québec: Bibliothèque de la Législature, Assemblée nationale, 1974. iii, 206 p. (Bibliographie et documentation / Bibliothèque de la Législature du Québec ; 3)
Note: Comprend le rapport et certains travaux particuliers (études et synthèses), liste des mèmoires présentés, travaux fournis par le secteur de la recherche (dossiers, cahiers documentaires, groupes ethniques, monographies, information, démographie, études spéciales).

Localisation: OONL.

6292 **Manitoba. Environment Protection Board**
Publications: Environment Protection Board, September 1970 – May 1974. Winnipeg: Environment Protection Board, 1974. [21] l.
Note: Approx. 60 entries.– Includes newsletters (published monthly, dealing selectively with specific environmental topics), interim reports, proceedings, brochures.
Location: OONL.

6293 **Mississauga Public Library**
Ontario government publications in the Mississauga Public Library: an annotated checklist of selected holdings. [Mississauga, Ont.]: Mississauga Public Library, 1974. 24 p.
Note: 58 entries.– Lists and describes topical pamphlets, statistical and general business information, government planning, municipal government publications.
Location: OONL.

— 1975 —

6294 **Canada. Department of Agriculture. Library**
Publications of the Canada Department of Agriculture, 1867-1974. 2nd rev. ed. [Ottawa: Information Canada], 1975. vii, 341 p.
Note: Includes all publications issued by the Department from 1867 to 1973.– Excludes papers published in scientific journals, reprints, unnumbered contributions, confidential or restricted documents, unedited manuscripts or unprocessed papers.
Titre en français: *Publications du Ministère de l'Agriculture du Canada, 1867-1974.*
Previous edition: Minter, Ella S.G. ..., *1867-1959.* Queen's Printer, 1963. 387 p.
Location: OONL.

6295 **Canada. Energy, Mines and Resources Canada. Earth Physics Branch**
Index of geophysical publications, series, and contributions of the Dominion Observatory and its successor the Earth Physics Branch of the Department of Energy, Mines and Resources, Canada through December, 1974, with addenda. Ottawa: Earth Physics Branch, 1975. 92 p.
Note: Location: OONL.

6296 **Canada. Information Canada**
Selections: federal government and international publications for educators. Ottawa: Information Canada, 1974-1975. 2 vol.
Note: Titre en français: *Titres: choix de publications fédérales et internationales à l'usage des éducateurs.*
Location: OONL.

6297 **Canada. Information Canada**
Titres: choix de publications fédérales et internationales à l'usage des éducateurs. Ottawa: Information Canada, 1974-1975. 2 vol.
Note: English title: *Selections: federal government and international publications for educators.*
Localisation: OONL.

6298 **Canada. Ministère de l'Agriculture. Bibliothèque**
Publications du Ministère de l'Agriculture du Canada, 1867-1974. [Ottawa: Information Canada], 1975. v, 136 p.
Note: Comprend toutes les publications du Ministère de 1867 à 1973.– Elle ne comprend pas toutefois les articles publiés dans les revues scientifiques, les tirés à part, les communications non numérotées, les documents

confidentiels ou secrets, ni les textes non publiés.
English title: *Publications of the Canada Department of Agriculture, 1867-1974.*
Édition antérieure: Minter, Ella S.G. *Publications of the Canada Department of Agriculture, 1867-1959.* Queen's Printer, 1963. 387 p.
Localisation: OONL.

6299 **Kronström, Denis**
"Liste sélective de publications parlementaires québécoises."
Dans: *Bulletin: Bibliothèque de l'Assemblée nationale du Québec*; Vol. 6, no 1 (juin 1975) p. 22-34.; ISSN: 0701-6808.
Note: Localisation: OONL.

6300 **MacTaggart, Hazel I.**
Publications of the Government of Ontario, 1956-1971: a checklist. Toronto: Ministry of Government Services, 1975. xi, 410 p.
Note: Approx. 4,200 entries.– Includes publications of departments, boards, other issuing agencies.– Most documents were examined and locations are given.– Excludes maps, posters, items relating to internal administration, newsletters, staff magazines, bills, office consolidations, acts/regulations separately printed, extracts reprinted from government publications, reprints of articles written by government officials, publications of provincially-supported educational institutions.
Location: OONL.

6301 **Saskatchewan. Department of Mineral Resources**
Catalogue of maps and publications [Province of Saskatchewan, Department of Mineral Resources]. Regina: Province of Saskatchewan, Department of Mineral Resources, 1975. 103 p.: maps, chart.
Note: Contains a comprehensive list of maps, reports, charts, regulations, statistical publications available from Publications Office, Department of Mineral Resources.– This catalogue and supplements supersede all previous issues.
Supplements:
Supplement to Catalogue of maps and publications, 1975. 1978. vi, 33 p.: maps. (Miscellaneous report series ; 78-9; ISSN: 0837-4457).
Catalogue of maps, publications and services. Saskatchewan Energy and Mines. 1988. 107 p. (Miscellaneous report / Saskatchewan Energy and Mines ; 88-7; ISSN: 0827-830X).
Location: OONL.

— 1976 —

6302 **Bishop, Olga B.**
Publications of the Government of Ontario, 1867-1900. Toronto: Ministry of Government Services, 1976. xi, 409 p.
Note: Approx. 2,000 entries.– Includes laws and statutes.– Lists serials and special publications.– Contains a history of each branch of government, as it applies to issuance of reports.– Locations are provided for most documents.
Location: OONL.

6303 **Canada. Energie, mines et ressources Canada. Division de la gravité et de la géodynamique**
Liste des publications 1948-1975 [Energie, mines et ressources Canada, Division de la gravité et de la géodynamique]. Ottawa: Energie, mines et ressources Canada, Direction de la physique du globe, Division de la gravité et de la géodynamique, 1976. 28 p.

Note: Regroupe toutes les publications de la Division de la gravité de l'Observatoire fédéral parues entre 1948 et avril 1970, de la Direction de la physique du globe entre avril 1970 et décembre 1975.
Localisation: OONL.

6304 **Salter, E.C.**
Newfoundland Forest Research Centre publications, 1950-1976. St. John's: Newfoundland Forest Research Centre, 1976. 59 l. (Newfoundland Forest Research Centre Information report ; 140; ISSN: 0704-7657)
Note: Approx. 500 entries.
Previous edition: *Bibliography of forest research, Newfoundland region.* Canadian Forestry Service, 1971. 44 l.
Location: OONL.

6305 **Thériault, J.–Yvon**
Les publications parlementaires du Québec depuis 1792. Québec: Assemblée nationale du Québec, 1976. ix, 37 p.: fac.–sim.; ISBN: 0-7754-2494-3.
Note: Localisation: OONL.

— 1977 —

6306 **Backhaus, Christine E.**
Royal commissions and commissions of inquiry in Alberta, 1905-1976. Edmonton: Legislature Library, 1977. [37] p.
Note: 82 entries.– Includes inquiries made under "The Public Inquiries Act" of Alberta, inquiries jointly appointed by Alberta and one or more other provincial governments when Alberta was a participant.– Excludes inquiries by departmental and Legislative Assembly commissions and committees.– Chronological arrangement.
Supplement: ..., *1977-1986.* [Edmonton: Legislature Library, 1986]. 2 l.
Location: OONL.

6307 **Canada. Environment Canada. Atmospheric Environment Service**
Atmospheric Environment Service publications in hydrometeorology and marine applications/Service de l'environnement atmosphérique publications su l'hydrométéorologie et les applications. Downsview, Ont.: Atmospheric Environment Service, Environment Canada, 1977. 42 p.
Note: Approx. 500 entries.– Reports and scientific papers on hydrometeorological, marine and water resources subjects published by employees of Atmospheric Environment Service from 1954 to July 1977.– Text in English and French/texte en français et en anglais.
Location: OONL.

6308 **McGill University. McLennan Library. Government Documents Department**
Guide to parliamentary publications of the province of Quebec. Rev. ed. [Montreal]: Government Documents Department, McLennan Library, McGill University, 1977. 11 p.
Note: Previous edition: 1973. 11 p.
Location: OONL.

6309 **Newfoundland Information Service**
List of publications offered by Government of Newfoundland and Labrador. St. John's: Newfoundland Information Service, 1974-1977. 11 vol.; ISSN: 0383-5189.
Note: Checklist of publications available for general distribution from the Government of Newfoundland.

Location: OONL.

6310 **W.A.C. Bennett Library**
British Columbia government publications. Burnaby, B.C.: Simon Fraser University Library, 1977. iii, 66 p. (Bibliography / W.A.C. Bennett Library ; GOV DOC 3)
Note: Location: OONL.

— 1978 —

6311 **Canada. Fisheries and Environment Canada**
Quarterly notice of new publications [Fisheries and Environment Canada]/Bulletin trimestriel des publications [Pêches et environnement Canada]. Ottawa: Fisheries and Environment Canada, 1976-1978. 7 vol.; ISSN: 0701-7197.
Note: Published from September 1976 to March 1978.
Previous edition: *Monthly notice of new publications/Avis mensuel: nouvelle publications.* 1974-1976.; ISSN: 0701-7200.
Supplements: *Notice of publications: contents/Bulletin des publications: sommaire.* Environment Canada, 1978-1983.; ISSN: 0225-6983.
Location: OONL.

6312 **Canada. Ministère d'État aux Affaires urbaines**
Liste des publications du MEAU. [Ottawa]: Le Ministère, 1978. 27, 27 p.: ill.; ISBN: 0-662-50013-X.
Note: Texte en français et en anglais disposé tête-bêche.– Titre de la p. de t. additionnelle: *List of MSUA publications.*
Localisation: OONL.

6313 **Canada. Ministry of State for Urban Affairs**
List of MSUA publications. [Ottawa]: The Ministry, 1978. 27, 27 p.: ill.; ISBN: 0-662-50013-X.
Note: Text in English and French with French text on inverted pages.– Title of additional title-page: *Liste des publications du MEAU.*
Location: OONL.

6314 **Canadian government publications: catalogue/ Publications du gouvernement canadien: catalogue.**
Ottawa: Information Canada, 1953-1978. 26 vol.; ISSN: 0318-675X.
Note: Annual list of publicly available parliamentary and departmental publications issued by the Government of Canada during the year: statutes, bills, House of Commons and Senate committee proceedings and reports, monographs and serials published by various agencies, boards, councils, commissions.– Appended list of periodicals and subscription services.– Arranged in two sections: one English, one French, with a bilingual general index and an index to periodicals.– Cumulation of *Daily checklist of government publications*, and *Canadian government publications, monthly catalogue.*
Previous editions:
Canadian government publications, consolidated annual catalogue. Queen's Printer, 1954. xvi, 578 p.
Publications du gouvernement du Canada: catalogue général. Imprimeur de la Reine, 1954. xvi, 402 p.
Government publications, annual catalogue. King's Printer, 1943-1948. 6 vol. (Supplements, 1949-1952).
Catalogue of official publications of the Parliament and government of Canada. King's Printer, 1928-1939.
Price list of government publications. 1895-1927.
Continued by: *Government of Canada publications: quarterly catalogue.* 1979- .; ISSN: 0709-0412.– In the same volume sequence, beginning with vol. 27, no. 1 (Jan./Mar. 1979).
Microform: Microfiche version available from Micromedia, Toronto.

6315 **Canadian government publications: monthly catalogue/ Publications du gouvernement canadien: catalogue mensuel.** Ottawa: Supply and Services Canada, 1953-1978. 26 vol.; ISSN: 0008-3690.
Note: Monthly listing of all publicly available Canadian government publications.– Cumulated annually as *Canadian government publications: catalogue/Publications du gouvernement canadien: catalogue.*
Location: OONL.

6316 **Ontario Geological Survey. Geoscience Data Centre**
Index to published reports and maps, Division of Mines, 1891 to 1977. Toronto: Ontario Ministry of Natural Resources, 1978. xv, 408 p.: maps. (Ontario Geological Survey Miscellaneous paper ; 77; ISSN: 0704-2752)
Note: Covers and itemizes about 4,100 serial and non-serial reports, maps and other publications: annual reports (1891-1970); annual statistical reports (1968-1973); bulletins; geoscience reports and maps; reports of the Mineral Resources Branch (and predecessors); selected miscellaneous publications.
Supplement: *Index to published reports and maps, Mines and Minerals Division, 1978-1986.* 1987. 406 p. (Ontario Geological Survey Paper ; 77).
Location: OONL.

6317 **Thwaites, James D.**
La documentation et les archives du Conseil régional de développement de l'Est du Québec. Québec: Institut supérieur des sciences humaines, Université Laval, 1978. xvii, 383 p. (Cahiers de l'ISSH, Collection Instruments de travail / Institut supérieur des sciences humaines, Université Laval ; no 23)
Note: 2,530 entrées.– Rapports et documents produit par le C.R.D.E.Q.– Couvre la période depuis la fondation en mai 1967 jusqu'à décembre 1976.
Localisation: OONL.

6318 **Tooth, John**
Looking for Manitoba government publications: an annotated bibliography of books and pamphlets. [Winnipeg]: Library, Department of Education, [1978]. ix, 267 p.
Note: Lists all Manitoba government publications in print at time of publication, with the exception of audio-visual titles.
Location: OONL.

— 1979 —

6319 **British Columbia. Aquatic Plant Management Program**
List of publications prepared and in preparation by the British Columbia Aquatic Plant Management Program. Victoria: Environmental Studies Division, Ministry of Environment, 1979. 12 l.
Note: Location: OONL.

6320 **British Columbia. Ministry of Lands, Parks and Housing. Parks and Outdoor Recreation Division. Library**
An annotated bibliography of research reports, 1974-79. Victoria: The Ministry, 1979. 19 l.
Note: Location: OONL.

6321 **Canada. Department of Supply and Services**
Selected titles published by Government of Canada departments and agencies. Ottawa: Department of Supply and Services, 1974-1979. 10 vol.; ISSN: 0384-9759.
Note: Text in English and French with French text on

inverted pages.– Title of additional title-page: *Titres choisies publiés par les ministères et agences du Gouvernement du Canada.*
Location: OONL.

6322 **Canada. Ministère des approvisionnements et services**
Titres choisis publiés par les ministères et agences du Gouvernement du Canada. Ottawa: Ministère des approvisionnements et services, 1974-1979. 10 vol.; ISSN: 0384-9767.
Note: Texte en français et en anglais disposé tête-bêche.– Titre de la p. de t. additionnelle: *Selected titles published by Government of Canada departments and agencies.*
Localisation: OONL.

6323 **Kogon, Marilyn H.**
Selected Ontario government publications for schools and libraries. [Toronto]: Ontario Library Association : Ministry of Government Services, 1979. 22 p.: ill.; ISBN: 0-7743-4216-1.
Note: Previous editions:
Selected free Ontario government publications for children and young adults. Toronto: 1977. 27 p.; ISBN: 0-8896-9006-5. 1976. [28] p.
Location: OONL.

6324 **Québec (Province). Éditeur officiel du Québec**
Catalogue de l'Éditeur officiel du Québec. Québec: Éditeur officiel du Québec, 1974-1979. 5 vol.; ISSN: 0316-1560.
Note: Éditions antérieures:
Publications – Bureau de l'Éditeur officiel du Québec/ Publications – Office of the Quebec Official Publisher. 1969-1973. 5 vol.; ISSN: 0316-1579.
Publications en vente au Bureau de l'Imprimeur de la Reine/ Publications on sale at the Office of the Queen's Printer. 1966-1968. 3 vol.
Localisation: OONL.

6325 **Swanick, Eric L.**
Canadian provincial government publications of interest to planners: a selective introductory bibliography. Monticello, Ill.: Vance Bibliographies, 1979. 13 p. (Public administration series: Bibliography ; P-256; ISSN: 0193-970X)
Note: Approx. 170 entries.– Lists publications relating to economics and management, education, energy, housing, land use, natural resources, recreation, social conditions, transportation.– Includes a list of bibliographies.
Location: OONL.

— 1980 —

6326 **Canada. Energy, Mines and Resources Canada. Information-EMR**
Index of selected publications, 1979 [Energy, Mines and Resources Canada]/Répertoire des publications choisies, 1979 [Énergie, mines et ressources Canada]. Ottawa: Energy, Mines and Resources Canada, 1980. 254 p.; ISBN: 0-662-50689-8.
Note: 1,377 entries.– Reports, pamphlets, maps, speeches, statements and news releases, selection of scientific and technical reports on energy, minerals and earth sciences published by Department of Energy, Mines and Resources, primarily in 1976-1979.– Text in English and French/texte en français et en anglais.
Location: OONL.

6327 **Georgian Bay Regional Library System**
Statistics Canada: union list of holdings for Barrie, Owen Sound and Orillia public libraries. [Barrie, Ont.]: The System, 1980. iii, 21 l.
Note: Location: OONL.

6328 **Répertoire analytique des publications gouvernementales du Québec.** Québec: Centre de documentation, Ministère des communications, 1976-1980. 3 vol.; ISSN: 0706-9057.
Note: Notices bibliographiques disposées par ordre alphabétique de titres sous des thèmes correspondant aux différents secteurs de l'activité gouvernementales.– Quatre index: auteurs, titres, descripteurs, identificateurs.– Irrégulier: vol. 1 (1974/75); vol. 2 (1976/77); vol. 3 (1978/79).– Petit divergence de titre.
Localisation: OONL.

6329 **Waintman, Susan; Tampold, Ana**
Ontario royal commissions and commissions of inquiry, 1867-1978: a checklist of reports. Toronto: Legislative Library, Research and Information Services, 1980. viii, 74 p.
Note: 177 entries.– Excludes departmental inquiries, studies related to commissions.– Arranged chronologically by date of appointment.– Indexes: names of commissioners, subjects (topics investigated by commissions; locations, people, societies or organizations that were subject of report).
Supplement: ... , 1979-1984: a checklist of reports. 1985. ix, 17 p.; ISBN: 0-7729-0041-8.
Location: OONL.

— 1981 —

6330 **Bishop, Olga B.**
Canadian official publications. Oxford; Toronto: Pergamon Press, 1981. x, 297 p. (Guides to official publications / Pergamon Press ; vol. 9); ISBN: 0-08-024697-4.
Note: Guide to the use of federal government publications.– Includes documents related to Canadian parliamentary government, federal-provincial relations, official indexes, parliamentary proceedings, parliamentary papers, acts/bills, commissions of inquiry and task forces, policy papers, non-parliamentary publications, reference books, statistics.
Location: OONL.

6331 **British Columbia. Ministry of Environment. Information Services Branch**
Publications list [BC Ministry of Environment]. Victoria: Province of British Columbia, Ministry of Environment, 1981. 10 l.
Note: Location: OONL.

6332 **Lyttle, Norman A.; Gillespie-Wood, Janet**
Index to assessment reports, 1864-1980 [Nova Scotia Department of Mines and Energy]. Halifax: Department of Mines and Energy, Province of Nova Scotia, 1981. vii, 109 p.: map. (Nova Scotia Department of Mines and Energy report ; 81-4; ISSN: 0821-8188); ISBN: 0-88871-029-1.
Note: Approx. 4,000 entries.– Bibliographic index to data contained in non-confidential mineral exploration assessment reports of the Nova Scotia Department of Mines and Energy.– Information includes commodity type, geographic location, county, province, property licence holder, report title, abbreviated description of

report contents, authors, date written.
Previous edition: Gregory, Diane J. *Index to mineral assessment reports to January 1977*. 1977. v, 380 p. (Nova Scotia Department of Mines and Energy report ; 77-2).
Supplement: *...* , *1981-1985*. 1986. xi, 178 p. (Nova Scotia Department of Mines and Energy report ; 86-2).
Location: OONL.

6333 **Lyttle, Norman A.; Gillespie-Wood, Janet**
Index to publications, open file reports and theses, 1862-1980 [Nova Scotia, Department of Mines and Energy]. Halifax: Province of Nova Scotia, Department of Mines and Energy, 1981. vii, 202 p.: map. (Province of Nova Scotia, Department of Mines and Energy report ; no. 81-6); ISBN: 0-88871-030-5.
Note: Approx. 2,000 entries.– Listing of acts and regulations, annual reports, bulletins, economic geology series, information series, memoirs, pamphlets, papers, published maps, open file reports, theses on geoscience of Nova Scotia.
Previous edition: Gregory, Diane J. *Index to open file reports to January 1978*. 1978. 27, 39 p.
Supplements:
Lyttle, Norman A.; Freeman, Janette M. *Author index to Nova Scotia Department of Mines and Energy assessment reports, open files, publications and theses, 1981-1990*. 1991. vii, 508 p.
Subject index to NSDME assessment reports, open files, publications and theses, 1981 to 1990 [microform]. 1991. 21 microfiches.
Location: OONL.

6334 **Manitoba. Legislative Library**
Manitoba government publications, 1970-1974: a checklist compiled in the Legislative Library. Winnipeg: Queen's Printer, 1981. 153 p.
Note: Location: OONL.

6335 **Musées nationaux du Canada**
Catalogue des publications [Musées nationaux du Canada]. Ottawa: Musées nationaux du Canada, 1979-1981. 6 vol.; ISSN: 0708-2916.
Note: English title: *Catalogue of publications [National museums of Canada]*.
Localisation: OONL.

6336 **National Museums of Canada**
Catalogue of publications [National Museums of Canada]. Ottawa: National Museums of Canada, 1979-1981. 6 vol.; ISSN: 0708-2886.
Note: Titre en français: *Catalogue des publications [Musées nationaux du Canada]*.
Location: OONL.

6337 **Taylor, Graham; Hardy, Roger**
Selected bibliography of CANMET publications pertaining to the activities of the Canadian Carbonization Research Association (CCRA), 1965-1980 [microform]. Ottawa: Canada Centre for Mineral and Energy Technology, 1981. 1 microfiche (14 fr.). (Microlog ; 90-04509)
Note: Listing of reports, papers and articles published or written by CANMET (formerly Mines Branch) in connection with the research and coal evaluation activities of CCRA, particularly the making of blast furnace coke from metallurgical coals.
Location: OONL.

— 1982 —

6338 **Alberta. Alberta Environment. Research Management Division**
List of reports [Alberta Environment, Research Management Division]. [Edmonton]: Research Management Division, [1982]. [62] p.
Note: 270 entries.– Alberta Oil Sands Environmental Research Program wide distribution reports and limited distribution reports, Research Management Division reports, Research Secretariat reports, AOSERP open file reports.
Supplement: 1988. 44 p.
Location: OONL.

6339 **Bennett, Judith Antonik**
Royal commissions and commissions of inquiry under the Public Inquiries Act in British Columbia, 1943-1980: a checklist. Victoria: Province of British Columbia, Legislative Library, 1982. 37 p.; ISBN: 0-7718-8305-6.
Note: 203 entries.
Location: OONL.

6340 **British Columbia. Government Information Services**
Provincial government literature: an updated guide to material available to the general public by the various ministries. Victoria: British Columbia Government Information Services, 1982. 55 p.
Note: Location: OONL.

6341 **Canada. Archives publiques**
Liste des publications des Archives publiques du Canada. Ottawa: Archives publiques Canada, 1974-1982. 8 vol.; ISSN: 0828-1505.
Note: Les livraisons de 1983-1984 n'ont pas été publiées.– Texte en français et en anglais disposé tête-bêche.– Titre de la p. de t. additionnelle: *List of publications of the Public Archives of Canada*.
Localisation: OONL.

6342 **Canada. Parks Canada**
Bibliography: Manuscript report series nos. 1-430: unedited manuscripts of the Parks Canada research divisions/Bibliographie: Travaux inédits nos 1-430: manuscrits inédits des divisions de recherches de Parcs Canada. [Hull, Quebec]: Parks Canada, [1982]. 83 p.
Note: 594 entries.– Listing of unedited, unpublished research reports dealing with archaeology, architecture, history and material culture.– Reports appear in the language of the author (English or French), are not translated.– Some of these are later edited, translated and published in the *Canadian Historic Sites*, or *History and Archaeology* series.– Entries in this publication provide this information.– Text in English and French/texte en français et en anglais.
Location: OONL.

6343 **Canada. Public Archives**
List of publications of the Public Archives of Canada. Ottawa: Public Archives of Canada, 1974-1982. 8 vol.; ISSN: 0828-1505.
Note: Issues for 1983-1984 not published.– Text in English and French with French text on inverted pages.– Title of additional title-page: *Liste des publications des Archives publiques du Canada*.
Location: OONL.

6344 **Canada. Statistics Canada. User Services Division**
Historical catalogue of Statistics Canada publications, 1918-1980. Ottawa: Statistics Canada, 1982. 337 p.; ISBN:

0-660-10964-6.

Note: Complete record of all catalogued publications of Statistics Canada and Dominion Bureau of Statistics.– Excludes technical papers, memoranda, working papers.

Titre en français: *Catalogue rétrospectif des publications de Statistique Canada, 1918-1980.*

Previous edition: Canada. Bureau of Statistics. Canada Year Book, Handbook and Library Division. *Historical catalogue of Dominion Bureau of Statistics publications, 1918-1960: Catalogue rétrospectif des publications du Bureau fédéral de la statistique, 1918-1960.* Dominion Bureau of Statistics, 1966. xiv, 298 p.

Supplement: Supplemented by annual Statistics Canada catalogue.

Location: OONL.

6345 **Canada. Statistique Canada. Division de l'assistance-utilisateurs**

Catalogue rétrospectif des publications de Statistique Canada, 1918-1980. Ottawa: Statistique Canada, 1982. 348 p.; ISBN: 0-660-90777-1.

Note: Énumération complète de toutes les publications figurant au catalogue de Statistique Canada et du Bureau fédéral de la statistique.– Exclut documents techniques, mémoires, documents de travail.

English title: *Historical catalogue of Statistics Canada publications, 1918-1980.*

Édition antérieure: *Historical catalogue of Dominion Bureau of Statistics publications, 1918-1960: Catalogue rétrospectif des publications du Bureau fédéral de la statistique, 1918-1960.* Bureau fédéral de la statistique; 1966. xiv, 298 p.

Supplément: Version annuelle du *Catalogue* de Statistique Canada.

Localisation: OONL.

6346 **Canada. Water Pollution Control Directorate**

Water Pollution Control Directorate publications/Les publications de la Direction générale de la lutte contre la pollution des eaux. Hull, Quebec: The Directorate, 1975-1982. 7 vol.; ISSN: 0703-6094.

Note: Includes the Environmental Protection Service Report series, miscellaneous reports, speeches and papers, reports published jointly by Environment Canada and the Ontario Ministry of the Environment under the Canada-Ontario Agreement on Great Lakes Water Quality, SCAT series of research reports (Sewage collection and treatment reports).

Location: OONL.

6347 **Canada Centre for Mineral and Energy Technology**

Catalogue of CANMET publications. Ottawa: Canada Centre for Mineral and Energy Technology, Technology Information Division, 1978-1982. 7 vol.; ISSN: 0707-560X.

Note: Contains CANMET reports, papers published in or submitted to periodicals and presentations, divisional and program reports, contract research reports, research agreement program reports, literature surveys and translations in mineral sciences, energy research, mining research, physical metallurgy research.– Text in English and French with French text on inverted pages.– Title of additional title page: *Catalogue des publications de CANMET.*

Location: OONL.

6348 **Centre canadien de la technologie des minéraux et de l'énergie**

Catalogue des publications de CANMET. Ottawa: Centre canadien de la technologie des minéraux et de l'énergie, Division de l'information technologique, 1978-1982. 7 vol.; ISSN: 0707-560X.

Note: Compilation des publications et des rapports préparés par le personnel scientifique et technique de CANMET et les rapports de recherche effectuée à contrat par les agences extérieures pour le CANMET.– Principaux thèmes traités: sciences minérales, recherche énergétique, recherche minière, métallurgie physique.– Texte en français et en anglais disposé tête-bêche.– Titre de la p. de t. additionelle: *Catalogue of CANMET publications.*

Localisation: OONL.

6349 **Cusack, Carla**

Bibliographie des sources fédérales de données à l'exception de Statistique Canada, 1981. Ottawa: Statistique Canada, Division de l'assistance-utilisateurs, Section de la documentation de référence, 1982. viii, 198 p.; ISBN: 0-660-90811-5.

Note: Comprend les sources des données socio-économiques diffusées périodiquement par les organismes et ministères fédéraux: commissions et conseils fédéraux, et quelques sociétés de la Couronne.

English title: *Bibliography of federal data sources excluding Statistics Canada, 1981.*

Localisation: OONL.

6350 **Cusack, Carla**

Bibliography of federal data sources excluding Statistics Canada, 1981. Ottawa: Statistics Canada, User Services Division, Reference Products Section, 1982. viii, 189 p.; ISBN: 0-660-11045-8.

Note: Brings together sources of social and economic data which are produced on a regular basis by federal departments and agencies, including a cross-section of commissions, boards and crown corporations.

Titre en français: *Bibliographie des sources fédérales de données à l'exception de Statistique Canada, 1981.*

Location: OONL.

6351 **Gourdeau, Monique F.**

Documents sessionnels de l'Assemblée législative du Québec (1960-1970). Québec: Bibliothèque de l'Assemblée nationale, 1982. 277 p. (Bibliographie et documentation / Bibliothèque de l'Assemblée nationale du Québec ; 9)

Note: 1,840 entrées.

Localisation: OONL.

6352 **Powell, Karen L.**

Reference guide to Alberta government committees, 1905-1980. Edmonton: Alberta Legislative Library, Cooperative Government Library Services, 1982. ca. 150 p.

Note: Listing of Alberta departmental and interdepartmental committees, with titles of reports, compilers, dates of issue.

Location: OONL.

6353 **Québec (Province). Bureau de la statistique du Québec. Centre d'information et de documentation**

Répertoire de données et de publications statistiques québécoises. Québec: Centre d'information et de documentation du Bureau de la statistique du Québec, 1982. 191 p.; ISBN: 2-550-02734-5.

Note: Approx. 200 entrées.– Publications et données du BSQ et les publications produites par les ministères ou

organismes gouvernementaux.
Localisations: OONL.

— 1983 —

6354 **Barnes, Eleanor; Juozapavicius, Danguole**
Select committees of the Legislative Assembly of Ontario, 1867-1978. Toronto: Legislative Library, Research and Information Services, 1983. x, 88 p.; ISBN: 0-7743-8080-2.
Note: 109 entries.– Records the reports of 109 select committees of the Legislative Assembly present during the period from Confederation to 1978.– Subject matter ranges from Agricultural marketing to Youth, Gambling laws to Nuclear energy.
Location: OONL.

6355 **British Columbia. Littoral Resources Unit**
List of publications prepared and in preparation by the Littoral Resources Unit. Victoria: Water Management Branch, Ministry of Environment, 1983. 17 l.
Note: Publications listed include reports and bulletins prepared by the Littoral Resources Unit from 1972 to 1982 on topics related to aquatic plant distribution, ecology and growth in British Columbia.
Previous edition: *List of publications prepared and in preparation by the British Columbia Aquatic Plant Management Program. 1979. 12 l.*
Location: OONL.

6356 **Checklist of publications associated with IDRC and recorded in AGRIS, 1975-1982.** Ottawa: International Development Research Centre, c1983. xi, 67 p.; ISBN: 0-88936-390-0.
Note: Publications produced or supported by the International Development Research Centre in the fields of agriculture, forestry, fisheries, food science, rural development.
Location: OONL.

6357 **Greater Vancouver Regional District**
Publications and maps for sale. Vancouver: Greater Vancouver Regional District, 1983. 26 p.
Note: Approx. 100 entries.– Catalogue of publications and maps produced by officials of the Greater Vancouver Regional District on various topics related to planning and development.
Location: OONL.

6358 **Griffiths, K.B.**
Forest Pest Management Institute bibliography (1977-1982). Sault Ste. Marie, Ont.: Forest Pest Management Institute, Canadian Forestry Service, 1983. i, 60 p. (Forest Pest Management Institute Information report ; FPM-X-60; ISSN: 0704-772X); ISBN: 0-662-13122-3.
Note: Approx. 400 entries.– Lists all Forest Pest Management Institute Information reports and journal articles published from formation of FPMI in 1977.– Subjects include biological control agents, physiological and genetic mechanisms, complementary research, application technology, pest products, environmental impact and chemical accountability.
Titre en français: *Bibliographie de l'institut pour la répression des ravageurs forestiers (1977-1985).*
Supplements:
Forest Pest Management Institute bibliography (1982-1985). 1985. i, 20 p.; ISBN: 0-662-14777-4.
Jamieson, K.B. *F.P.M.I. bibliography, 1985-1990/I.R.R.F. liste des publications pour les années 1985-1990.* 1991. 76 p.; ISBN: 0-662-58317-5.

Location: OONL.

6359 **National Research Council Canada. Division of Building Research**
List of publications [National Research Council Canada. Division of Building Research]/Liste des publications [Conseil national de recherches du Canada, Division des recherches sur le bâtiment]. Ottawa: The Division, 1947-1983. 36 vol.; ISSN: 0382-1439.
Note: Annual with cumulations:
...: 1947-1959 inclusive. 1959. 35 p.
...: 1947-1962 inclusive. 1962. 60 p.
...: 1947-1971/...: 1947-1971. [s.d.]. 178 p.
...: 1972-1977/...: 1972-1977. 1978. 64 p.
Continued by: Institute for Research in Construction (Canada). *List of publications/Liste des publications.* 1984-. vol.; ISSN: 0835-9083.– Annual.
Location: OONL.

6360 **Ontario. Ministère des services gouvernementaux**
Catalogue des publications en français du gouvernement de l'Ontario. Toronto: Ministère des services gouvernementaux, 1979-1983. 5 vol.; ISSN: 0706-2923.
Note: Cessé avec vol. 5, no 4 (décembre 1984).
Localisation: OONL.

6361 **Québec (Province). Ministère de l'éducation. Direction des études économiques et démographiqes**
Liste des publications de la Direction des études économiques et démographiques de 1977 à 1982. [Québec]: La Direction, 1983. 24 p.; ISBN: 2-550-05928-X.
Note: Approx. 150 entrées.– Trois catégories: études et analyses; statistiques; répertoires et annuaires.
Localisation: OONL.

6362 **Québec (Province). Ministère des affaires sociales. Service de l'informathèque**
Monographies et publications officielles (Gouvernement du Québec. Ministère des affaires sociales. Informathèque). Sainte-Foy: Gouvernement du Québec, Ministère des affaires sociales, [1976-1983]. 8 vol.; ISSN: 0833-4811.
Note: Comprend des publications en anglais.
Localisation: OONL.

6363 **Université de Sherbrooke. Service de bibliothèques**
Liste des périodiques gouvernementaux. Éd. provisoire. Sherbrooke, Québec: Le Service, 1983. 106 p.
Note: Comprend des publications en français et en anglais, principalement des publications du gouvernement du Québec.
Localisation: OONL.

— 1984 —

6364 **Bishop, Olga B.**
Publications of the province of Upper Canada and of Great Britain relating to Upper Canada, 1791-1840. Toronto: Ontario Ministry of Citizenship and Culture, 1984. vii, 288 p.; ISBN: 0-7743-8931-1.
Note: Approx. 1,000 entries.
Location: OONL.

6365 **Nova Scotia. Legislative Library**
Nova Scotia royal commissions and commissions of inquiry, 1849-1984: a checklist. 3rd ed. Halifax: The Library, 1984. 39 p.
Note: Approx. 90 entries.
Previous editions:
Nova Scotia royal commissions and commissions of enquiry appointed by the Province of Nova Scotia, 1977-1973. 1973. 23

l.
A finding list of royal commissions appointed by the Province of Nova Scotia, 1908-1954. 1956. 4 l.
Location: OONL.

6366 **Québec (Province). Ministère de l'environnement. Centre de documentation**
Répertoire des publications scientifiques et techniques du Ministère de l'environnement. [2e éd.]. [Québec]: Ministère de l'environnement, Direction des communications et de l'éducation, Centre de documentation, 1984. 64 p.; ISBN: 2-550-11030-7.
Note: Approx. 700 entrées.
Édition antérieure: 1983. 57, [5] p.; ISBN: 2-550-10408-0.
Localisation: OONL.

— 1985 —

6367 **Arsenault, B.**
Bibliographie de l'Institut pour la répression des ravageurs forestiers (1977-1985). Sault Ste. Marie, Ont.: Institut pour la répression des ravageurs forestiers, Service canadien des forêts, 1985. ii, 30 p. (Rapport d'information / Institut pour la répression des ravageurs forestiers ; FPM-X-60F; ISSN: 0827-1119); ISBN: 0-662-93784-8.
Note: Approx. 75 entrées.– Rapports d'information, notes techniques, revues des programmes.
English title: *Forest Pest Management Institute bibliography (1977-1982).*
Supplément: Jamieson, K.B. *F.P.M.I. bibliography (1985-1990)/I.R.R.F. liste des publications pour les années 1985-1990.* 1991. 76 p.; ISBN: 0-662-58317-5.
Localisation: OONL.

6368 **British Columbia. Ministry of Industry and Small Business Development**
Publications list [British Columbia Ministry of Industry and Small Business Development]. Victoria: Province of British Columbia, Ministry of Industry and Small Business Development, [1980-1985]. 4 vol.; ISSN: 0711-835X.
Note: Irregular.
Location: OONL.

6369 **Comité fédéral-provincial sur la statistique minérale (Canada). Groupe de travail sur les publications**
Répertoire des publications sur la statistique minérale: publications et enquêtes fédérales et provinciales au Canada. Ottawa: Ministère de l'énergie, des mines et des ressources Canada, 1985. v, 47, v, 41 p.; ISBN: 0-662-53978-8.
Note: Texte en français et en anglais disposé tête-bêche.– Titre de la p. de t. additionnelle: *Catalogue of mineral statistics: federal and provincial publications and surveys in Canada.*
Localisation: OONL.

6370 **Communauté urbaine de Québec (Québec)**
Répertoire des documents produits dans le cadre de l'élaboration du schéma d'aménagement. Québec: La Communauté, [1985]. 86 p.; ISBN: 2-89216-007-3.
Note: 79 entrées.– Rapports techniques, études, documents de travail et cartes.
Localisation: OONL.

6371 **Fast, Louise**
Statistics Canada publications on microfiche, 1850-1980. [Toronto]: Micromedia, [1985]. 1 vol. (in various pagings).; ISBN: 0-88892-5136-5.
Note: User's guide to the "Statistics Canada publications on microfiche" collection, compiled from the holdings lists of this collection.
Location: OONL

6372 **Federal-Provincial Committee on Mineral Statistics (Canada). Publications Task Force**
Catalogue of mineral statistics: federal and provincial publications and surveys in Canada. Ottawa: Department of Energy, Mines and Resources, 1985. v, 41, 47, v p.; ISBN: 0-662-53978-8.
Note: Text in English and French with French text on inverted pages.– Title on added title page: *Répertoire des publications sur la statistique minérale: publications et enquêtes fédérales et provinciales au Canada.*
Location: OONL.

6373 **Gagné, Raymond**
Publications parlementaires québécoises: catalogue collectif. Québec: Bibliothèque, Assemblée nationale, 1985. [26] f. (Bibliographie et documentation / Bibliothèque de l'Assemblée nationale du Québec ; no 19; ISSN: 0821-1175)
Note: Localisation: OOP.

6374 **Morrison, B.A.; Thuns, A.**
Summary of projects and publications, 1960-1985 [Engineering and Statistical Research Institute, Agriculture Canada]/Sommaire des projets et des publications, 1960-1985 [Institut de recherche technique et statistique, Agriculture Canada]. Ottawa: Engineering and Statistical Research Institute, Research Branch, Agriculture Canada, 1985. 369 p. (Engineering and Statistical Research Institute Contribution ; no. I-780)
Note: 1,760 entries.– Publications of the Engineering and Statistical Research Institute of the Department of Agriculture: research in agricultural mechanization, farm buildings, energy, food engineering, electronics, instrumentation, engineering technology and statistics.– Text in English and French/texte en français et en anglais.
Location: OOSS.

6375 **National Research Council Canada. Fire Research Section**
List of publications, Fire Research Section, 1955-1985/ Liste des publications, Section d'étude de feu, 1955-1985. Ottawa: The Section, 1985. 43 p.
Note: Approx. 400 entries.– Research related to fire-related characteristics of materials and products, fire processes, techniques for fire-safety design, development of fire protective measures.– Text in English and French/ texte en français et en anglais.
Location: OON.

— 1986 —

6376 **Bates, D.; Gillmeister, D.**
Ontario Tree Improvement and Forest Biomass Institute publications, 1980-1985: an annotated bibliography. Toronto: Ontario Ministry of Natural Resources, c1986. ii, 31 p. (Forest Research report / Ontario Ministry of Natural Resources ; no. 114; ISSN: 0301-3924); ISBN: 0-7729-1342-0.
Note: 206 entries.– Research reports, papers and journal articles written by staff of Ontario Tree Improvement and Forest Biomass Institute between 1980 and 1985.
Location: OONL.

6377 **Canada. Library of Parliament. Information and Reference Branch**
Green papers, 1971-1986/Livres verts, 1971-1986. Ottawa: Library of Parliament, Information and Reference Branch, 1986. 54, [10] l.
Note: 47 entries.– For the purposes of this compilation, a green paper is an official document sponsored by Ministers of the Crown issued to invite public comment on an issue prior to policy formation.
Location: OONL.

6378 **Canada. Library of Parliament. Information and Reference Branch**
White papers, 1939-1986/Livre blancs, 1939-1986. Ottawa: Library of Parliament, Information and Reference Branch, 1986. 60, [9] l.
Note: 55 entries.– For the purposes of this compilation, white papers are official documents presented by Ministers of the Crown which state and explain the government's policy on a certain issue.
Location: OONL.

6379 **Canada. Transport Canada. Library and Information Centre**
Transport Canada publications catalogue/Transports Canada catalogue des publications. Ottawa: Transport Canada, 1981-1986. 9 vol.; ISSN: 0823-5171.
Note: Irregular.– Ceased with no. 9 (1986).– Includes English and French publications.
Previous edition: *Transport Canada publications catalogue and selected ongoing research and development projects/ Transports Canada, catalogue des publications et liste sélective des projets de recherche et développement en cours.* 1978-1980. 3 vol.; ISSN: 0702-0473.
Location: OONL.

6380 **Fortier, Monique**
Les commissions parlementaires à l'Assemblée nationale, 1980-1985. [Québec]: Assemblée nationale du Québec, Bibliothèque, Division de l'indexation et de la bibliographie, 1986. 218 p. (Bibliographie et documentation / Bibliothèque de l'Assemblée nationale du Québec ; 24); ISBN: 2-551-06669-7.
Note: 896 entrées.– Thèmes principaux: le gouvernement, les droits individuels, les services, la culture et l'éducation.
Localisation: OONL.

6381 **Maillet, Lise**
Provincial royal commissions and commissions of inquiry, 1867-1982: a selective bibliography/ Commissions royales provinciales et commissions d'enquête, 1867-1982: bibliographie sélective. Ottawa: National Library of Canada, 1986. xvii, 254 p.; ISBN: 0-660-53123-2.
Note: 767 entries.– Text in English and French/texte en français et en anglais.
Location: OONL.

6382 **Ontario. Ministry of Industry, Trade and Technology**
In print: publications available from the Ontario Ministry of Industry, Trade and Technology. Toronto: Province of Ontario, The Ministry, 1986. 21 l.; ISSN: 0836-8430.
Note: Location: OONL.

— 1987 —

6383 **British Columbia. Petroleum Resources Division**
Catalogue of publications, maps, and services [Petroleum Resources Division]. Victoria: British Columbia Ministry of Mines and Petroleum Resources, 1982-1987. 3 vol.; ISSN: 0831-4055.
Note: Previous edition: *Catalogue of publications, maps & services available through the [British Columbia] Petroleum Resources Branch.* 1971-1981. 10 vol.; ISSN: 0703-6264.– Anuual.
Location: OONL.

6384 **Canada. Environment Canada. Lands Directorate**
Lands Directorate publications. Ottawa: Lands Directorate, 1977-1987. [9] vol.; ISSN: 0707-2023.
Note: Irregular.– Listings include "Canada Land Inventory reports," "Land Use in Canada series," "Working paper series," "Fact sheets," "Ecological land classification series," "Map folios," "Canada Land Data System reports."- Text in English and French with French text on inverted pages.– Title of additional title-page: *Publications: Direction générale des terres.*
Location: OONL.

6385 **Canada. Environnement Canada. Direction générale des terres**
Publications: Direction générale des terres. Ottawa: Direction générale des terres, 1977-1987. [9] vol.; ISSN: 0707-2023.
Note: Irrégulier.– Comporte des listes: "Inventaire des terres du Canada: rapports et cartes," "Rapports sur la politique fédérale sur l'utilisation des terres," "Série de l'utilisation des terres au Canada," "Série de documents de travail," "Série de la classification écologique du territoire," "Dossiers cartographiques," "Cartes."- Texte en français et en anglais disposé tête-bêche.– Titre de la p. de t. additionnelle: *Lands Directorate publications.*
Localisation: OONL.

6386 **Nova Scotia. Legislative Library**
Publications of the Province of Nova Scotia, quarterly checklist. Halifax: Legislative Library, 1980-1987. 7 vol.; ISSN: 0228-0299.
Note: Quarterly listing of the published documents of departments and agencies of the Province of Nova Scotia.– Vol. 1, no. 1 (June 1980) – Vol. 7, no. 4 (March 1987).
Location: OONL.

6387 **Yapa, A.C.; Mitchell, M.H.**
Bibliography, 1979-1985 [Petawawa National Forestry Institute]/Liste des publications pour les années 1979-1985 [Institut forestier national de Petawawa]. Chalk River, Ont.: Petawawa National Forestry Institute, Canadian Forestry Service, 1987. i, 150 p. (Information report / Petawawa National Forestry Institute ; PI-X-70E/ F; ISSN: 0714-3354); ISBN: 0-662-55451-5.
Note: Approx. 250 entries.– Text in English and French/ texte en français et en anglais.
Supplements:
Ballantyne, B.A.; Mitchell, M.H. *Bibliography, 1986-1987/ Liste des publications, 1986-1987.* 1989. vi, 70 p. (Information report ; PI-X-87E/F; ISSN: 0714-3354); ISBN: 0-662-56488-X.
Boross, Pierre A.; Mitchell, M.H. *Bibliography, 1988-1990/ Bibliographie, 1988-1990.* 1991. vi, 125 p. (Information report ; PI-X-106E/F; ISSN: 0706-1854); ISBN: 0-662-58651-4.
Location: OONL.

— 1988 —

6388 **Canada. Environment Canada. Canadian Parks Service. Socio-Economic Branch**
Reports from Parks Service socio-economic surveys, 1960-1988/Rapports des enquêtes socio-économiques du Service canadien des parcs, 1960-1988. Ottawa: Environment Canada, Canadian Parks Service, 1988. i, 41 l. (Canadian Parks Service Reference list ; no. 2)
Note: Location: OOFF.

6389 **Canada. Inland Waters Directorate. Water Quality Branch**
Publications [Water Quality Branch]/Publications [Direction de la qualité des eaux]. Ottawa: Environment Canada, 1988. x, 49 p.; ISSN: 0710-8737.
Note: 58 entries.– Interpretive reports, data management reports, precipitation studies, reference publications.
Online access: *AQUAREF* database, available through CAN/OLE, CISTI.
Previous editions:
1987. xii, 69 p.; ISBN: 0-662-56471-5.
1985. vi, 39 p.; ISBN: 0-662-54889-2.
1983. vi, 24 p.; ISBN: 0-662-53421-2.
Bibliography of Water Quality Branch publications. 1978.; ISSN: 0225-431X.
Location: OONL.

6390 **Canadian Government Publishing Centre**
Consolidated list of serials of the Government of Canada: (includes the serials that appear on the Weekly checklist). Hull, Quebec: Canadian Government Publishing Centre, 1988. 43 l.
Note: Titre en français: *Liste générale des publications en série du gouvernement du Canada.*
Location: OONL.

6391 **Centre d'édition du gouvernement du Canada**
Liste générale des publications en série du gouvernement du Canada: (comprend les publications en série signalées dans la Liste hebdomadaire). Hull, Québec: Centre d'édition du gouvernement du Canada, 1988. 55 f.
Note: English title: *Consolidated list of serials of the Government of Canada.*
Localisation: OONL.

6392 **Québec (Province). Ministère des communications. Bibliothèque administrative**
Liste mensuelle des publications du gouvernement du Québec. Québec: Direction générale des publications gouvernementales, Ministère des communications, 1981-[1988]. 7 vol.; ISSN: 0714-5993.
Note: Mensuelle, mars 1981-décembre 1987.– Publications officielles regroupées par ministères et organismes et classées dans l'ordre alphabétique de titre.– Index des titres et index des titres annuel.
Localisation: OONL.

6393 **Sander, F.**
St. Andrews Biological Station publications, 1977-86. St. Andrews, N.B.: Biological Sciences Branch, Department of Fisheries and Oceans, 1988. iv, 32 p. (Canadian manuscript report of fisheries and aquatic sciences ; no. 1960; ISSN: 0706-6473)
Note: 848 entries.– Compilation of all publications produced by research programs at St. Andrews Biological Station, 1977-1986, arranged chronologically, and within each year, alphabetically by author.– Préface en français.

Location: OONL.

— 1989 —

6394 **Agence canadienne de développement international**
Catalogue des publications de l'Agence canadienne de développement international. Hull, Québec: Direction générale des affaires publiques, Agence canadienne de développement international, c1989. 24, 24 p.: ill.; ISBN: 0-662-56873-7.
Note: Texte en français et en anglais disposé tête-bêche.– Titre de la p. de t. additionnelle: *Publications catalogue of the Canadian International Development Agency.*
Localisation: OONL.

6395 **Canada. Tourism Canada**
Bibliography of research publications [Tourism Canada]. [Ottawa]: Industry, Science and Technology Canada, [1989]. 14, 14 p.: ill.
Note: Comprehensive listing of tourist trade survey reports produced by Tourism Canada.– Title of additional title-page: *Répertoire des publications de recherche [Tourisme Canada].* – Text in English and French with French text on inverted pages.
Location: OONL.

6396 **Canada. Tourisme Canada**
Répertoire des publications de recherche [Tourisme Canada]. [Ottawa]: Industrie, Sciences et Technologie Canada, [1989]. 14, 14 p.: ill.
Note: Documents publiés par la Direction de la recherche de Tourisme Canada.– Texte en français et en anglais disposé tête-bêche.– Titre de la p. de t. additionnelle: *Bibliography of research publications [Tourism Canada].*
Localisation: OONL.

6397 **Canada Centre for Mineral and Energy Technology. Library and Documentation Services Division**
CANMET publications in print/Publications de CANMET disponibles. [Ottawa]: The Division, 1989. [116] p.
Note: Lists CANMET publications currently in print: report series, special publication series, monographs and occasional publications.– Arranged in subject divisions: coal, energy excluding coal, general, materials engineering, mineral processing, mining engineering.– Excludes divisional or laboratory reports, contract reports, notes of oral presentations, journal articles contributed by CANMET staff members.– Text in English and French/ texte en français et en anglais.
Location: OONL.

6398 **Canadian International Development Agency**
Publications catalogue of the Canadian International Development Agency. Hull, Quebec: Public Affairs Branch, Canadian International Development Agency, c1989. 24, 24 p.: ill.; ISBN: 0-662-56873-7.
Note: Text in English and French with French text on inverted pages.– Title of additional title-page: *Catalogue des publications de l'Agence canadienne de développement international.*
Location: OONL.

6399 **Murphy, Joan; Poulin, Michelle**
Centre de foresterie des Laurentides publications, 1980-1988/Laurentian Forestry Centre publications, 1980-1988. Sainte-Foy, Québec: Forêts Canada, 1989. vi, 44 p. (Rapport d'information / Centre de foresterie des Laurentides ; LAU-X-86B; ISSN: 0835-1589); ISBN: 0-662-56745-5.

Note: Approx. 600 entrées.– Documents publiés par Forêts Canada, Région du Québec: rapports d'information, feuillets d'information, monographies, guides d'aménagement des terrains boisés privés, articles de revues, de symposiums, d'ateliers, de périodiques spécialisés ou vulgarisateurs et les bulletins.– Nom antérieur de la collectivité: Centre de recherches forestières des Laurentides/Laurentian Forest Research Centre.– Texte en français et en anglais/text in English and French.
Supplément: Bilodeau, Colleen; Poulin, Michelle. ... , 1989-1991/... , 1989-1991. 1992. 30 p. (Rapport d'information / Centre de foresterie des Laurentides ; LAU-X-1008).
Localisation: OONL.

6400 **Québec (Province). Office de planification et de développement du Québec**
Répertoire des publications de l'Office de planification et de développement du Québec. [Québec]: Service des communications de l'O.P.D.Q., 1989. viii, 68 p.; ISBN: 2-550-19951-0.
Note: Approx. 600 entrées.– Comprend toutes les publications réalisées par l'OPDQ depuis sa création en 1968: recherches, études, enquêtes, inventaires: les plans, programmes et projets de développement économique et social et d'aménagement du territoire.
Localisation: OONL.

6401 **Rochon, Denis**
Forestry Canada publications, 1986-1988/Publications de Forêts Canada, 1986 à 1988. Ottawa: Forestry Canada, 1989. 63 p.; ISBN: 0-66-566838-9.
Note: Information reports, journal articles, symposium proceedings, other publications by staff of Forestry Canada institutes and research centres.– Text in English and French/texte en français et en anglais.
Location: OONL.

6402 **Tedford, Douglas E.; Triplehorn, Julia H.; Brûlé, Monique L.**
Annotated list of indexes to Canadian provincial geological publications (including the Yukon and Northwest Territories). Ottawa: Energy, Mines and Resources Canada, 1989. ii, 26, 25, ii p.
Note: Approx. 180 entries.– Historical publications, publication lists, additional bibliographies for each province and territory.– Text in English and French with French text on inverted pages.– Title of additional title-page: *Liste annotée des index aux publications géologiques provinciales canadiennes (incluant le Yukon et les Territoires du Nord-Ouest).*
Location: OONL.

6403 **Tedford, Douglas E.; Triplehorn, Julia H.; Brûlé, Monique L.**
Liste annotée des index aux publications géologiques provinciales canadiennes (incluant le Yukon et les Territoires du Nord-Ouest). Ottawa: Énergie, Mines et Ressources Canada, 1989. ii, 25, 26, ii p.
Note: Approx. 180 entrées.– Publications historiques, listes de publications, autres bibliographies pour toutes les provinces et les territoires.– Texte en français et en anglais disposé tête-bêche.– Titre de la p. de t. additionnelle: *Annotated list of indexes to Canadian provincial geological publications (including the Yukon and Northwest Territories).*

Localisation: OONL.

— 1990 —

6404 **Gélinas, Pat**
Catalogue of mineral statistics: federal and provincial publications and surveys in Canada. [Ottawa]: Energy, Mines and Resources Canada, 1990. v, 45, 47, v p. (Mineral policy sector internal report ; MRI 90-1); ISBN: 0-662-57967-4.
Note: Text in English and French with French text on inverted pages.– Title of additional title page: *Répertoire traitant de la statistique des minéraux: publications et enquêtes fédérales-provinciales au Canada.*
Previous edition: 1985. v, 41, 47 v p. (Mineral policy sector internal report ; MRI 85-1); ISBN: 0-662-53978-8.
Location: OONL.

6405 **Gélinas, Pat**
Répertoire traitant de la statistique des minéraux: publications et enquêtes fédérales-provinciales au Canada. [Ottawa]: Énergie, mines et ressources Canada, 1990. v, 47, 45, v p. (Secteur de la politique minérale rapport interne ; MRI 90-1); ISBN: 0-662-57967-4.
Note: Texte en français et en anglais disposé tête-bêche.– Titre de la p. de t. additionnelle: *Catalogue of mineral statistics: federal and provincial publications and surveys in Canada.*
Édition antérieure: 1985. v, 47, 41, v p. (Rapport interne du sector de la politique minérale ; MRI 85-1); ISBN: 0-662-53978-8.
Localisation: OONL.

6406 **Ontario. Ministry of Transportation and Communications. Research and Development Branch**
Research & development publications catalogue [Ontario Ministry of Transportation and Communications]. Downsview: Research and Development Branch, Ontario Ministry of Transportation, 1988-1990. 3 vol.; ISSN: 0846-2542.
Note: Annual.
Location: OONL.

6407 **Robitaille, André**
Bibliographie annotée des documents produits par la Division Écologie du Service de l'inventaire forestier, 1987-1990. Charlesbourg, Québec: Division de l'écologie, 1990. 14 p.
Note: 39 entrées.
Localisation: OONL.

6408 **Van Haaften, Jami**
An index to selected Canadian provincial government publications: for librarians, teachers and booksellers. Roslin, Ont.: J. Van Haaften, 1990. 1 vol. (loose-leaf).
Note: Selection of free or low-cost government publications grouped in eight broad subject categories: agriculture, culture, education, energy, environment, health and safety, natural resources, tourism and recreation.
Supplement: 1992- . vol.; ISSN: 1193-9370.– Biennial.
Location: OONL.

— 1991 —

6409 **Bates, D.; Gillmeister, D.**
Ontario Forest Research Institute publications, 1980-1991 (an annotated bibliography). Sault Ste. Marie: Ontario Forest Research Institute, 1991. ii, 74 p.; ISBN: 0-772-99396-3.
Note: Supplement: Ontario Ministry of Natural

Resources, 1991- . vol.; ISSN: 1189-5624.– Annual.
Location: OONL.

6410 **British Columbia. Geological Survey Branch**
NTS location and author index to publications of the British Columbia Geological Survey Branch. Victoria: B.C. Ministry of Energy, Mines and Petroleum Resources, 1991. vi, 304 p.: map.
Note: Location: OONL.

— 1992 —

6411 **Conseil économique du Canada**
Catalogue des publications [Conseil économique du Canada]. Ottawa: Conseil économique du Canada, 1981-1992. 10 vol.; ISSN: 0828-4350.
Note: Texte en français et en anglais disposé tête-bêche.– Titre de la p. de t. additionnelle: *Catalogue of publications [Economic Council of Canada]*.
Localisation: OONL.

6412 **Economic Council of Canada**
Catalogue of publications [Economic Council of Canada]. Ottawa: Economic Council of Canada, 1981-1992. 10 vol.; ISSN: 0828-4350.
Note: Text in English and French with French text on inverted pages.– Title of additional title-page: *Catalogue des publications [Conseil économique du Canada]*.
Location: OONL.

6413 **Petsche-Wark, Dawna; Johnson, Catherine**
Royal commissions and commissions of inquiry for the provinces of Upper Canada, Canada and Ontario, 1792 to 1991: a checklist of reports. Toronto: Ontario Legislative Library, 1992. ix, 174 p.; ISBN: 0-77299-327-0.
Note: Location: OONL.

6414 **Sage, Richard; Weir, Aileen**
Select committees of the assemblies of the provinces of Upper Canada, Canada and Ontario, 1792 to 1991: a checklist of reports. Toronto: Ontario Legislative Library, 1992. xi, 431 p.; ISBN: 0-772-99326-2.
Note: Location: OONL.

6415 **Zaldokas, Daiva O.; Aird, Debra L.**
Abstracts of Fisheries management reports, technical circulars and project reports of the Fisheries Branch. Vancouver: B.C. Environment, Fisheries Branch, 1992. 56 p. (Fisheries technical circular / B.C. Fisheries Branch ; no. 91); ISBN: 0-77261-641-8.
Note: Location: OONL.

— Ongoing/En cours —

6416 **Alberta. Alberta Education**
Publications catalogue [Alberta Education]. Edmonton: Central Support Services, Alberta Education, 1991-. vol.; ISSN: 0846-0183.
Note: Annual.– Lists publications produced by Alberta education: information documents (news releases, task force reports, annual reports, bulletins, research reports, policy papers); legal documents, service documents.
Previous editions:
Alberta Education publications. 1987-1990. 3 vol.; ISSN: 0837-7618.– Annual.
Publications list [Alberta Education]. [1983-1986]. 3 vol.; ISSN: 0837-760X.– Irregular.– Issue for 1984 not published.
Publications annual list [Alberta Education]. [1974-1975]. 2 vol.; ISSN: 0837-7596.– Issues for 1976-1982 not published.
Alberta. Department of Education. *Publications: annual list [Alberta Department of Education]*. 1953-1973. 20 vol.;

ISSN: 0837-7588.– Annual.
Location: OONL.

6417 **Alberta. Alberta Energy**
General publications [Alberta Energy, Alberta Forestry]. Edmonton: Alberta Energy, 1987-. vol.; ISSN: 0832-6886.
Note: Annual.– General materials produced by the department dealing with Alberta energy, fish and wildlife, forestry, land, outdoor activities, surveying and mapping.
Previous edition: *General publications of Alberta Energy and Natural Resources*. 1980-1986. 6 vol.; ISSN: 0711-1274.– Annual, 1985-1986; two issues yearly, 1980-1984.
Location: OONL.

6418 **Alberta. Alberta Energy**
Technical publications [Alberta Energy, Alberta Forestry]. Edmonton: Alberta Energy, 1987-. vol.; ISSN: 0832-6894.
Note: Annual.– Lists technical documents produced by the department dealing with Alberta energy, fisheries, forestry, land, resource management, surveying and mapping, wildlife.
Previous edition: *Technical publications of Alberta Energy and Natural Resources*. 1981-1986. 5 vol.; ISSN: 0711-1282.– Annual.
Location: OONL.

6419 **Alberta. Alberta Environment. Research Management Division**
Publications catalogue [Alberta Environment, Research Management Division]. [Edmonton]: Research Management Division, Alberta Environment, 1986-. vol.; ISSN: 0833-4706.
Note: Cumulated edition published in 1986 lists all publications produced by the Division, including those published prior to 1980, when the agency was called the Research Secretariat.
Previous edition: *Publications: Research Management Division*. 1983-1985. 3 vol.; ISSN: 0833-4692.
Supplements: Updates are issued annually, and *New publications bulletins* are issued periodically.
Location: OONL.

6420 **Alberta. Alberta Labour. Support Services Division**
Publications catalogue: Alberta Labour. Edmonton: Alberta Labour, Support Services Division, 1987-. vol.; ISSN: 0835-1678.
Note: Annual.
Location: OONL.

6421 **Alberta. Energy Resources Conservation Board**
Catalogue: publications, maps, services [Alberta Energy Resources Conservation Board]. Calgary: Energy Resources Conservation Board, [1987]-. vol.; ISSN: 0844-8523.
Note: Annual.– Lists publications and maps related to energy and energy resource development in Alberta: Acts and regulations, ERCB serial publications, guides, ERCB reports; maps (oil, gas and pipeline, table of formations, coal, electricity, geological).
Previous editions:
Publications, maps and services: catalogue. 1976-1986. 10 vol.; ISSN: 0702-3510.
Catalogue of publications, services and maps. 1958-1975. 14 vol.; ISSN: 0568-9007.
Location: OONL.

6422 **Alberta. Public Affairs Bureau**
Alberta government publications. Edmonton: Alberta Public Affairs Bureau, 1973-. vol.; ISSN: 0840-4976.
Note: Annual listing of official publications of Alberta government departments and agencies, documents published in the current year and serials, including annual reports.– Generated from SPIRES on-line database GAP (Government of Alberta Publications), which includes bibliographic records and library locations of Alberta government publications, including periodicals, dating from 1905 to the present (on-line availability on items published since 1980).– Title varies: *Publications catalogue.* 1973-1987. 15 vol.; ISSN: 0316-392X.
Location: OONL.

6423 **Alberta. Public Affairs Bureau**
Alberta government publications quarterly list. [Edmonton]: Alberta Public Affairs Bureau, Publication Services, [1991]-. vol.; ISSN: 1184-9851.
Note: Current listing of Alberta government publications, including serials and annual reports that have commenced publication, or been discontinued in the quarter covered.
Location: OONL.

6424 **Alberta. Public Affairs Bureau**
List of Alberta publications and legislation. [Edmonton]: Alberta Public Affairs Bureau, 1987-. vol.; ISSN: 0837-7375.
Note: Annual.– Catalogue of Alberta statutes, regulations and selected departmental publications.– Arrangement is alphabetical by title of statute or regulation.– Includes an index to legislative publications by subject and act.
Location: OONL.

6425 **Alberta Research Council**
Publications list [Alberta Research Council]. Edmonton: Alberta Research Council, 1986-. vol.; ISSN: 0833-4218.
Note: Irregular.– Every 3 or 4 years.
Previous edition: *List of publications.* 1968-1981. 8 vol.; ISSN: 0701-5127.– Issues for 1982-1985 not published.
Location: OONL.

6426 **Annuaire du Canada.** Ottawa: Statistique Canada, 1906-. vol.; ISSN: 0316-8557.
Note: Annuel (irrégulier).– Volumes de 1913 à 1946 comporte une liste des publications officielles.
Localisation: OONL.

6427 **British Columbia. Geological Survey Branch**
Reports, maps and geoscience databases [issued by the British Columbia Geological Survey Branch]. Victoria: Geological Survey Branch, [1989]-. vol.; ISSN: 0847-3676.
Note: Annual.
Location: OONL.

6428 **British Columbia. Mineral Resources Division**
Catalogue of publications, maps, and services [British Columbia Mineral Resources Division]. Victoria: Province of British Columbia, Ministry of Energy, Mines and Petroleum Resources, Mineral Resources Division, 1984-. vol.; ISSN: 0831-4047.
Note: Annual.– Includes listings for Bulletin series, Paper series, Open file maps and reports, Preliminary map series, Aeromagnetic map series, Assessment report series.
Previous editions:
Publications and maps. 1982-1983. 2 vol.; ISSN: 0826-4171.

Publications and maps. Mineral Resources Branch, 1979-1980. 2 vol.; ISSN: 0226-7349.
Publications and maps. Department of Mines and Petroleum Resources, 1971-1978. 7 vol.; ISSN: 0703-6280.
List of publications. Department of Mines and Petroleum Resources, 1960-1971. 12 vol.
List of publications. Department of Mines, 1952-1959. 7 vol.
Location: OONL.

6429 **British Columbia. Ministry of Agriculture and Food**
Publications catalogue [British Columbia Ministry of Agriculture and Food]. Victoria: The Ministry, 1986-. vol.; ISSN: 0837-6190.
Note: Annual.
Previous editions:
Publications list. 1981-1984. 4 vol.; ISSN: 0821-9125.– Issue for 1985 not published.
Publications list [Ministry of Agriculture]. Ministry of Agriculture, 1977-1980. 4 vol.; ISSN: 0821-9109.
British Columbia. Department of Agriculture. *Publications of the British Columbia Department of Agriculture.* 1973-1975. 3 vol.; ISSN: 0821-9117.
British Columbia. Department of Agriculture. *List of publications.* 1954-[1972]. Irregular.
Location: OONL.

6430 **British Columbia. Ministry of Forests**
List of publications [British Columbia Ministry of Forests]. Victoria: Province of British Columbia, Ministry of Forests, 1989-. vol.; ISSN: 1185-2968.
Note: Irregular.
Location: OONL.

6431 **British Columbia. Queen's Printer**
Queen's Printer publications catalogue [British Columbia]. Victoria: Province of British Columbia, Queen's Printer, 1983-. vol.; ISSN: 0824-9628.
Note: Previous editions:
Queen's Printer publications price list. 1980-1983. 3 vol.; ISSN: 0710-3107.
Price list of printed documents issued from the Office of the Queen's Printer. 1941-1979. [35] vol.; ISSN: 0708-6075.– Ceased with issue for February 1, 1979.
Location: OONL.

6432 **British Columbia government publications.** Victoria: Legislative Library, 1983-. vol.; ISSN: 0824-8516.
Note: Annual.– Cumulation of the monthly publication: *British Columbia government publications monthly checklist.*– First issue: 1982.
Location: OONL.

6433 **British Columbia government publications monthly checklist.** Victoria: Legislative Library, 1970-. vol.; ISSN: 0316-0823.
Note: Location: OONL.

6434 **Canada. Archives nationales**
Publications [Archives nationales du Canada]. Ottawa: Archives nationales du Canada, 1985-. vol.; ISSN: 0844-711X.
Note: Texte en français et en anglais disposé tête-bêche.– Titre de la p. de t. additionnelle: *Publications [National Archives of Canada].*
Localisation: OONL.

6435 **Canada. Atomic Energy Control Board**
Publications catalogue: Atomic Energy Control Board/ Catalogue des publications: Commission de contrôle de l'énergie atomique. Ottawa: Atomic Energy Control

Board, Office of Public Information, 1979-. vol.; ISSN: 0711-9917.

Note: Includes publications in English and French/ comprend des publications en français et en anglais.

Location: OONL.

6436 **Canada. Bureau des traductions. Direction de la terminologie et des services linguistiques**

Liste des publications [Bureau des traductions]. Ottawa: Secrétariat d'État du Canada, Direction générale de la terminologie et des services linguistiques, 1989-. vol.; 0848-4546.

Note: Annuel.– Texte en français et en anglais disposé tête-bêche.– Titre de la p. de t. additionnelle: *List of publications [Translation Bureau].*

Éditions antérieures:

1985-[1988]. 2 vol.; ISSN: 0848-4538.

Liste des publications [Bureau des traductions]/List of publications [Translation Bureau]. [19- -1985].; ISSN: 1193-1086.

Localisation: OONL.

6437 **Canada. Conseil du Trésor**

Liste des publications [Conseil du Trésor du Canada]. [Ottawa]: Division des communications, Conseil du Trésor du Canada, 1979-. vol.; ISSN: 0837-6476.

Note: Annuel.– Constitue le répertoire mis à jour des documents publiés par le Conseil du Trésor et vous indique où vous les procurer.– Texte en français et en anglais disposé tête-bêche.– Titre de la p. de t. additionnelle: *List of publications [Treasury Board of Canada].*

Localisation: OONL.

6438 **Canada. Energy, Mines and Resources Canada. Mineral Policy Sector**

Publications catalogue of the Mineral Policy Sector/ Répertoire des publications du Secteur de la politique minérale. Ottawa: Energy, Mines and Resources Canada, 1986-. vol.; ISSN: 0832-7904.

Note: Annual.– Text in English and French/texte en français et en anglais.

Location: OONL.

6439 **Canada. Environmental Protection Directorate**

Publications [Environmental Protection Directorate, Environment Canada]/Publications [Direction générale, protection de l'environnement, Environnement Canada]. Ottawa: The Directorate, 1986-. vol.; ISSN: 0839-8267.

Note: Annual.– Lists the Environmental protection series technical reports by subject: airborne pollutants, hazardous wastes, refrigeration and air conditioning, etc.; EnviroTIPS manuals (Environmental and Technical Information for Problem Spills) on planning of spill counter-measures; publications and reports published jointly by Environment Canada and other government agencies.

Previous edition: Canada. Environmental Protection Service. *Environmental Protection Service publications/Les publications du Service de la protection de l'environnement.* [1976]-1985. 10 vol.; ISSN: 0839-8259.– Annual.

Location: OONL.

6440 **Canada. Forestry Canada**

Forestry Canada publications/Publications de Forêts Canada. Ottawa: Forestry Canada, 1989-. vol.; ISSN: 0846-6459. (Information report / Forestry Canada; ISSN: 0705-324X)

Note: Previous editions:

Forestry Canada publications, 1986-1988/Publications de forêts Canada, 1986 à 1988. 63 p.; ISBN: 0-662-56838-9.

Publications [Canadian Forestry Service]/Publications [Service canadien des forêts]. Ottawa: Canadian Forestry Service, 1982-[1986]. 4 vol.; ISSN: 0715-0687.– Annual.

Location: OONL.

6441 **Canada. Health and Welfare Canada**

Publications [Health and Welfare Canada]. Ottawa: Health and Welfare Canada, 1986-. vol.; ISSN: 0837-4635.

Note: Irregular.

Location: OONL.

6442 **Canada. Labour Canada**

Publications catalogue [Labour Canada]. Ottawa: Labour Canada, 1989-. vol.; ISSN: 0848-3280.

Note: Annual.– Text in English and French with French text on inverted pages.– Title of additional title-page: *Catalogue des publications [Travail Canada].*

Previous editions:

Publications [Department of Labour]. [1983]-1986. 3 vol.; ISSN: 0848-3272.– Annual.

Publications [Canada Department of Labour]. 1968-[1982]. 14 vol.; ISSN: 0848-3264.– Annual.

Department of Labour publications. 1967.; ISSN: 0226-059X.

Location: OONL.

6443 **Canada. National Archives**

Publications [National Archives of Canada]. Ottawa: National Archives of Canada, 1985-. vol.; ISSN: 0844-711X.

Note: Text in English and French with French text on inverted pages.– Title of additional title page: *Publications [Archives nationales du Canada].*

Location: OONL.

6444 **Canada. Statistics Canada. Library**

Listing of supplementary documents/Liste de documents supplémentaires. Ottawa: Statistics Canada, 1981-. vol.; ISSN: 0228-5134.

Note: Annual.– First issue, 1980.– Inventory of supplementary Statistics Canada documents publicly available, including technical papers, memoranda, discussion and working papers.– Issues for 1987-1990 not published.– Text in English and French/texte en français et en anglais.

Location: OONL.

6445 **Canada. Statistics Canada. Library Services Division**

Statistics Canada catalogue. Ottawa: Statistics Canada, 1988-. vol.; ISSN: 0838-4223.

Note: Annual listing of publications, maps, census products, electronic products (CANSIM database, microdata files), geographic products and services.

Titre en français: *Catalogue de Statistique Canada.*

Previous editions:

Current publications index. 1986. 152 p.; ISSN: 0832-8331.

Canada. Statistics Canada. Business, Provincial and Municipal Relations Division. 1983-1985. 3 vol.; ISSN: 0317-770X.

Canada. Statistics Canada. User Services Division. 1981-1982. 2 vol.; ISSN: 0317-770X.

Canada. Statistics Canada. User Advisory Services Division. 1972-1980. 6 vol.; ISSN: 0317-770X.

Canada. Dominion Bureau of Statistics. *DBS Catalogue/ Catalogue du BFS.* Dominion Bureau of Statistics, 1968-1971. 2 vol.; ISSN: 0590-5699.

Canada. Dominion Bureau of Statistics. *Canadian government publications [Dominion Bureau of Statistics]/ Publications du gouvernement canadien [Bureau fédéral de la statistique]*. Dominion Bureau of Statistics, 1964. xxvii, 288 p.; ISSN: 0844-6830.

Canada. Dominion Bureau of Statistics. *Current publications of the Dominion Bureau of Statistics*. Dominion Bureau of Statistics, 1950-1960. 8 vol.; ISSN: 0844-6822.

Canada. Dominion Bureau of Statistics. *Publications of the Dominion Bureau of Statistics, including reports, bulletins, press releases, etc.* Dominion Bureau of Statistics, 1943-1948. 4 vol.; ISSN: 0844-6814.

Canada. Dominion Bureau of Statistics. *List of publications including reports, bulletins, press releases, etc.* Dominion Bureau of Statistics, 1925-1934. 3 vol.; ISSN: 0844-6806.

Canada. Dominion Bureau of Statistics. *Reports, bulletins, press releases, etc. issued by the Dominion Bureau of Statistics*. Dominion Bureau of Statistics, 1922-1923. 2 vol.; ISSN: 0844-6792.

Location: OONL.

6446　**Canada. Statistique Canada. Services de la bibliothèque**

Catalogue de Statistique Canada. Ottawa: Statistique Canada, 1988-. vol.; ISSN: 0838-4231.

Note: Annuel.– Liste des publications, cartes, produits de recensement, produits électroniques (CANSIM), produits et services géographiques.

English title: *Statistics Canada catalogue*.

Éditions antérieures:
Répertoire des publications. 1986. 168 p.; ISSN: 0832-834X.
Canada. Statistique Canada. Division des relations avec les entreprises, les provinces et les municipalités. *Statistique Canada catalogue*. 1983-1985. 3 vol.; ISSN: 0382-2648.
Canada. Statistique Canada. Division de l'assistance-utilisateurs. *Statistique Canada catalogue*. 1980-1982. 3 vol.; ISSN: 0382-2648.
Catalogue [Statistique Canada]. 1976-1979. 2 vol.; ISSN: 0318-3130.
Statistique Canada catalogue. 1975. 287 p.; ISSN: 0318-3130.

Localisation: OONL.

6447　**Canada. Translation Bureau. Terminology and Linguistic Services Directorate**

List of publications [Translation Bureau]. Ottawa: Department of the Secretary of State of Canada, Terminology and Linguistic Services Directorate, 1989-. vol.; ISSN: 0848-4546.

Note: Annual.– Text in English and French with French text on inverted pages.– Title of additional title-page: *Liste des publications [Bureau des traductions]*.

Previous editions:
Terminology and Linguistic Services Branch, 1985-[1988]. 2 vol.; ISSN: 0848-4538.

Location: OONL.

6448　**Canada. Travail Canada**

Catalogue des publications [Travail Canada]. Ottawa: Travail Canada, 1989-. vol.; ISSN: 0848-3280.

Note: Annuel.– Texte en français et en anglais disposé tête-bêche.– Titre de la p. de t. additionnelle: *Publications catalogue* [Labour Canada].

Éditions antérieures:
Publications [Ministère du travail]. [1983]-1986. 3 vol.; ISSN: 0848-3272.– Annuel.

Les publications du Ministère du travail du Canada. 1968-[1982]. 14 vol.; ISSN: 0848-3264.– Annuel.
Les publications du Ministère du travail. 1967.; ISSN: 0226-059X.

Localisation: OONL.

6449　**Canada. Treasury Board**

List of publications [Treasury Board of Canada]. [Ottawa]: Communications Division, Treasury Board of Canada, 1979-. vol.; ISSN: 0837-6476.

Note: Annual.– Current publications of Treasury Board of Canada, with instructions on how to obtain them.– Text in English and French with French text on inverted pages.– Title of additional title-page: *Liste des publications [Conseil du Trésor du Canada]*.

Location: OONL.

6450　**Canada year book.** Ottawa: Statistics Canada, 1906-. vol.; ISSN: 0068-8142.

Note: Volumes for 1913-1946 list Canadian government publications.

Location: OONL.

6451　**Forintek Canada Corporation**

List of publications [Forintek Canada]/Liste des publications [Forintek Canada]. Ottawa: Forintek Canada Corporation, 1981-. vol.; ISSN: 0227-101X.

Note: Previous editions:
List of publications available from Eastern Forest Products Laboratory, Western Forest Products Laboratory. 1965-1976.; ISSN: 0700-2521.
List of publications of the Forest Products Research Branch. [1962-1965].; ISSN: 0576-1859.
List of publications of the Forest Products Laboratories of Canada. Forestry Branch, 1951-1962.; ISSN: 0821-8935.

Location: OONL.

6452　**Government of Canada publications: quarterly catalogue/Publications du gouvernement du Canada: catalogue trimestriel.** Hull, Québec: Supply and Services Canada, 1979-. vol.; ISSN: 0709-0412.

Note: Listing of all publicly available Canadian government publications issued during the quarter.– Contains all documents listed in the *Weekly checklist* and the *Special list*.– Includes parliamentary publications (statutes, bills, committee proceedings and reports of House and Senate, Library of Parliament Research Branch publications); departmental publications (monographs and serials published by departments, agencies, boards, commissions, councils, etc.).– Index sections are cumulated annually.– Continues *Canadian government publications catalogue*, which was published daily, monthly, annually from 1953 to 1978.

Location: OONL.

6453　**Institute for Research in Construction (Canada)**

List of publications [Institute for Research in Construction]/Liste des publications [Institut de recherche en construction]. Ottawa: Institute for Research in Construction (Canada), 1984-. vol.; ISSN: 0835-9083.

Note: Annual.– Title varies: 1987-1988, *List of IRC publications/Liste des publications de l'IRC*; ISSN: 0840-2035; From 1991, *Publications catalogue/Catalogue des publications*; ISSN: 1185-9628.

Location: OONL.

6454　**Manitoba. Department of Natural Resources. Library**

Annotated bibliography of the renewable resource publications of the Manitoba Department of Natural

Resources. Winnipeg: The Library, 1980-. vol. (Manitoba Department of Natural Resources Manuscript report series ; ISSN: 0715-0504)

Note: Annual list of books, periodical articles, manuscript reports from Fisheries, Forestry, Parks, Surveys and Mapping, Water Resources and Wildlife Branches of Manitoba Department of Natural Resources.

Location: OONL.

6455 **Manitoba. Geological Services Branch**
Publications price list [Manitoba Energy and Mines, Geological Services Branch and Mines Branch]. Winnipeg: The Branches, 1985-. vol.; ISSN: 0845-101X.

Note: Previous editions:
Information services & publications catalogue [Geological Services Branch and Mines Branch]. 1981-1984.; ISSN: 0715-2892.
Publications catalogue [Mineral Resources Division]. 1968-1979.; ISSN: 0225-9427.

Location: OONL.

6456 **Manitoba. Legislative Library**
Manitoba government publications: monthly checklist/ Publications du gouvernement du Manitoba: liste mensuelle. Winnipeg: Manitoba Culture, Heritage and Recreation, 1975-. vol.; ISSN: 0318-1200.

Note: Monthly.– Some issues have title: *Manitoba government publications for the month of ... : monthly checklist.*– Text in English only, 1975-1988; text in English and French, 1989- .
Previous edition: *Manitoba government publications received in the Legislative Library.* 1971-1974. 13 vol.; ISSN: 0318-1219.

Location: OONL.

6457 **Manitoba. Legislative Library**
Manitoba government publications. Winnipeg: Legislative Library, 1975-. vol.; ISSN: 0701-7553.

Note: Annual.

Location: OONL.

6458 **Manitoba. Office of the Queen's Printer**
Statutory publications, price list/Publications officielles, liste des prix. [Winnipeg]: Manitoba Culture, Heritage and Citizenship, 1991-. vol.; ISSN: 1185-9652.

Note: Catalogue of acts and regulations, bills, votes and proceedings, journals, Manitoba Law Reform Commission reports, special sets (on various subjects, e.g. Family law).– Text in English and French/texte en français et en anglais.

Location: OONL.

6459 **Manitoba. Water Standards and Studies Section**
Bibliography of Water Standards Section publications. [Winnipeg]: The Section, [1983]-. vol.; ISSN: 0836-9763. (Water Standards and Studies reports; ISSN: 0830-1735)

Note: Lists manuscript reports, water quality assessment reports, water quality data reports, miscellaneous information papers.

Location: OONL.

6460 **Microlog: Canadian research index/Microlog: index de recherche du Canada.** Toronto: Micromedia, 1979-. vol.; ISSN: 0839-1289.

Note: Monthly with annual cumulations.– Lists and describes Canadian federal, provincial, municipal publications, professional associations, special interest groups; research papers in physical, natural, social sciences; policy papers; annual reports.– Main access is

by title.– Indexing provides access by subjects, corporate or individual authors, series titles, microfiche collection.– English and French documents are indexed and abstracted in both languages.– Online service available. *MIC-Microlog: Canadian research index online.*– Online service through: CAN/OLE, InfoGlobe, iNet 2000.– Available on CD-ROM: *Microlog on CD,* with semi-annual updating.– From 1979 to 1986, title was *Microlog index.*

Supercedes:
Profile index. 1973-1978. 6 vol.; ISSN: 0316-4608.
Publicat index. 1977-1978. 2 vol.; ISSN: 0384-9813.
Urban Canada. 1977-1978. 2 vol.; ISSN: 0384-9821.
Continues: Canadian Council on Urban and Regional Research. *Urban & regional references, 1945-1969.* (Supplements to 1976).

Location: OONL.

6461 **New Brunswick. Legislative Library. Government Documents Section**
New Brunswick government documents annual catalogue/Publications gouvernementales du Nouveau-Brunswick Catalogue annuel. Fredericton: [Legislative Library], 1956-. vol.; ISSN: 0548-4006.

Note: Annual.– Checklist of New Brunswick government documents received at the Legislative Library during the calendar year: official publications (laws, statutes, bills, Legislative Assembly documents, advisory committees and commissions, etc.); departmental publications; others (Council of Maritimes Premiers, Atlantic Lottery Corporation, Atlantic Provinces Transportation Commission).– Cumulates the *Quarterly list.*– Text in English and French/texte en français et en anglais.

Location: OONL.

6462 **New Brunswick. Legislative Library. Government Documents Section**
New Brunswick government publications, quarterly list/ Publications du gouvernement du Nouveau-Brunswick, liste trimestrielle. Fredericton: The Library, 1986-. vol.; ISSN: 0830-1085.

Note: Checklist of all New Brunswick government documents received at the Legislative Library during the quarter.– Text in English and French/texte en français et en anglais.

Location: OONL.

6463 **Northwest Territories. Department of Culture and Communications**
Publications catalogue [Government of the Northwest Territories]. Yellowknife: Northwest Territories, Culture and Communications, 1986-. vol.; ISSN: 0837-4406.

Note: Irregular.– Lists in alphabetical order, by departments and agencies, all publicly available publications (reports, pamphlets, booklets) of the Government of the Northwest Territories.– Maps, internal publications, speeches are not included.
Previous editions:
Northwest Territories. Department of Information. 1979-1985. 7 vol.; ISSN: 0837-6557.
Government publications catalogue, Northwest Territories. 1977.; ISSN: 0701-9831.

Location: OONL.

6464 **Nova Scotia. Legislative Library**
Publications of the Province of Nova Scotia. Halifax: Legislative Library, 1967-. vol.; ISSN: 0550-1792.

Note: Annual listing of published output of provincial

government departments, agencies, and crown corporations: books, periodicals, reports, studies, pamphlets, brochures, flyers.– Excludes internal or confidential reports.– Also generally excluded are press releases, posters, wall maps.– Arranged in two sections: official publications (gazettes, bills, statutes, regulations, debates, journals); departmental publications by name of issuing agency, board or commission.

Location: OONL.

6465 **Nova Scotia. Legislative Library**

Publications of the Province of Nova Scotia, monthly checklist. Halifax: Legislative Library, 1987-. vol.; ISSN: 0835-6513.

Note: Monthly listing of published output of provincial government departments, agencies, and crown corporations: books, periodicals, reports, studies, pamphlets, brochures, flyers.– Excludes internal or confidential reports, press releases, posters, wall maps.

Previous editions:

Publications of the Province of Nova Scotia quarterly checklist. 1980-1987. 7 vol.; ISSN: 0228-0299.

Nova Scotia government publications. 1978-1980. 2 vol.; ISSN: 0713-0821.

Location: OONL.

6466 **Nova Scotia Government Bookstore**

Publications catalogue: Nova Scotia Government Bookstore. Halifax, N.S.: Information Division, Department of Government Services, 1974-. vol.: ill.; ISSN: 0228-0175.

Note: Imprint varies: 1974-1980, Nova Scotia Communications and Information Centre.

Location: OONL.

6467 **Ontario. Legislative Library. Checklist and Catalogue Service**

Ontario government publications annual catalogue/ Publications du gouvernement de l'Ontario: catalogue annuel. Toronto: Ontario Ministry of Government Services, 1973-. vol.; ISSN: 0227-2628.

Note: Annual listing from 1972 of all publicly available legislative and departmental publications issued by the Government of Ontario.– Cumulates the contents of the *Monthly checklist*, with some additions and changes.– Press releases and publications of an internal nature are not included.– Title varies: 1972-1978, *Ontario government publications/Publications du gouvernement de l'Ontario.–* Text in English and French/texte en français et en anglais.

Location: OONL.

6468 **Ontario. Legislative Library. Checklist and Catalogue Service**

Ontario government publications monthly checklist/ Publications du gouvernement de l'Ontario: liste mensuelle. Toronto: Printing Services Branch, Ministry of Government Services, 1971-. vol.; ISSN: 0316-1617.

Note: Monthly listing of all publicly available legislative and departmental publications issued by the Government of Ontario.– Cumulated in *Ontario government publications/Publications du gouvernement de l'Ontario,* 1972-1978, and *Ontario government publications annual catalogue/Publications du gouvernement de l'Ontario: catalogue annuel,* 1979- .– Text in English and French/ texte en français et en anglais.

Location: OONL.

6469 **Prince Edward Island. Island Information Service**

P E I provincial government publications checklist. Charlottetown: Island Information Service, 1976-. vol.; ISSN: 0380-6685.

Note: Monthly.

Location: OONL.

6470 **Québec (Province). Ministère des communications. Bibliothèque administrative**

Liste annuelle des périodiques du gouvernement du Québec. Québec: Gouvernement du Québec, Direction générale des publications gouvernementales, Bibliothèque administrative, 1983-. vol.; ISSN: 0712-6905.

Note: Localisation: OONL.

6471 **Québec (Province). Ministère des communications. Bibliothèque administrative**

Liste bimestrielle des publications du gouvernement du Québec. Québec: Ministère des communications, Bibliothèque administrative, 1988-. vol.; ISSN: 0840-7908.

Note: Publications officielles regroupés par ministères et organismes et classées dans l'ordre alphabétique de titre.– Comprend des publications anglais.

Localisation: OONL.

6472 **Saskatchewan. Legislative Library**

Checklist of Saskatchewan government publications. Regina: Legislative Library of Saskatchewan, 1976-. vol.; ISSN: 0705-4122.

Note: Listing of publicly available legislative and departmental publications.– Monthly with annual cumulations.

Location: OONL.

6473 **Saskatchewan. Saskatchewan Agriculture and Food**

Publications list [Saskatchewan Agriculture and Food]. Regina: Saskatchewan Agriculture and Food, 1978-. vol.; ISSN: 0837-435X.

Note: Annual.– Some issues have title: *Saskatchewan Agriculture's publication list.*

Location: OONL.

6474 **Special list of Canadian government publications/Liste spéciale des publications du gouvernement canadien.** Ottawa: Department of Supply and Services, 1969-. vol.; ISSN: 0700-2882.

Note: Irregular.– Numbering begins each year with no. 1.– Text in English and French/texte en français et en anglais.

Title varies: *Special list of government publications/Liste spéciale des publications fédérales.* Information Canada, 1969-1976.; ISSN: 0700-2890.

Location: OONL.

6475 **Weekly checklist of Canadian government publications/ Liste hebdomadaire des publications du gouvernement canadien.** Hull, Québec: Supply and Services Canada, 1978-. no.; ISSN: 0706-4659.

Note: Weekly listing of publicly available Canadian parliamentary and departmental publications.

Previous editions:

Daily checklist of Canadian government publications/Liste quotidienne des publications du gouvernement canadien. 1976-1978.; ISSN: 0700-2904.– Numbering begins each year with no. 1.

Daily checklist of government publications/Liste quotidienne des publications fédérales. Ottawa: Information Canada,

1952-1976.; ISSN: 0318-6768.– Numbering begins each year with no. 1.
Location: OONL.

Maps

Cartes

— 1872 —

6476 **Harrisse, Henry**
Notes pour servir à l'histoire, à la bibliographie et à la cartographie de la Nouvelle-France et des pays adjacents, 1545-1700. Paris: Tross, 1872. xxxiii, 367 p.
Note: 374 entrées.
Microforme: ICMH collection de microfiches ; no 05394; ISBN: 0-665-05394-0. 5 microfiches (219 images).
Réimpressions:
Amsterdam: Meridian, 1976. xxxiii, 367 p.; ISBN: 9-0604-1102-1. Localisation: OOCC.
New York: Argonaut Press, 1966. xxxiii, 367 p.
Dubuque, Iowa: W.C. Brown, [1962]. xxxiii, 367 p.
Localisation: OONL.

— 1875 —

6477 **Baldwin, Charles Candee**
Early maps of Ohio and the West. Cleveland: [s.n.], 1875. 25 p. (Western Reserve and Northern Ohio Historical Society Tract ; no. 25)
Note: Cartographic essay with a chronological listing of maps from 1529 to 1808.
Microform: CIHM Microfiche series ; no. 27235; ISBN: 0-665-27235-9. 1 microfiche (16 fr.).
Location: OONL.

— 1876 —

6478 **Scadding, Henry**
"On the early gazetteer and map literature of western Canada."
In: *Canadian Journal of Science, Literature and History*; Vol. 15, no. 1 (April 1876) p. 23-45.; ISSN: 0381-8624.
Note: Bibliographic essay, with annotated list of geographic publications (atlases, surveys, gazetteers), of Canada West (Ontario).
Location: OONL.

— 1884 —

6479 **Marcou, Jules; Marcou, John Belknap**
Mapoteca geologica americana: a catalogue of geological maps of America (North and South), 1752-1881, in geographic and chronologic order. Washington: G.P.O., 1884. 184 p. (United States Geological Survey Bulletin ; vol. 2, no. 7)
Note: 924 entries.– Includes Canadian references.
Microform: CIHM Microfiche series ; no. 19028; ISBN: 0-665-19028-X. 2 microfiches (98 fr.).
Location: BVAU.

— 1885 —

6480 **Marcel, Gabriel**
Cartographie de la Nouvelle France. Paris: Maisonneuve et Leclerc, 1885. 41 p.
Note: 114 entrées.– "Supplément de M. Henry Harrisse sur le même sujet."- "Publié avec des documents inédits."
Microforme: ICHM collection de microfiches ; no 09537; ISBN: 0-665-09537-6. 1 microfiche (30 images).
Localisation: OONL.

— 1886 —

6481 **United States. Hydrographic Office**
Catalogue of charts, plans, sailing directions, and other publications of the United States Hydrographic Office. Washington: G.P.O., 1886. 163 p.: map.
Note: Canadian listings are included in sections on Newfoundland and Grand Banks, Labrador, Gulf of St. Lawrence, Nova Scotia, Bay of Fundy and Georges Bank, British America and Alaska, Arctic Ocean.
Microform: CIHM Microfiche series ; no. 55911; ISBN: 0-665-55911-9. 2 microfiches (92 fr.).
Location: QQS.

6482 **Winsor, Justin**
The Kohl collection of maps relating to America. Cambridge, Mass.: Issued by the Library of Harvard University, 1886. 70 p. (Bibliographical contributions / Harvard University Library ; no. 19)
Note: Includes Canadian references.
Microform: CIHM Microfiche series ; no. 59565; ISBN: 0-665-59565-4. 1 microfiche (39 fr.).
Location: QQL.

— 1891 —

6483 **Dionne, Narcisse-Eutrope**
"Cartographie de la Nouvelle-France au XVIe siècle."
Dans: *La Nouvelle-France de Cartier à Champlain, 1540-1603.* Québec: Darveau, 1891. P. 213-255.
Note: Microforme: ICMH collection de microfiches ; no 02717; ISBN: 0-665-02717-6. 5 microfiches (210 images).
Localisation: OONL.

— 1892 —

6484 **France. Bibliothèque nationale**
Catalogues des documents géographiques exposés à la Section des cartes et plans de la Bibliothèque nationale. Paris: J. Maisonneuve, 1892. 77 p.
Note: En tête du titre: "Quatrième centenaire de la découverte de l'Amérique."
Microforme: ICMH collection de microfiches ; no 06643; ISBN: 0-665-06643-0. 1 microfiche (49 images).
Localisation: OOA.

6485 **Harrisse, Henry**
The discovery of North America: a critical, documentary, and historical investigation, with an essay on the early cartography of the New World, including descriptions of two hundred and fifty maps or globes, existing or lost, constructed before the year 1536.... London: H. Stevens, 1892. xii, 802 p.: ill., maps.
Note: Microform: CIHM Microfiche series ; no. 06774; ISBN: 0-665-06774-7. 10 microfiches (458 fr.).
Reprint: Amsterdam: N. Israel, 1969. xii, 802 p., xxliii l. of pl. (some folded): maps.
Location: OOA.

— 1898 —

6486 **Phillips, P. Lee**
Alaska and the Northwest part of North America, 1588-1898: maps in the Library of Congress. Washington:

G.P.O., 1898. 119 p.
Note: Approx. 750 entries.– Includes maps of British
Columbia and the Yukon.
Microform: CIHM Microfiche series , no. 15894, ISBN. 0-
665-15894-7. 2 microfiches (68 fr.).
Location: OOA.

— 1912 —

6487 Canada. Public Archives
Catalogue of maps, plans and charts in the map room of
the Dominion Archives. Ottawa: Government Printing
Bureau, 1912. xii, 685 p. (Publications of the Canadian
Archives ; no. 8)
Note: 4,190 entries.– Classified and indexed by H.R.
Holmden, in charge of the Map Division.
Location: OONL.

— 1922 —

6488 Canada. Geographic Board
Catalogue of the maps in the collection of the Geographic
Board. Ottawa: Acland, Printer to the King, 1922. 100 p.:
ill., maps.
Note: Approx. 1,700 entries.– Coverage from seventeenth
century to January 1922.– Arranged in six sections,
including Dominion, provinces and regions.– Includes
lists of international boundary maps, atlases of Canada.
Previous edition: 1918. 50 p.
Supplement: Catalogue of maps of Canada published between
January 1, 1922 and December 31, 1924. Ottawa: Acland,
1925. 19, [1] p.
Location: OONL.

— 1923 —

6489 Toronto. Public Library
Map collection of the Public Reference Library of the city
of Toronto, Canada. Toronto: Public Library, 1923. 111 p.
Note: "Includes the collection presented by the late Mr.
John Ross Robertson."- Compiled by May MacLachlan.
Location: OOCC.

— 1934 —

6490 Canada. Department of the Interior. Topographical and
Air Survey Bureau
Catalogue of maps, plans and publications distributed by
the Topographical and Air Survey Bureau. 6th ed.
Ottawa: King's Printer, 1934. 24 p.: map (folded).
Note: Previous editions:
Canada. Topographical Survey. Catalogue of maps, plans
and publications of the Topographical Survey. 1930. 23 p.
Canada. Topographical Survey. Catalogue of maps, plans
and publications of the Topographical Survey. 1927. 19 p.
Canada. Topographical Survey. Maps, plans and
publications of the Topographical Survey of Canada. 1925.
16 p.
Canada. Topographical Surveys Branch. List of maps and
publications issued by the Topographical Surveys Branch and
available for distribution. 1922. 15 p.
Location: OONL.

— 1937 —

6491 Ontario. Department of Mines
Index of geological maps accompanying annual reports,
volumes 1 to 45, 1891 to 1936. Toronto: King's Printer,
1937. 41 p.: folded map (in pocket). (Ontario Department
of Mines Bulletin ; no. 110)
Note: Compiled by P.A. Jackson.
Location: OONL.

— 1938 —

6492 Gilroy, Marion
A catalogue of maps, plans and charts in the Public
Archives of Nova Scotia. Halifax. Public Archives of
Nova Scotia, 1938. 95 p. (Public Archives of Nova Scotia
Bulletin, vol. 1, no. 3)
Note: Location: NSHMS.

— 1939 —

6493 Canada. Department of Mines and Resources. Surveys
and Engineering Branch
1939 catalogue of maps, plans and publications. Ottawa:
Patenaude, Printer to the King, 1939. 55 p.: maps (folded).
Note: Listing of map series by province: national
topographic series, air navigation charts and strip maps,
sectional maps of western Canada, old geographic series,
land classification and soil maps, township development
plans; reports, pamphlets, index maps.
Supplement: 1942. 30 p.
Location: OONL.

— 1944 —

6494 Benson, Lillian Rea
"Historical atlases of Ontario: a preliminary check-list."
In: Ontario Library Review; Vol. 28, no. 1 (February
1944) p. 45-53.; ISSN: 0030-2996.
Note: Listing of 31 atlases for 29 Ontario counties or
groups of counties, most of which were printed between
1875 and 1881.
Location: OONL.

6495 Winnipeg Art Gallery Association
Catalogue of a selection of early views, maps, charts and
plans of the Great Lakes, the far West, the Arctic and
Pacific Oceans. Montreal: Canada Steamship Lines
Limited, 1944. 22 p.: ill., maps.
Note: "From the William H. Coverdale collection of
historical Canadiana at the Manoir Richelieu, Murray
Bay, P.Q. Exhibited by the Winnipeg Art Gallery Associa-
tion, in the Art Gallery, the Winnipeg Auditorium,
February 1st to February 29th, 1944." Cover title: The last
frontier.
Location: OHM.

— 1946 —

6496 Canada. Department of Mines and Resources. Bureau
of Geology and Topography
Published maps (1917-1946 inclusive). Ottawa: Bureau of
Geology and Topography, 1946. i, 119 p.
Note: Previous edition: Published maps (1917-1930
inclusive). Ottawa: King's Printer, 1931. 16 p.
Location: OONL.

— 1947 —

6497 Faessler, Carl
Cross-index to the maps and illustrations of the Geological Survey and Mines Branch (Bureau of Mines) of
Canada, 1843-1946 (incl.). Quebec: Laval University,
1947. 525 p. (Contributions / Université Laval, Département de géologie et de minéralogie ; no 75)
Note: Supplement: First supplement, 1946-1956, to Cross-
index .... 1956. (Contributions (Université Laval, Département de géologie et de minéralogie) ; no 118).
Location: ACU.

— 1948 —

6498 Université Laval. Institut d'histoire et de géographie
Collection de cartes anciennes et modernes pour servir à
l'étude de l'histoire de l'Amérique et du Canada.

[Québec: s.n.], 1948. viii, 91 f.: cartes.
Note: Localisation: OONL.

— 1949 —

6499 **Rousseau, Jacques**
"La cartographie de la région du Lac Mistassini: essai bibliographique."
Dans: *Revue d'histoire de l'Amérique française*; Vol. 3, no 2 (septembre 1949) p. 289-312.; ISSN: 0035-2357.
Note: 116 entrées.
Localisation: AEU.

— 1953 —

6500 **Drake, Everett N.**
Historical atlases of Ontario: a condensed checklist. Toronto: [s.n.], 1953. [2] p.
Note: From Lochhead.– No location.

— 1954 —

6501 **Canada. Department of Mines and Technical Surveys. Surveys and Mapping Branch. Canadian Hydrographic Service**
Catalogue of Canadian Hydrographic Service nautical charts and sailing directions for inland waters of Canada including the Great Lakes ... and other Canadian government publications of interest to mariners. Ottawa: Department of Mines and Technical Surveys, 1954. vi, 15 [i.e., 26] p.: maps.
Note: Location: OONL.

— 1955 —

6502 **Canada. Department of Mines and Technical Surveys. Surveys and Mapping Branch. Canadian Hydrographic Service**
Catalogue of Canadian Hydrographic Service nautical charts, tidal and current publications, sailing directions and other Canadian government publications of interest to mariners. Ottawa: Queen's Printer, 1914-1955. 15 vol.
Note: Title varies: 1928-1935: *Catalogue of marine charts, sailing directions and tidal information*; 1936-1948: *Catalogue of nautical charts, sailing directions, tidal information*.
Location: OOP.

— 1956 —

6503 **Canada. Department of Mines and Technical Surveys. Geographical Branch**
Canadian maps, 1949 to 1954. Ottawa: [s.n.], 1956. vii, 82 p. (Bibliographical series / Canada Department of Mines and Technical Surveys, Geographical Branch ; no. 16)
Note: Selected bibliography of maps of Canada, provinces and territories, published by federal and provincial governments and other agencies; comprehensive list of map sheets of various federal topographic series.– Excludes detailed geological map sheets, hydrographic charts, some special subject maps.
Supplement: ... , *1955-1956*. Ottawa: 1958. iv, 40 p.
Location: OONL.

6504 **Canada. Public Archives. Map Division**
Sixteenth-century maps relating to Canada: a checklist and bibliography. Ottawa: The Archives, 1956. 283 p.: facsims.
Note: 830 entries.
Titre en français: *Cartes géographiques du seizième siècle se rapportant au Canada: liste préliminaire et bibliographie*.
Location: OONL.

— 1957 —

6505 **Whebel, C.F.J.**
"Printed maps of Upper Canada, 1800-1864: a select bibliography."
In: *Ontario History*; Vol. 49, no. 3 (Summer 1957) p. 139-144.; ISSN: 0030-2953.
Note: 8 entries.
Location: OONL.

— 1958 —

6506 **Canada. Archives publiques. Division des Cartes géographiques**
Cartes géographiques du seizième siècle se rapportant au Canada: liste préliminaire et bibliographie. Ottawa: Archives publiques Canada, 1958. xxvii, 305 p.: fac-sim.
Note: 830 entrées.
English title: *Sixteenth-century maps relating to Canada: a checklist and bibliography*.
Localisation: OONL.

— 1959 —

6507 **Brun, Christian F.**
Guide to the manuscript maps in the William L. Clements Library. Ann Arbor: University of Michigan, 1959. xiii, 209 p.: maps.
Note: Includes historical maps relating to Canada, chiefly p. 1-49.
Location: OONL.

— 1964 —

6508 **Ganong, William F.**
Crucial maps in the early cartography and place-nomenclature of the Atlantic coast of Canada. Toronto: Published by the University of Toronto Press in cooperation with the Royal Society of Canada, 1964. xvii, 511 p.: maps, port. (Special publications / Royal Society of Canada ; 7)
Note: Location: OONL.

— 1966 —

6509 **Nova Scotia. Community Planning Division**
Municipal map index: Nova Scotia. Halifax, N.S.: The Division, [1966]. 10, [56] l.
Note: Location: OONL.

6510 **Québec (Province). Services géologiques**
Liste des cartes publiées par les Services géologiques/ List of maps published by the Geological Services. Québec: [s.n.], 1966. 15 p.
Note: Localisation: OONL.

— 1967 —

6511 **Skelton, Raleigh Ashlin; Tooley, R.V.**
The marine surveys of James Cook in North America, 1758-1768, particularly the survey of Newfoundland: a bibliography of printed charts and sailing-directions. London: Map Collectors' Circle, 1967. 32, [14] p.: facsims. (Map Collectors' Circle ; Vol. 4, no. 37)
Note: 23 entries.– Describes all known editions of original charts and associated tracts of sailing-directions compiled and printed from the North American surveys made by James Cook between 1758 and 1768.
Location: OONL.

6512 **Thomas, Morley K.; Anderson, S.R.**
Guide to the climatic maps of Canada. Toronto: Meteorological Branch, Department of Transport, 1967. 1 vol. (in various pagings).
Note: Contains a national, regional and provincial listing of climatic maps, with complete bibliographical informa-

tion on each map in part 3, arranged alphabetically by author.

Location: OON.

6513 **Tooloy, R.V.**
French mapping of the Americas: the De l'Isle, Buache, Dezauche succession (1700-1830). London: Map Collectors' Circle, 1967. 39, [24] p.: facsims. (Map Collectors' Circle ; Vol. 4, no. 33)
Note: 115 entries.– Description of maps relating to America published by Guillaume De l'Isle and his successors.
Location: OONL.

— 1968 —

6514 **Stuart-Stubbs, Basil**
Maps relating to Alexander Mackenzie: a keepsake distributed at a meeting of the Bibliographical Society of Canada. Vancouver: [s.n.], 1968. [36] l.: ill., maps.
Note: Carto-bibliography of Alexander Mackenzie.
Location: OONL.

— 1969 —

6515 **Mullins, W.J.; Fogwill, W.D.; Greene, B.A.**
Province of Newfoundland and Labrador: map index: geological, geophysical and related maps to December 31, 1969. [St. John's, Nfld.]: Mineral Resources Division, Department of Mines, Agriculture and Resources, 1969. 59 p.: ill. (Information circular / Newfoundland Mineral Resources Division ; no. 13)
Note: Location: OONL.

6516 **Wheat, James Clements; Brun, Christian F.**
Maps and charts published in America before 1900: a bibliography. New Haven: Yale University Press, 1969. xxii, 215 p.: maps.
Note: 915 entries.– Includes a small section (p. 13-20) listing maps of Canadian locations published in the United States prior to 1800: separate maps and charts, illustrations in books and pamphlets, maps published in atlases, almanacs, magazines.
Location: OONL.

— 1970 —

6517 **Canada. Archives publiques. Division de la collection nationale de cartes et plans**
Le Canada par les cartes: [catalogue]. [Ottawa: Archives Publiques, 1970]. [30], [28] p.
Note: 102 entrées.– Exposition de cartes géographiques, choisies pour illustrer le rôle de la cartographie au cours de cinq siècles d'histoire canadienne.– Texte en français et en anglais disposé tête-bêche.– Titre de la p. de t. additionnelle: *Canada in maps.*
Localisation: OONL.

6518 **Canada. Public Archives. National Map Collection**
Canada in maps. [Ottawa: Public Archives, 1970]. [28], [30] p.
Note: 102 entries.– Items in an exhibition of maps selected to illustrate the role of mapping in five centuries of Canadian history.– Text in English and French with French text on inverted pages.– Title of additional title-page: *Le Canada par les cartes.*
Location: OONL.

6519 **Kidd, Karole**
"Bibliography of computer mapping."
In: *A computer atlas of Ottawa-Hull (with a bibliography of computer mapping)*, by D.R.F. Taylor and D.H. Douglas. Ottawa: Department of Geography, Carleton University, 1970. P. 45-68.
Note: Location: OONL.

6520 **May, Betty**
County atlases of Canada: a descriptive catalogue/Atlas de comtés canadien: catalogue descriptif. [Ottawa]: National Map Collection, Public Archives of Canada, 1970. xii, 192 p.: ill., maps.
Note: Location: OONL.

6521 **Sudbury Public Library**
Sudbury maps. Sudbury: Sudbury Public Library, 1970. 6 l.
Note: Location: OONL.

6522 **Warkentin, John; Ruggles, Richard I.**
Historical atlas of Manitoba: a selection of facsimile maps, plans and sketches from 1612 to 1969. Winnipeg: Historical and Scientific Society of Manitoba, 1970. xvi, 585 p.: facsims.
Note: 312 entries.
Location: OONL.

— 1971 —

6523 **Clarke, John**
"Documentary and map sources for reconstructing the history of the reserved lands in the western district of Upper Canada."
In: *Canadian Cartographer*; Vol. 8, no. 2 (December 1971) p. 75-83.; ISSN: 0008-3127.
Note: Location: OONL.

6524 **O'Dea, Fabian**
The 17th century cartography of Newfoundland. Toronto: B.V. Gutsell, Department of Geography, York University, 1971. vi, 48 p.: ill., maps. (Cartographica Monograph ; no. 1)
Note: Location: OONL.

6525 **Québec (Province). Service de la photogrammétrie et de la cartographie**
Répertoire des cartes géographiques et des photographies aériennes. Québec: Le Service, 1971. 31 l.: cartes (coul.).
Note: Localisation: OONL.

6526 **Scollie, Frederick Brent**
Fort William, Port Arthur, Ontario, and vicinity, 1857-1969: an annotated list of maps in Toronto libraries. Thunder Bay, Ont.: [s.n.], 1971. 67 l.: maps.
Note: 158 entries.– Carto-bibliography of Thunder Bay region: general maps, specialized atlases, hydrographic charts, soils, forests, geology.
Location: OOA.

— 1972 —

6527 **Carleton University. Department of Geography. Map Library**
Ottawa area resources held by the Map Library. Ottawa: [s.n.], 1972. 1 vol. (unpaged).
Note: Location: OOCC.

6528 **Charbonneau, André**
"Cartobibliographie de Jean-Baptiste-Louis Franquelin."
Dans: *Cahiers de la Société bibliographique du Canada*; Vol. 11 (1972) p. 39-52.; ISSN: 0067-6896.
Note: 48 entrées.– Liste des cartes de Franquelin: cartes signées, cartes attribuées à Franquelin, cartes de l'Atelier de Québec, collaboration.
Localisation: OONL.

6529 **Harvey, Fernand**
Inventaire des cartes socio-économiques sur le Québec, 1940-1971. Québec: Institut supérieur des sciences humaines, Université Laval, 1972. vi, 44 f. (Cahiers de l'ISSH, Collection Instruments de travail / Institut supérieur des sciences humaines, Université Laval ; no 5)
Note: 312 entrées.
Localisation: OONL.

6530 **Verner, Coolie**
Explorers' maps of the Canadian Arctic, 1818-1860. Toronto: B.V. Gutsell, Department of Geography, York University, 1972. 84 p.: [6] folded l. of pl., maps. (Monograph / Department of Geography, York University ; no. 6)
Note: 158 entries.– Cartographic documents depicting development of geographical knowledge about Canadian Arctic.– Maps are grouped by expedition that produced them, arranged chronologically under date of publication of first map printed from the expedition.– Information provided includes title, engraver, imprint, size, location.
Location: OONL.

6531 **Winearls, Joan**
"Federal electoral maps of Canada, 1867-1970."
In: *Canadian Cartographer*; Vol. 9, no. 1 (June 1972) p. 1-24.; ISSN: 0008-3127.
Note: Checklist of federal electoral maps from 1867 to 1970, together with the redistribution acts to which they pertain, preceded by an essay on the redistribution process and a commentary on the maps.
Location: OOAG.

— 1973 —

6532 **Bouchard, Louis-Marie**
"Répertoire des cartes géographiques non-autonomes du Saguenay-Lac-St-Jean."
Dans: *Protée*; Vol. 2, no 3 (mai 1973) p. 21-41; vol. 3, no 1 (décembre 1973) p. 43-67.; ISSN: 0300-3523.
Note: Localisation: OONL

6533 **McGill University. Department of Rare Books and Special Collections**
Nineteenth-century maps and atlases of Montreal in the collections of the Rare Book Department of the McGill University Library. [Montreal: McGill University Library, 1973]. 6, [1] l.
Note: Approx. 35 entries.
Location: OONL.

6534 **Projet Colique**
Cartes urbaines du Québec. Québec: Le Projet, 1973. 4 t. en 5 vol.
Note: En tête du titre: "Université du Québec, Institut national de la recherche scientifique, Urbanisation; Université Laval, Bibliothèque, Cartothèque."
Localisation: QQLA.

— 1974 —

6535 **Benson, Lillian Rea**
"The Illustrated historical atlases of Ontario with special reference to H. Belden & Co."
In: *Aspects of nineteenth-century Ontario: essays presented to James J. Talman*, edited by F.H. Armstrong, H.A. Stevenson and J.D. Wilson. London, Ont.: Published in association with the University of Western Ontario by University of Toronto Press, 1974. P. 267-277.; ISBN: 0-8020-2061-5.

Note: Listing of original publications and reprint publications of Ontario county atlases, with background essay.
Location: OONL.

6536 **Canada. Department of Energy, Mines and Resources. Surveys and Mapping Branch**
Catalogue of published maps [Canada Surveys and Mapping Branch]/Catalogue des cartes publiées [Canada Direction des levés et de la cartographie]. Ottawa: Department of Energy, Mines and Resources, 1974. 362 p.: maps (some in colour).
Note: Listing of topographical maps, national park maps, aeronautical charts, thematic maps, atlases and atlas loose sheets, gazeteers and teaching aids.– Text in English and French/texte en français et en anglais.
Location: OONL.

6537 **Canada. Public Archives. National Map Collection**
Telecommunications: the Canadian experience: an annotated list of maps/Télécommunications: l'expérience canadienne: une liste explicative des cartes. Ottawa: National Map Collection, Public Archives of Canada, 1974. 90 p.: maps.
Note: 90 entries.– Annotated carto-bibliography of thematic maps relating to telecommunications in Canada.– Information elements: date, title, imprint, insets and illustrations, physical description.– Text in English and French/texte en français et en anglais.
Location: OONL.

6538 **Canadian Wildlife Service (Western Region). Library**
A catalogue of the permanent map collection, Western Regional Library, Canadian Wildlife Service. Edmonton: Canadian Wildlife Service, Western Region, 1974. v, 24 l.
Note: Approx. 100 entries.– Collection includes county and municipality maps for the prairie provinces, maps of surficial geology, watersheds, precipitation and wildlife habitat.– List includes all maps catalogued to June, 1974.
Location: OONL.

6539 **Deslongchamps, Bernard; Duchesneau, Serge; Larue, Gilles**
Le domaine agricole du Québec: répertoire de cartes. Québec: Ministère de l'agriculture, Service des études économiques, [1974]. 139 p.: cartes (certaines en coul.).
Note: Localisation: QQLA.

6540 **Nagy, Thomas L.**
Ottawa in maps: a brief cartographical history of Ottawa, 1825-1973/Ottawa par les cartes: brève histoire cartographique de la ville d'Ottawa, 1825-1973. Ottawa: National Map Collection, Public Archives Canada, 1974. ii, 87 p.: ill., maps.
Note: Approx. 300 entries.– Chronological arrangement.– Detailed notes on selection of 30 maps.
Location: OONL.

6541 **Poulin, Guy; Cadieux, Francine**
Index to township plans of the Canadian West/Index de plans des cantons de l'Ouest canadien. Ottawa: Public Archives of Canada, National Map Collection, 1974. xvii, 69 p.: ill., maps.
Note: Index to about 20,000 township plans of the West.– Text in English and French/texte en français et en anglais.
Location: OONL.

6542 **Québec (Province). Service de la cartographie**
Cartes géologiques publiées: index de localisation/ Published geological maps: location index. Québec: Le

Service, 1974. v, 57 p.
Note: Localisation: QQLAS.

6543 Union list of atlases: Provincial Archives, Simon Fraser University, University of British Columbia, U.B.C Special Collections, University of Victoria, Vancouver City Archives, Vancouver Public Library. [S.l.]: Triul [Tri-university Libraries of British Columbia], 1974. 155, 17 l.
Note: Approx. 1,850 entries.
Location: OONL.

6544 Woodward, Frances M.
Fire insurance plans of British Columbia municipalities: a checklist. [S.l.: s.n.], 1974. 23 p.
Note: Approx. 200 entries.– Covers 1885 to the 1950s.– Provides information about size, scale, locations.
Location: OONL.

— 1975 —

6545 Artibise, Alan F.J.; Dahl, Edward H.
Winnipeg in maps, 1816-1972/Winnipeg par les cartes, 1816-1972. Ottawa: National Map Collection, Public Archives of Canada, 1975. 80 p.: maps.
Note: 31 entries.– Chronological arrangement.– Detailed notes.– Text in English and French/texte en français et en anglais.
Location: OONL.

6546 Dahl, Edward H., et al.
La Ville de Québec, 1800-1850: un inventaire de cartes et plans. Ottawa: Musées nationaux du Canada, 1975. ix, 413 p.: ill., cartes, plans. (Musée national de l'homme Collection mercure; Division de l'histoire dossier ; no. 13; ISSN: 0316-1900)
Note: Inventaire de 315 cartes de la ville de Québec, conservées aux Archives publiques du Canada; répertoire de 388 cartes provenant de divers dépôts d'archives à Québec; une étude sur l'evolution de la ville entre 1800 et 1850, avec illustrations; 75 reproductions de cartes.– Summary in English.
Localisation: OONL.

6547 Dubreuil, Lorraine
List of atlases in the University Map Collection. Montreal: McGill University, University Map Collection, [1975]. vii, 45 p. (Publication / University Map Collection, McGill University ; no. 1)
Note: 478 entries.
Location: OONL.

6548 Ross, Tim
Montreal maps: an annotated list. [Montreal]: McGill University, University Map Collection, 1975. 28 p.: maps. (Publication / University Map Collection, McGill University ; no. 2)
Note: 71 entries.
Location: OONL.

6549 Saunders, Elizabeth; Hale, Elizabeth
The W.A. Pugsley Collection of Early Maps of Canada, McGill University Library Map Collection: a catalogue. Montreal: McGill University, Department of Rare Books and Special Collections, 1975. 16 l.
Note: Location: ACU.

6550 Shields, Gordon
List of arctic and subarctic maps in the McGill University Map Collection. Montreal: McGill University, Centre for Northern Studies and Research, University Map Collection, 1975. 166 p.

Note: Location: OONL.

6551 U.S.–Canadian Map Service Bureau
Official eastern North America map and chart index catalog. Noonah, Wis.: U.S. Canadian Map Service Bureau, c1975. 186 p.: col. maps.
Note: Includes topographical maps, special interest maps (geophysical, land use, historic, and glacier maps, Canadian national parks), hydrographic charts and publications.
Location: OONL.

6552 U.S.–Canadian Map Service Bureau
Official western North America map and chart index catalog. Neenah, Wis.: U.S.–Canadian Map Service Bureau, c1975. 226 p.: col. maps.
Note: Includes topographical maps, special interest maps (geophysical, land use, historic, alpine and glacier maps, Canadian national parks), hydrographic charts and publications.
Location: OONL.

— 1976 —

6553 British Columbia. Ministry of Environment. Surveys and Mapping Branch
Map and air photo catalogue. Victoria: The Branch, 1976. [30] p.: maps.
Note: Location: OONL.

6554 Canada. Public Archives. National Map Collection
Catalogue of the National Map Collection, Public Archives of Canada, Ottawa, Ontario/[Catalogue de la Collection nationale de cartes et plans, Archives publiques du Canada, Ottawa, Ontario]. Boston: G.K. Hall, 1976. 16 vol.; ISBN: 0-8161-1215-0.
Note: National Map Collection contained approximately 750,000 items when this catalogue was produced in 1976.– About 10 to 15 percent of the collection is described here, mainly maps issued in separate sheet form or from atlases and books.– Text in English and French/texte en français et en anglais.
Location: OONL.

6555 Donkin, Kate; Finch, Rita
Union list of atlases in Ontario universities. Toronto: Council of Ontario Universities, 1976. [14], 253 p.
Note: 3,193 entries.– Canadian listings total 384 entries.– Geographic arrangement, with subject index for theme atlases.
Location: OONL.

6556 Maddick, Heather
County maps: land ownership maps of Canada in the 19th century/Cartes de comtés: cartes foncières du Canada au XIXe siècle. Ottawa: National Map Collection, Public Archives of Canada, 1976. vi, 94 p.: maps.; ISBN: 0-662-00108-7.
Note: 58 entries.– Maps are from Ontario (32), Quebec (4), Nova Scotia (18), Prince Edward Island (1).– Information includes compiler, publisher, engravers, printers, size, insets, views.
Location: OONL.

6557 Phillips, W. Louis; Stuckey, Ronald L.
Index to plant distribution maps in North American periodicals through 1972. Boston: G.K. Hall, 1976. xxxvii, 686 p.; ISBN: 0-8161-0009-8.
Note: Approx. 28,500 entries culled from 268 North American periodicals published by botanical, biological, and natural history societies, colleges and universities,

museums, herbaria, botanical gardens and arboreta.– Information includes name of taxon mapped, periodical reference, geographical distribution, type of map, author of article.– Contains a separate list of maps found in 160 published books, arranged geographically according to area of covered.
Location: OONL.

6558 **Tessier, Yves**
Catalogue collectif des atlas des cartothèques du Québec. Québec: [Bibliothèque de l'Université Laval, 1976. ix, 134, iii, 27, iv, 76 f.: carte.
Note: 1,662 entrées.
Localisation: OONL.

— 1977 —

6559 **Alberta. Alberta Municipal Affairs. Planning Support Services Branch**
Maps of Alberta municipalities: index. [Edmonton]: Planning Branch, Department of Municipal Affairs, 1977. [123] l.: maps.
Note: Lists compiled maps, planimetric maps, Indian reserves, agency boundaries, lakes.
Location: OONL.

6560 **Hayward, Robert J.**
Fire insurance plans in the National Map Collection/ Plans d'assurance-incendie de la Collection nationale de cartes et plans. Ottawa: Public Archives, 1977. xxvi, 171 p.: ill. (some in colour), plans.; ISBN: 0-662-01609-2.
Note: Location: OONL.

6561 **Nova Scotia. Department of Lands and Forests**
A book of maps: land use and natural resources of Nova Scotia. Halifax: Department of Lands and Forests, 1977. iv, 48 p.
Note: Location: NSHL.

6562 **Peterson-Hunt, William S.; Woodruff, Evelyn L.**
Union list of Sanborn fire insurance maps held by institutions in the United States and Canada: volume 2 (Montana to Wyoming; Canada and Mexico). Santa Cruz, Calif.: Western Association of Map Libraries, 1977. xv, 201 p. (Occasional paper / Western Association of Map Libraries ; no. 3)
Note: Includes listings for British Columbia only.
Location: OONL.

— 1978 —

6563 **Québec (Province). Ministère des richesses naturelles**
Répertoire des cartes et levés de géochimie et de dépôts meubles au Québec. Québec: Service de la géochimie, Direction des levés géoscientifiques, Ministère des richesses naturelles, 1978. 39 p.
Note: Localisation: OONL.

6564 **Root, John D.**
Index to geological, bedrock topography, soils, and groundwater maps of Alberta. [Edmonton]: Alberta Research Council, 1978. 66 p. (Earth sciences report / Alberta Research Council ; 77-3)
Note: Covers maps published from 1924.
Location: OONL.

6565 **Verner, Coolie**
Cook and the cartography of the north Pacific: an exhibition of maps for the conference on Captain James Cook and his times, April 1978. Burnaby, B.C.: Simon Fraser University, 1978. vi, 35 p.
Note: Location: OONL.

6566 **Withycombe, B.; Fogwill, W.D.**
Map index 1969-1977 of geological and geochemical maps of the Island of Newfoundland: (supplement to 1969 map index). St. John's: Government of Newfoundland and Labrador, Mineral Development Division, 1978. 147 p.: maps. (Report / Government of Newfoundland and Labrador, Mineral Development Division ; 78-2)
Note: Location: OONL.

— 1979 —

6567 **Oppen, William A.**
The Riel rebellions: a cartographic history/Le récit cartographique des affaires Riel. Toronto: Published by the University of Toronto Press in association with the Public Archives of Canada and the Canadian Government Publishing Centre, c1979. x, 109 p.: ill., maps.; ISBN: 0-8020-2333-9.
Note: 63 entries.– Reproduction and listing of archival maps, plans, charts related to the Red River Insurrection of 1869-70, and Riel Rebellion of 1885.– Select bibliography.– Text in English and French/texte en français et en anglais.
Location: OONL.

6568 **Québec (Province). Direction générale des eaux. Service des relevés**
Répertoire des cartes bathymétriques. Québec: Direction générale des eaux, 1979. vi, 114 p.; ISBN: 2-550-00089-7.
Note: Approx. 1,800 entrées.– Le programme d'inventaire des lacs du Québec comprend une série de renseignements relativement à l'identification, à la morphométrie, à la bathymétrie, à l'hydrométrie du lac inventorié.
Localisation: OONL.

6569 **Tessier, Yves**
"La documentation cartographique dans l'enseignement de la géographie au Québec: liste sélective de documents utiles."
Dans: *Didactique-géographie*; No 11 (hiver 1979) p. 47-51.; ISSN: 0318-6555.
Note: Localisation: OONL.

— 1980 —

6570 **British Columbia. Ministry of Energy, Mines and Petroleum Resources**
Index to bedrock geological mapping, British Columbia: including publications of the Geological Survey of Canada, British Columbia Ministry of Energy, Mines and Petroleum Resources, and journal articles, theses, and company reports. Victoria, B.C.: Province of British Columbia, Ministry of Energy, Mines and Petroleum Resources, 1980. [ca. 100] l.: map.; ISBN: 0-771-99295-5.
Note: Location: OONL.

6571 **Milette, Denise McFadden; Milette, Jean-Luc**
Répertoire de cartes autonomes sur l'Ontario français. Ottawa: Centre de recherche en civilisation canadienne-française, Université d'Ottawa, 1980. iv, 39 p. (Documents de travail du Centre de recherche en civilisation canadienne-française ; 17)
Note: 109 entrées.
Localisation: OONL

6572 **Mitchell, Bruce W.**
Selected thematic maps of man's activities in Canada's watersheds/Cartes thématiques des activités de l'homme dans les bassins hydrographiques du Canada. Ottawa:

Statistics Canada, Office of the Senior Adviser on Integration, Economic Statistics Section, 1980. 88 p.
Note: 58 entries.– Text in English and French/texte en français et en anglais.
Location: OONL.

— 1981 —

6573 **Acres Consulting Services Limited**
Bibliography of oceanographic atlases covering Canadian ocean waters. Ottawa: Department of Fisheries and Oceans, 1981. v, 99 p.: maps. (Marine Environment Data Service Contractor report ; no. 6)
Note: 167 entries.– Annotated list of atlases containing primarily physical oceanographic material from Canadian waters.– Includes a group of parameter maps (waves, currents, etc.).– Section outlining information sources includes a listing of bibliographies, databases, government agencies, periodicals.– Résumé en français.
Location: OONL.

6574 **Canada. Public Archives. National Map Collection**
Maps of Indian reserves and settlements in the National Map Collection/Cartes et réserves et agglomérations indiennes de la Collection nationale de cartes et plans. Ottawa: National Map Collection, Public Archives Canada, 1980-1981. 2 vol.: ill., facsims.; ISBN: 0-662-50525-5 (Vol. 1); 0-662-51523-4 (Vol. 2).
Note: Vol. 1: *British Columbia*. xx, 157 p.– Lists significant cartographic documents within holdings of National Map Collection relating to Indian affairs in British Columbia: Indian land sales maps, Indian Affairs survey records plans, maps from Commission Respecting Indian Lands in British Columbia, maps from Indian Claims Commission, maps from other federal government departments and agencies, general reference maps.– Excludes architectural material relating to Indian affairs.
Vol. 2: *Alberta, Saskatchewan, Manitoba, Yukon Territory, Northwest Territories*. xxiv, 153 p.– Includes maps which can be used in studies of particular reserves, as well as a selection of more general material relating to Indian affairs in Canada.– Excludes maps relating specifically to the Riel rebellions.– Compiled by Linda Camponi.– Text in English and French/texte en français et en anglais.
Location: OONL.

6575 **Jolicoeur, Jovette**
Inventaire des cartes de la végétation pour la région des Cantons de l'Est. Sherbrooke, Québec: Université de Sherbrooke, Département de géographie, 1981. 74 f. (Bulletin de recherche / Université de Sherbrooke, Département de géographie ; no 54)
Note: 68 entrées.
Localisation: OONL.

6576 **Nicholson, Norman L.; Sebert, L.M.**
The maps of Canada: a guide to official Canadian maps, charts, atlases and gazetteers. Folkestone: Dawson, 1981. x, 251 p.: ill., maps.; ISBN: 0-7129-0911-7.
Note: Outline of the mapping of Canada, with description and listing of various map series, thematic maps, hydrographic charts, provincial map series, atlases.
Location: OONL.

6577 **Québec (Province). Direction générale du domaine territorial**
Répertoire des cartes, plans et photographies aériennes. [Québec]: Ministère de l'énergie et des ressources, Direction générale du domaine territorial, 1981. 136 p.:

ill., cartes.; ISBN: 2-551-06408-2.
Note: Éditions antérieures:
Québec (Province). Service de l'arpentage. Direction des communications, Ministère de l'énergie et des ressources, 1981. 145 p.: ill., cartes.
Le Service de l'information du Ministère des terres et forêts, 1978. 135 p.: ill., cartes.
Localisation: OONL.

6578 **SansCartier, L.; Keeley, J.R.**
Oceanographic atlases of Canadian waters: a bibliography. Ottawa: Department of Fisheries and Oceans, 1981. v, 84 p.: maps. (Marine Environment Data Service Technical report ; no. 10)
Note: 224 entries.– Extends work of Acres Consulting Services' *Bibliography of oceanographic atlases covering Canadian ocean waters* (Ottawa: 1981) to compile a list of atlases containing physical oceanographic information about Canadian waters.– Includes parameter maps (waves, currents, etc.).– Résumé en français.
Location: OONL.

6579 **Verreault-Roy, Louise**
Répertoire cartographique de la Mauricie, 1800-1950. [Trois-Rivières]: Groupe de recherche sur la Mauricie, Université du Québec à Trois-Rivières, 1981. vii, 246 p. (Cahier / Groupe de recherche sur la Mauricie, Université du Québec à Trois-Rivières ; no 5); ISBN: 2-9800058-4-3.
Note: 1,034 entrées.– Les seigneuries et les cantons, les comtés, les municipalités, La ville de Trois-Rivières, les réserves indiennes, cartes thématiques, les atlas.
Localisation: OONL.

— 1983 —

6580 **Biron, Guy; Gagnon, France**
Info-carto 02: répertoire cartobibliographique sur la région 02 et Moyen Nord. [Chicoutimi, Québec]: U.Q.A.C., 1983. v f., 261 p.: cartes.
Note: Approx. 200 entrées.– Région administrative du Saguenay-Lac-Saint-Jean et la région géographique du Moyen Nord: cartes géographiques, cartes anciennes, atlas et recueils, guides d'excursions et plan d'aménagement et d'urbanisme.
Localisation: OONL.

6581 **Index to bedrock geological mapping, British Columbia: including publications of the Geological Survey of Canada, British Columbia Ministry of Energy, Mines and Petroleum Resources, and journal articles, theses, and company reports.** [Victoria]: Province of British Columbia, Ministry of Energy, Mines and Petroleum Resources, 1983. 45 p.: map.; ISBN: 0-7719-9295-5.
Note: List of geological mapping of British Columbia according to the National Topographic System location.– Covers to 1982, with additions to 1983.– Geological mapping defined as map representation of bedrock features, exposed or inferred, over a given area, and derived from fieldwork and/or compilation.– Excludes articles which simply reproduce a previously published geological map, and mapping of a generalized nature.
Location: OONL.

6582 **Nova Scotia. Department of Municipal Affairs. Community Planning Division**
Nova Scotia map index. Halifax, N.S.: The Division, 1983. 116 p.: ill., maps.

Note: Location: OOAG.

6583 **Tessier, Yves**
Carto-03: répertoire cartobibliographique sur la région de Québec. [Québec]: Cartothèque, Bibliothèque de l'Université Laval, 1983. 269 p.: ill.; ISBN: 2-9200310-01-1.
Note: Approx. 600 cartes et 30 atlas.– Cartes géographiques, cartes anciennes, cartes autonomes de la Commission d'aménagement de la Communauté urbaine de Québec, 1970-1976, atlas.
Localisation: OONL.

— 1984 —

6584 **Hébert, John R.**
Panoramic maps of cities in the United States and Canada: a checklist of maps in the collections of the Library of Congress, Geography and Map Division. 2nd ed. Washington: Library of Congress, 1984. v, 181 p.: ill.; ISBN: 0-8444-0413-6.
Note: 1,726 entries.– Identifies manuscript and printed maps of cities in 47 states, District of Columbia and 9 Canadian provinces, including photocopies of originals in other repositories than Library of Congress.– Information provided includes artists, publishers, lithographers/ printers, map size.– Revised by Patrick E. Dempsey.
Previous edition: 1974. v, 118 p.; ISBN: 0-8444-0114-5.– 1,117 entries.
Location: OONL.

— 1985 —

6585 **Lefebvre, Marie, et al.**
Répertoire des documents cartographiques et photographiques sur la région de Trois-Rivières (04). Trois-Rivières: Cartothèque, Université du Québec à Trois-Rivières, 1985. vii, 377 p.: ill., cartes.
Note: Localisation: OONL.

6586 **Lépine, Pierre; Berthelette, Josée**
Documents cartographiques depuis la découverte de l'Amérique jusqu'à 1820: inventaire sommaire. Montréal: Bibliothèque nationale du Québec, 1985. xiii, 383 p.: cartes.; ISBN: 2-551-06545-3.
Note: Approx. 1,500 entrées.– Documents cartographiques sont composés en partie d'originaux et partie de reproductions: fac-similés imprimés et édités, reproductions photographiques et microcopies: atlas, cartes individuelles.– Index toponymique, index chronologique des atlas.
Localisation: OONL.

— 1986 —

6587 **Dufour, Daniel**
Répertoire cartobibliographique de Charlevoix. Baie-Saint-Paul [Québec]: Société d'histoire de Charlevoix, 1986. xvi, 345 p. (Instruments de recherche / Société d'histoire de Charlevoix ; no 1); ISBN: 2-9800595-0-1.
Note: 973 entrées.– Comprend trois parties: les cartes anciennes (période de 1600 à 1880), les cartes géographiques (période de 1881 à 1986), et les atlas.
Localisation: OONL.

6588 **Ontario. Ministry of Municipal Affairs. Research and Special Projects Branch**
Maps: a map index for community planning in Ontario. [Toronto]: The Branch, 1986. iii l., 130 p.: ill., maps.; ISBN: 0-7729-1025-1.
Note: Deals with mapping interpretation and application issues, with samples of maps with information on scales, sources, coverage, features and publishers.– Categories

include base mapping for planning, administration, social and economic, land use, transportation, geology and mining, climate, recreation, natural resources.
Location: OONL.

— 1987 —

6589 **Canadian maps and atlases, 1984-1987: an exhibition of the National Archives of Canada/Cartes et atlas canadiens, 1984-1987: une exposition des Archives nationales du Canada.** [Ottawa]: National Archives of Canada, c1987. [96] l.
Note: Maps, atlases, cartographic books, periodicals, brochures.– Text in English and French/texte en français et en anglais.
Location: OONL.

— 1988 —

6590 **Courville, Serge; Labrecque, Serge**
Seigneuries et fiefs du Québec: nomenclature et cartographie. Québec: CÉLAT, 1988. 202 p.: ill. (Dossier toponymiques / CÉLAT ; 18); ISBN: 2-920576-22-4.
Note: Localisation: OONL.

6591 **Dubreuil, Lorraine**
Early Canadian topographical map series: the Geological Survey of Canada, 1842-1949. Ottawa: Association of Canadian Map Libraries and Archives, 1988. vi, 71 p.: maps. (Occasional papers of the Association of Canadian Map Libraries and Archives ; no. 1); ISBN: 0-9690682-8-X.
Note: Approx. 450 entries.
Location: OONL.

6592 **Michaud, Yves B.**
Répertoire cartobibliographique sur la région de l'est du Québec. [Rimouski]: Cartothèque, Université du Québec à Rimouski, 1988. iii, 336 p.: cartes.
Note: Énumère toutes les cartes du Bas Saint-Laurent, de la Gaspésie et des îles-de-la-Madeleine conservées à la Cartothèque de l'Université du Québec à Rimouski.
Localisation: OONL.

— 1989 —

6593 **Dubreuil, Lorraine**
Sectional maps of western Canada, 1871-1955: an early Canadian topographic map series. Ottawa: Association of Canadian Map Libraries and Archives, 1989. vi, 57 p.: ill. (Occasional papers / Association of Canadian Map Libraries and Archives ; no. 2); ISBN: 0-969-0682-9-8.
Note: Approx. 225 entries.
Location: OONL.

6594 **Peters, Diane E.**
Atlases in W.L.U. Library. [Waterloo, Ont.]: The Library, Wilfrid Laurier University, 1989. vi, 117 p.; ISBN: 0-921821-06-9.
Note: Approx. 1,000 entries.– Canada, provinces, counties of Ontario, world atlases, other countries, thematic (climate, resources, etc.).
Location: OONL.

6595 **Woods, Cheryl A.**
U.W.O. Map Library: atlas collection. London: Department of Geography, University of Western Ontario, 1989. vii, 124 p.; ISBN: 0-7714-1078-6.
Note: Approx. 1,850 entries (about 375 Canadian).
Location: OONL.

— 1991 —

6596 **Canadian maps and atlases, 1987-1990: an exhibition of the National Archives of Canada/Cartes et atlas canadiens, 1987-1990: une exposition des Archives** nationales du Canada. [Ottawa]: National Archives of Canada, c1991. [90] p.

Note: 57 entries.– Historical maps, contemporary maps, atlases and map folios, cartographic literature, map catalogues.– Text in English and French/texte en français et en anglais.

Location: OONL.

6597 **Dubreuil, Lorraine**
Standard topographical maps of Canada, 1904-1948. Ottawa: Association of Canadian Map Libraries and Archives, 1991. vi, 31 p.: maps. (Occasional papers of the Association of Canadian Map Libraries and Archives ; no. 3); ISBN: 0-9695062-0-1.

Note: Location: OONL.

6598 **Winearls, Joan**
Mapping Upper Canada, 1780-1867: an annotated bibliography of manuscript and printed maps. Toronto: University of Toronto Press, c1991. xli, 986 p.: maps.; ISBN: 0-8020-2794-6.

Note: Listing of all significant and autonomous maps (manuscript and printed) of Upper Canada between the years 1780 and 1867.– Maps cover regions, rivers, lakes, districts and counties, cities and towns (including maps of major parts of cities).– Includes printed maps from books and atlases.– Types of maps and surveys include reconnaissance and exploration manuscript maps, township surveys, military maps, road maps, maps of canals and navigation, nautical charts, international boundary surveys, topical maps, county and district maps, town and city maps.– Excludes maps for individual urban features (buildings and cemeteries), and small parts of cities.– All records include date of production, bibliographical statement, physical description, endorsements, annotation, library locations.– Indexes: name, subject, title.

Location: OONL.

— 1992 —

6599 **Bobrowsky, Peter T.; Giles, Tim; Jackaman, Wayne**
Surficial geology map index of British Columbia. Victoria: Province of British Columbia, Geological Survey Branch, 1992. 1 vol. (in various pagings): ill., maps.; ISBN: 0-771-89156-3.

Note: Catalogue of economic and physical geology maps for British Columbia.

Location: OONL.

6600 **Dubreuil, Lorraine**
Canada's militia and Defence maps, 1905-1931. Ottawa: Association of Canadian Map Libraries and Archives, 1992. vi, 44 p.: ill., maps.; ISBN: 0-9695062-3-6.

Note: Location: OONL.

6601 **Morgan, W.C.; Wheeler, J.O.**
Cartes géologiques du Canada: histoire et évolution. [Ottawa]: Énergie, Mines et Ressources Canada, [1992]. 46 p.

Note: Catalogue d'une exposition de cartes géologiques du Canada à l'occasion du 150e anniversaire de la Commission géologique du Canada.

English title: *Geological maps of Canada: history and evolution.*

Localisation: OOAMA.

6602 **Morgan, W.C.; Wheeler, J.O.**
Geological maps of Canada: history and evolution. [Ottawa]: Energy, Mines and Resources Canada, [1992]. 41 p.

Note: 99 entries.– Catalogue of exhibition of geological maps of Canada to mark the 150th anniversary of the Geological Survey of Canada.

Titre en français: *Cartes géologiques du Canada: histoire et évolution.*

Location: OOAMA.

— 1993 —

6603 **Kershaw, Kenneth A.**
Early printed maps of Canada. I. 1540-1703. Ancaster, Ont.: Kershaw Publishing, 1993. vi, 320 p.: maps.; ISBN: 0-9697184-0-3.

Note: 321 entries.

Location: OONL.

Audio-visual Materials

Documents audio-visuels

— 1952 —

6604 **National Film Board of Canada**
Canadian travel film library: 16mm motion picture films.
Ottawa: National Film Board of Canada, 1952. 27 p.
Note: Location: OONL.

— 1953 —

6605 **National Film Board of Canada**
Catalogue of films produced by the National Film Board
of Canada available in Australia. [Ottawa: Queen's
Printer, 1953]. 73, [1] p.
Note: Approx. 400 entries.
Location: OONL.

— 1954 —

6606 **National Film Board of Canada**
Canadian travel and wildlife films. Ottawa: National
Film Board of Canada, 1954. 31 p.
Note: Location: OONL.

— 1965 —

6607 **Canada. Department of Forestry. Information and
Technical Services**
Catalogue of Canadian forestry and other resource films/
Films canadiens sur les forêts et autres ressources
renouvelables. Ottawa: Queen's Printer, 1965. vii, 32 p.
Note: Approx. 150 entries dealing with forest
management, conservation and ecology, forest fire
control, entomology and pathology, logging, pulp and
paper industry, recreational use of forest regions.– Text
in English and French/texte en français et en anglais.
Location: OONL.

— 1968 —

6608 **Centre national des arts (Canada)**
Catalogue: films sur les arts d'interprétation. Ottawa: Le
Centre, 1968. 18, 24 p.
Note: Texte en français et en anglais disposé tête-bêche.–
Titre de la p. de t. additionnelle: *Catalogue: films on the
performing arts.*
Localisation: OONL.

6609 **National Arts Centre (Canada)**
Catalogue: films on the performing arts. Ottawa: The
Centre, 1968. 24, 18 p.
Note: Text in English and French with French text on
inverted pages.– Title of additional title-page: *Catalogue:
films sur les arts d'interprétation.*
Location: OONL.

6610 **National Film Board of Canada**
Filmstrips and slides: catalogue. Ottawa: Queen's
Printer, 1952-1968. [9] vol.
Note: Lists filmstrips, 8 mm. film loops, media kits, slide
sets, overhead projectuals.
Titre en français: *Catalogue des films fixes.*
Continued by: *Media catalogue.* 1969-1977. [9] vol.; ISSN:
0382-3393.
Location: OONL.

6611 **Office national du film du Canada**
Catalogue des films fixes. Ottawa: Impr. de la Reine,
1952-1968. [9] vol.
Note: "Films en boucle 8 mm, films fixes, jeux de
diapositives, ensembles de média, transparents pour
rétroprojecteur".
English title: *Filmstrips and slides: catalogue.*
Suivi de: *Catalogue de média.* 1969-1977. [9] vol.; ISSN:
0382-3407.
Localisation: OONL.

— 1969 —

6612 **McGill University. Archives**
A preliminary guide to motion pictures in the University
Archives collections, McGill University. Montreal:
McGill University, 1969. 19 l.
Note: Location: OONL.

— 1971 —

6613 **Walser, Lise**
Répertoire des longs métrages produits au Québec, 1960-
1970. Montréal: Conseil québécois pour la diffusion du
cinéma, 1971. 110 p.
Note: Contient tous les films de plus de 60 minutes
produits au Québec entre janvier 1960 et décembre
1970.– Les films sont groupés par année de production.
Localisation: OONL.

6614 **Water films.** 2nd ed. Ottawa: Secretariat, Canadian National Committee, International Hydrological Decade,
[1971]. 194 p.
Note: 455 entries.– Films about hydrology and related
fields: meteorology, groundwater, snow and ice,
glaciology, geomorphology, hydraulics, water quality,
conservation, oceanography, hydroelectric projects.–
Compiled by the National Science Film Library of the
Canadian Film Institute.
Previous edition: 1968 (reprinted with revisions, 1969). v,
93 p.– 186 entries.
Location: OON.

— 1972 —

6615 **Hamelin, Lucien; Walser, Lise**
Cinéma québécois: petit guide. Montréal: Conseil
québécois pour la diffusion du cinéma, 1972. 47 p.: ill.
Note: Comprend bio-filmographies de cinéastes,
addresses des organismes et compagnies de distribution,
références bibliographiques.
Localisation: OONL.

6616 **National Science Film Library (Canada)**
A catalogue of films on the medical sciences/Catalogue
des films sur les sciences médicales. Ottawa: Canadian
Film Institute, 1972. vi, [25], 144 p.
Note: Approx. 700 entries.– Information provided:
country, year of production, length, language versions
available, producer or sponsor, scientific advisor, descrip-
tion of content.– Many Canadian references.– Text in
English and French/texte en français et en anglais.
Location: OONL.

6617 **Reid, Alison**
Canadian women film-makers: an interim filmography. Ottawa: Canadian Film Institute, 1972. [12] l. (Canadian Film Archives, Canadian filmography series ; no. 8)
Note: Approx. 150 entries.– Covers to end of 1971.– Includes television producers.– Excludes films by women students, first-time directors.
Location: OONL.

— 1973 —

6618 **Canadian Centre for Films on Art**
Catalogue: films on art. Ottawa: Canadian Centre for Films on Art, 1965-1973. 10 vol.
Note: Titre en français: *Catalogue, films sur l'art et sujets connexes*.
Location: OONL.

6619 **Centre canadien du film sur l'art**
Catalogue, films sur l'art et sujets connexes. Ottawa: Centre canadien du film sur l'art, 1965-1973. 10 vol.
Note: Title in English: *Catalogue: films on art*.
Localisation: OONL.

6620 **Université de Montréal. Bibliothèque des sciences humaines et sociales. Médiathèque**
Liste des enregistrements sur cassettes et sur rubans magnétoscopiques que possède la médiathèque. [Montréal]: Bibliothèque des sciences humaines et sociales, Université de Montréal, 1973. 37 f.
Note: Approx. 150 entrées.– Conférences, tables rondes, rencontres d'écrivains, interviews, pièces de théâtre, etc.
Localisation: OONL.

6621 **University of British Columbia. Library**
Catalogue of oral history phonotapes in University of British Columbia libraries. Vancouver: Reynoldston Research and Studies Oral History Programmes, c1973. xi, 30 p.
Note: 250 entries (representing 800 hours of tape).– Focus on British Columbia.– Topics covered: cultural communities of B.C., 1900-1973, including Doukhobor, Finnish, French Canadian, Japanese, Jewish, Native Indian; role of women in B.C.; organizers of labour unions; lumber and mining industries.
Location: OONL.

— 1974 —

6622 **Zimmerly, David W.**
Museocinematography: ethnographic film programs of the National Museum of Man, 1913-1973. Ottawa: National Museums of Canada, 1974. vii, 103 p.: ill. (National Museum of Man Mercury series, Ethnology Division paper ; no. 11)
Note: Contains a listing of current ethnographic film holdings in the Ethnology Division, NMM, with detailed descriptions of selected ethnographic films, compiled by Johanne Cadieux and Maria Folan, and biographic and bibliographic notes on selected filmmakers (George H. Wilkins, Harlan I. Smith, Richard S. Finnie).
Location: OONL.

— 1975 —

6623 **Association des cinéastes amateurs du Québec**
Répertoire de films amateurs du Québec. Montréal: Association des cinéastes amateurs du Québec, [1975]. [49] f.
Note: Localisation: OONL.

6624 **Douglas College. Library**
AV: a selective bibliography of non-print materials in the health sciences with emphasis on nursing. New Westminster, B.C.: Douglas College Library, 1975. i, 286 l.
Note: Approx. 1,500 entries.
Location: OONL.

6625 **Metropolitan Toronto Library. Audio-Visual Services**
Filmography: Indians of North America. Toronto: Audio-Visual Services, Metropolitan Toronto Library, 1975. 16 p.
Note: Location: OONL.

6626 **National Film Board of Canada**
A catalogue of films projecting women. Toronto: National Film Board of Canada, [1975]. 57 p.: ill.
Note: Two sections: "Subjects:" women and their bodies, images and stereotypes, portraits, social and political context, woman as prime socializer, psychological; "Women filmmakers."- "This catalogue was conceived, researched and written by the women of the National Film Board in Ontario."- On cover: *Projecting women*.
Location: OONL.

6627 **Rousseau, Camille; Alexandre, Claude; Labrecque, Olivette**
Répertoire des films accessibles aux jeunes scientifiques. Montréal: Conseil de la jeunesse scientifique, 1975. vi, 147 p.
Note: 464 entrées.
Localisation: OONL.

— 1976 —

6628 **Burgess, Jean**
An annotated list of 16mm films in the Regional Library, Canadian Wildlife Service, Edmonton. Edmonton: Canadian Wildlife Service, Western & Northern Region, 1976. iii, 25 p.
Note: Location: OONL.

6629 **McQuillan, Barry H.**
A resource list of multi-media materials on ethnicity and multi-culturalism. [Toronto: s.n.], 1976. 47 p.
Note: Approx. 400 entries.– Films, videotapes, audio tapes, filmstrips, multi-media kits, tranparencies, charts, simulation games on ethnic groups and ethnic relations appropriate for use in high schools.
Location: OONL.

— 1977 —

6630 **Canadian Centre for Films on Art**
Films on art: a source book. New York: Watson-Guptill Publications; Ottawa: Canadian Film Institute, 1977. 220 p.; ISBN: 0-8230-1780-X.
Note: Approx. 450 entries.– Films include television series, curriculum films, works by independent filmmakers, documents of exhibitions, lives and works of individual artists produced mainly in Canada, Britain, France, and the United States.– Indexes: subject, artist, title.– Directory of sources.
Location: OONL.

6631 **Cinémathèque québécoise**
Index de la production cinématographique canadienne/ Index of Canadian film production. Montréal: Cinémathèque québécoise, Musée du cinéma, 1976-1977. 2 vol.; ISSN: 0702-777X.
Note: Annuel.– "Films publiés dans la revue *Nouveau cinéma canadien: New Canadian Film*."- Texte en français et en anglais/text in English and French.
Localisation: OONL.

6632 **Demers, Pierre**
"Le patrimoine cinématographique du Saguenay-Lac-Saint-Jean."
Dans: *Focus*; Vol. 1, no 2 (juin 1977) p. 28-31.; ISSN: 0705-5579.
Note: Localisation: OONL:

6633 **Ontario Federation of Labour. Resource Centre**
Labour film list. [Don Mills] Ont.: Ontario Federation of Labour Resource Centre, [1977]. 54, [6] l.
Note: Approx. 150 entries.– Topics include automation, collective bargaining, grievance and arbitration, human rights, safety and health, strikes, labour movement: aims/function/structure, political education, women, youth.
Location: OONL.

— 1978 —

6634 **McIntyre, John**
"Bibliographie de films en langue française."
Dans: *Canadian Modern Language Review*; Vol. 34, no. 2 (January 1978) p. 211-220.; ISSN: 0008-4506.
Note: Localisation: AEU.

6635 **Ojibway-Cree Resource Centre**
Audio-visual bibliography [Ojibway-Cree Resource Centre]. [Timmins, Ont.: Ojibway-Cree Resource Centre], 1978. ii l., 45 p.
Note: Approx. 280 entries.– Audio tapes, video recordings, films, filmstrips, phonograph records on native culture, education, music, government relations, history, socio-economic development.
Location: OONL.

6636 **Québec (Province). Cinémathèque**
Catalogue des documents audiovisuels, 1978. Québec: Cinémathèque, 1978. 380 p.
Note: Localisation: OONL.

6637 **Télévision communautaire de Rivière-du-Loup**
Répertoire des documents audio-visuels. Rivière-du-Loup, Québec: Télévision communautaire de Rivière-du-Loup, 1978. 91 f.
Note: Publié en collaboration avec l'Éditeur officiel du Québec.
Localisation: OONL.

— 1979 —

6638 **Browne, Colin**
Motion picture production in British Columbia: 1898-1940: a brief historical background and catalogue. Victoria: British Columbia Provincial Museum, 1979. 381 p. (British Columbia Provincial Museum Heritage record ; no. 6; ISSN: 0701-9556); ISBN: 0-7718-8136-3.
Note: 1,131 entries.– Information provided includes producers, directors, photographers, length, gauge (35 mm., etc.), tint (black & white/colour), sound or silent, current state of film, descriptive notes.
Location: OONL.

6639 **Calder, Carol**
Multimedia resources for educational administrators. Toronto: Library, Reference and Information Services, Ontario Institute for Studies in Education, 1979. vi, 126 p. (Current bibliography / Ontario Institute for Studies in Education ; no. 12)
Note: Approx. 400 entries.– Nonprint materials include 16mm films, videotapes, audiotapes, multimedia kits, filmstrips and simulations.– Emphasis on topics of interest in planning workshops or seminars, training of new administrators and development and awareness of

administrators already in the field.– Topics include collective bargaining, decision making, evaluation of staff, leadership, management styles and methods, organization development, time management.
Location: OONL.

6640 **Page, James E.**
Seeing ourselves: films for Canadian studies. Montreal: National Film Board of Canada, 1979. v, 210 p.: ill.; ISBN: 0-772-20001-7.
Note: "A project of the National Film Board's Education Support Program."
Location: OONL.

6641 **Southwestern Regional Library System (Ont.)**
Video catalogue: Southwestern Library System. Windsor, Ont.: Board of the Southwestern Regional Library System, [1979]. iii, 416 p.; ISSN: 0706-439X.
Note: Approx. 1,500 entries.
Location: OONL.

— 1980 —

6642 **Donald, Gail**
Media materials: a Can. Lit. collection. Peterborough, Ont.: CANLIT, 1980. 35 p.
Note: Approx. 300 entries.– Films, audiotapes, records and video recordings relating to Canadian literary works and various themes such as women, family, politics, education, history, influence of the United States.
Previous edition: 1977. 40 p.
Location: OONL.

6643 **Mental health filmography.** [Toronto]: Audio Visual Services, Metropolitan Toronto Library Board, 1980. ii, 29 p.
Note: Approx. 170 entries.– Topics include child growth and development, adults and family life, special problems (child abuse, alcoholism, crime and delinquency, drug abuse, mental illness, suicide).
Location: OONL.

6644 **Rothwell, Helene de F.**
Canadian selection: filmstrips. Toronto: University of Toronto Press, c1980. xvi, 537 p.; ISBN: 0-8020-4586-3.
Note: Approx. 1,800 entries.– Listing of English- and French-language filmstrips for children and young adults.– Annotations in English only.
Location: OONL.

6645 **Rothwell, Stephen J.**
Multi-media on Indians and Inuit of North America, 1965-1980/Documents audio-visuels sur les Indiens et les Inuit de l'Amérique du Nord, 1965-1980. [Ottawa]: Inuit and Indian Affairs Program, Public Communications and Parliamentary Relations Branch, [1980]. 244 p.
Note: Approx. 1,000 entries.– Text in English and French/texte en français et en anglais.
Previous edition: *Films on Indians and Inuit of North America, 1965-1978/Films sur les Indiens et les Inuit de l'Amérique du Nord, 1965-1978*. 1978. xxxiv, 255 p.
Location: OONL.

— 1981 —

6646 **Dryden, Jean E.**
Voices of Alberta: a survey of oral history completed in Alberta up to 1980. Edmonton: Alberta Culture, Historical Resources Division, 1981. vi, 430 p.
Note: Survey contains three parts: numerical listing of holdings in each collection, alphabetical listing of all informants interviewed, alphabetical listing of all

subjects, places, and persons mentioned in the tapes. Revised alphabetical listing by subjects, people and places covered published in July, 1982.
Voix Albertaines, supplément français à *Voices of Alberta*, compile par Raymond Lanteigne. Edmonton: 1983. ix, 124 p.
Location: OONL.

6647 **Québec (Province). Ministère de l'éducation. Direction générale des réseaux**
Catalogue des documents audio-visuels [Gouvernement du Québec, Ministère de l'éducation, Direction générale des réseaux]. Trois-Rivières: Gouvernement du Québec, Ministère de l'éducation, Direction générale des réseaux, 1981. 133 p.; ISBN: 2-550-04736-2.
Note: 108 entrées.
Localisation: OONL.

6648 **Rozon, René**
Répertoire des documents audiovisuels sur l'art et les artistes québécois. Montréal: Bibliothèque nationale du Québec: Ministère des Communications, Direction générale du cinéma et de l'audiovisuel, 1981. 319 p.; ISBN: 2-550-00965-7.
Note: 758 entrées.– Renferme cinq genres de documents: films, films fixes, diapositives, diaporamas et bandes vidéo sur les sujets: architecture, artisanat, cinéma, danse, design, documents d'artistes, musique, peinture, photographie, sculpture.– Cinq index: des séries, des titres, des artistes, des réalisateurs et des distributeurs.
Localisation: OONL.

6649 **Thiele, Judith C.**
Funstuff: a selected bibliography of recreational and leisure reading talking books in the Crane collection. Vancouver, B.C.: Charles Crane Memorial Library, University of British Columbia, 1981. 41 p.; ISBN: 0-88865-185-6.
Note: Approx. 800 entries.– Emphasis on Canadian materials: fiction and non-fiction titles by Canadian writers or published in Canada, in both official languages: children's literature, adult fiction, adult non-fiction: anthropology, art and literature, biography, ecology and economics, history/politics/law, humor, practical works, psychology/sociology/philosophy/religion; books in progress.
Location: OONL.

— 1982 —

6650 **Canadian Film Institute**
Multiculturalism film and video catalogue/Répertoire des films et vidéos sur le multiculturalisme. Ottawa: The Institute, 1982. 89 p.; ISBN: 0-919096-12-3.
Note: Approx. 800 entries.– Edited by Margaret Britt.– Text in English and French/texte en français et en anglais.
Location: OONL.

6651 **Nadon, Claude**
Audiovidéographie pour l'enseignement du français aux adultes: de l'éducation de base au secondaire V: films de format 16mm, films en boucle 8mm, audio-visions, jeux de diapositives, disques, rubans magnétiques, ensembles multi media. [Québec]: Gouvernement du Québec, Direction générale de l'éducation des adultes, [1982]. 320 p.
Note: Inventaire critique des documents audio-visuels mis à la disposition des professeurs de français qui travaillent avec des étudiants adultes.

Localisation: OONL.

6652 **Ontario. Ministry of Agriculture and Food**
16 mm motion picture films produced by Ontario government ministries: a publication of the Council of Communications Directors. Toronto: The Ministry, 1980-1982. 3 vol.; ISSN: 0824-4413.
Note: Covers from 1955 to 1983.– Annotated listing of documentaries, animated films and dramatizations produced by Ontario government ministries.
Location: OONL.

6653 **Zaporzan, Shirley; Klymasz, Robert B.**
Film and the Ukrainians in Canada, 1921-1980: a filmography index of film titles and bibliography with supplementary appendices. Edmonton: Canadian Institute of Ukrainian Studies, University of Alberta, 1982. xi, 76 p.: ill., [17] l. of pl. (Research report / Canadian Institute of Ukrainian Studies ; no. 1)
Note: 110 entries.– Includes filmstrips and videotapes.– Bibliography contains 74 entries: books, periodical and newspaper articles.
Location: OONL.

— 1983 —

6654 **Laplante, Michelle**
Répertoire des productions audio-visuelles sur la condition féminine. Québec: Conseil du statut de la femme, 1983. xix, 206 p.; ISBN: 2-550-02964-X.
Note: Approx. 350 entrées.– Documents produits sous forme de vidéo, film, diaporama sur les thèmes: adolescence, condition de vie des femmes, création, économie, féminisme et mouvements de femmes, relations homme/femme, santé, santé mentale, socialisation, éducation, travail, violence.
Localisation: OONL.

6655 **Manitoba. School Library Services**
Focal point: a bibliography of non-print resources for the visual arts. Winnipeg: Manitoba School Library Services, 1983. iv, 76 p. (Manual / Manitoba School Library Services ; 5-83)
Note: Location: OONL.

— 1984 —

6656 **British Columbia. Ministry of Agriculture and Food**
Film & slide catalogue [BC Ministry of Agriculture and Food]. Victoria: Province of British Columbia, Ministry of Agriculture and Food, [1984]. 38 p.; ISBN: 0-77260-095-3.
Note: Location: OONL.

6657 **Canadian Film Institute**
Multiculturalism multimedia catalogue, 1984/Répertoire des multimedia sur le multiculturalisme, 1984. Ottawa: Canadian Film Institute, 1984. 64 p.; ISBN: 0-919096-25-5.
Note: Listing of filmstrips (captioned, sound), slide sets, audio cassettes, annotated tape manuscripts, slide-tape presentations related to multiculturalism, race relations, customs and traditions, folklore and folktales, immigrants and immigration, music, individual ethnic groups.– Editor, research coordinator: M.S. Kiely.– Published in cooperation with Multiculturalism Canada.– Text in English and French/texte en français et en anglais.
Location: OONL.

6658 **Faucher, Carol**
La production française à l'ONF: 25 ans en perspectives. Montréal: Cinémathèque québécoise, c1984. 80 p.: ill. (Dossiers de la Cinémathèque / Cinémathèque

québécoise ; no 14); ISBN: 2-89207-027-9.
Note: Localisation: OONL.

6659 **William R. Perkins Library**
Canadiana: nonprint resources held in Perkins Library.
[Durham, N.C.]: Duke University, 1984. [7], 54 l.
Note: Includes audio and video recordings on political,
social and cultural aspects of Canadian life collected to
support Canadian studies courses: music and spoken
word in English, French and Spanish languages.
Location: OONL.

— 1985 —

6660 **British Columbia. Ministry of Provincial Secretary and
Government Services. Recreation and Sport Branch**
Recreation and Sport film library catalogue. [Victoria]:
Recreation and Sport Branch, Ministry of Provincial
Secretary and Government Services, 1985. 80 p.; ISBN: 0-
7726-0296-4.
Note: Approx. 350 entries.– Lists documentary films on
recreation, fitness and health, first aid, water safety,
coaching, athletic competition, specific sports held at the
Recreation and Sport Branch film library.– Includes Can-
adian and British Columbia references.
Location: OONL.

6661 **British Columbia. Provincial Educational Media Centre**
Media resources: Agriculture. Richmond: B.C. Ministry
of Education, Provincial Educational Media Centre, 1985.
v, 67 p.; ISBN: 0-7726-0362-6.
Note: List of videotapes and films available from the
PEMC; teaching aids to support agriculture curriculum
in British Columbia schools, colleges and universities.
Location: OONL.

— 1986 —

6662 **Le catalogue de la cinémathèque nationale des
relations industrielles.** [Ottawa]: Office national du film
du Canada, c1986. 21, 31 p.; ISBN: 0-662-54352-1.
Note: Approx. 200 entrées.– Films sur les questions
ouvrières par la société Radio-Canada, l'Office national
du film et Travail Canada portant sur la sécurité et
l'hygiène au travail, formation des cadres, questions
relatives à la situation de la femme, la qualité de la vie au
travail, négociation collective et le processus de présentation des griefs.– Texte en français et en anglais disposé
tête-bêche.– Titre de la p. de t. additionnelle: *National
industrial relations film catalogue.*
Disponible en ligne: *FORMAT*, le base de données de
l'ONF pour les moyens audiovisuels.
Localisation: OONL.

6663 **Duffy, Dennis**
Camera west: British Columbia on film, 1941-1965:
including new information on films produced before
1941. Victoria: Sound and Moving Image Division,
Provincial Archives, c1986. ix, 318 p.: ill.; ISBN: 0-7718-
8479-6.
Note: 1,082 entries for the 1941-1965 period.– 252 entries
for the pre-1941 period.– Includes filmed programs
produced for television.– Excludes TV commercials,
filmed program inserts, TV news clips.
Location: OONL.

6664 **Media for minds: educational resources from CBC
Enterprises.** Montreal: CBC Enterprises, 1986. vi, 133, 67,
vi p.: ill.; ISBN: 0-88794-249-0.
Note: Educational films, video recordings, transcripts,
music, audio products produced by the Canadian

Broadcasting Corporation/Société Radio Canada.– Text
in English and French with French text on inverted
pages.– Title of additional title-page: *Télé-formation:
catalogue des ressources éducatives des Entreprises Radio-
Canada.*
Location: OONL.

6665 **National industrial relations film catalogue.** [Ottawa]:
National Film Board of Canada, c1986. 31, 21 p.; ISBN: 0-
662-54352-1.
Note: Approx. 150 entries.– Labour-related films from
the Canadian Broadcasting Corporation, National Film
Board, Labour Canada.– Topics include occupational
health and safety, training, women's issues, quality of
working life, collective bargaining, grievance processes.–
Text in English and French with French text on inverted
pages.– Title of additional title-page: *Le catalogue de la
cinémathèque nationale des relations industrielles.*
Online access: *FORMAT*, the NFB database for audio-
visual materials.
Location: OONL.

6666 **Télé-formation: catalogue des ressources éducatives des
Entreprises Radio-Canada.** Montréal: Entreprises Radio-
Canada, 1986. vi, 67, 133, vi p.; ISBN: 0-88794-249-0.
Note: Matériel didactique (films, vidéocassettes, cassettes
audio, musique), productions radio ou télé de la Société
Radio-Canada.– Texte en français et en anglais disposé
tête-bêche.– Titre de la p. de t. additionnelle: *Media for
minds: educational resources from CBC Enterprises.*
Localisation: OONL.

6667 **Wyman, Doreen**
Bibliography of law-related AV material. 2nd ed.
Edmonton: Legal Resource Centre, Faculty of Extension,
University of Alberta, c1986. 162 p.
Note: Approx. 600 entries.– Subjects include business
and consumer law, criminal law, family law, housing,
juvenile delinquency, legal education, legal history, legal
process, native rights, prison and reform, sexual assault,
women and the law.
Previous edition: Sy, San San. *Audio-visual resources: law
and law-related.* c1980. 186 p.– Approx. 400 entries.
Location: OONL.

— 1987 —

6668 **Canadian Association of Children's Librarians**
Canadian films for children and young adults. Ottawa:
Canadian Library Association, c1987. 33 p.; ISBN: 0-
88802-219-0.
Note: Approx. 150 entries.– Films made in Canada or
made in other countries if the producer/director/actors
are Canadians or if the film is about a Canadian subject.
Location: OONL.

6669 **Dick, Ernest J.**
Catalogue des fonds sur la Société Radio-Canada
déposés aux Archives publiques. [Ottawa]: Archives
publiques Canada, c1987. viii, 141, 125, viii p.; ISBN: 0-
662-54911-2.
Note: Texte en français et en anglais disposé tête-bêche.–
Titre de la p. de t. additionnelle: *Guide to CBC sources at
the Public Archives.*
Localisation: OONL.

6670 **Dick, Ernest J.**
Guide to CBC sources at the Public Archives. [Ottawa]:
Public Archives Canada, c1987. viii, 125, 141, viii p.;
ISBN: 0-662-54911-2.

Note: Text in English and French with French text on inverted pages.– Title of additional title-page: *Catalogue des fonds sur la Société Radio-Canada déposés aux Archives publiques.*
Location: OONL.

6671 **Kiely, Michael Sean**
Perspectives on the forest sector: an evaluative guide to forestry audio-visuals/Perspectives sur le secteur forestier: guide des instruments audio-visuels et des études sur la foresterie. Ottawa: Canadian Film Institute, 1987. iv, 33 p.; ISBN: 0-919096-31-X.
Note: 60 entries.– Canadian films dealing with issues related to forestry, including acid rain, forest management, ecosystems, fire, reforestation, logging and social history.– Text in English and French/texte en français et en anglais.
Location: OONL.

6672 **Normandeau, André; Vauclair, Martin**
"Film library on prisons in Canada/Filmographie canadienne sur la prison."
In: *Canadian Journal of Criminology*; Vol. 29, no. 1 (January 1987) p. 84-120.; ISSN: 0704-9722.
Note: 50 entries.
Location: OONL.

6673 **Turner, D. John**
Canadian feature film index, 1913-1985/Index des films canadiens de long métrage, 1913-1985. [Ottawa]: Public Archives Canada, National Film, Television and Sound Archives, c1987. xx, 816 p.; ISBN: 0-660-53364-2.
Note: 1,222 entries.– Information about the films includes titles (main title, alternative title(s), unused titles); technical details related to the making of the film (film stock, laboratory, dialogue); principal participants (producers, directors, technicians, actors); cost and running time; distribution and release; Archives' holdings.– Feature film is defined as "any audio-visual document (motion picture) available on a film support, irrespective of content, running more than 60 minutes".– Text in English and French/texte en français et en anglais.– Texte français: Micheline Morisset.
Location: OONL.

— 1988 —

6674 **Moscovitch, Arlene**
Focus on Canada: a film and video resource handbook for secondary level social studies. Montreal: The Film Board, [1988]. ii, 122 p.: ill.; ISBN: 0-7722-0133-1.
Note: Approx. 200 entries selected from a collection of 3,000, with emphasis on Canadian history and contemporary issues.
Location: OONL.

6675 **National Film Board of Canada**
Women breaking through: a cross-curriculum A-V resource guide for secondary school. Montreal: National Film Board of Canada, 1988. 28 p.; ISBN: 0-7722-0128-5.
Note: 128 entries.
Location: OONL.

6676 **Québec (Province). Office des personnes handicapées**
300 documents audiovisuels sur les personnes handicapées. Québec: L'Office, 1988. [9], 99 p.; ISBN: 2-551-08229-3.
Note: 335 entrées.– Films, vidéogrammes, montages audiovisuels traitent de différent aspects de la situation des personnes handicapées.– Tous ces documents

proviennent de la base DAVID de la Centrale des bibliothèques du Québec, et de la base FORMAT de l'Office national du film du Canada.
Localisation: OONL.

— 1989 —

6677 **British Columbia. Library Services Branch**
National catalog of audiobooks. Victoria, B.C.: Ministry of Provincial Secretary and Government Services, Library Services Branch, 1979-1989. 11 vol.
Note: Annual.
Location: OONL.

6678 **Canada. Department of Indian Affairs and Northern Development**
On film: a film catalogue [Indian Affairs and Northern Development]. Ottawa: The Department, 1989. 72, 32 p.
Note: Approx. 400 entries.– Films and videos in English, French and native languages available at Department of Indian Affairs and Northern Development headquarters on all aspects of native life.– Text in English and French with French text on inverted pages.– Title of additional title-page: *Filmographie: catalogue des films.*
Location: OONL.

6679 **Canada. Indian and Northern Affairs Canada. Communications Service Program**
Audio visual resources catalogue, Manitoba Region/ Catalogue de documents audio-visuels, Région du Manitoba. Ottawa: Indian and Northern Affairs Canada, [1989]. [2], ix, 25 p.
Note: Annotated listing of films and video recordings about native North Americans.– Text in English and French/texte en français et en anglais.
Location: OONL.

6680 **Canada. Ministère des affaires indiennes et du nord canadien**
Filmographie: catalogue des films [Ministère des affaires indiennes et du nord canadien]. Ottawa: Le Ministère, 1989. 32, 72 p.
Note: Approx. 400 entrées.– Films et vidéos sur les autochtones au Canada en français, anglais, langues autochtones disponible à l'Administration centrale du ministère des Affaires indiennes et du Nord canadien.– Texte en français et en anglais disposé tête-bêche.– Titre de la p. de t. additionnelle: *On film: a film catalogue.*
Localisation: OONL.

6681 **Canada. Solicitor General Canada. Ministry Library and Reference Centre**
AV catalogue [Solicitor General Canada]/Catalogue AV [Solliciteur général Canada]. [Ottawa]: Solicitor General Canada, Ministry Library and Reference Centre, [1989]. [iv], 153, 75 p.
Note: Lists audio-cassettes and video-cassettes available for loan from the Ministry Library on subjects relating to crime and criminals, corrections, administration of justice.– Text in English and French/texte en français et en anglais.
Location: OONL.

6682 **Canadian Police College. Law Enforcement Reference Centre**
Audio visual catalogue: Law Enforcement Reference Centre, Canadian Police College/Catalogue audio-visuel: Centre de documentation policière, Collège canadien de police. Ottawa: The Centre, 1989. 2, ii, 220 p.
Note: Approx. 750 entries.– Motion pictures, video

recordings, slide presentations dealing with Royal Canadian Mounted Police, police-related audio-visual material (organizational, operational, bombs and terrorism, computer security), crime prevention and related subjects (vandalism, rape, physical abuse, alcoholism, drugs), management and supervision.– Text in English and French/texte en français et en anglais.
Location: OONL.

6683 **Hesch, Rick, et al.**
Our home and native land: a film and video resource guide for aboriginal Canadians. Ottawa: National Film Board, 1989. iv, 34 p.: ill.; ISBN: 0-7722-0158-7.
Note: Approx. 100 entries.– English films and videos produced by the National Film Board which are oriented towards social action and based on native culture.– Topics include aboriginal rights, land claims and sovereignty, native community issues, native women, legends, arts and crafts.
Location: OONL.

6684 **Justice Institute of British Columbia. Resource Centre**
Audio visual catalogue [Justice Institute of British Columbia]. Vancouver, B.C.: The Centre, 1989. 119, 37, 8 p.; ISSN: 0835-9962.
Note: Films, videos, audiotapes, slides dealing with the law, courts, police, corrections, and related topics.– Arranged in three main sections: Alphabetical title listing, which contains the descriptive information (running time, producer, date of production, etc.); Subject index; Series index.
Supplement: September 1991-. vol; ISSN: 1187-5453.
Location: OONL.

6685 **National Film Board of Canada**
The family violence audio-visual catalogue/Catalogue de documents audiovisuels sur la violence dans la famille. 2nd ed. Montreal: National Film Board of Canada, [1989]. ix, 97 p.; ISBN: 0-7722-0148-X.
Note: Listing with descriptive annotations of films, videotapes, filmstrips and audio-tape-slide presentations dealing with child abuse and neglect, spouse abuse and elder abuse.– Text in English and French/texte en français et en anglais.– Online access: *FORMAT database*, a national information system for Canadian audio-visual materials managed by NFB, available through UTLAS.
Previous edition: 1986. vii, 58 p.; ISBN: 0-7722-0506-X.
Location: OONL.

6686 **New Brunswick Human Rights Commission**
Human rights: a guide to audio visual resources. Fredericton: The Commission, 1989. 110 p.
Note: Approx. 300 entries.– Films, video recordings, filmstrips relating to various human rights issues: age, disability, race, religion, sexual orientation, etc.– Coded for suggested audience levels and applications.– Prepared by Jane C. Williams.
Location: OONL.

6687 **Threlfall, William**
Audiovisual materials concerning the care, use, behaviour and general biology of animals. St. John's, Nfld.: Memorial University of Newfoundland, 1989. i, 353 p. (Memorial University of Newfoundland Occasional papers in biology ; no. 13; ISSN: 0702-0007)
Note: Lists audio-visual aids and software ranging from laboratory-oriented work to wildlife films, from pro-use to no use of animals in research.– Topics include animal

rights and welfare, anatomy and dissection, anaesthesia, animal behaviour (including human), diseases, ecology, endangered species, human biology, laboratory animal biology, surgery, wildlife biology.
Location: OON.

— 1990 —

6688 **Alberta. Alberta Family and Social Services. Library Services**
Audio-visual catalogue [Alberta Family and Social Services]. Edmonton: Library Services, Alberta Family and Social Services, 1990. 69 l.
Note: Annotated list of films, sound and video recordings dealing with social issues and problems held by Alberta Family and Social Services Library.– Topics include adoption and foster care, family violence, handicapped, child welfare, parenting, income support, divorce, alcoholism.
Location: OONL.

6689 **Alberta. Alberta Occupational Health and Safety. Library Services Branch**
Health and safety on the job: audio-visual catalogue. Edmonton: The Branch, 1990. 27, xiv, 83 p.
Note: Annotated list of films and videos held by Alberta Audio-Visual Services dealing with occupational health and safety issues from Canadian, American, British and other sources.
Location: OONL.

6690 **Québec (Province). Ministère de l'énergie et des ressources**
Répertoire des documents audiovisuels du Ministère de l'énergie et des ressources, 1990-1991. Québec: Gouvernement du Québec, Ministère de l'énergie et des ressources, Direction des communications, 1990. 26 p.; ISBN: 2-550-20843-9.
Note: Édition antérieure: 1987. 21 p.; ISBN: 2-550-17393-7.
Localisation: OONL.

6691 **Quigley, E.P.**
Fisheries Development Division video-tape library catalogue. [Ottawa]: Fisheries and Oceans Canada, 1990. iv, 14 p.
Note: 71 entries.– Lists video recordings relating to the fisheries available from libraries and DFO offices in the Newfoundland region.
Location: OONL.

— 1991 —

6692 **Films et vidéos documentaires pour adolescents et adultes: 11299 documents pour les 12 ans et plus.** Montréal: Services documentaires Multimedia, [1991]. xiii, 1629 p.: ill. (Guides Tessier); ISBN: 2-89059-114-X.
Note: 11,299 entrées.– Films et vidéos documentaires de langue française produits au Québec (8,241), ailleurs au Canada (1,403), aux États-Unis, en France, en Grande-Bretagne, en Belgique.– La période couverte est de 1971 à novembre 1990.– Index: noms (auteurs et maisons de production), titres, sujets, collections, distributeurs.– Base de données: DAVID (Documents AudioVisuels Disponibles), accès via SDM, UTLAS, iNet.– Disponible: microfiches et CD-ROM.
Localisation: OONL.

6693 **National Film Board of Canada**
The NFB film guide: the productions of the National Film Board of Canada from 1939 to 1989. Montreal: The Board, c1991. clvii, 960 p., [72] p. of pl.: ill., ports.; ISBN:

0-660-56485-8 (set).
Note: 4,475 English-language films produced by NFB, 437 bibliographic references (books, theses, articles, government reports and research studies) on the NFB.– Film titles in alphabetical order, with information provided about release, series and version titles, date of production, running time, title code, colour/black and white indicator, credits, subject description, sponsors.– Indexes: subject, director, producer, production year.
Titre en français: *Le répertoire des films de l'ONF: la production de l'Office national du film du Canada de 1939 à 1989.*
Location: OONL.

6694 **Office national du film du Canada**
Le répertoire des films de l'ONF: la production de l'Office national du film du Canada de 1939 à 1989. Montréal: L'Office, c1991. clvii, 758 p., [72] p. de pl.: ill., portr.; ISBN: 0-660-56485-8 (série).
Note: 3,355 films en français de l'ONF, 437 références bibliographiques sur l'ONF (livres, thèses, articles de périodiques, rapports gouvernementaux, étude de recherche).– Les titres des films sont énuméres par ordre alphabétique.– Pour chaque film: titre, série et version, date de production, durée, code titre, indicateur de film couleur/noir et blanc, la générique, description du sujet, noms des commanditaires, etc.– Index des sujets, séries, réalisateurs, producteurs, année de production.
English title: *The NFB film guide: the productions of the National Film Board of Canada from 1939 to 1989.*
Localisation: OONL.

6695 **Répertoire des documents écrits et audiovisuels relatifs à la famille.** [Québec]: Gouvernement du Québec, Ministère de l'éducation, Direction de la coordination des réseaux, c1991. iii, 188 p.; ISBN: 2-550-15520-3.
Note: Documents d'origine exclusivement québécoise publiés depuis 1980, divise en deux parties, la bibliographie et la liste des documents audiovisuels: (1) documents écrits: instruments de travail, ouvrages généraux, ouvrages spécialises (droit, santé, sexualité, etc.); (2) documents audiovisuels: liste des films, documents vidéo et des diaporamas relatifs à la famille.– Liste des distributeurs.
Localisation: OONL.

— 1992 —
6696 **British Columbia. Parks Library**
Audio-visual catalogue [BC Parks Library]. [Victoria, B.C.]: The Library, 1992. x, 56 p.; ISBN: 0-7726-1564-0.
Note: Approx. 300 entries.– Audio cassettes, films, slide tapes, video recordings.– Title index.
Previous edition: 1990. viii, 30 l.; ISBN: 0-7726-0801-6.
Location: OONL.

6697 **Broderick, Corinne; Lawton, Janet; Greenaway, Nora**
Video mosaic: an elementary guide to multicultural videos and films. Vancouver: Vancouver School Board, Staff Development Division, 1992. 37 p.: ill.; ISBN: 1-55031-368-1.
Note: Location: OONL.

6698 **Canada. Multiculturalism and Citizenship Canada**
Film, video, and audio productions [supported by Multiculturalism programs, 1973-1992]/Productions cinématographiques, vidéos et sonores [Programmes de Multiculturalisme, 1973-1992]. Ottawa: Multiculturalism and Citizenship Canada, c1992. vii, 83 p.; ISBN: 0-662-

59315-4.
Note: Text in English and French/texte en français et en anglais.
Location: OONL.

— Ongoing/En cours —
6699 **Alberta. Provincial Film Library**
Resource catalogue [Alberta Provincial Film Library]. [Edmonton]: Alberta Public Affairs Bureau, 1983-. vol.; ISSN: 0823-3306.
Note: Catalogue lists all audio-visual resources held by the Provincial Film Library, including 16 mm. films, video tapes, filmstrips, slide sets, many accompanied by audio-cassettes, recordings, discussion guides, scripts.– Subjects covered include health, sports, tourism, family violence, consumer affairs, nutrition, safety, various topics relating to Alberta.– Some issues have title: *Audio-visual resource catalogue.*
Location: OONL.

6700 **Alberta Educational Communications Corporation**
Audio-visual catalogue [Alberta Educational Communications Corporation]. Edmonton: Alberta Educational Communications Corporation, 1984-. vol.; ISSN: 0836-8244.
Note: Irregular.– Lists materials produced or acquired by ACCESS Network for use by educators in Alberta.– Mainly Canadian subjects, with emphasis on western Canada.
Location: OONL.

6701 **Alberta Educational Communications Corporation**
Video catalogue [Alberta Educational Communications Corporation]. Edmonton: Alberta Educational Communications Corporation, [1982]-. vol.; ISSN: 0827-8814.
Note: Irregular.– Lists programs produced or acquired by ACCESS Network for use by educators in Alberta.– Titles index with series title, curriculum subject.– Subject (curriculum) index, videos are annotated, with information provided regarding length, colour, date of production.
Location: OONL.

6702 **Canadian Coast Guard College. Library**
Audio-visual catalogue [Canadian Coast Guard College Library]/Catalogue de matériel audio-visuel [Garde côtière canadienne, Bibliothèque du collège]. [Sydney, N.S.]: The Library, [1985]-. vol.; ISSN: 0837-2500.
Note: Text in English and French/texte en français et en anglais.
Location: OONL.

6703 **Film-video Canadiana/Film-vidéo Canadiana.** Montreal: Published by the National Film Board of Canada for National Library of Canada; National Archives of Canada, Moving Image and Sound Archives; La Cinémathèque québécoise: musée du cinéma, 1988-. vol.; ISSN: 0836-1002.
Note: Biennial.– First issue, 1985/86.– Lists Canadian films and videos by Canadian production companies or independent producers, as well as co-productions with foreign companies, short films and TV productions released for general distribution.– Information includes title, year of production, running time, format, director/producer, production company/sponsor, synopsis.– From 1948 to 1964, films produced in Canada were listed in the *Canadian Index to Periodicals and Documentary*

Films.– Canadian films were listed in the national bibliography *Canadiana* from 1964 to 1976, at which time the CFI's *Film Canadiana* became the principal source for information on films produced in Canada.– Information is stored in FORMAT, a national, bilingual information system for audio-visual materials developed by the National Film Board, and is available online through UTLAS and QL Systems.– Text in English and French/texte en français et en anglais.

Previous editions:

Film Canadiana, 1983-1984. National Film Board of Canada, 1986. x, 550 p.; ISSN: 0015-1173.

Film Canadiana, 1980-1982. National Film Board of Canada, 1984. viii, 455 p.; ISBN: 0-7722-0084-X.

Film Canadiana. Canadian Film Institute, 1969-1980. 12 vol.; ISSN: 0015-1173.

Location: OONL.

6704 **Manitoba. Department of Agriculture**
Audio-visual catalogue [Manitoba Department of Agriculture]. Winnipeg: Manitoba Department of Agriculture, 1978-.   vol.; ISSN: 0704-9676.
Note: Irregular.
Location: OONL.

6705 **Metropolitan Toronto Reference Library**
One-half inch VHS videocassettes in the Audio Visual Services Department collection. Toronto: Metropolitan Toronto Reference Library, 1990-. vol.; ISSN: 0840-7134.
Note: Annual.– Listing of video recording collection arranged in two sections: "Title and series;" "Subject," with information provided: producer, distributor, date of production, running time, brief abstract, colour or black & white, audience level.
Location: OONL.

6706 **National Film Board of Canada. Reference Library**
Books on film and television in the Reference Library of the National Film Board of Canada/Livres sur le cinéma et la télévision se trouvant à la Bibliothèque de l'Office national du film du Canada. Montreal: The Library, 1992- . vol.
Note: Volume 1: *Production, production technology and distribution/Production, technologie de production et distribution.*– ISBN: 0-7722-0395-4.– 1,067 entries.– First of a projected 3-volume bibliography on film, video and television.– On cover: Life Long Learning Training Committee.– Text in English and French/texte en français et en anglais.
Location: OONL.

6707 **Québec (Province). Ministère des forêts**
Répertoire des documents audiovisuels [Ministère des forêts (Québec)]. Charlesbourg: Gouvernement du Québec, Ministère des forêts, 1991-.   vol.; ISSN: 1187-905X.
Note: Biennal.
Localisation: OONL.

6708 **Vancouver Community College. Advanced Education Media Acquisitions Centre**
Video catalogue [Advanced Education Media Acquisitions Centre]. Vancouver: The Centre, c1991-. vol.; ISSN: 1183-8663.
Note: Annual.
Location: OONL.

Catalogues/Collections

— 1844 —

6709 **Rich, Obadiah**
Catalogue of books relating to North and South America, including also voyages round the world, collections of voyages and travels, &c., being the duplicates of Mr. Rich's American collection. London: O. Rich, 1844. 48 p.
Note: 817 entries.– Sections on the Arctic, Canada, Newfoundland, Hudson Bay.
Location: OONL.

— 1845 —

6710 **Canada. Legislature. Legislative Council. Library**
Alphabetical catalogue of the Library of the Hon. the Legislative Council of Canada: authors and subjects. Montreal: J. Starke, 1845. 252 p.
Note: Microform: CIHM Microfiche series ; no. 47681; ISBN: 0-665-47681-7. 3 microfiches (135 fr.).
Location: QQS.

— 1846 —

6711 **Canada. Legislature. Legislative Assembly. Library**
Catalogue of books in the Library of the Legislative Assembly of Canada. Montreal: [s.n.], 1846. 123, xxi p.
Note: Microform: CIHM Microfiche series ; no. 43439; ISBN: 0-665-43439-1. 2 microfiches (78 fr.).
Location: OONL.
Previous edition: Kingston, Ont.: [s.n.], 1842. 76 p.
Microform: CIHM Microfiche series ; no. 45659; ISBN: 0-665-45659-X. 1 microfiche (42 fr.).
Location: QQS.

6712 **Natural History Society of Montreal**
Catalogue of the library and museum of the Natural History Society of Montreal. Montreal: Lovell & Gibson, 1846. 40 p.
Note: Microform: CIHM Microfiche series ; no. 39509; ISBN: 0-665-39509-4. 1 microfiche (24 fr.).
Location: OONL.

6713 **Rich, Obadiah**
Bibliotheca americana nova: a catalogue of books relating to America, in various languages, including voyages to the Pacific and round the world, and collections of voyages and travels printed since the year 1700, compiled principally from the works themselves, by O. Rich. London: Rich and Sons, 1846. 2 vol.
Note: Approx. 5,500 entries.– Vol. 1 is a reissue of the *Bibliotheca americana nova* published as an independent work in 1835 (with half-title Pt. 1: 1701 to 1800) and its Supplement, first published in 1841.– Vol. 2 is a reissue of two parts, issued in 1844 and 1846, covering literature of 1801-1830 and 1831-1844 respectively.– A third volume was announced, to consist of supplement and general index, but never published.– Includes numerous references to France in Canada and the Americas, Hudson Bay, Arctic regions, Quebec, Upper Canada, Cape Breton.
Microform: Vol. 1: CIHM Microfiche series ; no. 47301; ISBN: 0-665-47301-X. 6 microfiches (275 fr.).– Vol. 2:

CIHM Microfiche series ; no. 47302; ISBN: 0-665-47302-8. 5 microfiches (233 fr.).
Reprint: New York: B. Franklin, [1964]. 2 vol. (Burt Franklin bibliography and reference series ; 43).
Location: OONL.

— 1858 —

6714 **Canada. Library of Parliament**
Catalogue of the Library of Parliament/Catalogue de la Bibliothèque du Parlement. Toronto: J. Lovell, 1857-1858. 2 vol.
Note: Vol. 1: *General Library/Ouvrages générale*. 1074 p.; Vol. 2: *Works relating to America, pamphlets and manuscripts, index to authors and subjects/Ouvrages relatifs à l'Amérique*. viii, 1075-1895 p.
Microform: CIHM Microfiche series ; no 48985; ISBN: 0-665-48984-6. (set). 12 microfiches (563 fr.).
Previous edition: *Catalogue of books in the Library of Parliament*. Quebec: J. Lovell's Steam Printing Establishment, 1852. vi p., 2 l., [11]-130 p.
Microform: CIHM Microfiche series ; no. 36084; ISBN: 0-665-36084-3. 2 microfiches (71 fr.).
Supplement: *Supplementary catalogue of the Library of Parliament: books added to the Library since 25th February, 1858/Supplément au catalogue de la Bibliothèque du Parlement: livres ajoutés à la Bibliothèque depuis le 25 février 1858*. 1860. 26 p.
Microform: CIHM Microfiche series ; no. 47828; ISBN: 0-665-47828-3. 1 microfiche (18 fr.).
Location: OONL.

6715 **Canadian Institute. Library**
Catalogue of the library of the Canadian Institute. Toronto: J. Lovell, 1858. 23 p.
Note: Microform: CIHM Microfiche series ; no. 44304; ISBN: 0-665-44304-8. 1 microfiche (16 fr.).
Location: OTU.

6716 **Young Men's Christian Association (Halifax, N.S.)**
Catalogue of books in the library of the Halfax Young Men's Christian Association. Halifax, N.S.: Library and Reading Rooms, 1858. 24 p.
Note: Microform: CIHM Microfiche series ; no. 08798; ISBN: 0-665-08798-5. 1 microfiche (17 fr.).
Location: NSHL.

— 1859 —

6717 **Nova Scotia. Legislative Council. Library**
Catalogue of books in the Legislative Council Library. Halifax, N.S.: [J. Bowes and Sons], 1859. 35 p.
Note: Microform: CIHM Microfiche series ; no. 10401; ISBN: 0-665-10401-4. 1 microfiche (38 fr.).
Previous edition: *Catalogue of books in the library of the Legislative Council*. J.S. Thompson, 1852. 24 p.
Microform: CIHM Microfiche series ; no. 10405; ISBN: 0-665-10405-7. 1 microfiche (27 fr.).
Location: NSHL.

— 1860 —

6718 **Canada. Library of Parliament**
Catalogue of the Library of Parliament: part I: law, legislation, political and social science, commerce and statistics, with index/Catalogue de la Bibliothèque du Parlement: 1re partie: droit et économie politique, suivi d'un index. Ottawa: Printed by Maclean, Roger & Co., 1860. [7], 552, 255 p.
Note: Text in English and French/texte en français et en anglais.
Microform: CIHM Microfiche series ; no. 61311; ISBN: 0-665-61311-3. 9 microfiches (426 fr.).
Location: OONL.

— 1862 —

6719 **Catalogue de la bibliothèque de feu L'Hon. Dominique Mondelet, juge de la Cour supérieure.** [S.l.: Plinguet & Laplante, 1862]. 14 p.
Note: "Cette bibliothèque contient une collection d'ouvrages rares et précieux sur la jurisprudence et sur l'histoire du Canada."
Microforme: ICMH collection de microfiches ; no 54192; ISBN: 0-665-54192-9. 1 microfiche (11 images).
Localisation: OONL.

— 1867 —

6720 **Canada. Library of Parliament**
Alphabetical catalogue of the Library of Parliament: being an index to the classified catalogues printed in 1857, 1858 and 1864, and to the books and pamphlets since added to the Library up to 1st October, 1867/ Catalogue alphabétique de la Bibliothèque du Parlement: comprenant l'index des catalogues méthodiques publiés en 1857, 1858 et 1864 et celui des livres et brochures ajoutés à la Bibliothèque depuis cette dernière époque jusqu'au 1er octobre, 1867. Ottawa: G.E. Desbarats, 1867. 496 p.
Note: Preliminary matter in English and French/matière préliminaire en français et en anglais.
Previous edition: ... : *being an index to the classified catalogues printed in 1857 and 1858, and to the books since added to the Library, up to 1st March, 1862/... : comprenant l'index des catalogues méthodiques publiés en 1857 et 1858, des livres ajoutés à la Bibliothèque depuis cette époque jusqu'au 1[e]r mars 1862.* Hunter, Rose, 1862. 313 p.
Location: OONL.

— 1869 —

6721 **Québec (Province). Bibliothèque de la Législature**
Catalogue alphabétique de la Bibliothèque de la Législature de Québec. [S.l.]: P.G. Delisle, [1869]. 51 p.
Note: Microforme: ICMH collection de microfiches ; no 53484; ISBN: 0-665-53484-1. 1 microfiche (30 images).
Suppléments:
Supplément au catalogue de la Bibliothèque de la Législature. Lévis, Québec: [s.n.], 1874. 18 p.
Microforme: ICMH collection de microfiches ; no 61058; ISBN: 0-665-61058-0. 1 microfiche (14 images).
Deuxième supplément au catalogue alphabétique de la Bibliothèque de la Législature. Québec: [s.n.], 1875. 183, [1] p.
Microforme: ICMH collection de microfiches ; no 61042; ISBN: 0-665-61042-4. 2 microfiches (98 images).
Localisation: OONL.

— 1870 —

6722 **Catalogue of rare and curious books including the collection of M. [i.e. Monsieur] Tross: comprising important works relating to America and the Indies ....** London: [s.n.], 1870. 64 p.
Note: Microform: CIHM Microfiche series ; no. 40144; ISBN: 0-665-40144-2. 2 microfiches (92 fr.).
Location: OONL.

— 1872 —

6723 **Ontario. Legislative Library**
Catalogue of the library of the Parliament of Ontario. Toronto: Hunter, Rose, 1872. iv, 93, [1], xxxvi p.
Note: Microform: CIHM Microfiche series ; no. 55912; ISBN: 0-665-55912-7. 2 microfiches (25 fr.).
Location: OONL.

— 1873 —

6724 **Literary and Historical Society of Quebec. Library**
Catalogue of books in the library of the Literary and Historical Society of Quebec. Quebec: Printed by the "Morning Chronicle", 1873. v, 195, iv, [43] p.
Note: Microform: CIHM Microfiche series ; no. 32822; ISBN: 0-665-32822-2. 3 microfiches (132 fr.).
Previous editions:
1864. vi, 114, [22] p.
Catalogue of the library. Printed by A. Coté, 1845. 44 p.
Microform: CIHM Microfiche series ; no. 47017; ISBN: 0-665-47017-7. 1 microfiche (31 fr.).
Supplement: *Hand list of additions to the library, 1900-1914.* The Society, 1914. 142 p.
Location: OOP.

— 1874 —

6725 **Académie commerciale catholique de Montréal**
Catalogue de la bibliothèque de l'Académie commerciale catholique et de l'École polytechnique de Montréal. Montréal: *La Minerve*, 1874. 126 p.
Note: Inclut les sections: "Histoire du Canada," "Brochures sur le Canada," "Géographie et voyages."
Microforme: ICMH collection de microfiches ; no 54294; ISBN: 0-665-54294-1. 2 microfiches (70 images).
Localisation: QQS.

— 1875 —

6726 **Ontario. Legislative Library**
Catalogue of the library of the Parliament of Ontario. Toronto: Hunter, Rose, 1875. viii, 308 p.
Note: Subject arrangement.– Includes sections listing works of Canadian history and topography, Canadian pamphlets, Canadian federal and provincial legislation, Canadian newspapers.
Microform: CIHM Microfiche series ; no. 55913; 0-665-55913-7. 4 microfiches (168 fr.).
Location: OONL.

— 1879 —

6727 **Canada. Library of Parliament**
Index to the catalogue of the Library of Parliament: part II: general library/Index du catalogue de la Bibliothèque du parlement: IIe partie: bibliothèque générale. Ottawa: Printed by the Citizen Printing and Publishing Co., 1879. xi, [1], 683 p.
Note: Alphabetical index of authors and subjects.– Paging refers to Library of Parliament catalogue volumes.– Text in English and French/texte en français et en anglais.
Microform: CIHM Microfiche series ; no. 61312; ISBN: 0-

665-61312-1. 8 microfiches (364 fr.).
Location: QONL.

6728 **Catalogue of pamphlets of the Library of the Legislature of Quebec.** Quebec: [s.n.], 1879. 119 p.
Note: Microform: CIHM Microfiche series ; no. 61040; ISBN: 0-665-61040-8. 3 microfiches (65 fr.).
Location: OONL.

6729 **Moore, George Henry**
The Jesuit relations, etc. New York: Printed for the Trustees [Lenox Library], 1879. 19 p. (Contributions to a catalogue of the Lenox Library ; no. 2)
Note: Microform: CIHM Microfiche series ; no. 08559; ISBN: 0-665-08559-1. 1 microfiche (15 fr.).
Location: OONL.

6730 **Québec (Province). Bibliothèque de la Législature**
Catalogue of pamphlets of the Library of the Legislature of Quebec /Catalogue des brochures de la Législature de Québec. Quebec: [s.n.], 1879. 119 p.
Note: Text in English and French/texte en français et en anglais.
Microform: CIHM Microfiche series ; no. 61040; ISBN: 0-665-61040-8. 2 microfiches (65 fr.).
Location: OOA.

— 1880 —

6731 **Acadia College. Library**
Catalogue of the Library of Acadia College. Wolfville, N.S.: [s.n.], 1880. 37 p.
Note: Microform: CIHM Microfiche series ; no. 05848; ISBN: 0-665-05848-9. 1 microfiche (22 fr.).
Previous edition: 1877. 28 p.
Microform: CIHM Microfiche series ; no. 08500; ISBN: 0-665-08500-1. 1 microfiche (19 fr.).
Location: OONL.

— 1881 —

6732 **Ontario. Legislative Library**
Catalogue of the library of the Parliament of Ontario: with alphabetical indexes of authors and of subjects, 1881. Toronto: Printed by C.B. Robinson, 1881. xi, [2]-558 p.
Note: Compiled by John Watson.
Microform: CIHM Microfiche series ; no. 54074; ISBN: 0-665-54074-4. 7 microfiches (299 fr.).
Location: OONL.

— 1882 —

6733 **O'Callaghan, Edmund Bailey**
Catalogue of the library of the late E.B. O'Callaghan, M.D., LL.D., historian of New York. New York: Taylor, 1882. 223 p.: port.
Note: 2,474 entries.– Sale catalogue.– Numerous listings of works pertaining to voyages of discovery, New France, Quebec, Canada, Jesuit relations.– Alphabetic arrangement, no index.
Microform: CIHM Microfiche series ; no. 11494; ISBN: 0-665-11494-X. 3 microfiches (122 fr.).
Location: OONL.

— 1883 —

6734 **Club canadien (Montréal, Québec). Bibliothèque**
Club canadien de Montréal: catalogue de la bibliothèque. Montréal: L. Perrault, 1883. 66, [1] p.
Note: Microforme: ICMH collection de microfiches ; no 01117; ISBN: 0-665-01117-2. 1 microfiche (40 images).
Localisation: QQL.

6735 **Halifax Garrison Library**
Rules and catalogue of the Halifax Garrison Library. Halifax, N.S.: J.W. Dolan, 1883. 134 p.
Note: Microform: CIHM Microfiche series , no. 53181; ISBN: 0-665-53181-8. 2 microfiches (80 fr.).
Previous edition: J. Munro, 1835. 58, [2] p.
Microform: CIHM Microfiche series ; no. 64450; ISBN: 0-665-64450-7. 1 microfiche (42 fr.).
Location: OOA.

— 1884 —

6736 **A Catalogue of books: chiefly relating to English and American history and antiquities ... presented to the University of McGill College, Montreal, by Peter Redpath, 1864-1884.** Cambridge: Macmillan and Bowes, 1884. 134 p.
Note: Microform: CIHM Microfiche series ; no. 54143; ISBN: 0-665-54143-0. 2 microfiches (76 fr.).
Location: OKQ.

— 1885 —

6737 **Dunn, Oscar**
Catalogue d'une bibliothèque canadienne: ouvrages sur l'Amérique et en particulier sur le Canada. Québec: [s.n.], 1885. 38 p.
Note: Microforme: ICMH collection de microfiches ; no 07107; ISBN: 0-665-07107-8. 1 microfiche (26 images).
Édition antérieure: *Catalogue d'une bibliothèque canadienne: ouvrages sur l'Amérique et en particulier sur le Canada collectionnés par M. Oscar Dunn.* C. Darveau, 1880. 28 p.
Microforme: ICMH collection de microfiches ; no 05951; ISBN: 0-665-05951-5. 1 microfiche (18 images).
Localisation: OTU.

6738 **Haight, Willet Ricketson**
Catalogue of a valuable collection of books and pamphlets relating to Canada and America, and the fine arts: being the second portion of the library of Frederick Broughton, late manager of the Great Western Railway .... Toronto: Hunter, Rose, 1885. 8, 44 p.
Note: Listing from Lochhead.– No location.

6739 **Toronto. Public Library**
Catalogue of books and pamphlets presented to the Toronto Public Library by John Hallam. Toronto: C.B. Robinson, 1885. 76 p.
Note: Approx. 2,000 entries.– Includes a number of Canadian references.
Microform: CIHM Microfiche series ; no. 26189; ISBN: 0-665-26189-6. 1 microfiche (44 fr.).
Location: OHM.

— 1887 —

6740 **Bibliotheca Canadensis: a catalogue of a very large collection of books and pamphlets relating to the history, the topography, the manners and customs of the Indians, the trade and government of North America ....** Toronto: R.W. Douglas, 1887. 79, [1] p.
Note: Microform: CIHM Microfiche series ; no. 68318; ISBN: 0-665-68318-9. 1 microfiche (46 fr.).
Location: NSWA.

6741 **Scadding, Henry**
Catalogue of the contents of a log shanty book-shelf in the pioneers' "Simcoe" Lodge, Exhibition Park, Toronto, 1887. Toronto: [s.n.], 1887. 7 p.
Note: Microform: CIHM Microfiche series ; no. 13228; ISBN: 0-665-13228-X. 1 microfiche (7 fr.).
Location: OONL.

— 1889 —

6742 **Toronto. Public Library**
A subject catalogue, or, Finding list of books in the Reference Library, with an index of subjects and personal names. Toronto: Murray, 1889. xxvii, 381 p.; ISBN: 0-665-26192-6.
Note: "Including additions made up to February 1st, 1889."
Microform: CIHM Microfiche series ; no. 26192; ISBN: 0-665-26192-6. 5 microfiches (216 fr.).
Location: OHM.

— 1890 —

6743 Catalogue of the library of James Stephenson, Esq., Montreal, Canada: a large, interesting and varied collection of books and pamphlets ... among which may be noted a great number of publications relating to Canada, its settlement, history and present condition .... New York: D. Taylor, 1890. 142 p.
Note: 2,191 entries.
Microform: CIHM Microfiche series ; no. 25124; ISBN: 0-665-25124-6. 2 microfiches (80 fr.).
Location: QMBM.

6744 **Nova Scotia. Legislative Library**
Catalogue of the books in the Legislative Library of Nova Scotia: authors, titles, and subjects. Halifax: Nova Scotia Printing Co., 1890. vi, 292 p.
Note: Compiled by Francis Blake Crofton, librarian.
Microform: CIHM Microfiche series ; no. 52602; ISBN: 0-665-52602-4. 4 microfiches (160 fr.).
Previous edition: 1876. 159, 3, 4 l.
Supplements:
"Supplementary catalogue of books, 1890-93." In: *Annual report of the Library Commissioner and Librarian for the year 1892-93.* 1894. P. 5-45.
"Supplementary catalogue of books, 1894-97." In: *Annual report ... for the year 1896-97.* 1898. P. 6-38.
"Supplementary catalogue of books, 1898-1901." In: *Annual report ... for the year 1900-1901.* 1902. P. 5-28.
"Supplementary catalogue of books, 1902-1907." In: *Annual report ... for the year 1907.* 1908. P. 1-47.
"Supplementary catalogue of books, 1908-1911." In: *Annual report ... for the year 1911.* 1912. P. 1-71.
"Supplementary catalogue of books, 1923-1930." In: *Annual report ... for the year 1930.* 1931. P. 1-130.
Location: OONL.

6745 **Ontario. Department of Education**
Catalogue of the books relating to Canada: historical and biographical in the library of the Education Department for Ontario, arranged according to topics and in alphabetical order. Toronto: Warwick, 1890. 122 p.
Note: Approx. 2,000 entries.
Location: OONL.

— 1895 —

6746 **Boosé, James Rufus**
Catalogue of the library of the Royal Colonial Institute. London: The Institute, 1895. clv, 543 p.
Note: Previous editions:
1886. 179 p.
Unwin, 1881. 29 p.
Supplement: *First supplementary catalogue of the library of the Royal Colonial Institute.* 1901. cclxxvlii, 793 p.
Location: OONL.

6747 Catalogue of the valuable historical library of Charles Lindsey, F.R.S.C. of Toronto, Canada: consisting of early Canadian history, laws, voyages, travels and discoveries, scarce political history and documents, rare Canadian imprints, historical and political pamphlets .... Boston: C.F. Libbie, 1895. 90 p.
Note: Microform: CIHM Microfiche series ; no. 04781; ISBN: 0-665-04781-9. 1 microfiche (53 fr.).
Location: QMBM.

— 1897 —

6748 Catalogue de livres canadiens de la bibliothèque de feu M. Faucher de St.–Maurice. [Québec]: C. Darveau, 1897. 22 p.
Note: "2000 volumes, collection d'ouvrages canadiens très rares..."
Microforme: ICMH collection de microfiches ; no 11763; ISBN: 0-665-11763-9. 1 microfiche (18 images).
Localisation: QMBM.

6749 **Catalogue of the American library of the late Mr. George Brinley of Hartford, Conn.** Hartford, Conn.: Lockwood & Brainard, 1878-1897. 5 vol.
Note: Microform:
Vol. 1: CIHM Microfiche series ; no. 07398; ISBN: 0-665-07398-4. 5 microfiches (221 fr.).
Vol. 2: CIHM Microfiche series ; no. 07399; ISBN: 0-665-07399-2. 3 microfiches (119 fr.).
Vol. 3: CIHM Microfiche series ; no. 07400; ISBN: 0-665-07400-X. 3 microfiches (108 fr.).
Vol. 4: CIHM Microfiche series ; no. 07401; ISBN: 0-665-07401-8. 3 microfiches (143 fr.).
Vol. 5: CIHM Microfiche series ; no. 07402; ISBN: 0-665-07402-6. 2 microfiches (94 fr.).
Location: OONL.

— 1898 —

6750 **Bibliothèque paroissiale de Notre-Dame et du Cercle Ville-Marie**
Catalogue des livres de la bibliothèque paroissiale de Notre-Dame et du Cercle Ville-Marie. Montréal: [s.n.], 1898. viii, 282 p.
Note: Microforme: ICMH collection de microfiches ; no 01062; ISBN: 0-665-01062-1. 4 microfiches (171 images).
Localisation: OTUTF.

6751 Catalogue de livres canadiens de la bibliothèque de feu M. C.C. Morency. [Québec: s.n.], 1898. 16 p.
Note: 345 entrées.
"Collection d'ouvrages canadiens très rares, ... grand nombre d'ouvrages très précieux sur le Canada, brochures très rares, encyclopédies, etc."
Microforme: ICMH collection de microfiches ; no 34050; ISBN: 0-665-34050-8. 1 microfiche (14 images).
Localisation: OTUTF.

6752 **Institut canadien de Québec. Bibliothèque**
Catalogue de la bibliothèque de l'Institut canadien de Québec. Québec: Dussault & Proulx, 1898. 315 p.
Note: Microforme: ICMH collection de microfiches ; no 09720; ISBN: 0-665-09720-4. 4 microfiches (167 images).
Éditions antérieures:
... , septembre 1881. 1881. 133 p.
Microforme: ICMH collection de microfiches ; no 09721; ISBN: 0-665-09721-2. 2 microfiches (74 images).
Institut canadien de Québec: acte d'incorporation, règlememts du Bureau de direction et catalogue. 1870. 45 p.
Microforme: ICMH collection de microfiches ; no 07511;

ISBN: 0-665-07511-1. 1 microfiche (27 images).
Catalogue méthodique des livres de la bibliothèque de l'Institut canadien de Québec. 1852. 32 p.
Microforme: ICMH collection de microfiches ; no 45677; ISBN: 0-665-45677-8. 1 microfiche (21 images).
Suppléments:
... : *Premier supplément.* 1903. 136 p.
... : *Deuxième supplément.* Impr. Chassé, 1906. 19 p.
Localisation: OOU.

— 1900 —

6753 **Catalogue of books in the library of late Right Hon. Sir John A. Macdonald.** Ottawa: [s.n.], 1900. 69 p.
Note: Microform: CIHM Microfiche series ; no. 09333; ISBN: 0-665-09333-0. 1 microfiche (42 fr.).
Location: OOA.

— 1904 —

6754 **Masson, Louis François Rodrigue**
Catalogue of the late Hon. L.R. Masson's magnificent private library: to be sold at public auction on Saturday, Monday, Tuesday, 9th, 11th, 12th April 1904, at 2:30 and 7:45 p.m. each day, at the residence, 286 Prince Arthur Street, Montreal, Canada. [Montreal]: Imp. La Patrie, 1904. 153 p.
Note: 2,371 entries.– Canadiana: p. 51-153.
Location: OONL.

— 1906 —

6755 **Bourinot, Sir John George**
The library of the late Sir John Bourinot containing rare books, pamphlets and maps relating to the progress of geographical discovery and the history of Canada, including many relating to the American Revolution and the history of America in colonial times. New York: Anderson Auction, 1906. [2], 175, [1] p.
Note: 1,576 entries.
Location: OONL.

— 1913 —

6756 **Gagnon, Philéas**
Essai de bibliographie canadienne: inventaire d'une bibliothèque comprenant imprimés, manuscrits, estampes, etc., relatifs à l'histoire du Canada et des pays adjacents: avec des notes bibliographiques. Québec: L'Auteur, 1895-1913. 2 vol.: ill., fac-sims.
Note: Vol. 1: 5,018 entrées; vol. 2: 2,841 entrées.
Titre de vol. 2: *Essai ... ajoutés à la collection Gagnon, depuis 1895 à 1909 inclusivement, d'après les notes bibliographiques et le catalogue de l'auteur.* Préface de l'échevin Victor Morin. Publié par la cité de Montréal sous la direction de Frédéric Villeneuve, Bibliothécaire en Chef. Montréal: 1913.
Microforme:
Vol. 1: ICMH collection de microfiches ; no 03756; ISBN: 0-665-03756-2. 8 microfiches (385 images).
Vol. 2: ICMH collection de microfiches ; no 03757; ISBN: 0-665-03757-0. 6 microfiches (257 images).
Localisation: OONL.

— 1916 —

6757 **Canada. Archives publiques**
Catalogue des brochures, journaux et rapports dans les Archives publiques du Canada, 1611-1867, avec index. 2e éd. [Ottawa: Impr. du Roi, 1916]. 471 p.
Note: 2,931 entrées.– Compilé par Norman Fee.
Édition antérieure: *Catalogue des brochures, journaux et rapports déposés aux Archives canadiennes, 1611-1867, suivi*

d'un index. 1911. 230 p.– 1,454 entrées.
English title: *Catalogue of pamphlets, journals and reports in the Public Archives of Canada, 1611-1867, with index.*
Localisation: OONL.

6758 **Canada. Public Archives**
Catalogue of pamphlets, journals and reports in the Public Archives of Canada, 1611-1867. 2nd ed. Ottawa: Taché, 1916. 471 p.
Note: 2,931 entries.– Chronological listing, with index.– Prepared by Norman Fee.
Titre en français: *Catalogue des brochures, journaux et rapports dans les Archives publiques du Canada, 1611-1867, avec index.*
Previous edition: 1911. 230 p.– 1,454 entries.
Location: OONL.

— 1931 —

6759 **Acadia University. Library**
Catalogue of books, manuscripts, maps and documents in the William Inglis Morse Collection, 1926-1931. London: Curwen, 1931. vi, 85 p.: front.
Note: Location: OONL.

6760 **Morin, Victor**
The American portion of the historical library of Victor Morin, comprising American voyages and explorations, Canadiana, Indian manuscripts by Jesuit fathers, Jesuit relations, etc., sold by his order. New York: American Art Association, Anderson Galleries, 1931. 72 p., 2 l. of pl.: ill.
Note: 337 entries.
Microform: Montréal: Bibliothèque national du Québec, 1987. 1 microfiche.
Location: OONL.

— 1932 —

6761 **Canada. Public Archives**
Catalogue of pamphlets in the Public Archives of Canada: with index; prepared by Magdalen Casey, Librarian/Catalogue des brochures aux Archives publiques du Canada: avec index; préparé par Magdalen Casey, Bibliothécaire. Ottawa: King's Printer, 1931-1932. 2 vol. (Publications of the Public Archives of Canada ; no. 13)
Note: Vol. 1: 1493-1877.– 4,260 entries.– Chronological arrangement.– Reproduces verbatim full title page of each pamphlet, with note on format and pagination.– Author and subject indexes.– Vol. 2: 1878-1931.– 5,812 entries.– Chronological arrangement.– Author and subject indexes.– Text in English and French/texte en français et en anglais.
Location: OONL.

6762 **Québec (Province). Bibliothèque de la Législature**
Catalogue de la bibliothèque de la Législature de la province de Québec. Québec: Paradis, Imprimeur du Roi, 1932. xxxii, 293 p.
Note: Préparé sous la direction de l'Honorable T.–D. Bouchard.– "Première partie contient tous les ouvrages canadiens, moins ceux ayant trait au droit."
Éditions antérieures:
Québec: Bibliothèque de la Législature, 1903. 746 p.
1884. 258 p.
Microforme: ICMH collection de microfiches ; no 61041; ISBN: 0-665-61041-6. 3 microfiches (138 images).
Catalogue de la bibliothèque de la Législature de Québec. Lévis: [s.n.], 1873. 536 p.– Compilé par L. Pamphile

Lemay.
Microforme: ICMH collection de microfiches ; no 61038; ISBN: 0-665-61038-6. 6 microfiches (284 images).
Localisation: OONL.

— 1933 —

6763 **Stewart, Sheila I.**
A catalogue of the Akins Collection of books and pamphlets. Halifax: Imperial Publishing Co., 1933. 206 p. (Publications of the Public Archives of Nova Scotia ; no. 1)
Note: Approx. 2,000 entries.– Thomas Beamish Akins Collection of historical books and pamphlets relating principally to British North America.
Location: OONL.

— 1937 —

6764 **Royal Commonwealth Society. Library**
Subject catalogue of the Library of the Royal Empire Society, formerly Royal Colonial Institute, by Evans Lewin. [London: The Society], 1930-1937. 4 vol.
Note: Vol. 3: *The Dominion of Canada and its provinces, The Dominion of Newfoundland, The West Indies and colonial America.* [London]: 1932. xix, 822 p.– Approx. 25,000 entries on Canada.
Location: OONL.

— 1938 —

6765 **Acadia University. Library**
A catalogue of the Eric R. Dennis collection of Canadiana in the library of Acadia University. Wolfville, N.S.: The University, 1938. [vi], 212 p.
Note: Approx. 5,500 entries.– Covers from 1618 to the 1930s.– Excludes reprints and extracts from periodicals, transactions of societies, railway guide books, election leaflets and pamphlets, most federal government publications.
Location: OONL.

— 1949 —

6766 **Harvard University. Library**
The Canadian collection at Harvard University. Cambridge, Mass.: Harvard University Printing Office, 1944-1949. 6 vol.
Note: Edited by William Inglis Morse.
Location: OOCC.

— 1953 —

6767 **Nova Scotia Research Foundation**
A catalogue of books in the library of Nova Scotia Research Foundation. Halifax, N.S.: Imperial Press, 1953. 62 p.
Note: Approx. 1,500 entries.
Location: OONL.

— 1961 —

6768 **New York Public Library. Reference Department**
Dictionary catalog of the history of the Americas. Boston: G.K. Hall, 1961. 28 vol.
Note: Approx. 600,000 entries.– Reproduction of catalogue cards of comprehensive collection of Canadiana.– Includes books, periodical articles, essays in collections.– Excludes biography, guidebooks, economic history, naval history, slavery, genealogy, maps, broadsides, newspapers, manuscripts.– Dictionary arrangement provides access by author, title, subject.
Supplement: ... . *First supplement.* 1973. 9 vol.; ISBN: 0-8161-0771-8. Covers all additions up to December 31, 1971.

Location: OONL.

6769 **Royal Commonwealth Society. Library**
Biography catalogue of the Library of the Royal Commonwealth Society. London: Royal Commonwealth Society, 1961. xxiii, 511 p.
Note: Books, articles, archival material, government publications.– Books published to fall of 1960, periodicals to end of 1959.– Includes personal bibliographies in addition to materials of strictly biographical nature.– Collective bibliographies arranged in geographic divisions with index to individual biographies.
Location: OONL.

— 1963 —

6770 **Philipps-Universität Marburg. Universitätsbibliothek**
Katalog der Kanada-Bibliothek: Stand Frühjahr 1963. Marburg: Der Bibliothek, 1963. 75 p.
Note: Approx. 1,350 entries.
Location: OONL.

— 1964 —

6771 **Great Britain. Colonial Office. Library**
Catalogue of the Colonial Office Library, London. Boston: G.K. Hall, 1964. 15 vol.
Note: 176,000 entries.– Books, pamphlets, reports, government publications, periodical articles and titles concerning present and former countries of the Commonwealth with imprint dates from mid-seventeenth century.– Excludes legislation, official gazettes, departmental reports, estimates, debates, treaties, sessional papers.
Supplements:
First supplement: .... 1967. v, 894 p.– 18,900 entries.– Materials added from 1963 to the end of August 1967.
Second supplement: Catalogue of the Colonial Office Library (Foreign and Commonwealth Office), London. 1972. 2 vol.; ISBN: 0-8161-0843-9.– 25, 557 entries.– Lists materials added from September 1967 to the end of April 1971.
Location: OONL.

— 1965 —

6772 **Lande, Lawrence M.**
The Lawrence Lande Collection of Canadiana in the Redpath Library of McGill University; a bibliography, collected, arranged and annotated by Lawrence Lande, with an introduction by Edgar Andrew Collard. Montreal: Lawrence Lande Foundation for Canadian Historical Research, 1965. xxxv, 301 p.: ill., facsims., maps.
Note: 2,328 entries.– Books, pamphlets, broadsides, maps, manuscripts, letters, relating to Canada, mainly before Confederation; western Canada up to 1900.
Supplement: *Rare and unusual Canadiana: first supplement to the Lande bibliography.* Montreal: McGill University; 1971. xx, 779 p.: facsims. (Lawrence Lande Foundation for Historical Research ; no. 6).
Location: OONL.

— 1966 —

6773 **Canadian Broadcasting Corporation. Research Department. Library**
CBC Research Library: a classified list of books held, October 1966. Ottawa: [s.n.], 1966. v, 122 p.
Note: Emphasis on aspects of broadcasting and communication, with substantial listings in fields of education, psychology, history, science, statistics.– Includes publications in English and French.
Location: OONL.

— 1967 —

6774 Cameron, William J.; McKnight, George
Robert Addison's library: a short-title catalogue of the books brought to Upper Canada in 1792 by the first missionary sent out to the Niagara frontier by the Society for the Propagation of the Gospel. Hamilton, Ont.: Printed at McMaster University for the Synod of the Diocese of Niagara, 1967. liv, 98 p.: ill., facsims.
Note: Location: OONL.

6775 Langhammer, Else Birgit
The William Palmer Witton Canadian collection. Hamilton, Ont.: [s.n.], 1967. 24, 14, [13] l.
Note: Location: OONL.

— 1968 —

6776 Harvard University. Library
Canadian history and literature: classification schedule, classified listing by call number, alphabetical listing by author or title, chronological listing. Cambridge, Mass.: Published by the Harvard University Library, distributed by the Harvard University Press, 1968. 411 p. (Widener Library shelflist ; 20)
Note: Approx. 10,200 entries.– Works on Canadian civilization, government and administration, religious affairs, geography and travel, literature in English and French, literary histories, anthologies, works by and about individual authors.
Location: OONL.

— 1971 —

6777 Royal Commonwealth Society. Library
Subject catalogue of the Royal Commonwealth Society, London. Boston, Mass.: G.K. Hall, 1971. 7 vol.
Note: Vol. 5: *The Americas*. xxiii, 713 p.– 15,000 entries on Canada, provinces and territories.– Vol. 7: *Biography, voyages and travels, World War I, World War II*. iii, 382 p.– Approx. 10,000 entries.– Extensive listings relating to Canada.– Books, pamphlets, official publications, periodical articles, chapters in books.
Supplement: ... : *First supplement*. 1977. 2 vol.; ISBN: 0-8161-0075-6 (set).– 11,700 entries.– Additions to the Library between March 1971 and December 1976.
Location: OONL.

6778 Spratt, Albert A.
The Ruth Konrad Collection of Canadiana: a descriptive catalogue. [Mississauga, Ont.]: Mississauga Public Library Board, 1971. 100 p.
Note: 647 entries.– Emphasis on four general areas: Pre-Confederation Ontario (pioneer life, Indians, Loyalists, War of 1812); southern Ontario local histories and area studies; Canadian literature pre-1945; Canadian art.– Includes books, brochures, manuscripts, documents, maps, broadsides, photographs related to Peel County, works by local writers and artists.
Location: OONL.

— 1972 —

6779 Université d'Ottawa. Bibliothèque générale. Informathèque
Catalogue des pamphlets et brochures de type Canadiana: projet O1 – CRC. [Ottawa]: Informathèque, Bibliothèque générale, 1972. ii, 130 f.
Note: 1,050 entrées.– La période couverte est de 1612 à 1971.
Localisation: OONL.

— 1975 —

6780 Université d'Ottawa. Centre de recherche en civilisation canadienne-française. Bibliothèque
Livres conservés au Centre de recherche en civilisation canadienne-française. Ottawa: Centre de recherche en civilisation canadienne-française, Université d'Ottawa, [1975]. 19 f. (Documents de travail du Centre de recherche en civilisation canadienne-française ; 3)
Note: 150 entrées.– Ouvrages de référence et volumes de base relatifs à l'histoire et la littérature du Canada français.
Localisation: OONL.

— 1977 —

6781 McMaster University. Library
Canadian pamphlets: a subject listing of the holdings of McMaster University Library. Hamilton, Ont.: McMaster University Library, 1976-1977. 3 vol.
Note: Approx. 2,800 entries, arranged in 415 numbered subject categories, with an author/title index.– Deals with aspects of Canadian history, literature, social conditions, political development over a period of 150 years.– Includes local histories, some French-Canadian pamphlets.– 250 items are dated pre-Confederation.– Based on a catalogue prepared by Susan Bellingham.– Compiled by Charlotte Stewart and Renu Barrett.
Published as three special numbers of *McMaster University Library Research News*: Vol. 3, no. 6 (December 1976); vol. 4, no. 1 (April 1977); vol. 4, no. 2 (July 1977).
Location: OONL.

— 1978 —

6782 Ducharme, Jacques, et al.
Inventaire des brochures conservées au Service des archives, 1771-1967. [Montréal]: Université du Québec à Montréal, Secrétariat général, 1978. 431 p. (Publication / Service des archives, Université du Québec à Montréal ; no 5)
Note: 2,425 titres de brochures, dont la plupart ont été publiées au Canada et traitent de sujets d'intérêt canadien.– Index: chronologique, auteurs.
Localisation: OONL.

6783 Québec (Province). Bibliothèque de la Législature. Service de référence
La collection de Pierre-Joseph-Olivier Chauveau, premier ministre du Québec, 1867-1873: exposition à la Bibliothèque de l'Assemblée nationale du Québec. Québec: Bibliothèque de l'Assemblée nationale, Service de référence, 1978. 38 p.: ill.
Note: 53 entrées.– Exposition de la collection des livres de Pierre-Joseph-Olivier Chauveau présenté à l'occasion des fêtes du patrimoine.– Section IV: "Ouvrages européens sur l'Amérique et sur le Québec, XVIe-XIXe siècles."- Section V: "Ouvrages et imprimés québécois, XVIIIe-XIXe siècles."
Localisation: OONL.

— 1979 —

6784 Canada. Public Archives. Library
Catalogue of the Public Archives Library/Catalogue de la Bibliothèque des Archives publiques. Boston, Mass.: G.K. Hall, 1979. 12 vol.; ISBN: 0-8161-0316-X.
Note: Reproduction of author-title catalogue and a chronological catalogue of the pamphlet collection.– Printed primary and secondary source material covering traditional areas of Canadian history: books on

cartography, discoveries and explorations of New France and North America; journals and diaries of early explorers, missionaries, travellers; works on politics, commerce, education, transportation, religion, works of biography.
Location: OONL.

— 1980 —

6785 **Maurey, Pierre**
"Lowry's library: an annotated catalogue of Lowry's books at the University of British Columbia."
In: *Malcolm Lowry Newsletter*; No. 7 (Fall 1980) p. 3-10.; ISSN: 0228-8427.
Note: Location: OONL.

— 1981 —

6786 **Pulp and Paper Research Institute of Canada**
List of library books and periodicals [Pulp and Paper Research Institute of Canada]. Pointe Claire, Quebec: The Institute, 1981. 254 p.
Note: Previous editions:
1972. iii, 210 p.
1967. v, 145 p.
1964. iii, 131 p.
Location: NBFU.

— 1982 —

6787 **Le Moine, Roger**
Le catalogue de la bibliothèque de Louis-Joseph Papineau. Ottawa: Centre de recherche en civilisation canadienne-française, Université d'Ottawa, 1982. 140 p. (Documents de travail du Centre de recherche en civilisation canadienne-française ; 21)
Note: 3,087 entrées.– Comprend les sections: "Droit du Bas-Canada et du Canada," et "Bibliotheca americana par ordre méthodique."
Localisation: OONL.

6788 **Ryder, Carolyn**
The Coutts collection: a selected descriptive bibliography. Calgary: University of Calgary Libraries, Special Collections Division, 1982. 36 p.: ill., facsim. (Occasional paper / University of Calgary Libraries, Special Collections Division ; no. 8); ISBN: 0-88953-034-3.
Note: 58 entries.– Emphasis on Canadiana.– Detailed descriptive annotations, including distinguishing traits of Coutts collection copy.
Location: OONL.

— 1984 —

6789 **York University (Toronto, Ont.). Libraries**
Catalogue: Canadian pamphlet collection/Catalogue: Collection des brochures canadiennes. Toronto: York University Libraries, 1984. 3 vol.
Note: Approx. 5,500 entries.– Pamphlets published primarily in Ontario and Quebec from about 1900 to 1969.– Includes brochures, leaflets, propaganda and religious tracts, broadsides, pamphlets of 100 pages or less.
Location: OWA.

— 1985 —

6790 **Olivier, Réjean**
Catalogue de la collection François Lanoue, prêtre, auteur et historien, faisant partie de la bibliothèque de la famille Olivier de Joliette. Joliette, Québec: R. Olivier, 1985. 18 f.; ISBN: 2-920249-91-6.
Note: 48 entrées.
Localisation: OONL.

— 1988 —

6791 **Université de Montréal. Service des bibliothèques. Collections spéciales**
Catalogue de la collection de Canadiana Louis Melzack. Montréal: Direction des services aux usagers, Service des bibliothèques, Université de Montréal, 1988. 3 vol.: ill., facsims.; ISBN: 0-88529-064-X.
Note: 3,706 entrées.– La section des imprimés, qui constitue la plus grande partie du catalogue, renferme des volumes, des brochures et des proclamations publiés pour la plupart au Canada, aux 18e et 19e siècles. La langue française et d'autres langues y sont représentées, mais la majorité des monographies est en anglais.– Comprend les livres de piété, des ordonnances, des ouvrages sur l'éducation et la jurisprudence, des almanachs, périodiques, manuscrits.
Localisation: OONL.

— 1989 —

6792 **Université de Montréal. Service des bibliothèques. Collections spéciales**
Catalogue des imprimés de la Collection Baby. Montréal: Direction des services aux usagers, Service des bibliothèques, Université de Montréal, 1989. 3 vol.: ill., fac-sims.; ISBN: 2-911185-00-8.
Note: 3,252 entrées.– Tome I: *Description bibliographique complète.*– Tome II et III: *Index*: auteur, titre, chonologique, illustrations, thématique.
Localisation: OONL.

— 1990 —

6793 **Holyoke, Francesca**
The Maritime Pamphlet Collection: an annotated catalogue. Fredericton, N.B.: University of New Brunswick Libraries, 1990. x, 241, 38 p.: ill.
Note: 1,502 entries.
Location: OONL.

— 1991 —

6794 **Ralph Pickard Bell Library**
The Edgar and Dorothy Davidson Collection of Canadiana at Mount Allison University. Sackville, N.B.: Centre for Canadian Studies, Mount Allison University, 1991. xxiv, 418 p.: ill.; ISBN: 0-919107-30-3.
Note: 579 entries.– Listing of rare first edition books and imprints from the seventeenth through the nineteenth centuries, arranged in five major subject divisions: "French and French influence," "English and English influence," "Exploration of the Arctic," "Western frontier," "Early Canadian imprints to 1820."- Indexes: author-title, subject, genre, maps, cartographer, illustrator, publisher, printer, bookplate and inscription.
Location: OONL.

6795 **Raymond H. Fogler Library**
The Canadian collection of the Fogler Library, University of Maine: a preliminary guide to research materials. Orono, Me.: The Library, 1991. i, 49 p.
Note: Location: OONL.

Individuals

Particuliers

Individuals

Particuliers

6796 **Abbott, Maude Elizabeth**
Publications of ... [Maude Elizabeth Abbott]. [S.l.: s.n.],
1940. 2 vol.
Note: Vol. 1: nos. 1-57, 1899-1923; vol. 2: nos. 58-103, 1924-
1940.
Location: QMMM.

6797 **Hulchanski, John David**
Thomas Adams: a biographical and bibliographical
guide. [Toronto]: Department of Urban and Regional
Planning, University of Toronto, 1978. 42 p. (Papers on
planning and design / Department of Urban and
Regional Planning, University of Toronto ; no. 15)
Note: Approx. 350 entries.– Works published by Adams
(books and articles) about Canadian housing and
planning, housing and planning in general, architecture,
land, transportation, zoning.
Location: OONL.

6798 **Judd, William W.**
Annotated catalogue and index of columns on nature
written by John W. Agnos (1927-1991) for *London Free
Press*, 1989-1991. London, Ont.: Phelps Publishing, 1991.
20 p.
Note: Location: OONL.

6799 **"William John Alexander: check-list of writings."**
In: *University of Toronto Quarterly*; Vol. 14, no. 1 (October
1944) p. 32-33.; ISSN: 0042-0247.
Note: Location: AEU.

6800 **Ami, Henri Marc**
List of contributions to geology, palaeontology, &c., by
Mr. H.M. Ami, of the Geological Survey of Canada,
Ottawa, from 1882 to 1901. [Montreal: Printed by the
Canada Engraving & Lithographing Co., 1901]. 15 l.
Note: 207 entries.– Books, contributions to scientific and
mining journals, book reviews, obituaries, papers read at
various societies.
Location: OONL.

6801 **Campbell, C.A.**
"Bibliography of Major André."
In: *The crisis of the revolution: being the story of Arnold and
André*, by William Abbatt. New York: W. Abbatt, 1899. P.
[101]-111.
Note: Microform: CIHM Microfiche series ; no. 01178;
ISBN: 0-665-01178-4. 4 microfiches (156 fr.).
Location: OTU.

6802 **Martel, Jacinthe**
"Bibliographie analytique d'Hubert Aquin, 1947-1982."
Dans: *Revue d'histoire littéraire du Québec et du Canada
français*; No 7 (hiver-printemps 1984) p. 80-229.; ISSN:
0713-7958.
Note: 1,199 entrées.– Bibliographies, biographie, oeuvres
d'Aquin, études et critiques.
Supplément.: "Mise à jour (1983-1984) de la bibliographie
d'Hubert Aquin". No 10 (été-automne 1985) p. 75-112.
Localisation: OONL.

6803 **Martel, Jacinthe**
Bibliographie analytique d'Hubert Aquin, 1947-1980
[microforme]. [Montréal]: Service des Archives,
Université de Montréal, 1984. 1 bobine de microfilm.
Note: 1,092 entrées.– "Bibliographies," "Biographie,"
"Oeuvres d'Aquin" (romans, nouvelles, articles, oeuvres
dramatiques, filmographie, emissions de radio ou de
télévision, conférences et discours, entrevues), "Études et
critiques."
Mémoire (M.A.), Université de Montréal.
Localisation: OONL.

6804 **Duke, David**
Violet Archer. Don Mills, Ont.: PRO Canada, 1983. 15 p.:
music, port.
Note: Bio-bibliography.– List of works, p. 6-13.–
Discography, p. 13.
Location: OONL.

6805 **Hartig, Linda Bishop**
Violet Archer: a bio-bibliography. New York:
Greenwood Press, 1991. viii, 153 p.: port. (Bio-
bibliographies in music ; no. 41; ISSN: 0742-6968); ISBN:
0-313-26408-2.
Note: 569 entries.– Contains four sections: "Biography,"
"Works and performance," "Discography," and
"Bibliography."- The bibliography is an annotated list of
writings about Archer's life and works, including
reviews of performances and recordings.
Location: OONL.

6806 **Fairbanks, Carol**
"Margaret Atwood: a bibliography of criticism."
In: *Bulletin of Bibliography*; Vol. 6, no. 2 (April-June
1979) p. 85-90.; ISSN: 0190-745X.
Note: Location: OONL.

6807 **Horne, Alan J.**
"A preliminary checklist of writings by and about
Margaret Atwood."
In: *Canadian Library Journal*; Vol. 31, no. 6 (December
1974) p. 576-592.; ISSN: 0008-4352.
Note: Location: OONL.

6808 **Horne, Alan J.**
"A preliminary checklist of writings by and about
Margaret Atwood."
In: *Malahat Review*; No. 41 (January 1977) p. 195-222.;
ISSN: 0025-1216.
Note: Listing of books, contributions to books,
periodicals, introductions to books by other authors,
recordings, writing about Atwood and her work, book
reviews, selected list of anthologies with contributions by
Atwood.– Excludes newspaper articles.
Location: OONL.

6809 **Horne, Alan J.**
"Margaret Atwood: an annotated bibliography (prose)."
In: *The annotated bibliography of Canada's major authors*,
Vol. 1, edited by Robert Lecker and Jack David.
Downsview, Ont.: ECW Press, 1979. P. 13-49.; ISBN: 0-

920802-02-8.
Note: 264 entries.– Works by Atwood: books and manuscripts, contributions to periodicals, books and anthologies; works about Atwood: books, articles, theses, interviews, book reviews.
Location: OONL.

6810 **Horne, Alan J.**
Margaret Atwood: an annotated bibliography (prose). [Downsview, Ont.]: ECW Press, 1979. P. 13-46.; ISBN: 0-920763-48-0.
Note: 264 entries.– Works by Atwood: books and manuscripts, contributions to periodicals, books and anthologies; works about Atwood: books, articles, theses, interviews, book reviews.
Extract from: *The annotated bibliography of Canada's major authors*, Vol. 1, edited by Robert Lecker and Jack David.
Location: OONL.

6811 **Horne, Alan J.**
Margaret Atwood: an annotated bibliography (poetry). Downsview, Ont.: ECW Press, c1980. P. 13-53.; ISBN: 0-920763-49-9.
Note: 482 entries.– Works by Atwood: books, broadsides, manuscripts, contributions to periodicals and books, audio and audio-visual recordings, graphic work; works about Atwood: books, articles, theses, interviews, book reviews.
Extract from: *The annotated bibliography of Canada's major authors*, Vol. 2, edited by Robert Lecker and Jack David.
Location: OONL.

6812 **Horne, Alan J.**
"Margaret Atwood: an annotated bibliography (poetry)."
In: *The annotated bibliography of Canada's major authors*, Vol. 2, edited by Robert Lecker and Jack David. Toronto: ECW Press, 1980. P. 13-53.; ISBN: 0-920802-40-0.
Note: 482 entries.– Works by Atwood: books, broadsides, manuscripts, contributions to periodicals and books, audio and audio-visual recordings, graphic work; works about Atwood: books, articles, theses, interviews, book reviews.
Location: OONL.

6813 **McCombs, Judith; Palmer, Carole L.**
Margaret Atwood: a reference guide. Boston: G.K. Hall, 1991. xxxi, 735 p.; ISBN: 0-8161-8940-4.
Note: Approx. 2,000 entries.– Chronological listing of writings about Atwood from 1962 to 1988.– Includes articles in literary journals, newspaper articles, books, essays, theses, interviews and reviews.
Location: OONL.

6814 **Hayne, David M.**
"Bibliographie critique des *Anciens Canadiens* (1863) de Philippe-Joseph Aubert de Gaspé."
Dans: *Cahiers de la Société bibliographique du Canada*; Vol. 3 (1964) p. 38-60.; ISSN: 0067-6896.
Note: Liste par ordre chronologique des éditions des *Anciens Canadiens*, traductions en langue anglaise, reproductions partielles.– Liste par ordre alphabétique d'auteurs des principaux livres et articles consacrés aux *Anciens Canadiens*.
Localisation: OONL.

6815 **Pleins feux sur Claude Aubry, 1949-1979/Something about Claude Aubry, 1949-1979.** [Ottawa: Bibliothèque publique d'Ottawa, [1979]. 5 f.
Note: Localisation: OONL.

6816 **Brault, Lucien**
Francis-J. Audet et son oeuvre: bio-bibliographie. Ottawa: [Imprimerie Leclerc], 1940. 92 p.: portr.
Note: Manuscrits, livres, brochures, collaborations, publications de sociétés, articles de revues et journaux.
Localisation: OONL.

6817 **Sirko, Hlib**
Essai de bio-bibliographie du R.P. Thomas-André Audet, o.p. Montréal: [s.n.], 1959. xxxiii, 68 f. port.
Note: Livres, articles, études, recensions, sermons, imprimés ou manuscrits par Audet.
Localisation: OONL.

6818 **Mansbridge, Francis**
"Margaret Avison: a checklist."
In: *Canadian Library Journal*; Vol. 34, no. 6 (December 1977) p. 431-436.; ISSN: 0008-4352.
Note: Works of Avison (books, anthologies, uncollected poems, book reviews), writings about Avison (articles, book reviews, theses).
Location: OONL.

6819 **Mansbridge, Francis**
"Margaret Avison: an annotated bibliography."
In: *The annotated bibliography of Canada's major authors*, Vol. 6, edited by Robert Lecker and Jack David. Toronto: ECW Press, 1985. P. 13-66.; ISBN: 0-920802-93-1.
Note: 422 entries.– Works by Avison: books (poetry, history, compilation, biography, translation), criticism, manuscripts, contributions to periodicals and books (poems, translations and adaptations, essays, book reviews, movie reviews, letters, short stories), audio-visual material; works about Avison: book, articles and sections of books, theses and dissertations, interviews, poems, selected book reviews.
Location: OONL.

— B —

6820 Alfred Goldsworthy Bailey: a checklist of his work and related criticism. Fredericton, N.B.: Department of Public Relations and Development, University of New Brunswick, 1978. vii, 31 p.
Note: Approx. 400 entries.– Works by Bailey: books, works edited, poems, articles, essays and pamphlets, book reviews, sound recordings; reviews of Bailey's work, biographical references.– Compiled and edited by the Reference Department, Harriet Irving Library.– Biographical sketch of Bailey by Francis A. Coghlan.
Location: OONL.

6821 **Bibliographie de M.C. Baillairgé: extraite du volume des "Transactions" pour 1894, de la Société royale du Canada: addenda jusqu'à ce jour, Québec, mai 1899.** [Québec: s.n., 1899]. xv p.
Note: Microforme: ICMH collection de microfiches ; 07068; ISBN: 0-665-07068-3. 1 microfiche (12 images).
Localisation: OONL.

6822 **Olivier, Réjean**
Notre polygraphe québécois: Frédéric-Alexandre Baillairgé, prêtre. L'Assomption [Québec]: Collège de l'Assomption, Bibliothèque, 1976. 43 f.: fac-sim.
Note: Sixième partie: "Bibliographie des oeuvres de Baillairgé classées par ordre chronologique."
Localisation: OONL.

6823 **Watson, Lawrence W.**
"Francis Bain, geologist."
In: *Proceedings and Transactions of the Royal Society of*

Canada; Series 2, vol. 9, section 4 (1903) p. 135-142.; ISSN: 0316-4616.

Note: Location: AEU.

6824 **Mertens, Susan**
Michael Conway Baker. Don Mills, Ont.: PRO Canada, 1984. 7, [1] p.: music, port.

Note: Bio-bibliography.– List of works, p. 5-[8].– Discography, p. [8].

Location: OONL.

6825 **Drumbolis, Nicky**
Nelson Ball cited: a bibliophilography from stock. Toronto: Letters Book Shop, [1992]. [182] p.: ill.; ISBN: 0-921688-03-2.

Note: 441 entries.– Annotated listing of works by Ball: separate works, contributions to books and periodicals, translations, edited publications, productions, booklists; works about Ball: reviews, publication announcements, biographical references, bibliographical references.– Includes an index of poems published in books and pamphlets.

Location: OONL.

6826 **Cardin, Clarisse**
Bio-bibliographie de Marius Barbeau, précédée d'un hommage à Marius Barbeau par Luc Lacourcière et Félix-Antoine Savard. [Montréal]: Éditions Fides, 1947. 96 p.

Note: 755 entrées.

Localisation: OONL.

6827 **Cardin, Clarisse**
"Bio-bibliographie de Marius Barbeau."
Dans: *Archives de folklore*; Vol. 2 (1947) p. 17-96.; ISSN: 0085-5243.

Note: Localisation: OONL.

6828 **Katz, Israel J.**
"Marius Barbeau, 1883-1969: [Bibliography of ethnomusicological works]."
In: *Ethnomusicology*; Vol. 14, no. 1 (January 1970) p. 129-142.; ISSN: 0014-1836.

Note: Chronological listing, 1915-1965, of Barbeau's contributions to ethnomusicology.

Location: OONL.

6829 **Landry, Renée**
Bibliographie de Marius Barbeau. [Ottawa]: Musée national de l'Homme, 1969. 16 f.

Note: 174 entrées.– Comprend manuscrits, livres et brochures, tiré à part, articles (revues et journaux).

Localisation: OONL.

6830 **Summers, Frances J.; Pouliot, Thérèse**
"Bibliographie de Yves Beauchemin."
Dans: *Voix et Images*; Vol. 12, no 3 (printemps 1987) p. 416-428.; ISSN: 0318-9201.

Note: Oeuvres d'Yves Beauchemin (romans, contes et nouvelles, films, articles divers); articles sur Beauchemin et ses oeuvres.

Localisation: AEU.

6831 **Goulet, Jean**
"L'oeuvre littéraire juridique de Monsieur le professeur Marie-Louis Beaulieu."
Dans: *Cahiers de droit*; Vol. 9, nos 3-4 (1967-68) p. 341-348.; ISSN: 0007-974X.

Note: 75 entrées.

Localisation: OONL.

6832 **Bélanger, Lise-Anne**
Bio-bibliographie de Michel Beaulieu, écrivain, 1941-1985 [microforme]. Montréal: Service des archives, Université de Montréal, 1988. 1 bobine de microfilm.

Note: Bibliographie analytique, 1959-1985: livres, livres d'artistes, poèmes et prose (publiés dans des recueils collectifs, anthologies, revues, journaux), articles de critiques, textes et adaptations radiophoniques, traductions, bibliographie sur Beaulieu et son oeuvre, documents audiovisuels.

M.A. en études françaises, Université de Montréal, 1987.

Location: OONL.

6833 **MacMillan, Rick**
John Beckwith. Don Mills, Ont.: PRO Canada, 1983. 11 p.: port.

Note: Bio-bibliography.– List of works, p. 6-10.– Discography, p. 11.

Location: OONL.

6834 **Wolfenden, Madge**
"Alexander Begg versus Alexander Begg."
In: *British Columbia Historical Quarterly*; Vol. 1, no. 2 (April 1937) p. 133-139.; ISSN: 0706-7666.

Note: Biographies and bibliographies of Begg the journalist (founder and editor of the *British Columbia Mining Record*, 1895-1897) and Begg the historian (author of *History of British Columbia from its earliest discovery to the present time*. Toronto: Briggs, 1894).

Location: OONL.

6835 **Scientific publications of Robert Bell, B.A.Sc., M.D., L.L.D., F.R.S.C., assistant director of the Geological Survey, 1857-1894.** [S.l.: s.n.], 1894. 12 p.

Note: Microform: CIHM Microfiche series ; no. 00211; ISBN: 0-665-00211-4. 1 microfiche (11 fr.).

Location: OONL.

6836 **Sokoloff, B.A.; Posner, Mark E.**
Saul Bellow: a comprehensive bibliography. Folcroft, Pa.: Folcroft Press, c1971. 49 l.

Note: Approx. 450 entries.– Primary sources (books, short fiction, articles, reviews, interviews) and secondary sources (reviews, books, biographical material, general criticism) of Canadian-born Nobel laureate Bellow.– Limited edition: 150 copies.

Location: OONL.

6837 **Arai, Mary Needler**
"Publications by Edith and-or Cyril Berkeley."
In: *Journal of the Fisheries Research Board of Canada*; Vol. 28, no. 10 (October 1971) p. 1365-1372.; ISSN: 0008-2686.

Note: Location: AEU.

6838 **Frederick Harris Music Co. Limited**
A complete catalogue of the published works of Boris Berlin. Oakville, Ont.: [s.n.], 1965. 8 p.: port.

Note: Location: OONL.

6839 **"Bio-bibliographie [Gérard Bessette]."**
Dans: *Québec littéraire*; No 1 (1974) p. 155-166.; ISSN: 0384-9406.

Note: Localisation: OONL.

6840 **Spencer, Nigel**
"Louis Riel and Norman Bethune: a critical bibliography."
In: *Moosehead Review*; Vol. 3, no. 1 (1982) p. 48-60; No. 7 (1983) p. 29-47.; ISSN: 0228-7404.

Note: Annotated listing of historical, literary and theatrical works about Riel and Bethune.– Includes fiction, poetry, drama, video and film.

Location: OONL.

6841 Walker, Byron Edmund
"List of the published writings of Elkanah Billings, F.G.S., palaeontologist to the Geological Survey of Canada, 1856-1876."
In: *Canadian Record of Science*; Vol. 8, no. 6 (July 1901) p. [366]-388.
Note: Location: OON.

6842 Walker, Byron Edmund
List of the published writings of Elkanah Billings, F.G.S., palaeontologist to the Geological Survey of Canada, 1856-1876. [S.l.: s.n., 1901]. P. [366]-388.
Note: Extract from the *Canadian Record of Science*, Vol. 8, no. 6, for July, 1901, issued 10th August, 1901.
Location: OONL.

6843 Harrison, Dallas
"Sandra Birdsell: an annotated bibliography."
In: *Essays on Canadian Writing*; No. 48 (Winter 1992-1993) p. 170-219.; ISSN: 0316-0300.
Note: 235 entries.
Location: OONL.

6844 Noel-Bentley, Peter
Earle Birney: an annotated bibliography. Downsview, Ont.: ECW Press, c1983. [115] p.; ISBN: 0-920763-50-2.
Note: 1,023 entries.– Works by Birney: books (novels, poetry, stories and sketches, criticism), manuscripts, contributions to periodicals and books, radio material, audio recordings; works about Birney: books, articles and sections of books, theses, books reviews.
Extract from: *The annotated bibliography of Canada's major authors*, Vol. 4, edited by Robert Lecker and Jack David.
Location: OONL.

6845 Noel-Bentley, Peter
"Earle Birney: an annotated bibliography."
In: *The annotated bibliography of Canada's major authors*, Vol. 4, edited by Robert Lecker and Jack David. Downsview, Ont.: ECW Press, c1983. P. 13-128.; ISBN: 0-920802-52-4.
Note: 1,023 entries.– Works by Birney: books (novels, poetry, stories and sketches, criticism), manuscripts, contributions to periodicals and books, radio material, audio recordings; works about Birney: books, articles and sections of books, theses, book reviews.
Location: OONL.

6846 Noel-Bentley, Peter; Birney, Earle
"Earle Birney: a bibliography in progress, 1923-1969."
In: *West Coast Review*; Vol. 5, no. 2 (October 1970) p. 45-53.; ISSN: 0043-311X.
Note: Writings by Birney: books (poetry, novels, criticism, editions); individual items (poems, stories, selected articles and essays); writings about Birney: selected articles, book reviews, biographical information.
Location: OONL.

6847 Performing Rights Organization of Canada
Keith Bissell. Don Mills, Ont.: PRO Canada, 1988. 19 p.
Note: Bio-bibliography.– List of compositions, p. 6-17.– Discography, p. 17-18.
Location: OONL.

6848 Yukon Archives
Martha Louise Black: a bibliography of sources available in the Yukon Archives. Whitehorse: Yukon Archives, 1983. ii, 9 l.; ISBN: 1-55018-039-8.
Note: Location: OONL.

6849 Colombo, John Robert
Blackwood's books: a bibliography devoted to Algernon Blackwood. Toronto: Hounslow Press, 1981. 119 p.; ISBN: 0-88882-055-0.
Note: 58 entries.– Documents Blackwood's work in English language.– Lists impressions, reprints, new editions, in such types of works as autobiography, plays, novels, children's fantasies, story collections.– Appendix gives details of Blackwood's years in Canada and influence on his work, Canadian settings and allusions.
Location: OONL.

6850 Boivin, Aurélien; Robert, Lucie; Major-Lapierre, Ruth
"Bibliographie de Marie-Claire Blais."
Dans: *Voix et Images*; Vol. 8, no 2 (hiver 1983) p. 249-295.; ISSN: 0318-9201.
Note: Oeuvres de Blais, études sur Blais et son oeuvre.
Localisation: AEU.

6851 Fabi, Thérèse
"Biobibliographie: Marie-Claire Blais."
Dans: *Présence francophone*; No 4 (printemps 1972) p. 209-216.; ISSN: 0048-5195.
Note: Localisation: OONL.

6852 Ricouart, Janine
"Bibliographie sur Marie-Claire Blais."
Dans: *Quebec Studies*; Vol. 10 (Spring-Summer 1990) p. 51-59.; ISSN: 0737-3759.
Note: Localisation: OONL.

6853 Duff, Wendy
"Bibliography of the writings of Phyllis Ruth Blakeley."
In: *Nova Scotia Historical Review*; Vol. 7, no. 2 (1987) p. 88-100.; ISSN: 0227-4752.
Note: Listing of the published writings of former Nova Scotia Provincial Archivist Phyllis Blakeley: books, articles (including a separate listing for articles written under pseudonym of Ruth Blake), book reviews, contributions to books and encyclopedias.
Location: AEU.

6854 Blanchard, Raoul
"Liste des travaux de Raoul Blanchard."
Dans: *Cahiers de géographie de Québec*; Vol. 3, no 6 (avril-septembre 1959) p. 35-45.; ISSN: 0007-9766.
Note: Principaux ouvrages de Blanchard, 1902 à juin 1958.
Localisation: OONL.

6855 Brethour, Ross
A Max Boag discography. Aurora, Ont.: Nomadic Record Co., [1981]. 14 l.
Note: Bio-discography of Canadian dance band leader and double bassist Max Boag (also known by pseudonym Harry Glenn).
Location: OONL.

6856 Brunet, Jean
Bio-bibliographie du Révérend père Léo Boismenu. Montréal: Éditions Pilon, 1953. 64 p.: portr.
Note: 125 entrées.
Localisation: OONL.

6857 Caparros, Ernest
"Jean-Charles Bonenfant (1912-1977)."
Dans: *Cahiers de droit*; Vol. 20, nos 1-2 (mars 1979) p. 7-46.; ISSN: 0007-974X.
Note: Bio-bibliographie de Bonenfant.– L'oeuvre juridique: droit constitutionnel, droit parlementaire, esquisses biographiques, collaboration dans des

dictionnaires et encyclopédies, préfaces, chroniques dans le journal *l'Action*, chroniques bibliographiques, chroniques sur le droit québécois.
Localisation: OONL.

6858 **Carlson, Roy L.**
"C.E. Borden's archaeological legacy."
In: *BC Studies*; No. 42 (Summer 1979) p. 3-12.; ISSN: 0005-2949.
Note: Review of Borden's published works: papers on culture history, field work reports, reviews, newsletter articles, popular articles, manuscripts.
Location: AEU.

6859 **Vann, Margaret Jean**
A bibliography and selected source material for the study of Paul-Émile Borduas and his relationship to other French Canadian automatists. [Winnipeg: University of Manitoba], 1964. xi, 98 l.: ill.
Note: Books, periodical articles, reproductions in periodicals, newspaper articles, pamphlets, manuscripts and press releases, films, letters.– Record of Borduas' participation in art exhibitions.– Thesis, Bachelor of Fine Arts, University of Manitoba, 1964.
Location: OONG.

6860 **Pavlovic, Myrianne**
"Bibliographie de Monique Bosco."
Dans: *Voix et Images*; Vol. 9, no 3 (printemps 1984) p. 55-82.; ISSN: 0318-9201.
Note: Écrits de Bosco (romans, récits, nouvelles et textes, poèmes, texte dramatique, textes radiophoniques, communications, articles dans les revues et journaux); études et critiques.
Localisation: AEU.

6861 **Robert, Véronique**
Walter Boudreau. Don Mills, Ont.: PRO Canada, 1984. 7 p.: music, port.
Note: Bio-bibliography.– List of works, p. 5-7.– Discography, p. 7.
Location: OONL.

6862 **Bergevin, André**
"Les oeuvres de Bourassa: index par sujet des ouvrages, articles et conférences."
Dans: *Action nationale*; Vol. 43, no 1 (janvier 1954) p. 199-244.; ISSN: 0001-7469.
Note: Localisation: OONL.

6863 **Bergevin, André; Nish, James Cameron; Bourassa, Anne**
Henri Bourassa: biographie, index des écrits, index de la correspondance publique 1895-1924. Montréal: Éditions de l'Action nationale, 1966. lxii, 150 p.
Note: Ouvrages, brochures, articles, conférences, discours parlementaires, correspondance.
Localisation: OONL.

6864 **Nguyên, Vy-Khanh**
Robert Bourassa. Québec: Division de la référence parlementaire, Bibliothèque de l'Assemblée nationale, 1986. 16 f. (Bibliographie / Bibliothèque de l'Assemblée nationale du Québec ; ISSN: 0836-9100)
Note: Approx. 100 entrées.– Écrits de Bourassa et documentation sur Bourassa (monographies, articles de périodiques).
Localisation: OONL.

6865 **Bibliothèque nationale du Canada**
Arthur S. Bourinot. Ottawa: Bibliothèque nationale du Canada, 1971. 30, 30 p.: ports.
Note: 190 entrées.– Catalogue d'exposition. Texte en français et en anglais disposé tête-bêche.– Titre de la p. de t. additionnelle: *Arthur S. Bourinot*.
Localisation: OONL.

6866 **National Library of Canada**
Arthur S. Bourinot. Ottawa: National Library of Canada, 1971. 30, 30 p.: ports.
Note: 190 entries.– Exhibit catalogue chronicles life of Bourinot, with listing of many works and memorabilia.– Text in English and French with French text on inverted pages.– Title of additional title-page: *Arthur S. Bourinot*.
Location: OONL.

6867 **Hélène de Rome, soeur**
Bibliographie analytique de l'oeuvre du Révérend père Jean Bousquet o.p., lecteur en théologie, précédée d'une biographie. Québec: [s.n.], 1964. 56 f.
Note: Édition limitée à 103 exemplaires dactylographiés.
Localisation: OONL.

6868 **"Bibliography of works by James Bovell."**
In: *Pioneers of Canadian science: symposium presented to the Royal Society of Canada in 1964*, edited by George F.G. Stanley. Toronto: University of Toronto Press, 1966. P. 136-137.
Note: Location: OONL.

6869 **Miki, Roy Akira**
A record of writing: an annotated and illustrated bibliography of George Bowering. Vancouver: Talonbooks, 1990. xviii, 401 p.: ill., facsims.; ISBN: 0-88922-263-0.
Note: 1,883 entries.– Covers from 1953 to December 1988.– Includes books and pamphlets by and edited by Bowering, periodical contributions, works in translation; works about Bowering; major manuscript collections.
Location: OONL.

6870 **Rose, Damaris; Galois, Robert; Wolfe, Jeanne**
"John Bradbury, 1942-1988: bibliographie."
Dans: *Cahiers de géographie de Québec*; Vol. 32, no 87 (décembre 1988) p. 373-374.; ISSN: 0007-9766.
Note: 29 entrées.
Localisation: OONL.

6871 **Béland, Madeleine**
"[François-Joseph Brassard]: bibliographie."
Dans: *Saguenayensia*; Vol. 25, nos 1-2 (janvier-Mars 1983) p. 17-25.; ISSN: 0581-295X.
Note: Articles de revues, périodiques, encyclopédies et dictionnaires, articles de journaux, émissions radiophoniques, travaux folkloriques, oeuvre musicale.
Localisation: AEU.

6872 **Chamberland, Roger**
"Bibliographie de Jacques Brault."
Dans: *Voix et Images*; Vol. 12, no 2 (hiver 1987) p. 256-264.; ISSN: 0318-9201.
Note: Poésie, roman, nouvelles, essai, édition critique, théâtre, études sur l'oeuvres de Brault.
Localisation: AEU.

6873 **Latourelle, René**
"Liste des écrits Saint Jean de Brébeuf."
Dans: *Revue d'histoire de l'Amérique française*; Vol. 3, no 1 (juin 1949) p. 141-147.; ISSN: 0035-2357.
Note: Cinq sections: "*Relations* et extraits de *Relations*,"

"Correspondance, latine et française," "Notes spirituelles," "Ouvrages en langue huronne," "Écrits perdus."
Localisation: AEU.

6874 **Robert, Véronique**
Brégent, Michel-Georges. Don Mills, Ont.: PRO Canada, 1984. 7 p.: music, port.
Note: Bio-bibliography.– List of works, p. 4-6.– Discography, p. 7.
Location: OONL.

6875 **Fowke, V.C.**
"Publications of G.E. Britnell."
In: *Canadian Journal of Economics and Political Science*; Vol. 28, no. 2 (May 1962) p. 289-291.; ISSN: 0315-4890.
Note: Location: AEU.

6876 **Falaise, Noël**
"Biographie et bibliographie de Benoît Brouillette."
Dans: *Cahiers de géographie de Québec*; Vol. 17, no 40 (avril 1973) p. 5-34.; ISSN: 0007-9766.
Note: Approx. 300 entrées.– Volumes et brochures, collaboration à des ouvrages; cartes d'enseignement; articles de périodiques; communications scientifiques; notes, chroniques, etc.; comptes rendus de livres et notices signalétiques.
Localisation: AEU.

6877 **Staines, David**
"E.K. Brown (1905-1951): the critic and his writings."
In: *Canadian Literature*; No. 83 (Winter 1979) p. 176-189.; ISSN: 0008-4360.
Note: Location: AEU.

6878 **Johnston, G.H.**
"Roger James Evan Brown, 1931-1980."
In: *Arctic*; Vol. 34, no. 1 (March 1981) p. 95-99.; ISSN: 0004-0843.
Note: Includes a bibliography listing scientific and technical papers, miscellaneous reports, notes, etc., mainly on the subject of permafrost.
Location: OONL.

6879 **Lesser, Gloria**
"Biography and bibliography of the writings of Donald William Buchanan (1908-1966)."
In: *Journal of Canadian Art History*; Vol. 5, no. 2 (1981) p. 129-136.; ISSN: 0315-4297.
Note: Books, articles, exhibition catalogues, reports.
Location: AEU.

6880 **Weinrich, Peter**
A select bibliography of Tim Buck, general secretary of the Communist Party of Canada, 1929-1962. Toronto: Progress Books, 1974. xv, 50 p., [7] l. of pl.; ISBN: 0-919396-24-0.
Note: 124 entries.– Books, leaflets and pamphlets by Tim Buck, selection of publications relating to sedition trial, 1931-1932.– Illustrations include reproductions of covers of books, pamphlets, broadsides.
Location: OONL.

6881 **University of Western Ontario. Libraries**
Richard Maurice Bucke: a catalogue based upon the collections of the University of Western Ontario Libraries. London [Ont.]: Libraries, University of Western Ontario, 1978. xv, 126 p.: [3] l. of pl., facsims., ports.; ISBN: 0-7714-0004-7.
Note: 828 entries.– Manuscripts, published works of Bucke (books, pamphlets, articles, letters), documents about or relating to Bucke (bibliographies and catalogues, biographical and critical writings).– Edited by Mary Ann Jameson.
Location: OONL.

6882 **Orange, John Charles**
Ernest Buckler: an annotated bibliography. Downsview, Ont.: ECW Press, c1981. P. 13-56.; ISBN: 0-920802-51-0.
Note: 342 entries.– Works by Buckler: novels, short stories, prose poems, manuscripts, contributions to periodicals and books, letters, radio and television plays; works about Buckler: books, articles, theses, interviews, book reviews.
Extract from: *The annotated bibliography of Canada's major authors*, Vol. 3, edited by Robert Lecker and Jack David.
Location: OONL.

6883 **Orange, John Charles**
"Ernest Buckler: an annotated bibliography."
In: *The annotated bibliography of Canada' major authors*, Vol. 3, edited by Robert Lecker and Jack David. Downsview, Ont.: ECW Press, c1981. P. 13-56.; ISBN: 0-920802-23-0.
Note: 342 entries.– Works by Buckler: novels, short stories, prose poems, manuscripts, contributions to periodicals and books, letters, radio and television plays; works about Buckler: books, articles, theses, interviews, book reviews.
Location: OONL.

6884 **Dalcourt, Gabrielle**
"Checklist of books by Mabel Burkholder."
In: *Douglas Library Notes*; Vol. 20, no. 1-2 (Fall 1971) p. 29.; ISSN: 0012-5717.
Note: Location: OONL.

— C —

6885 **Winship, George Parker**
Cabot bibliography. Providence, R.I.: [s.n.], 1897. 71 p.
Note: Microform: CIHM Microfiche series ; no. 34388; ISBN: 0-665-34388-4. 1 microfiche (40 fr.).
Location: OONL.

6886 **Winship, George Parker**
Cabot bibliography: with an introductory essay on the careers of the Cabots based upon an independent examination of the sources of information. London: Stevens; New York: Dodd, Mead, 1900. lii, 180 p.
Note: "Sources of information regarding John and Sebastian Cabot, including works written or printed during the XVI century, containing references to the Cabots. Including also modern works whose chief value is due to the contemporary documents relating to Cabot, which they contain."
Reprint: New York: B. Franklin; [1967]. (Burt Franklin bibliographical and reference series ; no. 99); (American classics in history and social science ; no. 14).
Microform: CIHM Microfiche series ; no. 34286. ISBN: 0-665-34286-1. 3 microfiches (126 fr.).
Location: OONL.

6887 **Kendle, Judith**
"Morley Callaghan: an annotated bibliography."
In: *The annotated bibliography of Canada's major authors*, Vol. 5, edited by Robert Lecker and Jack David. Downsview, Ont.: ECW Press, 1984. P. 13-177.; ISBN: 0-920802-68-0.
Note: 1,359 entries.– Works by Callaghan: books (novels, stories, juvenile fiction, memoirs, plays), audio material, manuscripts, contributions to periodicals and books,

radio contributions, television contributions; Works about Callaghan: books, articles and sections of books, theses and dissertations, dramatic adaptations and screenplays, selected book, play and film reviews.
Location: OONL.

6888 **Latham, David**
"A Callaghan log."
In: *Journal of Canadian Studies*; Vol. 15, no. 1 (Spring 1980) p. 18-29.; ISSN: 0021-9495.
Note: Chronological listing of Morley Callaghan biographical and literary events to 1979, includes book and periodical publication and production of plays.– Contains a selected checklist of books, articles and theses on Callaghan's work.
Location: AEU.

6889 **Staines, David**
"Morley Callaghan: the writer and his writings."
In: *The Callaghan Symposium*. Ottawa: University of Ottawa Press, 1981. P. 111-121. (Reappraisals: Canadian writers); ISBN: 2-7603-4387-1.
Note: Chronological listing of Callaghan works, 1926-1979.
Location: OONL.

6890 **Klinck, Carl F.**
Complete bibliography of Wilfred Campbell, 1858-1918. [S.l.: s.n.], 1943. 32 p.
Note: Companion to the author's *Wilfred Campbell, a study in late provincial Victorianism*. Toronto: Ryerson Press, 1942. 289 p.
Location: OOCC.

6891 **Wicken, George**
"William Wilfred Campbell (1858-1918): an annotated bibliography."
In: *Essays on Canadian Writing*; No. 9 (Winter 1977-1978) p. 37-47.; ISSN: 0316-0300.
Note: Books of poetry by Campbell, poetry anthologies edited by Campbell, drama, social history, travel, essays and reviews, manuscripts, criticism, theses.
Location: AEU.

6892 **"J.M.S. Careless: select bibliography."**
In: *Old Ontario: essays in honour of J.M.S. Careless*, edited by David Keane and Colin Read. Toronto: Dundurn Press, 1990. P. 321-326.; ISBN: 1-55002-060-9.
Note: Chronological listing of works by and about Careless, 1945-1989.
Location: OONL.

6893 **Morse, William Inglis**
Bliss Carman: bibliography, letters, fugitive verses and other data. Windham, Conn.: Hawthorn House, 1941. 86 p.: ill., facsim., ports.
Note: Bibliography: p. 29-49.
Location: OONL.

6894 **Sherman, Frederic F.**
"A check list of first editions of the works of Bliss Carman."
In: *Bliss Carman*, by Odell Shepard. Toronto: McClelland and Stewart, 1923. P. 171-184.
Note: 107 entries.
Location: OONL.

6895 **Sorfleet, John R.**
"A primary and secondary bibliography of Bliss Carman's work."
In: *Bliss Carman: a reappraisal*, edited by Gerald Lynch.

Ottawa: University of Ottawa Press, c1990. P. 193-204. (Reappraisals: Canadian writers ; 16); ISBN: 0-7766-0286-1.
Note: Primary sources in chronological sequence (books and pamphlets, volumes edited); selected secondary sources in chronological sequence.
Location: OONL.

6896 **Roy, Antoine**
"Bibliographie de M. L'Abbé Ivanhoë Caron."
Dans: *Culture*; Vol. 3, (1942) p. 91-94.; ISSN: 0317-2066.
Note: Localisation: AEU.

6897 **Turpin, Marguerite**
Life and work of Emily Carr (1871-1945): a selected bibliography. Vancouver: School of Librarianship, University of British Columbia, 1965. 20 p.: ill.
Note: Location: OONL.

6898 **Soublière, Roger**
"Bibliographie [Roch Carrier]."
Dans: *Nord*; No 6 (automne 1976) p. 145-152.; ISSN: 0315-3789.
Note: Localisation: OONL.

6899 **Baxter, James Phinney**
A memoir of Jacques Cartier, sieur de Limoilou: his voyages to the St. Lawrence, a bibliography and a facsimile of the manuscript of 1534 with annotations, etc. New York: Dodd, Mead, 1906. ix, 464 p., [9] l. of pl. (3 folded): ill., maps (3 folded, 1 col.), port., facsims.
Note: Location: OONL.

6900 **Nichol, bp**
"A chronological checklist of published work by Barbara Caruso, 1964-1985."
In: *Open Letter*; Series 6, no. 4 (Spring 1986) p. 79-92.; ISSN: 0048-1939.
Note: Location: AEU.

6901 **Martin, Gérard**
"Bibliographie sommaire des écrits sur Samuel de Champlain."
Dans: *Bulletin des recherches historiques*; Vol. 65, no 3 (juillet-septembre 1959) p. 51-62.
Note: 140 entrées.
Localisation: OONL.

6902 **Ducrocq-Poirier, Madeleine**
"Robert Charbonneau [biographie: bibliographie]."
Dans: *Présence francophone*; No 4 (printemps 1972) p. 112-119.; ISSN: 0048-5195.
Note: Localisation: OONL.

6903 **"Bibliographie de M. Hubert Charbonneau."**
Dans: *Bulletin de l'Association des démographes du Québec*; Vol. 3, no 4 (décembre 1974) p. 34-40.
Note: Localisation: OONL.

6904 **Morley, William F.E.**
"A bibliographical study of Charlevoix's *Histoire et description générale de la Nouvelle France*."
In: *Papers of the Bibliographical Society of Canada*; Vol. 2 (1963) p. 21-45.; ISSN: 0067-6896.
Note: Part I describes editions and translations of the *Histoire* and the *Journal*.– Part II lists excerpts, abstracts, reviews, and works or parts of works based on Charlevoix.– Chronological arrangement.
Location: OONL.

6905 **"Bibliographie de François Charron."**
Dans: *Voix et Images*; Vol. 16, no 3 (printemps 1991) p. 469-480.; ISSN: 0318-9201.

Note: Approx. 200 entrées.– Oeuvres de Charron: volumes, poèmes, articles critiques ou essais parus dans des périodiques; mémoire; entrevues; études.
Localisation: AEU.

6906 **Laurin, Clément**
"Bibliographie de Jean-Olivier Chenier."
Dans: *Cahiers d'histoire de Deux-Montagnes*; Vol. 5, no 2 (octobre 1982) p. 58-66.; ISSN: 0226-7063.
Note: Localisation: OONL.

6907 **Performing Rights Organization of Canada**
Brian Cherney. Don Mills, Ont.: PRO Canada, 1988. 7 p.
Note: Bio-bibliography.– List of compositions, p. 4-7.– Discography, p. 7.
Location: OONL.

6908 **Legris, Renée**
"Bibliographie [Robert Choquette]."
Dans: *Robert Choquette*. Montréal: Fides, 1972. P. 51-64. (Dossiers de documentation sur la littérature canadienne-française ; 8)
Note: Localisation: OONL.

6909 **MacDonald, Ruth**
"Leonard Cohen."
In: *Bulletin of Bibliography*; Vol. 31, no. 3 (July-September 1974) p. 107-110.; ISSN: 0007-4780.
Note: Location: OONL.

6910 **Whiteman, Bruce**
Leonard Cohen: an annotated bibliography. Downsview, Ont.: ECW Press, c1980. P. 55-95.; ISBN: 0-920763-52-9.
Note: 387 entries.– Works by Cohen: books (novels and poetry), manuscripts, contributions to periodicals and books, audio recordings; works about Cohen: books, articles and sections of books, theses, interviews, book and record reviews.
Extract from: *The annotated bibliography of Canada's major authors*, Vol. 2, edited by Robert Lecker and Jack David.
Location: OONL.

6911 **Whiteman, Bruce**
"Leonard Cohen: an annotated bibliography."
In: *The annotated bibliography of Canada's major authors*, Vol. 2, edited by Robert Lecker and Jack David. Downsview, Ont.: ECW Press, c1980. P. 55-95.; ISBN: 0-920802-40-0.
Note: 387 entries.– Works by Cohen: books (novels and poetry), manuscripts, contributions to periodicals and books, audio recordings; works about Cohen: books, articles and sections of books, theses, interviews, book and record reviews.
Location: OONL.

6912 **Gould, Allan Mendel**
A critical assessment of the theatre criticism of Nathan Cohen with a bibliography and selected anthology. Toronto: York University, 1977. ix, 424 l.
Note: Thesis, Ph.D., York University, 1977.
Microform: Canadian theses on microfiche ; no. 33632. 5 microfiches.
Location: OONL.

6913 **Scollard, Robert J.**
A bibliography of the writings of Charles Collins. Toronto: Basilian Press, 1974. 24 p. (Historical bulletin ; no. 9)
Note: Location: OONL.

6914 **Fauchon, André**
"Bibliographie de l'oeuvre de Maurice Constantin-Weyer."
Dans: *Cahiers franco-canadiens de l'Ouest*; Vol. 1, no 1 (printemps 1989) p. 49-70.; ISSN: 0843-9559.
Note: Romans, essais, nouvelles, biographies; ouvrages en collaboration; ouvrages traduit par Constantin-Weyer; appendices, avant-propos, introductions et préfaces.
Localisation: OONL.

6915 **Willis, Stephen C.**
Alexis Contant: catalogue. Ottawa: Bibliothèque nationale du Canada, 1982. v, 91, 87, v p.: ill.; ISBN: 0-660-51891-0.
Note: 119 entrées.– Catalogue des oeuvres musicales, enregistrements sonores, bibliographie, fonds d'archives, avec index des titres et les premières lignes, index des auteurs et des compositeurs.– Texte en français et en anglais disposé tête-bêche.– Titre de la p. de t. additionnelle: *Alexis Contant: catalogue*.
Localisation: OONL.

6916 **Willis, Stephen C.**
Alexis Contant: catalogue. Ottawa: National Library of Canada, 1982. v, 87, 91, v p.: ill.; ISBN: 0-660-51891-0.
Note: 119 entries.– Exhibit catalogue listing musical works of Contant, with section of sound recordings, bibliography, archival sources, index of titles and first lines, index of authors and composers.– Text in English and French with French text on inverted pages.– Title of additional title-page: *Alexis Contant: catalogue*.
Location: OONL.

6917 **Beddie, M.K.**
Bibliography of Captain James Cook R.N., F.R.S. Sydney: Council of the Library of New South Wales, 1970. xvi, 894 p.; ISBN: 0-7240-9999-9.
Note: 4,808 entries.– Includes a section on the third voyage, the search for the Northwest Passage, 1776-1780: manuscripts, printed accounts, books and articles.
Location: OONL.

6918 **British Columbia Library Association. Bibliography Committee**
Captain James Cook. [Vancouver: The Association], 1935-1936. [3], 7 p.
Note: Approx. 100 entries.
Location: BVIPA.

6919 **Holmes, Maurice**
Captain James Cook, R.N., F.R.S.: a bibliographical excursion. London: F. Edwards, 1952. 103 p., [11] l. of pl.: facsims.
Note: Previous edition: *An introduction to the bibliography of Captain James Cook, R.N.* 1936. 59 p.
Reprint: *Captain James Cook: a bibliographical excursion.* New York: B. Franklin, 1968. 103 p.: facsims. (Burt Franklin bibliography and reference series ; 262).
Location: OONL.

6920 **Leduc, Jean**
"La vie et l'oeuvre de Jean-Pierre Cordeau, 1922-1971."
Dans: *Union médicale du Canada*; Vol. 101, no 12 (décembre 1972) p. 2641-2645.; ISSN: 0041-6959.
Note: Localisation: OONL.

6921 **Dunn, Margo**
"A preliminary checklist of the writings of Isabella Valancy Crawford."
In: *The Crawford Symposium*, edited by Frank M. Tierney.

Ottawa: University of Ottawa Press, 1979. P. 141-155.; ISBN: 2 7603-4385-5.

Note: Major collections and editions, poetry, prose (fairy stories, short fiction, novels), criticism (articles and chapters in books, reviews), theses.

Location: OONL.

6922 **Suo, Lynne**
"Annotated bibliography on Isabella Valancy Crawford."
In: *Essays on Canadian Writing*; No. 11 (Summer 1978) p. 289-314.; ISSN: 0316-0300.

Note: Works of Crawford: books (prose, poetry), manuscripts, selected contributions to anthologies; books about Crawford: articles and sections of books, theses, reviews, unpublished works.

Location: AEU.

6923 **Condemine, Odette; Wyczynski, Paul**
Octave Crémazie, 1827-1879: Émile Nelligan: 1879-1941. Ottawa: National Library of Canada, 1979. 97, 107 p.: ports.; ISBN: 0-662-50530-1.

Note: 201 entries.– Exhibition catalogue lists and describes written, pictorial and sound documents to illustrate the poets life and work.– Includes bibliography for Crémazie and Nelligan.– Text in English and French/ texte en français et en anglais.

Location: OONL.

6924 **Rousseau, Jacques**
Le docteur J.–A. Crevier, médecin et naturaliste, 1824-1889: étude biographique et bibliographique. [Montréal: s.n.], 1940. 96 p.: ill.

Note: 166 entrées.– "Extrait des *Annales de l'ACFAS*, volume 6, 1940".

Localisation: OONL.

6925 **Rousseau, Jacques**
"Le docteur J.–A. Crevier, médecin et naturaliste, 1824-1889: étude biographique et bibliographique."
Dans: *Annales de l'ACFAS*; Vol. 6 (1940) p. 173-269.; ISSN: 0066-8842.

Note: 166 entrées.

Localisation: OONL.

— D —

6926 **Thomson, Inga; Dafoe, Marcella**
"Bibliography of J.W. Dafoe, 1866-1944."
In: *Canadian Journal of Economics and Political Science*; Vol. 10, no. 2 (May 1944) p. 213-215.; ISSN: 0315-4890.

Note: Location: OONL.

6927 **University of Manitoba. Department of Archives, Manuscripts and Rare Books**
Register of the John Wesley Dafoe collection. Winnipeg: Department of Archives, Manuscripts and Rare Books, University of Manitoba Libraries, 1979. 64 l. port.

Note: Diaries, correspondence, speeches, editorials, articles, memoranda, reports.– Topics include: British Empire, Canadian nationalism, journalism, Canadian and Manitoba politics, Liberal Party, Rowell-Sirois Commission.

Location: OONL.

6928 **Beauregard, Ludger**
"Pierre Dagenais: une biobibliographie."
Dans: *Cahiers de géographie de Québec*; Vol. 27, no 71 (septembre 1983) p. 149-163.; ISSN: 0007-9766.

Note: Ouvrages de Dagenais: volumes, articles de revue, encyclopédie, cartes pédagogiques, chroniques et comptes rendus.

Localisation: AEU.

6929 **Marie-de-Sion, soeur**
Bibliographie analytique précédée d'une biographie du Rév. père Jean-Paul Dallaire, s.j. Saint-Damien. École normale N.D. du Perpétuel-Secours, 1960. 106 p.

Note: Localisation: OTU.

6930 **"Catalogue of printed books and tracts, by the late Alexander Dalrymple."**
In: *Biographical memoir of Alexander Dalrymple, Esq.: late hydrographer to the Admiralty*. London: [s.n.], 1816. P. 201-204.

Note: 59 entries.

Microform: CIHM Microfiche series ; no. 17416; ISBN: 0-665-17416-0. 1 microfiche (18 fr.).

Location: BVIPA.

6931 **Flemington, Frank**
"Annie Charlotte Dalton (1865-1938): biographical note and bibliography."
In: *Canadian Author and Bookman*; Vol. 22, no. 3 (September 1946) p. 42-44.; ISSN: 0008-29337.

Note: Location: AEU.

6932 **Potvin, Fernand**
"Saint Antoine Daniel, martyr canadien: bibliographie."
Dans: *Revue d'histoire de l'Amérique française*; Vol. 8, no 3 (décembre 1954) p. 395-414.; ISSN: 0035-2357.

Note: Manuscrits, guides, sources contemporaines, sources imprimées, ouvrages généraux, articles de périodiques.

Localisation: AEU.

6933 **Daniells, Laurenda**
"The Canadian scholar: Roy Daniells: vita and bibliography."
In: *English Studies in Canada*; Vol. 5, no. 4 (Winter 1979) p. xii-xix.; ISSN: 0317-0802.

Note: Listing of books, contributions to books, edited works, articles in periodicals, published lectures, introductions, review articles, poems in journals, poems in anthologies, miscellaneous, works about Daniells.

Location: OONL.

6934 **"Bibliographie des publications de Pierre Dansereau de 1972 à ce jour."**
Dans: *Géographie physique et quaternaire*; Vol. 39, no 1 (1985) p. 4-6.; ISSN: 0705-7199.

Note: Localisation: OONL.

6935 **Dansereau, Pierre**
"Bibliographie des publications de M. Pierre Dansereau/ Bibliography of the publications of Mr. Pierre Dansereau."
Dans: *Revue canadienne de géographie*; Vol. 11, nos 2-3 (1957) p. 115-123.; ISSN: 0316-3022.

Note: Localisation: AEU.

6936 **Dansereau, Pierre**
"Bibliographie des publications de Pierre Dansereau/ Bibliography of the publications of Pierre Dansereau."
Dans: *Revue de géographie de Montréal*; Vol. 22, no 1 (1968) p. 65-68.; ISSN: 0035-1148.

Note: Localisation: AEU.

6937 **Davidson, John**
A Scottish emigrant's contribution to Canada: record of publications and public lectures, 1911-1961. [Vancouver: s.n., 1961]. 1 vol. (in various pagings).

Note: Biographical sketch and chronological listing of publications and lectures, mainly in the field of botany

and gardening.
Location: OONL.

6938 **Benson, Eugene**
"Robertson Davies: a chronology and checklist."
In: *Canadian Drama*; Vol. 7, no. 2 (1981) p. 3-12.; ISSN: 0317-9044.
Note: Lists all books and parts of books, information about premières of plays and their publication.– Emphasis on Davies' career as dramatist.
Location: OONL.

6939 **Roper, Gordon**
"A Davies log."
In: *Journal of Canadian Studies*; Vol. 12, no. 1 (February 1977) p. 4-19.; ISSN: 0021-9495.
Note: Chronological listing of Robertson Davies' biography and writings to 1977, with a check-list of selected books, articles and theses about Davies' work.
Location: AEU.

6940 **Ryrie, John**
Robertson Davies: an annotated bibliography. [Downsview, Ont.: ECW Press, c1981]. P. 57-279.
Note: 2,422 entries.– Works by Davies: novels, drama, sketches, criticism, essays, addresses, articles, manuscripts, audio-visual material; works about Davies: articles and sections of books, theses and dissertations, audio-visual material, book reviews.
Extract from: *The annotated bibliography of Canada's major authors*, Vol. 3, edited by Robert Lecker and Jack David.
Location: OONL.

6941 **Ryrie, John**
"Robertson Davies: an annotated bibliography."
In: *The annotated bibliography of Canada's major authors*, Vol. 3, edited by Robert Lecker and Jack David. Downsview, Ont.: ECW Press, c1981. P. 57-279.; ISBN: 0-920802-23-0.
Note: 2,422 entries.– Works by Davies: novels, drama, sketches, criticism, essays, addresses, articles, manuscripts, audio-visual material; works about Davies: articles and sections of books, theses and dissertations, audio-visual material, book reviews.
Location: OONL.

6942 **Markham, Albert Hastings**
The voyages and works of John Davis, the navigator. London: Printed for the Hakluyt Society, 1880. xcv, 392 p.: ill., maps. (Works issued by the Hakluyt Society ; no. 59)
Note: Microform: CIHM Microfiche series ; no. 11194; ISBN: 0-665-11194-0. 6 microfiches (269 fr.).
Location: OKQ.

6943 **Ami, Henri Marc**
"Bibliography of Dr. George M. Dawson."
In: *George Mercer Dawson*, by B.J. Harrington. Minneapolis: Geological Pub. Co., [1901]. P. 67-86.
Note: Listing from Lochhead.– No location.

6944 **Ami, Henri Marc**
"Bibliography of Dr. George M. Dawson."
In: *American Geologist*; Vol. 28 (1901) p. 76-86.; ISSN: 0190-518X.
Note: Location: OOG.

6945 **Ami, Henri Marc**
Biographical sketch of George Mercer Dawson. Ottawa: Ottawa Printing Co., 1901. 31 p.
Note: Bibliography of Dr. George M. Dawson, p. 21-31.–

Chronological listing of publications from 1870 to 1901. Reissued, with addition of bibliography from the *Ottawa Naturalist*, Vol. 15, no. 2 (May 1901) P. 43-52.
Location: OONL.

6946 **Ami, Henri Marc**
"Bibliography of Dr. George M. Dawson."
In: *Proceedings and Transactions of the Royal Society of Canada*; Series 2, vol. 8, section 4 (1902) p. 192-201.; ISSN: 0316-4616.
Note: Chronological listing from 1870 to 1901.
This bibliography was also published in *The Canadian Record of Science*, vol. 8, no. 8 (July 1902) p. 503-516, and in *The Ottawa Naturalist*, vol. 15, no. 9 (December 1901) p. 202-213.
Location: AEU.

6947 **Ami, Henri Marc**
"Bibliography of Sir John William Dawson."
In: *Ottawa Naturalist*; Vol. 13, no. 12 (March 1900) p. 279-294.; ISSN: 0316-4411.
Note: Chronological listing from 1841 to 1877.
Location: OONL.

6948 **Ami, Henri Marc**
"Memoir of Sir J. William Dawson: bibliography."
In: *Geological Society of America Bulletin*; Vol. 11 (1900) p. 557-580.; ISSN: 0016-7606.
Note: Location: OTY.

6949 **Ami, Henri Marc**
"Sir John William Dawson. A brief biographical sketch."
In: *American Geologist*; Vol. 26 (July 1900) p. 1-48.; ISSN: 0190-518X.
Note: Location: OTU.

6950 **Ami, Henri Marc**
Sir John William Dawson. A brief biographical sketch. [Minneapolis: s.n., 1900]. 57 p.
Note: Excerpt from *American Geologist*, Vol. 26, no. 1 (July 1900) P. 1-48, with corrections and additions to the bibliography.
Microform: CIHM Microfiche series ; no. 02192; ISBN: 0-665-02192-5. 1 microfiche (36 fr.).
Location: OONL.

6951 **Ami, Henri Marc**
"Bibliography of Sir John William Dawson."
In: *Proceedings and Transactions of the Royal Society of Canada*; Series 2, vol. 7, section 4 (1901) p. 15-44.; ISSN: 0316-4616.
Note: Chronological listing from 1842 to 1901.
Listing from 1841 to 1877 contained in the *Ottawa Naturalist*, vol. 13, no. 12 (March 1900) p. 279-294.
Location: AEU.

6952 **Chamberland, Roger; Gervais, André**
"Bibliographie de Roger Des Roches."
Dans: *Voix et Images*; Vol. 13, no 2 (hiver 1988) p. 280-289.; ISSN: 0318-9201.
Note: Oeuvres de Des Roches (volumes, prose et poèmes publiés en revues et non repris en livre, musique rock et cinéma, textes pour la radio, entrevues à la radio, conférences); études sur les oeuvres.
Localisation: AEU.

6953 **Bosa, Réal**
"Bibliographie des oeuvres publiées de Edmond Desrochers."
Dans: *Livre, bibliothèque et culture québécoise: mélanges offerts à Edmond Desrochers, s.j.* Montréal: ASTED, 1977. P.

47-62.; ISBN: 0-88606-000-1.

Note: Localisation: OONL

6954 **Michaud, Irma**
"Antonin Dessane, 1826-1873."
Dans: *Bulletin des recherches historiques*; Vol. 39, no 2 (février 1933) p. 73-76.
Note: Notice biographique suivie de la liste de ses oeuvres.
Localisation: OONL.

6955 **Villemaire, Fernande**
Bio-bibliographie de Narcisse-E. Dionne. Québec: Bibliothèque nationale du Québec, 1983. xiii, 102 p. (Bibliographie et documentation / Bibliothèque nationale du Québec ; 15)
Note: 256 entrées.– Livres et brochures (ouvrages personnels de l'auteur, ouvrages de collaboration, collaboration à ouvrage collectif, préface); articles de revues et de journaux.– Préparé en 1945 par Mme Villemaire dans le cadre du cours de bibliothéconomie de l'Université de Montréal.
Localisation: QRUQR.

6956 **Pincoe, Grace**
"Arthur Garratt Dorland 1887-1979: a bibliography."
In: *Canadian Quaker History Newsletter*; No. 25 (November 1979) p. 32-38.; ISSN: 0319-3934.
Note: Chronological listing of books, pamphlets, articles.
Location: AEU.

6957 **Robitaille, Alphéda**
"Hommage à un historien: Antonio Drolet, 1904-1970: bibliographie."
Dans: *Archives*; Vol. 2 (juillet-décembre 1970) p. 32-42.; ISSN: 0044-9423.
Note: Localisation: OONL.

6958 **Manseau, Édith; Blanchette, Louise; Dumas, Céline**
"Bibliographie de Réjean Ducharme."
Dans: *Voix et images*; Vol. 8, no 3 (printemps 1983) p. 535-567.; ISSN: 0318-9201.
Note: Oeuvres, extraits, lettres, chansons de Ducharme; études et critiques sur Ducharme et son oeuvre.
Localisation: AEU.

6959 **Wenek, Karol W.J.**
Louis Dudek: a check-list. Ottawa: Golden Dog Press, 1975. vi, 54 p.; ISBN: 0-919614-15-9.
Note: Approx. 650 entries.– Covers the period from December 1936 to December 1974.– Includes works by Dudek, works about Dudek (biographical material, criticism and comment, reviews).
Location: OONL.

6960 **Ames, Michael M.**
"A note on the contributions of Wilson Duff to northwest coast ethnology and art."
In: *BC Studies*; No. 31 (Autumn 1976) p. 3-11.; ISSN: 0005-2949.
Note: Bio-bibliographical essay and list of Duff's publications.
Location: AEU.

6961 **Boivin, Aurélien; Robert, Lucie**
"Bibliographie de Guy Dufresne."
Dans: *Voix et Images*; Vol. 9, no 1 (automne 1983) p. 59-81.; ISSN: 0318-9201.
Note: Oeuvres (radio, télévision, cinéma, à la scène, publications); études sur Dufresne et son oeuvre.
Localisation: AEU.

6962 **Bayard, Caroline**
"A Raoul Duguay bibliography."
In: *Open Letter*; Series 3, no. 8 (Spring 1978) p. 37-43.; ISSN: 0048-1939.
Note: 97 entries.
Location: AEU.

6963 **Larivière-Derome, Céline**
Inventaire des documents Edmond Dyonnet conservés au Centre de recherche en civilisation canadienne-française. Ottawa: Centre de recherche en civilisation canadienne-française, Université d'Ottawa, 1976. 51 p. (Documents de travail du Centre de recherche en civilisation canadienne-française ; 5)
Note: Le fonds Edmond Dyonnet couvre la période 1898-1954.– Documents concerne la carrière artistique et professorale de Dyonnet: notes biographiques, correspondance, photographies, articles.
Location: OONL.

— E —

6964 **Ray, Margaret**
"Pelham Edgar: a bibliography of his writings."
In: *Across my path*, edited by Northrop Frye. Toronto: Ryerson Press, 1952. P. 163-167.
Note: Location: OONL.

6965 **Ouellet, France**
Inventaire sommaire du fonds Robert Elie. Montréal: Bibliothèque nationale du Québec, Ministère des affaires culturelles, 1988. 140 p. ill.; ISBN: 2-550-16398-2.
Note: Comprend: Oeuvres de Robert Elie: articles de journaux et de revues, romans, nouvelles, poésie, théâtre, scénarios, conférence et notes de conférence, études et essais; correspondance; papiers personnels; coupures de presse.
Localisaton: OONL.

6966 **Wengle, Annette**
"Marian Engel (née Passmore): an annotated bibliography."
In: *The annotated bibliography of Canada's major authors*, Vol. 7, edited by Robert Lecker and Jack David. Toronto: ECW Press, 1987. P. 11-113.; ISBN: 0-920802-11-1.
Note: 772 entries.– Works by Engel: books (novels, stories, children's books, criticism), editorial work, audio-visual material, manuscripts, contributions to periodicals and books; works about Engel: books, theses, articles and sections of books, adaptations, interviews, selected book reviews.
Location: OONL.

6967 **"Bibliography of Robert England."**
In: *Canadian Ethnic Studies*; Vol. 8, no. 2 (1976) p. 29-33.; ISSN: 0008-3496.
Note: Books and brochures, articles by England; biographical references.
Location: OONL.

6968 **Doumato, Lamia**
Arthur C. Erickson. Monticello, Ill.: Vance Bibliographies, 1984. 11 p. (Architecture series: Bibliography ; A-1244; ISSN: 0194-1356); ISBN: 0-89028-094-0.
Note: Writings by Erickson (books, articles, contributions), books and articles on Erickson and his work, listing of awards and honours.
Location: QQLA.

6969 **Wade, Jill**
A bibliography of literature on Arthur C. Erickson. Winnipeg: University of Manitoba Libraries, 1973. iii, 20 l. (Bibliography series / University of Manitoba Libraries ; no. 1)
Note: Approx. 120 entries.– Listing of periodical articles by and about Erickson, books and reports, letters.
Location: OONL.

6970 **Lalonde, Émile**
Bio-bibliographie de Monseigneur Antoine d'Eschambault, p.d., diocèse de Saint-Boniface, Manitoba. Saint-Boniface: Collège de Saint-Boniface, 1962. xi, 104 p.: portr.
Note: Localisation: OTU.

6971 **Giesbrecht, Herbert**
"A bibliography of books and articles authored and edited by Dr. David Ewert: 1953-1987."
In: *The Bible and the Church: essays in honour of Dr. David Ewert*, edited by A.J. Dueck, H.J. Giesbrecht, V.G. Shillington. Winnipeg: Kindred Press, c1988. P. 251-274.; ISBN: 0-919797-88-1.
Note: Location: OONL.

— F —

6972 **Olivier, Réjean**
Quarante ans dans le Grand Nord: bio-bibliographie du père Eugène Fafard, O.M.I., natif de Saint-Cuthbert, comté de Bernier. L'Assomption, Québec: Collège de L'Assomption, Bibliothèque, 1981. 18 f.; ISBN: 2-920248-95-2.
Note: 17 entrées.
Localisation: OONL.

6973 **"Bibliographie de Jean-Charles Falardeau."**
Dans: *Recherches sociographiques*; Vol. 23, no 3 (septembre-décembre 1982) p. 429-437.; ISSN: 0034-1282.
Note: Approx. 200 entrées.– Études et articles, études et articles en collaboration, livres, livres en collaboration, traduction, comptes rendus de livres.
Localisation: AEU.

6974 **Wales, Katherine**
"Sir Robert Alexander Falconer: chronological bibliography."
In: *University of Toronto Quarterly*; Vol. 13, no. 2 (January 1944) p. 167-174.; ISSN: 0042-0247.
Note: Location: AEU.

6975 **Maine, Michael**
Robert Farnon discography. Leicester: Robert Farnon Appreciation Society, 1977. [87] p.
Note: Listing of recordings of Canadian composer, arranger and conductor Robert Farnon.– Categories include instrumental recordings conducted by Farnon, accompaniments directed by Farnon, arrangements, film scores.
Location: OONL.

6976 **Paquet, Gilles**
"Bio-bibliographie d'Albert Faucher."
Dans: *Actualité économique*; Vol. 59, no 3 (septembre 1983) p. 397-400.; ISSN: 0001-771X.
Note: Localisation: BVAU.

6977 **Renault, Raoul**
Faucher de Saint-Maurice: son oeuvre. Québec: Brousseau, 1897. 16 p.
Note: Microforme: ICMH collection de microfiches ; no 04928; ISBN: 0-665-04928-5. 1 microfiche (14 images).

Localisation: OONL.

6978 **Harkins, Edwin**
Maynard Ferguson: a discography. [S.l.]: E. Harkins, c1976. iv, 73 l.
Note: Phonograph record listing of Canadian jazz trumpeter Maynard Ferguson.
Location: OONL.

6979 **Scollard, Robert J.**
The diaries and other papers of Michael Joseph Ferguson, C.S.B.: a bibliography. Toronto: Basilian Press, 1970. 36 p. (Basilian historical bulletin ; no. 5)
Note: Location: OONL.

6980 **Smith, Karen**
"Bibliography of the works of Charles Bruce Fergusson."
In: *Collections of the Nova Scotia Historical Society*; Vol. 40 (1980) p. 193-202.; ISSN: 0383-8420.
Note: Listing of books, articles, book reviews, contributions to *Dictionary of Canadian Biography*.
Location: AEU.

6981 **Cantin, Pierre**
"Nouvelle contribution à la bibliographie des écrits de Jacques Ferron."
Dans: *Revue d'histoire littéraire du Québec et du Canada français*; No 2 (1980-1981) p. 115-135.; ISSN: 0713-7958.
Note: Comprend trois parties: titres ajoutés (livres, périodiques); titres corrigés ou complétés; titres retirés.
Localisation: AEU.

6982 **Cantin, Pierre**
"Bibliographie sélective de Jacques Ferron."
Dans: *Voix et Images*; Vol. 8, no 3 (printemps 1983) p. 464-475.; ISSN: 0318-9201.
Note: Oeuvres de Ferron; études sur Ferron et son oeuvres.
Localisation: AEU.

6983 **Cantin, Pierre**
Jacques Ferron, polygraphe: essai de bibliographie suivi d'une chronologie. Montréal: Éditions Bellarmin, 1984. 548 p.; ISBN: 2-89007-574-5.
Note: 4,318 entrées.– Oeuvres inédites, imprimés (livres, textes publiés dans des périodiques, préfaces/introductions/présentations, écrits épars, textes et extraits repris en diverses publications, traductions, transcriptions d'entrevues), oeuvres jouées, enregistrées ou adaptées, interviews, tables rondes, études et documents sur l'homme et l'oeuvre, émissions de radio et de télévision, filmographie.
Localisation: OONL.

6984 **Monette, Guy J.A.**
Introduction à l'oeuvre de Ja[c]ques Ferron: [bibliographie]. [Kingston, Ont.]: Association des professeurs de français des universités et collèges canadiens, 1982. 23 p.
Note: 207 entrées.– "Oeuvres de Ferron" (romans, récits, soties, pièces de théâtre, contes, traductions, interviews et films); "Critiques de l'oeuvres de Ferron" (livres, thèses, parties de livres, articles).
Localisation: OONL.

6985 **Potvin, Diane**
"Bibliographie des écrits de Jacques Ferron."
Dans: *Études françaises*; Vol. 12, 3-4 (octobre 1976) p. 353-383.; ISSN: 0014-2085.
Note: Livres, périodiques, 1942 à 31 décembre 1975.
Localisation: OONL.

6986 Roberts, Carol; Macdonald, Lynne
Timothy Findley. an annotated bibliography. Toronto: ECW Press, 1990. x, 136 p.; ISBN: 1-55022-112-4.
Note: 534 entries.– Works by Findley (novels, short stories, plays, play productions, films, audio-visual material, manuscripts, contributions to periodicals and books, book reviews, radio and television material; works about Findley (articles and sections of books, theses and dissertations, interviews, reviews of books, plays, television, films).
Location: OONL.

6987 McMullen, Lorraine
"A checklist of the works of May Agnes Fleming."
In: *Papers of the Bibliographical Society of Canada*; Vol. 28 (1989) p. 25-37.; ISSN: 0067-6896.
Note: Chronological listing of works of New Brunswick born novelist May Agnes Fleming, 1857-1915: short stories, serialized short fiction, novels.
Location: OONL.

6988 Marie-Magloire-des-Anges, soeur
Bio-bibliographie de M. l'abbé Ovila Fournier, L.Sc., professeur à l'Institut de biologie de l'Université de Montréal, 1935-1955. Montréal: Cercles des jeunes naturalistes, 1962. xx, 89 p.: portr.
Note: Localisation: OONL.

6989 British Columbia Library Association. Bibliography Committee
Simon Fraser. [Vancouver: The Association], 1935. 3 p.
Note: 24 entries.
Location: BVIPA.

6990 Hudon, Dominique
Bibliographie analytique et critique des articles de revues sur Louis Fréchette, 1863-1983. Québec: Centre de recherche en littérature québécoise, Université Laval, 1987. 269 p. (Collection "Bibliographies" / Centre de recherche en littérature québécoise, Université Laval ; no 2); ISBN: 2-920801-08-2.
Note: 324 entrées.– Trois parties: "La critique du vivant de Louis Frechette (1863-1907);" "Articles nécrologiques (1908-1909);" "La critique aprés le décés de Frechette (1910-1983)."
Localisation: OONL.

6991 Klinck, George Alfred
"Bibliographie: Louis Fréchette."
Dans: *Revue d'histoire de l'Amérique française*; Vol. 7, no 1 (juin 1953) p. 132-146.; ISSN: 0035-2357.
Note: Manuscrits, livres et brochures, articles et revues, articles de journaux, ouvrages critiques sur Fréchette et son temps, lettres.
Localisation: AEU.

6992 "List of Dr F.E.J. Fry's publications."
In: *Journal of the Fisheries Research Board of Canada*; Vol. 33, no. 2 (February 1976) p. 341-343.; ISSN: 0008-2686.
Note: Location: AEU.

6993 Denham, Robert D.
Northrop Frye: an enumerative bibliography. Metuchen, N.J.: Scarecrow Press, 1974. vii, 142 p. (Scarecrow author bibliographies ; no. 14); ISBN: 0-8108-0693-2.
Note: Approx. 800 entries.– Listing of Frye's writings from October 1935 to June 1973, annotated list of secondary sources, list of reviews of Frye's books.
Location: OONL.

6994 Denham, Robert D.
"Northrop Frye: a supplementary bibliography."
In: *Canadian Library Journal*; Vol. 34, no. 3 (June 1977) p. 181-197.; ISSN: 0008-4352.
Note: Writings by Frye (listed chronologically), biographical essays and notices, writings about Frye's criticism, reviews of Frye's books.
Supplement: *Canadian Library Journal*; Vol. 34, no. 4 (August 1977) p. 301-302.
Location: OONL.

6995 Denham, Robert D.
Northrop Frye: an annotated bibliography of primary and secondary sources. Toronto: University of Toronto Press, c1987. xviii, 449 p.; ISBN: 0-8020-2630-3.
Note: Approx. 1,500 entries.– Primary sources: books, books edited, separately published monographs, reviews, essays, introductions, miscellaneous undergraduate writings, interviews, sound recordings/ films/videotapes, manuscripts, unpublished correspondence; secondary sources: books and collections of essays, essays, reviews, dissertations and theses, bibliographies, miscellaneous news stories.
Location: OONL.

6996 Grant, John E.
"A checklist of writings by and about Northrop Frye."
In: *Northrop Frye in modern criticism: selected papers from the English Institute*, edited by Murray Krieger. New York: Columbia University Press, 1966. P. 147-188.
Note: 149 numbered entries of works by Frye, with subject index.– Checklist of criticism of Frye's work, 1947 to 1965.– Excludes brief reviews, unpublished speeches and scripts, unsigned writings, routine university writing, contributions to encyclopedias.
Location: OONL.

— G —

6997 "Bibliographie de Madeleine Gagnon."
Dans: *Voix et Images*; Vol. 8, no 1 (automne 1982) p. 53-58.; ISSN: 0318-9201.
Note: Livres, fictions et poèmes parus dans des périodiques, articles; choix d'études consacrées aux écritures de Madeleine Gagnon.
Localisation: AEU.

6998 Grant, Judith Skelton; Malcolm, Douglas
"Mavis Gallant: an annotated bibliography."
In: *The annotated bibliography of Canada's major authors*, Vol. 5, edited by Robert Lecker and Jack David. Downsview, Ont.: ECW Press, 1984. P. 179-230.; ISBN: 0-920802-68-0.
Note: 599 entries.– Works by Gallant: books and manuscripts, contributions to periodicals and books; works about Gallant: books, articles and sections of books, theses, interviews, audio-visual material, book and play reviews.
Location: OONL.

6999 Malcolm, Douglas
"An annotated bibliography of works by and about Mavis Gallant."
In: *Essays on Canadian Writing*; No. 6 (Spring 1977) p. 32-52.; ISSN: 0316-0300.
Note: Works by Gallant: novels and novellas, short story collections, stories in anthologies, contributions to periodicals (stories, essays, feature articles (in *Standard Magazine*), book reviews, newspaper articles); writings

about Gallant: articles, sections of books, reviews of fiction and non-fiction.
Supplement: *Canadian Fiction Magazine*, No. 28 (1978) p. 115-133.– Updates the listing to the end of 1977.
Location: AEU.

7000 **Webster, John Clarence**
William Francis Ganong memorial. Saint John, N.B.: New Brunswick Museum, 1942. 31 p.: port.
Note: Bibliography, p. 19-31.– Papers by Ganong published in bulletins of Natural History Society of New Brunswick; botanical and general writings; historical monographs and papers; historical geographical documents relating to New Brunswick.
Location: OONL.

7001 **Guertin, Marcelle**
"L'oeuvre de Serge Garant."
Dans: *Canadian University Music Review: Revue de musique des universités canadiennes*; No. 7 (1986) p. 36-45.; ISSN: 0710-0353.
Note: Localisation: OONL.

7002 **Wyczynski, Paul**
"François-Xavier Garneau: aspects bibliographiques."
Dans: *Cahiers de la Société bibliographique du Canada*; Vol. 18 (1979) p. 55-77.; ISSN: 0067-6896.
Note: Oeuvre de Garneau: poésies, histoire, récit de voyage, journaux et articles de journaux, correspondance; études sur Garneau: renseignements généraux sur la vie, l'époque et l'oeuvre; renseignements sur la poésie.
Localisation: OONL.

7003 **Blais, Jacques**
"Documents pour servir à la bibliographie critique de l'oeuvre de Saint-Denys Garneau."
Dans: *Revue de l'Université Laval*; Vol. 18, no 5 (janvier 1964) p. 424-438.; ISSN: 0384-0182.
Note: 102 entrées.– Liste chronologique, 1937 à 1962.
Localisation: OONL.

7004 **Blais, Jacques**
"Bibliographie: [Saint-Denys Garneau]."
Dans: *De Saint-Denys Garneau*. Montréal: Fides, 1971. P. 53-65. (Dossiers de documentation sur la littérature canadienne-française ; 7)
Note: Localisation: OONL.

7005 **Blais, Jacques**
"Complément à une bibliographie de Saint-Denys Garneau."
Dans: *Études françaises*; Vol. 20, no 3 (hiver 1984-1985) p. 113-127.; ISSN: 0014-2085.
Note: Localisation: OONL.

7006 **Gratton, Claude**
Yvon Gauthier: écrits philosophiques: bibliographie chronologique, 1967-1985. Sorel [Québec]: Éditions artisanales, c1986. 31 p. (Brochures / Éditions artisanales ; no 3); ISBN: 2-920827-02-2.
Note: 98 entrées.
Localisation: OONL.

7007 **Imbeau, Gaston**
Claude Gauvreau, l'homme et l'oeuvre [microforme]: biobibliographie descriptive. [Montréal: Université de Montréal, Faculté des études supérieures], 1976. 1 bobine de microfilm.
Note: Textes publiés, textes inédits par Gauvreau, écrits sur Gauvreau.– Mémoire présenté à la Faculté des études supérieures en vue l'obtention de la Maîtrise des arts

(Études françaises).
Localisation: OONL.

7008 **Geddes, James**
Bibliography of Geddes publications. [S.l.: s.n.], 1934. 18 p.
Note: Location: OKQ.

7009 **Falardeau, Jean-Charles**
"Bibliographie de Léon Gérin."
Dans: *Recherches sociographiques*; Vol. 1, no 2 (avril-juin 1960) p. 139-157.; ISSN: 0034-1282.
Note: Oeuvres de Gérin: manuscrits, imprimés (livres, articles, collaborations à des ouvrages collectifs, articles de journaux, comptes rendus de livres); sources sur Gérin: sources bibliographiques, études, commentaires, comptes rendus.
Localisation: AEU.

7010 **Lavoie, Pierre**
"Bio-bibliographie [commentée sur Jean-Claude Germain]."
Dans: *Jeu*; No 13 (automne 1979) p. 105-141.; ISSN: 0382-0335.
Note: Comprend quatre parties: biographie, théâtrographie, autre textes de Germain (critiques, essais, poèmes, préfaces, textes en prose), études sur Germain et son oeuvre.
Localisation: OONL.

7011 **Vaillancourt, Roseline**
"Bibliographie: Jean-Claude Germain."
Dans: *Voix et Images*; Vol. 6, no 2 (hiver 1981) p. 189-204.; ISSN: 0318-9201.
Note: Oeuvres de Germain: pièces publiées, pièces et spectacles inédits, articles et chroniques de Germain sur le théâtre, préfaces; études et documents sur Germain et son oeuvre.
Localisation: AEU.

7012 **Chamberland, Roger**
"Bibliographie de Roland Giguère."
Dans: *Voix et Images*; Vol. 9, no 2 (hiver 1984) p. 75-89.; ISSN: 0318-9201.
Note: Oeuvres de Giguère, études générales, thèses, études particulières.
Localisation: AEU.

7013 **Cimon, Renée**
"Bibliographie de Roland Giguère."
Dans: *Barre du jour*; No 11-13 (décembre 1967-mai 1968) p. 173-196.; ISSN: 0005-6057.
Note: Localisation: OONL.

7014 **Drumbolis, Nicky**
In the works: back roads to next spring's Gerry Gilbert bibliography. Toronto: Letters Book Shop, 1991. [370] p.: ill.; ISBN: 0-921688-01-6.
Note: Location: OONL.

7015 **Wyczynski, Paul**
Albert Laberge, 1871-1960: Charles Gill, 1871-1918. Ottawa: National Library of Canada, 1971. 42, 42 p.
Note: 200 entries.– Catalogue of exhibit at National Library marking the centenary of births of Gill and Laberge lists writings and artifacts, with descriptive notes.– Text in English and French with French text on inverted pages.– Title of additional title-page: *Albert Laberge, 1871-1960: Charles Gill, 1871-1918*.
Location: OONL.

7016 **Wyczynski, Paul**
Albert Laberge, 1871-1960: Charles Gill, 1871-1918.
Ottawa: Bibliothèque nationale du Canada, 1971. 42, 42 p.
Note: 200 entrées.– Catalogue d'exposition souligne le
centenaire de la naissance de Gill et Laberge, liste des
oeuvres.– Texte en français et en anglais disposé tête-
bêche.– Titre de la p. de t. additionnelle: *Albert Laberge,
1871-1960: Charles Gill, 1871-1918.*
Localisation: OONL.

7017 **Kershaw, G.P.**
"Don Allyn Gill (1934-1979)."
In: *Arctic*; Vol. 33, no. 1 (March 1980) p. 215-219.; ISSN:
0004-0843.
Note: Includes a selected bibliography of books, papers
and articles by Gill.
Location: AEU.

7018 **McGrath, Margaret**
Étienne Gilson: a bibliography/Étienne Gilson: une
bibliographie. Toronto: Pontifical Institute of Mediaeval
Studies, c1982. xxviii, 124 p. (Étienne Gilson series ; no. 3;
ISSN: 0708-319X); ISBN: 0-88844-703-5.
Note: 1,210 entries.– Works by Gilson (founder of the
Pontifical Institute of Mediaeval Studies, University of
Toronto): monographs, works edited, anthologies,
scholarly and general interest articles, book reviews;
works about Gilson: monographs, theses, scholarly and
general articles, memorials and obituaries; non-printed
materials.– Text in English and French/texte en français
et en anglais.
Location: OONL.

7019 **Chassé, Béatrice**
Bibliographie d'une thèse: le notaire Girouard, patriote et
rebelle. [Québec: Université Laval, 1974]. [22] f.
Note: Sources manuscrites, sources imprimées de Jean-
Joseph Girouard, notaire, portraitiste, député de Deux-
Montagnes de 1831 à 1837 et actif dans le mouvement
révolutionnaire.
Localisation: QQLA.

7020 **Sutherland, Fraser**
John Glassco: an essay and bibliography. Downsview,
Ont.: ECW Press, c1984. 121 p.; ISBN: 0-920802-78-8.
Note: 277 entries.– Works by Glassco: books, books
edited, contributions to books and periodicals,
translations, radio broadcasts.– Works about Glassco:
articles and sections of books, profiles and interviews,
radio interviews, awards and honours, reviews.
Location: OONL.

7021 **Roy, Antoine**
"Bibliographie des travaux historiques du Père Archange
Godbout, o.f.m. (1886-1960)."
Dans: *Bulletin des recherches historiques*; Vol. 66, no 4
(octobre-novembre-décembre 1960) p. 69-83.
Note: Localisation: OONL.

7022 **Freeman, Richard Broke; Wertheimer, Douglas**
Philip Henry Gosse: a bibliography. Folkestone, Kent:
Dawson, 1980. xviii, 148 p., 3 l. of pl.: ill., port.; ISBN: 0-
7129-0935-4.
Note: 466 entries.– Books and pamphlets, contributions
to serials, biographies of Gosse.
Location: OONL.

7023 **Maheux, Arthur**
Les trois Gosselin. Québec: [s.n.], 1946. 11 p.
Note: Location: OHM.

7024 **Carnet bibliographique des publications de M. l'Abbé
Auguste Gosselin: petit souvenir à l'occasion de ses
noces d'or sacerdotales, 30 septembre, 1866-1916.**
Québec: Laflamme, 1916. 24 p.
Note: 97 entrées.– Articles de journaux et de revues,
brochures, volumes.
Localisation: OONL.

7025 **"Glenn Gould discography/Discographie de Glenn
Gould."**
In: *Musicanada*; No. 46 (June 1981) p. 2.
Note: Location: OONL.

7026 **Pincoe, Ruth**
Glenn Gould: catalogue raisonné du Fonds Glenn Gould.
Ottawa: Bibliothèque nationale du Canada, 1992. 2 vol.:
ill.; ISBN: 0-660-57327-X (ensemble).
Note: Vol. 1 comprend une section des renseignements
bibliographiques sur les écrits de Gould, p. 14-51, et une
liste des oeuvres et des arrangements musicaux de
Gould, p. 53-60.– Vol. 2 inclut une bibliographie sélective
(livres et articles sur Gould), p. 231-260, et une
discographie, p. 261-287.– Texte en français et en anglais
disposé tête-bêche.– Titre de la p. de t. additionnelle:
Glenn Gould: descriptive catalogue of the Glenn Gould Papers.
Localisation: OONL.

7027 **Pincoe, Ruth**
Glenn Gould: descriptive catalogue of the Glenn Gould
Papers. Ottawa: National Library of Canada, 1992. 2 vol.:
ill.; ISBN: 0-660-57327-X (set).
Note: Vol. 1 includes a section providing bibliographic
information on writings by Gould, p. 13-49, and a list of
musical compositions and arrangements, p. 51-58.– Vol. 2
contains a selected bibliography of books and articles
about Gould, p. 223-253, and a discography, p. 255-280.–
Text in English and French with French text on inverted
pages.– Title of additional title page: *Glenn Gould:
catalogue raisonné du Fonds Glenn Gould.*
Location: OONL.

7028 **Doumato, Lamia**
A bibliography of the writings of Alan Gowans.
Monticello, Ill.: Vance Bibliographies, 1984. 13 p.
(Architecture series: Bibliography ; A-1280; ISSN: 0194-
1356); ISBN: 0-89028-170-X.
Note: Approx. 100 entries.– Books, pamphlets,
contributions, exhibition catalogues, essays, periodical
and newspaper articles, book reviews dealing with
Canadian and American architectural history, commerci-
al arts.
Location: OOPAC.

7029 **Rompkey, Ronald George**
Sir Wilfred Thomason Grenfell (1865-1940): a selective
bibliography (annotated and including periodical items).
St. John's: Memorial University of Newfoundland, 1965.
20 l.
Note: Lists books and articles by and about Grenfell.
Location: NFSM.

7030 **Barbeau, Victor; Rémillard, Juliette; Dionne, Madeleine**
L'oeuvre du chanoine Lionel Groulx: témoignages, bio-
bibliographie. Montréal: Académie canadienne-française,
1964. 197 p.: ill.
Note: L'oeuvre historique (ouvrages, brochures, cours);
l'oeuvre oratoire (sermons, allocutions, discours
patriotiques, conférences); divers (poésies, articles, contes
et romans, volumes en collaboration, lettres);

témoignages critiques sur Groulx et son oeuvre.
Localisation: OONL.

7031 **Desaulniers, Robert**
Catalogue des manuscrits de Lionel Groulx (1892-1922). Outremont, Québec: Fondation Lionel-Groulx, Centre de recherche Lionel-Groulx, 1987. viii f., 396 p.; ISBN: 2-980070-3-X-2.
Note: 577 entrées.– Deux parties et quatre index: notices descriptives des manuscrits de Groulx, par ordre chronologique; textes publiés de Groulx; index des titres des manuscrits, titres des publications; index onomastique et thèmatique des manuscrits, et celui des publications.
Localisation: OONL.

7032 **Rémillard, Juliette**
"Lionel Groulx: bibliographie (1964-1979)."
Dans: *Revue d'histoire de l'Amérique française*; Vol. 32, no 3 (décembre 1978) p. 465-524.; ISSN: 0035-2357.
Note: Localisation: OONL.

7033 **Miska, John P.**
Frederick Philip Grove: a bibliography of primary and secondary material. Ottawa: Microform Biblios, 1984. 32 l. (Canlit bibliographic series / Microform Biblios ; no. 3)
Note: 360 entries.– Works by and about F.P. Grove: novels, stories, poems, published and in manuscript; translations and editions; bibliographies, books, monographs, papers, theses, journal articles.
Location: OONL.

7034 **University of Manitoba. Department of Archives, Manuscripts and Rare Books**
Register of the Frederick Philip Grove collection. Winnipeg: Department of Archives, Manuscripts and Rare Books, University of Manitoba Libraries, 1979. 65 l.: port.
Note: Lists correspondence, published books and novels, unpublished books and novels, published and unpublished short stories, poems, published and unpublished articles, newspaper clippings, biographical material, photograph collection, microfilm collection, bibliographies.
Location: OONL.

7035 **Curat, Hervé; Menay, Lionel**
Gustave Guillaume et la psycho-systématique du langage: bibliographie annotée. Québec: Presses de l'Université Laval, 1983. ix, 235 p. (Cahiers de psycholmécanique du langage); ISBN: 2-7637-7029-0.
Note: 1,534 entrées.– Monographies, articles, comptes rendus: travaux de Gustave Guillaume, travaux des disciples et des critiques de Guillaume.
Localisation: OONL.

7036 **Guillet, Edwin C.**
Bio-bibliography of Dr. Edwin C. Guillet. Kingston, Ont.: Douglas Library, Queen's University, 1970. 23 p. (Douglas Library Occasional papers ; no. 3)
Note: Location; OONL.

7037 **Allison, L.M.; Keitner, W.J.R.**
"Ralph Gustafson: a bibliography in progress, 1929-1972." In: *West Coast Review*; Vol. 9, no. 1 (June 1974) p. 29-38.; ISSN: 0043-311X.
Note: Lists works by Gustafson (books of poetry, editions, individual poems, short stories, literary criticism); works about Gustafson (biography, articles, reviews).

Location: OONL.

— H —

7038 **"Bibliographie: Philippe Haeck (1969-1980)."**
Dans: *Voix et Images*; Vol. 6, no 3 (printemps 1981) p. 373-380.; ISSN: 0318-9201.
Note: 156 entrées.– Liste chronologique des oeuvres de Haeck, principales lectures sur Haeck.
Localisation: AEU.

7039 **Ivan Halasz de Beky: a bibliography.** Toronto: Ivan Bush, 1983. [24] p.
Note: 79 entries.– Works of University of Toronto librarian Halasz de Beky: bibliographies, bibliographical essays related to the Hungarian holdings of the library.
Location: OONL.

7040 **Anderson, John Parker**
"Bibliography [Thomas Chandler Haliburton]."
In: *Haliburton: a centenary chaplet*. Toronto: Published for the Haliburton Club, King's College, Windsor, N.S. [by] W. Briggs, 1897. P. 107-116.
Note: Microform: CIHM Microfiche series ; no. 09277; ISBN: 0-665-09277-6. 2 microfiches (70 fr.).
Location: OONL.

7041 **O'Brien, A.H.**
"Haliburton: a sketch and bibliography."
In: *Proceedings and Transactions of the Royal Society of Canada*; Series 3, vol. 3, section 2 (1909) p. 43-66.; ISSN: 0316-4616.
Note: Location: AEU.

7042 **Publications de Louis-Edmond Hamelin: professeur de géographie et directeur du Centre d'études nordiques.** Québec: Université Laval, 1969. 51 f.
Note: Localisation: QQLA.

7043 **Liste des publications de Louis-Edmond Hamelin, professeur de géographie et chercheur du Centre d'études nordiques, Université Laval, Québec.** [S.l.: s.n.], 1975. 68 l.
Note: Approx. 600 entrées.– Géographie, sciences humaines et économiques, textes administratifs et informatifs, matériel pédagogique et audio-visuel, recensions d'ouvrages et notices signalétiques.
Localisation: OONL.

7044 **Hamelin, Louis-Edmond**
"Bibliographie des publications de Louis-Edmond Hamelin."
Dans: *Revue de géographie de Montréal*; Vol. 23, no 1 (1969) p. 75-82; vol. 23, no 2 (1969) p. 179-185.; ISSN: 0035-1148.
Note: Localisation: AEU.

7045 **Foss, Brian; Singer, Loren**
"J. Russell Harper, O.C., D.Litt., D.F.A., F.R.S.C.: a chronological bibliography."
In: *Journal of Canadian Art History*; Vol. 7, no. 2 (1984) p. 106-112.; ISSN: 0315-4297.
Note: Location: AEU.

7046 **Fancy, Margaret**
Lawren Phillips Harris: a bibliography. Sackville, N.B.: Ralph Pickard Bell Library, Mount Allison University, c1979. x, 52 p. (Bibliography series / Ralph Pickard Bell Library, Mount Allison University ; no. 2); ISBN: 0-88828-028-9.
Note: Approx. 650 entries.– Articles and speeches by Harris, articles and books about Harris and his work, exhibitions and catalogues, list of works: paintings,

drawings, serlgraphs.
Location: OONL.

7047 **Growoll, Adolf**
Henry Harrisse: biographical and bibliographical sketch.
New York: Printed for the Dibdin Club by the Key Print.
House, 1899. 13 p. (Dibdin Club leaflets ; no. 3)
Note: Microform: CIHM Microfiche series ; no. 07147;
ISBN: 0-665-07147-7. 1 microfiche (14 fr.).

7048 **Émond, Maurice**
"Introduction à l'oeuvre d'Anne Hébert: [bibliographie
sommaire]."
Dans: *Québec français*; No 32 (décembre 1978) p. 37-40.;
ISSN: 0316-2052.
Note: Localisation: OONL.

7049 **Paterson, Janet**
"Bibliographie critique des études consacrées aux romans
d'Anne Hébert."
Dans: *Voix et images*; Vol. 5, no 1 (automne 1979) p. 187-
192.; ISSN: 0318-9201.
Note: Localisation: OONL.

7050 **Paterson, Janet**
"Bibliographie d'Anne Hébert."
Dans: *Voix et Images*; Vol. 7, no 3 (printemps 1982) p. 505-
510.; ISSN: 0318-9201.
Note: Oeuvres d'Anne Hébert, études sur les romans
(ouvrages, articles, thèses).
Localisation: AEU.

7051 **Russell, D.W.**
"Anne Hébert: an annotated bibliography."
In: *The annotated bibliography of Canada's major authors*,
Vol. 7, edited by Robert Lecker and Jack David. Toronto:
ECW Press, 1987. P. 115-270.; ISBN: 0-920802-11-1.
Note: 809 entries.– Works by Hébert: books (poetry,
novels, novellas and stories, drama, literary criticism),
film scenarios and collaborations, audio-visual material,
radio work, manuscripts, contributions to periodicals
and books (children's stories and plays, essays,
journalism); works about Hébert: books, articles and
sections of books, theses and dissertations, interview and
profiles, selected book, film, play reviews.
Location: OONL.

7052 **Maria Chapdelaine: évolution de l'édition 1913-1980.**
Montréal: Bibliothèque nationale du Québec, 1980. 80 p.,
23 f de pl.: ill. (certaines en coul.).; ISBN: 2-550-01473-1.
Note: 250 entrées.– Catalogue publié lors de l'exposition
par la Bibliothèque nationale du Québec, automne 1980,
à l'occasion du centenaire de la naissance de Louis
Hémon.– Inclut toutes les formes d'adaptations (pièces
de théâtre, films, radiophoniques) et tous les supports
d'impression (bandes magnétiques, bandes dessinées,
textes en braille).– Comprend deux index: 1. éditeurs,
préfaciers, traducteurs, adaptateurs, illustrateurs; 2.
langues, des publications et de leurs éditeurs.– Exclut les
critiques de l'oeuvre ou de l'auteur.
Localisation: OONL.

7053 **Houston, C. Stuart; Bechard, Marc J.**
"A.D. Henderson, Alberta's foremost oologist, 1878-1963."
In: *Blue Jay*; Vol. 48, no. 2 (June 1990) p. 85-96.; ISSN: 0006-
5099.
Note: Includes list of writings by and about Henderson.
Location: OONL.

7054 **Cameron, William J.**
A bibliography in short-title catalog form of seventeenth
and eighteenth century editions of the writings of Louis
Hennepin, Recollet explorer and missionary. [London:
University of Western Ontario], 1982. 15 l. (WHSTC
Bibliography ; no. 1; ISSN: 0712-9289); ISBN: 0-7714-0332-
1.
Note: Location: OONL.

7055 **Hugolin, père**
Bibliographie du père Louis Hennepin, récollet: les
pièces documentaires. Montréal: [Imprimerie des
franciscains], 1937. xxvii, 238 p., [2] f. de pl.: fac-sim.,
portr.
Note: 204 entrées.
Localisation: OONL.

7056 **Hugolin, père**
"Étude bibliographique et historique sur la morale
pratique du jansénisme du P. Louis Hennepin, récollet."
Dans: *Mémoires de la Société royale du Canada*; Série 3, vol.
31, section 1 (1937) p. 127-149.; ISSN: 0316-4616.
Note: Localisation: AEU.

7057 **Neill, Edward Duffield**
The writings of Louis Hennepin, Recollect Franciscan
missionary. Minneapolis: [s.n.], 1880. 10 p.
Note: Microform: CIHM Microfiche series ; no. 42023;
ISBN: 0-665-42023-4. 1 microfiche (14 fr.).
Location: OONL.

7058 **Paltsits, Victor Hugo**
"Bibliographical data."
In: *A new discovery of a vast country in America*, by Louis
Hennepin. Chicago: McClurg, 1903. P. xlv-lxiv.
Note: Location: OONL.

7059 **Porter, Peter Augustus**
Father Hennepin: an attempt to collect every edition of
his works: a brief bibliography thereof. Niagara Falls,
N.Y.: [s.n.], 1910. 17 p.
Note: Location: OOP.

7060 **Porter, Peter Augustus**
The works of Father Hennepin: a catalogue of the
collection brought together by Peter A. Porter of Niagara
Falls, N.Y. New York: Dodd & Livingston, 1910. 13 p.
Note: 58 entries.
Location: OONL.

7061 **Shea, John Gilmary**
Bibliography of Hennepin's works. New York: J.G. Shea,
1880. 13 p.
Note: Location: OONL.

7062 **Sabin, Joseph**
A list of the editions of the works of Louis Hennepin and
Alonso [i.e. Antonio] de Herrera: extracted from *A diction-
ary of books relating to America*. New York: J. Sabin, 1876.
16 p.
Note: Microform: CIHM Microfiche series ; no. 09269;
ISBN: 0-665-09269-5. 1 microfiche (14 fr.).
Location: OONL.

7063 **Lebel-Péron, Suzanne**
"Liste des publications de Monsieur Jacques Henripin."
Dans: *Bulletin de l'Association des démographes du Québec*;
Vol. 2, no 1 (mars 1973) p. 17-22.
Note: Localisation: OONL.

7064 **Maud, Ralph**
"Bio-bibliography of Charles Hill-Tout."
In: *The Salish people: the local contribution of Charles Hill-*

Tout. Vancouver: Talon Books, 1978. Vol. 4, p. 17-32.; ISBN: 0-88922-151-0.

Note: Location: OONL.

7065 **"John W. Holmes: a select bibliography."**
In: *An acceptance of paradox: essays on Canadian diplomacy in honour of John W. Holmes*, edited by Kim Richard Nossal. Toronto: Canadian Institute of International Affairs, 1982. P. 197-202. (Contemporary affairs / Canadian Institute of International Affairs ; 49); ISBN: 0-919084-39-7.

Note: Lists works published since Holmes's departure from the Department of External Affairs in 1960.– Excludes book reviews, unpublished speeches, newspaper articles.

Location: OONL.

7066 **Struthers, J.R. (Tim)**
"A bibliography of works by and on Hugh Hood."
In: *Essays on Canadian Writing*; Nos. 13/14 (Winter/Spring 1978-1979) p. 230-294.; ISSN: 0316-0300.

Note: Works by Hood: books and manuscripts, contributions to newspapers, periodicals, books, anthologies, theses and dissertations directed or adjudicated by Hood; works about Hood: books, articles, theses, selected book reviews.

Location: OONL.

7067 **Struthers, J.R. (Tim)**
"Hugh Hood: an annotated bibliography."
In: *The annotated bibliography of Canada's major authors*, Vol. 5, edited by Robert Lecker and Jack David. Downsview, Ont.: ECW Press, 1984. P. 231-353.; ISBN: 0-920802-68-0.

Note: 673 entries.– Works by Hood: books (novels, short stories, sketches, non-fiction, criticism), manuscripts, contributions to periodicals and books, audio-visual material; works about Hood: books, theses and dissertations, interviews and profiles, audio-visual material, dramatic adaptations, selected book reviews.

Location: OONL.

7068 **Lewis, David**
Louis Hooper: the Harlem years: a bio-discographical dossier. Montreal: Montreal Vintage Music Society, 1989. 26 l.; ISBN: 1-895002-01-X.

Note: 122 entries listing Canadian jazz pianist Louis Hooper recordings in New York between 1923 and April, 1929, most featuring Hooper as accompanist to vocalists. Reprinted from the *Montreal Vintage Music Society Bulletin*, No. 205 (May 2, 1989) P. 9-34.

Location: OONL.

7069 **Lamb, William Kaye**
F.W. Howay: a bibliography. Vancouver: William Hoffer and Stephen Lunsford, 1982. [38] p.: port.

Note: 293 entries.– Reprinted from: *British Columbia Historical Quarterly*; Vol. 8, no. 1 (January 1944) in an edition of 200 copies by William Hoffer and Stephen Lunsford.– Includes a biographical sketch.

Location: OONL.

7070 **Elliott, Shirley B.**
"Joseph Howe: 1804-1873: a bibliography compiled in the Legislative Library."
In: *Journal of Education*; Vol. 1, no. 1 (series 6) (Fall 1973) p. 31-36.; ISSN: 0022-0566.

Note: Location: OONL.

7071 **Nelson, Debra**
E.J. Hughes: a bibliography. Surrey, B.C.: Surrey Art Gallery, c1984. 52 p.; ISBN: 0-920181-09-0.

Note: References to reproductions, reviews, articles on B.C. artist E.J. Hughes in newspapers, exhibition catalogues, periodicals and books.

Location: OONL.

7072 **Hugolin, père**
Bibliographie du R.P. Hugolin. Montréal: [Imprimerie des franciscains], 1932. 50 p.

Note: 70 livres et brochures, approx. 270 articles et autres écrits.

Localisation: OONL.

— I —

7073 **Ward, Jane**
"The published works of H.A. Innis."
In: *Canadian Journal of Economics and Political Science*; Vol. 19, no. 2 (May 1953) p. 233-244.; ISSN: 0315-4890.

Note: Location: AEU.

— J —

7074 **Innis, Harold Adams**
"William T. Jackman, 1871-1951: [publications]."
In: *Canadian Journal of Economics and Political Science*; Vol. 18, no. 2 (May 1952) p. 202-204.; ISSN: 0315-4890.

Note: Location: AEU.

7075 **Hugolin, père**
Bibliographie et iconographie du serviteur de Dieu le R.P. Frédéric Janssoone, o.f.m., 1838-1916. Québec: Imprimerie Franciscaine missionaire, 1932. 62 p.

Note: 278 entrées.– Cinq parties: "Les livres et brochures du P. Frédéric," "Ses écrits dans les périodiques," "Les écrits sur le Père Frédéric," "L'iconographie du P. Frédéric," "Ses manuscrits."

Localisation: OONL.

7076 **Wollock, Jeffrey**
"Stinson Jarvis: a bio-bibliography."
In: *Papers of the Bibliographical Society of Canada*; Vol. 8 (1969) p. 23-60.; ISSN: 0067-6896.

Note: Reviews works of Jarvis, lists works dealing with life and work of Jarvis (1854-1926), "Toronto-born author of six books, several short stories, and numerous essays and articles."
Supplement: "Further bibliography of Stinson Jarvis". In: *Papers of the Bibliographical Society of Canada*; Vol. 14 (1975) p. 79-89.– 82 entries.

Location: OONL.

7077 **Balikci, Asen**
"Bio-bibliography of Diamond Jenness."
In: *Anthropologica*; No. 4 (1957) p. 37-46.; ISSN: 0003-5459.

Note: Chronological listing of writings of Jenness from 1916 to 1956: books, articles, conference papers, museum bulletins.

Location: AEU.

7078 **Collins, Henry B.; Taylor, William E.**
"Diamond Jenness (1889-1969)."
In: *Arctic*; Vol. 23, no. 2 (June 1970) p. 71-81.; ISSN: 0004-0843.

Note: Includes *Jennessiana*, p. 78-81, a partial list of writings of Jenness, 1916 to 1970.

Location: AEU.

7079 **De Laguna, Frederica**
"Bibliography of Diamond Jenness."
In: *American Anthropologist*; Vol. 73, no. 1 (February

1971) p. 251-254.; ISSN: 0065-6941.
Note: Chronological checklist, 1916-1970.
Location: OONL.

7080 **"Ouvrages du père Jetté."**
Dans: *Vie oblate life*; Vol. 33, no 4 (décembre 1974) p. 235-239.; ISSN: 0318-9392.
Note: Localisation: OONL.

7081 **Belton, Eric J.**
Bibliography of published writings of Dr. Harry G. Johnson. [Thunder Bay, Ont.]: Library, Lakehead University, 1979. 69 p.
Note: Approx. 1,000 entries.– Four sections: "Books, pamphlets, lectures (arranged alphabetically)," "Published writing, other than reviews" (arranged chronologically)," "Signed reviews (arranged by year of publication)," "Unpublished manuscripts."
Location: OONL.

7082 **Judd, William W.**
Catalogue of documents pertaining to the life and activities of William Wallace Judd, professor emeritus (zoology), University of Western Ontario, deposited in the Regional History Library, University of Western Ontario, London, Ontario, Canada. London, Ont.: Phelps, 1989. 65 p., 2 l.
Note: 608 entries of published material.– Includes list of publications by Judd dating from 1940 to 1989: papers, journal articles, studies.
Location: OONL.

— K —

7083 **"Writings by Helmut Kallmann."**
In: *Musical Canada: words and music honouring Helmut Kallmann*, edited by John Beckwith and Frederick A. Hall. Toronto: University of Toronto Press, 1988. P. 315-324.; ISBN: 0-8020-5759-4.
Note: Books, major articles, prefaces, short dictionary articles, bibliographical compilations, editorial contributions, reviews, concert program notes from 1949 to 1987.
Location: OONL.

7084 **Robert, Lucie**
"Bibliographie de Naïm Kattan."
Dans: *Voix et Images*; Vol. 11, no 1 (automne 1985) p. 45-54.; ISSN: 0318-9201.
Note: Oeuvres de Kattan: volumes et chapitres de volumes, articles de périodiques; études sur Kattan et son oeuvre.
Localisation: AEU

7085 **Schmidt, Jeanette G.**
J.R. Kidd: a bibliography of his writings. Toronto: Department of Adult Education and the R.W.B. Jackson Library, Ontario Institute for Studies in Education, 1988. xi, 47 p.; ISBN: 0-7744-9809-9.
Note: Approx. 450 entries.– Books, articles, tapes, papers, speeches relating to various aspects of adult education.
Location: OONL.

7086 **Grant, Madeline**
William Lyon Mackenzie King: a bibliography. Prelim. ed. [Waterloo, Ont.]: Department of History, University of Waterloo, 1974. 28 l.
Note: Approx. 560 entries.– Monographs and articles by King; monographs, articles, dissertations about King.
Location: OOP.

7087 **Grant, Madeline**
"William Lyon Mackenzie King: a bibliography."
In: *Mackenzie King: widening the debate*, edited by John English and W.O. Stubbs. Toronto: Macmillan of Canada, c1977. P. 221-253.; ISBN: 0-7705-1529-0.
Note: Lists published materials by and about Mackenzie King.– Excludes unpublished materials, manuscripts, articles from most newspapers or newsmagazines, official handouts.
Location: OONL.

7088 **Brady, Elizabeth**
"A bibliographical essay on William Kirby's *The Golden Dog*, 1877-1977."
In: *Papers of the Bibliographical Society of Canada*; Vol. 15, (1976) p. 24-48.; ISSN: 0067-6896.
Note: Detailed description of six editions of Kirby's novel, including various impressions and issues: collation, contents, text, typography, illustrations, paper, casing, locations, notes.
Location: OONL.

7089 **"40 years of Kirkconnell: titles and selected articles."**
In: *Acadia Bulletin*; Vol. 47, no. 1 (January 1961) p. 19-23; vol. 48, no. 1 (January 1962) p. 22-25.; ISSN: 0044-5843.
Note: Location: OONL.

7090 **Canadian Library Association. Reference Section**
40 years of Kirkconnell: titles and selected articles. [Ottawa: s.n., 1962]. iii, 13 l.
Note: 370 entries.– Books, pamphlets, offprints; works in collaboration; contributions to collective works; articles.– Section of press comments on Kirkconnell works. Extract from the *Acadia Bulletin*, vol. 47, no. 1 (January 1961) p. 19-23, and vol. 48, no. 1 (January 1962) p. 22-25.
Location: OONL.

7091 **Perkin, J.R.C.; Snelson, James B.**
Morning in his heart: the life and writings of Watson Kirkconnell. [Hantsport, N.S.]: Published for Acadia University Library by Lancelot Press, 1986. viii, 371 p.: ill., port.; ISBN: 0-88999-304-1.
Note: 1,800 entries.– Works by Kirkconnell: books and pamphlets, translations, serial contributions (articles, addresses, poems); chapters, sections in books by someone else; prefaces, forewords, etc.; reviews of Kirkconnell's works, bibliographic sources.
Location: OONL.

7092 **Smucker, Donovan E.**
"Walter Klassen: a bibliography."
In: *Conrad Grebel Review*; Vol. 9, no. 3 (Fall 1991) p. 345-351.; ISSN: 0829-044X.
Note: 87 entries.– Books, articles, chapters in books, pamphlets, book reviews.
Location: OONL.

7093 **Caplan, Usher**
"A.M. Klein: a bibliography and index to manuscripts."
In: *The A.M. Klein symposium*, edited by Seymour Mayne. Ottawa: University of Ottawa Press, 1975. P. 87-122.; ISBN: 0-7766-4382-7.
Note: Listing of Klein's published and unpublished writings: poetry, fiction, drama, essays and articles, book reviews, translations, edited material.
Location: OONL.

7094 **Dietz, Hanns-Bertold**
Lothar Klein. Don Mills, Ont.: PRO Canada, 1983. 11 p.: music, port.

Note: Bio-bibliography.– List of works, p. 4-9.– Discography, p. 10.
Location: OONL.

7095 **Thomas, Clara**
"Carl Klinck: indefatigable Canadian: a Carl F. Klinck bibliography."
In: *Journal of Canadian Fiction*; Vol. 2, no. 3 (Summer 1973) p. 5-8.; ISSN: 0047-2255.
Note: Biographical note accompanied by list of books, bulletins, articles on early Canadian literature, reviews, work in progress.
Location: AEU.

7096 **Parker, J.H.**
"The published works of George A. Klinck."
In: *Canadian Modern Language Review*; Vol. 30, no. 3 (March 1974) p. 201-205.; ISSN: 0008-4506.
Note: Location: AEU.

7097 **Judd, William W.**
Catalogue of columns on natural history, "Nature's diary", by Alfred Brooker Klugh (1882-1932), published in the *Farmer's Advocate*, 1912 to 1925, at London, Ontario, Canada. London, Ont.: Phelps, 1986. ii l., 42 p.
Note: 597 entries.
Location: OONL.

7098 **Burke, Anne**
"Raymond Knister: an annotated checklist."
In: *Essays on Canadian Writing*; No. 16 (Fall-Winter 1979-1980) p. 20-61.; ISSN: 0316-0300.
Note: Works by Knister: books and manuscripts, contributions to periodicals, books, anthologies; works about Knister and his work: articles, sections of books, letters, theses, selected book reviews.– Index of critics listed in the bibliography.
Location: AEU.

7099 **Burke, Anne**
Raymond Knister: an annotated bibliography. [Downsview, Ont.: ECW Press, c1981]. P. 281-322.; ISBN: 0-920763-54-5.
Note: 350 entries.– Works by Knister: poetry and prose, manuscripts, contributions to books and periodicals; works about Knister: articles and sections of books, theses and dissertations, letters, audio recordings, book reviews.
Extract from: *The annotated bibliography of Canada's major authors*, Vol. 3, edited by Robert Lecker and Jack David.
Location: OONL.

7100 **Burke, Anne**
"Raymond Knister: an annotated bibliography."
In: *The annotated bibliography of Canada's major authors*, Vol. 3, edited by Robert Lecker and Jack David. Downsview, Ont.: ECW Press, c1981. P. 281-322.; ISBN: 0-920802-23-0.
Note: 350 entries.– Works by Knister: poetry and prose, manuscripts, contributions to books and periodicals; works about Knister: articles and sections of books, theses and dissertations, letters, audio recordings, book reviews.
Location: OONL.

7101 **Ray, Margaret**
Raymond Knister: a bibliography of his works. [Toronto]: Published under the auspices of the Bibliographical Society of Canada, [1950]. 8 p.
Note: Approx. 90 entries.– Extract from: Livesay,

Dorothy. *Collected poems of Raymond Knister*. Toronto: Ryerson Press, 1949.
Location: OONL.

7102 **Lecker, Robert**
"An annotated bibliography of works by and about Robert Kroetsch."
In: *Essays on Canadian Writing*; Nos. 7/8 (Fall 1977) p. 74-96.; ISSN: 0316-0300.
Note: Works by Kroetsch: books, contributions to periodicals and anthologies; writings about Kroetsch: articles, interviews, sections of books, book reviews.
Location: AEU.

7103 **Lecker, Robert; Maracle, Kathleen**
"Robert Kroetsch: an annotated bibliography."
In: *The annotated bibliography of Canada's major authors*, Vol. 7, edited by Robert Lecker and Jack David. Toronto: ECW Press, 1987. P. 271-402.; ISBN: 0-920802-11-1.
Note: 596 entries.– Works by Kroetsch: books (novels, poetry, memoir, criticism, travel book, books edited), broadside, editorial work, audio-visual material, manuscripts, contributions to periodicals and books; works about Kroetsch; books, articles and sections of books, theses and dissertations, interviews and profiles, adaptations, selected book reviews.
Location: OONL.

7104 **Fudge, Evelyn**
"A selected list of the writings of E. Cockburn Kyte."
In: *Ernest Cockburn Kyte: a tribute*, edited by William F.E. Morley. Kingston, Ont.: Douglas Library, Queen's University, 1970. P. 23-25.
Note: Location: OONL.

— L —

7105 **Smith, Donald; Tétreault, Josée**
"Bibliographie de Gilbert La Rocque."
Dans: *Voix et Images*; Vol. 15, no 3 (printemps 1990) p. 387-394.; ISSN: 0318-9201.
Note: Oeuvres de La Rocque (volumes, articles de périodiques, entrevues); études sur La Rocque et son oeuvre.
Localisation: AEU.

7106 **Mercier, Marguerite**
"Pierre Gaultier de Varennes, Sieur de La Verendrye: bibliographie."
Dans: *Revue d'histoire de l'Amérique française*; Vol. 3, no 4 (mars 1950) p. 623-627.; ISSN: 0035-2357.
Note: Localisation: AEU.

7107 **Wyczynski, Paul**
Albert Laberge, 1871-1960: Charles Gill, 1871-1918. Ottawa: Bibliothèque nationale du Canada, 1971. 42, 42 p.
Note: 200 entrées.– Catalogue d'exposition souligne le centenaire de la naissance de Gill et Laberge, liste des oeuvres.– Texte en français et en anglais disposé tête-bêche.– Titre de la p. de t. additionnelle: *Albert Laberge, 1871-1960: Charles Gill, 1871-1918.*
Localisation: OONL.

7108 **Wyczynski, Paul**
Albert Laberge, 1871-1960: Charles Gill, 1871-1918. Ottawa: National Library of Canada, 1971. 42, 42 p.
Note: 200 entries.– Catalogue of exhibit at National Library marking the centenary of births of Gill and Laberge lists writings and artifacts, with descriptive notes.– Text in English and French with French text on inverted pages.– Title of additional title-page: *Albert*

Laberge, 1871-1960; Charles Gill, 1871-1918.
Location: OONL.

7109 **Olivier, Réjean**
Le père Albert Lacombe, O.M.I. (1827-1916) ...
bibliographie signalétique et chronologique de ses écrits,
comprenant articles de périodiques, brochures, livres et
manuscrits. L'Assomption [Québec]: Collège de
l'Assomption, Bibliothèque, 1983. 86 f., ill., ports.; ISBN:
2-920248-81-2.
Note: 203 entrées.– Oeuvres du père Lacombe;
principales sources sur la vie et les oeuvres du père
Lacombe.
Localisation: OONL.

7110 **"Oeuvres de Guy Lafond."**
Dans: *Voix et Images*; Vol. 4, no 2 (décembre 1978) p. 187-
188.; ISSN: 0318-9201.
Note: Publications, poèmes détachés, articles, émissions
(radio, télévision); publications et thèse concernant
l'oeuvre de Lafond.
Localisation: AEU.

7111 **Cameron, William J.**
A bibliography in short-title catalog form of eighteenth
century editions of the writings of Louis Armand de Lom
d'Arce, Baron de Lahontan. [London: University of
Western Ontario], 1982. iii, 14 l. (WHSTC Bibliography ;
no. 6 ; ISSN: 0712-9289); ISBN: 0-7714-0363-1.
Note: Location: OONL.

7112 **Greenly, Albert Harry**
"Lahontan: an essay and bibliography."
In: *Papers of the Bibliographical Society of America*; Vol. 48,
no. 4 (1954) p. 334-389.; ISSN: 0006-128X.
Note: Location: OONL.

7113 **Paltsits, Victor Hugo**
Bibliography of the writings of Baron Lahontan.
[Montreal]: Édition du Bouton d'Or, [1978]. [li]-xciii p.
Note: Introduction, notes and index by Reuben Gold
Thwaites.
Location: OONL.

7114 **Evans, Gwynneth; Hawkins, Elizabeth; Honeywell,
Joan**
"Bibliography of the published works of William Kaye
Lamb."
In: *Archivaria*; No. 15 (Winter 1982-1983) p. 131-144.;
ISSN: 0318-6954.
Note: Lists monographs, edited works and introductions,
periodicals and series edited, articles, encyclopaedia
articles, book reviews, works in progress.
Location: AEU.

7115 **Gratton, Claude**
Yvan Lamonde: historien de la culture: essai de
bibliographie, 1965-1984. Nouv. version rev., augm. et
corr. Sorel, Québec: Éditions Artisanales, 1986. 47 f.;
ISBN: 2-920827-04-9.
Note: Livres, articles paru dans les revues spécialisées
(philosophie, histoire), articles parus dans les collectifs,
comptes-rendus dans les revues spécialisées et journaux,
réplique, lettres ouvert, rapports de recherche, interview,
textes radiophoniques et participations télévisuelles,
tapuscrits.
*Édition antérieure: ... : bibliographie chronologique, 1965-
1984.* 1985. [44] p.; ISBN: 2-920827-01-4.
Localisation: OONL.

7116 **Bentley, D.M.R.**
"Archibald Lampman (1861-1899): a checklist."
In: *Essays on Canadian Writing*; No. 5 (Fall 1976) p. 36-49.;
ISSN: 0316-0300.
Note: Description of public collections of Lampman
materials in Canada, listing of Lampman works: poetry,
prose; selected reviews of Lampman's poems, obituaries,
etc., studies, including theses, dealing with Lampman
and his work.
Location: AEU.

7117 **Wicken, George**
Archibald Lampman: an annotated bibliography.
Downsview, Ont.: ECW Press, c1980. P. 97-146.; ISBN: 0-
920763-55-3.
Note: 370 entries.– Works by Lampman: books (poetry
and prose), manuscripts, essays and short stories, letters,
anthology contributions; works about Lampman: books,
articles and sections of books, theses and dissertations,
book reviews.
Extract from: *The annotated bibliography of Canada's major
authors*, Vol. 2, edited by Robert Lecker and Jack David.
Location: OONL.

7118 **Wicken, George**
"Archibald Lampman: an annotated bibliography."
In: *The annotated bibliography of Canada's major authors*,
Vol. 2, edited by Robert Lecker and Jack David.
Downsview, Ont.: ECW Press, c1980. P. 97-146.; ISBN: 0-
920802-38-9.
Note: 370 entries.– Works by Lampman: books (poetry
and prose), manuscripts, essays and short stories, letters,
anthology contributions; works about Lampman: books,
articles and sections of books, theses and dissertations,
book reviews.
Location: OONL.

7119 **Noizet, Pascale**
"Bibliographie de Suzanne Lamy."
Dans: *Voix et Images*; Vol. 13, no 1 (automne 1987) p. 70-
80.; ISSN: 0318-9201.
Note: Oeuvres, chapitres de volumes, articles de
périodiques et de journaux, communications et
productions radiophonique/télévisuelle; articles sur
Lamy et son oeuvre.
Localisation: AEU.

7120 **Bates, Hilary**
"A bibliography of Fred Landon."
In: *Ontario History*; Vol. 62, no. 1 (March 1970) p. 5-16.;
ISSN: 0030-2953.
Note: 241 entries.– Chronological listing of works of
Landon: books, articles, pamphlets, papers, typewritten
manuscripts.– Excludes newspaper articles which
appeared principally in the *London Free Press, Farmer's
Advocate, Western University Gazette*.– Includes reviews of
Landon's writings.
Location: AEU.

7121 **Lajoie, Yvan**
"Essai de bibliographie des oeuvres de Rina Lasnier."
Dans: *Liberté*; No 108 (novembre-décembre 1976) p. 143-
154.; ISSN: 0024-2020.
Note: Liste de publications et des manuscrits de Rina
Lasnier à l'exception des poèmes.– Ouvrages et études
consacrés à l'auteur.
Localisation: OONL.

7122 **Buss, Helen M.**
"Margaret Laurence: a bibliographical essay."
In: *American Review of Canadian Studies*; Vol. 11, no. 2 (Autumn 1981) p. 1-14.; ISSN: 0272-2011.
Note: Location: AEU.

7123 **Lacroix, Jean-Michel**
"A selected bibliography on Margaret Laurence."
In: *Études canadiennes: Canadian studies*; No. 11 (1981) p. 155-164.; ISSN: 0153-1700.
Note: Works by Laurence, critical studies in chronological order.
Location: OONL.

7124 **Nancekivell, Sharon**
"Margaret Laurence: bibliography."
In: *World Literature Written in English*; Vol. 22, no. 2 (Autumn 1983) p. 263-284.; ISSN: 0093-1705.
Note: Primary texts: Manawaka cycle, African fiction, children's fiction, uncollected short stories, poems, travel writing, literary criticism, essays, manuscripts, audio-visual adaptations, interviews; secondary sources: books and articles on Laurence.
Location: OONL.

7125 **Warwick, Susan J.**
"A Laurence log."
In: *Journal of Canadian Studies*; Vol. 13, no. 3 (Fall 1978) p. 75-83.; ISSN: 0021-9495.
Note: Chronological listing of Margaret Laurence biographical and literary events to 1978: books, articles by Laurence; books and articles about Laurence, including theses (completed or in progress).
Location: AEU.

7126 **Warwick, Susan J.**
"Margaret Laurence: an annotated bibliography."
In: *The annotated bibliography of Canada's major authors*, Vol. 1, edited by Robert Lecker and Jack David. Downsview, Ont.: ECW Press, 1979. P. 447-101.; ISBN: 0-920802-02-8.
Note: 374 entries.– Works by Laurence: books, contributions to periodicals, newspapers, books and anthologies; works about Laurence: books, articles, theses and dissertations, interview, awards and honours, book reviews.
Location: OONL.

7127 **Arndt, John; Woeller, Richard**
A Laurier bibliography. Waterloo, Ont.: Library, Wilfrid Laurier University, c1973. 24 p.: port.; ISBN: 0-88920-002-5.
Note: Approx. 100 entries.– Includes works by Laurier: books, articles, political papers, personal papers, letters; works about Laurier: books, articles, theses.
Location: OONL.

7128 **Stewart, Marjorie J.**
"Sir Wilfrid Laurier; a contribution towards a bibliography."
In: *Ontario Library Review*; Vol. 15, no. 2 (November 1930) p. 59-61.; ISSN: 0030-2996.
Note: Writings by Laurier, works about Laurier: books, parts of books, periodical articles.
Location: OONL.

7129 **"Bibliographie sur Calixa Lavalée et 'O Canada'."**
Dans: *Passe-Temps*; Vol. 39, no. 864 (août 1933) p. 42.; ISSN: 0384-5737.
Note: 25 entrées.

Localisation: OONL.

7130 **Bennett, Joy; Polson, James**
Irving Layton, a bibliography, 1935-1977. Montreal: Concordia University Libraries, 1979. iv, 200 p.; ISBN: 0-9690101-0-9.
Note: Lists published materials: Layton's work in every known edition (poetry, prose, plays, stories, correspondence); critical material (articles reviews, theses, bibliographies).
Location: OONL.

7131 **Mayne, Seymour**
"Irving Layton: a bibliography-in-progress, 1931-1971."
In: *West Coast Review*; Vol. 7, no. 3 (January 1973) p. 23-32.; ISSN: 0043-311X.
Note: Works by Layton: books (poetry and prose, editions, edited material), individual items (poems, stories, articles and essays, selected published correspondence); writings about Layton: selected articles, reviews and other writing, biographical information.
Location: AEU.

7132 **MacDonald, Marjorie Anne**
Robert Le Blant, historien et chef de file de la recherche sur les débuts de la Nouvelle-France: bibliographie commentée. Saint John: Musée du Nouveau-Brunswick, 1986. 30, 28 p.; ISBN: 0-919-32637-4.
Note: 50 entrées.– Comprend: livres, articles par Le Blant, publié et en préparation.– Texte en français et en anglais disposé tête-bêche.– Titre de la p. de t. additionnelle: *Robert Le Blant: seminal researcher and historian of early New France: a commented bibliography.*
Localisation: OONL.

7133 **MacDonald, Marjorie Anne**
Robert Le Blant, seminal researcher and historian of early New France: a commented bibliography. Saint John: New Brunswick Museum, 1986. 28, 30 p.; ISBN: 0-919-32637-4.
Note: 50 entries.– Includes books and articles by Le Blant, published and in preparation.– Text in English and French with French text on inverted pages.– Title of additional title-page: *Robert Le Blant, historien et chef de file de la recherche sur les débuts de la Nouvelle-France: bibliographie commentée.*
Location: OONL.

7134 **"Select bibliography of Stephen Leacock's contributions to the social sciences."**
In: *Canadian Journal of Economics and Political Science*; Vol. 10, no. 2 (May 1944) p. 228-230.; ISSN: 0315-4890.
Note: Location: AEU.

7135 **Curry, Ralph L.**
"Stephen Leacock: the writer and his writings."
In: *Stephen Leacock: a reappraisal*, edited by David Staines. Ottawa: University of Ottawa Press, c1986. P. 133-160. (Reappraisals: Canadian writers ; 12); ISBN: 0-7766-0146-6.
Note: Chronological listing of Leacock writings, 1887-1947.
Location: OONL.

7136 **Lomer, Gerhard Richard**
Stephen Leacock: a check-list and index of his writings. Ottawa: National Library of Canada, 1954. 153 p.: ill.
Note: Listing of books, pamphlets, essays, sketches, articles, manuscripts.– Covers material traced to the end of 1950.

7137 **McGill University. Library School**
A bibliography of Stephen Butler Leacock. Montreal: [s.n.], 1935. 31 p., [4] p. of pl.: ill., ports.
Note: Approx. 225 entries.– Lists works of Leacock under various topics: biography, humour, political science, sports, etc.; works about Leacock: reported addresses, biography and criticism, interviews, portraits, reviews.
Location: OONL.

7138 **Félix Leclerc, 1914-1918: bibliographie et dossier La Presse.** Montréal: Services documentaires Multimedia, 1988. 36 p.: ill., portr.; ISBN: 2-89059-330-4.
Note: Oeuvres de Félix Leclerc, ouvrages sur Leclerc, documents audiovisuels.
Localisation: OONL.

7139 **Samson, Jean-Noël**
"Bibliographie [Félix Leclerc]."
Dans: *Félix Leclerc.* Montréal: Fides, 1967. P. 79-87. (Dossiers de documentation sur la littérature canadienne-française ; 2)
Note: Localisation: OONL.

7140 **Tremblay, Monique; Provencher, Luc**
Félix Leclerc: bibliographie. [S.l.]: Collège d'enseignement général et professionnel François-Xavier-Garneau, 1990. 27 f.; ISBN: 2-920910-02-7.
Note: Approx. 250 entrées.– Articles, monographies, ouvrages généraux, documents audiovisuels.
Localisation: OONL.

7141 **Saddlemyer, Ann**
"A checklist of the publications of Clifford Leech."
In: *University of Toronto Quarterly*; Vol. 45, no. 3 (Spring 1976) p. 246-261.; ISSN: 0042-0247.
Note: Location: AEU.

7142 **Hare, John**
"A bibliography of the works of Léon Pamphile Lemay (1837-1918)."
In: *Papers of the Bibliographical Society of America*; Vol. 57, no. 1 (1963) p. 50-60.; ISSN: 0006-128X.
Note: Location: AEU.

7143 **Pellerin, Maurice; Gallichan, Gilles**
Pamphile Le May, bibliothécaire de la Législature et écrivain. Québec: Bibliothèque de l'Assemblée nationale, 1986. iii, 141 p.: ill., port. (Bibliographie et documentation / Bibliothèque de l'Assemblée nationale du Québec ; 21)
Note: 483 entrées.– Oeuvres de Lemay, articles sur Lemay et son oeuvre, biographie, index des titres.
Localisation: OONL.

7144 **Renault, Raoul**
Bibliographie de Sir James M. Lemoine. Québec: Brousseau, 1897. 11 p.
Note: Extrait du *Courrier du livre*, janvier-mars 1897, t. 1, nos 9-11, p. 141-146.
Microforme: ICMH collection de microfiches ; no 12329; ISBN: 0-665-12329-9. 1 microfiche (12 images).
Localisation: OONL.

7145 **Cayouette, Jacques; Blondeau, Marcel**
"Bibliographie d'Ernest Lepage."
Dans: *Bulletin de la Société botanique du Québec*; No 4 (1982) p. 3-19.; ISSN: 0228-975X.
Note: 126 entrées.– La période couverte est de 1935 à 1980.
Localisation: QMM.

7146 **Devanney, Burris; Campbell, Sandra; Di Nardo, Domenico**
"Kenneth Leslie: a preliminary bibliography."
In: *Canadian Poetry*; No. 5 (Fall/Winter 1979) p. 105-116.; ISSN: 0704-5646.
Note: Lists books of poetry, individual poems, anthologized poems, pamphlets, selected editorials from *Protestant Digest* and *The Protestant*, selected articles, book reviews, miscellaneous prose.– Selected articles, reviews about Leslie.
Location: AEU.

7147 **Service de diffusion sélective de l'information de la Centrale des bibliothèques**
René Lévesque, 1922-1987. Montréal: Le Service, 1987. 15 p. (DSI/CB ; no 105; ISSN: 0825-5024); ISBN: 2-89059-310-X.
Note: 168 entrées.– Monographies, articles de périodiques et journaux, documents audiovisuels.
Localisation: OONL.

7148 **Ricketts, Alan Stuart**
Dorothy Livesay: an annotated bibliography. Downsview, Ont.: ECW Press, c1983. [75] p.; ISBN: 0-920763-57-X.
Note: 773 entries.– Works by Livesay: poetry, broadsides, short stories, criticism, manuscripts, contributions to periodicals and books, audio recordings; works about Livesay: articles and sections of books, theses and dissertations, films, interviews, book reviews.
Extract from: *The annotated bibliography of Canada's major authors*, Vol. 4, edited by Robert Lecker and Jack David.
Location: OONL.

7149 **Ricketts, Alan Stuart**
"Dorothy Livesay: an annotated bibliography."
In: *The annotated bibliography of Canada's major authors*, Vol. 4, edited by Robert Lecker and Jack David. Downsview, Ont.: ECW Press, c1983. P. 129-203.; ISBN: 0-920802-52-4.
Note: 773 entries.– Works by Livesay: poetry, broadsides, short stories, criticism, manuscripts, contributions to periodicals and books, audio recordings; works about Livesay: articles and sections of books, theses and dissertations, films, interviews, book reviews.
Location: OONL.

7150 **Fancy, Margaret**
"To remember a landscape: a checklist of the works of Douglas Lochhead."
In: *The Red jeep and other landscapes: a collection in honour of Douglas Lochhead*, edited by Peter Thomas. Sackville, N.B.: Centre for Canadian Studies, Mount Allison University, 1987. P. 91-108.; ISBN: 0-86492-063-6.
Note: Books by Lochhead, books and series edited by Lochhead, poems in anthologies and journals, articles, pamphlets, book reviews, introductions, prefaces, readings; works printed by Lochhead; selected reviews of Lochhead's work, selected biographical and critical works.
Location: OONL.

7151 **Foshay, Toby Avard**
John Daniel Logan (1869-1929) [microform]: biography, bibliography and checklist of the Logan papers in the Acadia University Library. Ottawa: National Library of Canada, 1981. 3 microfiches (Canadian theses on microfiche ; 49143; ISSN: 0227-3845); ISBN: 0-31501-286-2.

Note: Location: OONL.

7152 **Lomer, Gerhard Richard**
List of publications by Gerhard R. Lomer. [Ottawa: s.n.], 1960. 5 l.
Note: Location: OONL.

7153 **Roy, Yvonne; Lemaire, Estelle**
Anselme Longpré: bio-bibliographie. [Montréal: Centre Les Compagnons de Jésus et de Marie], 1984. 206 p.: portr.
Note: Localisation: OONL.

7154 **Hugolin, père**
Bio-bibliographie du R.P. Ephrem Longpré, O.F.M. Québec: Imprimerie franciscaine missionnaire, 1931. 40 p.
Note: 123 entrées.
Localisation: OONL.

7155 **Parent, Édouard**
"Bibliographie du P. Éphrem Longpré, O.F.M."
Dans: *Culture*; Vol. 27 (1966) p. 276-289.; ISSN: 0317-2066.
Note: 288 entrées.– Livres et articles de revues, articles publiés dans des dictionnaires religieux, recensions de volumes, ouvrages en collaboration, préfaces de volumes.
Localisation: AEU.

7156 **Caron, Fabien**
"Bibliographie d'Albert Peter Low."
Dans: *Cahiers de géographie de Québec*; Vol. 9, no 18 (avril-septembre 1965) p. 179-181.; ISSN: 0007-9766.
Note: Localisation: OONL.

7157 **MacDermaid, Anne**
"A select list of publications by A.R.M. Lower."
In: *His own man: essays in honour of Arthur Reginald Marsden Lower*, edited by W.H. Heick and Roger Graham. Montreal: McGill-Queen's University Press, 1974. P. 163-182.; ISBN: 0-7735-0202-2.
Note: Chronological listing (1915-1973) of published books and articles by A.R.M. Lower.– Excludes early student newspaper articles, book reviews, most letters to newspapers.
Location: OONL.

7158 **Birney, Earle; Lowry, Marjerie**
"Malcolm Lowry (1909-1957): a bibliography."
In: *Canadian Literature*; No. 8 (Spring 1961) p. 81-88; no. 9 (Summer 1961) p. 80-84; no. 11 (Winter 1962) p. 90-95; no. 19 (Winter 1964) p. 83-89.; ISSN: 0008-4360.
Note: 364 entries.– Works by Lowry: stories and novellas, novels, poetry, articles and reviews, letters, radio adaptations, unpublished material; works about Lowry: critical, biographical, bibliographical.
Location: OONL.

7159 **New, William H.**
Malcolm Lowry: a reference guide. Boston: G.K. Hall, c1978. xxix, 162 p. (Reference publication in literature); ISBN: 0-8161-7884-4.
Note: Approx. 1,000 entries.– Directory of manuscript collections, major writings by Lowry; translations of Lowry's major writings; writings about Lowry and his work, 1927 to 1976.
Location: OONL.

7160 **Woolmer, J. Howard**
A Malcolm Lowry catalogue, with essays by Perle Epstein and Richard Hauer Costa. New York: J. Howard Woolmer, 1968. 64 p.
Note: 219 entries.
Location: OONL.

7161 **Woolmer, J. Howard**
Malcolm Lowry: a bibliography. Revere, Pa.: Woolmer/Brotherson, 1983. xvi, 183 p.: ill.; ISBN: 0-913506-12-5.
Note: Books and pamphlets by Lowry, contributions by Lowry to books by, or edited by, others, contributions to periodicals, translations of Lowry's work into foreign languages, radio and television programs and films, song lyrics, recordings.
Location: OONL.

7162 **Yandle, Anne; Amor, Norman L.**
"Bibliography [Malcolm Lowry]."
In: *Malcolm Lowry Newsletter*; No. 5 (Fall 1979) p. 2-8; no. 7 (Fall 1980) p. 22-25; no. 9 (Fall 1981) p. 35-38; no. 11 (Fall 1982) p. 21-23; no. 13 (Fall 1983) p. 35-38; no. 15 (Fall 1984) p. 68-71; nos. 17/18 (Fall 1985-Spring 1986) p. 145-150; nos. 19-20 (Fall 1986-Spring 1987) p. 151-156; nos. 23/24 (Fall 1988-Spring 1989) p. 160-167; no. 26 (Spring 1990) p. 53-57; no. 28 (Spring 1991) p. 50-70; nos. 29-30 (Fall-Spring 1992) p. 103-121.; ISSN: 0228-8427.
Note: Title varies: *Malcolm Lowry Review*; No. 15 (Fall 1984)-nos. 29-30 (Fall-Spring 1992); ISSN: 0828-5020.
Location: BVAS.

7163 **Braide, Janet**
"John Lyman: a bibliography of his writings."
In: *Journal of Canadian Art History*; Vol. 4, no. 2 (1977/1978) p. 130-140.; ISSN: 0315-4297.
Note: Location: AEU.

— M —

7164 **Bellingham, Susan**
Isabel Ecclestone Mackay bibliography. Waterloo, Ont.: University of Waterloo Library, c1987. xiii, 77 p. (University of Waterloo Library bibliography ; no. 15: ISSN: 0829-948X); ISBN: 0-920834-01-9.
Note: Describes or lists publications of Mackay and includes critical, biographical and manuscript material relating to Mackay.– Attempts to list all periodical and anthology appearances of her work.– Based on Mackay Collection in Dana Porter Library, University of Waterloo.
Location: OONL.

7165 **Cameron, Elspeth**
Hugh MacLennan: an annotated bibliography. Downsview, Ont.: ECW Press, 1979. P. 103-153.; ISBN: 0-920763-58-8.
Note: 625 entries.– Works by MacLennan: books, pamphlets, manuscripts, contributions to books, periodicals and anthologies; works about MacLennan: books, articles and sections of books, theses, interviews, awards and honours, book reviews.
Extract from: *The annotated bibliography of Canada's major authors*, Vol. 1, edited by Robert Lecker and Jack David.
Location: OONL.

7166 **Cameron, Elspeth**
"Hugh MacLennan: an annotated bibliography."
In: *The annotated bibliography of Canada's major authors*, Vol. 1, edited by Robert Lecker and Jack David. Downsview, Ont.: ECW Press, 1979. P. 103-153.; ISBN: 0-920802-02-8.
Note: 625 entries.– Works by MacLennan: books, pamphlets, manuscripts, contributions to periodicals, books and anthologies; works about MacLennan: books, articles and sections of books, theses and dissertations, interviews, awards and honours, books reviews.

Location: OONL.

7167 **Cameron, Elspeth**
"A MacLennan log."
In: *Journal of Canadian Studies*; Vol. 14, no. 4 (Winter 1979/
80) p. 106-121.; ISSN: 0021-9495.
Note: Chronological listing of Hugh MacLennan
biographical and literary events to 1978: books, articles
by MacLennan; selected books, articles, theses, sections
of books about MacLennan.
Location: AEU.

7168 **Gunn, Gertrude E.**
"William Stewart MacNutt: a bibliography, 1932-1983."
In: *Acadiensis*; Vol. 14, no. 1 (Autumn 1984) p. 146-154.;
ISSN: 0044-5851.
Note: Chronological listing of MacNutt's work.
Location: AEU.

7169 **Svacek, Victor**
"Crawford Brough Macpherson: a bibliography."
In: *Powers, possessions and freedoms: essays in honour of C.B.
Macpherson*, edited by Alkis Kontos. Toronto: University
of Toronto Press, c1979. P. 167-178.; ISBN: 0-8020-5474-9.
Note: Contains a listing of all scholarly publications of
Macpherson, to September 1979: books, articles, review
articles, chapters in books, book reviews, arranged
chronologically within each category.– Translations,
revised editions, and reprints are noted with the original
work.– Excludes correspondence, reported versions of
addresses, speeches, interviews.
Location: OONL.

7170 **Pendzey, Luba**
Paul Robert Magocsi: a bibliography, 1965-1985. Toronto:
Chair of Ukrainian Studies, University of Toronto, 1985.
28 p.; ISBN: 0-7727-5106-4.
Note: 154 entries.
Location: OONL.

7171 **Lortie, Lucien**
Bibliographie analytique de l'oeuvre de L'Abbé Arthur
Maheux, précédée d'une biographie. Québec: [s.n.], 1942.
159 p.: portr.
Note: 505 entrées.– Manuscrits, livres et brochures,
préface, ouvrages en collaboration, articles de revues et
journaux, traductions, éditions.
Localisation: OONL.

7172 **Léger, Lauraine**
"Bibliographie: oeuvres d'Antonine Maillet."
Dans: *Revue de l'Université de Moncton*; Vol. 7, no 2 (mai
1974) p. 83-90.; ISSN: 0316-6368.
Note: Localisation: AEU.

7173 **Boivin, Aurélien**
"Bibliographie d'André Major."
Dans: *Voix et Images*; Vol. 10, no 3 (printemps 1985) p. 70-
89.; ISSN: 0318-9201.
Note: Oeuvres, textes radiophoniques et télévisuels,
nouvelles et récits, préfaces; histoires et l'études
générales.
Localisation: AEU.

7174 **Daveluy, Marie-Claire**
"Bibliographie: Jeanne Mance, 1606-1673."
Dans: *Revue d'histoire de l'Amérique française*; Vol. 8, no 2
(septembre 1954) p. 292-306; vol. 8, no 3 (décembre
1954) p. 449-455; vol. 8, no 4 (mars 1955) p. 591-606.;
ISSN: 0035-2357.
Note: Vie et survie; écrits personnels de Mance (textes

narratifs, textes diplomatiques); note sur les ouvrages
des contemporains de Mance; écrits modernes;
biographies de Mance.
Localisation: AEU.

7175 **Potvin, Claudette**
"Bibliographie de Jovette Marchessault."
Dans: *Voix et Images*; Vol. 16, no 2 (hiver 1991) p. 272-280.;
ISSN: 0318-9201.
Note: Oeuvres de Marchessault: volumes, articles de
périodiques; études sur Marchessault et son oeuvres;
divers: film, spectacles, expositions, radio-télévision.
Localisation: AEU.

7176 **Pelletier, Louise**
"Bibliographie: Gilles Marcotte, 1955-1979."
Dans: *Voix et Images*; Vol. 6, no 1 (automne 1980) p. 35-
49.; ISSN: 0318-9201.
Note: Approx. 300 entrées.– Liste classés par ordre
chronologique: romans, critique littéraire, préfaces, textes
pour la radio et télévision.– Exclut critique sur Marcotte
et son oeuvre.
Localisation: AEU.

7177 **Jamet, A.**
"Bibliographie [de Marie de l'Incarnation]."
Dans: *Revue d'histoire de l'Amérique française*; Vol. 1, no 2
(septembre 1947) p. 308-312.; ISSN: 0035-2357.
Note: Manuscrits, imprimés, études (biographies, essais).
Localisation: OONL.

7178 **Wilcox-Magill, Dennis William; Helmes-Hayes,
Richard C.**
"Complete bibliography of Leonard Charles Marsh."
In: *Journal of Canadian Studies*; Vol. 21, no. 2 (Summer
1986) p. 59-66.; ISSN: 0021-9495.
Note: Books, chapters in books, articles and journalism,
booklets and reports, collaborations, book reviews,
lectures/symposia.
Location: AEU.

7179 **Brethour, Ross**
Discography of Ralph Marterie. Aurora, Ont.: R.
Brethour, [1979]. 9 l.
Note: Location: OONL.

7180 **Trew, Johanne**
The Rodolphe Mathieu collection at the National Library
of Canada: an annotated catalogue. Ottawa: National
Library of Canada, 1989. 158 p.; ISBN: 0-315-44440-1.
Note: Includes music manuscripts, writings (published
and unpublished) by and about Mathieu, concert
programmes, correspondence, photographs, bills,
receipts, legal documents, news clippings.– Bibliography.
Thesis, M.A., Musicology, McGill University, 1987.
Location: OONL.

7181 **Greig, Peter E.**
John McCrae, 1872-1918: selected sources/John McCrae,
1872-1918: ressources choisies. Ottawa: National Defence
Library Services, 1990. 15 p. ill., facsim.
Note: Approx. 20 entries.– Works by and about McCrae,
versions of In Flanders Fields, index of titles and first
lines of McCrae's poems.– Text in English and French/
texte en français et en anglais.
Location: OONL.

7182 **Cansino, Barbara**
Diana McIntosh. Don Mills, Ont.: PRO Canada, 1988. 7 p.
Note: Bio-bibliography.– List of compositions, p. 5-7.–
Discography, p. 7.

Location: OONL.

7183 **MacGillivray, Royce**
Sandy Fraser: a bibliography of the writings of John Everett McIntosh (1876-1948) in *The Farmer's Advocate* under the pen name of Sandy Fraser. Waterloo, Ont.: R. MacGillivray, 1991. 106 l.; ISBN: 0-9695129-0-2.
Note: Approx. 750 entries.– Listing of articles and letters to the editor.
Location: OONL.

7184 **The Writings of Marshall McLuhan: listed in chronological order from 1934 to 1975: with an appended list of reviews and articles about him and his work.** Fort Lauderdale, Fla.: Wake-Brook House, c1975. 101, [4] p.: port.; ISBN: 0-87482-078-2.
Note: Location: OONL.

7185 **"Robert McQueen, 1896-1941: [bibliography]."**
In: *Canadian Journal of Economics and Political Science*; Vol. 7, no. 2 (May 1941) p. 281-283.; ISSN: 0315-4890.
Note: Location: AEU.

7186 **Waines, W.J.**
"Bibliography of Professor Robert McQueen."
In: *Manitoba Arts Review*; Vol. 2 (Spring 1941) p. 47-50.
Note: Chronological listing from 1933 to 1941 of articles, briefs, reports, reviews.
Location: NBFU.

7187 **Olivier, Réjean**
Bio-bibliographie de Monsieur Jean-Baptiste Meilleur, 1796-1878, médecin, auteur, fondateur du Collège de l'Assomption, 1832 et premier superintendant de l'Instruction publique dans le Bas-Canada, 1843-1855. Joliette [Québec]: R. Olivier, 1982. 55 p.: ill., fac-sims.; ISBN: 2-920249-54-1.
Note: 27 entrées.
Localisation: OONL.

7188 **Greig, Peter E.**
"A checklist of primary source material relating to Fleury Mesplet."
In: *Papers of the Bibliographical Society of Canada*; Vol. 13 (1974) p. 49-74.; ISSN: 0067-6896.
Note: Chronological listing of manuscripts, documents, imprints of Montreal printer Fleury Mesplet, including references to projected works.
Location: OONL.

7189 **McLachlan, R.W.**
"Fleury Mesplet, the first printer at Montreal."
In: *Proceedings and Transactions of the Royal Society of Canada*; Series 2, vol. 12, section 2 (1906) p. 197-230.; ISSN: 0316-4616.
Note: Location: AEU.

7190 **Marin, Armand**
L'honorable Pierre-Basile Mignault. Montréal: Fides, 1946. 132 p. (Bibliographies d'auteurs canadiens d'expression française)
Note: 79 entrées.– Ouvrages de Mignault: manuscrits, livres et brochures, articles de revues et de journaux, arrêts de la Cour suprême, mémoires et plaidoyers; sources générales.
Localisation: OONL.

7191 **Brouillette, Benoît**
"Bibliographie des ouvrages d'Émile Miller."
Dans: *Revue canadienne de géographie*; Vol. 4 (1950) p. 94-96.; ISSN: 0316-3032.
Note: Localisation: AEU.

7192 **Esdras Minville: bio-bibliographie.** Montréal: [s.n.], 1972. 15 f.
Note: Localisation: OONL.

7193 **Latham, Sheila**
W.O. Mitchell: an annotated bibliography. [Downsview, Ont.: ECW Press, c1981]. P. 323-364.
Note: 435 entries.– Works by and about Mitchell: novels, stories, plays, radio and television works, screenplays, audio recordings and speeches, articles, theses, interviews, reviews of books and theatrical performances. Extract from: *The annotated bibliography of Canada's major authors*, Vol. 3, edited by Robert Lecker and Jack David.
Location: OONL.

7194 **Latham, Sheila**
"W.O. Mitchell: an annotated bibliography."
In: *The annotated bibliography of Canada's major authors*, Vol. 3, edited by Robert Lecker and Jack David. Downsview, Ont.: ECW Press, c1981. P. 323-364.; ISBN: 0-920802-23-0.
Note: 435 entries.– Works by and about Mitchell: novels, stories, plays, radio and television works, screen plays, audio recordings and speeches, articles, theses, interviews, reviews of books and theatrical performances.
Location: OONL.

7195 **Hugolin, père**
Bibliographie du R.P. Joachim-Joseph Monfette, o.f.m. Québec: Imprimerie franciscaine missionaire, 1931. 42 p.
Note: 434 entrées.
Localisation: OONL.

7196 **Garner, Barbara Carman; Harker, Mary**
"Anne of Green Gables: an annotated bibliography."
In: *Canadian Children's Literature*; No. 55 (1989) p. 18-41.; ISSN: 0319-0080.
Note: 82 entries.– Books, theses, scholarly periodical articles, popular periodical articles, reviews.
Location: AEU.

7197 **Russell, Ruth Weber; Russell, D.W.; Wilmshurst, Rea**
Lucy Maud Montgomery: a preliminary bibliography. Waterloo, Ont.: University of Waterloo Library, c1986. xxiii, 175 p. (University of Waterloo Library bibliography ; no. 13; ISSN: 0829-948X); ISBN: 0-920834-42-6.
Note: 1,989 entries.– Works by Montgomery: novels, poems, letters, published journals, autobiography, translations, adaptations for other media, archival holdings; works about Montgomery: books, theses, articles, chapters of books, audio-visual studies, selected articles from reference books, selected newspaper articles, book reviews, film and theatre reviews.
Location: OONL.

7198 **Wilmshurst, Rea**
"L.M. Montgomery's short stories: a preliminary bibliography."
In: *Canadian Children's Literature*; No. 29 (1983) p. 25-34.; ISSN: 0319-0080.
Note: Location: OONL.

7199 **Wilmshurst, Rea**
A bibliography of L.M. Montgomery's short stories, poems, and miscellaneous articles. [Toronto: R. Wilmshurst], c1985. 201 p.
Note: 1,033 entries.– Lists only stories, poems, articles intended for publication.– Includes a magazine index and a chronological index, Montgomery's ledger lists of

stories and poems sold, with amount she received for each.

Location: NBFU.

7200 **Carrière, Gaston**
"Adrien-Gabriel Morice, o.m.i. (1859-1938): essai de bibliographie."
Dans: *Revue de l'Université d'Ottawa*; Vol. 42, no 3 (juillet-septembre 1972) p. 325-341.; ISSN: 0041-9206.
Note: Localisation: AEU.

7201 **Robert, Jacques**
"Bibliographie et index de Gérard Morisset."
Dans: *A la découverte du patrimoine avec Gérard Morisset*. Québec: Ministère des affaires culturelles, 1981. P. 229-255.; ISBN: 2-551-04204-6.
Note: 347 entrées.– Volumes, volumes en collaboration, journaux, périodiques.– Index analytique par Monique Cloutier.
Localisation: OONL.

7202 **Ommanney, C. Simon L.**
"Selected bibliography of the publications of Fritz Müller for the period 1954-1980."
In: *Arctic*; Vol. 34, no. 2 (June 1981) p. 196-198.; ISSN: 0004-0843.
Note: Location: AEU.

7203 **Cook, D.E.**
"Alice Munro: a checklist (to December 31, 1974)."
In: *Journal of Canadian Fiction*; No. 16 (1976) p. 131-136.; ISSN: 0047-2255.
Note: Listing of books, short stories, anthologies.– Writings about Munro: book reviews, articles, biographical sketches.
Location: AEU.

7204 **Struthers, J.R. (Tim)**
"Some highly subversive activities: a brief polemic and a checklist of works on Alice Munro."
In: *Studies in Canadian Literature*; Vol. 6, no. 1 (Spring 1981) p. 140-150.; ISSN: 0380-6995.
Note: 115 entries.– Articles and sections of books, theses, interviews and profiles.
Location: AEU.

7205 **Thacker, Robert**
"Alice Munro: an annotated bibliography."
In: *The annotated bibliography of Canada's major authors*, Vol. 5, edited by Robert Lecker and Jack David. Downsview, Ont.: ECW Press, 1984. P. 354-414.; ISBN: 0-920802-68-0.
Note: 360 entries.– Works by Munro: books, audio-visual material, manuscripts, contributions to periodicals and books, television scripts; works about Munro: articles and sections of books, bibliographies, theses and dissertations, dramatic adaptations, awards and honours, selected book reviews.
Location: OONL.

7206 **"A Munro bibliography."**
In: *Journal of Education*; Vol. 1, no. 3 (series 6) (Spring 1974) p. 23-24.; ISSN: 0022-0566.
Note: Books, articles, reviews, reports and addresses by Henry Fraser Munro, Nova Scotia Superintendent of Education, 1926-1949.
Location: OONL.

— N —

7207 **Samson, Jean-Noël**
"Bibliographie d'Émile Nelligan."

Dans: *Émile Nelligan*. Montréal: Fides, [1968]. P. 95-104. (Dossiers de documentation sur la littérature canadienne-française ; 3)
Note: Localisation: OONL.

7208 **Wyczynski, Paul**
"Bibliographie d'Émile Nelligan."
Dans: *Études françaises*; Vol. 3, no 3 (août 1967) p. 285-298.; ISSN: 0014-2085.
Note: Localisation: OONL.

7209 **Wyczynski, Paul**
Bibliographie descriptive et critique d'Émile Nelligan. Ottawa: Éditions de l'Université d'Ottawa, 1973. 319 p. (Bibliographies du Canada français ; no 1); ISBN: 0-7766-3951-X.
Note: 1,419 entrées.– Sept sections: "L'oeuvre de Nelligan (manuscrits et imprimés)," "Ouvrages, articles et documents signés," "Articles anonymes," "Chronologie des écrits sur Nelligan," "Poèmes en hommage à Nelligan," "Discographie," "Filmographie."
Localisation: OONL.

7210 **Archibald, R.C.**
"Bibliography of the life and works of Simon Newcomb."
In: *Proceedings and Transactions of the Royal Society of Canada*; Series 2, vol. 10, section 3 (1905) p. 79-109.; ISSN: 0316-4616.
Note: Location: AEU.

7211 **Lecker, Robert**
"An annotated bibliography of works by and about John Newlove."
In: *Essays on Canadian Writing*; No. 2 (Spring 1975) p. 28-53.; ISSN: 0316-0300.
Note: Works by Newlove: books, anthologies, contributions to periodicals (poems, stories), audio recordings, translations by Newlove, translations of Newlove's work; writings about Newlove: articles, sections of books, book reviews.
Location: AEU.

7212 **Lecker, Robert; O'Rourke, David**
"John Newlove: an annotated bibliography."
In: *The annotated bibliography of Canada's major authors*, Vol. 6, edited by Robert Lecker and Jack David. Toronto: ECW Press, 1985. P. 67-128.; ISBN: 0-920802-93-1.
Note: 531 entries.– Works by Newlove: books, broadsides, audio-visual material, editorial work, manuscripts, contributions to books and periodicals (poems, stories, poetry translations, articles, reviews), librettos; works about Newlove: articles and sections of books, thesis, interviews, selected book reviews.
Location: OONL.

7213 **Nichol, bp**
"Published autotopography [checklist of bpNichol's complete works in all genres]."
In: *Essays on Canadian Writing*; No. 1 (Winter 1974) p. 39-46.; ISSN: 0316-0300.
Note: Books, pamphlets, magazines containing poems, anthologies edited by Nichol; periodicals edited by Nichol, exhibitions, reviews and criticism by Nichol; reviews and criticism about Nichol.
Location: AEU.

7214 **Room 302 Books (Firm)**
Room 302 Books, list #4: bpNichol, a ranging. Toronto: Room 302 Books, 1987. [16] p.
Note: Bibliography of works written and published by

bp Nichol.
Location: OONL.

— O —

7215 Randall, Melanie
"The published writings of Mary O'Brien: an annotated bibliography."
In: *Resources for Feminist Research*; Vol. 18, no. 3 (September 1989) p. 107-110.; ISSN: 0707-8412.
Note: Location: AEU.

7216 Arnold, Richard
"Howard O'Hagan: an annotated bibliography."
In: *Silence made us visible: Howard O'Hagan and Tay John*, edited by Margery Fee. Toronto: ECW Press, 1992. P. 128-157.; ISBN: 1-55022-167-1.
Note: Location: OONL.

7217 Olivier, Réjean
Catalogue descriptif et chronologique des oeuvres éditées, composées et compilées par Réjean Olivier contenant une courte notice biographique. Joliette [Québec: s.n.], 1981. iii, 56 p.: ill.; ISBN: 2-920249-50-9.
Note: 52 entrées.
Édition antérieure: *Catalogue chronologique des oeuvres éditées par Réjean Olivier*. 1976. 13 f.
Localisation: OONL.

7218 Olivier, Réjean
Vingt ans de recherches artistiques, bibliographiques, biographiques, culturelles, historiographiques et historiques pour mettre en valeur la région de Lanaudière ou Catalogue descriptif et chronologique des oeuvres éditées, composées et compilées par Réjean Olivier. 2e éd. L'Assomption [Québec]: Collège de l'Assomption, Bibliothèque, 1984. 115 f.: ill.; ISBN: 2-920248-64-2.
Note: 114 entrées.
Édition antérieure: 1983. 80 p.; ISBN: 2-920249-66-5.
Localisation: OONL.

7219 Olivier, Réjean
Bibliographie chronologique des oeuvres de Réjean Olivier publiées par la maison Édition privée et la Bibliothèque du Collège de L'Assomption, et cataloguées par la Centrale des bibliothèques. L'Assomption, Québec: Collège de L'Assomption, Bibliothèque, 1985. 13 f.; ISBN: 2-920248-35-9.
Note: 28 entrées.
Localisation: OONL.

7220 Olivier, Réjean
Les écrits d'un bibliothécaire, auteur, bibliophile, bibliographe et historien de 1967 à 1988. Joliette [Québec]: [s.n.], 1988. 51, 35 p. (Collection Oeuvres bibliophiliques de Lanaudière ; no 18); ISBN: 2-920904-21-3.
Note: 154 entrées.
Localisation: OONL.

7221 Olivier, Réjean
"Catalogue chronologique des livres publiés par Réjean Olivier."
Dans: *Je viens causer des livres* .... Joliette, Québec: Édition privée, 1990. P. 249-313.; ISBN: 2-92090-423-X.
Note: Localisation: OONL.

7222 Olynyk, Nadia M.
Roman Rakhmanny: a bibliographic guide to selected works. Winnipeg: Ukrainian Academy of Arts and Sciences in Canada, 1984. 24 p. (Ukrainian Academy of Arts and Sciences in Canada Bibliography ; no. 1: 21)
Note: 204 entries.– Chronological listing from 1945 to 1982 of writings of Ukrainian-Canadian columnist and publicist Rakhmanny: published and unpublished material, radio broadcast commentaries in non-Ukrainian languages.– Some of these writings were published under Rakhmanny's real name, Roman Olynyk, or other bylines: Romain D'Or and R.R.
Location: OONL.

7223 Brady, Judith
"Michael Ondaatje: an annotated bibliography."
In: *The annotated bibliography of Canada's major authors*, Vol. 6, edited by Robert Lecker and Jack David. Toronto: ECW Press, 1985. P. 129-205.; ISBN: 0-920802-93-1.
Note: 583 entries.– Works by Ondaatje: books, broadsides, dramatic productions, editorial work, manuscripts, contributions to periodicals and books; works about Ondaatje: articles and sections of books, thesis, interviews, selected book, film and play reviews.
Location: OONL.

7224 Woodward, Frances M.
"Margaret Anchoretta Ormsby: publications."
In: *BC Studies*; No. 32 (Winter 1976-1977) p. 163-169.; ISSN: 0005-2949.
Note: Approx. 100 entries.– Books, articles, encyclopaedia articles, book reviews and review articles, unpublished work.
Location: AEU.

7225 Abbott, Maude Elizabeth
"Classified bibliography of Sir William Osler's Canadian period (1868-1885)."
In: *Sir William Osler: memorial number, the "Canadian Medical Association Journal," July 1920*. Montreal: Canadian Medical Association, 1920. P. 103-123.
Note: Location: OONL.

7226 Abbott, Maude Elizabeth
Classified and annotated bibliography of Sir William Osler's publications: (based on the chronological bibliography by Minnie Wright Blogg). 2nd ed., rev. and indexed. Montreal: Medical Museum, McGill University, 1939. xiii, [2], 163 p.: ill., facsims., 2 port. (incl. front.).
Note: Extract: "Reprinted, with additions, from the Sir William Osler memorial volume of the International Association of Medical Museums (Bulletin no. IX) 1926, p. 473-605."
Location: OOCC.

7227 Blogg, Minnie Wright
Bibliography of the writings of Sir William Osler. Rev. and enl. ed. Baltimore: Blogg, 1921. 96 p.: ill.
Note: 1,195 entries.– Copy examined was microfilm-xerographic facsimile of original, produced in 1967 by University Microfilms, Ann Arbor, Mich.
Previous edition: "Bibliography of Sir William Osler, Bart., M.D., F.R.S." In: *Sir William Osler, Bart.: brief tributes to his personality* .... Johns Hopkins Press, 1920. P. 121-167.– 730 entries.
Location: OONL.

7228 Golden, Richard L.; Roland, Charles G.
Sir William Osler: an annotated bibliography with illustrations. San Francisco: Norman Publishing, 1988. xv, 214 p.: ill., ports. (Norman bibliography series ; 1); ISBN: 0-930405-00-5.
Note: 1,493 entries.– Listings arranged in categories:

natural science, including original research; pathology; clinical medicine; literary papers, history, biography, bibliography; medical education, societies, profession; public welfare activities; volumes edited; pseudonymous papers (an Egerton Yorrick Davis checklist); various editions, printings, translations of *The Principles of Medicine*; contents of composite volumes; unpublished works.
Location: OONL.

7229 **Nation, Earl F.; Roland, Charles G.; McGovern, John P.**
An annotated checklist of Osleriana. [Kent, Ohio]: Kent State University Press, 1976. xii, 289 p., [3] l. of pl.: ill.; ISBN: 0-87338-186-6.
Note: 1,367 entries.
Location: OONL.

7230 **Owen, Myra**
Dr. William Osler reprints in the Montreal General Hospital Archives: accession 1501:120, McGill University Archives. Montreal: University Archives, McGill University, 1973. ii, 47 l.
Note: Location: OONL.

7231 **"Bibliographie des oeuvres de Fernand Ouellette."**
Dans: *Voix et Images*; Vol. 5, no 3 (printemps 1980) p. 471-475.; ISSN: 0318-9201.
Note: Oeuvres de l'auteur: poésie, essai, roman.– Liste chronologique des poèmes et articles, 1974-1979.
Localisation: AEU.

— P —

7232 **"F. Hilton Page: Publications."**
In: *Dalhousie Review*; Vol. 69, no. 1 (Summer 1989) p. 173-175.; ISSN: 0011-5827.
Note: 35 entries.– Papers, reviews.
Location: AEU.

7233 **Orange, John Charles**
"P.K. Page: an annotated bibliography."
In: *The annotated bibliography of Canada's major authors*, Vol. 6, edited by Robert Lecker and Jack David. Toronto: ECW Press, 1985. P. 207-285.; ISBN: 0-920802-93-1.
Note: 668 entries.– Works by Page: books (novels, stories, drawings, books edited, scripts for film strips), manuscripts, contributions to periodicals and books, audio-visual material; works about Page: articles and sections of books, theses and dissertations, interviews, poems dedicated to Page, audio-visual material, selected book reviews.
Location: OONL.

7234 **Preston, Michele**
"The poetry of P.K. Page: a checklist."
In: *West Coast Review*; Vol. 3, no. 3 (February 1979) p. 12-17.; ISSN: 0043-311X.
Note: Location: AEU.

7235 **Lapointe, Raoul**
"Bibliographie: Articles et ouvrages concernant Rodolphe Pagé."
Dans: *Saguenayensia*; Vol. 29, no 3 (juillet-septembre 1987) p. 31-33.; ISSN: 0581-295X.
Note: Localisation: AEU.

7236 **"Bibliographie: Papineau (Louis-Joseph) 1786-1871."**
Dans: *Revue d'histoire de l'Amérique française*; Vol. 1, no 1 (juin 1947) p. 148-151.; ISSN: 0035-2357.
Note: Sources manuscrites; sources imprimées: biographies, ouvrages généraux, articles ou essai, périodiques, guides.

Localisation: AEU.

7237 **Pearson, Norman**
Lifetime list of publications: to 1st January 1972. [S.l.: s.n., 1972]. 19 l.
Note: 98 entries.– Books, refereed journals and chapters in books, reports, conference papers, newspaper articles, book reviews related to subjects of town planning, housing, urban renewal, land use, transportation.
Location: OONL.

7238 **Peel, Bruce Braden**
Bibliography of Bruce Braden Peel. Edmonton: [Peel], 1986. 18 p.
Note: 165 entries.
Location: OONL.

7239 **Ryder, Dorothy E.**
"Bruce Braden Peel: a preliminary bibliography."
In: *Papers of the Bibliographical Society of Canada*; Vol. 14 (1975) p. 14-16.; ISSN: 0067-6896.
Note: Books and pamphlets, periodical and newspaper articles, contributions to books and pamphlets.
Location: OONL.

7240 **Charland, Thomas**
"Bibliographie de l'Abbé Alexis Pelletier."
Dans: *Revue d'histoire de l'Amérique française*; Vol. 1, no 3 (décembre 1947) p. 463-469.; ISSN: 0035-2357.
Note: Brochures, articles de journaux.
Localisation: AEU.

7241 **Cormier, François; Lacroix, Yves**
"Oeuvres de Pierre Perrault."
Dans: *Voix et Images*; Vol. 3, no 3 (avril 1978) p. 371-378.; ISSN: 0318-9201.
Note: Articles au *Quartier-Latin*, émissions radiophoniques, dramatiques pour la télévision, dramatiques pour la scène, livres, articles, films.
Localisation: AEU.

7242 **Savoie, Donat**
"Bibliographie d'Émile Petitot: missionnaire dans le Nord-Ouest canadien."
Dans: *Anthropologica*; Vol. 13, nos. 1-2 (1971) p. 159-168.; ISSN: 0003-5459.
Note: 81 entrées.
Localisation: AEU.

7243 **Lapointe, Jean-Pierre; Levasseur, Jean**
"Bibliographie de Jacques Poulin."
Dans: *Voix et Images*; Vol. 15, no 1 (printemps 1989) p. 58-64.; ISSN: 0318-9201.
Note: Oeuvres de Poulin, articles de critique.
Localisation: AEU.

7244 **Laakso, Lila**
"E.J. Pratt: a preliminary checklist."
In: *Canadian Library Journal*; Vol. 34, no. 4 (August 1977) p. 273, 275+.; ISSN: 0008-4352.
Note: Works by Pratt: books and other separately published works, books containing contributions by Pratt, hymns, contributions to periodicals, anthologies with contributions by Pratt); writings about Pratt: books, addresses and parts of books, articles, theses, book reviews; shortlist of Pratt manuscripts.– Poetry title index.
Location: OONL.

7245 **Laakso, Lila**
"E.J. Pratt: a preliminary checklist of publications by and about him with a shortlist of manuscript collections."

In: *The E.J. Pratt symposium,* edited by Glenn Cleaver. Ottawa: University of Ottawa Press, 1977. P. 141-169. (Reappraisals: Canadian writers); ISBN: 0-7766-4384-3.
Note: Location: OONL.

7246 **Laakso, Lila, et al.**
E.J. Pratt: an annotated bibliography. Downsview, Ont.: ECW Press, c1980. P. 147-220.; ISBN: 0-920763-60-X.
Note: 446 entries.– Works by Pratt: books, broadsides, manuscripts, contributions to periodicals and books, audio recordings, anthology contributions; works about Pratt: books, articles and sections of books, theses, interviews, audio recordings, book reviews.
Added authors: Raymond Laakso, Moira Allen, Marjorie Linden.
Extract from: *The annotated bibliography of Canada's major authors,* Vol. 2, edited by Robert Lecker and Jack David.
Location: OONL.

7247 **Laakso, Lila, et al.**
"E.J. Pratt: an annotated bibliography."
In: *The annotated bibliography of Canada's major authors,* Vol. 2, edited by Robert Lecker and Jack David. Downsview, Ont.: ECW Press, c1980. P. 147-220.; ISBN: 0-920802-40-0.
Note: 446 entries.– Works by Pratt: books, broadsides, manuscripts, contributions to periodicals and books, audio recordings, anthology contributions; works about Pratt: books, articles and sections of books, theses, interviews, audio recordings, book reviews.– Additional contributors: Raymond Laakso, Moira Allen, Marjorie Linden.
Location: OONL.

7248 **Cassis, A.F.**
"A checklist of the publications of F.E.L. Priestley."
In: *Some reflections on Life and habit,* by Northrop Frye. Lethbridge, Alta.: University of Lethbridge Press, c1988. P. 36-47.
Note: Location: OONL.

7249 **Hair, Donald S.**
"A checklist of the publications of F.E.L. Priestley."
In: *English studies in Canada;* Vol. 1, no. 2 (Summer 1975) p. 139-143.; ISSN: 0317-0802.
Note: Listing of books, books edited, articles and contributions to books, reviews and review articles.
Location: OONL.

7250 **Demers, Pierre**
"Filmographie (sommaire) de l'abbé Proulx."
Dans: *Cinéma Québec;* Vol. 4, no 6 (1975) p. 22-31.; ISSN: 0319-4647.
Note: Liste chronologique, 1934-1961.
Localisation: OONL.

7251 **Micros, Marianne**
Al Purdy, an annotated bibliography. Downsview, Ont.: ECW Press, 1980. P. 221-277.; ISBN: 0-920763-61-8.
Note: 772 entries.– Works by Purdy: books (poetry, prose, broadsides), manuscripts, contributions to periodicals and books, audio recordings, radio and television plays; works about Purdy: articles and sections of books, theses, interviews, book and record reviews.
Extract from: *The annotated bibliography of Canada's major authors,* Vol. 2, edited by Robert Lecker and Jack David.
Location: OONL.

7252 **Micros, Marianne**
"Al Purdy, an annotated bibliography."
In: *The annotated bibliography of Canada's major authors,* Vol. 2, edited by Robert Lecker and Jack David. Downsview, Ont.: ECW Press, 1980. P. 221-277.; ISBN: 0-902802-40-0.
Note: 772 entries.– Works by Purdy: books (poetry, prose, broadsides), manuscripts, contributions to periodicals and books, audio recordings, radio and television plays; works about Purdy: articles and sections of books, theses, interviews, book and record reviews.
Location: OONL.

7253 **Fraser, J. Keith**
"Bibliography of D.F. Putnam."
In: *Revue canadienne de géographie;* Vol. 5 (1951) p. 48-49.; ISSN: 0316-3032.
Note: 32 entries.
Location: AEU.

— R —

7254 **Young, Alan R.**
Thomas Head Raddall: a bibliography. Kingston, Ont.: Loyal Colonies Press, 1982. xi, 71 p.; ISBN: 0-920832-08-3.
Note: 773 entries.– Works by Raddall: novels, short story collections, histories, memoirs, poetry, articles, manuscripts, radio and television broadcasts, bibliographies; works about Raddall: biographical material, criticism, reviews.
Location: OONL.

7255 **Young, Alan R.**
"Thomas H. Raddall: an annotated bibliography."
In: *The annotated bibliography of Canada's major authors,* Vol. 7, edited by Robert Lecker and Jack David. Toronto: ECW Press, 1987. P. 403-477.; ISBN: 0-920802-11-1.
Note: 591 entries.– Works by Raddall: books (novels, stories, histories, memoir), pamphlets, audio-visual material, manuscripts, contributions to periodicals and books (short stories, serials, excerpts from novels and histories, selection of reprinted anthology contributions, articles, reviews, poems), radio and television material; works about Raddall: books, bibliographies, articles and sections of books, theses and dissertations, interviews, adaptations, selected book reviews.
Location: OONL.

7256 **Blakeney, Sharon**
An annotated bibliography of the works of Silas Tertius Rand. Halifax, N.S.: Dalhousie University, 1974. viii, [69] l.
Note: Works of Silas Rand, nineteenth-century Baptist missionary to Micmacs.
Location: NSHPL.

7257 **Morley, William F.E.**
"A bibliographical study of John Richardson."
In: *Papers of the Bibliographical Society of Canada;* Vol. 4 (1965) p. 21-88.; ISSN: 0067-6896.
Note: 69 entries.– Detailed description of Richardson's works, with locations.– Alphabetical arrangement with chronological index.
Location: OONL.

7258 **Morley, William F.E.**
A bibliographical study of Major John Richardson. Toronto: Bibliographical Society of Canada, 1973. xxvii, 144 p.: facsims., port.
Note: 80 entries.– Monographic works, major serial

contributions to those periodicals which Richardson himself owned, edited and largely wrote (*Canadian Loyalist, Expositor, New Era*).
Location: OONL.

7259 **"Mordecai Richler: a selected bibliography."**
In: *Inscape*; Vol. 11, no. 2 (Spring 1974) p. 51-61.; ISSN: 0020-1782.
Note: Primary material: novels, books edited, collected essays, film scripts, radio and TV scripts, tapes, shorter fiction and journalism; secondary material: book reviews, discussions of Richler in other works, book length studies of Richler.
Location: OONL.

7260 **Darling, Michael**
Mordecai Richler: an annotated bibliography. [Downsview, Ont.: ECW Press, c1979]. P. 155-210.; ISBN: 0-920763-62-6.
Note: 589 entries.– Works by Richler: books and manuscripts; works about Richler: books, articles and sections of books, bibliography, theses and dissertations, interviews, book reviews.
Extract from: *The annotated bibliography of Canada's major authors*, Vol. 1, edited by Robert Lecker and Jack David.
Location: OONL.

7261 **Darling, Michael**
"Mordecai Richler: an annotated bibliography."
In: *The annotated bibliography of Canada's major authors*, Vol. 1, edited by Robert Lecker and Jack David. Downsview, Ont.: ECW Press, c1979. P. 155-210.; ISBN: 0-920802-02-8.
Note: 589 entries.– Works by Richler: books and manuscripts, works about Richler: books, articles and sections of books, bibliography, theses and dissertations, interviews, book reviews.
Location: OONL.

7262 **Bates, Stewart**
"Lothar Richter (1894-1948): [publications]."
In: *Canadian Journal of Economics and Political Science*; Vol. 15, no. 4 (November 1949) p. 544-545.; ISSN: 0315-4890.
Note: Location: AEU.

7263 **Arora, Ved**
Louis Riel: a bibliography. Rev. 2nd ed. Regina: Published by Saskatchewan Library Association with the co-operation of Saskatchewan Library, 1985. x, 193 p.; ISBN: 0-919059-13-9.
Note: 1,642 entries.– Books, theses, government publications, periodical articles, films, records and microfilms in French and English covering the period 1885 to 1985.– All materials on Riel, the Northwest Rebellion, the Red River Uprising and history of Métis people.
Previous edition: Provincial Library, Bibliographic Services, 1972. 66 p.
Location: OONL.

7264 **Dhand, Harry; Hunt, L.; Goshawk, L.**
Louis Riel: an annotated bibliography. Saskatoon: Research Resource Centre, College of Education, University of Saskatchewan, 1972. 41 p.
Note: Approx. 175 entries.– Books, periodical articles, booklets, government documents intended for classroom teachers at secondary and elementary levels.– Includes a section of French-language sources.
Location: OONL.

7265 **Lafontaine, Thérèse E.**
"Louis Riel: a preliminary bibliography, 1963-1968."
In: *Louis Riel & the Métis*, edited by A.S. Lussier. Winnipeg: Pemmican Publications, 1983. P. 129-162.; ISBN: 0-919143-16-4.
Note: Approx. 300 entries.– Bibliographies, books and pamphlets, articles, theses, facsimile editions, literary texts.– Excludes government documents, newspaper articles, review articles.
Location: OONL.

7266 **Rocan, Claude**
"Bibliography of works on Louis Riel/Bibliographie des ouvrages et articles sur Louis Riel."
In: *The collected writings of Louis Riel: Les écrits complèts de Louis Riel*, edited by George F.G. Stanley. Edmonton: University of Alberta Press, 1985. Vol. 5, p. 131-205.; ISBN: 0-88864-105-2.
Note: 443 entries.– Lists bibliographies, books, chapters in books and articles in collected works, journal articles, theses, government documents of Canada, Great Britain and the United States.
Location: AEU.

7267 **Samuda, Madeleine**
"Bibliographie sur Louis Riel."
Dans: *Cefco: Centre d'études franco-canadiennes de l'Ouest*; No 21 (octobre 1985) p. 15-21.; ISSN: 0226-0670.
Note: Localisation: AEU.

7268 **Spencer, Nigel**
"Louis Riel and Norman Bethune: a critical bibliography."
In: *Moosehead Review*; Vol. 3, no. 1 (1982) p. 48-60; No. 7 (1983) p. 29-47.; ISSN: 0228-7404.
Note: Annotated listing of historical, literary and theatrical works about Riel and Bethune.– Includes fiction, poetry, drama, video and film.
Location: OONL.

7269 **Hamel, Jacques**
"Bibliographie de Marcel Rioux."
Dans: *Sociologie et sociétés*; Vol. 17, no 2 (octobre 1985) p. 133-144.; ISSN: 0038-030X.
Note: Ouvrages; recueils, ouvrages collectifs et livres en collaboration; brochures et documents; préface à des ouvrages; entrevue, entretien et débat; contribution à des recueils et ouvrages collectifs; articles; comptes rendus de livres; études sur les travaux de Rioux.
Localisation: AEU.

7270 **Adams, John Coldwell**
"A preliminary bibliography [Charles G.D. Roberts]."
In: *The Sir Charles G.D. Roberts Symposium*, edited by Glenn Cleaver. Ottawa: University of Ottawa Press, 1984. P. 221-249. (Reappraisals: Canadian writers ; 10); ISBN: 0-7766-4390-8.
Note: Listing of poetry published in periodicals, poetry in collections, fiction published in periodicals, fiction in book form, non-fiction, selected biography and criticism (arranged chronologically).– Provides location of manuscripts, correspondence, etc.
Location: OONL.

7271 **"Publications of J. Lewis Robinson."**
In: *Studies in Canadian regional geography: essays in honor of J. Lewis Robinson*, edited by Brenton M. Barr. Vancouver: Tantalus Research, 1984. P. 8-18. (B.C. geographical series ; no. 37; ISSN: 0068-1571); ISBN: 0-919478-58-1.
Note: Chronological listing, 1943-1984, of Robinson

writings on aspects of Canadian geography.
Location: OONL.

7272 **Sears, Linda**
Canadian and international themes: Raymond Spencer Rodgers, a bio-bibliographical sketch. Mobile: Department of Political Science, University of South Alabama, 1966. 1 vol. (in various pagings).
Note: Location: OOP.

7273 **"Bibliography of published books and articles of the late Norman McLeod Rogers relating to history, economics, and political science."**
In: *Canadian Journal of Economics and Political Science*; Vol. 6, no. 3 (August 1940) p. 477-478.; ISSN: 0315-4890.
Note: Location: AEU.

7274 **Struthers, J.R. (Tim); Hogan, Lesley; Orange, John Charles**
"A preliminary bibliography of works by Leon Rooke."
In: *Canadian Fiction Magazine*; No. 38 (Special Leon Rooke issue) (1981) p. 148-164.; ISSN: 0045-477X.
Note: 176 entries.
Location: AEU.

7275 **Turek, Victor**
"A Bibliography of the writings of William J. Rose."
In: *Canadian Slavonic Papers*; Vol. 4 (1959) p. 1-30.
Note: 320 entries.– Chronological listing (1903-1959) of books, pamphlets, articles, translations, prefaces by Slavonic studies scholar William J. Rose.
Location: OONL.

7276 **Latham, David**
Sinclair Ross: an annotated bibliography. Downsview, Ont.: ECW Press, c1981. P. 365-395.; ISBN: 0-920763-63-4.
Note: 176 entries.– Works by Ross: novels, short stories, contributions to books and periodicals, audio-visual material; works about Ross: articles and sections of books, theses, audio-visual material, book reviews.
Extract from: *The annotated bibliography of Canada's major authors*, Vol. 3, edited by Robert Lecker and Jack David.
Location: OONL.

7277 **Latham, David**
"Sinclair Ross: an annotated bibliography."
In: *The annotated bibliography of Canada's major authors*, Vol. 3, edited by Robert Lecker and Jack David. Downsview, Ont.: ECW Press, 1981. P. 365-395.; ISBN: 0-920802-23-0.
Note: 176 entries.– Works by Ross: novels, short stories, contributions to books and periodicals, audio-visual material; works about Ross: articles and sections of books, theses, audio-visual material, book reviews.
Location: OONL.

7278 **Rousseau, Jacques**
Curriculum vitae et bibliographie [Jacques Rousseau]. [Montréal: s.n., 1970]. 75 f.
Note: Localisation: QQLA.

7279 **Ludovic, frère**
Bio-bibliographie de Mgr Camille Roy, P.A., V.G., recteur de l'Université Laval. Québec: [Imprimé pour la Procure des Frères des Écoles Chrétiennes], 1941. 180 p.
Note: 306 entrées.– Manuscrits, livres et brochures, préfaces, ouvrages en collaboration, éditions, articles de revues et de journaux; sources sur l'auteur: livres et brochures, articles de revues et journaux.
Localisation: OONL.

7280 **Samson, Jean-Noël**
"Bibliographie [Gabrielle Roy]."
Dans: *Gabrielle Roy*. Montréal: Fides, 1967. P. 83-90. (Dossiers de documentation sur la littérature canadienne-française ; 1)
Note: Oeuvre de Gabrielle Roy: romans, reportages, nouvelles, contes, récits, divers, interviews, études.
Localisation: OONL.

7281 **Socken, Paul**
"Gabrielle Roy: an annotated bibliography."
In: *The annotated bibliography of Canada's major authors*, Vol. 1, edited by Robert Lecker and Jack David. Downsview, Ont.: ECW Press, 1979. P. 213-263.; ISBN: 0-920802-02-8.
Note: 372 entries.– Works by Roy: novels, short stories, contributions to periodicals, books, anthologies; works about Roy: books, selected articles and sections of books, theses and dissertations, interviews, awards and honours, book reviews.
Location: OONL.

7282 **Socken, Paul**
Gabrielle Roy: an annotated bibliography. Downsview, Ont.: ECW Press, 1979. P. 213-263.
Note: 372 entries.– Works by Roy: novels, short stories, contributions to anthologies, essays; works about Roy: books, selected articles and sections of books, theses, interviews, awards and honours, book reviews.
Extract from *The annotated bibliography of Canada's major authors*, Vol. 1, edited by Robert Lecker and Jack David.
Location: OONL.

7283 **Martin, Gérard**
Bio-bibliographie de Joseph-Edmond Roy. Lévis [Québec]: Société d'histoire régionale de Lévis, 1984. 115 p.; ISBN: 2-920281-015.
Note: 180 entrées.– Livres et brochures (ouvrages personnels, collaboration à des ouvrages collectifs), revues et journaux.– Index alphabétique de chaque ouvrage ou article, par titre, sujet, mot typique.
Localisation: OONL.

7284 **Vézina-Demers, Micheline; Grégoire-Reid, Claire**
Catalogue des oeuvres musicales du fonds Léo Roy. Québec: Atelier de Musicographie, 1987. viii, [2], 143 p.: fac.–sim., port.; ISBN: 2-9801120-0-3.
Note: 1,345 entrées.– Deux parties: oeuvres originales; harmonisations: musique instrumentale, musique orchestrale, musique vocale.– Les oeuvres sont classées par ordre chronologique.– Index: alphabétique, chronologique, onomastique.
Localisation: OONL.

7285 **Roy, Antoine**
L'oeuvre historique de Pierre-Georges Roy: bibliographie analytique. Paris: Jouve, 1928. xxxi, 268 p.
Note: Localisation: OONL.

7286 **J.B. Rudnyckyj repertorium bibliographicum, 1933-1983.** Ottawa: Ukrainian Language Association, [1984]. 296 p.: facsims., port.
Note: 2,102 entries.– "Compiled and published by students and friends of the author on occasion of the 50th anniversary of his scholarly activities." (Chairman of the Editorial Committee: Ol'ha Woycenko).
Location: OONL.

7287 **Mandryka, Mykyta I.**
Bio-bibliography of J.B. Rudnyckyj. Winnipeg: Ukrainian Free Academy of Sciences, 1961. 72 p. (Ukrainian Free Academy of Sciences: Series: Ukrainian Scholars ; no. 10)
Note: 751 entries.
Location: OONL.

7288 **"Jane Rule: a bibliography."**
In: *Canadian Fiction Magazine*; No. 23 (Autumn 1976) p. 133-138.; ISSN: 0045-477X.
Note: Works by Rule: novels, short stories, criticism and social comment, articles, book reviews; works about Rule: profiles, book reviews.
Location: AEU.

— S —

7289 **Huls, Mary Ellen**
Moshe Safdie, Canadian architect: a bibliography. Monticello, Ill.: Vance Bibliographies, 1985. 6 p. (Architecture series: Bibliography ; A-1470; ISSN: 0194-1356); ISBN: 0-890286-00-0.
Note: Location: OON.

7290 **Boutilier, Helen R.**
"A bibliography of the printed writings of Walter Noble Sage."
In: *British Columbia Historical Quarterly*; Vol. 17, no. 1/2 (January-April 1953) p. 127-137.; ISSN: 0706-7666.
Note: 125 entries.– Chronological list of works by Sage from 1916 to 1952.– Excludes newspaper articles and publications presented under auspices of Anglican Church or Masonic Lodge.
Location: OONL.

7291 **"Bibliography of R.A. Samek."**
In: *Dalhousie Law Journal*; Vol. 9, no. 2 (June 1985) p. 469-470.; ISSN: 0317-1663.
Note: Location: AEU.

7292 **Thérèse-du-Carmel, soeur**
Bibliographie analytique de l'oeuvre de Félix-Antoine Savard. Montréal: Fides, c1967. 229 p.: port.
Note: 911 entrées.
Localisation: OONL.

7293 **Adams, Stephen**
"A bibliography of R. Murray Schafer."
In: *Open Letter*; Fourth Series, nos. 4-5 (Fall 1979) p. 235-244.; ISSN: 0048-1939.
Note: Chronological catalogue of musical works, books, pamphlets, translations of books and pamphlets, periodical articles, film, selected secondary sources.
Location: AEU.

7294 **Adams, Stephen**
R. Murray Schafer. Don Mills, Ont.: PRO Canada, 1983. 15 p.: music, port.
Note: Bio-bibliography.– List of works, p. 6-12.– Discography, p. 12-14.
Location: OONL.

7295 **Adams, Stephen**
R. Murray Schafer. Toronto: University of Toronto Press, 1983. x, 240 p., [6] p. of pl.: ill., music, ports. (Canadian composers ; no. 4; ISSN: 0316-1293); ISBN: 0-8020-5571-0.
Note: Appendix 1: "Compositions by R. Murray Schafer."- Appendix 2: "Discography."- Includes a bibliography, p. 227-233.
Location: OONL.

7296 **Gerson, Carole**
"The piper's forgotten tune: notes on the stories of D.C. Scott and a bibliography."
In: *Journal of Canadian Fiction*; No. 16 (1976) p. 138-143.; ISSN: 0047-2255.
Note: Location: AEU.

7297 **Kelly, Catherine E.**
"Selected bibliography: [Duncan Campbell Scott]."
In: *The Duncan Campbell Scott Symposium*, edited by K.P. Stich. Ottawa: University of Ottawa Press, 1980. P. 147-155. (Reappraisals: Canadian writers); ISBN: 2-7603-4386-3.
Note: Primary sources (manuscripts and papers), collected poetry, separate private printings of poetry, fiction, collected short stories, miscellaneous prose; secondary sources.
Location: OONL.

7298 **"Bibliography of the works of F.R. Scott/Bibliographie des oeuvres de F.R. Scott."**
In: *McGill Law Journal*; Vol. 30, no. 4 (October 1985) p. 635-643.; ISSN: 0024-9041.
Note: Location: OONL.

7299 **Still, Robert**
F.R. Scott: an annotated bibliography. Downsview, Ont.: ECW Press, c1983. [61] p.; ISBN: 0-920763-65-0.
Note: 658 entries.– Works by Scott: books (poetry, social and political subjects, books edited, translation), contributions to books and periodicals, published addresses, letters; works about Scott: articles and sections of books, theses, interviews, book reviews.
Extract from: *The annotated bibliography of Canada's major authors*, Vol. 4, edited by Robert Lecker and Jack David.
Location: OONL.

7300 **Still, Robert**
"F.R. Scott: an annotated bibliography."
In: *The annotated bibliography of Canada's major authors*, Vol. 4, edited by Robert Lecker and Jack David. Downsview, Ont.: ECW Press, c1983. P. 205-265.; ISBN: 0-920802-52-4.
Note: 658 entries.– Works by Scott: books (poetry, social and political subjects, books edited, translation), contributions to books and periodicals, published addresses, letters; works about Scott: articles and sections of books, theses, interviews, book reviews.
Location: OONL.

7301 **Bouchard, René; Saulnier, Carole**
"Bio-bibliographie de Robert-Lionel Séguin."
Dans: *La vie quotidienne au Québec: histoire, métiers, techniques et traditions: mélanges à la mémoire de Robert-Lionel Séguin*. Sillery: Presses de l'Université du Québec, 1983. P. 51-85.; ISBN: 2-7605-0338-0.
Note: Localisation: OONL.

7302 **Ami, Henri Marc**
Sketch of the life and work of the late Dr. Alfred R.C. Selwyn ... Director of the Geological Survey of Canada from 1869 to 1894. [Minneapolis, Minn.: s.n., 1903]. 24 p., 1 l. of pl.: port.
Note: Excerpt from *American Geologist*, Vol. 31 (January 1903).– Bibliography: p. 16-24.
Location: OONL.

7303 **Ami, Henri Marc**
"Sketch of the life and work of the late Dr. Alfred R.C. Selwyn ... Director of the Geological Survey of Canada

from 1869 to 1894."
In: *American Geologist*; Vol. 31 (January 1903) p. 1-21.;
ISSN: 0190-518X.
Note: Location: OOG.

7304 **Ami, Henri Marc**
"Sketch of the life of Dr. A.R.C. Selwyn, C.M.G.:
bibliography."
In: *Proceedings and Transactions of the Royal Society of
Canada*; Series 2, vol. 10, section 4 (1904) p. 173-205.;
ISSN: 0316-4616.
Note: Location: OONL.

7305 **Roberts, F.X.**
"A bibliography of Robert William Service, 1874-1958."
In: *Four Decades of Poetry, 1890-1930*; Vol. 1, no. 1 (January
1976) p. 76-85.; ISSN: 0308-0889.
Note: Lists collections of poetry, poems published
separately in periodicals, prose works (fiction,
autobiography); items about Service: articles, theses,
books; portraits.
Location: OONL.

7306 **Neill, R.F.**
"Adam Shortt: a bibliographical comment."
In: *Journal of Canadian Studies*; Vol. 2, no. 1 (February
1967) p. 53-61.; ISSN: 0021-9495.
Note: Articles, reports, reviews by Shortt; articles about
Shortt; notebooks; typescripts.
Location: AEU.

7307 **Bonnelly, Claude**
"Bibliographie de Émile Simard de 1946 à 1969."
Dans: *Laval théologique et philosophique*; Vol. 25, no 2
(1969) p. 168-170.; ISSN: 0023-9054.
Note: Localisation: OONL.

7308 **Marie-Raymond, soeur**
Bio-bibliographie du R.P. Georges Simard, o.m.i.
[Montréal]: Beauchemin, [1939]. 64 p.: port.
Note: Approx. 300 entrées.– Manuscrits, imprimés (livres
et brochures), préfaces, collaboration aux revues et aux
journaux; ouvrages sur Simard: livres et brochures,
articles de revues et journaux.
Localisation: OONL.

7309 **"O.D. Skelton, 1878-1941: [bibliography]."**
In: *Canadian Journal of Economics and Political Science*; Vol.
7, no. 2 (May 1941) p. 276-278.; ISSN: 0315-4890.
Note: Location: AEU.

7310 **Kalish, Jana**
Josef Skvorecky: a checklist. [Toronto]: University of
Toronto Library, 1986. iv, 232 p.; ISBN: 0-7727-6000-4.
Note: Primary sources: first editions of fiction, non-fiction, literary works in periodicals, non-literary
contributions to periodicals, works edited, translations,
broadcasts; secondary sources: in books, periodicals,
interviews, reviews.– Covers the period to Fall, 1983.
Location: OOCC.

7311 **Burke, Anne**
A.J.M. Smith: an annotated bibliography. Downsview,
Ont.: ECW Press, c1983. [104] p.; ISBN: 0-920763-66-9.
Note: 815 entries.– Works by Smith: books and
manuscripts, contributions to periodicals and books,
addresses, audio-visual material; works about Smith:
books, articles, theses, interviews, book reviews.
Extract from: *The annotated bibliography of Canada's major
authors*, Vol. 4, edited by Robert Lecker and Jack David.
Location: OONL.

7312 **Burke, Anne**
"A.J.M. Smith: an annotated bibliography."
In: *The annotated bibliography of Canada's major authors*,
Vol. 4, edited by Robert Lecker and Jack David.
Downsview, Ont.: ECW Press, c1983. P. 267-370.; ISBN: 0-
920802-52-4.
Note: 815 entries.– Works by Smith: books and
manuscripts, contributions to periodicals and books,
addresses, audio-visual material; works about Smith:
books, articles, theses, interviews, book reviews.
Location: OONL.

7313 **Darling, Michael**
A variorum edition of the poems of A.J.M. Smith with a
descriptive bibliography and reference guide. Toronto:
York University, 1979. ix, 589 l.
Note: Thesis, Ph.D., York University, 1979.
Microform: Canadian theses on microfiche ; no. 42137. 7
microfiches.
Location: OONL.

7314 **Darling, Michael**
A.J.M. Smith: an annotated bibliography. Montréal:
Véhicule Press, c1981. 228 p.; ISBN: 0-919890-34-2.
Note: 760 entries.– Works by Smith: books and
pamphlets, first appearance contributions to books,
contributions to periodicals, anthologies, translations;
works about Smith: criticism, book reviews; appendix of
works wrongly attributed to Smith.
Location: OONL.

7315 **Leechman, Douglas**
"Bibliography of Harlan I. Smith."
In: *Bulletin (National Museum of Canada)*; No. 112 (1949) p.
8-14.; ISSN: 0068-7944.
Note: Chronological listing, 1889 to 1936, of published
archaeological writings of Harlan Ingersoll Smith.
Location: OONL.

7316 **Performing Rights Organization of Canada**
Harry Somers. Don Mills, Ont.: PRO Canada, 1983. 15 p.:
music, port.
Note: Bio-bibliography.– List of works, p. 6-10.–
Discography, p. 10-13.
Location: OONL.

7317 **Whiteman, Bruce**
Collected poems of Raymond Souster: bibliography.
[Ottawa]: Oberon Press, c1984. 240 p.; ISBN: 0-88750-528-
7.
Note: 650 entries.– Books, books edited, separately
published poems, separately published prose,
translations, tapes and records, contributions to
anthologies, secondary literature.
Location: OONL.

7318 **Mercer, Eleanor**
"The writings of Frederic H. Soward."
In: *Empire and nations, essays in honour of Frederic H.
Soward*, edited by Harvey L. Dyck and H. Peter Krosby.
Toronto: University of Toronto Press in association with
the University of British Columbia, 1969. P. 219-228.;
ISBN: 0-8020-1652-9.
Note: Chronological listing (1923-1968) of books, articles,
reviews, contributions.
Location: OONL.

7319 **Fancy, Margaret**
A bibliography of the works of George Francis Gillman
Stanley. Sackville, N.B.: Ralph Pickard Bell Library,

Mount Allison University, c1976. 52 p. (Bibliography series / Ralph Pickard Bell Library, Mount Allison University ; no. 1)
Note: 303 entries.– Works by Stanley and reviews of Stanley's books.
Location: OONL.

7320 **Varma, Prem**
"Robert Stead: an annotated bibliography."
In: *Essays on Canadian Writing*; No. 17 (Spring 1980) p. 141-204.; ISSN: 0316-0300.
Note: 406 entries.– Works by Stead: novels, poetry, manuscripts, articles and miscellaneous prose, poems, drama, contributions to periodicals and newspapers; works about Stead and his work: sections of books, articles, theses, interviews, selected book and poem reviews.
Location: AEU.

7321 **Mattila, Robert W.**
A chronological bibliography of the published works of Vilhjalmur Stefansson. Hanover, N.H.: Dartmouth College Libraries, c1978. xii, 66 p.
Note: 457 entries.– Books, books with contributions by Stefansson, contributions to periodicals and newspapers.– Substantial Canadian content.
Location: OONL.

7322 **Fullerton, Carol**
"George Stewart, Jr.: a bibliography."
In: *Papers of the Bibliographical Society of Canada*; Vol. 25 (1986) p. 97-108.; ISSN: 0067-6896.
Note: Approx. 200 entries.– Books and monographs, articles, reviews, short stories, lectures, journals published by Stewart; newspapers and journals edited by Stewart; unpublished papers.
Location: OONL.

7323 **Malchelosse, Gérard**
Benjamin Sulte et son oeuvre: essai de bibliographie des travaux historiques et littéraires (1860-1916) de ce polygraphe canadien, précédé d'une notice biographique. Montréal: Pays laurentien, 1916. 78 p. (Collection laurentienne)
Note: Localisation: OONL.

7324 **Morgan, Henry J.**
The writings of Benjamin Sulte. Milwaukee: Keogh, 1898. 13 p.: port.
Note: "Writings of Benjamin Sulte, magazine articles, and pamphlets," p. 8-13.
Microform: CIHM Microfiche series ; no. 64563; ISBN: 0-665-64563-5. 1 microfiche (11 fr.).
Location: OONL.

— T —

7325 **Bates, Hilary**
"Bibliography of the academic and journalistic writings of James J. Talman."
In: *Aspects of nineteenth-century Ontario: essays presented to James J. Talman*, edited by F.H. Armstrong, H.A. Stevenson and J.D. Wilson. London, Ont.: Published in association with the University of Western Ontario by University of Toronto Press, 1974. P. 334-350.; ISBN: 0-8020-2061-5.
Note: 298 entries.– Chronological listing, 1927 to 1972.
Location: OONL.

7326 **McAtee, W.L.**
"Ornithological publications of Percy Algernon Taverner, 1895-1945."
In: *Bulletin (National Museum of Canada)*; No. 112 (1949) p. 102-113.; ISSN: 0068-7944.
Note: Location: OONL.

7327 **Clark, Robert**
Keith Tedman. Don Mills, Ont.: PRO Canada, 1988. 7 p.
Note: Bio-bibliography.– List of compositions, p. 5-6.
Location: OONL.

7328 **Bouchard, René**
Filmographie d'Albert Tessier. Montréal: Éditions du Boréal Express, 1973. 179 p.: ill., portr. (Documents filmiques du Québec ; 1)
Note: Localisation: OONL.

7329 **Girard, Hélène**
"Bibliographie de France Théoret."
Dans: *Voix et Images*; Vol. 14, no 1 (automne 1988) p. 57-69.; ISSN: 0318-9201.
Note: Oeuvres de Théoret: volumes, mémoire et thèse, ouvrages en collaboration, articles de périodiques et de journaux, communications/entretiens radiophoniques; études sur Théoret et son oeuvre.
Localisation: AEU.

7330 **Biron, Luc-André**
Bio-bibliographie de Charles-Yvon Thériault, journaliste (1948-1956). Trois-Rivières: [s.n.], 1961. xi, 105 p.: portr., fac-sim.
Note: 497 entrées.– Manuscrits, livres et brochures, articles, analyses et critiques.
Localisation: OOA.

7331 **Bérubé, Renald**
"Bibliographie des oeuvres de Yves Thériault."
Dans: *Voix et images*; Vol. 5, no 2 (hiver 1980) p. 241-243.; ISSN: 0318-9201.
Note: Localisation: OONL.

7332 **Carrier, Denis**
Bibliographie analytique d'Yves Thériault, 1940-1984. Québec: Centre de recherche en littérature québécoise, Université Laval, 1985. 326 p. (Collection "Bibliographies" / Centre de recherche en littérature québécoise, Université Laval ; no 1); ISBN: 2-920801-02-3.
Note: 1,848 entrées.– Oeuvres par Thériault: manuscrits, imprimés (livres, publications dans les périodiques et les livres), textes radiophoniques, textes télévisuels (téléthéâtres, adaptations, sketches), tables rondes, conférences, discographie, filmographie; études sur Thériault: bio-bibliographies, livres et chapitres de livres, thèses, articles, comptes rendus, émissions radiophoniques et télévisées.
Localisation: OONL.

7333 **Provencher, Louise-Marie**
"Bibliographie: Adrien Thério."
Dans: *Voix et Images*; Vol. 7, no 1 (automne 1981) p. 57-76.; ISSN: 0318-9201.
Note: Manuscrits et les oeuvres imprimées (livres et brochures, contes parus dans les anthologies, articles et contes dans les revues et journaux), participation à des émissions de radio et de télévision.
Localisation: AEU.

7334 **McKay, Jean**
"A Colleen Thibaudeau checklist."
In: *Brick: a Journal of Reviews*; No. 5 (Winter 1979) p. 71-

78.; ISSN: 0382-8565.
Note: Chronological listing of published poems and short stories by Thibaudeau.
Location: AEU.

7335 **Darling, Michael**
"Clara Thomas: a bibliography."
In: *Essays on Canadian Writing*; No. 29 (Summer 1984) p. 232-239.; ISSN: 0316-0300.
Note: Approx. 80 entries.– Books, contributions to books, articles, book reviews.
Location: AEU.

7336 **Bourinot, Arthur S.**
Edward William Thomson (1849-1924): a bibliography with notes and some letters. Ottawa: The Author, 1955. 28 p.
Note: Location: OONL.

7337 **Lavoie, Pierre**
"Bibliographie commentée [de Michel Tremblay]."
Dans: *Voix et Images*; Vol. 7, no 2 (hiver 1982) p. 225-306.; ISSN: 0318-9201.
Note: Oeuvres: théâtrographie (oeuvres originales, adaptations), filmographie, bibliographie (romans, contes, nouvelles, divers); études sur Tremblay et son oeuvre.
Localisation: AEU.

7338 **Gagnon-Arguin, Louise; Perron, Normand**
"Mgr Victor Tremblay: bibliographie sommaire."
Dans: *Saguenayensia*; Vol. 21, nos 5-6 (novembre-décembre 1979) p. 177-180.; ISSN: 0581-295X.
Note: Localisation: AEU.

7339 **Canada. Library of Parliament. Information and Reference Branch**
Pierre Elliott Trudeau: select bibliography/Pierre Elliott Trudeau: bibliographie sélective. Ottawa: The Branch, 1982. 29 l.
Note: Approx. 200 entries.– Chronological list of books, parts of books, articles, speeches, interviews by Trudeau from 1944 to 1982.
Location: BVAS.

7340 **Savard, Pierre**
"Présentation de Marcel Trudel."
Dans: *Revue de l'Université d'Ottawa*; Vol. 47, nos 1-2 (janvier-avril 1977) p. 6-13.; ISSN: 0041-9206.
Note: Liste des ouvrages, articles, préfaces, comptes rendus.
Localisation: OONL.

7341 **MacMillan, Rick**
Robert Turner. Don Mills, Ont.: PRO Canada, 1983. 11 p.: music, port.
Note: Bio-bibliography.– List of works, p. 5-8.– Discography, p. 8-9.
Location: OONL.

7342 **Barnard, Henry G.**
"Victor Witter Turner: a bibliography (1952-1975)."
In: *Anthropologica*; Vol. 27, nos. 1-2 (1985) p. 207-233.; ISSN: 0003-5459.
Note: Approx. 225 entries.– Annotated chronological listing of Turner's books and articles, with citations for reviews of books and abstracts of articles.
Location: AEU.

7343 **Manning, Frank E.**
"Bibliography of Victor Witter Turner (1975-1986)."
In: *Anthropologica*; Vol. 27, nos. 1-2 (1985) p. 235-239.;

ISSN: 0003-5459.
Note: Chronological listing of books and articles of Turner, with citations for reviews of books and abstracts of articles.
Location: AEU.

7344 **Blanchard, Robert G.**
The first editions of John Buchan: a collector's bibliography. Hamden, Conn.: Archon Books, 1981. xi, 284 p.; ISBN: 0-208-01905-7.
Note: 1,331 entries.– Books and pamphlets, edited works, contributions to books, uncollected contributions to periodicals and public documents, contributions to *The Spectator*.
Location: OONL.

7345 **Bower, William J.**
A rough check list of the first editions of John Buchan (Lord Tweedsmuir). [Bronxville, N.Y.: s.n., 1939]. [12] l.
Note: Approx. 150 entries.– Compiled by William J. Bower with the assistance of Paul Lemperly, Louis C. Stoneman and C. Hopkinson.– Mimeograph of typescript.
Location: OONL.

7346 **Hanna, Archibald**
John Buchan, 1875-1940: a bibliography. Hamden, Conn.: Shoe String Press, 1953. xi, 135 p.
Note: 403 entries.– All editions and translations of Buchan's works: books and pamphlets, contributions to books, contributions to periodicals; writings about Buchan.
Location: OONL.

7347 **Queen's University (Kingston, Ont.). Douglas Library. Buchan Collection**
A checklist of works by and about John Buchan in John Buchan Collection. [Rev. & augm.]. Boston: G.K. Hall, 1961. 38, 24 p.: ill., port.
Note: 317 entries.– Manuscript and published writings of Buchan: fiction, major prose other than fiction, minor prose, poetry, works compiled, edited by Buchan; works about Buchan: bibliographies, autobiography, letters, biography and criticism, books dedicated to Buchan.
Location: OONL.

— U —

7348 **Penlington, Norman**
"Bibliography of the writings of Frank H. Underhill."
In: *On Canada: essays in honour of Frank H. Underhill*. Toronto: University of Toronto Press, 1971. P. 131-192.; ISBN: 0-8020-1725-8.
Note: Chronological list (1911-1970) of writings of Frank Underhill: books, articles, extracts, editorials, essays, reviews, speeches, broadcasts.
Location: OONL.

— V —

7349 **Chamberland, Roger; Noizet, Pascale**
"Bibliographie de Michel van Schendel."
Dans: *Voix et Images*; Vol. 11, no 2 (hiver 1986) p. 256-261.; ISSN: 0318-9201.
Note: Oeuvres, chapitres de volumes, articles de périodiques, textes journalistiques et radiophoniques, traductions, études à consulter.
Localisation: AEU.

7350 **British Columbia Library Association. Bibliography Committee**
Captain Vancouver. [Vancouver: The Association], 1935. 3 p.

Note: 41 entries.

Location: BVIPA.

7351 **Rudnyckyj, Jaroslav Bohdan**
"Ivan Velyhorskyj (1889-1955) [selected bibliography of writings]."
In: *Orbis: bulletin international de documentation linguistique*; Vol. 4, no. 2 (1955) p. 571-573: port.; ISSN: 0030-4379.
Note: Biographical sketch (obituary) and list of publications.

7352 **Gagné, Marc**
Gilles Vigneault: bibliographie descriptive et critique, discographie, filmographie, iconographie, chronologie. Québec: Presses de l'Université Laval, 1977. xxxii, 976 p.: ill., fac.–sims.; ISBN: 0-7746-6799-0.
Note: 4,802 entrées.
Localisation: OONL.

7353 **Robert, Lucie**
"Bibliographie de Yolande Villemaire."
Dans: *Voix et Images*; Vol. 11, no 3 (printemps 1986) p. 455-462.; ISSN: 0318-9201.
Note: Oeuvres de Villemaire: volumes, ouvrages en collaboration, theses, articles de périodiques; études sur Villemaire.
Localisation: AEU.

7354 **"Bibliographie chronologique de Jean-Paul Vinay, 1939-1974."**
Dans: *Vingt-cinq ans de linguistique au Canada: hommage à Jean-Paul Vinay*. Montréal: Centre éducatif et culturel, c1979. P. 109-123.; ISBN: 2-7617-0019-8.
Note: Localisation: OOCC.

7355 **Cercle linguistique de Montréal**
Jean-Paul Vinay: bibliographie chronologique, 1936-1962. [Montréal]: Cercle linguistique de Montréal, 1963. 16 p.
Note: 156 entrées.
Localisation: OONL.

7356 **Robert, Véronique**
Claude Vivier. Don Mills, Ont.: PRO Canada, 1984. 7, [1] p.: music, port.
Note: Bio-bibliography.– List of works, p. 5-7.– Discography, p. 7-[8].
Location: OONL.

— W —

7357 **Ricou, Laurence R.**
"Miriam Waddington: a checklist, 1936-1975."
In: *Essays on Canadian Writing*; No. 12 (Fall 1978) p. 162-191.; ISSN: 0316-0300.
Note: Location: AEU.

7358 **Ricou, Laurence R.**
"Miriam [Dworkin] Waddington: an annotated bibliography."
In: *The annotated bibliography of Canada's major authors*, Vol. 6, edited by Robert Lecker and Jack David. Toronto: ECW Press, 1985. P. 287-388.; ISBN: 0-920802-93-1.
Note: 1,019 entries.– Works by Waddington: books (poetry, stories, criticism, books edited), broadsides, audio-visual material, manuscripts, contributions to periodicals and books; works about Waddington: articles and sections of books, thesis, interviews and profiles, selected book reviews.
Location: OONL.

7359 **Spafford, Shirley**
"Norman Ward: a selected bibliography."
In: *The Canadian House of Commons: essays in honour of Norman Ward*, edited by John C. Courtney. Calgary: University of Calgary Press, c1985. xv, 217 p.; ISBN: 0-919813-31-3.
Note: Approx. 175 entries.– Books, reports, revised and edited books, contributions to books, journals and encyclopedias, book reviews.
Location: OONL.

7360 **Harting, Lynn**
Peter Ware. Don Mills, Ont.: PRO Canada, 1988. 7 p.
Note: Bio-bibliography.– List of compositions, p. 7-8.– Discography, p. 8.
Location: OONL.

7361 **"Bibliographie: Sylvia Truster Wargon."**
Dans: *Bulletin de l'Association des démographes du Québec*; Vol. 2, no 4 (décembre 1973) p. 52-53.
Note: Localisation: OONL.

7362 **Frey, Cecelia**
"Phyllis Webb: an annotated bibliography."
In: *The annotated bibliography of Canada's major authors*, Vol. 6, edited by Robert Lecker and Jack David. Toronto: ECW Press, 1985. P. 389-448.; ISBN: 0-920802-93-1.
Note: 477 entries.– Works by Webb: books (poetry, criticism), broadsides, audio-visual material, radio and television work, manuscripts, contributions to periodicals and books; works about Webb: articles and sections of books, interviews, selected book reviews.
Location: OONL.

7363 **Healey Willan centennial year 1980: [first of his choral compositions].** Toronto: International Music Sales, 1979. [4] p.
Note: Location: OONL.

7364 **Bryant, Giles**
Healey Willan catalogue. Ottawa: National Library of Canada, 1972. 174 p.: ill., music, ports.
Note: Listing of 784 works by Willan: dramatic music, vocal music, chamber music, piano/organ music, masses, canticles, motets, anthems, carols, hymns, secular choral music, songs; sound recordings, films, bibliography.– Text in English and French/texte en français et en anglais.
Supplement: 1982. viii, 51 p.; ISBN: 0-662-51783-0.
Location: OONL.

7365 **Royal Canadian College of Organists**
Healey Willan. Toronto: Royal Canadian College of Organists, 1979. 34 p.: ill., port.
Note: Bio-bibliography.– List of works, p. 21-26.
Location: OONL.

7366 **Risk, R.C.B.**
"Books, articles, case comments and reviews: John Willis."
In: *Dalhousie Law Journal*; Vol. 9, no. 3 (December 1985) p. 551-554.; ISSN: 0317-1663.
Note: Location: AEU.

7367 **McComb, Bonnie Martyn**
"Ethel Wilson: a bibliography, 1919-1977."
In: *West Coast Review*; Vol. 14, no. 1 (June 1979) p. 38-43; vol. 14, no. 2 (October 1979) p. 49-57; vol. 14, no. 3 (January 1980) p. 58-64; vol. 15, no. 1 (June 1980) p. 67-72.; ISSN: 0043-311X.
Note: Primary sources: novels, excerpts from novels, short stories, articles and essays; secondary sources

(critical studies, theses); book reviews.– Appendices: list of sources which contain reviews not listed in the bibliography; chronological list of Wilson's publications.
Location: OONL.

7368 **McComb, Bonnie Martyn**
"Ethel Wilson: an annotated bibliography."
In: *The annotated bibliography of Canada's major authors*, Vol. 5, edited by Robert Lecker and Jack David. Downsview, Ont.: ECW Press, 1984. P. 415-480.; ISBN: 0-920802-68-0.
Note: 447 entries.– Works by Wilson: books (novels, short stories), audio material, manuscripts, contributions to periodicals and books; works about Wilson: book, articles and sections of books, bibliographies, theses and dissertations, interviews, audio-visual material, selected book reviews.
Location: OONL.

7369 **Leechman, Douglas**
"Bibliography of W.J. Wintemberg, 1899-1947."
In: *Bulletin (National Museum of Canada)*; No. 112 (1949) p. 38-41.; ISSN: 0068-7944.
Note: Archaeological writings of W.J. Wintemberg.
Location: OONL.

7370 **Panofsky, Ruth**
Adele Wiseman: an annotated bibliography. Toronto: ECW Press, 1992. xviii, 130 p., [1] p. of pl.: ill.; ISBN: 1-55022-103-5.
Note: 703 entries.– Works by Wiseman: novels, plays, poetry, book reviews, excerpts and manuscripts; works about Wiseman: reviews, newspaper articles, journal articles, sections of books, theses and biographical entries.
Location: OONL.

7371 **"William C. Wonders: bibliography of published work, 1948-1989."**
In: *A world of real places: essays in honour of William C. Wonders*, edited by P.J. Smith and E.L. Jackson. Edmonton: Department of Geography, University of Alberta, c1990. P. 207-210.; ISBN: 0-88864-762-X.
Note: Location: OONL.

7372 **Astbury, Effie C.**
Casey A. Wood (1856-1942): a bio-bibliography. Montreal: Graduate School of Library Science, McGill University, 1981. vi, 66 p. (McGill University Graduate School of Library Science Occasional papers ; 7)
Note: 345 entries.
Location: OONL.

7373 **Meikle, W. Duncan**
"A bibliography of George M. Wrong."
In: *Papers of the Bibliographical Society of Canada*; Vol. 14 (1975) p. 90-114.; ISSN: 0067-6896.
Note: Chronological listing from 1884 to 1940 of articles, addresses, reviews, books and edited works.
Location: OONL.

7374 **Wales, Katherine; Murray, Elsie McLeod**
"A bibliography of the works of George M. Wrong."
In: *Canadian Historical Review*; Vol. 29, no. 3 (September 1948) p. 238-239.; ISSN: 0008-3755.
Note: Chronological list from 1892 to 1940.
Location: AEU.

— Y —

7375 **Ian Young: a bibliography, 1962-1980.** Toronto: Pink Triangle Press, 1981. 58 p.: ill., pl. (Canadian Gay Archives publication ; no. 3); ISBN: 0-920430-08-2.

Note: Approx. 540 entries.– Lists work by and about Young: books and chapbooks, broadsides/posters/poemcards, contributions to anthologies, contributions to periodicals, articles about Young and his work.
Addendum: "Checklist of *Catalyst* titles," edited by Ian Young.
Location: OONL.

INDEXES

INDEX

Authors

Auteurs

Allen, David E. 2580
Allen, Don H. 1750
Allen, E. 5490
Allen, Gerald L. 1752
Allen, Harold Don 3475
Allen, Joel Asaph 5302
Allen, Marie-France 3364
Allen, Moira 7246, 7247
Allen, Patrick 1949
Allen, Richard 0511, 4559
Allen, Robert S. 2016, 4104, 4105
Allington-Baker, Amanda 4106
Allison, L.M. 7037
Allix, Beverley 1441
Alsène, Éric 4379
Alston, Sandra 0047
Altfest, Karen C. 4215
Amaratunga, T. 5418
Ambeault, Georgia 6277
Ambroise, Antoine 3663
American Foundation for the Blind 5869
American Geophysical Union 5028
American Society of Genealogists 1934
Ames, Michael M. 6960
Amesse, Fernand 2668, 5820, 5821
Amey, L.J. 1615
Ami, Henri Marc 4729, 4730, 4731, 4732, 4736, 6800, 6943,
   6944, 6945, 6946, 6947, 6948, 6949, 6950, 6951, 7302, 7303, 7304
Amirault, P.A. 5017
Amor, Norman L. 0661, 7162
Amprimoz, Alexandre L. 1143, 1161
Amtmann, Bernard 0074, 0100, 0105, 1328, 1332
Amyot, Pierre 3476
Anand, T. 0619
Anctil, Pierre 1144, 2001
Andersen, Heather 2937
Andersen, Lorrie 3679
Andersen, Marguerite 3826, 3827
Anderson, Alan B. 0543, 1565
Anderson, Beryl L. 1589, 1721
Anderson, Daphne 3787
Anderson, Dennis 2644, 2645, 5209
Anderson, Duncan M. 1756
Anderson, E. William 4657
Anderson, Ethel E. 3530
Anderson, Grace M. 4141
Anderson, John C. 3120
Anderson, John Parker 7040
Anderson, M.K. 5716
Anderson, Roselyn 2835
Anderson, S.R. 5049, 6512
Anderson, William 4647
Anderson, Wolseley W. 4230
Andoniadis, Katherine L. 0689
Andrew, Caroline 2443, 3874
Andrews, Christina Ann 1368
Andrews, Donald Arthur 2171
Andrews, John T. 4813, 5142
Andrews, Martha 0651, 0660, 4813, 5142
Andrews, Thomas A. 5257
Angel, Michael 0542

Angers, Majëlla 4342
Anglin, Lise 5667
Anisef, Paul 3631, 3632
Anschutz, Martha 1591
Anthony, Geraldine 1125
Anthony, Linda 1459
Aoyagi, Akiko 4719
Appleby, J.A. 5266
Aquan-Yuen, R. Margaret 3348
Arai, H.P. 5491
Arai, Mary Needler 6837
Archambault, Guy 2773
Archambault, Jacques 0327
Archambault, Michèle 1106, 1224
Archambault, Roger 0832
Archibald, R.C. 7210
Archives ordinolingues (Canada) 1821
Arctic Institute of North America 0612, 4454, 5341
Arctic Institute of North America. Library 0616
Arctic Science and Technology Information System 0663, 5177
Argue, Robert 4804
Armstrong, Bryan C. 5781
Armstrong, C. 0582, 4781
Armstrong, Douglas 2127, 2617, 2811, 2812, 2813, 2817, 3743
Armstrong, F.H. 4380, 6535, 7325
Armstrong, Hamilton Fish 2424
Armstrong, Jim 4814
Armstrong, Judy B. 3961
Armstrong, Robert H. 5352
Armstrong, Simon 2191
Arnason, David 5909
Arndt, John 1563, 7127
Arndt, Karl J.R. 6017
Arnell, Susan 5036
Arnold, Richard 7216
Arnup, Katherine 3813
Arora, Ved 0532, 2128, 2594, 3931, 7263
Arrowsmith, David 2674, 2879
Arsenault, A. Bertrand 5687
Arsenault, B. 6367
Arsenault, Georges 0243
Arthur, George W. 5508
Arthur, James Richard 5491
Arthurs, H.W. 2115
Arthy, Iain 2517
Artibise, Alan F.J. 0165, 0166, 0522, 0526, 4363, 4380, 4390, 6545
Arts plastiques de Rimouski (Projet). Section recherche en
   histoire 0312, 0313
Ashley, Linda 0139
Ashmore, Peter 5210
Association canadienne d'éducation de langue française 3477
Association canadienne des éducateurs de langue française.
   Commission permanente de la langue parlée 1420
Association canadienne pour la santé, l'éducation physique et
   la récréation 1798
Association des cinéastes amateurs du Québec 6623
Association des directeurs de crédit de Montréal 3165
Association des institutions d'enseignement. Commission des
   bibliothécaires 3732
Association des littératures canadiennes et québécoise. Comité
   de recherche francophone 1126

Boyd, J.A. 3633
Boyd, Susan B. 2328
Boyer, Denis 0362
Boylan, Heather 6039
Boyle, Cornelius Breckinridge 4524
Boyle, Gertrude M. 0047
Bracher, Michael D. 3013
Bradberry, Carroll E. 5028
Bradford, J.D. 5160
Bradford, Martin R. 4805
Bradley, Ian L. 0680, 0687, 0850, 0851, 0858
Bradley, Kenneth 0080
Bradley, Patricia 0687
Bradshaw, Janice 0757
Brady, Elizabeth 7088
Brady, Judith 7223
Braide, Janet 7163
Braine, Linda 0245
Bramall, L. 5425
Bramhall, George 5725
Bramm, Susan 4818
Bramstedt, Wayne G. 4001
Bramwell, John R. 3548
Brand, Judith 3318
Brand, Rosemary 4407
Brander, Leo G. 5057
Brandt, Gail Cuthbert 3887
Brascoupé, Simon 4011
Brass, Allen E. 0734
Brassard, Charles 5197, 5198
Brassard, Denise 4012
Brassard, François 0830
Brassard, Guy R. 5541
Brassard, Hélène 4723
Brassard, Léo 0309
Brasseaux, Carl A. 2019
Brassinga, R.D. 4847
Brault, Helen 0239
Brault, Jean-Rémi 1618, 1688
Brault, Lucien 0427, 6816
Braun, Connie 3710
Brazeau, Marcel 4951
Brearly, Anne 5722
Breem, Wallace 2345
Breen, William J. 0147
Bregman, Alvan 0150
Brehaut, Willard 6070
Brereton, Thomas F. 4327
Brethour, Ross 6855, 7179
Breton, Jean-René 0415
Breton, Lise 3510, 3559, 3582, 3583, 3594, 3603, 3608, 3634
Breton, Marcel 4596
Breugelmans, René 5881, 6095
Brewer, Heather M. 5830
Breyfogle, Donna 4178
Bricker, Mary Anne 1996
Bridault, Alain 2728, 2729
Brideau, Monique 4318
Bridle, Paul 0216
Brière, Jean-Marie 2415, 2428, 5756
Brière, Roger 1751

Brierley, John E.C. 2111
Briggs, W.E. 4824
Bright, Norman F.H. 5740
Brighton, Wayne 3085
Bringhurst, Robert 1660
Brinkhurst, Ralph O. 5521
Brisson, Irène 0904
British Columbia Centennial Committee 4129
British Columbia Federation of Foster Care Associations 3234
British Columbia Library Association 5685, 6040
British Columbia Library Association. Bibliography Committee 0557, 0558, 1912, 6918, 6989, 7350
British Columbia Medical Library Service 5715
British Columbia Research Council 6250
British Columbia School Librarians' Association 1593
British Columbia School Trustees Association 3494
British Columbia Systems Corporation. Library Services 1661, 1676
British Columbia. Aquatic Plant Management Program 6319
British Columbia. Department of Agriculture. Publications Office 6273
British Columbia. Department of Consumer Services 2614
British Columbia. Department of Education. Division of Curriculum 0569
British Columbia. Department of Mines and Petroleum Resources 6257
British Columbia. Ecological Reserves Program 5230
British Columbia. Fish and Wildlife Branch 4888, 5365
British Columbia. Geological Survey Branch 6410, 6427
British Columbia. Government Information Services 6340
British Columbia. Legal Services Commission 2165
British Columbia. Library Services Branch 6677
British Columbia. Littoral Resources Unit 6355
British Columbia. Mineral Resources Division 6428
British Columbia. Ministry of Agriculture and Food 6429, 6656
British Columbia. Ministry of Education, Science & Technology. Continuing Education Division 3560
British Columbia. Ministry of Energy, Mines and Petroleum Resources 6570
British Columbia. Ministry of Environment. Information Services Branch 6331
British Columbia. Ministry of Environment. Surveys and Mapping Branch 6553
British Columbia. Ministry of Forests 5426, 6430
British Columbia. Ministry of Human Resources 1349, 3152, 3197, 3211, 3245
British Columbia. Ministry of Industry and Small Business Development 6368
British Columbia. Ministry of International Business and Immigration 0601
British Columbia. Ministry of Lands, Parks and Housing. Parks and Outdoor Recreation Division. Library 6320
British Columbia. Ministry of Municipal Affairs, Recreation and Culture 0599
British Columbia. Ministry of Provincial Secretary and Government Services. Recreation and Sport Branch 6660
British Columbia. Ministry of Transportation and Highways. Snow Avalanche Programs 4518
British Columbia. Parks Library 6696
British Columbia. Petroleum Resources Division 6383
British Columbia. Provincial Archives. Library 0578

British Columbia. Provincial Educational Media Centre 6661
British Columbia. Provincial Museum 4081, 6237
British Columbia. Provincial Museum. Department of Recreation and Conservation 5340, 5388
British Columbia. Queen's Printer 6431
British Columbia. Recreation and Sport Branch 1802
British Columbia. Recreation Division. Technical Services Unit 1803
British Columbia. Workmen's Compensation Board 2801
British Empire Exhibition (1924-1925: London, England) 0039
British Museum. Department of Printed Books 0007
British North America Philatelic Society 1760
Britt, Margaret 6650
Broadhead, Lee-Anne 2508
Brochu, Lucien 0899
Brochu, Serge 2359
Broderick, Corinne 6697
Brodeur, Denis 4875
Brodeur, Ghyslaine 4587
Brodeur, Léo A. 6113
Brodie, R.J. 5716
Brodo, Irwin M. 5509
Brodribb, Somer 3820
Brody, Bernard 2912
Bromberg, Erik 6058
Brook, Michael 5889
Brook, Robert C. 5608
Brooke, W. Michael 3396
Brooks, I.R. 3511
Brosseau, Marc 3059
Broten, Delores 1637
Broughton, Dawn 2034
Brouillette, Benoît 2961, 7191
Brousseau, Francine 0774
Brown, A.F.C. 5717
Brown, Ann Duncan 0053
Brown, Barbara E. 2780
Brown, Brian E. 3374
Brown, Charles R. 2101, 2104, 2110
Brown, Elizabeth P. 4920
Brown, Gail 2183
Brown, Gerald R. 0106
Brown, Jennifer M. 3031
Brown, M.P. Sharon 0643
Brown, Marilyn 1800
Brown, Mary M.S. 1047
Brown, R.D. 5378
Brown, Roger J.E. 5073
Brown, S.A. 5428
Browne, Colin 6638
Browning, Clyde E. 6103
Brozowski, R.S. 0464
Bruce, Anthony Peter Charles 1984
Bruce, N.G. 4947, 6283
Bruce, Sharon G. 5706
Bruchet, Susan 6188
Bruck, Peter A. 0982, 2501
Brûlé, Monique L. 6402, 6403
Brumble, H. David 4023
Brumpton, Cynthia 3862
Brun, Christian F. 6507, 6516

Brundin, Robert E. 0148
Bruneau, André 2618, 2623
Bruneau, Hélène C. 4703, 4704
Bruneau, Pierre 2624
Bruneau, Sylvie 3584
Brunel, Pierre 5051
Brunelle, Lucie 5276
Bruner, John Clay 5557
Brunet, Jean 6856
Brunet, Manon 1722
Brunet, Raymond 1432
Brunet-Aubry, Lise 2147
Brunet-Lamarche, Anita 1189
Brunet-Sabourin, Manon 1630
Brunkow, Robert deV. 1553
Brunn, Stanley D. 6147
Bryant, Giles 7364
Bryce, Robert 3435
Brye, David L. 4216
Brym, Robert J. 3285
Bubic, Suzanne 2757
Buccini, Anne 0113
Buchanan, Jim 4002
Buchanan, Robert A. 5129, 5130
Buchignani, Norman 4179, 4220
Buckley, L.P. 3383
Bucknall, Brian D. 2115
Buckner, Phillip 2025
Bucksar, R.G. 0435
Budnick, Carol 1726
Buggey, Susan 0752
Bujea, Eleanor 3667
Bujold, Charles 2861
Bull, William Perkins 0045
Buller, Edward 0970
Bullock, Chris 1165
Bunn, Frank E. 5757
Buono, Yolande 0343, 0383
Burdenuk, Gene 1619
Burge, Elizabeth J. 3726
Burgess, Jean 6628
Burgess, Joanne 0412, 2929
Burgess, Larry 5518
Buri, Thomas 0586
Burk, C.F. 4775
Burk, William R. 5443
Burke, Anne 7098, 7099, 7100, 7311, 7312
Burke, Margaret 1396
Burke, Ronald J. 3863
Burkle, Eric F. 3549
Burnet, Jean R. 4248, 4249
Burnett, Mary 1061
Burns, Gordon R. 5493
Burpee, Lawrence J. 0280, 0994, 0995, 1898, 6214
Burr, S.V. 4832
Burrage, David 5767
Burrows, Sandra 6041, 6042
Burtch, Brian E. 3183
Burton, Melody C. 1677
Burton, Thomas L. 3159
Buschert, Karen 1866

Buss, Helen M. 7122

Busse, S. 5588

Bussières, Aline 0613

Butcher, G.A. 5472

Butcher, William W. 5998

Butler, Brian E. 3212

Butler, H. Julene 0785

Butler, J. 4771

Butler, K.C. 4851

Butler, Marian 0181, 0182

Butler, Phyllis 3711

Butler, T.H. 5344, 5362

Butling, Pauline 5972

Buttazzoni, Maria 2346, 2541

Butterfield, L.H. 3927

Butterfield, Rita 0110, 1062

Buyniak, Victor O. 4158

Byam, Barbara 3045

Byers, S.C. 5144, 5170

Byler, Mary Gloyne 4047

C.D. Howe Research Institute 2625

Cabatoff, Kenneth 2489

Caccia, Iva 2280, 2356

Cadieux, Andrée 3198

Cadieux, Francine 6541

Cadieux, Johanne 6622

Cadrin, Carmen 5013

Caine, T.W. 4864, 4865

Calder, Carol 6639

Calder, Kathryn 1976

Calderisi, Maria 0889, 0890, 0919, 0933

Caldwell, Gary 4217

Caldwell, George 2799

Calgary Board of Education. Media Services Group. Educational Media Team 3651

Calkins, Charles F. 0756

Calloway, Colin G. 4099

Camerlain, Lorraine 1179

Cameron, Elspeth 7165, 7166, 7167

Cameron, James J. 5781

Cameron, Judith M. 2216

Cameron, Nancy P. 0652, 4866

Cameron, Neville S.C. 4816

Cameron, William J. 0142, 2035, 2067, 2068, 6774, 7054, 7111

Cammaert, A.B. 4492

Camp, Charles L. 0537

Campbell, A.E. 4943

Campbell, Bonnie A. 5495

Campbell, C.A. 6801

Campbell, Catherine 0062

Campbell, Cindy 0801

Campbell, Craig A. 5427

Campbell, Dani Leigh 1689

Campbell, Elizabeth 5013

Campbell, Geraldine 0489, 0490

Campbell, Glen S. 5853

Campbell, Gordon 3414

Campbell, H.F. 2806

Campbell, Henry Cummings 0083, 0180, 1941

Campbell, K.W. 5242

Campbell, R. Wayne 5473, 5494, 5539

Campbell, Sandra 7146

Campbell, William Wilfred 1890

Camponi, Linda 6574

Canada Centre for Mineral and Energy Technology 5831, 6347

Canada Centre for Mineral and Energy Technology. Library and Documentation Services Division 6397

Canada Council. Research and Evaluation 0728

Canada Institute for Scientific and Technical Information 2615, 4628, 5966

Canada Land Inventory 1756

Canada Mortgage and Housing Corporation 4443

Canada Mortgage and Housing Corporation. Development Evaluation and Advisory Services Division 4381

Canada Oil and Gas Administration 4838

Canada. Agriculture Canada. Advisory Committee on Soil Survey 4705

Canada. Agriculture Canada. Economics Branch 4664

Canada. Agriculture Canada. Research Station (Saskatoon). Library 5086

Canada. Archives nationales 6434

Canada. Archives publiques 6341, 6757

Canada. Archives publiques. Division de la collection nationale de cartes et plans 6517

Canada. Archives publiques. Division des archives fédérales 0638

Canada. Archives publiques. Division des Cartes géographiques 6506

Canada. Atmospheric Environment Service 5074

Canada. Atmospheric Environment Service. Information Resource Centre 5979

Canada. Atomic Energy Control Board 6435

Canada. Bibliothèque du Parlement 0152

Canada. Bureau des traductions. Direction de la documentation 0149

Canada. Bureau des traductions. Direction de la terminologie et des services linguistiques 6436

Canada. Bureau fédéral de la statistique 2964

Canada. Bureau of Statistics. Education Division. Research Section 3387

Canada. Bureau of Statistics. Library 4445

Canada. Canadian Heritage 4296

Canada. Canadian Studies Directorate 0173

Canada. Civil Service Commission. Pay Research Bureau 2795

Canada. Commission de la Fonction publique. Direction générale du programme de la formation linguistique 1469

Canada. Commission of Conservation 6213

Canada. Commission of Inquiry Relating to Public Complaints, Internal Discipline and Grievance Procedure within the Royal Canadian Mounted Police 2140

Canada. Conseil du Trésor 6437

Canada. Consumer and Corporate Affairs Canada 3235

Canada. Department of Agriculture. Economics Division 4640

Canada. Department of Agriculture. Economics Division. Rural Sociology Unit 3080

Canada. Department of Agriculture. Engineering Research Service 4651

Canada. Department of Agriculture. Library 4668, 5928, 6294

Canada. Department of Citizenship and Immigration. Canadian Citizenship Branch 4128, 6063

Canada. Department of Citizenship and Immigration. Economic and Social Research Branch 4133

Canada. Department of Citizenship and Immigration. Library 4130

Canada. Department of Consumer and Corporate Affairs. Library 2117

Canada. Department of Energy, Mines and Resources. Gravity Division 6287

Canada. Department of Energy, Mines and Resources. Surveys and Mapping Branch 6536

Canada. Department of External Affairs 0216

Canada. Department of External Affairs. Information Division 0091

Canada. Department of External Affairs. Library Services Division 2525

Canada. Department of Forestry 4648

Canada. Department of Forestry and Rural Development. Information and Technical Services Division 6265

Canada. Department of Forestry. Information and Technical Services 6607

Canada. Department of Indian Affairs and Northern Development 6678

Canada. Department of Indian Affairs and Northern Development. Northern Regulatory Review 4848

Canada. Department of Indian and Northern Affairs. Indian and Inuit Affairs Program. Research Branch 4013

Canada. Department of Indian and Northern Affairs. Northern Social Research Division 3184

Canada. Department of Indian and Northern Affairs. Program Reference Centre 3963

Canada. Department of Industry, Trade and Commerce 0122

Canada. Department of Industry, Trade and Commerce. Foreign Investment Division 2595, 2603

Canada. Department of Industry, Trade and Commerce. Library 2583

Canada. Department of Justice 2253, 2331

Canada. Department of Labour. Accident Prevention Division. Technical Library 2828

Canada. Department of Labour. Economics and Research Branch 2576

Canada. Department of Manpower and Immigration 4142

Canada. Department of Manpower and Immigration. Occupational Research Section. Occupational Analysis Unit 2798

Canada. Department of Manpower and Immigration. Research Branch 2796

Canada. Department of Marine and Fisheries 6217

Canada. Department of Mines and Resources. Bureau of Geology and Topography 6496

Canada. Department of Mines and Resources. Surveys and Engineering Branch 6493

Canada. Department of Mines and Technical Surveys. Geographical Branch 1935, 2956, 2957, 2958, 2959, 2966, 2968, 4302, 4749, 4754, 5029, 6503

Canada. Department of Mines and Technical Surveys. Surveys and Mapping Branch. Canadian Hydrographic Service 6501, 6502

Canada. Department of National Health and Welfare 6235

Canada. Department of National Health and Welfare. Departmental Library Services 3142

Canada. Department of National Health and Welfare. Emergency Health Services Division 5570

Canada. Department of National Health and Welfare. Epidemiology Division 5565

Canada. Department of Public Printing and Stationery 6242, 6252, 6266

Canada. Department of Public Printing and Stationery. Documents Library 6247, 6248, 6249, 6261

Canada. Department of Regional Economic Expansion. Planning Division 2584

Canada. Department of Supply and Services 6321

Canada. Department of the Interior 2949

Canada. Department of the Interior. Natural Resources Intelligence Branch 6218

Canada. Department of the Interior. Topographical and Air Survey Bureau 6490

Canada. Department of the Secretary of State 2118

Canada. Department of the Secretary of State. Bilingualism Development Programme. Social Action Branch 3115

Canada. Department of the Secretary of State. Human Rights Directorate 2264

Canada. Department of the Secretary of State. Library 4231

Canada. Department of Trade and Commerce 0066

Canada. Direction des études canadiennes 0174

Canada. Dominion Bureau of Statistics 2965, 6445

Canada. Dominion Bureau of Statistics. Canada Year Book, Handbook and Library Division 6258

Canada. Emplois et immigration Canada. Analyse et développement–Professions et carrières 2841

Canada. Employment and Immigration Commission. Occupational and Career Analysis and Development 2842

Canada. Energie, mines et ressources Canada. Division de la gravité et de la géodynamique 6303

Canada. Energy, Mines and Resources Canada. Earth Physics Branch 6295

Canada. Energy, Mines and Resources Canada. Information-EMR 6326

Canada. Energy, Mines and Resources Canada. Mineral Policy Sector 6438

Canada. Environment Canada 5286

Canada. Environment Canada. Atmospheric Environment Service 6307

Canada. Environment Canada. Canadian Parks Service. Socio-Economic Branch 6388

Canada. Environment Canada. Land Use Studies Branch. Outdoor Recreation-Open Space Division 1769

Canada. Environment Canada. Lands Directorate 6384

Canada. Environmental Conservation Service 5221

Canada. Environmental Protection Directorate 6439

Canada. Environnement Canada. Direction générale des terres 6385

Canada. Fisheries and Environment Canada 6311

Canada. Forestry Canada 6440

Canada. Geographic Board 6488

Canada. Geological Survey 6209, 6210, 6211, 6216, 6229, 6231, 6244, 6245, 6253

Canada. Health and Welfare Canada 3185, 6441

Canada. Health and Welfare Canada. Departmental Library Services 3153, 3762

Canada. Health and Welfare Canada. Family Violence Prevention Division. National Clearinghouse on Family Violence 3319

Canada. Health Consultants Directorate 5610

Canada. Indian and Northern Affairs Canada. Communications Service Program 6679

Canada. Indian and Northern Affairs Canada. Departmental Library 5953, 5985

Canada. Indian and Northern Affairs Canada. Inuit Art Section 0727

Canada. Indian Claims Commission. Research Resource Centre 3964

Canada. Information Canada 6296, 6297

Canada. Inland Waters Directorate. Glaciology Division 5122

Canada. Inland Waters Directorate. Water Quality Branch 6389

Canada. Labour Canada 6442

Canada. Labour Canada. Library 5931, 5942

Canada. Legislature. Legislative Assembly. Library 1873, 6711

Canada. Legislature. Legislative Council. Library 6710

Canada. Library of Parliament 0059, 0153, 2373, 2384, 2557, 4884, 6714, 6718, 6720, 6727

Canada. Library of Parliament. Bibliographies and Compilations Section 2324, 2534, 3286

Canada. Library of Parliament. Information and Reference Branch 2018, 2227, 2282, 2434, 2457, 2461, 2502, 2658, 3800, 6377, 6378, 7339

Canada. Library of Parliament. Information and Technical Services Branch 2310, 2514

Canada. Lieux et parcs historiques nationaux. Section des publications de recherches 0805

Canada. Mines Branch 6219

Canada. Ministère d'État aux Affaires urbaines 6312

Canada. Ministère de l'Agriculture. Bibliothèque 6298

Canada. Ministère de la justice 2332

Canada. Ministère des affaires indiennes et du nord canadien 6680

Canada. Ministère des approvisionnements et services 6322

Canada. Ministère des travaux publics 2985

Canada. Ministry of State for Urban Affairs 6313

Canada. Multiculturalism and Citizenship Canada 3336, 4289, 6698

Canada. Multiculturalisme et citoyenneté Canada 3337

Canada. National Advisory Committee on Water Resources Research 5062

Canada. National Archives 6443

Canada. National Capital Commission 0126

Canada. National Historic Parks and Sites. Research Publications Section 0806

Canada. National Museum 6232

Canada. NOGAP Secretariat 4880

Canada. Ocean Science and Surveys 5458

Canada. Parks Canada 6342

Canada. Parks Canada. National Historic Parks and Sites Branch. Policy Co-ordination Division 1781

Canada. Parks Canada. Socio-Economic Division 1804, 1837

Canada. Public Archives 6206, 6343, 6487, 6758, 6761

Canada. Public Archives. Federal Archives Division 0639

Canada. Public Archives. Library 0061, 6784

Canada. Public Archives. Map Division 6504

Canada. Public Archives. National Map Collection 6518, 6537, 6554, 6574

Canada. Public Service Commission. Language Training Program Branch 1470

Canada. Public Service Commission. Staffing Programs Branch. Operations, Staffing Support and Services Division. Women's Programs Centre 3828

Canada. Public Service Staff Relations Board. Library 2690

Canada. Public Works Canada. Departmental Library 4330, 4331, 4344, 4345, 4346, 4357, 4358

Canada. Santé et Bien-être social Canada. Division de la prévention de la violence familiale. Centre national d'information sur la violence dans la famille 3320

Canada. Secrétariat d'État. Direction des droits de la personne 2254

Canada. Service de la conservation de l'environnement 5222

Canada. Solicitor General Canada. Ministry Library and Reference Centre 2333, 2334, 4115, 6681

Canada. Solicitor General Canada. Ministry Secretariat 3877, 4112

Canada. Solicitor General Canada. Programs Branch 2288

Canada. Statistics Canada 3000, 3036, 3055, 3071

Canada. Statistics Canada. Business, Provincial and Municipal Relations Division 6445

Canada. Statistics Canada. Housing, Family and Social Statistics Division. Target Groups Project 3849

Canada. Statistics Canada. Library 6444

Canada. Statistics Canada. Library Services Division 6445

Canada. Statistics Canada. User Advisory Services Division 6445

Canada. Statistics Canada. User Services Division 6344, 6445

Canada. Statistique Canada 3037, 3056, 3072

Canada. Statistique Canada. Division de l'assistance-utilisateurs 6345, 6446

Canada. Statistique Canada. Division des relations avec les entreprises, les provinces et les municipalités 6446

Canada. Statistique Canada. Division des statistiques sociales, du logement et des familles. Projet de groupes cibles 3850

Canada. Statistique Canada. Services de la bibliothèque 6446

Canada. Tourism Canada 6395

Canada. Tourisme Canada 6396

Canada. Translation Bureau. Terminology and Linguistic Services Directorate 6447

Canada. Transport Canada. Library and Information Centre 6379

Canada. Transport Canada. Surface 3167

Canada. Transport Canada. Transportation Development Centre 3246, 4487, 4488

Canada. Travail Canada 6448

Canada. Treasury Board 6449

Canada. Unemployment Insurance Commission. Library 2807

Canada. Wartime Information Board 6226

Canada. Water Pollution Control Directorate 6346

Canada. Women's Bureau 3888

Canadian Advertising Limited 5859

Canadian Association for Adult Education 1016, 2380, 3399

Canadian Association for Adult Education. Research Library 3381

Canadian Association for the Prevention of Crime 2166

Canadian Association in Support of the Native Peoples 3932, 3986

Canadian Association of Children's Librarians 3213, 6668

Canadian Association of Law Libraries 5977

Canadian Bankers' Association 2589

Canadian Book Information Centre 0129

Canadian Broadcasting Corporation 6288

Canadian Broadcasting Corporation. Research Department. Library 6773

Cardinal, Michel 4320
Cardinal, Robert 1596
Careless, Virginia 1988
Carile, Paolo 2043
Cariou, Mavis 0150
Carleton University. Carleton Archives 6114
Carleton University. Department of Geography 6165
Carleton University. Department of Geography. Map Library 6527
Carleton University. Library 2381, 2385
Carlino, Elvia 1346
Carlson, Alvar W. 0753
Carlson, Robert F. 5052
Carlson, Roy L. 6858
Carmichael, Wendy J. 0584
Carney, R.J. 3388
Caron, A. 1558
Caron, Diane 0368
Caron, Fabien 0299, 0626, 7156
Caron, Hélène 2730
Caron, Louise 3500
Carpenter, Carole Henderson 4567, 4580
Carpentier, Louise E. 3864
Carpentier, Robert 4792
Carr, Sheridan 0703, 0704
Carrier, Denis 3257, 7332
Carrier, Lois J. 2973, 5874
Carrier, Maurice 3503
Carrière, Gaston 1416, 1506, 1507, 1513, 3919, 3939, 7200
Carrière, Richard 3258, 3269, 4072
Carrigy, M.A. 4763
Carswell Company 0028
Carter, Connie 3838
Carter, James L. 3965
Carter, John C. 3635
Carter, John Lyman 4548
Carter, Neil M. 6267, 6284
Carter, Ruth C. 4548
Carter, Tom 4117
Cartigny, Sylvie 2412
Caruso, Barbara 1678
Caruso, Naomi 4201
Case, A.B. 4958
Casey, Magdalen 6761
Casno, Pierre 3523
Casno, Pierre 3562
Casper, Dale E. 0781, 0782
Cass-Beggs, Barbara 0863
Casselman, J.M. 5528
Casselman, Paul Hubert 2564
Cassidy, Frank 4082
Cassis, A.F. 7248
Castonguay, Lise 0377
Castonguay, Rachelle 0632, 4631
Catling, P.M. 5522
Caughey, Margaret 1391
Caughey, S.E. 5736
Cavanagh, Beverley 0831
Cavanagh, Joan 4849
Cawker, Ruth 1097
Cayford, J.H. 5345

Cayouette, Jacques 7145
Cebotarev, E.A. 3806
Celsie, Mary Jane 1741
Central Mortgage and Housing Corporation. Data and Information Group 0741
Central Mortgage and Housing Corporation. Library 0748, 4308, 4310, 5719
Centre canadien d'hygiène et de sécurité au travail 2863
Centre canadien d'information et de documentation en archivistique 1690
Centre canadien de la technologie des minéraux et de l'énergie 6348
Centre canadien du film sur l'art 6619
Centre d'édition du gouvernement du Canada 6391
Centre de musique canadienne au Québec 0904
Centre de recherche en histoire économique du Canada français 1971
Centre national des arts (Canada) 6608
Cercle linguistique de Montréal 7355
Ceska, Adolf 5483
Chabot, Josée 2528
Chabot, Juliette 1008
Chabot, Line 0774
Chackowsky, Leonard Eugene 4873
Chaison, Gary N. 2843
Chalifoux, Jean-Pierre 0093, 1032, 1037, 2394
Chalmers, Lex 3060
Chaloult, Michel 2378
Chamberlain, A.F. 4522, 4523
Chamberlain, Jane 5592
Chamberlain, K.E. 0715
Chamberlain, Simon B. 4314
Chamberland, Claire 3338
Chamberland, Constant-Alfred 3368
Chamberland, Diane 2527, 2544
Chamberland, Roger 6872, 6952, 7012, 7349
Chan, Janet B.L. 2357
Chance, David H. 3940
Chandler, Dorothy 2007
Chandrasekhar, S. 4239
Chao, Yen-pin 2242, 2347
Chapdelaine, Cécile 3604
Chapman, Geoffrey 1324
Chappell, Duncan 2243, 2244, 2311, 2312
Chappell, M.S. 5812, 5813
Charbonneau, André 6528
Charbonneau, Chantal 0730
Charbonneau, Hélène 1364
Charest, Marie-Claire 2213
Charest-Knoetze, Claire 0264
Charette, Jean-Yves 5276
Charland, Jean-Pierre 3605
Charland, Thomas 7240
Charlton, M. Jane 1391
Chartier, Armand B. 0279
Chartier, Jean-Pierre 3681
Chartier, Yves 0874
Chartrand, Francis 4874
Chartrand, Georges-Aimé 1588
Chassay, Jean-François 1290
Chassé, Béatrice 7019

Couturier, Gaston 0832
Cowan, Ann S. 0120
Cowell, Daryl William 4826, 5134
Cox, Bruce Alden 4092
Cox, Carole Ann 1793
Cox, Joseph P. 1741
Cox, Mark 0471
Cox, Sandra J. 0150, 2301
Craig, Béatrice 2081
Craig, Helen C. 1814, 6050
Cram, Jennifer 3652
Cramm, Karen M. 3121
Crane, Brian A. 2379
Crane, Nancy 0405
Cranmer-Byng, Alison 1175
Craven, Paul 2634
Craven, Rita 1454
Craven, Scott R. 5460
Crawford, Hewlette S. 5474
Crawford, Patricia 0749
Crawford, William 3259
Creelman, Gwendolyn 0265, 0854
Creelman, Jan 1699
Cregier, Sharon E. 4717
Crewe, Donald Martin 3606
Crime Writers of Canada 1300
Crispens, Charles G. 5331
Crochetière, Jacques 2037
Crofton, Francis Blake 6744
Crombie, Jean Breakell 0054, 0999
Cronk, Michael Sam 6172
Crooks, Grace 0440
Crosby, Louis S. 1744
Cross, Lowell M. 0821
Cross-Cultural Communication Centre 3778
Crossley, Diane 4427
Crossman, E.J. 5372, 5420, 5528
Crouch, Yvonne J. 2034
Crowhurst, Christine Marie 5645
Crowley, David F. 4314
Crown, Elizabeth Marie 2731
Crowther, Roy A. 5247, 5444
Cruger, Doris M. 6086
Crusz, Rienzi 0462, 2635
Crysdale, Stewart 1532
Cuddy, Mary Lou 0583
Cukier, Golda 4201, 5932
Cullen, Carman 2644, 2645
Cullen, Mary K. 0767
Cullingworth, J.B. 4393
Culver, Stephen John 5445
Cumming, Alice 0446
Cumming, Alister 3712
Cumming, Greta 2329, 2330
Cumming, Ross 0446
Cummings, Richard 1176
Cummins, Jim 3618
Cummins, Vivian 2779
Cunningham, Peter G. 4469
Cunningham, Rosella 5622
Curat, Hervé 7035

Currie, A. Blaine 3568
Curry, Ralph L. 7135
Curtis, Fred A. 4846
Curtis, Joanna B. 2902
Curtis, Lois 1346
Cusack, Carla 6349, 6350
Cusson, Maurice 2276
Cyr, André 0311
Cyr, Hermel 0228
Czaykowski, Bogdan 1246
Czetwertynska, Aniela 2169
D'Amore (L.J.) & Associates Ltd 5156
D'Amours, Isabelle 0942
D'Anglejan, Alison 1474, 3686
D'Souza, Colleen 5833
Dafoe, Elizabeth 0063
Dafoe, Marcella 6926
Dagenais, Huguette 3833
Dagg, A.I. 3794, 5427
Dahl, Edward H. 6545, 6546
Dahms, Moshie 1292
Dakin, John 4332
Dalcourt, Gabrielle 6884
Dale, Ronald J. 0451
Dale, Rosemary 0479
Daley, Bruce 0221
Dalgliesh, W.A. 5737
Dalhousie University. Institute of Public Affairs. Library 4359
Dalhousie University. Library 1594, 3920, 4146
Dalke, Paul D. 5348
Damien, Yvonne M. 4586
Dandurand, Liette 2257
Dandurand, Pierre 3713
Daniells, Laurenda 1831, 6933
Daniells, Lorna M. 2566
Danis, Jane 4601
Danks, H.V. 5461
Danky, James P. 5951
Dann, T.F. 5191
Dansereau, Bernard 2416, 2420
Dansereau, Pierre 6935, 6936
Daoust, Denise 1478
Daoust, Lucie 2192
Daoust, Paul 1434
Darling, Michael 7260, 7261, 7313, 7314, 7335
Darlington, Susan 2732
Dartmouth Regional Library 4839
Darton, Nelson Horatio 4728
Dassonville, Michel 6069
Dau, Christian P. 5409
Daugherty, Wayne 4055, 4056
Dave, Nand K. 5267
Daveluy, Marie-Claire 0292, 1938, 7174
Davey, Frank 1084
David, Hélène 2858
David, Jack 1302
Davidson, John 6937
Davidson, Nadean 1650
Davidson, R.B. 5472
Davidson-Arnott, Robin G.D. 4777
Davie, Cyril Francis 2100

Davie, Lynn 3653
Davies, G.K. 5730
Davies, Maureen 2512
Davies, R.W. 5366
Davies, Raymond Arthur 4127
Davies, W.H. 0515
Davis, Egerton Yorrick, pseud 7228
Davis, Harry Osmond 4762
Davis, John F. 0169
Davis, Lynne 4097
Davis, P.F. 2679
Davis, Shelton 4052
Davis, Stephen A. 4561, 4599
Dawson, C.A. 0608
Dawson, Irene J. 1950
Dawson, K.C.A. 4594
Dawson Brothers (Montreal, Quebec) 1576
Day, Alan Edwin 2054
Day, Dwane 4889
Day, Stephen 4152
Day, T.J. 5229
Daye, Peter Graeme 5446
De Billy, Marie-Claude 3663
De Groot, Pieter 5524, 5525
De Haas, Patricia 1438
De la Barre, Kenneth 0641, 3023, 3038
De Laguna, Frederica 7079
De Leeuw, J.H. 4452
De Leon, Lisa 0259
De March, B. 5389
De Pasillé, François B. 3124
De Plaen, Jacqueline 2169, 2193, 2246
De Stricker, Ulla 2751
De Valk, Alphonse 1537
De Varennes, Rosario 0079
De Veber, L.L. 3661
De Vries, John 4251, 4252, 4253, 4254
Deacon, James 2307, 2308
Deane, Marie 3753
Decarie, Graeme 0369
Dechêne, Paul 2844
Dechene, Verona M. 1071, 1096
Dechief, Helene A. 4447, 4478
Decore, Anne Marie 4024
DeCoste, Frederick Charles 3890
DeDuy, Anh 5784
Deer, A. Brian 3951, 3952, 3975, 3976, 3977
Defoe, Deborah 0472
DeGrâce, Eloi 0533
Degrange, J.E. 4711
Dehem, Roger 2781, 2782
Dekin, Albert A. 4572
Delisle, Claude E. 5223
Delisle, Jean 1445, 1472
Deller, June 3323
Delorme, R.J. 4860
Demers, Henri 2627, 4472
Demers, Pierre 0845, 6026, 6632, 7250
Dempsey, Hugh A. 4108
Dempsey, Patrick E. 6584
Denault, Bernard 1540, 2730

Dendwick, F.M. 4970
Denham, Robert D. 6993, 6994, 6995
Denike, C.C.E. 5041
Denis, Théophile 4740
Denison, P.J. 5148
Dennis, Janet Lenoir 4083
Dennison, John D. 3437
Denton, Vivienne 1365, 4255
Deosaran, Ramesh 3502
Derksen, A.J. 5455
Desai, R.L. 5727
Desaulniers, Robert 7031
Desbarats Advertising Agency 6002
Descarries, Francine 3869
Descent, David 3324
Deschamps, Isabelle 5838
Deschamps, Marcel 0953
Deschênes, Gaston 2504, 2659
Deschênes, Jean-Guy 4014, 4073, 4084
Deschênes, Marc 0980
Desgranges, Jean-Luc 5018
Desiree Bradley Library and Technical Services 5243
Desjardins, Joëlle 2309, 2335, 2515, 2536, 2543, 2733, 2734,
    2735, 2736, 3325, 3350, 4710, 5686
Desjardins, Marc 0398, 0399
Desjardins-MacGregor, Louise 1991
Desjarlais, Lionel 3503
Deslongchamps, Bernard 6539
Deslongchamps, Jocelyne 0354
Desmarteau, Leo M. 2802
Desrochers, Alain 1451, 3136, 4192
Desrochers, Edmond 1584, 1618
Desrosiers, Danielle 2455, 3351, 3898
Desrosiers, Denise 3032
Dessureault, Guy 3638
Désy, Marguerite 3564
Deutsch, M.M. 5419
Devanney, Burris 7146
Deverell, Alfred Frederick 3383
Devers, Charlotte M. 5957
Dew, Ian F. 0516, 3168
Dewailly, Éric 5279
Dewar, D. 5481
Dewar, Heather 5560
Deyell, Suzanne M. 3683
DeYoung, Marie 2871
Dhand, Harry 4321, 7264
Dhillon, Balbir Singh 5850, 5851
Di Nardo, Domenico 7146
Diamant, Isabell 5140
Diamond, Sara 2864
Dibb, Sandra 0517
Dick, Ernest J. 6669, 6670
Dick, T.A. 5558
Dick, Trevor J.O. 2636
Dickerhoof, Edward 2647
Dickinson, Gary 0579
Dickson, Constance 0214
Dickson, Heather 4082
Dietrich, B. 2950
Dietz, Hanns-Bertold 7094

Engineering Interface Limited 5776
English, Jennifer 5654
English, John 7087
English, M. 5280
Ennis, G.L. 4899
Enns, Carol 3538
Enns, Richard A. 0549
Enright, Catherine Theresa 5475
Enros, Philip Charles 4629
Envirocon Ltd. 4794
Environics Research Group 3105, 3106, 5579
Epp, Henry T. 4602
Epstein, Perle 7160
Ericson, Richard V. 2348, 3183
Erskine, Anthony J. 5359
Ervin, Alexander M. 0640
Espesset, Hélène 2808, 2816, 4500, 4501
États-Unis. Service d'information 2395
Etcheverry, Jorge 1270
Eterovich, Adam S. 4170
Ettlinger, John R.T. 0163
Evans, David 5380
Evans, David O. 5495
Evans, Gwynneth 3755, 6188, 7114
Evans, Judith E.M. 5658
Evans, Karen 0047, 4075
Evans, Mary 0461
Evert, F. 4935
Ewing, Guy 3685
Ewing, John 6212
Exposition de l'Empire britannique (1924-1925: Londres, Angleterre) 0040
Eyler, Phillip L. 0628
Eyre, D. 5752
Fabi, Thérèse 6851
Fabien, Claude 2139
Faessler, Carl 6497
Faghfoury, Nahid 3333, 3334
Fagnan, Vivianne M. 5688
Fahl, Ronald J. 4955
Fahmy-Eid, Nadia 3835
Fairbanks, Carol 3817, 6806
Fairley, Helen 0559, 0560
Falaise, Noël 6876
Falardeau, Jean-Charles 1514, 7009
Falby, Walter F. 4802
Falk, Gathie 0699
Fallis, B.W. 5180
Family Planning Federation of Canada 3116
Faminow, Merle Douglas 4722
Fancy, Margaret 0839, 7046, 7150, 7319
Fang, Jin Bao 5725
Faribault, Georges Barthélemi 1872
Farmer, Colin 2171
Farnell, Margaret B. 3200
Farrell, David M. 2793
Farson, Anthony Stuart 2336
Fast, Louise 6371
Fathi, Ashgar 5912
Fattah, E.A. 2152
Faucher, Carol 6658

Fauchon, André 3039, 6914
Faulds, Jon 2184
Faulkner, Mary S. 2490
Fauteux, Aegidius 3369
Favreau, Marc 5541
Fay, Terence J. 2474
Fearnley, Edel 0140, 0141
Feather, Joan 5700
Federal-Provincial Committee on Mineral Statistics (Canada). Publications Task Force 6372
Fédération des enseignantes et des enseignants de l'Ontario. Comité de la condition féminine 3271
Fedigan, Larry 3551, 3566
Fedynski, Alexander 6023
Fee, Margery 1097, 7216
Fee, Norman 6757, 6758
Féger, Robert 3297
Fehr, Helen 3933
Fehr, Laurene D. 5118
Feihl, John 0865
Feihl, O. 4963
Feit, Harvey A. 3934, 3978, 3979, 4555
Feldman, M. 4715
Feldman, Wendy A. 3788
Feller, M.C. 4974
Fellmann, Jerome D. 5938
Fellows, Jo-Ann 1976, 2024
Felsky, Martin 2292
Feltner, Charles E. 2020
Feltner, Jeri Baron 2020
Fenton, William Nelson 3927
Ferguson, D.S. 3401
Ferguson, Margaret 2259
Ferguson, W.O. 3388
Ferres, John H. 1098
Ferrier, Dorothy J. 6216
Ferrier, W.F. 6216
Ferris, Kathryn 3818
Festival international du livre (1er: 1969: Nice, France) 0092
Feuerwerker, Elie 5391
Ficke, Eleanore R. 5123
Ficke, John F. 5123
Field, Thomas Warren 3904
Field, William D. 5381
Filby, P. William 2026, 2069
Filiatrault, Johanne 5687
Filotas, Paul K.G. 6202
Filson, D.H. 5752
Filteau, J.O. 0012
Finch, Rita 6555
Findlay, Joanna 2214
Finegold, Ronald 4201
Fingas, M.F. 5124
Fink, Howard 0978
Finkel, Reeva 3752
Finley, E. Gault 3394, 3702
Finley, Jean C. 3654, 4843, 5194
Finn, Julia 0723
Finson, Shelley Davis 3891
Firth, Edith G. 1941, 6012
Fischer, Lewis R. 4503

Fisher, Gerald 0229
Fisher, Honey Ruth 3272
Fisher, Joel E. 1743
Fisher, John 1527
Fisher, Kathleen E. 2286
Fisher, Mary 2717
Fiszhaut, Gustawa M. 2973
Fitchko, J. 5232
Fitzpatrick, Connie 6289
Fitzpatrick, Diane E. 5701
Flack, David 1212
Fladmark, K.R. 4549
Flaherty, David H. 2226, 2266
Flaherty, Shelagh 2285
Flax, Judy 3038
Flem-Ath, Rand 2505
Fleming, Patricia Lockhart 0273, 0452, 0486, 1639
Flemington, Frank 6931
Flemming, Tom 5694
Flick, Frances Josephine 4920
Flint, John E. 0089
Flitton, Marilyn G. 1149
Florkow, David W. 2232
Flow, A.F. 1994
Foerstel, Hans 4349
Fogwill, W.D. 4798, 6515, 6566
Fohlen, Claude 1953
Folan, Maria 6622
Foley, Kathryn Shred 1474, 3686
Foley, Margaret 0265
Folk, Karen R. 3993
Fondation de l'arbre Canada 3219
Fontannaz-Howard, Lucienne 1331
Forcese, Dennis P. 3339
Ford, John 2865, 3819
Ford, Theresa M. 1342
Foreign Service Community Association. Committee on Mobility and the Family 3169
Forest, Paul 1816
Forest Engineering Research Institute of Canada 5007
Forest Fire Research Institute (Canada). Information Centre 4925
Forgay, Beryl 2349, 4869
Forget, Guy 6241
Forintek Canada Corporation 6451
Forkes, David 1776
Forrest, Anne 2634
Forrester, C.R. 4889
Forrester, W.D. 5047
Forsman, E.D. 5494
Forsyth, Joseph 0541, 6278
Fort Frontenac Library 5968
Fortier, André 0326
Fortier, John 0738
Fortier, Marcel 4121
Fortier, Monique 6380
Fortier, Y. 5736
Fortin, Benjamin 0453
Fortin, Donald 2596, 2604, 2605, 2606
Fortin, Jean-Luc 1732
Fortin, Marcel 1251, 1717

Fortin, Suzanne 0318
Fortuine, Robert 5573, 5577
Foshay, Toby Avard 7151
Foss, Brian 7045
Foster, Leslie A. 2369
Foster, Leslie T. 5104
Found, William C. 3015
Fournier, François 2468, 4964
Fournier, Marcel 0328, 0339
Fournier, Pierre 2676
Fournier, Sandy 4834
Fournier-Renaud, Madeleine 0975
Fowke, Edith 0833, 0863, 0910, 4567, 4580
Fowke, V.C. 4639, 6875
Fowle, Charles David 5149
Fowler, Terry A. 3684
Fox, Richard George 3095
Fox, W. Sherwood 5318
Fraker, P.N. 4936
Framst, G.E. 4665
France. Bibliothèque nationale 6484
Franco, Beatriz 3662
Frank, David 2904
Frank, Jackie 5668
Frank, K. Portland 5623
Frank, Peter G. 5484
Frank, Thomas F. 4652
Frankel, B. Gail 5608
Frankel-Howard, Deborah 3327, 3328
Franzin, William Gilbert 5496
Frappier, Monique 0334
Fraser, Alex W. 0491
Fraser, C.M. 5317
Fraser, Doreen E. 1541, 5635
Fraser, Ian Forbes 1004
Fraser, J. Keith 6116, 7253
Fraser, James H. 5225
Frayne, June 1326
Fréchette, Jean-Guy 4926
Frederick Harris Music Co. Limited 6838
Frederking, R. 5113
Fredriksen, John C. 2002, 2046
Free, Brian Michael 5233
Freedman, Gloria 3757
Freeman, Janette M. 6333
Freeman, Milton M.R. 5257
Freeman, Richard Broke 7022
Freemark, Kathryn 5560
Freer, Katherine M. 0573
French, R. 4853
French Institute in the United States 0285
Frey, Cecelia 7362
Fricker, Aubrey 4850
Frideres, James S. 4193
Fried, Bruce 5674
Fried, Jacob 3909
Friendly, Martha 3353
Friesen, Gerald 0534
Friesen, Jean 0542, 0590
Friesen, John W. 4015
Friesen, Richard J. 0633, 0634

Gilchrist, J. Brian 6043
Giles, Tim 6599
Giles, Valerie M.E. 3728
Gill, Dhara S. 0520
Gill, R.J. 4492
Gill, Theodore Nicholas 5302
Gillespie, C.R. 4771
Gillespie, Gilbert 0956
Gillespie, Kay M. 0551
Gillespie-Wood, Janet 4857, 6332, 6333
Gilliss, Geraldine 3623, 3656, 3657
Gillmeister, D. 6376, 6409
Gilroy, A.E. 3371
Gilroy, Marion 6492
Gimbarzevsky, Philip 4980
Gingras, André 2267
Ginn, R.M. 6074
Girard, Hélène 7329
Girard, Sonya 5636
Girouard, Laurie 2597
Giroux, Nicole 2720
Giroux, Richard 3489
Giuliani, Gary 2143
Gladman, Tina 3602
Gladstone, Jane 2348
Glazebrook, George P. de T. 2374
Glazier, Kenneth M. 6020
Glenbow-Alberta Institute 2125
Glenbow-Alberta Institute. Library 0508
Gnarowski, Michael 1023, 1040, 1130, 1590, 6137
Goard, Dean S. 0579
Godard, Barbara 1202, 3851
Godavari, Sigrun Norma 2681
Godfrey, David 0103
Godfrey, H. 5383
Goehlert, Robert 2538
Goeldner, C.R. 1752, 1764
Goertz, Richard O.W. 1528, 5884, 6098
Goff, T.W. 0233
Goggin, John Mann 4538
Goggio, Emilio 5867
Golant, Stephen 3089
Gold, Lorne W. 5097, 5823
Goldberg, Michael A. 2692
Golden, Richard L. 7228
Goldstein, Jay 4210
Gollop, Bernie 5549
Gomer, Mary 3195
Goodfellow, Gay 4481
Goodfellow, John 0561
Goodman, Millie 2590
Goodwillie, S.B. 5044
Goodwin, C. Ross 0644, 3038, 3654, 4843, 5181, 5182, 5196, 5796
Goodwin, Daniel Corey 2059
Goodyear, Carole D. 5477
Googins, Bradley 3260
Goorachurn, Lynn-Dell 1452
Gordon, Robert Macaire 2243, 2244
Gordon, Robert S. 1614
Gordon, W. Terrence 1449
Gordon Home Blackader Library 0733

Gorecki, Paul K. 2194
Görlach, Manfred 1463
Gorman, J.R. 4970
Gormely Process Engineering 4858
Goshawk, L. 7264
Gotell, Lise 3852
Gotthardt, Michael 0447
Gotthardt, Ruth 0447
Gottlieb, Amy 3813
Gottlieb, Lois C. 1150
Gough, C.J. 4232
Gould, Allan Mendel 6912
Goulet, Jean 2215, 6831
Goulet, Marcel 4964
Goulson, Cary F. 3592
Gourd, Benoît-Beaudry 0323, 4796
Gourdeau, Monique F. 6351
Gourdes, Irénée 1602
Govia, Francine 4256
Gowdey, C.D. 5564
Gower, Wendy 2866, 2919
Gowling, Linda 0319
Grace, Robert J. 4297
Graham, Bruce M. 5057
Graham, Katherine A. 4123
Graham, R. 1823, 5777
Graham, Roger 7157
Graham (D.W.) and Associates 3007
Grainger, Bruce 2013
Grains Group (Canada) 4460
Grammond, Madeleine 1560, 1562, 1569
Granatstein, J.L. 2025
Granberg, Charlotte 3024
Grande, Ellen 1336
Granger, Denise 5703
Granger Frères 0032
Grant, John E. 6996
Grant, Judith Skelton 6998
Grant, Linda 3238
Grant, Madeline 2405, 7086, 7087
Gras, N.S.B. 2562
Grasham, W.E. 2404
Grasmick, Harold G. 4041
Grasmick, Mary K. 4021
Gratton, Claude 7006, 7115
Gravel, Pierre 2421
Graves, Donald E. 2021
Gray, B.J. 5819
Gray, Viviane 3928
Grayson, Donald K. 5099
Great Britain. Colonial Office. Library 6771
Greater Vancouver Regional District 6357
Greater Vancouver Regional District. Planning Department 4374, 4391
Greco, Michael E. 4946
Green, Deirdre E. 5609
Green, Howard 4044
Green, Rayna 4045
Green, Vicki A. 3409
Greenaway, Nora 6697
Greenberg, A. Morley 2818

Greene, B.A. 6515
Greenfield, Katharine 1519
Greenly, Albert Harry 1930, 7112
Greenshields, H. 5732
Greenwood, Brian 4777
Greenwood-Church, Margo L. 3279
Greer, Marbeth 2124
Greer-Wootten, Bryn 0324
Grégoire-Reid, Claire 7284
Gregor, Jan 2506
Gregorovich, Andrew 1724, 4153, 4156, 4194, 4196, 4257
Gregory, Diane J. 4789, 6332, 6333
Gregory, Joel W. 3032
Gregory, Paul 0955, 3125
Gregory, Winifred 0050, 6004, 6220
Greig, Peter E. 0104, 1354, 6015, 7181, 7188
Grenier, A. 3075
Grenier, Ginette 0370
Grenier, M.G. 4851
Grewal, H. 5531
Gribenski, Jean 6151
Gridgeman, N.T. 5425
Griffin, Appleton Prentiss Clark 1878, 1879, 1880, 1896, 2558
Griffin, Meredith 4124
Griffin, P.J. 6244
Griffin-Allwood, Philip G.A. 1568
Griffing, T.C. 5444
Griffith, J.W. 4750
Griffiths, Curt Taylor 2274, 4109
Griffiths, K.B. 6358
Griffiths, K.J. 5404, 5447
Grimard, Jacques 0123, 0466
Grimble, D.G. 4990
Grmela, Sonia 2507
Grondines, Hélène 0925
Groot, C. 5517
Gross, Konrad 1203
Groulx, Lorraine 0709
Groupe chargé d'étudier les problèmes de santé mentale des immigrants et des réfugiés 5678
Groupe de travail sur la surveillance de la santé et de la sécurité dans les laboratoires 5647
Growoll, Adolf 7047
Gruchy, I.M. 5368
Grumet, Robert Steven 4004
Grünsteudel, Günther 0164
Guay, Donald 1765
Guay, Michelle 3170
Gue, Leslie R. 3410
Guédon, Marie-Françoise 0834
Guérin, Huguette 1490
Guertin, Marcelle 7001
Guilbeault, Claude 6285
Guilbeault, Marielle T. 3096
Guilbert, Honoré 1498
Guillet, Edwin C. 7036
Guillot, Andrée 3608
Guilmette, Bernadette 1237
Guilmette, Pierre 0951
Guimont, Pierre 0649
Guitard, André 1522

Gulbinowicz, Eva 3789
Gulick, Charles Adams 2789
Gullett, D.W. 5260, 5261
Gunn, Diane M. 1346
Gunn, Gertrude E. 7168
Gunn, Jonathan P. 3248
Gurstein, Michael 3988
Guse, Lorna 4595
Gushue, W.J. 3467
Gusset, Gérard 4560
Guthe, Alfred K. 4538
Gutman, G.M. 5679
Gutteridge, Paul 2082, 2607
Guttmann, David 4267
Guyot, Mireille 4546
Gwillim, J.C. 4735
Gwyn, Julian 1972
Haas, Marilyn L. 4046
Haberer, A. 4666
Habgood, Helen 5195
Habiak, Marilyn J. 3485
Hacia, Henry 5065
Hackett, Brenda 0454
Hackett, Christopher 0546
Haddad, April 3275
Hadeed, Henry 1326
Hady, Maureen E. 5951
Haeberlé, Viviane 0980
Haeussler, S. 5526, 5553
Hafstrom, Ole 0170, 5974
Hagler, Ronald 1396
Haight, Willet Ricketson 0024, 6738
Hainaux, René 0983
Hair, Donald S. 7249
Haire, Jennifer 1385
Haist, Dianne 2831, 3765
Hakim, Antjie 2462
Halary, Charles 2423
Hale, Elizabeth 6549
Hale, Linda Louise 0592, 0594, 0602, 3361, 3362, 3780, 3844
Halévy, Balfour 2338
Halifax City Regional Library 0213
Halifax City Regional Library. Reference Department 0249
Halifax Garrison Library 6735
Hall, Agnez 1640
Hall, E. 6245
Hall, Frederick A. 0825, 0931, 0933, 7083
Hall, R.J. 5588
Halliday, R.G. 4908
Hallsworth, Gwenda 0480, 0481, 0487
Halpert, Herbert 4590
Hambraeus, Bengt 0904
Hamel, Jacques 7269
Hamel, Lucie 3544
Hamel, Pierre 2445, 4379
Hamel, Réginald 1033, 1049, 1050, 1099, 1188, 3746
Hamelin, Colette L. 1511
Hamelin, Jean 0371, 1957, 1958, 2055, 2377, 6264
Hamelin, Louis-Edmond 0613, 1511, 2960, 7044
Hamelin, Lucien 6615
Hamelin, Marcel 2377

Heick, W.H. 7157
Heide, Cynthia 5731
Heidenreich, Barbara 4097
Heinke, Gary W. 5739
Heinrich, Albert C. 5913, 6104, 6117
Heissler, Ivar 0447, 0449
Heitz, Thomas R. 2232
Helen K. Mussallem Library 5625, 5988
Hélène de Rome, soeur 6867
Hellman, Florence S. 0053
Helm, June 3980, 4058
Helmes-Hayes, Richard C. 7178
Hemsley, Gordon D. 2510
Hemstock, C. Anne 0656
Henderson, George Fletcher 6262
Henderson, V. 5485
Hendricks, Klaus B. 1701, 1702
Hendrickson, O. 4976
Hendrix, Catrina 4402
Hendsey, Susanne 2626
Henley, Thomas J. 0628
Hennepin, Louis 7058
Henning, D.N. 3101
Henning, J. 0160
Henning, Joanne K. 6195
Henry, Ginette 5917
Henry, Jon Paul 1182
Henry, Ronald 2729
Henshel, Richard L. 2233
Heraldry Society of Canada. Library 2060
Herberg, Dorothy C. 3195
Herbert, Lynn 1719, 1721, 1725
Herisson, Michel R.P. 3953
Heritage Canada Conference on Area Conservation 0743
Heritage Ottawa 0750
Herman, Carlton M. 5405
Herman, Esther 0119, 0134
Herman, Michael John 2151
Hernandez, Marilyn J. 0513
Héroux, Réjean W. 1609
Herperger, Dwight 2339, 2351
Herrick, Ramona 1770, 1771, 1772, 1777, 3002
Herscovitch, Pearl 3051
Hesch, Rick 6683
Hess, Ernest 5865
Hessel, Peter 4223
Hétu, Jacques 0904
Heuring, L.G. 5464
Hewitt, A.R. 0064
Hewitt, Gordon C. 5314
Hickcox, E.S. 3473
Hickey, Michael Daniel 5726
Hicks, Brenda 6051
Hidy, Muriel E. 2565
Hidy, Ralph W. 2565
Hieatt, D.J. 4481
Higgins, Kenneth F. 5270
Higgins, Marion Villiers 0042, 0283, 6221
Hill, Stuart B. 4669, 4672
Hillard, Jane 2446
Hillman, M. 5392

Hillman, Thomas A. 3052
Hills, L.V. 5450
Hills, Steven C. 5016
Hiltz, Linda L. 5414
Hinke, C.J. 1350
Hinks, Yvonne 4837
Hippler, Arthur E. 3921, 3954
Hiratsuka, Y. 5490
Hirschfelder, Arlene B. 4031, 4047
Hiscock, Audrey M. 0245
Hiscock, Philip 0221
Historical and Scientific Society of Manitoba 0503
Hitchman, James H. 1998
Hlady, Walter M. 4540
Hobson, G.D. 4633
Hodge, Frederick Webb 3908
Hodge, William H. 3981
Hodgins, J. George 3367
Hodgins, James 5430
Hodgson, C.A. 5542
Hodgson, Maurice 2047
Hodson, Dean R. 6133
Hodson, P.V. 5467
Hoffman, Bernard G. 1936
Hogan, Brian F. 1566
Hogan, K. 0160
Hogan, Lesley 7274
Holcomb, Adele M. 0717
Holdsworth, Rosalynd 2022
Hole, Maureen 1480
Holland, Clive 0636
Holland, Susan 0436
Holland, William L. 2491, 2559
Hollett, Gary 0837
Holmberg, Robert George 5296
Holmden, H.R. 6487
Holmes, Alison 1829
Holmes, Janet 0705, 5768
Holmes, Marjorie C. 6227, 6230
Holmes, Maurice 6919
Holmes, R.M. 4641
Holroyd, Geoffrey L. 5514
Holste, Susanne 4516
Holt, Faye Reineberg 1297
Holway, Debra 4834
Holyoke, Francesca 6793
Holzmueller, Diana Lynn 3941
Hondius, E.H. 2131
Honeywell, D.M. 6114
Honeywell, Joan 7114
Honigmann, John J. 3912
Hooper, Tracey D. 5244
Hoos, Lindsay M. 5088, 5100, 5101
Hoover, Herbert T. 4005
Hope, S. 3016
Hôpital Rivière-des-Prairies. Bibliothèque du personnel 3146, 3147, 3171, 5659
Hopkinson, C. 7345
Hopkinson, Marvin W. 4463
Horbay, Z. 4165
Horguelin, Paul A. 1439

Horn, Charles 4109
Horne, A.J. 0080
Horne, Alan J. 6807, 6808, 6809, 6810, 6811, 6812
Horning, Lewis Emerson 0995
Horsman, Jennifer 3716
Horvath, Maria 1530
Hostetler, John A. 1525
Hostikka, S.A. 4954
Houghton, Conrad 4508
Hould, Claudette 0700
Houlden, Melanie G. 3844
Houle, France 2293
Houle, Ghislaine 0302, 0844, 1089, 1783, 3756
Houle, Gilles 3186
Houle, Guy 1228
House, Anthony B. 1443
Houston, C. Stuart 7053
Houyoux, Philippe 0375, 1090, 3148, 3539, 5924
Howard, Lynne M. 0644, 0645, 4843, 5196, 5234
Howard, Susan V. 0169
Howard, William 3260
Howay, F.W. 0555
Hoxie, Frederick E. 4116
Hoy, Eileen Monica 3384
Hoy, Helen 1204
Hrebenyk, B. 5224
Hristienko, Hank 4983
Hromadiuk, Bob 4291
Hruska, Jan 4775
Huang, Paul Te-Hsien 2119
Hubbard, William F. 3031, 4799, 4942, 4950
Hudon, Céline 0344
Hudon, Dominique 6990
Hudon, Jean-Paul 0713, 1145, 1221
Hudson's Bay Company 1913
Huff, Donald W. 1823, 3029
Huffman, James 0690, 2637, 3540, 3610, 5612
Huffman, Sybil 0690, 2637, 3540, 3610, 5612
Huggard, Turner 4224
Hughes, G.T. 4764
Hughes, Linda 5632
Hugolin, père 1495, 1496, 1497, 1498, 1500, 1501, 3076, 3077, 7055, 7056, 7072, 7075, 7154, 7195
Huizenga, Angie 0473
Hulbert, Tina G. 3541
Hulchanski, John David 3358, 4333, 4369, 4370, 4375, 4394, 4411, 4417, 6797
Hull, Jeremy 3611
Huls, Mary Ellen 7289
Hunka, Diane Lynne 5089
Hunston, Jeffrey R. 4574, 4608
Hunt, L. 7264
Hunt, Lynn J. 1212
Hunter, Andrew F. 4526
Hunter, Elizabeth 0423
Hunter, Isabel 5671
Huntsman, A.G. 5317
Huot, Diane 1460
Hurn, Nancy J. 0885
Hurst, James W. 1959
Husted, Deborah 0784

Huston, Barbara 0527
Huston, R.D. 5782
Hutcheson, Stephanie 0139
Hutchings, Mary 3752
Hutchinson, Elaine 2352
Hutchinson, Raymond 5431
Hymer, Stephen 2592
Hynes, Mary C. 6116
Hynes, Ronald 4321
Hynes, Susan 2696
Hyttenrauch, David 0708
Ibach, Stephanie 5510, 5511
Iezzoni, Massimo 2489
Ihde, A.J. 5324
Iles, Janet 0476
Imbeau, Gaston 7007
Imperial Tobacco Products Limited. Library 4658
Imprimerie générale A. Côté et Cie 0025
Indian and Eskimo Affairs Program (Canada). Education and Cultural Support Branch 3990
Indian-Eskimo Association of Canada 3411, 3914, 3922
Indians of Quebec Association. James Bay Task Force 5077
Indra, Doreen Marie 4225
Ing, Pearl 4406
Ingles, Ernest 0171
Ingram, David R. 0136
Ingram, Doreen 1171
Inkster, Tim 1662
Innis, Harold Adams 2560, 6054, 7074
Institut canadien d'éducation des adultes. Équipe de recherche 3107
Institut canadien de Québec. Bibliothèque 6752
Institut canadien de recherche sur les femmes 3903
Institut canadien pour la paix et la sécurité internationales 2556
Institut de la médecine du travail et des ambiances 5114
Institut de recherches politiques. Secrétariat du Colloque national 3671
Institut national canadien-français pour la déficience mentale 3108
Institute for Research in Construction (Canada) 6453
Institute for Research on Public Policy. National Forum Secretariat 3672
Institute for Research on Public Policy. Regional Employment Opportunities Program 2492
Institute of Occupational and Environmental Health 5115
International Commission for the Northwest Atlantic Fisheries 4885
International Development Research Centre (Canada) 2413
International Reference Group on Great Lakes Pollution from Land Use Activities 5150
Internationale Jugendbibliothek (Munich, Germany) 1366
Inuvik Scientific Resource Centre 4631
Ironside, Diana J. 3377
Irvine, Russell 1758
Irvine, Susan 0595
Irving, E. 1426
Irwin, Barbara I. 0467
Isbester, A. Fraser 2794
Issenman, Betty 4032
Isto, Sarah A. 3968

Ives, Edward D. 4534
Iwaasa, David B. 4171
Izzo, Herbert J. 5914
Jack, David Russell 5858
Jacka, Alan A. 3117
Jackaman, Wayne 6599
Jackel, Susan 3853
Jackson, E.L. 7371
Jackson, Kathryn 0801
Jackson, L.J. 4566
Jackson, P.A. 6491
Jackson, Robert J. 2547, 2548
Jackson, Robin 4173
Jaenen, Cornelius J. 2025
Jaffee, Georgina 3807
Jain, Sushil Kumar 0087, 1028, 1029, 1034, 1946, 4139, 4147
Jakle, John A. 3030, 4161
Jakubick, A.T. 4852
James, Charles Canniff 0992
James, I.R. 3485
Jameson, Mary Ann 1169, 1239, 6881
Jamet, A. 7177
Jamet, Virginie 2511
Jamieson, A.F. 0495
Jamieson, K.B. 6358, 6367
Jamieson, Kathleen 4048
Jandali, Tarek 5224
Janiak, Jane M. 4509
Janik, Sophie 3218, 3309
Janisch, Alice H. 6279
Janisch, H.N. 2294
Jansen, Vivian A. 2361
Janssen, Helen 2438
Janssen, Viveka K. 4211
Jaque, Mervyn H. 3149
Jarjour, Gabi 2753
Jarman, Lynne 0855
Jarrell, Richard A. 4626, 4627
Jarvi, Edith T. 0150, 0428, 2792
Jarvis, Eric 0475
Jarvis, J.M. 5347
Jasion, Pat 4152
Jaster, Marion C. 4751
Javitch, Gregory 3955
Jay-Rayon, Jean-Claude 1840
Jean, Claire 1557
Jean, Michel 5462
Jeffries, Fern 2132
Jeglum, J.K. 5440
Jenner, Catherine 2268
Jennings, Daniel T. 5432, 5474
Jensen, Karlo 5892
Jensen, Mary 3752
Jensen, Susan E. 4482
Jerabek, Esther 4174
Jetté, Sylvie 2017
Jeux olympiques, Montréal, Québec, 1976. Comité
    organisateur. Centre de documentation 1784
Jewett, Linda J. 2809
Job, A.L. 4773
Joba, Judith C. 4487, 4497, 4498

Jobling, J. Keith 6124
Johannessen, O.M. 5047
Johansson, M.P. 4653
Johansson, S. Ryan 4033
Johansson, T.S.K. 4653
John Bassett Memorial Library 0293, 0386
Johnsen, Julia E. 4444
Johnsen, Laila W. 4706
Johnson, B.C. 5406
Johnson, Basil 3923
Johnson, Bryan R. 4098
Johnson, Catherine 6413
Johnson, H.J. 4928
Johnson, J.K. 2025
Johnson, Jean-Michel 1862
Johnson, Jenny 3249
Johnson, Joy L. 5713
Johnson, Larry 5116
Johnson, Lee E. 5457
Johnson, Marion E. 4932
Johnson, Melvin W. 0776
Johnson, Ronald P. 5084
Johnson, Stephen R. 5393
Johnston, A.G. 6244
Johnston, Cynthia 4407
Johnston, G.H. 5744, 6878
Johnston, H. Kirk 5742
Johnston, J.M. 5327
Johnston, Joan L. 0681, 0688
Jolicoeur, Catherine 4550
Jolicoeur, Jovette 6575
Jolicoeur, Louis-Philippe 3163
Jonasson, Eric 4185
Jones, Barry C. 5407
Jones, David C. 3580
Jones, Ellen 1741
Jones, L. 5778
Jones, Linda M. 0177, 5959
Jones, Mary Jane 0617, 0618
Jones, Olive 5768
Jones, Peter 2529
Jones, Phyllis E. 5629
Jones, Richard C. 0443
Jones, Richard Edward 5235
Jones, Tim E.H. 4602
Jones, Winstan M. 3168
Jorgensen, E. 4624
Joseph, Gene 4119
Joy, Albert H. 5289
Joyal, Robert 5374
Joyes, Dennis C. 4568, 4602
Judd, William W. 5332, 5408, 5463, 6798, 7082, 7097
Jukelevics, Nicette 1091
Juliani, T.J. 2234
Julien, Germain 2404, 2417
Juozapavicius, Danguole 6354
Juricic, Zelimir B. 5893
Jurkovic, Joseph J. 0123
Jury, Elsie McLeod 4530
Justice Institute of British Columbia. Resource Centre 6684
Kabano, John 2360

Lambe, Lawrence M. 5313
Lambert, Elisabeth 5499
Lambert, Ronald D. 0372, 2418
Lambert, Rosalind 4350
Lamirande, Emilien 1512
Lamonde, Francine Neilson 6268
Lamonde, Yvan 0340, 0961, 1205, 1251, 1605, 1656, 1973, 1985, 2076
Lamont, Jane 0538
Lamontagne, Richard 0402
Lamothe, Emélie S. 5690
Lamping, Donna L. 5697, 5698
Lampron, Christiane 3303
Lamson, Cynthia 4909
Lamy, Jean-Christian 0361
Lamy, Nicole 2682, 2726
Lanari, Robert 0629, 0632, 3942
Lancaster, John E. 4667
Lanctot, Gustave 1923
Land, Bernard 5214
Land, Brian 2567, 2568, 2569, 2710, 2791
Land-related Information Systems Co-ordination Project 3033
Landar, Herbert 1436
Landau, Tammy 2290
Lande, Lawrence M. 0114, 0115, 0838, 1531, 1954, 2010, 2027, 2040, 2048, 2061, 2071, 2077, 2078, 3956, 6772
Landry, Charlotte 6033
Landry, Francine 3687, 3688
Landry, Kenneth 1063, 1164
Landry, Renée 6829
Landry, Yves 3068
Landsburg, June 3514
Lane, Chris 3752
Lane, Daniel E. 4914
Lane, E. David 5512
Lane, Kenneth 2326
Lane, Marion 2235
Lang, A.H. 4748
Lang, Reg 4376
Langer, William L. 2424
Langhammer, Else Birgit 6775
Langille, David 2501
Langlois, Pierre 1456
Langlois, Simon 3251
Langor, David William 5543
Langton, H.H. 1899
Lanning, Mabel M. 0561
LaNoue, George R. 6078
Lanteigne, Raymond 6646
Laperrière, Guy 0394, 2822
Laperrière, René 2890
Lapierre, André 1461
Lapierre-Adamcyk, Evelyne 3061
Lapkin, Sharon 3626
Laplante, Louise 0861, 0904
Laplante, Michelle 6654
Lapointe, Jean 4607
Lapointe, Jean-Pierre 7243
Lapointe, Michèle 4915, 5554
Lapointe, Raoul 0395, 7235
Lapointe, Serge 3172

Laporte, Gilbert 2765
Larivière-Derome, Céline 6963
Lark, J.G.I. 4898
Larkin, Lise 3584
Larned, Josephus Nelson 1893
Larochelle, André 5434, 5532, 5550
Laroque, Emma 3967
LaRose, André 3057, 5743
Larouche, Irma 1635, 2091
Larouche, Ursula 5297
Larrivée, Jean 0377, 2624
Larsen, R.W. 1748
Larter, Sylvia 3563
Larue, Gilles 6539
Lasalle, Pierre 4770
Lasserre, F. 4304
Latham, Barbara 3838
Latham, David 6888, 7276, 7277
Latham, Sheila 1153, 1726, 3757, 7193, 7194
Latourelle, René 6873
Laubitz, Diana R. 5544
Lauder, Kathleen 4360
Laugher, Charles T. 1192
Laurin, Christiane 5895
Laurin, Clément 0378, 6906
Laurin, Serge 0387
Lauzier, Suzanne 0302, 0844, 1783, 3523
Lavallée, Denis 0323
Lavallée, Laval 4350, 4360
Lavallée, Robert 5533, 5534
Laverdière, Camille 5054
Laverdière, Richard 4634
Lavoie, Amédée 1922
Lavoie, André 5499
Lavoie, Cécile 1601
Lavoie, Marc C. 4598
Lavoie, Pierre 0981, 0989, 7010, 7337
Law Reform Commission of Canada 2152
Law Society of Upper Canada. Library 2098
Lawrence, Bertha 0494
Lawrence, Jean 3275
Lawrence, Pauline 3004
Lawson, B.M. 4644
Lawson, Ian B. 2261
Lawton, Janet 6697
Lawton, Stephen B. 3568
Lawton-Speert, Sarah 3240
Laychuck, Julian L. 5896, 6097, 6125
Layton, Carol 3967
Layton, M. 5356, 5397, 5464
Lazarowich, Linda M. 4025
Le Moine, Roger 6787
Le Normand, J. 4680, 4681
Leach, Karen E. 5724
Leafloor, Lorne B. 6231
League of Canadian Poets 1254
Leaman, B.M. 5411
Leaney, Adelle J. 5172
Leavitt, Ferrin D. 5451
Lebeau, Mario 3341, 3342
Lebedynski, Linda 3752

Libick, Helen 6155
Liboiron, Albert A. 2391
Licht, Merete 1131
Liddell, Peter G. 4213
Liepner, Michael 2153
Lifschutz, E. 4148
Light, Beth 3796, 3801
Light, John D. 5815, 5816
Lightbown, Patsy 1462
Lillard, Charles 1132, 1154, 4957
Lillard, Richard G. 1038
Lilley, Doreen A. 4137
Lim, Eileen 1703
Lim, H.S. 5742
Lim, T.P. 5267
Lin, Suzane 3515
Lind, Terry 3178
Lindal, Walter J. 5897
Lindeburgh, S.B. 5008
Linden, Marjorie 1108, 7246, 7247
Lindsay, Doreen 0691
Linell, Kenneth A. 5744
Ling, Joyce 2588
Linteau, Paul-André 0306, 0311, 1980, 2012, 2086
Linton, D.A. 5545
Linzon, Samuel Nathan 5173
Lips, Hilary M. 3797
Lips, Thomas 3265
Lipton, S. 0160
Lister, Rota Herzberg 1193
Lisun, Luba 2183
Litchfield, Jack 0905
Literary and Historical Society of Quebec 1903
Literary and Historical Society of Quebec. Library 6724
Little, Barbara 3609
Littlefield, George Emery 3905
Litvak, I.A. 2581
Liu, Gwen 4180
Livermore, Ronald P. 0504
Llamas, José 5117
Lloyd, Hazel A. 5635
Loades, Peter 4241
Locas, Claude 3504
Loch, J.S. 5435, 5455
Lochhead, Douglas 0104, 0214, 1240
Locke, G.H. 0047, 5866
Lodhi, Abdul Q. 2296
Lohnes, Marilyn 1741
Lomer, Gerhard Richard 5860, 7136, 7152
Lonardo, Michael 2925, 2938
London Public Libraries and Museums (Ont.) 3289
Lonergan, David 5299
Long, B.F.N. 5277, 5278
Long, Peter 0652
Long, Robert James 0197
Longley, Richmond Wilberforce 5059
Loosely, Elizabeth W. 0052
Lord, Jules 0789, 0802
Lord, Michel 1296
Lort, John C.R. 0584
Lortie, Lucien 7171

Loslier, Sylvie 0696
Lotz, James 0435, 0656
Lougheed, W.C. 1479
Lounder, Shirley A. 2232
Lounds, John 4376
Lousier, J. Daniel 5009
Love, John L. 2173
Love, Mary 1455
Lover, John G. 2341
Loveridge, Donald Merwin 3019, 6031
Lovett, Robert Woodberry 2593
Lowenberg, Paul 4335
Lowry, Marjerie 7158
Lowther, Barbara J. 0575
Lubinsky, G.A. 5435
Lucas, Glenn 1534
Luce, Sally R. 2873
Lucyk, J.R. 3187
Ludewig, Hermann E. 1400
Ludgate, George 4506
Ludovic, frère 7279
Luethy, Ivor C.E. 4149
Lukawiecki, Teresa 3310
Lunn, Jean 6006, 6008
Lusignan, Lucien 1504
Lussier, A.S. 7265
Lusty, Terry 4015
Luttrell, Gwendolyn W. 4759
Lutz, John S. 0598, 0604
Lyle, Guy R. 1987
Lyn, D.E. 2608
Lynas, Lothian 5581
Lynch, F. Jennifer 2204
Lynch, Gerald 6895
Lynch, K.D. 5436
Lynch-Stewart, Pauline 5199, 5200
Lyndsay Dobson Books 1657
Lyttle, Brendan J. 0867
Lyttle, Norman A. 6332, 6333
MacBryde, Bruce 5382
MacDermaid, Anne 7157
MacDermot, Hugh Ernest 5864
Macdonald, Allan F. 0212
MacDonald, Bertrum H. 1736, 4632
MacDonald, Christine 0498, 6034, 6233
MacDonald, E. Grant 5774
MacDonald, Heather 2029
MacDonald, Janet 0656
Macdonald, John Stevenson 4998
Macdonald, Lynne 6986
Macdonald, Maggie 5609
MacDonald, Marjorie Anne 7132, 7133
MacDonald, Mary Lu 1283
Macdonald, R. Bruce 3670
MacDonald, Ruth 6909
MacDonald, V.N. 4351
Macdonald, William S. 0219, 5774
Macdougall, Donald V. 2154
MacDuff, Pierre 1186
MacFarlane, David S. 5225
Macfarlane, Dianne 2143

MacFarlane, Ivan C. 5328, 5733
MacFarlane, John 1817
MacFarlane, William Godsoe 0194
MacGibbon, Diana 4412
MacGillivray, Royce 7183
Macgregor, Robert 1631
Machalski, Andrew 1255, 4242
Machine Readable Archives (Canada) 1824
Machniak, Kazimierz 5126, 5395
MacInnis, Peggy 0940
Mack, Yvonne 2768
Mackaay, Ejan 2120
MacKay, A.H. 5315
MacKay, G. David M. 5725
Mackay, Margaret S. 5860
Mackay, Neilson A.M. 4457
Mackenzie, B.J. 5201
MacKenzie, Catharine 0150
MacKenzie, David 2072
MacKenzie, M.E. 1427, 3934
MacKenzie, Margaret 0098, 0509, 3440
Mackenzie River Basin Committee 5174
Mackey, William Francis 1444
MacKinnon, Fred R. 3276
Mackinnon, Moyra 4837
MacLachlan, May 6489
Maclachlan, Wills 5718
Maclaren, Virginia 3022
MacLean, Ian A. 1645, 1646
MacLean, Margaret 3640
Maclellan, Delphine C. 5437
MacLeod, Anne E. 2021
MacMechan, Archibald 0196
MacMillan, Jean Ross 0809
MacMillan, Keith 0846
MacMillan, Rick 6833, 7341
MacMillan, Robert 5958
Macmillan, Stuart 4910
Macnaughton, Elizabeth 0720
MacPhail, Cathy 0444
MacPherson, Arlean 4687
MacPherson, Lillian 3890
MacPike, E.F. 1006
Macri, Paula 4348
MacTaggart, Hazel I. 6251, 6300
Macyk, T. 5834
Maddaugh, Peter D. 2126
Maddick, Heather 6556
Madill, Dennis 4034, 4049, 4050, 4051, 4099
Madison, Charlotte 5957
Madsen, Nina 1336
Maerz, Norbert H. 4844
Mage, Julius A. 4671, 4700
Magee, Eleanor E. 0236, 0839
Magee, William Henry 1011
Magnan, Pierre 4915, 5513
Maguire, Robert K. 2874, 4384
Mah, Judy 0544
Mahant, Edelgard E. 2495
Maheux, Arthur 7023
Mahler, Gregory S. 2520

Mahy, Gérard D. 2981
Maidment, J.M. 4902
Mail, Patricia D. 4016
Mailhiot, Bernard 6075
Mailhot, José 3934, 4017, 4555
Mailhot, Laurent 0376, 1188
Mailhot, Yves 5552
Maillet, Antonine 4554
Maillet, Lise 1727, 6381
Maillet, Marguerite 1155, 1172, 1194, 1272, 1298
Mailloux, Pierre 0108
Maine, F.W. 5500
Maine, Michael 6975
Major-Lapierre, Ruth 6850
Makahonuk, Glen 2056
Makepeace, Charles E. 5721
Malchelosse, Gérard 7323
Malcolm, Douglas 6998, 6999
Malcolm, Ross 1825
Malcolm, Wyatt 4738
Malhotra, S.K. 5728
Mallea, John R. 3552, 4175
Mallen, Bruce E. 2581
Mallett, Graham 3609
Malpezzi, Frances M. 4054
Maltais, Claire 4226
Maltais, Madeleine 1981
Malycky, Alexander 1051, 1054, 1056, 1528, 4143, 4218, 5883, 5884, 5888, 5889, 5890, 5893, 5898, 5899, 5904, 6096, 6098, 6099, 6102, 6106, 6119, 6126
Mandryka, Mykyta I. 7287
Manégre, Jean-François 3717
Mangham, Colin R. 3354
Manitoba Genealogical Society. Library 2023
Manitoba Library Association 6037
Manitoba School Library Audio Visual Association 0506
Manitoba Women's Directorate 3730
Manitoba. Department of Agriculture 6704
Manitoba. Department of Consumer and Corporate Affairs and Environment 3203
Manitoba. Department of Education 3641, 4035
Manitoba. Department of Education. Library 3596, 4227
Manitoba. Department of Natural Resources. Library 6454
Manitoba. Energy Information Centre 5791
Manitoba. Environment Protection Board 6292
Manitoba. Geological Services Branch 6455
Manitoba. Instructional Resources Branch 1388
Manitoba. Instructional Resources Branch. Library 3729
Manitoba. Legislative Library 0065, 6334, 6456, 6457
Manitoba. Manitoba Education and Training 3723
Manitoba. Manitoba Education. Library 3703
Manitoba. Multiculture Educational Resource Centre 1487
Manitoba. Native Education Branch 3982
Manitoba. Office of the Queen's Printer 6458
Manitoba. Provincial Archives 2028
Manitoba. School Library Services 6655
Manitoba. Water Standards and Studies Section 6459
Manley, Frank 0943
Mann, Donald 4807
Manning, Edward W. 4692, 4693
Manning, Frank E. 7343

McCartney, Allan P. 5142
McCaughey, Claire 0706
McClure, Lynn 5710
McComb, Bonnie Martyn 7367, 7368
McCombs, Judith 6813
McConkey, Nancy 2146
McConnell, David 1835
McConnell, Ruth Ethel 3403
McCoomb, L.A. 4474
McCormick, W.A. 5449
McCoy, James Comly 0043, 1915
McCready, A.L. 1746
McCready, R.G.L. 4856
McCreath, Peter L. 4243
McCrossan, R.G. 4755
McCue, Harvey A. 4026
McCullough, Alan Bruce 4905, 4906
McCullough, Donna 0450
McCutcheon, Sarah 0691
McDiarmid, G.Y. 4351
McDiarmid, Garnet 3913
McDonald, David R. 4016
McDonald, Douglas Moore 2561
McDonald, L. 2608
McDonald, Michael 3082
McDonough, Irma 1351, 1378
McDougall, Don 2320, 2321
McDougall, Gordon H.G. 5209
McDougall, Keith A. 5514
McDowell, Linda 3785
McDowell, Marilyn E. 5661
McDowell, Marjorie 1312
McDowell, Patricia 4114
McEwen, Ruth 3739
McFarlane, Deborah 4862
McGahan, Elizabeth W. 0274
McGee, Harold Franklin, Jr. 4561
McGill University. Archives 1606, 6612
McGill University. Blackader Library of Architecture 4300
McGill University. Blacker-Wood Library of Zoology and Ornithology 5342
McGill University. Centre d'études canadiennes-françaises 0325
McGill University. Centre d'études canadiennes-françaises. Bibliothèque 1044
McGill University. Centre for Northern Studies and Research 0630
McGill University. Department of Rare Books and Special Collections 0382, 6533
McGill University. Faculty of Graduate Studies and Research 6090
McGill University. French Canada Studies Programme 2387
McGill University. Library School 0042, 7137
McGill University. McLennan Library. Government Documents Department 6308
McGill University. McLennan Library. Reference Department 0404, 1195, 1999
McGill University. Mechanical Engineering Research Laboratories 5723
McGillis, Joe R. 5514
McGinnis, Janice Dickin 2284

McGovern, John P. 7229
McGowan, Mark G. 1572
McGrath, J.T. 5765
McGrath, Margaret 7018
McGrath, Robin 1216, 1273
McGraw, Donna 2217
McHenry, Renée E. 4512
McHenry, Wendie A. 3174
McHoul, Alison 4038
McIlwaine, John 6198
McIlwraith, Thomas Forsyth 4542
McInnes, B.E. 5383
McIntosh, Robert Dale 0916
McIntyre, F. 4585
McIntyre, Janet Houghton 2011
McIntyre, John 6634
McIntyre, Lillian 3010
McIntyre, Sheila 1109
McIntyre, W. John 2011
McKay, H.B. 3103
McKay, Ian 0234
McKay, Jean 7334
McKay, Margaret 3811, 4497
McKean, Colin J.P. 5184
McKechnie, Gail 4109
McKechnie, Ruth 4486
McKeen, Carol A. 3863
McKenney, Daniel William 5019
McKenzie, Donald 5640
McKenzie, Karen 5934
McKillip, J.H. 4771
McKitrick, Ross 2756
McKnight, George 6774
McLachlan, R.W. 7189
McLaren, Duncan 6019
McLaren, William S. 4455
McLaren Atlantic Limited 5536
McLaughlin, W. Keith 2828, 5648
McLean, C.C. 5551
McLean, E.J. 5551
McLean, Isabel 0150
McLean, M.P. 4896
McLeay, D. and Associates Limited 5248, 5249
McLeish, Walter 5825
McLeod, Donald W. 1652, 3308, 5669
McLeod, Gordon Duncan 1085
McLeod, Keith A. 4167
McMahon, T.A. 5148
McMaster University. Library 6781
McMillan, Barclay 0862
McMullen, Lorraine 6987
McMurdo, John 4604
McMurray, J.G. 3421
McNally, Peter F. 1675, 1679, 1680
McNaught, Hugh 2184, 6029
McNeilly, Russell A. 2296
McNern, Janet 3894
McNicholl, Martin K. 5515, 5559
McNicol, R.E. 4896
McPhail, John Donald 5333
McPhail, Marjorie E. 4886

McPherson, Kathryn 3821
McPherson, Lynn 0656
McQuarrie, Jane 1371
McQuillan, Barry H. 6629
McQuitty, J.B. 4654
McRae, Douglas J. 4967
McRae, James Duncan 4688, 4689
McTavish, Isabella 2865
McTavish, Mary 2459
McTernan, D.J. 0413
Meagher, Heather 5568
Medin, Dean E. 5546
Mehlhaff, Carol J. 2494
Meikle, W. Duncan 7373
Meikle, William 5994
Meiklejohn, Christopher 3929, 5672, 5706
Meilicke, Carl A. 5626
Meister, Marilyn 5878
Melançon, Benoît 1229, 1274, 4277
Melançon, Carole 1230
Melançon-Bolduc, Ginette 4461
Melanson, Holly 1256
Melanson, Lloyd J. 0240
Meldrum, Janis 5236
Melenchuk, Allan Samuel 3674
Memorial University of Newfoundland. Learning Resources
    Council 3724
Memorial University of Newfoundland. Maritime History
    Group 0251
Ménard, Marleine 0402
Menay, Lionel 7035
Mendis, Asoka 4271
Mennie-de Varennes, Kathleen 0330, 1602, 1937, 1940, 2062
Menzies, Robert J. 2200
Mercer, Anne V. 1305
Mercer, Eleanor 7318
Mercer, G.W. 5582
Mercer, Paul 0840, 0868, 0877
Mercer, Tom 5939
Mercier, Diane 3648
Mercier, Jacques 2915
Mercier, Lucie 3808
Mercier, Marguerite 7106
Mercure, Gérard 1595
Meredith, Colin 3262, 3263
Merrens, Roy 4385, 4430, 4431
Merriman, J.C. 5183
Mertens, Susan 6824
Mes, Femmy 3265
Mescaniuk, Sheri 5210
Messely, Maryse 5691
Messieh, Shoukry N. 5453
Messier, Jean-Jacques 2003
Messier, Suzanne 3027
Metress, Seamus P. 4244, 4258
Metropolitan Toronto Library Board 1607
Metropolitan Toronto Library. Audio-Visual Services 6625
Metropolitan Toronto Library. Languages Centre 1433
Metropolitan Toronto Library. Languages Department 4233
Metropolitan Toronto Library. Reference Division. Business
    Department 2697, 2712

Metropolitan Toronto Library. Science and Technology Library
    5746
Metropolitan Toronto Reference Library 6705
Meyer, H.H.B. 2558
Meyer, R.F. 4822
Meyer, Ron H. 4458
Meyer, W.C. 6116
Meynen, Emil 4125
Mezei, Kathy 1480
Mezirow, Jack D. 3379
Michaud, Irma 6954
Michaud, Yves B. 6592
Michel, Bernard 5038
Michie, George H. 2963
Michon, Jacques 1729
Micmac-Maliseet Institute 4089
Micros, Marianne 7251, 7252
Middleton, J.E. 1891
Midgley, Ellen 3188
Miki, Roy Akira 6869
Miletich, John J. 2683, 2684, 4483, 4489, 5202, 5799
Milette, Denise McFadden 6571
Milette, Jean-Luc 0463, 6571
Milisauskas, Sarunas 4583
Millan, Carol A. 4675
Millar, Esther 5832
Millar, J.F.V. 0640
Miller, Alan V. 2218, 2845, 3175, 3176, 3802, 3819, 5653, 5669,
    5945, 5976
Miller, Ann H. 3614
Miller, Ann-Marie 3204
Miller, Clara G. 0467
Miller, Dallas K. 2278
Miller, E. Willard 2775
Miller, G. 4998, 5517, 5538
Miller, Genevieve 5569
Miller, Gordon 5118, 5136, 5137, 5415, 5422
Miller, Thomas W. 4321
Millette, Robert 0348
Milligan, G.C. 4747
Milligan, Janet 0474
Milliron, H.E. 5357
Mills, B.A. 4760
Mills, Judy 6091
Mills, Patricia A. 1684
Milne, David 0718, 2757
Milne, Henry 5409
Milne, William Samuel 1021
Milner, Philip 0241
Milton, Norma 4219
Minion, Robin 0646, 0647, 0650, 0653, 0654, 0711, 1361, 1362,
    1464, 1561, 3047, 4061, 4062, 4405, 4495, 4597, 4845, 4903,
    5216, 5226, 5227, 5501, 5502, 5503, 5504, 5808, 6180, 6185, 6186
Minter, Ella S.G. 6294, 6298
Mirza, Izhar 1483
Mischook, Muriel 3636
Miska, John P. 1076, 1173, 1257, 1284, 1294, 1670, 4245, 4655,
    4659, 4660, 4661, 4662, 4673, 4676, 4677, 5384, 5454, 5516,
    6127, 7033
Mississauga Public Library 6293
Mitchell, Alan Kenneth 5711

Mitchell, Bruce W. 6572
Mitchell, Elaine Allan 0608
Mitchell, James Kenneth 2972
Mitchell, Joan 4892
Mitchell, M.H. 6387
Mitchell, Mary E. 5977
Mitchell, William Bruce 4892, 5576
Mock, Karen R. 3642
Moeller, Roger W. 4570
Mohammed, Gina H. 5022
Moir, Elizabeth 0033
Moir, Lindsay 4108
Mokede, Ernestine 1346
Mokkelbost, Per B. 2703
Moldenhauer, John A. 0123
Moline, M. 5160
Moll, Marita 2832, 3526, 3542, 3554, 3570, 3571, 3572, 3573,
    3597, 3615, 3619, 3623, 3643, 3656, 3657, 3675
Mollica, Anthony 3633
Molnar, John Edgar 0049
Moloney, Nancy M. 6128
Molot, Maureen Appel 2540
Monenco Consultants Limited 5282
Monette, Guy J.A. 6984
Monette, René 4642
Money, Christine 1214
Mongeon, Jean 1819, 1820
Mongrain, Susan 0723, 4101, 4102
Monière, Denis 0364
Monk, Philip 0749
Monroe, Robin Lee 5825
Montagnes, Ramona 1381
Montigny-Pelletier, Françoise de 0407
Montminy, Jean-Paul 1532
Montreal Council of Social Agencies. Research Department
    3092
Montreal Engineering Company 5048
Montreal Health Libraries Association 5978
Monty, Vivienne 2609, 2776
Moody, B.H. 5017
Moody, Lois 0869
Moogk, Edward B. 0847, 0848
Moore, Barbara G. 3659
Moore, Gary C. 4978
Moore, George Henry 6729
Moore, Ian 5385
Moore, J.E. 4912
Moore, Kathryn E. 4846
Moore, Larry F. 2586, 2823, 3120
Moore, R.S. 4829
Moore, Rhonda D. 2243, 2244, 2311, 2312
Moran, S.R. 5834
Moreau, Bernice M. 4246
Morgan, Henry J. 0009, 0018, 7324
Morgan, Jane 3205
Morgan, K. 2354
Morgan, Kathryn Pauly 3855
Morgan, W.C. 6601, 6602
Mori, Monica 3322, 3894, 5705
Morin, Cimon 1796
Morin, Claire 5322

Morin, Gérald 5228
Morin, Marie-Josée 1716
Morin, Victor 6760
Morisette, Thomas 5010
Morisset, Micheline 6673
Morisset, Pierre 2982
Morley, E. Lillian 0422
Morley, Glen 0917
Morley, Marjorie 0500, 6234
Morley, William F.E. 0172, 0208, 0308, 0458, 6015, 6904, 7104,
    7257, 7258
Morrell, Michael R. 5393
Morrell, W.P. 1968
Morris, Dave M. 5016
Morris, John 2843
Morris, Sahlaa 5152, 5166, 5172
Morrison, B.A. 4701, 4715, 6191, 6374
Morrison, Doreen 4124
Morrison, Frances C. 3677
Morrison, Hugh M. 0055
Morrison, James H. 4228
Morrison, Linda 2367
Morse, Hazel G. 0198
Morse, Janice M. 5654
Morse, William Inglis 6766, 6893
Morton, Desmond 2087, 2088
Morton, S.M. 4864, 4865
Morton, William Markham 5352
Mortsch, Linda D. 0780, 4840, 5217, 5290, 5291
Moscovitch, Allan 3250
Moscovitch, Arlene 6674
Moskal, Susan 4090
Moss, Harold Charles 4643
Motard, Chantal 0385
Motiuk, Laurence 2392, 2405
Mottershead, D. 5542
Moulary-Ouerghi, Josiane 2480
Moulton, Donalee 0692
Mount, Graeme S. 2495
Mount Allison University. Canadian Studies Programme 1101
Mount Saint Vincent University. Library 1217, 3895
Moussette, Marcel 4560
Moyer, Sharon 2219, 2220
Moyles, Robert Gordon 1066, 1102
Moysa, Susan 4818
Moyse, Catherine M. 5144, 5170, 5468, 5810
Muhammad, A.F. 4624
Muise, D.A. 2025
Mukherjee, Arun P. 1231
Muldoon, Maureen 3798
Mullen, E.C. 2981
Mullens, Marjorie C. 4778
Mullins, W.J. 6515
Multicultural History Society of Ontario 4292
Munkittrick, Kelly Roland L.H. 4878
Munns, Edward Norfolk 4918
Munro, Douglas 4484
Munro, James 6212
Munro, K.M. 3890
Munro, Neil 1756
Munroe, Allan R. 3127

New Brunswick. Legislative Library. Government Documents Section 6461, 6462

New Brunswick. Water Resource Planning Branch 5250

New Play Centre 1110

New York Public Library 1914

New York Public Library. Reference Department 6768

Newfoundland Information Service 6309

Newkirk, G.F. 5475

Newman, Lynda 3248

Newman, Maureen 1094, 1440

Newman, Reg F. 4706, 4986

Newton, Arthur Percival 1907

Newton, Jennifer L. 3764, 3770, 3781

Newton, Keith 2837

Ngatia, Therese 4229

Nguyên, Vy-Khanh 2722, 4418, 6864

Nichol, bp 1068, 1133, 1678, 6900, 7213

Nichol, Paul 4721

Nicholls, H.B. 5386, 5398

Nicholson, Alison 5013

Nicholson, Frank H. 2997

Nicholson, H. Alleyne 4521

Nicholson, H.F. 4912, 5438

Nicholson, Norman L. 6576

Nickles, John M. 4527, 4883

Nicolas, Frank 6210

Nietfeld, Marie T. 5011

Nietmann, K. 4991

Niilo, Alan 5516

Nijholt, W.W. 5439

Nilson, Lenore 1379

Nininger, J.R. 4351

Nish, Elizabeth 1961

Nish, James Cameron 1944, 1961, 2577, 2578, 2587, 6863

Niswander, Jerry D. 5577

Noble, Willa J. 5537

Noël, François 6171

Noel-Bentley, Peter 6844, 6845, 6846

Noizet, Pascale 7119, 7349

Noland, T.L. 5022

Nollet, Jean 5824

Noonan, Gerald 1222

Nordin, Richard Nels 5184

Nordstrom, Lance O. 4986

Normand, Sylvio 2355, 2497

Normandeau, André 2144, 2276, 2362, 3290, 6672

Normandeau, Louise 3023

Norris, A.W. 4768

Norris, Ken 1135

North, George W. 5327

North, R.A. 2389

North York Public Library. Canadiana Collection 0478, 2000

Northern Alberta Development Council 0553

Northern Co-ordination and Research Centre (Canada) 0614

Northern Political Studies (Program) 0664

Northern Regulatory Review 2723

Northwest Territories. Department of Culture and Communications 6463

Norton, Judith A. 2089

Norwell, M.H. 5325

Noseworthy, Ann 5203

Nossal, Kim Richard 7065

Nouveau-Brunswick. Ministère de l'éducation 3627

Nova Scotia Government Bookstore 6466

Nova Scotia Museum 0224

Nova Scotia NewStart Incorporated 3113

Nova Scotia Provincial Library. Reference Services Section 1610

Nova Scotia Research Foundation 4618, 5387, 6767

Nova Scotia. Community Planning Division 6509

Nova Scotia. Department of Agriculture and Marketing. Marketing and Economics Branch. Co-operatives Section 2698

Nova Scotia. Department of Lands and Forests 5023, 6561

Nova Scotia. Department of Municipal Affairs. Community Planning Division 6582

Nova Scotia. Legislative Council. Library 6717

Nova Scotia. Legislative Library 0217, 0252, 6365, 6386, 6464, 6465, 6744

Nova Scotia. Senior Citizens' Secretariat 3291

Nowak, W.S.W. 4890, 4897

Nowosielski, Maryna 3206

Nyenhuis, Pat 3333, 3334

O'Bready, Maurice 0307, 6014

O'Brien, A.H. 7041

O'Bryan, Kenneth G. 3660

O'Callaghan, Edmund Bailey 1874, 1875, 6733

O'Callaghan, T.C. 6066

O'Dea, Agnes C. 0263

O'Dea, Fabian 6524

O'Dea, Shane 0768

O'Donnell, Brendan 0389, 0414

O'Dor, R.K. 5418

O'Driscoll, Robert 4258

O'Flanagan, J. 5716

O'Grady, K. 3020

O'Hara, Susan 4470

O'Leary, Timothy J. 3970, 4562

O'Neill, Patrick B. 0163, 1136, 1137, 1208

O'Reilly, Dorcas 2158

O'Reilly, Robert R. 3587, 3588

O'Riordan, Jonathan 5031

O'Rourke, David 7212

Oak, Lydia 1641, 2222

Oberlander, H. Peter 4304

Obermeir, Paule 4204

Ockert, Roy A. 2789

Oct. Lemieux et Cie. 0016

Office national du film du Canada 6611, 6694

Offshore Safety Task Force 4835

Ogaard, Louis A. 5465

Ogle, Robert W. 5899, 5904

Ojibway-Cree Resource Centre 4065, 6635

Okanagan Regional Library 0580

Oki, Diane 2517

Oldford, L. 5466

Oleson, Robert V. 2983

Oleson, T.J. 1927

Oliver, Kent D. 4646

Oliver, Peter 2025

Olivier, Daniel 1656, 2008, 4558

Olivier, Réjean 0130, 0303, 0304, 0335, 0373, 0390, 0984, 1185, 1233, 1556, 3691, 5885, 6790, 6822, 6972, 7109, 7187, 7217, 7218, 7219, 7220, 7221

Olivier, Yolande 0304

Olloy, Vanessa 5632

Olling, Randy 0441

Olson, David R. 3685

Olson, J.C. 4822

Olson, May E. 6017

Olver, C.H. 5505

Olvet, Jaan 5900

Olynyk, Nadia M. 7222

Ommanney, C. Simon L. 0655, 4877, 5185, 5218, 5271, 5272, 5283, 5284, 5285, 5298, 7202

Ontario Agricultural College. School of Agricultural Engineering 4649

Ontario Archaeological Society. Library 4576

Ontario Association for the Mentally Retarded 3158

Ontario College of Education. Department of Educational Research 6061

Ontario Economic Council 2671

Ontario Educational Communications Authority 5102

Ontario Federation of Labour. Resource Centre 6633

Ontario Genealogical Society 2049

Ontario Genealogical Society. Kingston Branch 2063

Ontario Genealogical Society. London Branch. Library 2057

Ontario Genealogical Society. Ottawa Branch. Library 1982

Ontario Geological Survey. Geoscience Data Centre 6316

Ontario Historical Society 0481

Ontario Institute for Studies in Education. Library. Reference and Information Services 3412, 3423, 3486

Ontario Library Association. School Libraries Division 5919

Ontario Research Foundation 4614

Ontario Teachers' Federation. Status of Women Committee 3278

Ontario Women's Directorate 2932

Ontario. Community Renewal Resource Centre 4396

Ontario. Department of Agriculture and Food 6269

Ontario. Department of Economics and Development. Office of the Chief Economist. Economic Analysis Branch 2582

Ontario. Department of Economics and Development. Regional Development Branch 4307

Ontario. Department of Education 3441, 3915, 6745

Ontario. Department of Mines 6254, 6260, 6491

Ontario. Department of Planning and Development. Community Planning Branch 6067

Ontario. Department of Public Records and Archives 3422

Ontario. Department of Revenue. Library 2397

Ontario. Legislative Library 6723, 6726, 6732

Ontario. Legislative Library. Checklist and Catalogue Service 6467, 6468

Ontario. Libraries and Community Information Branch 1372

Ontario. Ministère des services gouvernementaux 6360

Ontario. Ministry for Citizenship and Culture 1367

Ontario. Ministry of Agriculture and Food 6652

Ontario. Ministry of Agriculture and Food. Library 4695

Ontario. Ministry of Citizenship and Culture 4234

Ontario. Ministry of Citizenship. Citizenship Development Branch 3676

Ontario. Ministry of Community and Social Services. Children's Services Branch 5681

Ontario. Ministry of Community and Social Services. Ministry Library 3150

Ontario. Ministry of Education 3772, 3971

Ontario. Ministry of Education. Library 3469

Ontario. Ministry of Industry, Trade and Technology 6382

Ontario. Ministry of Labour. Library 1818, 2277, 2847, 2848, 2867, 2882, 2887, 2888, 2891, 2892, 2893, 2899, 2916, 3822

Ontario. Ministry of Labour. Library and Information Services 2759, 2907, 2908, 2917, 2921, 2922, 2926, 2927, 2931, 2939, 3865

Ontario. Ministry of Municipal Affairs and Housing. Library 0769

Ontario. Ministry of Municipal Affairs. Research and Special Projects Branch 6588

Ontario. Ministry of Transportation and Communications. Research and Development Branch 6406

Ontario. Ministry of Treasury and Economics 2693

Ontario. Ministry of Treasury and Economics. Library Services 2498, 2699, 2700, 2701, 2702, 2713, 2714, 2724, 2894, 3846, 4386

Ontario. Office of King's Printer 6215

Ontario. Royal Commission on Electric Power Planning 2662

Ontario. Royal Commission on Violence in the Communications Industry 0965

Oppen, William A. 6567

Orange, John Charles 6882, 6883, 7233, 7274

Ormsby, Margaret 0562

Ort, Karen 2391

Orton, Larry J. 3913

Ory, François 4126

Osborne, Reed 0454

Ostling, Kristen 2873

Ostrye, Anne T. 2725

Ott, Lenie 1381

Ottawa Public Library 2760, 3505, 5655

Ottawa Public Library. Reference Department 2247

Ottley, Horace 3419

Ouellet, Dominique 2728, 2729

Ouellet, Fernand 2025

Ouellet, France 6965

Ouellet, Francine 3303

Ouellet, Micheline 3718

Ouellet, Thérèse 0946

Ouimet, Laurent 2185

Overall, Christine 5699

Overboom, Fernande 5120

Overseas Institute of Canada 2393

Owen, Myra 7230

Owens, John N. 4987, 4988

Ozaki, Hiroko 1641, 1647, 1682, 1683, 1692, 1693

P.G. Whiting and Associates 2715

P.S. Ross & Partners 0518

Pacey, Margaret 0231

Pacific Forestry Centre 5024

Packard, Alpheus Spring 0193

Packman, Glen A. 5088

Padbury, Peter 2987

Page, Donald M. 2408, 2430

Page, Garnet T. 2799

Page, James E. 3957, 6640

Pagé, Pierre 0957, 1111

Pageau, Pierrette 3983

Pahulje, Dani 2352

Painchaud, Claude 2676

Petrelli, Robert 4419
Petro-Canada 5205
Petrolias, John A. 3109
Petsche-Wark, Dawna 6413
Pettersen, Annie 3881
Pettigrew, Teresa 4894
Pettipas, Leo F. 4571
Péwé, Troy L. 5073
Pfeifer, Wilma E. 5416
Phelps, Edward 0429, 0438
Phelps, V.H. 5377
Philip, L. 4175
Philipps-Universität Marburg. Universitätsbibliothek 6770
Phillips, David 0682
Phillips, David W. 5157, 5206, 5260, 5261
Phillips, Donna 0128
Phillips, Gillian 3896
Phillips, P. Lee 1891, 6486
Phillips, Sally 2345
Phillips, W. Louis 6557
Pianarosa, Albertina 1431
Piché, Victor 3032
Pichette, Jean- Pierre 4611
Pichora, Anne 2073
Pickin, Frances 4583
Picot, Jocelyne 5662
Pigeon, Marc 0300
Pihach, John D. 4235
Pillai, N.G. 2588
Pille, John M. 0898
Pilling, James Constantine 1403, 1404, 1405, 1406, 1407, 1408, 1409, 1410, 1411, 1428
Pilon, C.A. 4801
Pilote, Pierre 4874
Pincoe, Grace 1547, 6956
Pincoe, Ruth 7026, 7027
Pineau, Gaston 3476
Piontkovsky, Roman 4150
Pirie, A.J. 2341
Piush, Evelyn 6262
Pivato, Joseph 1196, 1261
Plant, Richard 0958, 0990
Plant, Sheila 5810
Plant Research Institute (Canada). Agrometeorology Section 4686
Plante, Denis 1621
Platnick, Phyllis 1223
Platzmann, Julius 1402
Plexman, C.A. 4992
Plourde, Marcel 1490
Plumptre, A.F.W. 3371
Pluscauskas, Martha 0110, 0181, 0182, 5962
Plympton, Charles William 1888
Pocius, Gerald L. 3292, 4588, 4605
Pogue, Laura A. 5370
Pohorecky, Zenon S. 4559
Poirier, André 2912
Poirier, Jean 0374, 4547
Poirier, Lucien 0908
Poirier, Marie 3839
Poirier, René 1709, 2761

Polegato, Lino L. 0218
Polis, Michel P. 4779
Polson, James 7130
Pomerleau, Luc 5958
Pontaut, Alain 1069
Poole, Ann 4513
Poon, C. 5818
Pope, Judy L. 1826, 1827
Pope, Lois 0656
Popham, Robert E. 4531, 4532, 4543, 5567
Poppe, Roger 3930
Poray-Wybranowski, Anna 0094
Port, Susan 0587, 1031
Porteous, J. Douglas 4319
Porteous, Janet S. 0044
Porter, Peter Augustus 7059, 7060
Posner, Mark E. 6836
Potter, Joy 3569
Potter, Kathy 4690
Potter, Paul 5936
Pottier, Bernard 1458
Potts, Randall C. 2431
Potvin, Claude 0255, 1318, 1321
Potvin, Claudette 7175
Potvin, Diane 6985
Potvin, Fernand 6932
Potvin, Gilles 0904
Potvin, Lise 5228
Potyondi, Barry 0534
Poulin, André 4439
Poulin, Guy 6541
Poulin, Martin 3224
Poulin, Michelle 6399
Poulin, Pierre 5470
Poulin, V.A. 4999
Pouliot, Richard 0320
Pouliot, Thérèse 6830
Pouliot-Marier, Colette 3251
Powell, John M. 5059
Powell, Karen L. 6352
Powell, M. 4317
Powell, Margaret S. 3040, 3062
Powell, Mary 3333, 3334
Powell, Stephen S. 3062
Powell, Wyley L. 4802
Power, Elizabeth A. 4878
Powter, Christopher Barrett 4830, 5186
Prairie Agricultural Machinery Institute (Canada) 4725
Pratt, Ethel M. 4756
Pratt, R.H.M. 4943, 5350
Press, Marian 3628
Pressman, Norman E.P. 4328, 4422
Preston, Caroline M. 5012
Preston, Michele 7234
Pretes, Michael 0659
Prevost, Gerald 0563
Price, G.M. 5736
Price, John A. 4092, 5905
Price, Lisa Sydney 3870
Price, S.F. 5590, 5603
Prichard, J. Robert S. 2194

Priddle, George Burton 5245
Priess, Peter J. 0754, 0755
Prime, Frederick 4727
Primrose, Lynne 3770
Prince, Tim 2738
Prince Edward Island. Island Information Service 6469
Prince Edward Island. Provincial Library 1636
Principe, Walter H. 1521
Pringle, John 4406
Proctor, George A. 0878
Programme des affaires indiennes et esquimaudes (Canada).
  Direction du soutien éducationel et culturel 3991
Project Child Care 3138
Projet Colique 6534
Prokopiw, Orysia L. 1054, 1056
Pronovost, Gilles 6145
Pross, Catherine 5262
Proto, Daniel 5081
Proudfoot, Geraldine 0471
Proulx, Jean-René 4068, 4079
Proulx, Jeanne 0094
Proulx, Serge 1664
Provencher, Léo 1778
Provencher, Louise-Marie 7333
Provencher, Luc 7140
Provost, Honorius 1505
Provost, Michelle 1343, 1374, 1377, 1392
Provost, Sylvie 1129
Prud'homme, François 1558
Public Legal Education Society of Nova Scotia. Schools
  Committee 2262
Publicité-Club de Montréal 2611
Pulp and Paper Research Institute of Canada 4923, 5826, 6786
Puls, Robert 5547
Pulyk, Marcia 3758
Purdham, James T. 5630
Pyszczyk, Heinz W. 4603
Quadling, C. 5105
Quance, Elizabeth J. 6172
Quantrell, James 2432
Quarles, Mervyn V. 1744
Québec (Province). Bibliothèque de l'Assemblée nationale
  2481, 2553
Québec (Province). Bibliothèque de la Législature 0350, 2145,
  6281, 6721, 6730, 6762
Québec (Province). Bibliothèque de la Législature. Service de
  documentation politique 2426
Québec (Province). Bibliothèque de la Législature. Service de
  référence 2437, 6783
Québec (Province). Bureau de l'Imprimeur de la Reine 6270
Québec (Province). Bureau de la statistique du Québec. Centre
  d'information et de documentation 6353
Québec (Province). Centrale des bibliothèques 4480
Québec (Province). Centrale des bibliothèques. Centre de
  bibliographie 3506, 5926
Québec (Province). Centre de services en communications.
  Service de médias 6030
Québec (Province). Cinémathèque 6636
Québec (Province). Comité permanent d'aménagement des
  ressources 6255
Québec (Province). Commission d'étude des problèmes
  juridiques de l'eau 5090

Québec (Province). Commission de toponymie 3053
Québec (Province). Conseil d'orientation économique 2575
Québec (Province). Conseil du statut de la femme 3766
Quebec (Province). Department of Mines 6243
Quebec (Province). Department of Natural Resources 6271
Quebec (Province). Department of Natural Resources. Mineral
  Deposits Service 4767
Québec (Province). Direction des énergies nouvelles 5769
Québec (Province). Direction générale de l'urbanisme et de
  l'aménagement du territoire 4399
Québec (Province). Direction générale des eaux. Service des
  relevés 6568
Québec (Province). Direction générale du domaine territorial
  6577
Québec (Province). Éditeur officiel du Québec 6286, 6324
Québec (Province). Ministère de l'éducation. Direction des
  communications 3616
Québec (Province). Ministère de l'éducation. Direction des
  études économiques et démographiqes 6361
Québec (Province). Ministère de l'éducation. Direction
  générale de la planification 6143
Québec (Province). Ministère de l'éducation. Direction
  générale des réseaux 6647
Québec (Province). Ministère de l'éducation. Service général
  des communications 3555
Québec (Province). Ministère de l'énergie et des ressources
  6690
Québec (Province). Ministère de l'énergie et des ressources.
  Direction générale de l'exploration géologique et minérale
  4836
Québec (Province). Ministère de l'environnement. Centre de
  documentation 6366
Québec (Province). Ministère de l'Industrie et du Commerce.
  Service de géographie 0288
Québec (Province). Ministère des affaires sociales. Service de
  l'informathèque 6362
Québec (Province). Ministère des communications.
  Bibliothèque administrative 0986, 5970, 6392, 6470, 6471
Québec (Province). Ministère des forêts 6707
Québec (Province). Ministère des mines 4752
Québec (Province). Ministère des richesses naturelles 4769,
  6272, 6563
Québec (Province). Ministère des richesses naturelles.
  Bibliothèque 0336
Québec (Province). Ministère des richesses naturelles. Direc-
  tion générale des eaux. Service de l'aménagement
  hydraulique 5055
Québec (Province). Musée d'art contemporain 1112
Québec (Province). Office d'information et de publicité 6256
Québec (Province). Office de planification et de développe-
  ment du Québec 6400
Québec (Province). Office des personnes handicapées 6676
Québec (Province). Office des ressources humaines. Direction
  de développement du personnel d'encadrement 2787
Québec (Province). Service de la cartographie 6542
Québec (Province). Service de la photogrammétrie et de la
  cartographie 6525
Québec (Province). Service des gîtes minéraux 4761
Québec (Province). Services géologiques 6510
Queen's University (Kingston, Ont.). Department of Industrial
  Relations 2788

Queen's University (Kingston, Ont.). Douglas Library 0044,
6015
Queen's University (Kingston, Ont.). Douglas Library. Buchan
Collection 7347
Queen's University (Kingston, Ont.). Industrial Relations
Centre. Research Reference Section 2824, 2825, 2826, 2827,
2838, 2839, 2840, 2850, 2851, 2852, 2853, 2854, 2855, 2941
Quennell, Michael 5696
Quigley, E.P. 6691
Quinlan, Barbara 2158
Quinn, David B. 4584
Quinton, R.G. 5728
Racey, G.D. 5000
Racine, Laurette 5321
Radovich, Milan M. 4172
Raduloff, Marianne 5901
Radvanyi, Andrew 4993
Radziminska-Lasalle, Jolanta 4770
Rafferty, J. Pauline 0595
Ragueneau, Paul 1993
Rahkra, A.S. 2685
Raines, Mary R. 4866
Rainey, Melvyn D. 3984
Ralph Pickard Bell Library 0265, 6794
Ralston, H. Keith 0590
Ramlalsingh, Roderick D. 4465
Ramrattan, Annette 3645
Ramsey, G.S. 4947
Randall, Melanie 3871, 3872, 7215
Rangel, Yolanda 2297
Rankin, Reita A. 0430
Rankin, Seth 3023
Rapoport, Joseph 0111
Rascoe, Jesse E. 4552
Raske, A.G. 5543
Ratté, Alice 3375
Ravel d'Esclapon, Rysia de 2114
Raveneau, Jean 3021, 6120
Rawkins, Reginald A. 2570
Rawlyk, George A. 1568
Rawson, Mary 4494
Rawson, S.G. 2294
Ray, Douglas 3662
Ray, Margaret 6964, 7101
Ray, Roger B. 3992
Ray, Susan L. 3360
Raymond, Jean-Claude 4485
Raymond H. Fogler Library 6795
Raynauld, André 2574
Raynauld, Françoy 3958
Razzolini, E.M. 4585
Read, Colin 6892
Read, Stanley E. 1831
Reade, J.G. 4909
Rede, L.T. 0001
Redekop, Calvin W. 1571
Redpath, D.K. 1779
Rees, D.L. 0464
Regan, Mary Margaret 5957
Regehr, T.D. 0511
Réginald Grigoire Inc. 3719

Regnier, Robert 3611
Reid, Alison 6617
Reid, Bob 1819, 1820
Reid, Crowther & Partners 3005
Reid, Darrel R. 2522
Reid, Dennis 0674
Reid, Doris 4012
Reid, Elspeth 6198
Reid, Jane 3838
Reid, Jean-Paul 2186, 4467
Reid, John 4570
Reid, L.D. 4452
Reid, Marianne E. 2298
Reid, R.L. 0556
Reilly, Nolan 0234
Reimer, Louise 1209
Reinecke, L. 4737
Rek, Joseph 0550
Relph, E.C. 5044
Relsted, Connie 0145
Rémillard, Juliette 7030, 7032
Remington, Cyrus Kingsbury 1884
Rempel, Judith Dianne 3304
Renaud, Wayne E. 5129, 5130
Renaud-Frigon, Claire 1626, 2158
Renault, Raoul 1889, 6977, 7144
Renewable Resources Consulting Services 5361
Renick, J.H. 5127
Rennie, P.J. 4995, 5001, 5006
Rentz, C.L. 4970
Reps, John W. 4403
Resnick, Gary 2202
Retfalvi, Andrea 0709
Revai, Elisabeth 6021
Revill (A.D.) Associates 3007, 3011
Reynolds, Grace 0058
Reynolds, Lorna 4258
Reynolds, Robert 2391, 2447
Reynolds, Roy 3424, 3516
Rheault, Marie 0337
Rhodenizer, Vernon Blair 1030, 1045
Ricard, François 1251
Ricci, Paolo F. 3022
Rich, Obadiah 0002, 6709, 6713
Richardson, James 4973, 5021
Richardson, Judith A. 5663
Richardson, R. Alan 4632
Richardson, W. George 4784
Richer, Julia 0110, 1053
Richer, Pierre 2017
Richer, Suzanne 4927, 4937, 4938, 4945
Richer-Lortie, Lyse 0904
Richeson, David 2025
Richeson, Meg 3102
Richling, Joanne 2909
Richmond, Anthony H. 2883
Ricketts, Alan Stuart 7148, 7149
Rico, José M. 2121
Ricou, Laurence R. 7357, 7358
Ricouart, Janine 6852
Riddell, B.E. 5480

Riddell, Janet 4879
Rideout, E. Brock 3395
Rider, Lillian M. 1653
Ridge, Marian F. 0656
Riedel, Walter E. 1174
Rigby, M.S. 5319
Riggs, H.C. 5028
Rightmire, Robert W. 1780
Riley, J.L. 5440
Riley, Marvin P. 1517
Rinfret, Gabriel-Édouard 0967
Riopel, Diane 5801
Rioux, Bernard 2810
Ripley, Diane Lorraine 4724
Ripley, Gordon M. 0448, 1305, 5962
Risk, R.C.B. 7366
Ritchie, J.R. Brent 2703
Rivard, Adjutor 1413, 1422
Riverin-Simard, Danielle 3544, 3574
Rivet-Panaccio, Colette 1596
Robb, Marion Dennis 0199
Roberge, Alain 0379
Roberge, Michel 1695
Roberge-Brassard, Jocelyne 3575
Robert, Georges-H. 1001
Robert, Jacques 7201
Robert, Jean-Claude 0311, 0334, 2085
Robert, Lucie 6850, 6961, 7084, 7353
Robert, Véronique 6861, 6874, 7356
Roberts, Albert E. 4778
Roberts, Carol 6986
Roberts, D.W.A. 5454
Roberts, Debra 2663
Roberts, F.X. 7305
Roberts, Hazel J. 2868, 3515
Roberts, Henry L. 2424
Roberts, Judy 5662
Roberts, R.P. 1453
Roberts, Wayne 2856
Roberts-Pichette, Patricia 5066
Robertson, Alex 0836, 0841, 0870
Robertson, Carolynn 1654, 1671, 1696, 1710, 1725, 2158
Robertson, George W. 4641
Robertson, Paul B. 4808
Robertson, Sheila M. 3121
Robertson, William Murdoch 4919
Robertson, Yves 2778, 5847
Robeson, Virginia R. 0132, 1994
Robichaud, Michèle 2248
Robichaud, Norbert 0268
Robidoux, Meridel D. 4945
Robillard, Renée 2769, 2777
Robins, G. Lewis 5358
Robins, Kathleen 5527
Robinson, Betty Belle 2953
Robinson, Christopher D. 1623, 4505
Robinson, Douglas 1648, 1665, 1666, 1672
Robinson, J.B. 4976
Robinson, Jill M. 1113
Robinson, Marjorie 2590
Robinson, Paul 0124, 1344, 3995

Robinson, Susan E. 5091
Robitaille, Alphéda 6957
Robitaille, André 6407
Robitaille, Denis 6188
Robitaille, J.A. 5552
Robitaille, Lucie 1418
Robson, Mark 1870
Robson, Robert 4413, 4432
Rocan, Claude 7266
Rochais, Gérard 3576
Rochefort, Alain 4513
Rochon, Denis 6401
Rochon, James 4470
Rockwood, Eleanor Ruth 0554
Rodgers, C.D. 5631
Rodgers, Evan 4338
Rodrigue, Denis 4592
Roger, Bernard 4607
Rogers, Amos Robert 0203, 1086
Rogers, Dorothy 4508
Rogers, Edward S. 4539
Rogers, Helen F. 0157, 0158, 1711, 1712, 3959
Rogers, Judith 2124
Rogers, Marion 1862
Rohrlick, Paula 3782
Rokala, D.A. 5672, 5706
Roland, Charles G. 5572, 5664, 5936, 7228, 7229
Rolfe, Brenda 3487
Rollins, Caron 4113
Rome, David 1022, 4132, 4154, 4204, 4260
Rompkey, Ronald George 7029
Ronald, K. 5410
Rondeau, Guy 5018
Ronning, Cheryl 4677
Room 302 Books (Firm) 7214
Rooney, Frances 3840
Roos, Arnold E. 4626, 4627
Root, John D. 6564
Roper, Gordon 6939
Rose, Damaris 6870
Roseman, Daniel 2464
Rosenbaum, H. 3425
Rosenberg, D.M. 5423
Rosenberg, Gertrude 2174, 3630
Rosenberg, Neil V. 0887
Roseneder, Jan 0513, 6173
Rosenfeld, William P. 2270
Rosenthal, Harald 5252
Ross, Aileen D. 4361
Ross, C.W. 5124
Ross, Elspeth 1393
Ross, R.R. 2146, 3103, 3160
Ross, Tim 6548
Rost, Betty 4818
Rosval, Sergei J. 6100
Rothbart, Linda S. 4514
Rothman, Joan 3909
Rothman, William A. 2805
Rothwell, Helene de F. 6644
Rothwell, Stephen J. 6645
Rotstein, Abraham 0103

Séminaire St-Joseph. Archives 4027

Semkow, Brian 2664, 3191

Semple, Shirley J. 5670

Senay, P.–E. 1001

Sendrovich, Pamela 5592

Senécal, André Joseph 0176, 0366, 0405

Senécal, Francine 2445

Senn, Harold A. 5325

Sereda, Peter J. 5800

Sergeant, David E. 5396

ServCom Côte-Nord (Québec) 3180

Service, Dorothy Jane 3784

Service de diffusion sélective de l'information de la Centrale des bibliothèques 0266, 0391, 0707, 0979, 1481, 1482, 1704, 1841, 2300, 2523, 2739, 2895, 3282, 3693, 3694, 5264, 5665, 5684, 5828, 7147

Sève, Nicole de 3119, 3442

Severance, Frank Hayward 1894

Severance, Henry Ormal 5861

Sevigny, David C. 2630

Seward, Shirley B. 2438

Sewell, W.R. Derrick 3192

Sexson, Terry N. 5259

Shaheen, Wali Alam 1483

Shand, Patricia Martin 0871, 0907, 0918, 0926, 0930

Shanks, Doreen 3617

Shannon, E.E. 5738

Shapson, Stanley M. 3443

Sharpe, Michel 0394

Sharrock, Susan R. 4080

Shea, Edward C. 3552

Shea, John Gilmary 7061

Shea, Mary 5138

Shearing, Clifford D. 2204, 2348

Sheehan, Michael M. 1523

Sheehy, Elizabeth A. 2328, 3858

Sheffield, Edward F. 3373

Sheffield, Nora Morrison 3373

Shek, Ben-Zion 1187

Shelton, Valerie 4323

Shepard, C. 5517

Shepard, Odell 6894

Sheppard, Stephen 1773, 1774, 1775

Sherman, Frederic F. 6894

Sherman, George 2065

Sherstone, David 4631

Shibata, Yuko 4183

Shiel, Suzanne 3046, 3063

Shields, Gordon 6550

Shilling, Barbara A. 3208

Shillington, V.G. 6971

Shindruk, Cheryl 4117

Shinn, J.H. 4711

Shortt, Adam 0036

Shoup, J.M. 5350, 5351, 5354

Shrimpton, D.M. 5401

Shrybman, Steven 5219

Shurtleff, William 4719

Shute, J.C.M. 4696

Sibbald, Ian Ramsay 4707

Sicotte, Evelyne 3130

Sidhu, S.S. 4958

Sidor, Nicholas 2447

Siemens, Catherine 1066

Siemens, Leonard Bernard 4645

Sigvaldadottir-Geppert, Margrét 1078

Sikstrom, Calvin 5139

Silvester, Elizabeth 6144

Silzer, V.J. 4352

Simard, Albert J. 4959

Simard, Carole 4397

Simard, Michel 2238

Simard, Sylvain 0112

Simcoe Public Library 0465

Simmins, Geoffrey 0803

Simon Fraser University. Library 2015, 2042, 2263, 2482, 4392

Simon Fraser University. Library. Humanities Division 1114

Simoneau, Gerald 0110

Simpson, Allan A. 4540

Simpson, Cathy 1395

Simpson, D.L. 5853

Simpson, Noreen 4512

Simpson-Lewis, Wendy 4486

Sims, H.P. 5186, 5345

Sims, R.A. 5134, 5440, 5487, 5488

Sinclair, Donald Michael 2382

Singer, Loren 0702, 6199, 7045

Singh, A. 3467

Singh, Ganda 4151

Singh, Irina G. 0656

Sirko, Hlib 6817

Sirois, Antoine 1238, 1276, 1277

Skelly, H.M. 5766

Skelton, A. 4680, 4681

Skelton, Raleigh Ashlin 6511

Skene, Gordon D. 4496

Skinner, Shirley 2225

Skvor, George J. 5887

Slade, Alexander L. 1726

Slavin, Suzy M. 0642

Slavutych, Yar 1234

Sletmo, Gunnar K. 4516

Sloane, D. Louise 0513

Slobodin, Richard 3973

Small, James M. 3491

Smalley, Ian J. 4844

Smandych, Russell Charles 2301

Smart, Anne 3759

Smeaton, B. Hunter 5912

Smiley, Alison 4505

Smirle, S.M. 5160

Smit-Nielsen, Hendrika 2022

Smith, Albert H. 3372

Smith, Anne Marie 5337, 6076

Smith, Annette L. 4785

Smith, B.A. 4474

Smith, Charles D. 2507

Smith, Charles Wesley 0568

Smith, Christine M. 5963

Smith, Clinton William 5848

Smith, Daniel W. 5781

Smith, Diane L. 4511

Warner, Morton M. 5601
Warren, I.H. 5722
Warren, Louise 1340
Warren, Nancy 3295
Warwick, Jack 2043
Warwick, Susan J. 7125, 7126
Washburn, Jon 0879
Washburn, Wilcomb E. 3927
Washburn & Gillis Associates Ltd. 5189
Wasserman, Paul 0119, 0134
Waterman, Nairn 2116
Waters, Joanne 1870
Waters, William G. 4496
Waters, William H. 5751
Waterston, Elizabeth 2004, 2079
Watkin, Gwyneth 3677
Watson, Donna J. 5060
Watson, G. Llewellyn 3884
Watson, John 6732
Watson, Lawrence W. 6823
Watson, M. 5787
Watson, Sereno 5304
Watson, W.B. 3101
Watt, Christine 1347
Watt, Frank A. 0069
Watt, Roy MacGregor (Mrs.) 1058
Watters, John G. 2303
Watters, Reginald Eyre 1036, 1072
Wawrzyszko, Aleksandra 1140
Weafer, Linda F. 4109
Wearing, J.P. 0964, 0977
Wearmouth, Amanda 6045
Weatherby Bibliographics 4499
Weaver, John 4356
Weaver, Robert 1052
Weaver, Sally M. 3950
Webb, Janis 4842
Webb, M.S. 5260, 5261
Webb, Margaret Alice 0054
Webber, Bert 0574
Weber, Eileen 0433
Webster, Ellen 0207
Webster, John Clarence 7000
Webster, Linda 0568
Webster, Peter M. 2304
Weeks, Thomas E. 2176
Weidmark, P.E. 5793
Weiler, John 4441
Weiner, Alan R. 2749
Weinman, Paul L. 3917
Weinrib, Alice 3731
Weinrich, Peter 2472, 6880
Weir, Aileen 6414
Weir, R.D. 5417
Weise, C.E. 5587, 5588, 5602, 5603
Weiss, Allan Barry 1265
Weissenborn, Helen F. 4753
Weist, Katherine M. 4080
Weitz, Margaret Collins 3799
Wellburn, G.V. 4994
Weller, Joan 1383, 5975

Wellman, Barry 4340, 4468
Wells, Lilian M. 3209
Wells, Peter G. 5132, 5187, 5188, 5468
Wellwood, Robert William 4921, 4929, 6076
Welwood, Ronald J. 0587
Wenek, Karol W.J. 6959
Wengle, Annette 6966
Wertheimer, Douglas 7022
Wertman, Paul 4969
Wertsman, Vladimir 4199, 4205
West, Allen Sherman 5519
Western Research & Development Limited 5096
Weston, Sydney Moss 6230
Westrheim, S.J. 5411, 5538
Whalen, Doreen 2319
Whaley, Sara S. 3751
Wheat, James Clements 6516
Whebel, C.F.J. 6505
Wheeler, J.O. 6601, 6602
Wheeler, Jean 1741
Wheeler, Linda 1815
Whitaker, Marilyn 4340, 4468
White, Anthony G. 0770, 0786, 0787, 0790, 0791, 0792, 0793, 0794, 0795, 0796, 0797, 0798, 0799, 0800, 2342
White, Bonney G. 4449
White, Charles A. 4521
White, Eleanor E. 4982
White, Louise 4028
White, Richard H. 4400
White, S. Richard 5060
Whiteaves, J.F. 5312
Whitehead, Paul C. 5608
Whitehurst, Anne 1701, 1702
Whiteman, Bruce 1674, 6910, 6911, 7317
Whiteside, Don 3947, 3948, 4010, 4022
Whitney, H.S. 5401
Whitney, Joan 4362
Whittingham, Michael David 2281
Whitworth, Fred E. 0055, 6228
Wick, Don C. 0527
Wicken, George 6891, 7117, 7118
Wickett, Samuel Morley 4299
Wickett, Tom 2379
Wickson, Ethelwyn 0052
Wiebe, Victor G. 1551
Wieler, Anne H. 5673
Wigmore, Judy 5141
Wigmore, Shirley K. 3380
Wigney, Trevor John 3737
Wikeem, Brian M. 4706, 4986
Wiktor, Christian 2135, 2271, 2369
Wilcox-Magill, Dennis William 7178
Wilde, G.J.S. 3100
Wildgoose, Annette 3159
Wiley, S.C. 1935
Wilford, David J. 4949
Wilhoit, Frances Goins 0988
Wilkie, Brian 5083
Wilkins, Diane 2987, 3344
Wilkins, James L. 2124
Willcock, A.J. 5005

Willey, R.C. 1749, 1750, 1753, 1807, 1838
William R. Perkins Library 6659
Williams, Alan F. 0136
Williams, C. Brian 2794, 2800
Williams, Carol 2834
Williams, D. Dudley 5556
Williams, Gaynor P. 5030, 5072, 5097
Williams, Gregory N. 4109
Williams, Jane C. 6686
Williams, John R. 5037
Williamson, Mary F. 0684, 0685, 0717, 0726, 5934
Williamson, Michael 3757
Williamson, Nancy J. 0813
Williamson & Company 0026
Willington, R.P. 4934
Willis, Stephen C. 0899, 6915, 6916
Willis, Tricia 3353
Williston, Samuel W. 5309, 5310
Willms, Sharon E. 3357, 3358
Willson, K.M. 2874
Wilman, Jean 0538
Wilmat, Lloyd H. 2983
Wilmshurst, Rea 7197, 7198, 7199
Wilson, C.R. 5729
Wilson, Catherine 0474
Wilson, Ian R. 4604
Wilson, J. Scott 5252
Wilson, J.D. 3413, 3580, 6535, 7325
Wilson, J.S. 0515
Wilson, Lucy Roberta 1579
Wilson, Margaret 2285
Wilson, Thomas A. 2194
Windthorst, Rolf E.B. 1059
Winearls, Joan 6531, 6598
Winks, Robin W. 1933
Winnipeg Art Gallery Association 6495
Winnipeg Public Library 0495, 1316
Winship, George Parker 6885, 6886
Winsor, Justin 6482
With, Peter K. 5892, 5898
Withler, Ruth Elinor 5480
Withycombe, B. 6566
Woeller, Richard 7127
Wolf, Carolyn E. 3993
Wolfart, H. Christoph 1457
Wolfe, Carol Anne 2860
Wolfe, J.S. 4709
Wolfe, Jeanne 0324, 6870
Wolfenden, Madge 6834
Wolff, Hans 1415
Wollock, Jeffrey 7076
Women's Health Clinic 5699
Wong, Betty 3670
Wong, Chuck 6141, 6162
Wong, R.K.W. 5280
Wong, Sandra Ann 3244
Wong, W.W. 4451
Wood, C.M. 5467
Wood, Dean D. 4190
Wood, John R. 3954
Wood, Marianna 0749

Wood, W.D. 2806, 6108
Woodcock, George 1105
Woodhead, Eileen 2704, 2705
Woodill, Gary 3232
Woodley, Elsie Caroline 3370
Woodruff, Evelyn L. 6562
Woods, C.S. 5360
Woods, Cheryl A. 6595
Woods, Lance B. 5627
Woodsworth, Anne 5907
Woodward, Agnes 3085
Woodward, Frances M. 0591, 0593, 0594, 3580, 6112, 6544, 7224
Woolbert, Robert Gale 2424
Woolford, Daniel 4298
Woolmer, J. Howard 7160, 7161
Worker's Compensation Board of British Columbia. Films and Posters Department 2928
Working Group on Health Surveillance and Laboratory Safety (Canada) 5649
Worobec, Christine 4203
Woroniuk, Carrie A. 0464
Wotherspoon, Shelagh 5671
Woycenko, Ol'ha 4136, 4165, 7286
Wren, Christopher 5207
Wright, Annie M. 1306
Wright, David M. 2818
Wright, Don 5197, 5198
Wright, Edgar Norman 3563
Wright, J.F. 6245, 6253
Wright, John 1577, 1578
Wright, Maureen 3041
Wright, Michael D. 4780
Wright, Thomas D. 4956
Writers' Development Trust. Atlantic Work Group 1115, 1116
Writers' Development Trust. British Columbia Work Group 1117, 1118
Writers' Development Trust. Ontario Work Group 1119, 1120
Writers' Development Trust. Prairie Work Group 1121, 1122
Writers' Development Trust. Quebec Work Group 1123, 1124
Wrong, George M. 1899
Würtele, Fred C. 1885
Wybouw, George 2910, 2923
Wyczynski, Paul 1024, 1099, 6923, 7002, 7015, 7016, 7107, 7108, 7208, 7209
Wylie, Alison 3885
Wylie, William N.T. 5815, 5816
Wyman, Doreen 6667
Wynn, Graeme 3074
Xeropaides, Micheline 0375
Yandle, Anne 7162
Yansouni, P.A. 4779
Yanz, Lynda 2878
Yapa, A.C. 6387
Yarranton, G.A. 5819
Yarranton, M. 5819
Yawney, Carole D. 4543
Yelle, André 2689
Yip, Gladys 4237
Yorio, Carlos Alfredo 3519
York University (Toronto, Ont.). Institute for Social Research 3050

York University (Toronto, Ont.). Libraries 6789
York University (Toronto, Ont.). Programme in Arts Administration 0679
Young, Alan R. 7254, 7255
Young, Brian 2286
Young, George 0598, 0604
Young, Judy 1200, 4214
Young, Rod 1714
Young, Stuart C. 5239
Young Men's Christian Association (Halifax, N.S.) 6716
Younger, Carolyn T. 3138
Yuan, Jing-dong 2779
Yuille, John C. 2320, 2321
Yukon Archives 0662, 2033, 2052, 4094, 6848
Yukon Indian Resource Centre 3949
Yukon Territory. Women's Directorate. Library 3897
Yundt, S.E. 4811
Yurkiw, Peter 1614
Yurkowski, M. 5520
Zalasky, H. 4962
Zaldokas, Daiva O. 6415
Zaporzan, Shirley 6653
Zaslow, Morris 2025
Zavitz, Carol 3781
Zekulin, Nicholas G.A. 5887
Zeman, Jarold K. 1568
Ziegler, Ronald M. 1797
Zilm, Glennis 0600, 1649, 5713
Zimmering, Suzann 1110, 1141
Zimmerly, David W. 6622
Zimmerman, Lothar 4221, 4274
Zinman, Rosalind 0357
Zins, Michael 2655
Zolobka, Vincent 4131
Zoltai, Stephen C. 4774
Zubrzycki, Pierre 5228
Zuckernick, Arlene 3706, 3707
Zuk, Ireneus 0923
Zureik, Elia 1698
Zysman, Ewa 0155

Titles

Titres

L'activité physique et la santé mentale: une bibliographie spécialisée de la base de données SPORT 1858

"L'activité professionnelle des femmes médecins au Québec: bibliographie/[Professional activity of female physicians in Québec: bibliography]" 3763

Activités de caractère historique subventionnées par Multiculturalisme Canada 2039

"Activités politiques des fonctionnaires: bibliographie annotée" 2403

"Activities in the field of German-Canadian studies and research/Aktivitäten im Bereich deutschkanadischer Studien und Forschung" 4222

"Adam Shortt: a bibliographical comment" 7306

L'adaptation de la main-d'oeuvre pour les années 1990: bibliographie sélective 2937

Addenda and corrigenda, 1974, to Subarctic Athapaskan bibliography, 1973 4058

Addenda to *A bibliography: television violence and its effect on the family* 0955

"Addenda to 'A bibliography of Canadian numismatics'" 1750

Additional references relating to reciprocity with Canada 2558

Additional references to reciprocity in trade between Canada and the United States of America 2557

Additions for the annotated bibliography of Cape Breton Highlands National Park 2978

Additions for the annotated bibliography of Terra Nova and Gros Morne National Parks 2984

Additions to the Annotated bibliography of Fundy National Park, sections IV & V 2981

Adele Wiseman: an annotated bibliography 7370

Administration de tests et évaluation du rendement des élèves au Canada 3656

L'administration municipale et les finances: une bibliographie annotée 4317

Administration publique canadienne: bibliographie 2404

L'administration scolaire et l'horaire modulaire flexible: une bibliographie/School administration and flexible modular scheduling: a bibliography 3456

Administrations publiques des Premières nations: bibliographie annotée 4121

"L'adolescent normal: une revue de la littérature récente pertinente à l'expérience de l'adolescent québécois" 3151

Adolescent pregnancy: a bibliography 3197

Adoption, special needs: a bibliography 3211

Adoption in brief: research and other literature in the United States, Canada and Great Britain, 1966-72: an annotated bibliography 3117

Adoption internationale, 1980-1989: bibliographie sélective et annotée 3325

"Adrien-Gabriel Morice, o.m.i. (1859-1938): essai de bibliographie" 7200

Adult basic education 3434

Adult education: an annotated bibliography 3491

Adult education theses, Canada 6158

Adult new readers: a bibliography of supplementary reading materials selected from the collection of the Windsor Public Library 3591

Advanced train control systems: a selective bibliography/ Systèmes d'automatisation de la marche des trains: bibliographie sélective 4508

Advanced wastewater treatment: a selective, coded bibliography 5738

Advances in CAD-CAM and robotics: NRC contributions: commentary and bibliography 5827

Advances in manpower management: a selected annotated bibliography 2823

Aeronautical sports, bicycling and cycling, equestrian sports, motor sports, target sports 1815

"Affirmative action: employment equity: a selected bibliography" 2921

After survival: a teacher's guide to Canadian resources 0124

The aged in Canadian society: select bibliography/Les vieillards dans la société canadienne: bibliographie sélective 3261

L'agent de développement pédagogique: bibliographie sommaire sur ses principales tâches dans un collège 3488

"Aging and the aged: an eclectic annotated resource list" 3346

Aging and the aged: list of selected publications from Health and Welfare Canada 3266

Aging and the aged in Nova Scotia: a list of writings from 1979 to 1985 3291

Agribusiness: an introductory bibliography 2619

Agricultural Energy Centre bibliography (including videotapes and displays) 4720

Agricultural labour in Canada and United States: a bibliography 2813

Agricultural meteorology: a brief literature review & bibliography 4641

Agricultural periodicals published in Canada, 1836-1960 5872

The agricultural use of marginal lands: a review and bibliography 4692

"AID: architect's information directory" 0804

Aide bibliographique pour l'étude du nouveau roman canadien-français 1100

Aide-mémoire en andragogie 3561

L'aide par les proches: mythes et réalités: revue de littérature et réflexions sur les personnes âgées en perte d'autonomie, leurs aidants et aidantes naturels et le lien avec services formels 3340

AIDS 1989: a bibliography of resources available from Manitoba Education Library 3703

AIDS resource directory 5707

Air pollution aspects of odorous substances: a literature survey 5103

Air tankers: a bibliography 4959

Air transportation 4509

"Aktivitäten im Bereich deutschkanadischer Studien und Forschung" 4222

Al Purdy, an annotated bibliography 7251, 7252

Alaska and the Northwest part of North America, 1588-1898: maps in the Library of Congress 6486

Alaska Highway, 1942-1991: a comprehensive bibliography of material available in the Yukon Archives & MacBride Museum 0662

Albert Laberge, 1871-1960: Charles Gill, 1871-1918 7015, 7016, 7107, 7108

Alberta, 1954-1979: a provincial bibliography 0536

Alberta authors and their books for children and young adults 1357

Alberta bibliography, 1980-1987 for adults and young adults 0544

Alberta bibliography: books by Alberta authors and Alberta publishers 0552

An annotated bibliography of studies related to the Windsor economy, 1975-1985 0484

An annotated bibliography of the Arctic charr (Salvelinus alpinus) with emphasis on aquaculture, commercial fisheries, and migration and movements 4910

An annotated bibliography of the balsam woolly aphid (Adelges piceae (Ratzeburg)) 5466

An annotated bibliography of the Banff National Park area 2995

An annotated bibliography of the British Army, 1660-1914 1984

An annotated bibliography of the Carnation Creek Fish-forestry Project, 1970 to 1988 4999

An annotated bibliography of the chain pickerel, Esox niger (Osteichthyes: Salmoniformes) 5372

Annotated bibliography of the college union 3668

Annotated bibliography of the eastern larch beetle, Dendroctonus simplex Leconte (Coleoptera: Scolytidae) 5543

An annotated bibliography of the effects of logging on fish of the western United States and Canada 5373

An annotated bibliography of the fishes of the Beaufort Sea and adjacent regions 5416

An annotated bibliography of the geology and geomorphology of the Rondeau Peninsula and environs 4807

Annotated bibliography of the literature on American Indians published in state historical society publications, New England and Middle Atlantic states 4031

An annotated bibliography of the literature on drinking and driving 3091

"Annotated bibliography of the McGill sub-arctic research papers (1954-1970)" 2994

Annotated bibliography of the McGill Sub-arctic Research papers and theses, 1954-1974 2997

An annotated bibliography of the muskellunge, Esox masquinongy (Osteichthyes: Salmoniformes) 5420

Annotated bibliography of the official languages of Canada/ Bibliographie analytique des langues officielles au Canada 1492

An annotated bibliography of the physical anthropology and human biology of Canadian Eskimos and Indians 3929

An annotated bibliography of the pike, Esox lucius (Osteichthyes: Salmoniformes) 5528

An annotated bibliography of the Quaternary geology and history for the Don Valley Brickworks 4860

Annotated bibliography of the Quaternary in Manitoba and the adjacent Lake Agassiz region (including archaeology of Manitoba) 4774

Annotated bibliography of the renewable resource publications of the Manitoba Department of Natural Resources 6454

Annotated bibliography of the salmonid embryo and alevin 5353

An annotated bibliography of the Sudbury area 0443

An annotated bibliography of the works of Silas Tertius Rand 7256

An annotated bibliography of Ukrainian literature in Canada: Canadian book publications, 1908-1985 1234

An annotated bibliography of unclassified reports issued by Defence Research Northern Laboratory, 1947-1965 5730

An annotated bibliography of unclassified reports issued by Defence Research Telecommunications Establishment, 1947-1969 5734

Annotated bibliography of underwater and marine park related initiatives in northern latitudes 1823

An annotated bibliography of western hemlock, Tsuga heterophylla (Raf.) Sarg. 5338

"An annotated bibliography of works by and about John Newlove" 7211

"An annotated bibliography of works by and about Mavis Gallant" 6999

"An annotated bibliography of works by and about Robert Kroetsch" 7102

An annotated bibliography of works on daily newspapers in Canada, 1914-1983/Une bibliographie annotée des ouvrages portant sur les quotidiens canadiens, 1914-1983 1697

An annotated bibliography of works related to the Edmonton Regional Planning Commission 4322

"Annotated bibliography of works written on the Supreme Court of Canada" 2109

Annotated bibliography on Arctic North American freshwater fishes 5333

Annotated bibliography on building for disabled persons 3101

Annotated bibliography on building for the handicapped 3101

Annotated bibliography on culture, tourism and multiculturalism 1847

Annotated bibliography on demand responsive scheduling systems 4476

Annotated bibliography on determination of teachers' salaries and effective utilization of teacher manpower 3426

Annotated bibliography on elk-livestock-range interactions in western Canada and northwestern U.S.A. specific to the management of elk and livestock within the Waterton Biosphere Reserve 5511

Annotated bibliography on engineering aspects of muskeg and peat (to 30 June 1969) 5733

An annotated bibliography on forest-range ecosystems in the Pacific Northwest 4986

Annotated bibliography on gifted children 3596

"An annotated bibliography on glacial chattermarks" 5054

Annotated bibliography on hydrology, 1941-1950 (United States and Canada) 5028

Annotated bibliography on hydrology (1951-54) and sedimentation (1950-54) United States and Canada 5028

Annotated bibliography on hydrology and sedimentation, 1959-1962 (United States and Canada) 5028

Annotated bibliography on hydrology and sedimentation, United States and Canada, 1955-58 5028

Annotated bibliography on Indian education 3409

Annotated bibliography on initial tree spacing 4935

"Annotated bibliography on Isabella Valancy Crawford" 6922

Annotated bibliography on Kluane National Park, Yukon Territory 2988

An annotated bibliography on laboratory buildings 0734

Annotated bibliography on metallic mineralization in the regions of Noranda, Matagami, Val-d'Or, Chibougamau 4767

Annotated bibliography on northern environmental engineering 5781

An annotated bibliography on planning for pedestrians 4338

Annotated bibliography on reproductive health hazards in the workplace in Canada 5676

An annotated bibliography on residential chimneys serving solid or liquid-fuel fired heating appliances 5720

Annotated bibliography on robotics 5824

Annotated bibliography on snow and ice problems 5044

The anti-psychiatry bibliography and resource guide 5623

Anti-racist education: kindergarten to senior 4: a bibliography of resources available from the Library, Instructional Resources Branch 3729

Antiques and restoration 0692

"Antonin Dessane, 1826-1873" 6954

"Aperçu bibliographique des travaux de l'Université de Montréal, 1960-1978" 2169

"Aperçu critique des principaux ouvrages pouvant servir à l'histoire du développement minier de l'Abitibi-Témiscamingue (1910-1950)" 4796

Aperçu de bibliophilatélie 1766

Aperçu du financement des universités: [bibliographie] 3579

Aperçu général sur les agressions sexuelles contre les enfants: résumé de 26 analyses de documentation et de projets spéciaux 3320

"Aperçu sur la recherche préhistorique au Québec" 4551

The Apex 8000 numerical 0841

Apicultural literature published in Canada and the United States 4653

APOA bibliography 5177

Apôtres de la plume: contribution des professeurs des facultés ecclésiastiques de l'Université d'Ottawa (1912 [i.e. 1932]-1951) à la bibliographie des Oblats de M.I. 1506

Applications of computer technology to law (1969-1978): a selected bibliography 2216

Applications of computer technology to law (1979-1982): a selected bibliography 2216

Applied climate bibliography for architects, planners, landscape architects and builders/Bibliographie de climatologie appliquée pour les architectes, les planificateurs, les paysagistes et les entrepreneurs et bâti-ment 0780

Appraisal of forest aesthetic values: an annotated bibliography 4946

Apprentissage assuré: bibliographie annotée 3582

"Apprentissage observationnel abstrait et éducation permanente: revue de littérature" 3574

Approches et méthodes de la recherche féministe: bibliographie multidisciplinaire 3833

Aquaculture/Aquiculture 4911

Aquatic sports, outdoor sports, wintersports 1815

Aquatic toxicity of pulp and paper mill effluent: a review 5248

Aquiculture 4911

"Arabic-Canadian periodical publications: a preliminary check list" 5912

Arabic-speaking immigrants in the United States and Canada: a bibliographical guide with annotation 4236

"An archaeological bibliography: the central and northern Great Plains prior to 1930" 4537

Archaeological bibliography for eastern North America 4570

An archaeological bibliography of the Maritime Provinces: works to 1984 4599

Archaeological field research in British Columbia: an annotated bibliography 4604

Archaeology and prehistory: the Saskatchewan case 4559

Archaeology in northern Canada 4597

Archibald Lampman: an annotated bibliography 7117, 7118

"Archibald Lampman (1861-1899): a checklist" 7116

Architecture canadienne: bibliographie 0748

L'architecture dans le *Canadian Illustrated News* et *L'Opinion publique*: inventaire des références 0774

Architecture et arts anciens du Québec: répertoire d'articles de revues disponibles à la Bibliothèque de la Faculté de l'aménagement, Université de Montréal 0746

Architecture in *Canadian Illustrated News* and *L'Opinion publique*: inventory of references/L'architecture dans le *Canadian Illustrated News* et *L'Opinion publique*: inventaire des références 0774

Architecture in Ontario: a select bibliography on architectural conservation and the history of architecture: with special relevance to the Province of Ontario: for "New Life for Old Buildings," a symposium sponsored jointly by Frontenac Historic Foundation and Ontario Heritage Foundation, Kingston, Ontario, September 9-12, 1976 0749

Architecture of Arctic regions: a selected bibliography 0786

The architecture of Calgary, Alberta, Canada: a selected bibliography 0787

The architecture of Ontario Province, Canada, Toronto metropolitan area: a selected bibliography 0790

The architecture of Quebec Province, Canada: Quebec metropolitan area: a selected bibliography 0791

The architecture of Toronto: a selected bibliography 0784

The architecture of Vancouver, British Columbia: a selected bibliography 0770

"Archival science bibliography, 1980-1986" 1690

Archival science bibliography, 1986-1988/Bibliographie en archivistique, 1986-1988 1723

Archival sources for the study of Finnish Canadians 4269

The Arctic 0658

Arctic air pollution bibliography 5096

Arctic and Antarctic regions 0663

Arctic archaeology: a bibliography and history 4572

Arctic bibliography 0627

"Arctic bibliography: a guide to current Arctic and Subarctic periodicals" 5973

The Arctic islands pipeline route: a bibliography of unpublish-ed Fisheries and Environment Canada reports 5136

Arctic petroleum transportation bibliography 4783

Arctic stream processes: an annotated bibliography 5155

Arctic transportation 4495

The ARDA catalogue [Agricultural Rehabilitation and Develop-ment Administration] 4648

Arms and disarmament: a bibliography of Canadian research, 1965-1980 2462

Around our lovely province 0213

"The arrival of Italian-Canadian writing" 1196

Art and architecture 0676

Art and architecture in Canada: a bibliography and guide to the literature to 1981/Art et architecture au Canada: bibliographie et guide de la documentation jusqu'en 1981 0726

The art and pictorial press in Canada: two centuries of art magazines 5934

Art et architecture au Canada: bibliographie et guide de la documentation jusqu'en 1981 0726

Arthur C. Erickson 6968

Arthur Charles Erickson's Canadian Chancery: a bibliography 0788

"Arthur Garratt Dorland 1887-1979: a bibliography" 6956

Arthur S. Bourinot 6865, 6866

Articles related to transportation in major economics journals, 1960-1971 4496

Avenues of research: a businessman's guide to sources of business information 2710

Aviation technology and pilot training program: bibliography 5753

L'Avortement 5665

L'avortement: bibliographie choisie 5596

Avortement: prises de position et aspects juridiques: bibliographie sélective et annotée 2322

Axel Heiberg Island bibliography 0655

"B.C. poets: a bibliography for 1970-75" 1092

Back injury prevention: a literature survey and compendium of programs and resources 5658

Backbenchers: a selected bibliography 2475

"Bacon and the fisheries of Newfoundland: a bibliographical ghost" 0206

Baffin Island Quaternary environments: an annotated bibliography 4813

La Baie James des amérindiens, bibliographie/Bibliography: native peoples, James Bay region 3934

Banff, Jasper, Kootenay and Yoho: an initial bibliography of the contiguous Canadian Rocky Mountains national parks 2995

Banking research from a Canadian perspective: an annotated bibliography 2703

Baptists in Canada, 1760-1990: a bibliography of selected printed resources in English 1568

The barn as an element in the cultural landscape of North America: a bibliography 0756

Bases de données canadiennes lisibles par machine: un répertoire et un guide 0157

A basic bibliography of musical Canadiana 0825

A basic bibliography on marketing in Canada 2581

Basic book list for Canadian schools 3400

Basic books in the mass media: an annotated, selected booklist covering general communications, book publishing, broadcasting, editorial journalism, film, magazines, and advertising 0988

Basic cataloguing tools for use in Canadian libraries 1589

A Basic legal collection for barristers and solicitors in British Columbia 2165

Basic list of current municipal documents: a checklist of official publications issued periodically since 1927 by the larger cities of the United States and Canada 4301

"Basic tax library" 2601

Basilian novitiates in Canada and the United States: an annotated bibliography 1526

Basilian serial publications, 1935-1969 5902

Battered wives: a select bibliography 3190

Bay of Fundy environmental and tidal power bibliography 5810

The Bay of Fundy tidal power project 5770

The Beatrice Hitchins Memorial Collection of Aviation History: catalogue 4463

La Beauce et un peu plus: bibliographie commentée, des ouvrages écrits sur la Beauce et la périphérie 0318

Beaufort E.I.S. bibliography 5196

The Beaufort Sea, Mackenzie delta, Mackenzie valley, and northern Yukon: a bibliographical review 0644

Beaver in western North America: an annotated bibliography, 1966 to 1986 5546

Beer and wine sales: different points of view: a selected bibliography 2717

Before the first day: teaching law for the first time: Nova Scotia resources 2262

Behavioral objectives: stating, defining, classifying, evaluating: a bibliography 3460

Behaviour modification 3480

Behaviour modification for the treatment of alcoholism: an annotated bibliography 5602

Behaviour modification with the offender: an annotated bibliography 2146

The Bella Coola River estuary: status of environmental knowledge to 1981: report of the Estuary Working Group, Fisheries and Oceans-Environment Joint Co-ordinating Committee on Environmental Affairs, Pacific and Yukon Region 5172

Beneficiation techniques applicable to Nova Scotian coals: a literature review 4829

Benjamin Sulte et son oeuvre: essai de bibliographie des travaux historiques et littéraires (1860-1916) de ce polygraphe canadien, précédé d'une notice biographique 7323

Benthic studies in Alice Arm and Hastings Arm, B.C. in relation to mine tailings dispersal 5486

The benzodiazepines-patterns of use: an annotated bibliography 5603

Besoins de logements des groupes spéciaux: une synthèse des recherches francophones 3341

The best of Children's choices 1379

Beyond the Arctic Circle: materials on Arctic explorations and travels since 1750 in the Special Collections and University Archives Division of the University of British Columbia Library 0661

"Beyond the basics in selecting Quebec literature" 1187

Beyond the textbook: a selected bibliography for the '80s 2006

The Bible and the Church: essays in honour of Dr. David Ewert 6971

Bibliografía de historia de América 2091

Bibliographia Canadiana 0109

Bibliographia invertebratorum aquaticorum canadensium 5544

"Bibliographia onomastica: Canada" 4544, 4547

Bibliographic directory of Amerindian authors in Quebec 4122

Bibliographic guide for translators, writers and terminologists 1445

"A bibliographic guide to French-Canadian literature" 1140

Bibliographic guide to North American history 2092

Bibliographic guide to North Bay and area 0464

Bibliographic guide to translation 1445

Bibliographic information on the Freshfield, Lyell and Mons glaciers, Alberta 5218

A bibliographic introduction to paralegals in two jurisdictions: Canada and the United States: 1970-1978 2209

Bibliographic list: reproductive technologies 5699

Bibliographic sources for travel and tourism research 1764

"Bibliographic sources on Ukrainian in the New World, listed chronologically" 1424

A bibliographic study of field agriculture in the Canadian prairie west 1870-1940 4674

A bibliographic survey of microeconomics reading materials in North American universities: a comparative study between Canada and the United States of America 2641

A bibliographic survey of publications of the Vineland Research Station, 1911-1986 4708

Bibliographie de guides et liste de dépôts d'archives 4068

"Bibliographie de Guy Dufresne" 6961

"Bibliographie de Jacques Brault" 6872

"Bibliographie de Jacques Poulin" 7243

"Bibliographie de Jean-Charles Falardeau" 6973

"Bibliographie de Jean-Olivier Chenier" 6906

"Bibliographie de Jovette Marchessault" 7175

"Bibliographie de la bataille de Saint-Eustache" 0378

Bibliographie de la bibliothèque [Association olympique canadienne] 1808

Bibliographie de la conversion au système métrique 2657

Bibliographie de la Côte-du-Sud 0393

Bibliographie de la Côte-Nord 0410

"Bibliographie de la critique" 1236

Bibliographie de la critique de la littérature québécoise dans les revues des XIXe et XXe siècles 1145

Bibliographie de la critique de la littérature québécoise et canadienne-française dans les revues canadiennes (1974-1978) 1249

Bibliographie de la critique des traductions littéraires anglaises et françaises au Canada: de 1950 à 1986 avec commentaires 1480

Bibliographie de la critique féminist[e] 3851

"Une bibliographie de la culture matérielle traditionnelle au Canada 1965-1982/ A bibliography of material culture in Canada 1965-1982" 4588

Bibliographie de la danse théâtrale au Canada 0951

Bibliographie de la documentation sur les carrières 2798

Bibliographie de la Gaspésie 0398

Bibliographie de la glaciologie 5185

"Bibliographie de la littérature canadienne pour la jeunesse: ..." 1381

"Bibliographie de la littérature canadienne pour la jeunesse: 1985" 1385

Bibliographie de la littérature outaouaise et franco-ontarienne 1180

"Bibliographie de la littérature récente en Ontario, en Acadie et dans l'Ouest canadien" 1228

Bibliographie de la Mauricie 0411

Bibliographie de la mécanique des glaces de rivières et de lacs/ Bibliography of river and lake ice mechanics 5038

Bibliographie de la néologie: 300 apports nouveax (1980-1987) 1489

Bibliographie de la néologie: nouveaux fragments (1980-1989) 1489

Bibliographie de la péninsule du Québec-Labrador 0299

Bibliographie de la philosophie au Canada: une[sic] guide à recherche 1570

Bibliographie de la poésie franco-canadienne 0993

"Bibliographie de la poésie franco-canadienne de l'Ouest" 1143

Bibliographie de la question universitaire Laval-Montréal, 1852-1921 3369

Bibliographie de la recherche sur les ressources hydrauliques 5062

Bibliographie de la réglementation des télécommunications au Canada 2294

Bibliographie de la Rive-Sud de Québec, (Lévis-Lotbinière) 0407

Bibliographie de la Société de Notre-Dame (1639-1663) accompagné de notes historiques et critiques 0292

"Bibliographie de la Société de Notre-Dame de Montréal (1639-1663) et de ses membres, accompagné de notes historiques et critiques" 1938

Bibliographie de la vie militaire au Canada, 1867-1967 2036

Bibliographie de la vie militaire au Canada, 1867-1983 2036

"Bibliographie de l'Abbé Alexis Pelletier" 7240

Bibliographie de l'Abitibi-Témiscamingue 0323

"Bibliographie de l'Acadie" 0222, 0223, 0230, 0235, 0238, 0244

Bibliographie de Lanaudière 0400

Bibliographie de langue française sur le droit d'auteur 2177

Bibliographie de l'art inuit 0727

"Bibliographie de l'art inuit canadien contemporain" 0697

Bibliographie de l'artisanat québécois 0712

Bibliographie de l'édition au Québec, 1940-1960 1669

Bibliographie de l'enseignement professionel au Québec, 1850-1980 3605

Bibliographie de l'enseignement supérieur au Canada 3378

"Bibliographie de Léon Gérin" 7009

Une bibliographie de l'habitation coopérative au Canada 4433

"Bibliographie de l'histoire de Hull: inventaire préliminaire" 0315

Bibliographie de l'histoire de l'éducation au Québec des origines à 1960 3539

Bibliographie de l'histoire du Québec et du Canada, 1946-1965/ Bibliography of the history of Quebec and Canada, 1946-1965 2058

Bibliographie de l'histoire du Québec et du Canada, 1966-1975 2012

Bibliographie de l'histoire du Québec et du Canada, 1976-1980/ Bibliography of the history of Quebec and Canada, 1976-1980 2044

Bibliographie de l'histoire du Québec et du Canada, 1981-1985/ Bibliography of the history of Quebec and Canada, 1981-1985 2080

Une bibliographie de l'histoire et du patrimoine de la région de la Capitale nationale 0126

Bibliographie de l'Ile Jésus 0380

Bibliographie de l'Institut pour la répression des ravageurs forestiers (1977-1985) 6367

Bibliographie de l'interprétation du patrimoine canadien, 1982 1817

Bibliographie de livres canadiens traduits de l'anglais au français et du français à l'anglais 1440

"Une bibliographie de livres pour enfants" 1335

"Bibliographie de l'oeuvre de Maurice Constantin-Weyer" 6914

"Bibliographie de M. Hubert Charbonneau" 6903

"Bibliographie de M. L'Abbé Ivanhoë Caron" 6896

Bibliographie de M.C. Baillairgé: extraite du volume des "Transactions" pour 1894, de la Société royale du Canada: addenda jusqu'à ce jour, Québec, mai 1899 6821

"Bibliographie de Madeleine Gagnon" 6997

"Bibliographie de Marcel Rioux" 7269

"Bibliographie de Marie-Claire Blais" 6850

"Bibliographie [de Marie de l'Incarnation]" 7177

Bibliographie de Marius Barbeau 6829

Bibliographie de météorologie forestière 4926

"Bibliographie de Michel van Schendel" 7349

"Bibliographie de Monique Bosco" 6860

"Bibliographie de Naïm Kattan" 7084

Bibliographie de pédagogie religieuse: introductions et commentaires 3386

Bibliographie de publications officielles relatives aux archives et à la gestion des documents 1617

Bibliographie de références sur la radiodiffusion canadienne 0963

Bibliographie sélective sur la contribution des usagers aux frais médicaux et le ticket modérateur 5633

Bibliographie sélective sur la procédure parlementaire 2384

"Bibliographie sélective sur la rééducation" 2179

Bibliographie sélective sur la répartition géographique des professionnels de la santé 5640

Une bibliographie sélective sur l'architecture au Canada 0771

Bibliographie sélective sur le bénévolat 3236

Bibliographie sélective sur le "burn-out": compilée à l'occasion de la journée internationale des femmes de 1989 3873

Une bibliographie sélective sur le choix, la planification, la mise en oeuvre, la gestion, l'évaluation et la préparation d'appels d'offre pour les systèmes intégrés de bibliothèques 1711

Bibliographie sélective sur le harcèlement sexuel 3225

Bibliographie sélective sur le viol 3264

Bibliographie sélective sur l'économie de l'énergie/Selective bibliography on the economics of energy 2726

Bibliographie sélective sur les actes médicaux inutiles 5643

Bibliographie sélective sur les communautés culturelles 4226

Bibliographie sélective sur les personnes âgées 3216

Bibliographie sélective sur les transferts internationaux de technologie 2668

Bibliographie sélective sur l'usage et l'abus des psychotropes par la population adulte 3217

Bibliographie signalétique: précipitations acides 5276

Bibliographie signalétique sur les précipitations acides 5276

Bibliographie sommaire de la Côte-du-Sud 0359

"Bibliographie sommaire des écrits sur Samuel de Champlain" 6901

"Bibliographie sommaire des études sur Montréal, 1958-1964" 0294

"Bibliographie sommaire des événements de 1837-1838" 1945

Bibliographie sommaire du Canada français, 1854-1954 1925

"Bibliographie sommaire sur la Confédération" 1944

Bibliographie sommaire sur la Côte-Nord et les régions circonvoisines 0337

"Bibliographie sommaire sur la profession de bibliothécaire" 1584

Bibliographie sommaire sur le port et le secteur riverain de Toronto 4430

Bibliographie sommaire sur les francophones hors Québec 1980-1989 4607

Bibliographie sommaire sur l'histoire de l'écriture féminine au Canada, 1769-1961 3746

Bibliographie spéciale sur les traités indiens canadiens et des autres sujets alliés 4007

"Bibliographie sur Calixa Lavalée et 'O Canada'" 7129

Bibliographie sur des questions actuelles 2394

"Bibliographie sur foyer nourricier et placement familial" 3124

Une bibliographie sur la banque au Canada 2589

Bibliographie sur la bibliotechnique 1602

Bibliographie sur la Bibliothèque nationale du Québec 1616

Bibliographie sur la Charte: une bibliographie annotée sur la Charte canadienne des droits et libertés 2280

"Bibliographie sur la Charte canadienne des droits et libertés" 2356

Bibliographie sur la construction dans les pays froids 5803

Bibliographie sur la coopération régionale 2550

Bibliographie sur la démographie récente des groupes ethno-linguistiques au Canada 4195

"Bibliographie sur la didactique de la géographie" 2974

Bibliographie sur la femme québécoise et le travail 3815

"Bibliographie sur la Francophonie" 2412

Bibliographie sur la glace de mer dans le Nord et autres sujets connexes 5160

Bibliographie sur la guignolée, Nöel, le jour de l'An, la quête de l'Enfant Jésus, l'Epiphanie et le temps des fêtes en général 4558

Bibliographie sur la main d'oeuvre, l'emploi et la formation dans le Nord canadien: aspects majeurs de la question 0641

Bibliographie sur la pollution de l'air des habitations 5275

Bibliographie sur la population du Manitoba 3039

Bibliographie sur la préhistoire de la psychiatrie canadienne au dix-neuvième siècle 5607

Bibliographie sur la propriété immobilière au Canada 2691

Bibliographie sur "la qualité totale" 2752

Bibliographie sur la sculpture québécoise 0678

Bibliographie sur la toponymie du Québec 3053

Bibliographie sur la ville de Joliette 0303

Bibliographie sur la violence à l'égard des enfants 3297

Bibliographie sur l'administration des Indiens du Canada et des États-Unis 3924

Bibliographie sur l'administration publique québécoise/ Quebec public administration: bibliography 2489

Bibliographie sur l'aide canadienne aux pays en voie d'expansion 2393

Bibliographie sur l'aide juridique au Canada 2186

Bibliographie sur l'aide juridique pour les handicapés/ Bibliography on legal aid for the handicapped 2230

Bibliographie sur l'aide juridique/Bibliography on legal aid 2228

Bibliographie sur le bassin de la Yamaska 5055

Bibliographie sur le camionnage 4485

Bibliographie sur le Code civil du Québec 2355

Bibliographie sur le delta du Mackenzie 0617

Bibliographie sur le développement régional/Bibliography on regional development 2706

Bibliographie sur le droit d'auteur: répertoires de centres gouvernementaux de documentation et de la bibliothèque de droit de l'Université Laval 2257

Bibliographie sur le droit des autochtones 2326

Bibliographie sur le formaldéhyde et la mousse isolante d'urée-formaldéhyde (MIUF)/Bibliography on formaldehyde and urea formaldehyde foam insulation (UFFI) 5804

Bibliographie sur le logement et les familles monparentales 4409

Bibliographie sur le loisir de plein air 1785

Bibliographie sur le phototrophisme des animaux marins 5349

Bibliographie sur le régionalisme dans les Maritimes et la collaboration entre les gouvernements 0267

Bibliographie sur le Saint-Laurent 0329

Bibliographie sur le saumon de la province de Québec 5321

Bibliographie sur le viol: et plus particulièrement sur la recherche au Canada dans ce domaine 2191

Bibliographie sur le zonage au Canada 4398

"Bibliographie sur l'éducation au Canada français" 3562

Bibliographie sur l'éducation au Québec 3404

Bibliographie sur l'éducation préscolaire 3616

Une bibliographie sur l'eider/A bibliography of eiders 5409

"Bibliographie sur l'enseignement de la géographie" 2954

Bibliographie sur l'enseignement supérieur 3585, 3599

muséographie et l'administration de musées et de galeries d'art 4565

Bibliography: archives course 1609

Bibliography: Canadian Petroleum Association publications 4867

Bibliography: Canadian political parties, 1791-1867, 1867- (including books, review articles, graduate theses and pamphlets) 2387

"Bibliography: Canadian refugee policy: a history" 3867

Bibliography: computer programs for creating a bibliography with accompanying KWIC index 1691

"A bibliography: development of the multicultural policy in Canada" 4173

Bibliography: energy-efficient community planning 4383

Bibliography: forestry 4948

Bibliography: glaciology of the St. Elias Range, Yukon Territory and Alaska 5122

Bibliography: history of north-eastern Ontario 0480

Bibliography: Indians and education 3411

Bibliography: Manuscript report series nos. 1-430: unedited manuscripts of the Parks Canada research divisions/ Bibliographie: Travaux inédits nos 1-430: manuscrits inédits des divisions de recherches de Parcs Canada 6342

Bibliography: native peoples, James Bay region 3934

Bibliography: occupational safety and health: selected holdings of Technical Library, Accident Prevention Division, Canada Department of Labour/Bibliographie: sécurité et hygiène professionnelles: choix de volumes de la Bibliothèque technique, Division de la prévention des accidents, Ministère du travail du Canada 2828

"Bibliography: recent publications relating to Canada's urban past/Bibliographie: contributions récentes à l'histoire urbaine du Canada" 4415

Bibliography: rehabilitation of pits, quarries, and other surface-mined lands 4811

"Bibliography: research on immersion education for the majority child" 3517

Bibliography: resource frontier communities 0621

Bibliography: scientific papers resulting from Canadian space and upper atmosphere research, 1969-1973 5751, 5761

Bibliography: scientific papers resulting from the Canadian upper atmosphere research program, 1965-1969 5751

Bibliography: some Canadian writings on the mass media/ Bibliographie: études canadiennes sur les mass media 0954

Bibliography: Symposium 1977: Prepared for Symposium 1977, The end of an era, 1880 – Canada – 1914/Bibliographie: Symposium 1977, La fin d'une époque, 1880 – Canada – 1914 0688

A bibliography: television violence and its effect on the family 0955

A bibliography: the long-range transport of air pollutants and acidic precipitation 5159

Bibliography: tourism research studies/Bibliographie: études de recherches de tourisme 1755

Bibliography: War of 1812-14 1890

Bibliography: women's studies in art in Canadian universities and schools of art, 1985 0717

"Bibliography (1758 to 1972) to the Staphylinidae of America north of Mexico (Coleoptera)" 5385

Bibliography and a résumé of current studies on fire history 4966

Bibliography and catalogue of the fossil vertebrata of North America 4528

Bibliography and general report 0031

"A bibliography and historical review of physical anthropology in Canada: 1848-1949" 4531, 4532

Bibliography and index of C.D. Howe Research Institute publications, 1958-1976 2625

Bibliography and index of coal in Saskatchewan and adjoining provinces and states 4801

Bibliography and index of North American Carboniferous brachiopods (1898-1968) 4548

Bibliography and literature review of the resource base of St. Lawrence Islands National Park 3007

A bibliography and selected source material for the study of Paul-Émile Borduas and his relationship to other French Canadian automatists 6859

Bibliography and some aspects of physical oceanography in the Gulf of St. Lawrence 5047

Bibliography compiled for A preliminary study on the environmental effects of various seabed exploitation schemes 5111

"Bibliography [Folklore]/Bibliographie [Folklore]" 4605

A bibliography for courses in the history of Canadian science, medicine, and technology 4627

A bibliography for examination of forms of training for scientific and technical work 1594

A bibliography for folklore studies in Nova Scotia 4561

Bibliography for professional development 3933

A bibliography for regional development: classified list of limited references 4307

A bibliography for the conservation of structures in Ottawa 0750

Bibliography for the study of British Columbia's domestic material history 1988

"Bibliography for the study of Eskimo religion" 1527

"Bibliography for Ukrainian researchers: resources at the Yorkton Public Library" 4235

Bibliography [Human rights and civil liberties] 2241

A bibliography in short-title catalog form of Canadiana in French, 1545-1631 2035

A bibliography in short-title catalog form of eighteenth century editions of the writings of Louis Armand de Lom d'Arce, Baron de Lahontan 7111

A bibliography in short-title catalog form of Jesuit relations, printed accounts of events in Canada, 1632-73, sent by Jesuit missionaries to France 2067

A bibliography in short-title catalog form of seventeenth and eighteenth century editions of the writings of Louis Hennepin, Recollet explorer and missionary 7054

"Bibliography [Malcolm Lowry]" 7162

Bibliography [Northern exploration] 0636

A bibliography of 19th century Ontario 0451

A bibliography of AECL publications on environmental research/Une bibliographie des publications de l'EACL sur les recherches écologiques 5163

A bibliography of AECL publications on reactor safety/Une bibliographie des publications de l'EACL sur la sûreté des réacteurs 5785

A bibliography of agricultural and rural restructuring 4721

Bibliography of agricultural research in central British Columbia, 1938-1979 4690

Bibliography of agriculture in northern Canada and the arctic tundra in Alaska, 1950-1970 4677

A bibliography of local history collection (Town of Simcoe and Haldimand-Norfolk region) at Simcoe Public Library 0465

Bibliography of lodgepole pine literature 5531

"A bibliography of loyalist source material in Canada" 1976

A bibliography of Loyalist source material in the United States, Canada, and Great Britain 2024

A bibliography of Macmillan of Canada imprints, 1906-1980: first supplement with corrigenda 1674

A bibliography of Macmillan of Canada imprints 1906-1980 1674

Bibliography of Major André 6801

A bibliography of major planning publications (May 1942 – December 1988) 4425

"Bibliography of Manitoba archaeology" 4540, 4571

A bibliography of Manitoba from holdings in the Legislative Library of Manitoba 0500

Bibliography of Manitoba geology, 1795 to 1988 4873

A bibliography of Manitoba local history: a guide to local and regional histories written about communities in Manitoba 0546

Bibliography of marine geoscience information, Pacific regions of Canada, 1900-1976 4797

Bibliography of masters and doctoral theses on Canadian industrial relations from 1967 to 1978 6108

A bibliography of master's theses in geography: American and Canadian universities 6129

"A bibliography of material culture in Canada 1965-1982" 4588

"Bibliography of material on the Supreme Court of Canada" 2151

Bibliography of material relating to southern Alberta published to 1970 0516

"Bibliography of materials at the Public Archives of Canada relating to the rebellion of 1837-1838" 1918

"Bibliography of materials available in the Women's Educational Resource Centre" 3820

A bibliography of materials for and about native people 3918

"Bibliography of materials in Fort William Public Library relating to Fort William, Port Arthur, and northwestern Ontario" 0430

Bibliography of McGill northern research, 1887-1975 0630

A bibliography of Mennonites in Waterloo County and Ontario 1571

Bibliography of mercury in Manitoba fish 5492

"Bibliography of Métis languages" 4107

"Bibliography of missionary activities and religious change in northwest coast societies" 4096

Bibliography of multistage sulphite pulping of various wood species 5735

Bibliography of New Brunswick geology, (1839 to 1988) 4876

"Bibliography of New England-Maritimes folklore, 1950-1957" 4534

Bibliography of New Quebec 0288

Bibliography of Newfoundland 0263

A bibliography of Newfoundland education 3467

Bibliography of Newfoundland history 0272

Bibliography of Newfoundland history books in print 0272

Bibliography of Newfoundland newspapers 6036

Bibliography of nickel 4756

A bibliography of NMR applications for forestry research 5012

Bibliography of non-sexist books 1327

"Bibliography of non-sexist children's books" 1323

"A bibliography of North American cherry fruit flies (Diptera: Tephritidae)" 5378

Bibliography of North American dipterology, 1878-1895 5309

"Bibliography of North American dipterology, 1878-1895" 5310

A bibliography of North American folklore and folksong 4535

A bibliography of North American Gasteromycetes: I. Phallales 5443

Bibliography of North American geology 4883

Bibliography of North American Indian mental health 5638

Bibliography of North American invertebrate paleontology 4521

A bibliography of North American paleontology, 1888-1892 4525

"Bibliography of North American Recent benthic foraminifera" 5445

Bibliography of North American shelterbelt research 4943

A bibliography of northern Manitoba 0549

Bibliography of northern North America and Greenland 3912

Bibliography of oceanographic atlases covering Canadian ocean waters 6573

Bibliography of oceanographic information for the inside waters of the southern British Columbia coast 5376

Bibliography of oil sands, heavy oils, and natural asphalts 4822

"A bibliography of Ontario archaeology" 4541

"A bibliography of Ontario directories to 1867" 0452

Bibliography of Ontario history, 1867-1976: cultural, economic, political, social 0467

The bibliography of Ontario history, 1976-1986/La bibliographie d'histoire ontarienne, 1976-1986 0487

Bibliography of "Operation Hazen," 1957-63 5034

Bibliography of "Operation Hazen-Tanquary," 1964-1967 5043

A bibliography of Oxford County 0461

A bibliography of Oxford County and the City of Woodstock, Ontario 0461

A bibliography of Pacific northwest herpetology 5473

A bibliography of papers and reports issued in the Census Field internal series: 1965-1977/Bibliographie des notes et des rapports publiés dans les séries internes du Secteur du recensement 3020

A bibliography of papers and reports published by the Defence Research Establishment Toronto (formerly the Defence Research Medical Laboratories) 1950-1971 5592

"A bibliography of papers on Cicindelidae published in The Canadian Entomologist, (1869-1979)" 5532

A bibliography of papers presented at the annual meetings of the Entomological Society of Alberta, 1953-1978 5448

"A bibliography of papers published on Cicindelidae in the Annual Reports and Proceedings of the Entomological Society of Ontario, 1871-1987" 5550

A bibliography of papers relevant to sanitary engineering practices in northern Saskatchewan townsites 5752

Bibliography of papers relevant to the scattering of thermal neutrons, 1963-1972 5743

A bibliography of parasites and diseases of fishes of Canada: 1879-1969 5355

A bibliography of parasites and diseases of Ontario wildlife 5479

"Bibliography of parliamentary government in Canada" 2370

Bibliography of pedogeography of Canada 4749

"A bibliography of periglacial studies in Quebec" 5042

A bibliography of periodical articles concerning the management and economics of water resources 5057

Bibliography on Saskatchewan uranium inquiries and the northern and global impact of the uranium industry 4869

Bibliography on sentencing in Canada 2141

"Bibliography on sexual harassment" 3812

A bibliography on silos: lateral pressure, field and model-measurements, theories 5775

A bibliography on snow and ice 5027

A bibliography on storm surges and seiches/Bibliographie sur les marées de tempête et les seiches 5217

Bibliography on student services at Canadian universities/ Bibliographie des services aux étudiants dans les universités canadiennes 3439

"Bibliography on Swedish settlement in Alberta, 1890-1930" 4211

Bibliography on technological forecasting and long range planning 5731

Bibliography on temporary shelter for battered women/ Bibliographie sur l'hébergement temporaire pour les femmes victimes de violence 3349

Bibliography on the application of reverse osmosis to industrial and municipal wastewaters 5742

"A bibliography on the arts and crafts of northwest coast Indians" 0680

A bibliography on the biochemistry, nutrition, and related areas of aquatic mammals and Arctic people to 1983 5520

A bibliography on the Canadian arctic 0614

"Bibliography on the Canadian Charter of Rights and Freedoms/Bibliographie sur la Charte canadienne des droits et libertés" 2356

Bibliography on the Cariboo District 0560

Bibliography on the Columbia River Basin 0557

Bibliography on the construction industry in Canada/ Bibliographie sur l'industrie de la construction au Canada 2708

Bibliography on the economic history and geography of the Great Lakes-St. Lawrence drainage basin 2967

A bibliography on the environmental impact of forest resource roads: a list 4958

Bibliography on the family from the fields of theology and philosophy 3082

Bibliography on the fate and effects of Arctic marine oil pollution 5239

A bibliography on the lateral strength of nails 5726

Bibliography on the limnology and fisheries of Canadian freshwaters 4912

Bibliography on the Parliament Buildings 0740

Bibliography on the physical characteristics of the Eastern Townships of Quebec, Canada 4776

"Bibliography on the sociology of women and work: 1970's" 3791

A bibliography on the white sturgeon, (Acipenser transmontanus) Richardson, 1836 5512

A bibliography on the wolverine Gulo gulo 5469

Bibliography on topics related to immigrant settlement and ethnic minority concerns (in the Canadian context) 4232

Bibliography on voluntarism: publications relevant to voluntarism and to the management of voluntary organizations 3295

A Bibliography on winter road construction and related subjects 4454

Bibliography on women: a resource for other disciplines/ Bibliographie sur les femmes: ouvrage de référence pour d'autres disciplines 3838

"Bibliography on women in Canada: non-fiction" 3739

Bibliography on zoning in Canada/Bibliographie sur le zonage au Canada 4398

Bibliography pertaining to environmental aspects of the James Bay Hydroelectric Development 5077

Bibliography pertinent to offshore energy exploration and development/Bibliographie concernant l'exploitation et la mise en valeur des ressources énergétiques en mer 4840

Bibliography re mobility of capital among Pacific Rim countries 2692

"Bibliography [recent publications relating to Canadian ethnic studies]" 4219, 4291

Bibliography related to Indian, Metis and non-status Indian socio-economic development 4011

A bibliography relating to African Canadian history 4278

A bibliography relating to constitutional and economic developments since the royal commission and the Newfoundland Act of 1933 2373

Bibliography relating to disaster nursing 5570

A bibliography relevant to crucifer-feeding flea beetle pests in Canada 5518

Bibliography series [Library and information science] 1741

Bibliography [Thomas Chandler Haliburton] 7040

A bibliography to Arctic grayling (Thymallus arcticus) 5472

Bibliography to the Report [Ontario Royal Commission on Electric Power Planning] 2662

"Bibliography [women and language]" 3826

Bibliograpie des travaux édités ou imprimés en Europe sur les Récollets du Canada 1501

Bibliohrafichnyi pokazhchyk ukraïnskoï presy poza mezhmy Ukraïny/Bibliographical index of the Ukrainian press outside Ukraine 6023

Bibliotheca Americana, or, A chronological catalogue of the most curious and interesting books, pamphlets, state papers, &c ... 0001

Bibliotheca americana: histoire, géographie, voyages, archéologie et linguistique des deux Amériques et des îles Philippines 0013

Bibliotheca americana nova: a catalogue of books relating to America, in various languages, including voyages to the Pacific and round the world, and collections of voyages and travels printed since the year 1700, compiled principally from the works themselves, by O. Rich 6713

Bibliotheca americana vetustissima: a description of works relating to America published between the years 1492 and 1551 0008

Bibliotheca americana. A dictionary of books relating to America, from its discovery to the present time. Begun by Joseph Sabin, continued by Wilberforce Eames, and completed by R.W.G. Vail for the Bibliographical Society of America 0049

Bibliotheca Canadensis, or, A manual of Canadian literature 0009

Bibliotheca Canadensis: a catalogue of a very large collection of books and pamphlets relating to the history, the topography, the manners and customs of the Indians, the trade and government of North America ... 6740

Bibliotheca hispano-americana: a catalogue of Spanish books ... : followed by a collection of works on the aboriginal languages of America 1401

Bibliotheca historica, or A catalogue of 5000 volumes of books and manuscripts relating chiefly to the history and literature of North and South America: among which is included the larger portion of the extraordinary library of the late Henry Stevens, senior, ... 0011

Bibliothèque américaine ou Catalogue des ouvrages relatifs à l'Amérique qui ont paru depuis sa découverte jusqu'à l'an 1700 0003

Bibliothèque canadienne: ou, Annales bibliographiques 0006

Bibliothèque de Canadiana [Expo 67] 0085

Bibliothèque du Centre de musique canadienne 0944

Bibliothèque du Conseil d'hygiène de la province de Québec: catalogue/Library of the Board of Health of province of Quebec: catalogue 5562

Une bibliothèque fondamentale d'une école d'immersion française: 7e – 9e années 3651

Bibliothèque Fort Frontenac: périodiques 5968

Bibliothèque ministérielle art et artistes indiens du Canada: une bibliographie 0723

Bibliothèque nationale du Canada: publications: une liste 1734

Bibliothèque nationale du Canada: une bibliographie 1635

Bibliothèque nationale du Canada présente livres canadiens pour l'exposition de la Bibliothèque nationale à Varsovie/ Biblioteka Narodoway Kanadzie przedstawia ksiezki [sic] Kanadyjskie na wystawie w Bibliotece Narodowej w Warszawie 0117

La bibliothèque paix et sécurité 2556

Bibliothèque universelle des voyages ou Notice complète et raisonnée de tous les voyages anciens et modernes dans les différentes parties du monde ... 1871

Bibliothèques: ressources et facilités: bibliographie choisie 1603

Les bibliothèques canadiennes à l'ère de l'automatisation: synthèse bibliographique 1970-1972 1596

Bibliothèques dans le domaine de la santé: bibliographie sélective 1641

Les bibliothèques de Edward et W.S. Maxwell dans les collections de la Bibliothèque Blackader-Lauterman d'architecture et d'art, Université McGill 0801

Bibliothèques des pénitenciers: une bibliographie 1717

Bibliothèques des sciences de la santé: bibliographie sélective, 1981-1984 1641

Les bibliothèques parlementaires: histoire, fonctions, services: bibliographie sélective et annotée 1732

Les bibliothèques personnelles au Québec: inventaire analytique et préliminaire des sources 1656

Les bibliothèques universitaires du Québec: essai de bibliographie 1633

Le bien-être social et économique: bibliographie sélective 3104

Big country: a bibliography of the history of the Kamloops Region & Southern Cariboo 0588

"Bilan de la recherche sur l'administration publique québécoise" 2417

Bilan des études spécifiques au site de Coteau-du-Lac 4582

Bilan des évaluations portant sur les services sociaux 3303

Bilan des recherches, Direction des services de recherche et de planification, 1972-1976 3513

Bilan des recherches ethnohistoriques concernant les groupes autochtones du Québec 4068

Bilingualism in the Americas: a bibliography and research guide 1417

Bilingualism in the federal Canadian public service 1450

Le bilinguisme canadien: bibliographie analytique et guide du chercheur 1444

Le bilinguisme chez l'enfant et l'apprentissage d'une langue seconde: bibliographie analytique/Child bilingualism and second language learning: a descriptive bibliography 1431

Bill 88: bibliography/Projet de loi 88: bibliographie 2552

A bio-bibliographical finding list of Canadian musicians and those who have contributed to music in Canada 0899

"Bio-bibliographie [commentée sur Jean-Claude Germain]" 7010

"Bio-bibliographie d'Albert Faucher" 6976

Bio-bibliographie de Charles-Yvon Thériault, journaliste (1948-1956) 7330

Bio-bibliographie de Joseph-Edmond Roy 7283

Bio-bibliographie de M. l'abbé Ovila Fournier, L.Sc., professeur à l'Institut de biologie de l'Université de Montréal, 1935-1955 6988

"Bio-bibliographie de Marius Barbeau" 6827

Bio-bibliographie de Marius Barbeau, précédée d'un hommage à Marius Barbeau par Luc Lacourcière et Félix-Antoine Savard 6826

Bio-bibliographie de Mgr Camille Roy, P.A., V.G., recteur de l'Université Laval 7279

Bio-bibliographie de Michel Beaulieu, écrivain, 1941-1985 [microforme] 6832

Bio-bibliographie de Monseigneur Antoine d'Eschambault, p.d., diocèse de Saint-Boniface, Manitoba 6970

Bio-bibliographie de Monsieur Jean-Baptiste Meilleur, 1796-1878, médecin, auteur, fondateur du Collège de l'Assomption, 1832 et premier superintendant de l'Instruction publique dans le Bas-Canada, 1843-1855 7187

Bio-bibliographie de Narcisse-E. Dionne 6955

Bio-bibliographie de Robert-Lionel Séguin 7301

Bio-bibliographie d'écrivains canadiens-français: une liste des bio-bibliographies présentées par les élèves de l'École de Bibliothécaires, Université de Montréal, 1937-1947 1008

Bio-bibliographie du R.P. Ephrem Longpré, O.F.M. 7154

Bio-bibliographie du R.P. Georges Simard, o.m.i. 7308

Bio-bibliographie du Révérend père Léo Boismenu 6856

"Bio-bibliographie [Gérard Bessette]" 6839

"Bio-bibliographie sommaire de la plupart des écrivains ayant participé à la Rencontre québécoise internationale des écrivains" 1163

Bio-bibliographies canadiennes-françaises 0094

Bio-bibliographies et bibliographies. Liste des travaux bibliographiques des étudiants en bibliothéconomie de l'Université de Montréal 0093

Bio-bibliography of Charles Hill-Tout 7064

"Bio-bibliography of Diamond Jenness" 7077

Bio-bibliography of Dr. Edwin C. Guillet 7036

Bio-bibliography of J.B. Rudnyckyj 7287

A bio-bibliography of Newfoundland songs in printed sources 0868

"Biobibliographie: Marie-Claire Blais" 6851

Biobibliography of publishing scientists in Ontario between 1914 and 1939 4629

Biochimie des écosystèmes des forêts tempérées: publications sur les inventaires et la dynamique de la biomasse et des éléments nutritifs 4984

Biodegradation of silicate and aluminosilicate minerals: a literature review 4847

Biogeochemistry of temperate forest ecosystems: literature on inventories and dynamics of biomass and nutrients/ Biochimie des écosystèmes des forêts tempérées: publications sur les inventaires et la dynamique de la biomasse et des éléments nutritifs 4984

Cordwood masonry construction: an annotated bibliography 0785

A core collection of materials on the disabled, suitable for public libraries: to observe the International year of disabled persons 3215

"Core French: a selected annotated resource list" 3633

Core reference for Manitoba schools, K-12: a selection guide for school libraries 1632

Correctional and criminological literature published in Canada 2137

Correctional literature published in Canada/Ouvrages de criminologie publiés au Canada 2137

Cost-benefit analysis and the economics of investment in human resources: an annotated bibliography 2806

Cost of living adjustments (COLA): a bibliography 2825

"Costume in Canada: an annotated bibliography" 4593

The costume of the North American Indian: an annotated bibliography of sources from journals 4025

Counter-terrorism: bibliography 2308

County atlases of Canada: a descriptive catalogue/Atlas de comtés canadien: catalogue descriptif 6520

County maps: land ownership maps of Canada in the 19th century/Cartes de comtés: cartes foncières du Canada au XIXe siècle 6556

"The County of Wellington: a bibliography" 0421

Coup d'oeil sur la littérature traitant du développement et de l'intégration des minorités ethnoculturelles 4252

Courrier du livre 0030

"A course in Canadian legal history" 2240

"Court exposé sur notre bibliographie générale des voyageurs au Canada" 1955

The Courtenay River estuary: status of environmental knowledge to 1978: report of the Estuary Working Group, Department of the Environment, Regional Board Pacific Region 5152

Cousin Cinderella: a guide to historical literature pertaining to Canadian women 3773

Le coût des soins médicaux 5692

The Coutts collection: a selected descriptive bibliography 6788

The Cowichan-Chemainus River estuaries: status of environmental knowledge to 1975: report of the Estuary Working Group, Department of the Environment, Regional Board Pacific Region 5098

CPV index [microform] 0153

La crainte du châtiment: la dissuasion 2148

Cranbrook Herald, 1900-1908 0565

CRAPE [Commission des Responsables de l'aide personnelle aux élèves] et documentation en bibliothèque: [bibliographie] 3622

Crawford Brough Macpherson: a bibliography 7169

The Crawford Symposium 6921

Creating success with native Indian students: a bibliographic source book on instructional strategies for teachers 3637

The credit system: an annotated bibliography 3487

CRIAW National Clearinghouse on New Reproductive Technologies: list of materials received to August 24, 1987 5699

Crime, criminal law and justice in Canadian history: a select bibliography, origins to 1940 2196

Crime in the country: a literature review of crime and criminal justice in rural areas 2283

Crime prevention: a selected bibliography 2143

Crime prevention literature: a catalogue of selected library holdings 2256

Criminal intelligence and security intelligence: a selective bibliography 2336

Criminal investigation: a selective literature review and bibliography 2243

Criminal justice research: a selective review 2229

Criminal justice statistical development: bibliography 2207

Criminologie canadienne: bibliographie commentée: la criminalité et l'administration de la justice criminelle au Canada/Canadian criminology: annotated bibliographie: crime and the administration of criminal justice in Canada 2174

"[Criminology: a bibliography]" 2144

Criminology: a reader's guide 2348

Crisis management: an annotated bibliography 2748

The crisis of the revolution: being the story of Arnold and André 6801

Critères d'identification des tâches à robotiser: revue de littérature 5801

Critères physiques en aménagement récréatifs à la campagne: recherches bibliographiques 1778

A critical assessment of the theatre criticism of Nathan Cohen with a bibliography and selected anthology 6912

"A critical discography of Canadian music/Une discographie critique de musique canadienne" 0895

A critical survey of recent geographical research on la Franco-Américanie 3064

Critical writings on Commonwealth literatures: a selective bibliography to 1970, with a list of theses and dissertations 1093

A critically annotated bibliography of works published and unpublished relating to the culture of French Newfoundlanders 0227

"Criticism of Canadian fiction since 1945: a selected checklist" 1098

La critique littéraire des oeuvres canadiennes-françaises dans le journal Le Canada, 1940-1946 [microforme]: bibliographie descriptive et analytique 1235

"Croatian-Canadian periodical publications: a preliminary check list" 5893

"Croatian imprints of Canada: a preliminary check list" 4162

Crop entomology [bibliography] 4659

Cropping systems: an evaluative review of the literature 4645

Cross cultural childrearing: an annotated bibliography 4237

Cross-cultural social work in Canada: an annotated bibliography 3195

Cross-index to the maps and illustrations of the Geological Survey and Mines Branch (Bureau of Mines) of Canada, 1843-1946 (incl.) 6497

Crow-Rate, the great debate: a historical bibliography 4482

Crowding and corrections: a bibliography 2281

Crown corporations in Canada: bibliography of material in the Library of the Ontario Ministry of Treasury, Economics and Intergovernmental Affairs 2631

Crucial maps in the early cartography and place-nomenclature of the Atlantic coast of Canada 6508

Cultural literacy in education: a literature review 3674

Culture and alcohol use: a bibliography of anthropological studies 4543

Le droit à la vie privée 2324

Le droit à la vie privée: bibliographie sélective 2324

Droit à l'information et protection des renseignements personnels: bibliographie 2273

Le droit d'auteur 2300

Le droit d'auteur: bibliographie sélective 2158

Le droit d'auteur: une bibliographie sélective 2222

"Droit de la concurrence et politique officielle au Canada, 1979-1982: une bibliographie" 2250

Le droit de vote des femmes au Québec: bibliographie sélective 3883

Drug education resources directory 3704

The Drug file: a comprehensive bibliography on drugs and doping in sport/Dossier dopage: une bibliographie complète sur les drogues et le dopage dans le sport 1868

Drug use and driving: a bibliography of the scientific literature on the effects of drugs other than ethanol on driving or simulated driving of automobiles, piloting or simulated piloting of aircraft, and driving-related mental and motor performance 5590

Du mot à l'image: guide de lectures pour une approche systématique de l'image fonctionnelle 3143

Dublin Public Libraries and the Canadian Embassy present an exhibition of Canadian books: Monday 15th-Wednesday 31st July 1991, Central Library, ILAC Centre 0175

The Duncan Campbell Scott Symposium 7297

Duncan-Cowichan District, V.I. 0563

Durability of building materials: a bibliography using a keyword guide 5800

E.J. Hughes: a bibliography 7071

"E.J. Pratt: a preliminary checklist" 7244

E.J. Pratt: a preliminary checklist of publications by and about him with a shortlist of manuscript collections 7245

E.J. Pratt: an annotated bibliography 7246, 7247

The E.J. Pratt symposium 7245

"E.K. Brown (1905-1951): the critic and his writings" 6877

EAMES bibliography 5181

"Earle Birney: a bibliography in progress, 1923-1969" 6846

Earle Birney: an annotated bibliography 6844, 6845

Early B.C. books: an overview of trade book publishing in the 1800s with checklists and selected bibliography related to British Columbiana 1649

Early bibles of America: being a descriptive account of bibles published in the United States, Mexico and Canada 1577

The early bibliography of the province of Ontario, Dominion of Canada, with other information. A supplemental chapter of Canadian archaeology 0420

"Early books and printing in British Columbia" 0600

Early Canadian children's books, 1763-1840: a bibliographical investigation into the nature and extent of early Canadian children's books and books for young people/Livres de l'enfance & livres de la jeunesse au Canada, 1763-1840: étude bibliographique 1328

Early Canadian topographical map series: the Geological Survey of Canada, 1842-1949 6591

"Early Canadiana" 0069

Early childhood education 3430

Early childhood education: bibliography 3508

The early Jewish presence in Canada: a book lover's ramble through Jewish Canadiana 4154

"The early literature of the Northwest coast" 0555

Early maps of Ohio and the West 6477

Early prayer books of America: being a descriptive account of prayer books published in the United States, Mexico and Canada 1578

Early printed maps of Canada. I. 1540-1703 6603

Early Toronto newspapers, 1793-1867: a catalogue of newspapers published in the Town of York and the City of Toronto from the beginning to Confederation 6012

Earth sciences of the Hudson Bay Lowland: literature review and annotated bibliography 4826

"East-Indian-Canadian periodical publications: a preliminary check list" 5910

East Indian immigration into Canada, 1880-1920: a bibliography 4137

East Indians in Canada: an essay with a bibliography 4147

Eastern Arctic Study: annotated bibliography 0643

Eastern Canadian boreal and sub-Arctic wetlands: a resource document 5291

Échange-renseignements: relevé d'études, de mémoires et de réalisations en action sociale 3199

L'École, son contexte social et le contexte de l'élève: relevé bibliographique commenté un vie d'une recherche 3575

L'école à aire ouverte: une bibliographie/Open schools: a bibliography 3457

The ecological effects of slashburning with particular reference to British Columbia: a literature review 4974

Ecological soil management: an annotated bibliography 4672

Écologie de l'archipel arctique canadien: bibliographie sélective 5178

Écologie et évaluation environnementale: bibliographie annotée 5192

L'écologie et la récupération des terres perturbées par l'activité minière: bibliographie sélective de la litérature[sic] canadienne 5165

L'écologie marine du Détroit de Lancaster et des eaux adjacentes: bibliographie commentée 5129

Ecology and environmental impact assessment: an annotated bibliography 5193

Ecology and management of the grassland and forested rangelands of interior British Columbia: an annotated bibliography 4972

The ecology and reclamation of lands disturbed by mining: a selected bibliography of Canadian references/L'écologie et la récupération des terres perturbées par l'activité minière: bibliographie sélective de la litérature[sic] canadienne 5165

Ecology of the Canadian Arctic Archipelago: selected references 5179

Economic development consultant reports: bibliography 3963

"Economic factors in the Pacific area: a review bibliography" 2559

Economic history of Canada: a guide to information sources 2636

Economic impacts of heritage institutions on the Canadian economy: bibliography 2715

Economic reports: a selected bibliography of economic reports produced by Ontario government departments 2582

Economics of forestry: a bibliography for the United States and Canada, 1940-1947 4920

Economics of immigration and racial discrimination: a literature survey (1970-1989) 4263

Economics of private woodlot management: a literature review/Les aspects économiques de l'aménagement des boisés privés: une étude documentaire 5020

État des recherches sur la pollution au Canada 5105

L'État et les personnes âgées, 1980-1991: bibliographie sélective et annotée 3352

Ethanol-alcohol from wastes: a literature review 5782

"Ethel Wilson: a bibliography, 1919-1977" 7367

Ethel Wilson: an annotated bibliography 7368

The ethical pharmaceutical industry and some of its economic effects: an annotated bibliography 2630

Ethics in sport: a specialized bibliography from the SPORT database/Éthique du sport: une bibliographie spécialisée de la base de données SPORT 1855

Éthique du sport: une bibliographie spécialisée de la base de données SPORT 1855

Ethnic and immigration groups: the United States, Canada, and England 4215

"Ethnic and multicultural materials for children's reading: bibliographical sources" 4255

Ethnic and native Canadian literature: a bibliography 1284

Ethnic and racial minorities in North America: a selected bibliography of the geographical literature 4161

Ethnic folklife dissertations from the United States and Canada, 1960-1980: a selected, annotated bibliography 6184

"Ethnic folklore in Canada: a preliminary survey" 4169

Ethnic groups: bibliography materials in M.E.R.C. 4227

Ethnic groups in British Columbia: a selected bibliography based on a check-list of material in the Provincial Library and Archives 4129

"Ethnic groups in Manitoba: a select bibliography" 4185

"The ethnic press in Ontario" 6032

Ethnic publications in Canada: newspapers, periodicals, magazines, bulletins, newsletters 5961

Ethnic studies in Canada 4215

"Ethnic themes in geographic research on western Canada" 4182

"Ethnica Canadiana: a select bibliography" 4180

Ethnicity and the mass media in Canada: an annotated bibliography 4276

Ethnocultural entrepreneurship: an overview and annotated bibliography 4271

Ethnographic bibliography of North America 3970

Ethnographic bibliography of northeastern North America 4561

"L'ethnologie juridique des Inuit: approche bibliographique critique" 3996

Étienne Gilson: a bibliography/Étienne Gilson: une bibliographie 7018

Étienne Gilson: une bibliographie 7018

Une étude bibliographique de l'utilisation, par les oiseaux, des habitats agricoles dans la région des Grands Lacs et du Saint-Laurent 5560

Étude bibliographique des publications du Bureau international du travail au Ministère du travail, Québec 6225

"Étude bibliographique et historique sur la morale pratique du jansénisme du P. Louis Hennepin, récollet" 7056

"Étude bibliographique sur les rapports de l'Association de la propagation de la foi à Montréal" 1508

"L'étude de l'agriculture québécoise: commentaires et bibliographie" 4670

Étude de l'aide de traceurs du déplacement de sédiments à grain fin dans les systèmes aquatiques: étude documentaire 5277

Étude de l'enseignement de l'anglais, langue seconde dans les écoles franco-ontariennes 3503

Étude des textes relatifs aux caractéristiques des eaux usées et aux techniques d'épuration dans l'industrie du traitement du bois 4960

Étude du plateau continental polaire: titres et résumés scientifiques publiés grâce au soutien de l'ÉPCP 4633

Étude et interprétation des ouvrages portant sur le prêt entre bibliothèques 1612

Les études autochtones au Canada: guide de recherche 4104

Études canadiennes: publications et thèses étrangères 0177

Études canadiennes-Canadian studies: books, atlases and other illustrative materials relating to social, political, economic and cultural affairs in Canada, selected from the holdings of the Library of the University of Birmingham: exhibition celebrating the designation of the university as a Regional Canadian Study Centre, May 1981, the Library, University of Birmingham, May 15th – May 22nd, 1981 0136

Les études de la femme à l'Université de Montréal: répertoire des mémoires et des thèses complétés de 1962 à 1983 (juin) 6167

Études d'impact socio-économique relatives à des projets de pipeline et à certains projets de developpement nordique: bibliographie 0632

Les études ethniques au Québec: bilan et perspectives 4217

Les Études féministes au Canada 3903

"Études psychologiques et socioculturelles de l'alcoolisme: inventaire des travaux disponibles au Québec depuis 1960" 3157

"Études réalisées pour la Commission Laurendeau-Dunton" 2401

"Les études sur la politique canadienne: une contribution modeste mais distincte" 2532

"Études sur le roman canadien-français: essai bibliographique" 1039

L'étudiant handicapé: vers une meilleure intégration au collège: bibliographie annotée 3594

"European Community-Canada relations: a selected bibliography, 1976-1981" 2464

European immigration and ethnicity in the United States and Canada: a historical bibliography 4216

Evaluating the arts in education: an annotated bibliography 3557

L'évaluation de l'apprentissage: bibliographie annotée 3583

L'évaluation des administrateurs: bibliographie 2606

L'évaluation des tâches: bibliographie annotée des documents disponibles à l'IRAT 2858

Evaluation instruments locally developed in Ontario: an annotated catalogue of material developed by school boards and other agencies 3548

Evaluation of impaired driver programs: a literature review 3178

Evaluation of student teachers 3522

An evaluative ethno-historical bibliography of the Malecite Indians 3953

Événements d'hier: recension de brochures et de plaquettes anciennes 1981

"Évolution de la maison rurale traditionnelle dans la région de Québec: bibliographie" 0742

Evolution des conceptions urbaines: bibliographie générale 4372

Guidelist of unpublished Canadian string orchestra music suitable for student performers 0926

Guides à l'intention des usagers des bibliothèques de collèges canadiens: liste des manuels et brochures conservés au Centre de documentation sur les bibliothèques 1655

Guides à l'intention des usagers des bibliothèques gouvernementales canadiennes: liste des manuels et brochures conservés au Centre de documentation sur les bibliothèques 1650

Guides de voyage au Québec 0391

Gun control: a bibliography since 1970: Canada, Great Britain, United States 2155

Gustave Guillaume et la psycho-systématique du langage: bibliographie annotée 7035

Gynocritics: feminist approaches to Canadian and Quebec women's writing 3851

Habitat bibliography: a selected bibliography of Canadian references on human settlements 4362

Habitudes de vie et santé: revue de la recherche 5651

"Haliburton: a sketch and bibliography" 7041

Halifax, N.S., social, economic and municipal studies, 1970-1980 0249

"Halifax in books" 0196

"'Hall of fame blocks women': re-righting literary history: women and B.C. literary magazines" 5972

"Halley's comet: a bibliography of Canadian newspaper sources, 1835-36 and 1910" 5811

The Hamilton working class, 1820-1977: a bibliography 2856

Handbook of Indians of Canada 3908

Handbook on climate data sources of the Atmospheric Environment Service 5261

Les handicapés, 1975-1986 3286

The handicapped, 1975-1986/Les handicapés, 1975-1986 3286

Handwriting: I. Instruction in handwriting in Ontario schools: II. Handwriting: an annotated bibliography 3568

Harp seals and hooded seals (Phoca groenlandica and Cystophora cristata): a guide to the scientific literature: prepared for Greenpeace Foundation of Canada 5482

Harry Somers 7316

"Hate literature and freedom of expression in Canada: an annotated bibliography" 2354

Hazardous substances in Canada: a selected, annotated bibliography 2683

Healey Willan 7365

Healey Willan catalogue 7364

Healey Willan centennial year 1980: [first of his choral compositions] 7363

Health, psychological and social factors: an annotated bibliography/La santé, les facteurs psychologiques et sociologiques: bibliographie annotée 1828

The health administrator's library: comprehensive bibliography of the materials available in the Canadian Hospital Association Library 5613

Health and disease of American Indians north of Mexico: a bibliography, 1800-1969 5577

Health and health education: selected references/Santé et éducation sanitaire: bibliographie choisie 5605

Health and safety aspects of visual display terminals: a comprehensive bibliography 5648

Health and safety hazards in the school environment 3675

Health and safety of laboratory workers in Canada: a review of the literature 5649

Health and safety of visual display terminals: a bibliography 5646

Health and safety on the job: audio-visual catalogue 6689

Health and social services administration: an annotated bibliography 5626

Health and well being of nurses with emphasis on health hazards in the nurses' work environment/Santé et bien-être des infirmières plus particulièrement sur risques en milieu infirmier 5606

Health care costs/Le coût des soins médicaux 5692

Health care sector unionization and collective bargaining: a bibliography, 1970-1977 2840

Health help: children's health information: a guide to national resources 5689

The health of the Eskimos: a bibliography, 1857-1967 5573

Health science libraries: selected references/Bibliothèques dans le domaine de la santé: bibliographie sélective 1641

Health sciences libraries: selected references, 1981-1984 1641

Heap leaching literature review 4858

The Helen F. McRae collection: a bibliography of Korean relations with Canadians and other western peoples, which includes a checklist of documents and reports, 1898-1975 1541

Hennepin, ses voyages et ses oeuvres 1886

Henri Bourassa: biographie, index des écrits, index de la correspondance publique 1895-1924 6863

Henry Harrisse: biographical and bibliographical sketch 7047

Heritage conservation: a selected bibliography, 1979 0757

Heritage history biography 2009

Heritage language education: a literature review 3618

Heritage language resources: an annotated bibliography 1487

Heritage languages: a bibliography 1459

Heritage of York: an historical bibliography, 1793-1840 0447

Heritage rivers bibliography: selected references from ARC Branch, Parks Canada card index 1794

Heures d'affaires dans les établissements commerciaux le dimanche: bibliographie 2740

Higher education with emphasis on nursing programs: selected references/Enseignement supérieur, principalement programmes d'enseignement infirmier: bibliographie choisie 3479

"Highlights of domestic building in pre-confederation Quebec and Ontario as seen through travel literature from 1763 to 1860" 0767

Highlights of research in sheep production in western Canada during the last thirty years 4712

Highways 4511

Hillbilly heaven: discography 0920

His own man: essays in honour of Arthur Reginald Marsden Lower 7157

Hispanic writers in Canada: a preliminary survey of the activities of Spanish and Latin-American writers in Canada 1255

Histoire de la profession infirmière au Canada: bibliographie sélective 5578

L'histoire des canaux du Québec: bilan et perspectives 4500

Histoire des communautés religieuses au Québec: bibliographie 1557

Histoire des femmes au Canada: bibliographie sélective/ Women's history in Canada: a selective bibliography 3899

L'histoire des idées au Québec, 1760-1960: bibliographie des études 2076

Impact of harvesting on forest environments and resources: a bibliography with abstracts 4942

Impact of harvesting on forest environments and resources: a review of the literature and evaluation of research needs 4942

The impact of logging on woodland caribou (Rangifer tarandus caribou): a literature review 4983

The impact of saline waters upon freshwater biota: a literature review and bibliography 5126

Impacts de la loi 90, L.R.Q. chap. P-41.1, dans la région de Québec: bibliographie concernant la protection du territoire agricole 4698

Impacts de la télématique sur l'aménagement et l'habitat: essai et bibliographie 4395

Impacts of forest harvesting and regeneration on forest sites 5009

Impacts of forest harvesting on physical properties of soils with reference to increased biomass recovery: a review 5003

Impacts of major pests on forest growth and yield in the prairie provinces and the Northwest Territories: a literature review 5017

Les imprimés dans le Bas-Canada, 1801-1840: bibliographie analytique 0298

"Imprimés en langues indiennes conservés aux Archives historiques Oblates, Ottawa" 3939

Improving durability of round timbers of some Canadian softwoods: an annotated bibliography 4944

Impurity limits for cast copper alloys: a literature survey of tin bronze 5763

The IMS directory of publications 5989

In cold blood: a directory of criminous books by members of the Crime Writers of Canada 1300

In print: publications available from the Ontario Ministry of Industry, Trade and Technology 6382

In review: Canadian books for children: 305 titles recommended, 1967-1972 1320

In review: Canadian books for young people 1351

In search of Canadian materials 0128

"In the library" 2786

In the mainstream: a bibliography on the disabled in Manitoba 3243

In the works: back roads to next spring's Gerry Gilbert bibliography 7014

Les incidences à terres de l'exploitation en mer des hydrocarbures: bibliographie annotée 5197

Income, income security and the Canadian welfare state, 1978-1987: a selected bibliography 3331

Income security: publications and sources of information/La sécurité du revenu: publications et sources de renseignements 2774

Income tax references/Références à la loi de l'impôt sur le revenu 2689

Incubateurs d'entreprises: bibliographie française et anglaise, 1986 2719

Independent study 3448

Independent study: a bibliography 3463

An index and guide to robotics research and development in Canada 5806

Index and list of titles, Fisheries Research Board of Canada and associated publications, 1900-1964 6267

Index and list of titles, Fisheries Research Board of Canada and associated publications, 1965-72 6284

Index and list of titles, publications of the Fisheries Research Board of Canada, 1901-1954 6240

Index de la production cinématographique canadienne/Index of Canadian film production 6631

Index de plans des cantons de l'Ouest canadien 6541

Index des Contributions du Département des Pêcheries 4887

Index des films canadiens de long métrage, 1913-1985 6673

Index des mémoires présentées à la Commission royale d'enquête sur l'enseignement dans la province de Québec, 1961-1963 3523

Index des organismes et répertoires féminins au Canada 3859

Index du catalogue de la Bibliothèque du parlement: IIe partie: bibliothèque générale 6727

Index général: recueil des traités du Canada, 1965-1974 6259

Index of BETT's reports 5814

Index of Canadian film production 6631

Index of Canadian literary theses (January 1969-September 1971): 1786 subjects 6113

Index of Canadian nursing research 5625

Index of Canadian nursing studies/Répertoire des études canadiennes sur les soins infirmiers 5625

Index of Canadian Tax Foundation publications to ... 2590

Index of geological maps accompanying annual reports, volumes 1 to 45, 1891 to 1936 6491

Index of geophysical publications, series, and contributions of the Dominion Observatory and its successor the Earth Physics Branch of the Department of Energy, Mines and Resources, Canada through December, 1974, with addenda 6295

Index of graduate theses in agricultural engineering and related fields 6191

Index of industrial relations literature 2941

Index of publications, 1948-1973 [Canada Department of Energy, Mines and Resources, Gravity Division] 6287

Index of publications of the Geological Survey of Canada (1845-1958) 6244

Index of research in northern Alberta sponsored by the Northern Alberta Development Council 0547

Index of selected articles from Canadian journals pertaining to the forest products industries, 1965-1967 4921

Index of selected publications, 1979 [Energy, Mines and Resources Canada]/Répertoire des publications choisies, 1979 [Énergie, mines et ressources Canada] 6326

Index of the lectures, papers and historical documents published by the Literary and Historical Society of Quebec, and also the names of their authors, together with a list of unpublished papers read before the society, 1829 to 1891 1885

"An index of theses relating to the history of the Anglican Church of Canada" 6077

Index of underground-environment dust reports: CANMET-Mining Research Laboratories, 1960-1985/Liste de rapports sur la poussière en milieu souterrain: CANMET-Laboratoires de recherche minière, 1960-1985 4851

Index of urban and regional studies, Province of Alberta, 1950-1974 4341

Index to annual reports of the Minister of Mines, 1937-1943: and bulletins 1-17, published by the Department of Mines, British Columbia 6257

Index to annual reports of the Minister of Mines of the Province of British Columbia for the years 1874 to 1936, inclusive 6257

Index to assessment reports, 1864-1980 [Nova Scotia Department of Mines and Energy] 6332

Index to BCSLA publications 1593

Index to bedrock geological mapping, British Columbia: including publications of the Geological Survey of Canada, British Columbia Ministry of Energy, Mines and Petroleum Resources, and journal articles, theses, and company reports 6570, 6581

Index to Canadian children's records 0913

Index to Canadian women's groups and directories 3860

Index to DIAND geology publications, Northwest Territories 4864

Index to DIAND geology publications, Yukon 4865

Index to federal scientific and technical contributions to forestry literature 1901-1971 4939

Index to geological, bedrock topography, soils, and groundwater maps of Alberta 6564

Index to Indian acts, 1876-1978/Répertoire des lois relatives aux Indiens, 1876-1978 4042

Index to Manuscript reports of the biological stations, no. 1-600, and Manuscript reports of the technological stations, no. 1-57, together with the titles of the papers in these two series 6238

Index to mineral assessment reports to January 1977 6332

Index to Ontario education research: ONTERIS 3612

Index to plant distribution maps in North American periodicals through 1972 6557

Index to publications, open file reports and theses, 1862-1980 [Nova Scotia, Department of Mines and Energy] 6333

Index to publications of the British Columbia Department of Mines: annual reports of the Minister of Mines, 1937 to 1953 and bulletins nos. 1 to 35 6257

Index to publications of the British Columbia Department of Mines and Petroleum Resources 6257

Index to published reports and maps, Division of Mines, 1891 to 1977 6316

Index to published reports and maps, Mines and Minerals Division, 1978-1986 6316

Index to reports of Geological Survey of Canada from 1927-50 6245

Index to reports of Geological Survey of Canada from 1951-59 6253

An index to selected Canadian provincial government publications: for librarians, teachers and booksellers 6408

Index to staff publications in the technical literature, 1968-1986 5826

Index to the archival publications of the Literary and Historical Society of Quebec, 1824-1924 1903

Index to the catalogue of the Library of Parliament: part II: general library/Index du catalogue de la Bibliothèque du parlement: IIe partie: bibliothèque générale 6727

An index to the described life histories, early stages and hosts of the macrolepidoptera of the continental United States and Canada 5371

Index to the publications of the Ontario Historical Society, 1899-1972 1979

An index to the publications of the staff of the Freshwater Institute, Winnipeg, 1974-75 5397

An index to the publications of the staff of the Freshwater Institute, Winnipeg; the Biological Station and Technological Unit, London; and the Central Biological Station, Winnipeg: 1944-1973 5397

An index to the publications of the staff of the western region, Department of Fisheries and Oceans, 1978-79 5397

Index to township plans of the Canadian West/Index de plans des cantons de l'Ouest canadien 6541

Index to Vernon Blair Rhodenizer's Canadian literature in English 1030

Index translationum. Répertoire international des traductions. International bibliography of translations 1494

Indian, Inuit, Métis: selected bibliography 1344

Indian, Metis and Inuit of Canada in theses and dissertations, 1892-1987 6197

"[Indian and Eskimo education, anthropology and the North: bibliography]" 3398

Indian claims in Canada: an introductory essay and selected list of Library holdings/Revendications des Indiens au Canada: un exposé préliminaire et une sélection d'ouvrages disponibles en Bibliothèque 3964

Indian education 3949

Indian history and claims: a research handbook 4037

Indian-Inuit authors: an annotated bibliography/Auteurs indiens et inuit: bibliographie annotée 3959

"Indian music of the Pacific northwest: an annotated bibliography of research" 0850

Indians, Indians, Indians: a selected bibliography and resource guide 4010

The Indians and Eskimos of North America: a bibliography of books in print through 1972 3943

"Indians and Metis of Manitoba: a bibliography" 4028

"Indians in Canada today: an annotated select bibliography" 3975

Indians of B.C. school package: book list and teacher's guide 3962

The Indians of Maine and the Atlantic Provinces: a bibliographical guide, being largely a selected inventory of material on the subject in the Society's library 3992

Indians of North America: methods and sources for library research 4046

Indians of North and South America: a bibliography based on the collection at the Willard E. Yager Library-Museum, Hartwick College, Oneonta, N.Y. 3993

Indians of the Americas: a bibliography 3945

The Indians of the Northeast: a critical bibliography 3998

The Indians of the subarctic: a critical bibliography 3980

Indians of the United States and Canada: a bibliography 4053

Les Indiens: une liste de livres à leur sujet 3991

Les Indiens en Amérique du Nord: au Québec, aux États-Unis 4027

Indigenous languages of Manitoba: a select bibliography 1454

Indigenous performing and ceremonial arts in Canada: a bibliography: an annotated bibliography of Canadian Indian rituals and ceremonies (up to 1976) 0970

L'indispensable en documentation: les outils de travail 1716

Indochinese refugees in Canada: a bibliography 4288

Industrial and labour relations in Canada: a selected bibliography 2794

Industrial arbitration in Canada, 1965-1973: a selective bibliography 2817

"Industrial relations and labour history" 2820

Industrial relations and the Canadian Charter of Rights: a bibliography 2918

Industrial relations in Canada 2832

5444
Literature review for biological monitoring of heavy metals in aquatic environments 4878

A literature review of aquatic macrophytes with particular reference to those present in Windermere Lake, British Columbia 5449

A literature review of bird use of farmland habitats in the Great Lakes-St. Lawrence region/Une étude bibliographique de l'utilisation, par les oiseaux, des habitats agricoles dans la région des Grands Lacs et du Saint-Laurent 5560

A literature review of deer damage and controls in the Pacific Northwest with special reference to British Columbia [microform] 4975

A literature review of Grasslands National Park, 1977-1981 3035

A literature review of life histories of some species of fish: rainbow smelt Osmerus mordax, gizzard shad Dorosoma cepedianum, paddlefish Polydon spathula, shovelnose sturgeon Scaphirhynchus platorynchus, pallid sturgeon Scaphirhynchus albus, and shortnose gar Lepisosteus platostomus, that may be introduced into the Hudson Bay watershed from the Missouri River watershed as a result of the Garrison Diversion 5455

A literature review of methods for handling solid residues arising from fuel recycle plant 5843

A literature review of ozone in the atmosphere and on interpretation of exceptionally high values of surface ozone recorded at Regina, Saskatchewan 5191

Literature review of personnel selection techniques: draft 2510

Literature review of previous oil pollution experience 5141

A literature review of research on the actions of drivers in emergencies 4481

A literature review of settlement behaviour of sanitary landfills and their application to Alberta 5787

Literature review of snow avalanche research 4518

Literature review of the controlled environment research completed on the sensitivity of coniferous tree species to air pollutants 5119

Literature review of the effects of persistent toxic substances on Great Lakes biota 5232

A literature review of the marine environment, Terra Nova National Park and adjacent bays 5203

Literature review of the occurrence of toxicity of metals in wild mammals 5207

Literature review of the studies on uptake, retention and distribution of radionuclides by the foetus 5690

Literature review of ultraviolet radiation systems and assessment of their use in aquaculture 4901

Literature review of wastewater characteristics and abatement technology in the wood and timber processing industry 4961

Literature review on fracture toughness of the heat-affected-zone 5765

Literature review on pollution deposition processes 5148

Literature review on the design of composite mechanically fastened joints/Revue de la documentation sur la conception des joints à liaison mécanique en composites 5818

Literature review on the disposal of drilling waste solids 5282

Literature review on the greenhouse effect and global warming 5280

Literature search on the growth of oysters as influenced by artificial diets and natural diets 5475

A literature survey of chemical oceanographic studies carried out in the Arctic 5110

Literature survey of papers dealing with the use of heat for keeping roads, sidewalks and parking areas free from snow and ice 4449

A literature survey on the application of computers to structural analysis 5728

The literatures of the world in English translation: a bibliography 1055

"Lithuanian-Canadian periodical publications: a preliminary check list" 5891

Littérature acadienne, 1960-1980: bibliographie 1177

"La littérature acadienne: bibliographie sélective" 1272

"Littérature acadienne (1874-1960): les oeuvres (liste chronologique)" 1155

La littérature au Canada en 1890 0019

"Littérature canadienne: une bibliographie avec commentaire" 1156

La littérature canadienne de langue anglaise 1259

La littérature canadienne de langue française 1248

"Littérature carcérale québécoise" 2147

Littérature criminologique publiée au Canada 2137

Littérature d'acadie: bibliographie 1172

La littérature de jeunesse au Canada français, bref historique, sources bibliographiques, répertoire des livres 1321

Littérature du Saguenay-Lac-Saint-Jean: répertoire des oeuvres et des auteurs 0360

Littérature en poche: collection "Petit format," 1944-1958: répertoire bibliographique 1299

Littérature enfantine canadienne pour les enfants jusqu'à dix ans 1341

"La littérature intime au Québec: éléments de bibliographie" 1157

La littérature montréalaise des communautés culturelles: prolégomènes et bibliographie 4277

Littérature pour la jeunesse: publications québécoises 1989 1386

"Littérature québécois pour la jeunesse: de solides acquis et un avenir prometteur" 1343

Littérature québécoise (romans, contes, nouvelles): bibliographie pour le 1er cycle du secondaire 1170

Littérature québécoise contemporaine 1190

La littérature québécoise et l'Amérique: guide bibliographique 1274

Litteratursogning: Canada almen bibliografi 0170

Litteratursogning: Canada tidsskrifter: en annoteret liste 5974

Litteratursongning: Canada Skonlitteratur pa engelsk: bibliografier, handboger, antologier 1278

"The little magazines of British Columbia: a narrative bibliography" 5878

"Living in and building up the Canadian city: a review of studies on the urban past" 4356

Living with dying: philosophical and psychological aspects of death and dying: a selected bibliography of printed and audio-visual material available at the Saskatoon Public Library 1548

Livre, bibliothèque et culture québécoise: mélanges offerts à Edmond Desrochers, s.j. 1618, 6953

Livre blancs, 1939-1986 6378

Le Livre canadien: premier Festival international du livre, Nice, 1969/Canadian books [International Book Festival, Nice, 1969] 0092

Le livre de mer: bibliographie commentée des livres de mer
 édités en français au Québec et au Canada et disponibles sur
 le marché 5299

Le livre québécois 1764-1975 0332

Livres à paraître 0185

Livres blancs et livres verts au Québec (1964-1984) 2504

Livres blancs et verts du Gouvernement du Québec (1960-1979)
 2504

Livres canadiens d'enfants : un trésor d'images: liste 1329

Livres canadiens d'hier et d'aujourd'hui: une exposition 0137

Livres canadiens pour la jeunesse 1378

"Livres canadiens pour la jeunesse canadienne" 1309

Livres canadiens sur les sports et les jeux pour la jeunesse: liste
 1348

Livres concernant le Canada 0073

Livres conservés au Centre de recherche en civilisation
 canadienne-française 6780

Livres d'artistes-femmes: une exposition de livres
 contemporains réalisés par des artistes canadiennes
 comprenant des "livres-objets" uniques ou des livres faisant
 partie d'éditions à petits tirages 0691

Livres de l'enfance & livres de la jeunesse au Canada, 1763-
 1840: étude bibliographique 1328

Livres de l'enfance & livres de la jeunesse au Canada, 1841-
 1867 1332

Livres d'images canadiens 1371

"Les livres d'images québécois" 1331

Les Livres disponibles canadiens de langue française/Canad-
 ian French books in print 0187

Livres du Canada 0122

Livres du Québec 0331, 0363

Les Livres du Québec: 40ième Foire du livre de Francfort, 5 au
 10 octobre 1988, Groupe Québec (Canada), Hall 4.1:A:906
 0403

Livres en langue française pour les jeunes 1364

Livres en langues autochtones dans les collections de livres
 rares de la Bibliothèque nationale du Canada 4070

Livres et auteurs canadiens: panorama de la production
 littéraire de l'année, 1961-1968 1043

Livres et auteurs d'Acadie 0266

Livres et auteurs québécois: revue critique de l'année littéraire,
 1969-1982 1207

"Livres et périodiques canadiens d'expression française publiés
 de 1946 à 1961/Canada's French language books and
 periodicals published from 1946 to 1961" 0291

Livres québécois, canadiens et américains antérieurs à 1878 de
 la bibliothèque Olivier 0130

Livres québécois pour enfants: une sélection de
 Communication-jeunesse 1374

Livres québécois pour jeunes de 10 à 13 ans 1341

Livres roses et séries noires: guide psychologique et
 bibliographique de la littérature de jeunesse 1311

Livres sur le cinéma et la télévision se trouvant à la
 Bibliothèque de l'Office national du film du Canada 6706

Livres verts, 1971-1986 6377

The lobster (Homaridae) and the lobster fisheries: an
 interdisciplinary bibliography 4890

Local histories of Alberta: an annotated bibliography 0538

Local histories of Ontario municipalities, 1951-1977: a
 bibliography, with representative trans-Canada locations of
 copies 0456

Local history in Manitoba: a key to places, districts, schools
 and transport routes 0546

Local history of the regional municipalities of Peel, York and
 Durham: an annotated listing of published materials located
 in the public libraries in the regional municipalities of Peel,
 York and Durham 0469

Local studies: Canada, Ontario, and the counties of Kent,
 Essex, Lanark and Renfrew 3015

"Lockers, the strap, liability and the law" 2231

Lodgepole pine: a bibliography 5426

The Log shanty book-shelf for 1898, the pioneer's predecessor,
 the red man of North and South America: works on his
 origin, history, habits and language 3906

Logement dans les réserves: bibliographie annotée 4060

Le logement et les personnes âgées: une bibliographie 3306

Logement sans but lucratif: une bibliographie 4426

Logging and mass wasting in the Pacific Northwest with application to the Queen Charlotte Islands, B.C.: a literature
 review 4994

"Logging fact and fiction: a bibliography" 4957

Logiciels éducatifs québécois 3690

Logiciels québécois d'applications professionnelles générales
 5828

Loi relative aux enquêtes sur les coalitions: bibliographie 2117

London, Ontario: Canadian urban information for federal land
 managment project 4345

London Branch Library holdings: a genealogical research aid
 2057

Lone parent families: a selected and annotated bibliography
 3201

Long range transportation of airborne pollutants: bibliography,
 1980-1984 5221

Looking for Manitoba government publications: an annotated
 bibliography of books and pamphlets 6318

Lothar Klein 7094

"Lothar Richter (1894-1948): [publications]" 7262

Louis "David" Riel & the North-West Rebellion: a list of
 references 1946

Louis Dudek: a check-list 6959

Louis Hooper: the Harlem years: a bio-discographical dossier
 7068

Louis Riel: a bibliography 7263

Louis Riel: a preliminary bibliography, 1963-1968 7265

Louis Riel: an annotated bibliography 7264

Louis Riel & the Métis 7265

"Louis Riel and Norman Bethune: a critical bibliography" 6840,
 7268

Louis Riel and the rebellions in the Northwest: an annotated
 bibliography of material in Special Collections, University of
 Saskatchewan Library 2056

Lower back care: an annotated bibliography/Soins pour les bas
 du dos: bibliographie annotée 1812

Lower Mainland Regional Planning Board publications 4374

"Lowry's library: an annotated catalogue of Lowry's books at
 the University of British Columbia" 6785

The Loyalist guide: Nova Scotian loyalists and their documents
 2029

Loyalist literature: an annotated guide to the writings on the
 Loyalists of the American Revolution 2016

Lucy Maud Montgomery: a preliminary bibliography 7197

Lutheran rites in North America [microform]: an annotated
 bibliography of the hymnals, altar books, and selected
 manuals produced by or for Lutherans in North America

from the late eighteenth century to the present 1573

M 'n N Canadiana: books by Canadians or about Canada: a national wedding present from Wm. Perkins Bull, K.C. to his son Michael Bull, B.A., Oxon., Barrister of the Inner Temple and his bride Noreen Hennessy, on the occasion of their visit (while on their honeymoon) to the parental home, Lorne Hall, Rosedale, Toronto, Canada, where Michael was born 0045

Mackenzie Delta bibliography 0618

Mackenzie King: widening the debate 7087

Mackenzie Mountains region bibliography 4828

"A MacLennan log" 7167

Made in Canada: artists in books, livres d'artistes 0731

"Made in Canada: texts and readers for Canadian criminology and criminal justice courses" 2206

Main d'oeuvre infirmière: références choisies 5611

Maintenir, rompre ou ... faire l'unité canadienne? Une bibliographie sur les aspects économiques de la Confédération 2622

Le maintien de l'acquis en langue seconde: bibliographie analytique 3696

Making better use of existing housing stock: a literature review 4394

Maladies chroniques et familles aidantes au Québec: une revue de la littérature 5702

Malcolm Lowry: a bibliography 7161

Malcolm Lowry: a reference guide 7159

"Malcolm Lowry (1909-1957): a bibliography" 7158

A Malcolm Lowry catalogue, with essays by Perle Epstein and Richard Hauer Costa 7160

Man builds – man destroys: a Canadian bibliographic supplement 5102

Management and economics journals: a guide to information sources 5929

Management and improvement of Saskatchewan rangeland: a selected bibliography 4691

"Management literature for librarians: an annotated list" 1599

The management of co-operatives: a bibliography 2737

Management science in the control and management of fisheries: an annotated bibliography 4914

Managing regional urban growth I: an annotated bibliography 4437

Managing regional urban growth II: review of government documents 4438

Managing technological change in manufacturing: an annotated bibliography of selected works 5840

"Mandatory retirement: a selected bibliography" 2927

Les mandats mondiaux de production: une revue de littérature 2694

Manitoba: a provincial look 0506

Manitoba: aquatic LRTAP data and bibliography 5258

Manitoba architecture to 1940: a bibliography 0751

Manitoba authors/Écrivains du Manitoba 0501

"Manitoba bibliography" 0551

"Manitoba bibliography of bibliographies" 0542

Manitoba bird studies, 1744-1983: a bibliography 5515

Manitoba bird studies: a bibliography of Manitoba ornithology 5515

Manitoba government publications 6457

Manitoba government publications, 1970-1974: a checklist compiled in the Legislative Library 6334

Manitoba government publications: monthly checklist/ Publications du gouvernement du Manitoba: liste mensuelle 6456

Manitoba government publications received in the Legislative Library 6456

Manitoba newspaper checklist with library holdings, 1859-1986 6037

Manitoba's research on aging: an annotated bibliography, 1950-1982 3241

Manpower management in Canada: a selected bibliography 2800

Manpower studies: a selected bibliography for policy and research 2796

Manpower training and retraining: a preliminary bibliography 2802

Manpower training and utilization in Canada, 1955-1970: a bibliography 2814

Manual brushing for forest vegetation management in British Columbia: a review of current knowledge and information needs 5015

Manuscripts and bulletins [National Historic Parks and Sites, Environment Canada] 0806

Manuscrits et bulletins [Lieux et parcs historiques nationaux, Environnement Canada] 0805

Les manuscrits et imprimés religieux au Québec, 1867-1960: bibliographie 1549

"Many called, but few chosen: a roll call of 350 outstanding Canadian books" 0057

Map and air photo catalogue 6553

Map collection of the Public Reference Library of the city of Toronto, Canada 6489

Map index 1969-1977 of geological and geochemical maps of the Island of Newfoundland: (supplement to 1969 map index) 6566

"Maple sugar: a bibliography of early records" 5324

Mapoteca geologica americana: a catalogue of geological maps of America (North and South), 1752-1881, in geographic and chronologic order 6479

Mapping Upper Canada, 1780-1867: an annotated bibliography of manuscript and printed maps 6598

Maps, plans and publications of the Topographical Survey of Canada 6490

Maps: a map index for community planning in Ontario 6588

Maps and charts published in America before 1900: a bibliography 6516

Maps of Alberta municipalities: index 6559

The maps of Canada: a guide to official Canadian maps, charts, atlases and gazetteers 6576

Maps of Indian reserves and settlements in the National Map Collection/Cartes et réserves et agglomérations indiennes de la Collection nationale de cartes et plans 6574

Maps relating to Alexander Mackenzie: a keepsake distributed at a meeting of the Bibliographical Society of Canada 6514

"Margaret Anchoretta Ormsby: publications" 7224

"Margaret Atwood: a bibliography of criticism" 6806

Margaret Atwood: a reference guide 6813

Margaret Atwood: an annotated bibliography (poetry) 6811, 6812

Margaret Atwood: an annotated bibliography (prose) 6809, 6810

"Margaret Avison: a checklist" 6818

Margaret Avison: an annotated bibliography 6819

"Margaret Laurence: a bibliographical essay" 7122

Margaret Laurence: an annotated bibliography 7126

"Margaret Laurence: bibliography" 7124

Maria Chapdelaine: évolution de l'édition 1913-1980 7052

Mariage et famille: inventaire préliminaire des fonds de la Bibliothèque nationale 3206

Marian Engel (née Passmore): an annotated bibliography 6966

Marine affairs bibliography: a comprehensive index to marine law and policy literature 2369

Marine biota of the NE Pacific: a bibliography emphasizing systematics and distribution 5419

The marine ecology of Lancaster Sound and adjacent waters: an annotated bibliography 5130

Marine mammal research in the Canadian Arctic 5396

"Marine parks bibliography" 3029

The marine surveys of James Cook in North America, 1758-1768, particularly the survey of Newfoundland: a bibliography of printed charts and sailing-directions 6511

Marine transportation and high Arctic development: a bibliography: scientific and technical research relevant to the development of marine transportation in the Canadian north 4479

Marine transportation in Canada and the U.S. Great Lakes region: a bibliography of selected references, 1950-1975 4465

Maritime energy education bibliography/Bibliographie sur les programmes d'éducation sur l'énergie dans les Maritimes 3602

The Maritime Pamphlet Collection: an annotated catalogue 6793

Maritime provinces water resources study, stage 1: appendix 1: bibliography 5048

"Marius Barbeau, 1883-1969: [Bibliography of ethnomusicological works]" 6828

Marius Barbeau et l'art au Québec: bibliographie analytique et thématique 0714

Le marketing en milieu muséal: une bibliographie analytique 0725

Le marketing et la bibliothèque spécialisée: bibliographie sélective 1710

Marketing the special library: a selective bibliography/Le marketing et la bibliothèque spécialisée: bibliographie sélective 1710

Marketing to farmers: an annotated bibliography 4652

Marriage and the family: preliminary check list of National Library holdings/Mariage et famille: inventaire préliminaire des fonds de la Bibliothèque nationale 3206

Martha Louise Black: a bibliography of sources available in the Yukon Archives 6848

Masinahikan: native language imprints in the archives and libraries of the Anglican Church of Canada 4075

Mass media bibliography: an annotated guide to books and journals for research and reference 0988

Master and bachelor theses in geography, 1965-1983 6165

Master's theses – northern Canada 6186

Master's theses and research essays accepted by Laurentian University between 1962 and June 1981, and held in the Main Library 6162

Masters theses in the pure and applied sciences accepted by colleges and universities of the United States and Canada 6208

"Material cultural research at Parks Canada" 4569

Material for a bibliography of North American mammals 5302

Material pertaining to women in the reference collection, Dana Porter Arts Library, University of Waterloo 3761

Materials for a history of the province of New Brunswick 0195

"Materials for Canadian history: the annals of towns, parishes, &c., extracted from church registers, and other sources" 1887

"Materials for the historical study of Canadian children's literature: a survey of resources" 1365

Materials of interest to school librarians: a bibliography for school librarians 1642

Matériaux pour une sociologie appliquée à la santé et sécurité du travail: bibliographie 2889

"Matériaux pour une sociologie politique du Canada français. III: Inventaire des sources" 2378

Matériel didactique canadien: sources de référence pédagogique pour les écoles ontariennes 3441

Matériel pédagogique sur la prévention de la violence utilisé dans les écoles: guide national 3727

Matériel pour une sociologie des maladies mentales au Québec 3126

Mauricie et centre du Québec: liste des journaux et périodiques régionaux 5924

La Mauricie et les Bois-Francs: inventaire bibliographique, 1760-1975 0346

Mavis Gallant: an annotated bibliography 6998

A Max Boag discography 6855

Maynard Ferguson: a discography 6978

McGill University thesis directory 6144

McKim's directory of Canadian publications 6007

Measuring unpriced values: an economic perspective and annotated bibliography for Ontario 5019

"La mécanisation de la construction: bibliographie" 5745

Media, peace and security: a working bibliography 2501

Media for minds: educational resources from CBC Enterprises 6664

"Media literacy bibliography" 3701

Media materials: a Can. Lit. collection 6642

Media resources: Agriculture 6661

Medical, social & political aspects of the acquired immune deficiency syndrome (AIDS) crisis: a bibliography 5669

Medical anthropology, social science, and nursing: a bibliography 4595

"Medical archives: an annotated bibliography" 1713

Medical information/Renseignements médicaux 5655

The medicare crisis in Saskatchewan (January 1, 1960 – July 31, 1962): a bibliography 5568

Medicinal and food plants of the North American Indians: a bibliography 5581

"The Meech Lake Accord: a comprehensive bibliography" 2339

Meech Lake Constitutional Accord/Entente constitutionnelle du Lac Meech 2318

A memoir of Jacques Cartier, sieur de Limoilou: his voyages to the St. Lawrence, a bibliography and a facsimile of the manuscript of 1534 with annotations, etc. 6899

"Memoir of Sir J. William Dawson: bibliography" 6948

"Mémoire de la Société Saint-Jean-Baptiste de Montréal sur l'éducation nationale: bibliographie sommaire" 3382

Mémoires et documents historiques: notice bibliographique 1889

Mémoires et thèses de linguistique et de traduction soutenus à l'Université de Montréal de 1943 à 1971 6153

Ojibway Resource Centre catalogue 4065

The Okanagan District 0562

Oklo natural reactors: geological and geochemical conditions: a review 4852

Old Ontario: essays in honour of J.M.S. Careless 6892

Older Canadian homeowners: a literature review 3248

Ombudsman: statut, rôle, pouvoirs, organisation: bibliographie 2536

Ombudsman bibliography 2451

On Canada: essays in honour of Frank H. Underhill 7348

On Canadian literature, 1806-1960: a check list of articles, books, and theses on English-Canadian literature, its authors, and language 1036

On film: a film catalogue [Indian Affairs and Northern Development] 6678

On-reserve housing: annotated bibliography 4066

On-site wastewater treatment bibliography [computer file] 5849

"On the early gazetteer and map literature of western Canada" 6478

Once upon a pedestal: multimedia list of material for reading, listening, and viewing prepared on the occasion of International Women's Year, 1975 3757

One-half inch VHS videocassettes in the Audio Visual Services Department collection 6705

The one-parent family: perspectives and annotated bibliography 3281

The one-parent family in the 1980s: perspectives and annotated bibliography, 1978-1984 3281

Ongoing and recently completed research studies concerned with the social implications of the development of communications systems in northern Canada 3184

Online retrieval of information: a comparison of different systems used to produce a bibliography on Ephemeroptera and pollution, 1969-78 5151

Onshore impacts of offshore hydrocarbon development: annotated bibliography 5198

Ontario, a bibliography for regional development: classified list of limited references 4307

Ontario and national marketing boards: a selected bibliography, 1955-1973 4665

Ontario and the Canadian North 0458

Ontario bicentennial and Toronto sesquicentennial: a selected bibliography of some holdings of the Canadiana Collection of the North York Public Library 0478

The Ontario Cabinet: a selected annotated bibliography 2490

Ontario Child Health Study: abstracts of research reports and literature reviews 5681

The Ontario colleges of applied arts and technology [microform]: a review and analysis of selected literature, 1965-1976 3581

The Ontario energy catalogue: a directory of who's doing what in energy in Ontario and a bibliography of materials on energy available in Ontario 4802

Ontario ethno-cultural newspapers, 1835-1972: an annotated checklist 6019

Ontario Forest Research Institute publications, 1980-1991 (an annotated bibliography) 6409

"L'Ontario français: guide bibliographique" 0466

Ontario Genealogical Society library holdings: housed with Canadiana Collection, North York Public Library 2049

Ontario government publications annual catalogue/ Publications du gouvernement de l'Ontario: catalogue annuel 6467

Ontario government publications in the Mississauga Public Library: an annotated checklist of selected holdings 6293

Ontario government publications monthly checklist/ Publications du gouvernement de l'Ontario: liste mensuelle 6468

Ontario renews bibliography: a listing of books, pamphlets and periodical information available from the Community Renewal Resource Centre 4396

Ontario royal commissions and commissions of inquiry, 1867-1978: a checklist of reports 6329

Ontario sediment-related literature: annotated bibliography 5240

Ontario since 1867: a bibliography 0467

The Ontario Textbook Collection catalogue, 1846-1970 [microform] 3628

Ontario Tree Improvement and Forest Biomass Institute publications, 1980-1985: an annotated bibliography 6376

Open area schools 3512

Open education: review of the literature and selected annotated bibliography 3471

Open learning and distance education in Canada 3707

Open plan: an annotated bibliography 3453

The open school: an annotated bibliography 3453

Open schools: a bibliography 3457

Optimisation dans manutention des conteneurs: une bibliographie sélective/Optimising container handling: a selective bibliography 4456

Optimising container handling: a selective bibliography 4456

Optimum class size? A review of the literature 3443

OR-OS [Outdoor Recreation-Open Space] reference system: component 1 (bibliographic file)/Système de référence PAGE [Plein-air-grand espaces]: composante no 1 (dossier bibliographique) 1769

or solo voice(s) in the libraries of the Canadian Music Centre/ Catalogue de musique canadienne pour orchestre, comprenant également les concertos ainsi que les oeuvres avec choeur ou soliste(s) disponible dans les bibliothèques du Centre de musique canadienne 0853

"Ordinateur et droit: bibliographie sélective" 2139

Les ordres religieux au Québec: bilan de la recherche: [bibliographie] 1554

"An ore body of note: theses and dissertations on Indians, Metis and Inuit at the University of Alberta" 6182

The Oregon question 0558

Les organes officiels des syndicats des enseignants québécois 3543

Organic agriculture: a bibliography 4679

Organisation policière: bibliographie sélective et annotée 2287

Organize for action: a reading guide for community participants 3121

Organized crime: a bibliography 2192, 2329

"Orientation bibliographique: [Océanographie de l'estuaire du Saint-Laurent]" 5153

"Orientation bibliographique sur la théorie des frontières interétatiques" 3001

"L'orientation des recherches historiques à Louisbourg" 1970

"Ornithological publications of Percy Algernon Taverner, 1895-1945" 7326

2027

"The political economy of Quebec: a selective annotated bibliography" 2484

Political parties and elections 2506

Political refugees and "displaced persons", 1945-1954: a selected bibliography and guide to research with special reference to Ukrainians 4207

Political-strategic aspects of Canadian Pacific policy: an annotated bibliography of periodical literature and government documents, 1965 to 1980 2466

La politique canadienne 2548

Politique de l'environnement: bibliographie sélective et annotée 5241

Politique de l'habitation: bibliographie sélective et annotée 4418

La politique des sciences, la recherche et le développement au Canada: bibliographie 4619

Politique et religion au Québec depuis 1960: bibliographie 1539

Politique étrangère canadienne: bibliographie 1972-1975 2421

Politique industrielle: bibliographie sélective et annotée 2734

Politiques d'emploi des gouvernements au Québec: inventaire, bibliographie, éléments d'évaluation 2884

Politiques d'immigration et d'accueil des réfugiés: bibliographie sélective et annotée 2527

Les politiques éducatives récentes au Québec: chronologie et bibliographie sélective annotée, 1977-1983 3663

Les politiques urbaines et régionales au Québec: éléments de bibliographie, 1940-1977 4379

Pollutant exposure and response relationships: a literature review: geological and hydrogeological aspects 5242

Pollution: bibliographie 5040

Pollution: bibliography/Pollution: bibliographie 5040

La pollution de l'air et les précipitations acides 5264

Pollution from land use activities in the Great Lakes basin: a selected bibliography 5161

Pollution in Alberta: a bibliography 5092

Polonica Canadiana: a bibliographical list of the Canadian Polish imprints, 1848-1957 4131

Polonica Canadiana ... , 1958-1970 4131

The poor in Vancouver: a preliminary checklist of sources 3145

"Popularized Canadian trials: a bibliography" 2154

La population du Québec: bibliographie démographique 3027

Pornography: a feminist survey 3841

Portrait de la littérature québécoise en toxicomanie 3338

"Portrait des journaux au Saguenay-Lac-Saint-Jean" 6026

Portraits de québécoises gestionnaires: une bibliographie annotée 3805

Les Portugais au Canada: une bibliographie 4295

The Portuguese in Canada: a bibliography/Les Portugais au Canada: une bibliographie 4295

"Post-graduate theses in Canadian literature: English and English-French comparative" 6142

"Post-graduate theses in Canadian literature: English and French comparative" 6118

"Post-graduate theses in Canadian universities on geologic research related to mineral deposits, 1983-1986" 6190

"Postmodern patchwork: some recent trends in the writing of women's history in Canada" 3887

"Pour l'histoire des communautés italiennes au Canada: essai bibliographique" 4272

Pour mieux connaître nos fondateurs: bibliographie pratique 1503

Pour parler des Amérindiens et des Inuit: guide à l'usage des professeurs du secondaire, histoire et géographie: bibliographie sélective commentée 4029

Pour suivre le théâtre au Québec: les ressources documentaires 0981

Pour une école nouvelle à Trois-Rivières: bibliographie annotée 3584

Poverty: an annotated bibliography and references 3085

Poverty in Canada and the United States: overview and annotated bibliography 3086

Powers, possessions and freedoms: essays in honour of C.B. Macpherson 7169

A practical guide to Canadian political economy 2709

Practical sampling of freshwater macrozoobenthos: a bibliography of useful texts, reviews and recent papers 5423

The practice of field instruction in social work: theory and process, with an annotated bibliography 3296

The practicum in teacher education 3450

La pratique de l'économie de l'éducation dans le Québec francophone de la dernière décennie, 1970-1980: une présentation bibliographique 3595

Pre-1900 Canadian directories: catalogue/La Collection de répertoires d'avant 1900: catalogue 5983

Pre-retirement bibliography: source book 3164

The pre-school visually impaired child: a guide for parents and practitioners: a selected, annotated bibliography 3188

Pre-service teacher education in Canada 3509

Pre-twentieth century literature of and about the Maritime Provinces: a bibliography of titles held in the special collections of Mount Allison University Library 0236

PRECIS: an annotated bibliography, 1969-1975 1623

PRECIS: an annotated bibliography, 1969-1977 1623

Précis d'histoire sur les Canadiens de race noire: sources et guide d'enseignement 4198

Prehistory of Canada: recommended general introductory reading 4608

Prejudice in educational material: a resource handbook 3527

A preliminary annotated bibliography for Pukaskwa National Park 2992

A preliminary annotated bibliography of L'Anse aux Meadows National Historic Park 2999

A preliminary annotated bibliography of literature on small mammals relevant to Elk Island National Park 5493

A preliminary annotated bibliography of Nahanni National Park and the South Nahanni Watershed, N.W.T. 2998

A preliminary annotated bibliography of the Stikine River country and its people 0586

A preliminary annotated bibliography on Georgia Strait fishes 5383

A preliminary annotated bibliography on muskeg 5328

Preliminary archaeology bibliography of Atlantic Canada and Maine 4561

Preliminary bibliographical inventory of sources in the history of science, technology and medicine in Canada to the twentieth century 4632

A preliminary bibliography [Charles G.D. Roberts] 7270

A preliminary bibliography for garden history in Canada 4714

A preliminary bibliography for historic artifact research in the Maritimes/Une bibliographie préliminaire sur les artefacts historiques pour les Maritimes 4598

"A preliminary bibliography of Canadian old time instrumental music books" 0887

Privacy and community: a selected community 4355
Privacy and data protection: an international bibliography 2266
Privacy as a factor in residential buildings and site development: an annotated bibliography 0736
Private policing: a bibliography 2132
Privatisation, 1986-1988: bibliographie sélective et annotée 2718
Privatisation: bibliographie sélective et annotée 2718
Privatisation des services de santé, 1985-1988: bibliographie sélective et annotée 5686
Privatization of correctional services: a select bibliography 2357
Probation: North American literature review (1971-1981) 2245
"Problèmes municipaux: liste bibliographique annotée" 4316
Problèmes politiques du Québec: répertoire bibliographique des commissions royales d'enquête présentant un intérêt spécial pour la politique de la province de Québec, 1940-1957 2376
Problems of immigrant women, past and present: a bibliography 3789
Problems of national defence: a study guide and bibliography 2379
Procédés de traitement et de conservation du maquereau: étude et bibliographie annotée 4893
Proceedings of the Workshop on the squid Illex illecebrosus: Dalhousie University, Halifax, Nova Scotia, May 1978: and a bibliography on the genus Illex 5418
Prodrome for a distributional check-list and bibliography of the recent marine mollusca of the west coast of Canada 5343
Production, production technology and distribution 6706
Production, technologie de production et distribution 6706
Production de semences forestières: revue bibliographiques et suggestions de recherche 4988
"La production des vingt dernières années en histoire de l'Église du Québec" 1536
La production française à l'ONF: 25 ans en perspectives 6658
Productions cinématographiques, vidéos et sonores [Programmes de Multiculturalisme, 1973-1992] 6698
La productivité dans le secteur public: les écrits récents, 1975-1982, sur le sujet, particulièrement ceux qui portent sur le Québec 2881
Productivity in Nova Scotia: a review of the literature and annotated bibliography 0219
Productivity trends: bibliography with selected annotations 2674
Products and services: reference 3055
Products and services of the 1981 census of Canada 3036
Produits et services: référence 3056
Produits et services du recensement du Canada de l981 3037
"[Professional activity of female physicians in Québec: bibliography]" 3763
Professional books for school librarians available from the Prince Edward Island Provincial Library 1636
Professional collection 1631
Professional development of core French teachers: selective review of general literature on inservice education and specific literature on inservice education of second language teachers 3658
Professional literature collection 1610
Professional reading materials 1610
Profile index 6460
Profiles in Canadian literature 1227
Programmation: bibliographie annotée 1833

Programme 04: cadre général de l'individualisation de l'enseignement professionnel: bibliographie sur l'élaboration, l'expérimentation et l'évaluation de programmes institutionnels 3520
Programme national de l'administration de la justice dans les deux langues officiels: publications 2327
Programme relatif à la pollution atmosphérique du Service canadien des forêts et bibliographie pertinente 5006
Programmed teaching and micro-teaching: a bibliography 3458
Programming: an annotated bibliography/Programmation: bibliographie annotée 1833
Progress of geological work in Canada during 1898 4730
Progress of geological work in Canada during 1899 4732
"Progress of geological work in Canada during 1898" 4729
"Progress of geological work in Canada during 1899" 4731
Project information exchange: an inventory of studies, briefs and social action projects/Échange-renseignements: relevé d'études, de mémoires et de réalisations en action sociale 3199
Projecting women 6626
Projet de loi 88: bibliographie 2552
Projet du musique "pop" canadienne: musique pour orchestre de compositeurs canadiens 0888
Projets de démonstration SCHL: un choix de notices bibliographiques annotées 4387
Projets de recherche canadiens en bibliothéconomie et sciences de l'information, une liste 1738
Les projets de recherche subventionnés par l'IMTA et les publications scientifiques qui en découlent, 1966-1976 5114
Promouvoir l'éducation interculturelle et l'éducation internationale: guide analytique des ressources éducatives de langue française 3648
Propaganda, mass media and politics [microform]: a computerized research bibliography 2427
La propension aux accidents: thésaurus et bibliographie 3148
Propriétés physico-mécaniques de l'écorce: une étude bibliographique 4964
"Prostitution in Canada: a bibliography" 3845
The protection of ornamental plants, 1979-April 1989: citations from AGRICOLA concerning diseases and other environmental considerations 4716
Protection of veneer logs in storage in eastern Canada: a survey of the literature 4963
Protestantism on the Prairies to 1977: an annotated bibliography of historical and biographical publications 1546
"Les Protestants en Nouvelle-France: bibliographie" 1544
La Province de Québec 0308
Province of Newfoundland and Labrador: map index: geological, geophysical and related maps to December 31, 1969 6515
Provincial and federal land use and land ownership policies and their potential impact on political, economic and social conditions in Canada 2621
A Provincial bibliography of literacy learning materials, curricula and reference documents 3725
Provincial government and politics 2506
Provincial government literature: an updated guide to material available to the general public by the various ministries 6340
Provincial-municipal relations in Canada 2397, 4315
Provincial royal commissions and commissions of inquiry, 1867-1982: a selective bibliography/Commissions royales provinciales et commissions d'enquête, 1867-1982: bibliographie sélective 6381

R. Murray Schafer 7294, 7295

"Rabelais et les traditions populaires en Acadie" 4554

Rabies: a select bibliography 5591

Radiation effects on living systems: a bibliography of AECL publications/Effets des rayonnements sur les organismes vivants: une bibliographie des publications de l'ÉACL 5797

Radio Frequency Spectrum Management Program evaluation: economic nature of the spectrum: a review of the literature 2755

Radioactive waste management in Canada: AECL research publications and other literature, 1953-1990/Gestion des déchets nucléaires au Canada: publications d'EACL recherche et autres documents, 1953-1990 5273

La radiodiffusion au Canada et au Québec: guide préliminaire de recherche 0961

Radiodiffusion et État: bibliographie des documents en langue française établie à l'intention du Groupe de travail sur la politique de la radiodiffusion 0980

Radiolyses pulsées: bibliographie complète, 1960-mars 1969 5732

Radon epidemiology: a guide to the literature 5680

Rafferty-Alameda Project environmental impact statement: bibliography 5251

Rail transport of coal: a selective bibliography/Transport du charbon par chemin de fer: bibliographie sélective 4504

Railroads 4510

"Ralph Gustafson: a bibliography in progress, 1929-1972" 7037

Range: a selected bibliography of research and information 4666

"A Raoul Duguay bibliography" 6962

A rape bibliography: with special emphasis on rape research in Canada/Bibliographie sur le viol: et plus particulièrement sur la recherche au Canada dans ce domaine 2191

Rapeseed and mustard: a selected bibliography 4687

"Rappel bibliographique [Centre de recherches sur l'eau]" 5117

Rapports concernant l'énergie (communication) publié par IRTS de 1973 à mai 1983 4701

Rapports des enquêtes socio-économiques du Service canadien des parcs, 1960-1988 6388

Rapports techniques concernant la prospection petrolière et gazière, 1920-1980 4817

Rationalisation des choix budgétaires: planning, programming, budgeting systems: une bibliographie 2643

La rationalisation des choix budgétaires: une bibliographie 2643

Raymond Knister: a bibliography of his works 7101

Raymond Knister: an annotated bibliography 7099, 7100

"Raymond Knister: an annotated checklist" 7098

Reaching agreement on urban development: an annotated bibliography/La recherche de consensus dans le développement urbain: bibliographie annotée 4441

Read: a selected list of Canadian books 0129

Read across Canada: creative activities for Canadian readers 1380

Read Canadian: a book about Canadian books 0103

Réadaptation des handicapés: guide populaire et bibliographie sélective 3142

Reader, lover of books, lover of heaven: a catalogue based on an exhibition of the book arts in Ontario 1644

A reader's guide to Canadian history 2025

A reader's guide to Quebec studies 0405

Reading development: a resource book for adult education 3609

Reading disability and crime – link and remediation: an annotated bibliography 3160

A reading guide to Canada in world affairs, 1945-1971 2405

"Reading in a second-foreign language: a bibliography 1974-1984" 3640

"Reading list on Canada and Montreal" 0277

Reading reference to social credit: a bibliography about the social credit movement. 2382

Reading references on ecological agriculture: eight annotated bibliographies 4669

Readings in Canadian library history 1675, 1679

Real estate development and market analysis: a selected bibliography/Aménagement des biens immobiliers et analyse du marché immobilier: bibliographie choisie 2660

The rebellion of 1837-38: a bibliography of the sources of information in the Public Reference Library of the City of Toronto, Canada 1904

Rebirth of feminism: a selected list 3759

Recension bibliographique: les maladies infectieuses dans les périodiques médicaux québécois du XIXe siècle 5682

Recent and recommended texts: a selective list for hospital libraries 5715

Recent Canadian glacier references, 1986-1988 5271

Recent Canadian Jewish authors and la langue française 1022

Recent developments in interlibrary loans: a select bibliography 1692

"Recent historical literature and the New England-Atlantic provinces region" 0210

"Recent literature on the history of Canadian architecture" 0739

Recent publications in Canadian native studies 4092

"Recent publications in Canadian women's history" 3801

"Recent publications in local history" 0535

"Recent publications in local history: New Brunswick" 0248

"Recent publications on Canadian art" 0722

"Recent publications récentes" 4636

"Recent publications relating to Canada" 0189

"Recent publications relating to Canadian ethnic studies" 4193, 4210

"Recent publications relating to the history of the Atlantic region" 0231, 0271, 0274

Recent publications supported by Multiculturalism and Citizenship Canada/Publications récentes subventionnées par Multiculturalisme et Citoyenneté Canada 4289

Recent trends and new literature in Canadian history 1933

La recherche académique et non-académique en éducation des adultes au Canada, 1970: un inventaire 3417

Recherche bibliographique: impacts culturels et linguistiques de la consommation de produits culturels étrangers (émissions de télévision et musique à la radio) 0985

La recherche de consensus dans le développement urbain: bibliographie annotée 4441

Recherche documentaire sur les professeurs du collégial 3638

La recherche en éducation des adultes au Canada, 1968: un inventaire 3399

"La recherche en gérontologie sociale au Québec: une originalité obscure ou une obscurité méritée?" 3305

"La recherche en histoire du Canada" 2085

"La recherche en mass-media au Québec" 0952

"La recherche en tourisme" 1852

Recherche et communiqué. Bibliographie annotée 1834

Recherche et développement en matière d'énergie éolienne au Conseil national de recherches du Canada, 1975-1985 5812

Recherche sur la consommation d'énergie: une bibliographie annotée 5209

La recherche sur les femmes au Québec: bilan et bibliographie 3808

La recherche sur les femmes cadres au Canada: une bibliographie annotée, 1980-1990 3879

"La recherche sur les Inuit du Nord québécois: bilan et perspectives" 4074

"La recherche sur l'histoire de l'imprimé et du livre québécois" 1605

La Recherche universitaire en communication au Québec, 1960-1986: bibliographie analytique des thèses et mémoires 6194

La recherche universitaire sur les femmes au Québec (1921-1980): répertoire des thèses de maîtrise et de doctorat déposées dans les universités du Québec 6166

"Recherches économiques récentes sur la province de Québec" 2574

"Recherches en éducation faites au Canada français" 6205

"Les recherches en psychologie sociale au Canada français (1946-1962)" 6075

Recherches et travaux connexes sur l'immersion de déchets en mer: bibliographie annotée 5170

"Les recherches religieuses au Canada français" 1514

Recherches sur l'adaptation des immigrants et les groupes ethniques: une bibliographie de thèses non publiées, 1920-1953 6063

Recherches sur l'adaptation des immigrants et les groupes ethniques: une bibliographie d'ouvrages publiées, 1920-1953 4128

Recherches sur le français de base: bibliographie analytique 1474

"Recherches sur les femmes et l'éducation formelle au Canada et au Québec publiées dans la période 1975-1986" 3866

Recherches urbaines et régionales au Canada: répertoire annoté 4389

Le récit cartographique des affaires Riel 6567

Le récit de voyage en Nouvelle-France: (FRA 6661): Cahier bibliographique 1993

Récits de voyages en Nouvelle-France au XVIIe siècle: bibliographie d'introduction 2043

Reclamation of disturbed alpine lands: a literature review 5281

Reclamation of lands disturbed by mining in mountainous and northern areas: a synoptic bibliography and review relevant to British Columbia and adjacent areas 4799

Recommended references to the flora of British Columbia 5388

Record of work of Electron Physics Section, 1949-1986 [i.e. 1985] 5817

A record of writing: an annotated and illustrated bibliography of George Bowering 6869

Records management: the Canadian contribution: a bibliography 1684

Le recours à des sanctions pénales contre la pollution de l'environnement: bibliographie choisie et commentée 2311

Recours à la télécopie pour la livraison des documents: les analyses des coûts: bibliographie sommaire 1693

Recreation and leisure data files 1824

Recreation and sport: technical resource index 1803

Recreation and Sport film library catalogue 6660

Recreation area maintenance and rehabilitation: a bibliography with abstracts 1771

Recreation policy bibliography 1781

Recreation residential developments: a review and summary of relevant material 1779

Recreation site development: a bibliography with abstracts 1773

Recreation trails in Canada: a comment and bibliography on trail development and use, with special reference to the Rocky Mountain national parks and proposed Great Divide Trail 1759

The recruitment, training and promotion of civil servants, French-speaking Third World and Canada: selective bibliography 2410

Recrutement, formation et promotion des fonctionnaires, Tiers-Monde francophone et Canada: bibliographie sélective/The recruitment, training and promotion of civil servants, French-speaking Third World and Canada: selective bibliography 2410

Recueil bibliographique sur les droits de l'enfant 2360

Recueil de documents pédagogiques préparées pour les classes d'immersion française, 1982-1984 3629

Recueil de références sur la télésanté au Canada 5662

Recueil des traités du Canada, 1928-1964 6259

The Red jeep and other landscapes: a collection in honour of Douglas Lochhead 7150

Red pine bibliography 5351

The reduction of winter-induced discomfort in Canadian urban residential areas: an annotated bibliography and evaluation 4422

Reference aids in Canadian history in the University of Toronto Library (Humanities and Social Sciences Division) 1975

Reference aids in international relations 2459

A reference and bibliographical guide to the study of English Canadian literature 1040

Référence et bibliographie en sciences pures et appliquées 4622

Reference guide to Alberta government committees, 1905-1980 6352

Reference guide to Canadian newspapers: a check list of major holdings in the library of the University of British Columbia 6022

A reference guide to English, American and Canadian literature: an annotated checklist of bibliographical and other reference materials 1060

The reference interview: a selective bibliography/L'entrevue de référence: bibliographie sélective 1671

"A reference list on Canadian folk music" 0863, 0910

Reference list on the subject of reciprocity in trade between Canada and the United States of America 2557

"Reference lists: Canada" 0023

Reference literature and general political readings 2506

Reference pamphlets listing, 1985-1986 4078

"Reference sources for the history of the Church of England in Upper Canada, 1791-1867" 1519

Reference sources on Canadian education: an annotated bibliography 3531

"Reference titles" 1735

Reference works for historians: a list of reference works of interest to historians in the libraries of the University of Ottawa 1972

Research on immigrant adjustment and ethnic groups: a bibliography of unpublished theses, 1920-1953/Recherches sur l'adaptation des immigrants et les groupes ethniques: une bibliographie de thèses non publiées, 1920-1953 6063

"Research on native peoples at the University of Saskatchewan" 6163

Research on youth: an annotated bibliography of selected current reports 3149

The research projects supported by IOEH and the scientific publications originating from them, 1966-1976 5115

Research record, 1947-1967 4618

Research related to native peoples at the University of Saskatchewan, 1912-1983 4043

Research results of projects funded by the Canadian Ethnic Studies Program, 1973-1988: a bibliography/Résultats des projets de recherche subventionnés par le Programme des études ethniques canadiennes, 1973-1988: une bibliographie 4296

Research review: North and South America wind effects on tall buildings 5737

Researcher's guide to British Columbia directories, 1901-1940: a bibliography & index 0604

The researcher's guide to British Columbia nineteenth century directories: a bibliography & index 0598

"Researching Canadian buildings: some historical sources" 0752

"Researching ceramics" 0720

Researching older Canadian companies at the Metropolitan Toronto Library 2697

Réseaux de bibliothèques de droit: une liste de références ... 1727

Réserve écologique de Tantaré: bibliographie annotée des travaux et d'acquisition de connaissances 5297

"La résidence secondaire et la région métropolitaine de Montréal: essai d'interprétation" 1853

Residential energy conservation: a selected bibliography of Canadian sources 5789

Resin acids and fatty acids of Canadian pulpwoods: a review of the literature 4941

Resource catalogue: family planning, sex education, population/Catalogue de ressources: le planning des naissances, l'éducation sexuelle, la population 3116

Resource catalogue [Alberta Provincial Film Library] 6699

Resource centers: a bibliography 1600

Resource Centre: bibliography of resource materials 4240

Resource development and indigenous peoples: a comparative bibliography 4052

Resource guide, eliminating racial discrimination in Canada: the challenge and the opportunity 3336

Resource guide for the War of 1812 2002

Resource guide of publications supported by multiculturalism programs, 1973-1992/Guide des publications subventionnées par les programmes du multiculturalisme, 1973-1992 4298

Resource list for a multicultural society 4181

A resource list of multi-media materials on ethnicity and multi-culturalism 6629

Resource material for social analysis of the Chignecto region: a preliminary bibliography 0233

Resource materials for traffic safety programs in elementary schools: a bibliography 3549

Resource reading list 1990: annotated bibliography of resources by and about native people 4114

Resources for a new age: a selected annotated bibliography on women and microtechnology/Ressources pour une ère nouvelle: bibliographie annotée d'ouvrages choisis concernant la femme et la microtechnologie 3828

Resources for North American studies: an annotated list of microform collections in Australian libraries relating to the United States and Canada 0147

Resources for teachers: local planning, development, environment 4349

Resources law bibliography 2224

"Resources on AIDS: the acquisition of instructional materials for schools" 3679

Responsabilité légale et négligence: une bibliographie spécialisée de la base de données SPORT 1865

Response of aspen suckering to pre-harvest stem treatments: a literature review 5004

Ressources canadiennes sur la famille: catalogue 3114

"Les ressources en éducation économique" 3607

Ressources pour une ère nouvelle: bibliographie annotée d'ouvrages choisis concernant la femme et la microtechnologie 3828

Résultats des projets de recherche subventionnés par le Programme des études ethniques canadiennes, 1973-1988: une bibliographie 4296

Retailing and wholesaling in Canada: information sources 2770

Retirement, mandatory retirement and pensions in Canada: an introductory bibliography 2667

Retirement: a bibliography, 1970-1979 3191

"A retrospective bibliography [on archives]" 1627

Revegetation in arctic and subarctic North America: a literature review 5116

Revegetation information applicable to mining sites in northern Canada 4800

Revendications des Indiens au Canada: un exposé préliminaire et une sélection d'ouvrages disponibles en Bibliothèque 3964

Revenus et langue au Québec: une revue des écrits 2695

Review and annotated bibliography of stream diversion and stream restoration techniques and associated effects on aquatic biota 5139

Review of Canadian aeronautical fatigue work, 1991-1993 5853

"A review of Canadian botany from 1800 to 1895" 5311

"A review of Canadian botany from the first settlement of New France to the nineteenth century" 5305

A review of crayfish literature relevant to the development of a crayfish industry in Saskatchewan 4904

Review of current information on Arctic cod (Boreogadus saida Lepechin) and bibliography 5506

"Review of economics text-books for use in Canadian high schools" 3371

Review of ethnohistorical research on the native peoples of Quebec 4079

Review of historical publications relating to Canada, 1896-1917-18 1899

A review of insects affecting production of willows 5519

A review of lake aeration as a technique for water quality improvement 5184

"Review of literature, science and art" 0018

A review of literature on the lateral shear strength of nail-timber connections 5729

A review of literature on the problem of blackening in cooked
   potatoes 4644
Review of literature related to clay liners for sump disposal of
   drilling waste 5834
A review of literature to 1975 of forest hydrology pertinent to
   the management of mountainous watersheds 4949
A review of paleobotanical studies dealing with the last 20,000
   years: Alaska, Canada and Greenland 5450
"A review of palynological studies in eastern Maritime
   Canada" 4765
A review of phase separation in borosilicate glasses, with
   reference to nuclear fuel waste immobilization/Examen de
   la séparation des phases dans les verres aux borosilicate qu-
   ant à l'immobilisation des déchets de combustible nucléaire
   5844
"Review of recent literature on Canadian-Latin American
   relations" 2495
Review of reports of growth and regeneration surveys in
   Canada, conducted by the Dominion Forest Service and the
   Commission of Conservation, 1918-36 4917
A review of research literature on forest fertilization 4922
"A review of selected materials in the educational history of
   western Canada" 3567
Review of silvicultural research: white spruce and trembling
   aspen cover types, Mixedwood Forest Section, Boreal Forest
   Region, Alberta-Saskatchewan-Manitoba 5347
A review of silviculture research in jack pine 5345
"A review of the historical and sociological literature on East
   Indians in Canada" 4179
A review of the international literature on mine spoil
   subsidence 4872
A review of the literature and field validation of the
   competencies of industrial and organizational trainers and
   educators 3653
Review of the literature concerning erosion and accretion of
   the Canadian shoreline of the Great Lakes 5145
A review of the literature of oil pollution with particular
   reference to the Canadian Great Lakes 5064
Review of the literature on apple by-products 4637
A review of the literature on attitudes and roles and their
   effects on safety in the workplace 2862
A review of the literature on health hazards of video display
   terminals 5630
Review of the literature on HIV infection and mental health
   5697
Review of the literature on home care 5610
Review of the literature on migrant mental health 5677
A review of the literature on the proposed Grasslands National
   Park 3019
A review of the literature relevant to rent regulation 4406
A review of water reconditioning re-use technology for fish
   culture, with a selected bibliography 4894
Reviews of the Young Offenders Act: a bibliography 2303
Revised annotated bibliography on the Dolly Varden char 5352
"Revised bibliography of Indian musical culture in Canada"
   0858
Revised biological literature review of Davis Strait [microform]
   5536
Revision and patriation of the Constitution 1965-1982: select
   bibliography/Révision et repatriement de la Constitution
   1965-1982: bibliographie sélective 2248

Revision constitutionnelle: bibliographie sélective 2227
Révision et repatriement de la Constitution 1965-1982:
   bibliographie sélective 2248
Revolutionary America, 1763-1789: a bibliography 2038
Revue bibliographique sur Pachypappa tremulae (L): un
   puceron des racines des plants de conifères en récipients
   5534
Revue critique de la littérature en français sur la coopération
   ouvrière de production dans les pays industrialisés, 1975-
   1983 2728
"Une revue critique de la littérature sur l'homosexualité avec
   une emphase sur la science et la mesure" 3118
Revue de la contamination dans la chaîne aquatique arctique:
   présentation de la banque de données 5279
Revue de la documentation sur la conception des joints à
   liaison mécanique en composites 5818
Revue de la documentation sur l'infection à VIH et la santé
   mentale 5698
Revue de la littérature et bibliographie des processus
   géologiques et des sédiments du Saint-Laurent 4875
Revue de la littérature sur le camionnage des produits
   forestiers en forêt 4933
Une revue de la littérature sur les relations avec les membres
   dans les coopératives (et les fédérations de coopératives)
   2677
Revue de littérature: le micro-ordinateur comme outil de vérifi-
   cation dans les cabinets d'experts-comptables 2754
Revue de littérature et bibliographie indexée sur la recherche-
   action chez les professeurs de niveau collégial 3650
Revue de littérature sur le rôle des activités d'apprentissage
   dans l'enseignement à distance 3688
Revue de littérature sur les coûts indirects des accidents du
   travail 2912
Revue de littérature sur les divers concepts de vergers à
   graines 5010
Revue de littérature sur les écrans cathodiques 5641
Revue de littérature sur les modèles et les stratégies de prestation de service communautaires offerts aux personnes âgées
   en perte d'autonomie fonctionnelle et mentale et à leurs
   aidants naturels 5703
Revue des documents de référence portant sur la santé mentale
   des migrants 5678
Revue des études sur la prévalence de la déficience mentale
   grave 5628
Revue des publications traitant des attitudes et des rôles et de
   leurs effets sur la sécurité du travail 2863
La Revue des revues de Recherches sociographiques:
   bibliographie 3122
Revue sélective des recherches en matière de justice pénale
   2237
"Les revues littéraires québécoises de l'université à la contre-
   culture" 5921
Richard Maurice Bucke: a catalogue based upon the collections
   of the University of Western Ontario Libraries 6881
Rideau Canal bibliography, 1972-1992 4520
Riel, Red River, and beyond: new developments in Métis his-
   tory 4099
The Riel rebellions: a cartographic history/Le récit
   cartographique des affaires Riel 6567
The right to privacy: select bibliography 2324
The right to privacy/Le droit à la vie privée 2324

The rights of indigenous peoples in international law: an annotated bibliography 2278

Riots: [a bibliography] 2160

Les risques pour la reproduction inhérants au milieu de travail au Canada: bibliographie annotée 5683

River ice jams: a literature review 5039

Road reference library: a catalogue of publications on roads and road transport 4448

Road reference library catalogue: supplement 1, August, 1961 4448

Robert Addison's library: a short-title catalogue of the books brought to Upper Canada in 1792 by the first missionary sent out to the Niagara frontier by the Society for the Propagation of the Gospel 6774

Robert Bourassa 6864

"Robert Charbonneau [biographie: bibliographie]" 6902

Robert Farnon discography 6975

Robert Kroetsch: an annotated bibliography 7103

Robert Le Blant, historien et chef de file de la recherche sur les débuts de la Nouvelle-France: bibliographie commentée 7132

Robert Le Blant, seminal researcher and historian of early New France: a commented bibliography 7133

"Robert McQueen, 1896-1941: [bibliography]" 7185

"Robert Stead: an annotated bibliography" 7320

Robert Turner 7341

"Robertson Davies: a chronology and checklist" 6938

Robertson Davies: an annotated bibliography 6940, 6941

The Rodolphe Mathieu collection at the National Library of Canada: an annotated catalogue 7180

"Roger James Evan Brown, 1931-1980" 6878

Le rôle des arts dans l'enseignement: bibliographie commentée 3558

Le role du député 2514

The role of government in providing child care facilities: a checklist of sources 3181

The role of organic compounds in salinization of Plains coal mining sites: a literature review 4816

The role of the backbencher/Le role du député 2514

Roll back the years: history of Canadian recorded sound and its legacy: genesis to 1930 0848

Roll compaction of metal powders: bibliography for period 1900 to 1973 5747

Roman canadien-français: évolution, témoignages, bibliographie 1026

"Le roman du XIXe siècle (1837-1895)" 1147

Le roman québécois, 1980-1983 1220

Roman Rakhmanny: a bibliographic guide to selected works 7222

"Romanian-Canadian periodical publications: a preliminary check list" 5914

The Romanians in America and Canada: a guide to information sources 4199

Romans policiers et histoires d'aventures canadiens pour la jeunesse: liste 1353

Romulus (Computer file)/Romulus (Fichier d'ordinateur) 5991

Romulus (Fichier d'ordinateur) 5991

Room 302 Books, list #4: bpNichol, a ranging 7214

Roots: genealogical resources in W.L.U. Library 2083

A rough check list of the first editions of John Buchan (Lord Tweedsmuir) 7345

A 'round the clock job: a selected bibliography on women's work at home in Canada 3821

Rowell's American newspaper directory 6001

Royal Canadian Mounted Police: a bibliography 2128, 2195

Royal Canadian Mounted Police: a bibliography of resource material 2125

Royal commissions and commissions of inquiry for the provinces of Upper Canada, Canada and Ontario, 1792 to 1991: a checklist of reports 6413

Royal commissions and commissions of inquiry in Alberta, 1905-1976 6306

Royal commissions and commissions of inquiry under "The Evidence Act" in Manitoba: a checklist 6234

Royal commissions and commissions of inquiry under the "Public Inquiries Act" in British Columbia, 1872-1942: a checklist 6227

Royal commissions and commissions of inquiry under the Public Inquiries Act in British Columbia, 1943-1980: a checklist 6339

Royalty and royal tours: a Canadian bibliography 2074

Le royaume du Saguenay: exposition de livres anciens 0402

Rules and catalogue of the Halifax Garrison Library 6735

The running Canadian bibliography: a consolidation, 1978-1984/Bibliographie courante d'ouvrages canadiens: une consolidation, 1978-1984 5668

Rural aging in Canada: an annotated bibliography 3280

Rural British Columbia: a bibliography of social and economic research 0579

Rural communication: information and innovation in farming: a literature review 4724

Rural sociology, farm related decision-making and the influence of environment on behaviour 3015

"Rural sociology in the United States and Canada: classified and annotated bibliography" 3079

The rural-urban fringe: a bibliography 4442

"Russian-Canadian imprints: a preliminary check list" 4150

"Russian-Canadian periodical publications: a preliminary check list" 5886

The Ruth Konrad Collection of Canadiana: a descriptive catalogue 6778

The Ryerson imprint: a check-list of the books and pamphlets published by The Ryerson Press since the foundation of the House in 1829 1580

Safety literature catalogue: the printed word works for safety 2801

"Saint Antoine Daniel, martyr canadien: bibliographie" 6932

Saint Joseph dans l'édition canadienne: bibliographie 1520

"Le Saint-Laurent: orientation bibliographique" 2971

Les saints Martyrs canadiens 1567

The Salish people: the local contribution of Charles Hill-Tout 7064

The sampling and analysis of airborne sulphates and nitrates: a review of published work and synthesis of available information 5176

Sanctions légales et dissuasion 2316

"Sandra Birdsell: an annotated bibliography" 6843

Sandy Fraser: a bibliography of the writings of John Everett McIntosh (1876-1948) in The Farmer's Advocate under the pen name of Sandy Fraser 7183

La santé, les facteurs psychologiques et sociologiques: bibliographie annotée 1828

Santé: bibliographie 5583

Santé et bien-être des infirmières plus particulièrement sur risques en milieu infirmier 5606

"A select bibliography of anthropology of British Columbia" 4557

Select bibliography of books by parliamentarians, as displayed at the National Library of Canada from Mar. 12, to Apr. 11, 1976/Bibliographie sélective de livres par des membres du parlement, en montre à la Bibliothèque nationale du Canada du 12 mars au 11 avril 1976 2425

"A select bibliography of Canadian decimal coins" 1807

"A select bibliography of Canadian numismatics" 1753

"A select bibliography of Newfoundland children's books, 1970-1990" 1395

Select bibliography of recent material on teaching machines and programmed learning 3384

"A select bibliography of South Asian poetry in Canada" 1231

"Select bibliography of Stephen Leacock's contributions to the social sciences" 7134

Select bibliography of the history of Canadian science, medicine and technology 4626

A select bibliography of the polar regions 0611

A select bibliography of Tim Buck, general secretary of the Communist Party of Canada, 1929-1962 6880

A select bibliography on alternatives to institutional care for the elderly 3150

Select bibliography on Canadian Indian treaties and related subjects/Bibliographie spéciale sur les traités indiens canadiens et des autres sujets alliés 4007

"Select bibliography on ethnic groups and inter-ethnic relations in Alberta: 1972-1974" 4168

A select bibliography on ethnicity and multiculturalism for high schools 4167

Select bibliography on higher education/Bibliographie sur l'enseignement supérieur 3585, 3599

"A select bibliography on indigenous peoples in Canada" 4118

Select bibliography on parliamentary procedure/Bibliographie sélective sur la procédure parlementaire 2384

"Select bibliography on post-war immigrants in Canada" 4144

Select bibliography on the history of British Columbia 0590

A select bibliography on the location of industry 2561

Select bibliography on travel in North America 1888

Select committees of the assemblies of the provinces of Upper Canada, Canada and Ontario, 1792 to 1991: a checklist of reports 6414

Select committees of the Legislative Assembly of Ontario, 1867-1978 6354

Select list of books, with references to periodicals, on reciprocity with Canada 2558

A select list of publications by A.R.M. Lower 7157

Select list of references on the annexation of Canada to the United States 2372

Select reading list on Canadian-Australian relations 2388

A selected, annotated bibliography concerning future needs in all levels and forms of native education in Alberta, Canada 3410

"A selected, annotated bibliography for Saskatchewan butterfly watchers" 5549

A selected, annotated bibliography of Canadian housing research, 1970-79 4382

"Selected and annotated bibliography of South Asians in Ontario" 4280

A selected and annotated bibliography on Indian self-government 4082

Selected and annotated bibliography on post-secondary education in Canada 3665

Selected and annotated bibliography on teaching and learning a second language with special emphasis on English as a second language 3503

A selected and annotated bibliography on the sociology of Eskimo education 3388

Selected and annotated bibliography on urbanization for Project Canada West 4321

Selected and annotated readings on planning theory and practice 3022

A selected and briefly annotated bibliography of sources relating to the Province of Nova Scotia and its major (and two minor) ethno-cultural groups 4187

A selected annotated bibliography for teacher training in Canada, 1976 3519

"Selected annotated bibliography of articles relevant to alternatives in librarianship" 1622

Selected annotated bibliography of asbestos resources in the United States and Canada 4753

Selected annotated bibliography of high-grade silica of the United States and Canada through December 1954 4751

Selected annotated bibliography of recent research on rural life on Prince Edward Island 0212

Selected annotated bibliography of research on part-time farming in Canada 4684

A selected annotated bibliography of rural Canada/ Bibliographie annotée du Canada rural 3168

A selected annotated bibliography of the climate of the Great Lakes 5065

Selected annotated bibliography on application of satellite images to thematic mapping 5795

Selected annotated bibliography on asphalt-bearing rocks of the United States and Canada, to 1970 4778

A selected annotated bibliography on the Filipino immigrant community in Canada and the United States 4273

Selected annotated references concerning timber wolf (Canis lupus) predation 5433

Selected architectural books published in Canada, 1974-1984 0778

"[Selected bibliographies on Canadian labour issues]" 2942

Selected bibliography: [Duncan Campbell Scott] 7297

A selected bibliography for aerial photograph interpretation of natural and cultural features 3016

A selected bibliography for garden history in Canada 4714

Selected bibliography of articles on oil and gas economics, 1986-1989 2753

Selected bibliography of Canadian forest literature, 1917-1946 4919

Selected bibliography of Canadian geography/Bibliographie choisie d'ouvrages sur la géographie au Canada 2968

"A selected bibliography of Canadian theatre and drama bibliographies and guides" 1199

A selected bibliography of Canadian water management (1965-April 1970) 5060

Selected bibliography of CANMET publications pertaining to the activities of the Canadian Carbonization Research Association (CCRA), 1965-1980 [microform] 6337

"Selected bibliography of Chilean writing in Canada" 1270

A selected bibliography of coastal erosion, protection and related human activity in North America and the British Isles 2972

Selected bibliography on the geology of Canadian deposits and occurrences of uranium and thorium 4795

A selected bibliography on the Peace and Athabasca rivers and the Peace-Athabasca Delta region 0502

A selected bibliography on the social and economic implications of electronic data processing 2576

A selected bibliography on Toronto's port and waterfront 4431

A selected bibliography on wage and price controls in Canada 2688

A selected bibliography on wage and salary administration, employee benefits and services and collective bargaining 2795

Selected books & journals for Manitoba health care facilities 5642

Selected Canadian agrometeorological publications 4686

Selected Canadian public health references of epidemiological significance 5565

"A selected checklist of Prairie poetry in English" 1167

Selected cities of the province of Quebec: Canadian urban information for federal land management project 4358

Selected free Ontario government publications for children and young adults 6323

"Selected Islandia bibliography, 1963-1973" 0220

A selected list of articles and papers on the climatology of the Upper Great Lakes published from 1960 to 1972 5074

Selected list of bibliographies 3233

Selected list of bibliographies on Indians of Canada 3976

A selected list of books and periodicals on industrial design 0667

A selected list of current government publications dealing with pollution 6289

Selected list of current materials on Canadian public administration 2385

A selected list of music reference materials 0823

A selected list of periodical literature on topics related to Canadian geography for the period 1930-1939 2957

A selected list of publications issued by the Ontario Ministry of Labour, 1955-1973 6282

A selected list of publications on the Indians of British Columbia 4081

A selected list of publications pertaining to the Indians of British Columbia 4081

Selected list of recent books and pamphlets on Canada 0053

A selected list of references on cost-cutting in house construction 5719

A selected list of the writings of E. Cockburn Kyte 7104

Selected list of war time pamphlets: No. 1-3 1920

Selected literature concerning birds in British Columbia 5340

Selected Ontario government publications for schools and libraries 6323

A selected reading list of books about the Arctic 0612

Selected readings on Canadian external policy, 1909-1959 2465

Selected references for Canadian hospital libraries, 1974-1980/ Bibliographie sélective à l'intention des bibliothèques d'hôpitaux canadiens, 1974-1980 1647

Selected references on abortion 5596

Selected references on Canadian Nurses' Association/ Bibliographie sélective on[sic] Association des infirmières et infirmiers du Canada 5617

Selected references on phosphorus removal 5078

Selected references with annotations for study of nurse manpower requirements 5611

Selected review of literature on adult female and male incest survivors 3360

Selected sources on aboriginal issues 4117

Selected sources on northern housing and related community infrastructure: an annotated bibliography 4432

Selected thematic maps of man's activities in Canada's watersheds/Cartes thématiques des activités de l'homme dans les bassins hydrographiques du Canada 6572

Selected titles published by Government of Canada departments and agencies 6321

"A selected western Canada historical resources bibliography to 1985" 0548

Selection aids for Saskatchewan schools: a bibliography for school libraries 1643

Sélection de livres français 0138

Sélection de publications sur les chemins de fer canadiens 4477

A selection of publications on the Indians of British Columbia 4081

A selection of publications on the native Indians of British Columbia with particular reference to the struggle for native rights 4069

Selection of teachers and student teachers 3533

Selections: federal government and international publications for educators 6296

Selections from the Canadiana collection of the Ontario Legislative Library 0154

A selective and annotated bibliography of Riding Mountain National Park 2983

"A selective annotated bibliography for the study of Newfoundland vertical-log structures with some comments on terminology" 0768

Selective annoted [sic] bibliography for the study of the Amerindians and Inuit: a guide for secondary school history and geography teachers 4084

Selective bibliography: terminology and related fields 1476

A selective bibliography of Canadian and international readings in arts administration and cultural development 0679

A selective bibliography of Canadian legal sources 2133

A selective bibliography of Canadian plays 1016

A selective bibliography of Canadiana of the prairie provinces: publications relating to western Canada by English, French, Icelandic, Mennonite, and Ukrainian authors 0495

A selective bibliography of ceremonies, dances, music & songs of the American Indian from books in the library of Gregory Javitch, with an annotated list of Indian dances 3955

A selective bibliography of important books, pamphlets and broadsides relating to Michigan history 1930

A selective bibliography of literature on revenue stamps 1748

Selective bibliography of materials relating to the geology of Calgary, Alberta and vicinity 4837

"Selective bibliography of North American commissions on criminal justice/Bibliographie sélective des commissions d'enquête nord-américaines en matière de justice pénale" 2362

A selective bibliography of publications on the Champlain Valley 0290

A selective bibliography of the lake trout, Salvelinus namaycush (Walbaum), 1784-1982 5505

A selective bibliography on human and civil rights 2127

A selective bibliography on the clothing and textile industry in Canada 2608

"Sir Wilfrid Laurier: a contribution towards a bibliography"
7128

Sir William Osler: an annotated bibliography with illustrations
7228

Le sirop d'érable: une bibliographie rétrospective, 1949-1971
4938

Site selection criteria and the principles of design for planning
recreational places: campgrounds: a bibliography with
abstracts 1775

Sitka spruce: a literature review with special reference to
British Columbia 5377

"Situation de la recherche sur la musique au Canada français"
0874

Situation de l'édition et de la recherche: littérature québécoise
ou canadienne-française 1126

Sixteenth century Canadiana in English: a bibliography in
short-title catalog form 2068

Sixteenth-century maps relating to Canada: a checklist and
bibliography 6504

The Skeena River estuary: status of environmental knowledge
to 1975: report of the Estuary Working Group, Department
of the Environment, Regional Board Pacific Region 5100

Sketch of the life and work of the late Dr. Alfred R.C. Selwyn ...
Director of the Geological Survey of Canada from 1869 to
1894 7302

"Sketch of the life and work of the late Dr. Alfred R.C. Selwyn
... Director of the Geological Survey of Canada from 1869 to
1894" 7303

"Sketch of the life of Dr. A.R.C. Selwyn, C.M.G.: bibliography"
7304

Skiing: an English language bibliography, 1891-1971 1776

Slavica Canadiana 4164

A slice of Canada: a list of Canadian books of interest to small
Alberta public libraries 0113

"Slovak-Canadian periodical publications: a preliminary check
list" 5882

Small aircraft crashworthiness 5825

Small and large group instruction: a bibliography 3464

Small business and entrepreneurship/Les petites entreprises et
l'entrepreneurship 2758

Small-scale technology for local forest development: an
annotated bibliography 4969

Smash the state: a discography of Canadian punk, 1977-92 0943

Snow and ice research in Canada, 1988 5272

Snow in Canada references (1988-1990) and recent work 5285

Snowshoe hares and forest plantations: a literature review and
problem analysis 4993

So we may know more about Canada, citizenship & democracy
2375

Social and economic studies 3969

Social and economic welfare: selected references/Le bien-être
social et économique: bibliographie sélective 3104

"Social and psychological aspects of the normal pregnancy
experience: a bibliography" 3797

Social aspects of urban transportation: a bibliographic review
4459

The social context of the new information and communication
technologies: a bibliography 1698

Social dimensions of environmental planning: an annotated
bibliography 5156

The social impacts of layoffs: an annotated bibliography 3202

Social protest from the left in Canada, 1870-1970 2472

Social psychology of Canada: an annotated bibliography 3100

The social psychology of inter-action contact and cross-cultural
communication: an annotated bibliography 4192

The social psychology of second language acquisition and
bilinguality: an annotated bibliography 3136

Social realism: [a resource guide for the teaching of Canadian
literature] 1115

Social science research on Asians in Canada 4220

Social service aspects of rehabilitation: a selective bibliography:
une bibliographie sélective 3131

Social studies year one: "Saskatchewan": bibliography, Division
two, resource materials 0519

Social work: a bibliography of bibliographies 3344

Social work: a bibliography of bibliographies in W.L.U. Library
3344

Social work: a bibliography of directories in W.L.U. Library
3332

La Société de Notre-Dame de Montréal, 1639-1663: son histoire,
ses membres, son manifeste 0292

La Société des écrivains canadiens: ses règlements, son action,
bio-bibliographie de ses membres 1005

Socio-economic development in Labrador: a select
bibliography 0261

Socio-economic factors pertaining to single-industry resource
towns in Canada: a bibliography with selected annotations
4384

Socio-economic impact studies relating to pipeline projects and
certain northern development projects: bibliography/Études
d'impact socio-économique relatives à des projets de
pipeline et à certains projets de developpement nordique:
bibliographie 0632

Sociologie de la famille et de la société québécoise:
bibliographie annotée, environ 750 titres 3194

"Sociologie du milieu carcéral, bibliographie sélective" 3290

"Sociology in Canada: a view from the eighties" 3339

Sociology of American Indians: a critical bibliography 4021

The sociology of Canadian Mennonites, Hutterites and Amish:
a bibliography with annotations 1542

The sociology of contemporary Quebec nationalism: an
annotated bibliography and review 0372

Soil science [bibliography] 4661

Soins infirmiers et services de santé, région du nord canadien:
bibliographie choisie 5586

Soins pour les bas du dos: bibliographie annotée 1812

Solstice de la poésie québécoise: poèmes, affiches,
vidéogrammes: une exposition itinérante 1112

Solvent abuse: an annotated bibliography with additional related citations 5587

The Somass River estuary: status of environmental knowledge
to 1980: report of the Estuary Working Group, Joint Fisheries
and Oceans-Environment Co-ordinating Committee on
Environmental Affairs, Pacific and Yukon Region 5166

"Some Canadian materials on women: a basic list" 3748

"Some highly subversive activities: a brief polemic and a
checklist of works on Alice Munro" 7204

Some implications of large-scale clearcutting in Alberta: a
literature review 4928

Some materials for the study of Nova Scotia architecture 0744

Some of the materials concerning the struggle for the Canadian
universities (other-wise known as "Americanization",
"takeover", "de-Canadianization of the universities") 3420

Sport and recreation for the disabled: an index of resource materials/Sport et loisir pour handicapés: un répertoire de la littérature 1830

Sport bibliography/Bibliographie du sport 1815

Sport et loisir pour handicapés: un répertoire de la littérature 1830

Sport et loisirs pour handicapés: une bibliographie, 1984-1989 1862

Sport legislation: Europe and North America: a specialized bibliography from the SPORT Database/Législation sportive: Europe et Amérique du Nord: une bibliographie spécialisée de la base de données SPORT 1867

Sport violence: a specialized bibliography from the SPORT database/Violence du sport: une bibliographie spécialisée de la base de données SPORT 1861

Sporting events and international competitions 1815

Sports and games in Canadian children's books: list/Livres canadiens sur les sports et les jeux pour la jeunesse: liste 1348

Les sports au Québec, 1879-1975: catalogue d'exposition 1783

Sports et loisirs: bibliographie, périodiques, films, diaporamas, organismes 1816

Spring habitats and their faunas: an introductory bibliography 5556

The spruce beetle, Dendroctonus rufipennis (Kirby): an annotated bibliography, 1885-1987 5545

Spruce budworms bibliography, with author and key word indices 5432

The Squamish River estuary: status of environmental knowledge to 1974: report of the Estuary Working Group, Department of the Environment, Regional Board, Pacific Region 5101

Square one: an index to CLE publications, 1978-1984- 2364

Le St-Laurent: bibliographie économique 4472

St. Andrews Biological Station publications, 1977-86 6393

The St. Andrew's chronicles: bibliography and notes 1545

St. John's bibliography, 1870-1914 0215

"St. Lawrence River ship canal" 4444

The Standard directory of newsletters 5992

Standard topographical maps of Canada, 1904-1948 6597

Standards for Canadian libraries: a bibliography 1725

Standards for Canadian libraries/Normes pour les bibliothèques canadiennes 1725

Standards for medical and dental equipment and materials: bibliography/Normes traitant des produits et du matériel à usage médical et dentaire: bibliographie 5636

Standards for music collections in medium-sized libraries 0817

Stany Zjednoczone Ameryki i Kanada w pismiennictwie polskim 1945-1985: bibliografia drukow zwartych 0155

Starting line-up: a directory of British Columbia writers for public libraries 0599

The state bibliography: an annotated bibliography on women and the state in Canada 3872

State of the art: research on the elderly, 1964-1972 3106

"Station touristique et temps partage: deux formes de villégiature" 1842

Statistics Canada: union list of holdings for Barrie, Owen Sound and Orillia public libraries 6327

Statistics Canada catalogue 6445

Statistics Canada publications on microfiche, 1850-1980 6371

Statistics published by provincial governments in Canada 3034

Statistique Canada catalogue 6446

Statistiques, études de marché et répertoires concernant l'industrie et l'exploitation forestières au Québec: une bibliographie 4996

Statistiques sur les bibliothèques canadiennes: une liste sélective des sources 1721

A status report and bibliography of cultural studies in the Canadian Arctic to 1976 0640

Statut de l'artiste: bibliographie sélective et annotée 0721

Le statut de réfugié au Canada: une bibliographie annotée 2507

Statutory publications, price list/Publications officielles, liste des prix 6458

Stephen Leacock: a check-list and index of his writings 7136

Stephen Leacock: a reappraisal 7135

Stephen Leacock: the writer and his writings 7135

"Stinson Jarvis: a bio-bibliography" 7076

STOL technology bibliography update 4452

Strategic minerals: a bibliography 4861

Streaming in Toronto and other Ontario schools: a review of the literature 3563

Street cars, subways and rapid transit: a Canadian bibliography 4424

Strength training for youth: a specialized bibliography from the SPORT database/Musculation pour les jeunes: une bibliographie spécialisées de la base de données SPORT 1869

Stress and coping: an annotated bibliography/Stress et stratégies d'adaptation: bibliographie annotée 1813

Stress et stratégies d'adaptation: bibliographie annotée 1813

The striped ambrosia beetle, Trypodendron lineatum (Oliver): an annotated bibliography 5439

The structure and dynamics of intra-urban labour markets: a diagnostic bibliography 2874

Student housing report: submitted by D.S. Ferguson to the Ontario Department of University Affairs, 1969, with bibliography and appendices 3401

Studies in Canadian regional geography: essays in honor of J. Lewis Robinson 7271

Studies in enterprise: a selected bibliography of American and Canadian company histories 2566

Studies in the book trade 1637

Studies of community patterns and planning in the counties of Peterborough, Victoria and Haliburton: a bibliographical guide to unpublished reports 4407

Studies of drinking in public places: an annotated bibliography 3272

"Studies of English Canadian literature" 1287

Studies related to British Columbia tourism: a bibliography with selected annotations 1800

The study of art in Canada 0685

"The study of British Columbia women: a quarter-century review, 1960-1984" 3844

Study of historical injustice to Japanese Canadians: text and bibliography 4279

The study of the future: a bibliography of material in the Library of the Ontario Ministry of Treasury, Economics and Intergovernmental Affairs 2654

Studying Nova Scotia: its history and present state, its politics and economy: a bibliography and guide 0225

Sub-doctoral theses on Canada: accepted by universities in the United Kingdom & Ireland, 1899-1986: together with a supplement to J.J. Dossick Doctoral research on Canada and Canadians, 1884-1983 6198

The subarctic Athabascans: a selected annotated bibliography 3954

Subarctic Athapaskan bibliography, 1973 4058

Subarctic Athapaskan bibliography, 1984 4058

Subject bibliography: native studies [bibliography of bibliographies] 4026

A subject bibliography of theses bibliographies held in Carleton University Library 6202

A subject catalogue, or, Finding list of books in the Reference Library, with an index of subjects and personal names 6742

Subject catalogue of CTF publications in print 3408

A subject catalogue of the Foundation's published material 2570

Subject catalogue of the Library of the Royal Empire Society, formerly Royal Colonial Institute, by Evans Lewin 6764

Subject catalogue of the Royal Commonwealth Society, London 6777

Subject classified literature references on effects of oil pollution in Arctic and subarctic waters 5140

Subject guide to native law cases and annotated text of the Indian Act of Canada 2272

Subject headings and subject access to children's literature: a bibliography covering materials issued 1975-1985/Vedettes-matière et accès par sujet à la littérature de jeunesse: une bibliographie qui traite des publications parues entre 1975 et 1985 1683

Subject index to NSDME assessment reports, open files, publications and theses, 1981 to 1990 6333

A subject index to the books in the Library of the Law Society of Upper Canada at Osgoode Hall, Toronto, January 1st, 1900 2098

Subventions agricoles, 1980-1987: bibliographie sélective et annotée 4710

The Sudbury basin: a guide to the local collection 0434

Sudbury maps 6521

Sudbury mining area: a selected bibliography 4810

A suggested buying guide to Canadian books for small Alberta libraries 0113

Summary of current research on snow and ice in Canada 5072

Summary of current research on snow and ice in Canada, 1976 5113

"Summary of developments in Canadian subject and area bibliography since 1974" 1653

Summary of projects and publications, 1960-1985 [Engineering and Statistical Research Institute, Agriculture Canada]/ Sommaire des projets et des publications, 1960-1985 [Institut de recherche technique et statistique, Agriculture Canada] 6374

"Sunday shopping legislation: a selected bibliography" 2759

Supervision et évaluation du personnel enseignant: bibliographie annotée 3455

Supplement to People and law: a bibliography of public legal education 2183

Supplementary bibliography [Edmonton Public Library, Western Canadiana Collection] 0541

"Supplementary bibliography of comparative Canadian literature (English-Canadian and French-Canadian)" 1277

"A supplementary bibliography on Newfoundland music" 0840

Supplementary list of publications of the Geological Survey, Canada 6211

"Sur la question nationale au Canada et au Québec" 2423

"Sur quelques bibliographies récentes" 1980

Surface water acidification literature review 5254

Surficial geology map index of British Columbia 6599

"Survey and annotated bibliography of curricula used by oral preschool programs" 3636

A survey and interpretation of the literature of interlibrary loan 1613

A survey and listing of Nova Scotia newspapers, 1752-1957: with particular reference to the period before 1867 6028

A survey of arts audience studies: a Canadian perspective, 1967-1984 0706

A survey of Canadian mining history 4784

"A survey of Canadian picture books in recent years" 1383

Survey of documents available for research in the Treaties and Historical Research Centre/Catalogue des documents au Centre de recherches historiques et d'étude des traités 4088

"A survey of hymnody in the Church of England in eastern Canada to 1909" 0819

Survey of leisure reading materials for A.B.E. students with emphasis on western Canada: a $500 collection 3560

A survey of literature on televised language instruction 3425

Survey of literature on the assessment of the pollution potential of the peat resource: final report submitted to Environment Canada 5189

A survey of literature on the lateral resistance of nails 5724

A survey of powder forging literature, 1960-1974 5766

Survey of research in music and music education in Canada 0860

A survey of the aboriginal populations of Quebec and Labrador 3909

A survey of the collection of Canadian statutes and subordinate legislation held in the Sir James Dunn Law Library 2176

A survey of the materials to be found in the Provincial Legislative Library, Alberta, for a study of Canadian history and more particularly that of western Canada 0494

Surveys of library collections in Canada, 1955-1981/Inventaire des collections des bibliothèques canadiennes, 1955-1981 1654

Suspended drivers in Ontario: license disqualification: a review of the literature 4505

Sustainable development and the entrepreneur: an annotated bibliography of small business development in circumpolar and developing regions 0659

Sustaining earth: a bibliography of the holdings of the Ecology Action Resource Centre, Halifax, Canada 5262

"Swedish-Canadian periodical publications: a preliminary check list" 5889

Sweet & Maxwell's complete law book catalogue 2110

Swimmers and sea birds 5504

"Swiss literature on Canada: a preliminary check list of imprints" 4149

A syllabus on Indian history and culture 3925

A synopsis of American fossil Bryozoa: including bibliography and synonymy 4527

Le syntagme terminologique: bibliographie sélective et analytique 1477

Synthèse historique de l'immersion française au Canada suivie d'une bibliographie sélective et analytique 3718

Système de référence PA-GE [Plein-air-grand espaces]: composante no 1 (dossier bibliographique) 1769

Le système métrique: liste bibliographique de guides, de manuels et de tables de conversion 2615

Systèmes d'automatisation de la marche des trains: bibliographie sélective 4508

Systems analysis in education 3415

T.F. Wood & Co's Canadian newspaper directory, containing accurate lists of all the newspapers and periodicals published in the Dominion of Canada and province of Newfoundland 5995

The T.M.E. system of feed evaluation: methodology, feed composition data and bibliography 4707

"Tableaux: périodiques littéraires et culturels du Québec depuis 1954" 5956

Tables provisoires du théâtre de Drummondville: index établi d'après les articles et les comptes rendus de presse parus dans les périodiques drummondvillois 0969

Taxe sur les produits et services (Phase II du Livre blanc sur la réforme fiscale): bibliographie sélective et annotée 2750

TDC publications, 1971-1982/Publications du CDT, 1971-1982 4488

Teacher and administrator evaluation 3597

Teacher autonomy and teacher decision making 3452

Teacher education programs for native people 3498

Teacher effectiveness research 3623

Teacher evaluation 3499

Teacher evaluation: an annotated bibliography 3478

Teacher handbook: resource materials: Native peoples of Manitoba 3982

Teacher resource book: western Canadian literature for youth 1342

Teacher stress 3615

Teacher workload 3542

Teacher's guide to resource materials in cross-cultural education: Part one: Indians, Eskimos and early explorers 3926

Teaching aids obtainable from departments of the government at Ottawa 3374, 6228

Teaching Canada: a bibliography 0116

Teaching Canadian studies: an evaluation of print materials, grades 1-13 0132

Teaching English as an additional language: annotated bibliography 3403

Teaching French as a second language in Canada 3554

Team sports, bowling sports and golf 1815

Team teaching: a bibliography 3459

Technical papers and technical memoranda issued by the Census Division, 1965-1968: an annotated list of studies and reports 2977

Technical publications [Alberta Energy, Alberta Forestry] 6418

Technical publications of Alberta Energy and Natural Resources 6418

Techniques d'administration: P.P.B.S., processus de prise de décision, gestion par les objectifs, analyse de problèmes, appliquées au monde de l'éducation: une bibliographie/School management: P.P.B.S., decision taking, M.B.O., problem solving: a bibliography 3461

Techniques d'intervention auprès des enfants d'âge préscolaire: dossier bibliographique ouvert au Centre de documentation du C.A.D.R.E. 3525

Techniques infirmières 5589

"Technological change and employment in Canada: a selected bibliography" 2892

Technological sovereignty: a selected bibliography with emphasis on Canada 2471

Technologie anaérobie: compte rendu des activités de recherche, de développement et de démonstration dans l'industrie agro-alimentaire et celle des pâtes et papiers 5830

Technologie et politique au Canada: bibliographie, 1963-1983 2485

Technology of mackerel fishery: bibliography and survey of literature 4891

Télé-formation: catalogue des ressources éducatives des Entreprises Radio-Canada 6666

Télécommunications: l'expérience canadienne: une liste explicative des cartes 6537

Telecommunications: the Canadian experience: an annotated list of maps/Télécommunications: l'expérience canadienne: une liste explicative des cartes 6537

Telecommunications and libraries: a selective bibliography for librarians/Télécommunications et bibliothèques: bibliographie sélective pour bibliothécaires 1666

Télécommunications et bibliothèques: bibliographie sélective pour bibliothécaires 1666

Télédétection des algues marines des côtes du Québec: 1 – Bibliographie mondiale annotée 5499

Telefacsimile transmission being used for document delivery: cost studies: an annotated bibliography/Recours à la télécopie pour la livraison des documents: les analyses des coûts: bibliographie sommaire 1693

Télématique et téléinformatique 1704

Telling our stories our way: a guide to good Canadian materials for women learning to read 3878

Témoins de la vie musicale en Nouvelle-France 0896

Le temps non-structuré: une bibliographie/Unstructured time: a bibliography 3462

The ten-year history and index of the Ontario Mineral Exploration Assistance Program (MEAP) 1971-1981 4832

"Ten years of Manitoba fiction in English: a selected bibliography" 1244

Ten years of northern research in Canada, 1974-1984/Dix ans de recherche nordique au Canada, 1974-1984 0649

Les tendances actuelles de la littérature de jeunesse en langue française: bibliographies d'ouvrages pour la jeunesse 1341

Tentative bibliography on filtration and some related subjects 5741

Tenure 3534

Teratogenic and chromosomal damaging effects of illicit drugs: an annotated bibliography with selected related citations involving the use of licit drugs 5588

A tercentennial contribution to a checklist of Kingston imprints to 1867 0457

Les terres et l'automobile: bibliographie sélective 4486

Terrestrial sediment transport into the marine environment of Canada: annotated bibliography and data 5229

Terrorism, 1970-1978, a bibliography 2197

Terrorism, 1980-1990: a bibliography 2353

Testing and evaluation of student achievement in Canada 3657

Textes et documents pour servir à l'étude de l'histoire économique et sociale de la Nouvelle-France 1960

Le théâtre à Nicolet, 1803-1969: bibliographie régionale 0976

Le théâtre canadien d'expression française: répertoire analytique des origines à nos jours 0967

Le théâtre canadien français: évolution, témoignages, bibliographie 0960

Towards a legal education and information program for native
people: a review of the literature and annotated bibliography
4006

Towns, wheels or wings? for resource development: an
annotated bibliography 4412

Township of York historical sources, volume 2: a descriptive
bibliography 0449

The toxicity of drilling fluid components to aquatic biological
systems: a literature review 5214

Tracing the movement of fine-grained sediment in aquatic
systems: a literature review 5278

Trade statistics with emphasis on Canada: a selected annotated
bibliography 2702

La tradition populaire québécoise: une base bibliographique
0368

Traditional knowledge and renewable resource management
in northern regions 5257

La traduction au Canada, 1534-1984/Translation in Canada,
1534-1984 1472

Traductions canadiennes 1493

Training, retraining, and labour market adjustment: an annotated bibliography of selected literature 2936

The training and employment of northern Canadians: an
annotated bibliography 3654

Transactions: indices to names of authors and subjects of the
papers presented to the Canadian Mining Institute, and the
antecedent provincial mining societies, 1891 to 1903 4734

"Transactions of the Canadian Mining Institute: Indices to
names of authors and subjects of the papers presented to the
Canadian Mining Institute, the Federated Canadian Mining
Institute, and the antecedent provincial mining societies,
1891 to 1903" 4733

Transferts de technologie Canada-Québec: bibliographie
annotée 2460

Transit: the nature and role of localized benefits: a selected
annotated bibliography 4494

Translation in Canada, 1534-1984 1472

"Translations of children's books in Canada" 1376

Translator's bibliography 1471

Transport à grande distance des polluants atmosphériques:
bibliographie 1980-1984 5222

Transport Canada publications catalogue and selected ongoing
research and development projects 6379

Transport Canada publications catalogue/Transports Canada
catalogue des publications 6379

Transport du charbon par chemin de fer: bibliographie
sélective 4504

Transport of solids in pipelines, with special reference to mineral ores, concentrates, and unconsolidated deposits (a
literature survey) 4773

Transport pour les handicapés: bibliographie 3167, 3189, 4471

Transportation for the disadvantaged: a bibliography/
Transport pour les handicapés: bibliographie 3167, 4471

Transportation for the mobility disadvantaged: a bibliography/
Transport pour les handicapés: bibliographie 3189

Transportation in British Columbia: a bibliography 4490

Transportation in Canada and the United States: a
bibliography of selected references, 1945-1969 4453

Transportation problems in Atlantic Canada: an introductory
bibliography 4475

Transports Canada, catalogue des publications et liste sélective
des projets de recherche et développement en cours 6379

Transports Canada catalogue des publications 6379

Travail, syndicalisme: bibliographie 2810

Travail de référence en commun: bibliographie sélective pour
bibliothécaires 1672

Le travail individuel de l'étudiant: une bibliographie/
Independent study: a bibliography 3463

Les travailleurs au Nouveau-Brunswick au 20ième siècle: un
guide au lecteur: bibliographie choisie et annotée 2904

Travailleurs du bâtiment [&] Personnel d'exploitation des
transports 2637

Travailleurs spécialisés des sciences sociales, membres du
clergé et enseignants 3540

Travaux en cours dans le domaine des sciences géologiques au
Canada 4881

Travaux en études régionales, résumés des mémoires de
maîtrise, 1980-1988 0406

Travaux historiques publiés depuis trente ans 1897

Travel in Canada: a guide to information sources 3043

Travel in the Maritime Provinces, 1750-1867 0252

The travellers: Canada to 1900: an annotated bibliography of
works published in English from 1577 2079

Trembling aspen bibliography 5350

The trend to the metropolis: bibliography 4312

Trente-quatre auteurs des provinces de l'Atlantique 0240

Trial bibliography: books and pamphlets relating to Canadian
railways in libraries of Montreal 4447

A trial bibliography of research pertaining to adult education
3385

"Tripartism" 2847

Les trois Gosselin 7023

Trucking 4514

True daughters of the North: Canadian women's history: an
annotated bibliography 3796

Tsunami: annotated bibliography 5294

Tsunamis: a selected bibliography 5131

Tulapai to Tokay: a bibliography of alcohol use and abuse
among native Americans of North America 4016

"Tune-book imprints in Canada to 1867: a descriptive
bibliography" 0862

"Tunebooks and hymnals in Canada, 1801-1939" 0932

Twenty-five years of Canadian publishing: W.H. Clarke: a
memorial exhibition, 1930-1955 1581

Tweny/20 1219

Twigg's directory of 1001 B.C. writers 0603

A two thousand item bibliography: the description, etiology,
diagnosis, and treatment of children with learning
disabilities or brain damage 3405

"Two year's work in Canadian poetry studies: 1976-1977" 1128

U.B.C. theses in forestry and related subject fields (1920-1967)
6093

U.S.–Canadian range management, 1935-1977: a selected
bibliography on ranges, pastures, wildlife, livestock, and
ranching 4683

U.S. and Canadian businesses, 1955 to 1987: a bibliography
2744

U.W.O. Map Library: atlas collection 6595

Ukraine and Ukrainian Canadians: books for high school,
college and public libraries 4194

"Ukrainian Canadian bibliography" 4135

"Ukrainian-Canadian creative literature: a preliminary check
list of imprints" 1054

"The view from the other side of the Atlantic" 0168

A view of university financing: [bibliography]/Aperçu du financement des universités: [bibliographie] 3579

Views and viewmakers of urban America: lithographs of towns and cities in the United States and Canada, notes on the artists and publishers, and a union catalog of their work, 1825-1925 4403

"The Vikings in America: a critical bibliography" 1927

La Ville de Québec, 1800-1850: un inventaire de cartes et plans 6546

The Vineer Organ Library 0900

Vingt ans de recherches artistiques, bibliographiques, biographiques, culturelles, historiographiques et historiques pour mettre en valeur la région de Lanaudière ou Catalogue descriptif et chronologique des oeuvres éditées, composées et compilées par Réjean Olivier 7218

Vingt-cinq ans de dramatiques à la télévision de Radio-Canada 0966

Vingt-cinq ans de géographie à l'Université de Sherbrooke, 1957-1982 3044

Violence and the media: a bibliography 0965

La violence au sein de la famille: une bibliographie sélective 3271

Violence au sein de la société: biobibliographie [sic] choisie 3288

Violence des spectateurs: une bibliographie spécialisée de la base de données SPORT 1860

Violence du sport: une bibliographie spécialisée de la base de données SPORT 1861

La violence familiale: examen des écrits théoriques et cliniques 3328

La violence familiale: une bibliographie des ressources ontariennes, 1980-1984 3269

La violence familiale: une bibliographie sélective 3351

Violence in society: a selective bibliography/Violence au sein de la société: biobibliographie [sic] choisie 3288

Violence prevention materials in the schools: a national listing 3730

Violet Archer 6804

Violet Archer: a bio-bibliography 6805

Virus diseases of small fruits: a bibliography, 1979-1981 4697

"Visible minority women and employment: a selected bibliography" 3822

"La vision chez les poissons: historique et bibliographie analytique" 5391

"Visits to Upper Canada, 1799-1867: a selected check-list of travel accounts in the Douglas Library" 1924

Visual display terminals: a selected bibliography/Les écrans cathodiques: une bibliographie sélective 5644

Voices of Alberta: a survey of oral history completed in Alberta up to 1980 6646

Voies de fait et mauvais traitements imposés aux femmes d'âge moyen et avancé par les conjoints et les enfants: bibliographie annotée 3302

Voix Albertaines 6646

"Volumes sur la faune du Québec" 5374

Volunteerism and volunteer administration: an annotated bibliography 3120

Volunteerism in corrections: a selected bibliography 2157

Volunteers and leadership bibliography 1801

The voyages and works of John Davis, the navigator 6942

Voyages et problèmes liés au décalage horaire: une bibliographie spécialisée de la base de données SPORT 5704

The W.A. Pugsley Collection of Early Maps of Canada, McGill University Library Map Collection: a catalogue 6549

W.O. Mitchell: an annotated bibliography 7193, 7194

W.W. Butcher's Canadian newspaper directory 5998

Wage-price control in Canada: an introductory bibliography 2651

Wage-price controls: a selected bibliography 2827

Walleye-sauger bibliography 5540

Walter Boudreau 6861

"Walter Klassen: a bibliography" 7092

The War of 1812: an annotated bibliography 2051

Wastewater Technology Centre: publications and presentations, 1972-1988 5837

The water balance in arctic and subarctic regions: annotated bibliography and preliminary assessment 5075

Water films 6614

Water Pollution Control Directorate publications/Les publications de la Direction générale de la lutte contre la pollution des eaux 6346

Water resources bibliography 5225

Water resources in New Brunswick: a preliminary bibliography 5250, 5256

Water resources of the Hudson Bay lowland: a literature review and annotated bibliography 5183

Waterborne preservative-treated railway ties: an annotated bibliography 5758

Weekly checklist of Canadian government publications/Liste hebdomadaire des publications du gouvernement canadien 6475

The welfare state in Canada: a selected bibliography, 1840 to 1978 3250

West Indians in Canada: a selective annotated bibliography 4145

"Western Canada: recent historical writing" 0525

Western Canada since 1870: a select bibliography and guide 0522

Wetland vegetation of the Prairie Pothole Region: research methods and annotated bibliography 5465

Wetlands and their role in treating acid mine drainage: a literature review 5267

"What's it like to be a woman artist? Selected bibliography" 0699

"What's new in second-language teaching: a selected annotated bibliography" 3731

What's QWL?: definition, notes, and bibliography 2837

Wheel-rail interaction: a selective bibliography/Interaction roue-rail: une bibliographie sélective 4499

"Where do we, should we, or can we sit? A review of Canadian foreign policy literature" 2540

Where is public participation going? An annotated bibliography focussing on Canadian experience 3192

Where it's at: pertinent publications on the arts 0708

Le whip: bibliographie sélective et annotée 2515

White collar crime: a bibliography 2214

White papers, 1939-1986/Livre blancs, 1939-1986 6378

Whole-tree harvest – nutrient relationships: a bibliography/ Exploitation des arbres entiers – rapport des éléments nutritifs: étude bibliographique 4985

Who's who in Canadian literature 1305

Women in the Canadian economy: an annotated selected bibliography 3745

Women in the labour force with an emphasis on the clerical and service occupations: a selected bibliography 3811

"Women in the library profession" 1604

Women with disabilities: documentation review and annotated bibliography 3889

Women's bookworks: a survey exhibition of contemporary artists' books by Canadian women including unique book-objects and printed editions/Livres d'artistes-femmes: une exposition de livres contemporains réalisés par des artistes canadiennes comprenant des "livres-objets" uniques ou des livres faisant partie d'éditions à petits tirages 0691

Women's education: a world view 3598

Women's history in Canada: a selective bibliography 3899

Women's labour history in British Columbia: a bibliography, 1930-1948 2864

Women's movement media: a source guide 3742

Women's resource catalogue 3901

Women's studies: a guide to reference sources 3825

Women's studies: video resource catalogue 3793

Women's studies research handbook: a guide to relevant research at the University of Waterloo 3880

Wood: fire behaviour and fire retardant: a review of the literature 5725

The Wood Buffalo National Park area: a bibliography 2986

Work and family employment policy: a selected bibliography 2934

Work and workers: an annotated bibliography for secondary schools 2909

Work camps and company towns in Canada and the U.S.: an annotated bibliography 2821

Work-related day care: an annotated bibliography 3238

Worker co-operatives: an international bibliography/Coopératives de travailleurs: une bibliographie internationale 2914

Workers' compensation: a bibliography 2903

Workers' health, safety and compensation: a preliminary bibliography of Canadian federal and provincial government commissions and inquiries 2846

Workers' participation: a bibliography of current books and articles 2834

Working women in the economic future: a selected bibliography with emphasis on Canada 3846

Workmen's compensation in Canada 2869

The works of Father Hennepin: a catalogue of the collection brought together by Peter A. Porter of Niagara Falls, N.Y. 7060

"Worksharing: jobsharing: a selected bibliography" 2893

A world bibliography of bibliographies, 1964-1974: a list of works represented by Library of Congress printed catalog cards: a decennial supplement to Theodore Besterman, "A world bibliography of bibliographies" 0082

A world bibliography of bibliographies, and of bibliographical catalogues, calendars, abstracts, digests, indexes and the like 0082

World bibliography of the redfishes and rockfishes (Sebastinae, Scorpaenidae) 5523

The World of Children's Books showcase: a selection of the best Canadian, British and American children's books: in celebration of the International Year of the Child 1979 1338

The world of high technology: a revised and expanded selective bibliography 5821

A world of real places: essays in honour of William C. Wonders 7371

World wide space law bibliography 2295

Writers of Newfoundland and Labrador: twentieth century 0259

Writings by Helmut Kallmann 7083

The writings of Benjamin Sulte 7324

The writings of Frederic H. Soward 7318

The writings of Louis Hennepin, Recollect Franciscan missionary 7057

The Writings of Marshall McLuhan: listed in chronological order from 1934 to 1975: with an appended list of reviews and articles about him and his work 7184

Writings on American history 2093

Writings on American history, 1962-73: a subject bibliography of articles 2093

Writings on American history, 1962-73: a subject bibliography of books and monographs 2093

Writings on Canadian English, 1792-1975: an annotated bibliography 1442

Writings on Canadian English, 1976-1987: a selective, annotated bibliography 1479

Writings relating to literacy: done at the Ontario Institute for Studies in Education 3715

"The year's exhibitions in Canada" 0709

"The year's work in Canadian poetry studies" 1239

"The year's work in Canadian poetry studies: 1978" 1148

"The year's work in Canadian poetry studies: 1979" 1169

Yellow walleye, Stizostedion vitreum vitreum (Mitchill): a literature review and bibliography 5395

"Yes, there is Canadian music." "Oui, notre musique existe!" 0827

The yews and taxol: a bibliography (1970-1991) 5711

You can say "no": an annotated resource guide for child abuse education 3318

The young crusaders: the Company of Young Canadians: a bibliography 3132

Yukon bibliography 0656

Yukon economic planning studies, 1965-1985: an annotated bibliography 0652

Yukon economic planning studies, 1986-1992: an annotated bibliography 0652

Yukon land and resource inventory: bibliographic index 0637

Yukon native history and culture: a bibliography of sources available at the Yukon Archives 4094

Yukon Women's Directorate Library containing a guide to using the library and library listings by category 3897

Yvan Lamonde: historien de la culture: essai de bibliographie, 1965-1984 7115

Yvon Gauthier: écrits philosophiques: bibliographie chronologique, 1967-1985 7006

Subjects : English

Matières : anglais

Aarhus universitet
—— Institut for engelsk filologi 0145
Abbott, Maude Elizabeth 6796
Abitibi region, Quebec 0310, 0323, 0354, 4796
Abortion 2322, 3233, 3798, 3896, 5585, 5596, 5665
Abstracting 1696
    See also Indexing
Abuse of the aged
    See Aged–Mistreatment
Académie commerciale catholique de Montréal 6725
Acadia 0200, 0205, 0222, 0223, 0230, 0235, 0238, 0244, 0255,
    0260, 0264, 0265, 0266, 0268, 1505, 1872, 2019, 4554, 4598, 5858
    See also New Brunswick; Nova Scotia
Acadia College
—— Library 6731
Acadia University 0198
—— Library 6759, 6765
Acadian literature 1138, 1155, 1172, 1177, 1194, 1228, 1272, 1298
Acadians 0204, 0232, 0243, 4596
ACCESS Network 6700, 6701
Accidents 3123
    See also Children–Accidents and injuries; Disasters;
    Shipwrecks; Sports–Accidents and injuries
—— Prevention 5658
    See also Nuclear reactors–Safety devices and measures;
    Safety education
—— Psychological aspects 3148
Accidents, Industrial 2803, 2912
    See also Explosions; Mine accidents and explosions;
    Worker's compensation
Accordion music 0901, 0940
Accountability
    See Responsibility
Accounting 2635, 2783
    See also Auditing
—— Automation 2754
Acculturation 3910, 3913, 3921, 4251, 4252, 4253, 4254
    See also Assimilation (Sociology); Ethnic relations; Race
    relations
Acid rain 4711, 4995, 5006, 5149, 5159, 5173, 5202, 5212, 5213,
    5223, 5231, 5238, 5242, 5243, 5247, 5254, 5258, 5264, 5276,
    5287, 5289, 5446
Acidity 5467
Acoustics, Architectural 0735
Acquired Immune Deficiency Syndrome
    See AIDS (Disease)
Actions and defences 3858
    See also Torts
Adam Shortt Library of Canadiana, University of
    Saskatchewan 4200
Adams, Thomas 6797
Adaptation (Psychology)
    See Adjustment (Psychology)
Addison, Robert, Library 6774
Adjustment (Psychology) 3169
Administration, Public 2381, 2385, 2404, 2410, 2417, 2489,
    2528, 2539, 2551, 4121
    See also Administrative agencies; Civil service; Decentraliza-
    tion in government; Government employees; Government
    investigations; Local government; Personnel management;
    Program evaluation

Administration of justice
    See Justice, Administration of
Administrative agencies 2439, 2448, 6279
Adolescence 1117, 3133, 3146, 3151, 3173
Adoption 3117, 3211, 3325
Adult education 1689, 3377, 3379, 3381, 3385, 3392, 3396, 3399,
    3417, 3428, 3432, 3434, 3476, 3491, 3530, 3544, 3560, 3561,
    3574, 3591, 3603, 3609, 3613, 3644, 3680, 6158, 6651
    See also Employees–Training; Frontier College; Labour–Edu-
    cation; Literacy education; Occupational training; Television
    in education; Vocational education
Advertising 2611
    See also Public relations; Women in advertising
Aerial photography
    See Photography, Aerial
Aerodynamics 5841
    See also Aviation
Aeronautic research 5818, 5825, 5846, 5853
Aeroplanes
    See Airplanes
Affirmative action programs 2913, 2920, 2921, 3852
Agassiz Centre for Water Studies 5759
Aged 1193, 3163, 3196, 3216, 3231, 3261, 3266, 3283, 3291, 3304,
    3347, 3352, 3807, 4267, 5673
    See also Old age; Retirement
—— Care and hygiene 3098, 3150, 3280, 3340, 3355, 5703, 5705
    See also Aged–Mistreatment; Aged–Physical fitness; Home
    care services; Long-term care of the sick
—— Housing 3150, 3248, 3254, 3306, 3326, 3335, 4308
—— Legal status, laws, etc 2260
—— Mental health 5663
—— Mistreatment 3287, 3301, 3302, 3310, 3314, 3343, 3359,
    6685
    See also Elder Abuse Resource Centre
—— Nutrition 3150, 3244
—— Physical fitness 1828, 1832, 1833, 1834, 1859
—— Quebec (Province) 3257
Aggressiveness (Psychology) 3363
    See also Violence
Aging 2260, 3105, 3106, 3241, 3244, 3252, 3256, 3266, 3283,
    3291, 3322, 3329, 3346, 3837, 3875, 3876, 3894
—— Social aspects 3350
Aging in Manitoba Project 3304
Agnos, John W. 6798
Agricultural engineering 4649, 4701, 4715, 6191, 6374
Agricultural industries 2619
Agricultural labour
    See Farm labour
Agricultural land 3026, 4442, 4678, 4688, 4689, 4698, 4700,
    4703, 4704, 5560
Agricultural machinery 4725
    See also Tillage
—— Marketing 4652
Agricultural meteorology 4641, 4686
    See also Plants, Effect of temperature on
Agricultural pests 4659, 4685, 4708
    See also Pest control; Plants–Diseases and pests
Agricultural policy 4718
    See also Land tenure; Rural planning
Agricultural production
    See Production, Agricultural

Agricultural Rehabilitation and Development Administration 4648
Agricultural research 1670, 4651, 4655, 4660, 4675, 4690, 4694, 4696, 4708, 4712, 4722, 5830, 6150
See also Tree breeding
Agricultural subsidies 4710
Agriculture 3049, 4638, 4646, 4668, 4671, 4677, 4684, 4692, 4693, 6177, 6294, 6298
See also Agronomy; Aquaculture; Crops; Farm labour; Farm manure; Farmers; Food supply; Homesteads; Irrigation; Land; Land utilization; Livestock; Organic farming; Part time farming; Plants, Protection of; Seeds; Soils; Women in agriculture
—— British Columbia 0579, 6273, 6429, 6656
—— —— Film catalogues 6661
—— Economic aspects 3015, 3168, 4640, 4664, 4709
See also Farm finance; Land tenure; Land values
—— Energy usage 4701, 4720
—— Environmental aspects 4669, 4711
—— History 2050, 4639
—— Information services 4724
—— Manitoba 4656
—— Ontario 4695, 6269
—— Periodicals 5872, 5906, 5915, 5944
—— Pollution 4654
—— Prairie provinces 4674, 4682
—— Quebec (Province) 4670, 4723, 6539
—— Saskatchewan 6473
—— Study and teaching 6661
Agriculture and state
See Agricultural policy
Agronomy 4642
Ahern, George 5563
AIDS (Disease) 3308, 3358, 3679, 3703, 5653, 5669, 5707, 5712
AIDS associated viruses 5697, 5698
Air freight service 4509
Air pilots 5753
Air pollution 4995, 5006, 5096, 5103, 5104, 5119, 5148, 5159, 5221, 5222, 5224, 5264, 5275
See also Acid rain; Dust; Odours; Ozone; Plants, Effect of air pollution on
—— Alberta 5168, 5242, 5246, 5247
—— Atlantic provinces 5238
—— Detection and monitoring 5176
—— Manitoba 5258
Airlines 4509
See also Air freight service
—— Non-scheduled operations 4489
Airplanes 5825
Airplanes in forest fire control 4959
Akwesasne Library and Cultural Center 3994
Alarms 2159
Alaska 4907
Alaska Highway 0662
Alberta 0516, 0522, 0536, 0540, 0541, 0544, 0547, 0552, 1142, 1551, 2352, 3149, 3196, 4240, 4666, 4699, 4711, 5092, 5429, 5530, 5559, 5771, 6278, 6699
See also Calgary, Alberta; Edmonton, Alberta; French Canadians in Alberta; Germans in Alberta; Lethbridge, Alberta
—— Alberta Education 6416
—— Alberta Energy 6417
—— Alberta Forestry, Lands and Wildlife 6417

—— Archaeology 4591
—— Department of Education 6416
—— Economic conditions 0518, 0520, 2632
—— Economic development 0553
—— Government departments 6352
—— History 0504, 0527, 0538, 0545, 3795, 4211, 4812, 6646
—— Imprints 0497
—— Maps 6421, 6559, 6564
—— Planning and development 4341
—— Politics and government 2382
—— Social conditions 0520
Alberta Band Association 0924
Alberta Environment
—— Research Management Division 6338
Alberta Hail Project
See Hail
Alberta Labour 6420
Alberta Oil Sands Environmental Research Program 4812, 5126, 5139, 5148, 5428, 5444, 6338, 6419
Alberta Playwrights' Network 1297
Alberta Research Council 4837, 6425
Alberta Society of Petroleum Geologists 4837
Alberta Weather Modification Board 5127
Alcohol and automobile drivers 3091, 3178
Alcohol and women 3747
Alcohol as fuel 5782
Alcohol drinking behaviour 3272, 4016, 4543, 4581
See also Temperance
Alcoholic beverages 1921, 6241
Alcoholics and alcoholism 3093, 3157, 5567, 5618
See also Skid row
—— Therapy 5602
Alcoholism and Drug Addiction Research Foundation of Ontario 5567
Alcoholism and employment 3260
Alexander, William John 6799
Algae 5387, 5389, 5499
See also Lichens; Plankton
Algonkian Indians 1457, 3953, 3980
See also Blackfoot Indians; Cree Indians; Micmac Indians; Montagnais Indians; Ojibway Indians
Algonkian languages 1406, 4063
Alienation (Social psychology) 3615
Allouez, Claude-Jean 1879, 1880
Almanacs 0276
Alpine flora 5370
Alpine lands 5281
Alternative press
See Underground press
Alzheimer's disease 5679
Amateurism (Sports) 1854
American Library Association 0041
American National Standards Institute 5636
American Society for Testing and Materials 5636
Americas 0001, 0002, 0005, 0013, 0049, 0190, 1935, 4546, 6709, 6713, 6722, 6733, 6749
See also North America
—— Discovery and exploration 0008, 1871, 1895, 6484, 6792
—— History 0003, 1872, 1873, 1876, 1995, 2086, 2093, 6736, 6768
Amherst Island, Ontario 0474

Ami, Henri Marc 6800
Amish 1542
Amphibia 5473
Amputees 5631
   See also Prosthesis
Anaerobic technology 5784, 5830
André, John 6801
Anglican Church of Canada 0819, 1515, 4075, 6077
Angling
   See Fishing
Animal Diseases Research Institute, Lethbridge 5516
Animal experimentation 6687
Animals 5424, 5547
   See also Insects; Invertebrates; Mammals; Reptiles;
   Vertebrates; Wildlife; Zoology
—— Diseases and pests 5516
   See also Rabies; Veterinary medicine
—— Habits and behaviour 4717
   See also Biotelemetry; Birds–Habits and behaviour;
   Fishes–Habits and behaviour
—— Stories 1352
—— Treatment 6687
   See also Animal experimentation; Trapping
Animals, Geographical distribution of
   See Geographical distribution of animals and plants
Anonyms and pseudonyms 0105
L'Anse aux Meadows National Historic Park 2999
Antennae (Electronics) 5734
Anthropogeography 3021, 6183
   See also Land settlement; Regionalism
Anthropology 0640, 3929, 4081, 4086, 4531, 4532, 4538, 4539,
   4542, 4543, 4546, 4557, 4559, 4563, 4564, 4573, 4574, 4581,
   4586, 4587, 4595, 6110, 6176, 6237, 6336
   See also Acculturation; Anthropogeography; Archaeology;
   Ethnography; Language and languages; Man, Prehistoric;
   Material culture; Women
Anti-combines legislation
   See Trusts, Industrial–Law
Anti-inflation Board 2638
Anticosti (Island) 0330
Antidepressants 5594
   See also Tranquillizing drugs
Antiques 0692, 2011, 5768
Antiquities 4538
Aphids 5466, 5533, 5534
Apples 4637
Aquaculture 4894, 4898, 4901, 4904, 4911, 5389, 5442, 5548
   See also Shellfish culture
Aquatic ecology 5095, 5138
Aquatic plants 5449, 6319, 6355
Aquin, Hubert 6802, 6803
Arabs 4283, 4284
Arabs in Canada 4236, 5912
Arbitration, Industrial 2793, 2817, 2826
   See also Collective bargaining; Grievance procedures;
   Industrial relations
Archaeology 4522, 4523, 4526, 4530, 4537, 4539, 4540, 4541,
   4546, 4549, 4559, 4560, 4561, 4562, 4563, 4564, 4566, 4568,
   4569, 4570, 4571, 4572, 4574, 4576, 4579, 4583, 4591, 4594,
   4597, 4598, 4599, 4602, 4608, 4609, 6172, 6342
   See also Anthropology; Excavations (Archaeology); Man,
   Prehistoric; Numismatics

Archer, Violet 6804, 6805
Architects 0748
Architectural acoustics
   See Acoustics, Architectural
Architecture 0676, 0681, 0688, 0689, 0702, 0726, 0733, 0737,
   0748, 0770, 0771, 0772, 0778, 0783, 0786, 0801, 0803, 0804,
   1988, 3868, 4605
   See also Architecture, Public; Buildings; Church architecture;
   Library architecture; Office buildings; School buildings;
   Sports facilities
—— Alberta 0787, 0792
—— Arctic regions 0763
—— Atlantic provinces 0799
—— British Columbia 0758, 0777, 0793
—— Conservation and restoration 0595, 0738, 0743, 0745,
   0747, 0749, 0750, 0754, 0755, 0757, 0761, 0782, 0805, 0806, 6152
   See also Historic houses, sites, etc
—— History 0739, 0752, 0766, 0774, 0776, 0777, 3030
—— Manitoba 0751, 0779, 0794
—— New Brunswick 0764
—— Newfoundland 0768, 0773
—— Northwest Territories 0800
—— Nova Scotia 0744, 0762
—— Ontario 0749, 0790, 0795
—— Periodicals 5934
—— Prince Edward Island 0796
—— Quebec (Province) 0742, 0746, 0789, 0791, 0798, 0802
—— Saskatchewan 0797
—— Yukon Territory 0800
Architecture, Domestic 0736, 0767, 0781
   See also Cottages; Country houses; Log construction; Vaca-
   tion houses
Architecture, Public 0788
Architecture and climate 0780, 4422, 5736, 5803, 5808
Architecture and energy conservation 4383
Architecture and the handicapped 0775, 3090, 3101, 3311, 3312
Archives 0527, 1609, 1614, 1621, 1625, 1627, 1638, 1690, 1706,
   1713, 1714, 1723, 1728, 6341, 6343
   See also Libraries; Manuscripts
—— Administration 1591, 1617, 1695
—— Laws, legislation, regulations, etc 2344
—— Periodicals 5980
Arctic char
   See Char (Fish)
Arctic Institute of North America 4833
Arctic Institute of North America Library 0616
Arctic islands
   See Islands of the Arctic
Arctic Ocean 5140, 5481
   See also Beaufort Sea
Arctic Petroleum Operators' Association 5177, 5536
Arctic Petroleum Operators' Association Project 5478
Arctic regions 0020, 0051, 0148, 0299, 0607, 0608, 0611, 0612,
   0613, 0614, 0616, 0626, 0627, 0630, 0640, 0642, 0643, 0645,
   0646, 0653, 0658, 0663, 0665, 0786, 1416, 1552, 1561, 2959,
   4479, 4495, 4597, 4631, 4633, 4783, 4820, 4833, 4880, 5075,
   5096, 5116, 5130, 5155, 5178, 5179, 5181, 5182, 5239, 5257,
   5279, 5396, 5461, 5527, 5739, 5973, 6180, 6185, 6186, 6495,
   6550, 6709
   See also Baffin Island; Greenland; Inuit; Northwest Passage;
   Tundras
—— Archaeology 4564, 4572
—— Discovery and exploration 0609, 0624, 0636, 0647, 0654,

0661, 2045, 2047, 2054, 6530
—— Geography 5052
—— Research 0648, 0649, 0651, 0655, 4843, 5034, 5043, 5110, 5520, 5730
   See also Eastern Arctic Study; Institute of Arctic and Alpine Research
—— Transportation 4473
Armed forces 2234
   See also Canada–Armed forces; United Nations–Armed forces
—— Demobilization 3078
Armed robbery 2276
Arnold, Frank B. 1191
Art 0670, 0676, 0677, 0682, 0684, 0686, 0702, 0722, 0726, 0733, 0801, 6335, 6336, 6738
   See also Book art; Design; Folk art; Graphic arts; Illustration of books and periodicals; Indians–Arts; Inuit–Art; Lithography; Photography; Sculpture
—— Catalogues 0703, 0704, 0730
—— Exhibitions 0694, 0709, 0732
—— Film catalogues 6618, 6619, 6630
—— Galleries and museums 0134, 0716, 4565, 5963
—— History and criticism 6199
—— Periodicals 5934
—— Quebec (Province) 0672, 0678, 0700, 0714, 6648
—— Study and teaching 0685, 0689, 6655
Art and feminism 0710, 0717
Art exhibition catalogues
   See Art–Catalogues
Art in movies 6630
Art objects
—— Conservation and restoration 0692
Arthropoda 5461
Artifacts 4603
Artificial intelligence 3060
   See also Simulation methods
Artists 0711, 0726
   See also Authors; Musicians; Women artists
—— Law 0695, 0721
Artists, Canadian 0670
   See also Group of Seven (Canadian Painters)
Artists' books
   See Book art
Arts 0018, 0683, 0690, 0708, 0713, 1847, 1848, 3557, 3558, 3847
   See also Architecture; Dancing; Indians–Arts; Music; Performing arts
—— Management 0679, 0724
—— Periodicals 5875, 5933
—— Research 0706, 0728
Arts and crafts 0681, 0688, 0712, 0746, 1792
   See also Ceramics; Folk art; Glassware
Arts and industry 0729
   See also Arts patronage
Arts and state 0679, 0719
   See also Canada Council
Arts patronage 0729
Asbestos 4753
—— Toxicology 5114, 5115
Asian Canadians 4208, 4220, 4225, 4268, 4280
Asphalt 4778, 4822
Assimilation (Sociology) 4253, 4254
   See also Acculturation; Ethnic relations; Minorities

Assiniboine Indians 4005
Association canadienne des bibliothécaires de langue française 1588
Association de la propagation de la Foi 1508
Association des institutions d'enseignement secondaire 3732
Association pour l'avancement de la recherche en musique du Québec 0912
Association québécoise de gérontologie 3257
Associations
—— British Columbia 0583
Astronomy 5760
   See also Comets; Meteorites
—— History 5811
Astrophysics 5760
Athabasca River 0502
Athapaskan Indians 1407, 1430, 3954, 3973, 3980, 4058, 4578
Atlantic Geoscience Centre 4850
Atlantic provinces 0106, 0144, 0198, 0208, 0209, 0214, 0222, 0223, 0229, 0230, 0235, 0236, 0238, 0244, 0253, 0265, 0267, 0919, 1192, 1295, 1509, 2550, 3004, 3992, 4089, 4187, 4475, 4534, 4538, 4561, 4570, 4705, 4909, 5436, 5522, 6765
—— Archaeology 4599
—— Economic history 0234
—— History 0210, 0231, 0252, 0271, 0274, 2089, 4055, 4056, 4598, 6793
—— Imprints 0273
—— Industries and resources 2579
Atlases 3043, 6494, 6500, 6520, 6533, 6535, 6543, 6547, 6555, 6558, 6569, 6573, 6576, 6578, 6583, 6586, 6589, 6594, 6595, 6596
   See also Maps
Atmosphere 5033, 5049, 5080, 5157, 5206, 5260, 5261, 6307
   See also Ionosphere; Meteorology; Ozone
Atmospheric greenhouse effect
   See Greenhouse effect, Atmospheric
Atmospheric ozone
   See Ozone
Atmospheric research 5026, 5751, 5761
Atomic Energy Control Board 5819, 6435
Atomic Energy of Canada Limited 5163, 5273, 5773, 5785, 5797, 5854
Atwood, Margaret 6806, 6807, 6808, 6809, 6810, 6811, 6812, 6813
Aubert de Gaspé, Philippe-Joseph 6814
Aubry, Claude 6815
Audet, Francis-J. 6816
Audet, Thomas-André 6817
Audiences 0706
Audio visual instruction 6664, 6666, 6700, 6701
   See also Television in education
Audio visual materials 3546, 6636, 6653, 6659, 6696, 6699, 6700
   See also Movies; Phonograph records; Slides (Photography); Video recordings
—— Agriculture 6656, 6661, 6704
—— Art 6648, 6655
—— Biology 6687
—— Education 6639, 6647, 6651
—— Forests and forestry 6707
—— History 6621
—— Labour 6662, 6665, 6689
—— Law 6667, 6681, 6684, 6686
—— Literature 6642
—— Medicine 6624
—— Multiculturalism 6629, 6650, 6657, 6697, 6698

—— Native studies 6635, 6645, 6679
—— Natural history 6628
—— Natural resources 6690
—— Naval art and science 6702
—— Police 6682
—— Social problems 6676, 6685, 6688
—— Sociology 6695
—— Women's studies 6654, 6675
Auditing 2754
    See also Accounting
Auditor General's Office 2440
Auroras 5226
Authors 6620
    See also Dramatists; Politicians as authors; Public lending
    rights (of authors); Women authors
Authors, Canadian 0009, 0599, 1007, 1070, 1084, 1089, 1159,
    1192, 1204, 1222, 1227, 1232, 1241, 1260, 1275, 1285, 1286,
    1302, 1305
    See also Authors, French Canadian; Crime Writers of
    Canada; Fredericton Tuesday Night Writers; Poets, Canadian
—— Alberta 0540, 0552, 1142
—— Atlantic provinces 0240, 0270
—— British Columbia 0566, 0603, 1154, 1182
—— Manitoba 0501, 0539, 1083, 1201
—— New Brunswick 0203
—— Newfoundland 0259
—— Nova Scotia 0197, 0241, 1045
Authors, French Canadian 0326, 0360, 0365, 1000, 1005, 1008,
    1012, 1019, 1043, 1049, 1064, 1099, 1103, 1163, 1185, 1205,
    1206, 1207
    See also Authors, Canadian; Dramatists, French Canadian;
    Poets, French Canadian
Autism 5670
Autobiography 1010, 1157, 1205, 3794, 4023, 4148
    See also Diaries
Automated teller machines 2681
Automation 5839
    See also Electronic data processing; Libraries–Automation;
    Office methods–Automation; Robots
—— Economic aspects 2575
—— Social aspects 1664, 1709, 2686
    See also Technology and labour
Automobile drivers 4505
    See also Alcohol and automobile drivers
Automobile driving 4481, 5590
Automobile industry
—— International aspects 2658
Automobile insurance
    See Insurance, Automobile
Automobile parking 4357
Automobiles 4486
    See also Taxicabs
Autonomy 2482, 2512
    See also Quebec (Province)–Autonomy and independence
Auyuittuq National Park 3011
Avalanches 4518
Aviation 5753
    See also Aerodynamics; Airplanes
—— History 4463
—— Laws and regulations 2106
—— Medical aspects 5564, 5566, 5704

Aviation research
    See Aeronautic research
Avison, Margaret 6818, 6819
Axel Heiberg Island 0655
B.C. Bookworld 0599
Baby, Georges, Collection 6792
Back 1812, 5658
Bacon, Francis 0206
Baffin Island 2980, 3011, 4813, 4833, 5142
Bailey, Alfred Goldsworthy 6820
Baillairgé, Charles 6821
Baillairgé, Frédéric-Alexandre 6822
Bain, Francis 6823
Baker, Michael Conway 6824
Ball, Nelson 6825
Bands (Music) 0859, 0898, 0924, 0930
    See also Orchestras
Banff National Park 5514
Banff School of the Environment 5156
Bank employees 2848
Banking laws and regulations 2650, 2681
Banks and banking 2589, 2626, 2703
    See also Interest rates
—— History 1749, 1750, 1838, 2010, 2027, 2040, 2048, 2061,
    2071
—— Small business loan programs 2720
—— Unions 2848
Banque royale (France) 2010
Baptist Church 1509, 1568
Barbarian Press 1700
Barbeau, Marius 0714, 6826, 6827, 6828, 6829
Bargaining
    See Negotiation
Bark 4964
Barns 0753, 0756
Barr Colony (Alta. and Sask.) 1987
Barreau de la province de Québec
—— Library 2094
Barren lands 2959
Barrette, Antonio 2469
Bars and bar rooms 3272
Basilian Fathers 1526, 5902
Bassoon music 0902
Battered wives
    See Wife abuse
Baum, L. Frank 1350
Beads 4577
Bears 5341
Beatrice Hitchins Memorial Collection of Aviation History
    4463
Beauce, Quebec 0318, 0415
Beauchemin, Yves 6830
Beaufort Sea 0644, 4866, 5196, 5216, 5393, 5416, 5478
Beaulieu, Marie-Louis 6831
Beaulieu, Michel 6832
Beavers 5428, 5546
Becker, A., Collection 4200
Beckwith, John 6833
Bedford Institute of Oceanography 5386, 5398
Bee culture 4653
Bees 5357

Building laws and regulations 2317
  See also Zoning
Building materials 0804, 5800
  See also Structural engineering
Building research 5716, 5726, 5729, 5744, 6359, 6453
  See also Institute for Research in Construction (Canada)
Building sites 4304
Buildings 0752
  See also Office buildings; School buildings
—— Acoustics
  See Acoustics, Architectural
—— Energy usage 0769, 5764, 5776, 5814
—— Preservation
  See Architecture–Conservation and restoration
Buildings and moisture 5807
Buildings Energy Technology Transfer Program 5814
Bulgarians in Canada 5901
Bull, Michael 0045
Bull, Noreen 0045
Buller Memorial Library 4646
Bumblebees
  See Bees
Bureau d'aménagement de l'Est du Québec 6263, 6268
Burkholder, Mabel 6884
Bus lines
  See Motor bus lines
Business 2571, 2594, 2626, 2635, 2707, 2746, 2760, 2780, 6108
  See also Commerce; Competition; Corporations;
  Entrepreneurship; Location in business and industry;
  Minorities and business; Small business
—— Directories 2741
—— Periodicals 5929, 5948, 5957
Business and labour 2847
Business and the arts
  See Arts and industry
Business districts 4336
Business education 3667
Business failures 2727
Business information 2599, 2710, 2741, 2751, 2785, 6280
Business intelligence 2778
  See also Trade secrets
Business literature 2580
Business management and organization 2646
  See also Arts–Management; Employees' representation in
  management; Management by objectives; Personnel manage-
  ment; Scheduling (Management)
Business men 2712
  See also Entrepreneurs
Business planning 2693
Business women 3863
  See also Women entrepreneurs; Women executives
Butterflies 5303, 5306, 5371, 5381, 5549
Byron Bog 5408
C.D. Howe Research Institute 2625
Cable television 0956
Cabot, John 6885, 6886
Cabot, Sebastian 6885, 6886
Calgary, Alberta 3298, 4591, 4837
—— Architecture 0787
Callaghan, Edmund Bailey, Library 6733
Callaghan, Morley 6887, 6888, 6889

Campbell, William Wilfred 6890, 6891
Campbell River estuary, British Columbia 5121
Camping 1775, 1785
  See also Outdoor life
Canada 0013, 0016, 0020, 0023, 0032, 0037, 0038, 0046, 0048,
  0051, 0052, 0053, 0055, 0057, 0059, 0063, 0067, 0073, 0076,
  0082, 0083, 0085, 0095, 0096, 0098, 0099, 0103, 0105, 0108,
  0113, 0125, 0144, 0146, 0147, 0148, 0151, 0155, 0168, 0169,
  0171, 0176, 0277, 0576, 1306, 1583, 1653, 1901, 2375, 6198,
  6674, 6738, 6743, 6745, 6751, 6754, 6765, 6766, 6775, 6779, 6795
  See also Federal-provincial relations
—— Annexation to the United States 2372
—— Appropriations and expenditures 2656
—— Armed forces 1947
—— Civilization 6780
—— Commerce 2702, 4516
—— —— Asia 2779
—— —— Pacific countries 2779
—— —— United States 2557, 2558, 2699, 2775
—— Commission of Conservation 6213
—— Constitution 1944, 2217, 2239, 2248, 2289, 2299, 2310,
  2318, 2319, 2335, 2339, 2351, 2455, 4087
—— Constitutional history 2102
—— Defences 2379, 2392, 6600
—— Department of Agriculture 1670, 6294, 6298
—— —— Economics Division 3080, 4640
—— Department of Energy, Mines and Resources 6326
—— —— Mineral Resources Division 6261
—— Department of Forestry 6248
—— Department of Forestry and Rural Development 6265
—— Department of Labour 6247, 6442, 6448
—— Department of National Health and Welfare
—— —— Physical Fitness Division 6235
—— Department of Northern Affairs and National Resources
  6249
—— Description and travel 2079
—— Discovery and exploration 0572, 1914, 1962, 1963, 6514
—— Dominion Bureau of Statistics 6258, 6445
—— Economic conditions 2560, 2563, 2618, 2622, 2709, 2711,
  2715, 2781, 2782, 3048, 3611, 6055, 6412
—— Economic history 2078, 2607, 2636
—— Economic policy 2625, 2706
  See also Economic Council of Canada
—— Environmental Protection Directorate 6439
—— Fisheries and Environment Canada 6311
—— Foreign opinion 0162
—— Foreign relations 0216, 2072, 2374, 2405, 2408, 2409, 2421,
  2424, 2430, 2436, 2465, 2466, 2467, 2508, 2517, 2524, 2525,
  2540, 2546
  See also Economic assistance, Canadian; Quebec
  (Province)–Foreign relations
—— —— Australia 2388
—— —— European Economic Community 2444, 2464
—— —— Latin America 2495
—— —— Union of Soviet Socialist Republics 2488
—— —— United States 2271, 2390, 2395, 2414, 2474, 2494
—— Forestry Canada 6401, 6440
—— French English relations 1123, 2380, 3115
—— Health and Welfare Canada 6441
—— History 0004, 0015, 0036, 0047, 0109, 0139, 0152, 0153,
  0189, 0278, 0494, 1212, 1574, 1575, 1873, 1882, 1889, 1893,
  1896, 1899, 1902, 1907, 1911, 1925, 1931, 1933, 1952, 1953,
  1958, 1961, 1968, 1975, 1994, 1999, 2006, 2009, 2012, 2015,

Centre d'essai des auteurs dramatiques 1186
Centre d'études nordiques, Université Laval 0623, 0626
Centre d'information sur l'enfance et l'adolescence inadaptées 3133
Ceramics 0720, 4598
Chamber music 0880, 0936
Chamberland, Paul 1089
Chambers of commerce 2568
Champagne, Claude 0904
Champlain, Samuel de 6901
Champlain Sea 4545, 4868
Champlain Valley 0290
Chapais, Thomas 1967
Chapais Collection (Department of Agriculture Library, Ottawa) 4668
Char (Fish) 4910, 5352, 5399, 5464, 5554
Charbonneau, Robert 6902
Charbonneau. Hubert 6903
Charles Crane Memorial Library, University of British Columbia 6649
Charlevoix, Pierre François Xavier de 6904
Charlevoix region, Quebec 0381, 6587
Charron, François 6905
Charter of Rights and Freedoms
    See Canadian Charter of Rights and Freedoms
Chateauguay region, Quebec 0367
Chauveau, Pierre-Joseph-Olivier, Collection 6783
Chemainus River estuary, British Columbia 5098
Chemical research 5740
Chemoreception 5498
Chenier, Jean-Olivier 6906
Cherney, Brian 6907
Cherries 5378
Chess 1806
Chewitt, W.C. & Company 1652
Chicoutimi, Quebec 0286
Chignecto region, New Brunswick 0233
Child abuse
    See Cruelty to children
Child mental health 5659
Child welfare 3353
    See also Day care; Foster home care; Homes, Institutional
Childbirth 3869, 5634
    See also Midwives
Children 3361
    See also Youth
—— Accidents and injuries 5666
—— Care and hygiene 3321
    See also Health education; Parent education
—— Growth and development 1793, 3146, 3205, 3624
—— Health 5681, 5689
—— History 3362
—— Hospital care 3182
—— Law 2235, 2360
    See also Parent and child (Law)
—— Management and training 3698, 4237
    See also Corporal punishment; Moral education; Safety education
—— Medical care 5708
—— Recreation 1816
    See also Play
—— Sexual behaviour 3363
—— Treatment 3317

    See also Cruelty to children; Sexual abuse of children
Children, Blind 3188
Children, Exceptional 3232, 3421, 3587, 3588
Children, Gifted 3596, 3614
Children, Handicapped 0872, 3173, 3210, 3213, 3227
    See also Socially handicapped children; Visually handicapped children
—— Education 3556
Children and death 3182
Children and parents
    See Parent child relationship
Children as witnesses
    See Witnesses
Children's allowances 3203
Children's literature 1306, 1320, 1323, 1324, 1326, 1327, 1328, 1329, 1332, 1333, 1334, 1337, 1338, 1342, 1345, 1346, 1348, 1349, 1350, 1351, 1352, 1353, 1354, 1355, 1357, 1361, 1362, 1363, 1365, 1366, 1368, 1369, 1370, 1372, 1375, 1378, 1379, 1380, 1381, 1382, 1384, 1385, 1387, 1388, 1390, 1391, 1393, 1394, 1395, 1396, 1397, 1398, 1399, 1683, 4255
    See also Children's poetry; Picture books for children
—— History and criticism 1312
—— Illustration
    See Illustration of books and periodicals
—— Themes 1389
—— Translations 1376
Children's literature, French 1322, 1364
Children's literature, French Canadian 1307, 1308, 1309, 1310, 1311, 1313, 1314, 1315, 1318, 1321, 1325, 1330, 1331, 1335, 1340, 1341, 1343, 1347, 1356, 1358, 1374, 1377, 1386, 1392, 1397, 1398
Children's music
—— Discography 0913
Children's periodicals 5975
Children's plays 1360
    See also Theatre, Children's
Children's poetry 1373
Children's rights 2360
Children's theatre
    See Theatre, Children's
Chilkoot Pass 0633, 0634
Chimneys 5720
Chinese in British Columbia 4129
Chinese in Canada 4208, 5896, 6097
Chippewa Indians
    See Ojibway Indians
Chlamydia infections 5684
Cholera 5660
Choquette, Robert 6908
Choral singing 0864, 0871, 0879
Christianity 1535
    See also Theology
Christmas 1233, 1354, 4558
Chromosome abnormalities 3095
Church, E.D., Collection 1895
Church and state 1524, 6078
Church architecture 0765
Church history 0250, 1523, 1528, 1529, 1534, 1536, 1546, 1552, 1563, 1566, 1574, 1575, 4212
    See also Missions; Saints
Church of England 1519

Churchill, Manitoba 0524
Churchill River Basin 0515
Chutes-de-la-Chaudière, Quebec 0407
Cinémathèque nationale (Québec) 6636
Cinémathèque québécoise-Musée du cinéma 0975
Cities and towns 4306, 4313, 4321, 4362, 4363, 4400, 4404, 6312, 6313, 6584
    See also Company towns; Geography, Urban; Neighbourhoods; New cities and towns; Sociology, Urban
——— Alberta 5224, 6559
——— British Columbia 4371, 4374, 4427
——— Growth 4314, 4437, 4438, 4440, 4441
——— History 0456, 4324, 4353, 4356, 4370, 4372, 4380, 4390, 4415, 4428
——— Northwest Territories 0629, 4405
——— Ontario 4396
——— Quebec (Province) 0281, 0286, 0301, 4309, 4342, 4358, 4420
——— Saskatchewan 4339, 5752
——— Western provinces 4429
Citizen participation
    See Social participation
Citizens' associations 3193
Citizenship 2496
City and town life 4403
City planning 3868, 4117, 4300, 4302, 4304, 4313, 4322, 4326, 4333, 4338, 4341, 4349, 4369, 4370, 4371, 4375, 4376, 4383, 4388, 4389, 4400, 4407, 4429, 6325, 6588
    See also Community development; Parks and playgrounds; Urban renewal; Zoning
Civil defence 5842
Civil law 2185
——— Quebec (Province) 2215, 2267, 2355
Civil rights 2127, 2233, 2241, 3527
    See also Canadian Charter of Rights and Freedoms; Free speech; Freedom of the press; Human rights; Privacy, Right of
Civil service 1450, 2410, 2498, 2824, 2881
    See also Government employees
Clams 5414
Clarinet music 0891
Clarke, Irwin & Company Limited 1581
Clarke, W.H. 1581
Clarke Institute of Psychiatry 5632
Class size 3443, 3464, 3466, 3542
Classroom management 3566
Clay soils 4844
Clergy 3540
    See also Priests
Climate 2997, 4840, 4979, 5033, 5049, 5065, 5080, 5157, 5206, 5253, 5260, 5261, 5290, 6512
    See also Architecture and climate; Palaeoclimatology
Climate and architecture
    See Architecture and climate
Climatology 5041, 5059, 5074
    See also Meteorology
Clothing and dress 4032
    See also Costume
Clothing industry 2608, 2731
Club canadien (Montréal, Québec)
——— Library 6734
Coaching (Athletics) 1815

Coal 4762, 4801, 4803, 4829, 5786, 6337
    See also Lignite
——— Transportation 4504
Coal liquefaction 5831
Coal mines and mining 4799
——— Environmental aspects 4816
Coast changes 2972, 5245
    See also Shore lines
Coats of arms
    See Heraldry
Cocaine 5667
Cod 4886, 5481, 5506, 5538
Cohen, Leonard 1089, 6909, 6910, 6911
Cohen, Nathan 6912
Coins 1780, 1807
Cold 5454
    See also Winter
Cold weather 5730, 5736, 5803, 5808
    See also Winter
Collective bargaining 2795, 2804, 2824, 2826, 2838, 2857, 2868, 2899, 2905, 2916, 3493
    See also Labour contracts
——— College professors and instructors 2839
——— Health workers 2805, 2840
——— Teachers 2832, 2839, 5923
Collective labour agreements 2868
Collectors and collecting 1796
College Administration Project 3454
Collège de l'Assomption 3691
Collège des Jésuites de Québec 4617
College education 3378, 3391, 3479, 3488, 3489, 3502, 3585, 3599, 3631, 3632, 3639, 3664, 3665, 3671, 3672, 3681, 6708
    See also Professional education
College libraries 1633, 1655, 1726, 1733
Collège militaire royal de St-Jean 1966
College professors and instructors 2868, 3427, 3638
    See also Women college professors and instructors
——— Salaries, pensions, etc 3492
College students 3439, 3668
Colleges and universities 3420, 3433, 3576, 3666
——— Administration 3454
——— Finance 3515, 3579
——— History 3440
——— International aspects 4696
——— Laws, legislation, regulations, etc 3390
——— Teaching 3593
Collins, Charles 6913
Colonies 1907
    See also France–Colonies; Great Britain–Colonies and protectorates
Columbia River Valley 0557
Comets 5811
Comics (Books, strips, etc) 1129, 5954, 5958
Commerce 1439, 2663, 2746
    See also Business; Free trade and protection; Tariff; Trading companies
——— Statistics 2702
Commercial crimes 2214, 2329
Commercial education
    See Business education
Commission on Declining School Enrolments in Ontario (CODE) 3570

Elgin County, Ontario 0448
Elie, Robert 6965
Elk 5348, 5369, 5511
Elk Island National Park 2989, 5493
Ellesmere Island 5034, 5043
Embassies (Buildings) 0788
Embryology 5353
   See also Reproduction
Emergencies
   See Accidents
Emergency Preparedness Canada 5842
Eminent domain 4316, 4335
Employee counselling 2866, 3260
Employee stock ownership plans 2853
Employees
  —— Attitudes 2862, 2863
  —— Dismissal 2867, 2931
   See also Layoff systems
  —— Fitness programs 1819
  —— Rating 2855
  —— Training 0641, 2917, 2936
   See also Occupational retraining
Employees' representation in management 2830, 2834
Employment 2743, 2819, 2823, 2845, 2884, 2892, 3654
   See also Discrimination in employment; Indians–Employ-
  ment; Part time employment; Unemployment;
  Women–Employment
Energy conservation
   See Power resources–Conservation
Energy Resources Conservation Board (Alberta) 6421
Engel, Marian 6966
Engelmann spruce 4931
Engineering 6201, 6208
   See also Agricultural engineering; Environmental engineer-
  ing; Materials engineering; Mechanical engineering; Military
  engineering; Reliability (Engineering); Sanitary engineering
  —— Dictionaries and encyclopaedias 1456
  —— Research 5730, 5733, 5739, 5823, 6374
Engineering and Statistical Research Institute, Agriculture
  Canada 4701, 6374
Engineering design 5744
Engineering Journal (Periodical) 5027
England, Robert 6967
English French relations
   See Canada–French English relations
English language 1095, 1437, 1441, 1442, 1463, 1479
  —— Dialects 1443
  —— Study and teaching 1470, 3403, 3503, 3547, 3676, 3678,
  3711, 3712
Entomological Society of Alberta 5448
Entomological Society of Ontario 5550
Entomology 4659, 4662, 4965, 5309, 5310, 5314, 5429, 5448
   See also Insects
Entrepreneurs 0659
   See also Women entrepreneurs
Entrepreneurship 2707, 2745, 2758, 4271
   See also Incubators (Entrepreneurship)
Environment 3856, 4349, 5063, 5102, 5133, 5135, 5143, 5146,
  5158, 5295, 5300, 5783, 6192
   See also Ecology
  —— Research 3060, 5105, 5230, 5274, 6338, 6419

Environment 2000 Program 5215
Environmental education 3604, 5263, 5292, 5301
   See also Outdoor education
Environmental engineering 5781, 5802, 5814, 6189
Environmental health 3675, 5675
   See also Occupational health and safety
Environmental impact analysis 0632, 3969, 5088, 5098, 5100,
  5106, 5107, 5121, 5152, 5166, 5172
Environmental law 2224
Environmental policy 3192, 5156, 5219, 5241, 5287
Environmental protection 4845, 5164, 5192, 5193, 5196, 5197,
  5198, 5231, 5251, 5255, 5262, 5269, 5361, 6292, 6366, 6439
  —— Economic aspects 2742, 5288
Equal employment opportunity
   See Affirmative action programs
Equal pay for equal work 2831, 2858, 2876, 2911, 2913, 2922,
  2933
Erickson, Arthur 0788, 6968, 6969
Erosion 2972, 4699, 4703, 4704, 4994, 5145
   See also Sedimentation and deposition
Eschambault, Antoine d' 6970
Eskimos
   See Inuit
Espionage 2505
Essays 1160
Essex County, Ontario 0428
Estonians in Canada 5900
Estuaries 5085
Etchemins, Quebec 0415
Ethanol 5782
Ethnic groups 0165, 1487, 3195, 3673, 4128, 4133, 4142, 4144,
  4153, 4156, 4161, 4167, 4169, 4176, 4177, 4180, 4181, 4182,
  4193, 4195, 4209, 4210, 4214, 4215, 4216, 4219, 4231, 4232,
  4234, 4238, 4241, 4251, 4252, 4253, 4254, 4255, 4262, 4275,
  4276, 4286, 4291, 4292, 5654, 6063, 6184, 6629, 6650, 6657
   See also Minorities
  —— Alberta 0538, 4168, 4240
  —— British Columbia 4129, 4282, 6621
  —— Manitoba 4185, 4227
  —— Nova Scotia 4187, 4228
  —— Ontario 4280
  —— Quebec (Province) 3364, 4217, 4226, 4277, 4285
Ethnic Newspaper Microfilming Project 6019
Ethnic periodicals 4143, 5880, 5881, 5882, 5883, 5884, 5886,
  5887, 5888, 5889, 5890, 5891, 5892, 5893, 5894, 5896, 5897,
  5898, 5900, 5901, 5908, 5910, 5912, 5914, 5935, 5941, 5960,
  5961, 5965
Ethnic press 1724, 4250, 5873, 5955, 6013, 6017, 6019, 6023,
  6032, 6047
Ethnic relations 4192, 4290, 4294
   See also Biculturalism; Intercultural education; Race relations
Ethnography 1936, 3909, 3970, 4036, 4573, 4584, 4609
  —— Film catalogues 6622
Ethnology 2883, 3996, 4100, 4555, 4561, 4578, 6335, 6336
   See also Anthropology; Ethnomusicology
Ethnomusicology 4612
Ethology 4717
The Etude (Periodical) 0835
European Economic Community
  —— Foreign relations
  —— —— Canada 2464

Foundations (Building) 5779
Fournier, Ovila 6988
France
—— Colonies 1905
France and Canada
   See Canada and France
Franchise system 2600, 2766, 2767
Franciscans 1496
Francoeur, Lucien 1089
Franklin, Sir John 2045, 2047
Franquelin, Jean-Baptiste-Louis 6528
Fraser, Sandy
   See McIntosh, John Everett (Sandy Fraser, pseud)
Fraser, Simon 6989
Fraser River estuary, British Columbia 5088, 5210
Fraser River Valley, British Columbia 0597
Frazil ice 5076
Fréchette, Louis 6990, 6991
Fredericton Tuesday Night Writers 1225
Free speech 1677, 2354
Free trade and protection 1850, 2557, 2558, 2699, 2739, 2743, 2756, 2757, 2762, 2916
   See also Tariff
Freedom of information 1677, 2210, 2273, 2415, 2441, 2446
   See also Government information
Freedom of the press 2123
Freemasons 1516, 1969, 4126
French American literature
   See Literature, French American
French Canadian literature
   See Literature, French Canadian
French Canadians 0062, 0086, 0289, 0319, 0382, 1524, 1925, 1943, 1989, 2008, 3109, 4607, 6780
   See also Acadians
—— Genealogy 2007
French Canadians in Alberta 0533
French Canadians in Manitoba 0507
French Canadians in Newfoundland 0227
French Canadians in Ontario 0453, 0463, 0466, 0470, 0477, 0482, 0488, 1180, 1228, 3503, 4611, 6571
French Canadians in Saskatchewan 0543
French Canadians in the United States 0320, 1144, 2001, 3064
French Canadians in the Western provinces 1228
French English relations
   See Canada–French English relations
French horn music 0938
French in America 2086
French in North America 1923, 1928
French language 1224, 1413, 1418, 1419, 1420, 1422, 1434, 1475, 1478, 1489, 6634
—— Gender 1473
—— Readers 3524
—— Study and teaching 1462, 1467, 1469, 1474, 3477, 3524, 3554, 3569, 3626, 3627, 3629, 3633, 3647, 3651, 3658, 3677, 3686, 3693, 3718
—— Textbooks 3535
French language books 0138
French language in Acadia 1466
French language in Ontario 1461
French language in Quebec 1412, 1435, 1438, 1447, 1481, 2323
French speaking countries 1152, 1482, 1763, 2406, 2412, 2509

Frères de l'instruction chrétienne 3655
Fresh water biology 5084, 5139, 5195, 5330, 5333, 5397, 5423, 5444, 5544, 5556
Friends, Society of 1547
Fringe benefits
   See Non-wage payments
Frontenac County, Ontario 0471
Frontier and pioneer life 3817
   See also Homesteads
Frontier College 3422
Frost damage 4962
Frozen ground 4754, 5037, 5042, 5066, 5073, 5268, 5284, 5739, 5744, 5779
Fruit flies 5378
Fruit trees
—— Diseases and pests 4697
Fry, F.E.J. 6992
Frye, Northrop 6993, 6994, 6995, 6996
Fuel research 5784, 5786, 5822
Fund raising 2628
Fundy, Bay of 5770, 5774, 5794, 5810
Fundy National Park 2981
Fungi 5443, 5537
   See also Mycology
Fungi, Pathogenic 4685
Fur bearing animals 5489
Fur industry
—— History 1909, 1913, 4579
   See also Hudson's Bay Company; North West Company
Fur trade 1898, 1906, 3952, 3982
Fur traders 1955, 2077
Furniture 1988, 2011
Future 2654, 2721, 2987, 3445, 3578
   See also Forecasts
Gagnon, Madeleine 6997
Gallant, Mavis 6998, 6999
Gambling 2329
   See also Lotteries
Games 1348, 1792
   See also Chess; Electronic games
Ganglia Press 1068
Gangs 2329
Ganong, William Francis 7000
Garant, Serge 0904, 7001
Garbage
   See Refuse and refuse disposal
Gardens and gardening 0789, 0802, 4663, 4713, 4714
   See also Greenhouses; Organic gardens and gardening
Garneau, François-Xavier 1967, 7002
Garneau, Saint-Denys 7003, 7004, 7005
Gas, Natural
—— British Columbia 6383
—— Offshore development 4823
—— Prospecting 4817, 4880
—— Yukon Territory 4866
Gas industry 2753, 4839
Gaspé Peninsula 0295, 0374, 0379, 0398, 5470
Gauthier, Yvon 7006
Gauvreau, Claude 7007
Gazetteers 3008, 5983, 6478
Geddes, James 7008

Geese, Wild 5390, 5460

Gélinas, Gratien 1090

Gendron Commission 6291

Genealogy 0258, 0491, 1919, 1929, 1934, 1937, 1940, 1982, 1996, 1997, 2000, 2008, 2014, 2022, 2023, 2026, 2028, 2041, 2049, 2052, 2057, 2062, 2063, 2066, 2073, 2075, 2082, 2083, 2090, 4224

Genetic engineering 5500
  See also Biotechnology

Geochemistry 4827

Geodesy 4745

Geoffroy, Louis 1089

Geographic Board of Canada (Canadian Permanent Committee on Geographical Names) 2966

Geographical distribution of animals and plants 3028, 5325, 6557

Geographical names
  See Names, Geographical

Geography 0011, 2946, 2950, 2952, 2955, 2956, 2957, 2958, 2960, 2963, 2968, 2973, 3014, 3015, 3017, 3044, 3060, 3069, 3070, 3075, 3856, 4182, 6103, 6116, 6129, 6133, 6147, 6160, 6165
  See also Dissertations, Academic–Geography; Economic geography; Information storage and retrieval systems–Geography; Maps; Physical geography
  —— Periodicals 5938
  —— Study and teaching 2954, 2961, 2974, 3051, 3059

Geography, Historical 2970, 3030, 3058, 3074, 6514
  —— Maps 6567

Geography, Human
  See Anthropogeography

Geography, Urban 4302, 4321, 4322, 4354, 4423

Geological maps
  See Maps, Geological

Geological Survey of Canada 4762, 4857, 6209, 6210, 6211, 6216, 6229, 6231, 6244, 6245, 6253, 6496, 6497, 6591

Geological surveys 4726, 4769

Geology 4727, 4728, 4729, 4730, 4731, 4732, 4733, 4734, 4736, 4737, 4738, 4748, 4762, 4768, 4782, 4817, 4819, 4833, 4838, 4877, 4883, 6066, 6190, 6209, 6210, 6211, 6216, 6231, 6244, 6245, 6253, 6295, 6326, 6402, 6403, 6496
  See also Glaciology; International Geological Correlation Program; Maps, Geological; Palaeontology; Petrology; Sediments (Geology); Submarine geology
  —— Alberta 4735, 4755, 4830, 4837, 4853, 6425, 6564
  —— Atlantic provinces 4772, 4777, 4871
  —— British Columbia 4735, 4755, 4781, 4879, 6410, 6427, 6428, 6570, 6581
  —— Manitoba 4746, 4747, 4758, 4760, 4766, 4774, 4826, 4873, 6455
  —— New Brunswick 4831, 4876
  —— Newfoundland 4771, 4798, 6515, 6566
  —— Northwest Territories 4755, 4793, 4813, 4820, 4828, 4864, 5227
  —— Nova Scotia 4789, 4821, 6333
  —— Ontario 4807, 4825, 4826, 4860, 6072, 6074, 6316, 6491
  —— Quebec (Province) 0336, 3024, 4740, 4769, 4776, 4836, 4874, 6510, 6563
  —— Research 4881
  —— Saskatchewan 4780
  —— Yukon Territory 2988, 4574, 4735, 4865

Geology, Stratigraphic 4805
  —— Pleistocene 4545, 4765
  —— Quaternary 4813, 4860, 4868

Geology, Structural 4841
  See also Geomorphology; Mountains

Geomorphology 3054, 4788, 5054

Geophysics 4744, 4769, 4838, 6068

Georges Bank 4908

Georgia, Strait of 5497

Georgian Bay Islands National Park 3012

Geriatrics 5579, 5598

Gérin, Léon 7009

Germain, Jean-Claude 7010, 7011

German language 1423

Germans in Alberta 4218

Germans in British Columbia 4213

Germans in Canada 0164, 0911, 1293, 1528, 4125, 4160, 4191, 4200, 4212, 4222, 4233, 4274, 5884, 6017, 6096

Germans in Ontario 4221, 4223

Germans in Saskatchewan 1565

Gerontology 3257, 5579, 5668, 5673

Gerontology, Social 3305

Ghosts 4550

Giguère, Roland 7012, 7013

Gilbert, Gerry 7014

Gill, Charles 7015, 7016

Gill, Don 7017

Gilson, Étienne 7018

Girouard, Jean-Joseph 7019

Glacier National Park 2996

Glaciers 5045, 5054, 5218, 5234, 5271
  See also Canadian Glacier Inventory; Moraines

Glaciology 2959, 2994, 2997, 5042, 5046, 5122, 5142, 5185, 5227, 5268

Glass 5768, 5844

Glassco, John 7020

Glassware 4598

Glenbow-Alberta Institute Library 0508

Glengarry County, Ontario 0491

Glenn, Harry
  See Boag, Max (Harry Glenn, pseud)

Global product mandating 2694

Global temperature changes 5280

Globe (Newspaper) 4022

Glyphosate 5265

Godbout, Archange 7021

Gold 4757, 4825

Gold mines and mining 4858
  —— British Columbia 4739
  —— Nova Scotia 4857

Goods and services tax 2750, 2768

Gordon Home Blackader Library 0733

Gosse, Philip Henry 7022

Gosselin, Amédée Edmond 7023

Gosselin, Auguste Honoré 7023, 7024

Gosselin, David 7023

Gould, Glenn 7025, 7026, 7027

Government administration
  See Administration, Public

Government agencies
  See Administrative agencies

Government and labour 2847

Government appropriations and expenditures 2713

Government corporations 2631, 2696, 6349, 6350
  See also Privatization of nationalized industry

Government employees 2824
—— Political activities 2403
Government information 2210, 2266, 2273, 2415, 2428, 2434
Government investigations 2121, 2362, 3592, 6381
    See also Royal commissions
—— Alberta 6306
—— British Columbia 6227, 6339
—— Manitoba 6234
—— Nova Scotia 6365
—— Ontario 6329, 6413
—— Quebec (Province) 2511, 6281
—— Saskatchewan 2396
Government publications 0154, 1617, 2130, 2798, 3266, 3283,
    3374, 4301, 4438, 5289, 6214, 6217, 6221, 6222, 6226, 6228,
    6241, 6246, 6248, 6266, 6275, 6276, 6277, 6289, 6290, 6296,
    6297, 6314, 6315, 6321, 6322, 6325, 6330, 6402, 6403, 6404,
    6405, 6408, 6426, 6450, 6452, 6460, 6474, 6475
—— Alberta 6236, 6278, 6422, 6423, 6424
—— British Columbia 6230, 6310, 6340, 6431, 6432, 6433
—— Great Britain 6212
—— Manitoba 6318, 6334, 6456, 6457
—— New Brunswick 6239, 6285, 6461, 6462
—— Newfoundland 6309
—— Northwest Territories 6463
—— Nova Scotia 6239, 6386, 6464, 6465, 6466
—— Ontario 2582, 3424, 6215, 6251, 6282, 6293, 6300, 6302,
    6323, 6354, 6360, 6364, 6413, 6414, 6467, 6468
—— Periodicals 6220, 6252, 6363, 6390, 6391
—— Prince Edward Island 6239, 6469
—— Quebec (Province) 2238, 6255, 6256, 6264, 6270, 6272,
    6280, 6281, 6286, 6299, 6305, 6308, 6324, 6328, 6351, 6366,
    6373, 6392, 6470, 6471
—— Saskatchewan 6233, 6472
Government purchasing
    See Purchasing, Government
Government secrecy
    See Official secrets
Governors-General 2018
Gowans, Alan 7028
Grading and marking (Students) 3412, 3472, 3487
    See also Students–Rating
Grain
—— Transportation 0524, 4460, 4482
Grain elevators 5775
Grandparent and child 1369, 1372
Graph theory 5788
Graphic arts 0696, 0702, 0726
    See also Printing
Graphic Publishers 1634
Grasslands National Park 3019, 3035
Gravestones 3292
Grayling 5472
Great Britain
—— Army 1984
—— Colonies and protectorates 1883, 6746
—— History 2042
—— Imprints 0172
—— Parliament 6212
—— Royal family 2074
Great Depression, 1929-1939 2053
Great Lakes 1346, 1992, 2020, 2967, 4446, 4450, 4464, 4465,
    4519, 4905, 4906, 5064, 5065, 5074, 5123, 5145, 5150, 5161,
    5232, 5245, 5290, 5330, 5477, 6495, 6501

Great Lakes Biolimnology Laboratory 5438
Great Lakes Forestry Centre 4992
Greeks in Canada 4206, 4266, 5894, 6124
Greenhouse effect, Atmospheric 5280
Greenhouses 4680, 4681, 4720
Greenland 0645
Grenfell, Sir Wilfred Thomason 7029
Grey County, Ontario 0476
Grief 1548
Grievance procedures 2875, 2887, 2919
Gros Morne National Park 2984
Groulx, Lionel 1967, 7030, 7031, 7032
Group of Seven (Canadian Painters) 0669, 0674
Groupe de recherche en développement de l'Est du Québec
    0377
Groups (Sociology) 3119, 3156
    See also Leadership; Social psychology
Grove, Frederick Philip 7033, 7034
Guaranteed annual income 2790
Guards 2132, 2159
Guelph, Ontario 0485
Guidebooks 0391, 3043, 3246
Guillaume, Gustave 7035
Guillet, Edwin C. 7036
Guitar music 0881
Gustafson, Ralph 7037
Haeck, Philippe 7038
Hail 5127
Halasz de Beky, Ivan 7039
Haldimand-Norfolk region, Ontario 0465
Haliburton, Thomas Chandler 7040, 7041
Haliburton County, Ontario 4407
Halifax, Nova Scotia 0196, 0249
—— Politics and government 4364
Halifax County, Nova Scotia 4821
Halifax Garrison Library 6735
Hallam, John 6739
Halley's comet
    See Comets
Halton region, Ontario 4378
Hamelin, Louis-Edmond 7042, 7043, 7044
Hamilton, Ontario 2856, 5332
Handicapped 2230, 3090, 3180, 3187, 3204, 3209, 3215, 3218,
    3220, 3222, 3235, 3237, 3243, 3247, 3249, 3286, 3309, 6676
    See also Architecture and the handicapped; Children,
    Handicapped; Mentally handicapped; Parents, Handicapp-
    ed; Socially handicapped; Sports for the handicapped;
    Women, Handicapped
—— Education 3442, 3541, 3546, 3594
—— Employment 2860, 2939, 3670
—— Housing 3214, 3229, 3341, 3342
—— Recreation 1767, 1830, 1862
—— Rehabilitation 3142, 3226
—— Sexual abuse 3316, 3356
—— Transportation 3167, 3189, 3246, 4471
Handwriting 3568
Hardware 0754, 0755
Harper, J. Russell 7045
Harris, Lawren 7046
Harrisse, Henry 7047
Harry Hawthorn Foundation for the Inculcation and Propaga-
    tion of the Principles and Ethics of Fly-Fishing 1831

—— Juvenile literature 1336, 1344, 1377
—— Languages 1400, 1401, 1402, 1404, 1405, 1406, 1407, 1408, 1409, 1410, 1411, 1414, 1415, 1416, 1425, 1427, 1428, 1430, 1433, 1452, 1454, 1457, 1458, 1464, 1491, 3907, 3911, 4070
   See also Algonkian languages
—— —— Texts 3919, 3939, 4063
—— Legal status, laws, etc 2172, 2272, 2274, 2278, 2326, 2337, 2349, 2350, 3928, 4030, 4042, 4069, 4093
—— Legends 3916, 4036, 4061, 4083
—— Manitoba 0549, 3974, 3982, 4028, 4595
—— Medical care 5639, 5710
—— Medicine 5581
—— Music 0834, 0850, 0858, 0876
—— New Brunswick 3989
—— Newspapers 5951, 6016, 6022
—— Northwest Territories 5257
—— Periodicals 5899, 5904, 5905, 5939, 5951, 5953, 5985
—— Population 4033
—— Quebec (Province) 3909, 3934, 3978, 4073, 4079, 4122, 4555
—— Religion and mythology 4036, 4061, 4096
—— Reserves 6574
—— Rights 4062
—— Rites and ceremonies 0970, 3955
—— Self-government 2512, 4082, 4087, 4101, 4121
—— Social conditions 4011, 4021, 4072
—— Study and teaching 3971
—— Treaties 4007, 4019, 4113
—— Urban residence 3988, 4001, 4041, 4117, 5710
—— Women 3782, 3886, 3897, 4045, 4048, 4085
—— Yukon Territory 3930, 4094
Indians and mass media 4067
Indians in literature 1283
Indochinese in Canada 4288
Industrial accidents
   See Accidents, Industrial
Industrial arbitration
   See Arbitration, Industrial
Industrial design
   See Design, Industrial
Industrial policy 2714, 2734
Industrial psychology
   See Psychology, Industrial
Industrial relations 2762, 2788, 2794, 2804, 2830, 2832, 2857, 2859, 2918, 2941, 6108, 6135
   See also Arbitration, Industrial; Collective bargaining; Labour laws and legislation; Labour management committees; Personnel management
—— Film catalogues 6662, 6665
—— Periodicals 5923
Industrial research
—— British Columbia 6250
Industrial safety
   See Occupational health and safety
Industries and resources 0589
Industry 0121, 2594, 2680, 2687, 2693
   See also Incentives in industry; Location in business and industry; Manufacturing industries
—— History 2593, 2697, 2744
—— Security measures 2159, 2661
—— Technology 5839
Industry and state 2313, 2314, 2439, 2722, 2723, 2847, 4848
   See also Deregulation of industry; Price regulation by government

Industry and the arts
   See Arts and industry
Infants
—— Nutrition 5645
Informal sector (Economics) 2678
Information display systems 5630, 5641, 5644, 5646, 5648
   See also Video monitors
Information science 1631, 1666, 1738, 1741
   See also Documentation; Electronic data processing
—— Study and teaching 1594
Information services 2785
   See also Libraries–Reference services; Machine-readable bibliographic data
Information storage and retrieval systems 0156, 0179, 0660
   See also Data transmission systems; Libraries–Automation; Machine-readable bibliographic data
—— Business and finance 2751
—— Geography 3033
—— Geology 4775
Information systems 1664, 1698, 1709, 2543, 2761, 4350, 4360
   See also Data transmission systems
Inheritance 2081
Inland water transportation 4515
Innis, Harold Adams 7073
Innovation (Economics) 5838
Insane, criminal and dangerous 3103
   See also Forensic psychiatry
Insects 5525
   See also Entomology
Inspection 2313, 2314
Institut agricole d'Oka 6150
Institut canadien de Québec
—— Library 6752
Institut canadien d'éducation des adultes 3680, 3689
Institut de recherche appliquée sur le travail 2858
Institut de recherche en droit public, Université de Montréal 2112
Institut d'histoire de l'Amérique française 2084
Institut national de la recherche scientifique (Québec) 3537
Institute for Computer Research, University of Waterloo 5832
Institute for Marine Dynamics (Canada) 5835
Institute for Research in Construction (Canada) 6453
Institute of Arctic and Alpine Research 0651
Institute of Occupational and Environmental Health 5114, 5115
Institute of Ocean Sciences, Ocean Ecology Division 5521
Institute of Pacific Relations 2491
Insurance 2749
Insurance, Automobile 2135
—— Quebec (Province) 2145
Insurance, Fire
—— Maps 6544, 6560, 6562
Insurance, Unemployment 2790, 2807
Insurance laws and regulations 2114
Intelligence 1426
Intelligence, Business
   See Business intelligence
Intelligence service 2336, 2505
   See also Secret service
Intercultural education 3552, 3620, 3642, 3648, 3673, 3674, 3692, 3721, 3729, 4175, 4190, 4242

Interest rates 2673

Intergovernmental relations 2391, 2447

Interior design 1988

Interlibrary loans 1612, 1613, 1692, 1693

Internal migration
    See Migration, Internal

International Commission for the Northwest Atlantic Fisheries 4885

International Development Research Centre 2413, 6356

International Geological Correlation Program 4819

International law 0611, 2180, 2271, 2278
    See also Boundaries; Maritime law; Territorial waters

International Organization for Standardization 5636

International relations 2405, 2408, 2430, 2459, 2467, 2508, 6174
    See also East-West relations; Nationalism; United Nations; War

International security 2501, 2535, 2555, 2556
    See also Disarmament; United Nations

International Sound Poetry Festival, Toronto 1133

Interprovincial relations 2522

Interracial relations
    See Race relations

Interviewing 1671

Inuit 0508, 0621, 0626, 0882, 1118, 1216, 1393, 1531, 3910, 3912, 3915, 3918, 3920, 3921, 3926, 3929, 3931, 3932, 3933, 3938, 3941, 3942, 3943, 3945, 3949, 3957, 3965, 3966, 3968, 3969, 3970, 3972, 3982, 3983, 3991, 3995, 3996, 3999, 4003, 4009, 4013, 4017, 4018, 4022, 4023, 4029, 4035, 4043, 4065, 4068, 4073, 4074, 4077, 4079, 4084, 4092, 4100, 4103, 4109, 4111, 4112, 4115, 4116, 4117, 4118, 4120, 4123, 4124, 4531, 4532, 4572, 4907, 5257, 6104, 6117, 6163, 6176, 6180, 6182, 6185, 6186, 6197, 6622, 6645, 6678, 6680
    —— Antiquities 4564, 4597
    —— Art 0668, 0671, 0687, 0697, 0698, 0711, 0712, 0727
    —— Claims 0643, 3987
    —— Costume and adornment 4032
    —— Education 3388, 3398, 3431
    —— Food 5661
    —— Health and hygiene 5573, 5661, 5672
    —— Juvenile literature 1344, 1377
    —— Languages 1403, 1428, 1436, 1454, 1464
    See also Inuktitut language
    —— Music 0831, 0876
    —— Periodicals 5913
    —— Religion and mythology 1527, 1561, 4061
    —— Women 3782, 4045

Inuit and mass media 4067

Inuit Tapirisat of Canada 3987

Inuktitut language 1403, 1455

Inuvik Scientific Resource Centre 4631

Inventory control 2752

Invertebrates 4521, 4524, 5389, 5423, 5444, 5544
    See also Insects; Molluscs; Protozoa; Worms

Investments, Canadian 2583

Investments, Foreign 2270, 2408, 2430, 2467, 2603, 2627, 2725
    See also Foreign Investment Review Agency; Foreign ownership

Ioleen A. Hawken Memorial Local History Collection, Owen Sound Public Library 0476

Ionization 5026

Ionosphere 5734

Irish in Canada 1959, 4157, 4186, 4224, 4241, 4258, 6128

Irish in Quebec 4297

Iron mines and mining 4863

Iroquois Indians 1404, 3917

Irrigation 4673, 5062

Islands of the Arctic 0619, 4793, 5136, 5137, 5178, 5179, 5185

Isozymes 4982

Italians in Canada 4261, 4272, 5888, 6102, 6139

Jackman, William T. 7074

James Bay Hydroelectric Project 3934, 3978, 3979, 5077, 5093

Janssoone, Frédéric 7075

Japan
    —— Foreign relations 2517

Japanese in British Columbia 4129

Japanese in Canada 2517, 4171, 4183, 4279, 6105

Jarvis, Thomas Stinson 7076

Jasper National Park 5514

Jazz music 0869, 0905

Jenness, Diamond 7077, 7078, 7079

Jesuits 1567, 1993
    —— History 1877
    —— Missions 1510, 1874, 1875, 1892, 1915, 1951, 2067, 6729, 6733

Jesus Island, Quebec 0380

Jetté, Fernand 7080

Jews 2962, 4126, 4148, 4155, 4247, 4267

Jews in Canada 0111, 1071, 4127, 4132, 4143, 4154, 4189, 4201, 4260, 4287, 5932, 6098

Jews in Quebec 4204

Joachim, Otto 0904

Job analysis 2858, 2876, 2913

Job hunting 2935

Job satisfaction 2829, 2861
    See also Quality of work life

Job training
    See Occupational training

Jogues, Isaac 1504

John Bassett Memorial Library 0293, 0386

John Orr Foster Reference Library 3112

Johnson, Daniel 2469

Johnson, Harry Gordon 7081

Joliette, Quebec 0303, 0304, 0335, 5885

Jolliet, Louis 1878

Joseph, saint 1520

Journalism, Labour 5931, 5942

Journals, Personal
    See Diaries

Judaism 4260

Judd, William W. 7082

Judges 2120
    See also Courts

Junior colleges
    See Community and junior colleges

Jurisdiction, Territorial 5090
    See also Territorial waters

Justice, Administration of 2169, 2174, 2178, 2199, 2207, 2225, 2229, 2234, 2236, 2237, 2238, 2274, 2283, 2288, 2301, 2331, 2332, 2333, 2343, 2348, 2349, 2350, 2361, 2362, 3267, 3268, 3877, 4109, 4115, 6681
    See also Courts; Criminal procedure; Law enforcement

Juvenile Crime Prevention Project 2255, 2256

1280
—— Manitoba 1243
—— Native authors 4122
—— Periodicals 1237, 5855, 5921, 5952, 5956
—— Translations 0097, 1028, 1046, 1124, 1440
—— Western provinces 1166
Literature and movies
    See Movies and literature
Literature and society 1027
Lithography 4403
Lithuanians in Canada 5891
Liturgies 1578
Livesay, Dorothy 1225, 7148, 7149
Livestock 4655, 4682, 4683, 4706, 5511
Livre d'ici (Periodical) 0185
Lobsters 4890, 5339
Local government 0439, 4427
    See also Metropolitan government; Municipal government;
    Provincial-municipal relations
Local history 1887, 3040
—— Alberta 0538, 0545, 2066
—— Atlantic provinces 0208
—— British Columbia 0602
—— Manitoba 0503, 0534, 0546
—— New Brunswick 0248
—— North, Canadian 0458
—— Nova Scotia 0250, 0258
—— Ontario 0456, 0458, 0469, 0476, 0489, 0490, 0491
—— Quebec (Province) 0284, 0308, 0328, 0339, 1916, 2014, 2037
—— Saskatchewan 0498, 0535
Local transit 4476
    See also Street railroads; Subways; Taxicabs
—— Finance 4494
Location in business and industry 2561, 2765
Lochhead, Douglas 7150
Lodge-pole pine 5426, 5531
Log construction 0768
Logan, John Daniel 7151
Loggers 2821
Logging
    See Lumbering
Lomer, Gerhard Richard 7152
London, Ontario 4345
Long-Range Transport of Air Pollutants Program 5159, 5221, 5222
Long-term care of the sick 5702
Longpré, Anselme 7153
Longpré, Ephrem 7154, 7155
Lotbinière, Quebec 0407
Lotteries 1787
Loucheux Indians 3930
Louisbourg (Fortress) 0738, 1970
Louisbourg National Historic Park 4585
Louisiana 2019
Lovell, John 0933
Low, Albert Peter 7156
Lower, Arthur Reginald Marsden 7157
Lower Saint Lawrence region, Quebec 0359
Lowry, Malcolm 7158, 7159, 7160, 7161, 7162
Lowry, Malcolm, Library 6785
Loyalists
    See United Empire Loyalists

Lumbering 1774, 4942, 4957, 4967
—— Environmental aspects 4928, 4949, 4978, 4983, 4994, 4998, 5009, 5373
Lutheran Church 1573
Lyman, John 7163
MacBride Museum 0662
Macdonald, Sir John Alexander, Library 6753
Machine-readable bibliographic data 1645, 1646
Mackay, Isabel Ecclestone 7164
Mackenzie, Alexander 6514
Mackenzie Mountains Region Baseline Study 4828
Mackenzie River region 0617, 0618, 4631, 5118, 5174, 5478, 5487, 5488
Mackerel 4891, 4893
MacLennan, Hugh 7165, 7166, 7167
Macmillan Company of Canada 1674
MacNutt, William Stewart 7168
Macpherson, C.B. 7169
Madawaska
—— History 0228
Mafia
    See Organized crime
Magdalen Islands 0305, 0344, 0399
Magnetism 5829
Magocsi, Paul Robert 7170
Maheux, Arthur 7171
Mail order catalogues
    See Catalogues, Mail order
Maillet, Antonine 7172
Major, André 7173
Maliseet Indians 3953, 4089
Mammals 5302, 5428, 5493, 5530
    See also Marine mammals
Man
—— Influence on nature 5257
Man, Prehistoric 4008, 4609
Man and the Biosphere Programme 5190
Management 2669, 2737, 2787, 4914
    See also Arts–Management; Business management and
    organization; Conflict management; Crisis management;
    Personnel management; Production management; Schedul-
    ing (Management); School management and organization
Management by objectives 2605
Mance, Jeanne 7174
Manitoba 0499, 0500, 0506, 0507, 0509, 0513, 0522, 0530, 0539, 0542, 0546, 0549, 0551, 0621, 3243, 4078, 4621, 5485, 5515
    See also Churchill, Manitoba; French Canadians in Manitoba;
    Winnipeg, Manitoba
—— Archaeology 4540, 4571, 4774
—— Department of Agriculture 6704
—— Department of Natural Resources 6454
—— Environment Protection Board 6292
—— Geological Services Branch 6455
—— History 0503, 0534, 0549, 1908, 1950, 3752
—— Laws, legislation, regulations, etc 6458
—— Maps 6522
—— Population 3039
—— Social policy 3304
Manitoba Energy Information Centre 5791
Manitoba Genealogical Society
—— Library 2023

Medicine, Popular 5685

Meech Lake Accord
See Canada–Constitution

Meilleur, Jean-Baptiste 7187

Melzack, Louis, Collection 6791

Memorial University of Newfoundland
—— Maritime History Group 0251

Men 3307
See also Women and men

Mennonites 0495, 1542, 1543, 1550, 1551, 1555, 1565, 1571, 4200
See also Amish

Mental health 1858, 2934, 5619, 5620, 5638, 5677, 5678, 5697, 5698
—— Film catalogues 6643

Mental health care 5614

Mental illness 3357
See also Autism; Depression, Mental; Learning disabilities
—— Prevention 5624
—— Social aspects 3126

Mentally handicapped 3108, 3112, 3161, 3208, 3237, 3245, 3273, 3365, 5628, 5650
See also National Institute on Mental Retardation
—— Sexual behaviour 3155, 3158

Mercure, Pierre 0904

Mercury pollution of rivers, lakes, etc 5091, 5492

Mesplet, Fleury 7188, 7189

Metallurgy 4757, 4779, 5721, 5740, 5747, 5763, 5766

Metals 5180, 5201, 5207, 5467, 5765
See also Heavy metals
—— Fatigue 5853
—— Refining 4863

Meteorites 4808

Meteorology 4926, 6307
See also Climatology

Métis 0543, 1393, 2343, 3938, 3945, 3950, 3982, 3995, 4015, 4022, 4028, 4030, 4035, 4043, 4065, 4073, 4078, 4095, 4103, 4109, 4111, 4112, 4115, 4117, 4123, 6106, 6119, 6163, 6176, 6182, 6197
—— Claims 4049, 4051
—— History 4099
—— Juvenile literature 1344
—— Languages 4107
—— Manitoba 3974
—— Periodicals 5899, 5904
—— Women 3782

Métis Rebellion, 1885
See Riel Rebellion, 1885

Metric Commission Canada 2657

Metric system 2615, 2657, 3475

Metropolitan areas 4312
See also Suburbs

Metropolitan government 3395

Metropolitan Toronto Bilingual Project 1607

Micmac Indians 3960, 4089

Microcomputers 1663, 1676

Microeconomics 2641

Microelectronics 3819

Microfiches 0167, 0694, 3477, 6371

Microfilms 3052, 5895, 6025
See also Books on microfilm; Newspapers on microfilm

Microforms 0352, 0419, 1595, 2368, 6035, 6040
See also Microfiches; Microfilms

Microorganisms 4976
See also Protozoa

Middlesex County, Ontario 5463

Midwives 5621

Mignault, Pierre-Basile 7190

Migration, Internal 3015, 3018, 3032, 3067, 3988
See also Labour mobility; Urban rural migration

Migration of birds
See Birds–Migration

Milfoil, Water
See Water milfoil

Military art and science
—— Periodicals 5870, 5968

Military engineering 2031, 2032

Military history 1966, 2021, 5572
See also Canada–History, Military; Naval history; Regimental histories

Military policy 2408, 2430, 2467

Military research 5592, 5730
See also Space research

Military strategy
See Strategy

Miller, Émile 7191

Miller, Henry C. 1634

Mine accidents and explosions 4859

Mine waste 4799, 4872, 4878, 5267, 5486

Mineral exploration 4827, 4832
See also Prospecting

Mineral industries 0643, 4735, 6261, 6326, 6438
—— Environmental aspects 4794, 4800, 4811, 4846, 4851, 4869, 4878, 5126, 5165
—— History 4784, 4796, 4810, 4857
—— Laws, legislation, regulations, etc 2723, 4848
—— Research 4870, 5740, 6347, 6348, 6397
See also Canada Centre for Mineral and Energy Technology
—— Statistics 6369, 6372, 6404, 6405
—— Technology 4773, 4856, 4858
—— Waste 5087

Mineral processing 5836

Mineralogy 4770, 4883

Minerals in diet 5547

Miners 2821, 2880

Mines and mineral resources 4733, 4734, 4819, 6190
See also Coal mines and mining; Gold mines and mining; Iron mines and mining; Ocean mining; Resource development
—— British Columbia 4781, 6257, 6428
—— Manitoba 4746, 4760, 6455
—— New Brunswick 4824, 4831
—— Nova Scotia 6332, 6333
—— Ontario 6254, 6260, 6316
—— Quebec (Province) 4752, 4761, 4767, 4874, 6243
—— Saskatchewan 6301

Minimum wage 2915

Minks 5428

Minorities 1459, 3109, 3253, 4159, 4161, 4289, 4294, 4296, 4298
See also Ethnic groups
—— Education 3538, 3552, 3618, 3692, 3700, 3717, 4175
See also Intercultural education
—— Film catalogues 6698
—— History 2039
—— Quebec (Province) 6171

Nurses and nursing 4595, 5570, 5586, 5589, 5593, 5606, 5615, 5616, 5617, 5622, 5629, 6624
   See also Canadian Nurses' Association; Home care services; School nursing
—— History 5578, 5713
—— Laws and legislation 2167
—— Periodicals 5988
—— Supply and demand 5611
—— Training 3428, 3479, 5604
Nursing research 5625
Nutrition 1857, 2620, 3220, 4718, 5392, 5661, 6177
   See also Aged–Nutrition; Infants–Nutrition; Vitamins
Nutrition education 3621
Oblates of Mary Immaculate 1416, 1499, 1506, 1507, 1512, 1513
O'Brien, Mary 7215
Obstetrics 5621
   See also Abortion; Childbirth; Pregnancy
Occult sciences 4575
   See also Parapsychology
Occupational health and safety 2801, 2828, 2846, 2862, 2863, 2889, 2902, 2928, 3675, 5606, 5615, 5619, 5620, 5646, 5647, 5648, 5649, 5658, 5676, 5683, 6689
   See also Accidents, Industrial; Hazardous substances
Occupational mobility 3169
Occupational retraining 2936, 3432
Occupational training 2799, 2802, 2814, 2937, 3654
   See also Employees–Training
Occupations 0690, 2637, 3540, 3610, 5612
   See also Career planning; Professions; Self employment
Ocean 4503, 5299
   See also Arctic Ocean; Pacific Ocean; Tides
Ocean mining 5111
Ocean pollution
   See Marine pollution
Oceanography 4479, 4743, 4840, 5047, 5051, 5112, 5130, 5153, 5205, 5337, 5376, 5383, 5386, 5398, 5437, 5458, 5497, 5796, 6573, 6578
   See also Dalhousie Ocean Studies Programme; Marine biology; Marine pollution
—— Research 5110
Odours 5103
Office buildings 5169
   See also Skyscrapers
Office methods
—— Automation 2576, 2679, 2686, 2754, 2910, 2923, 3819, 3828
Office workers 2838, 2873, 3811
Official secrets 2210, 2434
Offshore drilling structures 4840, 5796
—— Safety devices and measures 4835
O'Hagan, Howard 7216
Oil and Gas Conservation Board (Alberta) 6421
Oil industry
   See Petroleum industry
Oil pollution 5064, 5095, 5124, 5132, 5140, 5141, 5167, 5187, 5188, 5204, 5239, 5244
Oil sand
   See Bituminous sand
Oil shales 4824
   See also Bituminous sand
Oil spills
   See Oil pollution

Oil well drilling rigs 5282
   See also Offshore drilling structures
Ojibway Indians 3946, 3985
Oka, Quebec 0353
Okanagan District, British Columbia 0562
Old age 3098, 3305, 5579, 5627, 5657
   See also Aging; Retirement
Old growth forests 5013
Old Order Amish
   See Amish
Old people
   See Aged
Olivier, Réjean 3691, 7217, 7218, 7219, 7220, 7221
Olivier, Réjean, Library 6790
Olympic Games 1784, 1808
Olynyk, Roman (Roman Rakhmanny) 7222
Ombudsmen 2451, 2536
Ondaatje, Michael 7223
Online data base systems
   See Information storage and retrieval systems
Ontario 0106, 0436, 0438, 0439, 0442, 0443, 0446, 0448, 0454, 0461, 0464, 0471, 0473, 0485, 0488, 4307, 4629, 5231, 5430, 5479
   See also French Canadians in Ontario; Germans in Ontario; Hamilton, Ontario; Kingston, Ontario; Kitchener, Ontario; London, Ontario; Niagara Falls, Ontario; North Bay, Ontario; North York, Ontario; Ottawa, Ontario; Owen Sound, Ontario; Peterborough, Ontario; Sudbury, Ontario; Thunder Bay, Ontario; Toronto, Ontario; Windsor, Ontario
—— Archaeology 4526, 4530, 4539, 4541, 4576, 4594
—— Department of Agriculture and Food 6269
—— Department of Education
—— —— Library 3367, 6745
—— Department of Mines 6254, 6260
—— Directories 0452
—— Economic conditions 0459
—— Economic policy 2671
—— Genealogy 2034
—— Geography 1346, 6067, 6089
—— History 0420, 0421, 0424, 0425, 0429, 0431, 0447, 0449, 0451, 0455, 0456, 0462, 0467, 0476, 0478, 0480, 0481, 0487, 0491, 1519, 1904, 1924, 1979, 2063, 2081, 3413, 4212, 6523, 6789
—— Imprints 0457, 0486
—— Industries and resources 2582
—— Laws, legislation, regulations, etc 2099, 2226, 3390
—— Legislative Assembly 2475, 2476, 2493
—— —— Cabinet 2490
—— —— Committees 6354, 6414
—— Legislative Library 6723, 6726, 6732
—— Maps 6478, 6494, 6505, 6526, 6535, 6571, 6588, 6598
—— Ministry of Industry, Trade and Technology 6382
—— Ministry of Labour 6282
—— Ministry of Transportation and Communications 6406
—— Planning and development 4329
—— Royal Commission on Electric Power Planning 2662
—— Social conditions 3015, 3329
—— Statistics 2993
Ontario, Northern 0435, 0436, 0445, 0458, 0480, 0483, 4594, 5016, 6141
Ontario Agricultural College
—— School of Agricultural Engineering 4649
Ontario Archaeological Society
—— Library 4576

Remote control 5755
Remote sensing 3075, 4980, 5499, 5757, 5771, 5795
Renewable energy resources 5759, 5769
Renewable resources 4804, 4809, 4862, 5257, 6454
Rent laws 2205, 4393, 4406
Reports 0121
Representative government and representation 2398
Reproduction 3869, 3871, 3896, 5676, 5683
   See also Fertility, Human; Spawning
—— Technology 5691, 5699, 5714
Reptiles 5473
Research 0547, 2579, 4046, 4615, 4618
   See also Agricultural research; Biological research; Building
   research; Criminal research; Educational research; Military
   research; National Research Council Canada; Nursing
   research; Operations research; Social science research; Space
   research; Wildlife research
Research and development 2669, 4619
Resorts 1842
Resource-based communities 4412, 4413
   See also Company towns
Resource development 3049, 4052
Resources, Conservation of
   See Conservation of resources
Responsibility 2498
Restraint of trade 2194
   See also Monopolies; Price fixing
Retail trade 2764, 2770
   See also Franchise system; Stores
—— Hours of business 2740, 2759
Retirement 2667, 2927, 3164, 3191
Retirement income 2774
   See also Pensions; Registered retirement savings plans
Retraining, Occupational
   See Occupational retraining
Revegetation 4800, 5066, 5116
Revenue stamps 1745, 1748
Reverse osmosis 5742
Rich, Obadiah, Collection 6709
Richardson, John 7257, 7258
Richelieu County, Quebec 0356
Richler, Mordecai 7259, 7260, 7261
Richter, Lothar 7262
Rideau Canal 0471, 4520
Riding Mountain National Park 2983
Riel, Louis 1946, 2056, 7263, 7264, 7265, 7266, 7267, 7268
Riel Rebellion, 1885 1946, 2056, 6567
Rimouski, Quebec 0313
Rimouski County, Québec 0312
Riots 2160
Rioux, Marcel 7269
Rivers 1772, 1790, 1794, 4912, 5045, 5240, 6572
   See also Ice on rivers, lakes, etc; Mercury pollution of rivers,
   lakes, etc; Streams
Road construction 4454
—— Dictionaries and encyclopaedias 1456
Roads 4448, 4511, 5138
   See also Alaska Highway; Canadian Good Roads Association
—— History 0662, 1950
Roads and Bridges (Periodical) 5027
Robberies and assaults 2276
   See also Armed robbery

Roberts, Sir Charles G.D. 7270
Robertson Library 0254
Robinson, J. Lewis 7271
Robots 5801, 5805, 5806, 5820, 5821, 5824, 5827
Rock bursts
   See Mine accidents and explosions
Rock groups 0942
Rock mechanics 5793
Rock music 0943
Rocks 4742
   See also Mineralogy; Petrology
Rocky Mountains 2945, 2951, 2995, 5370
Rodgers, Raymond Spencer 7272
Rodolphe Joubert Collection, McGill University 0382
Rogers, Norman McLeod 7273
Roman Catholic Church 1500, 1503, 1514, 1518, 1522, 1523,
   1529, 1536, 1537, 1566, 1569, 1574, 1575, 5986
Romanians in Canada 4199, 5914
Rondeau Peninsula 4807
Rooke, Leon 7274
Rose, William J. 7275
Ross, Sinclair 7276, 7277
Rousseau, Jacques 7278
Routes of trade
   See Trade routes
Roy, Camille 7279
Roy, Gabrielle 1230, 7280, 7281, 7282
Roy, Joseph-Edmond 7283
Roy, Léo 7284
Roy, Pierre-Georges 7285
Royal Canadian Mounted Police 1088, 1281, 2103, 2125, 2128,
   2129, 2140, 2190, 2195, 2203, 6682
Royal College of Physicians and Surgeons of Canada 5656
Royal Colonial Institute
—— Library 6746
Royal commissions 2599, 2609, 3592, 6223, 6224, 6262, 6381
—— Alberta 6306
—— British Columbia 6227, 6339
—— Manitoba 6234
—— Nova Scotia 6365
—— Ontario 6329, 6413
—— Quebec (Province) 2376
—— Saskatchewan 2396
Royal Commonwealth Society
—— Library 6769, 6777
Royal Empire Society
—— Library 6764
Royal Society of Canada 0021, 0022
Royal Society of Canada Transactions 5027
Rudnyckyj, Jaroslav Bohdan 7286, 7287
Rule, Jane 7288
Rural education
   See Education, Rural
Rural life
   See Country life
Rural medical care
   See Medical care, Rural
Rural planning 3166, 3168, 4388, 4648, 4709, 4721
Rural sociology 3015
Rural women 3832
   See also Women in agriculture

Russians in Canada 4150, 4164, 5886, 6100
Ruth Konrad Collection 6778
Ryerson Press 1580
Sabin, Joseph 0190
Safdie, Moshe 7289
Safety devices and measures 3311, 3312
Safety education 3549
Sage, Walter Noble 7290
Saguenay-Lac-Saint-Jean, Quebec 0309, 0345, 0360, 0395, 0402, 0406, 4788, 6026, 6532, 6632
Sailing 6217, 6501, 6502
Saint Francis River (Quebec) 0336
Saint John River 5250
Saint Lawrence, Gulf of 2985, 3028, 5047, 5363
Saint Lawrence Islands National Park 3007
Saint Lawrence River 0329, 1914, 2971, 4875, 5051, 5061, 5071, 5112, 5153, 5552
Saint Lawrence River Valley 0337, 0359, 0393, 0407, 4472
Saint Lawrence Seaway 2971, 4444, 4446, 4450, 4461, 4465, 4472, 6242
Saint-Marcoux, Micheline Coulombe 0904
Sainte-Foy, Quebec 0349
Saints 1495, 1567, 1993
Sales contracts 2136
Sales tax 2750
Salishan Indians 1409
Salle Gagnon, Bibliothèque de la ville de Montréal 2008
Salmon 4999, 5318, 5321, 5334, 5379, 5412, 5456, 5480, 5513, 5517
Salmonidae 5353
Salted fish
    See Fish, Salted
Samek, R.A. 7291
Sand 4751
Sandstone 4751
Sanitary engineering 5752
Sarnia, Ontario 0438
Saskatchewan 0505, 0517, 0519, 0521, 0522, 0528, 0532, 1113, 1289, 1551, 1565, 4303, 4643, 4691, 5700
    See also French Canadians in Saskatchewan; Germans in Saskatchewan; Saskatoon, Saskatchewan
    —— Archaeology 4559, 4568, 4602
    —— Department of Mineral Resources 6301
    —— Economic conditions 3611
    —— History 0498, 0512, 0535, 0543, 5568
    —— Imprints 0496, 3722
    —— Maps 6301
    —— Saskatchewan Agriculture 6473
    —— Saskatchewan Energy and Mines 6301
    —— Social conditions 3252
Saskatchewan in literature 1034
Saskatchewan Rebellion, 1885
    See Riel Rebellion, 1885
Saskatchewan Research Council 4623
Saskatchewan River Basin 5032
Saskatoon, Saskatchewan 4158, 4330
Saturday Night (Periodical) 0835
Sault Sainte Marie, Michigan 0444
Sault Ste. Marie, Ontario 0444
Sault Ste. Marie Public Library 2075
Sauvé, Paul 2469

Savard, Félix-Antoine 7292
Saxophone music 0892
Scallops 5542
Scarborough, Ontario 0492
Schafer, R. Murray 7293, 7294, 7295
Scheduling (Management) 3456
Schefferville, Quebec 2994, 2997, 3024
Scholarly periodicals 5903
Scholarly publishing
    See University presses
School administrators 3597, 6639
School and the community 3494, 3501, 3521
School attendance 3550, 3570
School boards 3736
School buildings 3393, 3457, 5778
—— Energy usage 5147
School children
—— Transportation 3526
School discipline 3480, 3497, 3566
    See also Classroom management
School hygiene 5599
School librarians 1705, 3724
School libraries 0128, 0144, 0253, 1593, 1600, 1615, 1619, 1632, 1636, 1642, 1643, 1658, 1703, 1705, 3400, 3622, 3651, 5919, 5950
School management and organization 3395, 3456, 3461, 3473
    See also Class size; School administrators
School nursing 5599
School superintendents and principals 3619
Schools 3719
    See also Correspondence schools and courses; Nursery schools; Private schools
—— Accreditation and standards 3465
—— Employees 3423, 3447, 3449
—— Equipment and supplies 3393
—— Safety devices and measures 3675
Schools, Experimental 3453, 3512, 3584
Science 0018, 0121, 4614, 4615, 4617, 4622, 4625, 4634, 5580, 6208
    See also Feminism and science; Natural history; Technology
—— Film catalogues 6627
—— History 4626, 4627, 4632, 4636
—— Periodicals 5860, 5865, 5911, 5943, 5966
—— Study and teaching 3669
    See also Nature study
Science and feminism
    See Feminism and science
Science and state 4619
    See also Canada–Science and technology policy; Technology and state
Science fiction 1129, 1146, 1262, 1296
Scientific research 0649, 4623, 4631, 4633, 4635, 5535, 6425, 6767
    See also Institut national de la recherche scientifique (Québec)
Scientists 4629
Scotland 2022
Scots in Canada 1159, 6125
Scott, Duncan Campbell 7296, 7297
Scott, Francis Reginald 7298, 7299, 7300
Scott Polar Research Institute 0654
Sculpture 0678
Sea birds 5504
Sea ice 5029, 5160, 5234, 5235, 5283, 5298

Sea law
See Maritime law
Sea stories 5299
Seabed mining
See Ocean mining
Seal hunting 4900, 5452
Seals (Animals) 4900, 5410, 5482, 5503
Second language learning 1431, 3517, 3640
Second language teaching 3731
Secondary education
See Education, Secondary
Secret service 2336
Secret societies 1969
See also Freemasons
Sects 1535, 1559
See also Amish; Doukhobors; Hutterian brethren; Mennonites
Sedimentation and deposition 5028, 5046, 5145, 5227, 5229, 5240, 5277, 5278, 5438, 5741
See also Marine sediments
Sediments (Geology) 4772, 4843, 4875
Seed banks 5016
Seeds 5010
Séguin, Robert-Lionel 7301
Seigniorial tenure 2050, 6590
Seismology 4741, 4882, 6295
See also Volcanoes
Selenium 4759
Self-care, Health 5685
Self employment 2732
Self government
See Autonomy
Selkirk, Thomas Douglas, fifth Earl of 1908
Selkirk Settlement
See Red River Settlement
Selwyn, Alfred Richard Cecil 7302, 7303, 7304
Semantics 1449
Séminaire de Québec 1505
Senate
See Canada–Parliament–Senate
Senior citizens
See Aged
Sentences (Criminal procedure) 2141
Separatism
See Autonomy
Serbs in Canada 4164, 4172
Serial publications 5329, 5856, 5866, 5871, 5873, 5876, 5918, 5922, 5932, 5941, 5955, 5959, 5962, 5966, 5982, 5987, 5991, 6390, 6391
—— Agriculture 5928
—— Art 5963
—— Environment 5979
—— Forests and forestry 5916
—— Humanities 5993
—— Indians 5951
—— Natural history 5920
—— Religion 5902
—— Social sciences 5993
Seripress 1678
Service, Robert W. 7305
Service industries 2724, 3811
—— Management 2784

Severance pay 2867
Sewage purification 5252
Sewerage 5739
Sex and law 3890
See also Prostitution
Sex crimes 2202, 3127, 3154, 3343, 3356, 3870
See also Incest; Indecent assault; Rape
Sex differences 3659
Sex discrimination 1818
Sex discrimination against women 3505, 3816, 3881
Sex discrimination in language 1473
Sex discrimination in literature 1323, 1392
Sex education 3116, 3155, 3318, 3506, 3564, 3661
Sex role 1327, 1389
See also Women and men
Sexism
See Sex discrimination against women
Sexist language
See Sex discrimination in language
Sexual abuse of children 2320, 2321, 3228, 3240, 3242, 3264, 3293, 3318, 3319, 3320, 3870, 6685
Sexual behaviour 3223, 3233
See also Children–Sexual behaviour
Sexual deviation 3127
See also Incest; Pedophilia
Sexual harassment 3225, 3802, 3812, 3816, 3865
Sexual sterilization
See Sterilization, Sexual
Sharks 5407
Sheep 4712
See also Mountain sheep
Shellfish culture 5542
Sherbrooke, Quebec 0370
Shipbuilding 4503
Shipping 4464, 4465, 4473, 4479, 4492, 4497, 4498, 4503, 4506, 4516, 5175
Shipping lines 4519
Ships 4487
See also Ice breaking vessels
Shipwrecks 2020
Shoplifting 2122
Shore lines 5109, 5145, 5245
Short stories 1014, 1067, 1081, 1087, 1097, 1265
Short take-off and landing aircraft 4452
Shortt, Adam 7306
Shrimps 5362
Sick, The 3209
See also Terminal care
Signals and signalling 4457
Sikhs 4151
Silica 4751
Silicates 4847
Simard, Émile 7307
Simard, Georges 7308
Simcoe, Ontario 0465
Simcoe County, Ontario 0440, 0493
Similkameen Valley 0561
Simulation methods 3483
See also Econometrics
Singers 0942
Singing, Choral
See Choral singing

Single enterprise communities 4413
Single parent family 3171, 3201, 3253, 3281, 3294, 4402, 4409
Siouan Indians 1411, 3946, 4005
   See also Assiniboine Indians
Sipunculida 5484
Skeena River estuary, British Columbia 5100
Skelton, Oscar Douglas 7309
Skid row 3093
Skis and skiing 1776
Skvorecky, Josef 7310
Skyscrapers 5737
Slavs 4138
Slavs in Canada 4164
Slides (Photography) 0703, 0704, 6610, 6611
Small business 2707, 2758, 2776
   See also Franchise system; Self employment
—— Finance 2665, 2720
Smelt 5368
Smith, A.J.M. 7311, 7312, 7313, 7314
Smith, Harlan Ingersoll 6622, 7315
Smoking 3704, 3705, 5618
Snow 5027, 5072, 5097, 5113, 5208, 5272, 5285, 5809
   See also Avalanches
Snow and ice removal 4449, 5044
Social action 3199
Social alienation
   See Alienation (Social psychology)
Social and economic security 3331
Social change 3107
Social classes 3186, 3324
Social conditions 3300
Social credit 2382
Social history 1988, 2011, 3057, 3068, 3785, 5768
Social impact analysis 5774
Social isolation 3093
Social movements 2445, 2472, 3324
Social participation 2261, 3119, 3121, 3129, 3140, 3159, 3172,
   3192, 3193, 3333, 3334, 4333
Social policy 2394, 3022, 3114, 3199, 3250, 3267, 3268, 3352,
   4459
Social problems 3097, 6688
Social psychology 3100, 3136, 3308, 6075
   See also Alienation (Social psychology); Organizational
   behaviour; Stereotype (Psychology)
Social science research 0221, 3239, 4220
Social sciences 0055, 1361, 2483, 3050, 3540, 3770, 6121, 6674
—— Periodicals 5993
Social Sciences and Humanities Research Council of Canada
   0675
Social services 3224, 3274, 3330, 5626
—— Quebec (Province) 3303, 6362
Social surveys 3050
Social values 3484, 3536
   See also Public interest
Social welfare 3092, 3104, 3276
Social work 3081, 3131, 3195, 3221, 3332, 3344, 5964, 6080
—— Study and teaching 3296
Social work with minorities 3364
Social workers, Volunteer 3236
Socially handicapped 3113

Socially handicapped children 3133, 3406
Société de géographie de Québec 2943
Société de Notre-Dame de Montréal 0292, 1938
Société des écrivains canadiens 1005, 1019
Société des écrivains de la Mauricie 0396
Société des professeurs de géographie du Québec 3014
Société historique de Montréal 1956
Société littéraire et historique de Québec 0030
Sociolinguistics 1429, 1448, 1463
   See also Linguistic demography; Literature and society
Sociology 1532, 3099, 3107, 3113, 3285, 3290, 3339, 3791, 3834,
   4021, 4909, 5574, 5922, 6110, 6136, 6178
   See also Assimilation (Sociology); Economic sociology;
   Educational sociology; Groups (Sociology); Human
   relations; Network analysis (Sociology); Social psychology;
   Sociolinguistics
Sociology, Rural 0579, 2283, 3079, 3080, 3102, 3166, 4460
Sociology, Urban 3357, 4326
Software, Computer
   See Computer programs and programming
Soil, Frozen
   See Frozen ground
Soil erosion
   See Erosion
Soil mechanics 4764, 4844
   See also Rock mechanics
Soils 4643, 4650, 4661, 4672, 4676, 4691, 4703, 4704, 4705, 4749,
   4830, 4976, 5003, 5009, 6564
Solar energy 5769
Solvents 5132
Somass River estuary, British Columbia 5166
Somers, Harry 7316
Songs 0818, 0837, 0857, 0868, 0877
   See also Folk songs
Songs, French Canadian 0844, 0866, 0897, 0939, 4611
   See also Folk songs, French Canadian
Sound
—— Recording and reproducing 0847
Sound poetry
   See Poetry
Souster, Raymond 7317
South America
—— History 0011
Southwestern Regional Library System 6641
Soward, Frederic H. 7318
Soybean products 4719
Space flight 5760
Space law 2295
Space research 5751, 5761
Spatial analysis (Economic geography) 3021
Spawning 5456, 5477
Speaker (Legislative bodies) 2478
Special education 3571, 3573
Spectroscopy 5757
   See also Nuclear magnetic resonance spectroscopy; Plasma
   spectroscopy
Speech, Freedom of
   See Free speech
Speeches, addresses, etc 1015
Spiritual life 1569
Sports 1765, 1768, 1783, 1789, 1791, 1799, 1815, 1856, 6156
   See also Amateurism (Sports); Coaching (Athletics); Drugs in
   sports; Recreation; Violence in sports

Support (Domestic relations) 2305, 2306
Surrogate mothers 3896
Swans 5364
Swedes in Canada 4211, 4281, 5889
Swiss in Canada 4149
Syphilis 5684
System analysis 3415
Talking books 3366, 6649, 6677
Talman, James J. 6535, 7325
Tantaré ecology reserve 5297
Tape recordings 6620
   See also Oral history
Tar sand
   See Bituminous sand
Tariff 2653
   See also Free trade and protection
Task Force on Alternative Fuels 5822
Taverner, Percy Algernon 7326
Tax credits 2649
Tax reform 2609, 2736, 2738
Taxation 2570, 2590, 2601, 2656, 2786
   See also Excise tax; Goods and services tax; Income tax;
   Municipal taxation; Property tax; Sales tax
Taxicabs 4476
Taxol 5711
Taylor, Alfred James Towle 0661
Teachers 3447, 3452, 3493, 3615, 3643, 3650
   See also College professors and instructors
—— Certification 3660
—— Education 3483, 3486, 3498, 3509, 3519, 3576, 3660
—— Education in service 3495, 3658
—— Quebec (Province) 3474
—— Rating 3455, 3478, 3499, 3597
—— Recruiting 3533
—— Salaries, pensions, etc 3426, 3492
—— Supply and demand 3426
—— Tenure 3534
Teachers and students 2231
Teachers' unions 3407, 3543
   See also Canadian Teachers' Federation; Federation of
   Women Teachers in Ontario
Teaching 3408, 3438, 3459, 3488, 3514, 3540, 3545, 3555, 3572,
   3623, 3693, 3724
   See also Class size; School discipline
Teaching load 3542
Teaching materials 0055, 0073, 0116, 0124, 0127, 0132, 0143,
   0144, 0245, 0504, 0519, 0528, 0569, 0689, 0871, 0907, 0913,
   1083, 1115, 1116, 1117, 1118, 1119, 1120, 1121, 1122, 1123,
   1124, 1170, 1178, 1201, 1218, 1317, 1342, 1452, 1464, 1487,
   1600, 1642, 1643, 1994, 2006, 2065, 2153, 2206, 2262, 2612,
   2797, 2832, 2909, 2960, 2974, 3051, 3371, 3374, 3400, 3527,
   3602, 3635, 3647, 3679, 3727, 3730, 3768, 3772, 3785, 3915,
   3926, 3962, 3971, 3982, 3990, 4000, 4024, 4038, 4064, 4084,
   4167, 4190, 4197, 4243, 4294, 4349, 5146, 5158, 5292, 5950,
   6228, 6296, 6297, 6323, 6569, 6661, 6674
   See also Audio visual materials; Computers–Educational use;
   Movies in education; Television in education
Team learning approach in education 3459
Technical education 3520
   See also Vocational education
Technological change 1694, 2892, 2940, 5838, 5840

Technological forecasting 5731
Technology 4615, 5580, 5820, 5821
—— History 4626, 4627, 4632, 4636
—— Periodicals 5865, 5911, 5966
Technology and civilization 1698
Technology and labour 1709, 2804, 2849, 3828
Technology and state 2460, 2471, 2485
   See also Science and state
Technology transfer 2460, 2668
Tectonics
   See Geology, Structural
Tedman, Keith 7327
Teenage pregnancy 3197
Teeth, Artificial 5688
Tekakwitha, Kateri 0367
Telecommunication 0973, 0974, 1666, 3184, 4395, 5734, 5820,
   5821, 6537
   See also Communications satellites; Data transmission
   systems; Facsimile transmission
—— Laws and regulations 2294
Telemedicine 3184, 5662
Telemetry, Biological
   See Biotelemetry
Telephone directories 5983
Television
—— Data transmission systems 1648, 1704
Television broadcasting 0959, 0973, 0974
   See also Cable television; Canadian Radio-Television and
   Telecommunications Commission
—— Drama 0949, 0966, 0967, 1111
—— Programs 6669, 6670
   See also Violence in television programs
—— Serials 0966
—— Social aspects 0956, 0985
Télévision communautaire de Rivière-du-Loup 6637
Television in education 3425, 6664, 6666
Television production and direction 6706
Telidon
   See Television–Data transmission systems
Temiscamingue region, Quebec 0323, 4796
Temperance 1496, 3076, 3077
   See also Alcohol drinking behaviour
Terminal care 1548, 3182, 3358, 5705
Terminology 1476, 1477, 1484, 1486, 1489, 1490
Terra Nova National Park 2984, 5203
Territorial jurisdiction
   See Jurisdiction, Territorial
Territorial waters 4884
   See also Maritime law
Terrorism 2197, 2307, 2308, 2353, 2505
Tessier, Albert 7328
Textbooks 0132, 2960, 3059, 3371, 3413, 3527, 3535, 3628, 3655,
   3695, 5580
   See also French language–Textbooks
Textile industry 2608, 2731
—— Pollution 5094
Theatre 0962, 0964, 0977, 0991, 1176, 1199, 1208
   See also Drama; Movies
—— History 0948, 0958, 0990
—— Manitoba 0968
—— Quebec (Province) 0969, 0972, 0976, 0981, 1001, 1179

—— Diseases and pests   4940, 4952, 4975, 4993, 5017, 5380, 5401, 5439, 5466, 5471, 5490, 5519, 5524, 5525, 6358, 6367
   See also Spruce budworms
—— Layering 5529
Tremblay, Gilles   0904
Tremblay, Michel   7337
Tremblay, Victor   7338
Trent University   5208
Trials   2154
   See also Actions and defences; Witnesses
Trois-Rivières, Quebec   6585
—— Newspapers   6003
Trombone music   0922
Tross, Edwin, Library   6722
Trout   5356, 5399, 5400, 5456, 5468, 5505, 5517
Trucking
   See Motor truck freight service
Trudeau, Pierre Elliott   7339
Trudel, Marcel   7340
Trusts, Industrial
—— Law   2117, 2161, 2194, 2250, 2340
Trusts and trustees   5695
Tulameen Valley   0561
Tundras   4677, 5066
   See also Barren lands
Tune-books   0862, 0932
Turner, Robert   7341
Turner, Victor Witter   7342, 7343
Turtles   5473
Tweedsmuir, John Buchan, 1st baron   7344, 7345, 7346, 7347
Tyrrell Museum of Palaeontology   4606
Ukrainian Free Academy of Sciences   4616
Ukrainian language   1424
Ukrainian Museum of Canada   4259
Ukrainian studies   4165
Ukrainians   4207
Ukrainians in Canada   4135, 4136, 4140, 4158, 4163, 4164, 4166, 4188, 4194, 4196, 4203, 4205, 4235, 4259, 5873, 5883, 5955, 6023, 6099, 6149, 6653
Ukrainians in Ontario   4257
Ultraviolet radiation   4901
Underdeveloped areas
   See Developing countries
Underground economy   2678
Underground press   5907, 6022, 6024
Underhill, Frank H.   7348
Unemployed   2053
Unemployment   2895, 2909
—— Relief measures   2894
—— Social aspects   3202
Unemployment insurance
   See Insurance, Unemployment
Union catalogues
   See Catalogues, Union
Union des écrivains québécois   1206
Union nationale   2479, 2519
Union of Soviet Socialist Republics   0162
—— Foreign relations   2488
United Church of Canada   1541, 1564
United Empire Loyalists   1948, 1976, 1997, 2005, 2016, 2024, 2029, 2038

United Nations   2462
—— Armed forces   2380, 2529
United States   0013
   See also Alaska; French Canadians in the United States; New England; Oregon
—— Commerce   2775
—— Foreign relations   2516
—— History   2093
—— —— Revolution   2016, 2038
—— Hydrographic Office   6481
United States and Canada
   See Canada and the United States
Université de Moncton   6115
Université de Montréal   0093, 0094, 2169, 3369, 6085, 6136, 6153, 6167, 6170
—— Centre internationale de criminologie comparée   2144
—— Département de criminologie   2144
—— Département d'éducation physique   1845
—— Faculté de droit   2187
—— Groupe de recherche sur l'inadaptation juvénile   2144
—— Service des archives   1706
Université de Sherbrooke
—— Département de géographie   3044
Université du Québec   6200
Université du Québec à Montréal   6174
—— Service des archives   6782
Université laurentienne de Sudbury
—— Institut franco-ontarien   0482
Université Laval   6057, 6069, 6071, 6101, 6120, 6131, 6177, 6203
—— École de bibliothéconomie   0133
University of Alberta   6083, 6087, 6182, 6196
—— Library   0081
University of British Columbia   6093, 6785
—— Library   1831
University of Calgary   6173
University of Calgary Libraries
—— Special Collections Division   6788
University of Lethbridge Regional History Project   0527
University of Manitoba   3440
—— Center for Settlement Studies   0621
—— Department of Agricultural Economics and Farm Management   4656
University of New Brunswick   3427, 6178
University of New Brunswick Libraries   6793
University of Ottawa   1513, 6121
—— Centre of Criminology   2144
—— Library   6779
University of Saskatchewan   4043, 6140, 6163
—— Law Library   2107
University of Toronto   4497, 6067, 6091, 6172
—— Centre of Criminology   2144, 2223, 2290
—— Faculty of Management Studies   2646
—— Library School   0056
—— School of Social Work   6080
University of Waterloo   5832
University of Western Ontario   6067, 6089, 6160
—— Map Library   6595
University of Windsor   6094
University presses   1620
University teaching
   See Colleges and universities–Teaching

Water milfoil 5507, 6355

Water plants
   See Aquatic plants

Water pollution 5062, 5087, 5150, 5151, 5161, 5168, 5180, 5201, 5214, 5232, 5254, 5279
   See also Marine pollution; Mercury pollution of rivers, lakes, etc; Oil pollution
   —— Control 5078, 6346

Water Pollution Control Directorate 6346

Water purification 5228, 5252, 5742

Water resources development 5031, 5057, 5093, 5174, 5215, 5286, 5361

Water supply 5060, 5062, 5090, 5171, 5290, 6389
   —— Arctic regions 5052
   —— Atlantic provinces 5048
   —— Fluoridation 5576
   —— Manitoba 6459
   —— New Brunswick 5053, 5215, 5250, 5256
   —— Nova Scotia 5225
   —— Ontario 5183
   —— Quebec (Province) 5055, 5071, 5117
   —— Western provinces 5032

Waterfalls 0433

Waterfronts 4337, 4385, 4430, 4431, 4469

Waterloo County, Ontario 1222, 1571

Waterton Lakes National Park 2990, 5190

Waterways 1797
   See also Canals; Saint Lawrence Seaway

Webb, Phyllis 7362

Weed control 5015, 5451, 6355
   See also Herbicides

The Week (Periodical) 0835, 1127

Welding 5765

Welfare state 3250

Wellington County, Ontario 0421, 0485, 1222

West Coast Oil Ports Inquiry 5141

West in literature 1342

West Indians in Canada 4145

West Indies 4202

Western Canada Research Project 6083

Western Canadiana Collection 0541

Western hemlock 5338

Western provinces 0106, 0522, 0523, 2066, 4182, 4400, 6083, 6541
   See also French Canadians in the Western provinces; Prairie provinces
   —— Archaeology 4562
   —— History 0494, 0508, 0511, 0525, 0529, 0531, 0548, 1987, 2284, 2725, 4579
   —— Maps 6495, 6538, 6593

Wetlands 5199, 5200, 5259, 5267, 5290, 5291, 5465
   See also Marshes

Whales 4907, 5496, 5555

Whaling 4907

Wheel-rail interaction 4499

Whip (Politics) 2515

White spruce 4931

Wholesale trade 2764, 2770

Widener Library 6776

Wife abuse 3190, 3198, 3271, 3275, 3278, 3301, 3302, 3349, 3858, 3870, 6685

Wilderness areas 1777, 1797, 3002, 5230, 5297
   See also National parks and reserves

Wildlife 4683, 5066, 5207, 5259, 5361, 5374, 5406, 5424, 5514, 6628, 6687
   —— Diseases and pests 5479
   —— Film catalogues 6606

Wildlife conservation 5035, 5063

Wildlife management
   —— British Columbia 5365

Wildlife research 5396

Wilfrid Laurier University
   —— Library 0937

Wilkins, George H. 6622

Willan, Healey 7363, 7364, 7365

William Colgate Printing Collection 1582

William H. Coverdale Collection 6495

William Inglis Morse Collection 6759

William L. Clements Library 6507

William R. Perkins Library 6659

Willis, John 7366

Willow 5519

Wilson, Ethel 7367, 7368

Wind erosion
   See Erosion

Wind power 5750, 5812, 5813

Winds 5737

Windsor, Ontario 0428, 0484, 5675

Wine industry
   —— Laws and legislation 2717

Winnipeg, Manitoba 0513, 0514, 0526
   —— Maps 6545

Wintemberg, William John 7369

Winter 4422, 4454, 5454

Winthrop Pickard Bell Collection of Acadiana 0265

Wiseman, Adele 7370

Witnesses 2320, 2321

Witton, William Palmer, Library 6775

Wolverines 5427, 5469

Wolves 5433

Woman suffrage 3883

Women 3739, 3740, 3741, 3743, 3748, 3751, 3754, 3757, 3761, 3764, 3768, 3770, 3772, 3776, 3780, 3781, 3783, 3785, 3790, 3794, 3804, 3820, 3823, 3826, 3830, 3837, 3838, 3842, 3849, 3850, 3854, 3856, 3868, 3875, 3876, 3884, 3894, 3897, 3900, 3901, 6166, 6167, 6204, 6654, 6675
   See also Drugs and women; Indians–Women; Inuit–Women; Minority women; Policewomen; Rural women
   —— Books and reading 3878
   —— British Columbia 3844
   —— Directories 3859, 3860
   —— Economic conditions 3745, 3792, 3824, 3846
   —— Education
   See Education of women
   —— Employment 2930, 2932, 3737, 3738, 3769, 3777, 3791, 3811, 3815, 3816, 3819, 3822, 3828, 3829, 3846, 3873
   —— Film catalogues 6626
   —— History 3752, 3773, 3795, 3796, 3801, 3809, 3810, 3814, 3836, 3853, 3887, 3899
   —— Legal status, laws, etc 2328, 3784, 3858, 3861, 3872, 3890
   —— Manitoba 3752
   —— Mental health 3762
   —— New Brunswick 3750
   —— North America 4045

—— Occupations 3777
—— Quebec (Province) 3756, 3763, 3766, 3774, 3799, 3808, 3815, 3827, 3864, 4085
—— Social conditions 3737, 3807, 3821, 3834
See also Prostitution
Women, Handicapped 3840, 3889
Women and alcohol
See Alcohol and women
Women and crime 3779, 3843, 3848, 3877, 3898
Women and men 1856
See also Sex differences
Women and religion 3787, 3798, 3891
Women artists 0691, 0699, 0710
Women athletes 1818
Women authors 1065, 1108, 1109, 1125, 1150, 1214, 1264, 3746, 3851, 5972
Women college professors and instructors 3852
Women composers 0939
Women entrepreneurs 3879
Women executives 3744, 3765, 3786, 3805, 3863, 3879
Women immigrants 3778, 3789, 3839, 3857
Women in advertising 3881
Women in agriculture 3806, 3817, 3832
Women in labour unions 2888
See Women in trade unions
Women in literature 1109, 1116, 1193, 3817, 3851
Women in movies 3753, 3881
Women in politics 3749, 3755, 3767, 3788, 3800, 3862, 3882
Women in the arts 3760, 3847
Women in the mass media industry 3758
Women in the movie industry 6617
Women in trade unions 2864, 2873, 2878
Women librarians
See Librarians
Women musicians 0843, 0939
Women police officers
See Policewomen
Women's Educational Resource Centre 3820, 3896
Women's Institutes 0489, 0490, 3422
Women's organizations 3742
Women's periodicals
See Periodicals for women
Women's shelters
See Homes, Institutional
Women's sports
See Sports for women
Women's studies 0717, 3793, 3825, 3833, 3874, 3880, 3895, 3902, 3903, 6203
Wonders, William C. 7371
Wood 5725
—— Preservation 4944, 5758
Wood, Casey A. 7372
Wood Buffalo National Park 2986, 3006
Wood construction 0785, 5724
Woodlots 5020
Woodstock, Ontario 0461
Work 2797, 2861, 2934, 2940
See also Job satisfaction; Labour; Quality of work life
Work design 2844
Work environment 5619, 5620
Work injuries
See Accidents, Industrial

Work sharing
See Part time employment
Workers
See Labour
Worker's compensation 2846, 2869, 2903, 2928
Working conditions, Physical
See Work environment
World War, 1914-1918 1910
See also Canada–History–World War, 1914-1918
World War, 1939-1945 1920
See also Canada–History–World War, 1939-1945
Worms 5402, 5484
Writing 3683
Wrong, George M. 7373, 7374
Yamaska, Quebec 5055
Yew 5711
York Township, Ontario 0447, 0449
York University
—— Libraries 6789
York University Joint Program in Transportation 4497
Young, Ian 7375
Young adults' literature 0544, 1319, 1328, 1332, 1339, 1357, 1367, 1378, 1388, 1389, 1399
Young Men's Christian Association (Halifax, N.S.) 6716
Young Offenders Act
See Juvenile delinquency
Youth 1540, 3132, 3149, 3313, 3361
See also Adolescence; Students
—— Health and hygiene 1869
—— History 3362
—— Social conditions 3255
Youth crime
See Juvenile delinquency
Yugoslavs in Canada 4170
Yukon Archives 0662
Yukon River Basin 5489
Yukon Territory 0106, 0625, 0637, 0644, 0656, 2052, 4834, 4895, 4899, 5118, 5502
—— Archaeology 4574
—— Historic houses, sites, etc 0657
—— History 0610, 0633, 0634, 1977, 2033
—— Maps 6486
—— Planning and development 0652
Yukon Women's Directorate 3897
Zero base budgeting 2642
Zinc 4854, 4855
Zoning 3208, 4304, 4335, 4398
Zoology 5312, 5313, 5316, 5342, 6232
See also Entomology; Ornithology
Zooplankton
See Plankton

Subjects : French

Matières : français

Automatisation des bureaux 2576, 2679, 2686, 2754, 2910, 2923, 3819, 3828
Automobiles 4486
    Voir aussi Taxis
—— Conduite 4481, 5590
—— Conduite en état d'ivresse
    Voir Alcool et automobilistes
—— Industrie
—— —— Aspect international 2658
—— Stationnement 4357
Automobilistes 4505
    Voir aussi Alcool et automobilistes
Automobilistes et drogues
    Voir Drogues et automobilistes
Autonomie 2482, 2512
    Voir aussi Institut canadien de Québec–Bibliothèque; Québec (Province)–Autonomie et indépendance
Autothérapie 5685
Avalanches 4518
Avantages sociaux 2852
Avenir 2654, 2721, 2987, 3445, 3578
    Voir aussi Prévisions
Aveugles 5869
    Voir aussi Enfants aveugles
Avions 5825
—— Lutte contre les feux de forêt 4959
Avions au décollage et à l'atterrissage court 4452
Avison, Margaret 6818, 6819
Avocats 2115, 3861
    Voir aussi Techniciens judiciaires
Avortement 2322, 3233, 3798, 3896, 5585, 5596, 5665
Azote 4676
B.C. Bookworld 0599
Baby, Georges, Collection 6792
Bacon, Francis 0206
Baie de Fundy 5770, 5774, 5794, 5810
Baie d'Hudson 2949, 6709
Baie d'Hudson, Basses terres 0531, 0628, 4768, 4826, 5134, 5183, 5440
Bailey, Alfred Goldsworthy 6820
Baillairgé, Charles 6821
Baillairgé, Frédéric-Alexandre 6822
Bain, Francis 6823
Baker, Michael Conway 6824
Balance hydrique
    Voir Bilan hydrologique
Baleines 4907, 5496, 5555
—— Chasse 4907
Ball, Nelson 6825
Banc de Georges 4908
Bandes 2329
Bandes dessinées 1129, 5954, 5958
Banff School of the Environment 5156
Banlieues 4442
Banque royale (France) 2010
Banques 2589, 2626, 2703
    Voir aussi Taux d'intérêt
—— Droit 2650, 2681
—— Histoire 1749, 1750, 1838, 2010, 2027, 2040, 2048, 2061, 2071
—— Personnel 2848
—— Syndicats 2848

Banques des semences 5016
Barbarian Press 1700
Barbeau, Marius 0714, 6826, 6827, 6828, 6829
Barrages 5211, 5251, 5455
    Voir aussi Projet hydro-électrique de la Baie James; Rafferty-Alameda Project
Barreau de la province de Québec
—— Bibliothèque 2094
Barrette, Antonio 2469
Bas-Saint-Laurent, Québec 0359
Bases de données 0156, 0157, 0158, 0160, 0179, 0180, 0186
—— Affaires et finances 2751
—— Agriculture 4723
—— Sciences 4628
Basiliens 1526, 5902
Basson, Musique de 0902
Bateaux 1863, 1864
    Voir aussi Canots et canotage; Kayaks; Voile
Baum, L. Frank 1350
Beatrice Hitchins Memorial Collection of Aviation History 4463
Beauce, Québec 0318, 0415
Beauchemin, Yves 6830
Beaulieu, Marie-Louis 6831
Beaulieu, Michel 6832
Beaux-Arts
    Voir Art
Becker, A., Collection 4200
Beckwith, John 6833
Begg, Alexander (Historien) 6834
Begg, Alexander (Journaliste) 6834
Behaviorisme (Psychologie) 3089, 3095, 3173, 3460
    Voir aussi Agressivité (Psychologie); Comportement organisationnel; Motivation (Psychologie)
Belden, H. & Co. 6535
Bell, Robert 6835
Bella Coola (Fleuve), Estuaire du, Colombie-Britannique 5172
Belle-Isle, Détroit de 4100
Belleville, Ontario 1545
Bellow, Saul 6836
Béluga
    Voir Baleines
Bénéfices marginaux 2774, 2795, 2835, 2852
    Voir aussi Prestations de maternité
Bénévolat 1801, 2156, 2157, 2171, 3120, 3132, 3236, 3295
    Voir aussi Travailleurs bénévoles en service social
Benzodiazepine 5603
Beothuk (Indiens) 3958, 4089
Berkeley, Cyril 6837
Berkeley, Edith 6837
Berlin, Boris 6838
Bernard Amtmann Inc. 0074
Bessette, Gérard 6839
Bétail 4655, 4682, 4683, 4706, 5511
Bethune, Norman 6840
Bibaud, Michel 1967
Bible 3911
—— Publication et diffusion 1577
Bibliographie 0030, 0033, 0038, 0079, 1583, 1587, 1618, 1653, 1691
    Voir aussi Bibliothéconomie; Éditeurs et édition; Imprimerie; Indexation; Systèmes d'information

Bibliographies 0042, 0056, 0058, 0070, 0081, 0082, 0093, 0098, 0104, 0119, 0133, 0149, 0321, 0325, 0358, 0366, 0477, 0523, 0542, 0607, 0878, 1199, 1521, 1619, 1686, 1973, 1980, 2577, 3344, 3617, 3741, 3776, 3829, 3842, 3976, 4026, 4586, 5551, 6056, 6202, 6275, 6276

Bibliotechniciens 1602

Bibliothécaires 1584, 1604, 1719

—— Évaluation 1651

Bibliothécaires scolaires 1705, 3724

Bibliothéconomie 1588, 1597, 1601, 1610, 1611, 1622, 1624, 1628, 1631, 1636, 1716, 1718, 1730, 1734, 1739, 1741, 6953

  Voir aussi Bibliographie; Catalogage

—— Dictionnaires et encyclopédies 1626

—— Étude et enseignement 0119, 1594

—— Recherche 1738

Bibliothèque Blackader-Lauterman d'architecture et d'art 0801

Bibliothèque commémorative Buller 4646

Bibliothèque municipale de Longueuil 1081

Bibliothèque municipale de Mississauga 6778

Bibliothèque nationale du Canada 0131, 1635, 1730, 1734, 1761, 3206

—— Division des livres rares et des manuscrits 4070

Bibliothèque nationale du Québec 1616, 1731

Bibliothèque paroissiale de Notre-Dame et du Cercle Ville-Marie 6750

Bibliothèque scientifique nationale (Canada) 4619

Bibliothèques 0119, 1628, 1666, 1740, 4046, 4103

  Voir aussi Hôpitaux–Bibliothèques; Prisons–Bibliothèques; Réseaux de bibliothèques

—— Acquisitions 1665

—— Administration 1599

—— Architecture 0759, 1673, 1720

—— Automatisation 1596, 1645, 1646, 1663, 1665, 1703, 1711

—— Catalogues

  Voir Catalogues de bibliothèques

—— Collections 0144, 6759

—— Conseils d'administration 1667

—— Enquêtes 1654, 1708

—— Extension 1726

—— Finances 1586

—— Histoire 1635, 1675, 1679, 1680

—— Instructions aux usagers 1655, 1733

—— Normes 1725

—— Relations publiques 1659, 1707, 1710

—— Services 1726

—— Services aux personnes âgées 1699, 1712

—— Services de référence 1671, 1672

—— Statistiques 1721

—— Sûreté

—— —— Mesures 1687

Bibliothèques gouvernementales, administratives, etc 1650, 1670, 1732, 5981

Bibliothèques privées 1656, 6787

Bibliothèques publiques 1615, 1689

Bibliothèques régionales 1579

Bibliothèques scolaires 0128, 0144, 0253, 1593, 1600, 1615, 1619, 1632, 1636, 1642, 1643, 1658, 1703, 1705, 3400, 3622, 3651, 5919, 5950

Bibliothèques spécialisées

—— Marketing 1710

Bibliothèques universitaires 1633, 1655, 1726, 1733

Biculturalisme 1123

Bien-être social 3092, 3104, 3276

  Voir aussi Services sociaux

Bien Public (Périodique) 0972

Bilan hydrologique 5075

Bilinguisme 1417, 1426, 1431, 1444, 1450, 1451, 1462, 1485, 1492, 2327, 2380, 3136

  Voir aussi Enseignement bilingue

Billings, Elkanah 6841, 6842

Bio-bibliographies 0093, 0094, 0292, 1008, 1103, 1175, 1973

Biocon Research Limited 4799, 4950

Biodégradation 4847

Bioéthique 5691, 5708

  Voir aussi Animaux, Expérimentation sur les

Biogéographie

  Voir Distribution géographique des animaux et plantes

Biographie 0087, 0653, 0994, 2009, 2017, 2070, 2523, 2712, 3794, 6769

  Voir aussi Autobiographie

Biologie 5317, 5327, 6687

  Voir aussi Botanique; Écologie; Environnement; Sciences naturelles; Zoologie

—— Recherche 5319, 5425, 5438

Biologie d'eau douce 5084, 5139, 5195, 5330, 5333, 5397, 5423, 5444, 5544, 5556

Biologie marine 5349, 5375, 5419, 5436, 5437, 5458, 5478, 5486, 5521, 5536, 5544, 6393

Biomasse 5021, 5777

Biotechnologie 4856, 5820, 5821, 5847

  Voir aussi Génie génétique

Biotélémétrie 5754, 5845

Biotine 5575

Birdsell, Sandra 6843

Birkbeck College

—— Centre for Canadian Studies 0169

Birney, Earle 6844, 6845, 6846

Bishop's University Library 0386

Bison américain 5415, 5508

Bissell, Keith 6847

Black, Martha Louise 6848

Blacker-Wood Library of Zoology and Ornithology 5342

Blackwood, Algernon 6849

Blais, Marie-Claire 6850, 6851, 6852

Blakeley, Phyllis Ruth 6853

Blanchard, Raoul 6854

Boag, Max (Harry Glenn, pseud) 6855

Boeufs musqués 5326, 5457

Bois 5725

—— Conservation 4944, 5758

—— Construction 0785, 5724

Bois d'oeuvre 4944

Bois-Francs, Québec 0346, 0392

Boismenu, Léo 6856

Boissons alcoolisées 1921, 6241

Boivin, Henri-Bernard 0118

Bonenfant, Jean Charles 6857

Book Publishers' Association of Canada 0071

Borden, Carl E. 6858

Borduas, Paul-Émile 6859

Bosco, Monique 6860

Botanique 4646, 5304, 5305, 5311, 5315, 5320, 5322, 5323, 5382, 5403, 5424, 5430, 5483, 6232

  Voir aussi Fécondation des plantes; Paléobotanique; Plantes

Botanique médicale 5581

Bouche édentée 5688

Boudreau, Walter 6861

Boulanger, Trefflé, Collection 3446

Bourassa, Henri 6862, 6863

Bourassa, Robert 2469, 6864

Bourdons
   Voir Abeilles

Bourgeoys, Marguerite 1503

Bourinot, Arthur S. 6865, 6866

Bourinot, Sir John George, Bibliothèque 6755

Bousquet, Jean 6867

Bovell, James 6868

Bowering, George 6869

Brachiopodes fossiles 4548

Bradbury, John 6870

Brassard, François-Joseph 6871

Brasserie
   —— Droit 2717

Brault, Jacques 6872

Brébeuf, Jean de 1504, 6873

Brégent, Michel-Georges 6874

Brinley, George, Bibliothèque 6749

Briques 0747

Brise-glaces 4502, 5160

British Columbia Provincial Museum 5382, 6237

British Columbia Research Council 6250

British Columbia School Librarians' Association 1593

British North America Philatelic Society 1760

Britnell, George Edwin 6875

Brochet 5358, 5528

Brochures 0004, 0152, 0153, 0371, 1556, 1920, 1954, 1981, 3422, 6728, 6730, 6757, 6758, 6761, 6779, 6781, 6782, 6789, 6793

Bronfman Collection of Jewish Canadiana 4154

Bronze 5763

Broughton, Frederick, Collection 6738

Brouillette, Benoît 6876

Broussailles, Lutte contre les 5015

Brown, Edward Killoran 6877

Brown, Roger James Evan 6878

Broyage 4779

Bruce, Comté de, Ontario 0446, 0476

Bruit 4870
   —— Pollution 2684

Brunet, Michel 1967

Bryophytes 5541

Buchan, John
   Voir Tweedsmuir, John Buchan, 1st baron; Tweedsmuir, John Buchan, 1st baron

Buchanan, Donald William 6879

Bûcherons 2821

Buck, Tim 6880

Bucke, Richard Maurice 6881

Buckler, Ernest 6882, 6883

Budget 2399, 2643, 2672, 2713

Budget à base zéro 2642

Buildings Energy Technology Transfer Program 5814

Bulgares au Canada 5901

Bull, Michael 0045

Bull, Noreen 0045

Bureau d'aménagement de l'Est du Québec 6263, 6268

Bureau de l'Auditeur général 2440

Burkholder, Mabel 6884

Byron Bog 5408

C.D. Howe Research Institute 2625

Cabot, John 6885, 6886

Cabot, Sebastian 6885, 6886

Cadres (Personnel)
   —— Évaluation 2606
   —— Formation 2604, 2773
   —— Salaires, pensions, etc 2690

Cadres scolaires
   Voir Administrateurs scolaires

Cailles 5331

Calgary, Alberta 3298, 4591, 4837
   —— Architecture 0787

Callaghan, Edmund Bailey, Bibliothèque 6733

Callaghan, Morley 6887, 6888, 6889

Calmar 5418

Camionnage 4485, 4514

Campbell, William Wilfred 6890, 6891

Campbell (Fleuve), Estuaire du, Colombie-Britannique 5121

Camping 1775, 1785

Canada 0013, 0016, 0020, 0023, 0032, 0037, 0038, 0046, 0048, 0051, 0052, 0053, 0055, 0057, 0059, 0063, 0067, 0073, 0076, 0082, 0083, 0085, 0095, 0096, 0098, 0099, 0103, 0105, 0108, 0113, 0125, 0144, 0146, 0147, 0148, 0151, 0155, 0168, 0169, 0171, 0176, 0277, 0576, 1306, 1583, 1653, 1901, 2375, 6198, 6674, 6738, 6743, 6745, 6751, 6754, 6765, 6766, 6775, 6779, 6795
—— Annexion à les États-Unis 2372
—— Archives nationales 6434, 6443
—— Archives publiques 6341, 6343, 6757, 6758, 6761
—— —— Bibliothèque 1638, 6784
—— Bibliothèque du Parlement 6714, 6718, 6720, 6727
—— Bureau de la statistique 6445
—— Bureau des traductions 6436, 6447
—— Bureau fédéral de la statistique 6258
—— Civilisation 6780
—— Commerce 2702, 4516
—— —— Asie 2779
—— —— États qui bordent le Pacifique 2779
—— —— États-Unis 2557, 2558, 2699, 2775
—— Commission of Conservation 6213
—— Commission royale de la concentration économique 2639
—— Commission royale d'enquête sur le bilinguisme et le biculturalisme 2401
—— Commission royale sur les peuples autochtones 4123
—— Conditions économiques 2560, 2563, 2618, 2622, 2709, 2711, 2715, 2781, 2782, 3048, 3611, 6055, 6412
—— Conditions sociales 3050, 3100, 3137, 3324
—— Conseil du Trésor 2450, 6437, 6449
—— Conseil législatif
—— —— Bibliothèque 6710
—— Constitution 1944, 2217, 2239, 2248, 2289, 2299, 2310, 2318, 2319, 2335, 2339, 2351, 2455, 4087
—— Cour suprême 2109, 2151, 2163
—— Crédits budgétaires et dépenses 2656
—— Découverte et exploration 0572, 1914, 1962, 1963, 6514
—— Défense nationale 2379, 2392, 6600
—— Descriptions et voyages 2079
—— Direction des levés et de la cartographie 6536
—— Direction générale, protection de l'environnement 6439
—— Direction générale des terres 6384, 6385
—— Division des Mines 6219, 6261

Cocaïne 5667

Cohen, Leonard 1089, 6909, 6910, 6911

Cohen, Nathan 6912

Col Chilkoot 0633, 0634

Coléoptères 5385, 5401, 5434, 5439, 5471, 5518, 5524, 5532, 5543, 5550

Collecte de fonds 2628

Collection Chapais (Bibliothèque du Ministère de l'agriculture, Ottawa) 4668

Collection nationale de cartes et plans 6554

Collection Rodolphe Joubert, Université McGill 0382

Collectionneurs et collections 1796

College Administration Project 3454

Collège de l'Assomption 3691

Collège des Jésuites de Québec 4617

Collège militaire royal de St-Jean 1966

Collège royal des médecins et chirurgiens du Canada 5656

Collèges communautaires 3414, 3419, 3429, 3435, 3436, 3437, 3510, 3581

Colleges d'enseignement général et professionnel 3510

Collins, Charles 6913

Colloque national sur l'enseignement postsecondaire 3664, 3665, 3671, 3672

Colombie-Britannique 0522, 0556, 0557, 0561, 0568, 0569, 0570, 0574, 0576, 0578, 0580, 0583, 0585, 0586, 0587, 0588, 0589, 0591, 0592, 0593, 0596, 0597, 0599, 0605, 1110, 1132, 1154, 1800, 2285, 3031, 3780, 4034, 4129, 4458, 4490, 4706, 4972, 5085, 5230, 5340, 5388, 5483, 5537, 5539, 5553, 6058

Voir aussi Allemands en Colombie-Britannique; Chinois en Colombie-Britannique; Ile de Vancouver; Japonais en Colombie-Britannique; Kamloops, Colombie-Britannique; Vancouver, Colombie-Britannique

—— Antiquités 4604

—— Aquatic Plant Management Program 6319

—— Archéologie 4549, 4556

—— Cartes 6428, 6486, 6544, 6553, 6570, 6581, 6599

—— Climat 5041

—— Conditions sociales 3256, 3322, 6621

—— Department of Agriculture 6273, 6429

—— Department of Mines 6257, 6428

—— Department of Mines and Petroleum Resources 6257, 6428

—— Department of the Attorney-General 2100

—— Droit 2165, 2251

—— Frontières 0558

—— Géographie 3010

—— Geological Survey Branch 6410, 6427

—— Histoire 0554, 0555, 0567, 0571, 0572, 0575, 0577, 0584, 0590, 0595, 0602, 0701, 1512, 1962, 1963, 2864, 3956, 6112

—— Imprimés 0567, 0600, 0606, 1649, 1660, 1685, 4163

—— Industrie et ressources 0579

—— Lieux historiques 0757

—— Mineral Resources Division 6428

—— Ministry of Agriculture and Food 6429

—— Ministry of Environment 6331

—— Ministry of Forests 6430

—— Ministry of Industry and Small Business Development 6368

—— Parcs 1825, 6320, 6696

—— Petroleum Resources Division 6383

—— Politique et gouvernement 2382, 4427

—— Politique publique 2431

—— Provincial Archives 0916

—— Répertoires 0598, 0604

Colombie-Britannique dans la littérature 1178

Colonie Barr (Alb. et Sask.) 1987

Colonies 1907

Voir aussi France–Colonies; Grande-Bretagne–Colonies et protectorats

Colonisation des terres 0538, 1935, 4638, 6523

Cols blancs 2838, 2873

Voir aussi Employés de bureau

Columbia, Vallée de la 0557

Combustibles

—— Recherche 5784, 5786, 5822

Combustibles nucléaires 5773, 5843

Comètes 5811

Comités 6352

Comités de citoyens 3193

Comités patronal-ouvrier 2902

Commerce 1439, 2663, 2746

Voir aussi Affaires; Libre-échange et protectionnisme; Missions commerciales; Tarif douanier

—— Statistiques 2702

Commerce de détail 2764, 2770

Voir aussi Concessions (Commerce de détail)

—— Heures d'affaires 2740, 2759

Voir aussi Dimanche, Loi du

Commerce de gros 2764, 2770

Commission canadienne des droits de la personne 2363, 2365

Commission canadienne des transports 4462

Commission de contrôle de l'énergie atomique 5819, 6435

Commission de la fonction publique du Canada 2510

Commission de lutte contre l'inflation 2638

Commission de réforme du droit de l'Ontario 2136

Commission de système métrique Canada 2657

Commission des droits des indiens du Canada 3964

Commission Gendron 6291

Commission géologique du Canada 4762, 4857, 6209, 6210, 6211, 6216, 6229, 6231, 6244, 6245, 6253, 6496, 6497, 6591

Commission internationale des pêches de l'Atlantique Nord-Ouest 4885

Commission on Declining School Enrolments in Ontario (CODE) 3570

Commissions de réforme du droit 2298

Commissions parlementaires 2511, 6380

Commissions royales 2599, 2609, 3592, 6223, 6224, 6262, 6381

Voir aussi Enquêtes administratives

—— Alberta 6306

—— Colombie-Britannique 6227, 6339

—— Manitoba 6234

—— Nouvelle-Écosse 6365

—— Ontario 6329, 6413

—— Québec (Province) 2376

—— Saskatchewan 2396

Committee on Northern Population Research 3023, 3038

Common law 2252

Commonwealth 0064, 0080, 0089, 0099, 0686, 1968, 2345, 6771

Voir aussi Empire britannique

Communauté, Vie en 4340, 4355

Voir aussi Quartiers (Urbanisme)

Communauté urbaine de Québec (Québec) 6370

Communication 0986, 2633, 3187, 3553, 3689, 4340, 6194

Voir aussi Écriture; Langage et langues; Médias

—— Aspect social 3143, 4192

—— Industries 0954, 0988

—— Satellites 5734
Communications dans les organisations 2677
Communisme 2416
Community colleges
   Voir Collèges communautaires
Community Renewal Resource Centre (Ontario) 4396
Compagnie de la Baie-d'Hudson 1898, 1906, 1909, 1912, 1913, 3940, 4022
Compagnie de Pulpe de Chicoutimi 4971
Compagnie des Indes 2010, 2027, 2040, 2048
Compagnie des Jeunes Canadiens 3132
Compagnie du Nord-Ouest 1898
Compétence territoriale
   Voir Juridiction territoriale
Compo Company 0841, 0870
Comportement organisationnel 5838
   Voir aussi Communications dans les organisations
Comportement sexuel 3223, 3233
   Voir aussi Enfants–Comportement sexuel; Handicapés mentaux–Comportement sexuel; Perversion sexuelle
Composés organiques 4816
Compositeurs 0808, 0811, 0812, 0813, 0822, 0826, 0842, 0846, 0861, 0904, 0934, 0935, 0939
Comptabilité 2635, 2783
   Voir aussi Vérification comptable
—— Informatique 2754
Comptines 4529
Computer Communications Networks Group, University of Waterloo 5832
Concentration économique 2639
   Voir aussi Monopoles
Conception assistée par ordinateur 5827
Conception technique 5744
Concessions (Commerce de détail) 2600, 2766, 2767
Conchyliculture 5542
Concordia Radio Drama Project 0978
Concurrence 2194, 2250, 2340, 2765
Concurrence (Biologie) 5022
Conditionnement physique 1820, 1857, 1858, 6235
   Voir aussi Culturisme
Conditionnement physique des employés 1819
Conditions économiques 3300
Conditions sociales 3300
Conduite automobile
   Voir Automobiles–Conduite
Confédération canadienne, 1867
   Voir Canada–Histoire–Confédération, 1867
Conférence canadienne des arts 0679, 0719
Conférences, allocutions, etc 1015
Conflits d'intérêts (Administration publique) 2533
Congrès 0050
Congrès du travail du Canada 2896
Congrès international des américanistes 3907
Conseil canadien pour la réadaptation des handicapés 3247
Conseil de la radiodiffusion et des télécommunications canadiennes 0973, 0974
Conseil de recherche en sciences humaines du Canada 0675
Conseil des arts du Canada 0675, 0708
Conseil économique du Canada 6411, 6412
Conseil national de recherches Canada 4615, 5425, 5812, 5813
—— Division de génie mécanique 5841
—— Division de recherche en construction 6359
—— Section d'étude de feu 6375

Conseil régional de développement de l'Est du Québec 6317
Conseil scolaire de l'île de Montréal 3736
Conseils scolaires 3736
Conservatory Quarterly Review (Périodique) 0835
Consolidex Magnorth Oakwood Joint Venture 4833
Consommateurs 2612, 2613, 2616, 2632, 2644, 2645, 2655, 2769, 2777, 5209
—— Éducation 2614, 2716, 3165, 3204
—— Protection 2261
—— —— Droit 2208
Consommation (Économie politique) 2597
Constantin-Weyer, Maurice 6914
Constitutionnel (Périodique) 0972
Construction 0741, 5736, 5739, 5802
   Voir aussi Architecture
—— Chantiers
   Voir Chantiers de construction
—— Droit 2317
   Voir aussi Zonage
—— Histoire 2031, 2032
—— Industrie 2585, 2637, 2708
—— —— Normes 5852
—— —— Statistiques 2685
—— Matériaux 0804, 5800
—— Recherche 5716, 5726, 5729, 5744, 6359, 6453
   Voir aussi Institut de recherche en construction (Canada)
Construction, Technique de la 5728
Construction en bois rond 0768
Construction en pierre 0776
Construction navale 4503
Constructions 0752
   Voir aussi Édifices à bureaux
—— Consommation d'énergie 0769, 5764, 5776, 5814
Constructions et moiteur 5807
Constructions scolaires 3393, 3457, 5778
—— Consommation d'énergie 5147
Contact culturel
   Voir Acculturation
Contact Press 1590
Contant, Alexis 6915, 6916
Conteneurisation 4456, 4467
Contes 1014, 1067, 1081, 1087, 1097, 1265, 1356
Continuing Legal Education Society of British Columbia 2364
Contraintes (Mécanique) 5717
   Voir aussi Métaux–Fatigue
Contrats 2136, 3861
Contrats de travail 2899
   Voir aussi Conventions collectives
Contrats de vente 2136
Conventions collectives 2868
Conversation 1460
Cook, James 6511, 6565, 6917, 6918, 6919
Coopération 2550, 2564
Cooperative Commonwealth Federation 2433
   Voir aussi Nouveau parti démocratique
Coopératives 2573, 2610, 2652, 2659, 2677, 2698, 2728, 2729, 2730, 2737, 2914, 4097
Coopératives de logement
   Voir Logement coopératif
Copépodes 5367, 5476
Copp Clark Company 1350

Drogues 3704, 3705, 5583, 5594
  Voir aussi Botanique médicale; Tranquillisants
Drogues et automobilistes 5590
Drogues et femmes 3747, 5609
Drogues et jeunesse 2184
Drogues et sports 1868
Droit 0121, 2094, 2095, 2096, 2097, 2098, 2100, 2108, 2110, 2111,
  2116, 2131, 2133, 2142, 2150, 2153, 2164, 2170, 2173, 2182,
  2187, 2196, 2213, 2247, 2253, 2259, 2260, 2263, 2265, 2268,
  2285, 2286, 2304, 2325, 2338, 2352, 2364, 2366, 2367, 2368,
  3996, 6088, 6187, 6667, 6684, 6718, 6719
  Voir aussi Common law; Justice–Administration; Législation;
  Négligence; Responsabilité (Droit); Tribunaux
—— Bibliothèques 1727, 2165, 2176, 2189
—— Étude et enseignement 2115, 2172, 2183, 2206, 2262, 4006
—— Histoire 2126, 2226, 2240, 2284
—— Informatique 2120, 2139, 2216, 2292
—— Periodiques 5977
Droit civil 2185
  Voir aussi Charte canadienne des droits et libertés
—— Québec (Province) 2215, 2267, 2355
Droit communautaire
  Voir Aide juridique
Droit constitutionnel 2102, 2105, 2227, 2481
Droit d'auteur 1625, 2119, 2138, 2158, 2177, 2222, 2257, 2300
—— Musique 0807
Droit de la famille 2293, 2328, 3861
Droit de prêt public (des écrivains) 1681
Droit de propriété étrangère 4700
Droit du travail 2890, 2924
  Voir aussi Dimanche, Loi du
Droit ecclésiastique 1506
Droit et féminisme 2328, 3890
Droit international 0611, 2180, 2271, 2278
Droit maritime 2112, 2113, 2162, 2369, 4892, 5299
  Voir aussi Eaux territoriales
Droit pénal 2124, 2181, 2229, 2237, 2301, 2311, 2312, 2361, 2362
  Voir aussi Peine capitale; Procédure pénale
Droit spatial 2295
Droits civils 2127, 2233, 2241, 3527
  Voir aussi Charte canadienne des droits et libertés; Droits de
  l'homme; Liberté de la presse; Vie privée, Droit à la
Droits de l'homme 2118, 2127, 2130, 2211, 2241, 2254, 2264,
  2296, 2363, 2365, 3175, 3274, 3662, 6686
  Voir aussi Enfants–Droits
—— Droit 2258
Drolet, Antonio 6957
Drosophiles 5378
Drummondville, Québec 0333, 0351, 0969
Dubé, Marcel 1090
Ducharme, Réjean 6958
Dudek, Louis 6959
Duff, Wilson 6960
Dufresne, Guy 6961
Duguay, Raoul 1089, 6962
Dundas, Comté de, Ontario 0491
Dunn, Oscar, Bibliothèque 6737
Duplessis, Maurice 2469
Duval, Etienne F. 0984
Dyonnet, Edmond 6963
Dystrophie musculaire progressive 3237

Eastcoast Petroleum Operators' Association Safety Committee
  4835
Eastern Arctic Study 0643
Eau 5253, 6614
—— Approvisionnement 5060, 5062, 5090, 5171, 5290, 6389
—— —— Fluorure 5576
—— —— Manitoba 6459
—— —— Nouveau-Brunswick 5053, 5215, 5250, 5256
—— —— Nouvelle-Écosse 5225
—— —— Ontario 5183
—— —— Provinces de l'Atlantique 5048
—— —— Provinces de l'ouest 5032
—— —— Québec (Province) 5055, 5071, 5117
—— —— Régions arctiques 5052
—— Droit 2112
—— Pollution 5062, 5087, 5150, 5151, 5161, 5168, 5180, 5201,
  5214, 5232, 5254, 5279
  Voir aussi Mer–Pollution; Mercure, Pollution des rivières,
  lacs, etc par le; Poissons, Effet de la pollution sur les
—— —— Contrôle 5078, 6346
Eau souterraine 4830, 5037, 5125, 5126, 5242, 6564
Eaux territoriales 4884
  Voir aussi Droit maritime
Eaux usées 4960, 4961, 5738, 5742, 5837, 5849
—— Épuration 5252
Échecs 1806
École des hautes études commerciales de Montréal 2572
École et communauté 3494, 3501, 3521
École nationale d'administration publique (Québec) 2528, 2539
École polytechnique de Montréal 6189, 6201, 6725
Écoles 3719
  Voir aussi Cours par correspondance; Universités
—— Accréditation et normes 3465
—— Direction et organisation
  Voir Administration scolaire
—— Équipements et matériels 3393
—— Personnel 3423, 3447, 3449
—— Sécurité 3675
Écoles et musées
  Voir Musées et écoles
Écoles expérimentales 3453, 3512, 3584
Écoles maternelles 3699
Écoles privées 3528, 3634
Écoliers
—— Transport 3526
Écologie 0517, 1870, 4657, 4672, 5058, 5067, 5079, 5162, 5178,
  5179, 5236, 5262, 5293, 5295, 5297, 5438
  Voir aussi Environnement
—— Québec (Province) 5093
Écologie aquatique 5095, 5138
Écologie des prairies 3019, 4666, 4691, 5270, 5465
Écologie forestière 4926, 4934, 4936, 4946, 4956, 4974, 4976,
  4984, 4985, 4986, 5018, 5526, 5553
Écologie marine 5087, 5111, 5129, 5130, 5180, 5181, 5201, 5203
Écologie végétale 5449
Ecology Action Resource Centre (Halifax) 5262
Économétrie 2765
Économie domestique 3821, 3831
  Voir aussi Ménagers et ménagères
Économie du travail 2857
Économie politique 1439, 2382, 2560, 2623, 2709, 2733, 2780,
  2781, 2782, 3371, 6054, 6055, 6108
  Voir aussi Affaires; Commerce; Finances; Innovation

Haldimand-Norfolk, Région de, Ontario 0465
Haliburton, Comté de, Ontario 4407
Haliburton, Thomas Chandler 7040, 7041
Halifax, Comté d', Nouvelle-Écosse 4821
Halifax, Nouvelle-Écosse 0196, 0249
—— Politique et gouvernement 4364
Halifax Garrison Library 6735
Hallam, John 6739
Halley, Comète de
    Voir Comètes
Halton, Région de, Ontario 4378
Hamelin, Louis-Edmond 7042, 7043, 7044
Hamilton, Ontario 2856, 5332
Handicapés 2230, 3090, 3180, 3187, 3204, 3209, 3215, 3218,
    3220, 3222, 3235, 3237, 3243, 3247, 3249, 3286, 3309, 6676
    Voir aussi Architecture et les handicapés; Enfants
    handicapés; Femmes handicapées; Parents handicapés
—— Abus sexuel 3316, 3356
—— Éducation 3442, 3541, 3546, 3594
—— Emploi 2860, 2939, 3670
—— Logement 3214, 3229, 3341, 3342
—— Loisirs 1767, 1830, 1862
—— Réadaptation 3142, 3226
—— Transport 3167, 3189, 3246, 4471
Handicapés mentaux 3108, 3112, 3161, 3208, 3237, 3245, 3273,
    3365, 5628, 5650
    Voir aussi Institut national pour la déficience mentale
—— Comportement sexuel 3155, 3158
Handicapés sociaux 3113
Harcèlement sexuel 3225, 3802, 3812, 3816, 3865
Hareng 5453, 5491
Harmonies (Ensembles instrumentaux) 0859, 0898, 0924, 0930
Harper, J. Russell 7045
Harris, Lawren 7046
Harrisse, Henry 7047
Harry Hawthorn Foundation for the Inculcation and Propaga-
    tion of the Principles and Ethics of Fly-Fishing 1831
Harvard University
—— Bibliothèque 6766, 6776
Hathaway, Rufus, Collection 1002
Haut-Saint-Laurent, Québec 0409
Health of Aquatic Communities Task Force 5232
Heavy metal (Musique)
    Voir Musique rock
Hébert, Anne 7048, 7049, 7050, 7051
Hémiplégie 5687
Hémon, Louis 7052
Henderson, Archibald Douglas 7053
Hennepin, Louis 1501, 1879, 1880, 1884, 1886, 7054, 7055, 7056,
    7057, 7058, 7059, 7060, 7061, 7062
Henripin, Jacques 7063
Héraldique 1929, 2026, 2060, 2083
    Voir aussi Généalogie
Herbicides 4936, 5004, 5231
—— Effets nocifs 5265
Héritage 2081
    Voir aussi Actes d'administration
Herrera y Tordesillas, Antonio de 7062
Hétérocères 5303, 5306, 5308, 5371, 5380, 5404, 5447
Hétu, Jacques 0904
Hiboux 5494

Hill-Tout, Charles 7064
Histoire 0011, 0190, 0994, 1095, 1972, 1981, 2004, 4373, 5607,
    6084, 6733, 6756
    Voir aussi Biographie; Église–Histoire; Géographie historique
—— Sources 1942
    Voir aussi Archives
Histoire, Sociétés d' 0766, 1896
Histoire économique 1971, 2027, 2040, 2048, 2061, 2071, 2562,
    2565, 2593
    Voir aussi Grande Dépression, 1929-1939
Histoire locale 1887, 3040
—— Alberta 0538, 0545, 2066
—— Colombie-Britannique 0602
—— Histoire locale 0503
—— Manitoba 0534, 0546
—— Nord canadien 0458
—— Nouveau-Brunswick 0248
—— Nouvelle-Écosse 0250, 0258
—— Ontario 0456, 0458, 0469, 0476, 0489, 0490, 0491
—— Provinces de l'Atlantique 0208
—— Québec (Province) 0284, 0308, 0328, 0339, 1916, 2014, 2037
—— Saskatchewan 0498, 0535
Histoire maritime 1998, 2020, 5299
Histoire militaire 1966, 2021, 5572
    Voir aussi Canada–Histoire militaire; Régiments–Histoire
Histoire navale 1926
Histoire orale 0354, 2013, 6621, 6646
Histoire sociale 1988, 2011, 3057, 3068, 3785, 5768
Histoire urbaine 0456, 4324, 4353, 4356, 4370, 4372, 4380, 4390,
    4415, 4428
Historiens 1973
Hitchins, Fred H. 4463
Hiver 4422, 4454, 5454
Hockey 1762, 1788, 1841
    Voir aussi Coupe Stanley (Série); Ligue nationale de hockey
Hockey sur gazon 1841
Hollandais au Canada 5881, 6095
Holmes, John W. 7065
Homards 4890, 5339
Homme
—— Influence sur la nature 5257
Homme préhistorique 4008, 4609
Hommes 3307
    Voir aussi Dissimilitude des sexes; Femmes et hommes
Hommes d'affaires 2712
Homosexualité 0989, 2845, 3118, 3175, 3176, 3259, 3282, 5653,
    5976
    Voir aussi Lesbianisme
Hongrois (Langue) 1446
Hongrois au Canada 1257, 4184, 4245, 5890, 6127
Hood, Hugh 7066, 7067
Hooper, Louis 7068
Hôpitaux 5583
—— Administration 5613, 5695
—— Bibliothèques 1603, 1647, 5715
—— Consommation d'énergie 5772
—— Personnel 2805
Horaires variables de travail 2833
Howay, Frederic William 7069
Howe, Joseph 7070
Hughes, E.J. 7071

—— Yukon 3930, 4094
Indiens (Orientaux) au Canada 4137, 4147, 4179, 4239, 5910, 6122
Indiens dans la littérature 1283
Indiens et médias 4067
Indochinois au Canada 4288
Industrie 0121, 2594, 2680, 2687, 2693
  Voir aussi Stimulants dans l'industrie
—— Concentration
  Voir Concentration économique
—— Histoire 2593, 2697, 2744
—— Localisation 2561, 2765
—— Mesures de sécurité 2159, 2661
—— Technologie 5839
Industrie et arts
  Voir Arts et industrie
Industrie et État 2313, 2314, 2439, 2722, 2723, 2847, 4848
  Voir aussi Déréglementation de l'industrie
Industrie familiale 2732
Industrie forestière 2647, 4921, 4932, 6451
  Voir aussi Exploitation forestière
—— Aspect de l'environnement 4958, 4960, 4961
—— Québec (Province) 4996
Industrie pétrochimique 4785
Industries agricoles 2619
Industries culturelles 0693, 0718, 0724, 0729, 1844
Industries de haute technologie 5799
Industries et ressources 0589
Industries manufacturières 5840
Infections à chlamydia 5684
Infirmiers et infirmières 4595, 5570, 5586, 5589, 5593, 5606, 5615, 5616, 5617, 5622, 5629, 6624
  Voir aussi Association des infirmières et infirmiers du Canada; Soins infirmiers à domicile; Soins infirmiers à l'école
—— Droit 2167
—— Formation 3428, 3479, 5604
—— Histoire 5578, 5713
—— Offre et demande 5611
—— Périodiques 5988
Information, Systèmes de visualisation de l' 5630, 5641, 5644, 5646, 5648
  Voir aussi Terminal vidéo
Information, Traitement de l', chez l'homme 3212, 3696, 3697
Information gouvernementale 2210, 2266, 2273, 2415, 2428, 2434
  Voir aussi Dossiers publiques–Accès–Contrôle; Propagande
Informatique 1468, 1598
  Voir aussi Intelligence artificielle
—— Aspect sociale 2576
—— Étude et enseignement 3659
—— Terminologie 1465
Informatisation 1694
Ingénierie 6201, 6208
  Voir aussi Génie mécanique; Génie rural; Sanitation–Ingénierie
—— Dictionnaires 1456
—— Recherche 5730, 5733, 5739, 5823, 6374
Ingénierie militaire 2031, 2032
Innis, Harold Adams 7073
Innovation (Économie politique) 5838
Inondations 5128

Insectes 5525
  Voir aussi Entomologie
Inspection 2313, 2314
Installations sportives 1803
Institut agricole d'Oka 6150
Institut canadien de l'information scientifique et technique 4619
Institut canadien de microreproductions historiques 5982
Institut canadien de Québec
—— Bibliothèque 6752
Institut canadien de recherches en génie forestier 5007
Institut canadien de recherches sur les femmes 5699
Institut canadien de recherches sur les pâtes et papiers 4923, 5826, 6786
Institut canadien d'éducation des adultes 3680, 3689
Institut de dynamique marine (Canada) 5835
Institut de la médecine du travail et des ambiances 5114, 5115
Institut de recherche appliquée sur le travail 2858
Institut de recherche en construction (Canada) 6453
Institut de recherche en droit public, Université de Montréal 2112
Institut de recherche sur les feux de forêt (Canada) 4947, 6283
Institut de recherche technique et statistique, Agriculture Canada 6374
Institut de recherches techniques et statistiques, Agriculture Canada 4701
Institut des sciences de la mer, Division de l'écologie des océans 5521
Institut d'histoire de l'Amérique française 2084
Institut forestier national de Petawawa 4977, 6387
Institut militaire et civil de médecine de l'environnement 5592
Institut national de la recherche scientifique (Québec) 3537
Institut national pour la déficience mentale 3112
Institut océanographique de Bedford 5386, 5398
Institut pour la répression des ravageurs forestiers 6358, 6367
Institute for Computer Research, University of Waterloo 5832
Institute of Arctic and Alpine Research 0651
Institute of Pacific Relations 2491
Institutions et affaires religieuses 1526
Institutions financières 2567, 2700
  Voir aussi Banques; Marché monétaire
Instituts féminins 0489, 0490, 3422
Instruments à cordes 0918, 0926
Intelligence 1426
Intelligence artificielle 3060
Interaction roue-rail 4499
Intérêt public 2261
International Sound Poetry Festival, Toronto 1133
Inuit 0508, 0621, 0626, 0882, 1118, 1216, 1393, 1531, 3910, 3912, 3915, 3918, 3920, 3921, 3926, 3929, 3931, 3932, 3933, 3938, 3941, 3942, 3943, 3945, 3949, 3957, 3965, 3966, 3968, 3969, 3970, 3972, 3982, 3983, 3991, 3995, 3996, 3999, 4003, 4009, 4013, 4017, 4018, 4022, 4023, 4029, 4035, 4043, 4065, 4068, 4073, 4074, 4077, 4079, 4084, 4092, 4100, 4103, 4109, 4111, 4112, 4115, 4116, 4117, 4118, 4120, 4123, 4124, 4531, 4532, 4572, 4907, 5257, 6104, 6117, 6163, 6176, 6180, 6182, 6185, 6186, 6197, 6622, 6645, 6678, 6680
—— Alimentation 5661
—— Antiquités 4564, 4597
—— Art 0668, 0671, 0687, 0697, 0698, 0711, 0712, 0727
—— Costume et parure 4032
—— Éducation 3388, 3398, 3431
—— Femmes 3782, 4045

Lituaniens au Canada 5891

Liturgie 1578

Livesay, Dorothy 1225, 7148, 7149

Livre d'ici (Périodique) 0185

Livres

—— Choix 1619

—— Expositions 0039, 0040, 0041, 0068, 0072, 0077, 0078, 0099, 0117, 0122, 0175, 0207, 0402, 0403, 0731, 1252, 1585, 1685, 6783

—— Foires 0092

—— Histoire 1736

—— Industrie 1637, 1715, 1722

—— Mise en page artistique 0669, 1644, 1685

—— Prix 0148

Livres d'artistes 0137, 0691, 0700, 0731, 1592

Livres de poche 1299

Livres de prières 1578

Livres d'images pour enfants 1329, 1331, 1371, 1383

Livres en gros caractères 3366

Livres parlants 3366, 6649, 6677

Livres rares 0008, 0010, 0014, 0017, 0026, 0027, 0074, 0107, 0114, 0115, 0131, 6794

Livres sur microfilm 0489

Lochhead, Douglas 7150

Logan, John Daniel 7151

Logement 3298, 3868, 4314, 4320, 4348, 4352, 4362, 4365, 4367, 4368, 4369, 4371, 4375, 4396, 4404, 4408, 4409, 4418, 4426
    Voir aussi Indiens–Logement; Maisons mobiles; Projets de logement gouvernemental; Sans-logis

—— Aspect sociale 3358, 4382, 4402

—— Coûts
    Voir Coût de logement

—— Nord canadien 4432

—— Nouveau-Brunswick 4410

—— Ontario 4394

—— Recherche 4443

—— Statistiques 4421

Logement coopératif 4325, 4411, 4417, 4433, 4439

Logiciels 1691, 5767, 5828

Logiciels pédagogiques 3690

Loi sur les ressources en eau du Canada 5286

Lois

—— Application 2361
    Voir aussi Police

Loisir 1765, 6145

Loisirs 0690, 1755, 1756, 1758, 1769, 1781, 1785, 1786, 1790, 1792, 1794, 1798, 1800, 1802, 1821, 1824, 1826, 1827, 1840, 3049, 4937, 6156, 6320
    Voir aussi Enfants–Loisirs; Handicapés–Loisirs

—— Aspect économique 1835

—— Filmographies 6660

Loisirs, Centres de 1803
    Voir aussi Installations sportives

Loisirs, Zones de 1770, 1771, 1772, 1773, 1774, 1775, 1777, 1778, 1805, 1837

Lomer, Gerhard Richard 7152

London, Ontario 4345

Longpré, Anselme 7153

Longpré, Ephrem 7154, 7155

Lotbinière, Québec 0407

Loteries 1787

Loucheux (Indiens) 3930

Louisbourg (Forteresse) 0738, 1970

Louisiane 2019

Loups 5433

Loutres 5394, 5428

Lovell, John 0933

Low, Albert Peter 7156

Lower, Arthur Reginald Marsden 7157

Lowry, Malcolm 7158, 7159, 7160, 7161, 7162

Lowry, Malcolm, Bibliothèque 6785

Loyers

—— Législation 2205, 4393, 4406

Lyman, John 7163

MacBride Museum 0662

Macdonald, Sir John Alexander, Bibliothèque 6753

Machines agricoles 4725

—— Marketing 4652

Mackay, Isabel Ecclestone 7164

Mackenzie, Alexander 6514

Mackenzie, Région du 0617, 0618, 4631, 5118, 5174, 5478, 5487, 5488

Mackenzie Mountains Region Baseline Study 4828

MacLennan, Hugh 7165, 7166, 7167

Macmillan Company of Canada 1674

MacNutt, William Stewart 7168

Macpherson, C.B. 7169

Madawaska

—— Histoire 0228

Magasins 5776

Magnétisme 5829

Magocsi, Paul Robert 7170

Maheux, Arthur 7171

Maillet, Antonine 7172

Main-d'oeuvre 2586, 2800, 2823, 2857, 2884

—— Mobilité 2796

Maisons

—— Consommation d'énergie 0769, 5789

Maisons de plaisance 1779, 1853

—— Multipropriété 1842

Maisons mobiles 4347, 4377

Maisons rurales 0742

Major, André 7173

Malades 3209
    Voir aussi Soins en phase terminale

Maladies à herpèsvirus 5684

Maladies à virus 4667
    Voir aussi SIDA (Maladie)–Virus

Maladies infectieuses 5682

Maladies mentales 3357
    Voir aussi Apprentissage, Troubles de l'; Autisme; Dépression mentale

—— Aspect sociales 3126

—— Prévention 5624

Maladies transmises sexuellement 5684
    Voir aussi Infections à chlamydia; SIDA (Maladie); Syphilis

Maliseet (Indiens) 3953, 4089

Mammifères 5302, 5428, 5493, 5530

Mammifères marins 5396, 5520

Mance, Jeanne 7174

Mandats mondiaux de production 2694

Manitoba 0499, 0500, 0506, 0507, 0509, 0513, 0522, 0530, 0539, 0542, 0546, 0549, 0551, 0621, 3243, 4078, 4621, 5485, 5515
    Voir aussi Canadiens-français au Manitoba; Churchill, Manitoba; Winnipeg, Manitoba

Produits dangereux 2683, 4785, 5232
—— Transport 4491
Produits forestiers 4929
—— Transport 4933
Professeurs (Enseignement supérieur) 2868, 3427, 3638
    Voir aussi Femmes professeurs de l'enseignement supérieur
—— Salaires, pensions, etc 3492
Professions libérales 3610
Programmation (Mathématiques) 4311
Programme canadien de gestion des déchets radioactifs 5273
Programme de formation scientifique dans le Nord 4635
Programme des études ethniques canadiennes 4296
Programme EEMAE 5181
Programme internationale de corrélation géologique 4819
Programme sur l'homme et la biosphère 5190
Programme Transport à grande distance des polluants atmosphériques 5159, 5221, 5222
Programmes d'action positive 2913, 2920, 2921, 3852
Programmes d'alphabétisation 3577, 3591, 3715, 3716, 3720, 3725
Programmes de prêts pour petites et moyennes entreprises 2720
Programmes d'études 3496
—— Planification 3481
Project Canada West 4321
Projet hydro-électrique de la Baie James 3934, 3978, 3979, 5077, 5093
Projets de logement gouvernemental 4381, 4387, 4401, 4416
Propagande 2415, 2427
Propriété foncière 2621, 6556
Propriété immobilière
—— Valeur 4335
Prospecteurs 2880
Prospection 4748
Prostitution 2329, 3845
Protection civile 5842
    Voir aussi Abris antiatomiques
Protection civile Canada 5842
Protéines 5392
Protestantisme 1534, 1544, 1546
Protestations, manifestations, etc 2160, 2472, 3948
    Voir aussi Émeutes
Prothèses 5631
Prothèses myoélectriques 5693
Protozoaires 5405
Proulx, Maurice 7250
Provinces de l'Atlantique 0106, 0144, 0198, 0208, 0209, 0214, 0222, 0223, 0229, 0230, 0235, 0236, 0238, 0244, 0253, 0265, 0267, 0919, 1192, 1295, 1509, 2550, 3004, 3992, 4089, 4187, 4475, 4534, 4538, 4561, 4570, 4705, 4909, 5436, 5522, 6765
—— Archéologie 4599
—— Histoire 0210, 0231, 0252, 0271, 0274, 2089, 4055, 4056, 4598, 6793
—— Histoire économique 0234
—— Imprimés 0273
—— Industries et ressources 2579
Provinces de l'Ouest 0106, 0522, 0523, 2066, 4182, 4400, 6083, 6541
    Voir aussi Canadiens-français dans les provinces de l'ouest
—— Archéologie 4562
—— Cartes 6495, 6538, 6593
—— Histoire 0494, 0508, 0511, 0525, 0529, 0531, 0548, 1987, 2284, 2725, 4579

Provinces des prairies 0495, 0510, 0519, 1085, 1546, 2225, 3166, 3853, 4537
—— Climat 5059
—— Histoire 4080
Provinces des prairies dans la littérature 1113
Provincial Archives of Alberta 3795
Pruche occidentale 5338
Pseudonymes
    Voir Anonymes et pseudonymes
Psychanalyse 5637
Psychiatrie 5607, 5623, 5632
Psychiatrie médico-légale 2200, 2246
Psychologie 6062, 6065, 6094
    Voir aussi Agressivité (Psychologie); Ajustement (Psychologie); Behaviorisme (Psychologie); Masculinité (Psychologie); Motivation (Psychologie); Parapsychologie; Stéréotype (Psychologie)
—— Périodiques 5927
—— Recherche 3094
Psychologie criminelle 2246
Psychologie éducationnelle 3460
Psychologie industrielle 2862, 2863
Psychologie sociale 3100, 3136, 3308, 6075
    Voir aussi Aliénation (Psychologie sociale); Groupes sociaux; Mouvements sociaux
Psychopharmacologie 5582, 5609
    Voir aussi Antidépresseurs; Tranquillisants
Psychophysiologie 3209
Public Archives of Nova Scotia 6492
Publications en série 5329, 5856, 5866, 5871, 5873, 5876, 5918, 5922, 5932, 5941, 5955, 5959, 5962, 5966, 5982, 5987, 5991, 6390, 6391
—— Agriculture 5928
—— Art 5963
—— Environnement 5979
—— Forêts et sylviculture 5916
—— Indiens 5951
—— Religion 5902
—— Sciences humaines 5993
—— Sciences naturelles 5920
—— Sciences sociales 5993
Publications officielles 0154, 1617, 2130, 2798, 3266, 3283, 3374, 4301, 4438, 5289, 6214, 6217, 6221, 6222, 6226, 6228, 6241, 6246, 6248, 6266, 6275, 6276, 6277, 6289, 6290, 6296, 6297, 6314, 6315, 6321, 6322, 6325, 6330, 6402, 6403, 6404, 6405, 6408, 6426, 6450, 6452, 6460, 6474, 6475
—— Alberta 6236, 6278, 6422, 6423, 6424
—— Colombie-Britannique 6230, 6310, 6340, 6431, 6432, 6433
—— Grande-Bretagne 6212
—— Ile-du-Prince-Édouard 6239, 6469
—— Manitoba 6318, 6334, 6456, 6457
—— Nouveau-Brunswick 6239, 6285, 6461, 6462
—— Nouvelle-Écosse 6239, 6386, 6464, 6465, 6466
—— Ontario 2582, 3424, 6215, 6251, 6282, 6293, 6300, 6302, 6323, 6354, 6360, 6364, 6413, 6414, 6467, 6468
—— Périodiques 6220, 6252, 6363, 6390, 6391
—— Québec (Province) 2238, 6255, 6256, 6264, 6270, 6272, 6280, 6281, 6286, 6299, 6305, 6308, 6324, 6328, 6351, 6366, 6373, 6392, 6470, 6471
—— Saskatchewan 6233, 6472
—— Terre-Neuve 6309
—— Territoires du Nord-Ouest 6463

Velyhorskyj, Ivan 7351
Vente par catalogue 2763
Vents 5737
Vérification comptable 2754
Vermont Historical Society
—— Bibliothèque 1989
Verre 5768, 5844
Verrerie 4598
Vers 5402, 5484
Vertébrés 4528
    Voir aussi Amphibie; Mammifères; Oiseaux; Reptiles
Vêtements 4032
    Voir aussi Costume
—— Industrie 2608, 2731
Viande
—— Recherche 4722
Vibration 4870
Victimes d'actes criminels 3262, 3263, 3898
Victoria, Comté de, Ontario 4407
Vidéodisques 1668
Vidéos 1718, 6620, 6641, 6674, 6678, 6680, 6683, 6689, 6691,
    6692, 6697, 6700, 6701, 6703, 6705, 6708
Vidéotex
    Voir Télévision–Transmission de données
Vie des pionniers 3817
Vie familiale, Éducation à la 3624
Vie privée 2210, 2446, 2681, 4355
    Voir aussi Ordinateurs et vie privée
Vie privée, Droit à la 0736, 2266, 2273, 2324, 2346
Vie religieuse et monastique 1556
Vie rurale 0212, 0579, 3168, 3280, 4688, 4689, 4709
Vie spirituelle 1569
Vie urbaine 4403
Vieillards
    Voir Personnes âgées
Vieillesse 3098, 3305, 5579, 5627, 5657
Vieillissement 2260, 3105, 3106, 3241, 3244, 3252, 3256, 3266,
    3283, 3291, 3322, 3329, 3346, 3837, 3875, 3876, 3894
—— Aspect social 3350
Viel, Nicolas 1501
Vigneault, Gilles 7352
Vikings 1927
Villemaire, Yolande 7353
Villes 4306, 4313, 4321, 4362, 4363, 4404, 6312, 6313, 6584
    Voir aussi Sociologie urbaine
—— Alberta 5224, 6559
—— Aspect économique
    Voir Économie urbaine
—— Colombie-Britannique 4371, 4374, 4427
—— Croissance 4314, 4437, 4438, 4440, 4441
—— Géographie
    Voir Géographie urbaine
—— Histoire
    Voir Histoire urbaine
—— Ontario 4396
—— Provinces de l'ouest 4429
—— Québec (Province) 0281, 0286, 0301, 4309, 4342, 4358, 4420
—— Recherche 4389
—— Rénovation 3022, 4336, 4396
    Voir aussi Community Renewal Resource Centre (Ontario)
—— Saskatchewan 4339, 5752
—— Territoires du Nord-Ouest 0629, 4405

Villes fermées 0445, 2821, 4319, 4366, 4384, 4412, 4413
Villes nouvelles 4310, 4328
Vinay, Jean-Paul 6153, 7354, 7355
Vineland Research Station 4708
Vins
—— Industrie
—— —— Droit 2717
Viol 2191, 2202, 3154, 3264, 3858
Violence 3288, 3727, 3730
    Voir aussi Émeutes; Terrorisme
Violence au télévision 0955
Violence dans les mass media 0965
Violence dans les sports 1860, 1861
Violence exercée sur les femmes 3190, 3198, 3271, 3275, 3278,
    3301, 3302, 3349, 3858, 3870
Violence familiale 0955, 3269, 3271, 3278, 3287, 3297, 3327,
    3328, 3343, 3351, 6685
Vision 3212
Visites officielles 0029, 2074
Visons 5428
Vitamines 5575
Vivier, Claude 7356
Voie maritime du Saint-Laurent 2971, 4444, 4446, 4450, 4461,
    4465, 4472, 6242
Voies ferrées 4451
Voies ferrées abandonées 1795
Voies navigables 1797
Voile 6217, 6501, 6502
Vol à l'étalage 2122
Vol à main armée 2276
Vol spatiale 5760
Volailles
—— Maladies et fléaux 4667
Volcans 4786
Vols et assauts 2276
Vote 2398, 2473
    Voir aussi Référendum
Voyage 1752, 1764, 3043
    Voir aussi Guides touristiques (Manuels)
—— Filmographies 6604, 6606
Voyages 1871, 6709, 6713
Voyageurs 2077
Waddington, Miriam 7357, 7358
Wapiti 5348, 5369, 5511
Ward, Norman 7359
Ware, Peter 7360
Wargon, Sylvia Truster 7361
Warren C. Miller Collection 0448
Wastewater Technology Centre 5837
Water and Sewage (Périodique) 5027
Waterloo, Comté de, Ontario 1222, 1571
Webb, Phyllis 7362
Week (Périodique) 0835, 1127
Wellington, Comté de, Ontario 0421, 0485, 1222
West Coast Oil Ports Inquiry 5141
Western Canada Research Project 6083
Western Canadiana Collection 0541
Whip (Politique) 2515
Widener Library 6776
Wilfrid Laurier University
—— Bibliothèque 0937

APPENDICES

ANNEXES

Short Entry Section

Liste des notices abrégées

"40 years of Kirkconnell: titles and selected articles." In: *Acadia Bulletin*; Vol. 47, no. 1 (January 1961) p. 19-23; vol. 48, no. 1 (January 1962) p. 22-25.; ISSN: 0044-5843. [7089]

Aarhus universitet. Institut for engelsk filologi

Canadiana at the University of Aarhus: the Canadian collection of the library of the English Department, University of Aarhus, Denmark. Aarhus, Denmark: The English Department, 1985. 94 p. [0145]

Abbott, Maude Elizabeth

Classified and annotated bibliography of Sir William Osler's publications: (based on the chronological bibliography by Minnie Wright Blogg). 2nd ed., rev. and indexed. Montreal: Medical Museum, McGill University, 1939. xiii, [2], 163 p.: ill., facsims., 2 port. (incl. front.). [7226]

"Classified bibliography of Sir William Osler's Canadian period (1868-1885)." In: *Sir William Osler: memorial number, the "Canadian Medical Association Journal," July 1920*. Montreal: Canadian Medical Association, 1920. P. 103-123. [7225]

Publications of ... [Maude Elizabeth Abbott]. [S.l.: s.n.], 1940. 2 vol. [6796]

Abler, Thomas S.; Weaver, Sally M.

A Canadian Indian bibliography, 1960-1970. Toronto: University of Toronto Press, 1974. xii, 732 p., [2] l. of pl.: maps.; ISBN: 0-8020-2092-5. [3950]

Abouguendia, Z.; Haraldson, J.; Valby, J.

Management and improvement of Saskatchewan rangeland: a selected bibliography. [Saskatoon]: Saskatchewan Research Council, 1981. ii, 80 p. (Saskatchewan Research Council Technical report ; no. 112) [4691]

Aboussafy, David

Bibliography of seniors and the family research, 1980-1991. Vancouver: B.C. Council for the Family, 1991. 42 p.; ISBN: 1-895342-32-5. [3347]

Abraham, Diana; Gomer, Mary; Herberg, Dorothy C.

Cross-cultural social work in Canada: an annotated bibliography. Toronto: Multicultural Worker's Network, 1980. ii, 43 p. [3195]

Académie commerciale catholique de Montréal

Catalogue de la bibliothèque de l'Académie commerciale catholique et de l'École polytechnique de Montréal. Montréal: *La Minerve*, 1874. 126 p. [6725]

Acadia College. Library

Catalogue of the Library of Acadia College. Wolfville, N.S.: [s.n.], 1880. 37 p. [6731]

Acadia University. Centre of Leisure Studies

Volunteers and leadership bibliography. Wolfville, N.S.: Acadia University, Centre of Leisure Studies, 1981. 62 p. [1801]

Acadia University. Institute

Bibliography on Fundy tidal power. Wolfville, N.S.: Acadia University Institute, 1984. 19 p. [5794]

Acadia University. Library

Catalogue of books, manuscripts, maps and documents in the William Inglis Morse Collection, 1926-1931. London: Curwen, 1931. vi, 85 p.: front. [6759]

A catalogue of the Eric R. Dennis collection of Canadiana in the library of Acadia University. Wolfville, N.S.: The University, 1938. [vi], 212 p. [6765]

A catalogue of the Maritime Baptist historical collection in the Library of Acadia University. Kentville, N.S.: Kentville Pub. Co., 1955. 41 p. [1509]

Acres Consulting Services Limited

Bibliography of oceanographic atlases covering Canadian ocean waters. Ottawa: Department of Fisheries and Oceans, 1981. v, 99 p.: maps. (Marine Environment Data Service Contractor report ; no. 6) [6573]

Adam, Margaret Isabella; Ewing, John; Munro, James

Guide to the principal parliamentary papers relating to the Dominions, 1812-1911. Edinburgh: Oliver and Boyd, 1913. viii, 190 p. [6212]

Adamovich, L.; Willington, R.P.; Lacate, D.

Bibliography on forest roads and the environment. [S.l.: s.n.], 1973. 25 l. [4934]

Adams, David W.

The psychosocial care of the child and his family in childhood cancer: an annotated bibliography. [Hamilton, Ont.]: McMaster University Medical Centre, c1979. vi, 92, xiv p.; ISBN: 0-9690051-0-5. [3182]

Therapeutic abortion: an annotated bibliography. [Hamilton, Ont.]: McMaster University Medical Centre, 1973. 69, xi, [13] p. [5585]

Adams, Eric; Ing, Pearl; Pringle, John

A review of the literature relevant to rent regulation. Toronto: Ontario Commission of Inquiry into Residential Tenancies, 1986. 311, 2 p. (Research study / Ontario Commission of Inquiry into Residential Tenancies ; no. 2); ISBN: 0-77291-456-7. [4406]

Adams, Gary

"Fur trade archaeology in western Canada: a critical evaluation and bibliography." In: *Saskatchewan Archaeology*; Vol. 2, no. 1&2 (June/December 1981) p. 39-53.; ISSN: 0227-5872. [4579]

Adams, J.; Norwell, M.H.; Senn, Harold A.

"Bibliography of Canadian plant geography." In: *Transactions of the Royal Canadian Institute*; Vol. 16, no. 2 (July 1928)-Vol. 26, no. 2 (1947) [5325]

Adams, John

Canadian crustal stress data: a compilation to 1985. Ottawa: Division of Seismology and Geomagnetism, Earth Physics Branch, Energy, Mines and Resources Canada, 1985. 16, [63] l.: ill., maps. (Earth Physics Branch Open file ; no. 85-31) [4841]

Adams, John Coldwell

"A preliminary bibliography [Charles G.D. Roberts]." In: *The Sir Charles G.D. Roberts Symposium*, edited by Glenn Cleaver. Ottawa: University of Ottawa Press, 1984. P. 221-249. (Reappraisals: Canadian writers ; 10); ISBN: 0-7766-4390-8. [7270]

Adams, R.D.; El-Osta, M.L.; Wellwood, Robert William

Index of selected articles from Canadian journals pertaining to the forest products industries, 1965-1967. Vancouver: Faculty of Forestry, University of British Columbia, 1968. iv, 22 l. [4921]

Adams, Stephen

"A bibliography of R. Murray Schafer." In: *Open Letter*; Fourth Series, nos. 4-5 (Fall 1979) p. 235-244.; ISSN: 0048-1939. [7293]

R. Murray Schafer. Toronto: University of Toronto Press, 1983. x, 240 p., [6] p. of pl.: ill., music, ports. (Canadian composers ; no. 4; ISSN: 0316-1293); ISBN: 0-8020-5571-0. [7295]

R. Murray Schafer. Don Mills, Ont.: PRO Canada, 1983. 15 p.: music, port. [7294]

Adams, W. Peter

Field research on Axel Heiberg Island, N.W.T., Canada: bibliographies and data reports. Montreal: Centre for Northern Studies and Research, McGill University, 1987. i, 207 p.: ill., maps. (McGill Subarctic Research paper ; no. 41; ISSN: 0076-1982) (McGill Axel. Heiberg research report, Miscellaneous paper ; no. 2) (Trent University Department of Geography Occasional paper ; no. 12) [0655]

Ice, including snow research at Trent University ... with a bibliography for 1971-84. Peterborough, Ont.: Trent University, 1984. 13 p. [5208]

Adams, W. Peter; Barr, William

"Annotated bibliography of the McGill sub-arctic research papers (1954-1970)." In: *Revue de géographie de Montréal*; Vol. 27, no 4 (1973) p. 391-412.; ISSN: 0035-1148. [2994]

Adams, W. Peter; Barr, William; Nicholson, Frank H.

Annotated bibliography of the McGill Sub-arctic Research papers and theses, 1954-1974. Montreal: McGill University, 1974. iv, 98 p. (McGill Subarctic Research paper ; no. 26; ISSN: 0076-1982) [2997]

Adamson, Edith

Public library finance: a literature review. Ottawa: Canadian Library Association, 1962. ii, 9 l. (Occasional paper / Canadian Library Association ; no. 36) [1586]

Addison, Paul Andrew; Rennie, P.J.

The Canadian Forestry Service air pollution program and bibliography. Ottawa: Canadian Forestry Service, 1988. iii, 133 p. (Canadian Forestry Service Information report ; DPC-X-26E; ISSN: 0705-324X); ISBN: 0-662-16584-5. [4995]

Programme relatif à la pollution atmosphérique du Service canadien des forêts et bibliographie pertinente. Ottawa: Service canadien des forêts, 1990. iii, 116 p. (Rapport d'information / Service canadien des forêts ; DPC-X-26F; ISSN: 0705-324X); ISBN: 0-662-96463-2. [5006]

Addison, William D.

A preliminary annotated bibliography of Nahanni National Park and the South Nahanni Watershed, N.W.T. [S.l.]: Department of Indian Affairs and Northern Development, National Parks Branch, 1974. ii, 149 l. [2998]

Adshead, Gordon R.; Desrosiers, Danielle

Referendum. [Ottawa]: Ottawa Public Library, [1980]. 39 p. [2455]

Aeronautical and Mechanical Engineering Library (Canada)

Remote handling: a bibliography. Ottawa: The Library, 1976. 27 l. [5755]

Afendras, Evangelos A.; Pianarosa, Albertina

Le bilinguisme chez l'enfant et l'apprentissage d'une langue seconde: bibliographie analytique/Child bilingualism and second language learning: a descriptive bibliography. Québec: Presses de l'Université Laval, 1975. xxiii, 401 p. (Travaux du Centre international de recherche sur le bilinguisme ; F-4); ISBN: 0-7746-6751-6. [1431]

Agence canadienne de développement international

Catalogue des publications de l'Agence canadienne de développement international. Hull, Québec: Direction générale des affaires publiques, Agence canadienne de développement international, c1989. 24, 24 p.: ill.; ISBN: 0-662-56873-7. [6394]

Agence littéraire des éditeurs canadiens-français

Ouvrages canadiens-français et titres québécois traduits et publiés au Canada, traduits et publiés à l'étranger et-ou publiés à l'étranger. 2e éd. rev., corr., mise à jour. Montréal: Conseil supérieur du livre, 1971. 27 f. [0097]

Aging and the aged: list of selected publications from Health and Welfare Canada. [Ottawa]: Office on Aging, Policy, Planning and Information Branch, Health and Welfare Canada, [1985]. 63, 63 p. [3266]

Agricultural Energy Centre

Agricultural Energy Centre bibliography (including videotapes and displays). Guelph, Ont.: The Centre, 1990. 20 l. [4720]

Ahern, George

Catalogue of books: being the complete library of late Geo. Ahern, Quebec, the well-known collector of rare and valuable Canadiana and Americana medical books. Montreal: [s.n.], 1928. 124 p. [5563]

"AID: architect's information directory." In: *Canadian Architect*; (1971-) vol.; ISSN: 0008-2872. [0804]

AIDS resource directory. Ottawa: National AIDS Clearinghouse, Canadian Public Health Association, 1992. iv, 22, 22, iv p. [5707]

Aitken, Barbara B.

Local histories of Ontario municipalities, 1951-1977: a bibliography, with representative trans-Canada locations of copies. Toronto: Ontario Library Association, 1978. ix, 120 p.; ISBN: 0-88969-012-X. [0456]

Aitken, Barbara B.; Broughton, Dawn; Crouch, Yvonne J.

Some Ontario references and sources for the family historian. Rev. and enl. ed. Toronto: Ontario Genealogical Society, c1984. 56 p.; ISBN: 0-920036-14-7. [2034]

Akbari, Ather H.

Economics of immigration and racial discrimination: a literature survey (1970-1989). [Ottawa]: Policy & Research, Department of Multiculturalism and Citizenship, 1989. 63, 32 p. [4263]

Économique de l'immigration et de la discrimination raciale: une revue de la documentation (1970-1989). [Ottawa]: Politique et recherches, Ministère du Multiculturalisme et de la Citoyenneté, 1989. 32, 63 p. [4264]

Akmentins, Osvalds

"Latvian-Canadian periodical publications: a preliminary check list." In: *Canadian Ethnic Studies*; Vol. 5, no. 1/2 (1973) p. 213-220.; ISSN: 0008-3496. [5908]

Akwesasne Library and Cultural Center

Bibliography of Indian books at the Akwesasne Library and Cultural Center. New York: [The Library and Cultural Center], 1978. 56 p. [3994]

Alain, Jean-Marc

Le budget à base zéro-BBZ: une bibliographie. Sainte-Foy, Québec: Centre de documentation, ENAP, 1979. ii f, 68 p. [2642]

Perceptions du député: une bibliographie. [Sainte Foy, Québec]: Centre de documentation, École nationale d'administration publique, Université du Québec, 1979. 10 f. [2442]

La rationalisation des choix budgétaires: une bibliographie. [Sainte-Foy, Québec]: Centre de documentation, ENAP, 1979. iv, 120 p. [2643]

Alain, Jean-Marc; Bélanger, Jacqueline

Qualité de vie au travail et productivité: lexique et bibliographie. [Sainte-Foy, Québec]: ENAP, [1983]. 70 p.; ISBN: 2-92011-12-0. [2885]

Alam, Ann; Creelman, Jan; Parsons, Ruth

Public library service to senior citizens: an annotated bibliography of sources, 1979-1987. London, Ont.: School of Library and Information Science, University of Western

Ontario, 1988. 40 p. [1699]

Albala, Leila

Catalogue of Canadian catalogues: shop at home from hundreds of mail order sources. Chambly, Quebec: ALPEL, c1990. 128 p.: ill.; ISBN: 0-921993-03-X. [2763]

Alberta Band Association. Lending Library

A.B.A. Lending Library band catalogue. [Calgary: The Library, 1986]. 34 p. [0924]

Alberta Education Response Centre

Parent resources inventory. Edmonton: Alberta Education Response Centre, [1989]. 82 p. (in various pagings).; ISBN: 0-7732-0252-8. [3698]

Alberta Education. Planning and Policy Secretariat

Educational quality indicators: annotated bibliography. 2nd ed. Edmonton: Planning and Policy Secretariat, Alberta Education, 1990. vi, 107 p.; ISBN: 0-7732-0299-4. [3708]

Alberta Educational Communications Corporation

Audio-visual catalogue [Alberta Educational Communications Corporation]. Edmonton: Alberta Educational Communications Corporation, 1984-. vol.; ISSN: 0836-8244. [6700]

Video catalogue [Alberta Educational Communications Corporation]. Edmonton: Alberta Educational Communications Corporation, [1982]-. vol.; ISSN: 0827-8814. [6701]

Alberta Genealogical Society. Lethbridge and District Branch

Lethbridge genealogical resources. Lethbridge: Lethbridge and District Branch, Alberta Genealogical Society, 1988. 185 p.; ISBN: 0-919224-79-2. [2066]

Alberta Genealogical Society. Library

Alberta Genealogical Society Library holdings. [Edmonton]: Alberta Genealogical Society, [1989]-. vol.; ISSN: 0848-8762. [2090]

Alberta novelists. [Edmonton]: Alberta Culture, Library Services, 1979. 16 p. [1142]

Alberta Remote Sensing Centre

Specialists involved in remote sensing in Alberta and a bibliography of remote sensing in Alberta. Edmonton: Alberta Environment, 1979. 27, [1] p. [5771]

Alberta Research Council

Publications list [Alberta Research Council]. Edmonton: Alberta Research Council, 1986-. vol.; ISSN: 0833-4218. [6425]

Alberta Teachers' Association. English Council

Canadian books for schools: a centennial listing. Edmonton: English Council and School Library Council of the Alberta Teachers' Association, 1968. 63 p. [1317]

Alberta. Alberta Advanced Education and Manpower. Career Resources Branch

Pre-retirement bibliography: source book. Edmonton: The Branch, 1978. 26 p. [3164]

Alberta. Alberta Career Development and Employment

An annotated bibliography of books on job-search related subjects. Edmonton: Information Development and Marketing Branch, Alberta Career Development and Employment, 1991. 40 p. [2935]

Alberta. Alberta Consumer and Corporate Affairs. Research Section

Annotated bibliography of research papers [Alberta Consumer and Corporate Affairs, Research Section]. [Edmonton]: Alberta Consumer and Corporate Affairs, Management Secretariat, Research Section, 1978. 8, 6, 1 l. [2632]

A bibliography on consumer credit use and regulation. Edmonton: Alberta Consumer and Corporate Affairs. Research Section, 1975. ii, 27 l. [2613]

Alberta. Alberta Culture. Film & Literary Arts

Alberta authors and their books for children and young adults. Edmonton: Alberta Culture, 1984. i, 45 p.: ill. [1357]

Alberta. Alberta Culture. Library

Multicultural resources in the Alberta Culture Library: an annotated bibliography. [Edmonton]: Alberta Culture, 1986. 173 p. [4238]

Alberta. Alberta Education

Publications catalogue [Alberta Education]. Edmonton: Central Support Services, Alberta Education, 1991-. vol.; ISSN: 0846-0183. [6416]

Alberta. Alberta Education. Language Services

Blackfoot language and culture: a selective bibliography of supplementary learning resources (early childhood services-grade 12). Edmonton: Language Services, Alberta Education, 1991. v, 97 p.; ISBN: 0-7732-0501-2. [1491]

Alberta. Alberta Energy

General publications [Alberta Energy, Alberta Forestry]. Edmonton: Alberta Energy, 1987-. vol.; ISSN: 0832-6886. [6417]

Technical publications [Alberta Energy, Alberta Forestry]. Edmonton: Alberta Energy, 1987-. vol.; ISSN: 0832-6894. [6418]

Alberta. Alberta Environment. Communications Branch

Government environmental resource materials guide. 4th ed. Edmonton: Alberta Environment, 1980. iv, 213 p. [5158]

Alberta. Alberta Environment. Research Management Division

List of reports [Alberta Environment, Research Management Division]. [Edmonton]: Research Management Division, [1982]. [62] p. [6338]

Publications catalogue [Alberta Environment, Research Management Division]. [Edmonton]: Research Management Division, Alberta Environment, 1986-. vol.; ISSN: 0833-4706. [6419]

Alberta. Alberta Family and Social Services. Library Services

Audio-visual catalogue [Alberta Family and Social Services]. Edmonton: Library Services, Alberta Family and Social Services, 1990. 69 l. [6688]

Alberta. Alberta Labour. Support Services Division

Publications catalogue: Alberta Labour. Edmonton: Alberta Labour, Support Services Division, 1987-. vol.; ISSN: 0835-1678. [6420]

Alberta. Alberta Municipal Affairs. Planning Support Services Branch

Maps of Alberta municipalities: index. [Edmonton]: Planning Branch, Department of Municipal Affairs, 1977. [123] l.: maps. [6559]

Alberta. Alberta Occupational Health and Safety. Library Services Branch

Health and safety on the job: audio-visual catalogue. Edmonton: The Branch, 1990. 27, xiv, 83 p. [6689]

Alberta. Alberta Social Services and Community Health

Selected list of bibliographies. [S.l.: s.n., 1982]. [32] p. [3233]

Alberta. Alberta Task Force on Urbanization and the Future

Index of urban and regional studies, Province of Alberta, 1950-1974. Edmonton: Alberta Municipal Affairs, 1973-1975. 7 vol. [4341]

Alberta. Bureau of Statistics

Criminal justice statistical development: bibliography. [Edmonton]: Alberta Bureau of Statistics, 1980. ix, 91 p. [2207]

Alberta. Career Development and Employment. Immigration and Settlement Services.

Resource Centre: bibliography of resource materials. [Edmonton]: Alberta Career Development and Employment, Immigration and Settlement Services, [1987]. 38 p. [4240]

Alberta. Consumer Education and Information Resource Centre

Consumer education materials: an annotated list. Rev. ed. [Edmonton]: Alberta Consumer and Corporate Affairs, 1986. 161 p. [2716]

Alberta. Culture, Youth and Recreation. Libraries Division

A slice of Canada: a list of Canadian books of interest to small Alberta public libraries. 2nd ed. Edmonton: Alberta Culture, Youth and Recreation, Libraries Division, 1975. 250 p. [0113]

Alberta. Department of Education

A bibliography of materials for and about native people. Edmonton: Alberta Department of Education, 1970. i, 53 p. [3918]

Alberta. Energy Resources Conservation Board

Catalogue: publications, maps, services [Alberta Energy Resources Conservation Board]. Calgary: Energy Resources Conservation Board, [1987]-. vol.; ISSN: 0844-8523. [6421]

Alberta. Language Services Branch

English as a second language: a selective bibliography of supplementary learning resources. Edmonton: Alberta Education, Language Services Branch, 1988. v, 34 p.; ISBN: 0-7732-0072-X. [3678]

Alberta. Provincial Archives. Historical Resources Library

Alberta's local histories in the Historical Resources Library. 8th ed. [Edmonton]: The Library, 1989. 204 p.; ISSN: 1180-9442. [0545]

Native peoples of Alberta: a bibliographic guide. [Edmonton]: Alberta Culture and Multiculturalism, Historical Resources Division, 1988. 33 p.; ISBN: 0-919411-15-0. [4095]

Alberta. Provincial Film Library

Resource catalogue [Alberta Provincial Film Library]. [Edmonton]: Alberta Public Affairs Bureau, 1983-. vol.; ISSN: 0823-3306. [6699]

Alberta. Public Affairs Bureau

Alberta government publications. Edmonton: Alberta Public Affairs Bureau, 1973-. vol.; ISSN: 0840-4976. [6422]

Alberta government publications quarterly list. [Edmonton]: Alberta Public Affairs Bureau, Publication Services, [1991]-. vol.; ISSN: 1184-9851. [6423]

List of Alberta publications and legislation. [Edmonton]: Alberta Public Affairs Bureau, 1987-. vol.; ISSN: 0837-7375. [6424]

Alberta. Queen's Printer

Catalogue of Alberta government publications. Edmonton: 1955. 2 vol. [6236]

Alberta. Task Force on the Criminal Justice System and Its Impact on the Indian and Metis People of Alberta

Justice on trial: report of the Task Force on the Criminal Justice System and its Impact on the Indian and Metis People of Alberta. Edmonton: The Task Force, 1991. 6 vol.: ill. [2343]

Alderdice, D.F.; Bams, R.A.; Velsen, F.P.J.

Factors affecting deposition, development, and survival of salmonid eggs and alevins: a bibliography, 1965-1975. Nanaimo, B.C.: Pacific Biological Station, Fisheries and Marine Service, Department of Fisheries and the Environment, 1977. 276 p. (Fisheries and Marine Service Technical report ; no. 743; ISSN: 0701-7626) [5412]

Alderman, John K.

Uranium in coal and carbonaceous rocks in the United States and Canada: an annotated bibliography. Morgantown, W.Va.: West Virginia University, 1978. 21 p. [4803]

Alderson Gill & Associates

An annotated bibliography of maintenance and custody literature. [Ottawa]: Department of Justice Canada, Family Law Research, c1988. 99, 112 p.; ISBN: 0-662-55723-9. [2305]

Bibliographie annotée sur la documentation relative à la garde d'enfants et aux pensions alimentaires. [Ottawa]: Ministère de la justice Canada, Recherche en droit de la famille, c1988. 112, 99 p.; ISBN: 0-662-55723-9. [2306]

Alemdag, I.S.; Richardson, James

Annotated bibliography of ENFOR biomass reports 1979-1990/Bibliographie annotée des rapports ENFOR sur la biomasse 1979-1990. Ottawa: Forestry Canada, 1993. viii, 288 p. (Information report / ENFOR Secretariat, Forestry Canada ; ST-X-6); ISBN: 0-660-58853-6. [5021]

Alexander, Anne

Newfoundland offshore oil and gas exploration and development: a bibliography. St. Johns, Nfld.: Memorial University of Newfoundland, Centre for Newfoundland Studies, 1982. 9 p. [4823]

Alexander, Harriet Semmes

English language criticism on the foreign novel: 1965-1975. Athens: Swallow Press; Ohio University Press, c1989. 285 p.; ISBN: 0-8040-0907-4. [1266]

Alexander, Martin E.

Bibliography and a résumé of current studies on fire history. Sault Ste. Marie, Ont.: Great Lakes Forest Research Centre, 1979. 43 p.: map. (Great Lakes Forest Research Centre report ; O-X-304; ISSN: 0704-7797) [4966]

Alexandrin, Barbara; Bothwell, Robert

Bibliography of the material culture of New France. [Ottawa: National Museums of Canada, 1970]. vii, 32 p. (National Museum of Man publications in history ; no. 4) [1965]

Alfred Goldsworthy Bailey: a checklist of his work and related criticism. Fredericton, N.B.: Department of Public Relations and Development, University of New Brunswick, 1978. vii, 31 p. [6820]

Algonquin Regional Library System

The first Americans: an Indian, Eskimo resource list. 4th ed. [Parry Sound, Ont.]: Algonquin Regional Library System, 1979. 73 l. [3999]

AliNiazee, M.T.; Brown, R.D.

"A bibliography of North American cherry fruit flies (Diptera: Tephritidae)." In: *Bulletin of the Entomological Society of America*; Vol. 20, no. 2 (June 1974) p. 93-101.; ISSN: 0013-8754. [5378]

Allaire, Daniel

"La législation déléguée: liste annotée de documents disponibles à la bibliothèque." Dans: *Bulletin: Bibliothèque de l'Assemblée nationale du Québec*; Vol. 7, no 1 (avril 1976) p. 15-25.; ISSN: 0701-6808. [2419]

Allan, Charlotte E.

Bibliography of books and monographs printed and published in Nova Scotia, 1895-1920. Toronto: 1939. [4], 36 l. [0201]

Allan, Norman

"Some random notes on Manitoba architectural bibliography." In: *Bulletin (Society for the Study of Architecture in Canada)*; Vol. 11, no. 2 (June 1986) p. 9-10.; ISSN: 0712-8517. [0779]

Allard, François; Collister, Edward A.

Bibliographie sélective sur la contribution des usagers aux frais médicaux et le ticket modérateur. Québec: Ministère des affaires sociales, Service de l'informathèque, 1981. 14 f. (Série bibliographiques / Ministère des affaires sociales, Service de l'informathèque ; no 3; ISSN: 0713-0740) [5633]

Allard, Jacques

"Où en sont les études sur la littérature québécoise?" Dans: *Revue internationale d'études canadiennes*; No 1-2 (printemps-automne 1990) p. 115-134.; ISSN: 1180-3991. [1280]

Allen, David E.

Business books translated from English: 1950-1965. Reading, Mass.: Addison-Wesley Pub. Co., 1966. xiv, 414 p. [2580]

Allen, Don H.; Willey, R.C.

"Addenda to 'A bibliography of Canadian numismatics'." In: *Canadian Numismatic Journal*; Vol. 5, no. 1 (January 1960) p. 28-32.; ISSN: 0008-4573. [1750]

Allen, Harold Don

Metric update: selected items from a column on metric conversion and metric education. And, Metric bibliography for the Canadian teacher. Truro, N.S.: Nova Scotia Teachers College, [1974]. 9, 4 l. [3475]

Allen, Marie-France

Intervention interculturelle dans les services sociaux et de santé. Québec: Centre de recherche sur les services communautaires, 1993. 115, 16 f.; ISBN: 2-92100-856-4. [3364]

Allen, Patrick

"Confédération canadienne: bibliographie sommaire." Dans: *Revue d'histoire de l'Amérique française*; Vol. 21, no 3a (décembre 1967) p. 697-719.; ISSN: 0035-2357. [1949]

Allen, Robert S.

Loyalist literature: an annotated guide to the writings on the Loyalists of the American Revolution. Toronto: Dundurn Press, 1982. 63 p. (Dundurn Canadian historical document series: Publication ; no. 2); ISBN: 0-919670-61-X. [2016]

Allen, Robert S.; Tobin, Mary A.T.

Les études autochtones au Canada: guide de recherche. 3e éd. Ottawa: Centre de la recherche historique et de l'étude des traités, Direction générale des revendications globales, Affaires indiennes et du Nord canadien, 1989. iii, 197 p. [4104]

Native studies in Canada: a research guide. 3rd ed. Ottawa: Treaties and Historical Research Centre, Comprehensive Claims Branch, Indian and Northern Affairs Canada, 1989. iii, 195 p. [4105]

Allington-Baker, Amanda

Our home and native land: books about Canada's native peoples. Toronto: Canadian Book Information Centre, 1989. 32 p.: ill. [4106]

Allison, L.M.; Keitner, W.J.R.

"Ralph Gustafson: a bibliography in progress, 1929-1972." In: *West Coast Review*; Vol. 9, no. 1 (June 1974) p. 29-38.; ISSN: 0043-311X. [7037]

Allix, Beverley

Annotated bibliography of English for special purposes. Toronto: Newcomer Services Branch, Citizenship Division, Ontario Ministry of Culture and Recreation, 1978. 91 p. [1441]

Alsène, Éric; Hamel, Pierre; Patenaude, Jules

Les politiques urbaines et régionales au Québec: éléments de bibliographie, 1940-1977. Montréal: Faculté de l'aménagement, Université de Montréal, [1980]. 80 p. (Cahier de recherche / Faculté de l'aménagement, Université de Montréal ; URB 01) [4379]

Altfest, Karen C.

"Ethnic studies in Canada." In: *Ethnic and immigration groups: the United States, Canada, and England*. New York: Institute for Research in History: Haworth Press, c1983. P. 71-92.; ISBN: 0-917724-46-1. [4215]

Amaratunga, T.; Balch, N.; O'Dor, R.K.

Proceedings of the Workshop on the squid Illex illecebrosus: Dalhousie University, Halifax, Nova Scotia, May 1978: and a bibliography on the genus Illex. [Halifax, N.S.: Dalhousie University], 1978. 1 vol. (in various pagings). [5418]

Ambeault, Georgia, et al.

Union list of government documents. [S.l.: Sault Area International Library Association], 1972. 1 vol. (in various pagings). [6277]

Ambroise, Antoine; De Billy, Marie-Claude

Les politiques éducatives récentes au Québec: chronologie et bibliographie sélective annotée, 1977-1983. Québec: Université Laval, Département de science politique, 1987. iv, 127 p. (Cahiers du LABRAPS: Série études et documents ; vol. 2; ISSN: 0824-0736); ISBN: 2-89326-008-X. [3663]

American Foundation for the Blind

Periodicals of special interest to blind persons in the United States and Canada. New York: [s.n.], 1960. 48 p. [5869]

American Geophysical Union

Annotated bibliography on hydrology, 1941-1950 (United States and Canada). [Washington: U.S. Government Printing Office, 1952]. 408 p. (Notes on hydrologic activities, Bulletin / U.S. Federal Inter-Agency River Basin Committee, Subcommittee on Hydrology ; no. 5) [5028]

American Society of Genealogists

Genealogical research: methods and sources. Washington: The Society, 1960. viii, 456 p. [1934]

Ames, Michael M.

"A note on the contributions of Wilson Duff to northwest coast ethnology and art." In: *BC Studies*; No. 31 (Autumn 1976) p. 3-11.; ISSN: 0005-2949. [6960]

Amesse, Fernand

Bibliographie sélective sur les transferts internationaux de technologie. Montréal: École des hautes études commerciales, 1981. 43 f. (Cahiers du Centre d'études en administration internationale ; no 81-08; ISSN: 0709-986X) [2668]

Amesse, Fernand, et al.

L'univers des nouvelles technologies: une bibliographie sélective révisée et augmentée. Montréal: École des hautes études commerciales, 1987. 94 f.: ill. (Cahiers du Centre d'études en administration internationale ; no 87-09; ISSN: 0825-5822) [5820]

The world of high technology: a revised and expanded selective bibliography. Montreal: École des hautes études commerciales, 1987. 94 l.: ill. (Cahiers du Centre d'études en administration internationale ; no 87-09; ISSN: 0825-5822) [5821]

Amey, L.J.

"The combination school and public library: a bibliography with special emphasis on the Canadian experience." In: *Canadian Library Journal*; Vol. 33, no. 3 (June 1976) p. 263-267.; ISSN: 0008-4352. [1615]

Ami, Henri Marc

"Bibliography of Canadian geology and palaeontology." In: *Proceedings and Transactions of the Royal Society of Canada*; Series 2, vol. 7, section 4 (1901)-series 3, vol. 3, section 4 (1909) [4736]

"Bibliography of Dr. George M. Dawson." In: *George Mercer Dawson*, by B.J. Harrington. Minneapolis: Geological Pub. Co., [1901]. P. 67-86. [6943]

"Bibliography of Dr. George M. Dawson." In: *Proceedings and Transactions of the Royal Society of Canada*; Series 2, vol. 8, section 4 (1902) p. 192-201.; ISSN: 0316-4616. [6946]

"Bibliography of Dr. George M. Dawson." In: *American Geologist*; Vol. 28 (1901) p. 76-86.; ISSN: 0190-518X. [6944]

"Bibliography of Sir John William Dawson." In: *Ottawa Naturalist*; Vol. 13, no. 12 (March 1900) p. 279-294.; ISSN: 0316-4411. [6947]

"Bibliography of Sir John William Dawson." In: *Proceedings and Transactions of the Royal Society of Canada*; Series 2, vol. 7, section 4 (1901) p. 15-44.; ISSN: 0316-4616. [6951]

Biographical sketch of George Mercer Dawson. Ottawa: Ottawa Printing Co., 1901. 31 p. [6945]

List of contributions to geology, palaeontology, &c., by Mr. H.M. Ami, of the Geological Survey of Canada, Ottawa, from 1882 to 1901. [Montreal: Printed by the Canada Engraving & Lithographing Co., 1901]. 15 l. [6800]

"Memoir of Sir J. William Dawson: bibliography." In: *Geological Society of America Bulletin*; Vol. 11 (1900) p. 557-580.; ISSN: 0016-7606. [6948]

Progress of geological work in Canada during 1898. Ottawa: [s.n.], 1899. 4 p. [4730]

Progress of geological work in Canada during 1899. [Ottawa: s.n.], 1900. 15 p. [4732]

"Progress of geological work in Canada during 1898." In: *Ottawa Naturalist*; Vol. 13, no. 2 (May 1899) p. 52-55.; ISSN: 0316-4411. [4729]

"Progress of geological work in Canada during 1899." *Canadian Record of Science*; Vol. 8, no. 4 (July 1900) p. 232-246.; ISSN: 0383-0373. [4731]

"Sir John William Dawson. A brief biographical sketch." In: *American Geologist*; Vol. 26 (July 1900) p. 1-48.; ISSN: 0190-518X. [6949]

Sir John William Dawson. A brief biographical sketch. [Minneapolis: s.n., 1900]. 57 p. [6950]

Sketch of the life and work of the late Dr. Alfred R.C. Selwyn ... Director of the Geological Survey of Canada from 1869 to 1894. [Minneapolis, Minn.: s.n., 1903]. 24 p., 1 l. of pl.: port. [7302]

"Sketch of the life and work of the late Dr. Alfred R.C. Selwyn ... Director of the Geological Survey of Canada from 1869 to 1894." In: *American Geologist*; Vol. 31 (January 1903) p. 1-21.; ISSN: 0190-518X. [7303]

"Sketch of the life of Dr. A.R.C. Selwyn, C.M.G.: bibliography." In: *Proceedings and Transactions of the Royal Society of Canada*; Series 2, vol. 10, section 4 (1904) p. 173-205.; ISSN: 0316-4616. [7304]

Amor, Norman L.

Beyond the Arctic Circle: materials on Arctic explorations and travels since 1750 in the Special Collections and University Archives Division of the University of British Columbia Library. Vancouver: University of British Columbia Library, 1992. 36 p.: ill., maps. (Occasional publication / University of British Columbia Library, Special Collections and University Archives Division ; no. 1); ISBN: 0-88865-196-1. [0661]

Amprimoz, Alexandre L.

"Bibliographie de la poésie franco-canadienne de l'Ouest." Dans: *Cefco: Centre d'études franco-canadiennes de l'Ouest*; No 2 (mai 1979) p. 9-14.; ISSN: 0226-0670. [1143]

"French poets of western Canada: a selected checklist." In: *Essays on Canadian Writing*; Nos. 18/19 (Summer/Fall 1980) p. 320-321.; ISSN: 0316-0300. [1161]

Amtmann, Bernard

A bibliography of Canadian children's books and books for young people, 1841-1867/Livres de l'enfance & livres de la jeunesse au Canada, 1841-1867. Montréal: B. Amtmann, 1977. viii, 124 p. [1332]

A catalogue of the catalogues issued by Bernard Amtmann since 1948. Montreal: 1964. 20 p. [0074]

Contributions to a dictionary of Canadian pseudonyms and anonymous works relating to Canada/Contributions à un dictionnaire des pseudonymes canadiens et des ouvrages anonymes relatifs au Canada. Montreal: B. Amtmann, 1973. 144 p. [0105]

Contributions to a short-title catalogue of Canadiana. Montreal: [s.n.], 1971-1972. 22 parts. [0100]

Early Canadian children's books, 1763-1840: a bibliographical investigation into the nature and extent of early Canadian children's books and books for young people/ Livres de l'enfance & livres de la jeunesse au Canada, 1763-1840: étude bibliographique. Montréal: B. Amtmann, 1976. xv, 150 p.: facsim. [1328]

Amyot, Pierre; Pineau, Gaston

Éducation permanente: répertoire bibliographique, 1957-1972. Montréal: Université de Montréal, Service d'éducation permanente, Division de la recherche, 1974. v, 245 p. [3476]

Anctil, Pierre

"Bibliographie commentée sur les Franco-américains de la nouvelle-angleterre." Dans: *Cahiers de géographie de Québec*; Vol. 23, no 58 (avril 1979) p. 179-181.; ISSN: 0007-9766. [2001]

A Franco-American bibliography: New England. Bedford, N.H.: National Materials Development Center, 1979. ix, 137 p.: ill., map. [1144]

Andersen, Lorrie

"Resources on AIDS: the acquisition of instructional materials for schools." In: *School Libraries in Canada*; Vol. 8, no. 2 (Winter 1988) p. 25-28.; ISSN: 0227-3780. [3679]

Andersen, Marguerite

"Bibliography [women and language]." In: *Resources for Feminist Research*; Vol. 13, no. 3 (November 1984) p. 72-78.; ISSN: 0707-8412. [3826]

"Le Québec: féminisme contemporain et écrits de femmes (1970-1983): une bibliographie pilote." Dans: *Documentation sur la recherche féministe*; Vol. 12, no 4 (décembre/janvier 1983-1984) p. 18-28.; ISSN: 0707-8412. [3827]

Anderson, Alan B.

German, Mennonite and Hutterite communities in Saskatchewan: an inventory of sources. Saskatoon: Saskatchewan German Council, 1988. 17, 11, 4 p. [1565]

Guide to bibliographic sources in francophone communities in Saskatchewan/Guide des sources bibliographiques des communautés francophones de la Saskatchewan. Saskatoon: Research Unit for French-Canadian Studies, University of Saskatchewan, 1987. 10 p. (Research report / Research Unit for French-Canadian Studies, University of Saskatchewan ; no. 13) [0543]

Anderson, Beryl L.

Basic cataloguing tools for use in Canadian libraries. Ottawa: Canadian Library Association, 1968. 28 l. (Occasional paper / Canadian Library Association ; no. 59) [1589]

Anderson, Daphne; Connor, Mary

Women and the Christian faith: a selected bibliography and resource catalogue. [Vancouver]: Division of Mission in Canada, United Church of Canada, [1979]. 51 p. [3787]

Anderson, Dennis; Cullen, Carman

Energy research from a consumer perspective: an annotated bibliography. Ottawa: Consumer Research and Evaluation Branch, Consumer and Corporate Affairs Canada, 1979. 191 p.; ISBN: 0-662-10514-1. [2644]

Perspective du consommateur sur la recherche en matière d'énergie: une bibliographie annotée. Ottawa: Direction de l'évaluation et de la recherche en consommation, Consommation et corporations Canada, 1979. 191 p.; ISBN: 0-662-90307-2. [2645]

Anderson, Dennis; McDougall, Gordon H.G.

Consumer energy research: an annotated bibliography/ Recherche sur la consommation d'énergie: une bibliographie annotée. Ottawa: Policy Research, Analysis and Liaison Directorate, Policy Coordination Bureau, Consumer and Corporate Affairs Canada, c1984. 329 p.; ISBN: 0-662-62743-7. [5209]

Anderson, E. William; Harris, Robert W.

References on grazing resources and associated elements of the Pacific Northwest range ecosystems (Oregon, Washington, British Columbia). [S.l.: Pacific Northwest Section, Society for Range Management, 1973. 103 p. [4657]

Anderson, Ethel E.

Annotated A.B.E. bibliography. Toronto: Movement for Canadian Literacy, 1978. ii, 106 p.: graph.; ISBN: 0-920588-01-8. [3530]

Anderson, Grace M.

A selected bibliography on Portuguese immigration. Toronto: [s.n.], 1969. iv, 5 p. [4141]

Anderson, John C.; Moore, Larry F.

Volunteerism and volunteer administration: an annotated bibliography. [Vancouver, B.C.]: Voluntary Action Resource Centre, Volunteer Bureau of Greater Vancouver, [1974]. iv, 111 p. [3120]

Anderson, John Parker

"Bibliography [Thomas Chandler Haliburton]." In: Haliburton: a centenary chaplet. Toronto: Published for the Haliburton Club, King's College, Windsor, N.S. [by] W. Briggs, 1897. P. 107-116. [7040]

Anderson, Roselyn

Employee benefits: a selected bibliography. Toronto: Ontario Ministry of Labour, Research Library, 1977. 24 p. (Bibliography series / Ontario Ministry of Labour, Research Library ; no. 7) [2835]

Anderson, William

Bibliography of world literature on the strawberry, 1920-1962. [S.l.: s.n.], 1966. 2 vol. [4647]

Anderson, Wolseley W.

Caribbean orientations: a bibliography of resource material on the Caribbean experience in Canada. Toronto: Organization for Caribbean Canadian Initiatives and Williams-Wallace Publishers, 1985. xi, 238 p.; ISBN: 0-88795-037-X. [4230]

Andoniadis, Katherine L.

Canadian art publications: an annotated bibliography for the secondary school. [Victoria, B.C.]: Canadian Society for Education through Art, 1978. vi, 138 p. (Canadian Society for Education through Art Booklet ; no. 4) [0689]

Andrew, Caroline

"Espace et politique: le cas de Montréal: synthèse bibliographique." Dans: Revue canadienne de science politique; Vol. 12, no 2 (juin 1979) p. 369-383.; ISSN: 0008-4239. [2443]

"Laughing together: women's studies in Canada." In: International Journal of Canadian Studies; No. 1-2 (Spring-Fall 1990) p. 134-148.; ISSN: 1180-3991. [3874]

Andrews, Christina Ann

The immigrant experience in Canadian children's literature 1976 to 1985: an annotated bibliography. Edmonton: [s.n.], 1986. 65 l. [1368]

Andrews, Martha

"Computerized information retrieval and bibliographic control of the polar and-or cold regions literature: a review." In: Bulletin (Special Libraries Association, Geography and Map Division); No. 159 (March 1990) p. 21-42.; ISSN: 0036-1607. [0660]

List of publications, 1968-1985: Institute of Arctic and Alpine Research. Boulder, Colo.: Institute of Arctic and Alpine Research, University of Colorado, 1986. iv, 97 p. (Institute of Arctic and Alpine Research Occasional paper ; no. 42; ISSN: 0069-6145) [0651]

Andrews, Martha; Andrews, John T.

Baffin Island Quaternary environments: an annotated bibliography. Boulder, Colo.: Institute of Arctic and Alpine Research, University of Colorado, 1980. xi, 123 p.: maps. [4813]

"Bibliography of Baffin Island environments over the last 1000 years." In: Thule Eskimo culture: an anthropological perspective, edited by Allan P. McCartney. Ottawa: National Museums of Canada, 1979. P. 555-569. (Archaeological Survey of Canada Paper ; no. 88) [5142]

Andrews, Thomas A.

"Selected bibliography of native resource management systems and native knowledge of the environment." In: Traditional knowledge and renewable resource management in northern regions, edited by Milton M.R. Freeman and Ludwig N. Carbyn. Edmonton: Boreal Institute for Northern Studies, University of Alberta, 1988. P. 105-124. (Boreal Institute for Northern Studies Occasional paper ; no. 23); ISBN: 0-919058-68-X. [5257]

Angers, Majëlla

Liste de publications reliées aux 63 principales agglomérations du Québec. [Québec: Ministère des affaires municipales, 1975]. 63 p. (Collection du ministère des affaires municipales) [4342]

Anglin, Lise

Cocaine: a selection of annotated papers from 1880 to 1984. Toronto: Addiction Research Foundation of Ontario, c1985. xxvi, 223 p. (Bibliographic series / Addiction Research Foundation of Ontario ; no. 19; ISSN: 0065-1885); ISBN: 0-88868-114-3. [5667]

Anisef, Paul

L'accessibilité à l'enseignement postsecondaire au Canada: recension des ouvrages. Ottawa: Direction générale de l'aide à l'éducation, Secrétariat d'État du Canada, c1985. x, 267 p.; ISBN: 0-662-93490-5. [3631]

Accessibility to postsecondary education in Canada: a review of the literature. Ottawa: Education Support Branch, Department of the Secretary of State of Canada, 1985. x, 243 p.: ill.; ISBN: 0-662-14410-4. [3632]

An annotated bibliography of CED resources. Vancouver: Westcoast Development Group, 1991. 75 p.; ISBN: 0-921424-06-X. [4436]

An annotated bibliography of literature in the field of energy-efficient construction. [Toronto]: Canadian Home Builders' Association, 1985. 45 p. [5802]

Annotated bibliography of publications based on research supported by the Northern Scientific Training Program/ Bibliographie annotée des publications fondées sur des recherches par le Programme de formation scientifique dans le Nord. Ottawa: Northern Affairs Program, Office of the Northern Research and Science Advisor, 1985-. vol.; ISSN: 0837-3019. [4635]

Annotated bibliography of selected documents pertaining to water allocation and utilization in the Saskatchewan River Basin. [S.l.: s.n.], 1961. 82 p. [5032]

Annotated bibliography of the official languages of Canada/ Bibliographie analytique des langues officielles au Canada. [Ottawa]: Office of the Commissioner of Official Languages, [1991]. 53 p. [1492]

"Annotated bibliography of works written on the Supreme Court of Canada." In: *Osgoode Hall Law Journal*; Vol. 3, no. 1 (April 1964) p. 173-177.; ISSN: 0030-6185. [2109]

Annotated bibliography on reproductive health hazards in the workplace in Canada. [Ottawa]: Women's Bureau, Labour Canada, c1988. 74 p.; ISBN: 0-662-16236-6. [5676]

An annotated list of books about Indians for grades 9 to 13. Brantford: Woodland Indian Cultural Educational Centre, 1979. 67 l. [4000]

An annotated list of selected library materials for early French immersion, kindergarten – grade 7. Richmond, B.C.: Modern Languages Services Branch, Ministry of Education, 1982. vii, 312 p.; ISBN: 0-7719-9124-X. [3600]

An annotated list of selected library materials for early French immersion and programme-cadre: kindergarten/ Liste annotée de matériel bibliographique pour les programmes d'immersion et programme-cadre: maternelle. [Victoria, B.C.]: Modern Languages Services Branch, Ministry of Education, 1986. vi, 53 p. [3647]

An annotated list of selected library materials for late French immersion, grades 6 and 7. 2nd ed. Richmond, B.C.: Modern Languages Services Branch, Ministry of Education, 1982. iv, 175 l.; ISBN: 0-7719-9010-3. [3601]

Annuaire du Canada. Ottawa: Statistique Canada, 1906-. vol.; ISSN: 0316-8557. [6426]

Annual bibliography of the history of the printed book and libraries. The Hague: Martinus Nijhoff, 1970-. vol.; ISSN: 0303-5964. [1737]

Anschutz, Martha

A preliminary list of writings on Canadian archives and records management. Montreal: University Archives, McGill University, 1970. 27 l. [1591]

Anthony, Geraldine; Usmiani, Tina

"A bibliography of English Canadian drama written by women." In: *World Literature Written in English*; Vol. 17, no. 1 (April 1978) p. 120-143.; ISSN: 0093-1705. [1125]

Anthony, Linda

Heritage languages: a bibliography. Regina: Multicultural Council of Saskatchewan, c1983. 16 p. [1459]

Anthropological bibliography of the eastern seaboard. New Haven: Eastern States Archeological Federation, 1947-1963. 2 vol. [4538]

Appleby, J.A.; Scarratt, D.J.

Physical effects of suspended solids on marine and estuarine fish and shellfish, with special reference to ocean dumping: a literature review. Halifax: Fisheries and Oceans Canada, 1989. v, 33 p. (Canadian technical report of fisheries and aquatic sciences ; no. 1681; ISSN: 0706-6457) [5266]

Aquan-Yuen, R. Margaret

Homelessness in Canada: a selective bibliography. Waterloo, Ont.: University of Waterloo Library, 1991. vii, 29 p.; ISBN: 0-920834-15-9. [3348]

Arai, Mary Needler

"Publications by Edith and-or Cyril Berkeley." In: *Journal of the Fisheries Research Board of Canada*; Vol. 28, no. 10 (October 1971) p. 1365-1372.; ISSN: 0008-2686. [6837]

Archambault, Guy

Le perfectionnement des managers: une revue de la littérature: les années 80. Montréal: École des hautes études commerciales, 1991. 32 f. (Cahier de recherche / École des hautes études commerciales ; no 92-04; ISSN: 0846-0647) [2773]

Archambault, Michèle

"Les instruments de travail." Dans: *Études françaises*; Vol. 13, no 3-4 (octobre 1977) p. 191-218.; ISSN: 0014-2085. [1106]

Archibald, R.C.

"Bibliography of the life and works of Simon Newcomb." In: *Proceedings and Transactions of the Royal Society of Canada*; Series 2, vol. 10, section 3 (1905) p. 79-109.; ISSN: 0316-4616. [7210]

Archives ordinolingues (Canada)

Dossiers des données sur les loisirs et la récréation. Ottawa: Archives publiques Canada, 1983. vi, 63, 62, vi p.; ISBN: 0-662-52335-0. [1821]

Arctic bibliography. Montreal: McGill-Queen's University Press, 1953-1975. 16 vol.: folded col. maps.; ISSN: 0066-6947. [0627]

Arctic Institute of North America

A Bibliography on winter road construction and related subjects. Montreal: Arctic Institute of North America, 1972. 1 vol. (in various pagings). [4454]

A polar bear bibliography. Washington, D.C.: Arctic Institute of North America, 1966. 25 p. [5341]

A selected reading list of books about the Arctic. Montreal: Arctic Institute of North America, 1965. 6 l. [0612]

Arctic Institute of North America. Library

Catalogue of the Library of the Arctic Institute of North America, Montreal. Boston: G.K. Hall, 1968. 4 vol. [0616]

Arctic Science and Technology Information System

APOA bibliography. Calgary: Arctic Institute of North America, 1982. v, 113 p. (ASTIS occasional publication / Arctic Science and Technology Information System ; no. 1; ISSN: 0225-5170) [5177]

ASTIS bibliography [microform]. Calgary: Arctic Institute of North America, 1979-. microfiches (& 9 l. introductory notes); ISSN: 0226-1685. [0663]

Argue, Robert

Renewable energy resources: a guide to the literature. Ottawa: Renewable Energy Resource Branch, Department of Energy, Mines and Resources, c1978. 29 p.; ISBN: 0-662-00980-0. [4804]

Armstrong, Bryan C.; Cameron, James J.; Smith, Daniel W.

Annotated bibliography on northern environmental engineering. Hull, Quebec: Environment Canada, Environmental Protection Service, 1977-1981. 3 vol. (Economic and technical review reports / Environmental Protection Service; ISSN: 0713-9985); ISBN: 0-662-00558-9 (1974/75); 0-662-10321-1 (1976/77); 0-662-11638-0 (1978/79). [5781]

Armstrong, C.

"Geological and mining index to the Q.C.I." In: *Charlottes*; Vol. 3 (December 1974) p. 56-57.; ISSN: 0316-6724. [4781]

"A selected bibliography of maritime voyages to the Q.C.I." In: *Charlottes*; Vol. 3 (December 1974) p. 56.; ISSN: 0316-6724. [0582]

Armstrong, Douglas; Dworaczek, Marian

The compressed work week: a bibliography. [Toronto]: Ontario Ministry of Labour, Research Library, 1973. 28 p. [2811]

Industrial arbitration in Canada, 1965-1973: a selective bibliography. [Toronto]: Ontario Ministry of Labour, Research Library, 1974. 8 p. [2817]

Plant closures, terminations, and layoffs: a bibliography. Toronto: Ontario Ministry of Labour, Research Library, 1973. 29 l. [2812]

A selective bibliography on human and civil rights. [Toronto]: Ontario Ministry of Labour, Research Library, 1973. 20 l. [2127]

Women: a bibliography of materials held in the Research Library. [Toronto]: Ontario Ministry of Labour, Research Library, 1974. 81 p. [3743]

Armstrong, Douglas; Krestensen, Kristeen

Agricultural labour in Canada and United States: a bibliography. Toronto: Ontario Ministry of Labour, Research Library, 1973. 40 l. [2813]

Armstrong, F.H.; Artibise, Alan F.J.; Baker, Melvin

Bibliography of Canadian urban history. [Monticello, Ill.]: Vance Bibliographies, [1980]. 6 vol. (Public administration series: Bibliography ; P-538-P-543; ISSN: 0193-970X) [4380]

Armstrong, Jim

The Canadian energy bibliography. Toronto: Ontario Library Association, 1980. xiv, 146 p.; ISBN: 0-88969-017-0. [4814]

Armstrong, Judy B.

"Canadian Indians: a selective bibliography." In: *Ontario Library Review*; Vol. 59, no. 1 (March 1975) p. 10-19.; ISSN: 0030-2996. [3961]

Armstrong, Robert H.; Morton, William Markham

Revised annotated bibliography on the Dolly Varden char. Juneau: Alaska Department of Fish and Game, 1969. 108 p. (Research report / Alaska Department of Fish and Game ; no. 7; ISSN: 0732-8486) [5352]

Arnason, David

"Canadian literary periodicals of the nineteenth century." In: *Journal of Canadian Fiction*; Vol. 2, no. 3 (Summer 1973) p. 125-128.; ISSN: 0047-2255. [5909]

Arndt, John

Christianity in Canada: a bibliography of books and articles to 1985. Waterloo, Ont.: Library, Wilfrid Laurier University, 1987. 195 p.: ill. [1563]

Arndt, John; Woeller, Richard

A Laurier bibliography. Waterloo, Ont.: Library, Wilfrid Laurier University, c1973. 24 p.: port.; ISBN: 0-88920-002-5. [7127]

Arndt, Karl J.R.; Olson, May E.

The German language press of the Americas, 1732-1968: history and bibliography/Die deutschsprachige Presse der Amerikas, 1732-1968: Geschichte und Bibliographie. Pullach-München: Verlag Dokumentation, 1973. 2 vol.; ISBN: 3-7940-3421-X. [6017]

Arnell, Susan

A bibliography on ice in navigable waters in Canada, 1945-1964. Ottawa: National Research Council of Canada, 1965. 64 p. [5036]

Arnold, Richard

"Howard O'Hagan: an annotated bibliography." In: *Silence made us visible: Howard O'Hagan and Tay John*, edited by Margery Fee. Toronto: ECW Press, 1992. P. 128-157.; ISBN: 1-55022-167-1. [7216]

Arnup, Katherine; Gottlieb, Amy

"Annotated bibliography [Lesbianism]." In: *Resources for Feminist Research*; Vol. 12, no. 1 (March 1983) p. 90-105.; ISSN: 0707-8412. [3813]

Arora, Ved

Eskimos: a bibliography. Regina: Bibliographic Services Division, Provincial Library, 1972. 50 p. [3931]

Guide to sources of information on Canadian business and industry. Regina: Provincial Library, Bibliographic Services Division, [1972]. 11 p. [2594]

Louis Riel: a bibliography. Rev. 2nd ed. Regina: Published by Saskatchewan Library Association with the co-operation of Saskatchewan Library, 1985. x, 193 p.; ISBN: 0-919059-13-9. [7263]

Royal Canadian Mounted Police: a bibliography. Regina: Bibliographic Services Division, Provincial Library, 1973. iv, 42 p. [2128]

The Saskatchewan bibliography. Regina: Saskatchewan Provincial Library, 1980. ix, 787 p.; ISBN: 0-919059-00-7. [0532]

Arrowsmith, David

Part-time workers: a selected bibliography. Kingston, Ont.: Industrial Relations Centre, Queen's University, 1982. 5 p. (Mimeographed bibliography series / Industrial Relations Centre, Queen's University ; no. 20) [2879]

Productivity trends: bibliography with selected annotations. Kingston, Ont.: Industrial Relations Centre, Queen's University, 1982. 16 p. (Mimeographed bibliography series / Industrial Relations Centre, Queen's University ; no. 21) [2674]

Arsenault, B.

Bibliographie de l'Institut pour la répression des ravageurs forestiers (1977-1985). Sault Ste. Marie, Ont.: Institut pour la répression des ravageurs forestiers, Service canadien des forêts, 1985. ii, 30 p. (Rapport d'information / Institut pour la répression des ravageurs forestiers ; FPM-X-60F;

ISSN: 0827-1119); ISBN: 0-662-93784-8. [6367]

Arsenault, Georges

Bibliographie acadienne: bibliographie sélective et commentée préparée à l'intention des enseignants de l'Ile-du-Prince-Édouard. Summerside, P.E.I.: Société Saint-Thomas d'Aquin, 1980. 26 f. [0243]

Arthur, George W.

A buffalo roundup: a selected bibliography. Regina: Canadian Plains Research Center, c1985. xiv, 153 p. (Canadian plains bibliographies / Canadian Plains Research Center ; 2; ISSN: 0823-8936); ISBN: 0-88977-036-0. [5508]

Arthur, James Richard; Arai, H.P.

Annotated checklist and bibliography of parasites of herring (Clupea harengus L.). Ottawa: Department of Fisheries and Oceans, 1984. iv, 26 p. (Canadian special publication of fisheries and aquatic sciences ; 70; ISSN: 0706-6481); ISBN: 0-660-11659-6. [5491]

Arthurs, H.W.; Bucknall, Brian D.

Bibliographies on the legal profession and legal education in Canada. [Toronto: York University Law Library, 1969]. viii, 95 p. [2115]

Artibise, Alan F.J.

"Canadian urban studies." In: *Communiqué: Canadian Studies*; Vol. 3, no. 3 (April 1977) ; ISSN: 0318-1197. [4363]

Gateway city: documents on the City of Winnipeg, 1873-1913. Winnipeg: Manitoba Record Society, 1979. xiv, 288 p.: ill., maps. (Manitoba Record Society Publications ; vol. 5) [0526]

Interdisciplinary approaches to Canadian society: a guide to the literature. Montreal: Published for the Association for Canadian Studies by McGill-Queen's University Press, 1990. 156 p.; ISBN: 0-7735-0788-4. [0165]

"Pacific views of Canada: Canadian studies research in Asia-Oceania." In: *International Journal of Canadian Studies*; No. 1-2 (Spring-Fall 1990) p. 259-278.; ISSN: 1180-3991. [0166]

Western Canada since 1870: a select bibliography and guide. Vancouver: University of British Columbia Press, [c1978]. xii, 294 p.; ISBN: 0-7748-0090-9. [0522]

Artibise, Alan F.J.; Dahl, Edward H.

Winnipeg in maps, 1816-1972/Winnipeg par les cartes, 1816-1972. Ottawa: National Map Collection, Public Archives of Canada, 1975. 80 p.: maps. [6545]

Artibise, Alan F.J.; Stelter, Gilbert A.

Canada's urban past: a bibliography to 1980 and guide to Canadian urban studies. Vancouver: University of British Columbia Press, [c1981]. xxxix, 396 p.; ISBN: 0-7748-0134-4. [4390]

Arts plastiques de Rimouski (Projet). Section recherche en histoire

Bibliographie annotée d'articles de journaux du comté de Rimouski. Rimouski: [s.n.], 1972. x p., 412 f. [0312]

Répertoire bibliographique du comté de Rimouski. Rimouski: Secrétariat-Jeunesse, 1972. xii, 197 p. [0313]

Ashmore, Peter; Mescaniuk, Sheri

The Fraser River estuary study: an annotated bibliography. Vancouver: Environment Canada, Pacific Yukon Region, 1984. v, 20 l. [5210]

Association canadienne d'éducation de langue française

Liste des publications disponibles sur microfiche [Association canadienne d'éducation de langue française]. Québec: Association canadienne d'éducation de langue française, Service de diffusion de la documentation, 1974. 6 p. [3477]

Association canadienne des éducateurs de langue française. Commission permanente de la langue parlée

Éléments de bibliographie sur la langue parlée. Québec: Association canadienne des éducateurs de langue française, 1963. 11 p. (Publication / Association canadienne des éducateurs de langue française, Commission permanente de la langue parlée ; no 2) [1420]

Association canadienne pour la santé, l'éducation physique et la récréation

Répertoire des documents publiés en français sur les sciences de l'activité physique et les loisirs. Vanier, Ont.: Centre de documentation pour le sport, 1980. 441 p. [1798]

Association des cinéastes amateurs du Québec

Répertoire de films amateurs du Québec. Montréal: Association des cinéastes amateurs du Québec, [1975]. [49] f. [6623]

Association des directeurs de crédit de Montréal

Répertoire des instruments et activités d'éducation sur le crédit à la consommation. Montréal: L'Association, [1978]. 15 p. [3165]

Association des institutions d'enseignement. Commission des bibliothécaires

Répertoire de documents pédagogiques produits dans les établissements-membres de l'A.I.E.S. Montréal: Association des institutions d'enseignement secondaire, 1982-. vol. (f. mobiles). [3732]

Association des littératures canadiennes et québécoise. Comité de recherche francophone

Situation de l'édition et de la recherche: littérature québécoise ou canadienne-française. Ottawa: Centre de recherche en civilisation canadienne-française, Université d'Ottawa, 1978. 182 p. (Documents de travail du Centre de recherche en civilisation canadienne-française ; 18) [1126]

Association des universités et collèges du Canada

Bibliographie choisie et annotée sur l'enseignement postsecondaire au Canada. [Ottawa]: Comité du Colloque national, [1987]. 35, 31 p. [3664]

Association des universités partiellement ou entièrement de langue française

Catalogue de l'exposition des publications périodiques et grandes collections des universités de langue française. Montréal: AUPELF, 1971. 95 p. [5903]

Association du Québec pour les déficients mentaux

Répertoire audio-scripto-visuel en déficience mentale: bibliographie, documentation, ressources. Montréal: Association du Québec pour les déficients mentaux, 1983. 1 vol. (en pagination multiple). [5650]

Association féminine d'éducation et d'action sociale

Pendant que les hommes travaillaient, les femmes elles... : entre 1820 et 1950. Montréal: Guérin, [1978]. 405 p.: ill. [3774]

Association of Book Publishers of British Columbia

Books from British Columbia. Vancouver: The Association, 1976-. vol.; ISSN: 0823-8707. [0606]

Association of Canadian Bookmen

Books about Canada. Toronto: Association of Canadian Bookmen, [1936]. 25 p. [0048]

Association of Canadian Orchestras

Canadian "pops" music project: music for orchestra by Canadian composers/Projet du musique "pop" canadienne: musique pour orchestre de compositeurs canadiens. Toronto: The Association, 1981. [60] p. [0888]

Association of Universities and Colleges of Canada
Selected and annotated bibliography on post-secondary education in Canada. [Ottawa]: National Forum Committee, [1987]. 31, 35 p. [3665]

Association québécoise de gérontologie
Répertoire des recherches gérontologiques publiées ou en cours (1977-1982). [Montréal]: L'Association, 1984. ii, 33 l. [5657]

Association québécoise pour l'étude de l'imprimé. Comité de bibliographie
Bibliographie des études québécoises sur l'imprimé, 1970-1987. Montréal: Bibliothèque nationale du Québec, 1991. 124 p.: ill.; ISBN: 2-921241-00-5. [1722]

Astbury, Effie C.
Casey A. Wood (1856-1942): a bio-bibliography. Montreal: Graduate School of Library Science, McGill University, 1981. vi, 66 p. (McGill University Graduate School of Library Science Occasional papers ; 7) [7372]

Asted. Comité du droit d'auteur
Bibliographie de langue française sur le droit d'auteur. Montréal: Association pour l'avancement des sciences et des techniques de la documentation, 1978. 13 f. [2177]

ASTED. Congrès (1979: Montréal, Québec)
Les tendances actuelles de la littérature de jeunesse en langue française: bibliographies d'ouvrages pour la jeunesse. Montréal: Secrétariat de l'ASTED, 1980. 50 p.; ISBN: 2-89055-008-7. [1341]

Atkinson, H.J.
A bibliography of Canadian soil science. [Ottawa]: Research Branch, Canada Department of Agriculture, 1971. 303 p. (Canada Department of Agriculture Research Branch Publication ; 1452) [4650]

Atlantic book choice: recommended Canadian and regional titles for a junior-senior high school library collection. Halifax, N.S.: Canadian Learning Materials Centre, 1984. vi, 235 p. (Model Library Project / Canadian Learning Materials Centre ; vol. 2) [0144]

Atlantic provinces checklist: a guide to current information in books, pamphlets, magazine articles and documentary films relating to the four Atlantic Provinces: New Brunswick, Newfoundland, Nova Scotia, Prince Edward Island. Halifax, N.S.: Atlantic Provinces Library Association, 1958-1966; 1974. [0214]

Atlantic Provinces Economic Council
Bibliography of research projects [Atlantic Provinces Economic Council]. Fredericton, N.B.: Atlantic Provinces Research Board, 1965. iii, 102 l. [2579]

Atlantic Resource Planners
Annotated bibliography of Kouchibouguac National Park [microform]. Fredericton, N.B.: [s.n.], 1971. 2 microfiches (86 fr.). [2975]

Atlantic salmon references. Halifax: Maritimes Regional Library, Fisheries Service, 1971-1974. 2 vol. [5379]

"Atlantic soundings: a checklist of recent literary publications of Atlantic Canada." In: *Fiddlehead*; No. 135 (January 1983)-no. 159 (Spring 1989) [1267]

Atnikov, Pam, et al.
Out from the shadows: a bibliography of the history of women in Manitoba. [Winnipeg]: Manitoba Human Rights Commission, 1975. 64 p. [3752]

Atomic Energy of Canada Limited
List of publications [AECL]/Liste des publications [EACL]. Chalk River, Ont.: Atomic Energy of Canada Limited, 1987-

. vol.; ISSN: 0571-8104. [5854]

Atomic Energy of Canada Limited. Technical Information Services Branch
Radioactive waste management in Canada: AECL research publications and other literature, 1953-1990/Gestion des déchets nucléaires au Canada: publications d'EACL recherche et autres documents, 1953-1990. Chalk River, Ont.: Chalk River Laboratories, 1990. 217 p.; ISSN: 0067-0367. [5273]

Atton, F.M.; Johnson, Ronald P.; Smith, N.W.
Bibliography of limnology and aquatic fauna and flora of Saskatchewan. Regina: Saskatchewan Department of Tourism and Renewable Resources, 1974. vi, 34 p. (Fisheries report / Saskatchewan Department of Tourism and Renewable Resources ; no. 10) [5084]

Aubé, Pierre-Yvan
Bibliographie d'histoire régionale. Drummondville: P.–Y. Aubé, 1978. 118 f. [0351]

Aubin, Paul; Côté, Louis-Marie
Bibliographie de l'histoire du Québec et du Canada, 1946-1965/Bibliography of the history of Quebec and Canada, 1946-1965. Québec: Institut québécois de recherche sur la culture, 1987. 2 vol.; ISBN: 2-89224-098-0. [2058]
Bibliographie de l'histoire du Québec et du Canada, 1976-1980/Bibliography of the history of Quebec and Canada, 1976-1980. [Québec]: Institut québécois de recherche sur la culture, 1985. 2 vol.; ISBN: 2-89224-055-7. [2044]
Bibliographie de l'histoire du Québec et du Canada, 1981-1985/Bibliography of the history of Quebec and Canada, 1981-1985. Québec: Institut québécois de recherche sur la culture, 1990. 2 vol.; ISBN: 2-89224-142-1. [2080]

Aubin, Paul; Linteau, Paul-André
Bibliographie de l'histoire du Québec et du Canada, 1966-1975. Québec: Institut québécois de recherche sur la culture, 1981. 2 vol.; ISBN: 2-89224-003-4. [2012]
"Bibliographie d'histoire de l'Amérique française (publications récentes)." Dans: *Revue d'histoire de l'Amérique française*; Vol. 21, no 1 (juin 1967)-vol. 46, no 2 (automne 1992). [2086]

Aubrey, Irene E.
Animal world in Canadian books for children and young people: list/Le monde animal dans les livres de jeunesse canadiens: liste. Ottawa: National Library of Canada, 1983. 24 p.; ISBN: 0-662-52331-8. [1352]
Canadian children's books: a treasury of pictures: list/Livres canadiens d'enfants : un trésor d'images: liste. Ottawa: National Library of Canada, 1976. 18 p. [1329]
Un Choix de livres canadiens pour la jeunesse: supplément. Ottawa: Bibliothèque nationale du Canada, 1977-. vol.: ill.; ISSN: 0715-2604. [1397]
Mystery and adventure in Canadian books for children and young people: list/Romans policiers et histoires d'aventures canadiens pour la jeunesse: liste. Ottawa: National Library of Canada, 1983. 18 p.; ISBN: 0-662-52484-5. [1353]
Notable Canadian children's books: 1980-1984 cumulative edition/Un choix de livres canadiens pour la jeunesse: édition cumulative 1980-1984. Ottawa: National Library of Canada, 1989. 148 p.; ISBN: 0-660-54803-8. [1384]
Notable Canadian children's books: supplement. Ottawa: National Library of Canada, 1977-. vol.: ill.; ISSN: 0715-2604. [1398]
Pictures to share: illustration in Canadian children's books/

Images pour tous: illustration de livres canadiens pour enfants. 2nd ed. Ottawa: National Library of Canada, 1987. 59 p.; ISBN: 0-660-53763-X. [1375]

Sources of French Canadian children's and young people's books: list/Sources d'information sur les livres de jeunesse canadiens-français: liste. Ottawa: National Library of Canada, 1984. 18 p.; ISBN: 0-662-52892-1. [1358]

Sports and games in Canadian children's books: list/Livres canadiens sur les sports et les jeux pour la jeunesse: liste. Ottawa: National Library of Canada, 1982. 6 p.; ISBN: 0-662-51763-6. [1348]

Aubrey, Irene E.; Greig, Peter E.

Canadian children's books for Christmas: a selection of titles/Un choix de livres de jeunesse canadiens pour Noël. Ottawa: Ottawa Book Collectors, 1983. 37 p. [1354]

Audet, Clément; Lacas, Robert

Inventaire des travaux québécois de recherche et développement en énergie dans les universités, les sociétés d'état, les industries manufacturières. Sainte-Foy, Québec: Centre de recherche industrielle du Québec, 1980. 357 p. [4815]

Audet, Pierre H.

The Canadian consumer and the regulatory process: a bibliography/Le consommateur canadien et le pouvoir réglementaire: une bibliographie. Ottawa: Consumer and Corporate Affairs Canada, Library, 1980. 10 l. [2208]

"Competition law and public policy in Canada, 1979-1982: a bibliography/Droit de la concurrence et politique officielle au Canada, 1979-1982: une bibliographie." In: *Canadian Competition Policy Record*; Vol. 4, no. 4 (December 1983) p. 19-34.; ISSN: 0228-1961. [2250]

Audio key: the record, tape & compact disc guide. 3rd ed. Winnipeg: Audio Key Publications, 1987. x, 379 p.; ISSN: 9820-1691. [0927]

Audy, Réginald

Inventaire de documents de base pour les études d'aménagement et d'environnement. Sherbrooke, Québec: Département de géographie, Université de Sherbrooke, 1979. 69 f. (Bulletin de recherche / Université de Sherbrooke, Département de géographie ; no 47; ISSN: 0710-0868) [5143]

Auger, Michèle; Andersen, Heather

Labour force adjustment for the 1990's: selective bibliography/L'adaptation de la main-d'oeuvre pour les années 1990: bibliographie sélective. Ottawa: Employment and Immigration Library, 1992. [6], 52 p. [2937]

Auld, John W.

Canadian housing references, 1975-1977. Monticello, Ill.: Vance Bibliographies, 1978. 182 p. (Public administration series: Bibliography ; P-11; ISSN: 0193-970X) [4367]

Aumont, Gérard

"Bibliographie sur l'enseignement de la géographie." Dans: *Revue canadienne de géographie*; Vol. 4, nos 1-2 (janvier-avril 1950) p. 22-30.; ISSN: 0316-3032. [2954]

Auster, Ethel

Reference sources on Canadian education: an annotated bibliography. Toronto: Ontario Institute for Studies in Education, 1978. vii, 114 p. (Bibliography series / Ontario Institute for Studies in Education ; no. 3); ISBN: 0-7744-0163-X. [3531]

Austin, W.C.; Deutsch, M.M.

Marine biota of the NE Pacific: a bibliography emphasizing systematics and distribution. Cowichan Station, B.C.: Khoyatan Marine Laboratory, 1978. 9, 14, 453, 3, 207 columns (ca. 400 p.). [5419]

Avery, Ruth Butler; Conant, Mary Lou; Weissenborn, Helen F.

Selected annotated bibliography of asbestos resources in the United States and Canada. Washington: United States Government Printing Office, 1958. P. 817-865. (United States Geological Survey Bulletin ; 1019-L) [4753]

Avis, Walter S.; Kinloch, A.M.

Writings on Canadian English, 1792-1975: an annotated bibliography. Toronto: Fitzhenry & Whiteside, [1978]. 153 p.; ISBN: 0-88902-121-X. [1442]

Avison, Margaret

The research compendium: review and abstracts of graduate research, 1942-1962, published in celebration of the fiftieth anniversary of the School of Social Work, University of Toronto. [Toronto]: University of Toronto Press, [c1964]. viii, 276 p. [6080]

B.C. Hydro. Library Services

Bibliography on biological effects of electric and magnetic fields, 1980-1987: literature held in B.C. Hydro Library. Vancouver: Library Services, B.C. Hydro, 1988. 53 p.; ISBN: 0-7726-0779-6. [5829]

B.C. Law Library Foundation

A legal bibliography for lawyers of B.C. 2nd ed. Vancouver: The Foundation, 1983. 1 vol. (loose-leaf). [2251]

Baccanale, Diane

Programme 04: cadre général de l'individualisation de l'enseignement professionnel: bibliographie sur l'élaboration, l'expérimentation et l'évaluation de programmes institutionnels. St-Lambert [Québec]: Commission scolaire régionale de Chambly, Direction des services de recherche et de planification, 1977. 64 f. [3520]

Back, John

Electronic book-detection systems: an annotated bibliography from 1975-1986. Edmonton: [J. Back], 1987. 75 l. [1687]

Backhaus, Christine E.

Royal commissions and commissions of inquiry in Alberta, 1905-1976. Edmonton: Legislature Library, 1977. [37] p. [6306]

Badger, Carole, et al.

Enfin, je lis! Bibliographie sélective pour enfants de 7 à 10 ans. Montréal: Asted, 1978. 72 p.: ill. [1334]

Badone, L.; Spence, N.S.

Physical metallurgy and uses of gold: bibliography for the ten-year period 1950-1959/Métallurgie physique et usages de l'or: bibliographie pour la décade 1950-1959. Ottawa: Mines Branch, 1959. iii, 86 p. (Information circular / Mines Branch ; 116) [4757]

Baglole, Harry

Exploring Island history: a guide to the historical resources of Prince Edward Island. Belfast, P.E.I.: Ragweed Press, 1977. xi, 310 p.; ISBN: 0-920304-00-1. [0226]

Bähr, Dieter

A bibliography of writings on the English language in Canada: from 1857 to 1976. Heidelberg: Winter, 1977. xi, 51 p.; ISBN: 3-533-02565-9. [1437]

Bahr, Howard M.

Disaffiliated man: essays and bibliography on skid row, vagrancy, and outsiders. Toronto: University of Toronto Press, [1970]. xiv, 428 p. [3093]

Bailey, Susan F.

Women and the British Empire: an annotated guide to sources. New York: Garland, 1983. xiii, 185 p. (Garland reference library of social science ; vol. 159); ISBN: 0-8240-9162-0. [3814]

Baillairgé, Frédéric-Alexandre

La littérature au Canada en 1890. Joliette, Québec: s.n., 1891. vii, 352 p. [0019]

Baillie, Murray

The census in Canada. Halifax, N.S.: Patrick Power Library, 1983. ii, 7 p. (Government publications guide ; no. 1) [3042]

Municipal government in metropolitan Halifax: a bibliography. 2nd ed. Halifax, N.S.: Patrick Power Library, Saint Mary's University, 1977. vi, 51 p. [4364]

Statistics published by provincial governments in Canada. Halifax, N.S.: Patrick Power Library, c1982. 7 p. (Documents fact sheet / Patrick Power Library ; no. 3) [3034]

Baird, P.D.

"Expeditions to the Arctic." In: *Beaver*; Outfit 279 (March 1949) p. 44-46; outfit 280 (June 1949) p. 41-44; outfit 280 (September 1949) p. 44-48.; ISSN: 0005-7517. [0609]

Bakan, David; Eisner, Margaret; Needham, Harry G.

Child abuse: a bibliography. Toronto: Canadian Council on Children and Youth, 1976. xxi, 89 p.; ISBN: 0-9690438-6-4. [3141]

Baker, G. Blaine

"A course in Canadian legal history." In: *Now and Then: A Newsletter For Those Interested in History and Law*; Vol. 2, no. 2 (September 1982) p. 56-62.; ISSN: 0229-690X. [2240]

Baker, G. Blaine, et al.

Sources in the Law Library of McGill University for a reconstruction of the legal culture of Quebec, 1760-1890. [Montreal]: Faculty of Law and Montreal Business History Project, McGill University, 1987. ix, 276 p. [2286]

Baker, Gloria

Changing roles: a bibliography of materials reflecting the roles of males and females in society. Vancouver, B.C.: Vancouver School Board, Program Services, 1991. viii, 157 p.; ISBN: 1-55031-318-5. [1389]

Baker, Harold R.; Bantjes, June E.

Education for rural development: an annotated bibliography of selected references, with emphasis on the Prairie region of Canada. Saskatoon: Rural Development Education Program, Extension Division, University of Saskatchewan, 1978. ii, 38 p. (Publication / University of Saskatchewan, Extension Division, Rural Development Education Program ; 388) [3166]

Baker, J.L.; Baskerville, G.L.

Growth and yield of New Brunswick forest species: an annotated bibliography. [Fredericton, N.B.]: Faculty of Forestry, University of New Brunswick, 1985. iii, 371 p. [4981]

Baker, Melvin

Bibliography of Newfoundland history books in print. 6th ed. [St. John's, Nfld.]: Newfoundland Historical Society, c1991. 36 l. [0272]

St. John's bibliography, 1870-1914. [St. John's: Memorial University of Newfoundland], 1974. 6 l. [0215]

Bakker, Peter

"Bibliography of Métis languages." In: *Amsterdam Creole Studies*; Vol. 10, No. 56 (June 1989) p. 41-47. [4107]

Balan, Jars

"A selected bibliography of critical sources on Ukrainian-Canadian literature." In: *Canadian Review of Comparative Literature*; Vol. 16, no. 3/4 (September-December 1989) p.

759-762.; ISSN: 0319-051X. [1268]

Baldwin, Charles Candee

Early maps of Ohio and the West. Cleveland: [s.n.], 1875. 25 p. (Western Reserve and Northern Ohio Historical Society Tract ; no. 25) [6477]

Balikci, Asen

"Bio-bibliography of Diamond Jenness." In: *Anthropologica*; No. 4 (1957) p. 37-46.; ISSN: 0003-5459. [7077]

Ball, John L.

"Theatre in Canada." In: *Canadian Literature*; No. 14 (Autumn 1962) p. 85-100.; ISSN: 0008-4360. [0948]

Ball, John L.; Plant, Richard

A bibliography of Canadian theatre history, 1583-1975. [Toronto: Playwrights Co-op, c1976]. 160 p.: ill.; ISBN: 0-919834-02-7. [0958]

Bibliography of theatre history in Canada: the beginnings through 1984/Bibliographie d'histoire du théâtre au Canada: des débuts-fin 1984. Toronto: ECW Press, 1992. xxii, 445 p.; ISBN: 1-55022-120-5. [0990]

Ballak, A.J.F.

Bibliography of reports produced under the assessment program of the Canada-Ontario Forest Management Subsidiary Agreement, 1978-1986. Sault Ste. Marie, Ont.: Great Lakes Forestry Centre, 1987. 29 p. (Great Lakes Forestry Centre Information report ; O-X-386; ISSN: 0832-7122); ISBN: 0-662-15550-5. [4989]

Ballou, Patricia K.

Women: a bibliography of bibliographies. 2nd ed. Boston, Mass.: G.K. Hall, c1986. xv, 268 p.; ISBN: 0-81618-729-0. [3842]

Banci, Vivian A.

A bibliography on the wolverine Gulo gulo. Victoria: Published by the Ministries of Environment and Forests, 1982. i, 53 p. (Integrated Wildlife Intensive Forestry Research ; 9) [5469]

Bancroft, Bryce

Response of aspen suckering to pre-harvest stem treatments: a literature review. Victoria: Forestry Canada, 1989. vii, 55 p.: ill. (FRDA report / Canada-British Columbia Forest Resource Development Agreement ; 087; ISSN: 0835-0752); ISBN: 0-7726-1013-4. [5004]

Bandy, P.J.

A selection of publications on the native Indians of British Columbia with particular reference to the struggle for native rights. Victoria: Ministry of Environment, 1985. 25 l. [4069]

Banks, Joyce M.

Books in native languages in the rare book collections of the National Library of Canada/Livres en langues autochtones dans les collections de livres rares de la Bibliothèque nationale du Canada. Rev. & enl. ed. Ottawa: National Library of Canada, 1985. [xvii], 190 p.: facsims.; ISBN: 0-660-53030-9. [4070]

Banks, Margaret A.

"An annotated bibliography of statutes and related publications: Upper Canada, the Province of Canada, and Ontario 1792-1980." In: *Essays in the history of Canadian law*, edited by David H. Flaherty. Toronto: Published for the Osgoode Society by the University of Toronto Press, 1981. P. 358-404.; ISBN: 0-8020-3382-2. [2226]

Bannatyne, Barry B.

Bibliography of geology, palaeontology, industrial minerals, and fuels in the post-Cambrian regions of Manitoba, 1958 to 1965. Winnipeg: Province of Manitoba, Department of Mines and Natural Resources, Mines Branch, 1966. vii, 37 p. (Mines Branch publication / Province of Manitoba, Department of Mines and Natural Resources ; 66-1) [4766]

Bannatyne, Barry B.; Zoltai, Stephen C.; Tamplin, Morgan J.
Annotated bibliography of the Quaternary in Manitoba and the adjacent Lake Agassiz region (including archaeology of Manitoba). Winnipeg: Province of Manitoba, Department of Mines and Natural Resources, Geological Division, 1970. vi, 142 p. (Geological Paper / Province of Manitoba, Department of Mines and Natural Resources, Geological Division ; 2/70) [4774]

Baragar, W.R.A.
National report for Canada on volcanology. Ottawa: Energy, Mines and Resources Canada, 1975. 12 p. (Geological Survey of Canada Paper ; 75-37; ISSN: 0068-7650) [4786]

Baras, Étienne
A bibliography of underwater telemetry, 1956-1990. Ottawa: Department of Fisheries and Oceans, Communications Directorate, 1991. iv, 55 p. (Canadian technical report of fisheries and aquatic sciences ; no. 1819; ISSN: 0706-6457) [5845]

Barbeau, Victor
La Société des écrivains canadiens: ses règlements, son action, bio-bibliographie de ses membres. Montréal: Éditions de la Société des écrivains canadiens, 1944. 117 p. [1005]

Barbeau, Victor; Fortier, André
Dictionnaire bibliographique du Canada français. Montréal: Académie canadienne-française, 1974. 246 p.; ISBN: 0-969008-14. [0326]

Barbeau, Victor; Rémillard, Juliette; Dionne, Madeleine
L'oeuvre du chanoine Lionel Groulx: témoignages, bio-bibliographie. Montréal: Académie canadienne-française, 1964. 197 p.: ill. [7030]

Barbin, René
Bibliographie de pédagogie religieuse: introductions et commentaires. Montréal: Éditions Bellarmin, 1964. 275 p. [3386]

Bard, Thérèse
Techniques infirmières. Montréal: Centrale des bibliothèques, Centre de la bibliographie, 1974. 202 p. (Cahiers de bibliographie / Centrale des bibliothèques, Centre de la bibliographie ; no 3; ISSN: 0383-4344); ISBN: 0-88523-005-1. [5589]

Bard, Thérèse, et al.
Informatique: [bibliographie de base]. 3e éd. rev. et mise à jour. Montréal: Centre de la bibliographie, Centrale des bibliothèques, 1973. 147 p. (Cahiers de bibliographie / Centrale des bibliothèques, Centre de la bibliographie ; no 1; ISSN: 0383-4344); ISBN: 0-88523-002-7. [1598]

Barker, Gordon; Beaudry, Richard
Maintenir, rompre ou ... faire l'unité canadienne? Une bibliographie sur les aspects économiques de la Confédération. Ottawa: Conseil économique du Canada, 1977. iii, 130 p. (Conseil économique du Canada Document ; no 99); ISBN: 0-662-01291-7. [2622]

Barker, John
"Bibliography of missionary activities and religious change in northwest coast societies." In: Northwest Anthropological Research Notes; Vol. 22, no. 1 (Spring 1988) p. 13-57.; ISSN: 0029-3296. [4096]

Barker, Maurice
"L'adolescent normal: une revue de la littérature récente pertinente à l'expérience de l'adolescent québécois." Dans: Union médicale du Canada; Vol. 106, no 9 (septembre 1977) p. 1237-1242.; ISSN: 0041-6959. [3151]

Barkley, Murray
"Some recent publications relating to Loyalists." In: Loyalist Gazette; Vol. 17, no. 2 (Autumn 1979) p. 12; vol. 18, no. 1 (Spring 1980) p. 12; vol. 18, no. 2 (Autumn 1980) p. 12-13.; ISSN: 0047-5149. [2005]

Barlow, D.P.
Tsunami: annotated bibliography. Victoria: Province of British Columbia, Floodplain Management Branch, 1992. 28 p.; ISBN: 0-7726-1644-2. [5294]

Barnabé, Clermont
Personnel management: a bibliography/Gestion du personnel: une bibliographie. [LaSalle, Québec]: Gesper, Service des éditions, 1982. 194 p.; ISBN: 2-9800030-0-X. [2675]

Barnard, Henry G.
"Victor Witter Turner: a bibliography (1952-1975)." In: Anthropologica; Vol. 27, nos. 1-2 (1985) p. 207-233.; ISSN: 0003-5459. [7342]

Barnes, David H.
A preliminary annotated bibliography of L'Anse aux Meadows National Historic Park. Ottawa: Department of Indian Affairs and Northern Development, National Parks Branch, 1974. 65 l. [2999]

Barnes, Eleanor; Fisher, Mary
Beer and wine sales: different points of view: a selected bibliography. Toronto: Ontario Legislative Library, Research and Information Services, [1986]. 14 l. (Bibliographies and lists. New series / Ontario Legislative Library, Research and Information Services ; no. 14; ISSN: 0833-2150) [2717]

Barnes, Eleanor; Juozapavicius, Danguole
Select committees of the Legislative Assembly of Ontario, 1867-1978. Toronto: Legislative Library, Research and Information Services, 1983. x, 88 p.; ISBN: 0-7743-8080-2. [6354]

Barnes, John
"Canadian sports torts: a bibliographical survey." In: Canadian Cases on the Law of Torts; Vol. 8 (1979) p. 198-206.; ISSN: 0701-1733. [2188]

Barnes, T.H.; Price, S.F.
Drug use and driving: a bibliography of the scientific literature on the effects of drugs other than ethanol on driving or simulated driving of automobiles, piloting or simulated piloting of aircraft, and driving-related mental and motor performance. Toronto: Addiction Research Foundation of Ontario, 1974. xvii, 106 p. (Bibliographic series / Addiction Research Foundation of Ontario ; no. 7; ISSN: 0065-1885) [5590]

Barnett, Don C.; Dyer, Aldrich J.
"Research on native peoples at the University of Saskatchewan." In: Canadian Journal of Native Education; Vol. 10, no. 4 (Summer 1983) p. 12-22.; ISSN: 0710-1481. [6163]
Research related to native peoples at the University of Saskatchewan, 1912-1983. [Regina: University of Saskatchewan], 1983. vi, 163 p. [4043]

Barnett, Gregory; Perell, Paul

Selected bibliography on sale of goods (other than warranties) and selected aspects of general contract law, together with supplement. [Toronto]: Ontario Law Reform Commission, 1974. 29, ii, 24 l. (Ontario Law Reform Commission Research paper ; no. I.5) [2136]

Barnett, Le Roy

Shipping literature of the Great Lakes: a catalog of company publications, 1852-1990. East Lansing: Michigan State University Press, 1992. ix, 165 p.: ill., maps.; ISBN: 0-87013-317-9. [4519]

Barney, Robert Knight

The history of sport and physical education: a source bibliography. [London, Ont.]: D.B. Weldon Library, University of Western Ontario, 1979. 57 p.; ISBN: 0-7714-0098-5. [1789]

Barnstead, Winifred G.

"University of Toronto Library School bibliographies 1928-1948." In: *Ontario Library Review*; Vol. 32, no. 3 (August 1948) p. 230-240.; ISSN: 0030-2996. [0056]

Barnwell, Stephen

"Post-graduate theses in Canadian literature: English and English-French comparative." In: *Journal of Canadian Fiction*; Vol. 2, no. 2 (Spring 1973) p. 78-82; vol. 3, no. 2 (1974) p. 87-92;, no. 16 (1976) p. 144-157.; ISSN: 0047-2255. [6142]

Barr, Elinor

Annotated bibliography of English-language books and articles relating to the Swedish experience in Canada. Växjö [Sweden]: Swedish Emigrant Institute; Thunder Bay, Ont.: Singing Shield Productions [distributor], 1991. 79 p.: port. (Proceedings from the Swedish Emigrant Institute ; 4; ISSN: 0283-4065); ISBN: 0-96917-173-0. [4281]

Northwestern Ontario books: a bibliography: alphabetical by title, 1980s. [Thunder Bay, Ont.: Ontario Library Service Nipigon], 1987. 31 p.; ISBN: 0-9692949-0-5. [0483]

Barreau de la province de Québec. Bibliothèque

Catalogue de la bibliothèque du Barreau de Québec: livres français. Québec: A. Coté, 1876. 65 p. [2094]

Barrett, Jane R.; Beaumont, Jane

A bibliography of works on Canadian foreign relations, 1976-1980. Toronto: Canadian Institute of International Affairs, c1982. xii, 306 p.; ISBN: 0-919084-40-0. [2467]

Barrett, Jane R.; Beaumont, Jane; Broadhead, Lee-Anne

A bibliography of works on Canadian foreign relations, 1981-1985. Toronto: Canadian Institute of International Affairs, c1987. 157 p.; ISBN: 0-919084-57-5. [2508]

Barrett, Jane R.; McTavish, Mary

Reference aids in international relations. [Toronto]: University of Toronto Library, 1981. iv, 155 l. (Reference series / University of Toronto Library ; no. 25) [2459]

Barrie Public Library

Huronia: a selection of books and pamphlets on this historic region. [Barrie, Ont.]: Barrie Public Library, 1972. 9 l. [0442]

Barron, John P.

A selected bibliography of the Kodaly concept of music education. Willowdale, Ont.: Avondale Press; published in collaboration with the Kodaly Institute of Canada, c1979. 81 p.; ISBN: 0-9690452-7-1. [0873]

Barrow, Mark V.; Niswander, Jerry D.; Fortuine, Robert

Health and disease of American Indians north of Mexico: a bibliography, 1800-1969. Gainesville: University of Florida Press, 1972. xiii, 147 p.; ISBN: 0-8130-0331-8. [5577]

Barry, G.S.

Bibliography of geology of the Precambrian area of Manitoba, 1950-1957. Winnipeg: Province of Manitoba, Department of Mines and Natural Resources, Mines Branch, 1959. 39 p. (Mines Branch Publication / Province of Manitoba, Department of Mines and Natural Resources ; 57-3) [4758]

Barry, Thomas W.; Kear, Janet

A bibliography of the swans. [Edmonton: Canadian Wildlife Service, 1972]. 181 l. [5364]

Barteaux, Eleanor

Selected bibliography on problems of demobilisation, adjustment and rehabilitation of men and women from the armed forces. Ottawa: Made available by the Canadian Library Council and Wartime Information Board, 1944. 24 l. [3078]

Barter, Geraldine

A critically annotated bibliography of works published and unpublished relating to the culture of French Newfoundlanders. [St. John's]: Memorial University of Newfoundland, 1977. xiii, 52 l., [2] l. of pl. [0227]

Bartlett, Mark C.; Black, Fiona A.; MacDonald, Bertrum H.

The history of the book in Canada: a bibliography. Halifax, N.S.: Dalhousie University, School of Library and Information Studies, 1993. xi, [xii], 260 p.; ISBN: 0-9697349-0-5. [1736]

Barton, B.A.; Toth, L.T.

Physiological stress in fish: a literature review with emphasis on blood cortisol dynamics. Calgary: Alberta Energy and Natural Resources, 1980. 18 l. (Fisheries research report / Alberta Energy and Natural Resources ; no. 21) [5442]

Bartram, Peter Edward Raven

The Ontario colleges of applied arts and technology [microform]: a review and analysis of selected literature, 1965-1976. Ottawa: National Library of Canada, 1981. 4 microfiches (310 fr.). (Canadian theses on microfiche ; 47005; ISSN: 0227-3845) [3581]

Basran, Gurcharn S.

"East-Indian-Canadian periodical publications: a preliminary check list." In: *Canadian Ethnic Studies*; Vol. 5, no. 1/2 (1973) p. 43-45.; ISSN: 0008-3496. [5910]

"University research on East-Indian-Canadians: a preliminary check list of theses." In: *Canadian Ethnic Studies*; Vol. 5, no. 1/2 (1973) p. 41-42.; ISSN: 0008-3496. [6122]

Bastedo, Jamie

Annotated bibliography for the Waterton Lakes Biosphere Reserve, with discussion of management and research priorities. [Ottawa]: Canada-MAB, 1983. 2 vol.: ill., maps. [5190]

Bataille, Gretchen M.; Sands, Kathleen M.

American Indian women: a guide to research. New York: Garland, 1991. xvii, 423 p.; ISBN: 0-8240-4799-0. [3886]

Bates, D.; Gillmeister, D.

Ontario Forest Research Institute publications, 1980-1991 (an annotated bibliography). Sault Ste. Marie: Ontario Forest Research Institute, 1991. ii, 74 p.; ISBN: 0-772-99396-3. [6409]

Ontario Tree Improvement and Forest Biomass Institute publications, 1980-1985: an annotated bibliography. Toronto: Ontario Ministry of Natural Resources, c1986. ii, 31 p. (Forest Research report / Ontario Ministry of Natural Resources ; no. 114; ISSN: 0301-3924); ISBN: 0-

7729-1342-0. [6376]

Bates, Hilary

"A bibliography of Fred Landon." In: *Ontario History*; Vol. 62, no. 1 (March 1970) p. 5-16.; ISSN: 0030-2953. [7120]

"Bibliography of the academic and journalistic writings of James J. Talman." In: *Aspects of nineteenth-century Ontario: essays presented to James J. Talman*, edited by F.H. Armstrong, H.A. Stevenson and J.D. Wilson. London, Ont.: Published in association with the University of Western Ontario by University of Toronto Press, 1974. P. 334-350.; ISBN: 0-8020-2061-5. [7325]

Index to the publications of the Ontario Historical Society, 1899-1972. Toronto: Ontario Historical Society, 1974. x, 175 p. [1979]

Bates, Stewart

"Lothar Richter (1894-1948): [publications]." In: *Canadian Journal of Economics and Political Science*; Vol. 15, no. 4 (November 1949) p. 544-545.; ISSN: 0315-4890. [7262]

Baxter, James Phinney

A memoir of Jacques Cartier, sieur de Limoilou: his voyages to the St. Lawrence, a bibliography and a facsimile of the manuscript of 1534 with annotations, etc. New York: Dodd, Mead, 1906. ix, 464 p., [9] l. of pl. (3 folded): ill., maps (3 folded, 1 col.), port., facsims. [6899]

Bayard, Caroline

"A Raoul Duguay bibliography." In: *Open Letter*; Series 3, no. 8 (Spring 1978) p. 37-43.; ISSN: 0048-1939. [6962]

Bayefsky, Evelyn

"Women and the status of part-time work: a review and annotated bibliography." In: *Ontario Library Review*; Vol. 58, no. 2 (June 1974) p. 124-141; vol. 61, no. 2 (June 1977) p. 86-106.; ISSN: 0030-2996. [3769]

"Women and work: a selection of books and articles." In: *Ontario Library Review*; Vol. 56, no. 2 (June 1972) p. 79-90.; ISSN: 0030-2996. [3738]

Bazinet, Jeanne, et al.

Catalogue des biographies. Montréal: Société Radio-Canada. Bibliothèque, 1982. 1 vol. [2017]

Beak Consultants Limited

A literature review of Grasslands National Park, 1977-1981. Winnipeg: Parks Canada, 1982. iii, 28 p. [3035]

Beanlands, D. Bruce; Deacon, James

Contre-terrorisme: bibliographie. [Ottawa]: Solliciteur général Canada, Secrétariat du Ministère, [1988]. [iii], 362 p. (Rapport pour spécialistes / Solliciteur général Canada, Secrétariat du Ministère ; no 1988-14) [2307]

Counter-terrorism: bibliography. [Ottawa]: Solicitor General Canada, Ministry Secretariat, [1988]. ii, 361 p. (User report / Solicitor General Canada, Ministry Secretariat ; no. 1988-14) [2308]

Beattie, Kathleen G.; Bond, Wayne K.; Manning, Edward W.

The agricultural use of marginal lands: a review and bibliography. [Ottawa]: Lands Directorate, Environment Canada, 1981. v, 90 p.: ill., maps. (Working paper / Lands Directorate, Environment Canada ; no. 13; ISSN: 0712-4473); ISBN: 0-662-11454-8. [4692]

L'utilisation agricole des terres marginales: une rétrospective et une bibliographie. [Ottawa]: Direction générale des terres, 1981. v, 98 p.: ill., cartes. (Document de travail / Direction générale des terres, Environnement Canada ; no 13); ISBN: 0-662-91113-8. [4693]

Beatty, Carol Anne

Managing technological change in manufacturing: an annotated bibliography of selected works. London, Ont.: National Centre for Management Research and Development, University of Western Ontario, 1990. 37 p. (Working paper series / National Centre for Management Research and Development, University of Western Ontario ; no. NC 90-18) [5840]

Beatty, Carolyn

Directory of associate composers. Toronto: Canadian Music Centre, 1989. 1 vol. (loose-leaf).; ISBN: 0-921519-08-7. [0934]

Répertoire des compositeurs agrées. Toronto: Centre de musique canadienne, 1989. 1 vol. (f. mobiles); ISBN: 0-921519-09-5. [0935]

Beauchamp, Hélène

Bibliographie annotée sur le théâtre québécois pour l'enfance et la jeunesse, 1970-1983: suivie d'une Liste sélective d'articles de presse portant sur les productions de théâtre québécois pour l'enfance et la jeunesse, 1950-1980. Montréal: Université du Québec, 1984. 39 f. [1359]

Beauchesne, André; Mercier, Diane

Promouvoir l'éducation interculturelle et l'éducation internationale: guide analytique des ressources éducatives de langue française. Montréal: Conseil scolaire de l'île de Montréal, c1986. 2 vol. [3648]

Beaudette, L.A.; McCready, R.G.L.

Biotechnology bibliographies/Bibliographies de la biotechnologie. Ottawa: Canada Centre for Mineral and Energy Technology, c1987. v, 109 p. (CANMET Special publication / Canada Centre for Mineral and Energy Technology ; SP 86-2); ISBN: 0-660-53890-3. [4856]

Beaudoin-Ross, Jacqueline; Blackstock, Pamela

"Costume in Canada: an annotated bibliography." In: *Material History Bulletin*; No. 19 (Spring 1984) p. 59-92.; ISSN: 0703-489X. [4593]

Beaudry, Claude

"Catalogue des imprimés musicaux d'avant 1800 conservés à la bibliothèque de l'Université Laval." Dans: *Musical Canada: words and music honouring Helmut Kallmann*, edited by John Beckwith and Frederick A. Hall. Toronto: University of Toronto Press, 1988. P. 29-49.; ISBN: 0-8020-5759-4. [0931]

Beaudry, Jacques

Philosophie et périodiques québécois: répertoire préliminaire, 1902-1982. Trois-Rivières [Québec]: Éditions Fragments, 1983. 131 f. (Collection Les cahiers gris ; 2) [5949]

Beaudry, Lucille; Fournier, François; Villeneuve, Daniel

Le souverainisme politique au Québec, le Parti québécois et les courants indépendantistes 1960-1980, recueil bibliographique. Montréal: Département de science politique, Université du Québec à Montréal, 1982. 103 p. (Notes de recherche / Département de science politique, Université du Québec à Montréal ; no 22) [2468]

Beaulieu, André, et al.

La presse québécoise: des origines à nos jours. Québec: Presses de l'Université Laval, 1973-1990. 10 vol. [5971]

Beaulieu, André; Bonenfant, Jean-Charles; Hamelin, Jean

Répertoire des publications gouvernementales du Québec de 1867 à 1964. Québec: Impr. de la Reine, 1968. 554 p. [6264]

Beaulieu, André; Hamelin, Jean

"Idéologies au Canada français, 1850-1900: orientations bibliographiques." Dans: *Recherches sociographiques*; Vol. 10, no 2-3 (mai-décembre 1969) p. 449-463.; ISSN: 0034-1282. [1957]

Beaulieu, André; Hamelin, Jean; Bernier, Benoît
Guide d'histoire du Canada. Québec: Presses de l'Université Laval, 1969. xvi, 540 p. (Les Cahiers de l'Institut d'histoire ; 13) [1958]

Beaulieu, André; Morley, William F.E.
La Province de Québec. Toronto: University of Toronto Press, 1971. xxvii, 408 p. (Histoires locales et régionales canadiennes des origines à 1950 ; vol. II); ISBN: 0-8020-1733-9. [0308]

Beaumont-Moisan, Renée; Hudon, Céline
Bibliographie sur les Iles-de-la-Madeleine. Québec: Ministère des Terres et Forêts, Service de l'Information, Bibliothèque, 1977. [24] f. [0344]

Beaupré, Michel; Carpentier, Robert
Les karsts et les cavernes du Québec: bibliographie inventaire de la littérature spéléologique québécoise, 1822-1975. Montréal: Société québécoise de spéléologie, 1976. 77 f. (Collection "Documents" / Société québécoise de spéléologie) [4792]

Beauregard, Christian
An annotated bibliography of Canadian public finance (revenue side) 1946-1979: a first round. Montréal: Département de science économique et Centre de recherche en développement économique, Université de Montréal, [1980]. 222, [7] p. (Cahier / Département de science économique et Centre de recherche en développement économique, Université de Montréal ; 8004) [2656]

Beauregard, Ludger
"Pierre Dagenais: une biobibliographie." Dans: Cahiers de géographie de Québec; Vol. 27, no 71 (septembre 1983) p. 149-163.; ISSN: 0007-9766. [6928]

Beauregard, Micheline; Tessier, Yves
Répertoire bibliographique: thèses de doctorat et mémoires de maîtrise en rapport avec la condition des femmes reçus dans six universités du Québec, 1987-1991. Sainte-Foy, Québec: Chaire d'étude sur la condition des femmes, Université Laval, 1992. 113 p.; ISBN: 2-9801950-5-7. [6204]

Beauregard, Yves
Bibliographie du centre du Québec et des Bois-Francs. Québec: Institut québécois de recherche sur la culture, 1986. 495 p.: cartes. (Documents de recherche / Institut québécois de recherche sur la culture ; no 9; ISSN: 0823-0447); ISBN: 2-89224-061-1. [0392]

Beauvais, Gisèle D.; Lallier-Millot, Louise; St-Pierre, Normand
Bibliographie: cours en archivistique/Bibliography: archives course. [Ottawa]: Archives publiques du Canada, 1975. 123 f. [1609]

Beavis, Joan; Cumming, Greta
Organized crime: a bibliography. Ottawa: Law Enforcement Reference Centre, 1990. 39 l. [2329]
Policewomen: a bibliography, 1980-1990. Ottawa: Law Enforcement Reference Centre, 1990. 20 l. [2330]

Beavis, Mary Ann; Patterson, Jeffrey
A select, annotated bibliography on sustainable cities. Winnipeg: Institute of Urban Studies, University of Winnipeg, 1992. v, 93 p. (Bibliographica / Institute of Urban Studies, University of Winnipeg ; 4); ISBN: 0-920213-77-4. [4440]

Bebee, Charles N.
The protection of ornamental plants, 1979-April 1989: citations from AGRICOLA concerning diseases and other environmental considerations. Beltsville, Md.: United States Department of Agriculture, National Agriculture Library, 1989. 211 p. (Bibliographies and literature of agriculture ; no. 87) [4716]

Beck, Alfred Ernest
Bibliography of mercury in Manitoba fish. Winnipeg: Government of Manitoba, Water Standards and Studies Section, 1984. ii, 9 l. [5492]

Beckwith, John
"Canadian recordings: a discography." In: Canadian Library Association Bulletin; Vol. 12, no. 5 (April 1956) p. 182-183.; ISSN: 0316-6058. [0814]
"Tunebooks and hymnals in Canada, 1801-1939." In: American Music; Vol. 6, no. 2 (1988) p. 193-234.; ISSN: 0734-4392. [0932]

Bédard, Carole
Politique et religion au Québec depuis 1960: bibliographie. Québec: [s.n.], 1976. v, 69 f. [1539]

Bédard, Marc-André
"Les Protestants en Nouvelle-France: bibliographie." Dans: Cahiers d'histoire; No 31 (1978) p. 127-138. [1544]

Bédard, Robert
Clinique sociologique et profession de sociologue: bibliographie. Québec: Institut supérieur des sciences humaines, Université Laval, [1971]. 52 f. [3099]

Bédard, Roger J.
"Finances municipales: une bibliographie." Dans: Cités et villes; Vol. 6, no 5 (mai 1963) p. 43-47; vol. 6, no 6 (juin 1963) p. 43.; ISSN: 0009-7500. [4305]

Beddie, M.K.
Bibliography of Captain James Cook R.N., F.R.S. Sydney: Council of the Library of New South Wales, 1970. xvi, 894 p.; ISBN: 0-7240-9999-9. [6917]

Beers, Henry Putney
The French and British in the old Northwest: a bibliographical guide to archive and manuscript sources. Detroit: Wayne State University Press, 1964. 297 p. [1942]
The French in North America: a bibliographical guide to French archives, reproductions, and research missions. Baton Rouge: Louisiana State University Press, c1957. xi, 413 p. [1928]

Beesley, Ken B.
The rural-urban fringe: a bibliography. Peterborough, Ont.: Department of Geography, Trent University, 1993. ix, 89 p. (Occasional paper / Trent University, Department of Geography ; 15); ISBN: 0-921062-12-5. [4442]

Beeston, John; Cramm, Karen M.; Robertson, Sheila M.
Organize for action: a reading guide for community participants. Halifax: Institute of Public Affairs, Dalhousie University, 1974. vii, 32 l. (Dalhousie University Programmes in public administration ; no. 94) [3121]

Bégin, Diane
Bibliographie sur la femme québécoise et le travail. Montréal: École des hautes études commerciales, [1983]. 77 f. [3815]

Bégin, Diane; Harel-Giasson, Francine; Marchis-Mouren, Marie-Françoise
Portraits de québécoises gestionnaires: une bibliographie annotée. Montréal: École des hautes études commerciales, 1982. iii, 64 f. (Rapport de recherche / École des hautes

études commerciales ; no 82-07; ISSN: 0709-986X) [3805]

Beguet, Véronique

Les réfugiés indochinois au Canada: une bibliographie/ Indochinese refugees in Canada: a bibliography. Québec: Groupe d'études et de recherches sur l'Asie contemporaine, Université Laval, c1992. x, 72 p.; ISBN: 0-98024-072-9. [4288]

Beharry, Hamblin

Native education in Alberta: a selective bibliography. [Edmonton]: Policy and Planning Branch, Alberta Native Affairs, 1986. 25 l. [3649]

Béland, Denis

La Revue des revues de *Recherches sociographiques*: bibliographie. Québec: Université Laval, 1974. iii f., 384 p. (Cahiers de l'ISSH, Collection Instruments de travail / Institut supérieur des sciences humaines, Université Laval ; no 14) [3122]

Beland, François

"La recherche en gérontologie sociale au Québec: une originalité obscure ou une obscurité méritée?" Dans: *Canadian Journal on Aging: La revue canadienne du vieillissement*; Vol. 7, no 4 (hiver 1988) p. 257-292.; ISSN: 0714-9808. [3305]

Béland, Madeleine

"[François-Joseph Brassard]: bibliographie." Dans: *Saguenayensia*; Vol. 25, nos 1-2 (janvier-Mars 1983) p. 17-25.; ISSN: 0581-295X. [6871]

Béland, Mario

Marius Barbeau et l'art au Québec: bibliographie analytique et thématique. 2e éd. rev. et corr. [Sainte-Foy, Québec: CELAT], 1988. xi, 135 p.: ill.; ISBN: 2-920576-19-4. [0714]

Bélanger, Lise-Anne

Bio-bibliographie de Michel Beaulieu, écrivain, 1941-1985 [microforme]. Montréal: Service des archives, Université de Montréal, 1988. 1 bobine de microfilm. [6832]

Bélanger, Marcel; Trotier, Louis

L'urbanisation de la région de Montréal: essai de bibliographie analytique. Québec: Département de géographie, Université Laval, 1975. 93 p. [4343]

Bélanger, Pierre-A.

"Bibliographie générale sur les Iles-de-la-Madeleine." Dans: *Recherches sociographiques*; Vol. 11, no 3 (septembre-décembre 1970) p. 393-407.; ISSN: 0034-1282. [0305]

Bélanger, Pierre C.

Recherche bibliographique: impacts culturels et linguistiques de la consommation de produits culturels étrangers (émissions de télévision et musique à la radio). Québec: Direction de la coordination et des politiques, Ministère des communications, 1988. v, 75 p.; ISBN: 2-550-19006-8. [0985]

Bélanger, Yves; Fournier, Pierre; Painchaud, Claude

Guide bibliographique pour l'étude du capital québécois. [Montréal]: Département de science politique, Université du Québec à Montréal, 1982. 72 f. (Notes de recherche / Département de science politique, Université du Québec à Montréal ; no 24) [2676]

Bélisle, Alvine

"Children's literature in French-speaking Canada." In: *Canadian Children's Literature*; No. 4 (1976) p. 59-65.; ISSN: 0319-0080. [1330]

"Les écrivains canadiens racontent à nos jeunes." Dans: *Canadian Library Association Bulletin*; Vol. 1, no. 1 (August 1956) p. 32-34.; ISSN: 0316-6058. [1310]

"Notre héritage français: choix de livres sur le Canada français." Dans: *Canadian Library*; Vol. 20, no. 1 (July 1963) p. 26-28.; ISSN: 0316-604X. [1314]

Notre héritage française [sic]: choix de livres sur le Canada français. Ottawa: Association canadienne des bibliothèques, [1963]. [4] p. [1315]

Bélisle, Alvine, et al.

Guide de lecture pour les jeunes, 5 à 13 ans. Montréal: Association canadienne des bibliothécaires de langue française, 1973. 164 p. [1322]

Bélisle Gouault, Denise

Les femmes et le vieillissement au Canada: bibliographie annotée multidisciplinaire, 1975-1989. Ottawa: Chair conjointe en études des femmes, Carleton University: Université d'Ottawa, [1990]. xii, 133, 125, viii p.; ISBN: 0-9694670-0-1. [3875]

Women and aging in Canada: multidisciplinary annotated bibliography, 1975-1989. Ottawa: Joint Chair in Women's Studies, Carleton University: University of Ottawa, [1990]. viii, 125, 133, xii p.; ISBN: 0-9694670-0-1. [3876]

Bell, B.T.A.

Transactions: indices to names of authors and subjects of the papers presented to the Canadian Mining Institute, and the antecedent provincial mining societies, 1891 to 1903. Ottawa: Orme's Hall, 1904. 31 p. [4734]

"Transactions of the Canadian Mining Institute: Indices to names of authors and subjects of the papers presented to the Canadian Mining Institute, the Federated Canadian Mining Institute, and the antecedent provincial mining societies, 1891 to 1903." In: *Journal of the Canadian Mining Institute*; Vol. 6 (1903) p. 489-520.; ISSN: 0368-1688. [4733]

Bell, Dorothy, et al.

Canadian Black studies bibliography. [London, Ont.: s.n.], 1971. [108] l. [4152]

Bell, Emma H.

Bibliography of serials, topical cases, named reports, law reports, digests and statutes held by the University of Saskatchewan Law Library. Saskatoon: College of Law, University of Saskatchewan, 1962. 29 l. [2107]

Bell, Inglis Freeman

"Canadian literature, a checklist." In: *Canadian Literature*; No. 3 (Winter 1960)-no. 19 (Winter 1964) [1020]

Bell, Inglis Freeman; Gallup, Jennifer

A reference guide to English, American and Canadian literature: an annotated checklist of bibliographical and other reference materials. Vancouver: University of British Columbia Press, [c1971]. xii, 139 p.; ISBN: 0-7748-0002-X. [1060]

Bell, Inglis Freeman; Port, Susan

Canadian literature, Littérature canadienne, 1959-1963: A checklist of creative and critical writings. Bibliographie de la critique et des oeuvres d'imagination. [Vancouver]: Publications Centre, University of British Columbia, 1966. 140 p. [1031]

Bell, John

Canuck comics: a guide to comic books published in Canada. Montreal: Published and distributed to the comic book trade by Matrix Books; Downsview, Ont.: Distributed to the book trade by Eden Press, c1986. 154 p.: ill.; ISBN: 0-921101-00-7. [5958]

Bell, Leonard M.; Kallman, Ronald J.

The Cowichan-Chemainus River estuaries: status of environmental knowledge to 1975: report of the Estuary Working

Group, Department of the Environment, Regional Board Pacific Region. [Ottawa]: Environment Canada, [1975]. 328 p. (Special estuary series / Estuary Working Group, Department of the Environment, Regional Board, Pacific Region ; no. 4) [5098]

The Kitimat River estuary: status of environmental knowledge to 1976: report of the Estuary Working Group, Department of the Environment, Regional Board Pacific Region. [Ottawa]: Environment Canada, [1976]. 296 p. (Special estuary series / Estuary Working Group, Department of the Environment, Regional Board, Pacific Region ; no. 6) [5106]

The Nanaimo River estuary: status of environmental knowledge to 1976: report of the Estuary Working Group, Department of the Environment, Regional Board Pacific Region. [Ottawa]: Environment Canada, [1976]. xxix, 298 p., [1] l. of pl.: ill., maps. (Special estuary series / Estuary Working Group, Department of the Environment, Regional Board, Pacific Region ; no. 5) [5107]

Bell, Leonard M.; Thompson, James M.

The Campbell River estuary: status of environmental knowledge to 1977: report of the Estuary Working Group, Department of the Environment, Regional Board Pacific Region. [Ottawa]: Fisheries and Environment Canada, [1977]. xxxvi, 346 p., [2] l. of pl.: ill. (Special estuary series / Estuary Working Group, Department of the Environment, Regional Board, Pacific Region ; no. 7) [5121]

Bell, Marcus A.M., et al.

Pacific Rim National Park: an annotated bibliography. [Ottawa]: Social Science Federation of Canada, [c1981]. xii, 234 p.; ISBN: 0-920052-20-7. [3031]

Bell, Marcus A.M.; Beckett, Jennifer M.; Hubbard, William F.

Establishment of forests after logging in north central British Columbia: an annotated bibliography. Victoria, B.C.: Pacific Forest Research Centre, 1976. 178 p. (Pacific Forest Research Centre Information report ; BC-X-109; ISSN: 0705-3274) [4950]

Impact of harvesting on forest environments and resources: a review of the literature and evaluation of research needs. Victoria: Pacific Forest Research Centre, Canadian Forestry Service, 1974. v, 141 p. [4942]

Bell, W.; Hanmore, C.J.; Willcock, A.J.

Growth and yield of northwestern Ontario boreal (coniferous) forest species: an annotated bibliography. Thunder Bay: Northwestern Ontario Forest Technology Development Unit, 1989. iii l., 211 p. (Technical report / Northwestern Ontario Forest Technology Development Unit ; no. 31) [5005]

Bellamy, Patricia

Graduate schools and financial aid: a guide to reference sources in the Robarts Library. 3rd ed. [Toronto]: University of Toronto Library, 1987. 52 p. [3666]

Bellemare, Louis

L'information électronique au Québec: guide pratique des services d'information en ligne. Québec: Gouvernement du Québec, Direction des technologies de l'information, 1987. 93 p.; ISBN: 2-550-17536-0. [0156]

Bellerive, Georges

Nos auteurs dramatiques, anciens et contemporains: répertoire analytique. Québec: Garneau, 1933. 162 p. [1000]

"Nos auteurs dramatiques: leurs noms et leurs oeuvres." Dans: *Canada français*; Vol. 20, no 8 (avril 1933) p. 748-757. [1001]

Bellingham, Susan

A catalogue of the modern Canadian poetry collection in the Division of Archives and Special Collections. Hamilton, Ont.: University Library Press at McMaster University, 1973. [75] p. [1073]

Isabel Ecclestone Mackay bibliography. Waterloo, Ont.: University of Waterloo Library, c1987. xiii, 77 p. (University of Waterloo Library bibliography ; no. 15: ISSN: 0829-948X); ISBN: 0-920834-01-9. [7164]

Belton, Eric J.

Bibliography of published writings of Dr. Harry G. Johnson. [Thunder Bay, Ont.]: Library, Lakehead University, 1979. 69 p. [7081]

Bendwell, André

Bibliographie annotée du Parc national La Mauricie. [Ottawa: Direction des parcs nationaux et des lieux historiques, Ministère des affaires Indiennes et du Nord Canadien, 1971. ii, 127 f. [2976]

Benfey, Tillman J.

A bibliography of triploid fish, 1943 to 1988. West Vancouver, B.C.: Department of Fisheries and Oceans, Biological Sciences Branch, 1989. iv, 33 p. (Canadian technical report of fisheries and aquatic sciences ; no. 1682; ISSN: 0706-6457) [5548]

Benjamin, Steven M.

The German-Canadians: a working bibliography. Morgantown, W. Va.: Department of Foreign Languages, West Virginia University, 1979. 41 p. (Occasional papers of the Society for German-American Studies ; no. 1) [4191]

Bennett, Joy; Polson, James

Irving Layton, a bibliography, 1935-1977. Montreal: Concordia University Libraries, 1979. iv, 200 p.; ISBN: 0-9690101-0-9. [7130]

Bennett, Judith Antonik

Royal commissions and commissions of inquiry under the Public Inquiries Act in British Columbia, 1943-1980: a checklist. Victoria: Province of British Columbia, Legislative Library, 1982. 37 p.; ISBN: 0-7718-8305-6. [6339]

Bennett, Paul W.

"Beyond the textbook: a selected bibliography for the '80s." In: *Rediscovering Canadian history: a teacher's guide for the '80s.* Toronto: OISE Press, 1980. P. 154-180. (Curriculum series / Ontario Institute for Studies in Education ; 39); ISBN: 0-7744-0192-3. [2006]

Benson, Eugene

"Robertson Davies: a chronology and checklist." In: *Canadian Drama*; Vol. 7, no. 2 (1981) p. 3-12.; ISSN: 0317-9044. [6938]

Benson, John

"Canadian labour history: essay in bibliography." In: *Bulletin: Society for the Study of Labour History*; Vol. 51, no. 1 (1986) p. 18-24.; ISSN: 0049-1179. [2900]

Benson, Lillian Rea

"Historical atlases of Ontario: a preliminary check-list." In: *Ontario Library Review*; Vol. 28, no. 1 (February 1944) p. 45-53.; ISSN: 0030-2996. [6494]

"The Illustrated historical atlases of Ontario with special reference to H. Belden & Co." In: *Aspects of nineteenth-century Ontario: essays presented to James J. Talman*, edited by F.H. Armstrong, H.A. Stevenson and J.D. Wilson. London, Ont.: Published in association with the University of Western Ontario by University of Toronto Press, 1974. P. 267-277.; ISBN: 0-8020-2061-5. [6535]

Bentley, D.M.R.

"Archibald Lampman (1861-1899): a checklist." In: *Essays on Canadian Writing*; No. 5 (Fall 1976) p. 36-49.; ISSN: 0316-0300. [7116]

A checklist of literary materials in *The Week* (Toronto, 1883-1896). Ottawa: Golden Dog Press, 1978. vi, 161 p.; ISBN: 0-919611-30-2. [1127]

Bercaw, Louise O.; Hannay, A.M.; Colvin, Esther M.

Bibliography on land settlement with particular reference to small holdings and subsistence homesteads. Washington: United States Government Printing Office, 1934. iv, 492 p. (United States Department of Agriculture Miscellaneous publications ; no. 172) [4638]

Bergeron, Chantal, et al.

Répertoire bibliographique de textes de présentation générale et d'analyse d'oeuvres musicales canadiennes (1900-1980)/Canadian musical works 1900-1980: a bibliography of general and analytical sources. Ottawa: Association canadienne des bibliothèques musicales, c1983. xiv, 96 p. (Publications / Association canadienne des bibliothèques musicales ; no 3); ISBN: 0-9690583-2-2. [0908]

Bergeron, Chantal; Tessier, Mario

Bibliographie préliminaire sur le vidéodisque et les banques d'images. [Laval, Québec: s.n., c1985]. ii, 24 f. [1668]

Bergeron, Gérard

Problèmes politiques du Québec: répertoire bibliographique des commissions royales d'enquête présentant un intérêt spécial pour la politique de la province de Québec, 1940-1957. Montréal: [Institut de recherches politiques, Fédération libérale provinciale], 1957. xiii, 218 p. [2376]

Bergeron, Julien

Bibliographie du homard (Homarus americanus, Milne-Edwards et Homarus gammarus L.). Québec: Ministère de l'industrie et du commerce, 1965. 81 p. (Cahiers d'information / Station de biologie marine, Grande-Rivière ; no 34) [5339]

Bibliographie du saumon de l'Atlantique (Salmo salar L.). Québec: Ministère de la chasse et des pêcheries, 1962. 64 p. (Contributions / Ministère de la chasse et des pêcheries, Québec ; no 88) [5334]

Bergeron, Raymond

Bibliographical listing of studies conducted or supported by the Northern Affairs Program, Department of Indian Affairs and Northern Development, 1973-1984/Liste bibliographique des études effectuées ou appuyées par le Programme des affaires du Nord, Ministère des affaires indiennes et du Nord canadien. Ottawa: Indian and Northern Affairs Canada, 1985. ii, 203 p. [0648]

Bergeron, Raymond; Guimont, Pierre

Ten years of northern research in Canada, 1974-1984/Dix ans de recherche nordique au Canada, 1974-1984. Ottawa: Indian and Northern Affairs Canada, 1985. 1 vol. (115+ pages); ISBN: 0-662-54065-4. [0649]

Bergersen, Moira; Frigon, Claire

"Management literature for librarians: an annotated list." In: *Canadian Library Journal*; Vol. 30, no. 3 (May-June 1973) p. 227-233.; ISSN: 0008-4352. [1599]

Bergevin, André

"Les oeuvres de Bourassa: index par sujet des ouvrages, articles et conférences." Dans: *Action nationale*; Vol. 43, no 1 (janvier 1954) p. 199-244.; ISSN: 0001-7469. [6862]

Bergevin, André; Nish, James Cameron; Bourassa, Anne

Henri Bourassa: biographie, index des écrits, index de la correspondance publique 1895-1924. Montréal: Éditions de l'Action nationale, 1966. lxii, 150 p. [6863]

Berman, Gerald

Graph theory bibliography with two level key-word index. [Waterloo, Ont.]: University of Waterloo Press, [1983]. 2 vol.; ISBN: 0-88898-046-9. [5788]

Bernad, Marcel

Bibliographie des missionnaires oblats de Marie Immaculée. Liège: H. Dessain, 1922. 127 p. [1499]

Bernard, Claire

Legal aspects of research and clinical practice with children: selected Canadian legal bibliography/Questions de droit touchant la recherche et la pratique clinique auprès des enfants: bibliographie juridique canadienne sélective. Ottawa: National Council on Bioethics in Human Research, 1992. 15 p.; ISBN: 0-9696111-3-7. [5708]

Bernard, F.R.

Prodrome for a distributional check-list and bibliography of the recent marine mollusca of the west coast of Canada. Nanaimo, B.C.: Fisheries Research Board of Canada, 1967. xxiv, 261 p.: ill. (Fisheries Research Board of Canada Technical report ; no. 2; ISSN: 0068-7553) [5343]

A selected bibliography on the biological effects of ocean dumping. Nanaimo, B.C.: Pacific Biological Station, Research and Development Directorate, Department of the Environment, 1976. iii, 22 p. (Fisheries and Marine Service Technical report ; no. 628; ISSN: 0701-7626) [5108]

Bernhard, Paulette; Saint-Aubin, Diane

"Recherches en éducation faites au Canada français." Dans: *Revue des sciences de l'éducation*; Vol. 1. no 1 (printemps 1975)-vol. 18, no 3 (1992) [6205]

Bernier, Gaston

"Bibliographie parlementaire." Dans: *Bulletin: Bibliothèque de l'Assemblée nationale du Québec*; Vol. 12, no 3 (septembre 1982)-vol. 15, no 1 (janvier 1985) [2487]

"Carte electorale: modes de scrutin: liste bibliographique annotée." Dans: *Bulletin: Bibliothèque de l'Assemblée nationale du Québec*; Vol. 1, no 3 (octobre 1970) p. 20-31.; ISSN: 0701-6808. [2398]

"Études réalisées pour la Commission Laurendeau-Dunton." Dans: *Bulletin: Bibliothèque de l'Assemblée nationale du Québec*; Vol. 2, no 4 (octobre 1971) p. 43-53.; ISSN: 0701-6808. [2401]

"Parlements, parlementaires et parlementarisme: bibliographie sélective." Dans: *Bulletin: Bibliothèque de l'Assemblée nationale du Québec*; Vol. 5, nos 1-2 (janvier-avril 1974) p. 29-71.; ISSN: 0701-6808. [2411]

"Problèmes municipaux: liste bibliographique annotée." Dans: *Bulletin: Bibliothèque de l'Assemblée nationale du Québec*; Vol. 2, no 1 (janvier 1971) p. 33-61.; ISSN: 0701-6808. [4316]

Bernier, Gérald; Boily, Robert

Le Québec en transition: 1760-1867: bibliographie thématique. [Montréal: Association canadienne-française pour l'avancement des sciences, c1987]. 193 p. (Politique et économie / Association canadienne-française pour l'avancement des sciences ; no 5); ISBN: 2-89245-068-3. [0397]

Bernier, Hélène

"La fille aux mains coupées (conte-type 706): bibliographie." Dans: *Archives de Folklore*; Vol. 12 (1971) p. 175-183.; ISSN:

0085-5243. [4553]

Bernier, Hélène; Caron, Diane
La tradition populaire québécoise: une base bibliographique. [Québec]: Gouvernement du Québec, Ministère du loisir, de la chasse et de la pêche, 1981. v, 207 f. [0368]

Bernier, Robert; Gagnon, Rosette
Guide bibliographique: économique de la criminalité et planification des ressources de la justice criminelle/ Bibliographical guide: the economics of crime and planning of resources in the criminal justice system. Ottawa: Solliciteur général Canada, Division de la recherche, 1978. x, 488 p.; ISBN: 0-662-01554-1. [2178]

Bernstein, J.W.
Literature review of ultraviolet radiation systems and assessment of their use in aquaculture. Saskatoon: Saskatchewan Research Council, 1985. i, 39 l. (Saskatchewan Research Council Technical report ; no. 183) [4901]

Berry, John W.; Wilde, G.J.S.
Social psychology of Canada: an annotated bibliography. Kingston [Ont.]: 1971. iv, 96 p. [3100]

Berton, Pierre
A Klondike bibliography. [Kleinburg, Ont.]: 1958. 23 l. [0610]
"A Klondike gold rush bibliography." In: *Journal of Canadian Fiction*; Vol. 2, no. 3 (Summer 1973) p. 201-204.; ISSN: 0047-2255. [1977]

Bertrand, Camille
Bulletin bibliographique. Montréal: Bertrand, 1920-1926. 1 vol.; ISSN: 0703-8461. [0997]

Bertrand, Denis
Optimisation dans manutention des conteneurs: une bibliographie sélective/Optimising container handling: a selective bibliography. Montréal: Département de génie civil, Section transport, École polytechnique de Montréal, 1973. 25 f. [4456]

Bérubé, Renald
"Bibliographie des oeuvres de Yves Thériault." Dans: *Voix et images*; Vol. 5, no 2 (hiver 1980) p. 241-243.; ISSN: 0318-9201. [7331]

Beslin, Ralph
Education finance in Canada. Ottawa: Canadian Teachers' Federation, 1978. 13 p. (Bibliographies in education / Canadian Teachers' Federation ; no. 62); ISBN: 0-88989-040-4. [3532]
Selection of teachers and student teachers. Ottawa: Canadian Teachers' Federation, 1978. 23 p. (Bibliographies in education / Canadian Teachers' Federation ; no. 64); ISBN: 0-88989-048-X. [3533]
Tenure. Ottawa: Canadian Teachers' Federation, 1978. 14 p. (Bibliographies in education / Canadian Teachers' Federation ; no. 66); ISBN: 0-88989-053-6. [3534]

Besoushko, Wolodmyr; Rudnyckyj, Jaroslav Bohdan
Publications of Ukrainian Free Academy of Sciences, 1945-1955. Winnipeg: Ukrainian Free Academy of Sciences, 1955. 22 p. (Ukrainian Free Academy of Sciences. Series: UVAN chronicle ; no. 13) [4616]

Bessette, Émile; Hamel, Réginald; Mailhot, Laurent
Répertoire pratique de littérature et de culture québécoises. Montréal: Fédération internationale des professeurs de français, 1982. 63 p.; ISBN: 2-901106-02-1. [1188]

Besterman, Theodore
A world bibliography of bibliographies, and of bibliographical catalogues, calendars, abstracts, digests, indexes and the like. 4th ed. rev. and greatly enl. throughout. Lausanne: Societas Bibliographica, 1965-1966. 5 vol. [0082]

Bethune, C.J.S.
"Bibliography of Canadian entomology." In: *Proceedings and Transactions of the Royal Society of Canada*; Series 2, vol. 7, section 4 (1901)-series 3, vol. 10, section 4 (1916) [5314]

Betts, Margaret; Krestensen, Kristeen
A selected list of publications issued by the Ontario Ministry of Labour, 1955-1973. Toronto: Ontario Ministry of Labour, Research Library, 1973. 24 l. [6282]

Beugin, Sue
Law library guide for Alberta practitioners. Calgary: Canadian Bar Association, Alberta Branch, 1979. iv, 162 p. [2189]

Beyer, Herman G.
Technical papers and technical memoranda issued by the Census Division, 1965-1968: an annotated list of studies and reports. Ottawa: Dominion Bureau of Statistics, Census Division, 1971. 36 p. (Working paper, General series / Dominion Bureau of Statistics, Census Division ; no. 1) [2977]

Bezanson, Donald S.; Moyse, Catherine M.; Byers, S.C.
Recherches et travaux connexes sur l'immersion de déchets en mer: bibliographie annotée. Ottawa: Gouvernement du Canada, Ministère des pêches et des océans, 1981. 106 p. (Immersion de déchets en mer rapport ; no 2F; ISSN: 0226-3475); ISBN: 0-662-91334-5. [5170]
Research and related work on ocean dumping: an annotated bibliography. Ottawa: Department of Fisheries and Oceans, 1979. [2], 94 p. (Ocean dumping report / Canada Department of Fisheries and Oceans ; 2; ISSN: 0704:2701); ISBN: 0-662-10617-2. [5144]

Bhatia, Mohan
Canadian federal government publications: a bibliography of bibliographies. Saskatoon: University of Saskatchewan, 1971. 33 l. [6275]
Canadian provincial government publications: a bibliography of bibliographies. Rev. and enl. ed. Saskatoon: University of Saskatchewan, Library, 1971. 19 l. [6276]

Bianchini, Luciano
"University research on Italian-Canadians: a preliminary check list." In: *Canadian Ethnic Studies*; Vol. 2, no. 1 (June 1970) p. 117-119.; ISSN: 0008-3496. [6102]

Bianchini, Luciano; Malycky, Alexander
"Italian-Canadian periodical publications: a preliminary check list." In: *Canadian Ethnic Studies*; Vol. 2, no. 1 (June 1970) p. 121-126.; ISSN: 0008-3496. [5888]

Bibaud, Maximilien
Bibliothèque canadienne: ou, Annales bibliographiques. Montréal: Cérat et Bourguignon, [1858]. 52 p. [0006]
Mémorial des honneurs étrangers conférés à des Canadiens ou domiciliés de la puissance du Canada. Montréal: Beauchemin & Valois, 1885. 100 p. [1881]

Bibliografía de historia de América. Ottawa: General Reference and Bibliography Section, National Library of Canada, 1977-. vol.; ISSN: 0708-2185. [2091]

Bibliographic guide to North American history. Boston: G.K. Hall, 1977-. vol.; ISSN: 0147-6491. [2092]

A bibliographic introduction to paralegals in two jurisdictions: Canada and the United States: 1970-1978. Vancouver: Pacific Legal Education Association, c1980. vii, 47 p. [2209]

"Bibliographic sources on Ukrainian in the New World, listed chronologically." In: *Canadian Ethnic Studies*; Vol. 1, no. 2 (December 1969) p. 202-212.; ISSN: 0008-3496. [1424]

"Bibliographie: Papineau (Louis-Joseph) 1786-1871." Dans: *Revue d'histoire de l'Amérique française*; Vol. 1, no 1 (juin 1947) p. 148-151.; ISSN: 0035-2357. [7236]

"Bibliographie: Philippe Haeck (1969-1980)." Dans: *Voix et Images*; Vol. 6, no 3 (printemps 1981) p. 373-380.; ISSN: 0318-9201. [7038]

"Bibliographie: Sylvia Truster Wargon." Dans: *Bulletin de l'Association des démographes du Québec*; Vol. 2, no 4 (décembre 1973) p. 52-53. [7361]

Bibliographie analytique régionale: études sur l'Estrie: [étude preparée dans le cadre du projet ESTRAE et presentée à l'Office de planification et de développement du Québec]. [Sherbrooke, Québec]: Université de Sherbrooke, Centre de recherches en aménagement régional, 1972. ii, 220 p. [0314]

Bibliographie annotée des caractéristiques physiques de la côte nord de l'estuaire maritime et du golfe Saint-Laurent. [Ottawa: Ministère des travaux publics], 1972. 191 l. [5061]

Bibliographie C.L.E.F. Ottawa: Centre de référence de la documentation juridique de langue française en matière de Common Law, [1983]. 57 p. (en pagination multiple). [2252]

"Bibliographie chronologique de Jean-Paul Vinay, 1939-1974." Dans: *Vingt-cinq ans de linguistique au Canada: hommage à Jean-Paul Vinay*. Montréal: Centre éducatif et culturel, c1979. P. 109-123.; ISBN: 2-7617-0019-8. [7354]

"Bibliographie de François Charron." Dans: *Voix et Images*; Vol. 16, no 3 (printemps 1991) p. 469-480.; ISSN: 0318-9201. [6905]

"Bibliographie de Jean-Charles Falardeau." Dans: *Recherches sociographiques*; Vol. 23, no 3 (septembre-décembre 1982) p. 429-437.; ISSN: 0034-1282. [6973]

"Bibliographie de M. Hubert Charbonneau." Dans: *Bulletin de l'Association des démographes du Québec*; Vol. 3, no 4 (décembre 1974) p. 34-40. [6903]

Bibliographie de M.C. Baillairgé: extraite du volume des "Transactions" pour 1894, de la Société royale du Canada: addenda jusqu'à ce jour, Québec, mai 1899. [Québec: s.n., 1899]. xv p. [6821]

"Bibliographie de Madeleine Gagnon." Dans: *Voix et Images*; Vol. 8, no 1 (automne 1982) p. 53-58.; ISSN: 0318-9201. [6997]

Une bibliographie de sources historiques du district de Nipissing. North Bay, Ont.: Société historique du Nipissing, 1979. vi, 21 p. (Société historique du Nipissing Études historiques ; no 1) [0460]

Bibliographie des chroniques de langage publiées dans la presse au Canada. [Montréal]: Département de linguistique et philologie, Université de Montréal, [1975-1976]. 2 vol. [1434]

"Bibliographie des écrits féministes." Dans: *Canadian Women's Studies*; Vol. 1, no. 1 (Fall 1978) p.135-136.; ISSN: 0713-3235. [3775]

"Bibliographie des matériaux déposés aux Archives publiques du Canada concernant l'insurrection de 1837-1838." Dans: *Rapport sur les Archives publiques du Canada*; (1939) p. 63-138.; ISSN: 0701-7790. [1917]

"Bibliographie des oeuvres de Fernand Ouellette." Dans: *Voix et Images*; Vol. 5, no 3 (printemps 1980) p. 471-475.; ISSN: 0318-9201. [7231]

"Bibliographie des publications de Pierre Dansereau de 1972 à ce jour." Dans: *Géographie physique et quaternaire*; Vol. 39, no 1 (1985) p. 4-6.; ISSN: 0705-7199. [6934]

Bibliographie du Québec. Montréal: Bibliothèque nationale du Québec, 1970-. vol.; ISSN: 0006-1441. [0417]

"Bibliographie [La famille au Québec]." Dans: *Relations*; No 305 (mai 1966) p. 162-164.; ISSN: 0034-3781. [3084]

"Bibliographie [L'Église au Québec]." Dans: *Relations*; No 302 (février 1966) p. 63-68.; ISSN: 0034-3781. [1518]

Bibliographie pour les services de garde en milieu scolaire. Québec: Gouvernement du Québec, Ministère de l'éducation, 1989. 36 p.; ISBN: 2-550-14751-0. [3699]

"Bibliographie raisonnée de l'anthroponymie canadienne." Dans: *Mémoires de la Société généalogique canadienne-française*; No 9 (1958) p. 153-173.; ISSN: 0037-9387. [1929]

"Bibliographie [relative à la vie sociale, économique et politique au Québec]." Dans: *Relations*; No 309 (octobre 1966) p. 288-292.; ISSN: 0034-3781. [0296]

"Bibliographie relative au drapeau québécois." Dans: *Le drapeau québécois*, par Jacques Archambault et Eugénie Lévesque. Québec: Éditeur officiel du Québec, 1974. P. 62-75. [0327]

"Bibliographie [revues littéraires québécoises]." Dans: *Voix et Images*; Vol. 10, no 2 (hiver 1985) p. 173-176.; ISSN: 0318-9201. [5952]

Bibliographie sélective: terminologie et disciplines connexes/ Selective bibliography: terminology and related fields. [Ottawa]: Direction de la terminologie, Secrétariat d'État du Canada, c1988. vi, 87 p.; ISBN: 0-660-54120-3. [1476]

"Bibliographie sommaire des événements de 1837-1838." Dans: *Liberté*; Vol. 7, no 1-2 (janvier-avril 1965) p. 174-182.; ISSN: 0024-2020. [1945]

"Bibliographie sur Calixa Lavalée et 'O Canada'." Dans: *Passe-Temps*; Vol. 39, no. 864 (août 1933) p. 42.; ISSN: 0384-5737. [7129]

Bibliographie sur le développement régional/Bibliography on regional development. Moncton, N.-B.: Institut canadien de recherche sur le développement régional, 1985. iii, 348, 22 p.; ISBN: 0-88659-005-1. [2706]

"Bibliographie sur les relations extérieures du Canada/ Canadian foreign relations: a bibliography." Dans: *Chronique des relations extérieures du Canada*; (juillet-septembre 1989)-(juillet-septembre 1992) [2546]

Bibliographie sur les rivières du patrimoine: références choisies du fichier de la Direction des accords au sujet de la récréation et de la conservation, Parcs Canada. Ottawa: Parcs Canada, 1979. iv, 302 p. [1790]

"Bibliographies, Canadian and international." In: *Canadian Newsletter of Research on Women*; (1972-1978) ; ISSN: 0319-4477. [3776]

"Bibliographies on contributors [to *Prism International*]." In: *Prism International*; Vol. 18, no. 1 (Spring/Summer 1979) p. 118-123; vol. 18, no. 2 (Winter 1979-1980) p. 140-143; vol. 19, no. 1 (Spring 1980) p. 109-112.; ISSN: 0032-8790. [1162]

"Bibliography: Canadian refugee policy: a history." In: *Canadian Woman Studies*; Vol. 10, no. 1 (Spring 1989) p. 115-121.; ISSN: 0713-3235. [3867]

A bibliography: the long-range transport of air pollutants and acidic precipitation. Downsview, Ont.: LRTAP Program Office, Atmospheric Environment Service, Environment Canada, 1980. 95 p. [5159]

Bibliography: tourism research studies/Bibliographie: études de recherches de tourisme. [Ottawa]: Canadian Government Travel Bureau, 1970. 86 p. [1755]

Bibliography and literature review of the resource base of St. Lawrence Islands National Park. Ottawa: Indian and Northern Affairs, Ontario Region, Parks Canada, [1975]. 1 vol. (in various pagings): ill., maps. [3007]

"Bibliography of atmospheric ionization." In: *Canadian Geophysical Bulletin*; Vol. 4, no. 2 (April-June 1950) p. 1-10.; ISSN: 0068-8819. [5026]

"Bibliography of Canadian educational history/Bibliographie d'histoire de l'éducation canadienne." In: *Historical Studies in Education*; Vol. 2, no. 1 (Spring 1990) p. 189-195.; ISSN: 0843-5057. [3709]

"Bibliography of Canadian geophysics, 1951." In: *Canadian Geophysical Bulletin*; Vol. 4, no. 4 (Part 1) (October-December 1950) p. 1-49.; ISSN: 0068-8819. [4744]

"Bibliography of Canadian hydrology." In: *Canadian Geophysical Bulletin*; Vol. 3, no. 2 (April-June 1949) p. 1-10.; ISSN: 0068-8819. [5025]

A bibliography of Canadian material on freedom of information, individual privacy, and related topics. Ottawa: Canadian Committee for the Right to Public Information, 1980. 55 l. [2210]

"Bibliography of Canadian seismology." In: *Canadian Geophysical Bulletin*; Vol. 2, no. 2 (April-June 1948) p. 1-12.; ISSN: 0068-8819. [4741]

"A bibliography of current publications on Canadian economics." In: *Canadian Journal of Economics and Political Science*; (1935-1952) ; ISSN: 0315-4890. [2563]

Bibliography of hydrology. Canada, 1968-1970/Bibliographie d'hydrologie. Canada, 1968-1970. [Ottawa]: Department of the Environment and National Research Council, [1970]. v, 336 p. [5050]

A bibliography of informational pamphlets and brochures to assist in immigrant settlement. [Toronto]: Ontario Ministry of Citizenship, [1989]. 47 p.; ISBN: 0-7729-0946-6. [4265]

Bibliography of kind of business publications. [Regina, Sask.]: Saskatchewan Tourism and Small Business, 1985. iii, 119 p. [2707]

Bibliography of land resource information for 17 estuaries in British Columbia. Vancouver: Lands Directorate, Pacific Region, Environment Canada, 1974. 1 vol. (in various pagings): maps. [5085]

"Bibliography of materials at the Public Archives of Canada relating to the rebellion of 1837-1838." In: *Report of the Public Archives of Canada*; (1939) p. 63-138.; ISSN: 0701-7790. [1918]

A bibliography of Oxford County. [Woodstock, Ont.]: Oxford Historical Research Project, 1979. [8], 88 p.: maps. [0461]

"Bibliography of physical oceanography for Canada." In: *Canadian Geophysical Bulletin*; Vol. 3, no. 2 (April-June 1949) p. 11-25.; ISSN: 0068-8819. [4743]

"Bibliography of published books and articles of the late Norman McLeod Rogers relating to history, economics, and political science." In: *Canadian Journal of Economics and Political Science*; Vol. 6, no. 3 (August 1940) p. 477-478.; ISSN: 0315-4890. [7273]

"Bibliography of R.A. Samek." In: *Dalhousie Law Journal*; Vol. 9, no. 2 (June 1985) p. 469-470.; ISSN: 0317-1663. [7291]

"Bibliography of radioactivity of rocks in Canada." In: *Canadian Geophysical Bulletin*; Vol. 2, no. 2 (April-June 1948) p. 13-27.; ISSN: 0068-8819. [4742]

"Bibliography of recent publications [Newfoundland and Labrador]." In: *Newfoundland Studies*; (1985-) vol.; ISSN: 0823-1737. [0275]

"Bibliography of recommended works dealing with the R.C.M. Police." In: *Royal Canadian Mounted Police Quarterly*; Vol. 1, no. 2 (October 1933) p. 62.; ISSN: 0317-8250. [2103]

"Bibliography of Robert England." In: *Canadian Ethnic Studies*; Vol. 8, no. 2 (1976) p. 29-33.; ISSN: 0008-3496. [6967]

Bibliography of studies on older people in Alberta. [Edmonton]: Senior Citizens Bureau, Alberta Social Services and Community Health, 1980. 28 l. [3196]

"Bibliography of the Canadian mountain region." In: *Canadian Alpine Journal*; Vol. 9 (1918) p. 159-164; vol. 10 (1919) p. 101-102.; ISSN: 0068-8207. [2947]

"Bibliography of the collection of A. Becker at the Adam Shortt Library of Canadiana, University of Saskatchewan, Saskatoon, Canada." In: *Saskatchewan Genealogical Society Bulletin*; Vol. 12, no. 3 (September 1981) p. 124-135.; ISSN: 0048-9182. [4200]

"A bibliography of the Royal Canadian Mounted Police." In: *Saskatchewan Genealogical Society Bulletin*; Vol. 4, no. 3 (Summer 1973) p. 73-76.; ISSN: 0048-9182. [2129]

A bibliography of the Royal Canadian Mounted Police. Ottawa: Historical Section, R.C.M.P. Headquarters, 1979. 69 p., 7 l. [2190]

"Bibliography of the works of F.R. Scott/Bibliographie des oeuvres de F.R. Scott." In: *McGill Law Journal*; Vol. 30, no. 4 (October 1985) p. 635-643.; ISSN: 0024-9041. [7298]

"Bibliography of works by James Bovell." In: *Pioneers of Canadian science: symposium presented to the Royal Society of Canada in 1964*, edited by George F.G. Stanley. Toronto: University of Toronto Press, 1966. P. 136-137. [6868]

Bibliography on disabled children: a guide to materials for young people aged 3 to 17 years. Ottawa: Canadian Library Association, c1981. 50 p.; ISBN: 0-88802-159-3. [3210]

Bibliography on Maritime regionalism and multi-government partnerships/Bibliographie sur le régionalisme dans les Maritimes et la collaboration entre les gouvernements. Halifax, N.S.: Council of Maritime Premiers, 1988. 13 l. [0267]

Bibliography on metric conversion/Bibliographie de la conversion au système métrique. Ottawa: Metric Commission Canada, 1980. 130 p. [2657]

Biblioteca Centrală de Stat a Republicii Socialiste Românâ
Expositia de carte canadiana: catalog. Bucuresti: Tipografia Bibliotecii Centrale de Stat, 1972. 30 p.: ill., facsims. [0101]

Bibliotheca Canadensis: a catalogue of a very large collection of books and pamphlets relating to the history, the topography, the manners and customs of the Indians, the trade and government of North America .... Toronto: R.W. Douglas, 1887. 79, [1] p. [6740]

Bibliotheca hispano-americana: a catalogue of Spanish books ... : followed by a collection of works on the aboriginal languages of America. London: Trübner, 1870. 184 p. [1401]

Bibliothèque de la ville de Montréal
L'Alimentation traditionnelle au Canada: une bibliographie. Montréal: Ville de Montréal, Service de loisirs et du développement communautaire, 1988. 8 p.; ISBN: 2-89417-028-9. [1846]

Bibliothèque du Conseil d'hygiène de la province de Québec: catalogue/Library of the Board of Health of province of Quebec: catalogue. Montréal: [s.n.], 1897. 40 p. [5562]

Bibliothèque municipale de Loretteville
Gros plan sur le Québec: bibliographie analytique sur la question référendaire au Québec. [Loretteville, Québec]: Bibliothèque municipale de Loretteville, 1980. viii, 87 p. [2456]

Bibliothèque municipale de Mulhouse

Livres du Québec. Mulhouse, France: Mairie de Mulhouse, [1975]. 24 p. [0331]

Bibliothèque nationale du Canada

Arthur S. Bourinot. Ottawa: Bibliothèque nationale du Canada, 1971. 30, 30 p.: ports. [6865]

Catalogue de publications [Bibliothèque nationale du Canada]. Ottawa: La Bibliothèque, 1992. 30, 30 p.; ISBN: 0-662-59049-X. [1730]

Bibliothèque nationale du Québec

Catalogue de la Bibliothèque nationale du Québec: revues québécoises. Montréal: La Bibliothèque, 1981. 3 vol.; ISBN: 2-551-04239-9. (Édition complète). [5940]

Contes et légendes du Québec: liste de volumes localisés à la Bibliothèque nationale du Québec et exposés à la Bibliothèque municipale de Longueuil, du 16 au 25 août 1974. Montréal: Bibliothèque nationale du Québec, Service d'orientation du lecteur, 1974. 9 f. [1081]

Édition Erta: [exposition, mars-avril 1971]. Montréal: Ministère des affaires culturelles, 1971. 34 p.: ill. [1592]

Liste des thèses de l'Institut agricole d'Oka déposées à la Bibliothèque nationale du Québec. Montréal: La Bibliothèque, 1979. 25 f. [6150]

Le livre québécois 1764-1975. Montréal: Bibliothèque nationale du Québec, 1975. 182 p.: ill. [0332]

Publications éditées par la Bibliothèque nationale du Québec. Montréal: La Bibliothèque, 1992. 31 p.: ill.; ISBN: 2-550-26645-5. [1731]

Bibliothèque nationale du Québec. Bureau de la bibliographie rétrospective

Bibliographie du Québec, 1821-1967. [Québec]: Éditeur officiel du Québec, 1980-.   vol.; ISBN: 2-551-03716-6 (édition complète). [0418]

Bibliothèque nationale du Québec. Centre bibliographique

Bibliographie de bibliographies québécoises. Montréal: Bibliothèque nationale du Québec, 1979. 2 vol.; ISBN: 2-400-00074-3 (Édition complète). [0358]

Bibliothèque nationale du Québec. Service de microphotographie

Catalogue des microéditions [Service de microphotographie, Bibliothèque nationale du Québec]. Montréal: Ministère des affaires culturelles, Bibliothèque nationale du Québec, 1974-1978. 5 vol.; ISSN: 0384-9724. [0352]

Microéditions de la Bibliothèque: catalogue. Montréal: Bibliothèque nationale du Québec, 1979-.   vol.; ISSN: 0707-848X. [0419]

Bibliothèque nationale du Québec. Service des entrées

Liste des revues et journaux courants québécois reçus à la Bibliothèque nationale du Québec. Montréal: Bibliothèque nationale du Québec, 1976-1982. 10 no.; ISSN: 0707-7823. [5947]

Bibliothèque paroissiale de Notre-Dame et du Cercle Ville-Marie

Catalogue des livres de la bibliothèque paroissiale de Notre-Dame et du Cercle Ville-Marie. Montréal: [s.n.], 1898. viii, 282 p. [6750]

Bibliothèque publique d'Ottawa

Liens entre les générations: livres pour enfants qui mettant l'accent sur l'établissement de liens entre les générations. Toronto: Ministère des affaires civiques et culturelles de l'Ontario, 1986. 6 f. [1369]

Bibliothèque régionale du Haut-Saint-Jean

Découvrons le Nouveau-Brunswick: bibliographie sélective sur l'histoire du Nouveau-Brunswick/Discover New Brunswick: selective bibliography on New Brunswick history. Edmundston, N.-B.: La Bibliothèque, [1984]. 32 f. [0256]

Bickerstaff, A.; Hostikka, S.A.

Growth of forests in Canada. [Ottawa]: Canadian Forestry Service, Fisheries and Environment Canada, 1977. v, 197 p. (Forest Management Institute Information report ; FMR-X-98) [4954]

Bickerton, James; Gagnon, Alain-G.

Canadian politics. Ottawa: Canadian Studies Directorate, Department of the Secretary of State of Canada, 1992. 26, 28 p. (Canadian studies resource guides. Second series); ISBN: 0-662-58836-3. [2547]

La politique canadienne. Ottawa: Direction des études canadiennes, Secrétariat d'État du Canada, 1992. 28, 26 p. (Guides pédagogiques des études canadiennes. Deuxième collection); ISBN: 0-662-58863-3. [2548]

Biehl, Nancy

Gazetteers in the History Section and the Baldwin Room of the Metropolitan Toronto Central Library. [Toronto]: Metropolitan Toronto Central Library, 1975. 32 p. [3008]

Biggins, Patricia

An annotated bibliography of Canadian radio drama produced by CBC Vancouver between 1939 and 1945. Burnaby, B.C.: Simon Fraser University, 1974. 103 l. [1082]

Billings, Fred L.

Biotin: an annotated bibliography. Montreal: Hoffman-Laroche Limited, 1970. 241 l. [5575]

Billy, George J.

Shipping. Monticello, Ill.: Vance Bibliographies, 1990. 41 p. (Public administration series: Bibliography ; P-2880; ISSN: 0193-970X); ISBN: 0-7920-0540-6. [4506]

Bilodeau, Françoise

Bibliographie du théâtre canadien-français de 1900-1955. [S.l.: s.n.], 1956. 93 f. [0947]

Binda, Gilles G.

Ontario sediment-related literature: annotated bibliography. Ottawa: Environment Canada, Water Resources Branch, Inland Waters-Lands Directorate, Sediment Survey Section, 1987. iii, 250 p. [5240]

Binda, Gilles G.; Day, T.J.; Syvitski, J.P.M.

Terrestrial sediment transport into the marine environment of Canada: annotated bibliography and data. [Ottawa]: Environment Canada, Inland Waters Directorate, Water Resources Branch, [1986]. 1 vol. (in various pagings): ill., (1 map folded). [5229]

Bindoff, Stanley Thomas; Boulton, James T.

Research in progress in English and history in Britain, Ireland, Canada, Australia and New Zealand. London: St. James Press; New York: St. Martin's Press, 1976. 284 p.; ISBN: 0-900997-28-1. [1095]

"Bio-bibliographie [Gérard Bessette]." Dans: *Québec littéraire*; No 1 (1974) p. 155-166.; ISSN: 0384-9406. [6839]

"Bio-bibliographie sommaire de la plupart des écrivains ayant participé à la Rencontre québécoise internationale des écrivains." Dans: *Liberté*; No 84 (décembre 1972)-no 130 (juillet-août 1980) [1163]

Bircham, Paul D.; Bruneau, Hélène C.

La dégradation des terres agricoles de la prairie canadienne: guide des publications et bibliographie annotée. [Ottawa]:

Direction générale des terres, Environnement Canada, 1985. viii, 154 p. (Document de travail / Direction générale des terres, Environnement Canada ; no 37); ISBN: 0 662 93032-0. [4703]

Degradation of Canada's prairie agricultural lands: a guide to literature and annotated bibliography. [Ottawa]: Lands Directorate, Environmental Conservation Service, Environment Canada, 1985. viii, 137 p. (Working paper / Lands Directorate, Environment Canada ; no. 37; ISSN: 0712-4473); ISBN: 0-662-13797-3. [4704]

Birney, Earle; Lowry, Marjerie
"Malcolm Lowry (1909-1957): a bibliography." In: *Canadian Literature*; No. 8 (Spring 1961) p. 81-88; no. 9 (Summer 1961) p. 80-84; no. 11 (Winter 1962) p. 90-95; no. 19 (Winter 1964) p. 83-89.; ISSN: 0008-4360. [7158]

Biron, Guy; Gagnon, France
Info-carto 02: répertoire cartobibliographique sur la région 02 et Moyen Nord. [Chicoutimi, Québec]: U.Q.A.C., 1983. v f., 261 p.: cartes. [6580]

Biron, Jean-Pierre
Bibliographie sur le loisir de plein air. Trois-Rivières: Université du Québec à Trois-Rivières, 1977. 35 f. [1785]

Biron, Luc-André
Bio-bibliographie de Charles-Yvon Thériault, journaliste (1948-1956). Trois-Rivières: [s.n.], 1961. xi, 105 p.: portr., fac-sim. [7330]

Birt, Heather; Gladman, Tina
Maritime energy education bibliography/Bibliographie sur les programmes d'éducation sur l'énergie dans les Maritimes. Halifax, N.S.: Maritime Provinces Education Foundation, 1982. ix, 46 p. [3602]

Bishop, Olga B.
Canadian official publications. Oxford; Toronto: Pergamon Press, 1981. x, 297 p. (Guides to official publications / Pergamon Press ; vol. 9); ISBN: 0-08-024697-4. [6330]

"Checklist of historical works on western Ontario in the libraries of the University of Western Ontario." In: *Western Ontario Historical Notes*; Vol. 14, no. 1 (December 1957)-vol. 18, no. 1 (March 1962) [0431]

Publications of the Government of Ontario, 1867-1900. Toronto: Ministry of Government Services, 1976. xi, 409 p. [6302]

Publications of the government of the Province of Canada, 1841-1867. Ottawa: Queen's Printer, 1963. x, 351 p. [6246]

Publications of the governments of Nova Scotia, Prince Edward Island, New Brunswick, 1758-1952. Ottawa: National Library of Canada, 1957. vi, 237 p. [6239]

Publications of the province of Upper Canada and of Great Britain relating to Upper Canada, 1791-1840. Toronto: Ontario Ministry of Citizenship and Culture, 1984. vii, 288 p.; ISBN: 0-7743-8931-1. [6364]

Bishop, Olga B.; Irwin, Barbara I.; Miller, Clara G.
Bibliography of Ontario history, 1867-1976: cultural, economic, political, social. 2nd ed. Toronto: University of Toronto Press, [1980]. 2 vol. (Ontario historical studies series; ISSN: 0380-9188); ISBN: 0-8020-2359-2 (set). [0467]

Bishop, Yvonne, et al.
Index and list of titles, publications of the Fisheries Research Board of Canada, 1901-1954. Ottawa: Fisheries Research Board of Canada, 1957. xxi, 209 p. (Fisheries Research Board of Canada Bulletin ; no. 110) [6240]

Index to Manuscript reports of the biological stations, no. 1-600, and Manuscript reports of the technological stations,

no. 1-57, together with the titles of the papers in these two series. [S.l.]: Fisheries Research Board of Canada, 1956. 142 p. [6238]

Bisson, Réal; Poulin, Pierre
Les oiseaux de la Gaspésie: liste annotée et bibliographie. Percé, Québec: Club des ornithologues de la Gaspésie, 1982. 57 f.: carte. [5470]

Bisztray, George
Canadian-Hungarian literature: a preliminary survey. [Ottawa]: Department of the Secretary of State of Canada, Multiculturalism, 1988. 48 l.; ISBN: 0-662-16033-9. [1245]

Black, A.; Powell, M.
Municipal government and finance: an annotated bibliography/L'administration municipale et les finances: une bibliographie annotée. [Ottawa: Policy Planning Division, Central Mortgage and Housing Corporation, 1971]. 230 p. [4317]

Black, Dorothy Miller
Guide to lists of master's theses. Chicago: American Library Association, 1965. 144 p. [6081]

Black, John B.
Propaganda, mass media and politics [microform]: a computerized research bibliography. Toronto: Micromedia, c1977. 8 microfiches. [2427]

Black, Joseph Laurence
Canadian-Soviet relations, 1917-1985: a bibliography. Ottawa: Institute of Soviet and East European Studies, Carleton University, 1985. iv, 142 p. (Institute of Soviet and East European Studies bibliography ; no. 4) [2488]

Soviet perception of Canada, 1917-1987: an annotated bibliographic guide. Kingston, Ont.: Ronald P. Frye, c1989. ix, 139, xiv, 242 p. (Centre for Canadian Soviet Studies, Bibliographic series ; no. 1); ISBN: 0-919741-94-0. [0162]

Blackader-Lauterman Library of Architecture and Art
The libraries of Edward and W.S. Maxwell in the collections of the Blackader-Lauterman Library of Architecture and Art, McGill University/Les bibliothèques de Edward et W.S. Maxwell dans les collections de la Bibliothèque Blackader-Lauterman d'architecture et d'art, Université McGill. Montréal: Blackader-Lauterman Library of Architecture and Art, McGill University, 1991. iii, 110 p.; ISBN: 0-7717-0245-0. [0801]

Blackburn, Robert H.
A joint catalogue of the serials in the libraries of the city of Toronto. 5th ed. [Toronto]: University of Toronto Press, 1953. 602 p. [5866]

Bladen, M.L.
"Graduate theses in Canadian political science and economics." In: *Contributions to Canadian Economics*; Vol. 6 (1933) p. 62-69. [6055]

Blais, André
"Les études sur la politique canadienne: une contribution modeste mais *distincte*." Dans: *Revue internationale d'études canadiennes*; No 1-2 (printemps-automne 1990) p. 55-76.; ISSN: 1180-3991. [2532]

Blais, Jacques
"Bibliographie: [Saint-Denys Garneau]." Dans: *De Saint-Denys Garneau*. Montréal: Fides, 1971. P. 53-65. (Dossiers de documentation sur la littérature canadienne-française ; 7) [7004]

"Complément à une bibliographie de Saint-Denys Garneau." Dans: *Études françaises*; Vol. 20, no 3 (hiver 1984-1985) p. 113-127.; ISSN: 0014-2085. [7005]

"Documents pour servir à la bibliographie critique de l'oeuvre de Saint-Denys Garneau." Dans: *Revue de l'Université Laval*; Vol. 18, no 5 (janvier 1964) p. 424-438.; ISSN: 0384-0182. [7003]

Blakeney, Sharon
An annotated bibliography of the works of Silas Tertius Rand. Halifax, N.S.: Dalhousie University, 1974. viii, [69] l. [7256]

Blanchard, Jim
"A bibliography on mechanics' institutes with particular reference to Ontario." In: *Readings in Canadian library history*, edited by Peter F. McNally. Ottawa: Canadian Library Association, 1986. P. 3-18.; ISBN: 0-88802-196-8. [1675]

Blanchard, Raoul
"Liste des travaux de Raoul Blanchard." Dans: *Cahiers de géographie de Québec*; Vol. 3, no 6 (avril-septembre 1959) p. 35-45.; ISSN: 0007-9766. [6854]

Blanchard, Robert G.
The first editions of John Buchan: a collector's bibliography. Hamden, Conn.: Archon Books, 1981. xi, 284 p.; ISBN: 0-208-01905-7. [7344]

Blanchette, Jean-François; Bouchard, René; Pocius, Gerald L.
"Une bibliographie de la culture matérielle traditionnelle au Canada 1965-1982/A bibliography of material culture in Canada 1965-1982." Dans: *Canadian Folklore: Folklore canadien*; Vol. 4, no 1/2 (1982) p. 107-146.; ISSN: 0225-2899. [4588]

Blazina, Vesna
"Bibliographie sélective sur la rééducation." Dans: *Criminologie*; Vol. 11, no 1 (1978) p. 80-86.; ISSN: 0316-0041. [2179]

Blazuk, Julia, et al.
The music, art and drama of Commonwealth countries: a source book for secondary teachers. Edmonton: 1977. 73 p.: ill. [0686]

Blizzard, Flora Helena
West Indians in Canada: a selective annotated bibliography. Guelph [Ont.]: The Library, University of Guelph, 1970. 41 p. (Bibliographic series / University of Guelph Library ; no. 1) [4145]

Blodgett, Jean
"Bibliographie de l'art inuit canadien contemporain." Dans: *Art et l'artisanat*; Vol. 5, no 2 (1982) p. 1-35.; ISSN: 0706-0203. [0697]
"A bibliography of contemporary Canadian Inuit art." In: *About Arts and Crafts*; Vol. 5, no. 2 (1982) p. 1-35.; ISSN: 0706-0203. [0698]

Blogg, Minnie Wright
Bibliography of the writings of Sir William Osler. Rev. and enl. ed. Baltimore: Blogg, 1921. 96 p.: ill. [7227]

Bloomfield, Elizabeth
"Bibliography: recent publications relating to Canada's urban past/Bibliographie: contributions récentes à l'histoire urbaine du Canada." In: *Urban History Review: Revue d'histoire urbaine*; Vol. 10, no. 2 (October 1981)-vol. 16, no. 2 (October 1987) [4415]

Bloomfield, Elizabeth; Stelter, Gilbert A.
Guelph and Wellington County: a bibliography of settlement and development since 1800. [Guelph, Ont.]: Guelph Regional Project, University of Guelph, 1988. 329 p.: map.; ISBN: 0-88955-133-2. [0485]

Bloomfield, Janice; Harrison, Peter
The shorezone: an annotated bibliography. [Ottawa]: Environment Canada, Lands Directorate, 1976. 53 p. (Occasional paper / Environment Canada, Lands Directorate ; no. 12) [5109]

Blouin, Pierre, et al.
L'Institut canadien d'éducation des adultes et les communications, 1956-1987: bibliographie analytique. Sainte-Foy: Réseau québécois d'information sur la communication, c1988. 41 p.; ISBN: 2-921026-00-7. [3680]

Blount, Gail
Collective bargaining in Canadian education: an annotated bibliography. [Toronto]: Ontario Institute for Studies in Education, [c1975]. x, 38 p. (Bibliography series / Ontario Institute for Studies in Education ; no. 1); ISBN: 0-7744-0114-1. [3493]
Teacher evaluation: an annotated bibliography. Toronto: Library, Reference & Information Services, Ontario Institute for Studies in Education, 1974. x, 32 p. (Current bibliography / Ontario Institute for Studies in Education ; no. 8) [3478]

Blue Pond Collaborative
A union list of Nova Scotia newspapers: who has what for when and where. Halifax: [s.n.], 1987. xii, 432 p. [6038]

Blum, Eleanor; Wilhoit, Frances Goins
Mass media bibliography: an annotated guide to books and journals for research and reference. 3rd ed. Urbana: University of Illinois Press, c1990. viii, 344 p.; ISBN: 0-252-01706-4. [0988]

Blumenfeld, Hans
The trend to the metropolis: bibliography. Monticello, Ill.: Council of Planning Librarians, 1970. 9 l. (Council of Planning Librarians Exchange bibliography ; 144) [4312]

BMI Canada Limited
"Yes, there is Canadian music." "Oui, notre musique existe!". Montreal: 1971. 221 p. [0827]

Bobrowsky, Peter T.; Giles, Tim; Jackaman, Wayne
Surficial geology map index of British Columbia. Victoria: Province of British Columbia, Geological Survey Branch, 1992. 1 vol. (in various pagings): ill., maps.; ISBN: 0-771-89156-3. [6599]

Bogo, Marion
The practice of field instruction in social work: theory and process, with an annotated bibliography. Toronto: University of Toronto Press, 1987. xii, 167 p.: ill.; ISBN: 0-8020-6689-5. [3296]

Bogusis, Ruth; Blazek, Liba
Checklist of Canadian ethnic serials/Liste des publications en série ethniques du Canada. Ottawa: Newspaper Division, Public Services Branch, National Library of Canada, 1981. viii, 381 p.; ISBN: 0-660-50732-3. [5941]

Bohm, W.D.
"Finnish-Canadian periodical publications: a preliminary check list." In: *Canadian Ethnic Studies*; Vol. 1, no. 1 (1969) p. 5-6.; ISSN: 0008-3496. [5880]

Boilard, Gilberte
L'accès aux documents des organismes publics, 1980-1991: bibliographie sélective et annotée. Québec: Bibliothèque de l'Assemblée nationale, Division de la référence parlementaire, 1991. 81 p. (Bibliographie / Bibliothèque de l'Assemblée nationale du Québec ; no 41; ISSN: 0836-9100) [2344]
Avortement: prises de position et aspects juridiques:

bibliographie sélective et annotée. Québec: Bibliothèque de l'Assemblée nationale, Division de la référence parlementaire, 1909. 40 p. (Bibliographie / Bibliothèque de l'Assemblée nationale du Québec ; no 25; ISSN: 0836-9100) [2322]

Charte de la lange française (Loi 101): bibliographie annotée. 2e éd. Québec: Bibliothèque de l'Assemblée nationale, Division de la référence parlementaire, [1989]. 115 p. (Bibliographie / Bibliothèque de l'Assemblée nationale du Québec ; no 23; ISSN: 0836-9100) [2323]

Conflits d'intérêt, 1988-1990: bibliographie sélective. Québec: Bibliothèque de l'Assemblée nationale, Division de la référence parlementaire, 1990. 46 p. (Bibliographie / Bibliothèque de l'Assemblée nationale du Québec ; no 35; ISSN: 0836-9100) [2533]

Discipline de parti: bibliographie sélective et annotée. Québec: Division de la référence parlementaire, Bibliothèque de l'Assemblée nationale, 1988. 23 p. (Bibliographie / Bibliothèque de l'Assemblée nationale du Québec ; no 15; ISSN: 0836-9100) [2513]

Édition du livre au Québec, 1980-1990: bibliographie sélective et annotée. Québec: Bibliothèque de l'Assemblée nationale, Division de la référence parlementaire, 1990. 20 p. (Bibliographie / Bibliothèque de l'Assemblée nationale du Québec ; no 33; ISSN: 0836-9100) [1715]

Francophonie: bibliographie sélective et annotée. Québec: Bibliothèque de l'Assemblée nationale, Division de la référence parlementaire, 1987. 78 p. (Bibliographie / Bibliothèque de l'Assemblée nationale du Québec ; no 8; ISSN: 0836-9100) [2509]

Municipalités régionales de comté: bibliographie. Québec: Bibliothèque de l'Assemblée nationale, Division de la référence parlementaire, 1988. 12 p. (Bibliographie / Bibliothèque de l'Assemblée nationale du Québec ; no 18; ISSN: 0836-9100) [4420]

Organisation policière: bibliographie sélective et annotée. Québec: Bibliothèque de l'Assemblée nationale, Division de la référence parlementaire, 1987. 26 p. (Bibliographie / Bibliothèque de l'Assemblée nationale du Québec ; no 12; ISSN: 0836-9100) [2287]

Privatisation: bibliographie sélective et annotée. Québec: Bibliothèque de l'Assemblée nationale, Division de la référence parlementaire, 1986. 50 p. (Bibliographie / Bibliothèque de l'Assemblée nationale du Québec ; no 1; ISSN: 0836-9100) [2718]

Statut de l'artiste: bibliographie sélective et annotée. Québec: Bibliothèque de l'Assemblée nationale, Division de la référence parlementaire, 1990. 92 p. (Bibliographie / Bibliothèque de l'Assemblée nationale du Québec ; no 37; ISSN: 0836-9100) [0721]

Taxe sur les produits et services (Phase II du Livre blanc sur la réforme fiscale): bibliographie sélective et annotée. Québec: Division de la référence parlementaire, Bibliothèque de l'Assemblée nationale, 1989. 30 p. (Bibliographie / Bibliothèque de l'Assemblée nationale du Québec ; no 30; ISSN: 0836-9100) [2750]

Boilard, Gilberte; Buttazzoni, Maria

Guide de documentation politique. 2e éd. Québec: Bibliothèque de l'Assemblée nationale, 1991. 93 p. (Bibliographie et documentation / Bibliothèque de l'Assemblée nationale du Québec ; 20); ISBN: 2-551-12629-0. [2541]

Boilard, Gilberte; Desjardins, Joëlle

Clause nonobstant: (article 33 de la Charte canadienne des droits et libertés): bibliographie sélective et annotée. Québec: Division de la référence parlementaires, Bibliothèque de l'Assemblée nationale, 1988. 16 p. (Bibliographie / Bibliothèque de l'Assemblée nationale du Québec ; no 16; ISSN: 0836-9100) [2309]

Boilard, Gilberte; Dufresne, Nicole

Heures d'affaires dans les établissements commerciaux le dimanche: bibliographie. Québec: Bibliothèque de l'Assemblée nationale, Division de la référence parlementaire, 1988. 8 p. (Bibliographie / Bibliothèque de l'Assemblée nationale du Québec ; no 17; ISSN: 0836-9100) [2740]

Boilard, Gilberte; Fortin, Jean-Luc

Les bibliothèques parlementaires: histoire, fonctions, services: bibliographie sélective et annotée. Québec: Assemblée nationale, Direction générale de la bibliothèque, Service de la référence, 1992. 78 p. (Bibliographie / Bibliothèque de l'Assemblée nationale du Québec ; no 44; ISSN: 0836-9100) [1732]

Boily, Robert

Québec 1940-1969: bibliographie: le système politique québécois et son environnement. Montréal: Presses de l'Université de Montréal, 1971. xxii, 208 p.; ISBN: 0-8405-0153-6. [2402]

Boirat, Jean-Michel

"Le district à amas sulfurés polymétalliques de Bathurst-Newcastle (New-Brunswick, Canada) dans son environnement géotectonique: étude bibliographique." Dans: *Chronique de la recherche minière*; No 473 (décembre 1983) p. 3-24.; ISSN: 0182-564X. [4831]

Boismenu, Gérard; Ducatenzeiler, Graciela

Technologie et politique au Canada: bibliographie, 1963-1983. Montréal: Association canadienne-française pour l'avancement des sciences, [1984]. 194 p. (Cahiers de l'ACFAS / Association canadienne-française pour l'avancement des sciences ; no 25); ISBN: 2-89245-016-0. [2485]

Transferts de technologie Canada-Québec: bibliographie annotée. Montréal: Département de science politique, Université de Montréal, 1981. 96 p. (Notes de recherche / Département de science politique, Université de Montréal ; no 3) [2460]

Boisvert, Bernard D.

Rabies: a select bibliography. [S.l.: s.n.], 1974. ii, 64 p.] [5591]

Boisvert, Marcel

Inventaire d'un stock d'anciens manuels de français. Montréal: Programme de perfectionnement des maîtres de français du secondaire, Faculté des sciences de l'éducation, Université de Montréal, 1978. 207 p. (Didactique du français au secondaire / Faculté des sciences de l'éducation, Université de Montréal ; série 1, no 2) [3535]

Boivin, Aurélien

"Bibliographie d'André Major." Dans: *Voix et Images*; Vol. 10, no 3 (printemps 1985) p. 70-89.; ISSN: 0318-9201. [7173]

Le conte littéraire québécois au XIXe siècle: essai de bibliographie critique et analytique. Montréal: Fides, c1975. xxxviii, 385 p.; ISBN: 0-7755-0557-9. [1087]

Boivin, Aurélien; Bourgeois, Jean-Marc

Littérature du Saguenay-Lac-Saint-Jean: répertoire des oeuvres et des auteurs. Alma [Québec]: Éditions du Royaume, c1980. 147 p.: ill., fac.-sims.; ISBN: 2-920164-00-

7. [0360]

Boivin, Aurélien; Émond, Maurice; Lord, Michel
Bibliographie analytique de la science-fiction et du fantastique québécois, 1960-1985. Québec: Nuit blanche, 1992. 577 p. (Cahiers du Centre de recherche en littérature québécoise: Bibliographie; no 3); ISBN: 2-021053-07-1. [1296]

Boivin, Aurélien; Landry, Kenneth
"Guide bibliographique de la littérature québécoise." Dans: *Stanford French Review*; Vol. 4, no. 1-2 (Spring-Fall 1980) p. 265-285.; ISSN: 0163-657X. [1164]

Boivin, Aurélien; Robert, Lucie
"Bibliographie de Guy Dufresne." Dans: *Voix et Images*; Vol. 9, no 1 (automne 1983) p. 59-81.; ISSN: 0318-9201. [6961]

Boivin, Aurélien; Robert, Lucie; Major-Lapierre, Ruth
"Bibliographie de Marie-Claire Blais." Dans: *Voix et Images*; Vol. 8, no 2 (hiver 1983) p. 249-295.; ISSN: 0318-9201. [6850]

Boivin, Henri-Bernard
"Contribution à la bibliographie du Comté des Deux-Montagnes." Dans: *Cahiers d'histoire de Deux-Montagnes*; Vol. 1, no 1 (janvier 1978) p. 24-41.; ISSN: 0226-7063. [0353]
Littérature acadienne, 1960-1980: bibliographie. Montréal: Bibliothèque nationale du Quebec, 1981. 63 p.: ill.; ISBN: 2-550-01639-4. [1177]

Boivin, Henri-Bernard; Jean, Claire; Bosa, Réal
Histoire des communautés religieuses au Québec: bibliographie. Montréal: Bibliothèque nationale du Québec, 1984. 157, [16] p.: ill.; ISBN: 2-551-06457-0. [1557]

Bojanowski, Belle C., et al.
Research on aging in British Columbia: an annotated bibliography, 1950-1983. Burnaby: Gerontology Research Centre, Simon Fraser University, c1984. v, 139 p.; ISBN: 0-86491-036-3. [3256]

Bolduc, Anicette; Breton, Lise
Apprentissage assuré: bibliographie annotée. Montréal: Centre d'animation, de développement et de recherches en éducation, 1981. 31 p.; ISBN: 2-89169-005-2. [3582]

Bolduc, Jocelyn
Equipements touristiques et politiques de développement: Tiers-Monde francophone et Canada: bibliographie sélective/Tourist facilities and development policies: French speaking Third World and Canada: selective bibliography. Ottawa: Institut de coopération internationale, Université d'Ottawa, 1974. vi, 71 f. (Travaux et documents de l'I.C.I.; série C, no 7: bibliographies) [1763]

Bollinger, Irene
Northern development: people, resources, ecology, and transportation in the Yukon and the Northwest Territories: a bibliography of government publications with selected annotations. Monticello, Ill.: Council of Planning Librarians, 1974. 13 p. (Council of Planning Librarians Exchange bibliography; 643) [0625]

Bollman, Ray D.
Selected annotated bibliography of research on part-time farming in Canada. Monticello, Ill.: Vance Bibliographies, 1979. 64 p. (Public administration series: Bibliography; P-262; ISSN: 0193-970X) [4684]

Bolsenga, S.J.
River ice jams: a literature review. [Detroit]: Great Lakes Research Center, U.S. Lake Survey, 1968. iii, 568 p.: ill. [5039]

Bombas, Leonidas C.
Greeks in Canada (an annotated bibliography). [Montreal, Que.: Leonidas Bombas, 1982]. 139 p. [4206]
Ho Hell-enismos tou Kanada: mia bibliographik-e parousias-e/Canada's Hellenism: a bibliographic guide. Athens: Leonidas C. Bombas, 1989. 76 p. (Greek-Canadian documentation series) [4266]

Bonar Law Bennett Library
A catalogue of the Rufus Hathaway collection of Canadian literature, University of New Brunswick. Fredericton: [s.n.], 1935. vi, 53 p. [1002]

Bonavia, George
Ethnic publications in Canada: newspapers, periodicals, magazines, bulletins, newsletters. Ottawa: Department of the Secretary of State of Canada, 1987. xii, 158 p. [5961]
Répertoire des publications ethniques du Canada: journaux, périodiques, magazines, bulletins, lettres d'informations. Ottawa: Multiculturalisme et citoyenneté Canada, 1988. xii, 165 p. [5965]

Bond, J. Jameson
Selected bibliography on Eskimo ethnology with special emphasis on acculturation. Ottawa: Department of Northern Affairs and Natural Resources, Northern Administration and Lands Branch, 1956. 11 l. [3910]

Bond, Mary E.
Canadian directories, 1790-1987: a bibliography and place-name index/Annuaires canadiens, 1790-1987: une bibliographie et un index des noms de lieux. Ottawa: National Library of Canada, 1989. 3 vol.; ISBN: 0-660-54786-4 (set). [5967]

Boneca, Shirley; Clinton, Marshall
Child abuse materials available in northwestern Ontario: a finding aid. 2nd ed. Thunder Bay, Ont.: Lakehead University Library, 1986. ii, 30 p.; ISBN: 0-88663-005-3. [3284]

Bonenfant, Jean-Charles
"Matériaux pour une sociologie politique du Canada français. III: Inventaire des sources." Dans: *Recherches sociographiques*; Vol. 2, no 3-4 (juillet-décembre 1961) p. 483-566.; ISSN: 0034-1282. [2378]

Bonenfant, Jean-Claude
"Livres et périodiques canadiens d'expression française publiés de 1946 à 1961/Canada's French language books and periodicals published from 1946 to 1961." Dans: *Annuaire du Québec*; (1961) p. 265-289. [0291]

Bonnelly, Claude
"Bibliographie de Émile Simard de 1946 à 1969." Dans: *Laval théologique et philosophique*; Vol. 25, no 2 (1969) p. 168-170.; ISSN: 0023-9054. [7307]

Bonnor, G.M.
Forest sampling and inventories: a bibliography. Ottawa: Forest Management Institute, Canadian Forestry Service, Environment Canada, 1972. 27 p. (Forest Management Institute Internal report; FMR-24) [4930]

Bonville, Jean de
Communications: liste d'ouvrages disponibles à la Bibliothèque de l'Université Laval, 1974-1978. Québec: Bibliothèque de l'Université Laval, 1978. 417 p. [2633]

"Book notes." In: *Ontario History*; (1948-1979); ISSN: 0030-2953. [0462]

Book Publishers' Association of Canada
Books & music [presented by the Book Publishers' Association of Canada & the Canadian Music Publishers' Association, Stratford Festival, Canada, 1963]. Toronto: [s.n.],

1963. 30 p. [0071]

Booker, Alfred

Catalogue de raretés bibliographiques canadiennes. Montréal: [s.n.], 1869. 16 p. [0010]

"Books about Canada." In: *Canada Year Book*; (1965)-(1985) [0146]

"Books and pamphlets authored by Fellows [of Canadian Numismatic Research Society]." In: *Transactions of the Canadian Numismatic Research Society*; Vol. 16, no. 2 (Summer 1980)-vol. 23 (1987) [1839]

Books by Manitoba authors: a bibliography. [Winnipeg]: Manitoba Writers' Guild, [1986]. 88 p.; ISBN: 0-9692525-0-1. [0539]

Books in Canada, past and present: an exhibition/Livres canadiens d'hier et d'aujourd'hui: une exposition. Ottawa: National Library of Canada, 1982. 34 p.: ill.; ISBN: 0-662-51972-8. [0137]

Books of French Canada: an exhibit prepared for the annual meeting of the American Library Association, Toronto, June 1927 under the distinguished patronage of the Hon. Athanase David, Secretary of the Province of Quebec. Montreal: Louis Carrier, 1927. 47 p. [0041]

"Books on Canada." In: *American Review of Canadian Studies*; Vol. 3, no. 1 (Spring 1973)-vol. 8, no. 1 (Spring 1978) [0125]

"Books relating to the Hudson's Bay Company." In: *Beaver*; Outfit 265, no. 3 (December 1934) p. 55-60.; ISSN: 0005-7517. [1909]

Boone, Maurice P.

Union list of scientific and technical periodicals in libraries of the Maritime provinces and Newfoundland. Halifax: Imperial Press, 1951. 63 p. [5865]

Boosé, James Rufus

Catalogue of the library of the Royal Colonial Institute. London: The Institute, 1895. clv, 543 p. [6746]

Titles of publications relating to the British colonies, their government, etc., in connection with imperial policy. London: Imperial Federation League, 1889. 24 p. [1883]

Borden, John H.

Secondary attraction in the Scolytidae: an annotated bibliography. 3rd ed. Burnaby, B.C.: Pest Management Program, Department of Biological Sciences, Simon Fraser University, 1982. v 1., 185 p. (Pest management papers / Centre for Pest Management, Simon Fraser University ; no. 26; ISSN: 0703-7643); ISBN: 0-86491-027-4. [5471]

Borys, Ann Mari

"Swedish-Canadian periodical publications: a preliminary check list." In: *Canadian Ethnic Studies*; Vol. 2, no. 1 (June 1970) p. 191-192.; ISSN: 0008-3496. [5889]

Bosa, Réal

"Bibliographie des oeuvres publiées de Edmond Desrochers." Dans: *Livre, bibliothèque et culture québécoise: mélanges offerts à Edmond Desrochers, s.j.* Montréal: ASTED, 1977. P. 47-62.; ISBN: 0-88606-000-1. [6953]

Les ouvrages de référence du Québec: bibliographie analytique. [Québec]: Ministère des affaires culturelles du Québec, 1969. xiii, 189 p. [0302]

Boshyk, Yury; Balan, Boris

Political refugees and "displaced persons", 1945-1954: a selected bibliography and guide to research with special reference to Ukrainians. Edmonton: Canadian Institute of Ukrainian Studies, University of Alberta, 1982. xliv, 424 p. (Research report / Canadian Institute of Ukrainian Studies ; no. 2) [4207]

Boston, Janet Ellen Poth

Indians of B.C. school package: book list and teacher's guide. [Vancouver]: Educational Research Institute of British Columbia, [1975]. 46 p. (ERIBC reports / Educational Research Institute of British Columbia ; no. 75:7) [3962]

Bouchard, Daniel

Inventaire des périodiques de la bibliothèque du Ministère des terres et forêts. Québec: Ministère des terres et forêts, 1974. 118 f. [5916]

Bouchard, Louis-Marie

"Répertoire des cartes géographiques non-autonomes du Saguenay-Lac-St-Jean." Dans: *Protée*; Vol. 2, no 3 (mai 1973) p. 21-41; vol. 3, no 1 (décembre 1973) p. 43-67.; ISSN: 0300-3523. [6532]

Bouchard, Marie

Une revue de la littérature sur les relations avec les membres dans les coopératives (et les fédérations de coopératives). Montréal: École des hautes études commerciales, Centre de gestion des coopératives, 1982. 52 f. [2677]

Bouchard, R.–Jean

"Les premiers ministres du Québec de Duplessis à Lévesque: orientation bibliographique." Dans: *Bulletin: Bibliothèque de l'Assemblée nationale du Québec*; Vol. 12, no. 3 (Septembre 1982) p. 83-97.; ISSN: 0701-6808. [2469]

Bouchard, R.–Jean; Thériault, J.–Yvon

Sources de documentation politique à l'usage des parlementaires. 2e éd. Québec: Service de l'édition de l'Assemblée nationale du Québec, 1982. ii, 61 p. [2470]

Bouchard, René

Filmographie d'Albert Tessier. Montréal: Éditions du Boréal Express, 1973. 179 p.: ill., portr. (Documents filmiques du Québec ; 1) [7328]

Bouchard, René; Saulnier, Carole

"Bio-bibliographie de Robert-Lionel Séguin." Dans: *La vie quotidienne au Québec: histoire, métiers, techniques et traditions: mélanges à la mémoire de Robert-Lionel Séguin.* Sillery: Presses de l'Université du Québec, 1983. P. 51-85.; ISBN: 2-7605-0338-0. [7301]

Bouchard, Serge; Vincent, Sylvie

Pour parler des Amérindiens et des Inuit: guide à l'usage des professeurs du secondaire, histoire et géographie: bibliographie sélective commentée. [Québec]: Gouvernement du Québec, Coordination des activités en milieux amérindiens et inuit, Ministère de l'Éducation, 1982. 94 p.; ISBN: 2-550-05231-5. [4029]

Boucher, Suzanne

"Bibliographie de l'Acadie." Dans: *Cahiers: Société historique acadienne*; Vol. 10, no 1 (mars 1979) p. 56-69.; ISSN: 0049-1098. [0238]

Boucher de la Richarderie, Gilles

Bibliothèque universelle des voyages ou Notice complète et raisonnée de tous les voyages anciens et modernes dans les différentes parties du monde .... Paris: Treuttel et Würtz, 1808. 6 vol. [1871]

Boudreau, Gérald; Tournoux, Étienne

Guide de documentation sur les affaires et l'économique au Québec. Montréal: École des hautes études commerciales de Montréal, Bibliothèque, 1973. 28 f. [2602]

Boulanger, Jean-Claude

Bibliographie de la néologie: nouveaux fragments (1980-1989). Québec: Gouvernement du Québec, Office de la langue française, 1990. v, 192 p. [1489]

Boulanger, Jean-Claude; Gambier, Yves
Bibliographie fondamentale et analytique de la terminologie: 1962-1984. Québec: Centre international de recherche sur le bilinguisme, 1989. 104 p.; ISBN: 2-89219-207-2. [1484]

Boulanger, Jean-Claude; Nakos, Dorothy
Le syntagme terminologique: bibliographie sélective et analytique. Québec: Centre international de recherche sur le bilinguisme, 1988. 81 p. (Publication / Centre international de recherche sur le bilinguisme ; K-7); ISBN: 2-89219-193-9. [1477]

Boulet, Marie-France
Équité salariale: bibliographie sélective et annotée. Québec: Bibliothèque de l'Assemblée nationale, Division de la référence parlementaire, 1987. 71 p. (Bibliographie / Bibliothèque de l'Assemblée nationale du Québec ; no 9; ISSN: 0836-9100) [2911]

Politique de l'environnement: bibliographie sélective et annotée. Québec: Division de la référence parlementaire, Bibliothèque de l'Assemblée nationale, 1987. 41 p. (Bibliographie / Bibliothèque de l'Assemblée nationale du Québec ; no 11; ISSN: 0836-9100) [5241]

Boulizon, Guy
Livres roses et séries noires: guide psychologique et bibliographique de la littérature de jeunesse. Montréal: Beauchemin, 1957. 188 p. [1311]

Boulizon, Guy; Boulizon, Jeanne
Nos jeunes liront: 1000 titres de livres. Montréal: École des parents du Québec, 1948. 40 p. [1308]

Boult, Jean-Claude
"Bibliographie de l'histoire de Hull: inventaire préliminaire." Dans: *Asticou*; No 9 (septembre 1972) p. 31-42.; ISSN: 0066-992X. [0315]

Boult, Reynald
A bibliography of Canadian law/Bibliographie du droit canadien. New ed. Ottawa: Canadian Law Information Council, 1977. xxii, 661 p.; ISBN: 0-920358-00-4. [2164]

Boultbee, Paul G.
A central Alberta bibliography. [Red Deer]: Red Deer College Press, 1986. 58 p.; ISBN: 0-88995-031-8. [0540]

Bouquiniste
Le guide du lecteur canadien-français. [Montréal: Imprimerie judiciaire], 1965. 77 p.: ill. [1025]

Bourgeois, Annette E.
Bibliography on the Parliament Buildings. [Ottawa: Public Works Library, 1974]. 12 l. [0740]

Bourgeois, Donald J.
Annotated bibliography, public opinion and social policy. [Ottawa]: Ministry Secretariat, Solicitor General of Canada, [1985]. 3, 56, 4 p. (Programs Branch user report / Ministry Secretariat, Solicitor General Canada ; no. 1985-05) [3267]

Bibliographie annotée: opinion publique et politique sociale. [Ottawa]: Secrétariat du Ministère, Solliciteur général Canada, [1985]. 110 f. (Rapport pour spécialistes / Ministère du Solliciteur général Canada ; no 1985-05) [3268]

Bourget, Manon; Chiasson, Robert; Morin, Marie-Josée
L'indispensable en documentation: les outils de travail. La Pocatière, Québec: Documentor, 1990. viii, 201 p.; ISBN: 2-89123-110-4. [1716]

Bourinot, Arthur S.
Edward William Thomson (1849-1924): a bibliography with notes and some letters. Ottawa: The Author, 1955.

28 p. [7336]

Bourinot, Sir John George
"Bibliography of parliamentary government in Canada." In: *Annual report of the American Historical Association*; (1891) p. 390-407.; ISSN: 0065-8561. [2370]

Bibliography of the members of the Royal Society of Canada. [Ottawa: Printed by order of the Society], 1894. 79 p. [0021]

"Bibliography of the members of the Royal Society of Canada." In: *Proceedings and Transactions of the Royal Society of Canada*; Series 1, Vol. 12 (1894) p. 5-79.; ISSN: 0316-4616. [0022]

"[Cape Breton Island]: bibliographical, historical and critical notes." In: *Proceedings and Transactions of the Royal Society of Canada*; Series 1, vol. 9, section 2 (1891) p. 291-343.; ISSN: 0316-4616. [0192]

"Comparative politics: bibliographical and critical notes." In: *Proceedings and Transactions of the Royal Society of Canada*; Series 1, vol. 2, section 2 (1893) p. 95-108.; ISSN: 0316-4616. [2371]

The library of the late Sir John Bourinot containing rare books, pamphlets and maps relating to the progress of geographical discovery and the history of Canada, including many relating to the American Revolution and the history of America in colonial times. New York: Anderson Auction, 1906. [2], 175, [1] p. [6755]

Bourne, L.S.; Biernacki, C.M.
Urban housing markets, housing supply, and the spatial structure of residential change: a working bibliography. Toronto: Centre for Urban and Community Studies, University of Toronto, 1977. ii, 56 p. (University of Toronto Centre for Urban and Community Studies Bibliographic series report ; no. 6; ISSN: 0316-4691) [4365]

Bourneuf, Denise, et al.
"Une bibliographie de livres pour enfants." Dans: *Québec français*; No 30 (mai 1978) p. 40-44.; ISSN: 0316-2052. [1335]

Bourque, Christa; Lévesque, Paulette
List of DFO-sponsored publications, Science Branch, Gulf Region, 1982-1991/Liste des publications subventionnées par le MPO, Direction des sciences, Région du golfe, 1982-1991. Revised edition. Moncton, N.B.: Department of Fisheries and Oceans, 1992. i, 38 p. (Canadian manuscript report of fisheries and aquatic sciences ; no. 2173; ISSN: 0706-6473) [4916]

Boutet, Edgar
"Les journaux de Hull: des origines à 1955." Dans: *Asticou*; Nos 10-11 (mars 1973) p. 45-70.; ISSN: 0066-992X. [6018]

Bouthillette, Jean
Répertoire de la collection Trefflé Boulanger. Sherbrooke: Université de Sherbrooke, Bibliothèque générale, 1973. 72 f. (en foliotation multiple). [3446]

Bouthillette, Jean; Tardif-Robitaille, Louise
Revue de littérature et bibliographie indexée sur la recherche-action chez les professeurs de niveau collégial. Sherbrooke: Université de Sherbrooke, [1986]. 1 vol. (en pagination multiple). [3650]

Boutilier, Helen R.
"A bibliography of the printed writings of Walter Noble Sage." In: *British Columbia Historical Quarterly*; Vol. 17, no. 1/2 (January-April 1953) p. 127-137.; ISSN: 0706-7666. [7290]

Bower, William J.
A rough check list of the first editions of John Buchan (Lord Tweedsmuir). [Bronxville, N.Y.: s.n., 1939]. [12] l. [7345]

Bowers, Neal

Index to Canadian children's records. Bridgewater, N.S.: Lunenburg County District Teacher's Centre, c1984. 48 p. [0913]

Bowles, Roy T.; Brand, Rosemary; Johnston, Cynthia

Studies of community patterns and planning in the counties of Peterborough, Victoria and Haliburton: a bibliographical guide to unpublished reports. Peterborough, Ont.: Frost Centre for Canadian Heritage and Development Studies, Trent University, 1986. 106 p. (Frost Centre for Canadian Heritage and Development Studies Research bibliography ; no. 1) [4407]

Bowman, Fred

A bibliography of Canadian numismatics. [Ottawa: Canadian Numismatics Association, 1954]. 35, v l. [1747]

Canadian numismatic research index. [Lachine, Quebec]: 1969. 176 p. [1754]

Bowman, Fred; Willey, R.C.

"Bibliography of Canadian numismatics." In: *Canadian Numismatic Journal*; Vol. 4, no. 6 (June 1959)-vol. 4, no. 10 (October 1959) [1749]

Bowman, James

Big country: a bibliography of the history of the Kamloops Region & Southern Cariboo. [Burnaby, B.C.]: Simon Fraser University, Department of Sociology and Anthropology, 1977. 79 p.: ill., map. [0588]

Boyce, Gerald E.

The St. Andrew's chronicles: bibliography and notes. Belleville, Ont.: St. Andrew's Presbyterian Church, [1978]. 57 p.; ISBN: 0-921385-08-0. [1545]

Boyce, Helena

Pre-service teacher education in Canada. Ottawa: Canadian Teachers' Federation, 1976. 29 p. (Bibliographies in education / Canadian Teachers' Federation ; no. 58); ISBN: 0-88989-011-0. [3509]

Boyd, Gary L.

Review of the literature concerning erosion and accretion of the Canadian shoreline of the Great Lakes. Burlington, Ont.: Canada Centre for Inland Waters, 1979. iii, 24 p. (Canada Centre for Inland Waters Technical note series ; no. 80-1) [5145]

Boyd, J.A.; Mollica, Anthony

"Core French: a selected annotated resource list." In: *Canadian Modern Language Review*; Vol. 42, no. 2 (November 1985) p. 408-439.; ISSN: 0008-4506. [3633]

Boylan, Heather

Checklist and historical directory of Prince Edward Island newspapers, 1787-1986. Charlottetown: Public Archives of Prince Edward Island, 1987. 211 p. [6039]

Boyle, Cornelius Breckinridge

A catalogue and bibliography of North American mesozoic invertebrata. Washington: G.P.O., 1893. 315 p. [4524]

Bracher, Michael D.; Krishnan, P.

"Family and demography: a selected Canadian bibliography." In: *Journal of Comparative Family Studies*; Vol. 7, no. 2 (Summer 1976) p. 367-372.; ISSN: 0047-2328. [3013]

Bradford, J.D.; Moline, M.

Bibliography on northern sea ice and related subjects/ Bibliographie sur la glace de mer dans le Nord et autres sujets connexes. 2nd ed. Ottawa: Department of Fisheries and Oceans; Department of Transport, 1980. x, 194 p. (Canadian special publication of fisheries and aquatic sciences ; 45; ISSN: 0706-6481) [5160]

Bradford, Martin R.

An annotated bibliographic and geographic review of Pleistocene and Quaternary dinoflagellatoo[sic] cysts and acritarchs. Calgary: Shell Canada Resources, 1978. 191 p. (American Association of Stratigraphic Palynologists Contribution series ; no. 6) [4805]

Bradley, Ian L.

"A bibliography on the arts and crafts of northwest coast Indians." In: *BC Studies*; No. 25 (Spring 1975) p. 78-123.; ISSN: 0005-2949. [0680]

"Indian music of the Pacific northwest: an annotated bibliography of research." In: *BC Studies*; No. 31 (Autumn 1976) p. 12-22.; ISSN: 0005-2949. [0850]

"Revised bibliography of Indian musical culture in Canada." In: *Indian Historian*; Vol. 10, no. 4 (Fall 1977) p. 28-32.; ISSN: 0019-4840. [0858]

A selected bibliography of musical Canadiana. rev. ed. Victoria, B.C.: University of Victoria, [c1976]. 177 p.; ISBN: 0-88874-050-6. [0851]

Bradley, Ian L.; Bradley, Patricia

A bibliography of Canadian native arts: Indian and Eskimo arts, crafts, dance and music. [Agincourt, Ont.: GLC Publishers, c1977]. [6], 107, [2] p.; ISBN: 0-88874-051-4. [0687]

Bradshaw, Janice

Heritage conservation: a selected bibliography, 1979. [Victoria]: British Columbia Heritage Trust, [1980]. 71 p. (Technical paper series / British Columbia Heritage Trust ; no. 1; ISSN: 0229-9976); ISBN: 0-7719-9281-5. [0757]

Brady, Elizabeth

"A bibliographical essay on William Kirby's *The Golden Dog*, 1877-1977." In: *Papers of the Bibliographical Society of Canada*; Vol. 15, (1976) p. 24-48.; ISSN: 0067-6896. [7088]

Brady, Judith

"Michael Ondaatje: an annotated bibliography." In: *The annotated bibliography of Canada's major authors*, Vol. 6, edited by Robert Lecker and Jack David. Toronto: ECW Press, 1985. P. 129-205.; ISBN: 0-920802-93-1. [7223]

Braide, Janet

"John Lyman: a bibliography of his writings." In: *Journal of Canadian Art History*; Vol. 4, no. 2 (1977/1978) p. 130-140.; ISSN: 0315-4297. [7163]

Bramall, L.; Clay, P.P.F.; Gridgeman, N.T.

Personnel and publications in biological research at NRCC, 1929-1953. Ottawa: National Research Council of Canada, 1979. 183 p. (in various pagings). [5425]

Bramstedt, Wayne G.

North American Indians in towns and cities: a bibliography. Monticello, Ill.: Vance Bibliographies, 1979. 74 p. (Public administration series: Bibliography ; P-234; ISSN: 0193-970X) [4001]

Bramwell, John R.; Vigna, Roxy

Evaluation instruments locally developed in Ontario: an annotated catalogue of material developed by school boards and other agencies. Toronto: Ministry of Education, c1979. xiv, 281 p. [3548]

Brand, Judith

You can say "no": an annotated resource guide for child abuse education. [Victoria]: Province of British Columbia, Ministry of Education, c1989. 124 p.; ISBN: 0-7726-1066-5. [3318]

Brander, Leo G.; Graham, Bruce M.

A bibliography of periodical articles concerning the management and economics of water resources. Wolfville, N.S.: Department of Economics, Acadia University, 1971. 22 l. [5057]

Brandt, Gail Cuthbert

"Postmodern patchwork: some recent trends in the writing of women's history in Canada." In: *Canadian Historical Review*; Vol. 72, no. 4 (December 1991) p. 441-470.; ISSN: 0008-3755. [3887]

Brascoupé, Simon

Bibliography related to Indian, Metis and non-status Indian socio-economic development. Ottawa: Regional Economic Expansion, 1980. 148 p. [4011]

Brass, Allen E.

An annotated bibliography on laboratory buildings. Ottawa: Division of Building Research, National Research Council Canada, 1959. 17 l. [0734]

Brassard, Denise; Lévesque, Lise; Reid, Doris

Bibliographie sur les Amérindiens: une liste de documents répertoiriés au Saguenay-Lac St-Jean. [Jonquière, Québec: s.n.], 1980. xxxviii, 633 p. [4012]

Brassard, François

"French-Canadian folk music studies: a survey." In: *Ethnomusicology*; Vol. 16, no. 3 (September 1972) p. 351-359.; ISSN: 0014-1836. [0830]

Brassard, Léo

"Bibliographie commentée des travaux suscités par les Jeunes Explos dans la région du Saguenay." Dans: *Saguenayensia*; Vol. 13, no 4 (juillet-août 1971) p. 101-105.; ISSN: 0581-295X. [0309]

Brault, Helen, et al.

Sources of information: an annotated directory of vertical file materials of interest to libraries in Nova Scotia. Halifax, Nova Scotia: [University Libraries/School of Library Service, Dalhousie University], 1979. iii, 54 l. (Dalhousie University Libraries and Dalhousie University School of Library Service Occasional papers ; no. 25; ISSN: 0318-7403); ISBN: 0-7703-0161-4. [0239]

Brault, Jean-Rémi

Bibliographie des Éditions Fides, 1937-1987. Montréal: Fides, 1987. 299 p.; ISBN: 2-7621-1358-X. [1688]

Brault, Jean-Rémi; Auger, Roland

"La bibliographie au Québec." Dans: *Livre, bibliothèque et culture québécoise: mélanges offerts à Edmond Desrochers, s.j.* Montréal: ASTED, 1977. P. 161-190.; ISBN: 0-88606-000-1. [1618]

Brault, Lucien

"Bibliographie d'Ottawa." Dans: *Revue de l'Université d'Ottawa*; Vol. 24, no 3 (juillet-Septembre 1954) p. 345-375.; ISSN: 0041-9206. [0427]

Francis-J. Audet et son oeuvre: bio-bibliographie. Ottawa: [Imprimerie Leclerc], 1940. 92 p.: portr. [6816]

Braun, Connie

Bibliography of rural education in Canada. Brandon: WESTARC Group, [1990]. 61 p. [3710]

Brazeau, Marcel; Veilleux, Jean-Marc

Bibliographie annotée sur les effets de la fertilisation sur la production de cônes et de semences. [Sainte-Foy]: Service de la recherche, Direction générale des forêts, Ministère des terres et forêts du Québec, 1976. viii, 26 p. (Mémoire / Direction générale des forêts, Québec ; no 25) [4951]

Brearly, Anne; Warren, I.H.

Uranium nitrides: an annotated bibliography. Vancouver: Canadian Uranium Research Foundation, [1962]. 18 l. [5722]

Breem, Wallace; Phillips, Sally

Bibliography of Commonwealth law reports. London, England; New York: Mansell, 1991. xix, 332 p.; ISBN: 0-720-12023-3. [2345]

Breen, William J.; Marshall, Julie G.

Resources for North American studies: an annotated list of microform collections in Australian libraries relating to the United States and Canada. Bundoora, Vic.: Borchardt Library, La Trobe University, 1985. vi l., 86 p.; ISBN: 0-85816-595-3. [0147]

Brehaut, Willard

"A quarter century of educational research in Canada." In: *Ontario Journal of Educational Research*; Vol. 2, no. 2 (April 1960) p. 109-222.; ISSN: 0474-2117. [6070]

Brereton, Thomas F.

Planning and government in the National Capital: a selected bibliography on Ottawa, Canberra, and Washington. Monticello, Ill.: Council of Planning Librarians, 1973. 25 p. (Council of Planning Librarians Exchange bibliography ; 461) [4327]

Brethour, Ross

Discography of Ralph Marterie. Aurora, Ont.: R. Brethour, [1979]. 9 l. [7179]

A Max Boag discography. Aurora, Ont.: Nomadic Record Co., [1981]. 14 l. [6855]

Breton, Jean-René

Bibliographie de Beauce-Etchemin. Québec: Institut québécois de recherche sur la culture, 1993. 195 p.: cartes. (Documents de recherche / Institut québécois de recherche sur la culture ; no 33; ISSN: 0823-0447); ISBN: 2-89224-18-0. [0415]

Breton, Lise; Dufresne, Jean-Pierre

Enseigner aux adultes: bibliographie annotée. Montréal: Centre d'animation, de développement et de recherche en éducation, 1982. 143 p.; ISBN: 2-89169-025-2. [3603]

Breton, Lise; Roy, Jean-Luc

Le collège québécois: introduction bibliographique. Montréal: Centre d'animation, de développement et de recherche en éducation, 1976. xvii, 98 p. [3510]

L'enseignement privé au Québec: bibliographie annotée. Montréal: Centre d'animation, de développement et de recherche en éducation, 1985. 100 p.; ISBN: 2-89169-032-X. [3634]

L'enseignement professionnel: bibliographie annotée. Montréal: Centre d'animation, de développement et de recherche en éducation, 1980. 262 p.; ISBN: 2-89169-002-8. [3559]

L'évaluation de l'apprentissage: bibliographie annotée. Montréal: Centre d'animation, de développement et de recherche en éducation, 1981. 63 p.; ISBN: 2-89169-004-4. [3583]

Breugelmans, René

"Netherlandic-Canadian periodical publications: a preliminary check list." In: *Canadian Ethnic Studies*; Vol. 1, no. 1 (1969) p. 56-58.; ISSN: 0008-3496. [5881]

"University research on Netherlandic-Canadians: a preliminary check list of dissertations and theses." In: *Canadian Ethnic Studies*; Vol. 1, no. 1 (1969) p. 54-55.; ISSN: 0008-3496. [6095]

Brewer, Heather M.
Anaerobic technology: a review of research, development and demonstration activity in the agrifood and pulp and paper industries/Technologie anaérobie: compte rendu des activités de recherche, de développement et de démonstration dans l'industrie agro-alimentaire et celle des pâtes et papiers. Ottawa: Environment Canada, 1988. xiv, 105 p.; ISBN: 0-662-55802-2. [5830]

Breyfogle, Donna; Dworaczek, Marian
Blacks in Ontario: a selected bibliography, 1965-1976. Toronto: Ontario Ministry of Labour, Research Library, 1977. 27 p. (Bibliography series / Ontario Ministry of Labour, Research Library ; no. 8) [4178]

Bricker, Mary Anne
"Genealogical materials for public libraries." In: *Ontario Library Review*; Vol. 62, no. 3 (September 1978) p. 206-209.; ISSN: 0030-2996. [1996]

Bridault, Alain; Ouellet, Dominique
Revue critique de la littérature en français sur la coopération ouvrière de production dans les pays industrialisés, 1975-1983. Sherbrooke, Québec: Institut de recherche et d'enseignement pour les coopératives, Université de Sherbrooke, 1987. xv, 99 p. (Collection Essais / Institut de recherche et d'enseignement pour les coopératives, Université de Sherbrooke ; no 9; ISSN: 0832-6037) [2728]

Bridault, Alain; Ouellet, Dominique; Henry, Ronald
Inventaire analytique des recherches universitaires canadiennes sur les coopératives, 1970-1985/Analytical inventory of Canadian university research on cooperatives, 1970-1985. Montréal: Centre interuniversitaires de recherche, d'information et d'enseignement sur les coopératives, c1987. xi, 321 p.: ill.; ISBN: 2-920258-06-0. [2729]

Brideau, Monique; Doré, Gérald
Bibliographie du Québec métropolitain: rapport de recherche ézop-Québec. Québec (Ville): Conseil des oeuvres et du bien-être de Québec, 1971. 62 p. [4318]

A brief bibliography for a study of general naval history and the naval history of Canada. Ottawa: Department of National Defence, [1955]. 6 p. [1926]

Brière, Jean-Marie
L'information gouvernementale au Québec: bibliographie analytique. Québec: Edi-GRIC, c1977. 135 p. (Travaux et recherches GRIC ; 1; ISSN: 0703-1297) [2428]
L'information gouvernementale au Québec et au Canada: bibliographie analytique (texte provisoire). [Montréal]: Université de Montréal, Faculté des études supérieures, École de bibliothéconomie, 1975. 41 f. [2415]
Publications officielles canadiennes sur l'énergie atomique, la radioactivité et la sécurité: bibliographie signalétique. Montréal: Faculté des études supérieures, École de bibliothéconomie, Université de Montréal, 1976. 17 f. [5756]

Brière, Roger
"Esquisse bibliographique de géographie touristique." Dans: *Revue canadienne de géographie*; Vol. 16, nos 1/2/3/4 (1962) p. 57-68.; ISSN: 0316-3032. [1751]

Brierley, John E.C.
Bibliographical guide to Canadian legal materials. Montreal: Faculty of Law, McGill University, 1968. ii, 260 p. [2111]

Briggs, W.E., et al.
Dielectric properties of Albert County oil shale. Fredericton: New Brunswick Department of Natural Resources, Minerals and Energy Division, 1982. 37 p. (Open file report / New Brunswick Department of Natural Resources, Minerals and Energy Division ; 82-18; ISSN: 0712-4562) [4824]

Bright, Norman F.H.
Bibliography of high-temperature condensed states research published in Canada. Ottawa: Department of Energy, Mines and Resources, Mines Branch, 1960-1973. 13 vol.; ISSN: 0527-8023. [5740]

Bringhurst, Robert
Ocean paper stone: the catalogue of an exhibition of printed objects which chronicle more than a century of literary publishing in British Columbia. Vancouver, B.C.: William Hoffer, 1984. 111 p.: ill., facsims.; ISBN: 0-919758-07-X. [1660]

Brinkhurst, Ralph O.
The Ocean Ecology Division, Institute of Ocean Sciences: the first decade, 1976-86. Sidney, B.C.: Fisheries and Oceans Canada, 1986. v, 24 p. (Canadian technical report of hydrography and ocean sciences ; no. 72; ISSN: 0711-6764) [5521]

British Columbia Centennial Committee
Ethnic groups in British Columbia: a selected bibliography based on a check-list of material in the Provincial Library and Archives. Victoria: British Columbia Centennial Committee, 1957. 64 l. [4129]

British Columbia Federation of Foster Care Associations
Foster care training resource catalogue. [Vancouver]: The Federation, 1982. 1 vol. (in various pagings). [3234]

British Columbia government publications monthly checklist. Victoria: Legislative Library, 1970-. vol.; ISSN: 0316-0823. [6433]

British Columbia government publications. Victoria: Legislative Library, 1983-. vol.; ISSN: 0824-8516. [6432]

British Columbia in fiction. [Vancouver]: Education Services Group, Vancouver School Board, 1981. 14 p. [1178]

British Columbia Library Association
British Columbia newspapers: register of microform masters. Vancouver: British Columbia Library Association, 1987. 7 p. [6040]
Self health: a resource guide for healthy living. Vancouver: British Columbia Library Association, 1989. 69 p. [5685]

British Columbia Library Association. Bibliography Committee
Bibliography on the Columbia River Basin. [Vancouver: The Association], 1935. [2], 46, [3] p. [0557]
Captain James Cook. [Vancouver: The Association], 1935-1936. [3], 7 p. [6918]
Captain Vancouver. [Vancouver: The Association], 1935. 3 p. [7350]
Hudson's Bay Company. [Vancouver: The Association], 1935. [58] p. [1912]
The Oregon question. [Vancouver: The Association], 1935. [17] p. [0558]
Simon Fraser. [Vancouver: The Association], 1935. 3 p. [6989]

British Columbia Medical Library Service
Recent and recommended texts: a selective list for hospital libraries. Vancouver: British Columbia Medical Library Service, 1964-. vol.; ISSN: 0228-0647. [5715]

British Columbia Research Council
Publications of the British Columbia Research Council. Vancouver: British Columbia Research Council, 1964. 26 l. [6250]

British Columbia School Librarians' Association
Index to BCSLA publications. Vancouver: British Columbia School Librarians' Association, 1970-1972. 3 vol.; ISSN: 0227-3446. [1593]

British Columbia School Trustees Association
The community education collection. [Vancouver]: British Columbia School Trustees Association, [1975]. [66] l. [3494]

British Columbia Systems Corporation. Library Services
Bibliography on microcomputers. Victoria: Library Services, British Columbia Systems Corporation, 1984-1986. 3 vol.; ISSN: 0827-0376. [1676]

Bibliography on mini-microcomputers. [Victoria]: Library Services, British Columbia Systems Corporation, 1984. 27 p. [1661]

British Columbia. Aquatic Plant Management Program
List of publications prepared and in preparation by the British Columbia Aquatic Plant Management Program. Victoria: Environmental Studies Division, Ministry of Environment, 1979. 12 l. [6319]

British Columbia. Department of Agriculture. Publications Office
List of publications [British Columbia Department of Agriculture]. Victoria: Department of Agriculture, [1954]-1970. [16] vol. [6273]

British Columbia. Department of Consumer Services
Consumer bibliography. Victoria: Department of Consumer Services, 1975. [27] l. [2614]

British Columbia. Department of Education. Division of Curriculum
A bibliography on British Columbia for elementary and secondary schools. Victoria, B.C.: The Department, 1956. 8 l. [0569]

British Columbia. Department of Mines and Petroleum Resources
Index to publications of the British Columbia Department of Mines and Petroleum Resources. Victoria: Department of Mines and Petroleum Resources, 1966. vi, 142 p. [6257]

British Columbia. Ecological Reserves Program
List of reports and publications for ecological reserves in British Columbia. Victoria, B.C.: The Program, 1986. 1 vol. (loose-leaf): map.; ISBN: 0-7726-0515-7. [5230]

British Columbia. Fish and Wildlife Branch
List of fisheries publications, 1947-1969. Victoria: [s.n., 1969]. 14, [3] l. [4888]

List of wildlife publications, 1935-1972. Victoria, B.C.: 1972. 28 l. [5365]

British Columbia. Geological Survey Branch
NTS location and author index to publications of the British Columbia Geological Survey Branch. Victoria: B.C. Ministry of Energy, Mines and Petroleum Resources, 1991. vi, 304 p.: map. [6410]

Reports, maps and geoscience databases [issued by the British Columbia Geological Survey Branch]. Victoria: Geological Survey Branch, [1989]-.　vol.; ISSN: 0847-3676. [6427]

British Columbia. Government Information Services
Provincial government literature: an updated guide to material available to the general public by the various ministries. Victoria: British Columbia Government Information Services, 1982. 55 p. [6340]

British Columbia. Legal Services Commission
A Basic legal collection for barristers and solicitors in British Columbia. Vancouver, B.C.: Centre for Continuing Education, University of British Columbia, 1977. vii, 58 p. [2165]

British Columbia. Library Services Branch
National catalog of audiobooks. Victoria, B.C.: Ministry of Provincial Secretary and Government Services, Library Services Branch, 1979-1989. 11 vol. [6677]

British Columbia. Littoral Resources Unit
List of publications prepared and in preparation by the Littoral Resources Unit. Victoria: Water Management Branch, Ministry of Environment, 1983. 17 l. [6355]

British Columbia. Mineral Resources Division
Catalogue of publications, maps, and services [British Columbia Mineral Resources Division]. Victoria: Province of British Columbia, Ministry of Energy, Mines and Petroleum Resources, Mineral Resources Division, 1984-. vol.; ISSN: 0831-4047. [6428]

British Columbia. Ministry of Agriculture and Food
Film & slide catalogue [BC Ministry of Agriculture and Food]. Victoria: Province of British Columbia, Ministry of Agriculture and Food, [1984]. 38 p.; ISBN: 0-77260-095-3. [6656]

Publications catalogue [British Columbia Ministry of Agriculture and Food]. Victoria: The Ministry, 1986-. vol.; ISSN: 0837-6190. [6429]

British Columbia. Ministry of Education, Science & Technology. Continuing Education Division
Survey of leisure reading materials for A.B.E. students with emphasis on western Canada: a $500 collection. Victoria: The Division, [1980]. 46 p. [3560]

British Columbia. Ministry of Energy, Mines and Petroleum Resources
Index to bedrock geological mapping, British Columbia: including publications of the Geological Survey of Canada, British Columbia Ministry of Energy, Mines and Petroleum Resources, and journal articles, theses, and company reports. Victoria, B.C.: Province of British Columbia, Ministry of Energy, Mines and Petroleum Resources, 1980. [ca. 100] l.: map.; ISBN: 0-771-99295-5. [6570]

British Columbia. Ministry of Environment. Information Services Branch
Publications list [BC Ministry of Environment]. Victoria: Province of British Columbia, Ministry of Environment, 1981. 10 l. [6331]

British Columbia. Ministry of Environment. Surveys and Mapping Branch
Map and air photo catalogue. Victoria: The Branch, 1976. [30] p.: maps. [6553]

British Columbia. Ministry of Forests
List of publications [British Columbia Ministry of Forests]. Victoria: Province of British Columbia, Ministry of Forests, 1989-.　vol.; ISSN: 1185-2968. [6430]

Lodgepole pine: a bibliography. Victoria: British Columbia Ministry of Forests, [1979]. [25] p. [5426]

British Columbia. Ministry of Human Resources
Adolescent pregnancy: a bibliography. Victoria: Province of British Columbia, Ministry of Human Resources, 1980. 6 p. [3197]

Adoption, special needs: a bibliography. Victoria: Province of British Columbia, Ministry of Human Resources, 1981. 13 p. [3211]

A bibliography of children's literature in the library. Vancouver: British Columbia Ministry of Human

Resources, 1982. 40 p. [1349]

Child abuse: a bibliography. Victoria: Province of British Columbia, Ministry of Human Resources, 1977. 15 p. [3152]

Mental retardation: a basic reading list. Victoria: Province of British Columbia, Ministry of Human Resources, Library, 1983. 10 p. [3245]

British Columbia. Ministry of Industry and Small Business Development

Publications list [British Columbia Ministry of Industry and Small Business Development]. Victoria: Province of British Columbia, Ministry of Industry and Small Business Development, [1980-1985]. 4 vol.; ISSN: 0711-835X. [6368]

British Columbia. Ministry of International Business and Immigration

Immigration to British Columbia: a selected annotated bibliography. Victoria: Province of British Columbia, Ministry of International Business and Immigration, 1991. iii, 40 p.; ISBN: 0-77261-327-3. [0601]

British Columbia. Ministry of Lands, Parks and Housing. Parks and Outdoor Recreation Division. Library

An annotated bibliography of research reports, 1974-79. Victoria: The Ministry, 1979. 19 l. [6320]

British Columbia. Ministry of Municipal Affairs, Recreation and Culture

Starting line-up: a directory of British Columbia writers for public libraries. Victoria: Province of British Columbia, Ministry of Municipal Affairs, Recreation and Culture, [1990]. [59] l.: ill. [0599]

British Columbia. Ministry of Provincial Secretary and Government Services. Recreation and Sport Branch

Recreation and Sport film library catalogue. [Victoria]: Recreation and Sport Branch, Ministry of Provincial Secretary and Government Services, 1985. 80 p.; ISBN: 0-7726-0296-4. [6660]

British Columbia. Ministry of Transportation and Highways. Snow Avalanche Programs

Literature review of snow avalanche research. Victoria: Ministry of Transportation and Highways British Columbia, Snow Avalanche Programs, Maintenance Branch, 1991. 328 p. [4518]

British Columbia. Parks Library

Audio-visual catalogue [BC Parks Library]. [Victoria, B.C.]: The Library, 1992. x, 56 p.; ISBN: 0-7726-1564-0. [6696]

British Columbia. Petroleum Resources Division

Catalogue of publications, maps, and services [Petroleum Resources Division]. Victoria: British Columbia Ministry of Mines and Petroleum Resources, 1982-1987. 3 vol.; ISSN: 0831-4055. [6383]

British Columbia. Provincial Archives. Library

Dictionary catalogue of the Library of the Provincial Archives of British Columbia, Victoria. Boston: G.K. Hall, 1971. 8 vol.; ISBN: 0-8161-0912-5. [0578]

British Columbia. Provincial Educational Media Centre

Media resources: Agriculture. Richmond: B.C. Ministry of Education, Provincial Educational Media Centre, 1985. v, 67 p.; ISBN: 0-7726-0362-6. [6661]

British Columbia. Provincial Museum

Publications of the Provincial Museum. Victoria, B.C.: British Columbia Provincial Museum, 1955. P. 87-99. [6237]

A selected list of publications on the Indians of British Columbia. [Victoria]: British Columbia Provincial Museum, 1986. 65 p. [4081]

British Columbia. Provincial Museum. Department of Recreation and Conservation

Recommended references to the flora of British Columbia. Victoria, B.C.: Provincial Museum, 1975. 13 p. [5388]

Selected literature concerning birds in British Columbia. Victoria, B.C.: British Columbia Provincial Museum, 1965. 9 p. [5340]

British Columbia. Queen's Printer

Queen's Printer publications catalogue [British Columbia]. Victoria: Province of British Columbia, Queen's Printer, 1983-. vol.; ISSN: 0824-9628. [6431]

British Columbia. Recreation and Sport Branch

Community recreation bibliography. Victoria: Province of British Columbia, Recreation and Sport Branch, [1981]. iii, 38 p.; ISBN: 0-7719-8777-3. [1802]

British Columbia. Recreation Division. Technical Services Unit

Recreation and sport: technical resource index. Victoria, B.C.: Province of British Columbia, Ministry of Provincial Secretary and Government Services, Recreation and Fitness Branch, [1981]. 139 p.; ISBN: 0-7719-8506-1. [1803]

British Columbia. Workmen's Compensation Board

Safety literature catalogue: the printed word works for safety. Vancouver: B.C. Workmen's Compensation Board, [1969]. 32 p. [2801]

British Empire Exhibition (1924-1925: London, England)

Catalogue of Canadian books (English section): British Empire Exhibition, Wembley Park, 1925. 2nd and rev. ed. [London]: The Exhibition, 1925. 63 p. [0039]

British Museum. Department of Printed Books

Catalogue of the American books in the library of the British Museum at Christmas MdcccLvi. London: C. Whittingham, 1866. xxxii, 628, 14, 62, 17 p. [0007]

British North America Philatelic Society

Library list, 1972 [British North America Philatelic Society]. [Burlington, Ont.]: British North America Philatelic Society, 1972. 19 p. [1760]

Brochu, Serge

Bibliographie portant sur les drogues et les questions criminelles. Montréal: S. Brochu, 1993. 106 p. [2359]

Broderick, Corinne; Lawton, Janet; Greenaway, Nora

Video mosaic: an elementary guide to multicultural videos and films. Vancouver: Vancouver School Board, Staff Development Division, 1992. 37 p.: ill.; ISBN: 1-55031-368-1. [6697]

Brodeur, Léo A.; Naaman, Antoine

Répertoire des thèses littéraires canadiennes (janvier 1969-septembre 1971): 1786 sujets/Index of Canadian literary theses (January 1969-September 1971): 1786 subjects. [Sherbrooke, Québec]: Centre d'étude des littératures d'expression française, Université de Sherbrooke, [c1972]. 141 p. (Cahiers francophones / Centre d'étude des littératures d'expression française, Université de Sherbrooke ; 2) [6113]

Brodie, R.J.; O'Flanagan, J.; Anderson, M.K.

A bibliography of Canadian papers of interest in building research to June 30, 1951. Ottawa: Division of Building Research, National Research Council Canada, 1952. 43 l. (National Research Council Canada, Division of Building Research Bibliography ; no. 4) [5716]

Brodo, Irwin M.

Guide to the literature for the identification of North American lichens. Ottawa: National Museums of Canada,

National Museum of Natural Sciences, 1985. 39 p. (Syllogeus / National Museum of Natural Sciences ; no. 56; ISSN: 0704-576X) [5509]

Brody, Bernard; Létourneau, Yves; Poirier, André
Revue de littérature sur les coûts indirects des accidents du travail. Montréal: École de relations industrielles, Université de Montréal, 1987. 43 p. (Document de recherche / École de relations industrielles, Université de Montréal ; 87-13; ISSN: 0829-0121) [2912]

Bromberg, Erik
"A Bibliography of theses and dissertations concerning the Pacific Northwest and Alaska." In: *Pacific Northwest Quarterly*; Vol. 40, no. 3 (July 1949) p. 203-252.; ISSN: 0030-8803. [6058]

Brooke, W. Michael
Canadian adult basic education. Toronto: Canadian Association for Adult Education, [1968]. 49 l. (Trends / Canadian Association for Adult Education) [3396]

Brooks, I.R.
Native education in Canada and the United States: a bibliography. [Calgary]: Office of Educational Development, Indian Students University Program Services, University of Calgary, c1976. xi, 298 p. [3511]

Brosseau, Marc
Bibliographie annotée des manuels de géographie au Canada français, 1804-1985. Ottawa: Université d'Ottawa, Centre de recherche en civilisation canadienne-française, 1990. 61 p. [3059]

Broten, Delores; Birdsall, Peter
Studies in the book trade. Victoria, B.C.: CANLIT, c1980. 30 p.; ISBN: 0-920566-10-3. [1637]

Brouillette, Benoît
"Bibliographie des ouvrages d'Émile Miller." Dans: *Revue canadienne de géographie*; Vol. 4 (1950) p. 94-96.; ISSN: 0316-3032. [7191]
"Chronique pédagogique: les sources principales de documentation." Dans: *Revue canadienne de géographie*; Vol. 14, nos 1-4 (1961) p. 72-99.; ISSN: 0316-3032. [2961]

Brousseau, Francine; Chabot, Line
Architecture in *Canadian Illustrated News* and *L'Opinion publique*: inventory of references/L'architecture dans le *Canadian Illustrated News* et *L'Opinion publique*: inventaire des références. Ottawa: Parks Canada, 1984. 203 p.; ISBN: 0-662-53167-1. [0774]

Brown, A.F.C.
Experimental stress analysis in the U.S.A. and Canada: a review of recent improvements in methods of stress analysis and of applications in various fields, with a classified bibliography. London: H.M.S.O., 1956. vi, 22 p. (Overseas technical reports / Department of Scientific and Technical Research ; no. 1) [5717]

Brown, Barbara E.
Canadian business and economics: a guide to sources of information. 3rd ed. Ottawa: Canadian Library Association, c1992. xv, 675 p.; ISBN: 0-88802-256-5. [2780]

Brown, Brian E.
Teaching aids obtainable from departments of the government at Ottawa. Ottawa: Canadian Citizenship Council, 1950. 23 p. [3374]

Brown, Charles R.
"Bibliography of Quebec or Lower Canada laws." In: *Law Library Journal*; Vol. 19, no. 4 (January 1927) p. 90-109.; ISSN: 0023-9283. [2101]

Brown, Gerald R.
Canada: the provincial look. [Ottawa]: Canadian School Library Association, Canadian Library Association, 1973. 103 p. (in various pagings), [32] p.: ill. [0106]

Brown, M.P. Sharon
Eastern Arctic Study: annotated bibliography. Kingston, Ont.: Centre for Resource Studies, Queen's University, [c1984]. iv, 69 p.; ISBN: 0-88757-043-7. [0643]

Brown, Mary M.S.
"Annual bibliography of Commonwealth literature, ... : Canada." In: *Journal of Commonwealth Literature*; 1966 in no. 4 (December 1967) p. 46-62; 1967 in no. 6 (January 1969) p. 43-63.; ISSN: 0021-9894. [1047]

Brown, Roger J.E.; Péwé, Troy L.
Distribution of permafrost in North America and its relationship to the environment: a review, 1963-1973. Ottawa: National Research Council Canada, Division of Building Research, [1973]. [30] p. (National Research Council Canada, Division of Building Research Technical paper ; no. 411) [5073]

Browne, Colin
Motion picture production in British Columbia: 1898-1940: a brief historical background and catalogue. Victoria: British Columbia Provincial Museum, 1979. 381 p. (British Columbia Provincial Museum Heritage record ; no. 6; ISSN: 0701-9556); ISBN: 0-7718-8136-3. [6638]

Browning, Clyde E.
A bibliography of dissertations in geography, 1901-1969. Chapel Hill, N.C.: University of North Carolina at Chapel Hill, Department of Geography, 1970. 96 p. (Studies in geography / University of North Carolina at Chapel Hill, Department of Geography ; no. 1) [6103]

The Browning directory of Canadian business information. Toronto: Browning Associates, 1988. 1 vol. (in various pagings).; ISBN: 0-920411-03-7. [2741]

Bruce, Anthony Peter Charles
An annotated bibliography of the British Army, 1660-1914. New York: Garland Publishing, 1975. 255 p. (Garland reference library of social science ; vol. 14); ISBN: 0-8240-9988-5. [1984]

Bruce, N.G.
Forest fire control literature: an author bibliography of CFS publications. Ottawa: Forest Fire Research Institute, 1973. 1 vol. (loose-leaf). (Forest Fire Research Institute Miscellaneous report ; FF-Y-1) [6283]

Bruck, Peter A., et al.
Canadian broadcasting: a working bibliography. Ottawa: Centre for Communication, Culture and Society, Carleton University, 1986. iii, 284 p. [0982]

Bruck, Peter A.; Langille, David; Vardy, Jill
Media, peace and security: a working bibliography. Ottawa: Centre for Communication, Culture and Society, Carleton University, 1986. 34 p. [2501]

Brumble, H. David
An annotated bibliography of American Indian and Eskimo autobiographies. Lincoln: University of Nebraska Press, c1981. 177 p.; ISBN: 0-8032-1175-9. [4023]

Brumpton, Cynthia
A woman's place is in the House ... of Commons: an annotated bibliography. [Toronto: C. Brumpton], 1988. 42 p. [3862]

Brun, Christian F.
Guide to the manuscript maps in the William L. Clements Library. Ann Arbor: University of Michigan, 1959. xiii,

209 p.: maps. [6507]

Brundin, Robert E.

Price guide to books on Canada and the Canadian Arctic. 2nd ed. Edmonton: University of Alberta Printing Services, 1985. vii, 124 p.; ISBN: 0-88864-950-9. [0148]

Bruneau, André

Répertoire des sources d'information économique: Canada et États-Unis. Québec: Service de l'éducation économique, Direction des communications, Ministère de l'industrie et du commerce, 1976. 83 p.; ISBN: 0-775-42560-5. [2618]

Bruneau, André; Germain, Geneviève

Répertoire des sources d'information économique: Québec. 2e éd., rev. et mise à jour. Québec: Service de promotion de l'économique, Direction générale des services aux entreprises, Ministère de l'industrie et du commerce, 1977. 150 p.; ISBN: 0-775-42737-3. [2623]

Bruneau, Pierre; Larrivée, Jean

Bibliographie: les inégalités de développement régional, au Québec et au Canada. Rimouski: Groupe de recherche interdisciplinaire en développement de l'est du Québec, Université du Québec à Rimouski, c1977. xvi, 152 p. (Cahiers du GRIDEQ / Groupe de recherche interdisciplinaire en développement de l'est du Québec ; no 1) [2624]

Bruneau, Sylvie; Larkin, Lise

Pour une école nouvelle à Trois-Rivières: bibliographie annotée. [Trois-Rivières: s.n.], 1981. [3], iii, 100 f. [3584]

Brunel, Pierre

"Bibliographie choisie sur l'océanographie de l'estuaire du Saint-Laurent." Dans: *Revue de géographie de Montréal*; Vol. 24, no 3 (1970) p. 277-282.; ISSN: 0035-1148. [5051]

Bruner, John Clay

Bibliography of the family Catostomidae (Cypriniformes). Edmonton: Natural History Section, Provincial Museum of Alberta, 1991. viii, 213 p. (Natural history occasional paper / Provincial Museum of Alberta ; no. 14; ISSN: 0838-5971); ISBN: 0-7732-0539-X. [5557]

Brunet, Jean

Bio-bibliographie du Révérend père Léo Boismenu. Montréal: Éditions Pilon, 1953. 64 p.: portr. [6856]

Brunet, Raymond

Guide bibliographique de la traduction: à l'intention des usagers de la Bibliothèque des sciences humaines et sociales. Montréal: Bibliothèque des sciences humaines et sociales, Université de Montréal, 1975. iv, 119 p. [1432]

Brunet-Aubry, Lise

"Littérature carcérale québécoise." Dans: *Criminologie*; Vol. 9, nos 1-2 (1976) p. 191-195.; ISSN: 0316-0041. [2147]

Brunet-Lamarche, Anita

"Auteurs et oeuvres: bio-bibliographie." Dans: *Revue du Nouvel Ontario*; No 4 (1982) p. 21-43.; ISSN: 0708-1715. [1189]

Brunet-Sabourin, Manon

Documents pour une histoire de l'édition au Québec avant 1900: bibliographie analytique. Montréal: M. Brunet-Sabourin, 1979. vii, 278 f. [1630]

Brunkow, Robert deV.

Religion and society in North America: an annotated bibliography. Santa Barbara, Calif.: ABC-Clio, 1983.; ISBN: 0-87436-042-0. [1553]

Brunn, Stanley D.

Key word identifiers of theses and dissertations from departments of geography in Canada and the United States on land use, water use, resource conflict, resource policy, and facility location. Monticello, Ill.: Council of Planning Librarians, 1978. 71 p. (Council of Planning Librarians Exchange bibliography ; 1512) [6147]

Bryant, Giles

Healey Willan catalogue. Ottawa: National Library of Canada, 1972. 174 p.: ill., music, ports. [7364]

Brye, David L.

European immigration and ethnicity in the United States and Canada: a historical bibliography. Santa Barbara, Calif.: ABC-Clio Information Services, 1983. vii, 458 p.; ISBN: 0-87436-258-X. [4216]

Brym, Robert J.

"Anglo-Canadian sociology: bibliography." In: *Current Sociology*; Vol. 34, no. 1 (Spring 1986) p. 112-152.; ISSN: 0011-3921. [3285]

Buchanan, Jim

Canadian Indian policy: a bibliography. Monticello, Ill.: Vance Bibliographies, 1979. 34 l. (Public administration series: Bibliography ; P-189; ISSN: 0193-970X) [4002]

Buchanan, Robert A.; Renaud, Wayne E.

L'écologie marine du Détroit de Lancaster et des eaux adjacentes: bibliographie commentée. Ottawa: Affaires indiennes et du Nord [Canada], c1978. xxv, 378 p.: ill. (Étude environnementale / Affaires indiennes et du Nord Canada ; no 7); ISBN: 0-662-90550-4. [5129]

The marine ecology of Lancaster Sound and adjacent waters: an annotated bibliography. Ottawa: Indian and Northern Affairs Canada, c1978. xxiv, 262 p.; ISBN: 0-662-10188-X. [5130]

Buchignani, Norman

"A review of the historical and sociological literature on East Indians in Canada." In: *Canadian Ethnic Studies*; Vol. 9, no. 1 (1977) p. 86-108.; ISSN: 0008-3496. [4179]

"Social science research on Asians in Canada." In: *Asian Canadians: aspects of social change*, edited by K. Victor Ujimoto and Josephine Naidoo. [Guelph, Ont.: s.n., 1984]. P. 1-29. [4220]

Bucksar, R.G.

Bibliography of socio-economic development of northern Ontario (northwestern and northeastern regions), 1968. Ottawa: Canadian Research Centre for Anthropology; Toronto: Department of Treasury and Economics, Regional Development Branch, 1968. 112 l. [0435]

Buggey, Susan

"Researching Canadian buildings: some historical sources." In: *Histoire sociale: Social History*; Vol. 10, no 20 (novembre 1977) p. 409-426.; ISSN: 0018-2257. [0752]

Bujea, Eleanor

Business education practices and trends: a literature review. Regina: University of Regina, Saskatchewan Instructional Development & Research Unit, 1987. 52 l. (SIDRU Research report / Saskatchewan Instructional Development & Research Unit ; no. 4; ISSN: 0835-6580); ISBN: 0-77310-110-1. [3667]

Bujold, Charles

"Signification du travail et valeurs de travail: revue de la littérature canadienne de langue française." Dans: *Orientation professionnelle*; Vol. 16, no 1 (juin 1980) p. 5-47.; ISSN: 0030-5413. [2861]

Bull, William Perkins

M 'n N Canadiana: books by Canadians or about Canada: a national wedding present from Wm. Perkins Bull, K.C. to his son Michael Bull, B.A., Oxon., Barrister of the Inner Temple and his bride Noreen Hennessy, on the occasion of their visit (while on their honeymoon) to the parental home, Lorne Hall, Rosedale, Toronto, Canada, where Michael was born. [Toronto: W.P. Bull, 1933]. xxi, [171] p.: ill. [0045]

Buller, Edward

Indigenous performing and ceremonial arts in Canada: a bibliography: an annotated bibliography of Canadian Indian rituals and ceremonies (up to 1976). [Toronto: Association for Native Development in the Performing and Visual Arts, c1981]. x, 151 p. [0970]

Bulletin bibliographique sur la didactique des langues. Québec: Centre international de recherche sur le bilinguisme, 1987. xiv, 559 p. (Publication / Centre international de recherche sur le bilinguisme ; J-1); ISBN: 2-89219-183-1. [1467]

Bulletin bibliographique sur la linguistique appliquée à l'informatique. Québec: Centre international de recherche sur le bilinguisme, 1987. xiv, 116 p. (Publication / Centre international de recherche sur le bilinguisme ; K-3); ISBN: 2-89219-182-3. [1468]

Bulletin bibliographique sur le bilinguisme et le contact des langues. Québec: Centre international de recherche sur le bilinguisme, 1989. xvii, 534 p. (Publication / Centre international de recherche sur le bilinguisme ; J-2); ISBN: 2-89219-201-3. [1485]

Bullock, Chris; Peck, David

Guide to Marxist literary criticism. Bloomington: Indiana University Press, c1980. ix, 176 p.; ISBN: 0-253-13144-8. [1165]

Bunn, Frank E.

Remote sensing reflectance spectroscopy: a working bibliography. Rexdale, Ont.: Ph.D. Associates, 1976. ii, 350 l. [5757]

Burdenuk, Gene

Annotated guide to selection sources for secondary school resource centres. Toronto: Ontario Library Association, 1977. 30 p. [1619]

Burge, Elizabeth J.

Computer mediated communication and education: a selected bibliography. Toronto: Distance Learning Office, Ontario Institute for Studies in Education, 1992. i, 87 p. [3726]

Burgess, Jean

An annotated list of 16mm films in the Regional Library, Canadian Wildlife Service, Edmonton. Edmonton: Canadian Wildlife Service, Western & Northern Region, 1976. iii, 25 p. [6628]

Burgess, Joanne

"Exploring the limited identities of Canadian labour: recent trends in English-Canada and Quebec." In: *International Journal of Canadian Studies*; No. 1-2 (Spring-Fall 1990) p. 149-174.; ISSN: 1180-3991. [2929]

Burgess, Joanne, et al.

Clés pour l'histoire de Montréal: bibliographie. Montréal: Boréal, 1992. 247 p.; ISBN: 2-89052-486-8. [0412]

Buri, Thomas

A preliminary annotated bibliography of the Stikine River country and its people. Telegraph Creek, B.C.: T. Buri, 1976. 36 l. [0586]

Burk, William R.

A bibliography of North American Gasteromycetes: I. Phallales. Vaduz [Liechtenstein]: A.R. Gantner, 1980. xv, 216 p. (Bibliotheca mycologica ; band 73); ISBN: 3-7682-1262-9. [5443]

Burke, Anne

A.J.M. Smith: an annotated bibliography. Downsview, Ont.: ECW Press, c1983. [104] p.; ISBN: 0-920763-66-9. [7311]

"A.J.M. Smith: an annotated bibliography." In: *The annotated bibliography of Canada's major authors*, Vol. 4, edited by Robert Lecker and Jack David. Downsview, Ont.: ECW Press, c1983. P. 267-370.; ISBN: 0-920802-52-4. [7312]

Raymond Knister: an annotated bibliography. [Downsview, Ont.: ECW Press, c1981]. P. 281-322.; ISBN: 0-920763-54-5. [7099]

"Raymond Knister: an annotated bibliography." In: *The annotated bibliography of Canada's major authors*, Vol. 3, edited by Robert Lecker and Jack David. Downsview, Ont.: ECW Press, c1981. P. 281-322.; ISBN: 0-920802-23-0. [7100]

"Raymond Knister: an annotated checklist." In: *Essays on Canadian Writing*; No. 16 (Fall-Winter 1979-1980) p. 20-61.; ISSN: 0316-0300. [7098]

Burke, Ronald J.; McKeen, Carol A.

Women in management bibliography. London, Ont.: National Centre for Management Research and Development, University of Western Ontario, 1988. 185 p. (Working paper series / National Centre for Management Research and Development, University of Western Ontario ; no. NC 90-20) [3863]

Burkle, Eric F.

Resource materials for traffic safety programs in elementary schools: a bibliography. [Victoria, B.C.]: Division of Policy Development, Ministry of Education, Science and Technology, 1979. 19 p.; ISBN: 0-7719-8248-8. [3549]

Burnet, Jean R.

Multiculturalism in Canada. [Ottawa]: Canadian Studies Directorate, Department of the Secretary of State of Canada, c1988. 26, 29 p. (Canadian studies resource guides); ISBN: 0-662-56210-0. [4248]

Le multiculturalisme au Canada. [Ottawa]: Direction des études canadiennes, Secrétariat d'État du Canada, c1988. 29, 26 p. (Guides pédagogiques des études canadiennes); ISBN: 0-662-56210-0. [4249]

Burnett, Mary

"Annual bibliography of Commonwealth literature, 1970: Canada." In: *Journal of Commonwealth Literature*; Vol. 6, no. 2 (December 1971) p. 43-67.; ISSN: 0021-9894. [1061]

Burns, Gordon R.

A preliminary annotated bibliography of literature on small mammals relevant to Elk Island National Park. Edmonton: Canadian Wildlife Service, 1984. 69 p. [5493]

Burpee, Lawrence J.

"A Canadian bibliography of the year 1901." In: *Proceedings and Transactions of the Royal Society of Canada*; Series 2, vol. 8, section 2 (1902) p. 233-344.; ISSN: 0316-4616. [0994]

"A chapter in the literature of the fur trade." In: *Papers of the Bibliographical Society of America*; Vol. 5 (1910) p. 45-60.; ISSN: 0006-128X. [1898]

"Check-list of Canadian public documents." In: *Papers of the Bibliographical Society of America*; Vol. 8, no. 1-2 (1914) p. 51-56.; ISSN: 0006-128X. [6214]

"Quebec in books." In: *Proceedings and Transactions of the*

Royal Society of Canada; Series 3, vol. 18, section 2 (1924) p. 75-85.; ISSN: 0316-4616. [0280]

Burn, O.V.

The ten-year history and index of the Ontario Mineral Exploration Assistance Program (MEAP) 1971-1981. Toronto: Ontario Ministry of Natural Resources, 1983. v, 196 p.: ill., maps. (Ontario Geological Survey Miscellaneous paper ; 108; ISSN: 0704-2752); ISBN: 0-7743-8016-0. [4832]

Burrage, David, et al.

Catalogue of programs [McGill University, Computing Centre]. Montreal: McGill University, Computing Centre, 1978. 88 p. [5767]

Burrows, Sandra; Gaudet, Franceen

Checklist of indexes to Canadian newspapers. Ottawa: National Library of Canada, 1987. 148, 154 p.; ISBN: 0-660-53735-4. [6041]

Liste de contrôle des index de journaux canadiens. Ottawa: Bibliothèque nationale du Canada, 1987. 154, 148 p.; ISBN: 0-660-53735-4. [6042]

Burtch, Brian E.; Ericson, Richard V.

The silent system: an inquiry into prisoners who suicide and annotated bibliography. Toronto: Centre of Criminology, University of Toronto, 1979. ix, 113 p. (Research report / Centre of Criminology, University of Toronto); ISBN: 0-919584-43-8. [3183]

Burton, Melody C.

Freedom of access and freedom of expression: an annotated bibliography of recent Canadian periodical literature. Edmonton: 1986. iv, 69 l. [1677]

Business methods literature: a monthly classified index. Ottawa: Keith Business Library, 1959-1960. 10 no.; ISSN: 0380-4909. [2571]

Buss, Helen M.

"Margaret Laurence: a bibliographical essay." In: *American Review of Canadian Studies;* Vol. 11, no. 2 (Autumn 1981) p. 1-14.; ISSN: 0272-2011. [7122]

Butcher, G.A.; Davidson, R.B.

A bibliography to Arctic grayling (Thymallus arcticus). [Victoria, B.C.]: Ministry of Environment, Aquatic Studies Branch, 1982. 30 l. [5472]

Butcher, William W.

W.W. Butcher's Canadian newspaper directory. London: Printed by the *Speaker* Printing Co., 1886. 46 p. [5998]

Butler, Brian E.

"Canadian studies of visual information-processing: 1970-1980." In: *Canadian Psychology;* Vol. 22, no. 2 (April 1981) p. 113-128.; ISSN: 0708-5591. [3212]

Butler, J.; Bartlett, G.

Bibliography of the geology of Newfoundland and Labrador, 1814 through 1968. St. John's, Nfld.: Department of Mines, Agriculture and Resources, Mineral Resources Division, 1969. 273 p. (Bulletin / Newfoundland Mineral Resources Division ; 38) [4771]

Butler, Phyllis; Harris, Aphrodite

English as a second language bibliography: the holdings of the King Edward Campus Library, Vancouver Community College. Vancouver: Vancouver Community College Press, c1990. v, 63 p.; ISBN: 0-921218-29-X. [3711]

Butler, T.H.

A bibliography of the Dungeness crab, Cancer magister Dana. Nanaimo, B.C.: Fisheries Research Board of Canada, 1967. 12 p. (Fisheries Research Board of Canada Technical report ; no. 1; ISSN: 0068-7553) [5344]

Butling, Pauline

"'Hall of fame blocks women': re-righting literary history: women and B.C. literary magazines." In: *Open Letter;* Series 7, no. 8 (Summer 1990) p. 60-76.; ISSN: 0048-1939. [5972]

Buttazzoni, Maria

La vie privée et l'informatique: bibliographie sélective. Québec: Bibliothèque de l'Assemblée nationale, Division de la référence parlementaire, 1991. 44 p. (Bibliographie / Bibliothèque de l'Assemblée nationale du Québec ; no 43; ISSN: 0836-9100) [2346]

Butterfield, Rita

"Canadian literature: a checklist." In: *Canadian Literature;* No. 23 (Winter 1965)-no. 48 (Spring 1971) [1062]

Buyniak, Victor O.

"Ukrainian imprints of Saskatoon, Saskatchewan: a preliminary check list." In: *Canadian Ethnic Studies;* Vol. 5, no. 1/2 (1973) p. 341-357.; ISSN: 0008-3496. [4158]

Byam, Barbara

Bibliography of statistical sources: sources of information of interest to writers, publishers, librarians and book and periodical distributors in Canada. [Toronto]: Book & Periodical Development Council, 1984. [3] l., 45 p. [3045]

C.D. Howe Research Institute

Bibliography and index of C.D. Howe Research Institute publications, 1958-1976. [Montreal, Quebec: C.D. Howe Research Institute], 1977. viii, 75 p.; ISBN: 0-88806-027-0. [2625]

Cabatoff, Kenneth; Iezzoni, Massimo

Bibliographie sur l'administration publique québécoise/ Quebec public administration: bibliography. Montréal: Université Concordia, Département de science politique, [1985]. 146 p. (Notes de recherche / Programme de maîtrise en politiques et en administration publiques, Université Concordia); ISBN: 0-88947-010-3. [2489]

Caccia, Iva

"Bibliography on the Canadian Charter of Rights and Freedoms/Bibliographie sur la Charte canadienne des droits et libertés." In: *Canadian Human Rights Yearbook: Annuaire canadien des droits de la personne;* Vol. 2 (1984-1985) p. 379-435; vol. 3 (1986) p. 199-297; vol. 4 (1987) p. 253-298; vol. 5 (1988) p. 263-297; vol. 6 (1989-1990) p. 313-366; vol. 7 (1991-1992) p. 265-294.; ISSN: 0824-5266. [2356]

Cadieux, Andrée

Le phénomène de la femme battue: une bibliographie canadienne/Wife battering: a Canadian bibliography. Ottawa: Conseil consultatif canadien de la situation de la femme, 1980. 1 vol. (en pagination variée.) [3198]

Cadrin, Carmen; Campbell, Elizabeth; Nicholson, Alison

A bibliography on old-growth forests in British Columbia: with annotations and abstracts. Victoria: Province of British Columbia, Ministry of Forests, 1991. v, 261 p. (Land management report / British Columbia Ministry of Forests ; no. 72; ISSN: 0702-9861); ISBN: 0-7718-9000-1. [5013]

Caine, T.W., et al.

Index to DIAND geology publications, Northwest Territories. Ottawa: Indian and Northern Affairs Canada, 1988. 95 p.; ISBN: 0-662-16638-8. [4864]

Index to DIAND geology publications, Yukon. Ottawa: Indian and Northern Affairs Canada, 1988. 48 p.; ISBN: 0-662-16637-X. [4865]

Calder, Carol

Multimedia resources for educational administrators. Toronto: Library, Reference and Information Services, Ontario Institute for Studies in Education, 1979. vi, 126 p. (Current bibliography / Ontario Institute for Studies in Education ; no. 12) [6639]

Calderisi, Maria

L'édition musicale au Canada, 1800-1867. Ottawa: Bibliothèque nationale du Canada, 1981. x, 124, 128, x p.: fac-sim., musique.; ISBN: 0-660-50454-5. [0889]

"John Lovell (1810-93): Montreal music printer and publisher." In: *Musical Canada: words and music honouring Helmut Kallmann*, edited by John Beckwith and Frederick A. Hall. Toronto: University of Toronto Press, 1988. P. 79-99; facsim., music.; ISBN: 0-8020-5759-4. [0933]

"Music publishers in the Maritimes: 1801-1900." In: *APLA Bulletin*; Vol. 49, no. 2 (September 1985) p. 10-11.; ISSN: 0001-2203. [0919]

Music publishing in the Canadas, 1800-1867. Ottawa: National Library of Canada, 1981. x, 128, 124, x p.: facsims., music.; ISBN: 0-660-50454-5. [0890]

Caldwell, Gary

Les études ethniques au Québec: bilan et perspectives. Québec: Institut québécois de recherche sur la culture, 1983. 106 p.; ISBN: 2-89224-017-4. [4217]

Calgary Board of Education. Media Services Group. Educational Media Team

Une bibliothèque fondamentale d'une école d'immersion française: 7e – 9e années. [Calgary]: The Board, c1986. vi, 145 p. [3651]

Calkins, Charles F.

The barn as an element in the cultural landscape of North America: a bibliography. Monticello, Ill.: Vance Bibliographies, 1979. 20 p. (Architecture series: Bibliography ; A-84; ISSN: 0194-1356) [0756]

Cambridge history of the British Empire. New York: Macmillan; Cambridge: The University Press, 1929-1959. 8 vol. [1931]

Camerlain, Lorraine

"Chronologie fragmentaire des créations québécoises depuis 1975." Dans: *Jeu*; No 21 (1981) p. 129-169.; ISSN: 0382-0335. [1179]

Cameron, Elspeth

Hugh MacLennan: an annotated bibliography. Downsview, Ont.: ECW Press, 1979. P. 103-153.; ISBN: 0-920763-58-8. [7165]

"Hugh MacLennan: an annotated bibliography." In: *The annotated bibliography of Canada's major authors*, Vol. 1, edited by Robert Lecker and Jack David. Downsview, Ont.: ECW Press, 1979. P. 103-153.; ISBN: 0-920802-02-8. [7166]

"A MacLennan log." In: *Journal of Canadian Studies*; Vol. 14, no. 4 (Winter 1979/80) p. 106-121.; ISSN: 0021-9495. [7167]

Cameron, Nancy P.

Yukon economic planning studies, 1965-1985: an annotated bibliography. Whitehorse: Yukon Archives, 1986. vii, 317 p. [0652]

Cameron, Nancy P.; Raines, Mary R.

Hydrocarbon development: a Yukon perspective: an annotated bibliography of sources available in the Yukon Archives. Whitehorse: The Archives, 1986-1988. 2 vol.; ISBN: 1-55018-024-X (vol. 1); 1-55018-062-2 (vol. 2). [4866]

Cameron, Neville S.C.

The role of organic compounds in salinization of Plains coal mining sites: a literature review. Edmonton: Reclamation Research Technical Advisory Committee, Alberta Land Conservation & Reclamation Council, 1980. viii, 46 p.: ill. (Report / Reclamation Research Technical Advisory Committee, Alberta Land Conservation & Reclamation Council ; no. 80-3) [4816]

Cameron, William J.

A bibliography in short-title catalog form of Canadiana in French, 1545-1631. [London: University of Western Ontario], 1984. iii, 38 l. (WHSTC Bibliography ; no. 12; ISSN: 0712-9289); ISBN: 0-7714-0519-7. [2035]

A bibliography in short-title catalog form of eighteenth century editions of the writings of Louis Armand de Lom d'Arce, Baron de Lahontan. [London: University of Western Ontario], 1982. iii, 14 l. (WHSTC Bibliography ; no. 6 ; ISSN: 0712-9289); ISBN: 0-7714-0363-1. [7111]

A bibliography in short-title catalog form of Jesuit relations, printed accounts of events in Canada, 1632-73, sent by Jesuit missionaries to France. Rev. ed. [London: University of Western Ontario], 1988. vi, 60 p. (WHSTC Bibliography ; no. 12; ISSN: 0712-9289); ISBN: 0-7714-0519-7. [2067]

A bibliography in short-title catalog form of seventeenth and eighteenth century editions of the writings of Louis Hennepin, Recollet explorer and missionary. [London: University of Western Ontario], 1982. 15 l. (WHSTC Bibliography ; no. 1; ISSN: 0712-9289); ISBN: 0-7714-0332-1. [7054]

A short-title catalog of Canadiana in English: from Hakluyt to Hennepin, 1599-1698 in the Rare Book Room: la Réserve, the National Library of Canada: la Bibliothèque nationale du Canada. London: University of Western Ontario, 1983. v, 10 l. (WHSTC library catalog ; no. 14; ISSN: 0712-9297); ISBN: 0-7714-0452-2. [0142]

Sixteenth century Canadiana in English: a bibliography in short-title catalog form. [London: University of Western Ontario], 1988. vi, 27 p. (WHSTC Bibliography ; no. 52; ISSN: 0712-9289); ISBN: 0-7714-1036-0. [2068]

Cameron, William J.; McKnight, George

Robert Addison's library: a short-title catalogue of the books brought to Upper Canada in 1792 by the first missionary sent out to the Niagara frontier by the Society for the Propagation of the Gospel. Hamilton, Ont.: Printed at McMaster University for the Synod of the Diocese of Niagara, 1967. liv, 98 p.: ill., facsims. [6774]

Campbell, A.E.; Pratt, R.H.M.

Bibliography of North American shelterbelt research. Edmonton: Canadian Forestry Service, Department of the Environment, 1974. 52 p. (Northern Forest Research Centre Information report ; NOR-X-92; ISSN: 0704-7673) [4943]

Campbell, C.A.

"Bibliography of Major André." In: *The crisis of the revolution: being the story of Arnold and André*, by William Abbatt. New York: W. Abbatt, 1899. P. [101]-111. [6801]

Campbell, Catherine

Canada's two heritages: the effect of the two predominant heritages on the French Canadians and English Canadians as revealed in their writings of the present century: a bibliography to the end of 1952. London [Ont.]: Lawson Memorial Library, University of Western Ontario, 1954.

53 p. [0062]

Campbell, Dani Leigh

A preliminary examination of the development of the public library and its antecedents, as institutions of public education in Ontario, 1851-1950: an annotated bibliography of the evidence found in the legislation and government reports of the province. Edmonton: [D.L. Campbell], 1987. 42 l. [1689]

Campbell, Geraldine

Notes on microfilmed Tweedsmuir books. Ridgetown, Ont.: Federated Women's Institutes of Ontario, 1991. [25] l. [0489]

Notes on published [Tweedsmuir] books. Ridgetown, Ont.: Federated Women's Institutes of Ontario, 1991. [12] l. [0490]

Campbell, Gordon

The community college in Canada: an annotated bibliography. Calgary: Department of Educational Administration, University of Calgary, [c1971]. v, 82 p. (University of Calgary Department of Educational Administration Series on tertiary and continuing education) [3414]

Campbell, Henry Cummings

The Espial data base directory: a guide to current Canadian information contained in national and international data bases and data banks. Toronto: Espial Productions, 1987-. vol.; ISSN: 0834-3888. [0180]

How to find out about Canada. Oxford: New York: Pergamon Press, 1967. xiv, 248 p.: ill., facsims. [0083]

Campbell, K.W.

Pollutant exposure and response relationships: a literature review: geological and hydrogeological aspects. Calgary: Acid Deposition Research Program, 1987. 151 p.: ill., maps.; ISBN: 0-921625-09-X. [5242]

Campbell, R. Wayne, et al.

A bibliography of British Columbia ornithology. Victoria: British Columbia Provincial Museum, 1979-1988. 2 vol. (British Columbia Provincial Museum Heritage record; no. 7; ISSN: 0701-9556) [5539]

A bibliography of Pacific northwest herpetology. Victoria: British Columbia Provincial Museum, 1982. v, 152 p.: ill., maps. (British Columbia Provincial Museum Heritage record; no. 14; ISSN: 0701-9556); ISBN: 0-7718-8288-2. [5473]

Campbell, R. Wayne; Forsman, E.D.; Van Der Raay, B.M.

An annotated bibliography of literature on the spotted owl. Victoria: Province of British Columbia, Ministry of Forests, 1984. 115 p.: ill., map. (Land management report / British Columbia Ministry of Forests; no. 24; ISSN: 0702-9861); ISBN: 0-7718-8454-0. [5494]

Campbell, William Wilfred

Bibliography: War of 1812-14. [S.l.: s.n., 1900]. 38 l. [1890]

Canada, Newfoundland, Labrador and the Canadian Arctic: a selection of six hundred and fifty books, with 44 illustrations. London: Maggs Bros., 1939. 118 p., [38] p. of pl.: ill., facsims. [0051]

Canada and international peace and security: a bibliography covering materials from January 1985 through December 1989/Le Canada, la paix et la sécurité internationales: une bibliographie comprenant des documents de janvier 1985 à décembre 1989. Ottawa: Canadian Institute for International Peace and Security, 1990. v, 434 p.; ISBN: 0-660-55772-X. [2535]

Canada Centre for Mineral and Energy Technology

Bibliography of CANMET publications on coprocessing. Ottawa: Canada Centre for Mineral and Energy Technology, Energy Research Laboratories, 1988. iii, 44 p. [5831]

Catalogue of CANMET publications. Ottawa: Canada Centre for Mineral and Energy Technology, Technology Information Division, 1978-1982. 7 vol.; ISSN: 0707-560X. [6347]

Canada Centre for Mineral and Energy Technology. Library and Documentation Services Division

CANMET publications in print/Publications de CANMET disponibles. [Ottawa]: The Division, 1989. [116] p. [6397]

Canada Council. Research and Evaluation

The Canada Council Arts Research bibliography/Le Conseil des arts du Canada Répertoire des travaux de recherche sur les arts. [Ottawa]: Canada Council, 1988-1992. 3 vol.; ISSN: 0837-4910.; ISBN: 0-660-57315-6 (vol. 1); 0-660-57335-0 (vol. 2); 0-660-57477-2 (vol. 3). [0728]

Canada Institute for Scientific and Technical Information

Directory of Canadian scientific and technical databases/Répertoire des bases de données scientifiques et techniques au Canada. Ottawa: National Research Council Canada, 1984. 91, [15] p. [4628]

The Metric system: a bibliography of instructional guides, manuals and conversion tables/Le système métrique: liste bibliographique de guides, de manuels et de tables de conversion. Ottawa: CISTI, 1975. 8 l. [2615]

Union list of scientific serials in Canadian libraries/Catalog collectif des publications scientifiques dans les bibliothèques canadiennes. 12th ed. Ottawa: National Research Council of Canada, 1988. 3 vol.; ISSN: 0082-7657. [5966]

Canada Land Inventory

An initial bibliography on outdoor recreational studies in Canada with selected United States references/Une première bibliographie des études sur les loisirs de plein air au Canada, accompagnée d'un choix d'ouvrages de référence publiés aux États-Unis. Rev. ed. [Ottawa]: Canada Land Inventory, Department of Regional Economic Expansion, 1970. vi, 165, [109] l. [1756]

Canada Mortgage and Housing Corporation

Compendium of research [CMHC]/Compendium de recherche [SCHL]. Ottawa: Canada Mortgage and Housing Corporation, 1984-. vol.; ISSN: 0838-892X. [4443]

Canada Mortgage and Housing Corporation. Development Evaluation and Advisory Services Division

CMHC demonstration projects: a selected annotated bibliography. [Ottawa]: CMHC, Demonstration Analysis Division, [1980]. 66, 68 p., ii l.; ISBN: 0-660-90545-0. [4381]

Canada Oil and Gas Administration

Released geophysical and geological reports, Canada lands/Divulgation des rapports géophysiques et géologiques, des terres du Canada. Ottawa: Canada Oil and Gas Administration, 1984. 131 p.: ill., maps. [4838]

"Canada on records." In: *Musicanada*; No. 26 (January-February 1970) p. 2-15.; ISSN: 0580-3152. [0824]

Canada water year book, 1979-1980: references/Annuaire de l'eau du Canada, 1979-1980: références. Ottawa: Environment Canada, 1981. v, 69 p.; ISSN: 0708-4285.; ISBN: 0-662-51566-8. [5171]

Canada year book. Ottawa: Statistics Canada, 1906-. vol.; ISSN: 0068-8142. [6450]

Canada. Agriculture Canada. Advisory Committee on Soil Survey

Bibliography of soil survey and related works in Atlantic Canada/Bibliographie sur l'étude pédologique et oeuvres connexes au Canada atlantique. [Fredericton]: Atlantic Provinces Agricultural Services Coordinating Committee, 1985. v, 35 p. [4705]

Canada. Agriculture Canada. Economics Branch

A bibliography of Canadian agricultural economics papers/ Bibliographie des études canadiennes en économie agricole. Ottawa: Communications Unit, Economics Branch, Agriculture Canada, 1974. 65 p. [4664]

Canada. Agriculture Canada. Research Station (Saskatoon). Library

Pesticide application and spraying: a selected bibliography. Saskatoon: Agriculture Canada, 1974. 195 p. (Technical bulletin / Saskatoon Research Station, Agriculture Canada ; no. 2) [5086]

Canada. Archives nationales

Publications [Archives nationales du Canada]. Ottawa: Archives nationales du Canada, 1985-. vol.; ISSN: 0844-711X. [6434]

Canada. Archives publiques

Catalogue des brochures, journaux et rapports dans les Archives publiques du Canada, 1611-1867, avec index. 2e éd. [Ottawa: Impr. du Roi, 1916]. 471 p. [6757]

Liste des publications des Archives publiques du Canada. Ottawa: Archives publiques Canada, 1974-1982. 8 vol.; ISSN: 0828-1505. [6341]

Canada. Archives publiques. Division de la collection nationale de cartes et plans

Le Canada par les cartes: [catalogue]. [Ottawa: Archives Publiques, 1970]. [30], [28] p. [6517]

Canada. Archives publiques. Division des archives fédérales

Documents pour l'étude du Nord canadien. Ottawa: Archives publiques Canada, 1980. 24, 21 p.; ISBN: 0-662-50848-3. [0638]

Canada. Archives publiques. Division des Cartes géographiques

Cartes géographiques du seizième siècle se rapportant au Canada: liste préliminaire et bibliographie. Ottawa: Archives publiques Canada, 1958. xxvii, 305 p.: fac-sim. [6506]

Canada. Atmospheric Environment Service

A selected list of articles and papers on the climatology of the Upper Great Lakes published from 1960 to 1972. Downsview, Ont.: Atmospheric Environment Service, Hydrometeorology and Marine Applications Division, 1973. 17 l. [5074]

Canada. Atmospheric Environment Service. Information Resource Centre

Serials list (Atmospheric Environment Service)/Liste de périodiques (Service de l'environnement atmosphérique). Downsview: The Centre, 1992. 142 p. [5979]

Canada. Atomic Energy Control Board

Publications catalogue: Atomic Energy Control Board/ Catalogue des publications: Commission de contrôle de l'énergie atomique. Ottawa: Atomic Energy Control Board, Office of Public Information, 1979-. vol.; ISSN: 0711-9917. [6435]

Canada. Bibliothèque du Parlement

Brochures canadiennes index [microform]. [Ottawa: Micro Can, 1986]. 11 microfiches. [0152]

Canada. Bureau des traductions. Direction de la documentation

Répertoire des bibliographies [Bureau des traductions]/ Directory of bibliographies [Translation Bureau]. 4e éd. [Ottawa: Le Bureau], 1985. vii, 21 p. [0149]

Canada. Bureau des traductions. Direction de la terminologie et des services linguistiques

Liste des publications [Bureau des traductions]. Ottawa: Secrétariat d'État du Canada, Direction générale de la terminologie et des services linguistiques, 1989-. vol.; 0848-4546. [6436]

Canada. Bureau fédéral de la statistique

Publications de recensement du Canada de 1961: liste. Ottawa: Bureau fédéral de la statistique, [1962-1963]. 3 vol. [2964]

Canada. Bureau of Statistics. Education Division. Research Section

A bibliographical guide to Canadian education/Guide bibliographique de l'enseignement au Canada. [2nd ed.]. Ottawa: Queen's Printer, 1964. 55 p. [3387]

Canada. Bureau of Statistics. Library

Bibliographical list of references to Canadian railways, 1829-1938. Ottawa: [s.n.], 1938. 99 p. [4445]

Canada. Canadian Heritage

Research results of projects funded by the Canadian Ethnic Studies Program, 1973-1988: a bibliography/Résultats des projets de recherche subventionnés par le Programme des études ethniques canadiennes, 1973-1988: une bibliographie. Ottawa: Canadian Heritage, 1993. x, 78 p.; ISBN: 0-662-60103-3. [4296]

Canada. Canadian Studies Directorate

Decisions: projects funded from 1984 to 1989. Ottawa: The Directorate, c1991. 152 p.: ill.; ISBN: 0-662-19287-7. [0173]

Canada. Civil Service Commission. Pay Research Bureau

A selected bibliography on wage and salary administration, employee benefits and services and collective bargaining. [Ottawa: s.n., 1966]. ii, 80 l. [2795]

Canada. Commission de la Fonction publique. Direction générale du programme de la formation linguistique

Français langue seconde: catalogue/French as a second language: catalogue. [Ottawa]: La Commission, c1987. 63 p.: ill.; ISBN: 0-662-54691-1. [1469]

Canada. Commission of Conservation

Catalogue of publications [Commission of Conservation]. [Ottawa]: Commission of Conservation, 1913. 35 p. [6213]

Canada. Commission of Inquiry Relating to Public Complaints, Internal Discipline and Grievance Procedure within the Royal Canadian Mounted Police

A bibliography on public complaints against the police, internal police discipline and related topics. [Ottawa: 1975]. 196 p. [2140]

Canada. Conseil du Trésor

Liste des publications [Conseil du Trésor du Canada]. [Ottawa]: Division des communications, Conseil du Trésor du Canada, 1979-. vol.; ISSN: 0837-6476. [6437]

Canada. Consumer and Corporate Affairs Canada

Consumer sourcebook for the disabled/Sources d'informations du consommateur handicapé. Ottawa: Consumer and Corporate Affairs Canada, 1982. vi, 118 p.; ISBN: 0-662-52226-5. [3235]

Canada. Department of Agriculture. Economics Division

A list of published material by members of the Economics Division, 1930-1953. Ottawa: The Division, 1953.

44 p. [4640]

Canada. Department of Agriculture. Economics Division. Rural Sociology Unit

A chronological summary of papers, reports and publications in the field of rural sociology and socio-economics of the Economics Division, Canada Department of Agriculture, Ottawa, Ontario. Ottawa: 1960-1962. 3 vol. [3080]

Canada. Department of Agriculture. Engineering Research Service

Bibliography of Canadian development equipment for field plot mechanization and related laboratory work. Ottawa: Engineering Research Service, Canada Department of Agriculture, 1972. 12 p. [4651]

Canada. Department of Agriculture. Library

Chapais collection/Collection Chapais. [Ottawa]: Canada Department of Agriculture, 1976. xxi, 77 p.; ISBN: 0-662-00373-X. [4668]

Publications of the Canada Department of Agriculture, 1867-1974. 2nd rev. ed. [Ottawa: Information Canada], 1975. vii, 341 p. [6294]

Union list of serials in Canada Department of Agriculture libraries/Répertoire collectif des publications en série des bibliothèques du Ministère de l'agriculture du Canada. 2nd ed. Ottawa: Canada Department of Agriculture, 1977. 745 p.; ISBN: 0-662-01292-5. [5928]

Canada. Department of Citizenship and Immigration. Canadian Citizenship Branch

Research on immigrant adjustment and ethnic groups: a bibliography of published material, 1920-1953/Recherches sur l'adaptation des immigrants et les groupes ethniques: une bibliographie d'ouvrages publiées, 1920-1953. Ottawa: Research Division, Canadian Citizenship Branch, Department of Citizenship and Immigration, 1956. ii, 131 p. [4128]

Research on immigrant adjustment and ethnic groups: a bibliography of unpublished theses, 1920-1953/Recherches sur l'adaptation des immigrants et les groupes ethniques: une bibliographie de thèses non publiées, 1920-1953. Ottawa: Research Division, Canadian Citizenship Branch, Department of Citizenship and Immigration, 1955. [3], 31 p. [6063]

Canada. Department of Citizenship and Immigration. Economic and Social Research Branch

Citizenship, immigration and ethnic groups in Canada: bibliography of research, published and unpublished sources, 1920-1958/Citoyenneté, immigration et groupes ethniques au Canada: une bibliographie des recherches, sources publiées et non publiées, 1920-1958. Ottawa: [Queen's Printer], 1960. [8], 190, xix p. [4133]

Canada. Department of Citizenship and Immigration. Library

Canadian immigration and emigration, 1946-1957: a bibliography. Ottawa: [s.n.], 1958. 38 p. [4130]

Canada. Department of Consumer and Corporate Affairs. Library

Combines Investigation Act: selected references/Loi relative aux enquêtes sur les coalitions: bibliographie. [Ottawa]: Department of Consumer and Corporate Affairs, Library, 1970. 7 l. [2117]

Canada. Department of Energy, Mines and Resources. Gravity Division

Index of publications, 1948-1973 [Canada Department of Energy, Mines and Resources, Gravity Division]. Ottawa:

Information Canada, 1974. 22 p.: ill., maps (folded). [6287]

Canada. Department of Energy, Mines and Resources. Surveys and Mapping Branch

Catalogue of published maps [Canada Surveys and Mapping Branch]/Catalogue des cartes publiées [Canada Direction des levés et de la cartographie]. Ottawa: Department of Energy, Mines and Resources, 1974. 362 p.: maps (some in colour). [6536]

Canada. Department of External Affairs

Documents on relations between Canada and Newfoundland/Documents relatifs aux relations entre le Canada et Terre-Neuve. Ottawa: Department of External Affairs, 1974. 2 vol. (bound in 3): ill. (some folded), folded col. maps, ports. (Documents on Canadian external relations); ISBN: 0-660-52445-7. [0216]

Canada. Department of External Affairs. Information Division

A list of Canadian books for young people: for the guidance of those responsible for the selection of books for school libraries. Ottawa: Information Division, Department of External Affairs, 1969. 29 p. [0091]

Canada. Department of External Affairs. Library Services Division

"For the record: bibliography of recent publications on Canadian foreign relations." In: *International Perspectives;* (1980-1989) ; ISSN: 0381-4874. [2525]

Canada. Department of Forestry

The ARDA catalogue [Agricultural Rehabilitation and Development Administration]. Ottawa: Department of Forestry, 1965-1966. 3 vol. [4648]

Canada. Department of Forestry and Rural Development. Information and Technical Services Division

List of available publications [Canada Department of Forestry and Rural Development]. Ottawa: Queen's Printer, 1968. 93 p. [6265]

Canada. Department of Forestry. Information and Technical Services

Catalogue of Canadian forestry and other resource films/Films canadiens sur les forêts et autres ressources renouvelables. Ottawa: Queen's Printer, 1965. vii, 32 p. [6607]

Canada. Department of Indian Affairs and Northern Development

On film: a film catalogue [Indian Affairs and Northern Development]. Ottawa: The Department, 1989. 72, 32 p. [6678]

Canada. Department of Indian Affairs and Northern Development. Northern Regulatory Review

Some references relevant to regulation of industrial activity in the Canadian north, 1983 to 1986. [Ottawa]: The Review, 1986. 26, 10, 40, 35 l. [4848]

Canada. Department of Indian and Northern Affairs. Indian and Inuit Affairs Program. Research Branch

A listing of research reports: Research Branch. Ottawa: Department of Indian and Northern Affairs, 1980. 55 p. [4013]

Canada. Department of Indian and Northern Affairs. Northern Social Research Division

Ongoing and recently completed research studies concerned with the social implications of the development of communications systems in northern Canada. Ottawa: Northern Social Research Division, Department of Indian and Northern Affairs, 1979. [70] l. [3184]

Canada. Department of Indian and Northern Affairs. Program Reference Centre

Economic development consultant reports: bibliography. [Ottawa: Research Reference Service, Indian and Northern Affairs, Government of Canada, 1975]. 192 p. [3963]

Canada. Department of Industry, Trade and Commerce

Books from Canada/Livres du Canada. Ottawa: Department of Industry, Trade and Commerce, 1977. 1 portfolio. [0122]

Canada. Department of Industry, Trade and Commerce. Foreign Investment Division

Direct investment in Canada by non-residents: a selected bibliography to October 1973. Ottawa: Department of Industry, Trade and Commerce, Foreign Investment Division, 1973. 1 vol. (in various pagings). [2603]

The international enterprise: a selected bibliography to May 1972. Ottawa: The Division, 1972. 29, 22, 1 l. [2595]

Canada. Department of Industry, Trade and Commerce. Library

Canadian investment abroad: selected bibliography, 1956 to 1968. Ottawa: Department of Industry, Trade and Commerce, 1969. 4, 5 l. [2583]

Canada. Department of Justice

Bibliography of public legal information materials/ Bibliographie des documents juridiques de vulgarisation. [S.l.]: Department of Justice, 1983. 172 p. [2253]

The prevention of crime and the treatment of offenders: a source book of Canadian experiences. Ottawa: Communication and Public Affairs, Department of Justice Canada, c1990. vi, 74, 81, vi p.; ISBN: 0-662-57687-X. [2331]

Canada. Department of Labour. Accident Prevention Division. Technical Library

Bibliography: occupational safety and health: selected holdings of Technical Library, Accident Prevention Division, Canada Department of Labour/Bibliographie: sécurité et hygiène professionnelles: choix de volumes de la Bibliothèque technique, Division de la prévention des accidents, Ministère du travail du Canada. Ottawa: Labour Canada, Occupational Safety and Health, 1976. x, 144 p.; ISBN: 0-662-00154-0. [2828]

Canada. Department of Labour. Economics and Research Branch

A selected bibliography on the social and economic implications of electronic data processing. [Ottawa: s.n.], 1964. 75 l. [2576]

Canada. Department of Manpower and Immigration

Immigration, migration and ethnic groups in Canada: a bibliography of research, 1964-1968/Immigration, migration et groupes ethniques au Canada: une bibliographie de recherches, 1964-1968. Ottawa: [Queen's Printer], 1969. xiv, 56 p. [4142]

Canada. Department of Manpower and Immigration. Occupational Research Section. Occupational Analysis Unit

Bibliography of career information publications/ Bibliographie de la documentation sur les carrières. 2nd ed. Ottawa: Queen's Printer, 1968. 2 vol. [2798]

Canada. Department of Manpower and Immigration. Research Branch

Manpower studies: a selected bibliography for policy and research. Ottawa: Research Branch, Program Development Service, Department of Manpower and Immigration, 1966. 56 p. [2796]

Canada. Department of Marine and Fisheries

Catalogue of official Canadian government publications of use to mariners. Ottawa: King's Printer, 1924. 38 p. [6217]

Canada. Department of Mines and Resources. Bureau of Geology and Topography

Published maps (1917-1946 inclusive). Ottawa: Bureau of Geology and Topography, 1946. i, 119 p. [6496]

Canada. Department of Mines and Resources. Surveys and Engineering Branch

1939 catalogue of maps, plans and publications. Ottawa: Patenaude, Printer to the King, 1939. 55 p.: maps (folded). [6493]

Canada. Department of Mines and Technical Surveys. Geographical Branch

Bibliography of periodical literature on Canadian geography, 1930 to 1955. Ottawa: [Queen's Printer], 1959-1960. 6 parts. (Bibliographical series / Canada Department of Mines and Technical Surveys, Geographical Branch ; no. 22) [2958]

Canadian maps, 1949 to 1954. Ottawa: [s.n.], 1956. vii, 82 p. (Bibliographical series / Canada Department of Mines and Technical Surveys, Geographical Branch ; no. 16) [6503]

Canadian urban geography. Rev. ed. Ottawa: E. Cloutier, 1957. 100 p. (Bibliographical series / Canada Department of Mines and Technical Surveys, Geographical Branch ; no. 13) [4302]

Colonization and settlement in the Americas: a selected bibliography/Colonisation et peuplement dans les Amériques: bibliographie choisie. Ottawa: [Queen's Printer], 1960. 68 p. (Bibliographical series / Canada Department of Mines and Technical Surveys, Geographical Branch ; no. 25) [1935]

A list of periodical literature on topics related to Canadian geography for the period 1940-1950. Ottawa: 1954. vi, 131 p. (Bibliographical series / Canada Department of Mines and Technical Surveys, Geographical Branch ; no. 9) [2956]

Pedogeography of Canada. Rev. ed. Ottawa: [s.n.], 1956. 24 p. (Bibliographical series / Canada Department of Mines and Technical Surveys, Geographical Branch ; no. 12) [4749]

Selected bibliography of Canadian geography/Bibliographie choisie d'ouvrages sur la géographie au Canada. Ottawa: Queen's Printer, 1950-1966. 16 vol. (Bibliographical series / Canada Department of Mines and Technical Surveys, Geographical Branch ; nos. 2, 4-8, 10, 14-15, 17, 19, 23, 26-29, 32-33) [2968]

Selected bibliography on Canadian permafrost: annotations and abstracts. Ottawa: [Queen's Printer], 1958. 23 p. (Bibliographical series / Canada Department of Mines and Technical Surveys, Geographical Branch ; no. 20) [4754]

Selected bibliography on Canadian toponymy/Bibliographie choisie d'ouvrages sur la toponymie au Canada. Ottawa: [Queen's Printer], 1964. 27 p. (Bibliographical series / Canada Department of Mines and Technical Surveys, Geographical Branch ; no. 30) [2966]

Selected bibliography on periglacial phenomena in Canada: annotations and abstracts. Ottawa: [Queen's Printer], 1960. 22 p. (Bibliographical series / Canada Department of Mines and Technical Surveys, Geographical Branch) ; no. 24) [2959]

Selected bibliography on sea ice distribution in the coastal waters of Canada. Ottawa: [Queen's Printer], 1957. 50 p.:

maps (2 folded). (Bibliographical series / Canada Department of Mines and Technical Surveys, Geographical Branch , no. 18) [3029]

A selected list of periodical literature on topics related to Canadian geography for the period 1930-1939. Ottawa: 1954. iv l., 97 p. (Bibliographical series / Canada Department of Mines and Technical Surveys, Geographical Branch ; no. 11) [2957]

Canada. Department of Mines and Technical Surveys. Surveys and Mapping Branch. Canadian Hydrographic Service

Catalogue of Canadian Hydrographic Service nautical charts, tidal and current publications, sailing directions and other Canadian government publications of interest to mariners. Ottawa: Queen's Printer, 1914-1955. 15 vol. [6502]

Catalogue of Canadian Hydrographic Service nautical charts and sailing directions for inland waters of Canada including the Great Lakes ... and other Canadian government publications of interest to mariners. Ottawa: Department of Mines and Technical Surveys, 1954. vi, 15 [i.e., 26] p.: maps. [6501]

Canada. Department of National Health and Welfare

Featuring fitness: a catalogue of the publications of the Physical Fitness Division, Dept. of National Health and Welfare, Ottawa. Ottawa: The Department, 1954. 19 p. [6235]

Canada. Department of National Health and Welfare. Departmental Library Services

Rehabilitation and the handicapped: a layman's guide to some of the literature: a bibliography/Réadaptation des handicapés: guide populaire et bibliographie sélective. Ottawa: Health and Welfare Canada, 1976. x, 184 p. [3142]

Canada. Department of National Health and Welfare. Emergency Health Services Division

Bibliography relating to disaster nursing. Ottawa: Department of National Health and Welfare, 1965. 30 p. [5570]

Canada. Department of National Health and Welfare. Epidemiology Division

Selected Canadian public health references of epidemiological significance. [Ottawa: The Division], 1957. ii, 75 p. [5565]

Canada. Department of Public Printing and Stationery

Documents relating to the St. Lawrence Seaway Development Project, obtainable from the Queen's Printer, Ottawa. Ottawa: Department of Public Printing and Stationery, 1959. 2 l. (Price list / Department of Public Printing and Stationery ; no. 3) [6242]

List of Canadian government periodicals/Liste des périodiques du gouvernement canadien. Ottawa: Queen's Printer, 1965. 15 p. [6252]

Report of the Department of Public Printing and Stationery. Ottawa: Queen's Printer, 1887-1968. 62 vol. [6266]

Canada. Department of Public Printing and Stationery. Documents Library

Canadian government publications catalogue: Mines Branch and Mineral Resources Division, Energy, Mines and Resources/Publications du gouvernement canadien: Énergie, mines et ressources, Direction des mines et Division des ressources minérales. 3rd ed. Ottawa: Queen's Printer, 1967. 401 p. (Sectional catalogue series / Department of Public Printing and Stationery, Documents Library ; no. 12) [6261]

Canadian government publications relating to labour/ Publications du gouvernement canadien sur les sujets relatifs au travail. 3rd ed., 2e éd. bilingue. Ottawa: Queen's Printer, 1963. 337 p. (Canadian government publications sectional catalogue ; no. 10) [6247]

Canadian government publications sectional catalogue: Department of Forestry/Publications du Gouvernement canadien: Ministère des forêts. Ottawa: Queen's Printer, 1963. 137 p. (Canadian government publications sectional catalogue ; no. 13) [6248]

Northern Affairs and National Resources publications/ Publications: Nord canadien et ressources nationales. 2nd ed. Ottawa: Queen's Printer, 1963. 182 p. (Queen's Printer Sectional catalogue ; no. 11) [6249]

Canada. Department of Regional Economic Expansion. Planning Division

Regional development and economic growth: problems, analyses, and policies: select bibliography/Expansion régionale et croissance économique: problèmes, analyses et politiques: bibliographie choisie. Ottawa: 1969. 285 p. [2584]

Canada. Department of Supply and Services

Selected titles published by Government of Canada departments and agencies. Ottawa: Department of Supply and Services, 1974-1979. 10 vol.; ISSN: 0384-9759. [6321]

Canada. Department of the Interior

Bibliography on Hudson Bay: list of books and references contained in the Natural Resources Reference Library, Department of the Interior, Ottawa, March 24th, 1926. [S.l.: s.n., 1926]. 7 l. [2949]

Canada. Department of the Interior. Natural Resources Intelligence Branch

Catalogue of publications [Natural Resources Intelligence Branch]. Ottawa: King's Printer, 1929. 21 p. [6218]

Canada. Department of the Interior. Topographical and Air Survey Bureau

Catalogue of maps, plans and publications distributed by the Topographical and Air Survey Bureau. 6th ed. Ottawa: King's Printer, 1934. 24 p.: map (folded). [6490]

Canada. Department of the Secretary of State

Human rights research in Canada: a bibliography. Ottawa: Queen's Printer, 1970. 64 p. [2118]

Canada. Department of the Secretary of State. Bilingualism Development Programme. Social Action Branch

Selected bibliography on Anglophone-Francophone relations in Canada/Bibliographie choisie sur les relations anglophones-francophones au Canada. [Ottawa]: Department of the Secretary of State, 1973. 56 p. [3115]

Canada. Department of the Secretary of State. Human Rights Directorate

Human rights publications. [Hull, Quebec]: The Directorate, 1984. 7, 7 p. [2264]

Canada. Department of the Secretary of State. Library

Canadian ethnic groups bibliography/Bibliographie des groupes ethniques canadiens. 2nd ed. [Ottawa]: Secrétariat d'État du Canada, La Bibliothèque Department of the Secretary of State, The Library, [1985]. iv, 96 p. [4231]

Canada. Department of Trade and Commerce

Books sent to the Library, Canadian Pavilion, Brussels Universal and International Exhibition, 1958. Ottawa: [s.n.], 1958. [27] l. [0066]

Canada. Direction des études canadiennes
Décisions: projets subventionnées entre 1984 et 1989. Ottawa: La Direction, 1991. 152 p.; ISBN: 0-662-97228-7. [0174]

Canada. Dominion Bureau of Statistics
Publications of the 1961 census of Canada: list. Ottawa: Dominion Bureau of Statistics, [1962-1963]. 3 vol. [2965]

Canada. Dominion Bureau of Statistics. Canada Year Book, Handbook and Library Division
Historical catalogue of Dominion Bureau of Statistics publications, 1918-1960/Catalogue rétrospectif des publications du Bureau fédéral de la statistique, 1918-1960. Ottawa: Dominion Bureau of Statistics, DBS Library, 1966. xiv, 298 p. [6258]

Canada. Emplois et immigration Canada. Analyse et développement–Professions et carrières
Instruments d'orientation professionnelle. [Ottawa]: Emploi et immigration Canada, Analyse et développement–Professions et carrières, [1978]. [16, 16] p. [2841]

Canada. Employment and Immigration Commission. Occupational and Career Analysis and Development
Career guidance material. [Ottawa]: Employment and Immigration Canada, Occupational and Career Analysis and Development, [1978]. [16, 16] p. [2842]

Canada. Energie, mines et ressources Canada. Division de la gravité et de la géodynamique
Liste des publications 1948-1975 [Energie, mines et ressources Canada, Division de la gravité et de la géodynamique]. Ottawa: Energie, mines et ressources Canada, Direction de la physique du globe, Division de la gravité et de la géodynamique, 1976. 28 p. [6303]

Canada. Energy, Mines and Resources Canada. Earth Physics Branch
Index of geophysical publications, series, and contributions of the Dominion Observatory and its successor the Earth Physics Branch of the Department of Energy, Mines and Resources, Canada through December, 1974, with addenda. Ottawa: Earth Physics Branch, 1975. 92 p. [6295]

Canada. Energy, Mines and Resources Canada. Information-EMR
Index of selected publications, 1979 [Energy, Mines and Resources Canada]/Répertoire des publications choisies, 1979 [Énergie, mines et ressources Canada]. Ottawa: Energy, Mines and Resources Canada, 1980. 254 p.; ISBN: 0-662-50689-8. [6326]

Canada. Energy, Mines and Resources Canada. Mineral Policy Sector
Publications catalogue of the Mineral Policy Sector/Répertoire des publications du Secteur de la politique minérale. Ottawa: Energy, Mines and Resources Canada, 1986-. vol.; ISSN: 0832-7904. [6438]

Canada. Environment Canada
Canada Water Act publications, 1970-1990/Publications relatives à la Loi sur les ressources en eau du Canada, 1970-1990. [Ottawa]: Environment Canada, [1991]. xii, 197 p.: 1 col. map. [5286]

Canada. Environment Canada. Atmospheric Environment Service
Atmospheric Environment Service publications in hydrometeorology and marine applications/Service de l'environnement atmosphérique publications su l'hydrométéorologie et les applications. Downsview, Ont.: Atmospheric Environment Service, Environment Canada, 1977. 42 p. [6307]

Canada. Environment Canada. Canadian Parks Service. Socio-Economic Branch
Reports from Parks Service socio-economic surveys, 1960-1988/Rapports des enquêtes socio-économiques du Service canadien des parcs, 1960-1988. Ottawa: Environment Canada, Canadian Parks Service, 1988. i, 41 l. (Canadian Parks Service Reference list ; no. 2) [6388]

Canada. Environment Canada. Land Use Studies Branch. Outdoor Recreation-Open Space Division
OR-OS [Outdoor Recreation-Open Space] reference system: component 1 (bibliographic file)/Système de référence PAGE [Plein-air-grand espaces]: composante no 1 (dossier bibliographique). Ottawa: Environment Canada, Lands Directorate, 1975. 2 vol. [1769]

Canada. Environment Canada. Lands Directorate
Lands Directorate publications. Ottawa: Lands Directorate, 1977-1987. [9] vol.; ISSN: 0707-2023. [6384]

Canada. Environmental Conservation Service
Long range transportation of airborne pollutants: bibliography, 1980-1984. [Ottawa]: Environment Canada, Environmental Conservation Service, 1985. iii, 27 p.; ISBN: 0-662-13962-3. [5221]

Canada. Environmental Protection Directorate
Publications [Environmental Protection Directorate, Environment Canada]/Publications [Direction générale, protection de l'environnement, Environnement Canada]. Ottawa: The Directorate, 1986-. vol.; ISSN: 0839-8267. [6439]

Canada. Environnement Canada. Direction générale des terres
Publications: Direction générale des terres. Ottawa: Direction générale des terres, 1977-1987. [9] vol.; ISSN: 0707-2023. [6385]

Canada. Fisheries and Environment Canada
Quarterly notice of new publications [Fisheries and Environment Canada]/Bulletin trimestriel des publications [Pêches et environnement Canada]. Ottawa: Fisheries and Environment Canada, 1976-1978. 7 vol.; ISSN: 0701-7197. [6311]

Canada. Forestry Canada
Forestry Canada publications/Publications de Forêts Canada. Ottawa: Forestry Canada, 1989-. vol.; ISSN: 0846-6459. (Information report / Forestry Canada; ISSN: 0705-324X) [6440]

Canada. Geographic Board
Catalogue of the maps in the collection of the Geographic Board. Ottawa: Acland, Printer to the King, 1922. 100 p.: ill., maps. [6488]

Canada. Geological Survey
Annotated catalogue of and guide to the publications of the Geological Survey Canada, 1845-1917. Ottawa: King's Printer, 1920. 544 p.: maps. [6216]
Catalogue of publications of the Geological Survey of Canada. Ottawa: King's Printer, 1909. 181 p. [6211]
General index to reports, 1885-1906 [Geological Survey of Canada]. Ottawa: Government Printing Bureau, 1908. x, 1014 p. [6210]
General index to the [Geological Survey of Canada] Reports of progress, 1863 to 1884. Ottawa: Queen's Printer, 1900. 475 p. [6209]
Index of publications of the Geological Survey of Canada (1845-1958). Ottawa: Department of Mines and Technical

Surveys Canada, 1961. x, 378 p.: folded col. map (in pocket). [6244]

Index to reports of Geological Survey of Canada from 1927-50. Ottawa: Department of Mines and Technical Surveys Canada, 1962. viii, 723 p. [6245]

Index to reports of Geological Survey of Canada from 1951-59. Ottawa: Department of Mines and Technical Surveys Canada, 1965. xii, 379 p. [6253]

Publications (1909-1947 inclusive) of the Geological Survey and National Museum. Ottawa: Department of Mines and Resources, Mines and Geology Branch, 1948. 103 p. [6229]

Publications of the Geological Survey of Canada (1917-1952). Ottawa: Department of Mines and Technical Surveys, 1952. v, 82 p. [6231]

Canada. Health and Welfare Canada

Canadians ask about child day care: a bibliography/Les canadiens veulent se renseigner sur la garde de jour des enfants: une bibliographie. [Ottawa]: Health and Welfare Canada, [1979]. 16 p. [3185]

Publications [Health and Welfare Canada]. Ottawa: Health and Welfare Canada, 1986-. vol.; ISSN: 0837-4635. [6441]

Canada. Health and Welfare Canada. Departmental Library Services

Divorce: a bibliographical look at the world/Le divorce: bibliographie internationale. Ottawa: Health and Welfare Canada, 1977. vi, 183 p. [3153]

Women and mental health: a selective bibliography (1965-1975)/La femme et la santé mentale: une bibliographie choisie (1965-1975). Ottawa: Departmental Library Services, Health and Welfare Canada, 1976. ii, 48 p. [3762]

Canada. Health and Welfare Canada. Family Violence Prevention Division. National Clearinghouse on Family Violence

Child sexual abuse overview: a summary of 26 literature reviews and special projects. [Ottawa]: National Clearinghouse on Family Violence, Health and Welfare Canada, 1989. 30, [1], [1], 36 p.; ISBN: 0-662-56641-6. [3319]

Canada. Health Consultants Directorate

Review of the literature on home care. Ottawa: Health Consultants Directorate, 1977. viii, 93 p. [5610]

Canada. Indian and Northern Affairs Canada. Communications Service Program

Audio visual resources catalogue, Manitoba Region/Catalogue de documents audio-visuels, Région du Manitoba. Ottawa: Indian and Northern Affairs Canada, [1989]. [2], ix, 25 p. [6679]

Canada. Indian and Northern Affairs Canada. Departmental Library

List of Canadian native and northern periodicals held by the INAC Library/Liste des périodiques canadiens sur les autochtones et sur le Nord conservés à la bibliothèque du AINC. Ottawa: Indian and Northern Affairs Canada, 1989-. vol.; ISSN: 0843-6401. [5985]

List of Canadian native periodicals held by the INAC Library/Liste des périodiques canadiens sur les autochtones conservés à la bibliothèque des AINC. Ottawa: Indian and Northern Affairs Canada, 1983-1985. 2 vol.; ISSN: 0828-4342. [5953]

Canada. Indian and Northern Affairs Canada. Inuit Art Section

Inuit art bibliography/Bibliographie de l'art inuit. 2nd ed. Ottawa: The Section, 1992. 733, 69 p. [0727]

Canada. Indian Claims Commission. Research Resource Centre

Indian claims in Canada: an introductory essay and selected list of Library holdings/Revendications des Indiens au Canada: un exposé préliminaire et une sélection d'ouvrages disponibles en Bibliothèque. Ottawa: Research Resource Centre, Indian Claims Commission, [c1975]. viii, 278 p. [3964]

Canada. Information Canada

Selections: federal government and international publications for educators. Ottawa: Information Canada, 1974-1975. 2 vol. [6296]

Titres: choix de publications fédérales et internationales à l'usage des éducateurs. Ottawa: Information Canada, 1974-1975. 2 vol. [6297]

Canada. Inland Waters Directorate. Glaciology Division

Bibliography: glaciology of the St. Elias Range, Yukon Territory and Alaska. Vancouver, B.C.: Inland Waters Directorate, Pacific Region, 1977. 54 p. [5122]

Canada. Inland Waters Directorate. Water Quality Branch

Publications [Water Quality Branch]/Publications [Direction de la qualité des eaux]. Ottawa: Environment Canada, 1988. x, 49 p.; ISSN: 0710-8737. [6389]

Canada. Labour Canada

Publications catalogue [Labour Canada]. Ottawa: Labour Canada, 1989-. vol.; ISSN: 0848-3280. [6442]

Canada. Labour Canada. Library

Canadian labour papers currently received in the Labour Canada Library/Journaux syndicaux canadiens que reçoit actuellement la Bibliothèque de Travail Canada. [Ottawa]: Labour Canada, Library, 1978. 9 p. [5931]

Canadian labour papers on microfilm in the Labour Canada Library/Journaux syndicaux canadiens sur microfilm dans la bibliothèque de Travail Canada. [Ottawa]: Labour Canada, Library, 1981. 48 p. [5942]

Canada. Legislature. Legislative Assembly. Library

Catalogue of books in the Library of the Legislative Assembly of Canada. Montreal: [s.n.], 1846. 123, xxi p. [6711]

Catalogue of books relating to the history of America: forming part of the Library of the Legislative Assembly of Canada. Quebec: [s.n.], 1845. 29 p. [1873]

Canada. Legislature. Legislative Council. Library

Alphabetical catalogue of the Library of the Hon. the Legislative Council of Canada: authors and subjects. Montreal: J. Starke, 1845. 252 p. [6710]

Canada. Library of Parliament

Alphabetical catalogue of the Library of Parliament: being an index to the classified catalogues printed in 1857, 1858 and 1864, and to the books and pamphlets since added to the Library up to 1st October, 1867/Catalogue alphabétique de la Bibliothèque du Parlement: comprenant l'index des catalogues méthodiques publiés en 1857, 1858 et 1864 et celui des livres et brochures ajoutés à la Bibliothèque depuis cette dernière époque jusqu'au 1er octobre, 1867. Ottawa: G.E. Desbarats, 1867. 496 p. [6720]

Bibliography of Canadiana: a list of Canadian books and references for public libraries, universities, the film industry, and others. Ottawa: 1949. 28 l. [0059]

A bibliography relating to constitutional and economic developments since the royal commission and the Newfoundland Act of 1933. [Ottawa: The Library, 1949]. 10, [1] p. [2373]

Catalogue of the Library of Parliament: part I: law, legislation, political and social science, commerce and statistics, with index/Catalogue de la Bibliothèque du Parlement: 1re partie: droit et économie politique, suivi d'un index. Ottawa: Printed by Maclean, Roger & Co., 1860. [7], 552, 255 p. [6718]

Catalogue of the Library of Parliament/Catalogue de la Bibliothèque du Parlement. Toronto: J. Lovell, 1857-1858. 2 vol. [6714]

CPV index [microform]. [Ottawa: Micro Can, 1986]. 20 microfiches. [0153]

Index to the catalogue of the Library of Parliament: part II: general library/Index du catalogue de la Bibliothèque du parlement: IIe partie: bibliothèque générale. Ottawa: Printed by the Citizen Printing and Publishing Co., 1879. xi, [1], 683 p. [6727]

List of British and American official documents relating to the history of the fisheries controversy. Ottawa: [s.n.], 1888. 21 l. [4884]

Reference list on the subject of reciprocity in trade between Canada and the United States of America. Ottawa: Government Printing Bureau, 1910. 68 p. [2557]

Select bibliography on parliamentary procedure/ Bibliographie sélective sur la procédure parlementaire. Ottawa: The Library, 1965. 29 l. [2384]

Canada. Library of Parliament. Bibliographies and Compilations Section

Federal-provincial relations in Canada, 1970-1990/Les relations fédérales-provinciales au Canada, 1970-1990. Ottawa: Library of Parliament, 1990. 67 p. (Bibliographies / Library of Parliament Information and Technical Services Branch ; no. 195) [2534]

The handicapped, 1975-1986/Les handicapés, 1975-1986. Ottawa: Library of Parliament, Information and Reference Branch, 1986. 33 l. [3286]

The right to privacy/Le droit à la vie privée. Ottawa: Library of Parliament, Information and Technical Services Branch, 1989. 62 p. (Bibliographies / Library of Parliament, Bibliographies and Compilations Section ; no. 21) [2324]

Canada. Library of Parliament. Information and Reference Branch

Canada-U.S. automotive pact: select bibliography/Accord Canada-États-Unis sur les produits de l'industrie automobile: bibliographie sélective. Ottawa: Library of Parliament, Information and Reference Branch, 1980. 12 l. [2658]

Capital punishment/La peine de mort. Ottawa: Library of Parliament, 1986. 59 l. [2282]

Constitutional review: select bibliography/Revision constitutionnelle: bibliographie sélective. Ottawa: The Branch, 1981. 55 l. [2227]

Government secrecy and the public's right to know: select bibliography/Secrets d'État et le droit du public à l'information. Ottawa: Library of Parliament, 1978. 40 p. [2434]

Governors General of Canada, 1867-1981: a select bibliography/Les Gouverneurs généraux du Canada, 1867-1981: une bibliographie sélective. [Ottawa: Information and Reference Branch, Library of Parliament, 1982]. ii, 58 p.: ports. [2018]

Green papers, 1971-1986/Livres verts, 1971-1986. Ottawa: Library of Parliament, Information and Reference Branch, 1986. 54, [10] l. [6377]

The Office of prime minister: select bibliography/La fonction de premier ministre: bibliographie sélective. Ottawa: The Branch, 1981. 15 l. [2461]

Pierre Elliott Trudeau: select bibliography/Pierre Elliott Trudeau: bibliographie sélective. Ottawa: The Branch, 1982. 29 l. [7339]

The Senate/Le Sénat. Ottawa: Library of Parliament, 1986. 51 p. [2502]

The speakership: select bibliography/La fonction d'orateur ou de président: bibliographie sélective. Ottawa: The Branch, 1980. 31 l. [2457]

White papers, 1939-1986/Livre blancs, 1939-1986. Ottawa: Library of Parliament, Information and Reference Branch, 1986. 60, [9] l. [6378]

Women in Canadian politics and government, 1974-1980: select bibliography/Les femmes en politique au Canada, 1974-1980: bibliographie sélective. Ottawa: The Library, 1981. 49 p. [3800]

Canada. Library of Parliament. Information and Technical Services Branch

The Constitution since patriation/La Constitution depuis le rapatriement. Ottawa: The Library, 1988. 86 p. (Select bibliography / Library of Parliament ; no. 206A) [2310]

The role of the backbencher/Le role du député. Ottawa: Library of Parliament, 1988. 36 l. (Select bibliography / Library of Parliament, Information and Technical Services Branch ; no. 45) [2514]

Canada. Lieux et parcs historiques nationaux. Section des publications de recherches

Manuscrits et bulletins [Lieux et parcs historiques nationaux, Environnement Canada]. Ottawa: Environnement Canada, Parcs, 1987-. vol.; ISSN: 0840-2027. [0805]

Canada. Mines Branch

Catalogue of Mines Branch publications. Ottawa: Printer to the King, 1930. 29 p. [6219]

Canada. Ministère de la justice

Prévention du crime et traitement des délinquants: recueil de ressources sur les expériences canadiennes. Ottawa: Direction des communications et affaires publiques, Ministère de la justice du Canada, c1990. vi, 81, 74, vi p.; ISBN: 0-660-57687-X. [2332]

Canada. Ministère de l'Agriculture. Bibliothèque

Publications du Ministère de l'Agriculture du Canada, 1867-1974. [Ottawa: Information Canada], 1975. v, 136 p. [6298]

Canada. Ministère des affaires indiennes et du nord canadien

Filmographie: catalogue des films [Ministère des affaires indiennes et du nord canadien]. Ottawa: Le Ministère, 1989. 32, 72 p. [6680]

Canada. Ministère des approvisionnements et services

Titres choisis publiés par les ministères et agences du Gouvernement du Canada. Ottawa: Ministère des approvisionnements et services, 1974-1979. 10 vol.; ISSN: 0384-9767. [6322]

Canada. Ministère des travaux publics

Bibliographie annotée des caractéristiques physiques de la côte nord de l'estuaire maritime et du golfe Saint-Laurent. Ottawa: Ministère des travaux publics, 1972. 191 l. [2985]

Canada. Ministère d'État aux Affaires urbaines

Liste des publications du MEAU. [Ottawa]: Le Ministère, 1978. 27, 27 p.: ill.; ISBN: 0-662-50013-X. [6312]

Canada. Ministry of State for Urban Affairs

List of MSUA publications. [Ottawa]: The Ministry, 1978. 27, 27 p.: ill.; ISBN: 0-662-50013-X. [6313]

Canada. Multiculturalism and Citizenship Canada

Film, video, and audio productions [supported by Multiculturalism programs, 1973-1992]/Productions cinématographiques, vidéos et sonores [Programmes de Multiculturalisme, 1973-1992]. Ottawa: Multiculturalism and Citizenship Canada, c1992. vii, 83 p.; ISBN: 0-662-59315-4. [6698]

Recent publications supported by Multiculturalism and Citizenship Canada/Publications récentes subventionnées par Multiculturalisme et Citoyenneté Canada. Ottawa: Multiculturalism and Citizenship Canada, 1992. 21 p.: ill. [4289]

Resource guide, eliminating racial discrimination in Canada: the challenge and the opportunity. Ottawa: Multiculturalism and Citizenship Canada, 1990. 16, 16 p.; ISBN: 0-662-58008-7. [3336]

Canada. Multiculturalisme et citoyenneté Canada

Documents de référence, l'élimination de la discrimination raciale au Canada: le défi et la possibilité de le relever. Ottawa: Multiculturalisme et citoyenneté Canada, 1990. 16, 16 p.; ISBN: 0-662-58008-7. [3337]

Canada. National Advisory Committee on Water Resources Research

Bibliography of water resources research/Bibliographie de la recherche sur les ressources hydrauliques. [Ottawa: s.n.], 1972. 80 l. [5062]

Canada. National Archives

Publications [National Archives of Canada]. Ottawa: National Archives of Canada, 1985-. vol.; ISSN: 0844-711X. [6443]

Canada. National Capital Commission

A bibliography of history and heritage of the National Capital Region/Une bibliographie de l'histoire et du patrimoine de la région de la Capitale nationale. Rev. ed. [Ottawa]: National Capital Commission, 1978. xv, 310 l. [0126]

Canada. National Historic Parks and Sites. Research Publications Section

Manuscripts and bulletins [National Historic Parks and Sites, Environment Canada]. Ottawa: Environment Canada, Parks, 1987-. vol.; ISSN: 0840-2019. [0806]

Canada. National Museum

Publications of the National Museum of Canada, 1913-1951. Ottawa: Department of Resources and Development, National Parks Branch, 1952. vi, 127 p. [6232]

Canada. NOGAP Secretariat

NOGAP bibliography: Northern Oil and Gas Action Program. Ottawa: NOGAP Secretariat, Constitutional Development and Strategic Planning Branch, Indian and Northern Affairs Canada, 1986-1992. 4 vol.; ISSN: 0837-4988. [4880]

Canada. Ocean Science and Surveys

Pilot catalog of OSS marine data holdings. Ottawa: Department of Fisheries and Oceans, 1981. [58] l.: ill., maps. [5458]

Canada. Parks Canada

Bibliography: Manuscript report series nos. 1-430: unedited manuscripts of the Parks Canada research divisions/Bibliographie: Travaux inédits nos 1-430: manuscrits inédits des divisions de recherches de Parcs Canada. [Hull, Quebec]: Parks Canada, [1982]. 83 p. [6342]

Canada. Parks Canada. National Historic Parks and Sites Branch. Policy Co-ordination Division

Recreation policy bibliography. Ottawa: The Division, 1976. [44] l. [1781]

Canada. Parks Canada. Socio-Economic Division

Park fees reference list. Ottawa: Parks Canada, 1986. 10 l. [1837]

Tourism: background reading list of interest to Parks Canada. [Ottawa]: Socio-Economic Division, Parks Canada, 1981. 36 l. [1804]

Canada. Public Archives

Catalogue of maps, plans and charts in the map room of the Dominion Archives. Ottawa: Government Printing Bureau, 1912. xii, 685 p. (Publications of the Canadian Archives ; no. 8) [6487]

Catalogue of pamphlets, journals and reports in the Public Archives of Canada, 1611-1867. 2nd ed. Ottawa: Taché, 1916. 471 p. [6758]

Catalogue of pamphlets in the Public Archives of Canada: with index; prepared by Magdalen Casey, Librarian/Catalogue des brochures aux Archives publiques du Canada: avec index; préparé par Magdalen Casey, Bibliothécaire. Ottawa: King's Printer, 1931-1932. 2 vol. (Publications of the Public Archives of Canada ; no. 13) [6761]

List of publications of the Public Archives of Canada. Ottawa: Public Archives of Canada, 1974-1982. 8 vol.; ISSN: 0828-1505. [6343]

Canada. Public Archives. Federal Archives Division

Sources for the study of the Canadian North. Ottawa: Public Archives Canada, 1980. 21, 24 p.; ISBN: 0-662-50848-3. [0639]

Canada. Public Archives. Library

Catalogue of the Public Archives Library/Catalogue de la Bibliothèque des Archives publiques. Boston, Mass.: G.K. Hall, 1979. 12 vol.; ISBN: 0-8161-0316-X. [6784]

Canada. Public Archives. Map Division

Sixteenth-century maps relating to Canada: a checklist and bibliography. Ottawa: The Archives, 1956. 283 p.: facsims. [6504]

Canada. Public Archives. National Map Collection

Canada in maps. [Ottawa: Public Archives, 1970]. [28], [30] p. [6518]

Catalogue of the National Map Collection, Public Archives of Canada, Ottawa, Ontario/[Catalogue de la Collection nationale de cartes et plans, Archives publiques du Canada, Ottawa, Ontario]. Boston: G.K. Hall, 1976. 16 vol.; ISBN: 0-8161-1215-0. [6554]

Maps of Indian reserves and settlements in the National Map Collection/Cartes et réserves et agglomérations indiennes de la Collection nationale de cartes et plans. Ottawa: National Map Collection, Public Archives Canada, 1980-1981. 2 vol.: ill., facsims.; ISBN: 0-662-50525-5 (Vol. 1); 0-662-51523-4 (Vol. 2). [6574]

Telecommunications: the Canadian experience: an annotated list of maps/Télécommunications: l'expérience canadienne: une liste explicative des cartes. Ottawa: National Map Collection, Public Archives of Canada, 1974. 90 p.: maps. [6537]

Canada. Public Service Commission. Language Training Program Branch

English as a second language: ESL catalogue/Anglais langue seconde: catalogue ASL. [Ottawa]: Public Service

Commission of Canada, c1987. 32 p.: ill.; ISBN: 0-662-54931-7. [1470]

Canada. Public Service Commission. Staffing Programs Branch. Operations, Staffing Support and Services Division. Women's Programs Centre

Resources for a new age: a selected annotated bibliography on women and microtechnology/Ressources pour une ère nouvelle: bibliographie annotée d'ouvrages choisis concernant la femme et la microtechnologie. [Ottawa]: The Centre, 1984. 38 p. [3828]

Canada. Public Service Staff Relations Board. Library

Executive compensation: a selective bibliography/ Rémunération des cadres: une bibliographie sélective. Ottawa: Library, Public Service Staff Relations Board, 1983. 30 p. [2690]

Canada. Public Works Canada. Departmental Library

Canadian urban profiles: Saskatoon. [Ottawa]: The Library, [1974]. 13 l. (Public Works Library bibliography ; no. 11) [4330]

Kitchener, Ontario: Canadian urban information for federal land management project. [Ottawa]: The Library, [1975]. 6 l. (Public Works Library bibliography ; no. 32) [4344]

London, Ontario: Canadian urban information for federal land managment project. [Ottawa]: Public Works Library, [1975]. 10 l. (Public Works Library bibliography ; no. 62) [4345]

Mississauga. [Ottawa]: Public Works Library, [1975]. [11] l. (Public Works Library bibliography ; no. 24) [4346]

National capitals: Ottawa. [Ottawa]: The Library, [1974]. 3 parts. (Public Works Library bibliography ; no. 5) [4331]

Parking in urban Canadian centres. [Ottawa]: The Library, 1976. 6 l. (Public Works Library bibliography ; no. 74) [4357]

Selected cities of the province of Quebec: Canadian urban information for federal land management project. [Ottawa]: The Library, [1976]. 21 l. (Public Works Library bibliography ; no. 70) [4358]

Canada. Santé et Bien-être social Canada. Division de la prévention de la violence familiale. Centre national d'information sur la violence dans la famille

Aperçu général sur les agressions sexuelles contre les enfants: résumé de 26 analyses de documentation et de projets spéciaux. [Ottawa]: Centre national d'information sur la violence dans la famille, Santé et Bien-être social Canada, 1989. 36, [1], [1], 30 p.; ISBN: 0-662-56641-6. [3320]

Canada. Secrétariat d'État. Direction des droits de la personne

Publications relatives aux droits de la personne. [Hull, Québec]: La Direction, 1983. 7, 7 p. [2254]

Canada. Service de la conservation de l'environnement

Transport à grande distance des polluants atmosphériques: bibliographie 1980-1984. [Ottawa]: Environnement Canada, Service de la conservation de l'environnement, 1985. iii, 27 p.; ISBN: 0-662-93165-3. [5222]

Canada. Solicitor General Canada. Ministry Library and Reference Centre

AV catalogue [Solicitor General Canada]/Catalogue AV [Sollicteur général Canada]. [Ottawa]: Solicitor General Canada, Ministry Library and Reference Centre, [1989]. [iv], 153, 75 p. [6681]

Library catalogue of aboriginal resources/Ouvrages autochtones à la bibliothèque. Ottawa: Solicitor General Canada, Ministry Secretariat, 1991. 2, 109, 108 p.; ISBN: 0-662-58718-9. [4115]

Natives & criminal justice catalogue/Catalogue sur les autochtones et la justice pénale. [Ottawa]: Solicitor General Canada, Ministry Library and Reference Centre, 1990. 106 p. [2333]

Police: a reading list/La police: liste de lectures choisies. [Ottawa]: Solicitor General Canada, Ministry Library and Reference Centre, 1990. P. 1953-2078 [2334]

Canada. Solicitor General Canada. Ministry Secretariat

Aboriginal peoples collection/Collection sur les autochtones. [Ottawa]: Solicitor General Canada, Ministry Secretariat, [1990]. 3 l., 106, 107 p. (User report / Solicitor General Canada, Ministry Secretariat ; no. 1990-10); ISBN: 0-662-57664-0. [4112]

Women and criminal justice collection/Collection sur les femmes et la justice pénale. [Ottawa]: Solicitor General Canada, Ministry Secretariat, [1990]. 3 l., 134, 139 p. (User report / Solicitor General Canada, Ministry Secretariat ; no. 1990-11); ISBN: 0-662-57665-9. [3877]

Canada. Solicitor General Canada. Programs Branch

Bibliography of Canadian criminal justice history [microform]/Bibliographie sur l'histoire de la justice pénale au Canada [microforme]. Toronto: Micromedia, 1987. 5 microfiches. [2288]

Canada. Statistics Canada

1971 census catalogue, population, housing, agriculture, employment/Publications du recensement de 1971, population, logement, agriculture, emploi. Final ed. Ottawa: Statistics Canada, 1974. 70 p. [3000]

1991 census catalogue. Ottawa: Statistics Canada, 1993. ii, 239 p.: maps.; ISBN: 0-660-14252-X. [3071]

Products and services: reference. Ottawa: Statistics Canada, 1988. ix, 136 p.: ill., maps.; ISBN: 0-660-12252-9. [3055]

Products and services of the 1981 census of Canada. Ottawa: Statistics Canada, c1982. 147 p.: ill., maps. [3036]

Canada. Statistics Canada. Housing, Family and Social Statistics Division. Target Groups Project

Guide to Statistics Canada data on women. Ottawa: Statistics Canada, 1987. 113 p.; ISSN: 0835-6300. [3849]

Canada. Statistics Canada. Library

Listing of supplementary documents/Liste de documents supplémentaires. Ottawa: Statistics Canada, 1981-. vol.; ISSN: 0228-5134. [6444]

Canada. Statistics Canada. Library Services Division

Statistics Canada catalogue. Ottawa: Statistics Canada, 1988-. vol.; ISSN: 0838-4223. [6445]

Canada. Statistics Canada. User Services Division

Historical catalogue of Statistics Canada publications, 1918-1980. Ottawa: Statistics Canada, 1982. 337 p.; ISBN: 0-660-10964-6. [6344]

Canada. Statistique Canada

Catalogue de recensement de 1991. Ottawa: Statistique Canada, 1993. 242 p.: cartes.; ISBN: 0-660-93502-3. [3072]

Produits et services: référence. Ottawa: Statistique Canada, 1988. x, 144 p.; ISBN: 0-660-91852-8. [3056]

Produits et services du recensement du Canada de 1981. Ottawa: Statistique Canada, c1982. 153 p.: ill., cartes. [3037]

Canada. Statistique Canada. Division de l'assistance-utilisateurs

Catalogue rétrospectif des publications de Statistique Canada, 1918-1980. Ottawa: Statistique Canada, 1982. 348 p.; ISBN: 0-660-90777-1. [6345]

Canada. Statistique Canada. Division des statistiques sociales, du logement et des familles. Projet de groupes cibles
Guide des données de Statistique Canada sur les femmes. Ottawa: Statistique Canada, 1987. 115 p.; ISSN: 0835-6319. [3850]

Canada. Statistique Canada. Services de la bibliothèque
Catalogue de Statistique Canada. Ottawa: Statistique Canada, 1988-. vol.; ISSN: 0838-4231. [6446]

Canada. Tourism Canada
Bibliography of research publications [Tourism Canada]. [Ottawa]: Industry, Science and Technology Canada, [1989]. 14, 14 p.: ill. [6395]

Canada. Tourisme Canada
Répertoire des publications de recherche [Tourisme Canada]. [Ottawa]: Industrie, Sciences et Technologie Canada, [1989]. 14, 14 p.: ill. [6396]

Canada. Translation Bureau. Terminology and Linguistic Services Directorate
List of publications [Translation Bureau]. Ottawa: Department of the Secretary of State of Canada, Terminology and Linguistic Services Directorate, 1989-. vol.; ISSN: 0848-4546. [6447]

Canada. Transport Canada. Library and Information Centre
Transport Canada publications catalogue/Transports Canada catalogue des publications. Ottawa: Transport Canada, 1981-1986. 9 vol.; ISSN: 0823-5171. [6379]

Canada. Transport Canada. Surface
Transportation for the disadvantaged: a bibliography/Transport pour les handicapés: bibliographie. [Montréal]: Transport Canada, 1978. 34 p.; ISBN: 0-662-01775-7. [3167]

Canada. Transport Canada. Transportation Development Centre
Canadian travel guides for disabled persons, a bibliography. Montreal: Transport Canada. Transportation Development Centre, 1983. [3] p. [3246]
Ships navigating in ice: a selected bibliography. [Montreal]: Transport Canada, [1982]. x, 129 p. [4487]
TDC publications, 1971-1982/Publications du CDT, 1971-1982. Montreal: The Centre, 1982. 70 p. [4488]

Canada. Travail Canada
Catalogue des publications [Travail Canada]. Ottawa: Travail Canada, 1989-. vol.; ISSN: 0848-3280. [6448]

Canada. Treasury Board
List of publications [Treasury Board of Canada]. [Ottawa]: Communications Division, Treasury Board of Canada, 1979-. vol.; ISSN: 0837-6476. [6449]

Canada. Unemployment Insurance Commission. Library
A selective bibliography on unemployment insurance in Canada, Great Britain and the United States, 1960-1971/Bibliographie sélective de l'assurance-chômage au Canada, en Grande-Bretagne et aux États-Unis, 1960-1971. Ottawa: Unemployment Insurance Canada, 1972. 23 l. [2807]

Canada. Wartime Information Board
List of Dominion government publications. Ottawa: The Board, 1944-1945. 6 nos. [6226]

Canada. Water Pollution Control Directorate
Water Pollution Control Directorate publications/Les publications de la Direction générale de la lutte contre la pollution des eaux. Hull, Quebec: The Directorate, 1975-1982. 7 vol.; ISSN: 0703-6094. [6346]

Canada. Women's Bureau
List of publications [Canada. Women's Bureau]. Ottawa: Labour Canada, Women's Bureau, 1991. [1] p. [3888]

Canadian Advertising Limited
French newspapers and periodicals of Canada and the United States. Montreal: [s.n., 1913]. 92, [1] p.: (incl. advertisements). [5859]

Canadian Association for Adult Education
Discussion materials on Canadian unity. Ottawa: [1964]. [8] l. [2380]
Non-degree research in adult education in Canada, 1968: an inventory/La recherche en éducation des adultes au Canada, 1968: un inventaire. Toronto: Jointly published by Canadian Association for Adult Education; Ontario Institute for Studies in Education; Montréal: Institut canadien d'éducation des adultes, 1969. 103 p. [3399]
A selective bibliography of Canadian plays. Toronto: Commission for Continuous Learning, Canadian Association for Adult Education, 1957. 15 l. [1016]

Canadian Association for Adult Education. Research Library
The literature of adult education: a selected list of holdings from the the Research Library in Adult Education of the Canadian Association for Adult Education. [Toronto: Canadian Association for Adult Education, 1961]. xiv, 75 l. [3381]

Canadian Association for the Prevention of Crime
Publications [Canadian Association for the Prevention of Crime]. Ottawa: Canadian Association for the Prevention of Crime, 1977. 13, 13 p.: ill. [2166]

Canadian Association in Support of the Native Peoples
Books by native authors. Toronto: Canadian Association in Support of the Native Peoples, [1977]. 2, 7 l. [3986]
Publications list no. 18 [Canadian Association in Support of the Native Peoples]. Toronto: The Association, 1972. [16] p. [3932]

Canadian Association of Children's Librarians
Bibliography of disabled children. [Ottawa]: Canadian Library Association, 1981. 50 p. [3213]
Canadian films for children and young adults. Ottawa: Canadian Library Association, c1987. 33 p.; ISBN: 0-88802-219-0. [6668]

Canadian Bankers' Association
A bibliography of Canadian banking/Une bibliographie sur la banque au Canada. [Toronto: s.n., 1971]. 36 p. [2589]

"Canadian bibliography of geodesy." In: Canadian Geophysical Bulletin; Vol. 4, no. 4 (Part 2) (October-December 1950) p. 1-10.; ISSN: 0068-8819. [4745]

The Canadian book at the Frankfurt Book Fair, 1963. Ottawa: Queen's Printer, 1963. 41 p. [0072]

The Canadian book at the Frankfurt Book Fair in West Germany, 1965. Ottawa: Queen's Printer, 1965. 54 p. [0077]

Canadian Book Information Centre
Read: a selected list of Canadian books. Toronto: The Centre, [1979]. 24 l. [0129]

Canadian booklist. Toronto: Published by Quill & Quire in cooperation with the National Library, 1961-1964. 18 no.; ISSN: 0576-4696. [0075]

Canadian books in print. Author and title index. Toronto: University of Toronto Press, 1975-. vol.; ISSN: 0068-8398. [0181]

Canadian books in print. Subject index. Toronto: University of Toronto Press, 1975-. vol.; ISSN: 0315-1999. [0182]

Canadian books in print/Catalogue des livres canadiens en librairie. Toronto: University of Toronto Press, 1967-1974. 8 vol.; ISSN: 0702-0201. [0110]

Canadian Broadcasting Corporation
C B C publications catalogue. Toronto: Canadian Broadcasting Corporation, 1969-1974. 4 vol.: ill. [6288]

Canadian Broadcasting Corporation. Research Department. Library
CBC Research Library: a classified list of books held, October 1966. Ottawa: [s.n.], 1966. v, 122 p. [6773]

The Canadian catalogue of books published in Canada, about Canada, as well as those written by Canadians, with imprint 1921-1949 (consolidated English language reprint edition) with cumulated author index. [Toronto]: Toronto Public Libraries, 1967. 1 vol. (in various pagings). [0084]

Canadian Centre for Films on Art
Catalogue: films on art. Ottawa: Canadian Centre for Films on Art, 1965-1973. 10 vol. [6618]
Films on art: a source book. New York: Watson-Guptill Publications; Ottawa: Canadian Film Institute, 1977. 220 p.; ISBN: 0-8230-1780-X. [6630]

Canadian Centre for Information and Documentation on Archives
Archival science bibliography, 1986-1988/Bibliographie en archivistique, 1986-1988. Ottawa: The Centre, c1991. xii, 164 p.; ISBN: 0-662-58342-6. [1723]
Directory of newsletters relating to archival administration and records management, published in Canada/Annuaire de bulletins de nouvelles, concernant l'administration des archives et la gestion des documents, publiés au Canada. Ottawa: Canadian Centre for Information and Documentation on Archives, 1992. 8 l. [5980]

Canadian Centre for Occupational Health and Safety
A review of the literature on attitudes and roles and their effects on safety in the workplace. [S.l.]: Canadian Centre for Occupational Health and Safety, 1980. 54 p.; ISBN: 0-660-11374-0. [2862]

Canadian Children's Book Centre
Our choice: your annual guide to Canada's best children's books. Toronto: Canadian Children's Book Centre, 1985-1992. 8 vol.: ill.; ISSN: 1192-2125. [1394]

Canadian Church Historical Society
Bibliography of printed books relating to the history of the Anglican Church of Canada. [Toronto: s.n., 1963]. 11 l. [1515]

Canadian Coast Guard College. Library
Audio-visual catalogue [Canadian Coast Guard College Library]/Catalogue de matériel audio-visuel [Garde côtière canadienne, Bibliothèque du collège]. [Sydney, N.S.]: The Library, [1985]-.   vol.; ISSN: 0837-2500. [6702]

Canadian Coast Guard. Search and Rescue Branch
Directory of safe boating information. Ottawa: Canadian Coast Guard, c1991. 50, [15] p.; ISBN: 0-662-18627-3. [1863]

Canadian Conference of the Arts
Municipalities and the arts: inventory of municipal cultural material in the resource centre of the Canadian Conference of the Arts/Les municipalités et les arts: répertoire de la documentation sur les municipalités et la culture disponible au centre de ressources de la Conférence canadienne des arts. Ottawa: Canadian Conference of the Arts, 1989. 27 p. [0719]

Canadian Congress for Learning Opportunities for Women. Literacy Materials for Women Working Group
Telling our stories our way: a guide to good Canadian materials for women learning to read. Toronto: Canadian Congress for Learning Opportunities for Women, c1990. 101 p.: ill.; ISBN: 0-921283-08-3. [3878]

Canadian Construction Association. Manufacturers and Suppliers Council. Market Data Committee
Guide to construction industry market data. Ottawa: Canadian Construction Association, 1969. 105 p. [2585]

Canadian Council of Ministers of the Environment. Research Advisory Committee
National inventory of environmental research and development projects/Inventaire national des projets de recherche et développement sur l'environnement. Ottawa: The Council, 1990. xii, 488 p. (Report / Canadian Council of Ministers of the Environment ; CCME-R-TRE-022); ISBN: 0-662-57656-X. [5274]

Canadian Council of Resource Ministers
Pollution: bibliography/Pollution: bibliographie. [Montreal: s.n., 1968]. 74, 52 p. [5040]

Canadian Council on International Law
Canadian bibliography on international law, 1967-1977/ Bibliographie canadienne en droit international, 1967-1977. [Ottawa: Canadian Council on International Law, 1978]. iv, 53 p. [2180]

Canadian Council on Social Development
Project information exchange: an inventory of studies, briefs and social action projects/Échange-renseignements: relevé d'études, de mémoires et de réalisations en action sociale. Ottawa: Canadian Council on Social Development; United Way of Canada, 1970-1980. 9 vol.; ISSN: 0704-6693. [3199]

Canadian Council on Urban and Regional Research
Urban & regional references; [références] urbaines & régionales, 1945-1969. Ottawa: [The Council, 1970]. xi, 796 p.; ISBN: 0-919076-06-8. [4313]

Canadian Criminology and Corrections Association
Correctional literature published in Canada/Ouvrages de criminologie publiés au Canada. Ottawa: Canadian Criminology and Corrections Association, 1968-1974. 6 vol.; ISSN: 0070-0509. [2137]

Canadian Cultural Information Centre
Canadian cultural publications/Publications culturelles canadiennes. Ottawa: Canadian Cultural Information Centre, 1951-1965. 13 vol.; ISSN: 0576-5110. [5875]

Canadian directory of agriculture and food markets information and services. Ottawa: Agriculture Canada, Market Information Service, 1984. [144] p. [4702]

Canadian Education Association
Graduate theses in education, 1913-1952: partial list. Toronto: Canadian Education Association, 1952. 33, [1] p. [6060]
Registry of Canadian theses in education. Toronto: Canadian Education Association, 1959-1961. 15 nos. [6073]

Canadian Education Association. Research and Information Division
Education studies completed in Canadian universities. Toronto: Canadian Education Association, 1967-1968. 2 vol.; ISSN: 0424-5652. [3397]

Canadian environmental directory. Toronto: Canadian Almanac & Directory Pub. Co., 1991-.   vol.; ISSN: 1187-1202. [5300]

Canadian Federation of Mayors and Municipalities
Municipal reference library catalogue/Catalogue de la bibliothèque de la Fédération [des maires et des municipalités]. Montreal: Canadian Federation of Mayors and Municipalities, 1956-1965. 1 vol. (loose-leaf). [4306]

Canadian Federation of Music Teachers' Associations
A list of Canadian music. Toronto: Oxford University Press, 1946. 23 p. [0810]

Canadian Film Institute
Multiculturalism film and video catalogue/Répertoire des films et vidéos sur le multiculturalisme. Ottawa: The Institute, 1982. 89 p.; ISBN: 0-919096-12-3. [6650]
Multiculturalism multimedia catalogue, 1984/Répertoire des multimedia sur le multiculturalisme, 1984. Ottawa: Canadian Film Institute, 1984. 64 p.; ISBN: 0-919096-25-5. [6657]

Canadian Folk Music Society
A reference list on Canadian folk music. Rev. and updated ed. Calgary: Canadian Folk Music Society; Toronto: Canadian Music Centre, 1978. 16 p. [0863]

Canadian Geoscience Council
Current research in the geological sciences in Canada/Travaux en cours dans le domaine des sciences géologiques au Canada. Ottawa: Energy, Mines and Resources Canada, 1951-. vol.; ISSN: 0526-4553. [4881]

Canadian Good Roads Association
Road reference library: a catalogue of publications on roads and road transport. Ottawa: The Association, 1956. iv, 149 p. [4448]

Canadian Government Office of Tourism. Tourism Reference and Data Centre
Book catalogue of tourism research studies/Catalogue de livres des études de recherches de tourisme. Ottawa: Canadian Government Office of Tourism, 1980-1983. 5 vol.; ISSN: 0712-3469. [1822]

Canadian government publications: catalogue/Publications du gouvernement canadien: catalogue. Ottawa: Information Canada, 1953-1978. 26 vol.; ISSN: 0318-675X. [6314]

Canadian government publications: monthly catalogue/Publications du gouvernement canadien: catalogue mensuel. Ottawa: Supply and Services Canada, 1953-1978. 26 vol.; ISSN: 0008-3690. [6315]

Canadian Government Publishing Centre
Consolidated list of serials of the Government of Canada: (includes the serials that appear on the Weekly checklist). Hull, Quebec: Canadian Government Publishing Centre, 1988. 43 l. [6390]

Canadian graduate theses in the humanities and social sciences, 1921-1946/Thèses des gradués canadiens dans les humanités et les sciences sociales, 1921-1946. [Ottawa: King's Printer, 1951]. 194 p. [6059]

Canadian Historical Association
Register of post-graduate dissertations in progress in history and related subjects/Répertoire des thèses en cours portant sur des sujets d'histoire et autres sujets connexes. [Ottawa]: Canadian Historical Association, [1966]-. vol.; ISSN: 0068-8088. [6206]

Canadian Historical Association. Archives Section
Bibliography on copyright. [S.l.: s.n.], 1974. 15 p. [2138]

Canadian Hospital Association. Library
The health administrator's library: comprehensive bibliography of the materials available in the Canadian Hospital Association Library. Ottawa: Canadian Hospital Association, c1978. 144 p.; ISBN: 0-919100-15-5. [5613]

Canadian Housing Information Centre
Bibliography of External Research Program reports/Bibliographies des rapports du Programme de recherche à l'extérieur. Ottawa: The Centre, 1986. 20 p. [4408]
Bibliography on building in cold climates/Bibliographie sur la construction dans les pays froids. Ottawa: Canada Mortgage and Housing Corporation, 1985. 7 p. [5803]
Bibliography on housing for single-parent families/Bibliographie sur le logement et les familles monparentales. Ottawa: Canadian Housing Information Centre, Canada Mortgage and Housing Corporation, 1986. 6 p. [4409]
Bibliography on housing in Canadian municipalities/Bibliographie sur l'habitation dans les municipalités canadiennes. Ottawa: The Centre, 1985. 44 p. [4404]
Bibliography on indoor air pollution/Bibliographie sur la pollution de l'air des habitations. Ottawa: Canada Mortgage and Housing Corporation, 1990. 29 p. [5275]
Bibliography on native housing. Ottawa: The Centre, 1985. 11 p. [4071]
Bibliography on non-profit housing/Logement sans but lucratif: une bibliographie. Ottawa: The Centre, 1989. 19 p. [4426]
Bibliography on public housing in Canada/Bibliographie sur les habitations à loyer modéré au Canada. Ottawa: The Centre, 1984. 15 p. [4401]
Bibliography on public housing in Canada/Bibliographie sur les habitations à loyer modéré au Canada. Ottawa: Canada Mortgage and Housing Corporation, 1987. 40 p. [4416]
Bibliography on real estate in Canada/Bibliographie sur la propriété immobilière au Canada. Ottawa: The Centre, 1983. 13 p. [2691]
Bibliography on temporary shelter for battered women/Bibliographie sur l'hébergement temporaire pour les femmes victimes de violence. Ottawa: Canada Mortgage and Housing Corporation, 1991. 11 p. [3349]
Bibliography on the construction industry in Canada/Bibliographie sur l'industrie de la construction au Canada. Ottawa: The Centre, 1985. 16 p. [2708]
Bibliography on zoning in Canada/Bibliographie sur le zonage au Canada. Ottawa: The Centre, 1983. 5 p. [4398]
Housing and the elderly: a bibliography/Le logement et les personnes âgées: une bibliographie. Ottawa: The Centre, [1988]. 78 p. [3306]
Housing in New Brunswick: a bibliography. Ottawa: The Centre, [1986]. 5 p. [4410]
Residential energy conservation: a selected bibliography of Canadian sources. Ottawa: Canada Mortgage and Housing Corporation, 1983. 19 l. [5789]
A selected bibliography on architecture in Canada/Une bibliographie sélective sur l'architecture au Canada. Ottawa: The Centre, 1983. 18 p. [0771]
A selected bibliography on housing and services for the disabled/Choix d'ouvrages sur le logement et les services pour les handicapés. Ottawa: Canada Mortgage and Housing Corporation, 1981. 28 p.; ISBN: 0-662-51450-5. [3214]

Canadian Human Rights Commission
An annotated bibliography: analysis of television content. Ottawa: Canadian Human Rights Commission, 1976. 8, [55] l. [0959]

Bibliography on human rights/Bibliographie sur les droits de la personne. [Ottawa]: The Commission, 1980. iv, 262 p.; ISBN: 0-662-50837-8. [2211]

Publications of the Canadian Human Rights Commission. [Ottawa]: Canadian Human Rights Commission, 1982-. vol. [2363]

Canadian Institute for Historical Microreproductions

Canada, the printed record [microform]: a bibliographic register with indexes to the microfilm series of the Canadian Institute for Historical Microreproductions/Catalogue d'imprimés canadiens [microforme]: répertoire bibliographique avec index de la collection de microfiches de l'Institut canadien de microreproductions historique. Ottawa: The Institute, 1990. 2 vol. (loose-leaf: [40] p. + 285 microfiches); ISBN: 0-665-99966-6. [0167]

Catalogue of periodicals in CIHM's microfiche collection (as of June 1993)/Catalogue des périodiques dans la collection de microfiches de l'ICMH (à partir de juin 1993). Ottawa: The Institute, 1993. 77 p.; ISSN: 1194-9236. [5982]

Native studies collection: catalogue/La collection des études autochtones: catalogue. Ottawa: CIHM, 1993. xii, 222 p.; ISBN: 0-665-91353-2. [4120]

Pre-1900 Canadian directories: catalogue/La Collection de répertoires d'avant 1900: catalogue. Ottawa: CIHM, 1993. xi, 75 p.; ISBN: 0-665-91354-0. [5983]

Preliminary checklist of pre-1901 Canadian serials [microform]. Ottawa: Canadian Institute for Historical Microreproductions, 1986. xiii, 267 p.: (10 microfiches; 515 fr.); ISBN: 0-665-00000-6. [5959]

Canadian Institute for International Peace and Security

Peace and security bookshelf. [Ottawa]: The Institute, 1990-. vol.; ISSN: 1189-3680. [2555]

Canadian Institute of Child Health

Prenatal information in Canada: resources available on a national basis, 1981: major findings and recommendations. Ottawa: The Institute, 1981. xiv, 80 p. [5634]

Canadian Institute of International Affairs. Toronto. Men's Branch. Defence Study Group

Problems of national defence: a study guide and bibliography. Toronto: Canadian Institute of International Affairs, 1962. [1], 12, 14 l. [2379]

Canadian Institute. Library

Catalogue of the library of the Canadian Institute. Toronto: J. Lovell, 1858. 23 p. [6715]

Canadian Intergovernmental Conference Secretariat

Federal-provincial conferences on the Constitution, September 1978 – March 1987: list of public documents. [Ottawa]: The Secretariat, [1987]. 55, 2, 60, 2 p. [2289]

Canadian International Development Agency

Publications catalogue of the Canadian International Development Agency. Hull, Quebec: Public Affairs Branch, Canadian International Development Agency, c1989. 24, 24 p.: ill.; ISBN: 0-662-56873-7. [6398]

Canadian Labour Congress

Alphabetical list of Canadian Labour Congress briefs. [Ottawa: The Congress], 1985. 40 p. [2896]

Canadian Labour Congress. Educational Services

CLC Educational Services catalogue. [Ottawa]: The Congress, 1986. xi, 202 p. (loose-leaf). [2901]

Canadian Law Information Council

CLIC's legal materials letter. Bulletin d'information juridique. Ottawa: Canadian Law Information Council, 1977-1989. 12 vol.; ISSN: 0704-0393. [2325]

Canadian League of Composers

Catalogue of orchestral music (including works for small orchestra and band, concertos, vocal-orchestral and choral-orchestral works) composed by members of the Canadian League of Composers. Toronto: Canadian League of Composers, 1957. 58 p. [0815]

Canadian Learning Materials Centre

Atlantic book choice: recommended Canadian and regional titles for an elementary school library collection. [Halifax]: Canadian Learning Materials Centre, [1983]. 2 vol. [0253]

Canadian library–information science research projects, a list/Projets de recherche canadiens en bibliothéconomie et sciences de l'information, une liste. Ottawa: Library Documentation Centre, National Library of Canada, 1981-. vol.; ISSN: 0826-1903. [1738]

Canadian Library Association

[Exhibition of Canadian books. Catalogue]. [Ottawa: 1965]. i, 37 p. [0078]

Publications catalogue [Canadian Library Association]. Ottawa: Canadian Library Association, 1969-. vol.; ISSN: 0381-5862. [1739]

Canadian Library Association. Microfilm Committee

Canadian newspapers on microfilm catalogue/Catalogue de journaux canadiens sur microfilm. Ottawa: Canadian Library Association, 1959-1977. 1 vol. (loose-leaf). [6025]

Canadian Library Association. Reference Section

40 years of Kirkconnell: titles and selected articles. [Ottawa: s.n., 1962]. iii, 13 l. [7090]

Canadian Library Association. Young People's Section

Canadian books: a selection of books for young people's libraries. Ottawa: Canadian Library Association, 1960-1971. 16 vol.; ISSN: 0068-838X. [1319]

Canadian maps and atlases, 1984-1987: an exhibition of the National Archives of Canada/Cartes et atlas canadiens, 1984-1987: une exposition des Archives nationales du Canada. [Ottawa]: National Archives of Canada, c1987. [96] l. [6589]

Canadian maps and atlases, 1987-1990: an exhibition of the National Archives of Canada/Cartes et atlas canadiens, 1987-1990: une exposition des Archives nationales du Canada. [Ottawa]: National Archives of Canada, c1991. [90] p. [6596]

Canadian Masonic Research Association

List of papers read before the Association, May 9, 1949-Dec. 31, 1962. [Halifax, N.S.: s.n., 1963]. [7] p. [1516]

"Canadian materials on the arts." In: *Ontario Library Review;* Vol. 60, no. 4 (December 1976) p. 226-235.; ISSN: 0030-2996. [0683]

Canadian Mobile Home Association

Mobile home library index. Toronto: Canadian Mobile Home Association, [1975]. [70] p. (in various pagings). [4347]

Canadian Museums Association

Bibliography: an extensive listing of published material on the subjects of museology, museography and museum and art gallery administration/Bibliographie: un inventaire considérable de publications portant sur la muséologie, la muséographie et l'administration de musées et de galeries d'art. Ottawa: The Association, 1976. [235] p. (in various pagings: loose-leaf). [4565]

Canadian Music Centre

Almanac/Almanach. Toronto: The Centre, c1984. iii, 94 p.; ISSN: 0827-7575. [0914]

Canadian chamber music/Musique de chambre canadienne.

Toronto: The Centre, 1980. c. 900 p.; ISBN: 0-9690836-4-5. [0880]

Canadian compositions for band/Oeuvres canadiennes pour fanfare et harmonie. Toronto: The Centre, 1977. 5 l. [0859]

Canadian music for accordion/Musique canadienne pour accordéon. Toronto: The Centre, 1982. 14 p. [0901]

Canadian music for bassoon/Musique canadienne pour basson. Toronto: The Centre, 1982. 27 p. [0902]

Canadian music for clarinet/Musique canadienne pour clarinette. Toronto: The Centre, 1981. 45 p. [0891]

Canadian music for guitar/Musique canadienne pour guitare. Toronto: The Centre, 1980. 18 p. [0881]

Canadian music for saxophone/Musique canadienne pour saxophone. Toronto: The Centre, 1981. 20 p. [0892]

Canadian music for viola/Musique canadienne pour alto. Toronto: The Centre, 1981. 38 p. [0893]

Canadian vocal music: available on loan from the libraries of the Canadian Music Centre/Musique vocale canadienne: disponible aux musicothèques du Centre de musique canadienne. 3rd ed. Toronto: The Centre, 1976. 108 l. [0852]

Catalogue of Canadian choral music/Catalogue de musique chorale canadienne. Toronto: The Centre, 1978. [400] p.; ISBN: 0-9690836-2-9. [0864]

Catalogue of Canadian keyboard music available on loan from the library of the Canadian Music Centre/Catalogue de musique canadienne à clavier disponible à titre de prêt à la bibliothèque du Centre musical canadien. Toronto: The Centre, c1971. 91 p. [0828]

Catalogue of Canadian music for orchestra, including concertos and works with choir and/or solo voice(s) in the libraries of the Canadian Music Centre/Catalogue de musique canadienne pour orchestre, comprenant également les concertos ainsi que les oeuvres avec choeur ou soliste(s) disponible dans les bibliothèques du Centre de musique canadienne. Toronto: The Centre, 1976. ca. 500 p. [0853]

List of Canadian music inspired by the music, poetry, art and folklore of native peoples. Toronto: The Centre, 1980. 22 l. [0882]

List of Canadian operas (including operettas & stage works): December 1982, available from Canadian Music Centre/Liste des opéras canadiens (incluant opérettes et musique de scène): décembre 1982, disponible au Centre de musique canadienne. Toronto: The Centre, 1982. 20 p. [0903]

New works accepted into the library of the Canadian Music Centre from January 1, 1982 to December 31, 1982/Nouvelles oeuvres acceptées à la musicothèque du Centre de musique canadienne du 1er janvier, 1982 à 31 décembre, 1982. Toronto: The Centre, [1983]. 27 p.; ISSN: 0822-8264. [0909]

Some reference sources for information on Canadian composers/Ouvrages de références sur les compositeurs canadiens. Toronto: The Centre, 1975. 13 l. [0842]

Canadian Music Centre. Library

Acquisitions: Canadian Music Centre Library/Bibliothèque du Centre de musique canadienne. Toronto: The Centre, 1985-. vol.; ISSN: 0827-7567. [0944]

Canadian Music Library Association

Musical Canadiana: a subject index. Ottawa: Canadian Library Association, 1967. v, 62 p. [0820]

Standards for music collections in medium-sized libraries. Ottawa: Canadian Library Association, 1959. ii, 42 l. [0817]

Canadian Music Research Council

Survey of research in music and music education in Canada. [Victoria, B.C.: n.n.], 1977. 15 p. [0860]

Canadian National Railways. Headquarters Library

A selected bibliography on Canadian railways/Sélection de publications sur les chemins de fer canadiens. 8th ed. Montreal: [CN Library, Headquarters and St. Lawrence Region], 1980. 20 l. (Special series / CN Library, Headquarters and St. Lawrence Region ; no. 25) [4477]

Canadian Network on the Informal Economy

A bibliography on material pertinent to the informal economy/Bibliographie des sources de documentation sur l'économie informelle. Ottawa: Vanier Institute of the Family, 1982. 54, 2 p. [2678]

Canadian Numismatic Association

Library catalogue [Canadian Numismatic Association]. Stayner, Ont.: Canadian Numismatic Association, 1976. 70 p. [1782]

Canadian numismatic bibliography. Montreal: 1886. 16 p. [1742]

Canadian Nurses' Association

Abortion: selected references/L'avortement: bibliographie choisie. [Ottawa]: Canadian Nurses' Association, 1975. 23 l. [5596]

Accidents and accident prevention: selected bibliography/Accidents et prévention des accidents: bibliographie choisie. [Ottawa]: Canadian Nurses' Association, 1974. 15 l. [3123]

Community health services with emphasis on the nurses' role, including mental health aspect: selected references/Services communautaires de santé avec insistence [sic] particulière sur le rôle de l'infirmière, à l'inclusion de l'aspect de la santé mentale: bibliographie sélective. Ottawa: Canadian Nurses' Association, 1978. 43 p. [5614]

Continuing education: selected bibliography/L'éducation permanente: bibliographie choisie. [Ottawa]: Canadian Nurses' Association, 1972. 25 l. [3428]

Development of basic nursing education programs in Canada: selected references/Expansion des programmes d'enseignement infirmier de base au Canada: références choisies. Ottawa: Canadian Nurses' Association, 1976. 10 l. [5604]

Health and health education: selected references/Santé et éducation sanitaire: bibliographie choisie. [Ottawa]: Canadian Nurses' Association, 1976. 29 l. [5605]

Health and well being of nurses with emphasis on health hazards in the nurses' work environment/Santé et bien-être des infirmières plus particulièrement sur risques en milieu infirmier. [Ottawa]: Canadian Nurses' Association, 1976. 22 l. [5606]

History of nursing in Canada: selected references/Histoire de la profession infirmière au Canada: bibliographie sélective. Ottawa: Canadian Nurses' Association, 1972. 9 l. [5578]

Libraries: resources and facilities: selected references/Bibliothèques: ressources et facilités: bibliographie choisie. [Ottawa]: Canadian Nurses' Association, 1974. 29 l. [1603]

Midwifery: selected references/Obstétrique: bibliographie sélective. Ottawa: Canadian Nurses' Association, 1979. 21 p. [5621]

Nursing manpower: selected references/Main d'oeuvre infirmière: références choisies. [Ottawa]: Canadian Nurses' Association, 1977. 28 l. [5611]

Occupational health nursing: selected references/
L'infirmière d'entreprise: soins en médecine du travail:
bibliographie choisie. Ottawa: Canadian Nurses' Association, 1978. 27 p. [5615]

Public relations: selected bibliography/Relations publiques:
bibliographie choisie. [Ottawa]: Canadian Nurses' Association, 1975. 16 l. [5597]

Rehabilitation and the nurse: selected references/
L'infirmière et la réadaptation: bibliographie choisie.
[Ottawa]: Canadian Nurses' Association, 1978. 24 p. [5616]

Selected references on Canadian Nurses' Association/
Bibliographie sélective on[sic] Association des infirmières
et infirmiers du Canada. Ottawa: Canadian Nurses'
Association, 1978. 4 p. [5617]

Social and economic welfare: selected references/Le bien-
être social et économique: bibliographie sélective. Ottawa:
Canadian Nurses' Association, 1972. 45 p. [3104]

Canadian Nurses' Association. Library

Compilation of provincial nurses' acts and related legisla-
tion/Compilation des lois régissant les infirmières et de la
législation qui s'y rapporte. [Ottawa]: Canadian Nurses'
Association, 1977. 18 l. (in various foliations). [2167]

Family planning: selected references/Planification familiale:
bibliographie choisie. Ottawa: Canadian Nurses' Association, 1975. 35 l. [3134]

Geriatrics: selected references/La gériatrie: bibliographie
choisie. Ottawa: Canadian Nurses' Association, 1975.
48 p. [5598]

Higher education with emphasis on nursing programs:
selected references/Enseignement supérieur, principalement programmes d'enseignement infirmier:
bibliographie choisie. Ottawa: Canadian Nurses' Association, 1974. 43 l. [3479]

Nursing and northern health services: selected bibliography/
Soins infirmiers et services de santé, région du nord
canadien: bibliographie choisie. Ottawa: Canadian Nurses'
Association, 1973. 5 l. [5586]

School health: selected references/L'infirmière en santé
scolaire: bibliographie choisie. Ottawa: Canadian Nurses'
Association, 1975. 15 l. [5599]

Canadian Olympic Association. Library

Library bibliography [Canadian Olympic Association]/
Bibliographie de la bibliothèque [Association olympique
canadienne]. Montreal: Canadian Olympic Association,
1982. ii, 45, 1 l. [1808]

"Canadian ornithological bibliography." In: *Transactions of the
Canadian Institute*; Vol. 1 (1889-1890) p. 60-64.; ISSN: 0384-
823X. [5307]

Canadian Pacific Railway Company

Catalogue of Canadian books provided for the tour of the
Duke and Duchess of Cornwall and York. Montreal: [s.n.],
1901. 3 p. [0029]

Canadian Paraplegic Association

A core collection of materials on the disabled, suitable for
public libraries: to observe the International year of
disabled persons. Toronto: The Association, 1981. 30,
viii p. [3215]

Canadian Permanent Committee on Geographical Names

Native Canadian geographical names: an annotated
bibliography/La toponymie autochtone du Canada: une
bibliographie annotée. Ottawa: The Committee, 1993. v,
158 p.; ISBN: 0-660-58890-0. [3073]

Canadian Petroleum Association

Bibliography: Canadian Petroleum Association publications.
Calgary: Canadian Petroleum Association, 1988. xi,
37 p. [4867]

Canadian philatelic literature. Cobden, Ont.: A.L. McCready,
1951. 39 l. ill. [1745]

**Canadian plays for community theatres: a selected annotated
bibliography.** Rev. 2nd ed. [Edmonton]: Alberta Culture and
Multiculturalism, [1989]. 27 p. [1269]

**Canadian plays for young audiences: pre-school through
grade 13.** Toronto: Playwrights Union of Canada, [1984].
[26] p. [1360]

Canadian Police College. Law Enforcement Reference Centre

Audio visual catalogue: Law Enforcement Reference Centre,
Canadian Police College/Catalogue audio-visuel: Centre
de documentation policière, Collège canadien de police.
Ottawa: The Centre, 1989. 2, ii, 220 p. [6682]

Canadian printed books, 1752-1961: an exhibition. London:
Times Bookshop, 1961. 27 p. [0068]

**Canadian publications, books-periodicals, out of print, 1967-
1972/Publications canadiennes, livres-périodiques,
épuisées, 1967-1972.** Vancouver: Versatile Publishing, 1973.
xxxiv, 651, 185 p. [0107]

Canadian Pulp and Paper Association. Sulphite Committee

Bibliography of multistage sulphite pulping of various wood
species. Montreal: Technical section, Canadian Pulp and
Paper Association, 1971. 52 p. [5735]

**Canadian Radio-Television and Telecommunications
Commission**

A bibliography of basic books on Canadian broadcasting/
Bibliographie de références sur la radiodiffusion
canadienne. Ottawa: Canadian Radio-Television and
Telecommunications Commission, Library, 1977.
9 p. [0963]

Bibliography of CRTC studies. [Ottawa]: Canadian Radio-
Television and Telecommunications Commission, 1982. vi,
75, 77 p.; ISBN: 0-662-52054-8. [0973]

Canadian Radio-Television Commission

Bibliography: some Canadian writings on the mass media/
Bibliographie: études canadiennes sur les mass media.
Ottawa: Canadian Radio-Television Commission, c1974.
99 p. [0954]

A Canadian reading list. Toronto: National Committee for
Friendly Relations with Overseas Students, [1960].
12 p. [0067]

Canadian record catalogue/Catalogue de disques canadiens.
Toronto: Canadian Independent Record Production Association, 1982-1984. 2 vol. (loose-leaf); ISSN: 0714-8070. [0915]

Canadian record guide. Toronto: ECC Publications, 1958. 2
no.; ISSN: 0821-2163. [0816]

Canadian Recording Industry Association

Cancon releases. Toronto: Canadian Recording Industry
Association, 1975-1980. 6 vol.; ISSN: 0706-8255. [0883]

Canadian Rehabilitation Council for the Disabled

Compendium of information resources on physical disability. Toronto: Canadian Rehabilitation Council for the
Disabled, 1983. 1 vol. (in various pagings).; ISBN: 0-86500-
013-1. [3247]

Canadian Research Institute for the Advancement of Women

Canadian women's studies: feminist research. Ottawa:
Canadian Studies Directorate, 1993. 46, 50 p. (Canadian
studies resource guides. Second series); ISBN: 0-662-60010-
4. [3902]

Women and work: an inventory of research/La femme et le travail: un inventaire de recherches. Ottawa: The Institute, c1978. xvi, 85 p. [3777]

Canadian resources listing. [Edmonton]: Alberta Education, 1978. xix, 676 p.; ISSN: 0708-4439. [0127]

Canadian Rights and Liberties Federation
Bibliography [Human rights and civil liberties]. Ottawa: The Federation, [1982]. 208 p. [2241]

Canadian School Library Association
Basic book list for Canadian schools. Ottawa: Canadian Library Association, 1968-1969. 3 vol. [3400]

Canadian School Trustees' Association
Scholastic adaptation and cost effectiveness of programs for immigrant-refugee children in Canadian schools: [report and literature review]. [Ottawa]: Canadian School Trustees' Association, 1989. x l., 83, 33 p.; ISBN: 0-920632-229-7. [3700]

Canadian Sealers' Association
Bibliography of articles on seals and sealing published in the *Times* of London, 1960-1982. [S.l.]: Canadian Sealers' Association, [1983]. 52 p. [4900]

Canadian serials directory/Répertoire des publications sériées canadiennes. 3rd ed. Toronto: Reference Press, 1987. 396 p.; ISBN: 0-919981-10-0. [5962]

Canadian Society for Musical Traditions
Folk music catalogue: LP's, cassettes and books. Calgary: CSMT Mail Order Service, 1989-. vol.; ISSN: 1186-7523. [0945]

Canadian Society of Authors
Bibliography and general report. Toronto: 1902. 29 p. [0031]

Canadian Standards Association
Construction plus: a guide to CSA construction standards (plus 4000). 3rd ed. [Rexdale, Ont.]: Canadian Standards Association, c1993. vi, 368 p.; ISBN: 0-921347-31-6. [5852]
List of publications [Canadian Standards Association]. Rexdale, Ont.: Canadian Standards Association, 1951-1977. 26 vol.; ISSN: 0527-9771. [5762]

Canadian steel industry factbook. 2nd ed. Toronto: Canadian Steel Industry Research Association, 1983. 47 p.: ill. [5790]

Canadian studies bibliographies/Bibliographies des études canadiennes. [Ottawa]: External Affairs Canada, Bureau of Public Affairs, [1977]. 1 vol. (in various pagings). [0123]

Canadian Task Force on Mental Health Issues Affecting Immigrants and Refugees
Review of the literature on migrant mental health. [Ottawa]: Multiculturalism and Citizenship Canada, c1988. ii, 51 p.; ISBN: 0-662-16393-1. [5677]

Canadian Tax Foundation
Index of Canadian Tax Foundation publications to .... Toronto: Canadian Tax Foundation, 1965-1971. 2 vol.; ISSN: 0576-6214. [2590]

Canadian Teachers' Federation
Behaviour modification. Ottawa: Canadian Teachers' Federation, 1974. 34 p. (Bibliographies in education / Canadian Teachers' Federation ; no. 45) [3480]
Books about Canada/Livres concernant le Canada. Ottawa: 1963. [16] p. [0073]
Community colleges. Ottawa: Canadian Teachers' Federation, 1972. 61 p. (Bibliographies in education / Canadian Teachers' Federation ; no. 26) [3429]
Community schools. Ottawa: Canadian Teachers' Federation, 1977. 18 p. (Bibliographies in education / Canadian Teachers' Federation ; no. 60); ISBN: 0-88989-016-

1. [3521]
Continuing education for teachers. Ottawa: Canadian Teachers' Federation, 1975. 65 p. (Bibliographies in education / Canadian Teachers' Federation ; no. 53) [3495]
Curriculum development in Canada. Ottawa: Canadian Teachers' Federation, 1974. 16 p. (Bibliographies in education / Canadian Teachers' Federation ; no. 48) [3481]
Differentiated staffing. Ottawa: Canadian Teachers' Federation, 1973. 14 p. (Bibliographies in education / Canadian Teachers' Federation ; no. 36) [3447]
A directory of curriculum guides used in Canadian schools. Ottawa: Canadian Teachers' Federation, [1975]. ii, 92 p. [3496]
Disadvantaged children in Canada. Ottawa: Canadian Teachers' Federation, 1970. 15 p. (Bibliographies in education / Canadian Teachers' Federation ; no. 9) [3406]
Early childhood education. Ottawa: Canadian Teachers' Federation, 1972. 47 p. (Bibliographies in education / Canadian Teachers' Federation ; no. 28) [3430]
Elementary education. Ottawa: Canadian Teachers' Federation, 1974. 39 p. (Bibliographies in education / Canadian Teachers' Federation ; no. 43) [3482]
Evaluation of student teachers. Ottawa: Canadian Teachers' Federation, 1977. 76 p. (Bibliographies in education / Canadian Teachers' Federation ; no. 59); ISBN: 0-88989-015-3. [3522]
Histories of teachers' associations in Canada. Ottawa: Canadian Teachers' Federation, 1970. 6 p. (Bibliographies in education / Canadian Teachers' Federation ; no. 14) [3407]
Independent study. Ottawa: Canadian Teachers' Federation, 1973. 20 p. (Bibliographies in education / Canadian Teachers' Federation ; no. 38) [3448]
Industrial relations periodicals: a selected and annotated directory of general and teacher-oriented periodicals. Ottawa: Canadian Teachers' Federation, 1976. iii, 20 p.; ISBN: 0-88989-005-6. [5923]
Intercultural education: Indians and Eskimos of North America. Ottawa: Canadian Teachers' Federation, 1972. 35 p. (Bibliographies in education / Canadian Teachers' Federation ; no. 30) [3431]
Microteaching. Ottawa: Canadian Teachers' Federation, 1974. 14 p. (Bibliographies in education / Canadian Teachers' Federation ; no. 40) [3483]
Moral and values education. Ottawa: Canadian Teachers' Federation, 1974. 30 p. (Bibliographies in education / Canadian Teachers' Federation ; no. 44) [3484]
Open area schools. Ottawa: Canadian Teachers' Federation, 1976. 27 p. (Bibliographies in education / Canadian Teachers' Federation ; no. 56); ISBN: 0-88989-008-0. [3512]
Paraprofessional school personnel. Ottawa: Canadian Teachers' Federation, 1973. 24 p. (Bibliographies in education / Canadian Teachers' Federation ; no. 35) [3449]
The practicum in teacher education. Ottawa: Canadian Teachers' Federation, 1973. 65 p. (Bibliographies in education / Canadian Teachers' Federation ; no. 39) [3450]
School buildings and equipment: a bibliography. Ottawa: Canadian Teachers' Federation, 1967. 88 l. (Information note / Canadian Teachers' Federation ; no. 77) [3393]
School discipline. Ottawa: Canadian Teachers' Federation, 1975. 14 p. (Bibliographies in education / Canadian Teachers' Federation ; no. 49) [3497]
Secondary education. Ottawa: Canadian Teachers'

Federation, 1973. 21 p. (Bibliographies in education / Canadian Teachers' Federation ; no. 37) [3451]

Subject catalogue of CTF publications in print. Ottawa: Canadian Teachers' Federation, 1970. 8 l. [3408]

Systems analysis in education. Ottawa: Canadian Teachers' Federation, 1971. 29 p. (Bibliographies in education / Canadian Teachers' Federation ; no. 25) [3415]

Teacher autonomy and teacher decision making. Ottawa: Canadian Teachers' Federation, 1973. 10 p. (Bibliographies in education / Canadian Teachers' Federation ; no. 34) [3452]

Teacher education programs for native people. Ottawa: Canadian Teachers' Federation, 1975. 18 p. (Bibliographies in education / Canadian Teachers' Federation ; no. 55) [3498]

Teacher evaluation. Ottawa: Canadian Teachers' Federation, 1975. 26 p. (Bibliographies in education / Canadian Teachers' Federation ; no. 52) [3499]

Canadian theses 1947-1960/Thèses canadiennes 1947-1960. Ottawa: National Library of Canada, 1973. 2 vol. [6123]

"Canadian theses in psychology, ..." In: *Canadian Psychologist*; Vol. 4, no. 1 (January 1955) p. 4-7; vol. 5, no. 1 (January 1956) p. 5-9; vol. 6, no. 1 (January 1957) p. 4-7.; ISSN: 0008-4832. [6065]

"Canadian theses in psychology." In: *Canadian Journal of Psychology*; Vol. 3, no. 1 (March 1949)-vol. 8, no. 1 (March 1954) [6062]

Canadian theses [microform]/Thèses canadiennes [microforme]. Ottawa: National Library of Canada, 1984-. microfiches; ISSN: 0068-9874. [6207]

Canadian theses/Thèses canadiennes. Ottawa: Ministry of Supply and Services, 1962-1983. 15 vol.; ISSN: 0068-9874. [6164]

Canadian translations/Traductions canadiennes. Ottawa: National Library of Canada, 1987-. vol.; ISSN: 0835-2291. [1493]

Canadian Transport Commission. Research Branch

Publications available from the Canadian Transport Commission. [Ottawa]: Canadian Transport Commission, 1976. 79 p. [4462]

Canadian union catalogue of library materials for the handicapped [microform]/Catalogue collectif canadien des documents de bibliothèque pour les personnes handicapées [microforme]. Ottawa: National Library of Canada, 1985-. microfiches; ISSN: 0822-2576. [3366]

Canadian Universities Foundation

Select bibliography on higher education/Bibliographie sur l'enseignement supérieur. Ottawa: Canadian Universities Foundation, [1963-1981]. 18 vol.; ISSN: 0049-0091. [3585]

Canadian Urban Institute

Managing regional urban growth I: an annotated bibliography. Toronto: Canadian Urban Institute, 1991. xiv, 78, 3 p. (Urban focus series / Canadian Urban Institute ; 90-1; ISSN: 1183-2304); ISBN: 1-895446-00-7. [4437]

Managing regional urban growth II: review of government documents. Toronto: Canadian Urban Institute, 1991. iii, 54, 3 p. (Urban focus series / Canadian Urban Institute ; 90-2; ISSN: 1183-2304); ISBN: 1-895446-02-3. [4438]

Canadian Water and Wastewater Association

On-site wastewater treatment bibliography [computer file]. Ottawa: Canadian Water and Wastewater Association, c1992. 1 computer disk (5 1/4 in. + program user's manual: 15 p.); ISBN: 0-92912-808-7. [5849]

Canadian Welfare Council. Research Branch

The day care of children: an annotated bibliography. Ottawa: The Branch, 1969. 68 l. [3088]

Canadian Wildlife Service (Western Region). Library

A catalogue of the permanent map collection, Western Regional Library, Canadian Wildlife Service. Edmonton: Canadian Wildlife Service, Western Region, 1974. v, 24 l. [6538]

Canadiana: Canada's national bibliography: La bibliographie nationale du Canada. Ottawa: National Library of Canada, 1951-. vol.; ISSN: 0008-5391. [0184]

Canadiana 1867-1900, monographs [microform]: Canada's national bibliography/Canadiana 1867-1900, monographies [microforme]: la bibliographie nationale du Canada. [Ottawa]: National Library of Canada, 1980-. microfiches; ISSN: 1183-6849. [0183]

Canadiana library [Expo 67]/Bibliothèque de Canadiana [Expo 67]. Montreal: 1967. 4 vol. [0085]

Candy, R.H.

Review of reports of growth and regeneration surveys in Canada, conducted by the Dominion Forest Service and the Commission of Conservation, 1918-36. Ottawa: Department of Mines and Resources, Lands, Parks and Forests Branch, 1938. 50 p. [4917]

Canplan Oceanology Limited

A literature survey of chemical oceanographic studies carried out in the Arctic. Halifax, N.S.: Canplan Oceanology, 1976. 233 p. [5110]

The CANSCAIP companion: a biographical record of Canadian children's authors, illustrators and performers. Markham, Ont.: Pembroke Publishers, c1991. 296 p.: ports.; ISBN: 0-921217-58-7. [1390]

Cansino, Barbara

Diana McIntosh. Don Mills, Ont.: PRO Canada, 1988. 7 p. [7182]

Cantin, Gabrielle; Chené-Williams, Adèle

Aide-mémoire en andragogie. [Montréal]: Faculté des sciences de l'éducation, Université de Montréal, 1980. 79 p. [3561]

Cantin, Pierre

"Bibliographie sélective de Jacques Ferron." Dans: *Voix et Images*; Vol. 8, no 3 (printemps 1983) p. 464-475.; ISSN: 0318-9201. [6982]

Jacques Ferron, polygraphe: essai de bibliographie suivi d'une chronologie. Montréal: Éditions Bellarmin, 1984. 548 p.; ISBN: 2-89007-574-5. [6983]

"Nouvelle contribution à la bibliographie des écrits de Jacques Ferron." Dans: *Revue d'histoire littéraire du Québec et du Canada français*; No 2 (1980-1981) p. 115-135.; ISSN: 0713-7958. [6981]

Cantin, Pierre; Harrington, Normand; Hudon, Jean-Paul

Bibliographie de la critique de la littérature québécoise dans les revues des XIXe et XXe siècles. Ottawa: Centre de recherche en civilisation canadienne-française, Université d'Ottawa, 1979. 5 vol. (Documents de travail du Centre de recherche en civilisation canadienne-française ; 12-16) [1145]

Caparros, Ernest

"Jean-Charles Bonenfant (1912-1977)." Dans: *Cahiers de droit*; Vol. 20, nos 1-2 (mars 1979) p. 7-46.; ISSN: 0007-974X. [6857]

LISTE DES NOTICES ABRÉGÉES | 971

Caplan, Usher
"A.M. Klein: a bibliography and index to manuscripts." In: *The A.M. Klein symposium*, edited by Seymour Mayne. Ottawa: University of Ottawa Press, 1975. P. 87-122.; ISBN: 0-7766-4382-7. [7093]

Carayon, Auguste
Bibliographie historique de la Compagnie de Jésus ou Catalogue des ouvrages relatifs à l'histoire des Jésuites depuis leur origine jusqu'à nos jours. London: Barthes and Lowell, 1864. viii, 612 p. [1877]

Cardin, Clarisse
"Bio-bibliographie de Marius Barbeau." Dans: *Archives de folklore*; Vol. 2 (1947) p. 17-96.; ISSN: 0085-5243. [6827]
Bio-bibliographie de Marius Barbeau, précédée d'un hommage à Marius Barbeau par Luc Lacourcière et Félix-Antoine Savard. [Montréal]: Éditions Fides, 1947. 96 p. [6826]

Cardinal, Claudette
The history of Quebec: a bibliography of works in English. [Montreal]: Centre for the Study of Anglophone Quebec, Concordia University, 1981. vi, 202 p.; ISBN: 0-88947-002-2. [0369]

Cardinal, Clive H.
"Preliminary check list of studies on German-Canadian creative literature." In: *Canadian Ethnic Studies*; Vol. 1, no. 1 (1969) p. 38-39; vol. 2, no. 1 (June 1970) p. 63-69; vol. 5, no. 1/2 (1973) p. 91-93.; ISSN: 0008-3496. [1074]

Cardinal, Clive H.; Malycky, Alexander
"University research on German-Canadians: a preliminary check list of dissertations and theses." In: *Canadian Ethnic Studies*; Vol. 1, no. 1 (1969) p. 7-12.; ISSN: 0008-3496. [6096]

Cardinal, Linda; Lapointe, Jean; Thériault, J.-Yvon
"Bibliographie sommaire sur les francophones hors Québec 1980-1989." Dans: *Le déclin d'une culture: recherche, analyse et bibliographie: francophonie hors Québec, 1980-1989*, par Bernard Roger. Ottawa: Fédération des jeunes Canadiens français, c1990. P. 139-192.; ISBN: 0-921768-05-5. [4607]

Cardinal, Michel
Urbanisme et logement: bibliographie. Montréal: Conseil de développement social du Montréal métropolitain, 1972. 169 p.: ill. [4320]

Careless, Virginia
Bibliography for the study of British Columbia's domestic material history. Ottawa: National Museum of Canada, 1976. ii, 73 p.: ill. (National Museum of Man Mercury series, History Division paper; no. 20; ISSN: 0316-1900) [1988]

Cariou, Mavis; Cox, Sandra J.; Bregman, Alvan
Canadian selection: books and periodicals for libraries. 2nd ed. Toronto: Published for the Ontario Ministry of Citizenship and Culture and the Centre for Research in Librarianship, University of Toronto [by] University of Toronto Press, c1985. xvi, 501 p.; ISBN: 0-8020-4630-4. [0150]

Carleton University. Carleton Archives
Theses and research essays accepted by Carleton University between 1950 and November 1969, and held in MacOdrum Library. Ottawa: Carleton Archives, Library, Carleton University, 1972. 62 l. [6114]

Carleton University. Department of Geography
Master and bachelor theses in geography, 1965-1983. Ottawa: Carleton University, 1983. 57 p. [6165]

Carleton University. Department of Geography. Map Library
Ottawa area resources held by the Map Library. Ottawa: [s.n.], 1972. 1 vol. (unpaged). [6527]

Carleton University. Library
Selected list of current materials on Canadian public administration. Ottawa: Carleton University, Library, 1954-1965. 19 vol.; ISSN: 0528-1504. [2385]
Sources of information for research in Canadian political science and public administration: a selected and annotated bibliography prepared for the Department of Political Science and the School of Public Administration. Ottawa: The Library, 1964. 25 l. [2381]

Carlson, Alvar W.
"Bibliography on barns in the United States and Canada." In: *Pioneer America*; Vol. 10, no. 1 (June 1978) p. 65-71.; ISSN: 0032-0005. [0753]

Carlson, Roy L.
"C.E. Borden's archaeological legacy." In: *BC Studies*; No. 42 (Summer 1979) p. 3-12.; ISSN: 0005-2949. [6858]

Carnet bibliographique des publications de M. l'Abbé Auguste Gosselin: petit souvenir à l'occasion de ses noces d'or sacerdotales, 30 septembre, 1866-1916. Québec: Laflamme, 1916. 24 p. [7024]

Carney, R.J.; Ferguson, W.O.
A selected and annotated bibliography on the sociology of Eskimo education. Edmonton: Boreal Institute, University of Alberta, c1965. v, 59 l. (Occasional publication / Boreal Institute, University of Alberta; no. 2) [3388]

Caron, Fabien
"Bibliographie d'Albert Peter Low." Dans: *Cahiers de géographie de Québec*; Vol. 9, no 18 (avril-septembre 1965) p. 179-181.; ISSN: 0007-9766. [7156]

Caron, Fabien; Bouchard, Jacqueline
Bibliographie des travaux du Centre d'études nordiques. Québec: Université Laval, 1974. 26 l. [0626]

Caron, Hélène; Denault, Bernard
Bibliographie internationale: rapports états-coopératives. Sherbrooke, Québec: Institut de recherche et d'enseignement pour les coopératives, Université de Sherbrooke, 1987. vi, 65 f. (Collection Essais / Institut de recherche et d'enseignement pour les coopératives, Université de Sherbrooke; no 13; ISSN: 0832-6037) [2730]

Caron, Louise; Leblanc, Nicole J.
Vie étudiante et services aux étudiants: bibliographie commentée sur les services aux étudiants au niveau collégial, le personnel de ces services, la clientèle étudiant concernée. Québec: Ministère de l'éducation, Direction générale de la planification, 1975. 144 f. [3500]

Carpentier, Louise E.; Lequin, Lucie
"Bibliographie des écrits des femmes du Québec de 1945 à 1960." Dans: *Resources for Feminist Research*; Vol. 17, no. 4 (December 1988) p. 49-61.; ISSN: 0707-8412. [3864]

Carr, Sheridan
Catalogue of slides for sale to educational institutions. Ottawa: National Gallery of Canada, 1984. 75 p.; ISBN: 0-88884-513-8. [0703]
Répertoire de diapos en vente aux établissements d'éducation. Ottawa: Galerie nationale du Canada, 1984. 76 p.; ISBN: 0-88884-514-6. [0704]

Carrier, Denis
Bibliographie analytique d'Yves Thériault, 1940-1984. Québec: Centre de recherche en littérature québécoise, Université Laval, 1985. 326 p. (Collection "Bibliographies" /

Centre de recherche en littérature québécoise, Université Laval ; no 1); ISBN: 2-920801-02-3. [7332]

Répertoire des recherches gérontologiques publiées ou en cours (1977-1982). Montréal: Association québécoise de gérontologie, 1984. ii, 33 f. [3257]

Carrier, Lois J.

Checklist of Canadian periodicals in the field of education. Ottawa: Canadian Library Association, 1964. iii, 17 p. (Occasional paper / Canadian Library Association ; no. 44) [5874]

Carrière, Gaston

"Adrien-Gabriel Morice, o.m.i. (1859-1938): essai de bibliographie." Dans: *Revue de l'Université d'Ottawa*; Vol. 42, no 3 (juillet-septembre 1972) p. 325-341.; ISSN: 0041-9206. [7200]

Apôtres de la plume: contribution des professeurs des facultés ecclésiastiques de l'Université d'Ottawa (1912 [i.e. 1932]-1951) à la bibliographie des Oblats de M.I. Rome: Maison générale O.M.I., 1951. 32 p. [1506]

"Bibliographie des Oblats de langue française au Canada." Dans: *Études oblates*; Vol. 10, no 2 (avril-juin 1951) p. 140-152; vol. 10, no 4 (octobre-décembre 1951) p. 291-304.; ISSN: 0318-9384. [1507]

"Bibliographie des professeurs oblats des facultés ecclésiastiques de l'Université d'Ottawa (1932-1961)." Dans: *Revue de l'Université d'Ottawa*; Vol. 32 (1962) p. 81-104, 215-244.; ISSN: 0041-9206. [1513]

"Catalogue des manuscrits en langues indiennes conservés aux Archives historiques Oblates, Ottawa." Dans: *Anthropologica*; Vol. 12, no. 2 (1970) p. 151-179.; ISSN: 0003-5459. [3919]

"Contribution des Oblats de Marie Immaculée de langue française aux études de linguistique et d'ethnologie du Nord canadien." Dans: *Culture*; Vol. 12, no 2 (juin 1951) p. 213-226.; ISSN: 0317-2066. [1416]

"Imprimés en langues indiennes conservés aux Archives historiques Oblates, Ottawa." Dans: *Anthropologica*; Vol. 15, no 1 (1973) p. 129-151.; ISSN: 0003-5459. [3939]

Carrière, Richard, et al.

Native child abuse and neglect: a bibliography of Canadian resources. Sudbury, Ont.: Laurentian University, 1985. 29, vii p. [4072]

Carrière, Richard; Thomson, Ashley

Child abuse & neglect: a compendium of community resources/Enfance maltraitée et négligée: un répertoire des ressources communautaires. Sudbury, Ont.: Laurentian University, 1984. xiv, 39, 94, 12, xxiv p. [3258]

Family violence: a bibliography of Ontario resources, 1980-1984/La violence familiale: une bibliographie des ressources ontariennes, 1980-1984. Sudbury, Ont.: Laurentian University, 1985. xiv, 95 p. [3269]

Carrigy, M.A.

Athabasca oil sands bibliography (1789-1964). Edmonton: Research Council of Alberta, 1965. ix, 91 p. (Research Council of Alberta Preliminary report ; 65-3) [4763]

Carswell Company

Catalogue of Canadian publications including historical and general books, statutes and other government imprints, pamphlets, magazines and miscellaneous books. Toronto: Carswell, 1900. 71 p. [0028]

Carter, James L.

Canadian Eskimo in fact and fiction: a discursive bibliography. Toronto: Ontario Library Association,

School Libraries Division, 1975. 21 p. (Ontario Library Association School Library Division Monograph ; no. 4) [3965]

Carter, John C.

"Community museums and schools: an annotated bibliography of resource and reference materials." In: *History and Social Science Teacher*; Vol. 21, no. 2 (December 1985) p. 89-93.; ISSN: 0316-4969. [3635]

Carter, John Lyman; Carter, Ruth C.

Bibliography and index of North American Carboniferous brachiopods (1898-1968). Boulder, Colo.: Geological Society of America, 1970. x, 382 p. (Geological Society of America Memoir ; 128) [4548]

Carter, Neil M.

Index and list of titles, Fisheries Research Board of Canada and associated publications, 1900-1964. Ottawa: Fisheries Research Board of Canada, 1968. xviii, 649 p. (Fisheries Research Board of Canada Bulletin ; no. 164) [6267]

Index and list of titles, Fisheries Research Board of Canada and associated publications, 1965-72. Ottawa: Fisheries Research Board of Canada, 1973. vi, 588 p. (Fisheries Research Board of Canada Miscellaneous special publication ; 18) [6284]

Cartigny, Sylvie

"Bibliographie sur la Francophonie." Dans: *Études internationales*; Vol. 5, no 2 (juin 1974) p. 399-425.; ISSN: 0014-2123. [2412]

Caruso, Barbara; Nichol, bp

"A Seripress bibliography, 1971-1979." In: *Open Letter*; Series 6, no. 4 (Spring 1986) p. 71-77.; ISSN: 0048-1939. [1678]

Caruso, Naomi; Cukier, Golda; Finegold, Ronald

A preliminary guide to the Jewish Canadiana Collection of the Jewish Public Library. Montreal: Jewish Public Library, 1981. 24 p. [4201]

Casno, Pierre, et al.

"Bibliographie sur l'éducation au Canada français." Dans: *Revue des sciences de l'éducation*; Vol. 1, no 1 (printemps 1975)-vol. 6, no 2 (printemps 1980) [3562]

Casno, Pierre; Bernard, Jean-Paul; Lauzier, Suzanne

Index des mémoires présentées à la Commission royale d'enquête sur l'enseignement dans la province de Québec, 1961-1963. Montréal: Université de Montréal, Service des bibliothèques, Bibliothèque E.P.C., 1977. 51 f.; ISBN: 0-88529-021-6. [3523]

Casper, Dale E.

Canadian domestic architecture: trends and projects. Monticello, Ill.: Vance Bibliographies, 1987. 5 p. (Architecture series: Bibliography ; A-1772; ISSN: 0194-1356); ISBN: 1-55590-222-7. [0781]

Preserving Canadian architecture in the 1980's. Monticello, Ill.: Vance Bibliographies, 1987. 7 p. (Architecture series: Bibliography ; A-1771; ISSN: 0194-1356); ISBN: 0-55590-221-9. [0782]

Casselman, Paul Hubert

Coopération: bibliographie des ouvrages et des articles publiés en français au Canada jusqu'à la fin de 1947. Ottawa: Centre social, Université d'Ottawa, [1953]. vii, 191 p. [2564]

Cassidy, Frank; Dickson, Heather

A selected and annotated bibliography on Indian self-government. [Victoria, B.C.]: School of Public Administration, University of Victoria, 1986. 34 l. [4082]

Cassis, A.F.
"A checklist of the publications of F.E.L. Priestley." In: *Some reflections on Life and habit,* by Northrop Frye. Lethbridge, Alta.: University of Lethbridge Press, c1988. P. 36-47. [7248]

Castonguay, Rachelle; Lanari, Robert
Socio-economic impact studies relating to pipeline projects and certain northern development projects: bibliography/ Études d'impact socio-économique relatives à des projets de pipeline et à certains projets de developpement nordique: bibliographie. Ottawa: Northern Research Division, Department of Indian Affairs and Northern Development, 1977. 27 l. [0632]

Catalogue collectif des presses universitaires de langue française. Montréal: Association internationale des presses universitaires de langue française, c1977. 135 p.; ISBN: 0-919012-25-6. [1620]

Catalogue de la bibliothèque de feu L'Hon. Dominique Mondelet, juge de la Cour supérieure. [S.l.: Plinguet & Laplante, 1862]. 14 p. [6719]

Le catalogue de la cinémathèque nationale des relations industrielles. [Ottawa]: Office national du film du Canada, c1986. 21, 31 p.; ISBN: 0-662-54352-1. [6662]

Catalogue de l'édition au Canada français. Montréal: Conseil supérieur du livre, 1958-1970. 7 vol. [1053]

Catalogue de livres canadiens de la bibliothèque de feu M. C.C. Morency. [Québec: s.n.], 1898. 16 p. [6751]

Catalogue de livres canadiens de la bibliothèque de feu M. Faucher de St.–Maurice. [Québec]: C. Darveau, 1897. 22 p. [6748]

Catalogue de livres de droit et de jurisprudence de la province de Québec (ci-devant Bas-Canada). Montréal: Theoret, 1900. 48, viii p. [2097]

Catalogue des manuscrits et des imprimés en langues sauvages ainsi que des reliques indiennes, exposés à Québec à l'occasion du XVe Congrès international des américanistes, septembre 1906. Québec: Dussault & Proulx, 1906. 50 p. [3907]

Catalogue d'ouvrages historiques et littéraires sur le Canada. Québec: Filteau, 1885. 8 p. [0015]

Catalogue éducation physique et sports. Ste-Foy: Service des communications du Conseil des loisirs – région de Québec, 1979. 64 p. (Librairie loisirs et sports) [1791]

Catalogue loisirs, plein air et socio-culturel. Ste-Foy: Service des communications du Conseil des loisirs – région de Québec, 1979. 81 p. [1792]

Catalogue of a large and valuable collection of English and French books: belonging to a private gentleman, among which are to be found a considerable number of scarce and rare books relating to the early history of America. Quebec: [s.n.], 1860. 16 p. [1876]

"Catalogue of a valuable collection of Canadian books and rare pamphlets." In: *Papers of the Bibliographical Society of Canada;* Vol. 3 (1964) p. 61-99.; ISSN: 0067-6896. [0076]

A Catalogue of books: chiefly relating to English and American history and antiquities ... presented to the University of McGill College, Montreal, by Peter Redpath, 1864-1884. Cambridge: Macmillan and Bowes, 1884. 134 p. [6736]

Catalogue of books in the library of late Right Hon. Sir John A. Macdonald. Ottawa: [s.n.], 1900. 69 p. [6753]

Catalogue of books relating to America, including a large number of rare works printed before 1700. Amsterdam: [s.n.], 1850. 98, 103-104 p. [0005]

Catalogue of environmental education materials/Répertoire didactique sur l'environnement. Ottawa: Department of the Environment, 1979. 12 vol.; ISBN: 0-662-30603-3. [3146]

Catalogue of pamphlets of the Library of the Legislature of Quebec. Quebec: [s.n.], 1879. 119 p. [6728]

Catalogue of pamphlets relating to Canada. Montreal: Lovell and Gibson, 1843. 3 p. [0004]

A catalogue of plays by Canadian authors: (including a select list of other publishers' plays). London, Ont.: Peter L. Morris, 1935. 29 p. [1003]

"Catalogue of printed books and tracts, by the late Alexander Dalrymple." In: *Biographical memoir of Alexander Dalrymple, Esq.: late hydrographer to the Admiralty.* London: [s.n.], 1816. P. 201-204. [6930]

Catalogue of rare and curious books including the collection of M. [i.e. Monsieur] Tross: comprising important works relating to America and the Indies .... London: [s.n.], 1870. 64 p. [6722]

Catalogue of sports books, films & video tapes/Catalogue du sports livres, films et bandes magnétoscopique. Ottawa: Coaching Association of Canada, [1980]. 260 p.: ill. [1799]

Catalogue of the American library of the late Mr. George Brinley of Hartford, Conn. Hartford, Conn.: Lockwood & Brainard, 1878-1897. 5 vol. [6749]

Catalogue of the library of James Stephenson, Esq., Montreal, Canada: a large, interesting and varied collection of books and pamphlets ... among which may be noted a great number of publications relating to Canada, its settlement, history and present condition .... New York: D. Taylor, 1890. 142 p. [6743]

Catalogue of the valuable historical library of Charles Lindsey, F.R.S.C. of Toronto, Canada: consisting of early Canadian history, laws, voyages, travels and discoveries, scarce political history and documents, rare Canadian imprints, historical and political pamphlets .... Boston: C.F. Libbie, 1895. 90 p. [6747]

A catalogue of the William Colgate Printing Collection: books, pamphlets, drawings. Montreal: McGill University Library, 1956. 25 p. [1582]

Catalogue or List of manuscript documents, arranged, bound and catalogued under the direction of the commissioner of public records: together with a list of books of entry consisting of minutes of His Majesty's Council ... from year 1710 to year 1867, ... Halifax, N.S.: Commissioner of Public Works and Mines, 1886. 42 p. [0191]

Catholic press directory. New York: Catholic Press Association, 1923-. vol.; ISSN: 0008-8307. [5986]

Catling, P.M., et al.
Bibliography of vascular plant floristics for New Brunswick, Newfoundland (insular), and Nova Scotia. Ottawa: Research Branch, Agriculture Canada, 1986. 28 p. (Technical bulletin / Research Branch, Agriculture Canada ; 1986-3E); ISBN: 0-662-14627-1. [5522]

Cavanagh, Beverley
"Annotated bibliography: Eskimo music." In: *Ethnomusicology;* Vol. 16, no. 3 (September 1972) p. 479-487.; ISSN: 0014-1836. [0831]

Cavanagh, Joan
Federal energy R&D task 6: oil, gas & electricity: bibliography 1975-1986/R-D énergétique du gouvernement fédéral activité 6: pétrole, gaz et électricité: bibliographie 1975-1986. [Ottawa]: Office of Energy Research and Development, Energy, Mines and Resources

Canada, 1986. xiii, 148 p.; ISBN: 0-662-54699-7. [4849]

Cayford, J.H.; Chrosciewicz, Z.; Sims, H.P.
A review of silviculture research in jack pine. Ottawa: Queen's Printer, 1967. v, 255 p.: ill. [5345]

Cayouette, Jacques; Blondeau, Marcel
"Bibliographie d'Ernest Lepage." Dans: *Bulletin de la Société botanique du Québec*; No 4 (1982) p. 3-19.; ISSN: 0228-975X. [7145]

Cebotarev, E.A., et al.
"An annotated bibliography on women in agriculture and rural societies." In: *Resources for Feminist Research*; Vol. 11, no. 1 (March 1982) p. 93-180.; ISSN: 0707-8412. [3806]

Central Mortgage and Housing Corporation. Data and Information Group
Bibliography of background material on building in northern communities. Ottawa: Data and Information Group, Central Mortgage and Housing Corporation, 1974. [33] l. [0741]

Central Mortgage and Housing Corporation. Library
Canadian architecture: bibliography/Architecture canadienne: bibliographie. [Ottawa: Central Mortgage and Housing Corporation], 1976. 12 l. [0748]
Housing for the aged: bibliography. Ottawa: [s.n.], 1968. 17 l. [4308]
New towns bibliography. [S.l.: s.n.], 1969. 36 l. [4310]
A selected list of references on cost-cutting in house construction. Ottawa: Central Mortgage and Housing Corporation, 1957. 15 p. (Central Mortgage and Housing Corporation Library Reference list ; no. 5) [5719]

Centre canadien de la technologie des minéraux et de l'énergie
Catalogue des publications de CANMET. Ottawa: Centre canadien de la technologie des minéraux et de l'énergie, Division de l'information technologique, 1978-1982. 7 vol.; ISSN: 0707-560X. [6348]

Centre canadien d'hygiène et de sécurité au travail
Revue des publications traitant des attitudes et des rôles et de leurs effets sur la sécurité du travail. Hamilton, Ont.: Centre canadien d'hygiène et de sécurité au travail, 1980. 69 p.; ISBN: 0-660-91076-4. [2863]

Centre canadien d'information et de documentation en archivistique
"Bibliographie en archivistique, 1980-1986/Archival science bibliography, 1980-1986." Dans: *Archives*; Vol. 19, no 1-2 (juin-septembre 1987) p. 1-304.; ISSN: 0044-9423. [1690]

Centre canadien du film sur l'art
Catalogue, films sur l'art et sujets connexes. Ottawa: Centre canadien du film sur l'art, 1965-1973. 10 vol. [6619]

Centre de musique canadienne au Québec
Compositeurs au Québec. Montréal: Centre de musique canadienne au Québec, 1974-1982. 14 vol.: ill., portr. [0904]

Centre de recherche en histoire économique du Canada français
Documents, livres et journaux sur microfilms, microfiches et microcartes en dépôt au C.H.E. Montréal: Centre de recherche en histoire économique du Canada français, 1971. ii, 122 f. [1971]

Centre d'édition du gouvernement du Canada
Liste générale des publications en série du gouvernement du Canada: (comprend les publications en série signalées dans la Liste hebdomadaire). Hull, Québec: Centre d'édition du gouvernement du Canada, 1988. 55 f. [6391]

Centre national des arts (Canada)
Catalogue: films sur les arts d'interprétation. Ottawa: Le Centre, 1968. 18, 24 p. [6608]

Cercle linguistique de Montréal
Jean-Paul Vinay: bibliographie chronologique, 1936-1962. [Montréal]: Cercle linguistique de Montréal, 1963. 16 p. [7355]

Chabot, Juliette
Bio-bibliographie d'écrivains canadiens-français: une liste des bio-bibliographies présentées par les élèves de l'École de Bibliothécaires, Université de Montréal, 1937-1947. Montréal: [s.n.], 1948. 1 f., 12 p. [1008]

Chackowsky, Leonard Eugene
Bibliography of Manitoba geology, 1795 to 1988. Winnipeg: Mines Branch, Minerals Division, Manitoba Energy and Mines, 1989. iv, 221 p. (+ 5 microfiche in pocket). [4873]

Chaison, Gary N.; Cockburn, Leslie; Morris, John
Labour education: a bibliography of selected reading materials available at libraries in New Brunswick/ L'enseignement syndical: une bibliographie de matières choisies disponibles dans les bibliothèques du Nouveau Brunswick. Fredericton: Department of Extension and Summer Session[s], University of New Brunswick, c1978. ix, 62 p. [2843]

Chalifoux, Jean-Pierre
Bibliographie sur des questions actuelles. [Montréal]: Bibliothèque, Centre d'études canadiennes-françaises, McGill University, 1968. [34] f. [2394]
Bio-bibliographies et bibliographies. Liste des travaux bibliographiques des étudiants en bibliothéconomie de l'Université de Montréal. Montréal: Ministère des affaires culturelles du Québec, 1970. 60 p. [0093]
"Liste de sources bibliographiques relatives à la littérature canadienne-française." Dans: *Bulletin de l'Association canadienne des bibliothécaires de langue française*; Vol. 13, no 3 (septembre 1967) p. 137-141.; ISSN: 0004-5314. [1037]
Liste préliminaire de sources bibliographiques relatives à la littérature canadienne-française. Montréal: Bibliothèque, Centre d'études canadienne-françaises, McGill University, 1966. 7 f. [1032]

Chalmers, Lex
Expert systems in geography and environmental studies: an annotated review of recent work in the field. [Waterloo, Ont.]: Department of Geography, University of Waterloo, 1990. v, 92 p. (Occasional paper publication series / Department of Geography, University of Waterloo ; no. 10; ISSN: 0843-7383); ISBN: 0-921083-35-1. [3060]

Chamberlain, A.F.
"Contributions towards a bibliography of the archaeology of the Dominion of Canada and Newfoundland." In: *Annual Archaeological Report, Ontario*; Vol. 2 (1887-1888) p. 54-59; vol. 3 (1888-1889) p. 102-118; vol. 4 (1890-1891) p. 78-82. [4523]
Contributions towards a bibliography of the archaeology of the Dominion of Canada and Newfoundland. Toronto: [s.n.], 1880. 6 p. [4522]

Chamberlain, Jane; Sendrovich, Pamela; Turl, L.H.
A bibliography of papers and reports published by the Defence Research Establishment Toronto (formerly the Defence Research Medical Laboratories) 1950-1971. Downsview, Ont.: Defence and Civil Institute of Environmental Medicine, 1974. vii, 350 p. (DCIEM report / Defence and Civil Institute of Environmental Medicine ;

no. 74-R-1000) [5592]

Chamberlain, K.E.
Design in Canada, 1940-1987: a bibliography. [Richmond, B.C.: K. Chamberlain, c1988]. [48] p. [0715]

Chamberlain, Simon B.; Crowley, David F.
Decision-making and change in urban residential space: selected and annotated references. [Toronto]: Centre for Urban and Community Studies, University of Toronto, 1970. iii, 67 p. (University of Toronto Centre for Urban and Community Studies Bibliographic series ; no. 2; ISSN: 0316-4691) [4314]

Chamberland, Claire
Portrait de la littérature québécoise en toxicomanie. [Québec]: Ministère de la santé et des services sociaux, Direction générale de la planification et de l'évaluation, 1990. 2 vol.; ISBN: 2-550-20685-1 (vol. 1); 2-550-20686-X (vol. 2). [3338]

Chamberland, Constant-Alfred
Catalogue des ouvrages utiles à l'enseignement religieux. Québec: Université Laval, 1916. 63 p. [3368]

Chamberland, Roger
"Bibliographie de Jacques Brault." Dans: *Voix et Images*; Vol. 12, no 2 (hiver 1987) p. 256-264.; ISSN: 0318-9201. [6872]
"Bibliographie de Roland Giguère." Dans: *Voix et Images*; Vol. 9, no 2 (hiver 1984) p. 75-89.; ISSN: 0318-9201. [7012]

Chamberland, Roger; Gervais, André
"Bibliographie de Roger Des Roches." Dans: *Voix et Images*; Vol. 13, no 2 (hiver 1988) p. 280-289.; ISSN: 0318-9201. [6952]

Chamberland, Roger; Noizet, Pascale
"Bibliographie de Michel van Schendel." Dans: *Voix et Images*; Vol. 11, no 2 (hiver 1986) p. 256-261.; ISSN: 0318-9201. [7349]

Chan, Janet B.L.; Matthews, Catherine J.
Privatization of correctional services: a select bibliography. Toronto: Centre of Criminology, University of Toronto, 1992. 28 p. (Information paper / Centre of Criminology, University of Toronto ; no. 9); ISBN: 0-919584-70-5. [2357]

Chance, David H.
"Influences of the Hudson's Bay Company on the native cultures of the Colville District." In: *Northwest Anthropological Research Notes*; Vol. 7, no. 1 (part 2) (1973) p. 138-166.; ISSN: 0029-3296. [3940]

Chandler, Dorothy, et al.
A checklist of French-Canadian genealogical works at the Minnesota Historical Society Reference Library. St. Louis Park, Minn.: Northwest Territory French and Canadian Heritage Institute, 1980. v, 96 p. [2007]

Chandrasekhar, S.
"A bibliography on immigration from India to Canada and the Asian Indian immigrant communities in Canada." In: *From India to Canada: a brief history of immigration, problems of discrimination, admission and assimilation*, edited by S. Chandrasekhar. La Jolla, Calif.: Population Review Books, 1986. P. 175-205.; ISBN: 0-9609080-1-3. [4239]

Chants pour la liturgie: onze années de bibliographie canadienne (1968-1978): suivie d'un index général descriptif. Ste-Foy, Québec: Alpec, 1980. 59 p.; ISBN: 2-920198-00-9. [0884]

Chao, Yen-pin
Police literature: selected publications for a basic police library. Rev. ed. [Toronto]: Ontario Police College, 1982. iii, 61 l. [2242]

Policing in Ontario: a bibliography. Aylmer, Ont.: Ontario Police College, 1991. vi, 187 p. [2347]

Chapdelaine, Cécile
Bibliographie: activités éducatives à l'environnement. Québec: Ministère de l'éducation, Direction générale de l'éducation des adultes, 1982. 94 p. [3604]

Chapman, Geoffrey
"Canadian reference and information books for children." In: *Canadian Children's Literature*; Vol. 1, no. 1 (Spring 1975) p. 42-52; vol. 1, no. 2 (Summer 1975) p. 47-65.; ISSN: 0319-0080. [1324]

Chappell, Duncan; Gordon, Robert Macaire; Moore, Rhonda D.
Criminal investigation: a selective literature review and bibliography. Ottawa: Communication Division, Programs Branch, Solicitor General Canada, 1982. 68 p.; ISBN: 0-662-12031-0. [2243]
L'enquête criminelle: revue de documents choisis et bibliographie. Ottawa: Division de communications, Direction des programmes, Solliciteur général Canada, 1982. 78 p.; ISBN: 0-662-91634-4. [2244]

Chappell, Duncan; Moore, Rhonda D.
Le recours à des sanctions pénales contre la pollution de l'environnement: bibliographie choisie et commentée. Ottawa: Ministère de la justice Canada, 1988. xvii, 109, 93, xvii p. (Recherches sur la réglementation et l'observation); ISBN: 0-662-55688-7. [2311]
The use of criminal penalties for pollution of the environment: a selective and annotated bibliography of the literature. Ottawa: Department of Justice Canada, 1988. xvii, 93, 109, xvii p. (Studies in regulation and compliance); ISBN: 0-662-55688-7. [2312]

Chappell, M.S.
Recherche et développement en matière d'énergie éolienne au Conseil national de recherches du Canada, 1975-1985. Ottawa: Conseil national de recherches Canada, Division de l'énergie, Programme d'énergie éolienne, 1986. xi, 181 p.: ill. [5812]
Wind energy research and development at the National Research Council of Canada, 1975-1985. Ottawa: National Research Council Canada, Wind Energy Program, 1986. xi, 164 p.: ill. [5813]

Charbonneau, André
"Cartobibliographie de Jean-Baptiste-Louis Franquelin." Dans: *Cahiers de la Société bibliographique du Canada*; Vol. 11 (1972) p. 39-52.; ISSN: 0067-6896. [6528]

Charbonneau, Hélène
Livres en langue française pour les jeunes. Montréal: Bibliothèque municipale de Montréal, 1985. xiii, 382 p.; ISBN: 2-920374-00-1. [1364]

Charest-Knoetze, Claire; Lefrançois, Guy
L'Acadie, l'Acadie: bibliographie des ouvrages en bibliothèque. Edmundston, N.-B.: Bibliothèque, Centre universitaire Saint-Louis-Maillet, Université de Moncton, 1987. [90] f. [0264]

Charette, Jean-Yves
Bibliographie signalétique sur les précipitations acides. Québec: Environnement Canada, Conservation et protection, Région du Québec, 1990. v, 316 p. [5276]

Charland, Jean-Pierre; Thivierge, Nicole
Bibliographie de l'enseignement professionel au Québec, 1850-1980. Québec: Institut québécois de recherche sur la culture, 1982. 282 p. (Instruments de travail / Institut

québécois de recherche sur la culture ; no 3); ISBN: 2-89224-006-9. [3605]

Charland, Thomas

"Bibliographie de l'Abbé Alexis Pelletier." Dans: *Revue d'histoire de l'Amérique française*; Vol. 1, no 3 (décembre 1947) p. 463-469.; ISSN: 0035-2357. [7240]

Chartier, Armand B.

"Introduction bibliographique à la civilisation du Québec." Dans: *Contemporary French Civilization*; Vol. 3, no. 2 (Winter 1919) p. 265-296.; ISSN: 0147-9156. [0279]

Chartier, Jean-Pierre

Des difficultés d'apprentissage en milieu collégial: bibliographie. Shawinigan: Collège de Shawinigan, 1988. 142 p. (Collection: Repérer et aider des étudiants en difficulté d'apprentissage ; 2); ISBN: 2-9801095-1-7. [3681]

Chartier, Yves

"Situation de la recherche sur la musique au Canada français." Dans: *Bulletin du Centre de recherche en civilisation canadienne-française de l'Université d'Ottawa*; No 19 (décembre 1979) p. 1-14.; ISSN: 0045-608X. [0874]

Chartrand, Francis; Couture, Jean-François; Pilote, Pierre

Les gîtes de l'Abitibi du Nord-Ouest québécois: un inventaire des recherches récentes. Québec: Gouvernement du Québec, Service géologique du Nord-Ouest, 1989. 8 f. [4874]

Chartrand, Georges-Aimé

"Bibliographie des publications de l'A.C.B.L.F., 1943-1963." Dans: *Bulletin de l'Association canadienne des bibliothécaires de langue française*; Vol. 9, no 2 (juin 1963) p. 104-108.; ISSN: 0004-5314. [1588]

Chassay, Jean-François

Bibliographie descriptive du roman montréalais. Montréal: Groupe de recherche Montréal imaginaire, Centre d'études québécoises, Département d'études françaises, Faculté des arts et des sciences, Université de Montréal, 1991. 230 p.; ISBN: 2-9802632-0-6. [1290]

Chassé, Béatrice

Bibliographie d'une thèse: le notaire Girouard, patriote et rebelle. [Québec: Université Laval, 1974]. [22] f. [7019]

Chawla, Rani J.K.

Tsunamis: a selected bibliography. Ottawa: Marine Sciences Directorate, Department of Fisheries and the Environment, 1978. 4 p. (+ 2 microfiches in pocket): ill. (Manuscript report series / Marine Sciences Directorate ; no. 51) [5131]

"Checklist of Crown Colony imprints." In: *British Columbia Historical Quarterly*; Vol. 1, no. 4 (October 1937) p. 263-271; vol. 4, no. 2 (April 1940) p. 139-141; vol. 7, no. 3 (July 1943) p. 226-227.; ISSN: 0706-7666. [0567]

Checklist of publications associated with IDRC and recorded in AGRIS, 1975-1982. Ottawa: International Development Research Centre, c1983. xi, 67 p.; ISBN: 0-88936-390-0. [6356]

Cheda, Sherrill

"Bibliography of non-sexist children's books." In: *Canadian Newsletter of Research on Women*; Vol. 2, no. 1 (February 1973) p. 43-47.; ISSN: 0319-4477. [1323]

"Women and management: a selective bibliography, 1970-73." In: *Canadian Library Journal*; Vol. 31, no. 1 (January-February 1974) p. 18-20+.; ISSN: 0008-4352. [3744]

"Women in the library profession." In: *Emergency Librarian*; Vol. 1, no. 5-6 (June-August 1974) p. 28-32.; ISSN: 0315-8888. [1604]

Cheng, Ivy; Macgregor, Robert

Professional collection. Kingston [Ont.]: Lake Ontario Regional Library System, 1979. 88 p. [1631]

Cheng, Maisy; Wright, Edgar Norman; Larter, Sylvia

Streaming in Toronto and other Ontario schools: a review of the literature. [Toronto]: Board of Education for the City of Toronto, 1980. 76 p. (Research Service / Research Department, Toronto Board of Education ; no. 157; ISSN: 0316-8786) [3563]

Cherry, M.E., et al.

Gold: selected references. Toronto: Ontario Geological Survey, 1982. v, 69 p. (Ontario Geological Survey Open file report ; 5382) [4825]

Cheung, Gretchen

A preliminary list of photocopies in the collection of Collège militaire royal, St-Jean, P.Q., 1750-1917/Liste préliminaire de photocopies dans la collection du Collège militaire royal de St-Jean, Province de Québec, 1750-1917. St-Jean, Québec: Collège militaire royal, 1970. 10 l. [1966]

Cheverie, Carol Anne

A brief history and bibliography of the Fredericton Tuesday Night Writers, 1966-1983 [microform]. Ottawa: National Library of Canada, 1986. 2 microfiches (135 frames); ISBN: 0-315-25119-0. [1225]

Chew, Anne C.; Churchill, Arthur C.

References on the Great Lakes-Saint Lawrence waterway project. 2nd ed. Washington, D.C.: G.P.O., 1940. 189 p. (Bibliographical contributions / United States Department of Agriculture Library ; no. 30) [4446]

Child, Alan H.

"The history of Canadian education: a bibliographical note." In: *Histoire sociale: Social History*; No. 8 (November 1971) p. 105-117.; ISSN: 0018-2257. [3416]

Child, Philip, et al.

"Many called, but few chosen: a roll call of 350 outstanding Canadian books." In: *Canadian Author and Bookman*; Vol. 24, no. 2 (June 1948) p. 34-42.; ISSN: 0008-2937. [0057]

Child abuse: materials available from Manitoba Education Library. [Winnipeg]: Manitoba Education, Instructional Resources, 1985. 15 p. [3270]

Children's Book Centre

Canadian multicultural books for children and young adults. Toronto: Ontario Ministry of Citizenship and Culture, 1986. 14 l. [1370]

Chilton, C.E.

Bibliography compiled for *A preliminary study on the environmental effects of various seabed exploitation schemes*. [Ottawa]: Resource Management and Conservation Branch, Department of Energy, Mines and Resources, 1976. 28 l. [5111]

Choate, Ray

North American studies: a bibliography of reference materials relevant to the study of the United States and Canada. Bundoora [Australia]: La Trobe University Library, 1972. Approx. 200 p. (Library publications / La Trobe University Library ; no. 3) [0102]

Le Choc du passé: les années trente et les sans-travail: bibliographie sélective annotée. Québec: Institut québécois de recherche sur la culture, 1986. 185 p. (Documents de recherche / Institut québécois de recherche sur la culture ; no 11; ISSN: 0823-0447); ISBN: 2-89224-082-4. [2053]

Chodyniecki, JoAnn
A bibliography on corrections, 1970-1979. Ottawa: Correctional Service of Canada, Information and Research Analysis Division, 1980. 37 l. [2212]

Chojnacki, Wladyslaw; Chojnacka, Jadwiga
"Canadian items in Polish periodical literature: a bibliography for the period 1845-1958." In: *The Polish past in Canada*, edited by Victor Turek. Toronto: Printed by Polish Alliance Press, 1960. P. 17-56. (Polish Research Institute in Canada Studies ; 3) [4134]

Choko, Marc H.
Cent ans de crise du logement à Montréal: bibliographie chronologique. Montréal: Centre de recherches et d'innovation urbaines, Université de Montréal, 1978. 27 f. [4368]

Choquette, Diane
New religious movements in the United States and Canada: a critical assessment and annotated bibliography. Westport, Conn.: Greenwood Press, 1985. xi, 235 p. (Bibliographies and indexes in religious studies ; no. 5; ISSN: 0742-6836); ISBN: 0-313-28772-7. [1559]

Chorley & Bisset Ltd
Energy conservation in schools: review of Canadian and U.S. studies, surveys, programs and publications. Ottawa: Energy, Mines and Resources Canada, Conservation and Renewable Energy Branch, 1979. 86, [146] p. (Buildings series Publication ; no. 2a) [5147]

Choudhury, A.; Dick, T.A.
Parasites of lake sturgeon, Acipenser fulvescens (Chondrostei: Acipenseridae), with special reference to the coelenterate parasite, Polypodium hydriforme, in Acipenseriform fishes: an annotated bibliography. Winnipeg: Central and Arctic Region, Department of Fisheries and Oceans, 1991. iv, 15 p. (Canadian technical report of fisheries and aquatic sciences ; no. 1772; ISSN: 0706-6457) [5558]

Chouinard, Charles; Collister, Edward A.; Tardif, Jean-François
Bibliographie sélective sur les personnes âgées. Québec: Ministère des affaires sociales, Service de l'informathèque, 1981. 63 f. (Série bibliographiques / Ministère des affaires sociales, Service de l'informathèque ; no 4; ISSN: 0713-0740) [3216]

Chrétien, Muriette; Perret, Diana-Lynn
Répertoire des documents pédagogiques produits par les professeurs de droit du Québec. Montréal: Association des professeurs de droit du Québec, 1980. 33 f. [2213]

Christensen, Ernest Martin
Annotated bibliography of the college union. Ithaca, N.Y.: Association of College Unions-International, 1967-1987. 5 vol. (College unions at work) [3668]

Christensen, John O.
Acid rain and public policy: a selective bibliography of recent references. Monticello, Ill.: Vance Bibliographies, 1991. 15 p. (Public administration series: Bibliography ; P-3072; ISSN: 0193-970X); ISBN: 0-7920-0792-1. [5287]

Christie, R.L.
Publications on the geology of the Arctic islands (District of Franklin) by the Geological Survey of Canada. Rev. ed. Ottawa: Energy, Mines and Resources Canada, 1976. iii, 37 p.: maps. (Geological Survey of Canada Paper ; 76-28; ISSN: 0068-7650) [4793]

Chronic, John; Chronic, Halka
Bibliography of theses written for advanced degrees in geology and related sciences at universities and colleges in the United States and Canada through 1957. Boulder, Colo.: Pruett Press, 1958. 1 vol. (unpaged). [6066]

"Chronologie de la littérature français de l'Ouest canadien."
Dans: *Cefco: Centre d'études franco-canadiennes de l'Ouest*; No 6 (octobre 1980) p. 5-12.; ISSN: 0226-0670. [1166]

Chung, Yong-Seung; Dann, T.F.
A literature review of ozone in the atmosphere and on interpretation of exceptionally high values of surface ozone recorded at Regina, Saskatchewan. Downsview, Ont.: Atmospheric Research Directorate, 1983. 32 l. [5191]

Chunn, Dorothy E.
Bibliography on sentencing in Canada. Ottawa: [s.n.], 1975. 13 p. [2141]

Firearms control: a select bibliography. Toronto: Centre of Criminology, University of Toronto, 1977. 34 p.; ISBN: 0-919584-36-5. [2168]

Church, Elihu Dwight
A catalogue of books relating to the discovery & early history of North and South America, forming a part of the library of E.D. Church, compiled and annotated by George Watson Cole. New York: Dodd, Mead; [Cambridge University Press], 1907. 5 vol.: facsims. [1895]

Churchill, A.V.
An annotated bibliography of reports, 1951-1970: human factors wing [Defence Research Establishment, Toronto]. Ottawa: Defence Research Board, Department of National Defence, 1970. 183 p. [3094]

Cimon, Renée
"Bibliographie de Roland Giguère." Dans: *Barre du jour*; No 11-13 (décembre 1967-mai 1968) p. 173-196.; ISSN: 0005-6057. [7013]

Cinémathèque québécoise
Index de la production cinématographique canadienne/ Index of Canadian film production. Montréal: Cinémathèque québécoise, Musée du cinéma, 1976-1977. 2 vol.; ISSN: 0702-777X. [6631]

Ciolkosz, A.; Baranowska, T.
Selected annotated bibliography on application of satellite images to thematic mapping. Waterloo, Ont.: Department of Geography, University of Waterloo, 1984. x, 176 p. (Occasional paper publication series / Department of Geography, University of Waterloo; no. 2; ISSN: 0843-7386) [5795]

Citizen's Committee on Children
Children's choices of Canadian books. Ottawa: The Committee, 1979-1991. 7 vol.; ISSN: 0844-2932. [1391]

Clague, J.J., et al.
Bibliography of marine geoscience information, Pacific regions of Canada, 1900-1976. [Ottawa]: Energy, Mines and Resources Canada, 1977. 43 p. (Geological Survey of Canada Paper ; 77-22; ISSN: 0068-7650); ISBN: 0-660-00840-8. [4797]

Clancy, Pam
Square one: an index to CLE publications, 1978-1984-. Vancouver: Continuing Legal Education Society of British Columbia, c1985-. vol.; ISSN: 0830-9639. [2364]

Clancy, Peter
Northern Canada bibliography. Kingston, Ont.: Centre for International Relations, Northern Studies Programme, Queen's University, 1978. 99 p. [0635]

Clapp, Jane

Museum publications. New York: Scarecrow Press, 1962. 2 vol. [5335]

Museum publications. New York: Scarecrow Press, 1962. 2 vol. [4536]

Clark, Andrew H.

"Contributions to geographical knowledge of Canada since 1945." In: *Geographical Review*; Vol. 40, no. 2 (April 1950) p. 285-308.; ISSN: 0016-7428. [2955]

Clark, Diane

"La recherche en mass-media au Québec." Dans: *Bulletin de l'Association canadienne des bibliothécaires de langue française*; Vol. 18, no 4 (décembre 1972) p. 233-243.; ISSN: 0004-5314. [0952]

Clark, Donald Woodforde

Koniag-Pacific Eskimo bibliography. Ottawa: National Museums of Canada, 1975. vii, 97 p. (National Museum of Man Mercury series; ISSN: 0316-1854 : Archaeological Survey of Canada paper ; no. 35; ISSN: 0317-2244) [3966]

Clark, Edith

"Niagara Falls: a partial bibliography." In: *Bulletin of Bibliography*; Vol. 3, no. 6 (July 1903) p. 85-91.; ISSN: 0276-1602. [2944]

Clark, Jane

Reference aids in Canadian history in the University of Toronto Library (Humanities and Social Sciences Division). Toronto: Reference Department, University of Toronto Library, 1972. iii, 75 p. (Reference series / University of Toronto Library ; no. 14) [1975]

Clark, Lorenne M.G.; Armstrong, Simon

A rape bibliography: with special emphasis on rape research in Canada/Bibliographie sur le viol: et plus particulièrement sur la recherche au Canada dans ce domaine. Ottawa: Solicitor General Canada, Research Division, 1979. xii, 130 p.; ISBN: 0-662-50513-1. [2191]

Clark, Robert

Keith Tedman. Don Mills, Ont.: PRO Canada, 1988. 7 p. [7327]

Clarke, Arthur H.

Annotated list and bibliography of the abyssal marine molluscs of the world. Ottawa: Department of Northern Affairs and National Resources, 1962. vi, 114 p.: col. maps (on lining papers). (National Museum of Canada Bulletin ; no. 181) [5336]

Clarke, Irwin & Company Limited

Twenty-five years of Canadian publishing: W.H. Clarke: a memorial exhibition, 1930-1955. Toronto: 1955. 28 p. [1581]

Clarke, John

"Documentary and map sources for reconstructing the history of the reserved lands in the western district of Upper Canada." In: *Canadian Cartographer*; Vol. 8, no. 2 (December 1971) p. 75-83.; ISSN: 0008-3127. [6523]

Clarke, Lynn

An annotated bibliography of selected crime prevention resource materials. Victoria, B.C.: Juvenile Crime Prevention Project, 1983. i, 34 p. [2255]

Crime prevention literature: a catalogue of selected library holdings. Victoria, B.C.: Juvenile Crime Prevention Project, 1983. ii, 113 p. [2256]

Clarke, R. McV.

The effects of effluents from metal mines on aquatic ecosystems in Canada. Winnipeg: Freshwater Institute, Research and Development Directorate, Fisheries and Marine Service, Environment Canada, 1974. v, 150 p. (Fisheries and Marine Service Technical report ; no. 488; ISSN: 0701-7626) [5087]

Clarke, Thomas E.

R & D management bibliography, 1981. 3rd ed. Vancouver, B.C.: Stargate Consultants, c1981. 314 p.; ISBN: 0-9690-711-0-8. [2669]

Clarkson, Thora K.

Miners and prospectors of Canada: a bibliography. Toronto: Thora Clarkson, 1982. vi, 80 p.; ISBN: 0-9691318-0-1. [2880]

Selections from the Canadiana collection of the Ontario Legislative Library. Toronto: Ontario Legislative Library, 1986. v, 72 p. ill. facsims.; ISBN: 0-7729-1032-4. [0154]

Clavet, Jocelyn

La critique littéraire des oeuvres canadiennes-françaises dans le journal *Le Canada*, 1940-1946 [microforme]: bibliographie descriptive et analytique. Ottawa: Bibliothèque nationale du Canada, 1987. 2 microfiches (143 images): (ii, 135 p.); ISBN: 0-315-33745-1. [1235]

Clay, D.

Bibliography: computer programs for creating a bibliography with accompanying KWIC index. Moncton, N.B.: Fisheries and Oceans Canada, 1987. iii, 37 p. (Canadian manuscript report of fisheries and aquatic sciences ; no. 1910; ISSN: 0706-6473) [1691]

Clay, D.; Kenchington, T.J.

World bibliography of the redfishes and rockfishes (Sebastinae, Scorpaenidae). Moncton, N.B.: Fisheries and Oceans Canada, 1986. iii, 303 p. (Canadian technical report of fisheries and aquatic sciences ; no. 1429; ISSN: 0706-6457) [5523]

Clément, H.L.

Inventory of Newstart documents: répertoire de documents des sociétés de relance. Ottawa: Social and Human Analysis Branch, 1972. 1 vol. (in various pagings). [3432]

Clements, William M.; Malpezzi, Frances M.

Native American folklore, 1879-1979: an annotated bibliography. Athens, Ohio: Swallow Press, c1984. xxiii, 247 p.; ISBN: 0-8040-0831-0. [4054]

Clermont, Simonne

Liste des thèses et des mémoires de l'Université de Moncton. Moncton, N.-B.: Bibliothèque Champlain, Université de Moncton, 1972. 24 f. [6115]

Cleugh, T.R.; Russell, L.R.

Fisheries and fish related publications in Yukon Territory. Vancouver: Department of Fisheries and Oceans, 1980. [55] p. (Canadian technical report of fisheries and aquatic sciences ; no. 938; ISSN: 0706-6457) [4895]

Cliche, Mireille

Informatique: bibliographie sélective. Québec: Gouvernement du Québec, Office de la langue français, Direction de la recherche et du secrétariat, 1986. 134 p.; ISBN: 2-550-16720-1. [1465]

Clifford, John Charles

Inspection: a case study and selected references. Ottawa: Law Reform Commission of Canada, c1988. xi, 108, 117, xi p. (Administrative law series / Law Reform Commission of Canada); ISBN: 0-662-56316-6. [2313]

Les régimes d'inspection: étude de cas et bibliographie sélective. Ottawa: Commission de réforme du droit du Canada, c1988. xi, 117, xi, 108 p. (Série droit administratif / Commission de réforme du droit du Canada); ISBN: 0-662-56316-6. [2314]

Cloutier, Céline; Masson, Dominique

Femmes et structures urbaines: bibliographie multidisciplinaire. Montréal: Faculté de l'aménagement, Université de Montréal, 1989. vi f., 101 p. (Notes de recherche / Faculté d'aménagement, Université de Montréal ; AME 04) [3868]

Club canadien (Montréal, Québec). Bibliothèque

Club canadien de Montréal: catalogue de la bibliothèque. Montréal: L. Perrault, 1883. 66, [1] p. [6734]

Cluff, A.W.; Cluff, P.J.

Energy conservation in hospitals: review of the Canadian and U.S. studies, programs and publications. Ottawa: Energy, Mines and Resources Canada, 1979. 198 p. (Buildings series Publication ; no. 2d) [5772]

CM: Canadian materials for schools and libraries. Ottawa: Canadian Library Association, 1980-. vol.; ISSN: 0821-1450. [1399]

Co-operative College of Canada. Publications Committee

A guide to publications on co-operatives. Saskatoon: Co-operative College of Canada, [1974]. 56 p. [2610]

Coach House Press

Tweny/20. Toronto: Coach House Press, c1985. 142 p.; ISBN: 0-88910-295-3. [1219]

Coaching Association of Canada. Sport Information Resource Centre

Body composition and exercise: an annotated bibliography/ Composition corporelle et exercise: bibliographie annotée. Ottawa: The Centre, c1982. [5] p. [1809]

Dance aerobics: an annotated bibliography/Danse aérobie: bibliographie annotée. Ottawa: The Centre, c1982. [4] p. [1810]

Exercise and pregnancy: an annotated bibliography/ Exercice et grossesse: bibliographie annotée. Ottawa: The Centre, c1982. [7] p. [1811]

Lower back care: an annotated bibliography/Soins pour les bas du dos: bibliographie annotée. Ottawa: The Centre, c1982. [4] p. [1812]

Stress and coping: an annotated bibliography/Stress et stratégies d'adaptation: bibliographie annotée. Ottawa: The Centre, c1982. [4] p. [1813]

Coad, Brian W.

A bibliography of the sticklebacks (Gasterosteidae: Osteichthyes). Ottawa: National Museum of Natural Sciences, National Museums of Canada, 1981. 142 p. (Syllogeus / National Museum of Natural Sciences ; no. 35; ISSN: 0704-576X) [5459]

Coady, L.W.; Maidment, J.M.

Publications of the Fisheries Research Branch, Northwest Atlantic Fisheries Centre, St. John's Newfoundland: 1931 to 1984. St. John's, Nfld.: Fisheries Research Branch, Department of Fisheries and Oceans, 1985. v, 159 p. (Canadian manuscript report of fisheries and aquatic sciences ; no. 1790; ISSN: 0706-6473) [4902]

Coakley, John Phillip; Brodeur, Denis; Dionne, Jean-Claude

Revue de la littérature et bibliographie des processus géologiques et des sédiments du Saint-Laurent. Burlington, Ont.: Institut national de recherche sur les eaux, 1989. 58 f.: carte. [4875]

Coakley, John Phillip; Long, B.F.N.

Étude de l'aide de traceurs du déplacement de sédiments à grain fin dans les systèmes aquatiques: étude documentaire. Burlington, Ont.: Direction générale des eaux intérieures, Institut national de recherche sur les eaux, Centre canadien des eaux intérieures, 1990. v, 29 p. (Série scientifique, Étude / Direction générale des eaux intérieures, Institut national de recherche sur les eaux, Centre canadien des eaux intérieures ; no 174); ISBN: 0-662-96274-5. [5277]

Tracing the movement of fine-grained sediment in aquatic systems: a literature review. Burlington, Ont.: Inland Waters Directorate, 1990. v, 21 p. (Scientific series / Inland Waters Directorate, National Water Research Institute, Canada Centre for Inland Waters ; no. 174); ISBN: 0-662-18040-2. [5278]

Coan, Otis W.; Lillard, Richard G.

America in fiction: an annotated list of novels that interpret aspects of life in the United States, Canada, and Mexico. Palo Alto, Calif.: Pacific Books, 1967. viii, 232 p. [1038]

Cochrane, Donald B.

Moral-values education in Canada: a bibliography and directory, 1970-1977. Toronto: Publication Division, Ontario Institute for Studies in Education, 1978. 13 p. [3536]

Cockburn, Ilze

The open school: an annotated bibliography. Rev. ed. [Toronto]: Library, Reference & Information Services, Ontario Institute for Studies in Education, 1973. viii, 34 p. (Current bibliography / Ontario Institute for Studies in Education ; no. 4) [3453]

Codignola, Luca

Guide des documents relatifs à l'Amérique du Nord française et anglaise dans les archives de la Sacrée Congrégation de la Propagande à Rome, 1622-1799. Ottawa: Archives nationales du Canada, c1991. xi, 252 p.; ISBN: 0-660-93101-X. [1574]

Guide to documents relating to French and British North America in the archives of the Sacred Congregation "de Propaganda Fide" in Rome, 1622-1799. Ottawa: National Archives of Canada, c1991. xiii, 250 p.; ISBN: 0-660-13758-5. [1575]

"The view from the other side of the Atlantic." In: *International Journal of Canadian Studies*; No. 1-2 (Spring-Fall 1990) p. 217-258.; ISSN: 1180-3991. [0168]

Cohen, Sanford F.

Pollution from land use activities in the Great Lakes basin: a selected bibliography. Monticello, Ill.: Vance Bibliographies, 1980. 10 p. (Public administration series: Bibliography ; P-577; ISSN: 0193-970X) [5161]

Cohen, Yolande; Boucher, Andrée

Les thèses universitaires québécoises sur les femmes, 1921-1981. 2e éd. rev., corr. et augm. Québec: Institut québécois de recherche sur la culture, 1983. 121 p. (Instruments de travail / Institut québécois de recherche sur la culture ; no 7; ISSN: 0714-5608); ISBN: 2-89224-016-6. [6166]

Colbert, François; Turgeon, Normand

La commandite dans le domaine des arts et de la culture: bibliographie. Montréal: Chaire de gestion des arts, École des hautes études commerciales de Montréal, 1992. 152 p. (Cahiers de la Chaire de gestion des arts / École des hautes études commerciales de Montréal ; GA92-01; ISSN: 0847-5148) [0729]

Cole, Arthur Harrison

Finding-list of royal commission reports in the British Dominions. Cambridge, Mass.: Harvard University Press, 1939. 134 p. [6223]

Cole, Elizabeth B.; Mischook, Muriel

"Survey and annotated bibliography of curricula used by oral preschool programs." In: *Volta Review*; Vol. 87, no. 3 (April 1985) p. 139-154.; ISSN: 0042-8639. [3636]

Coleman, Brian

A bibliography of the social effects of nuclear power, 1945-1973. Vancouver: Policy and Long-term Planning, British Columbia Hydro and Power Authority, 1974. [6] l., 188 p. [5748]

Collectif de l'École de traducteurs et d'interprètes

Bibliographie du traducteur/Translator's bibliography. [Ottawa]: Presses de l'Université d'Ottawa, 1987. xiii, 332 p. (Cahiers de traductologie ; no 6); ISBN: 2-7603-0120-6. [1471]

Collectif Hommes et gars

Répertoire de la condition masculine. Montréal: Éditions Saint-Martin, 1988. 160 p.; ISBN: 2-89035-151-3. [3307]

College Administration Project

A catalogue of C A P publications. Edmonton: Department of Educational Administration, University of Alberta, 1973. v, 12 p. [3454]

The multi-campus: an annotated bibliography for Canadian colleges. [Edmonton: Department of Educational Administration], University of Alberta, 1972. ii, 22 p. [3433]

College Bibliocentre

Adult basic education. Don Mills, Ont.: College Bibliocentre, 1972. 2 vol. (Current awareness lists / College Bibliocentre) [3434]

Collège d'enseignement général et professionnel de Rivière-du-Loup. Centre d'étude régionale

Liste des documents disponibles au Centre d'étude régionale. Rivière-du-Loup [Québec]: Le Centre, 1983. 23 p. (Publications du Centre d'étude régionale ; no 1); ISBN: 2-920571-00-1. [0379]

Collette-Carrière, Renée

Les études de la femme à l'Université de Montréal: répertoire des mémoires et des thèses complétés de 1962 à 1983 (juin). [S.l.: s.n.], 1983. 58 p. [6167]

Collin, Wilbur; Bryce, Robert

Self-development readings for community college personnel: an annotated bibliography. Edmonton: Department of Educational Administration, Faculty of Education, University of Alberta, 1972. v, 38 p. [3435]

Collin, Wilbur; Konrad, Abram G.; Stewart, Peter

Understanding community colleges: a review of institutional research and related literature produced by community colleges in western Canada. Edmonton: Department of Educational Administration, University of Alberta, 1972. iv, 19 p. [3436]

Collins, Henry B.; Taylor, William E.

"Diamond Jenness (1889-1969)." In: *Arctic*; Vol. 23, no. 2 (June 1970) p. 71-81.; ISSN: 0004-0843. [7078]

Collins, Jim; Webb, Janis

Update of *A peat research directory for Canada*. Ottawa: National Research Council Canada, Peat Energy Program, 1985. vi, 381 p. [4842]

Collister, Edward A.

Bibliographie sélective sur le bénévolat. Québec: Ministère des affaires sociales, Service de l'informathèque, 1982. 27 p. (Série bibliographiques / Ministère des affaires sociales, Service de l'informathèque ; no 11; ISSN: 0713-0740) [3236]

Collister, Edward A.; Chouinard, Charles

Bibliographie sélective sur l'usage et l'abus des psychotropes par la population adulte. Québec: Ministère des affaires sociales, Service de l'informathèque, 1981. 25 p. (Série bibliographiques / Ministère des affaires sociales, Service de l'informathèque ; vol. 1, no 2; ISSN: 0713-0740) [3217]

Collister, Edward A.; Janik, Sophie

La personne handicapée: documentation québécoise. Drummondville: Gouvernement du Québec, Ministère des affaires sociales, Direction des communications, 1981. v, 210 p. [3218]

Colman, Mary Elizabeth

British Columbia books past and present. Victoria, B.C.: British Columbia Government Travel Bureau, 1957. 1 folder: ill., map. [0570]

Colombo, John Robert

Blackwood's books: a bibliography devoted to Algernon Blackwood. Toronto: Hounslow Press, 1981. 119 p.; ISBN: 0-88882-055-0. [6849]

Colombo, John Robert, et al.

CDN SF & F: a bibliography of Canadian science fiction and fantasy. Toronto: Hounslow Press, c1979. viii, 85 p.; ISBN: 0-88882-036-4. [1146]

Comeau, Adélard

"Bibliographie de l'Acadie." Dans: *Cahiers: Société historique acadienne*; Vol. 11, no 4 (décembre 1980) p. 367-382.; ISSN: 0049-1098. [0244]

Comeau, Robert; Lévesque, Michel

Le Parti québécois: bibliographie rétrospective. Québec: Bibliothèque de l'Assemblée nationale, 1991. 132 p. (Bibliographie et documentation / Bibliothèque de l'Assemblée nationale du Québec ; 38); ISBN: 2-551-12602-9. [2542]

Partis politiques et élections provinciales au Québec: bibliographie rétrospective (1867-1991). Québec: Bibliothèque de l'Assemblée nationale, 1992. x, 391 p.; ISBN: 2-551-12997-4. [2549]

Comité fédéral-provincial sur la statistique minérale (Canada). Groupe de travail sur les publications

Répertoire des publications sur la statistique minérale: publications et enquêtes fédérales et provinciales au Canada. Ottawa: Ministère de l'énergie, des mines et des ressources Canada, 1985. v, 47, v, 41 p.; ISBN: 0-662-53978-8. [6369]

Le commerce de détail et de gros au Canada: sources d'information. [Ottawa]: Division des services de distribution, Industrie, sciences et technologie Canada, 1990. 40 p.; ISBN: 0-662-95998-1. [2764]

Commercialization of amateur sport: a specialized bibliography from the SPORT database/Commercialisation du sport amateur: une bibliographie spécialisée de la base de données SPORT. Gloucester, Ont.: Sport Information Resource Centre, 1990. 12 l. (SportBiblio ; no. 4; ISSN: 1180-5269) [1854]

Commission canadienne des droits de la personne

Publications de la Commission canadienne des droits de la personne. [Ottawa]: Commission canadienne des droits de la personne, 1982-. vol. [2365]

Commission de réforme du droit du Canada

La crainte du châtiment: la dissuasion. Ottawa: Commission de réforme du droit du Canada, c1976. vii, 160 p. [2148]

Commission des écoles catholiques de Montréal. Bureau des bibliothèques scolaires
Jeunes, voulez-vous des livres? ... 4000 suggestions pour tous les âges, pour tout les goûts. 2e éd. Montréal: Bureau des bibliothèques scolaires, Services des études, Commission des écoles catholiques de Montréal, 1960. 318 p. [1313]

Commission scolaire régionale de Chambly. Direction des services de recherche et de planification
Bilan des recherches, Direction des services de recherche et de planification, 1972-1976. [Saint-Lambert, Québec: Commission scolaire régionale de Chambly, Direction des services de recherche et de planification, 1976]. [73] f.: ill., carte. [3513]

Communauté urbaine de Québec (Québec)
Répertoire des documents produits dans le cadre de l'élaboration du schéma d'aménagement. Québec: La Communauté, [1985]. 86 p.; ISBN: 2-89216-007-3. [6370]

Communication-jeunesse (Montréal, Québec)
Auteurs canadiens pour la jeunesse. Montréal: Communication-jeunesse, 1972-1975. 3 vol. [1325]
Littérature pour la jeunesse: publications québécoises 1989. Montréal: Communication-jeunesse, 1990. 58 p.; ISBN: 2-92045-304-1. [1386]

Communication-Québec. Centre de documentation
Répertoire bibliographique de la documentation dans l'Outaouais. Hull: Communication-Québec, 1972. 9 t. en 1 vol. [0316]

Communication Québec. Région de l'île de Montréal
Répertoire des médias ethniques de la région de Montréal. 5e éd. Montréal: Communication-Québec, île-de-Montréal, 1988. 83 f.; ISBN: 2-550-19251-6. [4250]

Community living and intellectual disability in Canada, 1980-1992: an annotated bibliography. North York, Ont.: Roeher Institute, 1993. vii, 278 p.; ISBN: 1-895070-39-2. [3365]

Complete catalogue of blue books relating to Canada and the Arctic regions from the earliest times to 1892. [S.l.: s.n., 1892]. 58 l. [0020]

Complete list of Canadian copyright musical compositions, entered from 1868 to January 19th, 1889, compiled from the official register at Ottawa. [Toronto: s.n., 1889]. [32] p. [0807]

Composers, Authors and Publishers Association of Canada
CAPAC presents 3000 all-time song hits, 1892-1963. Toronto: The Association, [1964]. 101 p. [0818]

Con, Ronald J.
"University research on Chinese-Canadians." In: Canadian Ethnic Studies; Vol. 1, no. 1 (1969) p. 1-2.; ISSN: 0008-3496. [6097]

Concordia University
Concordia University thesis directory. Montreal: Concordia University, 1979-1983. 2 vol.; ISBN: 0-88947-0006 (vol. 1); 0-88947-008-1 (vol. 2). [6168]

Condemine, Odette; Wyczynski, Paul
Octave Crémazie, 1827-1879: Émile Nelligan: 1879-1941. Ottawa: National Library of Canada, 1979. 97, 107 p.: ports.; ISBN: 0-662-50530-1. [6923]

Condon, Ann
An informal annotated bibliography of materials related to native land claims: with editorial comment from the files and library of Inuit Tapirisat of Canada. [Ottawa]: Department of Indian and Northern Affairs, [1977]. 1 vol. (in various pagings). [3987]

Condon, Richard G.
"Arctic bibliography: a guide to current Arctic and Subarctic periodicals." In: Arctic Anthropology; Vol. 27, no. 2 (1990) p. 113-122.; ISSN: 0066-6939. [5973]

Cone, Gertrude
A selective bibliography of publications on the Champlain Valley. [Plattsburgh, N.Y.: c1959]. viii, 144 p. [0290]

Confederation College. Native Programs Department
The native learner and distance education: annotated bibliography. Thunder Bay, Ont.: Confederation College, Native Programs Department, 1988. 43 l. [3682]

Conine, Tali A.
The parent who is disabled: a selected annotated bibliography on childbearing and childcaring with a physical or sensory disability. Vancouver: School of Rehabilitation Medicine, University of British Columbia, 1989. ii, 30 p.; ISBN: 0-88865-509-6. [3321]

Connatty, Brad
A bibliography of sustainable economic development literature available from the University of Calgary's MacKimmie Library. Calgary: Arctic Institute of North America, 1988. 55 p. [2742]

Connections: writers and the land. Winnipeg: Manitoba School Library Audio-Visual Association, 1974. viii, 136 p.: ill. [1083]

Connections two: writers and the land. Winnipeg: Manitoba School Library Audio-Visual Association, 1983. 123 p.; ISBN: 0-920082-009. [1201]

Connelly, M. Patricia
Women in the Canadian economy: an annotated selected bibliography. Toronto: Ontario Institute for Studies in Education, 1974. 24 l. [3745]

Connor, Cynthia
Women with disabilities: documentation review and annotated bibliography. Ottawa: Disabled Persons Participation Program, Department of the Secretary of State, 1991. 154, 15 p. [3889]

Connor, Sylvia
"Books of our northern North." In: British Columbia Library Quarterly; Vol. 34, no. 2-3 (October 1970-January 1971) p. 22-24.; ISSN: 0007-053X. [0622]

Conolly, L.W.; Wearing, J.P.
"Nineteenth-century theatre research: a bibliography." In: Nineteenth Century Theatre Research; Vol. 1, no. 2 (Autumn 1973)-vol. 5, no. 2 (Autumn 1977) [0964]

Conrad, Glenn R.; Brasseaux, Carl A.
A selected bibliography of scholarly literature on colonial Louisiana and New France. Lafayette: Center for Louisiana Studies, University of Southwestern Louisiana, c1982. 138 p.; ISBN: 0-940984-06-7. [2019]

Conseil canadien des ministres des ressources
Bibliographie juridique des eaux canadiennes: revue de la doctrine et de la jurisprudence/Legal bibliography on Canadian waters: review of publications and decisions of the courts. [Montréal]: Le Secrétariat, Conseil canadien des ministres des ressources, 1968. xiii, 359 p. [2112]

Conseil de la radiodiffusion et des télécommunications canadiennes
Bibliographie des études du C.R.T.C. [Ottawa]: Conseil de la radiodiffusion et des télécommunications canadiennes, 1982. vi, 77, 75 p.; ISBN: 0-662-52054-8. [0974]

Conseil économique du Canada
Catalogue des publications [Conseil économique du Canada]. Ottawa: Conseil économique du Canada, 1981-1992. 10 vol.; ISSN: 0828-4350. [6411]

CONSER Microfiche [microform]. Ottawa: National Library of Canada, 1979-.. microfiches; ISSN: 0707-3747. [5987]

Contandriopoulos, André-Pierre
"L'activité professionnelle des femmes médecins au Québec: bibliographie/[Professional activity of female physicians in Québec: bibliography]." Dans: *Bulletin: Corporation professionnelle des médecins du Québec*; Vol. 16, no 1 (janvier 1976) p. 42-43. [3763]

Contant, André
Supervision et évaluation du personnel enseignant: bibliographie annotée. Montréal: Centre d'animation, de développement et de recherche en éducation, 1973. iii, 32 f. [3455]

Conzen, Michael P.; Rumney, Thomas A.; Wynn, Graeme
A scholar's guide to geographical writing on the American and Canadian past. Chicago: University of Chicago Press, 1993. xiii, 741 p.: ill., maps.; ISBN: 0-226-11569-0. [3074]

Cook, D.E.
"Alice Munro: a checklist (to December 31, 1974)." In: *Journal of Canadian Fiction*; No. 16 (1976) p. 131-136.; ISSN: 0047-2255. [7203]

Cook, D.F.
"A survey of hymnody in the Church of England in eastern Canada to 1909." In: *Journal of the Canadian Church Historical Society*; Vol. 8, no. 3 (September 1965) p. 36-61.; ISSN: 0008-3208. [0819]

Cooke, Alan
"A bibliographical introduction to Sir John Franklin's expeditions and the Franklin search." In: *The Franklin era in Canadian Arctic history, 1845-1859*, edited by Patricia D. Sutherland. Ottawa: National Museum of Man, National Museums of Canada, 1985. P. 12-20. (National Museum of Man Mercury series; ISSN: 0316-1854 : Archaeological survey of Canada paper ; no. 131; ISSN: 0317-2244) [2045]

Cooke, Alan; Caron, Fabien
Bibliography of the Quebec-Labrador peninsula/ Bibliographie de la péninsule du Québec-Labrador. Boston: G.K. Hall, 1968. 2 vol. (viii, 430; [4], 383 p.). [0299]

Cooke, Alan; Holland, Clive
"Bibliography [Northern exploration]." In: *The exploration of northern Canada: 500 to 1920, a chronology*. Toronto: Arctic History Press, c1978. P. 447-505.; ISBN: 0-7710-2265-4. [0636]

Cooke, Esther
Canadian women in music: a bibliography of Canadian women composers and artists in the Alfred Whitehead Memorial Library. [Sackville, N.B.: Alfred Whitehead Memorial Library, 1975]. i, 8 p. [0843]

Cooke, Owen Arnold
The Canadian military experience, 1867-1983/Bibliographie de la vie militaire au Canada, 1867-1983. 2nd ed. Ottawa: Directorate of History, Department of National Defence, 1984. xix, 329 p. (Monograph series / Department of National Defence, Directorate of History ; no. 2); ISBN: 0-660-52649-2. [2036]

Cooke, Ronald J.
Canadian publications listings: a listing of daily newspapers, trade journals, and consumer magazines. Beaconsfield, Quebec: R.J. Cooke, [1982]. 24 p. [5948]

Cooley, Dennis
"A selected checklist of Prairie poetry in English." In: *Essays on Canadian Writing*; Nos. 18/19 (Summer/Fall 1980) p. 304-319.; ISSN: 0316-0300. [1167]

Cooney, Jane; Gervino, Joan; Hendsey, Susanne
"United States and Canadian business and banking information sources." In: *Law Library Journal*; Vol. 70, no. 4 (November 1977) p. 561-569.; ISSN: 0023-9283. [2626]

Cooper, Ian; Hulchanski, John David
Canadian town planning, 1900-1930: a historical bibliography. Toronto: Centre for Urban and Community Studies, University of Toronto, 1978. 3 vol. (Bibliographic series / Centre for Urban and Community Studies, University of Toronto ; no. 7-9; ISSN: 0316-4691) [4369]

Cooper, Mary; Mori, Monica
Annotated bibliography of B.C. publications on aging: 1984-1988. Vancouver: Gerontology Research Centre, Simon Fraser at Harbour Centre, c1989. 201 p.; ISBN: 0-86491-096-7. [3322]

Cooper, P.A.
Improving durability of round timbers of some Canadian softwoods: an annotated bibliography. Vancouver: Western Forest Products Laboratory, 1974. 20 p. (Information report / Western Forest Products Laboratory ; VP-X-128; ISSN: 0045-429X) [4944]

Waterborne preservative-treated railway ties: an annotated bibliography. Vancouver: Environment Canada, Forestry Directorate, Western Forest Products Laboratory, 1976. 12 p. (Information report / Western Forest Products Laboratory ; VP-X-143; ISSN: 0045-429X) [5758]

Coppens, Patrick
Littérature québécoise contemporaine. Québec: Gouvernement du Québec, Ministère de l'éducation, Direction générale des moyens d'enseignement; La Pocatière, Québec: Société du stage en bibliothéconomie de La Pocatière, [1982]. 77 p. (Bibliothèmes / Société du stage en bibliothéconomie de La Pocatière ; no 1; ISSN: 0229-639X); ISBN: 2-89123-084-1. [1190]

Ouvrages de base en littérature québécoise. Montréal: SDM, 1991. 60 p. (Services documentaires Multimedia ; no 178; ISSN: 0838-3189); ISBN: 2-89054-400-9. [1291]

La poésie québécoise, 1980-1983. Montréal: Service de diffusion sélective de l'information de la Centrale des bibliothèques, 1984. 84 p. (DSI/CB ; no 55; ISSN: 0825-5024); ISBN: 2-89059-255-3. [1210]

Le roman québécois, 1980-1983. Montréal: Service de diffusion sélective de l'information de la Centrale des bibliothèques, 1985. 71 p. (DSI/CB ; no 67; ISSN: 0825-5024); ISBN: 2-89059-267-7. [1220]

Corbeil, Christine; Descarries, Francine
Femmes, féminisme et maternité: une bibliographie sélective. [Montréal]: Université du Québec à Montréal, Centre de recherche féministe [et] Département de travail social, 1989. 79 p.; ISBN: 2-921080-03-6. [3869]

Core reference for Manitoba schools, K-12: a selection guide for school libraries. Winnipeg: Manitoba Department of Education, School Library Services, 1979. 59 p. (School library guide / Manitoba Department of Education, School Library Services ; no. 3) [1632]

Corke, S.E.
A selected, annotated bibliography of Canadian housing research, 1970-79. [Toronto]: Centre for Urban and Community Studies, University of Toronto, 1980. 264 p.

(Bibliographic series / Centre for Urban and Community Studies, University of Toronto ; no. 13; ISSN: 0316-4691); ISBN: 0-7727-1249-2. [4382]

Corley, Nora T.

A bibliography of expeditions to the Canadian Arctic 1576 to 1966: with special emphasis on the classics of Canadian exploration. Ottawa: Arctic Institute of North America, 1973. [100] l. [0624]

Travel in Canada: a guide to information sources. Detroit, Mich.: Gale Research Co., 1983. xxi, 294 p. (Geography and travel information guide series ; vol. 4); ISBN: 0-8103-1493-2. [3043]

Corley, Nora T., et al.

A selected bibliography on the Peace and Athabasca rivers and the Peace-Athabasca Delta region. Montreal: Arctic Institute of North America, 1971. [30] l. [0502]

Corley, Nora T.; Coulter, K.; Anand, T.

A selected bibliography on S.W. Devon Island (Radstock Bay and Maxwell Bay areas). Montreal: Arctic Institute of North America, 1970. [50] l.: map. [0619]

Corman, Linda

Community education in Canada: an annotated bibliography. Toronto: Ontario Institute for Studies in Education, c1975. xi, 55 p. (Bibliography series / Ontario Institute for Studies in Education ; no. 2); ISBN: 0-7744-0115-X. [3501]

Declining enrolments: issues and responses: an annotated bibliography. Toronto: Ontario Institute for Studies in Education, 1979. x, 82 p. (Current bibliography / Ontario Institute for Studies in Education ; no. 11) [3550]

Cormier, François; Lacroix, Yves

"Oeuvres de Pierre Perrault." Dans: *Voix et Images*; Vol. 3, no 3 (avril 1978) p. 371-378.; ISSN: 0318-9201. [7241]

Cormier, Normand, et al.

La chanson au Québec, 1965-1975. Montréal: Bibliothèque nationale du Québec, 1975. ix, 219 p. (Bibliographies québécoises / Bibliothèque nationale du Québec, Centre bibliographique ; no 3) [0844]

Correctional Service Canada

Legal documentation for institutional libraries in Canadian corrections services. [Ottawa: Correctional Service Canada], 1978. [4], 20 l. [2181]

Cortelyou, Catherine

Urban transportation. Monticello, Ill.: Vance Bibliographies, 1990. 52 p. (Public administration series: Bibliography ; P-2886; ISSN: 0193-970X); ISBN: 0-7920-0546-5. [4507]

Cossette, Claude; Tessier, Yves

Du mot à l'image: guide de lectures pour une approche systématique de l'image fonctionnelle. Québec: Groupe de recherche sur l'image fonctionnelle, École des arts visuels, Université Laval, 1976. 50 f. [3143]

Côté, André

Sources de l'histoire du Saguenay-Lac-Saint-Jean: Tome III: guide bibliographique. [Québec]: Centre de documentation, Direction de l'Inventaire des biens culturels, 1977. 273 p.: cartes. (Direction générale du patrimoine Dossier ; no 30) [0345]

Côté, Jean

"L'institution des donnés à Sainte-Marie-Des-Hurons: bibliographie." Dans: *Revue d'histoire de l'Amérique française*; Vol. 10, no 3 (décembre 1956) p. 448-453.; ISSN: 0035-2357. [1510]

Côté, Lise

Bibliographie sur la Bibliothèque nationale du Québec. Montréal. Ministère des affaires culturelles, Bibliothèque nationale du Québec, 1976. 6, 1, 4 p. [1616]

Côté, Pauline; Kabano, John

Recueil bibliographique sur les droits de l'enfant. Rimouski, Québec: Éditions GREME, 1993. 117 p.: ill. (Monographie / Université du Québec à Rimouski, Département des sciences de l'éducation); ISBN: 2-89241-113-0. [2360]

Cotnam, Jacques

Contemporary Quebec: an analytical bibliography. [Toronto]: McClelland and Stewart, [c1973]. 112 p.; ISBN: 0-7710-2249-2. [0322]

"Essai de guide bibliographique des études canadiennes-françaises." Dans: *Enseignement secondaire*; Vol. 46, no. 5 (novembre-décembre 1967) p. 318-351. [0086]

Cotterrell, Ann

"Listings: recent articles in Canadian studies." In: *British Journal of Canadian Studies*; Vol. 2, no. 1 (June 1987)-vol. 8, no. 1 (1993) [0178]

Couillard-Després, Azarie

"Aux sources de l'histoire de l'Acadie." Dans: *Mémoires de la Société royale du Canada*; Série 3, vol. 27, section 1 (1933) p. 63-81.; ISSN: 0316-4616. [0200]

Coulombe, Johanne; Gamache, Sylvie; Provost, Michelle

Le plaisir de lire sans sexisme: répertoire des livres québécois pour la jeunesse. Québec: Gouvernement du Québec, Ministère de l'éducation, 1991. 46 p.: ill.; ISBN: 2-550-15544-0. [1392]

Council of Maritime Premiers (Canada)

Bibliography on regional cooperation/Bibliographie sur la coopération régionale. Halifax, N.S.: Council of Maritime Premiers, 1992. 5 p.; ISBN: 0-920925-08-1. [2550]

Courchene, Melanie

Training, retraining, and labour market adjustment: an annotated bibliography of selected literature. Kingston, Ont.: Industrial Relations Centre, Queen's University, 1991. 62 p. (Bibliography series / Industrial Relations Centre, Queen's University ; no. 8; ISSN: 0075-613X); ISBN: 0-88886-285-7. [2936]

Cournoyer, Luce

Bibliographie sur l'aide juridique/Bibliography on legal aid. Ottawa: Centre national d'information et de recherche sur l'aide juridique, 1981. ix, 33 p.; ISBN: 0-919513-00-X. [2228]

Courrier du livre. Québec: Brosseau, 1897-1901. 5 vol. [0030]

Courtemanche, Johanne

La recherche sur les femmes cadres au Canada: une bibliographie annotée, 1980-1990. Montréal: Le Groupe Femmes, gestion et entreprises, 1990. v, 53 p.; ISBN: 2-9801355-1-8. [3879]

Courtois, Hélène

Essai de bibliographie sélective d'ouvrages et d'articles publiés en français relatifs au droit maritime privé anglais, américain et canadien. Chicago: University of Chicago Law School, 1968. 15 p. [2113]

Courville, Serge; Labrecque, Serge

Seigneuries et fiefs du Québec: nomenclature et cartographie. Québec: CÉLAT, 1988. 202 p.: ill. (Dossier toponymiques / CÉLAT ; 18); ISBN: 2-920576-22-4. [6590]

Couse, Keith; Matonovich, Rae T.

Probation: North American literature review (1971-1981). Regina: Prairie Justice Research, University of Regina, 1982. iv, 249 p.; ISBN: 0-7731-0051-2. [2245]

Cousineau, Douglas F.
Legal sanctions and deterrence. Ottawa: Department of Justice Canada, Research and Development Directorate, Policy, Programs and Research Branch, 1988. vii, 214 p. (Research reports of the Canadian Sentencing Commission; ISSN: 0836-1797); ISBN: 0-662-15879-2. [2315]

Sanctions légales et dissuasion. Ottawa: Ministère de la justice Canada, Direction générale de la recherche et du développement, Direction de la politique, des programmes et de la recherche, 1988. viii, 235 p. (Rapports de recherche de la Commission canadienne sur la détermination de la peine; ISSN: 0836-1800); ISBN: 0-662-94682-0. [2316]

Cousineau, Eric
Comparable worth: a list of readings. Kingston, Ont.: Industrial Relations Centre, Queen's University, 1987. 109 p. (Mimeographed bibliography series / Industrial Relations Centre, Queen's University ; no. 23); ISBN: 0-88886-168-0. [2913]

Couture, A.
Impurity limits for cast copper alloys: a literature survey of tin bronze. Ottawa: Canada Centre for Mineral and Energy Technology, 1977. iii, 67 p. (CANMET Report / Canada Centre for Mineral and Energy Technology ; 76-37); ISBN: 0-660-00987-0. [5763]

Couture, Denise, et al.
Matériaux pour une sociologie appliquée à la santé et sécurité du travail: bibliographie. Montréal: Centre d'information et d'aide à la recherche, Département de sociologie, Université de Montréal, 1984. xxii, 258 p. (Les Cahiers du CIDAR / Centre d'information et d'aide à la recherche, Département de sociologie, Université de Montréal ; no 5); ISBN: 2-920770-00-4. [2889]

Couture, Murielle, et al.
Catalogue [des volumes et des publications concernant le Nord-Ouest: Abitibi-Témiscamingue]. Rouyn, Québec: Information Abitibi-Témiscamingue, 1971. 2 vol. [0310]

Couturier, Gaston; Archambault, Roger
Chansons et thèmes. Montréal: Office des communications sociales, 1972. 96 f. [0832]

Cowan, Ann S.; Corcoran, Frank
"Museum publications." In: *Communiqué: Canadian Studies*; Vol. 2, no. 4/5 (May 1976) p. 11-34, 72-92.; ISSN: 0318-1197. [0120]

Cowell, Daryl William
Earth sciences of the Hudson Bay Lowland: literature review and annotated bibliography. Burlington, Ont.: Lands Directorate, Environment Canada, 1982. xii, 309 p. (Working paper / Lands Directorate, Environment Canada ; no. 18; ISSN: 0712-4473); ISBN: 0-662-11539-2. [4826]

Cox, Carole Ann
A comprehensive bibliography on children and play. Owen Sound, Ont.: Toy Yard, Owen Sound Public Library, 1979. 46 l. [1793]

Cox, Mark; Proudfoot, Geraldine
Pittsburgh Township, 1783-1948: an annotated bibliography of history sources. Kingston, Ont.: Pittsburgh Historical Society, [1982]. iii, 99 p.: maps. [0471]

Craig, Béatrice
"Bibliographie relative aux transmissions de patrimoine en Amérique du Nord." Dans: *Histoire sociale: Social History*; Vol. 23, no. 46 (novembre 1990) p. 269-270.; ISSN: 0018-

2557. [2081]

Craig, Helen C.
Bibliography of Canadian Boy Scout materials. [Fredericton, N.B.: H.C. Craig, 1982]. [6] 57 p.; ISBN: 0-9691055-0-9. [1814]

New Brunswick newspaper directory, 1783-1988/Répertoire des journaux du Nouveau-Brunswick, 1783-1988. Fredericton: Council of Head Librarians of New Brunswick, 1989. xxiv, 254 p.; ISBN: 0-9690287-3-3. [6050]

Cram, Jennifer; Cooke, Stefan
A bibliography on northern and native education. Montreal: Hochelaga Research Institute, 1986. 159 p. [3652]

Craven, Paul; Forrest, Anne; Traves, Tom
Canadian company histories: a checklist. [Downsview, Ont.: Social Science Division, York University], 1978. 5, [75] l. [2634]

Craven, Rita
Indigenous languages of Manitoba: a select bibliography. [Winnipeg]: Elizabeth Dafoe Library, University of Manitoba, 1982. 19 l. [1454]

Craven, Scott R.
The Canada goose (Branta Canadensis): an annotated bibliography. Washington, D.C.: U.S. Department of the Interior, Fish and Wildlife Service, 1981. 66 p. (Special scientific report: wildlife ; no. 231) [5460]

Crawford, Hewlette S.; Jennings, Daniel T.
Relationships of birds and spruce budworms: literature review and annotated bibliography. Washington, D.C.: Forest Service, U.S. Department of Agriculture, 1982. 38 p. (Bibliographies and literature of agriculture ; no. 23) [5474]

Crawford, Patricia; Monk, Philip; Wood, Marianna
Architecture in Ontario: a select bibliography on architectural conservation and the history of architecture: with special relevance to the Province of Ontario: for "New Life for Old Buildings," a symposium sponsored jointly by Frontenac Historic Foundation and Ontario Heritage Foundation, Kingston, Ontario, September 9-12, 1976. Toronto: Department of Fine Arts, University of Toronto, 1976. ix, 140 p.; ISBN: 0-88365-404-0. [0749]

Crawford, William
Homosexuality in Canada: a bibliography. 2nd ed. Toronto: Canadian Gay Archives, c1984. viii, 378 columns [iv, 189] p. (Canadian Gay Archives publication ; no. 9); ISBN: 0-9690981-3-8. [3259]

Creating success with native Indian students: a bibliographic source book on instructional strategies for teachers. [Victoria]: British Columbia Ministry of Education, Indian Education Branch, c1985. 45 p. [3637]

Creelman, Gwendolyn; Cooke, Esther; King, Geraldine L.
Canadian music scores and recordings: a classified catalogue of the holdings of Mount Allison University libraries. Sackville, N.B.: Ralph Pickard Bell Library, Mount Allison University, c1976. viii, 192 p. (Publications in music / Ralph Pickard Bell Library, Mount Allison University ; no. 3); ISBN: 0-88828-000-9. [0854]

Cregier, Sharon E.
Farm animal ethology: a guide to sources. North York, Ont.: Captus University Publications, 1989. xv, 213 p.; ISBN: 0-921801-40-8. [4717]

Crewe, Donald Martin
An annotated bibliography of published materials supplemental to the high school English program in Newfoundland [microform]. Ottawa: National Library of

Canada, 1982. 3 microfiches (228 fr.). (Canadian theses on microfiche ; 53323; ISSN: 0227-3845) [3606]

Crime Writers of Canada
In cold blood: a directory of criminous books by members of the Crime Writers of Canada. Toronto: Crime Writers of Canada, 1993. 43 p.; ISBN: 0-9696825-0-6. [1300]

Criminal justice research: a selective review. Ottawa: Solicitor General Canada, Communication Division, c1981. ii, 88 p.; ISBN: 0-662-11844-8. [2229]

Crispens, Charles G.
Quails and partridges of North America: a bibliography. Seattle: University of Washington Press, 1960. xii, 125 p. (University of Washington Publications in biology ; vol. 20) [5331]

Crochetière, Jacques; Dupont, L.
"Genèse des structures d'habitat dans les seigneuries du Québec: une bibliographie sélective." Dans: *Cahiers de géographie de Québec*; Vol. 28, nos 73-74 (avril-septembre 1984) p. 317-327.; ISSN: 0007-9766. [2037]

Crombie, Jean Breakell
A list of Canadian historical novels. Montreal: McGill University Library School, 1930. iv, 10 p. (McGill University publications, series VII: Library ; no. 21) [0999]

Crombie, Jean Breakell; Webb, Margaret Alice
Bibliography of Canadiana, 1944. Montreal: Sir George Williams College, 1945. 322 l. [0054]

Crooks, Grace
Huronia: a list of books and pamphlets concerning Simcoe County and the Lake Simcoe region. Barrie, Ont.: Simcoe County Historical Association, 1971. 10 l. [0440]

Cross, Lowell M.
A bibliography of electronic music. Toronto: University of Toronto Press, 1967. ix, 126 p. [0821]

Cross-Cultural Communication Centre
Bibliography of Centre's resources on immigrant women in Canada and their countries of origin. Toronto: Cross-Cultural Communication Centre, [1978]. 17 p. [3778]

Crossley, Diane
A bibliography on local government in British Columbia. Victoria: Province of British Columbia, Ministry of Municipal Affairs, Recreation and Culture, 1989. vi, 68 p.; ISBN: 0-7718-8762-0. [4427]

Crossman, E.J.
An annotated bibliography of the muskellunge, Esox masquinongy (Osteichthyes: Salmoniformes). Toronto: Royal Ontario Museum, 1978. 131 p. (Life sciences miscellaneous publications; ISSN: 0082-5093); ISBN: 0-88854-208-9. [5420]

Crossman, E.J.; Casselman, J.M.
An annotated bibliography of the pike, Esox lucius (Osteichthyes: Salmoniformes). Toronto: Royal Ontario Museum, 1987. xix, 386 p. (Royal Ontario Museum Life Sciences miscellaneous publications; ISSN: 0082-5093); ISBN: 0-88854-331-X. [5528]

Crossman, E.J.; Lewis, G.E.
An annotated bibliography of the chain pickerel, Esox niger (Osteichthyes: Salmoniformes). Toronto: Royal Ontario Museum, c1973. 81 p. (Royal Ontario Museum Life sciences miscellaneous publications; ISSN: 0082-5093); ISBN: 0-88854-146-5. [5372]

Crowhurst, Christine Marie; Kumer, Bonnie Lee
Infant feeding: an annotated bibliography. Toronto: Nutrition Information Service, Ryerson Polytechnical

Institute, 1982. 154 p.; ISBN: 0-919351-06-9. [5645]

Crown, Elizabeth Marie
Economics of textiles and clothing: a bibliography and selected readings. Edmonton: University of Alberta, 1987. 1 vol. (in various pagings): ill. [2731]

Crowther, Roy A.; Griffing, T.C.
A literature review and bibliography of factors affecting the productivity of benthic invertebrates in running waters and the use of trophic classification in aquatic energy studies. Edmonton: Alberta Oil Sands Environmental Research Program, 1980. xvi, 216 p.: ill. (some folded, some col.), maps (some folded). [5444]

Cruger, Doris M.
A list of doctoral dissertations on Australia, covering 1933-34 through 1964-65; Canada, covering 1933-34 through 1964-65; New Zealand, covering 1933-34 through 1964-65. Ann Arbor, Mich.: Xerox, 1967. 20 p. [6086]

Crusz, Rienzi
Business, a guide to select reference sources. Waterloo, Ont.: University of Waterloo Library, 1978. 50 p. (University of Waterloo Library bibliography ; no. 1; ISSN: 0829-948X); ISBN: 0-920834-00-0. [2635]

Crysdale, Stewart; Montminy, Jean-Paul
La religion au Canada: bibliographie annotée des travaux en sciences humaines des religions (1945-1970)/Religion in Canada: annotated inventory of scientific studies of religion (1945-1970). Downsview, Ont.: York University; Québec: Presses de l'Université Laval, 1974. viii, 189 p. (Histoire et sociologie de la culture ; no 8); ISBN: 0-7746-6687-0. [1532]

Cuddy, Mary Lou; Scott, James J.
British Columbia in books: an annotated bibliography. Vancouver: J.J. Douglas, 1974. 144 p.: ill., maps.; ISBN: 0-88894-066-1. [0583]

Cukier, Golda
Canadian Jewish periodicals: a revised listing. Montreal: Collection of Jewish Canadiana, Jewish Public Library, 1978. 38 p. [5932]

Cullen, Mary K.
"Highlights of domestic building in pre-confederation Quebec and Ontario as seen through travel literature from 1763 to 1860." In: *Association for Preservation Technology Bulletin*; Vol. 13, no. 1 (1981) p. 16-34.; ISSN: 0044-9466. [0767]

Cullingworth, J.B.
A bibliography on rent control. [Toronto]: Centre for Urban and Community Studies, 1982. 11 p. (University of Toronto Centre for Urban and Community Studies Bibliographic series ; no. 14; ISSN: 0316-4691); ISBN: 0-7727-1250-6. [4393]

Culver, Stephen John
"Bibliography of North American Recent benthic foraminifera." In: *Journal of Foraminiferal Research*; Vol. 10, no. 4 (October 1980) p. 286-302.; ISSN: 0096-1191. [5445]

Cumming, Alice; Cumming, Ross
Bibliography of Bruce. Port Elgin, Ont.: Alice & Ross Cumming in co-operation with Bruce County Library, 1973. 8 l. [0446]

Cumming, Alister
"An annotated bibliography of Canadian ESL materials." In: *TESL Canada Journal*; Special Issue 2 (June 1990) p. 1-64.; ISSN: 0826-435X. [3712]

Cummins, Jim
Heritage language education: a literature review. Toronto: Ontario Ministry of Education, c1983. v, 59 p.; ISBN: 0-7743-8375-5. [3618]

Cunningham, Peter G.
Canada's changing ports scene: an annotated classified bibliography. Toronto: University of Toronto-York University Joint Program in Transportation, 1978. 92 p. (University of Toronto-York University Joint Program in Transportation Research report; no. 54; ISSN: 0316-9456) [4469]

Cunningham, Rosella
Child abuse and family-centred care. Toronto: Faculty of Nursing, University of Toronto, c1979. 20 p. (Literature review monograph / Faculty of Nursing, University of Toronto; 1) [5622]

Curat, Hervé; Menay, Lionel
Gustave Guillaume et la psycho-systématique du langage: bibliographie annotée. Québec: Presses de l'Université Laval, 1983. ix, 235 p. (Cahiers de psycholmécanique du langage); ISBN: 2-7637-7029-0. [7035]

"Current bibliography [Sedimentary geology]." In: *Maritime Sediments*; (1965-1969); ISSN: 0025-3456. [4772]

Curry, Ralph L.
"Stephen Leacock: the writer and his writings." In: *Stephen Leacock: a reappraisal*, edited by David Staines. Ottawa: University of Ottawa Press, c1986. P. 133-160. (Reappraisals: Canadian writers; 12); ISBN: 0-7766-0146-6. [7135]

Curtis, Joanna B.
Joint workplace health and safety committees and worker participation: a selected bibliography. Hamilton, Ont.: Canadian Centre for Occupational Health and Safety, 1986. 51 p.; ISBN: 0-660-12076-3. [2902]

Cusack, Carla
Bibliographie des sources fédérales de données à l'exception de Statistique Canada, 1981. Ottawa: Statistique Canada, Division de l'assistance-utilisateurs, Section de la documentation de référence, 1982. viii, 198 p.; ISBN: 0-660-90811-5. [6349]

Bibliography of federal data sources excluding Statistics Canada, 1981. Ottawa: Statistics Canada, User Services Division, Reference Products Section, 1982. viii, 189 p.; ISBN: 0-660-11045-8. [6350]

Cyr, Hermel
Relevé de sources et d'ouvrages se rapportant au Madawaska des XVIIIe et XIXe siècles. [S.l.: s.n.], 1977. 43 f. [0228]

Czaykowski, Bogdan
Polish writing in Canada: a preliminary survey. [Ottawa]: Department of the Secretary of State of Canada, Multiculturalism, 1988. 57 l.; ISBN: 0-662-16030-4. [1246]

Dafoe, Elizabeth
Canada: nation of the new world: a book list. [S.l.: s.n.], 1954. 14 l. [0063]

Dagenais, Huguette
Approches et méthodes de la recherche féministe: bibliographie multidisciplinaire. Québec: Groupe de recherche et d'échange multidisciplinaire féministes, Université Laval, 1985. 60 p. (Cahiers de recherche du GREMF / Groupe de recherche et d'échange multidisciplinaire féministes, Université Laval; no 1); ISBN: 2-89364-000-X. [3833]

Dagg, A.I.
76 terrific books about women: an annotated list. Waterloo, Ont.: Otter Press, 1980. 24 p. [3794]

Dagg, A.I.; Campbell, Craig A.
An annotated bibliography on the status and ecology of the wolverine in Canada. [S.l.: s.n., 1979]. 1 vol. (in various pagings): map. [5427]

Dahl, Edward H., et al.
La Ville de Québec, 1800-1850: un inventaire de cartes et plans. Ottawa: Musées nationaux du Canada, 1975. ix, 413 p.: ill., cartes, plans. (Musée national de l'homme Collection mercure; Division de l'histoire dossier; no. 13; ISSN: 0316-1900) [6546]

Dahms, Moshie
"Annual bibliography of Commonwealth literature, ...: Canada." In: *Journal of Commonwealth Literature*; Vol. 16, no. 2 (February 1982)-vol. 26, no. 2 (1991) [1292]

Dakin, John; Manson-Smith, Pamela
Toronto urban planning: a selected bibliography, 1788-1970. Monticello, Ill.: Council of Planning Librarians, 1974. 31 p. (Council of Planning Librarians Exchange bibliography; 670) [4332]

Dalcourt, Gabrielle
"Checklist of books by Mabel Burkholder." In: *Douglas Library Notes*; Vol. 20, no. 1-2 (Fall 1971) p. 29.; ISSN: 0012-5717. [6884]

Dale, Ronald J.
Bibliography of 19th century Ontario. [Ottawa: s.n.], 1975. 101 p.; ISBN: 0-88884-582-0. [0451]

Dalgliesh, W.A.; Marshall, R.D.
Research review: North and South America wind effects on tall buildings. Ottawa: Division of Building Research, National Research Council Canada, [1972]. [16] p.: ill. (National Research Council Canada, Division of Building Research Technical paper; no. 401) [5737]

Dalhousie University. Institute of Public Affairs. Library
Municipal reference library catalogue. Halifax, N.S.: Institute of Public Affairs, Dalhousie University, 1957-1976. 6 no.; ISSN: 0316-5027. [4359]

Dalhousie University. Library
A bibliography for examination of forms of training for scientific and technical work. Halifax: Dalhousie University Library, 1972. 69 l. (Occasional paper / Dalhousie University Library; no. 1) [1594]

Blacks in Canada: representative source materials. Halifax: Dalhousie University Library, 1970. 10 l. [4146]

The Eskimos: representative sources. Halifax: Dalhousie University Library, 1970. 17 l. (Dalhousie University Library bibliographies) [3920]

Dalke, Paul D.
Bibliography of the elk in North America. Moscow: Idaho Cooperative Wildlife Research Unit, University of Idaho, 1968. 87 p. [5348]

Dandurand, Liette
Bibliographie sur le droit d'auteur: répertoires de centres gouvernementaux de documentation et de la bibliothèque de droit de l'Université Laval. [Québec]: Ministère des Affaires culturelles, Service gouvernemental de la propriété intellectuelle, 1983. 501 p. [2257]

Dandurand, Pierre
Les grandes orientations de la recherche en sociologie de l'éducation au Québec: un bilan bibliographique. Sainte-Foy, Québec: Université Laval, Laboratoire de recherche

en administration et politique scolaires, 1990. vi, 154 p. (Cahiers du LABRAPS: Série études et documents ; 6; ISSN: 0824-0736); ISBN: 2-89326-015-2. [3713]

Daniells, Laurenda
"The Canadian scholar: Roy Daniells: vita and bibliography." In: *English Studies in Canada*; Vol. 5, no. 4 (Winter 1979) p. xii-xix.; ISSN: 0317-0802. [6933]

Daniells, Lorna M.
Studies in enterprise: a selected bibliography of American and Canadian company histories. Boston: Baker Library, Harvard University Graduate School of Business Administration, 1957. xiv, 169 p. [2566]

Danis, Jane
"Bibliography of vertebrate palaeontology in Dinosaur Provincial Park." In: *Alberta*; Vol. 1, no. 1 (1988) p. 225-234. [4601]

Danks, H.V.
Bibliography of the Arctic arthropods of the nearctic region. Ottawa: Entomological Society of Canada, 1981. 125 p.; ISBN: 0-9690829-1-6. [5461]

Danky, James P.; Hady, Maureen E.
Native American periodicals and newspapers, 1828-1982: bibliography, publishing record, and holdings. Westport, Conn.: Greenwood Press, 1984. xxxii, 532 p.: ill., 49 p. of pl.; ISBN: 0-313-23773-5. [5951]

Dansereau, Bernard
"Documentation sur le Parti Communiste du Canada." Dans: *Histoire des travailleurs québécois: Bulletin RCHTQ*; Vol. 3, no 3 (octobre-novembre 1976) p. 19-25.; ISSN: 0315-7938. [2420]
"Inventaire préliminaire des documents relatifs au mouvement communiste du Canada." Dans: *Histoire des travailleurs québécois: Bulletin RCHTQ*; Vol. 2, no 3 (octobre-novembre 1975) p. 26-34.; ISSN: 0315-7938. [2416]

Dansereau, Pierre
"Bibliographie des pubications de M. Pierre Dansereau/ Bibliography of the publications of Mr. Pierre Dansereau." Dans: *Revue canadienne de géographie*; Vol. 11, nos 2-3 (1957) p. 115-123.; ISSN: 0316-3022. [6935]
"Bibliographie des publications de Pierre Dansereau/ Bibliography of the publications of Pierre Dansereau." Dans: *Revue de géographie de Montréal*; Vol. 22, no 1 (1968) p. 65-68.; ISSN: 0035-1148. [6936]

Daoust, Lucie
Organized crime: a bibliography. Ottawa: RCMP HQ Library, 1979. ii, 201 p. [2192]

Darling, Michael
A.J.M. Smith: an annotated bibliography. Montréal: Véhicule Press, c1981. 228 p.; ISBN: 0-919890-34-2. [7314]
"Clara Thomas: a bibliography." In: *Essays on Canadian Writing*; No. 29 (Summer 1984) p. 232-239.; ISSN: 0316-0300. [7335]
Mordecai Richler: an annotated bibliography. [Downsview, Ont.: ECW Press, c1979]. P. 155-210.; ISBN: 0-920763-62-6. [7260]
"Mordecai Richler: an annotated bibliography." In: *The annotated bibliography of Canada's major authors*, Vol. 1, edited by Robert Lecker and Jack David. Downsview, Ont.: ECW Press, c1979. P. 155-210.; ISBN: 0-920802-02-8. [7261]
A variorum edition of the poems of A.J.M. Smith with a descriptive bibliography and reference guide. Toronto: York University, 1979. ix, 589 l. [7313]

Darlington, Susan
Home business information. Montreal: Info-Recherche, 1987. 14 p. [2732]

Dartmouth Regional Library
Oil: gas bibliography. Dartmouth, N.S.: Dartmouth Regional Library, 1984. 20 l. [4839]

Darton, Nelson Horatio
Catalogue and index of contributions to North American geology, 1732-1891. Washington: U.S. Government Printing Office, 1896. 1045 p. (United States Geological Survey Bulletin ; no. 127) [4728]

Dassonville, Michel
"Répertoire des thèses présentées à la faculté des lettres de l'Université Laval, 1946-1956." Dans: *Culture*; Vol. 20, no 2 (juin 1959) p. 195-222.; ISSN: 0317-2066. [6069]

Daugherty, Wayne
Bibliographie choisie et annotée sur l'histoire des Indiens des Maritimes. Ottawa: Ministère des affaires indiennes et du nord, 1984. 25 p. [4055]
Select annotated bibliography on Maritime Indian history. Ottawa: Department of Indian and Northern Affairs, 1984. 22 p. [4056]

Dave, Nand K.; Lim, T.P.
Wetlands and their role in treating acid mine drainage: a literature review. [Ottawa]: Canada Centre for Mineral and Energy Technology, Mining Research Laboratories, 1989. i, 37 p. (Mining Research Laboratory Divisional report ; MRL-107-LS) [5267]

Daveluy, Marie-Claire
"Bibliographie: Jeanne Mance, 1606-1673." Dans: *Revue d'histoire de l'Amérique française*; Vol. 8, no 2 (septembre 1954) p. 292-306; vol. 8, no 3 (décembre 1954) p. 449-455; vol. 8, no 4 (mars 1955) p. 591-606.; ISSN: 0035-2357. [7174]
"Bibliographie de la Société de Notre-Dame de Montréal (1639-1663) et de ses membres, accompagné de notes historiques et critiques." Dans: *Revue d'histoire de l'Amérique française*; (1951-1963) ; ISSN: 0035-2357. [1938]
La Société de Notre-Dame de Montréal, 1639-1663: son histoire, ses membres, son manifeste. Montréal: Fides, [c1965]. 326, 127 p.: fac-sims. (Collection Fleur de lys) [0292]

Davey, Frank
From there to here: a guide to English-Canadian literature since 1960. Erin, Ont.: Press Porcepic, 1974. 288 p.: ill.; ISBN: 0-88878-036-2. [1084]

David, Hélène
L'évaluation des tâches: bibliographie annotée des documents disponibles à l'IRAT. Montréal: Institut de recherche appliquée sur le travail, Centre de documentation, [1979]. 11 p. (Centre de documentation bibliographie / Institut de recherche appliquée sur le travail ; no. 1) [2858]

Davidson, John
A Scottish emigrant's contribution to Canada: record of publications and public lectures, 1911-1961. [Vancouver: s.n., 1961]. 1 vol. (in various pagings). [6937]

Davie, Cyril Francis
Catalogue of the text-books, reports, digests, statutes, encyclopedias and periodicals, etc., which are to be found in the library of the Attorney-General's Department and in the Law Department of the library of the Legislative Assembly of the Province of British Columbia. Victoria, B.C.: King's Printer, 1909. vi, 117 p. [2100]

Davie, Lynn; Suessmuth, Patrick; Thomas, Alan M.

A review of the literature and field validation of the competencies of industrial and organizational trainers and educators. Toronto: Ontario Ministry of Education, 1986. iv, 40 p. (Review and evaluation bulletins / Ontario Ministry of Education; vol. 6, no. 2; ISSN: 0226-7306); ISBN: 0-7729-1549-0. [3653]

Davies, G.K.

An annotated bibliography of unclassified reports issued by Defence Research Northern Laboratory, 1947-1965. Ottawa: Defence Scientific Information Service, 1969. 68 p. (Defence Scientific Information Service Report; no. B-13) [5730]

Davies, R.W.

Annotated bibliography to the freshwater leeches (Hirudinoidea) of Canada. Nanaimo, B.C.: Pacific Biological Station, Fisheries Research Board of Canada, 1972. 15 p. (Fisheries Research Board of Canada Technical report; no. 306; ISSN: 0068-7553) [5366]

Davies, Raymond Arthur

Printed Jewish Canadiana, 1685-1900: tentative checklist of books, pamphlets, pictures, magazine and newspaper articles and currency, written by or relating to the Jews of Canada. Montreal: Lillian Davies, 1955. 56 p.: ill., ports., facsims. [4127]

Davies, W.H.; Wilson, J.S.

A picture primer on the Churchill River Basin. Saskatoon: Churchill River Study, 1975. 56 p.: ill., map. (Bulletin / Churchill River study, Missinipe probe; 7) [0515]

Davis, Harry Osmond

Canadian coal geology: an annotated, toponymic bibliography of Geological Survey of Canada publications, 1845-1962. London, Ont.: University of Western Ontario, 1964. xiv, 277 p. [4762]

Davis, John F.; Howard, Susan V.

Catalogue of Canadian holdings in Birkbeck College libraries. London: Birkbeck College, Centre for Canadian Studies, 1990. 86 p. [0169]

Davis, Lynne; Heidenreich, Barbara

Aboriginal economic development: an annotated bibliography. Peterborough, Ont.: LHD, 1988. 107 p. [4097]

Davis, P.F.; Stevenson, J.H.; Suttie, I.P.

Office automation: its impact on people, processes and procedures: selected resources. London, (Ont.): Department of Secretarial and Administrative Studies, Social Science Centre, University of Western Ontario, 1982. ix, [60] p.; ISBN: 0-7714-0383-6. [2679]

Dawson, Irene J.

"The Dawson route, 1857-1883: a selected bibliography with annotations." In: *Ontario History*; Vol. 59, no. 1 (March 1967) p. 47-55.; ISSN: 0030-2953. [1950]

Dawson, K.C.A.

"A history of archaeology in northern Ontario to 1983 with bibliographic contributions." In: *Ontario Archaeology*; No. 42 (1984) p. 27-92.; ISSN: 0078-4672. [4594]

Dawson Brothers (Montreal, Quebec)

Books published by Dawson Brothers. Montreal: Dawson Brothers, [1870]. 33, 3, [26] p. [1576]

Day, Alan Edwin

Search for the Northwest Passage: an annotated bibliography. New York: Garland, 1986. xiv, 632 p. (Garland reference library of social science; vol. 186); ISBN: 0-8240-9288-0. [2054]

Day, Dwane; Forrester, C.R.

A preliminary bibliography on the trawl fishery and groundfish of the Pacific coast of North America. [Ottawa: Information Canada, 1971]. 91 p. (Fisheries Research Board of Canada Technical report; no. 246; ISSN: 0068-7553) [4889]

Day care: a guide to reading/Garde de jour: guide du lecteur.

Ottawa: National Day Care Information Centre, 1975. 168 p. [3135]

Daye, Peter Graeme

Effects of ambient pH on fish: an annotated bibliography. St. Andrews, N.B.: Government of Canada, Fisheries and Oceans, 1980. iii, 28 p. (Canadian technical report of fisheries and aquatic sciences; no. 950; ISSN: 0706-6457) [5446]

De Groot, Pieter

Cone and twig beetles (Coleoptera: Scolytidae) of the genus Conophthorus: an annotated bibliography. Sault Ste. Marie, Ont.: Forest Pest Management Institute, Canadian Forestry Service, 1986. iii, 36 p. (Forest Pest Management Institute Information report; FPM-X-76; ISSN: 0704-772X); ISBN: 0-662-14986-6. [5524]

Diptera associated with cones and seeds of North American conifers: an annotated bibliography. Sault Ste. Marie, Ont.: Forest Pest Management Institute, Canadian Forestry Service, c1986. iii, 38 p. (Forest Pest Management Institute Information report; FPM-X-69; ISSN: 0704-772X); ISBN: 0-662-14533-X. [5525]

De Haas, Patricia

A bibliography of French-Canadian reference sources: literature and language/Bibliographie des ouvrages canadiens-français de référence: littérature et langue. Edmonton: University of Alberta Library, 1977. 8 f. [1438]

De la Barre, Kenneth

Northern population bibliography-Canada/Bibliographie sur les populations nordiques canadiennes. Calgary: Arctic Institute of North America, 1978. x, 167 p. [3023]

De la Barre, Kenneth; Harvey, Denise

Northern population bibliography-Canada II/Bibliographie sur les populations nordiques canadiennes-II. Calgary: Arctic Science and Technology Information System, 1982. xv, 97 p. (ASTIS occasional publication / Arctic Science and Technology Information System; no. 5; ISSN: 0225-5170); ISBN: 2-930393-00-6. [3038]

De la Barre, Kenneth; Harvey, Denise; Legat, Allice

A bibliography on labour, employment and training in the Canadian North: some important issues/Bibliographie sur la main d'oeuvre, l'emploi et la formation dans le Nord canadien: aspects majeurs de la question. Montréal: Committee on Northern Population Research: Comité de recherche sur les populations nordiques, c1983. xv, 106 p. (ASTIS occasional publication / Arctic Science and Technology Information System; no. 8; ISSN: 0225-5170); ISBN: 2-920393-02-2. [0641]

De Laguna, Frederica

"Bibliography of Diamond Jenness." In: *American Anthropologist*; Vol. 73, no. 1 (February 1971) p. 251-254.; ISSN: 0065-6941. [7079]

De Leeuw, J.H.; Reid, L.D.

"A bibliography of STOL technology." In: *An assessment of STOL technology*. Ottawa: Canadian Transport Commission, 1970. P. 101-V-71. (UTIAS Report / University of Toronto Institute for Aerospace Studies; no. 162;

ISSN: 0082-5255) [4452]

De Leon, Lisa
Writers of Newfoundland and Labrador, twentieth century. St. John's, Nfld.: Jesperson Press, 1985. 380 p.: ill.; ISBN: 0-920502-58-X. [0259]

De March, B., et al.
A compilation of literature pertaining to the culture of aquatic invertebrates, algae and macrophytes. Winnipeg: Freshwater Institute, Fisheries and Marine Service, Environment Canada, 1975. 2 vol. (Fisheries and Marine Service Technical report ; no. 576; ISSN: 0701-7626) [5389]

De Pasillé, François B.
"Bibliographie sur foyer nourricier et placement familial." Dans: *Famille*; Vol. 10, nos 110-111 (février-mars 1974) p. 4-25.; ISSN: 0046-3191. [3124]

De Plaen, Jacqueline
"Bibliographie générale sur la probation." Dans: *Criminologie*; Vol. 12, no 2 (1979) p. 101-105.; ISSN: 0316-0041. [2193]
"Psychiatrie légale et criminalité: bibliographie sélective." Dans: *Criminologie*; Vol. 15, no 2 (1982) p. 131-134.; ISSN: 0316-0041. [2246]

De Plaen, Jacqueline; Czetwertynska, Aniela
"Aperçu bibliographique des travaux de l'Université de Montréal, 1960-1978." Dans: *Criminologie*; Vol. 10, no 2 (1977) p. 93-107.; ISSN: 0316-0041. [2169]

De Stricker, Ulla; Dysart, Jane I.
Business online: a Canadian guide. Toronto: John Wiley in association with the Canadian Institute of Chartered Accountants, c1989. xv, 335 p.; ISBN: 0-471-79676-X. [2751]

De Valk, Alphonse
History collection: Canadian Catholic Church: catalogue/ Collection d'histoire: l'église catholique canadienne: catalogue. Saskatoon: St. Thomas More College, University of Saskatchewan, 1971-1975. 4 vol.; ISSN: 0315-3371. [1537]

De Varennes, Rosario
"Panorama de la bibliographie canadienne." Dans: *Bulletin de l'Association canadienne des bibliothécaires de langue française*; Vol. 11, no 1 (mars 1965) p. 13-17.; ISSN: 0004-5314. [0079]

De Vries, John
Analytical overview of the literature on ethno-cultural community development and integration. [Ottawa]: Policy & Research, Multiculturalism & Citizenship Canada, 1988. [11], 16 l. [4251]
Coup d'oeil sur la littérature traitant du développement et de l'intégration des minorités ethnoculturelles. [Ottawa]: Politiques et recherches, Multiculturalisme et citoyenneté, 1988. 16, [11] f. [4252]
L'intégration des communautés ethnoculturelles dans la société canadienne: bibliographie sélective. [Ottawa]: Multiculturalisme et Citoyenneté Canada, 1988. 117, 118 p. [4253]
The integration of ethno-cultural communities into Canadian society: a selected bibliography. [Ottawa]: Multiculturalism and Citizenship Canada, 1988. 118, 117 p. [4254]

Deane, Marie, et al.
"Women and film: a filmography." In: *Ontario Library Review*; Vol. 59, no. 1 (March 1975) p. 44-51.; ISSN: 0030-2996. [3753]

Dechêne, Paul
Le mouvement de restructuration du travail: bibliographie sélective commentée sur les nouvelles formes d'organisa-tion du travail. Québec: Direction générale de la recherche, Ministère du travail et de la main-d'oeuvre, 1978. x, 187 p. (Études et recherches / Québec Ministère du travail et de la main d'oeuvre, Direction générale de la recherche ; 3); ISBN: 0-775-43271-7. [2844]

Dechene, Verona M.
Liste de référence de la littérature canadienne-française dans les bibliothèques manitobaines/A checklist of French-Canadian literature in Manitoba libraries. Winnipeg: University of Manitoba Libraries, 1976. 317 p. (Bibliography series / University of Manitoba Libraries ; no. 2) [1096]

Dechief, Helene A.
A bibliography of published material and theses on Canadian railways/Liste des publications et thèses sur les chemins de fer canadiens. Montréal: CN Bibliothèque/ Library, 1980. 72 p.; ISBN: 0-86503-000-6. [4478]
Trial bibliography: books and pamphlets relating to Canadian railways in libraries of Montreal. [Montreal: H.A. Dechief], 1953. viii, 118 l. [4447]

Decore, Anne Marie, et al.
Native people in the curriculum. Edmonton: Alberta Education, 1981. ii, 143 p. [4024]

DeCoste, Frederick Charles; Munro, K.M.; MacPherson, Lillian
Feminist legal literature: a selective annotated bibliography. New York: Garland Publishing, 1991. x, 499 p. (Garland reference library of social science ; vol. 671); ISBN: 0-8240-7117-4. [3890]

DeDuy, Anh
Inventaire de la R&D sur l'hydrolyse enzymatique et la fermentation des matériaux lignocellulosiques en combustibles liquides et gazeux au Canada. Québec: Direction des programmes d'énergies nouvelles, Ministère de l'énergie et des ressources, Gouvernement du Québec, 1982. viii, 58 p. [5784]

Deer, A. Brian
Bibliography of the Cree, Montagnais, and Naskapi Indians. Rupert House: Cree-Way Project, 1974. [4, 68] l. [3951]
Bibliography of the history of the James Bay people relating to the Cree people. Rupert House: Cree-Way Project, 1974. 28 l. [3952]
"Indians in Canada today: an annotated select bibliography." In: *History and Social Science Teacher*; Vol. 12, no. 1 (Fall 1976) p. 46-49.; ISSN: 0316-4969. [3975]
Selected list of bibliographies on Indians of Canada. Ottawa: Library and Information Services, National Indian Brotherhood, 1976. [3] l. [3976]
Unpublished material by Indian organizations in Canada: a list of holdings in the National Indian Brotherhood library. Ottawa: Library & Info Services, National Indian Brotherhood, 1976. 41 p. [3977]

Defence and arms control/Défense et contrôle des armements. Ottawa: CSP Publications, 1986. xvi, 266 p. (Science and society: a directory to information sources ; vol. 1); ISBN: 0-9691021-3-5. [2503]

Defoe, Deborah
Kingston: a selected bibliography. 2nd ed. Kingston, Ont.: Kingston Public Library Board, 1982. 76 p. [0472]

DeGrâce, Eloi
Inventaire des documents sur les Franco-albertains. Edmonton: Archives provinciales de l'Alberta, 1981. 10 f. [0533]

Degree and non-degree research in adult education in Canada, 1970: an inventory/La recherche académique et non-académique en éducation des adultes au Canada, 1970: un inventaire. Toronto: Ontario Institute for Studies in Education; Canadian Association for Adult Education; Montréal: Institut canadien d'éducation des adultes; Université de Montréal, Faculté des sciences de l'éducation, 1971. 151 p. [3417]

Dehem, Roger
Canadian economics. [Ottawa]: Canadian Studies Directorate, Department of the Secretary of State of Canada, c1992. 22, 24 p. (Canadian studies resource guides. Second series); ISBN: 0-662-58839-8. [2781]
L'économie du Canada. [Ottawa]: Direction des études canadiennes, Secrétariat d'État du Canada, 1992. 24, 22 p. (Guides pédagogiques des études canadiennes. Deuxième collection); ISBN: 0-662-58839-8. [2782]

Dekin, Albert A.
Arctic archaeology: a bibliography and history. New York: Garland Publishing, 1978. 279 p. (Garland reference library of science and technology ; v. 1); ISBN: 0-8240-1084-1. [4572]

Delisle, Claude E.; Roy-Arcand, Line; Bouchard, Michel A.
Effets des précipitations acides sur les divers ecosystèmes: synthèse bibliographique. Québec: CINEP École polytechnique: Fondation canadienne Donner: Environnement Canada, Service de la protection de l'environnement, 1985. x, 307 p. [5223]

Delisle, Jean
La traduction au Canada, 1534-1984/Translation in Canada, 1534-1984. [Ottawa]: Presses de l'Université d'Ottawa, 1987. 436 p.: ill., ports.; ISBN: 2-7603-0182-6. [1472]

Delisle, Jean; Albert, Lorraine
Guide bibliographique du traducteur, rédacteur et terminologue/Bibliographic guide for translators, writers and terminologists. Éd. rev., corr. et augm. Ottawa: Éditions de l'Université d'Ottawa, 1979. 207 p. (Cahiers de traductologie ; no 1); ISBN: 2-7603-4651-X. [1445]

Deller, June
Family day care internationally: an annotated bibliography. [Toronto]: Child Care Branch, c1989. i, 49 p.; ISBN: 0-7729-5339-2. [3323]

Demers, Henri
Les investissements étrangers au Canada et au Québec: essai de bibliographie. Québec: Ministère de l'industrie et du commerce, Direction générale de l'administration, Centre de documentation, 1977. 83 p. [2627]
Le St-Laurent: bibliographie économique. [Québec]: Centre de documentation, Ministère de l'industrie et du commerce, 1979. 93 p. [4472]

Demers, Pierre
"Filmographie (sommaire) de l'abbé Proulx." Dans: Cinéma Québec; Vol. 4, no 6 (1975) p. 22-31.; ISSN: 0319-4647. [7250]
"Filmographie succincte de la musique traditionnelle au Québec." Dans: Cinéma Québec; Vol. 4, no 9-10 ([1975]) p. 29.; ISSN: 0319-4647. [0845]
"Le patrimoine cinématographique du Saguenay-Lac-Saint-Jean." Dans: Focus; Vol. 1, no 2 (juin 1977) p. 28-31.; ISSN: 0705-5579. [6632]
"Portrait des journaux au Saguenay-Lac-Saint-Jean." Dans: Focus; Vol. 1, no 6 (novembre 1977) p. 30-36.; ISSN: 0705-5579. [6026]

Dempsey, Hugh A.; Moir, Lindsay
Bibliography of the Blackfoot. Metuchen, N.J.: Scarecrow Press, 1989. viii, 245 p. (Native American bibliography series ; no. 13); ISBN: 0-8108-2211-3. [4108]

Denault, Bernard
"Jeunes et religion au Québec: revue des recherches." Dans: Cahiers de pastorale scolaire; No 6 (février 1976) p. 7-22. [1540]

Dendwick, F.M., et al.
Forest research bibliography, 1968-1975; with 1976-1979 supplement compiled by F.M. Dendwick and R.M. Waldron. Edmonton: Northern Forest Research Centre, Canadian Forestry Service, 1980. x, 64, 19 p. [4970]

Denham, Robert D.
"Northrop Frye: a supplementary bibliography." In: Canadian Library Journal; Vol. 34, no. 3 (June 1977) p. 181-197.; ISSN: 0008-4352. [6994]
Northrop Frye: an annotated bibliography of primary and secondary sources. Toronto: University of Toronto Press, c1987. xviii, 449 p.; ISBN: 0-8020-2630-3. [6995]
Northrop Frye: an enumerative bibliography. Metuchen, N.J.: Scarecrow Press, 1974. vii, 142 p. (Scarecrow author bibliographies ; no. 14); ISBN: 0-8108-0693-2. [6993]

Denike, C.C.E.
A bibliography of climatology for British Columbia. Vancouver: [s.n.], 1968. vi, 70 l. [5041]

Denison, P.J.; McMahon, T.A.; Kramer, J.R.
Literature review on pollution deposition processes. Edmonton: Alberta Oil Sands Environmental Research Program, 1979. xx, 264 p.: ill., map. (Alberta Oil Sands Environmental Research Program report ; no. 50) [5148]

Dennis, Janet Lenoir
An annotated bibliography of Canadian Plains Indian legends published in book form. Edmonton: [J.L. Dennis], 1986. 52 l. [4083]

Dennison, John D.; Tunner, Alex
The impact of community colleges: bibliography. Vancouver: B.C. Research, 1972. 142 p. (in various pagings). [3437]

Denton, Vivienne
"Ethnic and multicultural materials for children's reading: bibliographical sources." In: Canadian Children's Literature; No. 49 (1988) p. 27-29.; ISSN: 0319-0080. [4255]
"Materials for the historical study of Canadian children's literature: a survey of resources." In: Canadian Children's Literature; No. 38 (1985) p. 35-50.; ISSN: 0319-0080. [1365]

Deosaran, Ramesh
Educational aspirations, what matters? A literature review. Toronto: Research Department, Toronto Board of Education, 1975. 94 p. (Research Service / Research Department, Toronto Board of Education ; no. 135; ISSN: 0316-8786) [3502]

"Département de sociologie, Université de Montréal: maîtrise et doctorat, 1955-1975." Dans: Sociologie et sociétés; Vol. 7, no 2 (novembre 1975) p. 143-152.; ISSN: 0038-030X. [6136]

Desai, R.L.
"Photodegradation of cellulosic materials: a review of the literature." In: Pulp and Paper Magazine of Canada; Vol. 69, no. 16 (August 16, 1968) p. 53-61.; ISSN: 0380-2515. [5727]

Desaulniers, Robert
Catalogue des manuscrits de Lionel Groulx (1892-1922). Outremont, Québec: Fondation Lionel-Groulx, Centre de recherche Lionel-Groulx, 1987. viii f., 396 p.; ISBN: 2-980070-3-X-2. [7031]

Desbarats Advertising Agency
The Desbarats newspaper directory. Montreal: Desbarats Advertising Agency, 1901 [1932]. [6002]

Descent, David, et al.
Classes sociales et mouvements sociaux au Québec et au Canada: essai synthèse et bibliographie. Montréal: Éditions Saint-Martin, c1989. 206 p. (Cahiers du CIDAR / Centre d'information et d'aide à la recherche, Département de sociologie, Université de Montréal ; no 9); ISBN: 2-89035-154-8. [3324]

Deschamps, Isabelle
Current trends in technology-innovation literature: a new departure for the POM area. Montreal: École des hautes études commerciales, 1989. 66 l. (Rapport de recherche / École des hautes études commerciales ; no 89-01; ISSN: 0709-986X) [5838]

Deschamps, Marcel; Tremblay, Deny
Dossier en théâtre québécois: volume 1: bibliographie. [Jonquière]: Cegep de Jonquière, c1972. xii, 230 p. [0953]

Deschênes, Gaston
Livres blancs et livres verts au Québec (1964-1984). 3e éd. Québec: Bibliothèque de l'Assemblée nationale, 1986. 52 p.; ISBN: 2-551-106592-5. [2504]
Le mouvement coopératif québécois: guide bibliographique. [Montréal]: Éditions du jour, [c1980]. xxiii, 291 p.; ISBN: 2-89044-029-X. [2659]

Deschênes, Jean-Guy
Selective annoted [sic] bibliography for the study of the Amerindians and Inuit: a guide for secondary school history and geography teachers. [Québec]: Gouvernement du Québec, Ministère de l'Éducation, 1986. 110 p.; ISBN: 2-550-08669-4. [4084]

Deschênes, Marc; Haeberlé, Viviane; Tremblay, Nicole
Radiodiffusion et État: bibliographie des documents en langue française établie à l'intention du Groupe de travail sur la politique de la radiodiffusion. Québec: Département d'information et de communication, Université Laval, 1985. iv, 129 p. [0980]

Desiree Bradley Library and Technical Services
An annotated bibliography of literature related to acid deposition in western Canada. Vancouver: Environment Canada, Atmospheric Environment Service, Scientific Services Division, 1987. 101 p. [5243]

Desjardins, Joëlle
L'Accord du lac Meech: bibliographie sélective et annotée. 3e éd. [Québec]: Division de la référence parlementaire, Bibliothèque de l'Assemblée nationale, 1990. 68 p. (Bibliographie / Bibliothèque de l'Assemblée nationale du Québec ; no 21; ISSN: 0836-9100) [2335]
Adoption internationale, 1980-1989: bibliographie sélective et annotée. Québec: Bibliothèque de l'Assemblée nationale, Division de la référence parlementaire, 1989. 12 p. (Bibliographie / Bibliothèque de l'Assemblée nationale du Québec ; no 28; ISSN: 0836-9100) [3325]
L'informatique dans les parlements: bibliographie sélective et annotée. Québec: Bibliothèque de l'Assemblée nationale, Division de la référence parlementaire, 1991. 21 p. (Bibliographie / Bibliothèque de l'Assemblée nationale du Québec ; no 42; ISSN: 0836-9100) [2543]
Les nouveaux libéralismes économiques: bibliographie sélective et annotée. Québec: Bibliothèque de l'Assemblée nationale, Division de la référence parlementaire, 1987. 48 p. (Bibliographie / Bibliothèque de l'Assemblée

nationale du Québec ; no 4; ISSN: 0836-9100) [2733]
Ombudsman: statut, rôle, pouvoirs, organisation: bibliographie Québec: Bibliothèque de l'Assemblée nationale, Division de la référence parlementaire, 1990. 48 p. (Bibliographie / Bibliothèque de l'Assemblée nationale du Québec ; no 34; ISSN: 0836-9100) [2536]
Politique industrielle: bibliographie sélective et annotée. Québec: Bibliothèque de l'Assemblée nationale, Division de la référence parlementaire, 1987. 28 p. (Bibliographie / Bibliothèque de l'Assemblée nationale du Québec ; no 7; ISSN: 0836-9100) [2734]
Privatisation des services de santé, 1985-1988: bibliographie sélective et annotée. Québec: Bibliothèque de l'Assemblée nationale, Division de la référence parlementaire, 1989. 13 p. (Bibliographie / Bibliothèque de l'Assemblée nationale du Québec ; no 20; ISSN: 0836-9100) [5686]
Réforme de la taxe foncière: bibliographie sélective. Québec: Bibliothèque de l'Assemblée nationale, Division de la référence parlementaire, 1987. 10 p. (Bibliographie / Bibliothèque de l'Assemblée nationale du Québec ; no 6; ISSN: 0836-9100) [2735]
Réforme fiscale: bibliographie sélective et annotée. Québec: Bibliothèque de l'Assemblée nationale, Division de la référence parlementaire, 1987. 39 p. (Bibliographie / Bibliothèque de l'Assemblée nationale du Québec ; no 10; ISSN: 0836-9100) [2736]
Subventions agricoles, 1980-1987: bibliographie sélective et annotée. Québec: Bibliothèque de l'Assemblée nationale, Division de la référence parlementaire, 1987. 23 p. (Bibliographie / Bibliothèque de l'Assemblée nationale du Québec ; no 13; ISSN: 0836-9100) [4710]
Le vieillissement de la population, 1980-1991. Québec: Bibliothèque de l'Assemblée nationale, Division de la référence parlementaire, 1991. 39 p. (Bibliographie / Bibliothèque de l'Assemblée nationale du Québec ; no 39; ISSN: 0836-9100) [3350]
Le whip: bibliographie sélective et annotée. Québec: Bibliothèque de l'Assemblée nationale, Division de la référence parlementaire, 1988. 11 p. (Bibliographie / Bibliothèque de l'Assemblée nationale du Québec ; no 14; ISSN: 0836-9100) [2515]

Desjardins, Marc
Bibliographie de la Gaspésie. [Québec]: Institut québécois de recherche sur la culture, 1987. 436 p.: ill., cartes. (Documents de recherche / Institut québécois de recherche sur la culture ; no 16; ISSN: 0823-0447); ISBN: 2-89224-100-6. [0398]
Bibliographie des Iles-de-la-Madeleine. [Québec]: Institut québécois de recherche sur la culture, 1987. 281 p.: carte. (Documents de recherche / Institut québécois de recherche sur la culture ; no 13; ISSN: 0823-0447); ISBN: 2-89224-089-1. [0399]

Desjardins-MacGregor, Louise
Bibliographie annotée des études portant sur le régime français. Hamilton, Ont.: Department of Geography, McMaster University, 1977. 44 p. (Discussion paper / Department of Geography, McMaster University ; no. 10) [1991]

Desjarlais, Lionel; Carrier, Maurice
Étude de l'enseignement de l'anglais, langue seconde dans les écoles franco-ontariennes. [S.l.: s.n.], 1975. vi, 335 f.: ill. [3503]

Deslongchamps, Bernard; Duchesneau, Serge; Larue, Gilles

Le domaine agricole du Québec: répertoire de cartes. Québec: Ministère de l'agriculture, Service des études économiques, [1974]. 139 p.: cartes (certaines en coul.). [6539]

Deslongchamps, Jocelyne

Répertoire de la collection entrevues des pionniers de l'Abitibi-Témiscamingue. Rouyn: Université du Québec, Centre d'études universitaires dans l'Ouest québécois, Service des bibliothèques, 1978. 85, [9] f.: ill. (Publication du Centre des archives de l'Abitibi-Témiscamingue ; no 7) [0354]

Desmarteau, Leo M.

Manpower training and retraining: a preliminary bibliography. Ottawa: Department of Manpower and Immigration, 1969. 24 l. [2802]

Desrochers, Alain; Clément, Richard

The social psychology of inter-action contact and cross-cultural communication: an annotated bibliography. Quebec: International Center for Research on Bilingualism, 1979. 261 p. (International Center for Research on Bilingualism Publication ; B-83) [4192]

Desrochers, Alain; Smythe, Padric C.; Gardner, Robert C.

The social psychology of second language acquisition and bilinguality: an annotated bibliography. London: Department of Psychology, University of Western Ontario, 1975. [150] p. (Research bulletin / Department of Psychology, University of Western Ontario ; no. 340; ISSN: 0316-4675) [3136]

Desrochers, Edmond

"Bibliographie sommaire sur la profession de bibliothécaire." Dans: *Bulletin de l'Association canadienne des bibliothécaires de langue française*; Vol. 7, no 1 (mars 1961) p. 18-25.; ISSN: 0004-5314. [1584]

Desrosiers, Danielle

Family violence: a selective bibliography/La violence familiale: une bibliographie sélective. [Ottawa]: Supreme Court of Canada, 1991. 18 l. [3351]

Desrosiers, Danielle; Lalonde, Nathalie

Women and the criminal law: a selective bibliography of Canadian material/Les femmes et le droit criminel: une bibliographie sélective d'ouvrages canadiens. Ottawa: Library, Supreme Court of Canada, 1992. 20 l. [3898]

Desrosiers, Denise; Gregory, Joel W.; Piché, Victor

La migration au Québec: synthèse et bilan bibliographique. 2e éd. [Québec]: Gouvernement du Québec, Ministère de l'immigration, 1981. 106 p. (Études et documents / Gouvernement du Québec, Ministère de l'immigration ; no 2) [3032]

Dessureault, Guy

Recherche documentaire sur les professeurs du collégial. [Québec]: Gouvernement du Québec, Ministère de l'éducation, Direction de la recherche, 1981-1985. 3 vol.; ISBN: 2-550-04718-4 (vol. 1); 2-550-06197-7 (vol. 2); 2-550-07711-3 (vol. 3). [3638]

Désy, Marguerite

Education sexuelle: bibliographie. Montréal: Association des institutions d'enseignement secondaire, 1980. ii, 71 f. [3564]

Devanney, Burris; Campbell, Sandra; Di Nardo, Domenico

"Kenneth Leslie: a preliminary bibliography." In: *Canadian Poetry*; No. 5 (Fall/Winter 1979) p. 105-116.; ISSN: 0704-5646. [7146]

Deverell, Alfred Frederick

Canadian bibliography of reading and literature instruction (English) 1760 to 1959. Montreal: Copp Clark, [c1963]. viii, 241 p. [3383]

Dew, Ian F.

Bibliography of material relating to southern Alberta published to 1970. [Lethbridge, Alta.]: University of Lethbridge, Learning Resources Centre, 1975. viii, 407 p. [0516]

A selected annotated bibliography of rural Canada/Bibliographie annotée du Canada rural. [Ottawa]: Central Mortgage and Housing Corporation, [1978]. ix, 434 p.; ISBN: 0-662-02046-4. [3168]

Dewailly, Éric

Revue de la contamination dans la chaîne aquatique arctique: présentation de la banque de données. Sainte-Foy, Québec: Service Santé et environnement, Centre hospitalier de l'Université Laval, 1990. 21, [43] p.: ill., cartes.; ISBN: 2-921304-13-9. [5279]

Dewar, D., et al.

A bibliography of the arctic species of the Gadidae, 1982. Winnipeg: Government of Canada, Department of Fisheries and Oceans, 1983. iv, 29 p. (Canadian technical report of fisheries and aquatic sciences ; no. 1141; ISSN: 0706-6457) [5481]

Deyell, Suzanne M.

Literacy: a selected bibliography. Calgary: Educational Media Team, Professional Resource Centre, Instructional Programs Department, Calgary Board of Education, 1988. 40 p. (Professional Resource Centre bibliography / Calgary Board of Education ; no. 35) [3683]

Dhand, Harry; Hunt, L.; Goshawk, L.

Louis Riel: an annotated bibliography. Saskatoon: Research Resource Centre, College of Education, University of Saskatchewan, 1972. 41 p. [7264]

Dhand, Harry; Miller, Thomas W.; Hynes, Ronald

Selected and annotated bibliography on urbanization for Project Canada West. Saskatoon: Project Canada West: Saskatchewan Teacher's Federation, 1972. iii l., 47 p. [4321]

Dhillon, Balbir Singh

Reliability and quality control: bibliography on general and specialized areas. Gloucester, Ont.: Beta Publishers, 1992. ix, 313 p.; ISBN: 1-89560-300-5. [5850]

Reliability engineering applications: bibliography on important application areas. Gloucester, Ont.: Beta Publishers, 1992. viii, 241 p.; ISBN: 1-895603-01-3. [5851]

Diamond, Sara

Women's labour history in British Columbia: a bibliography, 1930-1948. [Vancouver, B.C.]: Press Gang Publishers, [c1980]. 80 p.; ISBN: 0-88974-033-8. [2864]

Dibb, Sandra

Northern Saskatchewan bibliography. Saskatoon: Institute for Northern Studies, University of Saskatchewan, 1975. xii, 80 p. (Maudsley memoir series / Institute for Northern Studies, University of Saskatchewan ; 2) [0517]

Dick, Ernest J.

Catalogue des fonds sur la Société Radio-Canada déposés aux Archives publiques. [Ottawa]: Archives publiques Canada, c1987. viii, 141, 125, viii p.; ISBN: 0-662-54911-2. [6669]

Guide to CBC sources at the Public Archives. [Ottawa]: Public Archives Canada, c1987. viii, 125, 141, viii p.; ISBN: 0-662-54911-2. [6670]

Dick, Trevor J.O.
Economic history of Canada: a guide to information sources. Detroit. Gale Research, c1978. xiii, 174 p. (Economics information guide series ; vol. 9); ISBN: 0-8103-1292-1. [2636]

Dictionnaire des oeuvres littéraires du Québec. Montréal: Fides, 1980-. vol.: ill., fac.–sim., ports.; ISBN: 2-7621-1190-0 (série). [1301]

Dietrich, B.
"Britisch-Nordamerika, besonders Kanada [Bibliographie von 1916-1930]." In: Geographisches Jahrbuch; 45 bd. (1930) S. 261-300.; ISSN: 0072-095X. [2950]

Dietz, Hanns-Bertold
Lothar Klein. Don Mills, Ont.: PRO Canada, 1983. 11 p.: music, port. [7094]

Dill, John; Macri, Paula
Current references relating to housing and land issues in Canada. Monticello, Ill.: Council of Planning Librarians, 1975. 33 p. (Council of Planning Librarians Exchange bibliography ; 842) [4348]

Dill, L.M.
Annotated bibliography of the salmonid embryo and alevin. Vancouver, B.C.: Department of Fisheries, 1969. 190 p. [5353]

Dindial, Frances A.
"A selected bibliography of people and places." In: Abegweit Review; Vol. 4, no. 1 (Spring 1983) p. 113-125.; ISSN: 0382-4632. [0254]

Dingle, J.R.
Procédés de traitement et de conservation du maquereau: étude et bibliographie annotée. Ottawa: Services des pêches et de la mer, 1978. viii, 69 p. (Service des pêches et de la mer Publication diverse spéciale ; 30F) [4893]
Technology of mackerel fishery: bibliography and survey of literature. Ottawa: Department of the Environment, Fisheries and Marine Service, 1976. viii, 63 p.: ill. (Fisheries and Marine Service Miscellaneous special publication ; 30) [4891]

Dingman, S. Lawrence
The water balance in arctic and subarctic regions: annotated bibliography and preliminary assessment. Hanover, N.H.: Corps of Engineers, U.S. Army, Cold Regions Research and Engineering Laboratory, 1973. 134 p. (Cold Regions Research and Engineering Laboratory, Special report ; 187) [5075]

Dion, Henriette
Histoire régionale: bibliographie. Drummondville, Québec: Bibliothèque, [Collège régional Bourgchemin], Campus de Drummondville, 1975. 27 f. [0333]

Dion, Judith
Alphabétisation: répertoire 1975-1989. Ottawa: Réseau national d'action éducation femmes, [1990]. 55 p.; ISBN: 0-9693724-5-0. [3714]

Dion, Louise
"L'Est du Québec: bibliographie 1966-1971." Dans: Cahiers de géographie de Québec; Vol. 16, no 37 (avril 1972) p. 130-139.; ISSN: 0007-9766. [0317]

Dionne, André
Bibliographie de l'Ile Jésus. [Québec]: Institut québécois de recherche sur la culture, 1983. 319, [4] p.: cartes. (Documents de recherche / Institut québécois de recherche sur la culture ; no 2; ISSN: 0823-0447); ISBN: 2-89224-035-2. [0380]

Dionne, Guy
L'État et les personnes âgées, 1980-1991: bibliographie sélective et annotée. 2e éd. [Québec]: Bibliothèque de l'Assemblée nationale, Division de la référence parlementaire, 1991. 21 p. (Bibliographie / Bibliothèque de l'Assemblée nationale du Québec; no 32; ISSN: 0836-9100) [3352]
Relations entre le Québec et les États-Unis: bibliographie. Québec: Bibliothèque de l'Assemblée nationale, Division de la référence parlementaire, 1988. 5 p. (Bibliographie / Bibliothèque de l'Assemblée nationale du Québec ; no 19; ISSN: 0836-9100) [2516]

Dionne, J.L.; Robertson, George W.; Holmes, R.M.
Agricultural meteorology: a brief literature review & bibliography. [Ottawa]: Experimental Farms Service, Canada Department of Agriculture, 1956. 59 p. [4641]

Dionne, Jean-Claude
"Bibliographie annotée du glaciel: aspects morpho-sédimentologiques / An annotated bibliography of "glaciel" studies: morpho-sedimentological aspects." Dans: Revue de géographie de Montréal; Vol. 23, no 3 (1969) p. 339-349.; ISSN: 0035-1148. [5046]
Bibliographie annotée sur les aspects géologiques du glaciel / Annotated bibliography on the geological aspects of drift ice. Ste-Foy: Centre de recherches forestières des Laurentides, Ministère de l'environnement, Service canadien des forêts, 1974. 122 p. (Rapport d'information / Centre de recherches forestières des Laurentides ; LAU-X-9; ISSN: 0835-1589) [4782]
"Bibliographie des dictionnaires, lexiques et vocabulaires du domaine des sciences de la terre." Dans: Revue de géographie de Montréal; Vol. 29, no 4 (1975) p. 367-373.; ISSN: 0035-1148. [4787]
"Bibliographie du périglaciaire du Québec, 1969-1989, incluant le glaciel pour la période 1960-1989." Dans: Géographie physique et quaternaire; Vol. 43, no 2 (1989) p. 233-243.; ISSN: 0705-7199. [5268]
"Bibliographie du périglaciaire du Québec/A bibliography of periglacial studies in Quebec." Dans: Revue de géographie de Montréal; Vol. 22, no 2 (1968) p. 175-180.; ISSN: 0035-1148. [5042]

Dionne, Narcisse-Eutrope
"Cartographie de la Nouvelle-France au XVIe siècle." Dans: La Nouvelle-France de Cartier à Champlain, 1540-1603. Québec: Darveau, 1891. P. 213-255. [6483]
Hennepin, ses voyages et ses oeuvres. Québec: R. Renault, 1897. 40 p. [1886]
Inventaire chronologique .... Québec: Société royale du Canada, 1905-1909. 4 vol. [0278]
Travaux historiques publiés depuis trente ans. Québec: Laflamme, 1909. 27 p. [1897]

Dionne, René
Bibliographie de la littérature outaouaise et franco-ontarienne. 2e éd. rev. et augm. Ottawa: Centre de recherche en civilisation canadienne-française, Université d'Ottawa, 1981. viii, 204 p. (Documents de travail du Centre de recherche en civilisation canadienne-française ; 10) [1180]
Canadian literature in French. [Ottawa]: Canadian Studies Directorate, Department of the Secretary of State of Canada, c1988. 31, 35 p. (Canadian studies resource guides); ISBN: 0-662-56209-7. [1247]
"Classiques de la littérature québécoise: essai de

bibliographie fondamentale." Dans: *Le Québécois et sa littérature*. Sherbrooke, Québec: Éditions Naaman; Paris: Agence de Coopération Culturelle et Technique, 1984. P. 407-424. (Collection littératures ; no 7); ISBN: 2-89040-299-1. [1211]

La littérature canadienne de langue française. [Ottawa]: Direction des études canadiennes, Secrétariat d'État du Canada, c1988. 35, 31 p. (Guides pédagogiques des études canadiennes); ISBN: 0-662-56209-7. [1248]

Répertoire des professeurs et chercheurs: littérature québécoise et canadienne française. 2e éd. Sherbrooke, Qué.: Éditions Naaman, 1980. 120 p.; ISBN: 2-89040-146-4. [1168]

"Le roman du XIXe siècle (1837-1895)." Dans: *Revue de l'Université d'Ottawa*; Vol. 49, nos 1-2 (janvier-avril 1979) p. 30-45.; ISSN: 0041-9206. [1147]

Dionne, René; Cantin, Pierre

"Bibliographie de la critique." Dans: *Revue d'histoire littéraire du Québec et du Canada français*; No 1 (1979)-no 14 (été-automne 1987) [1236]

Bibliographie de la critique de la littérature québécoise et canadienne-française dans les revues canadiennes (1974-1978). [Ottawa]: Presses de l'Université d'Ottawa, 1988. 480 p. (Histoire littéraire du Québec et du Canada français); ISBN: 2-7603-0147-8. [1249]

Direction générale de la condition féminine de l'Ontario

L'équité d'emploi: une bibliographie commentée. Toronto: Direction générale de la condition féminine de l'Ontario, 1990. 12, 16 f. [2930]

Direction générale de la main-d'oeuvre féminine du Manitoba

Matériel pédagogique sur la prévention de la violence utilisé dans les écoles: guide national. Winnipeg: Direction générale de la main-d'oeuvre féminine du Manitoba, 1992. 63, 59 p. [3727]

Directories of Canadian libraries/Répertoires des bibliothèques canadiennes. Ottawa: National Library of Canada, 1980-. vol.; ISSN: 0825-8899. (Bibliographies / Library Documentation Centre; ISSN: 0226-4226) [1740]

Directory of Canadian reports: a guide to Canadian report literature/Répertoire des rapports canadiens: guide des publications techniques canadiennes. Vancouver: Versatile, c1976. xxviii, 683 p. [0121]

Directory of Canadian scientific and technical periodicals: a guide to currently published titles/Répertoire des périodiques scientifiques et techniques canadiens: un guide de la littérature technique actuelle. 5th ed. Ottawa: National Science Library, National Research Council of Canada, 1973. vii, 49 p. [5911]

Directory of Canadian trade directories. Rev. ed. Toronto: Ontario Department of Trade and Development, Technical Information Centre, 1971. 1 vol. (unpaged). [2591]

Directory of education studies in Canada/Annuaire d'études en éducation au Canada. Toronto: Canadian Education Association, 1969-. vol.; ISSN: 0070-5454. [3733]

Directory of faculty publications, 1975-1979. Toronto: Faculty of Management Studies, University of Toronto, [1979]. 42 p. [2646]

Directory of industry data sources, the United States of America and Canada. Cambridge, Mass.: Ballinger, c1982. 3 vol.; ISBN: 0-88410-883-X (set). [2680]

Directory of information sources in Canada/Répertoire des sources d'information au Canada. Toronto: Micromedia, 1991-. vol.; ISSN: 0843-9494. [2785]

Disabilities resources library bibliography: a Canada community development project sponsored by Participation House, Brantford. [Brantford, Ont.: The House, 1982]. iv, 138 l. [3237]

District of Parry Sound bibliography. [Parry Sound, Ont.: s.n.], 1975-1976. 63 l. [0454]

Dobbs, R.C.

Regeneration of white and Engelmann spruce: a literature review with special reference to the British Columbia interior. Ottawa: Information Canada, 1972. 77 p. [4931]

Dobrowolsky, Helen

Fort Selkirk bibliography: a listing of sources for Fort Selkirk and the Yukon field force found in Yukon Archives & elsewhere. Whitehorse: Yukon Tourism, Heritage Branch, 1988. ii, 32 p. [0657]

Dobson, W.R.; Drinnan, R.L.

Harp seals and hooded seals (Phoca groenlandica and Cystophora cristata): a guide to the scientific literature: prepared for Greenpeace Foundation of Canada. [Vancouver: Greenpeace Foundation of Canada], 1983. 2 vol. [5482]

Dockstader, Frederick J.

The American Indian in graduate studies: a bibliography of theses and dissertations. New York: Museum of the American Indian, Heye Foundation, 1973-1974. 2 vol. (Contributions from the Museum of the American Indian, Heye Foundation ; vol. 25) [6132]

Dodds, Donald G.

Annotated bibliography of Cape Breton Highlands National Park. [Ottawa]: National and Historic Parks Branch, Department of Indian Affairs and Northern Development, 1971. 128 l. [2978]

Dodds, Donald G.; Swain, Richard J.

Bibliography of Kejimkujik National Park. [Ottawa: National and Historic Parks Branch, Department of Indian Affairs and Northern Development], 1971. [98] l. [2979]

Doe, Kenneth G.; Harris, Gary W.; Wells, Peter G.

A selected bibliography on oil spill dispersants. Ottawa: Environmental Protection Service, Fisheries and Environment Canada, 1978. 98 p. (Environmental Impact Control Directorate Economic and technical review report ; EPS-3-EC-78-2); ISBN: 0-662-01573-8. [5132]

Doelle, Leslie L.

Acoustics in architectural design: an annotated bibliography on architectural acoustics. Ottawa: National Research Council Canada, Division of Building Research, 1965. 543 p. (National Research Council Canada, Division of Building Research Bibliography ; no. 29) [0735]

Doerkson, Lorna

"Women and crime: a bibliography." In: *Resources for Feminist Research*; Vol. 14, no. 4 (December/January 1985-1986) p. 60-61.; ISSN: 0707-8412. [3843]

Doiron, Jean

Bibliographie acadienne. Halifax: Fondation d'éducation des provinces maritimes, [1985]. iv, 38 p. [0260]

Dominion Observatory (Canada)

Bibliography of seismology. Ottawa: F.A. Acland, 1929-. vol.; ISSN: 0523-2988. (Publications of the Dominion Observatory Ottawa) [4882]

Dominique, Richard; Deschênes, Jean-Guy

Bibliographie thématique sur les Montagnais-Naskapi. [Québec]: Direction générale du patrimoine, Ministère des affaires culturelles, 1980. 113 p.: cartes. (Direction générale du patrimoine Dossier ; no 48); ISBN: 2-550-01493-6. [4014]

Cultures et sociétés autochtones du Québec: bibliographie critique. Québec: Institut québécois de recherche sur la culture, 1985. 221 p.: cartes. (Instruments de travail / Institut québécois de recherche sur la culture ; no 11); ISBN: 2-89224-066-2. [4073]

Dominique, Richard; Trudel, François

"Bibliographie sur les relations entre anthropologie et histoire, et sur l'ethnohistoire." Dans: *Recherches amérindiennes au Québec*; Vol. 7, nos 3-4 (1978) p. 120-122.; ISSN: 0318-4137. [4573]

Donald, Gail

Media materials: a Can. Lit. collection. Peterborough, Ont.: CANLIT, 1980. 35 p. [6642]

Donaldson, Edward M.

Bibliography of fish reproduction, 1963-1974. West Vancouver, B.C.: Research and Resource Services Directorate, Fisheries and Marine Service, Department of Fisheries and the Environment, 1977. 3 vol. (Fisheries and Marine Service Technical report ; no. 732; ISSN: 0701-7626) [5413]

Donaldson, George; Fortin, Marcel

Prison libraries: a bibliography/Bibliothèques des pénitenciers: une bibliographie. Ottawa: Solicitor General Canada, Ministry Library and Reference Centre, 1990. 14 l. [1717]

Donaldson, Helen

A descriptive bibliography of manuscripts, pamphlets and books on education in Upper Canada particularly for the years 1791 to 1841. [S.l.: s.n.], 1953. x, 166 l. [3376]

Donelan, Rita P.; Landau, Tammy

Research in criminology by staff of the Centre of Criminology, January 1980 – December 1986. Toronto: Centre of Criminology, University of Toronto, c1987. 79 p.; ISBN: 0-919584-64-0. [2290]

Donkin, Kate; Finch, Rita

Union list of atlases in Ontario universities. Toronto: Council of Ontario Universities, 1976. [14], 253 p. [6555]

Donnelly, Joseph P.

Thwaites' *Jesuit Relations*: errata and addenda. Chicago: Loyola University Press, 1967. v, 269 p. [1951]

Donnelly, Michael W.; Arthy, Iain; Oki, Diane

Canada-Japan: a selected bibliography. [Toronto]: University of Toronto-York University Joint Centre for Asia-Pacific Studies and Nakasone Programme of the Japan Foundation, [1988]. ii, 36 l.; ISBN: 0-921309-82-1. [2517]

Donneur, André

Politique étrangère canadienne: bibliographie 1972-1975. [Montréal]: Université du Québec à Montréal, Département de science politique, 1976. iii, 50 f. (Notes de recherche / Département de science politique, Université du Québec à Montréal ; no 1) [2421]

Dooling, Peter J.; Herrick, Ramona

Lakeshore and surface waters for recreational use: a bibliography with abstracts. Vancouver: Park and Forest Recreation Resources, Faculty of Forestry, University of British Columbia, 1975. 14 l. (Recreation land use review Report ; no 3) [1770]

Recreation area maintenance and rehabilitation: a bibliography with abstracts. Vancouver: Park and Forest Recreation Resources, Faculty of Forestry, University of British Columbia, 1975. 23 l. (Recreation land use review Report ; no. 1) [1771]

Wild, scenic and recreational waterways: classification and management and water quality criteria for recreational use: a bibliography with abstracts. Vancouver: Park and Forest Recreation Resources, Faculty of Forestry, University of British Columbia, 1975. 20 l. (Recreation land use review Report ; no. 2) [1772]

Dooling, Peter J.; Sheppard, Stephen

Recreation site development: a bibliography with abstracts. Vancouver: Park and Forest Recreation Resources, Faculty of Forestry, University of British Columbia, 1975. 16 l. (Recreation land use review Report ; no. 5) [1773]

Silvicultural techniques favoring visual resource management in recreation use influence zones and intensive use recreation sites: visitor reactions to timber harvesting: a bibliography with abstracts. Vancouver: Park and Forest Recreation Resources, Faculty of Forestry, University of British Columbia, 1975. 20 l. (Recreation land use review Report ; no. 6) [1774]

Site selection criteria and the principles of design for planning recreational places: campgrounds: a bibliography with abstracts. Vancouver: Park and Forest Recreation Resources, Faculty of Forestry, University of British Columbia, 1975. 16 l. (Recreation land use review Report ; no. 4) [1775]

Dorais, Louis-Jacques

"La recherche sur les Inuit du Nord québécois: bilan et perspectives." Dans: *Études Inuit Studies*; Vol. 8, no 2 (1985) p. 99-115.; ISSN: 0701-1008. [4074]

Dorge, Lionel

Introduction à l'étude des Franco-Manitobains: essai historique et bibliographique. Saint-Boniface: La Société Historique de Saint-Boniface, 1973. v, 298 p. [0507]

Dorion, Henri

"Orientation bibliographique sur la théorie des frontières interétatiques." Dans: *Cahiers de géographie de Québec*; Vol. 18, no 43 (avril 1974) p. 248-265.; ISSN: 0007-9766. [3001]

Dornbusch, Charles Emil

The Canadian army, 1855-1965: lineages – regimental histories. Cornwallville, N.Y.: Hope Farm Press, 1966. viii, 179 p. [1947]

Dorney, Lindsay

Women's studies research handbook: a guide to relevant research at the University of Waterloo. 3rd ed., rev. and enl. Waterloo, Ont.: University of Waterloo Press, c1990. 88 p.; ISBN: 0-88898-100-7. [3880]

Dorotich, Daniel

A bibliography of publications of Canadian Slavists. Vancouver: University of British Columbia, 1967. 51 [2] l. [4138]

Dossick, Jesse J.

Doctoral research on Canada and Canadians, 1884-1983/ Thèses et doctorat concernant le Canada et les canadiens, 1884-1983. Ottawa: National Library of Canada, 1986. xv, 559 p.; ISBN: 0-660-53227-1. [6181]

Dostaler, Ann

Bibliographie sur l'aide juridique pour les handicapés/ Bibliography on legal aid for the handicapped. Ottawa: Centre national d'information et de recherche sur l'aide juridique, 1981. vii, 41 p.; ISBN: 0-919513-01-8. [2230]

Doucet, René; Boily, Jocelyn

Bibliographie annotée sur le marcottage de l'épinette noire. [Québec]: Gouvernement du Québec, Ministère de l'énergie et des ressources, Direction de la recherche et du développement, 1987. x, 32 p. (Mémoire / Service de la recherche appliquée, Direction de la recherche et du développement, Ministère de l'énergie et des ressources, Gouvernement du Québec; no 90); ISBN: 2-550-17281-7. [5529]

Doucet, Ronald

Bibliographie sur "la qualité totale". Québec: Direction des communications, Ministère de l'industrie, du commerce et de la technologie, 1989. viii, 150 p.; ISBN: 2-550-19860-3. [2752]

Doughty, Arthur George; Middleton, J.E.

Bibliography of the siege of Quebec in three parts by A. Doughty and J.E. Middleton with a list of plans by R. [sic] Lee Phillips of the Library of Congress, Washington. Quebec: Dussault & Proulx, 1901. 161 p.: facsim. [1891]

Doughty, Howard

"Industrial relations and labour history." In: Communiqué: Canadian Studies; Vol. 1, no. 3 (March 1975) p. 2-22.; ISSN: 0318-1197. [2820]

Douglas, George W.; Ceska, Adolf; Ruyle, Gloria G.

A floristic bibliography for British Columbia. Victoria: Information Services Branch, British Columbia Ministry of Forests, 1983. iv, 143 p. (Land management report / British Columbia Ministry of Forests; no. 15; ISSN: 0702-9861); ISBN: 0-7719-9190-8. [5483]

Douglas College

An annotated bibliography of adult basic education materials relevant to industrial and craft workers. Victoria: British Columbia, Ministry of Education, 1981. 25 p. [3586]

A bibliography of basic materials in the health sciences with emphasis on nursing. New Westminster, B.C.: Douglas College, 1974. 109 p. [5593]

Douglas College. Division of Libraries

Child care bibliography. New Westminster, B.C.: Douglas College, 1976. 99 l. [3144]

Douglas College. Institute of Environmental Studies

The environmental crisis: a bibliography of publications available in Douglas College Library. [New Westminster, B.C.]: Douglas College Institute of Environmental Studies, 1972. 31 l. [5063]

Douglas College. Library

AV: a selective bibliography of non-print materials in the health sciences with emphasis on nursing. New Westminster, B.C.: Douglas College Library, 1975. i, 286 l. [6624]

Doumato, Lamia

Arthur C. Erickson. Monticello, Ill.: Vance Bibliographies, 1984. 11 p. (Architecture series: Bibliography; A-1244; ISSN: 0194-1356); ISBN: 0-89028-094-0. [6968]

Arthur Charles Erickson's Canadian Chancery: a bibliography. Monticello, Ill.: Vance Bibliographies, 1989. 17 p. (Architecture series: Bibliography; A-2226; ISSN: 0194-1356); ISBN: 0-7920-0276-8. [0788]

A bibliography of the writings of Alan Gowans. Monticello, Ill.: Vance Bibliographies, 1984. 13 p. (Architecture series: Bibliography; A-1280; ISSN: 0194-1356); ISBN: 0-89028-170-X. [7028]

Contemporary architecture in Canada. Monticello, Ill.: Vance Bibliographies, 1987. 9 p. (Architecture series:

Bibliography; A-1893; ISSN: 0194-1356); ISBN: 1-55590-463-7. [0783]

Doutrelepont, Jean-François

"Les ressources en éducation économique." Dans: Vie pédagogique; No 21 (novembre 1982) p. 28-32.; ISSN: 0707-2511. [3607]

Dow, Charles Mason

Anthology and bibliography of Niagara Falls. Albany: Published by the State of New York, J.B. Lyon Co., printers, 1921. 2 vol., [49] l. of pl. (1 folded): ill. (some col.), maps, port. [2948]

Dow, Ian I.; O'Reilly, Robert R.

L'enfance en difficulté: une revue de la documentation. Toronto: Ministère de l'Éducation: Ministère des Collèges et Universités, c1981. 210 p.; ISBN: 0-7743-6747-4. [3587]

Exceptional pupils: a review of the literature. Toronto: Ministry of Education: Ministry of Colleges and Universities, c1981. 81 p.; ISBN: 0-7743-6746-6. [3588]

Dow, Robena M.

"The County of Wellington: a bibliography." In: Ontario Historical Society Papers and Records; Vol. 30, (1934) p. 96-105.; ISSN: 0380-6022. [0421]

Dowler, Linda

"Two year's work in Canadian poetry studies: 1976-1977." In: Canadian Poetry; No. 2 (Spring/Summer 1978) p. 111-126.; ISSN: 0704-5646. [1128]

"The year's work in Canadian poetry studies: 1978." In: Canadian Poetry; No. 4 (Spring/Summer 1979) p. 131-142.; ISSN: 0704-5646. [1148]

Dowler, Linda; Jameson, Mary Ann

"The year's work in Canadian poetry studies: 1979." In: Canadian Poetry; No. 6 (Spring/Summer 1980) p. 89-103.; ISSN: 0704-5646. [1169]

Doyle, Veronica M.

Homesharing matchup agencies for seniors: a literature review. Burnaby, B.C.: Gerontology Research Centre, Simon Fraser University, 1989. 46 p.; ISBN: 0-8649109-5-9. [3326]

Draayer, Ingrid

Sport bibliography/Bibliographie du sport. Ottawa: Sport Information Resource Centre, 1981-1982. 8 vol.; ISBN: 0-920678-02-5 (vol. 1); 0-920678-04-1 (vol. 2); 0-920678-06-8 (vol. 3); 0-920678-08-4 (vol. 4); 0-920678-10-6 (vol. 5); 0-920678-12-2 (vol. 6); 0-920678-14-9 (vol. 7); 0-920678-16-5 (vol. 8). [1815]

Drache, Daniel; Clement, Wallace

The new practical guide to Canadian political economy. Updated and expanded ed. Toronto: J. Lorimer, 1985. xxiv, 243 p.; ISBN: 0-88862-785-8. [2709]

Drake, Everett N.

Historical atlases of Ontario: a condensed checklist. Toronto: [s.n.], 1953. [2] p. [6500]

Drake, Paul Burton

Protestantism on the Prairies to 1977: an annotated bibliography of historical and biographical publications. Edmonton: [s.n.], 1978. vii, 114 l. [1546]

Drapeau, Arnold J.

Répertoire des mémoires de maîtrise et thèses de doctorat de l'École polytechnique, 1983-1987. Montréal: École polytechnique, 1990. iv, 224 p.; ISBN: 2-553-00203-3. [6201]

Répertoire des travaux de recherche en génie de l'environnement à l'École polytechnique de Montréal, 1964-1986. Montréal: Département de génie civil, École polytechnique de Montréal, 1987. 41 p. (Rapport technique / Département de génie civil, École polytechnique de Montréal ; no EPM. RT-07/10), ISBN: 2 553 00193 2. [6189]

Draper, Anne

Bibliographie sur le formaldéhyde et la mousse isolante d'urée-formaldéhyde (MIUF)/Bibliography on formaldehyde and urea formaldehyde foam insulation (UFFI). [Ottawa]: Centre sur la MIUF, 1985. iv, 82 p. [5804]

Draper, James A.

Adult education theses, Canada. Toronto: Department of Adult Education, Ontario Institute for Studies in Education, 1981. iv, 165 p. [6158]

Writings relating to literacy: done at the Ontario Institute for Studies in Education. Toronto: OISE, 1990. xi, 31 p. [3715]

Dreijmanis, John

Canadian politics, 1950-1975: a selected research bibliography. Monticello, Ill.: Council of Planning Librarians, 1976. 16 p. (Council of Planning Librarians Exchange bibliography ; 1105) [2422]

Drennan, D.M.; Quinton, R.G.; Malhotra, S.K.

A literature survey on the application of computers to structural analysis. Halifax: Nova Scotia Technical College, 1968. 52 p. [5728]

Dresser, John A.; Denis, Théophile

La géologie de Québec/Geology of Quebec. Québec: Paradis, Imprimeur du Roi, 1941. 3 vol.: ill., cartes. [4740]

Drew, Bernard A.

Lawmen in scarlet: an annotated guide to Royal Canadian Mounted Police in print and performance. Metuchen, N.J.: Scarecrow Press, 1990. xx, 276 p.: ill.; ISBN: 0-8108-2330-6. [1281]

Drolet, Antonio

Bibliographie du roman canadien-français, 1900-1950. Québec: Presses universitaires de Laval, 1955. 125 p. [1014]

"Ouvrages scientifiques de la bibliothèque du Collège des Jésuites de Québec." Dans: *Naturaliste canadien*; Vol. 82, nos 4-5 (avril-mai 1955) p. 102-107.; ISSN: 0028-0798. [4617]

Répertoire de la bibliographie canadienne (ouvrages imprimés). [Québec]: 1962. 36 f. [0070]

Drolet, Gaëtan

Bibliographie de publications officielles relatives aux archives et à la gestion des documents. Montréal: Faculté des études supérieures, École de bibliothéconomie, 1976. ii, 15 f. [1617]

Bibliographie sur la sculpture québécoise. [Montréal]: École de bibliothéconomie, Université de Montréal, 1974. 28 f. [0678]

Les bibliothèques universitaires du Québec: essai de bibliographie. [Québec]: Conférence des recteurs et des principaux des universités du Québec, 1979. 197 p.; ISBN: 2-920079-00-X. [1633]

Drolet, Gaëtan; Labrecque, Marie France

Les femmes amérindiennes au Québec: guide annotée des sources d'information. [Québec]: Laboratoire de recherches anthropologiques, Département d'anthropologie, Université Laval, 1986. vii, 100 p. (Collection "Outils pédagogiques" / Laboratoire de recherches anthropologiques, Département d'anthropologie, Université Laval ; no 2) [4085]

Drolet, Jacques

"Bibliographie concernant les congrès annuels de la S.P.G.Q. depuis sa fondation." Dans: *Didactique-géographie*; Nouv. série, no 4 (décembre 1976) p. 130-137.; ISSN: 0318-

6555. [3014]

Drouilly, Pierre

Les élections au Québec: bibliographie. Québec: Bibliothèque de l'Assemblée nationale, 1990. 62 p. (Bibliographie et documentation / Bibliothèque de l'Assemblée nationale du Québec ; 35); ISBN: 2-551-12406-9. [2537]

Drumbolis, Nicky

In the works: back roads to next spring's Gerry Gilbert bibliography. Toronto: Letters Book Shop, 1991. [370] p.: ill.; ISBN: 0-921688-01-6. [7014]

Nelson Ball cited: a bibliophilography from stock. Toronto: Letters Book Shop, [1992]. [182] p.: ill.; ISBN: 0-921688-03-2. [6825]

Drummond, Christina S.R.

Guide to accounting pronouncements & sources: a Canadian accountant's index of authoritative accounting and auditing literature including Canadian, international and relevant US and UK pronouncements. 3rd ed. Toronto: Canadian Institute of Chartered Accountants, 1992. 188 p.; ISBN: 0-88800-284-X. [2783]

Dryden, Jean E.

Some sources for women's history at the Provincial Archives of Alberta. [Edmonton]: Alberta Culture, Historical Resources Division, [1980]. viii, 189 p.: ill. (Provincial Archives of Alberta Occasional paper ; no. 2) [3795]

Voices of Alberta: a survey of oral history completed in Alberta up to 1980. Edmonton: Alberta Culture, Historical Resources Division, 1981. vi, 430 p. [6646]

Du Berger, Jean

Bibliographie du théâtre québécois de 1935 à nos jours. Québec: Université Laval, Département d'études canadiennes, 1970. 18 f. [0950]

"Bibliographie du théâtre québécois de 1935 à nos jours." Dans: *Nord*; Nos 4-5 (automne-hiver 1973) p. 207-228.; ISSN: 0315-3789. [1075]

Dubé, Carl

Annotated bibliography on culture, tourism and multiculturalism. [Ottawa: Department of Communications], 1988. 23, 25 p. [1847]

Bibliographie commentée sur la culture, le tourisme et le multiculturalisme. [Ottawa: Ministère des communications], 1988. 25, 23 p. [1848]

Dubé, Viateur, et al.

Bibliographie sur la préhistoire de la psychiatrie canadienne au dix-neuvième siècle. [Trois-Rivières, Québec]: Université du Québec à Trois-Rivières, Département de philosophie, 1976. xii, 117, 5 f. [5607]

Dublin Public Libraries

Dublin Public Libraries and the Canadian Embassy present an exhibition of Canadian books: Monday 15th-Wednesday 31st July 1991, Central Library, ILAC Centre. Dublin: The Central Library, 1991. 21 l. [0175]

Dubois, Bernard

Choix bibliographique sur la bande dessinée: ouvrages généraux, québécois, thèses. Sillery, Québec: B. Dubois, 1985. 32 f. [5954]

Dubois, J.M.M.

Vingt-cinq ans de géographie à l'Université de Sherbrooke, 1957-1982. Sherbrooke, Québec: Département de géographie, Université de Sherbrooke, 1983. 3 vol. (Bulletin de recherche / Université de Sherbrooke, Département de géographie ; no 65, 67/68, 76; ISSN: 0710-0868) [3044]

Dubois, J.M.M.; Dubois, Lise

Bibliographie sur les caractéristiques physiques des Cantons de l'Est, Province de Québec, Canada/Bibliography on the physical characteristics of the Eastern Townships of Quebec, Canada. Sherbrooke, Québec: Laboratoire de géographie physique, Département de géographie, Université de Sherbrooke, 1972. 74 f. (Bulletin de recherche / Université de Sherbrooke, Département de géographie ; no 3; ISSN: 0710-0868) [4776]

Dubois, Monique

Répertoire de chansons folkloriques. [Québec]: Gouvernement du Québec, Ministère de l'éducation, 1981. 65 p. (Document d'information / Gouvernement du Québec, Ministère de l'éducation ; 16-3505-03); ISBN: 2-550-04851-2. [0894]

Dubreuil, Lorraine

Canada's militia and Defence maps, 1905-1931. Ottawa: Association of Canadian Map Libraries and Archives, 1992. vi, 44 p.: ill., maps.; ISBN: 0-9695062-3-6. [6600]

Early Canadian topographical map series: the Geological Survey of Canada, 1842-1949. Ottawa: Association of Canadian Map Libraries and Archives, 1988. vi, 71 p.: maps. (Occasional papers of the Association of Canadian Map Libraries and Archives ; no. 1); ISBN: 0-9690682-8-X. [6591]

List of atlases in the University Map Collection. Montreal: McGill University, University Map Collection, [1975]. vii, 45 p. (Publication / University Map Collection, McGill University ; no. 1) [6547]

Sectional maps of western Canada, 1871-1955: an early Canadian topographic map series. Ottawa: Association of Canadian Map Libraries and Archives, 1989. vi, 57 p.: ill. (Occasional papers / Association of Canadian Map Libraries and Archives ; no. 2); ISBN: 0-969-0682-9-8. [6593]

Standard topographical maps of Canada, 1904-1948. Ottawa: Association of Canadian Map Libraries and Archives, 1991. vi, 31 p.: maps. (Occasional papers of the Association of Canadian Map Libraries and Archives ; no. 3); ISBN: 0-9695062-0-1. [6597]

Dubuc, J.-H.

Bibliographie des monographies paroissiales du diocèse de Sherbrooke. [Montréal: s.n., 1939]. 11 l. [0284]

Ducasse, Russell

Le mode de scrutin au Québec: synthèse, chronologie, vocabulaire et bibliographie, 1970-1982. Québec: Bibliothèque de l'Assemblée nationale, 1983. 85 p. (Bibliographie et documentation / Bibliothèque de l'Assemblée nationale du Québec ; 12); ISBN: 2-551-05364-1. [2473]

Ducharme, Jacques, et al.

Inventaire des brochures conservées au Service des archives, 1771-1967. [Montréal]: Université du Québec à Montréal, Secrétariat général, 1978. 431 p. (Publication / Service des archives, Université du Québec à Montréal ; no 5) [6782]

Ducharme, Jacques; Plante, Denis

Catalogue des ouvrages traitant d'archivistique et de sujets connexes. Montréal: Secrétariat général de l'Université de Montréal, 1977. v, 238 p. (Publication / Université de Montréal, Service des archives ; no 25) [1621]

Duchesnay, Lorraine

Vingt-cinq ans de dramatiques à la télévision de Radio-Canada. [Ottawa: Relations publiques, Services français, Société Radio-Canada], 1978. xxi, 684 p. [0966]

Duchesne, Louis; Messier, Suzanne; Sabourin, Conrad

La population du Québec: bibliographie démographique. [Québec]: Gouvernement du Québec, Conseil de la langue française, Direction des études et recherches, 1980. 206 p. (Documentation du Conseil de la langue française ; 2); ISBN: 2-551-03900-2. [3027]

Ducrocq-Poirier, Madeleine

"Robert Charbonneau [biographie: bibliographie]." Dans: *Présence francophone*; No 4 (printemps 1972) p. 112-119.; ISSN: 0048-5195. [6902]

Duesterbeck, Florence; Veeman, Nayda

Literacy materials produced in Saskatchewan: a bibliography. Saskatoon: Saskatchewan Literacy Network, 1991. 16 p.; ISBN: 0-919059-58-9. [3722]

Duff, Wendy

"Bibliography of the writings of Phyllis Ruth Blakeley." In: *Nova Scotia Historical Review*; Vol. 7, no. 2 (1987) p. 88-100.; ISSN: 0227-4752. [6853]

Duff, Wilson; Kew, Michael

"A select bibliography of anthropology of British Columbia." In: *BC Studies*; No. 19 (Autumn 1973) p. 73-121.; ISSN: 0005-2949. [4557]

Duffy, Dennis

Camera west: British Columbia on film, 1941-1965: including new information on films produced before 1941. Victoria: Sound and Moving Image Division, Provincial Archives, c1986. ix, 318 p.: ill.; ISBN: 0-7718-8479-6. [6663]

Dufour, Daniel

Répertoire cartobibliographique de Charlevoix. Baie-Saint-Paul [Québec]: Société d'histoire de Charlevoix, 1986. xvi, 345 p. (Instruments de recherche / Société d'histoire de Charlevoix ; no 1); ISBN: 2-9800595-0-1. [6587]

Dufour, Desmond

Inventaire des travaux publiés par le Service de la démographie scolaire au 1 avril 1981. [Québec]: Gouvernement du Québec, Ministère de l'éducation, Direction des études économiques et démographiques, 1981. 105 p. (Document hors série / Gouvernement du Québec, Ministère de l'éducation, Direction des études économiques et démographiques ; no 20); ISBN: 2-550-04459-2. [3589]

Dufour, Jules

Bibliographie thématique sur l'environnement. Québec: Service de la recherche et de l'évaluation, Musée de la civilisation, 1992. 50, [7] p. (Document / Service de la recherche et de l'évaluation, Musée de la civilisation ; no 7); ISBN: 2-551-12842-0. [5295]

"Géomorphologie du Saguenay et du Lac Saint-Jean: bibliographie." Dans: *Protée*; Vol. 4, no 1 (printemps 1975) p. 163-170.; ISSN: 0300-3523. [4788]

Dufresne, Nicole

Chartes, déclarations, recommandations et ententes concernant l'environnement: bibliographie sélective. Québec: Bibliothèque de l'Assemblée nationale, Division de la référence parlementaire, 1989. 17 p. (Bibliographie / Bibliothèque de l'Assemblée nationale du Québec ; no 31; ISSN: 0836-9100) [5269]

Développement durable: bibliographie sélective et annotée. Québec: Bibliothèque de l'Assemblée nationale, Division de la référence parlementaire, 1991. 23 p. (Bibliographie / Bibliothèque de l'Assemblée nationale du Québec ; no 8; ISSN: 0836-9100) [5288]

Gestion des déchets domestiques: bibliographie sélective et

annotée. Québec: Bibliothèque de l'Assemblée nationale, Division de la référence parlementaire, 1990. 39 p. (Bibliographie / Bibliothèque de l'Assemblée nationale du Québec ; no 36; ISSN: 0836-9100) [4434]

Référendums (1979-1989): bibliographie sélective et annotée. Québec: Bibliothèque de l'Assemblée nationale, Division de la référence parlementaire, 1989. 50 p. (Bibliographie / Bibliothèque de l'Assemblée nationale du Québec ; no 29; ISSN: 0836-9100) [2526]

Dufresne, Nicole; Chamberland, Diane

Le député québécois: bibliographie sélective et annotée. Québec: Bibliothèque de l'Assemblée nationale, Division de la référence parlementaire, 1991. 37 p. (Bibliographie / Bibliothèque de l'Assemblée nationale du Québec ; no 40; ISSN: 0836-9100) [2544]

Politiques d'immigration et d'accueil des réfugiés: bibliographie sélective et annotée. Québec: Bibliothèque de l'Assemblée nationale, Division de la référence parlementaire, 1989. 39 p. (Bibliographie / Bibliothèque de l'Assemblée nationale du Québec ; no 27; ISSN: 0836-9100) [2527]

Dugan, Sylvia A.

"Elementary French readers: a selective annotated bibliography." In: *Canadian Modern Language Review*; Vol. 33, no. 3 (January 1977) p. 379-393.; ISSN: 0008-4506. [3524]

Dugas, Jean-Yves

"Bibliographie commentée des études concernant le problème des gentilés au Québec et au Canada." Dans: *Onoma*; Vol. 26 (1982) p. 227-267.; ISSN: 0078-463X. [4589]

Duguid, Stephen; Fowler, Terry A.

Of books and bars: an annotated bibliography on prison education. Burnaby, B.C.: Institute for the Humanities, Simon Fraser University, 1988. 138 p.; ISBN: 0-86491-064-9. [3684]

Duhaime, Carole P.; Trudeau, Sylvain

La clientèle des musées d'art: une revue de littérature. Montréal: École des hautes études commerciales, 1988. 52 f. (Rapport de recherche / École des hautes études commerciales ; no 88-03; ISSN: 0709-986X) [0716]

Duhamel, Roger, et al.

"The literature of French Canada." In: *Canadian Author and Bookman*; Vol. 24, no. 4 (December 1948) p. 42-45.; ISSN: 0008-2937. [1009]

Duinker, Peter N.; Beanlands, Gordon E.

Écologie et évaluation environnementale: bibliographie annotée. Halifax, N.-É.: Institute for Resource and Environmental Studies, Dalhousie University, et Bureau fédéral d'examen des évaluations environnementales, 1983. 44, 40 p. [5192]

Ecology and environmental impact assessment: an annotated bibliography. Halifax, N.S.: Institute for Resource and Environmental Studies, Dalhousie University, in cooperation with Federal Environmental Review Office, 1983. 40, 44 p. [5193]

Duke, David

Violet Archer. Don Mills, Ont.: PRO Canada, 1983. 15 p.: music, port. [6804]

Duke, Dorothy Mary

Agricultural periodicals published in Canada, 1836-1960. [Ottawa]: Information Division, Canada Department of Agriculture, 1962. iv, 101 p. [5872]

Dulong, Gaston

"Bibliographie raisonnée du parler français au Canada." Dans: *Revue de l'Université Laval*; Vol. 15, no 5 (janvier 1961)-vol. 16, no 7 (mars 1962) [1419]

Dumais, Hélène

La féminisation des titres et du discours au Québec: une bibliographie. Québec: Groupe de recherche et d'échange multidisciplinaire féministe, Université Laval, [1987]. 35 p. (Cahiers de recherche du GREMF / Groupe de recherche et d'échange multidisciplinaire féministe, Université Laval ; 12); ISBN: 2-89364-012-5. [1473]

Dumas, Jean-Marc; Bergeron, Hélène; Hardy-Roch, Marcelle

L'enseignement professionnel court au Québec: bibliographie analytique. Ste-Foy, Québec: INRS-Éducation, 1981. 60, 2 f. [3590]

Dumas, Jean-Marc; Blais, Georgette

Répertoire des écrits de l'INRS-Éducation. Sainte-Foy, Québec: INRS-Éducation, [1978]. 45 f. [3537]

Dumont, Rob

Energy conservation in old and new buildings: bibliography. Saskatoon: College of Engineering, University of Saskatchewan, 1977. 84 p. [5764]

Dunbar, M.J.

Marine transportation and high Arctic development: a bibliography: scientific and technical research relevant to the development of marine transportation in the Canadian north. Ottawa: Canadian Arctic Resources Committee, 1980. v, 162 p.; ISBN: 0-919996-15-9. [4479]

Dunbar, M.J., et al.

The biogeographic structure of the Gulf of St. Lawrence. Montreal: McGill University, Marine Sciences Centre, 1980. 142 p.: maps. (Manuscript report / Marine Sciences Centre, McGill University ; no. 32; ISSN: 0828-1831) [3028]

Duncan, Barry

"Media literacy bibliography." In: *History and Social Science Teacher*; Vol. 24, no. 4 (Summer 1989) p. 210-215.; ISSN: 0316-4969. [3701]

Duncan, Robert J.; Quarles, Mervyn V.; Crosby, Louis S.

"Bibliography of Prince Edward Island [postage stamps]." In: *British North America Philatelic Society Year Book*; (1949) p. 11, 13-14. [1744]

Dunn, Christopher J.C.

Select bibliography: the Canadian Charter of Rights and Freedoms. St. John's, Nfld.: [s.n.], 1992. 16 l. [2358]

Dunn, Elizabeth; Stanlake, E.A.

The family Mustelidae: a bibliography. Victoria: Wildlife Research and Technical Services Section, Ministry of Recreation and Conservation, Province of British Columbia, 1978. 73 p. (Fish and Wildlife bulletin ; B-4) [5421]

Dunn, Margo

"A preliminary checklist of the writings of Isabella Valancy Crawford." In: *The Crawford Symposium*, edited by Frank M. Tierney. Ottawa: University of Ottawa Press, 1979. P. 141-155.; ISBN: 2-7603-4385-5. [6921]

Dunn, Oscar

Catalogue d'une bibliothèque canadienne: ouvrages sur l'Amérique et en particulier sur le Canada. Québec: [s.n.], 1885. 38 p. [6737]

DuPerron, William A.

Annotated research bibliography on rape. [Edmonton]: Correctional Justice Program, Grant MacEwan Community College, [1977]. 100 p. [3154]

Annotated research bibliography on the female offender. Edmonton: Grant MacEwan Community College, Correctional Justice Program, 1978. 157 p. [3779]

Dupont, L.

Répertoire des publications du Musée de la civilisation. Québec: Service de la recherche et de l'évaluation, Musée de la civilisation, 1992. 49 p. (Document / Service de la recherche et de l'évaluation, Musée de la civilisation ; no 10); ISBN: 2-551-12941-9. [4610]

Dupont, Pierrette

Répertoire bibliographique d'information scolaire et professionnelle. Sherbrooke: Faculté des sciences de l'éducation, Université de Sherbrooke, 1971. 109 f. [3418]

Dupras, André

Sexualité et éducation sexuelle des personnes déficientes mentales: bibliographie annotée. Montréal: Conseil du Québec de l'enfance exceptionnelle, 1977. 138 p. [3155]

Dupuis, Onil

L'administration scolaire et l'horaire modulaire flexible: une bibliographie/School administration and flexible modular scheduling: a bibliography. Montréal: Cogito, 1973. 17 f. [3456]

Le centre de ressources: une bibliographie/Resource centers: a bibliography. Montréal: Cogito, 1973. 16 f. [1600]

L'école à aire ouverte: une bibliographie/Open schools: a bibliography. Montréal: Cogito, 1973. 15 f. [3457]

L'enseignement micro-gradué ou programmé: une bibliographie/Programmed teaching and micro-teaching: a bibliography. Montréal: Cogito, 1973. 34 l. [3458]

L'enseignement par équipe: une bibliographie/Team teaching: a bibliography. Montréal: Cogito, 1973. 19 l. [3459]

Les objectifs pédagogiques: formulation, définition, classification, évaluation: une bibliographie/Behavioral objectives: stating, defining, classifying, evaluating: a bibliography. Montréal: Cogito, 1973. 30 f. [3460]

Techniques d'administration: P.P.B.S., processus de prise de décision, gestion par les objectifs, analyse de problèmes, appliquées au monde de l'éducation: une bibliographie/ School management: P.P.B.S., decision taking, M.B.O., problem solving: a bibliography. Montréal: Cogito, 1973. 34 l. [3461]

Le temps non-structuré: une bibliographie/Unstructured time: a bibliography. Montréal: Cogito, 1973. 16 f. [3462]

Le travail individuel de l'étudiant: une bibliographie/ Independent study: a bibliography. Montréal: Cogito, 1973. 23 l. [3463]

L'utilisation pédagogique des petits et grands groupes: une bibliographie/ Small and large group instruction: a bibliography. Montréal: Cogito, 1973. 17 f. [3464]

Dupuis, Susan L.; Perron-Croteau, Lise

List of archival literature in the Public Archives Library/ Répertoire d'ouvrages et articles traitant d'archivistique conservés à la Bibliothèque des Archives publiques. [Ottawa]: Public Archives Canada, 1980. 111 p. [1638]

Durand, Pierre

"L'étude de l'agriculture québécoise: commentaires et bibliographie." Dans: *Anthropologie et sociétés*; Vol. 1, no 2 (1977) p. 5-21.; ISSN: 0702-8997. [4670]

Durocher, René; Linteau, Paul-André

Histoire du Québec: bibliographie sélective (1867-1970). Trois-Rivières: Boréal Express, 1970. 189 p. [0306]

Duryea, Michelle LeBaron

Conflict and culture: a literature review and bibliography. Victoria, B.C.: UVic Institute for Dispute Resolution, c1992. ix, 176 p. [4290]

Duska, Leslie; Malycky, Alexander

"Hungarian-Canadian periodical publications: a preliminary check list." In: *Canadian Ethnic Studies*; Vol. 2, no. 1 (June 1970) p. 75-81.; ISSN: 0008-3496. [5890]

Dussault, Christiane

"Bibliographie du service social canadien-français." Dans: *Service social*; Vol. 10, no 3/vol. 11, no 1 (octobre 1961-avril 1962) p. 122-141.; ISSN: 0037-2633. [3081]

Dussault, Gilles

Le monde de la santé, 1940-1975: bibliographie. Québec: Institut supérieur des sciences humaines, Université Laval, c1975. vii f., 170 p. (Cahiers de l'ISSH, Collection Instruments de travail / Institut supérieur des sciences humaines, Université Laval ; no 17) [5600]

Dutil, Élisabeth; Filiatrault, Johanne; Arsenault, A. Bertrand

Répertoire d'évaluations des fonctions sensori-motrices chez l'hémiplégique. [Montréal]: Centre de recherche, Institut de réadaptation de Montréal, [c1989]. 16 f. [5687]

Dutilly, Arthème

Bibliography of bibliographies on the Arctic. Washington, D.C.: Catholic University of America, 1945. 47 p. (Catholic University of America Department of Biology publication ; no. 1 B) [0607]

Bibliography of reindeer, caribou and musk-ox. Washington, D.C.: Department of the Army, Environmental Protection Section, 1949. x, 462 p. [5326]

Duval, Marc

Bibliographie d'articles de périodiques sur la Côte-Nord. Sept-îles [Québec]: Éditions Infodoc, 1985. 149 f. [0384]

Incubateurs d'entreprises: bibliographie française et anglaise, 1986. Boucherville [Québec]: M. Duval, 1986. [8] l. [2719]

Duval, Raymond, et al.

Impacts de la loi 90, L.R.Q. chap. P-41.1, dans la région de Québec: bibliographie concernant la protection du territoire agricole. Québec: Centre de recherche en aménagement et en développement, Université Laval, 1983. 40 f. (Cahier spécial / Centre de recherche en aménagement et en développement, Université Laval ; no 9) [4698]

Duvall, D.

Real estate development and market analysis: a selected bibliography/Aménagement des biens immobiliers et analyse du marché immobilier: bibliographie choisie. [Ottawa: Public Relations and Information Services], Public Works Canada, [1980]. xiv, 143 p.; ISBN: 0-660-50582-7. [2660]

Dworaczek, Marian

The Canadian Bill of Rights and the Charter of Rights and Freedoms: a bibliography. Monticello, Ill.: Vance Bibliographies, 1987. 71 p. (Public administration series: Bibliography ; P-2207; ISSN: 0193-970X); ISBN: 1-55590-407-6. [2291]

Employment and free trade: a bibliography. Monticello, Ill.: Vance Bibliographies, 1988. 14 p. (Public administration series: Bibliography ; P-2482; ISSN: 0193-970X); ISBN: 1-55590-912-4. [2743]

Health and safety of visual display terminals: a bibliography. Toronto: Ontario Ministry of Labour Library, 1982. 32 l.

(Bibliographical guides to the sciences ; no. 5) [5646]

History of the Canadian labour unions: a selective bibliography. Monticello, Ill.: Vance Bibliographies, [1983] 7 p. (Public administration series: Bibliography ; P-1300; ISSN: 0193-970X); ISBN: 0-88066-710-9. [2886]

Human rights: a bibliography of government documents held in the Library. [Toronto]: Research Library, Ontario Ministry of Labour, 1973. 34 p. [2130]

Human rights legislation in Canada: a bibliography. Monticello, Ill.: Vance Bibliographies, 1983. 35 p. (Public administration series: Bibliography ; P-1145; ISSN: 0193-970X); ISBN: 0-88066-395-2. [2258]

Industrial relations and the Canadian Charter of Rights: a bibliography. Monticello, Ill.: Vance Bibliographies, [1988]. 11 p.; ISBN: 1-555907-70-9. [2918]

Job satisfaction: a selected bibliography. Toronto: Research Library, Ontario Ministry of Labour, 1976. 38 p. [2829]

Labour legislation in Canada: a bibliography. Monticello, Ill.: Vance Bibliographies, 1989. 150 p. (Public administration series: Bibliography ; P-2776; ISSN: 0193-970X); ISBN: 0-7920-0366-7. [2924]

Labour topics: a selected bibliography. Toronto: Ontario Ministry of Labour, Research Library, 1977. 78 p. (Bibliography series / Ontario Ministry of Labour, Research Library ; no. 9) [2836]

Manpower training and utilization in Canada, 1955-1970: a bibliography. Toronto: Ontario Ministry of Labour, Research Library, 1973. 21 l. [2814]

Minority groups in Metropolitan Toronto: a bibliography. [Toronto]: Ontario Ministry of Labour, Research Branch, Library, 1973. 57 p. [4159]

Women and the world of work: issues in the '80's: a selective bibliography, 1980-1982. Monticello, Ill.: Vance Bibliographies, 1983. 37 p. (Public administration series: Bibliography ; P-1243; ISSN: 0193-970X); ISBN: 0-88066-593-9. [3816]

Women at work: a bibliography of bibliographies. Monticello, Ill.: Vance Bibliographies, 1984. 18 p. (Public administration series: Bibliography ; P-1414; ISSN: 0193-970X); ISBN: 0-88066-894-6. [3829]

Workers' compensation: a bibliography. Monticello, Ill.: Vance Bibliographies, 1986. 38 p. (Public administration series: Bibliography ; P-1974; ISSN: 0193-970X); ISBN: 0-89028-934-4. [2903]

Dworaczek, Marian; Perry, Elizabeth

Labour-management cooperation: a selected bibliography. Toronto: Ontario Ministry of Labour, Research Library, 1976. 18 p. (Bibliography series / Ontario Ministry of Labour, Research Library ; no. 5) [2830]

Dwyer, John

The poor in Vancouver: a preliminary checklist of sources. Vancouver, B.C.: Dwyer, 1976. 76 l. [3145]

Dwyer, Melva J.

"Bibliography of British Columbia." In: *BC Studies*; No. 76 (Winter 1987-88)-no. 98 (Summer 1993) [0605]

A selected list of books and periodicals on industrial design. Vancouver, B.C.: University of British Columbia Library, 1958. 12 l. (Reference publication / University of British Columbia Library ; no. 13) [0667]

A selected list of music reference materials. Rev. ed. Ottawa: Canadian Library Association, 1969. 15 l. [0823]

Dyck, Ruth

"Ethnic folklore in Canada: a preliminary survey." In: *Canadian Ethnic Studies*; Vol. 7, no. 2 (1975) p. 90-101.; ISSN: 0008-3496. [4169]

Dyde, Dorothy F.

"History of Kingston and District: a selected list." In: *Ontario Library Review*; Vol. 34, no. 3 (August 1950) p. 226-228.; ISSN: 0030-2996. [0424]

Dyer, Aldrich J.

Indian, Metis and Inuit of Canada in theses and dissertations, 1892-1987. Saskatoon: University of Saskatchewan, c1989. 206, xxix, xl p.; ISBN: 0-88880-225-0. [6197]

"An ore body of note: theses and dissertations on Indians, Metis and Inuit at the University of Alberta." In: *Canadian Journal of Native Education*; Vol. 13, no. 2 (1986) p. 40-51.; ISSN: 0710-1481. [6182]

Dykstra, Gail S.

A bibliography of Canadian legal materials/Une bibliographie de documentation juridique canadienne. Toronto: Butterworths, 1977. xii, 113 p.; ISBN: 0-409-82824-6. [2170]

A bibliography of legal materials for non-law libraries. Toronto: York University Law Library, c1975. 55 p. [2142]

"Lockers, the strap, liability and the law." In: *Emergency Librarian*; Vol. 8, no. 3-4 (January-April 1981) p. 20-22.; ISSN: 0315-8888. [2231]

Dzubin, Alex X.

A selected bibliography of effects of dams, artificial impoundments and reservoirs on the aquatic bird resource. Saskatoon: Ecological Assessment Section, Canadian Wildlife Service, Prairie Migratory Bird Research Centre, 1984. 226 l. [5211]

Eady, David

Adult new readers: a bibliography of supplementary reading materials selected from the collection of the Windsor Public Library. [Windsor, Ont.]: Windsor Public Library, 1981. 25 l. [3591]

Eakins, W. George

"The bibliography of Canadian statute law." In: *Index to Legal Periodicals and Law Library Journal*; Vol. 1, no. 1 (January 1908) p. 61-78.; ISSN: 0023-9283. [2099]

Eales, J. Geoffrey

A bibliography of the eels of the genus Anguilla. St. Andrews, N.B.: Biological Station, Fisheries Research Board of Canada, 1967. 171 p. (Fisheries Research Board of Canada Technical report ; no. 28; ISSN: 0068-7553) [5346]

Ealey, David M.

A bibliography of Alberta mammalogy. [Edmonton]: Alberta Culture, Historical Resources Division, 1987. vii, 400 p.: map. (Natural history occasional paper / Provincial Museum of Alberta ; no. 8; ISSN: 0838-5971) [5530]

Ealey, David M.; McNicholl, Martin K.

A bibliography of Alberta ornithology. 2nd ed. Edmonton: Natural History Section, Provincial Museum of Alberta, 1991. vi, 751 p.: map. (Natural history occasional paper / Provincial Museum of Alberta ; no. 16; ISSN: 0838-5971); ISBN: 0-7732-0599-3. [5559]

Easson, A.J.

Canada and the European communities: selected materials. Kingston, Ont.: Centre for International Relations, Queen's University, 1979. iii l., 359 p. (Canada-Europe series ; no. 2/1979) [2444]

Ebbers, Mark A.; Colby, Peter J.; Lewis, Cheryl A.
Walleye-sauger bibliography. St. Paul: Minnesota Department of Natural Resources, 1988. 201 p. (Minnesota Department of Natural Resources Investigational report; no. 396) (Ontario Ministry of Natural Resources, Fisheries Branch Contribution; no. 88-02) [5540]

Echlin, Kim
Bibliography of Canadian Indian mythology. [Downsview? Ont.: s.n.], 1984. 48 col. [4057]

École des hautes études commerciales de Montréal
Contribution des professeurs de l'École des hautes études commerciales de Montréal à la vie intellectuelle du Canada ... : catalogue des principaux écrits. [Montréal]: 1960. iii, 132 f. [2572]

École des hautes études commerciales de Montréal. Groupe de recherche et de formation en gestion des arts
Bibliographie sélective et synthèses de documents: rapport préparé pour le Groupe d'études sur la formation professionnelle dans le secteur culturel au Canada. Montréal: Le Groupe, 1991. 156 f. [0724]

Écologie de l'archipel arctique canadien: bibliographie sélective. Ottawa: Affaires indiennes et du Nord, 1974-1982. 11 vol.; ISSN: 0715-8815. [5178]

Ecology of the Canadian Arctic Archipelago: selected references. [Ottawa]: Indian Affairs and Northern Development, 1974-1982. 11 vol.; ISSN: 0715-8807. [5179]

Economic Council of Canada
Catalogue of publications [Economic Council of Canada]. Ottawa: Economic Council of Canada, 1981-1992. 10 vol.; ISSN: 0828-4350. [6412]

Economic Council of Canada. Regional Development Research Team
Bibliography on local and regional development. Ottawa: Economic Council of Canada, 1990. iii, 86 p. [4435]

Edmonds, E.L.
An annotated bibliography on team teaching. [Charlottetown]: University of Prince Edward Island, [1972]. [89] p.; ISBN: 0-919013-03-1. [3438]

Edmonton Public Library
Of, by and about women: a bibliography for International Women's Year. [Edmonton: The Library, 1975]. [19] l. [3754]

Edmonton Public Library. Western Canadiana Collection
Supplementary bibliography [Edmonton Public Library, Western Canadiana Collection]. [Edmonton]: The Library, [1986]. iv, 184 p. [0541]

Edmonton Regional Planning Commission
An annotated bibliography of works related to the Edmonton Regional Planning Commission. [Edmonton: Edmonton Regional Planning Commission], 1972. 276 l. (in various foliations). [4322]

Educational Research Institute of British Columbia
Reports list [Educational Research Institute of British Columbia]. [Vancouver]: Educational Research Institute of British Columbia, 1976-. vol.; ISSN: 0706-9944. [3734]

ÉDUQ: bibliographie analytique sur l'éducation au Québec. [Québec]: Gouvernement du Québec, Ministère de l'éducation, Direction de la recherche, [1981]-. vol.; ISSN: 0712-4635. [3735]

Edward E. Ayer Collection
A bibliographical check list of North and Middle American Indian linguistics in the Edward E. Ayer Collection. Chicago: The Newberry Library, 1941. 2 vol. [1414]

Edwards, Barry
"A critical discography of Canadian music/Une discographie critique de musique canadienne." In: *Musicanada*; No. 46 (June 1981) p. 22-24; no. 47 (December 1981) p. 21-23.; ISSN: 0700-4745. [0895]

Edwards, Barry; Love, Mary
A bibliography of Inuit (Eskimo) linguistics in collections of the Metropolitan Toronto Library. Toronto: Metropolitan Toronto Library Board, Languages Centre, [1982]. iii, 36 p. [1455]

Edwards, Henry
Bibliographical catalogue of the described transformations of North American Lepidoptera. Washington: U.S.G.P.O., 1889. 147 p. [5306]

Edwards, Margaret H.; Lort, John C.R.
A bibliography of British Columbia: years of growth, 1900-1950. Victoria, B.C.: Social Sciences Research Centre, University of Victoria, 1975. x, 446 p.: maps (on lining papers).; ISBN: 0-9690418-3-7. [0584]

Edwards, Mary Jane
"Fiction and Montreal, 1769-1885: a bibliography." In: *Papers of the Bibliographical Society of Canada*; Vol. 8 (1969) p. 61-75.; ISSN: 0067-6896. [1048]

Egoff, Sheila; Bélisle, Alvine
Notable Canadian children's books/Un choix de livres canadiens pour la jeunesse. 2nd ed. Vancouver: Vancouver School Board, 1977. vii, 94 p. [1333]

Egoff, Sheila; Salman, Judith
The New republic of childhood: a critical guide to Canadian children's literature in English. Toronto: Oxford University Press, 1990. xiv, 378 p.: ill.; ISBN: 0-19-540576-5. [1387]

Eiber, Thomas G.; King, Marjorie
Forestry bibliography: theses, 1971-1983. Thunder Bay, Ont.: Lakehead University, 1983. 122 p. [6169]

Eichler, Margrit
"And the work never ends: feminist contributions." In: *Canadian Review of Sociology and Anthropology*; Vol. 22, no. 5 (December 1985) p. 619-644.; ISSN: 0008-4948. [3834]

An annotated selected bibliography of bibliographies on women. Ottawa: Association of Universities and Colleges of Canada, Committee on the Status of Women, c1973. 17 p. [3741]

Eichler, Margrit; Marecki, John; Newton, Jennifer L.
Women: a bibliography of special periodical issues (1960-1975). [Toronto]: Canadian Newsletter of Research on Women, c1976. 76 p. [3764]

Eichler, Margrit; Newton, Jennifer L.; Primrose, Lynne
"A bibliography of social science materials on Canadian women, published between 1950-1975." In: *Women in Canada*. Rev. ed., edited by Marylee Stephenson. Don Mills, Ont.: General Publishing, 1977. P. 275-360.; ISBN: 0-7736-1026-X. [3770]

Eiselt, Horst A.; Laporte, Gilbert; Thisse, Jacques-François
Competitive location models: a framework and bibliography. Montréal: Centre de recherche sur les transports, Université de Montréal, 1990. 34 l. (Publication / Centre de recherche sur les transports, Université de Montréal; no. 706) [2765]

Eisenbichler, W.
Genealogy at the Sault Ste. Marie Public Library. [Sault Ste. Marie, Ont.]: Sault Ste. Marie Public Library, 1989. 28 p. [2075]

Eisenhauer, J.H.

A partial bibliography on Branta bernicla. Lethbridge: University of Lethbridge, 1975. 10 p. [5390]

El-Kassaby, Yousry Aly; White, Eleanor E.

Isozymes and forest trees: an annotated bibliography. Victoria: Pacific Forest Research Centre, Canadian Forestry Service, 1985. 79 p. (Pacific Forest Research Centre Information report ; BC-X-267; ISSN: 0705-3274); ISBN: 0-662-14070-2. [4982]

El-Sabh, Mohammed I.

Bibliographie sur l'océanographie de l'estuaire du St-Laurent/Oceanographic bibliography for the St. Lawrence estuary. Rimouski, Québec: Section d'océanographie, Université du Québec à Rimouski, 1976. v f., 97 p.: cartes. [5112]

El-Sabh, Mohammed I.; Forrester, W.D.; Johannessen, O.M.

Bibliography and some aspects of physical oceanography in the Gulf of St. Lawrence. Montreal: Marine Sciences Centre, McGill University, 1969. 65 p.: ill., charts, maps. (Manuscript report / Marine Sciences Centre, McGill University ; no. 14; ISSN: 0828-1831) [5047]

Elder Abuse Resource Centre

Elder Abuse Resource Centre bibliography, May 1992: Canadian material. Winnipeg: Age & Opportunity, 1992. [17] p. [3359]

Elliott, A.R. (Firm)

Elliott's hand-book of medical, hygienic, pharmaceutical and dental journals of the United States and Canada. New York: A.R. Elliott, 1895. vi, 144 p. [5857]

Elliott, Lorris

The bibliography of literary writings by Blacks in Canada. Toronto: Williams-Wallace Publishers, 1986. 48 p.; ISBN: 0-88795-047-7. [1226]

Literary writing by Blacks in Canada: a preliminary survey. [Ottawa]: Department of the Secretary of State of Canada, Multiculturalism, 1988. 40 l.; ISBN: 0-662-16029-0. [1250]

Elliott, Shirley B.

"An historical review of Nova Scotia legal literature: a select bibliography." In: Dalhousie Law Journal; Vol. 8, no. 3 (1984) p. 197-212.; ISSN: 0317-1663. [2265]

"Joseph Howe: 1804-1873: a bibliography compiled in the Legislative Library." In: Journal of Education; Vol. 1, no. 1 (series 6) (Fall 1973) p. 31-36.; ISSN: 0022-0566. [7070]

Nova Scotia in books: a quarter century's gatherings, 1957-1982. Halifax, N.S.: Department of Education, Education Resources Services, 1986. [4], 110, [12] p.; ISBN: 0-88871-088-7. [0262]

"Novascotiana." In: Journal of Education; Vol. 7, no. 3, series 5 (June 1958)-no. 398 (September 1984) [0257]

Elliott, Shirley B.; Webster, Ellen

Nova Scotia in books, from the first printing in 1752 to the present time, commemorating the centennial of Confederation. Halifax, N.S.: Halifax Library Association in cooperation with the Nova Scotia Provincial Library, 1967. 40 p.: ill., facsims. [0207]

Ellis, Dormer

An overview of literature pertaining to the presentation of students for and placement in post-secondary studies [microform]. [Toronto]: Ontario Ministry of Education, [1980]. 4 microfiches. [3565]

Ellison, Suzanne

Bibliography of Newfoundland newspapers. St. John's, Nfld.: Memorial University of Newfoundland Library, 1985. 32 p.; ISBN: 0-88901-107-9. [6036]

Historical directory of Newfoundland and Labrador newspapers, 1807-1987. St. John's: Memorial University of Newfoundland Library, 1988. 175 p.; ISBN: 0-88901-158-3. [6046]

Elphège, père

Bibliographie franciscaine: nos périodiques, nos auteurs, 1931-1941. Montréal: [s.n.], 1941. 21 p. [1502]

Elson, J.A.

"The Champlain Sea: evolution of concepts, and bibliography." In: The Late quaternary development of the Champlain Sea basin, edited by N.R. Gadd. St. John's, Nfld.: Geological Association of Canada, 1988. P. 1-13.; ISBN: 0-919216-35-8. [4868]

Elsted, Crispin

Utile dulci: the first decade at Barbarian Press, 1977-1987: a history & bibliography. Mission, B.C.: Barbarian Press, c1988. 52 p.; ISBN: 0-920971-07-5. [1700]

Emard, Michel

"Bibliographie des Comtés-Unis de Prescott-Russell, Ontario." Dans: Ontario History; Vol. 72, no. 1 (March 1980) p. 49-55.; ISSN: 0030-2953. [0468]

Inventaire sommaire des sources manuscrites et imprimées concernant Prescott-Russell, Ontario. Rockland [Ont.]: M. Emard, 1976. 172 p.: cartes. [0455]

Emerson, Mabel E.

"Reference lists: Canada." In: Monthly Bulletin of the Providence Public Library; Vol. 1, no. 10 (October 1895) p. 176-180. [0023]

Emery, Alan R.

A review of the literature of oil pollution with particular reference to the Canadian Great Lakes. [Toronto]: Ontario Ministry of Natural Resources, 1972. ii, 63 p. (Research information paper / Ontario Ministry of Natural Resources ; no. 40) [5064]

Émond, Maurice

"Introduction à l'oeuvre d'Anne Hébert: [bibliographie sommaire]." Dans: Québec français; No 32 (décembre 1978) p. 37-40.; ISSN: 0316-2052. [7048]

Endres, Robin

"Women authors in Canada." In: Canadian Newsletter of Research on Women; Vol. 1, no. 2 (October 1972) p. 46-52.; ISSN: 0319-4477. [1065]

Energy information index, 1978/Répertoire de renseignements sur l'énergie, 1978. [Ottawa]: Energy, Mines and Resources Canada, c1978. 111 p. (Energy index series ; 78-1); ISBN: 0-662-01308-5. [4806]

Engineering Interface Limited

Energy conservation in retail stores: review of Canadian and U.S. studies, surveys, programs and publications. Ottawa: Renewable Energy Branch, Energy, Mines and Resources Canada, 1980. 1 vol. (in various pagings). (Buildings series Publication ; no. 2b) [5776]

English, M.; Wong, R.K.W.; Kochtubajda, B.

Literature review on the greenhouse effect and global warming. [Edmonton]: Alberta Department of Energy, 1990. 52 p.: ill. [5280]

Ennis, G.L., et al.

An annotated bibliography and information summary on the fisheries resources of the Yukon River basin in Canada. Vancouver: Water Use Unit, Habitat Management Division, Department of Fisheries and Oceans, 1982. v, 278 p. (Canadian manuscript report of fisheries and aquatic sciences ; no. 1657; ISSN: 0706-6473) [4899]

Enns, Carol

The education of new Canadians: an annotated bibliography. Toronto: Library, Reference and Information Services, Ontario Institute for Studies in Education, 1978. ix, 50 p. (Current bibliography / Ontario Institute for Studies in Education ; no. 10) [3538]

Enns, Richard A.

A bibliography of northern Manitoba. Winnipeg: University of Manitoba Press, 1991. 128 p. (Manitoba studies in native history occasional papers); ISBN: 0-88755-625-6. [0549]

Enright, Catherine Theresa; Newkirk, G.F.

Literature search on the growth of oysters as influenced by artificial diets and natural diets. Halifax: Biology Department, Dalhousie University, 1982. vii, 194 p.: ill. [5475]

Enros, Philip Charles

Biobibliography of publishing scientists in Ontario between 1914 and 1939. Thornhill, Ont.: HSTC Publications, c1985. xxxvi, 526 p. (Research tools for the history of Canadian science and technology ; no. 2; ISSN: 0715-9668); ISBN: 0-9690475-3-3. [4629]

Envirocon Ltd.

Environmental protection in strip mining. Calgary: Envirocon, 1976. 2 vol. [4794]

Environics Research Group

État des connaissances: recherches sur les personnes âgées de 1964 à 1972. Ottawa: Division de planification des politiques, Société centrale d'hypothèques et de logement, 1972. 69, 81 p. [3105]

The seventh age: a bibliography of Canadian sources in gerontology and geriatrics, 1964-1972/Le septième âge: une bibliographie des sources canadiennes de gérontologie et de gériatrie, 1964-1972. [Ottawa: Policy Planning Division, Central Mortgage and Housing Corporation], 1972. xvii, 290 p. [5579]

State of the art: research on the elderly, 1964-1972. Ottawa: Policy Planning Division, Central Mortgage & Housing Corporation, 1972. 81, 69 p. [3106]

Environment source book: a guide to environmental information in Canada: a joint project of the Department of the Environment, Ottawa and provincial and territorial environment and renewable resource departments. [Ottawa: Department of the Environment], c1978. 115 p.; ISBN: 0-662-01622-X. [5133]

"The environmental crisis: a select annotated list of books, films and magazine articles." In: *Ontario Library Review*; Vol. 55, no. 1 (March 1971) p. 21-26.; ISSN: 0030-2996. [5058]

The environmental reading list. Toronto: Pollution Probe Foundation, [1980]. [5] l.; ISBN: 0-919764-10-X. [5162]

Environmental resource book, 1986: environmental groups in Ontario and topical lists of their printed and audio-visual resources organized by issue category. Toronto: Ontario Environment Network, c1986. 42 p.: ill. [5231]

Environmental resource directory. [Toronto]: Public Focus, [1989]-. vol. (loose-leaf). [5301]

Erskine, Anthony J.

A preliminary catalogue of bird census studies in Canada/ Repertoire préliminaire des études de d'enombrement des oiseaux du Canada. Ottawa: Canadian Wildlife Service, 1971. 78 p. (Progress notes / Canadian Wildlife Service ; no. 20; ISSN: 0069-0023) (Cahiers de biologie / Service canadien de la faune ; no 20; ISSN: 0703-0967) [5359]

Esdras Minville: bio-bibliographie. Montréal: [s.n.], 1972. 15 f. [7192]

Espesset, Hélène

L'histoire des canaux du Québec: bilan et perspectives. [Ottawa]: Environnement Canada, Parcs, 1987. 36 p.: carte. (Bulletin de recherches / Environnement Canada Parcs ; no. 255; ISSN: 0228-1236) [4500]

History of Quebec canals: a review of the literature. [Ottawa]: Environment Canada, 1987. 17 p.: map. (Research bulletin / Environment Canada Parks ; no. 255; ISSN: 0228-1228) [4501]

Espesset, Hélène; Hardy, Jean-Pierre; Ruddell, Thierry

"Le monde de travail au Québec au XVIIIe et au XIXe siècles: historiographie et État de la question." Dans: *Revue d'histoire de l'Amérique française*; Vol. 25, no 4 (mars 1972) p. 499-539.; ISSN: 0035-2357. [2808]

Essai de bibliographie sur la filtration et quelques sujets connexes/Tentative bibliography on filtration and some related subjects. Montréal: École polytechnique, Département du génie civil, Section du génie de l'environnement, 1973. 123 f. [5741]

États-Unis. Service d'information

Choix de publications et de sources de renseignements en français sur les relations canado-américaines. Ottawa: Service d'information des États-Unis, 1968. 28, iii f. [2395]

Etcheverry, Jorge

"Selected bibliography of Chilean writing in Canada." In: *Canadian Review of Comparative Literature*; Vol. 16, no. 3/4 (September-December 1989) p. 863-865.; ISSN: 0319-051X. [1270]

Eterovich, Adam S.

A guide and bibliography to research on Yugoslavs in the United States and Canada. San Francisco: [s.n.], 1975. xiii, 187 p.; ISBN: 0-88247-341-7. [4170]

Ethics in sport: a specialized bibliography from the SPORT database/Éthique du sport: une bibliographie spécialisée de la base de données SPORT. Gloucester, Ont.: Sport Information Resource Centre, 1990. 10 l. (SportBiblio ; no. 1; ISSN: 1180-5269) [1855]

"The ethnic press in Ontario." In: *Polyphony*; Vol. 4, no. 1 (1982) p. 1-143.; ISSN: 0704-7002. [6032]

Ettlinger, John R.T.; O'Neill, Patrick B.

A checklist of Canadian copyright deposits in the British Museum, 1895-1923. Halifax, N.S.: Dalhousie University, School of Library Service, 1984-1989. 5 vol.; ISBN: 0-7703-0179-7 (v.1); 0-7703-0178-9 (v.2); 0-7703-9706-9 (v.3, pt. 1); 0-7703-9726-3 (v.3, pt.2); 0-7703-9730-1 (v.4, pt. 1); 0-7703-9736-0 (v.4, pt.2); 0-7703-9732-8 (v.5). [0163]

"Études sur le roman canadien-français: essai bibliographique." Dans: *Relations*; No 320 (octobre 1967) p. 278-279.; ISSN: 0034-3781. [1039]

Evans, David

A selected bibliography of North American literature on the European pine shoot moth. Victoria, B.C.: Canadian Forestry Service, 1974. 162 p. [5380]

Evans, David O.; Campbell, Bonnie A.

An annotated listing of original field data books and diaries of Ontario Fisheries Research Laboratory workers (1921-1948). [Toronto]: Ontario Ministry of Natural Resources, 1984. iii, 37 p. (Ontario fisheries technical report series ; no. 11; ISSN: 0227-986X); ISBN: 0-7743-8982-6. [5495]

Evans, Gwynneth
Women in federal politics: a bio-bibliography/Les femmes au fédéral: une bio-bibliographie. Ottawa: National Library of Canada, 1975. 81 p. [3755]

Evans, Gwynneth; Hawkins, Elizabeth; Honeywell, Joan
"Bibliography of the published works of William Kaye Lamb." In: *Archivaria*; No. 15 (Winter 1982-1983) p. 131-144.; ISSN: 0318-6954. [7114]

Evans, Judith E.M.
Back injury prevention: a literature survey and compendium of programs and resources. [Edmonton]: Alberta Worker's Health, Safety and Compensation, Occupational Health and Safety Division, 1984. iii, 101 p. [5658]

Evans, Karen
Masinahikan: native language imprints in the archives and libraries of the Anglican Church of Canada. Toronto: Anglican Book Centre, 1985. xxiii, 357 p.; ISBN: 0-919891-33-0. [4075]

Evert, F.
Annotated bibliography on initial tree spacing. Ottawa: Canadian Forestry Service, Department of the Environment, 1973. 149 p. (Forest Management Institute Information report ; FMR-X-50) [4935]

Ewing, Guy; Olson, David R.
The nature of literacy: a bibliography. Rev. ed. Toronto: McLuhan Program in Culture and Technology, University of Toronto, c1988. 74 p. (Working paper / McLuhan Program in Culture and Technology, University of Toronto ; no. 14); ISBN: 0-77275-915-4. [3685]

Explorations et enracinements français en Ontario, 1610-1978. [Toronto]: Ontario Ministère de l'Éducation, 1981.; ISBN: 0-7743-6187-5. [0470]

Exposition de documents d'histoire du Canada (1840-1880) à l'occasion du deuxième centenaire du Collège de Montréal avec l'aide financière de la Commission du Centenaire. Montréal: [s.n.], 1967. [24] p. [1952]

Exposition de l'Empire britannique (1924-1925: Londres, Angleterre)
Catalogue de livres canadiens (section française): Exposition de l'Empire britannique, Parc Wembley, Londres, 1925. Londres: l'Exposition, 1925. 38 p. [0040]

"F. Hilton Page: Publications." In: *Dalhousie Review*; Vol. 69, no. 1 (Summer 1989) p. 173-175.; ISSN: 0011-5827. [7232]

Fabi, Thérèse
"Biobibliographie: Marie-Claire Blais." Dans: *Présence francophone*; No 4 (printemps 1972) p. 209-216.; ISSN: 0048-5195. [6851]

Fabien, Claude
"Ordinateur et droit: bibliographie sélective." Dans: *Revue du barreau*; Vol. 34, no 5 (novembre 1974) p. 561-567.; ISSN: 0383-669X. [2139]

Faessler, Carl
Cross-index to the maps and illustrations of the Geological Survey and Mines Branch (Bureau of Mines) of Canada, 1843-1946 (incl.). Quebec: Laval University, 1947. 525 p. (Contributions / Université Laval, Département de géologie et de minéralogie ; no 75) [6497]

Fagnan, Vivianne M.
Edentulousness: a bibliography of published reports, surveys and analyses of rates and trends of complete and partial edentulousness and of personnel requirements to satisfy the needs of the edentate in North American, Western European and other populations. Sherwood Park,

Alta.: Alberta Denturist Society, 1989. vi, 30 p. [5688]

Fahl, Ronald J.
North American forest and conservation history: a bibliography. Santa Barbara, Calif.: Published under contract with the Forest History Society [by] A.B.C.–Clio Press, c1977. 408 p.; ISBN: 0-87436-235-0. [4955]

Fahmy-Eid, Nadia; Dumont, Micheline
"Bibliographie sur l'histoire de l'éducation des filles au Québec." Dans: *Documentation sur la recherche féministe*; Vol. 14, no 2 (juillet 1985) p. 45-70.; ISSN: 0707-8412. [3835]

Fairbanks, Carol
"Margaret Atwood: a bibliography of criticism." In: *Bulletin of Bibliography*; Vol. 6, no. 2 (April-June 1979) p. 85-90.; ISSN: 0190-745X. [6806]

Fairbanks, Carol; Sundberg, Sara Brooks
Farm women on the prairie frontier: a sourcebook for Canada and the United States. Metuchen, N.J.: Scarecrow Press, 1983. xiii, 237 p.: ill.; ISBN: 0-8108-1625-3. [3817]

Fairley, Helen
Bibliography of Prince George District. [Vancouver: British Columbia Library Association], 1935. 5 p. [0559]
Bibliography on the Cariboo District. [Vancouver: British Columbia Library Association], 1935. [1], 8 p. [0560]

Falaise, Noël
"Biographie et bibliographie de Benoît Brouillette." Dans: *Cahiers de géographie de Québec*; Vol. 17, no 40 (avril 1973) p. 5-34.; ISSN: 0007-9766. [6876]

Falardeau, Jean-Charles
"Bibliographie de Léon Gérin." Dans: *Recherches sociographiques*; Vol. 1, no 2 (avril-juin 1960) p. 139-157.; ISSN: 0034-1282. [7009]
"Les recherches religieuses au Canada français." Dans: *Recherches sociographiques*; Vol. 3, no 1-2 (janvier-août 1962) p. 209-228.; ISSN: 0034-1282. [1514]

Falk, Gathie
"What's it like to be a woman artist? Selected bibliography." In: *Capilano Review*; No. 24 (1982) p. 59-61.; ISSN: 0315-3754. [0699]

Fallis, B.W.; Klenner, W.E.; Kroeker, D.W.
Bibliography of trace metals (As, Cd, Hg, Pb, Zn) in marine ecosystems with emphasis on arctic regions, 1970-1980. Winnipeg: Government of Canada, Fisheries and Oceans, 1982. iv, 33 p. (Canadian technical report of fisheries and aquatic sciences ; no. 1087; ISSN: 0706-6457) [5180]

Family Planning Federation of Canada
Resource catalogue: family planning, sex education, population/Catalogue de ressources: le planning des naissances, l'éducation sexuelle, la population. [Toronto]: Family Planning Federation of Canada, [1973]. 52 p. [3116]

Family violence: an annotated bibliography. Halifax: Public Legal Education Society of Nova Scotia, c1986. 43 p.; ISBN: 0-88648-066-3. [3287]

Faminow, Merle Douglas
Bibliography of red meat research in Canada, 1980 to 1991. Winnipeg: Department of Agricultural Economics and Farm Management, University of Manitoba, 1991. iii, 43 p. (Occasional series / Department of Agricultural Economics and Farm Management, University of Manitoba ; no. 18) [4722]

Fancy, Margaret
A bibliography of the works of George Francis Gillman Stanley. Sackville, N.B.: Ralph Pickard Bell Library, Mount Allison University, c1976. 52 p. (Bibliography series /

Ralph Pickard Bell Library, Mount Allison University ; no. 1) [7319]

Lawren Phillips Harris: a bibliography. Sackville, N.B.: Ralph Pickard Bell Library, Mount Allison University, c1979. x, 52 p. (Bibliography series / Ralph Pickard Bell Library, Mount Allison University ; no. 2); ISBN: 0-88828-028-9. [7046]

"To remember a landscape: a checklist of the works of Douglas Lochhead." In: *The Red jeep and other landscapes: a collection in honour of Douglas Lochhead*, edited by Peter Thomas. Sackville, N.B.: Centre for Canadian Studies, Mount Allison University, 1987. P. 91-108.; ISBN: 0-86492-063-6. [7150]

Fang, Jin Bao; MacKay, G. David M.; Bramhall, George
Wood: fire behaviour and fire retardant: a review of the literature. Ottawa: Canadian Wood Council, 1966. 1 vol. (in various pagings). [5725]

Faribault, Georges Barthélemi
Catalogue d'ouvrages sur l'histoire de l'Amérique, et en particulier sur celle du Canada, de la Louisiane, de l'Acadie, et autres lieux, ci-devant connus sous le nom de Nouvelle-France; avec des notes bibliographiques, critiques et littéraires. En trois parties. Québec: Cowan, 1837. 207 p. [1872]

Farnell, Margaret B.
Screening procedures for the detection or prediction of child abuse: an annotated bibliography. [Toronto]: Centre of Criminology, University of Toronto, 1980. v, 29 p.; ISBN: 0-919584-47-0. [3200]

Farrell, David M.
The contracting out of work: an annotated bibliography. Kingston, Ont.: Industrial Relations Centre, Queen's University, 1965. v, 61 p. (Bibliography series / Industrial Relations Centre, Queen's University ; no. 1) [2793]

Farson, Anthony Stuart; Matthews, Catherine J.
Criminal intelligence and security intelligence: a selective bibliography. Toronto: Centre for Criminology, University of Toronto, 1990. vii, 77 p. (Bibliography / Centre of Criminology, University of Toronto ; no. 14); ISBN: 0-919584-66-7. [2336]

Fast, Louise
Statistics Canada publications on microfiche, 1850-1980. [Toronto]: Micromedia, [1985]. 1 vol. (in various pagings).; ISBN: 0-88892-5136-5. [6371]

Fathi, Ashgar; Smeaton, B. Hunter
"Arabic-Canadian periodical publications: a preliminary check list." In: *Canadian Ethnic Studies*; Vol. 5, no. 1/2 (1973) p. 1-4.; ISSN: 0008-3496. [5912]

Faucher, Carol
La production française à l'ONF: 25 ans en perspectives. Montréal: Cinémathèque québécoise, c1984. 80 p.: ill. (Dossiers de la Cinémathèque / Cinémathèque québécoise ; no 14); ISBN: 2-89207-027-9. [6658]

Fauchon, André
"Bibliographie de l'oeuvre de Maurice Constantin-Weyer." Dans: *Cahiers franco-canadiens de l'Ouest*; Vol. 1, no 1 (printemps 1989) p. 49-70.; ISSN: 0843-9559. [6914]
Bibliographie sur la population du Manitoba. [Saint-Boniface]: Collège universitaire de Saint-Boniface, 1982. iii, 64 f. (Travaux et documents de géographie / Collège universitaire de Saint-Boniface ; no 2) [3039]

Faulkner, Mary S.; Krueger, Donald R.
The Ontario Cabinet: a selected annotated bibliography. Toronto: Ontario Legislative Library, Research and Information Services, 1985. 5 l. (Bibliographies and lists. New series / Ontario Legislative Library, Research and Information Services ; no. 9; ISSN: 0833-2150) [2490]

Fauteux, Aegidius
Bibliographie de la question universitaire Laval-Montréal, 1852-1921. Montréal: Arbour & Dupont, 1922. 62 p. [3369]

Favreau, Marc; Brassard, Guy R.
Catalogue bibliographique des bryophytes du Québec et du Labrador. St. Jean, Terre-Neuve: Memorial University of Newfoundland, 1988. 114 p. (Memorial University of Newfoundland Occasional papers in biology ; no. 12; ISSN: 0702-0007) [5541]

Fay, Terence J.
"Canadian studies on the American relationship, 1945-1980." In: *American Review of Canadian Studies*; Vol. 13, no. 3 (Autumn 1983) p. 179-200.; ISSN: 0272-2011. [2474]

Federal-Provincial Committee on Mineral Statistics (Canada). Publications Task Force
Catalogue of mineral statistics: federal and provincial publications and surveys in Canada. Ottawa: Department of Energy, Mines and Resources, 1985. v, 41, 47, v p.; ISBN: 0-662-53978-8. [6372]

Fédération des enseignantes et des enseignants de l'Ontario. Comité de la condition féminine
La violence au sein de la famille: une bibliographie sélective. [Toronto]: La Fédération, [1985]. 24, 82 p.; ISBN: 0-88872-064-5. [3271]

Fedigan, Larry
Classroom management and achievement: a review of the literature. Edmonton: Planning and Research Branch, Alberta Education, 1980. 60 p. [3566]
School-based elements related to achievement: a review of the literature. Edmonton: Minister's Advisory Committee on Student Achievement, 1979. 112 p. [3551]

Fedynski, Alexander
Bibliohrafichnyi pokazhchyk ukraïnskoï presy poza mezhmy Ukraïny/Bibliographical index of the Ukrainian press outside Ukraine. [Cleveland]: Ukrainian Museum-Archives in Cleveland, 1966-1975. 9 vol.; ISSN: 0067-737X. [6023]

Fee, Margery; Cawker, Ruth
Canadian fiction: an annotated bibliography. Toronto: Peter Martin Associates, c1976. xiii, 170 p.; ISBN: 0-88778-134-9. [1097]

Féger, Robert; Gauthier, Marcelle
Bibliographie sur la violence à l'égard des enfants. Montréal: Commission des écoles catholiques de Montréal, Bureau de ressources en développement pédagogiques et en consultation personnelle, 1987. 129 p.; ISBN: 2-92076-638-4. [3297]

Fehr, Helen
Bibliography for professional development. Saskatoon: Indian and Northern Education Program, University of Saskatchewan, [1972]. 48, 15 l. [3933]

Feihl, John; Murphy, Brian
List of controversial and obscure CanCon material. Ottawa: B. Murphy, 1978. 13 l. [0865]

Feihl, O.
Protection of veneer logs in storage in eastern Canada: a survey of the literature. Ottawa: Eastern Forest Products

Laboratory, 1978. iii, 20 p. [4963]

Feit, Harvey A.

"Bibliographie [concernant la Baie James]." Dans: *Recherches amérindiennes au Québec*; Vol. 6, no 1 (printemps 1976) p. 61-64.; ISSN: 0318-4137. [3978]

James Bay debates: a bibliography. [Montreal]: Grand Council of Crees (of Quebec), 1976. 13 l. [3979]

Feit, Harvey A., et al.

La Baie James des amérindiens, bibliographie/Bibliography: native peoples, James Bay region. [Montréal]: s.n., 1972. 62 p.: carte. [3934]

Feit, Harvey A.; Mailhot, José

"La région de la Baie James (Québec): bibliographie ethnologique." Dans: *Recherches amérindiennes au Québec*; Vol. 2, Spécial 1 (juin 1972) p. 4-42.; ISSN: 0318-4137. [4555]

Feldman, Wendy A.

"Women in Canadian politics since 1945: a bibliography." In: *Resources for Feminist Research*; Vol. 8, no. 1 (March 1979) p. 38-42.; ISSN: 0707-8412. [3788]

Félix Leclerc, 1914-1918: bibliographie et dossier La Presse. Montréal: Services documentaires Multimedia, 1988. 36 p.: ill., portr.; ISBN: 2-89059-330-4. [7138]

Feller, M.C.

The ecological effects of slashburning with particular reference to British Columbia: a literature review. Victoria: Information Services Branch, B.C. Ministry of Forests, 1982. vii, 60 p. (Land management report / British Columbia Ministry of Forests ; no. 13; ISSN: 0702-9861); ISBN: 0-7719-8890-7. [4974]

Fellows, Jo-Ann; Calder, Kathryn

"A bibliography of loyalist source material in Canada." In: *Proceedings of the American Antiquarian Society*; Vol. 82 (1972) p. 67-270.; ISSN: 0044-751X. [1976]

Felsky, Martin

The CLIC bibliography of computers and the law, 1983-1986. Ottawa: Canadian Law Information Council, 1987. 106 p.; ISBN: 0-921481-12-8. [2292]

Feltner, Charles E.; Feltner, Jeri Baron

Great Lakes maritime history: bibliography and sources of information. Dearborn, Mich.: Seajay Publications, 1982. xii, 111 p. ill., port. [2020]

Fenton, William Nelson

American Indian and white relations to 1830: an essay & a bibliography. New York: Russell & Russell, [1971]. x, 138 p. (Needs and opportunities for study series) [3927]

Ferguson, D.S.

Student housing report: submitted by D.S. Ferguson to the Ontario Department of University Affairs, 1969, with bibliography and appendices. Toronto: Ontario Department of University Affairs, 1969. 111 p. [3401]

Ferguson, Margaret; Sy, San San

Legal materials for high school libraries in Alberta. Edmonton: Legal Resource Centre of Alberta, c1983. vi, 50 p.; ISBN: 0-919792-02-2. [2259]

Ferres, John H.

"Criticism of Canadian fiction since 1945: a selected checklist." In: *Modern Fiction Studies*; Vol. 22, no. 3 (Autumn 1976) p. 485-500.; ISSN: 0026-7724. [1098]

Ferris, Kathryn

"Child custody and the lesbian mother: an annotated bibliography." In: *Resources for Feminist Research*; Vol. 12, no. 1 (March 1983) p. 106-109.; ISSN: 0707-8412. [3818]

Festival international du livre (1er: 1969: Nice, France)

Le Livre canadien: premier Festival international du livre, Nice, 1969/Canadian books [International Book Festival, Nice, 1969]. Ottawa: Conseil des arts du Canada, 1969. 120 p. [0092]

Feuerwerker, Elie; Ali, M.A.

"La vision chez les poissons: historique et bibliographie analytique." Dans: *Revue canadienne de biologie*; Vol. 34, no 4 (décembre 1975) p. 221-285.; ISSN: 0035-0915. [5391]

Ficke, Eleanore R.; Ficke, John F.

Ice on rivers and lakes: a bibliographical essay. Reston, Va.: Quality of Water Branch, U.S. Geological Survey, 1977. v, 173 p. (U.S. Geological Survey Water resources investigations ; 75-95) [5123]

Field, Thomas Warren

An essay towards an Indian bibliography: being a catalogue of books relating to the history, antiquities, languages, customs, religion, wars, literature, and origin of the American Indians, in the library of Thomas W. Field. New York: Scribner, Armstrong, 1873. iv, 430 p. [3904]

Field, William D.; Dos Passos, Cyril F.; Masters, John H.

A bibliography of the catalogs, lists, faunal and other papers on the butterflies of North America north of Mexico arranged by state and province (Lepidoptera: Rhopalocera). Washington: Smithsonian Institution Press, 1974. 104 p. (Smithsonian contributions to zoology ; no. 157) [5381]

Filby, P. William

American & British genealogy & heraldry: a selected list of books. 3rd ed. Boston: New England Historic Genealogical Society, 1983. xix, 736 p.; ISBN: 0-8808200-4-7. [2026]

Passenger and immigration lists bibliography, 1538-1900: being a guide to published lists of arrivals in the United States and Canada. Detroit, Mich.: Gale Research, c1988. xi, 324 p.; ISBN: 0-8103-2740-6. [2069]

Film-video Canadiana/Film-vidéo Canadiana. Montreal: Published by the National Film Board of Canada for National Library of Canada; National Archives of Canada, Moving Image and Sound Archives; La Cinémathèque québécoise: musée du cinéma, 1988-. vol.; ISSN: 0836-1002. [6703]

Films et vidéos documentaires pour adolescents et adultes: 11299 documents pour les 12 ans et plus. Montréal: Services documentaires Multimedia, [1991]. xiii, 1629 p.: ill. (Guides Tessier); ISBN: 2-89059-114-X. [6692]

Filotas, Paul K.G.

A subject bibliography of theses bibliographies held in Carleton University Library. Ottawa: Carleton University, Library, 1990. 1 vol. (unpaged). [6202]

Filson, D.H.; Eyre, D.

A bibliography of papers relevant to sanitary engineering practices in northern Saskatchewan townsites. [Saskatoon: Saskatchewan Research Council], 1975. 12 l. [5752]

Filteau, J.O.

Catalogue de livres canadiens et de quelques ouvrages français sur le Canada anciens et modernes. St.-Roche de Québec: Laberge & Gingras, 1878. 22 p. [0012]

Findlay, Joanna

White collar crime: a bibliography. Ottawa: RCMP HQ Library, 1980. i, 105 p. [2214]

Fingas, M.F.; Ross, C.W.

An oil spill bibliography: March, 1975 to December, 1976. Ottawa: Fisheries and Environment Canada, 1977. 112 p.

(Economic and technical review report / Fisheries and Environment Canada ; EPS-3-EC-77-10); ISBN: 0-66200663-1. [5124]

Fink, Howard

Canadian national theatre on the air, 1925-1961: CBC-CRBC-CNR radio drama in English, a descriptive bibliography and union list. Toronto: University of Toronto Press, c1983. ix, 48 p. (+ 25 microfiches) (The Concordia Radio Drama Project); ISBN: 0-8020-0358-3. [0978]

Finley, E. Gault

Education in Canada: a bibliography/L'éducation au Canada: une bibliographie. Toronto: Published by Dundurn Press in cooperation with the National Library of Canada and the Canadian Government Pub. Centre, 1989. 2 vol.; ISBN: 1-55002-044-7 (vol. 1); 1-55002-047-1 (vol. 2). [3702]

Sources à consulter en vue d'une compilation bibliographique sur l'évolution de l'éducation au Canada français. [Montréal: Université McGill, 1967]. 60 f. [3394]

Finley, Jean C.

Bibliography of the Lancaster Sound resource management plan: supporting documentation. Calgary: Arctic Institute of North America, University of Calgary, 1983. iv, 13 p. (ASTIS occasional publication / Arctic Science and Technology Information System ; no. 11; ISSN: 0225-5170) [5194]

Finley, Jean C.; Goodwin, C. Ross

The training and employment of northern Canadians: an annotated bibliography. Calgary: Published under the auspices of the Environmental Studies Revolving Funds by the Arctic Institute of North America, c1986. xx, 206 p. (Environmental Studies Revolving Funds report ; no. 050); ISBN: 0-920-783-49-X. [3654]

Finson, Shelley Davis

Women and religion: a bibliographic guide to Christian feminist liberation theology. Toronto: University of Toronto Press, c1991. xix, 207 p.; ISBN: 0-8020-5881-7. [3891]

Firth, Edith G.

Early Toronto newspapers, 1793-1867: a catalogue of newspapers published in the Town of York and the City of Toronto from the beginning to Confederation. Toronto: Published by the Baxter Pub. Co. in co-operation with the Toronto Public Library, 1961. 31 p.: facsims. [6012]

Fischer, Lewis R.; Salmon, M. Stephen

Canadian maritime bibliography for 1987. Ottawa: Canadian Nautical Research Society, 1988. 86 p. [4503]

Fisher, Gerald

"Atlantic Canada studies." In: *Communiqué: Canadian Studies*; Vol. 3, no. 2 (January 1977) p. 2-68.; ISSN: 0318-1197. [0229]

Fisher, Honey Ruth

Studies of drinking in public places: an annotated bibliography. Toronto: Addiction Research Foundation of Ontario, c1985. x, 85 p. (Bibliographic series / Addiction Research Foundation of Ontario ; no. 18; ISSN: 0065-1885); ISBN: 0-88868-106-2. [3272]

Fisher, Joel E.

Bibliography of Canadian mountain ascents. [S.l.: The Author], 1945. 103 p. [1743]

Fisher, John

"Bibliography for the study of Eskimo religion." In: *Anthropologica*; Vol. 15, no. 2 (1973) p. 231-271.; ISSN: 0003-5459. [1527]

Fiszhaut, Gustawa M.; Carrier, Lois J.

Guide to reference materials in geography in the Library of the University of British Columbia. Vancouver: University of British Columbia Library, 1969. 92 p. (Reference publication / University of British Columbia Library ; no. 27) [2973]

Fitchko, J.

Literature review of the effects of persistent toxic substances on Great Lakes biota. Windsor, Ont.: International Joint Commission, Great Lakes Regional Office, 1986. vii, 256 p.: map. [5232]

Fitzpatrick, Connie

A selected list of current government publications dealing with pollution. Vancouver: University of British Columbia Library, 1974. ii, 77 p. (Reference publication / University of British Columbia Library ; no. 51) [6289]

Fitzpatrick, Diane E.

The history of birth control in Canada: a working bibliography. Monticello, Ill.: Vance Bibliographies, 1991. 9 p. (Public administration series: Bibliography ; P-3039; ISSN: 0193-970X); ISBN: 0-7920-0759-X. [5701]

Flack, David; Hunt, Lynn J.; Murray, Danielle

History through drama: sourcebook. [Ontario: s.n.], c1984. 125 p.; ISBN: 0-9691747-0-5. [1212]

Fladmark, K.R.

"Bibliography of the archaeology of British Columbia." In: *BC Studies*; No. 6-7 (Fall-Winter 1970) p. 126-151.; ISSN: 0005-2949. [4549]

Flaherty, David H.

Privacy and data protection: an international bibliography. White Plains, N.Y.: Knowledge Industry Publications, 1984. xxvi, 276 p.; ISBN: 0-86729-121-4. [2266]

Flem-Ath, Rand

Canadian security and intelligence: a bibliography, 1945-1985. Victoria, B.C.: University of Victoria, 1986. 47 l. [2505]

Fleming, Patricia Lockhart

Atlantic Canadian imprints, 1801-1820: a bibliography. Toronto: University of Toronto Press, c1991. xviii, 188 p.: ill.; ISBN: 0-8020-5872-8. [0273]

"A bibliography of Ontario directories to 1867." In: *Ontario Library Review*; Vol. 59, no. 2 (June 1975) p. 98-107.; ISSN: 0030-2996. [0452]

A history of publishing in Toronto, 1841-1978, with a descriptive bibliography of imprints. London, (Eng.): [s.n.], 1980. [1639]

Upper Canadian imprints, 1801-1841: a bibliography. Toronto: University of Toronto Press in co-operation with the National Library of Canada and the Canadian Government Publishing Centre, Supply and Services Canada, [c1988]. xviii, 555 p.; ISBN: 0-8020-2585-4. [0486]

Flemington, Frank

"Annie Charlotte Dalton (1865-1938): biographical note and bibliography." In: *Canadian Author and Bookman*; Vol. 22, no. 3 (September 1946) p. 42-44.; ISSN: 0008-29337. [6931]

Flemming, Tom; Kent, Diana

Sourcebook of Canadian health statistics. Toronto: Canadian Health Libraries Association, 1990. vi, 100 p.; ISBN: 0-9692171-2-9. [5694]

Flick, Frances Josephine; Brown, Elizabeth P.

Economics of forestry: a bibliography for the United States and Canada, 1940-1947. Washington, D.C.: United States Department of Agriculture Library, 1950. vi, 126 p. (Library list / United States Department of Agriculture

Library ; no. 52) [4920]

Flint, John E.

Books on the British Empire and Commonwealth. London. Published on behalf of the Royal Commonwealth Society by Oxford University Press, 1968. vi, 65 p. [0089]

Flitton, Marilyn G.

"Annual bibliography of Commonwealth literature, 1978: Canada." In: *Journal of Commonwealth Literature*; Vol. 14, no. 2 (December 1979) p. 42-62.; ISSN: 0021-98944. [1149]

Florkow, David W.; Heitz, Thomas R.; Lounder, Shirley A.

Case law reporting: a selected bibliography and checklist of Canadian law reporting studies. Ottawa: Canadian Law Information Council, [1981]. vi, 86 p. (CLIC Occasional paper ; no. 3); ISBN: 0-920358-05-5. [2232]

Foerstel, Hans

Resources for teachers: local planning, development, environment. [S.l.: s.n.], 1975. 24, 8 p.: ill. [4349]

Fogwill, W.D.; Hawkins, V.

Bibliography of the geology of Newfoundland and Labrador, 1969 to 1974. St. John's, Nfld.: Mineral Development Division, Department of Mines and Energy, Government of Newfoundland and Labrador, 1977. 258 p. [4798]

Fohlen, Claude

"Au Canada, un siècle après la Confédération." Dans: *Revue historique*; Vol. 238 (juillet-septembre 1967) p.135-146.; ISSN: 0035-3264. [1953]

Foley, Kathryn Shred; Harley, Birgit; D'Anglejan, Alison

"Research in Core French: a bibliographic review." In: *Canadian Modern Language Review*; Vol. 44, no. 4 (May 1988) p. 593-618.; ISSN: 0008-4506. [3686]

Research in core French: an annotated bibliography/ Recherches sur le français de base: bibliographie analytique. [Winnipeg]: Canadian Association of Second Language Teachers, 1987. v, 167 p.; ISBN: 0-921238-00-2. [1474]

Fondation de l'arbre Canada

Répertoire de la recherche et des projets pilotes réalisés au Canada sur l'enfance maltraitée et négligée: un rapport de recherches. [Ottawa]: Gouvernement du Canada, c1981. 369 p.; ISBN: 0-662-91348-5. [3219]

Fontannaz-Howard, Lucienne

"Les livres d'images québécois." Dans: *Documentation et bibliothèques*; Vol. 22, no 2 (juin 1976) p. 87-90.; ISSN: 0315-2340. [1331]

Forcese, Dennis P.

"Sociology in Canada: a view from the eighties." In: *International Journal of Canadian Studies*; No. 1-2 (Spring-Fall 1990) p. 35-53.; ISSN: 1180-3991. [3339]

Ford, John; McTavish, Isabella

Job sharing and work sharing: a selected bibliography. [Toronto]: Ontario Ministry of Labour, Library, 1980. 12 p. [2865]

Ford, John; Miller, Alan V.

Women, microelectronics, and employment: a selected bibliography. [Toronto]: Ontario Ministry of Labour, Library, 1983. 16 p. [3819]

Ford, Theresa M.

Teacher resource book: western Canadian literature for youth. Edmonton: Alberta Education, c1980. 576 p.; ISBN: 0-920794-07-6. [1342]

Foreign Service Community Association. Committee on Mobility and the Family

Mobility, cultural adaptation and the family: a selected annotated bibliography/Mobilité, adaptation culturelle et la famille: bibliographie commentée d'ouvrages choisis. Ottawa: Committee on Mobility and the Family, Foreign Service Community Association, 1978. iii, 47 p. [3169]

Forest, Paul

Sports et loisirs: bibliographie, périodiques, films, diaporamas, organismes. Montréal: Collège Marie-Victorin, 1982. 31, [1] p.; ISBN: 2-920279-08-4. [1816]

Forest Engineering Research Institute of Canada

FERIC publications, 1975-1989. Pointe-Claire, Quebec: FERIC, 1990. [40] p. [5007]

Forest Fire Research Institute (Canada). Information Centre

Document list [Forest Fire Research Institute]. Ottawa: Forest Fire Research Institute, Department of Fisheries and Forestry, 1969. 1 vol. (loose-leaf). [4925]

Forget, Guy

Bibliography of Canadian official publications on alcoholic beverages, 1921-1956. Ottawa: [s.n.], 1957. 1 vol. (unpaged). [6241]

Forintek Canada Corporation

List of publications [Forintek Canada]/Liste des publications [Forintek Canada]. Ottawa: Forintek Canada Corporation, 1981-. vol.; ISSN: 0227-101X. [6451]

Forkes, David

Skiing: an English language bibliography, 1891-1971. Vancouver: [s.n.], 1975. 53 l.; ISBN: 0-96909-020-X. [1776]

Forsyth, Joseph

Government publications relating to Alberta: a bibliography of publications of the government of Alberta from 1905 to 1968, and of publications of the government of Canada relating to the province of Alberta from 1867 to 1968. High Wycombe [S. Buckingham]: University Microfilms, [1972]. 8 vol. [6278]

Fort Frontenac Library

Fort Frontenac Library periodical holdings/Bibliothèque Fort Frontenac: périodiques. [Kingston, Ont.]: The Library, 1989. 120 p. [5968]

Forthcoming books/Livres à paraître. Ottawa: National Library of Canada, 1987-. vol.; ISSN: 1187-6301. [0185]

Fortier, John

"The Fortress of Louisbourg and its cartographic evidence." In: *Bulletin: Association for Preservation Technology*; Vol. 4, no. 1-2 (1972) p. 3-40.; ISSN: 0044-9466. [0738]

Fortier, Marcel; Taylor, Marianne

First Nations public administration: an annotated bibliography/Administrations publiques des Premières nations: bibliographie annotée. Ottawa: Indian Government Support Directorate, 1993. [11], 77 p.; ISBN: 0-662-59637-4. [4121]

Fortier, Monique

Les commissions parlementaires à l'Assemblée nationale, 1980-1985. [Québec]: Assemblée nationale du Québec, Bibliothèque, Division de l'indexation et de la bibliographie, 1986. 218 p. (Bibliographie et documentation / Bibliothèque de l'Assemblée nationale du Québec ; 24); ISBN: 2-551-06669-7. [6380]

Fortin, Benjamin; Gaboury, Jean-Pierre

Bibliographie analytique de l'Ontario français. [Ottawa]: Éditions de l'Université d'Ottawa, 1975. xii, 236 p. (Cahiers du Centre de recherche en civilisation canadienne-française ; 9); ISBN: 0-776-4089-5. [0453]

Fortin, Donald

Le développement des administrateurs et le perfectionnement: bibliographie. Montréal: Fédération des CEGEP, 1973. 14 f. [2604]

Le développement organisationnel et le changement planifié: bibliographie. Montréal: Fédération des CEGEP, 1972. 31 f. [2596]

La direction par objectifs: bibliographie. Montréal: Fédération des CEGEP, 1973. 12 f. [2605]

L'évaluation des administrateurs: bibliographie. Montréal: Fédération des CEGEP, 1973. 9 f. [2606]

Fortin, Marcel; Lamonde, Yvan; Ricard, François

Guide de la littérature québécoise. [Montréal]: Boréal, 1988. 155 p.; ISBN: 2-89052-248-2. [1251]

Fortin, Suzanne, et al.

La Beauce et un peu plus: bibliographie commentée, des ouvrages écrits sur la Beauce et la périphérie. Saint-Georges: [s.n.], 1972. 1 vol. (en pagination multiple). [0318]

Fortuine, Robert

The health of the Eskimos: a bibliography, 1857-1967. Hanover, N.H.: Dartmouth College Libraries, [1968]. 87 p. [5573]

Foshay, Toby Avard

John Daniel Logan (1869-1929) [microform]: biography, bibliography and checklist of the Logan papers in the Acadia University Library. Ottawa: National Library of Canada, 1981. 3 microfiches (Canadian theses on microfiche ; 49143; ISSN: 0227-3845); ISBN: 0-31501-286-2. [7151]

Foss, Brian; Singer, Loren

"J. Russell Harper, O.C., D.Litt., D.F.A., F.R.S.C.: a chronological bibliography." In: Journal of Canadian Art History; Vol. 7, no. 2 (1984) p. 106-112.; ISSN: 0315-4297. [7045]

Found, William C.

Environment, migration, and the management of rural resources. Monticello, Ill.: Council of Planning Librarians, 1976. 4 vol. (Council of Planning Librarians Exchange bibliography ; 1143, 1144, 1145, 1146) [3015]

Fournier, François; Goulet, Marcel

Propriétés physico-mécaniques de l'écorce: une étude bibliographique. Québec: Département d'exploitation et utilisation des bois, Université Laval, 1978. 44 f. (Notes de recherche / Département d'exploitation et utilisation des bois, Université Laval ; no 7) [4964]

Fournier, Marcel

Guide bibliographique Joliette-Lanaudière: [livres et journaux, 1847-1976]. Joliette [Québec]: Société historique de Joliette, 1976. 96 f.: fac.–sim. [0339]

Guide des monographies de paroisses de la région Joliette-Lanaudière. Chertsey, Québec: [s.n.], 1974. 30 f. [0328]

Fournier-Renaud, Madeleine; Véronneau, Pierre

Écrits sur le cinéma: bibliographie québécoise, 1911-1981. Montréal: Cinémathèque québécoise-Musée du cinéma, c1982. 180 p.: ill. (Dossiers de la Cinémathèque / Cinémathèque québécoise-Musée du cinéma ; no 9); ISBN: 2-89207-022-8. [0975]

Fowke, Edith

"Anglo-Canadian folksong: a survey." In: Ethnomusicology; Vol. 16, no. 3 (September 1972) p. 335-350.; ISSN: 0014-1836. [0833]

"A reference list on Canadian folk music." In: Canadian Folk Music Journal; Vol. 1 (1973) p. 46-56; vol. 6 (1978) p. 41-56; vol. 11 (1983) p. 43-60.; ISSN: 0318-2568. [0910]

Fowke, Edith; Carpenter, Carole Henderson

A bibliography of Canadian folklore in English. Toronto: University of Toronto Press, 1981. xx, 272 p.; ISBN: 0-8020-2394-0. [4580]

"A bibliography of Canadian folklore in English." In: Communiqué: Canadian Studies; Vol. 3, no. 4 (August 1977) p. 3-72.; ISSN: 0318-1197. [4567]

Fowke, V.C.

"An introduction to Canadian agricultural history." In: Canadian Journal of Economics and Political Science; Vol. 8, no. 1 (February 1942) p. 56-68.; ISSN: 0315-4890. [4639]

"Publications of G.E. Britnell." In: Canadian Journal of Economics and Political Science; Vol. 28, no. 2 (May 1962) p. 289-291.; ISSN: 0315-4890. [6875]

Fowle, Charles David; Baehre, Ralph K.

A bibliography on acid rain. Don Mills, Ont.: Federation of Ontario Naturalists, 1979. 27 p. [5149]

Fox, Richard George

The extra Y chromosome and deviant behavior: a bibliography. [Toronto]: Centre of Criminology, University of Toronto, 1970. 21 l. [3095]

Fox, W. Sherwood

"The literature of Salmo salar in Lake Ontario and tributary streams." In: Proceedings and Transactions of the Royal Society of Canada; Series 3, vol. 24, section 2 (1930) p. 45-55.; ISSN: 0316-4616. [5318]

Framst, G.E.

Ontario and national marketing boards: a selected bibliography, 1955-1973. Toronto: Economics Branch, Ontario Ministry of Agriculture and Food, 1974. 4 p. [4665]

France. Bibliothèque nationale

Catalogues des documents géographiques exposés à la Section des cartes et plans de la Bibliothèque nationale. Paris: J. Maisonneuve, 1892. 77 p. [6484]

Le franchisage au Canada: sources d'information. [Ottawa]: Direction générale des industries des services et des biens de consommation, Industrie, sciences et technologie Canada, 1990. 19, 19 p.; ISBN: 0-662-57349-8. [2766]

Franchising in Canada: information sources. [Ottawa]: Service Industries and Consumer Goods Branch, Industry, Science and Technology Canada, 1990. 19, 19 p.; ISBN: 0-662-57349-8. [2767]

Frank, David, et al.

The New Brunswick worker in the 20th century: a reader's guide: a selective annotated bibliography/Les travailleurs au Nouveau-Brunswick au 20ième siècle: un guide au lecteur: bibliographie choisie et annotée. Fredericton: Department of History, University of New Brunswick, 1986. 178 p. [2904]

Frank, Jackie; Schonfield, David

The running Canadian bibliography: a consolidation, 1978-1984/Bibliographie courante d'ouvrages canadiens: une consolidation, 1978-1984. Winnipeg: Canadian Association on Gerontology, [1985]. 1 vol. (in various pagings). [5668]

Frank, K. Portland

The anti-psychiatry bibliography and resource guide. 2nd ed., rev. & expanded. Vancouver: Press Gang, 1979. 159 p.; ISBN: 0-88974-008-9. [5623]

Frank, Peter G.

A checklist and bibliography of the Sipuncula from Canadian and adjacent waters. Ottawa: National Museum of Natural Sciences, 1983. 47 p.: ill., maps. (Syllogeus / National Museum of Natural Sciences ; no. 46; ISSN: 0704-576X) [5181]

Frank, Thomas F.; Tarte, Frank C.

Marketing to farmers: an annotated bibliography. Guelph, Ont.: School of Agricultural Economics and Extension Education, Ontario Agricultural College, University of Guelph, 1972. [43] l. [4652]

Frankel, B. Gail; Brook, Robert C.; Whitehead, Paul C.

Therapeutic communities for the management of addictions: a critically annotated bibliography. Toronto: Addiction Research Foundation, c1976. xvii, 204 p. (Bibliographic series / Addiction Research Foundation of Ontario ; no. 12; ISSN: 0065-1885); ISBN: 0-88868-021-X. [5608]

Frankel-Howard, Deborah

Family violence: review of theoretical and clinical literature. [Ottawa]: Policy, Communications and Information Branch, Health and Welfare Canada, 1989. 115, 129 p.; ISBN: 0-662-16951-4. [3327]

La violence familiale: examen des écrits théoriques et cliniques. [Ottawa]: Direction générale de la politique, des communications et de l'information, [1989]. 129, 115 p.; ISBN: 0-662-95439-4. [3328]

Franzin, William Gilbert

Bibliographies of beluga (Delphinapterus leucas), narwhal (Monodon monocerus) and walrus (Odobenus rosmarus) to June, 1982. Winnipeg: Government of Canada, Fisheries and Oceans, 1984. iv, 20 p. (Canadian manuscript report of fisheries and aquatic sciences ; no. 1740; ISSN: 0706-6473) [5496]

Frappier, Monique; Heap, Margaret; Robert, Jean-Claude

"Montréal dans les récits de voyage: bibliographie." Dans: *Rapport et travaux, 1973-1975: Groupe de recherche sur la société montréalaise au 19e siècle*. Montréal: Département d'histoire, Université du Québec à Montréal, 1975. 50 p.; ISSN: 0225-6959. [0334]

Fraser, Alex W.

Title guide of local histories for the counties of Glengarry, Dundas, Prescott, Stormont: including the HH-GGS titles. Lancaster, Ont.: Highland Heritage/Glengarry Genealogical Society, 1991. 83 p.: ill.; ISBN: 0-921307-40-3. [0491]

Fraser, Doreen E.; Lloyd, Hazel A.

The information needs of physiotherapists with a guide to physiotherapy collections for community general hospitals. Halifax: Dalhousie University Libraries, 1981. 72 p. (Occasional papers / Dalhousie University Libraries and Dalhousie University School of Library Service ; no. 13; ISSN: 0318-7403) [5635]

Fraser, Ian Forbes

Bibliography of French-Canadian poetry. Part 1: From the beginnings of the literature through the École littéraire de Montréal. New York: Institute of French Studies, Columbia University, c1935. vi, 105 p. [1004]

Fraser, J. Keith

"Bibliography of D.F. Putnam." In: *Revue canadienne de géographie*; Vol. 5 (1951) p. 48-49.; ISSN: 0316-3032. [7253]

Fraser, J. Keith; Hynes, Mary C.

List of theses and dissertations on Canadian geography/ Liste des thèses et dissertations sur la géographie du Canada. Ottawa: Lands Directorate, Department of the Environment, 1972. vi, 114 p. (Geographical paper / Lands Directorate, Department of the Environment ; no. 51) [6116]

Frayne, June; Laidley, Jennifer; Hadeed, Henry

Print for young Canadians: a bibliographical catalogue of Canadian fiction for children from 1825-1920. Toronto: [s.n.], 1975. x, 80 p.: ill. [1326]

Fréchette, Jean-Guy

Bibliographie de météorologie forestière. Québec: Éditeur officiel du Québec, 1969. 59 p. [4926]

Frederick Harris Music Co. Limited

A complete catalogue of the published works of Boris Berlin. Oakville, Ont.: [s.n.], 1965. 8 p.: port. [6838]

Frederking, R.

Summary of current research on snow and ice in Canada, 1976. Ottawa: National Research Council Canada, Associate Committee on Geotechnical Research, 1976. 52 p. (Associate Committee on Geotechnical Research Technical memorandum ; no. 118) [5113]

Fredriksen, John C.

Free trade and sailors' rights: a bibliography of the War of 1812. Westport, Conn.: Greenwood Press, c1985. xiii, 399 p. (Bibliographies and indexes in American history ; no. 2; ISSN: 0742-6828); ISBN: 0-313-24313-1. [2046]

Resource guide for the War of 1812. [S.l.: s.n.], c1979. vii, 156 p. [2002]

Free, Brian Michael

Bibliography of recycling. Edmonton: Environment Council of Alberta, 1986. 56 p. [5233]

Freeman, Richard Broke; Wertheimer, Douglas

Philip Henry Gosse: a bibliography. Folkestone, Kent: Dawson, 1980. xviii, 148 p., 3 l. of pl.: ill., port.; ISBN: 0-7129-0935-4. [7022]

Freemark, Kathryn; Dewar, Heather; Saltman, Jane

A literature review of bird use of farmland habitats in the Great Lakes-St. Lawrence region/Une étude bibliographique de l'utilisation, par les oiseaux, des habitats agricoles dans la région des Grands Lacs et du Saint-Laurent. Ottawa: Canadian Wildlife Service, 1991. [200] p. (in various pagings): map. (Technical report series / Canadian Wildlife Service ; no. 114; ISSN: 8031-6481); ISBN: 0-662-18398-3. [5560]

Freer, Katherine M.

Vancouver, a bibliography compiled from material in the Vancouver Public Library and the Special Collections of the University of British Columbia Library. [London, Eng.]: University of London, 1962. [ix], 234 l. [0573]

French Institute in the United States

Publications contemporaines de langue française aux États-Unis et au Canada; exposition. New York: French Institute, 1942. 45 p. [0285]

Frey, Cecelia

"Phyllis Webb: an annotated bibliography." In: *The annotated bibliography of Canada's major authors*, Vol. 6, edited by Robert Lecker and Jack David. Toronto: ECW Press, 1985. P. 389-448.; ISBN: 0-920802-93-1. [7362]

Fricker, Aubrey; Samson, A.L.

Bibliography of publications by staff of the Atlantic Geoscience Centre to December 1984. Dartmouth, N.S.: Fisheries and Oceans, 1986. v, 326 p. (Canadian data report of hydrography and ocean sciences ; no. 48; ISSN: 0711-6721) [4850]

Frideres, James S.

"Recent publications relating to Canadian ethnic studies." In: *Canadian Ethnic Studies*; Vol. 8, no. 2 (1976) p. 142-146; vol. 9, no. 2 (1977) p. 153-156; vol. 10, no. 2 (1978) p. 211-216;

vol. 11, no. 2 (1979) p. 148-153.; ISSN: 0008-3496. [4193]

Fried, Jacob

A survey of the aboriginal populations of Quebec and Labrador. Montreal: McGill University, 1955. iv, 121 p. (Eastern Canadian anthropological series ; no. 1) [3909]

Friendly, Martha; Willis, Tricia

Child care policy in Canada, 1990: selected topics: an annotated bibliography. Toronto: Childcare Resource and Research Unit, Centre for Urban and Community Studies, University of Toronto, 1991. 108 p. [3353]

Friends of the library: a bibliography. Regina: Provincial Library, Saskatchewan Education, 1989. 5 p. [1707]

Friesen, Gerald; Potyondi, Barry

A guide to the study of Manitoba local history. Winnipeg: Published by the University of Manitoba Press for the Manitoba Historical Society, c1981. 182 p.: ill.; ISBN: 0-88755-121-1. [0534]

Friesen, Jean; Angel, Michael

"Manitoba bibliography of bibliographies." In: *Manitoba History*; No. 12 (Fall 1986) p. 18-24 (Insert, 8 p.).; ISSN: 0226-5036. [0542]

Friesen, John W.; Lusty, Terry

The Metis of Canada: an annotated bibliography. [Toronto]: OISE Press, [c1980]. viii, 99 p.; ISBN: 0-7744-0215-6. [4015]

Friesen, Richard J.

The Chilkoot: a literature review. Ottawa: National Historic Sites Service, Department of Indian Affairs and Northern Development, 1977. iv, 111 p.: ill. (Manuscript report / National Historic Parks and Sites Branch ; 203) [0633]

The Chilkoot Pass: a preliminary bibliography. [Ottawa]: National Historic Parks and Sites Branch, Parks Canada, 1977. 36 p. (National Historic Parks and Sites Branch Research bulletin ; no. 50) [0634]

Frisken, Frances; Emby, Gwynneth

Social aspects of urban transportation: a bibliographic review. [Toronto]: University of Toronto/York University Joint Program in Transportation, 1975. 252 p. (University of Toronto-York University Joint Program in Transportation Research report ; no. 30; ISSN: 0316-9456) [4459]

Frittaion, Franco, et al.

"Bibliography of Canadian plays in English 1800-1945." In: *Canadian Drama*; Vol. 3, no. 1 (Spring 1977) p. 42-74.; ISSN: 0317-9044. [1107]

Fritz, Linda

Native law bibliography. 2nd ed. Saskatoon: University of Saskatchewan, Native Law Centre, 1990. ix, 167 p.; ISBN: 0-88880-233-6. [2337]

Subject guide to native law cases and annotated text of the Indian Act of Canada. Saskatoon: University of Saskatchewan Native Law Centre, 1985. 267 p. [2272]

Froeschle, Hartmut

Americana Germanica: Bibliographie zur deutschen Sprache und deutschsprachigen Literatur in Nord- und Lateinamerika. Hildesheim: Olms, 1991. xxi, 233 p. (Auslandsdeutsche Literatur der Gegenwart ; Band 15; ISSN: 0175-842X); ISBN: 3-487-08321-3. [1293]

"Deutschkanadische Bibliographie: eine auswahl." In: *German-Canadian Yearbook*; Vol. 1 (1973) p. 327-344.; ISSN: 0316-8603. [4160]

Froeschle, Hartmut; Zimmerman, Lothar

German Canadiana: a bibliography/Deutschkanadische bibliographie. Toronto: Historical Society of Mecklenburg Upper Canada, 1990. xix, 420 p.; ISBN: 1-895503-12-

4. [4274]

"The Germans in Ontario : a bibliography." In: *German-Canadian Yearbook*; Vol. 8 (1984) p. 243-279.; ISSN: 0316-8603. [4221]

Fudge, Evelyn

"A selected list of the writings of E. Cockburn Kyte." In: *Ernest Cockburn Kyte: a tribute*, edited by William F.E. Morley. Kingston, Ont.: Douglas Library, Queen's University, 1970. P. 23-25. [7104]

Fulford, Robert; Godfrey, David; Rotstein, Abraham

Read Canadian: a book about Canadian books. Toronto: James Lewis & Samuel, 1972. xi, 275 p.; ISBN: 0-88862-018-7. [0103]

Fuller, Anthony M.; Mage, Julius A.

A directory of part-time farming studies. Vol. 1: North America and W. Europe. Guelph, Ont.: Department of Geography, University of Guelph, 1977. v, 81 p. [4671]

Fullerton, Carol

"George Stewart, Jr.: a bibliography." In: *Papers of the Bibliographical Society of Canada*; Vol. 25 (1986) p. 97-108.; ISSN: 0067-6896. [7322]

Fulton, John

Keys and references to the marine copepoda of British Columbia. Nanaimo, B.C.: Fisheries Research Board of Canada, Pacific Biological Station, 1972. 63 p. (Fisheries Research Board of Canada Technical report ; no. 313; ISSN: 0068-7553) [5367]

Furse, Alison; Levine, Elyse

Food, nutrition and the disabled: an annotated bibliography. Toronto: Nutrition Information Service, Ryerson Polytechnical Institute Library, 1981. vii, 82 p.; ISBN: 0-919351-00-X. [3220]

Fyffe, L.R.; Blair, D.M.

Bibliography of New Brunswick geology, (1839 to 1988). Fredericton: Minerals and Energy Division, Department of Natural Resources and Energy, New Brunswick, 1989. i, 225 p. (Geoscience report / Minerals and Energy Division, Department of Natural Resources and Energy, New Brunswick ; 89-3; ISSN: 0838-2565) [4876]

Gabel, Gernot U.

Canadian literature: an index to theses accepted by Canadian universities, 1925-1980. Köln: Edition Gemini, 1984. 157 p.; ISBN: 3-922331-15-7. [6175]

Gabriel-de-l'Annonciation, soeur

Bibliographie analytique sur la méthodologie de l'histoire du Canada, 1950-1962. Québec: [s.n.], 1963. viii, 47 p. [1939]

Gadacz, René R.

Thesis and dissertation titles and abstracts on the anthropology of Canadian Indians, Inuit and Metis from Canadian universities, report 1, 1970-1982. Ottawa: National Museums of Canada, 1984. x, 128 p. (National Museum of Man Mercury series: Canadian Ethnology Service paper ; no. 95; ISSN: 0316-1862) [6176]

Gagné, Armand

Répertoire des thèses des facultés ecclésiastiques de l'Université Laval, 1935-1960. Québec: [s.n.], 1960. iii, 19 f. (Études et recherches bibliographiques / Université Laval ; no 2) [6071]

Gagné, Marc

Gilles Vigneault: bibliographie descriptive et critique, discographie, filmographie, iconographie, chronologie. Québec: Presses de l'Université Laval, 1977. xxxii, 976 p.: ill., fac.–sims.; ISBN: 0-7746-6799-0. [7352]

Gagné, Martine P.

Catalogue de la bibliothèque [Québec Ministère des richesse naturelles]. Québec. Éditeur officiel du Québec, 1971. 338 p. [4620]

Gagné, Oscar

L'oeuvre pédagogique des Frères de l'instruction chrétienne dans la province de Québec, 1886-1986. La Prairie [Québec]: Frères de l'instruction chrétienne, 1986. xiv, 229 p. (Cahiers du Regroupement des archivistes religieux ; no 2); ISBN: 2-9800558-0-8. [3655]

Gagné, Raymond

Publications parlementaires québécoises: catalogue collectif. Québec: Bibliothèque, Assemblée nationale, 1985. [26] f. (Bibliographie et documentation / Bibliothèque de l'Assemblée nationale du Québec ; no 19; ISSN: 0821-1175) [6373]

Gagnon, André

"Translations of children's books in Canada." In: *Canadian Children's Literature*; No. 45 (1987) p. 14-53.; ISSN: 0319-0080. [1376]

Gagnon, André; Gagnon, Anne

Canadian books for young people/Livres canadiens pour la jeunesse. 4th ed. Toronto: University of Toronto Press, c1988. 186 p.; ISBN: 0-8020-6662-3. [1378]

Gagnon, Claude-Marie

Bibliographie critique du joual, 1970-1975. Québec: Institut supérieur des sciences humaines, Université Laval, 1976. 117 f. (Cahiers de l'ISSH, Collection Instruments de travail / Institut supérieur des sciences humaines, Université Laval ; no 19) [1435]

Les manuscrits et imprimés religieux au Québec, 1867-1960: bibliographie. Québec: Université Laval, Institut supérieur des sciences humaines, c1981. 195 p. (Collection études sur le Québec ; no 12) [1549]

Gagnon, Claude-Marie; Provost, Sylvie

Bibliographie sélective et indicative de la paralittérature. Québec: Institut supérieur des sciences humaines, Université Laval, c1978. 88 f. (Cahiers de l'ISSH, Collection Instruments de travail / Institut supérieur des sciences humaines, Université Laval ; no 24) [1129]

Gagnon, Philéas

Catalogue d'ouvrages rares sur le Canada et les États-Unis. [S.l.: s.n.], 1886. 12 p. [0017]

Catalogue of rare old books: read attentively, English & French, Americana and miscellanies, but specially a Canadian collection. [Quebec: s.n., 1884]. 12 p. [0014]

Essai de bibliographie canadienne: inventaire d'une bibliothèque comprenant imprimés, manuscrits, estampes, etc., relatifs à l'histoire du Canada et des pays adjacents: avec des notes bibliographiques. Québec: L'Auteur, 1895-1913. 2 vol.: ill., fac-sims. [6756]

Gagnon, Solange; Brassard, Hélène

Répertoire des banques de données agricoles du Québec. Sainte-Foy, Québec: Groupe de gestion et d'économie agricoles, Comité collecte et accès à l'information technico-socio-économique, 1992. 152 f. [4723]

Gagnon-Arguin, Louise; Perron, Normand

"Mgr Victor Tremblay: bibliographie sommaire." Dans: *Saguenayensia*; Vol. 21, nos 5-6 (novembre-décembre 1979) p. 177-180.; ISSN: 0581-295X. [7338]

Gaida, Pranas; Baltgailis, Peter

"Lithuanian-Canadian periodical publications: a preliminary check list." In: *Canadian Ethnic Studies*; Vol. 2, no. 1 (June 1970) p. 151-155.; ISSN: 0008-3496. [5891]

Gajewsky, Stan

Accreditation: review of the literature and selected annotated bibliography. Montreal: Faculty of Education, McGill University, c1973. 58 l. (Reports in education / Faculty of Education, McGill University ; no. 1) [3465]

Class size: review of the literature and selected annotated bibliography. Montreal: Faculty of Education, McGill University, c1973. 58 l. (Reports in education / Faculty of Education, McGill University ; no. 2) [3466]

Gakovich, Robert P.; Radovich, Milan M.

Serbs in the United States and Canada: a comprehensive bibliography. [Minneapolis]: Immigration History Research Center, University of Minnesota, 1976. xii, 129 p.: ill. [4172]

Gale directory of databases. Detroit: Gale Research, 1993. 2 vol.; ISBN: 0-8103-5746-1 (set). [0179]

Gall, Q.; Birkett, T.

"Post-graduate theses in Canadian universities on geologic research related to mineral deposits, 1983-1986." In: *CIM Bulletin*; Vol. 80, no. 905 (September 1987) p. 88-100.; ISSN: 0317-0926. [6190]

Gallat-Morin, Élizabeth; Bouchard, Antoine

Témoins de la vie musicale en Nouvelle-France. Montréal: Ministère des affaires culturelles, Archives nationales du Québec, 1981. 74 p.; ISBN: 2-550-04322-0. [0896]

Gallichan, Gilles

"Essai bibliographique sur les débats parlementaires du Québec (1792-1963)." Dans: *Cahiers de la Société bibliographique du Canada*; Vol. 27 (1988) p. 54-79.; ISSN: 0067-6896. [2518]

Gallina, Paul

Electronic funds transfer: a bibliography. Ottawa: Socioscope, 1981. 94 p.; ISBN: 0-919539-02-5. [2670]

"Research in urban history 1987-1988." In: *Urban History Review: Revue d'histoire urbaine*; Vol. 18, no. 2 (October 1989) p. 166-175.; ISSN: 0703-0428. [4428]

Ganong, William F.

Crucial maps in the early cartography and place-nomenclature of the Atlantic coast of Canada. Toronto: Published by the University of Toronto Press in cooperation with the Royal Society of Canada, 1964. xvii, 511 p.: maps, port. (Special publications / Royal Society of Canada ; 7) [6508]

Materials for a history of the province of New Brunswick. [S.l.: s.n.], 1896. 21 p. [0195]

Garant, Louise

La déinstitutionnalisation en santé mentale: un tour d'horizon de la littérature. Québec: Ministère des affaires sociales, Secrétariat à la coordination de la recherche, 1985. 74 p. [3273]

Habitudes de vie et santé: revue de la recherche. Québec: Gouvernement du Québec, Ministère des affaires sociales, 1983. 108 p. (Évaluation des programmes / Gouvernement du Québec, Ministère des affaires sociales ; 11) [5651]

Revue des études sur la prévalence de la déficience mentale grave. Québec: Service des synthèses de recherche, Ministère des affaires sociales, 1980. 34 f. [5628]

Garant, Louise; Bolduc, Mario

L'aide par les proches: mythes et réalités: revue de littérature et réflexions sur les personnes âgées en perte d'autonomie, leurs aidants et aidantes naturels et le lien avec services formels. Québec: Gouvernement du Québec, Ministère de la santé et des service sociaux, Direction générale de la planification et de l'évaluation, 1990. xviii, 157 p. (Collection Études et analyses / Gouvernement du Québec, Ministère de la santé et des service sociaux, Direction générale de la planification et de l'évaluation ; 8); ISBN: 2-550-21000-X. [3340]

Garceau, Benoît
"La philosophie analytique de la religion: contribution canadienne 1970-1975." Dans: *Philosophiques*; Vol. 2, no 2 (octobre 1975) p. 301-339.; ISSN: 0316-2923. [1538]

Garde côtière canadienne. Direction de la recherche et du sauvage
Répertoire de documents sur la sécurité nautique. Ottawa: Garde côtière canadienne, c1991. 51, [15] p.; ISBN: 0-662-96718-6. [1864]

Gardner, Grant Allan; Szabo, Ildy
British Columbia pelagic marine Copepoda: an identification manual and annotated bibliography. Ottawa: Department of Fisheries and Oceans, 1982. vi, 536 p. (Canadian special publication of fisheries and aquatic sciences ; 62; ISSN: 0706-6481); ISBN: 0-660-11250-7. [5476]

Gardner, L., et al.
Alternative transportation fuels: review of research activity in Canada: report of the Task Force on Alternative Fuels, Associate Committee on Propulsion, National Research Council Canada/Combustibles de transport de remplacement: examen des travaux de recherche au Canada: rapport du Groupe de travail sur les combustibles de remplacement, Comité associé sur la propulsion, Conseil national de recherches du Canada. [Ottawa]: Division of Mechanical Engineering, National Research Council Canada, 1987. vii, 74, 64 p. (National Research Council Canada, Division of Mechanical Engineering report ; 1987-06) [5822]

Gardner, Robert C.; Desrochers, Alain
"Second-language acquisition and bilingualism: research in Canada (1970-1980)." In: *Canadian Psychology*; Vol. 22, no. 2 (April 1981) p. 146-161.; ISSN: 0708-5591. [1451]

Gareau, C.A.
Liste de livres canadiens rares et précieux: au nombre desquels se trouvent plusieurs incunables. Montréal: 1899. 15 p. [0027]

Garigue, Philippe
A bibliographical introduction to the study of French Canada. [Montreal]: Department of Sociology and Anthropology, McGill University, 1956. 133 p. [0289]

Garigue, Philippe; Savard, Raymonde
Bibliographie du Québec (1955-1965). Montréal: Presses de l'Université de Montréal, 1967. 227 p. [0297]

Garneau, Denyse
Selected bibliography on the geology of Canadian deposits and occurrences of uranium and thorium. Ottawa: Geological Survey of Canada, 1976. 41 p. (Geological Survey of Canada Paper ; 75-45; ISSN: 0068-7650) [4795]

Garner, Barbara Carman; Harker, Mary
"Anne of Green Gables: an annotated bibliography." In: *Canadian Children's Literature*; No. 55 (1989) p. 18-41.; ISSN: 0319-0080. [7196]

Garratt, John G.
The four Indian kings/Les quatre rois indiens. [Ottawa]: Public Archives Canada, 1985. xiv, 186 p.: ill., facsims.; ISBN: 0-660-53006-6. [4076]

Gascon, Denis; Roy, Paul-Martel
La productivité dans le secteur public: les écrits récents, 1975-1982, sur le sujet, particulièrement ceux qui portent sur le Québec. Montréal: Laboratoire de recherche sur l'emploi, la répartition et la sécurité du revenu, 1982. 12, 4 f. [2881]

Gaspari, Carol; Kernaghan, Helgi
Fund raising: the Canadian view, 1960-1976: a selective bibliography. [S.l.: s.n.], c1977. 45 p. [2628]

Gaudert, P.C.
Publications on composite materials (January 1983-June 1991). Ottawa: Institute for Aerospace Research, [1991]. i, 12 p. (Structures and Materials Laboratory Report ; LTR-ST-1833) [5846]

Gaudette, Micheline
Humanisation: bibliographie annotée. Montréal: Conseil de la santé et des services sociaux de la région de Montréal métropolitain, c1985. [62] p. [3274]

Gaudreau, Liette
"Bibliographie de l'édition au Québec, 1940-1960." Dans: *L'Édition littéraire au Québec de 1940 à 1960*. Sherbrooke, Québec: Département d'études françaises, Université de Sherbrooke, 1985. P. 179-208. (Cahiers d'études littéraires et culturelles ; no 9); ISBN: 2-89343-000-7. [1669]

Gaulin, Jean-Guy; Gaulin, André
"Petite discographie de la chanson québécoise." Dans: *Québec français*; No 29 (mars 1978) p. 32-36.; ISSN: 0316-2052. [0866]

Gauthier, Benoît
"Bibliographie du phytobenthos laurentin, Québec (1850-1975)." Dans: *Revue de géographie de Montréal*; Vol. 30, no 4 (1976) p. 359-366.; ISSN: 0035-1148. [5403]
Liste des périodiques en sciences naturelles au Québec. 2e éd. augm. Ste-Foy: Société linnéene du Québec, 1981. ix, 53 p.; ISBN: 2-920125-01-X. [5943]

Gauthier, Louis-Guy
CRAPE [Commission des Responsables de l'aide personnelle aux élèves] et documentation en bibliothèque: [bibliographie]. Montréal: Association des institutions d'enseignement secondaire, 1984. [29] f. [3622]
La généalogie: une recherche bibliographique. Précédée de Outils généalogique à la salle Gagnon de la Bibliothèque de la ville de Montréal, par Daniel Olivier. Montréal: Commissions des bibliothécaires: Association des institutions d'enseignement secondaire, 1980. xix, 150 p. [2008]
Littérature québécoise (romans, contes, nouvelles): bibliographie pour le 1er cycle du secondaire. Montréal: Association des institutions d'enseignement secondaire, 1980. vi, 8 f. [1170]

Gauthier, Monique
Bibliographie sur le phototrophisme des animaux marins. Grande-Rivière, Québec: Ministère de l'Industrie et du Commerce, Station de biologie marine, 1968. 73 p. (Cahiers d'information / Station de biologie marine, Grande-Rivière ; no 44) [5349]

Gauthier, Serge
Bibliographie de Charlevoix. [Québec]: Institut québécois de recherche sur la culture, 1984. 316 p.: cartes. (Documents de recherche / Institut québécois de recherche sur la culture ; no 3: ISSN: 0823-0447); ISBN: 2-89224-037-9. [0381]

Gauthier-Larouche, Georges
"Évolution de la maison rurale traditionnelle dans la région de Québec: bibliographie." Dans: *Archives de Folklore*; Vol.

15 (1974) p. 279-287.; ISSN: 0085-5243. [0742]

Gauvin, Lise

"Les revues littéraires québécoises de l'université à la contre-culture." Dans: *Études françaises*; Vol. 11, no 2 (mai 1975) p. 161-189.; ISSN: 0014-2085. [5921]

Gauvin, Lise; Mailhot, Laurent

Guide culturel du Québec. Montréal: Boréal Express, 1982. 533 p.: ill.; ISBN: 2-89052-044-7. [0376]

Geahigan, Priscilla C.

U.S. and Canadian businesses, 1955 to 1987: a bibliography. Metuchen, N.J.: Scarecrow Press, 1988. xi, 589 p.; ISBN: 0-8108-2186-9. [2744]

Gedalof, Robin

An annotated bibliography of Canadian Inuit literature. [Ottawa]: Indian and Northern Affairs Canada, [1979]. 108 p. [4003]

Geddes, James

"Bibliographical outline of French-Canadian literature." In: *Papers of the Bibliographical Society of America*; Vol. 8, no. 1-2 (1914) p. 7-42.; ISSN: 0006-128X. [0996]

Bibliography of Geddes publications. [S.l.: s.n.], 1934. 18 p. [7008]

Canadian French, the language and literature of the past decade, 1890-1900, with a retrospect of the causes that have produced them. Erlangen [Germany]: Junge & Sohn, 1902. 66 p. [1412]

Geddes, James; Rivard, Adjutor

Bibliographie du parler français au Canada: catalogue analytique des ouvrages traitant de la langue française au Canada. Paris: H. Champion; Québec: E. Marcotte, 1906. 99 p. (Publications de la Société du Parler français au Canada) [1413]

Geddes, James; Rivard, Adjutor; Dulong, Gaston

Bibliographie linguistique du Canada français. Québec: Presses de l'Université Laval; Paris: Librairie C. Klincksieck, 1966. xxxii, 166 p. (Bibliothèque française et romane. Série E: Langue et littérature françaises au Canada ; 1) [1422]

Geddie, Nancy

Bibliography on student services at Canadian universities/ Bibliographie des services aux étudiants dans les universités canadiennes. Ottawa: Association of Universities and Colleges of Canada, 1972. 69 p. [3439]

Gee, Joyce

Chinese Canadian bibliography. Toronto: Chinese Interpreter and Information Services, [1982]. 61 p. [4208]

Gélinas, Michel

Droit à l'information et protection des renseignements personnels: bibliographie. Sainte-Foy, Québec: Centre de documentation, École nationale d'administration publique, 1985. 56 p. (ENAP Collection bibliographie ; no 1) [2273]

Guide bibliographique en administration publique (Québec). Sainte-Foy, Québec: École nationale d'administration publique, 1992. 71 p.; ISBN: 2-920112-56-2. [2551]

Gélinas, Michel; Chabot, Josée

Liste cumulative des publications et rapports de recherche du personnel de l'ÉNAP. [Sainte-Foy, Québec]: École nationale d'administration publique, Université de Québec, 1989. 193 p.; ISBN: 2-920112-47-3. [2528]

Gélinas, Pat

Catalogue of mineral statistics: federal and provincial publications and surveys in Canada. [Ottawa]: Energy,

Mines and Resources Canada, 1990. v, 45, 47, v p. (Mineral policy sector internal report ; MRI 90-1); ISBN: 0-662-57967-4. [6404]

Répertoire traitant de la statistique des minéraux: publications et enquêtes fédérales-provinciales au Canada. [Ottawa]: Énergie, mines et ressources Canada, 1990. v, 47, 45, v p. (Secteur de la politique minérale rapport interne ; MRI 90-1); ISBN: 0-662-57967-4. [6405]

Gelmon, Sherril B.; Fried, Bruce

Multi-institutional arrangements and the Canadian health system. Ottawa: Canadian Hospital Association, 1987. v, 107 p.; ISBN: 0-919100-50-3. [5674]

Gémar, Jean-Claude

Bibliographie sélective du traducteur: droit et justice. Montréal: Linguatech, c1978. [283] p. (en pagination multiple). [2182]

Gémar, Jean-Claude; Horguelin, Paul A.

Bibliographie sélective du traducteur: commerce et économie. Montréal: Linguatech, c1977. 187 p. (pagination variée). [1439]

Gender issues in sport: a specialized bibliography from the SPORT database/L'équité dans le sport: une bibliographie spécialisée de la base de données SPORT. Gloucester, Ont.: Sport Information Resource Centre, 1990. 49 l. (SportBiblio ; no. 15; ISSN: 1180-5269) [1856]

Gendron, Gaétan

"Les métis et indiens sans statut du Québec: bibliographie sommaire." Dans: *Recherches amérindiennes au Québec*; Vol. 12, no 2 (1982) p. 138-139.; ISSN: 0318-4137. [4030]

A general bibliography of the Lancaster Sound-Baffin Bay region: comprised of citations and abstracts of research documents in the public domain at the Arctic Institute of North America. Calgary: Consolidex Magnorth Oakwood Joint Venture, 1983. xxviii, 207 p. [4833]

"Geographical publications: reviews and titles of books, papers, maps." In: *Geographical Review*; (1916-1918) ; ISSN: 0016-7428. [2946]

Georges, Robert A.; Stern, Stephen

American and Canadian immigrant and ethnic folklore: an annotated bibliography. New York: Garland Publishing, 1982. xix, 484 p. (Garland folklore bibliographies ; vol. 2); ISBN: 0-8240-9307-0. [4209]

Georgian Bay Regional Library System

Sélection de livres français. [Barrie, Ont.]: The System, 1982. 132 p. [0138]

Statistics Canada: union list of holdings for Barrie, Owen Sound and Orillia public libraries. [Barrie, Ont.]: The System, 1980. iii, 21 l. [6327]

Gephart, Ronald M.

Revolutionary America, 1763-1789: a bibliography. Washington: Library of Congress, 1984. 2 vol. (xl, 1672 p.), ill.; ISBN: 0-8444-0359-8 (vol. 1); 0-8444-0379-2 (vol. 2). [2038]

Germain, Élisabeth

Maladies chroniques et familles aidantes au Québec: une revue de la littérature. Matane, Québec: Centre local de services communautaires de Matane, 1991. vii, 106 p. [5702]

Les ordres religieux au Québec: bilan de la recherche: [bibliographie]. Québec: Groupe de recherche en science de la religion, Université Laval, 1983. iv, 80 p.: ill. (Études et documents en sciences de la religion: dossier documentaire ; 1) [1554]

German-Canadian Historical Association
"Activities in the field of German-Canadian studies and research/Aktivitäten im Bereich deutschkanadischer Studien und Forschung." In: *Canadiana Germanica*; No. 41 (April 1984) p. 25-37.; ISSN: 0703-1599. [4222]

Gerson, Carole
"The piper's forgotten tune: notes on the stories of D.C. Scott and a bibliography." In: *Journal of Canadian Fiction*; No. 16 (1976) p. 138-143.; ISSN: 0047-2255. [7296]

Gervais, Émile
Pour mieux connaître nos fondateurs: bibliographie pratique. Montréal: Bureau de propagande, 1942. 32 p. (Collection "Textes" / Bureau de propagande, Église catholique ; no 1) [1503]

Gervais, Gaétan; Hallsworth, Gwenda; Thomson, Ashley
The bibliography of Ontario history, 1976-1986/La bibliographie d'histoire ontarienne, 1976-1986. Toronto: Dundurn Press, 1989. xxxiv, 605 p.; ISBN: 1-55002-031-5. [0487]

Gervais, Gaétan; Thomson, Ashley; Hallsworth, Gwenda
Bibliographie: histoire du nord-est de l'Ontario/ Bibliography: history of north-eastern Ontario. Sudbury: La Société historique du Nouvel-Ontario, 1985. 112 p. (Documents historiques / Société historique du Nouvel-Ontario ; no 82) [0480]

Gesner, Edward
Bibliographie annotée de linguistique acadienne. Québec: Centre international de recherche sur le bilinguisme, 1986. 89 p. (Publication / Centre international de recherche sur le bilinguisme ; B-155); ISBN: 2-89219-166-1. [1466]

Gibbons, Dave R.; Salo, Ernest O.
An annotated bibliography of the effects of logging on fish of the western United States and Canada. Portland, Or.: Pacific Northwest Forest and Range Experiment Station, U.S. Department of Agriculture, 1973. 145 p. (USDA Forest Service General technical report ; PNW-10) [5373]

Gibeault, André
Canadian records: a discography & price guide of Canadian 45's and LP's from 1955 to 1975. St-Lambert, Québec: André Gibeault, 1987. 1 vol. (in various pagings). [0928]

Gibson, Rose Mary
Genealogical sources in the Douglas Library, Kingston, Ont. Ottawa: Ottawa Branch, Ontario Genealogical Society, 1978. 15, 2, 6, 4 p. [1997]

Giesbrecht, Herbert
"A bibliography of books and articles authored and edited by Dr. David Ewert: 1953-1987." In: *The Bible and the Church: essays in honour of Dr. David Ewert*, edited by A.J. Dueck, H.J. Giesbrecht, V.G. Shillington. Winnipeg: Kindred Press, c1988. P. 251-274.; ISBN: 0-919797-88-1. [6971]

The Mennonite Brethren: a bibliographic guide. 2nd ed. Fresno, Calif.: Board of Christian Literature, General Conference of Mennonite Brethren Churches, 1983. iv, 99 p. [1555]

Giesbrecht, Irene
The consumer crunch, or: meeting the challenge of rising prices. [Saskatoon]: Saskatoon Public Library, 1975. 21 p. [2616]

Giffen, A.V.
The occurrence and prevention of frazil ice blockage at water supply intakes: a literature review and field survey. [Toronto]: Ontario Ministry of the Environment, 1973. iii,

32 p. (Research Branch publication / Ontario Ministry of the Environment ; no. W 42) [5076]

Giguère, Richard; Elder, Jo-Anne
"Bibliographie sélective." Dans: *Voix et Images*; Vol. 10, no 1 (automne 1984) p. 59-65.; ISSN: 0318-9201. [1213]

Giguère, Rita; Larrivée, Jean; Castonguay, Lise
Répertoire de données compilées par le GRIDEQ. Rimouski: Université du Québec à Rimouski, 1982. viii, 137 p. [0377]

Gilbert, Anne
Mémoires et thèses en géographie humaine dans les universités canadiennes de langue française: 1975-1985. Montréal: Université de Montréal, Département de Géographie, 1986. 60 p. (Notes et documents / Département de Géographie, Université de Montréal ; no 86-01) [6183]

Gilbert, Charlotte
Répertoire bibliographique: auteurs Amérindiens du Québec/Bibliographic directory of Amerindian authors in Quebec. Saint-Luc, Québec: Centre de recherche sur la littérature et les arts autochtones du Québec, 1993. 46 p.; ISBN: 2-9803426-0-2. [4122]

Gilbert, F.F.; Brown, S.A.; Stoll, M.E.
Semi-aquatic mammals: annotated bibliography. Edmonton: Alberta Oil Sands Environmental Research Program, [1979]. xii, 167 p. (Alberta Oil Sands Environmental Research Program report ; no. 59) [5428]

Gilbert, S.R.
"British Columbia studies: basic references: selected bibliography." In: *Communiqué: Canadian Studies*; Vol. 1, no. 4 (May 1975) p. 2-7.; ISSN: 0318-1197. [0585]

Gilchrist, J. Brian
Inventory of Ontario newspapers, 1793-1986. Toronto: Micromedia, c1987. vi, 202, 72 p.; ISBN: 0-88892-596-4. [6043]

Giles, Valerie M.E.
Annotated bibliography of education history in British Columbia. Victoria: Royal British Columbia Museum, c1992. iii, 65 p. (Royal British Columbia Museum technical reports); ISBN: 0-7718-9188-1. [3728]

Gill, Dhara S.
A bibliography of socio-economic studies on rural Alberta, Canada. Monticello, Ill.: Council of Planning Librarians, 1977. 206 p. (Council of Planning Librarians Exchange bibliography ; 1260-1261-1262) [0520]

Gill, R.J.; Cammaert, A.B.
Ice control for Arctic ports and harbours. Montreal: Transportation Development Centre, Transport Canada, 1983. 2 vol. [4492]

Gill, Theodore Nicholas; Coues, Elliott; Allen, Joel Asaph
Material for a bibliography of North American mammals. Washington: U.S.G.P.O., 1877. P. [951]-1081. [5302]

Gillespie, Gilbert
Public access cable television in the United States and Canada: with an annotated bibliography. New York: Praeger, 1975. vii, 157 p. (Praeger special studies in U.S. economic, social and political issues); ISBN: 0-275-09980-6. [0956]

Gillespie, Kay M.
"Manitoba bibliography." In: *Manitoba History*; No. 6 (Fall 1983)-no. 24 (Fall 1992) [0551]

Gillespie-Wood, Janet
Gold in Nova Scotia: a bibliography of the geology, and exploration and mining histories from 1832-1986. Halifax:

Nova Scotia Department of Mines and Energy, 1987. xvi, 483 p.: map. (Nova Scotia Department of Mines and Energy report ; 87-02; ISSN: 0821-8188) [4857]

Gilliss, Geraldine; Moll, Marita

Administration de tests et évaluation du rendement des élèves au Canada. Ottawa: Fédération canadienne des enseignantes et des enseignants, 1986. 28, 172 p. (Bibliographies en éducation / Fédération canadienne des enseignantes et des enseignants ; no 80); ISBN: 0-88989-181-8. [3656]

Teacher effectiveness research. Ottawa: Canadian Teachers' Federation, 1984. 2 vol. (Bibliographies in education / Canadian Teachers' Federation ; nos. 77, 78); ISBN: 0-88989-160-5 (no. 77); 0-88989-161-3 (no. 78). [3623]

Testing and evaluation of student achievement in Canada. Ottawa: Canadian Teachers' Federation, 1986. 172, 28 p. (Bibliographies in education / Canadian Teachers' Federation ; no. 80); ISBN: 0-88989-181-8. [3657]

Gilroy, Marion

A catalogue of maps, plans and charts in the Public Archives of Nova Scotia. Halifax: Public Archives of Nova Scotia, 1938. 95 p. (Public Archives of Nova Scotia Bulletin, vol. 1, no. 3) [6492]

Gimbarzevsky, Philip

Remote sensing in forest damage detection and appraisal: selected annotated bibliography. Victoria: Pacific Forest Research Centre, 1984. 55 p. (Pacific Forest Research Centre Information report ; BC-X-253; ISSN: 0705-3274); ISBN: 0-662-13444-3. [4980]

Gingras, André; Perret, Diana-Lynn; Perret, Louis

Legal bibliography on the Québec civil law published in English. Ottawa: Éditions de l'Université d'Ottawa, 1984. P. [713]-760 [2267]

Ginn, R.M.

Bibliography of theses on the Precambrian geology of Ontario. [Toronto]: Ontario Department of Mines, 1961. ii, 49 l. (Miscellaneous paper / Ontario Department of Mines ; MP-2) [6074]

Girard, Hélène

"Bibliographie de France Théoret." Dans: *Voix et Images*; Vol. 14, no 1 (automne 1988) p. 57-69.; ISSN: 0318-9201. [7329]

Girard, Sonya

Standards for medical and dental equipment and materials: bibliography/Normes traitant des produits et du matériel à usage médical et dentaire: bibliographie. [Ottawa]: Standards Council of Canada, 1981. 16 l.; ISBN: 0-920360-18-1. [5636]

Girouard, Laurie

La consommation en dette: bibliographie. Montréal: Conseil de développement social du Montréal métropolitain, 1972. 2 vol. [2597]

Giroux, Nicole

Gestion du crédit aux P.M.E. dans les banques: revues de la littérature. Montréal: École des hautes études commerciales, 1986. 41 f. (Cahier / École des hautes études commerciales, Montréal ; 86-3); ISBN: 2-893600-70-0. [2720]

Gladstone, Jane; Ericson, Richard V.; Shearing, Clifford D.

Criminology: a reader's guide. Toronto: Centre of Criminology, University of Toronto, 1991. vi, 275 p.; ISBN: 0-919584-67-5. [2348]

Glazebrook, George P. de T.

"Bibliographical article: Canadian foreign policy in the twentieth century." In: *Journal of Modern History*; Vol. 21,

no. 1 (March 1949) p. 44-55.; ISSN: 0022-2801. [2374]

Glazier, Kenneth M.

A list of newspapers in the university libraries of the prairie universities of Canada. Rev. and enl. ed. Calgary: [University of Calgary Library], 1974. iii, 104 l. [6020]

Glenbow-Alberta Institute

Royal Canadian Mounted Police: a bibliography of resource material. Calgary: Glenbow-Alberta Institute, [1972]. 102 p. (Glenbow Archives publication series / Glenbow-Alberta Institute ; no. 5) [2125]

Glenbow-Alberta Institute. Library

Catalogue of the Glenbow historical library, the Glenbow-Alberta Institute Library, Calgary, Alberta. Boston: G.K. Hall, 1973. 4 vol.; ISBN: 0-8161-0994-X. [0508]

"Glenn Gould discography/Discographie de Glenn Gould."

In: *Musicanada*; No. 46 (June 1981) p. 2. [7025]

Gnarowski, Michael

A concise bibliography of English-Canadian literature. Rev. ed. Toronto: McClelland and Stewart, c1978. 145 p.; ISBN: 0-7710-3362-1. [1130]

"Contact Press, 1952-1967: a check list of titles." In: *Culture*; Vol. 30, no. 3 (September 1969) p. 227-232.; ISSN: 0317-2066. [1590]

A reference and bibliographical guide to the study of English Canadian literature. Ottawa: [s.n.], 1967. [1040]

Theses and dissertations in Canadian literature (English): a preliminary check list. Ottawa: Golden Dog Press, 1975. 41 p.; ISBN: 0-919614-12-4. [6137]

Goard, Dean S.; Dickinson, Gary

A bibliography of social and economic research pertaining to rural British Columbia. Ottawa: Regional Economic Expansion Canada, 1971. iv, 44 p. (Canada Land Inventory Project ; no. 49015) [0579]

Godard, Barbara

Bibliography of feminist criticism/Bibliographie de la critique féminist[e]. [Toronto]: ECW Press, [c1987]. 116 p.; ISBN: 0-920763-97-9. [3851]

Inventory of research in Canadian and Quebec literature/ Répertoire des recherches en littératures canadiennes et québécoises. Downsview, Ont.: York University, 1983. 126 p. [1202]

Godavari, Sigrun Norma

Electronic funds transfer: an annotated bibliography. [Ottawa: Canadian Home Economics Association], 1982. 78 p. [2681]

Goehlert, Robert

The Parliament of Canada: a select bibliography. Monticello, Ill.: Vance Bibliographies, 1990. 23 p. (Public administration series: Bibliography ; P-2957; ISSN: 0193-970X); ISBN: 0-7920-0657-7. [2538]

Goeldner, C.R.

Bibliographic sources for travel and tourism research. Burnaby, B.C.: Department of Economics and Commerce, Simon Fraser University, 1974. 22 l. [1764]

Goeldner, C.R.; Allen, Gerald L.

Bibliography of tourism and travel: research studies, reports and articles. Boulder, Colo.: Business Research Division, Graduate School of Business Administration, University of Colorado, [c1967]. vi, 71 l. [1752]

Goertz, Richard O.W.; Malycky, Alexander

"German-Canadian church history: Part II: Individual congregations: a preliminary bibliography." In: *Canadian Ethnic Studies*; Vol. 5, no. 1/2 (1973) p. 95-123.; ISSN: 0008-

3496. [1528]

Goff, T.W.

Resource material for social analysis of the Chignecto region: a preliminary bibliography. Sackville, N.B.: Chignecto Research Group of Mount Allison University, 1978. [6], 20 l. (Chignecto Research Group of Mount Allison University Internal note ; no. 7); ISBN: 0-88828-015-7. [0233]

Goggio, Emilio; Corrigan, Beatrice; Parker, J.H.

A bibliography of Canadian cultural periodicals (English and French from colonial times to 1950) in Canadian libraries. Toronto: Department of Italian, Spanish and Portuguese, University of Toronto, 1955. 45 p. [5867]

Golant, Stephen

Human behavior before the disaster: a selected annotated bibliography. [Toronto: Department of Geography, University of Toronto], 1969. 14 p. (Natural hazard research working paper / Department of Geography, University of Toronto ; no. 9) [3089]

Gold, Lorne W.

"Fifty years of progress in ice engineering." In: *Journal of Glaciology*; (Special Issue 1987) p. 78-85.; ISSN: 0022-1430. [5823]

Goldberg, Michael A.

Bibliography re mobility of capital among Pacific Rim countries. Vancouver: Institute of Asian Research, University of British Columbia, 1983. 64 p. (Working paper / Institute of Asian Research, University of British Columbia ; no. 5) [2692]

Golden, Richard L.; Roland, Charles G.

Sir William Osler: an annotated bibliography with illustrations. San Francisco: Norman Publishing, 1988. xv, 214 p.: ill., ports. (Norman bibliography series ; 1); ISBN: 0-930405-00-5. [7228]

Goldstein, Jay

"Recent publications relating to Canadian ethnic studies." In: *Canadian Ethnic Studies*; Vol. 12, no. 3 (1980) p. 171-176; vol. 13, no. 3 (1981) p. 173-175; vol. 14, no. 3 (1982) p. 140-146.; ISSN: 0008-3496. [4210]

Gollop, Bernie

"A selected, annotated bibliography for Saskatchewan butterfly watchers." In: *Blue Jay*; Vol. 47, no. 2 (June 1989) p. 83-88.; ISSN: 0006-5099. [5549]

Goodfellow, Gay; Hieatt, D.J.

A literature review of research on the actions of drivers in emergencies. Downsview, Ont.: Policy Planning and Research Division, Ontario Ministry of Transportation and Communications, 1981. 60 p. [4481]

Goodfellow, John; Lanning, Mabel M.

Similkameen Tulameen Valleys. [Vancouver: British Columbia Library Association], 1935. [8] p. [0561]

Goodwin, C. Ross

EAMES bibliography. Calgary: Arctic Institute of North America, 1982. vii, 38 p. (ASTIS occasional publication / Arctic Science and Technology Information System ; no. 6; ISSN: 0225-5170) [5181]

Norlands bibliography. Calgary: Arctic Institute of North America, 1982. iv, 10 p. (ASTIS occasional publication / Arctic Science and Technology Information System ; no. 7; ISSN: 0225-5170) [5182]

Goodwin, C. Ross, et al.

Cold ocean engineering bibliography. Calgary: Published jointly by the Arctic Science and Technology Information System and the Ocean Engineering Information Centre,

Memorial University of Newfoundland, 1984. vi, 169 p. (ASTIS occasional publication / Arctic Science and Technology Information System ; no. 12; ISSN: 0225-5170) (C-CORE publication ; no. 84-12) [5796]

Goodwin, C. Ross; Finley, Jean C.; Howard, Lynne M.

Ice scour bibliography. [Ottawa]: Environmental Studies Revolving Funds, 1985. xi, 99 p. (Environmental Studies Revolving Funds report ; no. 010); ISBN: 0-920783-09-0. [4843]

Goodwin, C. Ross; Howard, Lynne M.

The Beaufort Sea, Mackenzie delta, Mackenzie valley, and northern Yukon: a bibliographical review. Ottawa: Arctic Science and Technology Information System, 1984. v, 310 p.: map. [0644]

Goodwin, Daniel Corey

A checklist of secondary sources for planter studies. Prelim. ed. Wolfville, N.S.: Acadia University, Department of History, Planter Studies Committee, 1987. iv, 64 l. [2059]

Goodyear, Carole D., et al.

Atlas of the spawning and nursery areas of Great Lakes fishes. Washington, D.C.: U.S. Fish and Wildlife Service, Office of Biological Services, 1982. 14 vol. [5477]

Goorachurn, Lynn-Dell

Native languages: resources pertaining to native languages of Manitoba. [Winnipeg]: Province of Manitoba, Department of Education, 1981. i, 52 p. (Curriculum support series / Manitoba Department of Education) [1452]

Gordon, W. Terrence

Semantics: a bibliography, 1965-1978. Metuchen, N.J.: Scarecrow Press, 1980. xiv, 307 p.; ISBN: 0-8108-1300-9. [1449]

Gordon Home Blackader Library

A catalogue of books on art and architecture in McGill University Library and the Gordon Home Blackader Library of Architecture. 2nd and rev. ed. Montreal: McGill University Library, 1926. 192, [2] p.: front., port. (McGill University publications series ; no. 9) [0733]

Gorecki, Paul K.; Stanbury, W.T.

"Competition law and public policy in Canada, 1888-1979: a bibliography." In: *Canadian competition policy: essays in law and economics*, edited by J. Robert S. Prichard, W.T. Stanbury and Thomas A. Wilson. Toronto: Butterworths, 1979. P. 555-609.; ISBN: 0-409-85950-8. [2194]

Gormely Process Engineering

Heap leaching literature review. Ottawa: Indian and Northern Affairs Canada, 1987. 38, [7] p. (Environmental studies / Indian and Northern Affairs Canada ; no. 51); ISBN: 0-662-15946-2. [4858]

Gotell, Lise

"Employment equity for women in Canadian universities: a bibliography." In: *Resources for Feminist Research*; Vol. 16, no. 4 (December 1987) p. 48-49.; ISSN: 0707-8412. [3852]

Gottlieb, Lois C.; Keitner, Wendy

"Bird at the window: an annotated bibliography of Canadian fiction written by women, 1970-1975." In: *American Review of Canadian Studies*; Vol. 9, no. 2 (Autumn 1979) p. 3-56.; ISSN: 0272-2011. [1150]

Gough, C.J.

Bibliography on topics related to immigrant settlement and ethnic minority concerns (in the Canadian context). Victoria, B.C.: Inter-cultural Association of Greater Victoria, [1982-1985]. 2 vol. [4232]

Gould, Allan Mendel

A critical assessment of the theatre criticism of Nathan Cohen with a bibliography and selected anthology. Toronto: York University, 1977. ix, 424 l. [6912]

Goulet, Jean

"L'oeuvre littéraire juridique de Monsieur le professeur Marie-Louis Beaulieu." Dans: *Cahiers de droit*; Vol. 9, nos 3-4 (1967-68) p. 341-348.; ISSN: 0007-974X. [6831]

"The Quebec legal system." In: *Law Library Journal*; Vol. 73 (1980) p. 354-381.; ISSN: 0023-9283. [2215]

Goulson, Cary F.

A source book of royal commissions and other major governmental inquiries in Canadian education, 1787-1978. Toronto: University of Toronto Press, c1981. xxii, 406 p.; ISBN: 0-8020-2408-4. [3592]

Gourd, Benoît-Beaudry

"Aperçu critique des principaux ouvrages pouvant servir à l'histoire du développement minier de l'Abitibi-Témiscamingue (1910-1950)." Dans: *Revue d'histoire de l'Amérique française*; Vol. 30, no 1 (juin 1976) p. 99-107.; ISSN: 0035-2357. [4796]

Bibliographie de l'Abitibi-Témiscamingue. Édition préliminaire. Rouyn: Université du Québec, Direction d'études universitaires dans l'Ouest québécois (Nord-Ouest), 1973. x, 270 p. [0323]

Gourdeau, Monique F.

Documents sessionnels de l'Assemblée législative du Québec (1960-1970). Québec: Bibliothèque de l'Assemblée nationale, 1982. 277 p. (Bibliographie et documentation / Bibliothèque de l'Assemblée nationale du Québec ; 9) [6351]

Government of Canada publications: quarterly catalogue/ Publications du gouvernement du Canada: catalogue trimestriel. Hull, Québec: Supply and Services Canada, 1979- . vol.; ISSN: 0709-0412. [6452]

Govia, Francine; Lewis, Helen

Blacks in Canada: in search of the promise: a bibliographical guide to the history of Blacks in Canada. Edmonton: Harambee Centre Canada, 1988. [viii], 102 p.; ISBN: 0-921550-00-6. [4256]

Gowdey, C.D.; Pearce, J.W.

A selected bibliography of the open literature on aviation medicine, 1945-1955. Ottawa: Defence Research Board, Department of National Defence, 1955. x, 59 p. [5564]

Gower, Wendy

Employee assistance programs. Kingston, Ont.: Industrial Relations Centre, Queen's University, 1980. 21 p. (Mimeographed bibliography series / Industrial Relations Centre, Queen's University ; no. 16) [2866]

Grievance arbitration: a bibliography. Kingston, Ont.: Industrial Relations Centre, Queen's University, 1988. [4] p. (Mimeographed bibliography series / Industrial Relations Centre, Queen's University ; no. 24) [2919]

Gowling, Linda

Contemporary French Canada: a select bibliography. [Waterloo, Ont.]: Reference Department, Dana Porter Arts Library, University of Waterloo, 1972. 77 l. [0319]

"Graduate theses in Canadian history and related subjects." In: *Canadian Historical Review*; (1927-1965) ; ISSN: 0008-3755. [6082]

Graham, Katherine A.

Public policy and aboriginal peoples, 1965-1992. Volume 4, Bibliography. Ottawa: Royal Commission on Aboriginal Peoples, 1993. iv, 69 p.; ISBN: 0-660-58880-3. [4123]

Graham, R.

Biomass pyrolysis gasification bibliography/Bibliographie pyrolyse et gazeification de la biomasse. Ottawa: Eastern Forest Products Laboratory, Forintek Canada Corporation, 1980. v, 17 p. (Review report / Eastern Forest Products Laboratory, Forintek Canada Corporation ; RR502FF; ISSN: 0709-4523) [5777]

Graham, R.; Huff, Donald W.

Annotated bibliography of underwater and marine park related initiatives in northern latitudes. Hull, Quebec: Parks Canada, 1983. [120] l. [1823]

Grainger, Bruce

"Information sources for oral history in Canada." In: *Ontario Library Review*; Vol. 65, no. 2 (June 1981) p. 124-128.; ISSN: 0030-2996. [2013]

Grains Group (Canada)

Grain handling and transportation: a bibliography of selected references on transportation and rural sociology. [Ottawa]: Grains Group, 1975. iv, 102 l. [4460]

Grammond, Madeleine; Lacroix, Benoît

"Mort et religion traditionnelle au Québec: bibliographie." Dans: *Bulletin d'histoire de la culture matérielle*; No 23 (printemps 1986) p. 56-64.; ISSN: 0703-489X. [1562]

Granberg, Charlotte

Annotated bibliography of recent research undertaken in the Labrador-Ungava area, near Schefferville, Quebec. Montreal: Centre for Northern Studies and Research, McGill University for the McGill Subarctic Research Station, 1978. iii l., 63 p.: ill. (McGill Subarctic Research paper ; no. 28; ISSN: 0076-1982) [3024]

Grande, Ellen; Hansen, John Nørskov; Madsen, Nina

Nordamerikanske indianere i børnelitteraturen: en genrebeskrivelse. København: Danmarks Biblioteksskole, 1978. 146 p. (Danmarks biblioteksskoles A4-serie ; nr 5); ISBN: 87-7415-090-1. [1336]

Granger, Denise; Lefebvre, Christine

Revue de littérature sur les modèles et les stratégies de prestation de service communautaires offerts aux personnes âgées en perte d'autonomie fonctionnelle et mentale et à leurs aidants naturels. Montréal: Université de Montréal, Faculté des sciences infirmières, 1991. vii, 200 p. [5703]

Granger Frères

Bibliographie canadienne: catalogue annoté d'ouvrages canadiens-français. [Montréal: s.n., 1906]. 295, [1] p. [0032]

Grant, John E.

"A checklist of writings by and about Northrop Frye." In: *Northrop Frye in modern criticism: selected papers from the English Institute*, edited by Murray Krieger. New York: Columbia University Press, 1966. P. 147-188. [6996]

Grant, Judith Skelton; Malcolm, Douglas

"Mavis Gallant: an annotated bibliography." In: *The annotated bibliography of Canada's major authors*, Vol. 5, edited by Robert Lecker and Jack David. Downsview, Ont.: ECW Press, 1984. P. 179-230.; ISBN: 0-920802-68-0. [6998]

Grant, Linda; Sai-Chew, Patricia; Natarelli, Fausto

Work-related day care: an annotated bibliography. Toronto: Social Planning Council of Metropolitan Toronto, 1982. 26 l. [3238]

Grant, Madeline

William Lyon Mackenzie King: a bibliography. Prelim. ed. [Waterloo, Ont.]: Department of History, University of

Waterloo, 1974. 28 l. [7086]

"William Lyon Mackenzie King: a bibliography." In: *Mackenzie King: widening the debate*, edited by John English and W.O. Stubbs. Toronto: Macmillan of Canada, c1977. P. 221-253.; ISBN: 0-7705-1529-0. [7087]

Gras, N.S.B.

"Books and articles on the economic history of the United States and Canada." In: *Economic History Review*; Vol. 9, no. 2 (May 1939) P. 239-250; Vol. 10, no. 2 (November 1940) p. 185-192.; ISSN: 0013-0117. [2562]

Grasham, W.E.; Julien, Germain

Canadian public administration: bibliography/Administration publique canadienne: bibliographie. [Toronto]: Institute of Public Administration of Canada, [c1972]. 261 p. [2404]

Gratton, Claude

Yvan Lamonde: historien de la culture: essai de bibliographie, 1965-1984. Nouv. version rev., augm. et corr. Sorel, Québec: Éditions Artisanales, 1986. 47 f.; ISBN: 2-920827-04-9. [7115]

Yvon Gauthier: écrits philosophiques: bibliographie chronologique, 1967-1985. Sorel [Québec]: Éditions artisanales, c1986. 31 p. (Brochures / Éditions artisanales ; no 3); ISBN: 2-920827-02-2. [7006]

Graves, Donald E.; MacLeod, Anne E.

Nova Scotia military history: a resource guide. Halifax [N.S.]: Army Museum, Halifax Citadel, 1982. 106 p. [2021]

Gray, Viviane

Bibliography of periodicals and articles on law related to Indians and Eskimos of Canada. [Ottawa]: Legal Services, Department of Indian Affairs and Northern Development, [1971]. [89] p. [3928]

Grayson, Donald K.

A bibliography of the literature on North American climates of the past 13,000 years. New York: Garland Publishing, c1975. 206 p. (Garland reference library of natural science ; vol. 2); ISBN: 0-8240-9992-3. [5099]

Great Britain. Colonial Office. Library

Catalogue of the Colonial Office Library, London. Boston: G.K. Hall, 1964. 15 vol. [6771]

Greater Vancouver Regional District

Publications and maps for sale. Vancouver: Greater Vancouver Regional District, 1983. 26 p. [6357]

Greater Vancouver Regional District. Planning Department

Lower Mainland Regional Planning Board publications. Vancouver: Greater Vancouver Regional District, 1979. 31 p. [4374]

Publications [Greater Vancouver Regional District, Planning Department]. Vancouver: Greater Vancouver Regional District, Planning Department, 1981. 26 l. [4391]

Green, Deirdre E.; Macdonald, Maggie

Women and psychoactive drug use: an interim annotated bibliography. Toronto: Addiction Research Foundation of Ontario, c1976. x, 177 p. (Bibliographic series / Addiction Research Foundation of Ontario ; no. 11; ISSN: 0065-1885); ISBN: 0-88868-018-X. [5609]

Green, Howard; Sawyer, Don

The NESA bibliography annotated for native studies. Vancouver: The Tillacum Library, 1983. 122 p.; ISBN: 0-88978-168-0. [4044]

Green, Rayna

Native American women: a contextual bibliography. Bloomington: Indiana University Press, c1983. viii, 120 p.; ISBN: 0-253-33976-6. [4045]

Green, Vicki A.

Annotated bibliography on Indian education. [Vancouver]: Indian Education Resources Centre, University of British Columbia, [1970]. 33 p. [3409]

Greenberg, A. Morley; Wright, David M.

The variable work week: a selected bibliography, 1967-1974. [Toronto]: Human, Social and Environmental Factors Section, Research and Development Division, Ontario Ministry of Transportation and Communications, 1974. 25 p. [2818]

Greenfield, Katharine

"Reference sources for the history of the Church of England in Upper Canada, 1791-1867." In: *Journal of the Canadian Church Historical Society*; Vol. 9, no. 3 (September 1967) p. 50-74.; ISSN: 0008-3208. [1519]

Greenly, Albert Harry

"Lahontan: an essay and bibliography." In: *Papers of the Bibliographical Society of America*; Vol. 48, no. 4 (1954) p. 334-389.; ISSN: 0006-128X. [7112]

A selective bibliography of important books, pamphlets and broadsides relating to Michigan history. Lunenburg, Vt.: Stinehour Press, 1958. 165 p.: facsims. [1930]

Greenshields, H.; Seddon, W.A.

Pulse radiolysis: a comprehensive bibliography, 1960-March 1969/Radiolyses pulsées: bibliographie complète, 1960-mars 1969. Chalk River, Ont.: Atomic Energy of Canada, 1970. ii, 62 p.; ISSN: 0067-0367. [5732]

Greenwood, Brian; Davidson-Arnott, Robin G.D.

"Quaternary history and sedimentation: a summary and select bibliography." In: *Maritime Sediments*; Vol. 8, no. 3 (December 1972) p. 88-100.; ISSN: 0025-3456. [4777]

Greer-Wootten, Bryn; Wolfe, Jeanne

"Bibliographie sur Montréal et sa région/Bibliography on Montreal and region." Dans: *Revue de géographie de Montréal*; Vol. 27, no 3 (1973) p. 305-317.; ISSN: 0035-1148. [0324]

Gregor, Jan

Bibliographical guide to Canadian government and politics, 1968-1980. Monticello, Ill.: Vance Bibliographies, 1986. 9 vol. (Public administration series: Bibliography ; P-1918-P-1926; ISSN: 0193-970X) [2506]

Gregorovich, Andrew

Canadian ethnic groups bibliography: a selected bibliography of ethno-cultural groups in Canada and the Province of Ontario. Toronto: Department of the Provincial Secretary and Citizenship of Ontario, 1972. xvi, 208 p. [4156]

Canadian ethnic press bibliography: ethnic, multilingual and multicultural press of Canada selected bibliography. Toronto: Canadian Multilingual Press Foundation, 1991. 31 p.; ISBN: 0-88969-032-4. [1724]

Multiculturalism and ethnic groups in Canada: a brief bibliography. Toronto: 1971. 24 l. [4153]

Ukraine and Ukrainian Canadians: books for high school, college and public libraries. Toronto: Ucrainica Research Institute, 1979. 58 p. [4194]

"Ukrainian Canadiana: a selected bibliography of scholarly works 1970-1980." In: *Canadian Ethnic Studies*; Vol. 12, no. 2 (1980) p. 102-124.; ISSN: 0008-3496. [4196]

"Ukrainians in Ontario: a selected bibliography." In: *Polyphony*; Vol. 10 (1988) p. 271-285.; ISSN: 0704-7002. [4257]

Gregory, Diane J.

Bibliography of the geology of Nova Scotia. [Halifax]: Nova Scotia Department of Mines, 1975. vii, 237 p.: maps. [1789]

Gregory, Paul

A bibliography: television violence and its effect on the family. Montreal: [Abused Children – Violence in the Family Project, 1974]. 14 p. [0955]

Child abuse bibliography. Montreal: [Abused Children – Violence in the Family Project, 1974]. 42 l. [3125]

Gregory, Winifred

American newspapers, 1821-1936: a union list of files available in the United States and Canada. New York: H.W. Wilson, 1937. xvi, 791 p. [6004]

International congresses and conferences, 1840-1937: a union list of their publications available in libraries of the United States and Canada. New York: H.W. Wilson, 1938. 229 p. [0050]

List of the serial publications of foreign governments, 1815-1931. New York: H.W. Wilson, 1932. 720 p. [6220]

Greig, Peter E.

"A checklist of primary source material relating to Fleury Mesplet." In: *Papers of the Bibliographical Society of Canada*; Vol. 13 (1974) p. 49-74.; ISSN: 0067-6896. [7188]

John McCrae, 1872-1918: selected sources/John McCrae, 1872-1918: ressources choisies. Ottawa: National Defence Library Services, 1990. 15 p. ill., facsim. [7181]

Grenier, A.; Dubois, J.M.M.

Publications et recherches en géographie et télédétection à l'Université de Sherbrooke, 1957-1993. Sherbrooke, Québec: Université de Sherbrooke, Département de géographie et télédétection, 1993. iii, 250 p. (Bulletin de recherche / Université de Sherbrooke, Département de géographie et télédétection ; no 110-112; ISSN: 0710-0868) [3075]

Grenier, Ginette

Bibliographie annotée de l'histoire de Sherbrooke. Trois-Rivières: Cegep de Trois-Rivières, 1981. iv, 58 f. [0370]

Grenier, M.G.; Butler, K.C.

Index of underground-environment dust reports: CANMET-Mining Research Laboratories, 1960-1985/Liste de rapports sur la poussière en milieu souterrain: CANMET-Laboratoires de recherche minière, 1960-1985. Ottawa: Canada Centre for Mineral and Energy Technology, Energy, Mines and Resources Canada, 1986. vii, 13 p. (CANMET Special publication / Canada Centre for Mineral and Energy Technology ; SP 86-4); ISBN: 0-660-12240-5. [4851]

Grewal, H.

Bibliography of lodgepole pine literature. Edmonton: Northern Forestry Centre, Canadian Forestry Service, 1987. vi, 327 p. (Northern Forestry Centre Information report ; NOR-X-291; ISSN: 0704-7673); ISBN: 0-662-15647-1. [5531]

Gribenski, Jean

Thèses de doctorat en langue française relatives à la musique: bibliographie commentée/French language dissertations in music: an annotated bibliography. New York: Pendragon Press, 1979.; ISBN: 0-018728-09-6. [6151]

Griffin, Appleton Prentiss Clark

Bibliography of American historical societies (the United States and the Dominion of Canada). 2nd ed., rev. and enl. Washington: American Historical Association, 1907. 1374 p. (The Association reference series) [1896]

Discovery of the Mississippi, bibliographical account of the travels of Nicolet, Allouez, Marquette, Hennepin and La Salle in the Mississippi Valley. Boston: [s.n.], 1883. P. [190]-199, [273]-280, [1] folded l. of pl.: col. map. [1879]

"Discovery of the Mississippi, bibliographical account of the travels of Nicolet, Allouez, Marquette, Hennepin and La Salle in the Mississippi Valley." In: *Magazine of American History*; Vol. 9 (1883) p. 190-199, [273]-280.; ISSN: 0361-6185. [1880]

The discovery of the Mississippi: a bibliographical account, with a fac-simile of the map of Louis Joliet, 1674. To which is appended a note on the Joliet map by B.F. De Costa, with a sketch of Joutel's maps. New York: A.S. Barnes, 1883. 200 p., [1] folded l. of pl.: maps (1 col.). [1878]

Griffin-Allwood, Philip G.A.; Rawlyk, George A.; Zeman, Jarold K.

Baptists in Canada, 1760-1990: a bibliography of selected printed resources in English. Hantsport, N.S.: Published by Lancelot Press for Acadia Divinity College and the Baptist Historical Committee of the United Baptist Convention of the Atlantic Provinces, 1989. xix, 266 p. (Baptist heritage in Atlantic Canada: documents and studies ; 10); ISBN: 0-88999-399-8. [1568]

Griffith, J.W.

A bibliography of the occurrence of uranium in Canada and related subjects. Ottawa: [Queen's Printer], 1956. iii l., 34 p. (Geological Survey of Canada Paper ; 56-5) [4750]

Griffiths, Curt Taylor; Chunn, Dorothy E.

Circuit and rural court justice in the North: a resource publication. [Burnaby, B.C.]: Northern Conference, [c1985]. 1 vol. (in various pagings).; ISBN: 0-86491-046-0. [2274]

Griffiths, K.B.

Forest Pest Management Institute bibliography (1977-1982). Sault Ste. Marie, Ont.: Forest Pest Management Institute, Canadian Forestry Service, 1983. i, 60 p. (Forest Pest Management Institute Information report ; FPM-X-60; ISSN: 0704-772X); ISBN: 0-662-13122-3. [6358]

Griffiths, K.J.

A bibliography of gypsy moth literature. Sault Ste. Marie, Ont.: Great Lakes Forest Research Centre, 1980. 2 vol. [5447]

The parasites and predators of the gypsy moth: a review of the world literature with special application to Canada. Sault Ste. Marie, Ont.: Great Lake Forest Research Centre, 1976. 92 p. (Great Lakes Forest Research Centre report ; O-X-243; ISSN: 0704-7797) [5404]

Grimble, D.G.

"CANUSA publications useful to northeastern forest-land managers." In: *Northern Journal of Applied Forestry*; Vol. 4, no. 2 (1987) p. 105-109.; ISSN: 0742-6348. [4990]

Grondines, Hélène

Bibliographie analytique des monographies, des thèses et essais concernant la musicothérapie et conservés à la bibliothèque de l'Université Laval [microforme]. Ottawa: Bibliothèque nationale du Canada, 1986. 3 microfiches (227 images).; ISBN: 0-315-22621-8. [0925]

Gross, Konrad

"Literary criticism in German on English-Canadian literature: commentary and bibliography." In: *German-Canadian Yearbook*; Vol. 6 (1981) p. 305-310; vol. 7 (1983) p. 234-238.; ISSN: 0316-8603. [1203]

Groupe chargé d'étudier les problèmes de santé mentale des immigrants et des réfugiés
Revue des documents de référence portant sur la santé mentale des migrants. Ottawa: Multiculturalisme et citoyenneté Canada, c1988. iii, 55 p.; ISBN: 0-662-95221-9. [5678]

Groupe de travail sur la surveillance de la santé et de la sécurité dans les laboratoires
La santé et la sécurité dans les laboratoires: une étude de la documentation. Ottawa: Santé et bien-être social Canada, 1982. v, 46 p. [5647]

Growoll, Adolf
Henry Harrisse: biographical and bibliographical sketch. New York: Printed for the Dibdin Club by the Key Print. House, 1899. 13 p. (Dibdin Club leaflets ; no. 3) [7047]

Gruchy, I.M.; McAllister, Don E.
A bibliography of the smelt family, Osmeridae. Ottawa: Fisheries Research Board of Canada, 1972. 104 p. (Fisheries Research Board of Canada Technical report ; no. 368; ISSN: 0068-7553) [5368]

Grumet, Robert Steven
Native Americans of the Northwest Coast: a critical bibliography. Bloomington: Published for the Newberry Library [by] Indiana University Press, c1979. xvii, 108 p. (Newberry Library Center for the History of the American Indian, Bibliographical series); ISBN: 0-253-30385-0. [4004]

Grünsteudel, Günther
Canadiana-Bibliographie: Veröffentlichungen deutschsprachiger Kanadisten, 1980-1987. Bochum [Germany]: N. Brockmeyer, 1989. 89 p. (Kanada-Studien ; Bd. 1); ISBN: 3-88339-703-2. [0164]

"Guaranteed wages and supplemental unemployment benefits: an annotated bibliography with some historical notes." In: *Labour Gazette*; Vol. 56, no. 10 (October 1956) p. 1244-1249.; ISSN: 0023-6926. [2790]

Guay, Donald
Bibliographie québécoise sur l'activité physique, 1850-1973: hygiène, santé, éducation physique, sport, plein air, tourisme, loisirs. [Québec]: Éditions du Pélican, c1974. xix, 316 p. (Groupe de recherche sur l'histoire de l'activité physique ; 1); ISBN: 0-88514-009-5. [1765]

Guay, Michelle
Planification des naissances et développement professionnel: bibliographie. Québec: Laboratoire de recherche, École de service social, Université Laval, [1978]. v, 153 p. [3170]

Gue, Leslie R.
A selected, annotated bibliography concerning future needs in all levels and forms of native education in Alberta, Canada. [S.l.: s.n.], 1970. 25 l. [3410]

Guédon, Marie-Françoise
"Canadian Indian ethnomusicology: selected bibliography and discography." In: *Ethnomusicology*; Vol. 16, no. 3 (September 1972) p. 465-478.; ISSN: 0014-1836. [0834]

Guertin, Marcelle
"L'oeuvre de Serge Garant." Dans: *Canadian University Music Review: Revue de musique des universités canadiennes*; No. 7 (1986) p. 36-45.; ISSN: 0710-0353. [7001]

Guide Espial des banques de données canadiennes. Montréal: Services documentaires multimédia, 1989-. vol.; ISSN: 0849-1453. [0186]

Un guide index de la recherche et du développement en robotique au Canada. Ottawa: Conseil national de recherches Canada, Division de génie électrique, 1985. vii, 256 p. [5805]

A Guide to agricultural periodicals published in western Canada. Edmonton: Alberta Agriculture, Library, 1981. iv, 16 l. [5944]

"A guide to articles & architects." In: *Canadian Architect*; Vol. 12, no. 12 (December 1967) p. 51-60.; ISSN: 0008-2872. [0737]

Guide to the records of Royal and special commissions and committees of inquiry appointed by the Province of Saskatchewan. [Regina: Legislative Assembly Office, 1968]. 103 l. [2396]

Guilbeault, Claude
Guide des publications officielles de la Province de Nouveau-Brunswick, 1952-1970/Guide to official publications of the Province of New Brunswick, 1952-1970. Moncton: [s.n.], 1973. 382 l. [6285]

Guilbeault, Marielle T.
Famille québécoise: bibliographie. [Québec]: Université Laval, Bibliothèque, 1970. 37 f. [3096]

Guillet, Edwin C.
Bio-bibliography of Dr. Edwin C. Guillet. Kingston, Ont.: Douglas Library, Queen's University, 1970. 23 p. (Douglas Library Occasional papers ; no. 3) [7036]

Guillot, Andrée; Breton, Lise
L'enseignement à distance: bibliographie annotée. Montréal: Centre d'animation, de développement et de recherche en éducation, 1982. 75 p.; ISBN: 2-89169-027-3. [3608]

Guilmette, Bernadette
"Bibliographie du *Nigog*." Dans: *Le Nigog*. Montréal: Fides, 1987. P. 343-367. (Archives des lettres canadiennes ; Tome 7); ISBN: 2-7621-1381-4. [1237]

Guilmette, Pierre
Bibliographie de la danse théâtrale au Canada. Ottawa: Bibliothèque nationale du Canada, 1970. 150 p.: ill. [0951]

Guitard, André
Bibliographie choisie d'études récentes sur le prêtre. Montréal: Office national de clergé, 1969. 70 p. [1522]

Gulbinowicz, Eva
Problems of immigrant women, past and present: a bibliography. [Toronto]: Ministry of Labour Library, 1979. 45 p. [3789]

Gulick, Charles Adams; Ockert, Roy A.; Wallace, Raymond J.
History and theories of working-class movements: a select bibliography. Berkeley, Calif.: Published jointly by the Bureau of Business and Economic Research and Institute of Industrial Relations, University of California, Berkeley, [1955]. xix, 364 p. [2789]

Gunn, Gertrude E.
"William Stewart MacNutt: a bibliography, 1932-1983." In: *Acadiensis*; Vol. 14, no. 1 (Autumn 1984) p. 146-154.; ISSN: 0044-5851. [7168]

Gunn, Jonathan P.; Verkeley, Jacqueline; Newman, Lynda
Older Canadian homeowners: a literature review. [Ottawa]: Canada Mortgage and Housing Corporation, 1983. [8], 71, [14] p. [3248]

Gurstein, Michael
Urbanization and Indian people: an analytical literature review. [Ottawa]: Indian and Northern Affairs Canada, 1977. 44, [7] p. [3988]

Guse, Lorna; Koolage, William
Medical anthropology, social science, and nursing: a bibliography. 2nd ed., rev. Winnipeg: Department of Anthropology, University of Manitoba, 1984. xvii, 106 p. (University of Manitoba Anthropology papers ; no.

28) [4595]

Gushue, W.J.; Singh, A.

A bibliography of Newfoundland education. [St. John's]: Committee on Publications, Faculty of Education, Memorial University of Newfoundland, 1973. 22 l. [3467]

Gutteridge, Paul

Canadian economic history. Burnaby, B.C.: Simon Fraser University Library, 1973. 42 p. (Bibliography / Simon Fraser University Library ; no. 40) [2607]

Canadian genealogical resources: a guide to the materials held in Surrey Public Library. [Surrey, B.C.]: Surrey Public Library, 1990. 168 p.; ISBN: 0-9692197-1-0. [2082]

Guttmann, David

Jewish elderly in the English-speaking countries. New York: Greenwood Press, 1989. xvii, 140 p. (Bibliographies and indexes in gerontology ; no. 10); ISBN: 0-313-26240-3. [4267]

Guyot, Mireille

Bibliographie américaniste: archéologie et préhistoire, anthropologie et ethnohistoire. Paris: Musée de l'homme, 1967-1968. 248 f. [4546]

Gwillim, J.C.

"A partial bibliography of publications referring to the geology and mineral industry of Alberta, British Columbia, and the Yukon." In: *Canadian Mining Journal*; Vol. 29 (1908) p. 210-211, 242-243.; ISSN: 0008-4492. [4735]

Gwyn, Julian

Reference works for historians: a list of reference works of interest to historians in the libraries of the University of Ottawa. [Ottawa]: Central Library, University of Ottawa, 1971. iv, 131 l. [1972]

Haas, Marilyn L.

Indians of North America: methods and sources for library research. Hamden, Conn.: Library Professional Publications, 1983. xii, 163 p.; ISBN: 0-208-01980-4. [4046]

Habgood, Helen

Lake Wabamun literature review. [Edmonton]: Lake Wabamun Watershed Advisory Committee, 1983. x, 136 p., 6 folded l.: ill., maps. [5195]

Habiak, Marilyn J.; Baker, P.J.; James, I.R.

Learning disabilities: a select bibliography of resources. Edmonton: Department of Education, Edmonton Regional Office, 1974. 97 p. [3485]

Hacia, Henry

A selected annotated bibliography of the climate of the Great Lakes. Silver Spring, Md.: U.S. Environmental Data Service, 1972. iv, 70 p. (National Oceanic and Atmospheric Administration Technical memorandum ; EDS BS-7) [5065]

Hackett, Christopher

A bibliography of Manitoba local history: a guide to local and regional histories written about communities in Manitoba. 2nd ed. [Winnipeg]: Manitoba Historical Society, c1989. xvi, 156 p.; ISBN: 0-921950-00-4. [0546]

Haeussler, S.; Coates, D.

Autecological characteristics of selected species that compete with conifers in British Columbia: a literature review. Victoria: Information Services Branch, Ministry of Forests, c1986. vi, 180 p. (Land management report / British Columbia Ministry of Forests ; no. 33; ISSN: 0702-9861); ISBN: 0-7718-8482-6. [5526]

Haeussler, S.; Coates, D.; Mather, J.

Autecology of common plants in British Columbia: a literature review. [Victoria]: Forestry Canada; British Columbia Ministry of Forests, c1990. vi, 272 p. (Forest Resource Development Agreement report ; no. 158; ISSN: 0835-0752); ISBN: 0-7726-1270-6. [5553]

Hafstrom, Ole; Stenderup, Vibeke

Litteratursøgning: Canada almen bibliografi. Aarhus: Statsbiblioteket, 1990. 24 p. (Canadiana / Statsbiblioteket, Aarhus ; 3); ISBN: 87-7507187-8. [0170]

Litteratursøgning: Canada tidsskrifter: en annoteret liste. Aarhus: Statsbiblioteket, 1990. 22 p. (Canadiana / Statsbiblioteket, Aarhus ; 2); ISBN: 87-7507-183-5. [5974]

Haight, Willet Ricketson

Canadian catalogue of books. Part one. Toronto: Haight, 1896. 130 p. [0024]

Catalogue of a valuable collection of books and pamphlets relating to Canada and America, and the fine arts: being the second portion of the library of Frederick Broughton, late manager of the Great Western Railway .... Toronto: Hunter, Rose, 1885. 8, 44 p. [6738]

Hainaux, René; Leclerc, Nicole

Les Arts du spectacle: Canada: bibliographie des ouvrages en français publiées au Canada entre 1960 et 1985, concernant le théâtre, la musique, la danse, le mime, les marionnettes, les spectacles de variétés, le cirque, la radio et la télévision, le cinéma. Liège, Belgique: Recherches et formation théâtrales en Wallonie, 1986. 79 f. [0983]

Hair, Donald S.

"A checklist of the publications of F.E.L. Priestley." In: *English studies in Canada*; Vol. 1, no. 2 (Summer 1975) p. 139-143.; ISSN: 0317-0802. [7249]

Haist, Dianne

Equal pay for work of equal value: a selected bibliography. Toronto: Ontario Ministry of Labour, Research Library, 1976. 15 p. (Bibliography series / Ontario Ministry of Labour, Research Library ; no. 3) [2831]

Women in management: a selected bibliography, 1970-1975. Toronto: Ontario Ministry of Labour, Research Library, 1976. 18 p. (Bibliography series / Ontario Ministry of Labour, Research Library ; no. 4) [3765]

Halary, Charles; Mascotto, J.; Soucy, P.-Y.

"Sur la question nationale au Canada et au Québec." Dans: *Pluriel*; No 7 (1976) p. 87-96.; ISSN: 0336-1721. [2423]

Hale, Linda Louise

"Bibliography of British Columbia." In: *BC Studies*; No. 55 (Autumn 1982) p. 107-123.; ISSN: 0005-2949. [0592]

Selected bibliography of manuscripts and pamphlets pertaining to women held by archives, libraries, museums and associations in British Columbia. [S.l.: s.n.], c1978. [185] l. [3780]

Vancouver centennial bibliography: a project of the Vancouver Historical Society. [Vancouver]: Vancouver Historical Society, 1986. 4 vol. (xi, 1791 p.): ill., maps.; ISBN: 0-9692378-0-4 (set). [0594]

Hale, Linda Louise; Barman, Jean

British Columbia local histories: a bibliography. Victoria, B.C.: British Columbia Heritage Trust, 1991. 196 p.: map.; ISBN: 0-7718-9078-8. [0602]

Hale, Linda Louise; Houlden, Melanie G.

"The study of British Columbia women: a quarter-century review, 1960-1984." In: *Resources for Feminist Research*; Vol. 15, no. 2 (July 1986) p. 58-68.; ISSN: 0707-8412. [3844]

Halévy, Balfour; Tanguay, Guy

Inventory of Canadian secondary legal literature, 1970-1986. Ottawa: Canadian Legal Information Centre, 1990. vii,

115 p.; ISBN: 0-921481-21-7. [2338]

Halifax City Regional Library
Around our lovely province. 3rd ed. [Halifax]: Halifax City Regional Library, 1973. 32 p. [0213]

Halifax City Regional Library. Reference Department
Halifax, N.S., social, economic and municipal studies, 1970-1980. Halifax: The Library, 1981. 13 l. [0249]

Halifax Garrison Library
Rules and catalogue of the Halifax Garrison Library. Halifax, N.S.: J.W. Dolan, 1883. 134 p. [6735]

Hall, Agnez; Ruthven, Patricia; Swanick, Eric L.
An inventory of New Brunswick indexing projects/ Inventaire des projets d'indexation en cours au Nouveau-Brunswick. Fredericton: Council of Head Librarians of New Brunswick, 1980. 51 p.; ISBN: 0-9690287-1-7. [1640]

Hall, Frederick A., et al.
A basic bibliography of musical Canadiana. Toronto: [s.n.], 1970. 38 l. [0825]

Halliday, R.G., et al.
A history of Canadian fisheries research in the Georges Bank area of the northwestern Atlantic. Dartmouth, N.S.: Fisheries and Oceans Canada, 1987. iv, 37 p.: map. (Canadian technical report of fisheries and aquatic sciences ; no. 1550; ISSN: 0706-6457) [4908]

Halpert, Herbert
A Folklore sampler from the Maritimes: with a bibliographical essay on the folktale in English. St. John's: Published for the Centre for Canadian Studies, Mount Allison University by Memorial University of Newfoundland Folklore and Language Publications, 1982. xix, 273 p. (Bibliographical and special series / Centre for Canadian Studies, Mount Allison University ; no. 8); ISBN: 0-88901-086-2. [4590]

Hamel, Jacques
"Bibliographie de Marcel Rioux." Dans: *Sociologie et sociétés*; Vol. 17, no 2 (octobre 1985) p. 133-144.; ISSN: 0038-030X. [7269]

Hamel, Pierre; Léonard, Jean-François; Senécal, Francine
Bibliographie sur les mobilisations populaires à Montréal, 1960-1978. [Montréal]: Département de science politique, Université du Québec à Montréal, 1979. 98 p. (Notes de recherche / Département de science politique, Université du Québec à Montréal ; no 17) [2445]

Hamel, Réginald
Bibliographie des lettres canadiennes-françaises, 1965. Montréal: Les Presses de l'Université de Montréal, 1966. 111 p. [1033]

Bibliographie sommaire sur l'histoire de l'écriture féminine au Canada, 1769-1961. [Montréal]: Université de Montréal, 1974. 134 p. [3746]

Cahiers bibliographiques des lettres québécoises. Montréal: Centre de documentation des lettres canadiennes-françaises, Université de Montréal, 1966-1969. 4 vol. [1049]

"Un choix bibliographique des lettres québécoises (1764-1967)." Dans: *Revue d'histoire littéraire de la France*; Vol. 69, no 5 (septembre-octobre 1969) p. 808-821. [1050]

Hamel, Réginald; Hare, John; Wyczynski, Paul
Dictionnaire pratique des auteurs québécois. Montréal: Fides, c1976. xxv, 723 p.; ISBN: 0-7755-0597-8. [1099]

Hamelin, Jean, et al.
Guide du chercheur en histoire canadienne. Québec: Presses de l'Université Laval, 1986. xxxii, 808 p.; ISBN: 2-7637-7096-7. [2055]

Hamelin, Jean; Beaulieu, André; Gallichan, Gilles
Brochures québécoises, 1764-1972. [Québec]: Gouvernement du Québec, Ministère des communications, Direction générale des publications gouvernementales, c1981. vii, 598, [2] p.; ISBN: 2-551-03737-9. [0371]

Hamelin, Jean; Letarte, Jacques; Hamelin, Marcel
"Les élections provinciales dans le Québec: orientations bibliographiques." Dans: *Cahiers de géographie de Québec*; Vol. 4, no 7 (octobre 1959-mars 1960) p. 204-207.; ISSN: 0007-9766. [2377]

Hamelin, Louis-Edmond
"Bibliographie annotée concernant la pénétration de la géographie dans le Québec." Dans: *Cahiers de géographie de Québec*; Vol. 4, no 8 (avril-septembre 1960) p. 345-358.; ISSN: 0007-9766. [2960]

"Bibliographie des publications de Louis-Edmond Hamelin." Dans: *Revue de géographie de Montréal*; Vol. 23, no 1 (1969) p. 75-82; vol. 23, no 2 (1969) p. 179-185.; ISSN: 0035-1148. [7044]

Hamelin, Louis-Edmond; Bussières, Aline
Repertoire des travaux sur le nord publiés par le Centre d'études nordiques et l'Institut de géographie de l'Université Laval, 1953-1964. Québec: Université Laval, 1965. 42 f.: carte. (Centre d'études nordiques Travaux divers ; no 8) [0613]

Hamelin, Louis-Edmond; Hamelin, Colette L.
Quelques matériaux de sociologie religieuse canadienne. Montréal: Éditions du Lévrier, 1956. 156 p. (Collection Sociologie et pastorale ; 1) [1511]

Hamelin, Lucien; Walser, Lise
Cinéma québécois: petit guide. Montréal: Conseil québécois pour la diffusion du cinéma, 1972. 47 p.: ill. [6615]

Hamilton, L.
"German publications relating to Canada, 1914-1920." In: *Canadian Historical Review*; Vol. 1, no. 3 (September 1920) p. 281-282.; ISSN: 0008-3755. [1901]

Hamilton, W.D.; Spray, W.A.
Source materials relating to the New Brunswick Indian. Fredericton: Hamray Books, 1977. vii, 134 p.; ISBN: 0-920332-05-6. [3989]

Hamm, Carol A.
Annotations from the literature on prevention and early intervention in mental health. Saskatoon: Saskatchewan Health, 1979. viii, 66 p. [5624]

Hamm, Jean-Jacques
Psychanalyse et littérature: essai de bibliographie. [Kingston, Ont.]: Association des professeurs de français des universités et collèges canadiens, 1981. 21 p. (Fascicule pédagogique / Association des professeurs de français des universités et collèges canadiens ; no 3) [5637]

Hamoda, M.F.D.; Shannon, E.E.; Schmidtke, N.W.
Advanced wastewater treatment: a selective, coded bibliography. Burlington, Ont.: Wastewater Technology Centre, Environmental Protection Service, 1972. 132 p. (Technical appraisal report / Water Pollution Control Directorate ; EPS 3-WP-73-1) [5738]

Hancock, Kenneth; Houghton, Conrad; Rogers, Dorothy
Advanced train control systems: a selective bibliography/ Systèmes d'automatisation de la marche des trains: bibliographie sélective. Rev. 2nd ed. Montreal: Transportation Development Centre, 1990. viii, 75 p.: ill. [4508]

Handfield, Roger; Nollet, Jean

Bibliographie annotée en robotique/Annotated bibliography on robotics. Montréal: École des hautes études commerciales, 1987. 5 vol. (Rapport de recherche / École des hautes études commerciales ; nos 87-12-87-16; ISSN: 0709-986X) [5824]

Hanessian, John

A select bibliography of the polar regions. New York: American Universities Field Staff, c1962. 30 p. [0611]

Hanley, Annie Harvey (Ross) Foster

British Columbia authors' index. White Rock, B.C.: [1941]. 84, 29, [10] l. [0566]

Hann, Robert G.

Deterrence and the death penalty: a critical review of the research of Isaac Ehrlich. Ottawa: Research Division, Solicitor General of Canada, 1976. 96 p. [2149]

Hann, Russell G., et al.

Primary sources in Canadian working class history, 1860-1930. Kitchener, Ont.: Dumont Press, 1973. 169, [16] p. [2815]

Hanna, Archibald

John Buchan, 1875-1940: a bibliography. Hamden, Conn.: Shoe String Press, 1953. xi, 135 p. [7346]

Hanrahan, James

"A current bibliography of Canadian church history/ Bibliographie récente de l'histoire de l'église canadienne." In: *Canadian Catholic Historical Association. Study Sessions*; Vol. 37 (1970) p. 101-126; Vol. 38 (1971) p. 71-94; Vol. 39 (1972) p. 83-104; Vol. 40 (1973) p. 69-93.; ISSN: 0318-6172. [1529]

Harasymiw, Elaine Verchomin; Malycky, Alexander

"Ukrainian-Canadian creative literature: a preliminary check list of imprints." In: *Canadian Ethnic Studies*; Vol. 2, no. 1 (June 1970) p. 205-227.; ISSN: 0008-3496. [1054]

Harbec, Hélène

Guide bibliographique de l'Acadie, 1976-1987. [Moncton, N.-B.]: Centre d'études acadiennes, Université de Moncton, 1988. xvii, 508 p.; ISBN: 0-919691-30-7. [0268]

Harding, Anne D.; Bolling, Patricia

Bibliography of articles and papers on North American Indian art. Washington: United States Department of the Interior, Indian Arts and Crafts Board, 1938. 365 p. [0666]

Harding, Howard

Cochliobolus sativus (Ito & Kurib.) Drechsl. ex Dastur (imperfect stage: bipolaris sorokiniana (Sacc. in Sorok.) Shoem.): a bibliography. Saskatoon: Research Station, Research Branch, Agriculture Canada, 1979. ca. 300 p. [4685]

Harding, Jim; Forgay, Beryl

Breaking down the walls: a bibliography on the pursuit of aboriginal justice. [Regina]: Prairie Justice Research, University of Regina, 1991. 108 p. (Aboriginal Justice Series report ; no. 2); ISBN: 0-7731-0191-8. [2349]

Harding, Jim; Forgay, Beryl; Gianoli, Mary

Bibliography on Saskatchewan uranium inquiries and the northern and global impact of the uranium industry. Regina: Prairie Justice Research, School of Human Justice, University of Regina, 1988. 76 p. (In the public interest Research report ; no. 1); ISBN: 0-7731-0052-0. [4869]

Harding, Jim; Spence, Bruce

An annotated bibliography of aboriginal-controlled justice programs in Canada. [Regina]: Prairie Justice Research, University of Regina, 1991. 89 p. (Aboriginal Justice Series

report ; no. 3); ISBN: 0-7731-0190-X. [2350]

Hardisty, Pamela

Publications of the Canadian Parliament: a detailed guide to the dual-media edition of Canadian parliamentary proceedings and sessional papers, 1841-1970. Washington, D.C.: United States Historical Documents Institute, 1974. viii, 57 p.; ISBN: 0-88222-033-0. [6290]

Hardy, J. Stewart

"A review of selected materials in the educational history of western Canada." In: *Journal of Educational Thought*; Vol. 14, no. 2 (August 1980) p. 64-79.; ISSN: 0022-0701. [3567]

Hardy, Kenneth J.

Calgary archaeology, 1959-1980: a select annotated bibliography. Edmonton: Kenneth J. Hardy, 1982. vi, 57 p. [4591]

Hardy, René; Trépanier, Guy

Bibliographie de la Mauricie. Québec: Institut québécois de recherche sur la culture, 1991. 294 p. (Documents de recherche / Institut québécois de recherche sur la culture ; no 27; ISSN: 0823-0447); ISBN: 2-89224-159-6. [0411]

Hardy, René; Trépanier, Guy; Belleau, Jacques

La Mauricie et les Bois-Francs: inventaire bibliographique, 1760-1975. Montréal: Éditions du Boréal Express, [1977]. 389 p.: cartes. (Collection Mékinac ; 2); ISBN: 0-88503-062-1. [0346]

Hardy BBT Limited

Reclamation of disturbed alpine lands: a literature review. Edmonton: Land Conservation and Reclamation Council, Reclamation Research Technical Advisory Committee, 1990. xviii, 198 [13] p. (Alberta Land Conservation and Reclamation Council report ; no. RRTAC 90-7; ISSN: 0713-1232) [5281]

Hare, John

Bibliographie du roman canadien-français, 1837-1962. Montréal: Fides, [1965]. 82 p. [1026]

"Bibliographie du théâtre canadien-français (des origines à 1973)." Dans *Le théâtre canadien français: évolution, témoignages, bibliographie*. Montréal: Fides, c1976. P. 951-999. (Archives des lettres canadiennes ; Tome 5); ISBN: 0-7755-0583-8. [0960]

"A bibliography of the works of Léon Pamphile Lemay (1837-1918)." In: *Papers of the Bibliographical Society of America*; Vol. 57, no. 1 (1963) p. 50-60.; ISSN: 0006-128X. [7142]

Les Canadiens français aux quatre coins du monde: une bibliographie commentée des récits, de voyage, 1670-1914. Québec: Société historique du Québec, 1964. 215 p. (Cahiers d'histoire / Société historique du Québec ; no 16) [1943]

"Literary sociology and French-Canadian literature: a summary bibliography." In: *Culture*; Vol. 26 (1965) p. 419-423.; ISSN: 0317-2066. [1027]

Hare, John; Motard, Chantal; Vigneault, Robert

"Bibliographie représentative de la prose d'idées au Québec, des origines à 1980." Dans *L'essai et la prose d'idées au Québec*. Montréal: Fides, 1985. P. 783-921. (Archives des lettres canadiennes ; Tome 6); ISBN: 2-7621-1279-6. [0385]

Hare, John; Wallot, Jean-Pierre

Les imprimés dans le Bas-Canada, 1801-1840: bibliographie analytique. Montréal: Presses de l'Université de Montréal, 1967. xxiii, 381 p. [0298]

Harger-Grinling, Virginia A.

Aide bibliographique pour l'étude du nouveau roman canadien-français. [Regina]: University of Regina, [1976].

iii, 57 f. [1100]

Harkins, Edwin

Maynard Ferguson: a discography. [S.l.]: E. Harkins, c1976. iv, 73 l. [6978]

Harner, James L.

Literary research guide: a guide to reference sources for the study of literatures in English and related topics. New York: Modern Language Association of America, 1989. 737 p.; ISBN: 0-87352-182-X. [1271]

Harper, Alexander Maitland

A bibliography of Alberta entomology, 1883 to 1977. Edmonton: Alberta Agriculture, 1979. 101 p. [5429]

A bibliography of papers presented at the annual meetings of the Entomological Society of Alberta, 1953-1978. [Edmonton: s.n.], 1980. 56 p. [5448]

Harper, J. Russell

Historical directory of New Brunswick newspapers and periodicals. Fredericton: University of New Brunswick, c1961. xxii, 121 p.: facsim. [5871]

Harrigan, MaryLou

Quality of care: issues and challenges in the 90s: a literature review. Ottawa: Canadian Medical Association, 1992. xv, 218 p.; ISBN: 0-92016-950-3. [5709]

Harris, Chauncey Dennison

International list of geographical serials. 3rd ed., rev., expanded, and updated. Chicago: University of Chicago, Department of Geography, 1980. vi, 457 p. (University of Chicago Department of Geography Research paper ; no. 193; ISSN: 0069-3340); ISBN: 0-89065-100-0. [5938]

Harris, R. Colebrook

"Historical geography in Canada." In: *Canadian Geographer*; Vol. 11, no. 4 (1967) p. 235-250.; ISSN: 0008-3658. [2970]

Harris, Robin S.

An annotated list of the legislative acts concerning higher education in Ontario. Toronto: Innis College, University of Toronto, 1966. vi, 79 p. [3390]

A list of reports to the Legislature of Ontario bearing on higher education in the province. [Toronto]: Innis College, University of Toronto, 1966. v, 17 p. [3391]

Harris, Robin S.; Tremblay, Arthur

A bibliography of higher education in Canada/Bibliographie de l'enseignement supérieur au Canada. [Toronto]: University of Toronto Press; [Québec]: Presses Universitaires Laval, [c1960]. xxv, 158 p. (Studies in higher education in Canada ; no. 1/Études dans l'enseignement supérieur au Canada ; no 1) [3378]

Harrison, Alice W.

Checklist of United Church of Canada publications, 1925-1986. Halifax, N.S.: Atlantic School of Theology Library, 1987. 2 vol. [1564]

Harrison, Cynthia Ellen

Women in American history: a bibliography. Santa Barbara, Calif.: American Bibliographical Center–Clio Press, c1979-1985. 2 vol. (Clio bibliography series ; no. 5, 20); ISBN: 0-87436-260-1 (vol. 1); 0-87436-450-7 (vol. 2). [3836]

Women's movement media: a source guide. New York: Bowker, c1973. x, 269 p.; ISBN: 0-8352-0711-0. [3742]

Harrison, Dallas

"Sandra Birdsell: an annotated bibliography." In: *Essays on Canadian Writing*; No. 48 (Winter 1992-1993) p. 170-219.; ISSN: 0316-0300. [6843]

Harrison, David; Little, Barbara; Mallett, Graham

Reading development: a resource book for adult education. Victoria: Province of British Columbia, Ministry of Education, 1982. 89 p.; ISBN: 0-771-99240-8. [3609]

Harrison, Dick

"Mountie fiction: a reader's guide." In: *Royal Canadian Mounted Police Quarterly*; Vol. 40, no. 4 (October 1975) p. 39-46.; ISSN: 0317-8250. [1088]

Harrison, P.J., et al.

A bibliography of the biological oceanography of the Strait of Georgia and adjacent inlets, with emphasis on ecological aspects. Nanaimo, B.C.: Fisheries Research Branch, Department of Fisheries and Oceans, 1984. vi, 140 p.: map. (Canadian technical report of fisheries and aquatic sciences ; no. 1293; ISSN: 0706-6457) [5497]

Harrisse, Henry

Bibliotheca americana vetustissima: a description of works relating to America published between the years 1492 and 1551. New York: G. Philes, 1866. iv, 519 p. [0008]

The discovery of North America: a critical, documentary, and historical investigation, with an essay on the early cartography of the New World, including descriptions of two hundred and fifty maps or globes, existing or lost, constructed before the year 1536.... London: H. Stevens, 1892. xii, 802 p.: ill., maps. [6485]

Notes pour servir à l'histoire, à la bibliographie et à la cartographie de la Nouvelle-France et des pays adjacents, 1545-1700. Paris: Tross, 1872. xxxiii, 367 p. [6476]

Hart, Denise; Comeau, P.G.

Manual brushing for forest vegetation management in British Columbia: a review of current knowledge and information needs. Victoria: BC Ministry of Forests, 1992. vi, 36 p.: ill., maps. (Land management report / British Columbia Ministry of Forests ; no. 77; ISSN: 0702-9861); ISBN: 0-7718-9172-5. [5015]

Hart, Earl Paul

Science for Saskatchewan schools: a review of research literature, analysis, and recommendations. Regina: University of Regina, Saskatchewan Instructional Development & Research Unit, 1987. ii l., 205 p.: ill. (SIDRU Research report / Saskatchewan Instructional Development & Research Unit ; no. 7; ISSN: 0835-6580); ISBN: 0-77310-125-X. [3669]

Hart, Keith

An annotated bibliography of Canadian police history, 1651-1984. Edmonton: University of Alberta, Faculty of Library Science, 1985. 59 l. [2275]

Hart, Patricia W.

Local history of the regional municipalities of Peel, York and Durham: an annotated listing of published materials located in the public libraries in the regional municipalities of Peel, York and Durham. Richmond Hill: Central Ontario Regional Library System, 1980. 2 vol. [0469]

"North York history: a bibliography." In: *Ontario Library Review*; Vol. 47, no. 4 (November 1963) p. 174-176.; ISSN: 0030-2996. [0432]

Hartig, Linda Bishop

Violet Archer: a bio-bibliography. New York: Greenwood Press, 1991. viii, 153 p.: port. (Bio-bibliographies in music ; no. 41; ISSN: 0742-6968); ISBN: 0-313-26408-2. [6805]

Harting, Lynn
Peter Ware. Don Mills, Ont.: PRO Canada, 1988. 7 p. [7360]

Hartling, Philip L.
"A bibliographical selection of local history sources at the Public Archives of Nova Scotia." In: *Nova Scotia Historical Review*; Vol. 1, no. 2 (1981) p. 42-49.; ISSN: 0227-4752. [0250]

Hartman, Charles W.; Carlson, Robert F.
A bibliography of Arctic water resources. College, Alaska: Institute of Water Resources, University of Alaska, [1970]. 344, [194] p. (Report / University of Alaska, Institute of Water Resources ; no. IWR-11) [5052]

Hartson, Thalia, et al.
"Canada at work: a bibliography." In: *One World*; Vol. 5, no. 3 (February 1967) 24 p.; ISSN: 0475-0209. [2797]

Harvard University. Library
The Canadian collection at Harvard University. Cambridge, Mass.: Harvard University Printing Office, 1944-1949. 6 vol. [6766]
Canadian history and literature: classification schedule, classified listing by call number, alphabetical listing by author or title, chronological listing. Cambridge, Mass.: Published by the Harvard University Library, distributed by the Harvard University Press, 1968. 411 p. (Widener Library shelflist ; 20) [6776]

Harvey, D.C.
"Newspapers of Nova Scotia, 1840-1867." In: *Canadian Historical Review*; Vol. Vol. 26, no. 3 (September 1945) p. 279-301.; ISSN: 0008-3755. [6009]

Harvey, Daniel A.
A literature review of deer damage and controls in the Pacific Northwest with special reference to British Columbia [microform]. Ottawa: National Library of Canada, 1982. 3 microfiches (217 fr.): ill.; ISBN: 0-315-05548-0. [4975]

Harvey, Eileen M. Forestell; Mohammed, Gina H.; Noland, T.L.
A bibliography on competition, tree seedling characteristics and related topics. Sault Ste. Marie: Ontario Ministry of Natural Resources, 1993. iv, 117 p. (Forest research information paper ; no. 108; ISSN: 0319-9118); ISBN: 0-7778-0969-9. [5022]

Harvey, Fernand
"An annotated bibliography on the Irish in Quebec." In: *The Irish in Quebec: an introduction to the historiography*, by Robert J. Grace. Québec: Institut québécois de recherche sur la culture, 1993. P. 135-262. (Instruments de travail / Institut québécois de recherche sur la culture ; no 12; ISSN: 0714-0614) [4297]
Bibliographie de six historiens québécois: Michel Bibaud, François-Xavier Garneau, Thomas Chapais, Lionel Groulx, Fernand Ouellet, Michel Brunet. [Québec]: Institut supérieur des sciences humaines, Université Laval, 1970. 43 f. [1967]
Inventaire des cartes socio-économiques sur le Québec, 1940-1971. Québec: Institut supérieur des sciences humaines, Université Laval, 1972. vi, 44 f. (Cahiers de l'ISSH, Collection Instruments de travail / Institut supérieur des sciences humaines, Université Laval ; no 5) [6529]

Harvey, Fernand; Houle, Gilles
Les classes sociales au Canada et au Québec: bibliographie annotée. Québec: Institut supérieur des sciences humaines, Université Laval, c1979. 282 p. (Collection études sur le Québec ; no 11) [3186]

Harvey, Fernand; Samuel, Rodrigue
Matériel pour une sociologie des maladies mentales au Québec. Québec: Institut supérieur des sciences humaines, Université Laval, 1974. xiii, 143 p. (Cahiers de l'ISSH, Collection Instruments de travail / Institut supérieur des sciences humaines, Université Laval ; no 15) [3126]

Hattersley-Smith, G.
Bibliography of "Operation Hazen," 1957-63. Ottawa: National Defence Department, Defence Research Board, Directorate of Physical Research Geophysics, 1964. 5 p. [5034]
Bibliography of "Operation Hazen-Tanquary," 1964-1967. Ottawa: Defence Research Telecommunications Establishment (Canada), 1968. 10 p. [5043]

Haubrich, Dennis J.; McLeod, Donald W.
Psychosocial dimensions of HIV and AIDS: a selected annotated bibliography. Ottawa: Health and Welfare Canada, Federal Centre for AIDS, 1988. v, 163 p.; ISBN: 0-662-16641-8. [3308]

Hauck, Philomena
Sourcebook on Canadian women. Ottawa: Canadian Library Association, [c1979]. 111 p.: ill.; ISBN: 0-88802-126-7. [3790]

Haugen, Einar Ingvald
Bilingualism in the Americas: a bibliography and research guide. [Gainesville, Fla.]: American Dialect Society, 1956. 159 p. (Publication of the American Dialect Society ; no. 26) [1417]

Haughton, E.R.; Huston, R.D.; Billingsley, W.A.
Ethanol-alcohol from wastes: a literature review. Victoria: Province of British Columbia, Ministry of Environment, Waste Management Branch, 1981. iii, 57 p. (Report / Province of British Columbia, Ministry of Environment, Waste Management Branch ; no. 81-1) [5782]

Hawaleshka, O.; Stasynec, G.
Alternative energy: a bibliography of practical literature. Winnipeg: Agassiz Centre for Water Studies, University of Manitoba, 1976. vii, 54 l.: ill. (Agassiz Centre for Water Studies Research report ; no. 11) [5759]

Hawkes, Herbert Edwin
Exploration geochemistry bibliography to January 1981. Rexdale, Ont.: Association of Exploration Geochemists, c1982. xi, 388 p. (Association of Exploration Geochemists Special volume ; no. 11); ISBN: 0-9691014-1-4. [4827]

Hawkins, Ann
Bibliography: energy-efficient community planning. Toronto: Ontario Ministry of Energy, 1980. 28 p. [4383]

Hawley, Donna Lea
"Prostitution in Canada: a bibliography." In: *Resources for Feminist Research*; Vol. 14, no. 4 (December/January 1985-1986) p. 61-63.; ISSN: 0707-8412. [3845]
Women and aging: a comprehensive bibliography. Burnaby, B.C.: Gerontology Research Centre, Simon Fraser University, 1985. iii, 128 p. (Simon Fraser University Gerontology Research Centre Bibliography series 85-1); ISBN: 0-86491-048-7. [3837]

Hawley, Norma J.
A bibliography of AECL publications on environmental research/Une bibliographie des publications de l'EACL sur les recherches écologiques. Pinawa, Man.: Whiteshell Nuclear Research Establishment, 1980. 47 p. (AECL-6319-Rev. 1; ISSN: 0067-0367) [5163]
A bibliography of AECL publications on reactor safety/Une bibliographie des publications de l'EACL sur la sûreté des

réacteurs. Pinawa, Man.: Whiteshell Nuclear Research Establishment, 1982. 34 p. (AECL-6426-Rev. 1; ISSN: 0067-0367) [5785]

Fuel cycles: a bibliography of AECL publications. Pinawa, Man.: Atomic Energy of Canada Limited, Whiteshell Nuclear Research Establishment, 1979. 27 p. [5773]

Radiation effects on living systems: a bibliography of AECL publications/Effets des rayonnements sur les organismes vivants: une bibliographie des publications de l'ÉACL. Pinawa, Man.: Whiteshell Nuclear Research Establishment, Atomic Energy of Canada Limited, 1984. 45 p. [5797]

Haworth, S.E.; Cowell, Daryl William; Sims, R.A.
Bibliography of published and unpublished literature on the Hudson Bay Lowland. Ottawa: Canadian Forestry Service, Department of the Environment, 1978. 270 p.: maps. (Great Lakes Forest Research Centre report ; O-X-273; ISSN: 0704-7797) [5134]

Hawthorn, R.S.; McCormick, W.A.
A literature review of aquatic macrophytes with particular reference to those present in Windermere Lake, British Columbia. Vancouver: Province of British Columbia, Ministry of Environment, 1980. ii, 57 l. [5449]

Hay, Oliver Perry
Bibliography and catalogue of the fossil vertebrata of North America. Washington: United States Government Printing Office, 1902. 868, iii p. (United States Geological Survey Bulletin ; 179) [4528]

Hayashida, D.L.
Parks Canada visitor services: a bibliography. Ottawa: Interpretation and Visitor Services Division, National Parks Branch, Parks Canada, 1981. [5], 49 l. [1805]

Hayes, Janet; Souka, Jody
Violence in society: a selective bibliography/Violence au sein de la société: biobibliographie [sic] choisie. [Ottawa]: Ministry Secretariat, Solicitor General Canada, [1986]. 215 p. (Programs Branch user report / Ministry Secretariat, Solicitor General Canada ; no. 1986-24) [3288]

Hayes, Janice E.
Bibliography on Canadian feminist art. Montreal: Graduate School of Library and Information Studies, McGill University, 1986. 43 p. (McGill University Graduate School of Library and Information Studies Occasional papers ; 9) [0710]

Hayhurst, K.; Gutman, G.M.; Cooper, Mary
Non-medical aspects of Alzheimer's disease and related disorders: a comprehensive bibliography, 1960-1988. Burnaby, B.C.: Gerontology Research Centre, Simon Fraser University, 1988. [12], 309 p.; ISBN: 0-86491-072-X. [5679]

Hayne, David M.
Bibliographie analytique de la critique littéraire au Québec. [Kingston, Ont.]: Association des professeurs de français des universités et collèges canadiens, 1981. 15 p. (Fascicule pédagogique / Association des professeurs de français des universités et collèges canadiens ; no 4) [1181]

"Bibliographie critique des *Anciens Canadiens* (1863) de Philippe-Joseph Aubert de Gaspé." Dans: *Cahiers de la Société bibliographique du Canada*; Vol. 3 (1964) p. 38-60.; ISSN: 0067-6896. [6814]

"État actuel des études bibliographiques de la littérature canadienne-française (avant 1945)." Dans: *Revue de l'Université d'Ottawa*; Vol. 49, nos 1-2 (janvier-avril 1979) p. 14-25.; ISSN: 0041-9206. [1151]

"Preliminary bibliography of the literary relations between

Quebec and the francophone world." In: *Canadian Review of Comparative Literature*; Vol. 6, no. 2 (Spring 1979) p. 206-218.; ISSN: 0319-051X. [1152]

Hayne, David M.; Sirois, Antoine
"Preliminary bibliography of comparative Canadian literature (English-Canadian and French-Canadian)." In: *Canadian Review of Comparative Literature*; Vol. 3, no. 2 (Spring 1976)-vol. 14, no. 2 (June 1987) [1238]

Hayne, David M.; Tirol, Marcel
Bibliographie critique du roman canadien-français, 1837-1900. [Toronto]: University of Toronto Press, c1968. viii, 144 p.; ISBN: 0-8020-1541-7. [1042]

Haynes, Jane Banfield
Law and society: a bibliography. Downsview, Ont.: York University, Faculty of Arts, Division of Social Science, 1976. 20 l. [2150]

Haythorne, Owen; Layton, Carol; Laroque, Emma
Natives of North America: a selected bibliography to improve resource availability in native studies programs. [Edmonton]: Alberta Education, 1975. iii, 156 p. [3967]

Hayward, Robert J.
Fire insurance plans in the National Map Collection/Plans d'assurance-incendie de la Collection nationale de cartes et plans. Ottawa: Public Archives, 1977. xxvi, 171 p.: ill. (some in colour), plans.; ISBN: 0-662-01609-2. [6560]

Haywood, Charles
A bibliography of North American folklore and folksong. 2nd rev. ed. New York: Dover Publications, [1961]. 2 vol.: maps (on lining papers). [4535]

Hazelgrove, A.R.
A tercentennial contribution to a checklist of Kingston imprints to 1867. Kingston, Ont.: Special Collections, Douglas Library, Queen's University, 1978. xix, 118 p.: ill., facsim. (Douglas Library Occasional papers ; no. 5) [0457]

Healey Willan centennial year 1980: [first of his choral compositions]. Toronto: International Music Sales, 1979. [4] p. [7363]

Health, psychological and social factors: an annotated bibliography/La santé, les facteurs psychologiques et sociologiques: bibliographie annotée. Vanier, Ont.: Secretariat for Fitness in the Third Age, 1984. 24 p.; ISBN: 0-919963-23-4. [1828]

Health help: children's health information: a guide to national resources. Ottawa: Canadian Association of Paediatric Hospitals, 1989. vi, 93 p. [5689]

Heath, Dwight B.; Cooper, A.M.
Alcohol use and world cultures: a comprehensive bibliography of anthropological sources. Toronto: Addiction Research Foundation of Ontario, c1981. xv, 248 p. (Bibliographic series / Addiction Research Foundation of Ontario ; no. 15; ISSN: 0065-1885); ISBN: 0-88868-045-7. [4581]

Heath, Jean
Lone parent families: a selected and annotated bibliography. Vancouver: British Columbia Ministry of Education, Division of Continuing Education, 1980. 39 p. [3201]

Heath, Jeffrey M.
Profiles in Canadian literature. Toronto: Dundurn Press, 1980-1986. 6 vol., ill., ports.; ISBN: 0-919670-46-6 (vol. 1); 0-919670-50-4 (vol. 2); 0-919670-58-X (vol. 3); 0-919670-59-8 (vol. 4); 1-55002-001-3 (vol. 5); 1-55002-002-1 (vol. 6). [1227]

Hébert, Jacques; Bélanger, Johanne

Statistiques, études de marché et répertoires concernant l'industrie et l'exploitation forestières au Québec: une bibliographie. Québec: Ministère de l'énergie et des ressources, 1988. 30 f. (Études et bibliographies / Centre de documentation, Terres et forêts ; no 2; ISSN: 0838-2255) [4996]

Hébert, Jacques; Collister, Edward A.

Historique de la gestion des terres et des forêts au Québec: une bibliographie. 2e éd., rev. et augm. Québec: Ministère de l'énergie et des ressources, Direction des communications, Centre de documentation – Terres et forêts, 1988. iv, 149 p. (Collection: Études et bibliographies / Québec, Ministère de l'énergie et des ressources, Direction des communications, Centre de documentation: Terres et forêts); ISBN: 2-550-17778-9. [4997]

Hébert, John R.

Panoramic maps of cities in the United States and Canada: a checklist of maps in the collections of the Library of Congress, Geography and Map Division. 2nd ed. Washington: Library of Congress, 1984. v, 181 p.: ill.; ISBN: 0-8444-0413-6. [6584]

Hébert, Yves

Bibliographie de la Côte-du-Sud. [Québec]: Institut québécois de recherche sur la culture, 1986. 339 p.: cartes. (Documents de recherche / Institut québécois de recherche sur la culture ; no 8; ISSN: 0823-0447); ISBN: 2-89224-060-3. [0393]

Hedges, Donna M.; Wong, Betty; Macdonald, R. Bruce

Employment of the learning disabled: an annotated bibliography of resource materials for education and training. Vancouver: Vancouver Association for Children and Adults with Learning Disabilities, 1987. xi, 159 p.; ISBN: 0-9693284-0-0. [3670]

Hedley, Alan

Privacy as a factor in residential buildings and site development: an annotated bibliography. Ottawa: National Research Council Canada, Division of Building Research, 1966. 63 l. (National Research Council Canada, Division of Building Research Bibliography ; no. 32) [0736]

Hedley, D.G.F.

Catalogue of rockburst literature. [Ottawa]: Mining Research Laboratories, Energy, Mines and Resources Canada, 1987. ii, 32 p. (Mining Research Laboratories Divisional report ; MRL 87-50-LS) [4859]

Hedlin, Menzies & Associates

Annotated bibliography of socio-economic references for water quality management studies in the Saint John River Basin. Toronto: [s.n.], 1970. 164 l. [5053]

Heggie, Grace F.

Canadian political parties, 1867-1968: a historical bibliography. [Toronto]: MacMillan of Canada, [c1977]. 603 p.; ISBN: 0-7705-1341-7. [2429]

Heide, Cynthia

Bibliography on technological forecasting and long range planning. Ottawa: Defence Research Board, 1969. ix, 22 p. [5731]

Heinke, Gary W.

Bibliography of Arctic environmental engineering. Ottawa: Department of Indian Affairs and Northern Development, Northern Science Research Group, 1972. iii, 159 p. [5739]

Heinrich, Albert C.

"Periodical publications of Canada's Eskimos: a preliminary check list." In: Canadian Ethnic Studies; Vol. 5, no. 1/2 (1973) p. 51-56.; ISSN: 0008-3496. [5913]

"University research on Canada's Eskimos." In: Canadian Ethnic Studies; Vol. 2, no. 1 (June 1970) p. 31-33.; ISSN: 0008-3496. [6104]

"University research on Canada's Eskimos: a preliminary check list of theses." In: Northian; Vol. 8, no. 4 (March 1972) p. 29-30.; ISSN: 0029-3253. [6117]

Heissler, Ivar

Township of York historical sources, volume 2: a descriptive bibliography. [Weston, Ont.: s.n.], 1974. i, 224 l. [0449]

Helen K. Mussallem Library

List of Canadian nursing related periodicals. Ottawa: Canadian Nurses Association, 1987-. vol.; ISSN: 0844-0999. [5988]

Hélène de Rome, soeur

Bibliographie analytique de l'oeuvre du Révérend père Jean Bousquet o.p., lecteur en théologie, précédée d'une biographie. Québec: [s.n.], 1964. 56 f. [6867]

Helm, June

The Indians of the subarctic: a critical bibliography. Bloomington: Indiana University Press, [c1976]. viii, 91 p. (Newberry Library Center for the History of the American Indian, Bibliographical series); ISBN: 0-253-33004-1. [3980]

Helm, June; Kurtz, Royce

Subarctic Athapaskan bibliography: 1984. Iowa City: Department of Anthropology, University of Iowa, [1984]. i, 515 p. [4058]

Hemsley, Gordon D.; Park, Norman W.

Literature review of personnel selection techniques: draft. Ottawa: Public Service Commission of Canada, 1987. 110 p. [2510]

Henderson, George Fletcher

Federal royal commissions in Canada, 1867-1966: a checklist. Toronto: University of Toronto Press, c1967. xvi, 212 p. [6262]

Henderson, V.; Sawatsky, W.

Bibliography of vegetation studies in Manitoba. [Winnipeg]: Terrestrial Standards and Studies Section, Environmental Management Services Branch, Department of Environment and Workplace Safety and Health, [1983]. 33 l., map. (Terrestrial Standards and Studies report ; 83-6) [5485]

Hendricks, Klaus B.; Whitehurst, Anne

La conservation des documents photographiques: liste d'ouvrages de référence de base. [Ottawa]: Archives nationales du Canada, c1988. vi, 32, 32, vi p.; ISBN: 0-662-55591-0. [1701]

Conservation of photographic materials: a basic reading list. [Ottawa]: National Archives of Canada, c1988. vi, 32, 32, vi p.; ISBN: 0-662-55591-0. [1702]

Hendrickson, O.; Robinson, J.B.; Chatarpaul, L.

The microbiology of forest soils: a literature review. Chalk River, Ont.: Petawawa National Forestry Institute, Canadian Forestry Service, 1982. ii, 75 p.; ISBN: 0-662-12257-7. [4976]

Henley, Thomas J.; Eyler, Phillip L.

Hudson Bay Lowlands bibliography. Winnipeg: Natural Resource Institute, University of Manitoba, 1976. ix, 82 p., [1] l. of pl.: ill., maps. [0628]

Henning, D.N.
Annotated bibliography on building for disabled persons. Rev. ed. Ottawa: Division of Building Research, National Research Council Canada, 1971. 6 l. (National Research Council Canada, Division of Building Research Bibliography ; no. 26) [3101]

Henning, J.; Hogan, K.; Lipton, S.
"Databases for research in Canadian studies: humanities and related disciplines (preliminary list)." In: *Canadian Issues*; Vol. 10, no. 4 (1988) p. 77-109.; ISSN: 0318-8442. [0160]

Henry, Ginette
Répertoire des périodiques québécois. Montréal: Ministère des affaires culturelles, 1974. xiv, 248 p. [5917]

Henry, Jon Paul
A select bibliography and a biographical dictionary of B.C. poets, 1970-1980. [Vancouver]: 1981. 78 l. [1182]

Henshel, Richard L.
The Canadian civil liberties bibliography (indexed). 5th rev. ed., enl. [London, Ont.: Henshel], 1981. iv, 151 l. [2233]

Heraldry Society of Canada. Library
Bibliography of the heraldic library of the Heraldry Society of Canada, la Société héraldique du Canada, at the City of Ottawa Archives. [Ottawa]: Heraldry Society of Canada, 1987. 1 vol. (in various foliations); ISBN: 0-9693063-1-8. [2060]

Herbert, Lynn
Standards for Canadian libraries/Normes pour les bibliothèques canadiennes. Ottawa: National Library of Canada, 1991. 18 p. (Bibliographies / Library Development Centre ; no. 6; ISSN: 0847-2467) [1725]

Herisson, Michel R.P.
An evaluative ethno-historical bibliography of the Malecite Indians. Ottawa: National Museums of Canada, 1974. vii, 260 p. (National Museum of Man Mercury series: Ethnology Division paper ; no. 16) [3953]

Heritage Canada Conference on Area Conservation
Bibliography of Canadian materials relevant to heritage conservation. Ottawa: Heritage Canada, 1974. 16 l. [0743]

Heritage history biography. Toronto: Canadian Book Information Centre, 1980. [44] p. ill. [2009]

Heritage of York: an historical bibliography, 1793-1840. [York, Ont.: s.n.], 1973. 1 vol. (in various pagings). [0447]

Heritage Ottawa
A bibliography for the conservation of structures in Ottawa. Ottawa: Heritage Ottawa, 1976. 24 l. [0750]

Heritage rivers bibliography: selected references from ARC Branch, Parks Canada card index. Ottawa: Planning Division, ARC Branch, Parks Canada, 1979. 255 p. [1794]

Herman, Carlton M., et al.
Bibliography of the avian blood-inhabiting protozoa. St. John's: International Reference Centre for Avian Haematozoa, Department of Biology, Memorial University of Newfoundland, 1976. v, 123 p. [5405]

Herman, Michael John
"Bibliography of material on the Supreme Court of Canada." In: *Ottawa Law Review*; Vol. 8, no. 1 (Winter 1976) p. 102-103.; ISSN: 0048-2331. [2151]

Herperger, Dwight
"Constitutional reform in the post-Meech era: a select bibliography." In: *Canada: the State of the Federation*; (1991) p. 241-249.; ISSN: 0827-0708. [2351]
"The Meech Lake Accord: a comprehensive bibliography." In: *Canada: the State of the Federation*; (1990) p. 271-289.;

ISSN: 0827-0708. [2339]

Herrick, Ramona
Wilderness preservation in North America: a conspectus and annotated bibliography. Cornwall, Ont.: Parks Canada (Ontario Region), 1974. 255 p. [3002]

Herrick, Ramona; Dooling, Peter J.
Wilderness recreation management: a bibliography with abstracts. Vancouver: Park and Forest Recreation Resources, Faculty of Forestry, University of British Columbia, 1975. 29 l. (Recreation land use review Report ; no. 7) [1777]

Herscovitch, Pearl; Hauck, Philomena
"Geography and history skills: an annotated bibliography of recent Canadian teaching resources." In: *History and Social Science Teacher*; Vol. 22, no. 1 (Fall 1986) p. 30-34.; ISSN: 0316-4969. [3051]

Hesch, Rick, et al.
Our home and native land: a film and video resource guide for aboriginal Canadians. Ottawa: National Film Board, 1989. iv, 34 p.: ill.; ISBN: 0-7722-0158-7. [6683]

Hessel, Peter
"German immigration to the Ottawa Valley in the 19th century." In: *German-Canadian Yearbook*; Vol. 8 (1984) p. 67-94.; ISSN: 0316-8603. [4223]

Hewitt, A.R.
Guide to resources for Commonwealth studies in London, Oxford and Cambridge, with bibliographical and other information. London: Published for the Institute of Commonwealth Studies by Athlone Press, University of London, 1957. vii, 219 p. [0064]

Hickey, Michael Daniel
A bibliography on the lateral strength of nails. Halifax: Nova Scotia Technical College, Department of Civil Engineering, 1967. iv, 37 l. (Essays on timber & timber structures / Nova Scotia Technical College, Department of Civil Engineering ; no. 23) [5726]

Hidy, Ralph W.; Hidy, Muriel E.
"List of books and articles on the economic history of the United States and Canada." In: *Economic History Review*; Vol. 8 (2nd series), no. 2 (1955) p. 265-277.; ISSN: 0013-0117. [2565]

Higgins, Kenneth F., et al.
Annotated bibliography of fire literature relative to northern grasslands in south-central Canada and north-central United States. Brookings, S.D.: U.S. Fish and Wildlife Service, 1989. 20 p. [5270]

Higgins, Marion Villiers
Canadian government publications: a manual for librarians. Chicago: American Library Association, 1935. 582 p.: ill. [6221]

Hill, Stuart B.
Ecological soil management: an annotated bibliography. [Regina]: University of Regina, 1977. 32 p. [4672]

Hill, Stuart B., et al.
Reading references on ecological agriculture: eight annotated bibliographies. [Regina]: University of Regina, 1976. [56] p. (in various pagings). [4669]

Hillman, M.
Fish protein concentrate (FPC): a bibliography, 1970-1974/ Les concentrés de protéines du poisson: bibliographie, 1970-1974. Ottawa: Environment Canada, Library, 1975. 7 l. (Environment Canada Libraries Bibliography series ; 75-1) [5392]

Hillman, Thomas A.

Catalogue of census returns on microfilm, 1661-1891/ Catalogue de recensements sur microfilm, 1661-1891. Ottawa: Public Archives Canada, 1987. xv, 289 p.; ISBN: 0-660-53711-7. [3052]

Hills, L.V.; Sangster, E.V.

"A review of paleobotanical studies dealing with the last 20,000 years: Alaska, Canada and Greenland." In: *Climatic change in Canada*, edited by C.R. Harington. Ottawa: National Museum of Natural Sciences, National Museums of Canada, c1980. P. 73-224: ill., maps; ISSN: 0704-576X. [5450]

Hills, Steven C.; Morris, Dave M.

The function of seed banks in northern forest ecosystems: a literature review. Sault Ste. Marie: Ontario Ministry of Natural Resources, 1992. iii, 25 p.: ill. (Forest research information paper ; no. 107; ISSN: 0319-9118); ISBN: 0-7729-9722-5. [5016]

Hiltz, Linda L.

The ocean clam (Arctica islandica): a literature review. Halifax, N.S.: Technology Branch, Fisheries and Marine Service, 1977. 161, 16 p.: ill. (Fisheries and Marine Service Technical report ; no. 720; ISSN: 0701-7626) [5414]

Hinke, C.J.

Oz in Canada: bibliography. Vancouver: William Hoffer, c1982. 85 p. ill.; ISBN: 0-919758-00-2. [1350]

Hippler, Arthur E.

Eskimo acculturation: a selected annotated bibliography of Alaskan and other Eskimo acculturation studies. College, Alaska: Institute of Social, Economic and Governmental Research, University of Alaska, 1970. vi, 209 p. [3921]

Hippler, Arthur E.; Wood, John R.

The subarctic Athabascans: a selected annotated bibliography. [Fairbanks, Alaska]: Institute of Social, Economic and Government Research, University of Alaska, [1974]. 331 p. (in various pagings). (ISEGR report series / Institute of Social, Economic and Government Research, University of Alaska ; no. 39); ISBN: 0-88353-012-0. [3954]

Hirschfelder, Arlene B.

Annotated bibliography of the literature on American Indians published in state historical society publications, New England and Middle Atlantic states. Millwood, N.Y.: Kraus International Publications, c1982. xv, 356 p.: ill.; ISBN: 0-527-40889-1. [4031]

Hirschfelder, Arlene B.; Byler, Mary Gloyne; Dorris, Michael A.

Guide to research on North American Indians. Chicago: American Library Association, 1983. xi, 330 p.; ISBN: 0-8389-0353-3. [4047]

Hiscock, Audrey M.; Braine, Linda

Annotated bibliography of Newfoundland materials for school libraries, part 1–print. [St. John's, Nfld.]: Division of Instruction, Department of Education, 1980. 137 p. [0245]

Historical and Scientific Society of Manitoba

A checklist of centennial publications in Manitoba, 1967-1970. Winnipeg: [s.n.], 1971. 11 p. [0503]

History projects supported by Multiculturalism Canada/ Activités de caractère historique subventionnées par Multiculturalisme Canada. Ottawa: Multiculturalism Canada, 1984. 109 p.; ISBN: 0-662-53665-7. [2039]

Hitchman, James H.

"Pacific Northwest maritime history: a bibliographical survey." In: *Pacific Northwest themes: historical essays, in honor of Keith A. Murray*, edited by James W. Scott. Bellingham, Wash.: Center for Pacific Northwest Studies, Western Washington University, 1978. P. 17-33. [1998]

Hlady, Walter M.; Simpson, Allan A.

"Bibliography of Manitoba archaeology." In: *Manitoba Archaeological Newsletter*; Vol. 1, no. 3 (Fall 1964) p. 3-20; vol. 2, no. 3 (Fall 1965) p. 7-12; vol. 3, no. 3 (Fall 1966) p. 3-6.; ISSN: 0025-2190. [4540]

Hobson, G.D.; Voyce, J.

Polar Continental Shelf Project: titles and abstracts of scientific papers supported by PCSP/Étude du plateau continental polaire: titres et résumés scientifiques publiés grâce au soutien de l'ÉPCP. Ottawa: Energy, Mines and Resources Canada, 1974-1989. 8 vol.; ISSN: 0823-3543. [4633]

Hodge, Frederick Webb

Handbook of Indians of Canada. Ottawa: Parmalee, 1913. x, 632 p.: maps. [3908]

Hodge, William H.

A bibliography of contemporary North American Indians: selected and partially annotated with study guides. New York: Interland Publishing, 1976. xvi, 310 p.; ISBN: 0-87989-102-5. [3981]

Hodgins, J. George

Catalogue of the books relating to education and educational subjects, also to history, geography, science, biography and practical life in the library of the Education Department for Ontario arranged in topical and alphabetical order. Toronto: Warwick Brothers & Rutter, 1897. vi, 268 p. [3367]

Hodgins, James

A guide to the literature on the herbaceous vascular flora of Ontario, 1978. Toronto: Botany Press, [1979]. 73 p.: ill.; ISBN: 0-920395-02-3. [5430]

Hodgson, C.A.; Bourne, N.; Mottershead, D.

A selected bibliography of scallop literature. Nanaimo, B.C.: Department of Fisheries and Oceans, 1988. iv, 133 p. (Canadian manuscript report of fisheries and aquatic sciences ; no. 1965; ISSN: 0706-6473) [5542]

Hodgson, Maurice

"The literature of the Franklin search." In: *The Franklin era in Canadian Arctic history, 1845-1859*, edited by Patricia D. Sutherland. Ottawa: National Museum of Man, National Museums of Canada, 1985. P. 1-11. (National Museum of Man Mercury series; ISSN: 0316-1854 : Archaeological survey of Canada paper ; no. 131; ISSN: 0317-2244) [2047]

Hodson, Dean R.

A bibliography of dissertations and theses in geography on Anglo-America, 1960-1972. Monticello, Ill.: Council of Planning Librarians, 1974. 202 p. (Council of Planning Librarians Exchange bibliography ; 583, 584) [6133]

Hoffman, Bernard G.

Cabot to Cartier: sources for a historical ethnography of northeastern North America, 1497-1550. [Toronto]: University of Toronto Press, 1961. xii, 287 p.: ill., maps, facsim. [1936]

Hogan, Brian F.

"A current bibliography of Canadian church history/ Bibliographie récente de l'histoire de l'église canadienne." In: *Canadian Catholic Historical Association. Study Sessions*;

Vol. 42 (1975)-vol. 55 (1988) [1566]

Holcomb, Adele M.; Williamson, Mary F.

Bibliography: women's studies in art in Canadian universities and schools of art, 1985. [Lennoxville, Que.]: Distributed by Universities Art Association of Canada/ Association d'art des universités du Canada, 1988. 11 p. [0717]

Holdsworth, Rosalynd; Smit-Nielsen, Hendrika

Scottish genealogy: a bibliographical guide to selected sources in the University of Calgary Library, the LDS Genealogical Library (Calgary), and the Calgary Public Library. [Calgary]: Alberta Family Histories Society, [1982]. 51 p.; ISSN: 0228-9288. [2022]

Holland, William L.

"Economic factors in the Pacific area: a review bibliography." In: *Pacific Affairs*; Vol. 2, no. 6 (June 1929) p. 329-346.; ISSN: 0030-851X. [2559]

"Source materials on the Institute of Pacific Relations." In: *Pacific Affairs*; Vol. 58, no. 1 (Spring 1985) p. 91-97.; ISSN: 0030-851X. [2491]

Hollett, Gary

An annotated bibliography of songs, ballads and poetry either about Newfoundland or by Newfoundlanders. [St. John's: Centre for Newfoundland Studies, Memorial University of Newfoundland, 1973]. 20 l. [0837]

Holmberg, Robert George

Pulp mills and the environment: an annotated bibliography for northern Alberta. Athabasca: Athabasca University; Edmonton: Canadian Circumpolar Institute, University of Alberta : Environmental Research and Study Centre, University of Alberta, 1992. 32 p.; ISBN: 0-919737-06-4. [5296]

Holmes, Alison

Children's play spaces and equipment: bibliography, prepared by Alison Holmes for the Canadian Institute of Child Health's Task Force for the Development of Guidelines for Children's Play Spaces and Equipment. Ottawa: The Institute, 1984. 19 l. [1829]

Holmes, Janet

"Papers completed in North American decorative arts, graduate course, University of Toronto, 1968-82." In: *Material History Bulletin*; No. 20 (Fall 1984) p. 83-85.; ISSN: 0703-489X. [0705]

Holmes, Janet; Jones, Olive

"Glass in Canada: an annotated bibliography." In: *Material History Bulletin*; No. 6 (Fall 1978) p. 115-148.; ISSN: 0703-489X. [5768]

Holmes, Marjorie C.

Publications of the government of British Columbia, 1871-1947. [Victoria: King's Printer, 1950]. 254 p. [6230]

Royal commissions and commissions of inquiry under the "Public Inquiries Act" in British Columbia, 1872-1942: a checklist. [Victoria: King's Printer, 1945]. 68 p. [6227]

Holmes, Maurice

Captain James Cook, R.N., F.R.S.: a bibliographical excursion. London: F. Edwards, 1952. 103 p., [11] l. of pl.: facsims. [6919]

Holt, Faye Reineberg

Alberta plays and playwrights: Alberta Playwrights' Network catalogue. Calgary: Alberta Playwrights' Network, c1992. 80 p.; ISBN: 0-9695459-0-8. [1297]

Holway, Debra; Fournier, Sandy

A bibliography of Whitehorse Copper Belt material in the Yukon Archives. [Whitehorse]: Yukon Archives, c1983. [62] p.; ISBN: 1-55018-035-5. [4834]

Holyoke, Francesca

The Maritime Pamphlet Collection: an annotated catalogue. Fredericton, N.B.: University of New Brunswick Libraries, 1990. x, 241, 38 p.: ill. [6793]

Holzmueller, Diana Lynn

Multi media resource list: Indian and Eskimo culture in the North. Anchorage: University of Alaska, Center for Northern Educational Research, 1973. iii, 59 p. [3941]

Homelessness: a selected, annotated bibliography. Calgary: City of Calgary, Social Services Department, 1987. i, 31 l. [3298]

Hondius, E.H.; Peletier, W.M.

Amerikaanse en Canadese rechtslitteratur in Nederlandse bibliotheken: lijst van Amerikaanse en Canadese juridische tijdschriften, jurisprudentierverzamelingen, serie-en standaardwerken/American and Canadian law literature in Dutch libraries: location guide to holdings of American and Canadian law journals, law reports, serials, digests and standard works. Deventer [Netherlands]: Kluwer, 1973. 80 p.; ISBN: 90-268-0686-8. [2131]

Honigmann, John J.

Bibliography of northern North America and Greenland. [Chapel Hill]: University of North Carolina, Department of Anthropology, 1966. 19 l. [3912]

Hooper, Tracey D.; Vermeer, Kees; Szabo, Ildy

Oil pollution of birds: an annotated bibliography. Delta, B.C.: Canadian Wildlife Service, 1987. 180 p. (Technical report series / Canadian Wildlife Service ; no. 34; ISSN: 0831-6481); ISBN: 0-662-15904-7. [5244]

Hoos, Lindsay M.

The Skeena River estuary: status of environmental knowledge to 1975: report of the Estuary Working Group, Department of the Environment, Regional Board Pacific Region. [Ottawa]: Environment Canada, 1975. xxvi, 418 p.: maps. (Special estuary series / Estuary Working Group, Department of the Environment, Regional Board, Pacific Region ; no. 3) [5100]

Hoos, Lindsay M.; Packman, Glen A.

The Fraser River estuary: status of environmental knowledge to 1974: report of the Estuary Working Group, Department of the Environment, Regional Board Pacific Region. [Ottawa]: Environment Canada, 1974. xx, 518 p.: ill., maps. (Special estuary series / Estuary Working Group, Department of the Environment, Regional Board Pacific Region ; no. 1) [5088]

Hoos, Lindsay M.; Vold, Cecily L.

The Squamish River estuary: status of environmental knowledge to 1974: report of the Estuary Working Group, Department of the Environment, Regional Board, Pacific Region. [Ottawa]: Environment Canada, 1975. 361 p.: ill., maps. (Special estuary series / Estuary Working Group, Department of the Environment, Regional Board, Pacific Region ; no. 2) [5101]

Hoover, Herbert T.

The Sioux: a critical bibliography. Bloomington: Indiana University Press, 1979. xvi, 78 p. (Newberry Library Center for the History of the American Indian, Bibliographical series); ISBN: 0-253-34972-9. [4005]

Hope, S.

A selected bibliography for aerial photograph interpretation of natural and cultural features. Victoria, B.C.: British Columbia Forest Service, 1976. 25 p. (Land management report / British Columbia Forest Service ; no. 1) [3016]

Hôpital Rivière-des-Prairies. Bibliothèque du personnel

Développement personnel et social de l'enfant et de l'adolescent. Montréal: Hôpital Rivière-des-Prairies, 1976. 21 f. [3146]

L'enfant en foyer. Montréal: Hôpital Rivière-des-Prairies, 1976. 37 f. [3147]

La famille monoparentale. Montréal: Hôpital Rivière-des-Prairies, 1978. 20 f. [3171]

Prévention en santé mentale: bibliographie annotée. Montréal: Service audio-visuel, Hôpital Rivière-des-Prairies, 1984. 42 p. [5659]

Hopkinson, Marvin W.

The Beatrice Hitchins Memorial Collection of Aviation History: catalogue. London, Ont.: D.B. Weldon Library, University of Western Ontario, 1976. xix, 73 p.: ill., port. (Library bulletin / D.B. Weldon Library, University of Western Ontario ; no. 9) [4463]

Horn, Charles; Griffiths, Curt Taylor

Native North Americans: crime, conflict and criminal justice: a research bibliography. 4th ed. [Burnaby, B.C.]: Northern Justice Society, 1989. 275 p.; ISBN: 0-86491-074-6. [4109]

Horne, A.J.; Bradley, Kenneth

The Commonwealth today: a select bibliography on the Commonwealth and its constituent countries. [London]: Library Association, 1965. 107 p. (Library Association Special subject list ; no. 45) [0080]

Horne, Alan J.

Margaret Atwood: an annotated bibliography (poetry). Downsview, Ont.: ECW Press, c1980. P. 13-53.; ISBN: 0-920763-49-9. [6811]

"Margaret Atwood: an annotated bibliography (poetry)." In: *The annotated bibliography of Canada's major authors*, Vol. 2, edited by Robert Lecker and Jack David. Toronto: ECW Press, 1980. P. 13-53.; ISBN: 0-920802-40-0. [6812]

"Margaret Atwood: an annotated bibliography (prose)." In: *The annotated bibliography of Canada's major authors*, Vol. 1, edited by Robert Lecker and Jack David. Downsview, Ont.: ECW Press, 1979. P. 13-49.; ISBN: 0-920802-02-8. [6809]

Margaret Atwood: an annotated bibliography (prose). [Downsview, Ont.]: ECW Press, 1979. P. 13-46.; ISBN: 0-920763-48-0. [6810]

"A preliminary checklist of writings by and about Margaret Atwood." In: *Malahat Review*; No. 41 (January 1977) p. 195-222.; ISSN: 0025-1216. [6808]

"A preliminary checklist of writings by and about Margaret Atwood." In: *Canadian Library Journal*; Vol. 31, no. 6 (December 1974) p. 576-592.; ISSN: 0008-4352. [6807]

Horning, Lewis Emerson; Burpee, Lawrence J.

A bibliography of Canadian fiction (English). Toronto: Printed for the [Victoria University] Library by William Briggs, 1904. 82 p. (Victoria University Library publication ; no. 2) [0995]

Horsman, Jennifer

Facilitating literacy: an introductory guide to readings on study circles and group process. Toronto: Toronto Board of Education, Continuing Education Department, Adult Basis Education Unit, [1990]. 21 p.; ISBN: 1-895282-06-

3. [3716]

Horvath, Maria

A Doukhobor bibliography, based on material collected in the University of British Columbia Library. Vancouver: University of British Columbia Library, 1970-1973. 3 vol. [1530]

Hospital governance: an annotated bibliography from Canadian sources in the English language, 1980-1989. Don Mills, Ont.: Ontario Hospital Association, c1990. 56 p.; ISBN: 0-88621-142-5. [5695]

Hostetler, John A.

"A bibliography of English language materials on the Hutterian brethren." In: *Mennonite Quarterly Review*; Vol. 44 (1970) p. 106-113.; ISSN: 0025-9373. [1525]

Hould, Claudette

Répertoire des livres d'artistes au Québec, 1900-1980. Montréal: Bibliothèque nationale du Québec, 1982. 240 p.: ill. (certaines en coul.); ISBN: 2-550-02456-7. [0700]

Houle, France

La famille et le droit: bibliographie annotée. Montréal: Université de Montréal, Centre de recherche en droit public, 1987. 134 p. [2293]

Houle, Ghislaine

La femme et la société québécoise. Montréal: Bibliothèque nationale du Québec, Ministère des affaires culturelles, 1975. 228 p. (Bibliographies québécoises / Bibliothèque nationale du Québec, Centre bibliographique ; no 1) [3756]

Houle, Ghislaine; Lafontaine, Jacques

Écrivains québécois de nouvelle culture. Montréal: Bibliothèque nationale du Québec [Centre bibliographique], 1975. 137 p. (Bibliographies québécoises / Bibliothèque nationale du Québec, Centre bibliographique ; no 2) [1089]

Houle, Ghislaine; Lauzier, Suzanne; Cormier, Normand

Les sports au Québec, 1879-1975: catalogue d'exposition. Montréal: Bibliothèque nationale du Québec, 1976. xiii, 185 p.: ill. (Bibliographies québécoises / Bibliothèque nationale du Québec, Centre bibliographique ; no 4) [1783]

Houle, Guy

"Bibliographie de la littérature récente en Ontario, en Acadie et dans l'Ouest canadien." Dans: *Revue de l'Université d'Ottawa*; Vol. 56, no 3 (juillet-septembre 1986) p. 145-154.; ISSN: 0041-9206. [1228]

Houston, C. Stuart; Bechard, Marc J.

"A.D. Henderson, Alberta's foremost oologist, 1878-1963." In: *Blue Jay*; Vol. 48, no. 2 (June 1990) p. 85-96.; ISSN: 0006-5099. [7053]

Houyoux, Philippe

Bibliographie de l'histoire de l'éducation au Québec des origines à 1960. Trois-Rivières: Université du Québec à Trois-Rivières, 1978. viii, 227 p. (Publication / Université du Québec à Trois-Rivières, Bibliothèque ; no 18) [3539]

Mauricie et centre du Québec: liste des journaux et périodiques régionaux. Trois-Rivières: Université du Québec à Trois-Rivières, Bibliothèque, 1976. 41 f. [5924]

La propension aux accidents: thésaurus et bibliographie. Trois-Rivières: Université du Québec à Trois-Rivières, 1976. 116 f. (Publication / Université du Québec à Trois-Rivières, Bibliothèque ; no 11); ISBN: 0-885740-00-9. [3148]

Théâtre québécois: M. Dubé, J. Ferron, G. Gélinas, G. Lamarche, J. Languirand, A. Laurendeau, F. Leclerc, Y. Thériault: bibliographies de travail. Trois-Rivières, Québec: Université du Québec à Trois-Rivières,

Bibliothèque, Centre bibliographique, 1975. 175 f. (Publication / Université du Québec à Trois-Rivières, Bibliothèque ; no 6) [1090]

Howard, Lynne M.

Icebergs: a bibliography relevant to eastern Canadian waters. Ottawa: Environmental Studies Revolving Funds, 1986. xii, 277 p. (Environmental Studies Revolving Funds report ; no. 030); ISBN: 0-920783-29-5. [5234]

Issues of public interest regarding northern development [microform]: an annotated bibliography. Calgary: Pallister Resource Management Ltd., 1984. 8 microfiches (451 fr.). [0645]

Howard, Lynne M.; Goodwin, C. Ross

Beaufort E.I.S. bibliography. Calgary: Arctic Institute of North America, 1983. iv, 66 p. (ASTIS occasional publication / Arctic Science and Technology Information System ; no. 9; ISSN: 0225-5170) [5196]

Howay, F.W.

"The early literature of the Northwest coast." In: *Proceedings and Transactions of the Royal Society of Canada*; Series 3, vol. 18, section 2 (1924) p. 1-31.; ISSN: 0316-4616. [0555]

Hoxie, Frederick E.

Native Americans: an annotated bibliography. Pasadena, Calif.: Salem Press, c1991. xiii, 325 p.; ISBN: 0-89356-670-5. [4116]

Hoy, Eileen Monica

Select bibliography of recent material on teaching machines and programmed learning. Toronto: Ontario Educational Research Council, 1963. 18 p. [3384]

Hoy, Helen

Modern English-Canadian prose: a guide to information sources. Detroit: Gale Research, c1983. xxiii, 605 p. (American literature, English literature, and world literatures in English Information guide series ; vol. 38); ISBN: 0-8103-1245-X. [1204]

Hristienko, Hank

The impact of logging on woodland caribou (Rangifer tarandus caribou): a literature review. Winnipeg: Manitoba Natural Resources, 1985. i, 46 l. (Technical report / Manitoba Natural Resources ; 40 46) [4983]

Hromadiuk, Bob

"Bibliography [recent publications relating to Canadian ethnic studies]." In: *Canadian Ethnic Studies*; Vol. 16, no. 3 (1984)-vol. 24, no. 3 (1992) [4291]

Hruska, Jan; Burk, C.F.

Computer-based storage and retrieval of geoscience information: bibliography 1946-69. [Ottawa]: Department of Energy, Mines and Resources, [1971]. v, 52 p. [4775]

Huang, Paul Te-Hsien

Bibliography on copyright. 2nd ed. Halifax: T.-H. Huang, c1971. vi, 118 l. [2119]

Hubbard, William F.; Bell, Marcus A.M.

Reclamation of lands disturbed by mining in mountainous and northern areas: a synoptic bibliography and review relevant to British Columbia and adjacent areas. Victoria: [British Columbia Ministry of Mines and Petroleum Resources, Inspection Branch], 1977. iii, 251 p. [4799]

Hudon, Dominique

Bibliographie analytique et critique des articles de revues sur Louis Fréchette, 1863-1983. Québec: Centre de recherche en littérature québécoise, Université Laval, 1987. 269 p. (Collection "Bibliographies" / Centre de recherche en littérature québécoise, Université Laval ; no 2); ISBN: 2-

920801-08-2. [6990]

Hudon, Jean-Paul

Guide bibliographique des lettres françaises et québécoises à l'intention des étudiants de l'Université du Québec à Chicoutimi. [Chicoutimi]: Bibliothèque, Université du Québec à Chicoutimi, 1985. vii, 109 p.; ISBN: 2-920751-02-6. [1221]

Répertoire bibliographique d'articles de périodiques sur les arts en général: dépouillement de seize (16) revues disponibles à la bibliothèque de l'UQAC. [Chicoutimi]: Bibliothèque, Université du Québec à Chicoutimi, 1987. v, 87 p.; ISBN: 2-920751-05-0. [0713]

Hudson's Bay Company

List of books relating to Hudson's Bay Company. [London: Hudson's Bay Company], 1935. 13 p. [1913]

Huff, Donald W.

"Marine parks bibliography." In: *Park News*; Vol. 16, no. 4 (Winter 1980) p. 26-28.; ISSN: 0553-3066. [3029]

Huffman, James; Huffman, Sybil

Construction trades occupations & Transport equipment operating occupations/Travailleurs du bâtiment [&] Personnel d'exploitation des transports. Toronto: Guidance Centre, Faculty of Education, University of Toronto, c1978. 40 p. (Career information: a bibliography of publications about careers in Canada ; book 3); ISBN: 0-7713-0052-2. [2637]

Occupations in medicine and health. Toronto: Guidance Centre, Faculty of Education, University of Toronto, c1977. 29 p. (Career information: a bibliography of publications about careers in Canada ; book 1); ISBN: 0-7713-0048-4. [5612]

Occupations in social sciences, religion and teaching/ Travailleurs spécialisés des sciences sociales, membres du clergé et enseignants. Toronto: Guidance Centre, Faculty of Education, University of Toronto, c1978. 33 p. (Career information: a bibliography of publications about careers in Canada ; book 4); ISBN: 0-7713-0054-9. [3540]

Occupations in the arts, recreation, and equipment operation/Carrières dans les arts, les loisirs et l'outillage technique. Toronto: Guidance Centre, Faculty of Education, University of Toronto, c1978. 34 p. (Career information: a bibliography of publications about careers in Canada ; book 7); ISBN: 0-7713-0060-3. [0690]

Huffman, Sybil; Huffman, James

Career information: a bibliography of publications about careers in Canada. Toronto: Guidance Centre, Faculty of Education, University of Toronto, c1982. ix, 117 p.; ISBN: 0-7713-0104-9. [3610]

Huggard, Turner

An annotated list of resource material on the Irish in New Brunswick. Fredericton: [s.n.], 1984. iii, 53 l. [4224]

Hughes, G.T., et al.

Bibliography of soil dynamics and soil structure interaction during dynamic or similar loadings. Ottawa: Defence Research Board, Department of National Defence, 1965. iii, 106 p. (Report / Defence Research Board of Canada ; no. 170) [4764]

Hugolin, père

Bibliographie antonienne, ou, Nomenclature des ouvrages, livres, revues, brochures, feuilles, etc., sur la dévotion à S. Antoine de Padoue, publiés dans la province de Québec de 1777 à 1909. Québec: Impr. de l'Événement, 1910. 76 p. [1495]

Bibliographie des ouvrages concernant la tempérance: livres, brochures, journaux, revues, feuilles, cartes, etc., imprimés à Québec et à Lévis depuis l'établissement de l'imprimerie [1764] jusqu'à 1910, par le R.P. Hugolin. Québec: L'Événement, 1910. 165 p. [3076]

"Bibliographie des travaux édités ou imprimés en Europe sur les Récollets du Canada." Dans: *Mémoires de la Société royale du Canada*; Série 3, vol. 27, section 1 (1933) p. 87-109.; ISSN: 0316-4616. [1500]

Bibliographie du père Louis Hennepin, récollet: les pièces documentaires. Montréal: [Imprimerie des franciscains], 1937. xxvii, 238 p., [2] f. de pl.: fac-sim., portr. [7055]

Bibliographie du R.P. Hugolin. Montréal: [Imprimerie des franciscains], 1932. 50 p. [7072]

Bibliographie du R.P. Joachim-Joseph Monfette, o.f.m. Québec: Imprimerie franciscaine missionnaire, 1931. 42 p. [7195]

Bibliographie du Tiers-Ordre séculier de Saint François au Canada (province de Québec). Montréal: Ménard, 1921. 149 p. [1498]

Bibliographie et iconographie du serviteur de Dieu le R.P. Frédéric Janssoone, o.f.m., 1838-1916. Québec: Imprimerie Franciscaine missionnaire, 1932. 62 p. [7075]

Bibliographie franciscaine: inventaire des revues, livres, brochures des autres écrits publié par les franciscains du Canada de 1890 à 1915. Québec: Imprimerie franciscaine missionaire, 1916. 141 p. [1497]

Bio-bibliographie du R.P. Ephrem Longpré, O.F.M. Québec: Imprimerie franciscaine missionnaire, 1931. 40 p. [7154]

"Étude bibliographique et historique sur la morale pratique du jansénisme du P. Louis Hennepin, récollet." Dans: *Mémoires de la Société royale du Canada*; Série 3, vol. 31, section 1 (1937) p. 127-149.; ISSN: 0316-4616. [7056]

Les Franciscains et la croisade antialcoolique dans la province de Québec (Canada): aperçu sommaire de leurs travaux préparé pour le Chapître général de l'Ordre des frères mineurs. Montréal: [s.n.], 1915. xxix p. [1496]

Inventaire des travaux, livres, brochures, feuillets et autres écrits concernant la tempérance publiés par les pères franciscains du Canada de 1906 à 1915. Montréal: 1915. 50 p. [3077]

Notes bibliographiques pour servir à l'histoire des Récollets du Canada. Montréal: Impr. des Franciscains, 1932-1936. 6 vol. [1501]

Huizenga, Angie; Stuart, Rob; Scott, Judy
Our Prince Edward County: a source reference. Bloomfield, Ont.: [s.n.], 1982. vi, 214 p. [0473]

Hulbert, Tina G.
Educational resource materials for the hearing impaired: an annotated compilation for parents and teachers of deaf, deaf-blind and deaf multiply handicapped individuals. Victoria, B.C.: Ministry of Education, c1978. iii, 111 p. [3541]

Hulchanski, John David
Canadian town planning and housing, 1930-1940: a historical bibliography. Toronto: Centre for Urban and Community Studies, University of Toronto, 1978. 35 l. (Bibliographic series / Centre for Urban and Community Studies, University of Toronto ; no. 10; ISSN: 0316-4691) [4370]

Canadian town planning and housing, 1940-1950: a historical bibliography. [Toronto]: Centre for Urban and Community Studies, University of Toronto, 1979. 51 p. (Bibliographic series / Centre for Urban and Community

Studies, University of Toronto ; no. 12; ISSN: 0316-4691) [4375]

Citizen participation in planning: a comprehensive bibliography. [Toronto]: Department of Urban and Regional Planning, University of Toronto, 1974. 77 p. (Papers on planning and design / Department of Urban and Regional Planning, University of Toronto ; no. 2) [4333]

Co-operative housing in Canada: a comprehensive bibliography. Vancouver: University of British Columbia, School of Community and Regional Planning, 1986. iv, 14 p. (U.B.C. planning papers: bibliographies / University of British Columbia, School of Community and Regional Planning ; 4) [4411]

Cooperative housing in Canada. Chicago: Council of Planning Librarians, 1987. 14 p. (CPL bibliography / Council of Planning Librarians ; no. 191) [4417]

Making better use of existing housing stock: a literature review. Toronto: Ministry of Municipal Affairs and Housing, Housing Renovation and Energy Conservation Unit, 1982. 155, 7 p. [4394]

Thomas Adams: a biographical and bibliographical guide. [Toronto]: Department of Urban and Regional Planning, University of Toronto, 1978. 42 p. (Papers on planning and design / Department of Urban and Regional Planning, University of Toronto ; no. 15) [6797]

Hull, Jeremy; Murphy, Michael; Regnier, Robert
Underdevelopment and education: selected annotated resources for Saskatchewan and Canadian educators. Saskatoon: Division of Extension and Community Relations, University of Saskatchewan, c1982. 280 p.; ISBN: 0-88880-117-3. [3611]

Huls, Mary Ellen
Moshe Safdie, Canadian architect: a bibliography. Monticello, Ill.: Vance Bibliographies, 1985. 6 p. (Architecture series: Bibliography ; A-1470; ISSN: 0194-1356); ISBN: 0-890286-00-0. [7289]

Human settlement issues in British Columbia 1968-1978: a selected bibliography. [Vancouver]: Centre for Human Settlements, University of British Columbia, 1978. i, 36 l. (Occasional papers / Centre for Human Settlements, University of British Columbia; ISSN: 0706-2559) [4371]

Hunka, Diane Lynne
The effects of effluents from the Canadian plastics industry on aquatic organisms: a literature review. Winnipeg: Freshwater Institute, Research and Development Directorate, Fisheries and Marine Service, Environment Canada, 1974. v, 64 p. (Fisheries and Marine Service Technical report ; no. 473; ISSN: 0701-7626) [5089]

Hunston, Jeffrey R.
A bibliography of Yukon archaeology, anthropology, and Quaternary research. Burnaby, B.C.: Department of Archaeology, Simon Fraser University, 1978. 102 l. [4574]

Prehistory of Canada: recommended general introductory reading. Whitehorse: Yukon Tourism, Heritage Branch, 1991. ii, 28 l.; ISBN: 1-550-18167-X. [4608]

Hunter, Andrew F.
"Bibliography of the archaeology of Ontario." In: *Annual Archaeological Report, Ontario*; Vol. 10 (1896-1897) p. 98-116; vol. 12 (1897-1898) p. 67-87; vol. 15 (1900) p. 50-62. [4526]

Hunter, Elizabeth
"History of Ottawa and district: a selected list." In: *Ontario Library Review*; Vol. 33, no. 4 (November 1949) p. 342-344.;

ISSN: 0030-2996. [0423]

Hunter, Isabel; Wotherspoon, Shelagh

A bibliography of health care in Newfoundland. St. John's, Nfld.: Faculty of Medicine, Memorial University of Newfoundland, c1986. [158] p. (Occasional papers in the history of medicine ; no. 6); ISBN: 0-88901-113-3. [5671]

Huntsman, A.G.; Fraser, C.M.

"List of publications based on results obtained at the biological stations of Canada, 1901-1921." In: *Contributions to Canadian Biology: being studies from the biological stations of Canada*; No. 12 (1921) p. 167-183. [5317]

Huot, Diane; Coulombe, Raymonde

La classe de conversation en L2: une bibliographie sélective et descriptive. Québec: Centre international de recherche sur le bilinguisme, 1984. 308, 20 p. (Publication / Centre international de recherche sur le bilinguisme ; B-142); ISBN: 2-89219-150-5. [1460]

Hurn, Nancy J.

Listing of sheet music available from the CNE archives. Toronto: The Archives, [1980]. [14] l. [0885]

Hurst, James W.

"The Fenians: a bibliography." In: *Eire: Ireland*; Vol. 4, no. 4 (1969) p. 90-106.; ISSN: 0013-2683. [1959]

Husted, Deborah

The architecture of Toronto: a selected bibliography. Monticello, Ill.: Vance Bibliographies, 1987. 100 p. (Architecture series: Bibliography ; A-1911; ISSN: 0194-1356); ISBN: 0-1-55590-501-3. [0784]

Huston, Barbara, et al.

A preliminary guide to archival sources relating to southern Alberta. [Lethbridge, Alta.: Department of History, University of Lethbridge], 1979. iii, 21, [77] l. [0527]

Hutchinson, Elaine; Pahulje, Dani

Legal materials for Alberta public libraries. Edmonton: Legal Resource Centre, Faculty of Extension, University of Alberta, 1991. iv, 93 p. [2352]

Hutchinson, Raymond

"Liste des publications traitant de la faune Odonatologique du Québec de 1871 à 1979." Dans: *Cordulia*; Vol. 5, no 2 (juin 1979) p. 21-33.; ISSN: 0700-4966. [5431]

Hymer, Stephen

"La firme plurinationale: une bibliographie sélective." Dans: *Études internationales*; Vol. 2, no 1 (mars 1971) p. 115-129.; ISSN: 0045-2123. [2592]

Hynes, Susan; Krueger, Donald R.

Accountability and control of crown corporations: a selected bibliography. Rev. and expanded ed. [Toronto]: Ontario Legislative Library, Research and Information Services, 1984. 29 l. [2696]

Hyttenrauch, David

Where it's at: pertinent publications on the arts. [Windsor, Ont.]: Arts Council Windsor & Region, 1985. [12], 315 p. [0708]

Ian Young: a bibliography, 1962-1980. Toronto: Pink Triangle Press, 1981. 58 p.: ill., pl. (Canadian Gay Archives publication ; no. 3); ISBN: 0-920430-08-2. [7375]

Ibach, Stephanie

Annotated bibliography of Rocky Mountain bighorn sheep specific to the management of bighorn sheep in Kootenay National Park. Edmonton: Produced by Canadian Wildlife Service for Parks Canada, Western Region, 1985. i, 242 [40] p. [5510]

Annotated bibliography on elk-livestock-range interactions in western Canada and northwestern U.S.A. specific to the management of elk and livestock within the Waterton Biosphere Reserve. Edmonton: Canadian Wildlife Service, 1985. i, 115, [43] p. [5511]

Icebreakers and icebreaking (Jan 70 – May 87): citations from the NTIS bibliographic database. Springfield, Va.: National Technical Information Service, 1987. [4502]

Imbeau, Gaston

Claude Gauvreau, l'homme et l'oeuvre [microforme]: biobibliographie descriptive. [Montréal: Université de Montréal, Faculté des études supérieures], 1976. 1 bobine de microfilm. [7007]

Immigration to British Columbia: a selected annotated bibliography. [Victoria]: Province of British Columbia, Ministry of International Business and Immigration, 1991. iii, 40 p.; ISBN: 0-7726-1327-3. [4282]

Imperial Tobacco Products Limited. Library

Books and periodicals on tobacco: corporate library holdings. Montreal: Imperial Tobacco Products, 1973. ii, 33 l. [4658]

Imprimerie générale A. Côté et Cie

Catalogue avec quelques notes des livres, brochures, journaux, etc. sortis de l'Imprimerie générale A. Côté et Cie depuis sa fondation, le 1er décembre, 1842. 2e éd. [Québec]: A. Côté, 1898. 32 p. [0025]

The IMS directory of publications. Fort Washington, Pa.: IMS Press, 1986-. vol.; ISSN: 0892-7715. [5989]

In review: Canadian books for children: 305 titles recommended, 1967-1972. Toronto: Provincial Library Service, Ontario Ministry of Colleges and Universities, 1972. 45 p. [1320]

In review: Canadian books for young people. Toronto: Libraries and Community Information Branch, 1967-1982. 16 vol.; ISSN: 0019-3259. [1351]

"In the library." In: *Canadian Tax Journal*; (1953-) vol.; ISSN: 0008-5111. [2786]

Income security: publications and sources of information/La sécurité du revenu: publications et sources de renseignements. Montreal: Canadian Pension Conference, 1991. iv, 80 p. [2774]

An index and guide to robotics research and development in Canada. [Ottawa]: National Research Council Canada, Division of Electrical Engineering, 1985. vii, 238 p. [5806]

Index of BETT's reports. Ottawa: Energy, Mines and Resources Canada, 1986. 1 vol. (in various foliations). [5814]

Index of research in northern Alberta sponsored by the Northern Alberta Development Council. [Peace River, Alta.]: Northern Alberta Development Council, [1989]. 19 l.: map. [0547]

"An index of theses relating to the history of the Anglican Church of Canada." In: *Journal of the Canadian Church Historical Society*; Vol. 5, no. 2 (June 1963) p. [2-5].; ISSN: 0008-3208. [6077]

Index to bedrock geological mapping, British Columbia: including publications of the Geological Survey of Canada, British Columbia Ministry of Energy, Mines and Petroleum Resources, and journal articles, theses, and company reports. [Victoria]: Province of British Columbia, Ministry of Energy, Mines and Petroleum Resources, 1983. 45 p.: map.; ISBN: 0-7719-9295-5. [6581]

Index to Ontario education research: ONTERIS. Toronto: Ontario Ministry of Education, c1982. 2 vol.; ISBN: 0-7743-7110-2 (set). [3612]

Index translationum. Répertoire international des traductions. International bibliography of translations. Paris. Unesco, 1948-. vol., ISSN: 0073-6074. [1494]

Indian and Eskimo Affairs Program (Canada). Education and Cultural Support Branch

About Indians: a listing of books. 4th ed. [Ottawa]: Indian and Eskimo Affairs Program, Education and Cultural Support Branch, [c1977]. [382] p.: ill.; ISBN: 0-662-00714-8. [3990]

Indian-Eskimo Association of Canada

An annotated bibliography of books for libraries serving children of Indian ancestry. Toronto: [s.n.], 1968. 13 p. [3914]

Bibliographies of materials relating to the Canadian Indian. [S.l.: s.n., 1970]. [39] p. [3922]

Bibliography: Indians and education. Toronto: [s.n.], 1970. 7 p. [3411]

Indians of Quebec Association. James Bay Task Force

Bibliography pertaining to environmental aspects of the James Bay Hydroelectric Development. Montreal: Indians of Quebec Association; Northern Quebec Inuit Association, 1973. 62 l. [5077]

Indra, Doreen Marie

Southeast Asian refugee settlement in Canada: a research bibliography. Ottawa: Canadian Asian Studies Association, 1984. 29 p. [4225]

Ingles, Ernest

Canada. Oxford: Clio Press, c1990. xxx, 393 p.: map. (World bibliographical series / Clio Press ; 62); ISBN: 1-85109-005-3. [0171]

Ingram, Doreen

"Annual bibliography of Commonwealth literature, 1979: Canada." In: *Journal of Commonwealth Literature*; Vol. 15, no. 2 (December 1980) p. 59-86.; ISSN: 0021-9894. [1171]

Inkster, Tim

An honest trade: an exhibition of Canadian small press books printed and bound at the Porcupine's Quill in Erin, Ontario, 1974-1983. Erin, Ont.: Porcupine's Quill, 1984. [40] p.: ill.; ISBN: 0-88984-047-4. [1662]

Innis, Harold Adams

"Bibliography of research work in economics in Canadian universities." In: *Contributions to Canadian Economics*; Vol. 1 (1928) p. 69-85; vol. 2 (1929) p. 69-97; vol. 3 (1931) p. 53-56; vol. 4 (1932) p. 50-55. [6054]

"William T. Jackman, 1871-1951: [publications]." In: *Canadian Journal of Economics and Political Science*; Vol. 18, no. 2 (May 1952) p. 202-204.; ISSN: 0315-4890. [7074]

Innis, Harold Adams; Bladen, M.L.

"Bibliography of Canadian economics." In: *Contributions to Canadian Economics*; Vol. 1 (1928)-vol. 7 (1934) [2560]

Institut canadien de Québec. Bibliothèque

Catalogue de la bibliothèque de l'Institut canadien de Québec. Québec: Dussault & Proulx, 1898. 315 p. [6752]

Institut canadien de recherche sur les femmes

Les Études féministes au Canada. Ottawa: Direction des études canadiennes, 1993. 50, 46 p. (Guides pédagogiques des études canadiennes. Deuxième collection); ISBN: 0-662-60010-4. [3903]

Institut canadien d'éducation des adultes. Équipe de recherche

Bibliographie générale sur l'animation. Montréal: Institut canadien d'éducation des adultes, 1972. v, 71, 36 f. [3107]

Institut canadien pour la paix et la sécurité internationales

La bibliothèque paix et sécurité. [Ottawa]: L'Institut, 1990-. vol., ISSN: 1109-3699. [2556]

Institut de la médecine du travail et des ambiances

Les projets de recherche subventionnés par l'IMTA et les publications scientifiques qui en découlent, 1966-1976. Montréal: Institut de la médecine du travail et des ambiances, 1976. xiii, 172 p. [5114]

Institut de recherches politiques. Secrétariat du Colloque national

Bibliographie des documents déposés au Colloque national. [Ottawa]: Le Secrétariat, [1987]. 24, 24 p. [3671]

Institut national canadien-français pour la déficience mentale

Bibliographie [Institut national canadien-français pour la déficience mentale: Centre d'information sur l'enfance inadaptées]. Montréal: Institut national canadien-français pour la déficience mentale, 1972. 2 vol. [3108]

Institute for Research in Construction (Canada)

List of publications [Institute for Research in Construction]/ Liste des publications [Institut de recherche en construction]. Ottawa: Institute for Research in Construction (Canada), 1984-. vol.; ISSN: 0835-9083. [6453]

Institute for Research on Public Policy. National Forum Secretariat

Bibliography of documents displayed at the National Forum. [Ottawa]: The Secretariat, [1987]. 24, 24 p. [3672]

Institute for Research on Public Policy. Regional Employment Opportunities Program

Canadian regionalism and political culture: a bibliography. [Montreal]: The Institute, [1985]. vii, 52 p. [2492]

Institute of Occupational and Environmental Health

The research projects supported by IOEH and the scientific publications originating from them, 1966-1976. Montreal: Institute of Occupational and Environmental Health, 1976. xiii, 172 p. [5115]

International Commission for the Northwest Atlantic Fisheries

Guide to I.C.N.A.F. documents, proceedings, reports, and programs published or otherwise circulated up to 30 Sept. 1954. Dartmouth, N.S.: International Commission for the Northwest Atlantic Fisheries, [1954]. 17 l. [4885]

International Development Research Centre (Canada)

Publications of the International Development Research Centre, 1970-73/Publications du Centre de recherches pour le développement international, 1970-73. Ottawa: International Development Research Centre, c1974. 24 p. [2413]

International Reference Group on Great Lakes Pollution from Land Use Activities

Annotated bibliography of PLUARG reports. Windsor, Ont.: International Joint Commission, Great Lakes Regional Office, 1979. xii, 121 p. [5150]

Internationale Jugendbibliothek (Munich, Germany)

Canadian children's books at the International Youth Library, Munich. [Munich: The Library, 1985]. [200] p. [1366]

Inuvik Scientific Resource Centre

Bibliography of research publications, Inuvik Scientific Resource Centre: revised edition, 1964-1985/Bibliographie des travaux de recherche, Centre de ressources scientifiques d'Inuvik: édition révisée, 1964-1985. Ottawa: Indian and Northern Affairs Canada, 1986. vi, 125 p. [4631]

Inventaire des rapports d'intervention présentés à l'ÉNAP: septembre 1972-avril 1990. [Sainte-Foy, Québec]: École nationale d'administration publique, Direction de l'enseignement et de la recherche, Université de Québec, 1990. 1 vol. (en pagination multiple); ISBN: 2-920-112-48-1. [2539]

Inventaire des travaux de terminologie récents: publiés et à diffusion restreinte. Québec: Gouvernement du Québec, Office de la langue française, 1989. 429 p.; ISBN: 2-550-19816-6. [1486]

Inventory of data files on aging in Ontario. Toronto: Centre for Studies on Aging, University of Toronto, 1989. 1 vol. (in various pagings). [3329]

Irvine, Russell; Sealey, Gary
A bibliography of selected topics related to park and recreation planning and management. Toronto: Parks and Recreation Areas Branch, Division of Outdoor Recreation, Department of Lands and Forests, 1971. ii, 187 l. [1758]

Irvine, Susan; Rafferty, J. Pauline
British Columbia Heritage Trust Student Employment Program: selected bibliography, 1982-1985. [Victoria]: British Columbia Heritage Trust, 1986. 36 p.: ill. (Information series / British Columbia Heritage Trust ; 1); ISBN: 0-7726-0427-4. [0595]

Irving, E.
"The relation between bilingualism and measured intelligence: a bibliographical guide." In: Cahiers linguistiques d'Ottawa; No 1 (1971) p. 75-89.; ISSN: 0315-3967. [1426]

Isbester, A. Fraser; Coates, Daniel; Williams, C. Brian
Industrial and labour relations in Canada: a selected bibliography. Kingston, Ont.: Industrial Relations Centre, Queen's University, 1965. [ix], 120 p. (Bibliography series / Industrial Relations Centre, Queen's University ; no. 2; ISSN: 0075-613X) [2794]

Issenman, Betty
Sources for the study of Inuit clothing. Montreal: B. Issenman, 1982. 60 l. [4032]

Isto, Sarah A.
Cultures in the North: Aleut, Athabascan Indian, Eskimo, Haida Indian, Tlingit Indian, Tsimpshian Indian: multimedia resource list. Fairbanks: Alaska Educational Program for Intercultural Communication, Center for Northern Educational Research, University of Alaska, 1975. v, 46 p. [3968]

The Italian connection: 25 years of Canadian literature and Italian translation, 1963-1988. Toronto: Thomas Fisher Rare Book Library, University of Toronto, 1988. 24 p. [1252]

Ivan Halasz de Beky: a bibliography. Toronto: Ivan Bush, 1983. [24] p. [7039]

Ives, Edward D.; Kirtley, Bacil
"Bibliography of New England-Maritimes folklore, 1950-1957." In: Northeast Folklore; Vol. 1 (Summer 1958) p. 18-31; vol. 2 (Summer 1959) p. 18-24; vol. 3 (1960) p. 20-23.; ISSN: 0078-1681. [4534]

Iwaasa, David B.
The Japanese Canadians: a bibliography. [S.l.: s.n.], c1975. ii, 27 l. [4171]

Izzo, Herbert J.
"Romanian-Canadian periodical publications: a preliminary check list." In: Canadian Ethnic Studies; Vol. 5, no. 1/2 (1973) p. 245-249.; ISSN: 0008-3496. [5914]

J.B. Rudnyckyj repertorium bibliographicum, 1933-1983. Ottawa: Ukrainian Language Association, [1984]. 296 p.: facsims., port. [7286]

"J.M.S. Careless: select bibliography." In: Old Ontario: essays in honour of J.M.S. Careless, edited by David Keane and Colin Read. Toronto: Dundurn Press, 1990. P. 321-326.; ISBN: 1-55002-060-9. [6892]

Jack, David Russell
"Acadian magazines." In: Proceedings and Transactions of the Royal Society of Canada; Series 2, vol. 9, section 2 (1903-1904) p. 173-203.; ISSN: 0316-4616. [5858]

Jacka, Alan A.
Adoption in brief: research and other literature in the United States, Canada and Great Britain, 1966-72: an annotated bibliography. Windsor [Eng.]: National Foundation for Educational Research in England and Wales, 1973. 71 p.; ISBN: 0-85633-015-9. [3117]

Jackel, Susan
Canadian prairie women's history: a bibliographic survey. Ottawa: Canadian Research Institute for the Advancement of Women, 1987. P. 1-22. (The CRIAW papers / Canadian Research Institute for the Advancement of Women ; no. 14); ISBN: 0-919653-14-6. [3853]

Jackson, L.J.
"A bibliography of Huron-Petun archaeology." In: Ontario Archaeology; no. 28 (1976) p. 33-69.; ISSN: 0078-4672. [4566]

Jackson, Robin
"A bibliography: development of the multicultural policy in Canada." In: Canadian Library Journal; Vol. 33, no. 3 (June 1976) p. 237-243.; ISSN: 0008-4352. [4173]

Jaffee, Georgina; Nett, Emily M.
"Annotated bibliography on women as elders." In: Resources for Feminist Research; Vol. 11, no. 2 (July 1982) p. 253-288.; ISSN: 0707-8412. [3807]

Jain, Sushil Kumar
A classified guide to Canadian biographical sources. Windsor, Ont.: University of Windsor Library, 1967. 16 l. [0087]

East Indians in Canada: an essay with a bibliography. Windsor, Ont.: Canadian Bibliographic Centre, 1970. 25 l. (Unexplored fields of Canadiana ; vol. 3. Minorities in Canada series ; no. 2) [4147]

French Canadian literature in English translation: a short list compiled from the library catalogues of the Regina Campus Library. Regina: Regina Campus Library, University of Saskatchewan, 1965. 9 l. [1028]

Louis "David" Riel & the North-West Rebellion: a list of references. Regina: Regina Campus Library, University of Saskatchewan, 1965. 19 l. [1946]

The Negro in Canada: a select list of primary and secondary sources for the study of [the] Negro community in Canada from the earliest times to the present days. Regina: Regina Campus Library, University of Saskatchewan, 1967. 30 l. (Unexplored fields of Canadiana ; vol. 3. Minorities in Canada series ; no. 1) [4139]

Poetry in Saskatchewan: a bibliography. Regina, Sask.: University of Saskatchewan, 1965. 10 l. [1029]

Saskatchewan in fiction: a bibliography of works of fiction about Saskatchewan & fiction written by Saskatchewanians. Regina: Regina Campus Library, University of Saskatchewan, 1966. viii, 15 l. [1034]

Jakle, John A.

Ethnic and racial minorities in North America: a selected bibliography of the geographical literature. Monticello, Ill.: Council of Planning Librarians, 1973. 71 p. (Council of Planning Librarians Exchange bibliography; 459, 460) [4161]

Past landscapes: a bibliography for historic preservationists. Rev. ed. Monticello, Ill.: Vance Bibliographies, 1980. 68 p. (Architecture series: Bibliography; A-314; ISSN: 0194-1356) [3030]

Jakubick, A.T.; Church, W.

Oklo natural reactors: geological and geochemical conditions: a review. Ottawa: Atomic Energy Control Board, 1986. ii, 53 p. [4852]

James, Charles Canniff

A bibliography of Canadian poetry (English). Toronto: Printed for the [Victoria University] Library by William Briggs, 1899. 71 p. (Victoria University Library publication; no. 1) [0992]

Jameson, Mary Ann

"The year's work in Canadian poetry studies." In: *Canadian Poetry*; No. 8 (Spring/Summer 1981)-no. 20 (Spring/Summer 1987) [1239]

Jamet, A.

"Bibliographie [de Marie de l'Incarnation]." Dans: *Revue d'histoire de l'Amérique française*; Vol. 1, no 2 (septembre 1947) p. 308-312.; ISSN: 0035-2357. [7177]

Jamet, Virginie

Commissions et comités gouvernementaux et parlementaires du Québec, 1867-1986: liste bibliographique annotée. Québec: Bibliothèque de l'Assemblée nationale, 1987. iv, 186 p. (Bibliographie et documentation / Bibliothèque de l'Assemblée nationale du Québec; 26) [2511]

Jamieson, Kathleen

Native women in Canada: a selected bibliography. [Ottawa]: Social Sciences and Humanities Research Council of Canada, [1983]. 49 p.; ISBN: 0-662-12396-4. [4048]

Jandali, Tarek; Hrebenyk, B.

Urban air quality research needs in Alberta: a literature review and synthesis of available information. Edmonton: Alberta Environment, Research Management Division, 1985. xi, 188 p. (RMD report / Alberta Environment, Research Management Division; 85-33) [5224]

"Jane Rule: a bibliography." In: *Canadian Fiction Magazine*; No. 23 (Autumn 1976) p. 133-138.; ISSN: 0045-477X. [7288]

Janiak, Jane M.

Air transportation. Monticello, Ill.: Vance Bibliographies, 1990. 78 p. (Public administration series: Bibliography; P-2879; ISSN: 0193-970X); ISBN: 0-7920-0539-2. [4509]

Janik, Sophie

Bibliographie québécoise sur les personnes handicapées. [Québec]: Office des personnes handicapées, 1988. vii, 253 p.; ISBN: 2-551-08230-7. [3309]

Janisch, Alice H.

Publication of administrative board decisions in Canada. London, Ont.: Canadian Association of Law Libraries, 1972. xi, 66 l. [6279]

Janisch, H.N.; Rawson, S.G.; Stanbury, W.T.

Canadian telecommunications regulation bibliography/ Bibliographie de la réglementation des télécommunications au Canada. Ottawa: Canadian Law Information Council, 1987. xxii, 111 p.; ISBN: 0-9214810-6-3. [2294]

Janssen, Viveka K.

"Bibliography on Swedish settlement in Alberta, 1890-1930." In: *Swedish American Historical Quarterly*; Vol. 33, no. 2 (April 1982) p. 124-129.; ISSN: 0730-028X. [4211]

Jaque, Mervyn H.

Research on youth: an annotated bibliography of selected current reports. Edmonton: Alberta Recreation, Parks & Wildlife, Youth Development Division, 1976. 24 l. [3149]

Jarjour, Gabi

Bibliographie sélectionée des articles sur l'économie du pétrole et du gaz, 1986-1989/Selected bibliography of articles on oil and gas economics, 1986-1989. Québec: Groupe de recherche en économie de l'énergie et des ressources naturelles, Université Laval, 1989. viii, 96, 6 p. (Cahier / Groupe de recherche en économie de l'énergie et des ressources naturelles; 89-05) [2753]

Jarman, Lynne

Canadian music: a selected checklist, 1950-73: a selective listing of Canadian music from the Fontes artis musicae, 1954-73 based on the catalogued entries of Canadiana from 1950/La musique canadienne: une liste sélective, 1950-73: répertoire sélective de musique canadienne extrait de Fontes artis musicae, 1954-73 d'après les notices catalographiques de Canadiana depuis 1950. Toronto: University of Toronto Press, [1976]. xiv, 170 p.; ISBN: 0-8020-5327-0. [0855]

Jarrell, Richard A.; Roos, Arnold E.

A bibliography for courses in the history of Canadian science, medicine, and technology. 2nd rev. ed. Thornhill, Ont.: HSTC Publications, 1983. vi, 62 p. (Research tools for the history of Canadian science and technology; no. 1; ISSN: 0715-9668); ISBN: 0-9690475-2-5. [4627]

"Select bibliography of the history of Canadian science, medicine and technology." In: *Science, technology and Canadian history/Les sciences, la technologie et l'histoire canadienne*, edited by Richard A. Jarrell and Norman R. Ball. Waterloo, Ont.: Wilfrid Laurier University Press, 1980. P. 217-231.; ISBN: 0-88920-086-6. [4626]

Jarvi, Edith T.

Bibliography of Windsor and Essex County. [Rev. ed.]. [Windsor, Ont.]: Windsor Public Libraries, 1955. 35 l. [0428]

Labour in Canada: basic books for Canadian public libraries. Ottawa: Canadian Library Association, 1963. 13 p. (Occasional paper / Canadian Library Association; no. 40) [2792]

Jarvis, Eric; Baker, Melvin

"Clio in Hogtown: a brief bibliography." In: *Ontario History*; Vol. 76, no. 3 (September 1984) p. 287-294.; ISSN: 0030-2953. [0475]

Jarvis, J.M., et al.

Review of silvicultural research: white spruce and trembling aspen cover types, Mixedwood Forest Section, Boreal Forest Region, Alberta-Saskatchewan-Manitoba. Ottawa: Queen's Printer, 1967. iii, 189 p.: ill., map. [5347]

Jaster, Marion C.

Selected annotated bibliography of high-grade silica of the United States and Canada through December 1954. Washington: United States Government Printing Office, 1957. P. 609-673. (United States Geological Survey Bulletin; 1019-H) [4751]

Javitch, Gregory

A selective bibliography of ceremonies, dances, music & songs of the American Indian from books in the library of

Gregory Javitch, with an annotated list of Indian dances. Montreal: Osiris, 1974. 71 p. ill. [3955]

Jay-Rayon, Jean-Claude

Bibliographie plein-air: résumés d'ouvrages francophones québécois, 1972-1986. [Québec]: Loisir, chasse et pêche, Québec, 1987. xxi, 167 p.; ISBN: 2-550-17214-0. [1840]

Jean, Michel

Bibliographie-caribou (révision 1980). Québec: Ministère du loisir, de la chasse et de la pêche, 1981. iii, 139 p. [5462]

Jeffries, Fern

Private policing: a bibliography. Toronto: Centre of Criminology, University of Toronto, 1973. iii, 39 p.; ISBN: 0-919584-07-1. [2132]

Jenner, Catherine

Bibliography of legal materials for non-law libraries. Toronto: Ontario Ministry of Citizenship and Culture, c1984. iv, 158 p.; ISBN: 0-7743-8963-X. [2268]

Jennings, Daniel T., et al.

Spruce budworms bibliography, with author and key word indices. Orono, Me.: Canada-United States Spruce Budworms Program, School of Forest Resources, University of Maine at Orono, 1979. iii, 687 p. (Miscellaneous report / Life science and agriculture experimental station, University of Maine at Orono; no. 213; ISSN: 0094-436X) [5432]

Jensen, Karlo

"Danish-Canadian periodical publications: a preliminary check list." In: *Canadian Ethnic Studies*; Vol. 2, no. 1 (June 1970) p. 27-29.; ISSN: 0008-3496. [5892]

Jensen, Susan E.

Crow-Rate, the great debate: a historical bibliography. Edmonton: Library, Alberta Agriculture, 1981. 31 p. [4482]

Jerabek, Esther

Czechs and Slovaks in North America: a bibliography. New York: Czechoslovak Society of Arts & Sciences in America, 1976. 448 p. [4174]

Jet lag and travel: a specialized bibliography from the SPORT database/Voyages et problèmes liés au décalage horaire: une bibliographie spécialisée de la base de données SPORT. Gloucester, Ont.: Sport Information Resource Centre, 1991. 18 l. [5704]

Jeux olympiques, Montréal, Québec, 1976. Comité organisateur. Centre de documentation

Bibliographie traitent des jeux olympiques et sujets connexes: annexe "A". [Montréal]: Comité organisateur des jeux olympiques de 1976, Direction générale de l'administration, Centre de documentation, 1976. iv, 74 f. [1784]

Jewett, Linda J.

"The shortened work week: a selective bibliography." In: *Ontario Library Review*; Vol. 56, no. 4 (December 1972) p. 230-237.; ISSN: 0030-2996. [2809]

Job, A.L.

Transport of solids in pipelines, with special reference to mineral ores, concentrates, and unconsolidated deposits (a literature survey). Ottawa: Department of Energy, Mines and Resources, Mines Branch, 1969. vii, 96 p. (Mines Branch Information circular ; IC 230) [4773]

Joba, Judith C.

Guide to marine transportation information sources in Canada. 2nd ed. Montreal: Transport Canada, Development, 1985. vii, 308 p.; ISBN: 0-660-11970-6. [4497]

Répertoire des sources d'information sur le transport

maritime au Canada. 2e éd. Montréal: Centre de développement des transports, Tranports Canada, 1985. vii, 323 p.; ISBN: 0-660-91624-X. [4498]

Jobling, J. Keith

"University research on Greek-Canadians: a preliminary check list of theses." In: *Canadian Ethnic Studies*; Vol. 5, no. 1/2 (1973) p. 125-126.; ISSN: 0008-3496. [6124]

Johansson, S. Ryan

"The demographic history of the native peoples of North America: a selective bibliography." In: *Yearbook of Physical Anthropology*; Vol. 25 (1982) p. 133-152.; ISSN: 0096-848X. [4033]

Johansson, T.S.K.; Johansson, M.P.

Apicultural literature published in Canada and the United States. [New York: s.n.], c1972. 103 p. [4653]

John Bassett Memorial Library

Catalogue of the Eastern Townships historical collection in the John Bassett Memorial Library. Lennoxville, Quebec: Bishop's University Library, 1965. 38 p. [0293]

Lists of Eastern Townships material in the John Bassett Memorial Library. Lennoxville, Quebec: Bishop's University Library, 1985. 2 vol.; ISBN: 0-920917-01-1 (set). [0386]

"John W. Holmes: a select bibliography." In: *An acceptance of paradox: essays on Canadian diplomacy in honour of John W. Holmes*, edited by Kim Richard Nossal. Toronto: Canadian Institute of International Affairs, 1982. P. 197-202. (Contemporary affairs / Canadian Institute of International Affairs ; 49); ISBN: 0-919084-39-7. [7065]

Johnsen, Julia E.

"St. Lawrence River ship canal." In: *Reference Shelf*; Vol. 1, no. 3 (December 1922) p. 1-74. [4444]

Johnson, B.C.

Labrador wildlife bibliography. St. John's, Nfld.: Canadian Wildlife Service, 1976. 7 l. [5406]

Johnson, Basil

Bibliography of Indian history books. Toronto: Indian-Eskimo Association of Canada, 1970. 14 p. [3923]

Johnson, Bryan R.

The Blackfeet: an annotated bibliography. New York: Garland Publishing, 1988. xxiv, 231 p. (Garland reference library of social science ; vol. 441); ISBN: 0-8240-0941-X. [4098]

Johnson, H.J., et al.

Some implications of large-scale clearcutting in Alberta: a literature review. Edmonton: Canadian Forestry Service, Department of the Environment, 1971. 114 l. (Northern Forest Research Centre Information report ; NOR-X-6; ISSN: 0704-7673) [4928]

Johnson, Jenny

Bibliography of selected titles on disability and disabled persons: procedures and selected sources. [North York, Ont.]: North York Public Library, 1983. 12, 19, 6 l. [3249]

Johnson, Larry; Van Cleve, Keith

Revegetation in arctic and subarctic North America: a literature review. Hanover, N.H.: U.S. Army Cold Regions Research and Engineering Laboratory, 1976. iv, 32 p. (CRREL report / U.S. Army Cold Regions Research and Engineering Laboratory ; 76-15) [5116]

Johnson, Marion E.

Forest products pollution control annotated bibliography (excluding pulp and paper). Vancouver: Department of the Environment, Canadian Forestry Service, Western Forest Products Laboratory, 1972. 20 p. (Information report / Western Forest Products Laboratory ; VP-X-100; ISSN: 0045-429X) [4932]

Johnson, Melvin W

The cobblestone architecture of the Great Lakes region: an annotated bibliography. Monticello, Ill.: Vance Bibliographies, 1985. 46 p. (Architecture series: Bibliography ; A-1416; ISSN: 0194-1356); ISBN: 0-89028-446-6. [0776]

Johnson, Stephen R.; Adams, William J.; Morrell, Michael R.

The birds of the Beaufort Sea: an annotated bibliography. Edmonton: Canadian Wildlife Service, Department of the Environment, 1975. 169 p. [5393]

Johnston, G.H.

"Roger James Evan Brown, 1931-1980." In: *Arctic*; Vol. 34, no. 1 (March 1981) p. 95-99.; ISSN: 0004-0843. [6878]

Johnston, H. Kirk; Lim, H.S.

Bibliography on the application of reverse osmosis to industrial and municipal wastewaters. Ottawa: Information Canada, [1973]. iv, 117 p. (Research report / Research Program for the Abatement of Municipal Pollution under provisions of the Canada-Ontario Agreement on Great Lakes Water Quality ; no. 18) [5742]

Johnston, Joan L.

Bibliography: Symposium 1977: Prepared for Symposium 1977, The end of an era, 1880 – Canada – 1914/ Bibliographie: Symposium 1977, La fin d'une époque, 1880 – Canada – 1914. [S.l.: s.n., 1977]. 22 p. [0688]

Canada in the Victorian image, 1837-1887: a selective guide to reading. [Guelph, Ont.]: Library, University of Guelph, c1975. 15 p. (Bibliography series / University of Guelph Library ; no. 4) [0681]

Jolicoeur, Catherine

"Le vaisseau fantôme: légende étiologique: bibliographie." Dans: *Archives de Folklore*; Vol. 11 (1970) p. 307-325.; ISSN: 0085-5243. [4550]

Jolicoeur, Jovette

Inventaire des cartes de la végétation pour la région des Cantons de l'Est. Sherbrooke, Québec: Université de Sherbrooke, Département de géographie, 1981. 74 f. (Bulletin de recherche / Université de Sherbrooke, Département de géographie ; no 54) [6575]

Jonasson, Eric

"Ethnic groups in Manitoba: a select bibliography." In: *Generations: the Journal of the Manitoba Genealogical Society*; Vol. 3, no. 2 (Summer 1978) p. 47-55.; ISSN: 0226-6105. [4185]

Jones, Barry C.; Geen, Glen H.

Bibliography of spiny dogfish (Squalus acanthius L.) and related species. Nanaimo, B.C.: Fisheries and Marine Service, Environment Canada, 1976. 84 p. (Fisheries and Marine Service Technical report ; no. 655; ISSN: 0701-7626) [5407]

Jones, L.

Energy conservation in schools [bibliography]. Ottawa: Division of Building Research, National Research Council Canada, 1980. 5 p. (Bibliography / National Research Council Canada, Division of Building Research ; no. 43) [5778]

Jones, Linda M.

Canadian studies: foreign publications and theses/Études canadiennes: publications et thèses étrangères. 4th ed. Ottawa: International Council for Canadian Studies for External Affairs Canada: Conseil international d'études canadiennes pour Affaires extérieures Canada, 1992. xvii, 525 p.; ISBN: 0-9691862-7-4. [0177]

Jones, Mary Jane

Bibliographie sur le delta du Mackenzie. Ottawa: Imprimeur de la Reine et contrôleur de la papeterie, 1969. xiii, 108 p.: ill., carte. (Travaux de recherches sur le delta du Mackenzie ; 6) [0617]

Mackenzie Delta bibliography. Ottawa: Queen's Printer and Controller of Stationery, 1969. xiii, 119 p.: map. (Mackenzie Delta research project ; 6) [0618]

Jones, Peter

Peacekeeping: an annotated bibliography. Kingston, Ont.: R.P. Frye, c1989. xl, 152 p.; ISBN: 0-919741-15-0. [2529]

Jones, Phyllis E.

Nurses in Canadian primary health care settings: a review of recent literature. [Toronto]: Faculty of Nursing, University of Toronto, c1980. iv, 26 p. (Literature review monograph / Faculty of Nursing, University of Toronto ; 2); ISBN: 0-7727-3601-4. [5629]

Jones, Richard C.

An annotated bibliography of the Sudbury area. 2nd ed., rev. and enl. Sudbury, Ont.: Sudbury Public Library, 1972. 55 p. [0443]

Jones, Richard Edward

The petrology and stratigraphy of arctic sea ice and relationships to formational processes [microform]: a critical review of the literature. Ottawa: National Library of Canada, 1986. 2 microfiches (118 fr.) (Canadian theses ; TH-26631); ISBN: 0-315-26631-7. [5235]

Jones, Tim E.H.

Annotated bibliography of Saskatchewan archaeology and prehistory. Saskatoon: Saskatchewan Archaeological Society, 1988. ii, 196 p.; ISBN: 0-9691420-0-7. [4602]

Joseph, Gene

Sharing the knowledge: a First Nations resource guide. Vancouver: Legal Services Society of British Columbia, 1992. ix, 101 p.: ill.; ISBN: 0-919736-77-7. [4119]

Journaux, bulletins et revues de l'Amérique française hors Québec: répertoire. Québec: Secrétariat permanent des peuples francophones, 1983-. vol.; ISSN: 0846-2488. [5990]

Joy, Albert H.

Acid rain: a bibliography of Canadian federal and provincial government documents. Westport: Meckler, c1991. xxi, 237 p.; ISBN: 0-88736-527-2. [5289]

Joyal, Robert

"Volumes sur la faune du Québec." Dans: *Québec chasse et pêche*; Vol. 2, no 6 (mars 1973) p. 30-31. [5374]

Joyes, Dennis C.

"A bibliography of Saskatchewan archaeology, 1900-1975." In: *Saskatchewan Archaeology Newsletter*; Vol. 52, no. 4-5 (1977) p. 41-115.; ISSN: 0581-832X. [4568]

Judd, William W.

Annotated catalogue and index of columns on nature written by John W. Agnos (1927-1991) for *London Free Press*, 1989-1991. London, Ont.: Phelps Publishing, 1991. 20 p. [6798]

A bibliography of the natural history of Hamilton to the year 1950. Hamilton, Ont.: Hamilton Naturalists' Club, 1960. 27 p. [5332]

A bibliography of the natural history of Middlesex County, Ontario to the year 1980: with an historical introduction. London, Ont.: Phelps Publishing, 1981. 157 p.; ISBN: 0-920298-32-X. [5463]

Catalogue of columns on natural history, "Nature's diary", by Alfred Brooker Klugh (1882-1932), published in the *Farmer's Advocate*, 1912 to 1925, at London, Ontario, Canada. London, Ont.: Phelps, 1986. ii l., 42 p. [7097]

Catalogue of documents pertaining to the life and activities of William Wallace Judd, professor emeritus (zoology), University of Western Ontario, deposited in the Regional History Library, University of Western Ontario, London, Ontario, Canada. London, Ont.: Phelps, 1989. 65 p., 2 l. [7082]

Sources of information on the Byron Bog. [London, Ont.: s.n.], 1976. 10 l. [5408]

Jukelevics, Nicette

A bibliography of Canadian concrete, visual and sound poetry, 1965-1972 with an introduction [microform]. [Ottawa: Canadian Theses Division, National Library of Canada, c1975]. 2 microfiches: ill. (Canadian theses on microfiche ; 25376; ISSN: 0227-3845) [1091]

Juliani, T.J.; Talbot, C.K.

Military justice: a selected annotated bibliography. Ottawa: CRIMCARE, c1981. xii, 71 l.; ISBN: 0-919395-00-7. [2234]

Julien, Germain; Trudel, Denys

"Bilan de la recherche sur l'administration publique québécoise." Dans: *Recherches sociographiques*; Vol. 16, no 3 (septembre-décembre 1975) p. 413-438.; ISSN: 0034-1282. [2417]

Juricic, Zelimir B.; Malycky, Alexander

"Croatian-Canadian periodical publications: a preliminary check list." In: *Canadian Ethnic Studies*; Vol. 2, no. 1 (June 1970) p. 21-25.; ISSN: 0008-3496. [5893]

Jury, Elsie McLeod

"A guide to archaeological research in Ontario." In: *Ontario Library Review*; Vol. 34, no. 2 (May 1950) p. 123-133.; ISSN: 0030-2996. [4530]

Justice Institute of British Columbia. Resource Centre

Audio visual catalogue [Justice Institute of British Columbia]. Vancouver, B.C.: The Centre, 1989. 119, 37, 8 p.; ISSN: 0835-9962. [6684]

Kaill, Robert C.

Crime in the country: a literature review of crime and criminal justice in rural areas. [Ottawa]: Solicitor General Canada, Programs Branch, [1986]. 139 p. (Programs Branch user report / Ministry Secretariat, Solicitor General Canada ; 1986-39) [2283]

Kakabelaki, Helen

"Greek-Canadian periodical publications: a preliminary check list." In: *Canadian Ethnic Studies*; Vol. 2, no. 1 (June 1970) p. 71-74.; ISSN: 0008-3496. [5894]

Kalant, Oriana Josseau, et al.

Cannabis: health risks: a comprehensive annotated bibliography (1844-1982). Toronto: Addiction Research Foundation, 1983. xxxiv, 1100 p. (Bibliographic series / Addiction Research Foundation of Ontario ; no. 16; ISSN: 0065-1885); ISBN: 0-88868-081-3. [5652]

Kalant, Oriana Josseau; Kalant, Harold

Amphetamines and related drugs: clinical toxicity and dependence: a comprehensive bibliography of the international literature. Toronto: Addiction Research Foundation, c1974. xlviii, 210 p. (Bibliographic series / Addiction Research Foundation of Ontario ; no. 8; ISSN: 0065-1885) [5594]

Kalish, Jana

Josef Skvorecky: a checklist. [Toronto]: University of Toronto Library, 1986. iv, 232 p.; ISBN: 0-7727-6000-4. [7310]

Kaliski, S.F.

Labour turnover in Canada: a survey of literature and data. Kingston, Ont.: Industrial Relations Centre, Queen's University, 1981. iv, 27 p. (Research and current issues series / Industrial Relations Centre, Queen's University ; no. 41; ISSN: 0317-2546); ISBN: 0-88886-112-5. [2872]

Kallio, Edwin; Dickerhoof, Edward

Business data and market information sourcebook for the forest products industry. Madison, Wis.: Forest Products Research Society, 1979. viii, 215 p. [2647]

Kallmann, Helmut

Catalogue of Canadian composers. Rev. and enl. ed. [Toronto]: Canadian Broadcasting Corporation, [1952]. 254 p. [0812]

"A check-list of Canadian periodicals in the field of music." In: *Canadian Music Journal*; Vol. 1, no. 2 (Winter 1957) p. 30-36.; ISSN: 0576-5773. [5868]

"The German contribution to music in Canada: a bibliography." In: *German-Canadian Yearbook*; Vol. 7 (1983) p. 228-238.; ISSN: 0316-8603. [0911]

Kalman, Harold

"Recent literature on the history of Canadian architecture." In: *Journal of the Society of Architectural Historians*; Vol. 31, no. 4 (December 1972) p. 315-323.; ISSN: 0037-9808. [0739]

Kanada kankei hogo bunken mokuroku: 1977-1988. Tokyo: Nihon Kanada Gakkai, 1988. 150 p. [0161]

Kandiuk, Mary

French-Canadian authors: a bibliography of their works and of English-language criticism. Metuchen, N.J.: Scarecrow Press, c1990. xii, 222 p.; ISBN: 0-8108-2362-4. [1282]

Kannins, Malva, et al.

"The changing Canadian society." In: *Ontario Library Review*; Vol. 59, no. 3 (September 1975) p. 171-181.; ISSN: 0030-2996. [3137]

Kapoor, Sudersan

Research and publication in adult education. Toronto: Adult Education Department, Ontario Institute for Studies in Education, [1966]. 14 p. [3392]

Karal, Pearl

Parenting education for the young: a literature survey. Toronto: Ontario Ministry of Education, 1984. vi, 70 p.; ISBN: 0-7743-9195-2. [3624]

Karim, Karim H.

Images des Arabes et des Musulmans: recension de la recherche. Ottawa: Politiques et recherche, Secteur du multiculturalisme, Multiculturalisme et citoyenneté, 1991. 44 f. (Images des minorités: Recensions de la recherche) [4283]

Images of Arabs and Muslims: a research review. Ottawa: Policy & Research, Multiculturalism Branch, Multiculturalism & Citizenship, 1991. 44 l. (Images of minorities: Research reviews) [4284]

Karim, Karim H.; Sansom, Gareth

Bibliographie annotée sur les ethnies et les média au Canada. [Ottawa]: Politiques & Recherches, Secteur du multiculturalisme, Multiculturalisme et citoyenneté, 1990. 32, 30 f. [4275]

Ethnicity and the mass media in Canada: an annotated bibliography. [Ottawa]: Policy & Research, Multiculturalism Sector, Multiculturalism & Citizenship,

1990. 30, 32 l. [4276]

Karklins, Karlis; Sprague, Roderick

A bibliography of glass trade beads in North America. Moscow, Idaho: South Fork Press, 1980. 51 p. [4577]

Karrow, P.F.

Bibliography of theses on Ontario geology (Cambrian to Quaternary inclusive). Toronto: Ontario Department of Mines, 1960. 11 l. [6072]

Kasemets, Udo

Canavangard: music of the nineteen sixties and after series. Don Mills, Ont.: BMI Canada, c1968. 112 p.: ill., ports. [0822]

Kathman, R.D., et al.

Benthic studies in Alice Arm and Hastings Arm, B.C. in relation to mine tailings dispersal. Sidney, B.C.: Institute of Ocean Sciences, Fisheries and Oceans Canada, 1983. vii, 30, [28] p.: ill., maps. (Canadian technical report of hydrography and ocean sciences ; no. 22; ISSN: 0711-6764) [5486]

Katz, Brian J.

Arctic petroleum transportation bibliography. Winnipeg: Natural Resource Institute, University of Manitoba, 1974. v, 123 p. [4783]

Katz, Israel J.

"Marius Barbeau, 1883-1969: [Bibliography of ethnomusicological works]." In: *Ethnomusicology*; Vol. 14, no. 1 (January 1970) p. 129-142.; ISSN: 0014-1836. [6828]

Kealey, Gregory; McKay, Ian; Reilly, Nolan

"Canada's "eastern question": a reader's guide to regional underdevelopment." In: *Canadian Dimension*; Vol. 13, no. 2 (1978) p. 37-40.; ISSN: 0008-3402. [0234]

Kearney, Hélène

La planification différentielle de la main-d'oeuvre en service social: un relevé bibliographique. Montréal: Centre de services sociaux juifs à la famille, 1981. 30 f. [3221]

Keays, J.L.

Complete-tree utilization: an analysis of the literature. Vancouver, B.C.: Forest Products Laboratory, Canadian Forestry Service, Department of Fisheries and Forestry, 1971. 5 vol.: ill. (Canadian Forestry Service Information report ; VP-X-69,70,71,77,79) [4929]

Keillor, Elaine

A bibliography of items on music in Canada. [Toronto]: E. Keillor, c1972. 89 l. [0835]

Bibliography of items on music in Canada in *The Musical Courier*, 1898-1903. Ottawa: E. Keillor, 1979. 27 l. [0875]

Keleher, J.J.

Manitoba: aquatic LRTAP data and bibliography. Winnipeg: Water Standards and Studies Section, 1988. ii, 272 p. [5258]

Kellogg, Catherine

Speaking of food: an annotated bibliography of resources related to food issues. Toronto: FoodShare Metro Toronto, 1989. [132] p.; ISBN: 0-921030-06-1. [4718]

Kelly, Catherine E.

"Selected bibliography: [Duncan Campbell Scott]." In: *The Duncan Campbell Scott Symposium*, edited by K.P. Stich. Ottawa: University of Ottawa Press, 1980. P. 147-155. (Reappraisals: Canadian writers); ISBN: 2-7603-4386-3. [7297]

Kelly, Ross Ian; Barnett, R.S.; Delorme, R.J.

An annotated bibliography of the Quaternary geology and history for the Don Valley Brickworks. Toronto: Mines and Minerals Division, Ministry of Northern Development

and Mines, 1987. iv, 38 p. (Ontario Geological Survey Miscellaneous paper ; 135; ISSN: 0704-2752); ISBN: 0-7729-2505-4. [4860]

Kelly, Shirley; Stark, Richard

Sport and recreation for the disabled: an index of resource materials/Sport et loisir pour handicapés: un répertoire de la littérature. Ottawa: Sport Information Resource Centre, 1984. xxxi, 186 p.; ISBN: 0-920678-38-6. [1830]

Kelsall, John P.; Telfer, Edmund S.; Wright, Thomas D.

The effects of fire on the ecology of the boreal forest, with particular reference to the Canadian north: a review and selected bibliography. Ottawa: Canadian Wildlife Service, 1977. 58 p. (Canadian Wildlife Service Occasional paper ; no. 32); ISBN: 0-662-00638-0. [4956]

Kelso, Dianne R.; Attneave, Carolyn L.

Bibliography of North American Indian mental health. Westport, Conn.: Greenwood Press, 1981. xxviii, 411 p.: map.; ISBN: 0-313-22930-9. [5638]

Kempeneers, Marianne; Massé, Raymond

Les migrations antillaises: bibliographie sélective et annotée. [Montréal]: Centre de recherches caraïbes de l'Université de Montréal, c1981. 53 p. [4202]

Kemshead, Alison

Newfoundland: a bibliography of social, economic and political conditions. Monticello, Ill.: Vance Bibliographies, 1980. 33 p. (Public administration series: Bibliography ; P-449; ISSN: 0193-970X) [0246]

Prince Edward Island: a bibliography of social, economic, and political conditions. Monticello, Ill.: Vance Bibliographies, 1980. 16 p. (Public administration series: Bibliography ; P-529; ISSN: 0193-970X) [0247]

Kendle, Judith

"Morley Callaghan: an annotated bibliography." In: *The annotated bibliography of Canada's major authors*, Vol. 5, edited by Robert Lecker and Jack David. Downsview, Ont.: ECW Press, 1984. P. 13-177.; ISBN: 0-920802-68-0. [6887]

Kennedy, Alan; Carbyn, Ludwig N.

Selected annotated references concerning timber wolf (Canis lupus) predation. Edmonton: Canadian Wildlife Service, Western and Northern Region, 1979. 54 p. [5433]

Kenny, William M.

Literature of the Lakes. [S.l.: s.n., 1977]. 3 vol.; ISBN: 0-9203-3903-4 (vol. 1). [1992]

Kent, Duncan

British Columbia: a bibliography of industry, labour, resources & regions for the social sciences. Vancouver, B.C.: University of British Columbia Press, 1978. xi, 199 p.: ill., map. [0589]

Kent, Thomas D.

Mackenzie Mountains region bibliography. Ottawa: Environment Canada, Lands Directorate, 1982. 1 vol. (in various pagings): maps. [4828]

Kenyon, Robert; Sawka, Edward

Primary prevention of substance abuse: an annotated bibliography of related literature (1981-1987). [Edmonton]: Alberta Alcohol and Drug Abuse Commission, c1987. viii, 137, [12] p. [3299]

Kenyon, Walter Andrew

"A bibliography of Ontario archaeology." In: *Ontario Archaeology*; No. 9 (June 1966) p. 35-62.; ISSN: 0078-4672. [4541]

Kerber, Jordan E.

Coastal and maritime archaeology: a bibliography. Metuchen, N.J.: Scarecrow Press, 1991. viii, 400 p.; ISBN: 0-8108-2465-5. [4609]

Kerbrat, Hervé

Bibliographie sélective pour l'exportation. Montréal: École des hautes études commerciales, 1979. 36 p. (Cahiers du Centre d'études en administration internationale ; no 79-01; ISSN: 0709-986X) [2648]

Kerek, Andrew

Bibliography of Hungarian linguistic research in the United States and Canada. [New Brunswick, N.J.]: American Hungarian Foundation, c1979. 28 p. (Hungarian reference shelf ; 5) [1446]

Kermond, Lesley; Money, Christine

Commonwealth women novelists: catalogue of an exhibition of novels, critical works and biographies, held in the Exhibition Galleries of the Commonwealth Institute 5-22 January, 1983. London: Library & Resource Centre, Commonwealth Institute, c1984. iii, 26 p.; ISBN: 0-946140-05-7. [1214]

Kerr, Alastair

"The growth of architectural history in British Columbia." In: *Bulletin (Society for the Study of Architecture in Canada)*; Vol. 10, no. 1 (March 1985) p. 21-24.; ISSN: 0712-8517. [0777]

Kerr, Dale D.

Annotated bibliography on the rain screen principle. Ottawa: National Research Council Canada, Division of Building Research, [1985]. 35 p. (Bibliography / National Research Council Canada, Division of Building Research ; no. 45) [5807]

Kerr, Lillian B.

Bibliography of geology, palaeontology, industrial minerals, and fuels in the post-Cambrian regions of Manitoba to 1950. Winnipeg: Province of Manitoba, Department of Mines and Natural Resources, Mines Branch, 1951. 38 p. (Mines Branch publication / Province of Manitoba, Department of Mines and Natural Resources ; 51-2) [4746]

Kerr, W.B.

"Historical literature on Canada's participation in the Great War." In: *Canadian Historical Review*; Vol. 14, no. 4 (December 1933) p. 412-436; vol. 15, no. 2 (June 1934) p. 181-190.; ISSN: 0008-3755. [1910]

Kerr, W.K.

Bibliography of Canadian reports in aviation medicine, 1939-1945. [Ottawa]: Defence Research Board, Department of National Defence, 1962. 187 p. [5566]

Kerri, James N.

American Indians (U.S. and Canada): a bibliography of contemporary studies and urban research. Winnipeg: Department of the Secretary of State, Canadian Citizenship Branch, 1972. v l., 193 p. [3935]

Kershaw, G.P.

"Don Allyn Gill (1934-1979)." In: *Arctic*; Vol. 33, no. 1 (March 1980) p. 215-219.; ISSN: 0004-0843. [7017]

Kershaw, Kenneth A.

Early printed maps of Canada. I. 1540-1703. Ancaster, Ont.: Kershaw Publishing, 1993. vi, 320 p.: maps.; ISBN: 0-9697184-0-3. [6603]

Kerst, Catherine Hiebert

Ethnic folklife dissertations from the United States and Canada, 1960-1980: a selected, annotated bibliography. Washington: American Folklife Center, Library of Congress, 1986. vi, 69 p. (Publications of the American Folklife Center ; no. 12) [6184]

Kerur, Sharad

Factfinding, a dispute resolution procedure for collective bargaining: a review of the existing literature and an analysis of its use by school boards and teachers in Ontario. Kingston, Ont.: Industrial Relations Centre, Queen's University, 1986. xii, 109 [i.e. 119] p. (Research essay series / School of Industrial Relations, Queen's University ; no. 5); ISBN: 0-88886-136-2. [2905]

Kesteman, Jean-Pierre

"Les premier journaux du District de Saint-François (1823-1845)." Dans: *Revue d'histoire de l'Amérique française*; Vol. 31, no 2 (septembre 1977) p. 239-253.; ISSN: 0035-2357. [6027]

Ketilson, Lou Hammond; Korthuis, Bonnie; Boyd, Colin

The management of co-operatives: a bibliography. Saskatoon: Centre for the Study of Co-operatives, University of Saskatchewan, [1987]. 137 p. [2737]

Ketilson, Lou Hammond; Quennell, Michael

Community-based models of health care: a bibliography. Saskatoon: Centre for the Study of Co-operatives, University of Saskatchewan, 1990. 49 p. [5696]

Key people: writers in Atlantic Canada. Halifax, N.S.: Writers' Federation of Nova Scotia, 1990. 201 p.; ISBN: 0-920636-15-2. [0270]

Keyes, Charles Rollin

A bibliography of North American paleontology, 1888-1892. Washington: U.S.G.P.O., 1894. 251 p. [4525]

Khan, Nuzrat Yar

Urdu literature in Canada: a preliminary survey. [Ottawa]: Department of the Secretary of State of Canada, Multiculturalism, 1988. 45 l.; ISBN: 0-662-16028-2. [1253]

Khayatt, M. Didl; Brodribb, Somer

"Bibliography of materials available in the Women's Educational Resource Centre." In: *Resources for Feminist Research*; Vol. 12, no. 3 (November 1983) p. 32-45.; ISSN: 0707-8412. [3820]

Kidd, Karole

"Bibliography of computer mapping." In: *A computer atlas of Ottawa-Hull (with a bibliography of computer mapping)*, by D.R.F. Taylor and D.H. Douglas. Ottawa: Department of Geography, Carleton University, 1970. P. 45-68. [6519]

Kidd, Kenneth E.; Rogers, Edward S.; Kenyon, Walter Andrew

Brief bibliography of Ontario anthropology. Toronto: Royal Ontario Museum, University of Toronto, 1964. 20 p. (Art and Archaeology Occasional paper / Royal Ontario Museum ; 7) [4539]

Kiely, Michael Sean

Perspectives on the forest sector: an evaluative guide to forestry audio-visuals/Perspectives sur le secteur forestier: guide des instruments audio-visuels et des études sur la foresterie. Ottawa: Canadian Film Institute, 1987. iv, 33 p.; ISBN: 0-919096-31-X. [6671]

Kienzle, Bob

The Wood Buffalo National Park area: a bibliography. [Ottawa]: National and Historic Parks Branch, Department of Indian Affairs and Northern Development, 1972. xi, 61 l. [2986]

Kiessling, Jerry J.; Andrews, Donald Arthur; Farmer, Colin

An introduction to the CaVIC reports. Ottawa: Canadian Volunteers in Corrections Training Project, 1977. 7 p. [2171]

Killaly contributors: being an index to *Stuffed Crocodile* and Killaly chapbook contributors and a list of their recent publications, together with Twenty found poems signed on a floor by Frank B. Arnold. London, Ont.: Killaly Press, 1982. [48] p. (Killaly chapbooks, 5th series ; no. 1); ISBN: 0-920438-24-5. [1191]

Kim, Hyung-chan
Asian American studies: an annotated bibliography and research guide. New York: Greenwood Press, 1989. x, 504 p. (Bibliographies and indexes in American history ; no. 11; ISSN: 0742-6828); ISBN: 0-313-26026-5. [4268]

Kimmins, J.P., et al.
Biogeochemistry of temperate forest ecosystems: literature on inventories and dynamics of biomass and nutrients/ Biochimie des écosystèmes des forêts tempérées: publications sur les inventaires et la dynamique de la biomasse et des éléments nutritifs. Chalk River, Ont.: Petawawa National Forestry Institute, Canadian Forestry Service, 1985. xxi, 227 p. (Information report / Petawawa National Forestry Institute ; PI-X-47 E/F; ISSN: 0706-1854); ISBN: 0-662-53946-X. [4984]
Whole-tree harvest – nutrient relationships: a bibliography/ Exploitation des arbres entiers – rapport des éléments nutritifs: étude bibliographique. Chalk River, Ont.: Petawawa National Forestry Institute, Canadian Forestry Service, 1985. xi, 377 p. (Information report / Petawawa National Forestry Institute ; PI-X-60E-F; ISSN: 0714-3354); ISBN: 0-662-54154-5. [4985]

Kimmins, J.P.; Fraker, P.N.
Bibliography of herbicides in forest ecosystems. Victoria, B.C.: Canadian Forestry Service, 1973. 261 p. [4936]

Kimmitt, Marianne
The World of Children's Books showcase: a selection of the best Canadian, British and American children's books: in celebration of the International Year of the Child 1979. Edmonton: World of Children's Books Magazine: Alberta Culture, Library Services Branch, 1979. iii, 31 p.: ill. [1338]

King, Geraldine L.
Introductory bibliography of ground-water studies in New Brunswick, 1865-1977. Fredericton: Environment New Brunswick, 1977. iii, 25 l. [5125]

King, Harold Godfrey Rudolf
The Arctic. Oxford: Clio Press, c1989. xvi, 272, [3] p.: map. (World bibliographical series / Clio Press ; 99); ISBN: 1-85109-072-X. [0658]

Kingsford, William
The early bibliography of the province of Ontario, Dominion of Canada, with other information. A supplemental chapter of Canadian archaeology. Toronto: Rowsell & Hutchison; Montreal: Eben Picken, 1892. 140 p. [0440]

Kinloch, A.M.; House, Anthony B.
"The English language in New Brunswick and Prince Edward Island: research published, in progress, and required." In: *Journal of the Atlantic Provinces Linguistic Association*; Vol. 1 (1978) p. 34-45.; ISSN: 0706-6910. [1443]

Kinnell, Susan K.
People in history: an index to U.S. and Canadian biographies in history journals and dissertations. Santa Barbara, Calif.: ABC-Clio, c1988. 2 vol.; ISBN: 0-87436-493-0. [2070]

Kirby, Ronald E.; Lewis, Stephen J.; Sexson, Terry N.
Fire in North American wetland ecosystems and fire-wildlife relations: an annotated bibliography. Washington, D.C.: Fish and Wildlife Service, U.S. Department of the Interior, 1988. vi, 146 p.: ill. (Biological report / Fish and Wildlife Service, U.S. Department of the Interior ; 88:1) [5259]

Kirschbaum, J M
"Slovak-Canadian periodical publications: a preliminary check list." In: *Canadian Ethnic Studies*; Vol. 1, no. 1 (1969) p. 65-68.; ISSN: 0008-3496. [5882]

Kirsh, Harvey J.
Kirsh: selected bibliography of construction law writings in Canada. Toronto: Carswell, 1988. vii, 43 p.; ISBN: 0-459-31371-1. [2317]

Kiyooka, Harry M.
"University research on Japanese-Canadians: a preliminary check list of theses." In: *Canadian Ethnic Studies*; Vol. 2, no. 1 (June 1970) p. 127-128.; ISSN: 0008-3496. [6105]

Klancher, Donald James; Hearfield, J.D.
The Royal Canadian Mounted Police: a bibliography. [Ottawa]: RCMP, [1979]. 111 p. [2195]

Klaprat, D.A.; Hara, T.J.
A bibliography on chemoreception in fishes, 1807-1983. Winnipeg, Man.: Western Region, Department of Fisheries and Oceans, 1984. iv, 47 p. (+ 1 errata sheet). (Canadian technical report of fisheries and aquatic sciences ; no. 1268; ISSN: 0706-6457) [5498]

Klement, Susan
The elimination of architectural barriers to the disabled: a selected bibliography and report on the literature in the field. Toronto: Canadian Rehabilitation Council for the Disabled, 1969. ii l., 36 p. [3090]
"Selected annotated bibliography of articles relevant to alternatives in librarianship." In: *Canadian Library Journal*; Vol. 34, no. 2 (April 1977) p. 137-140.; ISSN: 0008-4352. [1622]

Klinck, Carl F.
"Annual bibliography of Commonwealth literature, ... : Canada." In: *Journal of Commonwealth Literature*; 1964 in no. 1 (September 1965) p. 27-43; 1965 in no. 2 (December 1966) p. 39-55.; ISSN: 0021-9894. [1035]
"Canadian literature in English: a select reading list." In: *Bulletin (Association for Commonwealth Literature and Language Studies)*; No. 4 (1967) 32 p. [1041]
Complete bibliography of Wilfred Campbell, 1858-1918. [S.l.: s.n.], 1943. 32 p. [6890]
"Post-graduate theses in Canadian literature: English and French comparative." In: *Journal of Canadian Fiction*; Vol. 1, no. 2 (Summer 1972) p. 68-73.; ISSN: 0047-2255. [6118]

Klinck, George Alfred
"Bibliographie: Louis Fréchette." Dans: *Revue d'histoire de l'Amérique française*; Vol. 7, no 1 (juin 1953) p. 132-146.; ISSN: 0035-2357. [6991]

Klippenstein, Lawrence
"Canadian Mennonite writings: a bibliographical survey, 1970-1980." In: *German-Canadian Yearbook*; Vol. 6 (1981) p. 284-293.; ISSN: 0316-8603. [1550]

Klodawsky, Fran; Spector, Aron N.; Hendrix, Catrina
Housing and single parents: an overview of the literature. [Toronto]: Centre for Urban and Community Studies, University of Toronto, 1984. 48 p. (University of Toronto Centre for Urban and Community Studies Bibliographic series ; no. 15; ISSN: 0316-4691); ISBN: 0-7727-1251-4. [4402]

Klos, Sheila M.; Smith, Christine M.
Historical bibliography of art museum serials from the United States and Canada. Tucson, Ariz.: Art Libraries Society of North America, 1987. 58 p. (Occasional papers

of the Art Libraries Society of North America ; no. 5; ISSN: 0730-7160); ISBN: 0-942740-04-1. [5963]

Klumph, S.G.; Haberer, A.
Range: a selected bibliography of research and information. Edmonton: Alberta Department of Energy and Natural Resources, Lands Division, 1975. vii, 201 p. [4666]

Klymasz, Robert B.
A bibliography of Ukrainian folklore in Canada, 1902-64. [Ottawa: Queen's Printer, 1968]. vi, 53 p. (National Museum of Canada Anthropology Papers ; no. 21) [4140]

Knafla, Louis A.
"Crime, criminal law and justice in Canadian history: a select bibliography, origins to 1940." In: *Law and society in Canada in historical perspective*, edited by D.J. Bercuson and Louis A. Knafla. Calgary: University of Calgary, c1979. P. 157-171. [2196]

Knapper, Christopher K.
"A decade review of college teaching research, 1970-1980." In: *Canadian Psychology*; Vol. 22, no. 2 (April 1981) p. 129-145.; ISSN: 0708-5591. [3593]

Knight, David B.; Davies, Maureen
Self-determination: an interdisciplinary annotated bibliography. New York: Garland Publishing, 1987. 254 p. (Canadian review of studies in nationalism ; vol. 8) (Garland reference library of social sciences ; vol. 394); ISBN: 0-8240-8495-0. [2512]

Knight, G.
Noise and vibration control in mines: index of research reports, 1972-1986/Bruits et vibration dans les mines: répertoire des rapports des recherche, 1972-1986. [Ottawa]: Mining Research Laboratories, Canada Centre for Mineral and Energy Technology, [1988]. ix, 12, xii, 11 p. (Mining Research Laboratories Divisional report ; MRL 88-5-LS) [4870]

Knight, Kenneth Drew; Nelson, James Gordon; Priddle, George Burton
Great Lakes shoreline resource management: a selected annotated bibliography. Waterloo, Ont.: Heritage Resources Centre, University of Waterloo, 1987. 43 p. (Occasional paper / Heritage Resources Centre, University of Waterloo ; 7; ISSN: 0829-0989); ISBN: 0-921245-12-2. [5245]

Knight, Kenneth W.
The literature of state budgeting in Australia, Canada, and the United States of America: a survey and select bibliography. St. Lucia, Queensland: University of Queensland Press, 1970. 51 p.; ISBN: 0-7022-0600-8. [2399]

Knight, Philip A.
Issues in law and aging: an annotated bibliography of legal literature. Winnipeg: Centre on Aging, University of Manitoba, 1983. 5, 3, 56 l. [2260]

Knight, Rolf
Work camps and company towns in Canada and the U.S.: an annotated bibliography. [Vancouver]: New Star Books, [c1975]. 80 p.; ISBN: 0-919888-60-7. [2821]

Knill, William Douglas, et al.
A classification of theses in education completed at the University of Alberta, 1929-1966. 3rd rev. ed. Edmonton: [s.n.], 1967. iv, 67 p. [6087]

Knopp, Edith
Bibliography of development education material produced by Canadian NGOs/Bibliographie du matériel sur l'éducation au développement produit par les ONG canadiennes.

Hull, Quebec: Canadian International Development Agency, Public Participation Program, 1984. iii, 70 p. [3625]

Knowlan, Anne McIntyre
The Fraser Valley: a bibliography. Abbotsford, B.C.: Fraser Valley College, [c1988]. vi, 132 p.: ill. [0597]

Koeneman, Joyce; Martinello, Gilda
Railroads. Monticello, Ill.: Vance Bibliographies, 1990. 26 p. (Public administration series: Bibliography ; P-2881; ISSN: 0193-970X); ISBN: 0-7920-0541-4. [4510]

Koester, C.B.
A bibliography of selected theses on [i.e. in] the library of the University of Alberta (Edmonton) relating to western Canada, 1915-1965. Edmonton: [s.n.], 1965. 21 l. [6083]

Kogon, Marilyn H.
Selected Ontario government publications for schools and libraries. [Toronto]: Ontario Library Association : Ministry of Government Services, 1979. 22 p.: ill.; ISBN: 0-7743-4216-1. [6323]

Kohler, Gernot; Hakim, Antjie; Bisci, Rosina
Arms and disarmament: a bibliography of Canadian research, 1965-1980. Ottawa: Operational Research and Analysis Establishment, Department of National Defence, 1981. xiii, 168 p. (ORAE extra-mural paper / Operational Research and Analysis Establishment, Department of National Defence ; no. 15) [2462]

Koltun, Lilly, et al.
"The photograph: an annotated bibliography for archivists." In: *Archivaria*; No. 5 (Winter 1977-1978) p. 124-140.; ISSN: 0318-6954. [1625]

Komorous, Hana
Union catalogue of British Columbia newspapers. Vancouver: British Columbia Library Association, 1987. 3 vol. [6044]

Konrad, Abram G.; Collin, Wilbur; Ottley, Horace
Community college research in western Canada: an annotated bibliography. Edmonton: Department of Educational Administration, Faculty of Education, University of Alberta, 1971. iv, 16 p. [3419]

Kortman, Gregory M.; Butler, H. Julene
Cordwood masonry construction: an annotated bibliography. Monticello, Ill.: Vance Bibliographies, 1987. 24 p. (Architecture series: Bibliography ; A-1797; ISSN: 0194-1356); ISBN: 0-55590-267-7. [0785]

Koshida, G.; Mortsch, Linda D.
Climate change and water level impacts on wetlands: a bibliography/Répercussions du changement climatique et du niveau des eaux sur les milieux humides: bibliographie. Downsview, Ont.: Canadian Climate Program, 1991. iv, 50 p. [5290]

Kossatz, V. Christine; Leavitt, Ferrin D.
The biology, and the chemical and cultural control of Canada thistle (Cirsium arvense): a bibliography for the Canadian prairies. Edmonton: Weed Control and Field Services Branch, Alberta Department of Agriculture, 1980. ii, 97 p. [5451]

Kossatz, V. Christine; Millan, Carol A.
Bibliography of the Northern Research Group. Beaverlodge, Alta.: Agriculture Canada, Research Station, 1978. 48, vii p.: map. [4675]

Kotin, David B.
"Graphic Publishers and the bibliographer: an introduction and checklist." In: *Papers of the Bibliographical Society of Canada*; Vol. 18 (1979) p. 47-54.; ISSN: 0067-6896. [1634]

Kotin, David B.; Rueter, Marilyn

Reader, lover of books, lover of heaven: a catalogue based on an exhibition of the book arts in Ontario. Willowdale, Ont.: North York Public Library, 1978-1981. 2 vol.: ill.; ISBN: 0-920552-01-3 (Vol. 1); 0-920552-02-1 (Vol. 2). [1644]

Kowand, Maureen

A bibliography of the river otter (Lutra canadensis). Edmonton: Canadian Wildlife Service, 1975. 27 l. [5394]

Kozak, Elaine

Applications of computer technology to law (1969-1978): a selected bibliography. Ottawa: Canadian Law Information Council, 1980. iii, 106 p. (Working paper / Canadian Law Information Council ; no. 4); ISBN: 0-920538-00-5. [2216]

Krause, F.F.; Collins, H.N.; French, R.

Bibliography of geological and engineering studies of the Cardium Formation and its hydrocarbon reservoirs. Calgary: Petroleum Recovery Institute, 1986. 1 vol. (looseleaf). [4853]

Krawczyk, Andrew, et al.

"Multicultural education bibliographies for elementary schools, secondary schools, and teachers." In: *Multiculturalism*; Vol. 10, nos. 2-3 (1986-1987) [3673]

Krawetz, Donna

The social impacts of layoffs: an annotated bibliography. Toronto: Social Planning Council of Metropolitan Toronto, 1980. 43 p. (Working papers for full employment ; no. 3) [3202]

Krayewski, Frances

Human rights in intergroup relations: a community approach. Toronto: Ontario Ministry of Labour, Research Branch, 1977. 13 p. (Bibliography series / Ontario Ministry of Labour, Research Branch ; no. 6) [3156]

Krech, Shepard

Native Canadian anthropology and history: a selected bibliography. Winnipeg: Rupert's Land Research Centre, University of Winnipeg, 1986. 214 p. [4086]

"Northern Athapaskan ethnology: an annotated bibliography of published materials, 1970-79." In: *Arctic Anthropology*; Vol. 17, no. 2 (1980) p. 68-105.; ISSN: 0066-6939. [4578]

Kreslins, Janis A.

Foreign affairs bibliography: a selected and annotated list of books on international relations, 1962-1972. New York: Published for the Council on Foreign Relations by R.R. Bowker Company, 1976. xxi, 921 p.; ISBN: 0-8352-0784-6. [2424]

Krogman, Ken K.

Annotated bibliography on soil erosion by wind applicable to southern Alberta. [Edmonton]: Soils Branch, Alberta Agriculture, 1983. 38 p. [4699]

Kronström, Denis

"La fonction d'orateur ou de président: bibliographie annotée." Dans: *Bulletin: Bibliothèque de l'Assemblée nationale du Québec*; Vol. 4, no 3 (juillet 1973) p. 31-61.; ISSN: 0701-6808. [2407]

"Liste sélective de publications parlementaires québécoises." Dans: *Bulletin: Bibliothèque de l'Assemblée nationale du Québec*; Vol. 6, no 1 (juin 1975) p. 22-34.; ISSN: 0701-6808. [6299]

Krotki, Joanna E.

Local histories of Alberta: an annotated bibliography. Edmonton: Department of Slavic and East European Studies, University of Alberta, 1983. xviii, 430 p. [0538]

Krouse, Howard Roy

Environmental sulphur isotope studies in Alberta: a review. Calgary: Acid Deposition Research Program, 1987. 89 p.; ISBN: 0-921625-05-7. [5246]

Krueger, Donald R.

Acid rain (part 1): a selected bibliography. Toronto: Ontario Legislative Library, Research and Information Services, 1984. 12 l. [5212]

Acid rain (part 2): a selected bibliography. Toronto: Ontario Legislative Library, Research and Information Services, 1984. 12 l. [5213]

Backbenchers: a selected bibliography. Toronto: Ontario Legislative Library, Research and Information Services, 1983. 4 l. (Bibliographies and lists / Ontario Legislative Library, Research and Information Services ; no. 83-02; ISSN: 0833-2142) [2475]

Business in the House: a selected bibliography. Toronto: Ontario Legislative Library, Research and Information Services, 1983. 3 l. (Bibliographies and lists / Ontario Legislative Library, Research and Information Services ; no. 83-09; ISSN: 0833-2142) [2476]

The Canadian Charter of Rights and Freedoms: a selected bibliography. Toronto: Ontario Legislative Library, 1984. 22 l. [2269]

Closure: an annotated bibliography. Toronto: Ontario Legislative Library, Research and Information Services, 1983. 3 l. (Bibliographies and lists / Ontario Legislative Library, Research and Information Services ; no. 83-07; ISSN: 0833-2142) [2477]

Legislative process in Ontario: a selected annotated bibliography. Toronto: Ontario Legislative Library, Research and Information Services, 1985. 5 l. (Bibliographies and lists. New series / Ontario Legislative Library, Research and Information Services ; no. 8; ISSN: 0833-2150) [2493]

Office of the Speaker: a selected bibliography. Toronto: Ontario Legislative Library, Research and Information Services, 1983. 4 l. (Bibliographies and lists / Ontario Legislative Library, Research and Information Services ; no. 83-03; ISSN: 0833-2142) [2478]

Quebec politics in historical and cultural perspective: a selected bibliography. Monticello, Ill.: Vance Bibliographies, 1981. 77 p. (Public administration series: Bibliography ; P-848; ISSN: 0193-970X) [2463]

Krummes, Daniel C.

Highways. Monticello, Ill.: Vance Bibliographies, 1990. 67 p. (Public administration series: Bibliography ; P-2885; ISSN: 0193-970X); ISBN: 0-7920-0545-7. [4511]

Kuehl, Warren F.

Dissertations in history: an index to dissertations completed in history departments of United States and Canadian universities, 1873-1960. [Lexington]: University of Kentucky Press, 1965. 249 p. [6084]

Kumar, Pradeep

Canadian industrial relations information: sources, technical notes and glossary. Kingston, Ont.: Industrial Relations Centre, Queen's University, 1979. viii, 166 p.; ISBN: 0-88886-101-X. [2859]

Kupsch, Walter Oscar

Annotated bibliography of Saskatchewan geology (1823-1970 incl.). Rev. ed. Regina: Department of Mineral Resources, Saskatchewan Geological Survey, 1973. xxiii, 421 p.: ill., maps. (Geological Survey report ; no. 9, revised edition,

1973) [4780]

"Nineteenth century geological writings and writers on the Canadian Arctic." In: *Musk-ox*; No. 28 (1981) p. 65-78.; ISSN: 0077-2542. [4820]

Kurtz, Norman R.; Googins, Bradley; Howard, William

Occupational alcoholism: an annotated bibliography. Toronto: Addiction Research Foundation of Ontario, c1984. xi, 218 p. (Bibliographic series / Addiction Research Foundation of Ontario ; no. 17; ISSN: 0065-1885); ISBN: 0-88868-101-1. [3260]

Kwamena, Felix A.; Brassard, Charles; Wright, Don

Les incidences à terres de l'exploitation en mer des hydrocarbures: bibliographie annotée. Ottawa: Service de la protection de l'environnement, Environnement Canada, 1983. iv, 123 p. (Rapport d'analyse économique et technique ; SPE 3-ES-83-4F); ISBN: 0-662-92198-4. [5197]

Onshore impacts of offshore hydrocarbon development: annotated bibliography. Ottawa: Environmental Protection Service, Environment Canada, 1983. iii, 108 p. (Economic and technical review report / Environmental Protection Service ; EPS 3-ES-83-4); ISBN: 0-662-12686-6. [5198]

Kydd, Donna L.

Towards a legal education and information program for native people: a review of the literature and annotated bibliography. [Saskatoon: Native Law Centre, University of Saskatchewan], 1979. vi, 73 p. [4006]

Kydd, Donna L.; Smith, Laurie J.

Legal information and education: an annotated bibliography. [Saskatoon: Native Law Centre, University of Saskatchewan], 1977. iv, 64 l. [2172]

L'Espérance, Jeanne

Vers des horizons nouveaux: la femme canadienne de 1870 à 1940. [Ottawa]: Archives publiques Canada, c1982. 69, 63 p.; ISBN: 0-662-52008-4. [3809]

The widening sphere: women in Canada, 1870-1940. [Ottawa]: Public Archives Canada, c1982. 63, 69 p.: ill.; ISBN: 0-662-52008-4. [3810]

L'Heureux, Lucie

Thèses et cours sur le Québec dans les institutions d'enseignement supérieur en France. Paris: Centre de coopération universitaire franco-québécoise, 1988. 159 p. [6193]

Laakso, Lila

"E.J. Pratt: a preliminary checklist." In: *Canadian Library Journal*; Vol. 34, no. 4 (August 1977) p. 273, 275+.; ISSN: 0008-4352. [7244]

"E.J. Pratt: a preliminary checklist of publications by and about him with a shortlist of manuscript collections." In: *The E.J. Pratt symposium*, edited by Glenn Cleaver. Ottawa: University of Ottawa Press, 1977. P. 141-169. (Reappraisals: Canadian writers); ISBN: 0-7766-4384-3. [7245]

Laakso, Lila, et al.

E.J. Pratt: an annotated bibliography. Downsview, Ont.: ECW Press, c1980. P. 147-220.; ISBN: 0-920763-60-X. [7246]

"E.J. Pratt: an annotated bibliography." In: *The annotated bibliography of Canada's major authors*, Vol. 2, edited by Robert Lecker and Jack David. Downsview, Ont.: ECW Press, c1980. P. 147-220.; ISBN: 0-920802-40-0. [7247]

L'abandon des voies ferrées au Canada: l'utilisation de historiques: bibliographie commentée. [Ottawa]: Parcs Canada, 1979. 97 p. [1795]

Labelle, Ronald; Beaulieu, Jean; Breton, Marcel

Inventaire des sources en folklore acadien. Moncton, N.–B.: Centre d'études acadiennes, Université de Moncton, 1984. viii, 194 p.: carte.; ISBN: 0-919241-20-4. [4596]

Laberge, Jacques

Impacts de la télématique sur l'aménagement et l'habitat: essai et bibliographie. Montréal: I.N.R.S.–Urbanisation, 1982. 73 p. (Études et documents / Institut national de la recherche scientifique ; 32); ISBN: 2-89228-032-X. [4395]

Laberge, Raymond

"Partis politiques québécois, 1968-1982: bibliographie sélective." Dans: *Bulletin: Bibliothèque de l'Assemblée nationale du Québec*; Vol. 13, no 1 (janvier 1983) p. 21-57.; ISSN: 0701-6808. [2479]

Labrie, Gisèle; Tremblay, Marc-André

"Études psychologiques et socioculturelles de l'alcoolisme: inventaire des travaux disponibles au Québec depuis 1960." Dans: *Toxicomanies*; Vol. 10, no 2 (avril-juin 1977) p. 85-135.; ISSN: 0041-0098. [3157]

Lacasse, Jean-Paul

"Les nouvelles perspectives de l'étude des frontières politiques: revue de quelques contributions récentes." Dans: *Cahiers de géographie de Québec*; Vol. 18, no 43 (avril 1974) p. 187-200.; ISSN: 0007-9766. [3003]

Lachance, André

Textes et documents pour servir à l'étude de l'histoire économique et sociale de la Nouvelle-France. Sherbrooke: Département d'histoire, Université de Sherbrooke, [1969]. 112 f. [1960]

Lacoste, Norbert

"Bibliographie sommaire des études sur Montréal, 1958-1964." Dans: *Recherches sociographiques*; Vol. 6, no 3 (septembre-décembre 1965) p. 277-281.; ISSN: 0034-1282. [0294]

Lacourcière, Luc

"Comptines canadiennes." Dans: *Archives de Folklore*; Vol. 3 (1948) p. 109-157.; ISSN: 0085-5243. [4529]

Lacroix, Benoît; Chrestien, Jean-Pierre

"Initiation bibliographique à la connaissance du Canada français." Dans: *Annales de Normandie*; Vol. 27, no 2 (juin 1977) p. 219-228.; ISSN: 0003-4134. [0347]

Lacroix, Benoît; Grammond, Madeleine

Canada: Tome 1: Le Québec. Turnhout (Belgique): Brepols; Montréal: Bellarmin, [1989]. 153 p. (La Piété populaire: répertoire bibliographique); ISBN: 2-89007-690-3. [1569]

Religion populaire au Québec: typologie des sources: bibliographie sélective (1900-1980). Québec: Institut québécois de recherche sur la culture, 1985. 175 p. (Instruments de travail / Institut québécois de recherche sur la culture ; no 10); ISBN: 2-89224-048-4. [1560]

Lacroix, Jean-Michel

Anatomie de la presse ethnique au Canada. [Bordeaux]: Presses universitaires de Bordeaux, 1988. 493 p.: ill.; ISBN: 2-85892-113-X. [6047]

"A selected bibliography on Margaret Laurence." In: *Études canadiennes: Canadian studies*; No. 11 (1981) p. 155-164.; ISSN: 0153-1700. [7123]

Lacroix, Lucien

Bibliographie 1975-1989, Service de la recherche [Centre de services sociaux de Québec]. Québec: Centre de services sociaux de Québec, 1989. 45 p. [3330]

Ladanyi, Branko
Literature review: field tests of foundations in permafrost. Montréal. École polytechnique de Montréal, 1980. 58 p : ill. [5779]

Laflèche, Guy
"Bibliographie analytique et critique des saints Martyrs canadiens." Dans: *Les saints Martyrs canadiens*. Laval, Québec: Singulier, 1988. P. 83-227.; ISBN: 2-920580-01-9. [1567]
Le récit de voyage en Nouvelle-France: (FRA 6661): Cahier bibliographique. Montréal: Université de Montréal, Département d'études françaises, 1977. v, 70 f. [1993]

Lafontaine, Suzanne
Canadian college library handbooks: a list of orientation materials held in the Library Documentation Centre / Guides à l'intention des usagers des bibliothèques de collèges canadiens: liste des manuels et brochures conservés au Centre de documentation sur les bibliothèques. Ottawa: National Library of Canada, 1983. 9 p. (Bibliographies / Library Documentation Centre; ISSN: 0226-4226) [1655]
Canadian government library handbooks: a list of orientation materials held in the Library Documentation Centre / Guides à l'intention des usagers des bibliothèques gouvernementales canadiennes: liste des manuels et brochures conservés au Centre de documentation sur les bibliothèques. Ottawa: National Library of Canada, 1982. 8 p. (Bibliographies / Library Documentation Centre; ISSN: 0226-4226) [1650]

Lafontaine, Thérèse E.
"Louis Riel: a preliminary bibliography, 1963-1968." In: *Louis Riel & the Métis*, edited by A.S. Lussier. Winnipeg: Pemmican Publications, 1983. P. 129-162.; ISBN: 0-919143-16-4. [7265]

Laforte, Conrad
Le catalogue de la chanson folklorique française. Nouv. éd. augm. et entièrement refondue. Québec: Presses de l'Université Laval, 1977-1987. 6 vol.: cartes. (Archives de folklore ; 18-23) [0929]
"Poétiques de la chanson traditionnelle française: bibliographie." Dans: *Archives de Folklore*; Vol. 17 (1976) p. 127-142.; ISSN: 0085-5243. [0856]

Lafortune, Andrée; Marchis-Mouren, Marie-Françoise
Revue de littérature: le micro-ordinateur comme outil de vérification dans les cabinets d'experts-comptables. Montréal: École des hautes études commerciales, 1989. 37 f. (Rapport de recherche / École des hautes études commerciales ; no 89-08; ISSN: 0709-986X) [2754]

Lafrenière, Gilles R.
Industrial security – Canada: bibliography. Ottawa: R.C.M.P. HQ Library, 1980. ii, 43 p. [2661]

Lafrenière, Normand
Bilan des études spécifiques au site de Coteau-du-Lac. Québec: Parcs Canada, 1981. [150] f. [4582]

Lahaise, Robert
Civilisation et vie quotidienne en Nouvelle-France: en 1000 diapositives, commentaire et bibliographie. Montréal: Guérin, [1973]. ix, 207 p. [1978]
Le Québec, 1830-1939: bibliographie thématique: histoire et littérature. LaSalle, Québec: Hurtubise HMH, 1990. 173 p.; ISBN: 2-89045-862-8. [0408]

LaHaye, Monique; Lefrançois, Richard
Répertoire de la recherche sociale au Québec, 1975-1981. Sherbrooke, Québec: Département de service social, Université de Sherbrooke, [1982]. 157 p. (Collection recherche sociale / Département de service social, Université de Sherbrooke ; no 2) [3239]

Laine, Edward W.
Archival sources for the study of Finnish Canadians. Ottawa: National Archives of Canada, 1989. vii, 104, 104 v p. (Ethnocultural guide series / National Archives of Canada); ISBN: 0-662-56435-9. [4269]
Sources d'archives sur les Finno-Canadiens. Ottawa: Archives nationales du Canada, 1989. v, 104, 104, vii p. (Collection des guides ethnoculturels / Archives nationales du Canada); ISBN: 0-662-56435-9. [4270]

Laird, Marshall
Bibliography of the natural history of Newfoundland and Labrador. London: Academic Press, 1980. lxxi, 376 p.: ill., maps.; ISBN: 0-12-434050-4. [5452]

Lajoie, Yvan
"Essai de bibliographie des oeuvres de Rina Lasnier." Dans: *Liberté*; No 108 (novembre-décembre 1976) p. 143-154.; ISSN: 0024-2020. [7121]

Lake Winnipeg, Churchill and Nelson Rivers Study Board (Canada)
Social and economic studies. Winnipeg: The Board, [1975]. 8 vol. in 12: ill., maps (some folded). [3969]

Lakhanpal, S.K.
Performance appraisal in libraries: a select annotated bibliography. Saskatoon: Collection Development, University of Saskatchewan Library, 1982. 37 l. [1651]
User education in North American academic libraries: a select annotated bibliography. Saskatoon: Collection Development Department, University of Saskatchewan Library, 1992. 5, 67, 17 l.; ISBN: 0-88880-271-4. [1733]

Lakos, Amos
Comparative provincial politics of Canada: a bibliography of select periodical articles, 1970-1977. Waterloo, Ont.: University of Waterloo Library, c1978. iii, 67 p. (University of Waterloo Library bibliography ; no. 2; ISSN: 0829-948X); ISBN: 0-920834-02-7. [2435]
Terrorism, 1970-1978, a bibliography. Waterloo, Ontario: University of Waterloo Library, 1979. vi, 73 p. (University of Waterloo Library bibliography ; no. 4; ISSN: 0829-948X); ISBN: 0-920834-06-X. [2197]
Terrorism, 1980-1990: a bibliography. Boulder: Westview Press, 1991. x, 443 p.; ISBN: 0-8133-8035-9. [2353]

Lakos, Amos; Cooper, Andrew F.
Strategic minerals: a bibliography. Waterloo, Ont.: University of Waterloo Library, 1987. ix, 132 p. (University of Waterloo Library bibliography ; no. 14; ISSN: 0829-948X); ISBN: 0-920834-44-2. [4861]

Lalonde, Émile
Bio-bibliographie de Monseigneur Antoine d'Eschambault, p.d., diocèse de Saint-Boniface, Manitoba. Saint-Boniface: Collège de Saint-Boniface, 1962. xi, 104 p.: portr. [6970]

Lalonde, Émile; Manseau, Edith
Guide bibliographique en sciences religieuses. 2e éd. rev. et augm. Trois-Rivières: Université du Québec à Trois-Rivières, [1974]. 31 f. (Publication / Université du Québec à Trois-Rivières, Bibliothèque ; no 1) [1533]

Lalonde, Francine

Bibliographie choisie sur les minorités francophones au Canada/Selected bibliography on Francophone minorities in Canada. [Ottawa]: Direction de la recherche et de la planification, Programme d'expansion du bilinguisme, Secrétariat d'État, 1972. 2 vol. [3109]

Lalonde, Girouard, Letendre & Associes

Bibliographie annotée: documents comprenant des données de base pour la région du Québec. [Montréal]: Environnement Canada, Direction générale régionale, Région du Québec, 1980. 340 f. [5164]

Lam, Van Be

L'immigration et les communautés culturelles du Québec, 1968-1990: bibliographie sélective annotée. Québec: Documentor, 1991. 142 p.; ISBN: 2-89123-114-7. [4285]

Lamarche, Rolande; Sabourin, Conrad

Psycholinguistique et sociolinguistique au Québec. [Montréal: Éditions fipf (Fédération internationale des professeurs de français)], 1974. 426 p. [1429]

Lamarche, Rolande; Tarrab, Elca; Daoust, Denise

Bibliographie de travaux québécois. [Québec]: Office de la langue française, c1988. 2 vol.; ISBN: 2-550-19244-3 (vol. 1); 2-550-19245-1 (vol. 2). [1478]

Lamarre, Patricia

Professional development of core French teachers: selective review of general literature on inservice education and specific literature on inservice education of second language teachers. Winnipeg: Canadian Association of Second Language Teachers, 1986. iii, 168 p.; ISBN: 0-921238-04-5. [3658]

Lamb, Eila; Nevison, Myrne

Annotated bibliography for guidance and counseling. Vancouver: Extension Department, University of British Columbia, [1969]. 26 l. [3402]

Lamb, William Kaye

F.W. Howay: a bibliography. Vancouver: William Hoffer and Stephen Lunsford, 1982. [38] p.: port. [7069]

"Seventy-five years of Canadian bibliography." In: *Proceedings and Transactions of the Royal Society of Canada*; Series 3, vol. 51, section 2 (1957) p. 1-11.; ISSN: 0316-4616. [1583]

Lambe, Lawrence M.

"Bibliography of Canadian zoology." In: *Proceedings and Transactions of the Royal Society of Canada*; Series 3, vol. 2, section 4 (1908)-series 3, vol. 7, section 4 (1913) [5313]

Lambert, Elisabeth; Lavoie, André; Dubois, Jean-Marie

Télédétection des algues marines des côtes du Québec: 1 – Bibliographie mondiale annotée. Québec: Gouvernement du Québec, Ministère de l'agriculture, des pêcheries et de l'alimentation, 1984. 44 p. (Cahier de l'information / Direction des pêches maritimes ; no 112); ISBN: 2-550-11666-6. [5499]

Lambert, Ronald D.

Nationalism and national ideologies in Canada and Quebec: a bibliography. rev. ed. [S.l.: s.n.], 1975. 144 l. [2418]

The sociology of contemporary Quebec nationalism: an annotated bibliography and review. New York: Garland Publishing, 1981. lxvi, 148 p. (Canadian review of studies in nationalism ; v. 2) (Garland reference library of social sciences ; v. 78); ISBN: 0-8240-9480-8. [0372]

Lambert, Rosalind; Lavallée, Laval

Bibliography on Canadian land market mechanisms and land information systems. Ottawa: Ministry of State for Urban Affairs, 1975. x, 50 p. (Urban paper / Canada Ministry of State for Urban Affairs ; A-76-1; ISSN: 0318-1286) [4350]

Lamirande, Emilien

"Unpublished academic literature concerning the Oblate missions of the Pacific coast." In: *Études oblates*; Vol. 16, no 4 (octobre-décembre 1957) p. 360-379.; ISSN: 0318-9384. [1512]

Lamonde, Francine Neilson

Répertoire bibliographique des documents du Bureau d'aménagement de l'est du Québec. Québec: Conseil d'orientation économique, Bureau d'étude en aménagement régional, 1968. ii, 118 p. (Planification du développement régional: série 1: Inventaire et méthodologie ; cahier 1-5) [6268]

Lamonde, Yvan

"Bibliographie des bibliographies des historiens canadiens-français du Québec." Dans: *Recherches sociographiques*; Vol. 12, no 2 (mai-août 1971) p. 237-248.; ISSN: 0034-1282. [1973]

Guide d'histoire du Québec. Sillery: Boréal Express, c1976. 94 p. (Collection Mékinac); ISBN: 0-88503-051-6. [0340]

L'histoire des idées au Québec, 1760-1960: bibliographie des études. Montréal: Bibliothèque nationale du Québec, 1989. 167 p.: ill., fac.–sim.; ISBN: 2-551-12140-X. [2076]

"Inventaire des études et des sources pour l'étude des associations 'litteraires' québécoises francophones au XIXe siècle (1840-1900)." Dans: *Recherches sociographiques*; Vol. 16, no 2 (mai-août 1975) p. 261-275.; ISSN: 0034-1282. [1985]

Je me souviens: la littérature personnelle au Québec, 1860-1980. Québec: Institut québécois de recherche sur la culture, 1983. 275 p. (Instruments de travail / Institut québécois de recherche sur la culture ; no 9; ISSN: 0714-0576); ISBN: 2-89224-028-X. [1205]

La radiodiffusion au Canada et au Québec: guide préliminaire de recherche. Montréal: Centre d'études canadiennes-françaises, McGill University, 1976. 8 f. [0961]

"La recherche sur l'histoire de l'imprimé et du livre québécois." Dans: *Revue d'histoire de l'Amérique française*; Vol. 28, no 3 (décembre 1974) p. 405-414.; ISSN: 0035-2357. [1605]

Lamonde, Yvan; Olivier, Daniel

Les bibliothèques personnelles au Québec: inventaire analytique et préliminaire des sources. Montréal: Ministère des Affaires culturelles, Bibliothèque nationale du Québec, 1983. 131 p. ill.; ISBN: 2-551-05267-X. [1656]

Lamontagne, Richard; Ménard, Marleine

Le royaume du Saguenay: exposition de livres anciens. Chicoutimi, Québec: Bouquinerie Jacques-Cartier, 1988. 42 p. [0402]

Lamothe, Emélie S.

Literature review of the studies on uptake, retention and distribution of radionuclides by the foetus. Ottawa: Atomic Energy Control Board, 1989. 23 p. [5690]

Lamping, Donna L.

Review of the literature on HIV infection and mental health. [Ottawa]: Health and Welfare Canada, 1990. iv, 66, 51, v, 2 p.; ISBN: 0-662-57720-5. [5697]

Revue de la documentation sur l'infection à VIH et la santé mentale. [Ottawa]: Santé et Bien-être social Canada, 1990. 2, v, 51, 66, iv p.; ISBN: 0-662-57720-5. [5698]

Lamson, Cynthia; Reade, J.G.

Atlantic fisheries and social sciences: a guide to sources. Halifax, N.S.: Fisheries and Oceans Canada, 1987. vi, 10 p.:

map. (Canadian technical report of fisheries and aquatic sciences ; no. 1549; ISSN: 0706-6457) [4909]

Lamy, Jean-Christian

Le Québec: guide documentaire élaboré par Jean-Christian Lamy avec le concours des bibliographes de la Centrale des bibliothèques du Québec. Paris: Centre national de documentation pédagogique, 1980. 108 p. (Collection guides documentaires / Centre national de documentation pédagogique ; no 7) [0361]

Lamy, Nicole

Bibliographie sur les maisons de commerce. Montréal: École des hautes études commerciales, 1982. 21 f. (Cahiers du Centre d'études en administration internationale ; no 82-10; ISSN: 0709-986X) [2682]

Lanari, Robert

"Bibliographie par village, de la population Inuit du Nouveau-Québec." Dans: *Recherches amérindiennes au Québec*; Vol. 3, nos 3/4 (1973) p. 103-125.; ISSN: 0008-3496. [3942]

Northwest Territories community bibliography/ Bibliographie par communauté Territoires du Nord-Ouest. Ottawa: Indian and Northern Affairs, 1976. 79 p.: map (folded).; ISBN: 0-662-00263-6. [0629]

Lancaster, John E.; Alexander, Dennis J.

Newcastle disease virus and spread: a review of some of the literature. Ottawa: Canada Department of Agriculture, 1975. 79 p.: ill., maps (2 folded). (Monograph / Canada Department of Agriculture ; no. 11) [4667]

Lanctot, Gustave

L'oeuvre de la France en Amérique du Nord: bibliographie sélective et critique. Montréal: Fides, 1951. 185 p. [1923]

Land, Bernard

The toxicity of drilling fluid components to aquatic biological systems: a literature review. Winnipeg: Freshwater Institute, Research and Development Directorate, Fisheries and Marine Service, Environment Canada, 1984. iv l., 33 p. (Fisheries and Marine Service Technical report ; no. 487; ISSN: 0701-7626) [5214]

Land, Brian

"Information desk: [Directory of publications issued by Canada's financial and investment community]." In: *Canadian Business*; Vol. 31, no. 9 (September 1958) p. 102, 104+.; ISSN: 0820-9510. [2567]

"Information desk: [Directory of publications issued periodically by chambers of commerce and boards of trade in Canada]." In: *Canadian Business*; Vol. 31, no. 11 (November 1958) p. 82, 84+.; ISSN: 0820-9510. [2568]

"Information desk: [list of city and trade directories published in Canada]." In: *Canadian Business*; Vol. 31, no. 4 (April 1958) p. 32, 37-44+.; ISSN: 0820-9510. [2569]

"Labor publications distributed in Canada." In: *Canadian Business*; Vol. 31, no. 6 (June 1958) p. 40, 42-45.; ISSN: 0820-9510. [2791]

Sources of information for Canadian business. 4th ed. Ottawa: Canadian Chamber of Commerce, 1985. iv, 108 p. [2710]

Land-related Information Systems Co-ordination Project

A consolidated bibliography on land-related information systems. Edmonton, Alta.: Treasury, Bureau of Statistics, 1981. iv, 408 p.; ISBN: 0-9690713-1-0. [3033]

Landar, Herbert

"An Innuit bibliography." In: *Papers on Eskimo and Aleut linguistics*, edited by Eric P. Hamp. Chicago: Chicago Linguistic Society, c1976. P. 108-139. [1436]

Lande, Lawrence M.

Canadian imprints a checklist. Montreal: McGill University, 1975. 62 p.: facsims. (Lawrence Lande Foundation for Canadian Historical Research ; no. 13); ISBN: 0-88940-029-6. [0114]

Canadian miscellanies: a checklist. Montreal: McGill University, 1975. 68 p.: facsims. (Lawrence Lande Foundation for Canadian Historical Research ; no. 12); ISBN: 0-88940-028-8. [0115]

A checklist of early music relating to Canada, collected, compiled and annotated by Lawrence M. Lande from his private library. Montreal: McGill University, 1973. 23 p.: facsims. (Lawrence Lande Foundation for Canadian Historical Research ; no. 8) [0838]

A checklist of printed and manuscript material relating to the Canadian Indian, also relating to the Pacific North West Coast. Montreal: McGill University, 1974. 78 p.: ill., facsims. (Lawrence Lande Foundation for Canadian Historical Research ; no. 9) [3956]

Confederation pamphlets: a checklist – liste abrégée. Montreal: McGill University, 1967. 67 p.: facsims. (1 folded in pocket). (Lawrence Lande Foundation for Canadian Historical Research ; no. 3) [1954]

The development of the voyageur contract (1686-1821): a monograph. Montreal: Lawrence Lande Foundation for Canadian Historical Research, 1989. xx, 151 p., [4] p. of pl.: ill., maps, facsims.; ISBN: 0-96941-850-7. [2077]

The founder of our monetary system, John Law, Compagnie des Indes & the early economy of North America: a second bibliography. Montreal: Lawrence Lande Foundation for Canadian Historical Research, McGill University, 1984. xxxix, 187, [1] p.: ill. facsims. [2040]

John Law, Banque royale & Compagnie des Indes: a bibliographical monograph. Montreal: [s.n.], 1980. 2 vol.: facsims. [2010]

John Law, early trade rivalries among nations and the beginnings of banking in North America: a sixth bibliography. Montreal: Lawrence Lande Foundation for Canadian Historical Research, 1988. xxi, 197 p.: ill. [2071]

John Law, the evolution of his system: a seventh bibliography. Montreal: Lawrence Lande Foundation for Canadian Historical Research, 1989. xl, 183 p.: ill.; ISBN: 0-9694185-1-5. [2078]

John Law, the French régime and the beginnings of exploration, trade and paper money in North America: a third bibliography. Montreal: Lawrence Lande Foundation for Canadian Historical Research, 1985. xii, 155 p.: ill. facsims. [2048]

John Law: the creditability of land and the development of paper money and trade in North America: a fifth bibliography. Montreal: Lawrence Lande Foundation for Canadian Historical Research, 1987. liii, 263 p.: ill. [2061]

The Lawrence Lande Collection of Canadiana in the Redpath Library of McGill University; a bibliography, collected, arranged and annotated by Lawrence Lande, with an introduction by Edgar Andrew Collard. Montreal: Lawrence Lande Foundation for Canadian Historical Research, 1965. xxxv, 301 p.: ill., facsims., maps. [6772]

The Moravian missions to the Eskimos of Labrador: a checklist of manuscripts and printed material from 1715 to 1967, supplemented by other works on the Eskimo of Canada. Montreal: McGill University, 1973. 32 p.: ill., facsims. (Lawrence Lande Foundation for Canadian Historical Research ; no. 7) [1531]

The political economy of New France: as developed by John Law, Compagnie des Indes & the French-Canadian traders: a bibliography, compiled by Lawrence M. Lande from manuscripts and printed material in his private collection. [Montreal: s.n.], 1983. xii, 98 p.: ill., facsims. [2027]

Landry, Charlotte
Franco-Albertan newspapers 1898-1982: a guide. Edmonton: [C. Landry], 1984. 65 l. [6033]

Landry, Francine
Bibliographie des documents québécois sur la reconnaissance des acquis extrascolaires. Montréal: Fédération des cégeps, 1988. 45 p. (Fonds et réflexions / Fédération des cégeps ; 15); ISBN: 2-89100-048-X. [3687]
Revue de littérature sur le rôle des activités d'apprentissage dans l'enseignement à distance. Montréal: Télé-université, Direction de la recherche et des études avancées, 1988. 47 p. (Notes de recherche / Direction de la recherche et des études avancées, Université du Québec); ISBN: 2-76240-078-3. [3688]

Landry, Renée
Bibliographie de Marius Barbeau. [Ottawa]: Musée national de l'Homme, 1969. 16 f. [6829]

Landry, Yves
"Bibliographie courante sur l'histoire de la population canadienne et la démographie historique au Canada/A current bibliography on the history of Canadian population and historical demography in Canada." Dans: *Histoire sociale: Social History*; Vol. 21, no 42 (novembre 1988)-vol. 25, no 50 (novembre 1992) [3068]

Landsburg, June; Lee, Linda
Annotated bibliography of print materials on instructional development and related matters. Ottawa: Carleton University, 1976. [1] l., 83 p. [3514]

Lane, Daniel E.
Management science in the control and management of fisheries: an annotated bibliography. Ottawa: Faculty of Administration, University of Ottawa, 1990. i, 32 p. (Working papers series / Faculty of Administration, University of Ottawa ; 90-6; ISSN: 0701-3086) [4914]

Lane, E. David
A bibliography on the white sturgeon, (Acipenser transmontanus) Richardson, 1836. Nanaimo, B.C.: Department of Fisheries and Oceans, 1985. iv, 33 p. (Canadian manuscript report of fisheries and aquatic sciences ; no. 1828; ISSN: 0706-6473) [5512]

Lane, Kenneth
Native land bibliography/Bibliographie sur le droit des autochtones. Ottawa: Library, Supreme Court of Canada, 1989. 19 l. [2326]

Lane, Marion
"Children's rights: an annotated bibliography." In: *Emergency Librarian*; Vol. 8, no. 3-4 (January-April 1981) p. 23-26.; ISSN: 0315-8888. [2235]

Lang, A.H.
A list of publications on prospecting in Canada and related subjects. Ottawa: Department of Mines and Technical Surveys, 1954. ii, 60 p. (Geological Survey of Canada Paper ; 54-1) [4748]

Lang, Reg; Lounds, John
Information resources for municipal energy planning and management. Downsview, Ont.: York University, Faculty of Environmental Studies, 1979. 125 p. (Working paper / York University Faculty of Environmental Studies ; no. 1) [4376]

Langhammer, Else Birgit
The William Palmer Witton Canadian collection. Hamilton, Ont.: [s.n.], 1967. 24, 14, [13] l. [6775]

Langlois, Pierre
Génie civil, travaux publics, terrassement, équipments de chantier et construction routière: bibliographies. Québec: Service des publications, Office de la langue française, 1982. 127 p.; ISBN: 2-551-04760-9. [1456]

Langor, David William; Raske, A.G.
Annotated bibliography of the eastern larch beetle, Dendroctonus simplex Leconte (Coleoptera: Scolytidae). St. John's: Newfoundland Forestry Centre, 1988. iii, 38 p. (Newfoundland Forestry Centre Information report ; N-X-266; ISSN: 0704-7657); ISBN: 0-662-16689-2. [5543]

LaNoue, George R.
A bibliography of doctoral dissertations undertaken in American and Canadian universities (1940-1962) on religion and politics. New York: National Council of the Churches of Christ in the United States of America, c1963. 49 p. [6078]

Laperrière, Guy
Bibliographie d'histoire des Cantons de l'Est/History of the Eastern Townships: a bibliography. 2e rev. et augm. éd. [Sherbrooke, Québec]: Département d'histoire, Université de Sherbrooke, 1986. 210 p. (Collection Histoire des Cantons de l'Est ; no 1); ISBN: 2-89343-006-6. [0394]
"Plan du cours: histoire du syndicalisme au Québec: bibliographie." Dans: *Histoire des travailleurs québécois: Bulletin RCHTQ*; Vol. 2, no 2 (juin-juillet 1975) p. 29-40.; ISSN: 0315-7938. [2822]

Laperrière, René
Bibliographie du droit du travail canadien et québécois, 1964-1983. Cowansville, Québec: Éditions Y. Blais, c1984. xv, 70 p.; ISBN: 2-89073-515-X. [2890]

Lapierre, André
"Bibliographie linguistique de l'Ontario français." Dans: *Cahiers linguistiques d'Ottawa*; No 12 (février 1984) p. 1-38.; ISSN: 0315-3967. [1461]

Lapierre-Adamcyk, Evelyne
"Bibliographie des travaux réalisés dans le cadre des enquêtes de fécondité au Québec, 1971 et 1976." Dans: *Cahiers québécois de démographie*; Vol. 9, no 1 (avril 1990) p. 139-141.; ISSN: 0380-1721. [3061]

Lapkin, Sharon, et al.
"Annotated list of French tests." In: *Canadian Modern Language Review*; Vol. 41, no. 1 (October 1984) p. 93-109.; ISSN: 0008-4506. [3626]

Laplante, Louise
Compositeurs canadiens contemporains. Montréal: Presses de l'Université du Québec, 1977. xxviii, 382 p.: [8] f. de pl., ill.; ISBN: 0-7770-0205-1. [0861]

Laplante, Michelle
Répertoire des productions audio-visuelles sur la condition féminine. Québec: Conseil du statut de la femme, 1983. xix, 206 p.; ISBN: 2-550-02964-X. [6654]

Lapointe, Jean-Pierre; Levasseur, Jean

"Bibliographie de Jacques Poulin." Dans: *Voix et Images*; Vol. 15, no 1 (printemps 1989) p. 58-64.; ISSN: 0318-9201 [7243]

Lapointe, Michèle

Modalités d'ensemencement pour l'omble de Fontaine: revue et analyse critique de la littérature, rapport. Québec: Direction de la gestion des espèces et des habitats, 1990. vi, 51 p.; ISBN: 2-550-21139-1. [5554]

Lapointe, Raoul

"Bibliographie: Articles et ouvrages concernant Rodolphe Pagé." Dans: *Saguenayensia*; Vol. 29, no 3 (juillet-septembre 1987) p. 31-33.; ISSN: 0581-295X. [7235]

Guide bibliographique sur la région du Saguenay-Lac-Saint-Jean. [Chicoutimi]: Université du Québec à Chicoutimi, Service de documentation en études et interventions régionales, 1986. 35 f.; ISBN: 2-920751-04-2. [0395]

Lapointe, Serge, et al.

L'animation sociale au Québec: bibliographie. Rimouski: Groupe de recherche interdisciplinaire en développement de l'est du Québec, Université du Québec à Rimouski, 1978. xiv, 91 p. (Cahiers du GRIDEQ / Groupe de recherche interdisciplinaire en développement de l'est du Québec ; no 4) [3172]

Larivière-Derome, Céline

Inventaire des documents Edmond Dyonnet conservés au Centre de recherche en civilisation canadienne-française. Ottawa: Centre de recherche en civilisation canadienne-française, Université d'Ottawa, 1976. 51 p. (Documents de travail du Centre de recherche en civilisation canadienne-française ; 5) [6963]

Larned, Josephus Nelson

The literature of American history: a bibliographical guide in which the scope, character, and comparative worth of books in selected lists are set forth in brief notes by critics of authority. Boston: Published for the American Library Association by Houghton Mifflin, 1902. 596 p. [1893]

Larochelle, André

"A bibliography of papers on Cicindelidae published in *The Canadian Entomologist*, (1869-1979)." In: *Cicindela*; Vol. 19, no. 2 (June 1987) p. 21-33.; ISSN: 0590-6334. [5532]

"A bibliography of papers published on Cicindelidae in the *Annual Reports and Proceedings of the Entomological Society of Ontario*, 1871-1987." In: *Cicindela*; Vol. 21, no. 3-4 (September-December 1989) p. 41-47.; ISSN: 0590-6334. [5550]

"Liste des publications traitant de la faune des Coléoptères carabidae du Québec de 1859 à 1979." Dans: *Cordulia*; Vol. 5, no 3 (septembre 1979) p. 41-63.; ISSN: 0070-4966. [5434]

LaRose, André

"Bibliographie courante sur l'histoire de la population canadienne et la démographie historique au Canada/A current bibliography on the history of Canadian population and historical demography in Canada." Dans: *Histoire sociale: Social History*; Vol. 12, no 23 (mai 1979)-vol. 21, no 41 (mai 1988) [3057]

Larose, André; Vanderwall, Jake

Bibliography of papers relevant to the scattering of thermal neutrons, 1963-1972. Hamilton, Ont.: McMaster University, c1973. 335 p. [5743]

Larouche, Irma

National Library of Canada: a bibliography/Bibliothèque nationale du Canada: une bibliographie. Ottawa: Reference and Bibliography Section, National Library of Canada, 1979. xxiii, 179 p.; ISBN: 0-660-50210-0. [1635]

Larouche, Ursula; Boudreau, Francis

Réserve écologique de Tantaré: bibliographie annotée des travaux et d'acquisition de connaissances. Québec: Ministère de l'environnement, Direction de la conservation et du patrimoine écologique, 1992. [4], i, 54 p.; ISBN: 2-550-26570-X. [5297]

Latham, Barbara; Carter, Connie; Reid, Jane

Bibliography on women: a resource for other disciplines/ Bibliographie sur les femmes: ouvrage de référence pour d'autres disciplines. Toronto: Canadian Studies Bureau, Association of Canadian Community Colleges, 1985. xviii, 64 p.; ill.; ISSN: 0228-8451. [3838]

Latham, David

"A Callaghan log." In: *Journal of Canadian Studies*; Vol. 15, no. 1 (Spring 1980) p. 18-29.; ISSN: 0021-9495. [6888]

Sinclair Ross: an annotated bibliography. Downsview, Ont.: ECW Press, c1981. P. 365-395.; ISBN: 0-920763-63-4. [7276]

"Sinclair Ross: an annotated bibliography." In: *The annotated bibliography of Canada's major authors*, Vol. 3, edited by Robert Lecker and Jack David. Downsview, Ont.: ECW Press, 1981. P. 365-395.; ISBN: 0-920802-23-0. [7277]

Latham, Sheila

Canadian poetry 1970-1979: a multi-media list. [Toronto]: Toronto Public Library, 1979. 16 p. [1153]

W.O. Mitchell: an annotated bibliography. [Downsview, Ont.: ECW Press, c1981]. P. 323-364. [7193]

"W.O. Mitchell: an annotated bibliography." In: *The annotated bibliography of Canada's major authors*, Vol. 3, edited by Robert Lecker and Jack David. Downsview, Ont.: ECW Press, c1981. P. 323-364.; ISBN: 0-920802-23-0. [7194]

Latham, Sheila; Freedman, Gloria; Williamson, Michael

Once upon a pedestal: multimedia list of material for reading, listening, and viewing prepared on the occasion of International Women's Year, 1975. [Toronto]: Young People's Service, Toronto Public Libraries, 1975. 13 p. [3757]

Latham, Sheila; Slade, Alexander L.; Budnick, Carol

Library services for off-campus and distance education: an annotated bibliography. Ottawa: Canadian Library Association, c1991. xxii, 249 p.; ISBN: 0-88802-257-3. [1726]

Latourelle, René

"Liste des écrits Saint Jean de Brébeuf." Dans: *Revue d'histoire de l'Amérique française*; Vol. 3, no 1 (juin 1949) p. 141-147.; ISSN: 0035-2357. [6873]

Laubitz, Diana R., et al.

Bibliographia invertebratorum aquaticorum canadensium. Ottawa: National Museum of Natural Sciences, National Museums of Canada, 1983-1988. 8 vol.; ISBN: 0-662-11272-5 (set). [5544]

Lauder, Kathleen; Lavallée, Laval

A Canadian bibliography of urban and regional information system activity. Ottawa: Ministry of State for Urban Affairs, [1976]. ix, 39 p. (Urban paper / Canada Ministry of State for Urban Affairs ; A-76-2; ISSN: 0318-1286) [4360]

Laugher, Charles T.

Atlantic Province authors of the twentieth century: a bio-bibliographical checklist. Halifax, N.S.: Dalhousie University, 1982. vi, 620 p. (Occasional papers / Dalhousie University Libraries and Dalhousie University School of Library Service ; no. 29; ISSN: 0318-7403); ISBN: 0-7703-0163-0. [1192]

Laurin, Christiane
Périodiques canadiens sur microfilms: liste des microfilms disponibles au Québec dans les bibliothèques universitaires et à la Bibliothèque nationale. Montréal: Ministère des affaires culturelles du Québec, 1970. 89 p. [5895]

Laurin, Clément
"Bibliographie de Jean-Olivier Chenier." Dans: *Cahiers d'histoire de Deux-Montagnes*; Vol. 5, no 2 (octobre 1982) p. 58-66.; ISSN: 0226-7063. [6906]
"Bibliographie de la bataille de Saint-Eustache." Dans: *Cahiers d'histoire de Deux-Montagnes*; Vol. 5, no 2 (octobre 1982) p. 10-14.; ISSN: 0226-7063. [0378]

Laurin, Serge; Lagrange, Richard
Bibliographie des Laurentides. [Québec]: Institut québécois de recherche sur la culture, 1985. 370 p.: cartes. (Documents de recherche / Institut québécois de recherche sur la culture ; no 7; ISSN: 0823-0447); ISBN: 2-89224-052-4. [0387]

Lavallée, Robert
Bibliographical review of Pachypappa tremulae (L): a root aphid of conifer seedlings in containers. Sainte-Foy, Quebec: Laurentian Forestry Centre, 1987. v, 16 p.: ill. (some col.). (Information report / Laurentian Forestry Centre ; LAU-X-73E; ISSN: 0835-1570); ISBN: 0-662-15184-4. [5533]
Revue bibliographique sur Pachypappa tremulae (L): un puceron des racines des plants de conifères en récipients. Sainte-Foy, Québec: Centre de recherches forestières des Laurentides, Service canadien des forêts, 1987. v, 16 p.: ill. (quelques coul.). (Rapport d'information / Centre de recherches forestières des Laurentides ; LAU-X-73F; ISSN: 0835-1589); ISBN: 0-662-94098-9. [5534]

Laverdière, Camille; Bernard, Claude
"Bibliographie annotée sur les broutures glaciaires/An annotated bibliography on glacial chattermarks." Dans: *Revue de géographie de Montréal*; Vol. 24, no 1 (1970) p. 79-89.; ISSN: 0035-1148. [5054]

Laverdière, Richard
Bibliographie commentée, l'arbre en tête. Québec: Gouvernement du Québec, Ministère des forêts, 1991. 68 p. [4634]

Lavoie, Amédée
Bibliographie relative à l'histoire de la Nouvelle-France, 1516-1700. Giffard, Québec: [s.n.], 1949. 81 f. [1922]

Lavoie, Cécile
312 volumes de bibliothéconomie et sciences connexes: liste bibliographique. Montréal: Fides, 1973. 27 p. [1601]

Lavoie, Marc C.
A preliminary bibliography for historic artifact research in the Maritimes/Une bibliographie préliminaire sur les artefacts historiques pour les Maritimes. Fredericton, N.B.: Archaeology Branch, Department of Tourism, Recreation and Heritage, New Brunswick, 1986. ii, 66 p. (Manuscripts in archaeology / Archaeology Branch, New Brunswick Department of Tourism, Recreation and Heritage); ISBN: 0-88838-354-1. [4598]

Lavoie, Pierre
"Bibliographie commentée [de Michel Tremblay]." Dans: *Voix et Images*; Vol. 7, no 2 (hiver 1982) p. 225-306.; ISSN: 0318-9201. [7337]
"Bio-bibliographie [commentée sur Jean-Claude Germain]." Dans: *Jeu*; No 13 (automne 1979) p. 105-141.; ISSN: 0382-0335. [7010]

Pour suivre le théâtre au Québec: les ressources documentaires. Québec: Institut québécois de recherche sur la culture, 1985. 521 p. (Documents de recherche / Institut québécois de recherche sur la culture ; no 4; ISSN: 0823-0447); ISBN: 2-89224-047-6. [0981]

Lavoie, Pierre; Lépine, Stéphane
"Théâtrographie: [théâtre et homosexualité au Québec]." Dans: *Jeu*; No 54 (1990) p. 127-133.; ISSN: 0382-0335. [0989]

Law Reform Commission of Canada
Fear of punishment: deterrence. Ottawa: Law Reform Commission of Canada, c1976. vii, 149 p. [2152]

Law Society of Upper Canada. Library
A subject index to the books in the Library of the Law Society of Upper Canada at Osgoode Hall, Toronto, January 1st, 1900. Toronto: Printed for the Law Society, 1900. 396 p. [2098]

Lawrence, Bertha
A survey of the materials to be found in the Provincial Legislative Library, Alberta, for a study of Canadian history and more particularly that of western Canada. Edmonton: 1936. 419 l. [0494]

Lawrence, Jean; Haddad, April
Wife abuse: a bibliography of materials available at the Justice Institute. Vancouver: Justice Institute of British Columbia, 1985. 8 l. [3275]

Lawrence, Pauline, et al.
Annotated bibliographies: Atlantic region national parks. Halifax, N.S.: Geomarine Associates, 1974. 4 vol. [3004]

Lawson, B.M.
A review of literature on the problem of blackening in cooked potatoes. Victoria, B.C.: Department of Agriculture, [1960]. 6 l. [4644]

Lawson, Ian B.
An annotated bibliography of public interest advocacy literature/Bibliographie annotée sur la défense de l'intérêt public. Ottawa: Research and Statistics Section, Policy Planning and Development Branch, Department of Justice Canada, 1983. iii, 233 p. [2261]

Lawton, Stephen B.; Currie, A. Blaine
Handwriting: I. Instruction in handwriting in Ontario schools: II. Handwriting: an annotated bibliography. Toronto: Ontario Ministry of Education, 1980. x, 174 p.; ISBN: 0-7743-4756-2. [3568]

Lawton-Speert, Sarah; Wachtel, Andy
Child sexual abuse and incest: an annotated bibliography. 2nd ed. Vancouver: United Way of the Lower Mainland, Social Planning and Research Department, 1982. iv, 42 p. (Working paper: Child Sexual Abuse Project / United Way of the Lower Mainland, Social Planning and Research Department ; 1) [3240]

Laychuck, Julian L.
"Chinese-Canadian periodical publications: a preliminary check list." In: *Canadian Ethnic Studies*; Vol. 2, no. 1 (June 1970) p. 15-20.; ISSN: 0008-3496. [5896]
"University research on Scottish-Canadians: a preliminary check list of theses." In: *Canadian Ethnic Studies*; Vol. 5, no. 1/2 (1973) p. 259-261.; ISSN: 0008-3496. [6125]

Lazarowich, Linda M.
The costume of the North American Indian: an annotated bibliography of sources from journals. [Winnipeg]: University of Manitoba, College of Home Economics, 1981. 9 l. [4025]

Le Moine, Roger
Le catalogue de la bibliothèque de Louis-Joseph Papineau. Ottawa: Centro do rochercho on civilisation canadienne-française, Université d'Ottawa, 1982. 140 p. (Documents de travail du Centre de recherche en civilisation canadienne-française ; 21) [6787]

Leach, Karen E.
A survey of literature on the lateral resistance of nails. Ottawa: Department of Forestry, 1964. 12 p. (Department of Forestry Publication ; no. 1085) [5724]

League of Canadian Poets
Who's who in the League of Canadian Poets. 3rd ed. Toronto: The League, 1988. 227 p.: ill.; ISBN: 0-9690327-4-9. [1254]

Leaney, Adelle J.; Morris, Sahlaa
The Bella Coola River estuary: status of environmental knowledge to 1981: report of the Estuary Working Group, Fisheries and Oceans-Environment Joint Co-ordinating Committee on Environmental Affairs, Pacific and Yukon Region. [Ottawa]: Environment Canada, 1981. xxxiv, 266 p.: maps. [5172]

Lebeau, Mario, et al.
Besoins de logements des groupes spéciaux: une synthèse des recherches francophones. [Ottawa]: Société canadienne d'hypothèques et de logement, 1990. 48, [32] p. [3341]
Special housing needs: a synthesis of French language research. [Ottawa]: Canada Mortgage and Housing Corporation, 1990. 48, [32] p. [3342]

Lebel, Clément
Documents de la Commission d'enquête sur la situation de la langue française et les droits linguistiques au Québec (Commission Gendron): bibliographie. Québec: Bibliothèque de la Législature, Assemblée nationale, 1974. iii, 206 p. (Bibliographie et documentation / Bibliothèque de la Législature du Québec ; 3) [6291]

Lebel, Marc
"Enseignement de la philosophie au Petit Séminaire de Québec (1765-1880)." Dans: *Revue d'histoire de l'Amérique française*; Vol. 18, no 3 (décembre 1964) p. 463-473; vol. 19, no 2 (septembre 1965) p. 323-328.; ISSN: 0035-2357. [3389]

Lebel, Maurice
Bibliographie des ouvrages publiés avec le concours du Conseil canadien de recherches sur les humanités et du Conseil des arts du Canada, 1947-1971. Ottawa: Conseil canadien de recherches sur les humanités, 1972. 45 p. [0675]
Thèses présentées à la Faculté des lettres de l'Université Laval, 1940-1947. Québec: Presses de l'Université Laval, 1947. 15 p. [6057]

Lebel-Péron, Suzanne
"Liste des publications de Monsieur Jacques Henripin." Dans: *Bulletin de l'Association des démographes du Québec*; Vol. 2, no 1 (mars 1973) p. 17-22. [7063]

Lebel-Péron, Suzanne; Péron, Yves
"Bibliographie chronologique sur la mortalité au Canada." Dans: *Cahiers québécois de démographie*; Vol. 7, no 2 (août 1978) p. 55-92.; ISSN: 0380-1721. [3025]
Bibliographie sur la démographie récente des groupes ethno-linguistiques au Canada. Calgary: Research Centre for Canadian Ethnic Studies, University of Calgary, 1979. iv, 52 p. (Canadian ethnic studies: Études ethniques au Canada / Research Centre for Canadian Ethnic Studies,

University of Calgary ; no 1) [4195]

LeBlanc, André E.
"Collegial education in Quebec: a bibliography." In: *McGill Journal of Education*; Vol. 20, no. 3 (Fall 1985) p. 273-280.; ISSN: 0024-9033. [3639]

LeBlanc, André E.; Thwaites, James D.
Le monde ouvrier au Québec: bibliographie rétrospective. Montréal: Presses de l'Université du Québec, 1973. xv, 283 p. (Collection Histoire des travailleurs québécois); ISBN: 0-7770-0061-X. [2816]

LeBlanc, Robert G.
"A critical survey of recent geographical research on la Franco-Américanie." In: *Le Québec et les francophones de la Nouvelle-Angleterre*. Sainte-Foy: Presses de l'Université Laval, 1991. P. 107-125. (Collection Culture française d'Amérique); ISBN: 2-7637-7273-0. [3064]

Leblanc, Thérèse
Les femmes: guide des ressources documentaires à Montréal, with an introduction for English-speaking users and an English-French index. [Montréal]: Éditions F. Huot, 1987. 110 p.; ISBN: 2-9800-808-0-2. [3854]

LeBlond, Robert
"Le Saint-Laurent: orientation bibliographique." Dans: *Cahiers de géographie de Québec*; Vol. 11, no 23 (septembre 1967) p. 419-464.; ISSN: 0007-9766. [2971]

Leboeuf, Jacques; Breton, Lise
L'étudiant handicapé: vers une meilleure intégration au collège: bibliographie annotée. Montréal: CADRE, 1981. 40 p.; ISBN: 2-89169-022-2. [3594]

LeBrasseur, Rolland, et al.
Worker co-operatives: an international bibliography/ Coopératives de travailleurs: une bibliographie internationale. Saskatoon: Centre for the Study of Co-operatives, University of Saskatchewan, [1987]. v, 68 p. [2914]

Lecker, Robert
"An annotated bibliography of works by and about John Newlove." In: *Essays on Canadian Writing*; No. 2 (Spring 1975) p. 28-53.; ISSN: 0316-0300. [7211]
"An annotated bibliography of works by and about Robert Kroetsch." In: *Essays on Canadian Writing*; Nos. 7/8 (Fall 1977) p. 74-96.; ISSN: 0316-0300. [7102]

Lecker, Robert; David, Jack
The annotated bibliography of Canada's major authors. Downsview, Ont.: ECW Press, 1979-. vol.; ISBN: 0-9208-0208-7 (set). [1302]

Lecker, Robert; Maracle, Kathleen
"Robert Kroetsch: an annotated bibliography." In: *The annotated bibliography of Canada's major authors*, Vol. 7, edited by Robert Lecker and Jack David. Toronto: ECW Press, 1987. P. 271-402.; ISBN: 0-920802-11-1. [7103]

Lecker, Robert; O'Rourke, David
"John Newlove: an annotated bibliography." In: *The annotated bibliography of Canada's major authors*, Vol. 6, edited by Robert Lecker and Jack David. Toronto: ECW Press, 1985. P. 67-128.; ISBN: 0-920802-93-1. [7212]

LeClair, B.P.
Selected references on phosphorus removal. Ottawa: Environment Canada, Environmental Protection Service, 1973. iii, 41 p. (Economic and technical review report / Water Pollution Control Directorate ; EPS 3-WP-73-2) [5078]

Leclerc, Charles

Bibliotheca americana: histoire, géographie, voyages, archéologie et linguistique des deux Amériques et des îles Philippines. Paris: Maisonneuve, 1878. vii, 424 p. [0013]

Leclerc, Pierre A.

Aperçu de bibliophilatélie. Québec: [s.n.], 1974. P. A-T, [5] p., [1] f. de pl.: fac-sim. [1766]

Lecompte, Louis-Luc

Enfance et adolescence inadaptées: catalogue des ouvrages de la collection des sciences du comportement. 3e éd. revue et augm. Montréal: Centre d'information sur la santé de l'enfant, Hôpital Sainte-Justine, 1978. vi, 300, [272] p. [3173]

"L'économie du tourisme." Dans: Notes du Centre d'études du tourisme; Vol. 8, no 1 (février 1988) p. 1-4.; ISSN: 0229-2718. [1849]

Lederer, K.M.

The nature of poverty: an interpretative review of poverty studies, with special reference to Canada. [Edmonton]: Human Resources Research Council, 1972. ii, 115 p. [3110]

Leduc, Jean

"La vie et l'oeuvre de Jean-Pierre Cordeau, 1922-1971." Dans: Union médicale du Canada; Vol. 101, no 12 (décembre 1972) p. 2641-2645.; ISSN: 0041-6959. [6920]

Leduc, Marcel

"Bibliographie sélective du monde ouvrier." Dans: Histoire des travailleurs québécois: Bulletin RCHTQ; Vol. 12, no 1 (hiver 1986) p. 13-45.; ISSN: 0315-7938. [2906]

"Complément bibliographique sur l'éducation des adultes." Dans: Histoire des travailleurs québécois: Bulletin RCHTQ; Vol. 8, no 2 (été 1982) p. 45-53.; ISSN: 0315-7938. [3613]

Leduc, Marcel; Vaisey, G. Douglas

"The Canadian labour bibliography/Bibliographie du mouvement ouvrier canadien." In: Labour: Le Travail; Vol. 8/9 (Autumn/Spring 1981/1982) p. 334-348; vol. 10 (Autumn 1982) p. 193-227; vol. 12 (Autumn 1983) p. 223-248; vol. 16 (Fall 1985) p. 245-270.; ISSN: 0700-3862. [2897]

Lee, Dorothy Sara

Native North American music and oral data: a catalogue of sound recordings, 1893-1976. Bloomington: Indiana University Press, c1979. xiv, 463 p.; ISBN: 0-25318-877-6. [0876]

Lee, Helen F. McRae Parker

The Helen F. McRae collection: a bibliography of Korean relations with Canadians and other western peoples, which includes a checklist of documents and reports, 1898-1975. Halifax, N.S.: School of Library Service, Dalhousie University, 1976. vii, 201 p. (Occasional papers / Dalhousie University School of Library Service ; no. 12); ISBN: 0-7703-0149-5. [1541]

Lee, Yam (Jim)

A review of research literature on forest fertilization. Victoria, B.C.: Department of Forestry and Rural Development, 1968. 40 p. [4922]

Lee-Whiting, Brenda B.

"A German-Canadian bibliography: studies on eastern Ontario." In: Canadiana Germanica; No. 35 (August 1982) p. 28-33.; ISSN: 0703-1599. [4212]

Leechman, Douglas

"Bibliography of Harlan I. Smith." In: Bulletin (National Museum of Canada); No. 112 (1949) p. 8-14.; ISSN: 0068-7944. [7315]

"Bibliography of W.J. Wintemberg, 1899-1947." In: Bulletin (National Museum of Canada); No. 112 (1949) p. 38-41.; ISSN: 0068-7944. [7369]

Lefebvre, Claude-Jean

"Bibliographie annotée des textes parus dans Arctic, de 1948 à 1969, sur le Nouveau-Québec, le Labrador et Baffin." Dans: Revue de géographie de Montréal; Vol. 25, no 1 (1971) p. 53-57.; ISSN: 0035-1148. [2980]

Lefebvre, Joan; Boulet, Francine

L'aménagement du territoire: bibliographie. Québec: Ministère des terres et forêts, Service de l'information, Bibliothèque, 1974. 55 f. [4334]

Lefebvre, Marie, et al.

Répertoire des documents cartographiques et photographiques sur la région de Trois-Rivières (04). Trois-Rivières: Cartothèque, Université du Québec à Trois-Rivières, 1985. vii, 377 p.: ill., cartes. [6585]

Lefebvre, Marie-Thérèse

"Répertoire des travaux universitaires sur la musique du Québec (1924-1984)." Dans: Canadian University Music Review: Revue de musique des universités canadiennes; No. 6 (1985) p. 45-67.; ISSN: 0710-0353. [6179]

Lefebvre, Monique

Techniques d'intervention auprès des enfants d'âge préscolaire: dossier bibliographique ouvert au Centre de documentation du C.A.D.R.E. Montréal: Centre d'animation, de développement et de recherche en éducation, 1977. 18 p. [3525]

A legal bibliography of the British Commonwealth of Nations. 2nd ed. London: Sweet and Maxwell, 1955-1964. 7 vol. [2110]

Legal Services Society of British Columbia

Publications catalogue [Legal Services Society of British Columbia]. Vancouver: Legal Services Society, 1983-. vol.; ISSN: 0825-5075. [2366]

Légaré, Benoît

Le marketing en milieu muséal: une bibliographie analytique. Montréal: École des hautes études commerciales, Chaire de gestion des arts, 1991. 179 f. (Cahiers de recherche de la Chaire de gestion des arts ; GA91-01B; ISSN: 0847-5148) [0725]

Légaré, Yves

Dictionnaire des écrivains québécois contemporains. Montréal: Québec/Amérique, c1983. 399 p.; ISBN: 2-89037-158-1. [1206]

Legendre, Victor

Musique canadienne: bibliographie. [Cap-Rouge, Québec]: Bibliothèque, Séminaire Saint-Augustin, 1970. 28 f. [0826]

Léger, Bernard

"Bibliographie de l'Acadie." Dans: Cahiers: Société historique acadienne; Vol. 9, no 1 (mars 1978) p. 38-43.; ISSN: 0049-1098. [0235]

Léger, Bernard; Léger, Raymond

"Bibliographie de l'Acadie." Dans: Cahiers: Société historique acadienne; Vol. 7, no 2 (juin 1976) p. 93-99.; ISSN: 0049-1098. [0223]

Léger, Lauraine

"Bibliographie: oeuvres d'Antonine Maillet." Dans: Revue de l'Université de Moncton; Vol. 7, no 2 (mai 1974) p. 83-90.; ISSN: 0316-6368. [7172]

Léger, Raymond

"Bibliographie de l'Acadie." Dans: Cahiers: Société historique acadienne; Vol. 8, no 2 (juin 1977) p. 93-96.; ISSN: 0049-1098. [0230]

Legere, Bill

Hillbilly heaven: discography. Mississauga, Ont.: B. Legere, 1985. 1 vol. (loose leaf). [0920]

[List of Canadian artists]. [S.l.: B. Legere], 1980. [180] l. [0886]

Leggat, Portia

A union list of architectural records in Canadian public collections/Catalogue collectif de recherche documentaire sur l'architecture provenant de collections publiques canadiennes. Montreal: Canadian Centre for Architecture, 1983. xxiii, 213 p. [0772]

Legge, Allan H.; Crowther, Roy A.

Acidic deposition and the environment: a literature overview. Calgary: Acid Deposition Research Program, 1987. ix, 235 p.: ill., map.; ISBN: 0-921625-13-8. [5247]

Legris, Renée

"Bibliographie [Robert Choquette]." Dans: *Robert Choquette*. Montréal: Fides, 1972. P. 51-64. (Dossiers de documentation sur la littérature canadienne-française ; 8) [6908]

Dictionnaire des auteurs du radio-feuilleton québécois. Montréal: Fides, 1981. 200 p.; ISBN: 2-7621-1090-4. [0971]

Legros, Dominique

"Bibliographie des Amérindiens de la Côte Nord-Ouest (1973-1982)." Dans: *Recherches amérindiennes au Québec*; Vol. 14, no 2 (1984) p. 57-70.; ISSN: 0318-4137. [4059]

Legros, Gisèle

Histoire des femmes au Canada: bibliographie sélective/ Women's history in Canada: a selective bibliography. Ottawa: Secrétariat d'État du Canada, Bibliothèque ministérielle, 1992. 16 p. [3899]

Lehmann, Cathy; Iles, Janet

A bibliography of the Ioleen A. Hawken Memorial Local History Collection of the Owen Sound Public Library: including materials on deposit from the Bruce and Grey Branch, Ontario Genealogical Society. Owen Sound, Ont.: The Library, 1984. 2, 108 l.; ISBN: 0-9691650-0-5. [0476]

Leidemer, Nelle L.

Geology of Halifax County: a selective bibliography. 2nd ed. Halifax, N.S.: University Libraries; School of Library Service, Dalhousie University, 1981. 60 p. (Occasional papers / Dalhousie University Libraries and Dalhousie University School of Library Service ; no. 5; ISSN: 0318-7403); ISBN: 0-7703-0142-8. [4821]

Leigh, Dawson M.

Huronia in print. Midland, Ont.: Huronia Historic Sites and Tourist Association, 1952. [9] l. [0426]

Leitch, Linda J.

Learning disabilities: review of the literature and selected annotated bibliography. Montreal: Faculty of Education, McGill University, c1973. 59 l. (Reports in education / Faculty of Education, McGill University ; no. 3) [3468]

Leith, Harry

Bibliography of books and articles on the relationship between science and pseudoscience. Toronto: York University, Department of Natural Sciences, Atkinson College, 1978. 61 p. [4575]

Leland, Marine; Hare, John

"French literature of Canada." In: *The literatures of the world in English translation: a bibliography*. Vol. 3, *The romance literatures* (Part 2: French literature), edited by George B. Parks and Ruth Z. Temple. New York: Ungar, [1970]. P. 576-590.; ISBN: 0-8044-3239-2. [1055]

Lelièvre, Francine

Bibliographie annotée de l'histoire humaine du Parc national Forillon, Gaspé, Québec: Direction des parcs nationaux et des lieux historiques, Ministère des Affaires indiennes et du Nord canadien, 1971. viii, 111 l. [1974]

Lemay, Henri-Paul

Bibliographie sur le Saint-Laurent. Saint-Foy: Institut national de la recherche scientifique, Université du Québec, 1974. iii, iv, 159 p. [0329]

Lemelin, Clément

La pratique de l'économie de l'éducation dans le Québec francophone de la dernière décennie, 1970-1980: une présentation bibliographique. Montréal: Département de science économique, Université de Québec à Montréal, 1981. 26, 15 f. (Cahier / Département de science économique, Université de Québec à Montréal ; no 8101) [3595]

Lemieux, Denise; Mercier, Lucie

La recherche sur les femmes au Québec: bilan et bibliographie. [Québec]: Institut québécois de recherche sur la culture, [1982]. 336 p. (Instruments de travail / Institut québécois de recherche sur la culture ; no 5); ISBN: 2-89-224-015-8. [3808]

Lemieux, Marthe

Essai d'une bibliographie sur la ville de Chicoutimi. Montréal: 1953. viii, 96 f. [0286]

LeMinh, Canh

Design management: bibliographie sélective. Montréal: École des hautes études commerciales, Bibliothèque, 1972. 52 f. (Sources d'information sur les problèmes nouveaux en relation avec les affaires) [2598]

Lemire, Maurice; Landry, Kenneth

Répertoire des spécialistes de littérature canadienne-française. [Québec]: Archives de littérature canadienne, Université Laval, 1971. vi, 93 p. [1063]

Lemoine, Réjean

"Les brochures publiées au XIXe siècle afin de lutter contre le choléra: essai bibliographique." Dans: *Cahiers du livre ancien du Canada français*; Vol. 1, no 2 (été 1984) p. 35-41.; ISSN: 0822-4315. [5660]

LeMoine, Sir James MacPherson

"Materials for Canadian history: the annals of towns, parishes, &c., extracted from church registers, and other sources." In: *Proceedings and Transactions of the Royal Society of Canada*; Series 2, vol. 3, section 2 (1897) p. 309-311.; ISSN: 0316-4616. [1887]

LeMoyne, Beryl

An annotated list of Quebec government documents for a business library. [Montreal]: Graduate School of Library Science, McGill University, 1972. ii, 13 l. (McGill University Graduate School of Library Science Occasional papers ; 2) [6280]

LeMoyne, Beryl; Millette, Robert

A Quebec bibliography. Montreal: ABQ/QLA, 1977. 10 p. [0348]

Lenentine, Beth L.

New Brunswick-Maine border water resources, water use and related data: an annotated bibliography. Dartmouth, N.S.: Environment Canada, Inland Waters Directorate, Atlantic Region, 1984. iv, 101 l.: map. [5215]

Lennoxville-Ascot Historical and Museum Society

Lennoxville-Ascot Historical and Museum Society: preliminary catalogue of documents, manuscripts and papers. Lennoxville, Quebec: The Society, 1985. 44 l. [0388]

Lenskyj, Helen

La femme, le sport et l'activité physique: recherche et bibliographie. 2e éd. Ottawa: Condition physique et sport amateur, c1991. 176 p.; ISBN: 0-660-92974-0. [3892]

Women, sport and physical activity: research and bibliography. 2nd ed. Ottawa: Fitness and Amateur Sport, c1991. 165 p.; ISBN: 0-660-13608-2. [3893]

Lenz, Karl

"Bibliography of geographic literature on Canada and its regions in the German language." In: *German-Canadian Yearbook*; Vol. 3 (1976) p. 291-302.; ISSN: 0316-8603. [3017]

Lepage, Francia G., et al.

Guide bibliographique: recherches historiques sur la ville de Sainte-Foy, 1534-1975. Sainte-Foy: Bureau de l'information de la Ville de Sainte-Foy, 1977. v, 207 p. [0349]

Lepage, Françoise; Boyer, Denis

Inventaire des documents de la Bibliothèque sur Hull et la région. Hull [Québec]: Bibliothèque municipale, 1980. [4], 172 f. [0362]

Lépine, Pierre; Berthelette, Josée

Documents cartographiques depuis la découverte de l'Amérique jusqu'à 1820: inventaire sommaire. Montréal: Bibliothèque nationale du Québec, 1985. xiii, 383 p.: cartes.; ISBN: 2-551-06545-3. [6586]

Lepkey, Gabriel

Législation et politique canadienne en matière de concurrence: la bibliographie d'un centenaire: 1889-1989/ Canadian competition law and policy: a centennial bibliography, 1889-1989. Ottawa: Bureau de la politique de concurrence, c1990. 252 p.; ISBN: 0-662-57571-7. [2340]

Lerner, Loren R.

"Recent publications on Canadian art." In: *Journal of Canadian Art History*; Vol. 10, no. 2 (1987) p. 169-178; vol. 13, no. 1 (1990) p. 98-111.; ISSN: 0315-4297. [0722]

Lerner, Loren R.; Williamson, Mary F.

Art and architecture in Canada: a bibliography and guide to the literature to 1981/Art et architecture au Canada: bibliographie et guide de la documentation jusqu'en 1981. Toronto: University of Toronto Press, 1991. 2 vol.: maps.; ISBN: 0-8020-5856-6 (set). [0726]

Leroux, Denise; Leduc, Diane

The aged in Canadian society: select bibliography/Les vieillards dans la société canadienne: bibliographie sélective. Ottawa: Library of Parliament, Information and Reference Branch, 1984. 17 l. [3261]

Leroux, Paul-André

"Une revue critique de la littérature sur l'homosexualité avec une emphase sur la science et la mesure." Dans: *Bulletin de l'Association pour l'analyse et la modification du comportement*; Vol. 3, no 2 (Juin 1973) p. 23-32. [3118]

Leroy, D.A.

Publications du Centre de foresterie du Nord, 1987-1990. Edmonton: Le Centre, 1991. vi, 30 p. (Rapport d'information / Centre de foresterie du Nord ; NOR-X-321F); ISBN: 0-662-97178-7. [5014]

Lessard, Marc-André

"Bibliographie des villes du Québec." Dans: *Recherches sociographiques*; Vol. 9, no 1/2 (1968) p. 143-209.; ISSN: 0034-1282. [4309]

"Les publications du B.A.E.Q." Dans: *Recherches sociographiques*; Vol. 8, no 3 (septembre-décembre 1967) p. 377-403.; ISSN: 0034-1282. [6263]

Lesser, Gloria

"Biography and bibliography of the writings of Donald William Buchanan (1908-1966)." In: *Journal of Canadian Art History*; Vol. 5, no. 2 (1981) p. 129-136.; ISSN: 0315-4297. [6879]

A lesson in history: Canadiana collected by Dr. Lawrence Lande/Une page d'histoire: livres et documents historiques de la collection Lawrence Lande. Ottawa: National Library of Canada: Public Archives Canada, 1980. 35 p.: ill., facsim.; ISBN: 0-662-50696-0. [0131]

"Letters in Canada." In: *University of Toronto Quarterly*; (1936-) vol.; ISSN: 0042-0247. [1303]

Letters in Canada. Toronto: University of Toronto Press, 1981-. vol.; ISSN: 0315-4955. [1304]

Léveillé, Lionel

Bibliographie sommaire de la Côte-du-Sud. La Pocatière, [Québec]: Cégep de La Pocatière, Service de l'éducation aux adultes, 1979. 66 p. [0359]

Levenson, Rosaline

Company towns: a bibliography of American and foreign sources. Monticello, Ill.: Council of Planning Librarians, 1977. 25 p. (Council of Planning Librarians Exchange bibliography ; 1428) [4366]

Lévesque, Albert

Répertoire des journaux et périodiques courants de langue française ou bilingues publiés au Canada à l'exception du Québec. Montréal: Association des responsables des bibliothèques et centre de documentation universitaires et de recherche d'expression française au Canada, 1993. xix, 73 p.; ISBN: 2-9802702-0-2. [5984]

Lévesque, Frédéric; Magnan, Pierre

Bibliographie annotée sur le saumon atlantique (Salmo salar) au stade post-fraie. Québec: Pêches et océans Canada, 1985. v, 42 p. (Rapport manuscrit canadien des sciences halieutiques et aquatiques ; no 1823; ISSN: 0706-6589) [5513]

Lévesque, Gaétan

Les facteurs déterminants du niveau des avantages sociaux: une revue de la littérature. Montréal: Institut de recherche et d'information sur la rémunération, 1987. vii, 67 f. [3300]

Lévesque, Michel

L'Union nationale: bibliographie. Québec: Assemblée nationale, Bibliothèque, 1988. 51 p. (Bibliographie et documentation / Bibliothèque de l'Assemblée nationale du Québec ; 31); ISBN: 2-551-12063-2. [2519]

Lévesque, Michel; Comeau, Robert

Le Parti libéral du Québec: bibliographie rétrospective (1867-1990). Québec: Bibliothèque de l'Assemblée nationale, 1991. xii, 198 p. (Bibliographie et documentation / Bibliothèque de l'Assemblée nationale du Québec ; no 39); ISBN: 2-551-12692-4. [2545]

Levine, Marc V.

"The language question in Quebec: a selected, annotated bibliography." In: *Québec Studies*; No. 8 (Spring 1989) p. 37-41.; ISSN: 0737-3759. [2530]

Levy, Adrian R.; Lechowicz, Martin J.

An annotated bibliography of research at Mont St. Hilaire, Quebec/Bibliographie annotée des recherches effectuées au Mont St-Hilaire (Québec). Ottawa: UNESCO Canada/ MAB Committee, 1987. 75, v p.: ill., map. (UNESCO Canada/MAB Report ; no. 18) [5535]

Lewis, David

Louis Hooper: the Harlem years: a bio-discographical dossier. Montreal: Montreal Vintage Music Society, 1989. 26 l.; ISBN: 1-895002-01-X. [7068]

Lewis, Grace S.

"Reports of Dominion and provincial royal commissions, together with a selection of reports of British royal commissions having a bearing on Canada." In: *Canada Year Book*; (1940) p. 1108-1116. [6224]

Lewis, Pamela

Radio Frequency Spectrum Management Program evaluation: economic nature of the spectrum: a review of the literature. Ottawa: Government of Canada, Department of Communications, Program Evaluation Division, 1989. vi, 43 p. [2755]

Leymarie, A. Léo

Exposition rétrospective des colonies françaises de l'Amérique du Nord: catalogue illustré. Paris: Société d'éditions géographiques, maritimes et coloniales, 1929. lxv, 312 p., 139 p. de pl.: ill. [1905]

LGL Limited Environmental Research Associates

The biological resources of the southeastern Beaufort Sea, Amundsen Gulf, northern Mackenzie delta and adjacent coastal areas [microform]: a selected annotated bibliography. Edmonton: LGL Limited, 1982. 12 microfiches (705 frames): negative, maps. (Arctic Petroleum Operators' Association Project ; no. 173) [5478]

Li, Kuo Lee

World wide space law bibliography. Montreal: Center for Research of Air and Space Law, McGill University, 1978-1987. 2 vol.; ISBN: 0-9692703-3-X. [2295]

Liability and negligence: a specialized bibliography from the SPORT database/Responsabilité légale et négligence: une bibliographie spécialisée de la base de données SPORT. Gloucester, Ont.: Sport Information Resource Centre, 1991. 15 l. (SportBiblio ; no. 11; ISSN: 1180-5269) [1865]

Libick, Helen

A bibliography of Canadian theses and dissertations in urban, regional and environmental planning, 1974-1979/ Une bibliographie canadienne des thèses et dissertations en planification urbaine, régionale et environnementale, 1974-1979. [Montreal]: Canadian Association of Planning Students, 1980. xv, 286 p. [6155]

Liboiron, Albert A.

Federalism and intergovernmental relations in Australia, Canada, the United States and other countries. Kingston, Ont.: Institute of Intergovernmental Relations, Queen's University, 1967. vi, 231 l. [2391]

"Le libre-échange et le champ récréotouristique." Dans: *Notes du Centre d'études du tourisme*; Vol. 8, no 6 (juillet 1988) p. 1-4.; ISSN: 0229-2718. [1850]

Licht, Merete

Et udvalg af bibliografier og monografier om Commonwealth litteratur i Det kongelige Bibliotek. København: Det Kongelige Bibliotek, 1978. 51 p. (Det Kongelige Bibliotek Fagbibliografier ; 8) [1131]

Liddell, Peter G.

A bibliography of the Germans in British Columbia. Vancouver: Canadian Association of University Teachers of German, 1982. 89 p. (CAUTG publications / Canadian Association of University Teachers of German ; no. 5); ISBN: 0-91994404-3. [4213]

Liepner, Michael; Chunn, Dorothy E.

The secondary school law programme: an annotated bibliography. Toronto: Centre of Criminology, University of Toronto, 1976. iii, 46 p.; ISBN: 0-919584-29-2. [2153]

Lifschutz, E.

Bibliography of American and Canadian Jewish memoirs and autobiographies in Yiddish, Hebrew and English. New York: YIVO Institute for Jewish Research, 1970. 75 p. [4148]

Light, Beth

"Recent publications in Canadian women's history." In: *Canadian Women's Studies*; Vol. 3, no. 1 (1981) p. 114-117.; ISSN: 0713-3235. [3801]

Light, Beth; Strong-Boag, Veronica

True daughters of the North: Canadian women's history: an annotated bibliography. [Toronto]: OISE Press, [1980]. v, 210 p. (Bibliography series / Ontario Institute for Studies in Education ; no. 5); ISBN: 0-7744-0185-0. [3796]

Light, John D.; Wylie, William N.T.

Guide pour la recherche sur l'histoire de la forge. Ottawa: Parcs Canada, 1986. 30 p.: ill. (Bulletin de recherches / Parcs Canada ; no 243; ISSN: 0228-1236) [5815]

A guide to research in the history of blacksmithing. Ottawa: Parks Canada, 1986. 27 p.: ill. (Research bulletin / Parks Canada ; no. 243; ISSN: 0228-1228) [5816]

Lightbown, Patsy

Bibliography of research on the acquisition of French L1 and L2. Quebec: International Center for Research on Bilingualism, 1984. ii, 27, xviii p. (International Center for Research on Bilingualism Publication ; B-132); ISBN: 2-89219-137-8. [1462]

Lillard, Charles

"Daylight in the swamp: a guide to the west coast renaissance." In: *Malahat Review*; No. 45 (January 1978) p. 319-340.; ISSN: 0025-1216. [1132]

"Fifty works of British Columbia fiction, 1908-1969." In: *Malahat Review*; No. 50 (April 1979) p. 23-26.; ISSN: 0025-1216. [1154]

"Logging fact and fiction: a bibliography." In: *Sound Heritage*; Vol. 6, no. 3 (1977) p. 73-77.; ISSN: 0316-2826. [4957]

Lilley, Doreen A.

East Indian immigration into Canada, 1880-1920: a bibliography. [Vancouver: University of British Columbia], 1966. 7 l. [4137]

Lim, Eileen

Automating the school library: a selective bibliography for librarians/L'informatisation des bibliothèques scolaires: une bibliographie sélective pour les bibliothécaires. Ottawa: National Library of Canada, 1988. 7 l. (Bibliographies / Library Documentation Centre; ISSN: 0226-4226) [1703]

Lin, Suzane; Roberts, Hazel J.

Financing universities in Canada: a bibliography/Le financement des universités au Canada: bibliographie. Ottawa: Association of Universities and Colleges of Canada, 1976. 7 p.; ISBN: 0-88876-044-2. [3515]

Lindal, Walter J.

"Icelandic-Canadian periodical publications: a preliminary check list." In: *Canadian Ethnic Studies*; Vol. 2, no. 1 (June 1970) p. 85-90.; ISSN: 0008-3496. [5897]

Lindeburgh, S.B.

Effects of prescribed fire on site productivity: a literature review. Victoria: B.C. Ministry of Forests, 1990. iv, 15 p.

(Land management report / British Columbia Ministry of Forests ; no. 66; ISSN 0702-9861); ISBN: 0-7718-8908-9. [5008]

Linden, Marjorie; Teeple, Diane
"The evolving role of Canadian women writers." In: *Ontario Library Review*; Vol. 61, no. 2 (June 1977) p. 114-131.; ISSN: 0030-2996. [1108]

Lindsay, Doreen; McCutcheon, Sarah
Women's bookworks: a survey exhibition of contemporary artists' books by Canadian women including unique book-objects and printed editions/Livres d'artistes-femmes: une exposition de livres contemporains réalisés par des artistes canadiennes comprenant des "livres-objets" uniques ou des livres faisant partie d'éditions à petits tirages. Montreal: Powerhouse Gallery, c1979. [ca. 100] p.: ill. [0691]

Linell, Kenneth A.; Johnston, G.H.
Engineering design and construction in permafrost regions: a review. Ottawa: Division of Building Research, National Research Council Canada, 1973. [23] p. (National Research Council Canada, Division of Building Research Technical paper ; no. 412) [5744]

L'Institut canadien d'éducation des adultes et les communications, 1956-1987: bibliographie analytique. Sainte-Foy, Québec: Réseau québecois d'information sur la communication, c1988. 41 p.; ISBN: 2-921026-00-7. [3689]

Linteau, Paul-André
"Sur quelques bibliographies récentes." Dans: *Revue d'histoire de l'Amérique française*; Vol. 28, no 1 (juin 1974) p. 105-112.; ISSN: 0035-2357. [1980]

Linteau, Paul-André; Thivierge, Jean
Montréal au 19e siècle: bibliographie. [Montréal]: Groupe de recherche sur la société montréalaise au 19e siècle, Université du Québec à Montréal, [1971]. viii, 79 f. [0311]

Linton, D.A.; Safranyik, L.
The spruce beetle, Dendroctonus rufipennis (Kirby): an annotated bibliography, 1885-1987. Victoria: Pacific Forestry Centre, 1988. 39 p.: ill. (Pacific Forestry Centre Information report ; BC-X-298; ISSN: 0830-0453); ISBN: 0-662-16210-2. [5545]

"L'Invasion du Canada, 1775-1776: esquisse bibliographique." Dans: *Cahiers d'histoire*; No 28 (1975) p. 225-228.; ISSN: 0008-008X. [1986]

Linzon, Samuel Nathan
An annotated bibliography, terrestrial effects of acidic precipitation. Toronto: Phytotoxicology Section, 1981. 181 p.; ISBN: 0-77437-087-4. [5173]

Lips, Hilary M.
"Social and psychological aspects of the normal pregnancy experience: a bibliography." In: *Resources for Feminist Research*; Vol. 9, no. 2 (July 1980) p. 72-77.; ISSN: 0707-8412. [3797]

"List of Dr F.E.J. Fry's publications." In: *Journal of the Fisheries Research Board of Canada*; Vol. 33, no. 2 (February 1976) p. 341-343.; ISSN: 0008-2686. [6992]

List of graduate theses in forestry and allied subjects accepted by Canadian universities, 1917-1956. [S.l.]: Pulp and Paper Research Institute of Canada, [1956]. [10] l. [6064]

Liste de référence des publications sur la construction domiciliaire. Ottawa: Affaires indiennes et du Nord Canada, Service techniques et marchés, 1984. 16 p. (Publications techniques des bandes) [5798]

Liste des bibliographies pour l'étude de l'Ontario français: dictionnaire des écrits de l'Ontario français. Sudbury [Ont.]: Université Laurentienne, 1984. ii, 48 p. (Document de travail / Université Laurentienne ; 1) [0477]

Liste des ouvrages subventionnés: soutien apporté à la diffusion du manuel scientifique, technique et médical francophone dans les universités du Québec (Entente franco-québécoise sur l'éducation). [S.l.: s.n.], 1972. 116 p. [5580]

Liste des publications de Louis-Edmond Hamelin, professeur de géographie et chercheur du Centre d'études nordiques, Université Laval, Québec. [S.l.: s.n.], 1975. 68 l. [7043]

Liste des revues littéraires françaises publiées en Canada depuis la cession 1763 jusqu'à 1883. [S.l.: s.n.], 1883. 1 f. [5855]

"Liste des thèses présentées à l'Institut d'histoire (Université de Montréal) 1947-1965." Dans: *Revue d'histoire de l'Amérique française*; Vol. 20, no 3 (décembre 1966) p. 515-521.; ISSN: 0035-2357. [6085]

Lister, Rota Herzberg
"Canadian plays in English about older women: a bibliography." In: *Resources for Feminist Research*; Vol. 11, no. 2 (July 1982) p. 238-240.; ISSN: 0707-8412. [1193]

Lisun, Luba
People and law: a bibliography of public legal education. Edmonton: Legal Resource Centre, University of Alberta Extension, 1978. 147 p. [2183]

Litchfield, Jack
The Canadian jazz discography: 1916-1980. Toronto: University of Toronto Press, c1982. 945 p.; ISBN: 0-8020-2448-3. [0905]

Literary and Historical Society of Quebec
Index to the archival publications of the Literary and Historical Society of Quebec, 1824-1924. Quebec: L'Événement, 1923. 215 p. [1903]

Literary and Historical Society of Quebec. Library
Catalogue of books in the library of the Literary and Historical Society of Quebec. Quebec: Printed by the "Morning Chronicle", 1873. v, 195, iv, [43] p. [6724]

Literary publications supported by Multiculturalism Canada/ Publications littéraires subventionnées par Multiculturalisme Canada. Ottawa: Multiculturalism Canada, 1984. 53 p.; ISBN: 0-662-53666-5. [1215]

Littlefield, George Emery
Catalogue of books and pamphlets relating to the American Indians. Boston: G.E. Littlefield, 1883. 24 p. [3905]

Liu, Gwen
"Ethnica Canadiana: a select bibliography." In: *Ontario Library Review*; Vol. 61, no. 3 (September 1977) p. 203-216.; ISSN: 0030-2996. [4180]

Livermore, Ronald P.
Bibliography of primary sources for classroom study of the history of Alberta [microform]. Calgary: University of Calgary, 1971. 1 reel of microfilm (x, 298 p.): ill., map, facsim. (Canadian theses on microfilm ; 10194) [0504]

"Livres canadiens pour la jeunesse canadienne." Dans: *École canadienne*; Vol. 24, no 7 (mars 1949) p. 446-448. [1309]

Les Livres disponibles canadiens de langue française/ Canadian French books in print. Outremont, Québec: Bibliodata, 1987-. vol.; ISSN: 0836-7078. [0187]

Les Livres du Québec: 40ième Foire du livre de Francfort, 5 au 10 octobre 1988, Groupe Québec (Canada), Hall 4.1:A:906. [S.l.]: SOGIC, Société générale des industries culturelles, Québec, [1988]. 81 p. [0403]

Livres du Québec. Montréal: Société de développement du livre et du périodique, 1980. 58 p. [0363]

Livres et auteurs canadiens: panorama de la production littéraire de l'année, 1961-1968. Montréal: [Éditions Jumonville], 1962-1968. 8 vol.: ill., ports.; ISSN: 0076-0153. [1043]

Livres et auteurs québécois: revue critique de l'année littéraire, 1969-1982. Québec: Presses de l'Université Laval, 1969-1983. 14 vol.: ill.; ISSN: 0316-2621. [1207]

Llamas, José

"Rappel bibliographique [Centre de recherches sur l'eau]." Dans: *Cahiers de Centreau*; Vol. 1, no 2 (1976) p. 1-66.; ISSN: 0702-7214. [5117]

Loades, Peter, et al.

Canada's multicultural mosaic. [Toronto]: Toronto Public Library, 1987. 16 p. [4241]

Locas, Claude

La réforme scolaire du Québec: bibliographie pour un bilan. [Québec]: Secrétariat, Direction générale de la planification, Ministère de l'éducation, 1975. 484 p. [3504]

Lochhead, Douglas

Bibliography of Canadian bibliographies/Bibliographie des bibliographies canadiennes. 2nd ed., rev. and enl. Toronto: Published in association with the Bibliographical Society of Canada by University of Toronto Press, 1972. xiv, 312 p.; ISBN: 0-8020-1865-3. [0104]

A checklist of nineteenth century Canadian poetry in English: the Maritimes. Preliminary ed. Sackville, N.B.: Centre for Canadian Studies, Mount Allison University, 1987. 75 l. [1240]

Lodhi, Abdul Q.; McNeilly, Russell A.

Human rights: sources and statutes. Fredericton, N.B.: Human Rights Research and Development, 1987. vii, 128 p.; ISBN: 0-920114-95-4. [2296]

Logement dans les réserves: bibliographie annotée. [Ottawa: Affaires indiennes et du Nord canadien], 1984. 24 f. [4060]

Logiciels éducatifs québécois. 3e éd. Montréal: Services documentaires multimedia, 1988. 146 p. (DSI/CB ; no 74; ISSN: 0825-5024); ISBN: 2-89059-346-0. [3690]

Lomer, Gerhard Richard

List of publications by Gerhard R. Lomer. [Ottawa: s.n.], 1960. 5 l. [7152]

Stephen Leacock: a check-list and index of his writings. Ottawa: National Library of Canada, 1954. 153 p.: ill. [7136]

Lomer, Gerhard Richard; Mackay, Margaret S.

A catalogue of scientific periodicals in Canadian libraries. Montreal: McGill University, 1924. xx, 255 p. [5860]

Lonardo, Michael

"The Canadian labour bibliography/Bibliographie du mouvement ouvrier canadien." In: *Labour: Le Travail*; Vol. 24 (Fall 1989) p. 95-218.; ISSN: 0700-3862. [2925]

Lonardo, Michael; Sweeny, Robert

"The Canadian labour bibliography/Bibliographie du mouvement ouvrier canadien." In: *Labour: Le Travail*; Vol. 26 (Fall 1990) p. 261-300; vol. 27 (Spring 1991) p. 371-423; vol. 28 (Fall 1991) p. 407-435; vol. 30 (Fall 1992) p. 339-367.; ISSN: 0700-3862. [2938]

London Public Libraries and Museums (Ont.)

Divorce: a multi-disciplinary approach. [London, Ont.]: London Public Libraries and Museums, [1986]. 13 p. [3289]

Lonergan, David

Le livre de mer: bibliographie commentée des livres de mer édités en français au Québec et au Canada et disponibles sur le marché. Bic, Québec: Isaac-Dion, 1993. 67 p.: ill.; ISBN: 2-9802497-2-6. [5299]

Long, Robert James

Nova Scotia authors and their work: a bibliography of the province. East Orange, N.J.: The Author, 1918. 312 [4] p. [0197]

Longley, Richmond Wilberforce; Powell, John M.

Bibliography of climatology for the Prairie provinces, 1957-1969. Edmonton: University of Alberta Press, 1971. 64 p. (University of Alberta studies in geography bibliographies ; 1); ISBN: 0-88864-002-1. [5059]

Loosely, Elizabeth W.; Wickson, Ethelwyn

"Canada: a reading guide and bibliography." In: *Booklist*; Vol. 37, no. 10 (February 1, 1941) p. 247-257. [0052]

Lord, Jules

Bibliographie analytique sur les grands domaines et jardins: Villa Bagatelle, Société d'histoire de Sillery. Sillery, Québec: J. Lord, 1990. 182 p. [0789]

Bibliographie sur les grands domaines de la Communauté urbaine de Québec: villas, jardins et cimetières-jardins. Québec: Institut québécois de recherche sur la culture, 1992. 129 p.: carte.; ISBN: 2-89224-175-8. [0802]

Lortie, Lucien

Bibliographie analytique de l'oeuvre de L'Abbé Arthur Maheux, précédée d'une biographie. Québec: [s.n.], 1942. 159 p.: portr. [7171]

Loslier, Sylvie

Répertoire sur les métiers d'art. Montréal: Centre de documentation Jean-Marie-Gauvreau, 1981. 50 f.; ISBN: 2-92027-300-0. [0696]

Lougheed, W.C.

Writings on Canadian English, 1976-1987: a selective, annotated bibliography. Kingston, Ont.: Strathy Language Unit, Queen's University, [1988]. xiii, 66 p. (Occasional papers / Strathy Language Unit, Queen's University ; no. 2); ISBN: 0-88911-510-9. [1479]

Lousier, J. Daniel

Impacts of forest harvesting and regeneration on forest sites. Victoria: British Columbia Ministry of Forests, 1990. x, 92 p. (Land management report / British Columbia Ministry of Forests ; no. 67; ISSN: 0702-9861); ISBN: 0-7718-8927-5. [5009]

Love, John L.

Bibliography of legal materials for the Ontario region of the Canadian Penitentiary Service: a purchasing selection aid. [S.l.: s.n.], 1977. 7 p. [2173]

Lover, John G.; Pirie, A.J.

Alternative dispute resolution for the community: an annotated bibliography. Victoria, B.C.: UVic Institute for Dispute Resolution, 1990. ix, 64 p.; ISBN: 1-550-58009-4. [2341]

Loveridge, Donald Merwin

A historical directory of Manitoba newspapers, 1859-1978. Winnipeg: University of Manitoba Press, c1981. 233 p.; ISBN: 0-887551-22-X. [6031]

A preliminary bibliography on the proposed Grasslands National Park. Winnipeg: Parks Canada, Department of Indian and Northern Affairs, 1977. 212 l. [3019]

Lovett, Robert Woodberry

American economic and business history information sources: an annotated bibliography of recent works pertaining to economic, business, agricultural, and labor history and the history of science and technology for the United States and Canada. Detroit: Gale Research, [1971]. 323 p. (Management information guide ; 23) [2593]

Lowenberg, Paul

Windfalls for wipeouts: an annotated bibliography on betterment recapture and worsenment avoidance techniques in the United States, Australia, Canada, England and New Zealand. [Monticello, Ill.: Council of Planning Librarians], 1974. 220 p. (Council of Planning Librarians Exchange bibliography ; 618-620) [4335]

Lowther, Barbara J.

A bibliography of British Columbia: laying the foundations, 1849-1899. [Victoria, B.C.: University of Victoria, 1968]. xii, 328 p. [0575]

Lubinsky, G.A.; Loch, J.S.

Ichthyoparasites of Manitoba: literature review and bibliography. Winnipeg: Western Region, Fisheries and Marine Service, Department of Fisheries and the Environment, 1979. vi, 29 p. (Fisheries and Marine Service Manuscript report ; no. 1513; ISSN: 0701-7618) [5435]

Lucas, Glenn

"Canadian Protestant church history to 1973." In: *Bulletin (United Church of Canada. Committee on Archives and History)*; No. 23 (1974) p. 5-50.; ISSN: 0824-5843. [1534]

Luce, Sally R.; Ostling, Kristen

"Women and white collar unions: an annotated bibliography." In: *Resources for Feminist Research*; Vol. 10, no. 2 (July 1981) p. 95-106.; ISSN: 0707-8412. [2873]

Lucyk, J.R.

Communications and the physically handicapped: a literature review with some policy implications. [Ottawa]: Broadcasting and Social Policy Branch, Department of Communications, 1979. ii, 48 p. [3187]

Ludewig, Hermann E.

The literature of American aboriginal languages. London: Trübner, 1858. xxiv, 258 p. (Trübner's bibliotheca glottica ; 1) [1400]

Ludovic, frère

Bio-bibliographie de Mgr Camille Roy, P.A., V.G., recteur de l'Université Laval. Québec: [Imprimé pour la Procure des Frères des Écoles Chrétiennes], 1941. 180 p. [7279]

Luethy, Ivor C.E.

"Swiss literature on Canada: a preliminary check list of imprints." In: *Canadian Ethnic Studies*; Vol. 2, no. 1 (June 1970) p. 245-248.; ISSN: 0008-3496. [4149]

Lukawiecki, Teresa

Elder abuse bibliography/Bibliographie sur les abus à l'égard des personnes âgées. [Ottawa]: National Clearing House on Family Violence, 1988. 87 p.; ISBN: 0-662-58951-3. [3310]

Lunn, Jean

"Bibliography of the history of the Canadian press." In: *Canadian Historical Review*; Vol. 22, no. 4 (December 1941) p. 416-433.; ISSN: 0008-3755. [6006]

"Canadian newspapers before 1921: a preliminary list." In: *Canadian Historical Review*; Vol. 25, no. 4 (December 1944) p. 417-420.; ISSN: 0008-3755. [6008]

Lusignan, Lucien

"Essai sur les écrits de deux martyrs canadiens." Dans: *Bulletin des recherches historiques*; Vol. 50, no 6 (juin 1944) p. 174-192. [1504]

Luttrell, Gwendolyn W.

Annotated bibliography on the geology of selenium. Washington, D.C.: United States Government Printing Office, 1959. P. 867-972. (United States Geological Survey Bulletin ; 1019-M) [4759]

Lutz, John S.; Young, George

The researcher's guide to British Columbia nineteenth century directories: a bibliography & index. [Victoria, B.C.]: Public History Group, University of Victoria, 1988. 162 p.; ISBN: 0-92127800-4. [0598]

Lyle, Guy R.

British emigration into the Saskatchewan valley: the Barr colony, 1903: its bibliographical foundation. [S.l.: s.n.], 1975. iv, 57 l. [1987]

Lyn, D.E.; McDonald, L.

A selective bibliography on the clothing and textile industry in Canada. Toronto: Ontario Ministry of Labour, Research Library, 1973. 5 l. [2608]

Lynas, Lothian

Medicinal and food plants of the North American Indians: a bibliography. New York: Library of the New York Botanical Garden, 1972. 21 p. [5581]

Lynch, K.D.

Partial bibliography of marine biomass resources of the Atlantic provinces. Halifax: Atlantic Research Laboratory, National Research Council of Canada, 1979. 60, [61] p. (Atlantic Research Laboratory Technical report ; no. 23) [5436]

Lynch-Stewart, Pauline

Changements d'utilisation des terres dans les milieux humides au sud du Canada: aperçu et bibliographie. Ottawa: Direction générale des terres, Environnement Canada, 1983. vii, 126 p. (Document de travail / Direction générale des terres, Environnement Canada ; no 26); ISBN: 0-662-92187-9. [5199]

Land use change on wetlands in southern Canada: review and bibliography. [Ottawa]: Lands Directorate, Environment Canada, 1983. 115 p. (Working paper / Lands Directorate, Environment Canada ; no. 26; ISSN: 0712-4473); ISBN: 0-662-12675-0. [5200]

Lyndsay Dobson Books

The Canadian private presses in print: a list of books & broadsides, posters and pamphlets, ephemera, etc. Grimsby, Ont.: Lyndsay Dobson Books, 1983. [50] p. [1657]

Lyttle, Brendan J.

A chartology of Canadian popular music: January 1965 to December 1976. [Toronto: RPM Music Publications, 1978]. 82 p. [0867]

Lyttle, Norman A.; Gillespie-Wood, Janet

Index to assessment reports, 1864-1980 [Nova Scotia Department of Mines and Energy]. Halifax: Department of Mines and Energy, Province of Nova Scotia, 1981. vii, 109 p.: map. (Nova Scotia Department of Mines and Energy report ; 81-4; ISSN: 0821-8188); ISBN: 0-88871-029-1. [6332]

Index to publications, open file reports and theses, 1862-1980 [Nova Scotia, Department of Mines and Energy]. Halifax: Province of Nova Scotia, Department of Mines and Energy, 1981. vii, 202 p.: map. (Province of Nova Scotia,

Department of Mines and Energy report ; no. 81-6); ISBN: 0-88871-030-5. [6333]

MacBryde, Bruce

"Bibliographical history of the botanical handbooks of the British Columbia Provincial Museum." In: *Syesis*; Vol. 7 (1974) p. 255-258.; ISSN: 0082-0601. [5382]

MacDermaid, Anne

"A select list of publications by A.R.M. Lower." In: *His own man: essays in honour of Arthur Reginald Marsden Lower*, edited by W.H. Heick and Roger Graham. Montreal: McGill-Queen's University Press, 1974. P. 163-182.; ISBN: 0-7735-0202-2. [7157]

MacDermot, Hugh Ernest

A bibliography of Canadian medical periodicals, with annotations. Montreal: Printed for McGill University by Renouf, 1934. 21 p. [5864]

Macdonald, Allan F.

Selected annotated bibliography of recent research on rural life on Prince Edward Island. Charlottetown, P.E.I.: Department of Sociology and Anthropology, University of Prince Edward Island, 1972. iv, 70 l. (P.E.I. community studies, report ; no. 1) [0212]

MacDonald, Christine

Historical directory of Saskatchewan newspapers, 1878-1983. Regina: Saskatchewan Archives Board, 1984. vi, 87 p.: ill., facsims. (Saskatchewan Archives Reference series ; 4); ISBN: 0-9691445-3-9. [6034]

"Jubilee local histories." In: *Saskatchewan History*; Vol. 8, no. 3 (Autumn 1955) p. 113-116; vol. 9, no. 1 (Winter 1956) p. 32-33; vol. 9, no. 3 (Autumn 1956) p. 110-115; vol. 11, no. 3 (Autumn 1958) p. 115-117.; ISSN: 0036-4908. [0498]

Publications of the governments of the North-West Territories, 1876-1905, and of the Province of Saskatchewan, 1905-1952. Regina: Legislative Library, 1952. 109 [1] p. [6233]

MacDonald, E. Grant; Macdonald, William S.

Fundy tidal power: a bibliography and guide to an assessment of its social impact. Halifax [N.S.]: Institute of Public Affairs, Dalhousie University, 1979. vi, 82 p.; ISBN: 0-88926-019-2. [5774]

Macdonald, John Stevenson; Miller, G.; Stewart, R.A.

The effects of logging, other forest industries and forest management practices on fish: an initial bibliography. West Vancouver, B.C.: Fisheries and Oceans Canada, 1988. iv, 212 p. (Canadian technical report of fisheries and aquatic sciences ; no. 1622; ISSN: 0706-6457) [4998]

MacDonald, Marjorie Anne

Robert Le Blant, historien et chef de file de la recherche sur les débuts de la Nouvelle-France: bibliographie commentée. Saint John: Musée du Nouveau-Brunswick, 1986. 30, 28 p.; ISBN: 0-919-32637-4. [7132]

Robert Le Blant, seminal researcher and historian of early New France: a commented bibliography. Saint John: New Brunswick Museum, 1986. 28, 30 p.; ISBN: 0-919-32637-4. [7133]

MacDonald, Mary Lu

"Chronological checklist: Canadian literary works about, or referring to, Indians: 1817-1850." In: *Canadian Literature*; No. 124-125 (Spring-Summer 1990) p. 106-109.; ISSN: 0008-4360. [1283]

MacDonald, Ruth

"Leonard Cohen." In: *Bulletin of Bibliography*; Vol. 31, no. 3 (July-September 1974) p. 107-110.; ISSN: 0007-4780. [6909]

Macdonald, William S.

Productivity in Nova Scotia: a review of the literature and annotated bibliography. Halifax, N.S.: Institute of Public Affairs, Dalhousie University, 1975. ix, 123 p.; ISBN: 0-88926-011-7. [0219]

Macdougall, Donald V.

"Popularized Canadian trials: a bibliography." In: *Gazette (Law Society of Upper Canada)*; Vol. 10, no. 3 (September 1976) p. 248-255.; ISSN: 0023-9364. [2154]

MacFarlane, David S.; Fraser, James H.

Water resources bibliography. Halifax: Province of Nova Scotia, Department of the Environment, 1985. ii, 111 p. [5225]

Macfarlane, Dianne; Giuliani, Gary

Crime prevention: a selected bibliography. [Toronto]: Centre of Criminology, University of Toronto, 1975. v, 78 p.; ISBN: 0-919584-19-5. [2143]

MacFarlane, Ivan C.

Annotated bibliography on engineering aspects of muskeg and peat (to 30 June 1969). Ottawa: National Research Council Canada, Division of Building Research, 1970. 1 vol. (in various pagings). (Bibliography / National Research Council Canada, Division of Building Research ; no. 39) [5733]

A preliminary annotated bibliography on muskeg. Ottawa: National Research Council Canada, Division of Building Research, 1955. 32 l. (National Research Council Canada, Division of Building Research Bibliography ; no. 11) [5328]

MacFarlane, John

The bibliography of Canadian heritage interpretation, 1982/ Bibliographie de l'interprétation du patrimoine canadien, 1982. Ottawa: Interpretation and Visitor Services Division, National Parks Branch, Parks Canada, [1982]. [37] l. [1817]

MacFarlane, William Godsoe

New Brunswick bibliography: the books and writers of the province. Saint John, N.B.: Sun Printing, 1895. 98 p. [0194]

MacGibbon, Diana

Towns, wheels or wings? for resource development: an annotated bibliography. [Victoria, B.C.]: Institute for Research on Public Policy, 1986. ix, 72 p. [4412]

MacGillivray, Royce

Sandy Fraser: a bibliography of the writings of John Everett McIntosh (1876-1948) in *The Farmer's Advocate* under the pen name of Sandy Fraser. Waterloo, Ont.: R. MacGillivray, 1991. 106 l.; ISBN: 0-9695129-0-2. [7183]

Machalski, Andrew

Hispanic writers in Canada: a preliminary survey of the activities of Spanish and Latin-American writers in Canada. [Ottawa]: Department of the Secretary of State of Canada, Multiculturalism, 1988. 51 l.; ISBN: 0-662-16031-2. [1255]

Multiculturalism in education resources: a user guide. [Ottawa]: Multiculturalism Sector, Department of the Secretary of State of Canada, 1987. 90 p. [4242]

Machine Readable Archives (Canada)

Recreation and leisure data files. [Ottawa]: Public Archives Canada, 1983. vi, 62, 63, vi p.; ISBN: 0-662-52335-0. [1824]

Machniak, Kazimierz

The effects of hydroelectric development on the biology of northern fishes (reproduction and population dynamics). Winnipeg: Freshwater Institute, Fisheries and Marine Service, Environment Canada, 1975. 4 vol. (Fisheries and Marine Service Technical report ; no. 527-530; ISSN: 0701-

7626) [5395]

The impact of saline waters upon freshwater biota: a literature review and bibliography. Edmonton: Alberta Oil Sands Environmental Research Program, 1977. 258 p.: map. (Alberta Oil Sands Environmental Research Program report ; no. 8) [5126]

MacInnis, Peggy

Guidelist of solo free bass accordion music suitable for student performers. Toronto: Canadian Music Centre, 1991. x, 92 p.; ISBN: 0-921519-05-2. [0940]

Mack, Yvonne

Goods and services tax: a reading list. Regina: Saskatchewan Legislative Library, 1990. 6 l. [2768]

Mackaay, Ejan

"Jurimétre, informatique juridique, droit de l'informatique: un résumé de la littérature." Dans: *Revue juridique Thémis*; No 1 (1971) p. 3-29.; ISSN: 0556-7963. [2120]

MacKay, A.H.

"Bibliography of Canadian botany." In: *Proceedings and Transactions of the Royal Society of Canada*; Series 2, vol. 7, section 4 (1901)-series 3, vol. 10, section 4 (1916) [5315]

Mackay, Neilson A.M.; Martin, Brian D.

Bibliography on railway signalling, 1960-1972. Kingston, Ont.: Canadian Institute of Guided Ground Transport, 1973. 50 l. (CIGGT report / Canadian Institute of Guided Ground Transport ; 73-9; ISSN: 0383-2449) [4457]

Mackenzie, B.J.

Bibliography of trace metals in marine and estuarine ecosystems, 1977-1981. Winnipeg: Government of Canada, Department of Fisheries and Oceans, 1983. iv, 20 p. (Canadian technical report of fisheries and aquatic sciences ; no. 1146; ISSN: 0706-6457) [5201]

MacKenzie, David

"Three sides of the same coin: some recent literature on Canada-Newfoundland relations in the 1940s." In: *Newfoundland Studies*; Vol. 4, no. 1 (Spring 1988) p. 99-104.; ISSN: 0823-1737. [2072]

Mackenzie, M.E.

"La Région de la Baie James (Québec): bibliographie linguistique." Dans: *Recherches amérindiennes au Québec*; Vol. 2, Spécial 1 (juin 1972) p. 43-49.; ISSN: 0318-4137. [1427]

MacKenzie, Margaret

Canadiana: a select bibliography of bibliographies in the Elizabeth Dafoe Library. Winnipeg: University of Manitoba Libraries, 1971. 4, 3 l. (Reference series / University of Manitoba Libraries ; no. 2) [0098]

A preliminary check-list of writings by native Manitobans and residents of Manitoba, and of material written about Manitoba and Manitobans. [Winnipeg: Elizabeth Dafoe Library, University of Manitoba, 1973]. 44 l. [0509]

The University of Manitoba almost one hundred years. Winnipeg: University of Manitoba Libraries, 1972. 26 l. (Reference series / University of Manitoba Libraries ; no. 5) [3440]

Mackenzie River Basin Committee

Sensitive areas: literature review: WATDOC references. [Edmonton: Environment Canada], 1981. 1 vol. (in various pagings): ill., maps. (Mackenzie River Basin Study report. Supplement ; 1; ISSN: 0227-0285); ISBN: 0-919425-02-X. [5174]

Mackey, William Francis

Le bilinguisme canadien: bibliographie analytique et guide du chercheur. Québec: Centre international de recherche sur le bilinguisme, 1978. [viii], 603 p. (Publication / Centre international de recherche sur le bilinguisme ; B-75) [1444]

MacKinnon, Fred R.

Annotated bibliography of social welfare in Nova Scotia. Halifax: Maritime School of Social Work, 1985. 221 p. [3276]

Maclachlan, Wills

List of articles, books, and reports on electrical shock and correlated subjects. Maple, Ont.: W. Maclachlan, 1956. 98 l. [5718]

MacLean, Ian A.

Inventaire des bases de données bibliographiques dans les établissements canadiens décernant des diplômes. Ottawa: Bibliothèque nationale du Canada, 1981. 1 vol. (en pagination multiple).; ISBN: 0-662-51478-5. [1645]

An inventory of bibliographic data bases in Canadian degree-granting institutions. Ottawa: National Library of Canada, 1981. 1 vol. (in various pagings).; ISBN: 0-662-51478-5. [1646]

MacLean, Margaret

"Reading in a second-foreign language: a bibliography 1974-1984." In: *Canadian Modern Language Review*; Vol. 42, no. 1 (October 1985) p. 56-66.; ISSN: 0008-4506. [3640]

Maclellan, Delphine C.

Theses and publications of the Marine Sciences Centre, 1964-1979. Montreal: Marine Sciences Centre, McGill University, 1979. 61 l. (Manuscript report / Marine Sciences Centre, McGill University ; no. 31; ISSN: 0828-1831) [5437]

MacMechan, Archibald

"Halifax in books." In: *Acadiensis*; Vol. 6, no. 2 (April 1906) p. 103-122; vol. 6, no. 3 (July 1906) p. 201-217.; ISSN: 0701-4368. [0196]

MacMillan, Jean Ross

"Music in Canada: a short bibliography." In: *Ontario Library Review*; Vol. 24, no. 4 (November 1940) p. 386-396.; ISSN: 0030-2996. [0809]

MacMillan, Keith; Beckwith, John

Contemporary Canadian composers. Toronto: Oxford University Press, 1975. xxiv, 248 p.: [4] l. of pl.; ISBN: 0-19-540244-8. [0846]

MacMillan, Rick

John Beckwith. Don Mills, Ont.: PRO Canada, 1983. 11 p.: port. [6833]

Robert Turner. Don Mills, Ont.: PRO Canada, 1983. 11 p.: music, port. [7341]

Macmillan, Stuart

An annotated bibliography of the Arctic charr (Salvelinus alpinus) with emphasis on aquaculture, commercial fisheries, and migration and movements. Winnipeg: Natural Resources Institute, University of Manitoba, 1987. 20 p. [4910]

Macnaughton, Elizabeth

"Researching ceramics." In: *Museum Quarterly*; Vol. 17, no. 4 (November 1989) p. 34-38.; ISSN: 0822-5931. [0720]

MacPhail, Cathy

A bibliography of works on the two Soos and their surroundings, giving locations of the libraries holding each title. [Sault Ste. Marie, Ont.]: Sault Area International Library Association, 1972. 94 l. (in various foliations). [0444]

MacPherson, Arlean
Rapeseed and mustard: a selected bibliography. Rev. ed. Winnipeg. Rapeseed Association of Canada, 1980. 150, [28] p. (Publication / Rapeseed Association of Canada ; no. 52) [4687]

MacPike, E.F.
"American and Canadian diaries, journals and notebooks: a short list." In: *Bulletin of Bibliography*; Vol. 18, no. 4 (May-August 1944) p. 91-92; vol. 18, no. 5 (September-December 1944) p. 107-115; vol. 18, no. 6 (January-April 1945) p. 133-135; vol. 18, no. 7 (May-August 1945) p. 156-158. [1006]

MacTaggart, Hazel I.
Publications of the Government of Ontario, 1901-1955: a checklist. Toronto: Printed and distributed by the University of Toronto Press for the Queen's Printer, 1964. xiv, 303 p. [6251]
Publications of the Government of Ontario, 1956-1971: a checklist. Toronto: Ministry of Government Services, 1975. xi, 410 p. [6300]

Maddaugh, Peter D.
A bibliography of Canadian legal history. Toronto: York University, 1972. xii, 77 p. [2126]

Maddick, Heather
County maps: land ownership maps of Canada in the 19th century/Cartes de comtés: cartes foncières du Canada au XIXe siècle. Ottawa: National Map Collection, Public Archives of Canada, 1976. vi, 94 p.: maps.; ISBN: 0-662-00108-7. [6556]

Madill, Dennis
Bibliographie annotée et choisie sur l'histoire et les revendications des Métis. [Ottawa]: Centre de la recherche historique et de l'étude des traités, Affaires indiennes et du Nord Canada, 1983. iii, 54 p.: carte. [4049]
Bibliographie choisie et annotée de la politique indienne et des revendications territoriales des Indiens de la Colombie-Britannique. Ottawa: Affaires indiennes et du Nord Canada, 1983. 28 p.: carte. [4050]
"Riel, Red River, and beyond: new developments in Métis history." In: *New directions in American Indian history*, edited by Colin G. Calloway. Norman: University of Oklahoma Press, 1988. P. 49-78. (D'Arcy McNickle Center bibliographies in American Indian history); ISBN: 0-80612-147-5. [4099]
Select annotated bibliography on British Columbia Indian policy and land claims. Ottawa: Department of Indian and Northern Affairs Canada, 1982. i, 27 p.: ill., map. [4034]
Select annotated bibliography on Métis history and claims. Ottawa: Treaties and Historical Research Centre, Indian and Northern Affairs Canada, 1983. 45 p.: map. [4051]

Maerz, Norbert H.; Smalley, Ian J.
The nature and properties of very sensitive clays: a descriptive bibliography. Waterloo, Ont.: University of Waterloo Library, 1985. x, 135 p.: ill. (University of Waterloo Library bibliography ; no. 12; ISSN: 0829-948X); ISBN: 0-920834-36-1. [4844]

Mage, Julius A.; Clemenson, Heather; Lee, Grant
Foreign ownership of farmland in Canada and the United States: legislative controls, literature review and bibliography. Guelph, Ont.: University School of Rural Planning and Development, University of Guelph, 1983. v, 59 l. (Publication (University School of Rural Planning and Development, University of Guelph) ; no. TSR-L10) [4700]

Magee, Eleanor E.
Pre-twentieth century literature of and about the Maritime Provinces: a bibliography of titles held in the special collections of Mount Allison University Library. Preliminary ed. [Sackville, N.B.]: Ralph Pickard Bell Library, Mount Allison University, c1978. iv, 25 p. (Maritime Studies Bibliography ; 2); ISBN: 0-88828-021-1. [0236]

Magee, Eleanor E.; Fancy, Margaret
Catalogue of Canadian folk music in the Mary Mellish Archibald Library and other special collections. [Sackville, N.B.]: Ralph Pickard Bell Library, Mount Allison University, [1974]. iv l., 88 p. (Library publications / Ralph Pickard Bell Library, Mount Allison University ; no. 5) [0839]

Magee, William Henry
A checklist of English-Canadian fiction, 1901-1950. [S.l.: s.n.], 1952. 65 p. [1011]

Magnan, Pierre; East, Pierre; Lapointe, Michèle
Modes de contrôle des poissons indésirables: revue et analyse critique de la littérature. Québec: Ministère du loisir, de la chasse et de la pêche, 1990. xi, 198 p. (Rapport technique / Québec Ministère du loisir, de la chasse et de la pêche); ISBN: 2-550-20959-1. [4915]

Maguire, Robert K.
Socio-economic factors pertaining to single-industry resource towns in Canada: a bibliography with selected annotations. Chicago, Ill.: Council of Planning Librarians, 1980. vi, 37 p. (CPL bibliography / Council of Planning Librarians ; no. 36); ISBN: 0-86602-036-5. [4384]

Maguire, Robert K.; Scott, Allen J.; Willson, K.M.
The structure and dynamics of intra-urban labour markets: a diagnostic bibliography. Toronto: University of Toronto-York University Joint Program in Transportation, 1981. 58 p. (University of Toronto-York University Joint Program in Transportation Research report ; no. 76; ISSN: 0316-9456) [2874]

Maheux, Arthur
Les trois Gosselin. Québec: [s.n.], 1946. 11 p. [7023]

Mahler, Gregory S.
Contemporary Canadian politics: an annotated bibliography, 1970-1987. New York: Greenwood Press, 1988. xiv, 400 p. (Bibliographies and indexes in law and political science ; no. 10; ISSN: 0742-6909); ISBN: 0-313-25510-5. [2520]

Mahy, Gérard D.
Annotated bibliography of Fundy National Park. Bathurst, N.B.: National and Historic Parks Branch, 1971. 91, [2] l. [2981]

Mail, Patricia D.; McDonald, David R.
Tulapai to Tokay: a bibliography of alcohol use and abuse among native Americans of North America. New Haven: HRAF Press, 1980. xv, 356 p. [4016]

Mailhiot, Bernard
"Les recherches en psychologie sociale au Canada français (1946-1962)." Dans: *Recherches sociographiques*; Vol. 3, no 1-2 (janvier-août 1962) p. 189-204.; ISSN: 0034-1282. [6075]

Mailhot, José
Les Amérindiens et les Inuit du Québec, des stéréotypes à la réalité: orientation bibliographique à l'usage des enseignants du primaire. [Québec]: Service de recherche et expérimentation pédagogique, Direction générale du développement pédagogique, Ministère de l'Éducation, [1980]. 81 p. (Études et documents: Collection "S.R.E.P." /

Service de recherche et expérimentation pédagogique); ISBN: 2-550-00969-X. [4017]

Maillet, Antonine

"Rabelais et les traditions populaires en Acadie." Dans: *Archives de Folklore*; Vol. 13 (1971) p. 189-196.; ISSN: 0085-5243. [4554]

Maillet, Lise

Provincial royal commissions and commissions of inquiry, 1867-1982: a selective bibliography/Commissions royales provinciales et commissions d'enquête, 1867-1982: bibliographie sélective. Ottawa: National Library of Canada, 1986. xvii, 254 p.; ISBN: 0-660-53123-2. [6381]

Maillet, Lise; Scott, Wendy

Law library networking: a list of references .../Réseaux de bibliothèques de droit: une liste de références .... Ottawa: National Library of Canada, 1991. 8 p. (Bibliographies / Library Development Centre ; no. 7; ISSN: 0847-2467) [1727]

Maillet, Marguerite

"Acadian literature: bibliography." In: *The Acadians of the Maritimes: thematic studies*. Moncton, N.B.: Centre d'études acadiennes, Université de Moncton, 1982. P. 513-549. [1194]

Bibliographie des publications d'Acadie, 1609-1990: sources premières et sources secondes. Moncton, N.-B.: Chaire d'études acadiennes, 1992. 389 p. (Collection Balises ; 2); ISBN: 2-921166-05-4. [1298]

"La littérature acadienne: bibliographie sélective." Dans: *Canadian Review of Comparative Literature*; Vol. 16, nos 3/4 (September-December 1989) p. 664-668.; ISSN: 0319-051X. [1272]

"Littérature acadienne (1874-1960): les oeuvres (liste chronologique)." Dans: *Revue de l'Université d'Ottawa*; Vol. 49, nos 1-2 (janvier-avril 1979) p. 92-98.; ISSN: 0041-9206. [1155]

"Littérature d'acadie: bibliographie." Dans: *Les Acadiens des Maritimes: études thèmatiques*. Moncton, N.B.: Centre d'études acadiennes, Université de Moncton, 1980. P. 557-594. [1172]

Mailloux, Pierre

Bibliographie annotée d'ouvrages de référence. Montréal: Ministère des affaires culturelles, 1973. ix, 131 p.: fac.–sim. [0108]

Maine, Michael

Robert Farnon discography. Leicester: Robert Farnon Appreciation Society, 1977. [87] p. [6975]

Makepeace, Charles E.

The non-atomic uses of uranium: a bibliography of metallurgical abstracts. Ottawa: [s.n.], 1960. xxxvii, 165 p.: ill. [5721]

Malchelosse, Gérard

Benjamin Sulte et son oeuvre: essai de bibliographie des travaux historiques et littéraires (1860-1916) de ce polygraphe canadien, précédé d'une notice biographique. Montréal: Pays laurentien, 1916. 78 p. (Collection laurentienne) [7323]

Malcolm, Douglas

"An annotated bibliography of works by and about Mavis Gallant." In: *Essays on Canadian Writing*; No. 6 (Spring 1977) p. 32-52.; ISSN: 0316-0300. [6999]

Malcolm, Ross

A selected bibliography on regional and community park topics with particular reference to British Columbia. [Victoria, B.C.]: Parks and Outdoor Recreation Division, Ministry of Lands, Parks and Housing, 1983. (unpaged). [1825]

Malcolm, Wyatt

"Bibliography of Canadian geology." In: *Proceedings and Transactions of the Royal Society of Canada*; Series 3, vol. 8, section 4 (1914) p. 287-315, 317-350; series 3, vol. 9, section 4 (1915) p. 279-305; series 3, vol. 10, section 4 (1916) p. 131-168.; ISSN: 0316-4616. [4738]

Mallea, John R.; Philip, L.

"Canadian cultural pluralism and education: a select bibliography." In: *Canadian Ethnic Studies*; Vol. 8, no. 1 (1976) p. 81-88.; ISSN: 0008-3496. [4175]

Mallea, John R.; Shea, Edward C.

Multiculturalism and education: a select bibliography. Toronto: Ontario Institute for Studies in Education; Ontario Ministry of Culture and Recreation, 1979. 290 p. (Informal series / Ontario Institute for Studies in Education ; 9); ISBN: 0-7744-5019-3. [3552]

Mallen, Bruce E.; Litvak, I.A.

A basic bibliography on marketing in Canada. [Chicago: American Marketing Association, c1966]. x, 119 p. (AMA bibliography series / American Marketing Association ; no. 13) [2581]

Maltais, Claire

Bibliographie sélective sur les communautés culturelles. Montréal: Ministère des Communautés culturelles et de l'Immigration, 1984. 65 p.; ISBN: 2-550-11284-9. [4226]

Maltais, Madeleine

Événements d'hier: recension de brochures et de plaquettes anciennes. Chicoutimi: Université du Québec à Chicoutimi, 1974. 235 f. [1981]

Malycky, Alexander

"German-Albertans: a bibliography." In: *German-Canadian Yearbook*; Vol. 6 (1981) p. 311-344; vol. 7 (1983) p. 239-325.; ISSN: 0316-8603. [4218]

"Norwegian-Canadian periodical publications: a preliminary check list." In: *Canadian Ethnic Studies*; Vol. 2, no. 1 (June 1970) p. 159-161.; ISSN: 0008-3496. [5898]

"A preliminary check list of studies on Ukrainian-Canadian creative literature: Part I. General studies." In: *Canadian Ethnic Studies*; Vol. 1, no. 1 (1969) p. 161-163.; ISSN: 0008-3496. [1051]

"Ukrainian-Canadian periodical publications: a preliminary check list." In: *Canadian Ethnic Studies*; Vol. 1, no. 1 (1969) p. 77-142.; ISSN: 0008-3496. [5883]

"University research on Canada's Indians and Métis." In: *Canadian Ethnic Studies*; Vol. 2, no. 1 (June 1970) p. 95-107.; ISSN: 0008-3496. [6106]

"University research on Canada's Indians and Métis: a preliminary check list." In: *Northian*; Vol. 8, no. 4 (March 1972) p. 31-37.; ISSN: 0029-3253. [6119]

"University research on Jewish-Canadians." In: *Canadian Ethnic Studies*; Vol. 1, no. 1 (1969) p. 40-43.; ISSN: 0008-3496. [6098]

"University research on Negro-Canadians: a preliminary check list of theses." In: *Canadian Ethnic Studies*; Vol. 5, no. 1/2 (1973) p. 225-227.; ISSN: 0008-3496. [6126]

"University research on Ukrainian-Canadians: a preliminary checklist of dissertations and theses." In: *Canadian Ethnic Studies*; Vol. 1, no. 1 (1969) p. 72-76.; ISSN: 0008-3496. [6099]

Malycky, Alexander; Cardinal, Clive H.

"German-Canadian periodical publications: a preliminary check list." In: *Canadian Ethnic Studies*; Vol. 1, no. 1

(1969) p. 13-30.; ISSN: 0008-3496. [5884]

Malycky, Alexander; Harasymiw, Elaine Verchomin

"A preliminary check list of studies on Ukrainian-Canadian creative literature: Part II. Specific studies." In: *Canadian Ethnic Studies*; Vol. 2, no. 1 (June 1970) p. 229-244.; ISSN: 0008-3496. [1056]

Mandryka, Mykyta I.

Bio-bibliography of J.B. Rudnyckyj. Winnipeg: Ukrainian Free Academy of Sciences, 1961. 72 p. (Ukrainian Free Academy of Sciences: Series: Ukrainian Scholars ; no. 10) [7287]

Manégre, Jean-François; Blouin, Louise

Le rendement scolaire des élèves des communautés culturelles: bibliographie commentée. Montréal: Conseil des communautés culturelles et de l'immigration, 1990. 29 p.; ISBN: 2-550-20816-1. [3717]

Mangham, Colin R.

Prevention in action: a bibliography of research, programs and resources in substance abuse prevention. [Victoria, B.C.]: Alcohol and Drug Program, Ministry of Labour and Consumer Services, c1991. 140 p.; ISBN: 0-7718-8996-8. [3354]

Manitoba Genealogical Society. Library

The library holdings of the Manitoba Genealogical Society, 1982. [Winnipeg]: The Society, [1982]. 2, [41], 3 p. [2023]

Manitoba Library Association

Manitoba newspaper checklist with library holdings, 1859-1986. [Winnipeg]: Manitoba Library Association, 1986. 106 p.; ISBN: 0-9692814-0-4. [6037]

Manitoba School Library Audio Visual Association

Manitoba: a provincial look. [Winnipeg: Manitoba School Library Audio Visual Association], 1972. 48 p. [0506]

Manitoba Women's Directorate

Violence prevention materials in the schools: a national listing. Winnipeg: Manitoba Women's Directorate, 1992. 59, 63 p. [3730]

Manitoba. Department of Agriculture

Audio-visual catalogue [Manitoba Department of Agriculture]. Winnipeg: Manitoba Department of Agriculture, 1978-. vol.; ISSN: 0704-9676. [6704]

Manitoba. Department of Consumer and Corporate Affairs and Environment

Children and money: a bibliography. Winnipeg: Manitoba, Department of Consumer and Corporate Affairs and Environment, 1980. 16 p. [3203]

Manitoba. Department of Education

Curriculum implementation in Manitoba: literature review. Winnipeg: Manitoba Education, Planning and Research, 1985. 12 p. [3641]

Native peoples: Department of Education resources pertaining to Indians, Inuit and Metis. [Rev. ed.]. [Winnipeg]: Province of Manitoba, Department of Education, 1982. vii, 287 p. (Curriculum support series / Manitoba Department of Education) [4035]

Manitoba. Department of Education. Library

Annotated bibliography on gifted children. Winnipeg: Manitoba Department of Education, Library, 1981. 7 p. [3596]

Ethnic groups: bibliography materials in M.E.R.C. Winnipeg: Manitoba Department of Education, Multiculture Educational Resource Centre, 1984. 8 p. [4227]

Manitoba. Department of Natural Resources. Library

Annotated bibliography of the renewable resource publications of the Manitoba Department of Natural Resources. Winnipeg: The Library, 1980-. vol. (Manitoba Department of Natural Resources Manuscript report series ; ISSN: 0715-0504) [6454]

Manitoba. Energy Information Centre

Energy answers bibliography: a subject guide to the literature available at the Manitoba Energy Information Centre. Winnipeg: The Centre, 1983. [106] p. (in various pagings). [5791]

Manitoba. Environment Protection Board

Publications: Environment Protection Board, September 1970 – May 1974. Winnipeg: Environment Protection Board, 1974. [21] l. [6292]

Manitoba. Geological Services Branch

Publications price list [Manitoba Energy and Mines, Geological Services Branch and Mines Branch]. Winnipeg: The Branches, 1985-. vol.; ISSN: 0845-101X. [6455]

Manitoba. Instructional Resources Branch

Images: a bibliography of Canadian children's and young adult literature. Winnipeg: Manitoba Education and Training, Instructional Resources Branch, 1990. 24 p. [1388]

Manitoba. Instructional Resources Branch. Library

Anti-racist education: kindergarten to senior 4: a bibliography of resources available from the Library, Instructional Resources Branch. Winnipeg: The Library, 1992. 7 p. [3729]

Manitoba. Legislative Library

Canadian imprints and books about Canada, 1949-1956. Winnipeg: The Library, [1957]. 71 l. [0065]

Manitoba government publications. Winnipeg: Legislative Library, 1975-. vol.; ISSN: 0701-7553. [6457]

Manitoba government publications, 1970-1974: a checklist compiled in the Legislative Library. Winnipeg: Queen's Printer, 1981. 153 p. [6334]

Manitoba government publications: monthly checklist/Publications du gouvernement du Manitoba: liste mensuelle. Winnipeg: Manitoba Culture, Heritage and Recreation, 1975-. vol.; ISSN: 0318-1200. [6456]

Manitoba. Manitoba Education and Training

Outdoor education resource catalogue. Winnipeg: Manitoba Education and Training, 1991. v, 95 p.; ISBN: 0-7711-1003-0. [3723]

Manitoba. Manitoba Education. Library

AIDS 1989: a bibliography of resources available from Manitoba Education Library. [Winnipeg]: Instructional Resources, Manitoba Education, 1989. 18 p.; ISBN: 0-7711-0804-4. [3703]

Manitoba. Multiculture Educational Resource Centre

Heritage language resources: an annotated bibliography. Winnipeg: Multiculture Educational Resource Centre, Manitoba Education, 1989. iv l., 89 p.; ISBN: 0-7711-0796-X. [1487]

Manitoba. Native Education Branch

Teacher handbook: resource materials: Native peoples of Manitoba. [Winnipeg]: Manitoba Native Education Branch; School Library Services Branch, Department of Education, [1976]. 99 p. [3982]

Manitoba. Office of the Queen's Printer

Statutory publications, price list/Publications officielles, liste des prix. [Winnipeg]: Manitoba Culture, Heritage and Citizenship, 1991-. vol.; ISSN: 1185-9652. [6458]

Manitoba. Provincial Archives

"Selected bibliography of genealogical publications." In: *Saskatchewan Genealogical Society Bulletin*; Vol. 14, no. 1 (February 1983) p. 27-35.; ISSN: 0048-9182. [2028]

Manitoba. School Library Services

Focal point: a bibliography of non-print resources for the visual arts. Winnipeg: Manitoba School Library Services, 1983. iv, 76 p. (Manual / Manitoba School Library Services ; 5-83) [6655]

Manitoba. Water Standards and Studies Section

Bibliography of Water Standards Section publications. [Winnipeg]: The Section, [1983]-. vol.; ISSN: 0836-9763. (Water Standards and Studies reports; ISSN: 0830-1735) [6459]

Manitoba's research on aging: an annotated bibliography, 1950-1982. [Winnipeg]: Manitoba Association on Gerontology, [1982]. v, 269 p. [3241]

Manley, Frank

Smash the state: a discography of Canadian punk, 1977-92. Westmount, Quebec: No Exit, 1993. vi, 138 p.: ill., ports.; ISBN: 0-9696631-0-2. [0943]

Mann, Donald; Coakley, John Phillip

An annotated bibliography of the geology and geomorphology of the Rondeau Peninsula and environs. [Waterloo, Ont.]: University of Waterloo, Department of Geography; Burlington, Ont.: Canada Centre for Inland Waters, Hydraulics Research Division, 1978. iii, 90 l.: map. [4807]

Manning, Frank E.

"Bibliography of Victor Witter Turner (1975-1986)." In: *Anthropologica*; Vol. 27, nos. 1-2 (1985) p. 235-239.; ISSN: 0003-5459. [7343]

Mansbridge, Francis

"Margaret Avison: a checklist." In: *Canadian Library Journal*; Vol. 34, no. 6 (December 1977) p. 431-436.; ISSN: 0008-4352. [6818]

"Margaret Avison: an annotated bibliography." In: *The annotated bibliography of Canada's major authors*, Vol. 6, edited by Robert Lecker and Jack David. Toronto: ECW Press, 1985. P. 13-66.; ISBN: 0-920802-93-1. [6819]

Manseau, Édith

Semaine des études québécoises, 1976: culture: bibliographie indicative. Trois-Rivières: Université du Québec à Trois-Rivières, [1976]. 7 f. [0341]

Manseau, Édith; Blanchette, Louise; Dumas, Céline

"Bibliographie de Réjean Ducharme." Dans: *Voix et images*; Vol. 8, no 3 (printemps 1983) p. 535-567.; ISSN: 0318-9201. [6958]

Mansfield, Arthur Walter; Smith, Thomas G.; Sergeant, David E.

Marine mammal research in the Canadian Arctic. Ste. Anne de Bellevue, Quebec: Arctic Biological Station, Fisheries and Marine Service, Department of the Environment, 1975. 23 l. (Fisheries and Marine Service Technical report ; no. 507; ISSN: 0701-7626) [5396]

Mantz, Douglas

Landscape in Canadian poetry: an annotated bibliography sampling the use of landscape in Canadian poetry, based upon the poetical works of major poets published in single-author book form between 1860 and 1960. Vancouver: [s.n.], c1981. 242 l. (TCP bibliography ; series 1, no. 1) [1183]

Maranda, Jeanne; Verthuy, Mair

"Québec feminist writing/Les écrits féministes au Québec." In: *Emergency Librarian*; Vol. 5, no. 1 (September-October 1977) p. 2-20.; ISSN: 0315-8888. [3771]

Marble, Allan Everett

A catalogue of published genealogies of Nova Scotia families. 2nd ed. Halifax: Genealogical Association of the Royal Nova Scotia Historical Society, 1984. 77 p. (Publication / Genealogical Association of the Royal Nova Scotia Historical Society ; no. 2) [2041]

Marcel, Gabriel

Cartographie de la Nouvelle France. Paris: Maisonneuve et Leclerc, 1885. 41 p. [6480]

Marchak, Nick

Assessing communication skills: a review of the literature: a study conducted under contract to Alberta Education, Edmonton, Alberta, Canada. Edmonton: Minister's Advisory Committee on Student Achievement, 1979. vii, 217 p.: ill. [3553]

Marchak, Patricia

"Canadian political economy [literature review]." In: *Canadian Review of Sociology and Anthropology*; Vol. 22, no. 5 (December 1985) p. 673-709.; ISSN: 0008-4948. [2711]

Marcotte, Alexandre

Bibliographie des travaux des laboratoires de biologie marine du gouvernement du Québec, 1938-1971. Québec: Direction générale des pêches maritimes, 1973. 131 p. (Cahiers d'information / Direction générale des pêches maritime, Direction de la recherche ; no 60) [5375]

Marcou, Jules; Marcou, John Belknap

Mapoteca geologica americana: a catalogue of geological maps of America (North and South), 1752-1881, in geographic and chronologic order. Washington: G.P.O., 1884. 184 p. (United States Geological Survey Bulletin ; vol. 2, no. 7) [6479]

Mardon, Jasper

Bibliography of references for Seminar on Basic Principles of Technical Papermaking: held at Lakehead University, Thunder Bay, Ontario, June 12, 13 and 14, 1974. Montreal: Technical Section, Canadian Pulp and Paper Association, [1974]. 64 p. [5749]

Margolis, L.

A bibliography of parasites and diseases of fishes of Canada: 1879-1969. Nanaimo, B.C.: Fisheries Research Board of Canada, 1970. 38 p. (Fisheries Research Board of Canada Technical report ; no. 185; ISSN: 0068-7553) [5355]

Maria Chapdelaine: évolution de l'édition 1913-1980. Montréal: Bibliothèque nationale du Québec, 1980. 80 p., 23 f de pl.: ill. (certaines en coul.).; ISBN: 2-550-01473-1. [7052]

Marie-de-Sion, soeur

Bibliographie analytique précédée d'une biographie du Rév. père Jean-Paul Dallaire, s.j. Saint-Damien: École normale N.D. du Perpétuel-Secours, 1960. 106 p. [6929]

Marie-Magloire-des-Anges, soeur

Bio-bibliographie de M. l'abbé Ovila Fournier, L.Sc., professeur à l'Institut de biologie de l'Université de Montréal, 1935-1955. Montréal: Cercles des jeunes naturalistes, 1962. xx, 89 p.: portr. [6988]

Marie-Raymond, soeur

Bio-bibliographie du R.P. Georges Simard, o.m.i. [Montréal]: Beauchemin, [1939]. 64 p.: port. [7308]

Marie-Ursule, soeur

"Civilisation traditionnelle des Lavalois: bibliographie." Dans: *Archives de Folklore*; Vol. 5-6 (1951) p. 391-395., ISSN: 0085-5243. [4533]

Marin, Armand

L'honorable Pierre-Basile Mignault. Montréal: Fides, 1946. 132 p. (Bibliographies d'auteurs canadiens d'expression française) [7190]

Marken, Jack W.

The Indians and Eskimos of North America: a bibliography of books in print through 1972. Vermillion, S.D.: Dakota Press, 1973. ix, 200 p.; ISBN: 0-88249-016-8. [3943]

Markham, Albert Hastings

The voyages and works of John Davis, the navigator. London: Printed for the Hakluyt Society, 1880. xcv, 392 p.: ill., maps. (Works issued by the Hakluyt Society; no. 59) [6942]

Markham, Susan E.

Research bibliography: the development of parks and playgrounds in selected Canadian Prairie cities, 1880-1930. Wolfville, N.S.: School of Recreation and Physical Education, Acadia University, 1989. 49 l. [4429]

Markotic, Vladimir

"Croatian imprints of Canada: a preliminary check list." In: *Canadian Ethnic Studies*; Vol. 5, no. 1/2 (1973) p. 19-25.; ISSN: 0008-3496. [4162]

Markowitz, Arnold L.

"Historic preservation: a survey of American and Canadian doctoral dissertations, 1961-1976." In: *Journal of Architectural Education*; Vol. 32, no. 3 (February 1979) p. 10-11.; ISSN: 0047-2239. [6152]

Marks, S.

Radon epidemiology: a guide to the literature. Washington, D.C.: U.S. Department of Energy, Office of Health and Environmental Research, 1988. iii, 136 p. [5680]

Marlatt, Daphne

"B.C. poets: a bibliography for 1970-75." In: *Communiqué: Canadian Studies*; Vol. 1, no. 4 (May 1975) p. 8-21.; ISSN: 0318-1197. [1092]

Marles, E.W.

Bibliography of oceanographic information for the inside waters of the southern British Columbia coast. Victoria, B.C.: Marine Sciences Directorate, Pacific Region, Environment Canada, 1973. 2 vol. maps. (Pacific marine science report; 73-1, 73-2) [5376]

Marsh, John S.

Recreation trails in Canada: a comment and bibliography on trail development and use, with special reference to the Rocky Mountain national parks and proposed Great Divide Trail. Monticello, Ill.: Council of Planning Librarians, 1971. 17 l. (Council of Planning Librarians Exchange bibliography; 175) [1759]

Marsh, Othniel Charles

Catalogue of official reports on geological surveys of the United States and British provinces. [S.l.: s.n.], 1867. 14 p. [4726]

Marshall, I.B.

The ecology and reclamation of lands disturbed by mining: a selected bibliography of Canadian references/L'écologie et la récupération des terres perturbées par l'activité minière: bibliographie sélective de la littérature[sic] canadienne. Enl. 2nd ed. [Ottawa]: Lands Directorate, Environment Canada, 1980. 64 p. (Working paper / Lands Directorate, Environment Canada; no. 1; ISSN: 0712-4473); ISBN: 0-662-50724-X. [5165]

Marshall, K.E.

A bibliography of the arctic charr, Salvelinus alpinus (L.) complex to 1980. Winnipeg: Western Region, Department of Fisheries and Oceans, 1981. iv, 68 p. (Canadian technical report of fisheries and aquatic sciences; no. 1004; ISSN: 0706-6457) [5464]

An index to the publications of the staff of the Freshwater Institute, Winnipeg; the Biological Station and Technological Unit, London; and the Central Biological Station, Winnipeg: 1944-1973. Winnipeg: Environment Canada, Fisheries and Marine Service, 1975. 94 p. (Fisheries and Marine Service Technical report; no. 505; ISSN: 0701-7626) [5397]

Online retrieval of information: a comparison of different systems used to produce a bibliography on Ephemeroptera and pollution, 1969-78. Winnipeg: Fisheries and Marine Service, Department of Fisheries and the Environment, 1979. vi, 18 p. (Fisheries and Marine Service Technical report; no. 878; ISSN: 0701-7626) [5151]

Marshall, K.E.; Keleher, J.J.

A bibliography of the lake trout, Cristivomer namaycush (Walbaum) 1929-1969. Winnipeg: Freshwater Institute, Fisheries Research Board of Canada, 1970. 60 p. (Fisheries Research Board of Canada Technical report; no. 176; ISSN: 0068-7553) [5356]

Marshall, K.E.; Woods, C.S.

A bibliography of Coregonid fishes. Winnipeg: Fisheries Research Board of Canada, 1971. 63 p. (Fisheries Research Board of Canada Technical report; no. 151; ISSN: 0068-7553) [5360]

Marsland, T.A.

An English language bibliography of computer chess. Edmonton: Department of Computing Science, University of Alberta, 1981. 42 (i.e. 21), 10 (i.e. 5) l. (Technical report / Department of Computing Science, University of Alberta; TR81-1) [1806]

Martel, Jacinthe

Bibliographie analytique d'Hubert Aquin, 1947-1980 [microforme]. [Montréal]: Service des Archives, Université de Montréal, 1984. 1 bobine de microfilm. [6803]

"Bibliographie analytique d'Hubert Aquin, 1947-1982." Dans: *Revue d'histoire littéraire du Québec et du Canada français*; No 7 (hiver-printemps 1984) p. 80-229.; ISSN: 0713-7958. [6802]

Martel, Yvon

Liste des publications scientifiques, des articles récents de vulgarisation et des projets actuels de recherches/List of scientific publications, recent extension articles and actual research projects. Lennoxville, Québec: Direction générale de la recherche, Agriculture Canada, 1981. 19 p. (Bulletin technique / Station de recherches Lennoxville; no 1; ISSN: 0319-9681) [4694]

Martijn, Charles A.

"Bibliographie préliminaire des Inuit de la Côte Nord du golfe Saint-Laurent, de la côte ouest de Terre-Neuve et du Labrador méridional: préhistoire et ethnohistoire/ Preliminary bibliography of the Inuit of the Gulf of St. Lawrence North Shore, the west coast of Newfoundland and southern Labrador: prehistory and ethnohistory." Dans: *Études Inuit Studies*; Vol. 4, nos 1-2 (1980) p. 201-232.; ISSN: 0701-1008. [4018]

"Canadian Eskimo carving in historical perspective:

bibliography." In: *Anthropos*; Vol. 59 (1964) p. 584-596.; ISSN: 0003-5572. [0668]

Martijn, Charles A.; Auger, Réginald

La présence autochtone dans le détroit de Belle-Isle, est du Canada: bibliographie préliminaire/The native presence in the Strait of Belle-Isle, eastern Canada: preliminary bibliography. Québec: Direction du Nouveau-Québec et service aux autochtones, Ministère des affaires culturelles, 1988. 49 p. [4100]

Martijn, Charles A.; Cinq-Mars, Jacques

"Aperçu sur la recherche préhistorique au Québec." Dans: *Revue de géographie de Montréal*; Vol. 24, no 2 (1970) p. 175-188.; ISSN: 0035-1148. [4551]

Martin, Carol

Canadian nomads: travel writing in the 20th century. Ottawa: National Library of Canada, 1991. 20, 20 p.; ISBN: 0-662-58147-4. [3065]

Des Canadiens nomades: récits de voyage du XXe siècle. Ottawa: Bibliothèque nationale du Canada, 1991. 20, 20 p.; ISBN: 0-662-58147-4. [3066]

Martin, Fred W., et al.

Therapeutic recreation in Canada: an annotated bibliography. [Waterloo, Ont.]: Therapeutic Recreation Information Centre, c1974. 68 p. (TRIC Information monograph series / Therapeutic Recreation Information Centre) [1767]

Martin, Gérard

"Bibliographie du siège de Québec (1759)." Dans: *Bulletin des recherches historiques*; Vol. 65, no 1 (janvier-mars 1959) p. 9-15. [1932]

"Bibliographie sommaire des écrits sur Samuel de Champlain." Dans: *Bulletin des recherches historiques*; Vol. 65, no 3 (juillet-septembre 1959) p. 51-62. [6901]

Bibliographie sommaire du Canada français, 1854-1954. Québec: Secrétariat de la Province de Québec, 1954. 104 p. [1925]

Bio-bibliographie de Joseph-Edmond Roy. Lévis [Québec]: Société d'histoire régionale de Lévis, 1984. 115 p.; ISBN: 2-920281-015. [7283]

Martin, Gwen L.

Neotechtonics in the Maritime Provinces. Ottawa: Atomic Energy Control Board, 1988. vii, 115 p. [4871]

Martin, Janis A.

An annotated bibliography of the literature on drinking and driving. Edmonton: Division of Alcoholism, Department of Health, Government of Alberta, 1969. 80, [4] p. [3091]

Martin, Maedythe J.; McGraw, Donna

Canadian constitutional reform: a checklist and index to the papers presented at Federal-Provincial conferences, 1976-1979. Toronto: Legislative Library, Research and Information Services, 1980. ii, 34 p. [2217]

Martin, Shirley A.; Makahonuk, Glen

Louis Riel and the rebellions in the Northwest: an annotated bibliography of material in Special Collections, University of Saskatchewan Library. Saskatoon: University of Saskatchewan Library, 1986. 145 p. [2056]

Martin, Sylvia

An annotated bibliography of recommended titles for public libraries in western Canada to support the reading needs of children in early French immersion programs. Edmonton: [s.n.], 1983. 50 l. [1355]

Marvin, Maureen Woodrow

"Annotated bibliography: women and drugs." In: *Canada's Mental Health*; Vol. 22, no. 3 (September 1974) p. 13-19.; ISSN: 0008-2791. [3747]

Mason, E.; Maine, F.W.

Tissue culture and micropropagation for forest biomass production: literature review. Ottawa: National Research Council of Canada, Division of Energy, 1984. vi, 81 p.: ill. [5500]

Massel, Jo Anne, et al.

Learning & growing: international year of disabled persons, 1981. [London, Ont.]: London Public Libraries and Museums, 1981. 46 p. [3222]

Massey, D. Anthony; Potter, Joy

A bibliography of articles and books on bilingualism in education. Ottawa: Canadian Parents for French, [1980]. [136] p. [3569]

Massey, Michael

Canadian repertoire manual for youth orchestras. Banff, Alta.: Canadian Association of Youth Orchestras, c1985. 1 vol. (loose-leaf). [0921]

Masson, Gaétan

Revue de la littérature sur le camionnage des produits forestiers en forêt. [S.l.: s.n.], 1972. 46 f. [4933]

Masson, Louis François Rodrigue

Catalogue of the late Hon. L.R. Masson's magnificent private library: to be sold at public auction on Saturday, Monday, Tuesday, 9th, 11th, 12th April 1904, at 2:30 and 7:45 p.m. each day, at the residence, 286 Prince Arthur Street, Montreal, Canada. [Montreal]: Imp. La Patrie, 1904. 153 p. [6754]

Masters theses in the pure and applied sciences accepted by colleges and universities of the United States and Canada. New York: Plenum Press, c1974-. vol.; ISSN: 0736-7910. [6208]

Mastrocola-Morris, Elaine

The assault and abuse of middle-aged and older women by their spouses and children: an annotated bibliography. [Ottawa]: National Clearing House on Family Violence, 1987. 5 p.; ISBN: 0-662-16663-9. [3301]

Voies de fait et mauvais traitements imposés aux femmes d'âge moyen et avancé par les conjoints et les enfants: bibliographie annotée. [Ottawa]: Centre national d'information sur la violence dans la famille, 1987. 6 p.; ISBN: 0-662-95363-4. [3302]

Matejcek, Jan

Catalogue of Canadian music suitable for community orchestras. Toronto: Canadian Music Centre, 1971. 40 [i.e. 46] l. [0829]

"Material cultural research at Parks Canada." In: *Material History Bulletin*; No. 2 (1977) p. 70-78.; ISSN: 0703-489X. [4569]

Matheson, Frances

Cranbrook Herald, 1900-1908. [Vancouver: British Columbia Library Association], 1935-1936. [2], 22 p. [0565]

Mathews, Robin

Some of the materials concerning the struggle for the Canadian universities (other-wise known as "Americanization", "takeover", "de-Canadianization of the universities"). [Ottawa: s.n., 1971]. 18 l. [3420]

Mathien, Thomas

Bibliography of philosophy in Canada: a research guide/ Bibliographie de la philosophie au Canada: une[sic] guide à recherche. Kingston, Ont.: R.P. Frye, c1989. 157 p. (Frye

library of Canadian philosophy supplementary ; vol. 1);
ISBN: 0-919741-74-6. [1570]

Matteau Beaumier, Murielle

Répertoire de chansons québécoises. [Québec]: Gouvernement du Québec, Direction générale du développement
pédagogique, 1981. 76 p.; ISBN: 2-550-04777-X. [0897]

Matthews, Catherine J.

Police stress: a selected bibliography concerning police stress
and the psychological evaluation and counseling of police.
Toronto: Centre of Criminology, University of Toronto,
1979. viii, 43 p.; ISBN: 0-919584-44-6. [2198]

Matthews, Catherine J.; Armstrong, Douglas

The food processing industry in Canada: a selected
bibliography, with particular emphasis on Ontario food
processing. [Toronto]: Ontario Ministry of Labour,
Research Library, 1975. 23 l. [2617]

Matthews, Catherine J.; Chunn, Dorothy E.

Congestion and delay in the criminal courts: a selected
bibliography. Toronto: Centre of Criminology, University
of Toronto, 1979. viii, 66 p.; ISBN: 0-919584-45-4. [2199]

Matthews, Catherine J.; Jansen, Vivian A.

Accountability in the administration of criminal justice: a
selective annotated bibliography. Toronto: Centre of
Criminology, University of Toronto, 1993. xi, 87 p.
(Bibliography / Centre of Criminology, University of
Toronto ; no. 16); ISBN: 0-919584-72-1. [2361]

Matthews, William

American diaries: an annotated bibliography of American
diaries written prior to the year 1861. Boston: Canner,
1959. 383 p. [1018]

Canadian diaries and autobiographies. Berkeley: University
of California Press, 1950. 130 p. [1010]

Mattila, Robert W.

A chronological bibliography of the published works of
Vilhjalmur Stefansson. Hanover, N.H.: Dartmouth College
Libraries, c1978. xii, 66 p. [7321]

Mattison, David

"British Columbia photographers of the nineteenth century:
an annotated, select bibliography." In: *BC Studies*; No. 52
(Winter 1981-1982) p. 166-170.; ISSN: 0005-2949. [0701]

Catalogues, guides and inventories to the archives of
Alberta, British Columbia, Northwest Territories, and the
Yukon Territory: a selected bibliography of publications,
1968-1990. Vancouver: Archives Associations of British
Columbia, 1991. 23 p. (Archives Association of British
Columbia Occasional paper series ; 91-01; ISSN: 1183-
8574); ISBN: 1-895584-00-0. [1728]

Matyas, Cathy

Entrepreneurship and new business enterprise: a resource
list. [Kingston, Ont.: Infomat, 1988]. 90 l. [2745]

Maud, Ralph

"Bio-bibliography of Charles Hill-Tout." In: *The Salish people:
the local contribution of Charles Hill-Tout*. Vancouver: Talon
Books, 1978. Vol. 4, p. 17-32.; ISBN: 0-88922-151-0. [7064]

A guide to B.C. Indian myth and legend: a short history of
myth-collecting and a survey of published texts.
Vancouver: Talonbooks, 1982. 218 p.; ISBN: 0-88922-189-
8. [4036]

Maughan, R.G.

Rail transport of coal: a selective bibliography/Transport du
charbon par chemin de fer: bibliographie sélective.
Montreal: Transportation Development Centre, 1989. vii,
79 p. [4504]

Maurey, Pierre

"Lowry's library: an annotated catalogue of Lowry's books at
the University of British Columbia." In: *Malcolm Lowry
Newsletter*; No. 7 (Fall 1980) p. 3-10.; ISSN: 0228-8427. [6785]

Mavrinac, Mary Ann

Guide to Canadian newspapers on microfilm in the D.B.
Weldon Library. London: University Library System,
University of Western Ontario, 1992. x, 150 p.; ISBN: 0-
7714-1371-8. [6052]

Maxwell, Janet, et al.

Resource list for a multicultural society. [Toronto]: Ministry
of Education; Ministry of Culture and Recreation, [1977].
viii, 626 p. [4181]

Maxwell, Karen A.

A guide to solo Canadian trombone literature available
through the Canadian Music Centre. Toronto: Canadian
Music Centre, 1985. i, 14 p. [0922]

Maxwell, William Harold; Brown, Charles R.

A complete list of British and colonial law reports and legal
periodicals arranged in alphabetical and in chronological
order with bibliographical notes [and] with a check list of
Canadian statutes. Toronto: Carswell, 1937. viii, 141,
59 p. [2104]

May, Betty

County atlases of Canada: a descriptive catalogue/Atlas de
comtés canadien: catalogue descriptif. [Ottawa]: National
Map Collection, Public Archives of Canada, 1970. xii,
192 p.: ill., maps. [6520]

May, Louise

A guide to labour records and resources in British Columbia.
Vancouver: Special Collections Division, University of
British Columbia Library, 1985. 197 p. [2898]

May, Lucille

"Music and composers of Canada." In: *Ontario Library Review*;
Vol. 33, no. 3 (August 1949) p. 264-270.; ISSN: 0030-
2996. [0811]

Mayer, Katia Luce

Criminologie canadienne: bibliographie commentée: la
criminalité et l'administration de la justice criminelle au
Canada/Canadian criminology: annotated bibliographie:
crime and the administration of criminal justice in Canada.
[Ottawa]: Solliciteur général Canada, Division de la
recherche, [1977]. xviii, 726 p. [2174]

Mayer-Renaud, Micheline; Berthiaume, Monique

Les enfants du silence: revue de la littérature sur la
négligence à l'égard des enfants. Montréal: Centre de
services sociaux du Montréal métropolitain, Direction des
services professionnels, 1985. 161, 12, 25 p. [3277]

Mayhew, Daniel R.

Motorcycle and moped safety: an annotated bibliography of
the library holdings of the Traffic Injury Research
Foundation of Canada. Ottawa: Traffic Injury Research
Foundation of Canada, 1983. v, 195 p. (TIRF reports /
Traffic Injury Research Foundation of Canada) [4493]

Mayne, Seymour

"Irving Layton: a bibliography-in-progress, 1931-1971." In:
West Coast Review; Vol. 7, no. 3 (January 1973) p. 23-32.;
ISSN: 0043-311X. [7131]

Mayrand, Pierre

Sources de l'art en Nouvelle-France. Québec: [s.n.], 1968.
36 p., [6] f. [0672]

Mays, Herbert J.

"Canadian Population Studies Group: report of research in progress." In: *Histoire sociale: Social History*; Vol. 7, no. 13 (May 1974) p. 165-173; vol. 8, no. 16 (November 1975) p. 350-357.; ISSN: 0018-2257. [3009]

Mazur, Carol; Pepper, Sheila

Women in Canada: a bibliography, 1965-1982. 3rd ed. Toronto: OISE Press, c1984. xxi, 377 p.; ISBN: 0-7744-0288-1. [3830]

McAllister, Don E.; Steigerwald, Michèle Bélanger

Bibliography of the marine fishes of Arctic Canada, 1771-1985. Ste. Anne de Bellevue, Quebec: Fisheries and Oceans Canada, 1986. v, 108 p.: map. (Canadian manuscript report of fisheries and aquatic sciences; no. 1909; ISSN: 0706-6473) [5527]

McAndrew, William J.; Elliott, Peter J.

Teaching Canada: a bibliography. Orono, Me.: New England-Atlantic Provinces-Quebec Center, University of Maine at Orono, [1975]. 102 p. [0116]

McAtee, W.L.

"Ornithological publications of Percy Algernon Taverner, 1895-1945." In: *Bulletin (National Museum of Canada)*; No. 112 (1949) p. 102-113.; ISSN: 0068-7944. [7326]

McBrien, Marlene; Buschert, Karen

An introductory guide to coastal paddling information sources. [Ottawa]: Visitor Activities Branch, National Parks, Canadian Parks Service, 1991. 25 p. [1866]

McCaffery, Steve; Nichol, bp

Sound poetry: a catalogue for the eleventh International Sound Poetry Festival, Toronto, Canada, October 14 to 21, 1978. Toronto: Underwhich Editions, [1978]. 111 p.: ill. [1133]

McCallum, John D.

Gun control: a bibliography since 1970: Canada, Great Britain, United States. [Waterloo, Ont.]: Library, Wilfrid Laurier University, 1976. iii, 19 p. [2155]

McCann, Bernard

Bibliographie annotée des sources d'information statistique sur l'habitation et les ménages. Québec: Société d'habitation du Québec, Direction de l'analyse et de la recherche, 1988. 73 p. [4421]

McCardle, Bennett

Bibliography of the history of Canadian Indian and Inuit health. Edmonton: Treaty and Aboriginal Rights Research (T.A.R.R.) of the Indian Association of Alberta, 1981. 89 p. [5639]

Canadian Indian treaties, history, politics and law: an annotated reading list. Ottawa: Treaty and Aboriginal Rights Research of the Indian Association of Alberta, 1980. 28 l. [4019]

Indian history and claims: a research handbook. [Ottawa]: Indian and Northern Affairs Canada, 1982. 2 vol.: ill., map. [4037]

McCarl, Henry N.; McConnell, David

Bibliography on economic analysis for parks and recreation. Monticello, Ill.: Vance Bibliographies, 1985. 28 p. (Public administration series: Bibliography; P-1709; ISSN: 0193-970X); ISBN: 0-89028-459-8. [1835]

McCaughey, Claire

A survey of arts audience studies: a Canadian perspective, 1967-1984. Ottawa: Research & Evaluation, Canada Council, 1984. v, 76, 20, 10 p. [0706]

McClure, Lynn, et al.

First nations urban health bibliography: a review of the literature and exploration of strategies. Winnipeg: Northern Health Research Unit, University of Manitoba, c1992. 89 p. (Monograph series / Northern Health Research Unit, University of Manitoba; no. 5); ISBN: 1-895034-04-3. [5710]

McComb, Bonnie Martyn

"Ethel Wilson: a bibliography, 1919-1977." In: *West Coast Review*; Vol. 14, no. 1 (June 1979) p. 38-43; vol. 14, no. 2 (October 1979) p. 49-57; vol. 14, no. 3 (January 1980) p. 58-64; vol. 15, no. 1 (June 1980) p. 67-72.; ISSN: 0043-311X. [7367]

"Ethel Wilson: an annotated bibliography." In: *The annotated bibliography of Canada's major authors*, Vol. 5, edited by Robert Lecker and Jack David. Downsview, Ont.: ECW Press, 1984. P. 415-480.; ISBN: 0-920802-68-0. [7368]

McCombs, Judith; Palmer, Carole L.

Margaret Atwood: a reference guide. Boston: G.K. Hall, 1991. xxxi, 735 p.; ISBN: 0-8161-8940-4. [6813]

McConnell, Ruth Ethel; Wakefield, P.

Teaching English as an additional language: annotated bibliography. Vancouver: Extension Department, University of British Columbia, 1969. 74 l. [3403]

McCoy, James Comly

Canadiana and French Americana in the library of J.C. McCoy: a hand-list of printed books. Montreal: Grasse, 1931. 87 p. [0043]

Jesuit relations of Canada, 1632-1673: a bibliography. Paris: Rau, 1937. xv, 310, [36] p.: front. (port.), ill. (facsims). [1915]

McCready, A.L.

Paper on Canadian philatelic literature. [Ottawa]: Ottawa Philatelic Society, 1952. [5] p. [1746]

McCreath, Peter L., et al.

Multiculturalism in the Maritimes: a teacher's resource guide. Tantallon, N.S.: Four East Publications, 1987. 49 p.; ISBN: 0-920427-14-6. [4243]

McCrossan, R.G., et al.

Annotated bibliography of geology of the sedimentary basin of Alberta and of adjacent parts of British Columbia and Northwest Territories, 1845-1955. Calgary: Alberta Society of Petroleum Geologists, 1958. xv, 499 p.: map (folded). [4755]

McCue, Harvey A.

Subject bibliography: native studies [bibliography of bibliographies]. [Peterborough, Ont.: s.n., 1981]. 10 l. [4026]

McCullough, Alan Bruce

Bibliographie annotée de travaux choisis sur l'historique des pêcheries commerciales des Grands Lacs canadiens. [Ottawa]: Parcs Canada, 1986. 20 p. (Bulletin de recherches / Parcs Canada; no. 238; ISSN: 0228-1236) [4905]

A select, annotated bibliography on the history of the commercial fisheries of the Canadian Great Lakes. [Ottawa]: Parks Canada, 1986. 20 p. (Research bulletin / Parks Canada; no. 238; ISSN: 0228-1228) [4906]

McCullough, Donna, et al.

Annotated bibliography: Peterborough and Lakefield. [S.l.: s.n.], 1974. 203 l.: ill., facsims., maps. [0450]

McDiarmid, Garnet

Culture contact, with special reference to the Indians of North America: an annotated bibliography. [Toronto]: Ontario Institute for Studies in Education, 1967. 214

l. [3913]

McDonald, Douglas Moore

A select bibliography on the location of industry. Montreal: McGill University, 1937. xi, 84 p. (Social research bulletin / McGill University ; no. 2) [2561]

McDonald, Michael

Bibliography on the family from the fields of theology and philosophy. Ottawa: Vanier Institute of the Family, 1964. vi, 95 l. [3082]

McDougall, Keith A.; McGillis, Joe R.; Holroyd, Geoffrey L.

Annotated wildlife references for Banff and Jasper National Parks. Edmonton: Canadian Wildlife Service, 1985. ii, 94 p. [5514]

McDowell, Marilyn E., et al.

Northern food habits, nutrition and health: an annotated bibliography. Halifax: Mount Saint Vincent University, 1984. 80 p. [5661]

McDowell, Marjorie

A history of Canadian children's literature to 1900, together with a checklist [microform]. Fredericton: University of New Brunswick, 1957. 1 reel (iii, 342 p.) [1312]

McEwen, Ruth

"Bibliography on women in Canada: non-fiction." In: *Canadian Newsletter of Research on Women*; Vol. 1, no. 2 (October 1972) p. 42-45.; ISSN: 0319-4477. [3739]

McFarlane, Deborah

Federal energy R&D, task 4: renewable energy bibliography, 1976-1986/R-D énergétique du gouvernement fédéral activité 4: énergies renouvelables bibliographie, 1976-1986. [Ottawa]: Office of Energy Research and Development, Energy, Mines and Resources Canada, [1987]. xii, 210 p.; ISBN: 0-662-54669-7. [4862]

McGahan, Elizabeth W.

"Recent publications relating to the history of the Atlantic region." In: *Acadiensis*; Vol. 21, no. 1 (Autumn 1991) p. 200-224; vol. 21, no. 2 (Spring 1992) p. 191-222; vol. 22, no. 2 (Spring 1993) p. 186-206.; ISSN: 0044-5851. [0274]

McGee, Harold Franklin, Jr.; Davis, Stephen A.; Taft, Michael

Three Atlantic bibliographies. [Halifax, N.S.]: Department of Anthropology, Saint Mary's University, 1975. 205 p. (Occasional papers in anthropology / Department of Anthropology, Saint Mary's University ; no. 1) [4561]

McGill University. Archives

Near-print publications of the McGill University Archives. Montreal: McGill University, 1974. 10 p. [1606]

A preliminary guide to motion pictures in the University Archives collections, McGill University. Montreal: McGill University, 1969. 19 l. [6612]

McGill University. Blackader Library of Architecture

Books on town planning: a reference collection on view in the Blackader Library of Architecture, McGill University Library, January to March 1926. Montreal: Mercury Press, 1926. 20 p. [4300]

McGill University. Blacker-Wood Library of Zoology and Ornithology

A dictionary catalogue of the Blacker-Wood Library of Zoology and Ornithology. Boston: G.K. Hall, 1966. 9 vol. [5342]

McGill University. Centre d'études canadiennes-françaises

Le Québec: guide bibliographique en histoire. [Montréal]: Centre d'études canadiennes-françaises; Service de la référence, Bibliothèque McLennan, Université McGill, 1973. 14 p. [0325]

McGill University. Centre d'études canadiennes-françaises. Bibliothèque

Bibliographie préliminaire de poésie canadienne-française. [Montréal: s.n.], 1968. 26 f. [1044]

McGill University. Centre for Northern Studies and Research

Bibliography of McGill northern research, 1887-1975. Montreal: Centre for Northern Studies and Research, McGill University, 1976. iv, 92 p.: folded col. map. (Information series / Centre for Northern Studies and Research, McGill University ; no. 1; ISSN: 0709-6364) [0630]

McGill University. Department of Rare Books and Special Collections

Catalogue of the Rodolphe Joubert Collection on French Canada in the Department of Rare Books and Special Collections. Montreal: McGill University Libraries, 1984. 321 p. [0382]

Nineteenth-century maps and atlases of Montreal in the collections of the Rare Book Department of the McGill University Library. [Montreal: McGill University Library, 1973]. 6, [1] l. [6533]

McGill University. Faculty of Graduate Studies and Research

List of McGill doctoral theses, 1907-1967. Montreal: McGill University, 1968. [6090]

McGill University. French Canada Studies Programme

Bibliography: Canadian political parties, 1791-1867, 1867- (including books, review articles, graduate theses and pamphlets). [Montreal: s.n., 1966]. 70 l. [2387]

McGill University. Library School

A bibliography of Canadian bibliographies compiled by the 1929 and 1930 classes in bibliography of the McGill University Library School under the direction of Marion V. Higgins. Montreal: [s.n.], 1930. iv, 45 p. (McGill University publications, series VII: Library ; no. 20) [0042]

A bibliography of Stephen Butler Leacock. Montreal: [s.n.], 1935. 31 p., [4] p. of pl.: ill., ports. [7137]

McGill University. McLennan Library. Government Documents Department

Guide to parliamentary publications of the province of Quebec. Rev. ed. [Montreal]: Government Documents Department, McLennan Library, McGill University, 1977. 11 p. [6308]

McGill University. McLennan Library. Reference Department

Canadian history: a student's guide to reference sources. [Montreal]: The Library, 1978. 52 p. [1999]

Canadian literature: a guide to reference sources. [Montreal]: McLennan Library, Reference Department, McGill University, 1982. 28 p. [1195]

Quebec studies: a guide to reference sources. [Montreal]: The Library, 1988. 21 p.; ISBN: 0-7717-0181-0. [0404]

McGill University. Mechanical Engineering Research Laboratories

Publications of the Mechanical Engineering Research Laboratories: McGill University. Montreal: McGill University, Mechanical Engineering Research Laboratories, 1962. 8 l. [5723]

McGinnis, Janice Dickin

"Bibliography of the legal history of western Canada." In: *Law and justice in a new land: essays in western Canadian legal history*, edited by Louis A. Knafla. Toronto: Carswell, 1986. P. 333-354.; ISBN: 0-459-38100-8. [2284]

McGowan, Mark G.

"Coming out of the cloister: some reflections on developments in the study of religion in Canada, 1980-1990." In:

International Journal of Canadian Studies; No. 1-2 (Spring-Fall 1990) p. 175-202.; ISSN: 1180-3991. [1572]

McGrath, J.T.
Literature review on fracture toughness of the heat-affected-zone. Ottawa: Canada Centre for Mineral and Energy Technology, 1977. vii, 48 p.: charts. (CANMET Report / Canada Centre for Mineral and Energy Technology ; 77-59); ISBN: 0-660-01582-X. [5765]

McGrath, Margaret
Étienne Gilson: a bibliography/Étienne Gilson: une bibliographie. Toronto: Pontifical Institute of Mediaeval Studies, c1982. xxviii, 124 p. (Étienne Gilson series ; no. 3; ISSN: 0708-319X); ISBN: 0-88844-703-5. [7018]

McGrath, Robin
Canadian Inuit literature: the development of a tradition. Ottawa: National Museum of Man, 1984. x, 230 p.: ill., maps. (Canadian Ethnology Service paper ; no. 94; ISSN: 0316-1862) [1216]

"A selected bibliography of Inuit literature." In: *Canadian Review of Comparative Literature*; Vol. 16, no. 3/4 (September-December 1989) p. 704-706.; ISSN: 0319-051X. [1273]

McHenry, Renée E.
Intercity bus lines. Monticello, Ill.: Vance Bibliographies, 1990. 21 p. (Public administration series: Bibliography ; P-2887; ISSN: 0193-970X); ISBN: 0-7920-0547-3. [4512]

McHenry, Wendie A.
A fostering bibliography: based on material collected in the Library, Ministry of Human Resources. [Victoria] B.C.: [Library], Ministry of Human Resources, 1978. 16 p.; ISBN: 0-7719-8095-7. [3174]

McHoul, Alison
Books to enjoy: a list for teachers on Indian reserves. Ottawa: Indian and Northern Affairs Canada, 1982. 23 p.: ill. [4038]

McIlwraith, Thomas Forsyth
"Bibliography of Canadian anthropology." In: *Bulletin (National Museum of Canada)*; No. 142 (1956)-no. 204 (1967) [4542]

McInnes, B.E.; Nash, F.W.; Godfrey, H.
A preliminary annotated bibliography on Georgia Strait fishes. Nanaimo, B.C.: Pacific Biological Station, 1974. 216 p. (Fisheries Research Board of Canada Manuscript report series ; no. 1332) [5383]

McIntosh, Robert Dale
Catalogue of the sheet music collection. Vancouver: Provincial Archives of British Columbia, 1984. 1 vol. (in various pagings). [0916]

McIntyre, John
"Bibliographie de films en langue française." Dans: *Canadian Modern Language Review*; Vol. 34, no. 2 (January 1978) p. 211-220.; ISSN: 0008-4506. [6634]

McIntyre, Lillian
Geography of British Columbia: a selected bibliography, 1930-1965. [Vancouver]: U.B.C. Library, Social Sciences Division, 1975. 59 l. [3010]

McIntyre, Sheila
"A bibliography of scholarship on literature on and by Canadian women." In: *Canadian Newsletter of Research on Women*; Vol. 6, no. 1 (February 1977) p. 99-114.; ISSN: 0319-4477. [1109]

McIntyre, W. John; McIntyre, Janet Houghton
"Canadian furniture: an annotated bibliography." In: *Material History Bulletin*; No. 11 (Fall 1980) p. 36-56.; ISSN: 0703-

489X. [2011]

McKay, Jean
"A Colleen Thibaudeau checklist." In: *Brick: a Journal of Reviews*; No. 5 (Winter 1979) p. 71-78.; ISSN: 0382-8565. [7334]

McKay, Margaret
Women in the labour force with an emphasis on the clerical and service occupations: a selected bibliography. Ottawa: Social Sciences and Humanities Research Council of Canada, 1982. 59 p.; ISBN: 0-662-12070-1. [3811]

McKenzie, Donald; Collister, Edward A.
Bibliographie sélective sur la répartition géographique des professionnels de la santé. Québec: Ministère des affaires sociales, Service de l'informathèque, 1981. 41 f. (Série bibliographiques / Ministère des affaires sociales, Service de l'informathèque ; no 6; ISSN: 0713-0740) [5640]

McKenzie, Karen; Williamson, Mary F.
The art and pictorial press in Canada: two centuries of art magazines. Toronto: Art Gallery of Ontario, 1979. 71 p.: ill.; ISBN: 0-919876-47-1. [5934]

McKim's directory of Canadian publications. Montreal: A. McKim, 1892-1942. ISSN: 0383-9451. [6007]

McKitrick, Ross
The Canada-U.S. Free Trade Agreement: an annotated bibliography of selected literature. Kingston, [Ont]: Industrial Relations Centre, Queen's University, [1989]. 27 p. (Bibliography series / Industrial Relations Centre, Queen's University ; no. 7; ISSN: 0075-613X); ISBN: 0-88886-223-7. [2756]

McLachlan, R.W.
"Fleury Mesplet, the first printer at Montreal." In: *Proceedings and Transactions of the Royal Society of Canada*; Series 2, vol. 12, section 2 (1906) p. 197-230.; ISSN: 0316-4616. [7189]

McLaren, Duncan
Ontario ethno-cultural newspapers, 1835-1972: an annotated checklist. Toronto: University of Toronto Press, 1973. xviii, 234 p.; ISBN: 0-8020-2066-6. [6019]

McLaren, William S.; Myers, Barry B.
Guided ground transportation: a review and bibliography of advanced systems. Ottawa: Transport Canada, Development, 1972. 515 p. [4455]

McLaren Atlantic Limited
Revised biological literature review of Davis Strait [microform]. Calgary: Arctic Petroleum Operators' Association, 1987. 3 microfiches (164 fr.). (Report / Arctic Petroleum Operators' Association ; APOA 138-8) [5536]

McLaughlin, W. Keith
Health and safety aspects of visual display terminals: a comprehensive bibliography. Edmonton: Occupational Health and Safety Library, Alberta Workers' Health, Safety and Compensation, [1982]. 28 l. (Occupational health and safety bibliographic series ; no. 7) [5648]

McLean, E.J.; McLean, C.C.; Donaldson, Edward M.
A partially annotated guide to selected fish bibliographies (1738-1988). West Vancouver: Fisheries and Oceans Canada, 1989. iv, 43 p.: ill. (Canadian technical report of fisheries and aquatic sciences ; no. 1717; ISSN: 0706-6457) [5551]

McLean, M.P.; McNicol, R.E.; Scherer, E.
Bibliography of toxicity test methods for the aquatic environment. Winnipeg: Department of Fisheries and Oceans, 1980. vi, 29 p. (Canadian special publication of fisheries and aquatic sciences ; 50; ISSN: 0706-6481) [4896]

McLeay, D. and Associates Limited

Aquatic toxicity of pulp and paper mill effluent: a review. Ottawa: Environment Canada, 1987. xlii, 191 p.; ISBN: 0-662-15335-9. [5248]

Enquête bibliographique sur la toxicité des effluents de l'industrie des pâtes et papiers pour les biocénoses aquatiques. Ottawa: Environnement Canada, 1987. xliii, 183, [12] p.; ISBN: 0-662-94212-4. [5249]

McLeod, Donald W.

"A chronological checklist of W.C. Chewitt and Company imprints." In: *Papers of the Bibliographical Society of Canada*; Vol. 21 (1982) p. 30-45.; ISSN: 0067-6896. [1652]

McLeod, Donald W.; Miller, Alan V.

Medical, social & political aspects of the acquired immune deficiency syndrome (AIDS) crisis: a bibliography. Toronto: Canadian Gay Archives, c1985. iii, 314 p. (Canadian Gay Archives publication; no. 10); ISBN: 0-9690981-2-X. [5669]

McLeod, Gordon Duncan

A descriptive bibliography of the Canadian prairie novel, 1871-1970. Winnipeg: University of Manitoba, 1974. xviii, 253 l. [1085]

McLeod, Keith A.

A select bibliography on ethnicity and multiculturalism for high schools. [Toronto: Faculty of Education, University of Toronto, 1974]. 24, 2 p. [4167]

McMaster University. Library

Canadian pamphlets: a subject listing of the holdings of McMaster University Library. Hamilton, Ont.: McMaster University Library, 1976-1977. 3 vol. [6781]

McMillan, Barclay

"Tune-book imprints in Canada to 1867: a descriptive bibliography." In: *Papers of the Bibliographical Society of Canada*; Vol. 16 (1977) p. 31-57; facsims., music.; ISSN: 0067-6896. [0862]

McMullen, Lorraine

"A checklist of the works of May Agnes Fleming." In: *Papers of the Bibliographical Society of Canada*; Vol. 28 (1989) p. 25-37.; ISSN: 0067-6896. [6987]

McMurdo, John

Archaeological field research in British Columbia: an annotated bibliography. [Victoria]: Province of British Columbia, Archaeology and Outdoor Recreation Branch, Resource Information Services Program, [c1989]. viii, 343 p.: ill., map.; ISBN: 0-7718-8563-6. [4604]

McMurray, J.G.

The exceptional student of secondary school age: a bibliography for psychology and education, 1960-1970. [London, Ont.]: J.G. McMurray, [1971]. viii, 138 l. [3421]

McNally, Peter F.

"Canadian library history in English, 1964-1984: a survey and evaluation." In: *Readings in Canadian library history*, edited by Peter F. McNally. Ottawa: Canadian Library Association, 1986. P. 19-30.; ISBN: 0-88802-196-8. [1679]

"Canadian library history in French, 1964-1984: a survey and evaluation." In: *Readings in Canadian library history*, edited by Peter F. McNally. Ottawa: Canadian Library Association, 1986. P. 31-39.; ISBN: 0-88802-196-8. [1680]

McNaught, Hugh

Newspapers of the modern Northwest Territories: a bibliographic study of their publishing history (1945-1978) and publishing record. Edmonton: Faculty of Library Science, University of Alberta, 1980. 106 l.: map. [6029]

McNaught, Hugh; Faulds, Jon

The non-medical use of drugs by minors: a bibliography of legislative materials of the governments of Alberta and British Columbia. Vancouver: Non Medical Use of Drugs Directorate, Health and Welfare Canada, 1978. vii, 62 p. [2184]

McNicholl, Martin K.

Manitoba bird studies, 1744-1983: a bibliography. [Winnipeg]: Manitoba Natural Resources, 1985. 290 p. [5515]

McPhail, John Donald

Annotated bibliography on Arctic North American freshwater fishes. Vancouver: Institute of Fisheries, University of British Columbia, 1960. 24 p. (Museum Contribution / Institute of Fisheries, University of British Columbia; no. 6) [5333]

McPhail, Marjorie E.

A selected bibliography of salt cod. Halifax, N.S.: Fisheries Research Board of Canada, 1957. iv, 30 p. (New series circular / Fisheries Research Board of Canada; no. 5) [4886]

McPherson, Kathryn

A 'round the clock job: a selected bibliography on women's work at home in Canada. Ottawa: Supply and Services Canada, 1983. 45 p.; ISBN: 0-662-12710-2. [3821]

McQuarrie, Jane; Dubois, Diane

Canadian picture books/Livres d'images canadiens. Toronto: Reference Press, 1986. xv, 217 p.; ISBN: 0-919981-12-7. [1371]

McQuillan, Barry H.

A resource list of multi-media materials on ethnicity and multi-culturalism. [Toronto: s.n.], 1976. 47 p. [6629]

McQuitty, J.B.; Barber, E.M.

An annotated bibliography of farm animal wastes. [Ottawa]: Water Pollution Control Directorate, Environmental Protection Service, 1972. vii, 522, [360] p. (Technical appraisal report / Water Pollution Control Directorate, Environmental Protection Service; EPS 3-WP-72-1) [4654]

McRae, Douglas J.

Prescribed burning in jack pine logging slash: a review. Sault Ste. Marie, Ont.: Great Lakes Forest Research Centre, 1979. 57 p.: ill. (Great Lakes Forest Research Centre report; O-X-289; ISSN: 0704-7797) [4967]

McRae, James Duncan

Les effets de l'établissement d'ex-citadins en milieu rural: une rétrospective de la littérature canadienne. [Ottawa]: Direction générale des terres, Environment Canada, 1980. v, 30 p. (Document de travail / Direction générale des terres, Environnement Canada; no 3) [4688]

The influence of exurbanite settlement on rural areas: a review of the Canadian literature. [Ottawa]: Lands Directorate, Environment Canada, 1980. v, 30 p. (Working paper / Lands Directorate, Environment Canada; no. 3; ISSN: 0712-4473); ISBN: 0-662-11085-4. [4689]

McTernan, D.J.

French Quebec: imprints in French from Quebec, 1764-1990, in the British Library: a catalogue/Le Québec français: imprimés en français du Québec, 1764-1990, à la British Library: catalogue. London: British Library, 1992. 2 vol.; ISBN: 2-551-12801-3 (vol. 1). [0413]

Meagher, Heather

The medicare crisis in Saskatchewan (January 1, 1960 – July 31, 1962): a bibliography. Regina: Legislative Library, 1963.

201 p. [5568]

"La mécanisation de la construction: bibliographie." Dans: *Industrialisation forum*; Vol. 4, no 2 (1973) p. 27-34.; ISSN: 0380-3945. [5745]

Media for minds: educational resources from CBC Enterprises. Montreal: CBC Enterprises, 1986. vi, 133, 67, vi p.: ill.; ISBN: 0-88794-249-0. [6664]

Medin, Dean E.; Torquemada, Kathryn E.
Beaver in western North America: an annotated bibliography, 1966 to 1986. Ogden, Utah: Intermountain Research Station, 1988. 18 p. (Intermountain Research Station General technical report ; INT-242) [5546]

Mehlhaff, Carol J.
Canada and the United States. Colorado Springs, Colo.: United States Air Force Academy Library, 1985. 45 p. (Special Bibliography series / United States Air Force Academy Library ; no. 69) [2494]

Meikle, W. Duncan
"A bibliography of George M. Wrong." In: *Papers of the Bibliographical Society of Canada*; Vol. 14 (1975) p. 90-114.; ISSN: 0067-6896. [7373]

Meikle, William
The Canadian newspaper directory, or, Advertisers' guide: containing a complete list of all the newspapers in Canada, the circulation of each, and all the information in reference thereto. Toronto: Blackburn's City Steam Press, 1858. 60 p. [5994]

Meiklejohn, Christopher
Annotated bibliography of the physical anthropology and human biology of Canadian Eskimos and Indians. [Toronto]: Department of Anthropology, University of Toronto, 1971. 169, xvi l. [3929]

Meiklejohn, Christopher; Rokala, D.A.
The native peoples of Canada: an annotated bibliography of population biology, health, and illness. Ottawa: Canadian Museum of Civilization, National Museums of Canada, 1986. vi, 564 p. (Canadian Museum of Civilization Mercury series: Archaeological Survey of Canada paper ; no. 134; ISSN: 0317-2244) [5672]

Meister, Marilyn
"The little magazines of British Columbia: a narrative bibliography." In: *British Columbia Library Quarterly*; Vol. 31, no. 2 (October 1967) p. 3-19.; ISSN: 0007-053X. [5878]

Melançon, Benoît
"Filmo-bibliographie: cinéma et littérature au Québec." Dans: *Revue d'histoire littéraire du Québec et du Canada français*; No 11 (hiver-printemps 1986) p. 167-221.; ISSN: 0713-7958. [1229]

La littérature montréalaise des communautés culturelles: prolégomènes et bibliographie. Montréal: Groupe de recherche Montréal imaginaire, Université de Montréal, 1990. 31 f. [4277]

La littérature québécoise et l'Amérique: guide bibliographique. Montréal: Centre de documentation des études québécoises, Université de Montréal, 1989. 39 p. [1274]

Melançon, Carole
Bibliographie descriptive et critique de la réception canadienne de *Bonheur d'occasion*, 1945-1983 [microforme]. Ottawa: Bibliothèque nationale du Canada, 1986. 5 microfiches.; ISBN: 0-315-2094-5. [1230]

Melançon-Bolduc, Ginette
"Bibliographie choisie sur la Voie maritime du Saint-Laurent entre 1967 et 1973." Dans: *Revue de géographie de Montréal*; Vol. 29, no 1 (1975) p. 61-68.; ISSN: 0035-1148. [4461]

Melanson, Holly
Literary presses in Canada, 1975-1985: a checklist and bibliography. Halifax, N.S.: Dalhousie University, School of Library and Information Studies, 1988. iii, 187 p. (Occasional papers / Dalhousie University School of Library and Information Studies ; no. 43; ISSN: 0318-7403); ISBN: 0-7703-9717-4. [1256]

Melanson, Lloyd J.
Thirty-four Atlantic provinces authors/Trente-quatre auteurs des provinces de l'Atlantique. Halifax, N.S.: Atlantic Provinces Library Association, 1979. 38 p.; ISBN: 0-920844-00-6. [0240]

Meldrum, Janis
Lake Superior bibliography: a compilation of references on the aquatic ecosystem. Houghton, MI.: Isle Royale National Park, 1986. ii, 95 l. [5236]

Melenchuk, Allan Samuel
Cultural literacy in education: a literature review. Regina: University of Regina, Saskatchewan Instructional Development & Research Unit, 1987. v l., 232 p.: ill. (SIDRU Research report / Saskatchewan Instructional Development & Research Unit ; no. 2; ISSN: 0835-6580); ISBN: 0-77310-108-X. [3674]

"Mémoire de la Société Saint-Jean-Baptiste de Montréal sur l'éducation nationale: bibliographie sommaire." Dans: *Action nationale*; Vol. 51, no 9-10 (mai-juin 1962) p. 834-839.; ISSN: 0001-7469. [3382]

"Mémoires et thèses de linguistique et de traduction soutenus à l'Université de Montréal de 1943 à 1971." Dans: *Vingt-cinq ans de linguistique au Canada: hommage à Jean-Paul Vinay*. Montréal: Centre éducatif et culturel, c1979. P. 125-135.; ISBN: 2-7617-0019-8. [6153]

Memorial University of Newfoundland. Learning Resources Council
Cooperative planning and teaching: annotated bibliography. St. John's, Nfld.: Learning Resources Council, Memorial University of Newfoundland, 1991. 5 p. [3724]

Memorial University of Newfoundland. Maritime History Group
Check list of research studies pertaining to the history of Newfoundland in the archives of the Maritime History Group. 5th ed. St. John's: Memorial University of Newfoundland, 1981. 38 p. [0251]

Mendis, Asoka
Ethnocultural entrepreneurship: an overview and annotated bibliography. Ottawa: Multiculturalism and Citizenship Canada, 1989. 52 l. [4271]

Mennie-de Varennes, Kathleen
Bibliographie annotée d'ouvrages généalogiques à la Bibliothèque du Parlement/Annotated bibliography of genealogical works in the Library of Parliament. Ottawa: Publiée à titre gracieux par la Bibliothèque du Parlement, 1963. 2 f. prélim., ix, 180 f. [1940]

Bibliographie annotée d'ouvrages généalogiques au Canada/Annotated bibliography of genealogical works in Canada. Markham, Ont.: Published by Fitzhenry & Whiteside in association with the National Library of Canada and the Canadian Government Publishing Centre, Supply and Services Canada, c1986-1987. 6 vol.; ISBN: 0-88902-911-3 (vol. 1); 0-88902-959-8 (vol. 2); 0-88902-905-9 (vol. 3); 0-88902-910-5 (vol. 4); 0-88902-986-5 (vol. 5); 0-88902-995-4 (vol. 6) [?06?]

Sources généalogiques tirées de "Canadiana"/Genealogical materials compiled from "Canadiana". Ottawa: Canadian Library Association, 1962. 21 p. (Occasional paper / Canadian Library Association ; no. 38) [1937]

Mennie-de Varennes, Kathleen; Gourdes, Irénée

Bibliographie sur la bibliotechnique. Québec: Ministère des terres et forêts, Bibliothèque, 1973. 26 f. [1602]

Mental health filmography. [Toronto]: Audio Visual Services, Metropolitan Toronto Library Board, 1980. ii, 29 p. [6643]

Menzies, Robert J.

Psychiatry and the judicial process: a bibliography. Toronto: Centre of Criminology, University of Toronto, 1979. 75 p.; ISBN: 0-919584-42-X. [2200]

Mercer, Eleanor

"The writings of Frederic H. Soward." In: *Empire and nations, essays in honour of Frederic H. Soward*, edited by Harvey L. Dyck and H. Peter Krosby. Toronto: University of Toronto Press in association with the University of British Columbia, 1969. P. 219-228.; ISBN: 0-8020-1652-9. [7318]

Mercer, G.W.

Non-alcoholic drugs and personality: a selected annotated bibliography. Toronto: Addiction Research Foundation, 1972. 77 p. (Bibliographic series / Addiction Research Foundation of Ontario ; no. 4; ISSN: 0065-1885) [5582]

Mercer, Paul

A bio-bibliography of Newfoundland songs in printed sources. St. John's: Memorial University of Newfoundland, 1978. xiii, 382 l. [0868]

Newfoundland songs and ballads in print, 1842-1974: a title and first-line index. St. John's, Nfld.: Memorial University of Newfoundland, 1979. 343 p.: ports. (Memorial University of Newfoundland Folklore and language publications, Bibliographical and special series ; no. 6); ISBN: 0-88901-038-2. [0877]

"A supplementary bibliography on Newfoundland music." In: *Canadian Folk Music Journal*; Vol. 2 (1974) p. 52-56.; ISSN: 0318-2568. [0840]

Mercer, Tom

"Quelques périodiques autochtones." Dans: *Recherches amérindiennes au Québec*; Vol. 9, no 4 (1980) p. 355-359.; ISSN: 0318-4137. [5939]

Mercier, Jacques

Les effets du salaire minimum sur l'emploi: revue de la littérature empirique américaine, canadienne et québécoise et estimations additionnelles pour le Québec. Québec: Département des relations industrielles, Université Laval, [1987]. i f., 106, [39] p. (Collection Instruments du travail / Département des relations industrielles, Université Laval ; 87-04); ISBN: 2-920259-08-3. [2915]

Mercier, Marguerite

"Pierre Gaultier de Varennes, Sieur de La Verendrye: bibliographie." Dans: *Revue d'histoire de l'Amérique française*; Vol. 3, no 4 (mars 1950) p. 623-627.; ISSN: 0035-2357. [7106]

Mercure, Gérard

"Microdocumentation: bibliographie." Dans: *Bulletin de l'Association canadienne des bibliothécaires de langue française*; Vol. 18, no 4 (décembre 1972) p. 263-266.; ISSN: 0004-5314. [1595]

Meredith, Colin

Compte rendu sommaire et bibliographie annotée sur les besoins des victimes d'actes criminels. [Ottawa]: Ministère du Solliciteur général du Canada, [1984]. 289 p. (Rapport pour spécialistes / Ministère du Solliciteur général Canada ; no 1984-18) [3262]

Overview and annotated bibliography of the needs of crime victims. [Ottawa]: Ministry of the Solicitor General of Canada, [1984]. 138 p. (Programs Branch user report / Ministry Secretariat, Solicitor General Canada ; no. 1984-18) [3263]

Merrens, Roy

Bibliographie sommaire sur le port et le secteur riverain de Toronto. [Toronto: Commission royale sur l'avenir du secteur riverain de Toronto, 1989. [13] p. (Documents de travail du Centre canadien de documentation sur le secteur riverain ; no 1; ISSN: 0847-3218) [4430]

A selected bibliography on Toronto's port and waterfront. [Toronto: Royal Commission on the Future of the Toronto Waterfront], 1989. [13] l. (Working papers of the Canadian Waterfront Resource Centre ; no. 1; ISSN: 0847-320X) [4431]

Urban waterfront redevelopment in North America: an annotated bibliography. Toronto: University of Toronto-York University Joint Program in Transportation, 1980. xxvii, 104 p. (University of Toronto-York University Joint Program in Transportation Research report ; no. 66; ISSN: 0316-9456) [4385]

Merriman, J.C., et al.

Water resources of the Hudson Bay lowland: a literature review and annotated bibliography. Sault Ste. Marie, Ont.: Canadian Forestry Service, Department of the Environment, 1982. 43 p.: map. (Great Lakes Forest Research Centre Information report ; 0-X-338; ISSN: 0704-7797); ISBN: 0-662-12028-0. [5183]

Mertens, Susan

Michael Conway Baker. Don Mills, Ont.: PRO Canada, 1984. 7, [1] p.: music, port. [6824]

Messely, Maryse

Les Nouvelles technologies de la reproduction: bibliographie sélective par sujets. Québec: Centre de documentation, Conseil du statut de la femme, 1989. 79 p.; ISBN: 2-550-19791-7. [5691]

Messieh, Shoukry N.

A bibliography of herring (Clupea harengus L.) in the northwest Atlantic. St. Andrews, N.B.: Fisheries and Environment Canada, 1980. iii, 25 p. (Fisheries and Marine Service Technical report ; no. 919; ISSN: 0701-7626) [5453]

Messier, Jean-Jacques

Bibliographie relative à la Nouvelle-France. [Montréal]: Éditions Univers: L'Aurore, c1979. 198 p.; ISBN: 2-89053-004-3. [2003]

Metress, Seamus P.

"The Irish in the Great Lakes: selected bibliography of sociohistorical sources." In: *Ethnic Forum*; Vol. 7, no. 1 (1987) p. 97-109.; ISSN: 0278-9078. [4244]

Metress, Seamus P.; Baker, William M.

"A bibliography of the history of the Irish in Canada." In: *The Untold story: the Irish in Canada*, edited by Robert O'Driscoll and Lorna Reynolds. Toronto: Celtic Arts of Canada, 1988. P. 977-1001.; ISBN: 0-921745-00-1. [4258]

Metropolitan Toronto Library Board

Checklist of books presented by the Quebec Government to the Provincial Library Service of Ontario/Répertoire des livres offerts par le gouvernment [sic] du Québec au Provincial Library Service de l'Ontario. Toronto: Metropolitan Toronto Library Board, 1974. 77 p. [1607]

Metropolitan Toronto Library. Audio-Visual Services
Filmography: Indians of North America. Toronto: Audio-Visual Services, Metropolitan Toronto Library, 1975. 16 p. [6625]

Metropolitan Toronto Library. Languages Centre
A bibliographical check-list of Canadian Indian linguistics in the Languages Centre of Metropolitan Toronto Central Library. Toronto: Languages Centre, Metropolitan Toronto Library Board, 1975. 31 p. [1433]

Metropolitan Toronto Library. Languages Department
A selected bibliography of German Canadiana in the Languages Department of the Metropolitan Toronto Library/Deutschkanadische bücher aus der Sammlung der Sprachenabteilung der Metropolitan Toronto Library. Toronto: The Department, 1985. 17 p. [4233]

Metropolitan Toronto Library. Reference Division. Business Department
Biographies on Canadian business people. Toronto: The Department, 1985. [3] l. (Bibliographies on business topics ; no. 9) [2712]
Researching older Canadian companies at the Metropolitan Toronto Library. Toronto: The Department, 1984. 18 p.: ill. (Bibliographies on business topics ; no. 8) [2697]

Metropolitan Toronto Library. Science and Technology Library
Bibliography of standards. [Toronto]: Metropolitan Toronto Library Board, [1973]. 15 p. [5746]

Metropolitan Toronto Reference Library
One-half inch VHS videocassettes in the Audio Visual Services Department collection. Toronto: Metropolitan Toronto Reference Library, 1990-. vol.; ISSN: 0840-7134. [6705]

Meyer, Ron H.
A selected bibliography on railways in British Columbia. Vancouver: Pacific Coast Branch, Canadian Railroad Historical Association, 1973. 2 vol. (B.C. rail guide / Canadian Railroad Historical Association, Pacific Coast Branch ; nos. 6 and 7) [4458]

Meynen, Emil
Bibliography on German settlements in colonial North America, especially on the Pennsylvania Germans and their descendants, 1688-1933. Leipzig: Harrassowitz, 1937. xxxvi, 636 p. [4125]

Mezei, Kathy
Bibliography of criticism on English and French literary translations in Canada: 1950-1986, annotated/ Bibliographie de la critique des traductions littéraires anglaises et françaises au Canada: de 1950 à 1986 avec commentaires. [Ottawa]: University of Ottawa Press, [1988]. 177 p. (Translation studies: Cahiers de traductologie ; 7); ISBN: 0-7766-0198-9. [1480]

Mezirow, Jack D.; Berry, Dorothea M.
The literature of liberal adult education, 1945-1957. New York: Scarecrow Press, 1960. x, 308 p. [3379]

Michaud, Irma
"Antonin Dessane, 1826-1873." Dans: *Bulletin des recherches historiques*; Vol. 39, no 2 (février 1933) p. 73-76. [6954]

Michaud, Yves B.
Répertoire cartobibliographique sur la région de l'est du Québec. [Rimouski]: Cartothèque, Université du Québec à Rimouski, 1988. iii, 336 p.: cartes. [6592]

Michel, Bernard; Triquet, Claude
Bibliographie de la mécanique des glaces de rivières et de lacs/Bibliography of river and lake ice mechanics. [Québec]: Université Laval, Faculté des sciences, Département de génie civil, Section mécanique des glaces, 1967. [250] l. [5038]

Michie, George H.
A select annotated bibliography of Canadian geography. Montreal: Canadian Association of Geographers, 1962. 19 p. (Canadian Association of Geographers Education Committee Bulletin ; no. 5; ISSN: 0068-8304) [2963]

Michon, Jacques
"Catalogue des Éditions de l'Arbre, 1941-1948." Dans: *Éditeurs transatlantiques: études sur les Éditions de l'Arbre, Lucien Parizeau, Fernand Pilon, Serge Brousseau, Mangin, B.D. Simpson.* Sherbrooke, Québec: Éditions Ex Libris, 1991. P. [185]-225.; ISBN: 2-89031-128-7. [1729]

Micmac-Maliseet Institute
The Micmac-Maliseet resource collection: a bibliographical listing. Fredericton: Micmac-Maliseet Institute, University of New Brunswick, 1987. 115 p. [4089]

Microcomputers in libraries: a bibliography. Regina: Bibliographic Services Division, Saskatchewan Provincial Library, 1984. 31 p.; ISBN: 0-919059-09-0. [1663]

Microlog: Canadian research index/Microlog: index de recherche du Canada. Toronto: Micromedia, 1979-. vol.; ISSN: 0839-1289. [6460]

Micros, Marianne
Al Purdy, an annotated bibliography. Downsview, Ont.: ECW Press, 1980. P. 221-277.; ISBN: 0-920763-61-8. [7251]
"Al Purdy, an annotated bibliography." In: *The annotated bibliography of Canada's major authors*, Vol. 2, edited by Robert Lecker and Jack David. Downsview, Ont.: ECW Press, 1980. P. 221-277.; ISBN: 0-902802-40-0. [7252]

Mid-Canada bibliography. [Toronto: Maclean-Hunter, 1970]. 141 l. (in various foliations). [0620]

Midgley, Ellen
The pre-school visually impaired child: a guide for parents and practitioners: a selected, annotated bibliography. Toronto: Ontario Foundation for Visually Impaired Children, 1979. 28 p. [3188]

Mieux vivre sa sexualité: qui consulter? quoi lire? Saint-Lambert, Qué[bec]: Éditions Héritage, 1981. 121 p.: ill.; ISBN: 0-7773-5508-6. [3223]

Miki, Roy Akira
A record of writing: an annotated and illustrated bibliography of George Bowering. Vancouver: Talonbooks, 1990. xviii, 401 p.: ill., facsims.; ISBN: 0-88922-263-0. [6869]

Miletich, John J.
Acid rain in Canada: a selected bibliography. Chicago, Ill.: Council of Planning Librarians, 1983. v, 21 p. (CPL bibliography / Council of Planning Librarians ; no. 124); ISBN: 0-86602-124-8. [5202]
Canadian high technology since 1980: a selected bibliography. Chicago, Ill.: Council of Planning Librarians, c1984. v, 26 p. (CPL bibliography / Council of Planning Librarians ; no. 135); ISBN: 0-86602-135-3. [5799]
Charter airline services in Canada: a selective bibliography. Monticello, Ill.: Vance Bibliographies, 1982. 5 p. (Public administration series: Bibliography ; P-980; ISSN: 0193-970X) [4489]

Hazardous substances in Canada: a selected, annotated bibliography. Chicago, Ill.: Council of Planning Librarians, 1982. v, 21 p. (CPL bibliography / Council of Planning Librarians ; no. 91); ISBN: 0-86602-091-8. [2683]

Light rail transit in Canada: a selected bibliography, 1970-1980. Chicago, Ill.: CPL Bibliographies, 1981. v, 10 p. (CPL bibliography / Council of Planning Librarians ; no. 62); ISBN: 0-86602-062-4. [4483]

Noise pollution in Canada: a selected bibliography, 1971-1981. Chicago, Ill.: Council of Planning Librarians, 1982. v, 14 p. (CPL bibliography / Council of Planning Librarians ; no. 77); ISBN: 0-86602-077-2. [2684]

Milette, Denise McFadden; Milette, Jean-Luc

Répertoire de cartes autonomes sur l'Ontario français. Ottawa: Centre de recherche en civilisation canadienne-française, Université d'Ottawa, 1980. iv, 39 p. (Documents de travail du Centre de recherche en civilisation canadienne-française ; 17) [6571]

Milette, Jean-Luc

Répertoire de brochures relatives à l'Ontario français. Ottawa: Centre de recherche en civilisation canadienne-française, Université d'Ottawa, 1979. 67 p. (Documents de travail du Centre de recherche en civilisation canadienne-française ; 9) [0463]

Milisauskas, Sarunas; Pickin, Frances; Clark, Charles

A selected bibliography of North American archaeological sites. New Haven, Conn.: Human Relations Area Files, 1981. 2 vol. (HRAFlex Books bibliography series ; N4-001) [4583]

Millar, Esther

Bibliography of technical reports in the fields of computer science and computer engineering issued at the University of Waterloo from 1967-1987. Waterloo, Ont.: University of Waterloo Library, c1988. x, 215 p. + 1 microfiche. (University of Waterloo Library bibliography ; no. 17; ISSN: 0829-948X); ISBN: 0-920834-07-8. [5832]

Millar, J.F.V.; Ervin, Alexander M.

A status report and bibliography of cultural studies in the Canadian Arctic to 1976. Saskatoon: Institute for Northern Studies, University of Saskatchewan, 1981. 113 p.: graphs. [0640]

Miller, Alan V.

Capital punishment as a deterrent: a bibliography. Monticello, Ill.: Vance Bibliographies, 1980. 10 p. (Public administration series: Bibliography ; P-452; ISSN: 0193-970X) [2218]

Gays and acquired immune deficiency syndrome (AIDS): a bibliography. Toronto: Canadian Gay Archives, 1983. ii, 67 l. (Canadian Gay Archives publication ; no. 7); ISBN: 0-9690981-0-7. [5653]

Homosexuality and employment: a selected bibliography. Toronto: Ontario Ministry of Labour, Research Branch, 1978. 111 p. (Bibliography series / Ontario Ministry of Labour, Research Branch ; no. 11) [2845]

Homosexuality and human rights: a selected bibliography. Toronto: Ontario Ministry of Labour, Research Branch, 1978. 67 p. (Bibliography series / Ontario Ministry of Labour, Research Branch ; no. 12) [3175]

Homosexuality in specific fields: the arts, the military, the ministry, prisons, sports, teaching, and transsexuals: a selected bibliography. Toronto: Ontario Ministry of Labour, Research Branch, 1978. 58 p. (Bibliography series / Ontario Ministry of Labour, Research Branch ; no. 13) [3176]

Lesbian periodical holdings in the Canadian Gay Archives as of June, 1981. Toronto: Canadian Gay Archives, 1981. 15 l. [5945]

Our own voices: a directory of lesbian and gay periodicals, 1890-1990. Toronto: Canadian Gay Archives, c1991. iv, 704 p. (Canadian Gay Archives publication ; no. 12); ISBN: 0-9690981-6-2. [5976]

Sexual harassment of women in the workplace: a bibliography with emphasis on Canadian publications. Monticello, Ill.: Vance Bibliographies, 1981. 22 p. (Public administration series: Bibliography ; P-801; ISSN: 0193-970X) [3802]

Miller, Ann H.

School based programme options for gifted secondary students with a review of the literature and existing programmes. Vancouver: Educational Research Institute of British Columbia, 1982. 45 p. (Reports / Educational Research Institute of British Columbia ; no. 82:25) [3614]

Miller, Ann-Marie

Consumer skills for disadvantaged adults: an annotated bibliography. Toronto: Ministry of Consumer and Commercial Relations, Consumer Information Centre, 1980. iii, 99 p.; ISBN: 0-7743-5547-6. [3204]

Miller, E. Willard

United States trade: United States, Canada, and Latin America: a bibliography. Monticello, Ill.: Vance Bibliographies, 1991. 33 p. (Public administration series: Bibliography ; P-3064; ISSN: 0193-970X); ISBN: 0-792007-84-0. [2775]

Miller, Genevieve

Bibliography of the history of medicine of the United States and Canada, 1939-1960. Baltimore: Johns Hopkins Press, [c1964]. xvi, 428 p. [5569]

Miller, Gordon

The American bison (Bison bison): an initial bibliography. Edmonton: Canadian Wildlife Service, 1977. vii, 89 p. [5415]

Canadian Wildlife Service studies in Canada's national parks: a bibliography. Edmonton: Canadian Wildlife Service, 1978. v, 179 p. [5422]

Miller, Gordon; Fehr, Laurene D.

A contribution to the bibliography of the Mackenzie River Valley and northern Yukon: a list of Environment Canada reports and studies. Edmonton: Canadian Wildlife Service, 1976. 149 l. [5118]

Milligan, G.C.

Bibliography of the geology of the Precambrian area of Manitoba to 1950. Winnipeg: Province of Manitoba, Department of Mines and Natural Resources, Mines Branch, 1951. 67 p. (Mines Branch publication / Province of Manitoba, Department of Mines and Natural Resources ; 51-1) [4747]

Milligan, Janet; Wilson, Catherine

Historical bibliography of Amherst Island. Kingston, Ont.: Kingston Branch, Ontario Genealogical Society, 1983. 10 p. [0474]

Milliron, H.E.

A monograph of the western hemisphere bumblebees (Hymenoptera: Apidae, Bombinae). Ottawa: Entomological Society of Canada, 1970. lii p. (Memoirs of the Entomological Society of Canada ; no. 65) [5357]

Mills, B.A.

Bibliography of geology, palaeontology, industrial minerals, and fuels in the post-Cambrian regions of Manitoba, 1950 to 1957. Winnipeg: Province of Manitoba, Department of Mines and Natural Resources, Mines Branch, 1959. 32 p. (Mines Branch Publication / Province of Manitoba, Department of Mines and Natural Resources ; 57-4) [4760]

Mills, Judy; Dombra, Irene

University of Toronto doctoral theses, 1897-1967: a bibliography. [Toronto]: Published for the University of Toronto Library by University of Toronto Press, [c1968]. xi, 186 p.; ISBN: 0-8020-3224-9. [6091]

Milne, David

Canada-United States free trade: a bibliography/Libre-échange entre le Canada et les États-Unis: une bibliographie. 5th ed. [Ottawa]: External Affairs and International Trade Canada, 1989. 147 p. [2757]

Canadian cultural industries: a bibliography/Industries culturelles canadiennes: une bibliographie. [Ottawa]: Library, Department of External Affairs, 1988. 47 p. [0718]

Milne, Henry; Dau, Christian P.

Une bibliographie sur l'eider/A bibliography of eiders. Québec: Ministère du tourisme, de la chasse et de la pêche, 1976. 225, 23 p. (Bulletin / Service de la Faune du Québec ; no 20) [5409]

Milne, William Samuel

Canadian full-length plays in English: a preliminary annotated catalogue. Ottawa: Dominion Drama Festival, c1964. viii, 47 p. [1021]

Milner, Philip

Nova Scotia writes. Antigonish, N.S.: FORMAC Publishing, 1979. 100 p.: ill.; ISBN: 0-88780-036-X. [0241]

Milton, Norma

"Bibliography [recent publications relating to Canadian ethnic studies]." In: *Canadian Ethnic Studies*; Vol. 15, no.3 (1983) p. 140-150.; ISSN: 0008-3496. [4219]

Minion, Robin

Archaeology in northern Canada. Edmonton: Boreal Institute for Northern Studies, University of Alberta, 1985. 63 p. (Boreal Institute for Northern Studies Bibliographic series ; no. 20; ISSN: 0824-8192); ISBN: 0-919058-54-X. [4597]

Arctic transportation. Edmonton: Boreal Institute for Northern Studies, University of Alberta, 1984. 138 p. (Boreal Institute for Northern Studies Bibliographic series ; no. 11; ISSN: 0824-8192); ISBN: 0-919058-45-0. [4495]

Aurora. Edmonton: Boreal Institute for Northern Studies, University of Alberta, 1985. 73 p. (Boreal Institute for Northern Studies Bibliographic series ; no. 24; ISSN: 0824-8192); ISBN: 0-919058-58-2. [5226]

Biographies – Canada. Edmonton: Boreal Institute for Northern Studies, University of Alberta, 1986. 122 p. (Boreal Institute for Northern Studies Bibliographic series ; no. 25; ISSN: 0824-8192) [0653]

Building construction in cold climates. Edmonton: Boreal Institute for Northern Studies, University of Alberta, 1985. 80 p. (Boreal Institute for Northern Studies Bibliographic series ; no. 17; ISSN: 0824-8192); ISBN: 0-919058-51-5. [5808]

Canadian national parks. Edmonton: Boreal Institute for Northern Studies, University of Alberta, 1985. 73 p. (Boreal Institute for Northern Studies Bibliographic series ; no. 22; ISSN: 0824-8192); ISBN: 0-919058-56-5. [3047]

Caribou and reindeer in Canada and Alaska. Edmonton:

Boreal Institute for Northern Studies, University of Alberta, 1984. 65 p. (Boreal Institute for Northern Studies Bibliographic series ; no. 3; ISSN: 0824-8192); ISBN: 0-919058-37-X. [5501]

Children's books. Part I, social sciences. Edmonton: Boreal Institute for Northern Studies, University of Alberta, 1984. 95 p. (Boreal Institute for Northern Studies Bibliographic series ; no. 7; ISSN: 0824-8192); ISBN: 0-919058-41-8. [1361]

Children's books. Part II, excluding social sciences. Edmonton: Boreal Institute for Northern Studies, University of Alberta, 1984. 122 p. (Boreal Institute for Northern Studies Bibliographic series ; no. 8; ISSN: 0824-8192); ISBN: 0-919058-42-6. [1362]

Communities and towns of the Northwest Territories. Edmonton: Boreal Institute for Northern Studies, University of Alberta, 1985. 100 p. (Boreal Institute for Northern Studies Bibliographic series ; no. 23; ISSN: 0824-8192); ISBN: 0-919058-57-4. [4405]

Doctoral dissertations: northern Canada. Edmonton: Boreal Institute for Northern Studies, University of Alberta, 1986. 84 p. (Boreal Institute for Northern Studies Bibliographic series ; no. 27; ISSN: 0824-8192); ISBN: 0-919058-61-2. [6185]

Fish and fisheries of northern Canada and Alaska. Edmonton: Boreal Institute for Northern Studies, University of Alberta, 1985. 81 p. (Boreal Institute for Northern Studies Bibliographic series ; no. 18; ISSN: 0824-8192) [4903]

Flora in the Yukon and NWT. Edmonton: Boreal Institute for Northern Studies, University of Alberta, 1984. 95 p. (Boreal Institute for Northern Studies Bibliographic series ; no. 10; ISSN: 0824-8192); ISBN: 0-919058-44-2. [5502]

Glacial deposition including moraines, drumlins and eskers. Edmonton: Boreal Institute for Northern Studies, University of Alberta, 1985. 98 p. (Boreal Institute for Northern Studies Bibliographic series ; no. 19; ISSN: 0824-8192); ISBN: 0-919058-53-1. [5227]

Hydroelectric development in northern regions. Edmonton: Boreal Institute for Northern Studies, University of Alberta, 1985. 78 p. (Boreal Institute for Northern Studies Bibliographic series ; no. 21; ISSN: 0824-8192); ISBN: 0-919058-55-8. [0650]

Ice in the Beaufort Sea. Edmonton: Boreal Institute for Northern Studies, University of Alberta, 1984. 78 p. (Boreal Institute for Northern Studies Bibliographic series ; no. 6; ISSN: 0824-8192); ISBN: 0-919058-40-X. [5216]

Inuit and Indian languages, including educational concerns and materials in these languages. Edmonton: Boreal Institute for Northern Studies, University of Alberta, 1985. 77 p. (Boreal Institute for Northern Studies Bibliographic series ; no. 16; ISSN: 0824-8192); ISBN: 0-919058-50-7. [1464]

Inuit art and artists. Edmonton: Boreal Institute for Northern Studies, University of Alberta, 1986. 80 p. (Boreal Institute for Northern Studies Bibliographic series ; no. 26; ISSN: 0824-8192); ISBN: 0-919058-48-5. [0711]

Land use in northern Canada and Alaska. Edmonton: Boreal Institute for Northern Studies, University of Alberta, 1984. 67 p. (Boreal Institute for Northern Studies Bibliographic series ; no. 2; ISSN: 0824-8192); ISBN: 0-919058-36-1. [0646]

Master's theses – northern Canada. Edmonton: Boreal Institute for Northern Studies, University of Alberta, 1986. 108 p. (Boreal Institute for Northern Studies Bibliographic series ; no. 28; ISSN: 0824-8192); ISBN: 0-919058-62-0. [6186]

Myths and legends. Edmonton: Boreal Institute for Northern

Studies, University of Alberta, 1984. 79 p. (Boreal Institute for Northern Studies Bibliographic series ; no. 5; ISSN: 0824-8192), ISBN. 0-919050-39-6. [4061]

Native rights in Canada. Edmonton: Boreal Institute for Northern Studies, University of Alberta, 1984. 102 p. (Boreal Institute for Northern Studies Bibliographic series ; no. 1; ISSN: 0824-8192); ISBN: 0-919058-35-3. [4062]

Nineteenth century expeditions in the Arctic and Canada. Edmonton: Boreal Institute for Northern Studies, University of Alberta, 1984. 98 p. (Boreal Institute for Northern Studies Bibliographic series ; no. 4; ISSN: 0824-8192); ISBN: 0-919058-38-8. [0647]

Offshore development in northern Canada and Alaska. Edmonton: Boreal Institute for Northern Studies, University of Alberta, 1985. 83 p. (Boreal Institute for Northern Studies Bibliographic series ; no. 14; ISSN: 0824-8192); ISBN: 0-919058-48-5. [4845]

Partial list of theses related to native peoples. Edmonton: Boreal Institute for Northern Studies, University of Alberta, 1985. 133 p. (Boreal Institute for Northern Studies Bibliographic series ; no. 13; ISSN: 0824-8192); ISBN: 0-919058-47-7. [6180]

Religions of the circumpolar north. Edmonton: Boreal Institute for Northern Studies, University of Alberta, 1985. 92 p. (Boreal Institute for Northern Studies Bibliographic series ; no. 15; ISSN: 0824-8192); ISBN: 0-919058-49-3. [1561]

Seals. Edmonton: Boreal Institute for Northern Studies, University of Alberta, 1984. 94 p. (Boreal Institute for Northern Studies Bibliographic series ; no. 9; ISSN: 0824-8192); ISBN: 0-919058-43-4. [5503]

Swimmers and sea birds. Edmonton: Boreal Institute for Northern Studies, University of Alberta, 1984. 79 p. (Boreal Institute for Northern Studies Bibliographic series ; no. 12; ISSN: 0824-8192); ISBN: 0-919058-46-9. [5504]

Minion, Robin; Saffran, Marion A.

20th century Canadian Arctic expeditions. Edmonton: Boreal Institute for Northern Studies, University of Alberta, 1986. 116 p. (Boreal Institute for Northern Studies Bibliographic series ; no. 29; ISSN: 0824-8192); ISBN: 0-919058-64-7. [0654]

Miska, John P.

Animal science [bibliography]. Lethbridge, Alta.: Agriculture Canada Research Station, [1972]. v, 25 l. (Bibliographic series / Canada Department of Agriculture Research Station, Lethbridge, Alberta ; no. 1) [4655]

Canadian prose written in English 1833-1980 [microform]: a bibliography of secondary material. Lethbridge, Alta.: Microform Biblios, 1980. 5 microfiches (Canadian literature bibliographic series ; no. 2); ISBN: 0-919279-00-7. [1173]

Canadian studies on Hungarians, 1886-1986: an annotated bibliography of primary and secondary sources. Regina: Canadian Plains Research Center, University of Regina, 1987. xiii, 245 p. (Canadian Plains bibliographies / Canadian Plains Research Center, University of Regina ; 1; ISSN: 0821-8936); ISBN: 0-88977-034-4. [4245]

Celebration 1910-1985: an annotated bibliography of Agriculture Canada, Libraries Division. Ottawa: The Division, 1985. vii, 35 p.; ISBN: 0-662-14437-6. [1670]

Crop entomology [bibliography]. Lethbridge, Alta.: Research Station, Canada Department of Agriculture, 1973. v, 34 l. (Bibliographic series / Canada Department of Agriculture Research Station, Lethbridge, Alberta ; no. 4) [4659]

Ethnic and native Canadian literature: a bibliography. 2nd

ed. Toronto: University of Toronto Press, 1990. xv, 445 p.; ISBN: 0-8020-5852-3. [1284]

Frederick Philip Grove: a bibliography of primary and secondary material. Ottawa: Microform Biblios, 1984. 32 l. (Canlit bibliographic series / Microform Biblios ; no. 3) [7033]

"Hungarian-Canadian creative literature: a preliminary check list of imprints." In: *Canadian Ethnic Studies*; Vol. 5, no. 1/2 (1973) p. 131-137.; ISSN: 0008-3496. [1076]

Hungarian writing in Canada: a bibliography of primary and secondary material. Ottawa: Microform Biblios, 1988. i, 45 l. (Canlit bibliographic series / Microform Biblios ; no. 5); ISBN: 0-919279-04-X. [1257]

Irrigation. Slough, Eng.: Commonwealth Agricultural Bureaux, 1976-1977. 4 vol. [4673]

Literature of Hungarian-Canadians. Toronto: Rákòczi Foundation, 1991. 143 p.; ISBN: 0-919279-07-4. [1294]

Nitrogen fixation 1970-1975: bibliography. Lethbridge, Alta.: Agriculture Canada Research Station, 1978. 18 l. [4676]

Plant pathology and plant science [bibliography]. Lethbridge, Alta.: Research Station, Canada Department of Agriculture, 1973. vi, 50, ix l. (Bibliographic series / Canada Department of Agriculture Research Station, Lethbridge, Alberta ; no. 2) [4660]

Soil science [bibliography]. Lethbridge, Alta.: Research Station, Canada Department of Agriculture, 1973. v, 35 l. (Bibliographic series / Canada Department of Agriculture Research Station, Lethbridge, Alberta ; no. 3) [4661]

"University research on Hungarian-Canadians: a preliminary check list of theses." In: *Canadian Ethnic Studies*; Vol. 5, no. 1/2 (1973) p. 127-128.; ISSN: 0008-3496. [6127]

Veterinary medical entomology [bibliography]. Lethbridge, Alta.: Research Station, Canada Department of Agriculture, 1973. iv, 19 l. (Bibliographic series / Canada Department of Agriculture Research Station, Lethbridge, Alberta ; no. 5) [4662]

Miska, John P.; Nelson, G.A.

Bibliography of decay of potato seed pieces, 1930-1973. Lethbridge, Alta.: Research Station, Agriculture Canada, 1974. v, 49, xix p. [5384]

Miska, John P.; Niilo, Alan

Animal diseases research, 1939-1985: a bibliography of research papers by ADRI scientists at Lethbridge. Ottawa: Agriculture Canada, 1985. 31 p. [5516]

Miska, John P.; Ronning, Cheryl

Bibliography of agriculture in northern Canada and the arctic tundra in Alaska, 1950-1970. Lethbridge: Agriculture Canada Research Station, 1978. 11 p. [4677]

"Missionaries vs. native Americans in the Northwest: a bibliography for re-evaluation." In: *Indian Historian*; Vol. 5, no. 2 (Summer 1972) p. 46-48.; ISSN: 0019-4840. [3936]

Mississauga Public Library

Ontario government publications in the Mississauga Public Library: an annotated checklist of selected holdings. [Mississauga, Ont.]: Mississauga Public Library, 1974. 24 p. [6293]

Mitchell, Alan Kenneth

The yews and taxol: a bibliography (1970-1991). Victoria: Pacific Forestry Centre, Forestry Canada, 1992. v, 31 p. (Pacific Forestry Centre Information report ; BC-X-338; ISSN: 0830-0453); ISBN: 0-662-19896-4. [5711]

Mitchell, Bruce W.

Selected thematic maps of man's activities in Canada's watersheds/Cartes thématiques des activités de l'homme dans les bassins hydrographiques du Canada. Ottawa: Statistics Canada, Office of the Senior Adviser on Integration, Economic Statistics Section, 1980. 88 p. [6572]

Mitchell, Elaine Allan

"Bibliography of the Canadian north." In: *The new North-west*, edited by C.A. Dawson. Toronto: University of Toronto Press, 1947. P. 315-334. [0608]

Mitchell, James Kenneth

A selected bibliography of coastal erosion, protection and related human activity in North America and the British Isles. [Toronto: Department of Geography, University of Toronto], 1968. 66 p. (Natural hazard research working paper / Department of Geography, University of Toronto ; no. 4) [2972]

Mitchell, Mary E.

Periodicals in Canadian law libraries: a union list. 6th ed. Vancouver: UBC Law Library, 1991. 332 p. [5977]

Mitchell, William Bruce

Fluoridation bibliography: background, behavioral and Canadian aspects. Waterloo, Ont.: Department of Geography, Division of Environmental Studies, University of Waterloo, 1971. 25 l. [5576]

Mitchell, William Bruce; Mitchell, Joan

Law of the sea and international fisheries management. Monticello, Ill.: Council of Planning Librarians, 1976. 48 p. (Council of Planning Librarians Exchange bibliography ; 1162) [4892]

Mock, Karen R.

"Multicultural early childhood education bibliography and resource list." In: *Multicultural preschool education: a resource manual for supervisors and volunteers*. Toronto: Ontario Ministry of Citizenship and Culture, 1985. P. 83-96.; ISBN: 0-7729-1093-6. [3642]

Moeller, Roger W.; Reid, John

Archaeological bibliography for eastern North America. New Haven: Eastern States Archeological Federation, 1977. xiii, 198 p. [4570]

Moir, Elizabeth

"List of books on Canadian bibliography in the reference department of the Toronto Public Library." In: *Library World*; Vol. 13, no. 52 (October 1910) p. 111-113.; ISSN: 0024-2616. [0033]

Moll, Marita

Declining enrolment. Ottawa: Canadian Teachers' Federation, 1980. 34 p. (Bibliographies in education / Canadian Teachers' Federation ; no. 72); ISBN: 0-88989-090-0. [3570]

L'éducation spéciale au Canada. Ottawa: Fédération canadienne des enseignants, 1980. 34, 137 p. (Bibliographies en éducation / Fédération canadienne des enseignants ; no 73); ISBN: 0-88989-093-5. [3571]

Health and safety hazards in the school environment. Ottawa: Canadian Teachers' Federation, 1987. 247 p. (Bibliographies in education / Canadian Teachers' Federation ; no. 81); ISBN: 0-88989-196-6. [3675]

Industrial relations in Canada. Ottawa: Canadian Teachers' Federation, 1976. 59 p. (Bibliographies in education / Canadian Teachers' Federation ; no. 57); ISBN: 0-88989-010-2. [2832]

Job sharing for teachers. Ottawa: Canadian Teachers' Federation, 1985. 30 p. (Bibliographies in education / Canadian Teachers' Federation ; no. 79); ISBN: 0-88989-180-X. [3643]

Part-time and substitute teaching. Ottawa: Canadian Teachers' Federation, 1980. 16 p. (Bibliographies in education / Canadian Teachers' Federation ; no. 71); ISBN: 0-88989-085-4. [3572]

Principals and vice-principals. Ottawa: Canadian Teachers' Federation, 1983. 138 p. (Bibliographies in education / Canadian Teachers' Federation ; no. 76); ISBN: 0-88989-148-6. [3619]

Pupil transportation and school bus safety in Canada. Ottawa: Canadian Teachers' Federation, 1977. 27 p. (Bibliographies in education / Canadian Teachers' Federation ; no. 61); ISBN: 0-88989-035-8. [3526]

Special education in Canada. Ottawa: Canadian Teachers' Federation, 1980. 137, 34 p. (Bibliographies in education / Canadian Teachers' Federation ; no. 73); ISBN: 0-88989-093-5. [3573]

Teacher and administrator evaluation. Ottawa: Canadian Teachers' Federation, 1981. 107 p. (Bibliographies in education / Canadian Teachers' Federation ; no. 74); ISBN: 0-88989-121-4. [3597]

Teacher stress. Ottawa: Canadian Teachers' Federation, 1982. 90 p. (Bibliographies in education / Canadian Teachers' Federation ; no. 75); ISBN: 0-88989-132-X. [3615]

Teacher workload. Ottawa: Canadian Teachers' Federation, 1978. 68 p. (Bibliographies in education / Canadian Teachers' Federation ; no. 63); ISBN: 0-88989-046-3. [3542]

Teaching French as a second language in Canada. Ottawa: Canadian Teachers' Federation, 1979. 95 p. (Bibliographies in education / Canadian Teachers' Federation ; no. 70); ISBN: 0-88989-067-6. [3554]

Moloney, Nancy M.

"University research on Irish-Canadians: a preliminary check list of theses." In: *Canadian Ethnic Studies*; Vol. 5, no. 1/2 (1973) p. 193-194.; ISSN: 0008-3496. [6128]

Molot, Maureen Appel

"Where do we, should we, or can we sit? A review of Canadian foreign policy literature." In: *International Journal of Canadian Studies*; No. 1-2 (Spring-Fall 1990) p. 77-96.; ISSN: 1180-3991. [2540]

Monenco Consultants Limited

Literature review on the disposal of drilling waste solids. Edmonton: Alberta Land Conservation and Reclamation Council, Reclamation Research Technical Advisory Committee, 1990. xii, 83 p. [5282]

Monette, Guy J.A.

Introduction à l'oeuvre de Ja[c]ques Ferron: [bibliographie]. [Kingston, Ont.]: Association des professeurs de français des universités et collèges canadiens, 1982. 23 p. [6984]

Monette, René

"Documentation sur la profession agronomique." Dans: *Agriculture*; Vol. 14, no 5 (septembre-octobre 1957) p. 162-164.; ISSN: 0002-1687. [4642]

Mongrain, Susan

Aboriginal self-government: a selective annotated bibliography. Ottawa: Departmental Library, Indian and Northern Affairs Canada, 1988. 11 l. [4101]

Land claims: a selected annotated bibliography on specific and comprehensive claims. [Ottawa]: Departmental Library, Indian and Northern Affairs Canada, 1988. 9 l. [4102]

Monière, Denis; Vachet, André
Les idéologies au Québec: bibliographie. 3e éd. rev. et augm. Montréal: Bibliothèque nationale du Québec, 1980. 175 p.; ISBN: 2-550-00821-9. [0364]

Monroe, Robin Lee; McLeish, Walter
Small aircraft crashworthiness. Montreal: Transportation Development Centre, 1987. 2 vol. [5825]

Montigny-Pelletier, Françoise de
Bibliographie de la Rive-Sud de Québec, (Lévis-Lotbinière). Québec: Institut québécois de recherche sur la culture, 1989. 263 p.: cartes. (Documents de recherche / Institut québécois de recherche sur la culture ; no 19; ISSN: 0823-0447); ISBN: 2-89224-122-7. [0407]

Montreal Council of Social Agencies. Research Department
Bibliographie des travaux de recherches dans le domaine du bien-être (1961-1967). Québec: Direction générale de la planification et de la recherche du Ministère de la famille et du bien-être social, 1969. 249 f. [3092]

Montreal Engineering Company
Maritime provinces water resources study, stage 1: appendix 1: bibliography. [Ottawa]: Atlantic Development Board, 1969. [95] p. (in various pagings). [5048]

Montreal Health Libraries Association
Union list of serials in Montreal health libraries/Catalogue collectif des périodiques dans les bibliothèques de santé de Montréal. 3rd ed. Montreal: INS Informatique, 1991. 285 p.; ISBN: 0-9801591-3-1. [5978]

Monty, Vivienne
A bibliography of Canadian tax reform. Toronto: York University Law Library, 1973. 66 l. [2609]
The Canadian small business handbook. 2nd ed. Don Mills, Ont.: CCH Canadian, 1991. x, 201 p.; ISBN: 0-88796-622-5. [2776]

Moody, B.H.; Amirault, P.A.
Impacts of major pests on forest growth and yield in the prairie provinces and the Northwest Territories: a literature review. Edmonton: Northern Forestry Centre, Forestry Canada, 1992. vi, 35 p. (Northern Forestry Centre Information report ; NOR-X-324; ISSN: 0704-7673); ISBN: 0-662-19535-3. [5017]

Moody, Lois
"Contemporary Canadian jazz recordings: a selected bibliography." In: *Jazz Ottawa*; No. 19 (September 1978) p. 7-10.; ISSN: 0383-9206. [0869]

Moogk, Edward B.
En remontant les années: l'histoire et l'héritage de l'enregistrement sonore au Canada, des débuts à 1930. Ottawa: Bibliothèque nationale du Canada, 1975. xii, 447 p.: ill., fac-sim., portr., disque (dans une pochette). [0847]
Roll back the years: history of Canadian recorded sound and its legacy: genesis to 1930. Ottawa: National Library of Canada, 1975. xii, 443 p.: ill., facsims., ports., phonodisc (in pocket). [0848]

Moore, Barbara G.
Equity in education: gender issues in the use of computers: a review and bibliography. Toronto: Ontario Ministry of Education, 1986. i, 68 p. (Review and evaluation bulletins: Education and technology series ; vol. 6, no. 1; ISSN: 0226-7306); ISBN: 0-7729-1543-1. [3659]

Moore, Gary C.
A report on the feasibility of harvesting timber within buffer zones: a literature review. Fredericton, N.B.: Department

of Natural Resources, 1983. iv, 138 l.; ISBN: 0-88838-538-2. [4978]

Moore, George Henry
The Jesuit relations, etc. New York: Printed for the Trustees [Lenox Library], 1879. 19 p. (Contributions to a catalogue of the Lenox Library ; no. 2) [6729]

Moore, Ian; Legner, E.F.
"Bibliography (1758 to 1972) to the Staphylinidae of America north of Mexico (Coleoptera)." In: *Hilgardia*; Vol. 42, no. 16 (December 1974) p. 511-547.; ISSN: 0073-2230. [5385]

Moore, Kathryn E.; Curtis, Fred A.
"Environmental management for pits and quarries: an annotated bibliography." In: *CIM Bulletin*; Vol. 78, no. 879 (July 1985) p. 78-82.; ISSN: 0317-0926. [4846]

Moore, Larry F.
Advances in manpower management: a selected annotated bibliography. Vancouver: Institute of Industrial Relations, University of British Columbia, 1975. vi, 69 p. [2823]
Guidelines for manpower managers: a selected annotated bibliography. Vancouver: Faculty of Commerce and Business Administration, University of British Columbia, [1969]. 82 p. (Monograph series / Faculty of Commerce and Business Administration, University of British Columbia ; no. 3) [2586]

Moore, R.S.
Beneficiation techniques applicable to Nova Scotian coals: a literature review. Halifax: Atlantic Research Laboratory, National Research Council Canada, 1982. 29, 30 p. (Atlantic Research Laboratory Technical report ; 39) [4829]

"Mordecai Richler: a selected bibliography." In: *Inscape*; Vol. 11, no. 2 (Spring 1974) p. 51-61.; ISSN: 0020-1782. [7259]

Moreau, Bernice M.
"Black Nova Scotian literature: a select bibliography." In: *Journal of Education*; No. 400 (1987) p. 46-50.; ISSN: 0022-0566. [4246]

Morgan, Henry J.
Bibliotheca Canadensis, or, A manual of Canadian literature. Ottawa: Printed by G.E. Desbarats, 1867. xiv, 411 p. [0009]
"Review of literature, science and art." In: *Dominion Annual Register and Review*; (1879)-(1886) [0018]
The writings of Benjamin Sulte. Milwaukee: Keogh, 1898. 13 p.: port. [7324]

Morgan, Jane
Parenting: an annotated bibliography. Toronto: Library, Reference and Information Services, Ontario Institute for Studies in Education, 1980. ix, 70 p. (Current bibliography / Ontario Institute for Studies in Education ; no. 13) [3205]

Morgan, K.
"Hate literature and freedom of expression in Canada: an annotated bibliography." In: *Canadian Law Libraries*; Vol. 16, no. 3 (August 1991) p. 91-96.; ISSN: 1180-176X. [2354]

Morgan, Kathryn Pauly
"Bibliography of recent feminist philosophy and theory." In: *Resources for Feminist Research*; Vol. 16, no. 3 (September 1987) p. 89-103.; ISSN: 0707-8412. [3855]

Morgan, W.C.; Wheeler, J.O.
Cartes géologiques du Canada: histoire et évolution. [Ottawa]: Énergie, Mines et Ressources Canada, [1992]. 46 p. [6601]
Geological maps of Canada: history and evolution. [Ottawa]: Energy, Mines and Resources Canada, [1992]. 41 p. [6602]

Mori, Monica

Palliative care of the elderly: an overview and annotated bibliography. Vancouver: Gerontology Research Centre, Simon Fraser University, 1991. v, 191 p.; ISBN: 0-86491-106-8. [5705]

Mori, Monica; McNern, Janet

Women and aging: an annotated bibliography, 1968-1991. Vancouver, B.C.: Gerontology Research Centre, Simon Fraser University, 1991. xi, 223 p.; ISBN: 0-86491-112-2. [3894]

Morin, Cimon

Canadian philately: bibliography and index, 1864-1973 / Philatélie canadienne: bibliographie et index, 1864-1973. Ottawa: National Library of Canada, 1979. xxi, 281 p.: ill., facsims.; ISBN: 0-660-50175-9. [1796]

Morin, Gérald; Potvin, Lise; Zubrzycki, Pierre

Bibliographie analytique et description des banques de données dans le cadre des recherches sur le programme d'assainissement des eaux du Québec. [Sainte-Foy, Québec]: ÉNAP, 1985. iii, 282 p. [5228]

Morin, Victor

The American portion of the historical library of Victor Morin, comprising American voyages and explorations, Canadiana, Indian manuscripts by Jesuit fathers, Jesuit relations, etc., sold by his order. New York: American Art Association, Anderson Galleries, 1931. 72 p., 2 l. of pl.: ill. [6760]

Morisette, Thomas

Revue de littérature sur les divers concepts de vergers à graines. Québec: Service de la régénération forestière, Ministère de l'énergie et des ressources, 1990. v, 32 f.; ISBN: 2-550-20488. [5010]

Morisset, Pierre

Bibliographie annotée sur l'histoire naturelle du Parc national Forillon (Québec). Québec: Parcs nationaux et des lieux historiques, 1971. 111 p. [2982]

Morley, E. Lillian

A Perth County bibliography. [Milverton, Ont.: Milverton Sun, 1948]. [14] p. [0422]

Morley, Glen

The Glen Morley collection of historical Canadian music of the nineteenth century: a catalogue of Canadian music published between 1832 and 1914. [Ottawa: Kingsmere Concert Enterprises, c1984]. 18 l. [0917]

Morley, Marjorie

A bibliography of Manitoba from holdings in the Legislative Library of Manitoba. Winnipeg: [s.n.], 1970. 267 p.: map. [0500]

Royal commissions and commissions of inquiry under "The Evidence Act" in Manitoba: a checklist. [Winnipeg: Legislative Library, 1952]. 11, 10 l. [6234]

Morley, William F.E.

The Atlantic provinces: Newfoundland, Nova Scotia, New Brunswick, Prince Edward Island. [Toronto]: University of Toronto Press, [c1967]. xx, 137 p.: maps, plans, facsims. (Canadian local histories to 1950: a bibliography ; vol. 1) [0208]

"A bibliographical study of Charlevoix's *Histoire et description générale de la Nouvelle France*." In: *Papers of the Bibliographical Society of Canada*; Vol. 2 (1963) p. 21-45.; ISSN: 0067-6896. [6904]

"A bibliographical study of John Richardson." In: *Papers of the Bibliographical Society of Canada*; Vol. 4 (1965) p. 21-88.; ISSN: 0067-6896. [7257]

A bibliographical study of Major John Richardson. Toronto: Bibliographical Society of Canada, 1973. xxvii, 144 p.: facsims., port. [7258]

Ontario and the Canadian North. Toronto: University of Toronto Press, c1978. xxxii, 322 p. (Canadian local histories to 1950: a bibliography ; vol. 3); ISBN: 0-8020-2281-2. [0458]

Morrell, W.P.

British overseas expansion and the history of the Commonwealth: a select bibliography. 2nd ed. London: Historical Association, 1970. 48 p. (Historical Association Helps for students of history ; no. 63) [1968]

Morris, Sahlaa, et al.

The Courtenay River estuary: status of environmental knowledge to 1978: report of the Estuary Working Group, Department of the Environment, Regional Board Pacific Region. [Ottawa]: Fisheries and Environment Canada, 1979. xxxii, 355 p.: ill. (Special estuary series / Estuary Working Group, Department of the Environment, Regional Board, Pacific Region ; no. 8) [5152]

The Somass River estuary: status of environmental knowledge to 1980: report of the Estuary Working Group, Joint Fisheries and Oceans-Environment Co-ordinating Committee on Environmental Affairs, Pacific and Yukon Region. [Ottawa]: Fisheries and Oceans Canada, 1980. 374 p. (Special estuary series / Estuary Working Group, Joint Fisheries and Oceans-Environment Co-ordinating Committee on Environmental Affairs, Pacific and Yukon Region ; no. 9) [5166]

Morrison, B.A.; Thuns, A.

A catalogue of Canadian graduate theses in agricultural engineering and related fields 1942-1986 / Répertoire des thèses maîtrise et de doctorat en génie rural ou autres domaînes connexes publiés au Canada de 1942 à 1986. Ottawa: Engineering and Statistical Research Centre, Research Branch, Agriculture Canada, 1987. 147 p. (Engineering and Statistical Research Centre Contribution ; no. I-946) [6191]

Energy reports (contributions) published by ESRI from 1973 to May 1983 / Rapports concernant l'énergie (communication) publié par IRTS de 1973 à mai 1983. Ottawa: Engineering and Statistical Research Institute, Research Branch, Agriculture Canada, 1983. 32 p. (Engineering and Statistical Research Institute Contribution ; no. I-501) [4701]

Summary of projects and publications, 1960-1985 [Engineering and Statistical Research Institute, Agriculture Canada] / Sommaire des projets et des publications, 1960-1985 [Institut de recherche technique et statistique, Agriculture Canada]. Ottawa: Engineering and Statistical Research Institute, Research Branch, Agriculture Canada, 1985. 369 p. (Engineering and Statistical Research Institute Contribution ; no. I-780) [6374]

Morrison, B.A.; Thuns, A.; Feldman, M.

List of engineering research contract reports under the DREAM, AERD and ERDAF programs of the Research Branch, 1973-1988 / Liste des rapports de contrats de recherches techniques réalisés au titre des programmes DREMA, RDGR et RDEAA de la Direction générale de la recherche de 1973-1988. Ottawa: Engineering and Statistical Research Centre, Research Branch, Agriculture Canada, 1988. iv, 179 p. [4715]

Morrison, Doreen

Native peoples: a guide to reference sources. Montreal: Humanities and Social Sciences Library Reference Department, McGill University, 1993. 28 p.; ISBN: 0-7717-0161-6. [4124]

Morrison, Hugh M.; Whitworth, Fred E.

A guide to reading on Canada for high school teachers and students of social studies. Ottawa: Canadian Council of Education for Citizenship, [1945]. 116 p. [0055]

Morrison, James H.

Common heritage: an annotated bibliography of ethnic groups in Nova Scotia. Halifax, N.S.: International Education Centre, Saint Mary's University, 1984. 130 p.: ill. [4228]

Morrison, Linda

A legal bibliography for lawyers of B.C. Vancouver: B.C. Law Library Foundation, 1983-. vol. (loose-leaf). [2367]

Morse, Hazel G.

"Acadia authors: a bibliography." In: *Acadia Bulletin*; Vol. 11, no. 11 (December 1922) p. 1-43.; ISSN: 0044-5843. [0198]

Morse, Janice M.; Tylko, Suzanne; English, Jennifer

Canadian cultures and health bibliography. Edmonton: University of Alberta, Faculty of Nursing, 1983. 16 l. [5654]

Morse, William Inglis

Bliss Carman: bibliography, letters, fugitive verses and other data. Windham, Conn.: Hawthorn House, 1941. 86 p.: ill., facsim., ports. [6893]

Morton, Desmond

Canadian history. [Ottawa]: Canadian Studies Directorate, Department of the Secretary of State of Canada, c1992. 31, 33 p. (Canadian studies resource guides. Second series); ISBN: 0-660-58837-1. [2087]

L'histoire du Canada. [Ottawa]: Direction des études canadiennes, Secrétariat d'État du Canada, c1992. 33, 31 p. (Guides pédagogiques des études canadiennes. Deuxième collection); ISBN: 0-660-58837-1. [2088]

Mortsch, Linda D.

Eastern Canadian boreal and sub-Arctic wetlands: a resource document. Ottawa: Environment Canada, Atmospheric Environment Service, 1991. xii, 169 p.: ill., maps (some folded). [5291]

Mortsch, Linda D.; Bolohan, Ken

Applied climate bibliography for architects, planners, landscape architects and builders/Bibliographie de climatologie appliquée pour les architectes, les planificateurs, les paysagistes et les entrepreneurs et bâtiment. Downsview, Ont.: Environment Canada, Atmospheric Environment Service, 1986. vi, 46 p. [0780]

Mortsch, Linda D.; Kalnins, Ingrid I.

A bibliography on storm surges and seiches/Bibliographie sur les marées de tempête et les seiches. Downsview, Ont.: Environment Canada, Atmospheric Environment Service, 1984. iii, 42 p. [5217]

Bibliography pertinent to offshore energy exploration and development/Bibliographie concernant l'exploitation et la mise en valeur des ressources énergétiques en mer. Downsview, Ont.: Environment Canada, Atmospheric Environment Service, 1984. iv, 102 p. [4840]

Moscovitch, Allan

The welfare state in Canada: a selected bibliography, 1840 to 1978. Waterloo, Ont.: Wilfrid Laurier University Press, c1983. xxiv, 246 p.; ISBN: 0-88920-114-5. [3250]

Moscovitch, Arlene

Focus on Canada: a film and video resource handbook for secondary level social studies. Montreal: The Film Board, [1988]. ii, 122 p.: ill.; ISBN: 0-7722-0133-1. [6674]

Moskal, Susan

Contemporary Canadian Indian statistics published by the federal government, 1960-1985: a selective bibliography and subject index to sources available in the University of Waterloo Library. Waterloo, Ont.: The Library, c1987. vii, 25 p. (University of Waterloo Library bibliography ; no. 16; ISSN: 0829-948X); ISBN: 0-920834-03-5. [4090]

Moss, Harold Charles

A partial bibliography of Saskatchewan soil science, 1921-1957. Saskatoon: Department of Soil Science, University of Saskatchewan, 1958. 25 p. [4643]

Motiuk, Laurence

Canadian Forces college reading guide for the study of war, national defence and strategy. [Ottawa: Department of National Defence, 1967]. vii, 345 p. [2392]

Motiuk, Laurence; Grant, Madeline

A reading guide to Canada in world affairs, 1945-1971. Toronto: Canadian Institute of International Affairs, c1972. x. 313 p. [2405]

Moulary-Ouerghi, Josiane; Villemaire, Carmen

Référendum québécois: bibliographie. Montréal: Éditions Bergeron, 1983. 276 p.; ISBN: 2-89247-113-3. [2480]

Moulton, Donalee

Antiques and restoration. Monticello, Ill.: Vance Bibliographies, 1979. 4 p. (Architecture series: Bibliography ; A-121; ISSN: 0194-1356) [0692]

Mount, Graeme S.; Mahant, Edelgard E.

"Review of recent literature on Canadian-Latin American relations." In: *Journal of Interamerican Studies and World Affairs*; Vol. 27, no. 2 (Summer 1985) p. 127-151.; ISSN: 0022-1937. [2495]

Mount Allison University. Canadian Studies Programme

A preliminary checklist of nineteenth century Canadian poetry in English. Sackville, N.B.: Canadian Studies Programme, Mount Allison University, 1976. 185 l. [1101]

Mount Saint Vincent University. Library

Catalogue of the Canadian drama collection in the Library of Mount Saint Vincent University, Halifax, Nova Scotia, 1984. Halifax, N.S.: The University, 1984. 29, 22, 62 p. [1217]

A guide to women's studies resources. [Halifax, N.S.]: The University, [1991]. 54 p.: ill.; ISBN: 1-895306-02-7. [3895]

Moussette, Marcel, et al.

"Bibliographie préliminaire pour la recherche en archéologie historique au Québec." Dans: *Recherches amérindiennes au Québec*; Vol. 4, no 4/5 (octobre-décembre 1974) p. 48-60.; ISSN: 0318-4137. [4560]

Moyer, Sharon

La déjudiciarisation dans le système judiciaire pour les jeunes et ses répercussions sur les enfants: recension de la documentation. [Ottawa]: Solliciteur général Canada, Division de la recherche, 1980. v, 296 p.; ISBN: 0-662-90708-6. [2219]

Diversion from the juvenile justice system and its impact on children: a review of the literature. [Ottawa]: Solicitor General Canada, Research Division, 1980. xix, 201 p.; ISBN: 0-662-10979-1. [2220]

Moyles, Robert Gordon

English-Canadian literature to 1900: a guide to information sources. Detroit: Gale Research, c1976. xi, 346 p. (American literature, English literature, and world literatures in English Information guide series ; vol. 6); ISBN: 0-8103-1222-0. [1102]

Moyles, Robert Gordon; Siemens, Catherine
English-Canadian literature: a student guide and annotated bibliography. Edmonton: Athabascan Publishing, 1972. 44 p. [1066]

Muhammad, A.F.; Jorgensen, E.
Natural history in the National Capital Region: a bibliography. Ottawa: Forest Management Institute, Canadian Forestry Service, Department of the Environment, 1974. 97 p. (Forest Management Institute Information report ; FMR-X-65) [4624]

Mukherjee, Arun P.
"A select bibliography of South Asian poetry in Canada." In: *World Literature Written in English*; Vol. 26, no. 1 (Spring 1986) p. 97-98.; ISSN: 0093-1705. [1231]

Muldoon, Maureen
Abortion: an annotated bibliography. New York; Toronto: E. Mellen Press, c1980. xv, [151] p. (Studies in women and religion ; vol. 3); ISBN: 0-88946-972-5. [3798]

Mullens, Marjorie C.; Roberts, Albert E.
Selected annotated bibliography on asphalt-bearing rocks of the United States and Canada, to 1970. Washington: U.S. Government Printing Office, 1972. iv, 218 p.: ill. (United States Geological Survey Bulletin ; 1352) [4778]

Mullins, W.J.; Fogwill, W.D.; Greene, B.A.
Province of Newfoundland and Labrador: map index: geological, geophysical and related maps to December 31, 1969. [St. John's, Nfld.]: Mineral Resources Division, Department of Mines, Agriculture and Resources, 1969. 59 p.: ill. (Information circular / Newfoundland Mineral Resources Division ; no. 13) [6515]

Multicultural History Society of Ontario
A guide to the collections of the Multicultural History Society of Ontario. Toronto: Multicultural History Society of Ontario, 1992. xx, 695 p.; ISBN: 0-91904-558-8. [4292]

Multilingual newspapers & periodicals in Ontario public libraries. [Toronto]: Ontario Ministry of Citizenship and Culture, [1986]. 124 p.; ISBN: 0-7729-0162-7. [5960]

Munkittrick, Kelly Roland L.H.; Power, Elizabeth A.
Literature review for biological monitoring of heavy metals in aquatic environments. Victoria: British Columbia Acid Mine Drainage Task Force, 1990. xi, 127 l.: ill. [4878]

Munns, Edward Norfolk
A selected bibliography of North American forestry. Washington: U.S. Government Printing Office, 1940. 2 vol. (United States Department of Agriculture Miscellaneous publications ; no. 364) [4918]

Munro, Douglas, et al.
The relationship between age-sex and accident involvement-severity: a literature survey. Toronto: University of Toronto-York University Joint Program in Transportation, 1981. v, 44 p. (University of Toronto-York University Joint Program in Transportation Working paper ; no. 10; ISSN: 0380-9889) [4484]

"A Munro bibliography." In: *Journal of Education*; Vol. 1, no. 3 (series 6) (Spring 1974) p. 23-24.; ISSN: 0022-0566. [7206]

Munroe, Allan R.
Research in sexual deviation and sexual offences: a bibliography. [Edmonton: Department of Psychological Services, Alberta Hospital], 1974. 86 p. [3127]

Murdoch, John
A bibliography of Algonquian syllabic texts in Canadian repositories. [Rupert House, Quebec]: Project ASTIC, 1984. xiii, 147 p.: ill.; ISBN: 0-920245-08-0. [4063]

Murdoch, Laurel
Bibliographie sélective concernant le bénévolat dans les services correctionnels. Toronto: Ministère des services correctionnels de l'Ontario, 1976. 21 f. [2156]

Volunteerism in corrections: a selected bibliography. Toronto: Ontario Ministry of Correctional Services, 1976. i, 20 l. [2157]

Murdoch, Laurel; Hillard, Jane
Freedom of information and individual privacy: a selective bibliography. [Toronto]: Commission on Freedom of Information and Individual Privacy, 1979. xii, 230 p. (Commission on Freedom of Information and Individual Privacy Research publication ; 12) [2446]

Murdock, George Peter; O'Leary, Timothy J.
Ethnographic bibliography of North America. 4th ed. New Haven: Human Relations Area Files Press, 1975. 5 vol.: maps. (Behavior science bibliographies); ISBN: 0-87536-205-2 (vol. 1); 0-87536-207-9 (vol. 2); 0-87536-209-5 (vol. 3); 0-87536-211-7 (vol. 4); 0-87536-213-3 (vol. 5). [3970]

Murphy, Joan; Poulin, Michelle
Centre de foresterie des Laurentides publications, 1980-1988/ Laurentian Forestry Centre publications, 1980-1988. Sainte-Foy, Québec: Forêts Canada, 1989. vi, 44 p. (Rapport d'information / Centre de foresterie des Laurentides ; LAU-X-86B; ISSN: 0835-1589); ISBN: 0-662-56745-5. [6399]

Murphy, Lynn
"Child abuse: an annotated bibliography." In: *Emergency Librarian*; Vol. 5, no. 4 (March-April 1978) p. 6-11.; ISSN: 0315-8888. [3177]

Housework: an annotated bibliography. Halifax, N.S.: International Education Centre, Saint Mary's University, 1984. [19] p. [3831]

Women and agriculture: an annotated bibliography. Halifax, N.S.: International Education Centre, Saint Mary's University, 1984. [12] p. [3832]

Murphy, Lynn; Hicks, Brenda
Nova Scotia newspapers: a directory and union list, 1752-1988. Halifax: School of Library and Information Studies, Dalhousie University, 1990. 2 vol.; ISBN: 0-7703-9742-5 (vol. 1); 0-7703-9744-1 (vol. 2). [6051]

Murray, Elsie McLeod
A check-list of early newspaper files located in local newspaper offices in western Ontario. London: University of Western Ontario, 1947. 23 l. (Western Ontario history nuggets ; 12) [6010]

Murray, Florence
"Canadian government catalogues and checklists." In: *Library Quarterly*; Vol. 6, no. 3 (July 1936) p. 237-262.; ISSN: 0024-2519. [6222]

Murray, Heather D.
Public lending right in Canada: a literature survey. Edmonton: H.D. Murray, 1986. v, 71 l. [1681]

Murray, J. Alex
An international business library bibliography. 4th ed. Waterloo, Ont.: Laurier Trade Development Centre, Wilfrid Laurier University, 1988. i, 78 p.; ISSN: 0834-3373 [2746]

Murtha, Peter A.; Greco, Michael E.
Appraisal of forest aesthetic values: an annotated bibliography. Ottawa: Canadian Forestry Service, 1975. v, 56 p. (Forest Management Institute Information report ; FMR-X-79) [4946]

Musée d'art contemporain de Montréal
Répertoire des catalogues du Musée d'art contemporain de Montréal, 1965-1990. Montréal: Le Musée, c1992. 87 p.: ill.; ISBN: 2-551-12880-3. [0730]

Musées nationaux du Canada
Catalogue des publications [Musées nationaux du Canada]. Ottawa: Musées nationaux du Canada, 1979-1981. 6 vol.; ISSN: 0708-2916. [6335]

Musique: liste de ressources pédagogiques, cycles intermédiaire et supérieur. [Toronto]: Ministère de l'Éducation, [1982]. iii, 43 p.: ill.; ISBN: 0-7743-7785-2. [0906]

Mutimer, Brian T.P.
Canadian graduating essays, theses and dissertations relating to the history and philosophy of sport, physical education and recreation. Rev. ed. Ottawa: Canadian Association for Health, Physical Education and Recreation, 1980. 35 p. [6156]

Myers, R. Holtby & Co.
R. Holtby Myers & Co.'s Complete catalogue of Canadian publications: containing carefully prepared lists of all the newspapers and periodicals published in the Dominion of Canada, giving circulation, age and other valuable information. Toronto: R. Holtby Myers, 1890. 29 p. [5856]

Myhal, Patricia J.
"A selected bibliography of the Foreign Investment Review Act." In: *Foreign investment review law in Canada*, edited by James M. Spence and William P. Rosenfeld. Toronto: Butterworths, 1984. P. 343-351.; ISBN: 0-4098-6300-9. [2270]

Myrand, Marie-Louise
Canada treaty series, 1928-1964/Recueil des traités du Canada, 1928-1964. Ottawa: Queen's Printer, 1966. 388 p. (Canadian government publications sectional catalogue ; no. 15) [6259]
National museums of Canada: publications/Musées nationaux du Canada: publications. Ottawa: Queen's Printer, 1970. 137 p. (Canadian government publications sectional catalogue ; no. 16) [6274]

Myres, Miles Timothy
An introduction to the literature of the effects of biocides on wildlife and fish: a select bibliography. Calgary: Department of Biology, University of Alberta at Calgary, 1964. 28, iii l. [5035]

Myroniuk, Halyna; Worobec, Christine
Ukrainians in North America: a select bibliography. St. Paul, Minn.: Immigration History Research Center, University of Minnesota; Toronto: Multicultural History Society of Ontario, [c1981]. 236, [24] p.; ISBN: 0-919045-04-9. [4203]

N.D. Lea & Associates
Transportation for the mobility disadvantaged: a bibliography/Transport pour les handicapés: bibliographie. Montreal: Transport Canada, Surface, 1979. 61 p. [3189]

Naaman, Antoine
Répertoire des thèses littéraires canadiennes de 1921 à 1976. Sherbrooke: Éditions Naaman, [1978]. 453 p. [6148]

Nadeau, Alphée
Bibliographie de base en astronomie, astronautique, astrophysique: documents textuels avec index correspondants. [La Pocatière: A. Nadeau, 1976]. ii, 101 p.: ill. [5760]

Nadeau, Charles
Saint Joseph dans l'édition canadienne: bibliographie. Montréal: Oratoire Saint-Joseph du Mont-Royal, 1967. v, 81 p. [1520]

Nadeau, Élise; Paquet, Dominik; Robertson, Yves
Les biotechnologies: bibliographie sélective. Québec: Conseil de la science et de la technologie, Centre de documentation, 1991. 73 p.; ISBN: 2-550-21871-X. [5847]

Nadeau, Johan
Entreprises internationales, transnationales et multinationales: bibliographie sélective et annotée. Québec: Bibliothèque de l'Assemblée nationale, Division de la référence parlementaire, 1988. 64 p. [2] f. (Bibliographie / Bibliothèque de l'Assemblée nationale du Québec ; no 26; ISSN: 0836-9100) [2747]

Nadeau, Lise
Pauvreté, province de Québec: bibliographie. Montréal: Ministère de la main-d'oeuvre et de l'immigration, Région du Québec, Bibliothèque régionale, 1974. 50 f. [3128]

Nadeau, Pierre
Santé: bibliographie. Montréal: Conseil de développement social du Montréal métropolitain, 1972. [95] p. [5583]

Nadel, Ira Bruce
Jewish writers of North America: a guide to information sources. Detroit, Mich.: Gale Research, c1981. xix, 493 p. (American studies information guide series ; vol. 8); ISBN: 0-8103-1484-3. [1184]

Nadkarni, Meena
Canadian legal materials in microform. Downsview, Ont.: York University Law Library in co-operation with the Canadian Association of Law Libraries, 1981-. vol. (looseleaf). [2368]
Citizenship in Canada: a retrospective bibliography. Monticello, Ill.: Vance Bibliographies, 1985. 29 p. (Public administration series: Bibliography ; P-1662; ISSN: 0193-970X); ISBN: 0-89028-372-9. [2496]

Nadon, Claude
Audiovidéographie pour l'enseignement du français aux adultes: de l'éducation de base au secondaire V: films de format 16mm, films en boucle 8mm, audio-visions, jeux de diapositives, disques, rubans magnétiques, ensembles multi media. [Québec]: Gouvernement du Québec, Direction générale de i'éducation des adultes, [1982]. 320 p. [6651]

Nagy, Thomas L.
Ottawa in maps: a brief cartographical history of Ottawa, 1825-1973/Ottawa par les cartes: brève histoire cartographique de la ville d'Ottawa, 1825-1973. Ottawa: National Map Collection, Public Archives Canada, 1974. ii, 87 p.: ill., maps. [6540]

Nakonechny, Patricia; Kishchuk, Marie
The monograph collections of the Ukrainian Museum of Canada: an integrated catalogue. Saskatoon: Ukrainian Museum of Canada, 1988. iv, 1174 p.; ISBN: 0-9693765-0-2. [4259]

Nancekivell, Sharon
"Margaret Laurence: bibliography." In: *World Literature Written in English*; Vol. 22, no. 2 (Autumn 1983) p. 263-284.; ISSN: 0093-1705. [7124]

Nantel, Jacques; Robillard, Renée

Le concept de la familiarité dans l'étude des comportements des consommateurs: une revue de la littérature. Montréal: Direction de la recherche, École des hautes études commerciales, 1991. ii, 44 f. (Cahier de recherche / Direction de la recherche, École des hautes études commerciales ; no 91-16; ISSN: 0846-0647) [2777]

Le concept de l'implication dans l'étude des comportements des consommateurs: une revue de la littérature. Montréal: École des hautes études commerciales, 1990. 59 f.: ill. (Rapport de recherche / École des hautes études commerciales ; 90-01; ISSN: 0709-986X) [2769]

Napier, Nina

"British Columbia: a bibliography of centennial publications, 1957-1959." In: *British Columbia Historical Quarterly*; Vol. 21 (1957-1958) p. 199-220.; ISSN: 0706-7666. [0571]

Narang, H.L.

Canadian masters' theses in reading education: an annotated bibliography. Regina: Faculty of Education, University of Saskatchewan, 1974. 77 l. [6134]

"Canadian research in Indian education." In: *Northian*; Vol. 11, no. 1 (Spring 1975) p. 11-12.; ISSN: 0029-3253. [6138]

Multicultural education: an annotated bibliography. Regina, Sask.: Multicultural Council of Saskatchewan, c1983. 28 p. [3620]

Narby, Jeremy; Davis, Shelton

Resource development and indigenous peoples: a comparative bibliography. Boston: Anthropology Resource Center, 1983. 32 p. [4052]

Naslund, Colin H.

Curriculum related Canadian consumer magazines for Alberta high school libraries: an annotated bibliography. Edmonton: [s.n.], 1983. 25, [62] l. [5950]

Nason, C.M.

A checklist of Canadian sources in criminal justice. Monticello, Ill.: Vance Bibliographies, 1981. 10 p. (Public administration series: Bibliography ; P-682; ISSN: 0193-970X) [2236]

Nation, Earl F.; Roland, Charles G.; McGovern, John P.

An annotated checklist of Osleriana. [Kent, Ohio]: Kent State University Press, 1976. xii, 289 p., [3] l. of pl.: ill.; ISBN: 0-87338-186-6. [7229]

National Arts Centre (Canada)

Catalogue: films on the performing arts. Ottawa: The Centre, 1968. 24, 18 p. [6609]

National Book League

Commonwealth in North America: an annotated list. 2nd rev. ed. London: National Book League and the Commonwealth Institute, 1971. 213 p.; ISBN: 0-85353-073-4. [0099]

National Committee for Research on Co-operatives

Bibliography of Canadian writings on co-operation, 1900 to 1959. Ottawa: Co-operative Union of Canada, 1960. 48 p. (Research paper / National Committee for Research on Co-operatives ; no. 1) [2573]

National Council of Jewish Women of Canada

Prejudice in educational material: a resource handbook. [Downsview, Ont.: National Council of Jewish Women of Canada], 1977. 18 p. [3527]

National Day Care Information Centre (Canada)

Day care services bibliography/Services de garde de jour: bibliographie. Ottawa: 1972. [74] l. [3111]

National Film Board of Canada

Canadian travel and wildlife films. Ottawa: National Film Board of Canada, 1954. 31 p. [6606]

Canadian travel film library: 16mm motion picture films. Ottawa: National Film Board of Canada, 1952. 27 p. [6604]

Catalogue of films produced by the National Film Board of Canada available in Australia. [Ottawa: Queen's Printer, 1953]. 73, [1] p. [6605]

A catalogue of films projecting women. Toronto: National Film Board of Canada, [1975]. 57 p.: ill. [6626]

The family violence audio-visual catalogue/Catalogue de documents audiovisuels sur la violence dans la famille. 2nd ed. Montreal: National Film Board of Canada, [1989]. ix, 97 p.; ISBN: 0-7722-0148-X. [6685]

Filmstrips and slides: catalogue. Ottawa: Queen's Printer, 1952-1968. [9] vol. [6610]

The NFB film guide: the productions of the National Film Board of Canada from 1939 to 1989. Montreal: The Board, c1991. clvii, 960 p., [72] p. of pl.: ill., ports.; ISBN: 0-660-56485-8 (set). [6693]

Women breaking through: a cross-curriculum A-V resource guide for secondary school. Montreal: National Film Board of Canada, 1988. 28 p.; ISBN: 0-7722-0128-5. [6675]

National Film Board of Canada. Reference Library

Books on film and television in the Reference Library of the National Film Board of Canada/Livres sur le cinéma et la télévision se trouvant à la Bibliothèque de l'Office national du film du Canada. Montreal: The Library, 1992-. vol. [6706]

National Gallery of Canada

National Gallery of Canada exhibition catalogues on microfiche, 1919-1959. Prelim. ed. [Ottawa]: McLaren Micropublishing, 1980. [51] l. [0694]

National Gallery of Canada. Library

Canadiana in the library of the National Gallery of Canada/Canadiana dans la bibliothèque de la Galerie nationale du Canada. Ottawa: The Gallery, 1967. [294] p. [0670]

Catalogue of the Library of the National Gallery of Canada, Ottawa, Ontario/[Catalogue de la Bibliothèque de la Galerie nationale du Canada, Ottawa, Ontario]. Boston: G.K. Hall, 1973. 8 vol.; ISBN: 0-8161-1043-3. [0677]

National Indian Brotherhood. Library

Annotated list of holdings [National Indian Brotherhood Library]. Ottawa: National Indian Brotherhood, 1973. 76 l. [3944]

National industrial relations film catalogue. [Ottawa]: National Film Board of Canada, c1986. 31, 21 p.; ISBN: 0-662-54352-1. [6665]

National Institute on Mental Retardation. National Reference Service

Catalogue of the John Orr Foster Reference Library. Downsview: The Institute, 1972. 142 p. [3112]

National Library of Australia

Select reading list on Canadian-Australian relations. Canberra: National Library of Australia, [1966]. 61 l. [2388]

National Library of Canada

Arthur S. Bourinot. Ottawa: National Library of Canada, 1971. 30, 30 p.: ports. [6866]

Made in Canada: artists in books, livres d'artistes. Ottawa: National Library of Canada, 1981-. vol.: ill. (some col.); ISSN: 0228-7749. [0731]

Manitoba authors/Écrivains du Manitoba. Ottawa: The Library, 1970. 1 vol. (unpaged). [0501]

Marriage and the family: preliminary check list of National Library holdings/Mariage et famille: inventaire préliminaire des fonds de la Bibliothèque nationale Ottawa: National Library of Canada, 1980. viii, 130 p.; ISBN: 0-662-51091-7. [3206]

National Library of Canada presents Canadian books for the exhibition at the National Library in Warsaw/ Bibliothèque nationale du Canada présente livres canadiens pour l'exposition de la Bibliothèque nationale à Varsovie/Biblioteka Narodowaw Kanadzie przedstawia ksiezki [sic] Kanadyjskie na wystawie w Bibliotece Narodowej w Warszawie. Ottawa: National Library of Canada, [1975]. 19 l. [0117]

The philatelic collection of the National Library of Canada/ La collection sur la philatelie de la Bibliothèque nationale du Canada. Ottawa: National Library, 1972. 36 l. [1761]

Publications catalogue [National Library of Canada]. Ottawa: The Library, 1992. 30, 30 p.; ISBN: 0-662-59049-X. [1734]

Romulus (Computer file)/Romulus (Fichier d'ordinateur). Ottawa: National Library of Canada, 1992-. compact disks; ISSN: 1188-8741. [5991]

Select bibliography of books by parliamentarians, as displayed at the National Library of Canada from Mar. 12, to Apr. 11, 1976/Bibliographie sélective de livres par des membres du parlement, en montre à la Bibliothèque nationale du Canada du 12 mars au 11 avril 1976. Ottawa: National Library of Canada, 1976. 4 l. [2425]

Theses of the Université de Montréal microfilmed since 1972/Thèses de l'Université de Montréal microfilmées depuis 1972. Ottawa: National Library of Canada, 1982-1983. 5 vol.; ISSN: 0713-5092. [6170]

Union list of Canadian newspapers [microform]/Liste collective des journaux canadiens [microforme]. Ottawa: National Library of Canada, 1988-. microfiches; ISSN: 0840-5832. [6053]

National Library of Canada. Collections Development Branch

Holdings of Canadian serials in the National Library/ Inventaire des publications canadiennes en série dans la Bibliothèque nationale. Ottawa: National Library of Canada, 1974. v, 278 p. [5918]

National Library of Canada. Newspaper Section

Union list of Canadian newspapers held by Canadian libraries/Liste collective des journaux canadiens disponibles dans les bibliothèques canadiennes. Ottawa: Newspaper Section, Serials Division, Public Services Branch, National Library of Canada, 1977-1988. 11 vol.: ill., facsim.; ISSN: 0840-5832. [6048]

National Library of Canada. Resources Survey Division

Checklists of law reports and statutes in Canadian law libraries/Listes de contrôle des recueils de jurisprudence et des statuts dans des bibliothèques de droit du Canada. Ottawa: National Library of Canada, 1977-1980. 4 vol. [2221]

National Library of Canada. Union Catalogue of Serials Division

Union list of serials in education and sociology held by Canadian libraries/Inventaire des publications en série dans les domaines de l'éducation et de la sociologie disponibles dans les bibliothèques canadiennes. Ottawa: National Library of Canada, Union Catalogue of Serials Division, 1975. xxxv, 221 p. [5922]

Union list of serials in fine arts in Canadian libraries/ Inventaire des publications en série dans la domaine des beaux-arts dans les bibliothèques canadiennes. Ottawa: National Library of Canada, 1978. vii, 236 p.; ISBN: 0-660-50131-7. [5933]

National Museums of Canada

Catalogue of publications [National Museums of Canada]. Ottawa: National Museums of Canada, 1979-1981. 6 vol.; ISSN: 0708-2886. [6336]

National program for the integration of the two official languages in the administration of justice: publications/ Programme national de l'administration de la justice dans les deux langues officiels: publications. Ottawa: Communications and Public Affairs, Department of Justice Canada, c1989. 24 p.; ISBN: 0-662-56864-8. [2327]

National Research Council Canada

Review of the literature on apple by-products. Ottawa: National Research Council Canada, 1930. 33 l. [4637]

National Research Council Canada. Associate Committee on Heat Transfer

Abstracts of completed graduate theses in heat transfer in Canadian universities, to December 1961. Ottawa: National Research Council Canada, 1963. 70 p. [6079]

National Research Council Canada. Division of Building Research

List of publications [National Research Council Canada. Division of Building Research]/Liste des publications [Conseil national de recherches du Canada, Division des recherches sur le bâtiment]. Ottawa: The Division, 1947-1983. 36 vol.; ISSN: 0382-1439. [6359]

List of publications on snow and ice. [Ottawa]: National Research Council Canada, Division of Building Research, [1985]. [106] p. [5809]

National Research Council Canada. Division of Electrical Engineering.

Record of work of Electron Physics Section, 1949-1986 [i.e. 1985]. [Ottawa]: National Research Council Canada, Division of Electrical Engineering, c1986. vii, 72 p. [5817]

National Research Council Canada. Division of Information Services

Publications of the National Research Council of Canada, 1918-1952. 3rd ed. Ottawa: [s.n.], 1953. 263 p. [4615]

National Research Council Canada. Division of Mechanical Engineering

Publications of the Division of Mechanical Engineering and the National Aeronautical Establishment. Ottawa: National Research Council Canada, 1965-1990. 8 no.; ISSN: 0077-5568. [5841]

National Research Council Canada. Fire Research Section

List of publications, Fire Research Section, 1955-1985/Liste des publications, Section d'étude de feu, 1955-1985. Ottawa: The Section, 1985. 43 p. [6375]

National Research Council Canada. Space Research Facilities Branch

A bibliography of Canadian space science, 1971-1975. Ottawa: Space Research Facilities Branch, National Research Council Canada, 1976. 79, 42 p. [5761]

National Science Film Library (Canada)

A catalogue of films on the medical sciences/Catalogue des films sur les sciences médicales. Ottawa: Canadian Film Institute, 1972. vi, [25], 144 p. [6616]

National Science Library (Canada)

List of medical and related journals held in the National Science Library, National Research Council, January 1966.

Ottawa: National Research Council of Canada, 1966. 92 p. [5877]

Scientific policy, research and development in Canada: a bibliography/La politique des sciences, la recherche et le développement au Canada: bibliographie. Rev. ed. Ottawa: National Research Council of Canada, 1970. 112 p. [4619]

National Science Library. Aeronautical and Mechanical Engineering Branch

Wind power: a bibliography. [Ottawa]: National Research Council Canada, 1974. 25 l. [5750]

Native Indian Pre-School Curriculum Research Project

Native Indian pre-school curriculum resources bibliography. Vancouver: Urban Native Indian Education Society, c1984. 107 p.: maps.; ISBN: 0-9691591-0-2. [4064]

Native People's Resource Centre (London, Ont.)

Catalogue: books, vertical files, videorecordings. London, Ont.: The Centre, [1982-1985]. [43] p. [4077]

Natural History Society of Montreal

Catalogue of the library and museum of the Natural History Society of Montreal. Montreal: Lovell & Gibson, 1846. 40 p. [6712]

Navet, Eric

"Introduction à une bibliographie analytique des cultures amérindiennes sub-arctiques." Dans: *Inter-Nord*; No. 16 (1982) p. 324-332.; ISSN: 0074-1035. [4039]

Nawwar, A.M.

Development of a research program for improving Arctic marine transportation technology: Volume III: Bibliography. Kanata, Ont.: Arctec Canada Limited, 1979. i, 41 p. [4473]

Neamtan, Judith; Paterson, Craig

Workers' health, safety and compensation: a preliminary bibliography of Canadian federal and provincial government commissions and inquiries. North Vancouver, B.C.: Capilano College Labour Studies Program, 1978. vii, 53 l. (Labour Studies Program Publication series / Capilano College Labour Studies Program ; no. 1) [2846]

Needs assessment of the library's community: a bibliography. Regina: Provincial Library, Saskatchewan Education, 1989. 7 p. [1708]

Neill, Edward Duffield

The writings of Louis Hennepin, Recollect Franciscan missionary. Minneapolis: [s.n.], 1880. 10 p. [7057]

Neill, R.F.

"Adam Shortt: a bibliographical comment." In: *Journal of Canadian Studies*; Vol. 2, no. 1 (February 1967) p. 53-61.; ISSN: 0021-9495. [7306]

Nelson, Debra

E.J. Hughes: a bibliography. Surrey, B.C.: Surrey Art Gallery, c1984. 52 p.; ISBN: 0-920181-09-0. [7071]

Nelson, Ruben

Canadian directory of futures services and resources. Ottawa: Square One Management, 1986. vii, 189 p.; ISBN: 0-9690393-4-4. [2721]

Nemec, Thomas F.

"The Irish emigration to Newfoundland: a critical review of the secondary sources." In: *Newfoundland Quarterly*; Vol. 69, no. 1 (July 1972) p. 15-24.; ISSN: 0014-1836. [4157]

The Irish emigration to Newfoundland: a critical review of the secondary sources. St. John's: [Memorial University of Newfoundland], 1978. 29 l. [4186]

Nesbitt, Bruce

"Canadian literature: an annotated bibliography/Littérature canadienne: une bibliographie avec commentaire." In: *Journal of Canadian Fiction*; Vol. 2, no. 2 (Spring 1973) p. 97-150; vol. 3, no. 4 (1975) p. 103-142; no. 17/18 (1976) p. 70-239; no. 23 (1979) p. 76-331.; ISSN: 0047-2255. [1156]

Canadian literature in English. [Ottawa]: Canadian Studies Directorate, Department of the Secretary of State of Canada, c1988. 41, 43 p. (Canadian studies resource guides); ISBN: 0-662-56134-1. [1258]

La littérature canadienne de langue anglaise. [Ottawa]: Direction des études canadiennes, Secrétariat d'État du Canada, c1988. 43, 41 p. (Guides pédagogiques des études canadiennes); ISBN: 0-662-56134-1. [1259]

Neufeld, Steve; Scott, Jude; D'Souza, Colleen

Automating Ontario museums: computers in museums, a selected bibliography. Toronto: Ontario Museum Association, c1988. 15 p. (Technical Leaflet / Ontario Museum Association ; no. 4); ISBN: 0-920402-10-0. [5833]

Neuman, Robert W.

"An archaeological bibliography: the central and northern Great Plains prior to 1930." In: *Plains Anthropologist*; No. 15 (February 1962) p. 43-57.; ISSN: 0032-0447. [4537]

Neumeyer, Ronald N.

The environmental effects of Canadian water diversion: a literature survey, 1985. Regina: Environment Canada, Inland Waters Directorate, 1986. iv, 87 p.: ill. [5237]

New, William H.

"Annual bibliography of Commonwealth literature, ... : Canada." In: *Journal of Commonwealth Literature*; No. 10 (December 1970)-vol. 13, no. 2 (December 1978) [1134]

Canadian writers, 1890-1920. Detroit, Mich.: Gale Research, 1990. xv, 472 p.: ill., facsims., ports. (Dictionary of literary biography ; vol. 92); ISBN: 0-8103-4572-2. [1285]

Canadian writers, 1920-1959. First series. Detroit, Mich.: Gale Research, 1988. xv, 417 p.: ill. (Dictionary of literary biography ; vol. 68); ISBN: 0-8103-1746-X. [1260]

Canadian writers, 1920-1959. Second series. Detroit, Mich.: Gale Research, 1989. xiii, 442 p.: ill. (Dictionary of literary biography ; vol. 88); ISBN: 0-8103-4566-8. [1275]

Canadian writers before 1890. Detroit, Mich.: Gale Research, 1990. xiv, 434 p.: ill., ports. (Dictionary of literary biography ; vol. 99); ISBN: 0-8103-4579-X. [1286]

Canadian writers since 1960. First series. Detroit, Mich.: Gale Research, 1986. xiii, 445 p.: ill. (Dictionary of literary biography ; vol. 53); ISBN: 0-8103-1731-1. [1232]

Canadian writers since 1960. Second series. Detroit, Mich.: Gale Research, 1987. xiii, 470 p.: ill., ports. (Dictionary of literary biography ; vol. 60); ISBN: 0-8103-1738-9. [1241]

"A checklist of major individual short story collections." In: *World Literature Written in English*; Vol. 11, no. 1 (April 1972) p. 11-13.; ISSN: 0093-1705. [1067]

Critical writings on Commonwealth literatures: a selective bibliography to 1970, with a list of theses and dissertations. University Park: Pennsylvania State University Press, [1975]. 333 p.; ISBN: 0-271-01166-1. [1093]

Malcolm Lowry: a reference guide. Boston: G.K. Hall, c1978. xxix, 162 p. (Reference publication in literature); ISBN: 0-8161-7884-4. [7159]

"Studies of English Canadian literature." In: *International Journal of Canadian Studies*; No. 1-2 (Spring-Fall 1990) p. 97-114.; ISSN: 1180-3991. [1287]

"New books." In: *Journal of Canadian Studies*; (1980-) vol.; ISSN: 0021-9495. [0188]

New Brunswick Human Rights Commission

Human rights: a guide to audio visual resources. Fredericton: The Commission, 1989. 110 p. [6686]

New Brunswick. Legislative Library

Aquaculture/Aquiculture. Fredericton: New Brunswick Legislative Library, 1988. 3 l. (Bibliography / New Brunswick Legislative Library) [4911]

Bill 88: bibliography/Projet de loi 88: bibliographie. Fredericton: New Brunswick Legislative Library, 1992. 4 p. (Bibliography / New Brunswick Legislative Library) [2552]

Employment equity/Équité en matière d'emplois. Fredericton: New Brunswick Legislative Library, 1988. 10 l. (Bibliography / New Brunswick Legislative Library) [2920]

Health care costs/Le coût des soins médicaux. Fredericton: New Brunswick Legislative Library, 1989. 8 l. (Bibliography / New Brunswick Legislative Library) [5692]

Meech Lake Constitutional Accord/Entente constitutionnelle du Lac Meech. Fredericton: Legislative Library, 1988. 6 l. [2318]

Regional development/Dévelopment regional. Fredericton: New Brunswick Legislative Library, 1988. 8 l. (Bibliography / New Brunswick Legislative Library) [0269]

Small business and entrepreneurship/Les petites entreprises et l'entrepreneurship. Fredericton: New Brunswick Legislative Library, 1989. 13 l. (Bibliography / New Brunswick Legislative Library) [2758]

New Brunswick. Legislative Library. Government Documents Section

New Brunswick government documents annual catalogue/ Publications gouvernementales du Nouveau-Brunswick Catalogue annuel. Fredericton: [Legislative Library], 1956-. vol.; ISSN: 0548-4006. [6461]

New Brunswick government publications, quarterly list/ Publications du gouvernement du Nouveau-Brunswick, liste trimestrielle. Fredericton: The Library, 1986-. vol.; ISSN: 0830-1085. [6462]

New Brunswick. Water Resource Planning Branch

Water resources in New Brunswick: a preliminary bibliography. Fredericton: Department of Municipal Affairs and Environment, Water Resource Planning Branch, 1987. 113 p. [5250]

New Play Centre

The catalogue: plays by British Columbia playwrights. Vancouver, B.C.: Athletica Press for New Play Centre, [c1977]. 40 p.; ISBN: 0-920294-00-6. [1110]

New reproductive technologies: a bibliography. Winnipeg: Manitoba Advisory Council on the Status of Women, 1990. 26 p. [5699]

New York Public Library

Canada: an exhibition commemorating the four-hundredth anniversary of the discovery of the Saint Lawrence by Jacques Cartier, 1534-1535: a catalogue with notes. New York: New York Public Library, 1935. 59 p. [1914]

New York Public Library. Reference Department

Dictionary catalog of the history of the Americas. Boston: G.K. Hall, 1961. 28 vol. [6768]

"Newfoundland architecture: a bibliography." In: *Bulletin (Society for the Study of Architecture in Canada)*; Vol. 8, no. 2 (June 1983) p. 20.; ISSN: 0712-8517. [0773]

Newfoundland Information Service

List of publications offered by Government of Newfoundland and Labrador. St. John's: Newfoundland Information Service, 1974-1977. 11 vol.; ISSN: 0383-5189. [6309]

Newman, Maureen; Stratford, Philip

"Bibliographie des livres canadiens en traduction: 1580-1974." Dans: *Meta*; Vol. 20, no 1 (mars 1975) p. 83-105.; ISSN: 0026-0452. [1094]

Newton, Arthur Percival, et al.

"Bibliographie d'histoire coloniale, 1900-1930 : Grande Bretagne et Dominions." Dans: *Bibliographie d'histoire coloniale, 1900-1930*. Paris: Société de l'histoire des colonies françaises, 1932. P. [103]-149. [1907]

Newton, Jennifer L.; Zavitz, Carol

Women: a bibliography of special periodical issues: volume II (updated through 1977). [Toronto]: Canadian Newsletter of Research on Women, c1978. vii, 280 p.; ISSN: 0319-4477. [3781]

Newton, Keith; Leckie, Norman

What's QWL?: definition, notes, and bibliography. Ottawa: Economic Council of Canada, 1977. iv, 124 p.; ISBN: 0-662-01346-8. [2837]

Ngatia, Therese

The Blacks in Canada: a selective annotated bibliography. [Edmonton: T. Ngatia, 1984]. 45 l. [4229]

Nguyên, Vy-Khanh

Déréglementation: bibliographie sélective et annotée. Québec: Bibliothèque de l'Assemblée nationale, Division de la référence parlementaire, 1986. 121 p. (Bibliographie / Bibliothèque de l'Assemblée nationale du Québec ; no 2; ISSN: 0836-9100) [2722]

Politique de l'habitation: bibliographie sélective et annotée. Québec: Bibliothèque de l'Assemblée nationale, Division de la référence parlementaire, 1987. 54 p. (Bibliographie / Bibliothèque de l'Assemblée nationale du Québec ; no 5; ISSN: 0836-9100) [4418]

Robert Bourassa. Québec: Division de la référence parlementaire, Bibliothèque de l'Assemblée nationale, 1986. 16 f. (Bibliographie / Bibliothèque de l'Assemblée nationale du Québec ; ISSN: 0836-9100) [6864]

Nichol, bp

"A chronological checklist of published work by Barbara Caruso, 1964-1985." In: *Open Letter*; Series 6, no. 4 (Spring 1986) p. 79-92.; ISSN: 0048-1939. [6900]

Ganglia Press index. Toronto: Ganglia Press, 1972. [49] p. [1068]

"Published autotopography [checklist of bpNichol's complete works in all genres]." In: *Essays on Canadian Writing*; No. 1 (Winter 1974) p. 39-46.; ISSN: 0316-0300. [7213]

Nichol, Paul

A bibliography of agricultural and rural restructuring. Guelph, Ont.: School of Rural Planning and Development, University of Guelph, 1990. 27 p. (Technical study / School of Rural Planning and Development, University of Guelph ; 134); ISBN: 0-88955-203-7. [4721]

Nicholls, H.B.; Sabowitz, N.C.

Reports by staff of the Bedford Institute of Oceanography, 1962-1973: list of titles and index. [Dartmouth, N.S.]: Bedford Institute of Oceanography, 1974. 126 p. (Bedford Institute of Oceanography Report series ; BI-R-74-4) [5386]

Nicholls, H.B.; Scott, Wendy
Publications by staff of the Bedford Institute of Oceanography, 1962-1974: list of titles and index. [Dartmouth, N.S.]: Bedford Institute of Oceanography, 1975. 113 p. (Bedford Institute of Oceanography Report series ; BI-R-75-7) [5398]

Nicholson, H.F.
List of the published and presented papers by the staff of the Great Lakes Biolimnology Laboratory, 1968-1978. [Ottawa]: Fisheries and Environment Canada, Fisheries and Marine Service, 1979. v, 30 l. (Fisheries and Marine Service Technical report ; no. 874; ISSN: 0701-7626) [5438]

Nicholson, H.F.; Moore, J.E.
Bibliography on the limnology and fisheries of Canadian freshwaters. Burlington, Ont.: Fisheries and Marine Service, 1974-1988. 10 vol. (Canadian technical reports of fisheries and aquatic sciences; ISSN: 0706-6457) [4912]

Nicholson, Norman L.; Sebert, L.M.
The maps of Canada: a guide to official Canadian maps, charts, atlases and gazetteers. Folkestone: Dawson, 1981. x, 251 p.: ill., maps.; ISBN: 0-7129-0911-7. [6576]

Nickles, John M.; Bassler, Ray S.
A synopsis of American fossil Bryozoa: including bibliography and synonymy. Washington: G.P.O., 1900. 663 p. (United States Geological Survey Bulletin ; no. 173) [4527]

Nietfeld, Marie T.; Telfer, Edmund S.
The effects of forest management practices on nongame birds: an annotated bibliography. Edmonton: Canadian Wildlife Service, c1990. v, 300 p. (Technical report series / Western & Northern Region, Canadian Wildlife Service ; no. 112; ISSN: 0831-6481); ISBN: 0-662-18315-0. [5011]

Nietmann, K.
Catalogue of Canadian forest inventory publications and manuals/Catalogue des manuels et publications de l'inventaire des forêts du Canada. Chalk River, Ont.: Canadian Forestry Service, c1987. 24 p. (Canadian Forestry Service Information report ; PI-X-76E/F; ISSN: 0714-3354); ISBN: 0-662-55501-5. [4991]

Nijholt, W.W.
The striped ambrosia beetle, Trypodendron lineatum (Oliver): an annotated bibliography. Victoria: Canadian Forestry Service, 1979. 35 p. (Pacific Forest Research Centre Report ; BC-X-121) [5439]

Nilson, Lenore
The best of Children's choices. Ottawa: Citizens' Committee on Children, 1988. vi, 114 p.; ISBN: 0-9690205-5-4. [1379]

Nininger, J.R.; MacDonald, V.N.; McDiarmid, G.Y.
Developments in the management of local government: a review and annotated bibliography. [Kingston, Ont.: School of Business, Queen's University at Kingston; Toronto: Ministry of Treasury, Economics and Intergovernmental Affairs], 1975. 79 p. (Local government management project: series D publications: periodic papers) [4351]

Nish, James Cameron
"Bibliographie des bibliographies relatives à l'histoire économique du Canada français." Dans: Actualité économique; Vol. 40, no 2 (juillet-septembre 1964) p. 456-466.; ISSN: 0001-771X. [2577]
"Bibliographie sommaire sur la Confédération." Dans: Action nationale; Vol. 54, no 2 (octobre 1964) p. 198-207.; ISSN: 0001-7469. [1944]

"Bibliographie sur l'histoire économique du Canada français." Dans: Actualité économique; Vol. 40, no 1 (avril-juin 1964) p. 200-209.; ISSN: 0001-771X. [2578]
Inventaire des documents relatifs à l'histoire économique du Canada français. Montréal: École des hautes études commerciales, 1967-1970. 14 fasc. [2587]

Nish, James Cameron; Nish, Elizabeth
Bibliographie pour servir à l'étude de l'histoire du Canada français. Montréal: Centre d'étude du Québec, Université Sir George Williams, 1966-1969. 5 vol. [1961]

Noble, Willa J., et al.
A second checklist and bibliography of the lichens and allied fungi of British Columbia. Ottawa: National Museum of Natural Sciences, c1987. 95 p.: ill., maps. (Syllogeus / National Museum of Natural Sciences ; no. 61; ISSN: 0704-576X) [5537]

Noël, François
Bibliographie des thèses et des mémoires sur les communautés culturelles et l'immigration au Québec. Montréal: Communautés culturelles et immigration Québec, 1983. ii, 43 p.; ISBN: 2-550-02925-9. [6171]

Noel-Bentley, Peter
Earle Birney: an annotated bibliography. Downsview, Ont.: ECW Press, c1983. [115] p.; ISBN: 0-920763-50-2. [6844]
"Earle Birney: an annotated bibliography." In: The annotated bibliography of Canada's major authors, Vol. 4, edited by Robert Lecker and Jack David. Downsview, Ont.: ECW Press, c1983. P. 13-128.; ISBN: 0-920802-52-4. [6845]

Noel-Bentley, Peter; Birney, Earle
"Earle Birney: a bibliography in progress, 1923-1969." In: West Coast Review; Vol. 5, no. 2 (October 1970) p. 45-53.; ISSN: 0043-311X. [6846]

Noizet, Pascale
"Bibliographie de Suzanne Lamy." Dans: Voix et Images; Vol. 13, no 1 (automne 1987) p. 70-80.; ISSN: 0318-9201. [7119]

Noonan, Gerald
Guide to the literary heritage of Waterloo and Wellington Counties from 1830 to the mid-20th century: an historical bibliography of authors and poets. Waterloo, Ontario: [Wilfrid Laurier University], 1985. 152 p.; ISBN: 0-9692184-0-0. [1222]

Nordin, Richard Nels; McKean, Colin J.P.
A review of lake aeration as a technique for water quality improvement. Victoria: Province of British Columbia, Ministry of Environment, Assessment and Planning Division, 1982. iv l., 30 p. (CAPD Bulletin / Province of British Columbia, Ministry of Environment, Assessment and Planning Division ; 22; ISSN: 0228-5304); ISBN: 0-7719-8888-5. [5184]

Nordstrom, Lance O.; Newman, Reg F.; Wikeem, Brian M.
An annotated bibliography on forest-range ecosystems in the Pacific Northwest. Victoria: Information Services Branch, Ministry of Forests, c1985. iv, 96 p. (Land management report / British Columbia Ministry of Forests ; no. 38; ISSN: 0702-9861); ISBN: 0-7718-8510-5. [4986]

Normand, Sylvio
Bibliographie sur le Code civil du Québec. Montréal: Wilson & Lafleur, 1991. x, 69 p.; ISBN: 2-89127-189-0. [2355]
Bibliographie sur les institutions parlementaires québécoises. Québec: Bibliothèque de l'Assemblée nationale, 1985. xiii, 90 p. (Bibliographie et documentation / Bibliothèque de l'Assemblée nationale du Québec ; 18); ISBN: 2-551-06573-9. [2497]

Normandeau, André
"[Criminology: a bibliography]." In: *Canadian Journal of Criminology and Corrections*, Vol. 17, no. 1 (January 1975) p. 110-131.; ISSN: 0315-5390. [2144]

"Selective bibliography of North American commissions on criminal justice/Bibliographie sélective des commissions d'enquête nord-américaines en matière de justice pénale." In: *Canadian Journal of Criminology*; Vol. 35, no. 3 (July 1993) p. 345-354.; ISSN: 0704-9722. [2362]

Normandeau, André; Cusson, Maurice
"Guide de lecteur sur le vol à main armée: si le coeur vous en dit!" Dans: *Criminologie*; Vol. 18, no 2 (1985) p. 147-154.; ISSN: 0316-0041. [2276]

Normandeau, André; Vauclair, Martin
"Film library on prisons in Canada/Filmographie canadienne sur la prison." In: *Canadian Journal of Criminology*; Vol. 29, no. 1 (January 1987) p. 84-120.; ISSN: 0704-9722. [6672]

"Sociologie du milieu carcéral, bibliographie sélective." Dans: *Revue canadienne de criminologie*; Vol. 28, no 4 (octobre 1986) p. 415-433.; ISSN: 0704-9722. [3290]

Noroît 1971-1986. Saint-Lambert, Québec: Éditions du Noroît, 1987. 78 p.: ill.; ISBN: 2-89018-160-X. [1242]

Norris, A.W.; Sanford, B.V.; Bell, R.T.
Bibliography on Hudson Bay Lowlands. Ottawa: Geological Survey of Canada, 1968. P. 47-118: chart, map. (Geological Survey of Canada Paper ; 67-60) [4768]

Norris, Ken
"Montreal English poetry in the seventies." In: *Contemporary Verse Two*; Vol. 3, no. 3 (January 1978) p. 8-13. [1135]

North, R.A.
Bibliography on Canadian government and politics. [Vancouver: s.n.], 1966. 47 l. [2389]

North York Public Library. Canadiana Collection
Genealogy and family history catalogue. [Downsview, Ont.]: North York Public Library, c1978. 96 p.; ISBN: 0-920552-00-5. [2000]

Ontario bicentennial and Toronto sesquicentennial: a selected bibliography of some holdings of the Canadiana Collection of the North York Public Library. [North York, Ont.]: North York Public Library, [1984]. 9 p. [0478]

Northern Alberta Development Council
List of current publications [Northern Alberta Development Council]. Peace River, Alta.: The Council, 1982-. vol.; ISSN: 0833-7918. [0553]

Northern Co-ordination and Research Centre (Canada)
A bibliography on the Canadian arctic. Ottawa: 1967. 10 p. [0614]

Northern Ontario: a selected bibliography relating to economic development in northern Ontario, 1969-1978. [Toronto]: Economic Development Branch, Ministry of Treasury, Economics and Intergovernmental Affairs, 1978. 51, [8] l. [0459]

Northern Political Studies (Program)
Northern politics review: an annual publication of Northern Political Studies Program. Calgary: University of Calgary, 1984-. vol.; ISSN: 0823-9576. [0664]

Northern Regulatory Review
Some references relevant to regulation of industrial activity in the Canadian north, 1983-1986. [Ottawa]: Indian and Northern Affairs Canada, 1986. 26, 10, 40, 35 p. [2723]

Northern titles: KWIC index. Edmonton: Boreal Institute for Northern Studies, University of Alberta, 1973-. vol.; ISSN: 0704-6839 [0665]

Northwest Territories. Department of Culture and Communications
Publications catalogue [Government of the Northwest Territories]. Yellowknife: Northwest Territories, Culture and Communications, 1986-. vol.; ISSN: 0837-4406. [6463]

Norton, Judith A.
New England planters in the Maritime provinces of Canada 1759-1800: bibliography of primary sources. Toronto: University of Toronto Press in association with Planter Studies Centre, Acadia University, c1993. xvii, 403 p.: map.; ISBN: 0-8020-2840-3. [2089]

Noseworthy, Ann
A literature review of the marine environment, Terra Nova National Park and adjacent bays. [St. John's, Nfld.: Whale Research Group, Memorial University of Newfoundland], 1983. 245 l.: ill. [5203]

Notices en langue française du *Canadian catalogue of books*, 1921-1949 avec index établi par Henri-Bernard Boivin. Montréal: Ministère des affaires culturelles, 1975. ix, 263, 199 p., 17 f. de pl.: ill. [0118]

Nouveau-Brunswick. Ministère de l'éducation
Répertoire des publications relatives à 'organisation de l'enseignement public et aux programmes d'enseignement en langue française dans la province du Nouveau-Brunswick. Fredericton: Gouvernement du Nouveau-Brunswick, Ministère de l'éducation, 1980-1984. 5 vol.; ISSN: 0825-690X. [3627]

Nouveau catalogue de livres de droit et de jurisprudence de la Librairie A. Périard: français, anglais, américains et canadiens. Montréal: A. Périard, 1891. 62 p. [2096]

Nova Scotia Government Bookstore
Publications catalogue: Nova Scotia Government Bookstore. Halifax, N.S.: Information Division, Department of Government Services, 1974-. vol.: ill.; ISSN: 0228-0175. [6466]

Nova Scotia Museum
Gleaning Nova Scotia's history: a bibliography for use in local history studies. Halifax, N.S.: Nova Scotia Museum, 1976. [12] l. [0224]

Nova Scotia NewStart Incorporated
Abstracts of reports [Nova Scotia NewStart Incorporated]. Yarmouth: Nova Scotia NewStart Incorporated, 1972. 40 l. [3113]

Nova Scotia Provincial Library. Reference Services Section
Professional reading materials. Halifax: Reference Services Section, Nova Scotia Provincial Libraries, 1975. 309 p. [1610]

Nova Scotia Research Foundation
A catalogue of books in the library of Nova Scotia Research Foundation. Halifax, N.S.: Imperial Press, 1953. 62 p. [6767]

Research record, 1947-1967. Halifax, N.S.: Nova Scotia Research Foundation, 1967. 69 p. [4618]

Selected bibliography on algae. Dartmouth, N.S.: Nova Scotia Research Foundation, 1952-1974. 14 vol.; ISSN: 0080-8571. [5387]

Nova Scotia. Community Planning Division
Municipal map index: Nova Scotia. Halifax, N.S.: The Division, [1966]. 10, [56] l. [6509]

Nova Scotia. Department of Agriculture and Marketing. Marketing and Economics Branch. Co-operatives Section
Co-operative bibliography. Truro, N.S.: Co-operatives Section, [1984]. 42 p. [2698]

Nova Scotia. Department of Lands and Forests
A book of maps: land use and natural resources of Nova Scotia. Halifax: Department of Lands and Forests, 1977. iv, 48 p. [6561]

Forest research report. Truro: Nova Scotia Department of Lands and Forests, 1987-. vol.; ISSN: 0845-1788. [5023]

Nova Scotia. Department of Municipal Affairs. Community Planning Division
Nova Scotia map index. Halifax, N.S.: The Division, 1983. 116 p.: ill., maps. [6582]

Nova Scotia. Legislative Council. Library
Catalogue of books in the Legislative Council Library. Halifax, N.S.: [J. Bowes and Sons], 1859. 35 p. [6717]

Nova Scotia. Legislative Library
Catalogue of the books in the Legislative Library of Nova Scotia: authors, titles, and subjects. Halifax: Nova Scotia Printing Co., 1890. vi, 292 p. [6744]

Nova Scotia royal commissions and commissions of inquiry, 1849-1984: a checklist. 3rd ed. Halifax: The Library, 1984. 39 p. [6365]

"Novascotiana: in-print titles as of May 1974." In: *Nova Scotia Historical Quarterly*; Vol. 4, no. 2 (June 1974) p. 179-205.; ISSN: 0300-3728. [0217]

Publications of the Province of Nova Scotia. Halifax: Legislative Library, 1967-. vol.; ISSN: 0550-1792. [6464]

Publications of the Province of Nova Scotia, monthly checklist. Halifax: Legislative Library, 1987-. vol.; ISSN: 0835-6513. [6465]

Publications of the Province of Nova Scotia, quarterly checklist. Halifax: Legislative Library, 1980-1987. 7 vol.; ISSN: 0228-0299. [6386]

Travel in the Maritime Provinces, 1750-1867. Halifax, N.S.: Nova Scotia Legislative Library, 1982. 14 l. [0252]

Nova Scotia. Senior Citizens' Secretariat
Aging and the aged in Nova Scotia: a list of writings from 1979 to 1985. [Halifax]: The Secretariat, 1986. ii, 10 l. [3291]

Nowak, W.S.W.
Inventory of post-graduate, honours and senior undergraduate reports on the fishery and fishing industry in the data banks owned by the compiler. [St. John's, Nfld.]: Department of Geography, Memorial University of Newfoundland, [1980]. 48 l. [4897]

The lobster (Homaridae) and the lobster fisheries: an interdisciplinary bibliography. St. John's: Memorial University of Newfoundland, 1972. 313 p. (Marine Sciences Research Laboratory Technical reports ; no. 6) [4890]

Nutrition and physical activity: a specialized bibliography from the SPORT database/Nutrition et l'activité physique: une bibliographie spécialisée de la base de données SPORT. Gloucester, Ont.: Sport Information Resource Centre, 1990. 12 l. (SportBiblio ; no. 9; ISSN: 1180-5269) [1857]

"O.D. Skelton, 1878-1941: [bibliography]." In: *Canadian Journal of Economics and Political Science*; Vol. 7, no. 2 (May 1941) p. 276-278.; ISSN: 0315-4890. [7309]

Oak, Lydia
Copyright: a selective bibliography/Le droit d'auteur: une bibliographie sélective. Ottawa: Library Documentation Centre, National Library of Canada, 1980. [8] p. [2222]

Health science libraries: selected references/Bibliothèques dans le domaine de la santé: bibliographie sélective. Ottawa: National Library of Canada, 1980. 5 p. (Bibliographies / Library Documentation Centre; ISSN: 0226-4226) [1641]

Oberlander, H. Peter; Lasserre, F.
Annotated bibliography: performance standards for space and site planning for residential development. Ottawa: National Research Council Canada, Division of Building Research, 1961. iv, 33 l. (National Research Council Canada, Division of Building Research Bibliography ; no. 19) [4304]

O'Bready, Maurice
Les Cantons de l'Est: début de bibliographie. [S.l.: s.n., 1970]. 12 f. [0307]

Les journaux publiés dans les Cantons de l'Est depuis 150 ans. Sherbrooke: [s.n.], 1965. 9 f. [6014]

O'Brien, A.H.
"Haliburton: a sketch and bibliography." In: *Proceedings and Transactions of the Royal Society of Canada*; Series 3, vol. 3, section 2 (1909) p. 43-66.; ISSN: 0316-4616. [7041]

O'Bryan, Kenneth G.
Requirements for the training and certification of teachers in early primary education: a review of the literature. Toronto: Ontario Ministry of Education, 1986. iv, 48 p.; ISBN: 0-7729-1255-4. [3660]

O'Callaghan, Edmund Bailey
Catalogue of the library of the late E.B. O'Callaghan, M.D., LL.D., historian of New York. New York: Taylor, 1882. 223 p.: port. [6733]

Jesuit relations of discoveries and other occurrences in Canada and the northern and western states of the Union, 1632-1672. New York: Press of the Historical Society, 1847. 22 p. [1874]

Relations des Jésuites sur les découvertes et les autres événements arrivés en Canada, et au nord et à l'ouest des États-Unis, 1611-1672. Montréal: Bureau des mélanges religieux, 1850. vi, 70 p. [1875]

Oct. Lemieux et Cie.
Catalogue, vente à l'encan d'une bibliothèque de livres rares et précieux par Oct. Lemieux & Cie: 2,000 volumes: ouvrages sur l'Amérique, et en particulier sur le Canada: droit, littérature, science, poésie, etc. .... [S.l.: s.n.], 1885. 24 p. [0016]

O'Dea, Agnes C.; Alexander, Anne
Bibliography of Newfoundland. Toronto: Published by University of Toronto Press in association with Memorial University of Newfoundland, c1986. 2 vol. (xx, 1450 p.): facsims.; ISBN: 0-8020-2402-5. [0263]

O'Dea, Fabian
The 17th century cartography of Newfoundland. Toronto: B.V. Gutsell, Department of Geography, York University, 1971. vi, 48 p.: ill., maps. (Cartographica Monograph ; no. 1) [6524]

O'Dea, Shane
"A selective annotated bibliography for the study of Newfoundland vertical-log structures with some comments on terminology." In: *Association for Preservation Technology Bulletin*; Vol. 13, no. 1 (1981) p. 35-37.; ISSN: 0044-9466. [0768]

O'Donnell, Brendan
Printed sources for the study of English-speaking Quebec: an annotated bibliography of works published before 1980.

Lennoxville, Quebec: Bishop's University, 1985. ii, 298 p. (Eastern Townships Research Centre series ; no. 2); ISBN: 0 920917 04 6. [0389]

Sources for the study of English-speaking Quebec: an annotated bibliography of works published between 1980 and 1990/Sources pour l'étude du Québec d'expression anglaise: bibliographie annotée d'ouvrages produit de 1980 à 1990. Lennoxville, Quebec: Eastern Townships Research Centre of Bishop's University with the assistance of the Secretary of State of Canada, 1992. li, 264 p.; ISBN: 0-662-58983-1. [0414]

"Oeuvres de Guy Lafond." Dans: *Voix et Images*; Vol. 4, no 2 (décembre 1978) p. 187-188.; ISSN: 0318-9201. [7110]

Office national du film du Canada

Catalogue des films fixes. Ottawa: Impr. de la Reine, 1952-1968. [9] vol. [6611]

Le répertoire des films de l'ONF: la production de l'Office national du film du Canada de 1939 à 1989. Montréal: L'Office, c1991. clvii, 758 p., [72] p. de pl.: ill., portr.; ISBN: 0-660-56485-8 (série). [6694]

Offshore Safety Task Force

Offshore Safety Task Force report to the EPOA:APOA Safety Committee: selected references. Calgary: Eastcoast Petroleum Operators' Association, 1983. 74 p. [4835]

Ogaard, Louis A.

Wetland vegetation of the Prairie Pothole Region: research methods and annotated bibliography. Fargo, N.D.: Agricultural Experimental Station, North Dakota State University, 1981. iv, 50 p. (North Dakota Research report ; no. 85) [5465]

Ogle, Robert W.; Malycky, Alexander

"Periodical publications of Canada's Indians and Métis: a preliminary check list." In: *Canadian Ethnic Studies*; Vol. 2, no. 1 (June 1970) p. 109-115.; ISSN: 0008-3496. [5899]

"Periodical publications of Canada's Indians and Métis: a preliminary check list." In: *Northian*; Vol. 8, no. 4 (March 1972) p. 39-43.; ISSN: 0029-3253. [5904]

O'Grady, K., et al.

A bibliography of papers and reports issued in the Census Field internal series: 1965-1977/Bibliographie des notes et des rapports publiés dans les séries internes du Secteur du recensement. Ottawa: Demographic Sector, Characteristics Division, Census Field, Statistics Canada, 1977. 1 vol. (in various pagings). [3020]

Oil and gas technical reports, 1920-1980/Rapports techniques concernant la prospection petrolière et gazière, 1920-1980. Ottawa: Indian and Northern Affairs Canada, 1980. 100 p.; ISBN: 0-662-51196-4. [4817]

Oil spill related research in the public domain at the Arctic Institute of North America: citations and abstracts: prepared through the Arctic Science and Technology Information System, Arctic Institute of North America, Calgary, Alberta at the request of The Consolidex Magnorth Oakwood Joint Venture in consultation with Pallister Resource Management Ltd. Calgary: Consolidex Magnorth Oakwood Joint Venture, 1983. xiii, 115 p. [5204]

Ojibway-Cree Resource Centre

Audio-visual bibliography [Ojibway-Cree Resource Centre]. [Timmins, Ont.: Ojibway-Cree Resource Centre], 1978. ii l., 45 p. [6635]

Ojibway Resource Centre catalogue. 2nd ed. [Timmins, Ont.]: The Centre, [1984]. 342, 262 p. [4065]

Okanagan Regional Library

British Columbia books. 3rd ed. Kelowna, B.C.: Okanagan Regional Library, 1971. 47 l. [0580]

O'Leary, Timothy J.

A preliminary bibliography of the archaeology of western Canada. [Calgary: s.n., 1975]. 23 l. [4562]

Oleson, Robert V.; Wilmat, Lloyd H.

A selective and annotated bibliography of Riding Mountain National Park. Winnipeg, Man.: [s.n.], 1971. 125, 168 l. [2983]

Oleson, T.J.

"The Vikings in America: a critical bibliography." In: *Canadian Historical Review*; Vol. 36, no. 2 (June 1955) p. 166-173.; ISSN: 0008-3755. [1927]

Oliver, Kent D.

Catalogue of the Buller Memorial Library/Catalogue de la Bibliothèque commémorative Buller. Ottawa: Research Branch, Canada Department of Agriculture, 1965. 84 p.: ill. [4646]

Olivier, Daniel

Bibliographie sur la guignolée, Nöel, le jour de l'An, la quête de l'Enfant Jésus, l'Epiphanie et le temps des fêtes en général. [Ste-Elisabeth, Québec: D. Olivier, 1973]. [12] f. [4558]

Olivier, Réjean

Bibliographie chronologique des oeuvres de Réjean Olivier publiées par la maison Édition privée et la Bibliothèque du Collège de L'Assomption, et cataloguées par la Centrale des bibliothèques. L'Assomption, Québec: Collège de L'Assomption, Bibliothèque, 1985. 13 f.; ISBN: 2-920248-35-9. [7219]

Bibliographie des journaux et périodiques de la ville de Joliette. Joliette, Québec: Société historique de Joliette, [1969]. 2 f. [5885]

Bibliographie sur la ville de Joliette. Joliette, Québec: Société historique de Joliette, 1969. 2 p. [0303]

Bibliographie sur Nöel et le temps des fêtes: établie à partir du catalogue de la collection de la famille Olivier de Joliette. Joliette, Québec: R. Olivier, 1986. 29 f. (Collection Oeuvres bibliophiliques de Lanaudière ; no 14); ISBN: 2-920249-98-3. [1233]

Bio-bibliographie de Monsieur Jean-Baptiste Meilleur, 1796-1878, médecin, auteur, fondateur du Collège de l'Assomption, 1832 et premier superintendant de l'Instruction publique dans le Bas-Canada, 1843-1855. Joliette [Québec]: R. Olivier, 1982. 55 p.: ill., fac-sims.; ISBN: 2-920249-54-1. [7187]

La boîte à prières: boîte de brochures conservées par la supérieure des Petites soeurs de la Sainte-Famille du Collège de L'Assomption et remises au bibliothécaire avant leur départ en 1980. L'Assomption, Québec: Collège de L'Assomption, Bibliothèque, 1983. 8 f.; ISBN: 2-920248-77-4. [1556]

"Catalogue chronologique des livres publiés par Réjean Olivier." Dans: *Je viens causer des livres* .... Joliette, Québec: Édition privée, 1990. P. 249-313.; ISBN: 2-92090-423-X. [7221]

Catalogue de la collection Etienne-F. Duval en théâtre québécois et français conservée à la bibliothèque du Collège de l'Assomption. Joliette, Québec: [s.n.], 1986. 164 p.: portr. (Collection Oeuvres bibliophiliques de Lanaudière ; no 15); ISBN: 2-920249-97-5. [0984]

Catalogue de la collection François Lanoue, prêtre, auteur et historien, faisant partie de la bibliothèque de la famille Olivier de Joliette. Joliette, Québec: R. Olivier, 1985. 18 f.; ISBN: 2-920249-91-6. [6790]

Catalogue de laurentiana, de canadiana et de livres anciens de la bibliothèque de la famille Olivier répertoriant 12,000 volumes et 120 collections de périodiques pour la plupart du Québec. Joliette [Québec: s.n.], 1981. 3 vol.; ISBN: 2-920249-00-2. [0373]

Catalogue descriptif et chronologique des oeuvres éditées, composées et compilées par Réjean Olivier contenant une courte notice biographique. Joliette [Québec: s.n.], 1981. iii, 56 p.: ill.; ISBN: 2-920249-50-9. [7217]

Le Collège de l'Assomption et son rayonnement dans les écrits et les éditions de Réjean Olivier, bibliothécaire. Joliette, Québec: [s.n.], 1988. 30 f.: ill. (Collection Oeuvres bibliophiliques de Lanaudière ; no 17); ISBN: 2-920904-20-5. [3691]

Les écrits d'un bibliothécaire, auteur, bibliophile, bibliographe et historien de 1967 à 1988. Joliette [Québec]: [s.n.], 1988. 51, 35 p. (Collection Oeuvres bibliophiliques de Lanaudière ; no 18); ISBN: 2-920904-21-3. [7220]

Le Lanaudois: bibliographie de la région de Lanaudière ou Extraits du catalogue de la collection de la famille Olivier de Joliette. Joliette [Québec: s.n.], 1985. 134 f., [12] f. de pl.: ill., fac-sims. (Collection Oeuvres bibliophiliques de Lanaudière ; no 15); ISBN: 2-920249-90-8. [0390]

Livres québécois, canadiens et américains antérieurs à 1878 de la bibliothèque Olivier. Joliette [Québec: s.n.], 1979. 37 f.; ISBN: 2-920249-04-5. [0130]

Notre polygraphe québécois: Frédéric-Alexandre Baillairgé, prêtre. L'Assomption [Québec]: Collège de l'Assomption, Bibliothèque, 1976. 43 f.: fac-sim. [6822]

Le père Albert Lacombe, O.M.I. (1827-1916) ... bibliographie signalétique et chronologique de ses écrits, comprenant articles de périodiques, brochures, livres et manuscrits. L'Assomption [Québec]: Collège de l'Assomption, Bibliothèque, 1983. 86 f., ill., ports.; ISBN: 2-920248-81-2. [7109]

Quarante ans dans le Grand Nord: bio-bibliographie du père Eugène Fafard, O.M.I., natif de Saint-Cuthbert, comté de Bernier. L'Assomption, Québec: Collège de L'Assomption, Bibliothèque, 1981. 18 f.; ISBN: 2-920248-95-2. [6972]

Répertoire des auteurs contemporains de la région de Lanaudière. Joliette, Qué.: Éditions Pleins Bords, c1981. 320 p.: ill.; ISBN: 2-89197-019-5. [1185]

Vingt ans de recherches artistiques, bibliographiques, biographiques, culturelles, historiographiques et historiques pour mettre en valeur la région de Lanaudière ou Catalogue descriptif et chronologique des oeuvres éditées, composées et compilées par Réjean Olivier. 2e éd. L'Assomption [Québec]: Collège de l'Assomption, Bibliothèque, 1984. 115 f.: ill.; ISBN: 2-920248-64-2. [7218]

Olivier, Réjean; Olivier, Yolande

Bibliographie chronologique des livres publiés à Joliette depuis sa fondation. Joliette, Québec: Société historique de Joliette, [1969]. 3 f. [0304]

Olling, Randy

A guide to research resources for the Niagara region. St. Catharines: Brock University, 1971. 299 p. [0441]

Olson, J.C.

"Bibliography of oil sands, heavy oils, and natural asphalts." In: *The future of heavy crude oils and tar sands*, edited by R.F. Meyer and C.T. Steele. New York: McGraw-Hill, c1981. P.

855-897.; ISBN: 0-7-0606650-9. [4822]

Olver, C.H.; Martin, N.V.

A selective bibliography of the lake trout, Salvelinus namaycush (Walbaum), 1784-1982. [Toronto]: Ontario Ministry of Natural Resources, 1984. iii, 109 p. (Ontario fisheries technical report series ; no. 12; ISSN: 0227-986X); ISBN: 0-7743-9061-1. [5505]

Olvet, Jaan

"Estonian-Canadian periodical publications: a preliminary check list." In: *Canadian Ethnic Studies*; Vol. 2, no. 1 (June 1970) p. 35-40.; ISSN: 0008-3496. [5900]

Olynyk, Nadia M.

Roman Rakhmanny: a bibliographic guide to selected works. Winnipeg: Ukrainian Academy of Arts and Sciences in Canada, 1984. 24 p. (Ukrainian Academy of Arts and Sciences in Canada Bibliography ; no. 1: 21) [7222]

Ommanney, C. Simon L.

Bibliographic information on the Freshfield, Lyell and Mons glaciers, Alberta. Ottawa: National Hydrology Research Institute, 1984. 9 p. [5218]

Bibliography of Canadian glaciology/Bibliographie de la glaciologie. Ottawa: National Hydrology Research Institute, Inland Waters Directorate, 1978-1982. 3 vol. (Inland Waters Directorate Report series ; no. 58,59,73) (Glacier inventory note ; no. 9,10,11; ISSN: 0713-2875) [5185]

Canadian lake, river and sea ice references (1991-1992) and recent work. Saskatoon: National Hydrology Research Institute, 1992. 120 p. (National Hydrology Research Institute Contribution ; no. 92037; ISSN: 0838-1992) [5298]

Current research in the earth sciences: NHRI report for May 1988-April 1989. Saskatoon: National Hydrology Research Institute, 1989. 35 l. [4877]

Floating ice in Canada references (1988-1990) and recent work. Saskatoon: National Hydrology Research Institute, 1990. 120 p. (National Hydrology Research Institute Contribution ; no. 90052; ISSN: 0838-1992) [5283]

Permafrost in Canada: references (1988-1990) and recent work. Saskatoon: National Hydrology Research Institute, 1990. 47 p. (National Hydrology Research Institute Contribution ; no. 90053; ISSN: 0838-1992) [5284]

Recent Canadian glacier references, 1986-1988. Saskatoon: Environment Canada, National Hydrology Research Institute, 1989. 22 l. (National Hydrology Research Institute Contribution ; no. 89001; ISSN: 0838-1992) [5271]

"Selected bibliography of the publications of Fritz Müller for the period 1954-1980." In: *Arctic*; Vol. 34, no. 2 (June 1981) p. 196-198.; ISSN: 0004-0843. [7202]

Snow and ice research in Canada, 1988. Saskatoon: National Hydrology Research Institute, [1989]. 13 l. (National Hydrology Research Institute Contribution ; no. 89038; ISSN: 0838-1992) [5272]

Snow in Canada references (1988-1990) and recent work. Saskatoon: Environment Canada, Conservation and Protection, Inland Waters Directorate, 1990. 53 p. [5285]

On-reserve housing: annotated bibliography. [Ottawa: Indian and Northern Affairs Canada], 1984. 24 l. [4066]

O'Neill, Patrick B.

Canadian plays: a supplementary checklist. Halifax, N.S.: Dalhousie University, University Libraries, School of Library Service, 1978. 69 l. (Occasional papers / Dalhousie University Libraries and Dalhousie University School of Library Service ; no. 19; ISSN: 0318-7403); ISBN: 0-7703-

0158-4. [1136]

"A checklist of Canadian dramatic materials to 1967." In: *Canadian Drama;* Vol. 8, no. 2 (1982) p. 173-303; vol. 9, no. 2 (1983) p. 369-506.; ISSN: 0317-9044. [1208]

"Unpublished Canadian plays, copyrighted 1921-1937." In: *Canadian Drama;* Vol. 4, no. 1 (Spring 1978) p. 52-63.; ISSN: 0317-9044. [1137]

Ontario Agricultural College. School of Agricultural Engineering

List of publications (School of Agricultural Engineering, University of Guelph). Guelph, Ont.: School of Agricultural Engineering, University of Guelph, 1966. 9 l. [4649]

Ontario Archaeological Society. Library

Library and archives [Ontario Archaeological Society], September 1979. Toronto: Ontario Archaeological Society, 1979. 26 p. [4576]

Ontario Association for the Mentally Retarded

Sexuality and the mentally handicapped: resource literature. Toronto: Ontario Association for the Mentally Retarded, [1977]. [14] l. [3158]

Ontario College of Education. Department of Educational Research

Theses in education: Ontario College of Education, University of Toronto since 1898: including theses in pedagogy from Queen's University, 1911-1925. Toronto: Department of Educational Research, Ontario College of Education, University of Toronto, [1952]. i, 32 l. (Educational research series / Department of Educational Research, Ontario College of Education, University of Toronto ; no. 20) [6061]

Ontario Economic Council

Annotated list of Ontario Economic Council research publications, 1974-1980. Toronto: The Council, 1981. [10], 57 p.; ISBN: 0-7743-6681-8. [2671]

Ontario Educational Communications Authority

Man builds – man destroys: a Canadian bibliographic supplement. Toronto: Ontario Educational Communications Authority, c1975. 48 p.: ill. [5102]

Ontario Federation of Labour. Resource Centre

Labour film list. [Don Mills] Ont.: Ontario Federation of Labour Resource Centre, [1977]. 54, [6] l. [6633]

Ontario Genealogical Society

Ontario Genealogical Society library holdings: housed with Canadiana Collection, North York Public Library. Toronto: The Society, c1985. 148 p.; ISBN: 0-920036-07-4. [2049]

Ontario Genealogical Society. Kingston Branch

Library holdings: housed with Kingston Public Library. Kingston, Ont.: The Branch, c1987. i, 44 p.; ISBN: 1-55034-002-6. [2063]

Ontario Genealogical Society. London Branch. Library

London Branch Library holdings: a genealogical research aid. London, Ont.: London Branch, Ontario Genealogical Society, c1986. 39 p. [2057]

Ontario Genealogical Society. Ottawa Branch. Library

Library holdings [Ontario Genealogical Society, Ottawa Branch]. Ottawa: The Society, [1974]. [23] p. [1982]

Ontario Geological Survey. Geoscience Data Centre

Index to published reports and maps, Division of Mines, 1891 to 1977. Toronto: Ontario Ministry of Natural Resources, 1978. xv, 408 p.: maps. (Ontario Geological Survey Miscellaneous paper ; 77; ISSN: 0704-2752) [6316]

Ontario Historical Society

Annual bibliography of Ontario history/Bibliographie annuelle d'histoire ontarienne. Sudbury, Ont.: Laurentian University, 1980-1986. 6 vol.; ISSN: 0227-6623. [0481]

Ontario Institute for Studies in Education. Library. Reference and Information Services

Differentiated staffing: an annotated bibliography. Toronto: Ontario Institute for Studies in Education, 1971. viii, 18 p. (Current bibliography / Ontario Institute for Studies in Education ; no. 3) [3423]

Elementary teacher education-certification: an annotated bibliography, 1963-1973. Toronto: Ontario Institute for Studies in Education, 1974. x, 44 p. (Current bibliography / Ontario Institute for Studies in Education ; no. 9) [3486]

Nongrading: an annotated bibliography. [Toronto]: Ontario Institute for Studies in Education, 1970. viii, 32 p. (Current bibliography / Ontario Institute for Studies in Education ; no. 1) [3412]

Ontario Library Association. School Libraries Division

Canadian periodicals for schools. Toronto: Ontario Library Association. School Libraries Division, 1974. [34] l. [5919]

Ontario Research Foundation

Scientific publications and papers by members of the staff of the Ontario Research Foundation covering the years 1929-1949. Toronto: [s.n., 1950]. 16 p. [4614]

Ontario Teachers' Federation. Status of Women Committee

Family violence: a selective bibliography. [Toronto]: The Federation, [1985]. 82, 24 p.; ISBN: 0-88872-064-5. [3278]

Ontario Women's Directorate

Employment equity: an annotated bibliography. Toronto: Ontario Women's Directorate, 1990. 16, 12 l. [2932]

Ontario. Community Renewal Resource Centre

Ontario renews bibliography: a listing of books, pamphlets and periodical information available from the Community Renewal Resource Centre. [Toronto]: Ontario Ministry of Municipal Affairs and Housing, 1982. 57, 21 p. [4396]

Ontario. Department of Agriculture and Food

Publications of the Ontario Department of Agriculture and Food. Toronto: Department of Agriculture and Food, 1968. 16 p. [6269]

Ontario. Department of Economics and Development. Office of the Chief Economist. Economic Analysis Branch

Economic reports: a selected bibliography of economic reports produced by Ontario government departments. Toronto: Ontario Department of Economics and Development, Office of the Chief Economist, Economic Analysis Branch, 1967. 28 l. [2582]

Ontario. Department of Economics and Development. Regional Development Branch

Ontario, a bibliography for regional development: classified list of limited references. 2nd ed. Toronto: Regional Development Branch, Department of Economics and Development, 1966. vi l., 126 p. [4307]

Ontario. Department of Education

Canadian curriculum materials: educational media for Ontario schools/Matériel didactique canadien: sources de référence pédagogique pour les écoles ontariennes. Toronto: 1972. 159 p. (Circular / Ontario Department of Education ; no. 15) [3441]

Catalogue of the books relating to Canada: historical and biographical in the library of the Education Department for Ontario, arranged according to topics and in alphabetical order. Toronto: Warwick, 1890. 122 p. [6745]

Multi-media resource list: Eskimos and Indians. [Toronto: s.n.], 1969. 50 p. [3915]

Ontario. Department of Mines

General index to the Reports of the Ontario Department of Mines. Toronto: Queen's Printer, 1921-1965. 7 vol. [6254]

Index of geological maps accompanying annual reports, volumes 1 to 45, 1891 to 1936. Toronto: King's Printer, 1937. 41 p.: folded map (in pocket). (Ontario Department of Mines Bulletin ; no. 110) [6491]

List of publications, 1891-1965 [Ontario Department of Mines]. Toronto: Queen's Printer, 1966. viii, 112 p.: ill., maps. (Ontario Department of Mines Bulletin ; no. 25) [6260]

Ontario. Department of Planning and Development. Community Planning Branch

Geographic theses: a bibliography. Toronto: The Branch, 1958. 25 p. [6067]

Ontario. Department of Public Records and Archives

A guide to pamphlets in the Ontario Archives relating to educational history, 1803-1967. [Toronto]: Department of History & Philosophy, Ontario Institute for Studies in Education, [1971]. iv, 104 p. (Educational record series / Department of History & Philosophy, Ontario Institute for Studies in Education ; no. 1) [3422]

Ontario. Department of Revenue. Library

Provincial-municipal relations in Canada. Toronto: Department of Revenue Library, 1969. 5 p. (Bibliography series / Ontario Department of Revenue Library ; no. 6) [2397]

Ontario. Legislative Library

Catalogue of the library of the Parliament of Ontario. Toronto: Hunter, Rose, 1875. viii, 308 p. [6726]

Catalogue of the library of the Parliament of Ontario: with alphabetical indexes of authors and of subjects, 1881. Toronto: Printed by C.B. Robinson, 1881. xi, [2]-558 p. [6732]

Catalogue of the library of the Parliament of Ontario. Toronto: Hunter, Rose, 1872. iv, 93, [1], xxxvi p. [6723]

Ontario. Legislative Library. Checklist and Catalogue Service

Ontario government publications annual catalogue/ Publications du gouvernement de l'Ontario: catalogue annuel. Toronto: Ontario Ministry of Government Services, 1973-. vol.; ISSN: 0227-2628. [6467]

Ontario government publications monthly checklist/ Publications du gouvernement de l'Ontario: liste mensuelle. Toronto: Printing Services Branch, Ministry of Government Services, 1971-. vol.; ISSN: 0316-1617. [6468]

Ontario. Libraries and Community Information Branch

Linking the generations: children's books with an inter-generational focus. Toronto: Ontario Ministry of Citizenship and Culture, 1986. 15 l. [1372]

Ontario. Ministère des services gouvernementaux

Catalogue des publications en français du gouvernement de l'Ontario. Toronto: Ministère des services gouvernementaux, 1979-1983. 5 vol.; ISSN: 0706-2923. [6360]

Ontario. Ministry for Citizenship and Culture

Canadian books for young adults. Toronto: Ontario Ministry for Citizenship and Culture, 1985. 26 l. [1367]

Ontario. Ministry of Agriculture and Food

16 mm motion picture films produced by Ontario government ministries: a publication of the Council of Communications Directors. Toronto: The Ministry, 1980-1982. 3 vol.; ISSN: 0824-4413. [6652]

Ontario. Ministry of Agriculture and Food. Library

Bibliography on northern Ontario agriculture. Toronto: The Library, 1982. 4 l. (Ontario Ministry of Agriculture and Food Library Special bibliography ; no. 1) [4695]

Ontario. Ministry of Citizenship and Culture

Multicultural information: a selected bibliography of materials available in the Ministry, November, 1985. Toronto: Ontario Ministry of Citizenship and Culture, 1985. ii, 84 p.; ISBN: 0-7729-0904-0. [4234]

Ontario. Ministry of Citizenship. Citizenship Development Branch

Holdings on early childhood education: English as a second language and related topics. Toronto: The Ministry, 1987. 46 p.; ISBN: 0-7729-2921-1. [3676]

Ontario. Ministry of Community and Social Services. Children's Services Branch

Ontario Child Health Study: abstracts of research reports and literature reviews. Toronto: The Ministry, c1988. v, 21 p. [5681]

Ontario. Ministry of Community and Social Services. Ministry Library

A select bibliography on alternatives to institutional care for the elderly. Toronto: Ministry of Community and Social Services, Ministry Library, 1976. 36 l. [3150]

Ontario. Ministry of Education

Girls and women in society: resource list. [Toronto]: Ministry of Education, [1977]. 21 p.: ill. [3772]

People of native ancestry: resource list for the primary and junior divisions. Toronto: Ontario Ministry of Education, 1975. 28 p. [3971]

Ontario. Ministry of Education. Library

Catalog of the teachers' professional collection/Catalogue des ouvrages de perfectionnement professionnel pour les enseignants. Sudbury: The Library, 1973. v, 499 p. [3469]

Ontario. Ministry of Industry, Trade and Technology

In print: publications available from the Ontario Ministry of Industry, Trade and Technology. Toronto: Province of Ontario, The Ministry, 1986. 21 l.; ISSN: 0836-8430. [6382]

Ontario. Ministry of Labour. Library

"Bibliographies prepared by the Ontario Ministry of Labour Library, 1970-1982." In: *Labour Topics*; Vol. 5, no. 12 (December 1982) p. 1-8.; ISSN: 0704-8874. [2882]

"Canadian Charter of Rights and Freedoms: a selected bibliography." In: *Labour Topics*; Vol. 8, no. 4 (April 1985) p. 1-6.; ISSN: 0704-8874. [2277]

"Collective bargaining and first contracts: a selected bibliography." In: *Labour Topics*; Vol. 8, no. 6 (June 1985) p. 1-2.; ISSN: 0704-8874. [2899]

"Free trade and collective bargaining: a selected bibliography." In: *Labour Topics*; Vol. 10, no. 7 (July 1987) p. 1-2.; ISSN: 0704-8874. [2916]

"Grievance arbitration: a selected bibliography." In: *Labour Topics*; Vol. 6, no. 9 (September 1983) p. 1-4.; ISSN: 0704-8874. [2887]

"Paid maternity leave: a selected bibliography." In: *Labour Topics*; Vol. 5, no. 2 (February 1982) p. 1-4; vol. 7, no. 9 (September 1984) p. 1-3.; ISSN: 0704-8874. [2891]

"Severance pay: a selected bibliography." In: *Labour Topics*; Vol. 3, No. 10 (October 1980) p. 1-3.; ISSN: 0704-8874. [2867]

"Sex discrimination in sports: a selected bibliography." In: *Labour Topics*; Vol. 5, no. 11 (November 1982) p. 1-4.; ISSN: 0704-8874. [1818]

"Technological change and employment in Canada: a

selected bibliography." In: *Labour Topics*; Vol. 7, no. 4 (April 1984) p. 1-4.; ISSN: 0704-8874. [2892]

"Triparusm." In: *Labour Topics*, Vol. 1, no. 4 (April 1978) p. 1-3.; ISSN: 0704-8874. [2847]

"Unionization of bank employees." In: *Labour Topics*; Vol. 1, no. 3 (March 1978) p. 1-2.; ISSN: 0704-8874. [2848]

"Visible minority women and employment: a selected bibliography." In: *Labour Topics*; Vol. 6, no. 8 (August 1983) p. 1-5.; ISSN: 0704-8874. [3822]

"Women in labour unions: a selected bibliography." In: *Labour Topics*; Vol. 6, no. 10 (October 1983) p. 1-4.; ISSN: 0704-8874. [2888]

"Worksharing: jobsharing: a selected bibliography." In: *Labour Topics*; Vol. 7, no. 11 (November 1984) p. 1-3.; ISSN: 0704-8874. [2893]

Ontario. Ministry of Labour. Library and Information Services

"Affirmative action: employment equity: a selected bibliography." In: *Labour Topics*; Vol. 11, no 9 (September 1988) p. 1-4.; ISSN: 0704-8874. [2921]

"Educational leave: a selected bibliography." In: *Labour Topics*; Vol. 10, no. 3 (March 1987) p. 1-4.; ISSN: 0704-8874. [2917]

"Electronic monitoring & surveillance in the workplace: a selected bibliography." In: *Labour Topics*; Vol. 9, no. 5 (May 1986) p. 1-2.; ISSN: 0704-8874. [2907]

"Employee dismissal – a Canadian perspective: a selected bibliography." In: *Labour Topics*; Vol. 13, no. 1 (January 1990) p. 1-4.; ISSN: 0704-8874. [2931]

"Employee pensions: a selected bibliography." In: *Labour Topics*; Vol. 12, no. 4 (April 1989) p. 1-4.; ISSN: 0704-8874. [2926]

"Employment equity and the disabled: a selected bibliography." In: *Labour Topics*; Vol. 15, no. 8-9 (September 1992) p. 1-4.; ISSN: 0704-8874. [2939]

"Mandatory retirement: a selected bibliography." In: *Labour Topics*; Vol. 12, no. 2 (February 1989) p. 1-3.; ISSN: 0704-8874. [2927]

"Part-time work: a selected bibliography." In: *Labour Topics*; Vol. 9, no. 7 (July 1986) p. 1-4.; ISSN: 0704-8874. [2908]

"Pay equity – a Canadian perspective: a selected bibliography." In: *Labour Topics*; Vol. 11, no. 4 (April 1988) p. 1-4.; ISSN: 0704-8874. [2922]

"Sexual harassment: a Canadian perspective: a selected bibliography." In: *Labour Topics*; Vol. 11, no. 7 (July 1988) p. 1-4.; ISSN: 0704-8874. [3865]

"Sunday shopping legislation: a selected bibliography." In: *Labour Topics*; Vol. 12, no. 1 (January 1989) p. 1-2.; ISSN: 0704-8874. [2759]

Ontario. Ministry of Municipal Affairs and Housing. Library

Energy conservation in housing and building: a bibliography: a listing of books, pamphlets and periodical information available from the Library. [Toronto]: Ontario Ministry of Municipal Affairs and Housing, 1981. 36, 20 p. [0769]

Ontario. Ministry of Municipal Affairs. Research and Special Projects Branch

Maps: a map index for community planning in Ontario. [Toronto]: The Branch, 1986. iii l., 130 p.: ill., maps.; ISBN: 0-7729-1025-1. [6588]

Ontario. Ministry of Transportation and Communications. Research and Development Branch

Research & development publications catalogue [Ontario Ministry of Transportation and Communications]. Downsview: Research and Development Branch, Ontario Ministry of Transportation, 1988-1990. 3 vol.; ISSN: 0846-2542. [6406]

Ontario. Ministry of Treasury and Economics

Declining industries: profiles and prospects: a selected bibliography, 1977-1983. Toronto: Ontario Ministry of Treasury and Economics, 1983. 13 p. [2693]

Ontario. Ministry of Treasury and Economics. Library Services

Budget and expenditure process and reforms: a bibliography with emphasis on Canada. Monticello, Ill.: Vance Bibliographies, [1985]. 16 p. (Public administration series: Bibliography ; P-1646; ISSN: 0193-970X); ISBN: 0-89028-336-2. [2713]

Canada-United States trade relations: issues and options. Monticello, Ill.: Vance Bibliographies, 1984. 9 p. (Public administration series: Bibliography ; P-1367; ISSN: 0193-970X); ISBN: 0-88066-827-X. [2699]

Canadian and provincial industrial policies – strategy debates since 1970: a bibliography. Monticello, Ill.: Vance Bibliographies, 1985. 28 p. (Public administration series: Bibliography ; P-1807; ISSN: 0193-970X); ISBN: 0-89028-637-X. [2714]

Financial services industry: emerging issues and trends, 1973-1984. Toronto: Ontario Ministry of Treasury and Economics, Library Services, 1984. [22] p. (T & E bibliographies / Ontario Ministry of Treasury and Economics, Library Services ; no. 9) [2700]

Job creation: alternative approaches: a selective bibliography. Toronto: Ontario Ministry of Treasury and Economics, Library Services, 1984. 14 p. (T & E Bibliographies / Ontario Ministry of Treasury and Economics, Library Services ; no. 8) [2894]

The new services economy: free trade, labour and technology issues. Monticello, Ill.: Vance Bibliographies, 1986. 54 p. (Public administration series: Bibliography ; P-2051; ISSN: 0193-970X); ISBN: 1-55590-091-7. [2724]

Pensions in the Canadian economy: a selected bibliography, 1973-1984. Toronto: Ontario Ministry of Treasury and Economics, Library Services, 1984. 19 p. [2701]

Public sector accountability: a selected bibliography with emphasis on Canada. Toronto: Ontario Ministry of Treasury and Economics, Library Services, 1985. 18 p. (T & E Bibliographies / Ontario Ministry of Treasury and Economics, Library Services ; no. 11) [2498]

Trade statistics with emphasis on Canada: a selected annotated bibliography. Monticello, Ill.: Vance Bibliographies, 1984. 12 p. (Public administration series: Bibliography ; P-1393; ISSN: 0193-970X); ISBN: 0-88066-863-6. [2702]

User fees for municipal services: a selected bibliography. Monticello, Ill.: Vance Bibliographies, 1980. 4 p. [4386]

Working women in the economic future: a selected bibliography with emphasis on Canada. Monticello, Ill.: Vance Bibliographies, 1986. 39 p. (Public administration series: Bibliography ; P-1999; ISSN: 0193-970X); ISBN: 0-89028-999-9. [3846]

Ontario. Office of King's Printer

Catalogue of publications issued by the government of Ontario (Revised to October 1st, 1917). Toronto: A.T. Wilgress, King's Printer, 1917. 16 p. [6215]

Ontario. Royal Commission on Electric Power Planning
Report of the Royal Commission on Electric Power Planning. Toronto: The Commission, 1980. 9 vol.; ISBN: 0-7743-4672-8 (set). [2662]

Ontario. Royal Commission on Violence in the Communications Industry
Violence and the media: a bibliography. Toronto: Royal Commission on Violence in the Communications Industry, [1977]. 171 p. [0965]

Oppen, William A.
The Riel rebellions: a cartographic history/Le récit cartographique des affaires Riel. Toronto: Published by the University of Toronto Press in association with the Public Archives of Canada and the Canadian Government Publishing Centre, c1979. x, 109 p.: ill., maps.; ISBN: 0-8020-2333-9. [6567]

Orange, John Charles
Ernest Buckler: an annotated bibliography. Downsview, Ont.: ECW Press, c1981. P. 13-56.; ISBN: 0-920802-51-0. [6882]

"Ernest Buckler: an annotated bibliography." In: *The annotated bibliography of Canada' major authors*, Vol. 3, edited by Robert Lecker and Jack David. Downsview, Ont.: ECW Press, c1981. P. 13-56.; ISBN: 0-920802-23-0. [6883]

"P.K. Page: an annotated bibliography." In: *The annotated bibliography of Canada's major authors*, Vol. 6, edited by Robert Lecker and Jack David. Toronto: ECW Press, 1985. P. 207-285.; ISBN: 0-920802-93-1. [7233]

"Orientation bibliographique: [Océanographie de l'estuaire du Saint-Laurent]." Dans: *Naturaliste canadien*; Vol. 106, no 1 (janvier-février 1979) p. 273-276.; ISSN: 0028-0798. [5153]

O'Riordan, Jonathan
A bibliography of Canadian writings in water resource management. [S.l.: s.n., 1960]. 1 vol. (in various pagings). [5031]

Ormsby, Margaret
The Okanagan District. [Vancouver: British Columbia Library Association], 1935. [1], 21 p. [0562]

Ory, François
Judéo-maçonnerie: petite bibliographie d'ouvrages surtout en français, à nos chers canadiens. Montréal: [s.n.], 1939. 17 p. [4126]

Ostrye, Anne T.
Foreign investment in the American and Canadian West, 1870-1914: an annotated bibliography. Metuchen, N.J.: Scarecrow Press, 1986. vii, 192 p.; ISBN: 0-8108-1866-3. [2725]

Ottawa Public Library
Business information/Information sur les affaires. [Rev. ed.]. [Ottawa]: The Library, 1989. 40 p. [2760]
Medical information/Renseignements médicaux. [Ottawa]: The Library, 1983. 15 p. [5655]
Sexism in education. [Ottawa: Ottawa Public Library], 1975. [12] p. [3505]

Ottawa Public Library. Reference Department
Legal reference materials at the Ottawa Public Library/ Documentation juridique au Service de consultation de la Bibliothèque publique d'Ottawa. Rev. and enl. ed. Ottawa: Reference Department, Ottawa Public Library, 1982. 58 p. [2247]

Ouellet, France
Inventaire sommaire du fonds Robert Elie. Montréal: Bibliothèque nationale du Québec, Ministère des affaires

culturelles, 1988. 140 p. ill.; ISBN: 2-550-16398-2. [6965]

Ouellet, Francine; Lampron, Christiane
Bilan des évaluations portant sur les services sociaux. Québec: Commission d'enquête sur les services de santé et les services sociaux, 1987. 91 p.; ISBN: 2-551-08489-X. [3303]

Ouellet, Micheline
Synthèse historique de l'immersion française au Canada suivie d'une bibliographie sélective et analytique. Québec: Centre international de recherche sur l'aménagement linguistique, 1990. vii, 261 p. (Publication / Centre international de recherche sur l'aménagement linguistique ; B-175); ISBN: 2-89219-212-9. [3718]

Ouellet, Thérèse
Bibliographie du théâtre canadien-français avant 1900. Québec: [Université Laval], 1949. 53 f. [0946]

Ouimet, Laurent
Bibliographie de droit civil: ouvrages généraux. Montréal: Université de Montréal, Service des bibliothèques, Bibliothèque de droit, 1978. 22 p.; ISBN: 0-88529-029-1. [2185]

"Ouvrages du père Jetté." Dans: *Vie oblate life*; Vol. 33, no 4 (décembre 1974) p. 235-239.; ISSN: 0318-9392. [7080]

"Ouvrages et articles publiés par les membres [de l'Association pour l'avancement de la recherche en musique du Québec]." Dans: *Cahiers de l'ARMUQ*; No 2 (mai 1983) p. 13-23.; ISSN: 0821-1817. [0912]

"Ouvrages sur le Canada." Dans: *Annuaire du Canada*; (1965)-(1985) [0151]

Overseas Institute of Canada
Bibliography on Canadian aid to the developing countries/ Bibliographie sur l'aide canadienne aux pays en voie d'expansion. Ottawa: Overseas Institute of Canada, 1967. 7, 4 l. [2393]

Owen, Myra
Dr. William Osler reprints in the Montreal General Hospital Archives: accession 1501:120, McGill University Archives. Montreal: University Archives, McGill University, 1973. ii, 47 l. [7230]

Owens, John N.; Blake, M.D.
Forest tree seed production: a review of the literature and recommendations for future research. Chalk River, Ont.: Petawawa National Forestry Institute, 1985. vi, 161 p.: ill. (Information report / Petawawa National Forestry Institute ; PI-X-53; ISSN: 0706-1854); ISBN: 0-662-14185-7. [4987]
Production de semences forestières: revue bibliographiques et suggestions de recherche. Chalk River, Ont.: Institut forestier national de Petawawa, 1986. iv, 216 p. (Rapport d'information / Institut forestier national de Petawawa ; PI-X-53F; ISSN: 0228-0736); ISBN: 0-662-93939-5. [4988]

Oxbridge directory of ethnic periodicals: the most comprehensive guide to U.S. & Canadian ethnic periodicals available. New York: Oxbridge Communications, c1979. 247 p.; ISBN: 0-91746-006-5. [5935]

Oxbridge directory of newsletters. New York: Oxbridge Communications, 1979-. vol.; ISSN: 0163-7010. [5992]

Ozaki, Hiroko
Interlibrary loan: a selected bibliography, 1982-1987/Le prêt entre bibliothèques: une bibliographie sélective, 1982-1987. Ottawa: National Library of Canada, 1987. 21 p. (Bibliographies / Library Documentation Centre; ISSN: 0226-4226) [1692]
Library services to prisoners in Canada: a bibliography/

Services de bibliothèques aux détenus au Canada: une bibliographie. Ottawa: National Library of Canada, 1986. 4 p. (Bibliographies / Library Development Centre, ISSN. 0847-2467) [1682]

Selected references for Canadian hospital libraries, 1974-1980/Bibliographie sélective à l'intention des bibliothèques d'hôpitaux canadiens, 1974-1980. Ottawa: National Library of Canada, 1981. 6 p. (Bibliographies / Library Documentation Centre; ISSN: 0226-4226) [1647]

Subject headings and subject access to children's literature: a bibliography covering materials issued 1975-1985 / Vedettes-matière et accès par sujet à la littérature de jeunesse: une bibliographie qui traite des publications parues entre 1975 et 1985. Ottawa: National Library of Canada, 1986. 4 l. (Bibliographies / Library Documentation Centre; ISSN: 0226-4226) [1683]

Telefacsimile transmission being used for document delivery: cost studies: an annotated bibliography/Recours à la télécopie pour la livraison des documents: les analyses des coûts: bibliographie sommaire. [Ottawa]: National Library of Canada, 1987. 5 p. (Bibliographies / Library Documentation Centre; ISSN: 0226-4226) [1693]

P.G. Whiting and Associates
Economic impacts of heritage institutions on the Canadian economy: bibliography. Ottawa: Canadian Museums Association, 1985. 54 l.; ISBN: 0-91910-618-8. [2715]

P.S. Ross & Partners
The economy of northern Alberta: a bibliography. [Edmonton]: Northern Development Group, Department of Business Development and Tourism, Government of Alberta, 1975. iii, 71 p. [0518]

Pacey, Margaret
"Recent publications relating to the history of the Atlantic region." In: *Acadiensis*; Vol. 7, no. 1 (Autumn 1977) p. 148-156.; ISSN: 0044-5851. [0231]

Pacific Forestry Centre
Reports and publications [Pacific Forestry Centre]. Victoria: Pacific Forestry Centre, 1985-. vol.; ISSN: 0846-6610. [5024]

Packard, Alpheus Spring
"Bibliography of books and articles relating to the geography and civil and natural history of Labrador." In: *The Labrador coast: a journal of two summer cruises to that region ... .* New York: Hodges, 1891. P. 475-501. [0193]

Padbury, Peter; Wilkins, Diane
The future: a bibliography of issues and forecasting techniques. Monticello, Ill.: Council of Planning Librarians, 1972. 102 p. (Council of Planning Librarians Exchange bibliography ; 279) [2987]

Page, Donald M.
A bibliography of works on Canadian foreign relations, 1945-1970. Toronto: Canadian Institute of International Affairs, c1973. 441 p. [2408]

A bibliography of works on Canadian foreign relations, 1971-1975. Toronto: Canadian Institute of International Affairs, c1977. ix, 300 p. [2430]

Page, Garnet T.; Caldwell, George
Inventory of research on adult human resource development in Canada, 1963-1968/Inventaire de la recherche sur le développement des ressources humaines adultes au Canada. [Ottawa]: Department of Regional Economic Expansion, [1968]. xxiii, 215 p. [2799]

Page, James E.
"Native studies: an introductory bibliography." In: *Communiqué. Canadian Studies*; Vol. 1, no. 1 (October 1974) p. 7-18.; ISSN: 0318-1197. [3957]

Seeing ourselves: films for Canadian studies. Montreal: National Film Board of Canada, 1979. v, 210 p.: ill.; ISBN: 0-772-20001-7. [6640]

Pagé, Pierre
Répertoire des oeuvres de la littérature radiophonique québécoise, 1930-1970. Montréal: Fides, c1975. 826 p.; ISBN: 0-7755-0533-1. [0957]

Pagé, Pierre; Legris, Renée
Répertoire des dramatiques québécoises à la télévision, 1952-1977: vingt-cinq ans de télévision à Radio-Canada, téléthéâtres, feuilletons, dramatiques pour enfants. Montréal: Fides, c1977. 252 p. (Archives québécoises de la radio et de la télévision ; vol. 3); ISBN: 0-7755-0664-8. [1111]

Pageau, Pierrette
Inuit du Nouveau-Québec: bibliographie. [Québec]: Centre de documentation, Service de l'inventaire des biens culturels, c1976. 175 f.: cartes. (Dossier / Centre de documentation, Service de l'inventaire des biens culturels ; 13) [3983]

Painchaud, Paul
Francophonie: bibliographie 1960-1969. Montréal: Presses de l'Université du Québec, 1972. xvii, 136 p.; ISBN: 0-7770-0034-2. [2406]

Relations extérieures du Canada et du Québec: bibliographie. Québec: Centre québécois de relations internationales, 1978. 53 p. [2436]

Pal, Gabriel
Annotated bibliography of publications concerning Canada's food growing capacity. [Guelph, Ont.]: University of Guelph, Library, 1978. ii, 8 p. (Bibliography series / University of Guelph Library ; no. 6) [4678]

A bibliography of publications concerning proved and potential energy resources in Canada, 1970-1974. [Guelph, Ont.]: University of Guelph, Library, c1975. 22 p. (Bibliography series / University of Guelph Library ; no. 5) [4790]

How to find information on Canadian natural resources: a guide to the literature. Ottawa: Canadian Library Association, 1985. 182 p.; ISBN: 0-88802-178-X. [4630]

Palfrey, Thomas R.; Coleman, Henry E.
Guide to bibliographies of theses, United States and Canada. 2nd ed. Chicago: American Library Association, 1940. 54 p. [6056]

Palko, Michael E.
Annotated guide to health instruction materials in Canada. 3rd ed. Ottawa: Canadian Health Education Specialists Society, 1972. iv, 89 p. [5584]

Palmegiano, E.M.
The British Empire in the Victorian press, 1832-1867: a bibliography. New York: Garland, 1987. xviii, 234 p. (Themes in European expansion ; vol. 8) (Garland reference library of social science ; vol. 389); ISBN: 0-8240-9802-1. [2064]

Palmer, Gregory
A bibliography of Loyalist source material in the United States, Canada, and Great Britain. Westport [Conn.]: Meckler, c1982. ix, 1064 p.; ISBN: 0-930466-26-8. [2024]

Paltiel, Freda L.

Poverty: an annotated bibliography and references. [Ottawa: Canadian Welfare Council], 1966. x, 136 p. [3085]

Paltsits, Victor Hugo

"Bibliographical data." In: *A new discovery of a vast country in America*, by Louis Hennepin. Chicago: McClurg, 1903. P. xlv-lxiv. [7058]

Bibliography of the writings of Baron Lahontan. [Montreal]: Édition du Bouton d'Or, [1978]. [li]-xciii p. [7113]

Pane, Remigio U.

"Doctoral dissertations on the Italian American experience completed in the United States and Canadian universities, 1908-1974." In: *International Migration Review*; Vol. 9, no. 4 (Winter 1975) p. 545-556.; ISSN: 0197-9183. [6139]

Pannekoek, Frits

"A selected western Canada historical resources bibliography to 1985." In: *Prairie Forum*; Vol. 15, no. 2 (Fall 1990) p. 329-374.; ISSN: 0317-6282. [0548]

Panofsky, Ruth

Adele Wiseman: an annotated bibliography. Toronto: ECW Press, 1992. xviii, 130 p., [1] p. of pl.: ill.; ISBN: 1-55022-103-5. [7370]

Pantazzi, Sybille

"Book illustration and design by Canadian artists 1890-1940, with a list of books illustrated by members of the Group of Seven." In: *Bulletin (National Gallery of Canada)*; Vol. 4, no. 1 (1966) p. 6-24: ill., facsims.; ISSN: 0027-9323. [0669]

Papst, M.H.; Ayles, G.B.; Lark, J.G.I.

Current bibliography of publications on waste heat utilization in aquaculture. Winnipeg: Government of Canada, Fisheries and Oceans, 1981. iv, 13 p. (Canadian manuscript report of fisheries and aquatic sciences ; no. 1598; ISSN: 0706-6473) [4898]

Paquerot, Sylvie

Éducation des adultes et développement régional: une étude exploratoire de la littérature nord-américaine (Québec exclu). Québec: Gouvernement du Québec, Ministère de l'éducation, Direction des politiques et des plans, 1985. 38, 15, 24 p.; ISBN: 2-550-08428-4. [3644]

Paquet, Gilles

"Bio-bibliographie d'Albert Faucher." Dans: *Actualité économique*; Vol. 59, no 3 (septembre 1983) p. 397-400.; ISSN: 0001-771X. [6976]

Paquet, Mario

L'intervention de groupe pour les personnes soutien de personne âgée en perte d'autonomie: bibliographie. Joliette, Québec: Département de santé communautaire de Lanaudière, 1991. 8 f.; ISBN: 2-920924-47-8. [3355]

Paquin, Benoît; Turgeon, Normand

La gestion de la qualité dans les entreprises de services: une bibliographie sélective/Quality management in the services industry: a selective bibliography. Montréal: Direction de la recherche, École des hautes études commerciales, 1992. 42 f. (Cahier de recherche: Working paper / Direction de la recherche, École des hautes études commerciales ; no 92-09; ISSN: 0846-0647) [2784]

Paradis, André; Naubert, Hélène

Recension bibliographique: les maladies infectieuses dans les périodiques médicaux québécois du XIXe siècle. [Trois-Rivières, Québec]: Centre de recherche en études québécoises, Université du Québec à Trois-Rivières, [1988]. 237 p. [5682]

Parent, Édouard

"Bibliographie du P. Éphrem Longpré, O.F.M." Dans: *Culture*; Vol. 27 (1966) p. 276-289.; ISSN: 0317-2066. [7155]

Parent, France; Cloutier, Renée

"Recherches sur les femmes et l'éducation formelle au Canada et au Québec publiées dans la période 1975-1986." Dans: *Recherches féministes*; Vol. 1, no 1 (1988) p. 129-148.; ISSN: 0838-4479. [3866]

Parent, Jean-Claude

Bibliographie commentée sur le régime seigneurial [microforme]. [Ottawa]: Parcs Canada, 1985. 4 microfiches (Parcs Canada Rapports sur microfiches ; no 220) [2050]

Parent, Raymond

Étude bibliographique des publications du Bureau international du travail au Ministère du travail, Québec. Québec: Le Ministère, 1943. 67, [3] p., [2] f. de pl.: ill. [6225]

Parke-Bernet Galleries

The celebrated collection of Americana formed by the late Thomas Winthrop Streeter. New York: [s.n.], 1969. 7 vol.: ill., facsims. (part col.). [0576]

Parker, Franklin

American dissertations on foreign education: a bibliography with abstracts: volume 1: Canada. Troy, N.Y.: Whitston Publishing, 1971. 175 p.; ISBN: 0-87875-013-4. [6109]

"Canadian education: a bibliography of doctoral dissertations." In: *McGill Journal of Education*; Vol. 2, no. 2 (Fall 1967) p. 175-182; vol. 3, no. 1 (Spring 1968) p. 63-70.; ISSN: 0024-9033. [6092]

Parker, Franklin; Parker, Betty June

Women's education: a world view. Westport, Conn.: Greenwood Press, 1979-1981. 2 vol.; ISBN: 0-313-23205-9 (set). [3598]

Parker, George L.

"A brief annotated bibliography of available titles in Canadian fiction, poetry, and related background material." In: *Twentieth Century Literature*; Vol. 16, no. 3 (July 1970) p. 217-224.; ISSN: 0041-462X. [1057]

Parker, J.E.; Anderson, S.R.

Guide to Canadian climatic data. Toronto: Meteorological Branch, Department of Transport, 1969. 1 vol. (in various pagings). [5049]

Parker, J.H.

"The published works of George A. Klinck." In: *Canadian Modern Language Review*; Vol. 30, no. 3 (March 1974) p. 201-205.; ISSN: 0008-4506. [7096]

Parker, James McPherson

Athabasca Oil Sands historical research project. Edmonton: Alberta Oil Sands Environmental Research Program, 1979. 3 vol.: ill., maps. [4812]

Parkin, Margaret L.

Index of Canadian nursing studies/Répertoire des études canadiennes sur les soins infirmiers. [Ottawa]: Canadian Nurses Association, 1979. 225, 97 p.; ISBN: 0-919108-00-8. [5625]

Parkin, Michael; Morrison, Frances C.; Watkin, Gwyneth

French immersion research relevant to decisions in Ontario. Toronto: Ontario Ministry of Education, c1987. 181 p. [3677]

Parnell, Pat

Serials list: Library, Prairie Migratory Bird Research Centre. Saskatoon: Canadian Wildlife Service, 1974. 23 l. [5920]

Parr, Richard T.

A bibliography of the Athapaskan languages. Ottawa: National Museums of Canada, 1974. xiii, 333 p.: map. (National Museum of Man Mercury series: Ethnology Division paper ; no. 14) [1430]

Passaris, Constantine E.A.

Canadian regional monetary policy: introduction and extensive bibliography. Monticello, Ill.: Council of Planning Librarians, 1977. 20 p. (Council of Planning Librarians Exchange bibliography ; 1402) [2629]

Paterson, Janet

"Bibliographie critique des études consacrées aux romans d'Anne Hébert." Dans: *Voix et images*; Vol. 5, no 1 (automne 1979) p. 187-192.; ISSN: 0318-9201. [7049]

"Bibliographie d'Anne Hébert." Dans: *Voix et Images*; Vol. 7, no 3 (printemps 1982) p. 505-510.; ISSN: 0318-9201. [7050]

Paterson, Laura A.

Annotated bibliography on Kluane National Park, Yukon Territory. Edmonton: Canadian Wildlife Service, 1972. 41 l. [2988]

Caribou bibliography. Edmonton: Canadian Wildlife Service, 1972. [76] l. [5369]

Patrickson, C.P.

Bibliography on blast protection. [Ottawa]: Public Works Canada, 1990. 1 vol. (in various pagings). [5842]

Patriquin, Larry

Income, income security and the Canadian welfare state, 1978-1987: a selected bibliography. [Ottawa]: Canadian Centre for Policy Alternatives, 1989. iii, 69; ISBN: 0-88627-976-3. [3331]

Patterson, Susan S.

Canadian Great Lakes shipping: an annotated bibliography. Toronto: University of Toronto-York University Joint Program in Transportation, 1976. 72 l. (University of Toronto-York University Joint Program in Transportation Research report ; no. 37; ISSN: 0316-9456) [4464]

Pauchant, Thierry C.

Crisis management: an annotated bibliography. Québec: Faculté des sciences de l'administration, Université Laval, 1988. 53 p. (Document spécial / Faculté des sciences de l'administration, Université Laval ; 88-110) [2748]

Pauls, D.R.; Moran, S.R.; Macyk, T.

Review of literature related to clay liners for sump disposal of drilling waste. Edmonton: Reclamation Research Technical Advisory Committee, 1988. xxiv, 61 p.: ill. (Report / Alberta Reclamation Research Technical Advisory Committee ; RRTAC 88-10) [5834]

Pauls, Jake L.

Life safety for people with disabilities: literature review. Ottawa: Public Works Canada, Architectural and Engineering Services, 1988. 75, 79 p. [3311]

La sécurité des personnes handicapés: étude bibliographique. Ottawa: Travaux publics Canada, Service d'architecture et de génie, 1988. 79, 75 p. [3312]

Pavlovic, Myrianne

"Bibliographie de Monique Bosco." Dans: *Voix et Images*; Vol. 9, no 3 (printemps 1984) p. 55-82.; ISSN: 0318-9201. [6860]

Pearce, D.C.

A bibliography on snow and ice. Ottawa: Division of Building Research, National Research Council, 1951. 69 l. (Bibliography / National Research Council Canada, Division of Building Research ; no. 1) [5027]

Pearlman, Rowena; Malycky, Alexander

"Jewish-Canadian periodical publications: a preliminary check list." In: *Canadian Ethnic Studies*; Vol. 1, no. 1 (1969) p. 44-49.; ISSN: 0008-3496. [4143]

Pearlstein, Toby; Dresley, Susan

General transportation. Monticello, Ill.: Vance Bibliographies, 1990. 69 p. (Public administration series: Bibliography ; P-2878; ISSN: 0193-970X); ISBN: 0-7920-0538-4. [4513]

Pearson, Norman

Lifetime list of publications: to 1st January 1972. [S.l.: s.n., 1972]. 19 l. [7237]

Pearson, Willis Barry

A bibliographical study of Canadian radio and television drama produced on the Canadian Broadcasting Corporation's national network, 1944-1967. [Saskatoon]: 1968. xix, 123 l. [0949]

Peckover, F.L.; Wong, W.W.

Annotated bibliography on track ballast to Dec. 1967. Montreal: Library Headquarters, Canadian National Railways, 1968. 43 l. (Special series / Canadian National Railways Library ; no. 43; ISSN: 0226-4889) [4451]

Pederson, Ann P., et al.

Coordinating healthy public policy: an analytic literature review and bibliography. [Ottawa]: Health and Welfare Canada, 1988. vi, 71 p. (Health Services and Promotion Branch Working paper ; HSPB 88-1); ISBN: 0-662-16702-3. [2521]

Coordination de la politique publique favorisant la santé: analyse documentaire et bibliographie. [Ottawa]: Direction générale des services et de la promotion de la santé, 1989. viii, 85 p. (Document de travail / Direction générale des services et de la promotion de la santé ; HSPB 88-1); ISBN: 0-662-95288-X. [2531]

Pederson, Beverley

Living with dying: philosophical and psychological aspects of death and dying: a selected bibliography of printed and audio-visual material available at the Saskatoon Public Library. Saskatoon: Saskatoon Public Library, 1980. 62 p. (in various pagings). [1548]

Peel, Bruce Braden

"Alberta imprints before 1900." In: *Alberta Historical Review*; Vol. 3, no. 3 (Summer 1955) p. 41-46.; ISSN: 0002-4783. [0497]

Bibliography of Bruce Braden Peel. Edmonton: [Peel], 1986. 18 p. [7238]

A bibliography of the prairie provinces to 1953, with biographical index. 2nd ed. Toronto: University of Toronto Press, c1973. xxviii, 780 p.; ISBN: 0-8020-1972-2. [0510]

"The Columbia drainage basin in Canada: a bibliographical essay." In: *Pacific Northwest Quarterly*; Vol. 52, no. 4 (October 1961) p. 152-154.; ISSN: 0030-8803. [0572]

"How the Bible came to the Cree." In: *Alberta Historical Review*; Vol. 6, no. 2 (Spring 1958) p. 15-19.; ISSN: 0002-4783. [3911]

"Saskatchewan imprints before 1900." In: *Saskatchewan History*; Vol. 6, no. 3 (Autumn 1953) p. 91-94.; ISSN: 0036-4908. [0496]

Pegis, Jessica; Gentles, Ian; De Veber, L.L.

Sex education: a review of the literature from Canada, the United States, Britain and Sweden. Toronto: Human Life Research Institute of Ottawa, 1986. 42 p.; ISBN: 2-92045-310-4. [3661]

Peitchinis, Stephen G.

Effects of technological changes on employment and educational and skill requirements: an annotated bibliography. Calgary: University of Calgary, 1978. 2, 63 l. (Studies on employment effects of technology) [2849]

Pellerin, Maurice; Gallichan, Gilles

Pamphile Le May, bibliothécaire de la Législature et écrivain. Québec: Bibliothèque de l'Assemblée nationale, 1986. iii, 141 p.: ill., port. (Bibliographie et documentation / Bibliothèque de l'Assemblée nationale du Québec; 21) [7143]

Pelletier, Jean Yves

Bibliographie sélective de l'Ontario français. 2e éd., rev., corr. et augm. [Ottawa]: Centre franco-ontarien de ressources pédagogiques, [c1989]. 65 p.; ISBN: 1-55043-221-4. [0488]

Pelletier, Jocelyn

"Activités politiques des fonctionnaires: bibliographie annotée." Dans: *Bulletin: Bibliothèque de l'Assemblée nationale du Québec*; Vol. 2, no 2 (avril 1971) p. 57-73.; ISSN: 0701-6808. [2403]

Pelletier, Louise

"Bibliographie: Gilles Marcotte, 1955-1979." Dans: *Voix et Images*; Vol. 6, no 1 (automne 1980) p. 35-49.; ISSN: 0318-9201. [7176]

Pelletier, Lyse

"Femmes, géographie et environnement: notes à propos de quelques titres." Dans: *Cahiers de géographie de Québec*; Vol. 31, no 83 (septembre 1987) p. 301-307.; ISSN: 0007-9766. [3856]

Pelletier, Sylvie

Bibliographie commentée sur le théâtre. Québec: Service de la recherche et de l'évaluation, Musée de la civilisation, 1992. 46 f. (Document / Service de la recherche et de l'évaluation, Musée de la civilisation ; no 8); ISBN: 2-551-12898-6. [0991]

Pelletier-Olivier, Yolande; Olivier, Réjean

Bibliographie joliettaine. L'Assomption [Québec]: Collège de l'Assomption, Bibliothèque, 1975. 62 f.: fac-sim. [0335]

Pembina Institute for Appropriate Development

The Canadian environmental education catalogue: a guide to selected resources and materials. Drayton Valley, Alta.: Pembina Institute for Appropriate Development, 1991. 1 vol. (in various pagings).; ISBN: 0-921719-07-8. [5292]

Pence, Alan R.

Bibliography of Canadian day care research/Bibliographie des études sur la garde des enfants au Canada. [Ottawa: Status of Women Canada], c1985. 51 p.; ISBN: 0-662-54141-3. [3279]

Pendzey, Luba

Paul Robert Magocsi: a bibliography, 1965-1985. Toronto: Chair of Ukrainian Studies, University of Toronto, 1985. 28 p.; ISBN: 0-7727-5106-4. [7170]

La pénétration et l'utilisation de l'informatique au Québec: guide bibliographique. [Québec]: Direction des technologies de l'information, Ministère des communications du Québec, c1987. 19 f.; ISBN: 2-550-17578-6. [1694]

Penhallow, D.P.

"A review of Canadian botany from 1800 to 1895." In: *Proceedings and Transactions of the Royal Society of Canada*; Series 2, vol. 3, section 4 (1897) p. 3-56.; ISSN: 0316-4616. [5311]

"A review of Canadian botany from the first settlement of New France to the nineteenth century." In: *Proceedings and Transactions of the Royal Society of Canada*; Vol. 5, section 4 (1887) p. 45-61.; ISSN: 0316-4616. [5305]

Penlington, Norman

"Bibliography of the writings of Frank H. Underhill." In: *On Canada: essays in honour of Frank H. Underhill*. Toronto: University of Toronto Press, 1971. P. 131-192.; ISBN: 0-8020-1725-8. [7348]

Pentland, David H.; Wolfart, H. Christoph

Bibliography of Algonquian linguistics. [Winnipeg]: University of Manitoba Press, 1982. xix, 333 p.; ISBN: 0-88755-128-9. [1457]

People Against Crime Together

Select annotated bibliography on abuse: child, domestic, elder, sexual, spouse, substance. Regina: People Against Crime Together, 1990. vi, 71 p.; ISBN: 0-9694625-0-6. [3343]

People's Library

People's Library bibliography, 1987-88. Winnipeg: Manitoba Indian Cultural Education Centre, 1987. 204 p. [4091]

Reference pamphlets listing, 1985-1986. [Winnipeg: The Library, 1985]. [128] p. [4078]

Pépin, Eugène

Bibliographie du droit aérien et questions connexes: 1957-1958/Bibliography of air law and related problems: 1957-1958. Montréal: [s.n.], 1959. 2 vol. [2106]

Percy, Kevin E.

Literature review of the controlled environment research completed on the sensitivity of coniferous tree species to air pollutants. Fredericton: Environment New Brunswick, 1976. [28] p. (in various pagings). (New Brunswick Department of the Environment Technical report series ; no. T-7601) [5119]

Performing Rights Organization of Canada

Brian Cherney. Don Mills, Ont.: PRO Canada, 1988. 7 p. [6907]

Harry Somers. Don Mills, Ont.: PRO Canada, 1983. 15 p.: music, port. [7316]

Keith Bissell. Don Mills, Ont.: PRO Canada, 1988. 19 p. [6847]

Périard, A. (Firm)

Catalogue of law books, Canadian, French, English and American: imported and for sale by A. Périard. Montreal: A. Périard, 1883. 36 p. [2095]

Periodical title comparison list: alphabetical listing of serial titles indexed in *Canadian Business Index, Canadian Education Index, Canadian Magazine Index, Canadian Periodical Index, Point de repère (édition abrégée)*. Toronto: Micromedia, 1989. 13 p. [5969]

Periodicals for natural resource management: a listing with some locations for economists, managers, and students working in areas dealing with the economic management of Canadian natural resources. [Toronto]: Natural Resources Information Center, Faculty of Management Studies, University of Toronto, [1976]. vii, 62, [5] l. (NR Publications / Natural Resources Information Center, Faculty of Management Studies, University of Toronto ; no. 1) [5925]

Perkin, J.R.C.; Snelson, James B.

Morning in his heart: the life and writings of Watson Kirkconnell. [Hantsport, N.S.]: Published for Acadia University Library by Lancelot Press, 1986. viii, 371 p.: ill., port.; ISBN: 0-88999-304-1. [7091]

Perkins, David; Tanis, Norman
Native Americans of North America: a bibliography based on collections in the libraries of California State University, Northridge. Metuchen, N.J.: Scarecrow Press, 1975. x, 558 p. ill.; ISBN: 0-8108-0878-1. [3972]

Perrault, Isabelle
Autour des jeunes: reconnaissance bibliographique. Québec: Institut québécois de recherche sur la culture, 1988. 422 p. (Documents de recherche / Institut québécois de recherche sur la culture ; no 17; ISSN: 0823-0447); ISBN: 2-89224-108-1. [3313]

Perret, Diana-Lynn
Répertoire des thèses de doctorat et de maîtrise soutenues dans les facultés de droit des universités du Québec et de l'Université d'Ottawa. 3e éd. [Ottawa]: Éditions de l'Université d'Ottawa, 1986. P. [947]-1030. [6187]

Perron, Bruno; Bonin, Bernard
Les mandats mondiaux de production: une revue de littérature. Montréal: École des hautes études commerciales, 1983. 42, [6] f. (Cahiers du Centre d'études en administration internationale ; no 83-04; ISSN: 0709-986X) [2694]

Perron, Monique
Bibliographie du Haut-Saint-Laurent (sud-ouest de la Montérégie). Québec: Institut québécois de recherche sur la culture, 1990. 318 p.: cartes. (Documents de recherche / Institut québécois de recherche sur la culture ; no 24; ISSN: 0823-0447); ISBN: 2-89224-140-5. [0409]

Perron, Normand
"Bibliographie: La Compagnie de Pulpe de Chicoutimi." Dans: Saguenayensia; Vol. 22, nos 3-4 (mai-août 1980) p. 184-186.; ISSN: 0581-295X. [4971]

Perron, Yolande; Rousseau, Raymond; Thériault, Jacques
Les organes officiels des syndicats des enseignants québécois. Québec: U.Q.A.R.–C.E.Q., 1978. ix, 901 p. [3543]

Perry, Lee
For the comtemplative man: a bibliography of works on angling and on game fish in the University of British Columbia Library. Vancouver: The Library, 1984. 130 p. [1831]

Pérusse, Lyne
Revue de littérature sur les écrans cathodiques. [Québec]: Département de santé communautaire, Hôpital du Saint-Sacrement, 1981. 81 f.; ISBN: 2-550-02265-3. [5641]

Peters, Diane E.
Atlases in W.L.U. Library. [Waterloo, Ont.]: The Library, Wilfrid Laurier University, 1989. vi, 117 p.; ISBN: 0-921821-06-9. [6594]
Music in Canada: a bibliography of resources in W.L.U. Library. Waterloo, Ont.: Library, Wilfrid Laurier University, 1991. 24 p.; ISBN: 0-921821-15-8. [0941]
Music reference and research materials in W.L.U. Library. Waterloo, Ont.: Library, Wilfrid Laurier University, 1990. v, 148 p.; ISBN: 0-921821-09-3. [0937]
Roots: genealogical resources in W.L.U. Library. Waterloo, Ont.: The Library, Wilfrid Laurier University, 1990. 161 p.; ISBN: 0-921821-05-0. [2083]
Social work: a bibliography of bibliographies in W.L.U. Library. Waterloo, Ont.: Library, Wilfrid Laurier University, 1990. 210 p.; ISBN: 0-921-821-11-5. [3344]
Social work: a bibliography of directories in W.L.U. Library. [Waterloo, Ont.]: The Library, Wilfrid Laurier University, 1989. 32 p.; ISBN: 0-921821-08-5. [3332]

Peters, Elizabeth
The central business district of Canadian cities: an interdisciplinary approach. Monticello, Ill.; Council of Planning Librarians, 1974. 31 p. (Council of Planning Librarians Exchange bibliography ; 625) [4336]
The Toronto waterfront: planning and development. Monticello, Ill.: Council of Planning Librarians, 1974. 6 p. (Council of Planning Librarians Exchange bibliography ; 624) [4337]

Peters, Evelyn J.
Aboriginal self-government in Canada: a bibliography, 1986. Kingston, Ont.: Institute of Intergovernmental Relations, Queen's University, c1986. ix, 112 p. (Aboriginal peoples and constitutional reform); ISBN: 0-88911-423-4. [4087]

Peterson, Everett B.; Peterson, N. Merle
Revegetation information applicable to mining sites in northern Canada. Ottawa: Supply and Services Canada, 1977. 405 p.: ill. (Environmental studies ; no. 3); ISBN: 0-662-01036-1. [4800]

Peterson, Everett B.; Peterson, N. Merle; Kabzems, R.D.
Impact of climatic variation on biomass accumulation in the boreal forest zone: selected references. Edmonton: Canadian Forestry Service, Northern Forest Research Centre, 1983. x, 355 p. (Northern Forest Research Centre Information report ; NOR-X-254; ISSN: 0704-7673); ISBN: 0-662-12895-8. [4979]

Peterson, Jean; Murphy, Lynn; MacDonald, Heather
The Loyalist guide: Nova Scotian loyalists and their documents. [Halifax]: Public Archives of Nova Scotia, [1983]. 272 p.; ISBN: 0-088871-044-5. [2029]

Peterson-Hunt, William S.; Woodruff, Evelyn L.
Union list of Sanborn fire insurance maps held by institutions in the United States and Canada: volume 2 (Montana to Wyoming; Canada and Mexico). Santa Cruz, Calif.: Western Association of Map Libraries, 1977. xv, 201 p. (Occasional paper / Western Association of Map Libraries ; no. 3) [6562]

Pethick, Jane
Battered wives: a select bibliography. [Toronto]: Centre of Criminology, University of Toronto, 1979. 114 p.; ISBN: 0-919584-41-1. [3190]

Pethick, Jane; Matthews, Catherine J.
Vandalism: a bibliography. Toronto: Centre of Criminology, University of Toronto, 1980. x, 79 p.; ISBN: 0-919584-46-2. [3207]

Petit album des auteurs des cantons de l'Est. Saint-Elie d'Orford, Qué.: Association des auteurs des Canton de l'Est, 1980. 126 p.: ill. [0365]

"Petite bibliographie québécoise sur les groupes nouveaux chrétiens." Dans: Relations; No 389 (janvier 1974) p. 13.; ISSN: 0034-3781. [1535]

Petrelli, Robert; Dubeau, Pierre
Guide bibliographique en gestion municipale. Sainte-Foy, Québec: École nationale d'administration publique, 1987. 278 p.; ISBN: 2-9800104-6-4. [4419]

Petro-Canada
Offshore Queen Charlotte Islands initial environmental evaluation. Calgary: Petro-Canada, [1983]. 3 vol. (loose-leaf): ill., maps. [5205]

Petsche-Wark, Dawna; Johnson, Catherine
Royal commissions and commissions of inquiry for the provinces of Upper Canada, Canada and Ontario, 1792 to 1991: a checklist of reports. Toronto: Ontario Legislative

Library, 1992. ix, 174 p.; ISBN: 0-77299-327-0. [6413]

Pettersen, Annie; Legault, Gaëtane
Bibliographie: femmes et médias. [Toronto]: Évaluation-Médias, [1990]. ii, 40 p.; ISBN: 2-9802007-1-9. [3881]

Pettigrew, Teresa, et al.
A review of water reconditioning re-use technology for fish culture, with a selected bibliography. St. Andrews, N.B.: Fisheries and Oceans Canada, 1978. iv, 19 p. (Fisheries and Marine Service Technical report ; no. 801; ISSN: 0701-7626) [4894]

Pettipas, Leo F.
"A bibliography of Manitoba archaeology." In: *Papers in Manitoba Archaeology*. Winnipeg: Department of Tourism, Recreation & Cultural Affairs, Historic Resources Branch, 1977. P. 55-74. (Miscellaneous papers / Historic Resources Branch, Manitoba Department of Tourism, Recreation & Cultural Affairs ; no. 4; ISSN: 0706-0483) [4571]

Pfeifer, Wilma E.
An annotated bibliography of the fishes of the Beaufort Sea and adjacent regions. [Fairbanks: University of Alaska], 1977. 76 p. (Biological papers of the University of Alaska ; no. 17) [5416]

Phelps, Edward
Bibliography of Lambton County and the City of Sarnia, Ontario. London, Ont.: General Library, University of Western Ontario, 1970. viii, 146 p.: ill., map. (University of Western Ontario Library Bulletin ; no. 8) [0438]
"Lambton County: some bibliographical notes." In: *Western Ontario Historical Notes*; Vol. 15, no. 4 (December 1959) p. 64-67.; ISSN: 0382-0157. [0429]

Phelps, V.H.
Sitka spruce: a literature review with special reference to British Columbia. Victoria, B.C.: Pacific Forest Research Centre, Canadian Forestry Service, 1973. 39 p. (Canadian Forestry Service Information report ; BC-X-83) [5377]

Philipps-Universität Marburg. Universitätsbibliothek
Katalog der Kanada-Bibliothek: Stand Frühjahr 1963. Marburg: Der Bibliothek, 1963. 75 p. [6770]

Phillips, David
"Fine arts and Canadian studies." In: *Communiqué: Canadian Studies*; Vol. 2, no. 1/2 (October 1975) p. 2-44.; ISSN: 0318-1197. [0682]

Phillips, David W.
A bibliography of Canadian climate, 1977-1981/ Bibliographie du climat canadien, 1977-1981. Ottawa: Environment Canada, Atmospheric Environment Service, 1983. 169 p.; ISBN: 0-660-52326-4. [5206]

Phillips, David W.; Gullett, D.W.; Webb, M.S.
Guide des sources des données climatiques du Service de l'environnement atmosphérique. 3e éd. Downsview, Ont.: Environnement Canada, Service de l'environnement atmosphérique, 1988. 1 vol. (en pagination multiple): ill., carte.; ISBN: 0-660-92270-3. [5260]
Handbook on climate data sources of the Atmospheric Environment Service. 3rd ed. Downsview, Ont.: Environment Canada, Atmospheric Environment Service, 1988. 276 p. (in various pagings): ill., map.; ISBN: 0-660-12735-0. [5261]

Phillips, Donna
In search of Canadian materials. Rev. ed. Winnipeg: Department of Education, 1978. iii, 336 p. [0128]

Phillips, Gillian
Reproduction: a guide to materials in the Women's Educational Resource Centre. Toronto: OISE Press, 1991. vi, 396 p. (WERC bibliography series / Women's Educational Resource Centre ; 1); ISBN: 0-7744-0373-X. [3896]

Phillips, P. Lee
Alaska and the Northwest part of North America, 1588-1898: maps in the Library of Congress. Washington: G.P.O., 1898. 119 p. [6486]

Phillips, W. Louis; Stuckey, Ronald L.
Index to plant distribution maps in North American periodicals through 1972. Boston: G.K. Hall, 1976. xxxvii, 686 p.; ISBN: 0-8161-0009-8. [6557]

Physical activity: annotated bibliography/Activité physique: bibliographie annotée. Ottawa: Secretariat for Fitness in the Third Age, 1984. 28 p.; ISBN: 0-919963-20-X. [1832]

Physical activity and mental health: a specialized bibliography from the SPORT database/L'activité physique et la santé mentale: une bibliographie spécialisée de la base de données SPORT. Gloucester, Ont.: Sport Information Resource Centre, 1990. 13 l. (SportBiblio ; no. 6; ISSN: 1180-5269) [1858]

Physical fitness in the third age: a specialized bibliography from the SPORT database/Condition physique du troisième âge: une bibliographie spécialisée de la base de données SPORT. Gloucester, Ont.: Sport Information Resource Centre, 1990. 18 l. (SportBiblio ; no. 5; ISSN: 1180-5269) [1859]

Pichette, Jean- Pierre
Le répertoire ethnologique de l'Ontario français: guide bibliographique et inventaire archivistique du folklore franco-ontarien. Ottawa: Presses de l'Université d'Ottawa, 1992. x, 230 p.: ill. (Histoire littéraire du Québec et du Canada français ; no 3); ISBN: 2-7603-0340-3. [4611]

Pichora, Anne
Genealogical reference sources at the National Library of Canada: a selective bibliography/Ouvrages de référence en généalogie à la Bibliothèque nationale du Canada: une bibliographie sélective. [Ottawa]: National Library of Canada, Reference and Information Services Division, 1988. 14 p. [2073]

Picot, Jocelyne; Roberts, Judy
A Canadian telehealth sourcebook/Recueil de références sur la télésanté au Canada. Ottawa: Canadian Hospital Association, c1984. 98 l. [5662]

Pigeon, Marc; Bernier, Gaston
"Le Québec contemporain: éléments bibliographiques." Dans: *Canadian Journal of Political Science*; Vol. 1, no. 2 (1968) p. 107-118.; ISSN: 0008-4239. [0300]

Pihach, John D.
"Bibliography for Ukrainian researchers: resources at the Yorkton Public Library." In: *Saskatchewan Genealogical Society Bulletin*; Vol. 16, no. 3 (July/September 1985) p. 127-129.; ISSN: 0048-9182. [4235]

Pillai, N.G.; Ling, Joyce
Regional development and economic growth: Canada: a select bibliography. Monticello, Ill.: Council of Planning Librarians, 1970. 23 l. (Council of Planning Librarians Exchange bibliography ; 143) [2588]

Pille, John M.
Catalogue of band music by Canadian composers. [Lennoxville, Quebec: J.M. Pille], c1981. 80 l. [0898]

Pilling, James Constantine

Bibliographies of the languages of the North American Indians. New York: AMS Press, 1973. 3 vol.; ISBN: 0-404-07390-5 (set). [1428]

Bibliography of the Algonquian languages. Washington: Government Printing Office, 1891. x, 614 p.: facsims. (Bulletin / Smithsonian Institution, Bureau of Ethnology ; no. 13; ISSN: 1066-1697) [1406]

Bibliography of the Athapascan languages. Washington: Government Printing Office, 1892. xiii, 125 p.: facsims. (Bulletin / Smithsonian Institution, Bureau of Ethnology ; no. 14; ISSN: 1066-1697) [1407]

Bibliography of the Chinookan languages (including the Chinook jargon). Washington: Government Printing Office, 1893. xiii, 81 p.: facsims. (Bulletin / Smithsonian Institution, Bureau of Ethnology ; no. 15; ISSN: 1066-1697) [1408]

Bibliography of the Eskimo language. Washington: Government Printing Office, 1887. v, 116 p.: facsims. (Bulletin / Smithsonian Institution, Bureau of Ethnology ; no. 1; ISSN: 1066-1697) [1403]

Bibliography of the Iroquoian languages. Washington: Government Printing Office, 1888. vi, 208 p., [1] folded l. of pl.: facsims. (Bulletin / Smithsonian Institution, Bureau of Ethnology ; no. 6; ISSN: 1066-1697) [1404]

Bibliography of the Muskhogean languages. Washington: Government Printing Office, 1889. v, 114 p. (Bulletin / Smithsonian Institution, Bureau of Ethnology ; no. 9; ISSN: 1066-1697) [1405]

Bibliography of the Salishan languages. Washington: Government Printing Office, 1893. xi, 86 p.: facsims. (Bulletin / Smithsonian Institution, Bureau of Ethnology ; no. 16; ISSN: 1066-1697) [1409]

Bibliography of the Siouan languages. Washington: Government Printing Office, 1887. v, 87 p. (Bulletin / Smithsonian Institution, Bureau of Ethnology ; no. 5; ISSN: 1066-1697) [1411]

Bibliography of the Wakashan languages. Washington: Government Printing Office, 1894. x, 70 p. (Bulletin / Smithsonian Institution, Bureau of Ethnology ; no. 19; ISSN: 1066-1697) [1410]

Pilon, C.A.

Bibliography and index of coal in Saskatchewan and adjoining provinces and states. Saskatoon: Saskatchewan Research Council, 1977. 85 p. (Saskatchewan Research Council Geology Division report ; no. 18) [4801]

Pincoe, Grace

"Arthur Garratt Dorland 1887-1979: a bibliography." In: Canadian Quaker History Newsletter; No. 25 (November 1979) p. 32-38.; ISSN: 0319-3934. [6956]

"Bibliography of historical material in Friends House Library, Toronto." In: Canadian Quaker History Newsletter; No. 3 (June 1973) p. 1-4; no. 6 (December 1973) p. 2-4; no. 8 (June 1974) p. 4-6; no. 12 (June 1975) p. 1-8; no. 22 (June 1978) p. 19.; ISSN: 0319-3934. [1547]

Pincoe, Ruth

Glenn Gould: catalogue raisonné du Fonds Glenn Gould. Ottawa: Bibliothèque nationale du Canada, 1992. 2 vol.: ill.; ISBN: 0-660-57327-X (ensemble). [7026]

Glenn Gould: descriptive catalogue of the Glenn Gould Papers. Ottawa: National Library of Canada, 1992. 2 vol.: ill.; ISBN: 0-660-57327-X (set). [7027]

Piontkovsky, Roman

"Russian-Canadian imprints: a preliminary check list." In: Canadian Ethnic Studies; Vol. 2, no. 1 (June 1970) p. 177-185.; ISSN: 0008-3496. [4150]

Pivato, Joseph

"The arrival of Italian-Canadian writing." In: Canadian Ethnic Studies; Vol. 14, no. 1 (1982) p. 127-137.; ISSN: 0008-3496. [1196]

Italian-Canadian writers: a preliminary survey. [Ottawa]: Department of the Secretary of State of Canada, Multiculturalism, 1988. 53 l.; ISBN: 0-662-16034-7. [1261]

Plant, Sheila

Bay of Fundy environmental and tidal power bibliography. 2nd ed. Dartmouth, N.S.: Fisheries and Oceans Canada, 1985. vi, 159, [270] p. (Canadian technical report of fisheries and aquatic sciences ; no. 1339; ISSN: 0706-6457) [5810]

Plant Research Institute (Canada). Agrometeorology Section

Selected Canadian agrometeorological publications. Ottawa: Agriculture Canada, [1966-1979]. 93 no.; ISSN: 0715-1772. [4686]

Platnick, Phyllis

Canadian poetry: index to criticisms, 1970-1979/Poésie canadienne: index de critiques, 1970-1979. [Ottawa]: Canadian Library Association, c1985. xxviii, 337 p.; ISBN: 0-88802-194-1. [1223]

Platzmann, Julius

Verzeichniss einer Auswahl Amerikanischer Grammatiken Wörterbücher, Katechismen, u.s.w. Leipzig: K.F. Köhler, 1876. 38 p. [1402]

Pleins feux sur Claude Aubry, 1949-1979/Something about Claude Aubry, 1949-1979. [Ottawa: Bibliothèque publique d'Ottawa, [1979]. 5 f. [6815]

Plexman, C.A.

Bibliography of Great Lakes Forestry Centre publications, 1983-1987. [Sault Ste. Marie, Ont.]: Great Lakes Forestry Centre, Canadian Forestry Service, 1987. [6], 95, [15] p. (Great Lakes Forestry Centre Information report ; O-X-388; ISSN: 0832-7122); ISBN: 0-662-15775-3. [4992]

Plumptre, A.F.W.; Gilroy, A.E.

"Review of economics text-books for use in Canadian high schools." In: Contributions to Canadian Economics; Vol. 7 (1934) p. 123-130. [3371]

Plympton, Charles William

Select bibliography on travel in North America. Albany: University of the State of New York, 1897. P. [37]-60. (New York State Library Bulletin; Bibliography ; no. 3) [1888]

Pocius, Gerald L.

"Bibliography [Folklore]/Bibliographie [Folklore]." In: Bulletin of the Folklore Studies Association of Canada; Vol. 8, nos 1/2 (May 1984)-vol. 13, nos 3/4 (November 1989) [4605]

"An introductory bibliography on cultural studies relating to death and dying in Canada." In: Material History Bulletin; No. 23 (Spring 1986) p. 53-55.; ISSN: 0703-489X. [3292]

Pogue, Laura A.

Bibliography on alpine vegetation in the Canadian Rockies. Edmonton: Canadian Wildlife Service, 1972. iii, 14 l. [5370]

Pohorecky, Zenon S.

"Archaeology and prehistory: the Saskatchewan case." In: A region of the mind: interpreting the western Canadian plains, edited by Richard Allen. Regina: Canadian Plains Studies Center, University of Saskatchewan, c1973. P. 47-72.; ISBN:

0-88977-008-5. [4559]

Poirier, Jean

Eléments de bibliographie: est du Québec. [Québec]: Ministère de l'éducation, Direction régionale du Bas-Saint-Laurent-Gaspésie, 1981. 86 f.; ISBN: 2-550-04310-3. [0374]

Poirier, Marie

Les femmes immigrées au Québec: bibliographie annotée. [Montréal]: Direction de la recherche, Ministère des Communautés culturelles et de l'immigration, c1985. 51 p.; ISBN: 2-550-11976-2. [3839]

Poirier, René; Cournoyer, Sylvie

Bibliographie thématique sélective sur l'économie de l'information/Thematic and selective bibliography on the information economy. Laval, Québec: Centre canadien de recherche sur l'information du travail, Direction de la recherche organisationnelle, 1989. 32 p.; ISBN: 0-662-57058-8. [2761]

L'impact des nouvelles technologies de l'information sur l'emplois et le travail: bibliographie thématique sélective/ New information technologies impact on employment and work: thematic and selective bibliography. Laval, Québec: Direction de la recherche organisationnelle, Centre canadien de recherche sur l'informatisation du travail, Ministère des communications du Canada, 1989. 192 p.; ISBN: 0-662-57057-X. [1709]

Polegato, Lino L.

Bibliography of reports, papers and studies prepared for the Strait of Canso area compiled for Nova Scotia Department of the Environment. [S.l.: s.n.], 1974. ca. 1000 p. (in various pagings): ill., maps. [0218]

Policewomen: a bibliography. Ottawa: R.C.M.P. Library, 1979. 42 l. [2201]

Polis, Michel P.; Yansouni, P.A.

Bibliographie annotée de la littérature concernant les processus de broyage. Montréal: École Polytechnique, Division d'automatique, 1972. 24 f. [4779]

Pontaut, Alain

Dictionnaire critique du théâtre québécois. Montréal: Leméac, 1972. 161 p. [1069]

Poon, C.

Literature review on the design of composite mechanically fastened joints/Revue de la documentation sur la conception des joints à liaison mécanique en composites. Ottawa: National Research Council Canada, 1986. vi, 63 p.: ill. (Aeronautical note / National Aeronautical Establishment ; NAE-AN-37) [5818]

Pope, Judy L.

A bibliographic survey of socio-economic studies relating to Canadian national heritage properties. Ottawa: Socio-economic Division, Program Management, Parks Canada, 1983. ix, 137 l. [1826]

Bibliographie sur les études socio-économiques relatives aux propriétés historiques du Canada. Ottawa: Division socio-économique, Direction de la gestion du programme, Parcs Canada, 1983. ix, 140 p. [1827]

Popham, Robert E.

"A bibliography and historical review of physical anthropology in Canada: 1848-1949." In: *Yearbook of Physical Anthropology*; Vol. 6 (1950) p. 161-184.; ISSN: 0096-848X. [4531]

"A bibliography and historical review of physical anthropology in Canada: 1848-1949." In: *Revue canadienne de biologie*; Vol. 9, no 2 (mai 1950) p. 175-198.; ISSN: 0035-

0915. [4532]

Popham, Robert E.; Schmidt, Wolfgang

A decade of alcoholism research: a review of the research activities of the Alcoholism and Drug Addiction Research Foundation of Ontario, 1951-1961. Toronto: Alcoholism and Drug Addiction Research Foundation, 1962. vii, 64 p. (Brookside monograph ; no. 3; ISSN: 0068-2853) [5567]

Popham, Robert E.; Yawney, Carole D.

Culture and alcohol use: a bibliography of anthropological studies. Toronto: Addiction Research Foundation of Ontario, 1967. v, 52 l. (Bibliographic series / Addiction Research Foundation of Ontario ; no. 1; ISSN: 0065-1885) [4543]

Poppe, Roger

Kutchin bibliography: an annotated bibliography of northern Yukon Kutchin Indians. Edmonton: Canadian Wildlife Service, 1971. 82 l. [3930]

Porteous, J. Douglas

The single-enterprise community in North America. Monticello, Ill.: Council of Planning Librarians, 1971. 18 p. (Council of Planning Librarians Exchange bibliography ; 207) [4319]

Porter, Peter Augustus

Father Hennepin: an attempt to collect every edition of his works: a brief bibliography thereof. Niagara Falls, N.Y.: [s.n.], 1910. 17 p. [7059]

The works of Father Hennepin: a catalogue of the collection brought together by Peter A. Porter of Niagara Falls, N.Y. New York: Dodd & Livingston, 1910. 13 p. [7060]

Potter, Kathy

Bibliography of agricultural research in central British Columbia, 1938-1979. Victoria, B.C.: Ministry of Agriculture, 1980. 96 p. [4690]

Pottier, Bernard

Bibliographie américaniste: linguistique amérindienne. Paris: Musée de l'homme, 1967-1982. 9 vol.; ISSN: 0067-690X. [1458]

Potts, Randall C.

Public policy and natural resources in British Columbia: a bibliography. Vancouver, B.C.: [s.n.], 1977. 1 vol. (unpaged). [2431]

Potvin, Claude

Acadiana 1980-1982: une bibliographie annotée/[Acadiana 1980-1982]: an annotated bibliography. Moncton, N.-B.: Éditions CRP, 1983. 110 p.; ISBN: 0-9690939-1-8. [0255]

La littérature de jeunesse au Canada français, bref historique, sources bibliographiques, répertoire des livres. Montréal: Association canadienne des bibliothécaires de langue française, 1972. 110 p. [1321]

"Sources bibliographiques sur la littérature enfantine au Canada français." Dans: *Bulletin de l'Association canadienne des bibliothécaires de langue française*; Vol. 16, no 2 (juin 1970) p. 55-61.; ISSN: 0004-5314. [1318]

Potvin, Claudette

"Bibliographie de Jovette Marchessault." Dans: *Voix et Images*; Vol. 16, no 2 (hiver 1991) p. 272-280.; ISSN: 0318-9201. [7175]

Potvin, Diane

"Bibliographie des écrits de Jacques Ferron." Dans: *Études françaises*; Vol. 12, 3-4 (octobre 1976) p. 353-383.; ISSN: 0014-2085. [6985]

Potvin, Fernand
"Saint Antoine Daniel, martyr canadien: bibliographie." Dans: *Revue d'histoire de l'Amérique française*; Vol. 8, no 3 (décembre 1954) p. 395-414.; ISSN: 0035-2357. [6932]

Poulin, André
Bibliographie sur les coopératives d'habitation à capitalisation. [Ottawa]: Société canadienne d'hypothèques et de logement, 1991. 13 p. [4439]

Poulin, Guy; Cadieux, Francine
Index to township plans of the Canadian West/Index de plans des cantons de l'Ouest canadien. Ottawa: Public Archives of Canada, National Map Collection, 1974. xvii, 69 p.: ill., maps. [6541]

Poulin, Martin; Tanguay, Marc
Bibliographie dans le domaine de la gestion des services sociaux (période recensée 1970-1980). Québec: Laboratoire de recherche, École de service social, Université Laval, 1981. xi, 81 f. (Rapports et outils de recherche / École de service social, Université Laval ; no 1) [3224]

Poulin, V.A.; Scrivener, James Charles
An annotated bibliography of the Carnation Creek Fish-forestry Project, 1970 to 1988. Nanaimo, B.C.: Pacific Biological Station, Biological Sciences Branch, Department of Fisheries and Oceans, 1988. iv, 35 p. (Canadian technical report of fisheries and aquatic sciences ; no. 1640; ISSN: 0706-6457) [4999]

Pouliot, Richard
Influences culturelles des États-Unis sur le Québec: état sommaire des travaux. Québec: Centre québécois de relations internationales: Institut canadien des affaires internationales, 1972. 21, 34 f. (Notes de recherche / Centre québécois de relations internationales ; no 4) [0320]

Pouliot-Marier, Colette; Langlois, Simon
Genres de vie et conditions de vie des ménages: bibliographie. Québec: Laboratoire de recherches sociologiques, Université Laval, 1983. 171 p. (Collection Outils de recherche / Laboratoire de recherches sociologiques, Université Laval ; cahier no 4); ISBN: 2-920495-13-5. [3251]

Powell, Karen L.
Reference guide to Alberta government committees, 1905-1980. Edmonton: Alberta Legislative Library, Cooperative Government Library Services, 1982. ca. 150 p. [6352]

Powell, Margaret S.; Powell, Stephen S.
"Bibliography of placename literature, United States and Canada, 1980-1988." In: *Names*; Vol. 38, nos. 1-2 (March-June 1990) p. 49-141.; ISSN: 0027-7738. [3062]

Powell, Mary; Faghfoury, Nahid; Nyenhuis, Pat
Encourager la participation du public: bref exposé et bibliographie choisie annotée. Ottawa: Conseil canadien de développement social, [1989]. 81 p.; ISBN: 0-88810-401-4. [3333]
Fostering public participation: a brief discussion and selected annotated bibliography. Ottawa: Canadian Council on Social Development, [1989]. iii, 73 p.; ISBN: 0-88810-383-2. [3334]

Powell, Wyley L.; Falby, Walter F.
The Ontario energy catalogue: a directory of who's doing what in energy in Ontario and a bibliography of materials on energy available in Ontario. Toronto: Ontario Library Association, 1977. 170, [24] p.; ISBN: 0-88969-011-1. [4802]

Powter, Christopher Barrett
A bibliography of baseline studies in Alberta: soils, geology, hydrogeology, groundwater. Edmonton: Alberta Department of the Environment, Research Management Division, [1982]. xvii, 97 p. (Reclamation Research Technical Advisory Committee report ; no. 82-2) [4830]

Prairie Agricultural Machinery Institute (Canada)
Publications [Prairie Agricultural Machinery Institute]. [Humboldt, Sask.]: Prairie Agricultural Machinery Institute, 1979-. vol.; ISSN: 0319-9398. [4725]

Pratt, Ethel M.; Cornwall, Henry R.
Bibliography of nickel. Washington, D.C.: United States Government Printing Office, 1958. P. 755-815. (United States Geological Survey Bulletin ; 1019-K) [4756]

"Presentable plays for use in Canada." In: *Ontario Library Review*; Vol. 13, no. 1 (August 1928) p. 14-46.; ISSN: 0030-2996. [0998]

Press, Marian; Adams, Susan
The Ontario Textbook Collection catalogue, 1846-1970 [microform]. Toronto: R.W.B. Jackson Library, Ontario Institute for Studies in Education, c1984. 12 microfiches. [3628]

Pressman, Norman E.P.
A comprehensive bibliography on new towns in Canada. Monticello, Ill.: Council of Planning Librarians, 1973. 22 p. (Council of Planning Librarians Exchange bibliography ; 483) [4328]
The reduction of winter-induced discomfort in Canadian urban residential areas: an annotated bibliography and evaluation. Ottawa: Canada Mortgage and Housing Corporation, 1988. 103 p. [4422]

Preston, Caroline M.; Rusk, Ann C.M.
A bibliography of NMR applications for forestry research. Victoria: Pacific Forestry Centre, Forestry Canada, 1990. vii, 42 p. (Pacific Forestry Centre Information report ; BC-X-322; ISSN: 0830-0453); ISBN: 0-662-17942-0. [5012]

Preston, Michele
"The poetry of P.K. Page: a checklist." In: *West Coast Review*; Vol. 3, no. 3 (February 1979) p. 12-17.; ISSN: 0043-311X. [7234]

Pretes, Michael
Sustainable development and the entrepreneur: an annotated bibliography of small business development in circumpolar and developing regions. Whitehorse: Department of Economic Development, Mines and Small Business, Government of the Yukon, 1989. vii, 52 l. [0659]

Prevost, Gerald
Duncan-Cowichan District, V.I. [Vancouver: British Columbia Library Association], 1935. [21] p. [0563]

Price, John A.
"Recent publications in Canadian native studies." In: *Native people, native lands: Canadian Indians, Inuit and Metis*, edited by Bruce Alden Cox. Ottawa: Carleton University Press, 1987. P. 266-298. (Carleton Library series ; no. 142); ISBN: 0-88629-062-7. [4092]
"US and Canadian Indian periodicals." In: *Canadian Review of Sociology and Anthropology*; Vol. 9, no. 2 (May 1972) p. 150-162.; ISSN: 0008-4948. [5905]

Price, Lisa Sydney
Patterns of violence in the lives of girls and women: a reading guide. Vancouver: Women's Research Centre, 1989. 97 p.; ISBN: 0-9692145-6-1. [3870]

Priess, Peter J.

An annotated bibliography for the study of building hardware. Ottawa: National Historic Parks and Sites Branch, Parks Canada, 1978. 79 p. (History and archaeology / National Historic Parks and Sites Branch ; 21); ISBN: 0-660-01775-X. [0754]

Bibliographie annotée pour l'étude de la quincaillerie du bâtiment. Ottawa: Parcs Canada, 1978. 80 p. (Histoire et archéologie / Direction des lieux et des parcs historiques nationaux ; 21); ISBN: 0-660-90035-1. [0755]

Prime, Frederick

A catalogue of official reports upon geological surveys of the United States and territories, and of British North America. Philadelphia: Sherman, 1879. 71 p. [4727]

Prince, Tim

Personal tax reform, 1970-1987: a selected bibliography of sources in the Legislative Library. Regina: Saskatchewan Legislative Library, 1987. 4 l. [2738]

Prince Edward Island. Island Information Service

P E I provincial government publications checklist. Charlottetown: Island Information Service, 1976-. vol.; ISSN: 0380-6685. [6469]

Prince Edward Island. Provincial Library

Professional books for school librarians available from the Prince Edward Island Provincial Library. Charlottetown: Prince Edward Island Provincial Library, 1979. 63, [9] p. [1636]

Principe, Walter H.

Bibliographies and bulletins in theology. Toronto: [s.n.], 1967. 44 l. [1521]

Proctor, George A.

Sources in Canadian music: a bibliography of bibliographies / Les sources de la musique canadienne: une bibliographie des bibliographies. 2nd ed. [Sackville, N.B.]: Ralph Pickard Bell Library, Mount Allison University, 1979. 36 p. (Publications in music / Ralph Pickard Bell Library, Mount Allison University ; no. 4); ISBN: 0-88828-027-0. [0878]

Programme des affaires indiennes et esquimaudes (Canada). Direction du soutien éducationel et culturel

Les Indiens: une liste de livres à leur sujet. 4e éd. [Ottawa]: Programme des affaires indiennes et esquimaudes, Direction du soutien éducationel et culturel, [1977]. [399] p.: ill. en coul.; ISBN: 0-662-00715-8. [3991]

Programming: an annotated bibliography/Programmation: bibliographie annotée. Vanier, Ont.: Secretariat for Fitness in the Third Age, 1984. 18 p.; ISBN: 0-919963-31-5. [1833]

Project Child Care

Family day care: an annotated bibliography. Toronto: Project Child Care, 1975. 38 p. (Project Child Care paper ; no. 1) [3138]

Projet Colique

Cartes urbaines du Québec. Québec: Le Projet, 1973. 4 t. en 5 vol. [6534]

Pronovost, Gilles

Répertoire des thèses de maîtrise et de doctorat sur le loisir au Québec (des origines à 1976). Trois-Rivières: Groupe de recherche en loisir, Université du Québec à Trois-Rivières, 1977. 85 f.; ISBN: 0-919718-01-9. [6145]

Pross, Catherine; Dwyer-Rigby, Mary

Sustaining earth: a bibliography of the holdings of the Ecology Action Resource Centre, Halifax, Canada. Halifax: School of Library and Information Studies, Dalhousie University, 1988. iv, 302 p. (Occasional papers / Dalhousie University School of Library and Information Studies ; no. 44; ISSN: 0318-7403); ISBN: 0-7703-9718-2. [5262]

Proulx, Jeanne

Bio-bibliographies canadiennes-françaises. Montréal: Université de Montréal, 1970. 59, [11] l. [0094]

Proulx, Serge; Harvey, Sylvie

"L'informatisation au Québec: sélection bibliographique." Dans: *Sociologie et sociétés*; Vol. 16, no 1 (avril 1984) p. 145-148.; ISSN: 0038-030X. [1664]

Provencher, Léo; Thibault, Jean-Claude

Critères physiques en aménagement récréatifs à la campagne: recherches bibliographiques. Sherbrooke: Université de Sherbrooke, Département de géographie, 1975. 56 f. (Bulletin de recherche / Université de Sherbrooke, Département de géographie ; no 23) [1778]

Provencher, Louise-Marie

"Bibliographie: Adrien Thério." Dans: *Voix et Images*; Vol. 7, no 1 (automne 1981) p. 57-76.; ISSN: 0318-9201. [7333]

A Provincial bibliography of literacy learning materials, curricula and reference documents. Vancouver: Literacy BC, 1991. 25 p.; ISBN: 0-9695709-0-2. [3725]

Provost, Honorius

"Le Séminaire de Québec et les missions d'Acadie." Dans: *Revue d'histoire de l'Amérique française*; Vol. 2, no 4 (mars 1949) p. 613-620.; ISSN: 0035-2357. [1505]

Provost, Michelle

"Littérature québécois pour la jeunesse: de solides acquis et un avenir prometteur." Dans: *Canadian Children's Literature*; No. 18/19 (1980) p. 72-94.; ISSN: 0319-0080. [1343]

Mieux connaître les Amérindiens et les Inuit en lisant avec les enfants: bibliographie sélective commentée. Québec: Gouvernement du Québec, Ministère de l'éducation, c1987. iii, 75 p.: carte.; ISBN: 2-550-13525-3. [1377]

Prud'homme, François

Les publications des Clercs de Saint-Viateur. Montréal: Clercs de Saint-Viateur, 1984. xxi, 344, 58 p.: ill., fac-sim. (Cahiers du Regroupement des archivistes religieux ; no 1); ISBN: 2-920597-00-X. [1558]

Public Legal Education Society of Nova Scotia. Schools Committee

Before the first day: teaching law for the first time: Nova Scotia resources. Halifax, N.S.: The Society, 1983. ii, 50 p.; ISBN: 0-88648-020-5. [2262]

Public participation: a general bibliography and annotated review of the Canadian experience. [S.l.: s.n., 1977]. iii, 129 p. [3159]

Publications de Louis-Edmond Hamelin: professeur de géographie et directeur du Centre d'études nordiques. Québec: Université Laval, 1969. 51 f. [7042]

"Publications of J. Lewis Robinson." In: *Studies in Canadian regional geography: essays in honor of J. Lewis Robinson*, edited by Brenton M. Barr. Vancouver: Tantalus Research, 1984. P. 8-18. (B.C. geographical series ; no. 37; ISSN: 0068-1571); ISBN: 0-919478-58-1. [7271]

Publicité-Club de Montréal

Bibliographie du monde des communicateurs. Montréal: Publicité-Club, 1974. 24 p. (Cahiers Publicité-Club de Montréal ; 3) [2611]

Pulp and Paper Research Institute of Canada

Index to staff publications in the technical literature, 1968-1986. Pointe-Claire, Quebec: The Institute, 1987.

102 p. [5826]

List of library books and periodicals [Pulp and Paper Research Institute of Canada]. Pointe Claire, Quebec: The Institute, 1981. 254 p. [6786]

List of Woodlands Research Department publications. Pointe Claire, Quebec: Pulp and Paper Research Institute of Canada, 1968. 14 p. (Woodlands Research index ; no. 36; ISSN: 0384-8663) [4923]

Puls, Robert

Mineral levels in animal health: bibliographies. Clearbrook, B.C.: Sherpa International, c1988. 334 p.; ISBN: 0-9694329-1-8. [5547]

Pulyk, Marcia

A bibliography of selected articles on women in the mass media. Ottawa: Canadian Radio-television and Telecommunications Commission, Library, 1975. iii, 43 l. [3758]

Purdham, James T.

A review of the literature on health hazards of video display terminals. Hamilton: Canadian Centre for Occupational Health and Safety, 1980. 18 p. [5630]

Quance, Elizabeth J.; Cronk, Michael Sam

"Museum studies dissertations at the University of Toronto: a selected bibliography." In: *Material Studies Bulletin*; No. 18 (Fall 1983) p. 50-54.; ISSN: 0703-489X. [6172]

Quantrell, James

Canada: federal provincial conferences of first ministers, 1887-1976: guide to microfiche edition. Toronto: Micromedia, 1977. 36 l. [2432]

Québec (Province). Bibliothèque de la Législature

Catalogue alphabétique de la Bibliothèque de la Législature de Québec. [S.l.]: P.G. Delisle, [1869]. 51 p. [6721]

Catalogue de la bibliothèque de la Législature de la province de Québec. Québec: Paradis, Imprimeur du Roi, 1932. xxxii, 293 p. [6762]

Catalogue des livres exposés au Musée de l'Assemblée nationale du Québec à l'occasion du 175e anniversaire de la Bibliothèque de la Législature. Québec: Bibliothèque de la Législature, 1977. 66 p.: ill. [0350]

Catalogue of pamphlets of the Library of the Legislature of Quebec /Catalogue des brochures de la Législature de Québec. Quebec: [s.n.], 1879. 119 p. [6730]

Commissions et comités d'enquêtes au Québec depuis 1867. Québec: Bibliothèque de la Législature, Assemblée nationale, 1972. vii, 95 p. (Bibliographie et documentation / Bibliothèque de la Législature du Québec ; 1) [6281]

Documents du Comité Gauvin. Québec: Bibliothèque de la Législature, Assemblée nationale, 1975. 119 p. (Bibliographie et documentation / Bibliothèque de la Législature du Québec ; 4) [2145]

Québec (Province). Bibliothèque de la Législature. Service de documentation politique

Bibliographie politique du Québec pour l'année 1975. Québec: Assemblée nationale, Bibliothèque de la Législature, 1976. xiii, 709 p. [2426]

Québec (Province). Bibliothèque de la Législature. Service de référence

La collection de Pierre-Joseph-Olivier Chauveau, premier ministre du Québec, 1867-1873: exposition à la Bibliothèque de l'Assemblée nationale du Québec. Québec: Bibliothèque de l'Assemblée nationale, Service de référence, 1978. 38 p.: ill. [6783]

Le référendum: bibliographie sélective et annotée. 2e éd. Québec: Bibliothèque de la Législature, 1978. x, 114 p. (Bibliographie et documentation / Bibliothèque de la Législature du Québec ; 6) [2437]

Québec (Province). Bibliothèque de l'Assemblée nationale

Bibliographie du Parlement du Québec. Québec: Les Publications du Québec, 1992. 119 p.; ISBN: 2-551-14961-4. [2553]

Liste des ouvrages conservés au Service de la reconstitution des débats. Québec: La Bibliothèque, 1983. iv, 40 p. [2481]

Québec (Province). Bureau de la statistique du Québec. Centre d'information et de documentation

Répertoire de données et de publications statistiques québécoises. Québec: Centre d'information et de documentation du Bureau de la statistique du Québec, 1982. 191 p.; ISBN: 2-550-02734-5. [6353]

Québec (Province). Bureau de l'Imprimeur de la Reine

Publications en vente au Bureau de l'Imprimeur de la Reine/ Publications on sale at the Office of the Queen's Printer. Québec: Imprimeur de la Reine, 1966-1968. 3 vol. [6270]

Québec (Province). Centrale des bibliothèques

Sécurité routière: inventaire préliminaire de la documentation disponible. Montréal: La Centrale, 1980. 85 f.; ISBN: 2-89059-013-5. [4480]

Québec (Province). Centrale des bibliothèques. Centre de bibliographie

Éducation sexuelle. Montréal: Centre de bibliographie de la Centrale des bibliothèques, 1975. 108 p. (Carnets de bibliographie / Centre de bibliographie de la Centrale des bibliothèques ; no 1); ISBN: 0-88523-015-9. [3506]

Périodiques pour les bibliothèques. Montréal: Centrale des bibliothèques, 1976. 273 p. (Sélections documentaires / Centrale des bibliothèques, Centre de bibliographie); ISBN: 0-88523-019-1. [5926]

Québec (Province). Centre de services en communications. Service de médias

Liste des journaux (quotidiens et hebdomadaires) et stations de télévision et de radio du Québec. Québec: Ministère des communications, 1980. 83 p. [6030]

Québec (Province). Cinémathèque

Catalogue des documents audiovisuels, 1978. Québec: Cinémathèque, 1978. 380 p. [6636]

Québec (Province). Comité permanent d'aménagement des ressources

Inventaire bibliographique préliminaire des publications du gouvernement du Québec relatives à l'aménagement du territoire. Québec: Administration ARDA-Québec, 1965. v f., 290 p. [6255]

Québec (Province). Commission de toponymie

Bibliographie toponymique du Québec. Éd. rev. et augm. Québec: Commission de toponymie, 1987. 160 p. (Dossiers toponymiques / Commission de toponymie du Québec ; 17); ISBN: 2-550-17744-4. [3053]

Québec (Province). Commission d'étude des problèmes juridiques de l'eau

Bibliographie annotée de la Commission d'étude des problèmes juridiques de l'eau: documents remis à la bibliothèque. Québec: Ministère des richesses naturelles, Service de la bibliothèque et des archives, 1974. xi, 96 p. [5090]

Québec (Province). Conseil d'orientation économique

Répercussions économico-sociales de l'automatisation: bibliographie analytique. Montréal: Le Conseil, 1963. 68

f. [2575]

Québec (Province). Conseil du statut de la femme

Les Québécoises: guide bibliographique suivi d'une filmographie. Québec: Éditeur officiel du Québec, 1976. 160 p. (Collection études et dossiers); ISBN: 0-7754-2451-X. [3766]

Quebec (Province). Department of Mines

Annotated list of publications of the Department of Mines of the province of Quebec, 1883-1960. Quebec: [s.n.], 1960. 116 p. [6243]

Quebec (Province). Department of Natural Resources

Catalogue of publications since 1883 [Quebec Department of Natural Resources]. Quebec: Quebec Department of Natural Resources, 1968. [128] p. (loose-leaf).: ill., map (folded). [6271]

Quebec (Province). Department of Natural Resources. Mineral Deposits Service

Annotated bibliography on metallic mineralization in the regions of Noranda, Matagami, Val-d'Or, Chibougamau. Quebec: Geological Services, 1967. xii, 284 p. (Special paper / Quebec Geological Services ; 2) [4767]

Québec (Province). Direction des énergies nouvelles

Sommaire de la littérature disponible en français dans le domaine des énergies nouvelles. Québec: Gouvernement du Québec, Direction générale de l'énergie, 1978. 31 p. [5769]

Québec (Province). Direction générale de l'urbanisme et de l'aménagement du territoire

Répertoire des informations du Gouvernement du Québec en matière d'aménagement du territoire. [Québec: Gouvernement du Québec, Direction générale de l'urbanisme et de l'aménagement du territoire], 1983. 352 p.: carte.; ISBN: 2-551-05584-9. [4399]

Québec (Province). Direction générale des eaux. Service des relevés

Répertoire des cartes bathymétriques. Québec: Direction générale des eaux, 1979. vi, 114 p.; ISBN: 2-550-00089-7. [6568]

Québec (Province). Direction générale du domaine territorial

Répertoire des cartes, plans et photographies aériennes. [Québec]: Ministère de l'énergie et des ressources, Direction générale du domaine territorial, 1981. 136 p.: ill., cartes.; ISBN: 2-551-06408-2. [6577]

Québec (Province). Éditeur officiel du Québec

Catalogue de l'Éditeur officiel du Québec. Québec: Éditeur officiel du Québec, 1974-1979. 5 vol.; ISSN: 0316-1560. [6324]

Publications: Bureau de l'Éditeur officiel du Québec/ Publications: Office of the Quebec Official Publisher. Québec: Éditeur officiel du Québec, 1969-1973. 5 vol.; ISSN: 0316-1579. [6286]

Québec (Province). Ministère de l'éducation. Direction des communications

Bibliographie sur l'éducation préscolaire. Québec: Direction générale du développement pédagogique, 1982. 42 p. (Guides pédagogiques du préscolaire); ISBN: 2-550-04984-5. [3616]

Québec (Province). Ministère de l'éducation. Direction des études économiques et démographiqes

Liste des publications de la Direction des études économiques et démographiques de 1977 à 1982. [Québec]: La Direction, 1983. 24 p.; ISBN: 2-550-05928-X. [6361]

Québec (Province). Ministère de l'éducation. Direction générale de la planification

Thèses et mémoires relatifs à l'éducation, 1969-1974. Québec: Ministère de l'éducation, Direction générale de la planification, 1976. 258 p. [6143]

Québec (Province). Ministère de l'éducation. Direction générale des réseaux

Catalogue des documents audio-visuels [Gouvernement du Québec, Ministère de l'éducation, Direction générale des réseaux]. Trois-Rivières: Gouvernement du Québec, Ministère de l'éducation, Direction générale des réseaux, 1981. 133 p.; ISBN: 2-550-04736-2. [6647]

Québec (Province). Ministère de l'éducation. Service général des communications

Références pédagogiques. Québec: Service général des communications, Ministère de l'éducation, 1976-1979. 4 vol.; ISSN: 0225-7254. [3555]

Québec (Province). Ministère de l'énergie et des ressources

Répertoire des documents audiovisuels du Ministère de l'énergie et des ressources, 1990-1991. Québec: Gouvernement du Québec, Ministère de l'énergie et des ressources, Direction des communications, 1990. 26 p.; ISBN: 2-550-20843-9. [6690]

Québec (Province). Ministère de l'énergie et des ressources. Direction générale de l'exploration géologique et minérale

Catalogue du fichier géologique. Québec: Ministère de l'énergie et des ressources, Service des publications géologiques, 1983. v, 143 p. [4836]

Québec (Province). Ministère de l'environnement. Centre de documentation

Répertoire des publications scientifiques et techniques du Ministère de l'environnement. [2e éd.]. [Québec]: Ministère de l'environnement, Direction des communications et de l'éducation, Centre de documentation, 1984. 64 p.; ISBN: 2-550-11030-7. [6366]

Québec (Province). Ministère de l'Industrie et du Commerce. Service de géographie

Bibliographie du Nouveau-Québec/Bibliography of New Quebec. Québec: Le Ministère, 1955. 321 p.: carte. (Publication / Québec Ministère de l'Industrie et du Commerce, Service de géographie ; no 1) [0288]

Québec (Province). Ministère des affaires sociales. Service de l'informathèque

Monographies et publications officielles (Gouvernement du Québec. Ministère des affaires sociales. Informathèque). Sainte-Foy: Gouvernement du Québec, Ministère des affaires sociales, [1976-1983]. 8 vol.; ISSN: 0833-4811. [6362]

Québec (Province). Ministère des communications. Bibliothèque administrative

Catalogue collectif des périodiques des bibliothèques gouvernementales du Québec, 1989. 4e éd. [Québec]: La Bibliothèque, [1989]. xviii, 932 p.; ISBN: 2-551-12182-5. [5970]

Liste annuelle des périodiques du gouvernement du Québec. Québec: Gouvernement du Québec, Direction générale des publications gouvernementales, Bibliothèque administrative, 1983-. vol.; ISSN: 0712-6905. [6470]

Liste bimestrielle des publications du gouvernement du Québec. Québec: Ministère des communications, Bibliothèque administrative, 1988-. vol.; ISSN: 0840-7908. [6471]

Liste mensuelle des publications du gouvernement du Québec. Québec: Direction générale des publications gouvernementales, Ministère des communications, 1981-[1988]. 7 vol.; ISSN: 0714-5993. [6392]

Répertoire des recherches faites par ou pour le Ministère des communications. 2e version. [Québec]: Ministère des communications, Direction générale de la coordination et des politiques, c1989. xiii, 128 p.; ISBN: 2-550-19262-1. [0986]

Québec (Province). Ministère des forêts

Répertoire des documents audiovisuels [Ministère des forêts (Québec)]. Charlesbourg: Gouvernement du Québec, Ministère des forêts, 1991-. vol.; ISSN: 1187-905X. [6707]

Québec (Province). Ministère des mines

Liste annotée des publications du Ministère des mines de la province de Québec, 1883-1957. Québec: Imprimeur de la Reine, 1957. 95 p. [4752]

Québec (Province). Ministère des richesses naturelles

Catalogue des publications depuis 1883 [Québec, Ministère des richesses naturelles]. Québec: [s.n.], 1968. 1 vol. (f. mobiles): ill., carte pliée. [6272]

Liste des documents de levés geophysiques aériens/List of airborne geophysical documents. Québec: Ministère des richesses naturelles, 1968. 49 p. [4769]

Répertoire des cartes et levés de géochimie et de dépôts meubles au Québec. Québec: Service de la géochimie, Direction des levés géoscientifiques, Ministère des richesses naturelles, 1978. 39 p. [6563]

Québec (Province). Ministère des richesses naturelles. Bibliothèque

Bibliographie du bassin de la rivière Saint-François. Québec: Gouvernement du Québec, Ministère des richesses naturelles, Service de la bibliothèque et des archives, 1975. 114 p. [0336]

Québec (Province). Ministère des richesses naturelles. Direction générale des eaux. Service de l'aménagement hydraulique

Bibliographie sur le bassin de la Yamaska. Québec: Ministère des richesses naturelles, 1970. 51 p.: carte. (Mission technique pour l'aménagement des eaux du bassin de la Yamaska, Rapport ; no 1) [5055]

Québec (Province). Musée d'art contemporain

Solstice de la poésie québécoise: poèmes, affiches, vidéogrammes: une exposition itinérante. Montréal: Musée d'art contemporain, 1977. [42] p.: ill. [1112]

Québec (Province). Office de planification et de développement du Québec

Répertoire des publications de l'Office de planification et de développement du Québec. [Québec]: Service des communications de l'O.P.D.Q., 1989. viii, 68 p.; ISBN: 2-550-19951-0. [6400]

Québec (Province). Office des personnes handicapées

300 documents audiovisuels sur les personnes handicapées. Québec: L'Office, 1988. [9], 99 p.; ISBN: 2-551-08229-3. [6676]

Québec (Province). Office des ressources humaines. Direction de développement du personnel d'encadrement

Bibliographie générale en management. Québec: Gouvernement du Québec, Office des ressources humaines, Direction de développement du personnel d'encadrement, 1983-. vol.; ISSN: 1181-8603. [2787]

Québec (Province). Office d'information et de publicité

Les publications gouvernementales du Québec. Québec: Office d'information et de publicité du Québec, 1965. [98] p. [6256]

Québec (Province). Service de la cartographie

Cartes géologiques publiées: index de localisation/Published geological maps. location index. Québec. Le Service, 1974. v, 57 p. [6542]

Québec (Province). Service de la photogrammétrie et de la cartographie

Répertoire des cartes géographiques et des photographies aériennes. Québec: Le Service, 1971. 31 l.: cartes (coul.). [6525]

Québec (Province). Service des gîtes minéraux

Bibliographie annotée sur les minéralisations métalliques dans les Appalaches du Québec: pour accompagner les cartes nos B-790, B-791, B-792. Québec: Le Service, 1963. vi, 106 p. [4761]

Québec (Province). Services géologiques

Liste des cartes publiées par les Services géologiques/List of maps published by the Geological Services. Québec: [s.n.], 1966. 15 p. [6510]

Quebec in books. Montreal: Unity Press, [1934]. 56 p.: ill. [0283]

Québec plays in translation: a catalogue of Québec playwrights and plays in English translation. Montreal: Centre des auteurs dramatiques, c1990. xii, 86 p.: ill.; ISBN: 2-920308-14-9. [1288]

"Le Québec touristique." Dans: *Notes du Centre d'études du tourisme*; Vol. 8, no 3 (avril 1988) p. 1-2.; ISSN: 0229-2718. [1851]

Queen's University (Kingston, Ont.). Department of Industrial Relations

A selected bibliography on industrial relations. Kingston, Ont.: Department of Industrial Relations, Queen's University, 1946. 77 p. (Bulletin / Queen's University Department of Industrial Relations ; no. 11) [2788]

Queen's University (Kingston, Ont.). Douglas Library

Canadiana, 1698-1900: in the possession of the Douglas Library, Queen's University, Kingston, Ontario. Kingston, Ont.: 1932. ii, 86 p. [0044]

Catalogue of Canadian newspapers in the Douglas Library, Queen's University. Kingston, [Ont.]: The Library, 1969. xxi l., 195 p. (Douglas Library Occasional papers ; no. 1) [6015]

Queen's University (Kingston, Ont.). Douglas Library. Buchan Collection

A checklist of works by and about John Buchan in John Buchan Collection. [Rev. & augm.]. Boston: G.K. Hall, 1961. 38, 24 p.: ill., port. [7347]

Queen's University (Kingston, Ont.). Industrial Relations Centre. Research Reference Section

Cafeteria, deferred and flexible compensation: a bibliography, 1970-1978. Kingston, Ont.: Industrial Relations Centre, Queen's University, 1978. 4 p. (Compensation bibliographies series / Industrial Relations Centre, Queen's University ; no. 7) [2850]

Collective bargaining and white collar employees: a bibliography, 1970-1977. Kingston, Ont.: Industrial Relations Centre, Queen's University, 1977. 10 p. [2838]

Collective bargaining in education in Canada: a bibliography, 1970-1977. Kingston, Ont.: Industrial Relations Centre, Queen's University, 1977. 6 p. [2839]

Collective bargaining in the public service of Canada: a bibliography. [Kingston, Ont.]: Industrial Relations Centre, Queen's University at Kingston, 1975. 18 p. [2824]

Compensation administration: a bibliography 1970-1978. Kingston, Ont.: Industrial Relations Centre, Queen's

University, 1978. 13 p. (Compensation bibliographies series / Industrial Relations Centre, Queen's University ; no. 5) [2851]

Cost of living adjustments (COLA): a bibliography. Kingston, Ont.: Industrial Relations Centre, Queen's University at Kingston, 1975. 9 l. [2825]

Employee benefits: a bibliography, 1970-1978. Kingston, Ont.: Industrial Relations Centre, Queen's University, 1978. 12 p. (Compensation bibliographies series / Industrial Relations Centre, Queen's University ; no. 10) [2852]

Employee stock options and employee stock ownership plans: a bibliography, 1970-1978. Kingston, Ont.: Industrial Relations Centre, Queen's University, 1978. 7 p. (Compensation bibliographies series / Industrial Relations Centre, Queen's University ; no. 8) [2853]

Final offer selection (FOS): a bibliography. Kingston, Ont.: Industrial Relations Centre, Queen's University, 1975. 7 l. [2826]

Health care sector unionization and collective bargaining: a bibliography, 1970-1977. Kingston, Ont.: Industrial Relations Centre, Queen's University, 1977. 9 p. [2840]

Index of industrial relations literature. Kingston (Ont.): Industrial Relations Centre, Queen's University, 1977-. vol.; ISSN: 0226-1537. [2941]

Pay for performance: a bibliography, 1970-1977. Kingston, Ont.: Industrial Relations Centre, Queen's University, 1978. 9 p. [2854]

Performance appraisal: a bibliography, 1970-1977. Kingston, Ont.: Industrial Relations Centre, Queen's University, 1978. 16 p. (Compensation bibliographies series / Industrial Relations Centre, Queen's University ; no. 2) [2855]

Wage-price controls: a selected bibliography. [Kingston, Ont.]: Industrial Relations Centre, Queen's University at Kingston, 1975. [10] p. [2827]

"La querelle de l'eau-de-vie sous le régime français: bibliographie." Dans: Revue d'histoire de l'Amérique française; Vol. 1, no 4 (mars 1948) p. 615-624; Vol. 2, no 1 (juin 1948) p. 138-140.; ISSN: 0035-2357. [1921]

Quigley, E.P.
Fisheries Development Division video-tape library catalogue. [Ottawa]: Fisheries and Oceans Canada, 1990. iv, 14 p. [6691]

Quill & Quire cumulative catalogue. Toronto: Quill & Quire, 1940-1968. vol. [0090]

Quinn, David B.
Sources for the ethnography of northeastern North America to 1611. Ottawa: National Museums of Canada, 1981. iv, 93 p. (National Museum of Man Mercury series: Canadian Ethnology Service paper ; no. 76; ISSN: 0316-1862) [4584]

Racey, G.D.
Moisture retaining materials for tree seedling packaging: a literature review. Maple, Ontario: Ontario Tree Improvement and Forest Biomass Institute, 1988. 16 p. (Forest Research report / Ontario Tree Improvement and Forest Biomass Institute ; 120; ISSN: 0301-3924); ISBN: 0-7729-3606-4. [5000]

Racine, Laurette
Bibliographie sur le saumon de la province de Québec. [Montréal: s.n., 1938]. 21 f. [5321]

Raduloff, Marianne
"Bulgarian-Canadian periodical publications: a preliminary check list." In: Canadian Ethnic Studies; Vol. 2, no. 1 (June 1970) p. 1-3.; ISSN: 0008-3496. [5901]

Radvanyi, Andrew
Snowshoe hares and forest plantations: a literature review and problem analysis. Edmonton: Northern Forestry Centre, 1987. vi, 17 p. (Northern Forestry Centre Information report ; NOR-X-290; ISSN: 0704-7673); ISBN: 0-662-15628-5. [4993]

Radziminska-Lasalle, Jolanta; Lasalle, Pierre
Une bibliographie sur les minéraux lourds/A bibliography of heavy minerals. Québec: Ministère des richesses naturelles du Québec, 1968. 56 p. [4770]

Rafferty-Alameda Project environmental impact statement: bibliography. [Regina]: Souris Basin Development Authority, [1987]. 53 l. [5251]

Rahkra, A.S.
Sources of economic and cost statistics for Canadian construction: a compilation. Ottawa: National Research Council Canada, Division of Building Research, 1982. iv, 37 p. (Bibliography / National Research Council Canada, Division of Building Research ; no. 44; ISSN: 0085-3828) [2685]

Rainey, Melvyn D.
Native American materials for school libraries. Vancouver: British Columbia School Librarians' Association, 1976. 17 p. (BCSLA Occasional paper / British Columbia School Librarians' Association ; no. 9) [3984]

Ralph Pickard Bell Library
Catalogue, the Winthrop Pickard Bell Collection of Acadiana. 2nd ed. Sackville, N.B.: Mount Allison University, 1987. 6 vol.; ISBN: 0-88828-061-0. [0265]

The Edgar and Dorothy Davidson Collection of Canadiana at Mount Allison University. Sackville, N.B.: Centre for Canadian Studies, Mount Allison University, 1991. xxiv, 418 p.: ill.; ISBN: 0-919107-30-3. [6794]

Ralston, H. Keith
"Select bibliography on the history of British Columbia." In: Historical essays on British Columbia, edited by Jean Friesen and H.K. Ralston. Toronto: Gage, 1980. P. 281-293.; ISBN: 0-7715-5694-2. [0590]

Ramlalsingh, Roderick D.
Marine transportation in Canada and the U.S. Great Lakes region: a bibliography of selected references, 1950-1975. Toronto: University of Toronto-York University Joint Program in Transportation, 1976. 32 l. (University of Toronto-York University Joint Program in Transportation Working paper ; no. 1; ISSN: 0380-9889) [4465]

Ramrattan, Annette; Kach, Nick
"Native education in Alberta: a bibliography." In: Canadian Journal of Native Education; Vol. 12, no. 2 (1985) p. 55-68.; ISSN: 0710-1481. [3645]

Ramsey, G.S.; Bruce, N.G.
Bibliography of departmental forest fire research literature. 3rd ed. Ottawa: Forest Fire Research Institute, Canadian Forestry Service, Department of the Environment, 1975. [138] p. (in various pagings). (Information report / Forest Fire Research Institute ; FF-X-2; ISSN: 0068-757X) [4947]

Randall, Melanie
"Feminist theory, political philosophy and the politics of reproduction: an annotated bibliography." In: Resources for Feminist Research; Vol. 18, no. 3 (September 1989) p. 111-122.; ISSN: 0707-8412. [3871]

"The published writings of Mary O'Brien: an annotated bibliography." In: Resources for Feminist Research; Vol. 18, no. 3 (September 1989) p. 107-110.; ISSN: 0707-8412. [7215]

The state bibliography: an annotated bibliography on women and the state in Canada. [Toronto: Ontario Institute for Studies in Education], 1989. 39 p. (Resources for feminist research Special publication) [3872]

Rangel, Yolanda
Le parrainage et la réunification de la famille: bibliographie annotée. [Québec]: Conseil des communautés culturelles et de l'immigration du Québec, 1987. [2], i, 34 f.; ISBN: 2-550-19148-X. [2297]

Rankin, Reita A.
"Bibliography of materials in Fort William Public Library relating to Fort William, Port Arthur, and northwestern Ontario." In: *Ontario Library Review*; Vol. 43, no. 2 (May 1959) p. 140-146.; ISSN: 0030-2996. [0430]

Rapoport, Joseph
Une liste abrégée sélective de Canadiana rare comprenent cent livres, mémoires et brochures imprimés pendant le 17e, 18e, et 19e siècle ainsi que plusieurs anciennes cartes géographiques de l'Amérique du Nord et des Canadas et contenant plus particulierement quelques items d'intérêt juif dans la bibliothèque privée de Joseph Rapoport/A selective checklist of rare Canadiana consisting of one hundred books, memoirs and pamphlets printed during the 17th, 18th & 19th century as well as several early maps of North America & of the Canadas and containing more particularly some items of Jewish interest in the private library of Joseph Rapoport. Montréal: Osiris, 1974. 58 p.: facsims. [0111]

Rascoe, Jesse E.
1200 treasure books: a bibliography. Fort Davis, Tex.: Frontier Book Co., 1970. 62 p. [4552]

Ratté, Alice; Gagnon, Gilberte
Bibliographie analytique de la littérature pédagogique canadienne-française. [Québec]: Association canadienne des éducateurs de langue française, 1952. 108 p. [3375]

Ravel d'Esclapon, Rysia de
"Bibliographie des assurances." Dans: *Revue juridique Thémis*; No 1 (1968) p. 77-86.; ISSN: 0556-7963. [2114]

Raveneau, Jean
"Liste des thèses de maîtrise (1960-1971) et mémoires de licence (1964-1971) présentés au Département de géographie de l'Université Laval et concernant l'Est du Québec." Dans: *Cahiers de géographie de Québec*; Vol. 16, no 37 (avril 1972) p. 122-129.; ISSN: 0007-9766. [6120]

Raveneau, Jean; Dion, Louise; Bélanger, Marcel
"Ouvrages récents (1973-1977) pertinents à la géographie culturelle." Dans: *Cahiers de géographie de Québec*; Vol. 21, nos 53-54 (septembre-décembre 1977) p. 309-318.; ISSN: 0007-9766. [3021]

Rawkins, Reginald A.
Guide to publications: a guide by subject and author to the publications of the Canadian Tax Foundation to December 31st, 1958. Toronto: Canadian Tax Foundation, 1959. 42 p. [2570]

Rawson, Mary
Transit: the nature and role of localized benefits: a selected annotated bibliography. Vancouver: Centre for Transportation Studies, University of British Columbia, 1983. 35 p.; ISBN: 0-919804-36-5. [4494]

Ray, Douglas; Franco, Beatriz
"Human rights in education: recently published Canadian sources and an index." In: *Canadian Journal of Education*; Vol. 11, no. 3 (Summer 1986) p. 364-382.; ISSN: 0380-

2361. [3662]

Ray, Margaret
"Pelham Edgar: a bibliography of his writings." In: *Across my path*, edited by Northrop Frye. Toronto: Ryerson Press, 1952. P. 163-167. [6964]
Raymond Knister: a bibliography of his works. [Toronto]: Published under the auspices of the Bibliographical Society of Canada, [1950]. 8 p. [7101]

Ray, Roger B.
The Indians of Maine and the Atlantic Provinces: a bibliographical guide, being largely a selected inventory of material on the subject in the Society's library. Portland: Maine Historical Society, 1977. [85] p. (Maine history bibliographical guide series) [3992]

Ray, Susan L.
Selected review of literature on adult female and male incest survivors. London, Ont.: HMS Press, 1992. [29] l.; ISBN: 0-9199578-5-4. [3360]

Raymond, Jean-Claude
Bibliographie sur le camionnage. Québec: Ministère des transports, 1981. 135 p.; ISBN: 2-550-02172-X. [4485]

Raymond H. Fogler Library
The Canadian collection of the Fogler Library, University of Maine: a preliminary guide to research materials. Orono, Me.: The Library, 1991. i, 49 p. [6795]

Raynauld, André
"Recherches économiques récentes sur la province de Québec." Dans: *Recherches sociographiques*; Vol. 3, no 1-2 (janvier-août 1962) p. 55-64.; ISSN: 0034-1282. [2574]

Raynauld, Françoy
A bibliography of the Beothuk culture of Newfoundland. Ottawa: National Museum of Man, Ethnology Division, 1974. iv, 14 l. [3958]

Razzolini, E.M.; McIntyre, F.
Bibliography of sources used in compiling and analyzing costume research and design information accumulated at the fortress of Louisbourg National Historic Park. [S.l.: s.n.], 1981. [27] l. [4585]

Read across Canada: creative activities for Canadian readers. Toronto: Canadian Children's Book Centre, 1988. 33 p.: ill. [1380]

A reader's guide to Canadian history. Toronto: University of Toronto Press, 1982. 2 vol.; ISBN: 0-8020-6442-6 (vol. 1).– 0-8020-6490-6 (vol. 2). [2025]

"Reading list on Canada and Montreal." In: *Library Journal*; Vol. 25 (March 1900) p. 120-141.; ISSN: 0000-0027. [0277]

"Recent publications in local history." In: *Saskatchewan History*; Vol. 17 (1964)-vol. 34, no. 2 (Spring 1981) [0535]

"Recent publications récentes." In: *Scientia canadensis*; (1984-) vol.; ISSN: 0829-2507. [4636]

"Recent publications relating to Canada." In: *Canadian Historical Review*; (1920-) vol.; ISSN: 0008-3755. [0189]

"La recherche en tourisme." Dans: *Notes du Centre d'études du tourisme*; Vol. 8, no 5 (juin 1988) p. 1-2.; ISSN: 0229-2718. [1852]

La Recherche universitaire en communication au Québec, 1960-1986: bibliographie analytique des thèses et mémoires. Sainte-Foy, Québec: Réseau québécois d'information sur la communication, c1988. xxiii, 222 p.; ISBN: 2-921026-01-5. [6194]

Recueil de documents pédagogiques préparées pour les classes d'immersion française, 1982-1984. Ottawa: Association canadienne des professeurs d'immersion: Canadian

Association for Immersion Teachers, [1982-1984]. 2 vol. [3629]

Rede, L.T.

Bibliotheca Americana, or, A chronological catalogue of the most curious and interesting books, pamphlets, state papers, &c .... London: Printed for J. Debrett ..., J. Sewell ..., R. Baldwin and J. Bew ..., and E. Harlowe ..., 1789. 271 p. [0001]

Redekop, Calvin W.

A bibliography of Mennonites in Waterloo County and Ontario. Waterloo, Ont.: Institute of Anabaptist and Mennonite Studies, Conrad Grebel College, University of Waterloo, c1989. 19 p. [1571]

Redpath, D.K.

Recreation residential developments: a review and summary of relevant material. [Ottawa]: Lands Directorate, Environment Canada, 1975. 32 p. (Occasional paper / Environment Canada, Lands Directorate ; no. 4) [1779]

Rees, D.L.; Topps, K.H.; Brozowski, R.S.

Bibliographic guide to North Bay and area. [North Bay, Ont.: Dept. of Geography, Nipissing University College], 1979. [22], 259 p.: ill., maps.; ISBN: 0-9690905-0-1. [0464]

"Reference titles." In: *Canadian Library Journal*; Vol. 44, no. 1 (February 1987)-vol. 49, no. 1 (February 1992) [1735]

Références écologiques: répertoire des sources d'information écologiques: une réalisation conjointe du ministère fédéral de l'Environnement et des ministères et services provinciaux et territoriaux de l'environnement et des ressources renouvelables. [Ottawa: Ministère de l'environnement], c1978. 124 p.; ISBN: 0-662-01622-8. [5135]

Référendum 80: répertoire de la presse. [Québec]: Directeur général des élections du Québec, [1985]. 3 vol.; ISBN: 2-551-06519-4 (éd. complète). [2499]

Regehr, T.D.

"Historiography of the Canadian plains after 1870." In: *A region of the mind: interpreting the western Canadian plains*, edited by Richard Allen. Regina: Canadian Plains Studies Centre, University of Saskatchewan, c1973. P. 87-101.; ISBN: 0-889770085. [0511]

Réginald Grigoire Inc.

Les facteurs qui façonnent une bonne école: rapport d'une recherche bibliographique sélective et analytique. Québec: Ministère de l'éducation, Direction générale de la recherche et du développement, 1990. 78 p.; ISBN: 2-550-15122-4. [3719]

Reid, Alison

Canadian women film-makers: an interim filmography. Ottawa: Canadian Film Institute, 1972. [12] l. (Canadian Film Archives, Canadian filmography series ; no. 8) [6617]

Reid, Bob; Mongeon, Jean

Employee fitness: an annotated bibliography/Condition physique de l'employé: bibliographie annotée. Ottawa: Coaching Association of Canada, Sport Information Resource Centre, c1982. [6] p. [1819]

Fitness motivation: an annotated bibliography/Motivation et conditionnement physique: bibliographie annotée. Ottawa: Sport Information Resource Centre, c1982. [5] p. [1820]

Reid, Darrel R.

Bibliography of Canadian and comparative federalism, 1980-1985. Kingston, Ont.: Institute of Intergovernmental Relations, Queen's University, c1988. vii, 492 p.; ISBN: 0-88911-451-X. [2522]

Reid, Dennis

A bibliography of the Group of Seven. Ottawa: National Gallery of Canada, 1971. 89 p. [0674]

Reid, Elspeth; McIlwaine, John

Sub-doctoral theses on Canada: accepted by universities in the United Kingdom & Ireland, 1899-1986: together with a supplement to J.J. Dossick *Doctoral research on Canada and Canadians, 1884-1983*. [London, Eng.]: British Association for Canadian Studies, 1989. iii, 10 p.; ISBN: 0-9509063-1-X. [6198]

Reid, Jean-Paul

Bibliographie de bibliographies sur les transports et domaines connexes/Bibliography of bibliographies on transportation and related fields. Montréal: Université de Montréal, Centre de recherche sur les transports, 1977. 65 l. (Université de Montréal Centre de recherche sur les transports Publication ; no 84) [4467]

Bibliography on legal aid in Canada/Bibliographie sur l'aide juridique au Canada. Montreal: National Legal Aid Research Centre, 1978. ii, 62 l. [2186]

Reid, Marianne E.

Enumerative bibliography of the University of Saskatchewan's holdings of Law Reform Commission publications for Australia, Canada, Great Britain and Scotland. [Saskatoon]: Publications Committee, University of Saskatchewan, 1987. 228 p.; ISBN: 0-88880-183-1. [2298]

Reid, R.L.

"British Columbia: a bibliographical sketch." In: *Papers of the Bibliographical Society of America*; Vol. 22, part 1 (1928) p. 20-44.; ISSN: 0006-128X. [0556]

Reimer, Louise

Canadian fiction classics: a booklist prepared in commemoration of the centennial year of the Toronto Public Library. [Toronto]: The Library, [1983]. 12 p. [1209]

Reinecke, L.

"Bibliography of Canadian geology for the years 1908 to 1911 (inclusive)." In: *Proceedings and Transactions of the Royal Society of Canada*; Series 3, vol. 6, section 4 (1912) p. 139-226.; ISSN: 0316-4616. [4737]

Rek, Joseph

Edmonton: an annotated bibliography of holdings in the Canadiana collection, Edmonton Public Library. 3rd updated ed. [Edmonton: Edmonton Public Library], 1991. 81 p. [0550]

Relph, E.C.; Goodwillie, S.B.

Annotated bibliography on snow and ice problems. Toronto: Department of Geography, University of Toronto, 1968. 14 p. (Natural hazard research working paper / Department of Geography, University of Toronto ; no. 2) [5044]

Rémillard, Juliette

"Lionel Groulx: bibliographie (1964-1979)." Dans: *Revue d'histoire de l'Amérique française*; Vol. 32, no 3 (décembre 1978) p. 465-524.; ISSN: 0035-2357. [7032]

Remington, Cyrus Kingsbury

The ship-yard of the Griffon: a brigantine built by René Robert Cavelier, sieur de La Salle, in the year 1679, above the falls of Niagara. Buffalo, N.Y.: [Press of J.W. Clement], 1891. 78 p. [1884]

Rempel, Judith Dianne

Annotated bibliography of papers, articles and other documents resulting from the Aging in Manitoba [Project]: 1971, 1976, 1983 cross-sectional and panel studies (Betty

Havens, Manitoba Health, Principal investigator).
[Winnipeg: Aging in Manitoba Project, Manitoba Health],
1987. 54 l. [0304]

Renaud-Frigon, Claire
Library and information science dictionaries and glossaries:
a selective list based on National Library of Canada
holdings/Dictionnaires et glossaires d'informatique et de
bibliothéconomie: liste sélective basée sur la collection de
la Bibliothèque nationale du Canada. Ottawa: National
Library of Canada, 1978. [13] p. [1626]

Renaud-Frigon, Claire; Robertson, Carolynn
Copyright: a selective bibliography/Le droit d'auteur:
bibliographie sélective. Ottawa: Library Documentation
Centre, National Library of Canada, 1976. 12, 10, 7, [1]
l. [2158]

Renault, Raoul
Bibliographie de Sir James M. Lemoine. Québec: Brousseau,
1897. 11 p. [7144]
Faucher de Saint-Maurice: son oeuvre. Québec: Brousseau,
1897. 16 p. [6977]
Mémoires et documents historiques: notice bibliographique.
Québec: Brousseau, 1897. 14 p. [1889]

Renewable Resources Consulting Services
A bibliography of wildlife studies for the Saskatchewan-
Nelson River Basin. [S.l.]: Canadian Wildlife Service,
Department of Environment, 1971. vii, 129 l. [5361]

Renick, J.H.
A bibliography of research on Alberta hailstorms and their
modification. Three Hills: Alberta Agriculture, 1977. 19 l.
(Alberta Weather Modification Board report ; no. 5) [5127]

Rennie, P.J.
Annotated bibliography of openly available published
reports, 1950 to 1987. [Ottawa: Canadian Forestry Service],
1988. iii, 80 p. [5001]

**Répertoire analytique des publications gouvernementales du
Québec.** Québec: Centre de documentation, Ministère des
communications, 1976-1980. 3 vol.; ISSN: 0706-9057. [6328]

**Répertoire annoté des publications des commissions
scolaires: documents pédagogiques et administratifs/
Annotated catalogue of school board publications:
pedagogical and administrative documents.** Montréal:
Conseil scolaire de l'île de Montréal, 1980-. vol.; ISSN: 0823-
275X. [3736]

**Répertoire bibliographique: thèses de doctorat et mémoires
de maîtrise en rapport avec la condition des femmes reçus
à l'Université Laval, 1987-1991.** [Sainte-Foy]: Chaire d'étude
sur la condition des femmes, Université Laval, [1991]. 16 p.;
ISBN: 2-9801950-2-2. [6203]

"Répertoire bibliographique." Dans: *Culture*; (1940-1970) ;
ISSN: 0317-2066. [0095]

**Répertoire de documents relatifs aux mesures d'accueil et de
francisation, au P.E.L.O. et l'éducation interculturelle:
préscolaire, primaire, secondaire.** Québec: Gouvernement
du Québec, Services aux communautés culturelles, 1988. 50,
[2] p.; ISBN: 2-550-14451-1. [3692]

Répertoire de documents sur la femme. 4e éd. [Ottawa]:
Secrétariat d'État, 1992. 60, 58 p.; ISBN: 0-662-59260-3. [3900]

Répertoire de l'édition au Québec. Montréal: Edi-Québec,
1972-1976. 3 vol.; ISSN: 0315-5943. [0342]

**Répertoire de matériel éducatif dans le domaine de
l'environnement.** Québec: Gouvernement du Québec,
Ministère de l'environnement, [1988]. 128 p.; ISBN: 2-550-
18724-5. [5263]

Répertoire de matériel éducatif en nutrition. [Montréal]:
Conseil scolaire de l'île de Montréal, [1983]. 1 vol. (f.
mobiles). [3621]

**Répertoire de périodiques québécois en santé et services
sociaux.** [Québec]: Service de l'évaluation, prévention et
services communautaires, Ministère de la santé et des
services sociaux, 1987. 2 f., 7, [270] p.: ill.; ISBN: 2-550-17408-
9. [5964]

Répertoire de ressources sur le sida. Ottawa: Centre national
de documentation sur le sida, Association canadienne de
santé publique, 1992. iv, 22, 22, iv p. [5712]

**Répertoire des documents écrits et audiovisuels relatifs à la
famille.** [Québec]: Gouvernement du Québec, Ministère de
l'éducation, Direction de la coordination des réseaux, c1991.
iii, 188 p.; ISBN: 2-550-15520-3. [6695]

**Répertoire des historiens et historiennes de l'Amérique
française.** Outremont [Québec]: Institut d'histoire de
l'Amérique française, 1990. [env. 250] p. [2084]

**Répertoire des publications des sociétés d'histoire et de
généalogie du Québec.** [Montréal]: Fédération des sociétés
d'histoire du Québec, 1979-1981. ISSN: 0228-3379. [2014]

**Répertoire des textes du Centre d'essai des auteurs
dramatiques.** Montréal: Cead, [1981]. 151 p.: ill. [1186]

Reps, John W.
Views and viewmakers of urban America: lithographs of
towns and cities in the United States and Canada, notes on
the artists and publishers, and a union catalog of their
work, 1825-1925. Columbia: University of Missouri Press,
1984. xvi, 570 p.: ill. (some col.); ISBN: 0-8262-0416-
3. [4403]

**Research and studies: an annotated bibliography/Recherche
et communiqué: bibliographie annotée.** Vanier, Ont.:
Secretariat for Fitness in the Third Age, 1984. 24 p.; ISBN: 0-
919963-20-X. [1834]

**A Research bibliography on immigration to British
Columbia.** Victoria: Immigration Policy Branch, Province of
British Columbia, 1992. ii, 50 p.; ISBN: 0-7726-1640-X. [4293]

Research bibliography on the cultural industries. [Ottawa:
Futures, 1979]. 86 p. (Arts research monograph ; no. 4) [0693]

**Research in criminology by staff of the Centre of
Criminology during the 1970's.** [Toronto]: Centre of
Criminology, University of Toronto, 1980. vi, 95 p.; ISBN: 0-
919584-53-5. [2223]

Resnick, Gary
An annotated bibliography of current research on rape and
other sexual offences. Toronto: Ontario Provincial
Secretariat for Justice, 1979. 94 p. [2202]

Resources law bibliography. [Calgary]: Canadian Institute of
Resources Law, c1980. xvi, 537 p.; ISBN: 0-919269-01-X. [2224]

Retailing and wholesaling in Canada: information sources.
[Ottawa]: Distribution Services Division, Industry, Science
and Technology Canada, 1990. 40 p.; ISBN: 0-662-17708-
8. [2770]

Retfalvi, Andrea
"Les expositions de l'année au Canada/The year's
exhibitions in Canada." Dans: *RACAR (Revue d'art
canadienne, Canadian Art Review)*; Vol. 5, no 1 (1978)-vol. 12,
no 1 (1985). [0709]

"A retrospective bibliography [on archives]." In: *Archivaria*;
Vol. 1, no. 1 (Winter 1975-76)-No. 6 (Summer 1978) [1627]

Revai, Elisabeth
Les périodiques de la collection Canadiana de Louis
Melzack: journaux de langue française. Montréal: Service

des collections des bibliothèques, Université de Montréal, 1974. iv, 59 f. [6021]

Review of historical publications relating to Canada, 1896-1917-18. Toronto: University of Toronto Press [etc.], 1897-1919. 22 vol. [1899]

Revill (A.D.) Associates
Annotated bibliography and literature review of Auyuittuq National Park. Belleville: A.D. Revill Associates, 1975. 3 vol. [3011]

Revue sélective des recherches en matière de justice pénale. Ottawa: Solliciteur général Canada, Division des communications, c1981. ii, 95 p.; ISBN: 0-662-91464-3. [2237]

Reynolds, Grace
"Bibliographies by Library School students." In: *Ontario Library Review*; Vol. 32, no. 2 (May 1948) p. 142-145.; ISSN: 0030-2996. [0058]

Reynolds, Robert; Sidor, Nicholas
Research in progress on Canadian federalism and intergovernmental relations: September, 1979. Kingston, Ont.: Institute of Intergovernmental Relations, Queen's University, c1979. 34 p. [2447]

Reynolds, Roy
A guide to periodicals and books relating to education in the Ontario Archives. [Toronto]: Department of History and Philosophy of Education, Ontario Institute for Studies in Education, c1976. iii l., 149 p. (Educational record series / Department of History and Philosophy of Education, Ontario Institute for Studies in Education ; 7) [3516]

A guide to published government documents relating to education in Ontario. [Toronto]: Department of History and Philosophy, Ontario Institute for Studies in Education, [1971]. i, 47 l. (Educational record series / Department of History and Philosophy, Ontario Institute for Studies in Education ; 2) [3424]

Rheault, Marie
Bibliographie sommaire sur la Côte-Nord et les régions circonvoisines. Sept-Iles: Bibliothèque municipale, [1975]. 36 f. [0337]

Rhodenizer, Vernon Blair
At the sign of the Hand and Pen: Nova Scotian authors. Toronto: Canadiana House, 1968. 42 p. [1045]

Canadian literature in English. [Montreal: Printed by Quality Press, c1965]. 1055 p. [1030]

Ricci, Paolo F.; Maclaren, Virginia
Selected and annotated readings on planning theory and practice. Ottawa: Department of Geography and Regional Planning, University of Ottawa, 1977. 72 p. (Research note / Department of Geography and Regional Planning, University of Ottawa ; no. 16) [3022]

Rich, Obadiah
Bibliotheca americana nova: a catalogue of books relating to America, in various languages, including voyages to the Pacific and round the world, and collections of voyages and travels printed since the year 1700, compiled principally from the works themselves, by O. Rich. London: Rich and Sons, 1846. 2 vol. [6713]

A catalogue of books relating principally to America: arranged under the years in which they were printed. London: O. Rich, 1832. 129 p. [0002]

Catalogue of books relating to North and South America, including also voyages round the world, collections of voyages and travels, &c., being the duplicates of Mr. Rich's American collection. London: O. Rich, 1844.

48 p. [6709]

Richardson, James
Black spruce research by the Canadian Forestry Service in Newfoundland. St. John's: Newfoundland Forest Research Centre, 1981. 36 l. (Newfoundland Forest Research Centre Information report ; N-X-206; ISSN: 0704-7657); ISBN: 0-662-11872-3. [4973]

Richardson, Judith A.
Mental health and aging: an annotated bibliography. Winnipeg: Centre on Aging, University of Manitoba, c1984. viii, 292 p.; ISBN: 0-920421-00-8. [5663]

Richardson, R. Alan; MacDonald, Bertrum H.
Science and technology in Canadian history: a bibliography of primary sources to 1914. Thornhill, Ont.: HSTC Publications, c1987. 105 microfiches + 1 pamphlet in loose-leaf binder (17 p.). (Research tools for the history of Canadian science and technology ; no. 3; ISSN: 0715-9668); ISBN: 0-9690475-4-1. [4632]

Richardson, W. George
A survey of Canadian mining history. [Montreal]: Canadian Institute of Mining and Metallurgy, 1974. iii, 115 p. (Special volume / Canadian Institute of Mining and Metallurgy ; 14) [4784]

Richer, Suzanne
Aménagement polyvalent de la forêt: une bibliographie rétrospective, 1960-1973. Sainte-Foy, Québec: Bibliothèque, Centre de recherches forestières des Laurentides, Service canadien des forêts, 1973. 30 p. (Document / Centre de recherches forestières des Laurentides, Bibliothèque ; no 2) [4937]

Publications scientifiques – scientific publications, Laboratoire de recherches forestières, région de Québec. Ste-Foy, Québec: Service canadien des forêts, Ministère des pêches et des forêts, 1970. [75] f. (Laboratoire de recherches forestières Rapports d'information ; Q-F-X-2) [4927]

Le sirop d'érable: une bibliographie rétrospective, 1949-1971. Sainte-Foy, Québec: Bibliothèque, Centre de recherches forestières des Laurentides, Service canadien des forêts, 1973. 5 p. (Document / Centre de recherches forestières des Laurentides, Bibliothèque ; no 1) [4938]

Richer, Suzanne; Robidoux, Meridel D.
Liste des publications scientifiques du personnel de recherche du CRFL. 2e éd. Ste-Foy, Québec: Centre de recherches forestières des Laurentides, 1974. 144 p. [4945]

Richeson, Meg
Canadian rural sociology bibliography. Monticello, Ill.: Council of Planning Librarians, 1971. 58 p. (Council of Planning Librarians Exchange bibliography ; 238) [3102]

Richling, Joanne
Work and workers: an annotated bibliography for secondary schools. Halifax, N.S.: Committee on Labour Education in the Schools, Henson College of Public Affairs and Continuing Education, Dalhousie University, 1986. 128 p. (Work and workers: a resource for teachers; ISSN: 0829-8955); ISBN: 0-7703-0966-6. [2909]

Richmond, Anthony H.
Comparative studies in the economic adaptation of immigrants in Canada: a literature review. Downsview, Ont.: York University, Institute for Behavioural Research, 1982. viii, 226 p.; ISBN: 0-919604-95-1. [2883]

Ricketts, Alan Stuart

Dorothy Livesay: an annotated bibliography. Downsview, Ont.: ECW Press, c1983. [75] p., ISBN. 0 920763 57 X. [7118]

"Dorothy Livesay: an annotated bibliography." In: *The annotated bibliography of Canada's major authors*, Vol. 4, edited by Robert Lecker and Jack David. Downsview, Ont.: ECW Press, c1983. P. 129-203.; ISBN: 0-920802-52-4. [7149]

Rico, José M.

"Commissions d'enquête sur la justice pénale au Canada." Dans: *Acta criminologica*; Vol. 4, (janvier 1971) p. 209-219.; ISSN: 0065-1168. [2121]

Ricou, Laurence R.

"Miriam [Dworkin] Waddington: an annotated bibliography." In: *The annotated bibliography of Canada's major authors*, Vol. 6, edited by Robert Lecker and Jack David. Toronto: ECW Press, 1985. P. 287-388.; ISBN: 0-920802-93-1. [7358]

"Miriam Waddington: a checklist, 1936-1975." In: *Essays on Canadian Writing*; No. 12 (Fall 1978) p. 162-191.; ISSN: 0316-0300. [7357]

Ricouart, Janine

"Bibliographie sur Marie-Claire Blais." Dans: *Quebec Studies*; Vol. 10 (Spring-Summer 1990) p. 51-59.; ISSN: 0737-3759. [6852]

Riddell, Janet

Information motherlode: geological source material for BC. Victoria: Province of British Columbia, Ministry of Energy, Mines and Petroleum Resources, Geological Survey Branch, 1990. 38 p. (Information circular / Province of British Columbia, Geological Survey Branch ; 1990-15; ISSN: 0825-5431); ISBN: 0-771-88965-8. [4879]

Rideout, E. Brock; Najat, Sandra

City school district reorganization: an annotated bibliography; centralization and decentralization in the government of metropolitan areas with special emphasis on the organization, administration and financing of large-city school systems. [Toronto]: Ontario Institute for Studies in Education, [c1967]. v, 93 p. (Educational research series / Ontario Institute for Studies in Education ; no. 1) [3395]

Rider, Lillian M.

"Summary of developments in Canadian subject and area bibliography since 1974." In: *Canadian Issues*; Vol. 4 (1982) p. 3-27.; ISSN: 0318-8442. [1653]

Riedel, Walter E.

"Verzeichnis kanadischer Literatur in deutscher Übersetzung." In: *Das literarische Kanadabild: eine Studie zur Rezeption kanadischer Literatur in deutscher Übersetzung.* Bonn: Bouvier, 1980. P. 116-140. (Studien zur Germanistik, Anglistik und Komparatistik ; Bd. 92; ISSN: 0340-594X); ISBN: 3-416-01544-4. [1174]

Rigby, M.S.

List of publications in connection with the work of the Biological Board of Canada 1922-1930. Ottawa: Biological Board of Canada, 1932. 22 p. (Biological Board of Canada Bulletin ; no. 28) [5319]

Rightmire, Robert W.

"A research bibliography for Canadian large cents." In: *Canadian Numismatic Journal*; Vol. 20, no. 6 (June 1975) p. 241-242.; ISSN: 0008-4573. [1780]

Riley, Marvin P.

The Hutterian Brethren: an annotated bibliography with special reference to South Dakota Hutterite colonies. Brookings: Sociology Department, Agricultural Experiment Station, South Dakota State University, 1965. 188 p.: map. [1517]

Rinfret, Gabriel-Édouard

Le théâtre canadien d'expression française: répertoire analytique des origines à nos jours. [Montréal]: Leméac, 1975-[1978]. 4 vol.; ISBN: 0-7761-9408-9. [0967]

Rioux, Bernard; Bernier, Lise

Travail, syndicalisme: bibliographie. Montréal: Conseil de développement social du Montréal métropolitain, 1972. 2 vol. [2810]

Ripley, Diane Lorraine; Rounds, Richard C.

Rural communication: information and innovation in farming: a literature review. Brandon, Man.: Rural Development Institute, Brandon University, 1993. vii, 65 p.: ill.; ISBN: 1-89539-713-8. [4724]

Ripley, Gordon M.

A bibliography of Elgin County and St. Thomas, Ontario. St. Thomas: [St. Thomas History Project], 1973. 55 l. [0448]

Risk, R.C.B.

"Books, articles, case comments and reviews: John Willis." In: *Dalhousie Law Journal*; Vol. 9, no. 3 (December 1985) p. 551-554.; ISSN: 0317-1663. [7366]

Les risques pour la reproduction inhérants au milieu de travail au Canada: bibliographie annotée. Ottawa: Bureau de la main-d'oeuvre féminine, Travail Canada, c1988. 84 p.; ISBN: 0-662-94929-3. [5683]

Ritchie, J.R. Brent; Mokkelbost, Per B.; Furlong, Carla B.

Banking research from a Canadian perspective: an annotated bibliography. [Montreal]: Institute of Canadian Bankers, 1984. viii, 519 p. [2703]

Riverin-Simard, Danielle

"Apprentissage observationnel abstrait et éducation permanente: revue de littérature." Dans: *Orientation professionnelle*; Vol. 16, no 4 (décembre 1980) p. 13-40.; ISSN: 0030-5413. [3574]

Riverin-Simard, Danielle; Hamel, Lucie; Couture, Francine

Bibliographie commentée sur l'apprenant-adulte. [Sainte-Foy, Québec]: INRS-Éducation: Téléuniversité, 1978. 14 f. [3544]

Rivet-Panaccio, Colette; Awad, Amal; Cardinal, Robert

Les bibliothèques canadiennes à l'ère de l'automatisation: synthèse bibliographique 1970-1972. Montréal: École de bibliothéconomie, Université de Montréal, 1972. 54 p. (Documentation en diagonale ; no 1) [1596]

Robb, Marion Dennis

Sources of Nova Scotian history, 1840-1867. Halifax, N.S.: Dalhousie University, 1927. 296 l. [0199]

Roberge, Michel

L'expertise québécoise en gestion des documents administratifs: bibliographie thématique et chronologique, 1962-1987. 1re éd. Saint-Augustin, Québec: Gestar, 1987. 1 vol. (en pagination multiple); ISBN: 2-9800920-0-2. [1695]

Roberge-Brassard, Jocelyne

L'École, son contexte social et le contexte de l'élève: relevé bibliographique commenté un vie d'une recherche. Ste-Foy, Québec: INRS-Éducation, 1980. 137 f. [3575]

Robert, Jacques

"Bibliographie et index de Gérard Morisset." Dans: *A la découverte du patrimoine avec Gérard Morisset*. Québec:

Ministère des affaires culturelles, 1981. P. 229-255.; ISBN: 2-551-04204-6. [7201]

Robert, Jean-Claude

"La recherche en histoire du Canada." Dans: *Revue internationale d'études canadiennes*; No 1-2 (printemps-automne 1990) p. 11-33.; ISSN: 1180-3991. [2085]

Robert, Lucie

"Bibliographie de Naïm Kattan." Dans: *Voix et Images*; Vol. 11, no 1 (automne 1985) p. 45-54.; ISSN: 0318-9201. [7084]

"Bibliographie de Yolande Villemaire." Dans: *Voix et Images*; Vol. 11, no 3 (printemps 1986) p. 455-462.; ISSN: 0318-9201. [7353]

Robert, Véronique

Brégent, Michel-Georges. Don Mills, Ont.: PRO Canada, 1984. 7 p.: music, port. [6874]

Claude Vivier. Don Mills, Ont.: PRO Canada, 1984. 7, [1] p.: music, port. [7356]

Walter Boudreau. Don Mills, Ont.: PRO Canada, 1984. 7 p.: music, port. [6861]

"Robert McQueen, 1896-1941: [bibliography]." In: *Canadian Journal of Economics and Political Science*; Vol. 7, no. 2 (May 1941) p. 281-283.; ISSN: 0315-4890. [7185]

Roberts, Carol; Macdonald, Lynne

Timothy Findley: an annotated bibliography. Toronto: ECW Press, 1990. x, 136 p.; ISBN: 1-55022-112-4. [6986]

Roberts, D.W.A.; Miska, John P.

Cold hardiness and winter survival of plants, 1965-1975. Slough, England: Commonwealth Agricultural Bureaux, 1980. ix, 407 p. (Commonwealth Bureau of Soils Special publication ; no. 8); ISBN: 0-85198-477-0. [5454]

Roberts, Debra

Selected bibliography on East-West commercial relations. Ottawa: East-West Project, Institute of Soviet and East European Studies, Carleton University, c1980. 134 p.; ISBN: 0-7709-0095-X. [2663]

Roberts, F.X.

"A bibliography of Robert William Service, 1874-1958." In: *Four Decades of Poetry, 1890-1930*; Vol. 1, no. 1 (January 1976) p. 76-85.; ISSN: 0308-0889. [7305]

Roberts, Hazel J.

Faculty collective bargaining in Canadian universities, 1974-1979/La négociation collective chez les professeurs des universités canadiennes, 1974-1979. Ottawa: Association of Universities and Colleges of Canada, Library, 1980. iii l., 44 p.; ISBN: 0-88876-066-3. [2868]

Roberts, R.P.; Blais, J.

"Bibliographie annotée de la didactique de la traduction et de l'interprétation/The didactics of translation and interpretation: an annotated bibliography." Dans: *Revue de l'Université d'Ottawa*; Vol. 51, no 3 (juillet-septembre 1981) p. 560-589.; ISSN: 0041-9206. [1453]

Roberts, Wayne, et al.

The Hamilton working class, 1820-1977: a bibliography. Hamilton, Ont.: McMaster University, Labour Studies Programme, 1978. 62 p. [2856]

Roberts-Pichette, Patricia

Annotated bibliography of permafrost-vegetation-wildlife-landform relationships. Ottawa: Canadian Forestry Service, Department of the Environment, 1972. 350 p. (Forest Management Institute Information report ; FMR-X-43) [5066]

Robertson, Alex

The Apex 8000 numerical. [Pointe Claire, Quebec: A. Robertson], 1974. vii, 58 l. [0841]

Canadian Compo numericals. Pointe Claire, Quebec: A. Robertson, 1978. v, 82 l. [0870]

Canadian Gennett and Starr-Gennett 9000 numerical. Pointe Claire, Quebec: [s.n.], 1972. iv, 30 l. [0836]

Robertson, Carolynn

A bibliography of standards relevant to indexing and abstracting and the presentation of information/ Bibliographie des normes relatives à l'analyse documentaire, à l'indexation et à la présentation de renseignements. Ottawa: National Library of Canada, 1987. 19 p. (Bibliographies / Library Documentation Centre; ISSN: 0226-4226) [1696]

Marketing the special library: a selective bibliography/Le marketing et la bibliothèque spécialisée: bibliographie sélective. Ottawa: National Library of Canada, 1989. 13 p. (Bibliographies / Library Development Centre ; no. 2; ISSN: 0847-2467) [1710]

The reference interview: a selective bibliography/L'entrevue de référence: bibliographie sélective. Ottawa: National Library of Canada, 1985. i, 9 p. (Bibliographies / Library Documentation Centre; ISSN: 0226-4226) [1671]

Surveys of library collections in Canada, 1955-1981/ Inventaire des collections des bibliothèques canadiennes, 1955-1981. Ottawa: National Library of Canada, 1982. i, 11 p. (Bibliographies / Library Documentation Centre; ISSN: 0226-4226) [1654]

Robertson, Paul B.

Bibliography of Canadian meteorite impact sites. Ottawa: Earth Physics Branch, Department of Energy, Mines and Resources, 1978. [28] p. [4808]

Robertson, William Murdoch

Selected bibliography of Canadian forest literature, 1917-1946. Ottawa: Department of Mines and Resources, Mines, Forests and Scientific Services Branch, 1949. 332 l. (in 3 parts). (Miscellaneous silvicultural research note / Canada Department of Mines and Resources, Mines, Forests and Scientific Services Branch ; no. 6) [4919]

Robertson, Yves

"Intelligence d'entreprise" et veille technologique: bibliographie sélective. Québec: Conseil de la science et de la technologie, Centre de documentation, 1991. 42 p.; ISBN: 2-550-22856-1. [2778]

Robeson, Virginia R.; Flow, A.F.

Documents in Canadian history: a teacher's guide. Toronto: Ontario Institute for Studies in Education, c1977. v, 33 p.: ill. (Curriculum series / Ontario Institute for Studies in Education ; 26); ISBN: 0-7744-0150-8. [1994]

Robeson, Virginia R.; Sylvester, Christine

Teaching Canadian studies: an evaluation of print materials, grades 1-13. Toronto: OISE Press, 1980. ix, 340 p. (Curriculum series / Ontario Institute for Studies in Education ; 40); ISBN: 0-7744-0184-2. [0132]

Robichaud, Michèle

Revision and patriation of the Constitution 1965-1982: select bibliography/Révision et repatriement de la Constitution 1965-1982: bibliographie sélective. Ottawa: Library of Parliament, Information and Reference Branch, 1982. 89, A4, B24 l. (Select bibliography / Library of Parliament, Information and Reference Branch ; no. 206) [2248]

Robins, G. Lewis

A bibliography of the pike perch of the genus Stizostedion (including the genus known as Lucioperca). Winnipeg: Freshwater Institute, Fisheries Research Board of Canada, 1970. 67 p. (Fisheries Research Board of Canada Technical report ; no. 161; ISSN: 0068-7553) [5358]

Robinson, Betty Belle

Bibliography of population and immigration, with special reference to Canada. [Hamilton, Ont.: McMaster University], 1949. 20 l. [2953]

Robinson, Christopher D.

PRECIS: an annotated bibliography, 1969-1977. 2nd ed. Toronto: C.D. Robinson, 1977. vi, 26 l. [1623]

Robinson, Christopher D.; Smiley, Alison

Suspended drivers in Ontario: license disqualification: a review of the literature. Toronto: Safety Coordination & Development Office, Ontario Ministry of Transportation, 1989. 27 l.; ISBN: 0-77295-871-8. [4505]

Robinson, Douglas

Automated acquisitions: a selective bibliography for librarians/Acquisitions automatisées: bibliographie sélective pour bibliothécaires. Ottawa: National Library of Canada, 1984. 10 p. (Bibliographies / Library Documentation Centre; ISSN: 0226-4226) [1665]

Cooperative reference: a selective bibliography for librarians/Travail de référence en commun: bibliographie sélective pour bibliothécaires. Ottawa: National Library of Canada, 1985. 5 p. (Bibliographies / Library Documentation Centre; ISSN: 0226-4226) [1672]

Telecommunications and libraries: a selective bibliography for librarians/Télécommunications et bibliothèques: bibliographie sélective pour bibliothécaires. Ottawa: National Library of Canada, 1984. 9 p. (Bibliographies / Library Documentation Centre; ISSN: 0226-4226) [1666]

Videotex: a selective bibliography for librarians/Le vidéotex: une bibliographie sélective pour les bibliothécaires. Ottawa: National Library of Canada, 1981. 12 p. (Bibliographies / Library Documentation Centre; ISSN: 0226-4226) [1648]

Robinson, Jill M.

Seas of earth: an annotated bibliography of Saskatchewan literature as it relates to the environment. Regina: Canadian Plains Research Center, University of Regina, 1977. x, 139 p.: ill., ports., 19 l. of pl. (Canadian Plains reports / Canadian Plains Research Center, University of Regina ; 2); ISBN: 0-88977-010-7. [1113]

Robinson, Paul

After survival: a teacher's guide to Canadian resources. Toronto: P. Martin Associates, c1977. 329 p.; ISBN: 0-88778-147-0. [0124]

Indian, Inuit, Métis: selected bibliography. Halifax, N.S.: Atlantic Institute of Education, 1980. 19 l. [1344]

Native writers and artists of Canada. Rev. ed. Halifax, N.S.: Atlantic Institute of Education, 1978. 29 p.: map. [3995]

Robinson, Susan E.; Scott, W.B.

A selected bibliography on mercury in the environment, with subject listing. Toronto: Royal Ontario Museum, 1974. 54 p. (Royal Ontario Museum Life sciences miscellaneous publications; ISSN: 0082-5093); ISBN: 0-88854-166-X. [5091]

Robitaille, Alphéda

"Hommage à un historien: Antonio Drolet, 1904-1970: bibliographie." Dans: Archives; Vol. 2 (juillet-décembre 1970) p. 32-42.; ISSN: 0044-9423. [6957]

Robitaille, André

Bibliographie annotée des documents produits par la Division Écologie du Service de l'inventaire forestier, 1987-1990. Charlesbourg, Québec: Division de l'écologie, 1990. 14 p. [6407]

Robitaille, Denis; Waiser, Joan

Theses in Canada: a bibliographic guide/Thèses au Canada: guide bibliographique. 2nd ed. Ottawa: National Library of Canada, 1986. xi, 72 p.; ISBN: 0-660-53228-X. [6188]

Robitaille, J.A.; Mailhot, Yves

Répertoire bibliographique des poissons d'eau douce et diadromes du Saint-Laurent, 1900-1987. Québec: Ministère du loisir, de la chasse et de la pêche, Direction de la gestion des espèces et des habitats, 1989. viii, 81 p.; ISBN: 2-550-20543-X. [5552]

Robitaille, Lucie

"Bibliographie: tableau approximatif des principaux ouvrages traitant de la langue française au Canada." Dans: Cahiers de l'Académie canadienne-française; Vol. 5 (1960) p. 139-156.; ISSN: 0065-0528. [1418]

Robson, Mark; Eagles, Paul F.J.; Waters, Joanne

Ecotourism: an annotated bibliography. Waterloo, Ont.: Department of Recreation and Leisure Studies, University of Waterloo, 1992. 59 p. (Occasional paper / Department of Recreation and Leisure Studies, University of Waterloo ; no. 19) [1870]

Robson, Robert

Canadian single industry communities: a literature review and annotated bibliography. Sackville, N.B.: Rural and Small Town Research Studies Program, Department of Geography, Mount Allison University, 1986. i, 148 p.: ill.; ISBN: 0-88828-055-6. [4413]

Selected sources on northern housing and related community infrastructure: an annotated bibliography. [Winnipeg]: Institute of Urban Studies, University of Winnipeg, 1989. ii, 84 p. (Bibliographica / Institute of Urban Studies, University of Winnipeg ; 1); ISBN: 0-920213-66-9. [4432]

Rocan, Claude

"Bibliography of works on Louis Riel/Bibliographie des ouvrages et articles sur Louis Riel." In: The collected writings of Louis Riel: Les écrits complèts de Louis Riel, edited by George F.G. Stanley. Edmonton: University of Alberta Press, 1985. Vol. 5, p. 131-205.; ISBN: 0-88864-105-2. [7266]

Rochais, Gérard

Bibliographie annotée de l'enseignement supérieur au Québec. Montréal: Commission d'étude sur les universités, 1979-1980. 2 vol.; ISBN: 2-550-00016-1 (édition complète). [3576]

Rochon, Denis

Forestry Canada publications, 1986-1988/Publications de Forêts Canada, 1986 à 1988. Ottawa: Forestry Canada, 1989. 63 p.; ISBN: 0-66-566838-9. [6401]

Rochon, James; O'Hara, Susan; Swain, Larry

Exposure to the risk of an accident: a review of the literature, and the methodology for the Canadian study. Ottawa: Transport Canada, Road Safety, 1978. 1 vol. (in various pagings). [4470]

Rockwood, Eleanor Ruth

Books on the Pacific northwest for small libraries. New York: H.W. Wilson, 1923. 55 p. [0554]

Rodgers, C.D.; Scott, Robert Nelson

The congenital upper-extremity amputee: a review of the literature with emphasis on early fittings of powered prostheses. Fredericton: Bio-Engineering Institute, University of New Brunswick, 1980. 24 l. [5631]

Rodgers, Evan

An annotated bibliography on planning for pedestrians. Toronto: University of Toronto-York University Joint Program in Transportation, 1974. 23, 3 p. (University of Toronto-York University Joint Program in Transportation Research Report ; no. 15; ISSN: 0316-9456) [4338]

Rodrigue, Denis

"Le cycle de Pâques au Québec et dans l'Ouest de la France." Dans: *Archives de Folklore*; Vol. 24 (1983) p. 313-329.; ISSN: 0085-5243. [4592]

Rogers, Amos Robert

American recognition of Canadian authors writing in English, 1890-1960. [Ann Arbor, Mich.: University Microfilms, 1974]. 2 vol. [1086]

Books and pamphlets by New Brunswick writers, 1890-1950. [Fredericton, N.B.: 1953]. vi, 73 l. [0203]

Rogers, Helen F.

Bases de données canadiennes lisibles par machine: un répertoire et un guide. Ottawa: Bibliothèque nationale du Canada, 1987. 140, 134 p.; ISBN: 0-660-53734-6. [0157]

Canadian machine-readable databases: a directory and guide. Ottawa: National Library of Canada, 1987. 134, 140 p.; ISBN: 0-660-53734-6. [0158]

Indian-Inuit authors: an annotated bibliography/Auteurs indiens et inuit: bibliographie annotée. Ottawa: National Library of Canada, 1974. 108 p. [3959]

Integrated systems: a selective bibliography on choosing, planning, implementing, managing, evaluating, and preparing RFPs for integrated library systems/Une bibliographie sélective sur le choix, la planification, la mise en oeuvre, la gestion, l'évaluation et la préparation d'appels d'offre pour les systèmes intégrés de bibliothèques. Ottawa: National Library of Canada, 1989. 6 p. (Bibliographies / Library Documentation Centre; ISSN: 0226-4226) [1711]

Library services for seniors: a selective bibliography/ Services de bibliothèque aux personnes âgées: une bibliographie sélective. [Ottawa]: National Library of Canada, 1989. 10 p. [1712]

Rohrlick, Paula; Pellatt, Anna

Canadian native women: an annotated bibliography. Montreal: Programme in the Anthropology of Development, McGill University, 1978. 146, 21 p. [3782]

Rokala, D.A.; Bruce, Sharon G.; Meiklejohn, Christopher

Diabetes mellitus in native populations of North America: an annotated bibliography. Winnipeg: Northern Health Research Unit, University of Manitoba, c1991. 221 p. (Monograph series / Northern Health Research Unit, University of Manitoba ; no. 4); ISBN: 1-895034-05-1. [5706]

Roland, Charles G.

"Annotated bibliography of Canadian military medical history: preliminary checklist." In: *Medical Services Journal Canada*; Vol. 23, no. 1 (January 1967) p. 42-59.; ISSN: 0368-9204. [5572]

Secondary sources in the history of Canadian medicine: a bibliography. Waterloo, Ont.: Hannah Institute for the History of Medicine, 1984. xxiii, 190 p.; ISBN: 0-88920-182-X. [5664]

Roland, Charles G.; Potter, Paul

An annotated bibliography of Canadian medical periodicals, 1826-1975. [Toronto]: Hannah Institute for the History of Medicine, c1979. xvii, 77 p.: ill., facsim.; ISBN: 0-7720-1243-1. [5936]

Rolfe, Brenda

The credit system: an annotated bibliography. Toronto: Library, Reference & Information Services, Ontario Institute for Studies in Education, 1974. x, 21 p. (Current bibliography / Ontario Institute for Studies in Education ; no. 6) [3487]

Rollins, Caron

"Canadian Indian treaties: a bibliography." In: *Canadian Law Libraries*; Vol. 15, no. 2 (April 1990) p. 68-72.; ISSN: 1180-176X. [4113]

Rome, David

A bibliography of Jewish Canadiana [microform]. Montreal: National Archives, Canadian Jewish Congress, 1988. 118 microfiches (ca. 55 fr. each) in binder with 3 printed l. [4260]

The early Jewish presence in Canada: a book lover's ramble through Jewish Canadiana. Montreal: Bronfman Collection of Jewish Canadiana, 1971. [163] l. [4154]

Jews in Canadian literature: a bibliography. rev. ed. Montreal: Canadian Jewish Congress and Jewish Public Library, 1964. 2 vol. [1022]

A selected bibliography of Jewish Canadiana. Montreal: Canadian Jewish Congress and The Jewish Public Library, 1959. 1 vol. (unpaged). [4132]

Rome, David; Nefsky, Judith; Obermeir, Paule

Les Juifs du Québec: bibliographie rétrospective annotée. Québec: Institut québécois de recherche sur la culture, 1981. xvi, 317 p. (Instruments de travail / Institut québécois de recherche sur la culture ; no 1); ISBN: 2-89224-004-2. [4204]

Rompkey, Ronald George

Sir Wilfred Thomason Grenfell (1865-1940): a selective bibliography (annotated and including periodical items). St. John's: Memorial University of Newfoundland, 1965. 20 l. [7029]

Ronald, K., et al.

An annotated bibliography on the Pinnipedia. Charlottenlund, Denmark: International Council for the Exploration of the Sea, 1976. 785 p. [5410]

Rondeau, Guy; Desgranges, Jean-Luc

Effets des perturbations naturelles et sylvicoles sur l'avifaune forestière: une synthèse bibliographique. Sainte-Foy, Québec: Service canadien de la faune, 1992. iv, 30 p. (Série de rapports techniques du Service canadien de la faune ; no 148; ISSN: 0831-6481); ISBN: 0-662-97394-1. [5018]

Room 302 Books (Firm)

Room 302 Books, list #4: bpNichol, a ranging. Toronto: Room 302 Books, 1987. [16] p. [7214]

Rooney, Frances

"[Women and disability]: bibliography/[Les femmes handicapées]: bibliographie." In: *Resources for Feminist Research*; Vol. 14, no. 1 (March 1985) p. 84-92.; ISSN: 0707-8412. [3840]

Root, John D.

Index to geological, bedrock topography, soils, and groundwater maps of Alberta. [Edmonton]: Alberta Research Council, 1978. 66 p. (Earth sciences report /

Alberta Research Council ; 77-3) [6564]

Roper, Gordon

A Davies log." In: *Journal of Canadian Studies*, Vol. 12, no. 1 (February 1977) p. 4-19.; ISSN: 0021-9495. [6939]

Rose, Damaris; Galois, Robert; Wolfe, Jeanne

"John Bradbury, 1942-1988: bibliographie." Dans: *Cahiers de géographie de Québec*; Vol. 32, no 87 (décembre 1988) p. 373-374.; ISSN: 0007-9766. [6870]

Roseman, Daniel

"European Community-Canada relations: a selected bibliography, 1976-1981." In: *Revue d'intégration européenne: Journal of European Integration*; Vol. 4, no. 3 (Spring 1981) p. 327-334.; ISSN: 0703-6337. [2464]

Rosenbaum, H.

A survey of literature on televised language instruction. Toronto: Ontario Educational Communications Authority, Research and Development Branch, 1971. 9 p. (Papers and reports concerning educational communications ; no. 11) [3425]

Rosenberg, D.M.

Practical sampling of freshwater macrozoobenthos: a bibliography of useful texts, reviews and recent papers. Winnipeg: Western Region, Fisheries and Marine Service, Department of Fisheries and the Environment, 1978. 15 p. (Fisheries and Marine Service Technical report ; no. 790; ISSN: 0701-7626) [5423]

Rosenberg, Gertrude

Distance education in the Canadian North: annotated bibliography. Ottawa: Association of Canadian Universities for Northern Studies, c1984. iv, [1], 28 l. (Occasional publication / Association of Canadian Universities for Northern Studies ; no. 12); ISBN: 0-9690987-7-4. [3630]

Rosenberg, Neil V.

"A preliminary bibliography of Canadian old time instrumental music books." In: *Canadian Folk Music Journal*; Vol. 8 (1980) p. 20-22.; ISSN: 0318-2568. [0887]

Roseneder, Jan

University of Calgary theses: a bibliography, 1959-1978. Calgary: University of Calgary Libraries, 1983. 2 vol. (Bibliography series / University of Calgary Libraries ; no. 2); ISBN: 0-88953-048-3. [6173]

Rosenthal, Harald; Wilson, J. Scott

An updated bibliography (1845-1986) on ozone, its biological effects and technical applications. Ottawa: Department of Fisheries and Oceans, 1987. vii, 249 p. (Canadian technical report of fisheries and aquatic sciences ; no. 1542; ISSN: 0706-6457) [5252]

Ross, Aileen D.

The people of Montreal: a bibliography of studies of their lives and behaviour. Montreal: Catholic Community Services, 1976. 30 l. [4361]

Ross, Elspeth

"Children's books on contemporary North American Indian, Native, Métis life: a selected bibliography of books and professional reading materials." In: *Canadian Children's Literature*; No. 61 (1991) p. 29-43.; ISSN: 0319-0080. [1393]

Ross, R.R.

Reading disability and crime – link and remediation: an annotated bibliography. [Ottawa: s.n.], 1977. 37 p. [3160]

Ross, R.R.; McConkey, Nancy

Behaviour modification with the offender: an annotated bibliography. Ottawa: [s.n.], 1975. 81 p. [2146]

Ross, R.R.; McKay, H.B.; Doody, K.

The psychopath: a partially annotated bibliography. [Waterloo, Ont.]: University of Waterloo, 1971. 162 p. [3103]

Ross, Tim

Montreal maps: an annotated list. [Montreal]: McGill University, University Map Collection, 1975. 28 p.: maps. (Publication / University Map Collection, McGill University ; no. 2) [6548]

Rosval, Sergei J.

"University research on Russian Canadians." In: *Canadian Ethnic Studies*; Vol. 1, no. 1 (1969) p. 59-60.; ISSN: 0008-3496. [6100]

Rothbart, Linda S.

Trucking. Monticello, Ill.: Vance Bibliographies, 1990. 63 p. (Public administration series: Bibliography ; P-2882; ISSN: 0193-970X); ISBN: 0-7920-0542-2. [4514]

Rothman, William A.

A bibliography of collective bargaining in hospitals and related facilities, 1959-1968. Ann Arbor: Institute of Labor and Industrial Relations, University of Michigan-Wayne State University, 1970. 106 p. [2805]

Rothwell, Helene de F.

Canadian selection: filmstrips. Toronto: University of Toronto Press, c1980. xvi, 537 p.; ISBN: 0-8020-4586-3. [6644]

Rothwell, Stephen J.

Multi-media on Indians and Inuit of North America, 1965-1980 / Documents audio-visuels sur les Indiens et les Inuit de l'Amérique du Nord, 1965-1980. [Ottawa]: Inuit and Indian Affairs Program, Public Communications and Parliamentary Relations Branch, [1980]. 244 p. [6645]

Rouillard, Eugène

Les premiers almanachs canadiens. Lévis: P.–G. Roy, 1898. 80 p. [0276]

Rouillard, Jacques

Guide d'histoire du Québec: du régime français à nos jours: bibliographie commentée. Laval, Québec: Méridien, 1993. 354 p.; ISBN: 2-89415-052-0. [0416]

Rouland, Norbert

"L'ethnologie juridique des Inuit: approche bibliographique critique." Dans: *Études Inuit Studies*; Vol. 2, no 1 (1978) p. 120-131.; ISSN: 0701-1008. [3996]

Rouleau, Ernest

Bibliographie des travaux concernant la flore canadienne, parus dans *Rhodora*, de 1899 à 1943 inclusivement, précédée d'un index alphabétique de tous les noms botaniques nouveaux proposés dans cette revue. Montréal: Université de Montréal, Institute botanique, 1944. 367 p. (Contributions de l'Institut botanique de l'Université de Montréal ; no 54) [5323]

Rousseau, Camille; Alexandre, Claude; Labrecque, Olivette

Répertoire des films accessibles aux jeunes scientifiques. Montréal: Conseil de la jeunesse scientifique, 1975. vi, 147 p. [6627]

Répertoire des volumes et des revues accessibles aux jeunes scientifiques. [Montréal]: Conseil de la jeunesse scientifique, 1975. xi, 553 p. [4625]

Rousseau, Denis

"L'édition en bibliothéconomie au Québec." Dans: *Livre, bibliothèque et culture québécoise: mélanges offerts à Edmond Desrochers, s.j.* Montréal: ASTED, 1977. P. 219-267.; ISBN: 0-88606-000-1. [1624]

Rousseau, Guildo

Contes et récits littéraires de la Mauricie, 1850-1950: essai de bibliographie régionale. Trois-Rivières, Québec: Éditions CEDOLEQ, [1982]. 178 p. (Guides bibliographiques / Éditions CEDOLEQ ; 8); ISBN: 2-89060-012-2. [1197]

Rousseau, Jacques

"La cartographie de la région du Lac Mistassini: essai bibliographique." Dans: *Revue d'histoire de l'Amérique française*; Vol. 3, no 2 (septembre 1949) p. 289-312.; ISSN: 0035-2357. [6499]

Curriculum vitae et bibliographie [Jacques Rousseau]. [Montréal: s.n., 1970]. 75 f. [7278]

Le docteur J.-A. Crevier, médecin et naturaliste, 1824-1889: étude biographique et bibliographique. [Montréal: s.n.], 1940. 96 p.: ill. [6924]

"Le docteur J.-A. Crevier, médecin et naturaliste, 1824-1889: étude biographique et bibliographique." Dans: *Annales de l'ACFAS*; Vol. 6 (1940) p. 173-269.; ISSN: 0066-8842. [6925]

Essai bibliographique sur la région du lac Mistassini. Montréal: [s.n.], 1954. 155 f. [0287]

Essai de bibliographie botanique canadienne. Montréal: Université de Montréal, Institut botanique, 1934. 101 p. (en pagination multiple). [5320]

Rousseau, Jacques; Gauvreau, Marcelle; Morin, Claire

Bibliographie des travaux botaniques contenus dans les *Mémoires et Comptes rendus de la Société royale du Canada*, de 1882 à 1936 inclusivement. Montréal: Institut botanique de l'Université de Montréal, 1939. 117 p. (Contributions de l'Institut botanique de l'Université de Montréal ; no 33) [5322]

Rousselle, Jean

Bibliographie sur les inondations: 1850-1976. Québec: Ministère des richesses naturelles, Direction générale des eaux, 1977. 2 vol. [5128]

Roux, Françoise

"La littérature intime au Québec: éléments de bibliographie." Dans: *Revue de l'Université d'Ottawa*; Vol. 49, nos 1-2 (janvier-avril 1979) p. 84-88.; ISSN: 0041-9206. [1157]

Rowat, Louise

A list of publications in the Ottawa ACLD Library. Ottawa: Ottawa Association for Children with Learning Disabilities, 1985. 73 p. [3646]

Rowell's American newspaper directory. New York: Rowell; Printers' Ink Publishing Co., 1869-1908. 40 vol. [6001]

Roy, Antoine

"Bibliographie de généalogies et histoires de familles." Dans: *Rapport de l'archiviste de la Province de Québec*; Vol. 21 (1940-1941) p. 95-332. [1919]

"Bibliographie de M. L'Abbé Ivanhoë Caron." Dans: *Culture*; Vol. 3, (1942) p. 91-94.; ISSN: 0317-2066. [6896]

"Bibliographie des monographies et histoires de paroisses." Dans: *Rapport de l'archiviste de la Province de Québec*; Vol. 18 (1937-1938) p. 254-364. [1916]

"Bibliographie des travaux historiques du Père Archange Godbout, o.f.m. (1886-1960)." Dans: *Bulletin des recherches historiques*; Vol. 66, no 4 (octobre-novembre-décembre 1960) p. 69-83. [7021]

"Court exposé sur notre bibliographie générale des voyageurs au Canada." Dans: *Bulletin des recherches historiques*; Vol. 69, no. 1 (janvier 1967) p. 21-24. [1955]

L'oeuvre historique de Pierre-Georges Roy: bibliographie analytique. Paris: Jouve, 1928. xxxi, 268 p. [7285]

Roy, Bernadette Kelly; Miller, Dallas K.

The rights of indigenous peoples in international law: an annotated bibliography. [Saskatoon]: University of Saskatchewan Native Law Centre, 1985. [x], 97 p.; ISBN: 0-88880-163-7. [2278]

Roy, G. Ross; Gnarowski, Michael

Canadian poetry: a supplementary bibliography. Quebec: Culture, 1964. 13 p. [1023]

Roy, J.-B.

"La presse agricole au Québec." Dans: *Agriculture*; Vol. 29, no 3 (septembre 1972) p. 20-22.; ISSN: 0002-1687. [5906]

Roy, Jean

Bibliographie sélective des sources générales de documentation juridique canadienne et québécoise. Montréal: Ecole de bibliothécaires, Université de Montréal, 1962. 75 f. [2108]

"Liste des thèses et mémoires de maîtrise, D.E.S. et doctorat des facultés de droit du Québec." Dans: *Revue du Barreau*; No 27 (1967) p. 680-687.; ISSN: 0383-669X. [6088]

Roy, Jean-Luc

L'enseignement privé: liste annotée de quelques documents récents. Montréal: Centre d'animation, de développement et de recherche en éducation, 1977. 14 p. [3528]

Roy, Jean-Luc; Contant, André

L'agent de développement pédagogique: bibliographie sommaire sur ses principales tâches dans un collège. Montréal: Centre d'animation, de développement et de recherche en éducation, 1974. 21 f. [3488]

Bibliographie annotée sur l'analyse institutionnelle. Montréal: Centre d'animation, de développement et de recherche en éducation, [1975]. v, 155 p. [3507]

Roy, Jean-Marie; Beaulieu, Gérard; Talbot, Claire

Index des *Contributions du Département des Pêcheries*. Québec: Direction des pêcheries, Ministère de l'industrie et du commerce, 1967. 54 p. [4887]

Roy, Mary L.

Inland water transportation. Monticello, Ill.: Vance Bibliographies, 1990. 32 p. (Public administration series: Bibliography ; P-2883; ISSN: 0193-970X); ISBN: 0-7920-0543-0. [4515]

Roy, Paul-Martel

Politiques d'emploi des gouvernements au Québec: inventaire, bibliographie, éléments d'évaluation. Montréal: Laboratoire de recherche sur l'emploi, la répartition et la sécurité du revenu, Université du Québec à Montréal, 1982. [4], 79 f. (Cahier / Laboratoire de recherche sur l'emploi, la répartition et la sécurité du revenu, Université du Québec à Montréal ; 8202) [2884]

Roy, Pierre-Georges

Bibliographie de la poésie franco-canadienne. Lévis, Québec: [s.n.], 1900. 14 p. [0993]

Bibliographie lévisienne. Lévis: [s.n.], 1932. 24 p. [0281]

"Bibliographie lévisienne." Dans: *Bulletin des recherches historiques*; Vol. 38, no 8 (août 1932) p. 449-470. [0282]

Roy, Yvonne; Lemaire, Estelle

Anselme Longpré: bio-bibliographie. [Montréal: Centre Les Compagnons de Jésus et de Marie], 1984. 206 p.: portr. [7153]

Roy, Zo-Ann

Bibliographie des contes, récits et légendes du Canada-français. Boucherville, Québec: Éditions Proteau, [1983]. 326 p.; ISBN: 2-920369-17-2. [1356]

Royal Canadian College of Organists
Healey Willan. Toronto: Royal Canadian College of Organists, 1979. 34 p.: Ill., port. [7365]

Royal Canadian Mounted Police. Library
Industrial security: a bibliography. Ottawa: The Library, 1976. ii, 142 p. [2159]
Police misconduct – Canada: a bibliography. Ottawa: The Library, 1979. iii, 121 p. [2203]
Riots: [a bibliography]. [Ottawa]: R.C.M.P., 1976. 204 p. [2160]

Royal College of Physicians and Surgeons of Canada
Library and archival holdings in the Roddick Room, 1983/ Contenu de la bibliothèque et archives dans la salle Roddick, 1983. [Ottawa]: The College, [1983]. 206 p. [5656]

Royal Commonwealth Society. Library
Biography catalogue of the Library of the Royal Commonwealth Society. London: Royal Commonwealth Society, 1961. xxiii, 511 p. [6769]
Subject catalogue of the Library of the Royal Empire Society, formerly Royal Colonial Institute, by Evans Lewin. [London: The Society], 1930-1937. 4 vol. [6764]
Subject catalogue of the Royal Commonwealth Society, London. Boston, Mass.: G.K. Hall, 1971. 7 vol. [6777]

Royick, Alexander
"Ukrainian imprints of British Columbia: a preliminary check list." In: Canadian Ethnic Studies; Vol. 5, no. 1/2 (1973) p. 293-301.; ISSN: 0008-3496. [4163]

Rozon, René
Répertoire des documents audiovisuels sur l'art et les artistes québécois. Montréal: Bibliothèque nationale du Québec: Ministère des Communications, Direction générale du cinéma et de l'audiovisuel, 1981. 319 p.; ISBN: 2-550-00965-7. [6648]

Rubin, Don; Cranmer-Byng, Alison
Canada's playwrights: a biographical guide. Toronto: Canadian Theatre Review Publications, c1980. 191 p.: ports.; ISBN: 0-920-644-49-X. [1175]

Rubin, Ken
Information guide on citizen action and corporate power. [Ottawa: s.n.], 1974. 36 l. [3129]

Rubio, Mary
"Canadian children's literature ... : a bibliography." In: Canadian Children's Literature; No. 21 (1981)-No. 35/36 (1984) [1363]

Rubio, Mary; Haire, Jennifer
"Annual bibliography [Canadian children's literature] ... / Bibliographie de la littérature canadienne pour la jeunesse: 1985." In: Canadian Children's Literature; No. 56 (1989) p. 52-73.; ISSN: 0319-0080. [1385]

Rubio, Mary; Montagnes, Ramona; Ott, Lenie
"Canadian children's literature: ... /Bibliographie de la littérature canadienne pour la jeunesse: ...." In: Canadian Children's Literature; 1982 in no. 44 (1986) p. 33-52; 1983 in no. 47 (1987) p. 29-56; 1984 in no. 52 (1988) p. 35-55.; ISSN: 0319-0080. [1381]

Rubio, Mary; Sorfleet, John R.
"Canadian children's literature ... : a bibliography." In: Canadian Children's Literature; 1976 in no. 13 (1979) p. 29-50; 1977 in no. 17 (1980) p. 27-55.; ISSN: 0319-0080. [1345]

Rudi, Marilynn J.
Atlantic Canadian literature in English: a guide to sources of information. Halifax, N.S.: Dalhousie University, School of Library and Information Studies, 1991. iii, 60 p. (Occasional papers / Dalhousie University School of Library and Information Studies ; no. 51; ISSN: 0318-7403); ISBN: 0-7703-9752-2. [1295]

Rudnicki, Diane
A bibliography of Canadian literature. Halifax, N.S.: Canadian Learning Materials Centre, 1984. 21 p. [1218]

Rudnyckyj, Jaroslav Bohdan
"Bibliographia onomastica: Canada." In: Onoma; Vol. 3 (1952)-vol. 12 (1966-1967) [4544]
"A bibliography of Ukrainian-Canadian press surveys." In: Papers of the Bibliographical Society of Canada; Vol. 2 (1963) p. 74-78.; ISSN: 0067-6896. [5873]
"Ivan Velyhorskyj (1889-1955) [selected bibliography of writings]." In: Orbis: bulletin international de documentation linguistique; Vol. 4, no. 2 (1955) p. 571-573: port.; ISSN: 0030-4379. [7351]
Slavica Canadiana. Winnipeg: Ukrainian Free Academy of Sciences, 1952-1973. 21 vol.; ISSN: 0583-5364. (Slavistica, Proceedings of the Institute of Slavistics of the Ukrainian Free Academy of Sciences ; no. 15, 18, 21, 24, 27, 30, 33, 36, 39, 42, 45, 48, 51, 54, 57, 60, 63, 66, 69, 72, 75) [4164]
"Ukrainian Canadian bibliography." In: Papers of the Bibliographical Society of Canada; Vol. 1 (1962) p. 44-48.; ISSN: 0067-6896. [4135]

Rudnyckyj, Jaroslav Bohdan, et al.
Ukrainica Canadiana. Winnipeg: Ukrainian Free Academy of Sciences, 1954-1973. 20 vol.; ISSN: 0503-1095. (Bibliography / Ukrainian Free Academy of Sciences ; no. 1-20) [4165]

Rudnyckyj, Jaroslav Bohdan; Poirier, Jean
"Bibliographia onomastica: Canada." In: Onoma; Vol. 13 (1968) P. 26-27; vol. 14 (1969) p. 513-515.; ISSN: 0078-463X. [4547]

Ruel, Ginette
Bibliographie sélective sur le viol. Québec: Service de la documentation, Ministère des affaires sociales, 1984. 53 f. [3264]

Ruel, Ginette; Collister, Edward A.
Bibliographie sélective sur le harcèlement sexuel. Québec: Ministère des affaires sociales, Service de l'informathèque, 1981. 20 f. (Série bibliographiques / Québec, Ministère des affaires sociales, Service de l'informathèque ; no 5; ISSN: 0713-0740) [3225]

Rumney, Thomas A.
The historical geography of Canada: a selected bibliography. rev., 2nd ed. Monticello, Ill.: Vance Bibliographies, 1988. 44 p. (Public administration series: Bibliography ; P-2480; ISSN: 0193-970X); ISBN: 1-55590-910-8. [3058]
The physical geography of Canada: climate, ice, water studies: a selected bibliography. Monticello, Ill.: Vance Bibliographies, 1987. 50 p. (Public administration series: Bibliography ; P-2275; ISSN: 0193-970X); ISBN: 1-55590-535-8. [5253]
The physical geography of Canada–geomorphology: a selected bibliography. Monticello, Ill.: Vance Bibliographies, 1987. 98 p. (Public administration series: Bibliography ; P-2241; ISSN: 0193-970X); ISBN: 1-55590-481-5. [3054]
A selected bibliography on the economic geography of Canada: agriculture, land use, resources, energy, development, recreation and tourism. Monticello, Ill.: Vance Bibliographies, 1985. 25 p. (Public administration series: Bibliography ; P-1761; ISSN: 0193-970X); ISBN: 0-89028-561-6. [3049]

A selected bibliography on the economic geography of Canada: industry, transportation, urban, and tertiary systems. Monticello, Ill.: Vance Bibliographies, 1985. 25 p. (Public administration series: Bibliography ; P-1762; ISSN: 0193-970X); ISBN: 0-89028-562-4. [3048]

The urban geography of Canada: a selected bibliography. 2nd ed. Monticello, Ill.: Vance Bibliographies, 1988. 74 p. (Public administration series: Bibliography ; P-2534; ISSN: 0193-970X); ISBN: 1-55590-994-9. [4423]

Runte, Hans R.

"Réquisitoire acadien." Dans: *Contemporary French Civilization*; Vol. 2, no. 2 (Winter 1978) p. 295-311.; ISSN: 0147-9156. [1138]

Russell, D.W.

"Anne Hébert: an annotated bibliography." In: *The annotated bibliography of Canada's major authors*, Vol. 7, edited by Robert Lecker and Jack David. Toronto: ECW Press, 1987. P. 115-270.; ISBN: 0-920802-11-1. [7051]

Russell, Hilary

A bibliography relating to African Canadian history. [Ottawa]: Historical Research Branch, National Historic Sites Directorate, 1990. 64 p. [4278]

Russell, L.R.

An annotated bibliography on steelhead trout and general salmonid ecology. Victoria, B.C.: Ministry of Environment, 1975. xi, 178, 66 p. [5400]

An annotated bibliography on the ecology of anadromous cutthroat trout and Dolly Varden char. Victoria: Province of British Columbia, Ministry of Environment, 1975. v, 86, 115 p. (Fisheries technical circular / British Columbia Ministry of Environment ; no. 17) [5399]

Russell, Marian

Annotated bibliographies: Terra Nova and Gros Morne National Parks. St. John's, Nfld.: [s.n.], 1971. iv, 244 l. [2984]

Russell, Phyllis J.

Guide to Canadian health science information services and sources. Ottawa: Canadian Library Association, c1974. ii, 34 p.; ISBN: 0-88802-103-8. [5595]

Russell, Ruth Weber; Russell, D.W.; Wilmshurst, Rea

Lucy Maud Montgomery: a preliminary bibliography. Waterloo, Ont.: University of Waterloo Library, c1986. xxiii, 175 p. (University of Waterloo Library bibliography ; no. 13; ISSN: 0829-948X); ISBN: 0-920834-42-6. [7197]

Ryan, Helen

Survey of documents available for research in the Treaties and Historical Research Centre/Catalogue des documents au Centre de recherches historiques et d'étude des traités. Rev. ed. Ottawa: Treaties and Historical Research Centre, 1986. v, 139 p. [4088]

Ryan, Joan

Bibliography on Canadian Indians, 1960-1972. Calgary: Department of Anthropology, University of Calgary, 1972. 117 l. [3937]

Ryan, Nancy E.

Rural aging in Canada: an annotated bibliography. Guelph, Ont.: Gerontology Research Centre, University of Guelph, c1985. iii, 150 p.; ISBN: 0-88955-033-6. [3280]

Rybczywski, Witold

"Bibliographie écologique." Dans: *Architecture concept*; Vol. 28, no 314 (mai 1973) p. 17,19.; ISSN: 0003-8687. [5079]

Ryder, Carolyn

The Coutts collection: a selected descriptive bibliography. Calgary: University of Calgary Libraries, Special Collections Division, 1982. 36 p.: ill., facsim. (Occasional paper / University of Calgary Libraries, Special Collections Division ; no. 8); ISBN: 0-88953-034-3. [6788]

Ryder, Dorothy E.

"Bruce Braden Peel: a preliminary bibliography." In: *Papers of the Bibliographical Society of Canada*; Vol. 14 (1975) p. 14-16.; ISSN: 0067-6896. [7239]

Canadian reference sources: a selective guide. 2nd ed. [Ottawa]: Canadian Library Association, 1981. viii, 311 p.; ISBN: 0-88802-156-9. [0135]

The Canadian West & the North: a bibliographical overview. [Toronto]; Edmonton: Published for the Bibliographical Society of Canada by the University of Alberta Library, 1978. 13 l. [0523]

Checklist of Canadian directories, 1790-1950/Répertoire des annuaires canadiens, 1790-1950. Ottawa: National Library of Canada, 1979. xvii, 288 p.; ISBN: 0-660-50409-X. [5937]

Ryrie, John

Robertson Davies: an annotated bibliography. [Downsview, Ont.: ECW Press, c1981]. P. 57-279. [6940]

"Robertson Davies: an annotated bibliography." In: *The annotated bibliography of Canada's major authors*, Vol. 3, edited by Robert Lecker and Jack David. Downsview, Ont.: ECW Press, c1981. P. 57-279.; ISBN: 0-920802-23-0. [6941]

Sabin, Joseph

A list of the editions of the works of Louis Hennepin and Alonso [i.e. Antonio] de Herrera: extracted from *A dictionary of books relating to America*. New York: J. Sabin, 1876. 16 p. [7062]

Sabin, Joseph; Eames, Wilberforce; Vail, R.W.G.

Bibliotheca americana. A dictionary of books relating to America, from its discovery to the present time. Begun by Joseph Sabin, continued by Wilberforce Eames, and completed by R.W.G. Vail for the Bibliographical Society of America. New York: 1868-1936. 29 vol. [0049]

Sabourin, Conrad; Lamarche, Rolande

Le français québécois: bibliographie analytique. Montréal: Service des publications, Office de la langue française, 1979. xv, 329 p.; ISBN: 2-551-03397-7. [1447]

Sabourin, Conrad; Lamarche, Rolande; Tarrab, Elca

La francité canadienne: bibliographie. Montréal: Université de Montréal, Faculté des sciences de l'éducation, 1985-1987. 2 vol.; ISBN: 2-920826-00-X (vol. 1); 2-920298-51-8 (vol. 2). [1475]

Sabourin, Conrad; Petit, Normand

Langues et sociétés: bibliographie analytique. Montréal: Service de publications, Direction des communications, Office de la langue française, 1979. xv, 583 p.; ISBN: 2-551-03303-9. [1448]

Saddlemyer, Ann

"A checklist of the publications of Clifford Leech." In: *University of Toronto Quarterly*; Vol. 45, no. 3 (Spring 1976) p. 246-261.; ISSN: 0042-0247. [7141]

Safranyik, L.; Shrimpton, D.M.; Whitney, H.S.

Mountain pine beetle bibliography. Victoria, B.C.: Canadian Forestry Service, Department of the Environment, 1975. 69 p. [5401]

Sage, Richard; Weir, Aileen

Select committees of the assemblies of the provinces of Upper Canada, Canada and Ontario, 1792 to 1991: a checklist of reports. Toronto: Ontario Legislative Library, 1992. xi, 431 p.; ISBN: 0-772-99326-2. [6414]

Saint-Denis, soeur
Gaspésiana. Montréal: Paris: Fides, [c1965]. xix, 180 p.: ill., fac sims., carte. [0295]

Saint-Germain, Richard; Bettinotti, Julia; Bleton, Paul
Littérature en poche: collection "Petit format," 1944-1958: répertoire bibliographique. Sherbrooke, Québec: Éditions Ex Libris, 1992. 336 p.: ill.; ISBN: 2-921061-05-8. [1299]

Saint-Hilaire, Gaston
Bibliographie de la Côte-Nord. Québec: Institut québécois de recherche sur la culture, 1990. 340 p.: 3 cartes pliées. (Documents de recherche / Institut québécois de recherche sur la culture ; no 26; ISSN: 0823-0447); ISBN: 2-89224-150-2. [0410]

Saint-Pierre, Céline; Rousseau, Thierry
Bibliographie thématique sur le travail et la technologie. Québec: Service de la recherche et de l'évaluation, Musée de la civilisation, 1992. 70 p. (Document / Service de la recherche et de l'évaluation, Musée de la civilisation ; no 6); ISBN: 2-55112-841-2. [2940]

Saint-Pierre, Henri; Giroux, Richard
Bibliographie annotée sur l'enseignement universitaire: volumes actuellement disponibles dans les différentes bibliothèques de l'Université Laval. Québec: Service de pédagogie universitaire, Université Laval, 1974. vii, 341 p. (Service de pédagogie universitaire bibliographie / Université Laval ; no 2) [3489]

Saint-Pierre, Jeanne-M.
"Choix de livres d'enfants se rapportant au Canada et à certains aspects de la vie canadienne." Dans: *Canadian Library Association Bulletin*; Vol. 3 (October 1946) p. 14-16.; ISSN: 0316-6058. [1307]

Saint-Pierre, Louise
Bibliographie québécoise de l'artisanat et des métiers d'art (1689-1985). [Québec]: Centre de formation et de consultation en métiers d'art, c1986. xxi, 205 p.; ISBN: 2-920790-01-3. [0712]

Saint-Yves, Maurice; Dion, Louise
"Bibliographie sur la didactique de la géographie." Dans: *Cahiers de géographie de Québec*; Vol. 14, no 31 (avril 1970) p. 117-147.; ISSN: 0007-9766. [2974]

Sainte-Jarre, Chantal
"Bibliographies concernant la problématique femme-philosophie." Dans: *Phi zéro*; Vol. 9, no 2 (février 1981) p. 149-157.; ISSN: 0318-4412. [3803]

Sainte-Pierre, Annette
"Bibliographie du théâtre français au Manitoba." Dans: *Cefco: Centre d'études franco-canadiennes de l'Ouest*; No 5 (mai 1980) p. 17-18.; ISSN: 0226-0670. [0968]

Salter, E.C.
Newfoundland Forest Research Centre publications, 1950-1976. St. John's: Newfoundland Forest Research Centre, 1976. 59 l. (Newfoundland Forest Research Centre Information report ; 140; ISSN: 0704-7657) [6304]

Saltiel, Marie-Louise
Référence et bibliographie en sciences pures et appliquées. [Montréal]: Librairie de l'Université de Montréal, 1973. 87 f. [4622]

Sameoto, D.
Review of current information on Arctic cod (Boreogadus saida Lepechin) and bibliography. [Dartmouth, N.S.]: Ocean Science and Surveys Atlantic, Fisheries and Oceans Canada, 1984. 71 p.: ill., maps. [5506]

Samoil, J.K.; Turtle, G.B.
Northern Forestry Centre publications, 1980-86. Edmonton: Northern Forestry Centre, Canadian Forestry Service, 1988. vi, 36 p. (Northern Forestry Centre Information report ; NOR-X-297; ISSN: 0704-7673); ISBN: 0-662-16058-4. [5002]

Samson, A.L., et al.
A selected bibliography on the fate and effects of oil pollution relevant to the Canadian marine environment/ Bibliographie sélective des travaux de recherche portant sur le devenir et les effets de la pollution par les hydrocarbures et pouvant s'appliquer au milieu marin canadien. 2nd ed. [Hull, Quebec]: Research and Development Division, Environmental Protection Service, Environment Canada, 1980. vii, 191 p. (Economic and technical review report / Research and Development Division, Environmental Protection Service, Environment Canada ; EPS-3-EC-80-5); ISBN: 0-662-51167-0. [5167]

Samson, Jean-Noël
"Bibliographie d'Émile Nelligan." Dans: *Émile Nelligan*. Montréal: Fides, [1968]. P. 95-104. (Dossiers de documentation sur la littérature canadienne-française ; 3) [7207]
"Bibliographie [Félix Leclerc]." Dans: *Félix Leclerc*. Montréal: Fides, 1967. P. 79-87. (Dossiers de documentation sur la littérature canadienne-française ; 2) [7139]
"Bibliographie [Gabrielle Roy]." Dans: *Gabrielle Roy*. Montréal: Fides, 1967. P. 83-90. (Dossiers de documentation sur la littérature canadienne-française ; 1) [7280]

Samson, Marcel
"La résidence secondaire et la région métropolitaine de Montréal: essai d'interprétation." Dans: *Notes du Centre d'études du tourisme*; Vol. 8, no 2 (mars 1988) p. 1-4.; ISSN: 0229-2718. [1853]

Samson, Marcelle Germain
Des livres et des femmes: bibliographie. Québec: Conseil du statut de la femme, 1978. 254 p. [3783]

Samuda, Madeleine
"Bibliographie sur Louis Riel." Dans: *Cefco: Centre d'études franco-canadiennes de l'Ouest*; No 21 (octobre 1985) p. 15-21.; ISSN: 0226-0670. [7267]

Sander, F.
St. Andrews Biological Station publications, 1977-86. St. Andrews, N.B.: Biological Sciences Branch, Department of Fisheries and Oceans, 1988. iv, 32 p. (Canadian manuscript report of fisheries and aquatic sciences ; no. 1960; ISSN: 0706-6473) [6393]

Sanderson, Paul
Artists' legal bibliography. Toronto: CARO (Canadian Artists' Representation Ontario), 1980. 9 l. [0695]
"Musicians' legal problems: a select and annotated bibliography of Canadian and comparative law related materials." In: *Queen's Law Journal*; Vol. 11 (1985) p. 90-133.; ISSN: 0316-778X. [2279]

Sandhu, H.S., et al.
Environmental sulphur research in Alberta: a review. Edmonton: Research Secretariat, Alberta Department of the Environment, 1980. viii, 90 p.: maps (some col.). [5168]

Sandvoss, Joachim
Canadian graduate theses in music and music education, 1897-1978. [S.l.: s.n., 1979]. [1], 38, [4] l. [6154]

Sandy Bay School. Library
Native studies materials bibliography, Sandy Bay School Library. Sandy Bay, Man.: The School, 1980. 40 l. [4020]

Sanfilippo, Matteo

"Pour l'histoire des communautés italiennes au Canada: essai bibliographique." Dans: *Annali accademici Canadesi*; Vol. 5 (1989) p. 115-132.; ISSN: 0394-1736. [4272]

Sanford, Cheryl

A bibliography of the Athabasca oil sands Fort McMurray, Alberta area: socio-economic and environmental studies, 1980 cumulated update. Edmonton: Alberta Department of the Environment, 1980. 341 p. [4818]

Canadian energy-environment education bibliography. [Edmonton]: SEEDS Foundation, [1981]. viii, 54 p. [5783]

Sanger, Ann; Tillotson, J.

Institute for Marine Dynamics reports, 1932-1985. St. John's, Nfld.: Institute for Marine Dynamics, 1988. ii, 142 p. [5835]

Sangster, D.F.

Bibliography of stratabound sulphide deposits of the Caledonian-Appalachian orogen. Ottawa: Geological Survey of Canada, 1980. 53 p. (Geological Survey of Canada Paper ; 79-27; ISSN: 0068-7650); ISBN: 0-660-10528-4. [4819]

Classification, distribution, and grade-tonnage summaries of Canadian lead-zinc deposits. Ottawa: Geological Survey of Canada, 1986. 68 p.: ill. (Geological Survey of Canada, Economic geology report ; 37; ISSN: 0317-445X); ISBN: 0-660-12152-2. [4854]

Classification, répartition et résumés des teneurs et des tonnages des gisements plombo-zincifères du Canada. Ottawa: Commission géologique du Canada, 1986. iv, 68 p.: ill. (certaines en coul.). (Commission géologique du Canada, Rapport de géologie économique ; 37; ISSN: 0317-445X); ISBN: 0-660-91774-2. [4855]

Sanmugasunderam, V.; Brassinga, R.D.; Fulford, G.D.

Biodegradation of silicate and aluminosilicate minerals: a literature review. Ottawa: Mineral Sciences Laboratories, 1985. ii, 33 l.: ill. [4847]

SansCartier, L.; Keeley, J.R.

Oceanographic atlases of Canadian waters: a bibliography. Ottawa: Department of Fisheries and Oceans, 1981. v, 84 p.: maps. (Marine Environment Data Service Technical report ; no. 10) [6578]

Sansfaçon, Jacques

Liste sélective de périodiques à l'intention des bibliothèques de collèges du Canada français. Montréal: Fédération des collèges classiques, 1967. 126 p. [5879]

Sansfaçon, Jacques; Legendre, Vianney

Bibliographie des titres des documents sériés ayant [été] publié sur les poissons, la pêche et les pêcheries du Canada/Bibliography of the titles of serial documents having [been] published on the fishes, fishing and fisheries of Canada. Montréal: Office de Biologie, Ministère de la Chasse et des Pêcheries, Province de Québec; Université de Montréal, 1957. xx. 107 f. [5329]

Sarker, Rakhal; McKenney, Daniel William

Measuring unpriced values: an economic perspective and annotated bibliography for Ontario. Sault Ste. Marie, Ont.: Forestry Canada, Great Lakes Forestry Centre, 1992. 29 p. (Great Lakes Forestry Centre Information report ; O-X-422; ISSN: 0832-7122); ISBN: 0-662-19923-5. [5019]

Saskatchewan aging: an annotated bibliography on research in Saskatchewan, 1945 to the present. Regina: Senior Citizens' Provincial Council, 1983. vi, 166 p. [3252]

Saskatchewan books! A selected annotated bibliography of Saskatchewan literature. Regina: Saskatchewan Writers Guild, c1990. 65 p.; ISBN: 0-9690387-7-1. [1289]

Saskatchewan Center for Community Studies

Developing Saskatchewan's community resources: annotated bibliography for community leaders. Saskatoon: University of Saskatchewan, Center for Community Studies, 1959. 17 l. [4303]

Saskatchewan Library Association

Saskatchewan publications. Regina: Saskatchewan Library Association, 1975-1977. 3 vol. [0521]

Saskatchewan Organization for Heritage Languages. Resource Centre

Saskatchewan Organization for Heritage Languages Resource Centre annotated bibliography. Regina: The Organization, 1991. vi, 160 p. (loose-leaf). [4286]

Saskatchewan Provincial Library

Library science video cassette resources in the Provincial Library. Regina: Provincial Library, Saskatchewan Education, 1990. ii, 39 p.; ISBN: 0-919059-52-X. [1718]

Saskatchewan Provincial Library. Bibliographic Services Division

Art and architecture. Regina: The Library, 1972. 93 p. [0676]

Books on library science. 2nd ed. Regina: The Library, 1972. 193 p. [1597]

Canadian fiction: a bibliography. Regina: Bibliographic Services Division, Provincial Library, 1973. 33 p. [1077]

Consumer affairs: bibliography. Regina: Saskatchewan Department of Consumer Affairs, Education and Information Branch, 1974. 66 l. [2612]

Education: a bibliography. Regina: Bibliographic Services Division, Provincial Library, 1973. 107 p. [3470]

Gardening: a bibliography. Regina: The Library, 1973. 29 p. [4663]

Hockey: a bibliography. Regina: Bibliographic Services Division, Provincial Library, 1973. 21 p. [1762]

Indians of the Americas: a bibliography. Regina: Bibliographic Services Division, Saskatchewan Provincial Library, 1973. 1 vol. (in various pagings). [3945]

Library trustees: a bibliography. [Regina]: Saskatchewan Provincial Library, [1984]. 7 p.; ISBN: 0-919059-07-4. [1667]

Organic agriculture: a bibliography. Regina: Saskatchewan Provincial Library, 1978. i, 59 p. [4679]

Planning library buildings: a selected bibliography. Regina: Bibliographic Services Division, Professional Services Branch, Saskatchewan Library, 1985. 38 p.; ISBN: 0-919059-11-2. [1673]

Rehabilitation of the handicapped: a bibliography. Regina: Saskatchewan Provincial Library, [1981]. i, [65] p. (in various pagings). [3226]

Saskatchewan history: a bibliography. Regina: Provincial Library, 1973. 23 p. [0512]

Saskatchewan homecoming '71: a bibliography. Regina: The Library, [1971]. 29 p. [0505]

Women: a selected bibliography. Regina: Bibliographic Services Division, Provincial Library, 1972. 52 p. [3740]

Women and politics. Regina: Provincial Library, 1976. ii, 19 l. [3767]

Saskatchewan Research Council

Saskatchewan Research Council reports, 1957-1972. [Saskatoon: The Council], 1973. 30, [7] l. [4623]

Saskatchewan. Department of Continuing Education. Program Development Branch

Annotated literacy bibliography. Regina: The Branch, 1980. 18 p. [3577]

Saskatchewan. Department of Education

Celebrate Saskatchewan: a bibliography of instructional resources. Regina, Sask.: The Department, 1979. iii, 60 p. [0528]

Materials of interest to school librarians: a bibliography for school librarians. Regina: Saskatchewan Education, 1980. 12 p. [1642]

Selection aids for Saskatchewan schools: a bibliography for school libraries. Regina: Saskatchewan Education, 1980. ii, 45 p. [1643]

Social studies year one: "Saskatchewan": bibliography, Division two, resource materials. Regina: Department of Education, Saskatchewan, 1975. vi, 40 p. [0519]

Saskatchewan. Department of Mineral Resources

Catalogue of maps and publications [Province of Saskatchewan, Department of Mineral Resources]. Regina: Province of Saskatchewan, Department of Mineral Resources, 1975. 103 p.: maps, chart. [6301]

Saskatchewan. Legislative Library

Annotated bibliography for the Special Committee on Rules and Procedures. [Regina]: The Library, 1992. 6 p. [2554]

Checklist of Saskatchewan government publications. Regina: Legislative Library of Saskatchewan, 1976-. vol.; ISSN: 0705-4122. [6472]

Saskatchewan. Legislative Library. Archives Division

Catalogue of newspapers on microfilm in the Legislative Library (Archives Division) and Provincial Archives of Saskatchewan. [Regina: Queen's Printer, 1958]. 15 p. [6011]

Saskatchewan. Saskatchewan Agriculture and Food

Publications list [Saskatchewan Agriculture and Food]. Regina: Saskatchewan Agriculture and Food, 1978-. vol.; ISSN: 0837-435X. [6473]

Saskatchewan. Saskatchewan Tourism and Small Business

Bibliography of tourism surveys and reports. Regina: Saskatchewan Tourism and Small Business, 1985. 25 p. [1836]

Saskatchewan. Urban Advisory Commission

Bibliography of programs for urban municipalities. Regina: Urban Advisory Commission, 1974. 130 l. (in various foliations). [4339]

Saskatoon Public Library

The conserver society: an annotated resource guide to selected books, films, periodicals & organizations. Saskatoon: Saskatoon Public Library, 1979. 80 p. [5154]

Something to chew on: Canadian fiction for young adults. Saskatoon: Saskatoon Public Library, 1979. 35 p. [1339]

Sater, John E.

Ice pressure ridges: a bibliography. Arlington, Va.: Arctic Institute of North America, 1981. [146] l. [5175]

Sauder, E.A.; Krag, R.K.; Wellburn, G.V.

Logging and mass wasting in the Pacific Northwest with application to the Queen Charlotte Islands, B.C.: a literature review. Victoria: Ministry of Forestry and Lands, 1987. vi, 26 p.: ill. (Forest Engineering Research Institute of Canada Special report ; no. SR-45) (Land management report / British Columbia Ministry of Forestry and Lands ; no. 53; ISSN: 0702-9861); ISBN: 0-7718-8606-3. [4994]

Sauer, Serge A.

"Russian-Canadian periodical publications: a preliminary check list." In: *Canadian Ethnic Studies*; Vol. 1, no. 1 (1969) p. 61-64.; ISSN: 0008-3496. [5886]

Sault College. Library Resource Centre

Aviation technology and pilot training program: bibliography. Sault Ste. Marie, Ont.: Sault College, Library Resource Centre, 1975. 17 p. [5753]

Bibliography: forestry. Sault Ste. Marie, Ont.: Sault College, Library Resource Centre, 1975. 26 p. [4948]

A broad look at education & related areas. Sault Ste. Marie, Ont.: Sault College, Library Resource Centre, 1978. a-f, 52 p. [3545]

Early childhood education: bibliography. Sault Ste. Marie, Ont.: Sault College, Library Resource Centre, 1975. 23 p. [3508]

Mental retardation counsellor: bibliography. Sault Ste. Marie, Ont.: Sault College, Library Resource Centre, 1977. 20 p. [3161]

Saunders, Elizabeth; Hale, Elizabeth

The W.A. Pugsley Collection of Early Maps of Canada, McGill University Library Map Collection: a catalogue. Montreal: McGill University, Department of Rare Books and Special Collections, 1975. 16 l. [6549]

Savage, Graham David; Runyon, K.L.

Economics of private woodlot management: a literature review/Les aspects économiques de l'aménagement des boisés privés: une étude documentaire. Fredericton: Forestry Canada, Maritimes Region, 1992. 111 p. (Information report / Forestry Canada, Maritimes Region ; M-X-182E-F; ISSN: 1192-0033); ISBN: 0-662-059100-3. [5020]

Savard, Jean-Guy

Bibliographie analytique de tests de langues/Analytical bibliography of language tests. 2e éd. rev. et augm. Québec: Presses de l'Université Laval, 1977. xiv, 570 p. (Travaux du Centre international de recherche sur le bilinguisme ; F-1); ISBN: 0-7746-6438-X. [3529]

Savard, Pierre

"Présentation de Marcel Trudel." Dans: *Revue de l'Université d'Ottawa*; Vol. 47, nos 1-2 (janvier-avril 1977) p. 6-13.; ISSN: 0041-9206. [7340]

"Un Quart de siècle d'historiographie québécoise, 1947-1972." Dans: *Recherches sociographiques*; Vol. 15, no 1 (janvier-avril 1974) p. 77-96.; ISSN: 0034-1282. [1983]

Savard, Réjean

L'enfant handicapé au Québec: bibliographie. Montréal: Bibliothèque nationale du Québec, 1981. 72 p.; ISBN: 2-550-01899-0. [3227]

Savoie, Donat

"Bibliographie d'Émile Petitot: missionnaire dans le Nord-Ouest canadien." Dans: *Anthropologica*; Vol. 13, nos. 1-2 (1971) p. 159-168.; ISSN: 0003-5459. [7242]

"Liste des publications indiennes, métis et esquimaudes." Dans: *Recherches amérindiennes au Québec*; Vol. 1, no 3 (juin 1971) p. 21-24.; ISSN: 0318-4137. [6016]

Sawada, Joel D.; Warner, Bing

Abstracts of fisheries management reports, technical circulars, and project reports of the Recreational Fisheries Branch, British Columbia Ministry of Environment, 1985-88. Vancouver: Province of British Columbia, Ministry of Environment, 1989. i, 55 p. (Fisheries technical circular / British Columbia Ministry of Environment ; no. 86); ISBN: 0-7726-0979-9. [4913]

Sawaie, Mohammed

Arabic-speaking immigrants in the United States and Canada: a bibliographical guide with annotation. Lexington, Ky.: Mazdâ Publishers, c1985. xxiv, 158 p.; ISBN: 0-939214-27-X. [4236]

Sawchuk, John P.

A natural resources bibliography for Manitoba. Winnipeg: Manitoba Department of Mines, Resources and Environmental Management, 1972. 1 vol. (in various pagings): map. [4621]

Sawchyn, W.W.

A review of crayfish literature relevant to the development of a crayfish industry in Saskatchewan. Saskatoon: Saskatchewan Research Council, 1985. iv, 64 l., [71] p.: ill. (Saskatchewan Research Council Technical report; no. 174) [4904]

Sawka, Edward; Lind, Terry

Evaluation of impaired driver programs: a literature review. Edmonton: AADAC, Program Development Division, [1978]. 9, [2] p. [3178]

Sawula, Lorne W.

A repository of primary and secondary sources for Canadian history of sport and physical education: prepared as a project for the History of Sport and Physical Activity Committee of C.A.H.P.E.R. [Halifax, N.S.]: Dalhousie University, School of Physical Education, 1974. 170 l. [1768]

Scace, Robert C.

Banff, Jasper, Kootenay and Yoho: an initial bibliography of the contiguous Canadian Rocky Mountains national parks. Ottawa: National and Historic Parks Branch, Department of Indian Affairs and Northern Development, 1973. 3 vol.: maps. [2995]

Glacier and Mount Revelstoke National Parks: an initial bibliography. Ottawa: National and Historic Parks Branch, Department of Indian Affairs and Northern Development, 1973. 173 l. [2996]

An initial bibliography of Prince Albert National Park. Calgary: Scace & Assoc., 1974. 69 l. [3005]

An initial bibliography of the Elk Island National Park area. Calgary, Alta.: [s.n.], 1972. xvi, 97 l.: ill. [2989]

An initial bibliography of Waterton Lakes National Park, with additional references to Waterton-Glacier: the international peace park. Calgary: [s.n.], 1972. xvii, 249 l. [2990]

An initial bibliography of Wood Buffalo National Park. Calgary: Scace & Assoc., 1974. 1 vol. (in various pagings). [3006]

Scadding, Henry

Catalogue of the contents of a log shanty book-shelf in the pioneers' "Simcoe" Lodge, Exhibition Park, Toronto, 1887. Toronto: [s.n.], 1887. 7 p. [6741]

The Log shanty book-shelf for 1898, the pioneer's predecessor, the red man of North and South America: works on his origin, history, habits and language. Toronto: Copp, Clark, 1898. 5 p. [3906]

"On the early gazetteer and map literature of western Canada." In: Canadian Journal of Science, Literature and History; Vol. 15, no. 1 (April 1876) p. 23-45.; ISSN: 0381-8624. [6478]

Scane, Joyce

"Selected bibliography of community papers concerning immigrant women in Canada: 1975-1986." In: Resources for Feminist Research; Vol. 16, no. 1 (March 1987) p. 47-53.; ISSN: 0707-8412. [3857]

Scantland, Anna Cecile

Study of historical injustice to Japanese Canadians: text and bibliography. Rev. ed. Vancouver: Parallel Publishers, c1990. 392 p.; ISBN: 0-9690710-3-5. [4279]

Scarborough Public Library Board

A history of the City of Scarborough: an annotated bibliography. Scarborough, Ont.: Scarborough Public Library Board, 1991. 174 p. [0492]

Schawb, Robert

The Church in northern Canada: a bibliography. Yellowknife: Northwest Territories Archives, [c1982]. 33 p. (Sources for Northwest Territories history; 2) [1552]

Schick-Swanson Library and Information Consultants Ltd

Pollution in Alberta: a bibliography. Edmonton: Schick-Swanson Library and Information Consultants, 1974. 31 p. [5092]

Schlesinger, Benjamin

Canadian family studies: a selected, annotated bibliography, 1970-1982. Chicago, Ill.: Council of Planning Librarians, [1983]. v, 45 p. (CPL bibliography / Council of Planning Librarians; no. 123); ISBN: 0-86602-123-X. [3253]

The Jewish family: a survey and annotated bibliography. [Toronto]: University of Toronto Press, [1971]. xii, 175 p.; ISBN: 0-8020-1749-5. [4155]

Jewish family issues: a resource guide. New York: Garland, 1987. xvi, 144 p. (Garland library of sociology; no. 10); ISBN: 0-8240-8460-8. [4247]

The multi-problem family: a review and annotated bibliography. 3rd ed. [Toronto]: University of Toronto Press, [c1970]. xii, 191 p.; ISBN: 0-8020-1726-6. [3097]

The one-parent family in the 1980s: perspectives and annotated bibliography, 1978-1984. 5th ed. Toronto: University of Toronto Press, c1985. 284 p.; ISBN: 0-8020-6565-1. [3281]

"La pauvreté: publications récentes." Dans: Service social; Vol. 14, no 1 (janvier-juin 1965) p. 98-106.; ISSN: 0037-2633. [3083]

Poverty in Canada and the United States: overview and annotated bibliography. [Toronto]: University of Toronto Press, 1966. xiii, 211 p. [3086]

Sexual abuse of children: a resource guide and annotated bibliography. Toronto: University of Toronto Press, 1982. xiii, 200 p.; ISBN: 0-8020-6481-7. [3242]

Sexual abuse of children: a selected annotated bibliography: 1937-1980. [Toronto]: Faculty of Social Work, University of Toronto, 1981. 74 l. [3228]

Sexual abuse of children in the 1980's: ten essays and an annotated bibliography. Toronto: University of Toronto Press, c1986. 210 p. [3293]

"Single parent families: a bookshelf: 1978-1985." In: Family Relations; Vol. 35, no. 1 (January 1986) p. 199-204.; ISSN: 0197-6664. [3294]

Schlesinger, Benjamin; Schlesinger, Rachel Aber

Abuse of the elderly: issues and annotated bibliography. Toronto: University of Toronto Press, [1988]. xxi, 188 p.; ISBN: 0-8020-6694-1. [3314]

Canadian families: a resource guide. Toronto: OISE Press-Guidance Centre, c1988. vii, 81 p. (Guidance series / Ontario Institute for Studies in Education; 3); ISBN: 0-7744-0337-3. [3315]

Schlichtmann, Hansgeorg

"Ethnic themes in geographic research on western Canada." In: Canadian Ethnic Studies; Vol. 9, no. 2 (1977) p. 9-41.; ISSN: 0008-3496. [4182]

Schmelz, Oskar
Jewish demography and statistics: bibliography for 1920-1960. Jerusalem: [s.n.], 1961. 1 vol. (in various pagings). [2962]

Schmidt, Jeanette G.
J.R. Kidd: a bibliography of his writings. Toronto: Department of Adult Education and the R.W.B. Jackson Library, Ontario Institute for Studies in Education, 1988. xi, 47 p.; ISBN: 0-7744-9809-9. [7085]

Schneider, Edgar W.
"A bibliography of writings on American and Canadian English (1965-1983)." In: *A bibliography of writings on varieties of English, 1965-1983*, compiled by Wolfgang Viereck, Edgar W. Schneider and Manfred Görlach. Amsterdam: John Benjamins, 1984. P. 89-223.; ISBN: 90-272-4861-3. [1463]

Schonfeld, Josef; Larsen, R.W.
A selective bibliography of literature on revenue stamps. Vancouver, B.C.: [s.n.], 1954. 34 p. [1748]

Schonfield, David; Stewart, Robert
A bibliography of Canadian research in gerontology, 1949-1970. [Calgary: University of Calgary], 1970. iii, 62 l. [3098]

Schooley, Hugh O.; Oldford, L.
An annotated bibliography of the balsam woolly aphid (Adelges piceae (Ratzeburg)). St. John's: Newfoundland Forest Research Centre, 1981. 97 p. (Newfoundland Forest Research Centre Information report ; N-X-196; ISSN: 0704-7657) [5466]

Schroeder, W.H.
Air pollution aspects of odorous substances: a literature survey. Ottawa: Air Pollution Control Directorate, Environment Canada, 1975. v, 53 p. (Economic and technical review report / Environmental Protection Service ; EPS 3-AP-75-1) [5103]

Schuette, H.A.; Schuette, Sybil C.; Ihde, A.J.
"Maple sugar: a bibliography of early records." In: *Transactions of the Wisconsin Academy of Sciences, Arts, and Letters*; Vol. 29 (1935) p. 209-236; vol. 38 (1946) p. 89-184.; ISSN: 0084-0505. [5324]

Schwebke, Paul
Canadian library resources: a bibliography. [Ottawa, Ont.: Paul Schwebke, c1975]. [1611]

Scientific publications of Robert Bell, B.A.Sc., M.D., L.L.D., F.R.S.C., assistant director of the Geological Survey, 1857-1894. [S.l.: s.n.], 1894. 12 p. [6835]

Scollard, Robert J.
Basilian novitiates in Canada and the United States: an annotated bibliography. Toronto: Basilian Press, 1972. 40 p. (Basilian historical bulletin ; no. 8) [1526]
Basilian serial publications, 1935-1969. Toronto: Basilian Press, 1970. 28 p.: facsims. (Basilian historical bulletin ; no. 1) [5902]
A bibliography of the writings of Charles Collins. Toronto: Basilian Press, 1974. 24 p. (Historical bulletin ; no. 9) [6913]
The diaries and other papers of Michael Joseph Ferguson, C.S.B.: a bibliography. Toronto: Basilian Press, 1970. 36 p. (Basilian historical bulletin ; no. 5) [6979]

Scollie, Frederick Brent
Fort William, Port Arthur, Ontario, and vicinity, 1857-1969: an annotated list of maps in Toronto libraries. Thunder Bay, Ont.: [s.n.], 1971. 67 l.: maps. [6526]
"Regional planning in Ontario: an introduction to the literature." In: *Ontario Library Review*; Vol. 57, no. 1 (March 1973) p. 5-14.; ISSN: 0030-2996. [4329]

Scott, Allen J.
A bibliography on combinatorial programming methods and application in regional science and planning. [Toronto]: Centre for Urban and Community Studies, University of Toronto, 1969. 23 l. (University of Toronto Centre for Urban and Community Studies Bibliographic series ; no. 1) [4311]

Scott, D.M.
An annotated bibliography (revised) of research on eye movements published during the period 1932-1962. Ottawa: Department of National Defence, Defence Research Medical Laboratories, 1965. 135 p. (DRML Publication / Defence Research Medical Laboratories ; no. 591) [5571]

Scott, Deborah
The junior kindergarten: an annotated bibliography. Toronto: Library, Reference & Information Services, Ontario Institute for Studies in Education, 1974. x, 21 p. (Current bibliography / Ontario Institute for Studies in Education ; no. 7) [3490]

Scott, Francis Reginald
Bibliography on constitutional law. [Montreal: Faculty of Law, McGill University, 1948]. [vii], 27, 5 l. [2105]

Scott, H.–A.
"Au berceau de notre histoire." Dans: *Mémoires de la Société royale du Canada*; Série 3, vol. 16, section 1 (1922) p. 39-74.; ISSN: 0316-4616. [1902]

Scott, Ian
Environmental theses from Atlantic Canada universities: a natural resource information base. Halifax: Atlantic Provinces Council on the Sciences, 1987. i, 80 p. [6192]

Scott, J.D., et al.
A review of the international literature on mine spoil subsidence. Edmonton: Alberta Land Conservation and Reclamation Council, 1988. xxiv, 36 p. (Report / Alberta Reclamation Research Technical Advisory Committee ; RRTAC 88-12) [4872]

Scott, Joyce
"A checklist of lodge and fraternal society material in the Regional History Collection." In: *Western Ontario Historical Notes*; Vol. 25, no. 2 (Spring 1970) p. 7-16.; ISSN: 0382-0157. [1969]

Scott, Kevin M.
Arctic stream processes: an annotated bibliography. Washington, D.C.: United States Government Printing Office, 1979. iii, 78 p. (Geological Survey Water-supply paper ; 2065) [5155]

Scott, Marianne
A selective bibliography of Canadian legal sources. Montreal: McGill University, Law Library, 1973. 29 l. (Bibliographical guides / McGill University Law Library ; no. 5) [2133]

Scott, Michael M.
A bibliography of western Canadian studies relating to Manitoba. Winnipeg: [Western Canada Research Council], 1967. 79 p. [0499]

Scott, Norlayne L.
In the mainstream: a bibliography on the disabled in Manitoba. Winnipeg: Library, Department of Education, 1982. xi, 102 p.; ISBN: 0-86497-063-3. [3243]

Scott, Robert Nelson; Childress, D.S.

A bibliography on myoelectric control of prostheses. Fredericton: Institute of Biomedical Engineering, University of New Brunswick, 1989. iii, 26 p. (UNB monographs on myoelectric prostheses ; no. 3); ISBN: 0-920114-51-2. [5693]

Scott, Wendy; Herbert, Lynn

Empowering librarians: meeting challenges of the 1990s/ Plein pouvoir aux bibliothécaires: relever les défis des années 1990. Ottawa: National Library of Canada, 1990. 18 p. (Bibliographies / Library Development Centre ; no. 3; ISSN: 0226-4226) [1719]

Scotton, Anne

Bibliography of all sources relating to the Cooperative Commonwealth Federation and the New Democratic Party in Canada. [S.l.]: Woodsworth Archives Project : Boag Foundation, c1977. 698 p. [2433]

Scrimgeour, J.H.C.; Vernadat, F.

Advances in CAD-CAM and robotics: NRC contributions: commentary and bibliography. Ottawa: National Research Council Canada, Division of Electrical Engineering, 1987. ix, 27 p. [5827]

Scrivener, James Charles; Butler, T.H.

A bibliography of shrimps of the family Pandalidae, emphasizing economically important species of the genus Pandalus. Nanaimo, B.C.: Fisheries Research Board of Canada, 1971. 42 p. (Fisheries Research Board of Canada Technical report ; no. 241; ISSN: 0068-7553) [5362]

Sealock, Richard B.; Sealock, Margaret M.; Powell, Margaret S.

Bibliography of place-name literature: United States and Canada. 3rd ed. Chicago: American Library Association, 1982. xii, 435 p.; ISBN: 0-8389-0360-6. [3040]

Searle, W.M.

An annotated bibliography of unclassified reports issued by Defence Research Telecommunications Establishment, 1947-1969. Ottawa: Defence Scientific Information Service, 1970. viii, 206 p. (Defence Scientific Information Service Report ; no. B14) [5734]

Sears, Linda

Canadian and international themes: Raymond Spencer Rodgers, a bio-bibliographical sketch. Mobile: Department of Political Science, University of South Alabama, 1966. 1 vol. (in various pagings). [7272]

Seaton, Elizabeth; Valaskakis, Gail

New technologies and native people in northern Canada: an annotated bibliography of communications projects and research. Montreal: Concordia University, 1984. 72 l. [4067]

Secrétariat des conférences intergouvernementales canadiennes

Conférences fédérales-provinciales sur la Constitution, septembre 1978 – mars 1987: liste des documents publics. [Ottawa]: Le Secrétariat, [1987]. 60, 2, 55, 2 p. [2299]

Sedgwick, Dorothy

A bibliography of English-language theatre and drama in Canada, 1800-1914. Edmonton: Nineteenth Century Theatre Research, 1976. 48 p.: ill. (Occasional publications / Nineteenth Century Theatre Research ; no. 1; ISSN: 0316-5329) [0962]

Sefton, Joan; Miller, Gordon

The Arctic islands pipeline route: a bibliography of unpublished Fisheries and Environment Canada reports. Ottawa: Department of Indian and Northern Affairs, 1978.

x, 154 p. (ESCOM Report ; no. AI-12) [5136]

L'itinéraire du pipeline des îles de l'Arctique: une bibliographie des rapports inédits du Ministère des Pêches et de l'Environnement. Ottawa: Programme écologique et social, Pipe-lines du Nord, 1978. ix, 153 p. (Rapport ESCOM ; no AI-12) [5137]

Segura, Pearl Mary

The Acadians in fact and fiction: a classified bibliography of writing on the subject of Acadians in the Stephens Memorial Library, Southwestern Louisiana Institute, Layfayette, Louisiana. Baton Rouge, La.: Department of Commerce and Industry, 1955. 88 p. [0204]

Selby, Joan Louise

A bibliography on co-operative housing in Canada/Une bibliographie de l'habitation coopérative au Canada. Ottawa: Co-operative Housing Foundation of Canada, 1989. xii, 121 p. (Research paper / Co-operative Housing Foundation of Canada ; 4); ISBN: 0-9690660-4-X. [4433]

Selby, Suzanne R.

"[Indian and Eskimo education, anthropology and the North: bibliography]." In: Musk-Ox; No. 4 (1968) p. i-103.; ISSN: 0077-2542. [3398]

Seldon-MacFarlane, Betty D.; Mills, Patricia A.

Records management: the Canadian contribution: a bibliography. London: Department of Secretarial and Administrative Studies, University of Western Ontario, 1986. 157 p.; ISBN: 0-7714-0652-5. [1684]

"Select bibliography of Stephen Leacock's contributions to the social sciences." In: Canadian Journal of Economics and Political Science; Vol. 10, no. 2 (May 1944) p. 228-230.; ISSN: 0315-4890. [7134]

Select bibliography on Canadian Indian treaties and related subjects/Bibliographie spéciale sur les traités indiens canadiens et des autres sujets alliés. [Ottawa]: Treaties and Historical Research Centre (PRE Group), Indian and Northern Affairs, 1979. [38] p. [4007]

"Select bibliography on ethnic groups and inter-ethnic relations in Alberta: 1972-1974." In: Canadian Ethnic Studies; Vol. 6, no. 1/2 (1974) p. 71-72.; ISSN: 0008-3496. [4168]

Select bibliography on higher education/Bibliographie sur l'enseignement supérieur. Ottawa: Association of Universities and Colleges of Canada, [1965-1981]. 17 vol.; ISSN: 0049-0091. [3599]

"Select bibliography on post-war immigrants in Canada." In: International Migration Review; Vol. 4, no. 1 (Fall 1969) p. 96-99.; ISSN: 0197-9183. [4144]

"[Selected bibliographies on Canadian labour issues]." In: Labour Topics; (1978-) vol.; ISSN: 0704-8874. [2942]

"A selected bibliography of Franco-manitoban writing." In: Prairie Fire; Vol. 8, no. 3 (Autumn 1987) p. 123-124.; ISSN: 0821-1124. [1243]

Selected bibliography of hydrology for the years ... annotated: Canada/Bibliographie choisie d'hydrologie des années ... annotée: Canada. Ottawa: National Research Council, Associate Committee on Geodesy and Geophysics, Subcommittee on Hydrology: Department of Energy, Mines and Resources, Inland Waters Branch, 1959-1968. 4 vol. [5045]

"Selected bibliography of literature on Canadian-American relations." In: International Organization; Vol. 28, no. 4 (Autumn 1974) p. 1015-1023.; ISSN: 0020-8183. [2414]

"A selected bibliography of literature relative to Eskimo art." In: Beaver; Outfit 298, no. 2 (Autumn 1967) p. 95-98.; ISSN: 0005-7517. [0671]

A selected bibliography on housing and services for the disabled/Choix d'ouvrages sur le logement et les services pour les handicapés. Ottawa: Canada Mortgage and Housing Corporation, 1981. 28 p.; ISBN: 0-662-51450-5. [3229]

Selected books & journals for Manitoba health care facilities. Winnipeg: Manitoba Health Libraries Association, 1981. vi, 48 l. [5642]

"Selected Islandia bibliography, 1963-1973." In: *Abegweit Review*; Vol. 1, no. 1 (March 1974) p. 66-67; vol. 2, no. 1 (Spring 1975) p. 110; vol. 2, no. 2 (Fall 1975) p. 150-151.; ISSN: 0045-3129. [0220]

Selected list of war time pamphlets: No. 1-3. Ottawa: Department of National War Services, 1941-1942. 3 vol. [1920]

Sell, Kenneth D.; Sell, Betty H.
Divorce in United States, Canada, and Great Britain: a guide to information sources. Detroit: Gale Research, c1978. xv, 298 p. (Social issues and social problems information guide series ; vol. 1); ISBN: 0-8103-1396-0. [3179]

Séminaire Saint-Augustin. Bibliothèque
Bibliographie sur l'éducation au Québec. [Cap-Rouge, Québec]: Bibliothèque du Séminaire Saint-Augustin, 1969. 42 f. (Document / Bibliothèque du Séminaire Saint-Augustin ; no 146) [3404]
Références bibliographiques d'auteurs canadiens. Cap-Rouge [Québec]: Séminaire Saint-Augustin, Bibliothèque, 1971. 55 f. [1064]

Séminaire St-Joseph. Archives
Les Indiens en Amérique du Nord: au Québec, aux États-Unis. Trois-Rivières, Québec: Les Archives, [1981]. 41 f. [4027]

Semkow, Brian
Pension reform in Canada: a bibliography with selected annotations. Kingston, Ont.: Industrial Relations Centre, Queen's University, 1980. 21 p. (Mimeographed bibliography series / Industrial Relations Centre, Queen's University ; no. 15) [2664]
Retirement: a bibliography, 1970-1979. Kingston, Ont.: Industrial Relations Centre, Queen's University, 1979. 72 p. [3191]

Senécal, André Joseph
Canada: a reader's guide: introduction bibliographique. Ottawa: International Council for Canadian Studies, c1991. xviii, 444 p.; ISBN: 0-9691862-4-X. [0176]
"Quebec studies: a guide to the bibliographies." In: *American Review of Canadian Studies*; Vol. 10, No. 2 (Autumn 1980) p. 85-88.; ISSN: 0272-2011. [0366]
A reader's guide to Quebec studies. Québec: Gouvernement du Québec, Ministère des affaires internationales, [1988]. xi, 145 p.; ISBN: 2-550-19125-0. [0405]

Sereda, Peter J.
Durability of building materials: a bibliography using a keyword guide. Ottawa: National Research Council Canada, Division of Building Research, 1984. [32] p. (DBR Paper / National Research Council Canada, Division of Building Research ; no. 1212; ISSN: 0167-3890) [5800]

ServCom Côte-Nord (Québec)
Bibliographie sur les personnes handicapées: documentation recueillie auprès des établissements de santé et de services sociaux de la Côte-Nord et auprès de la FRASC. Hautrive: CRSSS Côte-Nord, 1978. 67 f. [3180]

Service, Dorothy Jane
Women and the law: a bibliography of materials in the University of Toronto Law Library. 2nd ed. Toronto: [s.n.], 1978. i, 105 p. [3784]

Service de diffusion sélective de l'information de la Centrale des bibliothèques
L'Acadie. Montréal: Le Service, 1987. 2 vol. (DSI/CB ; 103, 104; ISSN: 0825-5024); ISBN: 2-89059-320-7 (série). [0266]
L'Avortement. Montréal: Le Service, 1984. 41 p. (DSI/CB ; no 54; ISSN: 0825-5024); ISBN: 2-89059-254-5. [5665]
Le chômage. Montréal: Le Service, 1984. 37 p. (DSI/CB ; no 17; ISSN: 0825-5024); ISBN: 2-89059-217-0. [2895]
Le droit d'auteur. Montréal: Le Service, 1987. 18 p. (DSI/CB ; no 89; ISSN: 0825-5024); ISBN: 2-89059-290-1. [2300]
L'enseignement du français au Québec. Montréal: Le Service, 1988. 27 p. (DSI/CB ; no 116; ISSN: 0825-5024); ISBN: 2-89059-323-1. [3693]
Le Français au Québec. Montréal: Le Service, 1988. 48 p. (DSI/CB ; no 115; ISSN: 0825-5024); ISBN: 2-89059-321-5. [1481]
La Francophonie. Montréal: Le Service, 1988. 34 p. (DSI/CB ; no 114; ISSN: 0825-5024); ISBN: 2-89059-321-5. [1482]
Guides de voyage au Québec. Montréal: Le Service, 1985. 63 p. (DSI/CB ; no 69; ISSN: 0825-5024); ISBN: 2-89059-269-3. [0391]
Le Hockey sur glace et sur gazon. Montréal: Le Service, 1987. 25 p. (DSI/CB ; no 101; ISSN: 0825-5024); ISBN: 2-89059-306-1. [1841]
L'Homosexualité. Montréal: Le Service, 1985. 50 p. (DSI/CB ; no 72; ISSN: 0825-5024); ISBN: 2-89059-272-3. [3282]
L'informatique et l'éducation: documents répertoriés dans ÉDUQ. Montréal: Le Service, 1988. 56 p. (DSI/CB ; no 108; ISSN: 0825-5024); ISBN: 2-89059-313-4. [3694]
Le Libre-échange Canada-États-Unis: bibliographie. Montréal: Le Service, 1987. 17 p. (DSI/CB ; no 96; ISSN: 0825-5024); ISBN: 2-89059-302-9. [2739]
Logiciels québécois d'applications professionnelles générales. 2e éd. Montréal: Le Service, 1987. 146 p. (DSI/CB ; no 76; ISSN: 0825-5024); ISBN: 2-89059-297-9. [5828]
Les MTS: les maladies transmises sexuellement, sauf le SIDA. Montréal: Le Service, 1988. 20 p. (DSI/CB ; no 113; ISSN: 0825-5024); ISBN: 2-89059-319-3. [5684]
La peinture québécoise. Montréal: Le Service, 1984. 90 p. (DSI/CB ; no 41; ISSN: 0825-5024); ISBN: 2-89059-241-3. [0707]
Personnalités politiques du Québec et du Canada. 2e éd. Montréal: Le Service, 1988. 43 p. (DSI/CB ; no 40; ISSN: 0825-5024); ISBN: 2-89059-330-4. [2523]
La pollution de l'air et les précipitations acides. 2e éd. Montréal: Le Service, 1988. 30 p. (DSI/CB ; no 56; ISSN: 0825-5024); ISBN: 2-89059-329-0. [5264]
René Lévesque, 1922-1987. Montréal: Le Service, 1987. 15 p. (DSI/CB ; no 105; ISSN: 0825-5024); ISBN: 2-89059-310-X. [7147]
Télématique et téléinformatique. Montréal: Le Service, 1988. 36 p. (DSI/CB ; no 120; ISSN: 0825-5024); ISBN: 2-89059-335-5. [1704]
Le théâtre québécois, 1980-1983. Montréal: Le Service, 1984. 54 p. (DSI/CB ; no 5; ISSN: 0825-5024); ISBN: 0-289059-205-7. [0979]

Sève, Nicole de
Animation sociale: bibliographie. Montréal: Conseil de développement social du Montréal métropolitain, 1973. [100] p. [3119]
Éducation: bibliographie, vol. 1, no 1. Montréal: Conseil de développement social du Montréal métropolitain, 1972. 84,

18 p. [3442]

Severance, Frank Hayward

"Contributions towards a bibliography of the Niagara Region: the Upper Canada rebellion of 1837-38." In: *Publications of the Buffalo Historical Society*; Vol. 5 (1902) p. [427]-495. [1894]

Severance, Henry Ormal

A guide to the current periodicals and serials of the United States and Canada. 5th ed. Ann Arbor, Mich.: G. Wahr, 1931. 432 p. [5861]

Sevigny, David C.

The ethical pharmaceutical industry and some of its economic effects: an annotated bibliography. Toronto: Addiction Research Foundation of Ontario, c1977. xiv, 521 p. (Bibliographic series / Addiction Research Foundation of Ontario ; no. 13; ISSN: 0065-1885) [2630]

Seward, Shirley B.; Janssen, Helen

Canadian development assistance: a selected bibliography, 1950-77. Ottawa: International Development Research Centre: Norman Paterson School of International Affairs, Carleton University, 1978. 62 p. (Norman Paterson School of International Affairs Bibliography series ; no. 6); ISBN: 0-88936-187-8. [2438]

Sewell, W.R. Derrick

Where is public participation going? An annotated bibliography focussing on Canadian experience. [Edmonton]: Environment Council of Alberta, [1979]. 146, [9] p. [3192]

Sexual assault: annotated bibliography of sexual assault literature. [Toronto]: Ontario Women's Directorate, [1990]. [12] p. [3345]

Shaheen, Wali Alam; Nasim, Anwar; Mirza, Izhar

Across continents: a review of Urdu language & literature in Canada. Ottawa: National Federation of Pakistani Canadians, 1988. 112 p.: ill. [1483]

Shand, Patricia Martin

Canadian music: a selective guidelist for teachers. Toronto: Canadian Music Centre, 1978. viii, 186 p.; ISBN: 0-9690836-0-2. [0871]

A guide to unpublished Canadian string orchestra music suitable for student performers. Ann Arbor, Mich.: University Microfilms International, 1984. 7 microfiches (687 fr.). [0918]

Guidelist of unpublished Canadian band music suitable for student performers. Toronto: Canadian Music Centre, 1987. xi, 76 p.; ISBN: 0-921519-01-X. [0930]

Guidelist of unpublished Canadian string orchestra music suitable for student performers. Toronto: Canadian Music Centre, 1986. viii, 138 p.; ISBN: 0-921519-00-1. [0926]

Musique canadienne: oeuvres choisies à l'intention des professeurs. Toronto: Centre de musique canadienne, 1982. viii, 133 p.; ISBN: 0-9690836-1-0. [0907]

Shanks, Doreen

Guide to bibliographies in education. [Winnipeg]: University of Manitoba, c1982. v, 144 p. (Monographs in education / University of Manitoba ; no. 7; ISSN: 0709-6313) [3617]

Shapson, Stanley M.

Optimum class size? A review of the literature. Toronto: Research Department, Toronto Board of Education, 1972. 18 p. (Research Service / Research Department, Toronto Board of Education ; no. 114; ISSN: 0316-8786) [3443]

Shea, John Gilmary

Bibliography of Hennepin's works. New York: J.G. Shea, 1880. 13 p. [7061]

Shea, Mary; Mathers, John S.

An annotated bibliography on the effects of roads on aquatic systems. Toronto: Ontario Ministry of Natural Resources; Ministry of Transportation and Communications, 1978. 55 p. [5138]

Shearing, Clifford D.; Lynch, F. Jennifer; Matthews, Catherine J.

Policing in Canada: a bibliography/La police au Canada: une bibliographie. Ottawa: Solicitor General Canada, Research Division, 1979. xiv, 362 p.; ISBN: 0-662-50540-9. [2204]

Sheehan, Michael M.

"A current bibliography of Canadian church history/ Bibliographie récente de l'histoire de l'église canadienne." In: *Canadian Catholic Historical Association. Study Sessions*; Vol. 32 (1965) p. 81-91; vol. 33 (1966) p. 51-67; vol. 34 (1967) p. 77-93; vol. 35 (1968) p. 117-135; vol. 36 (1969) p. 79-101.; ISSN: 0318-6172. [1523]

Sheehy, Elizabeth A.

Special defences for women: outline. Ottawa: National Association of Women and the Law, 1987. 5 p.; ISBN: 0-929049-22-5. [3858]

Sheehy, Elizabeth A.; Boyd, Susan B.

Canadian feminist perspectives on law: an annotated bibliography of interdisciplinary writings. Toronto: Resources for Feminist Research, Ontario Institute for Studies in Education, 1989. 79 p. [2328]

Sheffield, Edward F.; Sheffield, Nora Morrison

Educational and vocational guidance materials: a Canadian bibliography. Ottawa: Canadian Council of Education for Citizenship, 1946. 49 p. [3373]

Shek, Ben-Zion

"Beyond the basics in selecting Quebec literature." In: *Ontario Library Review*; Vol. 65, no. 2 (June 1981) p. 103-118.; ISSN: 0030-2996. [1187]

Shelton, Valerie

"Bibliography on Canadian urban policy." In: *Plan Canada*; Vol. 12, no. 1 (July 1972) p. 123-128.; ISSN: 0032-0544. [4323]

Shepard, C.; Miller, G.; Groot, C.

Migration and movements of Pacific salmon, Atlantic salmon, and steelhead trout: a bibliography, 1900-1982. Nanaimo, B.C.: Department of Fisheries and Oceans, Fisheries Research Branch, 1985. iv, 450 p. (Canadian technical report of fisheries and aquatic sciences ; no. 1413; ISSN:0706-6457) [5517]

Sherman, Frederic F.

"A check list of first editions of the works of Bliss Carman." In: *Bliss Carman*, by Odell Shepard. Toronto: McClelland and Stewart, 1923. P. 171-184. [6894]

Sherman, George

The Canada connection in American history: a guide for teachers: content backgrounders, teaching strategies, student materials and a multi-media bibliography. Plattsburgh, N.Y.: Center for the Study of Canada, SUNY Plattsburgh, 1987. vi, 199 l.: ill., maps. [2065]

Shibata, Yuko

"The Japanese Canadians: a bibliography." In: *The forgotten history of the Japanese-Canadians, volume one*. Vancouver: Published for the Japanese-Canadian History Group by New Sun Books, 1977. P. 23-85. [4183]

Shiel, Suzanne
Annotated bibliography of Canadian demography, 1983-1989. London, Ont.: Population Studies Centre, University of Western Ontario, c1990. 237 p.; ISBN: 0-7714-1184-7. [3063]

Shields, Gordon
List of arctic and subarctic maps in the McGill University Map Collection. Montreal: McGill University, Centre for Northern Studies and Research, University Map Collection, 1975. 166 p. [6550]

Shilling, Barbara A.
Exclusionary zoning: restrictive definitions of family: an annotated bibliography. Chicago: Council of Planning Librarians, 1980. x, 38 p. (CPL bibliography / Council of Planning Librarians ; no. 31) [3208]

Shindruk, Cheryl; Carter, Tom
Selected sources on aboriginal issues. Winnipeg: Institute of Urban Studies, University of Winnipeg, 1991. iv, 31 p. (Bibliographica / Institute of Urban Studies, University of Winnipeg ; 3); ISBN: 0-920213-55-3. [4117]

Ship Harbour proposed national park: a bibliography.
Halifax, N.S.: Dalhousie University, School of Library Service and University Library, 1972. 173 l. [2991]

Shortt, Adam; Doughty, Arthur George
Canada and its provinces: a history of the Canadian people and their institutions by one hundred associates. Archives ed. Toronto: Glasgow, Brook, 1914-1917. 23 vol. [0036]

Shoup, J.M.; Nairn, L.D.
Black spruce bibliography. Winnipeg: Canada Department of Fisheries and Forestry, 1969. 72 p. (Liaison and Services Note / Forest Research Laboratory, Winnipeg ; MS-L-6) [5354]

Shoup, J.M.; Nairn, L.D.; Pratt, R.H.M.
Trembling aspen bibliography. Winnipeg, Man.: Forest Research Laboratory, 1968. 81 l. [5350]

Shoup, J.M.; Waldron, R.M.
Red pine bibliography. Winnipeg: Canada Department of Forestry and Rural Development, 1968. 61 l.: ill. (Liaison and services note / Forest Research Laboratory, Winnipeg ; MS-L-1) [5351]

Shrybman, Steven
Environmental mediation: bibliographies. Toronto: Canadian Environmental Law Association, 1984. 19, 22 l. [5219]

Shurtleff, William; Aoyagi, Akiko
Bibliography of soya in Canada: 663 references from 1855 to 1989. Lafayette, Calif.: Soyfoods Center, 1989. 112 l. [4719]

Shute, J.C.M.
Ghana-Guelph bibliography. [Guelph, Ont.: s.n.], 1982. 20 l. [4696]

Sibbald, Ian Ramsay
The T.M.E. system of feed evaluation: methodology, feed composition data and bibliography. Ottawa: Research Branch, Agriculture Canada, 1986. 114 p. (Technical bulletin / Agriculture Canada, Research Branch ; 1986-4E); ISBN: 0-662-14628-X. [4707]

Sicotte, Evelyne
"Bibliographie sur les foyers nourriciers." Dans: *Famille*; Vol. 10, nos 110-111 (février-mars 1974) p. 26-36.; ISSN: 0046-3191. [3130]

Sidhu, S.S.; Case, A.B.
A bibliography on the environmental impact of forest resource roads: a list. St. John's: Newfoundland Forest Research Centre, 1977. 28 l. [4958]

Siemens, Leonard Bernard
Cropping systems: an evaluative review of the literature. Winnipeg: Faculty of Agriculture and Home Economics, University of Manitoba, 1963. vii, 89 p. (Technical bulletin / Faculty of Agriculture and Home Economics, University of Manitoba ; no. 1) [4645]

Sigvaldadottir-Geppert, Margrét
"Icelandic-Canadian creative literature: a preliminary check list of imprints." In: *Canadian Ethnic Studies*; Vol. 5, no. 1/2 (1973) p. 139-151.; ISSN: 0008-3496. [1078]

Sikstrom, Calvin; Martin, John A.
Review and annotated bibliography of stream diversion and stream restoration techniques and associated effects on aquatic biota. Edmonton: Alberta Oil Sands Environmental Research Program, 1978. xiv, 114 p.: ill. [5139]

The silent epidemic: childhood injuries: Canadian statistics (1978-82) and a selected bibliography of recent literature.
2nd ed. Ottawa: Canadian Institute of Child Health, 1984. ii, 54 p. [5666]

Silzer, V.J.
Housing rehabilitation and neighbourhood change: Britain, Canada and USA: an annotated bibliography. [Toronto]: Centre for Urban and Community Studies, University of Toronto, 1975. 72 p. (University of Toronto Centre for Urban and Community Studies Bibliographic series ; no. 5; ISSN: 0316-4691) [4352]

Simard, Albert J.
Air tankers: a bibliography. Ottawa: Forest Fire Research Institute, 1977. 79 p. (Forest Fire Research Institute Information report ; FF-X-62) [4959]

Simard, Carole; Choko, Marc H.; Collin, Jean-Pierre
Le développement urbain de Montréal, 1940-1960: bibliographie. Montréal: Institut national de la recherche scientifique, Université du Québec, 1982. 113 p. (Études et documents / Institut national de la recherche scientifique ; 35); ISBN: 2-89228-035-4. [4397]

Simard, Michel
Répertoire des documents parlementaires québécois relatifs à la justice pénale, 1867-1900. Montréal: École de criminologie, Université de Montréal, 1981. 111 f. (Cahiers de l'École de criminologie / Université de Montréal ; no 6) [2238]

Simard, Sylvain
"Bibliographie des écrits français sur le Canada." Dans: *Les Relations entre la France et le Canada au XIXe siècle*. Paris: Centre culturel canadien, 1974. P. 85-109. (Les Cahiers du Centre culturel canadien ; no 3); ISBN: 2-900434-03-3. [0112]

Simcoe Public Library
A bibliography of local history collection (Town of Simcoe and Haldimand-Norfolk region) at Simcoe Public Library. Simcoe, Ont.: Simcoe Public Library, 1979. 12 l. [0465]

Simmins, Geoffrey
Bibliography of Canadian architecture/Bibliographie d'architecture canadienne. Ottawa: Society for the Study of Architecture in Canada, 1992. 28 p.; ISBN: 0-919525-18-0. [0803]

Simon Fraser University. Library
Canadian history. [Burnaby, B.C.]: Simon Fraser University Library, 1981. 25 p. [2015]
Canadian law. Rev. ed. Burnaby, B.C.: Simon Fraser University Library, 1983. 34 p. (Bibliography / Simon Fraser

University Library ; GOV DOC 1) [2263]

The first British Empire: discovery & colonization, 1485-1775. [Burnaby, B.C.]: The Library, 1984. 29 p. (Simon Fraser University Library reference bibliography ; HIST 8) [2042]

Municipal politics and government. Burnaby, B.C.: Simon Fraser University Library, 1981. 24 p. (Bibliography / Simon Fraser University Library ; GOV DOC 6) [4392]

Separatism. Burnaby, B.C.: Simon Fraser University Library, 1983. 45 p. (Bibliography / Simon Fraser University Library ; POL 6) [2482]

Simon Fraser University. Library. Humanities Division

A bibliographical guide to French-Canadian literature/ Guide bibliographique de la littérature canadienne-française. [Burnaby, B.C.]: Simon Fraser University Library, Humanities Division, 1977. 33 p. [1114]

Simpson, Cathy

"A select bibliography of Newfoundland children's books, 1970-1990." In: *Canadian Children's Literature*; No. 66 (1992) p. 59-66.; ISSN: 0319-0080. [1395]

Simpson, D.L.

Review of Canadian aeronautical fatigue work, 1991-1993. Ottawa: National Research Council Canada, Institute for Aerospace Research, 1993. 94 p. (Structures and materials report / National Research Council Canada, Institute for Aerospace Research ; LTR-ST.1932) [5853]

Simpson-Lewis, Wendy; McKechnie, Ruth

Land and the automobile: a selected bibliography/Les terres et l'automobile: bibliographie sélective. [Ottawa]: Lands Directorate, Environment Canada, 1981. iv, 95 p. (Working paper / Lands Directorate, Environment Canada ; no. 12; ISSN: 0712-4473); ISBN: 0-662-51259-6. [4486]

Sims, H.P.; Powter, Christopher Barrett

Land surface reclamation: an international bibliography. Edmonton: Alberta Land Conservation and Reclamation Council, 1982. 2 vol. (Alberta Land Conservation and Reclamation Council report ; no. RRTAC 82-1; ISSN: 0713-1232) [5186]

Sims, R.A.; Murtha, Peter A.

Reindeer at Mackenzie: a selected annotated bibliography. Ottawa: Indian and Northern Affairs Canada, 1983. iv, 63 p.: ill., map. (Northern Affairs Program Environmental studies ; no. 31); ISBN: 0-662-12666-1. [5487]

Les rennes dans la région du Mackenzie: références choisies. Ottawa: Affaires indiennes et du Nord Canada, 1983. iv, 75 p.: ill., carte. (Programme des affaires du Nord Étude environnementale ; no 31); ISBN: 0-662-92180-1. [5488]

Sims, R.A.; Riley, J.L.; Jeglum, J.K.

Vegetation, flora and vegetational ecology of the Hudson Bay Lowland: a literature review and annotated bibliography. Sault Ste. Marie, Ont.: Great Lakes Forest Research Centre, 1979. 177 p. (Hudson Bay Lowland environment baseline studies report ; 0-X-297: ISSN: 0704-7797) [5440]

Sinclair, Donald Michael

Reading reference to social credit: a bibliography about the social credit movement. [Vancouver: s.n., 1964]. 26, 16 l. [2382]

Singer, Loren

"Canadian art history theses and dissertations/Mémoires et thèses en l'histoire de l'art au Canada." In: *Journal of Canadian art history*; Vol. 5, no. 2 (1981)-vol. 12, no. 2 (1989) [6199]

"Canadian art publications: history and recent develop-

ments." In: *Art Libraries Journal*; Vol. 8, no. 1 (Spring 1983) p. 4-57.; ISSN: 0307-4722. [0702]

Singh, Ganda

The Sikhs in Canada and California. Patiala [India]: Punjabi University, Department of Punjab Historical Studies, 1970. 22 l. [4151]

Sirko, Hlib

Essai de bio-bibliographie du R.P. Thomas-André Audet, o.p. Montréal: [s.n.], 1959. xxxiii, 68 f. port. [6817]

Sirois, Antoine, et al.

Bibliography of studies in comparative Canadian literature, 1930-1987/Bibliographie d'études de littérature canadienne comparée, 1930-1987. Sherbrooke, Québec: Département des lettres et communications, Université de Sherbrooke, 1989. 130 p. (Cahiers de littérature canadienne comparée / Département des lettres et communications, Université de Sherbrooke ; no 1); ISBN: 2-893-43-010-4. [1276]

Sirois, Antoine; Van Sundert, Maria

"Supplementary bibliography of comparative Canadian literature (English-Canadian and French-Canadian)." In: *Canadian Review of Comparative Literature*; Vol. 16, no. 1-2 (March-June 1989) p. 170-176.; ISSN: 0319-051X. [1277]

Skelly, H.M.

A survey of powder forging literature, 1960-1974. Ottawa: Canada Centre for Mineral and Energy Technology, c1977. ii, 166 p. (CANMET Report / Canada Centre for Mineral and Energy Technology ; 76-38); ISBN: 0-660-00975-7. [5766]

Skelton, A.; Le Normand, J.; Ghanimé, Linda

Méthodes de conservation d'énergie dans les serres canadiennes: aperçu général et bibliographie. Ste. Anne de Bellevue, Québec: Institut de recherches Brace, Collège Macdonald de l'Université McGill, 1978. 5 p. [4680]

Methods of energy conservation for Canadian greenhouses, outline and bibliography. Ste. Anne de Bellevue, Quebec: Brace Research Institute, Macdonald College of McGill University, 1978. 4 p. [4681]

Skelton, Raleigh Ashlin; Tooley, R.V.

The marine surveys of James Cook in North America, 1758-1768, particularly the survey of Newfoundland: a bibliography of printed charts and sailing-directions. London: Map Collectors' Circle, 1967. 32, [14] p.: facsims. (Map Collectors' Circle ; Vol. 4, no. 37) [6511]

Skinner, Shirley

Annotated bibliography of Consortium members' current research, and published and unpublished materials. [Regina: Prairie Justice Research Consortium, School of Human Justice, University of Regina], 1980. 26 l. [2225]

Skvor, George J.

"Czech-Canadian periodical publications: a preliminary check list." In: *Canadian Ethnic Studies*; Vol. 1, no. 1 (1969) p. 3.; ISSN: 0008-3496. [5887]

Slavin, Suzy M.

Polar regions: a guide to reference sources. Montreal: McLennan Library, Reference Department, McGill University, 1983. 12 p.; ISBN: 0-7717-0105-5. [0642]

Slavutych, Yar

An annotated bibliography of Ukrainian literature in Canada: Canadian book publications, 1908-1985. 2nd enl. ed. Edmonton: Slavuta, 1986. 155, 23 p.; ISBN: 0-919452-44-2. [1234]

Sletmo, Gunnar K.; Holste, Susanne
  The shipping and trade of Asia Pacific: trends and implications for Canada. Montréal. École des hautes études commerciales, Centre d'études en administration internationale, 1990. 2 vol.: ill., map. (Cahiers de recherche du Centre d'études en administration internationale ; no 90-16; ISSN: 0825-5822) [4516]

Sloane, D. Louise; Roseneder, Jan; Hernandez, Marilyn J.
  Winnipeg: a centennial bibliography. Winnipeg: Manitoba Library Association, 1974. xi, 140 p. [0513]

Slobodin, Richard
  "Canadian subarctic Athapaskans in the literature to 1965." In: Canadian Review of Sociology and Anthropology; Vol. 12, no. 3 (August 1975) p. 278-289.; ISSN: 0008-4948. [3973]

Small, James M.; Edey, J.H.
  Adult education: an annotated bibliography. Edmonton: Department of Educational Administration, Faculty of Education, University of Alberta, 1974. v, 24 p. [3491]

Smandych, Russell Charles; Matthews, Catherine J.; Cox, Sandra J.
  Canadian criminal justice history: an annotated bibliography. Toronto: University of Toronto Press, c1987. xviii, 332 p.; ISBN: 0-8020-5720-9. [2301]

Smart, Anne; Parnell, Pat
  Rebirth of feminism: a selected list. Saskatoon: Saskatoon Public Library, 1975. 11 [i.e. 21] p. [3759]

Smith, Albert H.
  A bibliography of Canadian education. Toronto: Department of Educational Research, University of Toronto, [c1938]. 302 p. (Department of Educational Research Bulletin / University of Toronto ; no. 10) [3372]

Smith, Anne Marie
  Guide to reference works in the aquatic sciences: a selected list of material to be found in the library of the University of British Columbia. Vancouver: University of British Columbia Library, 1962. 17 l. [5337]

Smith, Anne Marie; Wellwood, Robert William; Valg, Leonid
  Canadian theses in forestry and related subject fields, 1913-1962. [S.l: s.n.], 1962. [26] p. [6076]

Smith, Annette L.
  The effects of effluents from the Canadian petrochemical industry on aquatic organisms: a literature review. Winnipeg: Research and Development Directorate, Freshwater Institute, 1974. vi, 68 [i.e. 72] p. (Fisheries and Marine Service Technical report ; no. 472; ISSN: 0701-7626) [4785]

Smith, Charles D.; Grmela, Sonia
  Le statut de réfugié au Canada: une bibliographie annotée. Montréal: [s.n.], 1986. ii, 70 f. [2507]

Smith, Charles Wesley
  Pacific northwest Americana: a check list of books and pamphlets relating to the history of the Pacific northwest. Edition 3, revised and extended by Isabel Mayhew. Portland, Ore.: Binfords & Mort, 1950. 381 p. [0568]

Smith, Clinton William
  Analytical inductively coupled plasma mass spectrometry: advantages, limitations, research directions and applications: a literature review. Ottawa: Mineral Sciences Laboratories, 1991. 14 l. [5848]

Smith, Donald; Tétreault, Josée
  "Bibliographie de Gilbert La Rocque." Dans: Voix et Images; Vol. 15, no 3 (printemps 1990) p. 387-394.; ISSN: 0318-9201. [7105]

Smith, Dwight L.
  The American and Canadian west: a bibliography. Santa Barbara, Calif.. American Bibliographical Center Clio Press, c1979. xi, 558 p. (Clio bibliography series ; no. 6); ISBN: 0-87436-272-5. [0529]
  The history of Canada: an annotated bibliography. Santa Barbara, Calif.: ABC-CLIO Information Services, c1983. xi, 327 p. (Clio bibliography series ; no. 10); ISBN: 0-87436-047-1. [2030]
  Indians of the United States and Canada: a bibliography. Santa Barbara: ABC-Clio, c1974-1983. 2 vol. (Clio bibliography series ; no. 3, 9); ISBN: 0-87436-124-9 (vol. 1); 0-87436-149-4 (vol. 2). [4053]
  The War of 1812: an annotated bibliography. New York: Garland Pub., 1985. xxiv, 340 p. (Wars of the United States ; v. 3) (Garland reference library of social science ; v. 250); ISBN: 0-8240-8945-6. [2051]

Smith, Gaddis
  "Selected readings on Canadian external policy, 1909-1959." In: The growth of Canadian policies in external affairs. Westport, Conn.: Greenwood Press, 1981. P. 164-168.; ISBN: 0-313-22850-7. [2465]

Smith, Gordon S.
  A selected bibliography on international peace-keeping. Ottawa: Defence Research Board, Department of National Defence Canada, 1964. 24 p., 2 l. (Systems Analysis Group Memorandum ; 64:M.2) [2383]

Smith, Illoana M.
  Transportation in British Columbia: a bibliography. Vancouver: Centre for Transportation Studies, University of British Columbia, c1982. iv, 113 p.; ISBN: 0-919804-28-4. [4490]

Smith, John Bernhard
  A catalogue, bibliographical and synonymical of the species of moths of the Lepidopterous superfamily Noctuidae: found in boreal America. Washington: G.P.O., 1893. 424 p. (Bulletin / United States National Museum ; no. 44) [5308]

Smith, Julian A.
  "Halley's comet: a bibliography of Canadian newspaper sources, 1835-36 and 1910." In: Journal of the Royal Astronomical Society of Canada; Vol. 79, no. 2 (April 1985) p. 54-99.; ISSN: 0035-872X. [5811]

Smith, Karen
  "Bibliography of the works of Charles Bruce Fergusson." In: Collections of the Nova Scotia Historical Society; Vol. 40 (1980) p. 193-202.; ISSN: 0383-8420. [6980]

Smith, Leonard H.
  Nova Scotia, genealogy and local history: a trial bibliography. 2nd ed. Clearwater, Fla.: Owl Books, 1984. 98 p.; ISBN: 0-932022-28-6. [0258]

Smith, Lillian H.; Wright, Annie M.
  "Canada: a reading guide for children and young people." In: Booklist; Vol. 37, no. 16 (May 1, 1941) p. 417-428. [1306]

Smith, Lynn M.; Addison, Edward M.
  A bibliography of parasites and diseases of Ontario wildlife. Toronto: Ontario Ministry of Natural Resources, 1982. 267 p. (Wildlife research report / Ontario Ministry of Natural Resources ; no. 99) [5479]

Smith, Margaret; Waisberg, Barbara
  Pornography: a feminist survey. Toronto: Boudicca Books, 1985. 31 p. (Boudicca booklist ; 2); ISBN: 0-920223-01-X. [3841]

Smith, Margo L.; Damien, Yvonne M.

Anthropological bibliographies: a selected guide. South Salem, N.Y.: Redgrave, c1981. 307 p.; ISBN: 0-913178-63-2. [4586]

Smith, Mary Margaret; Pyszczyk, Heinz W.

A selected bibliography of historical artifacts: c. 1760-1920. Edmonton: Alberta Culture and Multiculturalism, Historical Resources Division, 1988. x, 325 p.: ill. [4603]

Smith, R.D. Hilton

"Northwestern approaches: the first century of books." In: *British Columbia Library Quarterly*; Vol. 32, no. 3 (January 1969) p. 3-67.; ISSN: 0007-053X. [1962]

Northwestern approaches: the first century of books. Victoria, B.C.: Adelphi Book Shop, 1969. 67 p. [1963]

Smith, R.M.

Bibliography of forest entomology research, 1927-77: Canadian Forestry Service, Prairies Region. Edmonton: Northern Forest Research Centre, Canadian Forestry Service, Environment Canada, 1978. ii, 34 p. (Northern Forest Research Centre Information report; NOR-X-212; ISSN: 0704-7673) [4965]

Bibliography of forest pathology research publications, western and northern region. Edmonton: Northern Forest Research Centre, Canadian Forestry Service, 1976. 37 l. [4952]

Smith, Ruell

"The alternative press in British Columbia." In: *British Columbia Library Quarterly*; Vol. 38, no. 3 (Winter 1975) p. 6-16.; ISSN: 0007-053X. [6024]

Canadian newspapers in the University of British Columbia Library. Rev. ed. Vancouver: University of British Columbia Library, 1974. [8], 91 p. (Reference publication / University of British Columbia Library; no. 52) [6022]

Smith, Shirleen

Bibliography of bowhead whales, whaling, and Alaskan Inupiat and Yupik whaling communities. Edmonton: Boreal Institute for Northern Studies, University of Alberta, 1986. v, 55 p. (Miscellaneous publications / Boreal Institute for Northern Studies, University of Alberta); ISBN: 0-919058-32-9. [4907]

Smith, Stephen L.J.; Blair, Marilyn

Information resources for students, scholars and researchers in outdoor recreation, University of Waterloo. [S.l: s.n.], 1977. 37 l. [1786]

Smith, T. Lynn

"Rural sociology in the United States and Canada: classified and annotated bibliography." In: *Current Sociology*; Vol. 6, no. 1 (1957) p. 24-75.; ISSN: 0011-3921. [3079]

Smith, Thomas G.; Hammill, Michael O.

A bibliography of the white whale, Delphinapterus leucas. Ste. Anne de Bellevue, Quebec: Fisheries and Oceans Canada, 1990. ii, 45 p. (Canadian manuscript report of fisheries and aquatic sciences; no. 2060; ISSN: 0706-6473) [5555]

Smitherman, Mary

"Canadian composers." In: *Ontario Library Review*; Vol. 15, no. 1 (August 1930) p. 3-6.; ISSN: 0030-2996. [0808]

Smithers, Anne B.; Ghanimé, Linda; Harington, C.R.

Climatic change in Canada, 4: annotated bibliography of quaternary climatic change in Canada. Ottawa: National Museums of Canada, National Museum of Natural Sciences, [1984]. 368 p.: ill., map. (Syllogeus / National Museum of Natural Sciences; no. 51; ISSN: 0704-576X) [5220]

Smits, C.M.M.

An annotated bibliography and information summary on the furbearer resource and trapping industry of the Yukon River Basin. Whitehorse: Wildlife Management Branch, Yukon Department of Renewable Resources, 1983. ii, 168 l. (Yukon River Basin Study Project report: Wildlife; no. 1, appendix 2) [5489]

Smucker, Donovan E.

The sociology of Canadian Mennonites, Hutterites and Amish: a bibliography with annotations. Waterloo, Ont.: Wilfrid Laurier University Press, c1977. xvi, 232 p.: ill.; ISBN: 0-88920-052-1. [1542]

"Walter Klassen: a bibliography." In: *Conrad Grebel Review*; Vol. 9, no. 3 (Fall 1991) p. 345-351.; ISSN: 0829-044X. [7092]

Snow, Dean R.

Native American prehistory: a critical bibliography. Bloomington: Published for the Newberry Library [by] Indiana University Press, c1979. xiv, 75 p. (Newberry Library Center for the History of the American Indian, Bibliographical series); ISBN: 0-253-33498-5. [4008]

Snow, Kathleen M.; Hauck, Philomena

Canadian materials for schools. Toronto: McClelland and Stewart, [c1970]. 200 p.; ISBN: 0-7710-8198-7. [0096]

Snyder, Ursula Kennedy

A selected and briefly annotated bibliography of sources relating to the Province of Nova Scotia and its major (and two minor) ethno-cultural groups. Halifax: St. Mary's University, [1978]. [30] l. [4187]

Snyder-Penner, Russel

"A select bibliography on indigenous peoples in Canada." In: *Conrad Grebel Review*; Vol. 9, no. 2 (Spring 1991) p. 171-178.; ISSN: 0829-044X. [4118]

So we may know more about Canada, citizenship & democracy. Ottawa: Canadian Citizenship Council, 1951. 14 l. [2375]

Sobsey, Richard, et al.

Annotated bibliography: sexual abuse and exploitation of people with disabilities. Edmonton: Severe Disabilities Program, Department of Educational Sociology, University of Alberta, 1988. 72 p. [3316]

Disability, sexuality, and abuse: an annotated bibliography. Baltimore; Toronto: P.H. Brookes Pub. Co., 1991. xii, 185 p.; ISBN: 1-55766-068-9. [3356]

Social dimensions of environmental planning: an annotated bibliography. Ottawa: Environment Canada, 1979. 206 p. (Office of the Science Advisor Report / Environment Canada; no. 17) [5156]

Social service aspects of rehabilitation: a selective bibliography: une bibliographie sélective. Ottawa: Health and Welfare Canada, Departmental Library Services, 1974. 67 p. [3131]

Société canadienne d'hypothèques et de logement. Division des services de consultation et d'évaluation du développement

Projets de démonstration SCHL: un choix de notices bibliographiques annotées. [Ottawa]: SCHL, Division de l'analyse de nouveaux concepts, [1980]. ii f., 68, 66 p.; ISBN: 0-660-90545-0. [4387]

Société canadienne pour la prévention du crime

Publications [Société canadienne pour la prévention du crime]. Ottawa: Société canadienne pour la prévention du crime, 1977. 13, 13 p.: ill. [2175]

Société de développement de la Baie James (Québec)

Développement hydroélectrique de la Baie James: développement de l'environnement. Montréal. Société d'énergie de la Baie James, 1974. 235 p.: ill. (certaines en coul.), cartes (certaines en coul.), graphiques. [5093]

Société de géographie de Québec

Bibliographie: la Société de géographie de Québec vient de publier un bulletin de ses travaux depuis 1893 jusqu'à 1897. [Québec: s.n., 1897]. 1 f. (verso blanc). [2943]

Société des écrivains canadiens

Bulletin bibliographique de la Société des écrivains canadiens. Montréal: Société des écrivains canadiens, 1937-1959. 23 vol.; ISSN: 0700-6756. [1019]

Répertoire bio-bibliographique de la Société des écrivains canadiens, 1954. Montréal: Éditions de la Société des écrivains canadiens, c1954. xviii, 248 p.: planches. [1012]

Société des écrivains de la Mauricie

Répertoire des publications des membres de la Société des écrivains de la Mauricie. Trois-Rivières, Québec: La Société: Distribution, Diffusion Collective Radisson, [1986]. 19 p.; ISBN: 2-9800582-0-3. [0396]

Société historique de l'Ouest du Québec

"Introduction bibliographique à l'histoire de l'ouest du Québec." Dans: *Asticou*; No 2 (janvier 1969) p. 15.; ISSN: 0066-922X. [1964]

Société historique de Montréal

Inventaire sommaire des documents historiques de la Société historique de Montréal. Montréal: [s.n.], 1968. 174 p. [1956]

Socio-economic development in Labrador: a select bibliography. [St. John's]: Department of Rural, Agricultural and Northern Development, Government of Newfoundland and Labrador, 1985. iv, 35 p. [0261]

Socken, Paul

"Gabrielle Roy: an annotated bibliography." In: *The annotated bibliography of Canada's major authors*, Vol. 1, edited by Robert Lecker and Jack David. Downsview, Ont.: ECW Press, 1979. P. 213-263.; ISBN: 0-920802-02-8. [7281]

Gabrielle Roy: an annotated bibliography. Downsview, Ont.: ECW Press, 1979. P. 213-263. [7282]

Sokoloff, B.A.; Posner, Mark E.

Saul Bellow: a comprehensive bibliography. Folcroft, Pa.: Folcroft Press, c1971. 49 l. [6836]

Sokoloff, Natalie J.

"Bibliography on the sociology of women and work: 1970's." In: *Resources for Feminist Research*; Vol. 8, no. 4 (1979) p. 48-74.; ISSN: 0707-8412. [3791]

Sokolyszyn, Aleksander; Wertsman, Vladimir

Ukrainians in Canada and the United States: a guide to information sources. Detroit, Mich.: Gale Research Company, [c1981]. xiv, 236 p. (Ethnic studies information guide series ; vol. 7); ISBN: 0-8103-1494-0. [4205]

Solar, I.I.; Donaldson, Edward M.; Douville, D.

A bibliography of gynogenesis and androgenesis in fish (1913-1989). West Vancouver, B.C.: Biological Sciences Branch, Department of Fisheries and Oceans, 1991. iv, 41 p. (Canadian technical report of fisheries and aquatic sciences ; no. 1788; ISSN: 0706-6457) [5561]

"Some Canadian materials on women: a basic list." In: *Communiqué: Canadian Studies*; Vol. 1, no. 2 (December 1974) p. 5-13.; ISSN: 0318-1197. [3748]

Some materials for the study of Nova Scotia architecture. [S.l.: s.n., 1975]. 3 l. [0744]

Soong, H.M.

Bibliography of land use planning law. Windsor, Ont.: University of Windsor, Faculty of Law Library, 1973. 37 l. [2134]

Soren, Richard

Political-strategic aspects of Canadian Pacific policy: an annotated bibliography of periodical literature and government documents, 1965 to 1980. Toronto: University of Toronto-York University Joint Centre on Modern East Asia, [1981]. 78 p. (Working paper series / University of Toronto-York University Joint Centre on Modern East Asia ; no. 7; ISSN: 0834-1664); ISBN: 0-921309-36-8. [2466]

Sorfleet, John R.

"A primary and secondary bibliography of Bliss Carman's work." In: *Bliss Carman: a reappraisal*, edited by Gerald Lynch. Ottawa: University of Ottawa Press, c1990. P. 193-204. (Reappraisals: Canadian writers ; 16); ISBN: 0-7766-0286-1. [6895]

Sorfleet, John R.; Rubio, Mary

"Canadian children's literature 1975: a bibliography." In: *Canadian Children's Literature*; No. 11 (1978) p. 29-58.; ISSN: 0319-0080. [1337]

Soroka, Diane

Education of native people in Canada: an annotated bibliography of the writings of native people about education. [S.l.: s.n.], 1972. 15 l. [3444]

Sotiron, Minko

An annotated bibliography of works on daily newspapers in Canada, 1914-1983/Une bibliographie annotée des ouvrages portant sur les quotidiens canadiens, 1914-1983. Montréal: M. Sotiron, 1987. viii, 288 p.; ISBN: 0-9693102-0-X. [1697]

Soublière, Roger

"Bibliographie [Roch Carrier]." Dans: *Nord*; No 6 (automne 1976) p. 145-152.; ISSN: 0315-3789. [6898]

Source list of publications on housing. Ottawa: Indian and Northern Affairs Canada, Technical Services and Contracts, 1983. 18 p. (Band technical publications) [5792]

Les sources d'information sur l'automatisation industrielle. [Québec]: Direction des communications, Ministère de l'industrie, du commerce et de la technologie, Gouvernement du Québec, 1989. 94 p.; ISBN: 2-550-19538-8. [5839]

South Central Regional Library System (Ont.)

"Prime resort" catalogue: a professional collection housed in the Hamilton Public Library. [Hamilton, Ont.]: South Central Regional Library System, 1978. 476 p. [1628]

Southam, Peter

Bibliographie des bibliographies sur l'économie, la société et la culture du Québec, 1940-1971. Québec: Institut supérieur des sciences humaines, Université Laval, 1972. vi [i.e. vii], 86 f. (Cahiers de l'ISSH, Collection Instruments de travail / Institut supérieur des sciences humaines, Université Laval ; no 6) [0321]

Southam, Peter; Barry, Francine

Caractéristiques de la pauvreté au Québec, 1940-1973: bibliographie. Québec: Institut supérieur des sciences humaines, Université Laval, 1975. v f., 221 p., 2 f. (Cahiers de l'ISSH, Collection Instruments de travail / Institut supérieur des sciences humaines, Université Laval ; no. 16) [3139]

Southern Ontario Library Service

First Nations 1989 annotated bibliography: a listing of books, videos for and approved by First Nations. London, Ont.:

Southern Ontario Library Service, 1989. iii, 27 p.; ISBN: 0-9693737-0-0. [4110]

Southwestern Regional Library System (Ont.)

Video catalogue: Southwestern Library System. Windsor, Ont.: Board of the Southwestern Regional Library System, [1979]. iii, 416 p.; ISSN: 0706-439X. [6641]

Spadoni, Carl

"Medical archives: an annotated bibliography." In: *Archivaria*; No. 28 (Summer 1989) p. 74-119.; ISSN: 0318-6954. [1713]

Spafford, Shirley

"Norman Ward: a selected bibliography." In: *The Canadian House of Commons: essays in honour of Norman Ward*, edited by John C. Courtney. Calgary: University of Calgary Press, c1985. xv, 217 p.; ISBN: 0-919813-31-3. [7359]

Sparrow, Christopher J.; Foster, Leslie T.

An annotated bibliography of Canadian air pollution literature. Ottawa: Air Pollution Control Directorate, Air Pollution Protection Service, Environment Canada, 1975. xiv, 270 p. (Economic and technical review report / Air Pollution Control Directorate, Air Pollution Protection Service, Environment Canada ; EPS 3-AP-75-2) [5104]

Spazzapan, P.; Ternowetsky, Gordon W.

"Comparative Canadian and Australian research in the social sciences: a bibliography." In: *Australian-Canadian Studies: an interdisciplinary social science review*; Vol. 1 (January 1983) p. 96-105.; ISSN: 0810-1906. [2483]

Special Libraries Association. Montreal Chapter

Union list of serials in Montreal and vicinity. Montreal: [s.n.], 1965. 1 vol. (unpaged). [5876]

Special Libraries Association. Special Committee on Municipal Documents

Basic list of current municipal documents: a checklist of official publications issued periodically since 1927 by the larger cities of the United States and Canada. New York: The Association, 1932. 71 p. [4301]

Special list of Canadian government publications/Liste spéciale des publications du gouvernement canadien. Ottawa: Department of Supply and Services, 1969-.   vol.; ISSN: 0700-2882. [6474]

Spectator violence: a specialized bibliography from the SPORT database/Violence des spectateurs: une bibliographie spécialisée de la base de données SPORT. Gloucester, Ont.: Sport Information Resource Centre, 1990. 10 l. (SportBiblio ; no. 2; ISSN: 1180-5269) [1860]

Spector, David

An annotated bibliography for the study of animal husbandry in the Canadian Prairie West, 1880-1925. Ottawa: National Historic Parks and Sites Branch, Indian and Northern Affairs Canada, 1978. 50 p. (National Historic Parks and Sites Branch Research bulletin ; no. 77) [4682]

A bibliographic study of field agriculture in the Canadian prairie west 1870-1940. [Ottawa]: National Historic Parks and Sites Branch, Parks Canada, 1977. 35 p. (National Historic Parks and Sites Branch Research bulletin ; no. 46) [4674]

Spehner, Norbert

Écrits sur la science-fiction: bibliographie analytique des études & essais sur la science-fiction publiés entre 1900 et 1987 (littérature-cinéma-illustration). Longueuil, Québec: Le Préambule, c1988. 534 p.; ISBN: 2-89133-092-7. [1262]

Speirs, J. Murray, et al.

Bibliography of Canadian biological publications. [Toronto]: Quebec Biological Bureau and the University of Toronto, [1949-1951]. 4 vol. [5327]

Spence, Alex

Police brutality in Canada: a bibliography of books, reports, magazine, journal and newspaper articles. Toronto: Infolib Resources, c1982. 47 l. [2249]

Spencer, Loraine; Holland, Susan

Northern Ontario: a bibliography. [Toronto]: University of Toronto Press, [c1968]. x, 120 p. [0436]

Spencer, Maureen J.

Shoplifting: a bibliography. Toronto: Centre of Criminology, University of Toronto, 1971. ii, 35 l. [2122]

Spencer, Nigel

"Louis Riel and Norman Bethune: a critical bibliography." In: *Moosehead Review*; Vol. 3, no. 1 (1982) p. 48-60; No. 7 (1983) p. 29-47.; ISSN: 0228-7404. [7268]

"Louis Riel and Norman Bethune: a critical bibliography." In: *Moosehead Review*; Vol. 3, no. 1 (1982) p. 48-60; No. 7 (1983) p. 29-47.; ISSN: 0228-7404. [6840]

Spitzer, Frank; Silvester, Elizabeth

McGill University thesis directory. Montreal: Faculty of Graduate Studies and Research, McGill University, 1976. 2 vol.; ISBN: 0-7735-0278-5. [6144]

Sport legislation: Europe and North America: a specialized bibliography from the SPORT Database/Législation sportive: Europe et Amérique du Nord: une bibliographie spécialisée de la base de données SPORT. Gloucester, Ont.: Sport Information Resource Centre, 1991. 16 l. [1867]

Sport violence: a specialized bibliography from the SPORT database/Violence du sport: une bibliographie spécialisée de la base de données SPORT. Gloucester, Ont.: Sport Information Resource Centre, 1990. 9 l. (SportBiblio ; no. 8; ISSN: 1180-5269) [1861]

Sprague, J.B.; Vandermeulen, J.H.; Wells, Peter G.

Oil and dispersants in Canadian seas: research appraisal and recommendations. Ottawa: Environment Canada, Environmental Protection Service, 1982. xiii, 185 p.: ill. (Environmental Impact Control Directorate Economic and technical review report ; EPS 3-EC-82-2); ISBN: 0-662-11995-9. [5187]

Le pétrole et les dispersants dans les mers baignant le littoral canadien: évaluation des recherches et recommandations. Ottawa: Environnement Canada, Service de la protection de l'environnement, 1982. xv, 199 p.: ill. (Direction générale du contrôle des incidences environnementales Analyse économique et technique, Rapport ; SPE 3-EC-82-2F); ISBN: 0-662-91605-0. [5188]

Spratt, Albert A.

"Efficient energy use: alternative energy sources: a bibliography." In: *Ontario Library Review*; Vol. 62, no. 1 (March 1978) p. 28-33.; ISSN: 0030-2996. [4809]

The Ruth Konrad Collection of Canadiana: a descriptive catalogue. [Mississauga, Ont.]: Mississauga Public Library Board, 1971. 100 p. [6778]

Spray, W.A.

"Recent publications in local history: New Brunswick." In: *Acadiensis*; Vol. 9, no. 2 (Spring 1980) p. 115-121.; ISSN: 0044-5851. [0248]

Springer, Nelson P.; Klassen, A.J.

Mennonite bibliography, 1631-1961. Scottdale, Pa.; Kitchener, Ont.: Herald Press, 1977. 2 vol.; ISBN: 0-8361-1208-3. [1543]

Sproat, Bonnie; Feather, Joan

Northern Saskatchewan health research bibliography. 2nd ed. Saskatoon: Northern Medical Services, Department of Family Medicine, University of Saskatchewan, c1990. x, 152 p.; ISBN: 0-88880-240-4. [5700]

Spry, D.J.; Wood, C.M.; Hodson, P.V.

The effects of environmental acid on freshwater fish with particular reference to the soft water lakes in Ontario and the modifying effects of heavy metals: a literature review. Burlington, Ont.: Department of Fisheries and Oceans, Great Lakes Biolimnology Laboratory, 1981. xi, 144 p. (Canadian technical report of fisheries and aquatic sciences ; no. 999; ISSN: 0706-6457) [5467]

Srivastava, V.M.

Fish of the Gulf of St. Lawrence: an unabridged bibliography. Dartmouth, N.S.: Fisheries Research Board of Canada, Marine Ecology Laboratory, Bedford Institute, 1971. 141 p. (Fisheries Research Board of Canada Technical report ; no. 261; ISSN: 0068-7553) [5363]

St-Amour, Jean-Pierre F.

L'Outaouais québécois: guide de recherche et bibliographie sélective. Hull, Québec: Université du Québec, Centre d'études universitaires dans l'Ouest québécois, [1978]. x, 178 p. [0355]

St Lawrence Seaway Development Corporation. Office of Information

Seaway bibliography. Washington, D.C.: St Lawrence Seaway Development Corporation, 1958. 1 vol. (in various pagings). [4450]

St-Pierre, Nicole; Ruel, Ginette

Bibliographie sélective sur la condition des femmes. [Québec]: Gouvernement du Québec, Ministère des affaires sociales, 1981. 16 f. [3804]

St. Clair, Barbara Elaine; Wong, Sandra Ann

Nutrition and aging: a selected bibliography. Toronto: Nutrition Information Service, Ryerson Polytechnical Institute, 1982. 128 p.; ISBN: 0-919351-05-0. [3244]

St. James, Man. Public Library

A bibliography of Canadiana. Centennial edition. [St. James, Man.]: 1967. 1 vol. (in various pagings). [0088]

St. James-Assiniboia Public Library

Winnipeg in print: a bibliography: books about Winnipeg or by Winnipeggers in the St. James-Assiniboia Public Library. [Winnipeg: St. James-Assiniboia Public Library], 1974. 59 p. [0514]

St. James Literary Society (Montreal, Quebec)

List of papers and debates presented before the St. James Literary Society, 1898-99 to 1954-55. Montreal: [s.n.], 1955. 87 p. [1015]

Stace-Smith, Richard; Matsumoto, T.

Virus diseases of small fruits: a bibliography, 1979-1981. Vancouver: Agriculture Canada, 1982. 20 p. [4697]

Staines, David

"E.K. Brown (1905-1951): the critic and his writings." In: Canadian Literature; No. 83 (Winter 1979) p. 176-189.; ISSN: 0008-4360. [6877]

"Morley Callaghan: the writer and his writings." In: The Callaghan Symposium. Ottawa: University of Ottawa Press, 1981. P. 111-121. (Reappraisals: Canadian writers); ISBN: 2-7603-4387-1. [6889]

Stamp, Robert M.

Royalty and royal tours: a Canadian bibliography. Toronto: Heritage Books, 1988. iv, 43 p. (Canadian Biblio-File series

publication ; 002); ISBN: 0-921342-02-0. [2074]

Street cars, subways and rapid transit: a Canadian bibliography. Toronto: Heritage Books, 1988. iv, 63 p. (Canadian Biblio-File series publication ; 001); ISBN: 0-921342-00-4. [4424]

Stanbridge, Joanne

"An annotated bibliography of Canadian poetry books written in English for children." In: Canadian Children's Literature; No. 42 (1986) p. 51-61.; ISSN: 0319-0080. [1373]

Stanbury, W.T.

"Anti-combines law and policy in Canada, 1888-1975: a bibliography." In: Canadian Business Law Journal; Vol. 1, no. 3 (August 1976) p. 352-374.; ISSN: 0319-3322. [2161]

Standish, J.T.; Commandeur, P.R.; Smith, R.B.

Impacts of forest harvesting on physical properties of soils with reference to increased biomass recovery: a review. Victoria: Pacific Forestry Centre, 1988. 24 p. (Pacific Forestry Centre Information report ; BC-X-301; ISSN: 0830-0453); ISBN: 0-662-16364-8. [5003]

Stanek, Edward

The Canadian Charter of Rights and Freedoms: a bibliography. Monticello, Ill.: Vance Bibliographies, [1987]. 10 p. (Public administration series: Bibliography ; P-2159; ISSN: 0193-970X); ISBN: 1-555903-19-3. [2302]

Native people: legal status, claims, and human rights: a bibliography. Monticello, Ill.: Vance Bibliographies, 1987. 18 p. (Public administration series: Bibliography ; P-2274; ISSN: 0193-970X); ISBN: 1-55590-534-X. [4093]

Stanek, Oleg

Aménagement de petites villes et de communautés rurales: bibliographie générale. Sherbrooke, Québec: Université de Sherbrooke, Département de géographie, 1980. 43 f. (Bulletin de recherche / Université de Sherbrooke, Département de géographie ; no 50; ISSN: 0710-0868) [4388]

Evolution des conceptions urbaines: bibliographie générale. Sherbrooke, Québec: Université de Sherbrooke, Département de géographie, 1978. 42 f. (Bulletin de recherche / Université de Sherbrooke, Département de géographie ; no 38) [4372]

L'influence de la localisation des logements sur la qualité de vie des personnes âgées: une bibliographie selectionée. Sherbrooke, Québec: Université de Sherbrooke, Département de géographie, 1983. 36 f. (Bulletin de recherche / Université de Sherbrooke, Département de géographie ; no 66) [3254]

Stanek, W.

Annotated bibliography of peatland forestry/Foresterie des régions de tourbières: bibliographie annotée. Ottawa: Environment Canada, Library, 1976. 205 p. (Environment Canada Libraries Bibliography series ; 76/1) [4953]

Stang, Anne

"School libraries, K to 9: an annotated bibliography on the role of the school library and teacher-librarian in the strategies of teaching and learning." In: School Libraries in Canada; Vol. 8, no. 3 (Spring 1988) p. 44-47.; ISSN: 0227-3780. [1705]

Stansby, Maurice Earl; Diamant, Isabell

Subject classified literature references on effects of oil pollution in Arctic and subarctic waters. Seattle, Wa.: Northwest and Alaska Fisheries Center, 1978. 201 p. [5140]

Stanton, Charles R.

Index to federal scientific and technical contributions to forestry literature 1901-1971. Ottawa: Canadian Forestry Service, Department of the Environment, 1973. 7 vol. [4939]

Stark, Richard, et al.

The Drug file: a comprehensive bibliography on drugs and doping in sport/Dossier dopage: une bibliographie complète sur les drogues et le dopage dans le sport. Gloucester, Ont.: Sport Information Resource Centre, 1991. vi, 179 p.; ISBN: 0-921817-10-X. [1868]

Sport and recreation for the disabled: a bibliography, 1984-1989/Sport et loisirs pour handicapés: une bibliographie, 1984-1989. Gloucester, Ont.: Sport Information Resource Centre/Centre de documentation pour le sport, 1990. ii, 209 p.; ISBN: 0-921817-08-8. [1862]

Stasko, Aivars B.

Underwater biotelemetry: an annotated bibliography. St. Andrews, N.B.: Biological Station, Fisheries and Marine Service, 1975. 31 p. (Fisheries and Marine Service Technical report ; no. 534; ISSN: 0701-7626) [5754]

"Station touristique et temps partage: deux formes de villégiature." Dans: *Notes du Centre d'études du tourisme*; Vol. 7, no 8 (février 1987) p. 1-4.; ISSN: 0229-2718. [1842]

Staton, Frances M.

"Some unusual sources of information in the Toronto Reference Library on the Canadian rebellions of 1837-8." In: *Papers and Records: Ontario Historical Society*; Vol. 17 (1919) p. 58-73.; ISSN: 0380-6022. [1900]

Stauffer, Ann Tholer

"The French-Americans and the French-Canadians: a select bibliography of materials in the Library of the Vermont Historical Society." In: *Vermont History*; Vol. 44, no. 2 (Spring 1976) p. 110-114.; ISSN: 0042-4161. [1989]

Stearns, Louise

Bibliography of Indians and Métis of Manitoba: preliminary draft. Winnipeg: [s.n.], 1975. [3] l. [3974]

Information Indian: [a list of books and other library materials about Cree Indians, Ojibway Indians, Sioux Indians]. Winnipeg: Manitoba Indian Brotherhood, 1973. 10 l. [3946]

Stebbings, Elizabeth

Native Indians in British Columbia: a selected annotated bibliography. [Vancouver: B.C. Hydro], 1978. iv, 69 p.: map. [3997]

Steckelberg, Warren Dean

Lutheran rites in North America [microform]: an annotated bibliography of the hymnals, altar books, and selected manuals produced by or for Lutherans in North America from the late eighteenth century to the present. Ottawa: National Library of Canada, 1990. 5 microfiches (Canadian theses ; no. 51212); ISBN: 0-315-51212-1. [1573]

Steele, Apollonia

Theses on English-Canadian literature: a bibliography of research produced in Canada and elsewhere from 1903 forward. Calgary: [University of Calgary Press], 1988. xxvi, 505 p.; ISBN: 0-919813-47-X. [6195]

Steep, Barbara J.

Drug education resources directory. Toronto: Addiction Research Foundation, c1989. 5 parts; ISBN: 0-88868-171-2 (set). [3704]

Répertoire des ressources éducatives sur les drogues: maternelle à fin du secondaire. Toronto: Fondation de la recherche sur la toxicomanie, c1989. xii, 63 p.; ISBN: 0-88868-171-1. [3705]

Steeves, Allan D.

A complete bibliography in sociology and a partial bibliography in anthropology of M.A. theses and Ph.D. dissertations completed at Canadian universities up to 1970. Ottawa: [s.n.], 1971. 83, 12 l. [6110]

Stefanski, M.J.

Characteristics and utilization of char: a literature survey. Halifax, N.S.: Atlantic Research Laboratory, National Research Council Canada, 1982. 33 p. (Atlantic Research Laboratory Technical report ; 40) [5786]

Circuitry instrumentation and process control: literature review. [Ottawa]: Canada Centre for Mineral and Energy Technology, 1988. 92 p. (Mineral Sciences Laboratories Division report ; MSL 88-112 LS) [5836]

Dewatering and self dewatering of concentrates. [Ottawa]: Mineral Sciences Laboratories, Canada Centre for Mineral and Energy Technology, 1987. iv, 72 l. (Mineral Sciences Laboratories Division report ; MSL 87-79 [IR]) [4863]

Stefansson Collection

Dictionary catalog of the Stefansson Collection on the Polar regions in the Dartmouth College Library. Boston: G.K. Hall, 1967. 8 vol. [0615]

Steinfirst, Susan

Folklore and folklife: a guide to English-language reference sources. New York: Garland, 1992. 2 vol. (Garland folklore bibliographies ; vol. 16); ISBN: 0-8153-0068-9 (set). [4612]

Stelter, Gilbert A.

Canadian urban history: a selected bibliography. Sudbury: Laurentian University Press, 1972. ii, 61 p. (Laurentian University social science research publication ; no. 2) [4324]

"Current research in Canadian urban history." In: *Urban History Review: Revue d'histoire urbaine*; No. 3 (1975) p. 27-36.; ISSN: 0703-0428. [4353]

Stelter, Gilbert A.; Rowan, John

Community development in northeastern Ontario: a selected bibliography. [Sudbury: Laurentian University Press, 1972]. 56 p. [0445]

Stenderup, Vibeke

Litteratursongning: Canada Skonlitteratur pa engelsk: bibliografier, handboger, antologier. Aarhus: Statsbiblioteket, 1989. 36 p. (Canadiana / Statsbiblioteket, Aarhus ; 1); ISBN: 87-7507-179-7. [1278]

Stephen, Marg

Alberta bibliography: books by Alberta authors and Alberta publishers. Edmonton: Young Alberta Book Festival Society, 1992. 73 p.; ISBN: 0-9693147-3-6. [0552]

Stephen, Marg; Mah, Judy

Alberta bibliography, 1980-1987 for adults and young adults. [Edmonton]: Young Alberta Book Festival Society, [1987]. 48 p.; ISBN: 0-9693147-0-1. [0544]

Stephenson, Mary Sue

Planning library facilities: a selected, annotated bibliography. Metuchen, N.J.: Scarecrow Press, c1990. ix, 249 p.; ISBN: 0-8108-2285-7. [1720]

Stephenson, Robert, et al.

Sudbury mining area: a selected bibliography. [Sudbury, Ont.]: Department of History, Laurentian University, [1978]. 29 p. [4810]

Sterns, Maurice A.; Hiscock, Philip; Daley, Bruce

Newfoundland and Labrador: social science research: a selected bibliography. St. John's, Nfld.: Department of Sociology, Memorial University of Newfoundland, 1975.

iii, 70 p. [0221]

Stevens, Alta Mae; McDowell, Linda

"Filling in the picture: resources for teaching about women in Canada." In: *History and Social Science Teacher*; Vol. 14, no. 1 (Fall 1978) p. 7-13.; ISSN: 0316-4969. [3785]

Stevens, Henry

Bibliotheca historica, or A catalogue of 5000 volumes of books and manuscripts relating chiefly to the history and literature of North and South America: among which is included the larger portion of the extraordinary library of the late Henry Stevens, senior, ... Boston: Houghton, 1870. xv, 234 p. [0011]

Stevens, Peter

Modern English-Canadian poetry: a guide to information sources. Detroit, Mich.: Gale Research, c1978. xi, 216 p. (American literature, English literature, and world literatures in English Information guide series ; vol. 15); ISBN: 0-8103-1244-1. [1139]

Stevens, R.D.S.

The sampling and analysis of airborne sulphates and nitrates: a review of published work and synthesis of available information. Ottawa: Environment Canada, Environmental Protection Service, 1981. ix, 46 p. (Air Pollution Control Directorate Surveillance report ; EPS 5-AP-82-14); ISBN: 0-662-12166-X. [5176]

Stevens, Thomas J.

"[Canadian military history]." In: *Communiqué: Canadian Studies*; Vol. 2, no. 3 (February 1976) p. 2-26.; ISSN: 0318-1197. [1990]

Stevens, Tina

1988 Native peoples annotated bibliography: a listing of books, films, videos, newspapers, journals for and approved by native people. London, Ont.: Ontario Library Service-Thames, c1988. iv, 93 p.; ISBN: 0-9693736-0-0. [4103]

Stevenson, H.A.

Public policy and futures bibliography: a select list of Canadian, American, and other book-length materials, 1970 to 1980, including highly selected works published between 1949 and 1969. Toronto: Ministry of Education, c1980. xvi, 413 p.: charts; ISBN: 0-7743-5231-0. [3578]

Stevenson, H.A.; Hamilton, William B.

Canadian education and the future: a select annotated bibliography, 1967-1971. London, Ont.: University of Western Ontario, c1972. 59 p. [3445]

Stevenson, Michael

Toronto and its metropolitan government: a bibliography. Monticello, Ill.: Vance Bibliographies, 1986. 18 p. (Public administration series: Bibliography ; P-1927; ISSN: 0193-970X) [4414]

Stewardson, Dawn; Thomas, Diane; Hughes, Linda

Mirrors of the mind: a comprehensive bibliography of publications by staff of the Clarke Institute of Psychiatry. [Toronto: Clarke Institute of Psychiatry, 1980]. 164 l. [5632]

Stewart, Alice R.

The Atlantic provinces of Canada: union lists of materials in the larger libraries of Maine. 2nd ed. [Orono, Me.]: New England-Atlantic Provinces-Quebec Center, University of Maine at Orono, 1971. 70 p. [0209]

"Recent historical literature and the New England-Atlantic provinces region." In: *Acadiensis*; Vol. 1, no. 1 (Autumn 1971) p. 90-93.; ISSN: 0044-5851. [0210]

Stewart, George

"Sources of early Canadian history." In: *Proceedings and Transactions of the Royal Society of Canada*; Series 1, vol. 3, section 2 (1885) p. 39-44.; ISSN: 0316-4616. [1882]

Stewart, Jean; Swan, J.O.

Nanaimo District, V.I. [Vancouver: British Columbia Library Association], 1935. [1], 14 p. [0564]

Stewart, Marjorie J.

"Sir Wilfrid Laurier: a contribution towards a bibliography." In: *Ontario Library Review*; Vol. 15, no. 2 (November 1930) p. 59-61.; ISSN: 0030-2996. [7128]

Stewart, Sheila I.

A catalogue of the Akins Collection of books and pamphlets. Halifax: Imperial Publishing Co., 1933. 206 p. (Publications of the Public Archives of Nova Scotia ; no. 1) [6763]

Still, Robert

F.R. Scott: an annotated bibliography. Downsview, Ont.: ECW Press, c1983. [61] p.; ISBN: 0-920763-65-0. [7299]

"F.R. Scott: an annotated bibliography." In: *The annotated bibliography of Canada's major authors*, Vol. 4, edited by Robert Lecker and Jack David. Downsview, Ont.: ECW Press, c1983. P. 205-265.; ISBN: 0-920802-52-4. [7300]

Stinson, Arthur

Canadians participate. [Ottawa]: Centre for Social Welfare Studies, Carleton University, 1979. 167 p.; ISBN: 0-7709-0054-2. [3193]

Citizen action: an annotated bibliography of Canadian case studies. Ottawa: Community Planning Association of Canada, 1975. 71 p. [3140]

Stinson, Shirley M.; Johnson, Joy L.; Zilm, Glennis

History of nursing beginning bibliography: a proemial list with special reference to Canadian sources. Edmonton: Faculty of Nursing, University of Alberta, 1992. vii, 97 p.; ISBN: 0-88864-772-7. [5713]

Stirrett, George M.

An annotated bibliography: Point Pelee National Park and the Point Pelee region of Ontario. [Ottawa]: National Parks Service, Dept. of Indian Affairs and Northern Development, [1968]. 76 p. [0437]

Stockerl, Edward C.; Kent, Robert L.

The distribution, identification, biology and management of Eurasian water milfoil: an Alberta perspective. [Edmonton]: Pesticide Chemicals Branch, Pollution Control Division, Alberta Environment, 1984. vii l., 89 p. [5507]

Stone, Leroy O.

"Bibliographie choisie sur la migration interne au Canada." Dans: *Cahiers québécois de démographie*; Vol. 5, no 3 (décembre 1976) p. 135-145.; ISSN: 0380-1721. [3018]

Stone, Martha B.; Kokich, George J.V.

A bibliography of Canadian demography. Ottawa: Dominion Bureau of Statistics, Census Division, 1966. 147 p. (Technical paper / Dominion Bureau of Statistics, Census Division ; no. 5) [2969]

Storch, Janet L.; Meilicke, Carl A.

Health and social services administration: an annotated bibliography. [Ottawa]: Foundation of the Canadian College of Health Service Executives, 1979. 112 p.; ISBN: 0-9690139-0-6. [5626]

Storck, Peter L.

A preliminary bibliography of early man in eastern North America, 1839-1973. Toronto: Royal Ontario Museum, 1975. 110 p. (Archaeology monograph / Royal Ontario

Museum ; 4); ISBN: 0-88854-158-9. [4563]

Storrie, Kathleen; Dykstra, Pearl

"Bibliography on sexual harassment." In: *Resources for Feminist Research*; Vol. 10, no. 4 (December 1981/January 1982) p. 25-32.; ISSN: 0707-8412. [3812]

Story, G.M.

"Bacon and the fisheries of Newfoundland: a bibliographical ghost." In: *Newfoundland Quarterly*; Vol. 65, no. 2 (November 1966) p. 17-18.; ISSN: 0380-5824. [0206]

Stothers, David M.; Dullabaun, Marlene A.

A bibliography of Arctic and sub-arctic prehistory and protohistory. Toledo, Ohio: Toldedo Area Aboriginal Research Club, 1975. iii, 58 p. (Toledo Area Aboriginal Research Bulletin Supplementary monograph ; no. 2) [4564]

Stott, Jon C.

Canadian books for children: a guide to authors & illustrators. Toronto: Harcourt Brace Jovanovich Canada, 1988. viii, 246 p.: ill.; ISBN: 0-7747-3081-1. [1382]

Stott, Margaret M.; Verner, Coolie

A trial bibliography of research pertaining to adult education. Vancouver, B.C.: Extension Department, University of British Columbia, 1963. ii, 29 l. [3385]

Strang, R.M.

Ecology and management of the grassland and forested rangelands of interior British Columbia: an annotated bibliography. Rev. ed. Victoria: Province of British Columbia, Ministry of Forests, Information Services Branch, c1980. v, 129 p. [4972]

Strasser, J.A.

Roll compaction of metal powders: bibliography for period 1900 to 1973. Ottawa: Department of Energy, Mines and Resources, Mines Branch, 1973. iii, 91 p. (Mines Branch Information circular ; IC 300) [5747]

Strasser, Jean; Dirksen, Jean

Festival of women in the arts: a multi-media list. Toronto: Metropolitan Toronto Library Board, 1975. 39 p. [3760]

Stratford, Philip

Bibliography of Canadian books in translation: French to English and English to French/Bibliographie de livres canadiens traduits de l'anglais au français et du français à l'anglais. 2nd ed. Ottawa: Humanities Research Council of Canada, 1977. xvii, 78 p. [1440]

"French-Canadian literature in translation." In: *Meta*; Vol. 13, no 4 (décembre 1968) p. 180-187.; ISSN: 0026-0452. [1046]

Strathern, Gloria M.

Alberta, 1954-1979: a provincial bibliography. Edmonton: University of Alberta, 1982. xv, 745 p.; ISBN: 0-88864-949-X. [0536]

Alberta newspapers, 1880-1982: an historical directory. Edmonton: University of Alberta Press, 1988. xxxi, 568 p.: ill., [8] p. of pl.; ISBN: 0-88864-137-0. [6049]

Navigations, traffiques & discoveries, 1774-1848: a guide to publications relating to the area now British Columbia. Victoria, B.C.: Social Sciences Research Centre, University of Victoria, 1970. xv, 417 p.: maps.; ISBN: 0-9690418-2-9. [0577]

Strathy, Peter; Overboom, Fernande

Natural resource management: a guide to reference and statistical materials for managers and economists. [Toronto]: Management Studies Library, Faculty of Management Studies, University of Toronto, 1976. vi, 107 p. (NR Publications / Faculty of Management Studies,

University of Toronto ; no. 2) [5120]

Strecker, Herman

Butterflies and moths of North America: ... with a full bibliography .... Reading, Pa.: B.F. Owen, 1878. [4], ii, 283 p. [5303]

Strength training for youth: a specialized bibliography from the SPORT database/Musculation pour les jeunes: une bibliographie spécialisées de la base de données SPORT. Gloucester, Ont.: Sport Information Resource Centre, 1991. 23 l. (SportBiblio ; no. 12; ISSN: 1180-5269) [1869]

Strong, Lisa L.

Contemporary books reflecting Canada's cultural diversity: a selective annotated bibliography for grades K-12. Vancouver: British Columbia Teacher-Librarians' Association, 1992. 120 p.: ill.; ISBN: 0-921140-20-7. [4294]

Strong-Boag, Veronica

"Cousin Cinderella: a guide to historical literature pertaining to Canadian women." In: *Women in Canada*. Rev. ed., edited by Marylee Stephenson. Don Mills, Ont.: General Publishing, 1977. P. 245-274.; ISBN: 0-7736-1026-X. [3773]

Struthers, J.R. (Tim)

"A bibliography of works by and on Hugh Hood." In: *Essays on Canadian Writing*; Nos. 13/14 (Winter/Spring 1978-1979) p. 230-294.; ISSN: 0316-0300. [7066]

"Hugh Hood: an annotated bibliography." In: *The annotated bibliography of Canada's major authors*, Vol. 5, edited by Robert Lecker and Jack David. Downsview, Ont.: ECW Press, 1984. P. 231-353.; ISBN: 0-920802-68-0. [7067]

"Some highly subversive activities: a brief polemic and a checklist of works on Alice Munro." In: *Studies in Canadian Literature*; Vol. 6, no. 1 (Spring 1981) p. 140-150.; ISSN: 0380-6995. [7204]

Struthers, J.R. (Tim); Hogan, Lesley; Orange, John Charles

"A preliminary bibliography of works by Leon Rooke." In: *Canadian Fiction Magazine*; No. 38 (Special Leon Rooke issue) (1981) p. 148-164.; ISSN: 0045-477X. [7274]

Stuart, Merrill M.

A bibliography of master's theses in geography: American and Canadian universities. Tualatin, Or.: Geographic and Area Study Publications, c1973. x, 275 p.; ISBN: 0-88393-001-3. [6129]

Stuart, Ross; Vincent, Thomas Brewer

A chronological index of locally written verse published in the newspapers and magazines of Upper and Lower Canada, Maritime Canada, and Newfoundland through 1815. Kingston, Ont.: Loyal Colonies Press, 1979. viii, 386 p.; ISBN: 0-920832-00-8. [1158]

Stuart-Stubbs, Basil

Étude et interprétation des ouvrages portant sur le prêt entre bibliothèques. Vancouver: University of British Columbia, Bibliothèque, 1975. 230 f. [1612]

Maps relating to Alexander Mackenzie: a keepsake distributed at a meeting of the Bibliographical Society of Canada. Vancouver: [s.n.], 1968. [36] l.: ill., maps. [6514]

A survey and interpretation of the literature of interlibrary loan. Vancouver: University of British Columbia Library, 1975. 158 l. [1613]

Stubley, Eleanor Victoria

A guide to solo french horn music by Canadian composers. Toronto: Canadian Music Centre, 1990. ix, 75 p.: ill., music.; ISBN: 0-921519-06-0. [0938]

A guide to unpublished Canadian brass chamber music suitable for student performers. Toronto: Canadian Music

Educators' Association, c1989. x, 106 p.; ISBN: 0-92151-902-8. [0936]

Studies related to British Columbia tourism: a bibliography with selected annotations. [Victoria, B.C.]: Ministry of Tourism in cooperation with the Ministry of Industry and Small Business Development and the Canadian Government Office of Tourism, [1980]. vi, 96, [11] l.: map. [1800]

Stuntz, Stephen Conrad

List of the agricultural periodicals of the United States and Canada published during the century July 1810 to July 1910. Wilmington, Del.: SR Scholarly Resources, 1973. vii, 190 p.; ISBN: 0-84201-500-0. [5915]

Sturino, Franc

Italian-Canadian studies: a select bibliography. [Toronto]: York University and Multicultural History Society of Ontario, [c1988]. 108 p. (Elia Chair publication series / York University and Multicultural History Society of Ontario ; no. 1); ISBN: 0-919045-37-5. [4261]

Stymeist, David H.; Salazar, Lilia; Spafford, Graham

A selected annotated bibliography on the Filipino immigrant community in Canada and the United States. Winnipeg: University of Manitoba, Department of Anthropology, 1989. xi, 131 p.: map. (University of Manitoba Anthropology papers ; no. 31) [4273]

Suchowersky, Celestin N.

"Ukrainian imprints of Edmonton, Alberta: a preliminary checklist." In: Canadian Ethnic Studies; Vol. 5, no. 1/2 (1973) p. 303-341.; ISSN: 0008-3496. [4166]

Sudbury Public Library

The Sudbury basin: a guide to the local collection. [Sudbury]: Sudbury Public Library, 1967. 17, [4] p. [0434]

Sudbury maps. Sudbury: Sudbury Public Library, 1970. 6 l. [6521]

Suen, Ling; Smith, B.A.; McCoomb, L.A.

Urban Transportation Research Branch directory: publications, computer programs, data tapes, audio-visual material/Direction de la recherche sur les transports urbains, répertoire: publications, ensemble de programmes, données en mémoire, matériel audio-visuel. [Ottawa]: Transport Canada, Surface, 1979. 49 p. [4474]

Sugunasiri, Suwanda H.J.

The search for meaning: the literature of Canadians of South Asian origin. [Ottawa]: Department of the Secretary of State of Canada, 1988. 215 p.; ISBN: 0-662-16032-0. [1263]

Sullivan, Elinor

A bibliography of Simcoe County, Ontario, 1790-1990: published works and post-graduate theses relating to the British colonial and post-Confederation periods: with representative locations. Penetanguishene, Ont.: SBI, 1992. 269 p.; ISBN: 0-969664-90-7. [0493]

Sullivan, Thomas Priestlay

Non-target impacts of the herbicide Glyphosate: a compendium of references & abstracts. Victoria: Canadian Forestry Service, 1988. iii, 46 p. (FRDA report / Canada-British Columbia Forest Resource Development Agreement ; 013; ISSN: 0835-0752); ISBN: 0-7726-0827-X. [5265]

Summers, Frances J.; Pouliot, Thérèse

"Bibliographie de Yves Beauchemin." Dans: Voix et Images; Vol. 12, no 3 (printemps 1987) p. 416-428.; ISSN: 0318-9201. [6830]

Suo, Lynne

"Annotated bibliography on Isabella Valancy Crawford." In: Essays on Canadian Writing; No. 11 (Summer 1978) p. 289-314.; ISSN: 0316-0300. [6922]

Surette, Paul; Bérubé, Claude

"Bibliographie de l'Acadie." Dans: Cahiers: Société historique acadienne; Vol. 6, no 1 (mars 1975) p. 48-57.; ISSN: 0049-1098. [0222]

Surry, Jean

An annotated bibliography for industrial accident research and related fields: a companion volume to Industrial accident research: a human engineering appraisal. Toronto: Occupational Health and Safety Division, Ontario Ministry of Labour, 1969. 159 p. [2803]

Surtees, Robert J.

Canadian Indian policy: a critical bibliography. Bloomington: Indiana University Press, [c1982]. ix, 107 p. (Newberry Library Center for the History of the American Indian, Bibliographical series); ISBN: 0-253-31300-7. [4040]

Sutherland, Betty

"The Canadian Rockies: a short bibliography." In: Public Libraries; Vol. 2, no. 5 (May 1915) p. 220-221. [2945]

Sutherland, Fraser

John Glassco: an essay and bibliography. Downsview, Ont.: ECW Press, c1984. 121 p.; ISBN: 0-920802-78-8. [7020]

Scotland here: a checklist of Canadian writers of Scottish ancestry. [Scotsburn, N.S.: F. Sutherland, 1979]. 13 l. [1159]

Sutherland, Jack R.

List of references on forest nursery-disease research in British Columbia. Victoria, B.C.: Pacific Forest Research Centre, Canadian Forestry Service, 1973. 11 p. (Pacific Forest Research Centre Internal report ; BC-45) [4940]

Sutherland, Neil; Barman, Jean; Hale, Linda Louise

Contemporary Canadian childhood and youth: a bibliography. Westport, Conn.: Greenwood Press, 1992. ix, 492 p.; ISBN: 0-31328-586-1. [3361]

History of Canadian childhood and youth: a bibliography. Westport, Conn.: Greenwood Press, 1992. ix, 486 p.; ISBN: 0-31328-585-3. [3362]

Sutton, Michael J.D.

Human impacts of office automation: a review of published information. Ottawa: Department of Systems and Computer Engineering, Carleton University, 1982. 33, 15, [28] p. [2686]

Sutton, R.M.D.; Quadling, C.

Inventory of pollution-relevant research in Canada/État des recherches sur la pollution au Canada. Ottawa: Environmental Secretariat, Division of Biological Sciences, National Research Council of Canada, 1975. 4 vol. [5105]

Sutyla, Charles M.

"Multicultural studies in Canada: a bibliography with introductory comments." In: Communiqué: Canadian Studies; Vol. 3, no. 1 (October 1976) p. 4-65.; ISSN: 0318-1197. [4176]

Svacek, Victor

"Crawford Brough Macpherson: a bibliography." In: Powers, possessions and freedoms: essays in honour of C.B. Macpherson, edited by Alkis Kontos. Toronto: University of Toronto Press, c1979. P. 167-178.; ISBN: 0-8020-5474-9. [7169]

Swain, D.P.; Derksen, A.J.; Loch, J.S.

A literature review of life histories of some species of fish: rainbow smelt Osmerus mordax, gizzard shad Dorosoma cepedianum, paddlefish Polydon spathula, shovelnose sturgeon Scaphirhynchus platorynchus, pallid sturgeon Scaphirhynchus albus, and shortnose gar Lepisosteus platostomus, that may be introduced into the Hudson Bay watershed from the Missouri River watershed as a result of the Garrison Diversion. [Winnipeg]: Manitoba Department of Natural Resources, 1980. x, 168 p.: map. (MS report / Fisheries Branch, Manitoba Department of Natural Resources ; 80-37) [5455]

Swain, Merrill

"Bibliography: research on immersion education for the majority child." In: *Canadian Modern Language Review*; Vol. 32, no. 5 (May 1976) p. 592-596.; ISSN: 0008-4506. [3517]

Swan, Eric P.

Resin acids and fatty acids of Canadian pulpwoods: a review of the literature. Vancouver: Department of the Environment, Canadian Forestry Service, Western Forest Products Laboratory, 1973. 21 p. (Information report / Western Forest Products Laboratory ; VP-X-115; ISSN: 0045-429X) [4941]

Swanick, Eric L.

Agribusiness: an introductory bibliography. Monticello, Ill.: Council of Planning Librarians, 1976. 11 p. (Council of Planning Librarians Exchange bibliography ; 1019) [2619]

The Bay of Fundy tidal power project. Monticello, Ill.: Vance Bibliographies, 1978. 5 p. (Public administration series: Bibliography ; P-117; ISSN: 0193-970X) [5770]

Bilingualism in the federal Canadian public service. Monticello, Ill.: Vance Bibliographies, 1980. 6 p. (Public administration series: Bibliography ; P-425; ISSN: 0193-970X) [1450]

British Columbia architecture: an introductory bibliography. Monticello, Ill.: Vance Bibliographies, 1980. 10 l. (Architecture series: Bibliography ; A-212; ISSN: 0194-1356) [0758]

The Canadian Anti-inflation Board: an introductory bibliography. Monticello, Ill.: Vance Bibliographies, 1978. 6 p. (Public administration series: Bibliography ; P-105; ISSN: 0193-970X) [2638]

Canadian federal regulatory agencies: an introductory bibliography. Monticello, Ill.: Vance Bibliographies, 1978. 7 p. (Public administration series: Bibliography ; P-104; ISSN: 0193-970X) [2439]

Canadian government purchasing policies: an introductory bibliography. Monticello, Ill.: Vance Bibliographies, 1980. 5 p. (Public administration series: Bibliography ; P-445; ISSN: 0193-970X) [2458]

Canadian immigration studies in the late 1960's and in the 1970's: an introductory bibliography. Monticello, Ill.: Council of Planning Librarians, 1976. 10 p. (Council of Planning Librarians Exchange bibliography ; 1179) [4177]

Canadian library architecture: an introductory bibliography. Monticello, Ill.: Vance Bibliographies, 1980. 10 p. (Architecture series: Bibliography ; A-189; ISSN: 0194-1356) [0759]

The Canadian lighthouse: an introductory bibliography with supplementary materials on lighthouses. Monticello, Ill.: Vance Bibliographies, 1980. 8 p. (Architecture series: Bibliography ; A-394; ISSN: 0194-1356) [0760]

Canadian lotteries: an introductory bibliography. Monticello, Ill.: Vance Bibliographies, 1978. 3 p. [1787]

Canadian provincial government publications of interest to planners: a selective introductory bibliography. Monticello, Ill.: Vance Bibliographies, 1979. 13 p. (Public

administration series: Bibliography ; P-256; ISSN: 0193-970X) [6325]

Canadian provincial regulatory agencies: an introductory bibliography. Monticello, Ill.: Vance Bibliographies, 1979. 5 p. (Public administration series: Bibliography ; P-227; ISSN: 0193-970X) [2448]

The Canadian Royal Commission on Corporate Concentration. Monticello, Ill.: Vance Bibliographies, 1978. 6 p. (Public administration series: Bibliography ; P-102; ISSN: 0193-970X) [2639]

Canadian small business financing: an introductory bibliography. Monticello, Ill.: Vance Bibliographies, 1980. 8 p. (Public administration series: Bibliography ; P-444; ISSN: 0193-970X) [2665]

Canadian tax credit systems: an introductory bibliography. Monticello, Ill.: Vance Bibliographies, 1979. 5 p. (Public administration series: Bibliography ; P-229; ISSN: 0193-970X) [2649]

Canadian trade missions: an introductory bibliography. Monticello, Ill.: Vance Bibliographies, 1980. 4 p. (Public administration series: Bibliography ; P-446; ISSN: 0193-970X) [2666]

Canadian writings on architecture for the disabled: an introduction to recent writings. Monticello, Ill.: Vance Bibliographies, 1984. 5 p. (Architecture series: Bibliography ; A-1281; ISSN: 0194-1356); ISBN: 0-89028-171-8. [0775]

Conservation architecture in Canada: an introductory bibliography. Monticello, Ill.: Vance Bibliographies, 1980. 7 p. (Architecture series: Bibliography ; A-174; ISSN: 0194-1356) [0761]

Current writings on Nova Scotia architecture: an introductory bibliography. Monticello, Ill.: Vance Bibliographies, 1980. 6 p. (Architecture series: Bibliography ; A-318; ISSN: 0194-1356) [0762]

Decentralization of government services in Canada. Monticello, Ill.: Vance Bibliographies, 1979. 5 p. (Public administration series: Bibliography ; P-300; ISSN: 0193-970X) [2449]

The energy situation: crisis and outlook, an introductory non-technical bibliography. Monticello, Ill.: Council of Planning Librarians, 1975. 34 p. (Council of Planning Librarians Exchange bibliography ; 742) [4791]

Housing and architecture in North American northern regions. Monticello, Ill.: Vance Bibliographies, 1980. 7 p. (Architecture series: Bibliography ; A-186; ISSN: 0194-1356) [0763]

Introductory bibliography on the Canadian Treasury Board. Monticello, Ill.: Vance Bibliographies, 1979. 3 p. (Public administration series: Bibliography ; P-303; ISSN: 0193-970X) [2450]

Land use studies in Canada during the 1970s: an introductory bibliography. Monticello, Ill.: Vance Bibliographies, 1979. 24 p. (Public administration series: Bibliography ; P-304; ISSN: 0193-970X) [3026]

Mobile homes in Canada: a revised bibliography. Monticello, Ill.: Vance Bibliographies, 1979. 9 p. (Public administration series: Bibliography ; P-301; ISSN: 0193-970X) [4377]

New Brunswick architecture: an introductory bibliography. Monticello, Ill.: Vance Bibliographies, 1980. 5 p. (Architecture series: Bibliography ; A-187; ISSN: 0194-1356) [0764]

New Brunswick regional development during the '60s and

the 70s: an introductory bibliography. rev. ed. Monticello, Ill.: Vance Bibliographies, 1979. 37 l. (Public administration series: Bibliography ; P-204; ISSN: 0193-970X) [0242]

The Office of the federal Canadian Auditor General: an introductory bibliography. Monticello, Ill.: Vance Bibliographies, 1978. 4 p. (Public administration series: Bibliography ; P-84; ISSN: 0193-970X) [2440]

Ombudsman bibliography. Monticello, Ill.: Vance Bibliographies, 1979. 39 p. (Public administration series: Bibliography ; P-302; ISSN: 0193-970X) [2451]

Public funding of political parties in Canada: an introductory bibliography. Monticello, Ill.: Vance Bibliographies, 1979. 5 p. (Public administration series: Bibliography ; P-212; ISSN: 0193-970X) [2452]

"Recent publications relating to the history of the Atlantic region." In: *Acadiensis*; Vol. 4, no. 2 (Spring 1975)-Vol. 19, no. 2 (Spring 1990) [0271]

Reform of the Canadian banking act: a selected bibliography. Monticello, Ill.: Vance Bibliographies, 1979. 5 p. (Public administration series: Bibliography ; P-228; ISSN: 0193-970X) [2650]

Registered retirement savings plans (RRSP'S) in Canada: an introductory selective bibliography. Monticello, Ill.: Vance Bibliographies, 1978. 4 p. (Public administration series: Bibliography ; P-83; ISSN: 0193-970X) [2640]

Religious architecture of Canada. Monticello, Ill.: Vance Bibliographies, 1980. 8 p. (Architecture series: Bibliography ; A-188; ISSN: 0194-1356) [0765]

Rent control in Canada: an introductory bibliography. Monticello, Ill.: Vance Bibliographies, 1979. 5 l. (Public administration series: Bibliography ; P-205; ISSN: 0193-970X) [2205]

Retirement, mandatory retirement and pensions in Canada: an introductory bibliography. Monticello, Ill.: Vance Bibliographies, 1980. 6 p. (Public administration series: Bibliography ; P-536; ISSN: 0193-970X) [2667]

Transportation problems in Atlantic Canada: an introductory bibliography. Monticello, Ill.: Vance Bibliographies, 1979. 6 p. (Public administration series: Bibliography ; P-166; ISSN: 0193-970X) [4475]

Wage-price control in Canada: an introductory bibliography. Monticello, Ill.: Vance Bibliographies, 1979. 17 p. (Public administration series: Bibliography ; P-213; ISSN: 0193-970X) [2651]

Workmen's compensation in Canada. Monticello, Ill.: Vance Bibliographies, 1980. 4 p. (Public administration series: Bibliography ; P-584; ISSN: 0193-970X) [2869]

Swanick, Eric L.; Whalen, Doreen

The Lake Meech Accord (Canadian constitution): a bibliography. Monticello, Ill.: Vance Bibliographies, 1988. 22 p. (Public administration series: Bibliography ; P-2421; ISSN: 0193-970X); ISBN: 1-55590-811-X. [2319]

Swanick, Lynne Struthers

Municipal administration in Canada: an introductory checklist of secondary sources. Monticello, Ill.: Vance Bibliographies, 1978. 12 p. (Public administration series: Bibliography ; P-95; ISSN: 0193-970X) [4373]

The role of government in providing child care facilities: a checklist of sources. Monticello, Ill.: Vance Bibliographies, 1978. 9 p. (Public administration series: Bibliography ; P-85; ISSN: 0193-970X) [3181]

Women and pensions: a checklist of publications. Monticello, Ill.: Vance Bibliographies, 1979. 9 p. (Public administration series: Bibliography ; P-273; ISSN: 0193-970X) [3792]

Women as administrators: selected bibliography. Monticello, Ill.: Vance Bibliographies, 1978. 16 p. (Public administration series: Bibliography ; P-86; ISSN: 0193-970X) [3786]

Women in Canadian politics and government: a bibliography. Monticello, Ill.: Council of Planning Librarians, 1974. 29 p. (Council of Planning Librarians Exchange bibliography ; 697) [3749]

"Women in New Brunswick: bibliography." In: *Emergency Librarian*; Vol. 2, no. 2 (December 1974) p. 19-21.; ISSN: 0315-8888. [3750]

The young crusaders: the Company of Young Canadians: a bibliography. Monticello, Ill.: Council of Planning Librarians, 1974. 16 p. (Council of Planning Librarians Exchange bibliography ; 566) [3132]

Swann, C.G.; Donaldson, Edward M.

Bibliography of salmonid reproduction 1963-1979 for the family Salmonidae; subfamilies Salmoninae, Coregoninae and Thymallinae. West Vancouver, B.C.: Resources Services Branch, Department of Fisheries and Oceans, 1980. iv, 221 p. (Canadian technical report of fisheries and aquatic sciences ; no. 970; ISSN: 0706-6457) [5456]

Swift, Karen

Knowledge about neglect: a critical review of the literature. Toronto: University of Toronto, Faculty of Social Work, 1988. 74, [9] p. (Working papers in social welfare in Canada ; 23; ISSN: 0710-0299) [3317]

Swyripa, Frances A.

Guide to Ukrainian Canadian newspapers, periodicals and calendar-almanacs on microfilm, 1903-1970. Edmonton: Canadian Institute of Ukrainian Studies, 1985. xv, 236 p. (Research report / Canadian Institute of Ukrainian Studies ; no. 8) [5955]

"Theses and dissertations on Ukrainian Canadians: an annotated bibliography." In: *Journal of Ukrainian Graduate Studies*; Vol. 3, no. 1 (Spring 1978) p. 91-110.; ISSN: 0701-1792. [6149]

Ukrainian Canadians: a survey of their portrayal in English-language works. Edmonton: University of Alberta Press, 1978. xiii, 169 p. (Alberta Library in Ukrainian-Canadian Studies); ISBN: 0-88864-050-1. [4188]

Sykes, William John

Canada: a reading list. Ottawa: Carnegie Public Library, 1933. 23 p. [0046]

Symansky, Judith

Canadian federal Royal Commissions of interest to business libraries, 1955-1970. Montreal: Graduate School of Library Science, McGill University, 1972. iii, 35 l. (McGill University Graduate School of Library Science Occasional papers ; 3) [2599]

Symons, I.J.

Northern development in Canada: the impact of change: economic, social, transportation and environmental: a bibliography. [Ottawa]: Lands Directorate, Environment Canada, 1976. ii, 124 l. [0631]

Systems Approach Ltd.

Transportation for the disadvantaged: a bibliography/ Transport pour les handicapés: bibliographie. Montreal: Transport Canada, Surface, 1978. 34 p.; ISBN: 0-662-01775-7. [4471]

Szabo, Eve

"Bibliography of British Columbia." In: *BC Studies*; No. 56 (Winter 1982-83)-no. 75 (Autumn 1987) [0596]

Széplaki, Joseph

Hungarians in the United States and Canada: a bibliography: holdings of the Immigration History Research Center of the University of Minnesota. [Minneapolis]: Immigration History Research Center, University of Minnesota, 1977. viii, 113 p. [2] l. of pl. (Ethnic bibliography series / Immigration History Research Center, University of Minnesota ; no. 2) [4184]

Szpakowska, Janina-Klara

Le Québec jeune, 1978-1983: mini-banque d'information bibliographique sur la condition sociale des québécois et québécoises de 13 à 25 ans. Montréal: École de bibliothéconomie, Université de Montréal, 1983. 368 p. (Publications de l'École de bibliothéconomie / Université de Montréal ; no 8); ISBN: 2-920-537-00-8. [3255]

Szucs, Lina

"University research on Polish-Canadians: a preliminary check list of theses." In: *Canadian Ethnic Studies*; Vol. 2, no. 1 (June 1970) p. 163-164.; ISSN: 0008-3496. [6107]

T.F. Wood & Co's Canadian newspaper directory, containing accurate lists of all the newspapers and periodicals published in the Dominion of Canada and province of Newfoundland. Montreal: T.F. Wood, 1876. 79 p. [5995]

"Tableaux: périodiques littéraires et culturels du Québec depuis 1954." Dans: *Voix et Images*; Vol. 10, no 2 (hiver 1985) p. 11-16.; ISSN: 0318-9201. [5956]

Taft, Michael

A regional discography of Newfoundland and Labrador, 1904-1972. [St. John's, Nfld.]: Memorial University of Newfoundland Folklore and Language Archive, 1975. xxx, 102 p. (Bibliographical and special series / Memorial University of Newfoundland Folklore and Language Archive ; no. 1) [0849]

Taghvai, Hassan; Lamy, Nicole

Bibliographie sélective sur l'économie de l'énergie/Selective bibliography on the economics of energy. Montréal: École des hautes études commerciales, 1986. 71 f. (Cahiers du Centre d'études en administration internationale no 86-05; ISSN: 0825-5822) [2726]

Taillon, Michèle

Inventaire de sources de données sur la main-d'oeuvre et l'emplois. Québec: Ministère de l'éducation, Direction générale de la planification, 1974. 150 p. (Documents éducation et emploi / Québec Ministère de l'éducation, Direction générale de la planification ; 4-15) [2819]

Talbot, Christiane

Index des organismes et répertoires féminins au Canada. Ottawa: Bureau de l'image de la femme dans la programmation, Société Radio-Canada, 1987. 65, 65 f. [3859]

Index to Canadian women's groups and directories. Ottawa: Office of the Portrayal of Women in Programming, Canadian Broadcasting Corporation, 1987. 65, 65 l. [3860]

Tallboy, Felicity

Open education: review of the literature and selected annotated bibliography. Montreal: Faculty of Education, McGill University, c1973. 109 l. (Reports in education / Faculty of Education, McGill University ; no. 4) [3471]

Talman, J.J.

"History of south western Ontario: a selected list." In: *Ontario Library Review*; Vol. 34, no. 2 (May 1950) p. 119-122; vol. 34, no. 4 (November 1950) p. 291-296.; ISSN: 0030-2996. [0425]

"The Newspaper press of Canada West, 1850-60." In:

Proceedings and Transactions of the Royal Society of Canada; Series 3, vol. 33, section 2 (1939) p. 149-174.; ISSN: 0316-4616. [6005]

Tanghe, Raymond

"Sources primordiales en bibliographie." Dans: *Cahiers de la Société bibliographique du Canada*; Vol. 1 (1962) p. 49-56.; ISSN: 0067-6896. [1587]

Tangri, Om P.

Transportation in Canada and the United States: a bibliography of selected references, 1945-1969. Winnipeg: Center for Transportation Studies, University of Manitoba, 1970. 2 vol. (Research report / University of Manitoba Center for Transportation Studies ; no. 5-6) [4453]

Tanner, Helen Hornbeck

The Ojibwas: a critical bibliography. Bloomington: Published for the Newberry Library [by] Indiana University Press, c1976. viii, 78 p. (Newberry Library Center for the History of the American Indian, Bibliographical series); ISBN: 0-253-34165-5. [3985]

Tanner, Väinö

A bibliography of Labrador (specially Newfoundland-Labrador). Helsingfors: [s.n.], 1942. 83 p. [0202]

Tapper, Lawrence F.

A guide to sources for the study of Canadian Jewry/Guide des sources d'archives sur les juifs canadiens. [Ottawa]: National Ethnic Archives, Public Archives Canada, 1978. 51 p.; ISBN: 0-662-50112-8. [4189]

Tarbox, George E.

Bibliography of graduate theses on geophysics in the U.S. and Canadian institutions. Golden, Colo.: Colorado School of Mines, 1958. vi, 55 p. [6068]

Tari, Andor J.; Clewes, Janet L.; Semple, Shirley J.

Annotated bibliography of autism, 1943-1983. Guelph: Ontario Society for Autistic Children, 1985. 454 p.; ISBN: 0-88955-035-2. [5670]

Tascona, J.

Grievance handling: issues and approaches: bibliography with selected annotations. Kingston, Ont.: Industrial Relations Centre, Queen's University, 1981. 12 p. (Mimeographed bibliography series / Industrial Relations Centre, Queen's University ; no. 17) [2875]

Job evaluation systems and pay discrimination: a bibliography with selected annotations. Kingston, Ont.: Industrial Relations Centre, Queen's University, 1981. 10 p. (Mimeographed bibliography series / Industrial Relations Centre, Queen's University ; no. 19) [2876]

Union mergers: bibliography with selected annotations. Kingston, Ont.: Industrial Relations Centre, Queen's University, 1981. 7 p. (Mimeographed bibliography series / Industrial Relations Centre, Queen's University ; no. 18) [2877]

Tawell, Rachel; Beaumont-Moisan, Renée

L'île d'Anticosti (bibliographie). Québec: Ministère des terres et forêts, Service de l'information, Bibliothèque, 1974. 43, 7, 14 p. [0330]

Taye, Haile Kebret

A compendium of recent research on migration. Ottawa: Canada Mortgage and Housing Corporation, 1991. 27 p. [3067]

Tayler, Anne Hamilton; Nelson, Megan Jane

From hand to hand: a gathering of book arts in British Columbia. Vancouver: Alcuin Society, 1986. 150 p.: ill. [1685]

Taylor, Adrienne
The native peoples of Canada: a checklist of uncatalogued material in the Canadiana Collection. [Toronto]: Canadiana Collection, North York Public Library, 1979. 69 l.: ill., maps. [4009]

Taylor, Billie Louise
An annotated bibliography of documentation relevant to acid precipitation in Atlantic Canada. Bedford, N.S.: Atmospheric Environment Service, 1986. iii, 77 p. [5238]

Taylor, Donna
The Great Lakes region in children's books: a selected annotated bibliography. Brighton, Mich.: Green Oak Press, c1980. xix, 481 p.; ISBN: 0-931600-01-4. [1346]

Taylor, Graham; Hardy, Roger
Selected bibliography of CANMET publications pertaining to the activities of the Canadian Carbonization Research Association (CCRA), 1965-1980 [microform]. Ottawa: Canada Centre for Mineral and Energy Technology, 1981. 1 microfiche (14 fr.). (Microlog ; 90-04509) [6337]

Taylor, Hugh A.
New Brunswick history: a checklist of secondary sources. Fredericton: Provincial Archives of New Brunswick, Historical Resources Administration, 1971. xii, 254 p. [0211]

Taylor, Peter
A literature review of methods for handling solid residues arising from fuel recycle plant. Pinawa, Man.: Whiteshell Nuclear Research Establishment, 1990. 19 p. [5843]
A review of phase separation in borosilicate glasses, with reference to nuclear fuel waste immobilization/Examen de la séparation des phases dans les verres aux borosilicate quant à l'immobilisation des déchets de combustible nucléaire. Pinawa, Man.: Whiteshell Nuclear Research Establishment, 1990. 48 p. [5844]

Taylor, Ruth
The non-graded school: an annotated bibliography. [Toronto]: Library, Reference & Information Services, Ontario Institute for Studies in Education, 1973. x, 40 p. (Current bibliography / Ontario Institute for Studies in Education ; no. 5) [3472]

Taylor, Sandra J.
Children: all different, all the same: a selected list of books available for loan through the Provincial Library System. Charlottetown: Prince Edward Island Provincial Library, 1979. 38 p. [3556]

Tedford, Douglas E.; Triplehorn, Julia H.; Brûlé, Monique L.
Annotated list of indexes to Canadian provincial geological publications (including the Yukon and Northwest Territories). Ottawa: Energy, Mines and Resources Canada, 1989. ii, 26, 25, ii p. [6402]
Liste annotée des index aux publications géologiques provinciales canadiennes (incluant le Yukon et les Territoires du Nord-Ouest). Ottawa: Énergie, Mines et Ressources Canada, 1989. ii, 25, 26, ii p. [6403]

Tega, Vasile
Franchising, 1960-1971: bibliographie internationale, sélective et annotée/Franchising, 1960-1971: an international, selective and annotated bibliography. Montréal: École des hautes études commerciales, Bibliothèque, 1972. vii, 64 p. [2600]
Management and economics journals: a guide to information sources. Detroit: Gale Research, c1977. xxiv, 370 p.; ISBN: 0-8103-0833-9. [5929]

Teillet, D.J.
A northern Manitoba bibliography. [Ottawa]: Regional Economic Expansion; [Winnipeg]: Manitoba Department of Mines, Natural Resources and Environment, 1979. iv, 82 p. (Technical report / Manitoba Department of Mines, Natural Resources and Environment ; 79-5) [0530]

Teixeira, Carlos; Levigne, Gilles
The Portuguese in Canada: a bibliography/Les Portugais au Canada: une bibliographie. Toronto: Institute for Social Research, 1992. v, 79 p.; ISBN: 1-55014-163-5. [4295]

Telang, S.A.
Surface water acidification literature review. Calgary: Acid Deposition Research Program, 1987. x, 123 p.; ISBN: 0-921625-03-0. [5254]

Télé-formation: catalogue des ressources éducatives des Entreprises Radio-Canada. Montréal: Entreprises Radio-Canada, 1986. vi, 67, 133, vi p.; ISBN: 0-88794-249-0. [6666]

Télévision communautaire de Rivière-du-Loup
Répertoire des documents audio-visuels. Rivière-du-Loup, Québec: Télévision communautaire de Rivière-du-Loup, 1978. 91 f. [6637]

Tellier, Sylvie
Chronologie littéraire du Québec, 1760 à 1960. Québec: Institut québécois de recherche sur la culture, 1982. 347 p. (Instruments de travail / Institut québécois de recherche sur la culture ; no 6); ISBN: 2-89224-024-7. [1198]

"Ten years of Manitoba fiction in English: a selected bibliography." In: *Prairie Fire*; Vol. 8, no. 3 (Autumn 1987) p. 124-125.; ISSN: 0821-1124. [1244]

Tennant, Robert D.
The quill-and-rail catalogue: a bibliographical guide to Canadian railroads. Halifax, N.S.: Tennant Publishing House, c1976. 92 p.; ISBN: 0-919928-00-5. [4466]

Tennyson, Brian
Cape Breton: a bibliography. Halifax, N.S.: Department of Education, Nova Scotia, 1978. vi, 114 p. [0237]

Terasmae, J.
"A review of palynological studies in eastern Maritime Canada." In: *Maritime Sediments*; Vol. 1, no. 2 (April 1965) p. 19-22.; ISSN: 0025-3456. [4765]

Ternaux-Compans, Henri
Bibliothèque américaine ou Catalogue des ouvrages relatifs à l'Amérique qui ont paru depuis sa découverte jusqu'à l'an 1700. Paris: Arthus-Bertrand, 1837. viii, 191, 16 p. [0003]

Tessier, Daniel
Bibliographie de Lanaudière. [Québec]: Institut québécois de recherche sur la culture, 1987. 270 p.: cartes. (Documents de recherche / Institut québécois de recherche sur la culture ; no 14; ISSN: 0823-0447); ISBN: 2-89224-097-2. [0400]

Tessier, Yves
Carto-03: répertoire cartobibliographique sur la région de Québec. [Québec]: Cartothèque, Bibliothèque de l'Université Laval, 1983. 269 p.: ill.; ISBN: 2-9200310-01-1. [6583]
Catalogue collectif des atlas des cartothèques du Québec. Québec: [Bibliothèque de l'Université Laval, 1976. ix, 134, iii, 27, iv, 76 f.: carte. [6558]
"La documentation cartographique dans l'enseignement de la géographie au Québec: liste sélective de documents utiles." Dans: *Didactique-géographie*; No 11 (hiver 1979) p. 47-51.; ISSN: 0318-6555. [6569]

Têtu, Horace

Historique des journaux de Québec. Nouv. éd., rev. augm. et annotée. Québec: [s.n.], 1889. 107 p. [5999]

Journaux de Lévis. 3e éd., rev. et augm. Québec: [s.n.], 1898. 29 p. [6000]

Journaux et revues de Montréal: par ordre chronologique. Québec: [s.n.], 1881. 16 p. [5996]

Journaux et revues de Québec: par ordre chronologique. Québec: [s.n.], 1883. 26 p. [5997]

Têtu-Bernier, P.; Allen, E.; Hiratsuka, Y.

Bibliography of western gall rust. Edmonton: Canadian Forestry Service, Northern Forest Research Centre, c1983. iv, 10 p. (Northern Forest Research Centre Information report ; NOR-X-250; ISSN: 0704-7673); ISBN: 0-662-12712-9. [5490]

Thacker, Robert

"Alice Munro: an annotated bibliography." In: *The annotated bibliography of Canada's major authors*, Vol. 5, edited by Robert Lecker and Jack David. Downsview, Ont.: ECW Press, 1984. P. 354-414.; ISBN: 0-920802-68-0. [7205]

Théâtre québécois: ses auteurs, ses pièces: répertoire du Centre d'essai des auteurs dramatiques. Outremont, Québec: VLB, c1989. xi, 307 p.: ill. [24] p. de pl.; ISBN: 2-89005-374-1. [0987]

Théberge, Jean-Yves

Bibliographie du Haut-Richelieu. Saint-Jean [Québec]: Service des moyens d'enseignement, Commission scolaire régionale Honoré-Mercier, 1978. 86 p. [0356]

Thérèse-du-Carmel, soeur

Bibliographie analytique de l'oeuvre de Félix-Antoine Savard. Montréal: Fides, c1967. 229 p.: port. [7292]

Thériault, J.–Yvon

Les publications parlementaires du Québec depuis 1792. Québec: Assemblée nationale du Québec, 1976. ix, 37 p.: fac.–sim.; ISBN: 0-7754-2494-3. [6305]

Thérien, Jean-Philippe

Relations Canada-Tiers Monde: bibliographie analytique, 1970-1987. Montréal: Département de science politique, Université de Montréal, 1988. iv, 63 p. (Notes de recherche / Département de science politique, Université de Montréal ; no 22) [2524]

Thérien, Robert; D'Amours, Isabelle

Dictionnaire de la musique populaire au Québec, 1955-1992. Québec: Institut québécois de recherche sur la culture, 1992. xxv, 580 p.: portr.; ISBN: 2-89224-183-9. [0942]

Theses in Canadian political studies: completed and in progress/Thèses canadiennes en science politique: complétées et en cours de rédaction. [Kingston, Ont.]: Canadian Political Science Association, [1971]. 71 p. [6111]

"Theses in geography completed for Department of Geography, University of Western Ontario." In: *Ontario Geography*; No. 1 (January 1967) p. 62-68.; ISSN: 0078-4850. [6089]

Theses related to planning. [Vancouver: University of British Columbia, Fine Arts Library], 1982. 124 p. [6161]

Thibault, Claude

Bibliographia Canadiana. Don Mills, Ont.: Longman Canada, 1973. lxiv, 795 p. [0109]

Canada's external relations, 1600-1969 [microform]: a bibliography /Les relations extérieures du Canada, 1600-1969 [microforme]: une bibliographie. Rochester, N.Y.: University of Rochester, 1973. 2 vol. (on 1 reel microfilm). [2409]

Thibault, Emilia

"L'Information et les problèmes de la liberté de la presse: bibliographie annotée." Dans: *Bulletin: Bibliothèque de l'Assemblée nationale du Québec*; Vol. 2, no 2 (avril 1971) p. 41-56.; ISSN: 0701-6808. [2123]

Thibault, Henri-Paul

"L'orientation des recherches historiques à Louisbourg." Dans: *Revue d'histoire de l'Amérique française*; Vol. 24, no 3 (décembre 1970) p. 408-412.; ISSN: 0035-2357. [1970]

Thibault, Marie-Thérèse

Bibliographie pour la conservation et la restauration de lieux et de bâtiments historiques. [Québec]: Ministère des affaires culturelles, Direction générale du patrimoine, Service de l'inventaire des biens culturels, Centre de documentation, 1975. iii, 43 p. (Direction générale du patrimoine Dossier ; no 1) [0745]

Thibault, Suzanne

Livres québécois pour enfants: une sélection de Communication-jeunesse. Montréal: Communication-jeunesse, 1986. 35 p.: ill. [1374]

Thiele, Judith C.

Funstuff: a selected bibliography of recreational and leisure reading talking books in the Crane collection. Vancouver, B.C.: Charles Crane Memorial Library, University of British Columbia, 1981. 41 p.; ISBN: 0-88865-185-6. [6649]

Thiele, Paul E.

Educational materials for the handicapped: a preliminary union list. Victoria: British Columbia Ministry of Education, 1978. 2 vol. [3546]

Thom, Douglas J., et al.

The hockey bibliography: ice hockey worldwide. [Toronto]: Ontario Institute for Studies in Education: Ministry of Culture and Recreation, Ontario, 1978. v, 153 p.: ill. (Bibliography series / Ontario Institute for Studies in Education ; no. 4); ISBN: 0-7744-0166-4. [1788]

Thom, Douglas J.; Hickcox, E.S.

A selected bibliography of educational administration: a Canadian orientation. Toronto: Canadian Education Association, 1973. v, 32 l. [3473]

Thomas, Clara

Canadian novelists, 1920-1945. Toronto: Longmans, Green, 1946. 129 p. [1007]

"Carl Klinck: indefatigable Canadian: a Carl F. Klinck bibliography." In: *Journal of Canadian Fiction*; Vol. 2, no. 3 (Summer 1973) p. 5-8.; ISSN: 0047-2255. [7095]

Our nature – our voices: a guidebook to English-Canadian literature. Toronto: New Press, 1972. ix, 175 p.: ill.; ISBN: 0-88770-618-5. [1070]

Thomas, J., et al.

"Aging and the aged: an eclectic annotated resource list." In: *Canadian Home Economics Journal*; Vol. 40, no. 3 (Summer 1990) p. 154-158.; ISSN: 0008-3763. [3346]

Thomas, Morley K.

A bibliography of Canadian climate, 1763-1957. Ottawa: Division of Building Research, National Research Council of Canada, 1961. 114 p. [5033]

A bibliography of Canadian climate, 1958-1971/ Bibliographie du climat canadien, 1958-1971. Ottawa: Information Canada, 1973. 170 p. [5080]

Thomas, Morley K.; Anderson, S.R.

Guide to the climatic maps of Canada. Toronto: Meteorological Branch, Department of Transport, 1967. 1 vol. (in various pagings). [6512]

Thomas, Morley K.; Phillips, David W.

A bibliography of Canadian climate, 1972-1976/ Bibliographie du climat canadien, 1972-1976. [Hull, Quebec]: Environment Canada, Atmospheric Environment Service, 1979. 135 p.; ISBN: 0-660-50220-8. [5157]

Thompson, Barbara

The effects of effluent from the Canadian textile industry on aquatic organisms: a literature review. Winnipeg: Environment Canada, Fisheries and Marine Service, Freshwater Institute, 1974. vi, 99 p. (Fisheries and Marine Service Technical report ; no. 489; ISSN: 0701-7626) [5094]

Thompson, Judy

Alcohol and drug research in Saskatchewan, 1970-1978: subject index and abstracts. [Regina]: Saskatchewan Alcoholism Commission, Research Division, 1978. [38] p. [5618]

Thompson, Lawrence Sidney

The new Sabin: books described by Joseph Sabin and his successors, now described again on the basis of examination of originals, and fully indexed by title, subject, joint authors, and institutions and agencies. Troy, N.Y.: Whitston Publishing, 1974-. vol. [0190]

Thomson, Bruce

Annotated bibliography of large organic debris (LOD) with regards to stream channels and fish habitat. Victoria: BC Environment, 1991. iii, 93 p. (MOE Technical report ; 32; ISSN: 0840-9730); ISBN: 0-771-89028-1. [5293]

Thomson, Inga; Dafoe, Marcella

"Bibliography of J.W. Dafoe, 1866-1944." In: *Canadian Journal of Economics and Political Science*; Vol. 10, no. 2 (May 1944) p. 213-215.; ISSN: 0315-4890. [6926]

Thomson, Jennifer

The law of the sea: with special reference to Canada: a select bibliography. Ottawa: Norman Paterson School of International Affairs, Carleton University, 1976. ii, 74 p. (Norman Paterson School of International Affairs Bibliography series ; no. 4) [2162]

Thomson, Murray; Ironside, Diana J.

A bibliography of Canadian writings in adult education. Toronto: Canadian Association for Adult Education, 1956. [ii], 56 p. [3377]

Thorington, J. Monroe

"A bibliography of the Canadian Rockies." In: *Canadian Alpine Journal*; Vol. 22 (1933) p. 230-231.; ISSN: 0068-8207. [2951]

Thornton, Russell; Grasmick, Mary K.

Sociology of American Indians: a critical bibliography. Bloomington: Indiana University Press, c1980. xi, 113 p. (Newberry Library Center for the History of the American Indian, Bibliographical series); ISBN: 0-253-35294-0. [4021]

Thornton, Russell; Sandefur, Gary D.; Grasmick, Harold G.

The urbanization of American Indians: a critical bibliography. Bloomington: Published for the Newberry Library [by] Indiana University Press, c1982. viii, 87 p. (Newberry Library Center for the History of the American Indian, Bibliographical series); ISBN: 0-253-36205-9. [4041]

Thouez, Jean-Pierre

Bibliographie de géographie urbaine. Sherbrooke: Université de Sherbrooke, Département de géographie, 1975. 67 f. (Bulletin de recherche / Université de Sherbrooke, Département de géographie ; no 22; ISSN: 0710-0868) [4354]

Thouin, Richard

Les bibliographies du cours de bibliothéconomie de l'Université Laval, 1947-1961 [microforme]: index. Montréal: Ministère des affaires culturelles, Bibliothèque nationale du Québec, 1980. 1 microfiche. [0133]

Threlfall, William

Audiovisual materials concerning the care, use, behaviour and general biology of animals. St. John's, Nfld.: Memorial University of Newfoundland, 1989. i, 353 p. (Memorial University of Newfoundland Occasional papers in biology ; no. 13; ISSN: 0702-0007) [6687]

Thunder Bay Environmental Project

The Thunder Bay environmental information index. Thunder Bay, Ont.: Thunder Bay Environmental Project, 1972. 99 p. [5067]

Thurlow and Associates

Annotated bibliography: Georgian Bay Islands National Park. [Ottawa]: Thurlow and Associates, 1975. vi, 197 l.: map. [3012]

Étude des textes relatifs aux caractéristiques des eaux usées et aux techniques d'épuration dans l'industrie du traitement du bois. Hull, Québec: Service de la protection de l'environnement, Environnement Canada, 1977. ix, 60 p.: ill. (Étude économique et technique, Rapport / Service de la protection de l'environnement, Environnement Canada ; EPS 3-WP-77-2); ISBN: 0-662-90231-9. [4960]

Literature review of wastewater characteristics and abatement technology in the wood and timber processing industry. Ottawa: Environmental Protection Service, Fisheries and Environment Canada, 1977. 70 p. (Economic and technical review report / Environmental Protection Service, Fisheries and Environment Canada ; EPS 3-WP-77-2); ISBN: 0-662-00514-7. [4961]

A preliminary annotated bibliography for Pukaskwa National Park. Ottawa: Thurlow and Associates, 1972. vi, 266, [7] l.: maps. [2992]

Thwaites, James D.

La documentation et les archives du Conseil régional de développement de l'Est du Québec. Québec: Institut supérieur des sciences humaines, Université Laval, 1978. xvii, 383 p. (Cahiers de l'ISSH, Collection Instruments de travail / Institut supérieur des sciences humaines, Université Laval ; no 23) [6317]

L'enseignant québécois: sources et études récentes. Québec: Institut supérieur des sciences humaines, Université Laval, 1973. x, 142 f. (Cahiers de l'ISSH, Collection Instruments de travail / Institut supérieur des sciences humaines, Université Laval ; no 8) [3474]

Thèses en sciences de l'éducation (universités du Québec et universités francophones ailleurs au Canada). Québec: Institut supérieur des sciences humaines, Université Laval, 1973. ii, 159 p. (Cahiers de l'ISSH, Collection Instruments de travail / Institut supérieur des sciences humaines, Université Laval ; no 9) [6130]

"Thèses récentes sur le travailleur, le syndicalisme et le patronat." Dans: *Histoire des travailleurs québécois: Bulletin RCHTQ*; Vol. 1, no 2 (février 1974) p. 18-20.; ISSN: 0315-7938. [6135]

Thwaites, Reuben Gold

The Jesuit relations and allied documents: travels and explorations of the Jesuit missionaries in New France, 1610-1791. Cleveland: Burrows Bros., 1896-1901. 73 vol.: ill., facsims., maps (some folded). [1892]

Tibbetts, Donald Cleveland

A bibliography on cold weather construction. Rev. ed. Ottawa: Division of Building Research, National Research Council Canada, 1971. 39 p. (National Research Council Canada, Division of Building Research Bibliography ; no. 10) [5736]

Tietz, Harrison Morton

An index to the described life histories, early stages and hosts of the macrolepidoptera of the continental United States and Canada. Sarasota, Fla.: Published by A.C. Allyn for the Allyn Museum of Entomology; Los Angeles: distributed by Entomological Reprint Specialists, 1972. 2 vol.; ISBN: 0-913492-01-9. [5371]

Tilson, Marie

Pipelines. Monticello, Ill.: Vance Bibliographies, 1990. 28 p. (Public administration series: Bibliography ; P-2884; ISSN: 0193-970X); ISBN: 0-7920-0544-9. [4517]

Times Bookshop (London, England)

Canadian printed books, 1752-1961: an exhibition. London: Times Bookshop, 1961. 27 p. [1585]

Tirman, Jean-Louis

"Répertoire des thèses de maîtrise en géographie présentées à l'Institut de géographie de l'Université Laval, d'octobre 1959 à novembre 1968." Dans: *Cahiers de géographie de Québec*; Vol. 13, no 30 (décembre 1969) p. 374-379.; ISSN: 0007-9766. [6101]

To, Minh Chau; Kryzanowski, Lawrence; Lessard, Michel

La performance des fonds mutuels: une revue de la littérature. Montréal: École des hautes études commerciales, 1990. 46 f. (Rapport de recherche / École des hautes études commerciales ; no 90-07; ISSN: 0709-986X) [2771]

To, Minh Chau; Kryzanowski, Lawrence; Roy, Vincent

Les anomalies dans les marchés des capitaux: une revue de la littérature. Montréal: École des hautes études commerciales, 1990. 55 f. (Rapport de recherche / École des hautes études commerciales ; no 90-06; ISSN: 0709-986X) [2772]

Tobin, Mary A.T.; Mongrain, Susan; Finn, Julia

Departmental Library Canadian Indian art and artists: a bibliography/Bibliothèque ministérielle art et artistes indiens du Canada: une bibliographie. Ottawa: Indian and Northern Affairs Canada, 1990. 26 p.; ISBN: 0-662-57509-1. [0723]

Tod, Dorothea D.; Cordingley, Audrey

"A bibliography of Canadian literary periodicals, 1789-1900." In: *Proceedings and Transactions of the Royal Society of Canada*; Series 3, vol. 26, section 2 (1932) p. 87-96.; ISSN: 0316-4616. [5863]

A check list of Canadian imprints, 1900-1925: preliminary checking edition/Catalogue d'ouvrages imprimés au Canada: liste à vérifier. Ottawa: Canadian Bibliographic Centre, Public Archives of Canada, 1950. 370 l. [0060]

Tokaryk, Tim T.; Storer, John E.; Nambudiri, E.M.V.

Selected bibliography of the Cretaceous-Tertiary boundary event, through 1989. Regina: Saskatchewan Museum of Natural History, c1992. 140 p. (Natural history contributions ; no. 11; ISSN: 0707-3887) [4613]

Tomlinson, Jackie

Sources of information for a listing of school libraries in Canada/Sources de renseignements sur les bibliothèques scolaires au Canada. Ottawa: National Library of Canada, 1983. 6 p. (Bibliographies / Library Documentation Centre; ISSN: 0226-4226) [1658]

Tooker, Elisabeth

The Indians of the Northeast: a critical bibliography. Bloomington: Indiana University Press, c1978. xi, 77 p. (Newberry Library Center for the History of the American Indian, Bibliographical series); ISBN: 0-253-33003-3. [3998]

Tooley, R.V.

French mapping of the Americas: the De l'Isle, Buache, Dezauche succession (1700-1830). London: Map Collectors' Circle, 1967. 39, [24] p.: facsims. (Map Collectors' Circle ; Vol. 4, no. 33) [6513]

Toomey, Kathleen M.; Willis, Stephen C.

Musicians in Canada: a bio-bibliographical finding list/ Musiciens au Canada: index bibliographique. Ottawa: Canadian Association of Music Libraries, 1981. xiv, 185 p. (Publications / Canadian Association of Music Libraries ; no. 1); ISBN: 0-9690583-1-4. [0899]

Tooth, John

Looking for Manitoba government publications: an annotated bibliography of books and pamphlets. [Winnipeg]: Library, Department of Education, [1978]. ix, 267 p. [6318]

Torjman, Sherri Resin

Mental health in the workplace: annotated bibliography. Toronto: Canadian Mental Health Association, 1978. iv, 78, 78, iii l. [5619]

La santé mentale et le lieu de travail: bibliographie annotée. Toronto: Association canadienne pour la santé mentale, 1978. iii, 78, 78, iv f. [5620]

Torn, M.S.; Degrange, J.E.; Shinn, J.H.

The effects of acidic deposition on Alberta agriculture. Calgary: Acid Deposition Research Program, 1987. xvi, 160 p.; ISBN: 0-921625-10-3. [4711]

"Toronto and York in literature." In: *York Pioneer and Historical Society Annual Report*; Vol. 86 (1954) p. 11-14.; ISSN: 0315-5269. [1013]

Toronto Board of Education. Language Study Centre

Bibliography of non-sexist books. Toronto: The Centre, 1975. 10 p. [1327]

Toronto Nutrition Committee

Food: economics and politics: an annotated bibliography. [Toronto]: The Committee, 1976. 13 p. [2620]

Toronto. Planning and Development Department. Research and Information Section

A bibliography of major planning publications (May 1942 – December 1988). Toronto: City of Toronto, Planning and Development Department, 1988. 89 p. [4425]

Toronto. Public Library

A bibliography of Canadiana: being items in the Public Library of Toronto, Canada, relating to the early history and development of Canada. Toronto: The Public Library, 1934. 828 p.: facsims. [0047]

Books and pamphlets published in Canada, up to the year eighteen hundred and thirty-seven, copies of which are in the Public Reference Library, Toronto, Canada. Toronto: Public Library, 1916. 76 p. [0035]

The Canadian North West: a bibliography of the sources of information in the Public Reference Library of the City of Toronto, Canada in regard to the Hudson's Bay Company, the fur trade and the early history of the Canadian North West. Toronto: Public Library, 1931. 52 p. [1906]

Catalogue of books and pamphlets presented to the Toronto Public Library by John Hallam. Toronto: C.B. Robinson, 1885. 76 p. [6739]

Experience Canada. 2nd ed. [Toronto]: The Library, 1982. 36 p. [0139]

Map collection of the Public Reference Library of the city of Toronto, Canada. Toronto: Public Library, 1923. 111 p. [6489]

The North West Passage, 1534-1859: a catalogue of an exhibition of books and manuscripts in the Toronto Public Library. Toronto: Baxter Publishing in co-operation with the Toronto Public Library, 1963. 26 p.: ill., facsims., maps, ports. [1941]

The rebellion of 1837-38: a bibliography of the sources of information in the Public Reference Library of the City of Toronto, Canada. [Toronto]: Public Library of Toronto, 1924. 81 p. [1904]

A subject catalogue, or, Finding list of books in the Reference Library, with an index of subjects and personal names. Toronto: Murray, 1889. xxvii, 381 p.; ISBN: 0-665-26192-6. [6742]

Toronto past and present: a multi-media list. rev. ed. [Toronto]: Toronto Public Library, 1984. 31 p. [0479]

Toronto. Public Library. Reference Division
Canadian books: an outline for the people. Toronto: Department of Education of Ontario, Public Libraries Branch, [1923]. 20 p. [0037]

Toth, Pierre
La prévision des faillites: revue de la littérature financière et méthodologie. Montréal: École des hautes études commerciales, c1986. 73 f., 8 p. (Cahier / École des hautes études commerciales, Montréal ; 86-1); ISBN: 2-893600-68-9. [2727]

Totosy de Zepetnek, Steven
"Literary works by German-speaking Canadians and their critical appraisal: a selected and annotated bibliography with an introduction." In: *Canadian Review of Comparative Literature*; Vol. 16, no. 3/4 (September-December 1989) p. 669-686.; ISSN: 0319-051X. [1279]

Tougas, Gérard
A checklist of printed materials relating to French-Canadian literature, 1763-1968/Liste de référence d'imprimés relatifs à la littérature canadienne-française, 1763-1968. 2nd ed. Vancouver: University of British Columbia Press, 1973. xvi, 174 p.; ISBN: 0-7748-0007-0. [1079]

Tourangeau, Rémi
Bibliographie du théâtre en Mauricie. Trois-Rivières: Centre de documentation en lettres québécoises, Université du Québec à Trois-Rivières, 1981. 2 vol.: ill. (Guides bibliographiques du théâtre québécois ; no 2, 4); ISBN: 2-89060-007-6 (Vol. 1); 2-89060-011-4 (Vol. 2). [0972]

Tables provisoires du théâtre de Drummondville: index établi d'après les articles et les comptes rendus de presse parus dans les périodiques drummondvillois. Trois-Rivières: Centre de documentation en lettres québécoises de l'Université du Québec à Trois-Rivières, 1980. 184 f. (Guides bibliographiques du théâtre québécois ; no 1); ISBN: 2-89125-001-X. [0969]

Le théâtre à Nicolet, 1803-1969: bibliographie régionale. Trois-Rivières, Québec: Éditions CÉDOLEQ, 1982. 394 p. (Guides bibliographiques du théâtre québécois ; no 5); ISBN: 2-89060-013-0. [0976]

"Tourisme, culture, régions." Dans: *Notes du Centre d'études du tourisme*; Vol. 7, no 11 (mai 1987) p. 1-4.; ISSN: 0229-2718. [1844]

Le Tourisme à Montréal: bibliographie annotée. [Montréal]: Centre d'études du tourisme, 1987. 138 p. [0401]

"Le tourisme à Montréal." Dans: *Notes du Centre d'études du tourisme*; Vol. 7, no 9 (mars 1987) p. 1-4.; ISSN: 0229-2718. [1843]

"Le tourisme ethno-culturel." Dans: *Notes du Centre d'études du tourisme*; Vol. 8, no 4 (mai 1988) p. 1-4.; ISSN: 0229-2718. [4262]

Tousignant, André
Données sur l'histoire régionale: bibliographie annotée avec index et autres sources de référence. [Châteauguay, Québec]: Société historique de la vallée de la Châteauguay/Chateauguay Valley Historical Society, 1980. viii, 151 p. [0367]

Toussaint, Adéline
Flore et faune canadiennes: inventaire de volumes et de documents audio-visuels au Canada français. [S.l.: s.n.], c1978. v, 66 p. [5424]

Towle, Edward L.
Bibliography on the economic history and geography of the Great Lakes-St. Lawrence drainage basin. Rochester, N.Y.: University of Rochester, 1964. 41 l. [2967]

Townsend, Vera S.; Maydell, Ursula M.
Computer network performance bibliography. Edmonton: Department of Computing Science, University of Alberta, 1980. 367 p. (Technical report / Department of Computing Science, University of Alberta ; TR80-2) (Alberta Research Council Contribution ; no. 1036) [5780]

Tracz, George S.
Annotated bibliography on determination of teachers' salaries and effective utilization of teacher manpower. Toronto: Department of Educational Planning, Ontario Institute for Studies in Education, 1971. 15 p. (Educational Planning Occasional papers / Ontario Institute for Studies in Education ; no. 10:71) [3426]

Research into academic staff manpower and salary issues: a selective bibliography. Toronto: Department of Educational Planning, Ontario Institute for Studies in Education, 1974. ii, 35 p. (Educational Planning Occasional papers / Ontario Institute for Studies in Education ; no. 73/74-7) [3492]

Trahan-Langlois, Lysette
Les facteurs associés à l'orientation des personnes âgées dans des établissements d'hébergement: une revue de la littérature. Québec: Gouvernement du Québec, Ministère de la santé et des services sociaux, Direction générale de la planification et de l'évaluation, 1989. xi, 100 p. (Collection Études et analyses / Gouvernement du Québec, Ministère de la santé et des services sociaux, Direction générale de la planification et de l'évaluation ; no 5); ISBN: 2-550-1961-8. [3335]

Tratt, Gertrude E.N.
A survey and listing of Nova Scotia newspapers, 1752-1957: with particular reference to the period before 1867. Halifax: School of Library Service, Dalhousie University, 1979. 193 p. (Occasional papers / Dalhousie University Libraries and Dalhousie University School of Library Service ; no. 21; ISSN: 0318-7403); ISBN: 0-7703-0160-6. [6028]

Tratt, Grace
Check list of Canadian small presses: English language. Halifax, N.S.: University Libraries; School of Library Service, Dalhousie University, 1974. 153 l. (Occasional

papers / Dalhousie University Libraries and Dalhousie University School of Library Service ; no. 6; ISSN: 0318-7403) [1608]

Tree Foundation of Canada
Inventory of Canadian research and demonstration projects on child abuse and neglect: a research report. [Ottawa]: Minister of Supply and Services Canada, 1981. 358 p.; ISBN: 0-662-11734-4. [3230]

Tremaine, Marie
A bibliography of Canadian imprints, 1751-1800. Toronto: University of Toronto Press, 1952. xxvii, 705 p.: facsim. [0061]

Tremblay, Jean-Marie
Sociologie de la famille et de la société québécoise: bibliographie annotée, environ 750 titres. Québec: Ministère de l'éducation, Service des programmes de la direction de l'enseignement collégial, 1979. 102 f. [3194]

Tremblay, Jean-Pierre
Bibliographie québécoise: roman, théâtre, poésie, chanson. Inventaire des Écrits du Canada français. [Cap-Rouge, Québec]: Educo média, 1973. 252 p. [1080]

"La chanson: essai bibliographique." Dans: *Cahiers de Cap-Rouge*; Vol. 4, no 4 (1976) p. 45-79.; ISSN: 0227-2822. [0857]

Tremblay, Louis-Marie
Bibliographie des relations du travail au Canada, 1940-1967. Montréal: Presses de l'Université de Montréal, 1969. ix, 242 p.; ISBN: 0-8405-0131-5. [2804]

Tremblay, Manon
La participation des femmes aux structures politiques électorales: une bibliographie. Québec: Groupe de recherche et d'échange multidisciplinaire féministe, Université Laval, 1990. 142 p. (Cahiers de recherche du GREMF / Groupe de recherche et d'échange multidisciplinaire féministe, Université Laval ; 35); ISBN: 2-89364-037-0. [3882]

Tremblay, Marc-Adélard
Bibliographie sur l'administration des Indiens du Canada et des États-Unis. [Québec: Université Laval], 1970. 76 f. [3924]

"L'État des recherches sur la culture acadienne." Dans: *Recherches sociographiques*; Vol. 3, no 1-2 (janvier-août 1962) p. 145-167.; ISSN: 0034-1282. [0205]

Tremblay, Monique; Provencher, Luc
Félix Leclerc: bibliographie. [S.l.]: Collège d'enseignement général et professionnel François-Xavier-Garneau, 1990. 27 f.; ISBN: 2-920910-02-7. [7140]

Tremblay-Matte, Cécile
La chanson écrite au féminin: de Madeleine de Verchères à Mitsou, 1730-1990. Laval, Québec: Éditions Trois, [1990]. 391 p.: ill. (Collection Trois Guinées); ISBN: 2-920887-16-5. [0939]

Trethewey, Paul
"Bibliography of the Supreme Court of Canada." In: *Osgoode Hall Law Journal*; Vol. 14, no. 2 (October 1976) p. 425-443.; ISSN: 0030-6185. [2163]

Trew, Johanne
The Rodolphe Mathieu collection at the National Library of Canada: an annotated catalogue. Ottawa: National Library of Canada, 1989. 158 p.; ISBN: 0-315-44440-1. [7180]

Triplehorn, Julia H.; Johnson, Lee E.
Muskox bibliography. Fairbanks: Institute of Arctic Biology, University of Alaska, 1980. 216 p. (Institute of Arctic Biology Occasional publications on northern life ; no.

3) [5457]

Trotter, Reginald George
"The bibliography of Canadian constitutional history." In: *Papers of the Bibliographical Society of America*; Vol. 22, part 1 (1928) p. 1-12.; ISSN: 0006-128X. [2102]

Canadian history: a syllabus and guide to reading. New and enl. ed. Toronto: Macmillan, 1934. xiv, 193 p. [1911]

Troy, Kathleen
Annotated bibliography of ESL testing. Toronto: Ministry of Culture and Recreation, Newcomer Services Branch, 1978. 49 p. [3547]

Trudel, François
Une bibliographie annotée sur le caribou (Rangifer tarandus) du Québec-Labrador. Québec: Ministère des affaires culturelles, Direction générale du patrimoine, 1979. 146 p.: ill. (Dossier / Direction générale du patrimoine, Québec ; 42) [5441]

Tuckermann, Walther
"Länderkunde der aussereuropäischen erdteile: Kanada und Neufundland [bibliographie von 1931-1939]." In: *Geographisches Jahrbuch*; 56 Bd. II (1941) p. 357-432.; ISSN: 0072-095X. [2952]

Tudor, Dean
"Basic tax library." In: *Ontario Library Review*; Vol. 56, no. 2 (June 1972) p. 95-99.; ISSN: 0030-2996. [2601]

Provincial-municipal relations in Canada. Monticello, Ill.: Council of Planning Librarians, 1970. 5 l. (Council of Planning Librarians Exchange bibliography ; 112) [4315]

Regional development and regional government in Ontario. Monticello, Ill.: Council of Planning Librarians, 1970. 53 l.: map. (Council of Planning Librarians Exchange bibliography ; 157) [0439]

Sources of statistical data for Ontario. Ottawa: Canadian Library Association, 1972. iv, 33 p.; ISBN: 0-88802-089-9. [2993]

Tupling, Donald
Canada: a dissertation bibliography/Canada: une bibliographie de dissertations. [Ann Arbor, Mich.]: University Microfilms International, [1980]. vi, 131 p. [6157]

Turcotte, Paul-André
"General selective bibliography on French-Canadian or Quebec nationalism/Bibliographie générale sélective sur le nationalisme canadien-français ou québécois." In: *Social Compass*; Vol. 31, no. 4 (1984) p. 427-438.; ISSN: 0037-7686. [2486]

Turek, Victor
"A Bibliography of the writings of William J. Rose." In: *Canadian Slavonic Papers*; Vol. 4 (1959) p. 1-30. [7275]

The Polish-language press in Canada: its history and a bibliographical list. Toronto: Polish Alliance Press, 1962. 248 p. (Polish Research Institute in Canada Studies ; 4) [6013]

Polonica Canadiana: a bibliographical list of the Canadian Polish imprints, 1848-1957. Toronto: Polish Alliance Press, 1958. 138 p. (Polish Research Institute in Canada Studies ; 2) [4131]

Turgeon, Bernard
Les horaires variable: examen de la littérature. Québec: Ministère du travail et de la main-d'oeuvre, Direction générale de la recherche, 1976. ii, 165 p.; ISBN: 0-7754-25-42-7. [2833]

Turnbull, Allen A.; Barefoot, John C.; Strickland, Lloyd H.
Privacy and community: a selected community. Ottawa: Carleton University, 1975. 27 l. [4355]

Turnbull, Christopher J.; Davis, Stephen A.
An archaeological bibliography of the Maritime Provinces: works to 1984. Halifax, N.S.: Council of Maritime Premiers, Maritime Committee for Archaeological Cooperation, 1986. 118 p. (Reports in archaeology / Council of Maritime Premiers, Maritime Committee for Archaeological Cooperation ; 6); ISBN: 0-88838-360-6. [4599]

Turner, D. John
Canadian feature film index, 1913-1985/Index des films canadiens de long métrage, 1913-1985. [Ottawa]: Public Archives Canada, National Film, Television and Sound Archives, c1987. xx, 816 p.; ISBN: 0-660-53364-2. [6673]

Turner, Larry
Rideau Canal bibliography, 1972-1992. Smiths Falls, Ont.: Friends of the Rideau, 1992. 37 p.; ISBN: 0-9696052-0-X. [4520]

Turpin, Marguerite
Life and work of Emily Carr (1871-1945): a selected bibliography. Vancouver: School of Librarianship, University of British Columbia, 1965. 20 p.: ill. [6897]

Twigg, Alan
Twigg's directory of 1001 B.C. writers. Victoria, B.C.: Crown Publications, 1992. 194 p.: ill., ports.; ISBN: 0-9696417-0-2. [0603]

Tymchuk, Alexander J.; Knights, Robert M.
A two thousand item bibliography: the description, etiology, diagnosis, and treatment of children with learning disabilities or brain damage. [Ottawa: s.n., 1969]. 186 l. [3405]

Tynen, Michael J.
A checklist and bibliography of the North American Enchytraeidae (Annelida: Oligochaeta). Ottawa: Natural Museum of Natural Sciences, National Museums of Canada, 1975. 14 p. (Syllogeus / Canadian Museum of Natural Sciences ; no. 9: ISSN: 0704-576X) [5402]

Tyrrell, Janice; Pawliuk, Nikki
Research directory '79, Halton region: a compilation of studies dealing with community services and concerns in the region of Halton. [Burlington, Ont.]: Halton Regional Social Planning Council, 1979. iii, 71 p. [4378]

Tyrrell Museum of Palaeontology
List of publications, by research, collections and library staff [Tyrrell Museum of Palaeontology]. Drumheller: Tyrrell Museum of Palaeontology, 1989. 16 l. [4606]

U.S.–Canadian Map Service Bureau
Official eastern North America map and chart index catalog. Neenah, Wis.: U.S.–Canadian Map Service Bureau, c1975. 186 p.: col. maps. [6551]
Official western North America map and chart index catalog. Neenah, Wis.: U.S.–Canadian Map Service Bureau, c1975. 226 p.: col. maps. [6552]

Uhlan, Miriam
Guide to special issues and indexes of periodicals. 3rd ed. Washington, D.C.: Special Libraries Association, c1985. vi, 160 p.; ISBN: 0-87111-263-9. [5957]

Ullom, Judith C.
Folklore of the North American Indians: an annotated bibliography. Washington: Library of Congress, 1969. 126 p. [3916]

Underwood, Lisa
Secondary level bibliographies: Canada studies, Canadian literature, multiculturalism. [Vancouver]: Education Services Group, Vancouver School Board, 1983. 51 p. (Curriculum resources / Education Services Group, Vancouver School Board ; 58) [0143]

Union des écrivains québécois
Les écrivaines du Québec. Montréal: L'Union, 1988. 53 p.: ill., portr.; ISBN: 2-920088-18-1. [1264]

Union list of atlases: Provincial Archives, Simon Fraser University, University of British Columbia, U.B.C. Special Collections, University of Victoria, Vancouver City Archives, Vancouver Public Library. [S.l.]: Triul [Tri-university Libraries of British Columbia], 1974. 155, 17 l. [6543]

Union list of manuscripts in Canadian repositories/Catalogue collectif des manuscrits des archives canadiennes. 2nd ed., rev. and enl. Ottawa: Public Archives Canada, 1975. 2 vol. [1614]

Union list of music periodicals in Canadian libraries/Inventaire des publications en série sur la musique dans les bibliothèques canadiennes. 2nd ed. Ottawa: Canadian Association of Music Libraries, 1981. 293 col. (Publications / Canadian Association of Music Libraries ; no. 2); ISBN: 0-9690583-0-6. [5946]

Union list of serials in Ontario government libraries/Liste collective des publications en série des bibliothèques du gouvernement de l'Ontario. 4th ed. Toronto: Ontario Government Libraries Council, 1992. [22], 339 p.; ISBN: 0-7729-9962-7. [5981]

Union list of serials in the social sciences and humanities held by Canadian libraries [microform]/Liste collective des publications en série dans le domaine des sciences sociales et humaines dans les bibliothèques canadiennes [microforme]. [Ottawa: National Library of Canada], 1981-. microfiches; ISSN: 0227-3187. [5993]

Union of Nova Scotia Indians
Bibliography of the Micmac Indians of Nova Scotia and related materials thereto. [Sydney, N.S.]: Union of Nova Scotia Indians, [1974]. [94] l. [3960]

United Empire Loyalists' Association of Canada. Dominion Council
Bibliography of the United Empire Loyalists at the Toronto Public Library. Toronto: [s.n.], 1966. 10 l. [1948]

United States. Air University. Library
Union list of military periodicals. Maxwell Air Force Base, Ala.: Air University Library, 1960. viii, 121 p. [5870]

United States. Department of Housing and Urban Development. Library and Information Division
Condominium and cooperative housing, 1960-1971: a bibliography of economic, financial and legal factors. Washington: Superintendent of Documents, U.S. Government Printing Office, 1972. v, 32 p. [4325]

United States. Environmental Protection Agency
Annotated bibliography of Lake Ontario limnological and related studies. Washington, D.C.: Office of Research and Monitoring, U.S. Environmental Protection Agency, 1973. 3 vol.: maps. (Ecological research series) [5081]

United States. Geological Survey
Bibliography of North American geology. Washington: United States Government Printing Office, 1907-. vol.; ISSN: 0740-6347. [4883]

United States. Hydrographic Office

Catalogue of charts, plans, sailing directions, and other publications of the United States Hydrographic Office. Washington: G.P.O., 1886. 163 p.: map. [6481]

United States. Information Service. Ottawa

A list of selected publications and sources of information on Canadian-American relations. Ottawa: 1966. 75 p. [2390]

United States. Library of Congress. Catalog Management and Publication Division

Newspapers in microform: foreign countries, 1948-1983. Washington: Library of Congress, 1984. xxv, 504 p. [6035]

United States. Library of Congress. Division of Bibliography

List of references on Canadian independence. Washington: Library of Congress, 1915. 2 l. [0034]

List of references on reciprocity. Washington: U.S. Government Printing Office, 1910. 137 p. [2558]

Select list of references on the annexation of Canada to the United States. Washington: Library of Congress, Division of Bibliography, [1909]. 8 l. [2372]

Selected list of recent books and pamphlets on Canada. [Washington]: 1941. 145 p. [0053]

United States. Water Resources Scientific Information Center

Lake Erie: a bibliography. Washington: U.S. Department of the Interior, Office of Water Resources Research, [1973]. iv, 240 p. [5082]

Lake Huron: a bibliography. Washington: U.S. Department of the Interior, Office of Water Resources Research, [1972]. iv, 95 p. [5068]

Lake Ontario: a bibliography. Washington: Water Resources Scientific Information Center, U.S. Department of the Interior, 1972. iv, 200 p. (Bibliography series / United States Water Resources Information Center ; WRSIC 72-212) [5069]

Lake Superior: a bibliography. Springfield, Va.: National Technical Information Service, United States Department of Commerce, [1972]. iv, 127 p. [5070]

Università di Pisa

Catalogo dei libri e dei periodici di interesse Canadese presso l'Università degli studi di Pisa a cura di Algerina Neri, Giovanni Pizzorusso. Pisa, [Italy]: Servizio Editoriale Universitario di Pisa, 1987. 168 p. [0159]

Université de Moncton. Centre d'études acadiennes

Inventaire général des sources documentaires sur les Acadiens. Moncton: Éditions d'Acadie, 1975-1977. 3 vol. [0232]

Université de Montréal. Bibliothèque de droit

Catalogue des oeuvres des professeurs de la Faculté de droit de l'Université de Montréal: exposition réalisée par la Bibliothèque de droit à l'occasion du centenaire de la Faculté de droit, 1878-1978. [Montréal]: Université de Montréal, Service de bibliothèques, Bibliothèque de droit, 1978. 23 f.; ISBN: 0-88529-028-3. [2187]

Université de Montréal. Bibliothèque des sciences humaines et sociales

Guide de la documentation en anthropologie: à l'intention des usagers de la Bibliothèque des sciences humaines et sociales. 2e éd., rev. et corr. [Montréal]: La Bibliothèque, 1981. xii, 105 p.: ill.; ISBN: 0-88529-036-4. [4587]

Guide de la documentation en lettres françaises et québécoises: à l'intention des usagers de la Bibliothèque des sciences humaines et sociales. 3e éd. rev., corr. et augm. [Montréal]: Université de Montréal, Bibliothèque des sciences humaines et sociales, 1985. vi, 166 p.; ISBN: 0-88529-040-2. [1224]

Guide de la documentation en science politique: à l'intention des étudiants, des chercheurs et des professeurs en science politique. [Montréal]: Université de Montréal, 1979. vii, 95 p.; ISBN: 0-88529-030-5. [2453]

Université de Montréal. Bibliothèque des sciences humaines et sociales. Médiathèque

Liste des enregistrements sur cassettes et sur rubans magnétoscopiques que possède la médiathèque. [Montréal]: Bibliothèque des sciences humaines et sociales, Université de Montréal, 1973. 37 f. [6620]

Université de Montréal. Bibliothèque EPC.

Liste des mémoires et des thèses en science de l'éducation, en psychologie et en communication disponibles à la Bibliothèque E.P.C.: licence, maîtrise, doctorat. Montréal: Service des bibliothèques, Université de Montréal, 1981. 2 vol.; ISBN: 0-88259-035-6. [6159]

Université de Montréal. Département d'éducation physique

Département d'éducation physique, Université de Montréal: rétrospective 1982 à 1987. Montréal: Le Département, 1987. 181 p. [1845]

Université de Montréal. École des relations industrielles

La libéralisation des échanges Canada-États-Unis et les relations industrielles au Québec, négocier l'avenir: bibliographie sommaire. Montréal: L'Université, 1989. 24 p. [2762]

Université de Montréal. Faculté de l'aménagement. Bibliothèque

Architecture et arts anciens du Québec: répertoire d'articles de revues disponibles à la Bibliothèque de la Faculté de l'aménagement, Université de Montréal. [S.l.: s.n.], 1975. 2, 92 p.; ISBN: 0-88529-003-8. [0746]

Université de Montréal. Service des archives

Bibliographie des publications du Service des archives. 6e éd., rev. et augm. Montréal: Université de Montréal, Service des archives, 1988. ii, 17 p. (Publication / Université de Montréal, Service des archives ; no 21); ISBN: 2-8911907-3-4. [1706]

Université de Montréal. Service des bibliothèques. Collections spéciales

Catalogue de la collection de Canadiana Louis Melzack. Montréal: Direction des services aux usagers, Service des bibliothèques, Université de Montréal, 1988. 3 vol.: ill., facsims.; ISBN: 0-88529-064-X. [6791]

Catalogue des imprimés de la Collection Baby. Montréal: Direction des services aux usagers, Service des bibliothèques, Université de Montréal, 1989. 3 vol.: ill., facsims.; ISBN: 2-911185-00-8. [6792]

Université de Sherbrooke. Bibliothèque générale

Coopératives et bibliothèque: guide d'utilisation des collections de la bibliothèque à l'intention des usagers oeuvrant dans le domaine des coopératives. [S.l.: s.n.], 1979. 29, 24 f. [2652]

Sens national, 1965: bibliographie de 400 articles et livres pour mieux comprendre les orientations nouvelles du sens national au Canada français. [Québec]: Association canadienne des éducateurs de langue française, 1965. 20 f. [2386]

Université de Sherbrooke. Groupe de recherche en histoire régionale

Bibliographie d'histoire des Cantons de l'Est. [Sherbrooke]: Département d'histoire, Université de Sherbrooke, 1975. 120 p. [0338]

Université de Sherbrooke. Service de bibliothèques

Liste des périodiques gouvernementaux. Éd. provisoire. Sherbrooke, Québec: Le Service, 1983. 106 p. [6363]

Université des sciences humaines de Strasbourg. Faculté des sciences historiques

Les Amériques, de la découverte à l'indépendance: exposition du 18 mars au 30 avril 1977: catalogue. Strasbourg, France: Bibliothèque nationale et universitaire, [1977]. xvii, 160 p.: ill. [1995]

Université d'Ottawa. Bibliothèque générale. Informathèque

Catalogue des pamphlets et brochures de type Canadiana: projet O1 – CRC. [Ottawa]: Informathèque, Bibliothèque générale, 1972. ii, 130 f. [6779]

Répertoire des thèses présentées à l'Université d'Ottawa dans le domaine des sciences sociales et des humanités: projet O3 – CE/Catalogue of social sciences and humanities theses presented at the University of Ottawa: O3 – CE project. [Ottawa]: Informathèque, Bibliothèque générale, 1972. v, 219 p. [6121]

Université d'Ottawa. Centre de recherche en civilisation canadienne-française. Bibliothèque

Livres conservés au Centre de recherche en civilisation canadienne-française. Ottawa: Centre de recherche en civilisation canadienne-française, Université d'Ottawa, [1975]. 19 f. (Documents de travail du Centre de recherche en civilisation canadienne-française ; 3) [6780]

Université d'Ottawa. Institut de Coopération Internationale

Recrutement, formation et promotion des fonctionnaires, Tiers-Monde francophone et Canada: bibliographie sélective/The recruitment, training and promotion of civil servants, French-speaking Third World and Canada: selective bibliography. Ottawa: L'Institut, 1973. vii, 98 f. (Travaux et documents de l'I.C.I. ; série C, no 3: bibliographies) [2410]

Université du Québec à Chicoutimi

Travaux en études régionales, résumés des mémoires de maîtrise, 1980-1988. [Chicoutimi]: Université du Québec à Chicoutimi, 1988. iv, 77 p. [0406]

Université du Québec à Montréal. Département de science politique

Sommaire des mémoires de maîtrise du Département de science politique. Montréal: Université du Québec à Montréal, 1983. 105 l. (Notes de recherche / Département de science politique, Université du Québec à Montréal ; no 25) [6174]

Université du Québec à Montréal. Service des recherches arctiques et sub-arctiques

Communications, Manitoba/Communications, Manitoba. Montréal: Université du Québec à Montréal, [1978]. 33 l. (Catalogue des coupures de presse, Collection Gardner ; catalogue 50) [0524]

Université du Québec à Trois-Rivières. Bibliothèque

Catalogue collectif régional: Mauricie et centre du Québec. Trois-Rivières: Université du Québec à Trois-Rivières, 1977-1981. 2 fasc. [0375]

Guide de périodiques en langue française: psychologie et éducation. Trois-Rivières: Université du Québec à Trois-Rivières, Bibliothèque, 1976. 24 f. (Publication / Université du Québec à Trois-Rivières, Bibliothèque ; no 9) [5927]

Liste de bio-bibliographies d'auteurs canadiens-français. Trois-Rivières: Université de Québec à Trois-Rivières, 1976. 17 f. [1103]

Université du Québec. Service du dossier étudiant. Section diplôme

Répertoire des mémoires et des thèses de l'Université du Québec, 1969-88. 4e éd. Sainte-Foy: Université du Québec, 1989. 534 p.; ISBN: 2-7628-1866-4. [6200]

Université laurentienne de Sudbury. Bibliothèque

Collection franco-ontarienne: catalogue. Version prélim. Sudbury [Ont.]: Université laurentienne de Sudbury, Institut franco-ontarien, 1986. xi, 106 p. [0482]

Université Laval. Bibliothèque

Catalogue des manuels scolaires québécois. 2e éd. Québec: Bibliothèque de l'Université Laval, [1988]. 2 vol.; ISBN: 2-920310-20-8. [3695]

Université Laval. Bureau de l'extension

Répertoire des thèses de maîtrise et de doctorat (1962-1984) Faculté des sciences de l'agriculture et de l'alimentation, Université Laval. Québec: Le Bureau, 1984. 1 vol. (en pagination multiple); ISSN: 0843-2937. [6177]

Université Laval. Centre de recherches sur l'eau

Bibliographie du Fleuve Saint-Laurent de Trois-Rivières à l'île-aux-coudres. Québec: Université Laval, 1972. [22] f. [5071]

Université Laval. Centre d'étude nordiques

Une décennie de recherches au Centre d'études nordiques, 1961-1970: résumés des principaux travaux publiés et manuscrits. Québec: Université Laval, 1971. 113 f. (Centre d'études nordiques Collection bibliographie ; no 4) [0623]

Université Laval. École des gradués

Répertoire des thèses, 1941-1973. 4e éd. [Québec]: Préparé par le Centre de documentation, Bibliothèque, pour l'École des gradués, Université Laval, 1973. 27, 186, 210 f. [6131]

Université Laval. Institut d'histoire et de géographie

Collection de cartes anciennes et modernes pour servir à l'étude de l'histoire de l'Amérique et du Canada. [Québec: s.n.], 1948. viii, 91 f.: cartes. [6498]

Universitet i Oslo. Amerikansk Institutt

List of books concerning the study of Canada at the American Institute, University of Oslo. Oslo: The University, 1982. 41, 15 p. [0140]

Universitet i Oslo. Romansk Institutt. Avdeling A (Fransk)

Liste de livres concernant l'étude du Canada à l'Institut des langues romanes, Section française, Université d'Oslo. Oslo: L'Université, 1982. 15, 41 p. [0141]

University Microfilms International. Dissertations Publishing

North American Indians: a dissertation index. Ann Arbor, Mich.: University Microfilms International, 1977. vii, 169 p.; ISBN: 0-8357-0134-4. [6146]

University of Alberta. Library

Bibliographies (national and trade) available in the Cameron Library. Edmonton: University of Alberta, 1965. iv, 65 l. [0081]

University of Alberta. Library. Special Collections Department

University of Alberta theses. Edmonton: University of Alberta Library, Special Collections Department, 1971-1988. 17 vol.; ISSN: 0315-5870. [6196]

University of Birmingham. Library

Études canadiennes-Canadian studies: books, atlases and other illustrative materials relating to social, political, economic and cultural affairs in Canada, selected from the holdings of the Library of the University of Birmingham: exhibition celebrating the designation of the university as a Regional Canadian Study Centre, May 1981, the Library, University of Birmingham, May 15th – May 22nd, 1981. Birmingham, England: Department of Geography, University of Birmingham, 1981. 35 p.: ill. [0136]

University of British Columbia. Department of Anthropology and Sociology

Bibliography of the archaeology of British Columbia. Vancouver: The Department, 1972. 31 l. [4556]

University of British Columbia. Faculty of Forestry

U.B.C. theses in forestry and related subject fields (1920-1967). Vancouver: The Faculty, 1968. 8 l. [6093]

University of British Columbia. Library

Catalogue of oral history phonotapes in University of British Columbia libraries. Vancouver: Reynoldston Research and Studies Oral History Programmes, c1973. xi, 30 p. [6621]

Exhibition catalogues [microform]. Vancouver: University of British Columbia Library, 1988-. microfiches; ISSN: 1181-3091. [0732]

French Canadian literature: La littérature canadienne française: a preliminary list of the holdings of the University of British Columbia Library. Vancouver: The Library, 1957. 68 l. [1017]

University of British Columbia. Library. Special Collections and University Archives Division

Canadian children's books, 1799-1939, in the Special Collections and University Archives Division, the University of British Columbia: a bibliographical catalogue. Vancouver: University of British Columbia, 1992. [391] p.: ill. (Occasional publication / University of British Columbia Library, Special Collections ; no. 2); ISBN: 0-88865-197-X. [1396]

University of British Columbia. Women's Resources Centre

Annotated bibliography for women's studies for high school students. Vancouver: Women's Resources Centre/ Daytime Program, Centre for Continuing Education, University of British Columbia, 1976. v, 126 p. [3768]

University of Calgary. Gallagher Library of Geology

Selective bibliography of materials relating to the geology of Calgary, Alberta and vicinity. Rev. ed. Calgary: Gallagher Library of Geology, University of Calgary, 1983. 8 p. [4837]

University of Manitoba. Center for Settlement Studies

Bibliography: resource frontier communities. [Winnipeg]: Center for Settlement Studies, University of Manitoba, 1969-1970. 3 vol. [0621]

University of Manitoba. Department of Agricultural Economics and Farm Management

Publications of Department of Agricultural Economics and Farm Management, University of Manitoba. Winnipeg: Department of Agricultural Economics and Farm Management, University of Manitoba, 1972. 8 p. [4656]

University of Manitoba. Department of Archives, Manuscripts and Rare Books

Register of the Frederick Philip Grove collection. Winnipeg: Department of Archives, Manuscripts and Rare Books, University of Manitoba Libraries, 1979. 65 l.: port. [7034]

Register of the John Wesley Dafoe collection. Winnipeg: Department of Archives, Manuscripts and Rare Books, University of Manitoba Libraries, 1979. 64 l. port. [6927]

University of Manitoba. Library

Literary works by Jewish writers in Canada in the Elizabeth Dafoe Library. Winnipeg: University of Manitoba Libraries, 1972. 21 l. (Reference series / University of Manitoba Libraries ; no. 4) [1071]

A selected bibliography of materials held in the libraries of the University of Manitoba pertaining to the history and historical geography of the Canadian Northwest, with particular reference to the Hudson Bay Lowlands, 1610-1930. [Winnipeg: University of Manitoba, 1979]. 103 p. [0531]

University of New Brunswick. Department of Sociology

Abstracts of master of arts theses, 1960 to 1984. Fredericton: The Department, 1984. iii, 136 p.; ISBN: 0-920114-66-0. [6178]

University of New Brunswick. Harriet Irving Library

Faculty publications, University of New Brunswick and St. Thomas University, 1970. [Fredericton, N.B.]: Harriet Irving Library, School of Graduate Studies, 1971. iii, 67 p. [3427]

University of Ottawa. Human Rights Research and Education Centre

Charter bibliography: an indexed bibliography on the Canadian Charter of Rights and Freedoms/Bibliographie sur la Charte: une bibliographie annotée sur la Charte canadienne des droits et libertés. Saskatoon: Canadian Human Rights Reporter, 1985. 62 p. [2280]

University of Saskatchewan

University of Saskatchewan postgraduate theses, 1912-1973. Saskatoon: University of Saskatchewan, 1975. 168 p. [6140]

University of Saskatchewan. Indian and Northern Curriculum Resources Centre

A syllabus on Indian history and culture. Saskatoon: The Centre, c1970. 46 l. [3925]

Teacher's guide to resource materials in cross-cultural education: Part one: Indians, Eskimos and early explorers. Saskatoon: University of Saskatchewn, 1970. 1 vol. (in various pagings). [3926]

University of Saskatchewan. Indian and Northern Education Program

Annotated bibliography of articles pertaining to native North Americans. [Saskatoon, Sask.: Indian and Northern Education Program, University of Saskatchewan, 1972]. 44 l. [3938]

University of Toronto. Centre for Urban and Community Studies

Annotated bibliography on demand responsive scheduling systems. Montreal: Transport Canada, 1979. ii, 173 p. (Taxi dispatch report series ; vol. 6) [4476]

University of Toronto. Faculty of Library and Information Science. Library

Bibliography series [Library and information science]. Toronto: The Library, 1983-. vol.; ISSN: 0838-7311. [1741]

University of Washington. Libraries

The dictionary catalog of the Pacific Northwest Collection of the University of Washington Libraries, Seattle. Boston: G.K. Hall, 1972. 6 vol.; ISBN: 0-8161-0985-0. [0581]

University of Waterloo. Library. Reference Department

Material pertaining to women in the reference collection, Dana Porter Arts Library, University of Waterloo. [Waterloo, Ont.]: Reference Department, Dana Porter Arts Library, University of Waterloo, 1975. 22 l. [3761]

University of Western Ontario. Cross-cultural Learner Centre

Annotated bibliography of environment-development issues. [London, Ont.]: London Cross Cultural Learner Centre, 1987. [54] p. [5255]

University of Western Ontario. Libraries
Richard Maurice Bucke: a catalogue based upon the collections of the University of Western Ontario Libraries. London [Ont.]: Libraries, University of Western Ontario, 1978. xv, 126 p.: [3] l. of pl., facsims., ports.; ISBN: 0-7714-0004-7. [6881]

University of Windsor. Data Bank Research Group
An annotated bibliography of studies related to health in Windsor and Essex County, 1977-1987. Windsor, Ont.: Data Bank Research Group, c1987. ii, 79 l. [5675]
An annotated bibliography of studies related to the Windsor economy, 1975-1985. Windsor, Ont.: Data Bank Research Group, 1987. ii, 43 l. [0484]

University of Windsor. Department of Psychology
Graduate research in psychology, 1961-1968. Windsor, Ont.: Department of Psychology, University of Windsor, 1968. v l., 67 p. [6094]

Urban and regional research in Canada: an annotated list/ Recherches urbaines et régionales au Canada: répertoire annoté. [Toronto]: Intergovernmental Committee on Urban and Regional Research, [1976-1980]. 3 vol.; ISSN: 0708-3823. [4389]

Urbas, Jeannette
From thirty acres to modern times: the story of French-Canadian literature. Toronto: McGraw-Hill Ryerson, 1976. xiv, 158 p.; ISBN: 0-07-082323-5. [1104]

Vadnay, Susan
A selected bibliography of research on Canadian Jewry, 1900-1980. Ottawa: [S. Vadnay], 1991. iv, 81 p. [4287]

Vagné-Lebas, Mireille
Irrationnel contemporain et survivance de la tradition au Québec. [Talence]: Maison des sciences de l'homme d'Aquitaine, 1986. 2 vol. (Publications de la M.S.H.A. / Maison des sciences de l'homme d'Aquitaine ; no 100); ISBN: 2-85892-104-0. [4600]

Vaillancourt, François; Lacroix, Robert
Revenus et langue au Québec: une revue des écrits. [Montréal]: Service des communications du Conseil de langue française, 1983. 32, 2 p. (Conseil de la langue française Notes et documents ; 27); ISBN: 2-550-02852-X. [2695]

Vaillancourt, Jean-Guy
"The political economy of Quebec: a selective annotated bibliography." In: Socialist Studies; (1983) p. 129-140.; ISSN: 0712-1970. [2484]

Vaillancourt, Roseline
"Bibliographie: Jean-Claude Germain." Dans: Voix et Images; Vol. 6, no 2 (hiver 1981) p. 189-204.; ISSN: 0318-9201. [7011]

Vaisey, G. Douglas
"Bibliography on Canadian labour history." In: Labour: Le Travail; Vol. 6 (Autumn 1980) p. 183-214.; ISSN: 0700-3862. [2870]
The labour companion: a bibliography of Canadian labour history based on materials printed from 1950 to 1975. Halifax: Committee on Canadian Labour History, [c1980]. 126 p. [2871]

Vaison, Robert
Nova Scotia past and present: a bibliography and guide. 2nd rev. and enl. ed. Halifax, N.S.: Nova Scotia, Department of Education, 1976. 164 p. [0225]
"Public financial administration in Canada: a bibliographic essay." In: Canadian Chartered Accountant; Vol. 96, no. 3 (March 1970) p. 164-168.; ISSN: 0008-316X. [2400]

Valade, Roxanne; Lips, Thomas; Mes, Femmy
"Bibliography on child abuse." In: Canada's Mental Health; Vol. 32, no. 2 (June 1984) p. B1-B8.; ISSN: 0008-2791. [3265]

Valence, Jocelyne; Belisle, Monique
Enfance et adolescence inadaptées: catalogue des ouvrages de la bibliothèque du C.I.E.A.I. Montréal: Centre d'information sur l'enfance et l'adolescence inadaptées, 1974. vi f., [69] p. [3133]

Valentini, Frances
"Literacy titles." In: Canadian Library Journal; Vol. 47, no. 3 (June 1990) p. 183-189.; ISSN: 0008-4352. [3720]

Vallée, Henri
Les journaux trifluviens de 1817 à 1933. Trois-Rivières: Éditions du Bien Public, 1933. 89 p. [6003]

Vallée, Jacqueline
Bibliographie sélective sur le "burn-out": compilée à l'occasion de la journée internationale des femmes de 1989. [Québec]: Ministère de la santé et des services sociaux, Direction générale de la planification et de l'évaluation, 1989. 23 f. (Collection méthodologie et instrumentation / Québec Ministère de la santé et des services sociaux, Direction générale de la planification et de l'évaluation ; no 1); ISBN: 2-550-19559-0. [3873]

Vallée, Jacqueline; Allard, François
Bibliographie sélective sur les actes médicaux inutiles. [Québec]: Ministère des affaires sociales, Service de l'informathèque, 1981. 18 f. (Série bibliographiques / Ministère des affaires sociales, Service de l'informathèque ; no 7) [5643]

Vallentine, John F.
U.S.–Canadian range management, 1935-1977: a selected bibliography on ranges, pastures, wildlife, livestock, and ranching. Phoenix, Ariz.: Oryx Press, 1978. xvii, 337 p.; ISBN: 0-912700-11-4. [4683]

Vallerand, Carole
La vieillesse au Québec: essai de bibliographie signalétique avec mention de localisation. [Québec]: Bibliothèque, Université Laval, 1981. 120 p. [3231]

Vallières, Gaétan; Grimard, Jacques
"L'Ontario français: guide bibliographique." Dans: Cahiers de géographie de Québec; Vol. 23, no 58 (avril 1979) p. 165-178.; ISSN: 0007-9766. [0466]

Vallières, Ginette; Herbert, Lynn
Canadian library statistics: a selective list of sources/ Statistiques sur les bibliothèques canadiennes: une liste sélective des sources. Ottawa: National Library of Canada, 1990. 10 p. (Bibliographies / Library Development Centre ; no. 4; ISSN: 0847-2467) [1721]

Valois, Robert
"Étude bibliographique sur les rapports de l'Association de la propagation de la foi à Montréal." Dans: Revue d'histoire de l'Amérique française; Vol. 4, no 4 (mars 1951) p. 560-567.; ISSN: 0035-2357. [1508]

Van der Bellen, Liana
"A checklist of books and articles in the field of the history of the book and libraries." In: Papers of the Bibliographical Society of Canada; Vol. 23 (1984) p. 84-99; vol. 25 (1986) p. 139-152.; ISSN: 0067-6896. [1686]

Van Haaften, Jami
An index to selected Canadian provincial government publications: for librarians, teachers and booksellers. Roslin, Ont.: J. Van Haaften, 1990. 1 vol. (loose-leaf). [6408]

Van Hoorn, L.

Index to Indian acts, 1876-1978/Répertoire des lois relatives aux Indiens, 1876-1978. [Ottawa]: Indian and Northern Affairs Canada, 1982. 48 p.: ill. [4042]

Van Leusden, Karen; St-Jean, Charles; Dubuc, Marcel

Canadian customs and excise: an annotated bibliography/ Douanes et accise du Canada: une bibliographie annotée. Ottawa: Revenue Canada, Customs and Excise, 1979. xii, 642 p.; ISBN: 0-662-50365-1. [2653]

Van Oosten, John

Great Lakes fauna, flora and their environment: a bibliography. Ann Arbor, Mich.: Great Lakes Commission, 1957. x, 86 p. [5330]

Van-The, Nhut

L'aspect humain du processus budgétaire: une revue de la littérature. Montréal: École des hautes études commerciales, 1981. 24 f. (Rapport de recherche / École des hautes études commerciales ; no 81-31; ISSN: 0709-986X) [2672]

Van Wagner, C.E.

Annotated bibliography of forest fire research at the Petawawa Forest Experiment Station, 1961-1979. Rev. ed. Chalk River, Ont.: Petawawa Forest Experiment Station, 1979. 21 p. (Petawawa Forest Experiment Station Information report ; PS-X-52) [4968]

Bibliographie annotée de la recherche sur les feux de forêt effectuée à la Station d'expérimentation forestière de Petawawa de 1961 à 1979. Chalk River, Ont.: Institut forestier national de Petawawa, 1982. i, 23 f. (Rapport d'information / Institut forestier national de Petawawa ; PS-X-52(F); ISSN: 0228-0736); ISBN: 0-662-91724-3. [4977]

Van Walleghem, Jean

Multicultural educational resources: an annotated bibliography. [Winnipeg]: Multiculture Educational Resource Centre, 1990. vi, 18 p.; ISBN: 0-7711-0936-9. [3721]

Vance, Mary

Historical society architectural publications: Canada. Monticello, Ill.: Vance Bibliographies, 1980. 37 p. (Architecture series: Bibliography ; A-179; ISSN: 0194-1356) [0766]

Selected architectural books published in Canada, 1974-1984. Monticello, Ill.: Vance Bibliographies, 1985. 62 p. (Architecture series: Bibliography ; A-1478; ISSN: 0194-1356); ISBN: 0-89028-608-6. [0778]

Vancouver Community College. Advanced Education Media Acquisitions Centre

Video catalogue [Advanced Education Media Acquisitions Centre]. Vancouver: The Centre, c1991-. vol.; ISSN: 1183-8663. [6708]

Vancouver Public Library. Science and Industry Division

Gold and gold mining in British Columbia. [Vancouver: British Columbia Library Association], 1936-1937. [2], 18 p. [4739]

Vanderwal, Andrew

Canadian development assistance, a selected bibliography, 1978-1984. Ottawa: Norman Paterson School of International Affairs, Carleton University, 1985. 39 p. (Norman Paterson School of International Affairs Bibliography series ; no. 7) [2500]

Vanier Institute of the Family

Canadian resources on the family: catalogue/Ressources canadiennes sur la famille: catalogue. Ottawa: Vanier Institute of the Family, 1972. 1 vol. (in various pagings). [3114]

An inventory of family research and studies in Canada, 1963-1967/Un inventaire des recherches et études sur la famille, au Canada [1963-1967]. Ottawa: The Institute, 1967. xiv, 161 p. [3087]

Perspectives on learning: a selected annotated bibliography/ Perspectives sur l'apprentissage: bibliographie sélective annotée. Ottawa: Vanier Institute of the Family, [1976]. 121 l. [3518]

Varieties of family lifestyles: a selected annotated bibliography: phase I: innovative lifestyles. Ottawa: Vanier Institute of the Family, [1977]. 98 p. [3162]

Vann, Margaret Jean

A bibliography and selected source material for the study of Paul-Émile Borduas and his relationship to other French Canadian automatists. [Winnipeg]: University of Manitoba], 1964. xi, 98 l.: ill. [6859]

Varin, Marie-Eve, et al.

Inventaire des travaux en cours et des projets de terminologie. [3e éd.]. [Québec]: Gouvernement du Québec, Office de la langue française, c1990. 202 p.; ISBN: 2-550-20568-5. [1490]

Varma, Prem

"Robert Stead: an annotated bibliography." In: *Essays on Canadian Writing*; No. 17 (Spring 1980) p. 141-204.; ISSN: 0316-0300. [7320]

Vechter, Andrea

Le maintien de l'acquis en langue seconde: bibliographie analytique. Ottawa: Commissariat aux langues officielles, 1988. ii, 91 p. [3696]

Second-language retention: an annotated bibliography. Ottawa: Office of the Commissioner of Official Languages, 1988. ii, 78 p. [3697]

Veillette, Denise

Bibliographie thématique sur la condition féminine. Québec: Laboratoire de recherches sociologiques, Université Laval, 1983. 255 p. (Collection Outils de recherche / Laboratoire de recherches sociologiques, Université Laval ; cahier 5); ISBN: 2-920495-15-1. [3823]

Veilleux, Bertrand

Bibliographie sur les relations entre l'Église et l'État au Canada français, 1791-1914. Montréal: La Bibliothèque, Centre d'Études canadiennes-françaises, 1969. 92 f. [1524]

Veitch, Isobel G.

Completed theses and undergraduate senior reports [Department of Geography, University of Western Ontario]. London: Department of Geography, University of Western Ontario, 1981. iv, 59 p. (Geographical papers / Department of Geography, University of Western Ontario ; no. 48; ISSN: 0706-487X); ISBN: 0-7714-0303-8. [6160]

Velikov, Velitchko

Provincial and federal land use and land ownership policies and their potential impact on political, economic and social conditions in Canada. Monticello, Ill.: Council of Planning Librarians, 1976. 22 p. (Council of Planning Librarians Exchange bibliography ; 993) [2621]

Venkateswarlu, Tadiboyina

A bibliographic survey of microeconomics reading materials in North American universities: a comparative study between Canada and the United States of America. Windson, Ont.: Department of Economics, University of Windsor, 1978. 48 p. (Discussion paper series /

Department of Economics, University of Windsor ; no. 51) [2641]

Labor and manpower economics library bibliography. Rev. 4th ed. Windsor, Ont.: University of Windsor, 1978. iv l., 114 p. [2857]

Verdun-Jones, S.N.

"Made in Canada: texts and readers for Canadian criminology and criminal justice courses." In: *Canadian Journal of Criminology*; Vol. 21, no. 1 (January 1979) p. 86-104.; ISSN: 0704-9722. [2206]

Vermeer, Rebecca Arrieta; Vermeer, Kees

The biological effects of oil pollution on aquatic organisms: a summarized bibliography. Ottawa: Pesticide Section, Canadian Wildlife Service, 1974. [4], 68 p. (Manuscript reports / Pesticide Section, Canadian Wildlife Service ; no. 31) [5095]

Verner, Coolie

Cook and the cartography of the north Pacific: an exhibition of maps for the conference on Captain James Cook and his times, April 1978. Burnaby, B.C.: Simon Fraser University, 1978. vi, 35 p. [6565]

Explorers' maps of the Canadian Arctic, 1818-1860. Toronto: B.V. Gutsell, Department of Geography, York University, 1972. 84 p.: [6] folded l. of pl., maps. (Monograph / Department of Geography, York University ; no. 6) [6530]

Verrall, Catherine; McDowell, Patricia

Resource reading list 1990: annotated bibliography of resources by and about native people. Toronto: Canadian Alliance in Solidarity with the Native Peoples, c1990. 157 p.; ISBN: 0-921425-03-1. [4114]

Verreault, Lucie; Taussig, Jeanne

Relations publiques et communication documentaire: revue de la littérature. Montréal: Asted, 1983. 51 p.; ISBN: 2-89055-055-9. [1659]

Verreault-Roy, Louise

Répertoire cartographique de la Mauricie, 1800-1950. [Trois-Rivières]: Groupe de recherche sur la Mauricie, Université du Québec à Trois-Rivières, 1981. vii, 246 p. (Cahier / Groupe de recherche sur la Mauricie, Université du Québec à Trois-Rivières ; no 5); ISBN: 2-9800058-4-3. [6579]

Vesely, J.A.

Highlights of research in sheep production in western Canada during the last thirty years. [Ottawa]: Research Branch, Agriculture Canada, 1987. i, 59 p. (Technical bulletin / Research Branch, Agriculture Canada ; 1987-4E; Lethbridge Research Station Contribution ; no. 11); ISBN: 0-662-15323-5. [4712]

Vézina, Germain

Québec métropolitain: répertoire bibliographique. [Québec]: Université Laval, Faculté de théologie, Centre de recherches en sociologie religieuse, 1968. 64 p. [0301]

Vézina-Demers, Micheline; Grégoire-Reid, Claire

Catalogue des oeuvres musicales du fonds Léo Roy. Québec: Atelier de Musicographie, 1987. viii, [2], 143 p.: fac.–sim., port.; ISBN: 2-9801120-0-3. [7284]

Vieillissement et personnes âgées: choix de publications de Santé et Bien-être social Canada. [Ottawa]: Santé et Bien-être social Canada, [1985]. 63, 63 p. [3283]

Vient de paraître: bulletin du livre au Canada français. Montréal: Beauchemin, 1965-1978. 14 vol.; ISSN: 0042-5656. [1629]

Viereck, Wolfgang

"German dialects spoken in the United States and Canada and problems of German-English language contact especially in North America: a bibliography." In: *Orbis: bulletin international de documentation linguistique*; Vol. 16, no. 2 (1967) p. 549-568.; ISSN: 0030-4379. [1423]

A view of university financing: [bibliography]/Aperçu du financement des universités: [bibliographie]. Ottawa: Association of Universities and Colleges of Canada, Library, 1980. 10 p. [3579]

Vigneault, Robert

"Bibliographie sélective de l'essai au Québec de 1895 à 1945." Dans: *Revue de l'Université d'Ottawa*; Vol. 49, nos 1-2 (janvier-avril 1979) p. 79-81.; ISSN: 0041-9206. [1160]

Villemaire, Fernande

Bio-bibliographie de Narcisse-E. Dionne. Québec: Bibliothèque nationale du Québec, 1983. xiii, 102 p. (Bibliographie et documentation / Bibliothèque nationale du Québec ; 15) [6955]

Villeneuve, G.–Oscar

Bibliographie climatologique du Québec. 2e éd. Québec: Ministère des richesses naturelles, Service de la météorologie, 1970. 17 p. [5056]

Villeneuve, Laurent; Riopel, Diane

Critères d'identification des tâches à robotiser: revue de littérature. Montréal: Département de génie industriel, École polytechnique de Montréal, 1984. ii, 34 f. (Rapport technique / Département de génie industriel, École polytechnique de Montréal ; EPM:RT-84-2) [5801]

Villeneuve, Paul Y.

Canadian geography. [Ottawa]: Canadian Studies Directorate, Department of the Secretary of State of Canada, 1992. 26, 28 p. (Canadian studies resource guides. Second series); ISBN: 0-662-58838-X. [3069]

La géographie du Canada. [Ottawa]: Direction des études canadiennes, Secrétariat d'État du Canada, 1992. 28, 26 p. (Guides pédagogiques des études canadiennes. Deuxième collection); ISBN: 0-662-58838-X. [3070]

Vinay, Jean-Paul

"Éléments de bibliographie de la traduction automatique." Dans: *Journal des traducteurs*; Vol. 10, no 3 (juillet-septembre 1965) p. 101-109. [1421]

Vinay, Jean-Paul; Avis, Walter S.; Rudnyckyj, Jaroslav Bohdan

"Linguistica Canadiana." In: *Journal of the Canadian Linguistic Association*; Vol. 1, no. 2 (October 1955)-vol. 15, no. 1 (Fall 1969) [1425]

Vincent, Charles; Burgess, Larry

Bibliographie sur les altises phytophages des crucifères au Canada/A bibliography relevant to crucifer-feeding flea beetle pests in Canada. Saint-Jean-sur-Richelieu, Québec: Agriculture Canada, 1985. 31 p. (Bulletin technique / Agriculture Canada ; no 22; ISSN: 0825-4559); ISBN: 0-662-53962-1. [5518]

Vincent, Elizabeth

Bibliographie choisie et commentée applicable à l'étude des techniques de construction du génie militaire en Amérique du Nord britannique, au XIXe siècle. [Ottawa]: Parcs Canada, 1983. 22 p. (Bulletin de recherches / Parcs Canada ; no 190; ISSN: 0228-1236) [2031]

A select annotated bibliography applicable to the study of the Royal Engineers building technology in nineteenth century British North America. [Ottawa]: Parks Canada,

1983. 20 p. (Research bulletin / Parks Canada ; no. 190; ISSN: 0228-1228) [2032]

Vincent, Sylvie; Proulx, Jean-René

Bilan des recherches ethnohistoriques concernant les groupes autochtones du Québec. [Québec]: Ministère des affaires culturelles du Québec, 1984. 5 vol.: carte. [4068]

Review of ethnohistorical research on the native peoples of Quebec. [Québec]: Direction régionale du Nouveau-Québec et Service aux autochtones, Ministère des affaires culturelles du Québec, 1985. 5 vol.; ISBN: 2-550-12263-1 (complete set). [4079]

Vincent, Thomas Brewer

An historical directory of Nova Scotia newspapers and journals before Confederation. Kingston, Ont.: Royal Military College of Canada, Department of English and Philosophy, 1977. vii, 67 p. [5930]

Vineer, Bill

The Vineer Organ Library. Ottawa: B. Vineer, [1981]. vi, 63 p. [0900]

Vineland Research Station. Library

A bibliographic survey of publications of the Vineland Research Station, 1911-1986. Vineland Station, Ont.: Agriculture Canada, Research Branch, [1986]. iv, 79 p. [4708]

Vinet, Alain

Epistémologie et sociologie de la médecine: bibliographie. Québec: Institut supérieur des sciences humaines, Université Laval, 1969. 51 f. (Cahiers de l'ISSH, Collection Instruments de travail / Institut supérieur des sciences humaines, Université Laval ; no 2) [5574]

Vinet, Bernard; Jolicoeur, Louis-Philippe

Bibliographie sur les personnes âgées: répertoire des livres et des périodiques de la collection de la Bibliothèque de l'Université Laval. Éd. provisoire. Québec: Bibliothèque de l'Université Laval, 1977. 167 f. (Guides bibliographiques / Bibliothèque de l'Université Laval ; 13) [3163]

Vinto Engineering Limited

Energy conservation in office buildings: review of Canadian and U.S. studies, surveys, programs and publications. Ottawa: Energy, Mines and Resources Canada, Conservation and Renewable Energy Branch, 1980. 178, 18, 14 p. (Buildings series) [5169]

"Visits to Upper Canada, 1799-1867: a selected check-list of travel accounts in the Douglas Library." In: *Douglas Library Notes*; Vol. 1, no. 3 (April 1952) p. [3-4].; ISSN: 0012-5717. [1924]

Visual display terminals: a selected bibliography/Les écrans cathodiques: une bibliographie sélective. Hamilton, Ont.: Canadian Centre for Occupational Health and Safety, 1981. 29 p.; ISBN: 0-660-52253-5. [5644]

Vlach, Milada; Buono, Yolande

Catalogue collectif des impressions québécoises, 1764-1820. Québec: Direction générale des publications gouvernementales, 1984. xxxiii, 251, 195 p.; ISBN: 2-551-08919-0. [0383]

Laurentiana parus avant 1821. Montréal: Bibliothèque nationale du Québec, 1976. xxvii, 416, 120 p. [0343]

Vlach, Milada; Gallichan, Gilles; Tessier, Louise

Le droit de vote des femmes au Québec: bibliographie sélective. Montréal: Bibliothèque nationale du Québec, 1990. 192 p.: ill.; ISBN: 2-551-12316-X. [3883]

Voisine, Nive

"La production des vingt dernières années en histoire de l'Église du Québec." Dans: *Recherches sociographiques*; Vol. 15, no 1 (janvier-avril 1974) p. 97-112.; ISSN: 0034-1282. [1536]

Volz, John R.

"Brick bibliography." In: *APT Bulletin*; Vol. 7, no. 4 (1975) p. 38-49.; ISSN: 0044-9466. [0747]

Vomberg, Elisabeth

Music for the physically disabled child: a bibliography. Toronto: E. Vomberg, 1978. 34 p. [0872]

Vomberg, Mac

Bibliography of legal materials on transportation of hazardous substances. Edmonton: Environmental Law Centre, 1982. 7 l.; ISBN: 0-921503-06-7. [4491]

Von Baeyer, Edwinna

L'histoire du jardinage au Canada: bibliographie sélective. Rév. et augm. éd. Ottawa: Direction des lieux et des parcs historiques nationaux, Environnement Canada–Parcs, 1987. 62 p.; ISBN: 0-662-94166-7. [4713]

A selected bibliography for garden history in Canada. Rev. and augm. ed. Ottawa: National Historic Parks and Sites Branch, Environment Canada, c1987. 62 p.; ISBN: 0-662-15269-7. [4714]

Vothi, Nhu-y

Bibliographie, forum sur la question économique. Québec: Gouvernement du Québec, Conseil du statut de la femme, [1983]. 128 p.: ill.; ISBN: 2-550-10446-3. [3824]

W.A.C. Bennett Library

British Columbia government publications. Burnaby, B.C.: Simon Fraser University Library, 1977. iii, 66 p. (Bibliography / W.A.C. Bennett Library ; GOV DOC 3) [6310]

Wachman, Constantin

An annotated bibliography on residential chimneys serving solid or liquid-fuel fired heating appliances. Ottawa: Division of Building Research, National Research Council Canada, 1957. 6 l. [5720]

Wachtel, Andy

Sexually intrusive children: a review of the literature. Vancouver: Greater Vancouver Mental Health Services, 1992. 58 p. [3363]

Urbanism and urban social organization: recent Canadian studies. Monticello, Ill.: Council of Planning Librarians, 1972. 23 p. (Council of Planning Librarians Exchange bibliography ; 348) [4326]

Wade, Jill

A bibliography of literature on Arthur C. Erickson. Winnipeg: University of Manitoba Libraries, 1973. iii, 20 l. (Bibliography series / University of Manitoba Libraries ; no. 1) [6969]

Manitoba architecture to 1940: a bibliography. Winnipeg: University of Manitoba Press, 1976. xvi, 109 p., [8] l. of pl.: ill.; ISBN: 0-88755-116-5. [0751]

Wagle, Iqbal

"Selected and annotated bibliography of South Asians in Ontario." In: *Polyphony*; Vol. 12 (1990) p. 137-151.; ISSN: 0704-7002. [4280]

Wagner, Anton

The Brock bibliography of published Canadian plays in English, 1766-1978. Toronto: Playwrights Press, c1980. xi, 375 p.; ISBN: 0-88754-157-7. [1176]

"A selected bibliography of Canadian theatre and drama

bibliographies and guides." In: *Canadian Theatre Review*; No. 34 (Spring 1982) p. 77-83.; ISSN: 0315-0836. [1199]

Wagner, Frances J.E.

Published references to Champlain Sea faunas 1837-1966 and list of fossils. Ottawa: Queen's Printer, 1967. v, 82 p. (Geological Survey of Canada Paper ; 67-16) [4545]

Wagner, Henry R.; Camp, Charles L.

The Plains & the Rockies: a critical bibliography of exploration, adventure, and travel in the American West, 1800-1865. San Francisco: John Howell-Books, 1982. xx, 745 p., [32] p. of pl.: ill.; ISBN: 0-910760-11-1. [0537]

Wai, Lokky

The native peoples of Canada in contemporary society: a demographic and socioeconomic bibliography. [London, Ont.]: Population Studies Centre, University of Western Ontario, [c1989]. i, 82 p.; ISBN: 0-7714-1060-3. [4111]

Wai, Lokky; Shiel, Suzanne; Balakrishnan, T.R.

Annotated bibliography of Canadian demography, 1966-1982. [London, Ont.]: Centre for Canadian Population Studies, University of Western Ontario, [c1984]. v, 314 p.; ISBN: 0-7714-0586-3. [3046]

Waines, W.J.

"Bibliography of Professor Robert McQueen." In: *Manitoba Arts Review*; Vol. 2 (Spring 1941) p. 47-50. [7186]

Waintman, Susan; Tampold, Ana

Ontario royal commissions and commissions of inquiry, 1867-1978: a checklist of reports. Toronto: Legislative Library, Research and Information Services, 1980. viii, 74 p. [6329]

Waiser, Joan

Women's studies: a guide to reference sources. [Montreal]: McGill University, McLennan Library, Reference Department, 1983. 22 p. [3825]

Wakil, F.A.

Law and women: a select bibliography of cross-national relevance. [Saskatoon: University of Saskatchewan, 1987]. viii, 94 p.; ISBN: 0-88880-189-0. [3861]

Wakil, S. Parvez

Reproduction, reproductive technologies, questions of law and ethics and the emergence of new family systems and policies in contemporary society: an annotated bibliography. Detroit, Mich.: Toronto: Farez-Savera, 1992. xiii, 66 p.; ISBN: 0-921230-03-6. [5714]

Waldon, Freda Farrell

Bibliography of Canadiana published in Great Britain, 1519-1763/Bibliographie des ouvrages sur le Canada publiés en Grande-Bretagne entre 1519 et 1763. Toronto: Published by ECW Press in collaboration with the National Library of Canada, c1990. lxv, 535 p.: port., facsims.; ISBN: 1-55022-087-X. [0172]

Wales, Katherine

"Sir Robert Alexander Falconer: chronological bibliography." In: *University of Toronto Quarterly*; Vol. 13, no. 2 (January 1944) p. 167-174.; ISSN: 0042-0247. [6974]

Wales, Katherine; Murray, Elsie McLeod

"A bibliography of the works of George M. Wrong." In: *Canadian Historical Review*; Vol. 29, no. 3 (September 1948) p. 238-239.; ISSN: 0008-3755. [7374]

Walker, Byron Edmund

List of the published writings of Elkanah Billings, F.G.S., palaeontologist to the Geological Survey of Canada, 1856-1876. [S.l.: s.n., 1901]. P. [366]-388. [6842]

"List of the published writings of Elkanah Billings, F.G.S.,

palaeontologist to the Geological Survey of Canada, 1856-1876." In: *Canadian Record of Science*; Vol. 8, no. 6 (July 1901) p. [366]-388. [6841]

Walker, Catherine

Pay equity: the Ontario experience. Toronto: Pay Equity Commission of Ontario, 1990. ii l., 14 p. (Selected bibliography / Pay Equity Commission of Ontario ; no. 5) [2933]

Walker, E.M.

"Bibliography of Canadian zoology." In: *Proceedings and Transactions of the Royal Society of Canada*; Series 3, vol. 8, section 4 (1914) p. 271-285; series 3, vol. 9, section 4 (1915) p. 307-318; series 3, vol. 10, section 4 (1916) p. 201-215.; ISSN: 0316-4616. [5316]

Walker, Elizabeth

"Mountaineering in Canada, 1960-1969: a bibliography of periodical literature." In: *Canadian Alpine Journal*; Vol. 53 (1970) p. 51-54.; ISSN: 0068-8207. [1757]

Walker, James W. St. G.

A history of Blacks in Canada: a study guide for teachers and students. Hull, Quebec: Minister of State, Multiculturalism, 1980. x, 181 p.; ISBN: 0-660-10735-X. [4197]

Précis d'histoire sur les Canadiens de race noire: sources et guide d'enseignement. Hull, Québec: Ministre d'État, Multiculturalisme, 1980. x, 197 p.; ISBN: 0-660-90535-3. [4198]

Walker, Karen

A legal collection for non-legal libraries in British Columbia. 4th ed. Vancouver: Library Services Program, Legal Services Society of British Columbia, 1986. 100 p.: ill.; ISBN: 0-77260-535-1. [2285]

Wallace, William Stewart

"The bibliography of Canadiana." In: *Canadian Historical Review*; Vol. 5, no. 1 (March 1924) p. 4-9.; ISSN: 0008-3755. [0038]

"The literature relating to the Selkirk controversy." In: *Canadian Historical Review*; Vol. 13, no. 1 (March 1932) p. 45-50.; ISSN: 0008-3755. [1908]

"The periodical literature of Upper Canada." In: *Canadian Historical Review*; Vol. 12, no. 1 (March 1931) p. 4-22.; ISSN: 0008-3755. [5862]

The Ryerson imprint: a check-list of the books and pamphlets published by The Ryerson Press since the foundation of the House in 1829. Toronto: Ryerson Press, [1954]. 141 p. [1580]

Walli, Gary; Schwaighofer, Joseph

A bibliography on silos: lateral pressure, field and model-measurements, theories. Toronto: Department of Civil Engineering, University of Toronto, 1979. 63 p. (Publication / Department of Civil Engineering, University of Toronto ; no. 79-05; ISSN: 0316-7968) [5775]

Walser, Lise

Répertoire des longs métrages produits au Québec, 1960-1970. Montréal: Conseil québécois pour la diffusion du cinéma, 1971. 110 p. [6613]

Walsh, Sandra A.

Canadian corporate and industry information. Monticello, Ill.: Vance Bibliographies, 1982. 13 p. (Public administration series: Bibliography ; P-950; ISSN: 0193-970X) [2687]

The Constitution of Canada and its amendment: a selected bibliography. Monticello, Ill.: Vance Bibliographies, 1981. 7 p. (Public administration series: Bibliography ; P-662;

ISSN: 0193-970X) [2239]

Crown corporations in Canada: bibliography of material in the Library of the Ontario Ministry of Treasury, Economics and Intergovernmental Affairs. Monticello, Ill.: Council of Planning Librarians, 1977. 2 l. (Council of Planning Librarians Exchange bibliography ; 1321) [2631]

Freedom of information in Canada: bibliography of material in the Ontario Ministry of Treasury, Economics and Intergovernmental Affairs Library. Monticello, Ill.: Vance Bibliographies, 1978. 5 p. (Public administration series: Bibliography ; P-26; ISSN: 0193-970X) [2441]

Interest rates, the recent Canadian experience: a selected bibliography. Monticello, Ill.: Vance Bibliographies, 1981. 6 p. (Public administration series: Bibliography ; P-799; ISSN: 0193-970X) [2673]

Quebec and Confederation: bibliography of material in the library of the Ontario Ministry of Treasury, Economics and Intergovernmental Affairs. Monticello, Ill.: Vance Bibliographies, 1979. 12 p. (Public administration series: Bibliography ; P-305; ISSN: 0193-970X) [2454]

A selected bibliography on wage and price controls in Canada. Monticello, Ill.: Vance Bibliographies, 1982. 7 p. (Public administration series: Bibliography ; P-1100; ISSN: 0193-970X); ISBN: 0-88066-310-3. [2688]

The study of the future: a bibliography of material in the Library of the Ontario Ministry of Treasury, Economics and Intergovernmental Affairs. Monticello, Ill.: Vance Bibliographies, 1979. 8 p. (Public administration series: Bibliography ; P-306; ISSN: 0193-970X) [2654]

Technological sovereignty: a selected bibliography with emphasis on Canada. Monticello, Ill.: Vance Bibliographies, 1982. 7 p. (Public administration series: Bibliography ; P-951; ISSN: 0193-970X) [2471]

Walters, John

An annotated bibliography of reports, theses, and publications pertaining to the campus and research forests of the University of British Columbia. Vancouver: Faculty of Forestry, University of British Columbia, 1968. viii, 71 p. [4924]

An annotated bibliography of western hemlock, Tsuga heterophylla (Raf.) Sarg. Vancouver: Faculty of Forestry, University of British Columbia, 1963. 86 p.: ill. [5338]

Walz, Joel

Annotated bibliography for developing oral proficiency in second and foreign languages. Québec: International Center for Research on Bilingualism, 1989. 63 p. (International Center for Research on Bilingualism Publication ; B-171); ISBN: 2-89219-200-5. [1488]

Ward, E. Neville; Watson, Donna J.; White, S. Richard

A selected bibliography of Canadian water management (1965-April 1970). Edmonton: Department of Geography, University of Alberta, 1971. 80 l. [5060]

Ward, Jane

"The published works of H.A. Innis." In: *Canadian Journal of Economics and Political Science*; Vol. 19, no. 2 (May 1953) p. 233-244.; ISSN: 0315-4890. [7073]

Ward, Megan

Evaluating the arts in education: an annotated bibliography. Ottawa: Government of Canada, Department of Communications, 1979. ii, 73 p. [3557]

Le rôle des arts dans l'enseignement: bibliographie commentée. Ottawa: Secrétariat d'État, 1979. ii, 73 p. [3558]

Ward, W. Peter

"Western Canada: recent historical writing." In: *Queen's Quarterly*; Vol. 85, no. 2 (Summer 1978) p. 271-288.; ISSN: 0033-6041. [0525]

Wardwell, Allen; Lebov, Lois

Annotated bibliography of Northwest Coast Indian art. New York: Library, Museum of Primitive Art, 1970. 25 p. (Primitive art bibliographies / Museum of Primitive Art Library ; no. 8) [0673]

Warkentin, John; Ruggles, Richard I.

Historical atlas of Manitoba: a selection of facsimile maps, plans and sketches from 1612 to 1969. Winnipeg: Historical and Scientific Society of Manitoba, 1970. xvi, 585 p.: facsims. [6522]

Warner, Morton M.

An annotated bibliography of health care teamwork and health centre development. [Vancouver]: Department of Health Care and Epidemiology, University of British Columbia, [1975]. vii, 274 p. [5601]

Warren, Louise

"Quelques livres québécois pour la jeunesse." Dans: *Dérives*; No 17-18 (1979) p. 95-102.; ISSN: 0383-7521. [1340]

Warren, Nancy

Bibliography on voluntarism: publications relevant to voluntarism and to the management of voluntary organizations. Toronto: Ontario Association of Volunteer Bureaux/Centres, 1986. x, 127 p.; ISBN: 0-7729-0381-6. [3295]

Warwick, Jack

"Récits de voyages en Nouvelle-France au XVIIe siècle: bibliographie d'introduction." Dans: *Scritti sulla Nouvelle-France nel seicento*. Bari, Italie: Adriatica, c1984. P. 283-319. (Quaderni del seicento francese ; 6) [2043]

Warwick, Susan J.

"A Laurence log." In: *Journal of Canadian Studies*; Vol. 13, no. 3 (Fall 1978) p. 75-83.; ISSN: 0021-9495. [7125]

"Margaret Laurence: an annotated bibliography." In: *The annotated bibliography of Canada's major authors*, Vol. 1, edited by Robert Lecker and Jack David. Downsview, Ont.: ECW Press, 1979. P. 447-101.; ISBN: 0-920802-02-8. [7126]

Washburn, Jon

CBC Choral Concert's 1979 Canadian choral records list. Vancouver: Canadian Broadcasting Corporation, 1979. 3, 16, 2 p. [0879]

Washburn & Gillis Associates Ltd.

Survey of literature on the assessment of the pollution potential of the peat resource: final report submitted to Environment Canada. Ottawa: National Research Council under the auspices of the Peat Forum, 1982. xv, 130 p. [5189]

Wasserman, Paul; Herman, Esther

Catalog of museum publications & media: a directory and index of publications and audiovisuals available from United States and Canadian institutions. 2nd ed. Detroit: Gale Research, 1980. xi, 1044 p.; ISBN: 0-8103-03880-4. [0134]

Library bibliographies and indexes: a subject guide to resource material available from libraries, information centers, library schools, and library associations in the United States and Canada. Detroit: Gale Research, 1975. ix, 301 p.; ISBN: 0-8103-0390-6. [0119]

Wastewater Technology Centre: publications and presentations, 1972-1988. Burlington, Ont.: Environment Canada, Conservation and Protection, Technology Development and Technical Services Branch, [1988]. 48 p. [5837]

Water films. 2nd ed. Ottawa: Secretariat, Canadian National Committee, International Hydrological Decade, [1971]. 194 p. [6614]

Water resources in New Brunswick: a preliminary bibliography. [Fredericton, N.B.]: Water Resource Planning Branch, Environmental Management, Land & Water Use Division, Department of Municipal Affairs and Environment, 1987. 113 p. [5256]

Waterman, Nairn
"Annotated bibliography of books on Canadian law published in 1968." In: *Osgoode Hall Law Journal*; Vol. 7, no. 1 (November 1969) p. 87-103.; ISSN: 0030-6185. [2116]

Waters, William G.
A bibliography of articles related to transportation in major economics journals, 1960-1981. Vancouver: Centre for Transportation Studies, University of British Columbia, 1984. [57] p. (Monographs / Centre for Transportation Studies, University of British Columbia) [4496]

Waters, William H.
Bibliography: scientific papers resulting from Canadian space and upper atmosphere research, 1969-1973. Ottawa: National Research Council Canada, 1974. 87 p. (Space Research Facilities Branch Report ; 081) [5751]

Waterston, Elizabeth
"Literature of exploration: Canadian travel books of the 1870's." In: *Studies in Canadian Literature*; Vol. 4, no. 2 (Summer 1979) p. 44-61.; ISSN: 0380-6995. [2004]

The travellers: Canada to 1900: an annotated bibliography of works published in English from 1577. Guelph, Ont.: University of Guelph, 1989. viii, 321 p., [12] l. of pl.: ill., map.; ISBN: 0-88955-170-7. [2079]

Watson, G. Llewellyn
Feminism and women's issues: an annotated bibliography and research guide. New York: Garland Pub., 1990. 2 vol.; ISBN: 0-8240-5543-8. [3884]

Watson, Lawrence W.
"Francis Bain, geologist." In: *Proceedings and Transactions of the Royal Society of Canada*; Series 2, vol. 9, section 4 (1903) p. 135-142.; ISSN: 0316-4616. [6823]

Watson, M.; Sego, David Charles Cletus; Thomson, S.
A literature review of settlement behaviour of sanitary landfills and their application to Alberta. Edmonton: Research Management Division, Alberta Environment, 1982. v, 82 p. (RMD report / Research Management Division, Alberta Environment ; RMD 81-20) [5787]

Watson, Sereno
Bibliographical index to North American botany, or, Citations of authorities for all the recorded indigenous and naturalized species of the flora of North America: with a chronological arrangement of the synonymy. Washington: Smithsonian Institution, 1878. vi, 476 p. (Smithsonian miscellaneous collections ; vol. 15) [5304]

Watt, Christine
Children's books in the French language and books about Quebec in English. Vancouver: Education Services Group, Vancouver School Board, 1981. 25 p. (Curriculum resources / Education Services Group, Vancouver School Board ; no. 40; ISSN: 0714-6124) [1347]

Watt, Frank A.
"Early Canadiana." In: *Book Collector*; Vol. 10, no. 1 (Spring 1961) p. 28-39.; ISSN: 0006-7237. [0069]

Watt, Roy MacGregor (Mrs.)
Catalogue of ranking plays. Ottawa: Ottawa Little Theatre, 1970. 9 p. [1058]

Watters, John G.
Reviews of the Young Offenders Act: a bibliography. [Ottawa]: Solicitor General Canada, Ministry Secretariat, [1987]. 84 p. (Programs Branch user report / Ministry Secretariat, Solicitor General Canada ; no. 1987-17) [2303]

Watters, Reginald Eyre
A checklist of Canadian literature and background materials, 1628-1960. 2nd ed., rev. and enl. Toronto: University of Toronto Press, 1972. xxiv, 1085 p.; ISBN: 0-8020-1866-1. [1072]

Watters, Reginald Eyre; Bell, Inglis Freeman
On Canadian literature, 1806-1960: a check list of articles, books, and theses on English-Canadian literature, its authors, and language. [Toronto]: University of Toronto Press, [c1966]. ix, 165 p.; ISBN: 0-8020-5166-9. [1036]

Wawrzyszko, Aleksandra
"A bibliographic guide to French-Canadian literature." In: *Canadian Library Journal*; Vol. 35, no. 2 (April 1978) p. 115-133.; ISSN: 0008-4352. [1140]

Wearing, J.P.
"Nineteenth-century theatre research: a bibliography." In: *Nineteenth Century Theatre Research*; Vol. 6, no. 2 (Autumn 1978)-vol. 10, no. 2 (Winter 1982) [0977]

Wearmouth, Amanda
Checklist of Yukon newspapers, 1898-1985. Whitehorse: Yukon Archives, 1987. iv, 47 p. [6045]

Weatherby Bibliographics
Wheel-rail interaction: a selective bibliography/Interaction roue-rail: une bibliographie sélective. Montreal: Transportation Development Centre, Transport Canada, 1986. iv, 131 p. [4499]

Weaver, John
"Living in and building up the Canadian city: a review of studies on the urban past." In: *Plan Canada*; Vol. 15, no. 2 (September 1975) p. 111-117.; ISSN: 0032-0544. [4356]

Weaver, Robert
"Annual bibliography of Commonwealth literature, 1968: Canada." In: *Journal of Commonwealth Literature*; No. 8 (December 1969) p. 89-106.; ISSN: 0021-9894. [1052]

Webber, Bert
The Pacific Northwest in books. [Tigard, Or.]: Lanson's, [1967]. 45 p.: ill. [0574]

Weber, Eileen
"Niagara Falls in history: a bibliography." In: *Ontario Library Review*; Vol. 47, no. 3 (August 1963) p. 107-111.; ISSN: 0030-2996. [0433]

Webster, John Clarence
William Francis Ganong memorial. Saint John, N.B.: New Brunswick Museum, 1942. 31 p.: port. [7000]

Webster, Peter M.
Fine print: a guide to law materials for Nova Scotians. 2nd ed. [Halifax, N.S.]: Public Legal Education Society of Nova Scotia, c1987. v, 99 p.; ISBN: 0-88648-076-0. [2304]

Weekly checklist of Canadian government publications/Liste hebdomadaire des publications du gouvernement canadien. Hull, Québec: Supply and Services Canada, 1978-. no.; ISSN: 0706-4659. [6475]

Weeks, Thomas E.

A survey of the collection of Canadian statutes and subordinate legislation held in the Sir James Dunn Law Library. Halifax, N.S.: Dalhousie University, 1977. ii, 71 p. [2176]

Weidmark, P.E.

"Bibliography of Canadian contributions in the field of rock mechanics." In: *CIM Bulletin*; (1963-1983); ISSN: 0317-0926. [5793]

Weiler, John; Bowering, Ann

Reaching agreement on urban development: an annotated bibliography/La recherche de consensus dans le développement urbain: bibliographie annotée. Ottawa: Canadian Centre for Livable Places, 1992. 36 p.; ISBN: 0-88814-046-0. [4441]

Weiner, Alan R.

The insurance industry: an information sourcebook. Phoenix: Oryx Press, 1988. ix, 278 p. (Oryx sourcebook series in business and management ; no. 16); ISBN: 0-89774-307-5. [2749]

Weinman, Paul L.

A bibliography of the Iroquoian literature, partially annotated. Albany: University of the State of New York, 1969. ix, 254 p. (Bulletin / New York State Museum and Science Service ; no. 411) [3917]

Weinrib, Alice

"What's new in second-language teaching: a selected annotated bibliography." In: *Canadian Modern Language Review*; Vol. 38, no. 1 (Autumn 1981)-vol. 49, no. 3 (April 1993) [3731]

Weinrich, Peter

A select bibliography of Tim Buck, general secretary of the Communist Party of Canada, 1929-1962. Toronto: Progress Books, 1974. xv, 50 p., [7] l. of pl.; ISBN: 0-919396-24-0. [6880]

Social protest from the left in Canada, 1870-1970. Toronto: University of Toronto Press, [c1982]. xxiii, 627 p.; ISBN: 0-8020-5567-2. [2472]

Weir, R.D.

Annotated bibliography of bird kills at man-made obstacles: a review of the state of the art and solutions. Ottawa: Canadian Wildlife Service, Ontario Region, [1977]. ii, 85 p. [5417]

Weise, C.E.

Behaviour modification for the treatment of alcoholism: an annotated bibliography. Toronto: Addiction Research Foundation of Ontario, c1975. xv, 275 p. (Bibliographic series / Addiction Research Foundation of Ontario ; no. 10; ISSN: 0065-1885); ISBN: 0-88868-013-9. [5602]

Solvent abuse: an annotated bibliography with additional related citations. Toronto: Addiction Research Foundation, [c1973]. x, 231 p. (Bibliographic series / Addiction Research Foundation of Ontario ; no. 5; ISSN: 0065-1885) [5587]

Weise, C.E.; Busse, S.; Hall, R.J.

Teratogenic and chromosomal damaging effects of illicit drugs: an annotated bibliography with selected related citations involving the use of licit drugs. Toronto: Addiction Research Foundation of Ontario, 1973. x, 175 p. (Bibliographic series / Addiction Research Foundation of Ontario ; no. 6; ISSN: 0065-1885) [5588]

Weise, C.E.; Price, S.F.

The benzodiazepines-patterns of use: an annotated bibliography. Toronto: Addiction Research Foundation of Ontario, c1975. xiii, 197 p. (Bibliographic series / Addiction Research Foundation of Ontario ; no. 9; ISSN: 0065-1885); ISBN: 0-88868-012-0. [5603]

Weiss, Allan Barry

A comprehensive bibliography of English-Canadian short stories, 1950-1983. [Toronto]: ECW Press, [c1988]. 973 p.; ISBN: 0-920763-67-7. [1265]

Weist, Katherine M.; Sharrock, Susan R.

An annotated bibliography of Northern Plains ethnohistory. Missoula, Mont.: Department of Anthropology, University of Montana, 1985. 299 p. (Contributions to anthropology / Department of Anthropology, University of Montana ; no 8) [4080]

Weitz, Margaret Collins

"An introduction to 'Les Québécoises'." In: *Contemporary French Civilization*; Vol. 5, no. 1 (Fall 1980) p. 105-129.; ISSN: 0147-9156. [3799]

Weller, Joan

"Canadian English-language juvenile periodicals: an historical overview, 1847-1990." In: *Canadian Children's Literature*; No. 59 (1990) p. 38-69.; ISSN: 0319-0080. [5975]

"A survey of Canadian picture books in recent years." In: *Canadian Children's Literature*; No. 52 (1988) p. 23-34.; ISSN: 0319-0080. [1383]

Wellman, Barry, et al.

Community, network, communication: an annotated bibliography. 2nd ed. Toronto: Centre for Urban and Community Studies, University of Toronto, 1974. 172 p. (Bibliographic series / Centre for Urban and Community Studies, University of Toronto ; no. 4) [4340]

Wells, Lilian M.

Chronic physical illness and disability: psychosocial perspectives: an annotated bibliography. [Toronto]: University of Toronto, Faculty of Social Work, 1980. 100 p. (University of Toronto Faculty of Social Work bibliographic series ; 1; ISSN: 0317-8382) [3209]

Wells, Peter G.; Moyse, Catherine M.

A selected bibliography on the biology of Salmo gairdneri Richardson (rainbow, steelhead, Kamloops trout), with particular reference to studies with aquatic toxicants. Dartmouth, N.S.: Contaminants and Assessments Branch, Environmental Protection Service, Atlantic Region, 1981. vi, 90 p. (Economic and technical review report / Environmental Protection Service ; EPS-3-AR-81-1) [5468]

Welwood, Ronald J.

Kootenaiana: a listing of books, government publications, monographs, journals, pamphlets, etc., relating to the Kootenay area of the Province of British Columbia and located in the libraries of Notre Dame University of Nelson, B.C. and-or Selkirk College, Castlegar, B.C., up to 31 March 1976. Nelson: Notre Dame University Library; Castlegar: Selkirk College Library, 1976. 167 p.: ill., maps. [0587]

Wenek, Karol W.J.

Louis Dudek: a check-list. Ottawa: Golden Dog Press, 1975. vi, 54 p.; ISBN: 0-919614-15-9. [6959]

Wengle, Annette

"Marian Engel (née Passmore): an annotated bibliography." In: *The annotated bibliography of Canada's major authors*, Vol. 7, edited by Robert Lecker and Jack David. Toronto: ECW

Press, 1987. P. 11-113.; ISBN: 0-920802-11-1. [6966]

Wertman, Paul
Small-scale technology for local forest development: an annotated bibliography. Vancouver: Forintek Canada Corp., Western Forest Products Laboratory, 1979. 189 p. (Review report / Western Forest Products Laboratory ; RR 1); ISBN: 0-86488-012-X. [4969]

Wertsman, Vladimir
The Romanians in America and Canada: a guide to information sources. Detroit: Gale Research, c1980. xvi, 164 p. (Ethnic studies information guide series ; vol. 5); ISBN: 0-8103-1417-7. [4199]

West, Allen Sherman
A review of insects affecting production of willows. St. John's: Newfoundland Forestry Centre, 1985. iv, 82 p. (Information report / Canadian Forestry Service, Newfoundland Forestry Centre ; N-X-232; ISSN: 0704-7657); ISBN: 0-662-14376-0. [5519]

Western Research & Development Limited
Arctic air pollution bibliography. Calgary: Western Research & Development, 1974. [65] l. [5096]

Westrheim, S.J.; Leaman, B.M.
A selected bibliography of northeastern Pacific rockfishes (Sebastes and Sebastolobus) other than Sebastes alutus. Nanaimo, B.C.: Pacific Biological Station, Fisheries and Marine Service, Environment Canada, 1976. iii l., 20 p. (Fisheries and Marine Service Technical report ; no. 659; ISSN: 0701-7626) [5411]

Westrheim, S.J.; Miller, G.
A partial bibliography of Pacific cod (Gadus macrophalus) in the north Pacific Ocean, through December 1985. Nanaimo, B.C.: Fisheries and Oceans Canada, 1987. iii, 55 p. (Canadian technical report of fisheries and aquatic sciences ; no. 1518; ISSN: 0706-6457) [5538]

Whaley, Sara S.; Eichler, Margrit
"A bibliography of Canadian and United States resources on women." In: *Women Studies Abstracts*; Vol. 2, no. 4 (Fall 1973) p. 1-104; vol. 3, no. 1 (Winter 1974) p. 1-106.; ISSN: 0049-7835. [3751]

Wheat, James Clements; Brun, Christian F.
Maps and charts published in America before 1900: a bibliography. New Haven: Yale University Press, 1969. xxii, 215 p.: maps. [6516]

Whebel, C.F.J.
"Printed maps of Upper Canada, 1800-1864: a select bibliography." In: *Ontario History*; Vol. 49, no. 3 (Summer 1957) p. 139-144.; ISSN: 0030-2953. [6505]

Whitaker, Marilyn; Wellman, Barry
A catalogue of participatory transportation planning cases: Canada and the United States. [Toronto]: Joint Program in Transportation, 1977. i, 83 p. (University of Toronto-York University Joint Program in Transportation Working paper ; no. 9; ISSN: 0380-9889) [4468]

White, Anthony G.
Architecture of Arctic regions: a selected bibliography. Monticello, Ill.: Vance Bibliographies, [1987]. 7 p. (Architecture series: Bibliography ; A-1840; ISSN: 0194-1356); ISBN: 1-555903-50-9. [0786]

The architecture of Calgary, Alberta, Canada: a selected bibliography. Monticello, Ill.: Vance Bibliographies, [1987]. 5 p. (Architecture series: Bibliography ; A-1842; ISSN: 0194-1356); ISBN: 1-555903-52-5. [0787]

The architecture of Ontario Province, Canada, Toronto metropolitan area: a selected bibliography. Monticello, Ill.: Vance Bibliographies, [1990]. 31 p. (Architecture series: Bibliography ; A-2339; ISSN: 0194-1356); ISBN: 0-792005-69-4. [0790]

The architecture of Quebec Province, Canada: Quebec metropolitan area: a selected bibliography. Monticello, Ill.: Vance Bibliographies, 1990. 7 p. (Architecture series: Bibliography ; A-2340; ISSN: 0194-1356); ISBN: 0-792005-70-8. [0791]

The architecture of Vancouver, British Columbia: a selected bibliography. Monticello, Ill.: Vance Bibliographies, 1982. 7 l. (Architecture series: Bibliography ; A-772; ISSN: 0194-1356) [0770]

Canadian architecture: Alberta: a selected bibliography. Monticello, Ill.: Vance Bibliographies, 1990. 8 p. (Architecture series: Bibliography ; A-2293; ISSN: 0194-1356); ISBN: 0-792004-43-4. [0792]

Canadian architecture: British Columbia: a selected bibliography. Monticello, Ill.: Vance Bibliographies, 1990. 16 p. (Architecture series: Bibliography ; A-2294; ISSN: 0194-1356); ISBN: 0-792004-44-2. [0793]

Canadian architecture: Manitoba: a selected bibliography. Monticello, Ill.: Vance Bibliographies, 1990. 7 p. (Architecture series: Bibliography ; A-2292; ISSN: 0194-1356); ISBN: 0-792004-42-6. [0794]

Canadian architecture: Ontario Province, Ottawa northward: a selected bibliography. Monticello, Ill.: Vance Bibliographies, 1990. 11 p. (Architecture series: Bibliography ; A-2319; ISSN: 0194-1356); ISBN: 0-792004-89-2. [0795]

Canadian architecture: Prince Edward Island Province: a selected bibliography. Monticello, Ill.: Vance Bibliographies, 1990. 5 p. (Architecture series: Bibliography ; A-2313; ISSN: 0194-1356); ISBN: 0-792004-63-9. [0796]

Canadian architecture: Saskatchewan Province: a selected bibliography. Monticello, Ill.: Vance Bibliographies, 1990. 5 p. (Architecture series: Bibliography ; A-2314; ISSN: 0194-1356); ISBN: 0-792004-64-7. [0797]

Canadian architecture: southwestern Quebec Province, Montreal area: a selected bibliography. Monticello, Ill.: Vance Bibliographies, 1990. 18 p. (Architecture series: Bibliography ; A-2318; ISSN: 0194-1356); ISBN: 0-792004-88-4. [0798]

Canadian architecture: the Maritime Provinces: a selected bibliography. Monticello, Ill.: Vance Bibliographies, 1990. 6 p. (Architecture series: Bibliography ; A-2291; ISSN: 0194-1356); ISBN: 0-792004-41-8. [0799]

Canadian architecture: Yukon and Northwest Territories: a selected bibliography. Monticello, Ill.: Vance Bibliographies, 1990. 5 p. (Architecture series: Bibliography ; A-2295; ISSN: 0194-1356); ISBN: 0-792004-45-0. [0800]

The Canadian Charter of Rights and Freedoms: a selected bibliography. Monticello, Ill.: Vance Bibliographies, 1990. 8 p. (Public administration series: Bibliography ; P-2907; ISSN: 0193-970X); ISBN: 0-792005-87-2. [2342]

White, Bonney G.
Literature survey of papers dealing with the use of heat for keeping roads, sidewalks and parking areas free from snow and ice. Ottawa: Division of Building Research, National Research Council Canada, 1957. 10 l. (Bibliography / National Research Council Canada,

Division of Building Research; no. 8; ISSN: 0085-3828) [4449]

White, Charles A.; Nicholson, H. Alleyne
Bibliography of North American invertebrate paleontology. Washington: G.P.O., 1878. 132 p. (Miscellaneous publications / United States Geological Survey; no. 10) [4521]

White, Louise, et al.
"Indians and Metis of Manitoba: a bibliography." In: *MSLAVA (Manitoba School Library Audio-visual Association Journal)*; Vol. 8, no. 3 (1981) p. 6-11.; ISSN: 0315-9124. [4028]

White, Richard H.
Human settlement issues in western Canada: a selected bibliography, 1975-1983. [Vancouver]: Centre for Human Settlements, University of British Columbia, 1983. iii, 48 l. (Occasional papers / Centre for Human Settlements, University of British Columbia ; 29; ISSN: 0706-2559) [4400]

Whiteaves, J.F.
"Bibliography of Canadian zoology, exclusive of entomology." In: *Proceedings and transactions of the Royal Society of Canada*; Series 2, vol. 7, section 4 (1901)-series 3, vol. 1, section 4 (1907) [5312]

Whiteman, Bruce
Collected poems of Raymond Souster: bibliography. [Ottawa]: Oberon Press, c1984. 240 p.; ISBN: 0-88750-528-7. [7317]
Leonard Cohen: an annotated bibliography. Downsview, Ont.: ECW Press, c1980. P. 55-95.; ISBN: 0-920763-52-9. [6910]
"Leonard Cohen: an annotated bibliography." In: *The annotated bibliography of Canada's major authors*, Vol. 2, edited by Robert Lecker and Jack David. Downsview, Ont.: ECW Press, c1980. P. 55-95.; ISBN: 0-920802-40-0. [6911]

Whiteman, Bruce; Stewart, Charlotte; Funnell, Catherine
A bibliography of Macmillan of Canada imprints 1906-1980. Toronto: Dundurn Press, 1985. xv, 474 p.; ISBN: 0-919670-89-X. [1674]

Whiteside, Don
Aboriginal people: a selected bibliography concerning Canada's first people. Ottawa: National Indian Brotherhood, c1973. i, 345 p.; ISBN: 0-919682-02-2. [3947]
An annotated bibliography of articles in *The Globe* (Toronto), related to Indians (Indians, Inuit and Half-breeds) from January 1, 1848 through January 16, 1867, with special attention to the Hudson's Bay Company. (Plus selected items, August through September 1876). Ottawa: Aboriginal Institute of Canada, 1980. 205 p. [4022]
Indians, Indians, Indians: a selected bibliography and resource guide. Ottawa: 1979. 3 vol. [4010]

Whiteside, Don; Cook, Cyndi
Contemporary Indian protests: reference aids–bibliographies. [Ottawa]: National Indian Brotherhood, 1973. 4 vol. [3948]

Whitney, Joan
Habitat bibliography: a selected bibliography of Canadian references on human settlements. Monticello, Ill.: Council of Planning Librarians, 1976. 98 p. (Council of Planning Librarians Exchange bibliography ; 1137-1138) [4362]

Whittingham, Michael David
Crowding and corrections: a bibliography. Toronto: [s.n.], 1985. 27 l. [2281]

Whitworth, Fred E.
Teaching aids obtainable from departments of the government at Ottawa. Ottawa: Canadian Council of Education for Citizenship, 1946. 17 p. [6228]

Who's who in Canadian literature. Teeswater, Ont.: Reference Press, 1983-. vol.; ISSN: 0715-9366. [1305]

Wicken, George
Archibald Lampman: an annotated bibliography. Downsview, Ont.: ECW Press, c1980. P. 97-146.; ISBN: 0-920763-55-3. [7117]
"Archibald Lampman: an annotated bibliography." In: *The annotated bibliography of Canada's major authors*, Vol. 2, edited by Robert Lecker and Jack David. Downsview, Ont.: ECW Press, c1980. P. 97-146.; ISBN: 0-920802-38-9. [7118]
"William Wilfred Campbell (1858-1918): an annotated bibliography." In: *Essays on Canadian Writing*; No. 9 (Winter 1977-1978) p. 37-47.; ISSN: 0316-0300. [6891]

Wickett, Samuel Morley
"Bibliography of Canadian municipal government." In: *Municipal government in Canada*. Toronto: [s.n.], 1907. P. [121]-128. [4299]

Wiebe, Victor G.
Alberta-Saskatchewan Mennonite and Hutterite bibliography, 1962-1981. Saskatoon: Mennonite Historical Society of Alberta and Saskatchewan, 1981. 10 p. [1551]

Wieler, Anne H.
Gerontological resources: a reference. Ottawa: Medical Services Branch, Indian & Inuit Health Services, 1986. 36 p. [5673]

Wigmore, Judy
Literature review of previous oil pollution experience. Vancouver: Environment Canada, Environmental Protection Service, 1978. vii, 20 p. (Regional program report / Environmental Protection Service ; 78-24) [5141]

Wigmore, Shirley K.
An annotated guide to publications related to educational research. Toronto: Ontario College of Education, Department of Educational Research, 1960. 26 l. (Educational research series / Department of Educational Research, Ontario College of Education ; no. 32) [3380]

Wigney, Trevor John
Education of women and girls in a changing society: a selected bibliography with annotations. [Toronto]: Department of Educational Research, University of Toronto, 1965. v, 76 p. (Educational research series / Department of Educational Research, University of Toronto ; no. 36) [3737]

Wikeem, Brian M.; Newman, Reg F.; Johnsen, Laila W.
A bibliography on range, forages and livestock management in British Columbia. Victoria: Research Branch, Ministry of Forests, 1985. ix, 121 p. (Land management report / British Columbia Ministry of Forests ; no. 32; ISSN: 0702-9861); ISBN: 0-7718-8483-4. [4706]

Wiktor, Christian
Automobile insurance publications. Halifax: Dalhousie University, Faculty of Law, 1973. xiii, 220 p. [2135]
Canadian bibliography of international law. Toronto: University of Toronto Press, 1984. xxiii, 767 p.; ISBN: 0-8020-5615-6. [2271]

Wiktor, Christian; Foster, Leslie A.
Marine affairs bibliography: a comprehensive index to marine law and policy literature. Halifax, N.S.: Dalhousie

Law School, 1980-.   vol.; ISSN: 0226-8361. [2369]

Wilcox-Magill, Dennis William; Helmes-Hayes, Richard C.

"Complete bibliography of Leonard Charles Marsh." In: *Journal of Canadian Studies*; Vol. 21, no. 2 (Summer 1986) p. 59-66.; ISSN: 0021-9495. [7178]

Wilford, David J.

A review of literature to 1975 of forest hydrology pertinent to the management of mountainous watersheds. Victoria, B.C.: Ministry of Forests, 1975. [3], 50 l.: ill. [4949]

Wilkie, Brian

Energy in Canada: a selective bibliographic review. Waterloo, Ont.: Faculty of Environmental Studies, University of Waterloo, [1973]. 14 p. (Occasional papers / Faculty of Environmental Studies, University of Waterloo ; no. 8; ISSN: 0317-8625) [5083]

Wilkins, James L.; Rogers, Judith; Greer, Marbeth

Legal aid in criminal matters: a bibliography. [Toronto]: Centre of Criminology, University of Toronto, 1971. ii, 63 l. [2124]

Willey, R.C.

"Bibliography of Canadian numismatics." In: *Canadian Numismatic Journal*; Vol. 6, no. 1 (January 1961)-vol. 31, no. 9 (October 1986) [1838]

"A select bibliography of Canadian decimal coins." In: *Canadian Numismatic Journal*; Vol. 22, no. 11 (December 1977) P. 493-494; Vol. 26, no. 4 (April 1981) p. 164-165.; ISSN: 0008-4573. [1807]

"A select bibliography of Canadian numismatics." In: *Transactions of the Canadian Numismatic Research Society*; Vol. 3, no. 2 (April 1967) p. 13-19.; ISSN: 0045-5202. [1753]

"William C. Wonders: bibliography of published work, 1948-1989." In: *A world of real places: essays in honour of William C. Wonders*, edited by P.J. Smith and E.L. Jackson. Edmonton: Department of Geography, University of Alberta, c1990. P. 207-210.; ISBN: 0-88864-762-X. [7371]

"William John Alexander: check-list of writings." In: *University of Toronto Quarterly*; Vol. 14, no. 1 (October 1944) p. 32-33.; ISSN: 0042-0247. [6799]

William R. Perkins Library

Canadiana: nonprint resources held in Perkins Library. [Durham, N.C.]: Duke University, 1984. [7], 54 l. [6659]

Williams, C. Brian

Manpower management in Canada: a selected bibliography. Kingston, Ont.: Industrial Relations Centre, Queen's University, 1968. 121 p. (Bibliography series / Industrial Relations Centre, Queen's University ; no. 3; ISSN: 0075-613X) [2800]

Williams, Carol

Workers' participation: a bibliography of current books and articles. Kingston, Ont.: Industrial Relations Centre, Queen's University, 1976. 18 p. [2834]

Williams, D. Dudley; Smith, Ian M.

Spring habitats and their faunas: an introductory bibliography. Ottawa: Biological Survey of Canada (Terrestrial Arthropods), 1990. ii, 156 p. (Biological Survey of Canada Document series ; no. 4); ISBN: 0-9692727-5-8. [5556]

Williams, Gaynor P.

Annotated bibliography on snow drifting and its control. Ottawa: Division of Building Research, National Research Council, [1974]. [43] p. (in various pagings). (National Research Council Canada, Division of Building Research Bibliography ; no. 42) [5097]

Frazil ice: a review of its properties with a selected bibliography. Ottawa: National Research Council Canada, Division of Building Research, 1959. 5 p. (National Research Council Canada, Division of Building Research Technical paper ; no. 81) [5030]

Summary of current research on snow and ice in Canada. Ottawa: National Research Council of Canada, Associate Committee on Geotechnical Research, 1972. 30 p. (Associate Committee on Geotechnical Research Technical memorandum ; no. 106) [5072]

Williams, John R.

Ground water in permafrost regions: an annotated bibliography. Washington: United States Government Printing Office, 1965. iii, 294 p.: map. (Geological Survey Water-supply paper ; 1792) [5037]

Williamson, Mary F.

Canadian art: a guide to reference sources. [Downsview, Ont.]: Scott Library, York University, 1976. 22 l. [0684]

The study of art in Canada. Toronto: York University Libraries, 1976. 23 l. [0685]

Williamson, Nancy J.

"Canadian music and composers since 1949." In: *Ontario Library Review*; Vol. 38, no. 2 (May 1954) p. 118-122.; ISSN: 0030-2996. [0813]

Williamson & Company

Catalogue of a valuable collection of Canadian books and rare pamphlets: includes some items of remarkable value and great scarcity, choice extra illustrated works, history, biography, travel, politics, geology, topography, agriculture, the Indian tribes, etc. : for sale at the affixed prices. Toronto: Printed for Williamson & Co. at the Robinson-Arbuthnot Press, 1898. 34 p. [0026]

Willis, Stephen C.

Alexis Contant: catalogue. Ottawa: Bibliothèque nationale du Canada, 1982. v, 91, 87, v p.: ill.; ISBN: 0-660-51891-0. [6915]

Alexis Contant: catalogue. Ottawa: National Library of Canada, 1982. v, 87, 91, v p.: ill.; ISBN: 0-660-51891-0. [6916]

Williston, Samuel W.

Bibliography of North American dipterology, 1878-1895. [S.l.: s.n.], 1896. P. 129-144. [5309]

"Bibliography of North American dipterology, 1878-1895." In: *Kansas University Quarterly*; Vol. 4, no. 3 (January 1896) p. [129]-144.; ISSN: 0885-4068. [5310]

Willms, Sharon E.; Bates, Joanna M.

Primary care for urban core disadvantaged patients: an annotated bibliography. Vancouver: Centre for Human Settlements, University of British Columbia, 1991. 30 p. (Housing and community planning series); ISBN: 0-88865-377-8. [3357]

Willms, Sharon E.; Hayes, Michael V.; Hulchanski, John David

Housing options for persons with AIDS: an annotated bibliography. Vancouver: Centre for Human Settlements, University of British Columbia, 1991. 16 p.; ISBN: 0-88865-375-1. [3358]

Wilmshurst, Rea

A bibliography of L.M. Montgomery's short stories, poems, and miscellaneous articles. [Toronto: R. Wilmshurst], c1985. 201 p. [7199]

"L.M. Montgomery's short stories: a preliminary bibliography." In: *Canadian Children's Literature*; No. 29 (1983) p. 25-34.; ISSN: 0319-0080. [7198]

Wilson, C.R.

A review of literature on the lateral shear strength of nail-timber connections. Halifax: Nova Scotia Technical College, Department of Civil Engineering, 1968. 45 l. (Essays on timber & timber structures / Nova Scotia Technical College, Department of Civil Engineering ; no. 25) [5729]

Wilson, J.D.

"Common school texts in use in Upper Canada prior to 1845." In: *Papers of the Bibliographical Society of Canada*; Vol. 9 (1970) p. 36-53.; ISSN: 0067-6896. [3413]

Wilson, Lucy Roberta

Regional and county library service in Canada: a bibliography. Ottawa: Canadian Library Association, 1949. 13 l. [1579]

Windthorst, Rolf E.B.

"German-Canadian creative literature: a preliminary check list of imprints." In: *Canadian Ethnic Studies*; Vol. 2, no. 1 (June 1970) p. 55-62.; ISSN: 0008-3496. [1059]

Winearls, Joan

"Federal electoral maps of Canada, 1867-1970." In: *Canadian Cartographer*; Vol. 9, no. 1 (June 1972) p. 1-24.; ISSN: 0008-3127. [6531]

Mapping Upper Canada, 1780-1867: an annotated bibliography of manuscript and printed maps. Toronto: University of Toronto Press, c1991. xli, 986 p.: maps.; ISBN: 0-8020-2794-6. [6598]

Winks, Robin W.

Recent trends and new literature in Canadian history. Washington: Service Center for Teachers of History, c1959. v, 56 p. (Publication / Service Center for Teachers of History ; no. 19) [1933]

Winnipeg Art Gallery Association

Catalogue of a selection of early views, maps, charts and plans of the Great Lakes, the far West, the Arctic and Pacific Oceans. Montreal: Canada Steamship Lines Limited, 1944. 22 p.: ill., maps. [6495]

Winnipeg Public Library

Canada in books for children. Winnipeg: [s.n.], 1967. 21 p. [1316]

A selective bibliography of Canadiana of the prairie provinces: publications relating to western Canada by English, French, Icelandic, Mennonite, and Ukrainian authors. [Winnipeg]: Winnipeg Public Library, 1949. 33 p. [0495]

Winship, George Parker

Cabot bibliography. Providence, R.I.: [s.n.], 1897. 71 p. [6885]

Cabot bibliography: with an introductory essay on the careers of the Cabots based upon an independent examination of the sources of information. London: Stevens; New York: Dodd, Mead, 1900. lii, 180 p. [6886]

Winsor, Justin

The Kohl collection of maps relating to America. Cambridge, Mass.: Issued by the Library of Harvard University, 1886. 70 p. (Bibliographical contributions / Harvard University Library ; no. 19) [6482]

Withler, Ruth Elinor; Healey, M.C.; Riddell, B.E.

Annotated bibliography of genetic variation in the family salmonidae. Nanaimo, B.C.: Department of Fisheries and Oceans, Fisheries Research Branch, Pacific Biological Station, 1982. v, 161 p. (Canadian technical report of fisheries and aquatic sciences ; no. 1098; ISSN: 0706-6457) [5480]

Withycombe, B.; Fogwill, W.D.

Map index 1969-1977 of geological and geochemical maps of the Island of Newfoundland: (supplement to 1969 map index). St. John's: Government of Newfoundland and Labrador, Mineral Development Division, 1978. 147 p.: maps. (Report / Government of Newfoundland and Labrador, Mineral Development Division ; 78-2) [6566]

Wolf, Carolyn E.; Folk, Karen R.

Indians of North and South America: a bibliography based on the collection at the Willard E. Yager Library-Museum, Hartwick College, Oneonta, N.Y. Metuchen, N.J.: Scarecrow Press, 1977. ix, 576 p.; ISBN: 0-8108-1026-3. [3993]

Wolfe, Carol Anne

Employment of the physically handicapped: a selected bibliography, 1970-1978. Toronto: Ontario Ministry of Labour, Research Branch, 1979. 42 p. (Bibliography series / Ontario Ministry of Labour, Research Branch ; no. 14) [2860]

Wolfe, J.S., et al.

Farm family financial crisis: annotated bibliography. Guelph, Ont.: University School of Rural Planning and Development, University of Guelph, 1986. ii, 43 p. (University School of Rural Planning and Development technical series ; 129); ISBN: 0-88955-136-7. [4709]

Wolfenden, Madge

"Alexander Begg versus Alexander Begg." In: *British Columbia Historical Quarterly*; Vol. 1, no. 2 (April 1937) p. 133-139.; ISSN: 0706-7666. [6834]

Wolff, Hans

"Bibliography of bibliographies of North American Indian languages still spoken." In: *International Journal of American Linguistics*; Vol. 13, no. 4 (October 1947) p. 268-273.; ISSN: 0020-7071. [1415]

Wollock, Jeffrey

"Stinson Jarvis: a bio-bibliography." In: *Papers of the Bibliographical Society of Canada*; Vol. 8 (1969) p. 23-60.; ISSN: 0067-6896. [7076]

Women and the arts: bibliography/Les femmes et les arts: bibliographie. [Ottawa: Canadian Conference of the Arts], c1986. iv, 67 l. [3847]

Women in conflict with the law: a selected bibliography. [Ottawa]: Ministry Secretariat, Solicitor General Canada, [1986]. 29 l. (Programs Branch user report / Ministry Secretariat, Solicitor General Canada ; no. 1986-36) [3848]

Women's resource catalogue. 4th ed. [Ottawa]: Secretary of State, Women's Program, c1992. 58, 60 p.; ISBN: 0-662-59260-3. [3901]

Women's studies: video resource catalogue. Toronto: Ontario Educational Communications Authority, 1979. 116 p. [3793]

Wong, Chuck

A checklist of university theses on northeastern Ontario/Répertoire des thèses sur le nord-est de l'Ontario. Sudbury, Ont.: Laurentian University Library, 1975. 45 l. [6141]

Master's theses and research essays accepted by Laurentian University between 1962 and June 1981, and held in the Main Library. Sudbury, Ont.: Laurentian University Library, 1982. 52 p. (Laurentian University Library special collections ; 2) [6162]

Wood, Dean D.

Multicultural Canada: a teachers' guide to ethnic studies. Toronto: Ontario Institute for Studies in Education, 1978.

vi, 138 p. (Curriculum series / Ontario Institute for Studies in Education ; 36); ISBN: 0-7744-0175-3. [4190]

Wood, W.D.; Campbell, H.F.
Cost-benefit analysis and the economics of investment in human resources: an annotated bibliography. Kingston, Ont.: Industrial Relations Centre, Queen's University, 1970. vii, 211 p. (Bibliography series / Industrial Relations Centre, Queen's University ; no. 5; ISSN: 0075-613X) [2806]

Wood, W.D.; Kelly, L.A.; Kumar, Pradeep
Canadian graduate theses, 1919-1967: an annotated bibliography (covering economics, business and industrial relations). Kingston, Ont.: Industrial Relations Centre, Queen's University, 1970. xiv, 483 p. (Bibliography series / Industrial Relations Centre, Queen's University ; no. 4; ISSN: 0075-613X) [6108]

Woodcock, George
Canadian poets, 1960-1973: a list. Ottawa: Golden Dog Press, 1976. x, 69 p.; ISBN: 0-919614-14-0. [1105]

Woodhead, Eileen
Bibliographie de catalogues commerciaux de l'est du Canada, 1800-1880. [Ottawa]: Parcs Canada, 1984. 26 p. (Bulletin de recherches / Parcs Canada ; no 217; ISSN: 0228-1236) [2704]
Bibliography of trade catalogues, 1800-1880, in eastern Canada. [Ottawa]: Parks Canada, 1984. 25 p. (Research bulletin / Parks Canada ; no. 217; ISSN: 0228-1228) [2705]

Woodill, Gary
Children with special needs: a manual of Canadian resources. Orillia, Ont.: Ptarmigan Publishing, 1981. 98 p.: ill.; ISBN: 0-9690349-0-3. [3232]

Woodley, Elsie Caroline
The history of education in the province of Quebec: a bibliographical guide. [S.l.: s.n.], 1932. 199 l. [3370]

Woods, Cheryl A.
U.W.O. Map Library: atlas collection. London: Department of Geography, University of Western Ontario, 1989. vii, 124 p.; ISBN: 0-7714-1078-6. [6595]

Woods, Lance B.
A bibliography of Canadian sources in gerontology, 1972-1978. Ann Arbor: Institute of Gerontology, University of Michigan, 1979. 26 l. [5627]

Woodsworth, Anne
The 'alternative' press in Canada: a checklist of underground, revolutionary, radical and other alternative serials from 1960. Toronto: University of Toronto Press, c1972. xi, 74 p.; ISBN: 0-8020-1940-4. [5907]

Woodward, Frances M.
"Bibliography of British Columbia." In: *BC Studies*; No. 1 (Winter 1968-69)-no. 54 (Summer 1982) [0593]
"British Columbia books of interest." In: *B.C. Historical News*; (June 1971-Summer 1981) ; ISSN: 0045-2963. [0591]
Fire insurance plans of British Columbia municipalities: a checklist. [S.l.: s.n.], 1974. 23 p. [6544]
"The history of education in British Columbia: a selected bibliography." In: *Schooling and society in twentieth century British Columbia*, edited by J.D. Wilson and David C. Jones. Calgary: Detselig Enterprises, c1980. P. 163-190.; ISBN: 0-920490-09-3. [3580]
"Margaret Anchoretta Ormsby: publications." In: *BC Studies*; No. 32 (Winter 1976-1977) p. 163-169.; ISSN: 0005-2949. [7224]
Theses on British Columbia history and related subjects in the Library of the University of British Columbia. Rev. and

enl. ed. Vancouver: University of British Columbia Library, 1971. 57 p. (Reference publication / University of British Columbia Library ; no. 35) [6112]

Woolford, Daniel
Resource guide of publications supported by multiculturalism programs, 1973-1992/Guide des publications subventionnées par les programmes du multiculturalisme, 1973-1992. Ottawa: Multiculturalism and Citizenship Canada, c1993. vii, 136 p.; ISBN: 0-662-59679-X. [4298]

Woolmer, J. Howard
Malcolm Lowry: a bibliography. Revere, Pa.: Woolmer/ Brotherson, 1983. xvi, 183 p.: ill.; ISBN: 0-913506-12-5. [7161]
A Malcolm Lowry catalogue, with essays by Perle Epstein and Richard Hauer Costa. New York: J. Howard Woolmer, 1968. 64 p. [7160]

Work and family employment policy: a selected bibliography. Victoria, B.C.: Work Well, 1990. 49 p. [2934]

Worker's Compensation Board of British Columbia. Films and Posters Department
Publications and posters catalogue: inform, educate, remind, protect. [Richmond, B.C.]: Films and Posters Department, Worker's Compensation Board of British Columbia, 1989. 24 l. [2928]

Working Group on Health Surveillance and Laboratory Safety (Canada)
Health and safety of laboratory workers in Canada: a review of the literature. Ottawa: Health and Welfare Canada, 1982. iii, 43 p. [5649]

Woycenko, Ol'ha
Ukrainian contribution to Canada's cultural life. Winnipeg: [s.n.], 1965. iv, 116 l. [4136]

Wren, Christopher
Literature review of the occurrence of toxicity of metals in wild mammals. Hull, Quebec: National Wildlife Research Centre, Canadian Wildlife Service, 1983. iv, 180, 29, [75] l. [5207]

Wright, John
Early bibles of America: being a descriptive account of bibles published in the United States, Mexico and Canada. New York: T. Whittaker, 1894. xv, 483 p. [1577]
Early prayer books of America: being a descriptive account of prayer books published in the United States, Mexico and Canada. St. Paul, Minn.: Press of Evans & Bissell, 1896. xv, 492 p.: ill., facsims., pl. [1578]

Wright, Maureen
Canadian statistics: a guide to sources of information. [Montreal]: McLennan Library, McGill University, Government Documents Department, 1982. 12 p. [3041]

Writers' Development Trust. Atlantic Work Group
Social realism: [a resource guide for the teaching of Canadian literature]. [Toronto]: Writers' Development Trust, [1977]. 68 p. [1115]
Women in Canadian literature: [a resource guide for the teaching of Canadian literature]. [Toronto]: Writers' Development Trust, [1977]. 93 p. [1116]

Writers' Development Trust. British Columbia Work Group
Coming of age in Canada: [a resource guide for the teaching of Canadian literature]. [Toronto]: Writers' Development Trust, [1977]. 52 p. [1117]
The North, native peoples: [a resource guide for the teaching of Canadian literature]. [Toronto]: Writers' Development

Trust, [1977]. 76 p. [1118]

Writers' Development Trust. Ontario Work Group

Action, adventure: [a resource guide for the teaching of Canadian literature]. [Toronto]: Writers' Development Trust, [1977]. 200 p. [1119]

Family relationships: [a resource guide for the teaching of Canadian literature]. [Toronto]: Writers' Development Trust, [1977]. 65 p. [1120]

Writers' Development Trust. Prairie Work Group

The immigrant experience: [a resource guide for the teaching of Canadian literature]. [Toronto]: Writers' Development Trust, 1977. 43 p. [1121]

New land, new language: [a resource guide for the teaching of Canadian literature]. [Toronto]: Writers' Development Trust, [1977]. 52 p. [1122]

Writers' Development Trust. Quebec Work Group

Images of biculturalism: [a resource guide for the teaching of Canadian literature]. [Toronto]: Writers' Development Trust, [1977]. 32 p. [1123]

Quebec literature in translation: [a resource guide for the teaching of Canadian literature]. [Toronto]: Writers' Development Trust, [1977]. 63 p. [1124]

"Writings by Helmut Kallmann." In: *Musical Canada: words and music honouring Helmut Kallmann*, edited by John Beckwith and Frederick A. Hall. Toronto: University of Toronto Press, 1988. P. 315-324.; ISBN: 0-8020-5759-4. [7083]

The Writings of Marshall McLuhan: listed in chronological order from 1934 to 1975: with an appended list of reviews and articles about him and his work. Fort Lauderdale, Fla.: Wake-Brook House, c1975. 101, [4] p.: port.; ISBN: 0-87482-078-2. [7184]

Writings on American history. Millwood, N.Y.: KTO Press, 1902- . vol.; ISSN: 0364-2887. [2093]

Würtele, Fred C.; Strachan, J.W.

Index of the lectures, papers and historical documents published by the Literary and Historical Society of Quebec, and also the names of their authors, together with a list of unpublished papers read before the society, 1829 to 1891. Quebec: Morning Chronicle, 1891. xlix p. [1885]

Wybouw, George; Kanaan, Richard

La bureautique et la productivité: revue de la littérature. Laval, Québec: Centre canadien de recherche sur l'information du travail, c1988. ii, 162 p.; ISBN: 0-662-94940-4. [2923]

Office automation and productivity: review of the literature. Laval, Quebec: Canadian Workplace Automation Research Centre, Organizational Research Directorate, 1986. ii, 165 p.; ISBN: 0-662-16252-8. [2910]

Wyczynski, Paul

Albert Laberge, 1871-1960: Charles Gill, 1871-1918. Ottawa: National Library of Canada, 1971. 42, 42 p. [7015]

Albert Laberge, 1871-1960: Charles Gill, 1871-1918. Ottawa: Bibliothèque nationale du Canada, 1971. 42, 42 p. [7107]

Albert Laberge, 1871-1960: Charles Gill, 1871-1918. Ottawa: National Library of Canada, 1971. 42, 42 p. [7108]

Albert Laberge, 1871-1960: Charles Gill, 1871-1918. Ottawa: Bibliothèque nationale du Canada, 1971. 42, 42 p. [7016]

"Bibliographie d'Émile Nelligan." Dans: *Études françaises*; Vol. 3, no 3 (août 1967) p. 285-298.; ISSN: 0014-2085. [7208]

Bibliographie descriptive et critique d'Émile Nelligan. Ottawa: Éditions de l'Université d'Ottawa, 1973. 319 p. (Bibliographies du Canada français ; no 1); ISBN: 0-7766-3951-X. [7209]

"François-Xavier Garneau: aspects bibliographiques." Dans:

Cahiers de la Société bibliographique du Canada; Vol. 18 (1979) p. 55-77.; ISSN: 0067-6896. [7002]

"Histoire et critique littéraires au Canada français: bibliographie." Dans: *Recherches sociographiques*; Vol. 5, no 1-2 (janvier-août 1964) p. 52-69.; ISSN: 0034-1282. [1024]

Wylie, Alison, et al.

"Philosophical feminism: a bibliographical guide to critiques of science." In: *Resources for Feminist Research*; Vol. 19, no. 2 (June 1990) p. 2-36.; ISSN: 0707-8412. [3885]

Wyman, Doreen

Bibliography of law-related AV material. 2nd ed. Edmonton: Legal Resource Centre, Faculty of Extension, University of Alberta, c1986. 162 p. [6667]

Yandle, Anne; Amor, Norman L.

"Bibliography [Malcolm Lowry]." In: *Malcolm Lowry Newsletter*; No. 5 (Fall 1979)-nos. 29-30 (Fall-Spring 1992) [7162]

Yanz, Lynda

"Women and unions: a bibliography." In: *Resources for Feminist Research*; Vol. 10, no. 2 (July 1981) p. 85-88.; ISSN: 0707-8412. [2878]

Yapa, A.C.; Mitchell, M.H.

Bibliography, 1979-1985 [Petawawa National Forestry Institute]/Liste des publications pour les années 1979-1985 [Institut forestier national de Petawawa]. Chalk River, Ont.: Petawawa National Forestry Institute, Canadian Forestry Service, 1987. i, 150 p. (Information report / Petawawa National Forestry Institute ; PI-X-70E/F; ISSN: 0714-3354); ISBN: 0-662-55451-5. [6387]

Yarranton, G.A.; Gray, B.J.; Yarranton, M.

Methodologies for evaluation of AECB regulatory program. Ottawa: Atomic Energy Control Board, 1986. vi, 296 p. [5819]

Yelle, André

Income tax references/Références à la loi de l'impôt sur le revenu. Toronto: Richard De Boo, c1982. 2 vol. (loose-leaf); ISBN: 0-88820-121-4. [2689]

Yip, Gladys

Cross cultural childrearing: an annotated bibliography. Vancouver: Centre for the Study of Curriculum and Instruction, University of British Columbia, c1985. 81 p. (Early childhood series / Centre for the Study of Curriculum and Instruction, University of British Columbia); ISBN: 0-88865-372-7. [4237]

Yorio, Carlos Alfredo

A selected annotated bibliography for teacher training in Canada, 1976. [Toronto]: Ministry of Culture and Recreation, Citizenship Branch, 1976. 12 p. [3519]

York University (Toronto, Ont.). Institute for Social Research

Canadian social science data archive. North York, Ont.: The Institute, 1985. 136 l.; ISBN: 0-919-76280-8. [3050]

York University (Toronto, Ont.). Libraries

Catalogue: Canadian pamphlet collection/Catalogue: Collection des brochures canadiennes. Toronto: York University Libraries, 1984. 3 vol. [6789]

York University (Toronto, Ont.). Programme in Arts Administration

A selective bibliography of Canadian and international readings in arts administration and cultural development. [Toronto]: Canadian Conference of the Arts, 1974. 24 l. [0679]

Young, Alan R.

"Thomas H. Raddall: an annotated bibliography." In: *The annotated bibliography of Canada's major authors*, Vol. 7, edited by Robert Lecker and Jack David. Toronto: ECW Press, 1987. P. 403-477.; ISBN: 0-920802-11-1. [7255]

Thomas Head Raddall: a bibliography. Kingston, Ont.: Loyal Colonies Press, 1982. xi, 71 p.; ISBN: 0-920832-08-3. [7254]

Young, George; Lutz, John S.

Researcher's guide to British Columbia directories, 1901-1940: a bibliography & index. Victoria, B.C.: Public History Group, University of Victoria, 1992. xviii, 255 p.; ISBN: 0-921278-08-X. [0604]

Young, Judy

"Canadian literature in the non-official languages: a review of recent publications and work in progress." In: *Canadian Ethnic Studies*; Vol. 14, no. 1 (1982) p. 138-149.; ISSN: 0008-3496. [1200]

"Some thoughts about the present state of bibliography in the area of Canadian ethnic studies." In: *Canadian Issues*; Vol. 4 (1982) p. 38-47.; ISSN: 0318-8442. [4214]

Young, Rod

"Labour archives: an annotated bibliography." In: *Archivaria*; No. 27 (Winter 1988-1989) p. 97-110.; ISSN: 0318-6954. [1714]

Young, Stuart C.

Bibliography on the fate and effects of Arctic marine oil pollution. Ottawa: Environmental Studies Revolving Funds, c1986. xii, 212 p. (Environmental Studies Revolving Funds report ; no. 026); ISBN: 0-920783-25-2. [5239]

Young Men's Christian Association (Halifax, N.S.)

Catalogue of books in the library of the Halfax Young Men's Christian Association. Halifax, N.S.: Library and Reading Rooms, 1858. 24 p. [6716]

Yuan, Jing-dong; Cummins, Vivian

Asian Pacific trade and Canada: a bibliography. Ottawa: Asian Pacific Research and Resource Centre, Carleton University, [1991]. 85 p. (Bibliography series / Asian Pacific Research and Resource Centre, Carleton University ; 1) [2779]

Yuille, John C.; King, Mary Ann; McDougall, Don

Child victims and witnesses: the social science and legal literatures. Ottawa: Department of Justice Canada, 1988. vii, 61, 67, vii p. (Studies on the sexual abuse of children in Canada); ISBN: 0-662-55765-4. [2320]

Enfants victimes et témoins: publications en droit et en sciences sociales. Ottawa: Ministère de la justice Canada, 1988. vii, 67, 61, vii p. (Études sur les agressions sexuelles contre les enfants au Canada); ISBN: 0-662-55765-4. [2321]

Yukon Archives

Alaska Highway, 1942-1991: a comprehensive bibliography of material available in the Yukon Archives & MacBride Museum. Whitehorse: Yukon Education, Libraries and Archives Branch, [1993]. iv, 83 p.: ill., map.; ISBN: 1-55018-558-6. [0662]

Dalton Trail: a bibliography of sources available at Yukon Archives. Whitehorse: Yukon, Education, Yukon Archives, 1983. 21 l.; ISBN: 1-55018-037-1. [2033]

Genealogy sources available at the Yukon Archives. Whitehorse: Yukon Archives, 1985. 11 l.; ISBN: 1-55018-041-X. [2052]

Martha Louise Black: a bibliography of sources available in the Yukon Archives. Whitehorse: Yukon Archives, 1983. ii, 9 l.; ISBN: 1-55018-039-8. [6848]

Yukon native history and culture: a bibliography of sources available at the Yukon Archives. Whitehorse: The Archives, 1987. ii, 65 p. [4094]

Yukon bibliography. Edmonton: Boreal Institute for Northern Studies, University of Alberta, 1964-1987. 11 vol. [0656]

Yukon Indian Resource Centre

Indian education. Whitehorse: Yukon Indian Resource Centre, 1973. 10 l.: ill. [3949]

Yukon land and resource inventory: bibliographic index. Whitehorse, Y.T.: Government of Yukon, 1979. 1 vol. (in various pagings). [0637]

Yukon Territory. Women's Directorate. Library

Yukon Women's Directorate Library containing a guide to using the library and library listings by category. [Whitehorse]: The Library, [1991]. 38 p.; ISBN: 1-55018-125-4. [3897]

Yundt, S.E.; Booth, G.D.

Bibliography: rehabilitation of pits, quarries, and other surface-mined lands. Toronto: Ontario Ministry of Natural Resources, 1978. vii, 27 p. (Ontario Geological Survey Miscellaneous paper ; 76; ISSN: 0704-2752) [4811]

Yurkowski, M.

A bibliography on the biochemistry, nutrition, and related areas of aquatic mammals and Arctic people to 1983. Winnipeg: Fisheries and Oceans Canada, 1985. iv, 236 p. (Canadian technical report of fisheries and aquatic sciences ; no. 1361; ISSN: 0706-6547) [5520]

Zalasky, H.

Bibliography of frost damage in tree nurseries. Edmonton: Northern Forest Research Centre, Canadian Forestry Service, Fisheries and Environment Canada, 1977. 8 l. [4962]

Zaldokas, Daiva O.; Aird, Debra L.

Abstracts of Fisheries management reports, technical circulars and project reports of the Fisheries Branch. Vancouver: B.C. Environment, Fisheries Branch, 1992. 56 p. (Fisheries technical circular / B.C. Fisheries Branch ; no. 91); ISBN: 0-77261-641-8. [6415]

Zaporzan, Shirley; Klymasz, Robert B.

Film and the Ukrainians in Canada, 1921-1980: a filmography index of film titles and bibliography with supplementary appendices. Edmonton: Canadian Institute of Ukrainian Studies, University of Alberta, 1982. xi, 76 p.: ill., [17] l. of pl. (Research report / Canadian Institute of Ukrainian Studies ; no. 1) [6653]

Ziegler, Ronald M.

Wilderness waterways: a guide to information sources. Detroit, Mich.: Gale Research, c1979. x, 317 p. (Sports, games, and pastimes information guide series ; no. 1); ISBN: 0-8103-1434-7. [1797]

Zilm, Glennis

Early B.C. books: an overview of trade book publishing in the 1800s with checklists and selected bibliography related to British Columbiana. [Burnaby, B.C.]: Simon Fraser University, 1981. xi, 303 p. [1649]

"Early books and printing in British Columbia." In: *AB Bookman's Weekly*; Vol. 85, no. 9 (February 26, 1990) p. 837-845.; ISSN: 0001-0340. [0600]

Zimmering, Suzann; Nesbitt, Bruce

"Canadian literature, 1971: an annotated bibliography: une bibliographie avec commentaire." In: *Essays on Canadian Writing*; No. 9 (Winter 1977-1978) p. 190-313.; ISSN: 0316-0300. [1141]

Zimmerly, David W.

Museocinematography: ethnographic film programs of the National Museum of Man, 1913-1973. Ottawa: National

Museums of Canada, 1974. vii, 103 p.: ill. (National Museum of Man Mercury series, Ethnology Division paper ; no. 11) [6622]

Zinman, Rosalind

"Selected bibliography on Quebec." In: *Canadian Review of Sociology and Anthropology*; Vol. 15, no. 2 (1978) p. 246-251.; ISSN: 0008-4948. [0357]

Zins, Michael, et al.

Consumer decision making: an annotated bibliography. [Ottawa]: Consumer Research and Evaluation Branch, Consumer and Corporate Affairs Canada, 1979. 398 p. [2655]

Zuckernick, Arlene

L'enseignement ouvert et la formation à distance au Canada. [Ottawa]: Secrétariat d'État du Canada, c1989. 51, 46 p. (Guides pédagogiques des études canadiennes); ISBN: 0-662-57210-6. [3706]

Open learning and distance education in Canada. Ottawa: Canadian Studies Directorate, Department of the Secretary of State of Canada, c1989. 46, 51 p. (Canadian studies resource guides); ISBN: 0-662-57210-6. [3707]

Zuk, Ireneus

The piano concerto in Canada (1900-1980): a bibliographic survey. Baltimore, Md.: Peabody Conservatory of Music, Peabody Institute of the Johns Hopkins University, 1985. xxxi, 429 l. [0923]

Zureik, Elia; Hartling, Dianne

The social context of the new information and communication technologies: a bibliography. New York: P. Lang, 1987. x, 310 p.; ISBN: 0-82040-413-6. [1698]

Zysman, Ewa

Stany Zjednoczone Ameryki i Kanada w pismiennictwie polskim 1945-1985: bibliografia drukow zwartych. Warszawa: Polski Instytut Spraw Miedzynarodowych, 1986. 272 p. [0155]

Serial Titles Searched

Publications en série: titres recherchés

AB Bookman's Weekly
Abegweit Review
About Arts and Crafts
Acadia Bulletin
Acadiensis
Acta criminologica
Action nationale
Actualité économique
Agriculture
Alberta Historical Review
Alberta
American Anthropologist
American Geologist
American Music
American Review of Canadian Studies
Amsterdam Creole Studies
Annales de l'ACFAS
Annales de Normandie
Annali accademici Canadesi
Annuaire du Canada
Annuaire du Québec
Annual Archaeological Report, Ontario
Annual report of the American Historical Association
Anthropologica
Anthropologie et sociétés
Anthropos
APLA Bulletin
APT Bulletin
Architecture concept
Archivaria
Archives de Folklore
Archives
Arctic Anthropology
Arctic
Art et l'artisanat
Art Libraries Journal
Association for Preservation Technology Bulletin
Asticou
Australian-Canadian Studies: an interdisciplinary
   social science review
B.C. Historical News
Barre du jour
BC Studies
Beaver
Blue Jay
Book Collector
Booklist
Brick: a Journal of Reviews
British Columbia Historical Quarterly
British Columbia Library Quarterly
British Journal of Canadian Studies
British North America Philatelic Society Year Book
Bulletin (Association for Commonwealth Literature
   and Language Studies)
Bulletin (National Gallery of Canada)
Bulletin (National Museum of Canada)
Bulletin (Society for the Study of Architecture in Canada)
Bulletin (Special Libraries Association, Geography
   and Map Division)
Bulletin (United Church of Canada. Committee on
   Archives and History)
Bulletin d'histoire de la culture matérielle
Bulletin de l'Association canadienne des bibliothécaires
   de langue française

Bulletin de l'Association des démographes du Québec
Bulletin de l'Association pour l'analyse et la
   modification du comportement
Bulletin de la Société botanique du Québec
Bulletin des recherches historiques
Bulletin du Centre de recherche en civilisation
   canadienne-française de l'Université d'Ottawa
Bulletin of Bibliography
Bulletin of the Entomological Society of America
Bulletin of the Folklore Studies Association of Canada
Bulletin: Association for Preservation Technology
Bulletin: Bibliothèque de l'Assemblée nationale du Québec
Bulletin: Corporation professionnelle des médecins du Québec
Bulletin: Society for the Study of Labour History
Cahiers d'histoire de Deux-Montagnes
Cahiers d'histoire
Cahiers de Cap-Rouge
Cahiers de Centreau
Cahiers de droit
Cahiers de géographie de Québec
Cahiers de l'Académie canadienne-française
Cahiers de l'ARMUQ
Cahiers de la Société bibliographique du Canada
Cahiers de pastorale scolaire
Cahiers du livre ancien du Canada français
Cahiers franco-canadiens de l'Ouest
Cahiers linguistiques d'Ottawa
Cahiers québécois de démographie
Cahiers: Société historique acadienne
Canada français
Canada Year Book
Canada's Mental Health
Canada: the State of the Federation
Canadian Alpine Journal
Canadian Architect
Canadian Author and Bookman
Canadian Business Law Journal
Canadian Business
Canadian Cartographer
Canadian Cases on the Law of Torts
Canadian Catholic Historical Association.
   Study Sessions
Canadian Chartered Accountant
Canadian Children's Literature
Canadian Competition Policy Record
Canadian Dimension
Canadian Drama
Canadian Ethnic Studies
Canadian Fiction Magazine
Canadian Folk Music Journal
Canadian Folklore: Folklore canadien
Canadian Geographer
Canadian Geophysical Bulletin
Canadian Historical Review
Canadian Home Economics Journal
Canadian Human Rights Yearbook: Annuaire canadien des
   droits de la personne
Canadian Issues
Canadian Journal of Criminology and Corrections
Canadian Journal of Criminology
Canadian Journal of Economics and Political Science
Canadian Journal of Education
Canadian Journal of Native Education
Canadian Journal of Political Science

Canadian Journal of Psychology
Canadian Journal of Science, Literature and History
Canadian Journal on Aging: La revue canadienne
   du vieillissement
Canadian Law Libraries
Canadian Library Association Bulletin
Canadian Library Journal
Canadian Library
Canadian Literature
Canadian Mining Journal
Canadian Modern Language Review
Canadian Music Journal
Canadian Newsletter of Research on Women
Canadian Numismatic Journal
Canadian Poetry
Canadian Psychologist
Canadian Psychology
Canadian Quaker History Newsletter
Canadian Record of Science
Canadian Review of Comparative Literature
Canadian Review of Sociology and Anthropology
Canadian Slavonic Papers
Canadian Tax Journal
Canadian Theatre Review
Canadian University Music Review: Revue de musique
   des universités canadiennes
Canadian Woman Studies
Canadian Women's Studies
Canadiana Germanica
Capilano Review
Cefco: Centre d'études franco-canadiennes de l'Ouest
Charlottes
Chronique de la recherche minière
Chronique des relations extérieures du Canada
Cicindela
CIM Bulletin
Cinéma Québec
Cités et villes
Collections of the Nova Scotia Historical Society
Communique: Canadian Studies
Conrad Grebel Review
Contemporary French Civilization
Contemporary Verse Two
Contributions to Canadian Biology: being studies
   from the biological stations of Canada
Contributions to Canadian Economics
Cordulia
Criminologie
Culture
Current Sociology
Dalhousie Law Journal
Dalhousie Review
Dérives
Didactique-géographie
Documentation et bibliothèques
Dominion Annual Register and Review
Douglas Library Notes
École canadienne
Economic History Review
Eire: Ireland
Emergency Librarian
English Studies in Canada
Enseignement secondaire
Essays on Canadian Writing

Ethnic Forum
Ethnomusicology
Études canadiennes: Canadian studies
Études françaises
Études internationales
Études Inuit Studies
Études oblates
Famille
Family Relations
Fiddlehead
Focus
Four Decades of Poetry, 1890-1930
Gazette (Law Society of Upper Canada)
Generations: the Journal of the Manitoba
   Genealogical Society
Geographical Review
Géographie physique et quaternaire
Geographisches Jahrbuch
Geological Society of America Bulletin
German-Canadian Yearbook
Hilgardia
Histoire des travailleurs québécois: Bulletin RCHTQ
Histoire sociale: Social History
Historical Studies in Education
History and Social Science Teacher
Index to Legal Periodicals and Law Library Journal
Indian Historian
Industrialisation forum
Inscape
Inter-Nord
International Journal of American Linguistics
International Journal of Canadian Studies
International Migration Review
International Organization
International Perspectives
Jazz Ottawa
Jeu
Journal des traducteurs
Journal of Architectural Education
Journal of Canadian Art History
Journal of Canadian Fiction
Journal of Canadian Studies
Journal of Commonwealth Literature
Journal of Comparative Family Studies
Journal of Education
Journal of Educational Thought
Journal of Foraminiferal Research
Journal of Glaciology
Journal of Interamerican Studies and World Affairs
Journal of Modern History
Journal of the Atlantic Provinces Linguistic Association
Journal of the Canadian Church Historical Society
Journal of the Canadian Linguistic Association
Journal of the Canadian Mining Institute
Journal of the Fisheries Research Board of Canada
Journal of the Royal Astronomical Society of Canada
Journal of the Society of Architectural Historians
Journal of Ukrainian Graduate Studies
Kansas University Quarterly
Labour Gazette
Labour Topics
Labour: Le Travail
Laval théologique et philosophique
Law Library Journal

Liberté
Library Journal
Library Quarterly
Library World
Loyalist Gazette
Magazine of American History
Malahat Review
Malcolm Lowry Newsletter
Manitoba Archaeological Newsletter
Manitoba Arts Review
Manitoba History
Maritime Sediments
Material History Bulletin
Material Studies Bulletin
McGill Journal of Education
McGill Law Journal
Medical Services Journal Canada
Mémoires de la Société généalogique canadienne-française
Mémoires de la Société royale du Canada
Mennonite Quarterly Review
Meta
Modern Fiction Studies
Monthly Bulletin of the Providence Public Library
Moosehead Review
MSLAVA (Manitoba School Library Audio-visual
    Association Journal)
Multiculturalism
Museum Quarterly
Musicanada
Musk-ox
Names
Naturaliste canadien
Newfoundland Quarterly
Newfoundland Studies
Nineteenth Century Theatre Research
Nord
Northeast Folklore
Northern Journal of Applied Forestry
Northian
Northwest Anthropological Research Notes
Notes du Centre d'études du tourisme
Nova Scotia Historical Quarterly
Nova Scotia Historical Review
Now and Then: A Newsletter For Those Interested in
    History and Law
One World
Onoma
Ontario Archaeology
Ontario Geography
Ontario Historical Society Papers and Records
Ontario History
Ontario Journal of Educational Research
Ontario Library Review
Open Letter
Orbis: bulletin international de documentation linguistique
Orientation professionnelle
Osgoode Hall Law Journal
Ottawa Law Review
Ottawa Naturalist
Pacific Affairs
Pacific Northwest Quarterly
Papers and Records: Ontario Historical Society
Papers of the Bibliographical Society of America
Papers of the Bibliographical Society of Canada

Park News
Passe-Temps
Phi zéro
Philosophiques
Pioneer America
Plains Anthropologist
Plan Canada
Pluriel
Polyphony
Prairie Fire
Prairie Forum
Présence francophone
Prism International
Proceedings and Transactions of the Royal Society of Canada
Proceedings of the American Antiquarian Society
Protée
Public Libraries
Publications of the Buffalo Historical Society
Pulp and Paper Magazine of Canada
Québec chasse et pêche
Québec français
Québec littéraire
Québec Studies
Queen's Law Journal
Queen's Quarterly
RACAR (Revue d'art canadienne, Canadian Art Review)
Rapport de l'archiviste de la Province de Québec
Rapport sur les Archives publiques du Canada
Recherches amérindiennes au Québec
Recherches féministes
Recherches sociographiques
Reference Shelf
Relations
Report of the Public Archives of Canada
Resources for Feminist Research
Revue canadienne de biologie
Revue canadienne de criminologie
Revue canadienne de géographie
Revue canadienne de science politique
Revue d'histoire de l'Amérique française
Revue d'histoire littéraire de la France
Revue d'histoire littéraire du Québec et du Canada
    français
Revue d'intégration européenne: Journal of European
    Integration
Revue de géographie de Montréal
Revue de l'Université d'Ottawa
Revue de l'Université de Moncton
Revue de l'Université Laval
Revue des sciences de l'éducation
Revue du barreau
Revue du Nouvel Ontario
Revue historique
Revue internationale d'études canadiennes
Revue juridique Thémis
Royal Canadian Mounted Police Quarterly
Saguenayensia
Saskatchewan Archaeology Newsletter
Saskatchewan Archaeology
Saskatchewan Genealogical Society Bulletin
Saskatchewan History
School Libraries in Canada
Scientia canadensis
Service social

Social Compass
Socialist Studies
Sociologie et sociétés
Sound Heritage
Stanford French Review
Studies in Canadian Literature
Swedish-American Historical Quarterly
Syesis
TESL Canada Journal
Toxicomanies
Transactions of the Canadian Institute
Transactions of the Canadian Numismatic Research Society
Transactions of the Royal Canadian Institute
Transactions of the Wisconsin Academy of Sciences,
    Arts, and Letters
Twentieth Century Literature
Union médicale du Canada
University of Toronto Quarterly
Urban History Review: Revue d'histoire urbaine
Vermont History
Vie oblate life
Vie pédagogique
Voix et images
Volta Review
West Coast Review
Western Ontario Historical Notes
Women Studies Abstracts
World Literature Written in English
Yearbook of Physical Anthropology
York Pioneer and Historical Society Annual Report